THE ROUGH GUIDE TO
INDIA

This eleventh edition updated by
**Nick Edwards, Marco Ferrarese, Lottie Gross,
Shafik Meghji,** ~~KINGSTON LIBRARIES~~
Martin Zatko

with additional co
Nina Meghji

ROUGH
GUIDES

Contents

A FATHER AND SON FISHING ON A TRADITIONAL BOAT NEAR ASSAM

Introduction to
India

India, it is often said, is not a country, but a continent. Stretching from the frozen summits of the Himalayas to the tropical greenery of Kerala, its expansive borders encompass an incomparable range of landscapes, cultures and people. Walk the streets of any Indian city and you'll rub shoulders with representatives of several of the world's great faiths, encounter temple rituals performed since the time of the Egyptian Pharaohs and spot onion-domed mosques erected centuries before the Taj Mahal, as well as quirky echoes of the British Raj on virtually every corner.

That so much of India's past remains discernible today is all the more astonishing given the pace of change since Independence in 1947. Spurred by the free-market reforms of the early 1990s, the **economic revolution** started by Rajiv Gandhi has transformed the country with new consumer goods, technologies and ways of life. Infrastructure has improved, too, making visiting the country easier than ever before. A growing number of cities boast gleaming new metro systems, and are linked by faster highways and speedier, more comfortable trains. The accommodation sector is blossoming, too, with homestays mushrooming in popularity and new breed of hostels opening up. Even your Indian visa can now be obtained online.

However, the presence in even the most far-flung market towns of ubiquitous wi-fi, the latest smartphones and Mahindra SUVs has thrown into sharp relief the **problems** that have bedevilled India since long before it became the world's largest secular democracy. More than twenty percent of India's inhabitants remain below the poverty line; no other nation on earth has slum settlements on the scale of those in Delhi, Mumbai and Kolkata, nor so many malnourished children, uneducated women and homes without access to clean water and waste disposal.

Many first-time visitors find themselves unable to see past such glaring disparities. Others come expecting a timeless ascetic wonderland and are surprised to encounter one of the most materialistic societies on the planet. Still more find themselves intimidated by what may seem, initially, an incomprehensible and bewildering continent. But for all its jarring juxtapositions, intractable paradoxes and frustrations, India remains an utterly compelling destination. Intricate and worn, its distinctive patina – the stream of life in its crowded bazaars, the ubiquitous filmi music, the pungent melange of diesel fumes, cooking spices, dust and dung smoke – casts a spell that few forget from the moment they step off a plane. Love it or hate it – and most travellers oscillate between the two – India will shift the way you see the world.

Where to go

The best Indian itineraries are the simplest. It just isn't possible to see everything in a single expedition, even if you spent a year trying. Far better, then, to concentrate on one or two specific regions and, above all, to be flexible. Although it requires a deliberate change of pace to venture away from the urban centres, rural India has its own very distinct pleasures. In fact, while Indian cities are undoubtedly adrenalin-fuelled, upbeat places, it is possible – and certainly less stressful – to travel for months around the Subcontinent and rarely have to set foot in one.

FACT FILE

- The Republic of India, whose capital is **Delhi**, is bordered by Afghanistan, China, Nepal and Bhutan to the north, Bangladesh and Myanmar (Burma) to the east and Pakistan to the west.
- It's the seventh largest country in the world, covering more than three million square kilometres, and is second only to China in terms of population, at more than **1.3 billion**. Hindus comprise eighty percent of the population, Muslims 14 percent, and there are millions of Christians, Sikhs, Buddhists and Jains. **Twenty-three official languages** are spoken, along with more than a thousand minor languages and dialects. Hindi is the language of more than forty percent of the population; English is also widely spoken.
- The **caste system** is pervasive and, although integral to Hindu belief, it also encompasses non-Hindus. It holds special sway in rural areas and may dictate where a person lives and what their occupation is.
- Eighty-one percent of males over 15 are **literate**, compared to 61 percent of females: 71 percent of the total adult population.
- Mawsynram, in the northeastern state of Meghalaya, is the **wettest place on Earth**, with an average annual deluge of 11,871mm.
- **Indian Railways** is India's largest employer, with around 1.4 million workers.
- Producing up to 2000 movies each year and turning over US$4 billion, India's **film industry** is the largest in the world, in terms of ticket numbers if not box office receipts.

The most-travelled circuit in the country, combining spectacular monuments with the flat, fertile landscape that for many people is archetypally Indian, is the so-called **Golden Triangle** in the north: Delhi itself, the colonial capital; Agra, home of the Taj Mahal; and the Pink City of Jaipur in **Rajasthan**. Rajasthan is probably the single most popular state with travellers, who are drawn by its desert scenery, the imposing medieval forts and palaces of Jaisalmer, Jodhpur, Udaipur and Bundi, and by its colourful traditional dress.

East of Delhi, the River Ganges meanders through some of India's most densely populated regions to reach the extraordinary holy Hindu city of **Varanasi**, where to witness the daily rituals of life and death focused around the waterfront *ghats* (bathing

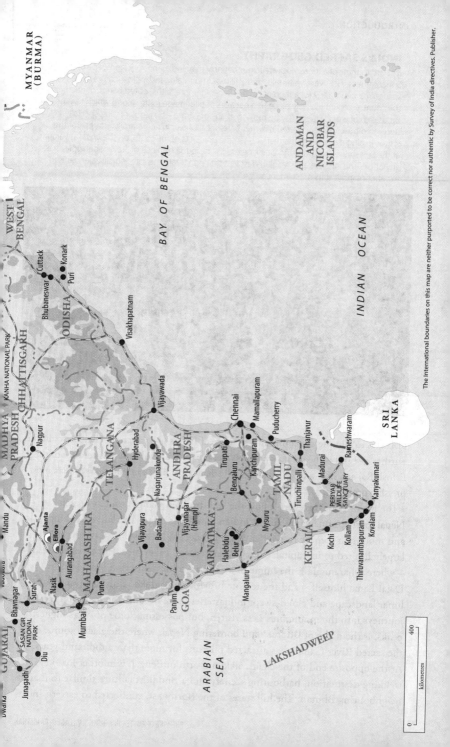

MYANMAR (BURMA)

WEST BENGAL

Cuttack

Konark

Bhubaneswar

Puri

ODISHA

BAY OF BENGAL

MADHYA PRADESH

KANHA NATIONAL PARK

CHHATTISGARH

Visakhapatnam

Nagpur

TELANGANA

Vijayawada

Hyderabad

ANDHRA PRADESH

Nagarjunakonda

Chennai

Mamallapuram

Mandu

Tirupati

Puducherry

Vijayapura

Badami

Bengaluru

Kanchipuram

MAHARASHTRA

Ajanta

Ellora

Vijayanagar (Hampi)

TAMIL NADU

Aurangabad

KARNATAKA

Halebidu

Belur

Mysuru

Tiruchirapalli

Thanjavur

Nasik

Surat

Pune

Madurai

Rameshwaram

Bhavnagar

SRI LANKA

GUJARAT

SASAN GIR NATIONAL PARK

Mumbai

Panjim

GOA

Mangaluru

PERIYAR WILDLIFE SANCTUARY

KERALA

Kanyakumari

Junagadh

Diu

Kochi

Kollam

Kovalam

Dwarka

Thiruvananthapuram

ARABIAN SEA

LAKSHADWEEP

INDIAN OCEAN

ANDAMAN AND NICOBAR ISLANDS

0   400

kilometres

INDIA'S SACRED GEOGRAPHY

It's hard to think of a more visibly religious country than India. The very landscape of the Subcontinent – its rivers, waterfalls, trees, hilltops, mountains and rocks – comprises a vast sacred geography for adherents of the dozen or more faiths rooted here. Connecting the country's countless holy places is a network of pilgrimage routes along which tens of thousands of worshippers may be moving at any one time – on regular trains, specially decorated buses, tinsel-covered bicycles, barefoot, alone or in noisy family groups. For the visitor, joining devotees in the teeming temple precincts of the south, on the *ghats* at Varanasi, at the Sufi shrines of Ajmer and Delhi, before the naked Jain colossi of Sravanabelagola, or at any one of the innumerable religious festivals that punctuate the astrological calendar is to experience India at its most intense.

places) is to glimpse the continuing practice of India's most ancient religious traditions. Further east still is the great city of **Kolkata**, the capital until early last century of the British Raj and now a teeming metropolis that epitomizes contemporary India's most pressing problems.

The majority of travellers follow the well-trodden Ganges route to reach Nepal, perhaps unaware that the **Indian Himalayas** offer superlative trekking and mountain scenery to rival any in the range. With travel in Kashmir still largely limited to its capital, Srinagar, and central valley area, **Himachal Pradesh** – where Dharamsala is the home of a Tibetan community that includes the Dalai Lama himself – and the remote province of **Ladakh**, with its mysterious lunar landscape and cloud-swept monasteries, have become the major targets for journeys into the mountains. Less visited, but possessing some of Asia's highest peaks, is the niche of **Uttarakhand** bordering Nepal, where the glacial source of the sacred River Ganges has attracted pilgrims for more than a thousand years. At the opposite end of the chain, **Sikkim**, north of Bengal, is another low-key trekking destination, harbouring scenery and a Buddhist culture similar to that of neighbouring Bhutan. The hill states of the **Northeast**, connected to eastern India

BREWING OPIUM TEA IN A BISHNOI VILLAGE IN RAJASTHAN

INDIAN RAILWAYS

India's **railways**, which daily transport millions of commuters, pilgrims, animals and hessian-wrapped packages between the four corners of the Subcontinent, are often cited as the best thing the British Raj bequeathed to its former colony. And yet, with its hierarchical legion of clerks, cooks, coolies, bearers, ticket inspectors, station managers and ministers, the network has become a quintessentially Indian institution.

Travelling across India by rail – whether you rough it in dirt-cheap second class, or pamper yourself with starched cotton sheets and hot meals in an a/c carriage – is likely to yield some of the most memorable moments of your trip. Open around the clock, the stations in themselves are often great places to watch the world go by, with hundreds of people from all walks of life eating, sleeping, buying and selling, regardless of the hour. This is also where you'll grow familiar with one of the unforgettable sounds of the Subcontinent: the robotic drone of the chaiwala, dispensing cups of hot, sweet tea.

by a slender neck of land, boast remarkably diverse landscapes and an incredible fifty percent of India's biodiversity.

Heading south from Kolkata along the coast, your first likely stop is Konark in **Odisha**, site of the famous Sun Temple, a giant carved pyramid of stone that lay submerged under sand until its rediscovery at the start of the twentieth century. **Tamil Nadu**, further south, has also retained its own tradition of magnificent architecture, with towering *gopura* gateways dominating towns whose vast temple complexes are still the focus of everyday life. Of them all, Madurai, in the far south, is the most stunning, but you could spend months wandering between the sacred sites of the Kaveri Delta and the fragrant Nilgiri Hills, draped in the tea terraces that have become the hallmark of south Indian landscapes. **Kerala**, near the southernmost tip of the Subcontinent on the western coast, is India at its most tropical and relaxed, its lush backwaters teeming with simple wooden craft of all shapes and sizes, and red-roofed towns and villages all but invisible beneath a canopy of palm trees. Further up the coast is **Goa**, the former Portuguese colony whose 100km coastline is fringed with beaches to suit all tastes and budgets, from upmarket package tourists to long-staying backpackers, and whose towns hold whitewashed Christian churches that could almost have been transplanted from Europe.

North of here sits **Mumbai**, an ungainly beast that has been the major focus of the nationwide drift to the big cities. Centre of the country's formidable popular movie industry, it reels along on an undeniable energy that, after a few days of acclimatization, can prove addictive. Beyond Mumbai is the state of **Gujarat**, renowned for the unique culture and crafts of the barren Kutch region.

On a long trip, it makes sense to pause and rest every few weeks. Certain places have fulfilled that function for generations, such as the Himalayan resort of **Manali**, epicentre of India's hashish-producing area, and the many former colonial hill stations that dot the country, from **Ootacamund (Ooty)**, in the far south, to that archetypal British retreat, **Shimla**, immortalized in the writing of Rudyard Kipling. Elsewhere, the combination of sand and the sea, and a picturesque rural or religious backdrop – such as at **Varkala** in Kerala, **Gokarna** in Karnataka, and the remoter beaches of Goa – are usually enough to loosen even the tightest itineraries.

When to go

India's weather is extremely varied, something you must take into account when planning your trip. The most influential feature of the Subcontinent's climate is the wet season, or **monsoon**. This breaks on the Keralan coast at the end of May, working its way northeast across the country over the following month and a half. While it lasts, regular and prolonged downpours are interspersed with bursts of hot sunshine, and the pervasive humidity can be intense. At the height of the monsoon – especially in the jungle regions of the northwest and the low-lying delta lands of Bengal – flooding can severely disrupt communications, causing widespread destruction. In the Himalayan foothills, landslides are common, and entire valley systems can be cut off for weeks.

By September, the monsoon has largely receded from the north, but it takes another couple of months before the clouds disappear altogether from the far south. The east coast of Andhra Pradesh and Tamil Nadu, and the south of Kerala, get a second

INDIAN FOOD

Indian cooking is as varied as the country itself, with dozens of distinctive regional **culinary traditions** ranging from the classic Mughlai cuisine of the north to the feisty coconut- and chilli-infused flavours of the south; these are often a revelation to first-time visitors, whose only contact with Indian food will probably have been through the stereotypical Anglo-Indian dishes served up in the majority of restaurants overseas. Best known is the cuisine of north India, with its signature biryanis, tandooris and rich cream- and yogurt-based sauces accompanied with thick naan breads, evidence of the region's long contact with Central Asia. The food of south India is light years away, exemplified by the ubiquitous vegetarian "meal" – a huge mound of rice served on a banana leaf and accompanied with fiery pickles – or by the classic masala dosa, a crisp rice pancake wrapped around a spicy potato filling. There's also a host of regional cuisines to explore – Punjabi, Bengali, Gujarati, Goan, Hyderabadi, Keralan and Kashmiri, to name just a few of the most distinctive – each of which has its own special dishes, spices and cooking techniques.

drenching between October and December, when the "northwest" or "retreating" monsoon sweeps in from the Bay of Bengal. By mid-December, however, most of the Subcontinent enjoys clear skies and relatively cool temperatures.

Mid-winter sees the most marked contrasts between the climates of north and south India. While Delhi, for example, may see frost and be ravaged by chill winds blowing off the snowfields of the Himalayas, the Tamil plains and coastal Kerala, more than 1000km south, still stew under fierce post-monsoon sunshine. As spring gathers pace, the centre of the Subcontinent starts to heat up again, and by late March thermometers nudge 33°C across most of the Gangetic Plains and Deccan plateau. Temperatures peak in May and early June, when anyone who can retreats to the hill stations. Above the baking Subcontinental land mass, hot air builds up and sucks in humidity from the southwest, causing the onset of the monsoon in late June, and bringing relief to millions of overheated Indians.

The best time to visit most places, therefore, is during the **cool, dry season**, between November and March. Delhi and Agra can be chilly but are mostly mild, while Varanasi, Rajasthan and Madhya Pradesh are ideal at this time, and temperatures in Goa and central India remain comfortable. The constant heat of the south becomes stifling in May and June, so aim to be in Tamil Nadu and Kerala between January and March. From May onwards, the Himalayas grow more accessible, and the trekking season reaches its peak in August and September while the rest of the Subcontinent is being soaked by the rains.

AVERAGE TEMPERATURES AND RAINFALL

	Jan	Feb	Mar	Apr	May	Jun	Jul	Aug	Sep	Oct	Nov	Dec
CHENNAI (TN)												
Max/min °C	28/20	31/21	33/23	36/26	38/27	37/27	35/26	34/26	34/25	32/24	29/22	28/21
Max/min °F	83/68	87/70	91/74	96/79	100/81	99/81	94/78	93/77	89/75	85/72	83/70	
Rainfall (mm)	28	33	5	13	38	71	122	137	160	157	152	152
DELHI												
Max/min °C	21/7	24/9	31/14	36/20	41/26	39/28	36/27	34/26	34/24	34/18	29/11	23/8
Max/min °F	70/63	75/48	88/57	97/68	106/79	102/82	97/81	93/79	93/75	93/64	84/52	73/46
Rainfall (mm)	23	18	13	8	13	74	180	173	117	10	3	10
KOLKATA (WB)												
Max/min °C	27/13	29/15	34/21	36/24	36/25	33/26	32/26	32/26	32/26	32/24	29/18	26/13
Max/min °F	81/55	84/59	93/70	97/75	97/77	91/79	90/79	90/79	90/79	90/75	84/64	79/55
Rainfall (mm)	10	31	36	43	140	297	325	328	252	114	20	5
MUMBAI (M)												
Max/min °C	28/19	28/19	30/22	32/24	33/27	32/26	29/25	29/24	29/24	32/24	32/23	31/21
Max/min °F	82/66	82/66	86/72	90/75	91/81	90/79	84/77	84/75	84/75	90/75	90/73	88/70
Rainfall (mm)	3	3	3	0	18	485	617	340	264	64	13	3
PANJIM (GOA)												
Max/min °C	32/19	32/21	32/23	33/25	33/26	30/24	29/24	28/24	29/24	32/24	33/22	32/21
Max/min °F	90/66	90/70	90/73	91/77	91/79	86/75	84/75	82/75	84/75	90/75	91/72	90/70
Rainfall (mm)	0	0	0	0	50	580	650	400	150	90	10	0

Author picks

Our authors have crossed the length and breadth of India in search of the most impressive monuments, sumptuous food and memorable journeys. Here's a list of their personal highlights.

Naga knees-up The spectacular Hornbill Festival, held near the town of Kohima in early December, brings together the tribes of Nagaland dressed in astonishingly beautiful finery for shows of martial arts, dance, archery and music (see page 861).

Microbrewery bars Beer aficionados should check out the new wave of small bars brewing their own fine ales and lagers. So far they're concentrated in Gurgaon (see page 118), Chandigarh (see page 539), Mumbai (see page 606) and Bengaluru (see page 1124), but expect that wave to swell.

The Buddha Trail Buddhism may be bigger elsewhere nowadays, but India is where it all began, and Buddhist pilgrims from across the world flock to sites such as Sarnath (see page 288), Kushinagar (see page 292), Bodhgaya (see page 817) and Nalanda (see page 821).

Masked trance Nothing encapsulates the otherworldly feel of the deep south like the masked spirit possession *theyyem* rituals enacted in villages around the town of Kannur, Kerala (see page 1115).

Toy trains A marvel of Victorian engineering, the "toy train" from Siliguri to Darjeeling (see page 415) is just one of India's amazing narrow-gauge mountain railways. The others run from Kalka to Shimla (see page 430), Pathankot to Joginder Nagar (see page 681), Neral to Matheran (see page 795) and Mettupalayam to Ooty (see page 1050).

Gilded vision Hypnotic *kirtans* (hymns) mingle to magical effect with the reflections of the Sikhs' holiest shrine in the shimmering Amrit Sarovar tank – an intoxicating image of spirituality (see page 533).

To the source Follow a winding dirt trail through the high Himalayas to the source of the sacred River Ganges, where yogis and sadhus bathe in icy water emanating from the snout of a glacier (see page 320).

Our author recommendations don't end here. We've flagged up our favourite places – a perfectly sited hotel, an atmospheric café, a special restaurant – throughout the Guide, highlighted with the ★ symbol.

THEYYAM RITUAL NEAR KUNNUR, KERALA

A SADHU STANDS IN A TREE POSE BY THE SOURCE OF THE RIVER GANGES

30

things not to miss

It's not possible to see everything India has to offer in one trip, and we don't suggest you try. What follows is a selective taste of the country's highlights: outstanding buildings, natural wonders, spectacular festivals and unforgettable journeys. All entries have a page reference to take you straight into the Guide, where you can find out more.

1 JAISALMER
See page 177
Honey-coloured citadel, emerging from the sands of the Thar Desert.

2 KANHA NATIONAL PARK
See page 383
Deep in the eastern tracts of Madhya Pradesh, this park is rich in animal and birdlife, including tigers and even the occasional leopard.

3 KONARK
See page 919
A colossal thirteenth-century temple, buried under sand until its rediscovery by the British.

4 GOKARNA
See page 1159
The beautiful beaches on the edge of this temple town are popular with budget travellers fleeing the commercialism of nearby Goa.

5 TAJ MAHAL
See page 240
Simply the world's greatest building: Shah Jahan's monument to love fully lives up to all expectations.

6 **THRISSUR PURAM**
See page 1107
More than one hundred sumptuously caparisoned elephants march in Kerala's biggest temple festival, accompanied by ear-shattering south Indian drum orchestras.

7 **KHAJURAHO**
See page 371
Immaculately preserved temples renowned for their uncompromisingly erotic carvings.

8 **KOCHI (COCHIN)**
See page 1093
This atmospheric harbourside is strung with elegant Chinese fishing nets.

9 **KEOLADEO NATIONAL PARK, BHARATPUR**
See page 228
Asia's most famous bird reserve, where millions of migrants nest each winter. The perfect antidote to the frenzy and pollution of nearby Agra and Jaipur.

10 **THIKSE**
See page 491
The most architecturally impressive of the many dramatic monasteries within striking distance of Leh.

11 ORCHHA
See page 367
This semi-ruined former capital of the Bundela rajas is an architectural gem, rising up through the surrounding forest.

12 VARANASI
See page 275
City of Light, founded by Shiva, where the bathing *ghats* beside the Ganges teem with pilgrims.

13 MEHRANGARH FORT, JODHPUR
See page 190
The epitome of Rajput power and extravagance, its apartments as sumptuous as the fort is imposing.

14 AMRITSAR
See page 532
The largest city in Punjab, and site of the fabled Golden Temple, the Sikhs' holiest shrine.

15 MAMALLAPURAM
See page 993
A fishing and stone-carving village, with magnificent boulder friezes, shrines and the sea-battered Shore Temple.

11

12

16 KATHAKALI
See page 1062
Kerala is the place to experience *kathakali* and other esoteric ritual theatre forms.

17 ELLORA CAVES
See page 660
Buddhist, Hindu and Jain caves, including the colossal Hindu Kailash temple, carved from a spectacular volcanic ridge at the heart of the Deccan plateau.

18 RATH YATRA, PURI
See page 915
Three colossal chariots with brightly coloured canopies are pulled by crowds of devotees through the streets of eastern India's holiest town.

19 GANGOTRI AND THE GAUMUKH GLACIER
See page 320
The holy and atmospheric village of Gangotri serves as a base for the trek into the heart of the Hindu faith – Gaumukh, the source of the Ganges.

20 HAMPI/ VIJAYANAGAR
See page 1165
The capital of a great Hindu empire, sacked five centuries ago to leave a site strewn with ruins and medieval sculptures.

17

21 UDAIPUR
See page 203
Arguably the most romantic city in India, with ornate Rajput palaces floating in the middle of two shimmering lakes.

22 PALOLEM
See page 740
Exquisite crescent-shaped beach in Goa's relaxed south, famous for its dolphins and local alcoholic spirit, *feni*.

23 DURGA PUJA
See page 753
An exuberant festival held in September or October, when every street and village erects a shrine to the goddess Durga. Kolkata has the most lavish festivities.

24 MANALI–LEH HIGHWAY
See page 468
India's epic Himalayan road trip, crossing some of the highest mountain passes in the world, is the most popular approach to Ladakh, and revered by motorbikers, cyclists and drivers alike.

25 PUSHKAR CAMEL MELA
See page 158
November sees the largest livestock market on earth, where thousands of Rajasthani herders in traditional costume converge on the desert oasis of Pushkar to trade and bathe in the sacred lake.

26 ZANSKAR
See page 507
A barren moonscape with extraordinary scenery and challenging trails over the high passes.

27 MADURAI
See page 1029
Definitive south Indian city, centred on a spectacular medieval temple.

28 DHARAMSALA
See page 430
Perched on the edge of the Himalayas, this is the home of the Dalai Lama and Tibetan Buddhism in exile.

29 BOATING ON THE BACKWATERS OF KERALA
See page 1080
Lazy boat trips wind through the lush tropical waterways of India's deep south.

30 FATEHPUR SIKRI
See page 255
The Mughal emperor Akbar's elegant palace complex now lies deserted on a ridge near Agra, but remains one of India's architectural masterpieces.

Tailor-made trips

India is simply too vast to explore in a single trip. It makes more sense to focus on one, two or perhaps three regions, depending on your time frame. The trips below give a flavour of what the country has to offer and what we can plan and book for you at ⓦroughguides.com/trips.

THE GOLDEN TRIANGLE

No other region of India packs in as many awe-inspiring monuments as the so-called "Golden Triangle" connecting Delhi, Agra and Jaipur. Allow at least a week to complete the circuit, with a diversion south to the tiger reserve at Ranthambore if you've time to spare.

❶ **Delhi** Start out at Shah Jahan's mighty Red Fort in Mughal Old Delhi, then work your way south through the medieval monuments of the city's southern suburbs. See page 80

❷ **Agra** Cross the Yamuna River by boat in the early morning for an unforgettable view of the Taj just after sunrise, then spend the rest of the day ticking off the city's other Mughal splendours. See page 239

❸ **Fatehpur Sikri** Overnight at a guesthouse below the deserted capital of Emperor Akbar to see its deep-red sandstone architecture at its most ethereal, in the diffuse light of dusk and dawn. See page 255

❹ **Keoladeo National Park** Bicycle safaris along the dirt tracks and banks that crisscross this teeming bird reserve offer a perfect antidote to the noise and traffic of India's northern cities. See page 228

❺ **Jaipur** Climb up to the ochre-walled palace of Amber Fort, before spending a day in the textile and gemstone bazaars of the Rajasthani capital – a riot of quintessentially Indian colour. See page 134

❻ **Shekhawati** Set on the fringes of the Thar Desert, the painted havelis (walled mansions) in the market towns of this once rich area make the ideal stopover on the journey back to Delhi. See page 159

AROUND THE "LAND OF KINGS"

India's dazzling desert state, Rajasthan, tends to be the destination of choice for most first-time travellers to India, and with good reason. You'll need at least a month to really do it justice, or three weeks at a pinch.

❶ **Jaipur** The Pink City, with its hectic streets and flamboyant Rajput architecture, is a real baptism of fire. Hilltop viewpoints such as the Tiger Fort and Monkey Temple offer welcome respite from the mayhem. See page 134

You can book these trips with Rough Guides, or we can help you create your own. Whether you're after adventure or a family-friendly holiday, we have a trip for you, with all the activities you enjoy doing and the sights you want to see. All our trips are devised by local experts who get the most out of the destination. Visit **www.roughguides.com/trips** to chat with one of our travel agents.

❷ Ranthambore If sighting a tiger is a priority, aim to spend at least a couple of nights at a camp near this world-famous reserve, where big cats prowl the shores of a ruin-studded lake. See page 225

❸ Pushkar Ringed by the white domes and sacred *ghats* of Hindu shrines, Pushkar makes a perfect base for leisurely desert walks and souvenir hunts. See page 153

❹ Udaipur Dine by candlelight on a haveli rooftop for the ultimate view of the Sisodia maharanas' fairytale palaces, rising from the banks of glassy Fateh Sagar lake. See page 203

❺ Jodhpur Perched on the rim of sheer sandstone cliffs, Rajasthan's most spectacular medieval fortress, Mehrangarh, towers above the warren-like old city painted a hundred shades of sky blue. See page 188

❻ Jaisalmer A long trip across the Thar is rewarded by the sublime vision of Jai Singh's yellow-stone citadel floating above the sand flats. Camel treks can take you deep into the surrounding desert. See page 177

❼ Bikaner Some quirky early twentieth-century architecture and a temple where thousands of rats run free are two vestiges of this city's former prominence on the trans-Thar caravan route. See page 170

❽ Nawalgarh After a succession of big cities, this small town on the fringes of the desert, famed for its elaborately painted merchants' houses, makes an enjoyable base for trips to nearby forts and havelis. See page 160

THE DEEP SOUTH

From the boulder-strewn plains of Tamil Nadu to the lush, intensely tropical coastal strip of Kerala, India's deep south offers a succession of dramatic landscapes and world-class historic monuments. You'll need at least three weeks to cover this route comfortably, or two at a rushed pace travelling with your own transport.

❶ Chennai The old colonial hub of Fort St George is the standout sight of the Tamil capital, but there's also a wealth of succulent southern cuisine on offer. See page 980

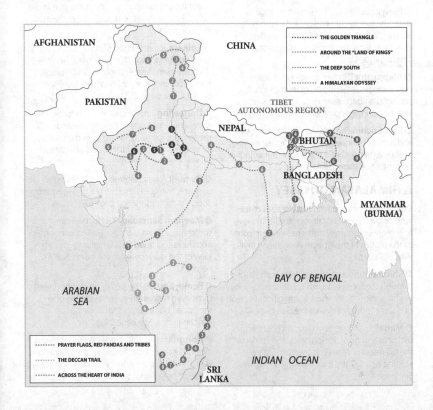

❷ Mamallapuram Sculpted a dozen or more centuries ago by the Pallava kings, Mamallapuram holds a tempting combination of ancient stonework and breezy tropical beaches. See page 993

❸ Puducherry Soak up the lingering Gallic ambience of France's former colony on the Coromandel Coast, ideally from the confines of a heritage hotel. See page 1007

❹ Thanjavur The mighty Brihadishwara Temple and famous collection of Chola bronzes in the town's art gallery make Thanjavur the perfect springboard for explorations of the Kaveri Delta region. See page 1020

❺ Tiruchirapalli (Trichy) Gaze from the summit of Trichy's exotic rock fort across the Kaveri River to the largest temple complex in India, on the island of Srirangam. See page 1025

❻ Madurai The shrine of the Fish-Eyed Goddess is Tamil Nadu's greatest living monument, renowned for its soaring, multicoloured, deity-encrusted gateway towers. See page 1029

❼ Periyar Scale the Western Ghat range to enter the jungles of Kerala's Cardamom Hills, where the Periyar Wildlife Sanctuary offers the chance to sight elephants from a punted raft. See page 1084

❽ Alappuzha This former colonial trading port provides the entry point for trips into the surrounding backwater region of Kuttanad – a watery world like no other in Asia. See page 1077

❾ Fort Cochin The heritage hotels, arty cafés and funky boutiques of Kerala's historic harbour town are the ideal end point for a tour of India's far south. See page 1094

A HIMALAYAN ODYSSEY

Experience the contrasting landscapes of the world's greatest mountain range with this two- to three-week journey from the northern plains to the fringes of the Tibetan Plateau and idyllic Vale of Kashmir.

❶ Shimla Trundle on the toy train from Kalka through the foothills to this quintessentially Raj-era hill station, from where a magnificent spread of distant snow peaks is visible. See page 413

❷ Manali Lush forests of deodar cedars, apple orchards and giant, ice-dusted summits flank the hill resort of Manali, in the Kullu Valley – starting point of the trans-Himalayan highway. See page 453

❸ Leh A breathless, two-day journey across a vast desert of scree and dizzying passes brings you to the capital of Ladakh, marooned in the high Indus Valley. See page 482

❹ The Ladakhi lakes Charter a jeep for the trip southeast to the hypnotically beautiful altitude lakes of Pangong Tso and Tso Moriri. See page 495

❺ Kargil Fairytale Buddhist monasteries and stupendous mountain scenery characterize the long haul to the mid-point on the journey to Kashmir, marked by this Shia Muslim market town. See page 505

❻ Srinagar Laze on the deck of a houseboat sipping spiced tea while the shadows lengthen on the surrounding mountainsides and *shikara* canoes filled with fruit and flowers paddle past. See page 510

PRAYER FLAGS, RED PANDAS AND TRIBES

Kolkata, the capital of West Bengal, is the launch pad for this classic trip through the tea estates around Darjeeling, Sikkim and Northeast India, a beautiful, predominantly Buddhist region in the lap of the Himalayas. You could cover the route in three weeks.

❶ Kolkata Join the flood of commuters crossing the Howrah Bridge, admire the spectacular monuments of the British Empire and discover one of India's tastiest regional cuisines. See page 752

❷ Darjeeling Amazing views of distant Kanchenjunga, a quaint Raj-era vibe and the famous Toy Train ride up from the plains account for the perennial appeal of India's principal tea hub. See page 790

❸ Rumtek A quiet alternative to the capital Gangtok, Rumtek is also the site of a spectacular Buddhist monastery. See page 838

❹ Maenam Sanctuary Tackle the lung-stretching, 1000m ascent of Maenam mountain from Ravangla town for a tantalizing panoramic view of the snow peaks to the north. See page 842

❺ Pemayangtse The poster boy for northeast Himalayan monasteries, Pemayangtse offers the added bonus of spectacular vistas of Kanchenjunga. See page 846

❻ Nongriat Hike 3000 steps to gape at the incredible double decker living root bridge, and stay the night to experience Khasi village life without the crowds. See page 875

❼ Tawang Stop by the Monpa villages of Bomdila and Dirang and their valleys strewn with century-old gompas, and then cross the glacial Sela Pass to reach the world's second biggest Buddhist monastery. See page 880

❽ Majuli Island Explore the world's largest, and shrinking, riverine island on a bicycle and meet the Mising and Assamese peoples that peacefully cohabit it. See page 869

❾ Dzukou Valley Short yet most rewarding hike to a high altitude valley of rolling green mounds between Nagaland and Manipur, blooming with a myriad colourful flowers in the wet season. See page 886

THE DECCAN TRAIL

Despite its extraordinary wealth of historic monuments, the Deccan region of central India sees comparatively few visitors. The rewards for those who do make it are considerable: a succession of astonishing temple sites, crumbling tombs, mosques and deserted capitals spanning sixteen centuries of civilization. Allow at least three weeks for this unforgettable trip.

❶ Hyderabad The convoluted ruins of medieval Golconda, on the outskirts of the city, followed by a climb of the Charminar ("Four Minarets") mosque and a slap-up Hyderabadi feast are the perfect preamble for what lies ahead. See page 933

❷ Bidar Resembling a town on the Central Asian Silk Route, Bidar's rambling fort-palace, madrasa, tombs and metal workshops recall this region's medieval Persian roots. See page 1181

❸ Vijayapura (Bijapur) For three centuries, Bijapur served as the capital of the Deccan. An unparalleled crop of monuments survive from the sixteenth and seventeenth centuries, including India's largest domed tomb, the mighty Gol Gumbaz. See page 1176

❹ Badami, Aihole and Pattadakal The Deccan's ancient Hindu heyday is represented by this trio of wonderful sites – a feast of enigmatic rock-cut caves, monkey-infested temples and tumbledown forts – in the middle of nowhere. See page 1181

❺ Hampi Rent a bicycle to explore the expansive, beautifully carved remains of medieval India's most splendid city, set amid a dreamy landscape of banana groves and boulder hills. See page 1165

❻ Gokarna This compact pilgrimage town on the Konkan coast holds plenty of traditional atmosphere, and a crop of gorgeous beaches around the headland to the south. See page 1159

❼ Goa For a self-indulgent spell soaking up the rays and surf of the Konkan, Goa's hard to beat. Aim for one of the less-developed resorts such as Agonda or Patnem in the south of the state. See page 696

ACROSS THE HEART OF INDIA

Travelling across central India from Mumbai on the Arabian Sea to Puri on the Bay of Bengal gives you the chance to see some of the country's most compelling attractions, relax by the beach, and then fly out from Kolkata. Realistically, you'll need a month for this route, though it could be done in three weeks at a canter.

❶ Mumbai Dynamic and exhilarating, this vast megalopolis bombards the senses with the extremes of urban India, and is an excellent place to sample some of the country's finest dining. See page 606

❷ Aurangabad A superb base from which to visit the breathtaking cave sculptures and carvings at Ellora and Ajanta. Check out, too, the city's own "false Taj", the Bibi-ka-Maqbara. See page 654

❸ Khajuraho Hidden away in India's very centre, this medieval temple complex is decorated with the most eye-popping array of erotica you'll find on any religious building anywhere. See page 371

❹ Lucknow Visit the now-ruined Residency in the capital of Uttar Pradesh, where a besieged British contingent famously held out for five months during the 1857 uprising. Don't leave without sampling the city's succulent *dum pukht* cuisine. See page 261

❺ Varanasi The spiritual capital of India, and one of the oldest cities on earth, where you can see bathing and cremations by the sacred River Ganges, and watch the kids fly their kites from your terrace while monkeys scurry around the rooftops. See page 275

❻ Bodhgaya The Buddha achieved enlightenment while sitting under a *bodhi* tree at Bodhgaya, one of a trio of sacred Buddhist sites within easy striking distance of Varanasi. See page 817

❼ Puri Home of the famous annual Jagannath "Car Festival" (Rath Yatra), Puri is also a low-key beach resort, popular with Indian families and Western backpackers, and an excellent place to recharge your batteries. See page 913

MUMBAI'S VICTORIA TERMINUS, ALSO KNOWN AS CST

Basics

Getting there

Although it's usually possible to arrive overland from neighbouring Nepal, Pakistan, Bangladesh and Bhutan, most visitors fly into India. There are numerous nonstop services from the UK, plus a few nonstop flights from North America and two from Australia. Most of these arrive at either Delhi or Mumbai, although from the UK it's also possible to reach Chennai, Hyderabad and Bengaluru without stopping.

Fares worldwide always depend on the season, with the highest being roughly from November to March, when the weather in India is best; fares drop during the shoulder seasons – April to May and August to early October – and you'll get the best prices during the low season, June and July. The most expensive fares of all are those coinciding with **Diwali** in October/November, when demand peaks as Indian emigrants travel home for holidays with their families.

For Goa or Kerala, you may find it cheaper to pick up a bargain **package deal** from a tour operator (see page 32). At the time of writing, in 2019, a government prohibition on **flight-only charters** had been lifted, and a restriction of 28 days on the period of time a charter ticket can cover had also been dropped. It was also now possible to buy one-way charter flights, but the law on such matters is always prone to change, so check when you are booking.

If arriving overland, the border with Nepal is the least problematic and most popular, with the best crossing located at Sunauli (a long early morning bus journey from Kathmandu). You can walk across the border here 24-hours a day, but vehicles only pass through between 6am and 10pm, and you'll need US dollars with you to pay for your visa. The Phuentsholing-Jaigaon border crossing is the best option for entering from Bhutan, and the Benapole-Petrapole crossing is the most popular for those coming from Bangladesh. The Pakistan border is one of the most heavily guarded in the world and there are just five crossing points, the best of which is at Wagah, where a daily lowering of the flags ceremony is a popular tourist attraction.

Flights from the UK and Ireland

It takes between eight and eleven hours to fly from the UK direct to India. A number of carriers fly nonstop from London Heathrow to Delhi and Mumbai; these currently include Air India (Ⓦairindia.com), Virgin Atlantic (Ⓦvirgin-atlantic.com) and British Airways (Ⓦba.com), who also fly nonstop to Chennai, Hyderabad and Bengaluru. Numerous other European and Middle Eastern carriers offer one-stop services via their home city in Europe or the Gulf. There are direct flights with Air India between Birmingham and Delhi, but if departing from elsewhere in the UK and **Ireland** you'll have to take an indirect flight, changing planes at either Heathrow or somewhere else in Europe, the Middle East or Asia. Both nonstop scheduled fares and flight-only charters usually start from around £450, although indirect routes, usually via the Gulf, can be found for as little as £330 return at slack times.

Flights from the US and Canada

India is on the other side of the planet from the US and Canada. If you live on the east coast it's quicker to travel via Europe, while from the west coast it's roughly the same distance (and price) whether you travel via Europe or the Pacific. There are currently nonstop flights from **New York** to Delhi and Mumbai on Air India and United (Ⓦunited.com). Otherwise, you'll probably stop over somewhere in Europe (most often London), the Gulf, or both. Nonstop flights take around 15–16 hours, with fares from New York to Mumbai/Delhi starting at around US$800, while indirect flights go from as little as US$660. Apart from Air India's new nonstop service from San Francisco to Delhi (16hr), you will have to change when travelling from the west coast, with fares starting at around US$900.

Air Canada (Ⓦaircanada.com) fly nonstop **from Toronto** to Delhi (14hr) from around Can$1100; otherwise you'll have to travel via a connecting city in the US, Europe or Asia with a minimum travel time of around 20 hours.

A BETTER KIND OF TRAVEL

At Rough Guides we are passionately committed to travel. We believe it helps us understand the world we live in and the people we share it with – and of course tourism is vital to many developing economies. But the scale of modern tourism has also damaged some places irreparably, and climate change is accelerated by most forms of transport, especially flying. We encourage our authors to consider the carbon footprint of the journeys they make in the course of researching our guides.

Flights from Australia, New Zealand and South Africa

Air India offer nonstop services to Delhi **from Melbourne and Sydney**, each taking around thirteen hours; otherwise you'll have to make at least one change of plane in a Southeast Asian hub city (usually Hong Kong, Kuala Lumpur, Singapore or Bangkok) with airlines like AirAsia or Fly Scoot. Flying from Melbourne or Sydney fares start from around Aus$900, while **from Auckland** the cheapest fares start at around NZ$1250; add on approximately NZ$200 for flights from Wellington or Christchurch.

There are no nonstop flights between **South Africa** and India, with most services routing via Addis Ababa, Nairobi or the Gulf. Fares start at around ZAR6000 return.

Round-the-world tickets

If India is only one stop on a longer journey, you might want to consider buying a **Round-the-World (RTW) ticket**. Some travel agents can sell you an "off-the-shelf" RTW ticket that will have you touching down in about half a dozen cities (Delhi and Mumbai feature on many itineraries); others will have to assemble one for you, which can be tailored to your needs but is apt to be more expensive. Prices start around £1600/US$2500 for a RTW ticket including India, valid for one year.

Packages and tours

Lots of operators run **package holidays** to India, covering activities ranging from trekking and wildlife-watching through to general sightseeing or just lying on the beach, not to mention more specialist-interest tours focusing on anything from motorbike adventures (see page 38) to food. In addition, many companies can also arrange **tailor-made tours** where you plan your own itinerary. Specialist trips such as trekking and tailor-made tours do not necessarily work out a lot more expensive than organizing everything independently, especially if you want a degree of comfort. Tour operators pay a lot less for better-class hotels and flights than you would, plus they save you time and hassle by knowing the best hotels, routes and sights to feature. On the other hand, a typical package tour can rather isolate you from the country, shutting you off in air-conditioned hotels and cars.

Agents and operators

TRAVEL AGENTS

North South Travel UK ☎ 01245 608 291, ⓦ northsouthtravel. co.uk. Friendly, competitive travel agency, offering discounted fares worldwide. Profits are used to support projects in the developing world, especially the promotion of sustainable tourism.

STA Travel UK ☎ 0333 321 0099, US ☎ 1 800 781 4040, Australia ☎ 134 782, New Zealand ☎ 0800 474 400, South Africa ☎ 0861 781 781; ⓦ statravel.co.uk. Worldwide specialists in independent travel; also student IDs, travel insurance, car rental, rail passes, and more. Good discounts for students and under-26s.

Trailfinders UK ☎ 020 7368 1200, Ireland ☎ 021 464 8800, Australia ☎ 1300 780 212; ⓦ trailfinders.com. One of the best-informed and most efficient agents for independent travellers.

Travel CUTS Canada ☎ 1 800 667 2887, US ☎ 1 800 592 2887; ⓦ travelcuts.com. Canadian youth and student travel firm.

USIT Ireland ☎ 01 602 1906, ⓦ usit.ie. Ireland's main student and youth travel specialists.

TOUR OPERATORS

Audley Travel UK ☎ 01993 838 450, ⓦ audleytravel.com. Tailor-made and small-group tours that use interesting accommodation (homestays, tented camps and heritage properties); they're also strong on wildlife.

Cox & Kings UK ☎ 020 3918 3311, ⓦ coxandkings.co.uk, US ☎ 1 800 209 0400; ⓦ coxandkings.com. Established in India in 1758, with upmarket group and private tours, many featuring Rajasthan and Agra, plus the *Palace on Wheels private rail journey*.

Exodus UK ☎ 0845 287 3644, Ireland ☎ 01 804 7153, US ☎ 1 844 227 9087, Canada ☎ 1 800 267 3347, Australia ☎ 1300 131 564, New Zealand ☎ 0800 838 747; ⓦ exodus.co.uk. Experienced specialists in small-group itineraries, treks and overland tours.

Explore Worldwide UK ☎ 020 3733 5532, US ☎ 1 844 227 9087, Australia ☎ 1300 151 564, New Zealand ☎ 0800 643 997; ⓦ explore.co.uk. Wide range of small-group adventure holidays with exceptional local guides.

G Adventures UK ☎ 0344 272 2060, ⓦ gadventures.co.uk, Ireland ☎ 01 697 1360, US ☎ 1 888 800 4100, Australia ☎ 1300 853 325, New Zealand ☎ 0800 333 415, ⓦ gadventures.com. Group tours for all budgets and ages, though some specifically geared towards 18–39-year-olds.

GeoEx US ☎ 1 888 570 7108, ⓦ geoex.com. Unusual group and customized tours, ranging from Tamil Nadu temple trips to Sikkim village walks.

High Places UK ☎ 0114 352 0060, ⓦ highplaces.co.uk. Sheffield-based trekking and mountaineering specialists; they also run an interesting sixteen-day tour through Kerala.

Insider Tours UK ☎ 07964 375 994, ⓦ insider-tours.com. Some of the most original, "hands-on" and ethical itineraries on the market, taking visitors to wonderful off-track corners of Kerala, Goa, the Northeast and elsewhere.

Intrepid UK ☎ 0808 274 5111, ⓦ intrepidtravel.com. Small group tours for varying budgets across India, including Rajasthan, South India and overland from Kathmandu to Delhi.

Kerala Connections UK ☎ 01892 722440, ⓦ keralaconnections. co.uk. Itineraries in Kerala, as well as Tamil Nadu, Karnataka, Goa and the Andamans, for a wide range of budgets.

Lakshmi Tours UK ☎ 01985 844183, India +91 98 2989 4435, ⓦ lakshmitoursindia.com/tours.htm. Special-interest tours (drawing, textiles, Ayurveda) for small groups, mostly focusing on Rajasthan and Kerala.

Mountain Kingdoms UK ☎ 01453 844400, ⓦ mountainkingdoms.co.uk. Quality treks in Sikkim, Garhwal, Himachal Pradesh, Ladakh and Arunachal Pradesh, plus a Kerala spice trail.

Myths and Mountains US ☎ 1 800 670 6984, ⓦ mythsandmountains.com. Special-interest trips (tailor-made or group) to some very unusual places, ranging from the mountains of Sikkim to deepest Gujarat, with the emphasis on culture, crafts and religion.

Peregrine UK ☎ 020 7206 0079, US ☎ 1 855 832 4859, Australia ☎ 1300 854 445; ⓦ peregrineadventures.com. Small-group wildlife and culture tours in Rajasthan and south India, plus trekking in Ladakh.

Pettitts Travel UK ☎ 01892 250039, ⓦ pettitts.co.uk. Established in 1988, India experts specialising in arranging unique and authentic tailor-made holidays to all regions of the country including Rajasthan, Kerala, Tamil Nadu and North East India.

SD Enterprises ☎ 020 8903 3411, ⓦ indiarail.co.uk. Run by Indian rail experts, SD Enterprises put together itineraries for independent travellers wanting to explore India by train, plus a range of non-choo choo choices.

Unwind Worldwide UK ☎ 0845 875 4010, ⓦ unwindworldwide. com. Wide range of group and tailor-made tours covering most of India.

Jules Verne UK ☎ 020 3131 6796, ⓦ vjv.co.uk. Classic heritage tours, including some by rail.

Entry requirements

Almost everyone requires a visa before travelling to India, though the process for obtaining a standard tourist visa has been streamlined a great deal in recent years, and online applications are now accepted for shorter visits. If you're going to study or work, you'll need to apply for a special student or business visa.

e-Tourist visas

Citizens of the UK, Ireland, the US, Canada, Australia, New Zealand, South Africa and many other countries can apply online for an **e-Tourist Visa** (eTV) through the Indian government's official online portal (ⓦ indianvisaonline.gov.in). These multiple-entry visas are valid for **one year** from the date of issue, allow a maximum stay of **90 days** during each visit, and must be secured at least four days (and no more than thirty days) before travel. You have to fill in the application, upload your

photo and pay the fee online, then carry a printed copy of the eTV with you to India; you'll be issued with your visa on arrival. Fees vary between zero and US$100, depending on your nationality, plus a small bank charge.

Tourist visas

Alternatively, or if you are a passport-holder from one of the few countries not covered by the eTV scheme, you can apply for a standard **tourist visa**, also valid for **one year** (or up to ten years for US citizens) from the date of issue, with a maximum stay during each visit of **180 days**. Fees are a princely £113 for UK citizens but vary greatly for other nationalities – check on the respective websites. You're asked to specify whether you need a single-entry or a multiple-entry visa; as the same rates apply to both, it makes sense to ask for the latter to cover all eventualities. Your passport will need to have at least 180 days' validity.

Visas in the UK, US, Canada and Australia are no longer issued by Indian embassies themselves, but by various third-party companies or subcontractors (see below), for a small additional fee. The firms' websites give all the details you need to make your application. Read the small print carefully and always **make sure you've allowed plenty of time**. Processing time is usually five working days but it's wiser to leave at least a week. **Postal applications** take a minimum of ten working days plus time in transit, and often longer.

Elsewhere in the world, visas are still issued by the relevant local embassy or consulate, though the same caveats apply. Bear in mind too that Indian high commissions, embassies and consulates observe Indian public holidays as well as local ones, so always check opening hours in advance.

Visa agencies

In many countries it's possible to pay a **visa agency** or "visa expediter" (see above) to process the visa on your behalf, which typically costs £60–70/US$100–120, plus the price of the visa. This is worth considering if you're not able to get to your nearest Indian High Commission, embassy or consulate yourself. Prices vary from company to company, as do turnaround times. Two weeks is about standard, but you can get a visa in as little as 24 hours if you're prepared to pay premium rates. For a full rundown of services, check the company websites, from where you can usually download visa application forms.

Visa extensions

It is no longer possible to **extend a tourist visa** in India, though exceptions may be made in special circumstances such as serious illness. Many travellers who want to spend more time in India go to a neighbouring country such as Nepal for a new visa when their old one expires, but there is no guarantee a new one will be issued right away, as you are not officially allowed to spend more than six months in the country within one year.

INDIAN EMBASSIES, HIGH COMMISSIONS, CONSULATES AND VISA-PROCESSING CENTRES ABROAD

Australia c/o VFS Global (ⓦ vfsglobal.com). Offices in all states and territories except Tasmania and NT – see website for contact details.

Canada c/o BLS International (ⓦ blsindia-canada.com). Nine offices countrywide – see website for contact details.

Ireland Embassy: 6 Leeson Park, Dublin 6 ⓣ 01 496 6787, ⓦ indianembassydublin.gov.in.

Nepal c/o Indian Visa Service Centre (IVSC), Kapurdhara Marg 336, Kathmandu ⓣ 01 4410 900, ⓦ indembkathmandu.gov.in.

New Zealand High Commission: Ranchhod Tower 102-112 Lambton Quay, Wellington ⓣ 04 473 6390, ⓦ hicomind.gov.in.

South Africa High Commission: 852 Francis Baard St, PO Box 40216, Arcadia 0007, Pretoria ⓣ 012 342 5392, ⓦ hcisouthafrica. in. Also consulates in Johannesburg, Cape Town and Durban.

Sri Lanka High Commission: 36–38 Galle Rd, Colombo 3 ⓣ 011 232 7587, ⓦ hcicolombo.gov.in; consulate: 31 Rajapihilla Mawatha, PO Box 47, Kandy ⓣ 081 222 3786, ⓦ ahcikandy.gov.in.

UK c/o VFS Global (ⓦ vfsglobal.com). Offices in twelve cities in Britain and Northern Ireland, including three in London – see website for contact details.

US c/o Travisa (ⓦ indiavisa.travisa.com). Offices in Washington, New York, San Francisco, Chicago, Houston and Atlanta – see website for contact details.

VISA AGENCIES

iVisa US ⓣ 1 756 574 6055, ⓦ ivisa.com. Additional offices in Spain and Peru.

CIBT Australia ⓣ 1902 211 133, Canada ⓣ 1 888 665 9956, UK ⓣ 0844 800 4650, US ⓣ 1 800 929 2428; ⓦ cibt.com.

Travel Document Systems US ⓦ traveldocs.com. Offices in Washington DC, Atlanta, Los Angeles, New York, San Francisco and Seattle.

Visa 24 UK ⓣ 0207 190 2999, ⓦ visa24.co.uk.

Visa Connection US & Canada ⓣ 1 416 506 8787, ⓦ visaconnection.biz.

Visa Genie UK ⓣ 020 571 0883, ⓦ visagenie.co.uk.

Getting around

Intercity transport in India may not be the fastest or the most comfortable in the world, but it's cheap and goes more or less everywhere. You generally have the option of train or bus, sometimes plane, and occasionally even boat. Transport around town comes in even more permutations, ranging in Kolkata, for example, from human-pulled rickshaws to a state-of-the-art metro system.

Whether you're on road or rail, public transport or your own vehicle, India offers the chance to try out some classics: narrow-gauge railways, steam locomotives, the Ambassador car and the Enfield Bullet motorbike – indeed some people come to India for these alone.

By train

Travelling by train is one of India's classic experiences. The national rail network covers almost the entire country; only a few places (such as the mountainous regions of Sikkim, Ladakh, Uttarakhand and most of Himachal Pradesh) are inaccessible by train. Although the railway system might look like chaos, it does work, and generally better than you might expect. Trains are often late, of course, sometimes by hours rather than minutes, but they do run, and when the train you've been waiting for rolls into the station, the reservation you made halfway across the country several weeks ago will be on a list pasted to the side of your carriage. You can now track live running statuses of trains with apps like Ixigo (ⓦ ixigo.com), as well as check fares on their website.

It's worth bearing in mind, with journeys frequently lasting twelve hours or more, that an **overnight train** can save you a day's travelling and a night's hotel bill, assuming you sleep well on trains. When travelling overnight, always padlock your bag to your bunk; an attached chain is usually provided beneath the seat of the lower bunk.

Types of train

There are three basic types of passenger train in India. You're most likely to use long-distance **intercity trains** (called "express" or "mail") along with the speedier "**super-fast**" air-conditioned trains – these include the long-established *Rajdhani* expresses, which link Delhi with cities nationwide, and *Shatabdi* expresses, daytime trains that connect major cities, mostly within an eight-hour travelling distance, plus the newer and faster still *Duronto* expresses, which also link major metropolitan areas and have fewer stops. There are also painfully slow local "**passenger**" trains, which stop everywhere, and which you'll only use if you want to get right off the beaten track. In addition to these three basic types of train, there are

RAIL RECORDS

Comprising 115,000km (71,000 miles) of track and over 10,000 locomotives, which transport an average of 23 million passengers every day, India's **rail network** is the second largest in the world, with a workforce of around 1.4 million.

One record the country's transport ministers are somewhat less proud of, however, is Indian Railways' **accident rate**. Between 2014 and 2017, a staggering 50,000 people died in railway-related incidents, including those killed while crossing the tracks, which makes this the most dangerous rail network in the world by a long chalk. Having said that, travelling by rail is considerably safer than using the buses. According to the most recent statistic, over 148,000 people died on the roads in 2015.

also a few dedicated **tourist trains** and other special services, such as the famous *Palace on Wheels* (see page 36) and the toy train to Darjeeling (see page 795).

Classes of train travel

Indian Railways distinguishes between no fewer than eight **classes** of travel. Different types of train carry different classes of carriage, though you'll seldom have more than four to choose from any one service. The simplest and cheapest class, used by the majority of Indians, is **second class** (II or "second seating"), which are mostly unreserved. These basic carriages have hard wooden seats and often become incredibly packed during the day – bearable for shortish daytime journeys, but best avoided for longer trips and (especially) overnight travel, unless you're exceptionally hardy or unusually poor. On the plus side, fares in second-class unreserved are so cheap as to be virtually free. It also represents a way of getting on a train at the last minute if you haven't been able to secure a reserved seat.

Far more civilized, and only around fifty percent more expensive, is regular **sleeper class** (SL) consisting of carriages of three-tiered padded bunks that convert to seats during the day. All seats in these carriages must be booked in advance even for daytime journeys, meaning that they don't get horrendously overcrowded like second-class unreserved, although there's usually still plenty going on, with itinerant chai- and coffee-sellers, travelling musicians, beggars and sweepers passing through the carriages. Overnight trips in sleeper compartments are reasonably comfy. **First class** (FC) consists of non-a/c seating in comfortable if ageing compartments of two to four berths, though this class is being phased out and is now seldom found.

The other five classes are all air-conditioned (available only on inter-city and super-fast trains). **A/c chair class** (CC) cars are found almost exclusively on super-fast services and consist of comfortable reclining seats; they're really designed for daytime

travel, since they don't convert to bunks, and aren't generally found on overnight services. *Shatabdi* expresses are made up entirely of chair-car carriages – ordinary a/c chair car and, for double the price, an **Executive a/c chair class** (EC) car.

There are three classes of air-conditioned sleepers. The cheapest, **a/c 3-tier** (AC3 or 3A), has open carriages with three-tier bunks – basically the same as second-class sleeper, except with a/c and bedding. Less crowded (and found on more services) is **a/c 2-tier** (AC2 or 2A), which has two-tier berths. Most comfortable of all is **a/c first-class** (AC1 or 1A), which consists of two-tier bunks in two- or four-person private compartments, complete with carpeting and relatively presentable bathrooms – although fares can work out more expensive than taking a plane.

Note that bed linen is provided free on most a/c services, while bottled water, snacks and simple meals are included in the ticket price of *Rajdhani*, *Shatabdi* and *Duronto* services.

Ladies' compartments now only exist on suburban trains in big cities, though the number of families travelling means that single women are at least unlikely to end up in a compartment with only men. You can always ask the ticket inspector to change your seat if you feel uncomfortable. Some stations also have ladies-only waiting rooms.

Timetables and fares

Fares, **timetables** and availability of berths can be checked online at Indian Railways' cumbersome website (ⓦ indianrail.gov.in), or via the more streamlined, privately run ⓦ cleartrip.com. Indian Railways' *Trains at a Glance* (₹70; updated twice a year) contains timetables of all inter-city and super-fast trains and is available from information counters and newsstands at all main stations.

All rail fares are calculated according to the exact **distance** travelled. *Trains at a Glance* prints a chart of fares by kilometres, and also gives the distance in kilometres of stations along each route in the timetables, making it possible to calculate what the basic fare will be for any given journey. By way of comparison, the cost for each class of travel for a ticket from New Delhi to Mumbai is approximately as follows: AC1 ₹4800; AC2 ₹3100; AC3 ₹2300; CC ₹800; SL ₹600; and II ₹350.

Reserving tickets

It's important to plan your train journeys in advance, as demand often makes it impossible to buy a long-distance ticket on the same day that you want to travel – although the Tatkal quota system (see below) has made life a little easier. Travellers following tight itineraries tend to buy their departure tickets from particular towns the moment they arrive to avoid having to trek out to the station again. At most large stations, it's possible to reserve tickets for journeys starting elsewhere in the country.

Online booking is best done via the privately run ⓦcleartrip.com, which accepts foreign Visa cards and MasterCards (with a 1.8 percent fee, plus an additional ₹20 booking charge); you will first have to register with them and Indian Railways (ⓦirctc.co.in) – check out ⓦseat61.com/India.htm for a clear explanation of this convoluted procedure. Bookings may be made from 120 days in advance right up to four hours before the scheduled departure time of the train. Cleartrip.com also handles Tatkal tickets (see below). Having booked your travel, you can then print out your own e-tickets, taking this along with some photo ID, such as a passport, when you board the train. A viable alternative to Cleartrip.com is ⓦmakemytrip. com, which also accepts some foreign credit cards, though you'll need a smartphone to download the app for train booking.

When **reserving a ticket in person** at a railway station, the first thing you'll have to do is fill in a little form at the booking office stating your name, age and sex, your proposed date of travel, and the train you wish to catch (giving the train's **name and number**). Most stations have computerized booking counters and you'll be told immediately whether or not seats are available. **Reservation offices** in the main stations are generally open from Monday to Saturday from 8am to 8pm with a short break for lunch, and on Sunday to 2pm. In larger cities, major stations have special tourist sections to cut queues for foreigners, with helpful English-speaking staff. Elsewhere, buying a ticket can often involve a longish wait, though women often have dedicated queues or can try simply walking to the head of the queue and forming their own "ladies' queue". A few stations also operate a number system of queueing, allowing you to repair to the chai stall until your number is called. A good alternative to queueing yourself is to get someone else to buy your ticket for you. Many **travel agents** will do this for a

small fee (typically around ₹50–100); alternatively, ask at your accommodation if they can sort it out.

Quotas and late-availability tickets

If there are no places available on the train you want, you have a number of choices. First, some seats and berths are set aside as a "**tourist quota**" – ask at the tourist counter of the reservations hall if you can get in on this, or else try the stationmaster. This quota is available in advance but usually only at major or originating stations. Failing that, other special quotas, such as one for "emergencies", only released on the day of travel, may remain unused – however, if you get a booking on the emergency quota and a pukka emergency or VIP turns up, you lose the reservation. Alternatively, you can stump up extra cash for a **Tatkal** ticket, which guarantees you access to a special ten percent quota on most trains, though certain catches and conditions apply. Bookable online and at any computerized office, these are released from 10am the day before the train departs, and there's a surcharge of ₹75–300, depending on the class of travel.

RAC – or "Reservation Against Cancellation" – tickets are another option, giving you priority if sleepers do become available. The ticket clerk should be able to tell you your chances. With an RAC ticket you are allowed onto the train and can sit until the conductor can find you a berth. The worst sort of ticket to have is a **wait-listed** one – identifiable by the letter "W" prefixing your passenger number – which will allow you onto the train (though not *Shatabdi*, *Rajdhani* or *Duronto* trains) but not in a reserved compartment; in this case go and see the ticket inspector (TTI) as soon as possible to persuade him to find you a place if one is free. For short journeys or on minor routes you won't need to reserve tickets in advance.

Luxury tourist trains

Inspired by the *Orient Express*, Indian Railways offers high-end holiday packages aboard luxury **tourist trains**. The flagship of the scheme is the **Palace on Wheels** (ⓦpalaceonwheels.net), with sumptuous ex-maharajas' carriages updated into modern air-conditioned coaches, still decorated with the original designs. An all-inclusive, eight-day whistle-stop tour (Sept–April weekly) starts at US$4550 per person for the full trip, with the cheapest rates off-season (Sept and April). Note that the train is often booked up for months ahead, so early reservations are advised.

The *Palace on Wheels* has proved so popular that it has spawned a number of similar heritage trains, including *Royal Rajasthan on Wheels* and *Maharajas' Express*. Details of all these tours, including fares, can be found on the *Palace on Wheels* website.

By plane

Considering the huge distances involved in getting around the country, and the time it takes to get from A to B, **flying** is an attractive option, despite the cost – the journey from Delhi to Chennai, for example, takes a mere 2 hours 30 minutes by plane compared to 36 hours on the train. Delays and cancellations can whittle away the time advantage, especially over small distances, but if you're short of time and plan to cover a lot of ground, flying can be a godsend. There was a proliferation of low-cost airlines in the early years of the millennium and after a few failures, most notably Kingfisher Airlines in 2012, a further crop has popped up in recent years. At the time of writing in 2019, Jet Airways had suspended all flights due to on-going financial issues, and look certain to permanently cease operations imminently.

Booking flights is most easily done online via the airline's website. Larger carriers also have offices in major cities, as well as at the airports they fly to; these are listed in the relevant guide chapters. Children under twelve pay half fare and under-twos (one per adult) pay ten percent.

DOMESTIC AIRLINES

Air Asia Ⓦ airasia.com.
Air India Ⓦ airindia.com.
Air India Express Ⓦ airindiaexpress.in.
GoAir Ⓦ goair.com
IndiGo Airlines Ⓦ goindigo.in.
SpiceJet Ⓦ spicejet.com.
Vistara Ⓦ airvistara.com.

By bus

Although trains are generally the most atmospheric and comfortable way to travel in India, there are some places, particularly in the Himalayas, not covered by the rail network, or where trains are inconvenient. By contrast, **buses** go almost everywhere, usually more frequently than trains (though mostly in daylight hours), and are also sometimes faster (including in parts of Rajasthan and other places without broad-gauge track). Going by bus also usually saves you the bother of reserving a ticket in advance.

Services vary enormously in terms of price and standard. Ramshackle **government-run buses**, packed with people, livestock and luggage, cover most routes, both short- and long-distance. In addition, popular routes between larger cities, towns and resorts are usually covered by **private buses**. These tend to be more comfortable, with extra legroom, tinted windows and padded reclining seats. Note, however, that smaller private bus companies may be only semilegal and have little backup in case of breakdown.

The description of the service usually gives some clue about the level of comfort. "Ordinary" buses usually have minimally padded, bench-like seats with upright backs. "Deluxe" or "Luxury" are more or less interchangeable terms but sometimes the term deluxe signifies a luxury bus past its sell-by date; occasionally a bus will be described as a "2 by 2" which means a deluxe bus with just two seats on either side of the aisle. When applied to government services, these may hardly differ from "ordinary" buses, but with private companies, they should guarantee a softer, individual seat. It's worth asking when booking if your bus will have a video or music system (a "video bus"), as their deafening noise ruins any chances of sleep. Always try to avoid the back seats – they accentuate bumpy roads.

Luggage travels in the hatch of private buses – for which you may have to part with about ₹10–20 for the safekeeping of your bags. On state-run buses, you can usually squeeze it into an unobtrusive corner, although you may sometimes be requested to have it travel on the roof (you may be able to travel up there yourself if the bus is too crowded, though it's dangerous and illegal); check that it's well secured (ideally, lock it there) and not liable to get squashed. Baksheesh is in order for whoever puts it up there for you.

In recent years, there has been a revolution in **online booking** services, which allow you to compare schedules and fares, buy tickets online and even to select your seat. Two of the best are Ⓦ makemytrip.com and Ⓦ redbus.in, both of which also have downloadable apps. Buying a bus ticket at the bus station is usually less of an ordeal than buying a train ticket, although at large city bus stations there may be twenty or so counters, assigned to different routes. When you buy your ticket you'll be given the registration number of the bus and, sometimes, a seat number. As at railway stations, women can form a separate, quicker, "ladies' queue".

You can usually only pay on board on most ordinary state buses, and at bus stands outside major cities. Prior booking is usually available and preferable for express and private services, and it's a good idea to check with the agent exactly where the bus will depart from. You can usually pay on board private buses too, though doing so reduces your chances of a seat.

By shared jeep

Another common and useful means of transport, especially in mountain areas, is **shared jeeps**, whose size and four-wheel drives are ideal for the bumpy terrain. These ply fixed routes and tend to depart at fairly fixed times from designated locations, usually in town centres. The number of passengers varies from six to ten, according to the type of vehicle and how willing the owner is to cram people in. The two most commonly used models are the Tata Sumo and Tempo Traveller.

Prices are fixed, although it's wise to check the going rate with an independent source if possible. Expect to pay roughly 50–100 percent more than the bus fare and note that it sometimes costs a bit more to sit in the prime front seat next to the driver. A typical fare from Jammu to Srinagar, for example, is ₹850. Jeeps can also be rented directly or through an agency for customized trips, sometimes of several days.

By boat

Apart from river ferries, few **boat services** run in India. The Andaman Islands are connected to Kolkata and Chennai by boat – as well as to each other (see page 960). Kerala has a regular passenger service with a number of services operating out of Alappuzha and Kollam, including the popular "backwater trip" between the two (see page 1080). The Sundarbans in the delta region to the south of Kolkata is only accessible by boat (see page 779).

By car

It is much more usual for tourists to be driven in India than it is for them to drive themselves; **car rental** firms operate on the basis of supplying **vehicles with drivers**. You can arrange them through any tourist office or taxi firm, and local taxi drivers hanging around hotels and city ranks are also available for day hire. Cars start around ₹2000 (£22/US$28) per day, which should include a maximum of 200km, with additional kilometres charged at around ₹10 per kilometre. On longer trips, the driver sleeps in the car, for which his firm may charge an additional ₹200–300. You should generally tip the driver around ₹200 per day, too. It is important to confirm exactly what the terms and costs of the rental are before you set off.

App-based ride-hailing services are widely used by locals in big cities and can be far cheaper than traditional cabs, but visitors should proceed with caution. While it's tempting to go for the easy fixed-price option, the quality of driver varies wildly. There are security concerns, too, as tension between taxi drivers and app-based drivers is rife, and there have been reports of violence. The situation is changing rapidly as drivers are demanding better working conditions and pay, so keep abreast of the local situation before

hailing a ride. Uber (ⓦuber.com) and Ola (ⓦolacabs. com) are the two most common apps and both require an internet connection to do the initial ordering. If you don't have a phone, hotel staff may be willing to order via their own devices and add the cost onto your bill.

Tourists still occasionally succumb to the romance of that quintessentially Indian automobile, the **Hindustan Ambassador** Mark IV, based on the design of the old British Morris Oxford. Sadly, however, the car's appalling suspension and back-breaking seats make it among the most uncomfortable rides in the world. All in all, you'll be much better off in a modern two- or four-door hatchback – ask your rental company for the options. Air-conditioning adds considerably to the rate, and with larger cars such as SUVs, the daily rate is higher and tends only to cover the first 80km, after which stiff additional per-kilometre charges apply.

Self-drive

A handful of big international chains offer **self-drive** car rental in India, but unless you've had plenty of experience on the country's notoriously dangerous roads, we strongly recommend you leave the driving to an expert. If you do drive yourself, expect the unexpected, and expect other drivers to take whatever liberties they can get away with. **Traffic** in the cities is particularly undisciplined; vehicles cut in and out without warning, and pedestrians, cyclists and cows wander nonchalantly down the middle of the road. In the country the roads are narrow, often in terrible repair, and hogged by overloaded Tata trucks that move aside for nobody, while something slow-moving like a bullock cart or a herd of goats can take up the whole road. It is particularly dangerous to drive at night – cyclists and cart drivers hardly ever have lights. If you are involved in an **accident**, it might be an idea to leave the scene quickly and go straight to the police to report it; mobs can assemble fast, especially if pedestrians or cows are involved.

By motorbike

Riding a **motorbike** in India is not for the faint-hearted. Besides the challenging road and traffic conditions (see above) with the resultant stress and fatigue, simply running an unfamiliar bike can become a nightmare.

Buying a motorbike in India is only for the brave. If it's an old classic you're after, the 350- or 500cc Enfield Bullet, sold cheapest in Puducherry on the Tamil Nadu coast, leads the field, with models becoming less idiosyncratic the more recent they are. If low price and practicality are your priorities, a smaller model from the likes of Bajaj, built in India but based on dependable old Japanese designs, may fit the bill if not the image. Delhi's Karol Bagh area is renowned for its motorcycle shops and rental agencies (see page 110). Obviously, you'll have to haggle over the price, but you can expect to pay half to two-thirds of the original price for a bike in reasonable condition. Given the right bargaining skills, you can sell it again later for a similar price – perhaps to another foreign traveller – by advertising it in hotels and restaurants. A certain amount of bureaucracy is involved in transferring vehicle ownership to a new owner but a garage should be able to put you on to a broker ("auto consultant") who, for a modest commission (around ₹1000–2000), will help you find a seller or a buyer and do the necessary paperwork.

Motorbike **rental** is available in many tourist towns and can be fun for local journeys, but the condition of the bike can be hit and miss. However, unless you know your stuff, this is a better strategy than diving in and buying a machine. Unlike with sales, it's in a rental outfit's interest to rent you a bike that works. Mechanically, the important thing to establish is the condition of the chain and sprockets, whether the machine starts and runs smoothly and, not least, whether both brakes and lights work (even so, riding at night is inadvisable). An in-depth knowledge of mechanics is not so necessary as every town has a bike mender who will be no stranger to Enfields.

A recommended firm in Delhi, both for purchasing bikes and for rental, is **Bulletwallas** (☎97 186 4 7447), at 7 Arakashan Rd, Multani Dhanda in the Paharganj district. An Aussie-run outfit, they specialize in Enfields, selling new, used and customized machines with only quality parts.

Without doubt the least stressful way of enjoying India on a motorbike, especially a temperamental but characterful Enfield, is joining one of several **motorbike tours**. They focus on the best locales with minimal traffic and amazing landscapes – the Himalayas, Rajasthan and Kerala – and remove much of the stress from what is still an adventure.

MOTORBIKE TOUR AGENCIES

Blazing Trails Tours UK ☎05603 666788, ☻blazingtrailstours. com.
Classic Bike Adventure India Goa 68467, ☻classic-bike-india. com.
Himalayan Roadrunners US ☎802 738 6500, ☻ridehigh.com.
Live India UK ☎07869 373 805, ☻liveindia.co.uk.
World On Wheels Australia ☎02 9970 6370, ☻ferriswheels. com.au.

By bicycle

In many ways a **bicycle** is the ideal form of transport in India, offering total independence without loss of contact with local people. You can camp out, though there are cheap lodgings in almost every village – take the bike into your room with you – and, if you get tired of pedalling, you can put it on top of a bus as luggage, or transport it by train.

Bringing a bike from abroad requires no special paperwork but spare parts and accessories may be of different sizes and standards in India, so you may have to improvise. Bring basic spares and tools, and a pump. **Buying a bike** in India couldn't be easier, since most towns have cycle shops and even entire markets devoted to bikes. The advantages of a local bike are that spare parts are easy to get, locally produced tools and parts will fit, and your bike will not draw a crowd every time you park it. Disadvantages are that Indian bikes tend to be heavier and less state-of-the-art than ones from abroad; mountain bikes are beginning to appear in cities and bigger towns, but with insufficient gears and a low level of equipment, they're not worth buying. Selling should be quite easy: you won't get a tremendously good deal at a cycle market but you may well be able to sell privately, or even to a rental shop.

Bicycles can be **rented** in most towns, usually for local use only, though better mountain bikes can be rented in some mountain areas: this is a good way to find out if your legs and bum can survive an Indian bike before buying one. Rates can be anything from ₹30 to ₹200 per day; you may have to leave a deposit or your passport as security. Several adventure-tour operators offer bicycle tours of the country (see page 32), with most customers bringing their own cycles.

As for **contacts**, International Bicycle Fund in the US (☎206 767 0848, ☻ibike.org) publishes information and offers advice on bicycle travel around the world and maintains a useful website. In India, the Cycling Federation of India (☎011 2375 3528, ☻cyclingfeder-ationofindia.org) is the main cycle-sports organization.

City transport

Transport around towns takes various forms. City **buses** can get unbelievably crowded, so beware of pickpockets, razor-carriers, pocket-slitters and "Eve-teasers" (see page 73); the same applies to **suburban trains** in Mumbai (Chennai is about the only other place where you might want to use trains for local city transport). Any visitor to Delhi or Kolkata will be amazed by the clean efficiency of the cities' two **metro** systems, with more under construction in Bengaluru, Chennai, Hyderabad, Jaipur, Lucknow and elsewhere.

You can also take **taxis**, usually rather battered Ambassadors (painted black and yellow in the large cities) and Maruti omnivans. With luck, the driver will agree to use the meter; in theory you're within your rights to call the police if he doesn't, but the usual compromise is to agree a fare for the journey before you get in. Naturally, it helps to have an idea in advance what the fare should be, though any figures quoted in this or any other guide should be treated as being the broadest of guidelines only. From places such as main stations, you may be able to find other passengers to share a taxi to the town centre. Many stations, and certainly most airports, operate **prepaid taxi schemes** with set fares that you pay before departure; more expensive prepaid limousines are also available. **App-based taxi-booking** companies are also making their presence felt, with Uber (ⓦ uber.com) now operating in 25 cities and India's own Ola (ⓦ olacabs.com) becoming very popular.

That most Indian of vehicles, the **auto-rickshaw** – commonly referred to as just an "auto" – is the front half of a motor scooter with a couple of seats mounted on the back. Cheaper than taxis, better at nipping in and out of traffic, and usually metered (although in many cities few drivers are willing to use them – you should agree a fare before setting off if that is the case), auto-rickshaws are a little unstable and their drivers often rather reckless but that's all part of the fun. In major tourist centres rickshaw-walas can, however, hassle you endlessly on the street, often shoving themselves right in your path to prevent you from ignoring them, and once you're inside may try to take you to several shops before reaching your destination. In general it is better to hail a rickshaw than to take one that's been following you, and to avoid those that hang around outside posh hotels. Apps for booking auto-rickshaws are even starting to appear. Some towns also have larger versions of auto-rickshaws known as **tempos** (or Vikrams), with six or eight seats behind, which usually ply fixed routes at flat fares.

Here and there, you'll come across horse-drawn carriages, or **tongas**. Tugged by underfed and often lame horses, these are the least popular with tourists. Slower and cheaper still is the **cycle rickshaw** – basically a glorified tricycle. Foreign visitors often feel uncomfortable about travelling this way; except in the major tourist cities, cycle rickshaw-walas are invariably emaciated pavement-dwellers who earn only a pittance for their pains. In the end, though, to deny them your custom on those grounds is spurious logic; they will earn even less if you don't use them. As a foreigner you'll probably be quoted grossly inflated fares, but ask yourself if it's really worth haggling over tiny sums, which they could probably do with more than you. Kolkata is the only city where rickshaw-walas continue to haul pukka rickshaws **on foot** (see page 768).

If you want to see a variety of places around town, consider renting a taxi, rickshaw or auto-rickshaw for the day. Find a driver who speaks English reasonably well and agree a price beforehand. You will probably find it a lot cheaper than you imagine: the driver will invariably act as a guide and source of local knowledge, so tipping is usually in order.

FIVE TOP BUDGET PLACES TO STAY

Backpacker Panda, Mumbai An excellent, modern hostel in the heart of Colaba. See page 631

Chachoo Palace, Srinagar Welcoming hotel right on the banks of Dal Lake. See page 514

Emerald Gecko, Havelock Island Laidback bamboo huts beside a pristine beach. See page 966

Garuda, Upper Pelling Favourite haunt of trekkers in Sikkim. See page 848

Walton's Homestay, Fort Cochin Beautifully converted mansion with lovely terrace and garden. See page 1101

Accommodation

There are far more Indians travelling around their own country at any one time – whether for holidays, on pilgrimages or for business – than there are foreign tourists, and a vast infrastructure of hotels and guesthouses caters for their needs. On the whole, accommodation, like so many other things in India, provides good value for money, though in the major cities, especially, there are luxury establishments that charge international prices for providing Western-style comforts and service. In recent years, there has also been a dramatic increase in the number of homestays in some parts of the country. Most places to stay now offer wi-fi and this should be assumed, unless otherwise stated in a specific listing in the guide.

Budget accommodation

While accommodation prices in India are generally on the up, there's still an abundance of inexpensive **hotels** and **hostels** catering for foreign backpackers,

ACCOMMODATION PRICES

Accommodation prices quoted throughout this guide are for the **cheapest double room during the main tourist season**, where one exists, but not for short spikes during peak periods, such as those that occur in the hill stations from April to July or in Rajasthan, Goa and Kerala over Christmas and New Year. Notable regional price fluctuations, including slack periods when great discounts can be had, are mentioned in the accommodation listings throughout the Guide chapters.

Where **two prices** are given, it denotes the cost of a double with shared bathroom first ("non-attached"), followed by the en-suite ("attached") option. **Dorm prices** per person are also quoted separately where applicable. If the review states that a hotel has some air-conditioned rooms, you can usually reckon on them costing 50–100 percent more than the non-a/c ones.

Not all hotels offer **single rooms**, so it can often work out more expensive to travel alone; in hotels that don't, you may be able to negotiate a slight discount. It's not unusual to find rooms with three or four beds, however – great value for families and small groups.

Like most other things in India, the price of a room may well be open to **negotiation**. If you think the price is too high, or if all the hotels in town are empty, try haggling. You may get nowhere – but nothing ventured, nothing gained.

Note that all hotels and guesthouses are required by law to have an official list of approved room prices. Some establishments, especially the cheaper ones, ignore this rule, while others do not display the rates. It is always worth asking for the "**tariff list**", if you cannot see it, as a starting point for any bargaining. In cheap hotels and hostels, you needn't expect any additions to your basic bill, but as you go up the scale, you'll find **taxes and service charges** creeping in, sometimes adding as much as a third on top of the original tariff. Service is generally ten percent, but taxes are a matter for local governments and vary from state to state. We have endeavoured to include tax in the prices throughout this guide, but readers should always check in advance to avoid nasty, and expensive, surprises.

---

tourists and less-well-off Indians. It's still easy to find a double room for ₹600–800, and rates outside big cities and tourist centres may fall as low as ₹300 (roughly £3/US$4.50). The rock-bottom option is usually in a dormitory of a hostel or lodge, where you may even pay less than ₹100. Even cheaper still are **dharamshalas**, hostels run by religious establishments and used by pilgrims (see page 43).

Budget accommodation varies from filthy fleapits to homely guesthouses and, naturally, tends to be cheaper the further you get off the beaten track. It's most expensive in Delhi, Mumbai, Goa and resorts of Kerala, where prices are at least double those for equivalent accommodation in most other parts of the country.

The cheapest rooms usually have flimsy beds and thin, lumpy mattresses. Most places now offer en-suite bathrooms (or "**attached**" rooms, as they're known locally) and hot water, either on tap or in a bucket, though shared showers and toilets with only cold water are still fairly common at the bottom of the range – in our reviews in the Guide we have assumed that establishments have attached rooms and noted exceptions. It's always wise to check out the state of the bathrooms and toilets before taking a room. Bedbugs and mosquitoes are other things to check for – splotches of blood around the bed and on the walls where people have squashed them are telltale signs.

If a **taxi or rickshaw driver** tells you that the place you ask for is full, closed or has moved, it's more than likely that it's because he wants to take you to a hotel that pays him commission – added, in some cases, to your bill. Hotel touts operate in many popular tourist spots, working for commission from the hotels they take you to; this can become annoying and they should be given a wide berth unless you are desperate.

Mid-range hotels

Even if you value your creature comforts, you don't need to pay through the nose for them. A large clean room, freshly made bed, your own spotless bathroom and hot and cold running water can still cost as little as ₹1000 (£10/US$15) in cheaper areas. Extras that bump up the price include local taxes (see box below), a TV, mosquito nets, a balcony and, above all, **air-conditioning**. Abbreviated in this book (and in India itself) as a/c, air-conditioning is not necessarily the advantage you might expect – in some hotels you can find yourself paying double for a system that is so dust-choked and noisy as to be more of a drawback than an advantage. Some offer **air-coolers** instead of a/c – these can be noisy and are less effective than full-blown a/c, but much better than just a fan. They're only found in drier climes as they don't work in areas

FIVE TOP LUXURY PLACES TO STAY

Chettinadu Mansion, Kanadukathan
Delightful heritage mansion containing many original features. See page 1037
Taj Falaknuma, Hyderabad Palatial luxury in the former nizam's residence. See page 940
Imperial, Delhi The capital's classiest hotel occupies an Art Deco building. See page 111
Lake Palace, Udaipur Lavishly converted palace in the middle of the lake. See page 202
Shergarh, Kanha National Park Eco-friendly and relaxing jungle hideaway. See page 385

of extreme humidity such as along the coasts of south India and the Bay of Bengal. Many medium-priced hotels also have attached restaurants, and also offer room service.

Most state governments run their own chain of hotels. They are usually good value but far less well run than comparable places in the private sector. We've reviewed such chain hotels throughout this guide. Bookings for state-run hotels can be made in advance through the state tourist offices throughout the country.

Upmarket hotels

Recent years have seen a proliferation in the number of luxury hotels throughout India, which charge ₹5000 and above. Roughly speaking, they fall into three categories. Pitched primarily at visiting businessmen, smart, Western-style hotels with air-conditioning and swanky interiors are to be found predominantly in towns and city centres. Because competition among them is rife, tariffs tend to represent good value for money, especially in the upper-mid-range bracket. Formal five-star chains such as Taj, India's premier hotel group, charge international rates – as most of their guests are on expense accounts or staying as part of discounted tour packages. Note that many top-end hotels offer significant **reductions to their rack rates** if you **book online**.

Holding more appeal for foreign visitors are the **heritage properties** that have mushroomed all across the country in recent years. Rajasthan started the trend, with old forts, palaces, hunting lodges, havelis and former hunting camps converted into accommodation for high-spending tourists. Brimming with old-world atmosphere, they deliver a

quintessentially Indian "experience", often in the most exotic locations, with turbaned bellboys and antique automobiles adding to the colonial-era ambience. Other states were quick to get in on the act, and these days you can stay in fabulous Tamil mansions; colonial tea bungalows in Coorg or the Nilgiris; wooden, gabled-roofed *tharavadus* (ancestral homes) in the Keralan backwaters; and Portuguese *palacios* in Goa. Quite a few wildlife sanctuaries also offer atmospheric, high-end accommodation in former hunting lodges, tented camps or treehouses, while down in Kerala, you can also experience the lakes and lagoons of the backwaters on a converted rice barge.

The third category, which is gaining in popularity in cities and touristic areas, is **boutique hotels**, modelled on Western lines. With much less of a corporate feel than business hotels, these tend to be smaller and place a greater emphasis on service and modern design features; some may occupy heritage properties.

Other options

Unsurprisingly, India has fully embraced the new global sharing economy and it's increasingly possible to find great places to stay via websites such as Ⓦ **airbnb.com** and Ⓦ **couchsurfing.org**. **Servas** (Ⓦ servas.org), established in 1949 as a peace organization, is also devoted to providing places in people's homes, representing more than six hundred hosts in India; you have to join before travelling by applying to the local Servas secretary (via the website).

Homestays, often as organized as hotels but with a far more personal touch, have been established for some time in places like Mumbai, Goa and Kerala. These have now spread far and wide, encompassing other states such as parts of Himachal Pradesh, Ladakh, Karnataka and Tamil Nadu. **Farmstays**, **rural villas** and **ecolodges** have also all mushroomed in popularity in recent years. None of these options are cheap, rarely costing less than ₹2000, but all aim to provide a more authentic experience, whether that is the chance to literally feel part of the family or to learn something about the local wildlife and environment, or even to participate in projects.

YMCAs and **YWCAs**, mostly confined to big cities, can be plusher and pricier than mid-range hotels. They are usually good value but are often full and some are exclusively single-sex. Official and non-official **youth hostels**, some run by state governments, are spread haphazardly across the country. They give HI cardholders a discount but rarely exclude non-members, nor do they usually impose daytime closing. Prices match the cheapest hotels; where there is a youth hostel, it usually has a dormitory and may well be the best budget accommodation available – which goes especially for the Salvation Army ones. A more modern, Western-style breed of **hostels** has started popping up in major cities and tourist destinations from Rajasthan to Tamil Nadu. These are aimed directly at backpackers and tend to provide better facilities than the old-style hostels, as well as pleasant communal areas ideal for socializing. Widespread chains include *Backpacker Panda* (Ⓦ backpackerpanda.com) and *Zostel* (Ⓦ zostel.com).

Camping is generally restricted to wildlife reserves, where the Forest Department lay on low-impact accommodation under canvas for visitors, and to beach resorts in which building is restricted by local coastal protection laws. Except on mountain treks, it's not usual simply to pitch a tent in the countryside. In some mountain areas, however, there are surprisingly upmarket **tent camps**, which provide spacious and luxurious options for staying in the great outdoors.

Many railway stations have "**retiring rooms**": basic private rooms with a bed and bathroom (some stations have dorms, too). They can be handy if you're catching an early morning train, and are usually among the cheapest accommodation available anywhere, but can be noisy. Retiring rooms cannot be booked in advance and are allocated on a first-come-first-served basis; just turn up and ask if there's a vacancy.

Finally, **religious institutions**, particularly Sikh *gurudwaras*, offer accommodation for pilgrims and visitors, which may include tourists; a donation is often expected, and certainly appreciated, but some of the bigger ones charge a fixed, nominal fee. Pilgrimage sites, especially those far from other accommodation, also have *dharamshalas* where visitors can stay – very cheap and very simple, usually with basic, communal washing facilities; some charitable institutions even have rooms with simple attached bathrooms. *Dharamshalas*, like *gurudwaras*, offer accommodation either on a donations system or charge a nominal fee, which can be as low as ₹25.

CHECKOUT TIMES

Checkout time is often noon, but confirm this when you arrive: some expect you out by 9am, but many others operate a 24hr system, under which you are simply obliged to leave by the same time as you arrived. Some places let you use their facilities after the official checkout time, sometimes for a small charge, while a few won't even let you leave your baggage after checkout unless you pay for another night.

Eating and drinking

Indian food has a richly deserved reputation as one of the world's great cuisines. Stereotyped abroad as the ubiquitous "curry", the cooking of the Subcontinent covers a wealth of different culinary styles, with myriad regional variations and specialities, from the classic creamy meat and fruit Mughlai dishes of the north through to the banana-leaf vegetarian thalis of the south.

For **vegetarians**, in particular, Indian food is a complete delight. Some of the Subcontinent's best food is meat-free, and even confirmed carnivores will find themselves tucking into delicious dhals and vegetable curries with relish. Most religious Hindus, and the majority of people in the south, don't eat meat or fish, while some orthodox Brahmins and Jains also avoid onions and garlic, which are thought to inflame the baser instincts. **Veganism** is not common, however; if you're vegan, you'll have to keep your eyes open for eggs and dairy products. Many eating places state whether they are vegetarian or non-vegetarian either on signs outside or at the top of the menu. The terms used in India (and throughout our eating listings) are "veg" and "non-veg". You'll also see "pure veg", which means that no eggs or alcohol are served. As a rule, **meat-eaters** should exercise caution in India: even when meat is available, especially in the larger towns, its quality can be poor, except in the best restaurants, and you won't get much in a dish anyway – especially in cheaper canteens where it's mainly there for flavouring. Hindus, of course, do not eat beef and Muslims shun pork, so you'll only find those in a few Christian enclaves such as the beach areas of Goa, and Tibetan areas. Note that what is called "mutton" on menus is in fact goat.

Where to eat

Broadly speaking, eating establishments divide into three main types: cheap and unpretentious local cafés (known variously as *dhabas*, *bhojanalayas* and *udupis*); Indian restaurants aimed at more affluent locals; and tourist restaurants. **Dhabas** and **bhojanalayas** are cheap cafés, where food is basic but often good, consisting of vegetable curry, dhal (a kind of lentil broth), rice or Indian bread (the latter more standard in the north) and sometimes meat. Often found along the sides of highways, *dhabas* traditionally cater to truck drivers – one way of telling a good *dhaba* is to

MORE ON FOOD AND DRINK
We give more advice on **drinking water** in the Health section (see page 50). There's a glossary of **food terms** in the Language section (see page 1227).

judge from the number of trucks parked outside. *Bhojanalayas* are basic eating places, usually found in towns (especially around bus stands and train stations) in the north and centre of the country; they tend to be vegetarian, especially those signed as "Vaishno". Both *dhabas* and *bhojanalayas* can be grubby – look them over before you commit yourself. The same is rarely true of their southern equivalent, **udupi** canteens, which offer cheap, delicious snacks such as masala dosa, *idli*, *vada* and rice-based dishes, all freshly cooked to order and served by uniformed waiters.

There are all sorts of **Indian restaurants**, veg and non-veg and typically catering to Indian businessmen and middle-class families. These are the places to go for reliably good Indian food at bargain prices. The more expensive Indian restaurants, such as those in five-star hotels, can be very expensive by local standards, but offer a rare chance to try top-notch classic Indian cooking, and still at significantly cheaper prices than you'd pay back home – assuming you could find Indian food that good.

Tourist restaurants, found across India wherever there are significant numbers of Western visitors, cater specifically for foreign travellers with unadventurous taste buds, serving up a stereotypical array of pancakes, omelettes, chips, muesli and fruit salad, along with a basic range of curries. The downside is that they tend to be relatively pricey, while the food can be very hit and miss – Indian spaghetti bolognese, enchiladas and chicken chow mein can be every bit as weird as you might expect. International-style **fast food**, including burgers (without beef – usually chicken or mutton) and pizzas, is also available in major cities. Some restaurants offer wi-fi access but it's still not the norm. National and international chains such as Café Coffee Day, McDonald's and Starbucks are reliable options for finding internet access with your meal; this guide highlights independent establishments where good wi-fi is available.

Indian food

The basic distinction in Indian food is between the cuisines of the north and south. **North Indian food** (which is the style generally found in Indian restaurants abroad) is characterized by its rich meat and vegetable dishes in thick tomato, onion and yogurt-based sauces, accompanied by thick breads. **South Indian food**, by contrast, is largely vegetarian, with spicy chilli and coconut flavours and lots of rice, either served in its natural state or made into one of the south's distinctive range of pancakes, such as the dosa, *idli* and *uttapam*, although coastal areas serve plenty of fish dishes.

What Westerners call a "curry" covers a huge variety of dishes, each made with a different masala, or mix of **spices**. Commonly used spices include chilli, turmeric, garlic, ginger, cinnamon, cardamom, cloves, coriander – both leaf and seed – cumin and saffron. Garam masala ("hot mix") is a combination of spices often added to a dish at the last stage of cooking to spice it up. **Chilli** is another key element in the Indian spice cabinet, but the idea that all Indian food is fiery hot is a complete myth. North Indian food, in particular, tends to be quite mildly spiced, often more so than Indian food in restaurants abroad. South Indian food can be hotter but not invariably so. If you can't take the heat, there are mild dishes such as korma and biryani where meat or vegetables are cooked with rice. Indians tend to assuage the effects of chilli with chutney, *dahi* (curd) or *raita* (curd with mint and cucumber, or other herbs and vegetables). Otherwise, beer is one of the best things for washing chilli out of your mouth; the essential oils that cause the burning sensation dissolve in alcohol, but not in water.

Vegetarian curries are usually identified (even on menus in English) by the Hindi names of their main ingredients, such as *paneer* (cheese), *alu* (potatoes), *chana* (chickpeas) or *mutter* (peas). **Meat curries** are more often given specific names such as korma or *dopiaza*, to indicate the kind of masala used or the method of cooking.

North Indian food

North Indian cooking has been heavily influenced by the various Muslim invaders who arrived in the Subcontinent from Central Asia and Persia. They gave Indian cooking many of its most popular dishes and accompaniments, such as the biryani and the

HOTEL OR RESTAURANT?
Somewhat confusingly, places serving traditional meals in India frequently call themselves "**hotels**", even though they do not offer accommodation. This is particularly common in the south, where you'll often come across men waving signs on roadsides advertising a "hotel", when it's no more than a lunch stop.

naan bread, as well as its relatively greater emphasis on meat compared to the south. The classic north Indian fusion of native and Central Asian influences (although it can be found as far south as Hyderabad) is so-called **Mughlai cooking**, the creation of the Mughal dynasty. Mostly non-veg, the food is mildly spiced but extremely rich, using ingredients such as cream, almonds, sultanas and saffron – the classic **korma** sauce is the best-known example.

The other big northern style is **tandoori**. The name refers to the deep clay oven (*tandoor*) in which the food is cooked. Tandoori chicken is marinated in yogurt, herbs and spices before cooking. Boneless pieces of meat, marinated and cooked in the same way are known as tikka; they may be served in a medium-strength masala (tikka masala), one thickened with almonds (*pasanda*), or in a rich butter sauce (*murg makhani* or butter chicken). Breads such as naan and *roti* are also baked in the *tandoor*.

A main dish – which may be a curry, but could also be a dry dish such as a kebab, or a tandoori dish without a masala – is usually served with a dhal and bread. Rice is usually an optional extra in north India and has to be ordered separately. **Bread** comes in a number of varieties, all of them flatbreads rather than loaves. **Chapatti** is a generic term for breads, but tends to refer to the simplest, unleavened type. It's usually made from wheat flour. The term **roti** is likewise generic, and a *roti* can be exactly the same as a chapatti, but the term tends to refer more to a thicker bread baked in a *tandoor*. In good Muslim cooking, delicately thin *rumali roti* ("handkerchief" bread) often accompanies rich meat and chicken dishes. **Naan** is leavened, thick and chewy, and invariably baked in a *tandoor*; it's a favourite in non-veg restaurants as it best accompanies rich meaty dishes. You may also come across fried breads, of which **paratha** (or *parantha*) is rolled out, basted with ghee, folded over and rolled out again several times before cooking, and often stuffed with ingredients such as potato (*alu paratha*); it's popular for breakfast. **Puris** are little fried puffballs. **Poppadum** (*papad*) is a crisp wafer made from lentil flour and is typically served as an appetizer.

Many restaurants also offer set meals, or **thalis**. A thali is a stainless-steel tray with a number of little dishes in it, containing a selection of curries, a chutney and a sweet. In the middle you'll get bread and usually rice. In many places, waiters will keep coming round with refills until you've had enough.

There's an enormous variety of regional cuisines across the north. **Bengalis** love fish and cook a mean *mangsho* (meat) curry as well as exotic vegetable dishes such as *mo-cha* – cooked banana flower. They also like

FIVE TOP PLACES TO EAT: NON-VEG

Ahdoo's, Srinagar A great place to sample rich meat-based Kashmiri *wazwan* cuisine. See page 516

Karim's, Old Delhi Atmospheric spot for tasty kebabs and mouthwatering Mughlai dishes. See page 113

Le Club, Puducherry A stylish touch of French *je ne sais quoi*. See page 1011

Paradise, Hyderabad Huge, plush restaurant serving wonderful biryanis and kebab dishes. See page 941

The Tibetan Kitchen, Leh Enjoy some of the best *thukpas* and *momos* you will find anywhere. See page 488

to include fish bones for added flavour in their vegetable curries – a nasty surprise for vegetarians. **Tibetans** and **Bhotias** from the Himalayas have a simple diet of *thukpa* (meat soup) and *momo* (meat dumplings), as well as a salty tea made with either rancid yak butter (where available) or with ordinary butter. In **Punjab** and much of northern India, home cooking consists of dhal and vegetables along with *roti* and less rice than the Bengalis. Food in **Gujarat**, predominantly veg, is often cooked with a bit of sugar. Certain combinations are traditional and seasonally repeated, such as *makki ki roti* (fried corn bread) with *sarson ka sag* (mustard-leaf greens) around Punjab and other parts of north India. *Baingan bharta* (puréed roast aubergine) is commonly eaten with plain yogurt and *roti*.

South Indian food

The food of south India is a world away from that of the north. Southern cooking also tends to use a significantly different repertoire of spices, with sharper, simpler flavours featuring coconut, tamarind, curry leaves and plenty of dried red and fresh green chillies. **Rice** is king, not only eaten in its natural form but also made into regional staples such as *idlis* (steamed rice cakes), *idiyyapams* (steamed rice-noodle cakes) and dosas (fermented rice-batter pancakes), such as the ubiquitous **masala dosa**, a potato curry wrapped in a crispy lentil-flour pancake. An alternative to the dosa is the *uttapam*, which is thicker, often with onions or another vegetable fried into its body. The lavish breads that are such a feature of north Indian cooking aren't usually available, apart from the fluffy little puri. Meat is comparatively uncommon in the brahmin-dominated temple towns of Tamil Nadu, but available throughout Kerala, where there are sizeable Christian and Muslim minorities.

FIVE TOP PLACES TO EAT: VEG OR SEAFOOD

Annalakshmi, Chennai Recipes with Ayurvedic properties are available in this beautifully decorated place. See page 991

Apoorva, Mumbai Top-quality Mangalorean coconut-based delights, especially seafood. See page 636

Jina Resort, Little Andaman Exquisite fish and veg dishes in a simple, friendly environment. See page 973

Kewpie's Kitchen, Kolkata Superb fish and seafood in a private home. See page 773

Sri Krishna Café, Mattancherry Pure-veg Keralan meals at bargain prices. See page 1102

Set meals are another common feature in the south, where they are generally referred to simply as "meals". They generally consist of a mound of rice surrounded by various vegetable curries, *sambhar* dhal, chutney and curd, and usually accompanied by puris and *rasam*, a thin, hot, peppery soup. Traditionally served on a round metal tray or thali (also found in north India), with each side dish in a separate metal bowl, set meals are sometimes presented on a section of banana leaf instead. In most traditional restaurants, you can eat as much as you want, and staff circulate with refills of everything.

In the south, even more than elsewhere, eating with your fingers is *de rigueur* and cutlery may be unavailable in cheap restaurants. Wherever you eat, remember to use only your **right hand**, and wash your hands before you start. Try to avoid getting food on the palm of your hand by eating with the tips of your fingers.

Snacks and street food

India abounds in **snacks** and **street food**. *Chana puri*, a chickpea curry with a puri (or sometimes another type of bread, a *kulcha*) to dunk, is a great favourite in the north; *idli sambhar* – lentil and vegetable sauce with rice cakes to dunk – is the southern equivalent. Street finger-food includes *bhel puris* (a Mumbai speciality consisting of a mix of puffed rice, deep-fried vermicelli, potato and crunchy puri with tamarind sauce), *pani puris* (the same puris dunked in peppery and spicy water – only for the seasoned), *bhajis* (deep-fried cakes of vegetables in chickpea flour), samosas (vegetables or occasionally meat in a pastry triangle, fried), and pakoras (vegetables or potato dipped in chickpea flour batter and deep-fried). In the south, you'll also come across the ever-popular *vada*,

a spicy deep-fried lentil cake which looks rather like a doughnut.

Kebabs are common in the north, most frequently *seekh* kebab, minced lamb grilled on a skewer, but also *shami* kebab, small minced-lamb cutlets. Kebabs rolled into griddle-fried bread, known as *kathi* or *kaati* rolls, originated in Kolkata but are now available in other cities as well. With all street snacks, though, remember that food left lying around attracts germs – make sure it's freshly cooked. Be especially careful with snacks involving water, such as *pani puris*, and cooking oil, which is often recycled. Generally, it's a good idea to acclimatize to Indian conditions before you start eating street food.

You won't find anything called "**Bombay mix**" in India, but there's no shortage of dry, spicy snack mixes, often referred to as *channa chur*. Jackfruit chips are sometimes sold as a savoury snack – though they are rather bland – and cashew nuts are a real bargain. Peanuts, also known as "monkey nuts" or *mumfuli*, usually come roasted and unshelled.

Non-Indian food

Chinese food is widely available throughout India. It's generally cooked by Indian chefs and isn't exactly authentic, except in the few Indian cities (most notably Kolkata) that have large Chinese communities, where you can get very good Chinese cuisine.

Tourist restaurants and backpacker cafés nationwide offer a fair choice of **Western food**, from unpretentious little bakeries serving cakes and sandwiches to smart tourist restaurants dishing up fine Italian cooking on candlelit terraces. However, quality is variable. Cities such as Delhi, Mumbai and Bengaluru are also home to a range of specialist non-Indian restaurants featuring Tex-Mex, Thai, Japanese, Italian and French cuisines – these are usually found in luxury hotels.

In addition to these places, international **fast-food** chains such as *Pizza Hut*, *Domino's*, *KFC* and *McDonald's* serve the same standard fare as elsewhere in the world at much cheaper prices.

Sweets

Most Indians have rather a sweet tooth and **Indian sweets**, usually made of milk, can be very sweet indeed. Of the more solid type, *penda i*, a kind of fudge made from milk which has been boiled down and condensed, varies from moist and delicious to dry and powdery. It comes in various flavours from plain creamy white to *pista* (pistachio) in livid green and is often sold covered with silver leaf (which you eat). Smoother-textured, round *penda* and thin diamonds of *kaju katli*, plus moist *sandesh* and the harder *paira*, both popular in Bengal, are among many other sweets made from *chhana* (boiled-down milk with whey). Crunchier *mesur* is made with chickpeas; numerous types of gelatinous halwa, not the Middle Eastern variety, include the rich *gajar ka halwa* made from carrots and cream.

Jalebis, circular orange tubes made of deep-fried treacle and dripping with syrup, are as sickly as they look. *Gulab jamuns*, deep-fried spongy dough balls soaked in syrup, are just as unhealthy. Another popular sweet is the round *ladoo*, essentially made from sugar, ghee and flour, though the ingredients may vary from region to region. Among Bengali sweets, widely considered to be the best are *rasgullas*, rosewater-flavoured cream-cheese balls floating in syrup. *Ras malai*, found throughout north India, is similar, but soaked in cream instead of syrup. Down south, *payasam* – a rice or vermicelli pudding flavoured with cardamom, saffron and nuts – is a popular dessert, with special versions served during major festivals.

Chocolate is improving rapidly in India and you'll find various Cadbury's and Amul bars. None of the various indigenous brands of imitation Swiss and Belgian chocolates are worth eating.

Among the large **ice-cream** vendors, Kwality (owned and branded as Wall's), Amul, Gaylord and Dollops stand out. Uniformed men push carts of ice cream around and the bigger companies have many imitators, usually quite obvious. Some have no scruples – stay away from water ices unless you have a seasoned constitution. Ice-cream parlours selling elaborate concoctions are very popular; Connaught Circus in Delhi has several. Be sure to try **kulfi**, a pistachio- and cardamom-flavoured frozen dessert which is India's answer to ice cream; bhang kulfi (popular during the festival of Holi) is laced with cannabis and has an interesting kick to it, but should be approached with caution.

Fruit

What fruit is available varies with region and season, but there's always a fine choice. Ideally, you should peel all fruit, including apples, or soak them in strong iodine or potassium permanganate solution for half an hour. Roadside vendors sell fruit which they often cut up and serve sprinkled with salt and even masala – don't buy anything that looks like it's been hanging around for a while.

Mangoes of various kinds are usually on offer but not all are sweet enough to eat fresh – some are used for pickles or curries. Indians are very picky about their mangoes, which they feel and smell before buying; if you don't know the art of choosing the fruit, you could be sold the leftovers. Among the species appearing at different times in the season, which lasts from spring to summer, look out for Alphonso and Langra. **Bananas** of one sort or another are also on sale all year round, and **oranges and tangerines** are generally easy to come by, as are sweet **melons** and thirst-quenching watermelons.

Tropical fruits such as coconuts, papayas (pawpaws) and pineapples are more common in the south, while things such as lychees and pomegranates are very seasonal. In the north, **temperate fruit** from the mountains can be much like that in Europe and North America, with strawberries, apricots and even rather soft apples available in season.

PAAN

You may be relieved to know that the red stuff you still occasionally see people spitting onto the streets isn't blood, but juice produced by chewing **paan** – a digestive, commonly taken after meals, and also a mild stimulant, found especially in the northeast, where it is fresh and much stronger.

Paan consists of chopped or shredded nut (always referred to as betel nut, though in fact it comes from the areca palm), wrapped in a leaf (which *does* come from the betel vine) that is first prepared with ingredients such as *katha* (a red paste), *chuna* (slaked white lime), *mitha masala* (a mix of sweet spices, which can be ingested) and *zarda* (chewing tobacco, not to be swallowed on any account, especially if made with *chuna*). The triangular package thus formed is wedged inside your cheek and chewed slowly. In the case of *chuna* and *zarda* paans, you should spit out the juice as you go.

Paan, and paan masala, a mix of betel nut, fennel seeds, sweets and flavourings, are sold by paan-walas, often from tiny stalls squeezed before shops. Paan-walas develop big reputations; those in the tiny roads of Varanasi are the most renowned, asking astronomical prices for paan made to elaborate specifications including silver and even gold foil. Paan is an acquired taste; novices should start off, and preferably stick with, the sweet and harmless *mitha* variety, which is perfectly all right to ingest.

Among less familiar fruit, the **chiku**, which looks like a kiwi and tastes a bit like a pear, is worth a mention, as is the watermelon-sized **jackfruit**, whose spiny green exterior encloses sweet, slightly rubbery yellow segments, each containing a seed. Individual segments are sold at roadside stalls.

Non-alcoholic drinks

India sometimes seems to run on **tea**, or chai, grown in Darjeeling, Assam and the Nilgiri Hills, and sold by chaiwalas on just about every street corner. Tea is usually made by putting tea leaves, milk and water in a pan, boiling it all up, straining it into a cup or glass with lots of sugar and pouring back and forth from one cup to another to stir. Ginger and/or cardamom are often added. If you're quick off the mark, you can get them to hold the sugar. English tea it isn't, but most travellers get used to it. Sometimes, especially in tourist spots, you might get a pot of European-style "tray" tea, generally consisting of a tea bag in lukewarm water – you'd do better to stick to the pukka Indian variety, unless, that is, you are in a traditional tea-growing area.

Coffee is becoming increasingly popular, with a growing number of cafés and restaurants now investing in proper coffee machines, especially in the major cities and tourist centres. There are now hundreds of branches of chains – *Café Coffee Day* (*CCD*) is by far the biggest, followed by *Barista* – and a growing number of independent outlets. In the south, coffee is just as common as tea, and generally far better than it is in the north. One of the best places to get it is in outlets of the *Indian Coffee House* chain, found in every southern town and occasionally in the north. A whole ritual is attached to the drinking of milky Keralan coffee in particular, poured in flamboyant sweeping motions between tall glasses to cool it down.

Soft drinks are ubiquitous. Coca-Cola and Pepsi have now largely replaced (or bought out) their old Indian equivalents such as Campa Cola and Thums Up, although you'll still find the pleasantly lemony Limca. All contain a lot of sugar but little else: adverts for Indian soft drinks have been known to boast "Absolutely no natural ingredients!" None will quench your thirst for long.

More recommendable is **water**, either treated or boiled tap water (see page 50) or bottled water (though quality may be suspect). You'll also find cartons of Frooti, Jumpin, Réal and similar brands of **fruit juice** drinks, which come in mango, guava, apple and lemon varieties. If the carton looks at all mangled, it is best not to touch it as it may have been recycled.

At larger stations, there will be a stall on the platform selling Himachali apple juice. Better still, green **coconuts**, common around coastal areas especially in the south, are cheaper than any of these and sold on the street by vendors who will hack off the top for you with a machete and give you a straw to suck up the coconut water (you then scoop out the flesh and eat it). You will also find street stalls selling freshly made sugar-cane juice: delicious, and not in fact too sweet, but not always safe healthwise.

India's greatest cold drink, **lassi**, is made with beaten curd and drunk either sweetened with sugar, salted, or mixed with fruit. Varying widely from smooth and delicious to insipid and watery, it is sold at virtually every café, restaurant and canteen in the country. Freshly made **milkshakes** are also commonly available at establishments with blenders. They'll also sell you what they call a fruit juice, but which is usually fruit, water and sugar (or salt) liquidized and strained; also, street vendors selling fresh fruit juice in less than hygienic conditions are apt to add salt and garam masala. With all such drinks, however appetizing they may seem, you should exercise great caution in deciding where to drink them.

Alcohol

Prohibition has been making something of a comeback in Modi's India and in 2016 Bihar joined Gujarat, Nagaland and Manipur in having a total alcohol ban for the general public. Other states such as Kerala, Tamil Nadu, Andhra Pradesh and some other states retain partial prohibition in the form of "dry" days, high taxes, very restrictive licences, and health warnings on labels.

Alcoholic enclaves in prohibition states can become major drinking centres: Daman and Diu in Gujarat, and Puducherry and Karaikal in Tamil Nadu are the main ones. Goa, Sikkim and Mahé (Kerala) join them as places where the booze flows especially freely and cheaply. Interestingly, all were outside the British Raj. Liquor permits – free, and available from Indian embassies, high commissions and tourist offices abroad, from tourist offices in Delhi, Mumbai, Kolkata and Chennai, at airports on arrival and even online – allow those travellers who bother to apply for one to evade certain restrictions in Gujarat.

Beer is widely available, if rather expensive by local standards. Price varies from state to state, but you can usually expect to pay around ₹100–240 for a 650ml bottle. A pub culture, not dissimilar to that of the West, has taken root among the wealthier classes in cities like Bengaluru and Mumbai and also in Delhi. Kingfisher, King's Black Label and Foster's are still the leading brands but there are plenty of others, and **microbreweries** are increasingly making their presence felt in some metropolitan areas (see page 118). The mainstream lagers tend to contain chemical additives, including glycerine, but are still fairly palatable if you can get them cold. In certain places, notably unlicensed restaurants in Tamil Nadu and Kerala, beer comes in the form of "special tea" – a teapot of beer, which you pour into and drink from a teacup to disguise what it really is.

A cheaper, and often delicious, alternative to beer in Goa and Kerala and other southern states is **toddy** (palm wine). In Bengal it is made from the date palm, and is known as *taddy*. Sweet and nonalcoholic when first tapped, it ferments within twelve hours. In the Himalayas, the Bhotia people (of Tibetan stock) drink *chang*, a beer made from millet, and one of the nicest drinks of all – *tumba*, where fermented millet is placed in a bamboo flask and topped with hot water, then sipped through a bamboo pipe.

Spirits usually take the form of "Indian Made Foreign Liquor" (IMFL), although the foreign liquor industry is expanding rapidly. Some Scotch, such as Seagram's 100 Pipers, is now being bottled in India and sold at a premium, as is Smirnoff vodka, among other known brands. Some of the brands of Indian whisky are not too bad and are affordable in comparison; gin and brandy can be pretty rough, while Indian rum is sweet and distinctive. In Goa, *feni* is a spirit distilled from coconut or cashew fruit. Steer well clear of illegally distilled *arak* (*araq*) however, which often contains methanol (wood alcohol) and other poisons. A look through the press, especially at festival times, will soon reveal numerous cases of blindness and death as a result of drinking bad hooch (or "spurious liquor" as it's called). Licensed country liquor, sold in several states under such names as *bangla*, is an acquired taste. Indian **wine** – despite the challenging climate – is improving with each year thanks to efforts of a few pioneering vineyards in Maharashtra and Karnataka such as Sula and Grover Zampa (see page 652). It's not as cheap as other Indian alcohol – expect to pay around ₹300 for a glass – but is a good alternative to the wildly overpriced foreign wine available in upmarket restaurants and luxury hotels.

Health

There are plenty of scare stories about the health risks of travelling in India, but in fact cases of serious illness are very much the exception rather than the rule. Standards of hygiene and sanitation have increased greatly over the past couple of decades and there's no reason you can't stay healthy throughout your trip – indeed many travellers now visit the Subcontinent without even experiencing the traditional dose of "Delhi belly". Having said that, it's still important to be careful, keep your resistance high and to be aware of the dangers of untreated water, mosquito bites and undressed open cuts. It's worth knowing, if you are ill and can't get to a doctor, that almost any medicine can be bought over the counter without a prescription.

Precautions

When it comes to **food**, be wary of dishes that appear to have been reheated. Anything boiled, fried or grilled (and thus sterilized) in your presence is usually all right, though seafood and meat can pose real risks if they're not fresh; anything that has been left out for any length of time, or stored in a fridge during a power cut, is best avoided. Raw unpeeled fruit and vegetables should always be viewed with suspicion, and you should steer clear of salads unless you know they have been washed in purified water.

Be vigilant about **personal hygiene**: wash your hands often, especially before eating. Keep all cuts clean, treat them with iodine or antiseptic (a liquid or dry spray is better in the heat) and cover them to prevent infection.

It's not just your stomach that needs protecting, though. India's **air pollution** reached an all-time high in 2018, with levels in Delhi quite literally off the government's pollution monitor chart. Big cities like Agra, Delhi, Lucknow and Srinagar are among the worst, but rural areas suffer too. It's most severe in the northern half of the country, and "pollution season" begins around October as a result of cooler temperatures and slow winds. Consider packing a facemask to filter the air as you breathe and avoid exercise like running or cycling in the worst-affected areas.

Advice on avoiding **mosquitoes** is offered under "Malaria" (see page 51). If you do get bites or itches, try not to scratch them: it's difficult, but infection and tropical ulcers can result if you do. Tiger Balm and even dried soap may relieve the itching.

Finally, especially if you are going on a long trip, have a **dental check-up** before you leave home.

Vaccinations

No **inoculations** are legally required for entry into India, but tetanus, typhoid and hepatitis A jabs are

WHAT ABOUT THE WATER?

One of the chief concerns of many prospective visitors to India is whether the water is safe to drink. Tap water is best avoided, even though locals happily gulp it down, but many hotels and restaurants have modern filtration systems that remove most of the risks. **Bottled water**, available in all but the most remote places, is an even safer bet, though it has a major drawback – namely the **plastic pollution** it causes. Visualize the size of the pile of plastic you'd leave behind after getting through a couple of bottles per day, then imagine that multiplied by millions and you have something along the lines of the amount of non-biodegradable landfill waste generated each year by tourists alone.

The best solution as regards your health and the environment is to purify your own water. **Chemical sterilization** using **chlorine** is completely effective, fast and inexpensive, and you can remove the nasty taste it leaves with neutralizing tablets or lemon juice.

Alternatively, invest in some kind of **purifying filter** incorporating chemical sterilization to kill even the smallest viruses. An ever-increasing range of compact, lightweight products are available these days through outdoor shops and large pharmacies, but pregnant women or anyone with thyroid problems should check that iodine isn't used as the chemical sterilizer.

recommended for travellers to many parts of the country, and it's worth ensuring that you are up to date with diphtheria, polio and other boosters. Vaccinations for hepatitis B, rabies, meningitis, Japanese encephalitis and TB are only advised if you're travelling to remote areas or working in environments with an increased exposure to infectious diseases.

Transmitted through contaminated food and water or through saliva, **hepatitis A** can lay a victim low for several months with exhaustion, fever and diarrhoea. Symptoms include yellowing of the whites of the eyes, general malaise, orange urine (though dehydration could also cause that) and light-coloured stools. If you think you have it, get a diagnosis as soon as possible, steer clear of alcohol, get lots of rest – and try to avoid passing it on. More serious is **hepatitis B**, transmitted like AIDS through blood or sexual contact.

Typhoid fever is also spread through contaminated food or water, but is rare in most parts of India. It produces a persistent high temperature with malaise, headaches and abdominal pains, followed by diarrhoea.

Cholera, spread the same way as hepatitis A and typhoid, causes sudden attacks of watery diarrhoea with cramps and debilitation. Again, this disease rarely occurs in India, breaking out in isolated epidemics; there is a vaccination but it offers very little protection. Most medical authorities now recommend immunization against meningococcal **meningitis (ACWY)** too. Spread by airborne bacteria (through coughs and sneezes for example), it is a very unpleasant disease that attacks the lining of the brain and can be fatal.

Rabies is widespread throughout the country, and the best advice is to give dogs and monkeys a wide berth – do not play with animals at all, no matter how

cute they might look. If you're bitten or scratched and it breaks the skin, immediately wash the wound gently with soap or detergent, apply alcohol or iodine if possible, and go straight away to the nearest hospital for an anti-rabies jab.

For up-to-the-minute information, make an appointment at a travel clinic. These clinics also sell travel accessories, including mosquito nets and first-aid kits.

MEDICAL RESOURCES FOR TRAVELLERS

International Society for Travel Medicine ⓦ istm.org. A full list of clinics worldwide specializing in travel health.

IN THE UK AND IRELAND

Hospital for Tropical Diseases Travel Clinic UK ☎ 020 3456 7891, ⓦ thehtd.org.

MASTA (Medical Advisory Service for Travellers Abroad) UK ☎ 0330 100 4200, ⓦ masta-travel-health.com. Dozens of clinics across the UK.

Tropical Medical Bureau Ireland ☎ 01 271 5200, ⓦ tmb.ie.

IN THE US AND CANADA

Canadian Society for International Health Canada ☎ 1 613 241 5785, ⓦ csih.org. Extensive list of travel health centres in Canada.

CDC US ☎ 1 800 232 4636, ⓦ cdc.gov. Official US government health site, including travel.

IN AUSTRALIA, NEW ZEALAND AND SOUTH AFRICA

Netcare Travel Clinics South Africa ☎ 082 911, ⓦ netcare.co.za. Travel clinics in South Africa.

Travellers' Medical & Vaccination Centre Australia ⓦ traveldoctor.com.au. Website listing travellers' medical and vaccination centres throughout Australia and New Zealand.

Heat trouble

The sun and the heat can cause a few unexpected problems. Before they've acclimatized, many people get a bout of **prickly heat rash**, an infection of the sweat ducts caused by excessive perspiration that doesn't dry off. A cool shower, zinc oxide powder (sold in India) and loose cotton clothes should help. **Dehydration** is another possible problem, so make sure you're drinking enough liquid, and drink rehydration salts frequently, especially when hot and/or tired. The main danger sign is irregular urination (only once a day for instance); dark urine definitely means you should drink more (although it could also indicate hepatitis).

The **sun** can burn, or even cause sunstroke; a high-factor sun block is vital on exposed skin, especially when you first arrive. A light hat is also a very good idea, especially if you're doing a lot of walking around in the sun.

Finally, be aware that overheating can cause **heatstroke**, which is potentially fatal. Signs are a very high body temperature, without a feeling of fever but accompanied by headaches and disorientation. Lowering body temperature (taking a tepid shower for example) and resting in an air-conditioned room is the first step in treatment; also take in plenty of fluids and seek medical advice if the condition doesn't improve after 24 hours.

Malaria

Though India has made some progress in its attempts to control **malaria**, the disease remains one of the Subcontinent's big killers. It's essential that you check with your doctor whether you'll need to take anti-malarial medication for your visit. The disease, caused by a parasite carried in the saliva of female *Anopheles* mosquitoes, can be found in many parts of India, and is especially prevalent in Odisha, Chhattisgarh and the northeast, although nonexistent in the high Himalayan regions (there's a useful malaria map of the country at ⓦ bit.ly/MalariaMap, showing varying levels of risk across the country). Malaria has a variable incubation period of a few days to several weeks, so you can become ill long after being bitten – which is why it's important to carry on taking the tablets even after you've returned home.

Ideas about appropriate **antimalarial medication** tend to vary from country to country and prophylaxis remains a controversial subject; it's important that you get expert medical advice on which treatment is right for you. In addition, resistance to established antimalarial drugs is growing alarmingly – none of the following provides complete protection, so avoiding being bitten in the first place remains important.

Chloroquine- and proguanil-resistant strains of malaria are particularly prevalent in **Assam and the northeast**; travellers to this region might consider taking a course of malarone, doxycycline or mefloquine instead.

The most established regime – widely prescribed in Europe, but not in North America – is a combination of **chloroquine** (trade names Nivaquin or Avloclor) taken weekly either on its own or in conjunction with a daily dose of **proguanil** (Paludrine). You need to start this regime a week before arriving in a malarial area and continue it for four weeks after leaving. In India chloroquine is easy to come by but proguanil isn't, so stock up before you arrive. **Mefloquine** (Lariam) is a stronger treatment. As a prophylactic, you need take just one tablet weekly, starting two weeks before entering a risk area and continuing for four weeks after leaving. Mefloquine is a very powerful and effective antimalarial, though there have been widely reported concerns about its side effects, including psychological problems.

Doxycycline is often prescribed in Australasia. One tablet is taken daily, starting a day or two before entering a malarial zone and continuing for four weeks after leaving. It's not suitable for children under ten and it can cause thrush in women, while three percent of users develop a sensitivity to light, causing a rash, so it's not ideal for beach holidays. It also interferes with the effectiveness of the contraceptive pill. **Malarone** (a combination of atovaquone and proguanil) is another alternative, which you only have to start taking two days before you enter a malarial zone and continue for just a week after leaving, meaning that, although it's expensive, it can prove economical for short trips.

Malarial symptoms

The first signs of malaria are remarkably similar to a severe **flu**, and may take months to appear: if you suspect anything go to a hospital or clinic for a blood test immediately. The shivering, burning fever and headaches come in waves, usually in the early evening. Malaria is not infectious, but some strains are dangerous and occasionally even fatal when not treated promptly, in particular, the chloroquine-resistant **cerebral malaria**. This virulent and lethal strain of the disease, which affects the brain, is treatable, but has to be diagnosed early. Erratic body temperature, lack of energy and aches are the first key signs.

Preventing mosquito bites

The best way of combating malaria is, of course, to avoid getting bitten: malarial mosquitoes are active from dusk until dawn and during this time you should use mosquito **repellent** and take all necessary precau-

A TRAVELLERS' FIRST-AID KIT

Below are items you might want to take, especially if you're planning to go trekking – all are available in India itself, at a fraction of what you might pay at home:

- Antiseptic cream
- Insect repellent and cream such as Anthisan for soothing bites
- Plasters/Band-Aids
- A course of Flagyl antibiotics
- Water sterilization tablets or water purifier
- Lint and sealed bandages
- Knee supports
- Imodium (Lomotil) for emergency diarrhoea treatment
- A mild oral anesthetic such as Bonjela for soothing ulcers or mild toothache
- Paracetamol/aspirin
- Multivitamin and mineral tablets
- Rehydration sachets
- Hypodermic needles and sterilized skin wipes

tions. Sleep under a mosquito net if possible, burn mosquito coils (widely available in India, but easy to break in transit) or electrically heated repellents such as All Out. An Indian brand of repellent called Odomos is widely available and very effective, though most travellers bring their own from home, usually one containing the noxious but effective compound DEET. DEET can cause rashes and a strength of more than thirty percent is not advised for those with sensitive skin. A natural alternative is citronella or, in the UK, Mosi-guard Natural, made from a blend of eucalyptus oils; those with sensitive skin should still use DEET on clothes and nets. Mosquito "buzzers" – plug-in contraptions that smoulder tablets of DEET compounds slowly overnight – are pretty useless, but wrist and ankle bands are as effective as spray and a good alternative for sensitive skin. Though active all night, female *Anopheles* mosquitoes prefer to bite in the evening, so be especially careful at that time. Wear long sleeves, skirts and trousers, avoid dark colours, which attract mosquitoes, and put repellent on all exposed skin.

Dengue fever and Japanese encephalitis

Another illness spread by mosquito bites is **dengue fever**, whose symptoms are similar to those of malaria, plus aching bones. There is no vaccine available and the only treatment is complete rest, with drugs to assuage the fever. **Japanese encephalitis**, a mosquito-borne viral infection causing fever, muscle pains and headaches, is most prevalent in wet, rural rice-growing areas. However, it only rarely affects travellers, and the vaccine isn't usually recommended unless you plan to spend much time around paddy fields during and immediately after the monsoons.

Intestinal troubles

Diarrhoea is the most common bane of travellers. When mild and not accompanied by other major symptoms, it may just be your stomach reacting to unfamiliar food. Accompanied by cramps and vomiting, it could well be food poisoning. In either case, it will probably pass of its own accord in 24–48 hours without treatment. In the meantime, it is essential to replace the fluids and salts you're losing, so take lots of water with oral rehydration salts (commonly referred to as ORS, or called Electrolyte in India). If you can't get ORS, use half a teaspoon of salt and eight of sugar in a litre of water, and if you are too ill to keep it down, seek medical help immediately. Travel clinics and pharmacies sell double-ended moulded plastic spoons with the exact ratio of sugar to salt.

While you are suffering, it's a good idea to avoid greasy food, heavy spices, caffeine and most fruit and dairy products. Some say bananas and papaya are good, as are *kitchri* (a simple dhal and rice preparation) and rice soup and coconut water, while curd or a soup made from Marmite or Vegemite (if you happen to have some with you) are forms of protein that can be easily absorbed by your body when you have the runs. **Drugs** like Lomotil or Imodium simply plug you up – undermining the body's efforts to rid itself of infection – though they can be useful if you have to travel. If symptoms persist for more than a few days, a course of antibiotics may be necessary; this should be seen as a last resort, following medical advice.

Sordid though it may seem, it's a good idea to look at what comes out when you go to the toilet. If your diarrhoea contains blood or mucus and if you are suffering other symptoms including rotten-egg belches and farts, the cause may be dysentery or giardia. With a fever, it could well be caused by bacillary dysentery, and may clear up without treatment. If you're sure you need it, a course of antibiotics such as tetracycline should sort you out, but they also destroy gut flora in your intestines (which help protect you – curd can replenish them to some extent). If you start a course, be sure to finish it, even after the symptoms have gone. Similar symptoms, without fever, indicate **amoebic dysentery**, which is much more serious, and can damage your gut if untreated. The usual cure is a course of Metronidazole (Flagyl) or Fasigyn, both antibiotics which may themselves make you feel ill, and must not be taken with alcohol. Symptoms of **giardia** are similar – including frothy stools, nausea and constant fatigue – for which the treatment is again Metronidazole. If you suspect that you have either of these, seek medical help, and only start on the Metronidazole (750mg three times daily for a week for adults) if there is definitely blood in your diarrhoea and it is impossible to see a doctor.

Finally, bear in mind that oral drugs, such as malaria pills and the Pill, are likely to be largely ineffective if taken while suffering from diarrhoea.

Bites and creepy crawlies

Worms may enter your body through skin (especially the soles of your feet) or food. An itchy anus is a common symptom, and you may even see them in your stools. They are easy to treat: if you suspect you have them, get some worming tablets such as Mebendazole (Vermox) from any pharmacy.

Biting insects and similar animals other than mosquitoes may also aggravate you. The obvious suspects are **bedbugs** – look for signs of squashed ones around beds in cheap hotels. An infested mattress can be left in the hot sun all day to get rid of them, but they often live in the frame or even in walls or floors. **Head** and **body lice** can also be a nuisance, but medicated soap and shampoo (preferably brought with you from home) usually see them off. Avoid **scratching bites**, which can lead to infection. Bites from ticks and lice can spread **typhus**, characterized by fever, muscle aches, headaches and, later, red eyes and a measles-like rash. If you think you have it, seek treatment (tetracycline is usually prescribed).

Snakes are unlikely to bite unless accidentally disturbed, and most are harmless in any case. To see one at all, you need to search stealthily – walk heavily and they usually oblige by disappearing. If you do get bitten, remember what the snake looked like (kill it if you can), try not to move the affected part, and seek medical help: antivenins are available in most hospitals. A few **spiders** have poisonous bites too. Remove **leeches**, which may attach themselves to you in jungle areas, with salt or a lit cigarette: never just pull them off.

Altitude sickness

At high altitudes, you may develop symptoms of **acute mountain sickness (AMS)**. Just about everyone who ascends to around 4000m or higher experiences mild symptoms, but serious cases are rare. The simple cure – descent – almost always brings immediate recovery.

AMS is caused by the fact that at high elevations there is not only less oxygen, but also lower atmospheric pressure. This can have all sorts of weird effects on the body: it can cause the brain to swell and the lungs to fill with fluid, and even bring on uncontrollable farting. The syndrome varies from one person to the next but symptoms include breathlessness, headaches and dizziness, nausea, difficulty sleeping and appetite loss. More extreme cases may involve disorientation and loss of balance, and the coughing up of pink frothy phlegm.

AMS strikes without regard for fitness – in fact, young people seem to be more susceptible, possibly because they're more reluctant to admit they feel sick and they dart about more energetically. Most people are capable of acclimatizing to very high altitudes but the process takes time and must be done in stages. The golden rule is not to go too high, too fast; or if you do, spend the night at a lower height ("Climb High, Sleep Low"). Above 3000m, you should not ascend more than 500m per day; take mandatory acclimatization days at 3500m and 4000m – more if you feel unwell – and try to spend these days day-hiking to higher altitudes.

The general symptoms of AMS can be treated with the drug acetazolamide (Diamox) but this is not advised as it will block the early signs of severe AMS, which can be fatal. It is better to stay put for a day or two, eat a high-carbohydrate diet, drink plenty of water (three litres a day is recommended), take paracetamol or aspirin for the headaches, and descend if the AMS persists or worsens. If you fly direct to a high-altitude destination such as Leh, be especially careful to acclimatize (plan for three days of initial rest); you'll certainly want to avoid doing anything strenuous at first.

Other precautions to take at high altitudes include avoiding alcohol and sleeping pills, drinking more liquid, and protecting your skin against UV solar glare.

HIV and AIDS

HIV/AIDS is as much of a risk in India as anywhere else, and in recent years the government has heeded

AYURVEDIC MEDICINE

Ayurveda, a Sanskrit word meaning the "knowledge for prolonging life", is a five-thousand-year-old holistic medical system that is widely practised in India. Ayurvedic doctors and clinics in large towns deal with foreigners as well as their usual patients, and some **pharmacies** specialize in Ayurvedic preparations, including toiletries such as soaps, shampoos and toothpastes.

Ayurveda assumes the fundamental sameness of self and nature. Unlike the allopathic medicines of the West, which depend on finding out what's ailing you and then killing it, Ayurveda looks at the whole patient: disease is regarded as a symptom of **imbalance**, so it's the imbalance that's treated, not the disease. Ayurvedic theory holds that the body is controlled by three forces, which reflect the forces within the self: *pitta*, the force of the sun, is hot, and rules the digestive processes and metabolism; *kapha*, likened to the moon, the creator of tides and rhythms, has a cooling effect and governs the body's organs; and *vata*, wind, relates to movement and the nervous system. The healthy body is one that has the three forces in balance. To diagnose an imbalance, the Ayurvedic **vaid** (doctor) responds not only to the physical complaint but also to family background, daily habits and emotional traits.

Imbalances are typically treated with herbal remedies designed to alter whichever of the three forces is out of whack. Made according to traditional formulae, using indigenous plants, Ayurvedic medicines are cheaper than branded or imported drugs. In addition, the doctor may prescribe various forms of yogic cleansing to rid the body of waste substances. To the uninitiated, these techniques will sound rather off-putting – for instance, swallowing a long strip of cloth, a short section at a time, and then pulling it back up again to remove mucus from the stomach. Ayurvedic **massage** with herbal oils is especially popular in Kerala where courses of treatments are available to combat a wide array of ailments.

WHO advice by setting up its own awareness and prevention campaigns. As elsewhere in the world, high-risk groups include prostitutes and intravenous drug users. It is extremely unwise to contemplate casual sex without a condom – carry some with you (preferably brought from home as Indian ones may be less reliable) and insist upon using them.

Should you need an **injection** or a **transfusion** in India, make sure that new, sterile equipment is used; any blood you receive should be from voluntary rather than commercial donor banks. If you have a shave from a barber, make sure he uses a clean blade and don't undergo processes such as ear-piercing, acupuncture or tattooing unless you can be sure that the equipment is sterile.

Getting medical help

Pharmacies can usually advise on minor medical problems, and most doctors in India speak English. Also, many hotels keep a **doctor** on call; if you do get ill and need medical assistance, take advice as to the best facilities around. Basic medications are made to Indian Pharmacopoea (IP) standards, and most medicines are available without prescription, but always check the sell-by date.

Hospitals have variable standards: private clinics and mission hospitals are often better than state-run ones but may not have the same facilities. Hospitals in big cities, including university or medical-school hospitals, are generally pretty good, and cities such as Delhi, Mumbai, Hyderabad and Bengaluru boast state-of-the-art medical facilities but at a price. Many hospitals require patients (even emergency cases) to buy necessities such as medicines, plaster casts and vaccines, and to pay for X-rays, before procedures are carried out. Remember to keep receipts for insurance reimbursements. **Government hospitals**, however, provide all surgical and after-care services free of charge and in most other state medical institutions charges are usually so low that for minor treatment the expense may well be lower than the initial "excess" on your insurance. You will, however, need a companion to stay, or you'll have to come to an arrangement with one of the hospital cleaners, to help you out in hospital – relatives are expected to wash, feed and generally take care of the patient. Beware of scams by private clinics in tourist towns such as Agra where there have been reports of overcharging and misdiagnosis by doctors to claim insurance money. Addresses of foreign consulates (who will advise in an emergency), as well as clinics and hospitals, can be found in the Directory sections in the accounts of major cities and towns in this book.

The media

With well over a billion people and a literacy rate approaching 75 percent, India produces in excess of a staggering 5000

daily papers in more than three hundred languages, plus another 40,000 journals and weeklies. There are a large number of English-language daily newspapers, both national and regional.

Newspapers and magazines

The most prominent of the **nationals** are the *Times of India* (W timesofindia.indiatimes.com), *The Hindu* (W thehindu.com), *The Deccan Herald* (W deccanherald. com), *The Hindustan Times* (W hindustantimes.com), *The Economic Times* (W economictimes.indiatimes. com) and the *New Indian Express* (W newindianexpress. com), usually the most critical of the government. All are pretty dry and sober, concentrating on Indian news, although Kolkata's *The Telegraph* (W telegraphindia. com) tends to have better coverage of world news than the rest. *The Asian Age* (W asianage.com), published simultaneously in Delhi, Mumbai, Kolkata and London is a conservative tabloid that sports a motley collection of the world's more colourful stories. The *Times of India*, *The Hindu* and *The Hindustan Times* provide the most up-to-date and detailed online news services.

India's press is the freest in Asia and attacks on the government are often quite outspoken. However, as in the West, most papers can be seen as part of the political establishment, and are unlikely to print anything that might upset the "national consensus".

There are also a number of *Time/Newsweek*-style **news magazines**, with a strong emphasis on politics. The best of these are *India Today* (W indiatoday.in) and *Frontline* (W frontline.in), published by *The Hindu*. Others include *Outlook* (W outlookindia.com), which presents the most readable, broadly themed analysis, and *The Week* (W theweek.in). As they give more of an overview of stories and issues than the daily papers, you will probably get a better insight into Indian politics, and most tend to have a higher proportion of international news, too. Also worth checking out are W samachar. com, one of the best news gateway sites, featuring headlines and links to leading Indian newspapers, and alternative news webzine W tehelka.com, famous for exposing corruption scandals in government.

Film **fanzines** and gossip mags are very popular – *Filmfare* (W filmfare.com) and the online-only *Screen* (W epaper.screenindia.com) are the best, though you'd have to be reasonably *au fait* with Indian movies to follow a lot of it. Other magazines and periodicals in English cover all sorts of popular and minority interests, so it's worth having a look through what's available. Expat-oriented bookstalls, such as those in New Delhi's Khan Market, stock slightly out-of-date and expensive copies of magazines like *Vogue*.

Foreign publications such as the *International Herald Tribune*, *Time* and *The Economist* are all available in the main cities, though it's easier (and cheaper) to read the day's edition for free online. For a read through the British press, try the British Council in Delhi, Mumbai, Kolkata, Chennai and six other cities; the USIS is the American equivalent. The UK's *Guardian* website (W guardian.co.uk/world/india) is one of the best online news resources, with an extensive archive of articles and an excellent dossier on Kashmir. Access is free.

Radio and TV

BBC World Service radio (W bbc.co.uk/worldservice) can be picked up at 94.3FM in most major cities, on short wave on frequencies ranging from 5790–15310kHz, and more sporadically on medium wave (AM) at 1413KHz (212m). It also broadcasts online. The Voice of America (W voa.gov) can be found on 15.75MHz (19) and (75.75MHz (39.5m), among other frequencies. Radio Canada (W rcinet.ca) broadcasts in English on 6165 and 7255KHz (48.6 and 41.3m) at 6.30–7.30am and on 9635 and 11,975 KHz (31 and 25m) at 8.30–9.30pm.

The government-run **TV company**, Doordarshan, which broadcasts a sober diet of edifying programmes, has tried to compete with the onslaught of mass access to **satellite TV**. The main broadcaster in English is Rupert Murdoch's Star TV network, which incorporates the BBC World Service and Zee TV (with Z News), a progressive blend of Hindi-oriented chat, film, news and music programmes. Star Sports, ESPN and Ten Sports churn out a mind-boggling amount of cricket, extensive coverage of English Premier League football, plenty of tennis and a few other sports. Other channels include CNN, the Discovery Channel, the immensely popular Channel V, hosted by scantily clad Mumbai models and DJs, and a couple of American soap and chat stations. There are now numerous local-language channels as well, many of them showing magnificently colourful religious and devotional programmes.

Festivals and holidays

Virtually every temple in every town or village across the country has its own festival. The biggest and most spectacular include Puri's Rath Yatra festival in June or July, the Hemis festival in Ladakh (also held in June or July), Pushkar's camel fair in November, Kullu's Dussehra, Madurai's

three annual festivals and, of course, the Kumbh Mela, held in turn at Prayagraj, Haridwar, Nasik and Ujjain. While mostly religious in nature, merrymaking rather than solemnity are generally the order of the day, and onlookers are invariably welcome. Indeed, if you're lucky enough to coincide with a local festival, it may well prove to be the highlight of your trip.

There isn't space to list every festival in every village across India here, but local festivals are featured at the start of each chapter and throughout the body of the Guide. The calendar below includes details of the main national and regional celebrations. Hindu, Sikh, Buddhist and Jain festivals follow the Indian **lunar calendar** and their dates therefore vary from year to year – we've given the lunar month (Magha, Phalguna, Chaitra, and so on), where relevant, in the listings below. The lunar calendar adds a leap month every two or three years to keep it in line with the seasons. Muslim festivals follow the **Islamic calendar**, whose year is shorter and which thus loses about eleven days per annum against the Gregorian.

In recent years, there has been an explosion in the number of contemporary, pop and fusion **music festivals**, as India develops a circuit something like the UK and other parts of Europe. Examples include Festa de Diu (ⓦfestadiu.com), Ragasthan (ⓦragasthan.com), Jodhpur RIFF (ⓦjodhpurriff.org) and Magnetic Fields (ⓦmagneticfields.in).

PRINCIPAL INDIAN HOLIDAYS

India has only four **national public holidays** as such: Jan 26 (Republic Day); Aug 15 (Independence Day); Oct 2 (Gandhi's birthday); and Dec 25 (Christmas Day). Each state, however, has its own calendar of public holidays; you can expect most businesses to close on the major holidays of their own religion. The Hindu lunar calendar months are given in brackets below.

Key: B=Buddhist; C=Christian; H=Hindu; J=Jain; M=Muslim; N=non-religious; P=Parsi; S=Sikh.

Jan–Feb (Magha)

N Hampi Utsav: Government-sponsored music and dance festival. See page 1123.

H Pongal (1 Magha): Tamil harvest festival celebrated with decorated cows, processions and *rangolis* (chalk designs on the doorsteps of houses). *Pongal* is a sweet porridge made from newly harvested rice and eaten by all, including the cows. The festival is also known as Makar Sankranti, and celebrated in Karnataka, Andhra Pradesh and the east of India.

H Sagar Mela: Pilgrims come from all over the country to Sagardwip, on the mouth of the Hooghly 150km south of Kolkata, to bathe during Makar Sankranti. See page 752.

N International Kite Festival/Uttarayan (Jan 14). Coinciding with Makar Sankranti, Ahmedabad (Gujarat) hosts the most spectacular of all of India's kite festivals. See page 556.

H Vasant Panchami (5 Magha): One-day spring festival in honour of Saraswati, the goddess of learning, celebrated with kite-flying, the wearing of yellow saris and the blessing of schoolchildren's books and pens by the goddess.

N Republic Day (Jan 26): A military parade in Delhi typifies this state celebration of India's republic-hood, followed on Jan 29 by the "Beating the Retreat" ceremony outside the presidential palace in Delhi.

H Teppa Floating Festival (16 Magha). Meenakshi and Shiva are towed around the Vandiyur Mariamman Teppakulam tank in boats lit with fairy lights – a prelude to the Tamil marriage season in Madurai, Tamil Nadu. See page 979.

N Elephanta Music and Dance Festival. Classical Indian dance performed with the famous rock-cut caves in Mumbai harbour as a backdrop.

Feb–March (Phalguna)

B Losar (1 Phalguna): Tibetan New Year celebrations among Tibetan and Himalayan Buddhist communities, especially at Dharamsala (HP).

H Shivratri (10 Phalguna): Anniversary of Shiva's *tandav* (creation) dance, and his wedding anniversary. Popular family festival but also a sadhu festival of pilgrimage and fasting, especially at important Shiva temples.

H Holi (15 Phalguna): Water festival held during Dol Purnima (full moon) to celebrate the beginning of spring, most popular in the north. Expect to be bombarded with water, paint, coloured powder and other mixtures; they can permanently stain clothing, so don't go out in your Sunday best.

N Khajuraho Festival of Dance: The country's finest dancers perform in front of Madhya Pradesh's famous erotic sculpture-carved shrines. See page 345.

N Goa Carnival: Goa's own Mardi Gras features float processions and *feni*-induced mayhem in the state capital, Panjim.

INDIAN WEDDINGS

You may, while in India, be lucky enough to be invited to a **wedding**. These are jubilant affairs, always scheduled on auspicious days. A Hindu bride dresses in red for the ceremony, and marks the parting of her hair with red *sindur* and her forehead with a bindi. She wears gold or bone bangles, which she keeps on for the rest of her married life. Although the practice is officially illegal, large dowries often change hands. These are usually paid by the bride's family to the groom, and can be contentious; poor families feel obliged to save for years to get their daughters married.

March–April (Chaitra)

H Gangaur (3 Chaitra): Rajasthani festival (also celebrated in Bengal and Odisha) in honour of Gauri (Parvati), marked with singing and dancing.

H Ramanavami (9 Chaitra): Birthday of Rama, the hero of the Ramayana, celebrated with readings of the epic and discourses on Rama's life and teachings.

C Easter (moveable feast): Celebration of the resurrection of Christ. Good Friday in particular is a day of festivity.

P Pateti Parsi new year, also known as Nav Roz, celebrating the creation of fire. Feasting, services and present-giving.

P Khorvad Sal (a week after Pateti): Birthday of Zarathustra (aka Zoroaster). Celebrated in the Parsis' fire temples, and with feasting at home.

April–May (Vaisakha)

HS Baisakhi (1 Vaisakha): To the Hindus, it's the solar new year, celebrated with music and dancing; to the Sikhs, it's the anniversary of the foundation of the Khalsa (Sikh brotherhood) by Guru Gobind Singh. Processions and feasting follow readings of the Granth Sahib scriptures.

H Chithirai: Lively procession at Madurai in Tamil Nadu. See page 979.

J Mahavir Jayanti (13 Vaisakha): Birthday of Mahavira, the founder of Jainism. The main Jain festival of the year, observed by visits to sacred Jain sites, especially in Rajasthan and Gujarat, and with present-giving.

H Puram: Frenzied drumming and elephant parades in Thrissur, Kerala. See page 1107.

B Buddha Jayanti (16 Vaisakha): Buddha's birthday. He achieved enlightenment and nirvana on the same date. Sarnath (UP) and Bodh Gaya (Bihar) are the main centres of celebration.

May–June (Jyaishtha)

H Ganga Dussehra (10 Jyaishtha): Bathing festival to celebrate the descent to earth of the goddess of the Ganges. See page 300.

June–July (Ashadha)

H Rath Yatra (2 Ashadha): Festival held in Puri (and other places, especially in the south) to commemorate Krishna's (Lord Jagannath's) journey to Mathura. See page 915.

H Teej (3 Ashadha): Festival in honour of Parvati to welcome the monsoon. Particularly celebrated in Rajasthan.

B Hemis Tsechu Held sometime between late June and mid-July, this spectacular Ladakh festival features *chaam* (lama dances) to signify the victory of Buddhism over evil. See pages 483 and 494.

July–Aug (Shravana)

H Naag Panchami (3 Shravana): Snake festival in honour of the *naga* snake deities. Mainly celebrated in Rajasthan and Maharashtra.

H Raksha Bandhan/Narial Purnima (16 Shravana): Festival to honour the sea god Varuna. Brothers and sisters exchange gifts, the sister tying a thread known as a *rakhi* to her brother's wrist. Brahmins, after a day's fasting, change the sacred thread they wear.

N Independence Day (Aug 15): India's biggest secular celebration, on the anniversary of Independence from the UK.

Aug–Sept (Bhadraparda)

H Ganesh Chaturthi (4 Bhadraparda): Festival dedicated to Ganesh, especially celebrated in Maharashtra. In Mumbai, huge processions carry images of the god to immerse in the sea. See page 609.

H Onam: Keralan harvest festival, celebrated with snake-boat races. The Nehru Trophy Snake Boat Race at Alappuzha (held on the 2nd Sat of Aug) is the most spectacular, with long boats crewed by 150 rowers (see page 1059).

H Janmashtami (23 Bhadraparda): Krishna's birthday, an occasion for fasting and celebration, especially in Agra, Gujarat, Mumbai, Mathura and Vrindavan (UP).

Sept–Oct (Ashvina)

H Dussehra/Dasara (1–10 Ashvina): Ten-day festival (usually two days' public holiday) associated with vanquishing demons, in particular Rama's victory over Ravana in the Ramayana, and Durga's over the buffalo-headed Mahishasura (particularly in West Bengal, where it is called Durga Puja). Dussehra (known as Dasara in south India) celebrations include performances of the Ram Lila (life of Rama). Best in Mysuru (Karnataka; see page 1138), Ahmedabad (Gujarat) and Kullu (Himachal Pradesh; see page 448). Durga Puja is best seen in Kolkata (see page 752) where it is an occasion for exchanging gifts, and every locality has its own competing street-side image.

N Mahatma Gandhi's Birthday (Oct 2): Solemn commemoration of independent India's founding father.

Oct–Nov (Kartika)

H Diwali (Deepavali) (15 Kartika): Festival of lights, and India's biggest, to celebrate Rama's and Sita's homecoming in the Ramayana. Festivities include the lighting of oil lamps and firecrackers, and the giving and receiving of sweets and gifts. Diwali coincides with Kali Puja, celebrated in temples dedicated to the wrathful goddess, especially in Bengal, and often accompanied by the ritual sacrifice of goats.

J Jain New Year (15 Kartika): Coincides with Diwali, so Jains celebrate alongside Hindus.

S Nanak Jayanti (16 Kartika): Guru Nanak's birthday marked by prayer readings and processions, especially in Amritsar and in the rest of the Punjab, and at Patna (Bihar).

Nov–Dec (Margashirsha or Agrahayana)

H Sonepur Mela World's largest cattle fair at Sonepur (Bihar). See page 815.

N Pushkar Camel Fair Camel herders don their finest attire for this massive livestock market on the fringes of the Thar Desert in Rajasthan. See page 131.

Dec–Jan (Pausa)

N Poush Mela (Dec 22–25): Held in Shantiniketan near Kolkata, this festival is renowned for its musical performances by Bauls (mystic minstrels; see page 752).

CN Christmas (Dec 25): Popular in Christian areas of Goa and Kerala, and in big cities.

Moveable

H Kumbh Mela: Major festival held at four holy cities in rotation, with each location hosting once every twelve years: Prayagraj (UP), Nasik (Maharashtra), Ujjain (MP) or Haridwar (Uttarakhand). The Prayagraj event is the most important and drew 120 million people in 2013; there are also Ardh (half) Kumbh Melas in between, with the most recent held in Prayagraj during early 2019. See page 269.

M Ramadan: The month during which Muslims may not eat, drink or smoke from sunrise to sunset, and should abstain from sex. Muslim areas tend to come alive in the evenings as locals break their fast after prayers (*iftar*) and shop for Id. Estimated future dates are: May 27 to June 25, 2017, May 16 to June 14, 2018, and May 6 to June 4, 2019.

M Id ul-Fitr: Feast to celebrate the end of Ramadan. The precise date of the festival depends on exactly when the new moon is sighted, and so cannot be predicted with complete accuracy. Estimated dates (though these may vary by a day or two) are: June 26, 2017, June 15, 2018, and June 5, 2019.

Sports

Cricket is by far the most popular sport in India, and a fine example of how something quintessentially British (well, English) has become something quintessentially Indian. Indian cricket now dominates the global game, responsible for as much as 80 percent of its revenue. Travellers to India will find it hard to get away from the game – it's everywhere, especially on television.

Cricketing heroes such as one-day and test captains (respectively) M.S. Dhoni and Virat Kohli live under the constant scrutiny of the media and public; expectations are high and disappointments acute. India versus Pakistan matches are especially emotive, with rivalries often spilling out into bloodshed. Besides

spectator cricket, you'll see games being played on open spaces all around the country.

Test matches are rare, but inter-state cricket is easy to catch – the most prestigious competition is the Ranji Trophy. Occasionally, in cities like Kolkata, you may even come across a match blocking a road, and will have to be patient as the players begrudgingly let your vehicle continue.

Football (soccer) has undergone a revolution since the establishment of the eight-team Indian Super League (ISL) in 2013, which attracts the fourth highest average attendances in the world as well as a massive TV audience. Teams employ high-profile coaches such as FC Goa's Brazilian legend Zico and Pune City's English ex-pro David Platt, while the players include a number of internationals, mostly from Africa. Goa and Kolkata have always been strongholds of the game, and Atlético de Kolkata won the inaugural trophy in 2014; but Chennaiyin FC surprised everyone by lifting it in 2015.

Horse racing can be a good day out, especially if you enjoy a flutter. The racecourse at Kolkata is the most popular, often attracting crowds of more than fifty thousand, especially on New Year's Day. There are several other racecourses around the country, mostly in larger cities such as Mumbai, Delhi, Pune, Hyderabad, Mysuru, Bengaluru and Ooty. Other (mainly) spectator sports include **polo**, originally from upper Kashmir, but taken up by the British to become one of the symbols of the Raj. Certain Rajasthani princes, such as the late Hanut Singh of Jodhpur, were considered to be the best polo players in the world between the 1930s and 1950s, but since the 1960s, when the privy purses were abolished, they have been unable to maintain their stables, and the tradition of polo has declined. Today, it's mainly the army who plays the game; the best place to catch a match is at the Delhi Gymkhana during the winter season. Polo, in more or less its original form, is still played on tiny

---

INDIA'S TWENTY20 VISION

Over the last ten years, the whole global cricket scene has been massively shaken up by the brashness and glamour of the **Indian Premier League** (ⓦiplt20.com), the world's biggest Twenty20 cricket tournament. Held annually in April and May since 2008, the IPL features a mix of young up-and-coming locals, established Indian players and international cricketing megastars such as AB de Villiers and Chris Gayle. Each of the league's eight city team franchises supplements their home-grown playing staff by signing up star "icon players", whose services are auctioned off via a series of sealed bids – records were broken in 2015 when Delhi Daredevils picked up master-blasting batsman Yuvraj Singh for a cool US\$2.4 million.

With such staggering sums of money changing hands, it's perhaps no surprise that the IPL has become as well known for its off-field controversies and financial irregularities as for the action and drama on the pitch. In 2013, three Rajasthan Royals players were arrested for spot-fixing and in 2015 both the Royals and Chennai Super Kings were booted out of the league for two years following revelations of match-fixing.

mountain ponies in Ladakh; a good place to see a game played in traditional style is in Leh during the Ladakh Festival in early September (see page 478).

After years in the doldrums, **field hockey**, which used to regularly furnish the country with Olympic medals, is making a strong comeback. The haul of medals dried up in the 1960s when international hockey introduced Astroturf – which was, and still is, a rare surface in India. However, hockey remains very popular, especially in schools and colleges and, interestingly, among the tribal girls of Odisha, who supply the Indian national team with a regular clutch of players. Having hosted the Hockey World Cup in 2010, India is due to stage the competition again in 2018.

Tennis in India has always been a sport for the middle and upper classes. The country has produced a number of world-class players, such as the men's duo of Mahesh Bhupati and Leander Paes, who briefly achieved a world number-one ranking in the men's doubles in 1999, but the brightest current star is undoubtedly Sania Mirza, the first Indian women to break into the singles top 50. After injury forced her to give up the solo game she shifted her attention to doubles and was ranked at number-one at the time of writing, having partnered Martina Hingis to three successive Grand Slam titles in 2015–16.

Volleyball is very popular throughout India, especially in the resorts of Goa. Standards aren't particularly high and joining a game is quite easy. Since the arrival on the Formula 1 scene of Kingfisher tycoon Vijay Malia's Force India team, **motor racing** has also grown in popularity and three Grand Prix races were hosted at the new track at Noida outside Delhi between 2011 and 2013, though tax disputes have led to the race being shelved since. **Golf** is widely followed, too, again among the middle classes; the second oldest golf course in the world is in Kolkata, and one of the highest in the world is at Shimla.

One indigenous sport you're likely to see in north India is **kabaddi**, played on a small (badminton-sized) court, and informally on any suitable open area. The game, with seven players in each team, consists of a player from each team alternately attempting to "tag" as many members of the opposing team as possible in the space of a single breath (cheating is impossible; the player has to maintain a continuous chant of "kabaddikabaddikabaddikabaddi" etc), and getting back to his/her own side of the court without being caught. The game can get quite rough, with slaps and kicks in tagging allowed, and the defending team must try to tackle and pin the attacker so as not to allow him or her to even touch the dividing line. Tagged victims are required to leave the court. Although still an amateur sport, kabaddi is taken very

seriously with state and national championships, and has featured in the Asian Games since 1990.

Popular with devotees of the monkey god, Hanuman, **Indian wrestling**, or *kushti*, has a small but dedicated following. Wrestlers are known as *pahalwaans* or "strong men" and can be seen exercising early in the morning with clubs and weights along river *ghats* such as those in Varanasi or Kolkata.

Trekking and outdoor activities

India offers plenty of opportunities for adventure sports, including trekking, mountaineering, whitewater rafting, caving and diving – just make sure you've got comprehensive insurance (see page 69) before getting stuck in.

Trekking

Though **trekking** in India is not nearly as commercialized as in neighbouring Nepal, the country can claim some of the world's most spectacular routes, especially in the Ladakh and Zanskar Himalayas, where the mountain passes frequently top 5000m. Himalayan routes are not all extreme, with relatively gentle short trails exploring the Singalila Range around Darjeeling, low-level forest walks through the rhododendron-clad hillsides of Sikkim and the well-beaten pilgrim trails of Garhwal. Trekking is also becoming more popular in the Western Ghats and Nilgiris of the south.

Hiring a **guide-cum-cook** is recommended whenever possible, especially on more difficult and less frequented routes, where the consequences of getting lost or running out of supplies could be serious. **Porters** (with or without ponies) can also make your trip a lot less arduous, and on longer routes where a week or more's worth of provisions have to be carried, they may be essential. You'll usually be approached in towns and villages leading to the trailhead by men touting for work. Finding out what the going day-rate is can be difficult, and you should expect to haggle.

If the prospect of organizing a trek yourself seems too daunting, consider employing a **trekking company** to do it for you. Agencies at places like Manali, Leh, Darjeeling and Gangtok are detailed in the Guide, while specialist tour operators abroad also offer trips based around trekking (see page 32). **Himachal Pradesh** is the easiest state in which to plan a trek. **Uttarakhand**

FIVE TOP TREKS

Naggar to the Parvati Valley via Malana Short but beautiful and culturally fascinating route in lush Himachal Pradesh. See page 458.

Padum to Lamayuru Legendary and tough (ten-day minimum) trek through the rugged Zanskar Range to Ladakh. See page 502.

The Dzongri Trail This eight-day hike through rhododendron forests and glaciers in Sikkim offers stunning views of Kanchenjunga. See page 847.

Amarnath Trek Medium-length hike to a cave with a natural ice lingam in the mountains of Kashmir. See page 517.

Kolukkumalai to Meesapulimalai Great three-day trek through tea plantations to the Western Ghats' second highest peak. See page 1091.

---

sees fewer trekkers, and there are plenty of opportunities to wander off the beaten track and either escape the hordes of pilgrims or, alternatively, to join them on their way to the sacred sites of the Char Dham. There are also exciting and exotic high-mountain trekking opportunities in the ancient Buddhist kingdoms of **Ladakh and Zanskar**, where trails can vary in length from relatively short four-day excursions to epics of ten days or more. At the eastern end of the Himalayas, **Darjeeling** makes a good base from which to explore the surrounding mountains. Neighbouring **Sikkim** has the greatest variations in altitude, from steamy river valleys to the third highest massif in the world. Shorter and less strenuous treks are available in the Ghats and the Nilgiri hills of **southern India**, with Munnar and Wayanad in Kerala, the Kodagu region of Karnataka and Ooty in Tamil Nadu proving the main springboards.

Having the right **equipment** for a trek is important, but high-tech gear isn't essential – bring what you need to be comfortable but keep weight to a minimum. You can rent equipment in places such as Leh and Darjeeling, but otherwise you'll have to buy what you need or bring it with you. Make sure everything (zips, for example) is in working order before you set off. Clothes should be lightweight and versatile, especially considering the range of temperatures you might encounter: dress in layers for maximum flexibility.

Mountaineering

Mountaineering is a more serious venture, requiring planning and organization; if you've never climbed, don't start in the Himalayas. Mountaineering institutes at Darjeeling, Uttarkashi and Dharamsala run training courses. The Nehru Institute of Mountaineering at Uttarkashi in Uttarakhand (ⓦ nimindia.net) is popular with foreigners: you can learn rock- and ice-climbing skills and expedition techniques for a fraction of what you'd pay in the West. Permission for mountaineering expeditions should be sought at least six months in advance from the Indian Mountaineering Federation in New Delhi (☏ 011 2411 1211, ⓦ indmount.org).

Skiing

Despite the mammoth spread of the Himalayas, **skiing** in India remains relatively undeveloped. The only options for organized skiing are the western Himalayas, in particular Uttarakhand, Himachal Pradesh and Kashmir; the eastern Himalayas have unreliable snowfall at skiing altitudes.

The ski area at **Auli**, near Joshimath in Uttarakhand (see page 323), has had money poured into it but suffers from a short season, limited (though cheap) skiing and nonexistent après-ski activity. In **Himachal Pradesh**, the skiing in the vicinity of Shimla is far too underdeveloped to warrant a detour, but the possibilities around Manali are more enticing because of the prospect of virgin powder: two or three surface tows operate in the Solang Nala for three months every winter (see box, page 456). By far the most promising prospect at present, however, is **Gulmarg** (see page 516) in Kashmir. On a plateau at 2600m, the former British hill station boasts the highest cable car in the world – and some of the most dependably fine powder snow to be had anywhere. Skiers are dropped at nearly 4000m by a French-built gondola, from where the off-piste possibilities are truly world class.

Whitewater rafting

Though not as well known as some of the mighty rivers of Nepal, the **rivers** Chenab and Beas in Himachal Pradesh, the Rangit and Teesta in Sikkim, the Zanskar and Indus in Ladakh, and the Ganges in Uttarakhand all combine exciting waters with magnificent scenery. Kullu, Manali, Leh, Gangtok and Rishikesh are among the main rafting centres. Prices start at around ₹2000 per day including food, but it's worth sounding out a few agents to find the best deals. For more details see the relevant accounts in the Guide.

Caving

Meghalaya has the best **caving** potential of all the Indian states. The three main areas are the East Khasi hills, the South Garo hills and the Jaintia hills (home to the 21.4km-long Krem Kotsati–Umlawan cave, the longest system in mainland Asia). Meghalaya Adventurers' Association in Shillong offers caving trips (see page 872).

Diving, snorkelling and other watersports

Because of the number of rivers draining into the sea around the Subcontinent, India's **coastal waters** are generally silt-laden and too murky for decent diving or snorkelling. However in many areas abundant hard coral and colourful fish make up for the relatively poor visibility. India also counts two beautiful tropical-island archipelagos in its territory, both surrounded by exceptionally clear seas. Served by well-equipped and reputable diving centres, the Andaman Islands and Lakshadweep offer world-class diving on a par with just about anything in Asia. Don't come here expecting rock-bottom prices though. India's dive schools cost at least as much as anywhere else, typically charging around US$70 for a two-tank outing, to US$270–300 for an open-water course.

For independent travellers, the most promising destination for both scuba diving and snorkelling is the **Andaman Islands** in the Bay of Bengal, around 1000km east of the mainland. Part of a chain of submerged mountains that stretch north from Sumatra to the coast of Myanmar (Burma), this isolated archipelago is ringed by gigantic coral reefs whose crystal-clear waters are teeming with tropical fish and other marine life. Havelock Island has by far the most dive centres, while its smaller neighbour Neil is slowly developing a scene; you can also dive on North Andaman or around Chiriya Tapu and Cinque Island, both accessed from Port Blair. If you want to do an open-water course, book ahead as places tend to be in short supply especially during the peak season, between December and February (see page 969).

Lakshadweep is a classic coconut-palm-covered atoll, some 400km west of Kerala in the Arabian Sea. The shallow lagoons, extensive coral reefs and exceptionally good visibility make this a perfect option for both first-timers and more experienced divers – though transportation and accommodation are very pricey (see page 1105).

PADI-approved dive schools also work out of a handful of resorts in **Goa**. Although the waters off the Goan coast have poor visibility, these schools take clients further south to an island off the shores of neighbouring Karnataka where conditions are much better.

Other niche watersports such as **kitesurfing**, which has a centre in Rameshwaram (see page 1038), are also beginning to make an appearance.

Camel trekking

The way to experience the desert in style is from the top of a camel. The one-humped Arabian camel, or dromedary, common in desert regions of Rajasthan, is well adapted to the terrain, with long double eyelashes to keep sand out of its eyes, nostrils that it can close, and broad, soft, padded feet that are ideal for walking on sand. Riding on a camel is smoother than riding on a horse because the camel moves its left and then right legs together, rather than front and then back legs, giving it a more rolling gait. They are usually docile, good-tempered animals, but the male goes into rut in spring, when it becomes rather grumpy and can kick and bite, and spit its regurgitated stomach contents in anger.

Camel treks can be arranged at Jaisalmer (see page 183), Bikaner (see page 174) and many other places

---

ELEPHANTS IN INDIA

Elephants play a central role in Indian life thanks to the Hindu god, Ganesha, and the animal's cultural importance throughout history. The country is home to around 50% of the world's wild Asian elephants, but it's also home to 20% of the continent's domesticated pachyderms. Some temples keep a captive elephant for religious reasons, and in some places in India such as the Amber Fort in Jaipur, elephant rides are a popular activity for tourists; however, for animal welfare reasons Rough Guides doesn't want to encourage this practice. While we will not recommend elephant rides in this Guide, the situation is not black and white. We will acknowledge where a temple keeps a captive elephant, but we would encourage you to learn more about the ethical implications before you decide whether to visit the sight and/or take an elephant ride. For more information, visit ⓦhttps://www.responsibletravel.com/holidays/elephant-conservation/travel-guide/elephant-sanctuaries-which-we-do-and-dont-support or ⓦroughguides.com/article/the-truth-about-elephant-tourism-in-asia (which has tips on what to look for in an ethical operation).

in Rajasthan. Some treks stick to the beaten track, and take you to the popular tourist sights. Others specialize in heading off deep into the desert for a feeling of isolation and remoteness. Typically, camel treks include two days in the saddle and a night spent camping in the desert, but you can opt for longer or shorter trips.

Yoga, meditation and ashrams

The birthplace of yoga and the spiritual home of the world's most famous meditation traditions, India offers unrivalled opportunities for spiritual nourishment, ranging from basic yoga and pranayama classes to extended residential meditation retreats.

Yoga is taught virtually everywhere in India and there are several internationally known centres where you can train to become a teacher. **Meditation** is similarly practised all over the country and specific courses are available in temples, meditation centres, monasteries and ashrams. **Ashrams** are communities where people work, live and study together, drawn by a common, usually spiritual, goal.

Details of yoga and meditation courses and ashrams are provided throughout the Guide. Most centres offer courses that you can enrol on at short notice, but many of the more popular ones (see page 63) need to be booked well in advance.

Yoga

Yoga (Sanskrit for "to unite" and root of the word "yoke") aims to help the practitioner unite his or her individual consciousness with the divine. This is achieved by raising awareness of one's self through spiritual, mental and physical exercises and discipline. **Hatha yoga**, the most popular form in the West, is based on physical postures called *asanas*, which stretch, relax and tone the muscular system of the body and also massage the internal organs. Each *asana* has a beneficial effect on a particular muscle group or organ, and although they vary widely in difficulty, consistent practice will lead to improved suppleness and health benefits. For serious practitioners, however, Hatha yoga is seen simply as the first step leading to more subtle stages of meditation which commence when the energies of the body have been awakened and sensitized by stretching and relaxing. Other forms of yoga include *raja* yoga,

which includes moral discipline, and *bhakti* yoga, the yoga of devotion, which entails a commitment to one's guru or teacher. *Jnana* yoga (the yoga of knowledge) is centred around the deep philosophies that underlie Hindu spiritual thinking.

Rishikesh, in Uttarakhand, is India's yoga capital, with a bumper crop of ashrams offering all kinds of courses (see page 310). The country's most famous teachers, however, work from institutes further south. **Iyengar** yoga is one of the most famous approaches studied today, named after its founder, B.K.S. Iyengar (a student of the great yoga teacher Sri Tirumalai Krishnamacharya), who died in 2014. Its main centre, the Ramamani Iyengar Memorial Yoga Institute, is in Pune, Maharashtra (Ⓦ bksiyengar.com), but there are many branches elsewhere. Iyengar's style is based upon precise physical alignment during each posture. With much practise, and the aid of props such as blocks, straps and chairs, the student can attain perfect physical balance and, the theory goes, perfect balance of mind will follow. Iyengar yoga has a strong therapeutic element and has been used successfully for treating a wide variety of structural and internal problems.

Ashtanga yoga is an approach developed by K. Pattabhi Jois of Mysuru (Ⓦ kpjayi.org; see page 1139), who also studied under Krishnamacharya. Unlike Iyengar yoga, which centres around a collection of separate *asanas*, Ashtanga links various postures into a series of flowing moves called *vinyasa*, with the aim of developing strength and agility. The perfect synchronization of movement with breath is a key objective throughout these sequences. Although a powerful form, it can be frustrating for beginners as each move has to be perfected before moving on to the next one.

The son of Krishnamacharya, T.K.V. Desikachar, established a third major branch in modern yoga, emphasizing a more versatile and adaptive approach to teaching, focused on the situation of the individual practitioner. This style became known as **Viniyoga**, although Desikachar has long tried to distance himself from the term. In the mid-1970s, he co-founded the Krishnamacharya Yoga Mandiram (Ⓦ kym.org), now a flagship institute in Chennai.

The other most influential Indian yoga teacher of the modern era has been Swami Vishnu Devananda, an acolyte of the famous sage Swami Sivanda, who established the International Sivananda Yoga Vedanta Center (Ⓦ sivananda.org), with more than thirty branches in India and abroad. **Sivananda**-style yoga tends to introduce elements in a different order from its counterparts – teaching practices regarded by others as advanced to relative beginners. This fast-forward approach has proved particularly popular with Westerners, who flock in their thousands to intensive introductory courses staged at centres all over India – the most renowned of them at Neyyar Dam, in the hills east of the Keralan capital, Thiruvananthapuram.

Meditation

Meditation is often practised after a session of yoga, when the energy of the body has been awakened, and is an essential part of both Hindu and Buddhist practice. In both religions, meditation is considered the most powerful tool for understanding the true nature of mind and self, an essential step on the path to **enlightenment**. In Vedanta, meditation's aim is to realize the true self as non-dual Brahman or godhead – the foundation of all consciousness and life. *Moksha* (or liberation – the nirvana of the Buddhists), achieved through disciplines of yoga and meditation, eventually helps believers release the soul from endless cycles of birth and rebirth.

Vipassana meditation (Wdhamma.org) is a technique, originally taught by the Buddha, whereby practitioners learn to become more aware of physical sensations and mental processes. Courses last for a minimum of ten days and are austere – involving 4am starts, around ten hours of meditation a day, no solid food after noon, segregation of the sexes, and no talking for the duration (except with the leaders of the course). Courses are free for all first-time students, to allow everyone an opportunity to learn and benefit from the technique. Vipassana is taught in nearly 75 centres throughout India.

Tibetan Buddhist meditation is attracting more and more followers around the world. With its four distinct schools, Tibetan Buddhism incorporates a huge variety of meditation practices, including Vipassana, known as *shiné* in Tibetan, and various visualization techniques involving the numerous deities that make up the complex and colourful Tibetan pantheon. India, with its large Tibetan diaspora, has become a major centre for people wanting to study Tibetan Buddhism and medicine. Dharamsala in Himachal Pradesh, home to the Dalai Lama and Tibetan government-in-exile, is the main centre for Tibetan studies (see page 430). Other major Tibetan diaspora centres in India include Darjeeling in West Bengal and Bylakuppe near Mysuru in Karnataka. For further details of courses available locally, see the relevant Guide chapters.

Ashrams and centres

Ashrams can range in size from just a handful of people to several thousand, and their rules, regulations and restrictions vary enormously. Some offer on-site accommodation, others will require you to stay in the nearest town or village. Some charge Western prices, others local prices, and some operate on a donation basis. Many ashrams have set programmes each day, while others are less structured, teaching as and when requested. In addition to these traditional Indian places to learn yoga and meditation techniques, dozens of smaller centres open in the coastal resorts of Goa and Kerala during the winter, several of them staffed by internationally famous teachers. The more prominent of these are listed below.

COURSES AND ASHRAMS

Ashiyana Tropical Retreat Centre Mandrem, Goa W ashiyana-yoga-goa.com. World-class yoga, massage, meditation and *satsang* tuition – from resident and visiting teachers – with treehouse accommodation and gorgeous views. See page 728.

Ashtanga Yoga Nilayam Gokulam, Mysuru, Karnataka ☎ 98801 85500, W ashtangayoganilayam.net. Run by students of Pattabhi Jois, and offering tuition in dynamic yoga, affiliated with martial arts. See page 1139.

Brahmani Centre Anjuna, Goa ☎ 99236 99378, W brahmaniyoga.com. Offers drop-in yoga classes – mainly Ashtanga, with a few taster sessions in other styles, plus *pranayama* and *bhajan* devotional singing – by top-notch teachers. See page 720.

Divine Life Society Garhwal, Uttarakhand ☎ 0135 2430040, W sivanandaonline.org. The original Sivananda ashram, with several retreats and courses on all aspects of yoga. See page 316.

International Society for Krishna Consciousness (ISKCON) Kolkata ☎ 033 247 3757; Vrindavan ☎ 0565 442478; Bengaluru ☎ 080 2357 8347; W iskcon.org. Large and well-run international organization with major ashrams and temples in Mayapur, north of Kolkata (see page 778), Vrindavan in west UP (see page 239), Bengaluru (see page 1127) and centres in numerous other locations, both in India and abroad. Promotes *bhakti* yoga (the yoga of devotion) through good deeds, right living and chanting – a way of life rather than a short course.

Osho Commune International Pune, Maharashtra ☎ 020 6601 9999, W osho.com. Established by the enigmatic Osho, this "Meditation Resort" is set in 31 acres of beautifully landscaped gardens and offers a variety of courses in personal therapy, healing and meditation. See page 686.

Prasanthi Nilayam Puttaparthy, Andhra Pradesh ☎ 08555 87390, W sathyasai.org. The ashram of Satya Sai Baba, one of India's most revered and popular gurus, who died in 2011. There is still a worldwide following of millions, with numerous international branches. Visitors sometimes comment on the strict security staffing and rigid rules and regulations. Cheap accommodation is available in dormitories or "flats" for four people. There is no need to book in advance, though you should phone to check availability (see page 951).

Purple Valley Centre Anjuna, Goa ☎ 0832 226 8364, W yogagoa. com. Lovely retreat now run by Sharath Rangaswamy, grandson of the illustrious Ashtanga guru, Shri K. Pattabhi Jois. See page 720.

Root Institute for Wisdom Culture Bodhgaya, Bihar ☎ 0631 220 0714, ⊕ rootinstitute.ngo. Regular seven- to ten-day courses on Tibetan Buddhism and meditation are held here (Oct–March), and there are facilities for individual retreats. Accommodation for longer stays should be booked well in advance. See page 819.

Saccidananda Ashram Thannirpalli, Kulithalai, near Tiruchirapalli, Tamil Nadu ☎ 04323 22260, ⊕ saccidanandaashramshantivanam.000webhostapp.com. Also known as Shantivanam (meaning Peace Forest in Sanskrit), it is situated on the banks of the sacred River Kaveri. Founded by Father Bede Griffiths, a visionary Benedictine monk, it presents a curious but sympathetic fusion of Christianity and Hinduism. Visitors can join in the services and rituals or just relax here. Accommodation is in simple huts dotted around the grounds and meals are communal. Very busy during the major Christian festivals.

Sivananda Yoga Vedanta Dhanwantari Ashram Neyyar Dam, Thiruvananthapuram, Kerala ☎ 94970 08432, ⊕ sivananda.org. in. An offshoot of the original Divine Life Society, this yoga-based ashram focuses on *asanas*, breathing techniques (*pranayama*) and meditation. They also run month-long yoga teacher-training programmes, but book well in advance. There are branches in Madurai, Chennai, Delhi, Uttarkashi and worldwide – see the website for details.

Tushita Meditation Centre McLeod Ganj, Dharamsala 176219, Himachal Pradesh ☎ 89881 60988, ⊕ tushita.info. Offers a range of Tibetan meditation courses. A ten-day course costs in the region of ₹5000; book well in advance.

Vipassana International Academy ⊕ dhamma.org. Runs a wide variety of 3- to 45-day courses in Vipassana meditation at 74 centres across India and more worldwide.

Culture and etiquette

Cultural differences extend to all sorts of little things. While allowances will usually be made for foreigners, visitors unacquainted with Indian customs may need a little preparation to avoid causing offence or making fools of themselves. The list of dos and don'ts here is hardly exhaustive: when in doubt, watch what the Indian people around you are doing.

Eating and the right-hand rule

The biggest minefield of potential faux pas has to do with **eating**. This is usually done with the fingers, and requires practice to get absolutely right. Rule one is: **eat with your right hand only**. In India, as right across Asia, the left hand is for wiping your bottom, cleaning your feet and other unsavoury functions (you also put on and take off your shoes with your left hand), while the right hand is for eating, shaking hands and so on.

Quite how rigid individuals are about this tends to vary, with brahmins (who, at the top of the hierarchical ladder, are one of the two "right-handed castes") and southerners likely to be the strictest. While you can hold a cup or utensil in your left hand, and you can get away with using it to help tear your chapatti, you should not eat, pass food or wipe your mouth with your left hand.

This rule extends beyond food. In general, do not pass anything to anyone with your left hand, or point at anyone with it either; and Indians won't be impressed if you put it in your mouth. In general, you should accept things given to you with your right hand – though using both hands is a sign of respect.

The other rule to beware of when eating or drinking is that your lips should not touch other people's food – *jhutha*, or sullied food, is strictly taboo. Don't, for example, take a bite out of a chapatti and pass it on. When drinking out of a cup or bottle to be shared with others, don't let it touch your lips, but rather pour it directly into your mouth. This custom also protects you from things like hepatitis. It is customary to wash your hands before and after eating.

Temples and religion

Religion is taken very seriously in India; it's important always to show due respect to religious buildings, shrines, images, and people at prayer. When entering a **temple or mosque**, remove your shoes and leave them at the door (socks are acceptable and protect your feet from burning-hot stone ground). Some temples – Jain ones in particular – do not allow you to enter wearing or carrying leather articles, and forbid entry to menstruating women. In the southern state of Kerala, most Hindu temples are closed to non-Hindus, but those that aren't require men to remove their shirts before entering (women must wear long dresses or skirts).

In a mosque, non-Muslims would not normally be allowed in at prayer time and women are sometimes not let in at all. In a Hindu temple, you are often not allowed into the inner sanctum; and at a Buddhist *stupa* or monument, you should always walk round clockwise (ie, with the *stupa* on your right). Hindus are very superstitious about taking photographs of images of deities and inside temples; if in doubt, desist.

Funeral processions are private affairs, and should be left in peace. In Hindu funerals, the body is normally carried to the cremation site within hours of death by white-shrouded relatives (white is the colour of mourning). The eldest son is expected to shave his head and wear white following the death of a parent. At Varanasi and other places, you may see cremations; such occasions should be treated with respect and photographs should not be taken.

Dress

Indian people are very conservative about dress. **Women** are expected to dress modestly, with legs and shoulders covered. Trousers are acceptable, but shorts and short skirts are offensive to many. **Men** should always wear a shirt in public, and avoid skimpy shorts away from beach areas. These rules are particularly important in temples and mosques. Cover your head with a cap or cloth when entering a *dargah* (Sufi shrine) or Sikh *gurudwara*; women in particular are also required to cover their limbs. Men are similarly expected to dress appropriately with their legs and head covered. Caps are usually available on loan, often free, for visitors, and sometimes cloth is available to cover up your arms and legs.

Never mind sky-clad Jains (see page 1210) or Naga Sadhus, **nudity** is not acceptable in India. Topless bathing is not uncommon in Goa (though it is in theory prohibited), but you can be sure the locals don't like it.

In general, Indians find it hard to understand why rich Westerners should wander round in ragged clothes or imitate the lowest ranks of Indian society, who would love to have something more decent to wear. Staying well groomed and dressing "respectably" vastly improves the impression you make on local people and reduces sexual harassment for women, too.

Other possible gaffes

Kissing and **embracing** are regarded in India as part of sex: do not do them in public. In more conservative areas (ie outside Westernized parts of big cities or tourist enclaves), it is still rare for couples to hold hands, though Indian men can sometimes be seen holding hands as a sign of "brotherliness". Be aware of your **feet**. When entering a private home, you should normally remove your shoes (follow your host's example); when sitting, avoid pointing the soles of your feet at anyone. Accidental contact with one's foot is always followed by an apology.

Indian English can be very formal and even ceremonious. Indian people may well call you "sir" or "madam", even "good lady" or "kind sir". At the same time, you should be aware that your English may seem rude to them. In particular, swearing is taken rather seriously, and casual use of the f-word is likely to shock.

Meeting people

Westerners have an ambiguous status in Indian eyes. In one way, you represent the rich sahib, whose culture dominates the world, and the old colonial mentality has not completely disappeared. On the other hand, as a non-Hindu, you are an outcaste, your presence in theory polluting to an orthodox or high-caste Hindu, while to members of all religions, your morals and your standards of spiritual and physical cleanliness are suspect.

As a traveller, you will constantly come across people who want to strike up a **conversation**. English not being their first language, they may not be familiar with the conventional ways of doing this, and thus their opening line may seem abrupt if at the same time very formal. "Excuse me, gentleman, what is your native place?" is a typical one. It is also the first in a series of questions that Indian men seem sometimes to have learnt from a single book in order to ask Western tourists. Some of the questions may baffle at first ("What is your qualification?" "Are you in service?"), some may be queries about the ways of the West or the purpose of your trip, but mostly they will be about your family and your job.

You may find it odd or even intrusive that complete strangers should want to know that sort of thing, but these subjects are considered polite conversation between strangers in India, and help people place one another in terms of social position. Your family, job, even income, are not considered "personal" subjects, and it is completely normal to ask people about them. Asking the same questions back will not be taken amiss – far from it. Being curious does not have the "nosey" stigma in India that it has in the West.

Things that Indian people, especially if they are older or more traditional, are likely to find strange about you are lack of religion (you could adopt one), travelling alone, leaving your family to come to India, being an unmarried couple (letting people think you are married can make life easier), and travelling second class or staying in cheap hotels when, as a tourist, you are relatively rich. You will probably end up having to explain the same things many times to many different people; on the other hand, you can ask questions too, so you could take it as an opportunity to ask things you want to know about India. English-speaking Indians and members of the large and growing middle class in particular are usually extremely well informed and well educated.

Shopping

No country in the world produces such a tempting array of arts and crafts as India. Intensely colourful, delicately worked, exquisitely ornate and immensely varied, India's crafts have the added advantage of being amazingly inexpensive. Every part of the country has its specialities – textiles in Rajasthan, metalwork in Karnataka, carpets in Kashmir, *thangkas* in Ladakh, leatherware in Maharashtra and batik in Odisha – but everywhere you'll see beautiful souvenirs that you'll find hard to resist buying. On top of that, all sorts of things (such as made-to-measure clothes or semi-precious gems) that would be vastly expensive at home are much more reasonably priced. Even if you lose weight during your trip, your baggage might well put on quite a bit – unless of course you post some of it home.

Where to shop

Quite a few items sold in tourist areas are made elsewhere and, needless to say, it's more fun (and cheaper) to pick them up at source. Best buys are noted in the relevant sections of the Guide, along with a few specialities that can't be found outside their regions. India is awash with **street hawkers**, often very young kids. Although they can be annoying and should be dealt with firmly if you are not interested, do not write them off completely as they sometimes have decent souvenirs at lower than shop prices and are open to hard bargaining.

Virtually all the state governments in India run handicraft **"emporia"**, most with branches in the major cities. Delhi, Kolkata, Chennai, Bengaluru, Varanasi and Patna also have **Central Cottage Industries Emporiums** (ⓦcottageemporium.in). Goods in these emporiums are generally of a high quality, even if their fixed prices are a little expensive, and they are worth a visit to get an idea of what crafts are available and how much they should cost.

Bargaining

Whatever you **buy** (except things like food, tickets and other daily items), you will almost always be expected to **haggle** over the price. Bargaining is very much a matter of personal style, but should always be light-hearted, never acrimonious. There are no hard and fast rules – it's really a question of how much something

is worth to you. It's a good plan, therefore, to have an idea of how much you want to pay. Bid low and let the shopkeeper argue you up. If they'll settle for your price or less, you have a deal. If not, you don't, but you've had a pleasant conversation and no harm is done.

Don't worry too much about the first quoted prices. Some people suggest paying a third of the opening price, but it really depends on the shop, the goods and the shopkeeper's impression of you. You may not be able to get the seller much below the first quote; on the other hand, you may end up paying as little as a tenth of it. If you bid too low, you may be hustled out of the shop for offering an "insulting" price, but this is all part of the game, and you'll no doubt be welcomed as an old friend if you return the next day. More often, however, if you start to walk away, the price will magically come down, so that's a useful tactic. "Green" tourists are easily spotted, so try and look like you know what you are up to, even on your first day, or leave it till later; you could wait and see what the going rate is first.

Haggling is a little bit like bidding in an auction, and similar rules apply. Don't start haggling for something if you know you don't want it, and never let any figure pass your lips that you are not prepared to pay – having mentioned a price, you are obliged to pay it. If the seller asks you how much you would pay for something and you don't want it, say so.

Sometimes rickshaw and taxi drivers stop unasked at shops where they get a small **commission** simply for bringing customers. In places like Jaipur and Agra where this is common practice, tourists sometimes even strike a deal with their drivers – agreeing to stop at five shops and splitting the commission for the time wasted. If you're taken to a shop by a tout or driver and you buy something, you pay around fifty percent extra. Stand firm if you have no appetite for such shenanigans. If you want a bargain, shop alone, and never let anybody on the street take you to a shop – if you do, they'll be getting a commission you'll be paying it.

Travelling with children

Travelling with kids can be both challenging and rewarding. Indians are very tolerant of children so you can take them almost anywhere without restriction, and they always help break the ice with strangers.

Most children will enjoy the vibrancy of just being in India, with festivals and temples likely to exert a special appeal. Similarly, you can't go far wrong taking them to beaches and wildlife sanctuaries, although not all Indian zoos are very happy places; the one in Mysuru (see page 1138) is an honourable exception. There are, however, relatively few attractions aimed especially at kids beyond a rash of rather cheesy family theme parks that have popped up in recent years, especially in areas popular with new Indian middle-class holiday-makers, such as the coast south of Chennai. On the other hand, the more modern museums are increasingly introducing interactive displays aimed at the young that are both educational and fun.

As for the difficulties of travel, the main problem with children, especially small ones, is their extra vulnerability. Even more than their parents, they need protection from the **sun**, unsafe drinking water, heat and unfamiliar food. All that **chilli** in particular may be a problem, even with older kids, if they're not used to it. Remember too, that **diarrhoea**, perhaps just a nuisance to you, could be dangerous for a child: rehydration salts (see page 52) are vital if your child goes down with it. Make sure too, if possible, that your child is aware of the dangers of **rabies**; keep children away from animals and consider a rabies jab.

For **babies**, nappies (diapers) are available in most large towns at similar prices to the West, but it's worth taking an additional pack in case of emergencies, and bringing sachets of Calpol or similar, which aren't readily available in India. And if your baby is on powdered milk, it might be an idea to bring some of that: you can certainly get it in India, but it may not taste the same. Dried baby food could also be worth taking – any café or chaiwala should be able to supply you with boiled water.

For touring, hiking or walking, child-carrier backpacks are ideal; some even come with mosquito nets these days. As for luggage, bring as little as possible so you can manage the kids more easily. If your child is small enough, a fold-up buggy is also well worth packing, even if you no longer use a buggy at home, as kids tire so easily in the heat. If you want to cut down on long train or bus journeys by flying, remember that children under 2 travel for ten percent of the adult fare, and under-12s for half-price.

Travel essentials

Costs

For Western visitors, India is still one of the world's less expensive countries. A little foreign currency can go a long way, and you can be confident of getting good value for your money, whether you're setting out to keep your budget to a minimum or to enjoy the opportunities that spending a bit more will make possible.

What you spend obviously depends on where you go, where you stay, how you get around, what you eat and what you buy. Outside the tourist resorts of Kerala and Goa, you can still survive on a **budget** of as little as ₹1000 (£10/US$15) per day, if you eat in local *dhabas*, stay in the cheapest hotels and don't travel too much. In reality, most backpackers nowadays tend to spend at least double that. On ₹2500 (£25/US$37.50) per day you'll be able to afford comfortable mid-range hotels, and meals in smarter restaurants, regular rickshaw or taxi rides and entrance fees to monuments. Spend over ₹6000 (£60/US$90) per day and you can stay in smart hotels, eat in the top restaurants, travel first class on trains and afford chauffeur-driven cars. Although it is possible to travel very comfortably in India, it's also possible to spend a great deal of money if you want to experience the very best the country has to offer, and there are plenty of hotels now charging US$500 per night, sometimes even more.

Budget **accommodation** is still very good value, however. Cheap double rooms start from around ₹400 (£4/US$6) per night, while a no-frills vegetarian **meal** in an ordinary restaurant will typically cost no more than ₹100. Long-distance **transport** can work out to be phenomenally good value if you stick to state buses and standard non-a/c classes on trains, but soon starts to add up if you opt for air-conditioned carriages on the super-fast inter-city services. The 200km trip from Delhi to Agra, for example, can cost anywhere from ₹73 (£0.73/US$1.10) in second-class unreserved up to ₹1203 (£12/US$18) in AC first-class.

Where you are also makes a difference: Mumbai is notoriously pricey, especially for accommodation, and Delhi is also substantially more expensive than most parts of the country. Upscale visitor accommodation in Kerala costs almost as much as it does in Europe, although fierce competition tends to keep prices at the lower end of the budget spectrum down in the tourist towns of Rajasthan. Out in the sticks, on the other hand, and particularly away from your fellow tourists, you will often find things incredibly cheap, though your choice will obviously be more limited.

Don't make any rigid assumptions at the outset of a long trip that your money will last for a certain number of weeks or months. On any one day it may be possible to spend very little, but cumulatively you won't be doing yourself any favours if you don't make sure you keep yourself well rested and properly fed. As a foreigner in India, you will find yourself penalized by double-tier entry prices to museums and historic sites (see box above) as well as in upmarket hotels and

ASI ENTRANCE FEES

The Archeological Survey of India (ASI), who manage many of India's most popular monuments, such as the Taj Mahal, currently operates a **two-tier entry system** at all its sites, whereby foreign visitors, including non-resident Indians (NRIs), pay a lot more than Indian residents. Some private attractions follow a similar policy; we've listed entrance fees for both foreigners and Indian residents (in parenthesis) throughout the Guide.

airfares, both of which are levied at a higher rate and in dollars.

Some independent travellers tend to indulge in wild and highly competitive **penny-pinching**, which Indian people find rather pathetic – they have a fair idea of what you can earn at home. Bargain where appropriate, but don't begrudge a few rupees to someone who is after all far worse off than you. Even if you get a bad deal on every rickshaw journey you make, it will only add a minuscule fraction to the cost of your trip. Remember what great value you are getting in most cases and that luxury items or services at home can be affordable here. At the same time, don't pay well over the odds for something if you know what the going rate is. Thoughtless extravagance can, particularly in remote areas that see a disproportionate number of tourists, contribute to inflation, putting even basic goods and services beyond the reach of local people.

Crime and personal safety

In spite of the crushing poverty and the yawning gulf between rich and poor, India is, on the whole, a **safe** country in which to travel. As a tourist, however, you are an obvious target for the tiny number of thieves (who may include some of your fellow travellers), and stand to face serious problems if you do lose your passport and money or bank cards. Common sense, therefore, suggests a few precautions.

Beware of crowded locations, such as packed buses or trains, in which it is easy for pickpockets to operate – slashing pockets or bags with razor blades is not unheard of in certain locations, and itching powder is sometimes used to distract the unwary. Don't leave valuables unattended on the beach when you go for a swim; backpacks in dormitory accommodation are also obvious targets, as is luggage on the roof of buses. Even monkeys rate a mention here, since it's not unknown for them to steal things from hotel

rooms with open windows, or even to snatch bags from unsuspecting shoulders.

Budget travellers would do well to carry a **padlock**, as these are usually used to secure the doors of cheap hotel rooms and it's reassuring to know you have the only key. You can also use them to lock your bag to seats or racks in trains, for which a length of chain also comes in handy. Don't put valuables in your luggage but keep them with you at all times. If your baggage is on the roof of a bus, make sure it is well secured. On trains and buses, the prime time for theft is just before you leave, so keep a particular eye on your gear then, beware of deliberate diversions, and don't put your belongings next to open windows. Remember that routes popular with tourists tend to be popular with thieves too. Druggings leading to theft and worse are rare but not unheard of, so you are best advised to politely refuse food and drink from fellow passengers or passing strangers, unless you are completely confident it's the family picnic you are sharing or have seen the food purchased from a vendor.

However, **don't get paranoid**; the best way of enjoying the country is to stay relaxed but with your wits about you. Crime levels in India are a long way below those of Western countries and violent crime against tourists is almost unheard of. Virtually none of the people who approach you on the street intend any harm: most want to sell you something (though this is not always made apparent immediately), some want to practise their English, others to chat you up, while more than a few just want to add your address to their book or have a snap taken with you. Anyone offering wonderful-sounding moneymaking schemes, however, is almost certain to be a con artist.

If you do feel threatened, it's worth looking for help. **Tourism police** are found sitting in clearly marked booths in the main railway stations, especially in big tourist centres, where they will also have a booth in the main bus station. In addition, they may have a marked booth outside major tourist sites.

Be wary of **credit-card fraud**; a credit card can be used to make duplicate forms by which your account is then billed for fictitious transactions, so don't let shops or restaurants take your card away to process – insist they do it in front of you or follow them to the point of transaction. It's not a bad idea to keep US$200 or so separately from the rest of your money, along with insurance policy number and phone number for claims, and a photocopy of the pages in your passport containing personal data and your Indian visa. This will cover you in case you do lose all your valuables.

If the worst happens and you get **robbed**, the first thing to do is report the theft as soon as possible to the local police. They are very unlikely to recover your belongings but you need a report from them in order to claim on your travel insurance. Dress smartly and expect an uphill battle – city cops in particular tend to be jaded from too many insurance scams.

Losing your passport is a real hassle, but does not necessarily mean the end of your trip. First, report the loss immediately to the police, who will issue you with the all-important "complaint form" that you need to be able to travel around and check into hotels, as well as claim back any expenses incurred in replacing your passport from your insurer. The next thing to do is telephone your nearest embassy or consulate in India. Normally, passports have to be applied for and collected in person, but if you are stranded, it is usually possible to arrange to receive the necessary forms in the post. However, you still have to go to the embassy or consulate to pick up your new passport. Emergency passports are the cheapest form of replacement, but are normally only valid for the few days of your return flight. If you're not sure when you're leaving India, you'll have to obtain a more costly full passport; these can only be issued by high commissions, embassies and larger consulates, although they can be arranged through consulates in Chennai, Kolkata, Mumbai or Panjim (Goa), and in the case of the UK, Bengaluru, Hyderabad and Ahmedabad.

Duty-free allowance

Anyone over 17 can bring in one US quart (0.95 litre – but nobody's going to quibble about the other 5ml) of spirits, or a bottle of wine and 250ml spirits; plus 200 cigarettes, or 50 cigars, or 250g tobacco. You may be required to register anything valuable on a tourist baggage re-export form to make sure you can take it home with you, and to fill in a currency declaration form if carrying more than US$10,000 or equivalent.

Electricity

Generally 220V 50Hz AC, though direct current supplies also exist, so check before plugging in. Most sockets are triple round-pin (accepting European-size double round-pin plugs). British, Irish and Australasian plugs will need an adaptor, preferably universal; American and Canadian appliances will need a transformer too, unless multivoltage. Power cuts and voltage variations are very common; voltage stabilizers should be used to run sensitive appliances such as laptops.

Insurance

It's imperative that you take out proper **travel insurance** before setting off for India. A typical travel insurance policy usually provides cover for the loss of baggage,

DRUGS

India is a centre for the production of **cannabis** and to a lesser extent **opium**, and derivatives of these drugs are widely available. **Charas** (hashish) is produced all along the Himalayas, while **ganja** (marijuana) is the more common form in the south. The use of cannabis is frowned upon by respectable Indians – if you see anyone in a movie smoking a chillum, you can be sure it's the baddie. Sadhus, on the other hand, are allowed to smoke it legally as part of their religious devotion to Shiva, who is said to have originally discovered its narcotic properties.

Bhang (a preparation made from marijuana leaves, which it is claimed sometimes contains added hallucinogenic ingredients such as *datura*) is legal and widely available in bhang shops: it is used to make sweets and drinks such as the notoriously potent bhang lassis which have waylaid many an unwary traveller. Bhang shops also frequently sell ganja, low-quality *charas* and opium (*chandu*), mainly from Rajasthan and Madhya Pradesh. Opium derivatives morphine and heroin are widespread too, with addiction an increasing problem among the urban poor. "Brown sugar" that you may be offered on the street is number-three heroin; Punjab has become notorious for its heroin problem, the drugs smuggled across the border from Pakistan. Use of other illegal drugs such as LSD, ecstasy and cocaine is largely confined to tourists in party locations such as Goa.

All of these drugs except bhang are strictly controlled under Indian **law**. Anyone arrested with less than five grams of cannabis, which they are able to prove is for their own use, is liable to a six-month maximum, but cases can take years to come to trial (two is normal, and eight not unheard of). Police raids and searches are particularly common in the Kullu and Parvati valleys (and on vehicles leaving them, especially at harvest time) and the beach areas of Goa. "Paying a fine now" may be possible on arrest (though it will probably mean all the money you have), but once you are booked in at the station, your chances are slim; a minority of the population languishing in Indian jails are foreigners on drugs charges.

ROUGH GUIDES TRAVEL INSURANCE

Rough Guides has teamed up with **WorldNomads.com** to offer great travel insurance deals. Policies are available to residents of over 150 countries, with cover for a wide range of adventure sports, 24hr emergency assistance, high levels of medical and evacuation cover and a stream of travel safety information. Roughguides.com users can take advantage of their policies online 24/7, from anywhere in the world – even if you're already travelling. And since plans often change when you're on the road, you can extend your policy and even claim online. Roughguides.com users who buy travel insurance with WorldNomads.com can also leave a positive footprint and donate to a community development project. For more information, go to ⓦ roughguides.com/travel-insurance.

tickets and – up to a certain limit – cash, as well as cancellation or curtailment of your journey. Most of them exclude so-called dangerous sports unless an extra premium is paid: in India this can mean scuba diving, whitewater rafting, windsurfing and trekking with ropes, though probably not jeep safaris. Many policies can be chopped and changed to exclude coverage you don't need – for example, sickness and accident benefits can often be excluded or included at will. If you do take medical coverage, ascertain whether benefits will be paid as treatment proceeds or only after return home, and whether there is a 24hr medical emergency number. When securing baggage cover, make sure that the per-article limit – typically under £500 – will cover your most valuable possession. If you need to make a claim, you should keep receipts for medicines and medical treatment, and in the event you have anything stolen, you must obtain an official statement from the police.

Internet

Broadband has now reached more or less everywhere, leading to a proliferation of **wi-fi** connections. The majority of hotels and guesthouses, at least those in touristic areas, will offer wi-fi, usually free but occasionally chargeable; we have noted exceptions in our accommodation reviews. Many cafés and restaurants also have wi-fi facilities and chains such as McDonald's, Café Coffee Day and Starbucks offer connection. The number of **internet outlets** has declined but you can usually still find somewhere with public computers in any sizeable town, charging from ₹20–40/hr in urban areas to as much as ₹300/hr in more remote places such as the Andaman Islands. Speeds can still be painfully slow and computers rather antiquated, making it difficult to load complex websites or to perform online transactions (like booking a train ticket).

Laundry

Although some hotels have washing machines and independent launderettes are starting to appear, most places still send laundry to a *dhobi*, either in-house or nearby. The *dhobi* will take your dirty washing to a *dhobi ghat*, a public clothes-washing area (the bank of a river for example), where it is shown some old-fashioned discipline: separated, soaped and given a damn good thrashing to beat the dirt out of it. Then it is hung out to dry in the sun and taken to the ironing sheds where every garment is endowed with razor-sharp creases and then matched to its rightful owner by hidden cryptic markings. Your clothes will come back absolutely spotless, though this kind of violent treatment does take it out of them: buttons get lost and eventually the cloth starts to fray.

Left luggage

Most stations in India have "cloakrooms" (sometimes called parcel offices) for passengers to leave their baggage. These can be extremely handy if you want to go sightseeing in a town and move on the same day. In theory, you need a train ticket to deposit luggage, but staff don't always ask; they may, however, refuse to take your bag if you can't lock it. If you lose your reclaim ticket expect a lot of bureaucracy before you can get your bag back. Many cloakrooms in large stations operate 24 hours but smaller ones may not. The standard charge is currently ₹15 for the first 24 hours, plus ₹20 per day afterwards.

LGBTQ travellers

The LGBTQ movement in India had a big win in 2018 when homosexuality was made legal again, having been made illegal by the conservative Modi government in 2013. However, homosexuality is not hugely open or widely accepted in India and prejudice is still ingrained, especially in conservative areas such as Rajasthan.

For **lesbians**, making contacts is difficult; even the Indian women's movement does not readily promote lesbianism as an issue that needs confronting. The only public faces of a hidden scene are the few organizations in major cities (see below). For **gay men**, homosexuality is no longer solely the preserve of the alternative scene of actors and artists, and is increasingly accepted by the upper classes, though Mumbai remains much more a centre for gay life than Delhi, let alone traditionalist Rajasthan. Despite the legal uncertainties, however, gay **pride** events and clubs are becoming more common in many cities; in recent years Delhi, Mumbai, Bengaluru, Chennai and some smaller cities have all hosted prides.

One **transgender** group of people you may come across are **hijras**, who were officially recognized as third gender by the Supreme Court in 2014. Many hijras are born with genitals that are neither fully male nor female, but some are male-to-female transsexual. They live in their own "families" and have a niche in Indian society, but not an easy one. At weddings, their presence is supposed to bring good luck, and they are usually given baksheesh for putting in a brief appearance. Generally, however, they have a low social status, face widespread discrimination, and many make a living by begging or prostitution.

LGBTQ CONTACTS AND RESOURCES

Chennai Dost Ⓦ facebook.com/chennaidost. Useful page aimed at the LGBTQ community in Chennai.

Galva-108 Ⓦ galva108.org. Interesting website set up by gay and lesbian Vaishnavas and Hindus.

Gay Bombay Ⓦ gaybombay.org. Comprehensive online resource for the LGBTQ community in Mumbai.

Gay Tours India Ⓦ gaytripindia.com. Tour operator specialising in tours for gay and lesbian travellers.

Gay Delhi Ⓦ gaydelhi.tripod.com. Weekly social meetings and other events for gay men in Delhi.

Humsafar Trust Ⓦ humsafar.org. Set up to promote safe sex among gay men, with lots of links and up-to-date information.

Indian Dost Ⓦ indiandost.com. LGBTQ networking and info.

Outright Action International Ⓦ outrightinternational.org. Latest news on the human rights situation for LGBTQ people worldwide, including regular bulletins on India.

Trikone Ⓦ trikone.org. Organization campaigning for LGBTQ rights in South Asia.

Maps

Getting good maps of India, in India, can be difficult. The government – in an archaic suspicion of cartography, and in spite of clear coverage of the country on Google – forbids the sale of detailed maps of border areas, which includes the entire coastline.

It therefore makes sense to bring a **full country map** of India with you. Freytag & Berndt produce the best country map, while Nelles covers parts of the country with 1:1,500,000 regional maps. These are generally excellent, but cost a fortune if you buy the complete set. Their double-sided map of the Himalayas is useful for roads and planning and has some detail but is not sufficient as a trekking map. Ttk, a Chennai-based company, publishes basic state maps which are widely available in India, and in some specialized travel and map shops in the UK such as Stanfords; these are poorly drawn but useful for road distances. The Indian Railways map at the back of the publication Trains at a Glance (see page 35) is useful for planning railway journeys.

If you need larger-scale **city maps** than the ones we provide in this guide you can sometimes get them from tourist offices, though the plans published free online at Google Maps (Ⓦ maps.google.com) or OpenStreetMap (Ⓦ openstreetmap.org) are vastly superior and many can be downloaded for offline use. Also try the Navmii app (Ⓦ navmii.com) for offline directions. Eicher (Ⓦ maps.eicherworld.com) has a growing series of glossy City Maps and city Road Maps produced in India and available at all good bookstores.

As for **trekking maps**, the US Army Map Service produced maps in the 1960s which, with a scale of 1:250,000, remain sufficiently accurate on topography, but are of course outdated on the latest road developments. Most other maps you can buy are based on these, and they're still the best available for most of the Himalayan regions. Leomann Maps (1:200,000) also cover the northwest Himalayan regions. These are not contour maps and are therefore better for planning and basic reference than for trekking. The Survey of India publishes a rather poor 1:250,000 series for trekkers in the Uttarakhand Himalayas – simplified versions of their own infinitely more reliable maps, produced for the military, which are absolutely impossible for an outsider to get hold of.

Money

India's unit of currency is the **rupee**, usually abbreviated ₹ and divided into a hundred paise. Almost all money is paper, with notes of 5, 10, 20, 50, 100, 500 and 1000 rupees. Coins in circulation are 1, 2, 5 and 10 rupees, the latter two gradually replacing the paper versions, plus (rarely seen) 50 paise. Note that it's technically illegal to take rupees in or out of India (although they are widely available at overseas forexes), so you might want to wait until you arrive before changing money.

Banknotes, especially lower denominations, can get into a terrible state. Don't accept torn banknotes, since no one else will be prepared to take them and you'll be left saddled with the things, though you can

EXCHANGE RATES

At the time of writing in early 2019, the **exchange rate** was approximately ₹90 to £1, ₹80 to €1 and ₹70 to US$1. You can check current exchange rates online at ⓦxe.com.

change them at the Reserve Bank of India and large branches of other big banks. Don't pass them on to beggars; they can't use them either, so it amounts to an insult.

Large denominations can also be a problem, as change is usually in short supply. Many Indian people cannot afford to keep much lying around, and you shouldn't necessarily expect shopkeepers or rickshaw-walas to have it (and they may – as may you – try to hold onto it if they do). Larger notes can be changed for smaller denominations at hotels and other suitable establishments.

ATMs and banking cards

The easiest way to access your money in India is with **plastic**, though It's a good idea to also have some backup in the form of cash. You will find **ATMs** at main banks in all major towns, cities and tourist areas, though your card issuer may well add a foreign transaction fee, and the Indian bank will also levy a small charge, generally around ₹25. Your card issuer, and sometimes the ATM itself, imposes limits on the amount you may withdraw in a day – typically ₹10,000–20,000.

Credit cards are accepted for payment at major hotels, top restaurants, some shops and airline offices, but virtually nowhere else. American Express, Master-Card and Visa are the likeliest to be accepted. Beware of people making extra copies of the receipt, in order to fraudulently bill you later; always insist that the transaction is made before your eyes.

Visa, American Express and some other financial institutions offer **prepaid cards** that you can load up with credit before you leave home and use in ATMs like a debit card – effectively replacing the increasingly defunct travellers' cheques.

One big downside of relying on plastic as your main access to cash, of course, is that cards can easily get lost or stolen, so take along a couple of alternatives if you can, keep an emergency stash of cash just in case, and make a note of your home bank's telephone number and website addresses for emergencies.

US dollars are the easiest **currency** to convert, with euros and pounds sterling not far behind. Major hard currencies can be changed easily in tourist areas and big cities, less so elsewhere. If you enter the country

with more than US$10,000 or the equivalent, you are supposed to fill in a currency declaration form.

Changing money

Changing money in regular **banks**, especially government-run banks such as the State Bank of India (SBI), can be a time-consuming business, involving lots of form-filling and queueing at different counters, so it's best to change substantial amounts at any one time. You'll have no such problems, however, with **private companies** such as Thomas Cook, American Express or forex agents. Major cities and main tourist centres usually have several **licensed currency exchange bureaux**; rates usually aren't as good as at a bank but transactions are generally a lot quicker and there's less paperwork to complete.

Outside **banking hours** (Mon–Fri 10am–2/4pm, Sat 10am–noon), large hotels may change money, probably at a lower rate, and exchange bureaux have longer opening hours. Banks in the arrivals halls at most major airports stay open 24 hours.

Wherever you change money, hold on to **exchange receipts** ("encashment certificates"); they will be required if you want to change back any excess rupees when you leave the country and to buy air tickets and reserve train berths with rupees at special counters for foreigners. The State Bank of India now charges for tax clearance forms.

Opening hours

Standard shop opening hours in India are Monday to Saturday 9.30am to 6pm, with Sunday openings increasingly common. Most big stores, at any rate, keep those hours, while smaller shops vary from town to town, region to region, and one to another, but usually keep longer hours. Government tourist offices are open Monday to Friday 9.30am to 5pm, Saturday 9.30am to 1pm, closed on the second Saturday of the month; state-run tourist offices are likely to be open Monday to Friday 10am to 5pm.

Phones

Since the mobile phone revolution, privately run phone **international direct-dialling** facilities – **STD/ISD** (Standard Trunk Dialling/International Subscriber Dialling) places – have become far less common so you can't always rely on finding one. In addition, calling from them will cost more than dialling from a mobile if you have an Indian SIM card. Most visitors bring their own phones and buy an Indian SIM to cover their trip (ensure your phone isn't locked to a specific network).

SIM cards are sold through most cellphone shops and network outlets, and there are often stalls located in airport arrivals terminals. You have to provide a photocopy of your passport (photo and visa pages), and you may be required to declare an Indian address, though the hotel you are staying in usually suffices. There is an initial connection fee ranging from ₹50 to ₹250, depending on the dealer and network.

Coverage varies from state to state, but the largest national network providers are best (Vodafone, Airtel and Idea) and have 3G connectivity. Once you have paid for the initial card, it can be topped up ("re-charged" as it's known) by amounts ranging from ₹10–1000, though only by paying specific amounts (check with the retailer) will you get the full amount in credits. You can also opt for a package including data, calls and texts. Call charges to the UK and US from most Indian networks cost ₹2–3 per minute. Also, ask your card supplier to turn on the "do not disturb" option, or you'll be plagued with spam calls and spam texts from the phone company.

Indian **mobile** numbers are ten-digit, starting with a 7, 8 or (most commonly) a 9. However, if you are calling from outside the state where the mobile is based (but not from abroad), you need to add a zero in front of that.

Calling an Indian mobile or landline from a UK landline, you can save a lot of money by dialling via a company such as Planet Talk (W planet-talk.co.uk), which requires no sign-up but uses an 0843 number, or better still by signing up cost-free with a VoIP provider such as 18185 (W 18185.co.uk). In the US you can make cheap calls via reasonable monthly deals on Phone.com (W phone.com).

Photography

Beware of pointing your camera at anything that might be considered "strategic", including airports and anything military. Remember to respect people's privacy and ask before you take a photo of any locals or religious men (you may occasionally be asked to pay a few rupees to the subject). More likely, you'll get people, especially kids, volunteering to pose and it's quite common for Indians to ask you to be in their snaps. Almost all photo shops can now transfer digital images onto a memory stick or CD – useful in order to free up memory space.

Post

Post can take anything from six days to three weeks to get to or from India, depending on where you are and the country you are posting to; ten days is about the norm. Most **post offices** are open Monday to Friday from 10am to 5pm and Saturday from 10am to noon, but town GPOs keep longer hours (usually Mon–Sat 9.30am–1pm & 2–5.30pm). **Stamps** are not expensive, but you'll have to stick them on yourself as they tend not to be self-adhesive (every post office keeps a pot of evil-smelling glue for this purpose). Aerogrammes and postcards cost the same to anywhere in the world. Ideally, you should also have mail franked in front of you.

Sending a parcel from India can be a performance. First take it to a tailor to have it wrapped in cheap cotton cloth, stitched up and sealed with wax. Next, take it to the post office, fill in and attach the relevant customs forms, buy your stamps, see them franked and dispatch it. Surface mail is incredibly cheap, and takes an average of six months to arrive – it may take half, or four times that, however. It's a good way to dump excess baggage and souvenirs, but don't send anything fragile this way.

Sexism and women's issues

India is not a country that provides huge obstacles to women travellers. In the days of the Raj, many upper-class women travelled through India alone, as did the female flower children of the hippie era. Plenty of women travel solo today, but few get through their trip without any hassle, so it's good to be prepared.

Indian streets are often dominated by male groups and you may find yourself subjected to incessant staring, whistling and cat-calling. Most of your fellow travellers on trains and buses will be men, who may start up most unwelcome conversations about sex, divorce and the freedom of relationships in the West. These cannot often be avoided, but demonstrating

---

CALLING HOME FROM ABROAD

To make an international call, dial the international access code (in India it's 00, then the destination's country code, before the rest of the number. Note that the initial zero is omitted from the area code when dialling the UK, Ireland, Australia and New Zealand from abroad.

Australia international access code + 61
New Zealand international access code + 64
UK international access code + 44
US and Canada international access code + 1
Ireland international access code + 353
South Africa international access code + 27

RAPE, MURDER AND AN "EVERYDAY EXPERIENCE"

On December 16, 2012, a 23-year-old female physiotherapy student and a male friend boarded a bus at Munirka in South Delhi. Unknown to her, the driver was on a joyride and the five other male passengers were his friends. Beating her friend unconscious, they gang-raped and brutally abused her in the back of the bus. They then dumped the unfortunate couple naked on a road near the airport. The rape victim was rushed to hospital with serious internal injuries, and was even flown for emergency treatment to Singapore, but ten days after the attack she died. The incident suddenly brought to public attention the high frequency of rape and sexual assault in Delhi, and sparked off violent protests that lasted for several days. The perpetrators were arrested and the government hurriedly brought in the death penalty for rape, but real change will need a shift in public attitudes. As another female medical student told the press, sexual harassment in Delhi is an "everyday experience" for women in the city. The shocking story of the rape, and subsequent protests, is retold in the powerful 2015 documentary *India's Daughter* (ⓦindiasdaughter.com).

In the aftermath, more rape cases gained publicity, perhaps because the victims were emboldened to report the crimes and the press eager to continue focusing on the now hot issue. In a celebrated case in Mumbai in 2013, for example, the perpetrators of a gang rape received the death penalty, reinforcing the shift in attitudes and legal action since the South Delhi incident.

Despite these horrific cases, India remains a generally safe destination, especially if sensible precautions are taken.

too much enthusiasm to discuss such topics can lure men into thinking that you are easy about sex, and the situation could become threatening. At its worst in larger cities, all this can become very tiring. You can get around it to a certain extent by joining women in public places.

If travelling with a man, expect Indian men to approach him (it will be assumed he is your husband) and talk about you quite happily as if you were not there. Beware, however, if you are (or look) of Indian origin with a non-Indian male companion: this may well cause you harassment, as you might be seen to have brought shame on your family by adopting the loose morals of the West.

In addition to staring and suggestive comments and looks, **sexual harassment**, or "Eve teasing" as it is bizarrely known, is likely to be a nuisance. It's not unlikely that you will get groped in crowds and not unusual to have men "accidentally" squeeze past you at any opportunity. It tends to be worse in cities than in small towns and villages, but being followed can be a real problem wherever you are.

Local women tend to dress modestly in items such as a *salwar kameez* with loose trousers, and many cover their hair (usually for religious reasons). Smoking or drinking in public may also cause unwanted attention.

You may see Indian women become mildly aggressive when offended (a slap or a punch on the arm, for example) – it might be effective but try this at your own risk. It will also likely attract attention and urge someone to help you, or at least deal with the offender – a man transgressing social norms is always out of line and any passer-by will want to let him know it.

Going to watch a Bollywood movie at the cinema is a fun and essential part of your trip to India but, at cheap cinemas especially, such an occasion is rarely without hassle. As an all-round rule, sticking to slightly more upmarket or touristy restaurants, bars and cinemas will likely result in less hassle.

Violent sexual assaults on tourists are extremely rare but the number of reported cases of rape is slowly rising, and you should always take precautions: avoid quiet, dimly lit streets and alleys at night, as well as remote rural locations; if you find a trustworthy rickshaw/taxi driver in the day keep him for the night journey. While Indian women are still quite timid about reporting rape – it is considered as much a disgrace to the victim as to the perpetrator – Western victims should always report it to the police. Letting other tourists, or locals, know of any incident in the hope that pressure from the community may uncover the offender and see him brought to justice is also likely to be effective.

The **practicalities of travel** take on a new dimension for solo female travellers. In hotels watch out for "peep-holes" in your door (and in common bathrooms), and note that tampons are not widely available outside main cities.

There are many situations in which it's beneficial to be a woman or group of women in India, though. For example, you might well be more welcome in some private houses than a group of Western males, and women frequently get preference at bus and railway stations where they can join a separate "ladies' queue", and use ladies' waiting rooms. On trains the enclosed ladies' compartments are peaceful havens (unless filled with noisy children); you could also try to share a berth section with a family where you are usually drawn into the security of the group and are less exposed to staring.

Time

India is all in one time zone and remains the same year round: GMT+5hr 30min. This makes it 5hr 30min ahead of London, 10hr 30min ahead of New York, 13hr 30min ahead of LA, 4hr 30min behind Sydney and 6hr 30min behind New Zealand; however, daylight saving time in those places will change the difference by an hour. Indian time is referred to as IST (Indian Standard Time, which cynics refer to as "Indian stretchable time").

Tipping and baksheesh

As a well-off visitor you'll be expected to be liberal with your **tips**. Low-paid workers in **hotels and restaurants** often accept lower pay than they should in the expectation of generous tips during the tourist season. Ten percent, or a simple rounding up, should be regarded as acceptable if you've received good service – more if the staff have really gone out of their way to be helpful. **Taxi and auto-rickshaw drivers** will not expect tips unless you've made unplanned diversions or stops. What to tip your driver at the end of long tours, however, is a trickier issue, especially if you've been forking out ₹150–200 for their daily allowance, as well as paying for meals. The simple answer is to give what you think they deserve, and what you can afford. Drivers working for tour operators, even more than hotel staff and waiters, depend on tips to get through the off-season (many are paid only ₹200–300 per day because their bosses know that foreign customers tend to tip well).

Alms giving (baksheesh) is common throughout India; people with disabilities and mutilations often congregate in city centres and popular resorts, where they survive from begging. In such cases a few coins up to ₹10–20 should be sufficient. Kids demanding money, pens, sweets or the like are a different case: yielding to any request only encourages them to pester others.

Toilets

Western-style toilets are becoming much more common in India now, especially in hotels and lodges in touristy areas, though you'll probably still come across a few traditional "squat" toilets – basically a hole in the ground. Paper, if used, often goes in a bucket next to the loo rather than down it. Instead, Indians use a jug of water and their left hand or the hose provided, a method you may also come to prefer, but if you do use paper, keep some handy, especially if staying in basic accommodation or going too far off the beaten track. Travelling is especially difficult for women as facilities are limited or nonexistent, especially when travelling by road rather than by rail. However, toilets in the a/c carriages of trains are usually kept clean, as are those in mid-range and air-conditioned restaurants. You might also find tourist toilets at every major historical site. For ₹5 you get water, mirrors, toilet paper and a clean sit-down loo.

Tourist information

The main tourist website for India is Ⓦ incredibleindia. org. The Indian government also maintains a number of **tourist offices abroad**, whose staff are usually helpful and knowledgeable; addresses and contact details can be found on Ⓦ bit.ly/IndiaTourismoffices. Other sources of information include the websites of Indian embassies and tourist offices, travel agents (who are in business for themselves, so their advice may not always be totally unbiased), and Indian Railways representatives abroad.

Inside India, both national and local governments run tourist information offices, providing general travel advice and handing out an array of printed material, from city maps to glossy leaflets on specific destinations. The Indian government's tourist depart-ment, whose main offices are on Janpath in New Delhi (see page 110) and opposite Churchgate railway station in Mumbai (see page 630), has branches in most regional capitals. These, however, operate independently of the state government information counters and their commercial bureaux are run by the state tourism development corporations, usually referred to by their initials (e.g. MPTDC in Madhya Pradesh, RTDC in Rajasthan, and so on), which offer a wide range of travel facilities, including guided tours, car rental and their own hotels. A list of state tourist office websites is given below.

Just to confuse things further, the Indian govern-ment's tourist office has a corporate wing, too. The Indian Tourism Development Corporation (ITDC) is responsible for the Ashok chain of hotels and operates tour and travel services, frequently competing with its state counterparts.

There's all sorts of information available about India **online** – we've listed the best websites in relevant places throughout the Guide. One particularly good general site is Ⓦ indiamike.com, which features lively chat rooms, bulletin boards, photo archives and banks of members' travel articles.

TRAVEL ADVICE

Australian Department of Foreign Affairs Ⓦ smartraveller.gov.au.
Canadian Department of Foreign Affairs Ⓦ voyage.gc.ca.
Irish Department of Foreign Affairs Ⓦ dfa.ie.
New Zealand Ministry of Foreign Affairs Ⓦ safetravel.govt.nz.
South African Department of Foreign Affairs Ⓦ dirco.gov.za.
UK Foreign & Commonwealth Office Ⓦ fco.gov.uk.
US State Department Ⓦ travel.state.gov.

STATE TOURISM WEBSITES

Andaman and Nicobar Islands Ⓦ go2andaman.com.
Andhra Pradesh Ⓦ aptdc.gov.in.
Arunachal Pradesh Ⓦ arunachaltourism.com.
Assam Ⓦ assamtourismonline.com.
Bihar Ⓦ bstdc.bih.nic.in.
Chandigarh Ⓦ chandigarhtourism.gov.in.
Chhattisgarh Ⓦ chhattisgarhtourism.net.
Daman Ⓦ daman.nic.in.
Diu Ⓦ diutourism.com.
Goa Ⓦ goa-tourism.com.
Gujarat Ⓦ gujarattourism.com.
Haryana Ⓦ haryanatourism.gov.in.
Himachal Pradesh Ⓦ hptdc.in.
Jammu & Kashmir Ⓦ jktourism.org.
Jharkhand Ⓦ jharkhandtourism.gov.in.
Karnataka Ⓦ karnatakatourism.org.
Kerala Ⓦ keralatourism.org.
Lakshadweep Ⓦ lakshadweeptourism.com.
Madhya Pradesh Ⓦ mptourism.com.
Maharashtra Ⓦ maharashtratourism.gov.in.
Manipur Ⓦ tourismmanipur.gov.in.
Meghalaya Ⓦ megtourism.gov.in.
Mizoram Ⓦ tourism.mizoram.gov.in.
Nagaland Ⓦ tourismnagaland.com.
Odisha Ⓦ orissa-tourism.com.
Puducherry Ⓦ tourism.puducherry.gov.in.
Punjab Ⓦ punjabtourism.gov.in.
Rajasthan Ⓦ rajasthantourism.gov.in.
Sikkim Ⓦ sikkimtourism.gov.in.
Tamil Nadu Ⓦ tamilnadutourism.org.
Telangana Ⓦ telanganatourism.gov.in.
Tripura Ⓦ tripuratourism.nic.in.
Uttarakhand Ⓦ uttarakhandtourism.gov.in.
Uttar Pradesh Ⓦ uptourism.gov.in.
West Bengal Ⓦ wbtourism.gov.in.

Travellers with disabilities

Disability is common in India; many conditions that would be curable in the West, such as cataracts, are permanent disabilities here because people can't afford the treatment. Those with disabilities are unlikely to receive the best treatment available, and the choice is usually between staying at home to be looked after by your family and going out on the street to beg for alms.

For **travellers with a disability**, this has its advantages and disadvantages. Disability doesn't get the same embarrassed reaction from Indian people that it does from some able-bodied Westerners. On the other hand, you'll be lucky to see a state-of-the-art wheelchair or a disabled loo, and the streets are full of all sorts of obstacles that would be hard for a blind or wheelchair-bound tourist to negotiate independently. Kerbs are often high, pavements uneven and littered, and ramps nonexistent. There are potholes all over the place and open sewers. Some of the more expensive hotels have ramps for the movement of luggage and equipment, but if that makes them accessible to wheelchairs, it is by accident rather than design. Nonetheless, the 1995 Persons with Disabilities Act specifies access for all to public buildings, and is sometimes enforced. A visit to Delhi by Professor Stephen Hawking in 2001 resulted in the appearance of ramps at several Delhi tourist sights including the Red Fort, Qutub Minar and Jantar Mantar, and most major Indian airports and metro systems have also been made a lot more accessible for chair users.

If you walk with difficulty, you will find India's many street obstacles and steep stairs hard going. Another factor that can be a problem is the constant barrage of people proffering things (hard to wave aside if you are, for instance, on crutches), and all that queueing, not to mention heat, will take it out of you if you have a condition that makes you tire quickly. A light, folding camp-stool is one thing that could be invaluable if you have limited walking or standing power.

Then again, Indian people are likely to be very helpful if, for example, you need their help getting on and off buses or up stairs. Taxis and rickshaws are easily affordable and very adaptable; if you rent one for a day, the driver is certain to help you on and off, and perhaps even around the sites you visit. If you employ a guide, they may also be prepared to help you with steps and obstacles.

If complete independence is out of the question, going with an able-bodied companion might be on the cards. There are some specialist operators for tourists with limited mobility – Enable Holidays (Ⓦ enableholidays.com) offer a good "Golden Triangle" tour, for example – and some mainstream package-tour operators try to cater for travellers with disabilities but you should always contact any operator and discuss your exact needs with them before making a booking. You should also make sure you are covered by any insurance policy you take out.

For more information about disability issues in India, check the government website ⓦ disabilityaffairs.gov.in.

Volunteering

It is illegal for a foreign tourist to work in India, although some obtain a business visa to work in TEFL, business or high-tech. Many visitors, however, do engage in some voluntary charitable work. Several charities welcome volunteers on a medium-term commitment, say over two months, but many places also welcome much shorter term, less formal involvement. As well as the list below, other local organizations are mentioned throughout the book.

If you want to spend your time working as a volunteer for an **NGO** (non-governmental organization), you should make arrangements well before you arrive by contacting the body in question, rather than on spec. Special visas are generally not required unless you intend to work for longer than six months. For information about which NGOs are operating across the country, log on to ⓦ csridentity.com/india/index.asp and select options from a drop-down list, or see what's available through the worldwide VSO organization at ⓦ vsointernational.org.

VOLUNTEERING RESOURCES

Animal Aid Unlimited ⓦ animalaidunlimited.org. Animal welfare group working to alleviate animal suffering in Udaipur, Rajasthan (see page 213). No special skills are required, though volunteers with veterinary knowledge are especially welcome.

Concern India Foundation ⓦ concernindiafoundation. org. Charitable trust supporting grassroots NGOs working with disadvantaged people, with offices in seven cities.

Darjeeling Children's Trust ⓦ darjeelingchildrenstrust.org. uk. UK-based charity, supporting eight primary schools, all within walking distance of the Chowrasta. Volunteers welcome for a week or more.

DISHA Foundation ⓦ dishafoundation.org. Jaipur-based resource centre for children with cerebral palsy and other disabilities. Needs donations, sponsors and volunteers with time or specific skills.

Goa Animal Welfare Trust (GAWT) ⓦ gawt.org. GAWT does sterling work with stray and mistreated animals, and welcomes volunteers in centres around Goa.

Indicorps ⓦ indicorps.org. US-based charity, contactable in Mumbai, with various projects for people of Indian origin to volunteer on.

Mandore Medical and Relief Society ⓦ mandore.com. Guesthouse which takes on volunteers for periods as short as a week to work in health awareness and education projects in rural areas around Jodhpur.

Mango Tree Goa ⓦ mangotreegoa.org. A British-run operation that works with disadvantaged children in Goa.

Mother Teresa of Calcutta Center ⓦ motherteresa.org. Charity that carries on the work of the most famous volunteer of them all (see page 764).

Salaam Baalak Trust ⓦ salaambaalaktrust.com. Charity working to help street children in in and around Delhi's Paharganj (see page 90).

Sambhali Trust ⓦ sambhali-trust.org. Jodhpur-based NGO dedicated to providing education, training and empowerment to girls and women from underprivileged backgrounds in rural Rajasthan.

Seva Mandir ⓦ sevamandir.org. Nonprofit organization working in tribal villages in the Udaipur district; takes interns to help with development projects.

Delhi

THE LOTUS TEMPLE, A BAHÁ'Í HOUSE OF WORSHIP

1 Delhi

Delhi is the symbol of old India and new.... Even the stones here whisper to our ears of the ages of long ago and the air we breathe is full of the dust and fragrances of the past, as also of the fresh and piercing winds of the present.
Jawaharlal Nehru

A buzzing international metropolis home to seventeen million people (and counting), sprawling Delhi is the capital of India, and also functions as the prime hub of wider South Asia. While this may conjure visions of urban chaos, and while those visions may be almost precisely accurate in teeming Paharganj and other older districts, much of the city is low-lying and surprisingly green, as best witnessed from the elevated sections of the excellent metro system. Delhi boasts a rich and varied history, and you'll come across tombs, temples and ruins dating back centuries; on the flip side of the coin, a burgeoning youth scene is exemplified by designer bars, chic cafés and decent clubs. The result is a city full of fascinating nooks and crannies that you could happily spend weeks, or even months, exploring.

From a tourist's perspective, Delhi is divided into two main parts. **Old Delhi** is the city of the Mughals and dates back to the seventeenth century. It's the capital's most frenetic quarter, and its most Islamic, a reminder that for more than seven hundred years Delhi was a Muslim-ruled city. Old Delhi's greatest monuments are undoubtedly the magnificent constructions of the Mughals, most notably the mighty **Red Fort**, and the **Jama Masjid**, India's largest and most impressive mosque.

To the south, encompassing the modern city centre, is **New Delhi**, built by the British to be the capital of their empire's key possession. A spacious city of tree-lined boulevards, New Delhi is also impressive in its own way. The **Rajpath**, stretching from **India Gate** to the Presidential Palace, is at least as mighty a statement of imperial power as the Red Fort, and it's among the broad avenues of New Delhi that you'll find most of the city's museums and its prime shopping area, centred around the elegant, colonnaded facades of **Connaught Place**. Meanwhile, at opposite ends of Lodi Road lie constructions marking two ends of the great tradition of Mughal garden tombs: **Humayun's Tomb**, its genesis, and **Safdarjang's Tomb**, its last gasp.

As the city expands, many shops, restaurants and other businesses are moving into **South Delhi**, the vast area beyond the colonial city; here, among the modern developments, you'll find some of Delhi's most ancient and fascinating attractions, including remains of the six cities that preceded Old Delhi, most notably the **Qutb Minar** and the rambling ruins of **Tughluqabad**.

Brief history

Delhi is said to consist of seven successive cities, with British-built New Delhi making an eighth. In truth, Delhi has centred historically on three main areas: **Lal Kot** and extensions to its northeast, where the city was located for most of the Middle Ages; **Old Delhi**, the city of the Mughals, founded by Shah Jahan in the seventeenth century; and **New Delhi**, built by the British just in time to be the capital of independent India.

Early Delhi

According to the Mahabharata, the heroic Pandavas had their capital at Indraprastha, near Purana Qila, circa 1450 BC. However, Delhi proper really got started in 1060 AD, when the **Tomars** (of the Rajput clan) founded **Lal Kot**, considered to be the first

HALL OF AUDIENCE, RED FORT

Highlights

❶ Red Fort Delhi's most famous monument, this imposing sandstone fort is a ghostly vestige of Mughal splendour. See page 85

❷ Rajpath The centrepiece of Lutyens' imperial New Delhi, this wide boulevard epitomizes the spirit of the British Raj. See page 94

❸ National Museum The country's finest museum, with exhibits from more than five thousand years of Indian culture. See page 95

❹ Humayn's Tomb An elegant red-brick forerunner of the Taj Mahal, whose lovely gardens offer an escape from the heat. See page 97

❺ Hazrat Nizamuddin A Sufi shrine in a deeply traditional Muslim quarter, where hypnotic

qawwali music is performed every Thursday. See page 97

❻ Khan Market and Hauz Khas Hit one – or both – of these trendy districts for a more contemporary take on things, and perhaps a sneak preview of the Delhi of the future. See page 100

❼ Qutb Minar Complex The ruins of Delhi's first incarnation, a thirteenth-century city dominated by an impressive Victory Tower. See page 101

❽ Parathe Wali Gali Teeming with people, this hugely atmospheric little Old Delhi alley features several small outlets making *parathas* to order – a cheap meal and a rich experience, all in one. See page 113

HIGHLIGHTS ARE MARKED ON THE MAP ON PAGE 82

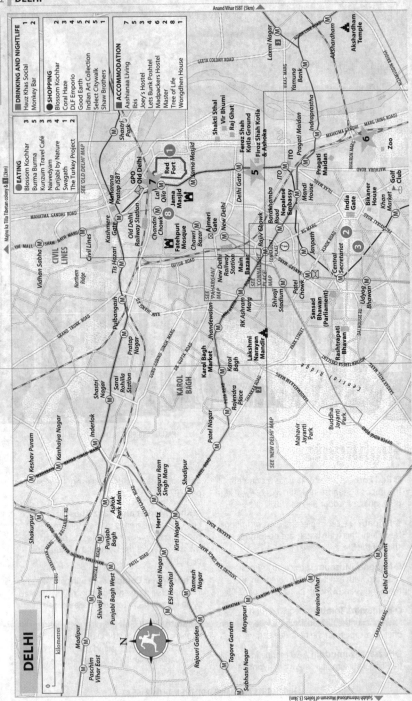

DELHI

EATING

Blossom Kochhar	3
Burma Burma	5
Kunzum Travel Café	3
Naivedyam	4
Punjabi by Nature	4
Swagath	1
The Turkey Project	2

DRINKING AND NIGHTLIFE

| Hauz Khas Social | 1 |
| Monkey Bar | 2 |

SHOPPING

Blossom Kochhar	2
Coral Haze	3
DLF Emporio	4
Indian Art Collection	5
Good Earth	2
Select Citywalk	5
Shaw Brothers	1

ACCOMMODATION

Aashianaa Living	7
Ibis	5
Joey's Hostel	3
Lets Bunk Poshtel	4
Madpackers Hostel	6
Master	2
Tree of Life	8
Wongdhen House	1

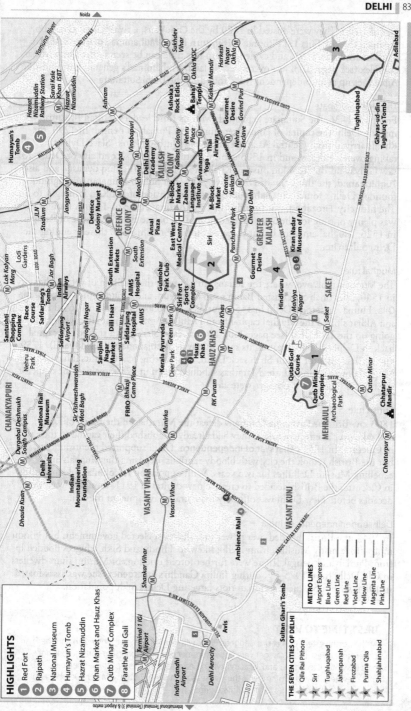

HIGHLIGHTS

1. Red Fort
2. Rajpath
3. National Museum
4. Humayun's Tomb
5. Hazrat Nizamuddin
6. Khan Market and Hauz Khas
7. Qutb Minar Complex
8. Parathe Wali Gali

THE SEVEN CITIES OF DELHI

1. Qila Rai Pithora
2. Siri
3. Tughluqabad
4. Jahanpanah
5. Firozabad
6. Purana Qila
7. Shahjahanabad

METRO LINES

Airport Express
Blue Line
Green Line
Red Line
Violet Line
Yellow Line
Magenta Line
Pink Line

1

city of Delhi. They were ousted in 1180 by the **Chauhans**, a rival Rajput clan who renamed the city Qila Lal Pithora. This in turn fell to **Muhammad of Ghor**'s Afghan Muslim armies in 1191, and evidence from this time can be seen in the Qutb Minar complex (see page 101); just over a decade later, Muhammad's general, Qutb-ud-din Aibak, set up as an independent ruler, founding the **Delhi Sultanate**.

The Delhi Sultanate

From 1211–36, the Sultanate expanded, with its third leader – Sultan Iltutmish – making Delhi the capital of lands stretching from Punjab to Bengal. In 1290, the **Khaljis** arrived from Central Asia, overthrowing Qutb-ud-din's "Slave Dynasty", taking over as sultans, and in 1303 commissioning **Siri**, the second city of Delhi. 1321 saw Ghiyas-ud-din Tughluq ousting Khaljis to found the Tughluq dynasty, and also **Tughluqabad**, the third city of Delhi; five years later Sultan Muhammad Tughluq founded Delhi's fourth city, **Jahanpanah**, as an extension of Lal Kot, joining it to Siri. The fifth city, **Firozabad**, was founded in 1354 during a time of decline, though there was plenty of time for the **Sayyids** to come and go before the First Battle of Panipat in 1526; Mughal emperor Babur defeated Sultan Ibrahim Lodi, thereby ending the Delhi Sultanate.

Mughal rule

The **Mughals** took over where the sultans left off, with the addition of yet another city: in 1540, Sher Shah Suri ousted Babur's son **Humayun**, and founded the sixth, **Purana Qila**. Humayun retook Delhi in 1556, but died the following year. In 1565, Humayun's son Akbar shifted the Mughal capital from Delhi to Agra, but just after work had got going on the Taj Mahal (see page 240), his grandson Shah Jahan shifted the capital back to Delhi in 1638, creating its seventh city at **Shahjahanabad** (Old Delhi). 1739 saw Persian emperor Nadir Shah sack Delhi, slaughtering 15,000 of its inhabitants as Mughal power crumbled; the Marathas subdued Delhi in 1784, making the emperor their vassal, but greater changes were afoot.

British rule

1803 saw Britain's **East India Company** defeat the Marathas in the Battle of Delhi, and take over as effective rulers; they had already established their capital to the east in Calcutta. In 1857's **First War of Independence**, Delhi supported the insurgents, but the British retook the city with bloody reprisals, deposing the Mughals and expelling Muslim Delhiites for two years. With opposition to colonial rule mounting in Calcutta, the British decided to create a new capital in 1911, though it was two decades before New Delhi was officially inaugurated as capital of the Raj.

Delhi under independent India

In 1947, the British handed over power to India's first elected government, but Hindu mobs drove many Muslims from Delhi; likewise, Hindu and Sikh refugees flooded in from Punjab and Bengal. There were further forced evictions of Muslim slum-dwellers in Old Delhi from 1975–77, during Indira Gandhi's **Emergency**; she was assassinated in 1984, with subsequent sectarian riots targeting Delhi's Sikh population.

BEST TIME TO VISIT

At the northwestern end of the Gangetic Plain, with the Himalayas to the north and the Thar Desert to its west, Delhi can get very hot in summer (April through June) and surprisingly cold in winter (December and January), when heavy fogs can disrupt train timetables quite severely. July to September is the wet season, making February, March, October and November optimum times to visit climate-wise.

FESTIVALS IN DELHI

Republic Day (Jan 26). Big, largely military parade on Rajpath, commemorating the adoption of India's constitution in 1950.

Garden Tourism Festival (Feb). Three-day flower and gardening show put on in one of Delhi's parks (the venue changes from year to year), with cultural and kids' activities.

International Mango Festival (July). A celebration of Indian mangoes held at Talkatora Stadium, with over five hundred varieties to try.

Id ul-Fitr (July/Aug). The area around the Jama Masjid becomes a huge market of live goats to be slaughtered for the annual Muslim festival.

Delhi International Arts Festival (Nov/Dec; Ⓦ dia.in). Lasting more than a week, DIAF is an extravaganza of music, dance and other arts from India and worldwide, held at venues around central New Delhi.

Qutub Festival (Nov/Dec). A three-day festival of arts and culture put on by Delhi Tourism around the Qutb Minar.

The twenty-first century has seen Delhi develop at an even greater pace than the rest of India. The first metro line opened in 2002 (though Kolkata had one in the 1980s), and the city proudly hosted the **Commonwealth Games** in 2010. This, however, was beset by substandard preparation; many competitors, appalled by the state of the Athletes' Village, demanded to be moved into hotels. 2013 saw the international reputation of Delhi – and India – sullied further, with the gang rape and murder of a student paramedic sparking worldwide protests.

These days, Delhi comes across as increasingly ambitious – its metro network now has eight lines (and counting), and at the time of writing, the city was considering bids for the 2030 Asian Games, and the 2032 Summer Olympics.

Old Delhi and around

Though it's not in fact the oldest part of Delhi, the seventeenth-century city of **Shahjahanabad**, built for the Mughal emperor Shah Jahan, is known as **OLD DELHI**. Construction began on the city in 1638, and within eleven years it was substantially complete, surrounded by more than 8km of ramparts pierced by fourteen main gates. It boasted a beautiful main thoroughfare, **Chandni Chowk**; an imposing citadel, the **Red Fort** (Lal Qila); and an impressive congregational mosque, the **Jama Masjid**. Today much of the wall has crumbled, and of the fourteen gates only four remain, but it's still a fascinating area, crammed with interesting nooks and crannies, though you'll need stamina, patience, time, and probably a fair few chai stops along the way to endure the crowds and traffic. The same is true of **Paharganj**, the district just across the rail tracks – somehow Delhi in a nutshell, despite being rather unrepresentative of the city as a whole.

The Red Fort

Netaji Subhash Marg • **Fort** Tues–Sun 9.30am–4.30pm • ₹600 (₹50) • Audio tour ₹118 • **Museums** 10am–5pm • Free (₹5) • Ⓜ Lal Quila

The largest of Old Delhi's monuments is **Lal Qila**, known in English as the **Red Fort** because of the red sandstone from which it was built. It was commissioned by Shah Jahan to be his residence and modelled on the fort at Agra. Work started in 1638, and the emperor moved in ten years later. The fort contains all the trappings you'd expect at the centre of Mughal government: halls of public and private audience, domed and arched marble palaces, plush private apartments, a mosque and elaborately designed gardens. The ramparts, which stretch for more than 2km, are interrupted by two gates – **Lahori Gate** to the west, through which you enter, and

Delhi Gate to the south. Shah Jahan's son, Aurangzeb, added barbicans to both gates. In those days, the Yamuna River ran along the eastern wall, feeding both the moat and a "stream of paradise" which ran through every pavilion. As the Mughal Empire declined, the fort fell into disrepair. It was attacked and plundered by the Persian emperor Nadir Shah in 1739, and by the British in 1857. Nevertheless, it remains an impressive testimony to Mughal grandeur. Keep your ticket stub, as you may have to show it several times.

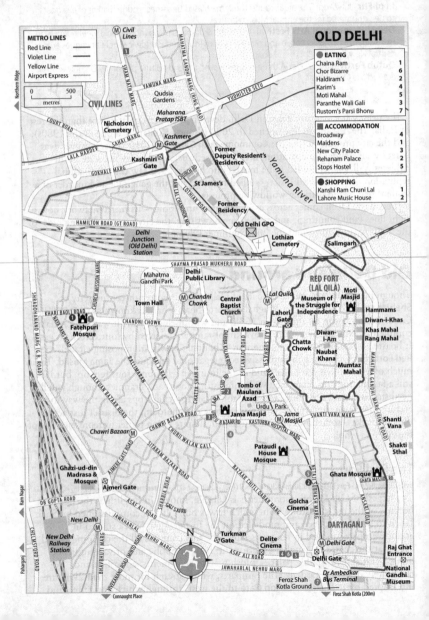

OLD DELHI

METRO LINES
Red Line
Violet Line
Yellow Line
Airport Express

0   500
metres

● **EATING**
Chaina Ram   1
Chor Bizarre   6
Haldiram's   2
Karim's   4
Moti Mahal   5
Paranthe Wali Gali 3
Rustom's Parsi Bhonu 7

■ **ACCOMMODATION**
Broadway   4
Maidens   1
New City Palace   3
Rehanam Palace   2
Stops Hostel   5

● **SHOPPING**
Kanshi Ram Chuni Lal 1
Lahore Music House   2

Chatta Chowk

The main entrance to the fort from Lahori Gate opens onto **Chatta Chowk**, a covered street flanked with arched cells that used to house Delhi's most talented jewellers, carpet-makers, goldsmiths and silk-weavers, but is now given over to souvenir-sellers. At the end, a path to the left leads to the **Museum of the Struggle for Independence**, depicting resistance to British rule.

Diwan-i-Am

The **Naubhat Khana** ("Musicians' Gallery") marked the entrance into the royal quarters. Beyond it, a path leads ahead through wide lawns to the **Diwan-i-Am**, or "Hall of Public Audience", where the emperor used to meet commoners and hold court. In those days it was strewn with silk carpets and partitioned with hanging tapestries. Its centrepiece is a marble dais on which sat the emperor's throne, backed by twelve panels inlaid with precious stones, mostly depicting birds and flowers. The most famous of them, in the middle at the top (and not easy to see), shows the mythological Greek Orpheus with his lute. The panels were made by a Florentine jeweller and imported from Italy, but the surrounding inlay work was done locally.

Mumtaz Mahal

The **Mumtaz Mahal**, south and east of the Diwan-i-Am, and probably used by princesses, now houses an **Archaeological Museum**, displaying manuscripts, paintings, ceramics and textiles, with a section devoted to the last Mughal emperor, Bahadur Shah II; exhibits include his silk robes and silver hookah pipe.

Rang Mahal

The pavilions along the fort's east wall face spacious gardens and overlook the banks of the Yamuna River. Immediately east of the Diwan-i-Am, **Rang Mahal**, the "Palace of Colour", housed the emperor's wives and mistresses. Originally, its ceiling was overlaid with gold and silver and reflected onto a central pool in the marble floor. Unfortunately, it was heavily vandalized while the British used it as an Officers' Mess after the 1857 uprising.

Khas Mahal

On the northern side of Rang Mahal, the marble **Khas Mahal** was the personal palace of the emperor, split into separate apartments for worship, sleeping and sitting. The southern chamber, **Tosh Khana** ("Robe Room"), has a stunning (though broken, at the time of writing) marble filigree screen on its north wall, surmounted by a panel carved with the scales of justice. The octagonal tower projecting over the east wall of the Khas Mahal was where the emperor appeared daily before throngs gathered on the riverbanks below.

Diwan-i-Khas

North of Khas Mahal, in the large **Diwan-i-Khas** ("Hall of Private Audience"), the emperor would address the highest nobles of his court. Today it's the finest building in the fort, a marble pavilion shaded by a roof raised on stolid pillars, which meet in ornate scalloped arches and are embellished with delicate inlays of flowers made from semiprecious stones. On the north and south walls you can still make out the inscription of a couplet in Persian attributed to Shah Jahan's prime minister, which roughly translates as: "If there be paradise upon this earthly sphere/It is here, oh it is here, oh it is here". More than just a paean, the verse refers to the deliberate modelling of the gardens on the Koranic description of heaven.

The hammams and Moti Masjid

A little further north are the **hammams**, or baths, sunk into the marble floor inlaid with patterns of precious stones, and dappled in jewel-coloured light that filters

1

through stained-glass windows. The western chamber contained hot baths while the eastern apartment, with fountains of rosewater, was used as a dressing room; access is not currently allowed to either interior.

Next to the hammams, the sweetly fashioned **Moti Masjid**, or Pearl Mosque, triple-domed in white marble, was added by Aurangzeb in 1659, but unfortunately the interior is closed to the public.

Kashmiri Gate and around

Just north of the tracks, **Kasmiri Gate** – also written as Kashmere Gate, the spelling used by its metro station – is these days of greatest significance for its jalopy of a bus. It's not the most pleasant of areas, but there are a couple of minor sights here if you've time to while away before your bus, or are changing metro lines.

Lothian Cemetery

Lothian Rd • Daily 10am–5pm • Free • Ⓜ Lal Quila

Netaji Subhash Marg leads north from the Red Fort and under a railway bridge to Old Delhi GPO. Just before the post office on the east side of the road, **Lothian Cemetery** was the burial ground for officers of the East India Company from 1808 until just after the 1857 uprising. Many locals believe that the ghost of one of these officers, a lovelorn fellow who shot himself in the head, wanders the cemetery at night.

St James's Church

Lothian Rd • Mon–Sat 9am–1pm & 2.30–4.45pm, Sun (for prayers) 9am–noon • Ⓜ Kashmere Gate

A few hundred metres north of the GPO is the rather fine cream-and-white baroque facade of **St James's Church**, commissioned in 1836 by **James Skinner**, the son of a Scottish Company-wala and a Rajput princess. Because of his mixed ancestry, and the increasing racism of the British regime, Skinner was refused a commission in the Company's army, but set up his own irregular cavalry unit and made himself pretty much indispensable. His victories over the forces of the maharaja of Jaipur and the great Sikh leader Maharaja Ranjit Singh eventually forced the Company to begrudgingly grant him the rank of Lieutenant Colonel and absorb his cavalrymen into its ranks. Skinner died in 1842 and is buried just in front of the altar.

Qudsia Gardens

Yamuna Marg • Daily 9am–5.30pm • Free • Ⓜ Kashmere Gate

The double-arched **Kashmiri Gate**, on the west side of Lothian Road just 300m north of St James's Church, was where the Mughal court would leave Delhi every summer bound for the cool valley of Kashmir. To its north is Maharana Pratap ISBT, beyond which, across the busy Lala Hardev Sahai Marg, the peaceful **Qudsia Gardens** are a fading remnant of the magnificent pleasure parks commissioned in the mid-eighteenth century by Queen Qudsia, favourite mistress of Muhammad Shah, and mother of Ahmed Shah. The park isn't visited in great numbers, and as such is not the best place for lone females.

Nicholson Cemetery

Lala Hardev Sahai Marg · Daily: summer 8am–6pm; winter 9am–5pm · Ⓜ Kashmere Gate

Just west of the Qudsia Gardens is Delhi's oldest burial ground, **Nicholson Cemetery**, named after Brigadier General John Nicholson, who was shot down at the Kashmiri Gate while leading the British attack to regain Delhi from the 1857 insurgents. It's mostly overgrown these days (bar the twenty-first-century graves at the west end), and you may have to prise open the gate yourself.

Paharganj

Just west of New Delhi station is the hectic, somewhat infamous **Paharganj** area; centred around its Main Bazaar, a great number of travellers call it home for much – or all – of their time in the city. It's a real love-it-or-hate-it area, packed with cheap

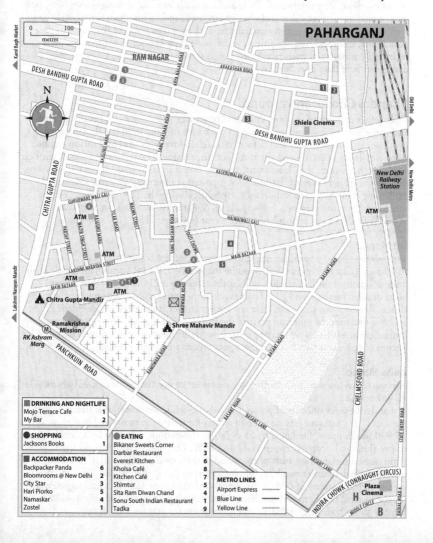

DRINKING AND NIGHTLIFE	
Mojo Terrace Cafe	1
My Bar	2

SHOPPING	
Jacksons Books	1

ACCOMMODATION	
Backpacker Panda	6
Bloomrooms @ New Delhi	2
City Star	3
Hari Piorko	5
Namaskar	4
Zostel	1

EATING	
Bikaner Sweets Corner	2
Darbar Restaurant	3
Everest Kitchen	6
Kholsa Café	8
Kitchen Café	7
Shimtur	5
Sita Ram Diwan Chand	4
Sonu South Indian Restaurant	1
Tadka	9

METRO LINES	
Airport Express	
Blue Line	
Yellow Line	

1

PAHARGANJ WALKING TOURS

Paharganj provides the first experience of the Subcontinent for many budget travellers, but there is also a less visible underside to life here, in the shape of the **street children**. Most are runaways who've left difficult homes, often hundreds of kilometres away; most sleep on the streets, and some inhale solvents to numb their pain. The **Salaam Baalak Trust** (W salaambaalaktrust.com), a local NGO, organizes walking tours of the area conducted by former street children. Tours last two hours and usually start at 10am (daily except Sun); there is no fixed price but a minimum donation of ₹300 is suggested; proceeds go towards providing shelter, education and healthcare for the children themselves.

hotels, restaurants, cafés and *dhabas*, and a busy fruit and vegetable market; it's also a paradise for shoestring shoppers seeking psychedelic clothing, joss sticks, bags and oils of patchouli or sandalwood. There aren't actually any major things to see here, but most would argue that Paharganj is a sight in itself, and its umpteen neon hotel signs look rather stunning by night, especially from the vantage point of the many rooftop restaurants, cafés and bars. Be sure to watch out for pickpockets, not to mention the racing motorbikes and auto-rickshaws, which somehow contrive to be even more dangerous here than elsewhere in Delhi.

Chandni Chowk and around

Old Delhi's main thoroughfare, **Chandni Chowk** was a sublime canal lined with trees and some of the most opulent bazaars in the whole of Asia, until the British paved over the canal after 1857 – and before India fell in love with the combustion engine. Auto-rickshaws operate along the road, but since traffic is extremely congested, the best way (in other words, the "least worst" way) to take it in is on foot. Along the way, look out for numbered "heritage buildings" signposted at intervals, with placards outside explaining their historical importance, especially during the 1857 uprising. Perhaps more notable is the presence, halfway along, of **Paranthe Wali Gali**, an alley that's arguably Delhi's most atmospheric place to eat (see page 113).

Lal Mandir

Daily 6am–noon & 6–9pm • Free but donations appreciated, especially for the bird hospital • M Lal Qila

At Chandni Chowk's eastern end, opposite the Red Fort, the **Lal Mandir** Jain temple is not quite as ornate as the Jain temples in Rajasthan (see pages 214 and 199), but it does boast detailed carvings, and gilded paintwork in the antechambers surrounding the main shrine. Remove your shoes and leave any leather articles at the kiosk before entering. The attached **bird hospital** puts into practice the Jain principle that all life is sacred by rescuing injured birds, with each type having its own ward; the sparrow ward is largely occupied by victims of ceiling fans, with which these poor critters frequently collide.

Jama Masjid

Urdu Bazaar Rd • Daily 7am–noon & 1.30–6.30pm • Entry free, photo permit ₹300; tower ₹300 (₹50) • No shorts, short skirts or sleeveless tops • M Jama Masjid

A wonderful piece of Mughal pomp, the red-and-white **Jama Masjid** is India's largest mosque – its courtyard is wide enough to accommodate the prostrated bodies of 25,000 worshippers. Designed by Shah Jahan, the mosque was built by a workforce of five thousand people between 1644 and 1656. Originally called Masjid-i-Jahanuma ("mosque commanding a view of the world"), this grand structure stands on Bho Jhala, one of Shahjahanabad's two hills, and looks east to the sprawling Red Fort, and down on the seething streets of Old Delhi. Broad, red-sandstone staircases lead to gateways on the eastern, northern and southern sides, where worshippers and visitors alike must remove their shoes (the custodian will guard them for you for a small tip).

Once inside the courtyard, your eyes will be drawn to the three bulbous marble domes crowning the **main prayer hall** on the west side (facing Mecca), fronted by a series of high cusped arches, and sheltering the mihrab, the central niche in the west wall indicating the direction of prayer. The pool in the centre is used for ritual ablutions. At each corner of the square yard, a slender minaret crowned with a marble dome rises to the sky, and it's worth climbing the **tower** (women must be accompanied by a man) south of the main sanctuary for a view over Delhi. In the northeast corner a white shrine protects a collection of Muhammad's relics, including his sandals, a hair from his beard and his "footprint" miraculously embedded in a marble slab.

Delhi Gate and around

The area around **Delhi Gate** is a symphony in two parts – to its west lies a scruffy slice of Old Delhi, and to its east a greener, quieter area featuring a museum and memorial pertaining to **Gandhi**, each within easy walking distance of each other. Together with the **Firoz Shah Kotla** ruins, it's possible to while away half a day here, and there are some good lunch spots around.

Raj Ghat

Mahatma Gandhi Marg • Daily 10am–8pm • Free • ⑩ Delhi Gate

When Shah Jahan established his city in 1638, its eastern edges bordered the Yamuna River, and a line of *ghats* – steps leading to the water – were installed along the riverbanks. *Ghats* have been used in India for centuries, for mundane things like washing clothes and bathing, but also for worship and funeral cremation. **Raj Ghat**, east of Delhi Gate – really more a park than a *ghat*, since the river is now some way to the east – is the place where Mahatma Gandhi was cremated, on the day after his assassination in 1948. The Mahatma's *samadhi* (cremation memorial), a low black plinth inscribed with his reputed last words – "Hai Ram", meaning "Oh God" – receives a steady stream of visitors, and he is remembered through prayers here every Friday evening at 5pm, and on the anniversaries of his birth and death (Oct 2 & Jan 30).

North of Raj Ghat, within the same park, memorials also mark the places where Jawaharlal Nehru (at **Shanti Vana**), his daughter Indira Gandhi (at **Shakti Sthal**), and his grandson Rajiv Gandhi (at **Vir Bhumi**) were cremated.

National Gandhi Museum

Jawaharlal Nehru Marg, opposite Raj Ghat's southwest corner • Tues–Sun 9.30am–5.30pm • Films in English Sat 4pm, in Hindi Sun 4pm • Free • ⓦ gandhimuseum.org • ⑩ Delhi Gate

The **National Gandhi Museum** houses some of the Mahatma's writings, as well as hundreds of photographs from his life and funeral, some of his old spinning wheels and leather sandals, and the blood-stained *dhoti* he was wearing when he was assassinated, together with one of the three bullets that killed him. At the top of the staircase you'll see four old telephones, and through their receivers you'll hear Gandhi's voice, which is quite entertaining in its own way. A half-hour film biography is shown alternatively in Hindi and English, and at weekends a longer film on Gandhi's political and personal life.

Firoz Shah Kotla

Mahatma Gandhi Marg, 1.5km south of Delhi Gate • Tues–Sun sunrise–sunset • ₹300 (₹25) • ⑩ Delhi Gate

Supposedly, Firoz Shah (sultan of Delhi from 1351 to 1358) had a whole fifth city of Delhi built in his name – Firozabad, founded in 1354. Today few traces survive of what was in any case probably never more than a suburb of the main city, but what does remain is the fortified palace of **Firoz Shah Kotla**, now a crumbling ruin with ornamental gardens. Its most incongruous and yet distinctive element is the third-century BC polished sandstone **Ashokan pillar**, carried down the Yamuna River by raft

1

from Ambala. For a reasonable view of the column, you'll need to climb to the top of the building, entering the compound through a gate on the west side, then mounting a stairway in the northeast corner. From the top you also get a view of the neighbouring mosque and *baoli* (step-well), as well as the lawns that make the site such a pleasant place to visit – plus an eponymous stadium, famed as Delhi's home of IPL cricket.

New Delhi

The modern area of **NEW DELHI**, with its wide, tree-lined avenues and solid colonial architecture, has been the seat of central government since 1931. At its hub, the royal mall, **Rajpath**, runs from the palatial **Rashtrapati Bhavan**, in the west, to the **India Gate** war memorial in the east. Its wide, grassy margins are a popular meeting place for families, picnickers and courting couples. North of the Rajpath lies busy **Connaught Place**, one of the city's most important hubs for dining and drinking; further south, **Khan Market** is a more chilled-out version of the same, with some great sights on its periphery.

Connaught Place and around

At the north edge of the new capital lies its thriving business centre, **Connaught Place** (more commonly referred to by locals as "CP"). With its classical colonnades, the area is radically different from the bazaars of Old Delhi, which it superseded; named after a minor British royal of the day, it takes the form of a circle, divided by eight radial roads and three ring roads into blocks lettered A–N, each crammed with restaurants, bars, shops, cinemas and the like. You'll get pestered regularly here, with gentlemen sidling up using the "approximo walk" and letting you know which block you're on – they usually want to usher you into a shop or travel agency, and are pretty harmless.

Hanuman Mandir
Baba Kharak Singh Marg • Daily 24hr • Free • ⓜ Rajiv Chowk

A short walk from the centre of CP is the area's largest temple, the **Hanuman Mandir**. Despite its busy location and throngs of devotees (especially on Tuesdays and Saturdays), some parts of the interior can be surprisingly calm. Look out for the crescent sitting atop the temple's spire – an Islamic motif rare in Hindu places of worship. It's also a popular place for tourists to plaster themselves with henna, and for Indians to consult the services of a clairvoyant.

Jantar Mantar
Sansad Marg • Daily sunrise–sunset • ₹300 (₹25) • ⓦ jantarmantar.org • ⓜ Rajiv Chowk or Shivaji Stadium

The **Jantar Mantar** was built in 1725, the first of five open-air observatories designed by the ruler of Jaipur, Jai Singh II, and a precursor to his larger one in Jaipur (see page 136). The huge slanting red-and-white stone structures, looming over palm trees and neat flowerbeds, were used to calculate time, solar and lunar calendars and astrological movements, achieving an admirable degree of accuracy.

Gurudwara Bangla Sahib
Ashok Rd • Daily 24hr • Free • Cover head and dress conservatively; deposit shoes at information centre • ⓦ dsgmc.in • ⓜ Shivaji Stadium

The vast, white marble structure of **Bangla Sahib Gurudwara** is Delhi's biggest Sikh temple, topped by a huge, golden, onion-shaped dome that's visible from some distance. The temple commemorates a 1664 visit to Delhi by the eighth Sikh guru, Hare Krishan, and welcomes visitors. Live devotional music (vocals, harmonium and tabla) is relayed throughout the complex, and everybody is invited to share a simple meal of dhal and chapattis, served three times daily.

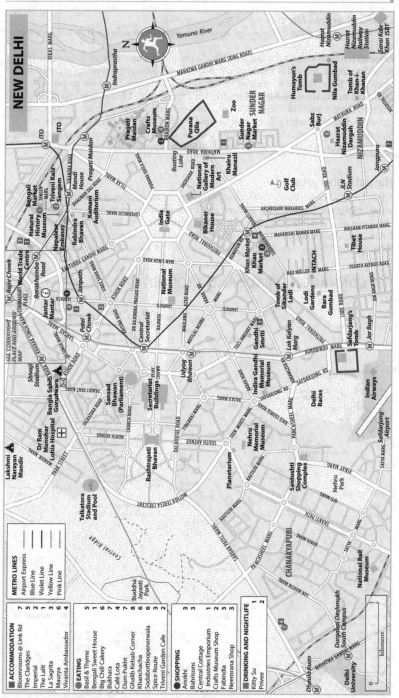

NEW DELHI

METRO LINES
Airport Express
Blue Line
Violet Line
Yellow Line
Pink Line

ACCOMMODATION
Bloomrooms @ Link Rd 7
The Claridges 5
Imperial 4
The Lalit 1
La Sagrita 3
Maurya 6
Vivanta Ambassador 4

EATING
Basil & Thyme 5
Bengali Sweet House 1
Big Chill Cakery 6
Bukhara 7
Café Lota 7
Dum Pukht 8
Ghalib Kebab Corner 4
Khanchacha 6
Sodabottleopenerwala 6
Spice Route 6
Triveni Garden Cafe 2

SHOPPING
Anokhi 3
Bahrisons 3
Central Cottage
Industries Emporium 1
Crafts Museum Shop 3
Fabindia 3
Neemrana Shop 3

DRINKING AND NIGHTLIFE
Kitty Su 1
Privee 2

1

Lakshmi Narayan Mandir

Mandir Marg • Daily 4.30am–1.30pm & 2.30–9pm • Free; deposit cameras, shoes and mobile phones at entrance • Ⓜ RK Ashram Marg or Shivaji Stadium

Lakshmi Narayan Mandir is a modern Hindu temple that also welcomes tourists. With its white, cream and red brick domes, it was commissioned by a wealthy merchant family, the Birlas (hence its alternative name, Birla Mandir). The main shrine is dedicated to Lakshmi, goddess of wealth (on the right), and her consort Narayana, aka Vishnu, the preserver of life (on the left, holding a conch). At the back is a tiny, ornate chamber decorated with coloured stones and mirrors and dedicated to Krishna, one of Vishnu's earthly incarnations. Devotional music is played throughout, and quotes from Hindu scriptures, many translated into English, adorn the walls.

Rajpath and around

Vijay Chowk, immediately in front of Rashtrapati Bhavan, leads into the wide, straight **Rajpath**, flanked with gardens and fountains that are floodlit at night, and the scene of annual **Republic Day** celebrations (Jan 26). The Rajpath runs east to **India Gate**; designed by Lutyens in 1921, the high arch – reminiscent of the Arc de Triomphe in Paris – commemorates ninety thousand Indian soldiers killed fighting for

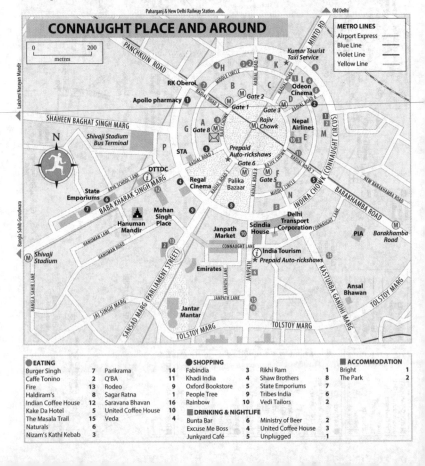

CONNAUGHT PLACE AND AROUND

● EATING			● SHOPPING				■ ACCOMMODATION	
Burger Singh	7	Parikrama	14	Fabindia	3	Rikhi Ram	1	Bright	1
Caffe Tonino	2	Q'BA	11	Khadi India	4	Shaw Brothers	8	The Park	2
Fire	13	Rodeo	9	Oxford Bookstore	5	State Emporiums	7		
Haldiram's	8	Sagar Ratna	1	People Tree	9	Tribes India	6		
Indian Coffee House	12	Saravana Bhavan	16	Rainbow	10	Vedi Tailors	2		
Kake Da Hotel	5	United Coffee House	10						
The Masala Trail	15	Veda	4	■ DRINKING & NIGHTLIFE					
Naturals	6			Bunta Bar	6	Ministry of Beer	2		
Nizam's Kathi Kebab	3			Excuse Me Boss	4	United Coffee House	1		
				Junkyard Café	5	Unplugged	1		

the British in World War I, and bears the names of more than three thousand British and Indian soldiers who died on the North-West Frontier and in the Afghan War of 1919. The extra memorial beneath the arch honours the lives lost in the Indo-Pakistan War of 1971.

Rashtrapati Bhavan

Rajpath • Tours of main buildings Thurs–Sun, museum Tues–Sun, gardens Aug–Mar Thurs–Sun • ₹50 each • Book tours at ⓦ rashtrapatisachivalaya.gov.in; bring passport • Ⓜ Central Secretariat

After King George V, emperor of India, decreed in 1911 that Delhi should replace Calcutta as the capital of India, the English architect **Edwin Lutyens** was commissioned to plan the new governmental centre. **Rashtrapati Bhavan**, the official residence of the president of India, is one of the largest and most grandiose of the Raj constructions, built by Lutyens and Herbert Baker between 1921 and 1929. Its majestic proportions can be appreciated on guided tours, the most interesting of which run around the main buildings, or (in season) the Mughal **gardens** at the west side (entrance via gate 35, accessed from Church Road); modelled on Mughal pleasure parks, the latter are a typically ordered square pattern of quadrants dissected by waterways and refreshed by fountains, including tennis courts, butterfly enclosures, vegetable and fruit patches, and a swimming pool.

National Museum

11 Janpath, just south of Rajpath • Tues–Sun 10am–5pm • ₹650 (₹20); includes a free audio tour (₹150 in English for Indian citizens), but you need to leave a passport, driving licence, credit card or ₹2000 deposit • Free guided tour Tues–Fri 10.30am & 2.30pm, Sat & Sun 11.30am, 2.30pm & 3pm • ⓦ nationalmuseumindia.gov.in • Ⓜ Udyog Bhawan

The **National Museum** provides a good overview of Indian culture and history. At a trot you can see the museum in a couple of hours, but to get the best out of your visit you should set aside at least half a day. Guided tours are available, though they cover a rather random selection of exhibits.

The most important displays are on the ground floor, kicking off in **room 4** with the Harappan civilization. The Gandhara sculptures in **room 6** betray some very obvious Greco-Roman influence, while **room 9** around the corner has some very fine bronzes, most especially those of the Chola period (from south India, between the ninth and the thirteenth centuries), and a fifteenth-century statue of Devi from Vijayanagar in south India. Among the late medieval sculptures in **room 10** is a fearsome, vampire-like, late Chola *dvarapala*, also from south India, and a couple of performing musicians from Mysore. **Room 12** is devoted to the Mughals, and in particular their miniature paintings – look out for two depicting the nativity of Jesus, a subject you might not expect. It's worth popping upstairs to the **Central Asian antiquities** collection, which includes a large number of paintings, documents, ceramics and textiles from Eastern Turkestan (now the Chinese province of Xinjiang) and the Silk Route, dating from between the third and twelfth centuries; another floor up are the **textile** exhibits, and an outstanding collection of **musical instruments**. On your way out, take a look at the massive twelve-tiered temple chariot from Tamil Nadu, an extremely impressive piece of woodwork in a glass shelter just by the southern entrance gate.

National Gallery of Modern Art

Jaipur House, India Gate • Tues–Sun 11am–6.30pm • ₹500 (₹20) • Free guided tours 11am, 1.30pm & 3.30pm • ⓦ ngmaindia.gov.in • Ⓜ Khan Market

Once the residence of the maharaja of Jaipur, the extensive **National Gallery of Modern Art** is a rich showcase of Indian contemporary art. The permanent displays, focusing on post-1930s work, exhibit many of India's most important modern pieces, including work by the "Bengali Renaissance" artists Abanendranath Tagore and Nandalal Bose, the great poet and artist Rabindranath Tagore, and Jamini Roy, whose work, reminiscent of Modigliani's, reflects the influence of Indian folk art. Also on show

1

are the romantic paintings and etchings of Thomas Daniell and his nephew William, British artists of the Bombay or Company School, which combined Indian delicacy with Western realism. The ground-floor galleries are used for temporary exhibitions.

Sunder Nagar and around

The affluent, low-key area around **Sunder Nagar** market makes quite a change from the rest of New Delhi; most of the cars you'll see parked here are large, foreign models, and some fellas wear designer shirts and loafers as they play cricket in the many small parks. The market itself has long been famed for handicrafts, replica "antiques" and jewellery, and there's a chic restaurant here (*Basil & Thyme*; see page 114), but for most visitors the prime attractions are just to the north, in the form of appealing **Purana Qila** fort – now illuminated rather pleasingly at night – and the excellent **Crafts Museum**.

Purana Qila

Mathura Rd • Daily sunrise–sunset • ₹300 (₹25) • Ⓜ Pragati Maidan, or buses from New Delhi railway station (gate 2)

The majestic fortress of **Purana Qila**, whose crumbling ramparts dominate busy Mathura Road, is thought to stand on the site of Indraprastha, the Pandava city of Mahabharata fame. Considered to be the sixth city of Delhi, it was begun by Humayun, the second Mughal emperor, as Din-Panah, and renamed Shergarh by Sher Shah Suri, who displaced him in 1540 and oversaw most of the construction.

Most of the fortress interior is taken up by pleasant lawns and gardens, but two important buildings survive. Of them, the **Qila-i-Kuhna Masjid** is one of Sher Shah's finest monuments. Constructed in 1541 in the Afghan style, it has five elegant arches, embellished with white and black marble to complement the red sandstone. The geometric patterns and carved Arabic calligraphy around the main doorway all represent a more sophisticated degree of decorative artwork than anything seen before in Delhi. Previous decorative carving on buildings had been in plaster, but here it's in stone, a more serious affair as it's obviously much harder to work.

The Purana Qila's other main building, the **Sher Mandal**, is a red-sandstone octagonal observatory and library built for Sher Shah. It was here in 1556 that the emperor Humayun died. He stumbled down its treacherously steep steps while hurrying to answer the muezzin's call to prayer, just a year after he had defeated Sher Shah's son Sikander Suri and regained power.

Crafts Museum

Pragati Maidan, Bhairon Marg • Tues–Sun 10am–1.30pm & 2–5pm • ₹200 (₹20) • Ⓦ nationalcraftsmuseum.nic.in • Ⓜ Pragati Maidan, or buses from New Delhi railway station (gate 2)

The **Crafts Museum** is a dynamic exhibition of the rural arts and crafts of India, divided into three sections. The **exhibition galleries** show a range of textiles, carvings, ceramics, painting and metalwork from across India, while the **village complex** displays an assortment of traditional homes from different parts of the country. The **craft demonstrations** do feature a few artisans actually at work, but mostly double as shops selling crafts typical of different Indian regions. There's also a library and the excellent *Café Lota* (see page 114), as well as a good **shop** (see page 120).

Nizamuddin and around

Most visit the **Nizamuddin** area in order to have a look at **Humayun's Tomb**, one of Delhi's foremost historical sights. However, there's a lot to be said for the self-contained *mahalla* (village) to the west of the tomb; with its meat-filled butchers, ancient mosques and tombs and relatively slow pace of life, it's so different from the surrounding city that to enter it is like passing through a time warp (or, given the attire of its populace, crossing into Pakistan). At its heart, surrounded by a tangle of narrow alleyways lined with shops and market stalls, lies one of Sufism's greatest shrines, the **Hazrat Nizamuddin Dargah**, which draws a constant stream of devotees from far and wide.

Humayun's Tomb

Off Mathura Rd; entrance on western side of complex • Daily sunrise–sunset • ₹600 (₹40) • Ⓜ Hazrat Nizamuddin, or prepaid auto from Connaught Place (₹75)

Close to the centre of Nizamuddin stands **Humayun's Tomb**, best photographed in late afternoon. Delhi's first Mughal mausoleum, it was constructed to house the remains of the second Mughal emperor, Humayun, and was built under the watchful eye of Haji Begum, his senior widow (and mother of Akbar), who camped here for the duration, and is now buried alongside her husband. The grounds were later used to inter several prominent Mughals, and served as a refuge for the last emperor, Bahadur Shah II, before his capture by the British in 1857.

The tomb's sombre, Persian-style elegance marks this as one of Delhi's finest historic sites. Constructed of red sandstone, inlaid with black and white marble, and set on a commanding podium looking towards the Yamuna River, it stands in the centre of the formal *charbagh*, or quartered garden. The octagonal structure is crowned with a double dome that soars to a height of 38m. Though it was the very first Mughal garden tomb – to be followed by Akbar's at Sikandra and, of course, the Taj Mahal at Agra (see page 240), for which it can be seen as a prototype – Humayun's mausoleum has antecedents in Delhi in the form of **Ghiyas-ud-din Tughluq's tomb** at Tughluqabad (see page 103), and that of **Sikandar Lodi** in Lodi Gardens (see page 98). It adopted its octagonal shape from the Taj, as well as the high central arch that was to become such a typical feature of Mughal architecture – you'll also see this style at Delhi's Jama Masjid (see page 90), for example.

Within the grounds southeast of the main mausoleum, another impressive square mausoleum, with a double dome and two graves bearing Koranic inscriptions, is that of Humayun's barber, a man considered to be important because he was trusted with holding a razor to the emperor's throat.

Nearby Hunayun's Tomb but outside the compound (so you'll have to walk right round for a closer look) stands the **Nila Gumbad** ("blue dome"), an octagonal tomb with a dome of blue tiles. It was supposedly built by one of Akbar's nobles to honour a faithful servant, and may possibly predate Humayun's Tomb. Additionally, the blue-domed structure in the middle of the road junction in front of the entrance to Humayun's tomb is a seventeenth-century tomb called **Sabz Burj** – the tiles on its dome are not original, but the result of a recent restoration.

Hazrat Nizamuddin Dargah

Boali Gate Rd; entrance at east side of compound, down some narrow alleys • Daily 24hr • Free • Leave footwear at the official area just by the entrance • Gawwali music usually Fri evenings; see Ⓦ nizamuddinaulia.org for latest timings

The marble *dargah* is the tomb of Sheikh Nizam-ud-din Aulia (1236–1325), fourth saint of the Chishtiya Sufi order founded by Khwaja Muin-ud-din Chishti of Ajmer (see page 151), and was built the year the sheikh died, but has been through several renovations, and the present mausoleum dates from 1562. Lattice screens and arches in the inner sanctum surround the actual tomb (closed to women), which is surrounded by a marble rail and a canopy of mother-of-pearl. Sheikh Nizam-ud-din's disciple, the poet and chronicler **Amir Khusrau** – considered to be the first Urdu poet and the founder of *khyal*, the most common form of north Indian classical music – lies in a contrasting red-sandstone tomb in front of his master's mausoleum. In the evenings **qawwali music** is performed here, in the form of chanting accompanied by a harmonium, *dholak* (barrel drum) and tabla (hand-drum). Its hypnotic rhythm is designed to lull its audience into a state of *mast* (spiritual intoxication), which is believed to bring the devotee closer to God. Spectators are welcome but should dress respectfully.

1

NIZAMUDDIN WALKING TOURS

The **Hope Project**, a self-help NGO for local slum-dwellers (☎011 2435 7081, ⓦhopeprojectindia.org), runs evening walking tours (1hr 30min) of Nizamuddin. They're best joined on days when you can go straight on to the *qawwali* session at the *dargah* afterwards (see above).

The oldest building in the area, the red-sandstone mosque of **Jamat Khana Masjid**, looms over the main *dargah* on its western side. It was commissioned in 1325 by Khizr Khan, the son of the Khalji sultan Ala-ud-din. It's a bit empty inside, bar some nice Koranic carving on the walls. Enclosed by marble lattice screens next to Amir Khusrau's mausoleum, the tomb of **Princess Jahanara**, Shah Jahan's favourite daughter, is topped by a hollow filled with grass in compliance with her wish to have nothing but grass covering her grave. Just east of the *dargah* compound, the elegant 64-pillared white marble **Chausath Khamba** was built as a mausoleum for the family of a Mughal politician who had been governor of Gujarat, and the building, with its low, wide form and elegant marble screens, bears the unmistakeable evidence of Gujarati influence. The compound is usually locked, but the caretaker should be on hand somewhere nearby to open it up should you want to take a closer look.

Southern New Delhi

A range of sights are dispersed throughout southern New Delhi, in the wide area between **Khan Market** and **Chanakyapuri**. Khan Market itself is a U-shaped affair, with restaurants, cafés and shops running along its fringes, and more of the same on the pedestrianized path running through its middle; it's like a far calmer, more refined version of CP. An easy walk away, you'll find Mughal tombs and a park full of ancient monuments, while pressing on west you can mop up a series of interesting museums: it's quite possible to see everything here in one full day.

Lodi Gardens

Lodi Rd, though entrances on all corners • Daily: April–Sept 5am–8pm; Oct–March 6am–8pm • Free • Ⓜ Khan Market or Jor Bagh, or a ₹80 auto ride from Connaught Place

If Delhi's noise and bustle are getting to you, make for the leafy, pleasant **Lodi Gardens**. A favourite with picnicking families, trysting couples and curious squirrels, they form part of a belt of fifteenth- and sixteenth-century monuments that now stand incongruously amid the golf greens and large bungalows of Delhi's elite. The park is especially full in the early mornings and early evenings, when fitness enthusiasts come to jog (or walk briskly) through the manicured gardens against a backdrop of medieval monuments. The gardens also contain the **National Bonsai Park**, which has a fine selection of diminutive trees, and a series of rose and herbal gardens. The best time to visit is at sunset, when the light is soft and the tombs are all lit up.

Near the centre of the gardens, the imposing **Bara Gumbad** ("large dome") is a square, late fifteenth-century tomb capped by the eponymous dome, its monotonous exterior relieved by grey and black stones and its interior adorned with painted stuccowork. **Shish Gumbad** ("glazed dome"), a similar tomb 50m north, still bears a few traces of the blue tiles liberally used to form friezes below the cornice and above the entrance; inside, meanwhile, you'll see plasterwork inscribed with ornate Koranic inscriptions.

The octagonal **tomb of Muhammad Shah** (ruled 1434–45) of the Sayyid dynasty stands 300m southwest of Bara Gumbad, surrounded by verandas and pierced by arches and sloping buttresses. In the northeast of the park, and enclosed within high walls and a square garden, the **tomb of Sikandar Lodi** (ruled 1489–1517) repeats the octagonal theme, with a central chamber – anointed daily, and copiously, by the pigeons – encircled by a veranda. Almost adjacent is the **Athpula** ("eight piers"), a sixteenth-century ornamental bridge, right by the park's northeastern exit.

Safdarjang's Tomb

Aurobindo Marg (opposite Lodi Rd) • Daily dawn–dusk • ₹300 (₹25) • ⓜ Jor Bagh

The two-storeyed tomb of **Safdarjang** was the very last of India's great Mughal garden tombs. Built between 1753 and 1774, it dates from the period after Nadir Shah's sacking of the city, by which time the empire was reduced to a fraction of its former size and most of the capital's grander buildings lay in ruins. Safdarjang was the Mughal nawab (governor) of Avadh who briefly became vizier before being overthrown for his Shi'ite beliefs. Emblematic of the decadence and degeneracy that characterized the twilight of the Mughal era, the mausoleum sports an elongated, tapered dome and absurdly ornate interior filled with swirling plasterwork. Facing east, it's at its most photogenic in the morning.

Gandhi Smriti

5 Tees January Marg • Tues–Sun (partially closed on 2nd Sat of each month) 10am–5pm • Free • ⓜ Race Course

A pilgrimage place of sorts, **Gandhi Smriti** is the house where the Mahatma lived his last days. He had come to Delhi to quell the sectarian rioting that accompanied Partition, but Hindu sectarian extremists hated him for protecting Muslims, and on January 30, 1948, one of them shot him dead. Visitors can view an exhibition about his life, and follow in his last footsteps to the spot where he died.

Indira Gandhi Memorial Museum

1 Safdarjang Rd • Tues–Sun 9.30am–4.45pm • Free • ⓜ Race Course

Despite her actions during the 1975–77 Emergency (see page 1198), Nehru's daughter, Indira Gandhi (no relation to the Mahatma), is still remembered by many with respect and affection. The **Indira Gandhi Memorial Museum** occupies the house where she was assassinated by her Sikh bodyguards in 1984; her bloodstained sari, chemically preserved, is on display, and there's a section devoted to her son Rajiv, including the clothes he was wearing when Sri Lankan Tamil separatists killed him in 1991.

Nehru Memorial Museum

Teen Murti Marg • **Museum** Tues–Sun 9am–5.30pm • Free • ⓦ nehrumemorial.nic.in **Planetarium** 40min astronomy shows in English Tues–Sun 11.30am & 3pm • ₹80 • ⓦ nehruplanetarium.org

The **Nehru Memorial Museum** occupies the former official residence of India's first prime minister, Jawaharlal Nehru, and is now preserved in his memory. One of Nehru's passions was astronomy, and there's a **planetarium** in the grounds of the house.

National Rail Museum

Service Rd, Chanakyapuri • Tues–Sun 10am–5pm • ₹100/50 weekends/weekdays; "Joy Train" ₹50/20 weekends/weekdays • ⓦ nrmindia. com • ⓜ Durgabai Deshmukh South Campus, on the pink line, but a short cab ride from easier-to-access yellow line stations including Lok Kalyan Marg

The cream of India's royal coaches and oldest engines are on permanent display at the **National Rail Museum** in the embassy enclave of Chanakyapuri. Some 27 locomotives and seventeen carriages – including the teak carriage of the maharaja of Mysore, trimmed in gold and ivory, and the cabin used by the Prince of Wales in 1876 – are kept in the grounds. A steam-hauled miniature "Joy Train" does a circuit of the grounds whenever it has enough passengers.

The covered section of the museum houses models of famous engines and coaches, displays of old tickets, and even the skull of an elephant hit by a train near Bombay in 1894. The pride of the collection, however, is a model of India's very first train, a steam engine that made its inaugural journey of 21 miles from Bombay to Thane in 1853.

1

South Delhi

Most of the early settlements of Delhi, including its first city at Qila Rai Pithora (around the Qutb Minar), are to be found not in "Old Delhi" but in **South Delhi**, the wide area south of Lutyens' carefully planned boulevards. The rapid expansion of suburban Delhi has swallowed up what was previously countryside, whole villages being embedded within it, and the area is now home to some of the city's newest and most happening locales, most pertinently **Hauz Khas Village**, a lakeside area filled with shops, bars and restaurants.

Hauz Khas

4km south of Safdarjang's Tomb • ⓜ Green Park

Set amid parks and woodland, the wealthy suburban development of **Hauz Khas** is typical of South Delhi in being a thoroughly modern area dotted with remnants of antiquity. The modern part takes the form of Hauz Khas Village, a shopping area packed with chic boutiques and smart restaurants. There's also a very pleasant deer park and a rose garden, but of most interest to visitors, apart from the upmarket **drinking** and **shopping** possibilities (see pages 118 and 119), are the ruins of a fourteenth-century reservoir at the western end of the village.

Sultan Ala-ud-din Khalji had the reservoir (or "tank") built in 1304 to supply water to his citadel at Siri, Delhi's "second city", and it became known as **Hauz-i-Alai**. Half a century later, it was expanded by Firoz Shah, who added a two-storey seminary and a mosque at its northern end. Among the anonymous tombs scattered throughout the area is that of Firoz Shah himself, directly overlooking the southern corner of the tank. Its high walls, lofty dome, and doorway spanned by a lintel with a stone railing outside are fine examples of Hindu Indian traditions effectively blended with Islamic architecture.

Siri

Just west of Panchsheel Forest • ⓜ Panchsheel Park

Siri itself was located a couple of kilometres east of Hauz Khas, and the remains of its ramparts can be seen from August Kranti Marg. Much of the site has been given over to parkland, which makes it pleasant enough to visit, but part of it was subsumed by a village built to house athletes competing in the 1982 Asian Games.

Greater Kailash and around

One of New Delhi's more affluent areas, **Greater Kailash** – increasingly referred to as "GK" by Delhi folk – is a sprawling, occasionally calm expanse featuring several component neighbourhoods, including trendy **Kailash Colony**, and the popular shopping district of **Lajpat Nagar**. East of Greater Kailash proper is delightful Astha Kunj Park; one of Delhi's most beautiful sights, the **Baha'i Temple**, sits pretty at its eastern end.

The Baha'i Temple

Off Lotus Temple Rd; entrance on eastern side of compound • Tues–Sun: April–Sept 9am–7pm; Oct–March 9am–5pm (you may be asked to wait briefly outside during services) • Free • ⓦ bahaihouseofworship.in • ⓜ Okhla NSIC

Often compared visually to the Sydney Opera House, Delhi's **Baha'i Temple** is an iconic piece of modern architecture that dominates the surrounding parkland and suburban sprawl. You'll be urged into single file on the approach to the temple, inching closer to the twenty-seven spectacular giant white petals of marble, forming the shape of an unfolding lotus, springing from nine pools, to symbolize the nine unifying spiritual paths of the Baha'i faith. Groups are allowed into the building in bursts and told to keep silent, though you can stay inside for as long as you like; each petal alcove contains an extract from the Baha'í holy scriptures. Set amid well-maintained gardens, the temple is at its most impressive at sunset; some of the prettiest views are from adjacent Astha Kunj Park, though there's sadly no way through the fence separating the park from the temple.

Ashoka's Rock Edict
Off Raja Dhirsain Marg • ⓂNehru Place

Ashoka's Rock Edict is a ten-line epigraph inscribed in ancient Brahmi script on a smooth, sloping rock. The rock, now protected by a shelter in its own little park, was used as a slide by neighbourhood kids until 1966, when local residents noticed the ancient inscription, which was promulgated by the Mauryan emperor Ashoka the Great in the third century BC and shows there must have been an important settlement nearby. It states that the emperor's exertions in the cause of dharma (righteousness) had brought the people closer to the gods, and that through their efforts this attainment could be increased even further.

Saket and around

Like Greater Kailash, **Saket** is a relatively well-to-do part of New Delhi, perhaps best exemplified by the large Select Citywalk Mall. Thanks to the presence of nearby sights – most pertinently the wonderful **Qutb Minar** monuments – it has long been on the tourist radar, though recent years have seen travellers making more use of the area itself, thanks to the opening up of several excellent places to stay.

Qutb Minar Complex

Ladha Sarai, Mehrauli • Daily sunrise–sunset • ₹600, or ₹550 if paying by card (₹30) • ⓂSaket

Above the foundations of Lal Kot, the "first city of Delhi" founded in the eleventh century by the Tomar Rajputs, stand the first monuments of Muslim India, known as the **Qutb Minar Complex**, 13km south of Connaught Place. Pride of place goes to the fluted red-sandstone tower of the **Qutb Minar** itself, which has become one of Delhi's most famous landmarks.

Covered with intricate carvings and deeply inscribed verses from the Koran, the **Qutb Minar** tapers upwards from ruins to a height of just over 72m. In times past it was considered one of the "Wonders of the East", second only to the Taj Mahal, but historian John Keay was perhaps more representative of the modern eye when he claimed that the tower had "an unfortunate hint of the factory chimney and the brick kiln; a wisp of white smoke trailing from its summit would not seem out of place".

Work on the Qutb Minar started in 1202; it was Qutb-ud-din Aibak's victory tower, celebrating the advent of the Muslim dominance of Delhi (and much of the Subcontinent) that was to endure until 1857. For Qutb-ud-din, who died four years after gaining power, it marked the eastern extremity of the Islamic faith, casting the shadow of God over east and west. It was also a minaret, from which the muezzin called the faithful to prayer. Only the first storey has been ascribed to Qutb-ud-din's own short reign; the other four were built under his successor Iltutmish, and the top was restored in 1369 under Firoz Shah, using marble to face the red sandstone.

The Quwwat-ul-Islam mosque
Adjacent to the tower lie the ruins of India's earliest extant mosque, **Quwwat-ul-Islam** ("the Might of Islam"), commissioned by Qutb-ud-din and built using the remains of 27 Hindu and Jain temples with the help of Hindu artisans; their

1

influence can be seen in the detail of the masonry and the indigenous corbelled arches. Steps lead to an impressive courtyard flanked by cloisters and supported by pillars unmistakeably taken from a Hindu temple and adapted to accord with strict Islamic law forbidding iconic worship – all the faces of the decorative figures carved into the columns have been removed. Especially fine ornamental arches, rising as high as 16m, remain of what was once the prayer hall. Beautifully carved sandstone screens, combining Koranic calligraphy with the Indian lotus, form a facade immediately to the west of the mosque, facing Mecca. The thirteenth-century Delhi sultan Iltutmish and his successors had the building extended, enlarging the prayer hall and the cloisters and introducing geometric designs, calligraphy, glazed tiles set in brick, and squinches (arches set diagonally to a square to support a dome).

In complete contrast to the mainly Islamic surroundings, an **Iron Pillar** (7.2m) stands in the precincts of Qutb-ud-din's original mosque, bearing fourth-century Sanskrit inscriptions of the Gupta period attributing it to the memory of King Chandragupta II (ruled 375–415 AD). Once topped with an image of the Hindu bird god, Garuda, the extraordinarily pure but rust-free pillar has puzzled metallurgists. Its rust resistance is apparently due to its phosphorous content – as much as one percent – which has acted as a chemical catalyst to create a protective layer of an unusual compound called misawite around the metal. The pillar was evidently transplanted here by the Tomars, but it's not known from where.

Alai Minar

The Khalji sultan Ala-ud-din had the mosque extended to the north, and aimed to build a tower even taller than the Qutb Minar, but his **Alai Minar** never made it beyond the first storey, which still stands, and is regarded as a monument to the folly of vain ambition. Ala-ud-din also commissioned the **Alai Darwaza**, an elegant mausoleum-like gateway with stone lattice screens, to the south of the Qutb Minar.

Archaeological Park

Anuvrat Marg, Mehrauli • Daily sunrise–sunset • Free • Ⓜ Saket or Qutab Minar, and a short walk from Qutb Minar itself; turn right out of the exit then right at the fork, and look for a small footpath to your right about 300m on

The area south of the Qutb Minar Complex, rich with remains from all sorts of historical periods, has been turned into a two hundred-acre **Archaeological Park**. Here, within a very pleasant stroll of each other, you'll find: the tomb of Ghiyas-ud-din Balban, one of the Slave Dynasty sultans (reigned 1265–87), believed to be the first building in India constructed with true arches; the beautiful 1528 mosque and tomb of the poet Jamali Kamali (you may need to find the caretaker to open up the tomb for you); and the octagonal Mughal tomb of Muhammad Quli Khan, one of Akbar's courtiers. This last was occupied in the early nineteenth century by Sir Thomas Metcalfe, the East India Company's resident at the Mughal court, who rather bizarrely converted it into a country house. The park contains more than eighty monuments, including tombs, mosques, gateways and *baolis*, dating from every century between the thirteenth and the twentieth.

Kiran Nadar Museum of Art

145 DLF South Court Mall • Tue–Sun 10.30am–6.30pm • Free • Ⓦ knma.in • Ⓜ Malviya Nagar

The **Kiran Nadar Museum of Art** became India's first private contemporary art museum when it opened in 2010, and it's still the biggest. Its main collection highlights artists from the decades around independence (anger, striving and joy, always good food for art), but exhibitions usually feature works of a more contemporary nature, often accompanied by artist talks, film screenings and the like – well worth the trip out to Saket, and if you've enjoyed the place, they've another wing just outside the city limits in Noida.

Further afield

A number of interesting sights – some architecturally or historically significant, others a little more quirky – lie dotted around the wide periphery of South Delhi, and with time on your hands it's certainly worth making the effort required to get to at least one or two of them. Over the river to the east is the striking, modern **Akshardham Temple**; south of the city centre you'll find **Tughluqabad**, the third city of ancient Delhi, and yet another massive temple; and out west, the **Sulabh International Museum of Toilets** has become a popular left-field sight.

Akshardham Temple

Noida Link Rd, Akshardham • Tues–Sun 9.30am–6.30pm • Free • No mirrors or electronic equipment, which should be deposited at the cloakroom outside, and no shorts or skirts above the knee • ⓦ akshardham.com • Ⓜ Akshardham

On the east side of the Yamuna River, the opulent **Akshardham Temple** was erected in 2005 by the Gujarat-based Shri Swaminarayan sect. The largest place of worship in India, the temple is also a stunning piece of art, embellished with wonderful carvings made using the same tools and techniques as in ancient times. The **main shrine** is surrounded by a pink sandstone relief (you must walk round it clockwise) whose theme is elephants – wild, domesticated or in legend. Inside, the centrepiece and main object of devotion is a 3m-high gold statue of the sect's founder, Bhagwan Shri Swaminarayan, attended by four disciples, and behind it are paintings depicting scenes from his life, and also personal objects such as his sandals and even some of his hair and nail clippings. The four subsidiary shrines are devoted to conventional Hindu gods.

Tughluqabad

Mehrauli–Badarpur Rd; the entrance is 1km east of the junction with Guru Ravidas Marg • Fort and tomb daily 7am–5pm • ₹100 (₹5), including tomb; free for Adilabad • Ⓜ Tughlakabad

Some 15km southeast of Connaught Place, a rocky escarpment holds the crumbling, 6.5km-long battlements of the third city of Delhi, **Tughluqabad**, built during the short reign of Ghiyas-ud-din Tughluq (1320–24). After the king's death the city was deserted, probably due to the lack of a clean water source nearby. The most interesting area is the high-walled **citadel** in the southwestern part of the site, though only a long underground passage, the ruins of several halls and a tower now remain.

The southernmost of Tughlaqabad's thirteen gates still looks down on a causeway, breached by the modern road, which rises above the flood plain to link the fortress with **Ghiyas-ud-din Tughluq's tomb**. The tomb is entered through a massive red-sandstone gateway leading into a courtyard surrounded by cloisters in the defensive walls. In the middle, surrounded by a well-kept lawn, stands the distinctive mausoleum, its sloping sandstone walls topped by a marble dome, and in its small way a precursor to the fine series of garden tombs built by the Mughals, which began here in Delhi with that of Humayun (see page 97). Inside the mausoleum are the graves of Ghiyas-ud-din, his wife and their son Muhammad Shah II. Ghiyas-ud-din's chief minister, Jafar Khan, is buried in the eastern bastion, and interred in the cloister nearby is the sultan's favourite dog.

The later fortress of **Adilabad**, built by Muhammad Shah II in much the same style as his father's citadel, and now in ruins, stands on a hillock to the southeast.

Chhatarpur Mandir

Main Chhattarpur Rd • Daily 6am–10pm • Free • ⓦ chhattarpurmandir.org • Ⓜ Chhattarpur

Some 7km south of CP as the crow flies, the sprawling seventy-acre Chhaatarpur Mandir complex, built in 1974, was the country's biggest until it was superseded by the Akshardham Temple. It isn't really so much a temple as a pleasant park-like compound, straddling the main road (there's a pedestrian underpass), with several temples within its boundaries. The site is overlooked by a red, 30m-high image of Hanuman, but

1

TRAVEL AGENTS AND TOUR OPERATORS

Don't book flights or excursions through any agency that you're directed to by a street tout, and note that many local agencies try their best to put forward the appearance of bona fide official tourist information offices. For **ticketing**, you may as well book your flights online these days (especially domestic), but agencies can come in handy for train and bus tickets.

Ashok Travels and Tours 3rd floor, Jeevan Vihar Building, 3 Sansad Marg ☎011 2374 8165, ⊕ attindiatourism.com. The India Tourism Development Corporation's commercial arm, Ashok Travels, sells excursions and air tickets.

Delhi Tourism Coffee Home, Baba Kharak Singh Marg ☎011 2336 5358, ⊕ delhitourism.gov.in. The DTTDC offers day-trips to Agra (daily; ₹1525) and three-day "Golden Triangle" excursions to Agra, Bharatpur Bird

Sanctuary (winter only) and Jaipur (every Tues & Fri; ₹6195, including accommodation).

Rajasthan Tourism Bikaner House, Pandara Rd ☎011 2338 3837 or ☎011 2338 6069, ⊕ rtdc.tourism. rajasthan.gov.in. Organizes package tours including wildlife tours and trips on the *Palace on Wheels* trains.

STIC G-55 Connaught Place ☎011 4620 6600, ⊕ statravel.co.in. Represents STA Travel in India, sells tickets and issues or renews ISIC cards.

there are lots of other sculptures too – some of them very good, and not all especially religious. The central temple is devoted to Ma Katyayani (Durga), and the whole development was financed by followers of a saintly guru known as Babaji, who died in 1998; although he forbade any personal reverence to him in his lifetime, his ashes are kept in a memorial temple here.

Sulabh International Museum of Toilets

Palam Dabri Larg • Mon–Sat 8am–8pm, Sun 10am–5pm • Free • ⊕ sulabhtoiletmuseum.org • ⊕ Dashrathpuri

A relatively new addition to the city's roster of sights, the **Sulabh International Museum of Toilets** has proven a bit of a hit, despite its slightly out-of-the-way location. The museum traces the history and evolution of human waste disposal, from the pit-toilets of the Harrapan civilisation to the modern day, via some highly decorative exhibits from the Victorian period.

ARRIVAL AND DEPARTURE   DELHI

Delhi's international airport is India's main point of arrival for overseas visitors, and the city also functions as north India's major transport hub, with four **long-distance railway** stations and three **intercity bus** terminals. Scores of travel agents (see page 104) sell bus and train tickets, while many hotels – budget or otherwise – will book them for you too. There's an ever-expanding network of internal flights, but it's still best to book these (for price reasons) and train tickets (for reasons of capacity) as far ahead as possible; at peak times such as Diwali, demand is very high.

BY PLANE

Indira Gandhi International Airport (☎0124 337 6000, ⊕ newdelhiairport.in), 20km southwest of the centre, IGI currently has three separate terminals (another three are planned). T1 and T2 are domestic terminals, while T3 is the main hub for international flights, plus Air India and Vistara domestic services. There are ATMs in all arrivals halls, but for currency exchange you'll get better rates in town. T2 and T3 are close to each

other (10min on foot), and there are free shuttle buses between T1 and T3, though only for those able to prove that they're transferring. As all over India, you will not be allowed into the terminal without a printout, or an e-ticket (phones and tablets both fine) with your name and destination visible.

GETTING INTO TOWN

By metro The quickest and easiest option is the Airport Express Link metro line, which takes travellers between the airport (T2 & T3) and New Delhi railway station (20min; ₹60) or Shivaji Stadium (for Connaught Place); note that the metro entrance is just east of the railway station (the opposite side to Paharganj). T1 is on the Magenta Line, which is useful for South Delhi; for the centre you can change to the Yellow Line at Hauz Khas, but in theory you're not allowed bulky luggage on either (see page 109). T1 is also connected by shuttle bus (₹30) to Aerocity station on the Airport Express line.

Taxis Taking a taxi is particularly advisable if you leave or arrive late at night. There are official prepaid taxi kiosks

A TAXI WAITS AT CONNAUGHT PLACE

1

RECOMMENDED TRAINS FROM DELHI

The trains below are recommended as the fastest and/or most convenient for specific cities, and run daily unless marked.

Destination	Name	No.	From	Departs	Arrives
Agra	Bhopal Shatabdi*	#12002	ND	6am	7.57am
	Taj Express	#12280	ND	6.45am	9.24am
	Gatimaan Express	#12050	HN	8.10am	9.50am (exc Fri)
	Kerala Express	#12626	ND	11.25am	2.05pm
Ahmedabad	Ashram Express	#12916	OD	3.20pm	7.40am+
	Adi SJ Rajdhani*	#12958	ND	7.55pm	9.40am+
Ajmer	Shatabdi Express*	#12015	ND	6.05am	12.45pm
	Ashram Express	#12916	OD	3.20pm	10.40pm
Attari (for Pakistan)	Delhi-Attari Express*	#14001	OD	11.10pm	7.15am+ (Sun & Wed)
Chandigarh	Kalka Shatabdi	#12011	ND	7.40am	11.05am
	Paschim Express	#12925	ND	11.05am	3.57pm
	Kalka Shatabdi	#12005	ND	5.15pm	8.35pm
Chennai	Tamil Nadu Express	#12622	ND	10.30pm	7.10am++
	GT Express	#12616	ND	6.40pm	6.20am++
Haridwar	Dehradun Shatabdi	#12017	ND	6.45am	11.30am
	Dehradun Janshatabd*	#12055	ND	3.20pm	7.33pm
Jaipur	Ajmer Shatabdi	#12015	ND	6.05am	10.40am
	Ashram Express	#12916	OD	3.20pm	8.25pm
Jhansi	Bhopal Shatabdi *	#12002	ND	6am	10.45am
Kolkata	Kolkata Rajdhani*	#12302	ND	4.55pm	9.55am+ (exc Fri)
	Sealdah Rajdhani*	#12314	ND	4.25pm	10.10am+
	Sealdah Duronto*	#12260	ND	7.40pm	12.45pm+ (Mon, Tues, Thurs, Fri)
Mumbai	Mumbai Rajdhani *	#12952	ND	4.25pm	8.15am
Udaipur	Mewar Express	#12963	HN	7pm	7.20am+
	Chetak Express	#12981	SR	7.40pm	7.50am+
Varanasi	Shiv Ganga Express	#12560	ND	6.55pm	7am+
	Swatantras Express	#12562	ND	8.40pm	8.25am+
	Manduadih Express	#12582	ND	10.35pm	11.10am+
Vasco da Gama (Goa)	Lakshadweep Express	#12618	HN	9.15am	8.30pm+

OD Old Delhi, ND New Delhi, HN Hazrat Nizamuddin, SR Sarai Rohilla
*a/c only, + next day, ++ two days later

at the airport arrivals areas; kiosk prices vary, but the fare will be around ₹450 to the city centre, with a 25 percent surcharge between 11pm and 5am. Many hotels and guesthouses offer pick-up services, which you'll find to be the smoothest and most reliable method of getting to your hotel from the airport; prices vary considerably, but expect ₹350–600, and the same for a return leg. Uber and other apps usually cost less.

Auto-rickshaws The auto-rickshaws waiting in line at the departure gate constitute the least reliable form of transport from the airport, especially at night, though they're cheaper than a taxi; fares are ₹200–250, while for the return a prepaid auto from CP costs ₹205.

BY TRAIN

Delhi has four major railway stations. All are notorious for theft: don't take your eyes off your luggage for a moment. Old Delhi, New Delhi and Anand Vihar stations are served by stops on the metro, but travelling on it with bulky baggage is prohibited (you may get away with it out of peak hours). Many southbound trains depart from New Delhi, but most trains to Rajasthan leave from either Old Delhi or Sarai Rohilla stations. Quite a few trains to south and central India leave from Hazrat Nizamuddin station, so check carefully when you buy your ticket. Bookings for all trains can be made at New Delhi station. **New Delhi station** At the eastern end of Paharganj, New Delhi station has two exits: take the Paharganj exit for

Connaught Place and most points south, and the Ajmeri Gate exit for Old Delhi. Both exits have prepaid auto-rickshaw booths (₹50 to CP, ₹80 to Chandni Chowk, plus ₹8 for large baggage). The station has an efficient booking office for foreign tourists (Mon–Sat 8am–8pm, Sun 8am–2pm), on the first floor of the departure building; bring your passport, and ignore touts' claims that it has moved or closed (see page 107).

Old Delhi station Officially called Delhi Junction, and west of the Red Fort, this well connected to the city by taxis, auto-rickshaws and cycle rickshaws, while Chandni Chowk – on the metro's Yellow Line – is just to the south. For autos there's a booth selling fixed-price prepaid tickets – Connaught Place is ₹80, plus ₹8 for baggage.

Hazrat Nizamuddin station Southeast of the centre (and a stop on the metro's Pink Line), serving most trains from Agra, and long-distance *Rajdhani Express* services from major cities nationwide. Connaught Place is a ₹105 ride (plus ₹8/piece of baggage) from the prepaid auto booth, though auto-walas often try to demand extra.

Sarai Rohilla station 4km west of Old Delhi station, serving some trains from Rajasthan. Prepaid autos to Connaught Place cost ₹80, and Shastri Nagar on the metro's Red Line is quite close.

Anand Vihar station One or two long-distance services arrive at this station in East Delhi, served by a metro station on the Blue Line, but it's expected to increase greatly in capacity in due course.

BY BUS

Buses are most useful for travelling to mountainous areas of neighbouring states that aren't served by trains, but may also be faster than trains on shorter routes. On longer routes there's usually a choice between the ramshackle state-run services and more comfortable private buses, which some see as potentially more dangerous as they travel faster and often overnight.

STATE BUSES

Maharana Pratap ISBT Also known as Kashmir Gate, this whopper of bus terminal north of Old Delhi railway station (Ⓜ Kashmere Gate, 20min and ₹100 from Connaught Place by prepaid auto) hosts all kinds of services, including most state-run intercity buses to and from the northern states, and many from Rajasthan, as well as an increasing number of private services. The place can be very confusing, and you should arrive well ahead of your scheduled departure time.

Destinations Amritsar (2–3 hourly; 8hr); Chandigarh (1–2 hourly; 5hr); Dehradun (every 30min; 6hr); Haridwar (every 30min; 5–7hr); Jammu (9 daily; 12hr); Manali (hourly; 13–15hr); Rishikesh (every 30min; 5hr 30min–7hr); Shimla (1 – 2 hourly; 8–10hr).

Anand Vihar ISBT Services for some Uttarakhand hill stations such as leave from this terminal in East Delhi (Ⓜ Anand Vihar). Take the Blue Line from Connaught Place, or a prepaid auto (₹125 plus ₹8 for baggage from CP).

Destinations Almora (4 daily; 12hr); Nainital (3 daily; 9hr); Ramnagar (for Corbett National Park; 18 daily; 7–8hr).

Sarai Kale Khan ISBT For destinations in Rajasthan, this terminal has the best services, including some deluxe buses. It's adjacent to Hazrat Nizamuddin railway station (see page 106), and also on the metro's Pink Line.

Destinations Ajmer (14 daily; 9hr); Jaipur (over 40 daily; 6hr); Jodhpur (4 daily; 12hr); Udaipur (3 daily; 20hr).

PRIVATE AND INTERNATIONAL BUSES

Private buses Private services depart from various areas, including Paharganj, Majnu Ka Tila, RK Ashram Marg metro

DELHI SCAMS

Delhi can be a headache for the first-time visitor because of scams to entrap the unwary. The old accommodation wheeze – whereby taxi drivers or touts tried to convince you that **the hotel you've chosen is full**, closed or has just burned to the ground so as to take you to one that pays them commission – has diminished of late, thanks to the fact that most travellers **reserve their accommodation in advance**; many hotels will arrange for a car and driver to meet you at your point of arrival, if you like. It's still prudent to **write down your taxi's registration number** (make sure the driver sees you doing it), as this can help for security purposes.

Outside **New Delhi railway station**, on **Connaught Place** and along **Janpath**, steer clear of phoney "tourist information offices" (which touts may try to divert you to), and never do business with any travel agency that tries to disguise itself as a tourist information office. For the record, India Tourism is at 88 Janpath, and the DTTDC is on Baba Kharak Singh Marg; all other "tourist offices" are private operators.

Finally, be aware that taxi, auto and rental-car drivers get a hefty **commission** for taking you to certain shops, which will be added to your bill should you buy anything. You can assume that auto-walas who accost you on the street do so with the intention of overcharging you, or of taking you to shops which pay them commission. Always hail a taxi or auto-rickshaw yourself, rather than taking one whose driver approaches you, and don't let them take you to places where you haven't asked to go.

1

DELHI METRO

Legend:
- Airport Express Line
- Blue Line
- Green Line
- Red Line
- Violet Line
- Yellow Line
- Magenta Line
- Aqua Line
- Pink Line
- Grey Line (under construction)
- Rapid MetroRail Gurgaon

Shaheed Sthal (New Bus Adda)
Hindon River
Arthala
Mohan Nagar
Shyam Park
Rajendra Nagar
Raj Bagh
Shaheed Nagar
Dilshad Garden
Jhilmil
Mansarovar Park
Shahdara
Seelampur
Welcome
East Azad Nagar
Krishna Nagar
Karkardooma Court
Karkardooma
Anand Vihar
I.P. Extension
Mandawali–West Vinod Nagar
Preet Vihar
Nirman Vihar
Laxmi Nagar
Akshardham
Yamuna Bank
Vaishali
U.P. Extension
Vinod Nagar East
Trilokpuri
Mayur Vihar Extension
Mayur Vihar Pocket I
New Ashok Nagar
Noida Sector 15
Noida Sector 16
Noida Sector 18
Botanical Garden
Noida City Centre
Golf Course
Noida Sector 34
Noida Electronic City
Noida Sector 62
Noida Sector 59
Noida Sector 61
Noida Sector 52
Sector 50
Sector 51
Sector 76
Sector 101
Sector 81
NSEZ
Sector 83
Sector 137
Sector 142
Sector 143
Sector 144
Sector 145
Sector 146
Sector 148
Depot Station
NOIDA
OKHLA Bird Sanctuary
Okhla Vihar
Jasola Vihar Shaheen Bagh
Kalindi Kunj
Okhla
Jamia Millia Islamia
Sukhdev Vihar
Govind Puri
Harkesh Nagar Okhla
Jasola Apollo
Sarita Vihar
Mohan Estate
Tughlakabad Station
Badarpur Border
Sarai
NHPC Chowk
Mewla Maharajpur
Sector 28
Badkhal Mor
Old Faridabad
Neelam Chowk Ajronda
Bata Chowk
Escorts Mujesar
Sant Surdas (Sihi)
Raja Nahar Singh
Nizamuddin
Hazrat
Ashram
Vinoba Puri
Lajpat Nagar
Moolchand
Kailash Colony
Nehru Place
Kalkaji Mandir
Nehru Enclave
Greater Kailash
Chirag Delhi
Hauz Khas
Malviya Nagar
Saket
Qutab Minar
Chhatarpur
Sultanpur
Ghitorni
Arjangarh
Guru Dronacharya
Sikanderpur
Phase 2
Phase 3
MG Road
IFFCO Chowk
HUDA City Centre
Belvedere Towers
Cyber City
DLF Phase 1
Sushant Lok
Sec 53–54
Sec 55–56
AIT Chowk
Moulsari Avenue
Shiv Vihar
Johri Enclave
Gokulpuri
Maujpur–Babarpur
Jaffrabad
Seelampur
Shastri Park
Kashmere Gate
Lal Quila
Jama Masjid
Delhi Gate
ITO
Mandi House
Pragati Maidan
Indraprastha
Yamuna Bank
Barakhamba Road
Rajiv Chowk
New Delhi
Chawri Bazar
Chandni Chowk
Civil Lines
Vidhan Sabha
Vishwavidyalaya
G.T.B. Nagar
Model Town
Azadpur
Adarsh Nagar
Jahangir Puri
Badli Mor
Rohini Sector 18
Samaypur Badli
Shiv Vihar
Central Secretariat
Patel Chowk
Udyog Bhawan
Lok Kalyan Marg
Jor Bagh
INA
Dilli Haat–INA
AIIMS
Green Park
Sarojini Nagar
Bhikaji Cama Place
R.K. Puram
Munirka
Vasant Vihar
Shankar Vihar
Terminal 1–IGI Airport
Sadar Bazar Cantt.
Palam
Dwarka
Dabri Mor
Janakpuri West
Dashrath Puri
Delhi Aerocity
Airport
Durgabai Deshmukh South Campus
Sir Vishweshwaraiah Moti Bagh
Bhikaji Cama Place
Naraina Vihar
Delhi Cantt.
Mayapuri
Rajouri Garden
ESI Hospital
Tagore Garden
Subhash Nagar
Tilak Nagar
Janakpuri East
Uttam Nagar East
Uttam Nagar West
Nawada
Dwarka Mor
Dwarka Sector 14
Dwarka Sector 13
Dwarka Sector 12
Dwarka Sector 11
Dwarka Sector 10
Dwarka Sector 9
Dwarka Sector 8
Dwarka Sector 21
Nangli
Najafgarh
Dhansa Bus Stand
Nangloi
Nangloi Railway Station
Rajdhani Park
Mundka
Mundka Industrial Area (MIA)
Ghevra Metro Station
Tikri Kalan
Tikri Border
Pandit Shree Ram Sharma
Bahadurgarh City
Brigadier Hoshiyar Singh
Peeragarhi
Udyog Nagar
Maharaja Surajmal Stadium
Nangloi
Paschim Vihar East
Paschim Vihar West
Madipur
Shivaji Park
Punjabi Bagh West
Punjabi Bagh
Shakur Pur
Netaji Subhash Place
Kohat Enclave
Pitampura
Rohini East
Rohini West
Rithala
Shalimar Bagh
Keshav Puram
Kanhaiya Nagar
Inderlok
Shastri Nagar
Pratap Nagar
Pulbangash
Tis Hazari
Ashok Park Main
Satguru Ram Singh Marg
Kirti Nagar
Shadipur
Moti Nagar
Ramesh Nagar
Rajdhani Park
Malis Park
Prashant Vihar
Rohini Sector 18
Majlis Park
Kalkaji
South Extension
Panchsheel Park
Chirag Delhi
Jangpura
Khan Market
Jawaharlal Nehru Stadium
Karol Bagh
Rajendra Place
Patel Nagar
Shadipur
Jhandewalan
Ramakrishna Ashram Marg
Jhilmil
LIT

station and the Red Fort; ticketing sites such as ⓦredbus. in are usually quite comprehensive with their schedule information. Popular destinations include Kullu, Manali and Dharamsala, which are not accessible by train, as well as Pushkar and the Uttarakhand hill stations. You can book tickets a day or two in advance through agencies in Paharganj or Connaught Place.

International buses Dr Ambedkar Terminal (near Delhi Gate) has services to Lahore in Pakistan (daily except Sun 6am; 12hr) and Kathmandu in Nepal (daily except Sun 10am; 28hr). You'll need to book at least a day ahead, and preferably more, and check in for the journey an hour early for Kathmandu and two hours (at 4am!) for Lahore (☎011 2331 8180, ⓦdtc.nic.in).

GETTING AROUND

Even with the addition of a very decent metro system, **public transport** in Delhi is still inadequate for the city's population and size, and increased car ownership is adding to the general chaos. **Cows** have been banned from much of central Delhi, but not the more traditional districts.

By metro Delhi's metro system (ⓦdelhimetrorail.com) is still expanding, with eight colour-coded lines so far – the choice of colours is curious to say the least, and it's easy to get confused between the Violet, Pink and Magenta lines (stay confusing, Delhi!). Fares are ₹10–60 depending upon distance travelled, and trains run from around 5am–midnight; during peak hours, trains can be very full indeed. If you're going to be using the metro a lot, it's worth getting a Smart Card (available at any metro station for ₹150, including ₹100 of credit); this gets a 10% discount from all fares, and will save you a lot of queuing (₹200 minimum recharge). Tourist Cards are also available (₹200 for a day's unlimited travel), but are unlikely to be worth your while. The metro is generally wheelchair accessible, and women have reserved carriages (either the first or last) to themselves. Children under 90cm (3ft) tall travel free if

accompanied by an adult. You'll have to go through security at all stations, and baggage weighing more than 15kg, or measuring more than 60cm x 45cm x 25cm, is prohibited, except on the Airport Express Line.

By bus With auto- and cycle rickshaws so cheap and plentiful, few tourists use Delhi's crowded buses, but they do prove useful from time to time, and some are even a/c. Fares are ₹5–20, and at the time of writing Smart Cards were not useable.

By auto-rickshaw Auto-rickshaws are often the most effective form of transport around Delhi. South of Connaught Place (where Janpath begins; see map p.94), as well as at stations and bus terminals, there are prepaid auto-rickshaw kiosks, charging certified official fares. Otherwise you'll need to negotiate a price before getting in; prices for foreigners vary according to your haggling skills, but as a sample fare, it should cost about ₹40–100 from Connaught Place to Old Delhi.

By cycle rickshaw Cycle rickshaws are not allowed in Connaught Place and parts of New Delhi, but are handy for short journeys to outlying areas and around Paharganj.

CITY TOURS

All five-star hotels offer their own packages, and some hotels in and around Paharganj, such as *Namaskar* and *Metropolis*, can arrange **city tours by taxi** for around ₹1000, which is good value when shared between three or four people. There are also **walking tours** of Paharganj (see page 90) and Nizamuddin (see page 98).

Delhi by Cycle ☎011 6464 5906, ⓦdelhibycycle. com. Five different three-and-a-half-hour bicycle tours (₹1850), mostly starting from Old Delhi's Delite Cinema, either at a bright-and-early 6.45am, or a more reasonable 1.15pm.

Delhi Tourism Coffee Home, Baba Kharak Singh Marg ☎011 2336 5358, ⓦdelhitourism.gov.in. Organizes a/c bus tours of New Delhi (Tue–Sun, 9am & 2.15pm; ₹290 each or ₹475 together, plus admission fees), starting outside their office. Depending on demand, they sometimes run a "Delhi by Evening" tour (₹300), which includes the sound-and-light show at the Red Fort (see page 88).

Delhi Transport Corporation Scindia House, Connaught Place ☎011 2375 2772, ⓦdtc.nic.in. Morning or afternoon tours (₹290 each, or ₹475 for

both), starting from Scindia House at 9.15am & 2.15pm, picking up at India Tourism on Janpath and the DTTDC kiosk on Baba Kharak Singh Marg.

HoHo At the kiosk, 100m southwest of the Delhi Tourism office on Baba Kharak Singh Marg, ☎011 4094 0000, ⓦhohodelhi.com. A hop-on, hop-off tour (5 daily, departing 8.30–11.30pm) on a circular route; tickets cost ₹1000 (₹500) for one day, or ₹1200 (₹600) for two days, and can be bought on the bus or from the DTTDC kiosk.

INTACH 71 Lodi Estate ☎011 2463 2267, ⓦintach delhichapter.org. The Indian National Trust for Art and Cultural Heritage runs heritage walks every weekend (₹200), though for schedules, their Facebook page is of more use than their website.

1

WHERE TO STAY IN DELHI

As if you didn't know already, Delhi is a rather big place, so it's important to give some thought to where you'd like to stay. Proximity to sights can be a factor, and prices vary by area, but you may also want to be near to a railway station – or to be somewhere far from the hubbub.

Few tourists stay in **Old Delhi**, which many find dirty, noisy and overcrowded, with hotels geared mostly to Indian visitors rather than foreigners. The hotels around Delhi station are particularly bad value, but there are a couple of good options. Just west of Old Delhi, and also New Delhi railway station, the **Paharganj** area is prime backpacker territory, with innumerable lodges offering inexpensive and mid-range accommodation. Some are good value; others offer very little for very little, and many suffer from slamming-door syndrome and people shouting till dawn, so choose carefully if you value peace and quiet. However, of all the areas in town to stay in, this is by far the most colourful.

New Delhi is focused on Connaught Place, but you pay a premium to stay here, so if you want value for money, stay elsewhere. South of "CP", grander hotels on and around Janpath and along Sansad Marg cater mainly for business travellers and tour groups, but there are some very good ones among them, and some charming outliers too.

More and more travellers are staying in **South Delhi**, a wide area home to some very pleasing mid-range hotels and guesthouses, and an increasing number of hostels for backpackers – the area is a great choice for those who want to stay somewhere quiet, and it makes an ideal introduction for those who've never been to Delhi (or even India) before.

They're also nippier than motorized traffic in Old Delhi. Rates should be roughly half that demanded by autos, but remember that your rickshaw-wala will be among Delhi's poorest citizens; see how hard they work, and unless they give you reason not to, be prepared to tip generously.

By taxi Delhi's taxis (white, or black and yellow) cost around 50% more than auto-rickshaws. Drivers belong to local taxi stands, where you can make bookings and fix prices; if you flag a taxi on the street you're letting yourself in for some haggling. A surcharge of around 25 percent operates between 11pm and 5am. The app-based taxi services Uber and Ola operate in Delhi, and can be as cheap as auto-rickshaws.

Chauffeur-driven cars For local sightseeing and journeys beyond the city confines, chauffeur-driven cars are very good value, especially for groups of three or four. Many budget hotels offer cars and drivers, as does Delhi Tourism (see page 104), and the booths at the southern end of the Tibetan Market on Janpath. Delhi Tourism rates are ₹2240/2800 for an 8/10hr day within Delhi (more in an a/c vehicle), which includes 80/100km mileage. Alternatively,

there's Kumar Tourist Taxi Service, K-14 Connaught Place (☎011 2341 5930, ⍟kumarindiatours.com). Driving yourself in Delhi can be dangerous, and is not advisable.

Car rental Driving yourself in Delhi can be dangerous, and is not advisable. If you do feel like giving it a go, try Avis, Khasra no. 802, K Block, Part II, Mahipalpur Extension ☎011 4155 5959 or ☎1860 500 0099; or Hertz, Plot 11a, Shivaji Marg, Moti Nagar ☎0124 301 4724.

Motorbike dealers The Karol Bagh area has many good bike shops selling new or secondhand Enfields. Reliable dealers include Inder Motors, 1744-A/55, Hari Singh Nalwa St, Abdul Aziz Rd (☎011 2875 0869, ⍟lallisingh.com; closed Mon); go two blocks east of Ajmal Khan Rd, turn right at the *chowki*, then take the third alley on the left.

By bicycle Cycling along the large avenues of New Delhi takes some getting used to and can be hazardous for those not used to chaotic traffic. Bicycle rental is hard to come by, but you can buy bikes pretty cheaply at Jhandewalan market (by Ⓜ Jhandewalan); alternatively join a bike tour (see page 104).

INFORMATION

Tourist information There are reasonably helpful Delhi Tourism offices at the international and domestic airports, railway stations and bus terminals, and India Tourism at 88 Janpath, just south of Connaught Place (Mon–Fri 9am–6pm, Sat 9am–2pm; ☎011 2332 0005 or ☎011 2332 0008), has information on historical sites, city tours, shopping and cultural events, as well as free city maps. DTTDC have a central office on Baba Kharak Singh Marg (daily 7am–9pm; ☎011 2336 5358,

⍟delhitourism.gov.in), plus a kiosk nearby. Beware of any other firms that look like or claim to be tourist offices (see page 107).

Listings It can be surprisingly hard to find decent info regarding upcoming exhibitions and cultural events; the most reliable listings can be found on Delhi Events (⍟delhievents.com), and there are some things worth seeing on the Insider.in website (⍟insider.in).

ACCOMMODATION

Delhi has a vast range of accommodation, from dirt-cheap lodges to extravagant international hotels. It's easy to **book rooms** online, even for cheaper places – even independent budget travellers are advised to book at least the first night in advance, since hauling a backpack from place to place around Paharganj is not only stressful, but will see you treated as a target by touts, whose advice is to be avoided in any case (see page 107).

HOTELS AND B&BS

OLD DELHI AND AROUND

★**Bloomrooms @ New Delhi** 8591 Arakashan Rd, Ram Nagar ☎ 011 4122 5666, ⓦ staybloom.com; ⓜ New Delhi; map p.89. A real cut above the other mid-range options in this area, with rooms somewhat akin to those of a Japanese business hotel – spotlessly clean, with everything in its right place. The rooms, the lobby and the pleasing upper-level courtyard are all painted white and fringed with yellow, which almost comes across as futuristic in scruffy Paharganj. ₹2000

Broadway 4/15A Asaf Ali Rd ☎ 011 4366 3600, ⓦ hotel broadwaydelhi.com; ⓜ Delhi Gate; map p.86. On the southern edge of Old Delhi, close to Delhi Gate, this mid-range hotel has a lot of old-fashioned charm and an excellent restaurant (Chor Bizarre; see page 113), plus a bar. Rooms are a little sombre, but they're clean and well equipped, and some look out to the Jama Masjid. Breakfast included. ₹3400

City Star 8718 DB Gupta Rd, Ram Nagar ☎ 011 4352 8111; ⓦ hotel-citystar.com; ⓜ New Delhi; map p.89. Good for a bit of comfort: rooms here are all well appointed and well maintained, with central a/c, and the "executive" ones are pretty huge. They've an on-site restaurant, and even a little gym. Rates include breakfast. ₹3800

Hari Piorko 4775 Main Bazaar, by Tooti Chowk ☎ 011 2358 7888 or ☎ 011 2358 7999, ⓦ hotelharipiorkodelhi. com; ⓜ RK Ashram Marg; map p.89. This bright hotel, slap-bang in the middle of the Paharganj action, with a balcony restaurant overlooking it all, generally gets a thumbs-up from budget travellers who don't want to slum it too much. The rooms, all attached, are nice and fresh, and there's lots of marble and mock stone cladding about the place. BB ₹1700

★**Maidens** 7 Sham Nath Marg, Civil Lines ☎ 011 2397 5464, ⓦ maidenshotel.com; ⓜ Civil Lines; map p.86. Stylish, understated luxury in a lovely old colonial mansion dating back to Company days; quiet and relaxing with comfortable period rooms, big bathrooms and leafy gardens as well as a swimming pool and a good restaurant. ₹7000

Rehanam Palace 1025 SF Pai Walan ☎ 011 4368 6255, ⓦ hotelrehanampalace.com; ⓜ Chawri Bazar; map p.86. Behind the Jama Masjid, in the heart of Old Delhi, this is a place that tries to please, and provides better value than more expensive places in the area. Nice, fresh rooms with a common veranda and a restaurant, but a rather slow elevator. ₹1700

NEW DELHI

Bright M-85, Connaught Place ☎ 011 4330 2222, ⓦ hotelbrightdelhi.in; ⓜ Rajiv Chowk or Barakhamba Road; map p.94. A former budget hotel reborn, given a new lease of life as an impressive upper-range option. Rooms are on the small side (some things just can't be changed), but feature tasteful silver decor with marble and mosaic-tile bathrooms, and the price includes breakfast. ₹7500

The Claridges 12 Aurangzeb Rd ☎ 011 3955 5000, ⓦ claridges.com; ⓜ Race Course; map p.93. One of Delhi's oldest and finest establishments, oozing elegant 1930s style from its facade to its rooms – and that includes the bathrooms. Facilities include three restaurants, a coffee shop, vodka bar and swimming pool. Breakfast included. ₹12,500

★**Imperial** Janpath ☎ 011 2334 1234, ⓦ theimperial india.com; ⓜ Janpath; map p.93. Delhi's classiest hotel, in a beautiful 1933 Art Deco building set amid large, palm-shaded gardens. The rooms are stylish, as is the cool lobby done out in cream and gold, while corridors double up as galleries exhibiting fascinating eighteenth- and nineteenth-century prints of India. Staff maintain just the right degree of courteousness, and there are a number of excellent restaurants including the renowned *Spice Route* (see page 115). Note that tax adds over a third to the listed price. ₹22,000

The Lalit Off Barakhamba Rd ☎ 011 4444 7777, ⓦ thelalit.com; ⓜ Barakhamba Rd; map p.93. A stylish, modern hotel, with cool, elegant rooms and a spacious lobby decorated with some impressive works of art, not to mention a 24hr bar and a 24hr café. It's pretty affordable, as far as the city's top hotels go, and expect hefty discounts when business is slack. ₹7500

La Sagrita 14 Sunder Nagar ☎ 011 2435 8572, ⓦ lasagrita.com; ⓜ Khan Market; map p.93. A former pension, now upgraded to a boutique hotel with lovely, spacious rooms (including two penthouse rooms with their own terraces), in a quiet, upscale neighbourhood. Wheelchair access, and buffet breakfast included. ₹6300

★**Master** R-500 New Rajendra Nagar ☎ 011 2874 1089, ⓦ master-guesthouse.com; ⓜ Karol Bagh; map p.82. Located in a fairly quiet residential neighbourhood, this is an excellent choice for those who have just landed in India – or who just want a change from Delhi's busier quarters. It's a lovely little pension-style guesthouse – comfortable, secure, friendly and family-run – with four a/c double rooms of different sizes and a secluded roof terrace. Located on the edge of the green belt just 10min by auto-

1

rickshaw from Connaught Place, and not far from the metro. Vegetarian meals available. BB ₹4250

Maurya Sardar Patel Marg, Chanakyapuri ☎011 2611 2233, ⓦitchotels.in/itcmaurya; map p.93. An extremely plush hotel on the edge of Chanakyapuri, opposite the Ridge forest, with an imposing range of luxury rooms and two of the best restaurants in Delhi (see page 114). It regularly hosts visiting heads of state (presidents Obama, Bush and Clinton have all stayed here, as have prime ministers of the UK, Canada, Australia and New Zealand). Promotional rates often available. BB ₹13,500

★ **The Park** 15 Sansad Marg ☎011 2374 3000, ⓦtheparkhotels.com; ⓜRajiv Chowk; map p.94. They don't come much snazzier than this place, just off Connaught Place, with its super-cool lobby, sleek, modern rooms, and bathrooms screened off by frosted glass walls. Service is snappy, the atmosphere relaxed, and all the facilities you'd expect are here, including a bar, good restaurant (see page 114) and pool. A cut above your run-of-the-mill five-star, and prices often dip to ₹8000. ₹11,000

SOUTH DELHI

★ **Aashianaa Living** 82 Gurdwara Rd ☎97161 5743; ⓜGreater Kailash; map p.82. Remarkably good value in this well-to-do area, this homely B&B provides most of the amenities you'd expect of a decent hotel room, providing that tricky mix of luxury and a personal touch at an extremely reasonable price. Breakfast included. ₹2200

Bloomrooms @ Link Rd 7 Link Rd, Jangpura ☎011 4122 5666, ⓦstaybloom.com; ⓜJangpura; map p.93. Like its sister establishment in Paharganj, this is modern affair with rooms following a sleek, white-and-yellow design scheme. It's just about the best-value place to stay in the entire New Delhi area, and set on the fringe of a rather charming – and almost entirely tourist-free – neighbourhood; Nizamuddin and Humayun's Tomb are both within walking distance. ₹2500

Ibis Asset #9, Hospitality District, Delhi Aerocity ☎011 4302 0202, ⓦaccorhotels.com; ⓜDelhi Aerocity; map p.82. Best value of the chain hotels – clean, reliable and handy for a night's sleep before your flight out. The rooms are well appointed and functional, with bed, desk and everything you need (the bathroom is a futuristic pod, not unlike a deluxe version of a portaloo), and there's a swimming pool. Prices usually up to ₹2000 under the rack rates. ₹6500

★ **Tree of Life** D-193, Saket ☎98102 77699, ⓦtree-of-life.in; ⓜSaket; map p.82. Friendly little B&B in a quiet neighbourhood close to the Qutb Minar and Archaeological Park, with seven immaculate and spacious rooms, a lounge and a kitchen – ideal if you're looking for somewhere clean and tranquil away from the hustle and bustle of the city centre, and perfect for first-time arrivals to Delhi. Breakfast included. ₹4900

Vivanta Ambassador Sujan Singh Park, off Subramaniam Bharti Marg ☎011 6626 1000, ⓦvivanta bytaj.com; ⓜKhan Market; map p.93. Low-key but well-run and classy, this is a friendly place with comfortably sized rooms and huge bathrooms, plus a couple of good restaurants and free use of the pool and health club at the nearby Taj Mahal hotel. Breakfast included. ₹13,000

HOSTELS AND BUDGET GUESTHOUSES

OLD DELHI AND AROUND

Backpacker Panda 22/1 Main Bazaar Rd ☎96438 23599, ⓦbackpackerpanda.com; ⓜRK Ashram Marg; map p.89. This hostel is worth a mention for its surprisingly cheap private rooms – the beds aren't the best, but the rooms are large, and ones with private bathrooms only cost ₹100 more. There's also a rooftop for drinking and socialising. Dorm ₹500, doubles ₹1000

Namaskar 917 Chandiwalan, off Main Bazaar ☎011 2358 2233, ⓦnamaskarhotel.com; ⓜRK Ashram Marg; map p.89. Popular family-run budget hotel off the Main Bazaar with a variety of attached rooms, some large with a/c (₹800), but not all the cheaper ones have outside windows. Staff are very attentive and helpful, and they also run car tours (see page 109). Currently the best value of the Paharganj cheapies. ₹500

New City Palace 726 Jama Masjid Motor Market ☎011 2327 9548, ✉newcitypalace@hotmail.com; ⓜChawri Bazar; map p.86. Though it doesn't live up to its billing of "a home for palatial comfort", this budget hotel is well situated, directly behind the Jama Masjid; reserve ahead if you want a room with a view. Rooms are usually clean (check before you pay), showers are hot and the best rooms have a/c, though not all the cheaper ones have outside windows; staff can be tetchy, and don't dare order anything from the restaurant. ₹700

Stops Hostel 4/23-B Asaf Ali Rd ☎011 4105 6226, ⓦstopshostels.com; ⓜDelhi Gate; map p.86. Decent hostel with a communal vibe where young travellers hang out together – no real surprise, since the surrounding area is more than a little scruffy. There's a kitchen on site for cooking, a bar for drinking, and activities such as guided walks; as with most hostels in the city, private rooms are overpriced. Breakfast included. Dorm ₹500, doubles ₹2500

★ **Wongdhen House** 15-A New Camp, just east of the main drag ☎011 2381 6689, ✉2wongdhenhouse@gmail. com; ⓜVidhan Sabha; map p.82. Friendly guesthouse with a choice of rooms, some overlooking the Yamuna River, just north of Paharganj in the Tibetan colony of Majnu Ka Tila. The cheapest ones have shared bathrooms, but there's solar-powered hot water and a good restaurant (Tibetan food, or breakfast items), plus a terrace with a great river view. ₹400

Zostel 5 Arakashan Rd ☎011 3958 9005, ⓦzostel. com; ⓜNew Delhi; map p.89. The best hostel option in Paharganj, with a range of decent dorms and affordable private rooms. The common areas are great for socialising, and there are games available if you need a way to break the ice. Breakfast included. Dorm ₹500, double ₹1500

NEW DELHI

Joey's Hostel 1/49 Lalita Park, Laxmi Nagar ☎98186 42824, ⓦjoeyshostel.com; Ⓜ Laxmi Nagar; map p.82. Located out across the river, this homely hostel is a good choice if you want to keep your distance from Delhi, but remain within a metro or cab ride of the centre; it's also within walking distance of Akshardham temple (see page 103). Dorms range from four to fourteen beds, and there's a good atmosphere, particularly when they throw barbecue parties up on the roof. Rates include breakfast. Dorm from ₹500, double ₹1800

SOUTH DELHI

Lets Bunk Poshtel T-40 Hauz Khas Village ☎97799 52158, ⓦletsbunk.live; Ⓜ Green Park; map p.82. An upper-end hostel, located in trendy Hauz Khas – the concept couldn't really lose, but thankfully it has been very well executed, with admirable thought put into everything from the lighting to the furnishings. Dorm ₹1000, double ₹4000

Madpackers Hostel 3rd floor, S-39A Panchseel Park ☎98186 71874; Ⓜ Hauz Khas; map p.82. Clean, friendly hostel, reasonably close to the metro (400m), and on a ring road with fast access to the airport. Dorms range from six- to twelve-bed, including one reserved for women only, and each has a bathroom. There's also a kitchen, communal spaces and a great roof terrace. Breakfast included. Dorm ₹700, double ₹2000

EATING

Most **restaurants** around Delhi close around 11pm, but this and the general vibe varies by neighbourhood. Many places deliver for a minimum price within 1–2 km, and if you feel like getting some long-distance room service, you can also order via apps such as Swiggy, Zomato and Uber Eats. There are also plenty of cool **cafés** knocking around.

RESTAURANTS AND EATERIES

OLD DELHI AND AROUND

Chor Bizarre Hotel Broadway, 4/15 Asaf Ali Rd ☎011 4366 3600, ⓦchorbizarre.com; Ⓜ Delhi Gate; map p.86. A wide selection of excellent Indian cuisine including specialities from around the country, but above all from Punjab and Kashmir – it's considered to have the best Kashmiri food in town, with dishes such as *gushtaba* (slow-cooked mutton in yogurt and cardamom; ₹550). The delightful, eccentric decor features a four-poster bed, sewing table and a servery made from a 1927 vintage Fiat. Daily noon–3.30pm & 7.30–11pm.

★ **Darbar Restaurant** 9003 Multani Dhanda Chowk ☎99996 61413; Ⓜ RK Ashram Marg; map p.89. A moderately-priced Paharganj veg restaurant, serving tasty thalis (₹210–240) and north Indian veg dishes such as *malai kofta* (₹245) as well as great golgappe (₹30). It's surprisingly attractive for the area, with tiled tables, mirrored walls, chandeliers, and smartly-dressed waiters. Daily 8.30am–11pm, meals noon–4pm & 7–11pm.

Everest Kitchen 1171/75 Main Bazaar ☎011 2356 1456; Ⓜ RK Ashram Marg; map p.89. The best of the rooftop restaurants clustered around the Paharganj Main Bazaar junction, and also the most distinctive – rather than serving the usual Western breakfasts, Israeli snacks and lame curries, they focus on Nepali and Tibetan food. Prices are cheap, and you'll probably pay under ₹250 per head. Daily 9am–11pm.

Karim's Gali Kababian, off Urdu Bazaar Rd ☎011 2326 4981, ⓦkarimhoteldelhi.com; Ⓜ Jama Masjid; map p.86. A perennial Delhi favourite, consisting of four eating halls (same kitchen) down a side street opposite the south gate of the Jama Masjid. The meat dishes are the best in the old city, at moderate prices, and including delicious fresh kebabs (₹65 each), hot breads and great Mughlai curries – a half portion of mutton korma will set you back ₹195. Daily 9am–11pm.

Kholsa Café 5024 Main Bazaar; Ⓜ RK Ashram Marg; map p.89. Tiny, long-established backpacker restaurant – a relic of the overland trail. Breakfasts here go for ₹140–160, and they still do hippie-traveller favourites such as banana pancakes (₹70). Daily 9am–11pm.

Moti Mahal 3704 Netaji Subhash Marg ☎011 2327 3011, ⓦmotimahal1947.com; Ⓜ Jama Masjid; map p.86. Renowned for its tandoori chicken, this basic-looking restaurant was one of the first Punjabi restaurants in town, and luminaries such as JFK, Indira Gandhi and Gordon Ramsey have all eaten here. Their speciality is *murg musallam* (chicken with kidney, egg and mincemeat; ₹450), and on occasion they also have live *qawwali* and *ghazal* music. Daily noon–12.30am.

★ **Paranthe Wali Gali** Off Chandni Chowk; Ⓜ Chandni Chowk; map p.86. Not a restaurant, but an alleyway – super-crowded though it may be, don't leave Delhi without eating here. Signed off Chandni Chowk, it's famed for *parathas* filled with anything from *paneer* and *gobi* to *mutter* and mooli, all cooked to order and served with a small selection of curries for ₹60–70. There are several basic, generations-old *paratha*-walas in the alley; *Pandit Gaya Prasad* at #34 has the best selection of fillings, including bitter gourd, cashew and even lemon. Daily 9am–11pm.

Rustom's Parsi Bhonu 2243 Raj Guru Marg ☎80107 75577; Ⓜ Delhi Gate; map p.86. If you're visiting Raj Ghat or the Gandhi Museum, this Parsi restaurant is just

1

down the road, and belies its compound location with exceptionally pretty colonial-style decor. Even without the breakfasts and starters, the choice of mains is quite prodigious, so they're best sampled in thali form – choose from veg, chicken, mutton, prawn and paneer (₹400–695), and maybe add a homemade raspberry soda. Daily 9am–10pm.

★ Shimtur 644 Moala Baoli, off Main Bazaar; ⓂRK Ashram Marg; map p.89. Meaning "shelter" in Korean, this secluded rooftop spot was designed as a haven for the Paharganj area's many Korean visitors. However, it has recently become extremely popular with young locals, on account of its affordable, acceptably authentic Korean food – try the ojingeo deop-bap (squid in a spicy sauce, on rice), or a tuna bibimbap. Most main dishes cost around ₹300, and you can drain a beer (or a soju, which at 19% ABV is like a diluted vodka; ₹600 per bottle) while you eat. Daily 10am–11pm.

★ Sita Ram Diwan Chand 2243 Raj Guru Marg ☎80107 75577; ⓂRK Ashram Marg; map p.89. If you're visited Paharganj without coming to this basic but extraordinarily popular place, you haven't really been to Paharganj at all. Chole bhature (spicy chickpeas and spongy bhatura bread) is the name of the game here, and the only thing on the menu, bar lassis and kulfi – portions are doled out for a meagre ₹35 (or a whopping ₹60 if you want two bhatura, rather than one), and eaten standing up, like a horse, from the tables out back. Cheap, tasty, extremely local, and highly recommended. Daily 8am–5pm.

Sonu South Indian Restaurant 8849/2 Multani Dhanda Chowk, off Desh Bandhu Gupta Rd, Ram Nagar ☎011 6800 6800; ⓂRK Ashram Marg; map p.89. Basic south Indian grub (masala dosa, idlis, vadas and the like) at low prices. A masala dosa goes for ₹70, a thali for ₹110–140. Daily 8am–11pm.

Tadka 4986 Ramdwara Rd (Nehru Bazaar) ☎011 3291 5216; ⓂRK Ashram Marg; map p.89. Safe dining in Paharganj: a clean, bright, modern little restaurant serving breakfast in the morning, then low-priced Indian veg dishes such as palak paneer or shahi (tomato) paneer (both ₹210). Daily 9am–10.30pm.

NEW DELHI

Basil & Thyme 28 Sundar Nagar ☎011 2435 7722, ⓦbasilandthyme.in; ⓂKhan Market; map p.93. Somewhat out of the way in the Sundar Nagar complex, this bistro-style restaurant offers Mediterranean dishes like moussaka, pastas and slow-roast lamb with apple and mint sauce (mostly ₹525–595 veg, ₹625–865 non-veg), and tasty desserts including tiramisu and lemon marscapone tart. Mon–Sat 11am–11pm.

Bukhara Maurya Hotel, Sardar Patel Marg, Chanakya-puri ☎011 2611 2233, ⓦitchotels.in/bukhara; map p.93. Delhi's top restaurant, specializing in succulently tender tandoori kebabs (₹2195 for a Peshwari lamb kebab, ₹2150 for tandoori pomfret), with a menu that's short but very sweet, and a kitchen separated from the eating area by a glass partition, so you can watch the chefs at work. Hillary and Bill Clinton are among the celebs who have flocked here. At lunchtime there's a set meal for ₹2600 veg/₹2800 non-veg. Daily 12.30–2.30pm & 7–11.30pm.

Burger Singh H-45 Connaught Place ☎87671 21212; ⓂRajiv Chowk; map p.94. Worth mentioning for the name alone, this is a relic of the pre-Westernization days. Most of the burgers (₹38–218) are pretty Indian in nature, with patties including mutton, chicken and veg options; save room for their spicy fries too. Daily 10am–1am.

Café Lota 2 Bhairon Marg ☎78389 60787; ⓂPragati Maidan; map p.93. Tucked into the Craft Museum complex (see page 96), this is an attractive little spot, and very popular with locals on account of it serving "fusion" food at reasonable prices – quite a rarity here. Some dishes hit the spot, others don't, but even if mustard fish tikka or jackfruit biryani don't float your boat, there'll be something of appeal on the menu (mains ₹395/530 veg/non-veg), and they've good coffee and saffron lassis. Tue–Sun 11.30am–10pm.

Caffe Tonino H-9 Connaught Place ☎78359 89939; ⓂRajiv Chowk; map p.94. Relaxed upper-level Italian joint popular with expats and local well-heeled sorts, even though it isn't all that pricey. It's particularly appealing for breakfast (₹255–385), with options ranging from meaty Sicilian omelettes to quinoa-flour pancakes; at other times go for their panini, pizzas or pasta dishes. Daily 8.30am–11pm.

Dum Pukht Maurya Hotel, Sardar Patel Marg, Chanakyapuri ☎011 2611 2233; map p.93. Bukhara isn't the only gourmet eatery in the Maurya Hotel: this place, which specializes in dum (slow-cooked casserole) Mughlai cuisine, is also among the city's best restaurants, offering super-elegant surroundings and absolutely punctilious service. The house speciality is raan-e-dum-pukht (₹3000), a dum-cooked leg of lamb so tender it falls off the bone and melts on the tongue. Daily 7–11.45pm.

Fire Park Hotel, 15 Sansad Marg ☎011 2374 3000; ⓂRajiv Chowk; map p.94. Scintillating if expensive modern restaurant whose contemporary Indian cuisine bears a strong hint of European influence. The menu is seasonal, with lighter dishes in summer, fierier ones in winter. Typical dishes include nasli nihari (slow-braised mutton, Delhi-style; ₹895) or Narangi black cod (orange-scented tandoori rock-cod; ₹995). Booking is advisable for the evening sitting, less so for lunchtime, which is cheaper too. Daily noon–3pm & 6.30–11.30pm.

Ghalib Kebab Corner Nizamuddin West, no phone; ⓂJawaharlal Nehru Stadium; map p.93. The Nizamuddin area has few reliable places to eat, but this little kebab shop is just the treat if you're in the area – and it's Nizamuddin through and through. Try some of their delicious mutton tikka rolls (₹150 for two). Daily 9am–11pm.

★ **Kake Da Hotel** 67 Municipal Market, Outer Ring, Connaught Place; ⓜ Rajiv Chowk; map p.94. A perennially popular diner that has become a real Delhi institution for unpretentious but reliably good Punjabi curries, mostly ₹230 a dish. Butter chicken and *palak* mutton are safe options, but if you really want to see your social media account catch fire, try a brain curry, or even gurde kapure, made with testicles; since you ask, the former "meat" has a delicate, melt-in-the-mouth texture and very little flavour, while if you have the balls to try it (so to speak), the latter has a taste and consistency similar to liver. Daily 12.30pm–12.30am.

Khanchacha 50 Khan Market ⓣ 92055 92801, ⓦ khanchacha.in; ⓜ Khan Market; map p.93. Specialising in delectable rolls, this simple-looking eatery is almost the anithesis of trendy, modern-day Khan Market, but the market was actually named after the restaurant – proof of the esteem that locals hold it in. Take your pick from a lengthy list of wrap-like rolls, including chicken tikka, mutton or veg aloo (₹220–260). Daily noon–11pm.

★ **The Masala Trail** 52 Janpath ⓣ 011 4359 3000; ⓜ Rajiv Chowk or Janpath; map p.94. Serving pure-veg street food from all over India to a retro Bollywood soundtrack, this is a fun place, and pleasingly cheesy. Colourful parasols – and an old scooter – dangle from the ceiling, while diners take their choice from a lengthy menu; the regional combos (₹210–345) are best if you're hungry, though their house speciality ginni dosas (₹220) are worth a shout, and the burst-in-your-mouth golgappe are a steal at ₹89. Daily 11am–11pm.

Nizam's Kathi Kebab Plaza Building, H-5 Connaught Place ⓣ 011 2332 1953, ⓦ nizams.com; ⓜ Rajiv Chowk; map p.94. Kebab rolls (mutton egg roll ₹180) are the speciality, but the biryanis (chicken biryani ₹320) are also superb in this little diner, an old-school place whose walls are hung with photos of CP in bygone times. Meals served daily noon–3.30pm & 7–11pm; snacks served in between.

Parikrama Kasturba Gandhi Marg ⓣ 011 2372 1616, ⓦ parikramarestaurant.com; ⓜ Rajiv Chowk or Janpath; map p.94. Indian (mainly tandoori), Chinese and Western cuisine in a revolving 24th-floor restaurant affording superb views over Delhi. Specialities include interesting appetisers such as *murg pasandey parikrama* (chicken breast stuffed with minced chicken and nuts in a cashew-nut sauce; ₹725), and there's a bar another floor up. Booking advisable at mealtimes. Daily 12.30–11pm.

Q'BA E-42/43 Connaught Place ⓣ 011 4517 3333, ⓦ qba. co.in; ⓜ Rajiv Chowk; map p.94. Stylish upmarket bar-restaurant on two floors and two terraces, with views over CP. Its "world cuisine" largely boils down to Indian, Italian and Thai, but the choice is still impressive, with a Goan fish

curry for ₹625, and paneer tikka tacos for ₹445), plus cheap local beer on draught. Daily 12.30–3pm & 7–11.30pm.

Rodeo A-12 Connaught Place ⓣ 011 2371 3781; ⓜ Rajiv Chowk; map p.94. Attractive establishment serving very decent Mexican food including tacos, enchiladas, fajitas and quesadillas; portions can be a little small, but they're lovingly made, and there are even some curious options fusing Indian and Mexican tastes. They also dole out pitchers of beer, *michelada* (beer with lime, salt and chilli; ₹225) and tequila slammers. Daily noon–12.30am.

Sagar Ratna K-15 Connaught Place ⓣ 011 2341 2470 ⓦ sagarratna.in; ⓜ Rajiv Chowk; map p.94. Ubiquitous Delhi chain serving good, inexpensive veg meals; this CP branch will ensure that travellers don't have to go too far out of their way. Daily 8am–11pm.

Saravana Bhavan 46 Janpath ⓣ 011 2331 7755; ⓜ Janpath; map p.94. Excellent low-priced south Indian snacks and meals, including thalis (noon–4pm & 7–10.30pm; ₹230) and quick lunches (10am–3pm; ₹170), as well as the usual dosas, *idlis* and *uttapams*. The mini tiffin (₹170) has a taste of everything. Daily 8am–11pm.

★ **Sodabottleopenerwala** 73B Khan Market ⓣ 98108 77701, ⓦ sodabottleopenerwala.in; ⓜ Khan Market; map p.93. Khan Market contains a branch of this lengthy-named Bombay legend, serving yummy Parsi breakfasts (most ₹245) and mains (from ₹340) in a stylish, tongue-in-cheek environment. Many of the staff are deaf or hard of hearing, so there's a flip-book on the table if you want to learn some sign language, and they've also a very healthy selection of alcoholic drinks. Daily noon–midnight.

Spice Route Hotel Imperial, Janpath ⓣ 011 2334 1234, ⓦ theimperialindia.com; ⓜ Janpath; map p.93. This beautifully decorated restaurant, rarefied and expensive, specializes in spicy Southeast Asian and Keralan cuisine. A sumptuous Thai tiger prawn curry will set you back ₹2300, a *nadan kozhi* (Keralan chicken curry with star anise) ₹1375, or there's a tasting menu for ₹7000. If you want to eat really well in the CP vicinity, this is one of your best bets. Daily 12.30–2.45pm & 7–11.45pm.

Veda H-27 Connaught Place ⓣ 011 4151 3535, ⓦ veda restaurants.com; ⓜ Rajiv Chowk; map p.94. Swanky restaurant that is heavy on the ambience (all smoochy red and black decor with low lights), though the food isn't at all bad either, with main dishes such as *makhani* chicken (₹625) and fish mooli (₹700). Daily noon–11.30pm.

SOUTH DELHI

★ **Burma Burma** Select CityWalk Mall, Saket ⓣ 011 4914 5807; ⓜ Malviya Nagar, ⓦ burmaburma.in; map p.82. By far the best choice in Saket, and very handy if you're visiting the nearby art museum, this Burmese restaurant is extremely attractive for a mall eatery. The menu simply bursts with tempting options; gorgeously-

1

presented mains such as Burmese curries or mohinga noodles cost around ₹460; there are plenty of teas to try too. Mon–Thurs noon–3.30pm & 6.45–11pm, Fri–Sun noon–11pm.

★ **Naivedyam** 1 Hauz Khas Village ☎011 4175 4984; ⓜGreen Park; map p.82. This beautiful, charmingly broody place is the most esteemed restaurant in the Hauz Khas area, creating such demand that there are now six other branches across Greater Delhi. They've a wide variety of South Indian food on offer at surprisingly low prices – try your hand at a dosa (from ₹155), uthappam five ways, or a very Insta-friendly thali (from ₹275). Daily 10am–10.30pm.

Punjabi by Nature T-305, 3rd floor, Ambience Mall, Nelson Mandela Marg, Vasant Vihar ☎011 4087 0196, ⓦpunjabibynature.in; map p.82. It's quite a haul from the centre (₹125 by prepaid auto from CP), but this restaurant has made a big name for itself among Delhi foodies with its fabulous Punjabi and north Indian cuisine. The Amritsari fish tikka (₹745) is succulent, but for something really special, try the *raan-e-Punjab* (leg of lamb; ₹1195). Daily noon–1am.

Swagath 14 Defence Colony Market ☎011 2433 0030; ⓜLajpat Nagar; map p.82. There are Indian and Chinese meat dishes on the menu of this stylish, intimate space, but ignore those and go for the Mangalore-style seafood – the Swagath special (chilli and tamarind), *gassi* (coconut sauce) and *malabari* (green masala) dishes are all great (all ₹775 with squid or ₹945 with prawns). Daily 11.30am–11.30pm.

The Turkey Project C-27 Defence Colony ☎011 4034 9066; ⓜMoolchand; map p.82. Relaxed venue specialising in Western dishes, including some meat choices involving the humble turkey. It pops up in some of the interestingly-named burgers – try the Lamb of God, which contains a lamb patty and turkey bacon (₹410); or the Supreme Leader, which is much the same, with a fried egg thrown in (₹450). Pizzas and pasta dishes round out the picture, and it's a decent place for coffee or a cold drink. Daily noon–11pm.

CAFÉS, SWEETSHOPS AND TEAROOMS

OLD DELHI

Bikaner Sweets Corner 9002 Multani Dhanda Chowk, just off Desh Bandhu Gupta Rd ☎011 2353 1322; ⓜRK Ashram Marg; map p.89. A wonderful sweets emporium, with all sorts of multi-coloured Bengali and Rajasthani confections (plain *barfi*, at ₹400/kg, is the least of them), plus tasty *namkeens* and savouries, including assorted veg samosas for ₹12–18. Daily 7.30am–10pm.

Chaina Ram 6499 Fatehpuri Chowk, next to Fatehpuri Mosque ☎011 2395 0747, ⓦchainaram.com; ⓜChandni Chowk; map p.86. Established in Karachi in

1901, and forced to relocate in 1947, this little shop is well known for its Sindhi-style sweets; the delicately aromatic Karachi *halwa* with almonds and pistachios (figure on ₹25 per piece) is the best in town. Daily 7am–10pm.

Haldiram's 1454 Chandni Chowk ☎011 4768 5114, ⓦhaldiramsonline.com; ⓜChandni Chowk; map p.86. Good branch of the low-priced snack chain, serving sweets and samosas downstairs, and drinks and snacks upstairs. If you've never tried one, the *raj kachori* (₹84), a crunchy pastry shell enclosing a tangy chickpea curry with yogurt, is a must. Daily 8.30am–10.30pm.

Kitchen Café Hotel Shelton, 5043 Main Bazaar; ⓜRK Ashram Marg; map p.89. This rooftop spot is more of a restaurant than a café – despite the name – but is best utilised as a café. The views are the best in Paharganj, the espresso here is the best in the area (₹70), and they do good banana pancakes (₹130). There's also a pool table, and unlike almost every other rooftop place in the area, a functional lift. Daily 24hr.

NEW DELHI

Bengali Sweet House Bengali Market ☎011 2332 2222; ⓜMandi House; map p.93. The Bengali Market isn't really a market, more a semi-circle of sweetie shops. This is the best, and almost like an Italian café in appearance thanks to its decor; their Bengali treats go for ₹25–30 each, or try the weird masala cola for ₹50. Daily 8am–11pm.

★ **Big Chill Cakery** 1B Khan Market ☎011 4175 7577; ⓜKhan Market; map p.93. Originally a single restaurant, Big Chill is quite apparently trying to colonize the whole of Khan Market. Their cakery wing is the most appealing of several options; styled like an English tearoom (though one, disappointingly, using paper plates and cups), they serve truly sinful-looking cupcakes, cheesecakes, brownies and pies (most ₹150–300). The cramped seating space will at least remind you to hold back a little on the calorie intake. Daily 8am–midnight.

Haldiram's L-6 Connaught Place ☎011 4768 5300, ⓦhaldiramsonline.com; ⓜRajiv Chowk; map p.94. Well-positioned branch of the sweet and snack house chain. Daily 10am–10pm.

Indian Coffee House 2nd floor, Mohan Singh Place Shopping Complex, Baba Kharak Singh Marg ☎011 2334 2994; ⓜRajiv Chowk; map p.94. When the Indian Coffee Board closed its coffee houses, a group of ex-workers formed a co-op to take them over; this branch, opened in 1957, was the first. A real relic of Nehruvian India, though sadly nowhere near as cool as it looks from outside, it serves coffee (from ₹36), snacks and basic meals to an eclectic cross-section of downtown New Delhi's daytime population, including a fair few hipsters. Daily 9am–9pm.

★ **Naturals** L-12 Connaught Place ☎011 6537 0007; ⓜRajiv Chowk; map p.94. If you're in need of a sugar fix on your way around CP, head for this ice-cream

WHERE TO EAT IN DELHI

Although your choice of which part of Delhi to eat in is likely to be dictated by where you're staying and what sights you choose to see, cheap transport prices enable access to the whole city's culinary scene.

Old Delhi's crowded streets contain numerous simple food-halls serving surprisingly good local dishes for next to nothing. Upmarket eating is thin on the ground, but some of the mid-range places serve food every bit as good as the posh restaurants elsewhere, and the sweets and snacks here are the best in town. There are now some good options in **Paharganj** too, though avoid the *dhabas* opposite New Delhi station.

Those seeking to dine in **New Delhi** usually make a bee-line for **Connaught Place** ("CP"), which has a real mix of upmarket restaurants, cheap and cheerful local options, and Western-style fast-food places. There's also a good emerging scene in **Khan Market**.

The enclaves and villages spread across the vast area of **South Delhi** offer countless eating options, and most of its upmarket shopping zones (Hauz Khas, Defence Colony, Ansal Plaza and the like) contain several good restaurants.

DELHI'S TOP TEN

Best for pan-Indian street food The Masala Trail (see page 115).
Best for testicle and brain curry Kake Da Hotel (see page 115).
Best for splashing the cash Bukhara (see page 114).
Best thalis Naivedyam (see page 116).
Best interior Spice Route (see page 115).
Best for Delhi street food Sita Ram Diwan Chand (see page 114).
Best food experience Paranthe Wali Gali (see page 113).
Best ice creams Naturals (see page 116).
Best for mutton rolls Khanchacha (see page 115).
Best for fancy coffee United Coffee House (see page 117).

DELHI CHAIN RESTAURANTS AND CAFÉS

Bikanervala ⓦ bikanervala.com. This family-friendly chain, now spread all over its home city of Delhi, serves snacks, ice creams, sweets and *namkeen*, all at reasonable prices.

Café Coffee Day ⓦ cafécoffeeday.com. India's answer to Starbucks, with branches all over Delhi, and even in Prague, Vienna and Kuala Lumpur. The coffee's decent, with cups going for ₹100–200.

Haldiram's ⓦ haldiramsonline.com. Though actually from Maharashtra, this chain has spread all over Delhi on account of its thick sweet lassis (₹90), *pao bhajis* (₹140), Indian sweeties (low-sugar and sugar-free options

usually available) and light Indian meals. There's a good branch in CP.

Keventer's ⓦ keventers.com. This milkshake chain is no modern creation, having been kicking about in one form or another since the 1920s; branches all over town sell shakes (from ₹80), made with ice cream and doled out in fetching little glass bottles.

Sagar Ratna ⓦ sagarratna.in. Delicious, inexpensive South Indian vegetarian food, with *vadas*, *idlis*, *ravas* and dosas (₹140–240), plus great Northern or Southern thalis (both ₹260). There's a conveniently located branch on CP.

parlour; delectable options include sitaphal (sugar apple), watermelon and lychee (all ₹70 per scoop), and sinfully divine mango ice-cream milkshakes (₹150). Daily 11am–midnight.

Triveni Garden Café 205 Tansen Marg ⓣ 99715 66904; ⓜ Mandi House; map p.93. Very popular with young, artsy sorts, this café's outdoor section looks over gardens and galleries. There's French press coffee (₹130) and sweet lassis (₹55), but if you've never had one, go for a jaljeera (₹80), which is something like a curry-flavoured cooler. Good desserts too, including beetroot helwa. Mon–Sat 10am–9pm, Sun noon–9pm.

United Coffee House E-15 Connaught Place ⓣ 011 2341 6075, ⓦ unitedcoffeehouse.in; ⓜ Rajiv Chowk; map p.94. By far the fanciest place for coffee in CP, with walls painted baby blue, salmon and gold; starched-collar waiters; and a whacking great chandelier dangling overhead. They've a global range of beans, including some from South Indian estates (₹169–269), and a clientele that's mainly moneyed locals. Daily 9.30am–11pm.

SOUTH DELHI

Blossom Kochhar 1 Hauz Khas Village ⓣ 011 4081 7655; ⓜ Green Park; map p.82. Set above a cosmetics shop (see page 121), and boasting an air of relaxed refinement, this is a delightful place for tea (from ₹60) and cake (from ₹180), or something more modern like a Nutella latte. Daily 11am–7pm.

Kunzum Travel Café T-49 Hauz Khas Village ☎ 99100 44476; Ⓜ Green Park; map p.82. Basic Hauz Khas café run by an Indian travel writer; full of photographs and books, and host to regular events, it's a good place to hobnob, though the drinks themselves (payment by donation) aren't always the best. Tue–Sun 11am– 7.30pm.

DRINKING AND NIGHTLIFE

With an ever-increasing number of pubs and clubs, Delhi's nightlife scene is in full swing. Loungey and industrial-chic **bars** with laidback music have become very popular, and quite a few have long happy hours; licensing laws mean that decent microbreweries are still thin on the ground, except across state lines in satellite cities such as **Gurgaon**, which is a short metro ride from Delhi. Come the weekend, the city's **clubs** really take off, but note that some places don't allow "stag entry" (men unaccompanied by women). Importantly, the **minimum drinking age** in Delhi is 25; this may be reduced to a less preposterous 21 at some point in the not too distant future. Lastly, there are plenty of seedy, almost exclusively male bars in Delhi; while female drinkers can attract unwanted attention anywhere, the establishments listed here can at least be described as relatively female-friendly.

BARS

OLD DELHI

★ **Mojo Terrace Café** 5096 Main Bazaar, Paharganj ☎ 99532 23744; Ⓜ RK Ashram Marg; map p.89. Few rooftop places in Paharganj serve alcohol, and very few bars in Paharganj could be described as "chilled". This place, then, is a real winner, with cool music pulsing from the speakers, and a clientele of local hipster sorts; small bottles of Kingfisher Strong go for just ₹150, and spirits are available too. You'll see the sign from the Main Bazaar Road, and then have to duck into a side-alley and spider up a dim staircase. Daily noon–1am.

My Bar 5136 Main Bazaar, Paharganj ☎ 98104 10411; Ⓜ RK Ashram Marg; map p.89. A large, lively and popular bar with loud dance music – and often people dancing, especially when the Bhangra songs come on. It's quite a fun hangout, and also serves food, although it's the cheap beer (from ₹180 for a 650ml bottle, or just ₹50 for a peg of local rum) that most people come for. Daily 11am–12.30am.

NEW DELHI

Bunta Bar 76 Janpath Rd ☎ 98107 47934; Ⓜ Rajiv Chowk or Janpath; map p.94. Industrial-chic space with a fun quirk – many of their cocktails (₹325) are served in distinctive soda bottles, with options such as thyme, cardamom and rose adding Indian flavours to the rum,

vodka and gin bases. Ladies' night on Thursdays, live bands on Fridays, Bollywood nights on Saturdays, and DJs from 8.30pm on other nights. Also a decent place for a hookah session (₹1500). Daily noon–12.30am.

Excuse Me Boss F-14 Connaught Place ☎ 87458 81999; Ⓜ Rajiv Chowk; map p.94. There are a clutch of bars on F-Block attempting to undercut each other's prices – good news for budget drinkers. At the time of writing this wasn't quite the cheapest of the cheap, but close enough, and certainly the best looking of the lot; draught beer goes from ₹80 (or get a whole tower for ₹500), and cocktails from ₹185. Daily 11.30am–12.30am.

★ **Junkyard Café** N-91 Connaught Place ☎ 95999 47643; Ⓜ Rajiv Chowk; map p.94. A large, fun venue in which cheap drinks are doled out by waiters wearing what look like orange Super Mario overalls, amid a panoply of tyres, crates and oil drums. A small Kingfisher will set you back ₹125, or go for their ₹435 Edison-bulb cocktails, including elderflower, rum, rosemary and lime (wasn't that a Simon & Garfunkel song?), served with dry ice billowing out the bottom. Live music most nights. Daily noon–1am.

Ministry of Beer M-44 Connaught Place ☎ 88000 12060; Ⓜ Rajiv Chowk; map p.94. This place looks promising, with its beer-making paraphernalia by the entrance, and line of taps on the counter. In reality, they usually only have bottles available (around ₹400 for domestic or cheaper international ones), but it's still a highly popular place, with an open-air courtyard out back, and an insanely noisy hookah lounge up top. Daily noon–1am.

United Coffee House E-15 Connaught Place ☎ 011 2341 6075, Ⓦ unitedcoffeehouse.in; Ⓜ Rajiv Chowk; map p.94. Though primarily a swanky café (see page 117), this is also an atmospheric place for an evening drink, with a range of well-made cocktails and highballs (₹500–600), plus a decent roster of wines and spirits. Daily 9.30am–11pm.

Unplugged L-23/7 Connaught Place ☎ 011 3310 7701; Ⓜ Rajiv Chowk; map p.94. With its gently-lit courtyard, this is one of the more visually pleasing places to drink in CP, and there's live music four nights a week (from 9.30pm onwards, Wed, Fri, Sat & Sun). Negative points include a rather boring drinks menu, from which your first few choices will usually be unavailable, and a tendency to turn away single males. Daily 11am–1am.

SOUTH DELHI

★ **Hauz Khas Social** 12 Hauz Khas Village ☎78386 52814, ⓦsocialoffline.in; ⓜGreen Park; map p.82. The undisputed uber-cool hub of this busy drinking area. There are several spaces to plonk yourself around this large, industrial-chic building, but for a quieter drink and a view of the lake, head on up to the terrace; much of the drinks list will be familiar, but try your hand at something more left-field, like the loaded goti sodas (₹340), the banarsi patiala (sugarcane juice and a triple shot of rum; ₹510), or the super-tall "Longest Island Iced Tea". Daily 11am–midnight.

Monkey Bar C-6 Vasant Kunj ☎011 4109 5155; ⓜVasant Vihar; map p.82. Claims to be a "gastrobar", but don't worry: set in a striking glass pyramid, this South Delhi venue is pretty cool, though to make the most of the unusual architecture it's actually best to get there before dark. DJs spin jolly retro sounds after sunset, and you can shoot a game of pool. Also does decent food. Daily noon–midnight.

CLUBS

NEW DELHI

Kitty Su Lalit Hotel, Fire Brigade Lane ☎011 444 7666, ⓦkittysu.com; ⓜBarakhamba Rd; map p.93. The only club in India to have made it onto *DJ Mag's* global Top 100, an opulent place split into four separate areas, each with their own vibe. Prices vary according to the night, but there's typically a ₹1000–2000 entry fee (ladies often free), and sometimes no "stag entry" allowed. Wed–Sun 10pm–1.30am, sometimes later.

Privee Eros Hotel, Ashoka Rd ☎82872 02020; ⓜJanpath; map p.93. Decent club that stands out for one big reason – it is open past 1am! This is where to go if you feel like dancing into the wee hours with all the "bad" boys and girls, plus the light and sound systems are pretty state-of-the-art. Usually ₹2000 entry fee per couple, sometimes no "stag entry" allowed. Wed–Sun 10pm–1.30am, sometimes later.

ENTERTAINMENT

DANCE AND DRAMA

Kamani Auditorium 1 Copernicus Marg ☎011 4350 3351–2, ⓦkamaniauditorium.org; ⓜMandi House. World-class auditorium hosting music, dance and theatrical performances (although the theatre is usually in Hindi). Their programme for the month is posted on their website.

Sangeet Natak Akademi Rabindra Bhavan, 35 Firoz Shah Rd ☎011 2338 7246, ⓦsangeetnatak.gov.in; ⓜMandi House. Delhi's premier performing arts institution, staging performances of classical dance and music from across India.

Triveni Kala Sangam 205 Tansen Marg ☎011 2371 9470; ⓜMandi House. A cultural complex incorporating two theatres and four art galleries, which puts on assorted dance shows and art exhibitions as well as running art, dance and music classes. There's also the excellent Triveni Terrace Café on site.

CINEMAS

Bollywood movies without subtitles are shown at some cinemas, and some also show the latest Hollywood movies in English (for a list of what films are currently on where and in which language, see ⓦfilmibeat.com). Tickets cost ₹80–400.

Odeon D-Block, Connaught Place ☎011 3954 1564; ⓜRajiv Chowk. The best cinema in CP, with a good selection of major Bollywood and Hollywood flicks, and a great bar upstairs for afterwards.

Shiela DB Gupta Rd ☎011 4350 4751; ⓜNew Delhi. There's usually only one film on at a time here (six showings through the day, and always Bollywood), but the exterior is highly attractive, and it's probably the best place in Delhi for a "local" movie-going experience.

SHOPPING

Although the traditional places to **shop** in Delhi are around **Connaught Place** (particularly the underground Palika Bazaar) and **Chandni Chowk**, a number of suburbs have emerged as fashionable shopping districts. To check prices and quality for crafts, you can't do better than the **state emporiums** on Baba Kharak Singh Marg, but beware of touts outside trying to sweet-talk you into visiting shops which pay them commission. Unlike the markets of Old Delhi, most shops in New Delhi take credit cards; in all bazaars and street markets, the rule is to **haggle**.

ART, ANTIQUES, CRAFTS AND JEWELLERY

For crafts and jewellery, the government emporiums on Baba Kharak Singh Marg should be your first stop, especially if you want to check prices. Paharganj and Janpath's Tibetan Market are good for trinkets such as cheap jewellery, decorated boxes and sandalwood carvings. For upmarket art, antiques (remember that to export anything more than a hundred years old you will need a permit) and jewellery, there's Sunder Nagar Market (map p.93).

Central Cottage Industries Emporium Jawahar Vyapar Bhawan, Janpath, opposite Imperial Hotel ☎011 2332 0439, ⓦcottageemporium.in; ⓜJanpath; map p.93. Popular and convenient government-run complex, with numerous floors of handicrafts, carpets, leather and reproduction miniatures at fixed (if fractionally high) rates. Jewellery ranges from tribal silver anklets to costume pieces and precious stones. Daily 10am–7pm.

1

Crafts Museum Shop Bhairon Marg ☎011 2337 1269; ⓜPragati Maidan; map p.93. The shop adjoining the Crafts Museum (see page 96) has an excellent selection of high-quality handicrafts, from terracotta horse figurines to dhurries, rugs and grass mats, combs made of ebony or *neem* wood, and wooden boxes inlaid with brass or copper. Not the cheapest prices you'll ever find (they're marked and fixed), but not inflated either, and certainly reliable in quality. Daily 9.30am–5.30pm.

Good Earth 9 Khan Market ☎011 2464 7175, ⓦgoodearth.in; ⓜKhan Market; map p.82. Fancy homeware at fancy prices, with tea and coffee mugs, incense holders and diffusers, lamps and the like, and almost all original designs – it's no exaggeration to state that some Delhi folk have decorated their entire home using this shop. Daily 11am–8pm.

Indian Art Collection 1 Hauz Khas Village ☎011 2685 1624; ⓜGreen Park; map p.82. Old Bollywood film posters are the speciality here, mostly in the ₹1000–5000 range. You can buy them framed, but it's generally easier to have them rolled up and slipped into a protective tube. They also sell a variety of superior bric-a-brac including old metal trays, maps and advertising placards – well worth a browse. Daily 11am–7pm.

Neemrana Shop A-26 Khan Market ☎011 4358 7183, ⓦneemranahotels.com; ⓜKhan Market; map p.93. This shop has a chic clientele and offers a range of clothes and a small collection of antiques and *objets d'art*. Mon–Sat 10am–8pm, Sun 11am–7pm.

State Emporiums Baba Kharak Singh Marg; ⓜRajiv Chowk; map p.94. The two wings of this building sell goodies from all over India, all lined up in a row – dodge the pests outside and take your pick from Kashmiri rugs, Odishan stone carvings, Rajasthani paintings and the like, all at fixed prices (and, since they're government-run establishments, there's more in the way of apathy than hard sell). Mostly Mon–Sat 11am–6pm.

Tribes India 9 Mahadev Rd ☎011 2334 1282, ⓦtribesindia.com; ⓜPatel Chowk; map p.94. Crafts by indigenous "tribal" peoples from across India, often very different from other traditional Indian products. It's a fair-trade outlet, guaranteeing a decent rate to the artisans who make the items on sale. Daily 10am–8pm.

BOOKS

Delhi can be a very good place to stock up on books, both new and used. On Sundays there's also Daryaganj Market by Delhi Gate in Old Delhi – an excellent place to search for book bargains.

Bahrisons 20 Khan Market ☎011 2469 4610; ⓜKhan Market; map p.93. The best bookstore in the Khan Market area, with its walls and shelves groaning under the weight of innumerable books, many pertaining to Delhi. Daily 10.30am–7pm.

Jacksons Books 5106 Main Bazaar, Paharganj ☎98990 89274; ⓜRK Ashram Marg; map p.89. The best address in Paharganj for used books – expect to find the sort of novels that backpackers like to read, plus travel guidebooks to India and neighbouring countries. Daily 10am–10pm.

Oxford Bookstore N-81 Connaught Place ☎011 4919 2092; ⓜRajiv Chowk; map p.94. Large, attractive all-round bookshop, selling a wide selection of fiction and non-fiction from India and elsewhere. There's even a decent café on site. Daily 10am–9.30pm.

CLOTHING AND FABRICS

Delhi's fabric and clothes shops sell anything from high-quality silks, homespun cottons, saris, Kashmiri shawls and traditional *kurta* pyjamas to multicoloured tie-dyed T-shirts and other hippie gear. For T-shirts and tie-dyed clothing, try Paharganj or the Tibetan Market off Janpath; stalls behind the latter sell lavishly embroidered and mirrored spreads from Rajasthan and Gujarat.

Anokhi 32 Khan Market ☎011 2460 3423, ⓦanokhi.com; ⓜKhan Market; map p.93. Hailing from Jaipur, this shop sells soft cotton and raw silk clothes and soft furnishings, and is particularly renowned for hand-block printed cottons combining traditional and contemporary designs. There are branches all over the city, but the best located is the one at Khan Market. Daily 10am–8pm.

Coral Haze D-24/385, 100 Ft Road, Chhattarpur Hills ☎98990 70747, ⓦcoralhaze.com; ⓜChhattarpur; map p.82. Embodying the air of its newly hipster-fied neighbourhood, this beautiful little shop sells fetching shoes with Indian motifs and patterns, all own-brand, at fair prices. Daily 11am–7.30pm.

DLF Emporio 4 Nelson Mandela Marg, Vasant Kunj ☎011 4611 6666, ⓦdlfemporio.com; ⓜVasant Vihar; map p.82. A designer-label mall whose ground floors feature all the international big-hitters; more interesting, however, is the third level, where the brightest lights in Delhi's burgeoning fashion scene – including AMPM, Ranna Gill and Namrata Joshipura – are all lined up for your perusal. Daily 11am–9pm.

Fabindia A-1 Connaught Place ☎011 4304 8295, ⓦfabindia.com; ⓜRajiv Chowk; map p.94. The best-located Delhi branch of this now international chain is located in CP, selling everything from furnishings and interiors to chic cotton clothing for men, women and children and wearable block-printed cottons, all sourced from villages across India. They also sell organic spices, jams and pickles. There's another handy branch in Khan Market (map p.93). Daily 10am–8.30pm.

Khadi India 24 Regal Building, Connaught Place ☎011 2336 0902, ⓦkvic.org.in; ⓜRajiv Chowk; map p.94. This government-run store is a great place to pick up hardy, lightweight travelling clothes. Reasonably priced, ready-made traditional Indian garments include *salwar kameez*, woollen waistcoats, pyjamas, shawls and caps, plus rugs, cloth by the metre, tea, incense, cards and tablecloths. Daily 10am–7.30pm.

People Tree 8 Regal Building, Sansad Marg, Connaught Place ☎ 011 2374 4877; Ⓜ Rajiv Chowk; map p.94. An interesting selection of alternative designs, with an emphasis on T-shirts, ethnic chic and jewellery. Mon–Sat 10.30am–7pm.

Rainbow 1 Janpath Market, Janpath ☎ 011 2332 8582; Ⓜ Rajiv Chowk; map p.94. A wide range of T-shirts with witty Indian designs and slogans – not designed for tourists particularly, but great as souvenirs. Daily 10.30am–8pm.

Shaw Brothers D-47 Ground Floor, Defence Colony ☎ 011 4123 2000, Ⓦ shawbrothersonline.com; Ⓜ Rajiv Chowk; map p.82. Upmarket purveyors of shawls, rugs, pashminas and silks. They also have a smaller but more conveniently located branch at Palika Bazaar, Connaught Place (see map, p.94). Daily 10am–9pm.

Vedi Tailors M-60 Connaught Place ☎ 011 2341 6901; Ⓜ Rajiv Chowk; map p.94. Originally established in Rangoon in 1926, this gents' tailor can run you up a made-to-measure suit for anything from ₹8000 to ₹30,000, depending on fabric and cut. They usually take a week, but for a little extra they can do it in 24hr. Mon–Sat 11am–8pm.

HERBAL PRODUCTS

Blossom Kochhar 1 Hauz Khas Village ☎ 011 4081 7655; Ⓜ Green Park; map p.82. Attractive shop selling essential oils (including gift packs), natural perfumes, joss sticks, scented candles and aroma diffusers. There's also a lovely tearoom on the upper level. Daily 10.30am–8pm.

SPORTS AND OUTDOOR ACTIVITIES

The recreational activity most likely to appeal to visitors in the pre-monsoon months has to be a dip in one of Delhi's **swimming pools**. Unfortunately most public pools require you to take out membership. Luxury hotels usually restrict their pools to residents, but may allow outsiders to join their health clubs.

SPECTATOR SPORTS

Delhi Races Kamal Ataturk Rd ☎ 011 2379 2869; Ⓜ Race Course. Regular horse racing Tues from 1.30pm, sometimes Thurs too. Entry usually ₹70, and mobile phones not always allowed inside (you can deposit them at the entrance).

Indian Premier League Ⓦ iplt20.com. The IPL is the world's most lucrative cricket competition, usually running through April & May. The Delhi Daredevils (Ⓦ delhidaredevils.com) have been a fixture since the birth of the league in 2008; catch them at the Feroz Shah Kotla ground (see map, p.82).

MALLS

Select Citywalk Saket District Centre, New Delhi ☎ 011 4211 4200; Ⓜ Malviya Nagar; map p.82. If you're in the mood for some Western-style retail therapy, or simply some new clothing from a label you're familiar with, this large, modern mall is a good choice. There's a great art gallery right next door, and good restaurants inside, including the wonderful Burma Burma (see page 115). Daily 10am–11pm.

MUSIC AND MUSICAL INSTRUMENTS

Lahore Music House 3705 Netaji Subhash Marg, Old Delhi ☎ 011 2327 1305; Ⓜ Jama Masjid; map p.86. Long-established North Indian musical instrument makers with a reputation for quality. Mon–Sat 11am–7pm.

Rikhi Ram G-8, Connaught Place ☎ 011 2332 7685, Ⓦ rikhiram.com; Ⓜ Rajiv Chowk; map p.94. Once sitar-makers to the likes of the late Ravi Shankar, and still maintaining an exclusive air, with prices to match. Check out the display of their own unique instrumental inventions. Mon–Sat noon–8pm.

SPICES

Kanshi Ram Chuni Lal 6628 Khari Baoli Rd ☎ 011 2395 0082, Ⓦ kcdryfruit.com; Ⓜ Chandni Chowk; map p.86. A good choice among the spice shops lining Khari Baoli's main drag, excellent for super-fresh big green cardamoms, fat black peppercorns and sackfuls of other spices, all sold by weight. Also good for a kilo or two of extra-strong Assam tea at good rates. Daily 10am–7pm.

OUTDOOR ACTIVITIES

Delhi Golf Club Dr Zakir Hussain Rd ☎ 011 2430 7100, Ⓦ delhigolfclub.org; Ⓜ Khan Market. Vaunted, historic, lovingly-designed course that was formerly the haunt of viceroys and princes (including the Agha Khan). Locals wait years – sometimes over a decade – for membership, but with prior reservation, foreigners can play a round for around ₹7000 (or ₹9250 on weekends).

Gulmohar Park Club Block C, Gulmohar Park ☎ 011 2686 8139, Ⓦ gulmoharcentre.com; Ⓜ Green Park. This is one of the only pools in the city allowing visitors to swim without becoming a member (₹275/hr); in addition, it's large and has a decent deep end. Open Apr–Dec.

Indian Mountaineering Foundation 6 Benito Juárez Marg (on the Delhi University campus) ☎ 011 2411 1211, Ⓦ indmount.org; Ⓜ Dhaula Kuan. Official organization governing mountaineering and permits throughout India. Some equipment can be rented here, there's an outdoor climbing wall, and you can get information on local crags and climbing groups.

COURSES AND ACTIVITIES

AYURVEDA AND YOGA

Kerala Ayurveda E-2 Green Park Extension ☎011 4175 4888, ⊕ayurvedancr.com; ⓜGreen Park. A "wellness centre" run by a Keralan firm marketing cosmetics and supplements based on Ayurvedic prescriptions. You can choose from a variety of treatments, including oil massages, for specific ailments or general wellbeing.

Sivananda Yoga A-41 Kailash Colony ☎011 3206 9070, ⊕sivananda.org.in; ⓜKailash Colony. Classes and courses in yoga at all levels. A single class costs ₹400, but courses and packages work out at rather less per class.

COOKING CLASSES

Gourmet Desire C-511 Sheik Sarai Phase 1 ☎011 4186 4006, ⊕gourmetdesire.com; ⓜHauz Khas. Cookery classes from ₹3450, including a meal (3–4hr). With advance warning they may be able to run market tours to buy the ingredients beforehand.

DANCE CLASSES

Delhi Dance Academy E-238 Amar Colony ☎011 4101 2909, ⊕delhidanceacademy.in; ⓜLady Shri Ram College. Large academy with all sorts of classes, but since you're travelling in India their Bollywood dance lessons may be most pertinent – beginners welcome.

LANGUAGE COURSES

HindiGuru H-5/1-2, Lower ground floor, Malviya Nagar ☎011 2668 1314, ⊕hindiguru.org; ⓜMalviya Nagar. Relaxed and easy-going language school offering courses in Hindi and other Indian languages at ₹500/hr.

Zabaan Language Institute A-15 Kailash Colony ☎96501 22722, ⊕zabaan.com; ⓜKailash Colony. This well-run, serious language school offers courses in Hindi, Urdu, Sanskrit and more, including four-week intensive Hindi courses with 60hr of teaching for ₹24,000 including tax.

DIRECTORY

Banks and exchange Almost every block on Connaught Place has an ATM, as do metro stations, and there are several along Chandni Chowk and Asaf Ali Rd in Old Delhi. You can also change money at numerous exchange offices in Connaught Place and Paharganj, and all major hotels have exchange facilities.

Embassies, consulates and high commissions Australia, 1/50-G Shanti Path, Chanakyapuri ☎011 4139 9900; Bangladesh, EP-39, Dr S. Radha Krishan Marg, Chanakyapuri ☎011 2412 1392; Canada, 7/8 Shanti Path, Chanakyapuri ☎011 4178 2000; China, 50-D Shanti Path, Chanakyapuri ☎011 2611 2345 (visa application office in Saket; see ⊕visaforchina.org); Ireland, C-17 Malcha Marg, Chanakyapuri ☎011 4940 3200; Malaysia, 50-M Satya Marg, Chanakyapuri ☎011 2415 9300; Maldives, C-31 Anand Niketan ☎011 4143 5701; Myanmar (Burma), 3/50-F Nyaya Marg, Chanakyapuri ☎011 2467 8822; Nepal, Barakhamba Rd ☎011 2347 6200; New Zealand, Sir Edmund Hillary Marg, Chanakyapuri ☎011 4688 3170; Pakistan, 2/50-G Shanti Path, Chanakyapuri ☎011 2611 0601; Singapore, E-6 Chandragupta Marg, Chanakyapuri ☎011 4600 0800; South Africa, B-18 Vasant Marg, Vasant Vihar ☎011 2614 9411; Sri Lanka, 27 Kautilya Marg, Chanakyapuri ☎011 2301 0201; Thailand, D-1/3 Vasant Vihar ☎011 4977 4100; UK, Shanti Path, Chanakyapuri ☎011 2419 2100; US, Shanti Path, Chanakyapuri ☎011 2419 8000.

Hospitals All India Institute of Medical Sciences (AIIMS), Ansari Nagar, Aurobindo Marg (☎011 2658 8500, ⊕aiims.edu), has a 24hr emergency service, as does Dr Ram Manohar Lohia Hospital, Baba Kharak Singh Marg (☎011 2334 8200, ⊕rmlh.nic.in). Private clinics include Indraprastha Apollo Hospital, Sarita Vihar, Delhi–Mathura Rd (☎011 2987 1090, ⊕apollohospdelhi.com). The US embassy maintains a list of hospitals and doctors on its website (⊕in.usembassy.gov).

Left luggage ₹15–20/day at the railway station cloakrooms, but you'll need ID and possibly a rail ticket. New Delhi station on the Airport Express Line also has a cloakroom, and most hotels offer left-luggage services to departing guests.

Money transfers Western Union and MoneyGram transfers can be picked up at post offices including the Old and New Delhi GPOs, and also the branch post office in Connaught Place (but Mon–Fri 10am–4pm only). Be sure to specify the correct post office.

Pharmacies Apollo, G-8 Connaught Place (☎011 2371 1838) and at New Delhi station (Ginger Hotel; ☎011 2323 2878) is open 24hr.

Police ☎100 (national number). Delhi has a dedicated squad of tourist police based at the airport, main stations and major tourist sights and hotel areas, whose aim is specifically to help tourists in trouble. If you need to involve the police, your hotel reception or the Government of India tourist office will direct you to the appropriate station.

Post offices Delhi GPO is in Old Delhi, Lothian Rd (north of the railway line), and not to be confused with New Delhi (Gole Market PO), on the roundabout at the intersection of Baba Kharak Singh Marg and Ashoka Rd. There is a branch office at A-6 Connaught Place (Mon–Sat 10am–7pm), and others all over the city.

Visa extensions and exit formalities Tourist visas cannot normally be extended, but in exceptional cases you may be able to get an exemption from the Ministry of

Home Affairs, Foreigners' Division (⊕ mha.gov.in). If your total stay will exceed six months, you will need to register at the Foreigner's Regional Registration Office (FRRO), East Block 8, Level 2, Sector 1, Ramakrishna Puram (Mon–Fri 9.30am–3pm; ☎ 011 2671 1443). Further information can be found at ⊕ boi.gov.in.

Rajasthan

PICHOLA LAKE, UDAIPUR

Rajasthan

Rajasthan, the "Land of Kings", is unquestionably king of colour in a land that's not exactly short of vivid quarters. Jaipur is known as the "Pink City" on account of its rosy facades and palaces, and Jodhpur likewise the "Blue City" thanks to its old town's sky-blue mass of cubic houses. Udaipur's limewashed waterside palaces gleam white by a distant vista of sawtooth hills, while Jaisalmer's golden fort stands proud over the shifting sands of the mighty Thar Desert. Then there are the Rajasthanis themselves, the ladies glinting with heavy silver anklets or circular golden nose ornaments, and the men bearing bulky red, yellow or orange turbans. Add to this the multi-faceted history of a mosaic of twenty-two feudal kingdoms, and the sum total is perhaps the most fascinating, absorbing state in India.

Rajasthan's extravagant **palaces**, **forts** and finely carved **temples** comprise one of the country's richest crops of architectural monuments. But these exotic buildings are not the only legacy of the region's prosperous and militaristic history. Rajasthan's strong adherence to tradition is precisely what makes it a compelling place to travel around. Swaggering moustaches, colourful turbans, pleated veils and mirror-inlaid saris may be part of the complex language of **caste**, but to most outsiders they epitomize India at its most exotic.

The route stringing together Rajasthan's four main staging posts has become one of the most heavily trodden tourist trails in India, and with good reason: **Jaipur**, the largest of the lot, has stacks to see; **Jodhpur** is smaller but perhaps even more distinctive; the magical desert city of **Jaisalmer**, out west, is largely built from local sandstone; and **Udaipur** down south is undeniably romantic. In addition, all are surrounded by a number of out-of-town sights; you could easily eat up a week in any of these cities, and you'll most likely emerge with a clear favourite.

Primary sights aside, it's easy to escape into more remote areas. Northwest of Jaipur, the desert region of **Shekhawati** is dotted with atmospheric market towns and innumerable richly painted havelis, while the desert city of **Bikaner** is also well worth a stopover for its fine fort, havelis and the unique "rat temple" at nearby Deshnok. The same is true of **Bundi**, in the far south of the state, with its magnificent, muralled fort and blue-washed old town, as well as the superbly prominent fort at **Chittaurgarh** nearby, not to mention the engaging hill station and remarkable Jain temples of **Mount Abu**.

Another attraction is Rajasthan's wonderful **wildlife sanctuaries**. Of these, the tiger sanctuary at **Ranthambore** is deservedly the most popular, while the **Keoladeo National**

BEST TIME TO VISIT

Rajasthan's climate reaches the extremes associated with desert regions, with temperatures topping 45°C during the hottest months of May and June. The **monsoon** breaks over central and eastern Rajasthan in July and usually continues until September, although in recent years rainfall has become increasingly unpredictable and sporadic. The fierce summer heat lingers until mid-September or October, when night temperatures drop considerably. The best time to visit is between November and February, when daytime temperatures rarely exceed 30°C; in midwinter, you'll need a shawl or thick jumper if you're outdoors at night.

PASSING JAISALMER FORT

Highlights

❶ **Savitri Temple, Pushkar** For optimum views of the famous lake and holy town, climb to the hilltop Savitri Temple. See page 155

❷ **Camel trekking** There's no better way to experience the Thar Desert than by riding a camel through it. See boxes, pages 174 and 183

❸ **Jaisalmer Fort** One of India's most beautiful forts, its massive, honey-coloured bastions enclosing a labyrinth of narrow streets dotted with sandstone havelis and temples. See page 179

❹ **Sunset, Jodhpur** Watch the sun set over the Blue City, with the day's final rays lighting its spectacular backdrop, the imperious Mehrangarh Fort. See page 190

❺ **Udaipur** The most romantic city in Rajasthan, if not all India: a fairy-tale ensemble of lakes, floating palaces and sumptuous Rajput architecture ringed by dramatic green hills. See page 203

❻ **Ranthambore National Park** One of the easiest places in the world to see tigers in the wild, thanks to its large and exhibitionist population of big cats. See page 225

❼ **Keoladeo National Park, Bharatpur** Flocks of rare birds – and birdwatchers – travel from across Asia and Europe each winter to visit this remarkable wetland sanctuary. See page 228

HIGHLIGHTS ARE MARKED ON THE MAP ON PAGE 128

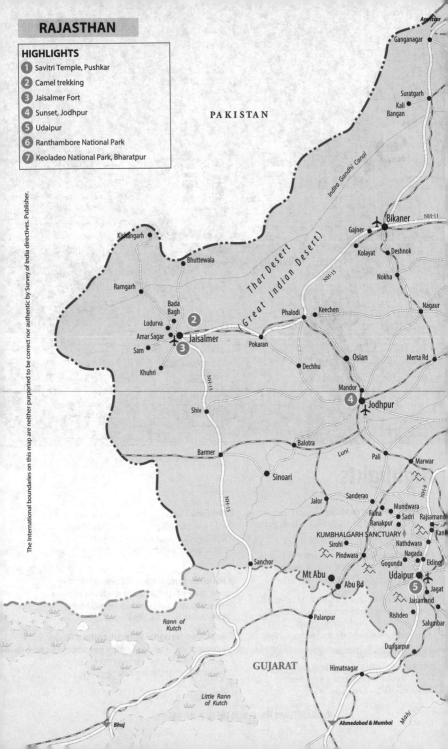

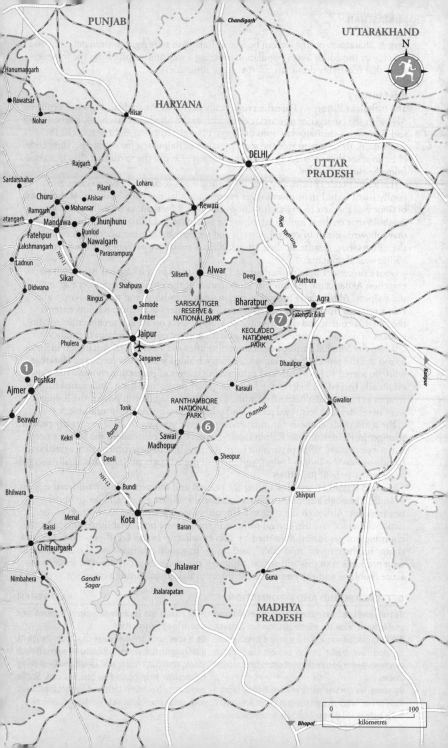

2

Park at **Bharatpur**, on the eastern border of Rajasthan near Agra, is unmatched in South Asia for its incredible avian population, offering a welcome respite from the frenetic cities that inevitably dominate most visitors' itineraries.

Brief history

The turbulent history of Rajasthan only really begins in the sixth and seventh centuries AD, with the emergence of warrior clans such as the Sisodias, Chauhans, Kachchwahas and Rathores – the **Rajputs** ("sons of Kings") Never exceeding eight percent of the population, they were to rule the separate states of **Rajputana** for centuries. Their code of honour set them apart from the rest of society – as did the myth that they descended from the sun and moon.

The Rajput codes of chivalry that lay behind endless clashes between clans and family feuds found their most savage expression in battles with Muslims. **Muhammad of Ghor** was the first to march his troops through Rajasthan, eventually gaining a foothold that enabled him to establish the **Sultanate** in Delhi. During the 350 years that followed, much of central, eastern and western India came under the control of the sultans, but, despite all their efforts, Rajput resistance prevented them from ever taking over Rajputana.

Ghor's successors were pushed out of Delhi in 1483 by the Mughal Babur, whose grandson **Akbar** came to power in 1556. Aware of the futility of using force against the Rajputs, Akbar chose instead to negotiate in friendship, and married Rani Jodha Bai, a princess from the Kachchwaha family of Amber. As a result, Rajputs entered the Mughal courts, and the influence of Mughal ideas on art and architecture remains evident in palaces, mosques, pleasure gardens and temples throughout the state.

When the Mughal empire began to decline after the accession of Aurangzeb in 1658, so too did the power of the Rajputs. Aurangzeb sided with a new force, the **Marathas**, who plundered Rajput lands and extorted huge sums of protection money. The Rajputs eventually turned for help to the Marathas' chief rivals, the **British**, and signed formal treaties as to mutual allies and enemies. Despite growing British power, the Rajputs were never denied their royal status, and relations remained largely amicable.

The nationwide clamour for Independence in the years up to 1947 eventually proved stronger in Rajasthan than Rajput loyalty; when British rule ended, the Rajputs were left out on a limb. With persuasion from the new Indian government they agreed one by one to join the Indian Union, and in 1949 the 22 states of Rajputana finally merged to form the state of **Rajasthan**.

Modern Rajasthan remains among the poorest and most staunchly traditional regions of India, although attempts to raise educational and living standards are gradually bearing fruit. Although the state still languishes somewhere near the bottom of the national literacy rate list, several major universities have been established and are now churning out graduates; Rajasthan has also crawled up India's GDP-per-capita list, and is now on the cusp of "mid-table", and rising. Irrigation schemes have also improved crop production in this arid region, although the severe threat of **drought** remains an acute problem, and the greatest single threat to Rajasthan's future prosperity.

GETTING AROUND AND INFORMATION   **RAJASTHAN**

By train and bus Trains connect all major cities and many smaller towns, while the reliable state-run bus company, RSRDC (ⓦ rsrtconline.rajasthan.gov.in), and various private operators have regular services between cities. Private companies tend to operate the most comfortable, modern coaches.

By plane You can save plenty of travel time by taking a flight or two. Jaipur receives plenty of flights from around India; Jodhpur and Udaipur both have decent connections; while Bikaner and Jaisalmer have recently opened their airports to passenger traffic.

On a tour Some turn their noses up at tours, though it's quite common for travellers in Rajasthan – especially those moving around as a couple or in a small group – to plump for one after weighing up their pros and cons. Smaller operators, such as Intense India Tours (ⓦ intenseindiatours. com), can be more conducive to individual requirements.

2

FESTIVALS AND FAIRS IN RAJASTHAN

Rajasthan's vibrant local costumes are at their most dazzling during the state's **festivals**. For dates of specific events, ask at tourist offices; most festivals fall on days determined by the lunar calendar.

Nagaur Cattle Fair (late Jan/early Feb). Thousands of farmers and around seventy thousand steers, cows and bullocks descend on Nagaur, south of Bikaner.

Desert Festival (Feb). Three-day event in Sam, near Jaisalmer. See page 188.

Elephant Festival (Feb/March). Parades of brightly painted elephants march through the streets of Jaipur, concluding with an extraordinary elephant-versus-*mahout* tug of war.

Mewar Festival (March/April). The ranas of Udaipur welcome the onset of spring with three days of traditional dances, the lighting of a sacred fire, and music by the city's famous bagpipe orchestra. Women play a prominent role.

Gangaur (March/April). In homage to Gauri, the consort of Lord Shiva, wives pray for their husbands, and unmarried girls wish for good suitors. At its best in Jaisalmer and Mount Abu.

Tilwara Cattle Fair (held over a fortnight in March or April). One of Rajasthan's biggest livestock markets, held at Tilwara, 93km southwest of Jodhpur.

Urs Ajmer Sharif (April/May). India's largest Islamic festival, held in Ajmer, an easy trip from the more popularly-visited town of Pushkar. See page 151.

Rani Sati Mela (Aug). Vast crowds gather in Jhunjhunu for a day of prayers and dances in memory of a merchant's widow who committed sati in 1595.

Pushkar Camel Fair (Nov). More than three hundred thousand visitors converge on the world's largest livestock market and Rajasthan's most colourful festival. See page 158.

Magnetic Fields (Dec; ⓦ magneticfields.in). A mite more modern than other festivals on this list, this three-day contemporary music and art event is held at the Alsisar Mahal in Shekhawati.

Alwar and around

Roughly halfway Delhi and Jaipur, the large, bustling town of **ALWAR** sprawls across a valley beneath one of eastern Rajasthan's larger and more impressive **forts**, whose massive ramparts straggle impressively along craggy ridges above. The town is mostly visited as a jumping-off point for Sariska National Park, though it has a number of fantastic attractions in its own right, including a fine palace, a string of colourful bazaars, and the gorgeous waterside Moosi Maharani Chhatri.

City Palace

Museum Tues–Sun 10am–5pm • ₹100 (₹20)

Alwar's principal attraction is its rambling and atmospheric **City Palace**, or Vinai Vilas Mahal, a sprawling complex of ornate but slightly dilapidated buildings, covered in crumbling ochre plaster and studded with endless canopied balconies. Most of the palace's innumerable rooms are now put to more mundane use as government offices; you'll often see lawyers prosecuting their business under the trees south of the main building.

The palace's time-warped **museum**, on the top floor, has extensive collections of weapons and miniature paintings, alongside a medley of objects belonging to former maharajas ranging from musical instruments to stuffed animals.

Steps at the left-hand end of the main facade lead up to a large, rather beautiful **tank**, flanked by symmetrical *ghats*, pavilions and a terrace on which stands the delicate **Moosi Maharani Chhatri**, built in memory of the mistress of Bhaktawar Singh, a local maharaja; after his death in 1815, she immolated herself on his funeral pyre.

Bala Qila

6km from Alwar by road, or 1–2hr each way on foot (take the path heading northwest from the city palace tank) • Daily 9am–5pm • ₹10 • The tourist office can arrange a 2hr 30min tour by gypsy for around ₹1300

Perched high above Alwar is **Bala Qila** fort, whose well-preserved walls climb dramatically up and down the thickly wooded hillsides that rise above the town. There's not much actually to see inside the fort – besides a temple and a few old cannons – but it's a pleasant walk up from town, with fine views and fresh hill breezes. It takes about two hours to make the return trip on foot up to the fort's outermost gate, or about twice that to reach the topmost point of the fortifications.

ARRIVAL AND INFORMATION   ALWAR

By train The railway station is on the eastern cusp of town, around 1.5km from the centre. Trains run to and from Delhi, Jaipur, Jodhpur, Ajmer and Ahmedabad. For Jaipur, the best service is the *Ajmer Shatabdi* #12015 (daily; dep. 8.42am, arr. 10.40am); for Delhi, the *Dee Double Decker* #12985 (daily; dep. 7.50am, arr. 10.30am) is the fastest service.
By bus Alwar's bus stand is right in the middle of town.

Buses depart for Bharatpur, many of them stopping at Deeg (every 15min; 4hr), Sariska (every 30min; 1hr 30min), Delhi (every 30min; 5hr) and Jaipur (hourly; 4hr).
Tourist information The helpful RTDC office is across the road, south of the railway station (Mon–Fri 10am–5pm; ☎ 0144 234 7348, ⊛ rajasthantourism.gov.in).

ACCOMMODATION

Aravali Clark's Inn Nehru Marg ☎ 0144 233 2883; map p.132. Recently redecorated with a wide variety of rooms (fan, air-cooled and a/c) and bar, gym and a guests-only pool in summer. Breakfast included. ₹3000
Ashoka Manu Marg ☎ 98288 33300; map p.132. Best of a cluster of more or less indistinguishable cheapies near the bus station, offering a range of simple but cheap, tolerably clean and reasonably comfortable fan and a/c rooms. It's on

a few of the main online booking engines, too. ₹800
Lemon Tree Shanti Kuni ☎ 0144 270 0600, ⊛ lemontreehotels.com; map p.132. Located to the south of town, this is Alwar's smartest hotel, with friendly and helpful staff. Rooms (all a/c) are bright, cosy and clean, with spotless modern bathrooms, and there's also a licensed bar and decent in-house restaurant. It's worth paying a little extra for buffet breakfast. ₹4500

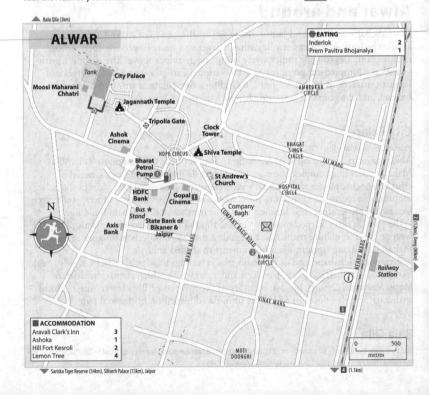

ALWAR

EATING
Inderlok	2
Prem Pavitra Bhojanalya	1

Bala Qila (3km)

Tank

City Palace

Moosi Maharani Chhatri

Jagannath Temple

AMBEDKAR CIRCLE

Tripolia Gate

Clock Tower

Ashok Cinema

BHAGAT SINGH CIRCLE

HOPE CIRCUS

Shiva Temple

JAI MARG

Bharat Petrol Pump

St Andrew's Church

HOSPITAL CIRCLE

HDFC Bank

Gopal Cinema

Company Bagh

N

Bus Stand

State Bank of Bikaner & Jaipur

COMPANY BAGH ROAD

Axis Bank

MANU MARG

NANGLI CIRCLE

NEHRU MARG

Railway Station

VINAY MARG

ACCOMMODATION
Aravali Clark's Inn	3
Ashoka	1
Hill Fort Kesroli	2
Lemon Tree	4

MOTI DOONGRI

0   500
metres

Sariska Tiger Reserve (34km); Siliserh Palace (13km); Jaipur

(13km); Deeg (80km)

(1.1km)

AROUND ALWAR

Hill Fort Kesroli 12km east of Alwar ☏ 0146 828 9352, ⓦ neemranahotels.com; map p.132. India's oldest heritage hotel, occupying a rugged fifteenth-century fort, impeccably restored and centred on a lush inner courtyard filled with plants and birds. Rooms are pleasantly rustic and have great views over Kesroli village and the surrounding countryside, as does the pretty pool. Discounts in summer. ₹3500

EATING

Alwar is famous throughout Rajasthan for its cavity-causing milk cakes (*palang torh*), which you can buy at the stalls around Hope Circus.

Inderlok Company Bagh Rd, near Nangli Circle ☏ 0144 270 0398; map p.132. Popular a/c vegetarian restaurant, serving good pan-India dishes, including unusual *paneer* varieties, along with a few Oriental mains. Mains ₹110–

150. Daily noon–3pm & 7–11pm.

Prem Pavitra Bhojanalya Shri Hans Tower ☏ 0144 233 5284; map p.132. This cosy little restaurant dishes up the best cheap food in town, with a very short menu of north Indian staples (mains from ₹75) such as *palek paneer* and *aloo paratha*. The entrance is easily missed. Daily 10am–10pm.

Siliserh Palace

15km south of Alwar • Daily, no set hours • ₹100 • Paddle boats ₹300 for 30min, motorboats ₹800 for 15min • ⓦ siliserhlake.com • Taxis from Alwar ₹3000–3500 return

Siliserh Palace is easily visited en route to or from Sariska if you've got your own vehicle (there's no public transport here). Maharaja Vijay Singh had the palace built in 1845 to win over a beautiful commoner, a certain Sheela, who agreed to marriage on the condition that she live within sight of her family's modest home. The whitewashed palace itself is fairly humdrum, but the Shangri-La setting, on the edge of a ten-square-kilometre lake ringed by jungle-clad hills, is idyllic. It's a nice spot to while away an afternoon, and you can rent out boats.

Sariska Tiger Reserve and National Park

Daily Oct–May 6–3.30pm • ⓦ fmdss.forest.rajasthan.gov.in • Park entry ₹565/person (₹100) in a 20-person canter or ₹600 (₹125) in a Gypsy (jeep). You rent vehicles from the entrance and pay an additional ₹250 (canter) or ₹350 (Gypsy) for the privilege plus ₹50/₹15 for a compulsory guide • Video permit ₹900

Alwar is the access point for **Sariska Tiger Reserve and National Park**, a former maharaja's hunting ground managed since 1979 by Project Tiger. Accustomed to being overshadowed by the more famous Ranthambore, Sariska was suddenly thrust into the headlines in 2005 when it was discovered that its tiger population, estimated at around 28 in 2003, had all but vanished due to poaching – one of India's biggest-ever conservation scandals. As a result, tigers were reintroduced to Sariska in 2008, with the arrival of one male and two females airlifted from Ranthambore, followed by a further two tigers in 2009 and 2010. Fortunately, these desperate measures have reaped rewards, and Sariska's current tiger currently stands at fourteen.

For birders and wildlife enthusiasts put off by the crowds and hassle of Ranthambore, Sariska's relative serenity comes as a welcome relief. The 881-square-kilometre sanctuary is home to abundant **wildlife** including sambar, *chital*, wild boar, nilgai and other antelopes, jackals, mongooses, monkeys, peacocks, porcupines, and numerous birds. The park is also dotted with a number of evocative ruins and other man-made structures, including the old **Kankwari Fort**, and a **Hanuman temple** deep within the park that gets surprisingly lively on Saturdays and Tuesdays, when Indian visitors are allowed into the park for free.

ARRIVAL AND DEPARTURE

SARISKA TIGER RESERVE

By bus The park lies 35km southwest of Alwar on the main Alwar–Jaipur road; buses between the two (every 30min; 1hr) will stop, on request, at the *Sariska Palace* hotel, a five minute walk from the park.

By taxi Alternatively, you may be able to arrange a taxi through a hotel in Alwar (around ₹3500 for the round trip), which also gives you time to visit Siliserh (see page 133) on the way back.

ACCOMMODATION

Tiger's Den ⊕0144 284 1342, ⊛rtdc.tourism. rajasthan.gov.in. Attractive, stone building hotel conveniently situated right next to the park entrance, with spacious, old-fashioned fan-cooled and a/c rooms, plus a nice garden. Rates are half-board. Licensed. **₹1750**

Sariska Palace A couple of minutes' drive down the main road from the park entrance ⊕011 2841 325,

⊛thesariskapalace.in. This former maharaja's residence has plenty of atmosphere, though rooms in the main building are surprisingly shabby given the hefty price, while those in the various modern annexes scattered around the grounds are poky and boring. There's also a pool (₹500 for non-guests), clay tennis court and large swathes of manicured lawns to loll around on. **₹8400**

Jaipur and around

A flamboyant showcase of Rajasthani architecture, **JAIPUR** has long been established on tourist itineraries as the third corner of India's "Golden Triangle", along with Agra and Delhi. At the heart of Jaipur lies the **Pink City**, the old walled quarter, whose **bazaars** rank among the most vibrant in Asia, renowned for their textiles, jewellery and Rajasthani handicrafts. For all its colour, however, Jaipur's heavy traffic, dense crowds and pushy traders make it a taxing place to explore, and many visitors stay just long enough to catch a train to more laidback destinations further west or south. If you can put up with the urban stress, however, the city's modern outlook and commercial hustle and bustle offer a stimulating contrast to many other places in the state.

Jaipur's attractions fall into three distinct areas. At the heart of the urban sprawl, the historic **Pink City** is where you'll find the fine City Palace and the Hawa Mahal. The leafier and less hectic area **south of the Pink City** is home to the Ram Niwas Gardens and Central Museum, while the city's **outskirts** are dotted with a string of intriguing relics of royal rule, most notably Nahargarh Fort, the cenotaphs at Royal Gaitor, and the temples (and monkeys) of Galta.

Additionally, forts, palaces, temples and assorted ruins from a thousand years of Kachchwaha history adorn the hills and valleys near Jaipur. The superb palace at **Amber** provides the most obvious destination for a day-trip, easily combined with a visit to the impressive fort of **Jaigarh**.

Brief history

Established in 1727, Jaipur is one of Rajasthan's youngest cities, founded by (and named after) **Jai Singh II** of the **Kachchwaha** family, who ruled a sizeable portion of northern Rajasthan from their fort at nearby Amber. The Kachchwaha Rajputs had been the first to ally themselves with the Mughals, in 1561, and, by the time of Jai Singh's accession, the free flow of trade, art and ideas had won them great prosperity. Jai Singh's fruitful 43-year reign was followed by an inevitable battle for succession, and the state was thrown into turmoil. Much of its territory was lost to Marathas and Jats, and the British quickly moved in to take advantage of Rajput infighting. Following Independence, Jaipur became **state capital** of Rajasthan in 1956.

Today, with a population of more than three million and as the tenth most populous city in the country, Jaipur is the state's most advanced commercial and business centre and its most prosperous city – some estimates put it among the world's fastest growing cities, with lively annual population growth, and gleaming new high-rises springing up on an almost weekly basis. Evidence of Jaipur's severe growing pains can be seen in older parts of the city, however, with creaking infrastructure and traffic-choked roads frequently approaching gridlock during the morning and evening rush hours.

The Pink City

At the heart of Jaipur lies Jai Singh's original city, popularly known as the **Pink City**, enclosed by walls and imposing gateways. Though certainly not all pink, many buildings here are painted a distinctively rosy colour – one that was actually intended to camouflage the poor-quality materials from which they were originally constructed. Chromatics aside, one of the Pink City's most striking features is its regular **grid-plan**, with wide, straight streets, broadening to spacious squares (*choupads*) at major intersections – a design created in accordance with the *Vastu Shastra*, a series of ancient Hindu architectural treatises. To make the most of your visit, buy a "composite" city ticket (see page 141).

City Palace

Daily 9.30am–5.30pm, last entry 5pm • ₹500 including audioguide (₹130); same ticket also valid for Jaigarh Fort at Amber if used within 24hr; on composite ticket (see page 141) • Palace at night ₹900 (₹450) • ⓦ royaljaipur.in

At the heart of the Pink City stands the magnificent **City Palace**, originally built by Jai Singh in the 1720s and having lost none of its original pomp and splendour. The royal family still occupies part of the palace, advancing in procession on formal occasions through the grand **Tripolia Gate** on its southern side. Less exalted visitors enter through a modest gate on the eastern side of the palace that leads into the first of the two main courtyards, centred on the elegant **Mubarak Mahal**. Built as a reception hall in 1899, the building now holds the museum's **textile collection**, housing some of the elaborately woven and brocaded fabrics that formerly graced the royal wardrobe. On the north side of the courtyard, the **Armoury** is probably the finest such collection in Rajasthan, a vast array of blood-curdling but often beautifully decorated weapons.

Diwan-i-Khas

Beyond the Mubarak Mahal, an ornate gateway flanked by a pair of fine stone elephants leads into the palace's second main courtyard, painted deep salmon pink. In its centre the raised **Diwan-i-Khas** (Hall of Private Audience) is an open-sided pavilion where important decisions of state were taken by the maharaja and his advisers. The hall contains two silver urns, or *gangajalis*, listed in the *Guinness Book of World Records* as the largest crafted silver objects in the world, each more than 1.5m high with a capacity of 8182 litres. When Madho Singh II went to London to attend the coronation of King Edward VII in 1901, he was so reluctant to trust the water in the West that he had these urns filled with Ganges water and took them along with him.

Pritam Niwas Chowk and the Chandra Mahal

Chandra Mahal entry ₹3000 (₹2500)

On the left (west) side of the courtyard, a small corridor leads through to the **Pritam Niwas Chowk**, or "Peacock Courtyard", adorned with four superbly painted doorways representing the four seasons. This courtyard also gives the best view of the soaring yellow **Chandra Mahal**, the residence of the royal family, who allow costly private tours of their quarters. Its heavily balconied seven-storey facade rises to a slope-shouldered summit, and views across the city from its peak are stunning. When the maharaja, Kumar Padmanabh Singh, is in residence his flag is flown from the topmost pavilion.

Diwan-i-Am

On the east side of the Diwan-i-Khas courtyard, beneath a large clock tower, sits the ornate **Sabha Niwas**, the Hall of Public Audience (or **Diwan-i-Am**), bare except for a pair of thrones in the middle and portraits of various former maharajas around the walls. Beyond here is the small **Diwan-i-Am courtyard**, with a collection of old carriages tucked into one end.

Jantar Mantar

Daily 9am–4.30pm, last entry 4pm · ₹200 (₹50), audioguide ₹150; on composite ticket (see page 141)

Immediately south of the City Palace lies the remarkable **Jantar Mantar**, a large grassy enclosure containing eighteen huge stone astronomical measuring devices constructed between 1728 and 1734 at the behest of Jai Singh, who invented many of them himself. Their strange, abstract shapes lend the whole place the look of a

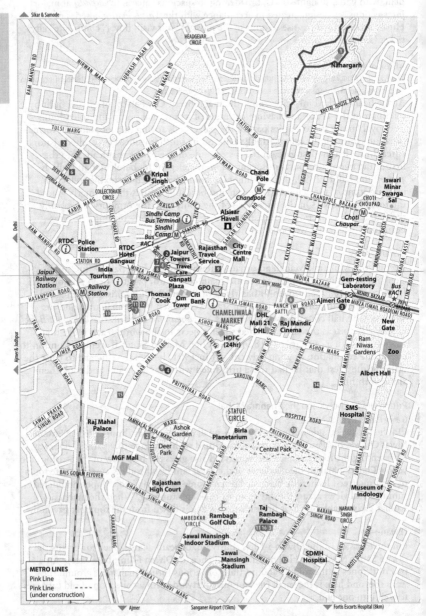

weird futuristic sculpture park. The Jantar Mantar is one of five identically named observatories created by the star-crazed Jai Singh across north India, including the well-known example in Delhi (see page 92), though his motivation was astrological rather than astronomical.

It's a very good idea to pay for the services of a **guide** to explain the workings of the observatory, which was able to identify the position and movement of stars and

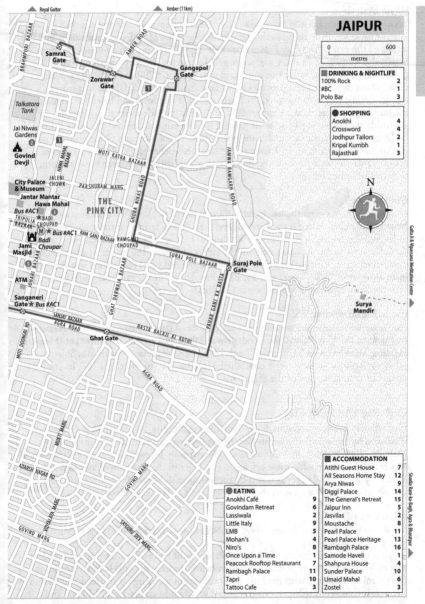

JAIPUR

2

0 — 600
metres

■ DRINKING & NIGHTLIFE	
100% Rock	2
#BC	1
Polo Bar	3

● SHOPPING	
Anokhi	4
Crossword	4
Jodhpur Tailors	2
Kripal Kumbh	1
Rajasthali	3

● EATING	
Anokhi Café	9
Govindam Retreat	6
Lassiwala	2
Little Italy	9
LMB	5
Mohan's	4
Niro's	8
Once Upon a Time	1
Peacock Rooftop Restaurant	7
Rambagh Palace	11
Tapri	10
Tattoo Cafe	3

■ ACCOMMODATION	
Atithi Guest House	7
All Seasons Home Stay	12
Arya Niwas	9
Diggi Palace	14
The General's Retreat	15
Jaipur Inn	5
Jasvilas	2
Moustache	8
Pearl Palace	11
Pearl Palace Heritage	13
Rambagh Palace	16
Samode Haveli	1
Shahpura House	4
Sunder Palace	10
Umaid Mahal	6
Zostel	3

planets, tell the time and even predict the intensity of the monsoon. Probably the most impressive of the observatory's constructions is the 27m-high sundial, the **Samrat Yantra**, which can calculate the time to within two seconds. A more original device, the **Jaiprakash Yantra**, consists of two hemispheres laid in the ground, each composed of six curving marble slabs with a suspended ring in the centre, whose shadow marks the day, time and zodiac symbol – vital for calculating auspicious days for marriage.

Hawa Mahal

Daily 9am–4.30pm, last entry 4pm · ₹200 (₹50), audioguide ₹150, guided tours ₹200; on composite ticket (see page 141)

Jaipur's most instantly recognizable landmark, the **Hawa Mahal**, or "Palace of Winds", stands to the east of the City Palace – it's best appreciated from the outside (or, even better, the rooftop of Tattoo Cafe; see page 144) during the early morning, when it glows orange-pink in the rays of the rising sun. Built in 1799 to enable the women of the court to watch street processions while remaining in purdah, its five-storey facade, decked out with hundreds of finely screened windows and balconies, makes the building seem far larger than it really is; in fact, it's little more than a facade. To get inside the palace itself you need to walk for five minutes around the rear of the building, following the lane that runs north from Tripolia Bazaar. Once inside, you can climb up the back of the facade to the screened niches from where the ladies of the court would once have looked down, and which still offer superb views over the mayhem of Jaipur below.

Govind Devji

Kanwar Nagar, near the Pradeep Rawat Memorial Hospital · Daily 4.30–11.30am & 5.45–9.30pm · Free · ⓦ govinddevji.net

North of the City Palace is the **Govind Devji**, the family temple of the maharajas of Jaipur. The temple is dedicated to Krishna in his character of Govinda, who is considered to be the guardian deity of the rulers of Jaipur. The principal shrine houses a sacred image of Govinda thought to be five thousand years old, which was brought from Vrindavan (near Agra) in 1735. Exit through the north gate and you'll be in the very pleasant, monkey-filled Jai Niwas Gardens.

Iswari Minar Swarga Sal

Tripolia Bazaar; entrance on side-road running parallel to main road · Daily 9.30am–4.30pm · ₹200 (₹50); on composite ticket (see page 141)

Just west of the City Palace, the slender **Iswari Minar Swarga Sal**, or **Ishwar Lat** (Heaven-Piercing Minaret), was built by Jai Singh II's son and successor, Iswari Singh, to celebrate a minor victory over a combined Maratha–Rajput force in 1747. Its summit offers the definitive view of the Pink City.

Outside the Pink City

Immediately south of the Pink City, the wide road leading out from New Gate is flanked by the surprisingly lush **Ram Niwas Gardens**, named after their creator, Maharaja Ram Singh (1835–80). Standing sentinel in among these gardens is the florid **Albert Hall**, while pressing on south again you'll get to the **Museum of Indology**. The Pink City is bookended to its north by the looming **Nahargarh**, while some distance to its east, and over a little rise, is the hugely enjoyable "**Monkey Palace**".

Albert Hall

Central Museum Daily 10am–5pm & 7–10pm · Day visits ₹300 (₹40), night visits ₹100, audioguide ₹177 (₹118); on composite ticket (see page 141) · ⓦ alberthalljaipur.gov.in

A prominent city landmark, the **Albert Hall** was built in 1867, exhibiting a whimsical mix of Venetian and Mughal styles (Italian below, Indian on top). It today houses the city's **Central Museum**, with the bulk of its collection focusing on regional and Indian themes, including fine displays of Jaipur pottery, Hindu statuary and Mughal and

Rajasthani miniature paintings, supported by an eclectic array of artefacts from around the globe – everything from Egyptian antiquities to decorative tiles from Stoke-on-Trent, with forays into Japan, Myanmar and Persia.

Museum of Indology

24 Gangawal Park, off Jawaharlal Nehru Road • Daily 8am–5pm • ₹500 (₹100) including guided tour

The **Museum of Indology** is home to assorted curiosities collected by the late Acharya Vyakul, stuffed into a rambling suburban house. Exhibits include oddities such as a map of India painted on a grain of rice, letters written on a hair and a glass bed, alongside other artefacts and literary treasures, all enjoyably arranged without any real organization.

Nahargarh

Daily 10am–6pm • ₹200 (₹50) • Taxis will charge around ₹300 to go up, but sometimes ₹200 to get back down; local youths will ask for around ₹100 each way on a scooter • Padao restaurant Entry ₹200 (₹100), including water, coffee, tea or soft drink

Teetering on the edge of the hills north of Jaipur is the dramatic **Nahargarh**, or "Tiger Fort", built by Jai Singh II in 1734 and offering superb views of Jaipur, best enjoyed at sunset. The fort's imposing walls sprawl for nearly 1km along the ridgetop and envelop a step-well among other features, but the only significant surviving structures within are the **palace apartments**, built inside the old fort by Madho Singh II between 1883 and 1892 as a love nest in which he kept his most treasured concubines away from the disapproving eyes of his courtiers and four official wives.

Four-wheeled vehicles can only get to the fort along a road that branches off Amber Road, a 13km-plus journey from Jaipur; as such taxis cost more than you'd expect, but it's fairly easy to walk the shorter – but steep and winding – road to the top. Try to avoid going up too late in the day or returning after dark; the fort is popular with delinquent teenagers and other unsavoury types, and the atmosphere can be a tad seedy at the best of times. Views of the sunset are pretty spectacular, either from the palace rooftop, various ramparts, or the *Padao Restaurant*, which charges for entry.

Royal Gaitor

Daily 9am–4.30pm • ₹30

On the northern edge of the city centre, the walled funerary complex of **Royal Gaitor** contains the stately marble mausoleums (chhatris) of Jaipur's ruling family. The compound consists of two main courtyards, each crammed full of imposing memorials. The first (and more modern) courtyard is dominated by the grandiose twentieth-century cenotaph of **Madho Singh II** (d. 1922), a ruler of famously gargantuan appetites, whose four wives and fifty-odd concubines bore him "around 125" children. The second, older, courtyard is home to the elaborate tomb of **Jai Singh II** (d. 1743), the founder of Jaipur and the first ruler to be interred at Gaitor.

On the ridgetop above Gaitor (reachable via a steep set of stairs) lies the **Ganesh Mandir**, the second of the city's two major Ganesh temples – a huge building instantly recognizable from the huge swastika painted on its side.

Galta Ji

3km east of Jaipur on foot • Daily sunrise–sunset • Free, camera ₹50, video camera ₹150; the temple is free, despite what ticket sellers may say about "donations" • 10km around the hills from Jaipur by vehicle (₹400 return by auto), or a stiff 20min walk over the rise from the eastern edge of the Pink City

Nestling in a steep-sided valley, the "Monkey Palace" of **Galta Ji** comprises a picturesque collection of 250-year-old temples squeezed into a narrow rocky ravine. Galta owes its sacred status in large part to a freshwater spring that seeps constantly through the rocks in the otherwise dry valley, keeping two **tanks** full. Surreally, these ponds are now the domain of more than five thousand macaque monkeys, which have earned Galta its nickname. For many tourists the sight of splashing locals – the tanks

2

> ## JAIPUR BUS SCAM
>
> Most buses arriving from Delhi or Agra skirt the southern side of the city, stopping briefly at Narain Singh Circle, where rickshaw-walas frequently board the bus and, with the connivance of the bus driver, announce that it's the end of the line ("bus going to yard") – a ploy to get you aboard their rickshaws and into a hotel that pays them commission.

are gender-segregated, and you'll always see fellas in the upper tank having a good gawp at the ladies down below – outstrips the attraction of the temples themselves, though the assorted shrines, dedicated variously to Krishna, Rama and Hanuman, are attractively atmospheric. It's also worth walking up to the spectacularly situated **Surya Mandir**, perched above the tanks on the ridgetop, which boasts dramatic views of the city below.

Sisodia Rani-ka-Bagh

11km east of Jaipur • Daily 8am–4.30pm • ₹200 (₹50)

On your way to Galta, if you're going by road, it's worth stopping off at the small royal pleasure palace and lush gardens of **Sisodia Rani-ka-Bagh**, built by Maharaja Sawai Jai Singh in 1728 as a gift to his second queen, Sisodia, a princess from Udaipur. The walls of the garden are adorned with Radha-Krishna murals and its design exhibits both Mughal and Indian influences.

ARRIVAL AND DEPARTURE   JAIPUR

Jaipur is Rajasthan's main **transport hub**, with frequent bus and train services to all major destinations around the state, as well as nationwide international air connections. Short journeys to destinations like Bharatpur, Ajmer (for Pushkar) and towns in Shekhawati are usually best made by bus; one exception is Sawai Madhopur, which is most easily reached by train.

By plane Jaipur's Sanganer airport (☎ 0141 225 0623) is 15km south of the city centre and is served by a number of international airlines, as well as numerous local carriers. There are regular airport buses to and from town (₹20); alternatively, a rickshaw will cost around ₹500, or a taxi under ₹1000.

Destinations Ahmedabad (4 daily; 1hr 20min); Bengaluru (7 daily; 2hr 25min); Bikaner (1 daily; 1hr); Chennai (3 daily; 2hr 30min); Delhi (8 daily; 1hr); Hyderabad (5 daily; 2hr); Jaisalmer (1 daily; 1hr 15min); Kolkata (4 daily; 2hr 15min); Mumbai (8 daily; 1hr 40min); Pune (2 daily; 1hr 50min); Udaipur (3 daily; 1hr).

By train The city's railway station, Jaipur Junction (☎ 0141 220 4536), lies 1.5km west of the Pink City. Bookings for trains should be made at least a day in advance at the reservations hall just outside the main station (Mon–Sat 8am–8pm, Sun 8am–2pm); go to the special foreigners'

counter. When departing, note that there's a nice little "executive lounge"; ₹195 gets you entry, water and a hot drink, and an extra ₹260 will allow a go at the buffet.

By bus State buses from all over Rajasthan and further afield pull in at the Inter-state Bus Terminal (also known as "Sindhi Camp") on Station Rd; you'll usually be fine just turning up (destinations are listed outside each cabin), perhaps bar direct buses to Pushkar, which leave daily at 4.15pm. For longer journeys, faster but less frequent deluxe Gold Line ("Volvo") and Silver Line government services guarantee seats, best reserved through your accommodation, though at the stations there's a dedicated booking hatch open 24hr. Many prefer the private buses, many of which leave from roads just south of Sindhi Camp; you can book tickets at the string of agents on Station Rd.

Destinations for private buses Agra (regular bar 7am–2pm gap; 4–6hr); Ajmer (3–5 hourly; 3hr); Bharatpur (regular bar 7am–2pm gap; 4hr); Bikaner (2–5 hourly; 5–6hr); Bundi (regular from 6pm; 3hr 15min–5hr); Chittaurgarh (regular from 7pm; 6hr); Delhi (1–5 hourly; 6hr); Jaisalmer (3 nightly; 12hr); Jodhpur (regular from 6pm; 6–7hr); Kota (regular from 6pm; 5hr); Pushkar (1–2 early morning; 3hr); Udaipur (2–4 hourly; 9hr).

GETTING AROUND

Jaipur is very spread out, and although it's possible to explore the Pink City on foot despite the crowds, you may need some form of transport to and from your hotel. It's best to avoid travelling during the morning and evening rush hours.

By rickshaw Auto-rickshaws are available all over the city. There are 24hr prepaid kiosks in front of the railway and bus stations, offering rates much cheaper than you're likely to get on the street – ₹500/₹300 for a full/half-day's rental, for example, or just ₹200 to Amber (or ₹400 for a roundtrip, including waiting time).

By taxi Cars with driver can be rented through most hotels or through any RTDC office, usually costing from ₹1300 for a half-day, or ₹2500/day. For private tours and taxi services, try the knowledgeable Shalutour (☎ 94123 42108, ⓦ shalutour.com), who charge from ₹2250/day.

By bus You're unlikely to want to navigate Jaipur by bus, but the #AC1 route is quite useful for getting to Amber (see page 146).

By metro Jaipur's metro system (ⓦ jaipurmetrorail.in) is quite modern, yet almost comically rubbish; trains on the single Pink Line are extraordinarily slow, and the primary use of most of the nine stations in use seems to be as public toilets for pigeons; in due course, two more stations will be added in the Pink City, which will make the system more useful (but probably still rubbish), and a second line has been proposed. Trains run every 10min from 6.30am to 9pm; tickets cost ₹6–17.

INFORMATION AND TOURS

Tourist information The RTDC (ⓦ rajasthantourism.gov. in) has tourist information offices at the railway station (daily 7am–10pm; ☎ 0141 220 0778); on MI Rd opposite the GPO (daily 10am–5pm; ☎ 0141 237 5466); and at the state bus terminal (daily 7am–10pm; ☎ 0141 220 6720). RTDC tours can be booked through any of these offices. There's an India Tourism (ⓦ tourism.rajasthan.gov.in) office at the *Khasa Kothi* hotel on MI Road (Mon–Fri 9.30am–6pm, Sat 9am–2pm; ☎ 0141 237 2200).

Attraction tickets A great-value way to see eight of Jaipur's biggest attractions (including Amber Fort, Jantar Mantar, Hawa Mahal, Nahargarh Fort and Albert Hall) is to buy a composite ticket for ₹1000 (₹300). You can buy these passes at the ticket offices of each named attraction, and they are valid for two consecutive days.

Guided tours One inexpensive, albeit very rushed, way to see Jaipur's main attractions is on one of the two guided tours run by the RTDC (9hr full-day tour ₹500; 5hr half-day tour if enough demand ₹400; entrance, camera and transport fees not included), which cram in most of the major city sights. They also run occasional "Pink City by Night" tours (6.30–10.30pm; ₹700), which include vegetarian dinner at Nahargarh Fort. Tours depart from, and can be booked through, any of the RTDC offices listed here. Lastly, despite the crowds, it can be pleasant to tour some parts of the city by bicycle; see ⓦ cyclinjaipur.com for guided tours (from ₹2000 per person).

ACCOMMODATION

Jaipur has a wide range of accommodation, mostly found west of the city centre, on or close to MI Rd and in the calm upmarket suburb of Bani Park. It's a good idea to book ahead, particularly around the Elephant Festival (first half of March). Note that almost all the places listed below offer free pick-up from the bus or train station.

LUXURY AND BOUTIQUE HOTELS

★ **Diggi Palace** SMS Hospital Rd ☎ 0141 237 3091, ⓦ hoteldiggipalace.com; map p.136. One of the city's most upmarket heritage hotels, occupying a characterful old haveli set amid huge gardens – home to squirrels and even peacocks, with such natural charm belying its

RECOMMENDED TRAINS FROM JAIPUR

All the following trains run daily.

Destination	Name	No.	Departs	Arrives
Abu Road	*Aravali Express*	19708	8.40am	4.40pm
Agra	*UDZ Kurj Express*	19666	6.15am	11am
Ajmer	*Shatabdi Express*	12015	10.45am	12.45pm
Alwar	*Shatabdi Express*	12016	5.50pm	7.50pm
Bikaner	*Bikaner Intercity*	12468	4.15pm	10.55pm
	Jodhpur Express	12307	12.45am	8am
Chittaurgarh	*Udaipur Express*	12992	2pm	7.05pm
Delhi	*Shatabdi Express*	12016	5.50pm	10.40pm
Jaisalmer	*Jaisalmer Express*	14659	11.45pm	11.45am
Jodhpur	*Ranikhet Express*	15014	11.10pm	5.45pm
	Ranthambore Express	12465	5pm	10.25pm
	Jaisalmer Express	14659	11.45pm	5am
Kota	*Mumbai Superfast*	12956	2.10pm	5.30pm
Sawai Madhopur	*Intercity Express*	12466	11.05am	1.15pm
Udaipur	*Udaipur SF Special*	09721	6.15am	1.30pm
	Udaipur Express	12992	2pm	9.30pm
Varanasi	*Sealdah Express*	12988	2.55pm	4.55pm

2

conveniently central location. Expect hefty online discounts on the ridiculous rack rates. ₹**11,000**

Jasvilas C-9, Sawai Jai Singh Highway, Bani Park ☎ 0141 220 4638, ⓦ jasvilas.com; map p.136. Welcoming family-run guesthouse in a gracious old suburban mansion, with spacious and comfortable a/c rooms, a lovely little pool and attractive enclosed gardens. ₹**6500**

★ **Rambagh Palace** Bhawani Singh Marg ☎ 0141 221 1919, ⓦ tajhotels.com; map p.136. This opulent palace complex, set amid 47 acres of beautiful gardens, is indisputably the grandest hotel in Jaipur, and one of the most romantic places to stay in India. Rooms are superbly equipped, with Rajasthani artworks, reproduction antique furniture and all mod cons. Facilities include a clutch of fine restaurants and bars (see page 143), indoor and outdoor pools, and a Jiva spa. Even if you can't afford to stay, call in for afternoon tea (₹2500/person). Check the website for discounts, especially in summer. ₹**45,000**

Samode Haveli Gangapole ☎ 0141 263 2370, ⓦ samode.com; map p.136. In an unbeatably central location on the northeastern edge of the Pink City, this superb old haveli is brimming with atmosphere, centred on an idyllic courtyard and with the prettiest pool in town. Rooms are a mishmash: it's worth paying a little more for a suite. In summer (May–Sept), rates can fall by forty percent. ₹**18,000**

Shahpura House Devi Marg, Bani Park ☎ 0141 408 9100, ⓦ shahpura.com; map p.136. Charismatic but affordable 200-year-old heritage hotel, superbly decorated throughout with lavish murals and Rajasthani architectural touches. Rooms all come with a/c, minibar and bathtub, and are attractively furnished with old wooden furniture; there's also a small pool. ₹**6000**

MID-RANGE HOTELS AND GUESTHOUSES

★ **All Seasons Home Stay** 63 Hathroi Fort, behind Vidhayakpuri Police Station ☎ 0141 236 9443, ⓦ allseasonshomestayjaipur.com; map p.136. The rooms in this family house each come with a/c, TVs, private bathrooms and garden-view terraces or balconies. Some also have attached kitchens, but better are the tasty home-cooked meals (₹breakfast 300, lunch or dinner ₹500). ₹**2000**

Arya Niwas Sansar Chandra Rd (behind Amber Tower) ☎ 0141 407 3450, ⓦ aryaniwas.com; map p.136. Dependable old haveli hotel arranged around a couple of intimate courtyards, with a lovely expanse of lawn and spacious veranda out front. Rooms are nicely furnished; all come with TVs and a/c, apart from a few air-cooled singles. They also offer city tours, including a 3hr guided stroll of the Pink City. ₹**2450**

The General's Retreat 9 Sardar Patel Marg, nr Chomu Circle ☎ 0141 237 7134, ⓦ generalsretreat.com; map p.136. Dating back to the 1960s, this quaint ex-general's mansion with lush garden is home to eleven clean, bright and cosy a/c rooms, adorned with old photographs, period furnishings and gorgeous Rajasthani fabrics, plus a convivial rooftop dining room. ₹**2900**

Jaipur Inn Shiv Marg, Bani Park ☎ 0141 220 1121, ⓦ jaipurinn.com; map p.136. Reliable, pleasantly old-fashioned lower-budget option, with comfortable and well-equipped rooms with TV and a/c (the rear garden rooms are nicest), plus breezy rooftop terrace and café. They've games to play, including ping-pong and Indian Monopoly, and they often offer Bollywood dance lessons. ₹**1500**

★ **Pearl Palace Heritage** 54 Gopal Bari, Lane no.2, Ajmer Rd ☎ 0141 237 5242, ⓦ pearlpalaceheritage. com; map p.136. Striking sister hotel to the excellent *Pearl Palace*, with a much more upmarket heritage theme – each of the spacious, painstakingly designed a/c rooms is highly unique and features traditional wooden doors, assorted artworks and artefacts. There's a superb sequence of stone carvings adorning the first-floor corridors – a miniature museum in itself. Rooms have TVs and spotless bathrooms, some of which feature Jacuzzi tubs. ₹**3000**

Umaid Mahal C-20/B-2 Bihari Marg, Bani Park ☎ 0141 220 1952, ⓦ umaidmahal.com; map p.136. Extravagantly decorated heritage-style modern hotel, with the shiniest front doors in the city – and once past them, virtually every surface covered in colourful traditional murals. The spacious a/c rooms are attractively furnished with antique-style wooden furniture, and there's also a nice basement pool and bar. Check website for discounts. ₹**2500**

HOSTELS AND BUDGET GUESTHOUSES

★ **Atithi Guest House** 1 Park House Scheme, just off MI Rd ☎ 0141 237 8679, ⓦ jatithijaipur.com; map p.136. Long-established red-brick guesthouse and still one of the nicer budget places in town, with pleasant, modern tiled rooms (air-cooled and a/c) and an attractive rooftop terrace. There's a smart café, and the popular restaurant *Mohan's* (see page 143) is a 2min stroll away. ₹**1200**

Moustache 7 Park House, near Ganpati Plaza ☎ 0141 403 4419, ⓦ moustachehostel.com; map p.136. Close to the bus station yet tucked into a tangle of quiet side-streets, this is an excellent choice, with well-informed staff, an attractive common area, and super-cheap dorm beds. What else could you want? Dorm ₹**350**

★ **Pearl Palace** Hari Kishan Somani Marg, Hathroi Fort ☎ 0141 237 3700, ⓦ hotelpearlpalace.com; map p.136. One of the best guesthouses in Rajasthan, with a selection of spotless and excellent-value, modern air-cooled and a/c rooms (a few with shared bathroom) attractively decorated with local arts and crafts, plus a mixed dorm. The well-drilled staff can take care of all your needs, and facilities include a silver shop and travel ticketing, plus an excellent rooftop restaurant (see page 143). Advance bookings recommended. Dorm ₹500, double ₹1100

Sunder Palace 46 Sanjay Marg, Hathroi Fort, Ajmer Rd ☎0141 236 0878, ⓦsunderpalace.com; map p.136. One of the city's standout budget options, with spotless, attractive local interiors and modern rooms (fan, air-cooled or a/c), all with sparkling attached bathrooms at very competitive prices. There's a choice of garden café or lively rooftop restaurant (see below), while the friendly and knowledgeable owners can also take care of money exchange, travel arrangements and anything else you're likely to think of. There's a souvenir shop, a book-swap library and a cushy day-room with games, TV and common shower for early/late arrivals. Advance bookings recommended. ₹600

★ **Zostel** 85A Rajamal Ka Talab, Pink City ☎011 3958 9005, ⓦzostel.com; map p.136. Finally, some decent accommodaiton in the Pink City! Part of a nationwide chain, this chilled hostel is a great place to stay, with a cushion-filled common room by reception, travel and culinary advice all over the place, and very decent dorm rooms. Dorm ₹450, double ₹1700

EATING

RESTAURANTS

Anokhi Café 2nd Floor, KK Square Mall, Prithviraj Rd ☎0141 400 7244; map p.136. If you've overloaded on curries and need a respite, this veggie-friendly, expat-heavy café attached to the Anokhi boutique (see page 144) is the perfect tonic. There's organic coffee (₹90), fresh juices, terrific cakes and cookies, plus sandwiches, falafels, bean burgers, pizzettas and amazing salads (mains ₹175–420). Most ingredients are sourced from their own organic farm. Daily 9.30am–7.30pm.

★ **Govindam Retreat** Udyog Kanwar Nagar, near Govind Devji temple ☎99299 49258; map p.136. There are few notable places to eat in the Pink City, so circle this one on your map – a charmingly decorated, second-floor place serving pure-veg Rajasthani dishes (most ₹180–300); try the sarso shag, like a garlicky palak paneer without the paneer, with a corn-based makha roti. They also sell cheaper South Indian dosas, *iddli* and *upmas*, and often offer a ₹500 lunch buffet, which is great if you're hungry. Daily 8.30am–10pm.

Little Italy KK Square Mall, Prithviraj Rd ☎0141 402 2444; map p.136. Svelte modern restaurant serving passable – if not particularly authentic – pizza, pasta, salads, risotto and a few Italian-style meat dishes, plus assorted Mexican snacks. Also has a selection of Indian wines. Mains around ₹400. Daily noon–11pm.

Mohan's 14 Motilal Atal Rd, opposite Hotel Neelam ☎0141 510 4299; map p.136. Cosy and unpretentious little veg restaurant near the bus station, popular with locals thanks to its well-prepared and excellent-value Indian food, with virtually everything under ₹90, and banana lassis for half that. There's not much room, so you might end up sharing a table. Daily 8am–10pm.

Niro's MI Rd ☎0141 237 4493, ⓦnirosindia.com; map p.136. This profusely mirrored restaurant has some of the best non-veg food in Jaipur, with Rajasthani specialities such as *sula* (lamb), *lal maans* (mutton) and *gatta* along with a big choice of tandoori dishes and other meat and veg curries, plus Western and Chinese. Try a goat brain masala, if you dare! Mains ₹400–600. Licensed. Daily 10am–4pm & 6–11pm.

Once Upon a Time Palace Complex, Nahargarh Fort ☎91160 48101; map p.136. While people usually head to the nearby Padao restaurant for sunset views (see page 139), this fort restaurant is far nicer, even though all the views are interior or courtyard-based. The food is a little dear, with Indian mains and tandoor dishes costing ₹650–900 – perhaps worth the splurge, and you'll almost never have to book ahead. Daily 11am–11pm.

★ **Peacock Rooftop Restaurant** Pearl Palace hotel, Hari Kishan Somani Marg ☎0141 237 3700; map p.136. The city's most appealing rooftop restaurant, with quirky original decor featuring cute metal chairs and striking peacock motifs. There's a big menu of veg and non-vegetarian North Indian options, all well prepared, with flavoursome sauces, crisp breads and cold beers, plus Chinese dishes and great burgers – try the "farmer's" one, a chicken patty with fried egg and bacon on top. It's a good idea to book ahead for dinner, since the place is particularly pretty after darm. Mains ₹200–500.

Rambagh Palace Bhawani Singh Marg ☎0141 221 1919, ⓦtajhotels.com; map p.136. Jaipur's most opulent hotel serves up a handful of memorable dining options. Choose between *Suarna Mahal*, offering Indian fine-dining (and afternoon tea from 3–6pm; ₹2500) in a superbly over-the-top, Neoclassical-style dining room, or tuck into Italian food at the more laidback *Steam* restaurant, built in and around the carriages of an old steam train in the hotel's grounds. Mains at both start at around ₹1200, and reservations are strongly recommended. Suvarna Mahal daily noon–midnight; Steam daily 6pm–midnight.

★ **Tapri** B4-E Prithviraj Rd ☎0141 236 0245; map p.136. A little out of the way, but so, so worth tracking down, this rooftop tearoom (see below for more on the tea) is one of the most enjoyable places to eat in Jaipur. Much of the menu is taken up with Indian street food, served in a manner far more beautiful than you'd ever see on the actual streets – samosas, *chana chaat*, dhal patties and the like, all super cheap at ₹150–300. The concept has really caught on with locals, and you'll most likely have to queue a while for a table. Daily 8am–10pm.

2

CAFES, TEAROOMS AND SNACKS

★ **Lassiwala** 312 MI Rd; map p.136. A Jaipur institution for its sublime lassis (large/small ₹60/30), served in old-style terracotta mugs, with eco-friendly wooden spoons. Its popularity has sparked a small lassi-wala-war, with two impostors setting up shop alongside – check for the correct street number (clearly displayed). Daily 7.30am until stock sold out (usually early afternoon).

LMB Johari Bazaar ☎0141 265 5844; map p.136. The sweet counter here outshines the restaurant, so come for the tooth-rotting goodies, not the mains next door. Try the famous *paneer ghewar* (honey-comb cake soaked in treacle) and piping hot *tikkis* in spicy mango sauce. Daily 8am–11.30pm.

Tapri B4-E Prithviraj Rd ☎0141 236 0245; map p.136.

An awesome place to eat (see above), this is, in theory, actually a tearoom, with all sorts of brews – including herbal and iced varieties – from India and abroad, going from ₹70 a cup. Daily 8am–10pm.

Tattoo Cafe 30 Hawa Mahal Rd ☎98280 65533; map p.136. An okay-ish cafe-restaurant with one gigantic claim to fame – its rooftop is the vantage point for many of the best shots of the Hawa Mahal (see page 138), which sits bang opposite. As such it's only really worth swinging by in the morning, before the movement of the sun puts the famous frontage into relatively dull shadow; the meals here are so-so and the service is slow, so stick to their drinks, which include lassis, shakes, smoothies and coffee (all ₹90–195). Daily 8am–11pm.

DRINKING AND NIGHTLIFE

100% Rock Hotel Shikha, R-14 Yudhister Marg ☎95711 11456; map p.136. Located in what's effectively Jaipur's best nightlife area (which isn't saying much – there are just a few bars), this is an appealing, slightly quirky spot. Most of the menu is filled with odd cocktails named after Janis Joplin, Bob Dylan or CCR songs (almost all ₹380), though despite this the music playing is mostly 80s and 90s rock; however, running contrary to the name of the place, when there are enough local guys about, things can go all Bollywood or Punjabi very fast. Happy hour runs pretty much all day; buy one, get one free, repeat. Daily 11am–midnight.

★ **#BC** Traditional Heritage Haveli, Gayatri Marg ☎0141 400 3300; map p.136. Although this cellar bar is a little hard

to find, to the degree that some people in the neighbourhood have no idea it's there, plenty of Jaipur folk know precisely where this place is – one reason why it's heaving most nights, especially for the DJ nights on Sat, and the live bands on Sun. The music's loud on weekday nights too, beers and cocktails are fairly priced at ₹400 or so, and almost everyone's sucking on various flavours of hookah (₹750). Daily 11am–1am.

Polo Bar Rambagh Palace, Bhawani Singh Marg ☎0141 221 1919, ⓦtajhotels.com; map p.136. For a truly enchanting evening, sink old-fashioned tipples in this memorable hotel's swanky, colonial-style bar. Hardly cheap, but quite surprisingly, not all that wallet-busting either. Daily noon–midnight.

SHOPPING

If you come across an Indian handicraft object or garment abroad, chances are it will have been bought in Jaipur. As a regular tourist, you'll find it harder to hunt out the best merchandise here, but as a source of souvenirs, perhaps only Delhi can surpass it. In keeping with Maharaja Jai Singh's original city divisions, different streets are reserved for purveyors of different goods. **Bapu Bazaar**, on the south side of the Pink City, is the best place for clothes and textiles, including Jaipur's famous **block-print** work and *bandhani* **tie-dye**. On the opposite side of town, along Amber Rd just beyond Zorawar Gate, rows of emporiums are stacked with gorgeous patchwork wall-hangings and **embroidery**; these places do a steady trade with bus parties of wealthy tourists, so be prepared to be hassled; haggle hard. For old-style Persian-influenced vases, along with tiles, plates and candleholders, visit the outlets of the city's renowned **blue potteries** along Amber Rd or the workshop of the late Kripal Singh (see below).

★ **Anokhi** 2nd Floor, KK Square Mall, Prithviraj Rd ⓦanokhi.com; map p.136. This is the place to buy high-quality "ethnic" Indian evening wear, *salwar kameez* and shirts. They also do lovely bedspreads, quilts, tablecloths and cushion covers. Daily 9.30am–8pm.

Crossword 1st Floor, KK Square Mall, Prithviraj Rd ☎0141 237 9400; map p.136. This big bookshop has a superb selection of English-language local fiction, and India-related titles. Daily 11am–9.30pm.

Jodhpur Tailors Moti Lal Atal Rd (behind Hotel Neelam) ☎93515 84026; map p.136. One of the best tailors in town. Hand-stitched suits run from around ₹8000, or you could just pick up a shirt (from ₹800), trousers (₹2000) or jodhpurs (₹2800). Mon–Sat 11.30am–8pm.

Kripal Kumbh Shiv Marg ⓦkripalkumbh.com; map p.136. The former workshop-cum-home of Jaipur's most famous ceramicist, the late Kripal Singh, full of attractive and affordable examples of the city's traditional blue-and-white pottery. They also claim to be the only workshop in Jaipur producing entirely lead-free pottery that can safely be used with hot food (as well as featuring colours such as red and orange, which are impossible with lead glazes). Daily 10am–8pm.

Rajasthali MI Rd, opposite Ajmeri Gate ⓦrajasthali.gov.in; map p.136. This large, government-run emporium gives you an idea of the range of handicrafts available and approximate costs – although you'll probably find similar items at cheaper prices in the Pink City bazaars. Mon–Sat 11am–7.30pm.

2

JEWELLERY AND GEMSTONES IN JAIPUR

The two best places for silver jewellery are **Johari Bazaar**, the broad street running north of Sanganeri Gate in the Pink City, and **Chameliwala Market**, just off MI Road in a tangle of alleyways. The latter also has the city's best selection of gems, though it's also a hard place to shop in peace, thanks to a particularly slippery breed of scam merchant, known locally as *lapkars*. These young men – usually smartly dressed and speaking excellent English – will regale you with beguiling tales about how you can buy gems in Jaipur and sell them back home for a massive profit. This is nonsense, of course, but by the time you realize this you'll be thousands of kilometres away with a handful of worthless cut-glass "gems" wondering where all the mysterious entries on your credit-card bill came from. If you're paying for gemstones or jewellery with a credit card in Jaipur, don't let it out of your sight.

There's a government-sponsored **gem-testing laboratory** (Mon–Fri & every first and third Sat of month 10am–5pm; ☎0141 256 8221) at the Gem and Jewellery Export Promotion Council, Rajasthan Chamber Bhavan, MI Rd near Ajmeri Gate, where you can have gemstones tested for authenticity. The cost is ₹1000 per stone, with reports delivered the following working day (or ₹1600 per stone for a same-day report if you deliver the stone before 1pm).

ENTERTAINMENT AND ACTIVITIES

Theme park Chokhi Dhani, 22km south of Jaipur on the Tonk Rd ☎0141277 0554, ⓦchokhanidhani.com. This Rajasthani theme-park-cum-restaurant attracts droves of well-heeled Jaipuris, especially at weekends, when the whole place gets wildly busy. The ₹900 entrance fee includes an evening meal plus access to a wide range of attractions (though tips are expected at many) – elephant, camel and bullock-cart rides, folk dances, puppet shows, magicians and chapatti-making demonstrations, to name just a few. When you've done with the entertainment, make for the mud-walled dining hall where you'll be sat on the floor and served an authentically original Rajasthani village thali quite unlike anything you'll find in the restaurants of Jaipur, with lots of rustic rural delicacies like cornflour chapattis, *gatta* and unusual curried vegetables. It's all a bit hokey, but fun. The higher entrance fee (₹1150) includes a meal in the posher a/c food hall. An auto will charge around ₹500 for the round trip. Daily 5–11pm.

★ **Cinema** The Raj Mandir Cinema (ⓦtherajmandir.com) on Bhagwan Das road is the place to go if you visit just one cinema while you're in India. Boasting a stunning Art Deco lobby and a 1500-seat auditorium, there are four screenings a day (usually at 12.30pm, 3.30pm, 6.30pm and 9.30pm). There's always a long queue for tickets (from ₹110, or ₹400 for a box), so get yours at least an hour before the show

starts – or, if possible, the day before. Hollywood movies are often shown in English during the first week of their release.

Events The Zee *Jaipur Literature Festival* (ⓦjaipurliterature festival.org) is one of Asia's biggest bookfests, held over five days in late January at the *Diggi Palace* hotel (see page 141). Jaipur's SMS Stadium (ⓦsmsstadium.com) hosts Indian Premier League cricket fixtures in season.

Meditation The Dhamma Thali Vipassana Centre (☎0141 268 0220, ⓦthali.dhamma.org), located in beautiful countryside on the road to Galta, is one of just fifty centres across the world set up to promote the practice of Vipassana meditation. Courses generally run for ten days (see website for schedule and details) and are free, but a donation is expected.

Swimming pools The nicest hotel pool currently open to non-guests is at the *Alsisar Haveli* (a pricey ₹400/hr; ☎0141 236 8290, ⓦalsisarhaveli.com); cheaper options include the pools at *Shahpura House* (₹300/3hr; see page 142).

Yoga Kalpana Yoga Homestay, 69 Harikishan Somani Marg (☎0141 237 3089, ⓦkalpyoga.com) offers proper courses in Bani Park; you don't actually have to stay here, but it helps. There are also free daily yoga classes from 6–7am at the Madhavanand Girls College, along Behari Marg (also in Bani Park), and 6.30–7.30am near the temple in Central Park (use Gate 3).

DIRECTORY

Banks and exchange There are stacks of ATMs around town, and many private exchange places in Jaipur (try Thomas Cook on MI Rd; Mon–Sat 9.30am–-5.30pm) offering more or less the same rates as the banks.

Hospitals For emergencies, the government-run SMS Hospital (☎0141 251 8422), on Sawai Ram Singh Rd, is best; treatment is usually free for foreigners, and it's open 24hr. Private hospitals include the Santokba Durlabhji

Memorial Hospital (Bhawani Singh Marg; ☎0141 256 6251, ⓦsdmh.in).

Left luggage The left luggage counter at the main bus station costs ₹50 per bag for 24 hours.

Police station The main police post is on Station Rd opposite the railway station (☎0141 220 2677, ⓦpolice. rajasthan.gov.in).

Post and couriers Jaipur's GPO is on MI Rd (Mon–Sat

2

HOT AIR BALLOONING

For bird's-eye views of the Pink City, Sky Waltz (☎ 97172 95801, ⊛ skywaltz.com) offers hot air balloon safaris (1hr; ₹13,000 including transfers) between April and February. They have a number of launch sites in and around the city including Amber and Samode, an hour north of Jaipur.

10am–6pm), and the DHL office is at G-8 Geeta Enclave, C Scheme, Vinobha Marg, behind Standard Chartered Bank (Mon–Sat 9.30am–7.30pm; ☎ 0141 236 1159).

Volunteering Local NGO TAABAR (⊛ taabar.org), opposite the railway station, provides street children and runaways with shelter, food and education, and also operates a mobile health clinic. Volunteers are welcome.

Amber

On the crest of a rocky hill 11km north of Jaipur, **AMBER** (or Amer) was the capital of the leading **Kachchwaha** Rajput clan from 1037 until 1727, when Jai Singh established his new city at Jaipur. Amber's palace buildings are less impressive than those at Jaipur, but the natural setting – perched high on a narrow rocky ridge above the surrounding countryside and fortified by natural hills and high ramparts – is unforgettably dramatic.

Visit Amber early in the day if you want to avoid the big coach parties; if you're there in the afternoon, stay on to watch the atmospheric Amber sound-and-light show from the lakeside Kesar Kiyari complex below the fort.

Below the palace, the atmospheric but little-visited **Amber town** is full of remnants of Kachchwaha rule. One of the most striking local landmarks is the unusual **Jagat Shiromani Temple**, a large and florid structure located to the south of Amer Road; built by Man Singh after the death in battle of his son and would-have-been successor, its shrine is topped by an enormous *shikhara* and fronted by an unusually large, two-storey *mandapa* with a curved roof inspired by those on Mughal pavilions.

The palace complex

Palace Daily 8am–6pm, last entry 5.30pm; Shri Sila Devi temple closed noon–4pm • ₹200 (₹25), audioguide ₹150 (₹100); on composite ticket (see page 141) • **Sound-and-light show** Daily 7.30pm in English (₹200); 8pm in Hindi (₹100) • ☎ 0141 253 0293, ⊛ amberfort.org

A path climbs from Amber village to Suraj Pole (Sun Gate) and the large **Jaleb Chowk** courtyard at the entrance to the main **palace complex**, where you'll find the ticket office and assorted official guides. On the left-hand side of the courtyard is the **Shri Sila Devi temple**, dedicated to Sila, an aspect of Kali. The statue within is one of the most revered in Jaipur, framed by an unusual arch formed from stylized carvings of banana leaves.

Next to the Shri Sila Devi temple, a steep flight of steps ascends to **Singh Pole** (Lion Gate), the entrance to the main palace. The architectural style is distinctly Rajput, though it's clear from the mirrored mosaics covering the walls that Mughal ideas also crept in.

Singh Pole leads into the first of the palace's three main courtyards, on the far side of which stands the **Diwan-i-Am** (Hall of Public Audience), constructed in 1639. This open-sided pavilion is notably similar in its overall conception to contemporary Mughal audience halls in Delhi and Agra, even if the architectural details are essentially Rajput.

Diagonally opposite, the exquisitely painted **Ganesh Pole** marks the entrance to a second courtyard, its right-hand side filled with a miniature fountain-studded garden, behind which lie the rooms of the **Sukh Mahal**, set into the side of the courtyard. The marble rooms here were cooled by water channelled through small conduits carved into the walls, an early and ingenious system of air-conditioning – the central room has a particularly finely carved example.

On the opposite side of the courtyard, the dazzling **Sheesh Mahal** houses what were the private chambers of the maharaja and his queen, its walls and ceilings decorated with intricate mosaics fashioned out of shards of mirror and coloured glass. On the far side of the courtyard beyond the Sheesh Mahal, a narrow stairwell winds up to the small **Jas Mandir**, decorated with similar mosaics and guarded from the sun by delicate marble screens.

From the rear of the Sheesh Mahal courtyard, a narrow corridor transports you into a further expansive courtyard at the heart of the **Palace of Man Singh I**, the oldest part of the palace complex. The buildings here are plain and austere compared to later structures, though they would originally have been richly decorated and furnished. The pillared *baradari* in the centre of the courtyard was once a meeting area for the maharanis, shrouded from men's eyes by flowing curtains.

Anokhi Museum of Hand Printing

Kheri Gate • Mid-July to May Tues–Sat 10.30am–5pm, Sun 11am–4.30pm • ₹30 • Camera ₹50, video camera ₹150 • ☎ 0141 2530226 • ⓦ anokhi.com/museum

The town is also home to the excellent **Anokhi Museum of Hand Printing**, a ten-minute walk northwest from the temple towards Sagar Lake (look out for the blue-and-white signs). Housed in an attractive old haveli, the museum has an interesting collection of hand block-printed textiles and garments, along with live demonstrations of printing and carving by resident craftsmen.

JAIGARH

Daily 9am–4.30pm • ₹200 (₹50) • A steep 15–20min climb on a path starting just below entrance to Amber palace • Jeeps around ₹500, including 2hr waiting time, from Amber town

Perched high on the hills behind Amber Palace, the rugged **Jaigarh** Fort offers incredible vistas over the hills and plains below. The fort was built in 1600, though as the Kachchwahas were on friendly terms with the Mughals, it saw few battles. At the centre of the fort, a small **museum** has the usual old maps and photographs, plus a selection of cannons dating back to 1588. None of them, however, can hold a candle to the immense **Jaivana** cannon, the largest in Asia, which sits in solitary splendour at the highest point of the fort, five minutes' walk beyond the museum. Needing one hundred kilos of gunpowder for a single shot, the Jaivana could supposedly hurl a cannonball 35km – though its true military value was never gauged since it was never fired in battle.

ARRIVAL AND INFORMATION   AMBER

It's a 15min uphill walk from the tourist office to the palace. encouraged.

Alternatively, you could rent a jeep; they hang out along the **By bus** You can pick up the #AC1 at Ajmeri Gate, Sanganeri main road and around the tourist office and charge ₹400 Gate or by the Hawa Mahal as it heads up to Amber (around for the return trip, including 1hr 30min waiting time. A 40min in moderate traffic; around ₹25).

fair number of tourists waddle up on an elephant, though **By auto-rickshaw** An auto from Jaipur will cost around given their treatment during "training", this cannot be ₹400 return, including a couple of hours' waiting time.

Samode

Palace entry ₹1000 for non-guests, redeemable against food and drink inside

Hidden among the Aravalli Hills 42km northwest of Jaipur, **SAMODE** is notable for its impeccably restored eighteenth-century **palace**, now an award-winning heritage hotel, the *Samode Palace* (non-guests have to pay to visit). Some three hundred steps lead up from the palace to a hilltop **fort**, with panoramic views.

ARRIVAL AND ACCOMMODATION   SAMODE

By bus and taxi Local buses to Samode depart Jaipur's Uncompromisingly romantic rooms covered with murals main bus station (Sindhi Camp) between 5am and 10pm and filled with antiques. It's popular with groups, but (every 30min; 2hr). Taxis (1hr) cost from ₹2800, including the lovely rooftop pool and Indian fusion restaurant is for waiting time. independent travellers only. Rates drop by 30 percent May–

★ **Samode Palace** ☎ 01423 240014, ⓦ samode.com. Sept. ₹29,000

Sanganer

SANGANER, 16km south of Jaipur, is the busiest centre for handmade **textiles** in the region, and the best place to watch traditional block printers in action. There are a couple of large factories here, but most of the printing is done as a cottage industry in family homes. The town itself has ruined palaces and a handful of elegant Jain **temples**, including the Shri Digamber temple near Tripolia Gate.

2

ARRIVAL AND DEPARTURE   SANGANER

By bus Government buses and minibuses to Sanganer from   or you can catch government bus #3A from Ajmeri Gate.
Jaipur run from Chand Pole via Ajmer Rd (every 15min; 1hr),

Tonk

Long seen as little more than a rest-stop between Jaipur and Bundi or Udaipur – indeed, the name of the *Midway* restaurant on Highway 12 bears witness to the main reason the city is on the tourist radar at all – the city of **TONK** nonetheless has more than enough to warrant stopping for a look around. As well as the large **Jama Masjid**, it's also a good starting point to discover the nearby Bisalpur Dam, gorgeous step-wells at Hadi Rani Kund, and the Govinddeoji Temple near the Dhakar Colony. The city has also found fame on account of being home to the largest hand-written *quran shareef* in the world, which is an impressive 125 inches long and 90 inches wide and contains 64 pages, each with 41 lines of immacualtely written text. Unfortunately, it's rarely put on display.

Jama Masjid
Moti Bagh Rd • Daily sunrise–sunset • Free

In the southern part of town, the beautiful **Jama Masjid** is one of the larger mosques in India, with *meenakari* – a metal-colouring decoration process – adorning the walls. The construction of the mosque dates back to 1246 when Amir Khan, the first Nawab of Tonk, started the project, which was later completed in 1298 by his son, Nawab Wazirudhoula.

ARRIVAL AND DEPARTURE   TONK

By bus Government buses (some non-a/c) run four times   A large number of buses between Jaipur and Bundi/Kota
daily from Jaipur's Durgapura bus stand and take two hours.   also stop off at Tonk.

Ajmer and around

The Nag Pahar ("Snake Mountain"), a steeply shelving spur of the Aravallis west of Jaipur, forms an appropriately epic backdrop for **AJMER**, home of the great Sufi saint **Khwaja Muin-ud-din Chishti**, who founded the Chishtiya Sufi order. His tomb, the **Dargah Khwaja Sahib**, remains one of the most important Islamic shrines in the world. The streams of pilgrims and dervishes (it is believed that seven visits here are the equivalent of one to Mecca) especially pick up during Muharram (Muslim New Year) and Eid, and for the saint's anniversary day, or **Urs Mela** (see page 151).

Although Ajmer's dusty modern roads are choked with traffic, the narrow lanes of the bazaars around the **Dargah Khwaja Sahib** retain an almost medieval character, especially around Naya Bazaar, home to lines of rose-petal stalls and shops selling prayer mats, beads, perfumes and lengths of gold-edged green silk offerings. Finely arched Mughal gateways still stand at the main entrances to the **old city**, whose skyscape of mosque minarets and domes is overlooked from on high by the crumbling **Taragarh** – for centuries India's most strategically important fortress.

While most of Rajasthan consisted of princely states, Ajmer fell under British rule, and colonial-era relics can be found scattered across the city, among them the **Jubilee**

clock tower opposite the railway station. The famous **Mayo College**, originally built as a school for princes and now a leading educational institution, is known in society circles as the "Eton of the East".

For Hindu pilgrims and foreign travellers, Ajmer is important primarily as a jumping-off place for **Pushkar**, a twenty-minute cab ride away, and most stay only for as long as it takes to catch transport out. As a day-trip from Pushkar, however, it's a highly worthwhile excursion, and as a stronghold of Islam, Ajmer is unique in Hindu-dominated Rajasthan.

Brief history

A fort was first established at Ajmer in the tenth century by local Rajput chieftain Ajay Pal Chauhan, whose clan, the Chauhans, went on to become the dominant power in eastern Rajasthan until they were beaten in 1193 by Muhammad of Ghor (see page 1177). The Delhi sultans allowed the Chauhans to carry on ruling as their tributaries, but in 1365, with Delhi on the wane as a regional power, Ajmer fell to the kingdom of Mewar (Udaipur).

During the sixteenth century, the city became the object of rivalry between Mewar and the neighbouring kingdom of Marwar (Jodhpur). The Marwaris took it in 1532, but the presence of Khwaja Muin-ud-din Chishti's *dargah* made Ajmer an important prize for the Muslim Mughals, and Akbar's forces marched in just 27 years later.

The Mughals held onto Ajmer for more than two centuries, but as their empire began to fragment, the neighbouring Rajput kingdoms once again started giving the city covetous looks. It was eventually taken in 1770 by the Marathas, who subsequently sold the city to the East India Company for ₹50,000 in 1818. Thus, while most of Hindu-dominated Rajasthan retained internal independence during the Raj, Ajmer was a little Muslim enclave of directly ruled British territory, only reunited with Jodhpur and Udaipur, its former overlords, when it became part of Rajasthan in 1956.

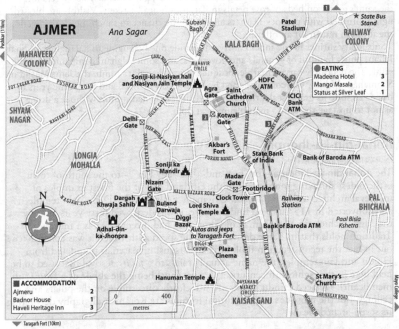

Dargah Khwaja Sahib

Dargah Bazaar • Daily 5am–midnight; tomb closed Fri–Wed 3–4pm, Thurs closed 2.30–3.30pm • *Qawwali* recitations from an hour or so before sunset–9pm • ⊕ dargahajmer.com

Housing the tomb of the revered Sufi saint, Khwaja Muin-ud-din Chishti, the **Dargah Khwaja Sahib**, or Dargah Sharif, is the most important Muslim shrine in India, attracting thousands of pilgrims each day. Founded in the thirteenth century, the *dargah* contains structures financed by many Muslim rulers, particularly the three great Mughals – Shah Jahan, Jahangir and, especially, Akbar, who came to the *dargah* to pray for a male heir and rewarded it with a new mosque when his wish was granted.

You enter the complex through the lofty **Nizam Gate**, donated by the nizam of Hyderabad in 1911. Once inside, you may be accosted by stern-looking young men claiming they are "official guides". In fact, they are *khadims*, hereditary priests who lead pilgrims through rituals in the *dargah* in exchange for donations. Their services are not compulsory, whatever they may say.

Beyond the Nizam Gate lies the smaller **Shajahani Gate**, commissioned by Shah Jahan. Carry on through this to reach a courtyard, from where steps lead up on the right to the **Akbari Masjid (Akbar's Mosque)**, built by a grateful Akbar following the birth of his son Salim, the future emperor Jahangir.

Just beyond the Shajahani Gate is a third gateway: the imposing, blue-and-green **Buland Darwaza**. After passing through it, you'll see, resting on raised platforms on either side, two immense cauldrons, known as **degs**, into which pilgrims throw money to be shared among the poor. The larger of the two, on the right, was donated by Akbar in 1567; the other was a gift from Jahangir upon his accession in 1605.

Beyond the *khanas* is an inner courtyard where the tomb of Khwaja Sahib lies inside the **Mazar Sharif**, a domed mausoleum made of marble. Nightly recitations of *qawwali* are held in the courtyard here, an exuberant form of religious singing, accompanied by harmonium and drums, which aims to lull the participants into a trance-like state called *mast*. The **tomb** inside is surrounded by silver railings and surmounted by a large gilt dome. Devotees file past carrying brilliant *chadars*, gilt-brocaded silk covers for the saint's grave, on beds of rose petals in flat, round head-baskets. Visitors are blessed, lightly brushed with peacock feathers and given the chance to touch the cloth covering the tomb in return for an offering.

Subsidiary shrines in the inner courtyard include one belonging to a daughter of Shah Jahan, plus a handful of generals and governors, and some Afghani companions of the saint. The delicately carved marble mosque behind the saint's tomb, the **Jama Masjid** or Shahjahani Masjid, was commissioned by Shah Jahan in 1628 and took nine years to build. Despite its grand scale, the emperor deliberately had it built without a dome so as not to upstage the saint's mausoleum next door.

Adhai-din-ka-Jhonpra

Andar Kot Rd • Daily dawn–dusk • Free

The **Adhai-din-ka-Jhonpra** – or "two-and-a-half-day hut" – to the south of town is the oldest surviving monument in the city, and one of the finest examples of medieval architecture in Rajasthan. Originally built in 660 AD as a Jain temple, and converted in 1153 into a Hindu college, it was destroyed forty years later by the Afghan chieftain Muhammad of Ghor, who had it renovated as a mosque. Tradition holds that its name derives from the speed with which it was constructed, but in fact the reconstruction took fifteen years, using materials plundered from Hindu and Jain temples; the name actually refers to a *fakirs'* festival that used to be held here in the eighteenth century, a *jhonpra* (hut) being the abode of a *fakir* (Sufi mendicant). Defaced Hindu motifs are still clearly discernible on the pillars and ceilings, but the mosque's most beautiful features are Koranic calligraphy decorating its seven-arched facade.

KHWAJA MUIN-UD-DIN CHISHTI AND THE URS MELA

Born in Afghanistan in 1156, **Khwaja Muin-ud-din Chishti**, India's most revered Muslim saint, began his religious career at the age of 13, when he distributed his inheritance among the poor and adopted the simple life of an itinerant Sufi *fakir* (the equivalent of the Hindu sadhu). On his travels, he soaked up the teachings of the great Central Asian Sufis, whose emphasis on mysticism, ecstatic states and pure devotion as a path to God were revolutionizing Islam during this period. Khwaja Sahib and his disciples settled in Ajmer at the beginning of the thirteenth century. Withdrawing into a life of meditation and fasting, he preached a message of renunciation, affirming that personal experience of God was attainable to anyone who relinquished their ties to the world. More radically, he also insisted on the fundamental **unity of all religions**: mosques and temples, he asserted, were merely material manifestations of a single divinity. Khwaja Sahib thus became one of the first religious figures to bridge the gap between India's two great faiths. After he died at the age of 97, his followers lauded the Bhagavad Gita as a sacred text, and even encouraged Hindu devotees to pray using names of God familiar to them, equating Ram with "Rahman", the Merciful Aspect of Allah – a spirit of acceptance which explains why **Khwaja Sahib's shrine** in Ajmer continues to be loved by adherents of all faiths.

The anniversary of Khwaja Sahib's death is celebrated with the **Urs Mela**, one of Rajasthan's most important religious festivals, held on the sixth day of the Islamic month of Rajab (around April). Pilgrims flock to the town to honour the saint with *qawwali* (Sufi devotional) chanting, while *kheer* (rice pudding) is cooked in huge vats at the *dargah* and distributed to visitors. At night religious gatherings called *mehfils* are held. It isn't really an affair for non-religious tourists, but the city does take on a festive air, with devotees from across the Subcontinent and beyond converging on Ajmer for the week leading up to it.

Akbar's Fort

Museum Rd; access is from western side of complex • **Museum** Tues–Sun noon–8pm • ₹100 (₹20)

The small but attractive **Akbar's Fort** encloses a rectangular pavilion made of golden sandstone; here, in 1616, Akbar's son Jahangir received Sir Thomas Roe, the first British ambassador to be granted an official audience, after four years of trailing between the emperor's encampments. Today, the old palace houses a small **museum**, displaying mainly Hindu and Jain statues.

Nasiyan Jain Temple

Prithivi Raj Marg • Daily 9am–5pm • ₹10, plus ₹1 for footwear stowage outside

Perhaps the most bizarre sight in Ajmer is the mirrored **Soniji-ki-Nasiya** hall adjoining the **Nasiyan Jain Temple**, or "Red Temple", in the heart of town. Commissioned in the 1820s by an Ajmeri diamond magnate, the Swarna Nagari "City of Gold" hall on the upper level contains a huge diorama-style display commemorating the life of Rishabha (or Adinath), the first Jain *tirthankara*. The glowing tableau, containing a tonne of gold, features a huge procession of soldiers and elephants carrying the infant *tirthankara* from Ayodhya to Mount Sumeru to be blessed, while musicians and deities fly overhead.

Ana Sagar

Laid out in the twelfth century, the artificial lake northwest of Ajmer known as **Ana Sagar** is worth a visit to see the exquisite marble pavilions called **baradaris**, or summer shelters, erected by Shah Jahan on the lake's eastern shore. Modelled on the Diwan-i-Am in Delhi's Red Fort, four of the five pavilions remain beautifully preserved, standing in the shade of trees and ornamental gardens laid out by Jahangir – particularly beautiful an hour before sunset.

2

RECOMMENDED TRAINS FROM AJMER

All the following trains run daily.

Destination	Name	No.	Departs	Arrives
Abu Road	*Yoga Express*	19032	6.50am	11.40am
	Aravali Express	19708	11.10am	4.40pm
Agra Fort	*Ajmer–Agra Superfast*	22987	6am	12.20pm
	Sealdah Express	12988	12.45pm	6.55pm
Alwar	*Ranikhet Express*	15013	12.10pm	5pm
	Ajmer Shatabdi	12016	3.45pm	7.50pm
Delhi	*Ashram Express*	12915	2.30am	10.10am
	Ranikhet Express	15013	12.10pm	9.10pm
Jaipur	*Sealdah Express*	12988	12.45pm	2.45pm
	Ajmer Shatabdi	12016	3.45pm	5.45pm
Jodhpur	*Ranikhet Express*	15014	1.35pm	5.45pm
Udaipur	*Udaipur Daily Special*	19665	1.25am	6.35am
	Jaipur–Udaipur Express	12992	4.10pm	9.30pm

ARRIVAL AND DEPARTURE

By train Ajmer's railway station is on the main Delhi–Ahmedabad railway line and slap-bang in the centre of town. The reservations hall (daily 8am–10pm) is on the first floor of the south wing; get there early in the morning to avoid queues or shell out a little extra for a travel agent.

By bus The State Bus Stand (☎0145 242 9398) lies 2km to the northeast of the train station on the Jaipur Rd – an auto-rickshaw from here into town costs around ₹100. The majority of travellers

visit Ajmer on a day-trip from Pushkar, but note that buses to and from Pushkar don't travel through the centre of Ajmer en route to the bus stand. State buses to Pushkar (40min; ₹16) depart roughly every 15min until about 8.30pm, and afterwards hourly until dawn; deluxe buses operate to Jaipur (5 daily; 5hrs) and Delhi (4 daily; 10hr). Seats on private buses – many of which have connecting services from Pushkar – can be reserved at travel agents along Kutchery Rd towards Prithviraj Marg.

ACCOMMODATION

Ajmer's hotels aren't great value; you're better off staying in Pushkar and visiting from there. Accommodation also tends to get chock-full during the Urs Mela (see page 151).

Ajmeru Off Prithviraj Marg, just inside Kotwali Gate ☎0145 243 1103, ⓦhotelajmeru.com; map p.149. This comfortable hotel is one of the best-value places to stay in town, with bright and well-kept fan, air-cooled and a/c rooms with attached bathrooms and cable TV. 24hr check-out. **₹1000**

Badnor House New Civil Lines, near RTDC Hotel Khadim ☎0145 262 7579, ⓦbadnorhouse.com; map p.149. Tucked into a residential area, this friendly homestay offers

clean modern rooms in a block away from the owner's house, all with a/c, attached bathrooms and TVs. **₹3000**

★ Haveli Heritage Inn Kutchery Rd, Phul Nawas ☎0145 262 1607, ⓦhaveliheritageinn.com; map p.149. In a house from the 1870s that was once used as the state HQ of the Indian Congress Party – Nehru and Gandhi both stayed here (in Room 2). It actually sounds grander than it is, but if you think of this as a pension rather than a haveli, you'll get the right idea – the big attractions are the peaceful atmosphere and the delightful family that runs it. Rooms (air-cooled and a/c) are bright, spacious and attractively furnished, and there's great home-cooking. **₹1450**

EATING

Note that none of the following serves alcohol; if you want a **drink**, find a local bottle shop.

Madeena Hotel Station Rd; map p.149. Muslim establishment serving tasty non-veg Mughlai curries, mostly involving "mutton" (ie goat), in the form of korma, *keema*, masala or biryani, in full or half portions (from ₹120) with freshly baked tandoori breads. There are also chicken, egg and veg options. Daily 9am–11pm.

★ Mango Masala Sardar Patel Marg ☎0145 242 2100, ⓦmangomasala.com; map p.149. Popular, rambling, studenty place serving all sorts, including meals like pizzas,

veg burgers and salads (₹90–200), shakes, sundaes and ice-cream sodas (₹150 or so), average coffee, and pastries like tasty little lemon tarts (₹30). Daily 11am–11pm.

Status at Silver Leaf Embassy Hotel, Jaipur Rd; map p.149. Tucked under street level, this sedate veg restaurant has tried its hardest to look plush, though it's usually quite empty. The food's good, though, with a big selection of curries (most around ₹180–350); the paneer *tufani*–a creamy number served on a hotplate–is highly recommended. Chinese and Italian dishes also available. Daily 8am–11pm.

Taragarh Fort

Daily sunrise–sunset • Free • 90min hike from Ajmer • Autos (around ₹550 return) and jeeps (₹100) leave from near Plaza Cinema on Diggi Chowk, west of the train station

Three kilometres to the southwest of Ajmer, and just visible on the ridge high above the city, **Taragarh** (the Star Fort) was for two thousand years the most important strategic objective for invading armies in northwest India. Any ruler who successfully breached its walls, rising from a ring of forbidding escarpments, effectively controlled the region's trade. The fort is now badly ruined but is still visited in large numbers by pilgrims, who come to pay their respects at what must be one of the few shrines in the world devoted to a tax inspector. The **Dargah of Miran Sayeed Hussein Khangsawar** honours Muhammad of Ghor's chief revenue collector, slain in the Rajput attack of 1202 when, following one of the fort's rare defeats, the entire Muslim population of the fort was put to the sword.

The best way of getting to Taragarh is to trek along the ancient paved pathway from Ajmer, with superb views across the plains and neighbouring hills; to pick up the trailhead, follow the lane behind the Dargah Khwaja Sahib, past the Adhai-din-ka-Jhonpra and on towards the saddle in the ridge visible to the south.

Pushkar

Relaxed little **PUSHKAR**, 15km northwest of Ajmer, has become one of Rajasthan's prime chill-out spots – small enough to minimalise that Indian city stress, yet with plenty to see and do (and, importantly, eat), travellers of a certain persuasion – typically young, hippie-ish types, mainly from France, Italy and Israel – often end up

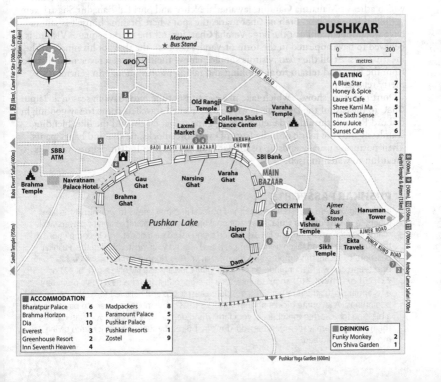

PUSHKAR

0   200
metres

● EATING

A Blue Star	7
Honey & Spice	2
Laura's Cafe	4
Shree Karni Ma	5
The Sixth Sense	1
Sonu Juice	3
Sunset Café	6

■ ACCOMMODATION

Bharatpur Palace	6	Madpackers	8
Brahma Horizon	11	Paramount Palace	5
Dia	10	Pushkar Palace	7
Everest	3	Pushkar Resorts	1
Greenhouse Resort	2	Zostel	9
Inn Seventh Heaven	4		

■ DRINKING

| Funky Monkey | 2 |
| Om Shiva Garden | 1 |

2

staying here for a week or more. Everything centres around the holy **lake**, surrounded by whitewashed temples and bathing *ghats*, and revered as one of India's most sacred sites: Pushkaraj Maharaj, literally "Pushkar King of Kings". There are also more than five hundred **temples** in and around Pushkar, although some, like the splendid **Vishnu Temple**, are out of bounds to non-Hindus; sat atop a hill southwest of town, **Savitri Temple** is of little historical or architectural importance, but makes a popular visit for its wonderful views out over the parched landscape.

According to legend, Pushkar came into existence when Lord Brahma, the Creator, dropped a lotus flower (*pushpa*) to earth from his hand (*kar*). At the three spots where the petals landed, water magically appeared in the midst of the desert to form three small blue lakes, and it was on the banks of the largest of these that Brahma subsequently convened a gathering of some 900,000 celestial beings – the entire Hindu pantheon. During the auspicious full-moon phase of October/November (the anniversary of the gods' mass meeting, or *yagya*), its waters are believed to cleanse the soul of all impurities, drawing pilgrims from all over the country. Alongside this annual religious festival, Rajasthani villagers also buy and sell livestock at what has become the largest **camel market** (*unt mela*) in the world, when more than 150,000 dealers, tourists and traders fill the dunes west of the lake.

The lake and ghats

Daily 24hr • Free • No footwear, smoking or photography allowed near ghats

Everything in Pushkar revolves around the **lake**. Five hundred beautiful whitewashed temples encircle the lake, connected to the water by 52 *ghats* – one for each of Rajasthan's maharajas, who built separate guesthouses in which to stay during their visits here. Primary among the *ghats* is **Gau Ghat**, sometimes called Main Ghat, from which ashes of Mahatma Gandhi, Jawaharlal Nehru and Shri Lal Bahadur Shastri were sprinkled into the lake. **Brahma Ghat** marks the spot where Brahma himself is said to have worshipped, while at the large **Varaha Ghat**, just off the market square, Vishnu is believed to have appeared in the form of Varaha (a boar), the third of his nine earthly incarnations. At all the *ghats*, visitors should remove their shoes at a reverential distance from the lake, and refrain from smoking and taking photos, though in general it's pretty relaxed.

Don't miss the "shows", which take place at sunset time most days in season at **Jaipur Ghat**, to the east of the lake; this is where free-spirited travellers come to say goodnight to Lord Ra with the aid of dancing, fire juggling, yoga, tai chi and the like, blending seamlessly into the fabric of India (sort of) with dreadlocks, tie-dye and baggy pants. Their posturing usually ends up of immense amusement to Indian visitors, which is great fun to watch in itself.

PUSHKAR PASSPORTS

Indian and Western tourists alike are urged by local Brahmin priests to worship at the lake; that is, to make **Pushkar Puja**. This traditional ritual involves the repetition of prayers while scattering rose petals into the lake, and then being asked for a donation. On completion of the puja, a red thread taken from a temple is tied around your wrist. Labelled the "Pushkar passport" by locals, this simple token means that you'll no longer attract pushy Pushkar priests and can wander unhindered onto the *ghats*. Indians usually give a sum of ₹21 or ₹31; ₹51 or, at most, ₹101 should suffice for a foreign tourist. (Hindus never give monetary gifts ending in "0"; the number "1" is considered auspicious and believed to symbolize new beginnings.) A favourite trick of phoney priests is to ask how much you want to pay, then say a blessing for assorted members of your family, and demand the amount you stated times the number of family members blessed; don't be bullied by such cheap tricks into giving any more than you agreed.

BRAHMA, SAVITRI AND GAYITRI

Although **Brahma**, the Creator, is one of the trinity of top Hindu gods, along with Vishnu (the Preserver) and Shiva (the Destroyer), his importance has dwindled since Vedic times and he has nothing like the following of the other two. The story behind his temple here in Pushkar serves to explain why this is so, and also reveals the significance of the temples here named after Brahma's wives, **Savitri** and **Gayitri**.

The story goes that Lord Brahma was to marry Savitri, a river goddess, at a sacrificial ritual called a *yagna*, which had to be performed at a specific, astrologically auspicious moment. But Savitri, busy dressing for the ceremony, failed to show up on time. Without a wife, the Creator could not perform the *yagna* at the right moment, so he had to find another consort quickly. The only unmarried woman available was a shepherdess of the untouchable Gujar caste named Gayitri, whom the gods hastily purified by passing her through the mouth of a cow (*gaya* means "cow", and *tri*, "passed through"). When Savitri finally arrived, she was furious that Brahma had married someone else and cursed him, saying that henceforth he would be worshipped only at Pushkar. She also proclaimed that the Gujar caste would gain liberation after death only if their ashes were scattered on Pushkar lake – a belief that has persisted to this day. After casting her curses, disgruntled Savitri flew off to the highest hill above the town. To placate her, it was agreed that she should have her temple on that hilltop, while Gayitri occupied the lower hill on the opposite, eastern side of the lake, and that Savitri would always be worshipped before Gayitri, which is exactly how pilgrims do it, visiting Savitri's temple first, and Gayitri's temple afterwards.

Brahma Temple

Daily 5am–1.30pm & 3pm–6pm • Free, bar small fee for footwear stowage outside

Pushkar's most important shrine, the **Brahma Temple**, houses a four-headed image of Brahma in its main sanctuary, and is one of the few temples in India devoted to him. Raised on a platform in the centre of a courtyard, the inevitably crowded chamber is surrounded on three sides by smaller subsidiary shrines topped with flat roofs providing views across the desert.

Savitri Temple

Daily 24hr • Free • Cable car 6am–7.30pm, ₹97 return

On the other side of town to the Brahma Temple, **Savitri Temple** sits on the summit of a nearby hill. The half-hour pant to the top (cable cars also available) is rewarded by matchless vistas over the town, surrounded on all sides by desert, and is best done before dawn, to reach the summit for sunrise, though it's also a great spot to watch the sun set. The temple itself is modern, but the image of Savitri is thought to date back to the seventh century.

ARRIVAL AND GETTING AROUND   PUSHKAR

By train Pushkar's railway station is to the northeast of town. The service running between Pushkar and Ajmer (daily bar Tues & Fri; 45min) is more of a tourist train; it departs Ajmer at 9.50am, and Pushkar at 4.15pm. For all other destinations, you need to take a train from Ajmer (see page 148).

By bus There are two bus stands; buses to Ajmer (every 15min or so; 40min) leave from the Ajmer Bus Stand in the east of town, while government and some private inter-city buses for destinations further afield leave from the Marwar Bus Stand (☎ 0145 242 9398), located to the north of town. Most of the latter also stop en route at Ajmer, which has

more connections, but it's not unknown for people who have bought tickets at agencies in Pushkar to find their seats double-booked when they try boarding in Ajmer; it's best to book in Ajmer itself. Lastly, some buses leave from outside private offices around Pushkar – basically, it's best to shop around.

Destinations from Marwar stand Bikaner (9 daily; 6hr 30min); Bundi (2 daily; 5hr); Delhi (2–4 daily, including overnight sleeper service; 10hr); Jaipur (2–4 daily; 3hr 30min); Jodhpur (1 daily plus 1 nightly; 6hr); Jaisalmer (2 nightly; 10hr).

By taxi Your accommodation will be able to call you a cab

2

to Ajmer, or book with an agency in town; expect to pay ₹300–500. Those same agencies advertise rates – very tempting if you're in a small group – to other destinations around Rajasthan, including Bundi (₹2600), Jaipur (₹1800), Jodhpur (₹2500) and Udaipur (₹3600).

Getting around There are very few cycle rickshaws and autos in Pushkar, so you'll probably have to walk to your hotel or hop on the back of a scooter. A number of

places around the Ajmer Bus Stand rent out scooters and motorbikes for around ₹300/day.

Travel agents EKTA Travels acts as Indian Railways' agent in Pushkar and can arrange tickets for train journeys out of any station in India for a ₹100 charge, and also handles bus and plane tickets. Their office is by the Ajmer bus stand (☎0145 277 2888).

ACCOMMODATION

Prices rise dramatically during the camel fair (see page 158), with increases of anything from two to five times the normal rate.

HOTELS

★ **Brahma Horizon** Off Panch Kund Rd ☎91161 09699, ⓦbrahmahorizon.com; map p.153. One of the town's newer options, this boutique hotel is rather wonderful – some of their supremely comfortable rooms face the pool, while after dark the others receive a snazzy not-too-distant-future pink glow from the lights outside. Staff are extremely well drilled, and rates include breakfast. ₹5800

Dia Next to Masters Paradise Resort, Panch Kund Rd ☎0145 277 2585, ⓦinn-seventh-heaven.com; map p.153. Gorgeous low-key sister-property to *Inn Seventh Heaven*; situated above the owner's home, the five attractively furnished rooms here feature breezy private balconies and terraces in a very peaceful location on the edge of town, around 500m from the Ajmer Bus Stand. ₹2400

Greenhouse Resort Kishanpura Rd, Tilore, about 8km from Pushkar ☎0145 230 0079, ⓦthegreenhouseresort. com; map p.153. A gorgeous eco-resort set in ten acres featuring twenty chic tents with attached bathrooms, pretty gardens, a huge pool, spa, licensed bar and an eco-styled restaurant. The resort's greenhouses supply the hotel with fresh veg, seasonal strawberries and roses. Packages available during the camel fair. ₹6000

★ **Inn Seventh Heaven** Chhoti Basti ☎0145 510 5455, ⓦinn-seventh-heaven.com; map p.153. Beautiful hotel in a 100-year-old haveli, mixing traditional and contemporary styles to memorable effect, with vine-draped balconies around a spacious interior courtyard and a range of beautifully furnished rooms. Rooms here really should cost a lot more than they do, and they've a decent restaurant (see page 157), as well as meditation sessions and massage options. ₹1350

Pushkar Palace Choti Basti ☎0145 277 3001, ⓦhotel pushkarpalace.com; map p.153. Attractive hotel occupying an old maharaja's palace in a plum position overlooking the lake. The place has lots of charm, with period-style rooms (most with lake views), a pretty courtyard and a rooftop restaurant, though one gets the

sense that the owners have rested on their laurels a tad. Rates include breakfast, but are exorbitant during the camel fair. ₹6000

Pushkar Resort Motisar Rd, Ganehra ☎0112 649 4531, ⓦsewara.com; map p.153. Tranquil resort, inconveniently situated 5km out of town in the desert, with forty a/c cottages in pristine gardens and a kidney-shaped pool. Their restaurant has a non-veg menu and an alcohol licence. Booking recommended. ₹4000

HOSTELS AND BUDGET HOTELS

Bharatpur Palace Main Bazaar ☎0145 277 2320, ⓔbharatpurpalace_pushkar@yahoo.co.in; map p.153. A bit basic and overpriced for what you get, but the location's wonderful, right on the lake, with views across the *ghats* from some rooms and delicious home-cooked meals. A couple of rooms have a/c; cheaper ones have shared bathrooms. ₹1200

★ **Everest** Near Main Gau (Ghandi Ghat) ☎0145 277 3417, ⓦpushkarhoteleverest.com; map p.153. Colourful, characterful guesthouse run by a friendly and knowledgeable family in a peaceful residential location above town. Rooms (all attached bathrooms, some a/c) are spotlessly clean, with modern bathrooms and a lovely rooftop restaurant. ₹600

★ **Madpackers** Off Panch Kund Rd ☎0145 277 3444; map p.153. Most of India's hostel chains have made a roost in Pushkar, and this is the best of the bunch, a beautifully decorated place with impactful haveli stylings – even the dorm rooms are gorgeous. It's *de rigueur* for guests to clamber up to the rooftop space for sunset. Rates include breakfast. Dorms ₹550, doubles ₹2400

Paramount Palace Bari Basti ☎0145 277 2428, ⓦpushkarparamount.com; map p.153. Relaxed guesthouse near the Brahma Temple with a mixed bag of rooms, all with fans and attached bathrooms. The upstairs rooms to the front with dusky pink balconies and stunning town views are lovely. Great rooftop restaurant. ₹500

Zostel Off Panch Kund Rd ☎011 3958 9004, ⓦzostel. com; map p.153. Above-average hostel which isn't quite as nice as Madpackers, on the same alley – then again, it's a bit cheaper, staff are perhaps better at organising special events, and with what may be the clincher for some, it does have a pool. Dorms ₹400, doubles ₹1800

RAJASTHAN'S ETHNIC MINORITIES

Like most Indian states, Rajasthan has a number of "tribal" peoples who live outside the social mainstream. Many are nomadic, and often called "Gypsies" – indeed the Romanies of Europe are thought to have originated among these Rajasthani Gypsy tribes. The most prominent are the **Kalbeliyas**, found largely in Pushkar. The Kalbeliyas discovered how to charm snakes, and they used to sing and dance for royalty, as they now do for tourists; but living on the margins of society, they suffer similar discriminations to their brethren in Europe.

The **Bhopas** are a green-eyed tribe of nomads who used to work as entertainers to the maharajas, and to this day they make a living as itinerant poets and storytellers. They are asked to perform particularly where someone is sick, as their songs are believed to aid recovery.

In the Jodhpur region, many tourists take an excursion into the countryside to visit the **Bishnoi** (see page 197), a religious rather than strictly ethnic group, whose tree-hugging beliefs chime with those of hippies in the West. Living in close proximity to them, though with a very different lifestyle, are the **Bhils**, great hunters who used to hire themselves out as soldiers in the armies of the Rajput kingdoms. They have their own language and religion, and their dances have become very popular, especially at Holi.

EATING

As Pushkar is sacred to Lord Brahma, all food within city limits is strictly veg: meat, eggs and alcohol are banned (at least, in theory). Pushkar's sweet speciality is **malpua**, which is basically a chapati fried in syrup, sold at sweetshops around town, and on Halwai Gali, the street directly opposite Gau Ghat.

A Blue Star Jammi Kund Rd ☎ 982 8355 263; map p.153. Peaceful painted restaurant on the outskirts of town serving good Israeli dishes such as falafel, hummus and aubergine pita wraps (around ₹140), plus shakshuka, toasted sandwiches and excellent wood-fired pizzas. Daily 9am–10pm.

★ **Honey & Spice** Laxmi Market, Main Bazaar ☎ 0145 510 55505; map p.153. Tucked into an alley, this is much more imaginative than your average Pushkar backpacker café, a simple-looking place with an eyebrow-raisingly creative health-food menu. Try one of their salad bowls (₹150–230), or "energising dishes" featuring ingredients such as brown rice, miso, yak cheese, tofu and shiitake mushrooms; gluten-free options are also available. For drinks, they've excellent cardamom coffee (₹80) or lassis made with saffron and almond, or fig, sesame and honey (all ₹85 or so). Daily 8am–6pm.

Laura's Cafe Main Bazaar ☎ 95291 05018; map p.153. Something a little different, this cafe-restaurant prides itself on Spanish food including paella and gazpacho, though oddly most customers opt for the pizzas and shakshukas they could have almost anywhere else in Pushkar. You'll pay ₹150–300 to fill up; lake views come free, and they sometimes (shhh!) have alcohol available. Daily 9am–11pm.

Shree Karni Ma Near Brahma Temple ☎ 98287 04942; map p.153. This is where a lot of Pushkar's Indian visitors come to eat, since it serves the best thalis (₹130–280) and veg curries in town. What's available depends on what vegetables are in season, but there's always a good selection. Daily 8am–10pm.

The Sixth Sense Inn Seventh Heaven, Chhoti Basti ☎ 0145 510 5455, ⓦ inn-seventh-heaven.com; map p.153. The stylish restaurant atop this lovely haveli (see page 156) has a carefully chosen range of Indian and Italian food made using fresh seasonal ingredients. Food is hauled up from ground level by pulley; have a go at a Rajasthani thali (₹350), or the interesting thali salads (₹250), which feature at least a dozen types of fruit and veg. Daily 8.30am–2.30pm & 6–10.30pm.

Sonu Juice Main Bazaar; map p.153. Almost every juice combination you can think of is sold at this little stall, along with great muesli (or even porridge with banana milk; ₹90), so it makes a great spot for breakfast. Small juices and shakes start at ₹35, or splash out ₹140 on the monster including strawberry, banana, dates, coconut, muesli, cocoa and smashed-up Oreos. Daily 7am–9pm.

Sunset Café East side of lake ☎ 0145 277 2382; map p.153. The perfect place to enjoy Pushkar's legendary lakeside sunsets and accompanying "shows", with great views – though the outside seats fill up quickly towards dusk – and a selection of juices, lassis and shakes (₹70–200); most people, sensibly, avoid the meals. Daily 7.30am–midnight.

DRINKING

Despite Pushkar's sacred status, it's usually quite possible to find places surreptitiously serving alcohol – options are limited, you may not get to see a menu as such, and your drink may arrive wrapped in something or disguised as something else, but this all makes for a rather pleasing speakeasy atmosphere.

2

KARTIKA PURNIMA AND PUSHKAR CAMEL FAIR

Hindus visit Pushkar year-round to take a dip in the redemptory waters of the lake, but there's one particular day when bathing here is believed to relieve devotees of all their sins. That day is the full moon (*purnima*) of the **Kartika** month (usually Nov). During the five days leading up to and including the full moon, Pushkar hosts thousands of celebrating devotees, following prescribed rituals on the lakeside and in the Brahma Temple.

At the same time, a huge, week-long **camel fair** is held west of the town, with hordes of herders from all over Rajasthan gathering to parade, race and trade more than forty thousand animals. With the harvest safely in the bag and the surplus livestock sold, the villagers have a little money to spend enjoying themselves, which creates a light-hearted atmosphere that's generally absent from most other Rajasthani livestock fairs, backed up with entertainments including camel races, moustache competitions and a popular funfair, complete with an eye-catching sequence of enormous big wheels.

The popularity of Pushkar's fair, which now attracts three hundred thousand people annually, has – inevitably – had an effect on the event, with camera-toting package tourists now bumping elbows with the event's traditional pilgrims and camel traders. But while the commercialism can be off-putting, the festive environment and coming together of cultures does produce some spontaneous mirth: in 2004, the second prize in the moustache contest was won by a Mancunian and nowadays the winning 'taches are so long that it is not uncommon for competitors to arrive with their moustaches rolled up into buns and fixed to the side of their faces before unleashing them and whipping them around in the air like a lasso.

INFORMATION

When to go The festival is held each November; for specific dates, see ⓦ pushkarfestivals.com. It's best to get here for the first two or three days to see the *mela* in full swing; by the final few days of the festival most of the buying and selling has been done and the bulk of the herders have packed up and gone home. The day before the festival officially starts is also good – pretty much all the traders and livestock have arrived, but there are relatively few tourists around.

Booking accommodation It's best to book a room as far ahead as possible, though if you arrive early in the day – and prepared to hunt – securing accommodation shouldn't be a problem. If you get stuck, you could try the *RTDC Tourist Village* close to the fairgrounds – ask at the tourist office or check ⓦ rtdc.in.

★ **Funky Monkey** Jamni Kund Rd ⓣ 98298 73439, ⓦ funkymonkeycafe.in; map p.153. This place started life as a tiny café in town; it's still there, but their new garden venue is a simply enchanting place to be at night. Dimly lit, it's decorated with 70s-rock paintings and posters, though the soundtrack is usually more blissed out, even dipping into dream pop, such as the likes of Mazzy Star and Cigarettes After Sex. The food – pizzas, pasta and the like – is merely okay, but knowing smiles and winks from the staff suggest that more interesting things are on offer, often including strong mojitos and Cuba Libres (₹200). Daily 9am–1am.

Om Shiva Garden Choti Basti ⓣ 0145 277 2305; map p.153. The most brazen of the restaurants serving alcohol (they often even have a signboard indicating so outside); cocktails cost around ₹300, and cans of Kingfishers ₹160, though you'll need to keep a tissue wrapped around the latter. The food's pretty good, too, with pizza and curries the best options. The atmosphere is pleasant, with sand to scrunch your toes in, and fairy lights and Tibetan prayer flags overhead, but unfortunately staff often try to rush diners when there's demand for their table. Daily 8am–11pm.

SHOPPING

Though it isn't a craft centre as such, Pushkar is a good place to pick up touristy souvenirs, with its shops conveniently strung out along the Main Bazaar. As well as lots of hippie-type clothes, T-shirts, silver jewellery and Hindi music, not to mention ceramic chillums (Pushkar's rival those of Hampi and Puducherry in the south), you'll find *lac* bangles, Rajasthani textiles, incense, essential oils and – always handy for a paint fight – Holi dyes. For new and used books, there's a slew of shops on the Main Bazaar, just south of Varaha Chowk.

ACTIVITIES

Camel and horse rides A number of places arrange short camel rides in the area around town; try Ambay Camel Safari (ⓣ 94146 67148) opposite Brahma Palace, who offer trips for around ₹350/hr. For longer trips in the desert around Pushkar, including rides on hardy Marwari steeds, it's better to go with specialists such as Babu Desert

Safari (w babudesertsafaripushkar.com), who run full-day excursions for ₹800, and overnight jaunts for ₹1750.

Dance The Colleena Shakti Dance Center (w colleenashakti. com) in the old Rangji Temple runs intensive courses in Odissi dance (Jan–May), plus drop-in sessions covering a range of styles.

Yoga and meditation Experienced teachers run yoga and meditation courses (3–30 days), and twice-daily Hatha yoga sessions, at Pushkar Yoga Garden (t 98282 79835, w pushkaryoga.org), in a nice area out of town on Vamdev Rd, behind the Sikh *gurudwara*.

Shekhawati

Northwest of Jaipur, the land becomes increasingly arid and inhospitable, with farms and fields gradually giving way to wind-blown expanses of undulating semidesert dotted with endless *khejri* trees and isolated houses enclosed in stockades of thorn. Although now something of a backwater, this region, known as **Shekhawati**, once lay on an important caravan route connecting Delhi and Sind (now in Pakistan) with the Gujarati coast, before the rise of Bombay and Calcutta diverted the trans-Thar trade south and eastwards. Having grown rich on trade and taxes, Shekhawati's Marwari merchants and landowning *thakurs* spent their fortunes competing with one another to build the grand, ostentatiously decorated **havelis** that still line the streets of the region's dusty little towns – an incredible concentration of mansions, palaces and cenotaphs plastered inside and out with elaborate and colourful **murals**. Wandering the streets of many of its towns, the mind marvels at just how grand these remote-feeling outposts must have looked back in the day.

Considering the wealth of traditional art here, and the region's proximity to Jaipur, however, most of Shekhawati still feels surprisingly far off the tourist trail; foreigners who pass this way tend to be older Europeans on group tours, which is understandable since travelling independently here can be time-consuming, and the region forms a logical start or finish line to a wider trip around Rajasthan. If you're doing Shekhawati under your own steam, it's a good idea to base yourself in one of the nicer, better-connected towns – such as **Nawalgarh** or **Mandawa** – and fan out from there; group tours tend to chalk off haveli after haveli, which can quickly start to feel repetitive, but for many the real pleasure of Shekhawati lies not in visiting specific places of interest, but simply strolling around, taking in the highly distinctive atmosphere.

ARRIVAL AND GETTING AROUND

SHEKHAWATI

By bus and jeep Getting around is best done by road. Regular local buses, often overcrowded, connect Shekhawati's main towns, while jeeps also shuttle between towns and villages, picking up as many passengers as they can cram in.

By train At the time of writing, the only decent train access to the region is on Delhi–Bikaner services, some of which (5 daily) stop at Ratangarh and Churu; there are also two daily services heading from Delhi to Jhunjhunu and Nawalgarh. The line from Churu to Jaipur has been out of action for

---

VISITING SHEKHAWATI'S HAVELIS

A number of Shekhawati's havelis, traditional townhouses common to the region, have now been restored and opened as museums, particularly in Nawalgarh. Most, however, remain in a state of picturesque dilapidation and are still occupied by local families, while others have been abandoned, and are now empty apart from a solitary **chowkidar** (caretaker-cum-guard). Visitors are welcome to look around inside some havelis in return for a small tip (₹30–50 is sufficient), while others remain closed to outsiders. If in doubt, just stick your head in the front door and ask, but remember that you're effectively entering someone's private home, so never go inside without permission. Visiting times are usually between sunrise and sunset. Be aware of "guide touts", who accost you on the street with offers of haveli tours. They might take you to a haveli or two, but they are not licensed guides, and their sole objective is to get you to a shop that pays them commission.

some time, but will hopefully reassume service before too long.

On a tour The majority of foreign visitors to Shekhawati go with a tour of some kind; you can book these with Delhi-based agencies such as Intense India Tours (⊕ intenseindiatours. com), though many of the havelis listed in this section offer their own tours once you're there, including options in Nawalgarh (see page 162) and Mandawa (see page 166).

Nawalgarh

At the centre of Shekhawati, surrounded by desert and *khejri* scrub, the lively little market town of **NAWALGARH** makes – along with nearby Mandawa – the most convenient and congenial base for exploring the region, with a bumper crop of painted havelis and a picturesque bazaar, along with a decent range of accommodation.

Podar Haveli Museum

Rambilas Podar Rd • Daily: summer 8am–8pm; winter 8.30am–6.30pm • ₹100 (₹80), camera ₹30, video camera ₹50 • ⊕ 01594 225 446, ⊕ podarhavelimuseum.org

The logical place to start a tour of Nawalgarh is on the east side of town at the magnificent Anandi Lal Podar Haveli, which now houses the **Podar Haveli Museum**. Built in 1920, this is one of the few havelis in Shekhawati to have been restored to its original glory, and boasts the most vivid murals in town, including steam trains, soldiers drilling with rifles, and a clever 3D-like panel of a bull's head that transmogrifies into that of an elephant as you move from left to right. There's also a mildly diverting series of **exhibits** showcasing aspects of Rajasthani life, including musical instruments, turbans and traditional costumes, and one hall has some fun models of Rajasthan's most famous forts.

Kamal Morarka Haveli Museum

Naya Bazaar • Daily 8am–6pm • ₹70 (free)

A short walk to the north of the Dr Ramnath A. Podar Haveli Museum lies the fine **Kamal Morarka Haveli Museum**, decorated with murals of Shiva, Parvati, Krishna and Jesus, plus a *baithak* complete with a fine old hand-pulled fan (*punkah*). Directly opposite the Morarka Haveli lies the eye-catching **Krishna (Gher Ka) Mandir**, dating from the mid-eighteenth century, a florid mass of delicate chhatris.

Bhagton ki Choti Haveli

Near Podar Gate • Daily 8am–6pm • ₹70

About 200m east of the Morarka Haveli, the unrestored, 150-year-old **Bhagton ki Choti Haveli** has an unusually varied selection of murals including a European-style angel and Queen Victoria (over the arches by the right of the main door). On the left, a *trompe-l'oeil* picture shows seven women in the shape of an elephant, while other pictures show Europeans riding bicycles, along with a steamboat and a train.

The fort

At the heart of town, the **fort** (Bala Qila) has more or less vanished under a clutch of modern buildings huddled around a central courtyard that now hosts the town's colourful vegetable market. The dilapidated building on the far left-hand side of the courtyard (by the Bank of Baroda) boasts a magnificent, eerily echoing **Sheesh Mahal**, covered in mirrorwork, which once served as the dressing room of the maharani of Nawalgarh, its ceiling decorated with pictorial maps of Nawalgarh and Jaipur. You'll have to pay ₹20–30 to see the room; if no one's around, ask at the sweet factory on the opposite side of the courtyard.

Surajmal Chhauchharia Haveli

Near Nansa Gate • Daily 8am–6pm • ₹70

JAISALMER'S PATWA HAVELI, ALSO KNOWN AS PAT-WON-KI HAVELI

2

Havelis dot the streets south and southeast of the Nansa Gate, one of the quietest and most atmospheric parts of town. These include the **Surajmal Chhauchharia Haveli**, whose murals feature two small pictures of Europeans floating past in a hot-air balloon. The painter took some playful licence as to the mechanics involved, with the passengers keeping their balloons aloft by blowing into them through small pipes. The place is poorly signed and a little hard to find by yourself; ask around.

ARRIVAL AND DEPARTURE
NAWALGARH

By train The railway station is 2.5km west of the town centre. Trains link Nawalgarh with Jhunjhunu (2–4 daily; 45min), Sikar (2–4 daily; 45min) and Delhi (2 daily; 6–7hr), and there are erratic services to Bikaner and Jaipur.

By bus Nawalgarh's bus and jeep stand is 1.5km west of the main area of interest, around ₹100 by auto-rickshaw to the town's various hotels and guesthouses. Few buses start or finish here, so schedules are usually best guesses, and for

destinations like Jaipur (3hr 30min) and Delhi (6hr 30min) you might as well just stand on the road and flag down whatever passes; there are also buses to Ajmer (7 daily; 3hr 30min) and Jodhpur (4 daily; 6hr 30min). Local buses (all 1–2 hourly), including services to Fatehpur (1hr 30min), Mandawa (1hr 30min) and Jhunjhunu (1hr) leave from the bus stand just past Baori Gate on the northern edge of town.

GETTING AROUND AND INFORMATION

Getting around For trips around the region, you can either jump on and off cheap, cramped village-to-village jeeps or rent a vehicle through *Apani Dhani* (see below) or the *Rajesh Jangid Tourist Pension* (see below). Cycles can also be rented at both of these places for ₹50/day.

Tours The owners of the *Apani Dhani* and the *Rajesh Jangid Tourist Pension* run socially responsible tours of Shekhawati

including jeep tours of nearby towns and other places of interest (₹1900–2500); walking tours of Nawalgarh (₹350/person); and tours by camel cart (₹1500/3hr). The *Roop Niwas Kothi* hotel also offers horseriding jaunts on its stable of pure-bred Marwari steeds (₹1000/hr), as well as short camel rides (₹800/hr) and more extended horse and camel safaris (see ⓦroyalridingholidays.com).

ACCOMMODATION

★ **Apani Dhani Eco Lodge** Northwest edge of town ☎0159 422 2239, ⓦapanidhani.com; map p.162.

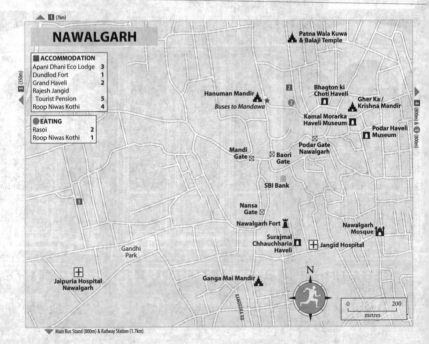

NAWALGARH

ACCOMMODATION
Apani Dhani Eco Lodge	3
Dundlod Fort	1
Grand Haveli	2
Rajesh Jangid Tourist Pension	5
Roop Niwas Kothi	4

EATING
Rasoi	2
Roop Niwas Kothi	1

Patna Wala Kuwa & Balaji Temple

Bhagton ki Choti Haveli

Gher Ka / Krishna Mandir

Hanuman Mandir

Buses to Mandawa

Kamal Morarka Haveli Museum

Podar Haveli Museum

Podar Gate Nawalgarh

Mandi Gate

Baori Gate

SBI Bank

Nansa Gate

Nawalgarh Fort

Nawalgarh Mosque

Surajmal Chhauchharia Haveli

Jangid Hospital

Gandhi Park

Jaipuria Hospital Nawalgarh

Ganga Mai Mandir

N

0   200
metres

Occupying a fetching cluster of mud-walled Rajasthani village-style huts (with clean attached bathrooms) dripping with bougainvillea, this eco-resort offers a perfect example of sustainable local tourism – 5% of room rates go to support environmental and educational projects, and local artisans earn some income through involvement in the resort's stimulating programme of craft and cultural activities. Guests share the premises with the owner's extended family, giving it the feel of a homestay, and rooms – especially those in the slightly more expensive superior category – have plenty of rustic charm. There's also excellent organic pure-veg food, with nearly all of the fresh produce plucked from the garden, as well as activities including tie-dye and cookery classes, plus tours (see above). No alcohol. Book ahead; you may find it locked otherwise. ₹1300

Grand Haveli Baori Gate ☎0159 422 5301, ⓦgrand haveli.com; map p.162. Occupying the beautifully restored, century-old Patnawalo ki Haveli, the individual rooms and suites here are a mixed bag; some feature *jharokas* and coloured frescoes, others are plain and poky – ask to see a couple first. Staff are not exactly on the ball here, and wi-fi is only available in the first courtyard (often full of mosquitoes), but there's a so-so licenced restaurant on site. ₹4000

Rajesh Jangid Tourist Pension On the western edge of town, just north of Maur Hospital ☎0159 422 4060, ⓦtouristpension.com; map p.162. Homely guesthouse offering simple but spotless and good-value rooms in a sociable Brahmin family home; all have solar-heated water and the most expensive boast beautiful murals. There's also excellent pure-veg food while activities include jeep tours (see above), Hindi classes and workshops in tie-dying, cooking and bangle-making. ₹1200

Roop Niwas Kothi 1km east of the town centre ☎0159 422 2008, ⓦroopniwaskothi.com; map p.162. This rambling Raj-era mansion has a certain faded elegance, old-fashioned rooms, a nice swimming pool and plenty of period charm at a fairly modest price. The restaurant's good, too (see below). ₹4500

OUT OF TOWN

Dundlod Fort Dundlod, 7km north of Nawalgarh ☎0159 425 2519, ⓦdundlod.com; map p.162. The tiny town of Dundlod is home to an old fort that has been turned into a heritage hotel; the rooms are a bit shabby and overpriced, though the public areas are atmospheric and it's a good place to organize horseriding tours (3–12 days) on one of the castle's thoroughbred mounts. ₹3500

EATING

There are very few decent places to eat in Nawalgarh, whose population mostly dines at home, or at the many, many puri stands dotted around the bazaar – there's a really good one just east of the Podar Gate (₹20).

Rasoi Just south of Grand Haveli ☎77260 00211; map p.162. At last, Nawalgarh has a proper restaurant! It's not bad, either, and popular with locals and domestic tourists, particularly at night, when fairy lights magic up the garden. Veg mains, including a lot of paneer choices, hover around the ₹300 mark; there are (oddly) Mexican dishes on the menu too, and cheap dosas (usually lunch only). Daily noon–9pm.

Roop Niwas Kothi 1km east of the town centre ☎0159 422 2008, ⓦroopniwaskothi.com; map p.162. Popular with passing coach parties as a post-sightseeing lunch stop, this elegant hotel (see above) has the most reliable restaurant in town, though sadly this isn't saying much. If a group's visiting, you can join the siege on the buffet counter (₹500), though there's an à la carte menu too. Daily noon–2.30pm & 7–9.30pm.

Parasrampura

Buses run to and from Nawalgarh (1–2 hourly; 1hr)

The serene hamlet of **PARASRAMPURA**, 20km southeast of Nawalgarh, is prettified by some of Shekhawati's oldest painted buildings. Monuments include the **Gopinath temple**, built in 1742, whose murals depict the torments of hell alongside images of the famous local Rajput ruler, Sardul Singh, with his five sons. Some of the paintings are unfinished, as the artists were diverted to decorate the chhatri of **Rajul Singh**, who died that same year. The large dome of this exquisite memorial contains a flourish of lively murals, once again including images of hell, and of Sardul Singh with his sons. Parasrampura's modest **fort** is on the west bank of the dry riverbed.

Jhunjhunu

Spreading in a mass of brick and concrete from the base of a rocky hill, Shekhawati's de facto capital of **JHUNJHUNU** is a busy and fairly unprepossessing town, though it preserves an interesting old central bazaar and a fine collection of painted havelis.

2

Jhunjhunu is usually visited as a day-trip from Nawalgarh or Mandawa, though it has a couple of decent accommodation options if you want to stay.

The large **Khetri Mahal** functions as the hub of tourist interest, and stretching east of the Khetri Mahal is Jhunjhunu's main bazaar, centred around **Futala Market**, a fascinating and hopelessly confusing tangle of narrow streets crammed with dozens of tiny, charmingly old-fashioned shops. Jhunjhunu's finest havelis are spread out along **Nehru Bazaar**, immediately east of the main bazaar.

Jhunjhunu is also a staging post for those on their way to the wonderful **Magnetic Fields festival**, which takes place in the nearby town of Alsisar each December (see page 131).

Khetri Mahal
West of Nehru Bazaar • Daily 10am–5pm • Free

Hidden away in the alleyways west of Nehru Bazaar is Jhunjhunu's most striking building, the magnificent **Khetri Mahal** of 1770, a superb, open-sided sandstone palace with cusped Islamic-style arches that wouldn't look out of place amid the great Indo-Islamic monuments of Fatehpur Sikri. The whole edifice seems incongruously grand amid the modest streets of central Jhunjhunu and is largely abandoned, save for the upper terraces that serve as impromptu open-air classrooms for local schoolchildren. A covered ramp, wide enough for horses, winds up to the roof, from where there are sweeping views over the town and across to the massive ramparts of the sturdy **Badalgarh Fort** (currently closed to the public) on a nearby hilltop.

Mohanlal Ishwardas Modi Haveli
North side of Nehru Bazaar • Daily 10am–5pm • ₹70

Further east down Nehru Bazaar, the **Mohanlal Ishwardas Modi Haveli** has a good selection of entertainingly naive portraits. Unusual oval miniatures of various Indian bigwigs frame the entrance to the zenana (women's courtyard), while in the zenana itself a long frieze of miniature portraits runs around the top of the arches showing assorted European and Indian personages sporting a range of flouncy costumes, silly hats and magnificent moustaches.

Bihari Ji Temple
South of Cloth Market Rd • Daily 6am–10pm • Free

To the northeast of Nehru Bazaar, the striking little **Bihari Ji Temple** features some of the oldest murals in Shekhawati, painted in 1776 in black and brown vegetable pigments, including a dramatic depiction inside the central dome of Hanuman's monkey army taking on the forces of the many-headed demon king Ravana.

Dargah of Kamaruddin Shah
West of Khetri Mahal • Daily sunrise–sunset • Free

At the foot of the craggy Nehara Pahar lies the **Dargah of Kamaruddin Shah**, an atmospheric complex comprising a mosque and madrasa arranged around a pretty courtyard (still retaining some of its original murals), with the ornate *dargah* (tomb) of the Sufi saint Kamaruddin Shah in the centre. Women must wear headscarves.

Mertani Baori
Near Pipli Circle • Daily 24hr • Free

North of the town centre lies the **Mertani Baori**, one of the region's most impressive step-wells. Constructed in 1783 by Mertani, the widow of Sardul Singh, this step-well is thought to be a staggering 30m deep.

Rani Sati Mandir
Off Rani Sati Rd • Daily 5am–1pm & 3–10.30pm • Free

To the northeast of town is the extraordinary **Rani Sati Mandir**, dedicated to a merchant's wife who committed sati in 1595. The shrine, with its enormous yet intricate facade, is reputedly the richest temple in the country after Tirupati in Andhra Pradesh – although similar claims are made for the Nathdwara temple (see page 214) – receiving hundreds of thousands of pilgrims each year and millions of rupees in donations. Its immense popularity bears witness to the enduring awe with which satis are regarded in the state.

ARRIVAL AND DEPARTURE

JHUNJHUNU | 2

By train The train station is around 1.5km southwest of the main bazaar, hosting services from Delhi (2 daily; 5hr 30min), Nawalgarh (2–4 daily; 45min) and Sikar (2–4 daily; 1hr 30min); as of mid-2019, there are no services to Bikaner or Jaipur, though these will be reintroduced in due course.
By bus The government bus stand (☎0159 223 2664) is just south of the town centre. There are frequent services to Nawalgarh (1–2 hourly; 1hr), Mandawa (every 45min; 45min–1hr) and towns throughout Shekhawati, as well as to Bikaner (4 daily; 5hr 30min), Jaipur (ever 30min; 4hr), Jodhpur (6 daily; 7hr), Ajmer (2 daily; 4hr) and Delhi (hourly, including a 9pm sleeper bus; 7hr).

GETTING AROUND AND INFORMATION

By rickshaw Jhunjhunu is quite spread out, and walking around can be tiring, but many of the streets of the old town are too narrow for cars; rickshaws operate as taxis, picking up as many passengers as they can.

Tours The *Jamuna Resort* offers full-day tours around Shekhawati by car or jeep for ₹2400, as well as shorter camel tours (2hr; ₹800/person) and three- to five-day cycling trips to local towns.

ACCOMMODATION

There are no good restaurants in town, and probably end up eating where you're staying.
Fresco Palace Paramveer Path, off Station Rd ☎0159 239 5233, ⊕hotelfrescopalace.com. Pleasant, modern hotel (although there aren't many frescoes in evidence), with comfortable, slightly chintzy rooms (all a/c) and a relaxing garden restaurant. ₹2500
Jamuna Resort Delhi–Sikar Rd ☎0159 223 2871. This village-style resort on the eastern edge of town comprises a cluster of thatch-roofed cottages (all a/c) set amid extensive grounds complete with pool and garden restaurant. The more expensive rooms are exquisitely decorated with mirrorwork and traditional murals. They also run courses in Indian cooking and art, plus free yoga classes. Also a good place to arrange tours (see above). ₹1000

Mandawa

Rising from a flat, featureless landscape roughly midway between Jhunjhunu and Fatehpur, **MANDAWA** was founded by the Shekhawats in 1755 and is now the most tourist-oriented place in Shekhawati, although the handicraft shops, touts and guides detract very little from the town's profusion of beautifully dilapidated mansions.

Naveti Haveli

Main Bazaar, now the SBI Bank • Daily 24hr (when gate unlocked) • Free

Tours usually begin with the **Naveti Haveli** on the main bazaar; it's now a bank, though the murals on its eastern side – you'll have to duck through a gate – are Mandawa's most entertaining, including well-preserved images of a bird-man attempting to take flight, the Wright Brothers' aeroplane, a man using a telephone and a strongman pulling a car. Excellent picture fodder.

Nand Lal Murmuria Haveli

West of Main Bazaar • Interior usually closed

A ten-minute walk west from here brings you to an interesting cluster of buildings centred around the **Nand Lal Murmuria Haveli**. The murals here are relatively modern, dating from the 1930s and executed in a decidedly flowery and sentimental style, perhaps influenced by contemporary European magazines, with images of various

Venetian scenes, George V, Nehru riding a horse and the legendary Maratha warrior Shivaji. Next door, the sun-faded **Goenka Double Haveli** (not to be confused with either of the other Goenka havelis nearby) is one of the largest and grandest in Mandawa, with two separate entrances and striking elephants and horses on the facade.

Gulab Rai Ladia Haveli

Southwest of fort, near Chobdar Haveli • Interior usually closed

The **Gulab Rai Ladia Haveli** is one of the finest in town. Its south-facing exterior wall is particularly interesting, with unusually racy (albeit modestly small) murals depicting, among other things, a Kama Sutra-like scene in a railway carriage. The interior of the haveli is entered via a grand ramp, with Belgian-glass mirrorwork over the finely carved door leading into the zenana (women's) courtyard.

Chokhani Double Haveli

South of Main Bazaar • Daily 9am–6pm • ₹50

A little south of town, the unusually large **Chokhani Double Haveli** (₹50) consists of two separate wings built for two brothers; look for the miserable British soldiers and chillum-smoking sadhu facing one another in the recess at the centre of the facade.

ARRIVAL AND INFORMATION   MANDAWA

By bus Buses from Jhunjhunu, Nawalgarh, Jaipur and Bikaner arrive at Subash Chowk, near Sonthaliya Gate in the east of town, except for the fast services that drop you at the highway junction (an auto into town should cost ₹70). From Fatehpur, most buses pull in at a stand in the centre, just off the main bazaar; both bus stands are within walking distance of most hotels. Jeeps ply the same routes from the same stands. There are frequent bus services to Jhunjhunu (every 30min; 1hr), Nawalgarh (every 30min; 45min) and Fatehpur (every 30min; 1hr), plus a handful of buses (mostly in the morning) to Jaipur (4hr), Bikaner (3hr 30min) and Delhi (6hr).

Tours Walking tours of Mandawa's havelis can be arranged through your hotel, from ₹200/person. Most guesthouses and hotels can also arrange trips out into the surrounding desert either by jeep or on horseback, on camel or in camel-drawn carts. Prices for all these activities vary wildly, but are usually cheapest if booked through *Shekhawati* hotel, who also rent bicycles for ₹50/hr. Classic Shekhawati Tours (☎01592 223144, ✉classicshekhamnd@yahoo.co.in), by the fort entrance, arranges more upmarket overnight tented camel safaris (₹5500), though you'll need to book a few days in advance.

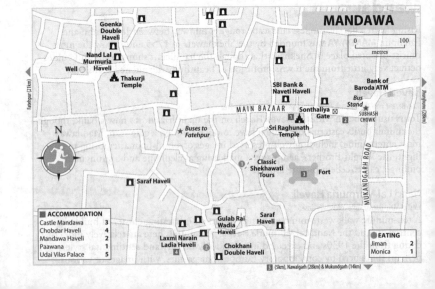

ACCOMMODATION

Castle Mandawa Inside the fort ☎0159 222 3124 or ☎0141 510 6081, ⊛castlemandawa.com; map p.166. Mandawa's fanciest accommodation, set in the old town fort, with an atmospheric mishmash of buildings around a sand-filled courtyard. All rooms are different – the Royal Suite is set in a turret – and so standards of comfort and decor vary. Amenities include a spa, gym, and an opulent pool surrounded by gardens. ₹6500

Chobdar Haveli Near Gulab Rai Wadia Haveli ☎93144 32690, ⊛hotelchobdarhaveli.com; map p.166. A dazzling white, late nineteenth-century, two-storey haveli in a quiet part of town with four spotless, colour-themed and well-furnished rooms (all a/c) featuring big beds and bright modern bathrooms with tubs. ₹4000

Mandawa Haveli Nr Sonthaliya Gate, Main Bazaar ☎0159 222 3088, ⊛hotelmandawahaveli.com; map p.166. Far and away Mandawa's most atmospheric heritage hotel, occupying a superb old haveli with original murals. Rooms are all a/c and have bags of period character, and there's a nice rooftop restaurant and garden. Rates discounted in summer by 20–40 percent. ₹2500

Paawana Main Bazaar ☎0159 222 3663, ⊛paawana haveli.com; map p.166. Modern building (done up with the obligatory murals) and offering attractively furnished a/c rooms at surprisingly affordable prices. There's a decent little mosaic-floor restaurant here, too, though it's basically only useful to in-house guests. ₹2800

Udai Vilas Palace Mukundgarh Rd, 5min drive south of Mandawa ☎94140 23378, ⊛uvpmandawa.com; map p.166. Upmarket resort hotel in a peaceful rural location, set amid three acres of landscaped grounds with fine desert views and accommodation in smart modern rooms. Facilities include a Keralan Ayurvedic spa, gym and pool. ₹5000

EATING

Jiman Shahi Palace, south of Main Bazaar ☎97853 69736, ⊛shahipalacemandawa.com; map p.166. Though a decent place to stay, the Shahi Palace is just outdone by rivals, in terms of its price range. However, its little restaurant makes a great pit-stop when you're touring the town (it's right opposite the Chokhani Double Haveli; see above), so pop in for a very yummy masala chai (₹40), or even a meal (veg and non-veg options ₹150–470). Daily 9am–9pm.

Monica West of the fort; map p.166. This rooftop restaurant (follow the signs from the entrance road to the fort) dishes up the best food in town, with well-prepared veg (mains ₹180–270) and non-veg (more like ₹350–450) Indian standards. It feels like home cooking, too, because as you'll notice on the way up, the place is patently a home. Daily 8am–10pm.

Fatehpur

Lying just off the NH-11 road, **FATEHPUR** is the closest town in Shekhawati to Bikaner, 116km west, and a convenient place to stop if you're taking the northern route across the Thar. The town itself is fairly scruffy and run-down, but it does have several elaborately painted mansions.

Le Prince Haveli

Near Chauhan Well, east of the town's main road • Daily 10am–7pm • ₹250 • ⊛leprincehaveli.com

Fatehpur's most celebrated muralled abode is the **Nadine Le Prince Haveli** near Chauhan Well, an 1802 mansion restored to its original splendour by its current owner, French artist Nadine Le Prince, who purchased the haveli in 1998 and has since opened it up as accommodation (see below). Some local aficionados complain about the manner in which the haveli has been restored – with large-scale repainting of murals, rather than the simple cleaning and preservation of existing art – but the overall effect is undeniably impressive, and the haveli as a whole is one of the few in Shekhawati where you get a real sense of how these lavish mansions would originally have looked.

Jagannath Singania Haveli

Churu–Sikar Road • Closed to visitors

Close to the Nadine Le Prince Haveli on Churu–Sikar Road, the imposing **Jagannath Singania Haveli** towers over the main road north. Most of the exterior paintings have faded; the best are on the western facade of the small building around the back, including Krishna and Radha framed by elephants and some heavily bewhiskered Europeans toting guns.

ARRIVAL AND DEPARTURE   FATEHPUR

By bus Fatehpur has two bus stands, near each other in the centre of town on the main Sikar–Churu (north–south) road. Buses from the government Roadways stand, furthest south, serve Jaipur (every 30min; 3hr 30min), Bikaner (every 30min; 3hr 30min–4hr) and Delhi (2 daily; 6hr). Private buses run from the stand further north along the bazaar to Mandawa (every 30min; 45min), Jhunjhunu (every 30min; 1hr), Mahansar (every 30min; 45min) and Ramgarh (every 30min; 30min). Arriving in Fatehpur, note that many buses stop at the NH-11 intersection, about 1km south of town.

ACCOMMODATION

★ **Le Prince Haveli** Near Chauhan Well ☎ 0157 123 3024. Before this delightful haveli (see above) opened up as accommodation, the only options in Fatehpur were awful; now it boasts one of Shekhawati's very best places to stay. It's a real beaut, with hints to its French ownership evident in the red-white-blue tricolore decoration. There are just over a dozen rooms, running the full gamut from tiny singles (₹1000) to opulent duplexes (₹6000), so it's made to suit any price range. There's an art studio and shop here, as well as a restaurant (mealtimes only), delightful pool and astonishingly well-stocked bar – when interns or regular guests arrive from overseas, they often bring a bottle of something with them. They're also able to organise tours by Royal Enfield; all in all, this is everything you could want from accommodation in this part of Rajasthan. **₹1800**

Mahansar

The relative inaccessibility of **MAHANSAR**, marooned amid a sea of scrub and drifting sand north of Mandawa, has ensured that its monuments remain among the least visited in the region, making the village a peaceful place to hole up for a day or two.

Sona ki Dukan Haveli

Centre of village • Daily, no set hours • Free, though tip expected • Ask around shops for the key

Otherwise known as the "Gold Shop Haveli", the **Sona ki Dukan Haveli** is home to Shekhawati's finest paintings. The murals in the entrance hall are the most striking, and depict the exploits of Rama, the incarnations of Vishnu and the life of Krishna, all painted in superb detail and picked out in lavish gold leaf (hence the haveli's name).

While you're here, it's also worth having a look at the nearby **Raghunath Mandir**, covered in colourful floral murals and offering good views over town from its chhatri-fringed rooftop.

ARRIVAL AND ACCOMMODATION   MAHANSAR

By bus or car Although driving is easily the best option, some daily services run to and from Nawalgarh (2hr 30min), Mandawa (1hr 30min) and Fatehpur (45min).
Narayan Niwas Castle Mahansar ☎ 0159 526 4322, ⓦ mehansarcastle.com. This quirky hotel, managed by Mahansar's royal family, is in a 1768 abode that's home to fourteen rooms of varying standards, including two memorably appointed heritage rooms, and some cheaper but still deeply atmospheric standard doubles (albeit stronger on period charm than creature comforts). **₹1600**

Ramgarh

RAMGARH, 20km north of Fatehpur, was founded in 1791 and developed as something of a status symbol by disaffected members of the wealthy Poddar merchant family, who made every effort for the town to outshine nearby Churu, which they left following a dispute with the local *thakur* over taxes. They succeeded in their aim: Ramgarh is one of the most beautiful – but also still one of the least-visited – towns in Shekhawati, with the usual fine havelis along with an exceptional array of religious architecture as well.

Starting from the bus stand on the west side of town, follow either of the two roads east into the town centre. After about five minutes' walk you'll reach the **Poddar family havelis**, which are close to the town's main square. Turn left here and head through the Churu Gate, beyond which the road is lined with a dense cluster of extraordinarily ornate temples and memorial chhatris erected by various members of the Poddar clan, their rooftops capped with a fantastical array of domes and arcades.

Poddar Family Havelis
Daily 8am–7pm • Free

The **Poddar family havelis** (daily 8am–7pm; free) are a superb cluster of ornate mansions decorated with scenes from local folk stories and a frequently repeated motif, comprising three fishes joined at the mouth, which is unique to Ramgarh. Just beyond here lies Ramgarh's main square, surrounded by the disintegrating remains of further lavishly painted havelis.

ARRIVAL AND ACCOMMODATION	RAMGARH
By jeep and bus Inter-village jeeps and buses run to Fatehpur (45min), Mandawa (1hr 30min) and Nawalgarh (2hr 30min) from the main Bissau–Ramgarh road. **By car** You can reach Ramgarh on day-trips from Fatehpur, Mandawa and Nawalgarh with your own vehicle, which is by far the quickest option. **Hotel Ramgarh Fresco** ☎ 0157 124 0595, ⚲ hotel	ramgarhfresco.com. A beautifully decorated haveli built around an open courtyard, this is the best option for accommodation in the town. There are fourteen nicely decorated rooms, and family-cooked meals (lunch ₹400, dinner ₹500) are served in the cute kitchen. The friendly owner also runs local walking tours. ₹2850

Lakshmangarh

The small town of **LAKSHMANGARH**, 20km south of Fatehpur, is another archetypal, but seldom visited, Shekhawati destination, its neat grid of streets (a layout inspired by that of Jaipur's Pink City) dotted with dozens of ornate havelis in various stages of picturesque decay. Lakshmangarh is dominated by its dramatic nineteenth-century **fort**, which crowns a rocky outcrop on the west side of town; it's now closed to the public, though you can walk up the steep track to the entrance to enjoy the fine views. Looking down from here you can see the extensive **Char Chowk Haveli** (Four-Courtyard Haveli), off to the left, the finest in town and one of the largest in Shekhawati.

ARRIVAL AND DEPARTURE	LAKSHMANGARH
By bus or car Numerous buses run from the station on Mukandgarh Rd to Fatehpur (45min), Sikar (1hr; where there's a train station), and Nawalgarh (1hr); you can also	reach Lakshmangarh on day-trips from these destinations with your own vehicle.

Churu

Twenty kilometres north of Ramgarh, at the northern tip of the Shekhawati region (and almost level with New Delhi), is the seldom-visited **CHURU**. Despite being largely overlooked by tourists, the city has plenty to offer, including the astonishing **Malji Ka Kamra**, a haveli with combined European Italian and Mughal architecture that was originally built by Marwari merchants and since renovated to its original turquoise colour. Around the corner is the **Surana Family Haveli**, also known as the **1100-window haveli**, built in the early 1870s, and in the main town square is the **clock tower**, built by the Lohia family in around 1890. Little remains of the old town fort except its legend: when, in 1813, the fort succumbed to a siege by the Raja of Bikaner, the occupier, Sheo Singh, killed himself by swallowing a diamond.

ARRIVAL AND ACCOMMODATION	CHURU
By train Churu is a stop on the main train line between Delhi (4–5 daily; 4–5hr) and Bikaner (5–7 daily; 2hr 30min–3hr 30min); the station is at the southern end of Nai Sarak, which runs through the middle of town.	**By bus** The main bus station is just outside the train station; services run to Jaipur (3 daily; 5hr), some stopping along the way at Fatehpur (1hr) and Sikar (2hr 30min). **Malji Ka Kamra** ☎ 0156 225 4514, ⚲ maljikakamra.

com. Easily the best accommodation and dining option in the city, this beautiful haveli has a number of attached rooms and suites (₹8000), all with air-conditioning and painstakingly restored murals, and some with enormous balconies looking out over the lawn and town beyond. There are walking tours of the town and cultural visits to wood-carving workshops, plus a non-veg Rajasthani cuisine restaurant. ₹5500

Bikaner and around

The bustling city of **BIKANER** has a decidedly frontier feel, perched as it is at the edge of the Thar, like a thirsty camel deciding whether or not to take the plunge and go all in. Dust swirls around this slightly overlarge place, getting into your mouth and hair, but though the city has little of the aesthetic magic of Jaisalmer, Jodhpur or Jaipur, it finds itself with a far more manageable number of tourists, and is worth a visit thanks to a number of worthy sights. Those just dropping by make a bee-line for the impressive **Junagarh Fort** and its brilliant museum; staying a night or two, however, will allow more freedom to explore the atmospheric **old city**, dotted with a rich array of quirky, early twentieth-century havelis, as well as making an expedition to a nearby **camel-breeding farm**, and the bizarrely fascinating, world-famous **rat temple** at Deshnok.

Junagarh Fort

Daily 10am–5.30pm (last entry 4.30pm) • ₹350 (₹50), camera ₹50, video camera ₹150 • Audioguide ₹350, though free English-speaking guides available • ☎ 0151 220 2297, ⓦ junagarh.org

Built at ground level and defended only by high walls and a wide moat, **Junagarh Fort** isn't as immediately imposing as the mighty hill forts elsewhere in Rajasthan, though its richly decorated interiors are as magnificent as any in the state. The fort was built between 1587 and 1593, and progressively enlarged and embellished by later rulers. For the tour, opt for the combined ticket that includes the audioguide, which is well-researched and insightful.

Entering the fort, look out for handprints set in stone near the second gate, **Daulat Pol**, which bear witness to the satis of various royal women. From here a passageway climbs up to the small Vikram Vilas courtyard, beyond which you'll find the main courtyard. Opening onto the main courtyard is the **Karan Mahal**, built in the seventeenth century to commemorate a victory over the Mughal emperor Aurangzeb and adorned with gold-leaf painting and an old *punkah* (fan). Next to here in the **Rai Niwas** are Maharaja Gai Singh's ivory slippers, one of Akbar's swords, and a representation of the Pisces zodiac sign which looks remarkably like a dinosaur in a headscarf.

Beyond here is the **Anup Mahal** (Diwan-i-Khas), the grandest room in the palace, with stunning red and gold filigree decorative painting and a red satin throne framed by an arc of glass and mirrors. The carpet was made by inmates of Bikaner jail – a manufacturing tradition that has only recently ceased. After such a hectic display of opulence, the blue **Badal Mahal** ("cloud palace"), built in the mid-nineteenth century for Maharaja Sardar Singh (1851–72), is pleasantly understated. Upstairs, a room exhibits beds of nails, sword blades and spear heads used by sadhus to demonstrate their immunity to pain; while across the terrace in the finely painted **Gaj Mandar** is the maharaja's chaste single bed and the maharani's more accommodating double.

The next part of the palace, the twentieth-century **Ganga Niwas**, created by Maharaja Ganga Singh (1887–1943), can be reached either via a long and labyrinthine passageway from the Gaj Mandar or, more directly, from the Vikram Vilas courtyard. This section of the palace is centred on the cavernous **Diwan-i-Am**, dominated by a World War I de Havilland biplane, a present from the British to Bikaner's state forces. The single aircraft is actually two half-planes, which were shot down during battle, then later fused together by the maharaja. Next door is the early twentieth-century office of Ganga Singh, followed by several further rooms stuffed full of guns and swords.

Prachina Museum

Junagarh Fort · Daily 9am–6pm · ₹100 (₹30), camera ₹50, video camera ₹150 · ⓦ prachinamuseum.org

Within the fort complex, the **Prachina Museum** houses a pretty collection of objects (glassware, crockery, cutlery and walking sticks) demonstrating the growing influence of Europe on Rajasthani style in the early twentieth century. A whole circa-1900 salon

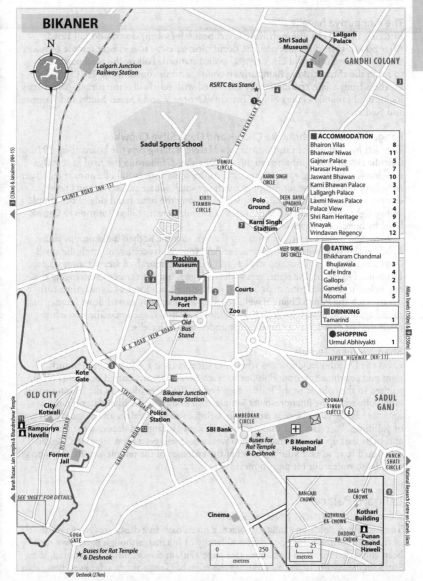

BIKANER

N

Lalgarh Junction
Railway Station

Shri Sadul
Museum

Lallgarh
Palace

GANDHI COLONY

RSRTC Bus Stand

Sadul Sports School

URMUL
CIRCLE

KARNI SINGH
CIRCLE

KIRTI
STAMBH
CIRCLE

DEEN DAYAL
UPADHYA
CIRCLE

Polo
Ground

Karni Singh
Stadium

VEER DURGA
DAS CIRCLE

Prachina
Museum

Junagarh
Fort

Courts

Old
Bus
Stand

Zoo

JAIPUR HIGHWAY (NH-11)

M G ROAD (KEM ROAD)

Kote
Gate

OLD CITY

City
Kotwali

STATION ROAD

Bikaner Junction
Railway Station

POONAN
SINGH
CIRCLE

SADUL
GANJ

Rampuriya
Havelis

Police
Station

AMBEDKAR
CIRCLE

OLD JAILROAD

GANGASHAR ROAD

SBI Bank

Buses for
Rat Temple
& Deshnok

P B Memorial
Hospital

PANCH
SHATI
CIRCLE

Former
Jail

SEE 'INSET' FOR DETAILS

RANGARI
CHOWK

DAGA-SITYA
CHOWK

KOTHRIAN
KA-CHOWK

Kothari
Building

Cinema

DADDHO
KA-CHOWK

Punan
Chand
Haweli

GOGA
GATE

Buses for Rat Temple
& Deshnok

0   250
metres

0   25
metres

Deshnok (27km)

ACCOMMODATION
Bhairon Vilas	8
Bhanwar Niwas	11
Gajner Palace	5
Harasar Haveli	7
Jaswant Bhawan	10
Karni Bhawan Palace	3
Lallgargh Palace	1
Laxmi Niwas Palace	2
Palace View	4
Shri Ram Heritage	9
Vinayak	6
Vrindavan Regency	12

EATING
Bhikharam Chandmal Bhujiawala	3
Cafe Indra	4
Gallops	2
Ganesha	1
Moomal	5

DRINKING
| Tamarind | 1 |

SHOPPING
| Urmul Abhivyakti | 1 |

S (32km) & Jaisalmer (NH-15)

GAJNER ROAD (NH-15)

Barah Bazaar, Jain Temples & Bhandreshwar Temple

Milan Travels (150m) & (550m)

National Research Centre on Camels (4km)

has been re-created, and there's also an interesting collection of Rajasthani textiles and clothing.

The old city

Bikaner's labyrinthine **old city** is notable for its profusion of unusual **havelis** whose idiosyncratic architecture demonstrates an unlikely fusion of indigenous sandstone carving with Art Nouveau and red-brick British municipal style. The city is confusing to navigate, so accept getting lost as part of the experience.

The Rampuriya havelis

Entering the old city through Kote Gate, bear left (south) down Old Jail Road. After 300m, turn right just past the florid pink gateway to a Hindu temple to reach the City Kotwali (the old city's central police station). Follow the road past here to reach the three striking **Rampuriya havelis**, commissioned in the 1920s by three brothers from a Jain trading family and faced with reliefs of a mixture of personages, including Maharaja Ganga Singh, Britain's George V and Queen Mary, and Krishna and Radha.

Rangari Chowk, Kothrion ka Chowk and Daga Sitya Chowk

Turn left just before the third Rampuriya Haveli, walking past the boarded-up 1918 **Golchha Haveli**, and continue roughly straight ahead, following the road as it makes two dog-legs to the right, to emerge after 100m onto a street full of ironmongers. Turn right here and continue for 300m to reach the small square called **Rangari Chowk**, centred on a neat white Hindu temple. Walk along the right-hand side of the temple and straight ahead you will see the small, triangular square called **Kothrion ka Chowk**, lined by handsome havelis.

Follow the road as it swings round to the left, past the **Kothari Building** (on your right), with five wonderfully extravagant Art Nouveau balconies, to reach the small **Daga Sitya Chowk**. A house on the left still has fading murals of steam trains, while Diamond House, on the right, gets wider as it goes up, each storey overhanging the one below it. Retrace your steps back to just before Kothrion ka Chowk, then turn left to reach the **Punan Chand Haveli**, boasting an amazingly carved floral facade. Turn round again and head back towards Kothrion ka Chowk, then take the first left to reach the large **Daddho ka Chowk**, surrounded by fine havelis.

Bhandreshwar Temple

Cross the Daddho ka Chowk to where the street ends at a T-junction, then turn right and continue for around 400m to reach **Barah Bazaar**, centred on a large pillar, painted in the colours of the Indian flag. Follow the street round to the left and you'll eventually reach the **Bhandreshwar Temple**; also known as the Bhandasar temple, it's unusual among Jain places of worship in being covered in a rich, almost gaudy, array of paintings. Porcelain tiles imported from Victorian England decorate the main altar, and steps lead up the unusually large tower, where you get a great view over the old city. You'll have to take your shoes off at the entrance of the temple and the steps up go outside, so watch out for pigeon mess.

Lallgarh Palace

Dr Karni Singhji Rd • ⓣ 0151 254 0201, ⓦ lallgarhpalace.com

The sturdy red-sandstone **Lallgarh Palace**, a green oasis in a dusty area to the north of the town centre, is home to the royal family of Bikaner, although parts have now been converted into a pair of hotels (see page 174), and its grounds also contain the **Shri Sadul Museum**. It was built during the reign of Ganga Singh, who lived here from

1902, and the sheer scale and profusion of the exterior decoration is impressive, even if it lacks the romantic allure of older Rajasthani palaces.

Shri Sadul Museum

Dr Karni Singhji Rd • Mon–Sat 10am–5.30pm • ₹50 (₹25), video camera ₹150

The **Shri Sadul Museum** houses an enormous and surprisingly engrossing collection of old photographs showing various viceregal visits, pictures of Ganga Singh at the signing of the Versailles Treaty and at royal processions, and plenty of awards, trophies and everyday royal possessions. At the start and end of the tour, there's also a full-size, beautifully preserved 1940s railway carriage to marvel at.

2

ARRIVAL AND INFORMATION

BIKANER AND AROUND

Bikaner is very spread out, with widely scattered accommodation. The RSRTC Bus Stand (☎0151 252 3800) is 1.5km north of town, near Lallgarh Palace; the old bus stand (used by some private buses) and railway station are both centrally located, although a few trains arrive at Lalgarh Junction, on the northwestern edge of town. An auto ride across town from the state bus stand to the railway station should cost ₹100 or less.

By plane Nal Airport (☎0151 254 0940) is located about 13km west of the city, and commenced flights in 2017, as part of Narendra Modi's airport-opening craze. There are currently flights to Delhi (1 daily; 1hr 10min) and Jaipur (1 daily; 1hr), with more potentially in the post; there's no bus service as yet, so you may have to grab a taxi (from ₹500).

By train The railway station, Bikaner Junction, is on Station Rd (☎0151 220 0131), just east of the old city. There are no direct trains to Ajmer, to which it's much easier to take the bus; to get to Jaisalmer, interchange at Jodhpur.

By bus Private buses are run by a handful of firms, most of which have offices at the Old Bus Stand on the south side of Junagarh Fort – shop around until you find a service that suits, or ask your accommodation to book tickets for you, usually for a small fee (₹100 or so). Most private services depart from outside these offices, though check when you book your ticket (there's also a newer private bus stand inconveniently located 5km north of town along the Ganganagar road; few operators use it, but you may well arrive there). The most comfortable long-distance buses are run by Milan Travels, west of town on Sadul Ganj (☎92142 01220), who also have several daily buses to Shekhawati; you could, alternatively, simply pay any agency for a ticket to Jaipur, and get off where appropriate.

Destinations Agra (3 daily; 12hr); Ajmer (7 daily; 6hr); Amritsar (1 daily; 15hr); Fatehpur (12 daily; 3hr); Delhi (6 daily; 8hr 30min–10hr); Jaipur (1–3 hourly; 5–7hr); Jaisalmer (2 daily; 7hr 45min); Jodhpur (1–2 hourly; 5hr); Phalodi (hourly; 3hr 30min); Pokaran (6 daily; 5hr); Udaipur (8 daily; 9–11hr).

ACTIVITIES AND INFORMATION

Bicycle rental Available for ₹60/hr from a couple of shacks just south of the main post office, opposite the southwest corner of the fort.

Camel and nature safaris Bikaner is a popular base for camel safaris and other nature trips (see page 174).

Festival Bikaner's colourful camel fair (usually mid-January) has the usual camel races and camel hairstyle competitions, plus dancing and firework displays. Most of the action takes place at the polo ground north of town, near the *Harasar Haveli* hotel (see below). Advance

RECOMMENDED TRAINS FROM BIKANER

All the following trains run daily.

Destination	Name	No.	Departs	Arrives
Abu Road	*Ranakpur Express*	14707	9.30am	7.27pm
	Ahmedabad Express	19224	12.45am	9.55am
Agra Fort	*Howrah Superfast*	22308	6.45pm	5.55am
Delhi	*Dee Intercity*	22471	9.30pm	5.25pm
	*Assam Express**	15910	7.50pm	7.20am
Jaipur	*Puri Express*	14709	4.40pm	11.20pm
	Leelan Express	12467	6am	12.35pm
Jodhpur	*Ranakpur Express*	14707	9.30am	2.15pm
	Barmer Express	14887	11am	4pm

*From Lalgarh Junction

2

CAMEL SAFARIS AND NATURE TOURS FROM BIKANER

Bikaner offers a good alternative to Jaisalmer as a starting point for **camel treks** into the Thar Desert. This eastern part of the desert, while just as scenic as the western Thar, is not nearly as congested with fellow trekkers, with the result that local people in the villages along the route don't wait around all day for the chance to sell Pepsi to tourists. Wildlife is also abundant, with plentiful blackbuck, nilgai and desert foxes.

Though your accommodation may be able to get you onto a camel (around ₹1500 for a few hours), if you'd like to make your own choice of **operator**, your options are somewhat limited. Treks have long been run by "Camel Man", based 5km east of the city at *Vijay* guesthouse (☎0151 223 1244, ⓦcamelman.com), but recent reports about his conduct and facilities have been less than encouraging. It's best to go with the far more central *Vinayak Desert Safari* (☎94144 30948, ⓦvinayakdesertsafari.com), based at the *Vinayak Guesthouse* (see page 175), most of whose tours are run by a trained zoologist. Options include jeep safaris (₹1500 – 2000 per person), camel safaris (day-trips ₹1600 per person including lunch, or ₹2000 overnight including accommodation and meals). Other trips include visits to remote Bishnoi villages. Safaris can be customized to focus on particular areas of interest, including specialized wildlife, birdwatching, snake-spotting and photographic tours.

accommodation booking is essential during this time.

Tourist information The helpful tourist office (Mon–Fri 10am–5pm; ☎0151 222 6701) is in the *RTDC Dholamaru*

Hotel at Pooran Singh Circle. Online, check out the informative ⓦrealbikaner.com.

ACCOMMODATION

Bikaner has a surprisingly large selection of hotels, though the cheap flophouses along Station Rd are insalubrious and best avoided.

Bhairon Vilas West of Junagarh Fort ☎0151 254 4751, ⓦhotelbhaironvilas.tripod.com; map p.171. Charming heritage hotel in an old royal haveli, surrounded by an attractive garden and kitted out with quirky antiques and family curios; an air of slight neglect hangs over the place, however, and staff can be apathetic. Rooms (all a/c and with TVs) are likewise a mixed bag; it's worth spending a little extra to get one of the more spacious and atmospheric heritage rooms. There's also a good restaurant, bijou bar and boutique. **₹2500**

Bhanwar Niwas Old City ☎0151 220 1043, ⓦbhanwar niwas.com; map p.171. Bikaner's most ostentatious haveli, built for a textile tycoon in the late 1920s and crammed with kitsch fittings and furniture, complete with a 1927 Buick in the lobby, an atmospheric *fin de siècle* dining room and an array of 25 memorably chintzy rooms. **₹6500**

Harasar Haveli Near Karni Singh Stadium ☎0151 220 9891, ⓦharasar.com; map p.171. Welcoming, medium-sized hotel with spotlessly clean and comfy rooms (all a/c), and a decent restaurant (see below). It often plays host to tour groups, hence the "cultural bash" put on each night, but this is both easy to ignore and actually kind of pleasant in its own way. Wi-fi doesn't reach all the rooms; if this is an issue, double check before you unpack your stuff. **₹2000**

Jaswant Bhawan Alakhsagar Rd ☎0151 254 8848, ⓦhoteljaswantbhawan.com; map p.171. Relaxing hotel in a nice old house built in 1926 for a prime minister,

very close to the station. Surprisingly quiet given the location, with very well priced, comfortable a/c rooms; it's worth paying a tiny bit more to upgrade to "deluxe" from the cheapest ones. **₹1200**

Karni Bhawan Palace Gandhi Colony, 1km east of Lallgarh Palace ☎0151 252 4701 or ☎1800 180 2933 or ☎1800 180 2944, ⓦhrhindia.com; map p.171. On the outside this place looks like an oversized English suburban house, but its interior is period and wonderful, with superb Art Deco suites (₹5500) in the main building, complete with original 1930s furniture (but don't bother with the standard rooms in the annexe). Some discounts in summer. **₹4500**

Lallgarh Palace Lallgarh Palace Complex ☎0151 254 0102, ⓦlallgarhpalace.com; map p.171. Set in the Lallgarh Palace complex, this is cheaper than its neighbour, the Laxmi Niwas (see below), and less grand, but it still makes for a thoroughly atmospheric place to stay. The halls can feel a little empty, but the rooms themselves are suitably opulent. **₹7500**

Laxmi Niwas Palace Lallgarh Palace Complex ☎0151 220 2777, ⓦlaxminiwaspalace.com; map p.171. The better of two palatial hotels in the Lallgarh Palace complex, offering large rooms with period English furniture. A large pool, reading room, bar with hunting trophies adorning the walls and a billiards room enhance the colonial feeling. The rack rates, though, are sky-high – you'll usually manage to get hefty discounts online, but if not, try the adjoining *Lallgarh Palace* (see above). **₹31,000**

Palace View Lallgarh Palace Campus ☎0151 254 3625, ⓦhotelpalaceview.com; map p.171. In a quiet location

2

to the north of town, *Palace View* has comfortable, clean and pleasantly old-fashioned rooms (most a/c), a homely little dining room and views of Lallgarh Palace. ₹1000

★ **Vinayak** Old Ginani ☎0151 220 2634, ⊛vinayak desertsafari.com; map p.171. Friendly and family run, this place offers simple but clean and cheap singles and doubles (all attached, some with hot-water bucket showers). Bicycles are complimentary, free cooking lessons are available (you pay only for the ingredients), and there are motorbikes for rent (₹400/day). Free 24hr pick-up from the train station is possible, and this is a good base for safaris (see page 174). ₹600

Vrindavan Regency Shiv Shakti Mall ☎0151 220 0446, ⊛hotelvrindavanregency.com; map p.171. The smartest of the cluster of hotels near the railway station, with its "business" atmosphere perhaps welcome if you've stayed in one too many havelis. 62 clean a/c rooms and suites (₹2500), plus a decent restaurant open until late, and

even a banquet hall and conference centre. ₹1900

OUT OF TOWN

Gajner Palace 32km southwest of Bikaner ☎0153 427 5061, ⊛heritagehotelsofindia.com; map p.171. This grand, red-sandstone affair was built in the early twentieth century as a hunting lodge for the maharajas of Bikaner. The ninety-room hotel overlooks a lake, and staff can arrange jaunts through the surrounding Gajner Wildlife Sanctuary. ₹9600

Shri Ram Heritage Sadulganj, 1.5 km east of the city centre ☎0151 252 2651, ⊛hotelshriramheritage.co.nf; map p.171. Friendly suburban hotel; the more expensive rooms (a/c from ₹1400) are spacious and very comfortably furnished, though the cheaper ones are a bit cramped. There's also a dorm, which you may well have to yourself, unless there's a youth group staying. Dorms ₹220, doubles ₹800

EATING

Bikaner is famous for sweets such as *kaju katli*, made with cashew nuts, and *tirangi*, a three-coloured confection made with cashews, almonds and pistachios.

Bhikharam Chandmal Bhujiawala Just off Station Rd on the road to Kote Gate; map p.171. Top *mithai* shop, known for its excellent Bengali and Rajasthani sweets. The English sign is small and easy to miss; look for maroon Hindi writing on a white block. Daily 8am–8pm.

Cafe Indra Udai Niwas, Rangmanch Rd ☎0151 222 3447; map p.171. Popular with foreign travellers and local hipsters, this is where to go for non-Indian food, such as burgers, pasta and American-style pizza (from ₹130). They also do good shakes (₹110–180), espresso (₹50), masala chai (₹40), and even Kashmiri kehwa (₹70); think about sitting indoors, since the outdoor section is occasionally ravaged by flies, and dominated by overloud music. Wed–Mon noon–10pm.

Gallops Court Rd ☎0151 320 0833; map p.171. Pleasant a/c restaurant opposite the fort; they've grown fat on the easy pickings of passing coach parties, but the

food's not bad, with a range of north Indian veg and non-veg standards, plus a few local specialities, served in big portions. Usually full of tour groups at lunchtime, though quieter and nicer in the evenings. Most mains between ₹300–400. Licensed, and they've a real espresso machine. Daily 10am–11pm.

Ganesha Bhairon Vilas ☎0151 254 4751; map p.171. The best place to drain a coffee in the fort area, decorated to the nines to an even greater degree than the Bhairon Vilas hotel (see above) in the same compound. ₹80 will get you a decent espresso, while various kinds of chai are available for even less. Daily 10am–2pm & 4–9pm.

Moomal Panchshati Circle, Sadul Ganj ☎0151 254 9575; map p.171. Popular with locals, this is the best restaurant in what counts as the (non-tourist) city centre. They serve sumptuous pan-Indian veg food – the cashew and cherry Moomal Special alone (₹300) is worth the trip, and will take you quite a while to finish. Daily 11am–4pm & 6–10.30pm.

DRINKING

There aren't many great places to drink in Bikaner; the options around the train station are a bit creepy and male-dominated, though there's a more relaxed (though still very male) local venue just west of the Harasar Haveli (see page 174).

Tamarind Bhairon Vilas ☎0151 254 4751; map p.171.

Spilling onto a tamarind-tree-shaded lawn, this restaurant isn't recommended as a place to eat, but the quirky atmosphere makes it a fantastic place to drink, with its dusky pink walls and black leather chairs. Beers from ₹300. Daily 8am–2pm & 7–10.30pm.

SHOPPING

Bikaner is famous for its skilled lacquerwork and handicrafts, and for its handwoven woollen *pattu* (a kind of shawl-cum-blanket).

Urmul Abhivyakti Ganganar Rd, near the bus stand ☎0151 252 2139; map p.171. Supported by the Urmul Trust

charity, this is the best place to buy *pattu* and the manager can arrange visits to villages to see how the textiles are woven by local women's co-ops. They don't pay commission to auto drivers, so don't believe anyone if they tell you that the shop's closed. Mon–Sat 9am–6pm, Sun 9am–1pm.

DIRECTORY

Banks and exchange There are banks with ATMs directly opposite the station, and plenty of others around town. Thomas Cook (Mon–Sat 9am–6pm), on the KEM Rd, changes currency.

Hospital Prince Bijoy Memorial (PBM) Hospital, Hospital Road near Ambedkar Circle (☎ 0151 222 6334).

Police Station Rd, directly opposite the station on Kote Gate (☎ 0151 252 2225, ☏ bikanerpolice.rajasthan.gov.in).

National Research Centre on Camels

Daily noon–6.30pm • ₹200 (₹50), camera ₹50; camel ride ₹100; guided tour ₹250 • Around ₹250 round trip from Bikaner by auto including waiting time • ☎ 0151 223 0183, ☏ nrccamel.icar.gov.in

What claims to be Asia's largest camel-breeding farm, the **National Research Centre on Camels** lies out in the desert, 10km southeast of the fort area. Bikaner is renowned for its famously sturdy beasts – the camel corps was a much-feared component of the imperial battle formation – but the growing proliferation of motor vehicles has severely reduced the camel's traditional role as the staple means of rural transport. It's best to take a guided tour of the farm; aim to arrive at around 3pm, soon after which you'll be wowed by the sight of hundreds of stampeding dromedaries arriving from the desert for their daily chow. A small **museum** showcases each species through a series of photographs. There's also a kiosk selling camel milk and milk-based products such as ice cream and "camel coffee"; many visitors make the journey here for a taste of the *kesar* (saffron) kulfi alone. There's also a small (camel) leather shop.

The temple of rats

Daily 5am–10pm • Free, ₹20 camera, ₹50 video camera, ₹10 for footwear stowage • Buses for Deshnok (every 15min or so; 45min) leave roughly every 15min from Bikaner's main bus stand • ₹500 by auto-rickshaw, including waiting time

The **Karni Mata Temple** in **DESHNOK**, 30km south of Bikaner, is one of India's most bizarre attractions. Step inside the Italian-marble arched doorway and everywhere you'll see free-roaming rats, known as *kabas*, which devotees believe are reincarnated souls saved from the wrath of Yama, the god of death (see page 176). The innermost shrine, made of rough stone and logs cut from sacred *jal* trees, houses the yellow-marble image of Karniji. This in turn is encased by a much grander marble building. Pilgrims bring offerings for the rats to eat inside the main shrine, and it's considered auspicious to eat the leftovers after they've been nibbled by the *kabas*. Some pilgrims spend hours searching for a glimpse of the temple's venerated white rat, while it's also considered fortunate for a rat to run over your feet (stand still for a while – preferably next to some food), but whatever you do don't step on one, or you'll have to donate a gold model of a rat to placate the deity. Shoes have to be removed at the gate – there's a little store across the street from the temple where you can leave them, after which you're free to wander among the rat droppings barefoot or in your socks.

THE DESHNOK DEVI

Members of the Charan caste of musicians believe that incarnations of the goddess Durga periodically appear among them, one of whom was **Karni Mata**, born at a village near Phalodi in 1387, who went on to perform miracles such as water divination and bringing the dead back to life, eventually becoming the region's most powerful cult leader. According to legend, one of Karni Mata's followers came to her because her son was grievously ill, but by the time they got to him, he had died. Karni Mata went to Yama, the god of the underworld, to ask for him back, but Yama refused. Knowing that of all the creatures upon the earth, only rats were outside Yama's dominion, Karni Mata decreed that all Charans would henceforth be reincarnated as rats, thus escaping Yama's power. It is these sacred rats (*kabas*) that inhabit the Deshnok temple.

Phalodi

The main highway and railway line wind in tandem east from Jaisalmer across the desert, separating at the small junction settlement of **PHALODI**, almost exactly midway between Jaisalmer and Bikaner. This scruffy salt-extraction colony is the jumping-off place for one of Rajasthan's most beautiful natural sights – the **demoiselle crane** breeding grounds at nearby Keechen.

ARRIVAL AND DEPARTURE   PHALODI

By train Phalodi Junction station is fairly central, near the police station on the road to Dechu. There are trains to Bikaner (2 daily; 2hr 30min), Jaisalmer (7 daily; 2hr 45min) and Jodhpur (4 daily; 3hr).

By bus There are hourly RSRTC departures to Bikaner (3hr 30min), Jaisalmer (3hr 30min) and Jodhpur (3hr 30min). The bus station is just off the Dechu road, near the train station. If you are only stopping for a few hours to see

Keechen's cranes, find out when the last bus leaves to your final destination.

On a tour If you'd like to see Keechen en route between Bikaner and Jaisalmer, contact *Vinayak Guesthouse* in Bikaner (see page 175), who can collect you in one and drop you off in the other, visiting Keechen and Gajner Wildlife Sanctuary en route.

ACCOMMODATION

Chetnya Palace Next to the old Jaisalmer Bus Stand ☎ 0292 522 3945. Its shabby rooms are uninspiring, but this is the best budget option in town. ₹800

Lal Niwas Dadhas Mohalla ☎ 992 8722 277, ⓦ lalniwas.

com. This three hundred-year-old red-sandstone haveli has been converted into a low-key heritage hotel, with 27 slightly dog-eared a/c rooms, and a tiny pool. ₹3900

Keechen

Around 6km east of Phalodi • From Phalodi, the best way to get to Keechen is to rent a bicycle from one of the stalls in town – a pleasant, mostly flat ride on well-surfaced roads; alternatively, jump in an auto-rickshaw (₹400) or taxi (₹800) for a tour

The village of **KEECHEN** hosts four thousand **demoiselle cranes** that migrate here each winter from their breeding grounds in Central Asia. Known locally as *kurja*, the birds are encouraged to return by the villagers, who scatter grain for them twice a day – a custom that has persisted for 150 years or more. Make sure you go at one of the feeding times (6–7am & 5–6pm) to witness at close quarters the staggering sight of the flock descending en masse, on a fenced-off area just outside the village.

Jaisalmer and around

In the remote westernmost corner of Rajasthan, **JAISALMER** is the quintessential desert town, its golden, sand-coloured ramparts rising out of the arid Thar like a scene from the *Arabian Nights*. Rampant commercialism may have dampened the romantic vision somewhat, but even with all the touts and tour buses, the town deservedly remains one of India's most popular destinations. Villagers – many dressed in voluminous red and orange turbans – still outnumber foreigners in the bazaar, while the exquisite sandstone architecture of the "Golden City" is quite unlike anything else in India.

The streets of Jaisalmer are flanked with numerous, pale honey-coloured facades, covered with latticework and floral designs, but the city's real showpieces are its **havelis**, commissioned by wealthy merchants during the eighteenth and nineteenth centuries. In addition, there are numerous sights out of town, as well as the desert itself – **camel safaris** are an extremely popular activity here, and most take the chance to spend at least one night out in the sands.

Brief history

Rawal Jaisal of the Bhati clan founded Jaisalmer in 1156 as a replacement for his less easily defensible capital at Lodurva. Constant wars with Jodhpur and Bikaner followed, as did conflict with the sultans of Delhi. In 1298, a seven-year siege of the fort by the

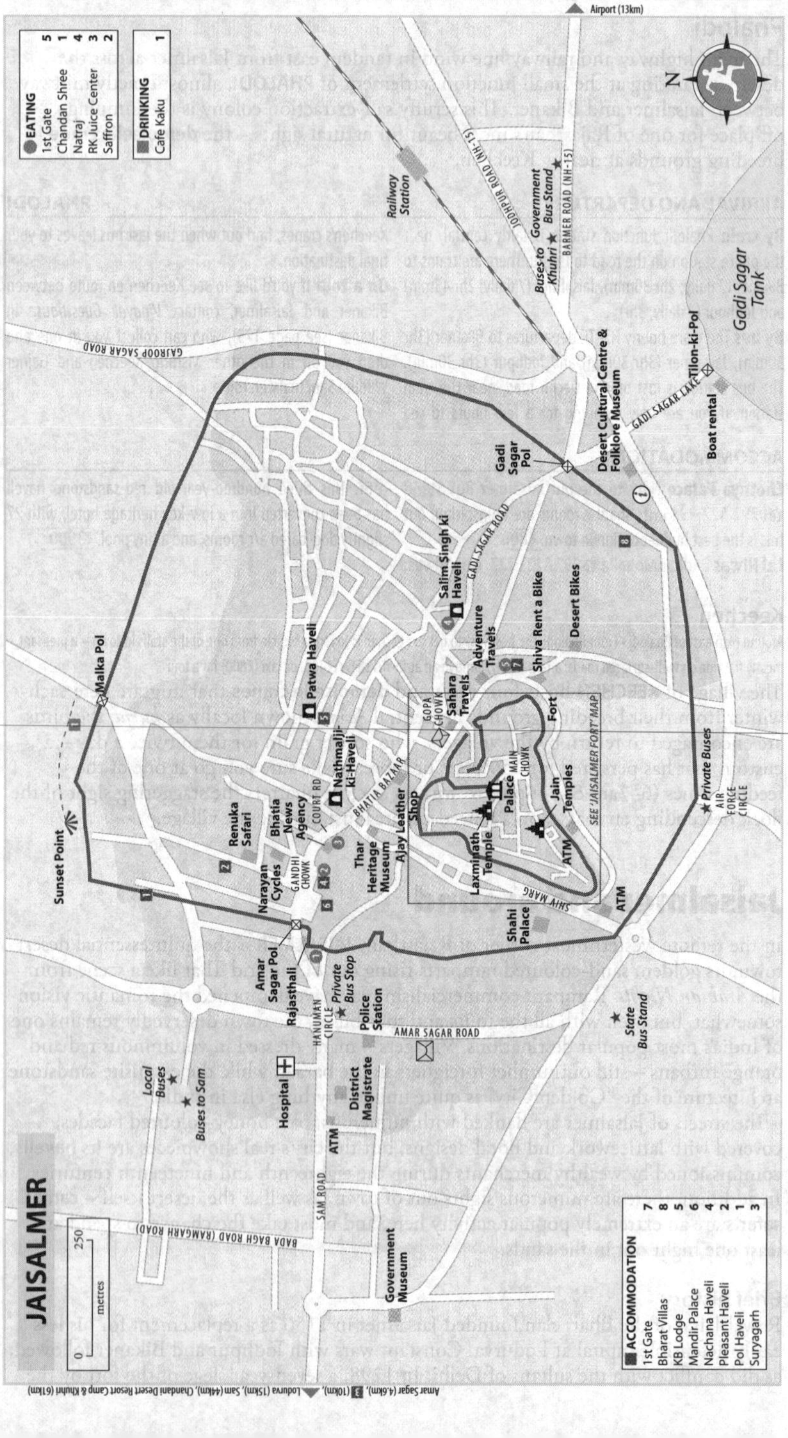

2

JAISALMER

▲ Airport (13km)

N

Railway
Station

Buses to
Khuhri ★

Government
Bus Stand

JODHPUR ROAD (NH-15)

BARMER ROAD (NH-15)

Gadi Sagar
Tank

GAJROOP SAGAR ROAD

Desert Cultural Centre &
Folklore Museum

GADI SAGAR LAKTlon-ki-Pol

Boat rental

Gadi
Sagar
Pol

GADI SAGAR ROAD

Salim Singh ki
Haveli

Malka Pol

Patwa Haveli

Adventure
Travels

Shiva Rent a Bike

Desert Bikes

Sunset Point

Renuka
Safari

Bhatia
News
Agency

COURT RD

Nathmalji-
ki-Haveli

GOPA
CHOWK

Sahara
Travels

SEE "JAISALMER FORT MAP"

Fort

Narayan
Cycles

GANDHI
CHOWK

Thar
Heritage
Museum

BHATIA BAZAAR

Ajay Leather
Shop

Palace MAIN
CHOWK

Jain
Temples

★ Private Buses

AIR
FORCE
CIRCLE

Amar
Sagar Pol

Rajasthali

HANUMAN
CIRCLE

Private
Bus Stop

Police Station

Laxminath
Temple

ATM

SHIV MARG

Shahi
Palace

ATM

★ Local
Buses

★ Buses to Sam

AMAR SAGAR ROAD

State
Bus Stand

Hospital

District
Magistrate

ATM

SAM ROAD

BADA BAGH ROAD (RAMGARH ROAD)

Government
Museum

0   250

metres

Amar Sagar (4.6km) ◀, 🚲 (10km) ◀, Lodurva (15km) ◀, Sam (44km) ◀, Chandani Desert Resort Camp & Khuhri (61km)

● EATING

1st Gate	5
Chandan Shree	1
Natraj	4
RK Juice Center	3
Saffron	2

■ DRINKING

| Cafe Kaku | 1 |

ACCOMMODATION

1st Gate	7
Bharat Villas	8
KB Lodge	5
Mandir Palace	6
Nachana Haveli	4
Pleasant Haveli	2
Pol Haveli	1
Suryagarh	3

forces of Ala-ud-din Khalji (see page 216) ended when the men of the city rode out to their deaths while the women committed *johar* sacrifice – although the Bhatis soon resumed their rule. The city was again besieged by Sultanate forces in 1326, resulting in another desperate act of *johar*, but Gharsi Bhati managed to negotiate the return of his kingdom as a vassal state of Delhi, after which it remained in Bhati hands.

In 1570 the ruler of Jaisalmer married one of his daughters to Akbar's son, cementing an alliance between Jaisalmer and the Mughal Empire. Its position on the overland route between Delhi and Central Asia made it an important trading post for goods such as silk, opium and spices, and the city grew rich on the proceeds, as the magnificent havelis of its merchants bear witness. However, the emergence of Bombay and Surat as major ports meant that overland trade diminished, and with it Jaisalmer's wealth. The death-blow came with Partition, when Jaisalmer's life-line trade route was severed by the new, highly sensitive Pakistani border. The city took on renewed strategic importance during the Indo-Pakistani wars of 1965 and 1971, and it is now a major **military outpost**, with jet aircraft regularly roaring past the ramparts.

Jaisalmer Fort

Daily 24hr • Free

Every part of Jaisalmer Fort is made of soft yellow Jurassic sandstone. Outside, the thick **walls**, punctuated with barrel-sided bastions, drop almost 100m to the town below, while inside narrow winding streets are flanked with carved golden facades. Two thousand people still live within its walls; seventy percent of them are Brahmins and the rest, living primarily on the east side, are predominantly Rajput. A paved road punctuated by four huge gateways winds up to the fort's **main chowk** (square) – large round stones lie atop the ramparts above the entrance, waiting to be pushed down on the heads of any approaching enemy. The main chowk was the scene of the three terrible acts of *johar* during the fourteenth and fifteenth centuries, when the women of the royal palace, which overlooks the chowk, had a huge fire built, and jumped from the palace walls into it.

Fort Palace Museum

Daily 9am–6pm; last tour 5pm • ₹500 (₹200) including audioguide (although you'll need to leave either a ₹2000 cash deposit or some ID), camera ₹100, video camera ₹200

The chowk is dominated by the **Palace of the Maharawal**, open to the public as the **Fort Palace Museum**. The palace's balconied, five-storey facade displays some of the finest masonry in Jaisalmer, while the ornate marble throne to the left of the palace entrance is where the monarch (known in Jaisalmer as the maharawal rather than the maharaja) would have addressed his troops.

Inside, the museum offers an intriguing snapshot of the life of Jaisalmer's potentates through the ages, with artefacts ranging from a fancy silver coronation throne to more homely items, such as the bed and thali dish of a nineteenth-century ruler. There's also an interesting array of other exhibits – from fifteenth-century sculptures (including an unusual bearded Rama) through to local stamps and banknotes, while the rooftop terrace gives unrivalled views over the city and the surrounding countryside.

Jain temples

Daily 8am–noon • ₹200 including camera/video fees (Indians free entry, ₹50 for camera/video)

The fort has a number of Hindu temples, including the venerable **Laxminath Temple** of 1494; however, none is as impressive as the complex of seven **Jain temples**. The temples, connected by small corridors and stairways, were built between the twelfth and fifteenth centuries with yellow and white marble shrines and exquisite sculpted motifs covering the walls, ceilings and pillars. Two of the seven temples are open between 8am and noon; the other five only open from 11am to noon, when the whole place gets overrun with coach parties, so it's best to visit before 11am to see the first two temples, then come back later to see the rest.

The old town

Jaisalmer's captivating **old town** surrounds the fort, and contains a few sights of its own, not least a series of delightful havelis. Despite the area's slightly labyrinthine layout, most tourists end up navigating precisely the same channels – as such, it's surprisingly easy to step away from the souvenir stand hawkers, and end up in a little slice of "real" Jaisalmer.

Thar Heritage Museum

Off Court Rd • Daily 9am–9pm • ₹100, ₹20 camera & video camera

In the centre of town, the modest little **Thar Heritage Museum** is one of Jaisalmer's more interesting museums. Showcasing the personal collection of a local historian, who may be on hand to explain some of the stories and customs behind the quirky array of local artefacts on display, exhibits range from bits of fossilized tree and old chillums through to camel regalia and antique musical instruments.

Nathmalji-ki-Haveli

Court Rd • Daily 8am–8pm • ₹50

Just north of Bhatia Bazaar, the **Nathmalji-ki-Haveli** was built in 1885 for Jaisalmer's prime minister by two brother stonemasons, one of whom built the left half, the other the right, as a result of which the two sides are subtly different. It's guarded by two

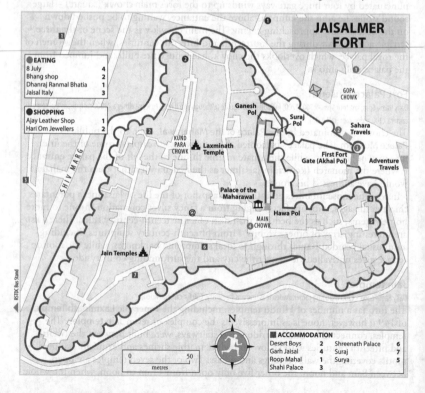

JAISALMER FORT

● EATING
8 July	4
Bhang shop	2
Dhanraj Ranmal Bhatia	1
Jaisal Italy	3

● SHOPPING
Ajay Leather Shop	1
Hari Om Jewellers	2

GOPA CHOWK

Ganesh Pol

Suraj Pol

Sahara Travels

SHIV MARG

KUND PARA CHOWK

Laxminath Temple

First Fort Gate (Akhai Pol)

Adventure Travels

Palace of the Maharawal

Hawa Pol

MAIN CHOWK

Jain Temples

RSTDC Bus Stand

N

0   50
metres

■ ACCOMMODATION
Desert Boys	2	Shreenath Palace	6
Garh Jaisal	4	Suraj	7
Roop Mahal	1	Surya	5
Shahi Palace	3		

elephants, and the first-floor bay window above the main doorway is surmounted by a frieze of little figures including elephants, horses, a steam train and a horse-drawn carriage. The place is basically a shop now, but it's still worth a look.

Patwa Haveli

Kumhar Para • Daily 8am–8pm • ₹50 **Government museums** Daily 10am–5pm • ₹200 (₹50) • **Kothari Patwa Haveli Museum** Daily 9am–6pm • ₹250 (₹100), video camera ₹90, camera ₹50 • ⓦ patwahaveli.com

The finely decorated **Patwa Haveli**, or Patwon-ki-Haveli, lies a couple of blocks north of the Nathmalji-ki-Haveli, its exterior a positive riot of exuberantly carved *jharokhas* (protruding balconies). The haveli was constructed in the first half of the nineteenth century by the Patwa merchants – five brothers from a Jain family who were bankers and traders in brocade and opium. There are actually five separate suites within the haveli; two are closed to visitors and two more, preserved in their original condition, are open as **government museums**. One, the **Kothari Patwa Haveli Museum**, has various traditional artefacts on display and replica mirrorwork on the walls, giving you some idea of how the haveli would originally have looked. As well as visiting the interior of the Patwa Haveli, it's worth taking a little stroll down the street whose entrance it bridges, to check out the stonework on four impressive neighbouring havelis.

Salim Singh ki Haveli

Asani Rd • Daily 8am–6pm • ₹70

The third of Jaisalmer's famous trio of havelis, the **Salim Singh ki Haveli**, lies on the east side of town and is immediately recognizable by the lavishly carved overhanging rooftop balcony that gives the whole building a strangely top-heavy appearance. Its upper floor, enclosed by an overhanging balcony, is best seen from the roof of *Natraj* restaurant (see page 185). Halfway up the building is a surprisingly good shop, with ornate pots and traditional "air fresheners" in the shape of animals, which use natural oils.

South of town

There are a couple of fairly minor sights just **south** of the old-town walls, including a museum hosting daily puppet shows, and **Gadi Sagar Tank**, one of the best of Jaisalmer's many sunrise and sunset spots.

Gadi Sagar Tank

Off Gadi Sagar Rd • Daily 24hr • Free • Boats ₹100 for 30min, Kashmiri shikaras ₹300 for 30min

South of the old town, through an imposing triple gateway, lies **Gadi Sagar Tank**, once Jaisalmer's sole water supply. Now flanked with sandstone *ghats* and temples, it's a peaceful place, staring out into the desert, and a good spot for watching the sun rise or set. You can also rent boats here for a spin on the water.

Desert Cultural Centre & Folklore Museum

Gadi Sagar Rd • Daily 10am–6pm • ₹50 (₹20), camera & video ₹50 (₹20) • Puppet shows daily 6.30pm & 7.30pm • ₹100 including museum entry

Local curiosities including musical instruments, fossils, tools, utensils and rare manuscripts are on display at the **Desert Cultural Centre & Museum**, next to the tourist office on the main road. The main exhibit is a cloth painting depicting the life of the local folk hero Pabuji, a legendary figure credited with introducing the camel to Rajasthan; the museum also recently absorbed various exhibits from the **Folklore Museum**, once located by the main gate of the Gadi Sagar Tank, including folk art and textiles, along with opium and betel nut paraphernalia. Of more interest to most visitors, however, are the **puppet shows** hosted each evening, with English narration.

2

ARRIVAL AND DEPARTURE JAISALMER

By plane Jaisalmer Airport, 14km west of town (₹500 by taxi, though your accommodation will often collect), was reopened to passenger services in 2017 – fantastic news for the town's tourist industry, since people living in Delhi and Mumbai can now visit for the weekend more easily. However, it's still mainly a military airport, and flights can get cancelled at short notice (even the evening before your scheduled departure); as well as keeping an eye out for emails from your airline, it's prudent to let your accommodation know your schedule, since they may hear updates while you're out gallavanting around the desert.
Destinations Ahmedabad (1–2 daily; 1hr 40min); Delhi (1 daily; 1hr 25min); Jaipur (1 daily; 1hr 15min); Mumbai (3–6 weekly; 1hr 35min).

By train Jaisalmer's railway station (☏0299 225 2354) is 2km east of the city on the Jodhpur Rd; an auto-rickshaw into town will cost around ₹100. The following trains run daily; for all other destinations, you're best off taking a bus. Note that night trains can get very cold – close to freezing in winter.
Destinations The daily #14660 *Jaisalmer–Delhi Express*, which departs at 4.45pm, stops at, among other places,

Pokaran (6.19pm), Phalodi (7.38pm), Osian (8.49pm), Jodhpur (10.45pm), Jaipur (4.50am), Alwar (7.14am) and New Delhi (11.15am). The #15013 *Ranikhet Express* takes a similar route, departing at 00.45am, arriving in Jodhpur at 6.20am and Delhi at 9.10pm. To Jodhpur, there's an extra train at 7am (#14809; 6hr); change here for Bikaner, Kolkata, Udaipur and the like.

By bus Most government buses (☏0299 225 1541) depart from the Government Bus Stand east of town on Barmer Rd, although early morning departures leave from the more conveniently located State Bus Stand at the southern end of Amar Sagar Rd; check when you buy your ticket. Private buses operate from Hanuman Circle and Air Force Circle, respectively west and south of the fort; tickets can be purchased from any of the numerous travel agents around town, such as Swagat Travels or Hanuman Travels, both just north of Hanuman Circle, or from Adventure Travels (see page 183).
Destinations Abu Rd (2 daily; 10hr 30min); Ajmer (3 daily; 10hr); Bikaner (2 daily; 6–8hr); Delhi (1 nightly; 15hr); Jaipur (7 daily; 11–14hr); Jodhpur (1–2 hourly; 5–6hr); Udaipur (3 daily; 12hr).

GETTING AROUND AND INFORMATION

Tourist information RTDC's tourist office (Mon–Sat 10am–5pm; ☏0299 225 2406), southeast of town near Gadi Sagar Pol, is just about passable, but your accommodation will quite possibly be of equal or better use.
Travel agents The excellent Adventure Travels (see page 183) can arrange bus, train and plane tickets for a modest commission; they also have currency exchange and can arrange hotel bookings.
Bicycle rental Narayan Cycles, on the street directly opposite *Nachana Haveli* hotel (100m up on the left, just where the street starts to bend); ₹50/hr.
Motorbike rental There are a couple of places south of Gopa Chowk including Desert Bikes (☏94141 50033) and

Shiva Rent a Bike (☏94620 94620), with bikes and scooters from ₹400/day, or ₹150/hr.
Festivals Jaisalmer's Desert Festival is held over three days at the full moon in the lunar month of Magha (in February). Unlike many of the region's other festivals, this is not a livestock fair, but a festival of performing arts, and generally a fun occasion, with folk dancing, turban-tying competitions, camel racing and craft bazaars. Main events are held at Dedansar Polo Ground. Room prices rise and hotels tend to get full at this time.
Swimming pool Non-guests can use the pools at the *Mandir Palace Hotel* (₹700/hr), and plenty of others in and around town.

ACCOMMODATION

Jaisalmer has plenty of accommodation, and fierce competition keeps prices low. The basic choice is between in one of the old places within the wonderfully atmospheric fort – but read "Jaisalmer in Jeopardy" first (see page 185) – or in one of the newer places outside, many of which are built in traditional sandstone and come with superb fort views. Most places offer free pick-up from the bus or railway stations, and the majority offer camel treks, which vary in standard and price.

IN THE FORT

Desert Boys ☏0299 225 0602, ⓦdesertboysguest house.com; map p.180. Friendly budget place with cheaper rooms downstairs (including a couple of bargain

singles with shared bathroom), and brighter rooms upstairs, some with fort views. They now have a second, far more luxurious location in the fort, boasting delightfully decorated rooms (from ₹2850). **₹800**
Garh Jaisal ☏0299 225 3836, ⓦhotelgarhjaisal.com; map p.180. Charming and efficiently run haveli with seven smart colour-themed rooms with balconies, a/c and superb views across town. Rates include breakfast, and coffee whenever you want, and their awesome roof terrace has arguably the best panoramas in the fort. Prices drop to around ₹3500 in off-season. **₹5500**
Shreenath Palace Near Jain temples ☏0299 225 2907, ⓦhotelinjaisalmer.com; map p.180. Atmospheric 450-year-old haveli – a former prime minister's abode –

CAMEL SAFARIS FROM JAISALMER

Few visitors who make it as far as Jaisalmer pass up the opportunity to go on a **camel trek**, which provides an irresistibly romantic chance to cross the barren sands and sleep under one of the starriest skies in the world. Sandstorms, sore backsides and camel farts aside, the safaris are usually great fun; treks normally last from one to four days, with **prices** varying from ₹750 to ₹2000 per night. The highlight is spending a night under the desert stars, and most travellers find that an overnight trip, departing around 3pm one day and returning the next at noon, is sufficient. Unfortunately, the price you pay is not an adequate gauge of the quality of services you get, and it pays to shop around and ask other travellers for recommendations. Make sure that you'll be provided with your own camel, an adequate supply of blankets (it can get very cold at night), food cooked with mineral water, and a campfire. You should also make sure that your operator is committed to either burning or removing all rubbish (including plastic bottles).

The traditional Jaisalmer camel safari used to head west out of town to Amar Sagar, Lodurva, Sam and Kuldhara (see page 186). Some operators still cover these areas, although encroaching development and crowds of other tourists (around Sam especially) mean that there is very little sense of the real desert hereabouts. The better operators are constantly seeking out new and unspoilt areas to trek through – this usually means an initial drive out of Jaisalmer of around 50–60km, though it's worth it to avoid the crowds. Longer seven- to ten-day treks to Pokaran, Barmer and Bikaner can also be arranged, though these shouldn't be attempted lightly.

Finally, don't book anything until you get to Jaisalmer. Touts trawl trains and buses from Jodhpur, but they usually represent dodgy outfits, or pretend to represent one of the well-established operators. Some offer absurdly cheap rooms (typically ₹100) if you agree to book a camel trek with them, and then rescind their offer of a room if you change your mind. Guesthouse noticeboards are filled with sorry stories of tourists who accepted. As a rule of thumb, any firm that has to tout for business – and that includes hotels – is worth avoiding.

SPECIALIST AGENCIES

Specialist agencies allow you to book direct through their offices in Jaisalmer. Reliable outfits include:

Adventure Travels Just south of the First Fort Gate ☎941 4149 176, ⓦadventurecamels.com. Serving tourists since the 1980s, this operator gets rave reviews for seeking out remote locations and providing fringe amenities, like real mattresses and sheets, plus hearty food and the chance to meet local villagers.

Chandani Desert Resort Camp Khuhri ☎0301 4274 005, ⓦchandanidesertresortcamp.in. Camel safaris that start near Dhoba village and climb up a sand dune for the sunset before continuing to a gorgeous resort of Swiss tents. Dinner around the campfire, music and dance shows included.

Sahara Travels Gopa Chowk ☎0299 225 2609, ⓦsaharatravelsjaisalmer.com. Dependable operator established in 1989, offering well-priced safaris with comfy cot beds, adequate blankets and a decent supply of food and drink.

HOTEL-ORGANIZED SAFARIS

Renuka Near Gandhi Chowk ☎029 9252 757, ⓦhotelrenuka.net. Friendly, reliable camel safaris at decent rates (₹1500 for a half-day trip, ₹2100 overnight including accommodation; ₹3000 for a three-day "deep desert" excursion). Guides speak decent English and facilities aren't bad, given the price. Thankfully you can book without having to stay at their poky guesthouse in town (see map, p.178).

Shahi Palace Off Shiv Marg ☎0299 225 5920, ⓦshahipalacehotel.com. As well as the regular overnight safaris (₹1950 per person), this hotel (see page 184) offers Swiss Tent accommodation by their very own private dune where, after a camel trek, the hosts cook a meal on a campfire under the stars. Not cheap (₹5000 for two), but definitely worth it.

run by a charming family. Rooms (all a/c) feature intricate archways, balconies and private bathrooms; the Rajasthani rooms are a bit stuffy, so it's worth splashing out on one of the charming suites. ₹2500

★**Suraj** ☎0299 225 1623, ⓦhotelsurajhaveli.com; map p.180. This superbly atmospheric haveli, dating back to 1526, is one of the nicest places to stay in the fort, with simple but characterful and hugely spacious heritage rooms

2

(all with fan only, though the more expensive ones are quite opulent) and a privileged rooftop view of the Jain temples. ₹1200

Surya East Fort Wall ☎ 94133 72888; map p.180. Cheapie providing some of the richest views in town – you'll probably spend more time gawping at the views, though their range of basic attached fan and a/c rooms (the more expensive ones have fine views) are decent enough. When demand is low, prices sometimes dip even lower than that stipulated here. ₹900

IN TOWN

★ **1st Gate** Dhibba Para ☎ 0299 225 4462, ⊛ 1stgate.in; map p.178. One of the newer options in town, this Italian-run boutique is really quite something. Its ten rooms are all gorgeous, wood-floored affairs with lovely bathrooms, and half of them face perhaps the most picturesque side of the fort. There's also a spa on site, as well as a little gym and sheltered pool (non-guests ₹500). Lastly, there's a great restaurant upstairs (see page 184). ₹7450

Bharat Villas Dhibba Para ☎ 0299 225 0715, ⊛ hotel bharatvillas.com; map p.178. Less than ten minutes' walk to the fort, this hotel has comfortable a/c rooms with TVs and attached bathrooms. The lovely rooftop restaurant has a great menu and a fantastic view of the fort. ₹1050

KB Lodge Opposite Patwa Haveli ☎ 0299 223 5833, ⊛ killabhawan.com; map p.178. An efficiently run, modern hotel a stone's throw from the havelis with just a handful of tastefully furnished yellow-walled rooms, ranging from fan-cooled ones to giant, sumptuously-decorated a/c affairs. Discounts in summer. ₹2450

Mandir Palace Gandhi Chowk ☎ 0299 225 2788, ⊛ mandirpalace.com; map p.178. Occupying part of the exquisite Mandir Palace, with pleasantly spacious rooms sporting discreet heritage touches, attractive public areas (including the fine old Durbar Hall, now housing a miniature museum) and a secluded pool. ₹8500

Nachana Haveli Gandhi Chowk ☎ 0299 225 1910, ⊛ nachanahaveli.com; map p.178. This venerable old haveli is one of the best choices in its class. The atmospheric ground-floor rooms (all a/c) are virtually windowless, and

some could do with a little love, but all have stone walls and are attractively decorated with antique fittings; the suites upstairs are brighter, and have fort views. There's also the good *Saffron* rooftop restaurant (see page 185). ₹4000

Pleasant Haveli Chainpura Rd ☎ 0299 225 3253; map p.178. A halfway house, price-wise, but there's nothing wrong with the rooms at this picturesque, ornately-fronted haveli, set on a calm street in the rather agreeable northwestern section of the old town. Free pick-up from train or bus stations. ₹2450

Pol Haveli Near Geeta Ashram, Dedansar Rd ☎ 0299 225 0131, ⊛ hotelpolhaveli.com; map p.178. Attractive guesthouse in a stylish little sandstone building. Rooms (fan or a/c) are neat and comfortable (although larger ones are slightly lacking in furniture), and there's a lovely rooftop terrace for idle lounging and fort-gazing. Free pick-up from train station. ₹750

Roop Mahal Off Shiv Marg ☎ 0299 225 1700, ⊛ hotel roopmahal.com; map p.180. Comfortable guesthouse in a good central location west of the fort, with bright, inexpensive, modern rooms (some with fort views and cheap a/c), helpful staff and a pleasant rooftop restaurant. There's also plenty of parking space. ₹450

★ **Shahi Palace** Off Shiv Marg ☎ 0299 225 5920, ⊛ shahipalacehotel.com; map p.180. Outstanding little hotel tucked just outside the fort in a stylish modern sandstone building with stunning fort views from the great rooftop terrace restaurant and immaculate rooms. The only caveat is that the cheaper rooms are a bit small – if your budget will stretch a bit, it's well worth coughing up for one of the superb larger a/c rooms (from ₹1850). ₹750

OUT OF TOWN

Suryagarh Off Sam Rd, 10km west of town ☎ 0299 226 9269, ⊛ suryagarh.com; off map p.178. If you value opulence and remoteness (hey, the desert is just as special as the fort, and even bigger), this is the best of the several luxury options dotted around Jaisalmer. There's occasionally a bit of a resort feel, but the pool, gym, yoga sessions and archery workshops will keep you entertained, and the on-site restaurants are excellent. ₹14,000

EATING

RESTAURANTS

1st Gate Dhibba Para ☎ 0299 225 4462, ⊛ 1stgate.in; map p.178. This rooftop restaurant of this boutique hotel (see page 184) is also a fantastic place to eat – given the Italian ownership, it makes sense that their pizzas and pasta dishes (₹360–500) are about as authentic as it gets in India. There are more surprising treats on the menu, including good gazpacho (great when the weather's hot; ₹180), and *dulce de leche* with cookies for afters (₹220). Oh, and the views are tremendous. Daily noon–10.30pm.

Chandan Shree Just south of Amar Sagar Pol, no phone; map p.178. No-frills restaurant serving up inexpensive veg curries (from ₹100) and thalis (₹140–175), as well as South Indian and Rajasthani specialities. They also do awesome makhaniya lassis (₹45). Daily noon–3.30pm & 7.30–11pm.

★ **Jaisal Italy** Inside first fort gate ☎ 0299 225 3504, ⊛ jaisalitaly.com; map p.180. Italian restaurant with great pasta dishes (from ₹210), served in heaped portions at reasonable prices, plus thin-crust pizzas, salads and great

2

JAISALMER IN JEOPARDY

Erected on a base of soft bantonite clay, sand and sandstone, the foundations of **Jaisalmer Fort** have been eroding in recent decades due to huge increases in water consumption, mainly related to tourism. At the height of the season, around 120 litres per head are pumped into the area – and due to problems with the drainage system, a large proportion of this water seeps back into the soil beneath the fort, weakening its foundations. The results have been disastrous. In 1998 six people died when an exterior wall gave way, and five more bastions fell in 2000 and 2001. Jaisalmer's fort has been listed among the World Monument Fund's most endangered sites.

An international campaign was set up to facilitate repairs throughout the fort, including assistance with upgrading underground sewerage. Despite the work so far carried out, however, some continue to think that the best way to save the fort would be to evacuate its two thousand inhabitants and start repairs to the drainage system from scratch, an expensive and time-consuming venture much opposed by the guesthouse owners inside, whose earnings depend on tourism.

Given all this, some people (and guidebooks) suggest that travellers **should avoid staying in the fort** in order to relieve pressure on its crumbling foundations. Unfortunately, this also has a serious side effect in that it deprives many local hoteliers – some of whom have been in the fort for decades, and who are in no way responsible for Jaisalmer's current plight – of a living. We have therefore continued to list certain guesthouses within the fort. All are long-established, low-impact, and occupy original and largely unmodified buildings. On the other hand, we haven't listed any of the fort's modern, custom-built hotels. Remember, too, that if you do stay in the fort, you can do your bit by minimizing your water usage as much as possible.

coffee (espresso ₹110). The superb terrace directly opposite the main ramparts is beautiful at night, though the interior is a beaut, too – set into the ramparts, it's a former sentry base, as the vertical slit-windows suggest. Daily 8.30am–10pm.

★ **Natraj** Opposite the Salim Singh ki Haveli ☎0299 225 2667; map p.178. There's no fort view from this upper-level restaurant (except one corner, from one or two tables, if you crane your neck). However, the local food is the best in town, with non-veg options including plenty of Rajasthani options – you're best off going for the scrummy Rajasthani thali (₹330), which gives you a little of all the local specialities, and will be served nice and spicy if you so desire. Licensed. Daily 8.30am–10pm.

Saffron Nachana Haveli, Gandhi Chowk ☎0299 225 2110; map p.178. Slightly upmarket rooftop haveli restaurant (see page 184), serving fine veg, tandoori and Mughlai food (mains ₹190–350). There's live music most nights, and this is the best time to visit, on account of the superlative fort views. Daily 8.30am–10pm.

CAFÉS AND SNACKS

8 July Main Chowk, in the fort ☎0299 225 2814; map p.180. Recommended for its privileged terrace view of the fort's bustling main chowk and palace rather than

for its food, though it has a good selection of smoothies, juices and lassis (try the awesome local variety, made with saffron, almond and cardamom; ₹140), as well as snacks such as delectable apple pie with custard (₹170). Homesick Brits/Aussies will love the Marmite/Vegemite-and-toast breakfast option, or the baked beans (in home-made sauce) on toast. Daily 5.30am–4pm; sometimes opens later.

Bhang shop Gopa Chowk; map p.180. If you like bhang – and be warned that it doesn't agree with everybody – this is one of the best places in the country to get it, with a whole menu of bhang-laced lassis (from ₹150) and cookies (minimum purchase of ten; ₹1500), and a choice of different strengths. Daily 9am–10pm.

Dhanraj Ranmal Bhatia Court Rd; map p.180. Wonderful, moist milk-based sweets (ladoos, barfi and the like), plus great samosas and mirchi badas; you can even watch them being made, as they do it all out front. You can get a little selection for under ₹100. Daily 9am–9pm.

RK Juice Center Bhatia Bazaar; map p.178. Wonderful freshly pressed juices (₹50) using whatever fruits are available on the day (usually including some or all of orange, pomegranate, pineapple, banana, carrot and ginger). They promise not to add ice or tap water (though they do use it to rinse out the juice extractor). Daily 7am–late.

DRINKING

Cafe Kaku Malka Pol ☎96727 03070; map p.178. Overlooking the city, and with a mighty (if slightly distant) view of the fort, this is your best bet for booze – wine and spirits are a bit pricey, but you can get a big bottle of

Kingfisher for ₹250. They've half a dozen low tables on cushion-covered platforms, all with winning views – a great place to smoke a hookah (₹1000), and for now at least, pleasingly off the tourist radar. Daily 10.30am–11pm.

SHOPPING

Jaisalmer is one of the best places in India to shop for souvenirs. Prices are comparatively high and the salesmen push hard, but the choice of goods is excellent – virtually the whole **fort** has now been turned into an enormous souvenir bazaar, while there are dozens of further places along **Bhatia Bazaar**. Jaisalmer is a particularly good place to pick up textiles, fabrics and leatherwork (including camel leather bags and shoes), as well as cheap hippie-style clothes.

Ajay Leather Shop 181 Fort Rd ☏ 96943 07055; map p.180. Perhaps the best choice for camel-leather goods, with staff light on hassle and big on conversation. If you're in town for a few days, they can dye some goods – laptop bags, handbags, purses, footwear and the like – the colour of your choosing. Daily 9am–9pm.

Hari Om Jewellers Sunset Point, inside the fort ☏ 94146 71025; map p.180. Well-located jewellery store, with a very decent selection at fair prices – just try to find it yourself, since even locals will try taking a commission if they show you the way. It's one of those places where you could pop in for a look, and emerge a couple of hours later, empty-handed but full of masala chai. Daily 10am–8pm.

DIRECTORY

Banks and exchange There are ATMs all over town, including some inside and outside Amar Sagar Pol, and a couple just outside the southern edge of the fort, plus a cluster of exchange bureaux in Gandhi Chowk.

Hospital The government T.B. Hospital is on Sam Rd, west of Hanuman Circle (☏ 0299 225 5627), but a better bet is the small, private Maheshwari Hospital off Sam Rd opposite the court and District Magistrate's office (☏ 0299 225 0024).

Police Just south of Hanuman Circle on Amar Sagar Rd (☏ 0299 225 2233).

Amar Sagar

Get there by rickshaw (₹400 return) or cycle from town • Adeshwar Nath Temple Daily dawn–dusk • ₹150, ₹100 camera, ₹150 video camera

Seven kilometres northwest of Jaisalmer is **AMAR SAGAR**, a small and peaceful town set around a large artificial lake (empty during the dry season) where you'll find the eighteenth-century Amar Singh Palace and three Jain temples, including the **Adeshwar Nath Temple**, commissioned in 1928 by a member of the same family who put up the Patwa Haveli in Jaisalmer.

Lodurva

There is just one bus a day to Lodurva (3pm), so taking a rickshaw or taxi is a more convenient and leisurely option (₹550/₹700 respectively for the round trip including stops at Amar Sagar and Bada Bagh) – or, if feeling energetic, you could cycle • Jain temples Daily 8am–5pm • ₹150

A further 10km northwest of Amar Sagar, **LODURVA** was the capital of the Bhati Rajputs from the eighth century until the twelfth, when it was sacked by Muhammad of Ghor, after which the Bhatis moved their capital to Jaisalmer. Only a few **Jain temples**, rebuilt in the seventeenth century, remain. The main temple, dedicated to Parshvanath, features an ornately carved 8m *toran* (arch), just inside the entrance to the main temple compound, perhaps the most exquisite in Rajasthan, plus a finely carved exterior.

Kuldhara

Daily sunrise–sunset • ₹10, vehicles ₹50 • No public transport; a jeep to Kuldhara costs ₹750 for the round trip

South of the Sam road, around 25km west of Jaisalmer, the ghost village of **KULDHARA** was one of 84 villages abandoned, for unknown reasons, simultaneously one night in 1825 by the Paliwal Brahmin community, which had settled here in the thirteenth century. The Paliwals' sense of industry and order is attested by their homes, each with its living quarters, guest room, kitchen and stables, and parking space for a camel; you can take an atmospheric stroll through them to the temple at the heart of the village. Kuldhara is a bit far from anything, but there's usually a little shop open near the entrance to the compound, and a drinks wagon 1.5km down the road into the complex.

2

THE BIRTHPLACE OF ATOMIC INDIA

Some 110km east of Jaisalmer, at the road and rail junctions between Jodhpur, Bikaner and the west, is the quiet and little-visited town of **POKARAN**. This became the centre of international attention in May 1998 when three massive **nuclear explosions** were detonated 200m beneath the sands of the Thar Desert, 20km northwest of the town, announcing India's arrival as one of the world's fully fledged atomic powers.

Sam

Daily bus (4pm, returning in morning) from local bus stand in Jaisalmer; jeeps/taxis about ₹1200/₹1750 for round trip

The huge, rolling sand dunes 40km west of Jaisalmer are known as **SAM**, though strictly this is the name of a small village further west. Unfortunately, the once pristine desert here has now vanished beneath endless tented camps, as around five thousand tourists descend daily to watch sunset and make merry in the desert. If you've come to the Thar in search of vast crowds, psychotic camel touts and endless piles of windblown plastic, then you'll be in seventh heaven. If not, the entire area is best given a wide berth. You can stay overnight here in one of the numerous tented camps, but this is not recommended.

Khuhri

Daily buses (3pm & 5pm, returning in morning) from just west of state bus stand in Jaisalmer; jeeps/taxis about ₹1200/₹1700 for round trip

A rather nicer place to watch the sun set over the dunes than Sam is the village of **KHUHRI**, 42km southwest of Jaisalmer. Many camel safaris either start here or pass through – most time their arrival so that tourists can see flamboyantly dressed local women arriving with large jugs on their heads to fill up with water at caste-specific wells. The village also has a certain charm – many of its homes are still made of mud and thatch rather than concrete, their exterior surfaces beautifully decorated with ornate white murals.

Unfortunately, tourist development has already eroded much of Khuhri's traditional character. Virtually every building has been converted into a guesthouse, while ugly new concrete buildings and endless signboards are beginning to mushroom on every available space, accompanied by the usual tide of discarded plastic and other rubbish.

ACCOMMODATION   KHUHRI

Badal House Call ahead for a pick-up at the bus stop ☏ 0810 733 9097. Despite the profusion of guesthouses in Khuhri (and upmarket tented camps around it), prices tend to be steep. If you do want to stay in the desert, you probably can't do better than the very simple but extremely peaceful *Badal House*. Owned by the charming Badul Singh, this welcoming homestay is a good place to chill out for a few days and get a feel of village life. You stay in huts or rooms and they can also arrange well-priced, authentic camel safaris (₹800/person). Full board. ₹850

Jodhpur and around

On the eastern fringe of the Thar Desert, **JODHPUR**, dubbed "the Blue City" after the colour-wash of its old townhouses, huddles below the mighty **Mehrangarh Fort**, the most spectacular citadel in Rajasthan, which dominates the cityscape from atop its huge sandstone plinth.

Blue originally denoted a high-caste Brahmin residence, resulting from the addition of indigo to lime-based whitewash, which was thought to protect buildings from insects, and to keep them cool in summer. Over time the colour caught on – there's now even a blue-wash mosque on the road from the Jalori Gate, south of the fort. However, don't arrive thinking that the whole city is blue – it's just part of the old city, and even here the hue is not totally dominant, vying with mauve for chromatic supremacy in some areas.

The bazaars of the old city, with different areas assigned to different trades, radiate out from the 1910 **Sardar Market** with its tall **clock tower**, a distinctive local landmark marking the centre of town. Most of the ramparts on the south side of the old city have been dismantled, leaving **Jalori Gate** and **Sojati Gate** looking rather forlorn as gates without a wall.

Jodhpur was once the most important town of Marwar, the largest princely state in Rajputana, and now has a population of around 1.3 million. Most people stay just long enough to visit the fort, though there's plenty to justify a longer visit. Getting lost in the blue maze of the old city you'll stumble across Muslim tie-dyers, puppet-makers and traditional spice markets, while Jodhpur's famed cubic roofscape, best viewed at sunset, is a photographer's dream.

Brief history

The **kingdom of Marwar** came into existence in 1381 when Rao Chanda, chief of the **Rathore** Rajput clan, seized the fort of Mandor (see page 196) from its former rulers, the Parihars. In 1459, the Rathore chief **Rao Jodha** moved from the exposed site at Mandor to a massive steep-sided escarpment, naming his new capital Jodhpur, after

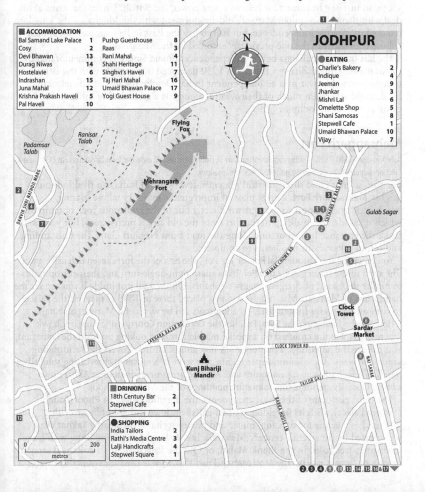

JODHPUR

ACCOMMODATION

Bal Samand Lake Palace	1	Pushp Guesthouse	8
Cosy	2	Raas	3
Devi Bhawan	13	Rani Mahal	4
Durag Niwas	14	Shahi Heritage	11
Hostelavie	6	Singhvi's Haveli	7
Indrashan	15	Taj Hari Mahal	16
Juna Mahal	12	Umaid Bhawan Palace	17
Krishna Prakash Haveli	5	Yogi Guest House	9
Pal Haveli	10		

EATING

Charlie's Bakery	2
Indique	4
Jeeman	9
Jhankar	3
Mishri Lal	6
Omelette Shop	5
Shani Samosas	8
Stepwell Cafe	1
Umaid Bhawan Palace	10
Vijay	7

Padamsar Talab

Ranisar Talab

Flying Fox

Mehrangarh Fort

DANTIH SHRI MATHUJI MARG

Gulab Sagar

SURHAID KA RASS RD

MANAK CHOWK RD

LAKHARA BAZAR RD

Clock Tower

Sardar Market

NAI SARAK

CLOCK TOWER RD

Kunj Bihariji Mandir

TAILOR GALI

BARKA HOUSE LN

DRINKING

18th Century Bar	2
Stepwell Cafe	1

SHOPPING

India Tailors	2
Rathi's Media Centre	3
Lalji Handicrafts	4
Stepwell Square	1

0 — 200 metres

2, 3, 4, 6, 10, 13, 14, 15, 16 & 17

2

FLYING FOX RIDES OVER THE BLUE CITY

For a bird's-eye view of the fort, you can fly its over courtyards, ramparts and lakes via **Flying Fox**, a network of six zipwires. The longest (and last) wire – known as the "Magnificent Marwar" – also gives amazing views of the Blue City itself. Tours are guided by an instructor and last about 90min. If you book online three days in advance, they usually offer a fifteen percent discount; the office is by the gardens inside the fort, but you don't have to pay the fort entry fee if you're heading here, so you can do your visit and your zipwiring at different times of day, if you so desire.

---

himself. His high barricaded fort proved virtually impregnable, and the city soon amassed great wealth from trade. The Mughals were keen to take over Jodhpur, and **Akbar** got his hands on the city in 1561, but he eventually allowed Marwar to keep its internal independence so long as the Rathore maharajas allied themselves to him.

In the eighteenth century, Marwar, Mewar (Udaipur) and Jaipur sealed a triple alliance to retain their independence against the Mughals, though the three states were as often at each other's throats as they were allied together. At the end of the century, **Maharaja Man Singh** found himself under pressure from the expanding Maratha Empire to his south, so in 1818 he turned for help to a new power, the **British**. Under the terms of his deal with them – not unlike Marwar's old arrangement with the Mughals – the kingdom retained its internal independence, but had to pay the East India Company an annual tribute equivalent to the one previously enforced by the Marathas.

The last but one maharaja before Independence, **Umaid Singh**, is commemorated by the immense Umaid Bhawan Palace. In 1930 he agreed in principle with the British to incorporate Marwar into an independent India. Despite the loss of official status, his descendants retain much of their wealth, alongside a great deal of influence and genuine respect in Jodhpur.

Mehrangarh Fort

Daily 9am–5pm • ₹600 (₹100) including audio tour if you leave ID, credit card or deposit; audio tour for Indian visitors costs ₹150; camera ₹100; video camera ₹200; elevator ₹50; guide ₹200 • ⓦ mehrangarh.org

For size, strength and sheer physical presence, few sights in India can rival Jodhpur's mighty **Mehrangarh Fort**, a great mass of impregnable masonry whose soaring, windowless walls appear to have grown directly out of the enormous rock outcrop on which it stands. The walk up to the fort from the old city is pretty steep, but you can reach the entrance by taxi or auto along the road from Nagauri Gate. The outstanding audio tour takes about two hours to complete.

You enter the fort through **Jai Pol** (or Jey Pol), the first of the fort's seven defensive gates. The sixth of the seven gates, **Loha Pol**, has a sharp right-angle turn and sharper iron spikes to hinder the ascent of charging enemy elephants. On the wall just inside it you can see the handprints of Maharaja Man Singh's widows, placed there in 1843 as they left the palace to commit sati on his funeral pyre – the last mass sati by wives of a Marwari maharaja.

Beyond the final gate, the **Suraj Pol**, lies the **Coronation Courtyard** (Shangar Chowk), where maharajas are crowned on a special marble throne. Looking up from the courtyard, you can see the fantastic *jali* (lattice) work that almost entirely covers the surrounding sandstone walls. The adjoining apartments now serve as a **museum** showcasing solid silver *howdahs* (elephant seats), palanquins and assorted armaments including Akbar's own sword. Upstairs are some fine **miniature paintings** of the Marwari school.

The most elaborate of the royal apartments, the magnificent 1724 **Phool Mahal** (Flower Palace), with its jewel-like stained-glass windows and gold filigree ceiling, was used as a venue for dancing, music and poetry recitals. The nearby **Takhat Vilas** was created by nineteenth-century Maharaja Takhat Singh, its ceiling hung with huge Christmas-tree balls. In the **Jhanki Mahal**, or Queen's Palace, there's a colourful array of cradles of former rulers. The **Moti Mahal** (Pearl Palace) was used for councils of state.

The five alcoves in the wall opposite the entrance are in fact concealed balconies where the maharaja's wives could listen in secretly on the proceedings.

Beyond the Moti Mahal is the **zenana**, or women's quarters. From here, take a walk south of the main complex; once through the gardens, you'll finally make it to the **Temple of Chamunda**, the city's oldest temple, dedicated to Jodhpur's patron goddess, an incarnation of Durga. Peek through the holes in the fortifications, and you'll get some spellbinding views over the Blue City.

Jaswant Thada

Off Fort Rd • Daily 9am–5pm • ₹30 (₹15); camera ₹25, video camera ₹50; guide ₹80

Some 500m north of the fort, and connected to it by road, **Jaswant Thada** is a pillared marble memorial to the popular ruler Jaswant Singh II (1878–95), who purged Jodhpur of bandits, initiated irrigation systems and boosted the economy. The cenotaphs of members of the royal family who have died since Jaswant are close to his memorial; those who preceded him are commemorated by chhatris at Mandor (see page 196). In the morning, this southwest-facing spot is an excellent place from which to photograph the fort.

Rao Jodha Desert Rock Park

Off Fort Rd • Daily: Apr–Sep 7am–6.30pm, Oct–Mar 8am–5.30pm • ₹100

If you're in the fort area, consider heading a little west to the new **Rao Jodha Desert Rock Park**, an undulating, grassy expanse spreading over 70 hectares – crazy though it may sound, visitors are advised to leave their mobile phone numbers at the ticket booth, just in case they get lost. This area was neglected for decades, partly on account of an infestation of thorny shrubs; there are still some here, but by and large this has been a resounding success, and the fort views are especially good in the evening.

Umaid Bhawan Palace

Circuit House Rd • Minimum fee for entry ₹3500, redeemable against food and drink • **Museum** Daily 9am–5pm • ₹100 (₹30), camera ₹50, video camera ₹100 • ⓦ tajhotels.com

Dominating the city's southeast horizon is the **Umaid Bhawan Palace**, a colossal Indo-Saracenic heap that kept three thousand labourers gainfully employed for sixteen years at a total cost of more than ₹9 million. The furniture and fittings for its 374 rooms were originally ordered from Maples in London during World War II, but were sunk by a U-boat en route to India. The maharaja was thus forced to turn to Stephen Norblin, a wartime Polish refugee, who gave the palace its fabulous Art Deco interiors.

The present incumbent, Maharaja Gaj Singh, occupies only one-third of the palace; the rest is given over to a luxury **hotel** (see page 195) and a rather dull **museum**,

---

SUNRISE AND SUNSET IN JODHPUR

Jodhpur being one of the most picturesque cities in Rajasthan – nay, India – many of its visitors want to see the place in the most spectacular light, which of course means the time around **sunrise** and **sunset**. The fort often plays a central role in photographic proceedings, but its opening times rule it out as an option; the nearby **Rao Jodha Desert Rock Park** closes later, and provides views of the sun's final rays flaring up the fort, as does **Singhoria Hill** (24hr; free) on the other side of the road. Popular with locals and independent travellers is the ridge south of the fort, often referred to as **Sunset Point**; although the trails leading up the promontory from the west and east are a little hard to find, you'll hunt them down in the end, and the views are colossal. Lastly, of course, your own accommodation may provide lovely views; failing that, head to restaurants such as Jeeman (see page 195) or Indique (see page 195).

2

containing assorted European crockery and glassware, plus a mildly entertaining gallery of clocks and barometers, some in the form of railway locomotives, lighthouses and windmills. Far more interesting (and expensive) is the palace itself, its Art Deco furniture and fittings nearly all original, enlivened with lashings of typically Rajasthani gilt and sweeping staircases. To see them, there's a hefty minimum fee.

ARRIVAL AND DEPARTURE
JODHPUR

Jodhpur stands at the nexus of Rajasthan's main tourist routes, with connections northeast to Jaipur, Pushkar and Delhi, south to Udaipur and Ahmedabad, and west to Jaisalmer. Buses for most destinations are faster than the train.

By plane Jodhpur's Civil Airport (☎ 291 251 2934) is 4km south of the city. A prepaid auto-rickshaw into town from the airport costs ₹200, taxis ₹500; Uber and Ola cabs usually cost ₹180–220.

Destinations Ahmedabad (2 daily; 1hr 20min); Delhi (4 daily; 1hr 25min); Mumbai (2 daily; 1hr 45min).

By train The railway station is on Station Rd, 300m south of Sojati Gate; there's a reservations office (Mon–Sat 8am–8pm, Sun 8am–2pm) just north of the station, behind the GPO. Note that there are no direct trains to Udaipur or

Chittaurgarh – it's much easier to catch the bus.

By bus Government buses leave from the Roadways (Raika Bagh) Bus Stand just east of the fort – turn up an hour or so before departure to buy a ticket. For timetable information, consult ☎ redbus.in. Most private buses leave from the stand on Pal Rd, 4km west of the centre (about ₹120 by auto); a few private buses leave from Kalpataru Cinema, 4km southwest of town (₹100 by auto). Private buses for Jaisalmer leave from Bombay Motors Circle, nearby, where they also drop off. You can book tickets on private buses at most travel agents and a lot of hotels (for a fee).

Destinations Agra (4 daily; 13hr); Ajmer (2–5 hourly; 4–6hr); Delhi (12 daily; 11–13hr); Jaipur (2–5 hourly; 7–9hr); Jaisalmer (1–2 hourly; 5hr); Udaipur (1–2 hourly; 4hr 30min–7hr).

GETTING AROUND AND INFORMATION

By taxi The Ola and Uber taxi-hailing apps work in Jodhpur, and prices are usually comparable to auto-rickshaws.

Motorcycle rental Jodhpur Travels on Station Rd (daily 6am–11pm; ☎ 946 0687 264, ☎ jodhpurtravels.com) has

motorbikes and mopeds for rent from ₹400/day.

Tourist information The tourist office (Mon–Fri 9.30am–6pm; ☎ 0291 254 5083) is next to the *RTDC Goomar Hotel* on High Court Rd.

ACTIVITIES

Cooking classes Numerous hotels in town offer cooking classes, but best are those at the *Rani Mahal* (see page 194); the classes themselves are free, and guests simply pay for the ingredients. South of town, *Indrashan* (see page 195) prides itself on cooking classes (₹1500) that draw amateur chefs from around the world.

Festivals Jodhpur's annual two-day Marwar Festival, held at the full moon of the Hindu month of Ashvina (mid-October) is a showcase of performing arts, mainly music and dance.

Flying Fox rides You can zoom over the Blue City on a series of zip-wires; tours (₹2000; ☎ flyingfox.asia) start more or less half-hourly from 9.30am–4.30pm.

ACCOMMODATION

Jodhpur has plenty of good accommodation in all price brackets, and happily the same can now be said of its main area of interest. Many guesthouses offer free pick-ups from the train or bus stations.

IN THE OLD TOWN AND CITY CENTRE

Cosy Bhram Puri, Chuna ki Chowki, Navchokiya ☎ 0291 261 2066, ☎ cosyguesthouse.com; map p.189. Friendly little guesthouse in a pretty blue-washed building buried deep in the maze of lanes in the west of the old city (call for free pick-up; it's tricky to find otherwise). Rooms (fan, air-cooled and a/c; a few with shared bathroom) are simple but neat and cosy, and there are killer views of the fort from the rooftop terrace. ₹750

Durag Niwas 1st Old Public Park Lane, Raika Bagh ☎ 0291 251 2385, ☎ durag-niwas.com; map p.189. Very friendly and well-run little place with cosy air-cooled and a/c rooms, all with private bathrooms, set around a peaceful courtyard. Also runs various programmes helping disadvantaged local women (half the guests are usually long-stay volunteers). LGBTQ friendly. ₹1200

Hostelavie Fort Rd ☎ 0291 261 1001, ☎ hostelavie.com; map p.189. The best, and best-located, of the hostel chain options, with decent dorm rooms – and rather overpriced private ones – augmented by free breakfast, laundry and instant coffee, and a sociable rooftop cafe-bar serving (a little oddly) Korean food. The friendly management are adept at organising tours. Dorms ₹400, doubles ₹1350

CAMELS IN THE DESERT NEAR JODPHUR

2

RECOMMENDED TRAINS FROM JODHPUR

All the following trains run daily. There's also the weekly *Thar Express* to Karachi in Pakistan (Sat at 1am; 24hr), which departs from Bagat Ki Kothi station, 4km south of the city.

Destination	Name	No.	Departs	Arrives
Abu Road	*Ahmedabad Express*	19224	5.55am	10.40am
	Ranakpur Express	14707	2.30pm	7.27pm
Agra Fort	*Howrah Superfast*	12308	8.15pm	5.55am
Ajmer	*Jodhpur–Indore Express*	54801	7.10am	12.35pm
Alwar	*Jaisalmer–Delhi Express*	14660	11.25pm	7.14am
Bikaner	*Ranakpur Express*	14708	9.50am	3.30pm
Delhi	*Mandor Express*	12462	7.45pm	6.40am
	Jaisalmer–Delhi Express	14660	11.25pm	11.15am
Jaipur	*Jaipur Intercity Express*	12466	5.55am	10.50am
	Mandor Express	12462	7.45pm	12.50am
Jaisalmer	*Ranikhet Express*	15014	6pm	11.25pm
	Jaisalmer Express	14810	11.40pm	6.10am
Sawai Madhopur	*Intercity Express*	12466	5.55am	1.15pm

★ **Juna Mahal** Ada Bazaar, off Daga St ☎0291 279 0366, ⊛junamahal.com; map p.189. This almost 500-year-old haveli has just five great-value boutique suites (all a/c) adorned with eye-catching artefacts, plus nice bathrooms and balconies. There's veg food and free pick-up from the railway station. ₹1550

Krishna Prakash Haveli Nayabas, Killikhana ☎0291 264 4077, ⊛kpheritage.com; map p.189. A little like a tourist hotel given a haveli-style makeover, this place may appear chintzy to some, but can come across as best-of-both-worlds to others. Rooms are pleasingly decorated with good wi-fi, and there's a cute, sheltered pool; the breakfast buffet is quite decent, and guests can dine up on the roof with a jaw-dropping view of the fort. ₹3000

Pal Haveli Near Gulab Sagar Lake ☎0291 329 3328, ⊛palhaveli.com; map p.189. Atmospheric heritage hotel in the heart of the old city with attractively furnished rooms and plenty of period character. Standard ("Royal Heritage") rooms are reasonably affordable, though the "Historical" suites (₹9500) are only slightly nicer, and almost twice the price. There's also a fabulous rooftop restaurant (see page 195), spa and bar. ₹6000

Pushp Guesthouse Near Manak Chowk ☎0291 264 8494, ⊛pushpguesthouse.com; map p.189. Tucked up a side alley in the heart of the Old City, and run by a friendly family, this place has five clean, jewel-coloured rooms (fan, a/c or air-cooled), a nice fabric-adorned rooftop café, and city views. ₹800

Raas Tunwarji-ka Jhalara ☎0291 263 6455, ⊛raasjodhpur.com; map p.189. At last, a real luxury option in the old town. Despite the location near the stepwell, there's a truly secluded air to proceedings, while buildings and decor are a quirky mix of old, old old, and modern. There's an old-site spa (but of course), a bar area overlooking the pool, and a dining room for in-house guests only – very exclusive. ₹21,000

★ **Rani Mahal** Navchokiya, Fort Rd ☎0291 263 9595, ⊛theranimahal.com; map p.189. Despite its location in a 450-year-old building, this is a relatively new accommodation option, yet already up there with the best in the city, with admirably switched-on management, and thirteen superlative rooms (six of which have marvellous antique wooden ceilings). Dua Lipa and assorted Bollywood stars have stayed here, as made evident by the wall of fame in the marvellously decorated lobby, which doubles as a restaurant; however, even this is trumped by the superlative views from the rooftop tables. ₹2200

★ **Shahi Heritage** Gandhi St, City Police district, off Katla Bazaar opposite Narsingh Temple ☎0291 262 3802, ⊛shahiguesthouse.net; map p.189. Welcoming family guesthouse occupying a quirky 350-year-old Mughal haveli, buried deep in the warren of lanes beneath the fort's southwest wall – and with superb views of it from the roof. The six rooms (all a/c) are brimming with character, decorated with a medley of quaint murals and assorted curios. Call for free pick-up, since it's difficult to find otherwise; breakfast included in the rates. ₹3000

Singhvi's Haveli Ramdevji-ka Chowk ☎0291 262 4293, ⊛singhvihaveli.com; map p.189. This family-run guesthouse and restaurant in a 500-year-old haveli rears up from the old town under the quieter western end of Mehrangarh Fort. The mishmash of rooms (all attached, some with a/c) range from cheap and cheerful doubles to a fabulous mirrorwork-adorned Maharani Suite. ₹1250

Yogi Guest House Manak Chowk, Old City ☎0291 264 3436, ⊛yogiguesthouse.com; map p.189. One of the more charming guesthouses located just north of Sardar Bazaar, with lovely blue decor and clean, comfy rooms (most with a/c) with wobbly old walls. There are excellent fort views from the rooftop restaurant. ₹800

FURTHER AFIELD

Bal Samand Lake Palace 8km north of Jodhpur along Mandore Rd ☎0291 4603 5500, ⓦjodhanaheritage. com; map p.189. Among the most attractive heritage hotels in the state, converted from the maharaja's lakeside summer palace, with ten beautiful "Palace Suites" in the main building – all huge, airy and exquisitely furnished – plus cheaper standard rooms in the palace's former stables, near reception. ₹7400

★ **Devi Bhawan** Ratanada Circle, Defence Laboratory Rd ☎0291 251 2215, ⓦdevibhawan.com; map p.189. Set in surprisingly lush gardens, this eighty-year-old refuge is home to spotless a/c rooms furnished with period fittings and colourful Rajasthani fabrics. The gorgeous pool is one of the nicest in town and there's a breezy restaurant that spills onto a terrace shaded by *neem* trees. ₹2700

Indrashan 593 High Court Colony, 3km south of town ☎0291 244 0665, ⓦindrashan.com; map p.189. Five cosy rooms in an authentic homestay in a quiet residential area, with sumptuous cooking classes. Non-guests are welcome for dinner if they call ahead. ₹2800

Taj Hari Mahal 5 Residency Rd, 1km south of town ☎0291 243 9700, ⓦvivantabytaj.com; map p.189. All the luxury you'd expect from a five-star *Taj* hotel, with swanky traditional-style decor, two good restaurants, a spa and good-sized pool, and spacious and attractively furnished rooms. ₹12,000

Umaid Bhawan Palace Circuit House Rd ☎0291 251 0101, ⓦtajhotels.com; map p.189. The maharaja of Jodhpur's princely pile (see page 191) ranks among the world's grandest hotels, with celebrity guests, lashings of trendy Art Deco and dark, marbled passageways. ₹US$1000

EATING

Local specialities include *mirchi bada*, a big chilli covered in wheatgerm and potato and then deep-fried like a pakora – you'll often find them served on trains on the way into and out of Jodhpur. You'll find these, and some of the town's most notable places to snack, around the clock tower, which is lit up rather kaleidoscopically at night; for Indian sweeties, try the shops at the western end of Mirchi bazaar.

RESTAURANTS

Indique Pal Haveli, near Gulab Sagar Lake ☎0291 329 3328, ⓦpalhaveli.com; map p.189. Atmospheric dining spot with tables on two levels of the rooftop, with stunning views of the fort, the Blue City and Umaid Bhawan Palace. The veg and non-veg food isn't quite as good as the view, but not bad at all – mainly Indian mains (₹350–600), including good Rajasthani options, but also lamb goulash, Thai curries, and Amritsari fish tikka. Licensed, too. Daily noon–3pm & 6–10.30pm.

Jeeman Navchokiya, Fort Rd ☎0291 263 9595, ⓦtheranimahal.com; map p.189. The in-house restaurant of the *Rani Mahal* (see page 194) offers excellent Indian meals (₹230–460), including plenty of Rajasthani options; the lobby level dining area is broodingly beautiful, though it's hard to pass up the opportunity to dine on the rooftop, especially around sunset, since the views are up there with the best in the city. Daily 10am–10pm.

Jhankar Choti Haveli, Makarana Mohalla ☎98280 31291; map p.189. The veg restaurant in this 500-year-old building spans three floors, with obligatory rooftop seating, but it's the enchanting court-yard garden restaurant that steals the show; sit under the shade of *neem* trees and dine on home-style Rajasthani specialities (₹180–300) such as *raboi* and *ker sangri*, perhaps best sampled in thali form, or Western treats such as banana pancakes (₹70). Daily 7am–11pm.

Stepwell Cafe By stepwell, Makarana Mohalla ☎0291 263 6455; map p.189. More of a restaurant than a cafe (although they do have an espresso machine, and staff who know how to operate it), this fancy spot has a quirky step-based menu. The "first step" starters are mostly Indian in nature but with some Western tweaks (₹130–290), "main step" mains are light affairs such as pasta dishes, mini calzone or dosas (₹190–350), and there are tasty desserts on the final step. Yet more steps link the main dining area to not one but two rooftop levels (somehow not a contradiction in terms), and all three have views of... a stepwell. Also a good bar (see page 196). Daily noon–10.30pm.

Umaid Bhawan Palace Circuit House Rd ☎0291 251 0101, ⓦtajhotels.com; map p.189. The opulent *Umaid Bhawan Palace* boasts various eating and drinking possibilities, though whatever you do you'll have to stump up a ₹3500 minimum charge, payable on entry and redeemable against anything you eat or drink (advance reservations for the restaurants are also strongly recommended) – although this at least gives you the chance to wander around the hotel's opulent Art Deco interior. *The Pillars* veranda café has sweeping views over the palace gardens and offers light snacks during the day. Full meals are available at the *Risala* multicuisine restaurant, set in a lavish, old-world European-style dining room, and at *The Pillars* at night. The Pillars 6.30am–11pm; Risala 1–3pm & 7.30–11pm.

Vijay Katla Bazaar ☎0291 264 9554; map p.189. You want local? You got local. This upper-floor hideyhole is one of precious few simple eateries in the Blue City, with a range of cheap, tasty mains like daal fry or kaju curry (from ₹80), plus fried cashews and carrot helwa in the winter. Daily 11am–11pm.

CAFES, SNACKS AND SWEETS

Charlie's Bakery Makarana Mohalla, no phone; map p.189. Part of the Stepwell Square boutique mall (see page 196), this interior courtyard cafe comes in handy if you want to escape the noise – a sonic refuge into which only the most insistent beeps and honks enter from street level. Pastries from ₹110, most coffees ₹150. Daily 10am–7pm.

Mishri Lal In the eastern arch of the south gate to Sardar Market; map p.189. The town's most famous purveyor of *makhania* lassi (₹35, or ₹40 from a clay cup), made with cream, yogurt, saffron and cardamom – deliciously rich and thick, you'll most likely be back for more the following day. Daily 8.30am–9pm.

Omelette Shop Eastern of the north gate to Sardar Market; map p.189. Legendary omelette stand with no fewer than 25 options (from just ₹30), including a tasty "Spanish" number made with potato. Unfortunately, the same hands used to make the omelettes are used to handle change; best not go here if you've just landed in India. Daily 10.30am–10pm.

Shani Samosas Clock Tower Rd; map p.189. Heaving with custom from the moment it opens its doors, this is the best place in town for *mirchi bada* (₹16), and you'll pay about the same price for the samosas or kachori. Daily 8am–8pm.

DRINKING

There are not many liquor stores in the old town, but you'll find one a short way south of the clock tower, on the west side of the road; they bring the shutters down at 7pm or so, but often serve until 9pm from a beer can-sized gap they conveniently leave open. Other places for a rooftop drink include Jeeman restaurant (see page 195) and Hostelavie (see page 192).

18th Century Bar Pal Haveli, near Gulab Sagar Lake ☎0291 329 3328, ⊛palhaveli.com; map p.189. There's a rather grand-looking bar – colonial chic? – in the

Pal Haveli (see page 194), with booze prices surprisingly reasonable; beers go for ₹250, and cocktails ₹250–350. Despite the fetching decor, more guests choose to drink up on the rooftop restaurant level (see page 195), especially for sundowners. Daily noon–10.30pm.

Stepwell Cafe By stepwell, Makarana Mohalla ☎0291 263 6455; map p.189. This sleek restaurant (see page 195) has a decent roster of Indian wines by the glass (from ₹520), as well as cocktails (₹490), and cheap local and pricey international spirits. Daily noon–10.30pm.

SHOPPING

Jodhpur's first-rate antique reproductions – everything from chests of drawers to sculptures of Jain *tirthankaras* – attract dealers from around the world; there's a line of shops selling them along Umaid Bhawan Palace Rd east of the Circuit House. Other good buys in town include textiles, patchwork bedcovers, *bandhani* (tie-dye) fabric and Jodhpur riding britches, as well as great spices from the many vendors in Mirchi Bazaar – it's ₹200/kg for most spices, ₹800/kg for garam or tea masala, or ₹220/gram for baby saffron, all much cheaper (and better quality) than the vendors around the clock tower.

India Tailors High Court Rd, 75m east of the junction with Nai Sarak; map p.189. Despite its small and unprepossessing appearance, this little shop can't be beaten for custom-made suits or Jodhpur riding britches, and counts the maharaja among its customers. Daily 10am–8pm.

Rathi's Media Centre Mohanpura, over the bridge ☎93140 40087; map p.189. Near the railway station, this formerly huge bookstore has been reduced to a fraction of its original size, but is still worth a look if you need a new novel, or a guidebook to neighbouring countries. Daily 10am–8.30pm.

Lalji Handicrafts Umaid Bhawan Palace Rd; map p.189. Huge warehouse-like shop stuffed with all sorts of unusual bric-a-brac including old enamel signs and colonial-era prints. Daily 9am–7pm.

Stepwell Square Makarana Mohalla; map p.189. Not a shop, but a small boutique mall, newly opened up in this increasingly trendy part of the city. The most notable outlets are Frazer and Haws silversmiths, and Via Jodhpur for fabrics, clothing and simple jewellery; there's also a decent little cafe here (see page 195). Daily 10am–7pm.

DIRECTORY

Banks and exchange Forex offices can be found north of the clock tower in Sardar Market and on Hanwant Vihar just north of Circuit House, and there are ATMs all over the place.
Hospital The best private hospital is the Goyal on Residency

Rd in the Sindhi Colony, 2km south of town (☎0291 243 2144, ⊛goyalhospital.in).
Police ☎0291 265 0777. There's a police tourist assistance booth by the clock tower in Sardar Market.

Mandor

Some 9km north of Jodhpur lies the sleepy village of **MANDOR**, home to a superb sequence of **royal cenotaphs** erected in memory of the kingdom's former rulers.

Mandor served as the capital of the Parihar Rajputs from the sixth century until 1381, when they were ousted by Rathore Rao Chauhan, and although the capital was moved to Jodhpur in 1459, the Marwari rulers continued to have their memorial cenotaphs (*dewals*) erected here. Temple-like in their sombre dark-red sandstone, the cenotaphs grew in size and grandeur as the Rathore kingdom prospered (the canopy-like chhatris next to them are for lesser royals). The largest is Ajit Singh's, built in 1724. His six queens, along with assorted mistresses, concubines, maids and entertainers – 84 women in all – committed sati on his funeral pyre.

At the end of the gardens, on the far side of the chhatris, you'll find the octagonal **Ek Thamba Mahal** (Single Pillared Palace), a three-storey pagoda-like affair built at the beginning of the eighteenth century for royal ladies to watch public events without breaking their purdah. Also interesting are the extensive remains of **Mandor Fort**, citadel of the Parihar and Rathore Rajputs when Mandor was their capital, reached via a flight of steps behind a mildly diverting museum.

ARRIVAL AND ACCOMMODATION

MANDOR

By bus Mandor can be reached on minibuses from the clock tower (7.30am–8.30pm; every 15min or so; ₹5).

Mandore Guest House Close to the gardens on Dadawari Lane ☎0291 254 5210, ⊛mandore.com. **₹2300**

It's actually more of a miniature resort than a guesthouse, with accommodation in a mix of air-cooled and a/c rooms and (rather dark) round huts set in a tree-studded garden.

The Bishnoi villages

Good and inexpensive tours of the Bishnoi villages are run by several guesthouses in Jodhpur including *Durag Niwas* and *Yogi's Guest House*; rates start at around ₹1200/person in a couple (slightly cheaper in groups of three or more)

Jodhpur's surroundings can be explored on organized "**village safaris**", which take small groups of tourists out into rural Rajasthan, usually stopping at four or five **Bishnoi villages** where you can taste traditional food, drink opium tea and watch crafts such as spinning and carpet-making. You might also spot nilgai (bluebull) antelopes and gazelles.

The Bishnois – a religious sect rather than an ethnic group in the usual sense – are among the world's earliest tree-huggers. Their origins go back to a drought in the year 1485. Observing that this was caused largely by deforestation, a guru by the name of Jambeshwar Bhagavan formulated 29 rules for living in harmony with nature and the environment – his followers are called Bishnoi after the Marwari word for 29. As well as enforcing strict vegetarianism, Jambeshwar's rules forbid the killing of animals or felling of live trees. In particular, Bishnoi hold the **khejri** tree sacred. In 1730, at the village of **Khejadali**, workers sent by the maharaja of Marwar to make lime for the construction of a palace started felling *khejri* trees to burn the local limestone. A woman by the name of Amrita Devi put her arms around a tree and declared that if they wanted to cut it down, they would have to cut her head off first. The leader of the working party ordered her decapitation, upon which her three daughters followed her example, and were similarly beheaded. Bishnoi people from the whole of the surrounding region then converged on the site to defend the trees – 363 of them gave their lives doing so. When news reached the maharaja, he ordered the felling to cease and banned cutting down trees and hunting animals in Bishnoi territory. Today, a small temple marks the place where all this happened, while in its grounds, 363 *khejri* trees commemorate the martyrs.

Although it is possible to go to Khejadali by bus, you'll be hard put to find a villager who speaks English, and it's a lot better to go with a tour group, which will also visit other villages. Most tours stop at Khejadali for lunch. This is sometimes followed by an **opium ceremony** in which opium is dissolved in water in a specially designed wooden vessel, and poured through a strainer into a second receptacle. The process is repeated twice more, and the resulting tea is drunk from the palm of a hand. Strictly speaking, it's illegal, but blind eyes are turned to this kind of traditional opium use, though in fact opium addiction is something of a social problem in rural Rajasthan.

2

Osian

Rajasthan's largest group of early Jain and Hindu temples lies on the outskirts of the small town of **OSIAN** (or **Osiyan**), 64km north of Jodhpur. The temples date from the eighth to the twelfth centuries when Osian was a regional trading centre. The town's ruler and population apparently converted to Jainism in the eleventh century, and the town is still an important Jain pilgrimage centre. Just south of the bus stop lies Osian's oldest collection of temples, centred on the **Vishnu and Harihara temples**, also built in the Pratihara period. The nine temples in this group retain a considerable amount of decorative carving, particularly in the surrounding friezes. However, most make a bee-line for the more diverting **Sachiya Mata Temple** and **Mahavira Jain Temple**.

Sachiya Mata Temple

Daily sunrise—one hour after sunset • ₹100 (₹50)

The town centre is dominated by the imposing twelfth-century **Sachiya Mata Temple**, overlooking the whole of Osian from its elevated hilltop position. At the very top of the complex, the main shrine to Sachiya (an incarnation of Durga) is unusually decorated with multicoloured mirrorwork and topped by a cluster of finely carved *shikharas*.

Mahavira Jain Temple

Daily 5am—10pm • ₹10 (free); ₹100 camera and video camera • No leather items permitted, and women should not enter while menstruating

A five-minute walk from the Sachiya Mata Temple lies Osian's most beautiful monument, the **Mahavira Jain Temple**. Built in the eighth century, renovated in the tenth, and restored quite recently, the temple's beautifully carved central shrine (which is somewhat ruined by the recently added metal staircase) is fronted by 28 pillars and surrounded by shrines to further *tirthankaras*. A trio of smaller temples lies nearby, including a pair of Surya temples and the unusual **Peeplaj Temple**, surrounded by gargoyle-like projecting elephants, along with a massive Pratihara-period (eighth and ninth centuries) step-well.

ARRIVAL AND INFORMATION

OSIAN

By bus Government buses from Jodhpur (hourly; 1hr 30min) drop you at the stand on the main road just south of town.

Tours Camel treks around Osian can also be arranged through the *Yogi* and *Cosy* guesthouses in Jodhpur; rates start at around ₹1000/person/day (minimum two people) plus transport costs (round trip by taxi from ₹1700).

ACCOMMODATION

Priest Bhanu Sarma Guesthouse Opposite the Mahavira temple ☏ 0292 227 4331. Run by the knowledgeable (Hindu) priest of the same name who looks after the (Jain) temple, rooms are basic but clean with shared

---

LEGEND OF THE THAR

Legend ascribes the **creation of the Thar** to Rama, hero of the Ramayana. In it, Rama, an earthly incarnation of the god Vishnu, has to rescue his wife Sita from the clutches of the demon Ravana, who is holding her on the island of Sri Lanka. To cross to the island, Rama loads his bow with a magical arrow that will dry up the ocean, but the sea god Sagara begs him not to shoot, offering him free passage instead. Well, says Rama, my bow is now drawn and must be shot, where shall I aim it? There is a sea to the north, replies Sagara, where evil-doers drink my water and hurt me; shoot your arrow there, and you'll be doing me a favour. So Rama takes aim and shoots, drying up the sea that Sagara has described, and creating the desert of Marwar ("Land of the Dead"). By Rama's special boon, this new land, though desert, is blessed, full of sweet herbs and fit for grazing cattle.

In fact, the legend would seem to be based on some degree of truth, for the fossil record shows that back in the Jurassic period (206–144 million years ago), the Thar was covered by sea. Indeed, you may notice that slabs of sandstone often bear tell-tale ripple marks showing that they once formed part of the seabed.

bathrooms and buckets for hot water. Priest Bhanu can act as a guide for the local temples and you can also arrange camel safaris and tours of local Bishnoi villages from here. ₹700 **Reggie's Camel Camp** Reservations c/o the

India Safari Club in Jodhpur on ☎0291 243 7023, ⊕camelcamposian.com. A comfortable and welcoming luxury hotel amid the desert on the outskirts of town, with carpeted a/c tents and a stunning pool. Full board. ₹13,000

Mount Abu

Rajasthan's only bona fide hill station, **MOUNT ABU** (1220m) is a major Indian resort, popular above all with honeymooners who flock here during the winter wedding season (Nov to March) and with visiting holidaymakers from nearby Gujarat. Mount Abu's hokey commercialism is aimed squarely at these local vacationers rather than foreign tourists, but the sight of lovestruck honeymooners shyly holding hands and jolly parties of Gujarati tourists on the loose lends the whole place a charmingly idiosyncratic holiday atmosphere quite unlike anywhere else in Rajasthan – and the fresh air is exhilarating after the heat of the desert plains. The town also occupies an important place in Rajput history, being the site of the famous *yagna agnikund* fire ceremony, conducted in the eighth century AD, from which all Rajputs claim mythological descent.

Note that during the peak months and at almost any major festival time (especially Diwali in November), and even during weekends, the town's population of thirty thousand mushrooms, room rates skyrocket, and peace and quiet are at a premium.

Nakki Lake

Pedalo rides ₹100/30min

At the centre of town, **Nakki Lake** is popular in the late afternoon for pony and pedalo rides. Of several panoramic viewpoints on the fringes of town above the plains, **Sunset Point** is the favourite – though the hordes of holidaymakers and hawkers also make it one of the noisiest and least romantic. **Honeymoon Point**, also known as **Anadhra-Ganesh Point** (after the adjacent temple) offers breathtaking views over the plain at any time of day, and tends to be more peaceful. 4pm is a good time to visit, but don't try to take clifftop paths between Sunset and Honeymoon points, as tourists have been mugged here.

Brahma Kumaris Museum

Off Nakki Lake Rd • Daily 8am–8pm • Free

The **Brahma Kumaris Museum**, between the polo ground and the lake, is devoted to the spiritual ideals of the Brahma Kumaris ("children of Brahma"), whose headquarters are situated nearby. The Brahma Kumaris preach that all religions reach for the same goal, but label it differently. Once through the "Gateway to Paradise", you'll be greeted by freakish, life-sized mannequins including blue monsters wielding long knives. Each personifies greed, sex-lust and other vestiges of the so-called "iron age" that temple leaders promise deliverance from. If it all sounds somewhat cultish you'll understand why many locals try to keep foreigners from falling into the sect's clutches.

Dilwara temples

Daily noon–6pm • Free, but donation requested; no photography, usual Jain temple restrictions apply • You can charter a jeep (₹200 one way or ₹300 return) from the junction at the north end of the polo ground, or take a place in a shared one (₹30) from just up the street • 1hr walk

The **Dilwara temples**, 3km northeast of Mount Abu, are some of the most beautiful Jain shrines in India. All five are made purely from marble, and the carving is breathtakingly intricate. Entrance to the temples is by guided tour only – you'll have to wait until sufficient people have arrived to make up a group – though once inside it's easy enough to break away and look around on your own.

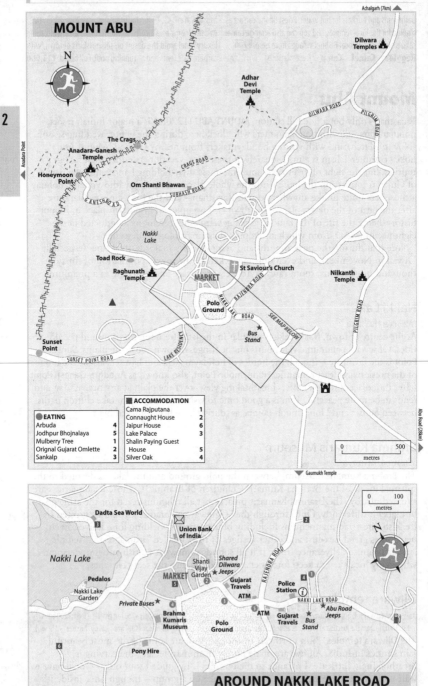

MOUNT ABU

Achalgarh (7km)

Dilwara Temples

Adhar Devi Temple

DILWARA ROAD

PILGRIM ROAD

The Crags

Anadara-Ganesh Temple

Honeymoon Point

Om Shanti Bhawan

SUBHASH ROAD

CRAGS ROAD

GANESH ROAD

Anadara Point

Nakki Lake

Toad Rock

Raghunath Temple

MARKET

St Saviour's Church

Nilkanth Temple

RAJENDRA ROAD

Polo Ground

NAKKI LAKE ROAD

SEE MAP BELOW

Bus Stand

PILGRIM ROAD

Sunset Point

SUNSET POINT ROAD

LAKE RESIDENCY

Abu Road (28km)

0 — 500 metres

Gaumukh Temple

● EATING
Arbuda	4
Jodhpur Bhojnalaya	5
Mulberry Tree	1
Orignal Gujarat Omlette	2
Sankalp	3

■ ACCOMMODATION
Cama Rajputana	1
Connaught House	2
Jaipur House	6
Lake Palace	3
Shalin Paying Guest House	5
Silver Oak	4

AROUND NAKKI LAKE ROAD

0 — 100 metres

Dadta Sea World

Union Bank of India

Nakki Lake

Pedalos

Nakki Lake Garden

Shanti Vijay Garden

Shared Dilwara Jeeps

Gujarat Travels

RAJENDRA ROAD

Police Station

ATM

MARKET

Private Buses

NAKKI LAKE ROAD

Abu Road Jeeps

Brahma Kumaris Museum

Polo Ground

ATM

Gujarat Travels

Bus Stand

Pony Hire

HIKING IN MOUNT ABU

Down in Mount Abu's market area, you gain little sense of the wonderfully wild **landscape** enfolding the town, but head for a few minutes up one of the many trails threading around the sides of the plateau, and it's easy to see why the area has inspired sages, saints and pilgrims for centuries. Unfortunately **hiking alone** is not recommended, as there have been robberies and even murders of unaccompanied visitors, and police will turn back anyone spotted heading out alone. There's also a chance of running into bears and leopards – bears, in particular, can be dangerous if surprised, or when with their young.

Good local **guides** are available from the *Shri Ganesh* hotel (see page 202), who run 3–4hr treks every morning (₹700/person); or the experienced "Charles" (⚙ mount-abu-treks.blogspot. com, contact via *Lake Palace* hotel, ☏ 94141 54854), who runs a range of half-day (from ₹500) and full-day (from ₹900) walking tours focusing on village life, wildlife spotting and local Ayurvedic plants, as well as overnight camping expeditions (₹1700, full board).

The oldest temple, the **Vimala Vasahi**, named after the Gujarati minister who funded its construction in 1031, is dedicated to Adinath, the first *tirthankara*. Although the exterior is simple – as, indeed, are the exteriors of all the temples here – inside not one wall, column or ceiling is unadorned, a prodigious feat of artistry that took almost two thousand labourers and sculptors fourteen years to complete. There are 48 intricately carved pillars inside, eight of them supporting a domed ceiling arranged in eleven concentric circles alive with dancers, musicians, elephants and horses, while a sequence of 57 subsidiary shrines run around the edge of the enclosure. In front of the entrance to the temple the so-called "Elephant Cell" (added after the construction of the temple itself in 1147) contains ten impressively large stone pachyderms. A more modest pair of painted elephants, along with an unusual carving showing stacked-up tiers of *tirthankaras*, flanks the entrance to the diminutive **Mahaveerswami Temple**, built in 1582, which sits by the entrance to the Vimala Vasahi.

The **Luna Vasahi Temple**, second of Dilwara's two great temples, was built in 1231, and is dedicated to Neminath, the 22nd *tirthankara*. It follows a similar plan to the Vimala Vasahi, with a central shrine fronted by a minutely carved dome and surrounded by a long sequence of shrines (a mere 48 this time). The carvings, however, are even more precise and detailed, especially so in the magnificently intricate dome covering the entrance hall.

The remaining two temples, both fifteenth-century, are less spectacular. The **Bhimasah Pittalhar Temple** houses a huge gilded image of the first *tirthankara*, Adinath, installed in 1468, which measures more than 2.5m high and weighs in at around 4.5 tonnes. The large three-storey **Khartar Vasahi Temple** (near the entrance to the temples) was built in 1458 and is consecrated to Parshvanath. The temple is topped by a high grey stone tower and boasts some intricate carving in places, though overall it's only a pale shadow of the earlier temples.

It's a pleasant walk up from town, though many opt for the sensible approach of ascending by jeep, then returning on foot.

Hindu temples

You can charter a jeep (₹1000 or so) to visit all temples

On the north side of town, en route to the Dilwara temples, a flight of more than four hundred steps climbs up to the **Adhar Devi Temple** (dedicated to Durga). The small main shrine is cut into the rocky hilltop and entered by clambering under a very low overhang. There are fine views from the terrace above, where there's another tiny shrine cut out of solid rock. The milk-coloured water of the **Doodh Baori** well at the foot of the steps is considered to be a source of pure milk (*doodh*) for gods and sages.

A further 8km northeast – not served by public transport, so you'll need to hire a jeep or a taxi – the temple complex at **ACHALGARH** is dominated by the **Achaleshwar**

2

Mahadeo Temple, believed to have been created when Lord Shiva placed his toe on the spot to still an earthquake. Its sanctuary holds a yoni stone with a hole in it that is said to reach into the netherworld. Nearby, the **Jamadagni Ashram** is site of the *yagna agnikund*, where the sage Vashishtha presided over the fire ritual that produced the four Rajput clans (the Parmars, Parihars, Solankis and Chauhans).

The lesser visited, but more dramatically situated, **Gaumukh Temple** lies 7km south of Mount Abu Town and is also not served by public transport. Standing at the head of a steep flight of 750 steps, the small pool inside the shrine – which continues to flow even during times of drought – is believed to hold water from the sacred Sarawati Ganga River. Pilgrims come here to perform puja, to invoke the blessings of India's two greatest *rishis* (sages), Vashishtha and Vishwamitra, who are thought to have meditated and debated here.

The last important Hindu pilgrimage site on Mount Abu is the Atri Rishi Temple at **Guru Shikar**, 15km northeast of town, which at 1772m above sea level marks the highest point in Rajasthan. You can enjoy superb panoramic vistas either from the temple itself, or from the food and drink stalls dotted around the site.

ARRIVAL AND INFORMATION   MOUNT ABU

Mount Abu is accessible only by road; the nearest railhead is at Abu Rd station, connected to town by bus. Entering Mount Abu, you have to pay a ₹50 entry fee (plus any additional charge for a car or jeep).

By train There's a train booking office (daily 8am–5pm) at the tourist office (see below). Buses to Abu Rd leave Mount Abu every hour between 6am and 9pm (45min; ₹100); jeeps leave when full (from next to the bus stand), and taxis can be hired at the corner by the *Jodhpur Bhojnalaya* restaurant for ₹500.

By bus Government buses run from the State Bus Stand on Nakki Lake Rd. Private buses are run by a string of operators along Nakki Lake Rd west of the State Bus Stand; Gujarat Travels is a reliable option. There are private services to

Ajmer (2 daily; 8hr), Ahmedabad (8 daily; 6hr 30min), Jaipur (2 daily; 10hr 30min), Jodhpur (3 daily; 7hr) and Udaipur (3 daily; 4hr).

Tourist information The RSTC Tourist Office (Mon–Sat 10am–1.30pm & 2–5pm; ☎02974 235151, ⊛rajasthan tourism.gov.in) is opposite the main bus stand.

Services The State Bank of India has an ATM in front of the tourist office, and there are plenty more between there and the polo ground.

Tours *Shri Ganesh* guesthouse runs forest treks and jeep tours (₹700 for the vehicle for 3–4hr) out to places like Achalgarh and Guru Shikar (see page 201 for more on hiking around Mount Abu).

ACCOMMODATION

The steady stream of pilgrims and honeymoon couples ensures that Mount Abu has plenty of hotels, lots of them offering luxuries for newlyweds in special "couple rooms". Prices rocket in high season (April–June & Nov–Dec), especially at weekends, reaching their peak during Diwali.

Cama Rajputana Adhar Devi Rd ☎0297 423 8205, ⊛camahotelsindia.com; map p.200. Popular with tour groups, this attractive resort-style place occupies a neatly refurbished colonial building in sprawling grounds. Rooms (all a/c) are cool and spacious, while the extensive facilities include a bar, billiard room and a big pool; rates include breakfast and dinner. ₹5200

★ **Connaught House** Rajendra Rd ☎0297 423 8560, ⊛jodhanaheritage.com; map p.200. Easily Mount Abu's most memorable accommodation option, occupying a time-warped colonial-era retreat set in a flower-filled garden with sweeping views. Rooms (all a/c) in the "cottage" are beautifully preserved, with period furniture and decor; those in the modern block on the hill above are much less atmospheric. Breakfast included. ₹7400

Jaipur House South of the lake ☎992 879 8383,

⊛jaipurhousemountabu.com; map p.200. A fine old summer palace perched on a hilltop above town, with some of the town's best and most spacious accommodation (and superb town views) in tastefully decorated suites with wooden furnishings – although the "deluxe" rooms, in an ugly modern block halfway down the drive, are dull and overpriced. ₹5500

Lake Palace Nakki Lake Rd ☎0297 423 7154, ⊛savshantihotels.com; map p.200. One of the town's best mid-range options, in a scenic position facing Nakki Lake, with good service and a range of well-maintained modern rooms (all a/c, the more expensive ones with lake view and balcony). ₹3800

Shalin Paying Guest House Sani Gaon ☎9413153593; map p.200. There aren't many recommendable budget options in town, but this homestay-style number has proven very popular with backpackers. Though the lake is just a few minutes away on foot, you're likely to get a good night's sleep here, thanks to its location in a quiet alley. A surprising level of attention has been put into the room decoration, though sadly many are afflicted by that very modern

RECOMMENDED TRAINS FROM ABU ROAD

All the following trains run daily.

Destination	Name	No.	Departs	Arrives
Ahmedabad	*Jammu Tawi Express*	19224	10.50am	3pm
Ajmer	*Aravali Express*	19707	9.40am	4.25pm
Delhi	*Swarna J Raj Express*	12957	8.50pm	7.30am
Jaipur	*Aravali Express*	19707	9.40am	6.55pm
Jodhpur	*Adi Jat Tawi Express*	19223	3.30pm	8.05pm
Mumbai	*Aravali Express*	19708	4.50pm	6.35am
	Surya Nagri Express	12479	11.27pm	11.35am

accommodation curse – windowed-off bathrooms affording zero privacy from whoever you're rooming with. ₹1500
Silver Oak 100m north of the main bus stand ☎946 1523 188, ⓦhotelsilveroak.com; map p.200. A warm welcome and spacious rooms (some with a/c and modern bathrooms) make this one of the best-value guesthouses in town; request one of the nicer front rooms, which open onto sunny garden terraces. ₹3000

EATING

Mount Abu's predominantly middle-class Gujarati visitors are typically hard to please when it comes to food, so standards are exceptionally high and prices low. Meat is rare; if you get carnivorous cravings, you could try a couple of non-veg Punjabi restaurants in the bazaar.

Arbuda Nakki Lake Rd ☎94144 49794; map p.200. Perennially popular spot with a huge veggie menu ranging from pizza, burgers and sandwiches through to Chinese, south Indian, Gujarati and Punjabi (mains from ₹120), as well as good fresh juices. Lightning-fast, friendly service and a popular, airy terrace. Daily 8am–10.30pm.

Jodhpur Bhojnalaya Nakki Lake Rd, opposite Bank of Baroda ☎0297 423 5382; map p.200. The best place in town for authentic Rajasthani veg food, heavy on ghee and spices. It's famous for its definitive *dhal bati churma* (a traditional Rajasthani dish consisting of baked wheatflour balls served with dhal and sweet *churma*; ₹130), and also has the usual big list of Indian veg dishes and thalis (₹190). Daily 11am–3pm & 7–11pm.

★**Mulberry Tree** Nakki Lake Rd ☎0297 4238 391, ⓦhotelhilltone.com; map p.200. The multi-cuisine non-veg restaurant at *Hotel Hilltone* is Mount Abu's smartest dining option, with tables neatly laid indoors or on the front lawn. From the open kitchen come Indian and Italian dishes (₹180–430) including sizzlers, pasta and steak. Licensed. Daily 8–10.30am, noon–3pm & 7.30–10.30pm.

Original Gujarat Omlette Nakki Lake Rd; map p.200. The place to go if you need an eggy snack; omelette sandwiches are ₹60 a go at this little shack – one of a few omelette sellers opposite the northern tip of the Polo Ground. Daily 8am–noon & 5–10pm.

Sankalp Opposite Hotel Samrat on Nakki Lake Rd ☎0297 423 5161, ⓦsankalponline.com; map p.200. Branch of a south Indian chain offering the usual dishes (*idlis*, dosas, *uttapams* and the like) in comfortable, modern a/c surrounds, with specialities such as veg pulao (₹110) or tomato masala *uthappa* (₹175), or if you really want to go to town, a metre-long dosa (₹550). Daily 8am–10pm.

Udaipur and around

Spreading around the shores of the idyllic Lake Pichola and backdropped by a majestic ring of craggy green hills, **UDAIPUR** seems to encapsulate India at its most quintessentially romantic, with its intricate sequence of ornately turreted and balconied palaces, whitewashed havelis and bathing *ghats* clustered around the waters of the lake – or, in the case of the *Lake Palace* hotel and Jag Mandir, floating magically upon them. Not that the city is quite perfect: insensitive lakeside development, appalling traffic along the **old city**'s maze of tightly winding streets and vast hordes of tourists mean that Udaipur is far from unspoilt or undiscovered. Even so, it remains a richly rewarding place to visit, and although it's possible to take in most of the sights in a few days, many people spend at least a week exploring the city and the various attractions scattered about the surrounding countryside.

North of the city are the historic temples of **Nagada**, **Eklingji**, **Nathdwara** and **Kankroli**, while to the northwest, en route to Jodhpur, lie the superb Jain temples of

Ranakpur and the rambling fort at **Kumbhalgarh**. Renting a car or motorcycle saves time, though local buses serve both routes.

Brief history

Udaipur is a relatively young city by Indian standards, having been established in the mid-sixteenth century by Udai Singh II of the **Sisodia** family, rulers of the state of **Mewar**, which covered much of present-day southern Rajasthan. The Sisodias are traditionally considered to be the foremost of all the Rajput royal dynasties. The present Sisodia maharana is the 76th in the unbroken line of Mewar suzerains, which makes the Mewar household the longest lasting of all royal families of Rajasthan, and perhaps the oldest surviving dynasty in the world.

The state of Mewar was established by Guhil in 568 AD. His successors set up their capital first at Nagda and then, in 734, at the mighty fort of Chittaurgarh, from where they established control over much of present-day southern Rajasthan. By the time **Udai Singh II** inherited the throne of Mewar in 1537, however, it was clear that Chittaurgarh's days were numbered. Udai began looking for a location for a new city, to be named Udaipur, eventually choosing a swampy site beside Lake Pichola, protected on all sides by outcrops of the Aravalli Range. The Mughal emperor Akbar duly captured Chittaurgarh after a protracted siege in 1568, but by then Udai was firmly established in his new capital, where he remained unopposed until his death in 1572. His son, the heroic **Pratap Singh**, continued to defy Akbar and spent much of his reign doggedly defending his kingdom's freedom against the overwhelming military muscle of the Mughal army.

Following Akbar's death, peace finally ensued, and the city – gradually emerging up around the city's grand **City Palace**, on the east shore of the lake – prospered until 1736, when Mewar suffered the first of repeated attacks by the **Marathas**, who gradually reduced the city to poverty until being finally driven off by the British in the early eighteenth century. The Sisodias from there on allied themselves to the British, while preserving their independence until 1947, when the famous old state of Mewar was finally merged into the newly created nation of India.

Lake Pichola

Udaipur's idyllic **Lake Pichola** provides the city's most memorable views, a beautiful frame for the City Palace buildings, havelis, *ghats*, temple towers and other structures which crowd its eastern side – best seen from a boat trip around the lake (see page 206). The lake's two **island palaces** are among Udaipur's most famous features, and each evening **Sunset Point**, near Amet Haveli, sees flocks of onlookers keen to snap the sun setting to the west, or the resultant illumination of the buildings east of the lake.

Jag Niwas

Lake Palace hotel • Closed to non-guests

Jag Niwas, now the *Lake Palace* hotel, was built in amalgamated Rajput-Mughal style as a summer palace during the reign of Jagat Singh (1628–52), after whom it was named. Unfortunately, as a security measure following the 2008 gun attacks in Mumbai, non-guests can no longer visit the hotel, which has often been called the most romantic hotel in the world; but you can see it as part of a boat ride around the lake.

Jag Mandir

Best visited as part of boat tour (see page 206) • Dinner ₹4000/3000 cover charge for couple/solo dinner

The **Jag Mandir** palace, on the island to the south, is arranged around a large garden guarded by stone elephants. The main building here is the **Gol Mahal**, which has detailed stone inlay work within its domed roof and houses a small exhibition on the history of the island. The young Shah Jahan once stayed here and was apparently so

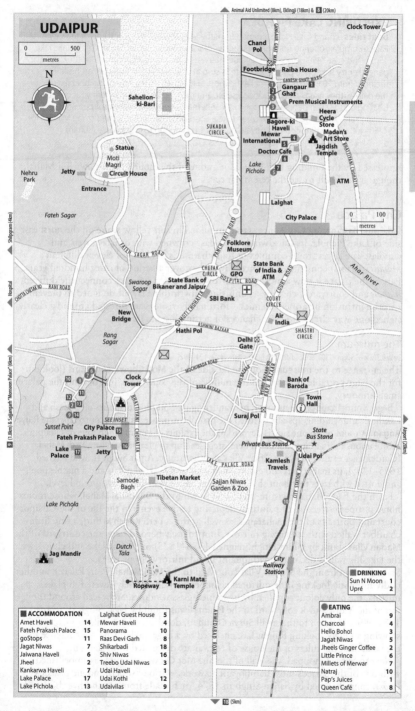

Animal Aid Unlimited (8km), Eklingji (18km) & 8 (20km)

UDAIPUR

0 ———— 500
metres

N

Sahelion-ki-Bari

SUKADIA CIRCLE

Statue
Moti Magri
Nehru Park
Jetty
Circuit House
Entrance

Fateh Sagar

SAHELI MARG

FATEH SAGAR ROAD

PANCH VATI ROAD

Swaroop Sagar

CHETAK CIRCLE

Folklore Museum

State Bank of India & ATM

GPO

State Bank of Bikaner and Jaipur

HOSPITAL ROAD

SBI Bank

New Bridge

Rang Sagar

Hathi Pol

MOTI CHOHATTA

ASHWINI BAZAAR

Air India

COURT CIRCLE

COURT ROAD

SHASTRI CIRCLE

Ahar River

Delhi Gate

MOCHIWADA ROAD

BABRI BAZAAR

BARA BAZAAR

Bank of Baroda

Clock Tower

SEE INSET

BHATTIANI CHOHATTA

Sunset Point
City Palace
Fateh Prakash Palace
Lake Palace
Jetty

Town Hall

Suraj Pol

State Bus Stand

Private Bus Stand

Kamlesh Travels

Udai Pol

Airport (20km)

Samode Bagh
Tibetan Market
Sajjan Niwas Garden & Zoo

LAKE PALACE ROAD

CITY STATION ROAD

Lake Pichola

Jag Mandir

Dutch Tala

Ropeway

Karni Mata Temple

City Railway Station

AHMEDABAD ROAD

9 (1.8km) & Sajjangarh "Monsoon Palace" (6km)

Shilpgram (4km)

Hospital

Chhitta Chetak Rd / Rani Road

18 (5km)

INSET:

Clock Tower

Chand Pol

Footbridge   Raiba House

GANGAUR GHAT MARG

GANESH GHAT MARG

Gangaur Ghat

Prem Musical Instruments

Heera Cycle Store

Bagore-ki-Haveli
Mewar International

Madan's Art Store

Jagdish Temple

Doctor Cafe

Lake Pichola

ATM

Lalghat

City Palace

0 ———— 100
metres

JAGDISH ROAD

BHATTIANI CHOHATTA

2

EXPLORING LAKE PICHOLA

Boat rides around Lake Pichola depart from the jetty towards the south end of the City Palace complex, offering unforgettable views of the various palaces. Circuits of the lake take 45min and cost ₹450 before 3pm or ₹800 afterwards, plus the additional fee for the City Palace general entry ticket (see page 206). All trips stop at the Jag Mandir. Tours depart hourly on the hour from 10am to 6pm; to make the most of them, sit on the side of the boat facing the palace (they usually run anticlockwise around the lake). You can also rent your own boat (seating up to seven people) here for ₹5300. Alternatively, on the waterfront between the *Jaiwana* and *Kankarwa* havelis, you can take a short boat ride (not stopping at Jag Mandir) for ₹250–400 (15–40min), or rent a private boat for ₹1500 for up to four people (30min).

---

impressed by the building that he used it as one of the models for his own Taj Mahal, though it's difficult to see the resemblance.

City Palace

Udaipur's fascinating **City Palace** stands moulded in soft yellow stone on the northeast side of Lake Pichola, its thick windowless base crowned with ornate turrets and cupolas. The largest royal complex in Rajasthan, it is made up of eleven different *mahals* (palaces) constructed by successive rulers over a period of three hundred years. Part of the palace is now a **museum**. Narrow low-roofed passages connect the different *mahals* and courtyards, creating a confusing, labyrinthine layout designed to prevent surprise intrusion by armed enemies – fortunately visitors are directed around a clearly signed one-way circuit, so your chances of getting lost are limited.

The museum

Daily 9.30am–5.30pm • ₹300; audioguide ₹200; guide ₹400 • ☎ 0294 241 9021

The entrance to the **museum** is on the far side of the **Moti Chowk** courtyard (look out for the large portable tiger-trap in the middle of the courtyard), just beyond the palace's small **armoury**.

Begin your circuit of the museum by wandering past propitious statues of Ganesh and Lakshmi, and winding upstairs to reach the first of the palace's myriad courtyards, the **Rajya Angan**. A room off to one side is devoted to the exploits of Pratap Singh, one of Udaipur's most famous military leaders. From here, steps lead up to pleasantly sylvan **Badi Mahal** (Garden Palace; also known as Amar Vilas after its creator, Amar Singh II, who reigned 1695–1755), its main courtyard embellished with finely carved pillars and a marble pool, and dotted with trees that flourish despite being built some 30m above ground level.

From the Badi Mahal, twisting steps lead down to the **Dilkushal Mahal**, whose rooms house a superb selection of paintings depicting festive events in the life of the Udaipur court and portraits of the maharanas, as well as the superb **Kanch ki Burj**, a tiny little chamber walled with red zigzag mirrors. Immediately beyond here, the courtyard of the **Madan Vilas** (built by Bhim Singh, reigned 1778–1828) offers fine lake and city views; the lakeside wall is decorated with quaint inlaid mirrorwork pictures.

Stairs descend from the Madan Vilas courtyard to the **Moti Mahal** (Pearl Palace), another oddly futuristic-looking little mirrored chamber, its walls entirely covered in plain mirrors, the only colour supplied by its stained-glass windows. Steps lead around the top of the Mor Chowk courtyard to the **Pitam Niwas** (built by Jagat Singh II, reigned 1734–90) and down to the small **Surya Choupad**, dominated by a striking image showing a kingly-looking Rajput face enclosed by a huge golden halo – a reference to the belief that the rulers of the house of Mewar are descended from the sun.

Next to Surya Choupad, the wall of the fine **Mor Chowk** courtyard is embellished with one of the palace's most flamboyant artworks, a trio of superb mosaic peacocks (*mor*), commissioned by Sajjan Singh in 1874, each made from around five thousand pieces of glass and coloured stone. On the other side of the courtyard is the opulent little **Manek Mahal** (Ruby Palace), its walls mirrored in rich reds and greens.

From the Manek Mahal, a long corridor winds past the kitsch apartments of the queen mother Shri Gulabkunwar (1928–73) and through the **Zenana Mahal** (Women's Palace), whose long sequence of rooms now houses a huge array of paintings depicting royal fun and frolics in Mewar. Continue onwards to emerge, finally, into the last and largest of the palace's courtyards, **Lakshmi Chowk**, the centrepiece of the Zenana Mahal. The museum exit is at the far end of the chowk, back where you came in.

Government Museum

Daily 10am–5pm • ₹100 (₹20) • ☎ 0294 241 9021, ⓦ museumsrajasthan.gov.in

The small **Government Museum**, opposite the entrance to the City Palace Museum, is of interest for its impressive sculpture gallery of pieces from Kumbhalgarh, including some outstanding works in black marble.

Durbar Hall

Crystal Gallery Daily 9am–6.30pm • ₹730 including audioguide and palace entry fee • No photography allowed

More interesting than the Government Museum in many ways – and certainly far more atmospheric – is the vast **Durbar Hall** in the Fateh Prakash Palace (the building immediately behind the main City Palace building, which now houses the *Fateh Prakash Palace* hotel). This huge, wonderfully time-warped Edwardian-era ballroom was built to host state banquets, royal functions and the like, and remains full of period character, complete with huge chandeliers, creaky old furniture and fusty portraits. In a gallery overlooking the hall is the eccentric **Crystal Gallery**, housing an array of fine British crystal ordered by Sajjan Singh in the 1880s and featuring outlandishly kitsch items including crystal chairs, tables and lamps – there's even a crystal hookah and a crystal bed. The extortionate entrance charge is a bit of a turn-off, though it does include an audioguide and non-alcoholic refreshments at the hotel's *Surya Dharshan Bar*.

Mewar sound-and-light show

Daily 7–8pm: May–Aug in Hindi; Sept–March in English • Seating at elevated Hathnal ki Chandni ₹550 in English (₹300 in Hindi); at ground-level in the Manek Chowk ₹250 in English (₹200 in Hindi) • Tickets only sold on same day, from 6pm

Every evening, fifteen years of history is revived at the palace, as special effects and commentary recount stories from the Kingdom of Mewar in a show called *The Legacy of Honour* (Yash ki Dharohar in Hindi). The Mewar sound-and-light show is held in Manek Chowk, and commentary is in English between September and April, and in Hindi for the rest of the year.

Jagdish Temple

City Palace Rd • Daily 5am–noon & 4–9pm • Free

Just north of the City Palace, **Jagdish Temple** is one of Udaipur's most popular and vibrant shrines. Built in 1652 and dedicated to Lord Jagannath, an aspect of Vishnu,

---

ACCESSING THE CITY PALACE

Note that to reach certain parts of the City Palace, including the *Fateh Prakash Palace* and *Shiv Niwas* hotels, the Durbar Hall, Crystal Gallery and the jetty for boats around Lake Pichola and over to the *Lake Palace* hotel, you'll have to pay ₹30 for a **general entrance ticket** to the City Palace complex. You don't have to buy this ticket if you're just visiting the City Palace Museum or the courtyard outside, or if you're actually staying at any of the three hotels; some staff at the ticket booth claim that the general ticket does not exist, and that you have to pay full entry, but if this is the case ask to speak to one of their colleagues.

its outer walls and towering *shikhara* are heavily carved with figures of Vishnu, scenes from the life of Krishna and dancing *apsaras* (nymphs). The circular *mandapa* leads to the sanctuary where a black stone image of Jagannath sits shrouded in flowers, while a small raised shrine in front of the temple protects a bronze Garuda. Subsidiary shrines to Shiva, Ganesh, Surya and Durga stand at each corner of the main temple.

Bagore-ki-Haveli

Gangaur Ghat Marg • **Museum** Daily 9.30am–5pm • ₹100 (₹50), camera ₹50, video camera ₹50 • **Shows** Daily 7–8pm • ₹150 (₹90), camera ₹150, video camera ₹150

North of Jagdish Temple, a lane leads to Gangaur Ghat and the **Bagore-ki-Haveli**, a 138-room lakeside haveli dating from 1751. A section of the building has been converted into a worthwhile **museum**, arranged on two floors around one of the rambling haveli's several courtyards. The upper floor has several immaculately restored rooms with original furnishings and artworks, plus some fine murals. The lower floor has rooms full of puppets, women's clothes, musical instruments, kitchen equipment and – the undisputed highlight – what is claimed to be the world's largest turban. Traditional **music and dance** shows are staged here each evening.

Folklore Museum

Panch Vati Rd • Daily 9am–6pm • ₹60 (₹40), camera ₹30, video camera ₹50 • Shows Daily noon & 6pm • ₹100 (₹80), camera ₹50, mobile phone ₹20

Just north of Chetak Circle in the new city, the hoary old **Folklore Museum** is home to a mildly interesting collection of exhibits covering the folk traditions of Rajasthan and India, with dusty displays of colourful masks, puppets and musical instruments. Short, amusing **puppet shows** (tip expected) are staged throughout the day on demand (the performers will probably hunt you down and drag you into the theatre shortly after your arrival), while there are two hour-long shows daily, with music, dancing and more puppets.

Sahelion-ki-Bari

Saheli Marg • Daily 8am–7pm • ₹50 (₹10)

The "garden of the maids of honour", **Sahelion-ki-Bari** was laid out by Sangram Singh (1710–34) as a summer retreat for the diversion and entertainment of the ladies of the royal household – though the fountains weren't installed until the reign of Fateh Singh (1884–1930). The walled gardens, attractive and formal, are centred on a peaceful courtyard enclosing a large pool; behind this, four elephant statues surround Udaipur's most striking fountain, a fanciful tiered creation that looks a bit like a huge, multicoloured cake stand.

Machlan Magra

Ropeway Daily 9am–9pm • ₹53 each way • ⓦ udaipurropeway.com

Just south of the old city, opposite Deen Dayal Park, ruby-red cable cars float up to the summit of Machlan Magra hill on the **Ropeway**. The panoramic views from its summit are stunning, taking in sights such as Lake Pichola, Jag Mandir and the Monsoon Palace – a particularly nice place to be at sunset. East of the Dutch Tala lake, a winding pathway provides an alternative ascent route used by pilgrims visiting the small hilltop Karni Mata temple; it's a fairly gentle walk through pleasant scenery.

Shilpgram

4km west of town • Daily 11am–7pm • ₹100 (₹30), camera/video camera ₹50 • ☏ 0294 243 1304, ⓦ shilpgram.in • Auto-rickshaw from Udaipur around ₹450 including waiting time

The popular rural arts and crafts centre of **Shilpgram** was set up to promote the traditional architecture, music and crafts of the tribal people of western India, with displays dedicated to the diverse lifestyles and customs of the region's rural population. Around thirty replica houses and huts in traditional style are arranged in a village-like compound, with examples of buildings from various states. Musicians, puppeteers and dancers – *hijras* (eunuchs) among them – hang out around the houses and strike up on the approach of visitors (tip expected), while you may also see people weaving, potting and embroidering as they would in their original homes – though most of the actual handicrafts on sale are fifth-rate, if that. Despite its honourable intentions, many tourists find the atmosphere contrived and resent the hustling by musicians and their ilk. Even so, it's well worth a visit if only for the scenic journey out along the road around Fateh Sagar Lake. It's best done by bicycle but you can also get there by auto-rickshaw.

Sajjangarh

Daily 9am–sunset, last entry 5pm • ₹300 (₹30), plus ₹100 for car shuttle up the hill or ₹150 with own car/taxi • Taxi from Udaipur around ₹450 round-trip

High on a hill 5km west of the city and inside the **Sajjangarh Wildlife Sanctuary**, the so-called "Monsoon Palace", **Sajjangarh**, was begun in 1883 by Maharana Sajjan Singh to serve as a summer retreat, complete with a nine-storey observatory from which the royal family proposed to watch the monsoon clouds travelling across the countryside below. Unfortunately, the maharana's untimely death the following year put paid to the planned observatory, and although the palace itself was finished by Singh's successor, Maharana Fateh Singh, it was found to be impossible to pump water up to it, and the whole place was abandoned shortly afterwards. The large though rather plain building is now a somewhat melancholy sight, but the views over Udaipur, more than 300m below, are unrivalled. The journey up to the palace takes a good fifteen minutes by taxi; really, the climb is too steep to tackle by bicycle, although some people try.

ARRIVAL AND DEPARTURE
UDAIPUR

By plane Maharana Pratap Airport (☏ 0294 265 5950) is located a full 20km east of Udaipur. Prepaid taxis from the airport cost ₹750; the journey costs ₹550 from the city.
Destinations Bangalore (2 daily; 2hr); Chennai (1 daily; 2hr 30min); Delhi (5 daily; 1hr 25min); Jaipur (2 daily; 55min); Mumbai (3 daily; 1hr 30min); Varanasi (1 daily; 1hr 40min).

By train Trains pull in at Udaipur City station, southeast of the city centre. Services from Udaipur are surprisingly limited; those listed here (see page 210) are the best of a bad bunch. Note that there are no direct services to Jodhpur; you'll have to change at Kota (or take a bus). You can save a trip to the station by booking tickets through travel agents in town (see page 210) for a surcharge of around ₹100, or your guesthouse, which will charge you about what you'd pay for a rickshaw to the station and back (₹200).

By bus Government buses leave from the main State Bus Stand at Udai Pol; from here prepaid autos cost ₹70 to the City Palace area. Private buses depart from across City Station Rd, and are a better option for longer and (especially) overnight journeys. It's easiest to book tickets for private buses through one of the many travel agents in town (usually for a surcharge of ₹50–100) or, for ease, through your hotel/guesthouse. If you want to book your own ticket you'll need to make a reservation with one of the bus company offices around Udai Pol – try the reliable Kamlesh Travels (☏ 0294 248 6549) who operate the best a/c sleeper coaches to Mumbai, Delhi and Jaipur. Local buses to destinations such as Nagda, Eklingji, Nathdwara and Kankroli leave regularly from the RSTRC bus stand; see the individual accounts for details.
Destinations Agra (5 daily; 12–17hr); Ahmedabad (2–5 hourly; 5hr); Ajmer (2–4 hourly; 4hr 30min–7hr); Chittaurgarh (every 15–30min; 3hr); Delhi (18 nightly; 14hr); Mumbai (21 nightly; 14hr); Jaipur (2–4 hourly; 7–9hr); Jaisalmer (4 nightly; 12hr); Jodhpur (1–3 hourly; 4–6hr); Mount Abu (3 daily; 3hr 15min).

GETTING AROUND

By auto-rickshaw Auto-rickshaws are the usual means of transport; there are no cycle rickshaws in town. Rickshaw sightseeing tours cost around ₹650 for 5–6hr.

Bicycle and motorbike rental Renting a bicycle is another possibility, although traffic around the city is bad. *Doctor Cafe*, near *Charcoal* restaurant (☏ 99295 07355),

2

RECOMMENDED TRAINS FROM UDAIPUR

All the following trains run daily.

Destination	Name	No.	Departs	Arrives
Ajmer	Chetak Express	12982	5.15pm	10.30pm
Bundi	Mewar Express	12963	6.15pm	10.36pm
Chittaurgarh	Mewar Express	12963	6.15pm	8.25pm
Delhi	Mewar Express	12964	6.15pm	6.35am
Jaipur	Ajmer Express	19666	10.20pm	5.45am
Kota	Mewar Express	12964	6.15pm	11.30pm
Mumbai	Bandra Express	22902/12996	9pm/9.35pm	1.30pm/2.20pm
Sawai Madhopur	Mewar Express	12964	6.15pm	12.45am

rents out bicycles for ₹100/day. They also have scooters (from ₹500/day) and Enfields (₹1100/day); you'll need to bring your passport and leave a hard-currency deposit.

INFORMATION

Tourist information The main tourist office (Mon–Sat 10am–5pm; ☏0294 241 1535, ⓦrajasthantourism.gov. in) is in Fateh Memorial on Airport Rd at Suraj Pol, on the east side of the city, with desks at the airport and railway station.

Tours Tours to Ranakpur, Kumbhalgarh, Nathdwara and Eklingji are offered by some of the innumerable travel agents dotted around the city centre (see below), as well as car rental with driver (usually around ₹2500/day for up to 250km).

Travel agents Virtually every shop and guesthouse around the Jagdish Temple seems to offer bus and rail ticketing. Reliable agents include Mewar International on Lalghat, which also stocks books; Gangaur Tour 'n' Travels, close by at 28 Gangaur Ghat (☏941 4160 476); and the travel agency inside the *Udai Niwas* hotel.

ACCOMMODATION

Most accommodation is on the east side of Lake Pichola, although there are a growing number of excellent places on the far more peaceful northwestern side of the lake, just across the bridge by Chand Pol.

OLD TOWN

Fateh Prakash Palace City Palace ☏0294 252 8016, ⓦheritagehotelsofindia.com; map p.205. The best location in the city, right in the heart of the City Palace complex, with prices to match. Most of the rooms have superb lake views, although some are rather small and characterless for the price. ₹17,000

★**Jagat Niwas** 23–25 Lalghat ☏0294 242 2860, ⓦjagatcollection.com; map p.205. Beautifully restored seventeenth-century haveli right on the lakeside, with 29 pleasant rooms (some with lake views) and a good restaurant (see page 212). The Raj rooms have lovely lakeside enclosed balconies, and are worth the splurge; all rates come with breakfast. ₹4550

★**Jaiwana Haveli** 14 Lalghat ☏0294 241 1103, ⓦjaiwanahaveli.com; map p.205. Good-value lakeside haveli accommodation with a range of spotless modern rooms; some have a/c, and the more expensive ones have fine lake views, as does the good rooftop restaurant. Best to book ahead. ₹4000

Jheel 52–56 Gangor Ghat ☏0294 242 1352, ⓦjheel guesthouse.com; map p.205. These neighbouring sister-guesthouses offer seven good-value rooms apiece (all with attached bathrooms); the older wing is home to more basic fan-cooled doubles (₹850) while those in the newer building come with a/c and superb lake views (some even have balconies). ₹2350

Kankarwa Haveli 26 Lalghat ☏0294 241 1457, ⓦkankarwahaveli.com; map p.205. Romantically restored haveli right on the waterfront. Not quite as pristine as the nearby *Jagat Niwas*, but equally atmospheric, with colourful antiquey rooms (all a/c; some with superb lake views) and an excellent guest-only rooftop veg restaurant. ₹4300

★**Lake Palace** Lake Pichola ☏0294 252 8800, ⓦtajhotels.com; map p.205. One of India's most famous hotels, sailing in magnificent isolation on its own island amid the serene waters of Lake Pichola. Accommodation is in a selection of luxurious rooms and suites, while facilities include a spa, pool, butler service and limousine rental. ₹35,000

Lalghat Guest House 33 Lalghat ☏0294 252 5301, ⓦlalghat.com; map p.205. One of the oldest guesthouses in Udaipur, and still going strong thanks to its superb lakeside position and cheapish rates. There's a mix of no-frills single and double rooms (some with shared bathrooms, some a/c, and a few with lakeside views), plus a nicer-than-average ten-person dorm, a bookshop and a food court. Dorms ₹500, doubles ₹1500

Mewar Haveli 34–35 Lalghat ☏0294 252 1140, ⓦmewarhaveli.com; map p.205. Spotless and well-run modern mid-range hotel in a very central location. The twelve rooms (some with a/c and lake views) are chintzy but comfortable, and there are further lake views from the attractive rooftop restaurant serving Rajasthani cuisine. ₹1850

Shiv Niwas City Palace ☎0294 252 8016, ⓦheritage hotelsofindia.com; map p.205. This upmarket heritage hotel trades on its superb location inside the City Palace complex, with grand public areas, a dreamy pool and a lavish spa. The viewless standard ("palace") rooms are disappointingly small and ordinary given the price tag; suites (₹22,000 to ₹40,000) are far more memorable, with genuine old-world atmosphere and marvellous lake views. Discounts in summer. ₹10,000

Treebo Udai Niwas Gangaur Marg ☎0294 241 4303, ⓦhoteludainiwas.com; map p.205. Bright, modern high-rise hotel with a range of smart, colourful rooms in various price categories (the more expensive ones have a/c and nice bathrooms). There's also a travel office, and a restaurant showing movies (7pm), although road noise and the periodic outbursts of massively amplified music from the nearby Jagdish Temple mean that it's not particularly peaceful. ₹1500

★ **Udai Haveli** 40 Gadia Devra, Ganesh Ghati ☎935 2506 701, ⓦudaihaveliguesthouse.com; map p.205. This excellent family-run guesthouse located up a quiet side-street near *Savage Garden* restaurant is one of the best-value cheapies in town. The nine rooms (a couple with shared bathrooms; ₹450) are neat and clean with bright, modern bathrooms. Delicious home-cooked food is served on the breezy rooftop. ₹650

NORTHWESTERN SIDE OF LAKE PICHOLA

★ **Amet Haveli** Chand Pol ☎0294 243 4009, ⓦamethaveliudaipur.com; map p.205. This fine old white haveli is one of the best lakefront properties in town. Rooms are beautifully decorated with traditional touches and come with a/c, TV and lake views, though you might want to spend a little more to get one of the superb suites, with big windows right over the water. Also home to *Ambrai* restaurant (see page 211) and a pool. ₹4000

goStops Ambari Rd ☎74288 88282, ⓦgostops.com; map p.205. Best of the city's chain hostels, elevating itself above the competition with a quiet location, excellent security, and a colourful common room. Activities on offer include cooking and painting classes, leather workshops and rooftop yoga sessions; on the downside, prices are higher than they probably should be, though rates do include a modest breakfast. Dorms ₹950, doubles ₹3000

Lake Pichola Piplia Haveli, Chand Pol ☎0294 243 1197, ⓦlakepicholahotel.in; map p.205. This long-established hotel's lakeside location and City Palace views are just about perfect, and prices quite reasonable. Don't bother with the viewless standard rooms, though. All 25 rooms have a/c and

TV. Also home to the excellent *Upre* rooftop restaurant, a massage centre and bar. ₹5100

★ **Panorama** Hanuman Ghat, Chand Pol ☎0294 243 1027 or ☎941 4352 523, ⓦpanoramaguesthouse. in; map p.205. Excellent budget hotel, efficiently run by friendly management and with cheap, cosy and great-value rooms (some with superb lake views and balconies; a few with a/c). There's a great rooftop spot where early arrivals can relax with the house tortoise, and also a nice rooftop restaurant with lovely lake views and good-value local cuisine plus pizza and pasta. Book ahead. ₹700

Udai Kothi Chand Pol ☎0294 243 2810, ⓦudaikothi. com; map p.205. Smart and spotless modern hotel in traditional style, with lots of flowery murals and chintzy architectural touches. Rooms all come with TV, a/c and plenty of slightly twee furnishings; there's a beautiful pool, gorgeous rooftop restaurant, spa and a lovely garden. ₹5500

OUTSIDE THE CITY CENTRE

★ **Raas Devi Garh** Delwara Village, 25km north of Udaipur ☎0295 328 9211, ⓦraasdevigarh.com; map p.205. Hidden away in the Aravalli Hills, a 40min drive north of Udaipur, this luxury hotel occupies the magnificent seventeenth-century Devi Garh palace, mixing traditional Rajasthani palace opulence with fresh, contemporary style to memorable effect. Facilities include a superb spa and a spectacular pool. Suites only; rates include breakfast. ₹22,000

Shikarbadi Goverdhan Vilas, 5km south of Udaipur on the NH-8 ☎0294 258 3201, ⓦheritagehotelsofindia. com; map p.205.Former royal hunting lodge with its own pool, garden restaurant, lake, deer park and stud farm – less ostentatious, and significantly cheaper, than the palaces in town. Suites (₹10,000) in the old 1930s block have more character than the newer a/c rooms. ₹4300

★ **Udaivilas** Haridasji Ki Magri ☎0294 243 3300, ⓦoberoihotels.com; map p.205. Udaipur's most opulent hotel and seen as one of the world's best, occupying a sprawling palace, embellished with acres of marble and a novel "moated pool" that flows around the outside of the main building. Suites come with semi-private infinity swimming pools and private butlers, and the spa is pure indulgence. ₹60,000

EATING

Many of Udaipur's tourist cafés screen the James Bond movie *Octopussy*, with its manic boat and auto-rickshaw chases round the city's landmarks, almost every evening at 7pm.

RESTAURANTS

Ambrai Amet Haveli, Chand Pol ☎0294 243 1085; map p.205. In a superlative lakeside setting facing the City

2

Palace and somehow the sunset too; though the cooking doesn't quite live up to the location, quality is usually decent from a menu featuring an extensive selection of north Indian veg and non-veg dishes (including top-notch tandooris), plus a few Chinese and European offerings. Even if you're not hungry, come for a sundowner and watch the sun set over the lake – and it'll have to be a drink, since a little oddly they don't serve food at that rather important time of day. Non-veg mains ₹350–700; licensed. Daily 7.30am–3pm & 7–10.30pm.

★**Charcoal** Pratap Bhawan, 12 Lal Ghat 87691 60106; map p.205. Something a little different, this rooftop (of course) restaurant specialises in grilled meat – the menu has a few quirky choices, like chicken satay (₹350), Greek souvlaki served with home-made tzatziki (lamb/pork ₹480/550), and plenty of paneer and veg (even vegan) options too. There are two levels; the upper one affords 360-degree views, and will see you get less smoke in the eyes. 8–11am, 1–3.30pm & 6–11pm.

Jagat Niwas 23–25 Lal Ghat 0294 242 2860; map p.205. Popular restaurant in the hotel of the same name (see page 210), serving up well-prepared north Indian standards (non-veg mains ₹275–365) and continental offerings such as chicken stroganoff, spaghetti bolognese and fish n' chips (all ₹525), with nice views over the lake – or two nice views, if you count the snazzy mirrored ceilings – from its comfy window seats. Daily 8am–10pm.

Little Prince Hanuman Ghat 90019 22643; map p.205. Right by the pedestrian bridge, and away from traffic in general, this is a good non-rooftop sunset spot, with good non-Indian food including sandwiches, pasta, Chinese, Israeli and Korean options (₹180–300). Daily 9am–10.30pm.

★**Millets of Merwar** Chand Pol 876 9348 440, milletsofmerwar.com; map p.205. Indulge in healthy cuisine (mains ₹170–260) in this rustic lake view café with vegan, organic and gluten-free options, including pasta, soups, thali, Indian and Thai curries, salads and corn/millet flour pizzas, plus shakes and juices. They also organize walks

to crafts villages (₹550) and offer water bottle refills for ₹10. Daily 8am–4pm & 6–10.30pm.

Natraj Station Rd 94147 57893; map p.205. Udaipur's top thali joint for more than twenty years, the original Natraj is in the Town Hall area but fiendishly hard to find; you may as well aim for their larger establishment, more or less opposite the railway station, where it's ₹240 for unlimited portions of veg curries, soups, dhal, curd and chapattis. Daily 10.30am–3.45pm & 6.30–10.30pm.

Queen Café Chand Pol 0294 243 0875; map p.205. This tiny, unpretentious little restaurant offers a refreshing alternative to Udaipur's mainstream tourist eateries, with an authentic taste of home-style vegetarian Indian cooking including mild banana, mango and pumpkin curries (from ₹70). At the time of writing they had two whole tables; the establishment may, in due course, move around the corner. Daily 7.30am–10.30pm.

CAFÉS AND SNACKS

★**Hello Boho!** 5/43 Gangaur Ghat 95300 95311; map p.205. While Jheels down the road (see below) gets way more custom, and is right by the lake, this is a far nicer place to hole up for a while – they've strong wi-fi, the service is friendly and the coffee (from ₹100) is the best in town, while welcome shade is provided through the day by the large tree outside. Toasties and other nibbles are available, written on the daily board. Daily 8am–11pm.

Jheels Ginger Coffee 56 Gangaur Ghat 94610 16511; map p.205. Grab one of the idyllic lakeside tables – separated from the water by nothing more than a few flowers – at this ground-floor café, which serves up all sorts of coffees and treats including sweet pies (₹110), muffins, sandwiches, and ice creams. Unfortunately, staff often act like they'd rather you weren't there; there's no wi-fi, either. Daily 8.30am–8pm.

Pap's Juices Satta Pole 97994 80101; map p.205. Tiny place with a mammoth range of excellent juices; try an ABC with ginger and mint, or a banana-date lassi (both ₹90). Good cereal, too. Daily 8.30am–8pm.

DRINKING

A few of the rooftop places around the lake are licensed – good news, particularly around sunset. For other entertainment, Bagore-ki-Haveli (see page 208) has nightly dance performances, while Shilpgram (see page 208) often hosts out-of-town performers.

Sun N Moon Treebo Udai Niwas, Gangaur Marg 0294 241 4303; map p.205. Sitting atop a hotel, this bar somehow has not one but several rooftop levels – the highest is only large enough to accommodate a single table.

Not the cheapest (cocktails ₹400, beer towers ₹750), but it's the only place in town with a reliable nightlife feel. Daily 8am–11pm.

Upré Lake Pichola Hotel, Chand Pol 0294 243 1197; map p.205. Chic, smart and surprisingly lush rooftop restaurant, though it's perhaps more notable for the licensed bar and plunge pool. Grab one of the lamplit balcony tables for the best views over the city and lake (beers and cocktails ₹300–550). Daily 8am–11pm.

SHOPPING

Udaipur is one of Rajasthan's top shopping destinations, with an eclectic array of local artisanal specialities along

with other crafts from across the state. The city's particular speciality is **miniature painting**, with numerous shops selling traditional Mewari-style works on paper and silk. Many places also do a good line in leather and cloth-bound **stationery** using handmade paper. Udaipur is well known for its **silver jewellery** – Jagdish St, Bara Bazaar and Moti Chohatta, around the clock tower, are home to lots of shops. Lalghat and the branches leading off it are home to plenty of **bookshops**.

ACTIVITIES AND CLASSES

Cooking lessons Available at numerous places around town. Try *Millets of Merwar* (see page 212), who charge ₹1000 for five recipes, including all materials.

Horseriding Various places around town offer horse-riding expeditions into the surrounding countryside. Princess Trails (☎ 98290 42012) specializes in extended, four- to eight-day safaris on thoroughbred Mewari mounts as well as jeep tours, hikes and horse-drawn carriage rides.

Music The Prem Musical Instrument shop (☎ 94143 43583), adjacent to the *Gangaur Palace* hotel, offer sitar and tabla lessons (₹400/hr) and can also arrange flute lessons, or musical appreciation classes if you just want to learn more about Indian music.

Painting lessons in traditional Indian painting are offered by many places around town; Madan's Art Store is a reliable option (₹400/hr).

Swimming pool The lovely pools at *Udai Kothi* and Shiv Niwas cost around ₹650/day for non-guests.

Volunteer work Animal Aid Unlimited in Badi Village, 8km northeast of the city (☏ animalaidunlimited.com), maintains a pet hospital where volunteers and visitors are encouraged. No special skills are required – just a willingness to work with animals, usually including street dogs, cows, donkeys, cats and monkeys.

Yoga Ashtanga Yoga Ashram, Raiba House, Chand Pol (☎ 93524 77577) has daily 90min Hatha yoga classes for all standards at 8.30am and 6pm (let them know you're coming a day in advance). Free, but donations are appreciated, with proceeds going to a local animal charity.

DIRECTORY

Banks and exchange There are ATMs all over the new city, plus a particularly handy 24hr machine on the street leading to the City Palace. Lots of places around Jagdish Temple offer forex.

Doctor Dr Virendra Bhandari (☎ 98290 91084) will visit hotels/guesthouses.

Hospital The private Aravalli Hospital is at 332 Ambamata Rd (☎ 0294 243 0222), or there's a large state hospital campus on the corner of Hospital Road and Collectorate Road, in the north of the city.

Nagada

Daily 10.30am–1pm & 3–7pm • Free • Regular buses leave for Kailashpuri (the Nagada turn-off) every 30min from Udaipur's main bus stand; Nagada is a further 3km away down this side road – rent a bicycle from the shop at the junction to get there, take an auto-rickshaw or walk • ₹900 return by taxi

Dating back to 626 AD, the ragged remnants of the ancient capital of Mewar, **NAGADA**, stand next to Bagela Lake, 20km northeast of Udaipur. Most of the buildings here were either destroyed by the Mughals or submerged by the lake, which has expanded naturally over the centuries. All that survives is a fine pair of tenth-century Vaishnavite temples known as **Saas-Bahu** – literally "mother-in-law" and "daughter-in-law". The more impressive mother-in-law temple has lost its *shikhara* (tower) but preserves a wealth of carving inside; while within the *mandapa*, a marriage area is marked by four ornate pillars, bearing images of the gods Brahma, Vishnu, Shiva and Surya to which couples are supposed to pay homage.

Eklingji

Main temple daily 10.30am–1.30pm & 5.30–8.30pm • Free • Frequent buses leave for Eklingji from Udaipur's main bus stand, dropping passengers off close to the temple

Returning to the main road, you can continue to **EKLINGJI** via the road or along a path that leads behind the old protective walls and downhill. Ask for directions at the bike shop. The god **Eklingji**, a manifestation of Shiva, has been the protective deity of the rulers of Mewar ever since the eighth century, when Bappa Rawal was bestowed with the title *darwan* (servant) of Eklingji by his guru. To this day, the maharana of Udaipur still visits the 108-temple complex every Monday evening (the day traditionally celebrated all over India as being sacred to Shiva) and the whole place is usually lively with local pilgrims seeking his blessings. The milky-white marble **main temple** is crowned by an elaborate two-storey *mandapa* guarded by stone elephants; inside, a four-faced black marble lingam marks the precise spot where Bappa Rawal received his accolade. Climb the small mountain behind the town for a gobsmacking view of the whole complex.

2 Nathdwara

Nathdwara is on NH-8, and sees a constant flow of buses en route north and south

The temple dedicated to Krishna – known also as **Nath**, the favourite avatar (incarnation) of Vishnu – at **NATHDWARA**, "Gateway to God", is one of the richest temples in India, and gets incredibly crowded during major religious festivals. It dates from the seventeenth century when a chariot laden with an image of Krishna – being carried from Mathura to Udaipur to save it from destruction by Aurangzeb – became stuck in the mud here. Its bearers interpreted the event as a divine sign, establishing the new **Shri Nathji Temple** where it had stopped.

The temple lies about 1km south of the town's bus stop, surrounded by a fascinating tangle of narrow streets where stalls display incense, perfumes and small Krishna statues. The temple opens for worship eight times daily, when the image is woken, dressed, washed, fed and put to bed. Don't miss the radiant *pichwai* paintings in the main sanctuary, made of hand-spun cloth and coloured with strong vegetable pigments. You could also ask a guide to show you the "footsteps of Krishna", a process that requires rubbing rose petals on the marble floor. It's occasionally closed to non-Hindus – check before you go.

Ranakpur

Main temple Daily noon–5pm • ₹100, includes camera or mobile with camera ₹100, video camera ₹100 • Free

Some 90km north of Udaipur, the spectacular **Jain temples** at **RANAKPUR** boast marblework on a par with that of the more famous Dilwara shrines at Mount Abu (see page 199). The temples are hidden away in a beautiful wooded valley, deep in the Aravalli Hills, originally gifted to the Jain community in the fifteenth century by Rana Kumbha, the Hindu ruler of Mewar.

The **main temple** was built in 1439 according to a strict system of measurement based on the number 72 (the age at which the founder of Jainism, Mahavira, achieved nirvana). The entire temple sits on a pedestal measuring 72 yards square and is held up by 1440 (72 x 20) individually carved pillars. Inside, there are 72 elaborately carved shrines, some octagonal in shape, along with the main deity (a 72-inch-tall image of the four-faced Adinath, the first *tirthankara*) encased in the central sanctum. The carving on the walls, columns and the domed ceilings is superb. Friezes depicting the life of the *tirthankara* are etched into the walls, while musicians and dancers have been modelled out of brackets between the pillars and the ceiling.

Three smaller temples nestle among the trees in the enclosure in front of the main temple and are free to enter. The most impressive is the **Parshwanath Temple**, around 100m from the main temple, with a small but finely carved shrine, while a further 100m walk brings you to the simpler **Neminath Temple**. Close by (a short walk across the car park) is a contemporary Hindu temple dedicated to **Surya**.

ARRIVAL AND DEPARTURE   RANAKPUR

By bus Ranakpur is a bumpy bus ride from Udaipur (hourly; 2hr 30min), or from Jodhpur (8 daily; 5hr) via the market town of Falna (the nearest railway station) on the NH-14, from where there are four daily buses to Abu Rd (5–6hr). Buses stop right outside the Jain temples, which are 2–4km from the hotels; if you're lucky, you might find an auto or jeep at the bus stop – if not you'll have to ring your hotel and ask to be picked up, or (worst-case scenario) walk.
By taxi Ranakpur can be visited as a day-trip from Udaipur, either on its own or in combination with nearby return

Kumbhalgarh; count on around ₹2400 for the return trip by car.

Trekking If you wish to visit Kumbhalgarh too, think about trekking between the two sites, a beautiful 25km hike through an unspoilt section of the Aravalli Hills. As Kumbhalgarh is on the top of the range, it's easier to hike down from there to Ranakpur; guides and rangers may be arranged at the hotels listed below for the 6hr uphill climb in the other direction.

ACCOMMODATION AND EATING

Accommodation in Ranakpur is expensive. There are no restaurants outside the hotels and guesthouses, although you can enjoy a delicious pure-veg thali lunch at the temple (noon–1.30pm) for a bargain ₹60.

Fateh Bagh 4km south of the temples ☎0293 428 6186, ⊚heritagehotelsofindia.com. Ranakpur's most authentic accommodation, a 200-year-old palace transported piece by piece for 50km, and rebuilt here. Rooms are comfy and characterful, and facilities include a pool, spa and Ayurveda centre. ₹7200

King's Abode 3km south of the temples ☎900 1999 491, ⊚kingsabode.in. Grey stone walls and a lush inner courtyard give this hotel plenty of character. Its 28 a/c double rooms are spacious and equipped with plenty of mod cons, while the higher-category rooms have private pools. There's a big swimming pool, Jacuzzi, spa and restaurant, and treks and nature walks can be arranged. ₹5000

Mana 5km south of the temples ☎900 1999 568, ⊚manahotels.in. Angular, Scandinavian-styled *Mana* is unashamedly modern and unlike anything else in Ranakpur, exhibiting plenty of timber, glass and steel. The chic rooms and cottages within the 3.5-acre garden all feature a/c, TVs and phones, plus bright modern bathrooms with tubs, while the slender infinity pool flows right into the restaurant/bar. ₹7000

Ranakpur Hill Resort 3km south of the temples ☎982 9157 303, ⊚ranakpurhillresort.com. Chintzy little resort with a range of great-value rooms (air-cooled and a/c) of varying standards, and some less appealing "Royal Hut" tents (Oct–March only). It also has a decent-sized pool and a small Ayurveda centre, and can arrange half-day horse safaris. Huts ₹4500, rooms ₹5500

Shivika Lake Hotel 2km south of the temples ☎742 8844 440. One of the few budget options in Ranakpur, although the rooms (some with a/c) are disappointingly shabby given the price. Local treks (₹600/person) and jeep safaris (₹850/person) can be arranged here and there's a gorgeously positioned swimming pool with forested lake backdrop. ₹1200

Kumbhalgarh

Fort Daily 8am–5.30pm • ₹125 (₹20) • **Sound-and-light show** (Hindi only) 7pm • ₹200 (₹100)

The remote hilltop fort of **Kumbhalgarh**, 80km north of Udaipur, is the most formidable of the 32 constructed or restored by Rana Kumbha of Chittaurgarh in the fifteenth century. Protected by a series of monumental walls and bastions, it was only successfully besieged once, when a confederacy led by Akbar poisoned the water supply. Aside from the fort itself, Kumbhalgarh is worth a visit to experience the idyllic Aravalli countryside, dotted with tribal villages and offering striking views.

The most memorable panorama of all is from the pinnacle of the rather plain **palace** building, crowning the summit of the fort, with striking bird's-eye views over the numerous Jain and Hindu **temples** clustered around the main gate and scattered over the hills below. The oldest are thought to date from the second century; the **tombs** of the great Rana Kumbha himself (murdered by his eldest son) and his grandson Prithviraj (poisoned by his brother-in-law) stand to the east. Some 36km of crenellated ramparts wind around the rim of the hilltop, and it's possible to walk around them in two comfortable days, sleeping rough or in tents; a guide is compulsory (from ₹1000/day). Be sure to take sufficient food and water.

Kumbhalgarh Wildlife Sanctuary

Daily 9am–6pm • ₹180 (₹20), camera ₹400, guide ₹200, jeep ride with guide ₹2200 including entry fees • ☎294 241 135

Lining the deep valley that plunges west from the fort down to the plains, the **Kumbhalgarh Wildlife Sanctuary** comprises a dense area of woodland that offers a refuge for wolves and leopards. With a local guide, you can trek through it to Ranakpur, a rewarding and easy hike of between four and five hours (the alternative is a long journey on an infrequent country bus). Entry **permits** are obtainable from the District Forest Officer at **Kelwara**, 7km down the road, though local guides – contactable through the hotels listed below, at local shops, or at the café just inside the fort gates – can obtain permits for you, and can walk the route with you or take you in a jeep.

ARRIVAL AND DEPARTURE
KUMBHALGARH

By taxi Kumbhalgarh and Ranakpur can easily be visited as a (longish) day-trip from Udaipur (around ₹2400 for the round trip by taxi for up to four people).

By shared jeep Otherwise, take a shared jeep from Chetak Circle to Kelwara, 7km down the road, from where you should be able to pick up a jeep or rickshaw to Kumbhalgarh.

ACCOMMODATION

The Aodhi 1km below the fort ☎0295 424 2341, ⓦheritagehotelsofindia.com. A peaceful and welcoming heritage hotel with stylishly furnished rooms (some with nice views), a big pool and jeep safaris to local villages. ₹8100

Club Mahindra Fort Kumbhalgarh, 5km down the Kelwara road ☎967 2723 444, ⓦclubmahindra.com. Upmarket hotel with 68 rooms, spa, and superb views from its pool and garden terrace. ₹2600

Chittaurgarh

The belt of hilly land east of Udaipur is the most fertile in Rajasthan, watered by several perennial rivers and guarded by a sequence of imposing forts perched atop the craggy ridges that crisscross the region.

The first major settlement you'll come across is the historic town of **CHITTAURGARH** (or **Chittor**), 115km northeast of Udaipur. Of all the former Rajput capitals, Chittaurgarh – former capital of the kingdom of Merwar before Udaipur – was the strongest bastion of Hindu resistance against the Muslim invaders and it is home to one of Rajasthan's most spectacular and historic forts, rising majestically above a verdant tapestry of plains. No less than three mass suicides (*johars*) were committed over the centuries by the female inhabitants of this honey-coloured **fort**. As a symbol of Rajput chivalry and militarism, only Jodhpur's Mehrangarh Fort compares.

Some visitors squeeze a tour of Chittaurgarh into a day-trip, or en route between Bundi and Udaipur, but it's well worth stopping overnight to give yourself plenty of time to explore the fort properly.

Brief history

The origins of Chittor Fort are obscure, but probably date back to the seventh century. It was seized by **Bappa Rawal**, founder of the Mewar dynasty, in 734, and remained the Mewar capital for the next 834 years, bar a couple of brief interruptions. Despite its commanding position and formidable appearance, however, Chittor was far from invincible, and was sacked three times over the centuries, by **Ala-ud-din-Khalji** (1303), **Sultan Bahadur Shah** (1535) and **Akbar** (1568). It was this last attack which convinced the then ruler of Mewar, Udai Singh, to decamp to a more remote and easily defensible site at Udaipur. Chittaurgarh was eventually ceded back to the Rajputs in 1616 on condition that it not be refortified, but the royal family of Mewar, by now firmly ensconced in Udaipur, never resettled here, and the entire fort, which once boasted a population of more than fifty thousand, still only houses a couple of thousand people.

The fort

Fort Daily 8am–6pm • ₹600 (₹40), video camera ₹25; plus ₹50/rickshaw; guide ₹250 **Museum** Daily except Fri 10am–5pm • ₹100 • **Sound-and-light show** daily 7pm; Fri & Tues in English • ₹200 (₹75) • Fort approximately 2km east of town; autos from bus/train stations should cost ₹200, or ₹450 return including waiting time

The entire **fort** is 5km long and 1km wide, and you could easily spend a whole day up here nosing around the myriad remains, although most visitors content themselves with a few hours. **Tours** of the fort are most easily made by auto-rickshaw; alternatively, take a rickshaw to the entrance and explore on foot. It's a long, steep climb up to the fort, but most of the roads on the plateau itself are flat.

The ascent to the fort, protected by massive bastions, begins at **Padan Pol** in the east of town and winds upwards through a further six gateways. The houses of those who still inhabit the fort are clustered to the north of the final gate, Ram Pol; if you have time, or simply don't want to pay to enter the historical part of the fort, this little village makes for worthwhile ambling, with refreshments (and food, if you book ahead) available at the Padmini Haveli (see page 218).

Palace of Rana Kumbha and around

Entering the fort, you first reach the slowly deteriorating fifteenth-century **Palace of Rana Kumbha** (reigned 1433–68), built by the ruler who presided over the period of Mewar's greatest prosperity. The main palace building still stands five storeys high, though it's difficult now to make much sense of the confusing tangle of partially ruined walls and towers. Every evening, hourly sound-and-light shows bring the palace to life, and recount the harrowing history – battles and stories – of the fort.

Opposite the palace stands the intricately carved fifteenth-century **Shingara Chauri Mandir**, a small but lavishly adorned Jain temple dedicated to Shantinath, the sixteenth *tirthankara*. Nearby, the modern **Fateh Prakash Palace**, a large, plain edifice built for the

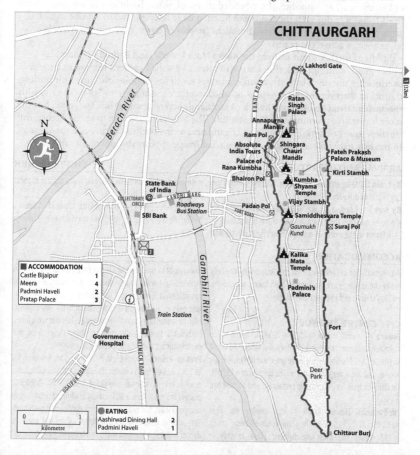

maharana of Udaipur in the 1920s, is home to a small **archeological museum**, containing a fine array of Jain and Hindu carvings recovered from various places around the fort.

A couple of hundred metres further on lies the imposing **Kumbha Shyama Temple**, constructed by (and named after) Rana Kumbha. A black statue of Garuda stands in its own pavilion in front of the shrine, while an image of Varaha, the boar incarnation of Vishnu, occupies a niche at the rear. A second shrine stands close by within the small walled enclosure, dedicated to **Meerabai**, a Jodhpur princess and poet famed for her devotion to Krishna.

The Vijay Stambh and beyond

The main road within the fort continues south to its focal point, **Vijay Stambh**, the soaring "tower of victory" erected by Rana Kumbha to commemorate his 1440 victory over the Muslim sultan Mehmud Khilji of Malwa. This magnificent sand-coloured tower, whose nine storeys rise 36m, took a decade to build; its walls are lavishly carved with mythological scenes and images from all Indian religions, including Arabic inscriptions in praise of Allah. You can climb the dark narrow stairs to the very summit for free by showing your fort entry ticket.

The area around the Vijay Stambh is littered with an impressive number of further remains, including a pair of monumental gateways and a number of florid temples, such as the superbly decorated **Samiddhesvara Temple**, whose shrine houses an image of the *trimurti*, a composite, three-headed image of Shiva, Brahma and Vishnu. A path leads from here down to the **Gaumukh Kund**, a large reservoir fed by an underground stream that trickles through carved mouths (*mukh*) of cows (*gau*) and commands superb views across the plains.

Buildings further south include the **Kalika Mata Temple**, and **Padmini's Palace**, its rather plain buildings enclosing a series of attractive walled gardens leading to a tower overlooking the small lake. The road continues south to the point once used for hurling traitors to their deaths, then returns north along the eastern ridge to **Suraj Pol** gate, with spectacular vistas across a patchwork of farmland. Several temples line the route, but the most impressive monument is **Kirti Stambh**. The inspiration for the tower of victory, this smaller "tower of fame" was built by Digambaras in the twelfth century as a monument to the first *tirthankara* Adinath, whose unclad image appears throughout its six storeys.

ARRIVAL AND DEPARTURE	CHITTAURGARH

By train Chittaurgarh's railway station is to the south of the city, a 20min drive from the fort.

By bus The Roadways (aka "Kothwali") Bus Stand is on the west bank of the Ghambiri and there is a station in Zink Nagar in the north of town; it hosts both private and state-run services, with the latter far more regular to most destinations in Rajasthan.

Destinations Ajmer (1–3 hourly; 5hr); Jaipur (1–3 hourly; 7–9hr); Kota (1–2 hourly; 4hr 30min); Udaipur (1–2 hourly; 2hr 30min).

ACCOMMODATION

Accommodation in Chittaurgarh is relatively pricey; the only really cheap places are the slightly grim hotels around the railway station and in the middle of town.

CITY CENTRE AND FORT

Meera Neemuch Rd ☏ 0147 224 0934, ⓦ hotelmeera chittaurgarh.com; map p.217. Recently renovated hotel in the centre of town, with a wide selection of fan and a/c rooms, and some very nicely decorated suites (from ₹3300); facilities include an inexpensive restaurant and a good bar. ₹1500

★ **Padmini Haveli** Anna Poorna Temple Rd, Fort ☏ 0147 224 1251, ⓦ thepadminihaveli.com; map p.217. Easily the most atmospheric place to stay in town, right in the heart of Chittor Fort. Run by a charming husband-and-wife team, this is authentic Rajasthani hospitality at its best, and the pure-veg food is excellent (see below). Rooms (all a/c) are characterful and adorned with beautiful fabrics and – unusually – Hermès sculptures; bathrooms feature solid granite sinks. Views from the rooftop sunset terrace are spectacular. ₹4000

Pratap Palace Opposite the GPO on Shri Gurukul Rd ☏ 0147 224 0099, ⓦ hotelpratappalacechittaurgarh.com; map p.217. Functional mid-range hotel, a bit shabby in places (and more than a little creepy at night, though largely in a good way), but with an attractive garden and good food. The smarter deluxe rooms are better value, and there's a decent non-veg restaurant that's also licensed. ₹2750

RECOMMENDED TRAINS FROM CHITTAURGARH

All the following trains run daily.

Destination	Name	No.	Departs	Arrives
Ajmer	Ratlam–Ajmer Express	19653	10.30am	1.55pm
Bundi	Kota Express	29019	3.45pm	5.43pm
Delhi	Mewar Express	12964	8.45pm	6.35am
Jaipur	Udaipur–Khajuraho Express	19666	12.30am	5.45am
	Udaipur–Jaipur Express	12991	8.20am	1.35pm
Udaipur	Udaipur City Express	19329	4.50pm	7.15pm

OUTSIDE THE CITY

Castle Bijaipur ☎0147 227 6351, ⊛castlebijaipur. co.in; map p.217. This lovely hotel occupies a superb sixteenth-century castle set in a tranquil and unspoilt rural location a 45min (32km) drive east of town. Rooms are decorated with traditional Rajasthani wooden furniture and artefacts, and there's a pool, library, Ayurvedic massages, daily group yoga and meditation sessions (individual tuition on request), plus cycle, jeep and horse safaris to nearby villages. They also have tented accommodation (₹5000) a few kilometres away in an even more remote rural location at Pangarh Lake. ₹6500

EATING

★**Aashirwad Dining Hall** Opposite Satkar Hotel ☎94141 10110; map p.217. Popular little veg thali joint (₹120, with free replenishments), now open for dinner as well as lunch. No English signage, but it's easy enough to spot. Daily 11.30am–3.30pm & 6.30–10.30pm.

Padmini Haveli Anna Poorna Temple Rd, Fort ☎0147 224 1251, ⊛thepadminihaveli.com; map p.217. Not just the best place to stay in the fort (see above), but the best place to eat, too. The pure-veg food is excellent, with lunch and dinner spreads going for ₹600 each; let them know you're coming at least the day before. Daily lunch & dinner.

Bundi

The walled town of **BUNDI**, 37km north of Kota, lies in the north of the former Hadoti state, shielded by jagged outcrops of the Vindhya Range. The site was the capital of the Hadachauhans, but although settled in 1241, 25 years before neighbouring Kota, Bundi never amounted to more than a modest market centre, and remains relatively untouched by modern development. The palace alone justifies a visit thanks to its superb collection of **murals**, while the well-preserved **old town**, crammed with crumbling havelis, picturesque old bazaars and a surprising number of flamboyant *baoris* or "step-wells" (giant water tanks designed to collect the precious monsoon rains), makes this one of southern Rajasthan's most appealing destinations – a fact recognized by the ever-increasing numbers of foreign tourists who are now visiting the place.

Garh Palace

Jodhpur's House of Strife, gray towers on red rock, is the work of giants, but the Palace of Bundi, even in broad daylight, is such a palace as men build for themselves in uneasy dreams – the work of goblins rather than men.
Rudyard Kipling

Daily 8am–6pm • ₹500 (₹180), video camera ₹100

Bundi's **palace** was one of the few royal abodes in Rajasthan untouched by Mughal influence, and its appearance is surprisingly homogenous considering the number of times it was added to over the years.

A short steep path winds up to the main gateway, **Hathi Pol**, surmounted by elephant carvings, beyond which lies the palace's principal courtyard. On the right-hand side, steps lead up to the **Ratan Daulat**, the early seventeenth-century Diwan-i-Am, or Hall of Public Audience, an open terrace with a simple marble throne overlooking the courtyard below.

2

At the far end of the Ratan Daulat, further steps lead down to the **Chhatra Mahal**. Go through the open-sided turquoise-fringed pavilion on the eastern side of the courtyard and the room beyond to reach a superb little **antechamber**, its every surface covered in finely detailed murals from the 1780s, embellished with gold and silver leaf. The opposite side of the courtyard is flanked by a pavilion with columns supported on the backs of quaint black trumpeting elephants.

From the Chhatra Mahal courtyard, a narrow flight of steps leads up to an even smaller courtyard flanked by the superbly decorated **Phool Mahal** (built in 1607, though the murals date from the 1860s), whose murals include a vast procession featuring regiments of soldiers in European dress and a complete camel corps.

From here, further narrow steps ascend to the **Badal Mahal** (Cloud Palace), home to what are often regarded as the finest paintings in the whole of southern Rajasthan. A vividly coloured ring of Krishnas and Radhas dance around the highest part of the vaulted dome, flanked by murals showing Krishna being driven to his wedding by Ganesh, and Rama returning from Sri Lanka to Ayodhya.

Chittra Sala

There are further outstanding murals in the **Chittra Sala**, just above the palace. At the rear left-hand corner of the garden, steps lead up to a small courtyard embellished with an outstanding sequence of paintings in an unusually muted palette of turquoises, blues and blacks, the majority devoted to magical depictions of scenes from the life of Krishna.

Taragarh Fort

Sunrise–sunset • Free with palace entry (₹25)

A steep twenty-minute climb above the Chittra Sala, the monkey-infested **Taragarh Fort** offers even more spectacular views over Bundi, its palace and the surrounding countryside. Upon passing through the second wooden gate, double back on yourself and go up the ramp to get onto the barracks for a great vantage point. Note that the path up can be tricky, even with decent footwear (flip-flops are not advisable), and a near-total lack of security means that solo females should probably give the climb a miss.

Raniji-ki-Baori

Southwest of Azad Park • Daily 9.45am–5pm • ₹200 (₹50), or ₹350 (₹75) including Sukh Mahal

South of the Old City is the rewarding **Raniji-ki-Baori**, one of Rajasthan's most spectacular step-wells. Built in 1699, this 46m-deep well is reached by a flight of steps punctuated by platforms and pillars embellished with sinuous S-shaped brackets and elephant capitals. As you descend, look for the beautifully carved panels showing the ten avatars of Lord Vishnu, which line the side walls. The nineteenth-century step-well of **Dhabhai-ka Kund** lies south of Ranji-ki-Baori; other notable Bundi *baoris* include the twin step-wells of **Nagar Sagar Kund**, near Chogan Gate, and **Bhora-ji-ka Kund**, to the west of town.

Sukh Mahal

Daily 9.45am–5pm • ₹200 (₹50), or ₹350 (₹75) including Raniji-ki-Baori • Around ₹120 return by auto from town to Sukh Mahal, ₹150 to Kshar Bagh

Northeast of the town on the southern shore of Jait Sagar lake is the pretty but now rather neglected **Sukh Mahal** – Rao Raja Vishnu Singh's summer palace – where Rudyard Kipling (who stayed here for a few months at the invitation of the raja) wrote parts of *Kim* and *The Jungle Book*. The building itself is closed to visitors but the gardens are pretty, and you can walk for a short distance along the lakeshore on either side of the palace. Some 1.5km further around the lakeshore, **Kshar Bagh** encloses sixty crumbling royal cenotaphs. If the door is locked, ask for the key at the chowkidar's hut on your left just after the gateway over the main road some 100m north of the cenotaphs.

ARRIVAL AND DEPARTURE

By train The railway station is around 5km south of town (₹150 or so by auto-rickshaw). Best for Kota is the *Mandasor Kota Express* #29019 (dep. 5.45pm, arr. 6.45pm), to Chittaurgarh the *Meerut City* #29020 (dep. 9.17am, arr. 11.35am), to Udaipur the *Mewar Express* #12963 (dep. 2.10am, arr. 7.20am), and to Sawai Madhopur the *Mandasor Kota Express* #29019 (dep. 5.45pm, arr. 9.10pm).

By bus Buses arrive in the southeast part of town near the post office, from where it's around ₹60 by auto-rickshaw to the palace and guesthouses. Heading south, there are regular buses to Kota (every 30min; 1hr), and services to Chittaurgarh (2 daily; 4hr) and Udaipur (3 daily; 6hr). Buses are the best way of reaching Ajmer (hourly; 4hr), Jaipur (every 30min; 5hr) and Jodhpur (5 daily; 8hr).

INFORMATION

Events The annual Bundi Festival takes place around mid-November, and is a celebration of Hadoti heritage with a very local, country-fair feel.

Tours Jovial archeology enthusiast "Kukki" (☏ 982 8404

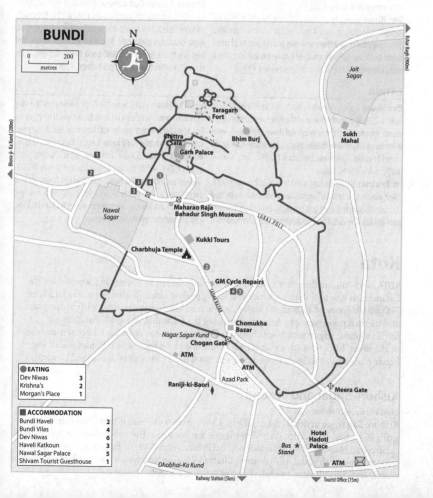

BUNDI

EATING
Dev Niwas	3
Krishna's	2
Morgan's Place	1

ACCOMMODATION
Bundi Haveli	2
Bundi Vilas	4
Dev Niwas	6
Haveli Katkoun	3
Nawal Sagar Palace	5
Shivam Tourist Guesthouse	1

2

527, ⓦ kukkisworld.com) runs engaging half-day and full-day tours (from ₹750) to prehistoric rock painting sites in Bundi's rural hinterland, plus visits to villages and vulture colonies.

ACCOMMODATION

★ **Bundi Haveli** 107 Balchand Para ☎0747 244 6716, ⓦ hotelbundihaveli.com; map p.221. Traditional old haveli given a stylish contemporary makeover, with beautifully furnished a/c rooms (many with *jharokhas*), and a decent restaurant (breakfast included in rates). Excellent value. ₹1150

★ **Bundi Vilas** Balchand Para ☎0747 244 4614, ⓦ bundivilas.com; map p.221. Tucked up against the palace's lower rampart walls, the seven charming rooms and suites (all a/c) of this 300-year-old family-run haveli are tastefully decorated and high on creature comforts. There's a pretty rooftop restaurant, and the rooftop suites are the most romantic in town. ₹4350

Dev Niwas Opposite Purani Kothwali ☎98290 42128, ⓦ jagatcollection.com; map p.221. This sociable guesthouse dates back three centuries and is home to 21 clean rooms and suites (all with attached bathrooms and a/c), plus a nice panoramic rooftop restaurant (see below). ₹1500

Haveli Katkoun Balchand Para ☎0747 244 4311, ⓦ katkounhavelibundi.com; map p.221. Guesthouse with gleaming marble floors and a range of spacious and smart single/double rooms, the best of which have a/c and palace views. Prices have increased in recent years, but you'll still often get generous discounts. ₹1600

Nawal Sagar Palace Balchand Para ☎98292 46541, ⓦ nawalsagarpalace.com; map p.221. Situated right beside the lake, this charming – but overpriced – hotel has spacious and clean heritage rooms (the more expensive with a/c and lake views), plus an emerald lawn and decent rooftop restaurant. ₹4000

Shivam Tourist Guesthouse Balchand Para ☎0747 244 7892, ⓦ shivam-bundi.co.in; map p.221. Extremely sociable little family guesthouse with friendly management, eight clean and pleasantly decorated attached rooms (the best on the upper floors) and good home-cooking (plus classes). Best in town at this price range. ₹500

EATING

Dev Niwas Opposite Purani Kothwali ☎98290 42128; map p.221. The most reliable of the hotel restaurants (just watch your head on the way up and down the stairs), with a menu of affordable Indian mains, including Rajasthani ones like gatta (₹165) and laal maas (₹255). Daily noon–3.15pm & 6.45–10.30pm.

★ **Krishna's** Sadar Bazaar ☎91660 46392; map p.221. "Best masala chai in India" sounds like a ridiculous claim, and it is, but this simple, hippy-painted spot is at least somewhere near the top. The constituent ingredients are pulverised with

a rock for almost every order (₹40), by a fellow with a very infectious grin – it takes a little while, but you'll be enjoying the scent long before you've touched your tea. A warning: come here once, and you'll be back again. Daily 8am–11pm.

Morgan's Place Kasera Paradise, near Surang Gate ☎0747 244 4679, ⓦ kaseraparadise.com; map p.221. The restaurant atop this hotel is the best in town, serving decent pasta and pizzas (₹300–400); veg and non-veg options are available, as are quirkier dishes such as lasagne, gnocchi and cannelloni. Daily 8am–11pm.

Kota

KOTA, a 45-minute drive from Bundi on a fertile plain fed by Rajasthan's largest river, the Chambal, is one of the state's dirtier and less appealing cities. With a population nudging 700,000, it is one of Rajasthan's major commercial and industrial hubs, with hydro, atomic and thermal power stations lining the banks of the Chambal, alongside Asia's largest fertilizer plant, whose enormous chimneys provide a not-so-scenic backdrop to many views of the town. Kota is worth a visit if only for its fine city palace, which houses one of the better museums in Rajasthan; while the old town has a commercial hustle and bustle.

Kishore Sagar and around

Chatra Vilas Gardens Daily 9am–7pm • ₹5

Kishore Sagar, an artificial lake built in 1346, gives some visual relief from the city's grim industrial backdrop, if its water levels are buoyant. The red-and-white palace in its centre, **Jag Mandir**, was commissioned by Prince Dher Deh of Bundi in 1346. On the eastern edge of the lake, the pleasing **Chatra Vilas Gardens** are an easy walk from the bus stand, and a good place to chill if you're waiting between services.

City Palace

Maharao Madho Singh Museum Daily 10am–5pm • Combined entrance to museum and palace ₹200 (₹100) including camera, video camera ₹100

On the southern side of the town centre, around 2km from the bus station, lies the **City Palace**, a well-preserved cluster of blue and pink royal residences; construction on them began in 1625 and continued sporadically until the early years of the twentieth century. The palace now houses the excellent **Maharao Madho Singh Museum**. The first room is filled with a selection of luxury items belonging to the maharaja, while diagonally across the courtyard lies the dazzling **Raj Mahal**, built by Rao Madho Singh (ruled 1625–49), richly decorated with paintings and mirrorwork, which served as the ruler's public audience hall. From the Raj Mahal, a corridor leads into a further sequence of rooms housing a well-stocked armoury and a small art gallery, and a depressing wildlife gallery, filled with the moth-eaten remains of various leopards and tigers.

Exit the museum then follow the steps up past the Raj Mahal to reach a series of finely painted palace buildings (you might need to ask one of the staff to open up the doors to the staircase for you). Three storeys up is the **Barah Mahal**, one of whose rooms is richly decorated with dozens of square miniatures placed together on the wall like tiles and depicting a range of religious and contemporary scenes, from Krishna lifting Mount Goverdhan to exotic-looking European ladies and gentlemen.

Chambal Gardens

Daily 9am–7pm • ₹50 • Boat rides ₹700/hr for up to five people

On the edge of the river, a few kilometres south of the fort, crocodiles and gharial sometimes sun themselves in a shallow pond in the **Chambal Gardens** (₹50), which also contains mini replicas of the new seven wonders of the world. Boats from here offer leisurely jaunts on the crocodile-infested River Chambal.

ARRIVAL AND INFORMATION
KOTA

Kota is a surprisingly large and sprawling city, and you'll need a rickshaw to cover the sights.

By train Kota Junction railway station is 2km to the north of town; from here you can take a rickshaw into the centre (₹100).

By bus Arriving at the central bus stand it's a long but feasible walk through the bustling main bazaar to the City Palace. Buses leave regularly to Ajmer (every 30min; 6hr), Bundi (every 30min; 45min–1hr), Chittorgarh (5 daily; 4hr), Jaipur (hourly; 5hr) and Udaipur (8 daily; 6hr). Services to Ajmer usually stop in Bundi en route and those to Udaipur sometimes stop at Chittaurgarh.

ACCOMMODATION AND EATING

Sukhdham Kothi Civil Lines ☎0744 232 0081, ⓦsukhdhamkothi.com. Marvellously atmospheric guesthouse located in a one-hundred-year-old stone mansion set amid extensive gardens. There are fifteen comfy rooms with old wooden furniture and assorted nineteenth-century bric-a-brac. Bar and restaurant on site. ₹2500

Umed Bhawan Palace Palace/Station Rd, Khelri Phatak ☎0744 232 5262, ⓦwelcomheritagehotels. com. Occupying a huge and rather ugly former royal residence, this fancy hotel offers upmarket comforts – and,

RECOMMENDED TRAINS FROM KOTA

All the following trains run daily.

Destination	Name	No.	Departs	Arrives
Chittaurgarh	Dehradun Express	29020	8.45am	11.35pm
Delhi	Golden Temple Mail	12903	11.05am	6.45pm
	Mewar Express	12964	11.35pm	6.35am
Jaipur	Jaipur Express	12955	8.55am	12.45pm
	Ranthambore Express	12465	12.35pm	4.45pm
Sawai Madhopur	Golden Temple Mail	12903	11.05am	12.25pm

yes, a fair bit of chintz – at a reasonable price. ₹7500 **Venus Plaza** Station Road ☏0968 018 7805. Basic but tidy hotel with air-conditioned rooms and attached bathrooms, as well as bunk beds in a mixed dorm makes this the best cheapie option. Dorms ₹500, doubles ₹1400

Sawai Madhopur and around

A scruffy, dusty little backwater, **Sawai Madhopur** wouldn't ordinarily receive any tourist attention at all – but then few scruffy, dusty little backwaters provide such easy access to wild **tigers**. No Indian nature reserve can guarantee a tiger sighting, but **Ranthambore National Park**, located just a few kilometres east of town, the odds are probably better than anywhere else: the park is relatively small and the resident tigers are famously unperturbed by humans, hunting in broad daylight and rarely shying away from cameras or jeep-loads of tourists. Combine the big cats' bravado with the park's proximity to the Delhi–Agra–Jaipur "Golden Triangle", and you'll understand why Sawai Madhopur attracts the number of visitors it does.

ARRIVAL AND INFORMATION
SAWAI MADHOPUR

By train Sawai Madhopur is served by trains on the main Mumbai–Delhi line, and is thus quite easily accessible. The station is right in the middle of the newer, commercial part of town.

By bus Buses from Sawai Madhopur are rarely better than the trains, though they usually depart from the Bundi stand,

east of the Main Bazaar (near the overpass).

Tourist information The friendly staff in the tourist office (Mon–Sat 10am–5pm; ☏07462 220808), located in the train station, hand out free maps of the town, and can advise on tiger tours.

ACCOMMODATION

Most of the area's numerous hotels and guesthouses are strung out along the 14km road between Sawai Madhopur's new town and the national park. Prices are significantly above average, and genuine budget accommodation is almost non-existent – hoteliers claim that they only really see six months' business every year, and therefore have to charge double prices.

AROUND SAWAI MADHOPUR

Raj Palace Resort Ranthambore Rd, just outside town ☏0746 222 4793, ⓦrajpalaceranthambhore.com. One of the best-value places in Ranthambore, with spacious and clean, modern a/c rooms in the main building and more homely a/c "cottages" on the other side of the garden, plus a pool and elegant restaurant (see page 225). ₹3800

Ranthambhore Bagh Ranthambore Rd, 2km from town ☏0746 222 1748, ⓦranthambhore.com. The upper-floor a/c rooms in this rambling hotel are average, but the twelve fabric-lined fully furnished en-suite tents (all with air-coolers and attached bathrooms; ₹4700) feel wonderfully authentic, and are scattered in a pretty garden; be sure to get one away from the road. ₹4200

Ranthambhore Palace Ranthambore Rd, just outside town ☏0746 222 0383, ⓦhotelranthambhorepalace. com. This relatively new high-rise is home to a selection of smart, well-furnished and good-value rooms with a/c, TVs and private modern bathrooms, plus a pleasant roof restaurant. ₹2000

★ **Vivanta Sawai Madhopur Lodge** Ranthambore Rd, just outside town ☏0746 222 0541, ⓦvivantaby

RECOMMENDED TRAINS FROM SAWAI MADHOPUR

All the following trains run daily.

Destination	Name	No.	Departs	Arrives
Ajmer	*Dayodai Express*	12181	9.40am	2.20pm
Bharatpur	*Golden Temple Mail*	12903	12.30pm	2.58pm
Delhi	*Raj Express*	12953	6.28am	10.55am
Jaipur	*Mumbai–Jaipur Express*	12955	10.40am	12.45pm
Jodhpur	*Ranthambore Express*	12465	2.35pm	10.25pm
Kota	*Intercity Express*	12466	1.25pm	2.55pm
Udaipur	*Mewar Express*	12963	11.58pm	7.20am

tajhotels.com. Occupying an atmospheric 1930s hunting lodge, this luxury heritage hotel has bags of charm, with pleasant leafy grounds and accommodation in beautifully appointed colonial-style rooms, plus a pool and attractive restaurant, home to extravagant daily lunch and dinner buffets. ₹19,000

Tiger Haveli Off Ranthambore Rd, 1km from town ☎ 99288 89936, ⊛ tigerhaveli.com. The best of the town's cheaper options, well geared to travellers, with helpful service and comfortably furnished rooms (some with a/c). The walk from town is tedious, but thankfully they have a decent on-site restaurant. ₹1000

THE ROAD TO RANTHAMBORE

Aman-i-Khás Sherpur village ☎ 0746 225 2052, ⊛ aman.com. Situated in a very quiet rural setting, this place rivals *Vanyavilas* (see below) for tasteful opulence (and even outdoes it for wallet-crunching expense). Accommodation is in ten superb, cavernous a/c luxury tents, and there's also a traditional step-well for swimming and a spa tent. Closed May–Sept. ₹85,000

★ **Khem Villas** Sherpur village ☎ 0746 225 2347,

⊛ khemvillas.com. Delightful eco-resort set amid ten acres of carefully nurtured wilderness that is home to abundant birdlife and other fauna. Accommodation is a mix of rooms, tents or stylish little cottages with private verandas and open-to-the-sky showers, and there's also home-grown organic vegetarian food and an interesting range of excursions. Full board. ₹16,000

Nahargarh Khilchipur Village, Ranthambore Rd, 2km south of park entrance ☎ 0746 225 2281, ⊛ nahargarh. com. Superbly theatrical-looking hotel, built in the style of an old-fashioned Rajput palace and looking every bit the regal retreat. Rooms are sumptuously decorated in traditional style and there's also a huge pool and licensed bar. ₹12,000

Oberoi Vanyavilas Ranthambore Rd, about 3.5km from town ☎ 0746 222 3999, ⊛ oberoihotels.com. Superbly stylish resort centred around a lavishly decorated restaurant specializing in royal Rajasthani cuisine. Scattered around the rustic grounds are beautifully equipped wooden-floored, hand-embroidered a/c tents with patios, an outdoor pool, lakeside spa and lookout tower. The rack rates are prohibitive, but you'll often get 40% or so off when booking online. ₹80,000

EATING

The area has few stand-out options for dining, and most people eat where they're staying.

★ **Asha's** Ranthambore Circle ☎ 0746 222 0340. Up on the first floor, this is a local joint for local families, serving absolutely wonderful pure-veg food at low prices. There's a full roster of paneer and veg curries on the menu, but it's hard to look past the thalis – the heavy Rajasthani one is dearest (₹250), but perhaps better (and certainly bigger) is

the stupendous VIP set (₹220). Daily 9am–11pm.

Raj Palace Resort Ranthambore Rd, just outside town ☎ 0746 222 4793, ⊛ rajpalaceranthambhore.com. Of all the hotel restaurants near town, this is the most reliable and easily accessible, with a decent mix of veg (₹150–300) and non-veg curries (₹300–400), and snacks served between mealtimes. Licenced. Daily 7am–3pm & 7–11pm.

Ranthambore National Park

With more than ninety thousand visitors a year, **Ranthambore National Park** is one of India's most popular national parks, and it can get ridiculously busy throughout the cool winter months, especially around Diwali and New Year. The summer months from April to June are a lot quieter, but obviously very hot. There are currently around seventy adult tigers in the park, plus healthy populations of *chital*, nilgai, jackals, leopards, jungle cats and a wide array of birds. The original core section of the national park is flanked by **buffer zones**, designed to provide space for the park's ever-expanding number of young, territory-seeking tigers.

ESSENTIALS   RANTHAMBORE NATIONAL PARK

Rules about visiting Ranthambore change frequently, but at present the number of vehicles allowed into the park is strictly limited to fifteen six-seater jeeps (also known as Gypsies) and 25 canters (open-top buses seating twenty people) being allowed in during each morning and afternoon session.

Tour times 3hr tours run every morning and afternoon; departure times vary slightly through the year, but usually leave 6–7am and 2–3pm. Dress in layers: early mornings can be surprisingly cold.

Prices High-season seats officially cost ₹1249 (₹509) in a canter and ₹1467 (₹727) in a jeep; prices include the park entrance fee, plus obligatory vehicle rental and guide fees; video cameras ₹900.

Booking If you want to book independently, make for the Tiger Reserve Tourist Centre (daily 5.30–6.30am & 12.30–1.30pm) near the *Tiger Safari* hotel, about 7km along Ranthambore Rd, where you can buy tickets for tours on the day. A much easier option is to book a seat in a jeep or canter through your hotel; it's a good idea to book your

2

CANTER OR GYPSY?

Obviously, most visitors prefer the much smaller and quieter jeeps ("Gypsies"), but demand usually outstrips supply. Your chances of seeing a tiger are roughly the same whether you're in a canter or a jeep because they take the same route, even though travelling by jeep may feel more like a "real" safari. You shouldn't have any problems getting a seat in a canter if you book the day before (except possibly during weekends between 1 Oct and 15 April, when five to eight canters are block-booked). If you want to go in a jeep it's best to book ahead, although you might get lucky, especially from around April through to June, when visitor numbers fall significantly. Your chances drop considerably around public holidays.

---

safari at the same time you book your room (or even before). You'll pay a surcharge for this, which can be anything from ₹200 for a seat in a canter booked through a cheaper hotel up to ₹2000 for a place in a jeep booked through a top-end establishment. At the time of writing, the otherwise-awful Ankur Resort (☏75686 19151, ⊕ankurresorts.com), just next to the Raj Palace (see page 224), was consistently offering cheaper prices than all agencies in town.

Zones The park is split into ten zones – five core zones (thought to be best for tiger spotting) and five buffer zones.

Zones are randomly allocated upon booking; if you are given the same one twice, you may be able to request a switch, but the final decision lies with the park authorities.

When to visit The core section of Ranthambore is closed annually from July 1 to September 30 with the exception of the four buffer zones, which remain open year-round. The best time to visit is during the dry season (Oct–March), when the lack of water entices the larger animals out to the lakeside. During and immediately after the monsoons they're more likely to remain in the forest.

Ranthambore Fort

Daily 6am–6pm • Best accessed on a tour; the tourist office in the railway station (see page 228) can organise taxi trips for ₹1000, including hotel pick-up and drop-off

It's well worth setting aside some time from the tigers to visit the dramatic **Ranthambore Fort**, set atop a rocky crag near the entrance to the national park, although in fact, since it's officially within the core zone, there's still the chance of spotting a tiger en route. The fort was founded in 944 by the Chauhan Rajputs and, following the decisive defeat of Prithviraj III by Muhammad of Ghor in 1192, became a key strategic focus in Rajput resistance to the expanding power of the Delhi Sultanate.

A few kilometres along the road into the park, a twisting flight of two hundred eroded stone steps leads up through gateways and crumbling fortifications to reach the fort, enclosed by some 7km of walls and bastions that snake around the ridgetop, offering fine views over the surrounding countryside. The numerous remains within the fort include a mosque, a large tank, assorted chhatris and several temples – the one dedicated to Ganesh is particularly revered, and people from all over the country write to the elephant-headed god's shrine here to invite him to their weddings.

Bharatpur and around

The walled town of **BHARATPUR** is just a stone's throw from the border with Uttar Pradesh – a mere 18km from the magnificent abandoned city of Fatehpur Sikri, and also within easy swiping distance of Agra. The town itself has an interesting mix of bazaars, palaces and temples, but the real reason to come here is to visit India's most famous bird sanctuary, the **Keoladeo National Park** (see page 228), on the town's southern edge, one of India's – if not the world's – top ornithological destinations.

Other than the moated **Lohagarh** at the centre of the city, and the aforementioned park, there's not all that much to see in Bharatpur. If you're bored, try tracking down the unusual **Ganga Mandir**, a large Hindu temple dedicated to the proprietary goddess of India's most sacred river (though the elaborately carved sandstone building looks a bit like a Neoclassical French chateau); the imposing **Jama Masjid**; or the finely embellished **Laxman Mandir**, dedicated to the family deity of the maharajas of Bharatpur. All three are somewhat neglected and of little interest, but on the plus side they're an easy walk from each other.

Lohagarh

Museum Tues–Sun noon–8pm • ₹100 (₹20), camera ₹50, video camera ₹100

Bharatpur was founded by the Jat king Surajmal, who constructed the virtually impregnable **Lohagarh** (Iron Fort) at the heart of town in 1732; time and modern development have had little effect on its magnificent 11km-long bastions and immense moat. You're most likely to enter the fort from the south, though it's worth having a look at the impressive **Ashtdhatu** (or Eight-Metal) **Gate**, named on account of the number of different metals that apparently went into the making of its extremely solid-looking doors.

The small but impressive fort is home to no less than three large royal palaces in various stages of dereliction, all built by the Jats between 1730 and 1850. The best preserved is the large orange **Kamra Khas Mahal**, on the west side of the fort, which now serves as the town's recently upgraded **museum**; the sculptures surrounding the fountain look of decidedly suspicious provenance, but the pretty upstairs level is home to a large collection of weapons, miniature paintings and regal memorabilia.

| ARRIVAL AND INFORMATION | BHARATPUR |

By train The railway station – on the main Delhi–Mumbai line – is a couple of kilometres northwest of the town centre, a ₹120 rickshaw ride from Keoladeo National Park and the nearby guesthouses. There are several daily trains to Agra Fort, including the *Agra Fort Superfast* #22987 (dep. 11am, arr. 12.20am); Sawai Madhopur and Kota, the best being the *Golden Temple Mail* #12904 (daily; dep. 10.25am, arr. 12.50pm in Sawai Madhopur and 2.20pm in Kota); and Jaipur, the best of which is the *Agra Fort Superfast* #22988 (dep. 3.40am, arr. 6.50am).

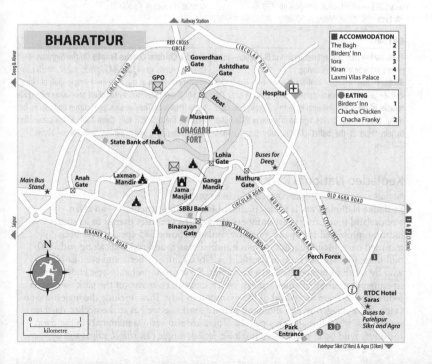

2

By bus Bharatpur's bus stand is in the west of town. If you're arriving from Fatehpur Sikri you'll save yourself time (and a rickshaw fare) by getting off the bus at the crossroads on the southeast side of town, near the park gates and close to guesthouses. There are services to Jaipur (6 daily; 4hr), Fatehpur Sikri (hourly; 30–45min) and Deeg (hourly; 1hr); for Agra (1hr) buses are frequent, and you may as well just flag down whatever comes along.

By taxi Bharatpur's reputation as a tourist-friendly oasis has made it an attractive base for day-trippers to Agra and the Taj Mahal – a day-trip by taxi to Agra and back should cost about ₹3500, all in.

Tourist information The town's tourist office (Mon–Sat 9.30am–6pm; ☎05644 222542, ☻bharatpur.rajasthan.gov. in) is at the crossroads east of the park entrance; around the back is a railway reservations office (Mon–Sat 8am–2pm).

ACCOMMODATION

All the town's best hotels and guesthouses are located near the entrance to Keoladeo National Park, on the southern edge of town and some 3km south of railway station. There's also an option in the park itself (see page 229).

The Bagh Agra–Achnera Rd, 1km past Laxmi Vilas Palace ☎0564 422 8333, ☻thebagh.com; map p.227. This idyllic upmarket hotel occupies a cluster of pink, low-rise buildings scattered around charbagh-style gardens that are home to more than fifty species of bird. Rooms are cool, spacious and attractively furnished, and there's also a spa and large pool. ₹7000

★**Birders' Inn** Off the highway, near the crossroads ☎0564 422 7346, ☻birdersinn.com; map p.227. The most inviting place in town, usually full of serious birdwatchers who gather nightly to compare checklists in the pleasant courtyard garden and superb a/c multi-cuisine restaurant (see below). All twenty-four a/c rooms are large, smart and excellent value. Free pick-up. ₹3000

★**Iora** 54 Gauri-Shankar Colony ☎98280 41294, ☻ioraguesthouse.com; map p.227. Owned by a friendly amateur photographer, the rooms here (air-cooled, or a/c for an extra ₹200) are a good size and comfortable with en suites. The attached cafe is lined with photography and books, and serves coffee, snacks and simple meals. ₹1100

★**Kiran** 364 Rajendra Nagar ☎0564 422 3845, ☻kiranguesthouse.com; map p.227. Run by an extremely friendly and helpful pair of brothers (one of whom is a certified naturalist), this place offers eight clean and comfortable fan-cooled, air-cooled and a/c rooms at rock-bottom prices. There's free collection and drop-off from the bus and train stations, plus binoculars for rent. ₹600

Laxmi Vilas Palace Agra Rd ☎0564 422 3523, ☻laxmivilas.com; map p.227. Former royal palace, set amid extensive grounds east of town with heated pool and spa including massage room. Reasonably priced a/c rooms complete with four-poster beds and other romantic, regal decorative touches. ₹6000

EATING

There are few independent restaurants in Bharatpur – most people eat where they're staying.

Birders' Inn Off the highway, near the crossroads ☎0564 422 7346, ☻birdersinn.com; map p.227. The reliable of the hotel restaurants, with a decent à la carte menu, though when there's a group in you may be tempted to join them at the buffet (₹550). Daily 9am–3pm & 7–10pm.

Chacha Chicken Chacha Franky Off the highway, near the crossroads ☎84331 51477; map p.227. You'll rarely see people dining at this extremely simple spot, but locals and highway users stop by to collect take-away with quite some frequency. They've a roster of curries and snacks, but best are the delicious rolls (from ₹60), which come filled with chicken, egg, veg or paneer. Daily 11am–10pm.

Keoladeo National Park

Daily sunrise–sunset • ₹500 (₹75), guides ₹250/hour, video camera ₹900 (₹600)

Keoladeo National Park is India's premier birdwatching sanctuary – an avian wonderland that attracts vast numbers of feathered creatures thanks to its strategic location, protected status and extensive wetlands. Some 385 species have been recorded here, including around two hundred year-round residents along with 190-odd migratory species from as far afield as Tibet, China, Siberia and even Europe, who fly south to escape the northern winter. Keoladeo is probably best known for its stupendous array of **aquatic birds**, which descend en masse on the park's wetlands following the dramatic arrival of the monsoon in July. These include the majestic saras crane and a staggering two thousand painted storks, as well as snake-necked darters, spoonbills, white ibis and grey pelican. There are also various **mammals** in the park, including wild boar, mongoose, antelope, jackal, jungle cat, chital, nilgai and sambar.

The **best time to visit** is following the monsoon (roughly Oct–March), when the weather is dry but the lakes are still full and the migratory birds in residence (although mists in December and January can hinder serious birdwatching). Most people chose to tour the park on a rickshaw, though cycling is advisable – the rickshaws are limited to one road going straight up and straight down, but on a bike you'll be away from people in no time, if you so desire, and you'll most likely surprise plenty of deer.

GETTING AROUND AND INFORMATION

KEOLADEO NATIONAL PARK

The park entrance is around 4km south of Bharatpur railway station, and within walking distance of most of the accommodation listed in Bharatpur (see page 228). A single road passes through the park, while numerous small paths cut around lakes and across marshes and provide excellent cover for birdwatching.

By rickshaw or van You can hire a cycle rickshaw for ₹150/hr; drivers are trained by the park authorities, and very clued up. Vans cost ₹300/hr, as do horse-drawn tongas.

By bicycle Although you can stroll through the park on foot, the best way to get around and cover more ground is by bicycle, available at the main entrance (₹50 for 4hr).

By boat During the winter, gondola-style boats (₹75/hr per person, minimum four people) offer short rides across the wetlands, assuming there's enough water.

Binoculars If you hire a guide, they'll probably have binoculars for you to borrow; if you choose to go it alone, try asking at your accommodation.

ACCOMMODATION AND EATING

Other than the *Bharatpur Forest Lodge*, there aren't any places for meals in the park, though there are refreshment kiosks at the beginning and end of the park road – whether they'll be open when you pass by is a different matter.

Bharatpur Forest Lodge 1km inside park ☏ 92127 77223, ⊛ bharatpurforestlodge.in. In a pleasantly sylvan setting inside the park (note that you'll have to pay one

day's park entrance fee for every night you stay here), this very sleepy hotel has fourteen spacious and comfortable, old-fashioned rooms with balconies overlooking the sanctuary, a pleasant garden out the back and a passable restaurant (mealtimes only). Relatively expensive, but the setting is pretty much unbeatable. ₹4000

Deeg

Served by **bus** from Bharatpur (every 30min; 1hr) and Alwar (hourly; 1hr)

Some 30km northwest of Bharatpur, the dusty little market town of **DEEG** is the unlikely home of one of eastern Rajasthan's most lavish **palaces**, a fascinating blend of Mughal and Hindu architectural styles constructed by the local Jat overlords in the mid-eighteenth century.

Deeg is easily visited as a day-trip from Bharatpur or Alwar, or en route between the two. There's nowhere particularly good to stay.

Jal Mahal

Sat–Thu 9am–5pm • ₹100 (₹10)

Deeg's extensive **Jal Mahal** comprises a large number of finely carved buildings, scattered around extensive *charbagh*-style gardens dotted with thirty-odd water jets – though sadly the water channels are usually dry, and the fountains are only switched on during local festivals.

As you enter the palace, the first and largest of the various *bhawans*, the **Gopal Bhawan**, lies immediately ahead, a spacious and plushly furnished hall that originally served as Surajmal's summer residence. Behind it lies the first of the palace's two large tanks, the **Gopal Sagar**. On the opposite side of the gardens lies the ornate **Kesav Bhawan**, or "Monsoon Palace", a richly carved, open-sided pavilion surrounded by a deep water channel dotted with hundreds of tiny fountains. This unusual structure was designed to re-create the cool ambience of the rainy season, with water released from rooftop pipes to imitate a shower of monsoon rain, while metal balls were agitated by further streams of pressurized water to simulate the sound of thunder. Immediately behind here is the second of the palace's **tanks**, its stepped *ghats* usually covered in washing laid out by local housewives, while beyond rise the enormous walls of the town's huge fort.

Uttar Pradesh

THE MAGNIFICENT TAJ MAHAL

Uttar Pradesh

Uttar Pradesh, "the Northern State" – formerly the United Provinces, but always UP – is the heartland of Hinduism and Hindi, dominating the nation in culture, religion, language and politics. A vast, steamy plain of the Ganges, it boasts a history that's very much the history of India, and its temples and monuments – Buddhist, Hindu and Muslim – are among the most impressive in the country.

Western UP, which adjoins Delhi, has always been close to India's centre of power. Its main city, **Agra**, once the Mughal capital, is home to the Taj Mahal, and a short hop from the abandoned Mughal city of Fatehpur Sikri. **Central UP** constituted the **Kingdom of Avadh**, the last centre of independent Muslim rule in northern India until the British unceremoniously took it over, fuelling the resentment that led to the 1857 uprising, in which its capital **Lucknow** (now UP's state capital) played such a celebrated role.

In **eastern UP** lies Hinduism's holiest city, the *tirtha* (crossing-place) of **Varanasi**, where it's believed death transports the soul to final liberation. Sacred since antiquity, it was frequented by Mahavira, the founder of Jainism, and also by Buddha, who preached his first sermon in nearby **Sarnath**.

Although UP was once a thriving centre of Islamic jurisprudence and culture, many Muslims departed during the years after Independence, and the Muslim population now comprises just eighteen percent. As the heart of what is known as the "cow belt" (equivalent to America's "bible belt"), UP has been plagued by caste politics and was for some years dominated by the Hindu sectarian BJP. It acquired an unfortunate reputation as the focus of bitter communal tensions, most notoriously in the wake of the 1992 destruction of the Babri Masjid mosque in **Ayodhya** (east of Lucknow, near Faizabad), which sparked off sectarian riots across India. In recent years, state politics have been dominated by two largely local left-wing parties, the socialist Samajwadi party (SP) and the mainly low-caste Bahujan Samaj party (BSP), but in the 2014 Lok Sabha election, the BJP made an almost clean sweep in UP.

Braj

The holy land of **BRAJ**, in the southwestern corner of the Gangetic valley, is the mythological land where Krishna – Vishnu's eighth earthly incarnation and a major character in the Mahabharata epic – spent his idyllic childhood. Early texts on Braj mention his birthplace Mathura, the forest tract of Vrindavan and the Yamuna River. In the sixteenth century, Krishna devotees "rediscovered" the geographical features and boundaries of the holy area.

Braj became, and remains, one of the most important pilgrimage centres for Krishna devotees, who tour, on foot, the twelve forests where he is supposed to have played.

BEST TIME TO VISIT

The best time to visit UP is October, just after the monsoon, when the climate is fresh and pleasantly warm. By the end of November it's getting chilly at night, and quite cold in December and January, when fog may cause train delays. By mid-January it starts to warm up, and by April it can be uncomfortably hot, with dusty dry winds. The arrival of the monsoon in June breaks the heat but can itself impede travel and other activities, with the possibility of flooding.

ON THE BANKS OF THE GANGES IN VARANASI

Highlights

❶ Taj Mahal One of the world's most beautiful buildings, and India's top tourist sight, marking the zenith and perfection of Mughal architecture, never fails to impress. See page 240

❷ Akbar's mausoleum, Sikandra The great Mughal's tomb looks just as it does in old miniatures, with tame monkeys and deer wandering in its ornamental gardens. See page 248

❸ Fatehpur Sikri An awesomely grand, deserted palace complex in what was once the imperial capital of Mughal India, straddling an arid ridge near the Rajasthani border. See page 255

❹ Kalinjar Fort In the dusty badlands on the southern edge of the state, and well off the usual tourist trail, this remote fort well repays the effort of getting to it. See page 274

❺ Varanasi Take a boat on the Ganges before dawn to watch the sun rise over India's most ancient and sacred city. See page 275

❻ Sarnath Evocative ruins on the site where the Buddha gave his first sermon. See page 288

HIGHLIGHTS ARE MARKED ON THE MAP ON PAGE 234

This great circular pilgrimage, known as the Ban Yatra (forest pilgrimage), can take several weeks. Less energetic or devout visitors just explore the major sites by bus.

Mathura

MATHURA, on the banks of the Yamuna River 141km south of Delhi and 58km northwest of Agra, is celebrated as the place where Krishna was born. Hindu mythology claims that it was founded by Shatrugna, the youngest brother of Ramayana hero and earlier Vishnu avatar Rama, while Mathura's earliest historical records date back around 2500 years. The city reached an early peak under the Indo-Bactrian Kushan people, whose greatest ruler Kanishka came to power in 78 AD. Its prosperity attracted such adventurers as the Afghan Mahmud of Ghazni, Delhi sultan Sikandar

UTTAR PRADESH

CHINA

TIBET
AUTONOMOUS REGION

HIGHLIGHTS

1 Taj Mahal
2 Akbar's mausoleum, Sikandra
3 Fatehpur Sikri
4 Kalinjar Fort
5 Varanasi
6 Sarnath

The International boundaries on this map are neither purported to be correct nor authentic by Survey of India directives. Publisher.

FESTIVALS IN UTTAR PRADESH

Magh Mela (Jan/Feb). Bathing festival held in Prayagraj (formerly Allahabad). the peripatetic, triennial Kumbh Mela took place in January 2019 and will be celebrated again in 2022 (see page 269).

Taj Mahotsav (Feb). Cultural festival put on by the tourist board in Agra's Shipgram craft market to showcase UP handicrafts.

Ramayan Mela (Feb/March). Celebration of the events in the Ramayana epic, held in Chitrakoot.

Dhrupad Mela (Feb/March). Classical music festival in Varanasi, centred on Tulsi Ghat.

Urs (May–June). Celebration of the life of the sufi saint Sheikh Salim Chisti, held in the Muslim month of Ramadan at Fatehpur Sikri's Jama Masjid.

Muharram (Aug/Sept). Lucknow sees particularly big processions to celebrate the Islamic new year.

Ganga Mahotsav (Oct/Nov). Celebration in Varanasi with candles lit along the *ghats* to pay homage to the River Ganges, held two weeks after Diwali, which is itself a major celebration in Varanasi.

3

Lodi and Mughal emperor Aurangzeb. The city's central landmark is the sandstone **Holi Gate**, at the junction of Agra Road, Chatta Bazar and Kotwali Road, with the old city to its north and the modern town to its south and west.

Vishram Ghat
Off Chatta Bazar

Mathura's **riverfront** is minute compared with Varanasi's. Each *ghat* has its temple, with shops selling Krishna dolls, outfits to dress them in, and other devotional paraphernalia. The most important of them is **Vishram Ghat**, the "ghat of rest", where Krishna is said to have recuperated after slaying his evil uncle Kamsa. Pilgrims performing a *parikrama* (round of the city's religious sites) start with a dip here. Shoes must be removed before entering the temple complex or visiting the *ghat*, no matter how muddy it is. Boats are on hand for river excursions (₹100 per boat for half an hour).

At the southern end of the *ghat*, **Sati Burj** is a three-storey sandstone tower decorated with carvings of birds and animals. It was commisioned in 1570 by Raja Bhagwan Das of Jaipur to honour his mother for committing sati (throwing herself onto her husband's funeral pyre), as good widows of the warrior class were supposed to do.

Dwarkadhish Temple
Chatta Bazar • Daily: summer 6.30–11am & 4–7.30pm; winter 6.30–11am & 3.30–7pm • Free (plus ₹10 for the shoe guardian)

Just north of the entrance to Vishram Ghat, the gaily painted **Dwarkadhish Temple** is dedicated to Krishna, under his aka of Dwarkadish ("King of Dwarka"). Mathura's most popular shrine, it is regularly packed out with devotees. The temple was commissioned by the treasurer of the state of Gwalior, one Seth Gokuldas Parikh, and dates from 1815.

Jama Masjid
Mandi Ramdas Rd at Chowk Bazar • Daily dawn (just before 1st prayer) to nightfall (after last prayer) • Free

On a plinth raised above street level in the middle of a bustling bazaar, Mathura's **Jama Masjid** (congregational mosque) was commissioned by Aurangzeb's local governor, Abd ul-Nabi Khan in 1662. It's long since lost its original glazed tiles, but still has its four original minarets and assorted outer pavilions. In front of the mosque is a picturesque little vegetable market.

Shri Krishna Janmasthan
Mathura–Vrindavan Rd • Daily: summer 5.30am–noon & 4–9.30pm; winter 6am–noon & 3–8.30pm • Free • No entry with phone or camera (these can be checked in at the cloakroom outside for ₹2) • ⓦ shrikrishnajanmasthan.net

Pretty much slap-bang in the centre of town, the **Shri Krishna Janmasthan** or Janmabhoomi complex, marks the birthplace of Krishna. Although the shops and shrines combine to produce a park-like atmosphere, nothing obscures the strong military presence – a reminder of underlying Hindu–Muslim tensions.

On entering the complex, you'll see a little **grotto** to your left, where you wander through and admire the slightly kitsch 3D tableaux illustrating the life of Krishna. In the **Kesava Deo Temple**, devotees and pilgrims pray to the image of Krishna. The temple was endowed by the Birla family of industrialists in 1965, the original having been razed on the orders of Aurangzeb in 1661 to build the neighbouring mosque. After Ayodha (see page 1199), it therefore became an obvious potential target for sectarian troublemakers – hence the heavy military presence.

Krishna's birthplace itself, known as the **Janmasthan**, is directly behind the mosque. In a low stone building, a cage-like surround signifies that Krishna was born in captivity, when his parents were prisoners of the tyrant King Kamsa. A stone slab marks the exact spot where he is thought to have been born.

Katra Masjid, the impressive mosque built on Aurangzeb's orders on the ruins of the original Kesava Deo Temple (which was itself built on the ruins of a Buddhist monastery), stands surrounded by barbed wire and watchtowers, its entrance to the west accessed from Mathura Road across a rail line. For the time being it remains closed to casual visitors, but if you want to try your luck, leave your phone, camera and any bags at the temple cloakroom, and bring your passport along; even then, it's unlikely the military will let you in as a tourist without a good reason.

Southwest of the temple complex the impressive stepped sandstone tank of **Potara Kund** is believed to have been used to wash Krishna's baby clothes.

Government Museum

Dampier Park • Tues–Sun 10.30am–4.30pm • ₹25 (₹5)

Close to the centre of Mathura in Dampier Park, the **Government Museum** places a particular emphasis on local Buddhist and Jain sculpture dating from the Kushan (first–third centuries AD) and Gupta periods (fourth–sixth centuries), known collectively as the Mathura School. The sculptures are typically hewn from spotted red sandstone and reflect the assimilation of early prehistoric religious cults within the successive Jain, Buddhist and Hindu pantheons. The museum's highlight, one of the finest examples of Gupta art, is a miraculously intact standing Buddha with a beautifully benign expression, an ornate halo and delicate fluted robes, making the Abhaya *mudra* (fearless) hand gesture. This and a seated Buddha, also in the museum, are thought to have been created by a

MATHURA AND VRINDAVAN

Vrindavan Railway Station

ISKCON Temple

BHAKTIVEDANTA SWAMI MARG

SEE 'VRINDAVAN' MAP FOR DETAILS

VRINDAVAN

MATHURA-VRINDAVAN MARG

N

Pagal Baba Temple

YAMUNA EXPRESSWAY LINK RD

Yamuna River

Delhi

DELHI ROAD

MATHURA-VRINDAVAN MARG

SEE 'MATHURA' MAP FOR DETAILS

MATHURA

NATIONAL HIGHWAY-MATHURA RD.

Yamuna River

MANDI ROAD

NATIONAL HIGHWAY-MATHURA RD.

Mathura Junction Railway Station

0   10

kilometres

Agra

monk named Dinna around 434 AD.
Kushana art on display includes a
headless image of King Kanishka in
a central Asian tunic and boots, and
some exquisite railings carved with
floral motifs and human figures.

ARRIVAL AND INFORMATION
MATHURA

By train The city's main rail station, Mathura
Junction, located 3km south of the centre, is served
by all trains plying the route between Delhi and Agra.
By bus The New Bus Stand, a kilometre south of
the centre on BSA College Road, has buses every
half-hour to Delhi, Agra and Vrindavan (15min), and
across the street you'll find shared autos and *tempos*
to Vrindivan for ₹20, the same as the bus fare (auto-
walas wanting you to hire them by yourself will
obviously be keen to disguise this fact from you).
Information The tourist office, in UP Tourism's *Rahi Hotel*

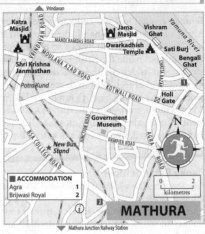

on Railway Station Road (Mon–Sat 10am–5pm; ☎0565
250 5351) provides good maps of Mathura and Vrindavan.

ACCOMMODATION

Agra Bengali Ghat ☎0565 241 3318, ✉agrahoyel2014@
gmail.com; map p.237. Modest little hotel, overlooking
the river in the old city and redolent of the atmosphere of the
ghats. The best rooms (₹900) are upstairs at the front. **₹500**

Brijwasi Royal SBI Crossing, Station Rd ☎88998
81881, ⊚brijwasihotels.com; map p.237. Modern hotel
with well-appointed rooms, all with a/c and TV, plus a bar, a
multicuisine veg restaurant and 24hr room service. **₹4250**

Vrindavan

VRINDAVAN, a dusty little town full of religious devotees, 11km north of Mathura,
attracts half a million pilgrims every year, mostly during the spring Holi festival,
which lasts for up to a month here, and during the two months of celebrations for the
birthdays of Krishna and his consort Radha, starting in August. Although Vrindavan
is in theory a *tirtha* or holy crossing place on the Yamuna, the town has in fact been
progressively abandoned by the river, as it meanders away from the original two-
kilometre-long waterfront – all but five of its 38 *ghats* are now without water. Neither is
there much trace of the forests of the Krishna legend, and only a few sacred basil groves
remain at the spot where he famously cavorted with a group of *gopis* (cowgirls), dancing
miraculously with all of them at the same time so that each thought she was his partner.
As a *tirtha*, Vrindavan attracts elderly Vaishnavites who believe that to die here earns
them instant *moksha* (nirvana). Along with its many *dharamshalas*, Vrindavan holds
several "widow houses", maintained
by wealthy devotees, which provide
food and shelter for widows, of whom
two thousand congregate twice daily
in the Mirabai Ashram to sing *bhajans*
(devotional songs).

Govind Dev Temple

Mathura Rd • Daily: summer 7am–noon & 3–8pm; winter
7.30am–12.30pm & 3.30–8.30pm • Free (plus ₹10 for the
shoe guardian) • ⊚ govinddevji.net

At the northern end of the Mathura–
Vrindavan road, the **Govind Dev**

Temple, erected in 1590 and known locally as "Govindji", was commissioned by Akbar's general Man Singh I, the Raja of Amber, and has quite a Rajasthani look about it. Built from the red sandstone so beloved of the Mughals, and dedicated to Govind Dev (another name for Krishna), it incorporates Hindu, Muslim and even European elements in its design. The stalactite-like embellishments give its facade a drippy, melting kind of feel. Within, it seems almost derelict: monkeys roam about at will, bats twitter in the ceiling, and it's rarely used devotionally. Originally seven storey high, Akbar's pious great-grandson Aurangzeb had the top floors dismantled as he didn't want it to be taller than any mosque. This act of bigoted vandalism has left it looking rather truncated, but it's still a beautiful building, and Vrindavan's most impressive temple by far.

Banke Bihari Temple

Banke Bihari Path (off Banke Bihari Bazar) • Daily: summer 7.45am–noon & 5.30–9.30pm; winter 8.45am–1pm & 4.30–8.30pm • Free • ⓦ bankeybihari.info

The **Banke Bihari Temple**, in the centre of town, is Vrindavan's most popular shrine, renowned for its impressive floral decorations. Its main deity, known as Biharji, is a black image of Krishna, apparently missing his flute. It is said to have materialized miraculously to the sixteenth-century poet, musician and guru Swami Haridas (at Nidhivan, just north of the Govind Dev Temple), but this temple wasn't built for it until 1864. A curtain in front of the image is opened and closed every few minutes because it is believed that looking at it for too long uninterrupted will make you lose consciousness.

Krishna Balaram Mandir

Bhaktivedanta Swami Marg, 1km west of the town centre • Daily: summer 4.10am–12.45pm & 4.30–8.45pm; winter 4.10am–12.45pm & 4–8.15pm • Free • ⓦ iskconvrindavan.com

The **Krishna Balaram Mandir** is the lavish temple complex of the International Society of Krishna Consciousness (ISKCON, commonly known as the Hare Krishnas). Built in Bengal Renaissance style with bright frescoes depicting episodes from Krishna's life, the complex incorporates a marble mausoleum in honour of the society's founder, Swami Prabhupada, who died in 1977. The image in the main temple is of Krishna and his brother Balaram, who are of course honoured with a lot of "hare" chanting, but do remain slightly on your guard here, as it's a favourite spot for pickpockets (and you don't need a guide, so don't be persuaded otherwise). Should you want further information about the ISKCON movement, plenty of books and pamphlets are available in numerous languages. There's also a restaurant and a guesthouse (see page 239).

Pagal Baba Temple

Mathura Road • Tableaux daily 7am–noon & 3–8pm • ₹5 (plus ₹10 for the shoe guardian)

South of town, the ten-storey white **Pagal Baba Temple** is mostly of interest for its puppet tableaux of scenes from the Mahabharata and the Ramayana, complete with moving parts and sound effects. The explanations are in Hindi only, so non-Hindi speakers can only guess at what they represent, although you'll know a lot of them if you're at all familiar with the two great epics. The tableaux teeter somewhere on the edge of being cute or just ridiculous, and some of them are even quite gruesome, but they're certainly worth the entrance fee.

ARRIVAL AND DEPARTURE   VRINDAVAN

By train Vrindavan has a station (hidden away in the centre of town, between Bhaktivedanta Swami Marg and the Mathura Road), and you can make computer bookings there, but it is not currently served by any trains.

By bus Buses, shared *tempos* and jeeps run out to Vrindavan from Mathura for Rs20 per head one-way.

ACCOMMODATION AND EATING

ISKCON Guest House Krishna Balaram Temple Complex, Bhaktivedanta Swami Marg ☎ 0565 254 0021, ⓦ ganpati.gkg@pamho.net; map p.237. Simple but spotlessly clean rooms in the guesthouse attached to the Krishna Balaram Temple (it's behind the temple and part of the complex, but there's a side door for 24hr access). They ask that you make reservations between 11am and 5pm, and it's a good idea to reserve ahead as it's often full. The restaurant serves decent veg meals, although they tone down the spices for the benefit of their largely Western devotees. No wi-fi. ₹950

Shubham Bhaktivedanta Swami Marg, just east of Vidyapeeth Crossing ☎ 0565 645 3288, ⓔ info@ shuibhamhotels.in; map p.237. A reasonable and very central hotel, with two slightly posher branches (*Shubham Holiday* and *Shubham Majesty*) just a stone's throw away. The lobby reeks of incense but the rooms are fresh and bright, although none of the hotel's branches have wi-fi. ₹1365

Agra

The splendour of **AGRA** – India's capital under the Mughals – remains undiminished, from the massive fort to the magnificent **Taj Mahal**. Along with Delhi, 204km northwest, and Jaipur in Rajasthan, Agra is the third apex of the "Golden Triangle", India's most popular tourist itinerary. Although it's possible to see Agra on a day-trip from Delhi, the Taj alone deserves so much more – a fleeting visit would miss the subtleties of its many moods, as the light changes from sunrise to sunset – while the city's other sights and Fatehpur Sikri can easily fill several days.

Most of the city's major Mughal monuments, including the Taj Mahal, are lined up along the banks of the **Yamuna River**, which bounds the city's eastern edge. They date from the later phase of Mughal rule and the reigns of Akbar, Jahangir and Shah Jahan – exemplifying the ever-increasing extravagance which, by Shah Jahan's time, had already begun to strain the imperial coffers and sow the seeds of political and military decline.

Brief history

Agra remained a minor administrative centre until 1504, when the Delhi sultan, **Sikandar Lodi**, moved his capital here to keep a check on the warring factions of his empire. The ruins of his city can still be seen on the Yamuna River's east bank. After defeating the last Lodi sultan, Ibrahim Lodi, at Panipat in 1526, **Babur**, the founder of the Mughal empire, sent ahead his son **Humayun** to capture Agra.

The city saw its heyday under Humayun's son, **Akbar the Great** (1556–1605), when Agra Fort was built, and it remained the empire's capital for more than a century. Even when **Shah Jahan**, Jahangir's son and successor, built a new city in Delhi – Shahjahanabad, now known as Old Delhi – his heart remained in Agra. He pulled down many of the earlier red-sandstone structures in the fort, replacing them with his trademark – exquisite marble buildings. The empire flourished under Shah Jahan's successor Aurangzeb (1658–1707), although his intolerance towards non-Muslims stirred up a hornets' nest and fatally fractured the empire. Agra was then occupied successively by the Jats, the Marathas and eventually the British.

AGRA ORIENTATION

Clustered around the Taj, the tangled little streets of **Taj Ganj** are home to most of the city's cheap accommodation and backpacker cafés. A couple of kilometres to the west, on the far side of the leafy Cantonment area, lies **Sadar Bazaar**, linked to Taj Ganj by Fatehabad Road, where you'll find many of the city's smarter places to stay, as well as numerous restaurants and crafts emporiums. Northwest of Taj Ganj lies **Agra Fort** and, beyond, the third of the city's main commercial districts, **Kinari Bazaar**, centred on the massive Jama Masjid.

The Taj Mahal

Described by Bengali poet Rabindranath Tagore as "a teardrop on the face of eternity", the **Taj Mahal** is undoubtedly the zenith of Mughal architecture. Volumes have been written on its perfection, and its image adorns countless glossy brochures and guidebooks; nonetheless, the reality never fails to overwhelm all who see it, and few words can do it justice.

The magic of the monument is strangely undiminished by the crowds of tourists who visit, as small and insignificant as ants in the face of the immense mausoleum. That said, the Taj is at its most alluring in the relative quiet of early morning, shrouded in mist and bathed with a soft red glow. As its vast marble surfaces fall into shadow or reflect the sun, its colour changes from soft grey and yellow to pearly cream and dazzling white. This play of light is an important decorative device, symbolically implying the presence of Allah, who is never represented in physical form. To really appreciate it fully however, you'd have to stick around from dawn until dusk.

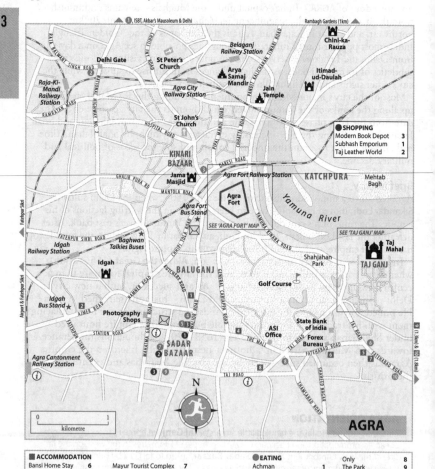

SHOPPING

Modern Book Depot	3
Subhash Emporium	1
Taj Leather World	2

AGRA

■ **ACCOMMODATION**

Bansi Home Stay	6	Mayur Tourist Complex	7
Clarks Shiraz	8	Sakura Guest House	2
Gateway	5	Tourists Rest House	1
GoStops Agra	9	Trident	10
Hilltop	4	Yamuna View	3

● **EATING**

Achman	1	Only	8
Chiman Lal Puri Wale	3	The Park	9
Choko Jeeman	2	Pinch of Spice	10
Dasaprakash	4	Sheroes Hangout	6
The Mandarin	5	Zorba the Buddha	7

THE TAJ MAHAL: A MONUMENT UNDER THREAT

Despite the seemingly impregnable sense of serenity and other-worldliness which clings to the Taj, in reality, India's most famous building faces **serious threats** from traffic and industrial pollution, and from the millions of tourists who visit each year. Marble is all but impervious to the onslaught of wind and rain that erodes softer sandstone, but it has no natural defence against the sulphur dioxide that lingers in a dusty haze and shrouds the monument. Sometimes the smog is so dense that the tomb cannot be seen from the fort. Sulphur dioxide is only one part of the problem: mixing with atmospheric moisture, it settles as sulphuric acid on the surface of the tomb, making the smooth white marble yellow and flaky, and forming a subtle fungus that experts have named "marble cancer". On top of that, increasing pollution levels in the Yamuna River are killing fish, and helping breed swarms of insects, whose droppings contribute to discolouring the Taj. The river's low level also threatens the Taj's wooden foundations, which need constant irrigation to avoid drying up and eventually collapsing.

The main sources of pollution are the continuous flow of **vehicles** along the national highways that skirt the city, and the seventeen hundred **factories** in and around Agra – chemical effluents belched out from their chimneys are well beyond recommended safety limits. Despite laws demanding the installation of pollution-control devices, the imposition of a ban on all petrol- and diesel-fuelled traffic within 500m of the Taj Mahal, and an exclusion zone banning new industrial plants from an area of 10,400 square kilometres around the complex, pollutants in the atmosphere have continued to rise.

Cleaning work on the Taj Mahal rectifies the problem to some extent, but the chemicals used will themselves eventually affect the marble – attendants already shine their torches on "repaired" sections of marble to demonstrate how they've lost their translucency. In November 2018, a BBC News feature reported that treating the Taj with a non-corrosive clay pack – something like a building-sized face-pack – to remove particle deposits from the marble makes the monument's surface rougher and more vulnerable to the dust storms that, thanks to climate change, sweep over Agra with an increasingly alarming frequency.

In a bid to save the Taj by reducing human impact, the Archaeology Survey of India introduced an additional ₹200 ticket cost on 10 December 2018. The extra cost applies to those accessing the main mausoleum; a three-hour limit to each entry was also set, along with a maximum quota of 4,000 tourists per day. Despite these efforts, the Taj's decade-long exposure to pollutants has yet to find a permanent solution.

Overlooking an increasingly polluted tract of the Yamuna River, the Taj Mahal stands at the northern end of a vast walled garden. Though its layout follows a distinctly Islamic theme, representing Paradise, it is above all a monument to romantic love. **Shah Jahan** built the Taj to enshrine the body of his favourite wife, Arjumand Bann Begum, better known by her official palace title, **Mumtaz Mahal** ("Chosen One of the Palace"), who died shortly after giving birth to her fourteenth child in 1631 – the number of children she bore the emperor is itself a tribute to her hold on him, given the number of other wives and concubines that the emperor would have been able to call on. The emperor was devastated by her death, and set out to create an unsurpassed monument to her memory – its name, "Taj Mahal", is simply a shortened, informal version of Mumtaz Mahal's palace title. Construction by a workforce of some twenty thousand men from all over Asia commenced in 1632 and took more than twenty years, not being completed until 1653. Marble was brought from Makrana, near Ajmer in Rajasthan, and semiprecious stones for decoration – onyx, amethyst, lapis lazuli, turquoise, jade, crystal, coral and mother-of-pearl – were carried to Agra from Persia, Russia, Afghanistan, Tibet, China and the Indian Ocean. Eventually, Shah Jahan's pious and intolerant son Aurangzeb seized power, and the former emperor was interned in Agra Fort, where as legend would have it he lived out his final years gazing wistfully at the Taj Mahal. When he died in January 1666, his body was carried across the river to lie alongside his beloved wife in his peerless tomb.

The Chowk-i-Jilo Khana

The south, east and west **entrances** all lead into the **Chowk-i-Jilo Khana** forecourt. The main entrance into the complex, an arched gateway topped with delicate domes and adorned with Koranic verses and inlaid floral designs, stands at the northern edge of Chowk-i-Jilo Khana, directly aligned with the Taj, but shielding it from the view of those who wait outside.

The charbagh

Once through the gateway from the Chowk-i-Jilo Khana, you'll see the Taj itself at the end of the huge **charbagh** (literally "four gardens"), a garden dissected into four quadrants by waterways (usually dry), evoking the Koranic description of Paradise, where rivers flow with water, milk, wine and honey. Introduced by Babur from Central Asia, *charbaghs* remained fashionable throughout the Mughal era. Unlike other Mughal mausoleums such as Akbar's (see page 248) and Humayun's (see page 97), the Taj isn't at the centre of the *charbagh*, but at the northern end, presumably to exploit its riverside setting.

The Taj

At the far end of the *charbagh*, steps lead up to the high-square marble platform on which the **mausoleum** itself sits, each corner marked by a tall, tapering minaret. To the west of the tomb is a domed red-sandstone **mosque** and to the east a replica **jawab**, put there to complete the architectural symmetry of the complex – it cannot be used as a mosque as it faces away from Mecca.

The Taj is essentially square in shape, with pointed arches cut into its sides and topped with a huge central dome that rises for over 55m, its height accentuated by a crowning brass spire almost 17m high. On approach, the tomb looms ever larger and grander, but not until you are close do you appreciate both its sheer size and the extraordinarily fine detail of relief carving, highlighted by floral patterns of precious

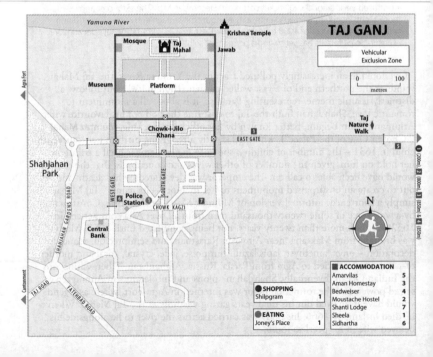

stones. Arabic verses praising the glory of Paradise fringe the archways, proportioned exactly so that each letter appears to be the same size when viewed from the ground.

The south face of the tomb is the main entrance to the **interior**: a high octagonal chamber whose weirdly echoing interior is flushed with pale light. A marble screen, decorated with precious stones and cut so finely that it seems almost translucent, protects the cenotaph of Mumtaz Mahal in the centre, perfectly aligned with the doorway and the distant gateway into the Chowk-i-Jilo Khana, and that of Shah Jahan crammed in next to it – the only object which breaks the perfect symmetry of the entire complex. The inlay work on the marble tombs is the finest in Agra, and no pains were spared in perfecting it – some of the petals and leaves are made of up to sixty separate stone fragments. Ninety-nine names of Allah adorn the top of Mumtaz's tomb, and set into Shah Jahan's is a pen box, the hallmark of a male ruler. These cenotaphs, in accordance with Mughal tradition, are only representations of the real coffins, which lie in the same positions in a crypt below.

The museum
In theory daily except Fri 9am–5pm (but sometimes closed for no apparent reason) • Free

The Taj's **museum**, in the enclosure's western wall, features exquisite miniature paintings, two marble pillars believed to have come from the fort and portraits of Mughal rulers including Shah Jahan and Mumtaz Mahal, as well as architectural drawings of the Taj and examples of *pietra dura* stone inlay work.

INFORMATION

Opening hours Daily except Fri sunrise–sunset.

Tickets ₹1300 (₹250 Indians – ₹50 without access to the main mausoleum – and ₹740 SAARC nationals); free for children below 15 years; ticket valid for one entrance and a maximum stay of three hours; also gives tax-free entry to other sites if used on the same day, giving ₹50 off the admission fee at Agra Fort, and ₹10 off at Sikandra, Itimad-ud-Daulah and Fatehpur Sikri. Ticket queues are longest at the west gate, shortest at the south gate; the east gate ticket office is 500m down the road, by the Shilpgram crafts village. You are not allowed to enter with food (and none is available inside), nor with a travel guidebook – these can be deposited at lockers near the entrances. Foreigners are given a free bottle of water and a pair of shoe covers on entry.

Night visits It's possible to see the Taj by moonlight on the night of the full moon itself and on the two days before and after. Four hundred visitors are admitted per night (in batches of fifty between 8pm and midnight, but not on Fridays or during Ramadan). Tickets (₹750 [₹510]) have to be purchased a day in advance from the ASI office, 22 The

TAJ MAHAL

Mall (Mon–Sat 10am–6pm; ☎ 0562 222 7261). If a viewing is cancelled, you get a refund.

Viewing the Taj for free You can see the Taj for free from a Taj Ganj hotel rooftop (many have restaurants with a Taj view), or by heading down the eastern side of the compound to a small Krishna temple by the river, where you can see the Taj, and also take a little boat ride (₹250–1000, depending on the size of your camera) to see it from the river. The view is breathtaking from Mehtab Bagh on the opposite bank of the river (daily sunrise–sunset; ₹300 [₹25]), especially at dawn. You cross the river on the road bridge north of Agra Fort, and turn right when you reach the far bank, following the metalled road until it enters the village of Katchpura and becomes a rough track that eventually emerges at a small *dalit* shrine on the riverside, directly opposite the Taj and next to the entrance of Mehtab Bagh. You can see the Taj from the garden's floodlit walkways, and from outside the gardens on the riverbank, but unfortunately you cannot access the gardens by boat from across the river by the Taj itself.

Agra Fort
Daily sunrise–sunset • ₹650, ₹600 on Friday (₹50, ₹40 on Friday), and ₹50 discount for foreigners on production of a Taj ticket for the same day

The high red-sandstone ramparts of **Agra Fort** dominate a bend in the Yamuna River 2km northwest of the Taj Mahal. Akbar laid the foundations of this majestic citadel, built between 1565 and 1573 in the form of a half-moon, on the remains of earlier Rajput fortifications. The structure developed as the seat and stronghold of the Mughal Empire for successive generations: Akbar commissioned the walls and gates, his grandson, Shah Jahan, had most of the principal buildings erected, and Aurangzeb, the last great emperor, was responsible for the ramparts.

The curved sandstone bastions reach a height of over 20m and stretch for around two and a half kilometres, punctuated by a sequence of massive gates (although only the **Amar Singh Pol** is currently open to visitors). The original and grandest entrance was through the western side, via the **Delhi Gate** and **Hathi Pol** or "Elephant Gate" (closed to the public), now flanked by two red-sandstone towers faced in marble, but once guarded by colossal stone elephants with riders which were destroyed by Aurangzeb in 1668. Access to this and to much of the fort is restricted, and only those parts open to the public are described here.

There's nowhere to buy drinks inside the fort, and exploring the complex can be thirsty work, so unless you're happy to take your chances at the public drinking taps, it's a good idea to take water in with you.

Diwan-i-Am and the great courtyard

Entrance to the fort is through the **Amar Singh Pol**, actually three separate gates placed close together and at right angles to each other to disorientate any potential attackers and to deprive them of the space in which to use battering weapons against the fortifications. From here a ramp climbs gently uphill flanked by high walls (another

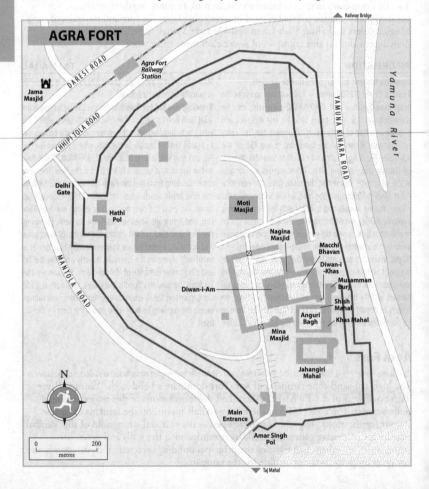

AGRA FORT

defensive measure), through a second gate to the spacious courtyard, with tree-studded lawns, which surrounds the graceful **Diwan-i-Am** ("Hall of Public Audience"). Open on three sides, the pillared hall, which replaced an earlier wooden structure, was commissioned by Shah Jahan in 1628. The elegance of the setting would have been enhanced by the addition of brocade, carpets and satin canopies for audiences with the emperor.

The ornate throne alcove – built to house a gem-encrusted Peacock Throne, which was eventually moved to Delhi, only to be looted from there by Nadir Shah and finishing up in Tehran – is inlaid in marble decorated with flowers and foliage in bas-relief, and connects to the royal chambers within. In front of the alcove, the **Baithak**, a small marble table, is where ministers would have sat to deliver petitions and receive commands. This is also where trials would have been conducted, and justice speedily implemented.

The area to the north of the Diwan-i-Am courtyard is, sadly, closed to visitors, though you can make out the delicate white marble domes and chhatris of the striking, if rather clumsily proportioned, **Moti Masjid** ("Pearl Mosque") rising beyond the courtyard walls, best seen from the Diwan-i-Am itself. Directly in front of the Diwan-i-Am an incongruously Gothic Christian tomb marks the **grave of John Russell Colvin**, lieutenant governor of the Northwestern Provinces, who died here during the 1857 uprising, when Agra's British population barricaded themselves inside the fort.

The royal pavilions

Heading through the small door to the left of the throne alcove in the Diwan-i-Am and climbing the stairs beyond brings you out onto the upper level of the **Macchi Bhavan** (Fish Palace), a large but relatively plain two-storey structure overlooking a spacious, grassy courtyard. This was once strewn with fountains and flowerbeds, interspersed with tanks and water channels stocked with fish on which the emperor and his courtiers would practise their angling skills, though the maharaja of Bharatpur subsequently removed some of its marble fixtures to his palace in Deeg, and William Bentinck (governor general from 1828 to 1835) auctioned off much of the palace's original mosaics and fretwork.

Nagina Masjid

On the north side of the courtyard (to the left as you enter) a small door leads to the exquisite little **Nagina Masjid** (Gem Mosque), made entirely of marble. Capped with three domes and approached from a marble-paved courtyard, it was commissioned by Shah Jahan for the ladies of the zenana (harem). At the rear on the right, a small balcony with beautifully carved lattice screens offers a discreet viewpoint from where members of the harem were able to inspect luxury goods – silks, jewellery and brocade – laid out for sale by merchants in the courtyard below, without themselves being seen.

The raised terrace on the far side of the Macchi Bhavan is adorned by two **thrones**, one black slate, the other white marble. The white one was used by Shah Jahan, the black one by the future emperor Jahangir to watch elephant fights in the eastern enclosure. It now serves, somewhat less gloriously, as a favoured perch for couples posing for photos against the backdrop of the distant Taj.

Diwan-i-Khas

To your right (as you face the river), a high terrace overlooking the Yamuna is topped with a sequence of lavish royal apartments designed to catch the cool breezes blowing across the waters below. The first is the delicate **Diwan-i-Khas** (Hall of Private Audience), erected in 1635, where the emperor would have received kings, dignitaries and ambassadors, and is one of the most finely decorated buildings in the fort, with paired marble pillars and peacock arches inlaid with lapis lazuli and jasper.

SOUND-AND-LIGHT SHOW

Every night after sunset (in English at 7pm in winter, 8.15pm or 8.30pm in summer; ₹220[₹70]), a **sound-and-light show** takes place at Agra Fort in front of the Diwan-i-Am. The show lasts an hour, during which time lights play on various parts of the fort as a commentary takes you through the history of the great Mughals. It's fun, but nothing spectacular. Tickets can be bought at the gate.

Mina Masjid

A passageway behind the Diwan-i-Khas leads to the tiny **Mina Masjid**, a plain white marble mosque built for Shah Jahan and traditionally said to have been used by him during his imprisonment here.

Musamman Burj

Beyond, the passageway leads to a two-storey pavilion known as the **Musamman Burj**, famous as the spot where he is said to have caught his last glimpse of the Taj Mahal before he died, and the most elaborately decorated structure in the fort. Its lattice-screen balustrade is dotted with ornamental niches and with exquisite *pietra dura* inlay covering almost every surface. In front of the tower a courtyard, paved with marble octagons, centres on a **pachisi board** where the emperor, following his father's example at Fatehpur Sikri (see page 255), played *pachisi* (a form of ludo) using dancing girls as pieces.

Anguri Bagh

Beyond the Musamman Burj, another large courtyard, the **Anguri Bagh** (Grape Garden), is a miniature *charbagh*, its east side flanked by the marble building known as **Khas Mahal** (Private Palace), possibly a drawing room or the emperor's sleeping chamber. The palace is flanked by two so-called **Golden Pavilions**, their curved roofs covered with gilded copper tiles in a style inspired by the thatched roofs of Bengali village huts.

In front of the Khas Mahal, steps descend into the northeast corner of the Anguri Bagh and the **Shish Mahal** (Glass Palace), where royal women bathed in the soft lamplight reflected from the mirrorwork mosaics that covered the walls and ceiling; the building is currently locked, so you can only peek in through the windows.

The Jahangiri Mahal

South of the Khas Mahal lies the huge **Jahangiri Mahal** (Jahangir's Palace), although the name is misleading since it was actually built for Jahangir's father, Akbar, and probably served not as a royal palace, but as a harem. Compared to the classic Mughal designs of the surrounding buildings, this robust sandstone structure has quite a few Hindu elements mixed up with traditional Mughal and Islamic motifs.

From the central courtyard, a gateway leads out through the main gateway into the palace, whose impressive facade shows a characteristic mix of Mughal and Indian motifs, with Islamic pointed arches and inlaid mosaics combined with Hindu-style overhanging eaves supported by heavily carved brackets. Immediately in front of the palace sits **Jahangir's Hauz** (Jahangir's Cistern), a giant bowl with steps inside and out, made in 1611 from a single block of porphyry and inscribed in Persian. Filled with rosewater, it would have been used by the emperor as a bathtub, and it's also believed that the emperor took it with him on his travels around the empire – though it seems difficult to credit this, given the bath's size and weight.

Jama Masjid

Jama Masjid Rd

Opposite Agra Fort, and overlooking Agra Fort railway station, is the city's principal mosque, the soaring red-sandstone **Jama Masjid** (Friday Mosque). Built in 1648, it was originally connected directly to the fort's principal entrance, the Delhi Gate, by a large courtyard, but the British ran a railway line between the two, leaving the mosque stranded in no-man's land on the far side of the tracks.

Standing on a high plinth above the chaotic streets of the surrounding bazaar (of which it affords fine views), the mosque is crowned by three large sandstone domes covered in distinctive zigzagging bands of marble. Five huge arches lead into the main prayer hall, topped by a prettily inlaid band of sandstone decorated in abstract floral patterns; inside, the mihrab is surrounded by delicate flourishes of Koranic script, inlaid in black, a design mirrored in the principal archway.

Kinari Bazaar

The space around the base of the mosque is now filled with the crowded – but refreshingly hassle-free – streets of **Kinari Bazaar**, a fascinating warren crammed full with shops and stalls, though the numbers of people, scooters, cycle rickshaws and cows pushing their way through the streets make exploring it a slow and tiring business. Opposite the northeast corner of the complex, look out for the **petha-walas**, purveyors of Agra's most famous sweet (see page 253).

Itimad-ud-Daulah

Moti Bagh • Daily sunrise–sunset • ₹310 (₹30)

On the east bank of the Yamuna River some 3km north of Agra Fort, the beautiful **Itimad-ud-Daulah** (pronounced "Atma Dolla"), is the tomb of Mirza Ghiyas Beg, *wazir* (chief minister) and father-in-law of Emperor Jahangir, who gave him the title of Itimad-ud-Daulah, or "Pillar of the State". The tomb is popularly known among Agra's rickshaw-walas as the "**Baby Taj**", and though it's much smaller and less successfully proportioned than its more famous relative, it does foreshadow the Taj in being the first building in Mughal Agra to be faced entirely in marble, with lavish use of *pietra dura* inlay to decorate its translucent exterior walls.

The tomb sits at the centre of a *charbagh* garden, though here entered from the eastern (rather than the usual southern) side, presumably to highlight its setting against the backdrop of the Yamuna River – another element of its design which anticipates that of the Taj. The building's undersized rooftop pavilion replaces the usual dome, and has four stocky minarets stuck onto each corner. However, these imperfections seem unimportant given the superbly intricate **inlay work** that covers virtually the entire tomb – an incredible profusion of floral and geometrical patterning in muted reds, oranges, browns and greys that give it the appearance of an enormous, slightly hallucinogenic experiment in medieval op-art. Elegant inlaid designs showing characteristic Persian motifs including wine vases, trees and honeysuckles adorn the arches of the four entrances, and the walls inside are covered in rather eroded and clumsily restored paintings of more vases, flowers and cypresses.

Chini-ka-Rauza

Around 1km north of Itimad-ud-Daulah is the **Chini-ka-Rauza**, built between 1628 and 1639 as the mausoleum of Afzal Khan, a Persian poet from Shiraz who was one of Shah Jahan's ministers. As befits his origins, Afzal Khan's tomb is of purely Persian design, the only such building in Agra.

Rambagh

Mahatma Gandhi Marg • Daily sunrise–sunset • ₹300 (₹25)

A kilometre or so north of the Chini-ka-Rauza, amid the dusty sprawl of northern Agra, the **Rambagh** gardens, dating from 1526, are one of the very few surviving remains in India from the reign of the Mughal dynasty's founder Babur. The gardens don't contain much in the way of architecture, and aren't very well maintained, but you can still see how they were laid out, as a square quartered by water channels following the Persian *charbagh* plan, which made it the prototype for all later Mughal gardens.

Akbar's mausoleum

Mathura Rd, Sikandra, 10km northwest of Agra • Daily sunrise–sunset • ₹310 (₹30) • Autos ₹120 each way, or take a Mathura-bound bus from Agra Fort Bus Stand

Given the Mughal tradition of magnificent tombs, it is no surprise that the mausoleum of the most distinguished Mughal ruler was one of the most ambitious structures of its time.

Akbar's mausoleum complex is entered via its huge **Buland Darwaza** (Great Gate), surmounted by four marble minarets, and overlaid with marble and coloured tiles in repetitive geometrical patterns, bearing the Koranic inscription "These are the gardens of Eden, enter them and live forever". Through the gateway, extensive, park-like **gardens** are divided by fine raised sandstone walkways into the four equal quadrants of the typical Mughal *charbagh* design. Langur monkeys may be seen along the path, while deer roam through the tall grasses, just as they do in the Mughal miniature paintings dating from the era when the tomb was constructed, lending the whole place a magically peaceful and rural atmosphere.

The mausoleum

The **mausoleum** itself sits in the middle of the gardens, at the centre of the *charbagh* and directly in front of Buland Darwaza. The entire structure is one of the strangest in Mughal Agra, its huge square base topped not by the usual dome but by a three-storey open-sided sandstone construction crowned with a solid-looking marble pavilion. The mishmash design may be attributable to Jahangir, who ordered changes in the mausoleum's design halfway through its construction, Akbar himself having neglected to leave finished plans for his mausoleum.

A high marble gateway in the mausoleum's southern facade frames an elaborate lattice screen shielding a small vestibule painted with rich sea-blue frescoes and Koranic verses. From here a ramp leads down into a large, echoing and absolutely plain subterranean **crypt**, lit by a single skylight, in the centre of which stands Akbar's grave, decorated with the pen-box motif, the symbol of a male ruler, which can also be seen on Shah Jahan's tomb in the Taj Mahal.

Mariam's Tomb

Daily sunrise–sunset • ₹300 (₹25)

Off the road on the opposite side, 1km north of Sikandra, lies the altogether more modest **Mariam's tomb**, last resting place of Mariam-uz-Zamani, a wife of Akbar and mother of Jahangir, who ordered the construction of this large mausoleum following her death in 1623. A weighty sandstone structure, with fine (though very eroded) carvings covering most of its exterior walls, the mausoleum belongs architecturally to the same style as Jahangir's palace in Agra Fort.

ARRIVAL AND DEPARTURE   **AGRA**

BY PLANE

Kheria airport, 7km southwest of town (☎ 0562 240 0844), has three weekly flights to Khajuraho (55min) and Varanasi (2hr 30min) with Air India.

BY TRAIN

Railway stations Agra has six stations, but visitors generally use only two of them. The busiest is Agra Canton-ment ("Cantt"), in the southwest, which serves

FORMER BRITISH RESIDENCY IN LUCKNOW THAT WAS BESIEGED DURING THE UPRISING OF 1857

RECOMMENDED TRAINS FROM AGRA

The trains below are recommended as the fastest and/or most convenient for specific cities. All those listed here run daily.

Destination	Name	No.	From	Departs	Arrives
Chennai	GT Express	#12616	AC	9.40am	6.20am++
	Tamil Nadu Express	#12622	AC	1.03am	7.10am+
Delhi	Karnataka Express1	#12627	AC	6.45am	10.30am
	Kerala Express1	#12625	AC	10.25am	1.45pm
	Gatimaan Express*2	#12049	AC	5.50pm	7.30pm (exc Fri)
	Shatabdi Express*1	#12001	AC	9.15pm	11.30pm
Gwalior	Shatabdi Express*	#12002	AC	8.02am	9.28am
	Punjab Mail	#12138	AC	8.35am	10.31am
Jaipur	Ajmer Intercity	#12195	AF	5.05am	9.30am
	Jaipur Express	#12403	AC	7.15am	12.50pm
Jhansi	Shatabdi Express*	#12002	AC	8.02am	10.43am
	Punjab Mail	#12138	AC	8.35am	12.25pm
Jodhpur	Howrah–Jodhpur Exp	#12307	AF	8.15am	6.35am+
Khajuraho	Khajuraho Express	#19666	AC	11.45am	7.50pm
	Sampark Kranti Exp	#22448	AC	11.10pm	6.35am+
Kolkata	Ajmer–Sealdah Exp	#12988	AF	7.25pm	4pm+
Udaipur	Udaipur Express	#19665	AC	5.40pm	6.45am+
Varanasi	Marudhar Express	#14854/64/66	AF	8.40pm	10.30am
Vasco da Gama	Goa Express	#12780	AC	5.33pm	6.30am++

AC Agra Cantonment, AF Agra Fort, *a/c only, + next day, ++ two days later
1 arrives New Delhi, 2 arrives Hazrat Nizamuddin

Delhi, Gwalior, Jhansi and most points south. Trains from Rajasthan pull in close to the Jama Masjid at Agra Fort station (a few also stop at Agra Cantt). Agra Cantt is more convenient for the hotels around Sadar Bazaar, while Agra Fort Station is slightly closer to the Taj Ganj area; both are a fair way from the hotels along Fatehabad Rd. There's a prepaid auto-rickshaw/taxi booth at Agra Cantonment station (₹130/200 to Taj Ganj); drivers may try to intercept you before you reach the prepaid booth so as to overcharge you or work some commission scam. Cycle rickshaws wait in the forecourt outside, but are slow if you're going to Fatehabad Rd or Taj Ganj. Cycle rickshaw and auto drivers may try to earn commission by taking you to a hotel of their choosing, and may therefore claim (falsely, of course) that the hotel of your choice is closed. Uber and Ola drivers are a far better option.

Tickets Train tickets, especially to the capital, should be booked several days in advance if possible at either Agra Cantonment or Agra Fort stations; both have computerized booking offices and separate tourist counters.

BY BUS

Travelling by bus along the Delhi–Agra–Lucknow Expressway saves time compared to doing the same journey by train; avoid using the Grand Trunk road though, or travelling to Jaipur on NH-11, as both roads see disconcertingly frequent accidents. Agra has three bus stands, but Agra Fort Bus Stand is now used for local services only.

Idgah Bus Stand, near Cantonment station in the southwest of town, has services to Fatehpur Sikri (every 30min; 1hr–1hr 30min), Delhi (every 30min; 5–6hr), Madhya Pradesh and Rajasthan. For Rajasthani destinations beyond Jaipur, take a bus to Jaipur (hourly; 5–6hr) and pick up a connecting service (an exception is Ajmer, which has three daily direct services, taking 9hr). One scam to be aware of on buses to Idgah, especially from Jaipur, is that they may make a stop in the suburbs, about 6km out, where auto-walas (often in collusion with the bus drivers) may claim that your vehicle has reached the end of the line, and that you need to disembark; if there are still Indian passengers on the bus, sit tight till you get to Idgah.

Transport Nagar ISBT, 12km north of town at Transport Nagar, just off the Delhi–Agra highway. Buses from here serve UP destinations such as Lucknow (15 daily; 9hr 30min) and Varanasi (daily; 14hr), as well as to Haridwar (12 daily; 10hr), Rishikesh (12 daily; 12hr) and Dehradun (12 daily; 13hr). An auto into town will cost some ₹300, but if you're really determined to get into Agra on the cheap, you can walk down to the highway and pick up a shared auto (₹10) to Baghwan Talkies, and a bus (₹25) from there to Sai ki Takia (the junction of Fatehpur Sikri Rd with Mahatma Gandhi Rd).

RSRTC buses Deluxe and a/c Rajasthan Roadways (RSRTC, bookable on ⊕rsrtc.com) nonstop services to Jaipur (9 daily; 4hr) leave from the forecourt of *Sakura Guest House*, next to the Idgah bus stand.

Private buses Hotels and travel agents can book seats on private buses to Delhi, Gwalior, Khajuraho, Lucknow and Nainital. The 12hr ride to Khajuraho (leaving at 5am) is a bit gruelling – it's better to take the train, or failing that, take a train to Jhansi (3hr) and pick up a bus there (5hr).

GETTING AROUND

Agra is very spread out and its sights too widely separated to get between them easily on foot, so you'll probably spend a fair amount of time in rickshaws or taxis. Getting from one part of the city to another can prove surprisingly time-consuming, and crossing from one side of the Yamuna River to the other is particularly tedious, with only two over-used and under-maintained bridges. Motorized vehicles are excluded from a small area around the Taj, supposedly to protect it from pollution. On rickshaws and taxis, haggle hard: Agra sees so many "fresh" tourists that drivers almost always quote significantly inflated prices to start with (the best policy, if a rickshaw driver names a silly price, is simply to walk away – they'll usually chase after you and offer a more realistic fare). Also, note that the main agenda for many rickshaw and taxi drivers is to get you into shops that pay them **commission**, added to your bill of course; if they offer you a ride for an absurdly low price, this is what their aim is. Always hail a ricksahaw or auto yourself rather than taking one that hustles you for business (almost invariably with the aim of overcharging you and/or working some kind of scam).

By cycle rickshaw Cycle rickshaws are good for short trips and provide a livelihood for some of the city's poorest inhabit-ants, as well as being cleaner and greener than autos, but are slow for long journeys, and rickshaw drivers are the biggest source of hassle in Agra – attempt to walk anywhere, and they will be constantly on your case; walking on the right-hand side of the street makes it harder for them to follow you. It's always wiser to hail a rickshaw of your own choice rather than go with a driver who pesters you (almost always with the intention of overcharging or working a commission scam).

By auto-rickshaw Auto-rickshaws are faster than cycle rickshaws, though the same caveats apply. Fares, including waiting time, are very reasonable if you haggle. Sample fares from Taj Ganj are ₹50 to Sadar Bazaar or Agra Fort, ₹120 to Agra Cantt station.

By taxi Taxis are handy for longer trips to Sikandra or Fatehpur Sikri; agree a fare before you set off. There are taxi ranks at the stations, or your hotel should be able to arrange a vehicle. Ola offers packages that take in most of Agra sites; a half day out should cost about ₹1300.

INFORMATION AND TOURS

Tourist information Agra has two tourist offices, India Tourism at 191 The Mall (Mon–Fri 9am–5.30pm, Sat 9am–2pm; ☎ 0562 222 6368), and UP Tourism at 64 Taj Rd (Mon–Sat 10am–5pm; ☎ 0562 222 6431).

Tours UP Tourism runs a whistlestop tour (daily except Fri) of Agra, aimed mainly at day-trippers from Delhi. The tour leaves the Cantonment station at 10.30am (coinciding with the *Taj Express* from Delhi), but depends on demand – call UP Tourism (☎ 0562 222 6368) to check whether it's running on any particular day. The full-day tour (₹3600 [₹750] including all entrance and guide fees) whisks you at breakneck speed around the Taj, Agra Fort and Fatehpur Sikri, ending at around 6pm in time for the *Taj Express* back to Delhi; you can also join the tour just for the afternoon visit to Fatehpur Sikri (₹1500 [₹550]). Tours can be booked either through the UP Tourism or India Tourism offices. The *Tourists Rest House* has a travel agency called Bag Packers (☎ 9997 113 228, ⊛ bagpackertravels.com), which can organize car rental with driver, day-trips to Fatehpur Sikri, Keoladeo and Bharatpur, and tailor-made tours of Agra and/or Rajasthan, starting from Agra or Delhi; they can also book train tickets and accept payment from foreign credit or debit cards.

ACCOMMODATION

Most budget travellers end up in **Taj Ganj**, the jumble of narrow lanes immediately south of the Taj. With their unrivalled rooftop views and laidback cafés, the hostels and guesthouses here can be great places to stay, although checkout time is usually 10am. There are more upmarket lodgings along **Fatehabad Rd**, southwest of Taj Ganj, while the leafier **Cantonment** area and the adjacent **Sadar Bazaar** have places to suit every budget.

TAJ GANJ

Amarvilas East Gate ☎ 0562 223 1515, ⊛ oberoihotels. com; map p.242. Easily the loveliest (and most expensive) hotel in Agra, virtually a work of art in its own right, constructed in a serene blend of Mughal and Moorish styles around a gorgeous *charbagh*-style courtyard water garden. Most rooms have Taj views. Facilities include a large pool, idyllic terraced gardens, two smart restaurants and a very chichi bar. ₹80,000

★ **Aman Homestay** Shilpgram road, on the inner lane behind Moustache Hostel ☎ 9536 440915 and 5622 331 234, ⊛ amanhomestayagra.com; map p.242. Boutique homestay run by a friendly family. All rooms are squeaky

3

clean, with huge king-sized beds and have the feel of a hotel in a much higher category. The rooftop rooms are the best (₹4080), set around a lovely veranda with views of the Taj. The downside is that breakfast costs an extra ₹350, and you can order dinner for ₹450. ₹2000

Bedweiser Near Shilpgram Parking, Taj East Gate Road ☎0562 223 1902, ⓦbedweiser.com; map p.242. Well-maintained backpacker hostel with a party vibe and an attractive reggae-themed rooftop — yet without Taj views. The four-bed dorms and doubles are all en suite and clean, but feel a little cramped without windows. It's within walking distance of the Taj, and the free Playstation corner will appeal to some. Dorms ₹400, Doubles ₹900

★ **Moustache Hostel** Taj East Gate Road ☎0562 233 0103, ⓦmoustachehostel.com; map p.242. The best hostel in town has a series of sparkling clean doubles, mixed (six-bed) and female-only (four-bed) dorms, with or without a/c (₹250). All have plush beds, reading lights and storage lockers below the bed frames. There's a restaurant with Taj views on the rooftop, tours, free luggage storage, and a chill-out area where guests can hang out until their bus/train. Dorms ₹₹300; doubles ₹1000

Shanti Lodge Chowk Kagzi ☎0562 233 1973, ⓔshantilodge2000@yahoo.co.in; map p.242. Popular backpacker lodge with superb Taj views from the rooftop restaurant, but a mixed bag of rooms – those in the annexe are newer and larger, but only one room (at ₹1500) has a Taj view. All are attached with hot water, however. Wi-fi doesn't work in all rooms. ₹400

Sheela 1/16B East Gate ☎0562 233 3074, ⓦhotelsheela agra.com; map p.242. Clean and spacious ground-floor rooms ranged around a lovely little garden, with fan, air-cooled and a/c options, friendly staff and a good restaurant. All rooms are attached, but the cheapest have hot water in buckets only, so it's worth paying ₹200 more for an upgrade. Wi-fi in the restaurant area only. Non a/c ₹900; a/c₹ ₹1450

Sidhartha West Gate ☎0562 233 0901, ⓦhotel sidhartha.com; map p.242. Bigger and better rooms than the other Taj Ganj budget joints, set around a restaurant in a leafy courtyard that includes fragments of Mughal-era walls. There are three grades of room, of which the top (₹1500) differs from the others only in having a/c, but all are sparkling, with attached bathrooms and 24hr hot water, and they upgrade them on a regular basis. ₹950

CANTONMENT AND SADAR BAZAAR

Clarks Shiraz 54 Taj Rd ☎0562 222 6121, ⓦhotel clarksshiraz.com; map p.240. Sprawling five-star in a pleasant Cantonment setting with small but cosy rooms, the more expensive of which have distant Taj views. Facilities include two restaurants, two bars, a swimming pool, an Ayurvedic massage centre and a health club. ₹5000

Hilltop 21 The Mall ☎0562 222 6836, ⓔhotelhilltop agra@yahoo.com; map p.240. Set in pleasant grounds

with peacocks and parrots, this place looks a bit ramshackle but the rooms are fine, and they're all good value, as is the restaurant. If you're utterly strapped for cash, you could go for the ultra-basic cell-like rooms with shared bath (₹300), and you can camp for ₹100/person. ₹500

Sakura Guest House 49 Old Igdah Colony, Ajmer Rd (near Idgah Bus Station) ☎0562 242 0169, ⓦhotelsakuraagra.com; map p.240. Well-run and good-value guesthouse on the west side of town. It doesn't look too inviting from the outside, but the rooms (of which there's quite a variety, including a/c rooms from ₹1000) are large, bright, spacious and nicely furnished, with hot water 6am–noon and 8pm–midnight, and the manager is extremely helpful and a mine of local information. The only drawback is the location: handy for Idgah bus and Cantonment train stations, but a bit of a hike from everywhere else. ₹700

★ **Tourists Rest House** Kutchery Rd, Baluganj ☎0562 246 3961, ⓦdontworrychickencurry.com; map p.240. One of Agra's top budget options, with a range of bright, competitively priced rooms around a tranquil leafy court-yard; all super-clean, and all attached with hot running water, some a/c (₹999). There's also free wi-fi, free bus and train reservations, and free pick-up from bus or train stations with a day's notice. ₹720

Yamuna View 6-B The Mall ☎0562 329 3777, ⓔsales@ hotelyamunaviewagra.com; map p.240. Conveniently central, low-key five-star. Rooms are stylish in an under-stated kind of way, and facilities include a pool, a bar and a couple of smart restaurants, including the *Mandarin* (see opposite), but wi-fi is available in the lobby area only. Breakfast included. ₹8000

FATEHABAD ROAD AND AROUND

Bansi Home Stay 18 Handicraft Nagar (off Fatehabad Rd) ☎0562 233 3033, ⓦbansihomestayagra.com; map p.240. Immaculate little place hidden away down a side street where the noise and bustle don't seem to penetrate and you're in a little oasis of quiet. The house is modern, the rooms spacious and sparkling, and the atmosphere warm and welcoming. And for those who want to smoke and drink, there's a grassy roof terrace, to which those activities are confined. Breakfast included. ₹3500

Gateway Fatehabad Rd ☎0562 660 2000, ⓦthe gatewayhotels.com; map p.240. Rooms at this stylish hotel (some with distant Taj views) are among the most attractive in Agra, while public areas are pleasantly plush and there's the usual range of five-star amenities including a pool. Discounts are usually available on the official rate. Breakfast included. ₹20,000

GoStops Agra 121 MMIG Taj Nagari Phase 1 ☎7428 882 828, ⓦgostops.com; map p.240. Another in the series of Agra's new swanky flashpacker hostels, GoStops has colourful doubles, top-of-the range dorms, a nice rooftop restaurant and social common areas — one even has a table football game. Breakfast included. Doubles ₹2500; dorms₹ ₹450

Mayur Tourist Complex Fatehabad Rd ☎0562 233 2302; map p.240. Dinky pagoda-like cottages with attached bathrooms around a large garden (generally peaceful, but often used for weddings Nov–Jan). Facilities include a multicuisine restaurant-cum-beer bar, and a swimming pool and health centre. ₹3000

Trident Tajnagri, Fatehabad Rd ☎0562 223 5000; ⓦtridenthotels.com; map p.240. A peaceful five-star, whose cheerful rooms (including one adapted for wheelchair users) are in low-lying buildings around a spacious garden with a large pool and multicuisine restaurant. Despite being located a couple of kilometres out of town, it's actually quite handy for the Taj's eastern entrance, with a direct road round the back of the hotel. Breakfast is included. ₹8,950

EATING

Agra is the home of **Mughlai cooking**, renowned for its rich cream- and curd-based sauces, accompanied by naan and tandoori breads roasted in earthen ovens, pulao rice dishes and milky sweets such as *kheer*. **Taj Ganj** has innumerable scruffy little travellers' cafés, though standards of hygiene are often suspect and the food is generally uninspiring, with slow service the norm. Taj Ganj's saving grace is the **rooftop cafés**, many with fine Taj views, which cap most of its buildings. Local **specialities** of Agra include *petha* (crystallized pumpkin) — the best is the Panchi brand, available at various outlets all over town, particularly in the row of *petha* shops in Kinari Bazaar along the northeast side of the Jama Masjid (past *Chimman Lal Puri Wale*). Look out too for *ghazak*, a rock-hard candy with nuts, and *dalmoth*, a crunchy mix made with black lentils. Agra's restaurants — including even apparently reputable places — are not immune to the epidemic of **credit-card fraud** (see opposite). It's best not to pay by credit card except in the city's five-star establishments, or, if you do, supervise the operation carefully.

Achman Agra–Delhi Highway (NH-2), Dayal Bagh, 5km out of town near Baghwan Talkies ☎0562 406 4401; map p.240. Veg restaurant highly rated among Agra folk in the know, famous for its *navratan* korma (a mildly spiced mix of nuts, dried fruit and *paneer*; ₹300) and *malai* kofta (₹250), as well as wonderful stuffed naans (₹90). Well off the tourist trail in the north of the city, but ideally placed for dinner on your way home from Sikandra (to which it's about halfway), and reachable by shared auto from Agra Fort bus station or Gwalior Rd. Daily noon–11pm.

★ **Chimman Lal Puri Wale** Opposite northeast wall of Jama Masjid ☎0562 246 1430; map p.240. An Agra institution for five generations now, this much-loved little café-restaurant looks a touch grubby from the outside, but serves delicious puri thalis, with two veg dishes and a sweet — all for ₹50. Ideal pit-stop after visiting the Jama Masjid. Daily 7am–10pm.

Choko Jeeman Delhi Gate, Raja Ki Mandi ☎0562 404 0338; ⓦchokoJeeman.com; map p.240. This cosy restaurant is adored by locals for its mouth-watering pure veg Rajasthani Thalis served in a relaxing bamboo-furnished bar area. Plates start at ₹180 with eight choices of vegetables, and you can re-fill as much as you want. Daily 11am–3.30pm and 6.30pm–10.30pm.

Dasaprakash Meher Cinema Complex, 1 Gwalior Rd, close to the Tourists Rest House ☎0562 246 3535, ⓦhoteldasaprakashagra.com; map p.240. Offshoot of a famous Chennai restaurant, serving a limited but top-notch menu of South Indian food, with special Mysore and spicy coriander versions of the masala dosa (₹180), thalis (₹190–220) and an extensive ice-cream menu — the hot fudge banana split (₹160) wins by a nose. Daily 12.30–11.45pm.

Joney's Place Chowk Kagzi, Taj Ganj ☎9837 339 686; map p.242. Oldest of the Taj Ganj travellers' cafés, going since 1978, and open early in case you need breakfast ahead of a dawn visit to the Taj. The house speciality is *malai kofta* (₹100), but they also do a pretty good vegetarian Mughlai biryani (₹90); their banana lassi (₹50) promises "no ice, no sugar, no water", and is so gloopy it comes with a spoon. Daily 5am–10pm.

The Mandarin Yamuna View hotel ☎0562 246 2990; map p.240. One of the best non-Indian restaurants in town, this stylish Chinese offers a possibly welcome change from Mughlai curries and masala dosas. The menu features a good selection of delicately prepared dishes like stir-fried vegetables in almond sauce (₹305) and crispy chicken in honey chilli (₹415), with the emphasis on light ingredients and subtle flavours. Daily noon–11pm.

Only 45/1 Mall Rd (at Phool Sayed Circle, the junction with Taj Rd) ☎0562 222 6834; map p.240. One of Agra's most popular north Indian restaurants, often packed with tourist groups and known for its well-prepared tandoori and Mughlai creations, though there's also a wide selection of more mainstream, north Indian meat and veg standards including a sumptuous chicken Mughlai (₹310) or *malai* kofta (₹295), plus a few Chinese and Continental offerings and lunchtime buffets (₹500). There's seating in an indoor a/c dining room or in the pleasant courtyard. Daily 7am–10pm.

The Park 183-A Taj Rd, Sadar Bazaar ☎94566 75101; map p.240. A long-established favourite with both locals and tourists, this simple a/c restaurant dishes up an excellent range of classic Mughlai chicken dishes, along with more mainstream tandooris and meat and veg curries accompanied by superb naan breads, plus a modest selection of Continental and Chinese favourites. Specialities include rogan josh (₹205) and chicken *badami* (with almonds; ₹240). Daily except Tues 11am–11pm.

Pinch of Spice 1076/2 Fatehabad Road ☏ 0562 404 5252 ⊛ pinchofspice.in; map p.240. Popular with local families, this slightly upmarket restaurant excels in almost all types of Indian cuisine. From veg and non-veg North and South Indian staples, to Chinese food and *momos*, tandoor specialties, continental food and pastas, it's an eclectic choice for a night out. A meal will set you back around ₹1000. Daily 9am–10.30pm.

★ **Sheroes Hangout** Kutchery Rd, Baluganj ☏ 0562 400 0401, ⊛ sheroeshangout.com; map p.240. Joyful, arty café-cum-library with a cause, run by women who are victims of acid attacks. Profits go toward supporting the work of the Chhanv Foundation. The food – from chicken sandwiches to roti and dhal concoctions –

and coffee are really delicious. Daily 9am–9pm.

Zorba the Buddha E-19 Shopping Arcade, Sadar Bazaar ☏ 0562 222 6091, ⊛ zorbarestaurantagra. com; map p.240. Aimed unashamedly at foreign tourists, though you'll find Indian people eating here too, this prettily decorated little place promises fruit and veg sterilized in boiling water, and no chilli unless you ask for it. They offer, along with Indian veg dishes, odd specialities such as a Hawaiian spree (vegetables and pineapple in pineapple sauce; ₹250) or a fiesta (vegetables in tomato and cashew sauce; ₹250), all generally tasty and well presented. They now have a non-veg branch downstairs too. July–May daily noon–10pm.

SHOPPING

Agra is renowned for its **marble** tabletops, vases and trays, inlaid with semiprecious stones in ornate floral designs, in imitation of those found in the Taj Mahal. It is also an excellent place to buy **leather**: Agra's shoe industry supplies all India, and its tanneries export bags, briefcases and jackets. **Carpets** and **dhurries** are manufactured here too, and traditional embroidery continues to thrive. *Zari* and *zardozi* are brightly coloured, the latter building up three-dimensional patterns with fantastic motifs; *chikan* uses more delicate overlay techniques. Shopping or browsing in Kinari Bazaar and Sadar Bazaar is fun, but be prepared to haggle; tourist emporiums are worth avoiding. A lot of private shops try to **disguise themselves** to look like state-run "cottage" or "handlooms" outlets – an indication of their level of integrity. Note also that Agra sees a large amount of **credit-card fraud**; be wary of ordering anything to be sent overseas, never let your credit card out of your sight, even for the transaction to be authorized, and make sure that all documentation is filled in correctly and fully so as not to allow unauthorized later additions. A list of stores against whom complaints have been lodged is maintained by the local police department. Remember that if you arrive at any shop in a rickshaw or taxi, the prices of anything you buy will be inflated (and not by just a little) to cover the driver's commission. If you're planning on buying, ask to be dropped off nearby, and then walk to the shop (not

allowing your driver to see where you are going).

Modern Book Depot 4 Taj Rd, Sadar Bazaar ☏ 0562 222 5695; map p.240. The best bookshop in town, with a wide selection of fiction and nonfiction in English. Daily except Tues 10.30am–9.30pm.

Shilpgram East Gate Road, by gate ticket office (500m east of Taj Ganj); map p.242. A state-sponsored open-air "crafts village" (ie, a market selling crafts to tourists). Expect to find the usual miniature Taj models and similar tourist souvenirs, plus arts and handicrafts from around India, enlivened with occasional live music and dance performances. Daily sunrise–sunset.

Subhash Emporium 18/1 Gwalior Rd, Sadar Bazaar ☏ 0562 222 5830 ⊛ facebook.com/Subhash EmporiumAgra; map p.240. If you want to buy *pietra dura* marble inlay work, this is the real deal, pricey but reliable, with genuine semi-precious stones (including lapis lazuli, turquoise, abalone and mother-of-pearl), as opposed to the plastic "stones" and alabaster "marble" sold in too many other places. Prices are "fixed" and high, but discounts are usually offered. Daily 9am–7pm.

Taj Leather World B-28 Shopping Arcade, Sadar Bazaar ☏ 0562 222 5076; map p.240. For leather shoes, wallets, handbags and jackets, all made locally in their own factory, this is an excellent place to check out the leather goods that Agra is known for. Daily 12.30–10pm.

DIRECTORY

Banks and exchange Banks included the State Bank of India on MG Rd north of Baluganj, with a branch just north of Fatehabad Rd in the Cantonment. There are private exchange offices in Taj Ganj, and in the Tourist Complex Area around *Amar Yatri Niwas* hotel.

Hospitals Clean and dependable private hospitals with English-speaking doctors: SR Hospital, Namenar Rd (☏ 0562 402 5200); GG Nursing Home, 106/2 Sanjay Place (☏ 0562 285 3952); Pushpanjali Hospital, Delhi Gate (☏ 0562 302 4004, ⊛ pushpanjalihospital.in). The District Hospital, MG

Rd, Chhipitola (☏ 0562 246 6099) gives free treatment, and may be preferable for minor injuries. Avoid backstreet clinics, even if recommended by your hotel manager, and in particular, if you fall ill with what appears to be food poisoning, do not go to a clinic or doctor suggested by someone in the restaurant concerned.

Internet There's plenty of internet access available around town, particularly in Taj Ganj; rates are typically ₹50/hr.

Photography A handful of places on MG Rd, a block north of The Mall, can download and burn digital images to disc.

Police There are police stations on Chowk Kagzi in Taj Ganj (☎0562 233 1015) and on Mahatma Gandhi Rd in Sadar Bazaar, slightly south of the intersection with Fatehpur Sikri Rd (☎0562 222 6561). Agra has a dedicated tourist police force to protect tourists; they can be contacted through UP Tourism or on ☎ 94544 02764, or in an emergency on ☎ 1073.
Post The Head Post Office is on The Mall, near India Tourism.
Swimming Non-guests can use the pools at the *Yamuna View* (₹500), Mayur Tourist Complex (₹400/2hr), and (near *Amar Yatri Niwas*) the *Amar* (₹500).

Fatehpur Sikri

The ghost city of **FATEHPUR SIKRI**, former imperial capital of the great Mughal emperor **Akbar**, straddles the crest of a rocky ridge on the Agra–Jaipur highway, 45km southwest of Agra and 21km east of Bharatpur. The city was built here between 1569 and 1585 as a result of the emperor's enthusiasm for the local Muslim divine **Sheikh Salim Chishti** (see page 259), though the move away from Agra may also have had something to do with Akbar's weariness of the crowds and his desire to create a new capital that was an appropriate symbol of imperial power. The fusion of Hindu and Muslim traditions in its architecture says a lot about the religious and cultural tolerance of Akbar's reign.

Fatehpur Sikri's period of pre-eminence was brief, however, and after 1585 it would never again serve as the seat of the Mughal emperor. The reasons for the **city's abandonment** remain enigmatic. The theory that the city's water supply proved incapable of sustaining its population is no longer widely accepted – even after the city had been deserted, the nearby lake to its northwest still yielded good water. A more likely explanation is that the city was simply the victim of the vagaries of the empire's day-to-day military contingencies. Shortly after the new capital was established, the empire was threatened by troubles in the Punjab, and Akbar moved to the more strategically situated Lahore to deal with them. These military preoccupations kept Akbar at Lahore for over a decade, and at the end of this period he decided, apparently for no particular reason, to return to Agra rather than Fatehpur Sikri. You, on the other hand, might decide to do the opposite: an increasing number of tourists are using Fatehpur Sikri as a base and travelling into Agra on day-trips.

The Royal Palace

Daily sunrise–sunset • ₹610 (₹50), video camera ₹25 • audio guide ₹113 (plus deposit of photo ID or ₹2000/$40/£40/€40) • Ⓦ fatehpursikri.gov.in

Shunning the Hindu tradition of aligning towns with the cardinal compass points, Akbar chose to construct his new capital following the natural features of the terrain, which is why the principal thoroughfare, town walls, and many of the most important buildings face southwest or northeast. The mosque and most private apartments do not follow the main axis, but face west towards Mecca, according to Muslim tradition, with the palace crowning the highest point on the ridge.

There are two **entrances** to the **Royal Palace** and court complex. Independent travellers mostly use the one on the west side, by Jodhbai's Palace; organized tours tend to use that on the east, by the Diwan-i-Am. Official **guides** offer their services at the booking office (₹450 for 2hr in a group of up to five people). There's nowhere to buy drinks in the palace, so take water in with you; you're not allowed to eat inside.

Diwan-i-Am

A logical place to begin a tour of the palace complex is the **Diwan-i-Am**, where important festivals were held, and where citizens could exercise their right to petition the emperor. Unlike the ornate pillared Diwan-i-Am buildings at the forts in Agra and Delhi, it is basically just a large courtyard, surrounded by a continuous colonnaded walkway with Hindu-style square columns and capitals, and broken only by the small pavilion, flanked by elaborately carved *jali* screens, in which the emperor himself

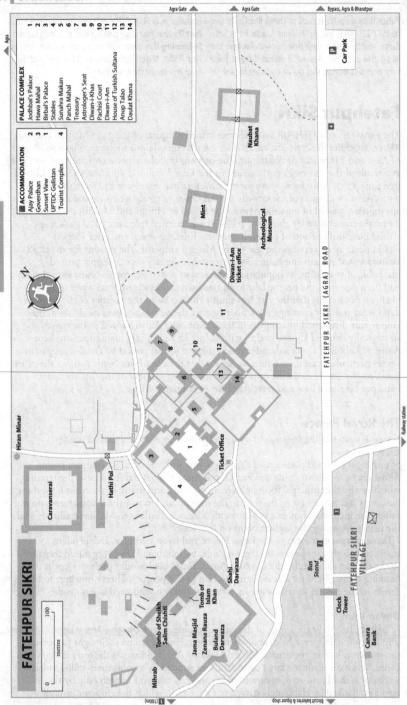

FATEHPUR SIKRI

0 — 100 metres

ACCOMMODATION
Ajay Palace ... 2
Goverdhan ... 3
Sunset View ... 1
UPTDC Gulistan Tourist Complex ... 4

PALACE COMPLEX
Jodhbai's Palace ... 1
Hawa Mahal ... 2
Birbal's Palace ... 3
Stables ... 4
Sunahra Makan ... 5
Panch Mahal ... 6
Treasury ... 7
Astrologer's Seat ... 8
Diwan-i-Khas ... 9
Pachisi Court ... 10
Diwan-i-Am ... 11
House of Turkish Sultana ... 12
Anup Talao ... 13
Daulat Khana ... 14

Agra Gate ▲   ▲ Agra Gate   ▲ Bypass, Agra & Bharatpur

Agra ▲

Car Park [P]

Naubat Khana

Mint

Archeological Museum

Diwan-i-Am ticket office

FATEHPUR SIKRI (AGRA) ROAD

Hiran Minar

Caravanserai

Hathi Pol

Ticket Office

Tomb of Sheikh Salim Chishti
Tomb of Islam Khan
Jama Masjid
Zenana Rauza
Buland Darwaza
Mihrab

Shahi Darwaza

Bus Stand ★

FATEHPUR SIKRI VILLAGE

Clock Tower

Canara Bank

Railway station ▶

Biscuit bakeries & liquor shop ▼   [1] (100m) ▼

would have sat – the position of the royal platform forced the emperor's subjects to approach him from the side in an attitude of humility.

The Diwan-i-Khas courtyard

A doorway in the northwest corner of the Diwan-i-Am leads to the centre of the *mardana* (men's quarters), a large, irregularly shaped enclosure dotted with a strikingly eclectic range of buildings. At the far (northern) end of the enclosure stands the tall **Diwan-i-Khas** ("Hall of Private Audience"), topped with four chhatris and embellished with the heavily carved Hindu-style brackets, large overhanging eaves and corbelled arches which are typical of the architecture of Fatehpur Sikri.

The interior of the building consists of a single high hall (despite the impression, from the outside that this is a two-storey building) centred on an elaborately corbelled column known as the **Throne Pillar**, supporting a large circular platform from which four balustraded bridges radiate outwards. Seated upon this throne, the emperor held discussions with representatives of diverse religions, aiming to synthesize India's religions into one. The pillar symbolizes this project by incorporating motifs drawn from Hinduism, Buddhism, Islam and Christianity.

Next to the Diwan-i-Khas lies the three-roomed **Treasury**, its brackets embellished by mythical sea creatures, guardians of the treasures of the deep; it's also known as Ankh Michauli, meaning hide and seek, which it's said was played here. In fact, both names are probably just fanciful inventions, and the building most likely served as a multipurpose pavilion which could be used for a variety of functions, as could most buildings in Mughal palaces. Attached to it is the so-called **Astrologer's Seat**, a small pavilion embellished with elaborate Jain carvings.

In the middle of the courtyard, separating the Diwan-i-Khas from the buildings on the opposite (south) side of the complex is the **Pachisi Court**, a giant board used to play *pachisi* (similar to ludo). Akbar is said to have been a fanatical player, using slave girls dressed in colourful costumes as live pieces. Abu'l Fazl, the court chronicler, related that at "times more than two hundred persons participated, and no one was allowed to go home until he had played sixteen rounds. This could take up to three months. If one of the players lost his patience and became restless, he was made to drink a cupful of wine. Seen superficially, this appears to be just a game. But His Majesty pursues higher objectives. He weighs up the talents of his people and teaches them to be affable."

House of the Turkish Sultana

Diagonally opposite the *pachisi* board, the **House of the Turkish Sultana** (or Anup Talao Pavilion) gained its name from the popular belief that it was the residence of one of Akbar's favourite wives, the Sultana Ruqayya Begum – though this seems unlikely given its location in the centre of the men's quarters. The name was probably made up by nineteenth-century guides to titillate early tourists, and the building is more likely to have served as a simple pleasure pavilion. Its superbly carved stone walls are covered with a profusion of floral and geometrical designs, plus some partially vandalized animal carvings.

South of here is the **Anup Talao** (Peerless Pool), a pretty little ornamental pond divided by four walkways connected to a small "island" in the middle – a layout reminiscent of the raised walkways inside the Diwan-i-Khas.

The Daulat Khana

Facing the Turkish Sultana's house from the other side of the Anup Talao are Akbar's former private sleeping and living quarters, the **Daulat Khana** ("Abode of Fortune"). The room on the ground floor with alcoves in its walls was the emperor's library, where he would be read to (he himself was illiterate) from a collection of fifty thousand manuscripts he allegedly took everywhere with him. Behind the library is the imperial sleeping chamber, the **Khwabgah** ("House of Dreams"), with an enormous raised bed in its centre.

AKBAR'S HAREM

Although remembered primarily for his liberal approach to religion, Akbar was typically Mughal in his attitudes to women, whom he collected in much the same way as a philatelist amasses stamps. At its height of splendour, the **royal harem** at Fatehpur Sikri held around five thousand women, guarded by a legion of eunuchs. Its doors were closed to outsiders, but rumours permeated the sandstone walls and several notable travellers were smuggled inside the Great Mughals' seraglios, leaving for posterity often lurid accounts of the emperors' private lives.

The size of Akbar's harem grew in direct proportion to his empire. With each new conquest, he would be gifted by the defeated rulers and nobles their most beautiful daughters, who, together with their maidservants, would be installed in the luxurious royal **zenana**. In all, the emperor is thought to have kept three hundred wives; their ranks were swollen by a constant flow of concubines (*kaniz*), dancing girls (*kanchni*) and female slaves (*bandis*), or "silver bodied damsels with musky tresses" as one chronicler described them, purchased from markets across Asia. Screened from public view by ornately pierced stone *jali* windows were women from the four corners of the Mughal empire, as well as Afghans, Turks, Iranians, Arabs, Tibetans, Russians and Abyssinians, and even one Portuguese, sent as presents or tribute.

The **eunuchs** who presided over them came from similarly diverse backgrounds. While some were hermaphrodites, others had been forcibly castrated, either as punishment following defeat on the battlefield, or after having been donated by their fathers as payment of backdated revenue – an all too common custom at the time.

Akbar is said to have consumed prodigious quantities of Persian wine, *araq* (a spirit distilled from sugar cane), bhang and opium. The lavish dance recitals held in the harem, as well as sexual liaisons conducted on the top pavilion of the Panch Mahal and in the zenana itself, would have been fuelled by these substances. Over time, Akbar's hedonistic ways incurred the disapproval of his highest clerics – the *Ulema*.

What life must actually have been like for the women who lived in Akbar's harem one can only imagine, but it is known that alcoholism and drug addiction were widespread, and that some also risked their lives to conduct illicit affairs with male lovers, smuggled in disguised as physicians or under heavy Muslim veils.

In fact, the notion that the harem was a gilded prison whose inmates whiled their lifetimes away in idle vanity and dalliance is something of a myth. Many women in the zenana were immensely rich in their own right, and wielded enormous influence on the court. Jahangir's wife, Nur Jahan, virtually ran the empire from behind the screen of purdah during the last five years of her husband's ailing reign, while her mother-in-law owned a ship that traded between Surat and the Red Sea, a tradition continued by Shah Jahan's daughter, who grew immensely wealthy through her business enterprises.

Panch Mahal

One of Fatehpur Sikri's most famous structures, the **Panch Mahal** or "Five-Storeyed Palace", looms northwest of here, marking the beginning of the **zenana** (women's quarters) which make up the entire western side of the palace complex. The palace tapers to a final single kiosk and is supported by 176 columns of varying designs; the ground floor contains 84 pillars – an auspicious number in Hindu astrology. The open spaces between the pillars were originally covered with latticed screens, so that ladies of the zenana could observe goings-on in the courtyard of the *mardana* below without themselves being seen.

The women's quarters

Directly behind the Panch Mahal, a courtyard garden was reserved for the zenana (harem). The adjoining **Sunahra Makan** (Golden House), also known as Mariam's House, is variously thought to have been the home of the emperor's mother or of Akbar's wife Mariam. It is enlivened by the faded remains of paintings on its walls (whose now vanished golden paint gave the pavilion its name), by the lines of verse penned by Abu'l Fazl, inscribed around the ceiling in blue bands, and by the quaint little carvings tucked into the brackets supporting the roof, including several elephants and a tiny carving of Rama attended by Hanuman (on the north side of the building, facing the zenana courtyard garden).

Solemnly presiding over the whole complex is the main harem, known as **Jodhbai's Palace**. The residence of several of the emperor's senior wives, this striking building is the grandest and largest in the entire city, and looks decidedly Hindu even in the eclectic context of Fatehpur Sikri, having been modelled after Rajput palaces such as those at Gwalior and Orchha.

On the north side of the palace, the **Hawa Mahal** ("Palace of the Winds"), a small screened tower with a delicately carved chamber, was designed to catch the evening breeze, while a raised covered walkway, lined with five large chhatris, leads from here to a (now vanished) lake.

Northwest of Jodhbai's Palace lies a third women's palace, known as **Birbal's Palace** – though this is another misnomer, as Birbal, Akbar's favourite courtier, was a man and would have been most unwelcome in the middle of the zenana. It's more likely to have been the residence of two of Akbar's senior wives.

Archeological Museum

Daily except Fri 9am–5pm • Free • Photography not allowed • Free half-hour film presentations at 9.30am, 12.30pm & 4pm

Housed in Akbar's old Treasury Building, the **Archeological Museum** has a small display of artefacts found in excavations on the site. Although the city itself is Mughal, there were settlements here going back some four thousand years, though all you'll see of the earliest ones are a few potshards. There was also evidently a Jain temple here in the ninth to twelfth centuries AD, and remains from that are rather more impressive, including a fine statue of Srutidevi Jaina Saraswati.

Jama Masjid

Daily dawn–dusk • Free

Southwest of the palace complex, with the village of Fatehpur Sikri nestling at its base, stands the **Jama Masjid** or Dargah Mosque, one of the finest in the whole of India. Unfortunately, pestilential self-appointed "guides" make it all but impossible to enjoy the place in peace. The mosque was apparently completed in 1571, before work on the palace commenced, showing the religious significance which Akbar accorded the entire site. This was due to its connections with the Sufi saint **Sheikh Salim Chishti**, who is buried here, and who played a crucial role in the founding of Fatehpur Sikri by prophesying the birth of a son to the emperor: when one of Akbar's wives, Rani Jodhabai, a Hindu Rajput princess from Amber, became pregnant, she was sent here until the birth of her son Salim, who later became the emperor Jahangir. Fatehpur Sikri was constructed in the saint's honour.

Buland Darwaza

The neck-cricking **Buland Darwaza** (Great Gate), a spectacular entrance scaled by an impressive flight of steps, was added around 1576 to commemorate Akbar's military campaign in Gujarat. Flanked by domed kiosks, the archway of the simple sandstone memorial is inscribed with a message from the Koran: "Said Jesus Son of Mary (peace be on him): The world is but a bridge – pass over without building houses on it. He who hopes for an hour hopes for eternity; the world is an hour – spend it in prayer for the rest is unseen." The numerous horseshoes nailed to the doors here date from the beginning of the twentieth century – an odd instance of British folk superstition in this very Islamic place.

Tomb of Sheikh Salim Chishti

The gate leads into a vast cloistered courtyard, far larger than in any mosque previously built in India. The **prayer hall**, on the west (left) side, is the focus of the mosque, punctuated by an enormous gateway. More eye-catching is the exquisite **Tomb of Sheikh Salim Chishti**, directly ahead as you enter the courtyard. Much of this was originally crafted in red sandstone and only later faced in marble: the beautiful lattice screens – another design feature probably imported from Gujarat, though it would later become a staple of Mughal architecture – are unusually intricate, with striking serpentine exterior brackets supporting the eaves.

ARRIVAL AND INFORMATION   FATEHPUR SIKRI

By train There are four daily trains from Fatehpur Sikri to Agra Fort (1hr–1hr 20min), and one to Agra Cantt (1hr), plus overnight services to Kota, Bundi and Chittaurgarh, and thrice-weekly to Lucknow and (though not conveniently timed) Mumbai. The station has a computer reservation office, and is a good place to make bookings as there isn't usually any queue.

By bus Buses to Agra's Idgah Bus Stand leave either from the crowded bus stand in the centre of the village (every 30min until 4.30pm; 1hr–1hr 30min) or from the bus stop on the bypass near Agra Gate, about 1.5km from town (about ₹20 by auto-rickshaw from the village, also connected by a ₹10 CNG bus to the palace entrance). At the bypass you'll also find buses to Jaipur (hourly; 4hr) and Bharatpur (hourly; 30–45min).

Services The *Hotel Goverdhan* will change dollars, pounds or euros (in cash or plastic), offers free tourist information and can arrange tours of Rajasthan.

ACCOMMODATION AND EATING

You'll probably **eat** where you stay. If you want to go out, try the *Goverdhan* or the *Ajay Palace* hotel. Fatehpur Sikri's delicious biscuits are not to be missed – you can savour them hot out of the oven each evening at the bakeries on the lane leading up from the village to the Jama Masjid.

Ajay Palace Agra Rd ☏05613 282950; map p.256. Simple hotel in the village, with small, plain rooms, all clean with attached bathrooms (though hot water comes in buckets). There's also a nice little rooftop terrace restaurant and good food. No wi-fi. **₹600**

★ **Goverdhan** Buland Gate Rd, just east of the bus stand ☏05613 282643, ⊕hotelfatehpursikriviews. com; map p.256. A wide range of well-kept rooms (all attached with hot running water) arranged around a neat lawn, with an upstairs veranda, good food (made with filtered water) and a friendly, helpful proprietor. **₹1200**

Sunset View 100m west of the Jama Masjid ☏94123 84416; map p.256. Backpacker guesthouse offering neat, clean (if basic) rooms and superb views over the Jama Masjid and the countryside beyond. Most rooms are attached, but hot water comes in buckets. They can also direct you on birdwatching walks in the surrounding area. **₹400**

UPTDC Gulistan Tourist Complex Agra Rd, 1km east of the village ☏05613 282490, ⊕rahigulistan@up-tourism. com; map p.256. A low-rise, modern building in red sandstone, which looks rather like an academic institution, and has decent if functional rooms set around a series of lawns, plus a restaurant, a pool room and a beer bar. **₹950**

Jhansi

Despite its seventeenth-century fort, the rail- and road-junction town of **JHANSI**, in an anomalous promontory of UP that thrusts south into Madhya Pradesh, is not much visited by tourists. Most stop only long enough to catch a connecting bus to **Khajuraho**, 175km southeast in Madhya Pradesh, but Jhansi is worth a visit in its own right. Like Avadh (see page 261), Jhansi was an independent state until the British summarily annexed it in 1854, and was consequently a major centre of support for the 1857 uprising, under the leadership of **Rani Lakshmibai**, its last ruler's widow, and the uprising's great heroine.

Jhansi Fort

Daily sunrise–sunset · ₹200 (₹5), video camera ₹25 · **Sound-and-light show** (English version) daily: April–Oct 8.45pm; Nov–March 7.45pm · ₹300 (₹50)

Dominating it all from a bare brown craggy hill, **Jhansi Fort**, built in 1613 by Bir Singh Joo Deo, raja of Orchha, is worth visiting primarily for the **views** from its ramparts. Rani Lakshmibai is supposed to have leapt over the west wall on horseback to escape the British, though she must have had a very athletic horse to do so. Inside the fort are a couple of unremarkable temples, plus an old cistern and the ruins of a palace.

Rani Lakshmi Mahal

Nehru Marg • Daily sunrise–sunset • ₹200 (₹5) • No photography allowed

Two minutes' walk from the roundabout below the fort, the **Rani Lakshmi Mahal** is a small stately home in "Bundela style" (lots of ornate balconies and domed roofs), built as a palace for the rani. The home was the scene of a brutal massacre in 1858, when British troops bayoneted all its occupants (they murdered some five thousand people in all after recapturing Jhansi from the insurgents).

ARRIVAL AND INFORMATION JHANSI

By train Jhansi is the most convenient main railway station for Orchha. The station is on the west side of town, 1.5km from the centre. There's a day train to Khajuraho, the #19666 *Udaipur–Khajuraho Express* (departs 3.30pm; arrives 7.50pm) and a night train, the #12448 *Sampark Kranti Express* (departs 2.25am; arrives 6.35am). Numerous trains serve Agra, mostly taking around 3hr, although the #12001 *Shatabdi Express* at 6.40pm takes only 2hr 30min. To Lucknow (5–8 daily; 5hr 15min–7hr 10min), the #11109 *Intercity Express* at 6.10am, arriving at 12.05pm, is the most convenient.

By bus The bus stand on the eastern edge of town – 1.5km from the centre, 3km from the station – has hourly departures for Khajuraho (5hr). It's generally better to take a shared *tempo* to

Orchha and an onward bus from there, or better still, go by train.

By tempo Shared *tempos* for Orchha (45min; ₹20) wait alongside the bus stand, but they tend to dry up around 5pm. An auto from Jhansi to Orchha will cost around ₹200.

Tourist information The UP Tourist Office at the *Hotel Veerangana* on Shivpuri Rd (Mon–Sat 10am–5pm; ☎0510 244 1267) provides town plans and information on Bundelkhand and the route to Khajuraho, but they often close up before time. At the station, UP Tourism have a kiosk on platform 1 (daily 10am–5pm, but may close briefly for breaks as it has a staff of only one), and MP Tourism have one next door (daily 10am–5pm; ☎0510 244 2622), with information about getting to Khajuraho.

ACCOMMODATION AND EATING

Jhansi Shastri Marg, Cantonment (opposite the GPO) ☎0510 247 0360, ⌨jhansihotel.com. Deluxe, supermodern, single-storey hotel whose stylish rooms give onto a lawn that's often used for receptions. There are even some "cottages", which are basically deluxe tents, in case you fancy a bit of glamping. No pool and no bar, however. **₹2500**

Nav Bharat Shastri Marg, Sadar Bazaar (300m up the street from Jhansi Hotel) ☎0510 247 0025. Veg or non-veg thalis, dosas, curries, burgers and sizzlers, served up fast-food-style. Thalis cost ₹150 veg, ₹170–180 non-veg. Daily except Tues 10am–10.30pm.

Raj Palace Shastri Marg, Cantonment (near the GPO) ☎0510 247 0554, ⌨hotelrajpalacejhansi@rediffmail.com. A friendly hotel in a quiet location. The rooms are quite spacious and presentable, and are all attached, but they don't all have widows, there's no wi-fi, and the cheaper rooms have hot running water 7am–noon only (though they'll do you a bucket of hot water any time outside those hours). **₹1200**

Sharma Sweets Shastri Marg, Sadar Bazaar (a few doors from Nav Bharat) ☎0510 247 1666. A good spot for a bit of *mithai* confectionery – the nutty dry fruit *ladoo* (₹30/piece) is wonderful. Daily 8am–10pm.

Lucknow

UP's state capital, **LUCKNOW**, is best remembered abroad for the ordeal of its British residents during a five-month **siege** of the Residency in 1857. Less remembered are the atrocities perpetrated by the British when they recaptured the city. Lucknow saw the last days of Muslim rule in India, and the summary British deposition in 1856 of Wajid Ali Shah, the last nawab of **Avadh**, was one of the main causes of the 1857 uprising.

Extraordinary sandstone **monuments**, now engulfed by modern Lucknow, still testify to the euphoric atmosphere of the Islamic Avadh's unique culture. European-inspired edifices, too, are prominent on the skyline, often embellished with flying buttresses, turrets, cupolas and floral patterns, but the brick and mortar with which they were constructed means that they are not ageing as well as the earlier stone buildings, and colonial Lucknow is literally crumbling away.

Brief history

Avadh (Oudh, as the British spelt it) broke away from the Mughal Empire in the mid-eighteenth century after its nawab, Safdarjang, was thrown out of office in Delhi for being a Shi'ite, but as the Mughal Empire declined, Avadh became the centre of Muslim power. Under the decadent later nawabs, the arts flourished. Lucknow, the Avadhi capital, became a magnet for artisans. Courtesans became poets, singers and dancers, and under the last nawab the amorous musical form called *thumri* emerged here (see page 1218). The city was also an important repository of Shi'a culture and Islamic jurisprudence, its Farangi Mahal law school attracting students from China and Central Asia.

The patronage of the Shi'ite nawabs also produced new expressions of the faith, notably in the annual **Muharram** processions. Held in memory of the martyrdom of Muhammad's grandson Hussain (the second Shi'ite Imam) at Karbala in Iraq, these developed into elaborate affairs with **tazia**, ornate paper reproductions of Hussein's Karbala shrine, being carried through the streets. During the rest of the year the *tazia* images are kept in Imambara (houses of the Imam); these range from humble rooms in poor Shi'ite households to the **Great Imambara** built by Asaf-ud-daula in 1784.

Hussainabad

In the west of the city, in the vicinity of Hardinge Bridge (or Pucca Pul) around "old" Lucknow, lie several crumbling relics of the nawabs of Avadh. Among them are two particularly impressive imambaras (great halls used for Shi'ite religious commemorations).

■ ACCOMMODATION						
Amber	8	Gemini Continental	2
Arif Castles	1	Go Awadh	4
Deep Avadh	7	La Place Sarovar Portico	3
Elora	5	Levana Suites	6

● EATING		
Dastarkhwan	3
Gannewala Café	2
Indian Coffee House	6
Jone Hing	7
Moti Mahal	7

MSH	8
Royal Café	1
Sakhawat's	4
Tunday Kababi	5

● SHOPPING		
Gangotri	1
Sugandhco	2

Bara Imambara

Hussainabad Rd • Daily sunrise–sunset, closed on Sun during Muharram • ₹500 (₹50), ticket includes Hussainabad Imambara and Picture Gallery

The **Bara Imambara** boasts one of the largest vaulted halls in the world – 50m long and 15m high. Flat on top, slightly arched inside, this imambara was built by Asaf-ud-daula in 1784 without the aid of a single iron or wooden beam; the roof was constructed using a technique known as *kara dena*, in which bricks are broken and angled to form an interlocking section and then covered with concrete – here several metres thick. The imambara is approached through what must have been an extravagant gate, now rather battered. Two successive courtyards lead from the gate to the imambara, on the left-hand side of which steps lead up to a fascinating labyrinth of chambers known as *bhulbhulaiya* – the "maze".

Overlooking the Bara Imambara from the south, the **Asfi Mosque** is set on a two-tiered arcaded plinth with two lofty minarets. Even though it is inside the Bara Imambara compound, it is closed to non-Muslims, but anyone can check out its exterior from the gardens adjoining it to the west.

Rumi Darwaza

Hussainabad Rd

Straddling the main road west of the Bara Imambara's entrance gates, the colossal **Rumi Darwaza** is an ornamental victory arch modelled on one of the gates to Asia Minor in Istanbul (known to the Islamic world in Byzantine times as "Rum"). Now decaying, it sports elaborate floral patterns and a few extraordinary trumpets; steps lead up to open chambers that command a general prospect of the monuments of Hussainabad.

Hussainabad Imambara and around

Hussainabad Rd • Same hours and ticket as Bara Imambara

A short distance west of the Rumi Darwaza, the lavish **Hussainabad Imambara** is also known as the Chhota (small) Imambara, or the Palace of Lights, thanks to its fairytale appearance when decorated and illuminated for special occasions. The raised bathing pool in front of it, which is approached via a spacious courtyard, adds to the overall atmosphere. A central gilded dome dominates the whole ensemble, busy with minarets, small domes and arches and even a crude miniature Taj Mahal. Built in 1837 by Muhammad Ali Shah, partly to provide famine relief through employment, the Imambara houses a silver-faced throne, plus the tombs of important Avadhi personalities. The dummy gate opposite the main entrance was used by ceremonial musicians, while the unfinished watchtower is known as the Satkhanda or "Seven Storeys", even though only four were ever constructed.

Beyond the Hussainabad Tank is the isolated 67-metre-high **Hussainabad clock tower**, an ambitious Gothic affair completed in 1887 which carries the largest clock in India. Southwest of the Hussainabad Imambara, and surrounded by ruins, are the two soaring minarets and three domes of the **Jama Masjid**. Commissioned by Muhammad Ali Shah, who ruled Avadh 1837–42, the mosque was only completed after his death.

Muhammad Ali Shah Art Gallery

Hussainabad Rd • Same hours and ticket as Bara Imambara

Close to the clock tower monolith lies **Taluqdar's Hall**, built by Muhammad Ali Shah to house the offices of the Hussainabad Trust and the dusty **Picture Gallery**, also known as the **Muhammad Ali Shah Art Gallery**. Arranged chronologically, the portraits of nawabs graphically demonstrate the decline of their civilization, as the figures become progressively portlier. In a famous image, the androgynous-looking last nawab, Wajid Ali Shah (1847–56), is shown in a daringly low-cut top that reveals his left nipple.

THE LUCKNOW RESIDENCY SIEGE

The insurgent sepoys who entered Lucknow on June 30, 1857, found the city rife with resentment against the recent British takeover of the kingdom of Avadh. The tiny and isolated **British garrison**, under the command of Sir Henry Lawrence, took refuge in the **Residency**, which became the focus of a fierce struggle.

Less than a third of the three thousand British residents and loyal Indians who crammed into the Residency survived the four-and-a-half-month siege. So unhygienic were their living conditions that those who failed to succumb to gangrenous and tetanus-infected wounds often fell victim to cholera and scurvy. While a barrage of heavy artillery was maintained by both sides, the insurgents attempted to tunnel under the defences and lay mines, but among the British were former tin-miners in the 32nd (Cornish) Regiment, who were far more adept at such things, and were able to follow the sounds of enemy chipping, defuse mines, and even blow up several sepoy-controlled buildings.

Morale remained high among the 1400 **noncombatants**, who included fifty schoolboys from La Martinière (see page 265), and class distinctions were upheld throughout. While the wives of European soldiers and non-commissioned officers, children and servants took refuge in the *tikhana* (cellar), the "ladies" of the Residency occupied the higher and airier chambers, until the unfortunate loss of one Miss Palmer's leg on July 1 persuaded them of the gravity of their predicament. Sir Henry Lawrence was fatally wounded the next day. The wealthier officers managed to maintain their own private hoard of supplies, living in much their usual style. Matters improved when, after three months, Brigadier-General Sir Henry Havelock arrived with reinforcements, and the normal round of visits and invitations to supper was resumed despite the inconvenient shortage of good food and wine. Not until November 17 was the siege finally broken by a force of Sikhs and Highlanders under Sir Colin Campbell. Their offers of tea, however, were turned down by the Residency women; they were used to taking it with milk, which the soldiers could not supply.

The Residency

Daily sunrise–sunset; museum daily except Fri 8am–4.30pm • ₹100 (₹5), video camera ₹25

The blasted **Residency** rests in peace amid landscaped gardens southeast of Hardinge Bridge – a battle-scarred ruin left exactly as it stood when the siege was finally relieved by Sir Colin Campbell on November 17, 1857 (see page 264). Its cannonball-shattered tower became a shrine to the tenacity of the British in India, and continued to be maintained as such even after Independence.

During the siege, every building in the complex was utilized for the hard-fought defence of the compound. The **Treasury**, on the right through the **Baillie Guard Gate**, served as an arsenal, while the sumptuous **Banqueting Hall**, immediately west, was a makeshift hospital, and the extensive single-storey **Dr Fayrer's House**, just south, housed women and children. Most of the original structures, such as **Begum Kothi**, were left standing to impede direct fire from the enemy. On the lawn outside Begum Kothi, a large cross honours the astute Sir Henry Lawrence, responsible for building its defences, who died shortly after hostilities began.

The pockmarked Residency itself holds a small **museum**. On the ground floor, the **Model Room**, the only one with its roof intact, houses a large model of the defences and of the Residency and a small but excellent collection of images, including etchings showing wall breaches blocked up with billiard tables and a soldier blacking up in preparation for a dash across enemy lines.

Hazratganj

With its shops and upmarket restaurants and hotels, and a concentration of banks and other services, **Hazratganj** is the modern centre of Lucknow. Though not as bustling as the older Kaiserbagh and Aminabad neighbourhoods to its west, Hazratganj still has quite a buzz, plus a handful of interesting sights.

Shah Najaf Imambara

Rana Pratap Marg (opposite *Carlton Hotel*) • Sat–Thurs 6am–6pm, Fri 6am–noon & 2–6pm • Free

With its huge dome, the **Shah Najaf Imambara**, named after the tomb of Ali in Iraq, is at its best when adorned with lights during the holy month of Muharram. Its musty interior holds some incredibly garish chandeliers used in processions, several *tazia*, and the silver-faced tomb of the decadent and profligate Ghazi-ud-din-Haidar (ruled 1814–27), buried with three of his queens.

Sikandrabagh

Rana Pratap Marg • **Botanical Gardens** Mon–Fri: April–Sept 5–9am; Oct–March 6–9am (last entry ticket sold 8.30am) • ₹1

The Imambara was commandeered as an insurgent stronghold in 1857, and the crucial battle that enabled the British to relieve the Residency was fought in the adjacent pleasure gardens of **Sikandrabagh** on November 16. It took one and a half hours of bombardment by Sir Colin Campbell's soldiers to breach the defences of the two thousand sepoys; then the Sikhs and 93rd Highlanders poured through. There was no escape for the terrified sepoys, some of whom are said to have believed the bloodstained, red-faced, kilted Scots to be the ghosts of a group of European women slaughtered at Kanpur earlier in the uprising. Driven against the north wall, the sepoys were either bayoneted or shot, and the dead and dying piled shoulder-high. Tranquil once again, Sikandrabagh is now home to the National Botanical Research Institute and the beautiful **Botanical Gardens**, with manicured lawns, conservatories, nurseries and herb, rose and bougainvillea gardens.

La Martinière

La Martinière Rd

Towards the east of Lucknow, an extraordinary chateau-like building has become almost a symbol of the city – **La Martinière** remains to this day an exclusive boys' school in the finest colonial tradition. It was built as a country retreat by Major-General Claude Martin, a French soldier-adventurer taken prisoner by the British in Puducherry. The enigmatic Martin later joined the East India Company, made his fortune in indigo, and served both the British and the nawabs of Avadh. The building is an outrageous but intriguing amalgam, crowned by flying walkways; Greco-Roman figures on the parapets give it a busy silhouette, gigantic heraldic lions gaze across the grounds, and a large bronze cannon graces the front. Martin himself is buried in the basement. During the uprising, La Martinière was occupied by insurgent forces, its boys having been evacuated to the Residency.

The zoo and State Museum

Rana Pratap Marg • **Zoo** Daily 8.30am–5pm • ₹60, video camera ₹50 • T8874 204 160 ⑫ lucknowzoo.com • **State Museum** Tues–Sun 10.30am–4pm • ₹5 (buy ticket at zoo entrance)

Close to the centre of Hazratganj, its grounds dotted with derelict Avadhi monuments, Lucknow's small **zoo** also serves as an amusement park with a miniature train to view the animals.

Inside the zoo, the **State Museum** exhibits delicate, speckled-red-sandstone sculpture from the Mathura School of the Kushana and Gupta periods (first to sixth centuries AD). Besides sculpture from Gandhara, Mahoba, Nalanda and Sravasti, it has a gallery of terracotta artefacts and even an Egyptian mummy. Musical instruments, paintings and costumes provide atmosphere in the Avadh gallery, while the natural history section is a taxidermist's dream.

ARRIVAL AND DEPARTURE **LUCKNOW**

By plane Amausi airport is 16km south of town on the Kanpur Rd (around ₹400 by taxi from the city centre, or ₹300 by Uber or Ola; it's served by the metro and connected to the Alambagh Inter State Bus Terminal and Charbagh Railway Station). Destinations include Delhi (with Air India and IndiGo), Mumbai (Go and IndiGo), Patna (IndiGo), Kolkata (IndiGo), Hyderabad (IndiGo) and Bengaluru (IndiGo).

By train Lucknow's busy railway station (with a computerized reservations office at the eastern end of its forecourt) is in Charbagh, 4km southwest of Hazratganj (₹100 by auto).

Note that Lucknow Junction (on the Northeastern Railway) is actually a separate station from the main one (just plain Lucknow, on the Northern Railway), and adjoins it to the west, at the end of the same forecourt; make sure you go to the right station to get your train. For Khajuraho, the #12533 *Pushpak Express* at 7.45pm reaches Jhansi at 1.30am, which ought to give you enough time to pick up the #12448/22448 *Sampark Kranti Express* at 2.25am, arriving in Khajuraho at 6.35am; if you want to play it safe, you can take the earlier #11110 *Intercity Express* at 4.40pm to reach Jhansi at 10.35pm.

By bus Most intercity buses operate from Charbagh ISBT, opposite Lucknow Junction station, which has hourly departures to Delhi (12hr), Gorakhpur (8hr) and Varanasi (9hr). A few buses use the more central Kaiserbagh Bus Stand (₹50 by cycle rickshaw from Hazratganj), which has departures to Dehradun (3 daily; 10hr 30min) and Haridwar (3 daily; 10hr). The Alambagh ISBT has direct links to Agra (hourly; 5hr) and Prayagraj (hourly; 3hr). Check routes and time tables at ⓦ upsrtconline.co.in.

GETTING AROUND

By tempo Multiseater *tempos* (Vikrams) ply regular routes such as from Charbagh to the GPO.

Car rental Cars (with driver) can be hired from Great Value Travels at *Hotel Clarks Avadh*, 8 MG Marg by Clarks Avadh Crossing (☏ 0522 262 7228), or UP Tours (see below) at the

Hotel Gomti (☏ 0522 261 2659).

Metro The current metro line runs from the airport in the south to Munshipulia in the north. At the time of writing, in 2019, an extension, running westward from Charbagh to Vasant Ganj was under consideration.

INFORMATION AND TOURS

Tourist information The UP Tourism office is inconveniently located at C-13 Vipin Khand in Gomti Nagar, 3km east of town (Mon–Fri 10am–5pm; ☏ 0522 230 4870), but they also have a kiosk in the station (daily 6am–9.30pm). If all you need is a town plan, you can pick one up from their tour agency, UP Tours at *Hotel Gomti*, 6 Sapru (Mon–Sat 9.30am–6.30pm; ☏ 0522 261 2659). Lucknow also has offices of both GMVN (for Garhwal, western Uttarakhand), at 4-7RF Khushnuma Complex, Bahadur Marg (☏ 0522 220 7844), and KMVN (for Kumaon, eastern Uttarakhand), at KMVN Uttarakhand Bhawan (near NTPC

Vibhutikhand), Gomti Nagar (☏ 0522 272 3960). There's a good information website about Lucknow at ⓦ lucknow.org.uk, and a listings site at ⓦ lucknowcity.org.in.

Tours Comprehensive daily city tours (₹850), which must be booked in advance through UP Tours (see above), and only run if they have three or more takers, leave the *Hotel Gomti* at 9.45am and return at 2.30pm. The price includes guide and entrance fees. A 2hr Heritage Walk starts bright and early at 7.30am daily in summer, 8am in winter (₹300) from Tile Wale Masjid north of Shah Najaf Imambara; for details contact Naved Zia on ☏ 94150 13047.

ACCOMMODATION

Amber Subhash Marg, Naka Hindola ☏ 0522 268 3201, ✉ amber.hotel@yahoo.in; map p.262. Good value near the station: a range of spacious rooms at different prices, all attached, most with a/c but a few just air-cooled. The cheapest rooms go quickly. 24hr checkout. **₹1500**

Arif Castles 4 Rana Pratap Marg ☏ 0522 409 8777, ⓦ arifcastles.com; map p.262. Quite well-appointed in marble, brass and light blue, this boutique hotel, as it describes itself, has cool rooms, a/c, cable TV and an Avadhi cuisine restaurant. Rates include breakfast. **₹2000**

Deep Avadh Aminabad Rd, Naka Hindola ☏ 0522 268 4381, ⓦ deephotels.com/deepavadh; map p.262. Good a/c rooms in various sizes with 24hr room service, as well as two restaurants, bar and travel desk, in an interesting part of town close to the station and on the edge of bustling Aminabad. 24hr checkout. **₹1800**

Elora 3 Lalbagh ☏ 0522 221 1307; map p.262. Popular place with a wide range of different rooms, including some with a/c (₹1200). Facilities include cable TV in all rooms, 24hr room service and a multi-cuisine restaurant, but no wi-fi. **₹800**

Gemini Continental 10 Rani Laximbai Marg, Hazratganj ☏ 0522 401 1111, ⓦ geminicontinental.

com; map p.262. Snazzy, upscale hotel in the centre of town. Spacious, modern rooms with great views, minibar, cable TV, a/c and 24hr room service. Buffet breakfast is included. **₹3800**

★ **Go Awadh** 5/39 Vishal Khand, Gomti Nagar ☏ 9161 034 777 ⓦ goawadh.com; map p.262. Lucknow's first hostel and co-working space, set in a quiet neighbourhood, is far from the city sights, but has spacious, squeaky clean, en suite doubles and dorms to suit every budget. The bamboo-furnished garden is the perfect place to relax. Booking in advance and online will save you a considerable amount. Doubles **₹2000**; dorms **₹700**

La Place Sarovar Portico 6 Shah Najaf Rd, Hazratganj ☏ 0522 405 5000, or toll-free ☏ 1800 111222, ⓦ sarovar hotels.com; map p.262. Small but smart, modern business hotel whose facilities include a business centre and executive offices, a rooftop bar-restaurant and a 24hr coffee shop, but no pool. Buffet breakfast included. Discounts usually available. **₹3500**

Levana Suites 72 Mahatma Gandhi Marg, Hazratganj ☏ 0522 410 1111; map p.262. Central and cosy hotel with large, well decorated rooms, a spa and a gym. On its creatively

RECOMMENDED TRAINS FROM LUCKNOW

The trains below are recommended as the fastest and/or most convenient for specific cities. All those listed here run daily.

Destination	Name	No.	From	Departs	Arrives
Agra Fort	*Marudhar Express*	#14853/63/55	L	12.30am	6.10am
Agra Cantt	*Intercity Express*	#12179	LJ	3.55pm	9.55pm
Dehradun	*Doon Express*	#13009	L	6.35pm	7.25am+
Delhi (ND)	*Shatabdi Express**	#12003	LJ	3.35pm	10.15pm
	Lucknow Mail	#12229	L	10.15pm	7.15am
Gorakhpur	*Katihar Express*	#15708	L	12.50am	5.45am
	Kushinagar Express	#11015	L	1.55am	7.10am
Jhansi	*Kushinagar Express*	#11016	L	12.40am	7.05am
	Gwalior Mail	#11123	L	11.50am	6.30pm
Kathgodam	*Bagh Express*	#13019	LJ	12.25am	9.30am
Kolkata	*Doon Express*	#13010	L	8.45am	6.55am+
	Howrah Mail	#13006	L	10.50am	7.20am+
Mumbai CST	*Pushpak Express*	#12533	L	7.45pm	8.05pm+
Prayagraj	*Intercity Express*	#14210	L	7.30am	11.45am
Ramnagar	*Dheradun Express*	#14265/55321	LJ	4.45pm	6.25am+
Varanasi	*Begampura Express*	#12238	L	7.20am	12.40pm
	Howrah Mail	#13006	L	10.50am	4.40pm

L: Lucknow main station (Northern Railway); LJ: Lucknow Junction (Northeastern Railway); ND: New Delhi station; *a/c only; + next day

3

decorated rooftop is *Elev8*, a swanky book café, and the first silent-disco in Lucknow, open from 6.30pm. **₹2500**

EATING

The rich traditional **Lucknavi cuisine** – featuring Mughlai dishes as well as the local *dum pukht* (steam casserole) style, sometimes known as *handi* after the pot it's cooked in – is available from food stalls throughout the city, in places such as Shami Avadh Bazaar, near the K.D. Singh Babu Stadium, the Chowk, Aminabad and behind the Tulsi Theatre in Hazratganj. Luknavi "kebabs" – extremely delicious – are in fact fried patties of very finely minced meat. The bazaars are the place to get Lucknow's popular breakfast speciality *paya-khulcha*, a spicy mutton soup served with hot breads.

Dastarkhwan China Gate ✆0522 262 5297; map p.262. One of a number of open-air diners in this little street by UP Press Club, with non-veg Mughlai dishes (such as rogan josh; ₹260), kebabs (₹120) and biryanis (₹260), with half portions available. Daily 1.30–10.30pm.

Gannewala Café 18/80 Indira Nagar (off Shah Najaf Rd, Hazratganj) ✆95591 88885, ⊛gannewala.com; map p.262. If you're tempted by street stalls selling cane juice but wary of drinking from them, this could be the place for you: a hygienic cane juice bar, where you can get a glass for ₹30 regular or ₹40 large, along with snacks (veg burger ₹50) and smoothies (₹85–95). Daily 11am–11pm.

Indian Coffee House Ashok Marg ✆0522 322 9556; map p.262. Once a hotbed of Lucknow's political intelligentsia, nick-named the "maternity ward" for the ideas it gave birth to, now reborn as a bright, new café serving excellent filter coffee (at ₹51) plus cakes, shakes, snacks and Avadhi, south Indian and Chinese food (veg thali ₹90–120, masala dosa ₹60). Daily 8am–10pm.

Jone Hing MG Marg, Hazratganj ✆93357 11772; map p.262. Chinese restaurant serving the usual sweet-and-sour, chop suey and chow mein, plus specialities such as Manchurian chicken lollipop (drumsticks in sauce; ₹290) or chilli fish (₹270). Daily 11am–10.45pm.

Moti Mahal 75 MG Marg, Hazratganj ✆0522 404 8101; map p.262. The sweet shop at the front has some great milky confec-tions, including sugar-free ones; the family restaurant upstairs serves excellent veg curries, including three types of *dum aloo* (Lucknavi, Banarsi or Kashmiri; ₹130–135). Daily 11am–11pm.

MSH Subhash Marg, at Station Rd, Charbagh ✆0522 404 8130; map p.262. Cheap *dhaba* opposite the station serving good dosas (₹60), veg curries and thalis (₹120). Daily 6am–10.30pm.

Royal Café 9–7 Shah Najaf Rd, Hazratganj ✆0522 402 3535; map p.262. A lively place that's popular among Lucknavi families. They have plenty of veg dishes, of course, but they tend to specialize in chicken, serving dishes such as Royal Café special chicken (with hard-boiled egg and dried fruit) or chicken *handi* (both ₹570 for a whole chicken, or ₹390 for half), and there are also Chinese and Continental dishes. Daily 10am–11.30pm.

Sakhawat's 2 Kaiserbagh Ave (behind Oudh Gymkana Club) ☎0522 321 1347, ⓦsakhawatrestaurant.com; map p.262. Highly acclaimed Avadhi restaurant and chefs' training school where they specialize in moderately priced Lucknavi cuisine, such as *shami* kebabs and mutton *musallam*. Daily except Sat & Sun 4.30–10.30pm.

★ **Tunday Kababi** Naaz Cinema Rd, just off Aminabad main chowk ☎93359 11858, ⓦtundaykababipvtltd. com; map p.262. For an authentic Avadhi gastronomic experience, head to this popular and inexpensive place (the best in a street of them), where tandoori chicken and kebabs are prepared out front and served up within. A plate of four kebabs will set you back ₹32 for beef, ₹70 for mutton. Daily 11.30am–11.30pm.

SHOPPING

Lucknow is also renowned for its **ittar** (or *attar*), concentrated perfume sold in small vials – an acquired (and expensive) taste. Small balls of cotton wool are daubed with the scent and placed neatly within the top folds of the ear; musicians believe that the aroma heightens their senses. Popular *ittar* include *ambar* from amber, *khus* from a flowering plant and rose-derived *ghulab*. A long-standing Lucknavi tradition of embroidery is **chikan**, in which designs are built up to form delicate floral patterns along edges on saris and on necklines and collars of *kurtas*; workshops can be found around the Chowk, the market area of old Lucknow, and shops and showrooms in Hazratganj (especially Janpath Market), Nazirabad and Aminabad.

Gangotri MG Marg, Hazratganj (half a block west of Lalbagh) ☎0522 262 4377; map p.262. The UP state crafts emporium has a variety of carvings, carpets, enamel ware, brass figurines, clothes and textiles. The fixed prices here are higher than those in the markets, but the quality is assured and you don't have to haggle. Mon–Sat 10.30am–7.30pm.

Sugandhco D-4 Janpath Market (on the south side of the market) ☎0522 262 1748, ⓦscentkart.com; map p.262. The smell of sweet perfume greets you as you enter this well-established dealer of top-whack own-brand *ittar* and incense, which is also sold in other shops around town. Mon–Sat noon–7.30pm.

DIRECTORY

Festivals November's Lucknow Festival (details from UP Tourism) is an opportunity to sample the city's vibrant traditions of music and dance.

Prayagraj (Allahabad) and around

The administrative and industrial city of **PRAYAGRAJ** – known as Allahabad until October 2018, when its pre-Mughal name was reinstated to highlight the city's role as a Hindu pilgrimage site – is 135km west of Varanasi and 227km southeast of Lucknow. **Prayag** means "confluence", the point where the Yamuna and Ganges rivers meet the mythical Saraswati River (see page 271). Sacred to Hindus, the **sangam** (which also means "confluence"), east of the city, is one of the great pilgrimage destinations of India. Prayagraj comes alive during its *melas* (fairs) – the annual **Magh Mela** (Jan/Feb), and the colossal **Maha Kumbh Mela**, held every twelve years (2025 and 2037 are the next ones).

Prayagraj is a pleasant city to visit, with vast, open riverside scenery, attractive street art, and good amenities, but is without major temples or monuments. At the junction of the fertile Doab, the "two-river" valley between the Yamuna and the Ganges, it did however possess a crucial strategic significance; its massive **fort**, built by the emperor Akbar in 1583, is still used by the military. Another Mughal, Jahangir's son Khusrau, was murdered here by his brother Shah Jahan, who went on to become emperor. Prayagraj was briefly the centre of power after the 1857 uprising, when the British moved the headquarters of their Northwestern Provinces here from Agra; the formal transfer of power from the East India Company to the Crown took place here the following year.

Central Prayagraj is split in two by the railway line, with the chaotic and congested **Old City** or **Chowk** south of Prayagraj Junction station, and the grid of the **Civil Lines** (the residential quarter of the Raj military town) to the north.

All Saints' Cathedral

Mahatma Gandhi Marg • Sun 9–11am

THE KUMBH MELA

Hindus traditionally regard river confluences (**sangams**) as auspicious places, and none more so than the one at Prayagraj, where the Yamuna and Ganges rivers meet the River of Enlightenment, the mythical subterranean Saraswati. According to legend, Vishnu was carrying a *kumbha* (pot) of *amrita* (nectar), when a scuffle broke out between the gods, and four drops were spilled. They fell to earth at the four *tirthas* of Prayag, Haridwar, Nasik and Ujjain. The event is commemorated every three years by the **Kumbh Mela**, held at each *tirtha* in turn; the Prayagraj sangam is known as Tirtharaja, the "King of *tirthas*", and its *mela*, the **Maha Kumbh Mela** or "Great" Kumbh Mela, is the greatest and holiest of all.

The largest religious fair in India, Maha Kumbh Mela was attended by an astonishing **120 million** pilgrims in 2013. The vast flood plains and riverbanks adjacent to the confluence were overrun by tents, organized in almost military fashion by the government, the local authorities and the police. The *mela* is especially renowned for the presence of an extraordinary array of religious ascetics – sadhus and *mahants* – enticed from remote hideaways in forests, mountains and caves. Once astrologers have determined the propitious bathing time or *kumbhayog*, the first to hit the water are legions of Naga Sadhus or Naga Babas, who cover their naked bodies with ash and wear their hair in dreadlocks. The sadhus, who see themselves as guardians of the faith, approach the confluence at the appointed time with all the pomp and bravado of a charging army.

Although the Kumbh Mela is only triennial, and not always in Prayagraj, there is a smaller annual bathing festival, the **Magh Mela**, held here every year in the month of Magha (Jan–Feb).

At the western end of the Civil Lines area, the yellow-and-red sandstone bulk of the Gothic **All Saints' Cathedral** was designed by Sir William Emerson, architect of Kolkata's Victoria Memorial. Work began in 1871, but wasn't completed until the 1920s. Much of its stained glass is still intact, and plaques provide interesting glimpses of Prayagraj in the days of the Raj, while flying buttresses and snarling gargoyles decorate the exterior. To see the inside, you'll need to come by during the Sunday service, which attracts quite large congregations, as do Masses at the flamboyant **St Joseph's Roman Catholic Cathedral**, a short distance northeast.

Prayagraj Museum

Kamla Nehru Marg • Tues–Sun 10.30am–4.30pm, closed the Sun following the 2nd Sat of the month • ₹500 (₹20), camera ₹1000

On the edge of the pleasant **Chandra Shekhar Azad Park**, the grounds of the **Prayagraj Museum** are dotted with pieces of ancient sculpture. Inside, you'll find early terracotta artefacts, eighth-century sculptures from the Buddhist site of Kaushambi, and a striking twelfth-century image from Khajuraho of Shiva and Parvati. A copious collection of modern Indian art includes work by Haldar, Sajit Khastgir and Rathin Mitra, as well as Jamini Roy, who was inspired by folk art. European paintings concentrate on spiritual themes, with bright, naive canvases by the Russian artist Nicholas Roerich, and pieces by the Tibetologist Lama Angarika Govinda. A natural history section features stuffed animals and birds, while photographs and documents cover the Independence struggle. North of the museum rise the nineteenth-century sandstone buildings of **Prayagraj University**, and the Gothic **Muir College**, built in 1870. A 61m-high tower accompanies domes clad with blue and white glazed tiles (some of which are missing), and a quadrangle with tall and elegant arches.

Anand Bhawan

Motilal Nehru Rd • **Museum** Tues–Sun 9.30am–5pm • ₹200 (₹15); no tickets sold 12.45–1.30pm **Planetarium** 11.30am, 12.30pm, 1.30pm, 2.30pm, 3.30pm, 4.30pm • ₹40, all in Hindi with a 30min lecture prior to the show

In beautiful grounds, 1km northeast of Allhabad museum, **Anand Bhawan**, an ornate Victorian building, crowned by a chhatri and with Indo-Saracenic effects finished in grey-and-white trim, was **Jawaharlal Nehru**'s boyhood home. It's now a museum, where visitors can peer through plate glass into the opulent interiors. More diverting than

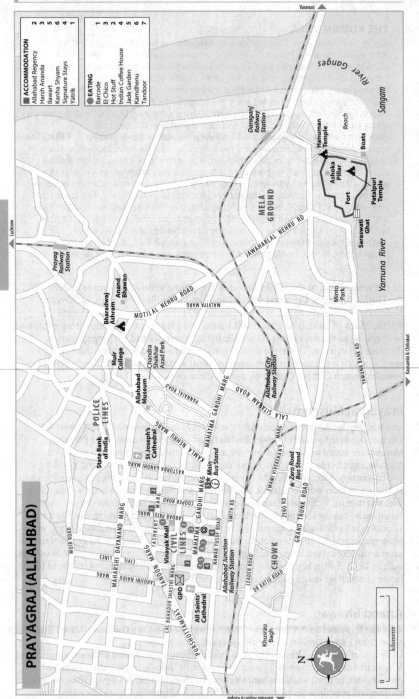

PRAYAGRAJ (ALLAHBAD)

■ ACCOMMODATION

Allahabad Regency	2
Harsh Ananda	3
Ilawart	5
Kanha Shyam	6
Signature Stays	4
Yatrik	1

● EATING

Barcode	1
El Chico	3
Hot Stuff	2
Indian Coffee House	4
Jade Garden	5
Kamdhenu	6
Tandoor	7

Nehru's spoons and trousers is the colonial court document of his trial for making salt. Nehru's daughter Indira Gandhi was born here, and Mahatma Gandhi (no relation) stayed when he visited the city. In the grounds, as at the Nehru Memorial Museum in Delhi, is a **planetarium**, which puts on six hour-long shows per day.

Khusrau Bagh
Leader Rd

A short way south of Prayagraj Junction railway station, a lofty gateway leads to the attractive walled gardens of **Khusrau Bagh**, where the remains of Jahangir's tragic son Khusrau rest in a simple sandstone mausoleum, completed in 1622. Khusrau made an unsuccessful bid for power that ended in death at the hands of his brother Shah Jahan, and is buried far from the centre of Mughal power. His mother's two-storey mausoleum is a short way west, beyond a tomb reputed to be that of his sister. Once Jahangir's pleasure garden, today much of Khusrau Bagh has been made into an orchard, famous for its guavas, and a rose nursery, but parts are unkempt and overgrown.

The river frontage

Most of Prayagraj's river frontage is along the Yamuna, where women perform *aarti* or evening worship at **Saraswati Ghat** by floating *diya* downstream. Immediately to the west, in **Minto Park**, a memorial marks the spot where, in 1858, the British Raj was born, as India officially passed from the East India Company to the Crown.

The fort

East of Saraswati Ghat, Akbar's **fort** is best appreciated from boats on the river (see box above). Much of it is still occupied by the military, and public access is restricted to the leafy corner around the **Patalpuri Temple**, approached through any of the three massive gates. Much of the superstructure is neglected; the **zenana** with its columned hall does survive, but its interior is closed to the public. At the main gate, a poorly restored, polished stone **Ashoka Pillar** is inscribed with the emperor's edicts and dated to 242 BC.

Hanuman Temple

Where the fort's eastern battlements meet the river, a muddy *ghat* is busy with boatmen jostling for custom from pilgrims heading to the sangam. Inland along the base of the fort, with the flood plain of the sangam to the right, a road leads past rows of stalls catering to pilgrims visiting the brightly painted **Hanuman Temple**. Unusually, the large sunken image of the monkey god inside is reclining rather than standing erect; during the annual floods the waters rise to touch his feet before once again receding.

THE SANGAM

Around 7km from the centre of the Civil Lines, overlooked by the eastern ramparts of the fort, wide flood plains and muddy banks protrude towards the sacred **sangam**. At the point at which the brown Ganges meets the greenish Yamuna, *pandas* (priests) perch on small platforms to perform puja and assist the devout in their ritual ablutions in the shallow waters. Beaches and *ghats* here are littered with the shorn hair of pilgrims who come to offer *pind* for their deceased parents, and women sit around selling cone-shaped pyramids of bright red and orange *tilak* powder.

Boats to the sangam, used by pilgrims and tourists alike, can be rented at the *ghat* immediately east of the fort. Depending on your bargaining skills, typical prices for a sixteen-seat boat are ₹300 (or ₹30 per head if you join a shared boat), but can soar to more than ₹2000 during the *melas*. On the way to the sangam, high-pressure aquatic salesmen loom up on the placid waters selling offerings such as coconuts for pilgrims to discard at the confluence. Once abandoned, the offerings are fished up and sold on to other pilgrims.

3

ARRIVAL AND DEPARTURE

By plane Bamrauli airport, 18km west on the Kanpur Rd, has daily flights to Delhi with Air India, Alliance Air, and IndiGo; four flights a week to Mumbai with Alliance Air; and one daily flight to Bangalore with IndiGo.

By train Prayagraj has four railway stations, but all express trains use Prayagraj Junction. Most hotels are nearby; be sure to use the right exit for the area where you plan to stay. Destinations include Delhi (22–27 daily; 7hr 12min–17hr 35min, including overnight #12559 *Shiv Ganga Express* dep. 10.30pm, arr New Delhi 8.10am), Agra (5–8 daily; 6hr 30min–11hr 15min, including #12987 *Sealdah–Ajmer Express* dep. 12.05pm, arr. Agra Fort 6.50pm), Lucknow (5–6 daily; 4hr 05min–8hr 15min, including #14215 *Ganga Gomti Express* dep. 6am, arr. 10.15am), Varanasi

PRAYAGRAJ AND AROUND

(13–23 daily; 2hr 35min–4hr 08min, fastest is the #12562 *Swatantrata Sainani Express* dep. 5.55am, arr. 8.30am) and Satna (for Khajuraho; 13–23 daily; 2hr 40min–3hr 15min including #12428 *Anand Vihar–Rewa Superfast Express* dep. 6.55am arr. 9.50am).

By bus The main bus stand is on MG Marg next to the *Hotel Ilawart*, with services to Varanasi (every 15min; 3hr 30min), Agra (every 15min; 7hr 30min), Lucknow (every 15min; 4hr) and Delhi (3 daily; 11hr). Because of their frequency, buses are more convenient than trains for the journey to Varanasi. Zero Road Bus Stand, south of the railway line, serves Mahoba, Satna and Chitrakut. Some private services, notably to Kaushambi, depart from Leader Road, just west of Prayagraj Junction station's south entrance.

GETTING AROUND AND INFORMATION

By rickshaw Cycle- and auto-rickshaws are the most common modes of transport; a trip to the sangam from the Civil Lines crossing costs around ₹100 (hang on to your vehicle for the return journey).

Car rental Car rental through general travel agencies such as Varuna in Tulsiani Plaza, next to *Harsh* hotel on MG Marg

(☏ 0532 256 1261, ✉ varunatravels@hotmail.com), costs in the region of ₹1800/day, plus mileage. UP Tours, next to *Ilawart* hotel on MG Marg, can also supply a car and driver.

Tourist information At *Ilawart* hotel, 35 MG Marg, Civil Lines (Mon–Sat 10am–5pm, but closed second Sat of the month; ☏ 0532 240 8873).

ACCOMMODATION

Allahabad Regency 16 Tashkent Marg ☏ 0532 240 7835, ⊕ hotelallahabadregency.in; map p.270. Nineteenth-century colonial bungalow with a good restaurant, a sauna, jacuzzi, swimming pool and gym. The rooms are very well done out, but a bit on the small side – it's worth paying ₹800 more for a suite-like "duplex" room. Breakfast included. **₹4500**

Harsh Ananda 118/116 MG Marg ☏ 0532 242 7697, ⊕ hotelharshananda.com; map p.270. An old colonial bungalow refurbished to make a very stylish hotel, with a lawn out front and fireplaces in some of the rooms, all of which are tastefully decorated in relaxing cream and brown tones. **₹3500**

Ilawart 35 MG Marg Civil Lines ☏ 0532 260 7440, ✉ rahiilawart@up-tourism.com; map p.270. The state-run "tourist bungalow" is an odd mix of grubby corridors and new, clean rooms, hot water (except 10am–1pm),

and no wi-fi, but good value on the whole, with a bar and restaurant, and handy for the bus stand. **₹2500**

Kanha Shyam Strachey Rd, Civil Lines ☏ 0532 256 0123, ⊕ hotelkanhashyam.com; map p.270. Classy four-star with quite stately rooms done out in burgundy. There's a lounge bar, 24hr coffee shop and a rooftop restaurant. Breakfast included. **₹4000**

Signature Stays MG Marg, next to Indian Coffee House ☏ 7986 502 393; map p.270. New business-focused hotel with modern rooms with all the amenities, including rain showers and plush mattresses. Booking online will likely get you a significant discount. **₹1600**

Yatrik 33 Sardar Patel Marg ☏ 0532 226 0921, ⊕ hotelyatrik.com; map p.270. Good upmarket choice: popular, well run and with a beautiful garden graced with elegant palms. 24hr check-out. Breakfast included. **₹5000**

EATING AND DRINKING

Barcode Sardar Patel Marg, opposite Grand Continental Hotel, ☏ 9839 951 333 ⊕ facebook.com/BarcodeAlld; map p.270. Popular lounge bar with wooden décor and cosy, dimly lit ambience, serving beers, cocktails and spirits. Check online for live music. Daily 10.30am–10.30pm.

El Chico 24 MG Marg ☏ 0532 242 0075 ⊕ elchico.in; map p.270. One of the city's best since 1964, a smart place with good Indian, Chinese and Western cuisine, including grills, sizzlers, Sichuan-style chicken (₹350) or baked fish in cheese sauce (₹400). Next door, El Chico Pastry Shop has a

mouth-watering array of cakes (from ₹60), waffles (₹100), sundaes (₹125), milkshakes and ice cream (₹75). Upstairs, the hip *El Chico Café* is the perfect place to relax with a cuppa while rubbing elbows with Prayagraj's young and trendy. Daily 9am–10.30pm.

Hot Stuff 21-C Sardar Patel Marg ☏ 75250 01221; map p.270. Fast-food-style diner popular with local youth, offering burgers (₹70, or ₹100 with Coke and fries), shakes (₹120), Chinese food and ice cream. They also do takeaways and deliver. Daily 10.30am–10.30pm.

Indian Coffee House MG Marg, set back from the road ☎0532 242 7211; map p.270. Prayagraj branch of the coffee co-op, serving great filter coffee and basic cheap snacks (masala dosa ₹60; nothing over ₹70) with no frills or pretensions. Daily 8am–9pm.

Jade Garden 123–127 MG Marg ☎0532 256 1408; map p.270. Small garden restaurant offering Chinese food of the chop suey, chow mein and sweet-and-sour variety, plus veg and non-veg Indian dishes. Lemon chicken, ginger chicken or chicken Manchurian are all ₹400. Daily 11am–11pm.

Kamdhenu 37 MG Marg, in the beautiful nineteenth-century Palace Theatre building ☎0532 256 0051 ⓦkamdhenusweet.in; map p.270. Famous Prayagraj sweet shop whose specialities include milk cake (₹20/piece), but their *anjeer* (fig) *barfi* (₹18/piece) is superb: subtly spiced and less cloyingly sweet than typical *mithai* confectionery. Daily 8am–10.30pm.

Tandoor 33 MG Marg ☎0532 242 7327; map p.270. Reliable non-veg restaurant, and one of the best places in the city for Indian food, serving all the tandoori classics including chicken tikka (₹150), kebabs and Mughlai curries (rogan josh; ₹150). Daily 10am–10.30pm.

DIRECTORY

Post office Prayagraj's main post office (known as the GPO or HPO) is at Sarojini Naidu Marg, near All Saints' Cathedral in the Civil Lines.

Around Prayagraj

Prayagraj makes a good base from which to venture into the remoter parts of **Bundelkhand** (see page 275) to the south. Destinations include the ancient city of Kaushambi, best taken in on a day-trip, the "mini-Varanasi" at Chitrakut, and the fort at Kalinjar.

Kaushambi

Just 63km southwest of Prayagraj, on the banks of the Yamuna, are the extensive ruins of **Kaushambi**, a major Buddhist centre where Buddha himself once preached. The city flourished between the eighth century BC and the sixth century AD; archeological evidence suggests even earlier habitation. According to legend, it was founded by descendants of the Pandavas, after floods destroyed their city of Hastinapur. Mud ramparts (originally faced with brick) tower over the fields, running along an irregular 6km perimeter, and sections remain of a defensive moat. Within the complex, excavations have revealed a paved road, brick houses, wells, tanks and drains, a monastery with cloisters, a large *stupa* and the ruins of a palace. The only standing feature is a damaged sandstone column ascribed to **Ashoka** – a second column, moved by the Mughals, now graces the gates of the fort at Prayagraj.

Chitrakut

The sprawling pilgrimage town of **CHITRAKUT** (also called **Sitapur**) is 128km southwest of Prayagraj, and easily accessible by both train and bus. Together with its twin town of **Karbi**, 8km east (where there are train connections to Prayagraj, Kolkata and Delhi), Chitrakut is a major Vaishnavite pilgrimage centre, like a smaller version of Varanasi, without the hustle. Most of its religious and leisure activity revolves around the charming central **Ramghat**, where boats with electric-blue mattresses and pillows create a pretty picture against a backdrop of ashrams and *ghats* to either side of the narrow, slow-moving river.

Kalinjar

About 88km southwest of Chitrakut, the abandoned star-shaped fortress of **KALINJAR** looks down on the Gangetic valley from the final escarpments of the craggy Vindhya hills, above the town of the same name. Much of the fort has been reclaimed by dry shrubby forest, populated by monkeys; once-grand avenues are now rocky footpaths that wind through the few crumbling yet ornately carved buildings that remain. Kalinjar has no tourist facilities to speak of – most of those who do come are either on day-trips from Chitrakut or Prayagraj, or stay in Banda, which is on major train and bus routes and is connected to Kalinjar by local buses.

Steep steps lead straight up for 3km from Kalinjar village to the fort's main gate, **Alam Darwaza**, but the southern **Panna Gate** has rock carvings depicting seven deer (like the fort's seven gates, these represent the then-known planets). Beneath **Bara Darwaza**, the

"Large Gate", in the artificial cave of Sita Sej, a stone couch dating from the fourth century holds some of Kalinjar's earliest inscriptions. The fort's colossal rambling **battlements** provide sweeping views of the Gangetic plain and the Vindhya hills.

ARRIVAL AND DEPARTURE

AROUND PRAYAGRAJ

Kaushambi Served by direct private buses departing from Leader Road in Prayagraj (see page 272). More reliably, there are buses every fifteen minutes from MG Marg bus stand to Saini (1hr 30min), where you can pick up a local bus, jeep or auto. Better still, get a taxi for the round trip from Prayagraj (around ₹2000 from Varuna Travels or UP Tours).

Chitrakut Buses from Prayagraj's Zero Road bus stand leave half-hourly until 8pm (3hr), continuing to Banda (for Kalinjar; 1hr).

Kalinjar Buses from Prayagraj's Zero Road bus stand, via Chitrakut, serve Banda (every 30min; 5hr), from where you can take a local bus or auto.

Varanasi

The great Hindu city of **VARANASI**, also known as **Banaras** or **Benares**, stretches along the River Ganges, its waterfront dominated by long flights of stone *ghats* where thousands of pilgrims and residents come for their daily ritual ablutions. Known to the devout as **Kashi**, the Luminous – the City of Light, founded by Shiva – Varanasi is one of the oldest living cities in the world. It has maintained its religious life since the sixth century BC in one continuous tradition, in part by remaining outside the mainstream of political activity and historical development of the Subcontinent, and stands at the centre of the Hindu universe, the focus of a religious geography that reaches from the Himalayan cave of Amarnath in Kashmir to India's southern tip at Kanyakumari, Puri to the east, and Dwarka to the west. Located next to a ford on an ancient trade route, Varanasi is among the holiest of all *tirthas* – "crossing places", that allow the devotee access to the divine and enable gods and goddesses to come down to earth. It has attracted pilgrims, seekers, *sannyasins* and students of the Vedas throughout its history, including sages such as Buddha, Mahavira (founder of the Jain faith) and the great Hindu reformer Shankara.

Anyone who dies in Varanasi attains instant *moksha*, or enlightenment. Widows and the elderly come here to live out their final days, finding shelter in temples, assisted by alms from the faithful. Western visitors since the Middle Ages have marvelled at the strangeness of this most alien of Indian cities: the tight mesh of alleys, the religious accoutrements, the host of deities – and the proximity of death.

The ghats

The great riverbanks at Varanasi, built high with eighteenth- and nineteenth-century pavilions and palaces, temples and terraces, are lined by stone steps – the **ghats** – which stretch along the whole waterfront, changing dramatically in appearance with the seasonal fluctuations of the river level. Each of the hundred *ghats*, big and small, is marked by a lingam, and occupies its own special place in the religious geography of the city. Some have

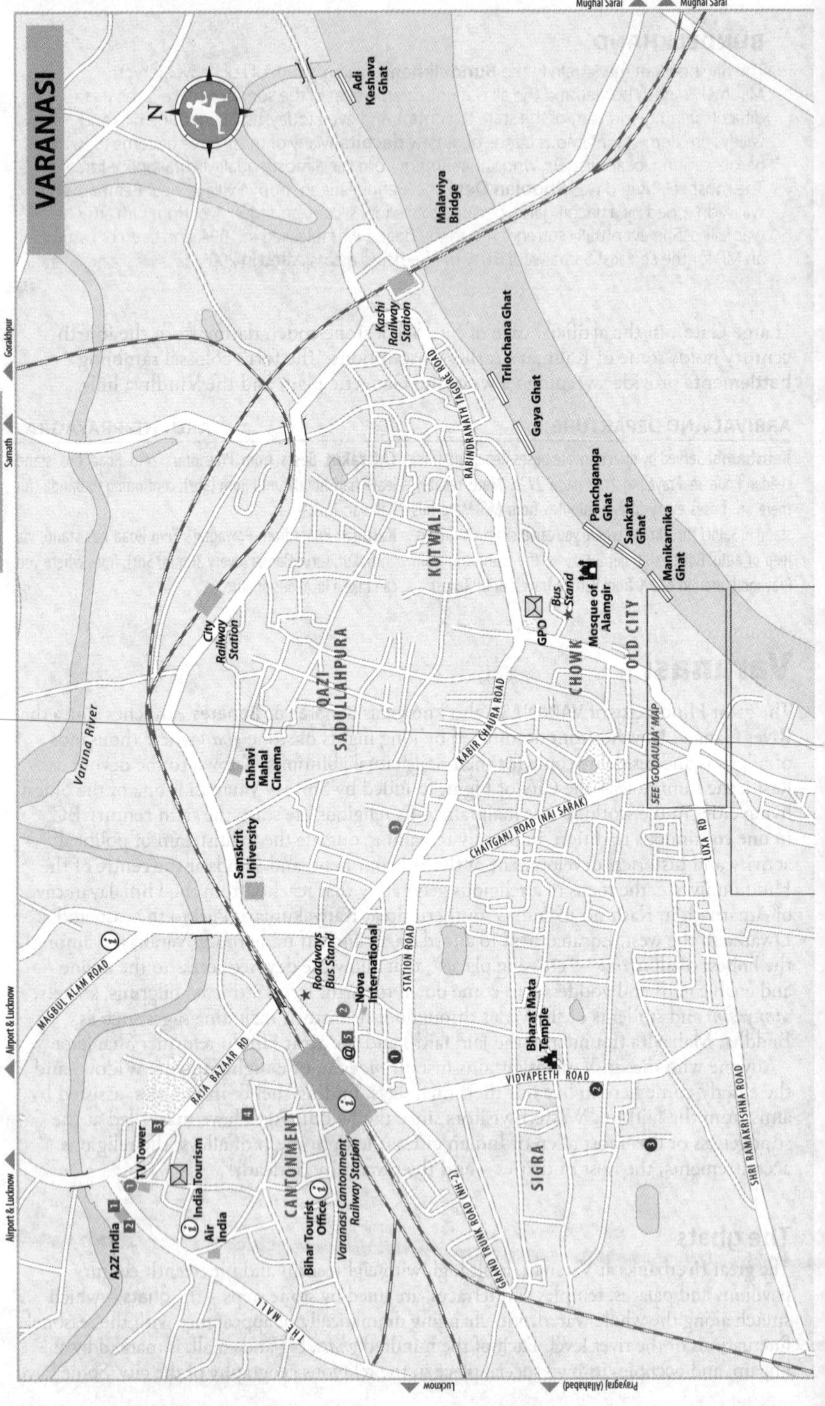

3

VARANASI

N

Mughal Sarai

Gorakhpur

Sarnath

Airport & Lucknow

Airport & Lucknow

Lucknow

Prayagraj (Allahabad)

Adi Keshava Ghat

Malaviya Bridge

Kashi Railway Station

Trilochana Ghat

Gaya Ghat

Panchganga Ghat

Sankata Ghat

Manikarnika Ghat

RABINDRANATH TAGORE ROAD

KOTWALI

City Railway Station

GPO

Bus Stand

Mosque of Alamgir

CHOWK

OLD CITY

QAZI SADULLAHPURA

KABIR CHAURA ROAD

SEE 'GODAULIA' MAP

Chhavi Mahal Cinema

Sanskrit University

Varuna River

CHAITGANJ ROAD (NAI SARAK)

LUKA RD

Roadways Bus Stand

Nova International

STATION ROAD

Bharat Mata Temple

VIDYAPEETH ROAD

MAGBUL ALAM ROAD

RAJA BAZAR RD

SIGRA

SHRI RAMAKRISHNA ROAD

TV Tower

India Tourism

A2Z India

Bihar Tourist Office

Varanasi Cantonment Railway Station

Air India

CANTONMENT

THE MALL

GRAND TRUNK ROAD (NH-2)

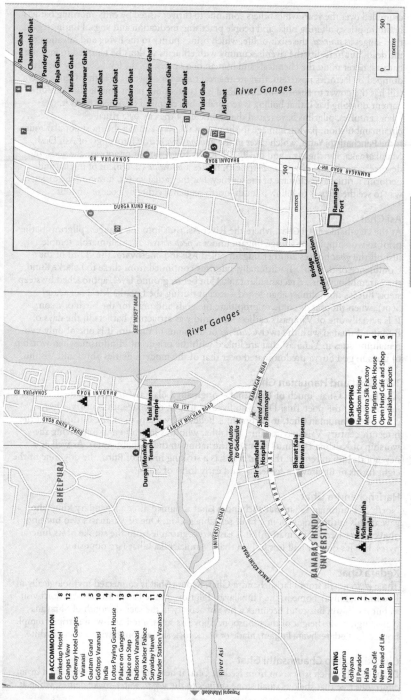

River Ganges

Rana Ghat
Chaumsathi Ghat
Pandey Ghat
Raja Ghat
Narada Ghat
Mansarowar Ghat
Dhobi Ghat
Chauki Ghat
Kedara Ghat
Harishchandra Ghat
Hanuman Ghat
Shivala Ghat
Tulsi Ghat
Asi Ghat

SONAPURA RD

BHADANI ROAD

DURGA KUND ROAD

RAMNAGAR ROAD NH-7

Ramnagar Fort

Bridge (under construction)

River Ganges

SEE 'INSET' MAP

SONAPURA RD

BHADANI ROAD

DURGA KUND ROAD

Tulsi Manas Temple

Durga (Monkey) Temple

ASI RD

SANKAT MOCHAN ROAD

BHELPURA

UNIVERSITY ROAD

Shared Autos to Godaulia

Shared Autos to Ramnagar

RAMNAGAR ROAD

Sir Sundarlal Hospital

Bharat Kala Bhawan Museum

NAISHCHANDRA MARG

New Vishwanatha Temple

BANARAS HINDU UNIVERSITY

PANCH KOSHI ROAD

River Asi

Prayagraj (Allahabad)

500 metres

0   500

■ **ACCOMMODATION**
Bunkedup Hostel	8
Ganges View	12
Gateway Hotel Ganges Varanasi	3
Gautam Grand	5
GoStops Varanasi India	10
Lotus Paying Guest House	4
Palace on Ganges	13
Palace on Step	7
Radisson Varanasi	9
Surya Kaiser Palace	1
Suryalday Haveli	2
Wander Station Varanasi	11
	6

● **SHOPPING**
Handloom House	2
Mehrota Silk Factory	1
Om Pilgrims Book House	4
Open Hand Café and Shop	5
Paraslakshmi Exports	3

● **EATING**
Annapurna	3
Ashiyana	1
El Parador	2
Haifa	7
Kerala Café	4
New Bread of Life	5
Vaatika	6

crumbled over the years while others continue to thrive, visited by early-morning bathers, brahmin priests offering puja, and people practising meditation and yoga. Hindus regard the Ganges as *amrita*, the elixir of life, which brings purity to the living and salvation to the dead, but in reality the river is scummy with effluent, so don't be tempted to join the bathers; never mind the chemicals and human body parts, it's the level of heavy metals, dumped by factories upstream, that are the real cause for concern. Whether Ganga water still has the power to absolve sin if sterilized is a contentious point among the faithful; current thinking has it that boiling is acceptable but chemical treatment ruins it.

For centuries, pilgrims have traced the perimeter of the city by a ritual circumambulation, paying homage to shrines on the way. Among the most popular routes is the **Panchatirthi Yatra**, which takes in the *pancha* (five) *tirthi* (crossings) of Asi, Dash, Manikarnaka, Panchganga, and finally Adi Kesh. To gain merit or appease the gods, the devotee, accompanied by a *panda* (priest), recites a *sankalpa* (statement of intent) and performs a ritual at each stage of the journey. For the casual visitor, however, the easiest way to see the *ghats* is to follow a south–north sequence either by boat or on foot.

Asi Ghat

At the clay-banked **Asi Ghat**, where the River Asi runs into the Ganges, pilgrims bathe prior to worshipping at a huge lingam under a *peepal* tree. A small marble temple just off the *ghat* houses another lingam called **Asisangameshvara**, the "Lord of the Confluence of the Asi". Traditionally, pilgrims continued from these to **Lolarka Kund**, the "Trembling Sun", a rectangular tank 15m below ground level, approached by steep steps, but it's now almost abandoned – except during the Lolarka Mela fair (Aug/Sept), when thousands come to propitiate the gods and pray for the birth of a son. It is actually one of Varanasi's earliest sites, and was attracting bathers in the days of Buddha. Equated with the twelve *adityas* or divisions of the sun, it is one of only two remaining sites in Varanasi that are linked with the origins of Hinduism, when worship of the sun god Surya predominated over that of the modern deities Shiva and Vishnu.

Tulsi Ghat and Hanuman Ghat

North of Asi Ghat, much of **Tulsi Ghat** – originally Lolarka *ghat*, but renamed in honour of the poet Tulsi Das, who lived nearby in the sixteenth century – has crumbled. **Hanuman Ghat**, to its north, is believed by many to be the birthplace of the fifteenth-century Vaishnavite saint, Vallabha, who was instrumental in reviving the worship of Krishna (Vishnu's human incarnation in the Mahabharata). As well as a new south Indian temple, the *ghat* also has a striking image of **Ruru**, the dog, one of the eight forms of **Bhairava**, a ferocious and early form of Shiva.

Harishchandra Ghat

North of Hanuman Ghat, **Harishchandra Ghat** is named after a legendary king who gave up his entire kingdom in a fit of self-abnegation. One of Varanasi's two **burning ghats** (*ghats* used for cremation), it is easily recognizable from the smoke of its funeral pyres, but it's quieter and less full-on than Manikarnika Ghat (see opposite).

Kedara Ghat

Three *ghats* north from Harishchandra Ghat, **Kedara Ghat** is connected mythologically to Kedarnath, Shiva's home in the Himalayas. Pilgrims on the Panchatirthi Yatra don't visit it, but it's always busy and becomes a hive of activity in the sacred month of Shravana (July/Aug), at the height of the monsoon. Above its steps, a red-and-white-striped temple houses the **Kedareshvara lingam**, made of black rock shot through with a vein of white.

Chauki Ghat to Chaumsathi Ghat

Chauki Ghat, which is next on from Kedara Ghat if heading north, is distinguished by an enormous tree that shelters small stone shrines to the *nagas*, water-snake deities, while at the unmistakeable **Dhobi** ("Laundrymen's") **Ghat**, clothes are still rhythmically pulverized in pursuit of purity. Beyond smaller *ghats* such as **Mansarowar**, named after the holy lake in Tibet, and **Narada**, honouring the divine musician and sage, lies **Chaumsathi Ghat**, where impressive stone steps lead up to the small temple of the **Chaumsathi** (64) **Yoginis**. Images of Kali and Durga in its inner sanctum represent a stage in the emergence of the great goddess as a single representation of a number of female divinities. Overlooking the *ghats* here is Peshwa Amrit Rao's majestic sandstone haveli (mansion), built in 1807 and currently used for religious ceremonies and occasionally as an auditorium for concerts.

Dashaswamedh Ghat
Dashaswamedh Ghat is Varanasi's most popular and accessible bathing *ghat*, with rows of *pandas* sitting on wooden platforms under bamboo umbrellas, masseurs plying their trade and boatmen jostling for custom. It's the second and busiest of the five *tirthas* on the Panchatirthi Yatra. Its **Brahmeshvara** lingam is supposed to have been planted by the god Brahma. South of here, a flat-roofed building houses the shrine of **Shitala**, which is likewise extremely popular, even in the rainy season when devotees have to wade to the temple or take a boat. Every night at 6.45pm the pompous *ganga aarti*, Varanasi's most popular blessing to the Ganges, takes place here.

Man Mandir Ghat to Lalita Ghat
Man Mandir Ghat is known primarily for its magnificent eighteenth-century observatory, built for the maharaja of Jaipur and equipped with ornate window casings. Pilgrims pay homage to the important lingam of Someshvara, the lord of the moon, alongside, before crossing **Tripurabhairavi Ghat** to **Mir Ghat** and the **New Vishwanatha Temple**, built by conservative brahmins who claimed that the main Vishwanatha lingam was rendered impure when Harijans (Untouchables) entered the sanctum in 1956. At Mir Ghat, the **Dharma Kupa**, the Well of Dharma, is surrounded by subsidiary shrines and the lingam of **Dharmesha**, where it is said that Yama, the Lord of Death, obtained his jurisdiction over all the dead of the world – except here in Varanasi.

To the north is **Lalita Ghat**, renowned for its **Ganga Keshava** shrine to Vishnu and the **Nepali Temple** (daily 4am–noon & 3–9pm; ₹20), a Kathmandu-style wooden structure which houses an image of **Pashupateshvara** – Shiva's manifestation at Pashupatinath, in the Kathmandu Valley – and sporting a small selection of erotic carvings.

Manikarnika Ghat
North of Lalita lies Varanasi's pre-eminent cremation ground, **Manikarnika Ghat**. Such grounds are usually held to be inauspicious, and located on the fringes of cities, but the entire city of Shiva is regarded as **Mahashamshana**, the "Great Cremation Ground", for the corpse of the entire universe. The *ghat* is perpetually crowded with funeral parties, as well as the **Doms**, its *dalit* guardians, busy and preoccupied with facilitating final release for those lucky enough to pass away here. Seeing bodies being cremated so publicly has always exerted a great fascination for visitors to the city, but photography is strictly taboo; even having a camera visible may be construed as intent, and provoke hostility. Touts and con merchants descend on tourists at the *ghat* explaining the finer metaphysical points of transmutation ("cremation is education") before subtly shifting to the practicalities of how much wood is needed to burn one body, the never-ending cycle of inflation and would you like to give a donation. The amounts written down in their "ledgers" are unbelievable.

Lying at the centre of the five *tirthas*, Manikarnika Ghat symbolizes both creation and destruction, epitomized by the juxtaposition of the sacred well of **Manikarnika Kund**, said to have been dug by Vishnu at the time of creation, and the hot, sandy ash-infused soil of cremation grounds where time comes to an end. In Hindu mythology, Manikarnika Kund predates the arrival of the Ganga and has its source deep in the Himalayas. Vishnu carved the *kund* (water tank) with his discus, and filled it with perspiration from his exertions in creating the world at the behest of Shiva. When Shiva quivered with delight,

---

BOAT TRIPS ON THE GANGES

All along the *ghats*, and especially at the main ones such as Dashaswamedh, the prices of **boat** (*bajra*) **rental** are highly inflated, with local boatmen under pressure from touts to fleece tourists and pilgrims. Renting a boat to catch the dawn in particular can be a bit of a free-for-all, and haggling is essential. There used to be an official rate, which everyone ignored, but it's now down to your bargaining skills. You'll get a far better rate (₹300/hr for a one- or two-person boat, ₹100/hr per person on a shared boat) if you walk up to Mir Ghat near the *Alka* hotel, where punters are thinner on the ground. Some small hotels and hostels offer special deals to their guests .

---

his earring fell into this pool, which as Manikarnika – "Jewelled Earring" – became the first *tirtha* in the world. Every year, after the floodwaters of the river have receded to leave the pool caked in alluvial deposits, the *kund* is re-dug. Its surroundings are cleaned and painted with bright folk art depicting the presiding goddess, **Manikarni Devi**.

Scindia Ghat

Bordering Manikarnika to the north is the picturesque **Scindia Ghat**, its tilted Shiva temple lying partially submerged in the river, after falling in as a result of the sheer weight of the *ghat*'s construction in the mid-nineteenth century. Above the *ghat*, several of Varanasi's most influential shrines are hidden within the tight maze of alleyways of the area known as **Siddha Kshetra** (the "Field of Fulfilment").

Panchganga Ghat to Adi Keshava Ghat

North of Lakshmanbala Ghat, with its commanding views of the river, lies one of the most dramatic – and contentious – *ghats*, **Panchganga**, dominated by Varanasi's largest riverside building, the great **Mosque of Alamgir**, known locally as Beni Madhav-ka-Darera. With its minarets now much shortened, the mosque stands on the ruins of the Bindu Madhava, a Vishnu temple that extended from Panchganga to Rama Ghat before it was destroyed by Aurangzeb and replaced with the mosque. Panchganga also bears testimony to more favourable Hindu–Muslim relations, being the site of the initiation of the medieval saint of the Sufi tradition, Kabir, the son of a humble Muslim weaver who is venerated by Hindus and Muslims alike. Along the riverfront lies a curious array of three-sided cells, submerged during the rainy season, some with lingams, others with images of Vishnu, and some empty and used for meditation or yoga. Above **Trilochana Ghat**, further north, is the holy ancient lingam of the three (*tri*)-eyed (*lochana*) Shiva. Beyond it, the river bypasses some of Varanasi's oldest precincts, now predominantly Muslim in character; the *ghats* themselves gradually become less impressive and are usually of the *kaccha* (clay-banked) variety. At **Adi Keshava Ghat** (the "Original Vishnu"), on the outskirts of the city, the Varuna River flows into the Ganga. Unapproachable during the rainy season, when it is completely submerged, the *ghat* marks the place where Vishnu supposedly landed as an emissary of Shiva, and stands on the original site of the city before it spread southwards. Around Adi Keshava are a number of Ganesha shrines.

The Old City

At the heart of Varanasi, between Dashaswamedh Ghat and Godaulia to the south and west and Manikarnika Ghat on the river to the north, lies the maze of ramshackle alleys that comprise the **Old City**, or Vishwanatha Khanda. The whole area buzzes with the activity of pilgrims, *pandas* and stalls selling offerings to the faithful, and there are lingams and shrines tucked into every corner. If you get lost just head for the river.

The Golden Temple and around

Accessed from Vishwanatha Mandir Lane to the north of Vishwanatha Gali, but closed to non-Hindus, the **Vishwanatha Mandir** temple complex, also called Visheshwara (the "Lord

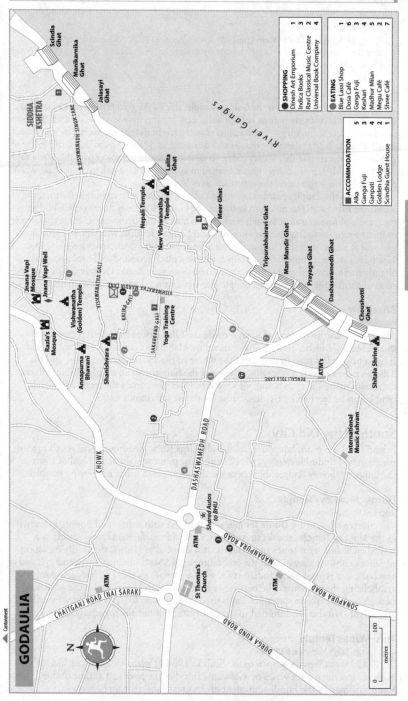

GODAULIA

● SHOPPING
Dinesh Art Emporium	1
Indica Books	3
Ravi Classical Music Centre	2
Universal Book Company	4

■ EATING
Blue Lassi Shop	1
Dosa Café	6
Ganga Fuji	3
Keshari	4
Madhur Milan	5
Megu Café	2
Shree Café	7

■ ACCOMMODATION
Alka	5
Ganga Fuji	3
Ganpati	4
Golden Lodge	2
Scindhia Guest House	1

> ### RAM LILA
>
> Varanasi is renowned for its **Ram Lila**, held during Dussehra (Oct), during which episodes from the Ramayana are re-enacted throughout the city and the maharaja sponsors three weeks of elaborate celebrations.

of All"), is popularly known as the **Golden Temple**, due to the gold plating on its massive spire. Because it is largely hidden behind walls, non-Hindus have to make do with glimpses of it from adjacent buildings. Vishwanatha's history has been fraught. Sacked by successive Muslim rulers, it was repeatedly rebuilt and destroyed; in 1785, Queen Ahilyabai Holkar of Indore built the temple that stands today. Its simple white domes tower over the **Jnana Vapi** ("Wisdom Well"), immediately north, housed in an open-arcaded hall built in 1828, where Shiva cooled his lingam after the construction of Vishwanatha.

Adjacent to the temple, guarded by armed police to protect it from Hindu fanatics, stands the **Jnana Vapi Mosque**, also known as the Great Mosque of Aurangzeb. Close by, the temple of **Annapurna Bhavani** is dedicated to Shakti, the divine female energy. Manifest in many forms, including the awesome Kali and Durga with their weapons and gruesome garlands of skulls, she's seen here as the provider of sustenance and carries a cooking pot. Nearby is a stunning image, faced in silver against a black surround, of **Shani** or Saturn. Slightly north, across the main road, the thirteenth-century **Razia's Mosque** stands atop the ruins of a still earlier Vishwanatha temple that was destroyed under the Sultanate.

Bharat Mata
Vidyapeeth Rd

About 3km northwest of Godaulia, outside the Old City, the modern temple of **Bharat Mata** ("Mother India"), inaugurated by Mahatma Gandhi, is unusual in that it has a huge relief map in marble of the whole of the Indian Subcontinent and the Tibetan plateau, with mountains, rivers and the holy *tirthas* all clearly visible. Pilgrims circumambulate the map before viewing it in its entirety from the second floor. The temple can be reached by rickshaw from Godaulia for around ₹100.

South of the Old City

Inland from the *ghats*, Sonapura Road and Durga Kund Road both lead south towards the Banaras Hindu University (BHU). The most popular sight at this end of town is the famous **Monkey Temple**, but there are also a couple of other interesting temples.

Durga (Monkey) Temple
Durga Kund Rd • Daily 4am–11pm

The nineteenth-century **Durga Temple** – stained red with ochre, and popularly known as the **Monkey Temple**, thanks to its aggressive and irritable monkeys – stands in a walled enclosure 4km south of Godaulia. It is devoted to Durga, the terrifying aspect of Shiva's consort, Parvati, and the embodiment of **Shakti** (divine female energy), and was built in a typical north Indian style, with an ornate *shikhara* in five segments, symbolizing the elements. The best views are from across Durga *kund*, the adjoining tank. A forked stake in the courtyard is used during some festivals to behead sacrificial goats. Non-Hindus are admitted to the courtyard, but not the inner sanctum.

Tulsi Manas Temple
Durga Kund Rd • Daily 5.30am–noon & 3.30–9pm

The **Tulsi Manas Temple** is open to all. Built in 1964 of white-streaked marble, its walls are inscribed with verses by Goswami Tulsidas, the poet and author of the Ramcharitmanas, the Hindi equivalent of the great Sanskrit epic Ramayana.

Bharat Kala Bhawan Museum

BHU campus • Mon–Sat 10.30am–4.30pm • ₹150 (₹10)

In the campus of the BHU, the **Bharat Kala Bhawan Museum** has a fabulous collection of miniature paintings, sculpture, contemporary art and bronzes. A gallery dedicated to the city of Varanasi, with a stunning nineteenth-century map, has a display of the recent Raj Ghat excavations and old etchings of the city. Along with Buddhist and Hindu sculpture and Mughal glass, further galleries are devoted to foreign artists who found inspiration in India, such as Nicholas Roerich and Alice Boner; the Bengali renaissance painter Jamini Roy, so influenced by folk art, is also well represented.

New Vishwanatha Temple

BHU campus • Daily 4am–noon & 1–9pm

The BHU campus is home to the **New Vishwanatha Temple**, distinguished by its lofty white-marble spire. The temple was the brainchild of Pandit Malaviya, founder of the BHU and a great believer in an egalitarian and casteless Hindu revival. It was financed by the Birlas, a wealthy Marwari industrial family. Although supposedly modelled on an original temple destroyed by Aurangzeb, the building displays characteristics of the new wave of temple architecture, amalgamating influences from various parts of India with a garish interior.

Ramnagar Fort

Ramnagar (south bank of the river) • Museum Daily 10am–5pm • ₹150 (₹20)

South of the *ghats*, on the opposite side of the river, the residence of the maharaja of Varanasi, **Ramnagar Fort** looks down upon the Ganges. The best views of the fortifications – especially impressive in late afternoon – are to be had from the bridge to the fort, which is reached by a road heading south from the BHU area. The fort can also be reached by chartering a boat from Dashaswamedh Ghat.

Inside, the fort bears testimony to the wealth of the maharaja and his continuing influence. A dusty and poorly kept **museum** provides glimpses of a decadent past: horse-drawn carriages, old motor cars, palanquins, ornate gilded and silver *howdahs* (elephant seats), hookahs, costumes and old silk in a sorry state are all part of the collection, along with an armoury, some minute ivory carvings, an astronomical clock and hunting trophies.

ARRIVAL AND DEPARTURE   VARANASI

By plane Babatpur airport is 22km northwest of the city (☎ 0542 262 2090). From Cantonment station, a prepaid taxi costs ₹650; a prepaid auto is ₹275 (or around ₹350 from town if you don't prepay). Uber and Ola may save you some rupees. Allow at least 90min from the Old City. Destinations: Delhi (10–11 daily with Air India, SpiceJet and IndiGo; 1hr 30min–1hr 45min); Mumbai (4 daily with IndiGo, Air India and SpiceJet; 2hr 20min).

By train Varanasi Cantonment (officially, Varanasi Junction) is the most conveniently located station, with prepaid auto and taxi booths, and a foreign tourists' reservations office (Mon–Sat 8am–8pm, Sun 8am–2pm). Many trains on the main east–west Delhi–Kolkata line bypass Varanasi but stop at Mughal Sarai, 17km east of town (₹300–400 by auto) and around 45min away by road or rail. There are retiring rooms at Mughal Sarai station and local buses or shared *tempos* to Varanasi (in Varanasi, pick them up at Roadways Bus Stand,

or directly across GT Rd). Trains from the north and east may stop at Varanasi City station before they reach Cantonment, but transport into town from there is sparser.

By bus Most buses terminate a couple of hundred metres east of the railway station along the main Grand Trunk Rd and at the Roadways Bus Stand (☎ 0542 220 3476). Buses from Nepal are met by the rickshaw mafia (see box above); going the other way, you have to change buses at the border anyway so there's no point buying a through ticket to Kathmandu – it's better to go to Sonauli, cross the border and buy an onward ticket in Nepal. For Prayagraj, good and regular buses from Varanasi make road a better option than rail. For Bihar on the other hand, buses are few and far between (with none at all to Patna), and road conditions not great, so rail is your best bet. Destinations PRayagraj (every 15min; 3hr 30min); Gorakhpur (hourly 5.30am–8.30pm; 7hr); Sonauli (hourly 5.30am–8.30pm; 10hr).

GETTING AROUND

By rickshaw Cycle rickshaws are the easiest way to get around Varanasi, and often defy death and traffic jams by

cycling up the wrong side of the road; a ride from Godaulia to Cantonment railway station costs around ₹60. Auto-

3

RECOMMENDED TRAINS FROM VARANASI

The trains below are recommended as the fastest and/or most convenient for specific cities. All those listed here run daily.

Destination	Name	No.	From	Departs	Arrives
Agra Fort	Marudhar Express	#14853/63/65	VJ	6.15pm	8.10am+ (5.25pm M, W & Sa)
	Howrah–Jodhpur Exp	#12307	MS	2.40am	3pm
Dehradun	Doon Express	#13009	VJ	10.30am	7.25am+
Delhi (ND)	Shiv Ganga Express	#12559	VJ	7.30pm	8.10am+
	Rajdhani Express*	#12309	MS	10.35pm	7.40am+
Gaya	Purshottam Express	#12802	MS	10.25am	1.35pm
Jaipur	Sealdah–Ajmer Exp	#12987	MS	9.50am	11.55pm
	Marudhar Express	#14853/63/65	VJ	6.15pm	12.05pm+ (5.25pm M, W & Sa)
Khajuraho	Khajuraho Link Exp	#21108	VJ	5.45pm	5.15am+ (M, W, Sa)
Kolkata (H)	Vibhuti Express	#12344	VJ	6.10pm	7.30am+
	Kalka Mail	#12312	MS	8.25pm	7.55am+
Mumbai (CST)	Mahanagri Express	#11094	VJ	11.20am	2.15pm+
Patna	Magadh Express	#12402	MS	7.55am	11.30am
	Brahmputra Mail	#14056	MS	11.45am	2.45pm
Ramnagar	Dehradun Express	#14265	VJ	8.25am	6.25am+
Satna	Lokmanyatilak Express	#11062/66	VJ	11.30pm	6.15am+

VJ: Varanasi Junction; MS: Mughal Sarai; ND: New Delhi station; H: Howrah station; *a/c only; + next day

rickshaws should be faster, but due to the volume of traffic they rarely are for short rides across town. Godaulia to the railway station should cost ₹90.

Car rental UP Tours at the Tourist Bungalow in Parade Kothi (☎ 0542 220 8545) can arrange car rental at around ₹3000/day (plus parking fees) for a car with driver within a 200km radius of Varanasi.

Motorcycles Mechanics and workshops specializing in Enfields are clustered in the Jagatganj area, near the Sanskrit University.

INFORMATION AND TOURS

Tourist information The main UP Tourism office is at Urban Haat, Sanskritik Sankul (Mon–Sat 10am–5pm; ☎ 0542 250 5033, ✉ up_tourism_varanasi@yahoo.co.in), though their tourist information counter (daily 7am–7pm; ☎ 0542 250 6670) inside the Cantonment railway station is their main office for giving out information – the boss, Uma Shankar, is extremely helpful and is backed up by a force of tourist police (same phone number) to defend tourists from crime. The India Tourism office is in the Cantonment district, away from the Old City and ghats, just off The Mall on Stranger Rd (Mon–Fri 9am–5.30pm, Sat 9am–2pm; ☎ 0542 250 1784). It gives out information on the whole of India, but staff can assist with booking

accommodation in Varanasi. They also maintain a booth at the airport (in principle open the same hours). The shabby Bihar Government tourist office at 3rd Floor, Hans Sarowar, Englishia Lane, Jawaharlal Nehru Market, Cantonment (☎ 0542 222 3821), is useful if you're heading east into that state. The local branch of the National Informatics Centre has some interesting information about Varanasi on their website at ⊕ varanasi.nic.in.

Travel agencies General travel agencies include the friendly Nova International, S-21/119C Shubhash Nagar, off Parade Kothi near the UP Tourist Bungalow (☎ 0542 220 8803), and A2Z India, S-20/51-5 Varunapul, The Mall (by Radisson hotel; ☎ 0542 250 0549).

ACCOMMODATION

Most of Varanasi's better and more expensive hotels lie on its peripheries, though to experience the full ambience of the city, stay close to the ghats and the lanes of the **Old City**, where top-floor rooms, with views and more light,

are generally the best. If you want to stay with a local family, ask at UP Tourism's station office about their **paying guesthouse** scheme.

GODAULIA

Alka D-3/23 Mir Ghat ☎0542 240 1681, ⓦhotelalkavns. com; map p.281. You'll need to book well ahead in high season (Oct–March), but this is a good mid-range riverside choice, with a variety of well-maintained quality rooms, plus a terrace and a pleasant little lawn overlooking the river, and Keralan ayurvedic spa treatments on hand. ₹900

Ganga Fuji D-7/21 Sakarkand Gali ☎0542 239 7444, ⓦgangafujihomevaranasi.com; map p.281. Well-run family guesthouse near the Golden Temple, with a range of tastefully decorated rooms, some with a/c (₹1550), and dorms. Scrupulously clean (though it's down a rather dirty alley) and the bathrooms are immaculate. Dorms ₹399; doubles ₹770

Ganpati D-3/24 Mir Ghat ☎0542 239 0057 or 9, ⓦganpatiguesthouse.com; map p.281. Rooms here – ideally booked in advance – overlook the Ganges or are arranged around a courtyard, and there's a restaurant and a sociable balcony overlooking the river. The 10am check-out time is a bit inconvenient, and you pay ₹800 extra for river views. ₹1699

Golden Lodge D-8/35 Kalika Gali, near Shanishvara ☎0542 239 8788, ⓔgoldenvaranasi@gmail.com; map p.281. Friendly staff, a range of attached and non-attached double rooms (plus some non-attached singles), and a pleasant roof terrace combine to make this a popular Old City budget choice. ₹400

Scindhia Guest House Manikarnika Ghat ☎0542 242 0319; map p.281. A range of rooms at this basic guesthouse right by the burning *ghats*, from non-attached singles (₹600) to super-deluxe a/c rooms with a balcony and river view (₹8000). The roof-top restaurant has good river views, and there's a higher top terrace with even better ones. ₹900

SOUTH OF GODAULIA, NEAR THE RIVER

Bunkedup Hostel D 24/12 Ward Dasashwamedh Pandey Ghat ☎0542 245 0508, ⓦbunkeduphostels. com; map p.276. The Varanasi franchise of this flash packer hostel offers very clean en-suite mixed and female dorms. There are privacy curtains, lockers, reading lights and two private doubles (₹2000) that are just a tad too small for the price. Breakfast is included and served on the social rooftop restaurant, from where you can see stunning Ganges views. They also run sunrise (₹200) and sunset (₹250) boat trips, which are a steal. ₹400

★ **Ganges View** Asi Ghat ☎0542 2313218, ⓦhotel gangesview.co.in; map p.276.In a lovely old house hung with paintings, the rooms are small but taste-fully and stylishly decorated (those on the upper storey have the best views, but cost rather more at ₹7000), and there's a wonderful big veranda looking out onto the river. Breakfast is included. ₹4500

Lotus Paying Guest House D32/141A Bangali Tola ☎0542 245 0095, ⓔlotuspayingguethouse@gmail. com; map p.276. Very clean budget guesthouse with spacious non-attached rooms, well-kept shared bathrooms and a friendly vibe, all within 3min walk from Godaulia and the main *ghat*. ₹600

Palace on Ganges B-1/158 Asi Ghat ☎0542 231 4304; map p.276. Luxury hotel on the Ganges, with 42 individually decorated rooms representing the states of India – the Gujarati room is particularly colourful. Facilities include central a/c, TV, minibar, tour desk and rooftop restaurant with live music nightly. Breakfast is included . ₹7000

Palace on Steps D-21/11 Rana Ghat ☎0542 245 0970, ⓦdwivedihotels.com.com; map p.276. Originally two hotels (separated by a big banyan tree), now combined to make one, in a building of which parts date back some three hundred years. There's a wide range of clean, comfortable rooms; the best include a dome turret room (#205 at ₹10,000), and some with balconies looking straight down onto the *ghats*. Breakfast is included. ₹2300

Suryaiday Haveli B-4/25 Shivala Ghat Road, Shivala Ghat ☎ 7800 490 390, ⓦsuryaidayhaveli.com; map p. 276. This *Amritara Resort* boasts fourteen deluxe rooms set around an inner courtyard renovated that once formed part of the residence of the Royal Family of Nepal. Packages include a complimentary arrival boat transfer from Assi

---

TOUT DODGING

Like Agra and Delhi, Varanasi is rife with **touts**, and you'll have to be careful of scams, especially on arrival. Many hotels pay a **commission** of up to eighty percent of the room rate (for every day you stay) to whoever takes you to the door – a cost that is passed on to you.

All English-speaking rickshaw drivers are part of this racket, and avoiding it takes persistence. At Cantonment railway station, you can phone your hotel of choice, who will send someone to pick you up (the tourist office will even do this for you). If you want to make your own way to the hotels of the old town, walk away from the bus or railway station to the main road, find a non-English-speaking cycle rickshaw driver, and ask to be taken to Godaulia, 3km southeast – a ₹60 ride. Rickshaws are unable to penetrate the maze of lanes around Vishwanatha Temple and are banned from the central part of Godaulia. Again, you can call a hotel from here to come and find you – if you attempt to get to a hotel yourself, touts may try to attach themselves and claim a commission on arrival. When trying to find hotels in the old town that don't pay commission to touts, it's common to hear that they have "burned down" or "flooded".

3

WHAT'S IN A NAME?

The **Mehrotra Silk Factory** (see page 288) is known for its integrity and the quality of its products, so a number of soundalike firms with names like Malhotra, Muhotra and Malahotra have sprung up to trap the unwary, and if you ask any rickshaw-wala to take you to the Mehrotra Silk Factory, they'll almost certainly take you to one of these spurious imitators, which pay them commission and are known for ripping off their customers. Similarly, popular lodges have faced competition from fly-by-night lookalike hotels that copy their names and pay commission to rickshaw-walas who divert customers to them (the rickshaw-walas who hustle you in the street are often intent on running some commission scam on you). So beware: if taking a rickshaw to your hotel, make sure it really is the one you want; better still, don't name the hotel and just ask for a nearby location such as Godaulia, and always hail a rickshaw yourself rather than taking one that offers you a ride. And never, ever, ask a rickshaw-wala to take you to a particular shop; Mehrotra Silk Factory is one of several stores and hotels that offer a free pick-up service for this very reason.

Ghat, one evening cruise to Dashaswamedh Ghat for the *Ganga Aarti*, and live traditional music shows. Breakfast and morning yoga classes included. ₹15,500

★ **Wander Station Varanasi** D 21/24 Rana Mahal Ghat ☎ 8881 114 118, ☻ wanderstationhostel.com; map p.276. Friendly and maniacally clean — shoes off at the door — hostel in an airy, well-managed building right off a peaceful *ghat*. The fully a/c dorms and doubles all have bathrooms and cool murals by local art students, together with privacy curtains, plush beds, reading lights, mini-fans and lockers. There's a nice rooftop restaurant serving free chai at 5pm, cheap boat rides, and a hearty breakfast (included) consisting of muesli, eggs, coffee and fresh fruits. Dorms ₹399; doubles ₹ ₹1200

CANTONMENT AND AROUND

Gateway Hotel Ganges Varanasi Nadesar Palace Grounds, Raja Bazaar Rd, ☎ 0542 666 0001, ☻ gateway.tajhotels. com/en-in/ganges-varanasi/; map p.276. The poshest *gaff* in town, set in vast grounds (good for birdwatching, especially early in the morning), with stately rooms, fine dining, a pool and fitness centre. Breakfast included. ₹21,000

Gautam Grand Parade Kothi ☎ 0542 220 8288, ☻ hotelgautamgrand@yahoo.co.in; map p.276. Good-value modern hotel near the station; the rooms (some a/c) are not huge, but they're reasonably well-kept, each with a balcony. There's also 24hr room service and the staff are eager to please. ₹300

GoStops Varanasi B 20/47 A-2, Vijayanagaram Colony, Bhelupur ☎ 742 888 2828, ☻ gostops.com/hostels/

hostels-varanasi; map p. 276. This friendly hostel is a 20min walk from the *ghats*, but has cheap and clean fourteen-bed dorms, with shared bathrooms that are somewhat inconveniently located on the roof, where one can also stay in one-man tents (₹199). The six (₹399) and eight-bed (₹499) en-suite dorms, together with the few private doubles, are better value. There's also a communal kitchen, city walks (some free, but not all), and a TV room with a library of movies. Breakfast is included. Dorm ₹299; doubles ₹2000

India 59 Patel Nagar ☎ 0542 250 7593, ☻ theindiahotel. com; map p.276. A three-star hotel that makes a pretty good attempt at being stylish. The rooms are carpeted, with attached bathrooms and a/c; and there's a health and fitness centre, a rooftop bar, basement lounge bar and a restaurant. Breakfast included. ₹4800

Radisson Varanasi The Mall ☎ 0542 250 1515 or 1800 1800 333, ☻ radisson.com/varanasiin; map p.276. One of Varanasi's best-value luxury places, with classy and well-appointed rooms, stylish but not huge, plus a swimming pool, free wi-fi, two restaurants, a bar and a coffee lounge. Large buffet breakfast included. ₹9000

Surya Kaiser Palace S-20/51, A5 The Mall ☎ 0542 250 8465, ☻ hotelsuryavns.com; map p.276. Well-run, comfortable and relaxing heritage property built in 1818 by Nepal's King Kaiser, arranged around a small lawn that doubles up as an alfresco restaurant. Rooms are small but well kept, with modern bathrooms, and many have balconies. Facilities include a pool (₹300 for non-guests), a decent restaurant and a bar. Breakfast is ₹450 extra. ₹3000

EATING

Most Old City **restaurants** are vegetarian and alcohol-free, but the Cantonment is less constrained, and some hotels have bars. Stomach disorders are common in Varanasi, so stick to bottled or treated water and be careful when choosing where you eat. After an early morning boat trip, try the traditional snack of *kachori*, savoury deep-fried pastry bread sold in the Old City next to the *ghats* — but avoid the chai stalls here, as the cups are often washed in river water.

GODAULIA

Blue Lassi Shop CK-12/1 Kachowri Gali Chowk ☎ 0542 240 1127; map p.281. Hole-in-the-wall shop whipping up excellent — yet overpriced — lassis (₹50–130) from plain, sweet or salted, through all kinds of fresh fruit varieties to a saffron lassi with dried fruits and nuts, mixed while you watch and served in clay pots. Right next door, ultra-basic Real Lassi dishes up equally delicious plain lassis for less than the price. Daily 9am–10pm (earlier if the curd runs out).

Dosa Café D-15/49 Manmandir, off Dashaswamedh Rd ☎ 9026 884 641; map p.281. Popular with both locals and foreigners, this spot dishes up the most divine semolina in all its most obvious, and frankly downright surprising – think chocolate – iterations. 10am–9.00pm, closed Wed.

★ **Ganga Fuji** D-5/8 Kalika Gali, Dashaswamedh ☎ 98396 14340; map p.281. Family-style home cooking, with live classical music from 7.30pm and a friendly host who guides diners through the menu. There are Chinese, Japanese and Continental options, but the north Indian dishes are the best, veg or non-veg, lightly spiced for the benefit of European tourists. A biryani goes for ₹120 veg, ₹240 with chicken. Daily 7.30am–10pm.

Keshari D-14/8, Teri Neem, off Dashaswamedh Rd ☎0542 240 1472; map p.281. The menu lists a huge variety of veg curries, "all items available". The *paneer* tomato (₹140) and the mushroom masala (₹180) are particular favourites, but every dish is delicious. Daily 9am–10.30pm.

Madhur Milan Dashaswamedh Rd, just past Vishwanatha Lane ☎ 95650 63977; map p.281. Cheap and very popular café, great for dosas, sweets, *kachoris* and samosas (₹10). Thalis ₹60–90. Daily 6.30am–11pm.

Megu Café D-8/1 Kalika Gali ☎ 92365 19262; map p.281. Down the alley leading to the *Golden Lodge* , this small place run by a Japanese-Indian couple (shoes off at the door), serves a short menu of Japanese treats including veg sushi rolls (₹150), veg tempura (₹150) and ginger chicken (₹160). Mon–Sat 10am–2.30pm & 5.30–8pm.

Shree Café D-15/2 Manmandir, off Dashaswamedh Rd ☎98391 98866; map p.281. Tiny tourist-oriented veg restaurant with an attractive restaurant full of beautiful black-and-white pictures of Varanasi. It's perfect to take a break with dosas (₹60), thalis (₹140), a small Mediterranean/Lebanese selection, or well-prepared Western comfort foods such as muesli (₹90) and pancakes – the coconut and nutella (₹200) is especially delicious. Daily 9am–10pm.

THE REST OF THE TOWN

Annapurna J-12/16A Ramkatora ☎0542 045 0955, map p.276. Gleaming multi-cuisine restaurant serving Continental, Subcontinental and Chinese veg food (thali ₹115–190); also does home delivery, and even delivers thalis at two hours' notice to any train passing through Varanasi (give train name and number, plus coach and seat number). Daily 9am–10.30pm.

Ashiyana Major Singh Place, Lt Rohan Marg, Cantonment ☎0542 250 3764; map p.276. Chinese and Indian meals, snacks and drinks served in an a/c lounge or on a rather noisy lawn. Try the chicken *dopiaza* (₹130), or chicken tikka masala (₹200). Daily 10.30am–10pm.

El Parador 17/331 Maldahia Rd (off Parade Kothi) ☎98394 33861; map p.276. Remarkable restaurant serving outstanding Mexican, Italian, Greek and French cuisine (including a lot of non-Indian vegetarian options) in a bistro atmosphere. You can get anything from a vegetarian moussaka (₹399) to a very non-veg filet mignon (₹599). All their pasta is homemade, and they have a bakery for bread and cakes, free wi-fi, and offer packed meals too. Daily 8am–10pm.

Haifa B-1/107 Asi Rd ☎0542 231 2960; map p.276. Laidback place serving approximations of Middle Eastern dishes – including hummus or *baba ghanouj* and pitta (₹130) – as well as the more usual Indian fare. The "Middle Eastern thali" (a selection of meze with pitta) is a great deal at ₹200. Daily 8am–10pm.

Kerala Café Durga Kund Rd, Bhelpura Thana ☎0542 227 5105; map p.276. A very popular south Indian restaurant with good snacks (dosas, *vadas*, *uttapams* and the like – a masala dosa will set you back ₹50) and there's *sambhar* rice or curd rice for ₹70. Daily 8am–10.15pm.

New Bread of Life B-3/322 Sonapura Rd ☎0542 227 5012; map p.276. Bakery providing brown bread, cinnamon rolls (₹70) and confectionery, with a small, clean restaurant serving Indian, Western and Chinese food, including chicken stroganoff and rice (₹250). Profits go to charity, but service is slow. Daily 7am–10pm.

★ **Vaatika** Asi Ghat ☎0542 801 9477, ⊕ pizzeria vaatika.in; map p.276. A leafy terrace right on the *ghat*, serving good pizza (₹230–400) and pasta (₹300–400), not to mention wonderful apple pies (₹100), plus espressos (₹70), freshly made juices and salads (all vegetables sterilized in permanganate, all water boiled and filtered). Daily 7.30am–10pm.

SHOPPING

Hustlers and rickshaw drivers are always keen to drag tourists into commission-paying stores, but avoiding those, **shopping in Varanasi** can be great, and it's worth seeking out the city's rich silk-weaving and brasswork. The best **areas to browse** are the Thatheri Bazaar (for brass), or Jnana Vapi and the Vishwanatha Gali in Godaulia with its Temple Bazaar (for silk brocade and jewellery). And of course, never go shopping with a guide, official or not, nor ask any guide or rickshaw-wala to take you to any shop.

CRAFTS

Dinesh Art Emporium D-5/5 Saraswati Phatak (a few doors from Golden Temple post office) ☎93361 50159; map p.281. Batik T-shirts, wall hangings and cushion covers, which they make themselves upstairs (if you're interested, they'll take you up for a look). Daily 10am–8pm.

Handloom House D-64/132K Sigra (off Vidyapeeth Rd) ☎0542 222 1742, ⊕ handloomhouse.in; map p.276. This government-run emporium offers fixed prices and assured quality on silk, cotton, saris, shirts, sheets and cushion covers. Mon–Sat 10am–8pm, Sun 11am–6pm.

Open Hand Café and Shop B-1/128-3 Dumraun Bagh Colony, Asi ⊕0542 236 9751, ⓦopenhand.in; map p.276. Near *Haifa* restaurant, this community-run project sells bed linen, clothes, bags and cards and it doubles up as a café, so you can enjoy filter coffee and chocolate cake while you shop. Mon–Sat 7.30am–8.30pm, Sun 7am–8pm.

SILK

Sales pitches tend to become most aggressive when it comes to silk. You need to be wary of the hard sell, and also to be aware that well-known reputable firms spawn crooked imitators using the same names to fool tourists.

3

★**Mehrotra Silk Factory** SC-21/72 Englishia Lane, off Station Rd near the railway station ⊕0542 220 0189, ⓦmehrotrasilk.in; map p.276. Highly recommended, and will happily run you up a shirt and deliver it to your hotel, as well as selling ready-made scarves, shawls and bed sheets at very good prices; they also have a branch at K-4/8A Lalghat, and offer free hotel or station pick-ups for customers, which is worth taking up (this shop is particularly plagued by spurious imitators, so carefully check the exact spelling of the shop name before entering, and on no account ask a rickshaw-wala or guide to bring you here, as they will almost certainly take you to a commission-paying and usually crooked imitator instead; see page 286). Daily 10am–8pm.

Paraslakshmi Exports D-61/16, Sidhgiribagh ⊕0542 241 1496; map p.276. A wide range of silk fabrics as well as scarves, shawls and bedspreads at fixed prices; offers free pick-ups for customers, and it is wise to take them up on this. Daily 10am–7pm.

MUSIC

Ravi Classical Music Centre D14/88 Tedineem (arrowed from the alley by Tripti Lodge on Dashaswamedh Rd) ⊕98389 74705; map p.281. A family firm three generations old making and selling sitars, tablas and other Indian classical instruments. They also offer lessons. Daily 10am–10pm.

BOOKS

Indica Books D-40/18 Madanpura Rd, Godaulia ⊕0542 245 0818, ⓦindicabooks.com; map p.281. A large selection of books on Hinduism, religious philosophy and what they call "Indology", including their own publications. There's also a good selection of Indian and foreign fiction and nonfiction in English at the front. Mon–Sat 10am–8pm.

Om Pilgrims Book House B-27/98 A-8, Nawabganj Rd, Durga Kund ⊕0542 231 4060, ⓦpilgrimsonlineshop.com; map p.276. A funny old place, a bit like a Victorian books emporium, in an old house, specializing in books on religion, particularly Buddhism, but also books on Varanasi and the Ganges, and even a few antiquarian books. Mon–Sat 10am–6pm.

Universal Book Company D40/60 Madanpura Rd, Godaulia ⊕0542 245 0042; map p.281. They pile the books high here, but there's a good selection, with lots of Indian literature, as well as books on Indian history, culture and religion, and they'll help you find what you need. Mon–Sat 10am–8.30pm.

DIRECTORY

Banks and exchange Several cheap hotels, as well as the upmarket ones, will change money. A2Z India by *Radisson* hotel (daily 8am–8pm) changes cash with a minimum of fuss.

Hospitals Sir Sunderlal Hospital, Benares Hindu University (⊕0542 230 9279, ⓦbhu.ac.in/ims/hospital); Shiv Prasad Gupta Hospital (government-run), Kabir Chaura (⊕0542 221 4723); Ram Krishna Mission Hospital, Luxa (⊕0542 245 1727).

Music The International Music Ashram, D33/81 Kalishpura, near Dasashwamedh Ghat in the Old City (⊕0542 245 2302, ⓔkeshvaraonayak@hotmail.com), is an excellent place to get a few lessons in tabla, sitar and theory and has rooftop concerts on Wednesday and Saturday at 8pm.

Pharmacies Every hospital has a neighbouring 24hr pharmacy.

Post The main post office in the Old City is on Kabir Chaura Rd near Kotwali police station at the top end of the Chowk district. The one in the Cantonment is off Raja Bazaar Rd near the big TV mast at its top end. Branch offices are located on the Mall in the Cantonment, on Dashaswamedh Rd near the river, and on Vishwanatha Mandir Lane north of *Ganga Fuji* restaurant.

Yoga There is a yoga institute at the Benares Hindu University, but the Yoga Training Cente (D-5/15 Shakarkand Lane, near Mir Ghat; ⊕99198 57895) in Godaulia is more central.

Sarnath

Ten kilometres north of Varanasi, the ruins and temples at **SARNATH** are a Buddhist pilgrimage centre, and also popular with day-trippers from Varanasi. It was here, around 530 BC, just five weeks after he had found enlightenment, that Buddha gave his first ever sermon. According to Buddhist belief, this set in motion the

Dharmachakra ("Wheel of Law"), a new cycle of rebirths and reincarnations leading eventually to ultimate enlightenment for everybody. During the rainy season, when Buddha and his followers sought respite from their round of itinerant teaching, they would retire to Sarnath. Also known as **Rishipatana**, the place of the *rishis*, or **Mrigadaya**, the deer park, Sarnath's name derives from Saranganatha, the Lord of the Deer.

Over the centuries, the settlement flourished as a centre of Buddhist (particularly Hinayana) art and teaching. Seventh-century Chinese pilgrim Xuan Zhang recounted seeing thirty monasteries, supporting some three thousand monks, and a life-sized brass statue of the Buddha turning the Wheel of Law, but Indian Buddhism floundered under the impact of Muslim invasions and the rise of Hinduism. Sarnath's expanding Buddhist settlement eventually dissolved in the wake of this religious and political metamorphosis. Except for the **Dhamekh Stupa**, much of the site lay in ruins for almost a millennium, prey to vandalism and pilfering, until 1834, when Alexander Cunningham, head of the Archaeological Survey, excavated the site. Today it is once more an important Buddhist centre, and its avenues house missions from all over the Buddhist world.

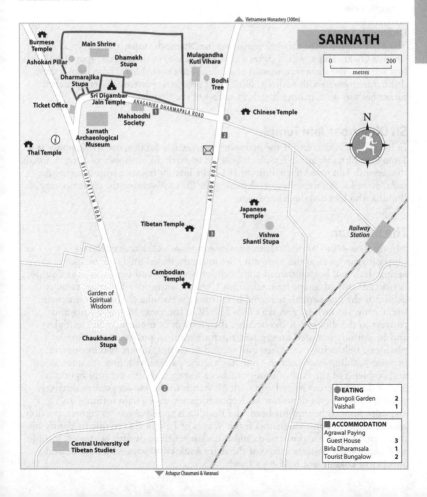

The main site

Daily sunrise–sunset • ₹200 (₹15), video camera ₹25 (ticket office just southwest of the site entrance, opposite museum)

Dominated by the huge bulk of the Dhamekh Stupa, the extensive archeological excavations of the main site of Sarnath are maintained within an immaculate park. As you enter from the southwest, the pillaged remains of the **Dharmarajika Stupa** lie immediately to the north: within its core the *stupa* holds a green marble casket containing relics of Buddha (Ashoka gathered these up from seven original locations and redistributed them among numerous *stupas* nationwide including this one) and precious objects, including decayed pearls and gold leaf. Commemorating the spot where the Buddha delivered his first sermon, Dharmarajika is attributed to the reign of Ashoka in the third century BC, but was extended a further six times.

Adjacent to Dharmarajika Stupa are the ruins of the **main shrine**, where Ashoka is said to have meditated. To the west stands the lower portion of an **Ashoka Pillar** – minus its famous capital, which is now housed in the museum. The ruins of four monasteries, dating from the third to the twelfth centuries, are also contained within the compound; all bear the same hallmark of a central courtyard surrounded by monastic cells.

Dhamekh Stupa

The most impressive of the site's remains is the **Dhamekh Stupa**, also known as the **Dharma Chakra Stupa**, which stakes a competing claim to be the exact spot of Buddha's first sermon. The *stupa* is composed of a cylindrical tower rising 33.5m from a stone drum, ornamented with bas-relief foliage and geometric patterns; the eight-arched niches halfway up may once have held statues of the Buddha.

Sri Digamber Jain Temple

In its own enclosure outside the main site, so accessible for free, the **Sri Digamber Jain Temple**, or Shreyanshnath Temple, is believed to mark the birthplace of Shreyanshnath, the eleventh Jain *tirthankara*. Built in 1824, the interior houses a large image of the saint, as well as attractive frescoes depicting the life of Mahavira, the contemporary of Buddha who founded the Jain religion.

The museum

Daily except Fri 9am–4.45pm • ₹5 (ticket office across the street); leave cameras and mobiles in lockers at the entrance

Opposite the gates to the main site, the **museum** is designed to look like a *vihara*. Its small but renowned collection of Buddhist and brahmanist antiquities consists mostly of sculpture made from Chunar sandstone. The most famous exhibit is the **lion capital**, removed here from the Ashoka column on the main site. Commissioned by Ashoka (273–232 BC), the great Mauryan king and convert to the dharma, it has become the emblem of modern India: four alert and beautifully sculpted lions guard the four cardinal points, atop a circular platform. Belonging to the first and second centuries AD are two impressive life-size standing *bodhisattvas* – one has a stone parasol with fine ornamentation and emblems of the faith. Among the large number of fifth-century figures is one of **Buddha**, cross-legged and with his hands in the *mudra* gesture. Perfectly poised, with his eyes downcast in deep meditation and a halo forming an exquisite nimbus behind his head, the Buddha is seated above six figures, possibly representing his companions, with the Wheel of Law in the middle to signify his first sermon. Later sculptures, dating from the tenth to twelfth centuries, include an exceptionally delicate image of the deity **Avalokiteshvara** with a lotus, and another of **Lokeshvara** holding a bowl.

Chaukhandi Stupa

Rishipattan Road • Daily sunrise–sunset • Free

The dilapidated brick remains of the **Chaukhandi Stupa**, 1km south of the main site, date from the Gupta period (300–700 AD), and are said to mark the spot where Buddha was reunited with the Panchavargiya Bikshus, his five ascetic companions who had previously deserted him. The *stupa*, standing atop a terraced rectangular plinth, is capped by an incongruous octagonal Mughal tower, which was built by Akbar in 1589 AD to commemorate his father's visit to the site.

Mulagandha Kuti Vihara

Anagarika Dharmapala Road • Daily: Feb–Nov 4–11.30am & 1.30–7.30pm; Dec & Jan 4–11.30am & 12.30–7.30pm • Free

Northeast of the Dhamekh Stupa, the lofty church-like **Mulagandha Kuti Vihara** monastery was built in 1931 with donations from the international Buddhist community. Run by the Mahabodhi Society, it drew devotees from all over the world to witness its consecration, and has become one of Sarnath's greatest attractions for pilgrims and tourists alike. The entrance foyer is dominated by a huge bell – a gift from Japan – and the interior houses a gilded reproduction of the museum's famous image of the Buddha, surrounded by fresco-covered walls depicting scenes from his life.

A little way east, shielded by a small enclosure, Sarnath's **bodhi tree** is an offshoot of the tree at Bodhgaya in Bihar, under which Buddha attained enlightenment. Sangamitra, Emperor Ashoka's daughter, took a branch from the original tree in 288 BC and planted it in Anuradhapura, in Sri Lanka, where its offshoots have been nurtured through the ages.

The grounds of the Mulagandha Kuti Vihar also contain a **deer park**, with enclosures for cheetals and black bucks, as well as a small zoo with a crocodile pond and aviaries.

ARRIVAL AND INFORMATION   SARNATH

By bus and auto-rickshaw Local bus services from GT Road outside Varanasi Cantonment station and opposite the bus stand have been suspended while roadworks have reduced much of the route to rubble, but shared autos to Sarnath still run for the same price (₹50), although some only run as far as Ashapur Chaumani, 2km south of Sarnath, from where you can walk or take a local rickshaw. A prepaid auto from Varanasi Cantonment station costs ₹200.

Tourist office UP Modern Recreation Centre (Mon–Sat 10am–5pm).

ACCOMMODATION

Agrawal Paying Guest House 14/91 Agrawal Ganj, Ashok Rd (opposite Tibetan Temple) ☎0542 259 5316, ✉agrawalpg@gmail.com; map p.289. Peaceful little guesthouse in a beautiful, well-kept garden with roses and starfruit trees. The rooms are immaculate, cool white with marble floors, all attached, but so far wi-fi only reaches the lobby (although they plan to extend it to the rooms too). It's worth paying ₹200 more for the bigger, brighter upstairs rooms. Wi-fi available, but coverage often not great in the rooms. ₹800

Birla Dharamsala Anagarika Dharmapala Rd ☎85746 33845, ✉nanda.baddegama@gmail.com; map p.289. One of a number of guesthouses run by religious institutions for pilgrims, this one is very central, spartan but clean, and subject to religious rules (no alcohol and no sex, for example). The rooms are attached and sleep up to five people. No wi-fi. ₹800

Tourist Bungalow Ashok Rd (opposite the post office) ☎0542 259 5965, ✉rahimrigdav@up-tourism.com; map p.289. The UP-state-run hotel is institutional and functional, but it's got large rooms, all attached, some a/c (₹1300), and a dorm. Dorm ₹200; double ₹900

EATING

Rangoli Garden SA-14/97 Ashok Rd (opposite the radio station) ☎0542 259 5325; map p.289. Just past Chukhandi Stupa, at the crossroad on the way from Varanasi, this is a very popular spot for good north and south Indian food and has an outdoor sitting area. Mains include chicken tikka masala (₹300) or, if you prefer it veg, *paneer* tikka masala (₹230). Mon–Sat 10am–10pm.

Vaishali At the junction of Anagarika Dharmapala Rd and Ashok Rd ☎96951 28901, ⚑vaishalirestaurant. com; map p.289. Upstairs restaurant with a choice of north Indian, south Indian or Chinese. You can get a masala dosa for ₹70, or *paneer* mushroom masala for ₹20. Daily 8am–10pm.

Gorakhpur

Some 230km north of Varanasi, **GORAKHPUR** rose to prominence as a waystation on a pilgrims' route linking Kushinagar (the place of Buddha's enlightenment) and **Lumbini** (his birthplace, across the border in Nepal), and is now known primarily as a gateway to Nepal. It was named after the Shaivite yogi **Gorakhnath**, and holds a large ashram and temple dedicated to him. Tourists and pilgrims tend to hurry through, their departure hastened by the town's infamous flies and mosquitoes. It does however, have a bustling bazaar, adequate amenities and a few passable hotels.

ARRIVAL AND INFORMATION GORAKHPUR

By plane The airport is 8km east of Gorakhpur towards Kushinagar. Taxis charge ₹400 into to`wn. Daily flights to Delhi are currently operated by Air India, IndiGo and SpiceJet.

By train Daily trains from Gorakhpur station in the city centre include the #12553 *Vaishali Express* at 5.05pm for Lucknow (arr. 10.05pm) and New Delhi (arr. 6.40am), and the #15018 *Gorakhpur–Lokmanyatilak Express* at 5.30am for Mumbai (arr. at Kurla 6.40pm next day) via Varanasi (arr. 10.45am). For Lucknow the #12531 *Intercity Express* may be more convenient (dep. 6.05am, arr. 11.05am).

By bus Gorakhpur has three bus stands. The Railway Bus Stand (200m up Station Rd, opposite the station, marked by a statue of Maharana Pratap Singh on horseback) is used by some services to Lucknow, and by buses to Kushinagar and the Nepalese border at Sonauli; for Kathmandu and Pokhara, see box below. The Kacheri Bus Stand, 1km southwest of the station, has buses to Prayagraj, Lucknow and Varanasi. Pedleyganj, 2km southeast of the station, is used by some Varanasi services.

By rickshaw Cycle rickshaws are the main means of transport around town.

Services The GPO is on Park Rd at Golghar.

ACCOMMODATION AND EATING

Gorakhpur **hotels** range from dingy flophouses near the station to mid-range places in Golghar (1km southwest) and Niyamachak (1.5km west). For **eating**, there's a row of cheap *dhabas* opposite the station.

Bobina Nepal Rd, Niyamachak ☎0551 233 6663, ⌨ bobina.hotelsinuttarpradesh.com. The public areas look a bit wind-swept, but this is a very good-value mid-range choice, with spacious a/c (₹3500) and non-a/c rooms, a decent restaurant and bar, and even a pool. Often full, so it's worth booking ahead. **₹2000**

Bobis Golghar ☎0551 233 2233. A multicuisine restaurant where lunch is served noon–3pm, supper 7–10.30pm, with snacks and cakes from the adjoining bakery served in-between times. A mutton curry here will set you back ₹205, a chicken curry ₹195, and there are also Chinese and Continental options. Daily 10am–10.30pm.

Clarks Grand Park Rd, near Golghar ☎0551 220 5015, ⌨ clarksgrand.in. Gorakhpur's most upmarket option, an unexciting but reliable business hotel with large rooms and a pool. Breakfast included. **₹6600**

Standard Station Rd, by the statue of Maharana Pratap Singh ☎0551 220 1439. Cleanest of the cheap hotels opposite the station. Rooms are attached, but hot water comes in a bucket. No wi-fi. **₹600**

Kushinagar

Set against a pastoral landscape 53km east of Gorakhpur, the small village of **KUSHINAGAR** is revered as the site of Buddha's death and cremation, and final liberation (**Mahaparinirvana**) from the cycles of death and rebirth. During his lifetime, **Kushinara**, as it was then called, was a small kingdom of the Mallas, surrounded by forest. It remained forgotten until the late nineteenth century, when archeologists began excavations based on the writings of seventh-century Chinese pilgrims.

Set in a leafy park in the heart of Kushinagar, the **Mahaparinirvana Temple** (or **Nirvana Stupa**; sunrise–sunset; free), dated to the reign of Kumaragupta I (413–455 AD), was extensively rebuilt by Burmese Buddhists in 1927. The large gilded **reclining Buddha** inside the shrine was reconstructed from the remains of an earlier Malla image. At the road crossing immediately southwest, the **Matha Kuwar** shrine holds a tenth-century Buddha made of blue schist rock, also covered in gilt. It's usually locked up (you can look in through the windows), but the caretaker may offer to open it up for you if he's around. Just round the corner, there's a **Buddha Museum** (Tues–Sat and most Sundays 10.30am–4.30pm;

GETTING TO NEPAL

Gorakhpur is a convenient jumping-off point for western **Nepal**, offering access to Pokhara and even Kathmandu. Through tickets to Kathmandu and Pokhara are not worth buying; they just limit your choices at the border and may even leave you without a connection at all. It's much better therefore to get a bus to Sonauli, walk across the border, and pick up onward transport connections on the other side.

Buses for Sonauli (3hr) depart from Gorakhpur's Railway Bus Stand between 4.30am and 9pm: deluxe buses leave from in front of the railway station. For onward destinations in Nepal, you'll need to get to Bhairawa, 5km north of the border post (around ₹20 by local bus, ₹50 by rickshaw). There are morning and evening buses and minibuses from Bhairawa to Kathmandu (8–9hr) and Pokhara (7–9hr), but set off early from Gorakhpur to get your connecting bus in daylight and enjoy the views.

Coming the other way, private buses for Gorakhpur leave Sonauli almost hourly in the mornings (5–11am).

ACCOMMODATION

Rahi Tourist Bungalow Maharaj Ganj, Sonauli (1km short of the border) ☎05522 238201, ✉rahinrajana@up-tourism.com. This UP state government-run hotel has a range of rooms, including a/c (₹700), and a dorm (₹100). There's more choice over the border in Nepal; and in Bhairawa, 4km up the road from the border, where the budget *Mt Everest* and more upmarket *Yeti* are popular options. **₹350**

VISAS AND MONEY

Multi-entry Nepalese visas are available at the border (US$25/40/100 for 15, 30 or 90 days, payable in US dollars, plus two passport photos). There is a State Bank of India on the Indian side of the border and moneychangers on the Nepalese side. Don't believe anyone saying it's illegal to enter Nepal with Indian Rupees – it's a scam to coax you into exchanging all your leftover money at lower rates.

₹10 (₹3), camera ₹20), housing a so-so collection of ancient Buddhist sculpture, not all original; the most interesting exhibits are the small pieces in a case of antiquities unearthed locally. The crumbling bricks of the **Ramabhar Stupa**, about 1.5km southeast of the main site (sunrise–sunset; free; around ₹75 for the roundtrip by rickshaw), are thought to be the original **Mukutabandhana Stupa**, erected to mark the spot where Buddha was cremated.

Today Kushinagar is rediscovering its roots as a centre of international Buddhism, and is home to several monasteries sponsored by Buddhists from Tibet, Burma, Thailand, Sri Lanka and Japan. The strikingly simple **Japanese Temple** consists of a single circular chamber housing a great golden image of Buddha, softly lit through small, stained-glass windows. In stark contrast, the recently constructed **Thai Monastery** is a large complex of lavish, traditionally styled temples and shrines.

ARRIVAL AND INFORMATION   KUSHINAGAR

By bus Regular buses link Kushinagar with Gorakhpur (1hr 30min). Buses drop you on the NH-28 highway at the junction with the road into town.

Tourist information UP Tourism maintains an office (Mon–Sat 10am–5pm but often closed for no particular reason; ☎05564 273045) at *Pathik Niwas*.

Tours India Tourism and UP Tourism run comprehensive tours of the whole "Buddhist Circuit" of Uttar Pradesh, which can be booked in Kushinagar, or at UP Tourism in Delhi. *Yama Café* organize a 13km hike to surrounding villages and holy sites (8am–4pm; ₹900/person including breakfast and lunch; minimum five people).

Services You can change money at the travel agent next to *Yama Café*, and at the *Lotus Nikko* hotel.

ACCOMMODATION AND EATING

Linh Son 300m from the NH-28 highway, on the left ☎99368 37270, ⊕linhsonnepalindiatemple.org. The bright, modern guesthouse attached to this resplendent Chinese-Vietnamese temple is one of the best in town, with clean, attached doubles with hot water. **₹600**

Lotus Nikko Next to the Japanese Temple ☎05564 273026, ⊕lotusnikkohotels.com. Very large rooms, more like suites, each with a sitting and eating area, make this Kushinagar's top hotel, but it's sometimes booked up by tour groups. **₹7300**

Uttarakhand

GARHWAL HIMALAYAS, AS SEEN FROM KUARI PASS

Uttarakhand

Northeast of Delhi, bordering Nepal and Tibet, the mountains of the Garhwal and Kumaon regions rise from the fertile sub-Himalayan plains. Together they form the state of Uttarakhand, which (as Uttaranchal) was shorn free from lowland Uttar Pradesh in 2000 after years of agitation. The region has its own distinct languages and cultures, and successive deep river valleys shelter fascinating micro-civilizations, where Hinduism and Buddhism meet animism. The snow peaks here rank among the most beautiful mountains of the inner Himalayas, forming an almost continuous chain that culminates in Nanda Devi, the highest mountain in India at 7816m.

Garhwal is the more visited region, busy with pilgrims who flock to its holy spots. At **Haridwar**, the Ganges thunders out from the foothills on its long journey to the sea. The nearby ashram town of **Rishikesh** is familiar from one of the classic East-meets-West images of the 1960s; it was where the Beatles came to stay with the Maharishi. From here pilgrims set off for the high temples of Char Dham – **Badrinath**, **Kedarnath**, **Yamunotri** and **Gangotri**, the source of the Ganges. Earthier pursuits are on offer at **Mussoorie**, a British hill station and now a popular Indian resort.

The less-visited **Kumaon** region remains largely unspoilt, and boasts pleasant small towns with panoramic mountain views, among them **Kausani**, **Ranikhet**, and the tiny hamlet of **Kasar Devi**, as well as the Victorian hill station of **Nainital**, where a lakeside promenade throngs with visitors escaping the heat of the plains. Further down, it's possible to stay inside **Corbett Tiger Reserve** and take a jeep safari to search for elusive wildlife. Both districts abound in classic treks, many leading through *bugyals* – summer pastures, where rivers are born and paths meet.

Brief history

The first known inhabitants of Garhwal and Kumaon were the **Kuninda** in the second century BC. A Himalayan tribal people practising an early form of Shaivism, they traded salt with Tibet and shared connections with contemporaneous Indo-Greek civilization. As evidenced by a second-century Ashokan edict at Kalsi in western Garhwal, Buddhism made some inroads in the region, but Garhwal and Kumaon remained Brahmanical. The Kuninda eventually succumbed to the **Guptas** around the fourth century AD, who, despite controlling much of the north Indian plains, failed to make a lasting impact here. Between the seventh and fourteenth centuries, the Shaivite **Katyuri** dominated lands around the modern-day **Baijnath** valley in Kumaon, where their stone temples still stand. As Brahmanical culture flourished, **Jageshwar** emerged as a major pilgrimage centre. In following centuries, Kumaon prospered further under the **Chandras**, who took learning and art to new levels, while Garhwal fell under the Panwar rajas. In 1803, the westward expansion of the Nepali Gurkhas engulfed both regions, but their brief rule ended with the Sugauli Treaty of 1816, resulting in annexation of both regions by the British.

BEST TIME TO VISIT

Uttarakhand is good to visit all year round except the peak winter and monsoon periods, especially in the upper tracts. During monsoons (July/August), heavy rains bring landslides, causing long transport delays, while snowfall in winter may lead to roadblocks. Summertime is pleasant, especially in the hills, though hill stations like Mussoorie and Nainital can get crowded in May/June.

Highlights

❶ **Char Dham** The pilgrim circuit to the four sacred sites of Garhwal reveals a cross-section of the Indian Himalayas' most superb scenery. See page 301

❷ **Ganga Aarti Haridwar** The spectacular nightly *aarti* ceremony in one of India's holiest cities sees thousands of devotees floating lamps down the Ganges. See page 306

❸ **Yoga in Rishikesh** This busy pilgrimage place on the banks of the icy Ganges is a renowned yoga and meditation centre. See page 310

❹ **Gangotri** Trek beyond the tree line to Gaumukh Glacier, source of the Ganges, where sadhus offer accommodation for spiritual retreats. See page 320

❺ **The Valley of Flowers** The lush meadows of this remote, hidden valley are a botanist's dream: come in monsoon season to see the flowers in full bloom. See page 326

❻ **Kuari Pass trek** A five-day trail through the upper reaches of Garhwal, offering stunning views of the Great Himalayan Watershed. See page 326

❼ **Corbett Tiger Reserve** Established in the 1930s, India's most famous nature reserve is renowned for its population of tigers. See page 330

HIGHLIGHTS ARE MARKED ON THE MAP ON PAGE 298

UTTARAKHAND

HIGHLIGHTS

1. Char Dham
2. Ganga Aarti Haridwar
3. Yoga in Rishikesh
4. Gangotri
5. The Valley of Flowers
6. Kuari Pass trek
7. Corbett Tiger Reserve

TIBET AUTONOMOUS REGION

Mana Pass

Komet (7756m)

Satopanth (7075m)

Mana

Badrinath ①

Nilkantha (6596m)

Sudarshan (6507m)

Nandanvan

Bhojbasa

Gomukh

Lanka ①

Bhaironghati

Tapovan

Bhagirathi (6856m)

Chaukhamba (7138m)

Gangotri ④

Shivling (6543m)

Gangotri Glacier

Harsil

Jogin (6465m)

Khatling Glacier

Kedarnath (6940m)

Madhmaheshwar

Har-ki-Dun

Swargarohini (6252m)

Khatling

Kedarnath ①

Rudranath

Osla

Bandarpunch (6316m) ①

Rambara

Gaurikund

Gopeshwar

Taluka

Yamunotri ①

Janki Chatti

Guptkashi

Sankri

Kharsali

Dodi Tal

Kalyani

Sonprayag

Okhimath

Chandrashila (3930m)

Netwar

Hanuman Chatti

Agoda

Uttarkashi

Gangi

Tunganath

Purola

GARHWAL

Ghuttu

Barkot

Budha Kedar

Nowgaon

Bhagirathi

Ghamsali

Rudraprayag

Deoban

Nag Tibba (3027m)

Sarkhanda Devi (3030m)

Srinagar

Chakrata

Dhanolti

New Tehri

Pauri

Tons

Chamba

Devaprayag

Mussoorie

Kalsi

Kunjapuri (2240m)

HIMACHAL PRADESH

Shimla & Chandigarh

Dehradun

Narendranagar

Nilkanth Mahadev

Rishikesh ③

Lansdowne

Kunnao

Chilla

RAJAJI NATIONAL PARK

②

Haridwar

Delhi

Bijnor

Roorkee

Yamunanagar

Saharanpur

UTTAR PRADESH

Ganges

The International boundaries on this map are neither purported to be correct nor authentic by Survey of India directives. Publisher.

FESTIVALS IN UTTARAKHAND

International Yoga Festival (March). Annual festival organized by Parmarth Niketan Ashram in Rishikesh (see page 310), with yoga classes, *mantras*, *kirtans*, plus lifestyle and healing programmes alongside cultural events.

Kumaoni Holi (March). In the hill tracts of Kumaon, Holi is a musical affair and takes various forms. At Baithki Holi, celebrations kick off in temple premises with traditional folk songs sung to a classical accompaniment. There's more singing at Khari Holi, celebrated mainly in rural areas. Mahila Holi is a women-only gathering.

Ganga Dussehra (May/June). A day devoted to worshipping the sacred Ganges, with devotees marking the occasion with a dip in the river and *aarti*. Hand-made Dussehra posters adorn the doors of temples and homes in Rishikesh, Haridwar and other towns along the river.

Bagwal or Devidhura Fair (August). Celebrated at the Varahi Devi temple at Devidhura, just south of Nainital. Amid folk songs and dances, two groups (*khams*) throw fruits and flowers at each other while protecting themselves with large wooden shields. Until 2013, it was stones that were pelted, and traditionally a priest would stop the ritual when it was ascertained that enough blood had been shed (equivalent to one man) to appease the goddess.

Nanda Devi Jaat (Aug/Sept). Dedicated to Uttarakhand's patron goddess, with an annual *jaat* (procession) and *melas* held in towns and villages with Nanda Devi shrines across Garhwal and Kumaon, including Almora, Nainital and Ranikhet.

The birth of Uttaranchal

Following Independence, Garhwal and Kumaon became part of Uttar Pradesh, but failure by the administration in Lucknow to develop the region led to increasingly violent calls for a **separate state**. The sympathetic high-caste BJP took up the separatist cause after coming to power in 1998, leading to the creation of a new state, originally called Uttaranchal, in 2000, and later reverting to its historical name, Uttarakhand, meaning "northern country", in 2007. The process of creating the new state was somewhat acrimonious, and deep cultural **differences** continue to characterize Garhwal and Kumaon.

On the environmental front, deforestation in the hills has led to a rapid loss of arable land, while global warming continues to shrink glaciers at an alarming rate. In June 2013, unprecedented rainfall caused devastating floods and landslides across north India, claiming thousands of lives and hitting Uttarakhand hardest of all. The tragedy, compounded by unscientific development – haphazard road-building, unregulated hotel construction on fragile river banks and the establishment of more than seventy hydroelectric projects in the state's watersheds – was regarded by environmentalists as a disaster waiting to happen. Ironically, it is drought and a scarcity of water that's increasingly having an impact on the state.

Dehradun

Capital of Uttarakhand, **DEHRADUN**, 255km north of Delhi, is pleasantly located at just below 700m, as the Himalayan foothills begin their dramatic rise, so it never gets too hot in summer, and snows rarely appear in winter. It stands at the centre of the 120km-long **Doon Valley**, hemmed in by the Yamuna to the west and the Ganges at Rishikesh to the east.

A popular retirement spot renowned for its elite institutions, the town dates its origins to 1676, when Guru Ram Rai, eldest son of the seventh Sikh Guru Har Rai ji, set up a *dera* (camp) in this tract of the *dun* or *doon* (valley). It was later occupied by Mughals and Gurkhas, but it's British influence that is most apparent.

More recently, driven by its status as state capital, increasing local and government investment has led to a commercial and IT boom in the city, but with much of the surrounding agricultural land swallowed up for development, Dehradun has becoming an urban sprawl with serious noise and traffic problems; it's particularly bad around the markets near the tall Victorian **clock tower**, and along Gandhi and Rajpur roads. Land grabbing – and the state-wide water shortage – also means that Dehradun's legendary high-quality basmati rice is fast becoming a rarity.

Darbar Guru Ram Rai Sahib

Daily 6am–7.30pm • ☎ 0135 2726698, ⊛ sgrrdarbar.org

The gateway, walls and ceilings of the seventeenth-century *gurudwara* of **Guru Ram Rai**, in the centre of town, are suffused with exquisite 200-year-old murals painted in Mughal style. The outer courtyard leads to the inner sanctum where the Guru's domed tomb stands in the centre. The annual raising of the *jhanda ji* (flagstaff) here, five days after Holi, is celebrated with great pomp.

Forest Research Institute Museum

3km northwest of the clock tower on Chakrata Rd • Mon–Fri 9.30am–1pm & 1.30–5pm • ₹40 • ☎ 0135 2759382, ⊛ fri.res.in/museum • Vikram #6 from Connaught Place

The chateau-like **Forest Research Institute**, an impressive red-brick, Raj-era structure completed in the 1920s, sits in sprawling grounds. The institute is devoted to the preservation of India's much-threatened woodlands, and is responsible for training most of India's forest officers. There's a large and interesting museum, split into six sections, with highlights including a section on timber showcasing wooden furniture and a slice of a 704-year-old deodar tree.

Mindrolling Monastery

Clement Town, 11km south of Dehradun • Daily 9am–noon & 2–7pm • Donation • ☎ 0135 264 0968, ⊛ mindrolling.org

Just outside Dehradun might seem an unlikely setting for one of the largest Buddhist centres in the world, but the serene **Mindrolling Monastery** is the focus of a Tibetan community in exile, here since the Uprising of 1959. The 185ft **Great Peace Stupa** has several floors and shrine rooms and the Dalai Lama was present when it was inaugurated in 2002.

International visitors interested in study and retreat established by Mindrolling Monastery can get in touch with the **Samten Tse Retreat Centre** in Mussoorie (☎0135 631267, ✉samtentseretreat@gmail.com).

GARHWAL AND THE CHAR DHAM YATRA

As the sacred land that holds the sources of the mighty Ganges and Yamuna rivers, **Garhwal** has been the heartland of Hindu identity since the ninth century when, in the wake of the decline of Buddhism in northern India, the reformer Adi Shankara incorporated many of the mountains' ancient shrines into the fold of Hinduism. He founded the four main **yatra** (pilgrimage) temples, deep within the Himalayas, known as the **Char Dham – Badrinath**, **Kedarnath**, **Gangotri** and **Yamunotri**. Each year, between May and November, once the snows have melted, streams of pilgrims penetrate high into the mountains, passing by way of **Haridwar** and **Rishikesh**, the land of yogis and ashrams.

For more than a millennium, the *yatris* (pilgrims) came on foot. However, the annual event has been transformed in the last few years; roads blasted by the military through the mountains during the war against China in the early 1960s are now the lifelines for a new form of motorized *yatra*. Eastern Garhwal in particular is getting rich, and the fabric of hill society is changing rapidly – visitors hoping to experience the old Garhwal should spend at least part of their time well away from the principal *yatra* routes. In addition to their spiritual significance, the hills have become a hub for **adventure sports**, offering all levels of trekking, whitewater rafting, paragliding, skiing and climbing.

ARRIVAL AND DEPARTURE

DEHRADUN

By bus The Inter-state Bus Terminal or ISBT is located 7km southwest of town, linked to the central railway station and budget hotels on Gandhi Rd by auto-rickshaw (₹200) or Vikram #5 (₹10). Buses to Mussoorie run from just north of the train station entrance.

Destinations Delhi (hourly, 7–9hr); Dharamsala (2 daily; 12hr); Haridwar (every 30min; 1hr 30min); Joshimath (daily 5pm; 12hr); Manali (daily 3pm; 14hr); Mussoorie (hourly; 1hr 30min); Nainital (6 daily; 8hr); Rishikesh (every 30min; 1hr); Shimla (daily 11pm; 8hr); Uttarkashi (daily 9pm; 9hr).

By train The station is off Gandhi Rd, 2km southwest of the clock tower. The best daily trains to Delhi are the overnight #14042 *Mussoorie Express* (departs 9.25pm; arrives Delhi 7.25am), the a/c #12018 *Dehradun Shatabdi* (departs 4.55pm; arrives New Delhi 10.50pm) and the #12056 *JNdls Janshatabdi* (departs 5.10am; arrives New Delhi 11.10am). The *Doon Express* #13010 is the most convenient option for Lucknow (departs 8pm; arrives 8.35am) as well as Varanasi (arrives 3.55pm) and Kolkata (arrives 6.55am the second morning). For Agra, the #14310 *Ujjaiyani Express* (Tues & Wed; departs 5.50am; arrives 4.40pm) is the fastest.

GETTING AROUND

By Vikram These blue, eight-seater auto-rickshaws are Dehradun's cheapest mode of transport; they are numbered by their routes and cost ₹5–10.

INFORMATION AND TOURS

Tourist information GMVN Tourist Office, *Hotel Drona*, 45 Gandhi Rd (Mon–Sat 10am–5pm; ☎0135 2653217, ⊕gmvnl.in). The KMVN Tourist Office is at the same premises (☎0135 274 9720, ⊕kmvn.gov.in). The GMVN's head office (74/1 Rajpur Rd; Mon–Sat 10am–5pm; ☎0135 2746817, ✉gmvn@sancharnet.in, ✉gmvn@gmvnl.in) books GMVN accommodation and tours throughout Garhwal.

Trekking and equipment Garhwal Adventure Tours (193 Araghar; ☎0135 2677769, ⊕garhwaladventure. com) is an experienced organization used to working with international tour groups. Equipment can be bought or hired from Cliff Climbers (51–61 Moti Bazaar; ☎0135 2651235, ⊕cliffclimbers.net), the best trekking and mountaineering equipment dealers in the region.

ACCOMMODATION

Many of Dehradun's mid-range **hotels** are strung along Rajpur Rd as it heads north to Mussoorie. Most budget accommodation can be found between the railway station and clock tower.

Hotel Aketa 113 1/2 Rajpur Rd ☎0135 274 3514, ⊕hotelaketadehradun.com. Around a 20min drive from the clock tower, and surrounded by trees, this is a great option for a clean and comfortable stay. The marble lobby sets a nice tone; rooms are large and well furnished. Breakfast is particularly good. ₹4000

Ashrey 10 Tyagi Rd ☎0135 262 3388, ⊕hotelashrey.in. In a quiet, but central spot, just a 3min walk south of Prince Chowk; the private lawn in front leads to well-furnished rooms with flatscreen TVs, some with a/c (₹3000). Their retro-themed *Sagar* restaurant features antiques and a vintage BSA motorbike and serves delicious north Indian and Chinese fare. ₹1500

Central Great Value 17 Rajpur Rd, opposite Gandhi Park ☎0135 265 3880, ⊕greatvaluehotel.com. Large, centrally located budget hotel, part of a well-run chain, with bright, spotless rooms, a multicuisine restaurant and a travel desk. ₹2200

Moti Mahal 7 Rajpur Rd ☎0135 265 1277, ⊕hotel motimahal.net. A bright, modern hotel with immaculate rooms, smart fittings and flatscreen TVs and a fancy restaurant next door. ₹1995

President 6 Astley Hall ☎0135 265 7082, ⊕hotel presidentdehradun.com. A luxury boutique hotel in contemporary style with classy rooms and a choice of fine-dining restaurants, covering cuisines as diverse as Lebanese and Mexican. ₹3500

★ **White House** 15/7 Subhash Rd ☎0135 265 6594. Atmospheric, peaceful, Art Deco Raj-era residence near the Astley Hall commercial complex, with a mix of a/c (₹1795) and non-a/c rooms, huge verandas, lofty ceilings, sturdy furniture and a friendly owner. Excellent pizzas, pastas and sandwiches are served at the cosy *Y Café*, and drop by the Purkal outlet, an NGO selling patchwork quilts and cushion covers made by local women. ₹2250

EATING AND DRINKING

Black Pepper 3 Astley Hall, Rajpur Rd ☎0135 265 7781, ⊕blackpepperdehradun.com. This cool, grotto-style restaurant appeals to families and bright young things, with a wide range of north and south Indian, Chinese and Continental meals. Try their chicken sizzler (₹475). The upstairs bar is equally inviting (beer ₹425) and happy hour is every day until 10pm. Daily 11am–11pm.

★ **Kumar Sweet Shop** MDDA Complex, Opposite GPO, clock tower ☎0135 265 5757. Established in 1957, this enduring sweetshop has a wide range of *mithai* (sweets) and snacks. The *rasmalai* (₹20), *kulfi* (₹75), carrot halwa and Mewa Bite (a dried-fruit milk sweet) are all highly recommended. *Kumar's* has a pure-veg branch 40m further north at 15-B Rajpur Rd (and not to be confused with the non-veg *Kumar Restaurant* nearby). Daily 9am–9pm.

Moti Mahal Moti Mahal hotel, 7 Rajpur Rd ☎0135 265 7307, ⊛hotelmotimahal.net. This sleek, a/c hotel restaurant serves excellent chicken, *paneer* and Chinese options. Favourites include chicken *karahi* (₹300), butter chicken (₹425) and chicken tikka masala (₹375). Daily 8am–11pm.

Tirupati 27-B Rajpur Rd ☎93581 10244. This clean, friendly multicuisine restaurant serves Chinese including chow mein (₹175) and spring rolls (₹210), but is particularly strong on south Indian dishes. A thali will set you back ₹190, or go for a masala dosa for ₹140 (they also have coconut, butter and paneer dosas). Daily 10am–10pm.

DIRECTORY

Banks and exchange A number of ATMs surround the clock tower.

Bookshop The famous Nataraj Green Bookshop (17 Rajpur Rd; Mon–Sat 10am–1.30pm & 3–8pm) has a fine stock of books on the environment and ecology and a good selection of titles by celebrated local author, Ruskin Bond.

Post office The GPO is on Rajpur Rd (Mon–Sat 10am–6pm).

Mussoorie

Spreading for 15km along a high serrated ridge, **MUSSOORIE** is the closest hill station to Delhi, just 278km north of the capital and 34km north of Dehradun, from where it is visible on a clear day. At an altitude of 2000m, it gives travellers from the plains their first glimpse of the snow-covered Himalayan **peaks** of western Garhwal, as well as dramatic views of the Doon Valley below.

A favoured retreat since the 1820s, Mussoorie is a highly popular weekend retreat for middle-class Indians up from the plains, with many of its Raj-era homes converted into heritage hotels. Many foreign visitors come to Mussoorie to **study** Hindi at the excellent Landour Language School, but the town also makes a handy base for **treks** into western Garhwal. Dominated by the long Bandarpunch Massif (6316m), with Swargarohini (6252m) in the west and the Gangotri group in the east, Mussoorie's mountain panorama forms a pleasant backdrop to the busy holiday town.

Mussoorie centres on the 2km pedestrian-only **Mall**, bookended by the town's two most lively hubs: Library Bazaar (also called Gandhi Chowk) to the west and Kulri Bazaar (or Picture Palace) to the east.

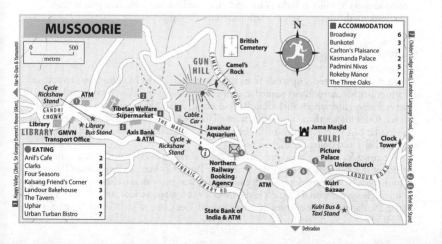

MUSSOORIE'S MOUNTAIN VIEWPOINTS

While Mussoorie's busy Mall faces away from the snows and towards Dehradun, a number of vantage points are within a short walk of the centre, offering glimpses of Himalayan giants such as Bandarpunch I (6316m) and II (6102m) and Kalanag Peak (6387m).

GUN HILL

The most popular of the town's viewpoints, **Gun Hill** (2024m) rises like a volcano over central Mussoorie, offering a superb Himalayan panorama (if you can see past the restaurants and old fair rides blocking the view). It can be ascended by a footpath forking up from the Mall, or by a 400m cable-car ride starting from the Ropeway station (10am–7pm; ₹125 return), halfway down the Mall.

CAMEL'S BACK ROAD

Rounding the northern base of Gun Hill is the pleasant 4km promenade of **Camel's Back Road**, a scenic northerly arch connecting Library and Kulri bazaars. Along the way are several worthy viewpoints, as well as the distinctive Camel's Rock and an old British cemetery – the resting place of British adventurer "Pahari" Wilson (closed to visitors).

SIR GEORGE EVEREST'S HOUSE

The 6km hike from Library Bazaar via Hathipaon hill to the former home and laboratory of **Sir George Everest** is rewarded with fantastic views of both the Himalayas and the Doon Valley. The whitewashed, abandoned house – The Park – was bought by the famous Welsh surveyor in 1833, and much of the work of the Great Trigonometric Survey of India, demarcating the boundaries of British India and measuring the height of the world's greatest peaks, took place here.

LAL TIBBA

Lal Tibba (Red Hill) is a steep and peaceful 5km climb east of the Mall on the slopes above Landour. As the vicinity's highest vantage point, it affords some of the best panoramic views of the Garhwal Himalayan range.

Happy Valley

2km west of the Library near Convent Hill (beyond LBSNAA and the polo ground)

Home to more than five thousand Tibetans, **Happy Valley** was the first Tibetan settlement in India following the Dalai Lama's 1959 escape from Tibet. Although the headquarters for the Tibetan government-in-exile moved to Dharamsala in 1960, Happy Valley remains a bastion of Tibetan culture, with a large school, a lively bazaar and numerous *gompas*, including the beautiful **Shedup Choephelling**, the first of its kind to be built in India, surrounded by gardens and fluttering prayer flags, overlooking the nearby hills of Hathipaon and Benog Tibba.

Landour

5km east of Kulri Bazaar

A road winding steeply upwards from the eastern end of the Mall leads to **Landour**, a former British cantonment named after the Welsh village of Llanddowror and home to several renowned writers including Ruskin Bond, Bill Aitkin and Allan Sealy. Landour is set 300m higher than Mussoorie, facing Tibet, with cooler air and cleaner surrounds; a circular bridle trail, locally called the *chukkar*, connects the three summits of Landour ridge, Lal Tibba being the highest point.

The town features colonial-era cottages and a thriving bazaar overflowing with relics of the Raj. Above Sister's Bazaar near St Paul's Church, is Char Dukan (literally "four shops"), a square dotted with cafés frequented by both travellers and townsfolk. Near Kellogg Memorial Church is the **Landour Language School** (☎0135 263 1487, ⊕landourlanguageschool.com; mid-Feb to mid-Dec), one of India's best for pupils of Hindi.

ARRIVAL AND DEPARTURE

By bus There are bus stands at either end of the Mall; the Library Bus Stand to the west and the Kulri Bus Stand (or Masonic Lodge Bus Stand) to the east. Buses from Dehradun arrive at both stands, though the former has more services heading towards Dehradun (hourly; 1hr 30min), buses to Barkot (2 daily; 4–5hr) for the Yamunotri trek and Sankri (7hr) via Nowgaon (3hr) for the Har-ki-Dun trek. The smaller Tehri Bus Stand, 5km east of the Mall, just beyond Landour, serves destinations to the east and northeast: for Uttarkashi, first head to Chamba (hourly; 4hr), from where regular buses ply to Gangotri (every 30min; 5hr).

By taxi Cars and shared taxis are available close to each bus stand. The taxi office 100m below the GMVN transport office, by the Library Bus Stand, serves Dehradun (₹1050), Delhi (₹8000), Gangotri and Uttarkashi (both ₹12,000), though it could be cheaper to organise a taxi through your hotel.

By train The Northern Railway Booking Office (Mon–Sat 8am–2pm; ☎ 0135 263 2846), near the post office, books train tickets from Dehradun, the nearest railhead, as does Sai Yatra (☎ 0135 263 5151), just west of *Tavern*.

GETTING AROUND

Vehicles are allowed on the Mall only to reach your hotel or destination (two-wheelers ₹100, four-wheelers ₹150; no entry 4–10.30pm), with single-trip permits available at the traffic barriers at either end.

Cycle rickshaws Cycle rickshaws ply the Mall from Library Bazaar to the Ropeway (₹50).

Motorbike rental Dhoom bike rental (☎ 0135 271 6227) are by the Library Bus stand.

INFORMATION

Tourist information The tourist bureau (Mon–Sat 10am–-5pm; ☎ 0135 263 2863), next to the cable car, offers booklets and brochures but little else.

Tours GMVN transport office (Mon–Sat 8am–5pm; ☎ 0135 263 1281), next to the Library Bus Stand, runs tours of the town and further afield. Trek Himalaya, on the steep street opposite the cable car (daily 11am–9pm; ☎ 0135 263 0491,

ⓦ trekhimalaya.com), and Yeti Outdoors, opposite *Hotel Hamers* (daily 9am–8.30pm; ☎ 99270 51112), can arrange treks.

Services There are several ATMs along the Mall. There's a post office towards the Kulri end of the Mall (Mon–Fri 9am–5pm, Sat 9am–4pm).

4

ACCOMMODATION

Mussoorie's high season runs from mid-May to mid-July, with June being the busiest (and costliest) month of the year – book far ahead at these times. Prices drop during the shoulder season which includes Christmas and New Year, April, May, Oct and Nov; rates are slashed by as much as fifty percent the rest of the year.

Broadway Camel's Back Rd ☎ 0135 263 2243; map p.303. Set in a rambling old nineteenth-century wooden building, this guesthouse is perched on the edge of Kulri Bazaar with charming, bright window boxes, lovely views and a friendly atmosphere. Great for budget travellers. No wi-fi. **₹1250**

Bunkotel Jhula Ghar, Mall Rd ☎ 0135 263 6958; map p.303. No-frills but neat and tidy place in an unbeatable location opposite the cable car offering rooms with 4–6 bunk beds in each. Dorms **₹1250**

Carlton's Plaisance Happy Valley Rd, 1.5km west of town ☎ 0135 263 2800, ⓦ carltonplaisance.com; map p.303. Atmospheric Raj-era house with a more modern annexe, both stuffed full of period memorabilia. Edmund Hillary stayed here and loved it. Lovely gardens and an ideal base for gentle rambles away from town. **₹4350**

★ **Kasmanda Palace** The Mall ☎ 0135 263 2424, ⓦ kasmandapalace.com; map p.303. A short, stiff climb up from the Mall leads to this beautiful ex-maharaja's

summer palace, bought from a British officer in 1915 and now a heritage hotel. Comfortable and quiet with lavish rooms, beautiful gardens and wall-mounted rhino heads. **₹7000**

★ **Padmini Nivas** The Mall ☎ 0135 263 1093, ⓦ hotel-padmininivas.com; map p.303. One of the oldest estates in Mussoorie, founded in the 1830s, and home to a former maharaja. Located just below the the Mall, with a beautiful rose garden and fruit trees, it offers excellent views and lovely rooms, most of them with a veranda. **₹5000**

Rokeby Manor Rajmandi, 5km from town in Landour ☎ 0135 263 1093, ⓦ rokebymanor.com; map p.303. A tastefully renovated 1840 bungalow with stunning views over Mussoorie, *Rokeby* exudes sheer class, with wood and stone interiors, old fireplaces and cosy rooms. Dine on gourmet Indian and Continental cuisine at *Emily's* restaurant, enjoy a cuppa at the *Tea Garden* or treat yourself to a spa treatment. Also runs the exclusive *Rokeby Residences*, a cluster of nearby 1800s cottages, and *Landour Bakehouse* on Sisters Bazaar. **₹10000**

The Three Oaks The Mall ☎ 0135 263 2225; map p.303. Friendly, clean place towering over the centre of the Mall, with a good restaurant and sunny terraces overlooking the Doon Valley – views that are even better from the rooms with balconies. **₹3000**

EATING

Anil's Café Char Dukan, 5km from town in Landour ☎0135 263 3783; map p.303. It's a bit of a ritual to stop here (first shop from corner) for ginger lemon honey tea (₹20), Maggi (instant noodles), *parathas* and bread omelette. Limited seating, both inside and outside. A selfie of Indian cricketer Sachin Tendulkar hangs as endorsement. Daily 7am–10pm.

Clarks The Mall, Kulri ☎0135 263 2393; map p.303. This multicuisine restaurant, housed in a nineteenth-century hotel with lofty ceilings and plush furnishings, offers separate menus for non-veg Indian and Chinese cuisine, a favourite being the chicken *Ra Ra* Punjabi (₹320). Daily 10am–10pm.

Four Seasons The Mall, Kulri; map p.303. Not as much fun as *The Tavern* across the street, but popular because of its old school vibe and good views. Don't miss the *murgh makhani* (butter chicken; ₹190/375 for half/full). Daily 11am–11pm.

★ **Kalsang Friend's Corner** The Mall, by the post office; map p.303. This cosy diner, decked with Chinese lanterns and Tibetan prayer flags, serves tasty Chinese, Indian and Thai dishes alongside hearty Tibetan food, including *momos* (₹119–199), *thukpas* (noodle soups; ₹139–189) and fried meat dishes such as pork *shaptak*

(₹239). Daily 11am–10.30pm.

Landour Bakehouse Sisters Bazaar, 5km from town in Landour ☎0135 263 5605; map p.303. This atmospheric 115-year-old building is the place to go if you want comforting cakes, cookies and tarts (red velvet cake ₹115, peanut butter cookies ₹150/4) and an espresso. Their crepes are delicious, too. Books written by local authors are sold here. Daily 8am–8pm.

The Tavern The Mall, Kulri; map p.303. Hip place near the Picture Palace, offering pricey Western, Thai, Chinese and Indian dishes, including chilli prawns (₹785) and sizzlers. There's a small bar upstairs with beers from ₹200–300 and live music nightly. Daily 11am–11pm.

Uphar Gandhi Chowk; map p.303. Clean and friendly north and south Indian veg food joint with an ice-cream bar (₹35/scoop). The speciality is Punjabi food; try the *sarson ka saag* (mustard curry) and *makki ki roti* (Indian corn bread; ₹145). Daily 12.30–4.30pm & 6.30–10.30pm.

Urban Turban Bistro The Mall, Kulri ☎084 492 84487; map p.303. This first-floor restaurant serves contemporary veg and non-veg Indian food and is a cut above its neighbours. Great staff and hospitality and uber cool decor. Try the charcoal grilled *momos* (veg *cheezara* ₹145). Daily 11am–11pm.

Haridwar

At **HARIDWAR** – the Gates (*dwar*) of God (*Hari*) – 214km northeast of Delhi, the **River Ganges** emerges from its final rapids past the Shivalik Hills to begin its long slow journey across northern India to the Bay of Bengal. Stretching for roughly 3km along a narrow strip of land between the craggy wooded hills to the west and the river to the east, Haridwar is revered by Hindus, for whom the **Har-ki-Pairi** *ghat* (literally the "Footstep of God") marks the exact spot where the river leaves the mountains. As a road and rail junction, Haridwar links the Gangetic plains with the mountains of Uttarakhand and their holy pilgrimage (*yatra*) network. Along with Nasik, Ujjain and Prayagraj, it is one of the four holy *tirthas* or "crossings" that host the massive **Kumbh Mela** festival (see page 269). Every twelve years (next due in 2022), millions of pilgrims come to bathe at a preordained moment in the turbulent waters of the channelled river around Har-ki-Pairi.

Har-ki-Pairi

Split by a barrage north of Haridwar, the **Ganges** flows through the town in two channels, divided by a long sliver of land. The natural stream lies to the east, while the embankment of the fast-flowing canal to the west holds the *ghats* and ashrams around **Har-ki-Pairi temple**. Bridges and walkways connect the various islands, and metal chains are placed in the river to protect bathers from being swept away.

The clock tower opposite Har-ki-Pairi *ghat* is an excellent vantage point, especially during evening worship. At both dawn and dusk, the spectacular ceremony of **Ganga Aarti** – devotion to the life-bestowing goddess Ganga – draws crowds of thousands. Lights float down the river and priests perform elaborate choreographed movements while swinging torches to the accompaniment of gongs and music. As soon as they've

HAR-KI-DUN VALLEY TREK

Tucked away in the northwest corner of Garhwal is the stunning "Valley of the Gods", reached by a relatively undemanding three-day (38km) trek from Sankri. A lush, forested valley striped with glacial streams from the snow-clad peaks of **Swargarohini** ("Ascent to Heaven"; 6252m) and **Bandarpunch** ("Monkey's Tail"; 6316m), Har-ki-Dun is home to the Himalayan black bear and the elusive snow leopard, and falls within the Govind Pashu Vihar National Park and Sanctuary (April–Nov; ₹600 for up to three days, nominal camping fees extra; head office in Purola; ☎01375 223433). Visitors are required to register in advance for an online permit, see ⓦ uttarkashi.nic.in).

The sparse local population traces its lineage back to the Mahabharata, and like the Pandavas of the epic, they practise a form of polyandry and follow intriguing religious customs, including witchcraft. Worship at Taluka's Duryodhana temple, for example, consists of throwing shoes at the idol; at Pakola, the image has its back to the congregation. Their distinctive alpine buildings have beautifully carved wooden doors and windows, with the mortar construction punctuated by wooden slats.

To reach the trailhead at **Sankri**, board a Yamunotri-bound bus from Mussoorie's Library Bus Stand and change at Nowgaon, 9km before Barkot, for a jeep to Sankri. On the way you'll pass the forest checkpoint at Neitwar, 13km before Sankri. The official trail begins here, although jeeps can continue to Taluka (1900m), 14km further along through deodar and sycamore woods. The second day's hike is 13km to **Seema**, just below the village of Osla (2559m), while the third day's hike is 14km to **Har-ki-Dun campsite** (3566m), an excellent base from which to explore the *bugyals* (high alpine meadows) below the Swargarohini to the east, and the Jaundhar Glacier, a day-trip to the northwest. Note that you'll need to take your own food to Har-ki-Dun as there are no *dhabas* after Seema; forest bungalows can be found at each campsite (Sankri, Taluka, Seema, Neitwar, Osla and Har-ki-Dun).

finished, the river shallows fill up with people looking for coins thrown in by the devout. The *ghat* area is free to visit, although a donation is required to visit the section at the bottom of the first staircase.

Haridwar's markets

Haridwar's teeming network of **markets** is the other main focus of interest. **Bara Bazaar**, at the top of town, is a good place to buy a *danda* (bamboo staff) for treks in the mountains. Stalls in the colourful **Moti Bazaar** in the centre of town, on the Jawalapur road, sell everything from clothes to spices.

Mansa Devi

Cable car daily: April–Oct 7am–7pm; Nov–March 8am–5pm; ₹163 return (or VIP ticket, with no waiting in line, ₹600)

High above Haridwar, on the crest of a ridge, the gleaming white *shikhara* of the **Mansa Devi** temple dominates both town and valley. In reverence to the goddess who grants all wishes, devotees tie threads to the branches of a nearby holy tree. The temple is reached by a four-seater **cable car** (known as "Udan Khatola") from a base station off Upper Road in the heart of town, or you can take a steep 1.5km walk. Early morning is the best time to visit; pedestrian traffic along the trail can become intense later in the day during *yatra* season and the queuing system for the cablecar gets chaotic. The upper shrines hold no great architectural interest and the priests are known to demand donations, though you do get excellent views along the river.

Chandi Devi

Cable car ₹263 return for both shrines (or VIP ticket, with no waiting in line, ₹600)

Rising above the opposite bank of the Ganges, about 4km to the south of Mansa Devi, is another hill, Neel Parvat, crowned by the hilltop temple of **Chandi Devi**. While its earliest roots trace back to the eighth century, the temple was built in 1929 by the king of Kashmir. It is reachable by a second cable car or by a 3km hike from Chandi *ghat*, which passes the impressive Kamraj ki-Kali temple on the way.

Bharat Mata Temple

5km north of Haridwar • ₹20 • Vikrams from next to *Shivalik* restaurant (₹10)

The modern, eight-storey, 55m **Bharat Mata temple**, dedicated to "Mother India", was inaugurated in 1983 by Indira Gandhi. Each of its various floors – connected by lifts – is dedicated to a celestial or political theme, and populated by lifelike images of heroes, heroines and Hindu deities.

ARRIVAL AND DEPARTURE   HARIDWAR

By bus Most buses depart from the Uttarakhand Roadways bus stand (☎01334 227037) at Rishikul on Railway Rd (departures listed below). Additionally, from the GMOU bus stand (about 200m south on Railway Rd) there are early morning buses in *yatra* season (May–Oct) to Gangotri (12hr), Kedarnath (10hr) and Badrinath (15hr), and from Nov–June there are hourly buses from the GMOU bus stand to Chilla (7am–1pm; 30min), for Rajaji National Park. Numerous private bus companies, clustered behind the GMVN tourist office, have services to major destinations

in the south. Konark on Jassa Ram Rd (☎01334 222630) has three daily services to Delhi (10.30am, 10pm & 11pm; 5–6hr).

Destinations Agra (8 daily; 12hr); Dehradun (every 30min; 1hr 30min); Delhi (10 daily; 5hr 20min); Lucknow (2daily; 10–12hr); Rishikesh (every 30min; 45min); Shimla (10 daily; 12–14hr).

By train Haridwar's railway station is on Railway Rd, just southwest of the centre. Major trains include the overnight #14042 *Mussoorie Express* (departs 11.25pm; arrives

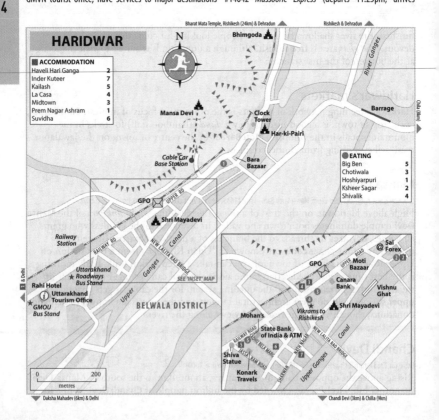

HARIDWAR

ACCOMMODATION	
Haveli Hari Ganga	2
Inder Kuteer	7
Kailash	5
La Casa	4
Midtown	3
Prem Nagar Ashram	1
Suvidha	6

● EATING	
Big Ben	5
Chotiwala	3
Hoshiyarpuri	1
Ksheer Sagar	2
Shivalik	4

Bharat Mata Temple, Rishikesh (24km) & Dehradun   Rishikesh & Dehradun

Bhimgoda

River Ganges

Mansa Devi

Clock Tower

Har-ki-Pairi

Barrage

Chila (8km)

Cable Car Base Station

Bara Bazaar

Railway Station

GPO

UPPER RD

Shri Mayadevi

Canal

New Lalita Rao Bridge

Ganges

Upper

SEE 'INSET' MAP

Uttarakhand Roadways Bus Stand

Rahi Hotel

Uttarakhand Tourism Office

GMOU Bus Stand

BELWALA DISTRICT

Sai @ Forex

GPO

UPPER ROAD

Moti Bazaar

Canara Bank

Vishnu Ghat

Shri Mayadevi

New Lalita Rao Bridge

Canal

Upper Ganges

Mohan's

Vikrams to Rishikesh

State Bank of India & ATM

Shiva Statue

Konark Travels

Railway Road

Jassa Ram Road

Jhru Bela Marg

Nath Nagar

Shamran

0   200
metres

Daksha Mahadev (6km) & Delhi   Chandi Devi (3km) & Chilla (9km)

4

Delhi 7.25am) and the a/c #12056 *Janshatabdi Express* (departs 6.30am; arrives New Delhi 11.15am); for Agra, the #18478 *Kalinga Utkal Express* (departs 6.10am; arrives 3.15pm); for Lucknow the #13010 *Doon Express* (departs 10.20pm; arrives 8.35am), which continues to Varanasi (arrives 3.55pm) and Kolkata (arrives Howrah Junction 6.55am second morning). Local trains on the branch line to Rishikesh aren't that useful in view of the excellent and more frequent road connections.

By Vikram Vikrams for Rishikesh (₹30) depart when full from next to *Shivalik* restaurant.

By taxi The Taxi Association near the railway station sets prices slightly higher than those quoted elsewhere, charging ₹1020 for a taxi to Rishikesh and ₹700 to Chilla. Travellers heading into the mountains should go to Rishikesh to pick up onward transport.

INFORMATION AND TOURS

Information Tourist information is available at a booth inside the station or from the more helpful GMVN tourist office at *Rahi Motel* on Railway Rd, southwest of the bus stand (Mon–Sat 10am–5pm; ☏ 01334 265304).

Tours Konark Travels, Jassa Ram Rd (daily 7am–9pm; ☏ 01334 222630, ⊕ konarktravels.com), offers tours of the state by bus or car; Mohan's (Mon–Sat 8am–10.30pm; ☏ 01334 220910/ ☏ 098 3710 0215, ⊕ mohansadventure.com), across from *Big Ben* restaurant, runs more adventure-based tours such as rafting, mountain biking and rock climbing.

ACCOMMODATION

Haveli Hari Ganga 21 Pilibhit House, Hanuman Ghat Rd ☏ 01334 226443, ⊕ havelihariganga.com; map p.308. A lovely haveli set up by two merchant brothers in 1917, converted into a beautiful heritage hotel with massage and spa rooms, a vegetarian restaurant and a private *ghat* for *aarti*. Suites with Ganges views cost ₹9000. **₹7000**

Inder Kuteer Sharwan Nath Nagar ☏ 01334 226336; map p.308. This friendly hotel near the river has small rooms with hot water and air-coolers (a/c rooms start at ₹2500), as well as a terrace with great rooftop views. Best value in this price range. **₹1500**

Kailash Shivmurti Chowk, Railway Rd ☏ 01334 227789, ⊕ hotelkailash.com; map p.308. Handy for the nearby railway station, the rooms here are all either air-cooled or a/c (₹1500). Most are beginning to show their age, though some have little balconies overlooking the busy street. Up to fifty percent discount off-season. **₹950**

La Casa Railway Rd, near Lalita Rao Bridge ☏ 096 3920 7070, ⊕ lacasahotels.in; map p.308. Within walking distance to the railway station, this nicely decorated twenty-room hotel provides a hearty breakfast if you're checking out early. Clean and comfortable, choose a deluxe or luxury room if you want a bit more space. **₹2000**

Midtown In an alley off Upper Rd, opposite Chotiwala restaurant ☏ 01334 227507, ⊕ midtownhotel.chobs.in; map p.308. The name fits at this centrally located hotel, set about midway between the transport hubs and Har-ki-Pairi *ghat*. It's a standard budget hotel, with clean rooms and friendly staff. Rooms at the front have balconies, while some have a/c (₹1600 upwards). Thirty percent discounts Nov–Feb. **₹950**

Prem Nagar Ashram Jawalapur Rd, 2km west of the station ☏ 01334 226345, ⊕ premnagarashram.com; map p.308. Calm and peaceful, if rather removed from town (₹10 by shared Vikram), this ashram has been around since 1944. Charming staff and clean, cheap rooms, most of which are en suite; a/c is extra. **₹600**

Suvidha Sharwan Nath Nagar, behind Chitra Talkies cinema ☏ 01334 227023, ⊕ hotelsuvidhadeluxe.com; map p.308. Comfortable place – though in need of a lick of paint – in a pleasant location near the river, away from the bustle of bazaars and main roads. If possible, view a few rooms and check you have 24hr hot water first. **₹1990**

EATING

As a holy city, Haridwar is strictly vegetarian and booze-free.

Big Ben Hotel Ganga Azure, Railway Rd ☏ 01334 220938, ⊕ hotelgangaazure.com; map p.308. Airy a/c restaurant with big windows overlooking a busy corner, offering a good range of veg curries, set meals, decent breakfasts (₹170–210) and a few Chinese and Continental dishes including cheese (₹190) and veg cutlets (₹160). Daily 8am–10.30pm.

Chotiwala Upper Rd; map p.308. Established in 1937, this dimly lit restaurant may no longer be the best in town but is still worth a visit for decent Indian food, Chinese and thalis (₹110–200). Daily 10am–11pm.

Hoshiyarpuri Upper Rd ☏ 01334 222603; map p.308.

Also established in 1937, this busy, friendly, Punjabi *dhaba*-like restaurant close to Har-ki-Pairi serves delicious Indian dishes such as *dal makhani* (₹110) and *baingan bharta* (₹120), *parathas* (₹40–60), lassi (₹50) and desserts like *kheer* (creamy rice pudding). Daily 8am–11pm.

Ksheer Sagar 21 Pilibhit House, Hanuman Ghat Rd; map p.308. The restaurant at *Haveli Hari Ganga* heritage hotel has great service and great food. They don't have an à la carte menu, but there's a huge buffet spread at breakfast and dinner (₹350/650) and a thali available at lunchtime. Daily 7am–10pm.

Shivalik Railway Rd ☏ 01334 226868; map p.308. Housed in the hotel of the same name, *Shivalik* offers

Chinese dishes and tasty south Indian snacks with worthy combo deals (₹170–225). The Continental breakfasts (₹200–250) and deluxe thali (₹175) are both good value. Daily 8am–10.30pm.

DIRECTORY

Banks and exchange Several banks with ATMs can be found along Railway Rd, including the State Bank of India and Canara Bank, both of which also change cash; there are more ATMs on Upper St, as well as Sai Forex for foreign exchange (☎ 01134 228483).

Post office The GPO is on Upper Rd (Mon–Sat 10am–5pm).

Rajaji National Park

Nov 15–June 15 daily 6–9am & 3–6pm • ₹600 (₹150) plus ₹500 (₹250) per vehicle or ₹1500 for a space in a jeep; mandatory local guide ₹300 • ⓦ rajajinationalpark.in

Rajaji National Park, part of the same forest belt as Corbett Tiger Reserve, 180km east, spans around 830 square kilometres of the Himalayan foothills immediately east and west of Haridwar. Of the park's eight **entry points**, the most useful are the main gates at **Chilla**, 9km east of Haridwar, and the gates at **Kunnao**, close to Rishikesh. Set beside the Ganges barrage and its massive electricity pylons, Chilla makes a relatively quiet base for explorations of the park. Meanwhile, **Chilla Beach** – occasionally used by large river turtles – lies within walking distance through the woods, 1km north along the Ganges.

Although largely surrounded by development and dotted with settlements of the **Van Gujjars**, a nomadic tribe whose summer homes have traditionally fallen within the park, for the time being Rajaji remains pristine and its wildlife resilient. Less developed than Corbett, it contains a similar range of fauna, most notably elephants, but also leopard and at least fourteen tigers at last count.

ARRIVAL AND GETTING AROUND
RAJAJI NATIONAL PARK

By bus and taxi Hourly buses (7am–1pm) run to Chilla from Haridwar's GMOU bus stand. Taxis charge ₹700 one way.

Jeep hire and safaris Jeeps can be hired by the gate in Chilla (3hr drive ₹3000–4000 for 1–5 people). Contact Mohan Adventure (see page 309) in Haridwar for safari bookings.

ACCOMMODATION

Camp King Elephant Four stone cottages and four tents with solar electricity, writing desk, veranda and attached bathroom with hot water. Packages include all meals, cycling trails with hampers and guided forest walks. No wi-fi. Bookings via the Forestry Department. **₹US$240**

Chilla Tourist Bungalow 5min walk from park gate, Chilla ☎ 01382 266678, ⓦ gmvnl.com. This GMVN bungalow, bookable through the GMVN tourist office in Haridwar (see page 309), offers clean and cosy deluxe a/c rooms with TV and hot water, two log huts (from ₹4500), dorms, a restaurant and gardens overlooking the dam. Staff can arrange jeep tours through the park. No wi-fi. Dorms **₹250**, doubles **₹2200**

Forest Rest Houses Scattered throughout the park itself

are ten simple forest resthouses, bookable through the Rajaji National Park Office in Dehradun (5/1 Ansari Marg; ☎ 0135 2621669) or Mohan's in Haridwar (see page 309). The one at Chilla is the largest, and the only one with meals available. No wi-fi. **₹2000**

V Resorts Gauhari Range, 10km before Chilla park gate ☎ 08130 777222, ⓦ vresorts.in. Located amid fields near the Chilla dam, this resort has sixteen rooms, each with a wildlife theme, hardwood floors and private balconies; half face a splash pool and the rest have views of the hills and forest. Local food is served in their restaurant, *Spice Walk*, and safaris, birding, trekking, mountain biking and yoga are all on offer; wi-fi is unreliable. **₹6200**

Rishikesh

RISHIKESH, 238km northeast of Delhi and just 24km north of Haridwar, huddles along the steep wooded banks of the fast-flowing Ganges as it exits the mountains of Garwhal to crash onto the plains. The centre for all manner of New Age and Hindu activity, its many ashrams continue to draw devotees and followers, with the large **Shivananda Ashram** in particular renowned as a yoga centre. Rishikesh is also emerging as an **adventure-sports** centre with rafting, trekking, mountaineering, zip-lining and bungee-jumping on offer.

Rishikesh has one or two ancient shrines, but its main role has always been as a way-station for *sannyasis*, yogis and travellers heading for the high Himalayas. The arrival of the Beatles, who came here to meet the Maharishi in 1968, triggered the lucrative expansion of the *yatra* pilgrimage circuit; these days it's easy to see why Ringo thought it was "just like Butlin's". The best times to visit are in winter and spring, when the mountain temples are shut by the snows – without the *yatra* razzmatazz, you get a sense of the tranquillity that was the original appeal of the place. At other times, a walk upriver leads easily away from the bustle to secluded spots among giant rocks ideally suited for yoga, meditation or an invigorating dip in the icy waters (though swimming is not advised owing to the fast currents).

The name Rishikesh applies to a loose association of distinct areas, encompassing several scattered hamlets on both sides of the river. The town of **Rishikesh** itself sprawls to the south of the Chandrabagha riverbed, home to Triveni Ghat, the train station, bus stand and the commercial and communications hubs. A short ride north of town, beyond Muni-ki-Reti, the Ram Jhula footbridge links **Swarg Ashram** on the east bank, while 2km further upstream near the village of Tapovan is a second footbridge, **Lakshman Jhula**. Both Swarg Ashram and Lakshman Jhula areas are largely traffic-free, spiritual hubs dotted with ashrams, temples, hotels and restaurants.

Triveni Ghat

Most pilgrims passing through Rishikesh en route to the Himalayan shrines of the Char Dham pause for a dip and puja at **Triveni Ghat**, at the southern end of Ghat Road, near the centre of town. The river looks especially divine during evening *aarti*, when *diya* lights (around ₹20) float on the water.

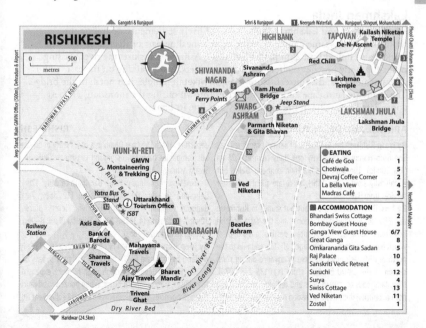

Bharat Mandir

Rishikesh's oldest temple, **Bharat Mandir** features a black stone image of Vishnu, believed to have been consecrated by the great ninth-century Hindu revivalist Shankara; the event is commemorated during Basant Panchami, the first day of spring. A sacred trio of entangled trees near the entrance represents the Hindu Trinity.

Swarg Ashram

The dense-knit complex of cafés, shops and ashrams collectively known as **Swarg Ashram**, opposite Shivananda Ashram, leans back on to the forest-covered hills where caves are still inhabited by sadhus. The most conspicuous of the area's many ashram-temples is **Parmarth Niketan**, whose large courtyard is crammed with brightly clad gods and goddesses. Next door is **Gita Bhavan**, which runs a free Ayurvedic dispensary (daily 8am– noon & 2–8pm); they also sell books, saris and *khadi* handloom cloth. The river can be crossed at this point either by the Ram Jhula footbridge or the nearby ferry (₹10).

Beatles' Ashram

1km south of Swarg Ashram • Daily 9am–4pm • ₹600 (₹150)

Set on a forested bluff high bluff above the river, the abandoned ashram of Maharishi Mahesh Yogi – locally known as **Chaurasi Kutiya** – is also known as the **Beatles' Ashram**, for it was here that the band and its entourage came to learn Transcendental Meditation from the enterprising guru, staying for up to six weeks (Ringo only lasted ten days, McCartney a month) in 1968 and penning over forty songs. Fringed by Rajaji National Park, the tranquil, ruined site was kept under lock and key by the Forest Department until 2015 and there isn't much too see except the **Beatles Cathedral Gallery**, with murals from when it reopened, and curious ovoid meditation huts, clad with smooth river pebbles.

Lakshman Jhula

Most travellers find **Lakshman Jhula**, a pair of lively settlements straddling the footbridge of the same name, to be the most appealing part of Rishikesh. The east bank is also linked by a 2km path from Swarg Ashram that skirts the river, passing beautiful sandy beaches sheltered by large boulders. Most striking on the east bank is the enormous, gaudy, thirteen-storey **Kailash Niketan Temple**, just north of the bridge. The dramatic landscape and turquoise river (brown during the monsoon) are best appreciated from one of the hippie cafés that line its banks.

ARRIVAL AND DEPARTURE | RISHIKESH

By train Rishikesh lies at the end of a small branch railway line from Haridwar, linked by one daily train at 7.25am (1hr 10min). The daily #54472 train connects Delhi, but is painfully slow (7am; 11hr); there are plenty of faster services from Haridwar.

By bus There are two important bus stands in Rishikesh: the ISBT (for lowland destinations) and the Yatra or Tehri Bus Stand (April–Oct for mountain destinations), both of which have recently been combined off Dehradun Rd to the north of Rishikesh town. Reserve in advance during *yatra* season at the GMOU booking office (☏0135 243 0076). Mountain roads are treacherous and tedious, landslides are not uncommon during the monsoon period, and only early departures reach the Char Dham in a day. Plenty of private bus companies have offices around Lakshman Jhula and Swarg Ashram.

Destinations Agra (6pm; 12hr); Badrinath (4 daily; 12hr); Dehradun (hourly; 1hr 30min); Delhi (12 daily; 7hr); Gangotri (5.30am; 11–12hr); Haridwar (every 30min; 30min); Kedarnath (4.30am; 10hr); Nainital (9am; 8–9hr); Uttarkashi (8 daily; 7–8hr).

By jeep Jeeps depart when full from the jeep stand (daily 4–8am) by the main GMVN office on Haridwar Bypass Rd, to the west of town. Although slightly more expensive than buses, they are much faster. When booked in advance through agencies, such as Sharma Travels (86 Haridwar Rd;

AROUND RISHIKESH: LOCAL WALKS

Plenty of paths wind through the forests around Rishikesh, offering walkers a welcome escape from the bustle of town. There's a chance of encountering wildlife along the way; keep a safe distance from wild elephants. Also, bring a guide or walking partner as there have been incidents of **robbery** along the trails.

NEERGARH WATERFALL

Just 3km north of High Bank along the Badrinath road, a left detour on a gravel path leads to the popular **Neergarh waterfall**. The moderately steep walk to the top is dotted with laidback cafés and numerous cascades and little pools, great for a swim. Entry ₹30.

NEELKANTH MAHADEV

Winding steeply through the forests from Swarg Ashram is an old, 10km pilgrim trail to the small Shiva shrine of **Neelkanth Mahadev**. It marks the spot where Lord Shiva once swallowed the poison that turned his throat blue, earning himself the nickname of Neelkanth, "the blue-throated one". The road that takes a long detour through the forest has made the small settlement a less peaceful retreat during *yatra* season. The trail offers some stunning vantage points, crossing a spur before the final descent to Neelkanth. One or both legs are often done by shared jeep (₹100/person), departing from the stand south of Ram Jhula Bridge.

KUNJAPURI

The small white Shakti temple of **Kunjapuri**, 10km north of town, stands at the sharp point of a conical hill 1645m high, with panoramic views of the high Himalayas to the north and Rishikesh and Haridwar to the south. A popular sunrise and sunset spot, it gets most traffic during the Navratri (April & Oct) and Dussehra (Oct) festivals. It's a 3–4hr hike from Lakshman Jhula, passing through pleasant countryside, or a short bus ride to Hindola Khal (every 15min from the Yatra Bus Stand), followed by a 3km (45min) walk uphill.

BEACHES

The motorable track running north of Lakshman Jhula passes several secluded beaches before arriving at the beautiful ashram of **Phool Chatti** (5km upstream), set at a bend in the river with sandy beaches including the famous **Goa Beach**. Giant boulders add drama, but swimming is hazardous due to strong undercurrents.

☏ 0135 243 0364), you may be able to arrange to be picked up from west-bank hotels.

GETTING AROUND

By Vikram and jeep Vikrams to Lakshman Jhula can be hired from Rishikesh's bus station for about ₹120 (₹20/person). On the east bank of the river, jeeps from the northern edge of Swarg Ashram connect to the centre of Lakshman Jhula (₹10).

By ferry Ferries cross the Ganges near Ram Jhula outside monsoon season (daily 7.30am–7pm; ₹10 one way, ₹15

By Vikram Vikrams to Haridwar depart from Dehradun Rd (₹40/person).

return).

By taxi There's a taxi booking office (☏ 0135 243 3861) run by the Garhwal Mandal Taxi Owners Association not far from the Ram Jhula bridge on the west bank. Reliable agencies include Ajay Travels (☏ 0135 243 0644) at *Hotel Neelkanth*, Haridwar Rd, and Mahayama Travels (☏ 0135 2432968) at the Urvasi Complex on Dehradun Rd.

INFORMATION

Information The Uttarakhand Tourist Office (Mon–Sat 10am–5pm; ☏ 0135 243 0209) is just north of the bus stands in the TFC Building. The GMVN (Mon–Sat 10am–-5pm; ☏ 0135 243 0799) has two offices: the larger Yatra Office is behind the jeep stand on Haridwar Bypass Rd,

Natraj Chowk, while a smaller Mountaineering and Trekking branch is on Lakshman Jhula Rd in Muni-ki-Reti (see page 316). Both provide local information, though they tend to push their own tours and accommodation.

ACCOMMODATION

Rishikesh town has a glut of hotels but also an excess of noise and pollution; the only reason to stay here is to be near the bus station. New Agers tend to prefer Swarg Ashram and the east bank of the river, away from the noise and near the ashrams, while backpackers head for the cheap little guesthouses of Lakshman Jhula or the huddle of hotels on High Bank.

Bhandari Swiss Cottage High Bank ☎ 0135 243 2939; ⊚ bhandariswisscottage.com; map p.311. This popular backpacker retreat has a range of good-value fan and a/c (₹1500) rooms spanning its three storeys; the priciest ones are on top for ₹1800. There's a cosy café and restaurant area with wi-fi, plus a nearby yoga class for ₹300. If it's full, the similarly priced *New Bhandari Swiss Cottage* (☎ 0135 243 5322) is a handy neighbour. ₹600

Bombay Guest House Lakshman Jhula, near taxi stand ☎ 78958 34900 or ☎ 0135 325 0038; map p.311. Basic accommodation with shared baths off a central courtyard; handy for exploring the unspoilt upper reaches of the river and popular with long-term travellers. The manager Manu rents bikes and arranges rafting. ₹400

Ganga View Guest House Lakshman Jhula ☎ 0135 244 0320; map p.311. A good-value choice among the many, generally similar, small budget hotels in the area – this one has nice fresh rooms, all with hot water, and it's set off the main drag, making it reasonably quiet. More expensive rooms are upstairs to the rear (₹400–450), while the best face the river and have balconies (₹500–600). A second location is 50m downstream. ₹300

Great Ganga Lakshman Jhula Rd, Muni-ki-Reti ☎ 0135 244 2243; ⊚ greatganga.com; map p.311. It's worth braving the steep pathway to reach this comfortable upmarket hotel. The spotless rooms have river-facing balconies, big windows and lovely views. If you really want to push the boat out, go for a twin-room suite (₹9800). There's also a spa, travel desk and multicuisine restaurant. They run another hotel nearby, *Vasundhara Palace*, with newer rooms (₹4600), though views aren't great. ₹4000

Omkarananda Gita Sadan Shivananda Nagar, Muni-ki-Reti near Ram Jhula Bridge ☎ 0135 243 6346, ⊚ oah.in/gita_sadan.htm; map p.311. Run by the ashram of the same name, this lovely all-a/c guesthouse has a relaxed atmosphere, plain but spacious and immaculately clean rooms, great views over the river towards Swarg Ashram from the upper rooms (₹2000), and even a four-person family suite (₹4000). Viewless rooms on the lower floor are the cheapest. ₹1000

Raj Palace Swarg Ashram, behind Parmarth Niketan ☎ 0135 244 0079, ⊚ hotel-raj-palace-rishikesh.hotelsgds.com; map p.311. Well-managed hotel popular with yoga students due to its location near the ashrams, two large yoga halls and rooftop café. The rooms are basic

but clean, all either air-cooled or a/c (₹1550), and there's a good travel desk and off-season discounts of up to fifty percent. ₹995

Sanskriti Vedic Retreat Near Shivanand Hospital, Ram Jhula ☎ 70604 49920, ⊚ sanskritivedicretreat.com; map p.311. Comfortable retreat close to Ram Jhula with large and well-appointed river-view rooms, an organic café and spa treatments. On a busy thoroughfare that's noisy during the day, but quiet at night. They offer yoga each morning and a great breakfast is included. ₹4500

Suruchi Opposite Yatra Bus Stand ☎ 0135 243 2602; map p.311. Friendly but rather bland budget hotel offering decent, carpeted a/c (₹975) and non-a/c rooms with hot water. There's also a basic restaurant and café downstairs, but the main attraction here is its convenient location for early Char Dham buses. ₹700

★ **Surya** Lakshman Jhula ☎ 0135 244 0211, ⊚ hotellaxmanjhula.com; map p.311. Just above *Café Coffee Day*, *Surya* is a backpacker favourite for its laidback vibe, location in the heart of Lakshman Jhula, and fantastic Ganges views. The best of its clean, marble-floored rooms are those facing the river (₹800–950) in front, though the darker back rooms are quieter. Wi-fi in reception only. ₹600

Swiss Cottage Chandrabhaga ☎ 0135 243 5012 or ☎ 094 1299 2856, ✉ shivgangamylove@rediff.com; map p.311. Rishikesh's first guest-house, founded in 1961 by Swami Brahmananda, disciple of Swami Shivananda. It's a small but peaceful haven with a friendly owner and assortment of rooms, some with a/c (₹1500) and good-value singles (₹500). Popular with long-term visitors so often booked up. ₹800

Ved Niketan Swarg Ashram ☎ 0135 243 0279, ✉ vedniketan@gmail.com; map p.311. Enormous orange ashram with manicured garden grounds on the east bank of the river, with cheap accommodation (single ₹200) popular with budget travellers. There are daily Hatha yoga classes (Mon–Sat 9–10.30am & 4–5.30pm) and Yoga Alliance-certified teacher-training programmes of 200hr duration on offer. ₹400

Zostel Rishikesh-Badrinath Hwy, Tapovan ☎ 0113 958 9003, ⊚ zostel.com; map p.311. India's coolest hostel chain has this spotless property with four- and eight-bed dorms and a compact double available. Bathrooms are a little worn but the laidback rooftop café and friendly atmosphere more than makes up for it. Plenty of organised activities, plus yoga and scooter hire. It's a steep 15min walk from the river. Dorms ₹350, doubles ₹1300

EATING

Café de Goa Above Kunwar Residency, Lakshman Jhula ☎ 0135 244 2490; map p.311. A friendly perch overlooking the Lakshman Jhula bridge and serving great Israeli and Continental dishes. It's most popular at breakfast

time (8–11am) when you cab get an English breakfast with coffee and juice for ₹230. Daily 8am–9pm.

Chotiwala Swarg Ashram ☎ 0135 2434070, ⊚ chotiwala.com; map p.311. Set up in 1958 by the

4

ADVENTURE ACTIVITIES IN RISHIKESH

Adventure activities have become one of Rishikesh's top draws, most notably **rafting**. Numerous river camps on the Ganges above Rishikesh operate from late September to June, with excursions ranging from half-day runs to extended camping/rafting expeditions (starting at around ₹900/person for a couple of hours).

Other activities include an 83m **bungee jump**, canyon swing and flying fox at Jumpin Heights' Jump Zone in Mohanchatti village, 16km from Tapovan, with transfer by coach from their booking office (☎0135 244 2100, ⊛jumpinheights.com), and a two-section **zipline** with India's zipline pioneers, Flying Fox (☎95689 43116, ⊛flyingfox.asia), over whitewater rapids of the Ganges at Shivpuri, 19km east of town. Most activities are only run outside the monsoon period (July–Sept).

TOUR OPERATORS

With the town's seasonal tourism boom has come a dramatic rise of unregulated tour and travel operators with no insurance cover for their drivers, cars or tourists. Ask for recommended **travel agents** at your hotel or at the tourist office, or try one of these reliable local firms.

De-N-Ascent Expeditions Lakshman Jhula Rd, Tapovan ☎0135 244 2354, ⊛kayakhimalaya.com. An experienced local operator (on the west bank of Lakshman Jhula), offering kayaking, rafting, mountain biking and trekking.

GMVN Mountaineering and Trekking Division Lakshman Jhula Rd, Muni-ki-Reti ☎0135 243 0799, ⊛gmvnl.in. Rents equipment and arranges guides for treks across Garhwal, as well as organising ski trips to Auli.

Red Chilli Lakshman Jhula Rd, Tapovan ☎0135 243 4021, ⊛redchilliadventure.com. Another reliable outfit for rafting, trekking, mountain biking and camping. River rafting expeditions run from three days to thirteen.

Agarwal brothers and split in 1995, the two neighbouring establishments with the same name vie for custom and constantly attempt to outdo each other, down to the emblematic *chotiwala* (braided man) sitting on a high chair outside each. Both places are large, busy and open early for breakfast; the extensive menus include express thalis (₹190–220), snacks, ice cream, sweets and cold drinks. Daily 7am–10pm.

Devraj Coffee Corner Lakshman Jhula, just west of the bridge ☎0135 244 2089; map p.311. Sharing shoulder space with Ganga Books Emporium, this is a great spot for a break: enjoy cinnamon rolls, muesli, fruit curd, apple strudel and superb cakes (₹80), or dine on pizzas, sizzlers, curries, burgers (₹170) or Mexican fare, while watching the Ganges and the pilgrims flow past. Daily 8am–9pm.

La Bella View Lakshman Jhula, east bank, near Om Hotel ☎94113 84485; map p.311. The Ganges view from the upstairs tables in the rooftop restaurant is only slightly better than the cosier, cushion-cl*ad downstairs area. The menu spans Indian to Israeli, with emphasis on Italian dishes like pasta al pesto (₹180) and pizza margherita (₹170). Daily 9am–10.30pm.

Madras Café Ram Jhula ☎0135 243 0934; map p.311. Set up in 1967 to cater to the south Indian tastes of Swami Sivananda's followers, this popular restaurant serves reason-ably priced *idli*, dosa and *sambhar* and excellent filter coffee. The "Himalayan Health Pulao" (₹180) is worth a try, made with vegetable sprouts and Ayurvedic herbs, as is the "Thali of the Kings" (₹190) and the house special wholewheat pancake (₹200), topped with mixed fruit, curd and honey. Daily 8am–9.30pm.

ASHRAMS, YOGA AND MEDITATION

Rishikesh has plenty of reputable ashrams welcoming students of yoga with courses of varying cost and duration – from one day to several months. Guests must be respectful of ashrams' strict rules governing conduct. Be warned that complaints of theft and harassment in ashrams are surprisingly common.

Parmarth Niketan Ashram Swarg Ashram ☎0135 244 0077, ⊛parmarth.com. This giant ashram right next to the river houses more than a thousand simple rooms with daily yoga classes, a range of yoga courses, nightly *aarti* ceremonies and a common dining hall. They also sponsor the International Yoga Festival in early March. Complaints about cleanliness are common and so visiting, rather than staying here, is probably best.

Phool Chatti Ashram 5km north of Lakshman Jhula ☎98977 30397, ⊛phoolchattiyoga.com. Peaceful ashram with lush gardens in a pristine setting far away from the noise of town. They specialize in seven-day, all-inclusive yoga and meditation retreats (from ₹8000/person), mostly aimed towards beginners and intermediate level.

Sivananda Ashram ☎ 0135 243 0040, ⓦ sivananda online.org. Large institution, with branches all over the world, run by the Divine Life Society and founded by Swami Sivananda (who passed into *maha samadhi* – final liberation – in 1963). It has a well-stocked library, a forest retreat and a charitable hospital. The most rigid schedule begins at 4am, with nearly constant lessons in meditation and yoga on offer. For long-term stays, contact the secretary three months in advance through their website. Stays are donation-based.

DIRECTORY

Banks and exchange Banks in town include the Bank of Baroda and the nearby Axis Bank, both on Dehradun Rd, with ATMs. There are also several banks with ATMs further north: on Lakshman Jhula Rd by the GMVN trekking office, on the east bank near Ram Jhula Bridge and in Swarg Ashram. Numerous travel agents in Lakshman Jhula will change cash.

Post office The main post office is on Ghat Rd near Triveni Ghat (Mon–Fri 10am–4pm, Sat 10am–1pm), with branch offices in Lakshman Jhula and near both sides of Ram Jhula Bridge.

Uttarkashi

The largest town in the interior of Garhwal, picturesque **UTTARKASHI** makes a convenient stopover to break up the road from Rishikesh (148km south) to Gangotri (100km northeast). Pilgrims often stop at the ancient **Kashi Vishwanath temple** in the heart of town, and discerning travellers are beginning to linger longer to hike the unspoiled trails of Garhwal's interior or to gear up for longer treks such as to Dodi Tal.

Occupying the flat and fertile valley floor of the Bhagirathi, Uttarkashi is no stranger to natural disasters; the town was hit by severe floods in 1978, an earthquake in 1991, a massive landslide in 2003, and further floods in 2013. Efforts have since been made to secure the hillside against landslides, but the bridge to Gangotri had to be rebuilt after the 2013 floods.

4

ARRIVAL AND DEPARTURE

UTTARKASHI

By bus All buses to and from Uttarkashi park on Gangotri Rd in the centre of town.

Destinations Chamba (every 30min; 5hr); Hanuman Chatti (2 daily; 7hr); Mussoorie (2 daily; 9hr); Rishikesh (9 daily; 8hr); Sangam Chatti (3 daily; 45min).

By jeep Shared jeeps depart from a jeep stand 500m north of the town centre, leaving when full for Gangotri (5am–2pm; 5hr). For Rishikesh (6hr), Haridwar (7hr) and other destinations south, another cluster of jeeps waits by the petrol station opposite *Bhandari Hotel*.

INFORMATION AND ACTIVITIES

Uttarkashi's busy and well-stocked market is ideal for picking up supplies before high-altitude treks.

Guides and trekking companies The town has an abundance of experienced mountain guides – most of them graduates of its highly esteemed Nehru Institute of Mountaineering (☎ 01374 222123, ⓦ nimindia.net), who run one-month mountaineering and adventure courses (₹14000). Specialist operators include Mount Support, BD Nautial Bhawan, Bhatwari Rd (☎ 01374 222419, ⓦ facebook.com/mountsupport), who also have equipment for rent and porters for hire.

Yoga Sivananda Kutir at Netala, 8km northeast on Gangotri Rd, offers month-long teacher-training courses (☎ 85478 81801, ⓦ sivananda.org.in).

ACCOMMODATION AND EATING

GMVN Tourist Bungalow Opposite District Collectorate ☎ 95680 06693, ⓦ gmvnl.com. A comfortable three-storey complex set around an attractive lawn in the heart of town. Rooms are clean and spacious with TVs and marble floors, and there's an attached dorm and restaurant. Prices come down slightly July–Oct and are slashed during low season (Nov–April). Dorms ₹280, doubles ₹1800

Hillview Gangotri Rd, 300m up from the bus stand. Set in the hotel of the same name, this is one of the best restaurants in town, offering an assortment of Chinese and Indian dishes as well as snacks and breakfasts. The veg thali is a good deal (₹80), but the special thali is even better (₹130). Daily 8.30am–10pm.

★ **Monal Tourist Home** 2km north of town ☎ 01374 222270, ⓦ monaluttarkashi.com. The best deal around, this welcoming guesthouse is run by Deependar Panwar, a graduate of the Nehru Institute of Mountaineering and a great source of local information. Both the A and B wings are clean and well kept, but the A wing is more attractive with more spacious rooms and a cosy veranda. Within Wing B is a bright,

---

THE DODI TAL TREK

One of Garhwal's classic hikes, the **Dodi Tal trek** links the Gangotri and Yamunotri regions without straying into high glacial terrain. It's relatively short and easy, but local villagers are keen to offer their services as porters or guides, taking hikers off the beaten track to visit the villages. Carry as much of your own food as possible and bring a tent.

From **Uttarkashi**, catch a morning bus (45min) or jeep heading to Sangam Chatti (1350m), from where it's a 7km climb through fields and woodland to **Agoda** (2286m), where you can set up camp or head to the *Tourist Bungalow* at the far end of the village. On the second day, follow the trail from Agoda as it climbs west of the Asi Ganga and zigzags steadily upwards through lush pine and spruce forests, with a smattering of chai shops en route. After 14km and a final undulation, you will reach the lake of **Dodi Tal** (3024m), set against a backdrop of thickly forested hills and said to be the spot where Lord Ganesha was both born and beheaded. Near the basic forest bungalow in the clearing are chai shops and areas for camping.

On the third day you'll make the 4km hike to Dharwa Top, following the well-marked path along (and often across) the stream that feeds Dodi Tal, which can get steep and entail scrambling, until you emerge above the tree line. A further 2km along, the trail heads left to a small pass, then zigzags up scree to **Dharwa Top** (4130m), the highest point of the trek, offering superb panoramas of the Srikanta Range. A leftward path beyond the top leads to camping and water, but if you've still got sufficient energy and daylight, you can continue along the main route, which takes about four more hours and 13km to rejoin the tree line at **Sima**, where there's basic hut accommodation.

The following day's beautiful 12km trail from Sima kicks off with a steep 1.5km scramble alongside a stream before easing past forest and *bugyal* (alpine meadow). A well-defined rocky path drops steadily through two villages and zigzags down to the Hanuman Ganga, finally emerging at **Hanuman Chatti** (see page 319), from where buses and jeeps connect with Barkot, Uttarkashi, Mussoorie and other points in Garhwal. The Dodi Tal trek can easily be tied in with hikes in the **Har-ki-Dun** (see page 307) and **Yamunotri** areas (see page 319).

---

big-windowed restaurant and sitting area, combined with a small library and a computer with internet access. ₹1200
Goat Village Dayara Bugyal, 45km from Uttarkashi ☎ 96392 31472. Off the Uttarkashi–Gangotri road – it's around 1hr 30min by taxi from town – this back to basics place doesn't have electricity (there's solar panels to charge phones etc.), but it does have an unbeatable rural location in the Garhwal Himalayas. Two private wooden cottages and group accommodation with bunk beds, plus space for tents. Dorms ₹2250, doubles ₹6500

DIRECTORY

Banks and exchange There are three ATMs in town: Bank of Baroda near Hillview on Gangotri Rd, and State Bank and PNB in the main market area.

Post office The post office (Mon–Sat 9.30am–5pm) is west of the main market, near the river.

The trek to Yamunotri

Cradled in a deep cleft in the lap of Bandarpunch, and thus denied mountain vistas, the temple of **Yamunotri** (3291m), 223km northeast of Rishikesh, marks the source of the Yamuna, India's second holiest river after the Ganges. The least dramatic but most beautiful of the four *dhams* (temples) of Garhwal, it's also the least spoiled and commercial. **Access** (mid-April to early Nov; exact dates vary annually) has become easier following road improvements; from the roadhead at Janki Chatti it's a mere 5km along a trail that follows the turbulent ice-blue river as it runs below rocky crags, with snowy peaks in the distance. The walk can also be combined with the **Dodi Tal trek** linking nearby Hanuman Chatti to Uttarkashi.

En route from the town of **Barkot**, there are several *chattis* (*serais* or inns) for pilgrims along the way, including Syana Chatti (27km before Yamunotri), Hanuman Chatti (13km) and Janki Chatti (6km).

Barkot

Situated 49km short of Yamunotri, among terraced fields and scenic apple orchards with views of the Bandarpunch range, **BARKOT** makes a great stopover to escape the *yatra* traffic. Tracing their origins to the Mahabharata, the local Rawain people – like the five Pandava brothers married to Draupadi – historically practised fraternal polyandry (marriage of multiple brothers to a single woman), a way of life still prevalent in rural areas.

Janki Chatti and around

The riverside hamlet of **HANUMAN CHATTI** (2400m) is the western terminus of the famous trek to Dodi Tal (see page 318); 7km beyond this is the enchanting little village of **JANKI CHATTI** (2475m), which marks the end of the motorable road from Rishikesh and the start of the trail to Yamunotri. While in Janki Chatti, it's worth making the 1km detour across the river to the traditional Garhwali village of **KHARSALI**, home to the *pandas* (pilgrim priests) of Yamunotri. Among the dry-stone buildings, with their beautifully carved wooden beams, stands a unique three-storey Shiva temple – dedicated to Someshwar, lord of the mythical intoxicant Soma.

Yamunotri

The 6km trail from Janki Chatti becomes steeper and more dramatic as it passes through rocky forested crags to reach **Yamunotri**. Built around three piping-hot sulphur springs by the river, Yamunotri's temple is new and architecturally uninteresting; it has to be completely rebuilt every few years due to the impact of heavy winter snows and monsoon rains. Its main shrine – actually part of the top spring, worshipped as the source of the river – holds a small silver image of the goddess Yamuna, bedecked with garlands. The daughter of Surya, the sun, and Sangya, consciousness, Yamuna is the twin sister of Yama, the lord of death; all who bathe in her waters are spared a painful end, while food cooked in the water is considered to be *prasad* (a divine offering). Most pilgrims bathe in the **hot spring** (free), which has separate pools for men and women.

Technically, the source of the Yamuna is the glacial lake of **Saptarishi Kund**, a hard, steep 12km trek up the mountain alongside the river that eases towards its end near the base of Kalinda Parbat. Both this trek and the route over the challenging Yamunotri Pass to Har-ki-Dun (see page 307) necessitate at least one day's acclimatization, adequate clothing and a guide, available from the GMVN tourist lodge in Yamunotri.

ARRIVAL AND DEPARTURE

THE TREK TO YAMUNOTRI

Barkot There are two daily buses to Barkot from Mussoorie (4–5hr) and several private buses from Rishikesh (6–7hr). All buses to Uttarkashi stop at Dharasu Bend, from where shared jeeps and buses ply to Barkot, which has frequent connections on to Hanuman Chatti (2hr 30min).

Hanuman Chatti During *yatra* season, Hanuman Chatti is connected by direct buses to Dehradun (8hr), Mussoorie (5hr 30min), Rishikesh (12hr), Gangotri (11hr) and Uttarkashi (7hr), although most services are for Barkot, from where there are more frequent connections available to all these destinations.

Janik Chatti Shared jeeps connect Janki Chatti with Hanuman Chatti (20min) and Barkot (2hr).

ACCOMMODATION AND EATING

In addition to the places below, there are GMVN tourist bungalows (@gmvnl.com), with dorms (from ₹170) and spartan rooms (from ₹500) at Barkot (☎01375 224236), Syana Chatti, Hanuman Chatti (☎96394 68793), Janki Chatti (☎01375 235639) and Phool Chatti (☎96394 68793).

BARKOT

Camp Nirvana Gangnani, 8km north of Barkot ☎96507 25842, @campnirvana.com. A peaceful eco-camp overlooking the river with twenty luxury tents, each with comfy beds, veranda and attached bathrooms. Village treks, fishing and local excursions organized. Rates include breakfast and dinner. Off-season discounts up to 30 percent. ₹5000

Yamunotri River Banks Resort Gangnani, 7km north of Barkot ☎98911 58725, ⓦyamunotriresorts.com. Riverside resort offering sixteen luxury tents with hot water, a multicuisine resturant and superb mountain views. Rates include breakfast and dinner. ₹4600

JANKI CHATTI

Atithi Niwas ☎97601 70011, ⓦhotelatithiniwas.com. One of the better hotels in town, with 33 double rooms that come with hot water, a basic restaurant and mountain views all around. Good off-season discounts. ₹2400

YAMUNOTRI

Several ashrams offer beds starting at around ₹300/person. Among the best of the ashrams are Ramananda, overlooking the temple, and Hanuman Mandir, run by the famous Rambharose Das, aka Nepali Baba. Otherwise, there's the Yamuna Ashram and the much smaller Kali Kamli Dharamshala.

Gangotri and the Gaumukh Glacier trek

Set amid tall deodar and pine forests at the head of the Bhagirathi gorge, 248km north of Rishikesh at 3140m, **Gangotri** is the most remote of Garhwal's Char Dham (see page 301) and the last place to stock up on supplies before heading up to the high altitudes. The jeep drive from Uttarkashi is breathtaking – in more ways than one – as it winds high above the Bhagirathi and crosses one of the world's highest bridges, over the gorge near **Lanka**. Although the wide Alaknanda, which flows past Badrinath, may have a better technical claim to be the main channel of the Ganges, Gangotri is for Hindus the spiritual source of the great river, while its physical source is the ice cave of **Gaumukh** on the Gangotri Glacier, 14km further up the valley. From here, the **River Bhagirathi** begins its tempestuous descent through a series of mighty gorges, carving great channels and cauldrons in the rock and foaming in whitewater pools.

Gangotri

Road accessible mid-April to early Nov

Although most of the nearby snow peaks are obscured by the desolate craggy mountains looming immediately above **GANGOTRI**, the town itself is redolent of the atmosphere of the high Himalayas, populated by a mixed cast of Hindu pilgrims and foreign trekkers. Across the Ganga River from the temple, a loose tangle of ashrams and guesthouses dwarfed by great rocky outcrops and huge trees leads down to **Dev Ghat**, overlooking the confluence with the Kedar Ganga. Near the centre of the town, webbed together by stone pathways and metal footbridges, is the impressive waterfall-fed pool of **Gaurikund**.

Gangotri temple

Gangotri's unassuming **temple**, overlooking the river just beyond a small market on the left bank, is one of India's holiest sites. Built early in the eighteenth century by the Gurkha general Amar Singh Thapa, the simple structure consists of a squat *shikhara* surrounded by four smaller replicas; it commemorates the legend of the goddess Ganga, brought to earth by King Bhagirath's penance to revitalize the ashes of his ancestors. Inside is a silver image of the goddess, while a slab of stone adjacent to the temple is venerated as **Bhagirath Shila**, the spot where the legendary king performed his meditation. Steps lead down to the main riverside *ghat*, where the devout bathe in the freezing waters of the river to cleanse their bodies and souls of sin.

ARRIVAL AND DEPARTURE	GANGOTRI

By bus and jeep The bus and jeep stands both lie just beyond the west entrance to town. Jeeps connect Gangotri to Uttarkashi (departing when full, 5.30am–2pm; 5hr), from where there are connections further south. During *yatra* season (May–Oct), early morning buses link Rishikesh (11hr) and Haridwar (12hr).

ACTIVITIES

Trekking Real Adventure, run by Deepak Rana (☎ 94101 78414, ⓦ realadventuregangotri.in), organizes treks to Tapovan, Dodi Tal and Kedarnath, among others, as well as lower-altitude winter treks, providing equipment and porters for hire.

ACCOMMODATION AND EATING

A number of *dhabas* and cafés on both sides of Gangotri's river serve thalis, good breakfasts and much-needed, warming chai. For pilgrims heading toward Gaumukh, the market area also marks the last chance to buy gloves and woolly hats. All hotels provide buckets of hot water for bathing (₹30).

Bhagirathi Sadan Across the river, 200m from the temple ☎ 94107 35573. A well-kept riverside option on the quieter side of the bridge, with small green rooms (plus a four-bed option; ₹1400) and a shared patio overlooking the river. Good off-season rates. A thali at the canteen costs ₹100–200. No wi-fi. **₹1000**

Gangaputra Guesthouse 200m east of jeep stand. Small hotel with six clean, green-carpeted double rooms sharing a cosy balcony over the main drag. The downstairs restaurant, serving north and south Indian food and equipped with a generator, is one of the town's best for thalis (₹100–150). No wi-fi. **₹800**

Krishna Restaurant 100m east of jeep stand ☎ 94101 99108. The cleanest and best restaurant in town, serving a good range of meals from cheesy pasta (₹130–300) to classic thalis (₹100–300). Daily 8.30am–9.30pm.

Gaumukh Glacier Trek

Mid-April to early Nov • ₹600 (₹150) for two days; ₹250 (₹50) per extra day; video camera ₹1500

A flight of steps beside the Gangotri temple begins the 20km trek to **Gaumukh Glacier**, one of the most beautiful and accessible glaciers in the inner Himalayas.

Leaving Gangotri, the trail rises gently above the north bank of the river, offering increasingly spectacular mountain vistas. Just 2km along at Kankhu is the **forest checkpoint**, where permits are inspected. About 7km further is the oasis of **Chirbasa**, where the skyline becomes dominated by magnificent buttresses and glass-like walls, culminating in the sharp pinnacles of Bhagirathi 3 (6454m) and Bhagirathi 1 (6856m). The path then climbs above the tree line, passing across a steep rocky area prone to landslides. Just around the bend, beyond a stream crossing, 5km from Chirbasa, is the cold grey hamlet of **Bhojbasa**, cowering in the shadows of the surrounding peaks. Most visitors spend a night here before the final push to the glacier.

From Bhojbasa, it's a further 4km up the giant boulder-strewn path to reach **Gaumukh** ("the cow's mouth"), bringing into view the beautiful **Shivling Peak** (6543m), the "Indian Matterhorn", and providing a closer look at the Bhagirathi peaks and the huge expanse of the Gangotri Glacier – 23km long, up to 4km wide and sweeping like a gigantic highway through the heart of the mountains. At the source, the river emerges with great force from a cavern in the glacier. The steadily retreating ice is in a constant state of flux, so the huge greyish-blue snout of the glacier continually changes appearance as chunks of ice tumble into the gushing water. Visitors are advised to keep 500m back from the glacier's mouth: many pilgrims have been crushed to death by falling ice while attempting to collect holy water. It's well worth braving the cold to reach Gaumukh for **sunrise**, though it's also rewarding in the afternoon, when the source is lit by the sun. From the glacier, most hikers return to Gangotri via Bhojbasa, while others may continue beyond the glacier to the meadow of Tapovan (6km) or further afield to the lake at Vasuki Tal.

> ## GAUMUKH GLACIER PERMITS
>
> Only 150 tourists are allowed on the Gaumukh Glacier trek each day; **permits** must be obtained in advance from either the District Forest Office in Uttarkashi (Mon–Sat 10am–5pm), 3km north of the bus stand near *Monal Tourist Home*, or, more conveniently, from the Gangotri office (daily 8–10am & 5–7pm), just above the jeep stand to the west of town; 120 are available at the former, the remainder at the latter. Come prepared with photocopies of the ID and visa pages of your passport so as not to let Gangotri's frequent power outages delay your trek.

In addition to **Bhojbasa**'s GMVN bungalow, you can stay at the popular Lal Baba Ashram or the quieter Ram Baba Ashram, both tented camps offering a snug bed for ₹300, common loo and meals. You can also camp for free down by the river but you'll need your own tent. At **Tapovan** the genial sadhu at Mauni Baba's Ashram, on a silent vow, provides bed, blanket and whatever he can rustle up in his small hut to travellers staying overnight. Donations and rations are welcome.

GMVN Tourist Bungalow Bhojbasa, 4km short of Gaumukh ☎ 0135 274687. Beds are available within the row of large, six-person canvas tents here, but there are no private rooms. Guests huddle in the small, friendly restaurant (thali ₹195), the warmest spot in Bhojbasa, which is also the place to arrange a mountain guide if you plan to cross the glaciers. ₹320

Kedarnath and around

It's hard to imagine a more dramatic setting for a temple than **Kedarnath** (3583m), 223km northeast of Rishikesh, which sits close to the source of the Mandakini overlooked by tumbling glaciers and giant buttresses of ice, snow and rock. The third of the sacred Char Dham sites, Kedarnath is among the most important shrines in the Himalayas and as one of India's twelve *jyotirlinga* – lingams of light – attracts hordes of Hindu pilgrims (*yatri*) in the summer months (open April–November only). The area makes a refreshing change from the rocky and desolate valleys of west Garhwal, with lush hanging gorges, terraced hillsides and abundant apple orchards.

In June 2013, however, Kedarnath was the epicentre of one of the worst Himalayan disasters in India. At the peak of the tourist season, continuous rain for five days and a cloudburst above the peak of Kedar Dome ruptured the Chorabari Glacier, 4km north, causing the Mandakini River to flood its banks. The ensuing flashflood wreaked havoc at Kedarnath and downstream as far as Rishikesh, with debris washing away hotels and other buildings, many illegally built on fragile riverbanks. According to official figures, over 5700 people died, though the actual toll of this "Himalayan tsunami" is much higher. With large chunks of the trail disappearing off the mountainside and the midway point at Rambara completely devastated, new trekking routes and a new tented base camp for pilgrims were created.

Gaurikund

Accessible early April to early Nov

The small but bustling town of **GAURIKUND**, at the end of the motorable road from the south, is revered as the place where Gauri, also called Parvati, paid her penance and eventually won the heart of Shiva. In town are a set of hot springs and a temple enshrining an image of Parvati, although the latter's religious significance far exceeds its visual appeal. For the vast majority, Gaurikund is most important as the main starting point of the trek up to the **temple of Kedarnath** (see page 323).

By bus and jeep As of 2016, only smaller vehicles are allowed up to Gaurikund. The jeep stand serves Rishikesh, Haridwar, Badrinath and Joshimath, although most head first to Rudraprayag (4hr), which is also served by regular buses from Haridwar and Rishikesh (every 30min). Connecting buses run to Sonprayag, 5km before Gaurikund.

ACCOMMODATION AND EATING

GMVN Tourist Bungalow Near Kedarnath trailhead ☎ 95680 06656. Gaurikund's most welcoming option, offering clean and cosy doubles with hot water on demand, and a mixture of squat and Western-style toilets. There's also a restaurant offering breakfasts, soups, salads and veg thalis (₹150). Dorms ₹220, doubles ₹990

The trek to Kedarnath

April to early Nov • Horses for the upward trek ₹1800; four-man *dholis* ₹3500

With the original trail to Kedarnath from Gaurikund via Rambara and Garur Chatti washed away in the 2013 floods, a new 15km route from Gaurikund, developed by the Indian Army and members of the Nehru Institute of Mountaineering (NIM), has now been opened. The new trail crosses a bridge where Rambara once was and then heads up via Jangal Chatti (4km away), Chhoti Linchuli and Badi Linchuli, before reaching the south face of Kedarnath peak (6940m) at the end of the valley. Alternative routes start from Chaumasi (18km) or Trijuginarayan (15km) to reach Kedarnath, which is also a good base for short treks to the beautiful lake of Vasuki Tal.

Kedarnath

Even before the tragedy of 2013, **KEDARNATH** was not a very attractive town – a cold, grey place almost unbearable at the height of the pilgrimage season (May, June & Sept). The central thoroughfare that stretches for 500m up to the temple was once lined with dozens of resthouses, *dharamshalas*, pilgrim shops and eateries. Barring the temple, little of the original Kedarnath remains, with a tented camp set up 500m south of the shrine. However, the sheer power of its location tends to sweep away any negative impressions, and it's always possible to escape to explore the incredible high-altitude scenery.

Kedarnath Temple

Although the surroundings and the compound wall of imposing **Kedarnath Temple** were destroyed, miraculously the shrine itself was not damaged: rocks that broke off from Kedar Dome blocked the floodwaters and diverted them around the temple. The temple was originally constructed by Adi Shankara in the ninth century. Built of stone with a large *mandapa* (fore-chamber), it houses an impressive stone image of Shiva's bull, Nandi. Within the inner sanctum, open to all, *pandas* (priests) sit around a rock considered to be Shiva's upraised bottom, left here as he plunged head-first into the ground in the form of a bull when fleeing Bhim, one of the Pandavas. Mendicant sadhus congregate in the elevated courtyard in front of the temple.

ACCOMMODATION AND EATING   KEDARNATH

GMVN Tourist Bungalow 500m before the temple **☎**01364 263228. The tourist bungalow at the new base camp is currently the only place to stay, a tented colony with ground beds in shared five-man tents. There's power and hot water available, but no wi-fi. ₹350

Shri Badrinath Kedarnath Mandi Samiti Just behind the temple. This canteen, run by the temple committee, serves curries and *aloo paratha*. Daily 5am–1am.

Joshimath

The scattered administrative town of **JOSHIMATH** clings to the side of a deep valley 250km northeast of Rishikesh, with tantalizing glimpses of the snow-capped peaks high above and the prospect, far below, of the road disappearing into a sunless canyon at Vishnu Prayag, the confluence with the Dhauli Ganga. Few of the pilgrims who pass through en route to Badrinath linger, but Joshimath has close links with **Adi Shankara**, the ninth-century reformer who attained enlightenment here beneath a mulberry tree before going on to establish **Jyotiramath**, one of the four centres of Hinduism (*dhams*) at the four cardinal points. The town itself consists of a long drawn-out **Upper Bazaar**, and, around 1km from the main market, a **Lower Bazaar** that holds the colourful Narsingh, Navadurga, Vasudev and Gauri Shankar **temples**. A 4km **cable car** (₹750 return) links the town to the slopes of **Auli**, one of India's better ski resorts, attracting visitors throughout the year for its views of the High Himalayas.

ARRIVAL AND DEPARTURE   JOSHIMATH

Despite considerable effort on the part of the military, the roads around Joshimath are notoriously prone to landslides during the monsoon season, making for routine delays.

By bus Buses depart from near the GMOU office in the centre of the main market, Upper Bazaar to Rishikesh (10hr) and Haridwar (11hr), stopping off in Karnaprayag (3hr 30min), from where there are frequent connections to Kumaon via Gwaldam. During *yatra* season, there are also regular buses from the Joshimath bus stand, just above the main market, to Govind Ghat (1hr) and Badrinath (2hr), as well as a daily service to Gaurikund (11hr).

By jeep The jeep stand is located beside the Joshimath bus stand, with jeeps departing when full for Govind Ghat (45min) and Badrinath (2hr), as well as down to Karnaprayag (3hr) and Rishikesh (9–10hr).

INFORMATION AND TOURS

Tourist information The tourist office (Mon–Fri & usually Sat 10am–5pm; ☎01389 222181) is by the GMVN block above Upper Bazaar.

Trekking and skiing Eskimo Adventure Company (☎97568 35647 or ☎01389 222864, ⌂eskimoadventure. com), opposite *Hotel Sriram* in the main market, and Himalayan Snow Runner (☎94120 82247 or ☎01389 222687, ⌂himalayansnowrunner.com), near the cable car west of Upper Bazaar, offer summer and winter trekking across Uttarakhand.

Banks and exchange There are two ATMs (PNB and SBI) in the main market.

ACCOMMODATION AND EATING

Dronagiri 1km west of main market ☎01389 222254, ⌂dronagirihotel.com. Although not the most central, this is the most comfortable hotel in town, offering a choice of rooms with good views, running hot water, a clean multi-cuisine restaurant, internet access and satellite TV. ₹1710

GMVN Tourist Rest House Up a short lane 400m from the Upper Bazaar ☎95680 06667. Centrally located, with basic but decent rooms (the deluxe ones are twice the price), a dorm and a café serving simple meals and veg thalis (₹100). The newer block, above the old and accessed by the lane opposite the GMOU office, is better (☎95680 06668; ₹2400), especially the rooms with front-facing views. No wi-fi. Dorm ₹250, doubles ₹1100

Auli D Food Plaza On the Upper Bazaar. Close to Punjab Bank, this is one of the many similar places serving standard veg and non-veg Indian fare, as well as some international dishes. The plastic-covered chairs and tables look like they were once quite grand and it's a local favourite. Cash only. Daily 9.30am–9.30pm.

Badrinath

Accessible May–Oct only

BADRINATH, "Lord of the Berries", just 40km from the Tibetan border, is the most popular of Garhwal's four main pilgrimage temples, and one of Hinduism's holiest sites. Founded by Shankara in the ninth century, it lies near the source of the Alaknanda, the main tributary of the holy Ganges. Badrinath's setting is dazzling, deep in a valley beneath the sharp, snowy pyramid of Nilkantha (6596m), but the town itself, sprawled to the south and east beyond the temple, is largely grubby and unattractive. Immediately south of the temple, on the west bank of the Alaknanda, is the old **village** of Badrinath, its traditional stone buildings and small market seeming like relics from a bygone age.

Badri Narayan

Strictly no photography inside the temple

Badrinath's **temple** is known as **Badri Narayan**, and is dedicated to Vishnu, said to have done penance in the mythical Badrivan ("Berry Forest") that once covered the mountains of Uttarakhand. Unusually, it is made of wood, and the entire facade is repainted each May after the snow has receded and the temple has reopened for the season. From a distance, its bright colours, which contrast strikingly with the concrete buildings, snowy peaks and deep blue skies, resemble a Tibetan *gompa*. Inside the temple, the black stone image of **Badri Vishal** is seated like a *bodhisattva* in the lotus position (some Hindus regard Buddha as an incarnation of Vishnu). *Pandas* sit around the cloisters carrying on the business of worship and a booth enables visitors to pay in advance for *darshan* chosen from a long menu.

This site, on the west bank of the turbulent Alaknanda, may well have been selected because of the sulphurous **Tapt Kund** hot springs on the embankment right beneath the temple, used for ritual bathing.

Mana

Local buses and taxis normally run the 4km from Badrinath to Mana but check the current situation before setting out

The main road north of Badrinath heads into border-sensitive territory, where the intriguing Bhotia village of **MANA** nestles at the road's end. It's also possible to walk to Mana along a clear footpath by the road. The village consists of a warren of small lanes and buildings piled virtually on top of each other; the local Bhotia people, Buddhists of Tibetan origin who formerly traded across the high Mana Pass, now tend livestock and ponies and sell yak meat and brightly coloured, handmade carpets. Past the village and over a natural rock bridge, a path leads up the true left bank of the river towards the mountain of Satopanth (7075m), to the base of the impressive 145m **waterfall** of **Vasudhara**, considered to be the source of the Alaknanda. Walking time is just an hour and a half and, unusually, there are no chai stalls en route.

ARRIVAL AND INFORMATION BADRINATH

By bus Badrinath's bus station is near the southern edge of town; buses depart from here every 2hr from 5.30am until 1.30pm to Joshimath (2hr), Rishikesh (12hr) and Haridwar (13hr), the later departures making an overnight halt en route to lowland destinations. During *yatra* season, one daily bus runs to Gaurikund (7am; 12–13hr).

By jeeps Shared jeeps depart from 5am until early afternoon from just outside the bus stand, connecting the same destinations as the buses.

Banks and exchange SBI has an ATM just across the bridge by the temple steps, though service is occasionally interrupted.

Internet There aren't many places with internet access and your best bet is wi-fi at the café at *Sarovar Portico* hotel.

ACCOMMODATION AND EATING

Badrinath is awash with rough, flea-bitten budget hotels strung along the main road. The most atmospheric area for cafés and chai shops is the old section around the temple, but the more commercial east bank holds a few more upmarket restaurants, along with numerous bog-standard *dhabas*.

GMVN Devlok Bazar 50m east of post office ☎ 95680 06651. Set closer to the action than most other hotels, *Devlok* has a somewhat institutional feel but spacious, pleasant rooms, a restaurant serving Marwari and Gujarati thalis (₹200), great views of Neelkanth and excellent local advice. No wi-fi. **₹2700**

Panchali Tourist Guest House Across from the south entrance to the bus station ☎ 94107 43596, ✉ rameshnaithani.05@gmail.com. This small family-run guesthouse, convenient for catching early buses heading south, has eight well-kept rooms with clean bathrooms, hot water buckets for ₹30 and a welcoming owner. **₹600**

Sarovar Portico 200m south of the bus station ☎ 93103 33317, ✇ sarovarhotels.com. Marking the southern entrance into town, this is Badrinath's poshest hotel, with plentiful amenities including a luxurious café-lounge. Rates include breakfast and wi-fi. **₹6500**

Hemkund and the Valley of Flowers

Trail to Ghangaria Open mid-April to early Nov · **Hemkund pilgrimage season** End May to end Sept · **Valley of Flowers National Park** June to early Oct daily 7am–5pm (last entry 2pm) · Three-day permit ₹650 (₹150)

Starting from the mountain hamlet of **Govind Ghat** (1800m), 28km south of Badrinath, an important pilgrim trail winds 15km up a steep stone path to the overgrown village of **Gangharia** (3048m), also known as Ghovind Dham. This one-street town is a stopover point for hundreds of Sikh pilgrims en route to Hemkund, as well as for a small trickle of visitors to the Valley of Flowers. Overnight stays are prohibited at both sites.

From Ghangaria, it is a further 6km trek along a steep path to reach the snow-melt lake of **Hemkund** (4329m). In the Sikh holy book, the Guru Granth Sahib, Govind Singh recalled meditating at a lake surrounded by seven high mountains; only in the twentieth century was Hemkund discovered to be that lake. A large *gurudwara* and a small shrine to Lakshmana, the brother of Rama, now stand alongside.

An alternative trail forks left from just above Ghangaria, climbing 5km to the mountain *bugyals* of the Bhyundar Valley – the **Valley of Flowers**. Starting at an altitude of 3352m, the valley was discovered in 1931 by the visionary mountaineer Frank Smythe, who named it for its multitude of rare and beautiful flora. The meadows are at their best during the monsoon, from mid-July until mid-August. Due to the no-camping rule, it is unfortunately impossible to explore the 10km valley in its entirety in the space of a day's hike from Ghangaria.

ARRIVAL AND DEPARTURE

HEMKUND AND THE VALLEY OF FLOWERS

TO GOVIND GHAT

By bus and jeep Buses and shared jeeps run frequently from early morning until mid-afternoon between Joshimath (45min) and Badrinath (1hr), stopping along Badrinath Rd at Govind Ghat, just above the trailhead.

ON TO GHANGARIA

By pony Beyond Govind Ghat, the road is motorable for a further 4km – shared Sumos (₹50/head) run to Pulna (2000m), from where you can travel by pony or mule (₹700 one way) to Ghangaria, 10km away.

KUARI PASS TREK

The old route over the **Kuari Pass** (4268m) in northeastern Garhwal, also called the Curzon Trail after the British viceroy who traversed parts of it in 1905, provides some stunning mountain views. Officially renamed the **Nehru Trail** after Independence, the popular five-day trek crosses the high ranges without entering the permanent snowline, making it an ideal expedition for those not equipped to tackle glacial terrain. Following alpine meadows, crossing several major streams and skirting the outer western edge of the Nanda Devi National Park, the trail affords excellent views of Trisul (7120m), the trident, Nanda Ghunti (6309m), and the elusive tooth-like Changabang (6864m), while to the far north on the border with Tibet rises the unmistakable pyramid of Kamet (7756m). Camping equipment is needed, especially on the pass; guides can be negotiated in Joshimath or Ghat.

Though the original trailhead lies much further south at Gwaldam, most people begin the trek at Ghat, which is connected by shared jeeps to Nandaprayag (1hr 15min). From Ghat, it's 62km to Auli, near Joshimath, crossing the Kuari Pass (3640m) on the sixth day, while an alternative ending takes you to the hot springs of Tapovan in the Dhauli Ganga Valley. The trek is best tackled from May to June and mid-September to November.

Using the Kuari Pass as a base, a climb to the peak of **Pangerchuli** (5183m), 12km up and down, is thoroughly recommended – the views from the summit reveal almost the entire route, including breathtaking mountain vistas. Although snow may be encountered on the climb, it is not a technical peak and no special equipment (save a good stick) is necessary. One descent from Kuari Pass is the picturesque and less abrupt 24km route through forest to the ski centre of **Auli** via Chitrakantha, while a worthy alternative is the gruelling, knee-grinding 22km descent down to the small village of **Tapovan**, overlooking the Dhauli Ganga and its hot-spring-fed tank, and connected by local transport to Joshimath, just 11km away.

By helicopter Helicopters operated by the Uttarakhand tourism department leave from Govind Ghat's helipad to Ghangaria, charging around ₹4000 per person.

INFORMATION AND PERMITS

Information The tourist information office in the centre of Ghangaria (daily 6pm–8pm) exists only to screen a nightly documentary on the Valley of Flowers (6pm; 20min; ₹20), provided the town's power is up and running.

Permits Three-day permits for the Valley of the Flowers can be bought from the ticket office, about 300m up the trail from Ghangaria towards Hemkund, to the left. Additional days are ₹250 (₹50) per day.

ACCOMMODATION

GMVN Tourist Guest House Ghangaria ☎ 75790 11005. This airy pink complex offers good value, with clean, spacious rooms set off the busy pathway towards the forested banks of the Pushpavati. No wi-fi. Dorms ₹280, doubles ₹1100

Priya Ghangaria ☎ 94129 53214. This basic hotel run by local expert Pratap Chauhan has a spacious shared balcony and decent, spotless rooms with clean bedding and white-tile bathrooms. The offering at the downstairs restaurant includes Garhwali dishes on request – *maruwa* (finger

millet) *roti*, *jholi* (seasoned curd curry) or *jhangora ki kheer* (sweet millet porridge; ₹90). Off-season discounts offered. No wi-fi. ₹1800

Shri Nanda Lokpal Palace Ghangaria ☎ 94120 54570. This three-storey block, just to the right of the trail as it reaches Ghangaria, houses clean, cosy rooms that are among the town's best. There's also a friendly owner, a handy generator and a restaurant serving pricey *jholi* (₹100). Hot water is ₹50/bucket. No wi-fi. ₹2750

Nainital

The small, peanut-shaped crater lake of Nainital, set in a mountain hollow at an altitude of 1938m, 277km north of Delhi, gives its name to the largest town in Kumaon. Discovered for Europeans in 1841 by Mr Barron, a wealthy sugar merchant, **NAINITAL** swiftly became a popular escape from the summer heat of the lowlands, and remains one of India's top hill stations. Throughout the year, and especially between March and July, hordes of tourists and honeymooners pack the **Mall**, a 1.5km promenade of restaurants, hotels and souvenir shops that links **Mallital** (head of the lake), the older, colonial part of Nainital at the north end, with **Tallital** (foot of the lake).

Nainital's position within striking range of the inner Himalayas – the peaks are visible from vantage points above town – makes it a good base for exploring Kumaon. When the town's commercialism gets a bit much, it's always possible to escape into the beautiful surrounding country, to lakes such as **Sat Tal** (23km away), where the foothills begin their sudden drop towards the plains to the south, or to the forested ridges around **Kilbury** (12km) and the old Shiva temple at **Mukteshwar** (51km), both of which offer stunning Himalayan vistas.

The Flats

The popular **Nainital Boat Club** stands at the edge of the large plain known as the **Flats**, the result of a huge landslide in 1880 that buried the *Victoria Hotel*, along with 150 people. Surrounded by the cheap and lively **Tibetan Market**, a **gurdwara**, the gleaming **Jama Masjid** and the rebuilt **Naina Devi Temple**, the Flats now hosts a large field for sporting events. A favourite pastime for day-trippers is to **rent a boat** (₹160) on the lake from next to the boat club, on the northwest corner.

High Altitude Zoo

A steep 1.5km climb from the southern end of the Mall • Tues–Sun 10am–4.30pm • ₹50, camera ₹25, video camera ₹200 • ☎ 05942 237927

Up in the hills of Sher ka Danda overlooking the town is Nainital's small **High Altitude Zoo**, home to exotic creatures such as Tibetan wolves, leopards and Himalayan black

> ### TRAVELLING IN KUMAON
>
> As the Shaivite temples of **Kumaon** do not attract the same fervour as their Garhwali equivalents, the region receives far less tourist traffic, its villages are largely unspoilt and its trekking routes unlittered. To the east, Kumaon's border with Nepal follows the Kali Valley to its watershed with Tibet; threading through it is the holy trail (foreigners must have a permit) to the ultimate pilgrimage site, Mount Kailash in Tibet, the abode of Shiva and his consort Parvati. Kumaon Mandal Vikas Nigam, or **KMVN** (🌐 kmvn.gov.in), runs the official tourist scene in Kumaon, reflecting the services of GMVN in Garhwal. Note that services in the region are sparse, with a capricious electricity supply, frequent power cuts and, outside of Nainital, very few banks that change cash.

bears. It's well managed, with detailed explanations in English and a tiny Shiva temple tucked away at the top.

Snow View and around

Cable car Daily: May & June 8am–8pm; July–April 10am–5pm • ₹150 return

A cable car climbs from near *Mayur Restaurant* on the Mall to **Snow View** (2270m), from where good views of the snow-clad peaks are most likely early in the morning (especially Oct–March). Otherwise it's a 2km hike along a choice of steep trails. The top gets overcrowded in season, with a carnival atmosphere of rides, stalls, go-karting, cafés and a promenade.

About halfway up to Snow View, conspicuous thanks to its abundant prayer flags, lies the small Tibetan *gompa* (temple) of **Gadhan Kunkyop Ling**, rebuilt in traditional *gompa* style. Beyond Snow View, trails lead on for 4km to **Naina Peak** (2611m), also called **China Peak**, the highest point around Nainital, with good views in all directions.

ARRIVAL AND DEPARTURE   NAINITAL

By bus Buses for most destinations run from Tallital Bus Stand in the south of town. Most buses to Ramnagar, however, depart from Sukhatal Bus Stand, west of Mallital, although two morning services also depart from Tallital. More connections throughout Kumaon are available from the nearby transport hubs of Bhowali (20min) and Haldwani (1hr 30min).

By jeep Shared jeeps congregate near the Tallital Bus Stand, linking Bhowali and Haldwani, as well as destinations further north in Kumaon such as Almora (3hr) and Ranikhet (2hr 30min).

Destinations Almora (daily; 3hr); Bhowali (every 30min; 20min); Delhi (9.30am & 9.30pm; 9hr); Haridwar (8 daily; 7–8hr); Kathgodam (every 30min; 30min); Ramnagar (6 daily; 3hr 40min); Ranikhet (daily; 3hr 30min); Rishikesh (8 daily; 8–9hr).

By train The Railway Reservation Office (Mon–Sat 9am–noon & 2–5pm, Sun 9am–2pm; ☎ 05942 231010) is by the Tallital Bus Stand. The nearest railway station is at Kathgodam (35km south; linked by regular buses), from where the #15014 *Ranikhet Express* connects Old Delhi (dep. 8.40pm; arr. 3.55am), the #14119 *Dehradun Express* connects Haridwar (dep. 7.45pm; arr. 2.45am) and Dehradun (arr. 4.20am), the #13020 *Bagh Express* connects Lucknow (dep. 9.55pm; arr. 5.55am), Gorakhpur (arr. 12.20pm), for crossings into Nepal, and Kolkata (arr. Howrah station 12.40pm on the second afternoon).

GETTING AROUND

Cycle rickshaw The cycle rickshaw stand is in Tallital; the journey from the Mall to Mallital costs ₹10.
Vehicle rental Bikes and motorbikes can be rented from *City Heart* hotel, while agencies along the Mall, among them KMVN Parvat Tours (see below) and Hina Tours (☎ 05942 235860 or ☎ 97190 30786, 🌐 hinatours.com), rent cars.

INFORMATION

Tourist information There's an Uttarakhand Tourism office on the Mall near Mallital (Mon–Sat 10am–5pm; ☎ 05942 237476), but you'll find better information online (🌐 nainitaltourism.com).
Tours, trekking and mountaineering The KMVN representative, Parvat Tours (Mon–Sat 10am–5pm; ☎ 05942

235656), organizes tours and books accommodation at KMVN lodges. For more advice on trekking and mountaineering, call in at Nainital Mountaineering Club, CRST Inter College Building (☎05942 235051), opposite *City Heart* hotel in Mallital, which offers mountain courses and climbing trips (Sept–June; starting at ₹1000 [₹500]).

ACCOMMODATION

As a holiday town, Nainital is full of hotels, but budget accommodation is hard to come by in season. Rates are highest between March and July, peaking in May and June. On the whole, rooms are cheaper in Tallital than in Mallital.

Ankur Plaza Opposite cable car station, Mallital ☎05942 239728, ⊛hotelankurplaza.com; map p.329. Steep prices in season and a steep climb up to it, but friendly management and a bargain off-season (doubles from ₹2000). Rooms are cosy, showing attention to detail if not great taste, and come with breakfast for two. **₹3750**

Ashok 100m from Tallital Bus Stand ☎05942 235721, ⊛ashoknainital.com; map p.329. Handy for early buses, this functional old-style hotel offers a range of decent, compact rooms, fine for a short stay, although its surrounds aren't as attractive as those in Mallital. Most room rates are cut by fifty percent during off-season. **₹2800**

★ **City Heart** Above Mallital rickshaw stand ☎05942 235228, ⊛cityhearthotelnainital.com; map p.329. This welcoming hotel has some of the best lake views in town, especially from the upper rooms and rooftop restaurant, all with cable TV and hot water (7–11am). The friendly owner, Pramod Pandey, is a great source of local information. Rates are much more reasonable in the off-season (from ₹1500). **₹3000**

Grand The Mall ☎05942 235008, ⊛thegrandnainital. com; map p.329. One of the first hotels to be built in Nainital (constructed in 1872), where time seems to stand still: there's plenty of period atmosphere in the large, high-ceilinged rooms, although some are showing their age a bit. The cheapest rooms are on the ground floor, featuring LCD TVs and quaint sitting rooms, though the first-floor ones have better views. **₹5400**

KMVN Tourist Bungalow 200m west of bus stand, Tallital ☎05942 231436; map p.329. Functional rooms that come with breakfast, and a cheap dorm, set in a quiet part of Tallital, a short walk from the bus stand. A lengthy set of stairs connects the upper rooms, which have great lake views. Good off-season discounts. Dorms **₹300**, doubles **₹3000**

Manu Maharani Mallital, 1.2km northwest from Nainital Boat Club ☎05942 237342, ⊛themanuaharani.com; map p.329. Barely a 15min walk from town, the sprawling hotel is a comfy perch with excellent service. Rooms on the ground floor have superb sitouts from which to savour scenic lake and valley views. Wholesome thali meals for ₹780 plus wide-ranging Western and Asian cuisine. **₹11,900**

The Naini Retreat Ayarpatta Slopes, 1km from the Mall ☎05942 235103 or ☎95550 88000, ⊛leisurehotels. in; map p.329. Beautifully situated high above the lake in extensive, immaculate grounds, this was the residence of the maharaja of Pilibhit. There's a great terrace for

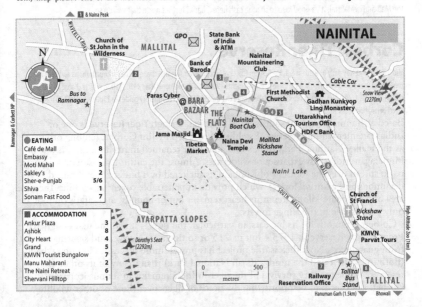

NAINITAL

EATING
Café de Mall	8
Embassy	4
Moti Mahal	3
Sakley's	2
Sher-e-Punjab	5/6
Shiva	1
Sonam Fast Food	7

ACCOMMODATION
Ankur Plaza	3
Ashok	8
City Heart	4
Grand	5
KMVN Tourist Bungalow	7
Manu Maharani	2
The Naini Retreat	6
Shervani Hilltop	1

barbecues, two restaurants, a café, bar and an Ayurvedic spa and wellness centre. Lake-facing rooms are more expensive. Breakfast included. ₹8750

Shervani Hilltop Mallital, 2km northwest from the Mall ☎05942 233800, ⓦshervanihotels.com; map p.329. Peaceful boutique hotel tucked into the hillside away from town. Smart, comfortable rooms are in cottages spread out among pretty gardens, with mountain views and excellent buffet breakfast and dinners. Shuttle service to/from town provided. ₹10,700

EATING

Café de Mall The Mall ☎05942 235527, ⓦcafedemall. com; map p.329. A restaurant and café with a small espresso (₹30) machine, and an open eating area overlooking the lake. The menu includes south Indian snacks, pizzas and sizzlers, plus thalis (₹250–290). Daily 9am–4pm & 5.30–10pm.

Embassy The Mall, Mallital ☎05942 235597; map p.329. One of Nainital's older favourites, with an attractive, wood-panelled interior and a small outdoor seating area. They are strongest on tandoori, Chinese and Tibetan dishes, but also offer sizzlers (₹340 upwards). Daily 9am–5pm & 7–11pm.

Moti Mahal The Mall, Mallital ☎05942 235515; map p.329. Among the favourites in town for Punjabi cuisine, *Moti Mahal* has a cosy set of booths and serves Chinese and Indian dishes (chicken curry ₹220) sandwiches and pizzas (vegetarian ₹215). Daily 9am–11pm.

Sakley's The Mall, Mallital ☎05942 235086; map p.329. Since 1944, cosy *Sakley's* has been serving posh if pricey international cuisine including breakfast pancakes (₹320), seafood dishes such as grilled fish with creamy lemon butter sauce (₹595) and chicken sizzlers (₹595). Alternatively, pop in for a very civilized tea with a pastry or slice of cake. Daily 10am–10pm.

Sher-e-Punjab The Mall; map p.329. Good non-veg Indian restaurant overlooking the Mall, with dishes including chicken and mutton *sagwala* (₹150) and butter chicken (₹350). A larger restaurant with the same name (but different owners) is near Bara Bazaar (daily 9am–11pm), and popular with locals, serving good thalis (₹90–140) and butter chicken for the same price as at the Mall restaurant. Daily 10.30am–10pm.

Shiva Bara Bazaar, Mallital ☎97197 24069; map p.329. Cheap, good and popular *dhaba* with tasty *matar paneer* (₹160) and mushroom dishes, among other veg options. Thalis range from ₹120–190. The next-door clone (to the right) is equally good. Daily 9am–11pm.

Sonam Fast Food Tibetan Market, Mallital; map p.329. Tiny but popular café in an alley behind the market, serving up hot plates of veg or mutton *momos* (₹60–80), chow mein (₹40–80) and *thukpa* (soup; ₹60), though there's not much in the way of seating. Daily 11am–9pm.

DIRECTORY

Banks and exchange There are a handful of ATMs along the Mall and in Mallital. It's a good idea to change cash here if you are moving on into the mountains, as there are few banks further north that will do so.

Corbett Tiger Reserve

Mid-June to mid-Nov daily 6–9.30am & 1.30–5.30pm (check at reception for seasonal changes in park hours); Jhirna and Dhela zones open year-round • Overnight fees: three days/two nights ₹900 (₹200); additional days ₹450 (₹100); vehicle charge ₹1500 (₹500) • Day visit (4hr) fees: permit fee ₹500 (₹200); vehicle charge ₹500 (₹250) • Mandatory guide fee ₹500 • ☎05947 251489, ⓦcorbettnationalpark.in

Based at Ramnagar, 63km southwest of Nainital, **Corbett Tiger Reserve** is one of India's premier wildlife reserves. Established in 1936 by Jim Corbett (among others) as the Hailey National Park, India's first, and later renamed in his honour, it is one of Himalayan India's last expanses of wilderness. Almost the entire 1288-square-kilometre park, spread over the foothills of Kumaon, is sheltered by a buffer zone of mixed deciduous and giant *sal* forests, which provide impenetrable cover for wildlife. The core area of 520 square kilometres at its heart remains out of bounds, and safaris on foot are only permissible in the fringe forests.

Corbett is famous for its big cats, in particular, the **tiger** – it was the first designated Project Tiger Reserve in 1973 – but its 215 or so tigers are elusive, and sightings are far from guaranteed. Nonetheless, the project has proven more successful in Uttarakhand (both in Corbett and the nearby Rajaji National Park) than in any of its other 48 reserves. While the very survival of the tiger in India remains in serious jeopardy, Corbett does seem to be prioritizing the needs of tigers over those of other wildlife and of tourists. Incidents of **poaching**, however, are not unheard of, though of late it's Corbett's **leopards** that have faced the most serious threat.

The reservoir within the park also shelters populations of **gharial**, a long-snouted, fish-eating crocodile, and large marsh **mugger crocodile**, as well as other reptiles. Jackal are common, and wild boar often run through the camps in the evenings. The grasslands around Dhikala are home to deer species such as the spotted **chital**, hog and barking **deer** and the larger **sambar**, while rhesus and common langur, the two main classes of Indian **monkey**, are both abundant, and happy to provide in-camp entertainment. Corbett also has spectacular birdlife, with nearly five hundred resident and migratory species, including around fifty species of raptors or **birds of prey**, among them the crested serpent eagle and the Himalayan grey-headed fishing eagle. Late spring (April–June) is the best time to see wildlife, when low water levels force animals into the open. The park is divided into six "eco-tourism zones" open for day-visits, of which by far the best for sighting big game is picturesque **Dhikala**, deep into the park near the reservoir and where visitors can stay overnight. Bijrani, Sonanandi, Jhirna, Durgadevi and **Dhela** are the other five zones, the last only opened to tourism only in 2014 and is slated for development, with a proposed tiger sanctuary and walking trails.

Ramnagar

Situated in the rich farm-belt of the terai, on the southeastern fringes of the great forests, the busy market town of **RAMNAGAR** is the administrative hub for Corbett Tiger Reserve and has plenty of budget accommodation. Permits and accommodation reservations are issued at the **reception office** (see page 333). There's little to do around Ramnagar itself except go **fishing**. At Lohachaur, 15km north along the River Kosi, good anglers are in with a chance of landing the legendary mahseer, a redoubtable battling river carp.

4

JIM CORBETT (1875–1955)

Hunter of man-eating tigers, photographer, conservationist and author, **Jim Corbett** was born in Nainital of English and Irish parentage. A childhood spent around the Corbett winter home just outside Kaladhungi (29km southeast of Ramnagar) instilled in young Jim a love for close communion with nature and an instinctive understanding of jungle ways.

Known locally as "Carpet Sahib", a mispronunciation of his name, Jim Corbett was called upon time and time again to rid the hills of Kumaon of **man-eating tigers** and leopards. Normally shy of human contact, such animals become man-eaters when infirmity brought upon by old age or wounds renders them unable to hunt their usual prey. Many of those killed by Corbett were found to have suppurating wounds caused by porcupine quills embedded deep in their paws.

One of Corbett's most memorable exploits was the killing of the **Champawat tiger**, which was responsible for a documented 436 human deaths, and was bold enough to steal its victims from the midst of human habitation. By the mid-1930s, though, Corbett had become dismayed with the increasing number of hunters in the Himalayas and the resultant decline in wildlife, and diverted his energies into conservation, swapping his gun for a movie camera and spending months capturing tigers on film. His adventures are described in books such as *My India*, *Jungle Lore* and *Man-Eaters of Kumaon*; Martin Booth's *Carpet Sahib* is an excellent biography of a remarkable man. Unhappy in post-Independence India, Jim Corbett retired to East Africa, where he continued his conservation efforts until his death at the age of eighty.

For a further glimpse into Corbett's life, head to his family's former winter retreat near Kaladhungi, which has been turned into the **Jim Corbett Museum** (Mon–Sat: summer 7am–6pm; winter 8am–5pm; ₹50 [₹10]).

Dhikala

Beautifully situated overlooking the Ramganga reservoir and the forested hills beyond, Corbett's main camp, **Dhikala**, lies 49km northwest of Ramnagar and 31km west of Dhangarhi Gate. As you can only stray beyond the confines of the camp on elephant-back or in a car or jeep, the whole place has something of the air of a military encampment. It's normally possible to see plenty of animals and birds from the Dhikala **watchtower**, a 1km wander down the path near the restaurant (turn left where the path meets a junction); bring binoculars, remain quiet and don't wear bright colours or perfume. *Chital*, sambar and various other deer species find refuge in the savannah grasslands known as the *chaur*, behind the camp to the south, and tigers are occasionally drawn in looking for prey.

ARRIVAL AND DEPARTURE
CORBETT TIGER RESERVE

The nearest town to Corbett Tiger Reserve is Ramnagar where you'll find the reserve Reception Office. Private vehicles are not allowed; visitors may enter the CTR in a registered 4WD, such as a Gypsy. Tours can be arranged in Ramnagar or any of the outlying resorts, but it is best to arrange this in advance.

RAMNAGAR

By train The railway station is 1km south of the town centre (beyond the *Corbett Kingdom* hotel); from here, the #25014 *Corbett Park Link Express* leaves at 10pm for Delhi Sarai Rohilla (arr. 4.56am). The #55322 *Ramnagar-Varanasi Express* leaves at 8.50pm, connecting with Lucknow (arr. 7.45am) and Varanasi (arr. 3.45pm). For faster trains and connections to other parts change at Moradabad (7 daily; 1–2hr).

By bus From the main bus stand (📞84760 07547) in the town centre, buses run to Bhowali (for Nainital; 2 daily; 3hr 30min), Delhi (every 15min; 7hr), Dehradun (every 30min; 7hr 30min) and Haridwar (24 daily; 6hr).

DHIKULI

Dhikuli (not to be confused with Dhikula) resorts offer pick-up from Ramnagar's bus and train stations, while auto-rickshaws charge ₹150–200.

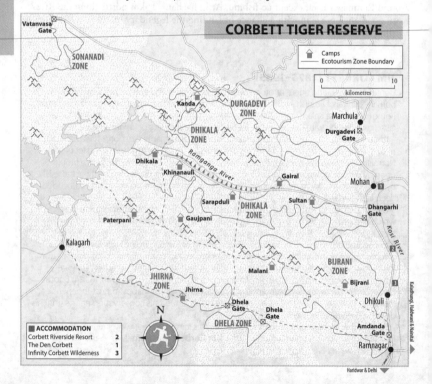

CORBETT TIGER RESERVE

Camps
Ecotourism Zone Boundary

0   10
kilometres

Vatanvasa Gate

SONANADI ZONE

Kanda

DURGADEVI ZONE

Marchula

DHIKALA ZONE

Durgadevi Gate

Dhikala

Ramganga River

Khinanauli

Gairal

Mohan

Sarapduli

Sultan

DHIKALA ZONE

Dhangarhi Gate

Paterpani

Gaujpani

Kosi River

Kalagarh

BIJRANI ZONE

JHIRNA ZONE

Malani

Bijrani

Dhikuli

Jhirna

Dhela Gate

Dhela Gate

N

DHELA ZONE

Amdanda Gate

Ramnagar

Kaladhungi, Haldwani & Nainital

ACCOMMODATION	
Corbett Riverside Resort	2
The Den Corbett	1
Infinity Corbett Wilderness	3

Haridwar & Delhi

PARK GATES

The closest of the various park gates from Ramnagar is at Amdanda (1km north) on the road to Bijrani (11km). Another useful gate is Dhangarhi (18km north of Ramnagar), which provides access to the park's northern and northwestern portions, including the main camp of Dhikala. Dhela Gate (20km west of Ramnagar) links Jhirna in the south of the park and in 2017, two further gates opened on the Garhwal-Kotdwar side of the park, closest to Delhi.

INTO THE PARK

Dhikala can only be accessed by those with an overnight reservation within the Dhikala camp, or on a day bus (Canter) tour organized via the reception centre. Other zones are accessible by jeep or bus (see below).

INFORMATION AND PERMITS

Information The CTR Reception Office (daily 10am–5pm; ☎ 05947 251489, ⓦ corbettonline.uk.gov.in) is about 100m to the north of the bus stand, on the opposite side of the road. There's also a visitors' centre (daily 10am–3pm) and museum at Dhangarhi Gate.

Park permits Permits should be organised at least 6 weeks in advance online at ⓦ corbettonline.uk.gov.in or by booking with a tour operator.

Banks and exchange There are several ATMs in Ramnagar, including Bank of Baroda on Ranikhet Rd and SBI at the train station.

TOURS AND GUIDES

Bus tours The park runs daily tours in sixteen-seater Canter buses (6am & noon; ₹3000 [₹1500]) to Dhikala from Ramnagar, providing the only means of reaching the camp without staying the night.

Safaris Jeeps to Bijrani, Jhirna, Dhela, Durgadevi and Sitabani (maximum six people) cost ₹7000 (₹4000) and can be arranged online or via your accommodation or a tour operator. Tigerland Safaris at Dhikuli (☎ 98976 55055, ⓦ tigerlandsafaris.com) is the longest established local operator; the owner, Pavan, is the go-to man for Corbett. Other operators can be found outside Ramnagar's bus stand. Be clear about what you're getting for your money: fuel, driver's accommodation and all safaris (4hr duration is standard) should all be included. A petrol 4WD, such as a Maruti Gypsy, is best as it is quiet and built for the terrain. Girish at *Govind* restaurant in Ramnagar (☎ 05947 251615) can also help arrange tours.

Guides All jeep safaris must be accompanied by a guide (₹500/day) – who may or may not be able to identify wildlife or speak English – allotted to your jeep by a rota system. If you require a guide with specific knowledge, contact the Field Director one month in advance with your request (☎ 05947 253977).

ACCOMMODATION

A number of self-contained **resorts** have sprung up on the fringes of Corbett, close to the town of **Dhikuli**, about 9km north of Ramnagar. These provide a higher standard of accommodation than in **Dhikala** or **Ramnagar** as well as guides for expeditions in the neighbouring forests, which can be as rich in wildlife as the park, minus all the restrictions and bureaucracy.

RAMNAGAR

Anand 100m south of the main bus stand ☎ 05947 254385. This modest option in the town's noisy centre offers clean, simple rooms, all with TV; larger ones with geyser water heaters cost ₹1200. There's a spotless little restaurant attached. ₹800

Corbett Kingdom 400m south of the bus stand ☎ 05947 253270, ⓦ corbettkingdom.com. Next to a none-too-clean irrigation ditch near the town centre, this flashy three-storey hotel is Ramnagar's best, offering a/c rooms with flatscreen TVs and big windows. The hotel's ample amenities include a multicuisine restaurant, travel desk and a small pool. ₹2500

Karan's Corbett Motel 1km south of the train station ☎ 98374 68933, ⓦ karanscorbettmotel.com. New setup in a leafy mango orchard with four neat rooms kitted out with air coolers (two bigger rooms cost ₹1500) and in-house restaurant. Friendly owner Karan arranges safaris and tours, besides pick-up from the town centre (otherwise a ₹80 auto-rickshaw ride). ₹1200

KMVN Tourist Lodge Next to CTR Reception Office, about 100m north of bus stand ☎ 05947 251225. As institutional as any KMVN lodge, in a central but relatively quiet location with a dorm and basic restaurant as well as spacious but spartan doubles, some with a/c (₹1900). Dorm ₹200, doubles ₹1400

DHIKALA

All accommodation within the park is bookable via the CTR Reception Office in Ramnagar; however, bookings (online or by telephone) for Dhikala should be made at least thirty days in advance (twenty for Indian nationals) during peak season. KMVN run a canteen for guests, *Parvat*, with both Indian and Western food available, while on the other side of the camp is a *dhaba* serving similar food.

Dhikala Forest Lodge ☎ 05947 251489, ⓦ dhikala

forestlodge.in. Surrounded by a small fence, the complex has 32 attached rooms spread across six wings with solar heating, plus a pair of twelve-bed dorms with bunk beds and common bathrooms. A veg buffet is served at the in-house restaurant. No wi-fi. Dorms ₹400, double ₹1250

DHIKULI RESORTS

Corbett Riverside Resort 11km north of Ramnagar ☏ 98111 09596, ⊚ corbettriverside.com; map p.332. A picturesque setting, 10km north of Ramnagar looking across the river to forest-covered cliffs. Amenities include a pool, volleyball court, billiards hall and a travel desk where you can arrange various safaris and horseback rides. The super-ritzy Presidential Suites along the river's edge (₹17,000) have verandas directly above the river beach. ₹6000

The Den Corbett 29km north of Ramnagar (9km beyond Dhangarhi Gate), Mohan ☏ 97566 07850; map p.332. Wood-panelled stone cottages in a leafy mango orchard above the Kosi River, complete with a curvaceous pool and a spa. There are good two-night/three-day package deals and off-season discounts. ₹5000

Infinity Corbett Wilderness 9km north of Ramnagar ☏ 96501 93662, ⊚ infinityresorts.com; map p.332. This ostentatious resort overlooks the Kosi and forested hills, with large comfortable rooms (facing the garden or river), a library, well-stocked bar, swimming pool, gym and spa. Safaris cost (a lot) extra. Activities include nature trails with the resort's own naturalists, jungle rides, fishing, trekking and films. Off-season ₹7000 with all meals. ₹11,600

Ranikhet

The small and deliberately undeveloped hill station of **RANIKHET** (1824m), 50km west of Almora, is essentially an army cantonment, home to the Kumaon Rifles. New construction is confined to the **Sadar Bazaar** area, while the rest of the town above it, climbing towards the crest of the hill, retains its peacefully pleasant atmosphere in the shade of tall pine woods. Forest trails abound, including a shortcut from the bazaar to the Mall (something of a misnomer, as it's a quiet road with few buildings apart from officers' messes), which starts just above the town and continues south for 3km along the wooded crest of the ridge.

KRC Shawl and Tweed Factory

Above the Narsingh Stadium Parade Ground, at the very start of the Mall • Mon–Sat 9am–7pm (winter 10am–6pm), Sun 10am–5pm • Free

The **KRC Shawl and Tweed Factory**, in an old church equipped with looms and wheels, allows visitors to watch the weavers in action, a fascinating display of concentration, dexterity and counting. The herringbone and hound's-tooth tweeds are sold in the shop next door (woollen items ₹700–1500).

ARRIVAL AND DEPARTURE   RANIKHET

By train There's a railway reservation office (Mon–Fri 9am–1pm & 2–4pm, Sat 9.30am–1pm & 2–3pm) next to the post office, handy for booking trains from the nearest station in Kathgodam.

By bus Buses from all over Kumaon, including the railway station at Kathgodam, 84km away, arrive at one of two stands on either end of the bazaar: the KMOU stand to the west at Gandhi Chowk, and the Uttarakhand Roadways stand (☏ 84760 07549) east of the bazaar. Long-haul buses to Delhi, Lucknow, Dehradun and Haridwar depart from the

UP Roadways stand, while all other regional destinations are served by the KMOU stand.

Destinations Dehradun (2 daily; 10hr); Delhi (4 daily; 11–12hr); Haldwani (10 daily; 4hr 30min); Kathgodam (6 daily; 3hr 30 min); Lucknow (2pm daily; 13–14hr); Ramnagar (1 daily; 4hr).

By jeep Shared jeeps depart when full from beside both bus stands for many of the same destinations, including Almora (2hr) and Haldwani (3hr).

GETTING AROUND

By jeep Shared jeeps leave when full for the Mall (₹10; 10min) from the small stand above Gandhi Chowk.

By taxi The taxi rank is just above the KMOU Bus Stand.

ACCOMMODATION AND EATING

If you're just passing through Ranikhet, the hotels in the   busy bazaar are sufficient, but the Mall is better for an extended stay. Eating choices are pretty limited; the best of them are within the better hotels, but there are a few good cafés and *dhabas* in the bazaar.

Chevron Ranikhet Club The Mall, 2km south of town centre ☎ 05966 220611, ⓦ chevronhotels.in. For a taste of Indian military life and a good dose of colonial nostalgia, take out a temporary membership of the Ranikhet Club (₹50/person/day) for a meal at the classy old restaurant (lunch till 3.30pm), which serves great sizzlers (₹260–290), or a drink at the bar; dress code is strictly formal. Guests can also use club facilities such as the tennis courts and billiards and cards rooms. The old rooms have been refurbished as well, but don't have as much character as the *Rosemount*. ₹3500

★ **Chevron Rosemount** 500m west of the Mall from the turn-off just south of Hotel Meghdoot ☎ 05966 221391, ⓦ chevronhotels.com. A beautifully restored 1897 colonial mansion, deep in the woods, all pine and teak with lovely rooms, a restaurant and gardens complete with tennis, croquet, badminton and snow views from the deckchairs on the lawn. ₹5000

Meghdoot The Mall, 3km south of town centre ☎ 05966 220475, ⓦ hotelmeghdootranikhet.in. Comfortable suites set back from balconies full of potted plants and flowers, with running hot water and room service, plus a good mid-range restaurant that serves up a range of tasty biryani (₹130–200), pulao and other non-veg dishes. Singles for ₹1400. ₹3000

DIRECTORY

Banks and exchange There are several ATMs in town, including one at the State Bank of India (Mon–Fri 10am–4pm).

Post office The main post office is on the Mall (Mon–Sat 9am–5pm), not far beyond the *Chevron Ranikhet Club*.

Almora

Spread out over a hilltop overlooking terraced fields, 67km north of Nainital, **ALMORA** (1646m) is Kumaon's official and cultural capital. Founded by the Chand dynasty in 1560, and occupied successively by the Gurkhas and the British, it remains a major market town, and has attracted an eclectic assortment of visitors over the years, including Swami Vivekananda, Timothy Leary and the Tibetologist author of *The Way of the White Clouds*, Lama Angarika Govinda. While many foreign visitors prefer the nearby traveller colony of Kasar Devi, around 8km north, Almora makes a practical base for regional excursions.

Almora bazaars

Although most of Almora's official business is conducted along the hectic **Mall**, the **bazaars**, immediately above and parallel to it along the crest of the saddle, hold much more of interest. These pedestrian-only flagstone lanes teem with local crowds in the evenings, while the faded, carved facades evoke a distant past. The most impressive example of the old architectural style is found at the Khazanchi Mohalla, which once belonged to the state treasurers. Stretching about 1.5km from Lal Bazaar to Thana Bazaar, the various markets offer everything from *khadi* (home-spun) cotton textiles to *tamta* (local copperware).

The temples

Towards the top of town, just north of the market area, a compound holds a group of Chand-period stone temples. The main one, a squat single-storey structure, is dedicated to **Nanda Devi**, the goddess embodied in the region's highest mountain. More typical of Kumaoni temple architecture are two larger Shaivite painted stone temples, capped with umbrella-like wooden roofs covering their stone *amalaka* (circular crowns). During September a large fair is held here in honour of Nanda Devi.

ARRIVAL AND DEPARTURE   **ALMORA**

By train There's a computerized railway reservation centre (Mon–Sat 9am–noon & 2–5pm) at the KMVN *Tourist Rest*

House hotel, on the Mall 1km west of the centre, useful for booking trains from the nearest railway station at

4

Kathgodam.

By bus Buses arrive and depart from a pair of nearby adjacent bus stands located in the middle of the Mall. Tickets for Kumaoni destinations can be bought from the KMOU office (☏ 94105 01878), while tickets for Dehradun, Haridwar and Delhi should be purchased from the UTC office (☏ 05962 230046), 50m east and down some steps by Deewan's Sweets.

Destinations Bageshwar (3 daily; 3hr 30min); Baijnath (2 daily; 2hr 30min); Bhowali (2 daily; 3hr 30min); Dehradun (2 daily; 12hr); Delhi (4 daily; 12hr); Haldwani (2 daily; 3hr); Haridwar (2 daily; 10hr); Kausani (2 daily; 2hr 30min).

By jeep The jeep stand is by the Bharat filling station on the Mall, just west of *Shikhar* hotel. Jeeps depart when full for Kasar Devi (15min), Binsar (1hr), Bageshwar (2hr), Ranikhet (2hr) and Kausani (2hr 30min).

INFORMATION AND TOURS

Tourist information The tourist office is next to the KMVN *Tourist Rest House* on Mall Rd (Mon–Sat 10am–5pm; ☏ 05962 230180).

Tours and treks The best places for taxi excursions, treks and other activities, or to hire equipment and guides, are

Discover Himalaya (☏ 94113 46550, ✉ bobbyalmora@ hotmail.com) and High Adventure (☏ 94120 44610, ✇ trekkinghimalayas.in), both on the Mall by *Hotel Kailas*.

Banks and exchange There are many ATMs along the Mall.

ACCOMMODATION

★ **Bansal Guest House** Lal Bazaar, at the top of the steep lane opposite Hotel Shikhar ☏ 05962 230864, ☏ 9927967002. Spotless, simple rooms with en suites (free hot bucket water), fantastic rooftop views and very friendly management, who'll deliver their renowned lassis (₹30) and *tikkis* (₹35) to your room. The top room is the largest and most attractive. **₹500**

Khim's Guest House Off Kasar Devi Rd, 3.5km north of Almora ☏ 94120 44865, ✇ khimsguesthouse.com. Laidback guesthouse favoured by old-school hippies, and a lovely place to chill out for a week or two. As well as standard doubles there are unattached single rooms for ₹350 and cottages with attached bathrooms (₹1500), plus an excellent library on the Himalayan region. **₹1000**

Savoy Mall Rd, 500m from the bus station ☏ 05942 238833, ✇ savoyhotelnainital.com/almora_savoy.php. Pistachio-green budget hotel with a view of the valley, conifer-covered hills and Himalayan peaks from the garden and upper balcony. Rooms on the first floor are sunnier, though the deluxe rooms are more spacious (₹2000). Gaudy furnishings but clean linen and a restaurant serving home-style Kumaoni food. **₹1000**

Shikhar The Mall, 150m northeast of the bus stand ☏ 05962 230253, ✇ hotelshikhar.in. Marking the centre of town, the huge *Shikhar* has a wide range of rooms at very reasonable prices (the more spacious deluxe rooms cost double), all with balconies. The gloomy but cavernous restaurant serves good food. **₹950**

EATING

Cafés and restaurants are strung along the Mall, especially around the bazaar area; locally grown and prepared Kumaon rice and black dhal are particularly delicious and for dessert try *singauri*, a milk sweet that's a local speciality.

Chatpat Chicken Corner The Mall, 300m west of the bus stand. Plain and simple, brightly lit place serving tasty roast chicken for under ₹100. Daily 11am–10.30pm.

Glory The Mall, near Shikhar Hotel ☏ 94123 14595.

Multicuisine café/restaurant, strong on north Indian cooking, with dishes from masala dosa (₹65) to butter chicken (half ₹200, full ₹350) as well as a smattering of Chinese food. Also good for breakfast. Daily 9am–10pm.

New Soni The Mall, near the bus stand. Excellent, Sikh-run *dhaba* famed for its chicken (half ₹150, full ₹300) and mutton dishes (₹200); it can get crowded. Daily 10am–10pm.

North of Almora

The scenic hills and forests north of Almora are home to a clutch of appealingly situated towns with ample opportunities for hiking. All the places covered below are accessible as day-trips from the regional capital, though also reward a longer stay for those with more time.

Kasar Devi

Spread among the cedar and rhododendron forest below the unassuming hilltop temple of Kasar Devi (of Swami Vivekananda fame), 8km north of Almora, is the pleasant hamlet of **KASAR DEVI**. Nicknamed "hippieland" by some of the locals, it plays host to a thriving long-term travellers' scene.

ARRIVAL AND DEPARTURE	KASAR DEVI

Shared jeeps run when full between Almora's jeep stand and Kasar Devi (15min; ₹30), dropping off passengers along Binsar Rd.

ACCOMMODATION AND EATING

Kasar Rainbow Yoga Retreat Off Binsar Rd, near Mohan's ☎05962 251105 or ☎97203 20664, ⓦ kasar rainbowyogaretreat.com. Reached by a small path off the main road, this guesthouse has undergone a swanky revamp and now focuses on yoga (and offers massage). Rooms have terraces with mountain views and there's a small library plus a spacious restaurant with organic food. The friendly owner, Sabu, can arrange treks to the surrounding villages. **₹5500**

Mohan's Binsar Retreat Binsar Rd ☎05962 251215, ⓦ mohansbinsarretreat.com. The pick of the lot, attracting both guests and non-guests to its breezy terrace café with lazy chairs overlooking the valley. Rooms come with fire-places and kettles, plus there's a good restaurant, housed in a gazebo. **₹5900**

New Dolma Binsar Rd ☎94120 44781, ⓦ dolma guesthouse.in. Run by Tibetans, *New Dolma* is perched above the road with a view of the Himalayas; you can enjoy *momos* (₹50), *thukpa* (₹60–75) and chow mein (₹50–75) on the broad outdoor terrace or inside the diner. The luridly coloured rooms have LCD TVs, a/c and good-quality beds. There's also a six-bed dorm upstairs. Dorms **₹250**, doubles **₹1000**

Rock House Café Kripal Guest House ☎09599 56814. A chilled out place with cushions strewn on the floor and great valley views. Freshly baked bread and proper coffee, as well as delicious burgers, chicken schnitzel and pizza. Daily 9am–10pm.

Binsar Wildlife Sanctuary

₹600 (₹150), vehicles ₹250 • No public transport; return taxi from Almora's jeep stand ₹1500

Binsar Wildlife Sanctuary, known locally as Jhandi Dhar ("hilltop"), 33km north of Almora and easily visited as a day-trip, rises in isolation to a commanding 2412m. Rich in alpine flora, ferns, hanging moss and wild flowers, and with over two hundred species of bird, it was once the summer capital of the Chandras, Kumaon's kings, though little of that era remains aside from the bulbous stone Shiva temple of **Bineshwar** (₹650 [₹250]), 3km below the summit. Most visitors come to see the 300km panorama of Himalayan peaks along the northern horizon, including, from west to east, Kedarnath, Chaukhamba, Trisul, Nandaghunti, Nanda Devi, Nandakot and Panchchuli. Closer at hand, you can enjoy quiet forest walks through oak and rhododendron woods.

ACCOMMODATION	BINSAR WILDLIFE SANCTUARY

Binsar Forest Retreat Ayarpani, 1km southwest of the sanctuary's Zero Point ☎70551 04971, ⓦ binsar forestretreat.com. Located in the middle of the wildlife sanctuary at an altitude of 2300m, with accommodation in luxurious tented cottages or a range of stone-floored, mud-walled rooms (₹9500–12,000) with views of the Trisul and Nandaghunti peaks. Meals ₹2000/day extra. **₹7000**

KMVN Tourist Rest House 2km before Zero Point ☎86500 02537. At the end of the road near the top of a steep hill, this KMVN place offers bland but comfortable wood-panelled rooms (upper-floor executive rooms ₹3000–4200). It runs on solar power and often goes dark in the evening: bring a torch. There's basic veg and non-veg food available. The mountain views from the broad garden terrace are wonderful. Wi-fi available only when the generator is switched on (5–8pm). **₹2400**

Jageshwar

JAGESHWAR, 25km northeast of Almora, is the very heart of Kumaon, a place where language and customs seem to have resisted change. An idyllic small river meanders through dark pines for 3km off the main road from **Artola**, stumbling onto a complex of 124 ancient shrines and temples that cluster at the base of venerable deodar trees. Jageshwar village retains much of its traditional charm, with stone-paved lanes and beautifully carved wooden doors and windows painted in green, turquoise and other striking colours. Good local **walks** include the steep 3km ascent through beautiful pine forests to the hamlet and stone temples of **Vriddha Jageshwar** (Old Jageshwar), with an extensive panorama from the mountains of Garhwal to the massifs of western Nepal. A trail from here leads 12km along an undulating ridge to Binsar; the trail finally emerges from the woods near the stone temple of **Bineshwar**.

ARRIVAL AND DEPARTURE JAGESHWAR

By bus A daily bus runs from Almora at noon (1hr 30min), returning from Jageshwar's main temple gate around 8am.

By taxi A return taxi from Almora costs about ₹1200.

ACCOMMODATION AND EATING

Tara Guest House Up the hill from Jageshwar Temple ☎ 05962 263068, ⊕ jageshwar.co.uk. This tiny, family-run block has nine basic rooms (three with hot showers) with twin beds and small patios overlooking the temple, in a quiet setting a few minutes off the road. Hot water, good breakfasts and thalis are provided by the friendly owner, who offers advice and guidance on local excursions. **₹800**

Kausani

Spread out east to west along a narrow pine-covered ridge 52km northwest of Almora, the village of **KAUSANI** has become a popular resort thanks to its spectacular Himalayan panorama. It's a simple day-trip from Almora, though as the peaks – Nanda Choti, Trisul, Nanda Devi and Panchchuli – are at their best at dawn and dusk, it's well worth an overnight stay. Up the hill from the town centre are several **ashrams**, including one that once housed Mahatma Gandhi, who walked here in 1929, thirty years before the road came through, and an observatory where you can admire the night sky (50m downhill from Anashakti Ashram; ₹100).

There are numerous possibilities for short **day-hikes** in the woods and terraced valleys around Kausani, among them the scenic hike to the Kausani Tea Estate (4km north), and the pleasant trail down the valley to the temples of **Baijnath** (10km). Further afield is the important pilgrimage site of **Bageshwar** and the trailhead for the Pindari Glacier, a few hours away in Song.

ARRIVAL AND INFORMATION KAUSANI

By bus and shared jeep Kausani is connected by regular buses and shared jeeps to Almora (every 30min; 2hr 30min) and Baijnath (hourly; 30min), from where buses continue to Bageshwar (1hr 30min) to the east and Gwaldam (1hr 30min) and Karnaprayag (3–4hr) to the northwest, for destinations in Garhwal.

Banks and exchange The State Bank of India has an ATM.

ACCOMMODATION AND EATING

Outside high season (April 15–June 15 & Oct 1–Nov 15), room rates are slashed roughly in half.

Anashakti Ashram Snow View Rd, looking down on the Mall ☎ 05962 258028. Guests prepared to observe house rules, such as attending compulsory prayers and not smoking, are welcome to stay at Gandhi's pleasant but spartan former ashram, run completely on solar power, for a donation. Either way, it's worth visiting the main prayer hall, which doubles as a Gandhi museum (daily 7am–noon & 4–6pm; free; no photos). No wi-fi.

★ **Uttarakhand Kausani** Up the steps 150m north of the bus stand ☎ 05962 258012, ⊕ uttarakhandkausani. com. This foreigner-friendly place is run by Vipin Upreti, a nature enthusiast and great source of information on hikes. Newly renovated, it has clean doubles and a broad terrace with fantastic Himalayan views; the first-floor rooms with satellite TV and flush bidet toilets are good value at ₹1550. The thatched-roof viewing tower, equipped with a telescope, rises above the hotel's *Garden Restaurant* – home to Kausani's only *tandoor* oven (full chicken ₹400). **₹1900**

Baijnath

At the bottom of the broad Garur Valley lies the quiet town of **BAIJNATH** (1126m), 16km north of Kausani and sprawled along the banks of the Gomti River. This was

PINDARI GLACIER TREK

One of the most accessible glaciers in the Kumaon region, the **Pindari Glacier** stretches more than 3km in length and almost 500m in width. Passing through pristine, high mountain country and a host of tiny Himalayan villages, the trail follows the Pindar River to its source, offering views along the way of the region's giants, among them Nanda Kot (6861m), Panwali Dwar (6663m) and Maiktoli (6803m).

Beginning and ending in **Song** (1600m), the trail covers about 90km round trip and takes six days to complete, crossing over the Dhakuri Pass (2680m) and beyond the final settlement of Khati to reach Zero Point at the edge of the Pindari Glacier (3660m). The whole route can be done teahouse style, as basic government lodges dot the trail. Camping equipment and sleeping bags are highly recommended. Near the glacier itself, you can stay with Swami Dharmanand or Babaji, whose NGO, Himalayan Villages Education And Development Program (w himved.org), pays the salaries of teachers at local schools threatened with closure.

Guides and porters are easily arranged in Song, connected to Bageshwar by jeeps (1hr 30min) and buses (2hr). The Pindari Glacier has also caught the attention of mountain-bikers: two-wheel tours are run by Mike McLean (w mountainbikekerala.com) in April and October.

once the capital city of the Katyur dynasty, which ruled much of Garhwal and Kumaon from the seventh to the fourteenth centuries; their stone temples, built between the ninth and twelfth centuries, still stand at a bend in the river. Eighteen towering shrines rise from the temple grounds, each a beautiful example of the medieval *nagara* style, the tallest of them devoted to Lord Shiva's form, Vaidyanath ("the Lord of Physicians"). The main temple, however, is devoted to Shiva's consort, Parvati, its 1.5m schist image of the goddess being one of the few in the complex to have withstood the ravages of time.

ARRIVAL AND DEPARTURE   BAIJNATH

By bus and jeep Regular buses and jeeps link Baijnath with Bageshwar (1hr), Kausani (30min) and Gwaldam (1hr 30min); jeeps and buses congregate 500m south of the temples, across the river.

ACCOMMODATION AND EATING

KMVN Tourist Rest House 200m north of the temples, off the main road to the left ☎ 86500 02548. A modern hotel in a quiet setting with large rooms with hot water, as well as two separate cottages (₹1250 and ₹1400), a four-bedded dorm, restaurant and garden area with good views of Trisul. Rates almost double in peak season. No wi-fi. Dorms ₹200, doubles ₹850

Bageshwar

Nestled 74km north of Almora, **BAGESHWAR** is one of Kumaon's most important pilgrimage towns, spread along the lush Gomti River valley. Pilgrims flock to its huddle of ancient temples, highlighted by the fifteenth-century Bagnath Temple, built by the Chandras, in the centre of town. Most foreign travellers use the town as a base for the Pindari Glacier trek (see page 339); Bageshwar's market is a great place to stock up on supplies.

ARRIVAL AND DEPARTURE   BAGESHWAR

By bus and jeep The bus and jeep stands are in the west of town, within a short walk of the town centre; regular buses connect Baijnath (1hr), Kausani (1hr 30min), Almora (3hr), Bhowali (6hr), Haldwani (7hr 30min) and Song (2hr) for the Pindari Glacier trek.

ACCOMMODATION AND EATING

KMVN Tourist Resthouse Tehsil Rd, 500m south of the bus station across a bridge ☎ 86500 02546. The basic rooms are passable, with large bathrooms and geysers, but it's worth paying extra for the deluxe rooms, which are carpeted and come with TV (₹900). The attached restaurant serves standard hot meals. Staff can get you sorted for the Pindari trek, as well as other regional excursions. No wi-fi. ₹700

Madhya Pradesh and Chhattisgarh

TIGER AT KANHA NATIONAL PARK

5 Madhya Pradesh and Chhattisgarh

Hot, dusty Madhya Pradesh is a vast landlocked expanse of scrub-covered hills, sun-parched plains and one third of India's forests. Stretching from beyond the headwaters of the mighty Narmada River to the fringes of the Western Ghats, it's a transitional zone between the Gangetic lowlands in the north and the high, dry Deccan plateau to the south. Despite its diverse array of exceptional attractions, ranging from ancient temples and hilltop forts to some of India's best tiger reserves, Madhya Pradesh receives only a fraction of the tourist traffic that pours between Delhi, Agra, Varanasi and the south. For those who make the effort, this gem of a state is both culturally rewarding and largely hassle-free. Meanwhile, the neighbouring state of Chhattisgarh is even further off the beaten trail but is now slowly opening up to tourism.

In the centre of Madhya Pradesh, the state capital **Bhopal**, though synonymous with industrial disaster (see page 349), has a vibrant Muslim heritage and some interesting museums. Nearby is **Sanchi**, one of India's most significant Buddhist sites. The hill station of **Pachmarhi**, meanwhile, has echoes of the Raj, numerous hiking routes and the little-visited Satpura National Park. In the north, the city of **Gwalior** has a stunning hilltop fort and is within striking distance of **Datia**'s Rajput palace, the Scindia family's mausoleums at **Orchha** and the atmospheric ruined capital of the Bundella rajas. Further east is the state's biggest attraction, the cluster of magnificent sandstone temples at **Khajuraho**, renowned for their intricate erotic carvings.

Western Madhya Pradesh is home to **Indore**, a modern city of industry. Though of little interest in itself, it's a good base for exploring **Mandu**, the romantic former capital of the Malwa sultans, the Hindu pilgrimage centres of **Omkareshwar** and **Maheshwar**, and the holy city of **Ujjain**, one of the sites of the Kumbh Mela (see box, page 269).

Nondescript **Jabalpur** is the biggest city in eastern Madhya Pradesh, a region that has few historic sites but does boast the **Kanha**, **Bandhavgarh** and **Pench** reserves, among the last strongholds for many endangered species, most notably the **tiger**. Alongside Orchha and Khajuraho, these parks are the only places in Madhya Pradesh or Chhattisgarh you're likely to meet more than a handful of foreign tourists.

In November 2000, sixteen districts seceded from eastern Madhya Pradesh to form the state of **Chhattisgarh**. Violent **Naxalite** (Maoist rebel groups) activity in the region, arising from the exploitation of the area's rich mineral resources (and of the tribal peoples who live on the land) has meant the state has until recently attracted a mere trickle of foreign visitors, but the ever diminishing violence means this may

---

BEST TIME TO VISIT

The best time to visit both states is during the relatively cool **winter** (Oct–March), though during the coldest months (Dec–Feb) it gets a bit chilly at night and in the early morning, and you may need a sweater or light jacket, especially in the upland areas. From April to June, daytime temperatures frequently exceed 40°C, but if you can stand the heat, this is the best time to catch glimpses of **tigers** in the national parks. The increasingly meagre **rains** finally sweep in from the southeast in late June or early July until September making the roads even more difficult than usual, though it's a good opportunity to see the waterfalls in the Bastar region of Chhattisgarh at their impressive full flow.

MANDU, ONCE THE FORTRESS CAPITAL OF THE MALWA SULTANATE

Highlights

❶ Sanchi India's finest Buddhist monument, Sanchi is a carefully restored *stupa* complex with intricately carved gateways. See page 352

❷ Pachmarhi Central India's only hill station, where you can trek to the top of a sacred Shaivite peak, hunt out prehistoric rock art or simply relax in the refreshingly cool air. See page 357

❸ Orchha Madhya Pradesh at its most exotic, Orchha boasts crumbling riverside tombs and ornate Rajput palaces amid lush, tranquil countryside. See page 367

❹ Khajuraho These renowned temples are swathed in thought-provoking erotic sculpture. Lost for centuries in thick jungle, they have since been beautifully restored. See page 371

❺ Kanha National Park The most famous of Madhya Pradesh's national parks, Kanha is archetypal Kipling country and teems with wildlife, most notably majestic tigers. See page 383

❻ Mandu A medieval fort on a plateau where the emperor got down to serious pleasure-seeking in his vast harem, theatre, steam baths and pavilions. See page 390

HIGHLIGHTS ARE MARKED ON THE MAP ON PAGE 344

5

soon change; the Chhattisgarh Tourism Board runs a string of well-located resorts and hotels, and independent hotels and tour operators are springing up in the most popular destinations. The state is particularly fascinating for its many tribal groups, particularly in the **Bastar** region, which also boasts beautiful landscapes. However, before travelling anywhere south of the capital, **Raipur**, you must obtain up-to-date information about the **state of security** around your intended destination – and travel with a guide if you want to head into the countryside. **Violent conflict** between Naxalite guerrillas and security forces and state-sponsored right-wing militias, although on the wane, continues to occasionally erupt in remote southern parts of the state.

Brief history

Any exploration of central India will be illuminated if you have a grasp of its long and turbulent history. Most of the marauding armies that have swept across the Subcontinent over the last two millennia passed through this corridor, leaving in their wake a bumper crop of monuments. The very first traces of settlement in Madhya Pradesh are the 10,000-year-old paintings on the lonely hilltop of **Bhimbetka**, near Bhopal. Aboriginal rock art was still being created here during the Mauryan emperor

MADHYA PRADESH & CHHATTISGARH

HIGHLIGHTS

1 Sanchi
2 Pachmarhi
3 Orchha
4 Khajuraho
5 Kanha National Park
6 Mandu

FESTIVALS IN MADHYA PRADESH

While Madhya Pradesh has one of the Kumbh Mela sites at Ujjain (see page 395), it won't be hosting it again till 2028. However, there are a couple of major **arts festivals**.

Chauragarh pilgrimage (Shivratri Mela; Feb/March). Tens of thousands of pilgrims and sadhus make the 23km climb up Chauragarh Mountain in Pachmarhi to see the all-powerful lingam. See page 359.

Khajuraho Festival of Dance (Feb; ⓦ khajurahodancefestival.com). One of India's premier dance events, this free festival features traditional and classical dance from all over India. See page 379.

Tansen Samaroh Festival (Nov/Dec; ⓦ tansensamaroh.com). A major four-day festival of Indian classical music to commemorate the life of the great sixteenth-century composer and musician Mian Tansen, held next to his tomb in Behat village, Gwalior.

Ashoka's evangelical dissemination of Buddhism, in the second century BC. Nearby **Sanchi** is this era's most impressive relic. By the end of the first millennium AD, central India was divided into several kingdoms. The Paramaras, whose ruler Raja Bhoj founded Bhopal, controlled the southern and central area, known as Malwa, while the Chandellas, responsible for some of the Subcontinent's most exquisite temples – most notably at **Khajuraho** – held sway in the north.

Muslim influence started to grow in the thirteenth century, and by the mid-sixteenth century the whole region was under **Mughal rule**, which left its mark on the architecture and culture of Mandu, Gwalior and Bhopal, in particular. The Marathas briefly took control before the arrival of the British in the seventeenth century. Under the **British**, the middle of India was known as the "Central Provinces", and administered jointly from Nagpur (now in Maharashtra), and the summer capital Pachmarhi.

Madhya Pradesh, or **MP**, only came into being after Independence, when the Central Provinces were amalgamated with a number of smaller princedoms. Since then, the state, more than ninety percent **Hindu** and with a substantial rural and **tribal** population, has remained far more stable than neighbouring Uttar Pradesh and Bihar. Major civil unrest between Hindus and Muslims was virtually unheard of until the **Bhopal riots** of 1992–93, sparked off by events in Ayodhya. Now Hindu–Muslim relations in MP are relatively cordial again, the state has turned to focus on the latest enemy – recurring **drought** across the poverty-stricken plains and the social and environmental consequences of the damming of the Narmada River. The state remains one of India's poorest, despite flourishing automotive, cement and soybean industries, and the state government sees **tourism** as one way of boosting Madhya Pradesh's economic prospects. The tourist board is always coming up with plans to make the state more accessible, including an intrastate air service (see below).

GETTING AROUND   MADHYA PRADESH

By bus Getting around Madhya Pradesh without your own vehicle normally involves a lot of bone-shaking and excruciatingly slow bus journeys. The state tourist authority, MP Tourism, used to run several very useful a/c coaches between popular tourist destinations, but these currently only run between Bhopal and Indore (7 daily) – check ⓦ mptourism.com for the latest situation.

By train For longer distances, trains are the best bet. The Central Railway, the main line between Mumbai and Kolkata, scythes straight through the middle of the state, forking at Itarsi Junction. One branch veers north towards Bhopal, Jhansi, Gwalior and Agra, while the other continues northeast to Varanasi and eastern India via Jabalpur. In the

far west, at Indore and the holy city of Ujjain, you can pick up the Western Railway, which heads up through eastern Rajasthan to Bharatpur and Delhi.

By taxi By far the most convenient way to travel around MP is by car. MP Tourism can arrange this from one of their offices – per day rates end up at around ₹2000–2500 – plus service tax, road tolls, permits and a ₹300–400 overnight charge for the driver if applicable.

By plane In an attempt to make the state more accessible, MP Tourism is introducing an intrastate air service linking local airports and using small prop airplanes; check ⓦ mptourism.com for details.

5 Bhopal

With around two million inhabitants, **BHOPAL**, Madhya Pradesh's capital, sprawls
out from the eastern shores of a huge artificial lake, its packed old city surrounded by
modern concrete suburbs and green hills. The nineteenth-century **mosques** emphasize its
enduring Muslim legacy, while the hectic **bazaars** of the walled old city are worth a visit.
Elsewhere, a couple of good archeological **museums** house hoards of ancient sculpture
and the lakeside **Bharat Bhavan** ranks among India's premier centres for performing and
visual arts. The **Museum of Man** on the city's outskirts is the country's most comprehensive
exhibition of *adivasi* houses, culture and technology; the nearby **Tribal Museum** focuses on
MP's adivasi groups. Despite all this, Bhopal will always be best known for the 1984 **gas
disaster**, which continues to cast a long shadow over the city and its people.

Bhopal has two separate centres. Spread over the hills to the south of the lakes,
the partially pedestrianized **New Market** area is a mix of shopping arcades, internet
cafés, ice cream parlours, cinemas and office blocks. Once you've squeezed through
the strip of land that divides the Upper and (smaller) Lower lakes, sweeping avenues,
civic buildings and gardens give way to the more heavily congested **old city**. This area
includes the **Jama Masjid** and the bazaar, centred on **Chowk**, a dense grid of streets
between the **Moti Masjid** and Hamidia Road. The art **galleries** and **museums** are on side
roads off New Market, or along the hilly southern edge of the Upper Lake.

Brief history

Bhopal's name is said to derive from the eleventh-century **Raja Bhoj**, who was
instructed by his court gurus to atone for the murder of his mother by linking up the

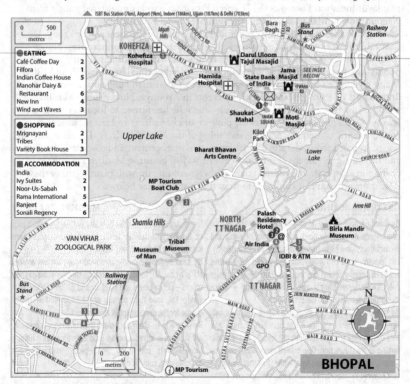

nine rivers flowing through his kingdom. A dam, or *pal*, was built across one of them, and the ruler established a new capital around the two resultant lakes – **Bhojapal**. By the end of the seventeenth century, **Dost Mohammed Khan**, an erstwhile general of Aurangzeb, had occupied the now deserted site to carve out his own kingdom from the chaos left in the wake of the Mughal Empire. The Muslim dynasty he established became one of central India's leading royal families. Under the Raj, its members were among the select few to merit the accolade of a nineteen-gun salute from the British. In the nineteenth century, Bhopal was presided over largely by female rulers, who revamped the city with noble civic works, including the three sandstone **mosques** that still dominate the skyline.

Today, Bhopal carries the burden of the appalling **Union Carbide factory gas disaster** of 1984 (see page 349), with residents quick to remind you of their continuing legal and medical plight. In 1992, **Hindu–Muslim rioting** broke out following the destruction of the Babri Masjid in Ayodhya. However, the many tales of Hindus sheltering their Muslim friends from the mobs at this time and vice versa demonstrate the long tradition of religious tolerance in the city. In recent years, Bhopal – and Madhya Pradesh in general – has remained true to its lenient nature, with little of the political and religious intolerance that afflicts many other north Indian states.

The bazaar

Chowk • Tues–Sun dawn–dusk

Bhopal's lively **bazaar** provides a welcome splash of colour after the dismal, traffic-filled streets around the railway station. Famous for *zarda*, purdah, *garda* and *namarda* (tobacco, veils, dust and eunuchs), it retains a strong Muslim ambience, with overhanging balconies intricately carved with Islamic geometric designs. Each of the narrow streets radiating from the central square specializes in a different type of merchandise, including Chanderi silk saris, bass drums and clarinets, tussar silk, silver jewellery and Bhopal's famous beaded purses. At the heart of the market loom the rich red-sandstone walls and stumpy minarets of the **Jama Masjid**, built in 1837 by Kudsia Begum.

Imam Square

Southwest of Chowk

Imam Square was once the epicentre of royal Bhopal. Nowadays, it's little more than a glorified traffic island, only worth stopping at to admire the **Moti Masjid** on its eastern edge. The "Pearl Mosque", erected in 1860 by Sikander Begum, Kudsia's daughter, is a diminutive and much less imposing version of Shah Jahan's Jama Masjid in Old Delhi, notable more for its slender, gold-topped minarets and sandstone cupolas than its size.

Lining the opposite, northern side of the square near the ceremonial archway is a more eccentric nineteenth-century pile. A fusion of Italian, Gothic and Islamic influences, the **Shaukat Mahal** was originally designed by a French architect. Unfortunately, both it and the elegant **Sadar Manzil** ("Hall of Public Audience") just west on Sultania Rd are now government offices and closed to visitors.

Darul Uloom Tajul Masajid

A 5min walk west of Imam Square • Daily except Fri dawn–dusk; closed during Id-ul-Fitr • Free

With its matching pair of colossal pink minarets soaring high above the city skyline, the **Darul Uloom Tajul Masajid** lives up to the epithet of "mother of all mosques", as denoted by the extra "a" in its name. Whether Bhopal's most impressive monument also deserves to be dubbed the biggest in India, as locals claim, is less certain. Work on the building commenced under Sultan Jehan Begum (1868–1901), the eighth

5

ruler of Bhopal. After the death of her domineering husband, the widow queen embarked on a spending spree that left the city with a postal system, new schools and a railway, but which all but impoverished the state – and the Tajul Masajid was never actually completed.

Birla Mandir Museum

East of the Lower Lake • Tues–Sun 10.30am–5.30pm • ₹100 (₹10)

The **Birla Mandir Museum** collection includes some of the finest stone sculpture in Madhya Pradesh, informatively displayed with explanatory panels in English in the main galleries. The museum is in a detached mansion beside Birla Mandir, the garish modern Hindu Lakshmi Narayan temple that stands high on Arera Hill overlooking the Lower Lake. Aside from the museum itself, the **temple gardens**, which overlook the city, are a fine place to watch the sunset.

The exhibition is divided between Vishnu, the mother goddesses and Shiva. The **Vishnu** section contains some interesting representations of the god's diverse and frequently bizarre reincarnations, while in the **Devi** gallery next door, a cadaverous Chamunda (the goddess Durga in her most terrifying aspect) stands incongruously amid a row of voluptuous maidens and fertility figures. The **Shiva** room, by contrast, is altogether more subdued. Finally, have a look at the replicas of the 3500-year-old **Harappan** artefacts encased under the stairs.

Bharat Bhavan Arts Centre

Lake View Rd, on the eastern tip of the Upper Lake • Tues–Sun: Feb–Oct 2–8pm; Nov–Jan 1–7pm • ₹10, free on Fri • ☎ 0810 305 4032, ⓦ bharatbhawan.org

The **Bharat Bhavan Arts Centre** is provincial India's pre-eminent arts centre. Inside Goan architect Charles Correa's campus of concrete domes and dour brickwork are temporary exhibitions as well as a large split-level **permanent collection** of modern Indian painting and sculpture. Rather incongruously placed amid the latter, look out for an eighteenth-century gilt-framed landscape by the Daniells – the uncle-nephew duo employed as a part of the Company school of painting during the Raj. Bharat Bhavan has a gallery devoted exclusively to **adivasi art**, in search of which talent scouts spent months roaming remote regions. Among their more famous discoveries was the Gond painter **Jangarh Singh Shyam**. Many of his works are on display here, along with a colourful assemblage of masks, terracotta, woodcarvings and ritual paraphernalia.

Museum of Man

Just off Shamla Hills Rd, south of the Upper Lake • Tues–Sun: March–Aug 11am–6.30pm; Sept–Feb 10am–5.30pm • ₹500 (₹30), vehicle ₹10, video ₹50 • ☎ 0821 244 8213 • A round-trip by auto-rickshaw from the city centre costs around ₹300 including waiting time

The story of India's indigenous minorities – the *adivasi*, literally "original inhabitants" – is all too familiar. Dispossessed of their land by large-scale development projects or exploitative moneylenders, the "tribals" have seen a gradual erosion of their traditional culture. The **Museum of Man**, or the Rashtriya Manav Sangrahalaya, is an enlightened attempt to redress the balance.

Overlooking New Market on one side and the majestic sweep of Upper Lake on the other, the 200-acre hilltop site includes a reconstructed Keralan coastal village and a winding trail where each tribal group from the state has contributed an interpretation of its own creation myth. A large exhibition hall draws on all the daily and ritual elements in the *adivasi* lifestyle, and dotted among the forest scrub are botanical trails, a research centre and a permanent open-air display of traditional *adivasi* buildings.

THE BHOPAL GAS TRAGEDY

At 12.05am on December 3, 1984, a lethal cloud of methyl isocyanate (MIC), a toxic chemical used in the manufacture of pesticides, exploded at the huge, US-owned **Union Carbide** plant on the northern edge of Bhopal.

Highly reactive, MIC must be kept under constant pressure at a temperature of 0°C – yet cost-conscious officials had reduced the pressure to save some US$70 a day. When water entered tank E-610 through badly maintained and leaking valves to contaminate the MIC, a massive reaction was triggered. Wind dispersed the gas throughout the densely populated residential districts and slums. There was neither a warning siren nor adequate emergency procedures in place, leaving the thick cloud of gas to blind and suffocate its victims. The leak killed 1600 instantly (according to official figures) and between 7000 and 10,000 in the aftermath, but the figure now totals well over 25,000 in the years since the incident. More than 500,000 people were exposed to the gas, of whom about one fifth have been left with chronic and incurable **health problems**, often passed on to children born in years following the tragedy. The water in the community pumps of the affected residential areas remains contaminated with dangerous toxic chemicals that seeped out from the now-deserted factory. Campaigners say the factory still contains thousands of tonnes of toxic waste.

EVADING RESPONSIBILITY

Though the incidence of TB, cancers, infertility and cataracts in the affected area remains way above the national average, the factory officials initially said the effect of MIC was akin to that of tear gas, causing only temporary health problems. They accepted moral **responsibility** for the accident, but blamed the Indian government for inadequate safety standards when it came to the issue of compensation. Only in 1989 did Union Carbide agree to pay an average of ₹25,000 to each adult victim – a paltry sum that didn't even cover loans for the medical bills in the first five years, let alone compensate for the loss of life and livelihoods and other consequences of the disaster. In 2001, the Bhopal Memorial Hospital and Research Centre opened to treat patients.

Despite both US and Indian former bosses being charged with serious offences – including manslaughter – the government and factory authorities had been keen to sweep the whole episode under the carpet. It took until June 2010 for some measure of justice to be dispensed, when a Bhopal court gave seven former factory employees two-year prison sentences for causing "death by negligence". The court also fined the former Indian unit of Union Carbide ₹500,000. NGOs and local campaigners dismissed the ruling as completely inadequate.

Warren Anderson, the former CEO of Union Carbide in the US, never faced justice; Anderson fled India to the US after the Indian court granted him bail and, although in 2002 a Bhopal court directed India's Central Bureau of Investigation to pursue his extradition, the US authorities refused to extradite him, and he died in a nursing home in Florida in 2014.

After much lobbying, the government in 2005 launched a legal case to recoup money from Dow Chemical, which bought Union Carbide in 2001 but denies ongoing liability. To date, little progress has been made but people in Bhopal continue to stage regular protests and rallies.

FIND OUT MORE

If you're interested in learning more about the disaster or **volunteering** your services, contact the Sambhavna Trust at Bafna Colony, Berasia Rd, Bhopal (☎0755 273 0914, ⊛bhopal.org). *Five Past Midnight in Bhopal* by Dominique Lapierre and Javier Moro, and the Booker Prize-nominated *Animal's People* by Indra Sinha are both highly recommended further reading, while the film *Bhopal: A Prayer for Rain*, starring Martin Sheen as Anderson, retold the story to mark the thirtieth anniversary in 2014.

Tribal Museum

Shamla Hills • Daily except Mon: Nov–Jan noon–7pm, rest of year noon–8pm • ₹100 (₹10) • ☎75526 61948, ⊛facebook.com/MPTribalMuseum

Best visited in conjunction with the nearby Museum of Man, the **Tribal Museum** is dedicated to the millions of adivasi people who live in Madhya Pradesh. It houses well-curated displays, traditional crafts, artworks and replica homes of the seven main tribal groups in the state. The museum also stages regular music and cultural performances.

5

Van Vihar Zoological Park

Lake View Rd, south of the Upper Lake • Daily except Tues 8am–6pm (summer 7am–7pm) • ₹200 (₹20) • For transport around the park, an auto-rickshaw is around ₹250 plus the ₹20 entrance fee for the driver

A trip to the **Van Vihar Zoological Park** ties in nicely with a visit to the Museum of Man next door – keep the same auto-rickshaw for the whole trip. The stars of the park are a couple of regal white tigers, but there are also gharial, leopards, Himalayan bears and lions. You can get a longer look at the 207 species of birds by taking a boat from the jetty, 500m northeast of the park gate.

ARRIVAL AND DEPARTURE   BHOPAL

By plane Bhopal's Raja Bhoj airport is 12km north of the city: a taxi to/from the city centre costs around ₹500, an auto-rickshaw roughly half that. Air India (☎0755 277 0480) has an office in Airlines House on Bhadbhada Rd, TT Nagar. Destinations Delhi (4 daily; 1hr 25min); Mumbai (4 daily; 1hr 35min).

By train The main railway station, Bhopal Junction, is close to the centre: to reach the hotel district, leave by the exit on platforms 4 or 5 and head to the busy corner of Hamidia Rd where there's a prepaid taxi and auto-rickshaw booth. The quickest and most convenient train to Delhi is the *Shatabdi Express* #12001 (daily 3.15pm; 8hr 15min), which travels via Jhansi (for Orchha/Khajuraho), Gwalior and Agra. One of the most convenient trains to Mumbai is the *Punjab Mail* #12138 (daily 4.55pm; 14hr 40min).

Destinations Agra (every 30min–1hr; 6–10hr); Delhi (every 30min–1hr; 8hr 15min–13hr 40min); Gwalior (every 30min–1hr; 4hr 20min–7hr 35min); Indore (6 daily; 4hr 5min–6hr 25min); Jabalpur (8 daily; 5hr 15min–12hr 20min); Jhansi (every 30min–1hr; 3hr 16min–6hr); Mumbai (roughly hourly; 12hr–16hr 45min); Varanasi (1–2 daily; 16hr 50min).

By bus The main state bus stand is the Inter-state Bus Terminal (ISBT), located just south of the airport, and 11km east of the railway station (around ₹150–200 by auto-rickshaw) on the Bairagarh Rd, is used by almost all bus services within and outside the state. However, in the mornings you can also use the more convenient Hamidia Rd bus stand which has services to/from Indore, Pachmarhi and Sanchi, and is a 10min walk southwest of the railway station.

Destinations Indore (every 30min; 4–5hr); Pachmarhi (every 2hr; 6hr 30min–7hr 30min); Sanchi (every 30min; 1hr 30min–2hr).

By MP Tourism bus MP Tourism currently runs an a/c coach service to Indore (7 daily; 4hr); tickets should be booked in advance, either online (ⓦmptourism.com) or at *Palash Residency*, about 200m northeast of the GPO is North TT Nagar, from where the buses arrive and depart.

GETTING AROUND AND INFORMATION

By auto-rickshaw Most of Bhopal's places of interest are so far apart that the best way of getting around is by auto-rickshaw, at about ₹700–800/day.

By taxi Taxis can be organized through your hotel, or MP Tourism at around ₹15–30/km (depending on vehicle; minimum 250km) either at one of their offices or by phoning their transport department direct on ☎0755 277 4340.

Tourist information The MP Tourism head office (Mon–Sat 9.30am–5.30pm; ☎0755 402 7100, ⓦmptourism. com) is inconveniently located in Paryatan Bhawan on Bhadbhada Rd, 2km south of New Market. There are also smaller branches at the railway station (platform 1 exit; daily 10am–5pm; ☎0755 274 6827) and at the airport (☎07552 646667; opens to meet incoming flights). You can book an MP Tourism tour, hotel or a/c bus to Indore at the booth (daily 8am–8pm; ☎0755 329 5040) at *Palash Residency* (see above).

Tours MP Tourism runs a city bus tour (Tues–Sun 11.30am –5pm; ₹120), which leaves from *Palash Residency*, and speed-boat trips (around ₹250/10–15min) on the Upper Lake.

ACCOMMODATION

If you're not bothered by traffic noise and fumes, **Hamidia Rd**, Bhopal's busy main thoroughfare, is the most convenient **place to stay**. Shoestring options are thin on the ground and even the dingiest dives will try to slap extra taxes and "service charges", though if you object strongly they may waive them. Most of Bhopal's top hotels are close to **Upper Lake** in the Shamla Hills area, a 15min ride from the railway station. At the time of writing in 2019, MP Tourism was in the process of transforming Bhopal's evocative Taj Mahal building into a "heritage hotel", which should be a memorable place to stay in the future.

India New Market ☎0755 255 4594; map p.346. Smoothly run by the *Indian Coffee House* cooperative (with one of its decent restaurants on site), this hotel has clean and comfortable mid-range a/c rooms with attached bathrooms, TVs and phones, though no wi-fi. It's very popular, so book in advance. **₹2600**

★**Ivy Suites** A. Nadir Colony, Shamla Hills ☎0755 423 5508, ⓦivysuites.com; map p.346. Tucked away in the city's most exclusive area, this wonderfully relaxed guesthouse has ten spacious rooms, each thoughtfully furnished with paintings, books and plants; those upstairs have ivy-filled balconies overlooking the Upper Lake. Rates include breakfast and they also serve lunch and dinner around 700 each. **₹5310**

Noor-Us-Sabah Palace Grounds, VIP Rd ✆0755 422 3333, ⬤noorussabahpalace.com; map p.346. The "Light of Dawn" is an impeccably renovated 1920s nawab's palace, perched on a hill overlooking the Upper Lake. Opulent rooms come with elegant mirrors, regal red furniture and private balconies, and there's a pool, spa, and a fine restaurant. **₹8000**

Rama International 2 Hamidia Rd ✆0755 274 0542; map p.346. Set back from the main road, and very popular with Indian tourists, this is a rambling, relatively peaceful hotel with clean and simple rooms (all attached, with fans;

a/c around ₹200 extra). **₹900**

Ranjeet 3 Hamidia Rd ✆0755 274 0500, ⬤ranjeet hotels.com; map p.346. Recently refurbished, the rooms here are bright and modern, with all mod cons and a/c, and rates include breakfast served in the reasonable restaurant downstairs. Rooms at the front can be very noisy, so ask for one at the back. 24hr checkout. **₹2125**

Sonali Regency Just off Hamidia Rd ✆0755 274 0880, ⬤hotelsonaliregency.com; map p.346. Quieter than the other hotels in the area, and although the cheapest rooms are boxy and the beds a bit hard, they all boast TVs and clean private bathrooms – ₹600 more will get you one with a/c and a comfy mattress. Nice touches like free newspapers, 24hr checkout and good service give *Sonali Regency* the edge over its similarly priced competitors nearby. **₹1100**

EATING

Decent restaurants are relatively thin on the ground. The larger hotels serve uniform multicuisine menus, while the canteens opposite the bus stand do thalis and *subzi*, rice and dhal for next to nothing. For **breakfast**, try the local favourites, *poha* (a steamed rice cake) and *katchori* (a fried, lentil-stuffed snack).

Café Coffee Day Lake View Rd ✆0755 266 0300, ⬤cafecoffeeday.com; map p.346. This outpost of the Indian chain has a great location overlooking the Upper Lake. The coffee (₹85–160) is good, too, and they also offer sandwiches, pastries and very chocolatey chocolate goodies. Daily 10am–11pm.

Filfora Opposite Koefiza Hospital, 18 Bada Colony ✆0755 425 6926; map p.346. Casual dining for the middle classes, this place serves up very good veg, and especially non-veg, Mughlai, Bhopali and south Indian dishes (with not-so-good Continental and Chinese options) in a plain but clean setting. Highly rated are the mutton *shami* (₹120) and *seekh* (₹180) kebabs, or for veggies the paneer butter masala (₹160). Daily 11am–11pm.

Indian Coffee House India hotel, New Market ✆0755 255 4594; map p.346. Aside from a couple of vintage coffee posters, the dining hall is nondescript, but the filter

coffee (₹18), south Indian breakfast options (from ₹50), thalis and service from the white-suited waiters are all excellent. Daily 8am–10.30pm.

Manohar Dairy & Restaurant Hamidia Rd ✆0755 422 3785, ⬤manohardairy.com; map p.346. Bustling fast-food-style veg joint where yellow-shirted waiters dish up a steady stream of *katchoris*, veggie burgers, pizzas and ice cream sundaes as well as thalis (₹140/₹180). There's also an attached sweet shop. South Indian snacks ₹15–115. Daily 8am–11pm.

New Inn Bhadbhada Rd, New Market ✆0755 422 3777; map p.346. Behind the glass frontage, incongruously decorated with a dragon motif, is a garish mix of yellow and orange walls and brown leather seats. Thankfully the keenly priced food – particularly the kebabs (₹115–220), Chinese chilli chicken (₹220) and the south Indian breakfast options (₹30–85) – is far better judged. Daily 8am–11pm.

Wind and Waves Lake View Rd ✆0755 266 1523; map p.346. While the standard MP Tourism menu (Indian, Chinese and some Continental dishes; mains ₹175-300) holds few surprises, the setting – conveniently close to the museums and boat club, and overlooking the Upper Lake – is appealing, and there's a bar upstairs. Daily 10.30am–10.30pm.

SHOPPING

Head to **Chowk** (bazaar Mon–Sat) for silk and silver. The **New Market** area has some bigger stores.

Mrignayani GTB Shopping Complex, Bhadbhada Rd, New Market ✆0755 422 6900, ⬤mrignayani.com; map p.346. The state-run, fixed-price Mrignayani has everything from batiks to bedspreads; there's also a branch on Hamidia Rd. Tues–Sun 11am–2.30pm & 3.30–8pm.

Tribes VIP Rd ✆0755 255 9687, ⬤tribesindia.com; map

p.346. Close to Moti Masjid, this national government-run store sells a selection of *adivasi* goods at fixed prices. As well as this branch, there's a smaller outlet in the same building as Mrignayani (above). Tues–Sun 11am–7pm.

Variety Book House Bhadbhada Rd, New Market ✆0755 255 4057; map p.346. Bhopal's best collection of English-language, fiction, non-fiction and magazines. Daily 10am–9.30pm.

DIRECTORY

Banks and exchange Only the main banks in New Market and the top hotels offer foreign exchange. ATMs are

common: the State Bank of India is by the GPO.
Hospital The central public Hamidia Hospital (✆0755

5

254 0222 or 0755 405 0450) is on Sultania Rd, between Imam Square and the Darul Uloom Tajul Masajid; for any non-emergency treatments you're better off at AIIMS teaching hospital (☏ 0755 290 2561 or 0755 298 2607, ⊛ aiimsbhopal.edu.in), on AIIMS Rd in Saget Nagar, which has a good reputation.

Post office The main GPO is just off Bhadbhada Rd, in New Market; there's also a GPO on Sultania Rd near the Darul Uloom Tajul Masajid.

Around Bhopal

A wealth of impressive ancient monuments lie within a couple of hours of Bhopal. To the northeast, the third-century-BC *stupas* at **Sanchi** are an easy day-trip. Its peaceful setting also makes an ideal base for visits to more *stupas* at **Satdhara** or **Udaigiri**'s rock-cut caves and the nearby Column of Heliodorus at **Besnagar**. South towards Hoshangabad and the Narmada Valley, the prehistoric cave paintings at **Bhimbetka** can be visited in a day by bus.

Sanchi

From a distance, the smooth-sided hemispherical object that appears on a hillock overlooking the main train line at **Sanchi**, 46km northeast of Bhopal, has the surreal air of an upturned satellite dish. In fact, the giant stone mound stands as testimony to a much older means of communing with the cosmos. Quite apart from being India's finest Buddhist monument, the **Great Stupa** is one of the earliest religious structures in the Subcontinent. It presides over a complex of ruined temples and monasteries that collectively provide a rich and unbroken record of the development of Buddhist art and architecture from the faith's first emergence in central India during the third century BC, until it was eventually squeezed out by the resurgence of Brahmanism during the medieval era.

Brief history

Unlike other famous Buddhist centres in eastern India and Nepal, Sanchi has no known connection with Buddha himself. It first became a place of pilgrimage when the Mauryan emperor **Ashoka**, who married a woman from nearby Besnagar (see page 356), erected a polished stone pillar and brick-and-mortar *stupa* here midway through the third century BC. The complex was enlarged by successive dynasties, but after the eclipse of Buddhism, Sanchi lay deserted and overgrown until its rediscovery in 1818 by General Taylor of the Bengal Cavalry. In the following years a swarm of heavy-handed treasure hunters invaded the site, yet the explorer Sir Alexander Cunningham was the only one to find anything more than rubble; in 1851, he unearthed two soapstone relic boxes, containing bone fragments and bearing the names of two of Buddha's most noted followers, Sariputra and Maha-Mogalanasa. Historians equated the discovery with "finding the graves of Saints Peter and Paul". The find transformed Sanchi, for centuries neglected, into a Buddhist place of pilgrimage once again.

By the 1880s, amateur archeologists had left the ruins in a sorry state. Deep gouges gaped from the sides of *stupas* 1 and 2, a couple of ceremonial gateways had completely collapsed and much of the masonry was plundered by local villagers. **Restoration work** made little impact until 1912, when the jungle was hacked away, the main *stupas* and temples rebuilt, lawns and trees planted and a museum erected to house what sculpture had not been shipped off to Delhi or London.

The Great Stupa

Daily sunrise–sunset• Main site ticket ₹500 (₹30), car ₹10

Floating serenely above a vast expanse of open plains, Sanchi's ruins have preserved the tranquillity that attracted the original occupants. Most visitors find a couple of hours sufficient to explore the site, though you could easily spend several days poring over the four exquisite gateways, or **toranas**, surrounding the Great Stupa. Paved walkways and steps lead around the hilltop enclosure, dotted with interpretive panels and shady trees.

Stupa 1, the **Great Stupa**, stands at the western edge of the plateau and is surrounded by some of the richest and best-preserved ancient sculpture you're likely to see in situ. Fragments of the original construction, a much smaller version built in the third century BC by Ashoka, lie entombed beneath the thick outer shell of lime plaster added a century later. The **Shungas** were responsible for the raised processional balcony, and the two graceful staircases that curve gently around the sides of the drum from the paved walkway at ground level, as well as the aerial-like *chhatra* and its square enclosure which crown the top of the mound. Four elaborate gateways were added by the **Satavahanas** in the first century BC, followed by the four serene meditating **Buddhas** that greet you as you pass through the main entrances. Carved out of local sandstone, these were installed during the Gupta era, around 450 AD, by which time figurative depictions of Buddha had become acceptable (elsewhere in Sanchi, Buddha is represented by an empty throne, a wheel, a pair of footprints and even a parasol).

As you move gradually closer to the *stupa*, the extraordinary wealth of sculpture adorning the **toranas** slips slowly into focus. Every conceivable space on the 8m upright posts and three curving cross-bars teems with delicate figures of humans, demigods and goddesses, birds, beasts and propitious symbols. In between are purely decorative panels and illustrations of heaven intended to inspire worshippers to lead meritorious lives on earth. Start with the *torana* on the south side, which is the oldest, and, as is the custom at Buddhist monuments, proceed in a clockwise direction around the *stupa*.

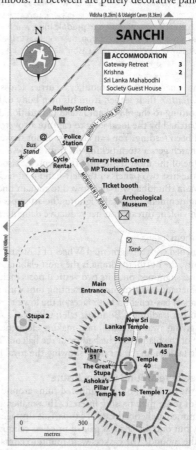

Southern torana

Opening directly onto the ceremonial staircase, the **southern torana** was the Great Stupa's principal entrance, as evidenced by the proximity of the stump of Ashoka's original stone pillar. Over the years, some of the panels with the best sculpture have dropped off the gateway (and are now housed in the site museum), but those that remain on the three crossbeams are still in reasonable condition. A carved frieze on the middle architrave shows Ashoka visiting a *stupa* in a traditional show of veneration. On the reverse side the scene switches to one of the Buddha's previous incarnations, the **Chhaddanta Jataka**, where the *bodhisattva* adopts the guise of an elephant who, in extreme selflessness, helps an ivory hunter saw off his own (six) tusks.

Western torana

The **western torana** collapsed during the nineteenth century, but has been skilfully restored and has some of Sanchi's liveliest sculpture. In the top

5

STUPAS

The hemispherical mounds known as **stupas** have been central to Buddhist worship since the sixth century BC, when Buddha himself modelled the first prototype. Asked by one of his disciples for a symbol to help disseminate his teachings after his death, Buddha took his begging bowl, teaching staff and a length of cloth – his only worldly possessions – and arranged them into the form of a *stupa*, using the cloth as a base, the upturned bowl as the dome and the stick as the projecting finial, or spire.

Originally, *stupas* were simple burial mounds, but as the religion spread, the basic components multiplied and became imbued with **symbolic significance**. The main dome, or **anda** – representing the "divine axis" linking heaven and earth – grew larger, while the wooden railings, or **vedikas**, surrounding it were replaced by massive stone ones. A raised ambulatory terrace, or **medhi**, was added to the vertical sides of the drum, along with two flights of stairs and four ceremonial entrances, carefully aligned with the cardinal points. Finally, crowning the tip of the *stupa*, the single spike evolved into a three-tiered umbrella, or **chhatra**, standing for the Three Jewels of Buddhism: the Buddha, the Law and the community of monks. The *chhatra*, usually enclosed within a low square stone railing, or **harmika**, formed the topmost point of the axis, directly above the reliquary in the heart of the *stupa*. Ranging from bits of bone wrapped in cloth to fine caskets of precious metals, crystal and carved stone, the reliquaries were the "seeds" and their protective mounds the "egg". Excavations of the 84,000 *stupas* scattered around the Subcontinent have shown that the solid interiors were also sometimes built as elaborate **mandalas** – symbolic patterns that exerted a beneficial influence over the *stupa* and those who walked around it. The ritual of circumambulation, or **pradakshina**, which enabled the worshipper to tap into cosmic energy and be transported from the mundane to the divine realms, was always carried out in a clockwise direction from the east, imitating the sun's passage across the heavens.

---

right panel, a troupe of monkeys scurries across a bridge over the Ganges, made by the *bodhisattva*, their leader, from his own body to help them escape a gang of soldiers. According to the **Mahakapi Jataka** (a traditional Buddhist tale), the troops were dispatched by the local king to capture a coveted mango tree from which the monkeys had been feeding. You can also just about make out the final scene, where the repentant monarch gets a stern ticking-off from the *bodhisattva* under a *peepal* tree.

One of the most frequently represented episodes from the life of Buddha features on the first two panels of the left-hand post facing the *stupa*. In the **Temptation of Mara**, Buddha, who has vowed to remain under the Bodhi tree until he attains enlightenment, heroically ignores the attempts of the evil demon Mara to distract him with violent threats and her seductive daughters.

Northern torana

Crowned with a fragmented Wheel of Law and two tridents symbolizing the Buddhist trinity, the **northern torana** is the most elaborate and best preserved of the four gateways. Scenes crammed onto its two vertical posts include Buddha performing an aerial promenade and a monkey presenting him with a bowl of honey. Straddling the two pillars, a bas-relief on both faces of the lowest crossbeam depicts the **Vessantara Jataka** (another traditional Buddhist tale), telling of a *bodhisattva*-prince banished by his father for giving away a magical rain-making elephant. A better view of the inner, south-facing side of the plaque can be had from the balcony of the *stupa*'s raised terrace. Note the little tableau on the far right showing the royal family trudging through the jungle.

Elsewhere around the enclosure

Of the dozens of other numbered ruins around the 400m enclosure, only a handful are of more than passing interest. The smaller, plainer but immaculately restored **Stupa 3**, immediately northeast of Stupa 1, is upstaged by its slightly older cousin in every way but one. In 1851, a pair of priceless reliquaries was discovered deep in the middle of the mound. The caskets were found to contain relics belonging to two of Buddha's closest disciples. In one, fragments of bone were encased with beads made from pearls, crystal, amethyst, lapis lazuli and gypsum, while on the lid, the initial of the saint they are thought to have belonged to, Sariputra, was painted in ink. Previously kept in London's British Museum, both are now in the new Buddhist temple outside the *stupa* enclosure and are brought out for public view for one day in late November.

Eastern torana

Leaning languorously into space from the right capital of the **eastern torana** is Sanchi's most celebrated piece of sculpture, the sensuous **salabhanjika**, or wood-nymph. The full-breasted fertility goddess is one of several such figures that once blessed worshipers as they entered the Great Stupa. Most of the others are now in museums in Los Angeles and London.

Panels on the inner face of the pillar below the *salabhanjika* depict scenes from the life of the Buddha, including his conception when the *bodhisattva* entered the body of his mother, Maya, in the form of a white elephant. The front face of the middle architrave picks up the tale some years later, when the young Buddha, represented by a riderless horse, makes his **great departure** from the palace where he grew up to begin the life of a wandering ascetic. The reverse side shows the fully enlightened Buddha, symbolized by an empty throne.

The eastern edge

From Stupa 3, pick your way through the clutter of pillars, small *stupas* and exposed temple floors nearby to the large complex of interconnecting raised terraces at the far **eastern edge** of the site. The most intact monastery of the bunch, **Vihara 45**, dates from the ninth and tenth centuries and has the usual layout of cells ranged around a central courtyard. Originally, a colossal, richly decorated sanctuary tower soared high above the complex, but this collapsed, leaving the inner sanctum exposed. The river goddesses Ganga and Yamuna number among the skilfully sculpted figures flanking the entrance to the shrine itself. Inside, Buddha still reigns supreme.

The enclosure's tenth-century eastern **boundary wall** is the best place from which to enjoy Sanchi's serene **views**. To the northeast, a huge, sheer-sided rock rises from the midst of Vidisha, near the site of the ancient city that sponsored the monasteries here (traces of the **pilgrimage** trail between Besnagar and Sanchi can still be seen crossing the hillside below). South from the hill, a wide expanse of well-watered wheatfields stretches off towards the angular sandstone ridges of the Raisen escarpment.

The southern area

The **southern area** of the enclosure harbours some of Sanchi's most interesting temples. Pieces of burnt wood dug from the foundations of **Temple 40** prove that the present apsidal-ended *chaitya* was built on top of an earlier structure contemporaneous with the Mauryan Stupa 1. **Temple 17** is a fine example of early Gupta architecture and the precursor of the classical Hindu design developed later in Orissa and Khajuraho.

Before leaving the enclosure, hunt out the stump of **Ashoka's Pillar** on the right of Stupa 1's southern *torana*. The Mauryan emperor erected columns like this all over the empire to mark sacred sites and pilgrims' trails. Its finely polished shaft was originally crowned with the magnificent lion capital now housed in the site museum. The inscription etched around its base is in the Brahmi script, recording Ashoka's edicts in Pali, the early Buddhist language and forerunner of Sanskrit.

The western slope

A flight of steps beside Stupa 1 leads down the **western slope** of Sanchi hill to the village, passing two notable monuments. The bottom portions of the thick stone walls of **Vihara 51** have been carefully restored to show its floorplan of 22 cells around a paved central courtyard. Further down, the second-century-BC **Stupa 2** stands on an artificial ledge, well below the main enclosure – probably because its relics were less important than those of *stupas* 1 and 3. The ornamental railings and gateways around it are certainly no match for those up the hill, although the carvings of lotus medallions and mythical beasts that decorate them are worth close scrutiny. The straps dangling from some of the horseriders' saddles are believed to mark the first appearance in India of stirrups.

Archeological Museum

Daily except Fri 10am–5pm • Entrance included in main site ticket (see page 352)

Sanchi's small **Archeological Museum**, to the left of the road up to the hilltop, houses a modest collection of artefacts, mostly fragments of sculpture, jewellery, pottery, weapons and tools. Its **main hall** contains the most impressive pieces, including the famous Ashokan lion-capital (see above) and two damaged *salabhanjikas* from the gateways of Stupa 1. Also of note are the distinctive Mathuran red-sandstone Buddhas.

ARRIVAL AND INFORMATION   SANCHI

By train There are trains between Bhopal and Sanchi (7–8 daily; 37min–1hr 33min); those travelling to Sanchi are much quicker than those travelling in the other direction. Both Sanchi and Vidisha (see page 356), 10km northeast and connected by plenty of local buses, see dozens of daily trains to/from Mumbai and Delhi.

By bus Buses from Bhopal to Sanchi (every 30min; 1hr 30min–2hr) depart from the Hamidia Rd bus stand

(mornings only) and the Inter-state bus stand. To catch a bus back to Bhopal, wait at the main crossroads and flag one down, and pray for a seat.

Services A handful of wooden stalls around the railway station constitute Sanchi's tiny bazaar, where you can rent bicycles (around ₹80/day) and use the internet café. Staff at the *Gateway Retreat* (see below) offer local information.

ACCOMMODATION

In addition to the **hotel restaurants**, *dhabas* and stalls in the bazaar serve inexpensive thalis (the *Jain Restaurant* is best). Don't miss the local speciality, sweet coconut *nariyal* samosas.

Gateway Retreat On the Bhopal–Vidisha Rd ☎ 07482 266723; map p.353. MP Tourism's accommodation option is Sanchi's smartest, with slightly overpriced whitewashed a/c rooms set in neatly tended grounds. It's often busy, so book ahead. There a reliable, if unexciting, restaurant here, as well as Sanchi's only bar, and they run a canteen on the road to the *stupa*, near the crossroads. ₹3060

Krishna Above the chemist on the Bhopal–Vidisha Rd ☎ 07482 266610; map p.353. This friendly, family-run place has the best set-up for backpackers, with clean tiled rooms (the best are at the back), squat or sit-down toilets and a roof terrace facing the *stupas*. ₹500

Sri Lanka Mahabodhi Society Guest House Near the railway station ☎ 07482 266699; map p.353. Low-cost accommodation – primarily aimed at visiting Buddhists, though other tourists are very welcome – offering spartan rooms with shared facilities facing a shady garden, and more comfortable a/c, attached rooms for around ₹1500. ₹200

Vidisha and around

The main reason to call in at the bustling market town of **VIDISHA**, a 56km train or bus ride from Bhopal, and also served by buses from nearby Sanchi, is to hop on an auto to the archeological site at **Udaigiri** and to visit the **district museum** where most of the best finds from Udaigiri – and the nearby Mauryan site of Besnagar – are kept.

District Museum

Behind the railway station in the east of town • Tues–Sun 10am–5pm • ₹50 (₹5) • if you're travelling to Udaigiri from Sanchi by auto, coming to the museum will add about ₹100 to the price

A worthwhile add-on to a trip to Udaigiri, Vidisha's **District Museum** displays some very fine statuary somewhat haphazardly around its gardens, and more formally inside several sprawling, badly lit galleries. The majority of its pieces, such as Kubera Yaksha, the 3m, pot-bellied male fertility figure in the hallway, are second-century Hindu artefacts unearthed at **Besnagar**, a small, underwhelming site 1km north of the Udaigiri turn-off on the road from Vidisha – most of the artefacts from the site have been moved here.

Udaigiri

6km west of Vidisha • Daily sunrise–sunset • Free • Take a round-trip auto-rickshaw ride from Vidisha (around ₹150–200) or Sanchi (around ₹350–400), rent a bike from one of the shops in Vidisha's bazaar or cycle from Sanchi, though this is more strenuous (1–2hr)

A modest collection of ruined temples and fifth-century rock-cut caves stand just 6km west of Vidisha at **Udaigiri**. The caves, many decorated by Hindu and Jain mendicants, lie scattered around a long, thin outcrop of sandstone surrounded by wheat fields.

Once you've left Vidisha, a left turn just after crossing the Betwa River leads along a gently undulating tree-lined avenue for 2–3km. As it approaches the hillside, the road takes a sharp left turn towards the village. Stop here, at the base of the near-vertical rock face, to climb a steep flight of steps to **Cave 19**, which has worn reliefs of gods and demons around the doorways, and a **Jain cave temple** on the northern edge of the ridge. Ask the chowkidar to unlock the doors for you.

The site's *pièce de résistance*, a 4m-high image of the boar-headed hero Varaha, stands carved into **Cave 5**. Vishnu adopted this guise to rescue the earth-goddess, Prithvi, from the churning primordial ocean. Varaha's left foot rests on a *naga* king wearing a hood of thirteen cobra heads, while the river goddesses Ganga and Yamuna hold water vessels on either side. In the background you can see Brahma and Agni, the Vedic fire-god. The scene is seen as an allegory of the Emperor Chandra Gupta II's conquest of northern India.

Bhimbetka

45km southeast of Bhopal • Daily sunrise–sunset • ₹100 (₹50) • Buses (hourly; 1hr) run from Bhopal's ISBT and Hamidia Rd bus stations (mornings only) and can drop you at the MP Tourism's *Highway Treat* (which has a restaurant and four rooms) from where it's 3.5km – the people at the mechanics can run you there and back on a bike for around ₹150–200 (includes 1hr waiting); alternatively, trains run from Bhopal to the town of Obaidullaganj, 7km from Bhimbetka, from where you can more easily find an auto-rickshaw (around ₹150–200) to take you to the site

Shortly after NH-12 peels away from the main Bhopal–Hoshangabad road, 45km southeast of Bhopal, a long line of boulders appears high on a scrub-covered ridge to the west. The hollows, overhangs and crevices eroded over the millennia from the crags of this malleable sandstone outcrop harbour one of the world's largest collections of **prehistoric rock art**. Discovered in 1957, **Bhimbetka** makes a fascinating day-trip.

Around half the thousand **shelters** so far catalogued along the 10km-long hilltop contain rock paintings, dating from three different periods. The oldest (around ten thousand years old) are green outline drawings of human figures and large red images of animals. The second, more prolific phase accounts for the bulk of Bhimbetka's rock art, and were created in the "Stone Age" – between 8000 and 5000 BC. These friezes depict dynamic hunting scenes full of rampaging animals, initiation ceremonies, burials, masked dances, sports, wars, pregnant women and a drinking party. Bhimbetka's third and final spate of cave painting took place during the early historic period; the stylized, geometric figures bear a strong resemblance to the art still produced by the region's *adivasi* groups.

From the car park at the top of the hill, a paved pathway winds through the jumble of rocks and fifteen caves containing the most striking of Bhimbetka's art. The chowkidars will show you around for a bit of baksheesh. Look out for the Paleolithic images in green, the wonderful "X-ray" animals filled in with cross-hatching and complex geometric designs, and the recurrent image of a bull chasing a human figure and a crab – believed to represent a struggle between the totemic heroes of three different tribes.

Pachmarhi

Among the last tracts of central India mapped by the British, the **Mahadeo Hills** weren't explored until 1857, when Captain J. Forsyth and his party of Bengal Lancers stumbled upon an idyllic saucer-shaped plateau at the heart of the range, strewn with huge boulders and crisscrossed by streams. Five years later a road was cut from the

5

railhead at **Piparia**, and by the end of the century **Pachmarhi** had become the summer capital of the entire Central Provinces, complete with a military sanatorium, churches, clubhouses, racecourse and polo pitch.

Aside from the faded Raj atmosphere and myriad walks and **hikes**, the main incentive to travel up here is in order to scramble around the surrounding forest in search of **prehistoric rock art** or to visit **Satpura National Park**, home to a handful of (elusive) tigers and leopards.

Pachmarhi town, more than 1000m above sea level, is clean, green and relaxed, despite the presence of a large military cantonment in its midst. It has retained a distinctly colonial ambience, enhanced by the elegant British bungalows and church spires that nose incongruously above the tropical tree line. In the evenings families stroll and picnic in the parklands, while army bands and scout troops march around the maidans.

Satpura National Park

Oct–mid June daily sunrise–sunset • On foot ₹150 (₹60), by jeep (up to six people) ₹1500 (₹660) plus vehicle rental around ₹2000; compulsory guides (₹360 for a half-day); entry permits, guides and jeeps are available from the Forestry Commission ticket office (Wed 9am–1pm, Thurs–Tues 9am–5pm), at Bison Lodge, 3km southwest of Pachmarhi town (near the roundabout)

The 524-square-kilometre **Satpura National Park**, dominated by the rugged Mahadeo Hills, is worth a visit to see Indian bison, barking deer, sambar, jackals and wild dogs, although you'll be very lucky to see any of the handful of tigers and leopards. **Bison Lodge**, where you find the **ticket office** for the park, also has a small museum with displays on the park's flora and fauna.

Pachmarhi Hill

Head to the whitewashed Muslim shrine in the Babu Lines area of town (1km southwest of the bus stand); from here it is a 15min climb to the summit

There is a fine panoramic view over the town on one side and the thickly forested valley of Jambu Dwip on the other from the top of **Pachmarhi Hill**. The craggy cliffs lining the north side of the uninhabited gorge below are riddled with hidden rock-shelters and caves.

Jata Shankar cave

The **Jata Shankar cave** is a thirty-minute walk along a well-beaten track from the Pachmarhi bus stand, twisting north from the main bazaar into the hillside through a narrow steep-sided canyon to this sacred cave, a prominent point in the Shivratri *yatra*. En route, in a small cluster of prehistoric rock-shelters and small cave temples just off the path (marked with white paint), look out for **Harper's cave**, named for its naturally formed seated figure of a man playing a harp. Beyond it, at the head of a dark chasm, the Jata Shankar cave itself lurks at the foot of a long flight of stone steps. The grotto's name, which literally means "Shiva's hairstyle", derives from the rock formation around a natural lingam on the damp cave floor, which supposedly resembles the god's matted dreadlocks.

SHIVRATRI MELA

Popular during the summer with Indian tourists, especially on long holiday weekends, Pachmarhi remains sleepy for much of the rest of the year. The big exception to this is during the annual **Shivratri Mela** (Feb/March), when thousands of pilgrims pour through en route to the top of nearby Chauragarh Mountain. The festival marks the anniversary of Shiva's *tandav* dance and his wedding anniversary.

5

THE PANDAV CAVES, FAIRY POOL AND BIG FALLS WALK

A two- to three-hour walk around the eastern fringes of the plateau strings together a small cluster of interesting sights. First head by road from Bison Lodge (see above) up to the **Pandav Caves** (2km), which occupy a knobbly sandstone hillock just east of the road between the ATC cantonment (an army training centre) and the petrol pump – usually with a handful of tour buses outside. Hindu mythology tells these five (*panch*) simple cells (*marhi*) sheltered the Pandava brothers of Mahabharata fame during their thirteen-year exile. Yet archeologists maintain a group of Buddhist monks excavated the bare stone chambers and pillared verandas around the first century BC. Rejoin the road in front of the caves and head around the back of the hill to the melancholy **British cemetery**. Beyond that, the road becomes a dirt track leading to a small car park.

If you plan to head on to **Apsara Vihar** ("Fairy Pool"), a popular bathing and picnic spot at the foot of a small waterfall, and then to the 107m-high **Rajat Prapat** (sometimes called the "Big Falls"), you will need to buy a park entry permit from the park office in Bison Lodge (see above). From the car park, take the footpath down the hill through the woods for about twenty minutes till the trail flattens out, and turn right at a fork to descend to Fairy Pool. A five-minute scramble over the boulders downstream brings you to Rajat Prapat. If you walk back to the fork and continue along the trail, a five-minute walk brings you to a railing from where you can get the best view of the falling water – Rajat Prapat in Hindi actually means "Silver Falls", after the colour of the water as the sunlight hits it. Beyond this point you will need a guide to find the 2km trail down to a deep, cold pool at the bottom.

Chauragarh

The 23km climb to the sacred summit of **Chauragarh Mountain**, on the south rim of the plateau, follows the main *yatra* trail used by pilgrims during the **Shivratri Mela** (see page 358). The first 11km can be covered by bike or taxi along the paved road. From the bazaar, head south across the lake towards the crossroads in front of the *Amaltas Hotel*, then take the road to **Mahadeo cave**, passing a vantage point above the narrow **Handi Kho** ravine, just before the road makes its first sharp descent at the turn-off for **Priyadarshini**, or "Forsyth's Point".

The **footpath** proper begins at the very bottom of the valley, after the road has plunged down a sequence of hairpin bends. Before setting off, make a brief diversion up the *khud* behind the modern **temple** to the Mahadeo cave, where pilgrims take a purifying dip in the cool spring water. From here, a path leads down from the car park, past a small Hanuman cave temple, and then it's a strenuous two-hour climb up an ancient trail to the top of the mountain, which is crammed with tens of thousands of worshippers and sadhus during the Shivratri festival. At the summit, where a temple houses the all-powerful Chauragarh lingam, a thicket of orange tridents surrounds a bright blue statue of Shiva. The views are suitably sublime.

ARRIVAL AND DEPARTURE
PACHMARHI

By train The nearest railway station is Piparia (or Pipariya), 52km northeast of Pachmarhi and on the Mumbai–Howrah line. If you're coming from Bhopal, you'll need to catch a connecting train from Itarsi Junction.

Destinations Itarsi Junction (every 30min–1hr; 1hr 8min–2hr 5min); Jabalpur (every 30min–1hr; 2hr 8min–4hr 21min); Nagpur (2–5 daily; 6hr 10min–7hr 30min); Satna (for Khajuraho; every 1–2hr; 4hr 52min–11hr 20min); Umaria (for Bandhavgarh National Park; 2 daily; 5hr 31min–6hr 52min).

By bus or shared jeep Regular buses travel between Bhopal's main bus station and Pachmarhi. Frequent buses and shared jeeps (every 30min or so; 1hr) shuttle between Piparia railway station and Pachmarhi.

Destinations Bhopal (every 2hr; 6hr 30min–7hr 30min); Indore (2 daily; 12–13hr); Nagpur (2–3 daily; 8–9hr).

By taxi Taxis start from around ₹5000 from Nagpur or Jabalpur, ₹4000 from Bhopal, ₹7500 from Indore or ₹1000 from Piparia.

GETTING AROUND

By jeep Any of the MP Tourism hotels can organize jeep rental (around ₹1500/day). Shared jeeps also do the rounds of Pachmarhi's main sights; a seat costs ₹150–250/day.

Bike rental Shops in the bazaar have a few bikes for rent (around ₹100–200/day); take a chain and padlock (bring your own) and hide the bike in the bushes while you are trekking to stop it being pinched.

5

INFORMATION AND TOURS

Tourist information The main MP Tourism information office (Mon–Fri 10am–7pm; ☎07578 252100) is next to *Amaltas* hotel near the military training area, Tehsil, on the far side of a lotus-filled lake, a 5min (about ₹50–60) jeep or auto-rickshaw ride south of the bus station. There's also a small information booth at the bus station (Mon–Fri 10am–5pm; ☎07578 252029).

Guides If you are considering any walks more ambitious than those mentioned in this account, it's worth investing in a local guide (see page 359) – contact the Forestry Commission ticket office at Bison Lodge (see below), a tour operator, or simply ask at your hotel.

Satpura Tours and Travels ☎94253 67365, ✉ shailendra.sahu84@yahoo.com. Based at *Saket* hotel (see below), Satpura Tours and Travels can organize guides from ₹400–600/day. The guides are young tribal men with expert local knowledge of the area, though they may not speak English, and the fees go directly to them and their villages. The agency also offers parasailing and can arrange rock climbing and homestays.

ACCOMMODATION

Accommodation in Pachmarhi is in short supply during the *melas*, over Christmas and New Year, and in May and June, when you should book well in advance. Outside of these times, it should be possible to negotiate a good discount almost everywhere. **Budget accommodation** centres on the bazaar (along Patel Marg), but most of the MP Tourism hotels are near Tehsil.

Amaltas Near Tehsil, around 1km southwest of the town centre ☎07578 252098, ⌨mptourism.com. The best-priced MP Tourism hotel in town, in an old British-built building with a collection of a/c "deluxe" (₹3290) renovated rooms with the odd flash of character such as a curved wall or marble fireplace. The standard a/c rooms, in a separate annexe, are less appealing. **₹2990**

★ **Evelyn's Own** Tehsil, near Golf View, around 2.5km southwest of the town centre ☎07578 252056 or ☎92786 00200, ✉ evelynsown@gmail.com. A colonial-era bungalow with homely rooms (they vary in quality, so ask to see a few), lush garden, small pool and tennis court. The real draw is the owner, former army colonel Bunny Rao and his wife Pramila. Both are a mine of information. **₹2000**

Forsyth Lodge 96km from Pachmarhi, near the village of Sarangpur, and opposite the Madai entrance to Satpura National Park ☎98100 93312, ⌨forsythlodge.com. Named after a pioneering British captain (see page 357), this wonderful lodge is set amid 44 acres of jungle. It has twelve beautiful cottages, a pool and well-trained staff and guides. Rates (listed for two people) include full board. **₹24,000**

Golf View Tehsil, overlooking the golf course, around 2.5km southwest of the town centre ☎07578 252115 or ☎91111 77793, ⌨golfview.in. One of Pachmarhi's smarter hotels, *Golf View* has classy attached rooms with 1920s-style furniture, fireplaces, high ceilings and modern features like tea-/coffee-makers and whirlpool baths. Outside you find manicured lawns, mango trees and, rather unexpectedly, a running track. Meals cost ₹550–750 extra each. **₹5500**

Rock-End Manor Near Tehsil, around 2km southwest of the town centre ☎07578 252079, ⌨mptourism.com. MP Tourism's well-restored British bungalow is a long-established favourite of visiting VIPs for its Raj-style rooms (they feel more like suites) and stately atmosphere. Easy chairs on the veranda offer views over the hills and the flower garden. Full board for two people **₹6300**

Saket Patel Marg, in the heart of the bazaar, a 5min walk from the bus stand ☎07578 252165, ⌨sakethotel. in. Friendly hotel offering clean rooms with TVs, attached bathrooms (some with squat toilets) and luminous stars on the ceilings. The more expensive ones (double the price) are bigger and have bath tubs, a/c and small balconies. There are smaller, less expensive guesthouses on the same road. **₹1800**

EATING

Khalsa Khalsa hotel, bottom end of bazaar, off the main road ☎07578 252298. A Sikh-run place with predictably good veg and non-veg Punjabi food (including a tasty Peshwari naan), plus a decent attempt at a Gujarati thali (mains from ₹150). The bizarre dining room features fake tree-trunk roof supports and fairy lights. Daily noon–3pm & 7–10.30pm.

Rock-End Manor Rock-End Manor hotel ☎07578 252079. All the MP Tourism properties have restaurants serving the solid but hardly earth-shattering north Indian and Chinese menu (mains ₹100–330), but the Raj-era charm here elevates it above the others. The dining hall is a bit poky, but you can dine out on the lovely veranda which has featured in many a Bollywood movie (though watch out for monkeys during the day). Daily noon–3pm & 8–10pm.

Gwalior

Straddling the main Delhi–Mumbai train line, **GWALIOR** is northern Madhya Pradesh's largest city and boasts one of India's most magnificent hilltop forts. The sandstone **citadel**, with its temples and palaces, peers down from the edge of a sheer-sided plateau above a haze of exhaust fumes and busy streets. The city's other unmissable attraction is the extraordinarily flamboyant **Jai Vilas Palace**, owned by the local ruling family, the **Scindias**. Their personalities and influence are everywhere, from the **chhatris** (cenotaphs) north of Jayaji Chowk to the excellent **Sarod Ghar** classical music museum. Despite its proximity to Agra, 119km north, Gwalior sees few foreign tourists and its drab modern centre lacks the charm of its nearby Rajasthani counterparts. That said, it is a worthwhile place to pause for a day, particularly around late November or early December, when the old **Mughal tombs** host one of India's premier classical music events, the **Tansen Samaroh Festival**.

Brief history

An inscription unearthed in a now-defunct sun temple suggests that Gwalior was first occupied in the sixth century BC by Hun invaders from the north. Local legend, however, attributes the founding of the fort to the Kuchwaha prince **Suraj Sen**, said to have been cured of leprosy during the tenth century by the hermit **Gwalipa** after whom the city is named. The Kuchwahas' successors, the Parihars, were brutally overthrown in 1232 by **Iltutmish**.

A third Rajput dynasty, the **Tomars**, retook Gwalior in 1398, ushering in the city's golden age. Under **Man Singh**, who ascended to the Tomar *gadi* (throne) in 1486, the hilltop gained the magnificent palaces and fortifications that were to earn it the epithet "the pearl in the necklace of the castles of Hind". Skirmishes with neighbouring powers dogged the Rajputs' rule until 1517, when the **Lodis** from Delhi besieged the fort for a second time and Man Singh was slain. Thereafter, Gwalior was ruled by a succession of Muslim overlords before falling to Akbar.

With the decline of the Mughals, Gwalior became the base of the most powerful of the four Maratha clans, the **Scindias**, in 1754. Twenty-six years later, British troops conquered the fort and Gwalior became a British feudatory state ruled by a succession of puppet rajas. The most famous of these, Jayaji Rao Scindia, remained loyal to the British during the 1857 uprising, although 6500 of his troops joined the opposing forces led by Tantia Tope and **Rani Lakshmi Bai** of Jhansi. Both rebel leaders were killed in the ensuing battle, and the maharaja quickly resumed his role as host of some of the grandest viceregal dinners, royal visits and tiger hunts ever witnessed by the Raj. The Scindias remained influential after Independence, and still live in Gwalior.

Gwalior Fort

North of the modern city • **Fort** Daily sunrise–sunset • ₹250 (₹75); guides ₹500/3hr for up to five people, though this is somewhat negotiable • **Sound-and-light show (in English)** Daily: March–Oct 8.30pm; Nov–Feb 7.30pm • ₹250 (₹75); tickets available from the fort or the MP Tourism office at *Tansen Residency* hotel

Gwalior's imposing **fort** sprawls over a 3km-long outcrop of sandstone. Its mighty turreted battlements encompass six palaces, three temples and several water tanks and cisterns, as well as a prestigious public school and a Sikh *gurudwara*.

Two routes wind up the hill. In the west, a driveable track just off Gwalior Road climbs the steep gorge of the **Urwahi Valley** to the **Urwahi Gate**, passing a line of rock-cut Jain statues along the way. The other, more accessible **Gwalior Gate** is on the northeast corner of the cliff. Official **guides** tout for trade at the Urwahi Gate and the cold-drinks shop at the entrance to the palace complex. There are nightly **sound-and-light shows** in the Man Singh Palace in Hindi and English.

Archeological Museum

Gujuri Mahal • Tues–Sun 10am–5pm • ₹200 (₹50)

A short walk north of the Gwalior Gate, just outside the fort compound, the modest Gujuri Mahal was built by Man Singh to woo his favourite rani, Mrignayani, when she was still a peasant girl. The elegant sandstone palace now houses the **Archeological Museum**, whose large collection of sculptures, inscriptions and paintings is well worth a

5

look, even if the labels are woefully uninformative. Highlights include the twin Ashoka lion capitals from Vidisha in gallery two, and gallery nine's erotic bas-relief; but the most famous exhibit is the exquisitely carved **salabhanjika**, a small female figurine, noted for her sensuous curves and sublime facial expression.

Man Singh Palace

South of the Gwalior Gate

Entered via the **Hathiya** ("elephant") **Paur** gateway, with its twin turrets and ornate blue tilework, the **Man Singh Palace** (sometimes called Man Mandir Palace) was declared "the noblest specimen of Hindu domestic architecture in northern India" by nineteenth-century explorer Sir Alexander Cunningham. Built between 1486 and 1517 by the Tomar ruler Man Singh, it's also known as the Chit Mandir ("Painted Palace") for the rich ceramic **mosaics** encrusting its facade. The best-preserved fragments of tilework, on its south side, can be seen from the bank left of the main Hathiya Paur gateway. Spread in luxurious bands of turquoise, emerald green and yellow across the ornate stonework are tigers, elephants, peacocks and crocodiles brandishing flowers.

By contrast, the **interior** of the four-storey palace is very plain. However, there are some fine pierced-stone *jali* screens, behind which the women of the palace would

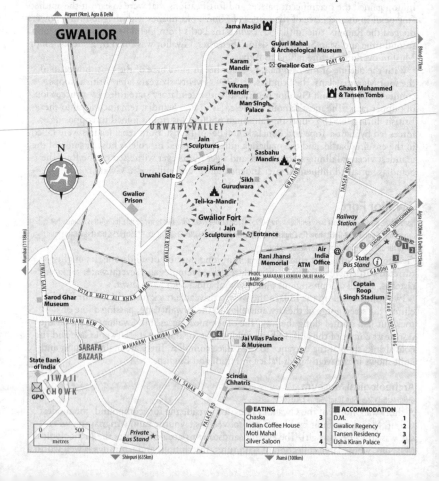

GWALIOR

Airport (9km), Agra & Delhi

Bhind (77km)

Jama Masjid

Gujuri Mahal & Archeological Museum

Karam Mandir

Gwalior Gate · FORT RD

Ghaus Muhammed & Tansen Tombs

Vikram Mandir

Man Singh Palace

URWAHI VALLEY

Jain Sculptures

Sasbahu Mandirs

Suraj Kund

Urwahi Gate

Sikh Gurudwara

Gwalior Prison

Teli-ka-Mandir

Gwalior Fort

Jain Sculptures · Entrance

Railway Station

GWALIOR ROAD

TANSEN ROAD

NH-3

GWALIOR ROAD

Rani Jhansi Memorial · ATM

Air India Office

@ · State Bus Stand · i

STATION RD (SURHASMARG)

STAND RD

Agra (120km) & Delhi (315km)

PHOOL BAGH JUNCTION · MAHARANI LAXMIBAI (MLB) MARG

GANDHI RD

MADHAV RAO SCINDIA MARG

Captain Roop Singh Stadium

Mumbai (1118km)

JIWAJI GANJ

USTAD HAFIZ ALI KHAN MARG

Sarod Ghar Museum

LAKSHMIGANJ NEW RD

SARAFA BAZAAR

MAHARANI LAXMIBAI (MLB) MARG

Jai Vilas Palace & Museum

JHANSI RD

State Bank of India

JIWAJI CHOWK

GPO

NAI SARAK RD

Scindia Chhatris

PALACE RD

0   500
metres

Private Bus Stand

● EATING		■ ACCOMMODATION	
Chaska	3	D.M.	1
Indian Coffee House	2	Gwalior Regency	2
Moti Mahal	1	Tansen Residency	3
Silver Saloon	4	Usha Kiran Palace	4

Shivpuri (635km)

Jhansi (100km)

assemble to receive instruction from Gwalior's great music gurus. The circular chambers in the lower storeys were once dungeons.

Teli-ka-Mandir and Suraj Kund
On the south side of the plateau, the 30m-tall **Teli-ka-Mandir** is the fort's oldest surviving monument. Dating from the mid-eighth century, it consists of a huge rectangular sanctuary tower capped with an unusual vaulted-arch roof, whose *peepal*-leaf shape derives from the *chaitya* windows of much earlier rock-cut Buddhist caves. In the aftermath of the 1857 Indian uprising, the Vishnu temple was used by the British as a soda factory, and restoration work continues. At the head of the Urwahi ravine, just north of the Teli-ka-Mandir, the **Suraj Kund** is the 100m-long tank whose waters are reputed to have cured the tenth-century ruler Suraj Sen, later Suraj Pal, of leprosy.

Sasbahu mandirs
At the eastern edge of the fort, the **Sasbahu**, or "mother-and-daughter-in-law", temples overlook the city near an unsightly TV mast. The larger one has a three-storey *mandapa* (assembly hall), supported by four intricate pillars, while the smaller one consists of an open-sided porch with a pyramidal roof. Both were erected late in the eleventh century and are dedicated to Vishnu.

Sikh gurudwara
South of the Sasbahu *mandirs*, the huge, gold-tipped, white-domed marble building to the south is a modern **Sikh gurudwara**, built to commemorate a Sikh hero who was imprisoned in the fort. Before entering, cover your arms, legs and head, remove your socks and shoes and wash your feet in the tank at the bottom of the steps.

Jain sculptures
Near the Urwahi Gate at the southern entrance to the fort, the sheer sandstone cliffs around the fort harbour some imposing rock-cut **Jain sculptures**. Carved between the seventh and fifteenth centuries, most of the large honey-coloured figures depict the 24 Jain teacher-saviours – the *tirthankaras*, or "Crossing Makers" – standing with their arms held stiffly at their sides, or sitting cross-legged, the palms of their hands upturned. Many lost their faces and genitalia when Mughal emperor Babur's iconoclastic army descended on the city in 1527.

The larger of the two main groups lines the southwestern approach to the fort, along the sides of the **Urwahi** ravine. The largest image, to the side of the road near Urwahi Gate, portrays Adinath, 19m tall, with decorative nipples, a head of tightly curled hair and drooping ears, standing on a lotus bloom beside several smaller statues. A little further from the fort, on the other side of the road, another company of *tirthankaras* enjoys a more dramatic situation, looking over a natural gorge. All have lost their faces, save a proud trio sheltered by a delicate canopy.

The third collection stands on the southeast corner of the plateau, overlooking the city from a narrow ledge. To get here, follow Gwalior Road north along the foot of the cliff from Phool Bagh junction, near the **Rani Jhansi memorial**, until you see a paved path winding up the hill from behind a row of houses on the left. Once again, the *tirthankaras*, which are numbered, occupy deep recesses hewn from the rock wall. One of the few not defaced by the Muslim invaders, no. 10, is still revered by Gwalior's small Jain community as a shrine.

The old town and south of the fort
A number of interesting Islamic monuments are tucked away down the narrow backstreets of Gwalior's predominantly Muslim **old town**, clustered around the north and northeast corners of the hill. One of the main landmarks in this area is the **Jama**

5

Masjid, erected in 1661, which stands close to the Gujuri Mahal near the main entrance to the fort.

Ghaus Mohammed and Tansen tombs

Off Tansen Rd, 1km east of the Jama Masjid • Daily 10am–5pm • Free

The city's most famous Muslim building is the sixteenth-century **Tomb of Ghaus Mohammed**, an Afghan prince who helped Babur take Gwalior Fort. It's a fine specimen of early Mughal architecture, and a popular local shrine. Elegant hexagonal pavilions stand at each of its four corners; in the centre, the large central dome retains a few remnants of its blue-glazed tiles. The tomb's walls are inlaid with exquisite pierced-stone *jali* screens.

The second and smaller of the tombs in the gardens is that of the famous Mughal singer-musician **Tansen**, one of the "Nine Jewels" of Emperor Akbar's court. Every year, performers and aficionados from all over India flock here for Gwalior's annual **Tansen Samaroh music festival** (see page 345). Local superstition holds that the leaves of the **tamarind tree** growing on the plinth nearby have a salutary effect on the singing voice, which is why its bottom branches have been stripped bare.

Jai Vilas Palace and Museum

Palace Rd, south of the fort • Tues–Sun: April–Sept 10am–4.45pm, Oct–March 10am–4.30pm • ₹800 (₹140) • ☎ 0751 237 2390, ⓦ jaivilasmuseum.org

The **Jai Vilas Palace** is one of India's most grandiose and eccentric nineteenth-century relics, although the lack of labelling and information can make for a frustrating visit. It was built in 1875 during the reign of Maharaja Jayaji Rao Scindia, who dispatched his friend Colonel Michael Filose on a grand tour of Europe to seek inspiration; Filose returned with a vast shipment of furniture, fabric, paintings, tapestries and cut glass, together with the blueprints for a building that borrowed heavily from Buckingham Palace, Versailles, Greek ruins and Italian-Baroque stately homes. The result is a shamelessly over-the-top blend of Doric, Tuscan and Corinthian architecture.

The Scindias, who still occupy part of the palace, have opened two wings to the public. The first wing, a **museum**, includes countless Mughal paintings, Persian rugs, gold and silver ornaments and antique furniture that belonged to the estate of Louis XVI before the French Revolution.

A still more extravagant wing lies across the courtyard from the museum. The **durbar hall** was where the maharaja entertained important visitors. A sweeping Belgian glass staircase leads from the lobby upstairs to the gargantuan assembly hall, which has the world's biggest chandeliers. At more than 3.5 tonnes apiece, they could not be installed until the strength of the roof had been tested with eight elephants. The rug lining the floor of the hall, woven by inmates of Gwalior jail, took twelve years to complete and, at over 40m in length, is the largest handmade carpet in Asia.

Sarod Ghar Museum

Ustad Hafiz Ali Khan Marg, Jiwaji Ganj, southwest of the fort • Tues–Sun 10am–1pm & 2–4pm • Free • ⓦ sarod.com

The **Sarod Ghar Museum** of music occupies the beautiful ancestral home of the Bangash family, whose ancestors, originally Afghan horse-traders who settled in India, produced a dynasty of musical virtuosos, including **Ustad Hafiz Ali Khan** and his son **Ustad Amjad Ali Khan**. The museum traces Gwalior's rich musical legacy, from Tansen, who performed in Mughal emperor Akbar's court, to the invention by Gulam Ali Khan Bangash of the **sarod**, whose ethereal tones accompany you as you progress through the galleries.

Scindia chhatris

Palace Rd, just south of the Jai Vilas Palace • Daily 10am–5pm • ₹50

Two characteristically ostentatious Scindia family tombs are found in the south of Gwalior. Inside a walled courtyard, the **Scindia chhatris** feature intricate stonework

RESTORED TEMPLES AT KHAJURAHO

5

and ornately painted scenes of life inside the nineteenth-century Maratha royal court. Built in 1817 to commemorate Maharaja Jiyaji Rao Scindia, the larger of the pair is most remarkable for the intricate outside panelling of interwoven flowers. The second chhatri is a more compact and finely detailed version of the former, constructed in 1843 for the recently departed Maharaja Janakaji Scindia; sculptures and carvings depict the hectic lifestyle of a king.

ARRIVAL AND INFORMATION   GWALIOR

By plane The airport, 12km north of the city (taxi to the centre around ₹600) is served by Air India (Maharani Laxmibai Marg; ☎0751 237 6872).

Destinations Delhi (2 weekly; 40min); Mumbai (3 weekly; 1hr 40min).

By train Gwalior's railway station lies in the east of the city, just off Station Rd and a short walk from numerous hotels. The quickest train to Delhi is the *Shatabdi Express* #12001 (daily 7.45pm; 3hr 45min), which travels via Agra (1hr 25min). Travelling in the opposite direction, the *Shatabdi Express* #12002 (daily 9.33) is the quickest train to both Jhansi (1hr 12min) and Bhopal (4hr 22min).

Destinations Agra (every 30min–1hr; 1hr 12min–3hr); Bhopal (every 30min–1hr; 4hr 30min–8hr 15min); Delhi (every 30min–1hr; 3hr 45min–7hr 50min); Indore (2–4 daily; 11hr 35min–14hr 12min); Jhansi (every 30min–1hr; 1hr 12min–5hr 15min); Khajuraho (1 daily; 6hr 10min).

By bus The state bus stand is around the corner from the railway station, just off Station Rd. The private bus stand,

inconveniently situated on the southwestern edge of Gwalior, is only worth considering if you are travelling long distances.

Destinations Agra (every 30min–1hr; 3hr–3hr 30min); Datia (every 30min–1hr; 1hr 30min–2hr); Jhansi (every 30min–1hr; 3hr 30min–4hr); Shivpuri (every 30min–1hr; 2hr 30min).

Tourist information MP Tourism has a useful office at *Tansen Residency* on Gandhi Rd (daily 10am–6pm; ☎0751 223 4557); it runs a daily bus tour of the city (8hr 30min; ₹120). There is also an MP Tourism booth in the railway station, platform 1 (daily 10am–5pm; ☎0751 404 0777).

Internet There are several internet cafés on Padav Rd, including Gwala's Cyber Zone.

Banks and exchange The State Bank of India, at the heart of the bazaar district near the GPO on Jayaji Chowk, changes foreign currency. There are numerous ATMs, including one next to the tourist office booth in the station and another on MLB Rd.

ACCOMMODATION

Standards at Gwalior's hotels are generally low, especially at the budget end. In addition, many shoestring hotels, particularly those near the railway station, refuse to take foreigners.

D.M. Link Rd, near the state bus stand ☎0751 234 2083; map p.362. Probably the best low-cost choice, with clean and quiet rooms; the cheaper ones are a little small, though, and have squat toilets – the bigger ones are around ₹200–300 more. **₹700**

Gwalior Regency Link Rd, near the state bus stand ☎0751 234 0670, ⊛hotelregencygroup.com; map p.362. Efficient, if not particularly friendly, mid-range hotel aimed primarily at business travellers. As well as

smart, modern, a/c attached rooms, there is a small pool, gym, coffee shop, a good restaurant and a bar-disco. **₹5000**

Tansen Residency 6A Gandhi Rd ☎0751 234 0370, ⊛mptourism.com; map p.362. This MP Tourism-run hotel is a reason-able choice for a night. Set in its own gardens, it has well-furnished a/c rooms, plus a pool, restaurant and bar. It's popular, so book in advance. **₹3415**

Usha Kiran Palace Jayendraganj, Lakshar ☎0751 244 4000, ⊛tajhotels.com; map p.362. Romantic 120-year-old palace set in nine acres of landscaped gardens. Charming rooms have Indian-style divans, 1930s-era furniture and silk cushions. There's a pool, spa and good restaurant (see below), and cookery and yoga classes are available. **₹13,150**

EATING

Chaska Ambience hotel, Railway station campus ☎0751 404 0341, ⊛ambiencegwalior.com; map p.362. Just outside the southern gate of the railway station, this clean fast-food-style veg outlet serves great south Indian snacks (₹60–120), pretty good sandwiches and burgers and more substantial combo meals (from ₹100). Daily 7am–10pm.

Indian Coffee House Station Rd; map p.362. Low-key place with white-turbaned waiters, it consistently produces the goods, from toast and filter coffee (from ₹18) and south

Indian breakfast options (from ₹50) to more substantial meals (₹90–330). Daily 8am–10.30pm.

Moti Mahal Gwalior Regency, Link Rd, near the state bus stand ☎0751 234 0670; map p.362. Serving Mughlai food at its best, this high-end chain was started by Kundan Lal Gujral, the so-called "father of tandoori cuisine", back in the 1920s. Famed for the signature *murg makhani* (₹), they also have good biryanis, *paneer lababdar* and other Punjabi favourites, mostly ₹250–475. Daily noon–11pm.

★ **Silver Saloon** Usha Kiran Palace, Jayendraganj, Lakshar ☎0751 244 4000, ⊛tajhotels.com; map p.362. If you can't afford to stay at the hotel (see above), a visit to its exemplary restaurant is the next best thing. gourmet Mughlai, Marathi, Nepalese and international dishes are served impeccably in evocative surroundings overlooking a verdant courtyard; expect to pay from ₹1000 for dinner. Daily 7am–11pm.

Datia

Constructed by Bir Singh Deo at the height of the Bundela "golden age", the little-visited majestic palace at **DATIA**, 30km northwest of Jhansi and 71km southeast of Gwalior, is one of India's finest Rajput buildings. Presiding over a mass of white- and blue-washed brick houses from its seat atop a rock outcrop, the 440-room, seven-storey **Bir Singh Deo Palace** (sometimes called Nrsing Dev Palace) stands in the east of town. Half the fun of visiting is trying to find a path from its pitch-black subterranean chambers, hewn out of the solid base of the hill for use during the hot season, to the rani's airy apartment on the top floor. In between, a maze of cross-cutting corridors, flying walkways, walls encrusted with fragments of ceramic tiles, latticed screens and archways, hidden passages, pavilions and suites of apartments lead you in ever-decreasing circles until you eventually run out of staircases. The views from the upper storeys are breathtaking. There are guides on hand, armed with torches, to show you around if you wish, and they can also open up some of the rooms that contain wall paintings (for a baksheesh of ₹50 or so).

ARRIVAL AND DEPARTURE   DATIA

By train Datia railway station, 2km southwest of the bus station, sits on the main Delhi–Mumbai train line, though services are fairly limited.

By bus The bus station is just south of the centre. Regular buses connect Datia with both Jhansi (every 30min–1hr;

1hr–1hr 30min) and Gwalior (every 30min–1hr; 1hr 30min–2hr). If you're coming from Shivpuri, 97km west, you'll need to change buses at Karera. An auto-rickshaw to the palace should cost no more than ₹120.

Orchha

An essential stop en route to or from Khajuraho, **ORCHHA** ("hidden place") certainly lives up to its name, residing amid a tangle of scrubby *dhak* forest 18km southeast of Jhansi. In spite of its tumbledown state, the fortified and now deserted medieval town remains an architectural gem, its guano-splashed temple *shikharas*, derelict palaces, havelis and weed-choked sandstone cenotaphs floating serenely above the banks of the River Betwa. Clustered around the foot of the exotic ruins, the sleepy village makes an excellent spot to unwind after the hassle of northern cities. However, it's now firmly established on the tour-group circuit, so try to spend a night or two here after the coach parties have moved off.

Brief history

After being chased by several generations of Delhi sultans from various capitals around central India, the Bundela dynasty finally settled at the former Malwan fort of **Orchha** in the fifteenth century. Work on Orchha's magnificent fortifications, palaces and temples was started by Raja **Rudra Pratap**, and continued after he was killed in 1531 trying to wrestle a cow from the clutches of a tiger. Thereafter, the dynasty's fortunes depended on the goodwill of their mighty neighbours, the **Mughals**. After being defeated in battle by Akbar, the proud and pious **Madhukar Shah** nearly signed his clan's death warrant by showing up at the imperial court with a red *tilak* smeared on his forehead – a mark at that time banned by the emperor. Madhukar's bold gesture, however, earned Akbar's respect, and the two became friends – an alliance fostered in the following years by Orchha's most illustrious raja.

5

During his 22-year rule, **Bir Singh Deo** erected 52 forts and palaces, including the citadel at Jhansi, the Bir Singh Deo Palace at Datia (see page 367) and many of Orchha's finest buildings. In 1627, he was killed by bandits while returning from the Deccan with a camel train full of booty. Afterwards, relations with the Mughals rapidly deteriorated, and the Bundelas eventually fled Orchha for the comparative safety of **Tikamgarh**. Apart from the *Sheesh Mahal*, now a hotel (see page 369), the magnificent monuments have lain virtually deserted ever since.

The main monuments

The ticket office is across the bridge, just east of the main market crossroads • Daily 8am–5.30pm • "Day passport" for all the main monuments ₹250 (₹10), camera ₹25, video camera ₹200, guides around ₹500 • **Sound-and-light show (in English)** Daily: March–Nov 7.30pm; Dec–Feb 6.30pm • ₹250 (₹100), children ₹150 (₹50)

The best-preserved of Orchha's scattered **monuments** – palaces, temples, tombs and gardens – lie within comfortable walking distance of the village and can be seen (at breakneck speed) in a day; to get the most out of a trip you should plan on staying the night. A **sound-and-light show** is held every night at the fort throughout the year.

Raj Mahal

Just beyond the bridge, the first building you come to across Orchha's medieval granite bridge is the well-preserved ruin of the royal palace, or **Raj Mahal**. Of the two rectangular courtyards inside, the second, formerly used by the Bundela ranis, is the most dramatic. Opulent royal quarters, raised balconies and interlocking walkways rise in symmetrical tiers on all four sides, crowned by domed pavilions and turrets; the apartments projecting into the quadrangle on the ground floor belonged to the most-favoured queens. As you wander around, look out for the fragments of mirror inlay and vibrant **painting** plastered over their walls and ceilings. Some of the friezes are in remarkable condition, depicting Vishnu's various outlandish incarnations, court and hunting scenes, and lively festivals.

Rai Praveen Mahal

Reached via a path that leads from the Raj Mahal around the northern side of the hill, the **Rai Praveen Mahal** is a small, double-storeyed brick apartment built by Raja Indramani for his concubine in the mid-1670s. The gifted poetess, musician and dancer Rai Praveen beguiled the Mughal emperor Akbar when she was sent to him as a gift, but was eventually returned to Orchha to live out her remaining days. Set amid the well-watered lawns of the **Anand Mahal gardens**, the building has a main assembly hall on the ground floor (used to host music and dance performances), a boudoir upstairs and cool underground apartments.

Saket Museum of Ramayana Correlogram

Tues–Sun 10am–5pm

A short walk south of the Raj Mahal, the small **Saket Museum of Ramayana Correlogram** has an intriguing collection of Hindu folk art from across India. Highlights include Mithila paintings (produced using paint made from cow's milk) from Bihar and colourful masks from Odisha and Uttar Pradesh.

Jahangir Mahal

South of the Rai Praveen Mahal, Orchha's most admired palace, the **Jahangir Mahal** was built by Bir Singh Deo as a monumental welcome present for the Mughal emperor when he paid a state visit here in the seventeenth century. Jahangir had come to invest his old ally with the sword of Abdul Fazal – the emperor's erstwhile enemy whom Bir Singh had murdered some years earlier. Entered through an ornate ceremonial gateway, the main, east-facing facade is still encrusted with turquoise tiles. Two stone elephants flank the stairway, holding bells in their trunks to announce the arrival of the raja, and there are three storeys of elegant hanging balconies, terraces, apartments and onion domes piled around a central courtyard. This palace, however, has a much lighter feel, with countless windows and pierced stone screens looking out over the exotic Orchha skyline to the west, and a sea of treetops and ruined temples in the other direction.

Sheesh Mahal

Just west of the Jahangir Mahal and built during the early eighteenth century, long after Orchha's demise, the **Sheesh Mahal** ("Palace of Mirrors") was originally intended to be an exclusive country retreat for the local raja, Udait Singh. Following Independence, the property was inherited by the state government, who converted it into a hotel. The rather squat palace stands between the Raj Mahal and the Jahangir Mahal, at the far end of an open-sided courtyard. Covered in a coat of whitewash and stripped of most of its Persian rugs and antiques, the building retains only traces of its former splendour, though there are stunning views from its upper terraces and turrets. If they're not occupied, check out the palatial suites (rooms 1 and 2), which contain original bathroom fittings.

Chhatris

Daily sunrise–sunset

A solemn row of pale brown weed-choked domes and spires perched above the river around 1km south of the market, the fourteen riverside **chhatris**, the cenotaphs of Bundelkhand's former rulers (including that of Bir Sing Deo), are Orchha's most melancholy ruins and best admired at sunrise or sunset.

Around the village

There are several interesting temples in the **village**, as well as a **nature reserve**. The more traditional market area, where local farmers come to sell their goods around the **Ram Raja Mandir** (west of the main street), is also worth a look, with several small dilapidated palaces dotted around the place that you can wander through (those bits that aren't squatted, anyway).

Ram Raja Mandir

Daily 8am–noon & 8–10pm • Free

The **Ram Raja Mandir** stands just west of the bazaar's main crossroads, in a cool marble-tiled courtyard. Local legend has it that Madhukar Shah constructed the building as a palace for his wife, Rani Ganesha, and it only became a temple after a Rama icon, which the queen had dutifully carried all the way from her home town of Ayodhya, could not be lifted from the spot where she first set it down; it remains there to this day, and the temple is a popular pilgrimage site.

Hardaul ka Baithak

Opposite the Ram Raja Mandir • No fixed opening times • Free

A path leads through the Mughal-style Phool Bagh ornamental garden to **Hardaul ka Baithak**, a grand pavilion where Bir Singh Deo's second son, Hardaul, ally of Jahangir and romantic paragon, once held court. Newlyweds come here to seek blessing from Hardaul, who, despite being poisoned by his jealous brother who accused him of intimacy with his sister-in-law, is thought to confer good luck. The tall towers rising above the gardens like disregarded bridge supports are *dastgirs* ("wind-catchers"), Persian-style cooling towers that provided air-conditioning for the neighbouring palace, Palkhi Mahal; they're thought to be the only ones of their kind surviving in India.

Chatturbuj Mandir

South of the market • No fixed opening times • Free

5

With its huge pointed *shikharas* soaring high above the village, **Chatturbuj Mandir** is the temple originally built to house Rani Ganesha's icon. In cruciform shape, representing the four-armed Vishnu, with seven storeys and spacious courtyards ringed by arched balconies, it epitomizes the regal Bundelkhand style, inspired by the Mughals, with Rajput, Persian and European touches. It's unusual for a Hindu temple, with few carvings and a wealth of space – perhaps to accommodate followers of the **bhakti** cult (a form of worship involving large congregations of people rather than a small elite of priests). You can climb up the narrow staircases between storeys to the temple's roof, pierced by an ornate *shikhara* whose niches shelter nesting vultures.

Orchha Nature Reserve

On the east side of the bridge, around 700m south of the market • Daily 8am–6pm • ₹150 (₹15)

The **Orchha Nature Reserve** is a good place to spend a spare morning or afternoon. Here you can take an idle wander or cycle along a peaceful nature trail (around 12km in length) in the company of monkeys and peacocks.

Lakshmi Narayan Mandir

Around 1km west of the village • No fixed opening times • Free

The solitary **Lakshmi Narayan Mandir** crowns a rocky hillock just under 1km west of Orchha village, at the end of a long, paved pathway. It takes around fifteen minutes to walk here from the market, for which you are rewarded with fine views and excellent seventeenth- and nineteenth-century paintings. For a small tip, the chowkidar will lead you through the galleries inside the temple. Look out for the frieze depicting the battle of Jhansi, in which the rani appears in an upper room of the fort next to her horse, while musket-bearing British troops scuttle about below. Elsewhere, episodes from the much-loved Krishna story crop up alongside portraits of the Bundela rajas and their military and architectural achievements, while a side pillar bears a sketch of two very inebriated English soldiers.

ARRIVAL AND DEPARTURE   ORCHHA

By tempo and bus Packed *tempos* and buses (departing when really full; 20–40min) shuttle between Jhansi bus station and Orchha's main crossroads, 18km away. If you're on a bus from Khajuraho/Bamitha to Jhansi you can ask to be dropped off at the turning on the main road, and pick up a *tempo* for the remaining 7km. If you're heading in the opposite direction, don't bank on being able to flag down a bus on the highway, as they're often full. Instead, get to Jhansi bus station, from where they depart. There is one daily bus direct from Jhansi to Khajuraho (the departure time fluctuates, so ask locally; 5hr), as well as numerous services between Jhansi and Bamitha, a 15min auto-rickshaw ride from Khajuraho.

By auto-rickshaw An auto-rickshaw between Jhansi and Orchha costs about ₹300 (more at night).

By taxi Taxis between Jhansi and Orchha charge around ₹500 (more at night); around ₹2500-2700 between Orchha and Khajuraho. The MP Tourism office (see below) and the better hotels can organize them for you.

By train Orchha's small railway station is 3.5km from the centre of the village (around ₹150 by auto-rickshaw or ₹10-15 if you don't mind sharing with at least a dozen other passengers). A single local train (5–6hr) trundles between Orchha and Khajuraho. It generally departs from Orchha in the morning, and returns from Khajuraho in the early afternoon – exact times fluctuate, so check locally. You can't book in advance, but there's usually no shortage of seats. Jhansi station has a far wider range of train services, including to and from Khajuraho (2 daily; 4hr 5min–8hr 20min).

INFORMATION

Tourist information The MP Tourism offices (daily 7am–10pm) at the *Sheesh Mahal* (☎ 07680 252624) and *Betwa Retreat* (☎ 07680 252618) can provide information and organize river-rafting trips (₹1300–2200).

Services A bike can be a useful way to get around Orchha;

several companies in town offer rental for around ₹100–250/day. The cybercafé next to *Bhola* restaurant offers internet and Skype access. Note that most of the smarter hotels will allow non-guests to use their pools for around ₹600.

ACCOMMODATION

Amar Mahal Bypass Rd, 100m north of chhatris ☎ 07680 252102, ⓦ amarmahal.com. A Mughal-themed hotel whose attached rooms, each with elegantly carved wooden beds and elaborately painted ceilings, are set around a series of peaceful, interlinked courtyards. As well as a restaurant, there's a pool and a mini spa (all open to non-guests). ₹6600

Betwa Retreat Off Tikamgarh Rd, 10min walk south of the market ☎ 07680 252618, ⊛ mptourism.com. An MP Tourism lodge with faded but tastefully decorated salmon-coloured cottages (including a Raj-style heritage one housed in an old shrine) and comfy a/c "Swiss" tents, each with a TV, fridge and marble bathroom set in a peaceful garden close to the river. There's a restaurant, bar and small pool. ₹2950

Bundelkhand Riverside Off Jhansi Rd, around 1km north of the market ☎ 07680 252612, ⊛ bundelkhandriverside.com. The former hunting lodge of Orchha's last maharaja, dating back to 1895, *Bundelkhand Riverside* has a blend of traditional Indian and British colonial architecture, spacious art-filled a/c attached rooms (most with river views), a good restaurant, a pool and nightly free culture shows at 7pm. ₹4500

Friends of Orchha ☎ 94107 62072, ⊛ orchha.org. This NGO offers homestays with local families; accommodation is basic, but the families provide food (breakfast ₹60, lunch/dinner ₹150 veg/₹250 non-veg) and the experience offers a wonderful insight into traditional Orchha life. ₹950

Ganpati Jhansi Rd, 300m north of the main crossroads ☎ 07680 252765. Welcoming, family-run hotel with a range of attached rooms set around a small garden, from where there are spectacular views of the old fortifications. All the rooms are clean (if a little scruffy); the more expensive have a/c and some boast vistas of their own. ₹1000

★ **Sheesh Mahal** Jehangir Mahal Rd, next to the Raj Mahal ☎ 07680 252624, ⊛ mptourism.com. The local raja's former country bolthole in the heart of the fort is now an atmospheric hotel with eight charming (and very good-value) a/c rooms and a personalized approach. If you can afford it, treat yourself to a romantic night in the Maharaja suite (₹7800) – perks include a vast marble bathtub and the ultimate loo with a view. Advance booking recommended. ₹3550

★ **Shri Mahant Guesthouse** Next to the Ram Raja Mandir entrance off the market crossroads ☎ 07680 252715. Backpacker stalwart in the heart of the action: the rooms are a little claustrophobic, and the most basic have squat toilets, but for double the price you get a/c, TV and Western-style toilets. There's also a small shared terrace overlooking the temple entrance which is great for people-watching (though pujas can be noisy). ₹600

EATING

Most of the **restaurants** in the centre of Orchha boast interchangeable, traveller-oriented menus and views across to the fort. If you want a bit more variety and some non-veg options, try the restaurants in the smarter hotels such as *Bundelkhand Riverside* (see above). The delicious local delicacy, *kalakand* (milk cake), can be bought from the small stalls in the market.

★ **Betwa Tarang** On the approach to the Fort Bridge. A first-floor veg restaurant with a good view of the fort and reasonable pizzas and pasta (₹250–320), as well as better and slightly cheaper Westernized Indian and Indianized Chinese dishes, and tasty, very filling thalis (₹140–350). Daily 7.30am–10pm.

Bhola On the approach to the Fort Bridge. Established, if rather scruffy little restaurant with an eclectic menu that jumps from Korean, Dutch and Israeli dishes to veg Indian staples, though the latter are much better – note that if you order a foreign dish and the owner recommends the pancakes instead, it means he doesn't cook the foreign dish well (and the pancakes are indeed excellent). Most dishes ₹50–150. Daily 8am–10pm.

Jharokha Sheesh Mahal hotel, Jehangir Mahal Rd, next to the Raj Mahal ☎ 07680 252624, ⊛ mptourism.com. Soak up the palace's evocative surroundings in the colonnaded dining hall, which has the usual MP Tourism menu, serving veg and non-veg food (standouts include the fish, chicken and egg curries for ₹130–220), a few local specialities, and live music and dancing in the evenings. Daily 8am–10pm.

Ram Raja On the approach to the Fort Bridge ☎ 07680 252697, ⊛ facebook.com/ramrajarestaurant. Cheerful little place with an extensive breakfast menu (served all day) that features hash browns , peanut butter or Nutella on toast and as many kinds of eggs as you can think of. They also serve simple veg Indian meals (₹110–₹250), *momos* and the best coffee in town. Daily 7am–10.30pm.

Khajuraho

The resplendent Hindu temples of **KHAJURAHO**, immaculately restored after almost a millennium of abandonment and neglect, and now a UNESCO World Heritage Site, are an essential stop on any itinerary of India's historic monuments. Famed for the delicate sensuality – and forthright **eroticism** – of their sculpture, they were built between the tenth and twelfth centuries AD and remain the greatest architectural achievement of the **Chandella** dynasty.

Waves of Afghan invaders soon hastened the decline of the Chandellas, however, who abandoned the temples for more secure ground shortly after they were built. The temples gradually fell out of use and by the sixteenth century had been swallowed by the surrounding jungle. It took "rediscovery" by the British in 1838 before these masterpieces were fully appreciated in India, let alone internationally. It is still not known exactly why the temples were built and there are a number of competing **theories** (see page 375); some say they are a "how to" guide for brahmin boys while others claim they symbolize the wedding party of Shiva and Parvati.

Some 400km southeast of Agra and the same distance west of Varanasi, Khajuraho might look central on maps of the Subcontinent, but remains almost as **remote** from the Indian mainstream as it was when the temples were built – which is presumably what spared them the depredations of the marauders, invaders and zealots who devastated so many early Hindu sites. However, trains now cross this extended flood plain, making Khajuraho much easier to visit today.

Khajuraho town

The sheer splendour of the temples rather overshadows **Khajuraho town**, which was largely built to service tourists – the original Khajuraho village is much sleepier and lies somewhat to the east. Still, if you stay a night or two, you'll discover a relaxed pace

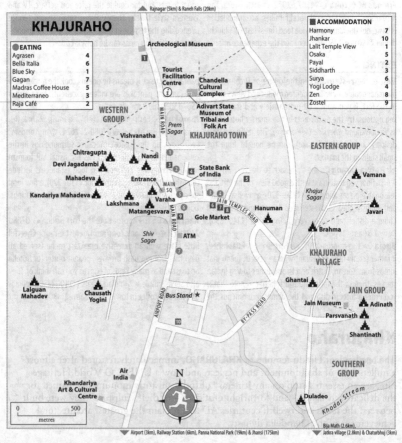

5

THE TEMPLES OF KHAJURAHO

The exquisite intricacy of the **temples** themselves – of which the most spectacular are **Kandariya Mahadeva**, **Vishvanatha** and **Lakshmana**, all in the conglomeration known as the **western group** – was made possible by the soft fawn-coloured sandstone used in their construction. Considering the propensity of such stone to crumble, they have withstood the ravages of time remarkably well. Much of the **ornate sculpture** adorning their walls is in such high relief as to be virtually three-dimensional, with strains of pink in the stone helping to imbue the figures with flesh-like tones. The incredible skill of the artisans is evident throughout, with friezes as little as 10cm wide crammed with naturalistic details of ornaments, jewellery, hairstyles and even manicured nails. To add to the beauty of the whole ensemble, the temples subtly change hue as the day progresses, passing from a warm pink at sunrise to white at midday and back to pink at sunset. Dramatic **floodlights** pick them out in the evening, and they glow white when the moon is out.

---

of life, especially in the evening when the open-air restaurants create a very sociable atmosphere. Visitor facilities are concentrated in the uncluttered avenues of the town; the gates of the western group of temples open immediately onto its **main square**, which is surrounded by hotels, cafés and curio shops where you should brace yourself for some hard selling.

Archeological Museum

North of the western group next to the *Lalit Temple View* hotel • Daily except Fri 10am–5pm • Free entry with a ticket for the western group of temples (see below); photography absolutely prohibited

The marble-floored **Archeological Museum** is principally noteworthy for a remarkable sculpture of a pot-bellied dancing Ganesh among a range of some of the best carvings and statues from the temples. Not all of the galleries were open at the time of writing, but there are many pieces arranged around the pleasant manicured gardens too.

Adivart State Museum of Tribal and Folk Art

Chandella Cultural Complex, just east of the Tourist Facilitation Centre • Tues–Sun noon–8pm • Free

Worth a quick visit, the **Adivart State Museum of Tribal and Folk Art** has a small but interesting collection of paintings, sculptures and artwork by Madhya Pradesh's many tribal groups. There is also a range of original paintings and prints for sale.

Temples: the western group

Entrance opposite the main square • Daily sunrise–sunset • ₹500 (₹30), camera ₹25; self-guided audio tour ₹120; smoking and lighters are prohibited and you'll be searched on the way in • Sound-and-light show (in English) Daily: March–Sept 7.30pm, Oct–Feb 6.30pm • ₹700 (₹250)

Stranded like a fleet of stone ships amid pristine lawns and flowerbeds fringed with bougainvillea, the **western group** of temples is Khajuraho's prime attraction. With the exception of **Matangesvara**, just outside the main complex, all are now virtually devoid of religious significance, and only spring back to life during Shivratri (see page 379). Visitors must remove their shoes before entering individual temples. An informative self-guided **audio tour** is available from the temple booking office, and there's a nightly **sound-and-light show** (55min). The site can get to be a bit of a scrum when the tour groups are in, so it's best to visit before 9am (when the rising sun illuminates the interiors of the temples), or around lunchtime.

Varaha

Just inside the complex a small open *mandapa* pavilion, built between the tenth and eleventh centuries, houses a huge, highly polished sandstone image of **Vishnu** as the boar – **Varaha**. Carved in low relief on its body, 674 figures in neat rows represent the major gods and goddesses of the Hindu pantheon. Lord of the earth, water and

5

heaven, the alert boar straddles Shesha the serpent, accompanied by what T.S. Burt (see box above) conjectured must have been the most beautiful form of **Prithvi**, the earth goddess – all that remains are her feet, and a hand on the neck of the boar. Above the image the lotus ceiling stands out in relief.

Lakshmana

Beyond Varaha, adjacent to the Matangesvara temple across the boundary wall, the richly carved **Lakshmana** temple, dating from around 950 AD, is the oldest of the western group. It stands on a high plinth covered with processional friezes of horses, elephants and camels, as well as soldiers, domestic scenes, musicians and dancers. Among explicit sexual images is a man sodomizing a horse, flanked by shocked female onlookers. The sheer energy of the work gives the whole temple an astounding sense of movement and vitality.

While the plinth depicts the human world, the temple itself, the *adhisthana*, brings one into contact with the celestial realm. Two tiers of carved panels decorate its exterior, with gods and goddesses attended by *apsaras*, "celestial nymphs", and figures in complicated sexual acts on the lower tier and in the recesses. Fine detail includes a magnificent dancing Ganesh on the south face, a master architect with his students on the east, and heavenly musicians and dancers.

The mandapa and inner sanctum

Successive pyramidal roofs over the *mandapa* and the porch rise to a clustered tower made of identical superimposed elements. Small porches with sloping eaves project from the *mandapa* and passageway, with exquisite columns, each with eight figures, at each corner of the platform supported by superb brackets in the form of *apsaras*. The inner sanctum, the *garbha griha*, is reached through a door whose lintel shows Vishnu's consort **Lakshmi**, accompanied by **Brahma** and **Shiva**; a frieze depicts the **Navagraha**, the nine planets. Inside, the main image is of Vishnu as the triple-headed, four-armed Vaikuntha, attended by his incarnations as boar and man-lion.

Kandariya Mahadeva

Sharing a common platform with other temples in the western corner of the enclosure, the majestic **Kandariya Mahadeva** temple, built between 1025 and 1050 AD, is the largest and most imposing of the western group. A perfect consummation of the five-part design instigated in Lakshmana and Vishvanatha, this Shiva temple represents the pinnacle of Chandellan art, its ornate roofs soaring dramatically to culminate 31m above the base in a *shikhara* consisting of 84 smaller replicas.

Kandariya Mahadeva is especially popular with visitors for the extraordinarily energetic and provocative erotica that ornaments its three tiers, covering almost every facet of the exterior. Admiring crowds can always be found in front of a particularly fine image of a couple locked in **mithuna** (sexual intercourse) with a maiden assisting on either side. One of Khajuraho's most familiar motifs, it seems to defy nature, with the male figure suspended upside down on his head; only when considered as if from above do the sinuous intertwined limbs begin to make sense.

The torana and the seven mothers

An elaborate garland at the entrance to the temple, carved from a single stone, acts as a *torana*, the ritual gateway of a marriage procession. Both inside and out, lavish and intricate images of gods, goddesses, musicians and nymphs celebrate the occasion; within the sanctuary a dark passage leads to its central *shivalingam*. Niches along the exterior contain images of **Ganesh**, **Virabhadra** and the **Sapta Matrikas**, the seven mothers responsible for dressing the bridegroom, Shiva. Wrathful deities and fearsome protectors, the seven consist of Brahmi, a female counterpart of Shiva, seated on the swan of Brahma; a three-eyed Maheshvari on Shiva's bull Nandi; Kumari; Vaishnavi, seated on the bird Garuda; Varahi, the female form of Vishnu as the boar; Narasimhi,

THE EROTIC ART OF KHAJURAHO

Prurient eyes have been hypnotized by the unabashed **erotica** of Khajuraho ever since its "rediscovery" in February 1838. A young British officer of the Bengal Engineers, **T.S. Burt**, had deviated from his official itinerary when he came upon the ancient temples all but engulfed by jungle. Frank representations of oral sex, masturbation and copulation with animals may have fitted into the mores of the tenth-century Chandellas, but, as Burt relates, were hardly calculated to meet with the approval of the upstanding officers of Queen Victoria:

"I found … seven Hindoo temples, most beautifully and exquisitely carved as to workmanship, but the sculptor had at times allowed his subject to grow a little warmer than there was any absolute necessity for his doing; indeed some of the sculptures here were extremely indecent and offensive … The palki (palanquin) bearers, however, appeared to take great delight at those, to them, very agreeable novelties, which they took care to point out to all present."

Burt found the inscription on the steps of the Vishvanatha temple that enabled historians to attribute the site to the Chandellas, and to piece together their genealogy, but it was several years before Major-General Sir Alexander Cunningham produced detailed plans of Khajuraho, drawing the distinction between "western" and "eastern" groups. Cunningham thought all the sculptures "highly indecent, and most of them disgustingly obscene".

TANTRIC CULTS TO CELESTIAL ENTERTAINMENT

The erotic images remain the subject of a disproportionate amount of controversy and debate among academics and curious tourists alike. The task of explanation is made more difficult by the fact that even the Chandellas themselves barely mentioned the temples in their literature, and the very name "Khajuraho" may be misleading, simply taken from that of the nearby village.

Among attempts to account for the sexual content of the carvings have been suggestions of links with **Tantric** cults, which use sex as a pivotal part of worship. Some claim they were inspired by the **Kama Sutra**, and similarly intended to serve as a manual on love, while others argue the sculptures were designed to entertain the gods, diverting their wrath and thus protecting the temples against natural calamities. Alternatively, the geometric qualities of certain images have been put forward as evidence that each represents a **yantra**, a pictorial form of a mantra, for use in meditation.

The sixteen large panels depicting sexual union that appear along the northern and southern aspects of the three principal temples – Kandariya Mahadeva, Lakshmana and Vishvanatha – are mostly concerned with the junction of the male and the female elements of the temples, the **mandapa** and the **garbha griha** (the "womb"). They might therefore have been intended as a visual pun, elaborated by artistic licence.

---

the female form of Vishnu as man-lion; and the terrifying Chamunda, the slayer of the *asuras* or "demons" Chanda and Munda, and the only one of the Sapta Matrikas who is not a female representation of a major male god.

Devi Jagadambi

North of Kandariya Mahadeva along the platform, the earlier **Devi Jagadambi** temple is a simpler structure, whose outer walls lack projecting balconies. Originally dedicated to Vishnu, its prominent *mandapa* is capped by a massive pyramidal roof. Three *bhandas* (belts) bind the *jangha* (body), adorned with exquisite and sensuous carvings; the erotica on the third is arguably Khajuraho's finest. Vishnu appears throughout the panels, all decorated with sinuous figures of nymphs, gods and goddesses, some in amorous embrace. Some consider the image in the temple sanctum to be a standing Parvati, others argue that it is the black goddess Kali, known here as Jagadambi.

Between Kandariya Mahadeva and Jagadambi, the remains of **Mahadeva** temple shelter a 1m-high lion accompanied by a figure of indeterminate sex. Recurring throughout Khajuraho, the highly stylized lion motif, seen here rearing itself over a kneeling warrior with drawn sword, may have been an emblem of the Chandellas.

5

Chitragupta

Beyond the platform, and similar to its southern neighbour, Jagadambi, the heavily (and in places clumsily) restored **Chitragupta** temple is unusual in being dedicated to **Surya**, the sun god. Ornate depictions of hunting scenes, nymphs and dancing girls accompany processional friezes, while on the southern aspect a particularly vigorous ten-headed Vishnu embodies all his ten incarnations. Within the inner chamber, the fiery Surya rides a chariot driven by seven horses. The small and relatively insignificant temple in front of Chitragupta, also heavily restored and now known as **Parvati**, may originally have been a Vishnu temple, but holds an interesting image of the goddess Ganga riding on a crocodile.

Vishvanatha

Laid out along the same lines as Lakshmana, **Vishvanatha**, in the northeast corner of the enclosure – the third of the three main western-group shrines – can be precisely dated to 1002 AD as the work of the ruler Dhangadeva. Unlike some other temples at Khajuraho, which may have changed their presiding deities, Vishvanatha is most definitely a Shiva temple, as confirmed by the open *mandapa* pavilion in front of the main temple, where a monolithic seated **Nandi** waits obediently. Large panels between the balconies once more show *mithuna*, with amorous couples embracing among the sensuous nymphs. Idealized representations of the female form include women in such poses as writing letters, playing music and cuddling babies. Decorative elephant motifs appear to the south of Vishvanatha, and lions guard its northern aspect.

Matangesvara

The simplicity of the **Matangesvara** temple, outside the complex gates, shows it to be one of Khajuraho's oldest structures, but although built early in the tenth century it remains in everyday use. Deep balconies project from the walls of its circular sanctuary, inside which a pillar-like *shivalingam* emerges from the pedestal yoni, the vulva – the recurring symbol of the union of Shiva. During the annual festival of Shivratri, the great wedding of Shiva and Parvati, the shrine becomes a hive of activity, drawing pilgrims for ceremonies that hark back to Khajuraho's distant past.

Chausath Yogini and around

Southwest of Shiv Sagar are the remains of the curious temple of **Chausath Yogini** – the "Sixty-Four Yoginis". Dating from the ninth century, it consists of 35 small granite shrines clustered around a quadrangle; there were originally 64 shrines, with the presiding goddess's temple at the centre. Only fourteen other temples, all in northern India, are known to have been dedicated to these wrathful and bloodthirsty female attendants of the goddess Kali. Around 1km further west lie the ruins of **Lalguan Mahadev**, a small temple dedicated to Shiva.

Temples: the eastern group

East of the town • Daily sunrise–sunset • Free

The two separate networks of temples that make up Cunningham's **eastern group** are reached via the two forks of the road east of the town. Although smaller than the western group temples, they feature workmanship that is equal or better, and are considerably less crowded. One is the tightly clustered **Jain group**, while slightly north are a number of shrines and two larger temples, **Vamana** and **Javari**, both dating from the late eleventh century.

The temples to the north

On the north side of Jain Temples Road a more modern temple is home to a 2m-high image of monkey god **Hanuman** that may predate all of Khajuraho's temples and shrines. As the road forks left along the eastern shore of the murky Khajur Sagar lake, at the edge

5

of Khajuraho village, it passes the remains of a single-room temple erroneously referred to as the **Brahma** temple. It is in fact a shrine to Shiva, as demonstrated by its *chaturmukha* – "four-faced" – lingam. While the eastern and western faces carry benign expressions, and the north face bears the gentler aspect of Uma, the female manifestation of Shiva, the ferocious southern face is surrounded by images of death and destruction. Crowning the lingam is the rounded form of **Sadashiva**, Shiva the Infinite at the centre of the cosmos.

Vamana temple

The largest of the Khajuraho village temples, **Vamana**, stands alone in a field. Erected slightly earlier than the nearby Javari, in a fully evolved Chandella style, Vamana has a simple uncluttered *shikhara* that rises in bands covered with arch-like motifs. Figures including seductive celestial nymphs form two bands around the *jangha*, the body of the temple, while a superb doorway leads to the inner sanctum, which is dedicated to Vamana, an incarnation of Vishnu.

On the way to the Jain group, the road runs near what survives of a late tenth-century temple, known as **Ghantai** for its fine columns sporting bells (*ghantai*), garlands and other motifs.

The Jain group temples
1.5km southeast of Jain Temples Rd

The temple of **Parsvanath**, dominating the walled enclosure of the **Jain group**, is probably older than the main temples of Khajuraho, judging by its relatively simple ground plan. Its origins are a mystery; although officially classified as a Jain monument, it may have been a Hindu temple that was donated to the Jains who settled here at a later date. Certainly, the animated sculpture of Khajuraho's other Hindu temples is well represented on the two horizontal bands around the walls, and the upper one is crowded with Hindu gods in intimate entanglements. Among Khajuraho's finest work, they include Brahma and his consort; a beautiful Vishnu; a rare image of the god of love, **Kama**, shown with his quiver of flower arrows embracing his consort **Rati**; and two graceful female figures. A narrow strip above the two main bands depicts celestial musicians playing cymbals, drums, stringed instruments and flutes. Inside, beyond an ornate hall, a black monolithic stone is dedicated to the Jain lord Parsvanath, inaugurated as recently as 1860 to replace an image of another *tirthankara*, Adinath.

Immediately north of Parsvanath, **Adinath**'s own temple, similar but smaller, has undergone drastic renovation. Three tiers of sculpture surround its original structure, of which only the sanctum, *shikhara* and vestibule survive; the incongruous *mandapa* is a much later addition. Inside the *garbha griha* stands the black image of the *tirthankara* Adinath himself. The huge 4.5m-high statue of the sixteenth *tirthankara*, **Shantinath**, in his newer temple, is the most important image in this working Jain complex. With its slender beehive *shikharas*, the temple attracts pilgrims from all over India, including naked sadhus.

Sculpture in the small circular **Jain Museum** (Mon–Sat dawn–6pm; ₹10), at the entrance to the Jain temples, includes stone carvings of all 24 *tirthankaras*.

Temples: the southern group
South of Khajuraho village • No fixed opening times • Free

Khajuraho's **southern group** consists of three widely separated temples. The nearest to town, **Duladeo**, is down the road south of the Jain group, 1.5km from the main town square. Built early in the twelfth century, Duladeo bears witness to the decline of temple architecture in the late Chandellan period, noticeable particularly in its sculpture. Nonetheless, its main hall contains some exquisite carving, and the angular rippled exterior of the main temple is unique to Khajuraho.

Across the Khodar stream and south along a small road leads through the small village of Jatkra from where a path leads west to the temple of **Bija Math**. The structure lay

5

below a suspiciously large mound of mud until 1998, when an excavation discovered the delicately carved platform. Unfortunately, the temple itself has disintegrated into the debris of ornate sculpture lying strewn around the site.

To get to the third, go back to Jatkra village and head south, past the Ram Spiritual Chai Shop until you get to the main road where you'll see the tapering temple of **Chaturbhuj**. A forerunner to Duladeo, built around 1100 AD and bearing some resemblance to the Javari temple of the eastern group, Chaturbhuj is plainer than Duladeo and devoid of erotica. A remarkable image of Vishnu, however, graces its inner sanctum. Either head back through Jatkra, or follow the main road west to where it meets Airport Road.

Raneh Falls

Around 22km northwest of Khajuraho • Daily dawn–dusk • ₹50 (there are additional charges if you want to bring an auto-rickshaw, car motorbike in with you) • An auto-rickshaw from Khajuraho costs around ₹450, including waiting time; a taxi costs around ₹1000

The **Raneh Falls** crash through a valley of black and pink basalt. Despite what you might be told, gharials (reptiles similar to crocodiles) are rarely seen here outside of the monsoon months, which is also when the falls are at their most spectacular (at other times they can be little more than a trickle). You can avoid the additional entry fees for auto-rickshaws and taxis by walking the 3.5km from the ticket office (around 45min).

ARRIVAL AND DEPARTURE

KHAJURAHO

By plane The airport is 5km south of the main square of Khajuraho town and served by Air India; taxis into town are pricey at around ₹400 though you can flag an auto-rickshaw from the main road for ₹100 or so.
Destinations Delhi (1–2 daily via Varanasi; 2hr 35min–2hr 50min); Varanasi (2 daily; 55min).
By train The railway station is 9km south of the town; a taxi into the centre costs around ₹500–600, an auto-rickshaw about ₹150. Tickets get booked up quickly, so plan well in advance. The only exception is the slow train to/from Orchha; tickets aren't available beforehand, but you can usually find a seat (note that you can also travel between Khajuraho and Orchha via Jhansi). For trains to a wider range of destinations, head to Satna, 125km east.
Destinations Agra (1 daily; 8hr 30min); Delhi (1 daily;

11hr 5min); Gwalior (1 daily; 6hr 15min); Jaipur (1 daily; 13hr 40min); Jaipur (1 daily; 13hr 25min); Jhansi (2 daily; 4hr 5min–8hr 20min); Orchha (3 daily; 4hr 20min–6hr); Udaipur (1 daily; 21hr 10min).
By bus The bus stand, less than 1km southeast of the main square, is within walking distance of most of the hotels but only has services to Bamitha (every 30min; 30min), 11km away on the main Indore highway, where you can find regular (usually full) services to Satna, Indore and even Jhansi. From Bamitha, (very) shared *tempos* and jeeps make the run up to Khajuraho or an auto-rickshaw costs around ₹100.
By taxi A taxi to Orchha costs around ₹3000 and to Satna ₹2000 or so. Ignore requests from drivers for extortionate "road tolls" and firmly agree a price first.

GETTING AROUND

By taxi Taxis and rental cars are available through most hotels and the *Raja Café* (see page 380). A day's sightseeing around Khajuraho costs about ₹1000–1500.
By auto-rickshaw Auto-rickshaws charge around ₹600 for a

full day of temple-spotting; cycle rickshaws cost about half this.
By bike Many places rent out bikes (around ₹100–200/ day), including Mohammad Bilal (☎98932 40074) on Jain Temples Rd, who will deliver a bike to your hotel.

INFORMATION AND TOURS

Tourist information The MP Tourism office, in the Tourist Facilitation Centre (daily except Sun and 2nd and 3rd Sat of the month 10am–5pm; ☎07686 274051), provides local information and can book accommodation (including homestays) and car rental.
Guides Guides certified by MP Tourism and/or India Tourism cost ₹750–1375 per half day tour of the Western

Group; there's a surcharge for tours in languages other than Hindi or English. Several recommended, highly experienced guides include Tantra expert Ganga, owner of the *Harmony* hotel (see below); Mr D.S. Rajput, Mr Mama and Mr Chandel, all three of whom can be contacted through the *Raja Café* (see page 380); and Anurag Shukla (☎94251 43963, ✉ mptskhajuraho@gmail.com).

ACCOMMODATION

For travellers coming from elsewhere in Madhya Pradesh,   Khajuraho's **touts** and commission system can be a shock.

5

FESTIVALS AND DANCE IN KHAJURAHO

Khajuraho is a bustling epicentre during **Phalguna** (Feb/March), when the festival of **Maha Shivratri** draws pilgrims from all over the region to commemorate the marriage of Shiva and Parvati. It also hosts one of India's premier dance events, the free **Khajuraho Festival of Dance** (Feb; ⓦkhajurahodancefestival.com). There are shows of traditional dances with live music from the local area at the Tourist Facilitation Centre (see page 378) nightly at 6.30pm (₹400), while the more commercial Khandariya Art and Cultural Centre (ⓣ07686 274031), 1km south of the town centre, hosts performances of dances (₹550) from across India most evenings; although the dancing is interesting, the music isn't live and they seem more interested in luring you into their overpriced shop.

Avoid going into **hotels** with taxi- or auto-rickshaw drivers and be firm about where you want to stay. The sheer number of hotels means competition is fierce, so standards are high across the board and substantial **discounts** can be negotiated. The MP Tourism office (see above) can organize **homestays** in nearby villages such as *Ram's* in Jatkra village (ⓣ098937 25885, ⓔram_jirai@yahoo.com; ₹600) or the slightly more comfortable *Bablu's Homestay* (ⓣ98930 18518, ⓦ khajuraho-homestay.jimdo.com; ₹700) just north of Jatkra in Nouri Purwa village.

Harmony Jain Temples Rd ⓣ07686 274135, ⓦhotel harmonyonline.com; map p.372. The Mediterranean influence in the design lends an air of spaciousness to this long-established hotel, which has a range of budget and mid-range attached rooms – each airy and clean – and a bird-filled courtyard. A/c rooms cost around ₹300 extra. **₹1310**

Jhankar By-Pass Rd ⓣ07686 274063, ⓦmptourism. com; map p.372. Away from the tourist and tout scrum near the western group, this well-kept, though dated, MP Tourism hotel is a big hit with Indian tourists. Clean a/c doubles are brightened up with paintings of the temples. **₹2705**

★**Lalit Temple View** Main Rd ⓣ07686 272111, ⓦthelalit.com; map p.372. If money is no object, this is the place to stay. Sumptuous rooms look out either towards the temples or the enticing pool and shaded groves of *mahua* trees. The spa treatments are a real selling point and include Ayurvedic and Thai massage and reflexology. **₹11,800**

Osaka Off Jain Temples Rd ⓣ07686 272839, ⓔosaka4 guest@ymail.com; map p.372. A decent budget choice, *Osaka* has a handful of large, faded, attached rooms with tiled floors. Rooms vary, so look at a few; some come with ancient a/c units for ₹200 extra. Mosquitoes can be a problem. **₹650**

Payal 1km across the fields northeast of the centre ⓣ07686 274064, ⓦmptourism.com; map p.372. Run

by MP Tourism, this sleepy hotel has pleasant gardens and an inviting pool. While the rooms, all with mini-verandas and either fans or a/c, could do with a spruce-up, they're comfortable and include breakfast. **₹2950**

Siddharth Opposite the western group ⓣ07686 274627, ⓔhotelsiddharth@rediffmail.com; map p.372. The staff at this mid-range hotel are amiable, but the attached rooms are a bit tired and frayed around the edges. Still, the a/c deluxe double (₹2700) at the front has wonderful temple views and the rooftop restaurant produces some of the town's best Indian food. **₹1200**

Surya Jain Temples Rd ⓣ07686 274145, ⓦhotelsurya khajuraho.com; map p.372. This popular and efficiently run hotel has clean and comfortable rooms (though hot water isn't available all day), a lush garden round which are more plush a/c rooms (₹1500), a book exchange, yoga and massage sessions, and an outdoor veg restaurant. **₹800**

★**Yogi Lodge** On a cul-de-sac between the row of shops behind Raja Café ⓣ07686 274158, ⓦyogilodge khajuraho.com; map p.372. The shoestring rooms here are attached and clean, though somewhat austere; the a/c rooms are better (₹900). But you can't argue with the price, nor the laidback hippy vibe with free yoga and meditation sessions, nor the well-priced rooftop restaurant. **₹500**

Zen Jain Temples Rd ⓣ07686 274228, ⓦhotelzen khajuraho.co.in; map p.372. The Zen-influenced garden complete with lotus ponds and pet rabbit is the focal point of this place, which has ageing but reasonable attached rooms with TVs and hot water. The on-site Italian restaurant serves great chocolate cake, and yoga and meditation classes (the latter free) are on offer. **₹1300**

Zostel Main Rd ⓣ92296 12255, ⓦzostel.com; map p.372. This India-wide hostel chain has arrived in Khajuraho, offering clean, brightly-coloured dorms and private rooms (the latter have attached bathrooms), plus a terrace to lounge around in, economical café, and communal kitchen. Dorms **₹500**, doubles **₹1600**

EATING

Many rooftop restaurants erroneously claim to have views of the evening sound-and-light shows (see page 373) – what you actually get are occasional flashes of light and a

muffled soundtrack.

Agrasen Jain Temples Rd; map p.372. The pot plant-filled, lantern-lit restaurant produces the typical traveller-

5

oriented menu with a little more flair than the norm; there's a lot of choice for breakfast, plus veg and non-veg thalis (₹200–400) and tasty lassis – try the coconut flavour. The Indian food is cooked to Western rather than local tastes, so ask if you want a bit more spice. Daily 6.30am–10.30pm.

Bella Italia Jain Temples Rd ☎98934 54795; ⓦfacebook.com/laBellaItaliaRestaurent; map p.372. The rooftop *Bella Italia* is a more economical alternative to *Mediterraneo* for thin-crust pizzas (₹240–370), home-made pastas (₹190–320) and crêpes (₹90–120). In the early evening, hundreds of parrots congregate in the neighbouring trees to make an almighty racket, before settling down for the night around 8pm. Daily 7.30am–10.30pm.

Blue Sky Main Rd ☎ 98188 00521; map p.372. While it's a bit of a tourist trap, this rooftop restaurant offers a unique experience: a table in a (slightly precarious) treehouse – just pay ₹50 extra and ring the bell for service. Even if you don't have a head for heights, the thalis and Indian and Chinese dishes aren't bad (₹50–250). The refreshing *jeevan rakshak ghol* (mineral water, lime juice, sugar and salt) is hard to beat on a hot day. Daily 7am–10pm.

Gagan Airport Rd ☎ 98933 45114; map p.372. This rooftop terrace and restaurant overlooking Shiv Sagar

Lake is ideal for a sundowner with cocktails or a Kingfisher. There's also a menu of traveller classics such as banana pancakes and other Indian and Chinese favourites (mains ₹60–290). Daily 9am–11pm.

Madras Coffee House Jain Temples Rd ☎94253 42194; map p.372. This modest, rather scruffy canteen is popular with locals and more recently foreign travellers (whose presence has pushed up the prices) for an authentic south Indian breakfast of dosas, *vadas* or *uttapams* (all ₹50–200) as well as thalis (from ₹200). Daily 8.30am–8.30pm.

★ **Mediterraneo** Jain Temples Rd ☎07686 272246; map p.372. Fairly authentic wood-fired, thin-crust pizzas (₹380–540), handmade pasta, home-baked bread, sweet and savoury crêpes , a superb Dutch-style apple pie and unparalleled espressos and cappuccinos make this the top joint in town. The specials on the board are often better than the pizza/pasta. Daily 7.30am–10pm.

★ **Raja Café** Main square ☎07686 272307; map p.372. A buzzing one-stop shop: as well as offering official guides, tours, a bookstore and the cleanest toilets in town, *Raja* also does a good line in Continental dishes (mains ₹150–450) such as *rösti*, mutton goulash and pizza as well as excellent, slightly cheaper Indian and Chinese options, Lavazza coffee and cold beer. Daily 8am–10pm.

DIRECTORY

Banks and exchange Foreign currency can be changed at the State Bank of India on the main square (Mon–Fri 10.30am–2.30pm & 3–4.30pm, Sat 10.30am–1.30pm); it

has an ATM opposite Shiv Sagar lake.

Post office The post office is in the Tourist Facilitation Centre (see page 378).

Panna National Park

37km south of Khajuraho • Mid-Oct to June daily except Wed 6.30–10am & 2.30–5pm • ₹2850 (₹1000) for a gypsy (open jeep) seating up to six tourists, plus ₹360/safari for a compulsory guide • All buses running along the busy Indore–Satna highway pass the park, though it's much easier and cheaper to go on a tour from Khajuraho; several hotels and travel agencies, including *Raja Café* (see above), offer safaris (around ₹2200–2500/gypsy, excluding entry and guide fees) • ⓦ pannatigerreserve.in

The chance of spotting **tigers** at the **Panna National Park** has greatly increased since the cats were relocated here from other parks after poachers killed off the entire population in 2006. There are currently around 35 tigers, though you'll still need a dose of luck to see one. Panna also boasts two hundred species of bird (it's a wonderful place for birders), as well as sloth bears, wolves and pythons and a waterfall. There are many tours available from Khajuraho, but for wildlife-spotting it's far better to stay a night at one of the lodges close to the park.

ACCOMMODATION   PANNA NATIONAL PARK

Madla Jungle Camp Next to the park's Madla gate ☎ 07732 275275, ⓦmptourism.com. Run by MP Tourism, this lodge offers accommodation in comfortable (though not particularly attractive) "Swiss" tents with a/c and attached bathrooms, as well as reliable, if unexciting meals. Staff can help arrange safaris. **₹3600**

Sarai at Toria Near Toria village, 700m north of the

road bridge, that leads across the river to the park gates ☎ 98917 96671, ⓦsaraiattoria.com. Run by a wildlife expert and photographer and a renowned conservation biologist, this ecofriendly lodge on the west bank of the River Ken is the best place to stay in the area, with a collection of delightful cottages. Rates include full board and activities, but not safaris. **₹24,960**

Jabalpur and around

After running in tandem across an endless expanse of wheatfields and tribal villages, the main Kolkata-to-Mumbai road and train lines converge on eastern Madhya Pradesh's largest city. However, **JABALPUR**, 330km east of Bhopal, is only really worth visiting en route to the **Marble Rocks**, gouged by the Narmada River nearby, or to the national parks and tiger reserves, **Kanha**, **Bandhavgarh** and **Pench**, all half a day's journey away.

Rani Durgawati Museum

2km west of the railway station, near Russel Chowk • Tues–Sun 10am–5pm • ₹100 (₹10), camera ₹50, video camera ₹200

If you have some time to kill in Jabalpur, visit the **Rani Durgawati Museum**, which houses a predictable assortment of ancient temple sculpture, bronze plates and seals recording regional dynastic histories, plus a better than you might expect display on the state's *adivasi* minorities.

Madan Mahal and Tilwara Ghat

Five kilometres west of the railway station in the direction of the Marble Rocks, the main highway skirts a large moraine of enormous granite boulders on the top of which stand the ruins of the **Madan Mahal** – a fortress-cum-pleasure-palace built by the Gond ruler Madan Shah in 1116. A short excursion 7km south on the Nagpur road takes you to an impressive bridge spanning the Narmada River. Known locally as **Tilwara Ghat**, the handful of shrines near the water's edge below marks one of the sacred places where Mahatma Gandhi's ashes were scattered.

Marble Rocks

Metrobus runs from Jabalpur to Marble Rocks (daily every 30min 6am–6pm; 30–40min) from the bus stand outside the platform 6 exit at the railway station (more packed local buses leave, on a similar schedule, from outside the main Jabalpur Medical College bus station); all arrive at the stand near the Dhuandhar Waterfall, a 10min walk (around ₹50 by auto-rickshaw) from accommodations – you can also get from Jabalpur to Bheraghat on excruciatingly slow and packed *tempos* (around 45min), on faster auto-rickshaws (around ₹300) or, if you can find one, by taxi (around ₹800)

Around 20km west of Jabalpur, the Narmada River suddenly narrows, plunges over a series of dramatic waterfalls, then squeezes through a seam of milky white marble before continuing on its westward course across the Deccan. The 30m cliffs and globulous shapes worn by the water out of the rock may not be so spectacular, but the **Marble Rocks**, known locally as **Bheraghat (or Bhedaghat)**, are a good place to while away an idle afternoon.

Bheraghat village

Bheraghat village itself, overlooking the gorge, is a sleepy little place, with few signs of activity beyond the ringing of chisels in the workshops of its many **marble-carvers**. Most pieces on display in the shopfronts are heavy-duty Hanumans, *shivalingams* and various deities, destined for sites around India. Bheraghat is also something of a **religious site**. At the southern end of town, from the fork in the river, 107 stone steps lead up to the tenth-century **Mandapur temple**, a circular building known for the 64 beautifully carved Tantric goddesses, or Chausath Yogini, which stand in its enclosure.

Dhuandhar Waterfall

No opening hours • Free • Cable car Daily 10.30am–6pm • ₹85 return trip • Buses from Jabalpur arrive here (see below)

Beyond the Mandapur temple, at the far end of the gorge, the **Dhuandhar Waterfall**, or "Smoke Cascade", is particularly dramatic after the monsoons. For the best views, unobstructed by the many day-trippers who crowd the viewing platform, there's a short cable car that runs over the falls (entrance on the path down).

5

BOAT TRIPS FROM BHERAGHAT

From Bheraghat's main street, a flight of steps leads down to the river and the **ghats**, from where **rowing boats** (₹25–50/head on a shared basis; ₹300–600 for the whole boat) ferry visitors up the gorge, although these don't run during the monsoon (July to mid-Oct). Avoid the boatmen who try and squeeze in 25 passengers. Once underway, the boatman begins his spiel, in Hindi, pointing out the more interesting **rock formations**. The most appreciative noises from the other passengers are not reserved for the "monkey's leap" (jumped over by Hanuman on his way to Lanka), but for the places used as Bollywood film locations. Look out for the enormous **bees' nests** dangling from the crevices in the rock. The formations are floodlit after dark.

ARRIVAL AND INFORMATION

By plane The airport is 21km northwest of the city centre; taxis to Jabalpur cost around ₹800–900, an auto-rickshaw around half that. Flights are run by Air India and SpiceJet.
Destinations Delhi (2 daily; 1hr 55min); Mumbai (1 daily; 2hr 5min).

By bus The busy Interstate Bus Terminus (better known simply as the ISBT) is around 6km northwest of the railway station (an autorickshaw into the city centre costs approximately ₹100).
Destinations Kisli/Khatia (for Kanha National Park; 3 daily; around 6hr); Mandla (every 30min–1hr; 3hr).

By train The railway station is 2km east of the centre; an auto-rickshaw costs around ₹40–60. For Khajuraho, you need to catch one of the early trains to Satna, from where you can take an onward bus. To reach Bandhavgarh National Park, take a train to Umaria, from where regular shared jeeps and taxis head to the park gate.
Destinations Bhopal (8–10 daily; 5hr 30min–11hr 15min); Delhi (3–5 daily; 13hr 55min–18hr 5min); Indore (2 daily; 10hr–13hr 47min); Mumbai (every 1–2hr; 14hr–21hr

39min); Nagpur (4–5 daily; 8hr 35min–9hr 50min); Patna (9-10 daily; 11hr 31min–17hr 50min); Satna (every 30min–1hr; 2hr 30min–4hr); Umaria (3 daily; 2hr 45min–3hr 50min); Varanasi (every 1–2hr; 9hr 30min–12hr 20min).

Car rental A car for a one-way trip to Kanha National Park costs around ₹3500. Most hotels can organize one, or try MP Tourism (see below). Note that taxis are not common in Jabalpur and so are often more expensive than usual.

Tourist information The MP Tourism office is inside the main arrivals hall at the railway station (Mon–Sat 11am–5pm; ☎07612 677290, ⓦmptourism.com); there's also a counter at the airport (☎ 07686 274648; opens to meet incoming flights). It runs boat cruises (daily 8am–7pm; 2–3hr; ₹120–150) on the Narmada River up to the Vergi Dam, 35km away.

Banks and exchange Change cash at the State Bank of India, around 1km west of the railway station, or at the *Rishi Regency* hotel opposite, which has a 24hr exchange counter. Note that there are a few ATMs but no exchange facilities at the tiger reserves.

ACCOMMODATION AND EATING

JABALPUR
India Near Karamchand Chowk ☎0761 248 0093, ✉icwcsltdjbp@rediffmail.com. Owned by the cooperative behind the *Indian Coffee House* chain – and run with the same quiet professionalism – this hotel has well-appointed, very clean attached rooms with TVs and phones. 24hr checkout. **₹1800**

Indian Coffee House India hotel, near Karamchand Chowk ☎0761 248 0093. This branch offers top Chinese, south and north Indian meals and snacks (veg ₹40-120, non-veg ₹80–320), and filter coffee (₹18). There are four other branches around town, including one just south of the railway station on Sadar Rd, all with the same menu. Daily 8am–10.30pm.

Kalchuri Residency Residency Rd ☎0761 267 8491, ⓦmptourism.com. MP Tourism's welcoming hotel, just south of the railway station in the Civil Lines area of town, has careworn but ample a/c rooms, plus a pool, a decent restaurant and a bar. **₹4700**

Narmada Jacksons Civil Lines ☎0761 402 5800, ⓦnarmadajacksons.com. The smartest place to stay in

Jabalpur has a stately entrance and lobby, and bland business-traveller-orientated attached rooms (the bathrooms could do with some modernization). There's also a pool, Ayurvedic spa, sauna, steam room and restaurant. **₹8350**

Utsav Russel Chowk ☎0761 401 7269, ⓦhotelutsav.com. While *Utsav*'s keenly priced rooms are pretty grungy, their attached bathrooms, TVs and phones help to make them acceptable for a night, and a step up from the fleapits round the station. It's on the corner of a busy junction, so bring earplugs. 24hr checkout; no wi-fi. **₹900**

MARBLE ROCKS
Motel Marble Rocks Just off the road out to the falls ☎0761 283 0424, ⓦmptourism.com. MP Tourism's pleasant motel occupies a converted colonial bungalow, complete with veranda, garden and easy chairs around a small pool from which to enjoy the vistas. The slightly more expensive tent rooms (₹4236) also have great views down the gorge, as does the restaurant. **₹3882**

Kanha National Park

5

Widely considered the greatest of India's wildlife reserves, **Kanha National Park** encompasses some 940 square kilometres of deciduous forest, savanna grassland, hills and gently meandering rivers – home to hundreds of species of birds and animals, including **tigers**. Despite the arduous overland haul to the park, few travellers are disappointed by its beauty, which is particularly striking at dawn. Tiger sightings are not guaranteed, but even a fleeting glimpse of one should be considered a great privilege. Moreover, the wealth of other creatures and some of central India's most quintessentially Kiplingesque countryside make it a wonderful place to spend a few days.

From the main gates, at **Kisli** in the west, and **Mukki**, 35km away in the south, a complex network of driveable dirt tracks fans out across the park, taking in a good cross section of its diverse terrain. Which animals you see from your open-top jeep largely depends on where your guide decides to take you. Kanha is perhaps best known for the broad sweeps of grassy rolling meadows, or **maidans**, along its river valleys, which support large concentrations of deer. The park has several different species, including the endangered "twelve-horned" **barasingha** (swamp deer), plucked from the verge of extinction in the 1960s. The ubiquitous **chital** (spotted deer – the staple diet of Kanha's tigers) congregates in especially large numbers during the rutting season in early July, when it's not uncommon to see several thousand at one time.

The **woodlands** carpeting the spurs of the Maikal Ridge that taper into the core zone from the south consist of *sal*, teak and moist deciduous forest oddly reminiscent of northern Europe. Troupes of langur monkeys crash through the canopy, while **gaur**, the world's largest wild cattle, forage through the fallen leaves; years of exposure to snap-happy humans seem to have left the awesome, hump-backed bulls impervious to camera flashes, but it's still wise to keep a safe distance. Higher up, you may catch sight of a **dhole** (wild dog) as well as porcupines, pythons, sloth bears, wild boar, mouse deer or the magnificent **sambar**. You might even spot a **leopard**, although these shy animals tend to steer well clear of vehicles. Kanha also supports an exotic and colourful array of **birds**, including Indian rollers, bee-eaters, golden orioles, paradise flycatchers, egrets, some outlandish **hornbills** and numerous kingfishers and birds of prey.

FROM HUNTERS TO POACHERS

Central portions of the Kanha Valley were designated a wildlife sanctuary in 1933. Previously, the whole area was one enormous viceregal hunting ground, its game the exclusive preserve of high-ranking British army officers and civil servants seeking trophies for their colonial bungalows. Not until the 1950s though, after a particularly voracious hunter bagged thirty tigers in a single shoot, did the government declare Kanha a bona fide national park. Kanha was one of the original participants in Indira Gandhi's **Project Tiger** (see page 1215), which helped numbers recover. The forest department claims there are around 78 tigers, but guides and naturalists say 40 to 45 is a more accurate estimate (for most of India's tiger reserves, halving the official figures will generally give you a more realistic idea). As part of a long-term project, the park has expanded to encompass a large protective buffer zone – a move not without its opponents among the local tribal community, who depend on the forest for food and firewood. Over the years, the authorities have had a hard time reconciling the needs of the villagers with the demands of conservation and tourism; but for the time being at least, an equitable balance seems to have been struck.

Yet serious **challenges** remain: although poaching is now largely under control here, it still remains a threat; illegal timber-felling continues; the buffer zone is increasingly being encroached upon; and there is little effort to check the growth of new hotels. There have also been problems when the big cats have strayed outside the park's boundaries and killed cattle and some local villagers have responded by leaving out poison. Visit the website of campaign organization Travel Operators for Tigers (⑩ toftigers.org) to find out what role travellers can play in protecting India's tigers.

5

ONLINE BOOKING FOR THE TIGER RESERVES

Top-end, mid-range and even some budget lodges at Kanha, Bandhavgarh (see page 385), Pench (see page 387), Satpura (see page 358) and Panna (see page 380) will take care of your **park entry ticket** if you have booked with them in advance – this is by far the easiest option and is strongly recommended. However, if you're planning to look for a place to stay on arrival (or are staying at a budget lodge that can't or won't book a ticket for you), you'll need to book an entry ticket yourself via the **MP Online website** (Ⓦforest.mponline.gov.in). Tickets are limited, so do this as far **in advance** as possible, especially during the high season (Nov–Feb).

After selecting the relevant park, you can choose which area of that park you want to book a safari slot for and whether you want a morning or afternoon safari. On the form itself, in the "Vehicle" category, select "light motorised vehicle (LMV)", though note that this doesn't mean that your vehicle is booked; you will still need to organize one via your lodge (something, again, that is worth doing in advance).

Kanha's tigers

Kanha's **tigers** are its biggest draw, and the jeep drivers and guides, who are well aware of this, scan the sandy tracks for pug marks and respond to the agitated alarm calls of nearby animals. Although the Kanha zone has been a prime site for spotting tigers in the past, at the time of research sightings here were less common here than in Kisli, Sarhi and Mukki. If you're intent on **seeing a tiger**, plan on spending three nights at the park and taking around five excursions; the cats are most often spotted lounging among camouflaging brakes of bamboo or in the tall elephant grass lining streams and waterholes.

ARRIVAL AND DEPARTURE   KANHA NATIONAL PARK

The easiest way to get to Kanha is via Jabalpur (see page 381), which is well connected by air and rail to most other parts of the country. It is also possible to travel via Nagpur, 226km away, which has a busy railway station and airport.

By bus Daily buses leave Jabalpur for Kisli (via Mandla) at 6.30–17am, 10.30–11am and noon–112.30pm (around 6hr). All stop briefly at the barrier in Khatia, 4km down the road from Kisli. Buses back to Jabalpur leave Khatia at 6am, 8am and 1.30pm. There are more frequent departures in both directions from Mandla (2hr from Kanha, 3hr from Jabalpur). There are also daily buses to/from Nagpur (6hr 30min) from nearby Balaghat. To get from the Khatia gate to the Mukki gate, you'll have to take the single daily noon bus to Bahihar (3hr), from where it's 15km to Mukki.

By taxi A taxi to/from Jabalpur costs around ₹3500 one way, or ₹1500 to/from Khatia gate to the Mukki gate. Locally, Javid (Ⓣ94254 17249) is a reliable driver.

INFORMATION

Opening hours Kanha is open daily except Wed afternoon from Oct until the monsoon arrives at the end of June (daily sunrise–11am & 3/4pm–sunset; the park is also open for night-time safaris at certain times of the year).

Entry fees ₹1500/safari for the Kanha, Kisli, Sarhi and Mukki zones of the park, ₹100 for the Khatia, Khapa or Sijhora zones or ₹1750 for a night-time patrol for a jeep seating up to six tourists, plus ₹360/safari for a compulsory guide. Note that prices are scheduled to rise 10 percent every year. Entry tickets should be booked as far in advance as possible (see page 384). For the shorter afternoon safaris, it is best to book a ticket for a zone that is close to your hotel – the Kisli, Sari and Kahna zones are close to the Khatia gate, while the Mukki zone, predictably enough, is close to the Mukki gate.

Jeep rental If you're not staying on a "Jungle Plan" package (see below) you will have to hire an open-top jeep – or "gypsy" (around ₹2000 for an afternoon safari) to get around the park. These are available through most hotels, private operators in Khatia or at the main gates: try and get a group together and book at least a day in advance. Jeeps can comfortably seat four people (excluding the guide and driver), although you can squeeze in six at a push. At the time of research, a maximum of 140 vehicles were allowed into the park/day; this number is likely to be reduced in the future. Note that walking inside the park is strictly forbidden.

Money There is an ATM close to the Khatia gate, and another in Bahihar, 15km from the Mukki gate, but it is still worth bringing some money with you.

When to visit During peak season (Nov–Feb), the nights and early mornings can get very cold, and there are frequent frosts, so bring warm clothing. The heat between March and June keeps visitor numbers down, but tiger sightings are more common then, when the cats are forced to come out to the waterholes and streams.

ACCOMMODATION

MP Tourism has two lodges in **Kisli**, atmospherically situated inside the park proper, and one close to the **Mukki** gate. Private hotels outside the west gate, in and around the village of **Khatia**, range from walk-in budget lodges to five-star resorts, while those close to Mukki are generally high-end places; all should be booked several days in advance (and at least four months in the high season). However, at any hotel it's worth asking about discounts. The Khatia hotels are scattered along a 6km stretch of road that sees very little traffic during the day, so make sure you are dropped off at the right place. Avoid visiting during **Indian holidays** such as Diwali and Holi, when hotels are packed. A few hotels offer **"Jungle Plan"** packages; these include accommodation, food and safaris and are only slightly more expensive for two people than for one. Assume all the resorts have restaurants, libraries, provide free bicycles, have in-house naturalists/guides (who can take you on cultural/nature tours outside the park), and all prices include full board for two people unless stated.

AROUND KISLI GATE

Baghira Log Huts/Tourist Hotel Kisli ☎07649 277227 or ☎07649 277310, ⓦmptourism.com. MP Tourism's *Baghira Log Huts*, in the core zone, has spacious a/c chalets with private bath; nos. 1–8 overlook a meadow where animals come to graze. The *Tourist Hotel* next door has a 24-bed dorm. Dorm ₹1500, doubles ₹6800

Kipling Camp 4km south of Khatia ☎07649 277218, reservations ☎011 6519 6377, ⓦkiplingcamp.com. A British-run camp in a secluded forest location offering five-star comfort, plus the company of Tara, the elephant made famous by Mark Shand's book (see page 1221). Beautiful cottages have exposed wooden beams, cane chairs and private verandas, some of which overlook a small watering hole where animals often visit. There's also a great photo-lined bar with a well-stocked library. ₹26,000

Pugmark Resort Khatia ☎07649 277291, ⓦpugmark-resort.com. This family-run resort, set in overgrown gardens with a campfire at the centre, and a birdwatching tower, has cheerful and comfortable rooms, with fans or a/c (₹500 extra). There's also an attractive restaurant, open to non-guests. It's a winding 10min walk from the main gate from where you can follow the signs. "Jungle Plan" for two ₹4130

Van Vihar Khatia, signposted 300m east from Khatia Gate ☎0940 781 0850,ⓦvanvihar.com. Stalwart budget choice with variable rooms that could be cleaner: the cheapest are pretty shabby, but the more expensive a/c ones (₹2600) are acceptable for the price. Meals and trips not included, but staff can help organize park entry tickets and jeep rental. ₹1900

AROUND MUKKI GATE

Chitvan 2km from Mukki gate ☎08860 518887, ⓦchitvan.com. In a peaceful (and a little hard-to-find) location surrounded by fields, the attractive *Chitvan* is accessed via a small bridge over a lily pond. As well as spacious, tasteful rooms, it has a lovely swimming pool, a mini-spa with Ayurvedic massage, vegetable and herb gardens, and 14 acres of grounds ideal for an idle wander or a birdwatching session. ₹14,800

Kanha Safari Lodge Mukki ☎07636 290715, ⓦmptourism.com. MP Tourism's tree-filled lodge on the quieter side of the park overlooks the river and has pristine a/c rooms with blue-tiled bathrooms, kettles and (rather redundant) TVs in villa-style buildings, plus a park information centre. ₹4710

★ **Shergarh** 4km from Mukki gate ☎90981 87346, ⓦshergarh.com. Katie and Jehan Bhujwala run an intimate, environmentally friendly and socially responsible camp of luxury tents, each with a smart attached bathroom and private veranda. Outstanding service and thoughtful touches (such as personal hot water bottles for chilly early morning safaris) create a wonderfully serene environment. The excellent chef makes use of organic produce from the camp's butterfly-filled gardens, while the small lake in the centre is home to kingfishers and cormorants. Quite simply, it's one of the finest places to stay in India. "Jungle Plan" for two ₹21,000

Singinawa 15km from Mukki gate ☎07636 200031, bookings ☎012 4490 8610, ⓦsinginawajunglelodge.com. Top-end lodge that combines an eco-friendly "plastic-free" ethos with luxury: accommodation is in tasteful isolated cottages (some with wheelchair access) in 100 acres of wildlife-filled grounds. There's also a lovely pool and organic food, and a small museum about the local tribes. It's decorated throughout with fantastic tribal art (the owner has a gallery in Delhi). "Jungle Plan" for two ₹20,000

Bandhavgarh National Park

Madhya Pradesh's second national park, **Bandhavgarh**, tucked away in the hilly northeast of the state, has one of the highest relative densities of **tigers** of any of India's reserves and shelters some fascinating ruins. Although it's a long haul to Bandhavgarh from either Jabalpur (195km) or Khajuraho (237km), it's worth it – not only to track tigers but also, as all the accommodation is close to the park gates, to watch the array of birdlife from the comfort of your lodge.

5

CALL OF THE WILD

For serious wildlife enthusiasts, there are a few very experienced naturalists in Tala, who can be contacted through your hotel. S.K. Tiwari of **Skay's Camp** (☎94253 31209, ⊛skayscamp.in) specializes in nature photography, and has an impressive knowledge of Indian flora and fauna.

Though there are flat grassy maidans in the south of the park, Bandhavgarh is predominantly rugged and hilly, with *sal* trees in the valleys, and mixed forest in the upper reaches, which shelter a diverse avian population. Bandhavgarh's headquarters and main gate are in the village of **Tala**, connected to Umaria, 32km southwest, by a road slicing through the park's narrow midriff.

On the whole, jeep safaris tend to stick to the core area where the chances of spotting a **tiger** (there are estimated to be more than 70) are high. Deer species include gazelle, barking deer, nilgai (blueball) and *chital* (spotted deer). Sloth bears, porcupines, sambar and muntjac also hide away in the forest, while hyenas, foxes and jackals appear occasionally in the open country. If you're very fortunate, you may catch sight of an elusive leopard. Look out too for some very **exotic birds**, including red jungle fowl, white-naped woodpecker, painted spurfowl and long-billed vultures.

The crumbling ramparts of the **fort** crown a hill in the centre of the park, 300m above the surrounding terrain. Its ramparts offer spectacular views and the best birdwatching in the park. Beneath the fort are a few modest temples, the rock-cut cells of monks and soldiers, and a massive stone Vishnu reclining on his cobra near a pool that dates from the tenth century. Tigers may be found in the area; they're more likely to stick to the lower levels, and there are no instances of people actually being harmed by tigers here or even suddenly coming across them – but the risks are real nonetheless.

Brief history

Legend dates the construction of Bandhavgarh's hilltop **fort** to the time of the epic Ramayana (around 800 BC). Excavations of caves tunnelled into the rock below the fort have revealed inscriptions scratched into the sandstone in the first century BC, from which time Bandhavgarh served as a base for a string of dynasties, including the **Chandellas**, responsible for the Khajuraho temples. They ruled here until the **Bhagels** took over in the twelfth century, staking a claim to the region that is still held by their direct descendant, the maharaja of Rewa. The dynasty shifted to Rewa in 1617, allowing Bandhavgarh to be slowly consumed by forest, bamboo and grasslands that provided prime hunting ground for the Rewa kings. The present maharaja ended his hunting days in 1968 when he donated the area to the state as parkland. In 1986, two more chunks of forest were added to the original core zone, giving the park a total area of 448 square kilometres.

ARRIVAL AND DEPARTURE

BANDHAVGARH NATIONAL PARK

By train The closest station to Bandhavgarh is Umaria, which is linked to the park by shared jeeps and taxis (around ₹1000), as well as a couple of morning buses (1hr). For trains going west to Mumbai and east to Kolkata or Chennai you'll need to head another 64km west to Katni, where there are more frequent trains going north too.

Destinations Agra (1–4 daily; 10hr 28min–13hr 49min); Bhopal (3 daily; 8hr 48min–14hr 20min); Delhi (2–4 daily; 13hr 43min–17hr 44min); Gwalior (1–3 daily; 9hr 2min–11hr 4min); Indore (1 daily; 17hr 59min); Jabalpur (3 daily; 2hr 38min–4hr 4min); Jhansi (2–4 daily; 6hr 56min–9hr 34min); Satna (for connections to Khajuraho; 4–5 daily; 2hr 59min–4hr 43min); Varanasi (2–3 daily; 11–12hr).

By taxi Travelling by taxi to and from Khajuraho or Jabalpur takes roughly 5hr and costs around ₹3600–4000.

INFORMATION

Opening times Bandhavgarh is open daily except Wed afternoon from mid-Oct until the end of June. You are most likely to see wildlife in the hotter months between March and June, when thirsty tigers and their prey are forced out to the waterholes and the park's three perennial streams; the heat can be trying at this time, however. Visiting in the cooler months, when wildlife viewing is still good, is more comfortable.

Entry fees The park headquarters is a few kilometres south of the village (daily except Wed; ☎07653 222214). Admission is ₹1500/safari for a jeep seating up to six tourists (in the core Tala zone where sightings are more common),

plus ₹360/safari for a compulsory guide. Note that prices are scheduled to rise 10 percent every year. It's possible to book online (see page 384).

Jeeps Jeeps (gypsies) seating up to six people (₹2200–2500/safari) can be booked at the park headquarters or more easily through your hotel.

ACCOMMODATION AND EATING

Most of Bandhavgarh's hotels, all of which are in and around **Tala**, cater for travellers on a higher budget, and some offer **"Jungle Plan"** packages (see page 385). The only places to eat outside the hotels are the basic and inexpensive *dhabas* on Tala's main road.

Bandhavgarh Jungle Lodge Close to the river ☎07627 265317, ⓦbandhavgarhjunglelodge.com. The rustic (but eminently comfortable) mud-walled huts with thatched roofs and brown and beige interiors, lush gardens and enthusiastic staff give this lodge plenty of character. Deer can often be seen at the nearby meadow. "Jungle Plan" for two ₹US$530

Tiger's Den Resort Opposite the petrol station on Umaria Rd ☎07838 966645, ⓦtigerdenbandhavgarh.com. This efficient and friendly lodge has a cluster of large cottages with soothing decor (some with bathtubs) in flower-filled gardens, plus an atmospheric wooden dining room, spa and pool. ₹9350

Tiger Trails 2.5km beyond Tala; book through Indian Adventures ☎022 2640 6339, ⓦindianadventures.com.

One of the better-value deals in Tala: cosy cottages have tiled roofs and exposed brickwork, while the alfresco dining room overlooks a little lake, which is great for birdwatching. Full-board ₹10,000

★ **Treehouse Hideaway** Ketkiya Village ☎0124 297 0497, ⓦtreehousehideaway.com. Blending seamlessly into the surrounding jungle, these stunning treehouses, made from local materials, are far removed from anything you may have played in as a child, combining top-end comforts with a sense of adventure. The camp has 21 acres of forest and even its own watering hole, which is sometimes visited by tigers. "Jungle Plan" for two ₹35,000

White Tiger Forest Lodge Umaria Rd, next to the barrier over the main road ☎07627 265366, ⓦmptourism.com. MP Tourism's large complex has snug a/c and air-cooled attached rooms, linked by raised walkways, plus a restaurant and bar. Rooms 17–21 are in cottages with verandas overlooking the river, which attracts myriad birds and – very occasionally – tigers. Full board ₹5300

Pench Tiger Reserve

Straddling both MP and Maharashtra (and far quieter than its more famous counterparts), **Pench Tiger Reserve** has an estimated fourteen to sixteen **tigers** and sightings are relatively common. The 758-square-kilometre park, made up largely of tropical deciduous forest, is also home to leopards, jackals, deer and 285 species of bird.

ARRIVAL AND DEPARTURE · PENCH TIGER RESERVE

By bus or shared jeep Daily buses link Jabalpur (192km; every 2–3hr; 5hr) and Nagpur (92km; every 2–3hr; 2hr 30min) with Khawasa, from where you can catch a shared jeep the 12km to Turia, which is 2km away from the main

gates and most of the hotels.

By taxi A taxi from Jabalpur will cost around ₹4000. From Nagpur it will cost in the region of ₹3000.

INFORMATION

Opening times The park is open daily except Wed, dawn to dusk, from Oct to end of June.

Entry fees The park headquarters is near Turia (daily except Wed; ☎09212 777223, ⓦpenchtiger.co.in). Admission costs ₹2640 (₹1320) for a jeep seating up to six tourists, plus

₹360/safari for a compulsory guide. It is possible to book in advance online (see page 384).

Jeeps Jeeps (₹2000–2200/safari) can be booked at the park headquarters or through your hotel; it's worth doing this in advance.

ACCOMMODATION

Kipling's Court Turia ☎07695 232830, ⓦmptourism.com. This MP Tourism-run lodge offers no-nonsense lodgings in fan-cooled and a/c rooms (₹5888), as well as twelve great-value dorm beds, plus pleasant grounds, a bar

and a small pool. Full board; dorm ₹1780, doubles ₹5416

Pench Jungle Camp Avarghani village, 2km west of Turia ☎07695 232817, ⓦpenchjunglecamp.com. Luxury tents with wicker furniture and attached bath-

5

rooms, a handful of appealing cottages, some more traditional hotel rooms, plus a pool and spa offering massages and reflexology. Price includes full board and nature walks; safaris are extra. **₹12,800**

Indore

The state's economic powerhouse and the biggest city in western Madhya Pradesh, **INDORE** is huge, modern and pretty dull. If you find yourself with time to kill en route to or from **Mandu**, 98km southwest, however, you could stop and check out a couple of worthwhile sights.

Indore's sights lie west of the railway line, in and around the **bazaar**. Two broad thoroughfares, MG Road and Jawahar Marg, form the north and south boundaries of this cluttered and chaotic district, which is interrupted in the east by the confluence of the Saraswati and Khan rivers. The city's principal landmark is the eighteenth-century former Holkar palace of **Raj Wada**, which presides over a palm-fringed square in the heart of the city and boasts a seven-storey gateway. Most of the palace collapsed after a fire in 1984, and only the facade and a temple survive.

Kanch Mandir

Off Jawahar Marg, in the clothes bazaar • Daily 6am–sunset • Free, no photography

The Jain **Kanch Mandir** or "Mirror Temple", deep in the bazaar district, is one of the city's more eccentric religious monuments; surprisingly, for a faith renowned for its austerity, the interior is decked with multicoloured glass **mosaics**.

Central Museum Indore

Near the GPO on AB Rd • Tues–Sun 10am–5pm • ₹100 (₹10)

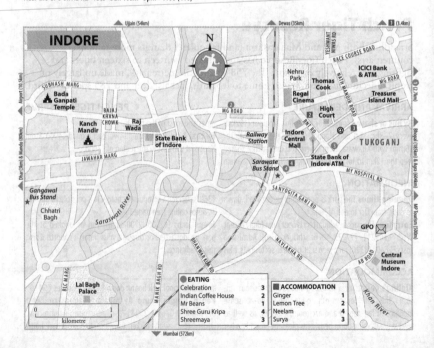

The **Central Museum Indore** houses Holkar-era swords, shields and armour, as well as terracotta, coins, paintings and fossils from throughout Madhya Pradesh. There is also a smaller selection of modern art and religious sculptures.

Lal Bagh Palace

Just off BLC Marg • Tues–Sun 10am–5pm • ₹250 (₹10)

The **Lal Bagh Palace** is an extravagant Neoclassical creation. Given a limitless budget, its British designers produced a vast stately home dripping with Doric columns, gilt stucco, crystal chandeliers and replica Rococo furniture. The Lal Bagh's main entrance is via a pair of grandiose wrought-iron gates, modelled on those at Buckingham Palace. Inside, a vast array of family heirlooms is housed in the former durbar hall, banquet rooms and the ballroom. Check out the jewel-encrusted portrait of Tukoji Rao (1902–25) – the ruler responsible for completing the palace – in the billiards room.

ARRIVAL AND INFORMATION INDORE

By plane Devi Ahilyabai Holkar Airport is 11.5km west of the city centre; a prepaid taxi from the booth in the arrivals hall into town costs around ₹400–500.

Destinations Ahmedabad (1 daily; 1hr 15min); Delhi (7–8 daily; 1hr 25min); Mumbai (4–5 daily; 1hr 15min); Nagpur (1 daily; 1hr); Raipur (2 daily; 1hr 10min).

By train The railway station is right in the city centre; two branches of the Western Railway connect Indore to cities in northern India.

Destinations Agra (2–4 daily; 12hr 55min–16hr); Ahmedabad (1–2 daily; 10hr); Bhopal (7–9 daily; 3hr 50min–6hr 5min); Delhi (2–3 daily; 13hr 6min–20hr 10min); Gwalior (2–4 daily; 11hr–12hr 10min); Jabalpur (2 daily; 10hr–13hr 10min); Jaipur (2 daily; 9hr 55min–10hr 45min); Jhansi (1–3 daily; 9hr 17min–10hr 30min); Mumbai (2–3 daily; 12hr 49min–14hr 20min); Ujjain (roughly hourly; 1hr 20min–2hr 30min).

By bus The main bus stand, Sarawate, is a short walk south from platform 1 of the railway station beyond the overpass; regular buses to Bhopal and Omkareshwar depart from here. Other buses – including those to Ujjain, Dhamnod (for connections to Maheshwar), Mandu and Dhar (connected to Mandu by buses every 30min) – depart from the Gangawal bus stand, 3km west.

Destinations Bhopal (every 30min; 4–5hr); Dhamnod (every 30min–1hr; 2–3hr); Dhar (every 30min–1hr; 2hr); Mandu (2 daily; 3hr 30min–4hr); Omkareshwar (every 30min–1hr; 3–4hr); Ujjain (every 30min–1hr; 1hr 30min–2hr).

By taxi Taking a taxi is much easier than struggling on the local buses and cost around ₹1700 to Ujjain or ₹2300 for one to Mandu, Maheshwar or Omkareshwar.

Tourist information The MP Tourism office (Mon–Sat 10am–6pm; ☏0731 2499566), close to St Paul's High School on Agricultural College Rd, provides the usual services, and is where the MP Tourism a/c coach departs for Indore (7 daily; 4hr).

ACCOMMODATION

Most of Indore's **hotels** cater for business visitors and are scattered around the prosperous suburb of **Tukoganj**. Budget travellers should ignore the dire lodges opposite the bus stand, and head for the better-value hotels along **Chhoti Gwaltoli**, just east of the railway station beneath the big Patel flyover (though note that not all are willing to accept foreign travellers).

Ginger AB Rd, near Shanivar Darpan ☏1860 266 3333, ⓦgingerhotels.com; map p.388. The Indore outpost of this chain ofmid-range hotels is a reliable choice: service is efficient, the attached rooms have flatscreen TVs, and there is a *Café Coffee Day* on site. The only downside is the location, a 10–15min (6km) auto-rickshaw ride north of the railway station. ₹3700

★ **Lemon Tree** RNT Rd ☏0731 442 3232, ⓦlemon treehotels.com; map p.388. With a bright yellow exterior, smart service and sleek attached rooms set around a vast atrium decorated with modern art, this is the pick of Indore's top-end hotels. There's a restaurant, café, sports bar and fitness centre, and the rooms have nice touches like ergonomic chairs and orthopedic mattresses. Discounts of 30–50 percent online. ₹5400

Neelam 33/2 Patel Bridge Corner ☏0731 246 6001, ☏251 8774; map p.388. Despite its location on a dingy alley, this is the best of the budget options. Lining a central courtyard, the compact rooms with tiny attached bathrooms (some have squat toilets) are pretty clean and have TVs and phones. 24hr checkout. ₹850

Surya 5/5 Nath Mandir Rd ☏0731 251 7701, ⓦsurya indore.com; map p.388. While the rooms at this established mid-range hotel are showing their age, they're still comfortable, particularly those in the "executive" class (well worth the extra ₹400 or so). Service is good, and there's an excellent multi-cuisine restaurant and bar. ₹3900

5

EATING

Celebration RNT Rd, in the annexe to the right of the Shreemaya hotel ☏0731 252 6666; map p.388. A hygienic bakery and café renowned for its sweet goodies, including cavity-inducing Black Forest , pineapple and chocolate truffle cakes (from ₹50 a slice), as well as south Indian snacks such as *katchoris*. Daily 7.30am–10.15pm.

Indian Coffee House Next to Rampura Building, off MG Rd ☏0731 243 2226; map p.388. Waiters in turbans and cummerbunds serve quality south Indian veg breakfasts, north Indian meals) and filter coffee (from ₹18). Other branches on BJ Nagar and the DAVV College campus. Mains ₹70–280. Daily 7.30am–10pm.

Mr Beans 100 Saket Nagar ☏0731 428 5050, ⓦmrbeans.in; map p.388. A gorgeous, stylish café-restaurant ideal for wiling away an afternoon or evening, Mr Beans has top notch coffee (from ₹55), as well as a globetrotting menu that features everything from baked brie to chicken schnitzel, pizzas to shepherd's pie (mains ₹200–555). Daily 10am–11pm.

Shree Guru Kripa 54 Vijay Nagar, opposite Bombay Hospital; map p.388. Popular veg joint serving up value-for-money dishes in a smart, clean and spacious dining hall: try one of the tasty paneer dishes (mains ₹155–185). There's another branch near the bus station. Daily 11am–11pm.

★ **Shreemaya** Shreemaya hotel, 12 RNT Rd ☏0731 423 4888; map p.388. Adjoining veg and non-veg restaurants with curvy Art Deco-style ceilings, frosted glasswork and mouthwatering north and south Indian food: the vast chicken biryani (₹400), *missi roti* and – if you have any space left – chocolate brownie and ice cream (₹165) are not to be missed. Daily 7am–11pm.

DIRECTORY

Banks and exchange The State Bank of Indore has a foreign exchange office opposite their main branch on Raj Wada, and has an ATM on RNT Rd. ICICI Bank, 576 MG Rd, and Thomas Cook (☏07316 454533, ⓦthomascook.in), Yeshwant Niwas Rd, are efficient alternatives. There are countless other ATMs throughout the city.

Travel agents President Travels at *President* hotel, 163 RNT Rd (☏0731 253 3472) is a reliable operator.

Mandu

Set against the rugged Vindhya hills, the medieval ghost town of **MANDU**, 98km southwest of Indore, is one of central India's most atmospheric monuments. This tranquil backwater sees far fewer visitors than it deserves, save for the busloads of exuberant Indian day-trippers on weekends. Visit at the height of the monsoons, when the rocky plateau and its steeply shelving sides are carpeted with green vegetation, and you'll understand why the Malwa sultans christened their capital **Shadiabad** – "City of Joy".

Even during the relentless heat of the dry season, the **ruins** are an exotic spectacle. Elegant Islamic palaces, mosques and mausoleums crumble beside large medieval reservoirs and precipitous ravines, while below, an endless vista of scorched plains and tiny villages stretches off to the horizon. Mandu can be visited as a day-trip from Indore, but you'll enjoy it more if you spend a night or two, giving you time not only to explore the ruins, but also to witness the memorable sunsets over the Narmada Valley.

Mandu's monuments derive from a unique school of **Islamic architecture** that flourished here, and at Dhar, between 1400 and 1516. The elegantly simple buildings are believed to have exerted a considerable influence on the Mughal architects responsible for the Taj Mahal. Mandu's platform, a 23-square-kilometre plateau, is separated from the body of hills to the north by the **Kakra Khoh** ("deep ravine"). A narrow causeway forms a natural bridge across the gorge, carrying the present road across and up via a series of subsidiary gates to the fort's modern entrance, beside the original, Delhi Gate.

Brief history

Archeological evidence suggests the remote hilltop was fortified around the sixth century AD, when it was known as Mandapa-Durga, or "Durga's hall of worship" – later corrupted to "Mandu". Four hundred years later, the site gained in strategic importance when the powerful **Paramaras** moved their capital from Ujjain to Dhar, 35km north. Yet the plateau's natural defences proved unable to withstand persistent attacks by the Muslim invaders and the fort eventually fell to the sultans of Delhi in 1305.

While the Sultanate was busy fending off the Mongols on their northern borders a century or so later, Malwa's Afghan governor, Dilawar Khan Ghuri, seized the chance to establish his own independent kingdom. He died after just four years on the throne, however, leaving his ambitious young son at the helm. During **Hoshang Shah**'s illustrious 27-year reign, Mandu was promoted from pleasure resort to royal capital, and acquired some of the finest Islamic monuments in Asia.

Mandu's golden age continued under the **Khaljis**, who took over from the Ghuri dynasty in 1436. Another building boom and several protracted wars later, Mandu settled down to a lengthy period of peace and prosperity under **Ghiyath Shah** (1469–1500). He amassed a harem of fifteen thousand courtesans, and a bodyguard of one thousand women, whom he accommodated in the appropriately lavish Jahaz Mahal. The sybaritic sultan was poisoned by his son shortly after his 80th birthday. His successor, Nasir Shah, died ten years later, and Mandu, dogged by feuds and the threat of rebellion, became an easy target for the militaristic sultan of Gujarat, who invaded in 1526. In the centuries that followed, control over the fort and its rapidly decaying monuments passed between a succession of independent rulers and the Mughals. By the time King James I's ambassador, **Sir Thomas Roe**, followed the mobile court of Emperor Jahangir here in 1617, most of the city lay in ruins, its mansions and tombs occupied by Bhil villagers whose descendants continue to scratch a living from the surrounding fields.

Royal Enclave

Daily except Fri sunrise–sunset • ₹200 (₹15), video camera ₹25

Reached via the lane that leads west off the village square is the **Royal Enclave**. Just inside the entrance is a bookshop and a small **museum** (free) with a modest collection

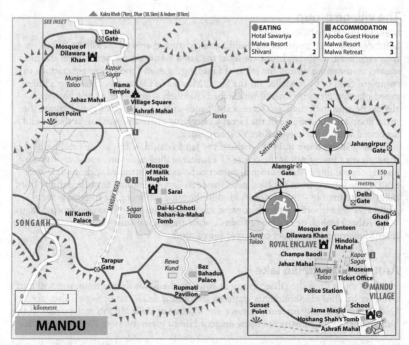

5

of stone carvings and pottery fragments. The Royal Enclave is dominated by Ghiyath Shah's majestic **Jahaz Mahal**, or "Ship Palace". The name derives from its unusual shape and elevated situation on a narrow strip of land between two large water tanks. A rooftop terrace, crowned with four domed pavilions, overlooks **Munja Talao** lake to the west, and the square, stone-lined **Kapur Sagar** to the east. From the northern balcony, you also get a good view of the geometric sandstone bathing pools.

The next building along the lane is the **Hindola Mahal**, or "Swing Palace" – so-called because its distinctive sloping walls supposedly look as though they are swaying from side to side. The design was, in fact, purely functional, intended to buttress the graceful but heavy stone arches that support the ceiling inside. At the far end of the T-shaped assembly hall, a long-stepped ramp allowed the sultan to reach the upper storey on elephant-back.

Champa Baodi

Sprawling over the northern shores of Munja Talao are the dilapidated remains of a second royal pleasure palace. The **Champa Baodi** boasts an ingeniously complex ventilation and water-supply system, which kept its dozens of subterranean chambers cool during the long Malwan summers. Immediately to the north stands the venerable **Mosque of Dilawara Khan**, dating from 1405. The chunks of Hindu temple used to build its main doorway and colonnaded hall are still very evident.

The **Hathi Pol**, or "Elephant Gate", with its pair of colossal, half-decapitated elephant guardians, was the main entrance to the Royal Enclave but is now closed. To reach the edge of the plateau and the grand **Delhi Gate** you will have to return to the bazaar and follow the road out of Mandu. Built around the same time as Dilawara Khan's mosque, this great bastion, towering over the cobbled road in five sculpted arches, is the most imposing of the twelve that stud the battlements along the fort's 45km perimeter.

The village group

Daily sunrise–sunset • ₹200 (₹15), video camera ₹25

Some of the fort's best-preserved buildings are clustered **around the village**. Work on the magnificent pink-sandstone mosque, the **Jama Masjid** on the west side of the main square, commenced during the reign of Hoshang Shah and took three generations to complete. Said to be modelled on the Great Mosque in Damascus, it rests on a huge raised plinth pierced by rows of tiny arched chambers – once used as cells for visiting clerics. Beyond the ornate *jali* screens and bands of blue-glazed tiles that decorate the main doorway, you emerge in the Great Courtyard, where a prayer hall at the far end is decorated with finely carved Koranic inscriptions.

Hoshang Shah's tomb (c.1440), behind the Jama Masjid, is this group's real highlight. It stands on a low plinth at the centre of a square-walled enclosure, and is crowned by a squat central dome and four small corner cupolas. Now streaked with mildew and mud washed down from the bats' nests inside its eaves, the tomb is made entirely from milky-white marble – the first of its kind in the Subcontinent. The interior is very plain, save the elaborate pierced-stone windows that illuminate Hoshang's sarcophagus.

The **Ashrafi Mahal**, or "Palace of Coins", was a theological college (madrasa) that the ruler Muhammad Shah later converted into a tomb.

Around Sagar Talao lake

Heading south from the village group en route to the Rewa Kund group, you will find a further handful of monuments scattered around the fields east of Sagar Talao lake. Dating from the early fifteenth century, the **Mosque of Malik Mughis** is the oldest of the bunch, once again constructed using ancient Hindu masonry; note the turquoise tiles

A SANDSTONE CENOTAPH AT ORCHHA

5

and fine Islamic calligraphy over the main doorway. The high-walled building opposite was a *caravanserai*, where merchants and their camel trains would rest during long treks across the Subcontinent. A short way south, the octagonal tomb known as the **Dai-ki-Chhoti Bahan-ka-Mahal** looms above the surrounding fields from a raised plinth, still retaining large strips of the blue ceramic tiles that plastered most of Mandu's beautiful Afghan domes.

The Rewa Kund group

Daily sunrise–sunset • ₹200 (₹15), video camera ₹25

The road to the **Rewa Kund Group** heads past herds of water buffalo grazing on the muddy foreshores of the lake, then winds its way gently through a couple of Bhil villages towards the far southern edge of the plateau; stately old baobabs line the roadside, like giant upturned root vegetables. The **Rewa Kund** itself, an old stone tank noted for its curative waters, lies 6km south of the main village. Water from it used to be pumped into the cistern in the nearby **Baz Bahadur Palace**. Bahadur, the last independent ruler of Malwa, retreated to Mandu to study music after being trounced in battle by Rani Durgavati. Legend has it that he fell in love with a Hindu singer named Rupmati, whom he enticed to his hilltop home with an exquisite palace. The couple eventually married, but did not live happily ever after. When Akbar heard of Rupmati's beauty, he dispatched an army to Mandu to capture her and the long-coveted fort. Bahadur managed to slip away, but his bride, left behind in the palace, poisoned herself rather than fall into the clutches of the attackers.

Rupmati Pavilion

The romantic **Rupmati Pavilion**, built by Bahadur for his bride-to-be, rests on a ridge high above the Rewa Kund; beneath its lofty terrace, the plateau plunges a sheer 300m to the Narmada Valley. The view is breathtaking, especially at sunset or on a clear day.

ARRIVAL AND DEPARTURE
MANDU

By bus Although there are a couple of direct buses to Mandu from Indore (2 daily; 3hr 30min–4hr), it's often quicker to travel to Dhar (every 30min–1hr; 2hr) and pick up one of the local services to Mandu (every 30min; 1hr) from there. For Maheshwar or Omkareshwar, take the 9am or 9.30am bus to Dhamnod (2hr 30min) and change there,

or else you're looking at multiple bus changes
By taxi A taxi to Mandu from Indore should cost around ₹2200, and ₹1000–1200 to Maheshwar. A reliable (and inexpensive) taxi driver in Mandu is Sanu (☎99533 45418), who also runs tours and rents out bicycles.

GETTING AROUND

By bike and taxi If you don't have your own vehicle, the most pleasant way of getting around the fort and its widely dispersed monuments is by bicycle – around ₹100/day from

Malwa Resort (see opposite), or Ritik Bicycle Shop, near *Shivani* restaurant. Alternatively, rent a taxi for a complete tour (around ₹1000).

ACCOMMODATION

Ajooba Guest House Around 1km south of the village ☎99935 35625; map p.391. The quietest of the village's three budget guesthouses, this old-school travellers' haunt has five basic, non-attached blue-painted concrete rooms (the beds are concrete too) with no hot water or wi-fi. Despite being just metres from the road, it's a very peaceful spot, with fields behind, and mellow owners. ₹250
Malwa Resort 2km south of the village ☎07292 263235, ⓦmptourism.com; map p.391. This MP Tourism-run hotel is by some distance the most comfortable

choice in town. It has a collection of a/c cottages, many with lake-facing verandas and separate seating and dressing areas and fridges. There's also a good restaurant and a bar. ₹3900
Malwa Retreat 300m north of the main square ☎07292 263221, ⓦmptourism.com; map p.391. The ageing air-cooled and a/c rooms at this MP Tourism-run hotel are clean and compact, with partial views of the gorge, more comfortable "Swiss" tents and thirty good-value dorm beds. Dorms ₹300, doubles ₹1790, tents ₹3530

EATING

Hotal Sawariya Just south of the Jama Masjid; map p.391. This basic family-run roadside *dhaba* is often called *Karuba's* after the white-*lunghi*ed patriarch who presides over proceedings, perched atop the clay chapatti oven. Always busy with locals and long-term visitors despite a limited menu of veg thali, samosas, pakoras and outstanding curd/lassi. The locals eat it all very spicy, but they will happily tone it down a tad if you struggle with the heat. You can eat well here for less than ₹80. Daily 7am–11pm.

Malwa Resort 2km south of the square ☎07292 263235, ⓦmptourism.com; map p.391. One of the smarter restaurants in town, serving the usual MP Tourism menu: meat and veg Indian and Chinese dishes, with a few Continental options thrown in for good measure (mains ₹90–380). They also serve local specialities such as *dalbafle*, deep-fried balls of yellow dhal, and have a dinner buffet. Daily 8–10am, noon–3pm & 7–10.30pm.

Shivani Halfway between the square and the Nagar Panchayat barrier; map p.391. Not the best, but this modest restaurant has a wider range of food than most of its competitors in Mandu, with dishes from north and south India (mains ₹60–170), as well as tasty Gujarati-style thalis. It's near the bus stop, so is a good place to get your bearings. Daily 9am–9pm.

Ujjain

On the banks of the sacred Shirpa River, **UJJAIN**, 55km north of Indore, is one of India's seven holiest cities. Like Haridwar, Nasik and Prayag, it plays host every twelve years to the country's largest religious gathering, the **Kumbh Mela** (see page 269), which has in the past drawn an estimated thirty million pilgrims here to bathe. Outside festival times, Ujjain is great for people-watching, as pilgrims and locals alike go about their daily business. Around the main temples, you see modern Hinduism at its most kitsch, with all types of devotional paraphernalia, gaudy lighting and plastic flower garlands for sale. At the *ghats*, women flap wet saris dry, children splash in the water, and pujaris ply their trade beneath the rows of riverside shrines. A mini-Varanasi Ujjain is not, but the temples rising behind the *ghats* are majestic at dusk, and with the ringing of bells and incense drifting around, this atmospheric place can feel timeless.

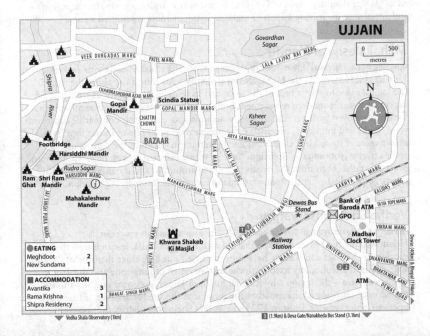

5

The Western Railway cuts straight through the **centre** of Ujjain, forming a neat divide between the spacious and affluent residential suburbs to the south and the more interesting, densely packed streets northwest of the station. Unless you spend all day wandering through the **bazaar**, sightseeing in Ujjain usually means treading the **temple trail**, with a brief foray south of the *ghats* to visit the **Vedha Shala observatory**. Minor temples of note include Harsiddhi Mandir, which Hindu mythology identifies as the spot where Parvati's elbow fell to earth while Shiva was carrying her burning body from the sati pyre, and Gopal Mandir, a blend of late Maratha Mughal domes, Moorish arches and a lofty Hindu sanctuary tower – the sanctum's silver-plated doors were fitted by Mahaji Scindia, who rescued them from Lahore after they were carried off by Muslim looters.

Brief history

Excavations north of Ujjain have yielded traces of settlement as far back as the eighth century BC. The ancient city was a major regional capital under the Mauryans (Ashok was once governor here), when it was known as **Avantika** and lay on the main trade route linking northern India with Mesopotamia and Egypt. According to Hindu mythology, Shiva later changed its name to **Ujjaiyini**, "He Who Conquers With Pride", to mark his victory over the demon king of Tripuri. Chandra Gupta II, renowned for his patronage of the arts, also ruled from here in the fourth and fifth centuries AD. Among the Nava Ratna, or "Nine Gems", of his court was the illustrious Sanskrit poet **Kalidasa**, whose much-loved narrative poem *Meghduta* ("Cloud Messenger") includes a lyrical evocation of the city. (**E.M. Forster** visited Ujjain in 1914, determined to get an idea of what it looked like in Kalidasa's day. He soon admitted defeat, declaring: "Old buildings are buildings, ruins are ruins.")

Most of Ujjain's temples were razed in 1234 by Iltutmish, of the Delhi Slave Dynasty. Thereafter, the Malwan capital was governed by the sultans of Mandu, the Mughals, and **Raja Jai Singh** from Jaipur, who designed the Vedha Shala observatory (Ujjain straddles the Hindu first meridian of longitude). Ujjain's fortunes have declined since the early eighteenth century, except for a sixty-year renaissance between the arrival of the Scindias in 1750 and their departure to Gwalior. Today, nearby Indore dominates the region's industrial activity, leaving Ujjain to make its living by more traditional means.

Mahakaleshwar Mandir

Overlooking the river • Daily 6am–11.30pm • Free, though you can pay ₹250 for a ticket that allows you to jump the lengthy queues

Ujjain's chief landmark, the **Mahakaleshwar Mandir**, crowning a rise above the river, is the logical place to start a tour of the town and its temples. Its gigantic saffron-painted sanctuary tower, a modern replacement built by the Scindias in the nineteenth century for one destroyed by Iltutmish in 1234, soars high above a complex of marble courtyards, water tanks and fountains, advertising the presence below of one of India's most powerful *shivalingams*. Housed in a claustrophobic subterranean chamber, the deity is one of India's twelve **jyotirlinga** – "lingam of light" – whose essential energy, or *shakti*, is "born of itself", rather than from the rituals performed around it, and is considered particularly potent, especially by Tantric followers, due to its unusual south-facing position.

Vedha Shala observatory

1km southwest of the railway station • Daily 8am–6pm • ₹100 (₹20); guides are free, though they may expect a tip

Ujjain was the birthplace of mathematical astronomy in India, research into the motion of the stars and planets having been carried out here since the time of Ashoka. Later, Hindu astronomers fixed both the **first meridian** of longitude and the Tropic of Cancer here – the reason why Raja Jai Singh of Jaipur, governor of Malwa under the Mughal emperor Mohammad Shah, chose it as the site for another of his surreal open-air observatories. Built in 1725, the **Vedha Shala observatory** overlooks the Shirpa

River. The complex is smaller than its more famous cousins in Delhi and Jaipur, the Jantar Mantars, but remains in excellent condition with very informative guides and labelling. Local astronomers still use its five instruments to formulate ephemeredes (charts predicting the positions of the planets), which you can buy at the site.

ARRIVAL AND INFORMATION   UJJAIN

By train The station, which sits on both branches of the Western Railway, is in the centre of town.

Destinations Bhopal (every 1–2hr; 2hr 40min–5hr 10min); Gwalior (4–5 daily; 9hr 18min–13hr 25min); Indore (roughly hourly; 1hr 20min–2hr 30min); Jabalpur (2–3 daily; 9hr 5min–13hr 30min); Jaipur (4–7 daily; 8hr 16min–15hr); Mumbai (3–4 daily; 10hr 30min–12hr 45min).

By bus Just northeast of the railway station is the Dewas bus stand, which sees services to and from Bhopal, Dhar (for connections to Mandu and Maheshwar) and Omkareshwar. The inconvenient Deva Gate/Nanakheda bus stand, next to MP Tourism's *Avantika*, 2km south of town, serves Indore.

Destinations Bhopal (every 15–30min; 5–6hr); Dhar (4 daily; 4hr); Indore (every 15–20min; 1hr 30min–2hr); Omkareshwar (5 daily, including a handy service at 9am; 3hr–3hr 30min).

Tourist information The useful MP Tourism office is near the Mahakaleshwar Mandir (daily 9am–6pm; ☎ 0734 255 2263).

GETTING AROUND

By auto-rickshaw or bicycle Ujjain is fairly spread out, so you'll need to get around by auto-rickshaw or by renting a bicycle (around ₹100/day) from the shop opposite the Dewas bus stand.

By taxi Taxis (around ₹2000–2500/day) can be arranged through the MP Tourism office (see above) or at *Avantika* (see below).

ACCOMMODATION

Avantika Off Lal Bahadur Shastri Marg, 2km south of town ☎ 0734 251 1398, ⌨ mptourism.com; map p.395. Also known as *Yatri Niwas*, this MP Tourism-run hotel has an institutional feel. The best bet for shoestring travellers is the partitioned dorm, which has comfortable beds and clean sheets; a/c private rooms are fine but overpriced. There's a decent restaurant, too. Dorm ₹400, doubles ₹1390

Rama Krishna Station Rd (Subhash Marg), opposite the railway station ☎ 0734 255 7012, ⌨ hotelramakrishna.co.in; map p.395. A notch above the other flophouses in the station area, the largish but tired rooms have smallish attached bathrooms with fairly reliable hot water; there are also better a/c options (around ₹350 extra) and dorm beds. The entrance is upstairs from their decent attached restaurant (see below). Dorms ₹200, doubles ₹650

Shipra Residency University Rd ☎ 07342 551495, ⌨ mptourism.com; map p.395. A tranquil, white-tiled courtyard is the centrepiece of this MP Tourism-run hotel (just about the best in town), around which are comfortable a/c rooms with fancy quilts. Good restaurant and bar. ₹4240

EATING

Ujjain suffers from a dearth of decent places to eat. There's a cluster of **food stalls** by the clock tower, but, as with the inexpensive *dhabas* opposite the railway station, you should only frequent the most popular ones.

Meghdoot Shipra Residency, University Rd ☎ 0734 255 1495, ⌨ mptourism.com; map p.395. Typical MP Tourism menu – veg and non-veg Indian, tandoori and Chinese dishes, plus a few Western options – in relaxed surroundings, plus Ujjain's widest choice of alcoholic drinks. From around ₹350/head. Daily 11pm–3pm and 7pm–10.30pm.

New Sundama Rama Krishna hotel, Station Rd (Subhash Marg), opposite the railway station ☎ 0734 255 7012; map p.395. A good option if you've just decamped from the train, this is the cleanest place near the station, serving well-priced veg and vegan Punjabi standards (₹60–130) such as *paneer tikka*, and (not as good) south Indian snacks in its pleasant diner-style interior. Daily 7am–11pm.

Maheshwar

Overlooking the north bank of the mighty Narmada River, 91km southwest of Indore, **MAHESHWAR** was the site of King Kartvirajun's ancient capital, **Mahishmati**, a city mentioned in both the Mahabharata and Ramayana. In the eighteenth century, Maharani **Ahilya Bai** built a palace and several temples here, giving the town a new lease of life. Today, it's a prominent port of call on the Narmada Hindu pilgrimage circuit, but well off the tourist trail.

5

The ghats

The waterfront **ghats** below an old sandstone palace make a quintessentially Indian spectacle. Parties of *yatris* take holy dips, while pujaris and groups of sadhus sit around murmuring prayers under raffia sunshades. For the best view of them, head for the overhanging balcony of the eighteenth-century **Ahilya Bai Mandir**, reached via steps under the facade of the palace behind.

Rehwa Society workshops

Palace and fort complex • Mon–Fri 10am–5pm • Free • ⊛ rehwasociety.org

The palace and fort complex houses the workshops of the **Rehwa Society**, established by the maharani 250 years ago to promote the local handloom industry; Maheshwari **saris** are famous for their distinctive patterns and high quality. Today you can visit the weavers' workshops – though most of the town's four thousand weavers actually work from home. Though descendants of the old ruling family still occupy parts of the building, a couple of rooms around the entrance courtyard have been given over to a small, eminently missable museum.

ARRIVAL AND DEPARTURE
MAHESHWAR

By bus All roads leading to Maheshwar are in a terrible state. If you're travelling from Indore, you'll need to change buses at the market town of Dhamnod.
Destinations Dhamnod (every 30min; 15min); Dhar (every 30min; 1hr 30min); Omkareshwar (every 30min–1hr; 1hr 30min).

By taxi A taxi from Indore costs around ₹2200, from Ujjain ₹3500.

ACCOMMODATION AND EATING

★**Ahilya Fort** On the banks of the river ☎011 4155 1575, ⊛ahilyafort.com. This heritage hotel is run by the son of the last maharaja of Indore. The sixteenth-century fort houses gorgeously ornate rooms with stone walls and colonial-era furnishings. There's a pool and lovely gardens, and exquisite food is served in the restaurant, around the swimming pool or in the courtyard (open to non-guests who reserve in advance). Only luxury Maharajah tents have a/c, though (around ₹1000/night more), and there's a two-night minimum stay. ₹38,000

Akash Deep Rest House Down an alley to the right of the fort car park, at the bottom of the hill ☎07283 273326. In the centre of town, this welcoming place has rather threadbare attached rooms (some with partial views of the fort). It's clean enough, and acceptable for a night if you're on a tight budget. ₹400
Narmada Retreat 1km outside town ☎83499 94784, ⊛mptourism.com. MP Tourism-run hotel with decent a/c rooms, comfortable "Swiss" tents (₹3300) and cosy cottages (₹3260), as well as an appealing restaurant. Bring mosquito repellent and a net. ₹3295

Omkareshwar

East of the main river crossing at Barwaha, the Narmada River dips southwards, sweeps north again to form a wide bend, and then forks around a 2km-long wedge-shaped outcrop of sandstone. Seen from above, the island, cut by several deep ravines, bears an uncanny resemblance to the "Om" symbol. This, coupled with the presence on its sheer south-facing side of a revered *shivalingam*, has made **OMKARESHWAR**, 77km south of Indore, one of central India's most **sacred Hindu sites**.

Since ancient times, pilgrims have flocked here for *darshan* and a holy dip in the river, while the town's remoteness and loaded religious feel also long made it a favourite with hard-core Western and Israeli dope-heads – though the town's modernization has made it less attractive to that crowd in recent years. Despite its changes – and the contentious **Omkareshwar dam** (completed in 2007), which led to the displacement of many thousands of people from nearby villages – the place manages to retain an authentic atmosphere among its temples, wayside shrines, bathing places and caves, which are strung together by an old paved pilgrims' trail.

The prominent white *shikhara* that soars above the **Shri Omkar Mandhata Mandir** is a relatively new addition to the dense cluster of buildings on the south side of the island. Below it, the ornate pillars in the assembly hall, or *mandapa*, are more representative of the shrine's great antiquity. Myths relating to the origins of the deity in the low-ceilinged sanctum date back to the second century BC. One of India's twelve **jyotirlinga** ("lingams of light"), it is said by Hindus to have emerged spontaneously from the earth after a struggle between Brahma, Vishnu and Shiva.

The parikrama

Traditionally, the **parikrama** (circular tour) of Omkareshwar begins at the *ghats* below Shri Mandhata and proceeds clockwise **around the island**. The walk takes at least a couple of hours, so carry plenty of water.

Triveni Sangam and the Gaudi Somnath Temple

The first section of the trail is a leisurely thirty-minute stroll from the footbridge to the pebble-strewn western tip of the island, where you'll find a small chai stall and a couple of insignificant shrines. The **Triveni Sangam**, or "Three-rivers Confluence", is an especially propitious bathing place where the Narmada River forks as it merges with the Kaveri River.

From here, the path climbs above the fringe of fine white sand lining the northern shore until it reaches level ground. The ruins of the **Gaudi Somnath Temple** stand in the middle of the plateau, surrounded by a sizeable collection of sculpture mounted on concrete plinths. The sanctuary houses a colossal *shivalingam*, attended by an equally huge Nandi bull.

At this point, drop down a steep flight of steps to the village, or continue east towards the old fortified town that crowned the top of the island before it was ransacked by Muslims in the medieval era. Numerous chunks of temple sculpture lying discarded among the rubble include a couple of finely carved gods and goddesses, used for shade by families of langur monkeys.

Surajkund Gate and the Siddhesvara Temple

After scaling the sides of a gully, the trail leads under the large ornamental archway of the **Surajkund Gate**, flanked by 3m figures of Arjun and Bheema, two of the illustrious Pandava brothers. The tenth-century **Siddhesvara Temple** stands five minutes' walk away to the south, on a patch of flat ground overlooking the river. Raised on a large plinth decorated with rampaging elephants, it has some fine *apsaras*, or celestial dancers, carved over its southern doorway.

Of the two possible routes back to the village, one takes you along the top of the plateau before dropping sharply down, via another ruined temple and the **maharaja's palace**, to the Shri Mandhata temple. The other follows a flight of steps to the riverbank, and then heads past a group of sadhus' caves to the main *ghats*.

ARRIVAL AND DEPARTURE   **OMKARESHWAR**

From the bus stand at the top of the village on the main road, the road heads east and down the hill (left at the fork), where Omkareshwar's only street runs 400m downhill to a ramshackle **square**, where you'll find most

5

of the *dharamshalas* and chai shops, and a handful of stalls hawking lurid puja paraphernalia (including the excellent stylized maps taken home by pilgrims as souvenirs). To **get to the island** itself, cross the high concrete footbridge or take one of the flat-bottomed ferries that shuttle between the *ghats* crouched at the foot of the river gorge.
By train Omkareshwar Road is the nearest railhead, but

only slow passenger services stop here. Barwaha, on the north bank of the Narmada River, is the closest mainline railway station.
By bus Buses are generally more convenient than trains. Destinations Dhamnod (every 30min; 3hr 30min); Indore (every 30min–1hr; 3hr); Maheshwar (every 30min–1hr; 1hr 30min); Ujjain (1 daily; 3hr–3hr 30min).

ACCOMMODATION AND EATING

Ganesh Guest House Near Tirole Kunbi Patel, from where a dozen signs will eventually lead you there through the backstreets ☎ 07280 271370. This friendly place has a cool traveller vibe, good views and a "foreign tourists only" policy, though the attached rooms are very spartan. Its restaurant, *Third Eye*, has a veg menu featuring so-so pizza and pasta, a sprinkling of much better Israeli and Indian dishes (₹70–160

), tasty pancakes and some great Tibetan *momos* (steamed dumplings) and *thukpas* (hearty soups). **₹400**
Narmada Resort On the hill above Nagar Ghat ☎ 07280 271455, ⏏ mptourism.com. This MP Tourism-run place is the smartest option in town. It has plain, slightly worn, but clean attached rooms with air coolers or a/c (for ₹3530) plus a reliable restaurant (with a great terrace) and bar. **₹1445**

Chhattisgarh

The little-visited state of **Chhattisgarh** has remained off the tourist radar for decades, but as it slowly opens up to tourists it's ripe for exploration. Main sights include **Amarkantak** – just over the border in MP, but better accessed through Chhattisgarh, this is one of the least-visited major Hindu holy sites in India, and offers a pleasant, hassle-free way to experience an important pilgrimage destination – and the nearby **Achanakmar Wildlife Sanctuary**, the only place in the state where tigers can be spotted. Meanwhile, in the south, the tribal heartland of **Bastar** is rich in cultural and natural attractions. The easiest way to travel in and out of the state is by train via **Raipur**, the state's busy and scruffy capital – but there's little to see there otherwise.

In addition to the major sights there are many other places worth a visit – for full details, contact the Chhattisgarh Tourism Board (see below). In the north, for example, 85km east of Raipur, **Sirpur**, the region's former capital and now a village, has a few fine fifth- to eleventh-century Buddhist and Hindu temples. Sirpur borders the hilly **Barnawapara Wildlife Sanctuary**, which offers the chance to see leopards and even elephants. Way up in the north, towards Patna in UP, the state's hill station, **Mainpat** offers relief from the hot season and has a sizeable Tibetan population. Meanwhile, just across the state border from Kanha in MP, exquisite erotic carvings based on the Kama Sutra can be seen on the eleventh-century *nagar*-style temples at **Bhoramdeo**, which make those at Khajuraho seem tame by comparison.

ARRIVAL AND INFORMATION

Arrival and departure The best way in or out of the state is by train via Raipur.
Destinations Delhi (2–4 daily; 19hr–27hr 45min); Gwalior (2–4 daily; 14hr 50min–21hr 35min); Jabalpur (1 daily; 9hr 20min); Kolkata (7–10 daily; 13hr–16hr 50min).
Getting around Chhattisgarh's public transport system and roads are even worse than in MP, so it's best to use a private car (around ₹3500–5000/day including overnight charges for the driver). Private buses are your best bet

between urban centres.
Tourist information Chhattisgarh Tourism Board (Mon–Fri 10am–5pm; ☎ 0771 422 4600, ⏏ chhattisgarhtourism. net) is a good source of information. They can organize private cars and accommodation, and should hold copies of the useful guide *Experience Chhattisgarh on the Road* by Thommen Jose (also available online). Ice Cubes Travel (☎ 09303 048400, ⏏ icecubes.in), also in Raipur, organizes private cars and tours.

Amarkantak

Perched 1048m up on the top of the Maikal Hills between Madhya Pradesh and northeastern Chhattisgarh, the small low-key town of **AMARKANTAK** – also known as Teerthraj or **"King of Pilgrimages"** – is the source of two of India's great rivers, the **Narmada** (one of the seven holy rivers of Hinduism) and the **Sone**. (The town is actually located in Madhya Pradesh, but is commonly accessed via Pendra Road railway station in Chattisgarh.) One legend (among many) has it that the Narmada and the Sone rivers were to be married, but the Sone spurned Narmada and so, distraught, she changed her course westwards and vowed to remain a virgin, while the Sone carried on east and married another – Narmada Devi remains one of the very few bachelorette Hindu goddesses.

In addition to the two major sites are many major Hindu and Jain **temples** – with several new ones being built in an attempt to cash in on the town's increasing attractiveness to religious tourists. In the surrounding area you can visit **Kabir Chabutra**, one of the most sacred sites of the Kabir religion, along with a number of small **waterfalls**.

Narmada Udgam
Daily sunrise–9pm • Free

The **source of the Narmada River** is within the walled **Narmada Udgam** temple complex at the centre of town; this is the main focus for the hundreds of pilgrims who come here daily for their ritual ablutions. Though not especially impressive architecturally, it has retained its spiritual atmosphere, with the devout bathing in large ponds filled with spring waters from the stone Gao Mukh (cow's mouth) spout. Reflected in the waters are 22 whitewashed temples, most of them dedicated to Narmada Devi. Those on the south side are the oldest, built by the eleventh-century Kalachuri king Karnadevi.

Sonmuda
1.5km southeast of the centre • Daily sunrise–9pm • Free

Down a long flight of stairs from the road lies the **source of the Sonmuda River**, a modest, pink-painted temple complex where the River Sone (or Son) also trickles out from a stone Gao Mukh, under the watchful gaze of a particularly sinister black-painted statue of the god Sone Dev, who wears a garland of skulls, and holds a *trishul* and freshly decapitated head in his hands. The complex clings to a hill high on the east-facing escarpment; if you follow the path further down the hill, you'll be rewarded with a magnificent view out over the jungle hills of the Achanakmar Wildlife Sanctuary (see page 402), and see the incipient river cascading down the cliffs.

Ancient Temples of Kalachuri
Next to Narmada Udgam • Daily sunrise–9pm • Free

Next to Narmada Udgam lie the well-preserved **Ancient Temples of Kalachuri**, a small group of sixth-century buildings in the curvilinear *nagara* style. These are perhaps the most photogenic of the town's monuments, surrounded by pretty and well-maintained gardens.

Sarvodaya Jain temple
Daily sunrise–9pm • Free

On the hill to the south of town is the construction site of the **Sarvodaya Jain temple**. This looks set to be pretty impressive, with stone carving equal to the ancients' and a 3m-high, 28-tonne metal statue of Bhagawan Adinatha which is the heaviest such statue in the world. Started in 2003, construction is due to continue for a few more years yet, but you can wander around inside and watch stone-carvers in action. The 20-crore rupee project has, however, been heavily criticized as hypocritical by impoverished local tribals.

Shri Yantra Mandir
Midway between Narmada Udgam and Sonmuda • Daily sunrise–9pm • Free

The Tantric **Shri Yantra Mandir** has been under construction since the late 1980s. Its gate, crowned by the four faces of the Mother Goddess, makes perhaps the most

5

striking image of all the temples here, reminiscent of temples at Angkor Wat in Cambodia. It's estimated that it will take at least another decade to complete, but you can usually have a mooch around inside unless the builders are doing something major.

Kabir Chabutra

5km southwest of Amakantak on the Bilaspur road • Daily dawn–dusk • Donation expected (either money or food)

One of the most significant sites for the Kabir religion, the tiny **Kabir Chabutra** monastery, hidden just off the main road and within the forest, is where fifteenth-century itinerant mystic poet and saint Kabir produced many of his writings. It's an amazingly peaceful spot, with a small pond (Kabir Kund) in which people say mysterious white strands appear daily at around 8.30–9.30am – supposedly the goddess Narmada Devi came here to wash the saint's feet in milk. Otherwise, there's not a lot to do apart from enjoy the tranquillity and talk to the three elderly monks (one speaks some English), who will happily show you≈the saint's stone bucket and explain something about their little-known faith.

ARRIVAL AND DEPARTURE
AMARKANTAK

By train The nearest railway station is Pendra Road, 17km northeast of Amarkantak and connected by buses (every 30min) or auto-rickshaw (around ₹350).

Destinations Bilaspur (every 1–2hr; 1hr 50min–4hr 24min); Delhi (2–4 daily; 16hr 2min–20hr 55min); Jabalpur (2–4 daily; 5hr 23min–7hr 40min); Raipur (6–8 daily; 3hr 45min–5hr 5min).**By bus** To get in and out of Amarkantak by bus, you'll have to head to Jabalpur in MP (see page

381) or Bilaspur to the east in Chhattisgarh. They're slow, arduous (though scenic) journeys and you're far better off travelling by train. The bus to/from Bilaspur, does, however, stop at both gates of the Achanakmar Wildlife Sanctuary (see page 402). The bus station is in the north of town, around 1km from the centre.

Destinations Bilaspur (3 daily; 5–6hr); Jabalpur (6–7 daily; 6–8hr).

GETTING AROUND

By taxi To see the sights outside town, or the Achanakmar Wildlife Sanctuary – though you can get there by bus (see opposite) – a taxi is best. Cars (around ₹2000/day) can be

organized easily through either the *Holiday Homes* resort in Amarkantak or *Sonbadra Tourist Resort* at Amodob, 14km south.

ACCOMMODATION AND EATING

There's not a lot of high-end accommodation or eating in Amarkantak; a few cheaper guesthouses and *dhabas* can be found along the road from the bus station to the centre of town.

Holiday Homes Near the Sarvodaya Jain temple 📞07629 269416, 🌐mptourism.com. MP Tourism

hotel with en-suite rooms and "Swiss cottage" tent accommodation (the latter start from ₹2940) that also boast heaters, which you'll need during the chilly winter nights. The acceptable restaurant provides the standard MP Tourism menu of Indian, Chinese and Continental dishes for around ₹300/head. **₹2700**

Achanakmar Wildlife Sanctuary

Midway between Amarkantak and Bilaspur, **Achanakmar Wildlife Sanctuary** is linked to the Kanha Tiger Reserve by a wildlife corridor, and is the only sanctuary in Chhattisgarh where **tigers** can be seen – around 18 to 24 are believed to have migrated here from Kanha, though sightings are actually rare and you're more likely to spot a **leopard**. The 557-square-kilometre park, made up of moist deciduous forest, largely *sal*, teak and bamboo, is also home to numerous bison, spotted dear, gaur, wild dogs, hyena and more than 150 species of bird.

As this sanctuary has few visitors, it is much wilder than the big-name parks in MP, and being bumped around in the back of a jeep while it hacks through the dense jungle hills is a far more authentic safari experience. The animals, however, are less used to seeing vehicles and far more nervous and prone to running away. Still, even if you don't see any big cats, most safaris end with a visit to one of the five watchtowers dotted around the park, from which the views of the jungle are sublime, especially at sunset.

NAXALITE MILITANTS IN THE BASTAR REGION

The Bastar region is one of the last remaining places where the anti-government Naxalites are found, though only in the deep forest and remote areas. Dantewada district, southwest of Jagdalpur is the main one, but nowhere listed this guide is in that area. Though as a foreign tourist you should have no problems – no foreigner has ever been targeted or harmed by the local Naxalites, who limit their attacks to security forces and police – you should take care to get the latest **information** before visiting and it is strongly advised that you use your own transport and take a **local guide** if travelling outside Jagdalpur or off the main roads.

As well as the wildlife, there are 22 **tribal villages** within the park (Gond and Baiga tribes), from where most of the guides come from – your accommodation can arrange cultural visits to these.

ARRIVAL AND DEPARTURE
ACHANAKMAR WILDLIFE SANCTUARY

By bus The NH-8 passes straight through the park and between Amarkantak and Bilaspur with a single morning and evening bus passing through each way.

By taxi Hiring a taxi from Jabalpur will cost around ₹3800, or about ₹2800 from Nagpur.

INFORMATION

Opening times The park is open daily from Nov to June (safaris 6–9am & 3–6pm). Its headquarters and main gate is at Lamni, around 40km south of Amarkantak and 60km northwest of Bilaspur, though a new gate is slated to open soon at Amodob, just 14km south of the former.

Entry fees ₹2000 (₹600), and vehicle entry fee of ₹2000 (₹500), so a total of ₹4000 (₹1100)/jeep seating up to six

tourists, plus ₹300/safari for a compulsory guide.

Jeeps Jeeps (around ₹2200/safari) can be booked at the park gates or more easily through your accommodation; it's worth doing this in advance as they only have four at each.

Services There are only a very few basic shops within the park, and the nearest ATMs are in Bilaspur or Amarkantak, so bring plenty of snacks and cash.

ACCOMMODATION

Baiga Resort Shivtarai village, a few kilometres south of the Lamni gate ☎ 99076 76753 or ☎ 98933 66225, ⌨ tigersofachanakmar.org. Very good value resort in the middle of the park, with comfortable and well-kept a/c rooms, and an adventure playground – they get lots of youth groups at weekends. **₹900**

Sonbadra Tourist Resort Amodob, 14km from Amarkantak ☎ 0771 422 4600, ⌨ chhattisgarhtourism.net. Near the new Amodob gate, this Chhattisgarh Tourism-run resort is one of the better-priced mid-range options in the park, offering twelve pleasant, comfortable cottages with verandas overlooking a small stream. The restaurant serves decent food. **₹3000**

Jagdalpur and around

Located 285km south of Raipur, the small town of **JAGDALPUR** is the main settlement of the **Bastar region**. This is the heartland of the Chhattisgarh tribals, who make up seventy percent of the population, many still living in the surrounding forests. Though there are few sights in town, you can experience the living **tribal culture** by visiting one of the nearby villages. Here locals produce traditional handicrafts and hold their **haat bazaars** which are quite extraordinary events – the women dress in their most colourful finery to sell even more colourful produce while the men drink *salfi* (the local brew) and occasionally watch cockfighting. Jagdalpur is also close to the **Kangar Valley National Park**, which contains not only wildlife but also the stepped **Tirathgarh Waterfall** and the **Kutsumar Cave**, the longest in India. To the northeast, you'll find the impressive horseshoe **Chitrakote Falls**.

Bastar Palace

Civil Lines, 1km north of the centre • Daily 10am–6pm • Free • ☎ 07782 226222

The main attraction in town is the sprawling 80-year-old **Bastar Palace**, the grandest of the state's Raj-era palaces. Unless you opt to stay in one of their

5

eye-wateringly expensive suites (if you have to ask you can't afford it), you'll only be able to visit the one "museum" room that's open to the public; here you can learn something of the extremely turbulent history of local Kakatiya rulers, the Dev family, whose descendants still occupy some of the palace's hundred rooms today.

Anthropological Museum

1km west of the centre along the Chitrakote road • Mon–Sat 10am–5.30pm • ₹10 • ☎ 07782 229356

The **Anthropological Museum**, within the Archaeological Survey of India compound, contains a colourful ethnographic snapshot of the local tribal cultures, including handicrafts, weapons, musical instruments and ingenious jungle implements, as well as information on local traditions such as the *haat* bazaar and *ghotul* system of courting.

Kangar Valley National Park

Main entrance and ticket office at the Kutumusar Gate, 27km south of Jagdalpur • Nov–June daily 8am–4pm • ₹150 (₹25), vehicle entry ₹50, compulsory guide ₹75, plus lights for the caves (₹25)

The 200-square-kilometre **Kangar Valley National Park**, around 30km southwest of town, is set in a rugged landscape of densely forested hills and limestone karst. Among several local cave systems, the **Kutsumar Cave** is the largest and the only one currently open to visitors. From the main park entrance a 10km rough jungle track winds through the *sal* and teak trees to a small car park where a very narrow entrance leads you 37m down a spiral staircase to the 337m-long cave. Here you can see alien-like formations of stalagmites and stalactites, as well as the pool of icy water where pasty-white blind fish live.

A far better tarmac road leads 4km in the other direction to the much-visited **Tirathgarh Waterfall**, where water cascades serenely down 27m over seven steps in the black rock. If you want to get away from the day-trippers, try climbing up to the small shrines on top of a basalt stack from where you can appreciate the lovely sight in relative peace.

If you have time, ask your guide to take you to one of the tribal settlements in the park, such as **Nagalsar** village where the modern world has had little impact; residents still live in mud huts and, idiosyncratically, the men shave the front of their heads but sport long ponytails. Apart from on the way to and from these sights, there currently isn't any opportunity for real nature trekking or seeing the park's large mammals such as leopard and bison. However, **birders** will have more luck spotting one of the park's 150-odd species; keep an ear open for the human-like wails and whistles of the state bird, the endangered Bastar Hill myna.

If possible, avoid visiting the park at weekends when it's overcrowded with local day-trippers. If you do come at this time, aim to make a side trip to the chaotic Sunday **haat bazaar** near the thirteenth-century Shiva temple at **Chingitarai**, around 10km from Tirathgarh Waterfall.

Chitrakote Falls

43km northeast of Jagdalpur • No opening times • Free; boats around ₹100/hr

Although just 32m high, the horseshoe-shaped **Chitrakote Falls** are one of the most impressive of its kind in India. For most of the year the force of the waters – the 300m-wide Indravati River is funnelled into seven separate flows – creates a peaceful susurration, but during and shortly after the rainy season it is at its thundering full flow, creating vast plumes of mist in which rainbows appear. This is, obviously, a massive draw for local day-trippers; to avoid being overwhelmed by crowds, visit mid-week, early morning or just before sunset. For an adventurous excursion, the local fishermen will take you out in a boat at the top of the falls, often quite close to the precipice.

ARRIVAL AND INFORMATION

The easiest ways in and out of Jagdalpur are via the state capital Raipur (by bus, taxi or train), or by train via Visakhapatnam in Andhra Pradesh, or Kolkata. To get around the local area – apart from to Chitrakote (served by local buses every 30min) – you will need a **car**; buses are poor or nonexistent to most points of interest outside of town and locals cram into any vehicle available.

By train Jagdalpur's railway station is about 1km south of the centre. Facilities are limited.

Destinations Kolkata (1–2 daily; 25hr 18min–26hr); Raipur (3 weekly; 15hr 30min); Visakhapatnam (2 daily; 8hr–10hr 15min).

By bus Slow and uncomfortable state buses to Raipur leave from the main bus stand, 200m east of the railway station

(every 15min; 10–12hr); Mahendra Travels' regular daytime and sleeper buses (7–8hr; ⓦmahendrabus.in) are a better option.

By taxi Hiring a taxi to/from Raipur will cost around ₹4000–6000; to/from Nagpur or Hyderabad it's more like ₹11,000–12,000.

Tourist information Jagdalpur's tourist information centre (Mon–Sat 10am–6pm; ☎09993 854165) is about 2km west of the town on the Chitrakote road, behind Jhanka Talkies. Staff can help organize guides, such as the well-connected Awesh Ali (☎09425 244925; around ₹1500/day) and cars (around ₹1500/8hr).

ACCOMMODATION AND EATING

There are several places to sleep and eat in Jagdalpur, mostly concentrated along the roads from the bus and train stations, with a few better resorts slightly out of town.

Dandami Resort Just down the river from Chitrakote Falls ☎0771 422460, ⓦchhattisgarhtourism.net. The Chhattisgarh Tourism-run resort at the falls is one of the better establishments in the region, with comfortable cottages and tents set among well-kept gardens; both cost

the same but the cottages are better located overlooking the river, and four have views towards the falls. ₹2200

Shradha Suman Civil Lines, just north of the Danteswari Temple ☎07782 231204. Best of the budget choices in town, this clean and simple hotel is well run by friendly staff, and has a veg restaurant. They can also help arrange tours and transport. ₹950

Himachal Pradesh

SPITI VALLEY

Himachal Pradesh

Ruffled by the lower ridges of the Shivalik Range in the far south, cut through by the Pir Panjal and Dhauladhar ranges in the northwest, and dominated by the great Himalayas in the north and east, Himachal Pradesh (HP) is India's most popular and easily accessible hill state. Sandwiched between the Punjab and Tibet, its lowland orchards, subtropical forests and maize fields peter out in the higher reaches where pines cling to the steep slopes of mountains whose inhospitable peaks soar in rocky crags and forbidding ice fields to heights of more than 6000m.

Together with deep gorges cut by rivers crashing down from the Himalayas, these mountains form natural boundaries between the state's separate districts. Each has its own architecture, from rock-cut shrines and *shikhara* temples to colonial mansions and Buddhist monasteries. Roads struggle against the vagaries of the climate to connect the larger settlements, which are way outnumbered by remote villages, many of which are home to seminomadic **Gaddi** and **Gujjar** shepherds.

An obvious way to approach the state is to head north from Delhi to the state capital, **Shimla**, beyond the lush and temperate valleys of **Sirmaur**. The former summer location of the British government, Shimla is a curious, appealing mix of grand homes, churches and chaotic bazaars, with breathtaking views. The main road **northeast** from Shimla tackles a pass just north of **Narkanda**, then follows the River Sutlej east towards **Sarahan**, with its spectacular wooden temple, before entering the eastern district of **Kinnaur**, much of which is accessible only to those holding **Inner Line permits** (see page 413). Kinnaur becomes more austere and barren as it stretches east to the Tibetan plateau, its beauty enhanced by delicate timber houses, temples and fluttering prayer flags.

Another road from Shimla climbs slowly northwest to **Mandi**, a major staging post for the state. To the north is Himachal's most popular tourist spot, the **Kullu Valley**, an undulating mass of terraced fields, orchards and forests overlooked by snowy peaks. Its epicentre is the continuously expanding tourist town of **Manali** – long a favourite hangout of Western hippies – set in idyllic mountain scenery and offering trekking, whitewater rafting and relaxing hot springs in nearby **Vashisht**. The sacred site of **Manikaran** in the Parvati Valley also has hot sulphur-free springs.

Beyond the Rohtang Pass – soon to be the Rohtang tunnel – in the far north of Kullu district, the high-altitude desert valleys of **Lahaul and Spiti** stretch beneath massive snow-capped peaks and remote settlements with Tibetan *gompas* dotting the landscape. **Permits** are needed for travel through to Kinnaur, but **Ki**, **Kaza** and **Tabo** have unrestricted access, as does the road through Lahaul to Leh in Ladakh.

Visitors to the densely populated **Kangra Valley** west of Manali invariably make a beeline for **Dharamsala**, or more properly **McLeod Ganj**, whose large community of

---

BEST TIME TO VISIT

Being a mountainous state, Himachal Pradesh is generally best visited between late March and mid-November, as it is freezing cold and snowy for much of the **winter** and few facilities remain open in the more remote parts of the state such as Spiti. The main **high season** from April to June, though blessed with clear skies, is also when the touristic parts of the state are at their most crowded and expensive, thus not ideal. The **monsoon** can make it extremely cloudy and wet, especially in places like Shimla and Dharamsala, for much of July and August. So the best time to visit overall is at the end of the monsoon in September and October, when the skies are mostly clear again, the days still warm and the nights not too chilly.

THE TOY TRAIN, WHICH RUNS FROM KALKA TO SHIMLA

Highlights

❶ **The toy train** A rattly ride through verdant mountain scenery from Kalka to the Raj-era hill station of Shimla. See page 415

❷ **Kalpa** This relaxing hillside village of apple orchards and atmospheric temples is Kinnaur's prime spot and affords views of the stunning Kinner-Kailash massif. See page 424

❸ **Rewalsar** Buddhist pilgrimage site based around a sacred lake, with monasteries, temples, caves and hermitages. See page 427

❹ **Dharamsala/McLeod Ganj** Home of the Dalai Lama, the famous Tibetan enclave is an ever-popular place for meditation retreats, trekking and chilling out. See page 430

❺ **Bharmour** This remote mountain village amidst the rich trekking areas of Dhauladhar and Lahaul is a true gem, with a lively square punctuated by ancient temples. See page 444

❻ **Naggar** This laidback village high up on the side of the Kullu Valley is home to the fascinating Roehrich Gallery and a great place to enjoy sweeping views. See page 452

❼ **Spiti Valley** Tiny Tibetan villages and beautiful white *gompas* dot Spiti's astonishing, weathered landscape. See page 463

❽ **Manali–Leh Highway** The second-highest road in the world, passing through a vast wilderness between Himachal's honeymoon capital and barren Ladakh. See page 468

HIGHLIGHTS ARE MARKED ON THE MAP ON PAGE 410

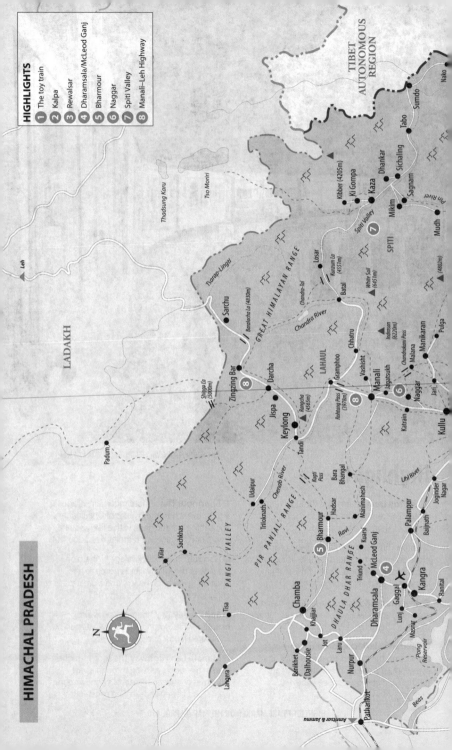

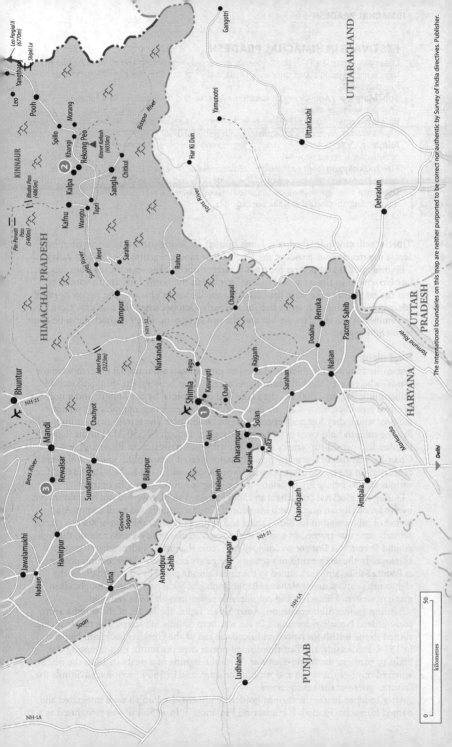

The international boundaries on this map are neither purported to be correct nor authentic by Survey of India directives. Publisher.

6

FESTIVALS IN HIMACHAL PRADESH

Losar (late Jan to late Feb). Tibetan New Year, marked with dancing and music in areas with large Buddhist populations, principally Dharamsala/McLeod Ganj (see page 430) and Spiti (see page 463).

Suhi Mata (early April). Four-day local festival celebrating the legend of Rani Sunena in Chamba. See page 442.

Baisakhi (usually April 13). Fairs are held throughout the state and people take dips in holy waters. Women are especially prominent with colourful dress.

Minjar (early Aug). A week-long riot of singing and dancing in Chamba to celebrate the growth of maize. See page 442.

Flaich Ukhayang (Sept, date varies). Colourful festival of flowers throughout Kinnaur (see page 421), marked by a procession of the village deity and goat sacrifice.

Dussehra (late Sept to late Oct). Important throughout India, in Himachal this ten-day festival is particularly spectacular in Kullu. See page 445.

Tibetan exiles includes the Dalai Lama himself. Trekking paths lead north from here across the treacherous passes of the Dhauladhar mountains into the **Chamba Valley**.

Finding guides and porters for **treks** is rarely difficult. The season runs from July to late November in the west, and to late October in the north and east. In **winter**, all but the far south of the state lies beneath a thick blanket of snow. The region north of Manali is accessible only from late June to early October when the roads are clear. Even in **summer**, when the days are hot and the sun strong, northern Himachal can be beset with chilly nights.

Brief history

The earliest known inhabitants of the area now known as Himachal Pradesh were the **Dasas**, who entered the hills from the Gangetic plain between the third and second millennium BC. By 2000 BC the Dasas had been joined by the **Aryans**, and a number of tribal republics, known as *janapadas*, began to emerge in geographically separate regions, where they fostered separate cultural traditions. The terrain made it impossible for one ruler to hold sway over the whole region, though by 550 AD Hindu Rajput families had gained supremacy over the northwestern districts of Bharmour and Chamba, just two of the many princely states created between the sixth and sixteenth centuries. Of these, the most powerful was **Kangra**, where the Katoch Rajputs held off various attacks before finally falling to the Mughals in the sixteenth century.

During the medieval era, **Lahaul and Spiti** remained aloof, governed not by Rajputs, but by the Jos of Tibetan origin, who introduced Tibetan customs and architecture. After a period of submission to Ladakh, Lahaul and Spiti came under the rajas of **Kullu**, a central princely state that reached its apogee in the seventeenth century. Further south, the region around **Shimla** and **Sirmaur** was divided into more than thirty independently governed *thakurais*. In the late seventeenth century, the newly empowered **Sikh** community, based at **Paonta Sahib** (Sirmaur), added to the threat already posed by the Mughals. By the eighteenth century, under **Maharaja Ranjit Singh**, the Sikhs had gained strongholds in much of western Himachal, and considerable power in both Kullu and Spiti.

Battling against Sikh expansion, Amar Singh Tapur, the leader of the **Gurkha** army, consolidated Nepalese dominion in the southern Shimla hill states. The *thakurai* chiefs turned to the **British** for help, and forced the last of the Gurkhas back into Nepal in 1815. Predictably, the British assumed power over the south, thus tempting the Sikhs to battle in the **Anglo-Sikh War**. With the signing of a treaty in 1846 the British annexed most of the south and west of the state, and in 1864 pronounced Shimla the summer government headquarters.

After Independence, the regions bordering present-day Punjab were integrated and named Himachal Pradesh ("Himalayan Provinces"). In 1956 HP was recognized as a

Union Territory and ten years later the modern state was formed, with Shimla as its capital. Despite being a political unity, Himachal Pradesh is culturally very diverse. With more than ninety percent of the population living outside the main towns, and many areas remaining totally isolated during the long winter months, Himachal's separate districts maintain distinct customs, architecture, dress and agricultural methods. Though Hinduism dominates, there are substantial numbers of Sikhs, Muslims and Christians, and Lahaul, Spiti and Kinnaur have been home to Tibetan Buddhists since the tenth century. This may explain why the state has traditionally been a **stronghold** for the more inclusive Congress Party, although recent years have seen the BJP take office.

6

Shimla and around

SHIMLA, Himachal's capital, is India's largest and most famous hill station, where much of the action in Rudyard Kipling's colonial classic *Kim* took place. While the city is a favourite spot for Indian families and honeymooners, its size does little to win it popularity among Western tourists. It is however, a perfect halfway house between the plains and the Kullu Valley. It's also the starting post for forays into the remoter regions of Kinnaur and Spiti.

Whether you travel by road or rail from the south, the last stretch of the climb up to Shimla seems interminable. Deep in the foothills of the Himalayas, the hill station is approached via a sinuous route that winds from the plains at **Kalka** across nearly 100km of precipitous river valleys, pine forests, and mountainsides swathed in maize terraces and apple orchards. It's not hard to see why the British chose this inaccessible site as their summer capital. At an altitude of 2159m, the crescent-shaped ridge over which it spills is blessed with perennially cool air and superb **panoramas**.

Southeast of Shimla, **Kasauli** is a peaceful place to break your journey from Chandigarh in Punjab, while nearby **Nalagarh Fort** has been converted into the finest hotel in the state. The southernmost area of the state, **Sirmaur**, is Himachal's most fertile area, with the major Sikh shrine in **Paonta Sahib** as a noteworthy sight.

Northeast of Shimla, the apple-growing centre of **Narkanda** and **Sarahan**, site of the famous **Bhimakali temple**, set against a backdrop of the majestic Himalayas, can be visited in a two- or three-day round trip from Shimla, or en route to Kinnaur via the characterless transport hub of **Rampur**.

RESTRICTED AREAS AND INNER LINE PERMITS

Foreigners travelling between Sumdo in Spiti and just east of Spillo in Kinnaur – where the road passes within a few kilometres of Western Tibet – require **Inner Line permits**, valid for travel through the border districts. Officially you are required to travel in a group of four or more, but in practice that is never enforced – though in most places you officially have to apply as part of a group.

Inner Line permits are valid for fourteen days and available from **Shimla**, **Manali**, **Kullu**, **Rampur**, **Kaza** and **Rekong Peo**. If travelling independently, you're best off applying at **Kaza** (see page 463) where you can do the legwork yourself and obtain a permit in an hour or two at no charge. In the other five locations officials normally insist that you can only apply as a group of four through a travel agent – fees are ₹350–400 per person, although these agents are very creative in manufacturing the requisite numbers. Wherever you apply, you will need to provide two photographs and photocopies of your passport and visa.

When travelling through restricted areas, you should never take photographs of military installations or sensitive sites such as bridges. Stick to the main route and you should have no problems with officialdom.

6

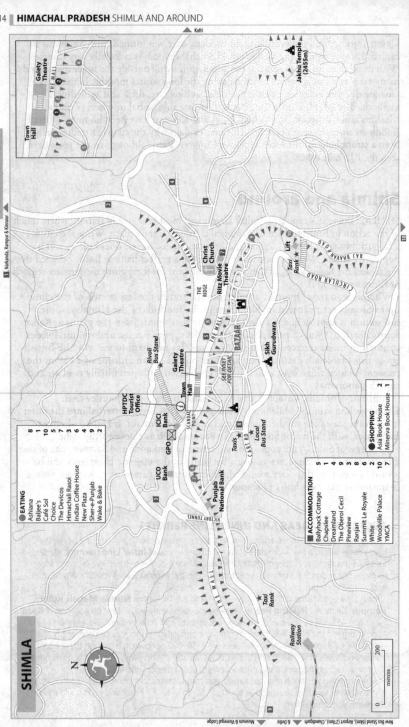

SHIMLA

Kufri

Jakhu Temple (2455m)

Galety Theatre

THE MALL

Town Hall

Narkanda, Rampur & Kinnaur

RAJ BHAVAN ROAD

CIRCULAR ROAD

Taxi Rank ★

Lift ★

Christ Church

THE RIDGE

Ritz Movie Theatre

Sikh Gurudwara

TALLARI BAZAAR

THE MALL

BAZAAR

Rivoli Bus Stand ★

Galety Theatre

SEE INSET FOR DETAIL

Town Hall

HPTDC Tourist Office

SCANDAL POINT

ICICI Bank ⊠

GPO ⊠

Taxis ★

Local Bus Stand ★

CART RD

UCO Bank 🏦

Punjab National Bank

VICTORY TUNNEL

THE MALL

Taxi Rank ★

Railway Station

N

0   200   metres

New Bus Stand (6km), Airport (23km), Chandigarh & Delhi

Museum & Viceregal Lodge

● **EATING**
Ashiana	8
Baljee's	1
Café Sol	10
Choice	5
The Devicos	3
Himachali Rasoi	6
Indian Coffee House	4
New Plaza	9
Sher-e-Punjab	2
Wake & Bake	7

■ **ACCOMMODATION**
Ballyhack Cottage	5
Chapslee	1
Dreamland	4
The Oberoi Cecil	9
Pineview	3
Ranjan	8
Summit Le Royale	6
White	2
Woodville Palace	10
YMCA	7

● **SHOPPING**
Asia Book House	2
Minerva Book House	1

THE VICEROY'S TOY TRAIN

Until the construction of the **Kalka–Shimla Railway**, the only way to get to the Shimla hill station was on the so-called **Cart Road** – a slow, winding trail trodden by lines of long-suffering porters and horse-drawn tongas. By the time the 96km narrow-gauge line was completed in 1903, 103 tunnels, 24 bridges and 18 stations had been built between Shimla and the railhead at Kalka, 26km northeast of Chandigarh. These days, buses may be quicker, but a ride on the "toy train" is far more memorable – especially if you travel first-class, in one of the glass-windowed rail cars. Hauled along by a tiny diesel locomotive, they rattle at a leisurely pace through stunning scenery, taking between five and a half and seven hours to reach Shimla.

Along the route, you'll notice the guards exchanging little leather pouches with staff strategically positioned on the station platforms. The bags they receive in return contain small brass discs, which the drivers slot into special machines to alert the signals ahead of their approach. "**Neal's Token System**", in place since the line was first inaugurated, is a fail-safe means of ensuring that trains travelling in opposite directions never meet face to face on the single-track sections of the railway.

Brief history

Named after its patron goddess, Shamla Devi (a manifestation of Kali), the tiny village that stood on this spot was "discovered" by a team of British surveyors in 1817. Glowing reports of its beauty and climate gradually filtered to the imperial capital, Calcutta, and within two decades the settlement had become the Subcontinent's most fashionable summer resort. The annual migration was finally rubber-stamped in 1864, when Shimla – by now an elegant town of mansions, churches and cricket pitches – was declared the Government of India's official hot-season HQ. With the completion of the **Kalka–Shimla Railway** in 1903, Shimla lay only two days by train from Delhi. Its growth continued after Independence, especially after becoming state capital in 1966.

Today, Shimla is still a major holiday resort, popular mainly with nouveau riche Punjabis and Delhi-ites who flock here in their thousands during the May–June run-up to the monsoons, and then again in October, when many Bengalis also visit. Its faded colonial charm also appeals to foreigners looking for a taste of the Raj. The burra- and memsahibs may have moved on, but Shimla retains a decidedly **British feel**: pukka Indian gentlemen in tweeds stroll along The Mall smoking pipes, while neatly turned-out schoolchildren scuttle past mock-Tudor shopfronts and houses with names like Braeside. At the same time, the pesky monkey troupes and chaotic mass of corrugated iron rooftops that make up Shimla's **bazaar** lend an unmistakeably Indian aspect to the town. Note that the entire town is a no-smoking zone.

The Ridge

Although Shimla and its satellite districts sprawl over the flanks of five or more hills, the centre is fairly compact, on and immediately beneath a shoulder of high ground known as "**The Ridge**". Shimla's busy social scene revolves around the broad and breezy piazza that straddles The Ridge, overlooking rippling foothills with the jagged white peaks of the Pir Panjal and Great Himalayan ranges on the horizon. It is said all water that drains off the north side of The Ridge ends up in the Arabian Sea, while from the south side it ends up in the Bay of Bengal. During high season it is a hive of activity, with entertainment provided by brass bands, pony rides and a giant screen showing sporting events. The Victorian Gothic spire of **Christ Church** is Shimla's most prominent landmark. The **stained-glass windows**, the finest in British India, depict (from left to right) Faith, Hope, Charity, Fortitude, Patience and Humility. There is still a service in English at 9am every Sunday. At the other end of The Ridge, **Scandal Point** is the focus of Shimla's famous mid-afternoon meet when crowds gather here to gossip.

The Mall

From The Ridge, a tangle of roads and lanes tumbles down in stages, each layer connected to the next by stone steps. **The Mall**, the main pedestrian thoroughfare, curves around the south slope of the hill. Flanked by a long row of unmistakeably British half-timbered buildings, Shimla's main shopping street was, until World War I, strictly out-of-bounds to all "natives" except royalty and rickshaw-pullers. These days, rickshaws, man-powered or otherwise, are banned and non-Indian faces are in the minority. The quintessentially colonial **Gaiety Theatre** (ⓦgaiety.in) was renovated in 2008 and puts on regular performances and exhibitions, now billing itself as a Heritage Cultural Complex.

The bazaar

Walk down any of the narrow lanes leading off The Mall, and you're plunged into a warren of twisting backstreets. Shimla's **bazaar** is the hill station at its most vibrant – a maze of dishevelled shacks, brightly lit stalls and minarets, cascading in a clutter of corrugated iron to the edge of Cart Road. Apart from being a good place to shop for authentic souvenirs, this is also one of the few areas of town that feels Himalayan: multicoloured Kullu caps (*topis*) bob about in the crowd, alongside the odd Lahauli, Kinnauri or Tibetan face.

The state museum

1.5km west of the centre via The Mall – take the right fork at the first intersection after the *Classic* hotel and left at the second, from where it is signposted • Tues–Sun 10am–1pm & 2–5pm, closed 2nd Sat of month • ₹100 (₹30), camera ₹100 (₹50)

The HP **state museum** is well worth the effort to get to. The ground floor of the elegant colonial mansion is given over largely to temple sculpture, and a gallery of magnificent **Pahari miniatures** – examples of the last great Hindu art form to flourish in northern India before the deadening impact of Western culture in the early nineteenth century. The Mughal-influenced Pahari or "Hill" school is renowned for subtle depictions of romantic love, inspired by scenes from Hindu epics. Among the museum's **paintings** are dozens of Mughal and Rajasthani miniatures and a couple of fine "Company" watercolours, produced for souvenir-hunting colonials by the descendants of the Mughal and Pahari masters. The *fakirs*, itinerant sadhus and mendicants they depict could have leapt straight from the pages of Kipling. One room is devoted to Mahatma Gandhi, packed with photos of his time in Shimla and amusing cartoons of his political relationship with the British.

THE HIKE TO JAKHU TEMPLE

The early-morning hike up to **Jakhu**, or "Monkey", **Temple** is something of a tradition in Shimla. The top of the hill (2455m) on which it stands offers a superb panorama of the Himalayas – particularly breathtaking before the cloud gathers later in the day. The relentlessly steep climb takes thirty to 45 minutes. The path starts just left of Christ Church; during the season, all you need do is follow the crowds.

After the hard walk up, the temple itself, a red-and-yellow-brick affair crammed with fairy lights and tinsel, comes as something of an anti-climax, although the new 30m-tall orange concrete statue of **Hanuman** is an impressive sight. The shrine inside houses what are believed to be the footprints of Hanuman himself. Legend has it that the monkey god, adored by Hindus for his strength and fidelity, rested on Jakhu after collecting healing Himalayan herbs for Rama's injured brother, Lakshmana. Watch out for the troupes of mangy monkeys around the temple. Pampered by generations of pilgrims and tourists, they have become real pests; hang on to your bag and don't flash food. Hold onto your specs too – one or two monkeys have even been trained to swipe them from unsuspecting victims' faces and turn them over to a local, who will hand them back ... for a small fee, of course.

The Viceregal Lodge

3km west of the centre • Daily 9am–5pm; guided tours on the hour except 1 & 2pm •House ₹100 (₹50), gardens ₹20

Shimla's single most impressive colonial monument is the old **Viceregal Lodge**, summer seat of British government until the 1940s and today home to the **Institute of Advanced Studies**. The solid grey mansion, built in Elizabethan style with a lion and unicorn set above the entrance porch, surveys trimmed lawns fringed by pines and flowerbeds – the grounds and the exterior of the lodge are most impressive. Inside is looking a little tired, with only a few rooms on the ground floor open to the public: a vast teak-panelled entrance hall, an impressive library (formerly the ballroom) and the guest room. The **conference room**, hung with photos of Nehru, Jinnah and Gandhi, was the scene of crucial talks in the run-up to Independence. On the stone terrace to the rear of the building, a plaque profiles and names the peaks visible in the distance.

6

Prospect Hill

The short hike up to **Prospect Hill** (2176m), a popular picnic spot, ties in nicely with a visit to the Viceregal Lodge. By cutting through the woods to the west of the mansion, you can drop down to a busy intersection known as **Boileauganj**, from where a tarmac path climbs steeply up to the small shrine of Kamana Devi, which affords fine views.

ARRIVAL AND DEPARTURE   SHIMLA

Wherever you arrive in Shimla, you'll be mobbed by **porters**. Most of the town is pedestrianized, and seriously steep, so you may be glad of the extra help to carry your gear, but it's better to politely refuse their offer to tout you a hotel.

By plane Shimla's airport lies 20km southwest of town on the Mandi road at Jubarhati. In 2017, after five years with no flights, Air India started a daily route between Shimla and Delhi (9.30am; 1hr 15min). Note that antiquated facilities and frequent bad weather cause frequent delays.

By train The train station is a 15min walk southwest of The Mall. The toy train connects Shimla with Kalka, where you can change onto the main broad-gauge line for Chandigarh and Delhi, the best services being the *Himalayan Queen* #14096 at 4.50pm or the faster *Shatabdi Express* #12012 at 5.45pm, both arriving in Delhi around 10pm. Toy train services depart from Shimla at 10.30am, 2.25pm, 4.25pm, 5.40pm and 6.15pm, while from Kalka they leave at 4am,

5.10am, 5.30am, 6am and 12.10pm; they should take around 5hr each, though it's often longer. Reservations for onward journeys from Kalka can be made at Shimla station (☏ 0177 265 2915, enquiries ☏ 131) or the booking booth next to the tourist office.

By bus Long-distance buses use the new multilevel bus stand 6km southwest of the centre, on the Chandigarh road. Frequent minibuses link it to the Local Bus Stand on Cart Rd. Services include Chandigarh (every 15min; 4hr), Delhi (hourly; 10hr), Mandi (12 daily; 5hr), Kullu (8 daily 7–8hr), Dharamsala (4 daily; 9–10hr), Manali (8 daily; 8–9hr), Sarahan (3 daily; 7–8hr) and Rekong Peo (6 daily; 9–10hr). HPTDC run a deluxe bus to Manali (8am) and a/c Volvo bus to Delhi (10pm); both depart from more central Victory Tunnel and tickets should be booked at least a day in advance at the tourist office, while state bus tickets can be reserved at the adjacent ticket counter (Mon–Sat 10am– 4.30pm) or at the bus stand.

GETTING AROUND

By taxi Taxis are the best way to get to the pricier hotels on the outskirts. The main Vishal Himachal Taxi Union rank (☏ 0177 265 7645) is 1km east of the Local Bus Stand, at the

bottom of the lift (₹10 each way) that connects the east end of Cart Rd with The Mall. Another, more central, taxi rank can be found just above the Local Bus Stand on Cart Rd.

INFORMATION AND TOURS

Tourist information The HPTDC main tourist office (daily: high season 9am–8pm; low season 9am–6pm; ☏ 0177 265 2561, ⊕ hptdc.in) is located on The Ridge near Scandal Point. It organizes whistle-stop sightseeing tours to destinations around Shimla, including Narkanda, and offers limited advice on local walks. To venture into the more remote and challenging regions such as Kinnaur and Spiti,

check out our recommended mountaineering and trekking agencies on The Mall (see page 419).

Walking tours Shimla Walks (☏ 94595 19620, ⊕ shimlawalks.com) organize guided walks around Shimla and the surrounding area.

6

ACCOMMODATION

Unsurprisingly for a state capital that is also a major holiday destination, **accommodation** is costlier than average. In May and June prices soar and it's essential to book in advance. At other times, most places are willing to bargain.

Ballyhack Cottage The Ridge ☎ 80913 00076, ⓦ ballyhackcottage.com; map p.414. Steps from Christ Church is one of the first houses built in Shimla, a historic lodge with breath-taking Himalaya views from the lawns. Choose the family suite (Deodar) from the five antique-filled rooms, as those on the lower ground floor can be damp. Breakfast is hearty and other home-cooked meals can be ordered in advance. ₹6000

Chapslee Between Lakkar Bazaar and Long Wood ☎ 0177 280 2542, ⓦ chapslee.com; map p.414. Exclusive, beautiful old manor house set in its own grounds on the edge of town and stuffed with antiques, plus a library, card room, tennis court and croquet lawn. Half-board, payment by credit card only. ₹24,000

★ **Dreamland** The Ridge, above Christ Church ☎ 0177 265 3005, ⓦ hoteldreamlandshimla.com; map p.414. Welcoming and excellent value during the low season especially; all rooms are clean, with hot showers and cable TV. The pricier rooms boast fantastic views over to the Himalayas. Large restaurant on the top floor; plus a helpful on-site travel agency. Wi-fi in the lobby only. ₹1500

The Oberoi Cecil The Mall ☎ 0177 280 4848, ⓦ oberoi hotels.com; map p.414. Raj-era building, frequented by Rudyard Kipling among others. It is now an opulent chain hotel somewhat devoid of historic character, but with fabulous service and an indoor heated pool. Advance online discounts. ₹14,000

Pineview Mythe Estate, on the far side of Victory Tunnel ☎ 0177 265 8604; map p.414. A rather ugly block but in a decent location near north-facing apple orchards, with a wide choice of comfortable attached rooms and some suites. ₹1000

Ranjan Just above the Old Bus Stand ☎ 0177 265 2818; map p.414. Originally built in 1907, this large white building is showing its age but few places are cheaper. The attached rooms are large if tatty, with some original fittings and common balconies supported by wooden columns. ₹750

Summit Le Royale Jakhoo Rd ☎ 0177 265 1002, ⓦ summithotels.in; map p.414. Modern and functional hotel offering great views from high above The Ridge and a variety of smart rooms of varying sizes, all with nice furnishings. Rather overpriced but bargaining is possible. ₹4000

White Lakkar Bazaar ☎ 0177 265 5276, ⓦ hotelwhite simla.com; map p.414. Well-managed hotel with light rooms over-looking the Himalayas. Gleaming white marble and woodwork everywhere. The deluxe suite is excellent. Fixed prices all year. ₹2400

Woodville Palace Raj Bhavan Rd ☎ 0177 262 3919, ⓦ woodvillepalacehotel.com; map p.414. A 20min walk south from Christ Church, this elegant – though slightly faded – 1930s mansion boasts huge rooms and suites, period furniture, lawns and a badminton court. ₹18,000

YMCA The Ridge, up the steps to the left of the Ritz movie theatre ☎ 0177 265 0021, ⓔ ymcashimla@ yahoo.co.in; map p.414. Large rooms, including seven attached. In-house dining hall (breakfast is included except Jan–March) and sun-terrace, along with cable TV, snooker tables, table tennis and internet café. It can be a little gloomy and damp, but it's a great location for the price. Dorms ₹400, doubles ₹1000

EATING

Few **restaurants** in Shimla retain any colonial ambience but standards have improved and a number of decent places complement the hotel restaurants, while the many **bakeries** and ice-cream parlours offer comfort for the sweet-toothed. For a really cheap and filling meal, try the fried potato patties (*tikki*) or chickpea curry and puris (*channa batura*) at one of the snack bars that line the steps opposite the Gaiety Theatre. Alternatively, the bazaar is good for cheap *dhabas*.

Ashiana The Ridge ☎ 0177 265 8464; map p.414. Touristy HPTDC restaurant in a converted bandstand offering views of the Mall and mainly non-veg Indian food, including tasty chicken *makhanwalla*, plus pizzas and a few Chinese dishes. Mains mostly ₹180–300. Daily 9am–10pm.

Baljee's The Mall ☎ 0177 281 4054; map p.414. This hectic coffee house does a roaring trade in snacks, sweets and ice cream in the evenings especially. The *Fascination* restaurant upstairs offers a good selection of Indian and Chinese dishes for around ₹150–250, as well as sausage, egg and chips. Daily 11.30am–11pm.

Café Sol The Mall, on the roof of Combemere Hotel ☎ 0177 252 2242; map p.414. Slick neon-lit cylindrical structure, good for reasonable Italian, Mexican and Thai dishes (₹180–500), as well as standard Indian food and tasty bakery items. Main dishes from ₹250 to over ₹1000 for an Aussie steak. Wi-fi. Daily 11am–10.30pm.

Choice Middle Bazaar, down the steps from Baljee's ☎ 0177 329 4626; map p.414. Tiny Chinese and Tibetan restaurant with warm red walls and an exhaustive menu of delicious veg and non-veg dishes such as *momos* and chow mein for ₹50–100. Daily noon–10.30pm.

The Devicos The Mall ☎ 0177 280 6335, ⓦ thedevicos. com; map p.414. The fairly plush restaurant downstairs does south Indian snacks for less than ₹100 and full-on Indian non-veg portions for ₹200–400. The ground floor is occupied by a *Coffee Day* franchise and there's a bar upstairs.

Daily 10am–10.30pm.

★ **Himachali Rasoi** 54 Middle Bazaar ☎0177 265 2386; map p.414. A tiny and cosy spot with just two veg *dham thalis* (a traditional Himachal festive spread) on the menu, that alternate depending on the day of the week (full ₹219, half ₹171). The smoked spiced black lentil dish is divine. Sides and sweets are available too, or you can pop in for a warm spiced lassi or herbal tea. Free delivery until 6pm. Daily noon–10pm.

★ **Indian Coffee House** The Mall ☎0177 265 2982; map p.414. Atmospheric, faded café with colonial ambience, offering the usual range of veg snacks such as masala dosa for ₹55, and attentive waiter service to the predominantly male clientele, who linger over coffee and put the world to rights. A must visit when in Shimla. Daily 8am–9pm.

New Plaza 60/1 Middle Bazaar, down the steps beside Himani's ☎0177 265 5438; map p.414. Popular family restaurant. Good-value food including tasty meat sizzlers and other non-veg curries for around ₹250–300. Daily 10am–10.30pm.

Sher-e-Punjab The Mall ☎0177 280 3538; map p.414. The best of the simple restaurants of the same name at the eastern end of The Mall is the *dhaba* down the stairs. Hearty portions of spicy beans, chickpeas and dhal at ₹50–80, plus inexpensive meat and fish. Daily 7am–10.30pm.

Wake & Bake The Mall ☎0177 281 3146; map p.414. Hip modern café/restaurant, with smart wooden booths and mostly non-Indian items such as hummus and pitta for ₹190 or full English breakfast for ₹300. Wi-fi. Daily 9.30am–10pm.

DIRECTORY

Banks and exchange Various ATMs line The Mall, many on Scandal Point, while cash can be exchanged at the Punjabi National Bank and one or two agents.

Bookshops Asia Book House (☎0177 281 2217) and Minerva Book House (☎0177 280 3078), both on The Mall, stock a wide range of paperbacks and reference titles.

Hospitals Indira Gandhi Medical College Hospital (☎0177 280 4251, ☏igmcshimla.edu.in); INDUS hospital, 6km from the ISBT at Mount Jakhoo (☎0177 284 1401).

Permits Inner Line permits (see page 413) are issued at the Additional District Magistrate's office (Mon–Sat 10am–-5pm, closed 2nd Sat of month; ☎0177 265 7005),

a short way below The Mall, but it saves a lot of hassle to apply through a travel agency.

Pharmacies Indu Medical, The Mall (9am–8pm).

Post The GPO (Mon–Sat 10am–6pm) is near Scandal Point on The Mall.

Travel agents Reliable operators on The Mall include City Travels, near Scandal Point (☎94180 20899, ☏citytravelshimla@gmail.com) and Great Himalayan Travels (☎0177 265 8934, ☏ghtravels.com). The *YMCA* (see page 418) also organizes treks and jeep safaris, as does Silver Dreams at the *Dreamland* hotel (see page 418).

Kasauli

Though it sees few Western tourists, the small, slow-paced town of **KASAULI**, cradled by pine forests 77km southwest of Shimla, and with a touch of Raj architecture, makes a good stop-off on the way to or from Delhi. Crisscrossed by spindly cobbled streets, spreading along low ridges carpeted with forests and flower-filled meadows, Kasauli offers an abundance of gentle short strolls, such as the one to nearby Sanawar, or the scenic longer trek to Kalka, railhead for the toy train to Shimla.

ARRIVAL AND DEPARTURE   KASAULI

By train The nearest railway station is 11km away at Dharampur on the Kalka–Shimla toy train line.

By bus There are frequent buses from Dharampur and direct hourly services from Shimla.

ACCOMMODATION AND EATING

Gian Post Office Rd, downhill from the bazaar near the Lower Mall ☎01792 272244. Fairly basic yet attractive hotel, whose high-ceilinged rooms all have fireplaces, carpets and balconies, in true faded Raj style. The restaurant does a limited range of Indian, Chinese and Continental

cuisine. No wi-fi. ₹800

Ros-Common Lower Mall ☎01792 272005, ☏kasauli@ hptdc.in. Overpriced state-run hotel with reasonable rooms of different prices and a standard restaurant. A more modern annexe is 500m away. ₹2200

Nalagarh

NALAGARH is an excellent place to break the journey between Delhi and Kullu, as it lies 60km from Chandigarh and just 12km off the main Chandigarh–Mandi road. Now an emerging industrial region, the town was capital of the medieval state of **Hindur**, founded by the Chandella Rajputs in 1100 AD. It is one outstanding feature is imposing **Nalagarh Fort**, now converted into the classiest heritage hotel in Himachal Pradesh.

ARRIVAL AND DEPARTURE
NALAGARH

By bus Nalagarh is most easily reached by bus from Chandigarh (every 1–2hr; 2hr).

ACCOMMODATION

★**The Fort Resort** ☎01795 223179/ 98115 59496, ⓦnalagarh.in. Accommodation is in beautifully maintained suites, each with period furniture, and surprisingly good value. An atmospheric lounge bar overlooks terraced grounds with a tennis court, croquet lawn and swimming pool, and an Ayurvedic clinic offers massage. Breakfast included. ₹4500

Paonta Sahib

On the border with Uttarakhand, the town of **PAONTA SAHIB**, where pastel-yellow houses are packed tightly into the cobbled streets, holds an important shrine dedicated to **Guru Gobind Singh**, the tenth Sikh guru, who lived here in the late 1680s.

ARRIVAL AND DEPARTURE
PAONTA SAHIB

By bus Paonta Sahib provides good bus connections for travel between Shimla and points in Uttarakhand such as Mussoorie, Dehradun, Haridwar and Rishikesh.

ACCOMMODATION

The Yamuna ☎01704 222341, ✉paonta@hptdc. in. HPTDC hotel, on the banks of the River Yamuna, with pleasant rooms, a restaurant serving the predictable range of Indian and Chinese dishes, and a bar. ₹700

Narkanda

A three-hour (65km) bus ride northeast of Shimla, the scruffy hill town of **NARKANDA** (2725m) makes a reasonable resting point on the bumpy, six-hour journey to Sarahan, and has a number of *dhabas* around the bazaar where you can grab a snack. This former staging post on the Hindustan–Tibet caravan route acts as the roadhead and main market town for the area's widely dispersed apple- and potato-growers. There are some good rambles through the cedar forests that surround the town, and great **views** of the Himalayas. **Hatu Peak** (3143m), crowned by a lonely hilltop **Durga temple**, 7km east of town, looks out over the River Sutlej winding far below, and a string of white-tipped mountains to the north and east.

ARRIVAL AND DEPARTURE
NARKANDA

By bus Narkanda has good bus connections with Shimla (every 30min–1hr; 3hr) and the towns of Kinnaur.

ACCOMMODATION AND EATING

The Hatu On a hillside above town ☎01782 242430, ⓦhotelhatu.tripod.com. Fairly smart HPTDC hotel with large well-appointed rooms and great views from the manicured lawns. Also has ski equipment for rent, cable TV and a bar. ₹1300

Mahamaya Palace Above the main road ☎01782 242448, ⓦhotelmahamayapalace.com. Spruced up Alpine-style hotel with lots of wood panelling, spacious rooms, a huge deluxe suite and a decent restaurant. The downstairs back rooms are best value and still have great views. ₹880

Negi Dhaba (New Himalayan Dhaba) Middle of the bazaar ☎01782 242426. By far the best place to eat, with modern wooden seating and fine valley views. Various thalis from ₹80–200 and a smart new coffee machine. Daily 7am–10pm.

Sarahan

Secluded **SARAHAN**, erstwhile summer capital of the Bhushar rajas, sits astride a 2000m ledge above the River Sutlej, near the Shimla–Kinnaur border. Set against a

BLOOD SACRIFICE IN SARAHAN

The **Bhimakali** deity, a local manifestation of the Hindu goddess Kali/Durga (see page 1208), has for centuries been associated with **human sacrifice**. Once every decade, until the disapproving British intervened in the 1800s, a man was killed here as an offering to the *devi*. Following a complex ceremony, his newly spilled blood was poured over the goddess's tongue for her to drink, after which his body was dumped in a deep well inside the temple compound. If no victim could be found, it is said that a voice would bellow from the depths of the pit, which is now sealed up.

The tradition of blood sacrifice continues in Sarahan to this day, albeit in less extreme form. During the annual **Astami** festival, two days before the culmination of **Dussehra**, a veritable menagerie of birds and beasts are put to the knife, including a water-buffalo calf, sheep, goat, fish, chicken, crab, and even a spider. The gory spectacle draws large crowds, and is a memorable alternative to the Dussehra procession in Kullu, which takes place at around the same time in mid-October.

6

spectacular backdrop, the village harbours one of the northwestern Himalayas' most exotic spectacles – the **Bhimakali temple**. With its two multitiered sanctuary towers, elegantly sloping slate-tiled roofs and gleaming golden spires, it is the most majestic early timber temple in the Sutlej Valley – an area renowned for housing holy shrines on raised wooden platforms. Although most of the structure dates from the early twentieth century, parts are thought to be more than eight hundred years old.

A pair of elaborately decorated metal doors lead into a large courtyard flanked by rest rooms and a small carved-stone **Shiva shrine**. After ascending to a second, smaller yard, you pass another golden door, also richly embossed with mythical scenes, beyond which the innermost enclosure holds the two **sanctuary towers**. The one on the right houses musical instruments, flags, paladins and ceremonial weapons, some of which are on show in the small "museum" in the corner of the courtyard. Non-Hindus who want to climb to the top of the other, more modern tower (no photography) to view the highly polished gold-faced deity must don one of the saffron or red caps, available at the entrance. Bhimakali herself is enshrined on the top floor, decked with garlands of flowers.

ARRIVAL AND DEPARTURE   SARAHAN

By bus There are several daily direct buses and many more local services from Jeori, 17km below Sarahan on the busy main road between Rampur and Kinnaur.

On foot Keen walkers might fancy ambling along the well-worn mule track to Sarahan from Jeori.

ACCOMMODATION

Monal Behind the temple ☎ 98822 06557. Simple, friendly guesthouse, which offers a choice of rather compact but clean attached or non-attached rooms. No wi-fi. ₹300/₹500

The Srikhand Opposite the temple ☎ 01782 274234, ✉ sarahan@hptdc.in. The building is an incongruous concrete monster but its rooms are reasonable and it has a delightful garden and a restaurant serving good veg meals on a relaxing terrace. Dorms ₹200, doubles ₹1800

Temple Guest House In the lower temple courtyard ☎ 01782 274248. The rooms are basic but pleasant and the dingy basement dorm offers some of the cheapest beds in the Himalayas. Dorms ₹100, doubles ₹600

Trehan's Main road ☎ 98166 87605, ⌨ hoteltrehan sarahan.com. Welcoming hotel that looks down the valley from the sheer mountainside and offers spacious attached rooms with attractive moulded ceilings and TV. Serves passable food too. ₹900

Kinnaur

Before 1992, the remote backwater of **KINNAUR**, a rugged buffer zone between the Shimla foothills and the wild western extremity of Chinese-occupied Tibet, was strictly off-limits

6

TREKKING IN KINNAUR

Unfrequented mountain trails crisscross Kinnaur, offering **treks** ranging from gentle hikes to challenging climbs over high-altitude passes. The routes along the **Sutlej Valley**, punctuated with government resthouses and villages, are feasible without the aid of ponies, but away from the main road you need to be completely self-sufficient. **Porters** can usually be hired in Rampur, Rekong Peo and the Baspa/Sangla Valley except in early autumn (Sept/Oct), when they're busy with the apple harvest.

THE KINNER-KAILASH CIRCUIT

The five- to seven-day *parikrama* (circumambulation) of the majestic Kinner-Kailash massif, a sacred pilgrimage trail, makes a spectacular trek for which you won't need an Inner Line permit. The circuit starts at the village of **MORANG**, on the left bank of the Sutlej, served by buses from Tapri or Rekong Peo. A track, passable by jeep, runs southeast from here to **Thangi**, the trailhead, and continues through Rahtak, over the **Charang La** pass (5266m) to **Chitkul** in the Baspa/Sangla Valley. The trail then follows the river down to the beautiful village of **Sangla**, from where a couple of worthwhile day-hikes can be made – to **Kamru fort** behind the village, or the steep ascent to the **Shivaling La** pass, from where there are superb views of Raldang (5499m), the southernmost peak on the Kinner-Kailash massif. The final stage passes through the lower Baspa/Sangla Valley, via Shang and Brua to **Karcham**, which overlooks the NH-22 highway. The best time for the Kinner-Kailash *parikrama* is between July and October; August is the most popular month with local pilgrims.

KAFNU TO KAZA, VIA THE PIN VALLEY

This challenging route across the Great Himalayan range, via the Kalang Setal glacier and the Shakarof La pass, is a dramatic approach to Spiti and the **Pin Valley**, and no restrictions apply. The trail, which is very steep, snow-covered, and hard to follow in places, should definitely not be attempted without ponies, porters, adequate gear and a reliable **guide**. It starts in earnest at Kafnu village, now connected to Wangtu on the main road by a paved surface, continuing via Mulling, Phustirang (3750m), and over the **Bhaba Pass** (4865m), a gruelling slog through snowfields, before dropping down into the beautiful and isolated **Pin Valley**. You can then trek onwards or get a vehicle to **Kaza** (see page 463). More of this route may become paved as the delayed Wangtu–Mudh road project painfully progresses.

CHITKUL TO HAR-KI-DUN

This ten-day trek to **Garhwal** (see page 301) passes along the edge of the Inner Line and is subject to restrictions. Starting from **Chitkul** and crossing the River Baspa to Doaria, the route then climbs up a side valley to follow a lateral moraine up to the Zupika Gad and then a steep ascent – the final section of which is up a crevassed glacier – to the **Borsu Pass** (5300m). The other side of the pass is down a steep snow- and boulder-field requiring some scrambling; you arrive a few days later in the beautiful valley of **Har-ki-Dun** in Garhwal. A guide is essential.

THE OLD HINDUSTAN–TIBET ROAD FROM KALPA TO THE RUPA VALLEY

Another route to consider is the relatively easy five-day trek starting at **Kalpa** and following the old Hindustan–Tibet road through the remote hamlets of upper Kinnaur (permits needed), past Shi Asu to the Rupa Valley. The views along the route are superb and the villagers are extremely hospitable. The road, now crumbling in places, is also ideal for mountain biking.

to tourists. Although visitors are now allowed to travel through the "**Inner Line**", and on to Spiti, Lahaul and the Kullu Valley, permits are still required (see page 413). Other areas of Kinnaur, notably the **Baspa Valley** (also called Sangla Valley) and the sacred **Kinner-Kailash** massif visible from the mountain village of **Kalpa**, are completely open.

Straddling the mighty River Sutlej, which rises on the southern slopes of Mount Kailash, Kinnaur has for centuries been a major trans-Himalayan corridor. Merchants travelling between China and the Punjabi plains passed through on the **Hindustan–Tibet caravan route**, stretches of which are still used by villagers and trekkers. The bulk of the traffic that lumbers east towards the frontier, however, uses the newer NH-22, which veers north into Spiti just short of the ascent to Shipki La pass, on the Chinese border, which remains closed.

In the well-watered, mainly Hindu west of the region, the scenery ranges from subtropical to almost Alpine: wood-and-slate villages, surrounded by maize terraces and orchards, nestle beneath pine forests and vast blue-grey mountain peaks. Further east, largely beyond the reach of the monsoons, it grows more austere, and glaciers loom on all sides. **Buddhism** arrived in Kinnaur with the tenth-century kings of Guge, who ruled what is now southwestern Tibet. When **Rinchen Zangpo** (958–1055), the "Great Translator" credited with the "Second Spreading" of the faith in Guge, passed through, he left behind several monasteries and a devotion to a pure form of the Buddhist faith that has endured here for nearly one thousand years. In the sixteenth century, after Guge had fragmented into dozens of petty fiefdoms, the **Bhushar kings** took control of Kinnaur. They remained in power throughout the British Raj, when this was one of the battlegrounds of the espionage war played out between agents of the Chinese, Russian and British empires – the "Great Game" evocatively depicted in the novels of Rudyard Kipling.

Rekong Peo

East of Jeori, the road climbs high above the Sutlej into ever more remote territory, traversing sheer ravines on cable bridges, while tiny wooden villages, each with a pagoda-roofed temple, cling to the mountainsides. At **Wangtu** bridge, the trailhead for the Kinnaur–Pin Valley–Kaza trek (see page 466), the highway switches to the north bank of the river. Further east there is a long-term detour at Tapri because of road subsidence, which ends near the sturdy metal bridge beside the huge Karcham Dam hydroelectric project. The route to **Sangla** and the rest of the Baspa Valley (which is also known as Sangla Valley) lies across the bridge to the south, while the main highway continues to **REKONG PEO**, district headquarters of Kinnaur. Its batch of concrete houses and government buildings around a small maidan, 7km above the main road, gives it the air of an upstart frontier settlement. Apart from its moderately interesting **bazaar**, the only reason to stop is to buy trekking supplies, find a connection to Kalpa or obtain an Inner Line **permit** (see page 413).

ARRIVAL AND INFORMATION | REKONG PEO

By bus Buses drop off and pick up at the bend in the main bazaar before proceeding up the hill on the Kalpa road for 2km to the main bus stand, which can be reached on foot by the 500m path from the end of ITBP Rd. There are services almost hourly to Shimla (9–10hr), early morning departures direct to Mandi and Kaza (10–11hr), and direct buses to Chandigarh, Amritsar and Delhi. Several morning buses run to Sangla (2hr), some continuing to Chitkul, and there are minibuses every 15–20min to Kalpa.

Tourist information The Tourist Info Centre (Mon–Sat 10am–5pm; ☎ 01786 222857) is in the open courtyard below the bazaar bus stop. This is also the official agent for Inner Line permits – they charge ₹350 but can take your photo and make copies of your passport as part of the service. A similar service and other helpful travel advice is available from adjacent The Monk Travels (☎ 98055 30056, ⌨ themonktravels.com).

ACCOMMODATION AND EATING

There are a surprising number of **hotels** lining the upper side of the main bazaar, although most of these are rather overpriced. Those further up the hill and on side roads offer better value.

Fairyland On the road immediately above the main bazaar ☎ 98174 11040, ✉ hotelfairyland@gmail.com. Most easily accessed via the steps beside *Cafeteria Roof*, *Fairyland*'s modest but clean attached rooms have TV and great views of Kinner-Kailash. Generous portions in the restaurant. No wi-fi. ₹**400**

Little Chef On the corner of the main bazaar ☎ 94180 92237. Brightly coloured mosaic table tops complement a wide-ranging menu of forgettable Indian, Chinese and Continental dishes in the ₹120–300 range. They do have a nice view from the balcony and filter water to refill your bottle. Daily 9am–9.30pm.

Mehfil ITBP Rd ☎ 94180 07799. Enjoying a central location but slightly removed from the bustling bazaar, this hotel has a range of attached rooms with TV and partial mountain views. ₹**600**

Vikas Bar & Restaurant In the middle of the main bazaar ☎ 94181 20411. Fairly basic place that does good local food such as soup, dhal, aloo gobi, pakora and mutton cari for ₹180. Daily 7am–10pm.

Kalpa (Chini)

KALPA can be reached by the twisting 9km road from Rekong Peo or on foot along various steep tracks. Its narrow atmospheric lanes, crammed with rickety wooden shops, and dramatic location, high above the right bank of the Sutlej, make it by far the most attractive base in the immediate vicinity. The ancient Tibetan *gompa* here was founded by Rinchen Zangpo, and there is also a small Shiva temple. The village and its growing number of hotels are quite spread out up the hill, which is festooned with apple orchards, and along the roads that radiate from the centre. Facing the village, the magnificent **Kinner-Kailash** massif sweeps 4500m up from the valley floor. The mountain in the middle, Jorkaden (6473m), is the highest, followed by the sacred summit of Kinner-Kailash (6050m) to the north, and the needle point of Raldang (5499m) in the south.

ARRIVAL AND DEPARTURE
KALPA (CHINI)

By bus Minibuses between Kalpa and Rekong Peo run every 15–20min; there are three daily buses to Shimla (7.40am, 11.30am & 2.30pm) and one to Sangla and Chitkul (8.30am).

ACCOMMODATION AND EATING

Apart from the hotel **restaurants**, there are just a few basic *dhabas* and tea houses. Hotel prices double in May, June and October.

Apple Pie On the upper road ☎88606 88496, ⊛hotel applepie.com. Friendly place, painted brilliant white and containing three floors of nicely furnished, sizeable rooms with attractive artwork. Good restaurant too. ₹2100

Blue Lotus Guest House In the village centre ☎01786 226001, ✉khokanroy.bluelotus@gmail.com. This mundane concrete block offers the most central budget accommodation in Kalpa, with rooms priced according to their view. The decent restaurant opens later than most. Daily 7am–10.30pm. ₹600

★ **Kinner Villa** On the upper road ☎01786 226006, ⊛kinnervilla.com. Expanded in 2012, this is the biggest resort around, with sleek, refurbished rooms, spotless bathrooms and a grassy lawn out front. Fine restaurant too. ₹2000

Rakpa Regency On the upper road ☎01786 226587/ 80453 25503. Large hotel, popular with holiday-makers from Bengal, set in pleasant grounds. The front rooms have balconies with splendid views and there's a huge upstairs terrace. ₹1000

The Baspa Valley

Hemmed in by the pinnacles of Kinner-Kailash to the north and the high peaks of the Garhwal range to the south, the 70km **River Baspa** rises in the mountain wilderness along the Indo-Tibetan border to flow through what was until recently one of Kinnaur's most beautiful and secluded areas. Much of the lower reaches of the valley below Sangla are now dominated by a massive and ugly hydroelectric plant but beyond Sangla the scenery remains unspoilt. Although the head of Baspa Valley (which is also known as Sangla Valley) is technically closed to tourists, there are still plenty of walking opportunities through side valleys. There are no official tourist offices nor any ATMs or banks that offer exchange in the Baspa/Sangla Valley, although you may be able to pay in foreign currency or exchange small amounts at the pricier hotels.

Sangla

The valley's largest settlement, **SANGLA**, makes an excellent base to visit nearby **Kamru** village, 25 minutes' walk above Sangla, with its warren of lanes and slate-roofed stone houses, and its wood-and-stone gable-roofed **fort**. Tibetan prayer flags flutter in the breeze and the inhabitants retain Buddhist funerary rites, although they are now mostly Hindu and no longer read Tibetan. The inner sanctum of the **temple** below the fort is off-limits to visitors unless a goat is paid for and sacrificed.

ARRIVAL AND DEPARTURE
SANGLA

By bus Sangla is served by 2–3 daily buses from Shimla, Rekong Peo and Kalpa. Two daily buses continue to Chitkul (noon & 2.30pm).

ACCOMMODATION

From late September through October Sangla fills up with Bengali holiday-makers so hotel options are increasing every year; the best **places to stay** are mostly dotted around the village outskirts.

Baspa Guest House Beside the bridge into town ☎ 98058 41254. This moderately attractive building with a flowery courtyard has a variety of attached doubles, the more expensive ones with cable TV, but all at the basic end of the scale. ₹600

Café 42 At the far end of the bazaar ☎ 98203 02881, ✉ cafe42sangla@gmail.com. Two very well-appointed rooms, with plans for expansion. The cosy café offers snacks all day for ₹100–200 and mains such as chicken at lunch and dinner. ₹1200

Igloo Nature Camp 1km north of the village ☎ 88946 10946. The most conveniently located of several luxury eco-camps in the Baspa/Sangla Valley also organizes trekking tours. The spacious Swiss tents have attached bathrooms and there's a large mess tent. Breakfast included. ₹4200

Sangla Resorts 300m south of the village ☎ 01786 242401, ✉ arunbhagat.negi@gmail.com. Perched on a hillock above apple orchards, this pleasant hotel has attached rooms of varying sizes and a dormitory. Dorms ₹200, doubles ₹900

EATING

Ashiana Cafe In the middle of the bazaar ☎ 98058 41254. No-nonsense upstairs restaurant serving a standard range of Indian and Chinese main courses at a snip – non-veg items in the ₹80–100 range. Also open for breakfast. Daily 6am–10pm.

Tibetan Cafe In the middle of the bazaar ☎ 96252 91706. As the name suggests, this tiny place specializes in inexpensive *momos*, *thukpa* and chow mein for just ₹60–80. Two balcony tables overlook the bazaar. Daily 7.30am–8pm.

Chitkul

Twenty-five kilometres beyond Sangla, **CHITKUL** is as far up the valley as you can officially go, although the checkpoint at the far end of the village that marks the start of the guarded Inner Line is now unmanned and guides sometimes lead trekkers further up the valley. However, it's still better not to wander too far unaccompanied. Visible above the village, which is set on a rise with dramatic views of the opening valley, a trail winds steeply up to a huge saddle below the **Charang La pass** – the route of the Kinner-Kailash pilgrimage circuit (see page 422).

ARRIVAL AND DEPARTURE   CHITKUL

By bus There are several daily buses to Sangla (1hr), of which at least one or two go on to Rekong Peo and even Kalpa.

ACCOMMODATION AND EATING

★ **The Kinner Heights** Opposite the bus stand ☎ 98056 28801. Friendly Nepali-run place with fairly simple but clean attached rooms and uninterrupted views along the valley. No wi-fi. ₹800

Shahensha Resort Far end of the village ☎ 98168 03505. One of the new breed of resorts, painted blue and white, with smart rooms and balconies giving views along the river valley. No wi-fi. ₹1500

Thakur Guesthouse Near the bus stand ☎ 89882 09604. Old-fashioned wooden building with a mixture of pretty basic rooms, some of which are attached. The upper storey affords fine views. No wi-fi. ₹400/₹700

Upper Kinnaur

Inner Line permits are required beyond the dull hamlet of **Spillo** for **upper Kinnaur**, the remote region east of Rekong Peo. Sparsely inhabited and increasingly bare, by the time the NH-22 has crossed the metal bridge beyond **Pooh** and starts to spiral up the greyish-brown slopes towards **Nako**, the terrain bears much more resemblance to Spiti or Ladakh than the greener Sutlej Valley.

Pooh and around

Several hours by road from Rekong Peo and within a day's hike of the frontier, the small town of **POOH**, perched 4km above the main road, is the first main settlement you encounter. Evidence from inscriptions suggest that Pooh was, in the eleventh century, an important trading centre that fell under the influence of the Tibetan

6

kingdom of Guge when the Great Translator, Rinchen Zangpo, travelled through the area. The temple here is devoted to Sakyamuni, with wooden columns supporting a high ceiling and a circumambulatory path around the altar.

Beyond Pooh, the road bends north, crossing the muddy Sutlej for the last time at **Khab**, where it meets the turquoise waters of River Spiti. To the northeast, Kinnaur's highest peak, **Leo Pargial II** (6770m), rises in a near-vertical 4000m wall which marks the border with Tibet and overlooks the old Indo-Tibet road at the **Shipki La pass** (5569m). The NH-22 continues north through the barren wastes of the Hanglang Valley, very similar to parts of Ladakh.

ARRIVAL AND DEPARTURE
POOH AND AROUND

By bus Very few buses go right up to Pooh, though you can get off anywhere along the main road below.

ACCOMMODATION

Om Guest House In the village centre ☏ 01785 232601. The best of the extremely limited choice here, the *Om* has decent rooms, two dorms and a good restaurant serving all the usual Indian and Chinese favourites. No wi-fi. Dorms ₹300, doubles ₹800

Nako

NAKO, the valley's largest village, nestling high above the River Spiti at 3640m around a small artificial **lake**, is now on the main Rekong Peo–Kaza road, which was redirected uphill to avoid the infamous **Malling Slide**. Unfortunately, the road still gets blocked during bad weather, as do many other points on the Kinnaur–Spiti circuit. In the northwest corner of the village, the eleventh-century complex of the **Nako Chokhor** (arrange entry through the Youth Club tent above the bus stand; ₹50) is attributed to Rinchen Zangpo; although it's in desperate need of restoration, its exquisite interior paintings are comparable to those in Alchi (see page 501). The finest building of all is the Serkhang or "Golden Hall", dedicated to the Tathagatas or Supreme Buddhas.

ARRIVAL AND DEPARTURE
NAKO

By bus/taxi One daily bus and numerous jeeps leave for Kaza via Tabo and for Rekong Peo.

ACCOMMODATION

Lake View Guest House Beside the lake ☏ 01785 236041, ⌨ lakeviewhotel.com. Enjoying by far the most scenic location, the attached rooms in this brightly painted place are fairly simple, but clean and comfortable and large. Buffet breakfast and dinner, plus sublime views. ₹1200

Reo Purguil Near the bus stand ☏ 94594 94111. Best of the central trio of guest-houses, where all rooms have bathrooms (with hot water) and balconies. The restaurant is the best in town too. ₹900

Northwest Himachal

From Shimla the main road winds west and north to the riverside market town of **Mandi**, an important crossroads linking the Kullu Valley and the hills to **the northwest**. The rolling foothills on this side of the state are warmer and more accessible than Himachal's eastern reaches, though less dramatic and considerably lower. The area sees little tourism outside **Dharamsala**, the British hill station turned Tibetan settlement, home to the Dalai Lama. Dharamsala is an excellent base for treks over the soaring Dhauladhar Range to the **Chamba Valley**, which harbours uniquely styled Hindu temples in **Bharmour** and **Chamba**. South of Chamba, the fading hill station of **Dalhousie** still has a certain ex-Raj charm, and is popular with Indian tourists who arrive in droves during the hot season and trek in the surrounding mountains.

The following section traces the River Beas and NH-21 as they weave from Mandi to Dharamsala, linking a string of quiet mountain towns and villages. While most visitors make the six-hour journey to Dharamsala in one go, those with more time can detour to sacred **Rewalsar**, just outside Mandi, or stop in the **Kangra Valley** to pick up the narrow-gauge train that trundles through patchwork fields and light forest to **Kangra**, just an hour away from Dharamsala and jumping-off point for a couple of little-visited places of interest.

Mandi

The junction town of **MANDI**, 158km north of Shimla, straddles the River Beas, its riverside *ghats* dotted with stone temples where sadhus and pilgrims pray. Once a major trading post for Ladakhis heading south – *mandi* means market – the town still bustles with commercial activity, now centred on the attractive **Indira Market** and its sunken garden, in the centre of the town square. A collection of sixteenth-century Nagari-style temples sits above the town on **Tarna Hill**. On the summit is the main Kali temple, decorated with garish paintings of the fierce mother goddess draped in skulls and blood.

6

ARRIVAL AND DEPARTURE   MANDI

By bus The bus stand is 500m across the river on the east bank. There are departures every 30min or so for Rewalsar, Kullu, Manali and Pathankot, roughly hourly for Baijnath, Dharamsala and Shimla, with more frequent connections in Bilaspur.

ACCOMMODATION AND EATING

Evening Plaza South side of the main square ☎ 01905 225123, ✉ malhotralalji@hotmail.com. Typically functional business hotel, which has a range of slightly worn rooms of differing sizes, some with a/c and either bucket hot water or a shower. ₹600

Raj Mahal North side of the main square ☎ 01905 222401, ⊕ rajmahalpalace.com. This period-furnished palace, set in spacious shady gardens on an embankment, has spacious rooms, a good restaurant and an atmospheric gentlemen's bar. ₹1600

The Regent Palms Northeast corner of the main square ☎ 01905 222777. Smart, modern business hotel with spacious, well-furnished rooms. Cool a/c restaurant with subdued lighting, serving ample portions of Indian, Chinese and some Continental cuisine for ₹150–300. Daily 7am–10pm. ₹1800

Shiva South side of the main square ☎ 01905 224211. The interior rooms are mostly windowless and not much cheaper than the far lighter ones facing the square. It's a decent budget option and food is available by room service. ₹500

Rewalsar

If you've any interest in Buddhism it's worth taking a detour to **REWALSAR** (Tso Pema in Tibetan), 24km southeast of Mandi, where three **Tibetan monasteries** (Nyingma, Drikung Kagyu and Drukpa Kagyu) mark an important place of pilgrimage. There are also Sikh and Hindu temples here, all of which draw a steady stream of pilgrims and tourists. The devout complete a *chora* around the small sacred lake and along narrow lanes full of shrines and stalls selling Tibetan curios, before lounging beneath the prayer flags on the lake's grassy fringes.

It's believed that Padmasambhava left many footprints and handprints in rocks and caves up in the hills around the lake, and steep paths lead up from the lake to **caves** that are used today as isolated meditation retreats. Of the three monasteries around the lake, **Tso-Pema Ogyen Heruka Gompa** is the most venerated and atmospheric; check out the tree planted in 1957 by the Dalai Lama, who visited India that year – two years before his exile from Tibet – to celebrate the 2500th anniversary of the Buddha's birth. Towering dramatically over the lake and visually dominating the Rewalsar setting is the large but much newer **Drukpa Kagyu Zigar Gompa**.

For **Hindus**, Rewalsar is regarded as the abode of the sage Lomas, for whose sake the lake was created with waters from the Ganga and Yamuna. Three small temples dedicated to Krishna, Lomas and Shiva, along with a Nandi bull statue and lakeside

6

ghats, reflect Rewalsar's Hindu connections. The voracious carp that scrap for treats thrown into the water by visitors are quite a sight too.

On the west shore, the Sikh **gurudwara** attracts pilgrims retracing the steps of Guru Gobind Singh, who came here in 1702; this is one of the few sites associated with his life in Himachal. To the south a small **sanctuary** protects deer and Himalayan black bears.

ARRIVAL AND DEPARTURE
REWALSAR

By bus There are buses about every 30min from Mandi (1hr). **By taxi** Taxis ply back and forth between Rewalsar and Mandi for around ₹600 and it's easy to organise one to or from Dharamsala (expect to pay around ₹3000).

ACCOMMODATION AND EATING

There are several small but reasonable Tibetan restaurants near the lake, which serve *thukpa*, *momos* and noodles, and *dhabas* along the main road serving north Indian food.

CG Homestay Near the post office, south of the lakeshore ☏ 09882 744092. A real homestay with a welcoming family and home-cooked meals cooked with produce from the garden. Rooms are simple, but quiet and clean and it's around a 10min walk to the lake. Plenty of local info on offer, too. Check ahead about what's included in the rate. ₹700

Emaho Café At the entrance to Drikung Kagyu Gompa ☏ 01905 240243. Colourful modern café run by monks, offering a tasty range of cakes and snacks, as well as fine teas and coffees. Free wi-fi. Daily 9am–9pm.

Nyingma Gompa Northwest lakeshore ☏ 01905 280226. Pretty basic cell-like rooms, many with lake views and some with attached bathrooms, in the peaceful monastery buildings. No wi-fi. ₹400

The Tourist Inn A short way back from the north shore ☏ 01905 240252, ✉ rewalsar@hptdc.in. Both blocks of this HPTDC hotel have fairly comfortable rooms with hot showers, although there are no views. ₹600

Baijnath

Although the nondescript village of **Joginder Nagar** is the eastern terminal of the Kangra Valley Railway, **BAIJNATH**, 21km further northwest, is perhaps a better spot to pick up the toy train, as more services originate here and it gives you a chance to visit the **Baidyanath Shiva temple**, parts of which are intricately carved and believed to date from 804 AD.

Kangra and around

Although most travellers bypass **KANGRA** on their way to Dharamsala, 18km further north, it's worth a brief detour. Kangra's crumbling, overgrown **fort** (daily 9am–5pm; ₹300 [₹150] with audio guide) was damaged by an earthquake in 1905 and is now inhabited by screeching green parrots that flit through a few simple temples still tended by priests. High gates, some British-built, span a cobbled path to the deserted ramparts. To get here, head 3km south on the road to Jawalamukhi, then turn up the 1km access road just before the bridge.

Masrur

Daily sunrise–sunset • ₹100 (₹5)

Thirty-five kilometres southwest of Kangra, the tiny village of **MASRUR** is the only place in the Himalayas with **rock-cut Hindu temples** similar to, though nowhere near as impressive or well-preserved, those at Ellora in Maharashtra (see page 660). The fifteen temples, devoted to Ram, Lakshman and Sita, were hewn from natural rock in the ninth and tenth centuries.

Jawalamukhi

A simple whitewashed temple in the otherwise nondescript town of **JAWALAMUKHI**, 35km south of Kangra, protects one of north India's most important Hindu shrines.

6

THE KANGRA VALLEY RAILWAY

India has five of the twenty or so vintage "toy trains" or narrow-gauge mountain railways in the world – three in the Himalayas and two of these in Himachal Pradesh. Most famous is the Kalka–Shimla line (see page 415), but the little-known 163km **Kangra Valley Railway** is also a magnificent engineering feat. Unlike the Kalka line, with its 103 tunnels and tortuous switchbacks, engineers of this route preferred bridges – 950 in all, many of which are still considered masterpieces – that give passengers uninterrupted views all the way from Pathankot to Joginder Nagar. Although it's slower than the equivalent road journey, the scenery along the way is far more impressive, particularly the stretch between Kangra and Mangwal.

There are six trains daily from Pathankot, departing between 2.15am and 5.45pm; four terminate at Baijnath (6hr 30min–7hr), while two go all the way to Joginder Nagar (10hr). In the opposite direction there are departures from Joginder Nagar at 8am and 12.20pm, and four more from Baijnath between 4.15am and 5.30pm. All services pass through Kangra.

The sanctuary, crowned with a squat golden spire, contains a natural blue gas flame emitted from the earth, revered as a manifestation of the goddess of fire, Jawalamukhi.

ARRIVAL AND DEPARTURE

KANGRA AND AROUND

By bus Buses from all over the Kangra Valley and further afield pull into the bus stand 1km north of the town centre, where there are frequent connections to Dharamsala, as well as hourly services to both Masrur and Jawalamukhi.

By toy train Kangra can also be reached from Pathankot (see page 531) and Joginder Nagar by the narrow-gauge railway (see page 430).

ACCOMMODATION AND EATING

Jwalaji On the outskirts of Jawalamukhi ☎01970 222280, ✉jawalaji@hptdc.in. One of the better HPTDC hotels, with a range of spacious rooms, a dormitory, a full-service restaurant and a snack bar. Dorms ₹200, doubles ₹1400

Preet On the road to the bus stand, Kangra ☎01892 265260. The best rooms at this functional hotel are on the first floor, alongside a cosy little terrace. The restaurant is quite average. ₹600

Dharamsala and McLeod Ganj

Home to the Dalai Lama and Tibetan government in exile, and starting point for some exhilarating treks into the high Himalayas, **DHARAMSALA**, or more correctly, its upper town **McLEOD GANJ**, is one of Himachal's most irresistible destinations. Spread across wooded ridges beneath the stark rock faces of the Dhauladhar Range, the town is divided into two distinct and separate sections, separated by 10km of perilously twisting road and almost 1000m in altitude. Originally a British hill station, **McLeod Ganj** has been transformed by the influx of **Tibetan refugees** fleeing Chinese oppression in their homeland. Tibetan influence here is subsequently very strong, with temples, schools, monasteries, nunneries, meditation centres and the most extensive library of Tibetan history and religion. As well as playing host to hordes of foreign and domestic tourists, McLeod Ganj is a place of pilgrimage that attracts Buddhists and interested parties from all over the world, including Hollywood celebrities such as Richard Gere and Uma Thurman. Many people visit India specifically to come here, and its relaxed and friendly atmosphere can make it difficult to leave.

Despite heavy snows and low **temperatures** between December and March, McLeod Ganj receives visitors throughout the year. Summer brings torrential rains – this being the second wettest place in India – that return in bursts for much of the year. Daytime temperatures can be high, but you'll need warm clothes for the chilly nights.

Dharamsala

It's easy to see why most visitors bypass **Dharamsala** itself, a haphazard jumble of shops, offices and houses that spreads along several kilometres of gradually rising road. Apart from a couple of moderately lively bazaars, the only place of interest is the **Museum of Kangra Art** (Tues–Sun 10am–5pm; ₹50 [₹10]), which contains a small collection of Kangra miniatures and some modern art.

McLeod Ganj and around

The ever-expanding settlement of **McLeod Ganj** extends along a pine-covered ridge with valley views below and the near vertical walls of the Dhauladhar Range towering behind. Despite being named after David McLeod, the Lieutenant Governor of Punjab when the hill station was founded in 1848, little evidence of British occupation remains. The focal point of McLeod Ganj is its Buddhist **temple**, ringed with spinning red-and-gold prayer wheels. Today, Indian residents are outnumbered by Tibetans, who bedeck their ramshackle buildings with fluttering prayer flags: McLeod Ganj is not simply a political haven for them, but also home to their spiritual leader, the Dalai Lama, and to the Tibetan government in exile.

It's easy to **find your way around** McLeod Ganj. At its northern end, the main road up from Dharamsala arrives at a small chowk, from which all other roads radiate. These include Temple Road and Jogiwara Road, which run closely parallel and constitute a double main strip, before splitting up and leading to the Dalai Lama's residence and main jeep route to Dharamsala respectively. Other smaller roads lead northeast to the village of Dharamkot, the Tushita Retreat Meditation Centre and to Dal Lake, and east to the hamlet of Bhagsu.

The Dalai Lama's Residence

Temple Rd

The Dalai Lama settled temporarily in McLeod Ganj in 1960; five and a half decades later he's still here, and his **Residence** on the south edge of town has become his permanent home in exile. His own quarters are modest and most of the walled compound overhanging the valley

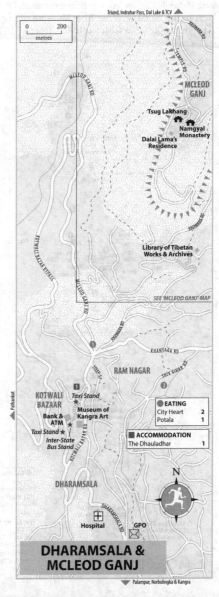

6

is taken up by government offices. In front of the private enclosure, Dharamsala's main Buddhist temple, **Tsug Lakhang**, shelters images of Sakyamuni (the historical Buddha), Padmasambhava (who introduced Buddhism to Tibet) and Avalokitesvara (the *bodhisattva* of compassion) seated in meditation postures, surrounded by offerings from devotees. Most afternoons (barring Sunday) monks from the nearby **Namgyal monastery** hold fierce but disciplined debates in the courtyard opposite the temple.

The Tibet Museum

Temple Rd • Tues–Fri & Sun 9am–5pm • Free; documentary screenings ₹10

Next to the monastery, the **Tibet Museum** displays in graphic detail the plight of the Tibetan people since China invaded Tibet in 1950. Using photographs and video clips,

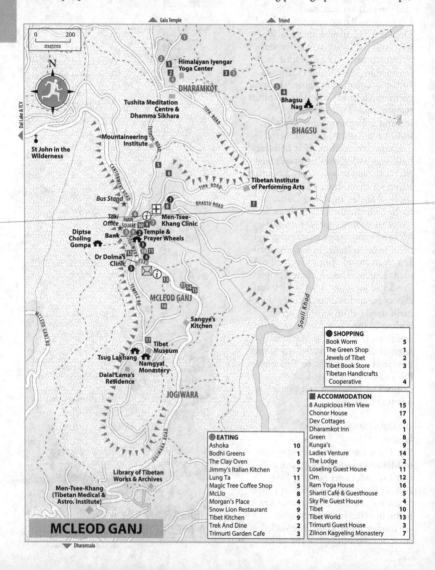

SHOPPING

Book Worm	5
The Green Shop	1
Jewels of Tibet	2
Tibet Book Store	3
Tibetan Handicrafts Cooperative	4

ACCOMMODATION

8 Auspicious Him View	15
Chonor House	17
Dev Cottages	6
Dharamkot Inn	1
Green	8
Kunga's	9
Ladies Venture	14
The Lodge	2
Loseling Guest House	11
Om	12
Ram Yoga House	16
Shanti Café & Guesthouse	5
Sky Pie Guest House	4
Tibet	10
Tibet World	13
Trimurti Guest House	3
Zilnon Kagyeling Monastery	7

EATING

Ashoka	10
Bodhi Greens	1
The Clay Oven	6
Jimmy's Italian Kitchen	7
Lung Ta	11
Magic Tree Coffee Shop	5
McLlo	8
Morgan's Place	4
Snow Lion Restaurant	9
Tibet Kitchen	3
Trek And Dine	2
Trimurti Garden Cafe	3

MCLEOD GANJ

MEETING HIS HOLINESS THE DALAI LAMA

The **Dalai Lama** is in great demand. Tibetans fleeing their homeland come to him for blessing and reassurance; monks and nuns from all over India and Nepal look to him for spiritual guidance; and an ever-increasing number of Westerners arrive in Dharamsala hoping for a moment of his attention. As His Holiness no longer conducts public audiences, most visitors should count on attending one of his **public teachings**, which are advertised well in advance by the Office of His Holiness The Dalai Lama (Thekchen Choeling, McLeod Ganj; ☎01892 221343, ⓦdalailama.com). **Private audiences** are granted to a select few and can only be arranged by writing at least four months in advance. The Dalai Lama's secretary receives hundreds of such letters each day and each case is reviewed on its merits.

6

the self-guided tour describes how Tibetan freedom fighters, backed by the CIA, waged an impossible guerrilla war against China that lasted into the 1970s. The upstairs hall features profiles of the museum curators – all refugees and ex-political prisoners – and a memorial to the 1.2 million Tibetans who have died in the conflict.

Kora Circuit

Open 24hr • Free

After paying homage to the Buddha inside, devotees complete a *kora*, a circumambulation of the temple complex (clockwise, starting at the trailhead downhill and to the left of the temple entrance), turning the numerous prayer wheels to send prayers out in all directions. Tibetan prayer flags flutter in the breeze in the hushed forest, and it feels a million miles from the clamour of town.

Library of Tibetan Works and Archives

Jogiwara Rd • Mon–Sat 9am–1pm & 2–5pm; closed 2nd & 4th Sat of month • Museum ₹10 • ☎01892 222467, ⓦtibetanlibrary.org

The **Library of Tibetan Works and Archives** has one of the world's most extensive collections of original Tibetan manuscripts of sacred texts and prayers, books on all aspects of Tibet, information on Indian culture and architecture and a rich archive of historical photos. Decorated with bright Tibetan motifs, it is housed in the Tibetan Central Administration compound, below the southern end of McLeod Ganj. Tibetan language and philosophy **courses** are held each weekday, and a small **museum** on the first floor of the library displays Buddhist statues, finely moulded bronzes and mandalas (symmetrical images, used in meditation to symbolize spiritual journeys and the pattern of the universe).

Men-Tsee-Khang (Tibetan Medical & Astro. Institute)

Jogiwara Rd • Daily 9am–1pm & 2–5pm • Free • Museum ₹5 • ☎01892 223113, ⓦmen-tsee-khang.org

Just down the road from the library compound, the small **Men-Tsee-Khang (Tibetan Medical & Astro. Institute)** is staffed by monks who diagnose symptoms by examining the eyes, pulse and urine, and prescribe pills made of herbs, precious stones and sometimes animal products, mixed on particularly auspicious lunar dates. You can also have your horoscope prepared here but you need to know the exact time you were born and have at least five thousand rupees to spare. A small but fascinating on-site **museum** has displays on Tibetan medicine, as well as related *thangkas* and medical specimens. There's a smaller clinic on the Dharamkot side of McLeod Ganj.

Dharamkot and around

From the Dhamma Sikhara the road continues to **Dharamkot**, starting point for walks to **Triund** (2975m) and treks over the high passes to the Chamba Valley. Taking one of the paths down through the wooded slopes north of the main road to Dharamkot brings you to the small, murky **Dal Lake**, the scene of an animal fair and Shaivite festival in September. It stands behind the **Tibetan Children's Village** (TCV), a huge

6

complex providing education and training in traditional handicrafts for around two thousand students, many of whom are orphans or have been brought to safety by parents who have returned to Tibet.

Dharamkot itself has grown in recent years and become a particular favourite hangout with Israeli travellers, offering an increasing number of cheap guesthouses and chill-out cafés from which to enjoy the scenery. To the south, the creeping development has almost joined the village to the upper reaches of much busier Bhagsu.

Tushita Meditation Centre and Dhamma Sikhara

Tushita Rd • **Tushita** Mon–Sat 9.30–11.30am & 12.30–4pm • ☎ 89881 60988, ⓦ tushita.info • **Dhamma Sikhara** Registration Mon–Sat 4–5pm • ☎ 01892 221309/ 09218 414051, ⓦ sikhara.dhamma.org

Continuing up the road from the Mountaineering Institute you approach two Buddhist retreat centres, both beautifully situated in the same peaceful neck of the woods (literally): the **Tushita Meditation Centre** was founded in 1972 by Lama Thubten Zopa Rinpoche, while nearby is **Dhamma Sikhara**, a Theravada Vipassana centre. Meditation courses and drop-in sessions are held at both centres; there's an hour-long morning guided mediation at Tushita (9.30am).

Bhagsu

Bhagsu Road heads east from McLeod Ganj's main square, skirting the hillside for 2km before reaching the village of **Bhagsu** with its ancient Shiva temple. The last few years have seen big changes here, with the construction of numerous hotels catering primarily for the domestic tourist market. Consequently, it's become too busy for the taste of many foreigners, although the new string of cafés lining the road up the hill are still popular hangouts, while the older ones near the temple complex are

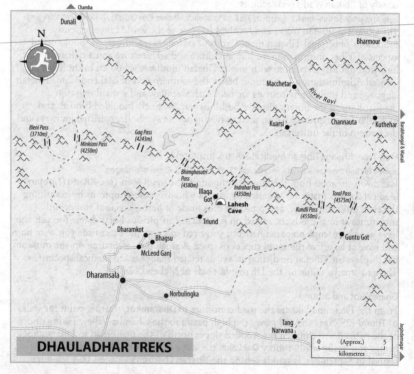

DHAULADHAR TREKS

TREKKING FROM DHARAMSALA

Dharamsala is one of the most popular starting points for **treks** over the rocky ridges of the Dhauladhar Range, which rise steeply from the Kangra Valley to 4600m. Trails pass through forests of deodar, pine, oak and rhododendron, cross streams and rivers and wind along vertiginous cliff tracks passing the occasional lake waterfall and glacier. You can easily tackle the well-worn path to Triund by yourself, but for longer treks, unless you are very experienced you'll need a guide, as the routes are steep and memorial stones testify to those who didn't make it. Despite the availability of rough huts and caves, it's best to take a tent. The best **season** to trek here is from September to November, when the worst of the monsoon is over and before it gets too cold. The **Mountaineering Institute** on the road to Dharamkot (Tushita Rd; Mon–Sat 10am–1.30pm & 2–5pm; closed 2nd Sat of month; ☎01892 221787) provides information on the region, including books and maps on the Dhauladhar Range, and can help arrange guides and porters: winter climbing should only be attempted by mountaineers experienced in using crampons and ice axes.

DHARAMSALA TO TRIUND

A popular outing from Dharamsala is the one-day trek to **Triund**, which is steep and hard going in places, but the trail is easy to follow and there are tea shops dotted along the way. Take an auto-rickshaw or taxi from Dharamshala to Dharamkot and – with the entrance to Tushita Meditation Centre on your left and the water tank on your right – follow the narrow road 50m around the back of the tank to find the trailhead. The path winds through a shady pine forest for thirty minutes before coming out on the rough jeep road to Gallu Devi Temple and the surrounding tea shops (open daily from around 7am). The trail then goes on to navigate steep rocky terrain for 9km to a grassy plateau at Triund, with its astonishing and unexpected view of the Dhauladhar Range. Most people are content to take it easy here, and there are rudimentary camps if you wish to stay overnight, but it's possible to push up to the snowline and still get back in one day. Avoid walking around the rocks behind the camps, as sadly, a lot of the area is used by tourists as an outdoor toilet.

DHARAMSALA TO CHAMBA OVER INDRAHAR PASS

The most frequented route from Dharamsala to the Chamba Valley, over the **Indrahar Pass** (4350m), is arduous in places, but most trekkers manage it in around five days. The first section is the 3–4 hours from Dharamkot to Triund (see above). From here the path climbs to **Laqa Got**, and then on a seriously steep section up to the knife-edged Indrahar Pass where, weather permitting, you'll enjoy breathtaking views south to the plains and north to the snowy Pir Panjal peaks and Greater Himalayas. The descent is difficult in places and will take you via the Gaddi villages of **Kuarsi** and **Channauta** to the main road, from where you can pick up transport to Bharmour and Chamba by road.

OTHER ROUTES FROM DHARAMSALA TO CHAMBA

Several **other routes** cross the Dhauladhar Range, including the **Toral Pass** (4575m) which starts from **Tang Narwana** (1150m), 10km from Dharamsala. The most difficult route north is the five- or six-day trek across **Bhimghasutri Pass** (4580m), covering near-vertical rocky ascents, sharp cliffs and dangerous gorges. A much easier four- or five-day trek from Dharamsala crosses **Bleni Pass** (3710m) in the milder ranges to the northwest, weaving through alpine pastures and woods and crossing a few streams, before terminating at **Dunali**, on the Chamba road.

frequented more by Indian tourists and pilgrims. Beyond the temple a path meanders up the boulder-strewn slopes of a small stream up to a **waterfall**. If you're interested in studying tabla (and sitar or flute), contact Ashoka at the *Trimurti Guest House* (see page 438); he runs the **Trimurti International Music School** from his home. Note that in the past there have been occasional **attacks** on women walking between Bhagsu and McLeod Ganj, usually at night.

Tibetan Institute of Performing Arts

Mon–Sat 9am–noon & 1–5pm, closed 2nd & 4th Sat of month • ☎ 01892 221478, ⓦ tipa.asia

The **Tibetan Institute of Performing Arts** was founded in 1959 to preserve the Tibetan identity in exile. Around 150 people live on its campus, in the forests above McLeod Ganj overlooking Bhagsu, including artists, teachers, musicians and administrators. The TIPA troupe perform traditional *lhamo* operas, which derive from ancient masked dance dramas, and have played a morale-building role at Tibetan refugee camps throughout India, while also sharing Tibet's cultural heritage with international audiences. Visit its office or check online for information on upcoming events and tours.

The Norbulingka Institute

8km from Dharamsala, near the village of Sidpur • Daily shuttle buses from *Chonor House* (see page 437), ₹110 (₹50), free guided tour on request • Daily 9am–5.30pm (workshops & offices closed Sun & second Sat of month) • ☎ 01892 246402, ⓦ norbulingka.org

The **Norbulingka Institute** is dedicated to preserving literary and artistic Tibetan culture. The complex of Tibetan-style buildings, built in 1985, is set amid peaceful Japanese gardens, and centres on the two-storey **Deden Tsuglakhang temple**, which houses 1173 images of the Buddha and frescoes of the fourteen Dalai Lamas in the upper gallery. The gilded copper statue of Sakyamuni in the hall downstairs is the largest of its kind outside Tibet. Elsewhere in the complex, the **Losel Doll Museum** shows colourful dioramas packed with traditionally clothed dolls and there's a delightful café.

ARRIVAL AND DEPARTURE

MCLEOD GANJ AND DHARAMSALA

By plane Dharamsala's airport is 12km south at Gaggal. There are two daily flights to Delhi (1hr 45min). A taxi between the airport and McLeod Ganj costs ₹900.

By bus State-run buses from Gaggal (every 30min; 30min), Shimla (4 daily; 10–11hr), Manali (3 daily; 10hr), Mandi (4 daily; 8–9hr), Pathankot (nearest railhead; every 30min; 3hr), Kangra (every 30min; 30min) and Delhi (6–8 daily; 15–16hr) pull into the bus stand on the south side of Dharamsala, though a very few private and deluxe buses from Delhi and Manali continue to McLeod Ganj.

GETTING AROUND

By taxi A shared minibus (₹15) between McLeod Ganj and Dharamsala takes just 15min. Taxi unions have fixed prices and a vehicle from McLeod Ganj to Dharamsala costs ₹250. Auto-rickshaws travel frequently from McLeod Ganj Bus Stand to Bhagsu (₹50) and the chai shop at Dharamkot (₹70).

By bus From 7.45am onwards numerous buses run between Dharamsala and McLeod Ganj (30min).

On foot To reach McLeod Ganj from Dharamsala, there is a steep 3km track that starts from the end of Temple Rd, passing the Tibetan Library and Secretariat.

By motorbike Two-wheelers can be rented from some agents, such as Himalayan Journey (see page 439); a moped costs around ₹400/day, an Enfield Bullet ₹800/day.

INFORMATION

Tourist information McLeod Ganj's tourist office (Mon–Fri 10am–5pm, Sat 10am–2pm), on South End, provides basic accommodation and transport information. A good source of general info, news and local listings is ⓦ mcllo. com or the free monthly news sheet *Contact*.

Tibetan Secretariat An information centre in Dharamsala's Tibetan Secretariat, beside the entrance to the compound, provides up-to-date news about the Tibetan community in Tibet and around the world.

ACTIVITIES

Numerous courses are available in McLeod Ganj, including dharma teachings, Tibetan language, Hindi, ancient Thai massage, yoga, tabla, karate, Xi Gung, Tai Chi, reiki, and Indian vegetarian and Tibetan cookery.

Buddhism and Tibetan language Free classes on dharma are given in translation by Buddhist monks from 11am until noon most weekdays at the Library of Tibetan Works and Archives. Philosophy courses and three-month Tibetan language courses (beginning March, June & Sept) are also run from the library (contact the Secretary for Tibetan Studies; ☎ 01892 222467).

Cookery courses Several places, such as *Sangye's Kitchen* (daily 10am–noon & 4–6pm; ₹300; ☎ 98161 64540) near the post office on Jogiwara Rd, offer Tibetan cooking lessons.

Meditation Tushita Meditation Centre has drop in meditation sessions (Mon–Sat 9.30am) and organises Tibetan Buddhist meditation courses and retreats (ⓦtushita.info). Courses range from short retreats of eight to ten days to an intensive three-month summer purification retreat (Vajrasattva). The Dhamma Sikhara Vipassana Centre (ⓦdhamma.org), next door, follows teachings more akin to Theravada Buddhism. It runs ten-day silent retreats and daily sittings.

Volunteering An excellent resource for a variety of volunteer jobs is Volunteer Tibet (ⓦvolunteertibet.org), whose office is opposite the Yong Ling School, Jogiwara Rd on the left past the post office. It welcomes volunteer teachers.

Yoga The Himalayan Iyengar Yoga Centre (ⓦhiyogacentre. com) in Dharamkot runs five-day courses in Hatha yoga, starting every Weds, mid-March to Oct, as well as longer retreats. Drop-in 1hr yoga lessons, taught by volunteers, take place at 9am & 5pm Mon–Fri at Tibet World (see page 437).

ACCOMMODATION

Finding accommodation is only a problem during Losar, the Tibetan New Year (Feb/March). Almost all foreign visitors stay in the upper town, **McLeod Ganj**, so there is little reason to stay in **Dharamsala** itself. Those planning long-term stays often head to the small settlements of **Bhagsu** or more peaceful **Dharamkot**, where there is a mixture of rooms in family houses and a growing number of hotels, serving Indian tourists and hippie travellers.

MCLEOD GANJ

8 Auspicious Him View Jogiwara Rd ☎01892 220567, ⓦ8aushimview.com; map p.432. Fifteen spotless rooms, tastefully decorated with Tibetan art and wood panelling, in a spanking-new block. Café and juice bar downstairs. Breakfast included. ₹3000

★**Chonor House** Temple Rd ☎01892 221006, ⓦnorbulingka.org; map p.432. Part of the Norbulingka Institute for Tibetan Culture, with very well presented rooms decorated by artists, combining traditional Tibetan decor with modern comfort. There's also wi-fi and an excellent restaurant with garden seating. All proceeds go to Norbulingka. ₹4500

Green Bhagsu Rd ☎01892 221200, ⓦgreenhotel.in; map p.432. Wide range of well-kept, comfortable rooms, with valley views, a good restaurant and on-site herbal products shop. Deservedly popular for being one of the better backpacker havens. ₹1300

Kunga's Bhagsu Rd ☎01892 221180; map p.432. Clean and centrally located with some non-attached rooms and a fantastic sun deck; larger rooms and suites are spacious and light, with big balconies. Views aside, the best thing about this place is *Nick's Italian Restaurant*, which the rooms are above and below – the newer block is below. ₹1800

Ladies Venture Jogiwara Rd ☎98162 35648, ⓔshantiazad@yahoo.co.in; map p.432. Well-appointed rooms of varying size, some with shared bathrooms, in a welcoming budget hotel. Quiet location but questionable cleanliness, especially in the dorm. Fixed price year-round. Dorms ₹250, doubles ₹400/₹600

Loseling Guest House Off Jogiwara Rd ☎01892 220085; map p.432. Simple monastery-owned lodge, plain and reasonably well maintained with good views from an open roof terrace. Upstairs rooms are best and most in demand. Staff are sometimes extremely uncommunicative. No wi-fi. ₹500

Om Down the path from the main chowk ☎98163 29985, ⓔdorpan68@yahoo.com; map p.432. Simple, quiet and very friendly lodge on the western edge of town. A variety of rooms; the cheapest ones share squat toilet bathrooms and hot showers. The upper terrace and sociable restaurant are popular spots at sunset. ₹400/₹800

Ram Yoga House Surya Hotel Rd, behind Norbu House ☎98164 09053, ⓦramyogahouse.com; map p.432. A modern block with large bright rooms and unbeatable views from the deluxe options (along with a kitchenette). Service can be grudging and the reality doesn't meet the chilled out hippie pictures online – there was no yoga when we visited, but you could use the rooftop room for practice. Ring ahead to be met on arrival, as it's hard to find. ₹1000

Shanti Café & Guesthouse Tushita Rd ☎98053 10685, ⓦfacebook.com/shantishanticafe/; map p.432. Very welcoming lodge with a few colourful, compact rooms, a couple of which have attached bathrooms. The café is nicely decorated and has chill-out cushions. ₹400/₹600

Tibet Bhagsu Rd ☎01892 221426, ⓦhoteltibetdhasa. com; map p.432. Popular and central hotel with the superb *Snow Lion* restaurant (see page 438); the downstairs valley-facing rooms offer the best value. Prices are fixed all year. ₹1000

Tibet World Jogiwara Rd ☎98169 99928, ⓦtibetworld. org; map p.432. This guesthouse-cum-cultural centre has simple rooms with twin beds, the costlier ones with great views. Various activities, yoga sessions and cultural events are organized. ₹800

Zilnon Kagyeling Monastery Bhagsu Rd ☎98827 45575, ⓔzklmonastery77@gmail.com; map p.432. Basic and extremely cheap single and double rooms with shared facilities in an active *gompa*. Great quiet location and rooftop café. No wi-fi. ₹300

BHAGSU

★**Sky Pie Guest House** Off the left turning as you approach the temple ☎01892 220497, ⓦskypie guesthouse.in; map p.432. Friendly and lively place with standard attached budget rooms in the old block and smarter ones with TV and balconies in the new block. ₹600

Trimurti Guest House Upper Bhagsu towards Dharamkot ☏01892 221364/ 09816 869144 ⌨trimurti garden.in; map p.432. A few rooms, all with shared bathrooms, in a quiet family place with a lawn, garden café and colourful shrine. The owner runs a small music school, too. ₹600

DHARAMKOT

Dev Cottages Down the path towards Bhagsu from the main junction ☏98164 87080, ⌨devcottage.com; map p.432. Smart and spacious cottages, comfortably furnished and blessed with fine valley views and outdoor space. ₹1800

Dharamkot Inn On the main road through the village ☏01892 221308, ⌨dharamkotinn.com; map p.432.

EATING

While eating options in Dharamsala are fairly perfunctory, McLeod Ganj and its satellites are renowned for relaxed **restaurants** serving traveller staples and Tibetan dishes such as *thukpa* and *momos*, as well as fresh-baked Tibetan bread and cakes. There's not much nightlife but alcohol is available in a few places.

MCLEOD GANJ

Ashoka Jogiwara Rd ☏01892 221589; map p.432. Good spicy Indian food, as well as Chinese, Continental and Israeli dishes are served on two indoor levels and on a pleasant roof terrace for ₹150–300. Try the *karai* chicken. Daily 9am–10.30pm.

The Clay Oven Tipa Rd ☏98161 16862; map p.432. First-floor restaurant with a narrow balcony overlooking the street. You can enjoy decent Nepali, Tibetan, Thai and Italian cuisine here, with *moktuk* (swimming *momos*) for ₹130 or pepperoni pizza for ₹300. Daily 10.30am–10pm.

Jimmy's Italian Kitchen Bhagsu Rd ☏98162 97093; map p.432. Hip Western-style upstairs café decorated with classic film posters. Good salads, baked potatoes, lattes and home-made desserts, when ingredients are available; dinners mainly ₹160–280. Daily 9am–10pm.

Lung Ta Jogiwara Rd ☏01892 220689; map p.432. Japanese vegetarian place with a constantly changing menu that usually includes miso soup, sushi, tempura vegetables and tofu steak; daily set menus ₹200. Profits go to assisting former Tibetan political prisoners. Mon–Sat noon–2.30 & 5.30–8.30pm.

McLlo Main chowk ☏01892 221280; map p.432. Garish, neon-lit building overlooking the square. Large selection of good Western food from ₹150, with more complex dishes, such as baked fish with tomatoes and olives, going for ₹370. The second-floor bar serves beer, local cider, wine and spirits. Daily 11am–midnight.

Sturdy white block with two wings, offering a range of rooms of varying sizes and comfort levels. The pricier upper-storey ones have balconies with superb views. ₹800

★ **The Lodge** Down the path towards Bhagsu from the main junction ☏96251 77478, ⌨thelodgedharamsala. com; map p.432. Almost a boutique-style hotel, with classy furniture and decoration in all rooms, plus big flat-screen TVs. ₹800

DHARAMSALA

The Dhauladhar Off Kotwali Bazaar ☏01892 224926, ✉dharamshala@hptdc.in; map p431. Institutional-feeling HPTDC place with spacious attached rooms with constant hot water and balconies giving superb views over the plains to the south. Plus a good mid-priced restaurant, bar, garden terrace and lawns. ₹1800

★ **Snow Lion Restaurant** Jogiwara Rd ☏01892 221289; map p.432. If you're in need of proper coffee, this place has an entire menu page devoted to freshly brewed beans (starting at ₹60 for espresso). Breakfast is a particular standout, with pancakes, smoothies and all-veggie set breakfasts (big breakfast ₹235). Chilled out jazz soundtrack, comfy booths and efficient service. Daily 7am–9pm.

★ **Tibet Kitchen** Corner of Jogiwara Rd and the main chowk ☏97362 54543; map p.432. Expertly run and stylishly decorated three-level restaurant-cum-café. The huge menu includes pan-Asian noodles, Italian and, most impressively, Bhutanese *datse* dishes such as pork *paa* and others in the spicy cheese *datse* sauce for ₹120–240. Daily 10am–10pm.

BHAGSU

Magic Tree Coffee Shop Up the left turning as you approach the temple ☏97367 27275; map p.432. Cosy little spot with a proper espresso machine, a modest selection of cakes and a mixture of rock and ethnic vibes. Daily 8am–11pm.

Trimurti Garden Cafe Upper Bhagsu towards Dharamkot ☏01892 221364 or ☏09816 869144 ⌨trimurtigarden.in; map p.432. This little hideaway vegetarian cafe is a 15min walk from Bhagsu and surrounded by trees – bring a torch at night. Thalis, salads and homemade bread and cakes are on the menu, plus lassi and herbal tea. You can top up your bottle with filter water, too. Daily 8am–9pm.

DHARAMKOT

Bodhi Greens Near the main junction ☏94184 55066, ⌨facebook.com/bodhigreens; map p.432. Laidback vegan cafe beloved by local yogis. Breakfast is served until noon and you can order a massive fresh fruit bowl with nuts, seeds and coconut cream (₹200) or scrambled tofu (₹140). Later in the day, soups, wraps, Buddha bowls and Indian dishes (₹120–200) are lovingly prepared, or just stop in for a peanut butter shake, *kombucha* or pot of masala chai. Daily 9am–10pm.

★ **Morgan's Place** Down the path towards Bhagsu ☎78338 63447; map p.432. Imaginatively designed place with an outdoor terrace, serving excellent pizza, Indian and Israeli dishes for ₹220–270, plus divine desserts such as apple crumble. Daily 9am–11pm.

Trek And Dine Near the main junction ☎97363 65156; map p.432. Typically colourful spot with wall hangings and a cushioned corner, serving a range of inexpensive

breakfasts, salads, pizza, pasta and Mexican dishes for around ₹200–250. Daily 9am–11pm.

DHARAMSALA

City Heart Near Kotwali Bazaar ☎01892 225290; map p.431. There's a basic ground-floor canteen and slightly more comfortable upstairs room. The food is mainly Bengali and tandoori, with some Chinese cuisine; all dishes around ₹70–220, chicken thali ₹180. Daily 9am–10.30pm.

Potala Near Kotwali Bazaar ☎86793 68859; map p.431. Very authentic Tibetan family restaurant tucked into a tiny upstairs room. Staples such as *thukpa* or *momos* go for just ₹60–100. Daily 9am–9pm.

SHOPPING

Stalls and little shops along the main streets stock Tibetan trinkets, inexpensive warm clothing, incense, prayer bells, rugs and books.

Book Worm South End ☎01892 221465 or ☎94182 23988, ⊛facebook.com/bookworm.mcleod/; map p.432. Small but well-stocked bookshop opposite the tourist office, specializing in Buddhism, language and literature. Daily 9.30am–6pm.

The Green Shop Bhagsu Rd; map p.432. Eco-conscious place, selling recycled painted cards, hand-painted T-shirts, books on the environment and filtered boiled water for ₹10. Tues–Sun 10am–5pm.

Jewels of Tibet Jogiwara Rd ☎01892 220767; map

p.432. This place is crammed with high-quality jewellery, ornaments and other colourful souvenirs such as prayer flags and incense sticks. Daily 10am–7.30pm.

Tibet Book Store Jogiwara Rd ☎01892 221317; map p.432. A good place to browse for works on Tibetan Buddhism and other religions, as well as coffee-table specials, travel titles and novels. Daily 10am–7.30pm.

Tibetan Handicrafts Cooperative Jogiwara Rd ☎01892 221415; map p.432. This large handicrafts shop sells *thangkas* of all sizes, along with prayer flags, local garments, plus various ornaments and Buddhist paraphernalia. Mon–Sat 9.30am–5pm.

DIRECTORY

Banks and exchange The Punjab National Bank (Mon–Fri 10am–2pm, Sat 10am–noon) in McLeod Ganj will change cash, as will the upper branch of State Bank of India in Dharamsala. There are three ATMs and several authorized exchange agencies in McLeod Ganj.

Cinema A tiny cinema on Jogiwara Rd shows Hollywood flicks, sometimes with a Tibetan or Indian theme. There's a more comfortable Gold Cinema (⊛goldcinema.co) in Dharamsala, too.

Donations For enquiries about the Tibetan settlement, call in either at the Welfare Office on Bhagsu Rd in McLeod Ganj or directly at the Reception Centre below the post office,

where donations of clothes, books, blankets and pens for new Tibetan arrivals are always gratefully accepted.

Hospitals The Tibetan Delek Hospital (☎01892 222053, ⊛delekhospital.org/delek), south of the Secretariat, is one of the best hospitals in the state and has Western doctors on call.

Travel agents General agents for all services include Himalayan Journey (☎94154 50940, ⊛himalayanjourney. in), Tibet Tours & Travels (☎01892 221283), both on Jogiwara Rd, Ways Tours & Travels on Temple Rd (☎01892 221910) and Windhorse Tours & Travels on Bhagsu Rd (☎01892 220416, ⊛windhorsetravels.com).

Dalhousie

The quiet, relaxed hill station of **DALHOUSIE** spreads over five low-level hills at the western edge of the Dhauladhar Range. While the town itself, mostly modern hotels interspersed with Raj-era buildings and low-roofed stalls, is unremarkable, the pine-covered slopes around it are intersected with paths and tracks ideal for short, undemanding walks.

Dalhousie owes its name to Lord Dalhousie, Governor General of Punjab (1849–56), who was attracted by the cool climate to establish a sanatorium here for the many British, who, like himself, suffered ill health. Early in the twentieth century, it was

6

a popular alternative to crowded, expensive Shimla, but thereafter declined. Today Dalhousie is a favourite summer retreat for holidaying Punjabis, but receives only a handful of Western tourists, few of whom stay for more than a day or two. A small population of Tibetans has lived here since the Tibet uprising in 1959.

The town is spread over a series of hills with winding roads and steep paths connecting the two focal points, the chowks. **Gandhi Chowk**, with its restaurants and post office, is the busiest section. From here The Mall and Garam Sarak dip and curve 2km to **Subhash Chowk**, at the top end of the largely Muslim Sadar Bazaar. Both chowks have unusual grandstand-style seating, ideal for people-watching. North of here, the bus stand and information office mark the main road out of town.

ARRIVAL AND INFORMATION
DALHOUSIE

By bus Dalhousie is usually approached by bus from Pathankot in the Punjab, 80km southwest (every 30min–1hr; 3hr 30min), or through the Himalayan foothills from Dharamsala (2–3 daily; 6hr) and Shimla (1–2 daily; 13–14hr), both via Nurpur. Transport to Chamba (2hr 15min) usually goes via Banikhet, though four buses also travel via Khajjiar. Taxis to either chowk from the bus stand cost a rather steep ₹100.

Tourist information The tourist information office (Mon–Sat 10am–5pm; ☎01899 242136), 50m from the bus stand, provides transport information.

ACCOMMODATION

Numerous **hotels** cater for Dalhousie's hot-season hordes and it is only between April and June that prices really shoot up.
Crags Garam Sarak Rd, 400m from Subhash Chowk ☎01899 242124, ⓦhotelcrags.com; map p.440. A quiet hotel, run by an old gentleman, with old-fashioned but comfortable wood-partitioned rooms, a large terrace, tasty food (if pre-arranged) and great views down to the plains. ₹1500
Pearl On the hill above Subhash Chowk ☎01899 240269, ⓦhotelpearldalhousie.com; map p.440. Rambling modern hotel with various levels, affording splendid views. The rooms are spacious and colourful, with flat-screen TVs and fridges. Huge discounts on rack rates out of high season. Wi-fi in lobby only. ₹2400
Sky Ways Court Rd, 100m from Subhash Chowk ☎01899 242818; map p.440. Rather characterless concrete building but the fairly large attached rooms with cable TV are good value and have uninterrupted views. ₹800
Youth Hostel 300m behind the dhabas from the bus stand ☎01899 242189, ⓦyouthhosteldalhousie.com; map p.440. Well-organized and extremely clean hostel, which has fifteen-bed dorms and attached doubles. Dorms ₹200, doubles ₹400
Zostel Kholpukhar, 5km from town ☎01139 589006, ⓦzostel.com; map p.440. A 10min drive from Gandhi Chowk

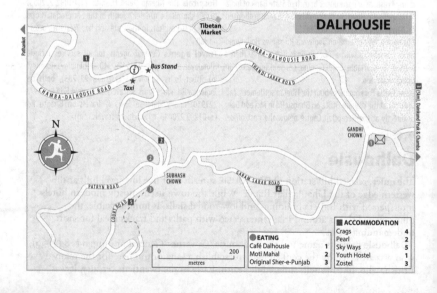

DALHOUSIE

Tibetan Market

CHAMBA–DALHOUSIE ROAD

Bus Stand

THANDI SARAK ROAD

CHAMBA–DALHOUSIE ROAD

Taxi

N

GANDHI CHOWK

PATRYN ROAD

SUBHASH CHOWK

GARAM SARAK ROAD

COURT ROAD

0 — 200
metres

EATING
Café Dalhousie — 1
Moti Mahal — 2
Original Sher-e-Punjab — 3

ACCOMMODATION
Crags — 4
Pearl — 2
Sky Ways — 5
Youth Hostel — 1
Zostel — 3

lands you in the middle of nowhere at this fun, modern hostel with views of snow-clad mountains from the terrace (where they light a bonfire most nights) and a restaurant with board games and a screen for films. There's an en-suite double and four- or eight-bed dorms, all of which get chilly at night. Great place to organise treks and overnight camping. Dorms ₹400, doubles ₹2200

EATING

Most hotels have their own restaurants, numerous *dhabas* crowd the chowks, and there are some independent **places to eat**. If you want to grab something close to the bus stand, head to the Tibetan Market for *momos* from a hole-in-the-wall joint.

Café Dalhousie Gandhi Chowk; map p.440. Atmospheric place with a standard menu of south Indian, Tandoori and Chinese dishes (from ₹100 for a giant dosa to ₹450 for a whole tandoori chicken). Service can be slow, but it's a good spot for people watching. Daily noon–9.30pm.

Moti Mahal Subhash Chowk ☎01899 242134; map p.440. Fairly functional restaurant with indoor and courtyard seating, which does a decent selection of Indian and Chinese dishes such as American chop suey for around ₹200, as well as cheaper snacks like masala dosa. Daily 9am–10pm.

Original Sher-e-Punjab Just below Subhash Chowk ☎01899 242213; map p.440. The most established and reliable of three adjacent establishments with very similar names. Best for rich and tasty non-veg dishes for ₹180–300. Unusually, it has a big screen for sports events. Daily 9am–10pm.

Around Dalhousie

From Dalhousie the road east zigzags through forests to the trailhead for **Dainkund Peak**, which is blanketed with snow in winter, and **Khajjiar**, a popular local day out, before descending through terraced mountain slopes to **Chamba**, perched above the rushing River Ravi. It's a slow and relaxed place with some fascinating temples and a small art museum. **Bharmour**, three hours further east by bus and the final settlement on the road into the mountains, holds even more splendid Hindu temples – both towns make good bases for **treks** into the remote **Pangi Valley**. Note that they are often sunny and warm when Dalhousie is shrouded in rain clouds during monsoon.

Dainkund Peak

The highest peak close to Dalhousie is **Dainkund Peak** at 2755m. It's a steep scramble up from the road to an initial viewpoint and then the trail follows the ridgeline for a couple of miles to the peak and **Pohlani Mata Temple** with its stunning views of the Dhauladhar and Pir Panjal ranges. Most tourists turn around here, but with a guide (or a compass), it's possible to continue three off-the-beaten-track miles to **Jot Pass**, passing the occasional shepherd hut and roughly following a mule trail.

Khajjiar

Heading east towards Chamba, the road descends through deodar forests to the meadow of **Khajjiar** where the small twelfth-century temple of **Khajjinag** looks down over a vast rolling green with a small lake cupped in the centre. Khajjiar is a popular day-trip from Dalhousie for Indian tourists who come to take pony rides. It is also possible to make a stop at **Kalatop Wildlife Sanctuary** (sunrise–sunset; ₹200 per vehicle), 10km before Khajjiar, a thickly forested area that is home to barking deer, Himalayan bear and rich birdlife. The road beyond Khajjiar dips across denuded and terraced hillsides down towards Chamba.

ARRIVAL AND DEPARTURE KHAJJIAR

By bus Prince Travels at the bus stand in Dalhousie runs a tourist bus to Khajjiar and Chamba, departing at 10am and returning to Dalhousie at 6.30pm; in addition, four Chamba-bound state buses travel via Khajjiar (1hr 15min) every day.

Chamba

Shielded on all sides by high mountains, **CHAMBA** was ruled for an entire millennium by kings descended from Raja Sahil Verma, who founded it in 920 AD and named

6

CHAMBA FESTIVALS

Chamba's annual four-day **Suhi Mata Festival**, in early April, commemorates Rani Sunena, the wife of the tenth-century Raja Sahil Verma. A curious legend relates that when water from a nearby stream failed to flow through a channel supposed to divert it to the town, local brahmins advised Raja Verma that either his son or his wife would have to sacrifice themselves. The queen obliged; she was buried alive at the head of the channel, and the water flowed freely. Only women and children participate in the festival, dancing on the *chaugan* before processing with an image of Champavati (Rani Sunena's daughter who gave her name to the town) and banners of the clan's solar emblem to the Suhi Mata temple in the hills behind the town.

Minjar, a week of singing and dancing at the start of August to celebrate the growth of maize, is also peculiar to Chamba. Its climax comes on the last day, when a rowdy procession of locals, Gaddis and Gujjars, dressed in traditional costumes, leaves the palace and snakes down to the riverbank, where bunches of maize are thrown into the water. Before Independence, locals followed a custom whereby a male buffalo was pushed into the river; its drowning was an auspicious sign but if the beast managed to swim to the opposite bank bad fortune was expected for the coming year.

it after his daughter Champavati. Unlike Himachal states further south, it was never formally under Mughal rule and its distinct Hindu culture remained intact until the first roads were built to Dalhousie in 1870. When the state of Himachal Pradesh was formed in 1948, Chamba became the capital. Today, few foreign visitors make it out here, passing through before or after trekking, or stopping off to see the unique **temples**.

The *chaugan*, a large green used for sports, evening strolls and festive celebrations, marks the centre of town, overlooked by the imposing old **Rang Mahal** palace, now a government building.

Bhuri Singh museum

Tues–Sun 10am–5pm • Free

At the south end of the *chaugan*, the **Bhuri Singh museum** holds a reasonable display of local arts and crafts. Its eighteenth- and nineteenth-century **Kangra miniature paintings**, depicting court life, amorous meetings and men and women smoking elaborate hookahs, are much bolder than their Mughal-influenced Rajasthani equivalents. The museum's best feature is its small cache of **rumals**. Made by women since the tenth century, *rumals* are like embroidered paintings, depicting scenes from popular myth. Today just a few women continue this tradition, but a weaving centre in the old palace is attempting to revitalize the art.

The temples

The intimate complex of **Lakshmi Narayan temples**, behind Dogra Bazaar west of the *chaugan*, is of a style found only in Chamba and Bharmour. Three of its six earth-brown temples are dedicated to Vishnu and three to Shiva, all with profusely carved outer walls and curious curved *shikharas*, topped with overhanging wooden canopies and gold pinnacles added in 1678 in defiance of Aurangzeb's order to destroy all Hindu temples in the hill states. Niches in the walls contain images of deities, but many stand empty, some statues lost in the earthquake of 1905 and others looted more recently.

Entering the compound, you're confronted by the largest and oldest temple, built in the tenth century and enshrining a marble idol of Lakshmi Narayan. The buxom maidens flanking the entrance to the sanctuary, each holding a water vessel, represent the goddesses Ganga and Yamuna, while inside a frieze depicts scenes from the Mahabharata and Ramayana. Temples dedicated to Shiva fill the third courtyard. In the inner sanctuary, you'll see sturdy brass images of Shiva, Parvati and Nandi, inlaid with silver and copper brought from mines nearby. Outside the temple complex, **coppersmiths** manufacture curved ceremonial trumpets and brass hookahs.

Of Chamba's other temples, the most intriguing is the tenth-century **Chamunda Devi temple** high above the town in the north, a steep half-hour climb up steps that begin near the bus stand. Decorated with hundreds of heavy brass bells and protecting a fearsome image of the bloodthirsty goddess Chamunda, the temple is built entirely of wood, and commands an excellent view up the Ravi Gorge. Back in town, south of the *chaugan* near the post office, the small, lavishly carved eleventh-century **Harirai temple** contains a smooth brass image of Vaikuntha, the triple-headed aspect of Vishnu.

ARRIVAL AND INFORMATION
CHAMBA

By bus Buses arrive at the cramped bus stand in the north of town.
Destinations Amritsar (1–3 daily; 8hr); Banikhet (every 30min; 2hr); Bharmour (every 30min–1hr; 3hr); Dharmsala (2 daily; 8–9hr); Pathankot (hourly; 5hr 30min); Shimla (2 daily; 15–16hr).

Tourist information The uninspiring tourist office (Mon–Sat 10am–5pm; ☎01899 224002) is part of the *Iravati* complex.

ACCOMMODATION AND EATING

Chamba has a fair number of mostly grubby budget **lodges** and cheap **restaurants**. Try the local speciality, *madhra*, a rich, oily and slightly bitter mix of beans and curd.
Chamunda View Below the bus stand ☎01899 224067. The pick of the budget lodges, having had a recent makeover. The compact attached rooms are comfortable enough. ₹800

City Heart Above the far end of the chaugan ☎01899 225930, ⓦhotelcityheartchamba.com. The best hotel in town is a modern affair, with fairly smart attached rooms

---

TREKS AROUND CHAMBA AND BHARMOUR

The most popular treks from Chamba lead south over the **Dhauladhar** via the Minkiani or Indrahar pass to Dharamsala. **Equipment** can be rented and porters and **guides** hired in Chamba and Bharmour. Mani Mahesh Travels in Chamba (☎01899 222507, ⓦhimalayanlap.com) organizes and equips treks.

TREKS IN THE PANGI VALLEY TO LAHAUL

Few trekkers make it to the spectacular, all but inaccessible **Pangi Valley**, between the soaring Greater Himalayan Range in the north and the Outer Himalayan Range in the south. Several peaks within it have never been climbed, and onward paths lead to Kashmir, Lahaul and Zanskar. The trek to Lahaul takes nine or ten days from **Traila** (90km north of Chamba) via Satraundhi (3500m) over the Sach Pass to Killar, Sach Khas, and finishing in Purthi from where you can take a bus via Tindi to **Udaipur**. Buses run from here to Keylong, capital of Lahaul, for connections northwards to Leh or south over the Rohtang Pass and down to Manali.

TREKS FROM BHARMOUR

Trekking routes lead north from **Bharmour** (2130m) over the Pir Panjal Range across passes that are covered with snow for most of the year. The challenging six- to seven-day trek over **Kalichho Pass** (4990m), "the Abode of Kali", ends in the village of **Triloknath**, whose ancient temple to three-faced Shiva is sacred to both Hindus and Buddhists. Buses run from here to Udaipur, and on to Keylong and Manali.

Another demanding five- to six-day route crosses the **Kugti Pass** (5040m). From **Hadsar**, an hour by bus from Bharmour, the path follows the River Budhil for 12km to **Kugti**, then up to **Kuddi Got**, a vast flower-filled meadow (4000m). The next stage, over the pass, requires crampons and ice axes for an incredibly taxing six-hour climb. Having enjoyed views of the towering peaks of Lahaul and Zanskar from the summit, you plummet once again to the head of a glacier at **Khardu**, continuing down to Raape, 7km from **Shansha**, which is linked to Udaipur and Keylong by road.

Finally, a delightful three-day trek to the sacred lake of **Manimahesh** (4183m) starts from and returns to Hadsar. The awesome Manimahesh Kailash massif, with its permanent glaciers and ice fields, overlooks the lake.

and probably the best restaurant too. ₹2880
The Iravati The nearest corner of the chaugan to the bus stand ☎01899 222671, ✉chamba@hptdc.

in. HPTDC hotel offering comfortable, carpeted attached rooms with cable TV and a reliable, if unexciting, restaurant. ₹1400

Bharmour

BHARMOUR is a delightful small town, made up of of slate-roofed houses, apple trees and small maize fields, draped across a verdant ridge above the river and shadowed on all sides by high snowy peaks. This gem of a place is well worth the effort to travel the extra distance from Chamba and you are likely to be rewarded by being the only foreigner in town. From the bus stand, the main street winds up through the bazaar area to the picturesque main square, which is dominated by the magnificent **Chaurasi temple complex**.

The temples, whose curved *shikharas* dominate the large, neatly paved central square, are more dramatic and better preserved than their rivals at Chamba. The sanctuaries are unlocked only for puja in the mornings and evenings, permitting a glimpse of bold bronze images of Shiva, Narsingh, Ganesh and Parvati, unchanged since their installation in the seventh and eighth centuries when Bharmour was capital of the surrounding mountainous region. A life-sized bronze Nandi bull, draped in a colourful cloth, stands under a shelter in front of the main Shiva temple, while a giant 25m deodar tree towers over the temple from behind.

The complex comes particularly alive around the **evening puja time**, when the whole town seems to crowd into the square, playing games, dancing to impromptu live music, or even taking their sheep for a walk on leads.

ARRIVAL AND INFORMATION BHARMOUR

By bus There are frequent bus connections with Chamba (every 30min–1hr; 3hr), far fewer with Dalhousie.
Tourist information There is no official tourist office

but Bharmour Trekking by the bus stand (☎98164 55505, ⓦbharmourtrekking.com) provides a full trekking service and other useful advice.

ACCOMMODATION AND EATING

Except during the September pilgrimage when everywhere is booked up, you can easily find **rooms** at the handful of hotels and guesthouses. **Food** is mainly available in the string of small *dhabas* and restaurants lining the main road between the bus stand and the square.
Bharmour View Above the main bazaar, near the bus stand ☎01895 225090. Modern(ish) hotel with huge windows offering sweeping views from the pricier front rooms. Oddly, there's a waterfall running through the back

of the building. ₹1000
Chourasi Main bazaar ☎01895 225615. Pretty basic restaurant on the ground floor of a mundane hotel but the veg and non-veg thalis for ₹80–120 are filling enough and there's a ₹60 set breakfast. Daily 8am–10pm.
Kuki Guest House Middle of the main bazaar ☎88949 98015, ⓦfacebook.com/kghotelbharmour84. Friendly place with cosy attached rooms, the front ones having small balconies and partial valley views. ₹800

The Kullu Valley

The majestic **KULLU VALLEY** is cradled by the Pir Panjal to the north, the Parvati Range to the east, and the Barabhangal Range to the west. This is Himachal at its most idyllic, with roaring rivers, pretty mountain villages, orchards and terraced fields, thick pine forests and snow-flecked ridges. The valley extends 80km north from the mouth of the perilously steep and narrow **Larji Gorge**, near Mandi, to the foot of the **Rohtang Pass** – gateway to Lahaul and Ladakh.

In spite of the changes wrought by roads, immigration and, more recently, mass tourism, the Kullu Valley's way of life is maintained in countless timber and stone villages. Known as **paharis** ("hill people"), the locals – high-caste landowning Thakurs, and their (low-caste) sharecropping tenant farmers – still sport the distinctive Kullu cap, or *topi*. The women, meanwhile, wear colourful headscarves and *puttoos* fastened with silver pins and chains. Venture into the lush meadows above the tree line and you'll cross paths with nomadic **Gaddi** shepherds.

Most tourists make a beeline for **Manali** after a gruelling bus ride from Leh or Delhi. With its vast choice of hotels and restaurants, there is something here for everyone. Still an evergreen hippie hangout, it's India's number-one honeymoon spot, and is also popular with outdoors enthusiasts taking advantage of the fine **trekking**. Few travellers actually stay in **Kullu town** and the only real attraction is the annual **Dussehra festival** in October. Flights from Delhi to Bhuntur, just south of Kullu, offer a welcome but weather-dependent alternative to the long overnight bus journeys. To the north, **Naggar**'s castle, ancient temples and relaxed guesthouses make a pleasant change from the claustrophobic concrete of modern Manali, as do **Manikaran**'s sacred hot springs, up the spectacular **Parvati Valley**.

Brief history

Known in the ancient Hindu scriptures as **Kulanthapitha**, or "End of the Habitable World", the Kullu Valley for centuries formed one of the major trade corridors between Central Asia and the Gangetic plains, and local rulers, based first at **Jagatsukh** and later at Naggar and Sultanpur (now Kullu), were able to rake off handsome profits from the through traffic. This trade monopoly, however, also made it a prime target for invasion, and in the eighteenth and early nineteenth centuries the Kullu rajas were forced to repulse attacks by both the raja of Kangra and the Sikhs, before seeing their lands annexed by the British in 1847. Over the following years, colonial families crossed the Jalori Pass from Shimla, making the most of the valley's alpine climate to grow the **apples** that, along with **cannabis** cultivation, today form the mainstay of the rural economy. The first road, built in 1927 to export the fruit, spelled the end of the peace and isolation, prompting many settlers to pack up and leave long before Independence. The population expanded again in the 1950s and 1960s with an influx of **Tibetan refugees**.

Kullu

KULLU, the valley's capital since the mid-seventeenth century, became district headquarters after Independence. Despite being the region's main market and transport hub it has been eclipsed as a tourist centre by Manali, 40km north. Kullu is noisy, polluted and worlds away from the tranquil villages that peer down from the surrounding hillsides, even though a bypass now diverts some of the traffic from the centre. Kullu makes a handy **transport hub** if you're travelling onwards to the Parvati Valley, and there are several **temples** dotted around town, some of which provide fine valley views. In October, when the entire population of the valley comes to town to celebrate **Dussehra**, the city takes on a life of its own. The town is also the centre for the manufacture of the valley's famous **shawls**, handwoven on looms from lamb's wool, angora or pashmina and increasing in price accordingly.

The temples

Kullu's most famous temple, the **Raghunathji Mandir** is home to a sacred statue of Lord Raghunathji, a manifestation of Rama, brought to Kullu by Raja Jagat Singh in the mid-seventeenth century. The raja had been advised by his priests to install the sacred icon here and crown it king in his place, and to this day the Kullu rajas consider themselves mere viceroys of Raghunathji, the most powerful *devta* in the valley and the focus of the Dussehra procession. The temple is tucked away behind the Kullu rajas' **Rupi Palace** above the bus station. Half an hour's walk further up, the paved trail leads beyond the village of Sultanpur to a high ridge, with excellent views over the River Beas to the snow peaks in the east. **Vaishno Devi Mandir**, a small cave-temple that houses an image of the goddess Kali (Durga), is a stiff 3km further on.

6

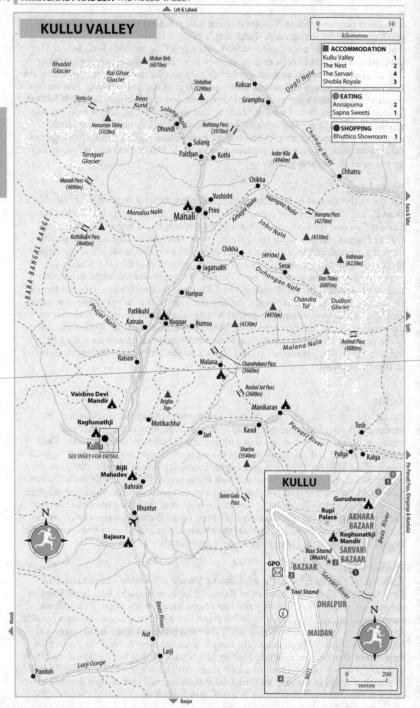

KULLU VALLEY

■ ACCOMMODATION	
Kullu Valley	1
The Nest	2
The Sarvari	4
Shobla Royale	3
● EATING	
Annapurna	2
Sapna Sweets	1
● SHOPPING	
Bhuttico Showroom	1

0   10
kilometres

Leh & Lahaul

Bhadal Glacier
Rai Ghar Glacier
Mukar Beh (6070m)
Shitidhar (5290m)
Koksar
Dugli Nala
Tentu La
Beas Kund
Solang Nala
Gramphu
Chandra River
Hanuman Tibba (5928m)
Dhundi
Rohtang Pass (3978m)
Tantgari Glacier
Solang
Palchan
Kothi
Indar Kila (4940m)
Chhatru
Manali Pass (4880m)
Vashisht
Chikha
Hampta Nala
Manalsu Nala
Prini
Manali
Arbojit Nala
Hampta Pass (4270m)
Jobri Nala
Kaza & Tabo
Kathikuhri Pass (4640m)
Chikha
(4330m)
Serai
(4910m)
Indrasan (6220m)
Jagatsukh
Duhangan Nala
Deo Tibba (6001m)
Haripur
Chandra Tal
Dudion Glacier
Spiti
Patlikuhl
Phojal Nala
Naggar
Rumsu
(4970m)
(4330m)
Katrain
Malana Nala
Animal Pass (4880m)
Raison
Malana
Chandrakani Pass (3660m)
Vaishno Devi Mandir
Rashol Jot Pass (2600m)
Brighu Top
Manikaran
Tosh
Raghunathji
Motikachha
Kullu
SEE INSET FOR DETAIL
Jari
Kasol
Parvati River
Pulga
Kalga
Pin Parvati Pass, Khirganga & Nainital
Bijli Mahadev
Shacha (3540m)
Bahrain
Tainti Galu Pass
Bhuntur
N
Bajaura
Mandi
Aut
Larji
Larji Gorge
Pandoh
Banjar

KULLU

Gurudwara
Rupi Palace
AKHARA BAZAAR
Beas River
Raghunathji Mandir
Bus Stand (Main)
SARVARI BAZAAR
BAZAAR
GPO
Sarvari River
Taxi Stand
DHALPUR
i
MAIDAN
N

0   200
metres

Another important temple, the **Bijli Mahadev Mandir**, stands 8km southeast of town, atop the bluff that overlooks the sacred confluence of the Beas and Parvati rivers. Although it's closer to Bhuntur than Kullu, you have to approach the temple via the Akhara Bazaar–Tapu suspension bridge and a well-worn track south along the left bank of the Beas. Bijli Mahadev is renowned for its extraordinary **lingam**. Bolts of lightning, conducted into the inner sanctum by means of the 20m, trident-tipped pole, are said to periodically shatter the icon, which later, with the help of invocations from the resident pujari, magically reconstitutes itself. From the temple, which has a basic resthouse, there are superb panoramic views of the Parvati and Kullu valleys and Himachal's highest peaks.

6

ARRIVAL AND DEPARTURE   KULLU

By plane The single daily flight to Kullu from Delhi arrives in Bhuntur, 30min south of Kullu by bus.

By bus All long-distance buses pull in at the main bus stand in Sarvari Bazaar, on the north side of the Sarvari River. Local services heading north also drop and pick up passengers at the top of Dhalpur maidan. There are direct services to Manali (1hr 30min) every 15min and hourly via Naggar (2hr), a far more scenic route. In 2017, an eco-friendly electric bus started plying the route between Kullu and Manali and is expected to operate up to four times daily. Frequent southbound buses via Bhuntur pass right outside the airport.

By taxi Taxis to the airport are exorbitant (₹450) and should be booked in the union office (☎01902 222322) on the main road close to the tourist office.

INFORMATION

Tourist information HPTDC's tourist office (daily 10am–6pm, until 9pm April–June; ☎01902 222349), on the west side of Dhalpur maidan, can book tickets on HPTDC's deluxe buses to Delhi, Shimla and Chandigarh.

Permits The District Commissioner's office near Dhalpur maidan (Mon–Sat 10am–5pm, closed 2nd Sat of month; ☎01902 222727) issues Inner Line permits (see page 413) but you need to apply through a travel agent. Try Harisons Travels at Akhara Bazaar (☎01902 224899, ⊛harisonstravels.in).

ACCOMMODATION

Kullu has a reasonable choice of **accommodation**, although prices can double during high season and even quadruple for Dussehra.

Kullu Valley Akhara Bazaar ☎01902 222223, ⊛hotelkulluvalley.com; map p.446. Smart, brightly lit modern hotel, whose rooms are nicely furnished and spacious; most boast bath-tubs. The cheaper ones without tubs are great value. **₹990**

The Nest Next to the bus stand ☎01902 222685, ⊛hotelthenest.com; map p.446. The best hotel by the bus stand but suffers from noise. Clean, good-value attached doubles; two of the pricier second-floor rooms have tubs. The downstairs restaurant is a good option between buses. **₹900**

The Sarvari South of the maidan and up a small lane ☎01902 222471; map p.446. HPTDC chain hotel in a quiet location with a range of rooms in two blocks. Good valley views, Ayurvedic massage, a restaurant and bar. **₹2200**

Shobla Royale Dhalpur ☎01902 222800, ⊛shoblaroyale.com; map p.446. Kullu's top hotel, fully refurbished in recent years. Large, lavishly decorated and furnished rooms, a good mixed-cuisine restaurant, a games room and a relaxing lawn. **₹2950**

EATING

There are few bona fide **restaurants** outside the hotels but a predictable host of *dhabas* and chai stalls.

★**Annapurna** Akhara Bazaar ☎01902 224162; map p.446. Very simple restaurant serving superb vegetarian dishes, mostly under ₹100, from both ends of the country, including fine masala dosas. There's a baked goods and sweet counter outside. Daily 7.30am–10pm.

Sapna Sweets Akhara Bazaar ☎01902 222744; map p.446. The name is slightly misleading as this popular pure-veg place does a range of traditional Himachal thalis (*dham*), samosas and dosas, as well as sweet items. It suffers from the usual copycats so check the phone number on the sign. Daily 7am–10pm.

SHOPPING

Bhuttico Showroom Sarvari Bazaar, near the bus stand ☎01902 224445, ⊛bhutticoshawl.com; map p.446. The most central of several outlets around town, with others in Manali and further afield. This is the best place to buy high-quality, fairly priced shawls, Kullu caps, jackets and other woven items. Daily 9am–8pm, closes 7pm in winter.

6

DUSSEHRA IN THE VALLEY OF THE GODS

In the Kullu region, often dubbed the **"Valley of the Gods"**, the village deity reigns supreme. No one knows how many *devtas* and *devis* inhabit the hills south of the Rohtang Pass, but nearly every hamlet has one. The part each one plays in village life depends on his or her particular **powers**; some heal, others protect the "parish" borders from evil spirits, summon the rains, or ensure the success of the harvest. Nearly all, however, communicate with their devotees by means of **oracles**. When called upon to perform, the village shaman, or *gaur* – drawn from the lower castes – strips to the waist and enters a trance in which the *devta* uses his voice to speak to the congregation. The deity, carried out of the temple on a ceremonial palanquin, or *rath*, rocks back and forth on the shoulders of its bearers as the *gaur* speaks. His words are always heeded, and his decisions final; the *devta*-oracle decides the propitious dates for marriages, and for sowing crops, and arbitrates disputes.

DUSSEHRA

The single most important outing for any village deity is **Dussehra**, which takes place in the town of **Kullu** every October after the monsoons. Although the week-long festival ostensibly celebrates Rama's victory over the demon-king of Lanka, Ravana, it is also an opportunity for the *devtas* to reaffirm their position in the grand pecking order that prevails among them – a rigid hierarchy in which the Kullu raja's own tutelary deity Rama, alias **Raghunathji**, is king.

On the tenth day of the new, or "white" moon in October, between 150 and 200 *devtas* make their way to Kullu to pay homage to Raghunathji. As befits a region that holds its elderly women in high esteem, the procession proper cannot begin until **Hadimba**, the grandmother of the royal family's chief god, arrives from the Dunghri temple in Manali. Like her underlings, she is borne on an elaborately carved wooden *rath* swathed in glittering silk and garlands, and surmounted by a richly embroidered parasol, or *chhatri*. Raghunathji leads the great **procession** in his six-wheeled *rath*. Hauled from the Rupi Palace by two hundred honoured devotees, the palanquin lurches to a halt in the middle of Kullu's maidan, to be circumambulated by the raja, his family, and retinue of priests. Thereafter, the festival's more secular aspect comes to the fore. **Folk dancers** perform for the vast crowds, and the maidan is taken over by market stalls, snake charmers, astrologers, sadhus and tawdry circus acts. The revelries finally draw to a close six days later on the full moon, when the customary **blood sacrifices** of a young buffalo, a goat, a cock, a fish and a crab are made to the god.

Kullu's Dussehra, now a major tourist attraction, has become increasingly staged and commercialized. Book accommodation well in advance, and be prepared for a crush if you want to get anywhere near the *devtas*.

The Parvati Valley

Hemmed in by giant-pinnacled mountain peaks, the **Parvati Valley**, which twists west from the glaciers and snowfields on the Spiti border to meet the Beas at Bhuntur, is the Kullu Valley's longest tributary. It's a picturesque place, with quiet hamlets perching precariously on its sides amid lush terraces and old pine forests. Though the landscape around **Jari** has been scarred by the ugly **Malana hydro project**, there is strong local pressure to at least camouflage the site. Visitors to the valley are an incongruous mix – a combination of Western hippies (especially Israelis), young Indian backpackers and van-loads of Sikh pilgrims bound for the *gurudwara* at **Manikaran**, 32km northeast of the Beas–Parvati confluence. Crouched at the foot of a gloomy ravine, this ancient religious site, sacred to Hindus as well as Sikhs, is famous for the **hot springs** that bubble out of its stony riverbanks.

To make the most of Parvati's stunning scenery you'll have to **hike**. Two popular trails thread their way up the valley: one heads north from the fascinating hill village of **Malana** (see page 458), over the Chandrakhani Pass to Naggar; the other follows the River Parvati east to another sacred hot spring and sadhu hangout, **Khirganga**, which is becoming increasingly popular with hippie travellers. The trail continues from Khirganga to **Mantalai** with its Shiva shrine and over the awesome 5400m Pin–Parvati

BUDDHIST MONK AT DRIKUNG KAGYU

pass into **Spiti**. This serious snowfield is riddled with crevasses and takes several hours to cross. A guide is absolutely essential (see page 458).

GETTING AROUND	THE PARVATI VALLEY

By bus Buses, some of them from Kullu, leave Bhuntur at least hourly for Manikaran (1hr 30min), passing through Jari and Kasol en route. The last bus back to Kullu, via Bhuntur, leaves around 6pm.

Jari and around

Spilling down the south side of the Parvati Valley, **JARI**, 15km from Bhuntur, looks across to the precipitous Malana nala in the north, and to the snow-flecked needles of the Baranagh Range on the eastern horizon. Like many of its lookalike cousins, the tatty settlement supports a small transient population of stoned Westerners, attracted by the top-quality *charas*. Those wanting a shortcut to **Malana** (see page 458) can rent a vehicle up to the Malana hydro project roadhead, from where the village is a mere 4km trek.

Jari's unspoilt and far more attractive satellite village of **Mateura**, just ten minutes' walk up the hill from the main road, has spectacular views over the Parvati Range and is home to the small but important **Kali Anagha temple**.

ACCOMMODATION AND EATING	JARI AND AROUND

Om Shiva On the left-hand side as you enter Jari ☎ 98161 47800. The rooms are rather basic in this simple but welcoming guesthouse, but all have attached bathrooms. No wi-fi. ₹500

Rooftop Restaurant & Guest House Upper side of Matheura ☎ 01902 275434. The rooms here are fairly small and basic, but the real draw is the roof terrace overlooking the village, which serves the best food in the area. No wi-fi. ₹600

Village Guest House Centre of Matheura village ☎ 01902 276070. A traditional wooden-balconied house, whose immaculate rooms have spotless bathrooms and satellite TV. Set in a wonderful garden, it's deservedly popular year-round. ₹700

Kasol

Beyond Jari, the road winds down towards the rushing grey-green Parvati, which it meets at **KASOL**, a pleasant village straddling a mountain stream and surrounded by forest. Kasol has grown in popularity, and now has a large resident population of *charas*-smoking travellers, most of whom are Israelis – earning it the nickname of "little Israel" from the locals. A trickle of trekkers also plod through on their way to or from the pass of Rashol Jot (2440m), a hard day's climb up the north side of the valley which provides an alternative approach to Malana and the Chandrakhani route to the Kullu Valley.

ACCOMMODATION AND EATING	KASOL

Accommodation ranges from basic rooms in village houses and simple lodges to more organized hotels, while Kasol's travellers' **cafés** are cheap and plentiful.

★ **Alpine Guest House** Off the main road, by the river bank ☎ 01902 273710, ⊛ alpineguesthouse.in. Attractive two-storey building with spacious attached rooms, set in wooded grounds by the river. Warm and welcoming atmosphere too. ₹1200

Café Rock'n'Roll On the Jari side of the village ☎ 70283 09425. First-floor rooftop café serving a variety of drinks and meals in a convivial atmosphere, such as the "Thai sexy spice salad" for ₹140 and steaks for ₹230–280. *Momos* are deservedly popular, too. Daily 9am–11pm.

Deep Forest Up the hill just before the bridge ☎ 01902 273048, ⊛ deepforestkasol@yahoo.in. The nondescript and functional attached rooms here are nothing like as spectacular as the views which the hotel's slight elevation give it. Large outdoor terrace and restaurant. ₹1000

Moondance Restaurant and Bakery Just beyond the bridge ☎ 98161 53681. Choose between interior seating and a nicely terraced courtyard overlooking the river. All the travellers' favourites such as pancakes and shakes are available for ₹100–300, plus there are board games to play. Daily 8am–10.30pm.

Sandhya Kasol 400m along the road to Manikaran ☎ 01902 273745, ⊛ sandhyahotels.in. Pleasantly situated away from the centre, this upmarket hotel has comfortable deluxe rooms and wildly fluctuating rates that mean good deals off-season. There's a *Coffee Day* franchise on the premises. ₹3650

PARVATI DISAPPEARANCES

Over the last two decades the Parvati Valley has seen the mysterious **disappearance** of at least twenty travellers. Most were travelling alone, although one incident in August 2000 involved three campers who were brutally attacked in their tent, thrown into the gorge and left for dead – one survived. Most of the vanished have never been found, including a Polish national and an American, both of whom were last seen in Manali, in 2015 and 2016 respectively. Several theories have been put forward to explain these disappearances, from drug-related accidents on the treacherous mountain trails, to attacks by bears or wolves or foul play by the numerous cannabis cultivators in the region; some even claim that the disappeared may have joined secret cults deep in the mountains. Most likely, however, they were victims of bandit attacks, motivated solely by money, with the wild waters of the River Parvati conveniently placed for disposing of bodies. Individual travellers should **take heed** and only use recognized guides on treks across the mountains. Don't attempt solo treks – even along the relatively simple trail over the Chandrakhani Pass between Naggar and Malana and the straightforward trek to the hot springs at Khirganga. There are many trekking agencies in Kullu and Manali who can put you in touch with a reputable guide.

6

Sasi Restaurant Just before the bridge ☎ 97363 68505. Blessed with a riverside location and gaily painted stone walls, and serving food from breakfast and snacks to filling Indian, Chinese and Western meals for ₹80–220. Daily 8am–11pm.

Manikaran

Just 4.5km along the pleasantly wooded main road beyond Kasol, clouds of steam billowing from the rocky riverbank herald the Parvati Valley's chief attraction. Hindu mythology identifies **MANIKARAN** as the place where the serpent king Shesha stole Parvati's earrings, or *manikara*, while she and her husband Shiva were bathing in the river. When interrogated, the snake flew into a rage and snorted the earrings out of his nose. Ever since, boiling water has poured out of the ground. The site is also venerated by Sikhs, who have erected a massive concrete *gurudwara* over the springs.

Boxed in at the bottom of a vast, sheer-sided chasm, Manikaran is a damp, dark and claustrophobic place where you're unlikely to want to spend more than a night. Most of the action revolves around the springs themselves, reached via the lane that leads through the village from the footbridge. On the way, check out the finely carved pale-grey stone **Rama temple** just beyond the main square, and the pans of rice and dhal cooking in the steaming pools on the pavements. Down at the riverside **Shiva shrine**, semi-naked **sadhus** sit in the scalding waters smoking chillums. Sikh pilgrims, meanwhile, make their way to the atmospheric **gurudwara** nearby, where they take a purifying dip in the underground pool, sweat in the hot cave and then congregate upstairs to listen to musical recitations from the Sikhs' holy book, the Guru Granth Sahib. If you visit, keep your arms, legs and head covered; tobacco is prohibited inside the complex.

ACCOMMODATION AND EATING   MANIKARAN

Except during May and June, when Manikaran fills up with Punjabi visitors, **accommodation** is plentiful and inexpensive. Most hotels have a steaming indoor hot tub, which tends to leave them feeling rather damp. **Food**, which is strictly veg, is mostly found in local *dhabas*.

Fateh Guest House In an alley near the Rama temple ☎ 98168 94968. All the small and simple rooms have hot showers and TVs at this welcoming family guesthouse, the best value in town. The owner has a mountain resthouse a 1hr walk away. No wi-fi. ₹400

Royal Palace On the main road before the turn-off to the bus stand ☎ 98173 73033, ⓦ royalpalacekasol.com. On the road to Kasol, this snazzy brick hotel has large rooms with TVs and balconies with river views. ₹2500

Sharda Classic Beside the bus stand ☎ 98164 77680. Airy hotel rooftop restaurant, serving good Indian veg dishes for ₹80–140, plus items such as half lemon chicken for ₹270. Daily 8am–10pm.

Sharma Guest House At the gurudwara end of the bazaar ☎ 98162 73742. Simple lodge with basic rooms, the best of those near the *gurudwara*. It now also has the smarter *New Sharma* nearby. ₹400

6

Naggar

Stacked up the lush, terraced lower slopes of the valley as they sweep towards the tree line from the left bank of the Beas, **NAGGAR** is the most scenic and accessible of the hill villages between Kullu and Manali, roughly 20km from each. Clustered around an old **castle**, this was the regional capital before the local rajas decamped to Kullu in the mid-1800s. A century or so later, European settlers began to move in. Seduced by the village's ancient **temples**, peaceful setting and unhurried pace, visitors often find themselves lingering in Naggar – a far less hippified village than those further north – longer than they intended. Numerous tracks wind up the mountain to more remote settlements, providing a choice of enjoyable **hikes**.

Naggar is a very pleasant place, often sadly overlooked by travellers making a beeline for Manali. The relaxed atmosphere, refreshing elevation, stunning views and a variety of interesting sites combine to make it an excellent spot to while away a few days.

The castle

Since it was erected by Raja Sidh Singh (c.1700), Naggar's central **castle**, astride a sheer-sided bluff, has served as palace, colonial mansion, courthouse and school. It is now a hotel, but non-residents can wander in for ₹20 to admire the views from its balconies. Built in the traditional "earthquake-proof" *pahari* style (layers of stone bonded together with cedar logs), the castle has a central courtyard, a small shrine and a shop selling local handicrafts downstairs. The **Jagti Patt temple**'s amorphous deity, a triangular slab of rock strewn with rose petals and rupee notes, is said to have been borne here from its home on the summit of Deo Tibba by a swarm of wild honeybees – the valley's *devtas* in disguise.

Nicholas Roerich Gallery

Daily April–Oct 10am–1pm & 1.30–6pm; Nov–March 10am–1pm & 1.30–5pm • ₹100 (₹50); ticket includes admission to Urusvati-Himalayan Folk Art Museum • ☎ 01902 248590

Perched on the upper outskirts of the village, the **Nicholas Roerich Gallery** houses an exhibition of paintings by and photographs of its former occupier, the Russian artist, writer, philosopher, archeologist, explorer and mystic, as well as works by his equally talented son Svetoslav. Around the beginning of the twentieth century, Roerich's atmospheric landscape paintings and esoteric philosophies – an arcane blend of Eastern mysticism and *fin de siècle* humanist-idealism – inspired a cult-like following in France and the United States. Financed by donations from devotees, Roerich was able to indulge his obsession with Himalayan travel, eventually retiring in Naggar in 1929 and dying here eighteen years later. The beautifully landscaped gardens contain his *samadhi* memorial.

Urusvati-Himalayan Folk Art Museum

Daily April–Oct 10am–1pm & 1.30–6pm; Nov–March 10am–1pm & 1.30–5pm • Admission included with Nicolas Roerich Gallery

A path winds further up from the Nicholas Roerich Gallery above the road through the forest for around 100m to **Urusvati-Himalayan Folk Art Museum**. Founded by Roerich's wife in 1928, the museum has a collection of local folk art, costumes, more of Roerich's paintings, several paintings by his Russian followers, and a gallery of Russian folk art.

The temples

The largest and most distinctive of Naggar's ancient Hindu **temples** and shrines, the wooden pagoda-style **Tripuri Sundri** stands in a small enclosure at the top of the village, just below the road to the Roerich Gallery. Like the Dunghri temple in Manali, it is crowned with a three-tiered roof, whose top storey is circular. Its *devta* is the focus of an annual *mela* (mid-May) in which deities from villages are brought in procession to pay their respects.

Ten minutes' walk further up the hill – follow the stone steps that lead right from the road – brings you to a clearing where the old stone **Murlidhar** (Krishna) **Mandir** looks down on Naggar, with superb views up the valley to the snow peaks around Solan and the Rohtang Pass. Built on the ruins of the ancient town of Thawa, the shrine, set in a large courtyard, is strictly off-limits to non-Hindus.

Finally, on your way to or from the bus stand at the bottom of the village, look out for the finely carved stone *shikharas* of the **Gaurishankar Mandir**. Set in its own paved courtyard below the castle, this Shiva temple, among the oldest of its kind in the valley, houses a living lingam, so slip off your shoes before approaching it.

ARRIVAL AND DEPARTURE NAGGAR

Naggar village proper, its sights and accommodation lie some way above the small bazaar on the main road where the buses pull in. If you have your own vehicle, you can drive all the way up to the Roerich Gallery at the top of the village.

By bus Naggar is equidistant (21km) from Kullu and Manali and connected to both by hourly buses along the scenic east

bank of the Beas. More frequent and faster services in either direction along the west bank can be joined at Patlikuhl, from where taxis and auto-rickshaws climb the 6km up to Naggar.

On foot You can walk from Patlikuhl on the old mule track – a hike of at least 1hr.

INFORMATION

Guides If you are thinking of trekking around Naggar, you are advised to use guides, especially if crossing the Chandrakhani Pass to Malana (see page 458). Himalayan Mountain Treks at *Poonam Mountain Lodge* (see below)

have equipment, porters and guides, although you need to make clear what is included in the price and chase them up on punctuality. Local guides are also easy to find, though make sure they are reputable.

ACCOMMODATION

★ **Alliance Guest House** Halfway between the village and the Roerich Gallery ☎01902 248263, ☎alliancenaggar.com. Popular French-owned guesthouse with three categories of accommodation: simple, clean rooms with shared bathrooms, medium-sized traditional wooden attached rooms and smarter rooms in the new building on the upper level. Also a small lending library and lovely outdoor patio. ₹600

The Castle Upper end of village ☎01902 248316, ☎kullu@hptdc.in. Atmospheric castle, now one of HPTDC's signature hotels, with well-furnished attached doubles, some offering superb views from spacious wooden balconies. The restaurant is also good. ₹1400

Poonam Mountain Lodge Below the castle ☎94181 49827, ☎poonammountain.in. Cosy doubles, three with

fireplaces for winter stays, in a largely wooden structure with a wraparound balcony beside the family house. Food is available on request. Knowledgeable if rather over-bearing owner. ₹800

Ragini Cottages 250m from the castle ☎09318 585385, ☎raginicottagesnaggar.com. Run by a Belgian-Indian couple who also have a place in Goa, *Ragini* offers large suites (two-bed with kitchenette ₹4000) or en-suite rooms, all with valley or castle views. Breakfast and dinner on request and plenty of help with planning treks or jeep/motorbike tours. ₹1800

Sheetal Hotel 50m from the castle ☎01902 248250, ☎hotelsheetal.com. The wood-panelled rooms in this ochre-coloured hotel are comfortable, with TV and balconies. There's also a decent rooftop restaurant and some nearby cottages are available. ₹900

EATING

At Hall Estate Just before the Roerich Gallery ☎01902 248590. Operated by the Roerich Trust, this rather institutional place has basic snacks and veg meals, mostly under ₹150, and excellent valley views. Daily 10am–6pm.

Nightingale – The Italian Restaurant 400m from the castle ☎01902 248168. Friendly restaurant serving excellent fusion Italian cuisine and rainbow trout specials

in a traditional dining room or on their terrace with a view. Daily 10am–10pm.

★ **Ragini Hotel Rooftop** Next to the Sheetal Hotel ☎01902 248185. The upstairs restaurant serves fine food, including superb grilled trout with a fine garlic lemon sauce for ₹350 and some Mexican dishes. There is a pleasant café downstairs. Daily 7am–10.30pm.

Manali

Himachal's main tourist resort, **MANALI**, stands at the head of the Kullu Valley, 108km north of Mandi. Despite lying at the heart of the region's highest mountain range, it remains easily accessible by road from the plains; after one hour on a plane and a short hop by road, or sixteen hours on a bus from Delhi, you could be staring from your hotel veranda across apple orchards and thick pine forests to the snowfields of Solang Nala, which shine a tantalizing stone's throw away to the north. Manali has become increasingly popular with domestic tourists (more than five million annually), and now greets an eclectic mix of honeymooners, holiday-makers, hippies, trekkers and traders.

The Manali that lured travellers in the 1970s has certainly changed, although the majestic mountain scenery, thermal springs and quality *charas* can still be enjoyed. **Old Manali** retains some of its atmosphere, and the village of **Vashisht** across the valley, with its increasing number of guesthouses and cafés, has become a popular place to chill out. For those preferring to venture into the mountains, Manali makes an ideal **trekking** base for short hikes and serious expeditions, and countless agencies can help put a package together for you. The relaxing hotels in Manali's cleaner, greener outskirts, and dozens of sociable cafés and restaurants ranged around a well-stocked **bazaar**, provide a welcome relief from the rigours of the mountain trails. As well as treks around Manali you can also explore the Kullu Valley (see page 444).

The Mall

Manali's main street, **The Mall**, quite unlike its namesake in Shimla, is a noisy scene of constant activity, fronted by the bus stand, several shopping markets, travel agents, and a line of hotels and restaurants. It's a great place to watch the world go by – locals in traditional caps, Tibetan women in immaculate rainbow-striped pinafores, Nepali porters, Buddhist monks, the odd party of Zanskaris swathed in fusty woollen *gonchas*, souvenir-hunting Indian tourists and a curious mix of Westerners. The grid of streets behind The Mall is curiously known as **Model Town**, though it is hardly a paradigm of town planning.

The bazaar

Manali's days as an authentic *pahari* bazaar ended when the mule trains were superseded by Tata trucks, but it's still great for souvenir **shopping**. Woollen goods are the town's real forte, particularly the brilliantly patterned **shawls** for which the Kullu Valley is famous. Genuine pure-wool handloom shawls with embroidered borders start at around ₹1000, but those made from finest pashmina cost a good five thousand rupees. Shop around and check out the fixed-price factory shops to get an idea of what's available (see page 460).

Elsewhere around the bazaar, innumerable stalls are stacked with handwoven goods and pillbox Kullu **topis**. Those with gaudy multicoloured up-turned flaps and gold piping are indigenous to the valley, but you can also pick up the plain-green velvet-fronted variety favoured by Kinnauris. Manali's other specialities are **Tibetan curios** such as prayer wheels, amulets, *dorjees* (thunderbolts) and masks, musical instruments and *thangkas*. Few of the items hawked as antiques are genuine but it takes an expert eye to spot a fake. The same applies to silver **jewellery** inlaid with turquoise and coral, which can nonetheless be attractive and relatively inexpensive.

The Hadimba Temple

Resting on a wide stone platform fifteen minutes' walk northwest of the bazaar, the **Hadimba Temple** is Manali's oldest shrine and the seat of Hadimba (or "Hirma Devi"), wife of Bhima. Considered to be an incarnation of Kali, Hadimba is worshipped in times of adversity, and also plays a key role in the Dussehra festival (see page 448). Hadimba is supposed to have given the kingdom of Kullu to the forefathers of the rajas of Kullu, and in veneration and affection the family to this day refer to her as "grandmother". The massive triple-tiered wooden pagoda, crowned by crimson pennants and a brass ball and trident (Shiva's *trishul*), dates from 1553, and is a replica of earlier ones that burned down in successive forest fires. The facade writhes with wonderful woodcarvings of elephants, crocodiles and folk deities. Entered by a door surmounted by wild ibex horns, the gloomy **shrine** is dominated by several large

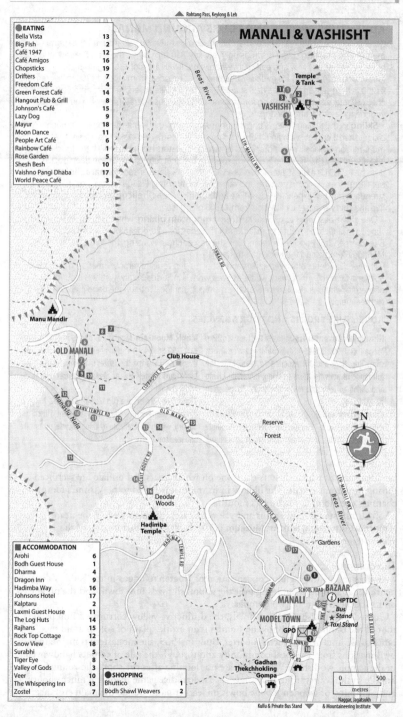

Rohtang Pass, Keylong & Leh

MANALI & VASHISHT

● EATING

Bella Vista	13
Big Fish	2
Café 1947	12
Café Amigos	16
Chopsticks	19
Drifters	7
Freedom Café	4
Green Forest Café	14
Hangout Pub & Grill	8
Johnson's Café	15
Lazy Dog	9
Mayur	18
Moon Dance	11
People Art Café	6
Rainbow Café	1
Rose Garden	5
Shesh Besh	10
Vaishno Pangi Dhaba	17
World Peace Café	3

■ ACCOMMODATION

Arohi	6
Bodh Guest House	1
Dharma	4
Dragon Inn	9
Hadimba Way	16
Johnsons Hotel	17
Kalptaru	2
Laxmi Guest House	11
The Log Huts	14
Rajhans	15
Rock Top Cottage	12
Snow View	18
Surabhi	5
Tiger Eye	8
Valley of Gods	3
Veer	10
The Whispering Inn	13
Zostel	7

● SHOPPING

Bhuttico	1
Bodh Shawl Weavers	2

Beas River

VASHISHT

Temple & Tank

LEH-MANALI HWY

JHINGI RD

Manu Mandir

OLD MANALI

Club House

CLUBHOUSE RD

Manalsu Nala

MANU TEMPLE RD

OLD MANALI RD

Reserve

Forest

N

CIRCUIT HOUSE RD

Deodar Woods

Hadimba Temple

HADIMBA TEMPLE RD

CIRCUIT HOUSE RD

Beas River

LEH-MANALI HWY

Gardens

BAZAAR

SCHOOL ROAD

HPTDC

MANALI

Bus Stand

★ Taxi Stand

MODEL TOWN

GPO

MODEL TOWN RD

THE MALL

GOMPHA RD

OLD KULLU HWY

Gadhan Thekchhokling Gompa

GOMPA RD

0   500

metres

Kullu & Private Bus Stand

Naggar, Jagatsukh & Mountaineering Institute

6

ADVENTURE SPORTS AND TOURS AROUND MANALI

Considering the fierce whitewater that thrashes down the Kullu Valley during the spring melt, Manali's **rafting** scene is surprisingly low-key. Raft trips down the River Beas are offered between the end of May and early July, when water levels are highest, beginning at Piridi (above Bhuntur) around 15km downstream at Jhiri. The price (from around ₹700 in low season, ₹1200 in high season for half a day) should include food, lifejackets, helmets and return travel; check exactly what you're paying for, as some unscrupulous operators expect you to make your own way back after the trip.

Skiing in the Solang Valley is popular from January to April – but the slope isn't much bigger than a cricket pitch and there is no proper ski centre (see ⓦ skihimalayas.net). A multi-million dollar ski resort proposed by foreign investors has repeatedly been blocked and it looks unlikely that facilities will be improved in the near future; if you have deep pockets then heli-skiing is a great alternative. The valley is also a popular spot for **paragliding** (₹2700 per flight), rock climbing, zorbing and especially **canyoning** (₹2100 for half a day). For a less strenuous burst of expensive adrenaline and stunning views, **helicopter rides** of between five and thirty minutes can be had from ₹2500 per person.

One of the best ways to explore Kullu is by **mountain biking**, which is possible from mid-June to mid-October; rental costs around ₹1000/day for a European bike, with a guide, which is recommended. Popular routes include the descent from Rohtang, the forest trail to the Bijli Mahadev Temple and the back road to Naggar.

Numerous agents offer jeep safaris and other guided tours to remote areas such as Lahaul, Spiti and Ladakh – prices vary wildly, as does what is included, so always shop around. Most of these operations also run treks on the most popular local routes (see page 458) and further afield.

ADVENTURE SPORTS AND TOUR AGENCIES

Himalayan Adventurers Opposite the tourist office, Manali ⓣ 01902 253050, ⓦ himalayanadventurers.com. Rup Negi and his experienced team offer the full range of activities from trekking, mountain biking and skiing to jeep and motorbike tours. There's even birdwatching.

Choppertrip ⓣ 09871 658111 or ⓣ 07895947233, ⓦ choppertrip.com. Choppertrip operates ten-minute helicopter "joyrides" from Manu Allaya Resort Spa helipad.

Magic Mountain Jagatsukh, 6km south of Manali ⓣ 98160 56934, ⓦ magicmountainadventures.com. Owner Raju Sharma specializes in mountain biking and leads tours himself. He can also arrange trekking, skiing and jeep safaris.

Tiger Eye Adventure Old Manali ⓣ 01902 251092, ⓦ tigereyeadventure.com. Very efficient Dutch-run agency, which runs reliable trekking, bicycle, motorbike and jeep tours.

boulders, one of which shelters the stone on which goats and buffalo are sacrificed during important rituals. The hollow in its middle, believed to be Vishnu's footprint, channels the blood to Hadimba's mouth.

Soft-drinks stands, curio stalls and yak rides cater for visitors while the nearby **Himachal Culture and Folk Art Museum** (₹10) displays detailed models of the valley's temples.

The gompas

Manali harbours the highest concentration of **Tibetan refugees** in the Kullu Valley, hence the prayer flags fluttering over the approach roads into town, and the presence, on its southern edge, of two **gompas**.

Capped with polished golden finials, the distinctive yellow corrugated-iron pagoda roof of the **Gadhan Thekchhokling Gompa** is an exotic splash of colour amid the ramshackle huts of the Tibetan quarter. Built in 1969, the monastery is maintained by donations from the local community and through the sale of **carpets** handwoven in the temple workshop. When they are not looking after the **shop**, the young lamas huddle in the courtyard to play *cholo* – a Tibetan dice game involving much shouting and slamming of wooden *tsampa* bowls on leather pads. Beside the main entrance, a roll of honour recounts the names of Tibetans killed during the violent political demonstrations that wracked China in the late 1980s.

The smaller and more modern of the two **gompas** stands nearer the bazaar, in a garden that in late summer blazes with sunflowers. Its main shrine, lit by dozens of bare electric bulbs and filled with fragrant Tibetan incense, houses a colossal gold-faced Buddha, best viewed from the small room on the first floor.

Old Manali

Old Manali, the village from which the modern town takes its name, lies 2km north of The Mall, on the far side of the Manalsu Nala. Built in the old *pahari* style, most of the houses of Old Manali have heavy stone roofs and wooden balconies hung with bushels of drying herbs and tobacco. Unlike its crowded, concrete offspring, the settlement retains an unhurried and traditional feel for most of the year, despite prolific tourist development. The vast majority of the travellers who cram into the many guesthouses and laidback restaurants during the warmer months are Westerners, although the freak element is not as noticeable as before – they prefer Vashisht and the Parvati Valley – and the consumption of *charas* more discreet. In the wake of the tourists come the Kashmiris, Rajasthani tailors and other opportunists, eager to make good business before returning to Goa in the autumn.

To get here, head north up Old Manali Road, bear right at the fork in the road, and keep going until you reach the iron bridge across the river. A pleasant alternative route during daylight hours is through the forested Nature Park (daily: summer 9am–7pm; winter 9am–5pm; ₹10), which starts on the right-hand side of the Old Manali Road, not far north of The Mall. The village proper is clustered on top of a steeply shelving ledge of level ground above the nala. It is also known as **Manaligarh** after its ancient citadel – now a ruined fort surrounded by a patchwork of maize terraces and deep-green orchards. At the centre of the village is an unusual, brash new temple dedicated to **Manu**, who laid the foundations of Hindu law, as well as *varna* or "colour" – the basis of the caste system. Inscribed stones dating from the Middle Ages embedded into the concrete paving reveal the site's antiquity. Although Manali itself is considered safe, women should be wary of walking along the lane from town to Old Manali after dark; it has been the scene of several **rapes** over the last two decades.

ARRIVAL AND DEPARTURE   MANALI

By bus Most Volvo/private buses pull into the bus stand 300m south of the State Bank of India at the bottom of town, while government ISBT/HRTC buses use the main bus stand in the middle of The Mall. There is the usual mixture of ordinary and deluxe services.

Destinations Delhi (8–10 daily; 16–17hr); Dharamsala (2 daily; 9–10hr); Kaza (1 daily; 12–13hr); Keylong (6 daily; 5–6hr); Kullu (every 15min; 1hr 30min–2hr); Mandi (hourly; 4–5hr); Naggar (hourly; 1hr); Shimla (7 daily; 8–9hr).

Railway booking There's an official Indian Railways reservation booth (Mon–Sat 8am–5pm, Sun 9am–2pm) next to the tourist office.

GETTING AROUND

By motorbike Reliable, well-serviced Enfields can be rented for ₹800–1200/day from Hardev Motors on the road to Vashisht (☎ 98160 82825, ⊕ hardevmotors.com).

By taxi Manali's Taxi Operators' Union kiosk (☎ 01902 252450) lies just up from the tourist office; the taxis have fixed rates, which are sometimes negotiable off-season. You can book single seats in jeeps and Tempo Traveller taxis to Leh (17–19hr; ₹1600–2000) and Kaza (10–11hr; ₹1000); numerous travel agents book the former, while the *Kiran Guest House* (near the State Bank of India; ☎ 01902 253066) is the best sales and departure point for Kaza.

INFORMATION

Tourist information The functional but not over-helpful tourist office (Mon–Sat 10am–5pm, sometimes longer hours April–June; ☎ 01902 252175) is at the north end of The Mall. You can make reservations for all state-run hotels at the HPTDC office (☎ 01902 253531), two doors down.

Permits If you want to get an Inner Line permit (see page 413) in Manali, you must do so through a registered travel agent (see page 456).

6

TREKS AROUND MANALI AND THE KULLU VALLEY

The Kullu Valley's spectacular alpine scenery makes it perfect for **trekking**. Trails are long and steep, but more than repay the effort with superb views, varied flora and the chance to visit remote hill stations. Within striking distance of several major trailheads, **Manali** is the most popular place to begin and end treks. While **package deals** (around ₹2500/person for three days with a group of four) offered by the town's many agencies can save time and energy, it is relatively easy to organize your own trip with maps and advice from the tourist office and the Mountaineering Institute at the bottom end of town. Porters and horsemen can be sought out in the square behind the main street. Always take a reliable **guide**, especially on less-frequented routes, as you cannot rely solely on **maps**. Some trekkers have reported difficulties when descending from the Bara Bangal Pass, as maps don't do the terrain justice.

The optimum trekking **season** is right after the monsoons (mid-Sept to late Oct), when skies are clear and pass-crossings easier. From June to August, you run the risk of sudden, potentially fatal snow, or view-obscuring cloud and rain. There are several good trekking agencies in Manali (see page 456).

MANALI TO BEAS KUND

The relatively easy trek to Beas Kund, a glacial lake at the head of Solang nala, is the region's most popular short hike. Encircled by 5000m-plus peaks, the well-used campground beside the lake, accessible in two days from Manali, makes a good base for side-trips up to the surrounding ridges and passes.

From **Palchan**, a village thirty minutes north of Manali by bus, follow the jeep track up the valley to **Solang**, site of a small ski station, resthouse and the Mountaineering Institute's log huts. The next two hours take you through pine forests and grassy meadows to the campground at **Dhundi** (2743m). A more strenuous walk of five to six hours the next day leads to **Beas Kund**. The hike up to the **Tentu La** Pass (4996m) and back from here can be done in a day, as can the descent to Manali via Solang.

MANALI TO LAHAUL, VIA THE HAMPTA PASS

The three-day trek from the Kullu Valley over the Hampta Pass to Lahaul, the old caravan route to Spiti, is a classic. Rising to 4330m, it is high by Kullu standards; do not undertake it without allowing good time to acclimatize. **Day one**, from the trailhead at **Jagatsukh** or Hampta (both villages near Manali) to the campground above **Sethen**, is an easy hike (4–5hr) up the verdant, forested sides of the valley. **Day two** (5hr) brings you to **Chikha**, a high Gaddi pasture below the pass; stay put for a day or so if you're feeling the effects of altitude. The ascent (700m) on **day three** to the **Hampta Pass** (4330m) is gruelling, but the views from the top – of Indrasan and Deo Tibba to the south, and the moonscape of Lahaul to the north – are sublime recompense. It takes six to seven hours of relentless rock-hopping and stream-crossing to reach **Chhatru**, on the

ACCOMMODATION

There are three main **accommodation** areas in Manali. Most longer-stay budget places are clustered in **Old Manali**, while many of Manali's classic hotels with gardens and character are dotted around the **northern and western outskirts**. In **central Manali**, numerous mid-range business and honeymoon hotels cluster on and behind The Mall. Tariffs rocket to at least double in most Manali hotels during **high season** (April–June), when you might want to check out availability at the Manali Hoteliers Association on The Mall (☎01902 253059). At most other times, competition keeps rates well down.

OLD MANALI

Dragon Inn Down the lane from Manu Temple Rd ☎01902 252790, ⓦdragoninnmanali.com; map p.455. Newer hotel with brash exterior but comfortable, spacious attached rooms with hot water and balconies. The top floor of the new block has some great wooden-floored duplexes. Also a fine restaurant and travel centre. ₹1550

Laxmi Guest House On the lane beyond Dragon ☎01902 253569; map p.455. Small, friendly place with rickety wooden rooms, which stay cheap even in high season. The attached ones cost little more. Largely uninterrupted valley views and a small garden are the best features. No wi-fi. ₹400

Rock Top Cottage Up the stepped path just past Lazy Dog, Manu Temple Rd ☎09805 601545, ⓦrocktop-cottage-cafe.business.site; map p.455. Decent attached and non-attached rooms, with grubby walls but clean bathrooms and fine views. You can camp in the lovely garden. ₹400

★ **Tiger Eye** Signposted down the lane towards the

floor of the Chandra Valley. From here, you can turn east towards Koksar and the **Rohtang Pass**, or west past the world's largest glacier, **Bara Shigri**, to **Batal**, the trailhead for the Chandratal–Baralacha trek (see page 466).

NAGGAR TO MALANA VIA THE CHANDRAKHANI PASS AND ONWARDS

The trek to Jari in the Parvati Valley from Naggar, 21km south of Manali, is quintessential Kullu Valley trekking, with superb scenery and fascinating villages. The round trip can be completed in three days, but you may be tempted to linger in **Malana** and explore the surrounding countryside. A **guide** is essential for several reasons: the first stage of the trek involves crossing a maze of grazing trails; Malana is culturally sensitive and requires some familiarity with local customs; and a number of people have **disappeared** in the Parvati Valley in recent years under suspicious circumstances (see page 451). The descent to the Parvati Valley is too steep for pack ponies, but porters are available in Naggar through the guesthouses (see page 453).

The trail leads through the village of Rumsu and then winds through wonderful old-growth forests to a pasture just above the tree line, which makes ideal camping ground. From here, a climb of 4km takes you to the **Chandrakhani Pass** (3660m), with fine views west over the top of the Kullu Valley to the peaks surrounding Solang nala and north to the Ghalpo mountains of Lahaul. Some prefer to reach the base of the pass on the first day and then camp below the final ascent.

The inhabitants of **MALANA**, a steep 7km descent from the pass, are known for their frostiness and staunch traditions. Plans by regional developers to extend a paved road here are vehemently opposed by the insular locals. Although notions of **caste pollution** are not as strictly adhered to as they once were, you should observe a few basic "**rules**" in Malana: approach the village quietly and respectfully; stick to paths at all times; keep away from the temple; and above all, don't touch anybody or anything, especially children or houses. If you do commit a cultural blunder, you'll be expected to make amends: usually in the form of a ₹1500 payment for a sacrificial offering of a young sheep or goat to the village deity, **Jamlu**, one of the most powerful Kullu Valley gods. His **temple**, open to high-caste Hindus only, is decorated with lively folk carvings, among them images of soldiers – the villagers claim to be the area's sole remaining descendants of Alexander the Great's army. Popular **places to stay** include the *Renuka Guesthouse*, which has hot water, and the *Himalaya Guesthouse*, run by the former village headman. The owner of *Santu Ram's* is an authority on local trails. All the guesthouses offer simple meals and rooms cost ₹500 or less. The official camping ground lies 100m beyond the village spring.

The **final stage** of the trek takes you down the sheer limestone sides of Malana nala to the floor of the Parvati Valley – a precipitous 12km drop that is partially covered by a switchback road. From the hamlet of **Rashol**, you have a choice of three onward routes: either head east up the right bank of the river to **Manikaran** (see page 451); follow the trail southwest to the sacred **Bijli Mahadev Mandir**; or climb the remaining 3km up to the road at **Jari**, from where regular buses leave for Bhuntur, Kullu and Manali.

top of village ☎01902 252718, ⓦtigereyeadventure.com; map p.455. Peaceful, modern family guesthouse run by a friendly Indian–Dutch couple. Immaculate rooms and balconies with great views, plus a TV and w-fi in the comfy lounge. Well worth the little extra. ₹1000

Veer On the lane beyond Dragon ☎01902 252410, ⓔveerguesthouse@hotmail.com; map p.455. The functional rooms are in two blocks separated by a leafy garden and communal eating area. Some non-attached singles and some rooms with a/c and TV. ₹800

Zostel Off Manu Temple Rd at the top of the village ☎01139 589003, ⓦzostel.com; map p.455. This mountain-view hostel with clean and comfy four-bed dorms, twin and double rooms is one of the best in the Zostel chain. Shared areas are laidback and welcoming, tours and activities are well organised and the on-site café does great food. No card payments. Dorms ₹500, doubles ₹2200

NORTHERN AND WESTERN OUTSKIRTS

Hadimba Way Log Huts area ☎01902 251522; map p.455. Best value of the several places in this relatively quiet enclave near the Hadimba Temple. Unusually, the upstairs rooms are cheaper than those on the ground floor, but in all the rooms check the linen to make sure it's clean. ₹1100

The Log Huts Overlooking Manalsu Nala ☎01902 253225, ⓔmanali@hptdc.in; map p.455. Luxurious but overpriced timber holiday cottages tucked away in the woods, with one or two double bedrooms, kitchens and most comforts including cable TV. ₹6000

Rajhans Between Old Manali Rd and Log Huts area ☎01902 252209, ⓦhotelrajhansmanali.in; map p.455. Stylish four-storey brick building with valley views from the more luxurious higher rooms and suites; all attached with TV. ₹2000

The Whispering Inn Club House Rd ☎01902 253253, ⓦthewhisperinginn.com; map p.455. Billing itself as a Swiss style chalet, this upmarket place adds personal touches to the well-furnished rooms. It also has a restaurant, two bars and a café. ₹5000

CENTRAL MANALI
★ **Johnsons Hotel** Circuit House Rd ☎01902 253764, ⓦjohnsonshotel.in; map p.455. Three-star comfort in an old colonial building. Spacious and neat wooden-floored rooms over-look the garden; the carpeted downstairs rooms are cheaper, with wood-burning heaters for winter. ₹5000

Snow View Model Town Rd ☎01902 253084, ⓦhotel snowviewmanali.com; map p.455. Large, functional hotel with comfort-able, decent-sized rooms, mainly aimed at business travellers. Facilities include cable TV and 24hr room service. ₹2200

EATING

Manali's wide range of **restaurants** reflects the town's melting-pot credentials: Tibetan *thukpa* joints stand cheek-by-jowl with south Indian coffee houses, Gujarati thali bars and Nepalese-run German pastry shops. Old Manali joints offer traveller-friendly **breakfasts** of eggs, porridge, pancakes, toast and jam, as well as a variety of cuisines.

OLD MANALI
Café 1947 Near the bridge ☎94184 61969; map p.455. Hip modern joint with a classy menu featuring mostly Italian dishes and burgers for ₹250–500. Live music most nights. Daily noon–11pm.

Drifters Manu Temple Rd ☎98160 05950; map p.455. Trendy hotel café-restaurant with low tables and cushions downstairs, plus an outdoor terrace. Serves grilled trout with the trimmings for around ₹350, somewhat less for other Indian, Chinese and Western dishes. Daily 9am–11pm.

Hangout Pub & Grill Just off Manu Temple Rd ☎98175 14062; map p.455. This popular hangout does a line in burgers from ₹160, pasta from around ₹200 and desserts such as banoffee pie. Home-made cider is available. Trance and disco vibes. Daily 9am–11pm.

Lazy Dog Manu Temple Rd ☎01902 254277; map p.455. Popular restaurant overlooking the river, beautifully decorated and fine for hanging out, if you like loud Western music. The menu includes a wide range of Indian, Chinese and Continental dishes such as sizzlers for ₹200–400. Daily 11am–11pm.

Moon Dance Manu Temple Rd ☎98162 01046; map p.455. Popular garden café and meeting place above the river with a varied menu that includes Indian, Israeli and Italian dishes for ₹150–250. Daily 9am–midnight.

People Art Café Manu Temple Rd ☎97367 87568; map p.455. Split-level restaurant, the lower part having crayons to draw with. Dishes like *sirniki* (curd fritters) and *draniki* (potato pancakes) make a change, plus they do fine Western breakfasts (₹200 for a full English with chicken sausages). Daily 8.30am–11pm.

★ **Shesh Besh** Manu Temple Rd ☎98829 37320; map p.455. This self-proclaimed "fresh & funky" joint boasts colourful artwork and river views. Breakfast options include sausage and bacon, while the delicious non-veg mains only cost ₹150–300. Daily 8am–11pm.

CENTRAL AND NORTHWEST MANALI
Bella Vista Log Hut Rd, just across the bridge from Old Manali ☎98166 99663; map p.455. This snazzy place is a self-billed Spanish café, with a range of tapas, although it has as many Italian main courses and wood-fired pizza for ₹300–450. Daily 8am–10.30pm.

★ **Café Amigos** North end of The Mall ☎98161 18765; map p.455. Wooden tables, colourful pottery, chilled-out world music and a fantastic range of cakes, brownies and apple pie, as well as main meals for around ₹250. Superb coffee, too. Daily 8am–10pm.

Chopsticks The Mall ☎01902 252639; map p.455. Very popular Tibetan-run restaurant with favourites such as *momos* for ₹120–180, plus Japanese dishes, fine filter coffee and muesli, fruit and curd. Daily 9am–10pm.

Green Forest Café Off Log Hut Rd ☎98053 42350; map p.455. Small local restaurant with some outdoor patio seating, serving the best *momos* and *thukpas* in Manali for under ₹100, plus pizza. Daily 9am–8.30pm.

Johnson's Café Johnson Hotel, Old Manali Rd ☎01902 253023; map p.455. A great café, with garden seating and an inviting menu including beer, fresh trout and crème caramel. Some items cost ₹400–600 but they're worth it. Daily 9am–11pm.

Mayur Mission Rd, just off The Mall ☎01902 252316; map p.455. Exciting and extensive Indian menu featuring dishes from all over the Subcontinent for ₹150–400 – try the excellent jalfrezi. Candles, serviettes and classical Indian music create a pleasant vibe. Daily 9am–11pm.

Vaishno Pangi Dhaba School Rd, just off The Mall ☎94186 60693; map p.455. One of the best cheap joints, serving a range of north and south Indian snacks such as masala dosa from around ₹80 and Punjabi thali from ₹140. Daily 8am–11pm.

SHOPPING

Bhuttico On The Mall opposite the tourist office ☎01902 252196, ⓦbhutticoshawl.com; map p.455. The most famous of the weaver co-operatives offers a huge range of shawls and other woven items. Daily: summer

9am–8pm; winter 9am–7pm.

Bodh Shawl Weavers Just off The Mall south of the bus stand ☎ 01902 260229, ⊛ bodhshawls.com; map p.455. Factory outlet offering high-quality woven and embroidered shawls. Daily 9.30–7pm.

Vashisht

Famous for its sweeping valley views and sulphurous hot-water springs, the ever-expanding village of **VASHISHT**, 3km northeast of Manali, is an amorphous jumble of traditional timber houses and modern concrete cubes, divided by paved courtyards and narrow muddy lanes. It is the epicentre of the local budget travellers' scene, with a good choice of guesthouses and cafés, with more of an alternative feel than Old Manali has these days. The tranquil and traditional atmosphere is only interrupted by the occasional rave that takes place in the woods, or if the weather is poor, in one or two obliging hotels.

The only place for a **hot soak** is in the bathing pools of Vashisht's ancient temple (free), which is far more atmospheric anyway. Divided into separate sections for men and women, they attract a decidedly mixed crowd of Hindu pilgrims, Western hippies, semi-naked sadhus and groups of local kids.

Vashisht boasts two old stone **temples**, opposite each other above the main square and dedicated to the local patron saint Vashishta, guru of Raghunathji. The smaller of the two opens onto a partially covered courtyard and is adorned with elaborate woodcarvings. Those lining the interior of the shrine, blackened by years of oil-lamp and *dhoop* smoke, are worth checking out.

ARRIVAL AND DEPARTURE   VASHISHT

There are no buses to Vashisht, so most people arrive on foot or by auto-rickshaw from Manali for around ₹100. Cheaper shared electric taxis are now plying this route, too.

ACCOMMODATION

Vashisht is packed with budget **guesthouses**, many of them old wooden buildings with broad verandas and uninterrupted vistas up the valley. A few larger **hotels** offer good-value, mid-range rooms. The only time you'll not be spoilt for choice is during high season (May–June).

Arohi On the main road into the village ☎ 01902 254421, ⊛ arohiecoadventures.com; map p.455. Immaculate rooms with cable TV, intercom and balconies overlooking the river. Rates are open to negotiation. Their agency can arrange various activities. **₹800**

Bodh Guest House In the lane just beyond the temple ☎ 01902 254165, ⊛ facebook.com/BodhGuestHouse; map p.455. Sociable, bright blue and white guesthouse with smallish but cosy rooms, all with common bathrooms. Extra charge for wi-fi access. **₹100**

★ **Dharma** A 5min walk up behind the temples ☎ 01902 252354, ⊛ hoteldharmamanali.com; map p.455. Most rooms at this large hotel complex have fantastic views, as does the marble terrace with a swing and loungers. There's even a tiny swimming pool, filled by the hot springs. **₹600**

Kalptaru Overlooking the temple tanks ☎ 01902 253031; map p.455. You can't get any closer to the baths – with great-value rooms, all attached, with hot showers. Small garden and veranda from which to watch the bathers. **₹500**

Surabhi Halfway up the main road ☎ 01902 252796, ⊛ surabhihotel.in; map p.455. The airy, smart newer rooms upstairs are all nicely furnished and all have views of the valley. The cheaper ground-floor rooms are colder and darker. **₹1000**

Valley of Gods On the main road into the village ☎ 97362 50440, ⊛ hotelvalleyofgods.com; map p.455. One of the smartest options, whose west-facing rooms all have attached bathrooms and superb views from their spacious balconies. Plenty of attractive wood panelling and upmarket furnishings. **₹3000**

EATING AND DRINKING

★ **Big Fish** On the main road, opposite the temples ☎ 88940 04509, ⊛ bigfishrestaurant.wordpress.com; map p.455. Upstairs restaurant serving trout for around ₹300 and more adventurous stuff such as Thai. Choose between the airy terrace and cushioned chill-out zone. Daily 7am–midnight.

Freedom Café On the main road into village ☎ 89883 15364; map p.455. Floor seating and a grassy deck with good views; the Indian food is mostly in the ₹150–250 range, while tandoori trout goes for ₹400. Daily 7.30am–11pm.

6

Rainbow Café Above the bathing tank ☎ 98160 95744; map p.455. Sociable hangout offering traveller-friendly staples such as pancakes, pasta and spring rolls, mostly ₹100–250, with terrace views of the temple tanks. Daily 7.30am–11.30pm.

Rose Garden On the main road into village ☎ 01902 253417; map p.455. A genuine Italian chef cooks up proper recipes from the old country and other parts of Europe, such as pasta for ₹350 and chicken escalope for ₹450. Ingredients are local and organic where possible. Daily 10am–10pm.

World Peace Café On the main road, above the Surabhi hotel ☎ 98160 42796; map p.455. Standard Indian and Western menu and prices but also Turkish coffee, movies, board games and frequent live gigs. Has a roof terrace too. Daily 7am–11pm.

Lahaul and Spiti

Few places on earth can mark so dramatic a change in landscape as the **Rohtang Pass**. To one side, the lush green head of the Kullu Valley; to the other, an awesome vista of bare, chocolate-coloured mountains, hanging glaciers and snowfields that shine in the dazzlingly crisp light, with just flecks of flora deep in the valley to soften the stark image. Until now, heavy snow between late October and late March has always closed the pass and sealed off the district of **Lahaul and Spiti** each winter, not to mention year-round maintenance and the occasional landslide following heavy rain. However, from the end of 2019, the region will no longer be so inaccessible. Nearly 2000m beneath the pass the longest tunnel in India will connect Himachal's largest district – named after its two subdivisions, which are, in spite of their numerous geographical and cultural similarities, distinct and separate regions – with the rest of India.

Lahaul

Lahaul, sometimes referred to as the Chandra-Bhaga Valley, is the region that divides the Great Himalayas and Pir Panjal ranges. Its principal river, the Chandra, rises deep in the barren wastes below the **Baralacha Pass**, and flows south, then west towards its confluence with the River Bhaga near Tandi. Here, the two rivers become the Chenab, and crash north out of Himachal to Kishtwar in Kashmir. Being closer to what rains the monsoon brings across the Rohtang Pass from the south, Lahaul's **climate** is less arid than in Ladakh and Zanskar to the north and as a consequence, the key highway passes of Rohtang La and Baralacha La are more prone to early snow than the higher examples further north. Despite such difficulties, Lahaulis, a mixture of Buddhists and Hindus, enjoy one of the highest per capita incomes in the Subcontinent. Using glacial water channelled through ancient irrigation ducts, Lahauli farmers manage to coax a bumper crop of **seed potatoes** from their painstakingly fashioned terraces. The region is also the sole supplier of **hops** to India's breweries, and harvests prodigious quantities of wild herbs, used to make perfume and medicine. Much of the profit generated by these cash crops is spent on lavish jewellery, especially seed-pearl necklaces and coral- and turquoise-inlaid silver plaques, worn by the women over ankle-length burgundy or fawn woollen dresses. Lahaul's traditional costume and Buddhism are a legacy of the Tibetan influence that has permeated the region from the east.

Keylong

Lahaul's largest settlement and the district headquarters, **KEYLONG**, 114km north of Manali, is the last significant settlement on the long road journey to Ladakh. Although of little interest itself, the town lies amid superb scenery, within a day's climb of three Buddhist **gompas**. A couple of **stores** in the busy market sell trekking supplies – useful if you are heading off to Zanskar.

Lahauli Buddhists consider it auspicious to make a clockwise circumambulation – known as the **Rangcha Parikarma** – of the sacred **Rangcha Mountain** (4565m), which overlooks the confluence of the Bhaga and Chandra rivers. A well-worn trail that makes a long and arduous day-hike from Keylong, the route is highly scenic, and takes in the large **Khardung Gompa** along the way. A rough motorable road leads to Khardung (10km), but closer to Keylong and on the same side of the valley are two quiet and picturesque *gompas* high up the mountainside, **Shasher Gompa** (3km) and **Gungshal Gompa** (5km).

ARRIVAL AND INFORMATION

By bus There are six buses daily to Manali, the first one leaving at 5.30am and the last at 1.30pm. Note that onward transport to Leh can be difficult to arrange in high season (July & Aug), as most buses are full by the time they get to Manali, though the 5.30am one does start here.

Services There are two ATMs, although it's wiser to have a stock of cash in case they are not working.

ACCOMMODATION AND EATING

Chanderbhaga On the main road, 1km towards Darcha ☎ 01900 222393, ✉ keylong@hptdc.in. Comfortable but bland and typically overpriced HPTDC hotel. Half-board included with the more expensive rooms. HPTDC buses overnight at the tent camp. Dorms ₹400, doubles ₹2100.

Gyespa The Mall ☎ 01900 222207. Neat three-storey hotel, which has compact but comfortable attached rooms with hot showers and a good multicuisine restaurant. Smarter new sister hotel near the bus stand. ₹700

Nordaling Guest House On a path between the main road and the bus stand ☎ 01900 222294, ✆ nordalingkeylong.in. Welcoming lodge that has bright, reasonably spacious rooms with bathrooms and cable TV, plus a decent restaurant. ₹800

Tashi Deleg Just above the bazaar ☎ 01900 222450, ✉ hotel_tashideleg@yahoo.in. Large place with great valley views, comfortable and sizeable rooms, plus a rooftop café serving a range of favourites. ₹1250

Spiti

From its headwaters below the **Kunzum La** pass, the River Spiti runs 130km southeast to within the flick of a yak's tail of the border with Tibet, where it meets the Sutlej. The valley itself, surrounded by huge peaks with an average altitude of 4500m, is one of the highest and most remote inhabited places on earth – a desolate, barren tract scattered with tiny mud-and-timber hamlets and lonely lamaseries. Until 1992, Spiti in its entirety lay off-limits to foreign tourists. Now, only its far southeastern corner falls within the **Inner Line** – which leaves upper Spiti, including the district headquarters **Kaza**, freely accessible from the northwest via Lahaul. If you are really keen to complete the loop through the restricted area to or from Kinnaur (see page 421), you will need a **permit** (see page 413). The last main stop before reaching the restricted zone is the famed **Tabo** *gompa*, which harbours some of the oldest and most exquisite Buddhist art in the world.

Northwestern Spiti

From Grampoo, where the road along the Spiti Valley forks east from the Manali–Leh Highway, you have to bump along a wide but rough track for the first 80km. However, the gorge, waterfalls, snowy peaks and not least, the white-knuckle ascent over Kunzum La pass, make for a mind-boggling entry into the region. Near the pass it's possible with your own vehicle to detour 12km north to the small but picturesque **Chandertal Lake** (4300m). Soon after crossing Kunzum La, the track reaches the sprawling village of **Losar** (4113m), where you have to sign in at a police checkpoint. There are a couple of basic guesthouses and a few *dhabas* but little reason to stay here. From this point the track becomes a patchily surfaced road for the last section to Kaza.

Kaza and around

KAZA, 76km southeast of the Kunzum Pass, and 201km from Manali, is the subdivisional headquarters of **Spiti**. Overlooking the north bank of the River Spiti, it's the region's least picturesque town, but as the main market and roadhead it's a good base from which to head off on two- or three-day treks to monasteries and remote

6

villages such as Kibber. Rates for porters and ponymen are comparable to those in Kullu. It is also possible to trek to Dhankar (32km) and on to Tabo (43km).

The town is divided into two parts by an almost dry creek that trickles into the River Spiti. On the west side, **New Kaza** is rather lacking in character but does boast a colourful modern monastery, just above the main road, which then loops round the head of the gorge towards the bus stand on the far side of **Old Kaza**. The old village is also accessible from New Kaza by a low footbridge, from the opposite side of which the bazaar winds down through a maze of alleys to the bus stand, passing most of the town's facilities on the way.

ARRIVAL AND DEPARTURE
KAZA AND AROUND

By bus There is one daily departure for Manali (5am; 12–13hr) and two for Tabo (2hr) at 7.30am and 2pm, the first of which goes all the way to Shimla (20–22hr) via Rekong Peo (11–12hr). The only bus to Mudh (2hr 30min) in the Pin Valley leaves daily at 3pm, returning the next morning.

Likewise, there is a 4.15pm departure to Kibber that returns next day.

By taxi Jeeps are plentiful around the bus stand and cost roughly ₹2500 return for the Pin Valley or Tabo and ₹1350 for Kibber via Ki.

ACCOMMODATION

Amazingly, Kaza has about fifty mostly simple **places to stay**, spread roughly equally between New and Old Kaza, so bargaining down the rather inflated prices can produce good results.

Khangsar Hotel Main road, New Kaza ☎ 01906 222276. This pleasant hotel has large, comfortable attached rooms, most with TV, and a decent restaurant. The back block is a little cheaper and it's worth viewing a few rooms first. Its nearby sister hotel *Deyzor* can take any overspill. No wi-fi. ₹800

The Parasol Retreat 200m below the monastery, New Kaza ☎ 94188 45187. Modern building whose attractive rooms have soft furnishings and most have sweeping views. The attached agency runs camping tours and activities. ₹1200

★ **Sakya Abode** Main road near the creek, New Kaza ☎ 94182 08987, ⌨ sakyaabode.com. This attractive place, built in traditional monastic style around a grassy lawn, offers smartish rooms and a cheap dorm. It organizes

meditation retreats and adventure activities. Dorms ₹250, doubles ₹1100

Tashi Delek Off Main Bazaar, near the bus stand ☎ 94596 66088. Conveniently placed for early morning departures, this ochre-coloured lodge has basic attached rooms. Those at the back have the best views. No wi-fi. ₹600

★ **Taste of Spiti Delek** Opposite Old Circuit House, Main Bazaar, Old Kaza ☎ 94184 39294, ⌨ spitiecosphere. com. Nicely located, eco-friendly building that runs on wind and solar energy. There's a range of simple attached rooms, whose water is solar-heated. The restaurant serves delicious fusion food, mixing local and world recipes and it's all run by community social enterprise Ecosphere. ₹800

Zangchuk Guest House Near the creek, Old Kaza ☎ 01906 222705. The attached rooms and facilities are pretty small and very basic but there are excellent views from its peaceful terrace. No wi-fi. ₹800

EATING AND DRINKING

Chandertal Cafe Main Bazaar, Old Kaza ☎ 94189 72250. Simple Tibetan canteen serving great *thentuk*, *thukpa* and *momos*, all for under ₹100. Check out the amusing and incongruous Rasta mural. Daily 6am–9pm.

Mahaboudha Main Bazaar, Old Kaza ☎ 94185 37545. Light upstairs restaurant with fine views from its large windows. It offers reasonable Indian and Chinese, including tasty pork dishes for ₹150–250. Daily 7am–9pm.

Sherab Food Corner Right below the monastery, New

Kaza ☎ 94595 24121. Tiny and ultra-basic Tibetan joint, where you can get a superb non-veg *thukpa* for just ₹70, as well as *momos* and chow mein. Daily 6.30am–8pm.

★ **Sòl Café** Main Bazaar, Old Kaza ☎ 94188 60099, ⌨ spitiecosphere.com. Artistically decorated and run solely on solar power by Ecosphere upstairs, you can get a few savoury snacks such as chaat and *tsampa* nachos with cheese dip, plus great cakes, handmade chocolates, juices, teas and coffee. Daily 9am–7pm.

DIRECTORY

Permits Those continuing on to Kinnaur can get a free Inner Line permit (see page 413) from the Additional Deputy Commissioner's office in New Kaza (Mon–Sat 9am–1pm & 2–5pm; closed 2nd Sat).

Travel agents Spiti Holiday Adventure (☎ 94186 38071, ⌨ spitiholidayadventure.com) is the most reliable travel agent and also offers currency exchange, while Ecosphere (☎ 94188 60099, ⌨ spitiecosphere.com) has free water refills, a network of homestays, trekking and wildlife info, plus opportunities for volunteering and learning local skills.

Ki Gompa

Set against a backdrop of snow-flecked mountains and clinging to the sides of a windswept conical hillock, **Ki Gompa** is a picture-book example of Tibetan architecture and one of Himachal's most exotic spectacles. Founded in the sixteenth century, Ki is the largest **monastery** in the Spiti Valley, supporting a thriving community of lamas whose Rinpoche, Lo Chien Tulkhu from Shalkar near Sumdo, is said to be the current incarnation of the "Great Translator" Rinchen Zangpo. His glass-fronted quarters crown the top of the complex, reached via stone steps that wind between the lamas' houses below. A labyrinth of dark passages and wooden staircases connects the prayer and assembly halls, home to collections of old *thangkas*, weapons, musical instruments, manuscripts and devotional images (no photography). Many of the rooms have seen extensive renovation since an earthquake struck in 1975; a prayer hall, dedicated by the Dalai Lama, was also added in 2000. During the new moon towards late June or early July, Ki hosts a large **festival** celebrating the "burning of the demon" when *chaam* dances are followed by a procession to the ritual ground below the monastery where a large butter sculpture is set on fire.

ARRIVAL AND DEPARTURE   KI GOMPA

By bus The daily bus from Kaza arrives around 5pm and continues   to Kibber. The return to Kaza passes through about 8am.

ACCOMODATION

Ki Gompa Guesthouse In the monastery ☏ 94186 26613. The monks rent out a few extremely basic, cell-like rooms in the monastery. Simple meals are included but there is only cold water. No wi-fi. ₹400

Tashi Khangsar Guesthouse After the first bend in the road towards Kibber ☏ 01906 226277. Small, friendly and clean guesthouse with very simple rooms, most with shared bathrooms. No wi-fi. ₹250/₹500

Kibber

KIBBER (4205m) is among the highest settlements in the world with a driveable road and electricity. Jeep tracks, satellite dishes and the odd tin-roofed government building aside, its smattering of a hundred or so old Spitian houses is truly picturesque. Surrounded in summer by lush green barley fields, Kibber also stands at the head of a trail that picks its way north across the mountains, via the high glaciated **Parang La** pass (5600m) to Ladakh. Before the construction of roads into the Spiti Valley, locals used to lead ponies and yaks this way to trade in Leh bazaar. Some Manali-based trekking companies (see page 456) offer a seventeen-day trek from here to the lake of **Tso Moriri** in Ladakh (see page 496) and on to Leh.

ARRIVAL AND DEPARTURE   KIBBER

By bus Taking the 4.15pm bus from Kaza to Kibber (1hr) means you have to spend the night.
Other options Alternatively you could rent a jeep, hitch

with a tour group, or forego transport altogether and walk the 16km of trails, although the outbound trip is nearly all uphill.

ACCOMMODATION

Norling Opposite the school ☏ 01906 200091. Typical of the handful of congenial lodges but slightly nicer than the adjoining *Rainbow* and with a better restaurant. Most rooms have common hot bucket bathrooms. No wi-fi. ₹300/₹500

Serkong In the centre of the village ☏ 01906 200156. Very quaint traditional rooms, all with common bathrooms, and a nice roof terrace for relaxing over a snack or tea in the sun. ₹300

Dhankar

Nearly a third of the way between Kaza and Tabo, near the meeting of the Pin and Spiti rivers, a rough road veers off to the east for 8.5km to Dhankar. The

6

TREKKING IN LAHAUL AND SPITI

Although parts of the old trade routes to Ladakh and Tibet are now sealed with tarmac, most of this remote and spectacular region is still only accessible on foot. Its trails, though well frequented in high season, are long, hard and high, so you must be self-sufficient and have a guide. Pack-horses and provisions are most readily available in **Manali**, or in **Keylong** and **Darcha** (Lahaul) and **Kaza** (Spiti) if you can afford to wait a few days. A good rope for river crossings will be useful, particularly in summer when the water levels are at their highest.

The **best time** to trek is July to early September, when brilliant blue skies make this an ideal alternative to the monsoon-prone Kullu Valley. By late September, the risk of snowfall deters many visitors from the longer expeditions. Whenever you leave, allow enough time to acclimatize to the **altitude** before attempting any big passes: AMS (Acute Mountain Sickness) claims victims here every season (see page 53).

LAHAUL: DARCHA TO PADUM VIA THE SHINGO LA PASS

The most popular trek is from **Darcha** over the **Shingo La** pass (5000m) to **Padum** in Zanskar. The trail passes through **Kargyak**, the highest village in Zanskar, and follows the Kargyak Valley down to its confluence with the Tsarap at **Purne**. There is a small café, shop, and camping ground here and it's a good base for the side trip to **Phuktal gompa**, one of the most spectacular sights in Zanskar. During the high season (July & Aug), a string of chai stall/tent camps spring up at intervals along the well-worn trail through the Tsarap Valley to Padum, meaning that you can manage without a guide or ponies from here on. Do not bank on finding food and shelter here at the start or end of the season.

LAHAUL: BATAL TO BARALACHA PASS

Lahaul's other popular trekking route follows the River Chandra north to its source at the **Baralacha Pass** (4920m) and makes a good extension to the Hampta Pass hike (see page 458). Alternatively, catch a Kaza bus from Manali to the trailhead at **Batal** (3960m) below the **Kunzum La** (4551m). The beautiful milky-blue **Chandratal** ("Moon") **Lake** is a relentless ascent of 7hr from Batal, with stunning views south across the world's longest glacier, **Bara Shigri**, and the forbidding north face of the **White Sail** massif (6451m). The next campground is at **Tokping Yongma** torrent. **Tokpo Yongma**, several hours further up, is the second of the two big side-torrents and is much easier to ford early in the morning; from here it is a steady climb up to the Baralacha Pass. You can then continue to Zanskar via the Phirtse La, or pick up transport (prearranged if possible) down to Keylong and Manali or onwards to Leh.

SPITI: KAZA VIA THE PIN VALLEY TO MANIKARAN OR WANGTU

One of the best treks in **Spiti** is up the **Pin Valley**. The track alongside the River Pin, which passes a string of traditional settlements and monasteries, is now motorable as far as Mudh, around 40km south of Kaza. Over the next few years it is expected to be paved right through to Wangtu, but for now it forks beyond Mudh into two walking paths: the northern path over the Pin–Parvati Pass (5400m) to **Manikaran** in the Parvati Valley (see page 451), and the southern one to Wangtu in **Kinnaur** via the Bhaba Pass (4865m). The last section to Wangtu itself has also fallen to the roadbuilders, so you might decide just to hitch a ride.

Dhankar Gompa (daily 8am–6pm; ₹25) on the uppermost peak behind the village of **DHANKAR** (3890m) is famed for its brilliant murals, probably painted in the seventeenth century, depicting the life of the Buddha. Although some of the work has been vandalized, the scenes depicting the Buddha's birth, rebirth and life in Kapilavastu and his rejection of worldly ways are spectacular. The *gompa*, much of which is in a sad state of repair and on the World Monument Fund's list of the hundred most endangered sites, also affords superb views down to the confluence of the main River Spiti and the Pin tributary.

ARRIVAL AND DEPARTURE	DHANKAR

By taxi/on foot Dhankar is not on a bus route so you'll have to take a taxi from Sichaling on the road to Tabo (₹250) or walk – the shortcut starts from the storm shelter by the main road under the *gompa* 3km before Sichaling.

ACCOMMODATION

Dhankar Gompa guesthouse In the monastery. The much improved monastery guesthouse has simple rooms, the non-attached with hot water, plus a dorm and terrace restaurant. No wi-fi. ₹500

Tenzin Homestay Above the monastery near the Old Fort ☎ 94592 70036. Welcoming family homestay with small, cosy rooms, all with shared baths, and splendid views across the valley. Food included. No wi-fi. ₹700

Pin Valley

Thirty minutes east of Kaza a bridge at Attargu crosses the Spiti and begins a 156km run up the **PIN VALLEY** to **Gulling**, above which stands the important Nyingma *gompa* of Gungri, believed to date back to the eighth or ninth century. Across the river lies the slightly larger settlement of **Sagnam**. At the head of the valley, a rough road veers slightly southwest to **Mikim** and the **Pin Valley National Park** (unrestricted free access), which starts beyond the hamlet of **Phukchong** and is home to the ibex, red fox and snow leopard. Beyond Sagnam the road deteriorates rapidly, but vehicles can push ahead another 14km to **Mudh**, an enchanting hamlet with a tiny nunnery that peers over a breathtaking valley flanked at its end by the pyramid-shaped Tordang Mountain.

ARRIVAL AND DEPARTURE	PIN VALLEY

By bus There is one bus from Kaza at 3pm, which returns the following morning.

ACCOMMODATION

The Hermitage On the edge of Phukchong ☎ 94184 39294. By far the most comfortable place to stay in the valley, with neat attached rooms. It is primarily a meditation retreat. Half-board ₹3000

Himalayan Pin Parvati Guest House Mudh village centre ☎ 94185 71167. Probably the best of the several simple guesthouses, with plain but clean rooms, all with common baths, and good healthy food. No wi-fi. ₹600

Shambala Guesthouse Sagnam village centre

☎ 01906 224221. The best of the small bunch at this delightful riverside location, with small but clean rooms and well-kept shared facilities. ₹500

Tara Guest House On the edge of Mudh ☎ 89880 62293, ⓦ facebook.com/Taraguesthousespiti. Providing simple meals and a warm family welcome, the *Tara* is another good option. All rooms are basic, although the more expensive have are en suite. Meals included. ₹1800

Tabo

One of the main reasons to brave the rough roads of Spiti is to get to **Tabo Gompa**, 43km east of Kaza. The mud-and-timber boxes of the old *gompa* that nestle on the steep north bank of the Spiti may look drab, but the multihued murals and stucco sculpture they contain are some of the world's richest and most important ancient Buddhist art treasures – the link between the cave paintings of Ajanta (see page 666) and the more exuberant Tantric art that flourished in Tibet five centuries or so later. According to an inscription in its main assembly hall, the monastery was established in 996 AD, when **Rinchen Zangpo** was disseminating dharma across the northwestern Himalayas. In addition to the 158 Sanskrit Buddhist texts he personally transcribed, the "Great Translator" brought with him a retinue of Kashmiri artisans to decorate the temples. The only surviving examples of their exceptional work are here at Tabo, at Alchi in Ladakh, and Toling and Tsaparang *gompas* in Chinese-occupied western Tibet.

The new *gompa*, inaugurated by the Dalai Lama in 1983, houses nearly fifty lamas and a handful of *chomos* (nuns), some of whom receive training in traditional painting techniques under a *geshe*, or teacher from eastern Tibet. Visitors are welcome to attend daily 6.30am puja. It's also worth exploring the caves across the main road, one of which houses more paintings, but you need to be let in by the *gompa* caretaker.

6

6

The Chogskhar

Daily 8am–5pm; unrestricted access to grounds • Donation

Enclosed within a mud-brick wall, Tabo's **Chogskhar**, or "sacred enclave", contains eight temples and 24 *chortens* (*stupas*). The largest and oldest structure in the group, the **Sug La-khang**, which includes the **Z'al** (House of Treasures), stands opposite the main entrance. Erected at the end of the tenth century, the "Hall of the Enlightened Gods" was conceived in the form of a three-dimensional mandala, whose structure and elaborately decorated interior functions as a mystical model of the universe complete with deities. There are three distinct bands of detail – the lower-level paintings depict episodes in the life of the Buddha and his previous incarnations; above are stucco gods and goddesses; and the top of the hall is covered with meditating Buddhas and *bodhisattvas*. Bring a torch to see the full detail of the murals.

The other temples date from the fifteenth and eighteenth centuries. Their contents illustrate the development of Buddhist iconography from its early Indian origins to the Chinese-influenced opulence of medieval Tibetan Tantricism that still, in a more lurid form, predominates in modern *gompas*.

ARRIVAL AND DEPARTURE   TABO

By bus Two buses per day travel to Kaza, the 3am departure going all the way to Manali. In the opposite direction, a bus passes through at around 9.30am on its way from Kaza to Rekong Peo in Kinnaur and on to Shimla.

ACCOMMODATION AND EATING

Café Kunzom Top In the village centre ☎ 94592 70055. Choose between the flowery courtyard and cushioned interior to enjoy tasty vegetarian food, including various types of Tibetan *tsampa*, curries and Western dishes such as rostis, all ₹60–150. Daily 7am–10pm.

Maitreya Regency In the village centre ☎ 94594 83103, ⓦ maitreyaregencytabo.in. Friendly family-run hotel with twelve large, bright and comfortable rooms spread over two floors. The convivial restaurant (which has a section with traditional Spitian low tables) does great *momos* and other food. ₹2500

Millennium Monastic Guest House Outside the main monastery gates ☎ 01906 223333. The official monastery guesthouse is run by monks and has simple rooms, some attached, and a dorm. Also has a simple restaurant. No-wi-fi. Dorms ₹250, doubles ₹400

★ **Sidharth** On the road to the bus stand ☎ 94185 81203, ⓔ dk22902@gmail.com. Bright new two-storey hotel with decent-sized rooms, all beautifully decorated and comfortably furnished. Small restaurant downstairs. ₹1400

Tashi Khangsar Hotel Between the monastery and the river ☎ 01906 233346, ⓔ vaneetrana23@gmail.com. Reasonably spacious and excellent-value rooms and a lovely large garden, with a parachute canopy for shade. Camping might be possible if you ask. ₹600

The Manali–Leh Highway

Since it opened to foreign tourists in 1989, the famous **Manali–Leh Highway** has replaced the old Srinagar–Kargil route as the most popular approach to Ladakh. In summer, a stream of vehicles set off from the Kullu Valley to travel along the second-highest road in the world, which reaches a dizzying altitude of 5328m at Tanglang La. Its surface varies wildly from fairly smooth asphalt through potholes of differing depths to dirt tracks sliced by glacial streams, traversing a starkly beautiful lunar wilderness. Depending on road conditions and type of vehicle, the 485km journey can take anything from seventeen to thirty hours' actual driving. Bus drivers invariably stop for a short and chilly night in one of the spartan **tent camps** along the route. These, however, are few and far between after September 15, when the highway officially closes; in practice, all this means is that the Indian government won't airlift you out if you get trapped in snow. Yet some companies run regardless of this until the passes become blocked by snowfall in late October. Note also that if it's a heavy monsoon the unpaved parts of the road can get extremely muddy in July and August especially and that landslides can cut off sections of road and cause severe delays. Details on **transport** between Manali (see page 453) and Leh (see page 482) are covered in the respective town accounts – all-year-round travel will be possible once the **Rohtang Tunnel** opens at the end of 2019.

Manali to Keylong

Once out of **Manali**, the road begins its long ascent of the **Rohtang Pass** (3978m) and, annoyingly, often gets clogged only an hour or so up, when trucks get bogged down in wet weather; it's not uncommon to have an unscheduled wait of up to four hours when this happens. This frustration may soon become a thing of the past, however, if the long-planned **Rohtang Tunnel** is completed by its revised schedule of 2019. The 8.8km feat of engineering will save 60km of twisting road and shave a couple of hours off the journey. Until the tunnel opens, buses pull in for breakfast (or brunch) 17km before the pass at a row of makeshift *dhabas* at **Marhi** (3360m). Though not all that high by Himalayan standards, the pass itself is one of the most treacherous in the region and every year locals and tourists alike are caught unawares by sudden weather changes – hence Rohtang's name, which literally means "piles of dead bodies". The road descends from Rohtang to the floor of the **Chandra Valley**, finally reaching the river at **Koksar**, little more than a scruffy collection of chai stalls with a **checkpoint** where you have to enter passport details in a ledger – one of several such stops on the road to Leh. The next few hours are among the most memorable on the entire trip. Bus seats on the left are best, as the road runs across the northern slopes of the valley through the first Buddhist settlements, hemmed in by towering peaks and hanging glaciers towards **Keylong** (see page 462). The HPTDC super-deluxe and some other buses break the journey here, leaving the bulk of the journey to the second day (the opposite obviously applies when travelling to Manali from Leh).

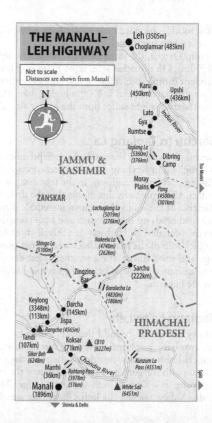

Keylong to Sarchu

Beyond Keylong, the Bhaga Valley broadens, but its bare sides support very few villages. At **DARCHA**, a lonely cluster of dry-stone huts and dingy tent camps, plus another checkpoint, the landscape is still fairly green. All buses stop here for passengers to grab a hot bowl of Tibetan *thukpa* from a wayside *dhaba*. There's little else to do in Darcha, though the Shingo La trailhead – the main trekking route north to Zanskar (see page 507) – is on the outskirts. If you are not on one of the through Manali–Leh buses, you're better off stopping at **JISPA**,

6

CYCLING THE MANALI–LEH HIGHWAY

Touring cylists revere the Manali–Leh highway as one of the most challenging road rides in the world and each summer up to five hundred intrepid two-wheelers set off to attempt the nearly 500km route, which requires at least a week to complete, plus more time for acclimatization. While the **gradients** are rarely unrideable, the two-day ascents, rough tracks over the **passes** and, most crucially, the **altitude** demand respect and some preparation.

Hauling a fully laden bike up 50km climbs to well over 5000m may sound daunting, but the exhilaration can be rewarding – especially if you're set up to camp rather than relying on the noisy, dirty parachute camps. You'll need wind- and waterproof clothing, a warm fleece, sunglasses and headwear, plus a good supply of high-energy snacks like the blocks of peanut brittle found in the bazaars. A water filter increases your autonomy too as you'll drink at least three litres a day. Check your bike has a suitably low gearing for crawling up the passes (most MTBs will), and that you have near-new brake pads for the long descents that follow, as well as a secure baggage system. As for clothing, choose quick-drying items that will wick away sweat before it brings on exposure on a chilly pass.

Most riders set off from Manali (1900m) and take eight to ten days to get to Leh (3500m). However, starting in Leh gives you a chance to acclimatize before you set off, and involves less climbing (but no less drama). Whichever direction you take, don't fret too much about you or your bike packing up halfway, as you'll always be able to hitch a lift. If riding alone is not for you, choose between numerous **mountain-bike tour operators** in Manali (see page 456). For more information, see ⓦ himalayabybike.com.

7km south, a pleasant little village with ample camping along the river as well as the route's one proper hotel.

From Darcha, the surfaced road climbs steadily northeast to the **Baralacha La** pass (4950m). On the other side, some buses stop for the night at **SARCHU**, where the state-run tent camp is preferable to several more expensive camps dotted along the road. Note that Sarchu Serai is 2500m higher than Manali, and travellers coming straight from Manali might suffer from the higher altitude here.

Sarchu to Taglang La

Sarchu packs up for the season from September 15. Northbound buses that haven't overnighted in Keylong thereafter press on over **Lachuglang La** (5019m), the second highest pass on the highway, to the tent camp at **PANG** (4500m), which stays open longer. Unfortunately, this means that the drive through one of the most dramatic stretches of the route, through an incredible canyon, is in darkness. North of Pang, the road heads up to the fourth and final pass, the **Taglang La**, the highest point on the Manali–Leh Highway at a literally breathtaking 5328m. Drivers pull in for a quick spin of the prayer wheels and a brief photo session alongside the altitude sign and small shrine. If the weather's clear enough, you can gaze north beyond the multicoloured tangle of prayer flags across Ladakh to the Karakoram Range, just visible on the horizon.

Taglang La to Leh

Thirty kilometres beyond the pass is **Rumtse**, the first Ladakhi village. There are two basic guesthouse-cum-*dhabas* here, located opposite a store selling unperishable snacks. Just down the road the next village of **Gya** has a health clinic (with oxygen) and just back below the tree line, **Lato** has a particularly nice campsite in season, as well as a basic lodge. At **Upshi**, the road reaches the dramatic Indus Valley, tracing the **Indus River** past slender poplars, sprawling army camps and ancient monasteries. Traffic builds as you approach **Choglamsar**, then climb the final dusty 10km to **Leh** (see page 482) – past the world's highest golf course – through the modern outskirts to the haberdashers, canny traders and wrinkled apricot-sellers of Leh's Main Bazaar.

ACCOMMODATION AND EATING   THE MANALI–LEH HIGHWAY

There are only very sparse accommodation options north of Keylong (see page 462), mostly at very basic **tent camps**, with the odd equally basic **guesthouse** thrown in. The one exception is the hotel listed below. Most of these places can rustle up simple **meals** and there are a few tented *dhabas* along the route too. If you are on a government bus, accommodation at the *Chanderbhaga* in Keylong (see page 463) is organized for you, whichever direction you are travelling in.

Hotel Ibex-Jispa Main Rd, Jispa ☏ 98160 36860, ⓦ hotelibexjispa.in. Incongruously large four-storey building with twenty-seven smart deluxe rooms and a twenty-bed dorm. Staff can arrange adventure activities. June to mid-Oct. Dorms ₹400, doubles ₹2200

6

Jammu and Kashmir

SHANTI STUPA, LEH

Jammu and Kashmir

India's northernmost and fifth-largest state, Jammu and Kashmir (usually shortened to J&K) is also one of its most mountainous, and quite staggeringly beautiful – think Himalayan peaks reflected in alpine lakes, and 5000m-plus passes which take the breath away in more ways than one. The most wretchedly beautiful spots – and the overwhelming majority of travellers – are to be found in lofty Ladakh, though there's some stunning scenery in Kashmir proper too. Safer than it has been for years (though it's still something to check on before your visit), Kashmir provides some wonderful trekking opportunities, as well as offering more sedentary beauty from the vantage point of a shikara or houseboat on Srinagar's picture-perfect, mountain-encircled Dal Lake.

7

Though in theory a single state, J&K is effectively split three ways in terms of culture and geography. Funnily enough, most people focus on neither Jammu or Kashmir, but the entity unheralded in the name of the state – adorable **Ladakh**, an extremely mountainous area with an altitude mostly over 3000m, and inhabitants who generally speak Ladakhi, a Tibetan tongue, and follow a strain of Tibetan Buddhism. Ladakh can prove hard to access overland for much of the year, thanks to the region's harsh climate, though many choose to brave the tortuous route from Manali in Himachal Pradesh, or the easier one from Srinagar to the west. Ladakh's enchanting capital, **Leh**, is surrounded by numerous villages dominated by venerable monasteries, such as **Thikse**, **Hemis** and **Lamayuru**. Exquisite areas worth the bumpy detours involved in reaching them from Leh include the icy lakes of **Pangong Tso** and **Tso Moriri**, as well as the almost surreal **Nubra Valley**, with its sand dunes and wandering camels.

There's a large Muslim population in the western half of Ladakh, though this increases to over 95 percent once across the "border" to **Kashmir**, a green belt of largely mountainous land whose people mostly speak Kashmiri, a language which, to some,

---

BEST TIME TO VISIT

J&K's harshest climate is in **Ladakh**, with passes into the region open only between late June and late October, when the sun is at its strongest and the weather, at least during the day, pleasantly warm. Although it is officially a high-altitude desert, recent years have seen increasing bouts of rain in July and August, sometimes making trekking difficult. From November onwards, temperatures drop fast, often plummeting to minus 40°C between December and February, when the only way in and out of Zanskar is along the frozen surface of the river. Note that nearly all hotels and guesthouses are closed from some time in October until April, while many garden restaurants only open in the peak summer months.

Kashmir is at its best (though also at its busiest and most expensive) during late March and mid-May, when spring flowers abound, and from September to early November, with its golden days and chillier nights. Although the region's climate is less harsh than Ladakh and the road up from Jammu kept open by the army, the winter months see some seriously subzero temperatures and heaps of snow. By contrast, as much of the Kashmir Valley (including Srinagar itself) is well under 2000m in altitude, high summer can be surprisingly hot, sometimes topping 35°C. It can also get quite wet in July and August.

Sitting at the top of the plains, the **Jammu** area can be visited at any time of year, though it can get extremely hot and humid between April and August and rather cold and foggy in the middle of winter.

TSO MORIRI, A HIGH-ALTITUDE LAKE IN THE HIMALAYAS

Highlights

❶ **Leh** Medieval streets, a Tibetan-style palace, bazaars and looming snowy peaks. See page 482

❷ **Thikse** Along with Lamayuru and Hemis, the Indian Himalayas' most impressive monastery complex. See page 491

❸ **Tso Moriri** This exquisite high-altitude lake inhabited by nomadic herders features snow-fringed desert mountains and rare migratory birds. See page 496

❹ **Nubra Valley** Sand dunes, Bactrian camels and views of the mighty Karakorams await across one of the world's highest driveable roads. See page 496

❺ **Alchi** Wonderful painted murals and stucco images are hidden behind the simple exterior of this ancient monastery. See page 501

❻ **Zanskar** Walled in by the Himalayas, during the winter this isolated valley can only be reached by following the frozen river route. See page 507

❼ **Kashmir Valley** This lush swathe of green is once more attracting visitors to trekking bases such as Pahalgam and Sonamarg. See page 509

❽ **Dal Lake** Lounging on a Kashmiri houseboat, surrounded by waterlilies, kingfishers and a stunning mountain range – unforgettable. See page 511

HIGHLIGHTS ARE MARKED ON THE MAP ON PAGE 476

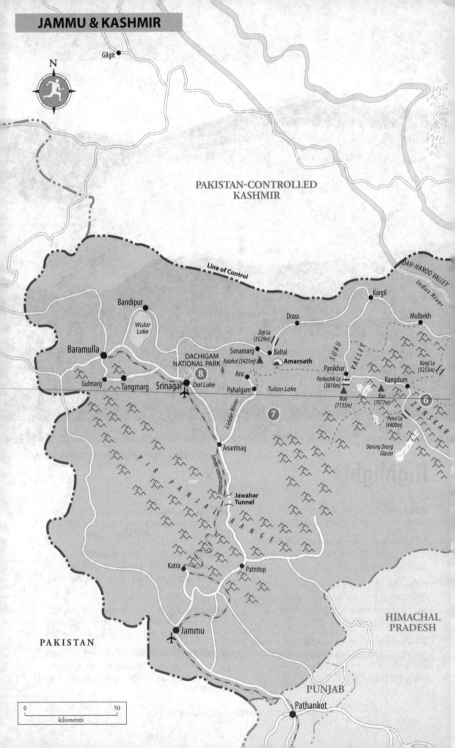

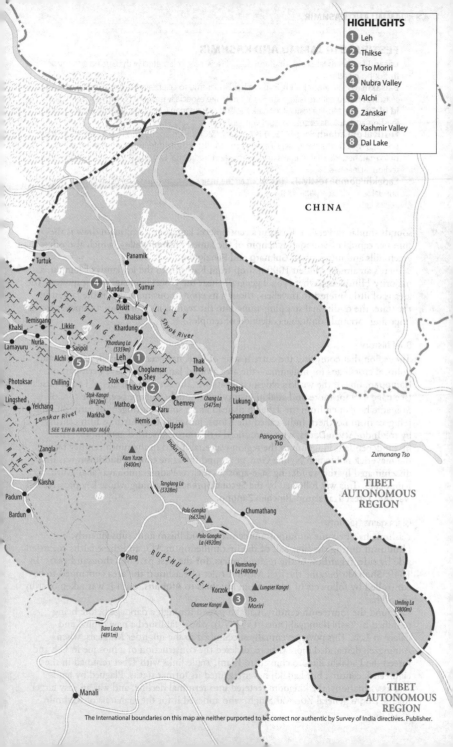

HIGHLIGHTS

1 Leh
2 Thikse
3 Tso Moriri
4 Nubra Valley
5 Alchi
6 Zanskar
7 Kashmir Valley
8 Dal Lake

CHINA

Turtuk
Panamik
Sumur
Hundur
Diskit
Khalsar
NUBRA VALLEY
Khardung
Shyok River
LADAKH RANGE
Temisgang
Likkir
Khalsi
Nurla
Khardung La
(5359m)
Lamayuru
Saspol
Alchi
Leh
Choglamsar
Shey
Thak
Thok
Photoksar
Spitok
Stok
Thikse
Chilling
Stok-Kangri
(6120m)
Matho
Karu
Chemrey
Chang La
(5475m)
Tangse
Lingshed
Yelchang
Zanskar River
Markha
Hemis
Lukung
Zangla
SEE 'LEH & AROUND' MAP
Upshi
Spangmik
Indus River
Pangong
Tso
Zumunang Tso
Karsha
Kam Yurze
(6400m)
Padum
Bardun
Tanglang La
(5328m)
TIBET
AUTONOMOUS
REGION
Polo Gongka
(6632m)
Chumathang
Pang
RUPSHU VALLEY
Polo Gongka
La (4920m)
Namshang
La (4800m)
Bara Lacha
(4891m)
Korzok
Lungser Kangri
Chamser Kangri
Tso
Moriri
Umling La
(5800m)
Manali
TIBET
AUTONOMOUS
REGION

The International boundaries on this map are neither purported to be correct nor authentic by Survey of India directives. Publisher.

FESTIVALS IN JAMMU AND KASHMIR

Losar (Late Jan to late Feb). Tibetan/Ladakhi New Year, celebrated with dancing and music throughout Ladakh.

Baisakhi (Usually April 13/14). Fairs are held in Jammu to celebrate the north Indian harvest season in Hindu culture (see page 57). Women are especially prominent, with colourful dress.

Id ul-Fitr. The Muslim festival to mark the end of Ramadan (see page 58) is celebrated with feasting and various events throughout Kashmir.

Festival of Ladakh Sept 1–15. This popular J&K Tourism-sponsored two-week event, held principally in Leh, is designed to extend the tourist season. It features archery contests, polo matches, Bactrian camels from Nubra and traditional Ladakhi dance along with some tedious speeches.

Ladakhi gompa festivals. Just about all the major *gompas* (monasteries) in Ladakh hold annual festivals (see page 483).

---

sounds similar to Persian. Kashmir's centrepiece, largest city and main draw is the summer capital of **Srinagar**, lynchpin of the famed **Kashmir Valley**, which also offers the green hills and meadows of **Gulmarg** and **Pahalgam**.

There's an almost sudden 1000m drop from Kashmir to the lowlands of **Jammu**, a majority-Hindu area where you'll generally hear the Dogri language being spoken. The area is of little interest to travellers, though its eponymous main city is the largest in the state; the traditional stepping-stone into the region, it's worthy of a stopover for its imposing fort and admirable collection of temples.

Brief history

The region that comprises the current state of J&K has been a cultural, religious and political crossroads for millennia – the area around Jammu may have been part of **Harappan**, one of the world's oldest civilizations. The first inhabitants of Ladakh itself (see page 479 for more on Ladakhi history) are thought to have been a mixture of nomadic herdsmen from the Tibetan plateau and a small contingent of early Buddhist refugees from northern India called the Mons, joined in the fourth or fifth century by the Indo-Aryan **Dards**, who introduced irrigation and settled agriculture. The first independent kingdom in the region was established in the ninth century by the maverick nobleman Nyima Gon, at around the same time as **Buddhism** was first disseminated by the wandering sage-apostles such as Padmasambhava (alias Guru Rinpoche). This was followed by the **Second Spreading**, among whose key proselytizers was the "Great Translator" **Rinchen Zangpo**.

Islam gains traction

Kashmir had become an important centre of Buddhism and, subsequently, Hinduism during the first half of the first millennium AD, and these faiths coexisted side by side, regardless of the region's rulers, for the best part of a thousand years. In 1349, **Shah Mir** became the first Muslim ruler of Kashmir; the area continued to be controlled by followers of Islam, from **Mughals** to **Afghans**, until it was taken over by the Sikhs.

Around the fourteenth century, Ladakh passed through a dark age before being reunified by **Tashi Namgyal** (ruled 1555–70), who established a new capital and palace at Leh. This power eventually succumbed to the mightier Mughals, when Aurangzeb demanded more tribute, ordered the construction of a mosque in Leh and forced the Ladakhi king to convert to Islam. Trade links with Tibet resumed in the eighteenth century, but Ladakh never regained its former status. Plagued by feuds and assassinations, the kingdom teetered into terminal decline, and was an easy target for the **Dogra** general Zorawar Singh, who annexed it for the maharaja of Kashmir in 1834.

J&K under Indian rule

J&K became a component state of independent India in 1948, following the first of the three Indo-Pak wars fought in the region. Tensions over the disputed Line of Control still flare up sporadically (see page 480), and when you consider the proximity of China, another old foe who annexed a large chunk of Ladakh in 1962, it's easy to see why this is India's most sensitive border zone. There is also a degree of internal friction. Long dissatisfied with the state government in Srinagar, a unified group of Ladakhi Buddhist and Muslim parties formed the **Ladakh Union Territory Front** in 2002, to push for separation from J&K and gain Union Territory recognition from Delhi; this merged with the BJP in 2010, leading to a heavy defeat by Congress in elections, though they emerged with a clear majority in the subsequent 2015 elections.

Across wider J&K, there have been alternative periods of Presidential rule – under the direct authority of central government – and control by the BJP-aligned People's Democratic Party (PDP), whose policy of collaborating with the Modi central government has dismayed many. There was a period of optimism under the Congress-aligned National Conference, with young Omar Abdullah as Chief Minister (2009–15), though chaos followed the premature death of PDP Chief Minister Mufti Mohammed Sayeed, who was succeeded by his daughter, Mehbooba Mufti (2016–18). Presidential rule was reinstated following Mufti's resignation in 2018, with elections for a new Chief Minister scheduled for mid-to-late 2019.

7

Ladakh

Ladakh (La-Dags – "land of high mountain passes") is mainland India's most remote and sparsely populated region, a high-altitude **desert** cradled by the Karakoram and Great Himalaya ranges and crisscrossed by myriad razor-sharp peaks and ridges. Variously described as "Little Tibet" or "the last Shangri-La", and culturally and administratively separate from the rest of India, this area is one of the last enclaves of Mahayana **Buddhism**, which has been its principal religion for nearly a thousand years. This is most evident in Ladakh's medieval monasteries: perched on rocky hilltops and clinging to sheer cliffs, these **gompas** are both repositories of ancient wisdom and living centres of worship.

RESTRICTED AREAS AND PERMITS

Parts of Ladakh are still inaccessible to casual tourists, and some of its most popular areas require **permits** to visit (photo ID only for Indian tourists), the cost of which includes an environmental fee. These include the **Nubra Valley** north of Leh (see page 496); the area around **Pangong Tso**, the lake to the east of Leh (see page 495); and the region of **Rupshu** with the lake of **Tso Moriri**, to the southeast of Leh (see page 496).

Permits are issued by the Deputy Commissioner's Office in Leh but the office deals only through Leh's many **tour operators** (see page 487), who charge a **fee** – usually around ₹550–660 per head. As the areas in question are served by infrequent public transport, you may well choose to use a tour operator anyway. In theory, permits are only issued to groups of at least two people accompanied by a guide, but in practice travel agents are generally happy to issue permits to solo individuals travelling independently, though you'll have an imaginary friend (usually somebody applying at the same time) listed on the permit to fulfil the official requirement. As long as your name and passport number are on the permit, the checkpoints are quite relaxed about how many of you there are. You will need two photocopies of the relevant pages of your passport and visa. Provided you apply in the morning, permits are usually issued on the same day, though don't bank on this. Once you have your permit, which is valid for seven days and covers all restricted areas, make at least five copies before setting off because officers at checkpoints sometimes like to keep a copy when you report in. If you go on an organized trip, however, the driver takes care of all this and you may never even handle your permit.

The highest concentration of monasteries is in the **Indus Valley** near **Leh**, the region's capital. Set in a sublime landscape and crammed with hotels, guesthouses and restaurants, this atmospheric little town, a staging post on the old Silk Route, is most visitors' point of arrival, and an ideal base for side-trips. North of Leh, across **Khardung La**, one of the highest driveable passes in the world, lies the valley of **Nubra**, where sand dunes carpet the valley floor. It is also possible to visit the great wilderness around the lake of **Tso Moriri** in **Rupshu**, southeast of Leh, and to glimpse Tibet from the shores of **Pangong Tso** in the far east of Ladakh. For all these areas you will, however, need a permit (see page 479). West of Leh, beyond the windswept **Fatu La** and **Namika La** passes, Buddhist prayer flags peter out as you approach the predominantly Muslim district of **Kargil**. Ladakh's second largest town, at the mouth of the breathtakingly beautiful **Suru Valley**, is the jumping-off point for **Zanskar**, the vast wilderness in the far south of the state that forms the border with Lahaul in Himachal Pradesh.

7

THE KASHMIR CONFLICT

The Himalayan region of **Kashmir** is the main reason why India and Pakistan have remained bitter enemies for most of the seventy or so years since Independence. The region's troubles date from Partition, when the ruling Hindu Maharaja Hari Singh opted to join India rather than Pakistan, and the geopolitical tug-of-war over the state has soured relations between the two countries ever since, at least until the last few years.

The conflict in Kashmir has taken two forms: firstly, a **military confrontation** between the Pakistani and Indian armies along the de facto border – on three occasions leading to fully fledged war (in 1947, 1965 and 1999); and, secondly, a violent **insurgency-cum-civil war** since 1989, during which both Kashmiri and foreign Muslim fighters have launched various attacks against Indian military and civilian targets inside Kashmir itself, leading to equally bloody reprisals by Indian security forces – a conflict which has now cost an estimated seventy thousand lives.

THE ROOTS OF THE PROBLEM

Following the cessation of hostilities in 1948, a UN resolution demanded that a plebiscite take place, allowing the Kashmiri people to decide their own future; this India has resolutely refused to hold. The Ceasefire Line, or so-called **Line of Control (LoC)**, became the effective border between India and Pakistan; the third of Kashmir held by Pakistan is referred to by those who support independence from India as **Azad (Free) Kashmir**. India lost a further slice of Kashmiri territory to China during the 1962 conflict (see page 1198) before a resumption of hostilities with Pakistan during the **Second Indo-Pakistan War** of 1965 (see page 1198). Again, Kashmir was the focus of attention, though at the end of the war both sides returned to their original positions. The **Simla Agreement** of 1972 committed both sides to renounce force in their dealings with one another, and to respect the LoC and the de facto border between their two states.

INSURGENCY AND CIVIL WAR

Simmering Kashmiri discontent with Indian rule began to transform into **armed resistance** around 1989 – the arrival of mujahideen in the Kashmir Valley after the end of the war with Russia in Afghanistan is often blamed for the sudden surge of militancy. The key incident, however, was the unprovoked massacre, in 1990, of around one hundred unarmed protesters, by Indian security forces on **Gawakadal Bridge** in the capital, Srinagar. By the following year, violence and human rights abuses had become endemic, both in the Kashmir Valley itself and further south around Jammu. **Curfews** became routine, and thousands of suspected militants were detained without trial amid innumerable accusations of torture, the systematic rape of Kashmiri women by Indian troops, disappearances of countless boys and men, and summary executions. The conflict continued to ebb and flow throughout the 1990s, with regular atrocities on both sides, while the region's once-thriving tourist industry was dealt a massive blow when the extremist Al-Faran Muslim group kidnapped five tourists trekking near Pahalgam in 1995; one was beheaded and the others were never found.

At the end of the decade, the crisis brought India and Pakistan to the verge of yet another all-out war. With both countries now fully fledged **nuclear states**, Kashmir had become one of the

Traditionally beyond the reach of the monsoons, Ladakh receives little snow, especially in the valleys, and even less rain (sometimes as little as 100mm per year). Only the most frugal methods enable its inhabitants to **farm** the thin sandy soil, frozen solid for eight months of the year and scorched for much of the other four. In recent years, however, **climate change** has meant even drier winters and less snow; the consequent loss of snowmelt has put pressure on traditional farming and irrigation, resulting in a real risk of drought, though this has been offset to some extent by increased rainfall during the summer months.

ARRIVAL AND GETTING AROUND
LADAKH

Two legendary "highways" connect Ladakh with the rest of India: the **Srinagar–Leh road**, and the route up from **Manali**, almost 500km south. These two, plus the rough road from Kargil to Padum in Zanskar, also link the majority of Ladakh's larger settlements with the capital.

By plane These days, the majority of visitors arrive at Leh airport, though doing so can raise the risk of altitude sickness (see page 484).

world's most dangerous geopolitical flashpoints. In May 1999, at least eight hundred Pakistani-backed mujahideen crept across the LoC near **Kargil** and began to occupy Indian territory. India moved thousands of troops and heavy artillery into the area, and swiftly followed up with an aerial bombardment. The conflict was contained, and by July the Indian army had retaken all ground lost to the militants. All-out war was only narrowly averted again in early 2003, after intense diplomatic pressure was brought to bear on both sides by US emissary **Colin Powell**. Within Kashmir, long-established organizations like the Jammu and Kashmir Liberation Front and the All Party Hurriyat Conference, which had traditionally adopted a secular and nationalist stance, were being increasingly eclipsed by militant Islamic and pro-Pakistani groups such as Lashkar-e-Toiba and Jaish-e-Mohammad.

THE ROAD TO PEACE?

The first signs of genuine rapprochement came in May 2003, when Indian prime minister Vajpayee made a **declaration of peace**, announcing that hundreds of Pakistanis detained since the Kargil War would be released. In 2004 and 2005 the Indian and Pakistani governments also held their first-ever talks with Kashmiri separatists, establishing a peaceful "road map" for progress in the region. Another round of Indo-Pak talks in 2005 resulted in, among other signs of progress, the inauguration of a fortnightly **bus service** between Srinagar and Muzaffarabad in Pakistani-controlled Kashmir, and in October the same year the Line of Control was opened up to speed up relief operations in the aftermath of a devastating **earthquake** in Pakistani Kashmir, which killed over seventy thousand. 2008 saw a downturn in Indo-Pak relations, first thanks to militant attacks in Kashmir, then to a minor issue regarding land transfer snowballing into giant protests; more unrest followed in 2010, then again in 2016, when the most recent curfews were imposed. However, relations have remained relatively cordial despite the chest-beating of the two main players: Indian nationalist PM Narendra Modi has not been not averse to the occasional bout of anti-Pakistani, Hindu fundamentalist-pleasing rhetoric, while his Pakistani counterpart Imran Khan was elected in 2018 on a rather anti-Indian ticket.

Tensions in the region threatened to boil over again in February 2019, when a suicide bombing by Jaish-e-Mohammad killed over forty Indian security personnel. India blamed Pakistan for the attack, who denied any involvement. In the ensuing weeks, both sides launched airstrikes against targets in each other's territories. India struck first, on February 26, against a supposed terrorist training camp in Pakistan-administered Kashmir, with Pakistan retaliating the next day, resulting in an Indian plane being shot down with its pilot taken prisoner. In the following days, tensions increased further and rhetoric was ramped up on both sides, before Pakistan returned the pilot on March 1, helping to diffuse the situation.

Various **long-term solutions** to the whole Kashmir issue have long being mooted, ranging from India's suggestion that the Line of Control might be converted into a permanent border, to Pakistan possibly being prepared to give up all claims to Kashmir should India allow the region some form of self-government. Kashmir's future looks fairly bright, although there remains the perpetual risk that a single violent incident could trigger a new phase of conflict.

7

7

By bus Services along the main Indus Valley highway are quite frequent and reliable, but become less so the further you get from Leh. Some services have been given as "summer-only"; the season generally runs Apr–Oct.

By jeep or taxi It is much easier to reach off-track side valleys and villages within a single day if you splash out on a jeep or minibus taxi, widely available in Kargil and Leh.

Trekking The alternative, more traditional way to get around the region is, of course, is by trekking.

Leh

As you approach **LEH** for the first time, via the sloping sweep of dust and pebbles that divides it from the floor of the Indus Valley, you'll have little difficulty imagining how the old trans-Himalayan traders must have felt as they plodded in on the caravan routes from Yarkhand and Tibet: a mixture of relief at having crossed the mountains

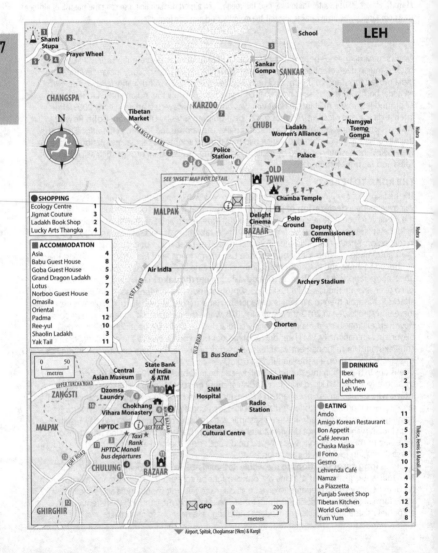

LEH

School

Shanti Stupa

Prayer Wheel

Sankar Gompa — SANKAR

CHANGSPA

KARZOO

Tibetan Market

CHANGSPA LANE

CHUBI

Ladakh Women's Alliance

Namgyel Tsemo Gompa

Police Station

Palace

OLD TOWN

SEE INSET MAP FOR DETAIL

Chamba Temple

MALPAK

Delight Cinema

Polo Ground

Deputy Commissioner's Office

SHOPPING
Ecology Centre	1
Jigmat Couture	3
Ladakh Book Shop	2
Lucky Arts Thangka	4

BAZAAR

Air India

Archery Stadium

ACCOMMODATION
Asia	4
Babu Guest House	8
Goba Guest House	5
Grand Dragon Ladakh	9
Lotus	7
Norboo Guest House	2
Omasila	6
Oriental	1
Padma	12
Ree-yul	10
Shaolin Ladakh	3
Yak Tail	11

Chorten

FORT ROAD

OLD ROAD

Bus Stand

Mani Wall

DRINKING
Ibex	3
Lehchen	2
Leh View	1

0   50
metres

Central Asian Museum

State Bank of India & ATM

UPPER TUKCHA ROAD

ZANGSTI

Dzomsa Laundry

Chokhang Vihara Monastery

MALPAK

HPTDC

IBEX ROAD

Taxi Rank

HPTDC Manali bus departures

CHULUNG

BAZAAR

MAIN BAZAAR

SNM Hospital

Radio Station

Tibetan Cultural Centre

EATING
Amdo	11
Amigo Korean Restaurant	3
Bon Appetit	5
Café Jeevan	1
Chaska Maska	13
Il Forno	8
Gesmo	10
Lehvenda Café	7
Namza	4
La Piazzetta	2
Punjab Sweet Shop	9
Tibetan Kitchen	12
World Garden	6
Yum Yum	8

GHIRGHIR

GPO

0   200
metres

Airport, Spitok, Choglamsar (9km) & Kargil

LADAKH FESTIVALS AND EVENTS

Most of Ladakh's Buddhist **festivals**, in which lamas perform masked **chaam** dance dramas in monastery courtyards, take place in January and February, when roads into the region are snowbound. This works out well for the locals, for whom the festivals relieve the tedium of the relentless winter, but it means that few outsiders get to experience some of the northern Himalayas' most vibrant and fascinating spectacles. Recently, however, a few of the larger *gompas* around Leh have followed the example of Hemis, and switched their annual festivals to the summer to attract tourists.

Gompas that hold their *chaams* (dance festivals) in winter or spring include **Matho** (mid-Feb to mid-March), **Spitok** (mid-Jan), **Thikse** (late Oct to mid-Nov) and **Diskit** (mid-Feb to early March) in Nubra.

SUMMER FESTIVALS

Hemis Tsechu: late June/early July. See page 492.
Karsha Gustor, Zanskar: late June/early July. See page 509.
Thak Thok Tsechu: late July/early Aug. See page 495.
Phyang Tsedup: late July/early Aug. See page 501.

OTHER EVENTS

Ice Hockey Ladakh Jan/Feb. Originally yet another attempt to set an altitudinal world record, it looks like this international ice hockey tournament – held with the temperature -35°C outside – may become an annual fixture in Leh.
Ladakh Marathon Sept. The "world's highest marathon" is a fun event – the main race and shorter events are held in Leh and the Indus valley, though the real nutters run 72km, including a summit of Khardung La (see page 497).

in one piece, and anticipation of a relaxing spell in one of central Asia's most scenic towns. Spilling out of a side valley that tapers north towards eroded snow-capped peaks and looks south towards the majestic **Stok-Kangri massif** (6120m), the Ladakhi capital sprawls from the foot of a ruined Tibetan-style **palace** – a maze of mud-brick and concrete flanked on one side by cream-coloured desert and on the other by a swathe of lush, irrigated farmland.

Despite being increasingly touristic, especially during the peak months of July and August, the abiding impression of Leh remains that of a lively yet laidback place – a great spot to unwind after a long journey. Attractions in and around the town itself include the former palace and **Namgyal Tsemo Gompa**, perched amid strings of prayer flags above the narrow dusty streets of the **old quarter**, whose layout has changed little since it was founded in the sixteenth century. A short walk north across the fields brings you to the small monastery at **Sankar**, which harbours accomplished modern Tantric murals and a thousand-headed Avalokitesvara deity. Leh is also a good base for longer **day-trips** out into the Indus Valley – among the string of picturesque villages and *gompas* within reach by bus are Shey (see page 490), site of a derelict seventeenth-century palace, and the spectacular Thikse Gompa (see page 491).

Brief history

Leh only became regional capital in the seventeenth century, when Sengge Namgyal shifted his court here from Shey, 15km southeast, to be closer to the head of the Khardung La–Karakoram corridor into China. The move paid off: within a generation the town had blossomed into one of the busiest markets on the Silk Road. Leh's prosperity, managed mainly by the Sunni **Muslim** merchants whose descendants live in its labyrinthine old quarter, came to an abrupt end with the closure of the Chinese border in the 1950s. Only after the Indo-Pak wars of 1965 and 1971, when India rediscovered the hitherto forgotten capital's strategic value, did its fortunes begin to look up. Today, khaki-clad *jawans* (soldiers) and their families from the nearby military

> ### ALTITUDE SICKNESS
>
> As Leh is 3500m above sea level, some travellers – and especially those who arrive by plane from Delhi – experience mild **altitude sickness** (see page 53). The best way to avoid the symptoms – persistent headaches, dizziness, insomnia, nausea, loss of appetite or shortness of breath – is to rest for at least 48 hours on arrival. Drink 3–4 litres of water a day, avoid alcohol, and don't exert yourself; try to walk more slowly than usual, especially when going uphill. For those suffering severely, **oxygen** is available at the Tourist Reception Centre on Ibex Rd (see page 487), where it costs ₹10 for a check-up and ₹50/30min if oxygen is required. For anything more serious, head to hospital (see page 489).

and air force bases are the mainstay of the local economy in winter, when **foreign visitors**, to whom the region was opened up in 1974, are few and far between. Leh has more than tripled in size since the advent of tourism, and is a far cry from the sleepy Himalayan town it was in the early 1970s.

The bazaar

After settling into a hotel or guesthouse, most visitors spend their first day in Leh soaking up the atmosphere of the **bazaar**. Eighty or so years ago, this bustling area was the busiest market between Yarkand and Kashmir – merchants from Srinagar and the Punjab would gather to barter for pashmina wool brought down by nomadic herdsmen from western Tibet, or for raw silk hauled across the Karakorams on Bactrian camels. These days, though the pedestrianized streets are awash with kitsch curio shops and handicraft emporiums, it retains a distinctly Central Asian feel. Even if you're not shopping for trekking supplies, check out the surviving **provision stores**, where bright pink, turquoise, and wine-red silk cummerbunds hang in the windows; tourists stick to the pedestrianized roads, but the local action is in side-alleys to the north and east, which also feature a few little markets.

Leh palace

Daily 9am–5pm • ₹300 (₹25)

Lording it over the old town from the top of a craggy granite ridge is the derelict **palace** of the sixteenth-century ruler Sengge Namgyal. A scaled-down version of the Potala in Lhasa, it's a textbook example of medieval Tibetan architecture, with gigantic sloping buttressed walls and projecting wooden balconies that tower nine storeys above the surrounding houses. Since the Ladakhi royal family left in the 1940s, damage inflicted by nineteenth-century Kashmiri cannons has caused large chunks of it to collapse. Despite recent restoration work, there's not much to see in the dark interior; most visitors spider up to the rooftop for lovely views out over Leh.

Namgyal Tsemo Gompa

Daily 24hr • Free • Gon-khang Daily 7–9am & 5–8pm • ₹20

Once you are acclimatized to the altitude, the stiff early-morning hike up to **Namgyal Tsemo Gompa**, the monastery perched precariously on the shale-covered crag above Leh palace, is a great way to start the day. Two trails lead up to "the Peak of Victory", whose twin peaks are connected by giant strings of multicoloured prayer flags: the first and most popular path zigzags across its south side from the palace road, while a second scales the more gentle northern slope via the north-Leh suburb of Chubi. This is the route followed by the lama from Sankar *gompa* (see page 485), who tends to the shrine each morning and evening. Alternatively, the place is accessible by road.

Approaching the *gompa* from the south, the first building you come to is the red-painted **Maitreya Temple**. Thought to date from the fourteenth century, the shrine houses a giant Buddha statue flanked by *bodhisattvas*. However, its wall paintings are modern and of less interest than those in the **Gon-khang** (temple of protector deities) at the top.

Central Asian Museum
Daily 10.30am–1pm & 2–5.30pm • ₹50

The **Central Asian Museum** is housed in a modern re-creation of a Lhasa mansion, with a gently tapering brick tower crowned by a wooden balustrade. It has a reasonable collection of artefacts, clothing and photographs that focus on the deep connections between Ladakh and the rest of Central Asia, forged through its position on the Silk Route.

Shanti Stupa
Daily sunrise–sunset • Free

Easily visible above Leh is the toothpaste-white **Shanti Stupa**, nearly 3km west of the bazaar by road. Inaugurated in 1985 by the Dalai Lama, the "Peace Pagoda", whose sides are decorated with gilt panels depicting episodes from the life of the Buddha, is one of several such monuments erected around India by a "Peace Sect" of Japanese Buddhists. It can be reached by car, or on foot via a steep flight of more than five hundred steps, which winds up from the end of Changspa Lane via the café just below the *stupa*. Its broad terrace makes an excellent spot to watch the sun rise or set, and is popular with early-morning yogis.

Sankar Gompa
Gompa Daily 7am–6pm • ₹50 • Museum Daily 9am–1pm & 2–7pm • ₹50

Nestled amid the shimmering poplar coppices and terraced fields of barley that extend up the valley behind Leh, **Sankar Gompa**, 2km north of the town centre, is among the most accessible monasteries in central Ladakh. You can get here either by car or on foot, the latter most agreeably through the fields behind the burgeoning tourist area of Karzoo.

The monastery is the official residence of the **Kushok Bakula**, Ladakh's head of the Gelug-pa sect. Above the **Du-khang** (main prayer hall) stands the *gompa*'s principal deity, Tara, in her triumphant, one-thousand-armed form as Dukkar, or "Lady of the White Parasol", presiding over a light, airy shrine room whose walls are adorned

---

CHORTENS AND MANI WALLS

Among the more visible expressions of Buddhism in Ladakh are the chess-pawn-shaped **chortens** at the entrance to villages and monasteries. These are the Tibetan equivalent of the Indian *stupa* (see page 354) – large hemispherical burial mounds-cum-devotional objects, prominent in Buddhist ritual since the third century BC. Made of mud and stone (now also concrete), many *chortens* were erected as acts of piety by Ladakhi nobles, and like their southern cousins, they are imbued with mystical powers and **symbolic significance**: the tall tapering spire, normally divided into thirteen sections, represents the soul's progression towards nirvana, while the sun cradled by the crescent moon at the top stands for the unity of opposites, and the oneness of existence and the universe. Some contain sacred manuscripts that, like the *chortens*, wither and decay in time, illustrating the central Buddhist doctrine of impermanence. Those enshrined in monasteries, however, generally made of solid silver and encrusted with semiprecious stones, contain the ashes or relics of revered *rinpoches* (incarnate lamas). Always circle a *chorten* in a clockwise direction: the ritual of circumambulation mimics the passage of the planets through the heavens and is believed to ward off evil spirits. Look out for the giant, brightly painted specimen between the bus station and Leh bazaar.

A short way downhill from the big *chorten*, near the radio station, stands an even more monumental symbol of devotion. The 500m **mani wall**, erected by King Deldan Namgyal in 1635, is one of several at important religious sites around Ladakh. Ranging from a couple of metres to more than 1km in length, the walls are made of hundreds of thousands of stones, each inscribed with prayers or sacred mantras – usually the invocation *Om Mani Padme Hum*: "Hail to the Jewel in the Lotus". It goes without saying that such stones should never be removed, and visitors should resist the urge to climb onto the walls to have photographs taken.

ENVIRONMENTAL ISSUES AND VOLUNTARY ORGANIZATIONS

Damage to the **environment** has become an issue of paramount importance in Ladakh. Although plastic bags are officially banned in Leh, as they clog up the vital river systems that the state so depends on, shopkeepers continue to use them. Plastic mineral-water bottles are a particular headache; you are advised to bring your own filtration system with you (see page 50), or refill plastic water bottles with filtered water, either at guesthouses or at the **Dzomsa Laundry**, near the main bazaar. As well as providing safe water and delicious local juices, this establishment provides a vital service in ecologically sound washing, using biodegradable detergent and water at a safe distance from habitation. It also serves as a co-op for rural, semiliterate people.

VOLUNTARY ORGANIZATIONS

With limited resources at their disposal, a handful of **voluntary organizations** battle to protect Ladakh's delicate environment and ancient culture, including the following.

17000ft ⊚ 17000ft.org. NPO aiming to strengthen education and employment opportunities in remote Ladakhi villages, with the aim of arresting the exodus of young folk to the cities.

Ladakh Ecological Development Group (LEDeG) ⊚ ledeg.org. Local NGO aiming to counter the negative impact of Western-style development by fostering economic independence and respect for traditional culture. Its headquarters are north of the main bazaar at the Ecology Centre (see page 489).

Local Futures ⊚ localfutures.org. Closely aligned to LEDeG, employing volunteers on the "Farm Project" in Ladakh to help local farmers maintain traditional farming methods.

Women's Alliance of Ladakh (WAL) ⊚ waladakh. org. Based in Chubi, north of central Leh, working to reinforce traditional Ladakhi culture. One of their more noticeable achievements was to ban plastic bags from Leh in 1998. The best time to visit them is during one of their festivals; see the website for details.

with a Tibetan calendar and tableaux depicting "dos and don'ts" for monks – some of which are very arcane indeed. Another flight of steps leads to the *gompa* **library** and, eventually, a roof terrace with fine views towards the north side of Namgyal Tsemo hill, and the valley to the south.

Right outside the *gompa*, the single-room **Ladakh Rocks & Minerals Museum** contains a thoughtfully laid out and labelled collection of geological samples from the region, including a huge chunk of sapphire.

ARRIVAL AND DEPARTURE LEH

By plane Leh airport is just 5km south of the city, on the main highway; a taxi into town costs ₹250–300.
Destinations Delhi (4–6 daily; 1hr 30min); Jammu (3 weekly; 1hr); Srinagar (1–2 daily; 45min).

By bus Long-distance services use the main bus station, a 15min walk or ₹80 taxi ride south of the bazaar, including the deluxe HPTDC buses to Manali (₹2900 including an overnight stop and three meals); tickets for the latter are available at the bus station, but best purchased at their office on Fort Rd (see map, p.482). Regional services often depart from the bus station too, local minibuses use a stop

near the archery stadium; see the relevant accounts for destinations around Leh.
Destinations Kargil (3–5 daily; 6hr); Manali (every 2–3 days in summer; 2 days); Srinagar (2–4 daily; 16hr).

By jeep Shared jeeps are widely used for transportation around Ladakh and to destinations further afield, such as Kargil (6hr; from ₹1000/person); Manali (16–18hr; ₹2200/person) and Srinagar (16hr; from ₹2500–3000/person). They're best booked through travel agencies, since the official taxi stands deal with full vehicles only.

GETTING AROUND

By taxi The main office of the Taxi Operators Co-operative (daily 6am–7pm; ☎ 01982 253039) is located near the tourist information centre, though most long-distance shared taxis depart from a yard opposite the bus station. Each driver carries a booklet (₹30) of fixed fares (see individual accounts for details) to just about

everywhere you might want to visit in Ladakh, taking into account waiting time, vehicle size and night halt charges.

Bike rental Mountain bikes can be rented from Ladakh Cycling (☎ 94195 63761) for ₹700/day, including helmet, repair kit and a spare inner tube. They also whisk riders up to the 5359m-high Khardung La pass (see page 497) by jeep (1hr 30min) for a fun cycle back to Leh (2–3hr; ₹1500/person, plus ₹400 for the permit if you don't have one).

Motorbikes Rates for motorized two-wheelers start at around ₹1000/day for an Enfield; always check the bikes carefully. There are numerous operators on the Old Leh Rd.

INFORMATION AND TOURS

Tourist office The highly informative J&K Tourist Reception Centre sits on Ibex Rd near the bazaar (June to mid-Sept Mon–Sat 9am–9pm, Sun 10am–5pm; mid-Sept to May Mon–Sat 10am–4pm; ☎01982 253462, ⍟jktourism.org).

Tour operators Innumerable agents around town offer trekking, jeep safaris and the like. Notable ones include Venture Ladakh on Changspa Lane (⍟ventureladakh.

in), who offer great trekking advice and have decent second-hand hiking boots to rent or buy; Wet N Wild Explorations on Fort Rd (⍟wetnwildexplorations.com), who specialize in rafting excursions (see page 500); and Ladakhi Women's Travel on Upper Tukcha Rd (⍟ladakhiwomenstravel.com), an agency run by and specializing in advice for women.

ACCOMMODATION

Leh is glutted with accommodation, much of it refreshingly neat and clean. Most places **close between October and April**; due to the short season prices do not fluctuate much, but you can bargain in the shoulder months. Most of the town's cheaper **guesthouses** are in the leafy areas of **Changspa** to the west and **Karzoo** to the north. Rooms in Leh's few **mid-range** and increasing number of **upmarket hotels** all come with piped hot water. Note that because of the early morning flight timings, checkout at most places is 9–10am.

Asia Changspa Rd ☎01982 253403, ⍟hotelasialadakh.com; map p.482. Large riverside guesthouse consisting of three blocks, the oldest of which has shared bathrooms. Sociable roof terrace-cum-café, as well as yoga, meditation, reiki, Pranic healing – plus a stuffed yak in reception. May–Oct. **₹800/₹2500**

Babu Guest House Near Delight Cinema, Old Town ☎01982 252419, ✉tamchos14@yahoo.co.in; map p.482. Friendly traditional, backstreet family guesthouse with a cute courtyard. The half-dozen cosy rooms are all non-attached. May–Oct. **₹500**

Goba Guest House Down path off Changspa Rd ☎95969 37530, ✉gobaguesthouse@gmail.com; map p.482. Well-maintained traditional house with a pleasant, farm-like garden and views of Shanti Stupa. Rooms are immaculate, and those in the newer block have attached bathrooms. Open all year. **₹500/₹800**

★**Grand Dragon Ladakh** Old Leh Rd ☎01982 257786, ⍟thegranddragonladakh.com; map p.482. Ladakh's top hotel, featuring professional service, extremely fancy rooms with comfortable beds (some with balconies too) and Ladakhi design flourishes, and an excellent dining hall with views of the mountains to the south. On site you'll also find a fitness centre, games room and souvenir shop; staff are adept at arranging tours to sights throughout the area. Open all year. **₹17,500**

Lotus Upper Karzoo ☎01982 250265, ⍟lotushotel.in; map p.482. The leafy location and laidback staff make this a relaxing and welcoming option. Decor is in traditional style with quality carvings and colourful fabrics, and the more expensive rooms have mountain views. Feb–Nov. **₹4400**

Norboo Guest House Upper Changspa ☎94193 40947; map p.482. One of the nicest budget joints in this popular riverside area, with views of Shanti Stupa. The seven rooms share three extremely clean bathrooms. May–Oct. **₹600**

Omasila Changspa Rd ☎01982 252119, ⍟hotelomasila.com; map p.482. Friendly, accommodating hotel, including suites and centrally heated rooms. The large terrace offers sweeping views, and the dining room serves excellent dishes featuring home-grown vegetables. Open all year. **₹4200**

Oriental Below the Shanti Stupa, Changspa ☎01982 253153, ⍟orientalhotel-ladakh.com; map p.482. Genuinely welcoming guesthouse with spotless rooms, free filtered water, superb views and nourishing home-cooked meals. Superb new hotel block (open in season only), with rooms costing more like ₹2000. Open all year. **₹1200**

Padma Ghrighir, off Fort Rd ☎01982 252630, ⍟padmaladakh.net; map p.482. Once a cheap backpacker spot, this is now decidedly middle-market, with an old wing featuring immaculate rooms with attached bathrooms, and a large modern building with even nicer rooms costing slightly more, and a rooftop restaurant; all offer views, mostly of the garden. Meals available; open all year. **₹2800**

Ree-yul Alley Lane off Upper Tuchpa Rd, Zangsti ☎96229 75939, ✉limbijal@rediffmail.com; map p.482. Tucked in a quiet corner of the centre, boasting a lovely courtyard and exquisitely carved woodwork, this convivial place has clean rooms, some with TV. Apr–Oct. **₹700**

★**Shaolin Ladakh** Sankar ☎01982 252903, ⍟shaolinladakh.com; map p.482. Set in a quiet area north of the bazaar, this is the best option in town at this price level, so long as you don't mind the 20min walk to and from the centre. The building curls around a delightful garden, bursting with flowers for much of the year, and even the standard rooms are lovely affairs with varnished-log ceilings and large windows. Apr–Sept. **₹2000**

Yak Tail Fort Rd ☎01982 252118, ⍟hotelyaktail.com; map p.482. Very attractive place with wood panelling and ornate wooden window-frames in its spotless rooms. The courtyard is surprisingly quiet, considering its proximity to busy Fort Rd. **₹3000**

7

EATING

Leh's thriving restaurant and café scene is run by a mixture of refugees, and businessmen from the rest of India looking to cash in. **Tibetan food** has a high profile alongside classic Indian and Chinese cuisine, plus there's an increasing range of European, Israeli and other international dishes to add variety; unfortunately, most restaurants try to serve absolutely everything, rather than focus on one food type in particular.

RESTAURANTS

Amdo 2nd floor of complex beside mosque, Main Bazaar ☎ 01982 253114; map p.482. Want to feel like one of the hippies from back in the day? This popular Tibetan restaurant has been here for decades, offering freshly prepared food that is generally excellent but can take up to half an hour to appear; try their range of *momos* (from ₹120), or some fried mutton thukpa noodles (₹150). Apr–Oct daily 10.30am–5.30pm.

Amigo Korean Restaurant Off Changspa Rd ☎ 01982 255057; map p.482. For something a little different, try this pretty place, designed along traditional Korean lines. The food isn't as authentic as it could be, but most meals still hit the spot, including doenjang jjigae (spicy soybean broth) and *bibimbap* (both ₹300); their ginger honey tea (₹50) may work wonders for those who've caught a cold. May–Sept daily 9am–9pm.

★ **Bon Appetit** Off a lane south of Changspa Rd ☎ 01982 251533; map p.482. One of the smartest places in town, and symptomatic of Leh's turn towards the trendy. Quirky dishes include black pepper paneer (₹250), mutton burgers (₹300) and Burmese and Thai fusion food, while the south-facing view – and the fact that alcohol is available – mean that it's perfect for a sunset meal and a drink. Aug–Oct daily 8am–10.30pm.

Café Jeevan Changspa Rd ☎ 94191 29157; map p.482. Very smart and clean pure-veg Sikh-run restaurant featuring a variety of cuisines in the ₹100–200 range. Lovely decor both downstairs and in the partially enclosed roof terrace. May–Sept daily 7am–11pm.

Chaska Maska South of Fort Rd ☎ 8629826082; map p.482. Cuisine from both ends of the Subcontinent, plus a few Western dishes. Best masala dosas in town (₹110), as well as items like peppered steak for ₹350. Apr–Oct daily 7am–11pm.

Il Forno LBA Complex, Zangshi ☎ 01982 258870; map p.482. It's somewhat refreshing to see a restaurant focusing on a single type of cuisine, even though they do have other options as well as their excellent Italian food. Pride of place goes to the lasagne selection, baked in a wood-fired over like their excellent pizzas (both from ₹350); pasta dishes available too (four shapes to choose from, plus gnocchi). Oh, and it has the best castle views in town. Apr–Oct daily 8.30am–10.30pm.

Gesmo Fort Rd ☎ 01982 251344; map p.482. Probably the most popular restaurant in town at the time of writing in 2019, this pretty spot has the typical "we serve everything" menu, but is perhaps most notable for the yak cheese specials, including yak-cheese veg *momos* (₹220), yak-cheese chicken pizza (₹350), and yak-cheese burgers (₹320). All of which begs the question: how does one milk a yak? Apr–Oct daily 8.30am–10.30pm.

La Piazzetta Changspa Rd ☎ 01982 253225; map p.482. Ambient courtyard with tented enclosures, candles and open fires creating a pleasant atmosphere. Most meals – non-veg Indian, Chinese, Thai and wood-fired pizza – cost ₹200–350, and it stays open later in the year than all other garden restaurants. Apr–Sept daily 10.30am–11.30pm.

Namza Zangsti Rd ☎ 94192 99111; map p.482. Tucked behind a clothing boutique of the same name, this is the place in which to try modern Ladakhi cuisine. Try the drapu dumplings, made with apricot kernel and walnut sauce (₹250); soups such as ayathuk, like a regular mutton soup with spicy chutney (₹300); or many other things besides. Seats face out over a small field. May–Sept daily 10am–10pm.

★ **Tibetan Kitchen** Down an alley off Fort Rd ☎ 96978 11510; map p.482. Considered by many, locals and visitors alike, to offer the best Tibetan food in town. Its success means higher prices, with mutton *thukpas* and *momos* (try the unusual tuna ones) around the ₹230 mark. Daily noon–10.30pm.

★ **World Garden** East end of Changspa Rd ☎ 72989 01597; map p.482. The usual Indian and Chinese staples, plus decent Italian and particularly good home-made falafel, hummus and chips (₹200) are available in this cool, shady garden with colourful fabric tents. May–Sept daily 8am–10.30pm.

CAFES, TEAROOMS AND SWEETS

Lehvenda Café 2nd floor of complex on corner of bazaar ☎ 80100 77124; map p.482. The best of many modern cafes in town, shading the competition with excellent coffee (from ₹100), a winning balcony view of the palace, steady wi-fi, and a generally congenial atmosphere. Open all year, daily 9am–9pm.

Punjab Sweet Shop Main bazaar, no phone; map p.482. Old-school tearoom where you can enjoy a glass of masala chai, a freshly-made samosa and a couple of sweets, and still get change from ₹100. Open all year, daily 8am–10pm.

★ **Yum Yum** LBA Complex ☎ 84938 54102; map p.482. The LBA complex is a hit with independent travellers – tucked between two roads, this courtyard has a few cheap places to snack, and the seating arrangement makes it easy to get chatting to people. This restaurant is the best and friendliest of the bunch, and most notable for its "French bakery" section; try the giant banana crumble (₹100) with some quality espresso (₹70). Apr–Oct daily 7am–10.30pm.

DRINKING

Beer is widely available in many of Leh's tourist restaurants, though it often has to be served surreptitiously. There's also a busy little liquor store just north of the Ibex bar.

★ **Ibex** Fort Rd ☎ 94191 89052; map p.482. If you feel like drinking somewhere more akin to Ladakh "back in the day", this bar will float your boat. Prices are super cheap (₹160 for a can of Kingfisher, ₹80 for a double shot of Old Monk rum), and the courtyard space – where the chairs are really, really comfy – facilitates the making of new friends. Open all year daily 9am–11pm.

Lehchen Zangsti Rd ☎ 99107 66617; map p.482. An

actual bar, and certainly the prettiest place to drink in town. The beer is overpriced, so it's best to go for the cocktails (₹400), some of which are extremely strong. Apr–Oct. Daily noon–11pm.

Leh View Main Bazaar ☎ 94697 73429; map p.482. This roof terrace has great views, and although it also a restaurant, it's a better bet for a drink than a meal; beers go for around ₹250, and double-shots of local spirits for ₹150, and they've hookahs to puff for ₹600. Mar–Oct. Daily 8.30am–11pm.

SHOPPING

Between June and September, Leh is swamped by almost as many transient Tibetan and Kashmiri **traders** as souvenir-hungry tourists. Most of the merchandise hawked in their temporary boutiques and stalls comes from outside the region: papier-mâché bowls, shawls and carpets from Srinagar, jewellery and miniature paintings from Jaipur, and "Himalayan" handicrafts, including *thangkas*, churned out in Nepal and by Tibetan refugees in Old Delhi. Prices tend to be high, so haggle hard, and don't be conned into shelling out for cleverly faked "antiques". Much of the "silver" on sale is in fact cheap white metal.

TRADITIONAL ARTEFACTS AND CLOTHING
For authentic Ladakhi souvenirs, try the outfitters and provision stores dotted along the main bazaar. There are also some genuine Ladakhi/Tibetan markets in the bazaar and along Changspa Lane. The lanes running off the bazaar towards Old Town are home to hole-in-the-wall seamstress shops that can produce custom-fit local clothing, including dapper stovepipe hats (*tibi*), hand-dyed Ladakhi robes (*goncha*), raw silk cummerbunds and tie-dyed rope-soled shoes (*pabbu*). The handicraft shops at the environmental organizations (see page 486) are also sources of quality traditional clothing, including hand-knitted woollen jumpers, shawls, hats and socks.

Ecology Centre Off Changspa Lane ☎ 01982 253221,

⊕ledeg.org; map p.511. As well as a small library, the Ecology Centre has a handicraft shop selling locally made clothes, *thangkas*, T-shirts, books and postcards. Open all year. Daily 10am–4pm, often closed weekends.

Jigmat Couture South of Fort Rd ☎ 01982 255065, ⊕jigmatcouture.org; map p.482. Modern takes on Ladakhi clothing – not the cheapest (most items ₹5000–12,000), but all made in Ladakh with local resources such as cashmere, yak and camel hair. Mar–Oct Mon–Sat 10.30am–7pm, Sun 2.30–7pm.

Lucky Arts Thangka South of Fort Rd ☎ 95968 01013; map p.482. Beautiful *thangkas* and other Tibetan artwork are on sale at this small shop. Mar–Oct Daily 10am–7pm.

BOOKS

There are quite a few bookshops dotted around the centre and along Changspa Lane; most have the usual selection of second-hand travellers' novels, but one or two offer a wider selection. In addition, the Ecology Centre's excellent library (see page 489) keeps books on everything from agriculture to Zen Buddhism.

Ladakh Book Shop Bazaar ☎ 01982 256464. Second-floor space crammed with books in English on Ladakhi and Tibetan religion and culture, plus travel and fiction sections. May–Sept daily 9.30am–9.30pm.

DIRECTORY

Banks You'll find an incredible number of banks with ATMs in the very centre of town, but very few outside it.
Hospital The poorly equipped SNM Hospital (☎ 01982 252014) is 1km south of the centre on Old Road. For urgent medical treatment, contact a doctor through any

upmarket hotel.
Laundry Dzomsa Laundry (see page 486).
Pharmacy Het Ram Vinay Kumar on the bazaar road sells a range of allopathic pills and potions.
Police ☎ 01982 252018, ☎ 100 for the operator.

Southeast of Leh: the Indus loop

Southeast of Leh, the Indus Valley broadens to form a fertile river basin. For some 35km, both sides are dotted with spectacular Buddhist monuments, and many travellers visit one, some or all of them on day-trips from Leh. The northeastern bank of the river has a better road, and sees most traffic; here you'll come across **Shey**, site of a ruined palace and giant brass Buddha, then the stunning monastery of **Thikse**. After crossing the Indus at Karu, you'll see **Hemis**, Ladakh's wealthiest monastery and the venue for one of the region's few summertime religious festivals; heading back to Leh, you can also mop up **Matho**, a gompa boasting superb views from its roof terrace; and **Stok Palace**, home of the Ladakhi monarchy. Note that there's accommodation outside or nearby most of these sights, giving travellers an easy chance to spend a night outside the "big" city; there are also places to eat dotted here and there.

GETTING AROUND	SOUTHEAST OF LEH: THE INDUS LOOP

By bus Buses are fairly regular on the northeastern side of the river, less so for sights on the southwestern side; advice is given at the top of each account.

By taxi The vast majority of travellers visit these sights by taxi; you could see them all for ₹2000, or just ₹1400 for the

"big three" of Shey, Thikse and Stok.

By rented vehicle This route is easy to do with a car – or, more temptingly, a motorbike – from Leh, and as such constitutes a good test-run if you're planning a more ambitious trip.

Shey

Buses from Leh (5 daily; 25min), or more regularly from Choglamsar • Taxis from Leh ₹450 one-way, ₹550 return

SHEY, 15km southeast of Leh and once the capital of Ladakh, is now all but deserted, the royal family having been forced to abandon it by the Dogras midway through the nineteenth century. Only a semi-derelict palace, a small *gompa* and a profusion of *chortens* remain, clustered around a bleached spur of rock that juts into the fertile floor of the Indus Valley. You can walk from Shey to Thikse monastery along a winding path that passes through one of Ladakh's biggest *chorten* fields, with hundreds of whitewashed shrines of varying sizes scattered across the surreal desert landscape.

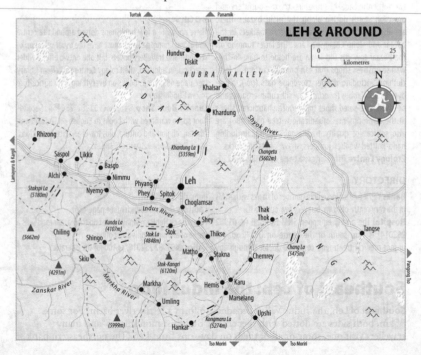

The palace

Buddha temple daily 6am–9pm • ₹30

The **palace**, a smaller and more dilapidated version of the one in Leh, sits astride the ridge, below an ancient fort. Crowned by a golden *chorten* spire, its pride and joy is the colossal metal Shakyamuni Buddha housed in its ruined split-level temple. Installed in 1633, the 12m icon allegedly contains a hoard of precious stones, mandalas and powerful charms. Entering from the second level, you come face to face with the massive Buddha, and a balcony allows you to survey the statue's torso. Preserved for centuries by thick soot from votary butter lamps, the gold-tinted murals coating the walls are among the finest in the valley.

Rock carving

Easily missed as you whizz past on the road is Shey's most ancient monument. The **rock carving** of the five Tathagata or "Thus gone" Buddhas, distinguished by their respective vehicles (*vahanas*) and hand positions (*mudras*), appears on a smooth slab of stone on the edge of the highway; it was probably carved soon after the eighth century, before the "Second Spreading" (see page 478). The large central figure with hands held in the gesture of preaching (turning the wheel of dharma), is the Buddha Resplendent, Vairocana, whose image is central in many of the Alchi murals (see page 501).

EATING	SHEY

Shilkhar On the main road ☎ 97973 10025. This no-frills restaurant offers a limited menu of Indian, Chinese and Western food, or local delights such as veggie *momos*, steamed or fried (₹130). Daily 8am–8pm.

Thikse

5 daily buses from Leh (40min; last one back leaves at 5pm), and more regularly from Choglamsar; you'll mostly likely have to hike up to the gompa from the main road • Taxis from Leh ₹700 one-way, ₹900 return • Walkable from Shey (see page 490) • Gompa daily 6am–6pm • ₹30

Ladakh's most photographed and architecturally impressive *gompa* is at **THIKSE**, 19km southeast of Leh. Founded in the fifteenth century, its whitewashed *chortens* and cubic monks' quarters rise in ranks up the sides of a craggy bluff, crowned by an imposing ochre- and red-painted temple complex whose gleaming golden finials are visible for kilometres in every direction.

Thikse's reincarnation as a major tourist attraction has brought it mixed blessings: its constant stream of summer visitors spoils the peace and quiet necessary for meditation, but the income generated has enabled the monks to invest in major refurbishments, among them the **Maitreya temple** immediately above the main courtyard. Inaugurated in 1980 by the Dalai Lama, the shrine is built around a gigantic, gold-faced Buddha-to-come, seated not on a throne as is normally the case, but in the lotus position. The bright murals on the wall behind, painted by monks from Lingshet *gompa* in Zanskar, depict scenes from Maitreya's life.

For most foreign visitors, however, the highlight of a trip to Thikse is the view from its lofty **roof terrace**. A patchwork of barley fields stretches across the floor of the valley, fringed by rippling snow-flecked desert mountains and a string of monasteries, palaces and Ladakhi villages. To enjoy this impressive panorama accompanied by primeval groans from the *gompa*'s gargantuan Tibetan trumpets – played on the rooftop at the 6–7am puja – you'll have to stay overnight or arrange an early taxi from Leh.

ACCOMMODATION AND EATING	THIKSE

Chamba Hotel Down by the road ☎ 01982 267005, ⊕ thiksay.org. Part of the monastery organization, this deluxe hotel offers reasonably comfortable rooms at rather inflated rates and a decent garden restaurant serving a varied menu from Tibetan food to pancakes, as well as a ₹330 buffet. April–Sept. **₹3300**

★ **Monastery Guesthouse** ☎ 01982 267385. The rooms behind the *gompa*'s simple restaurant are spacious and clean, and some have private bathrooms. This is one of Ladakh's most atmospheric places to stay, as you end up feeling part of the monastic community. **₹800/1200**

THE SUPERSTAR LAMA

While he hasn't yet been a major character in a Brad Bitt movie, **Jigme Pema Wangchen** – the 12th **Gyalwang Drukpa**, or head lama of the "Dragon" school of Tibetan Buddhism – is certainly the trendiest local lama of modern times, and has harvested more than 750,000 Facebook followers to date. Born in Himachal Pradesh in 1963, he has become an active environmental campaigner, often attempting to solve modern-day problems with ancient Buddhist thought with his "Live to Love" movement. However, it's his non-ancient acts which have caught the most attention, including what seems to be a fixation with getting into the Guinness Book of Records; his volunteers broke the "most trees planted simultaneously" record in 2012, and the "largest Ladakhi dance" and "highest ice hockey game" are among those to have fallen since. In 2016, with a cohort of 240 nuns, he cycled from Kathmandu to Hemis monastery in order to raise environmental awareness across the Himalayas – the bike he rode is now part of the monastery museum (see below).

7

Stakna

Direct bus from Leh daily at 4.30pm, returning at 7.30am the next day; alternatively, take any vehicle along the road and get off by the suspension bridge near the monastery • *Gompa* Daily 8am–7pm • ₹30

STAKNA, around 30km south of Leh, sits astride a rocky outcrop just west of the Indus. The *gompa* was founded in the late sixteenth century by the Bhutanese saint, Chosje Jamyang Palkar. Its main features are some dazzling recently painted Tantric murals and a few original murals and sandalwood statues – oh, and the wonderful mountainous backdrop.

Hemis

In summer usually one daily bus from Leh at 9am, and sometimes also 2pm; in winter there's one at 1pm on Mon, Wed & Sat • Taxis from Leh ₹1300 one-way, ₹1900 return • *Gompa* Daily 8am–1pm & 2–6pm • ₹50 • Museum Daily 8am–6pm • ₹100 (₹50)

Thanks to its famous festival – one of the few held in summer, when the passes are open – **HEMIS**, 45km southeast of Leh, is visited in greater numbers than any other *gompa* in Ladakh, even though it's certainly not the prettiest. At other times, the rambling and atmospheric seventeenth-century **monastery** can be disappointingly quiet: although it's one of the region's foremost religious institutions, only a skeleton staff of monks and novices are resident off-season. Still, the richly painted main hall is worth a look, as is the small **museum**, a winding subterranean hall with a modest collection of *thangkas*, masks and musical instruments. On your way down, look out for the bicycle on the wall, which was ridden all the way here from Kathmandu by **Jigme Pema Wangchen**, a rather rare breed of lama (see box above).

Each June or July (see page 483), hundreds of foreigners join the huge crowds of locals, dressed in their finest traditional garb, that flock to watch the colourful two-day pageant. Accompanied by cymbal crashes, drum rolls and periodic blasts from the temple trumpets, the culmination of the event on the second day is a frenzied dismemberment of a dummy, symbolizing the destruction of the human ego, and thus the triumph of Buddhism over ignorance and evil. Once every twelve years, the Hemis Festival also hosts the ritual unrolling of a giant *thangka*. The *gompa*'s prize possession, which covers the entire facade of the building, it was embroidered by women whose hands are now revered as holy relics. Decorated with pearls and precious stones, it will not be displayed again until 2028.

ACCOMMODATION AND EATING	**HEMIS**

You can find basic homestay accommodation in the village beneath the gompa; it'll cost around ₹500 for a room. **Hemis Gompa Restaurant** Below the monastery ☎ 96223 72915. This garden restaurant serves standard Indian and Chinese dishes – some good, some less so – for ₹120–200, and is a popular lunch spot for those touring the area. You can usually pitch a tent at the back, too. Daily 8am–8pm.

7

Matho

Buses from Leh daily at 9am & 3pm, and more regular minibuses from Choglamsar • Taxis from Leh ₹1000 one-way, ₹1300 return • *Gompa* Daily 9am–6pm • ₹50, including museum entry

MATHO, 27km south of Leh, straddles a spur at the mouth of an idyllic side-valley that runs deep into the heart of the Stok-Kangri massif. Though no less interesting or scenically situated than its neighbours, it sees comparatively few visitors. The *gompa* is the only representative in Ladakh of the **Sakyapa** sect, which held political power in thirteenth-century Tibet.

Despite its collection of 400-year-old *thangkas*, the monastery is best known for its **oracle festival**, Matho Nagran, held on the twenty-fifth and twenty-sixth day of the second Tibetan month (Feb/March). Two oracles, known as *rongzan*, are elected by lot every three years from among the sixty or so resident lamas. During the run-up to the big days, the pair fast and meditate in readiness for the moment when they are possessed by the spirit of the deity. Watched by crowds of rapt onlookers, they then perform all manner of death-defying stunts that include leaping blindfold around the *gompa*'s precipitous parapets while slurping kettlefuls of *chang*, and slashing themselves with razor-sharp sabres without drawing blood. The events are rounded off with colourful *chaam* dances in the monastery courtyard, and a question-and-answer session in which the *rongzan*, still under the influence of the deity, make prophecies about the coming year.

You can admire the costumes and masks worn by the monks during the festivals in Matho's small **museum**, tucked away behind the main prayer hall. Men are also permitted to visit the eerie **Gon-khang** on the roof, where the oracles' weapons and ritual garments are stored. The floor of the tiny temple is covered by a deep layer of barley brought as harvest offerings by local villagers.

Stok

Buses from Leh daily at 4.30am, with additional 8.30am summer service • Taxis from Leh ₹600 one-way, ₹750 return • *Museum* Daily 8am–6pm • ₹70 • *Gompa* Daily 9am–6pm • ₹50

Visible from Leh, at the head of a huge moraine, the elegant four-storey **Stok Palace** stands in the shadow of a TV mast, overlooking barley terraces studded with whitewashed farmhouses. Built early in the nineteenth century by the last ruler of independent Ladakh, it has been the official residence of the Ladakhi royal family since they were ousted from Leh and Shey two hundred years ago. The present queen mother – Deskit Wangmo, a former member of parliament – still lives here during the summer, and has converted one wing of her 77-room palace into a small **museum**. The fascinating collection comprises some of the royal family's most precious heirlooms, including exquisite sixteenth-century *thangkas* illuminated with paint made from crushed rubies, emeralds and sapphires. The *pièces de résistance*, however, are the *gyalmo*'s **peraks**; still worn on important occasions, the ancient headdresses – thought to have originated in Tibet – are encrusted with slabs of flawless turquoise (a full 401 pieces, on one of them), polished coral, lapis lazuli and nuggets of pure gold.

Stok gompa, twenty minutes' walk up the valley, boasts a collection of dance-drama masks and some lurid modern murals painted by lamas from Lingshet *gompa* in Zanskar, the artists responsible for the Maitreya statue in Thikse (see page 491).

ACCOMMODATION AND EATING   STOK

There's a cafeteria outside the entrance to the palace, good for refreshments with a grand view down towards Leh.
Skittsal 2km down the Choglamsar road ☎01982 242049, ⊚skittsal.com. Despite its panoramic valley views, this hotel seems unfeasibly large for such a remote location. The rooms are spacious but seriously overpriced. There's a so-so restaurant on site, too. May–Sept. **₹2600**

Eastern Ladakh: the lakes

To side-step your fellow tourists without spending a night away from Leh, head up the austerely beautiful tributary valley back on the opposite side of the river from Hemis to the *gompas* of **Chemrey** and **Thak Thok**, the latter built around a fabled meditation cave.

East of Thak Thok, the road crosses the Chang La pass and then veers east to the high mountain lake of **Pangong Tso**, most of which lies in Tibet. Far more relaxing and inviting is the vast wilderness of **Rupshu**, with trekking possibilities around the shores of **Tso Moriri**, in the deep south of Ladakh. Permits are required for these three areas (see page 479).

Chemrey

Gompa daily 8am–6pm • ₹50, including museum • Accessible on buses from Leh to Sakti (5 daily; 1hr 15min) • Taxis ₹1850 return from Leh

Clinging like a swallow's nest to the sides of a conical hill, the magnificent *gompa* of **CHEMREY** sees very few visitors because of its location – tucked up the side-valley that runs from Karu, below Hemis, to the Chang La pass into Pangong.

Founded in 1664 as a memorial to King Sengge Namgyal, the monastery is staffed by a dwindling community of around twenty Drugpa monks and their young novices. Its main **Du-khang**, off the courtyard on the lower level, boasts a fine silver *chorten* and a set of ancient Tibetan texts whose title pages are illuminated with gold-and-silver calligraphy. Upstairs in the revamped **Guru-La-khang** sits a giant brass statue of Padmasambhava. The museum on the top floor houses statues, *thangkas*, scrolls and utensils.

Thak Thok

Gompa daily 8am–6pm • ₹50 • Bus from Leh to Sakti (5 daily; 1hr 15min), then a 50min walk • Taxis ₹2150 return from Leh

Up the valley from Chemrey, and a few kilometres above the village of **Sakti**, **THAK THOK** (pronounced *Tak-Tak* and meaning "rock roof") *gompa* shelters a cave in which the apostle Padmasambhava is said to have meditated during his epic eighth-century journey to Tibet. Blackened over the years by sticky butter-lamp and incense smoke, the mysterious grotto is now somewhat upstaged by the monastery's more modern wings nearby. As well as some spectacular twentieth-century wall paintings, the **Urgyan Photan Du-khang** harbours a collection of multicoloured yak-butter candle-sculptures made by the head lama. For a glimpse of state-of-the-art Buddhist iconography, head to the top of Thak Thok village, where a shiny new temple houses a row of huge gleaming Buddhas, decked out in silk robes and surrounded by garish modern murals.

Apart from during the annual **festival** (see page 483), Sakti is a tranquil place, blessed with serene views south over the snowy mountains behind Hemis. There are plenty of ideal camping spots beside the river, although as ever you should seek permission before putting up a tent on someone's field.

Pangong Tso

Summer-only bus from Leh (6.30am Mon, Tue, Thurs & Sat; 5hr) to Spangmik village, returning around 7am the following day • Jeep safaris from Leh from ₹1700 per person, more if overnighting; 3-day trips including Nubra Valley ₹19,700 per vehicle

Pangong Tso, 154km southeast of Leh, is one of the largest saltwater lakes in Asia, a long, narrow strip of water stretching from Ladakh east into Tibet. Only a quarter of the 134km-long lake is in India, and the army, who experienced bitter losses along its shores in the war against China in 1962, jealously guard their side of the frontier. Until the mid-1990s, this area was off-limits to visitors, and tourists still need a permit to come here (see page 479). The lake, at an altitude of 4267m, with the dramatic glacier-clad Pangong Range to its south and the Changchenmo Range reflected in its deep blue-green waters to the north, measures 8km across at its widest point and provides a tantalizing view of Tibet in the distance, although the bitter winds blowing over the brackish water make it one of the coldest places in Ladakh. On the way here, your driver may stop to allow a photo-op with some local marmots, who are surprisingly comfortable in the presence of human beings.

7

ACCOMMODATION **PANGONG TSO**

There is basic accommodation and food at Spangmik but it is poor value, especially the hugely overpriced tent camp. Better deals can be had near other parts of the lake.

Padma Home Stay Where the road first meets the lake ☎94198 19078, ✉tonybuddhist@yahoo.co.in. Meals are included with the rooms, which vary in size but all have shared bathrooms. They also rent tents with full board. ₹1300

Tso Moriri

Summer-only bus from Leh (10th, 20th & 30th of month; 4hr 30min–5hr), returning the following morning • Jeep safaris from Leh start from ₹2000 per person (not including accommodation) for a three-day trip • Treks start from ₹3600 per day in a group of four, usually including transport, food and tents

Famous for the large herds of *kiang*, or wild ass, which graze on its shores, the lake of **Tso Moriri**, 210km southeast of Leh, lies in the sparsely populated region of **Rupshu**. You need a permit to travel here (see page 479). Twenty kilometres long, the lake nestles in a wide valley flanked by some of the highest peaks in Ladakh – **Lungser Kangri** (6666m) and **Chanmser Kangri** (6622m) – and is home to flocks of migratory *nangpa* or bar-headed geese, as well as occasional herds of pashmina goats and camps of nomadic herders.

7

Located on the shores of the lake at an altitude of 4595m, the only large village in the area is **Korzok**, a friendly place with a small *gompa*. To help protect the fragile ecosystem against the influx of tourists, a new directive stipulates that no habitation can be built within 700m of the shoreline. Visitors should bring their own food supplies and make sure they take all their rubbish away.

The open spaces around Tso Moriri make for some pleasant **trekking**, including the relatively easy – if you are acclimatized – three-day, 40km circuit of the lake. Another route gaining popularity is the trail from Rumtse near Upshi via Tso Kar to Tso Moriri. Some trekking operators in Manali and Leh can arrange more ambitious treks, such as following the ancient trade route linking **Spiti** to Tso Moriri and Leh via Kibber.

ACCOMMODATION **TSO MORIRI**

Accommodation is in local homestays dotted around the lake area and an overpriced tent colony or in Korzok, 1km back from the lake.

Lake View Just below Korzok bus stand ☎94193 45362, ⓦtsomoririhotellakeview.com. Refurbished guesthouse with smart modern rooms that maintain traditional touches and the lake views the name would suggest. Reasonable restaurant too. ₹4050

Northern Ladakh: the Nubra Valley

Until 1994, the lands north of Leh were off-limits to tourists and had been unexplored by outsiders since the nineteenth century. Now, the breathtaking **Nubra Valley**, unfolding beyond one of the world's highest stretches of driveable road as it crosses the **Khardung La** (5359m), can be visited with a seven-day **permit** (see page 479), which gives you enough time to explore the stark, cocoa-coloured terrain and trek out to one or two *gompas*. The valley's mountain backbone looks east to the Nubra River and west to the Shyok River, which meet amid sand dunes and boulder fields. To the north and east, the mighty Karakoram Range marks the Indian border with China and Pakistan. In these valleys the climate is relatively mild, though **dust storms** are common, whipping up sand and light debris in choking clouds above the broad riverbeds; the altitude is around 3100m, meaning that the risk of developing altitude sickness is quite low, especially if you've spent a day or two in Leh.

Before the region passed into the administrative hands of Leh, Nubra's ancient kings ruled from a palace in Charasa, atop an isolated hillock opposite **Sumur**, home to the valley's principal monastery. Further up the Nubra River, the hot springs of **Panamik**, once welcomed by footsore traders, can still be refreshing after a day on a bumpy bus. By the neighbouring Shyok River, **Diskit**, surveyed by a hillside *gompa*, lies just 7km from **Hundur**, known for its peculiar high-altitude double-humped Bactrian camels. Beyond, it is now possible to travel all the way north to the Muslim village of **Turtuk**.

ARRIVAL AND DEPARTURE

By bus There are two main routes from Leh. The main one is the daily 7.30am service to Diskit (6–7hr), from which Hundur is a short taxi ride (or a long walk) away; in summer, an additional weekly service (6.30am Sat; 9–10hr) goes all the way to Turtuk. The second is the summer-only service to Panamik (6.30am; 7–8hr), which passes Sumur on the way. You should always try to book your return journey as soon as you arrive.

By jeep Up to five people can rent a jeep and driver from Leh taxi rank or any tour operator (see page 487). A complete two-day itinerary, including a visit to Diskit and Panamik, costs ₹10,500 for the vehicle (and therefore from ₹1750 per person), or ₹19,700 for three days including Pangong Tso.

NORTH OF LEH: NUBRA VALLEY

GETTING AROUND

By bus There are usually a few daily services between Diskit and Panamik.

By taxi There are few jeeps or minibuses in the valley but you can negotiate day-trips from Diskit or Sumur up either of the river branches for around ₹1500, or around ₹2400 to go up both.

Khardung La

Day-trip from Leh and back ₹2700 per jeep • Operators such as Ladakh Cycling (see page 486) will drive you up and allow you to cycle back down to Leh

First things first – **KHARDUNG LA** is not the world's highest stretch of road, driveable or otherwise. There are at least two loftier places in Tibet, and another in Bolivia, while the highest of the lot opened in late 2017 in the southeast of Ladakh: Umling La, which tops out at just over 5800m (see map, p.490). Regardless, Khardung La is probably still the most dramatic of the lot, and it makes for an exciting journey. Most of the route north from Leh to Nubra is now good, metalled road, though there's still around 7km of rough, bus-battering surface either side of the pass; the ascent from Leh (1h 30min–2hr) is rapid, and on the way you may luck out and see planes landing at the airport, 20km away and a full 2km below – a wonderfully weird feeling. The altitude at the pass itself has been wrongly marked for years; the most "optimistic" reading has been replaced with a more reasonable one (5,480m), though it's still some way off the actual altitude of 5359m. After a few selfies and a cup of masala chai from the military café, most visitors are on their way – some back to Leh, others on to Nubra on a gentler road down. Due to its strategic importance as the military road to the battlefields of the Siachen Glacier, the road to Nubra is kept open all year round, but conditions can see it closed at any time – far more likely in the winter, of course.

Diskit

DISKIT is the largest and most appealing population centre north of Leh, and an ideal base for touring the valleys – everything listed here is within easy day-trip distance from Diskit. The town is centred on a bazaar, which courses downhill with its attendant buildings likewise dropping down in a step-like fashion. There's also an appealing old town, whose low, balconied houses lie below the main road.

Diskit gompa

Daily 7am–7pm • ₹30 • Walkable in 30min from main road, though most go up by taxi

Located by a decidedly non-ancient 30m seated Buddha statue is Diskit's picturesque **gompa**, built in 1420. After the long climb up from the main road, further steps up climb past the monks' quarters to the spooky **Gon-khang**, first of a group of temples. Local legend has it that a Mongol demon, a sworn enemy of Buddhism, was slain nearby, but his lifeless body kept returning to the *gompa*; you'll see what are reputed to be his wrinkled head and hand clasped by a pot-bellied protector deity at the back of the hall.

The diminutive **Lachung temple**, higher up, is the oldest here; soot-soiled murals face a huge Tsong-kha-pa statue, topped with a Gelug-pa yellow hat. In the heart of the *gompa*, the **Du-khang**'s remarkable mural, filling a raised cupola above the hall, depicts Tibet's Tashilhunpo *gompa*, where the Panchen Lama is receiving a long stream of visitors approaching on camels, horses and carts.

ACCOMMODATION DISKIT

Desert Himalaya Northeast edge of Diskit ☎98919 60222, ⓦdeserthimalayaresort.com. Upmarket glamping option just outside central Diskit, with a series of luxurious tents featuring beds, showers and toilet facilities. Good food, too. ₹8500

Olthang Close to the main road prayer wheel ☎01980 220025. Offers a range of smart rooms and camping for

₹500. Home-grown vegetables from the picturesque garden are served for dinner in the dining hall. ₹1500

Sunrise Diskit Just downhill from the main road prayer wheel ☎01980 220011. This simple place offers cheap rustic rooms, some with shared bathrooms, and a pleasant garden. ₹700

EATING AND DRINKING

★ **Bar & Restaurant** East of the central village crossroads, no phone. You'll have to look hard to find this place, for there's no sign – it's next to the western end of the mani wall by the Sten-del Hotel. The courtyard bar (nobody's here for the "restaurant" component) looks like it would be quite at home on a Thai island, right down to the bamboo walls and cool-looking staff; the customers,

though, are all earthy locals quaffing cans of Kingfisher (₹150), or supping shots of spirits. Daily 1–9pm.

Rinchen Sherpa At the top of the bazaar, no phone. An indisputably local place to eat, with veg momos and bowls of thukpa both going for ₹70. It's tucked into a cute little alley, and unsigned, so you may have to ask around. Daily 7am–8pm.

Hundur

Seven kilometres west of Diskit, in a wooded valley beyond some impressive **sand dunes**, is the village of **HUNDUR**. Despite a tiny population – even in season – the place is quite spread out, meaning that it lacks the vibe of Diskit; some, however, prefer the even more relaxed atmosphere. Its principal monastery lies just below the main road, near the bridge and the end of the bus route, but most visitors are here for the dunes.

The sand dunes

Daily 7am–7pm • ₹30 • Camel rides Summer only 9am–noon & 3.30pm–7pm • ₹200 for 15min, ₹600 for 1hr

The village is renowned for its herd of **Bactrian camels** (a vestige of its days on the old trans-Karakoram trade route), which you will invariably encounter if you walk towards the **sand dune** area that hems Hunder in to its east. Even if you don't want to ride one, you can go a-wandering by yourself, and there are usually ATVs for hire too.

ACCOMMODATION AND EATING HUNDUR

Goba Gueshouse 400m down from the roadside gompa ☎01980 221083, ⓦgobaguesthouse.gq. This friendly hangout is a quaint, low-key affair with good food, a sunny yard and hundreds of flowers. Some rooms have attached bathrooms. Apr–Oct. ₹1500

Snow Leopard Signposted off the main road at the back

of the village ☎01980 221097, ⓦsnowleopardhotel. com. Completely rebuilt in traditional style to become one of the smartest hotels in the valley, this offers beautifully furnished rooms with satellite TV, and a garden area to relax in. HB ₹3000

Turtuk

Almost 80km northwest of Hundur and only seven kilometres short of the Line of Control with Pakistan, the remote and enticing village of **TURTUK** only opened up to foreigners in 2009. The spectacular drive along the Shyok Valley is just as enjoyable as the sense of having arrived at the northernmost point you can reach in India. In fact, the village was in Pakistan until the 1971 war and is a gateway to the inaccessible Siachen Glacier. Despite being predominantly Muslim, Turtuk has a couple of small *gompas*, as well as the odd simple mosque.

ACCOMMODATION AND EATING TURTUK

Kharmang Guesthouse Just outside the village ☎91946 06200, ⓦkharmangguesthouse.yolasite.com. By far the most pleasant place in the area. The rooms are

all simply furnished with large panelled windows and the shared bathrooms are kept extremely clean. ₹900

Sumur

Beyond the confluence of the Shyok and Nubra rivers, **SUMUR** is a sleepy oasis spread over a large area – similar to Hunder, but without some of the charm. It is home to the valley's most influential monastery, **Samstem Ling gompa**, a pleasant 40min uphill walk behind the village. Built in 1841, the *gompa* accommodates just under a hundred Gelug-pa monks of all ages; if you want to catch the morning or evening puja, it's best to stay in town for the night.

ACCOMMODATION AND EATING | SUMUR

AO Guesthouse Centre of village, 100m from prayer wheel ☎ 94697 31976. Six of the basic doubles have attached baths, plus there's a relaxing garden, vegetarian café and camping for ₹200. **₹800**

Lchang Nang West of village ☎ 94192 16213, ⓦ lchangnang.com. Upscale option with great views of the mountains across the Nubra, featuring beautifully-decorated cottages set beside a lovely garden which makes a grand place to chill out. **₹4500**

Panamik

Twenty-two km up the valley from Sumur, **PANAMIK** (aka Pinchimik) is as far north as you can go up the Nubra Valley, a dusty hamlet overlooked by the pinpoint summit of Charouk Dongchen. Again, it's a somewhat spread-out place, though this time without any distinct centre; it has, however, found fame for its **hot springs**, with a few places to enjoy them around 1km south of the village. The sapphire Nubra runs to the west of the village, and splitting into wide rivulets at this point, it seems shallow and tame – it's not, and heed local advice not to ford it, as there have been several reported accidents involving travellers.

The hot springs

Main springs daily 9am–5pm • ₹30 • Oasis springs May–Sept 9am–5pm • ₹50

The main **hot spring** centre lies at the end of a dirt track, running a short way uphill from the main road, south of the village. It's cheap but rather underwhelming, with its two gender-segregated pools set in an ugly concrete building. More fun is the **Oasis Herbal Bath** centre nearby, on the other side of the main road; here at least a couple of the pools are out in the open, though it's open for less of the year.

Ensa gompa

A dot on the mountainside across the river, **Ensa gompa** is the main historical attraction in these parts, and now accessible by vehicle. The walking route, three hours each way, passes through the village and crosses a bridge beyond the vast boulder field 3km upstream, then joins a track above the river for around the same distance back again. Though the *gompa* is usually locked, the view from crumbling *chorten* rows nearby make the climb worthwhile.

ACCOMMODATION | PANAMIK

Hot Springs Guesthouse South end of village, on the main road ☎ 01980 247043. Set in a pleasant flower-filled garden fairly close to the springs, this one of the only places in town with attached bathrooms, although the rooms lack character. No wi-fi. **₹700**

West of Leh

Of the many *gompas* accessible by road **west of Leh**, only **Spitok**, piled on a hilltop at the end of the airport runway, and **Phyang**, which presides over one of Ladakh's most picturesque villages, are most easily visited on day-trips from the capital; however, **Likkir** and the temple complex at **Alchi**, with its wonderfully preserved eleventh-century murals, are also within range, though they're usually seen en route to or from **Kargil**. The 231km journey, which takes in a couple of high passes and some mind-blowing scenery, can be

> ## RAFTING AND KAYAKING IN LADAKH
>
> When water levels are high, between the end of June and late August, Leh's more entrepreneurial travel agents operate **rafting** trips on the Indus and Zanskar rivers. The routes are tame in comparison with Nepal's, but floating downstream in a twelve-seater rubber inflatable is a hugely enjoyable way to experience the rugged and beautiful landscape. Two different stretches of the River Indus are most commonly used: from **Phey** near Spitok to the Indus–Zanskar confluence at **Nyemo** (3hr), and from Nyemo to below the ancient temple complex at **Alchi** (2hr 30min). Experienced rafters may also want to try the more challenging route between Alchi and Khalsi, which takes in the 1km-long series of rapids at **Nurla**. The annual multiday expedition down the River Zanskar to the Indus is by far the most rewarding as it also includes the spectacular road approach to Padum. A popular shorter route on the Zanskar is from Chiling to Nyemo (3hr).
>
> Several adventure tour operators in Leh (see page 487) offer white-water rafting or kayaking on the Indus. **Trips** should be booked at least a day in advance; depending on how far from Leh you go, **prices** range from ₹1000–1800 per person for half-day trips (including transport; ₹200 or so extra for lunch). Make sure when you book that they include transport to and from the river, rental of life jackets and helmets, and meals, and that there is a waterproof strongbox for valuables.

completed in a single six-hour haul, slightly less by jeep. To do this stretch of road justice, however, you should spend at least a few days making short forays up the side-valleys of the Indus, where idyllic settlements and *gompas* nestle amid barley fields and mountains.

One of the great landmarks punctuating the former caravan route is the monastery of **Lamayuru**. Reached via a nail-biting sequence of hairpin bends as the highway climbs out of the Indus Valley to begin its meandering ascent of **Fotu La**, it lies within walking distance of some extraordinary lunar-like rock formations, at the start of the main trekking route south to Padum in Zanskar. Further west still, beyond the dramatic **Namika La** pass, **Mulbekh** is the last Buddhist village on the highway. From here on, *gompas* and *gonchas* give way to onion-domed mosques and flowing *salwar kameez*.

The Leh–Kargil road once struck fear into foreign travellers, though it's now a much smoother affair – only the section around Zoji La remains rough going, though landslides, rockfall and dodgy bridges remain constant sources of peril, and accidents remain common. In summer, **transport** along the highway is straightforward; getting to more remote spots, however, can be hard and it is worth considering getting a group together to rent a **jeep** from tour operators in Leh (see page 487).

Spitok

Taxi including Phyang ₹1200 return from Leh, or take any bus heading west along the main Srinagar highway

The *gompa* at **SPITOK**, rising incongruously from the end of the airport runway, makes a good half-day foray from Leh, 10km up the north side of the Indus Valley. Extremely picturesque, the fifteenth-century **monastery** tumbles down the sides of a steep knoll to a tight cluster of farmhouses and well-watered fields. Approached by road from the north, or from the south along a footpath that winds through Spitok village, its spacious rooftops command superb views. The main complex is of less interest than the **Palden Lumo** chapel, perched on a ridge above. Although visiting soldiers from the nearby Indian army barracks consider the deity inside the chapel to be Kali Mata, the key-keeper will assure visitors that what many consider to be the black-faced and bloodthirsty Hindu goddess of death and destruction is actually **Yidam Dorje Jigjet**. Coloured electric lights illuminate the cobwebbed chamber of veiled guardian deities whose ferocious faces are only revealed once a year. If you have a torch, check out the six-hundred-year-old paintings on the back wall, partially hidden by eerie *chaam* masks used during the winter festival season.

Phyang

Buses from Leh (3 daily at 9am, 2pm & 4.30pm), returning an hour later; however, the main highway, which has many more vehicles to and from Leh, is only a 30min walk away • Taxi including Spitok ₹1200 return • Gon-khang ₹30

A mere 17km west of Leh, the *gompa* at **PHYANG** looms large at the head of a secluded side-valley that tapers north into the Ladakh Range from the Srinagar highway. The *gompa* itself houses a fifty-strong community of lamas, but few antique murals of note, most of them having recently been painted over with brighter colours. Its only treasures are a small collection of fourteenth-century Kashmiri bronzes in the modern Guru-Padmasambhava temple and the light and airy **Du-khang**'s three silver *chortens*, one of which is decorated with a seven-eyed **dzi stone**. The gem, considered to be highly auspicious, was brought to Phyang from Tibet by the monastery's former head lama, whose ashes the *chorten* encases. Tucked away around the side, the shrine in the *gompa*'s gloomily atmospheric **Gon-khang** houses a ferocious veiled protector deity and an amazing collection of weapons and armour plundered during the Mongol invasions of the fourteenth century. Also dangling from the cobweb-covered rafters are several sets of yak horns, believed to be 900-year-old relics of the Bon cult.

Phyang's annual **festival**, Phyang Tsedup, held between mid-July and early August (see page 483) to coincide with the tourist season, is the second largest in Ladakh after the one held in Hemis (see page 492). Celebrated with the usual masked *chaam* dances, the event is marked with a ritual exposition of a giant 10m brocaded silk *thangka*.

Likkir

Bus from Leh in summer (1 daily at 4pm; 2hr), returning in the morning; the main highway, which has many more vehicles to and from Leh, is a 1hr walk away • Taxi including Alchi ₹3000 return from Leh • Museum Daily: summer daily 8am–1pm & 2–6pm, winter daily 10am–1pm & 2–4pm • ₹30

Five kilometres to the north of the main Leh–Srinagar highway, shortly before the village of Saspol, the large and wealthy *gompa* of **LIKKIR** is home to around one hundred monks and renowned for its 23m-high yellow statue of the Buddha-to-come that towers serenely above the terraced fields. The *gompa*, 3km up the valley from Likkir village, was extensively renovated in the eighteenth century and today shows little sign of the antiquity related to the site. There is a small **museum** in the complex, displaying some antique *thangkas* and other Buddhist paraphernalia. The *gompa* overlooks the starting point for the popular two-day hike to Temisgang via Rhizong, which provides a comparatively gentle introduction to trekking in Ladakh.

A pleasant break from the bustle of Leh, the village of Likkir itself offers a small but adequate choice of accommodation which, along with the sheer tranquillity of the surroundings, tempts many travellers to linger a few days.

ACCOMMODATION AND EATING   LIKKIR

Chhume Guest House Just behind the gompa ☏ 94692 00793. Basic place run by welcoming hosts, with carpeted, non-attached rooms and a homely lounge. **₹700**

★ **Norboo Spon Guesthouse** East side of the village

☏ 94199 91510, ⊛ thesimplife.com. Enjoy a unique homestay-style experience with full board in this out-of-the-way guesthouse, with simple non-attached rooms. **₹1800**

Alchi

Private buses from Leh at 8am (summer only, returning in the afternoon) and 4.30pm (year-round, returning in the morning); 2hr 30min • Taxi including Likkir ₹3000 return from Leh • Daily 8am–1pm & 2–6pm • ₹50

Driving past on the nearby Srinagar–Leh highway, you'd never guess that the spectacular sweep of wine-coloured scree 3km across the Indus from **Saspol** conceals one of the most significant historical sites in Asia. Yet the low pagoda-roofed **Chos-khor**, or "religious enclave", at **ALCHI**, 70km west of Leh, harbours an extraordinary wealth of ancient wall paintings and wood sculpture, miraculously preserved for more than nine centuries inside five tiny mud-walled temples. The site's earliest murals are regarded as the finest surviving examples of a style that flourished in Kashmir during

7

the "Second Spreading". Barely a handful of the monasteries founded during this era escaped the Muslim depredations of the fourteenth century; Alchi is both the least remote and most impressive of them all.

Legend tells that Rinchen Zangpo, the "Great Translator" (see page 478), stuck his walking stick in the ground here en route to Chilling and upon his return found it had become a poplar, an auspicious sign that made him build a temple on the spot. One tree near the entrance to the Chos-khor, denoted with a signboard, is symbolic of this event. The Chos-khor itself consists of five near-adjoining temples, various residential buildings and a scattering of large *chortens*, surrounded by a mud-and-stone wall. Most concentrate on the two oldest temples, the **Sumtsek** and the **Vairocana**, although the **Lotsa** and **Manjushree** shrines also boast colourful murals, and the latter a huge, brightly painted statue of the Buddha of Wisdom.

The Sumtsek

Standing to the left of the Du-khang, the **Sumtsek** marks the high watermark of early medieval Indian-Buddhist art. Its woodcarvings and paintings, dominated by rich reds and blues, are almost as fresh and vibrant today as they were nine hundred years ago when the squat triple-storey structure was built. The heart of the shrine is a

TREKKING IN LADAKH AND ZANSKAR

The ancient footpaths that crisscross **Ladakh** and **Zanskar** provide some of the most inspiring **trekking** in the Himalayas. Threading together remote Buddhist villages and monasteries, cut off in winter behind high passes whose rocky tops bristle with prayer flags, nearly all are long, hard and high – but never dull. Whether you make all the necessary preparations yourself, or pay an agency to do it for you, Leh (see page 487) is the best place to plan a trek; the **best time** is from June to September.

Most hikers arrange their trips as **package treks**, sold by agencies in Leh. Prices are pretty standard across the board, and in any case agencies often pool people together. For an idea of prices, Likkir to Temisgang is one of the shortest treks available, and will cost around ₹11,500 all in assuming a group of four or mow; Markha Valley expeditions, on the other hand, start at more like ₹26,000 for six days.

Trekking **independently** is straightforward if you don't mind haggling and are happy to organize the logistics yourself. To find ponies and guides, head for the Tibetan refugee camp at Choglamsar, 3km south of Leh; doing so can work out far cheaper than package tours from Leh. You can **rent equipment**, including high-quality tents (₹150–200 a day), sleeping bags (₹100–150), gas stoves (₹60–80), sleeping mats (₹30–80), duck-down jackets and boots (₹50–80 each), either through your chosen agency or at somewhere like Venture Ladakh (see page 487); if you're intending to climb Stok-Kangri you may need to dish out ₹100 for an ice axe. Also consider buying Indian equipment in the bazaar, and then later selling it on.

Minimize your impact in culturally and ecologically sensitive areas by being as **self-reliant** as possible, especially with food and fuel. Buying provisions along the way puts an unnecessary burden on the villages' subsistence-oriented economies, and encourages strings of unsightly "tea shops" (often run by outsiders) to sprout along the trails. Always burn kerosene, never wood – a scarce and valuable resource. Refuse should be packed up, not disposed of along the route, no matter how far from the nearest town you are, and plastics retained for recycling at the Ecology Centre in Leh (see page 489). Always bury your faeces and burn your toilet paper afterwards. Finally, do not defecate in the dry-stone huts along the trails; local shepherds use them for shelter during snowstorms.

For information about trekking to **Zanskar** from the south, see "Trekking in Lahaul and Spiti" (see page 466).

LIKKIR TO TEMISGANG

A driveable road along the old caravan route through the hills between **Likkir** and **Temisgang** makes a leisurely two-day hike, which takes in three major monasteries (Likkir, Rhizong and Temisgang) and a string of idyllic villages. The "Sham" trek, as you'll see it advertised, is a great

colossal statue of **Maitreya**, the Buddha-to-come, his head high in the second storey. Accompanying him are two equally grand **bodhisattvas**, their heads peering serenely down through gaps in the eaves. Each of these stucco statues wears a figure-hugging *dhoti*, adorned with different, meticulously detailed motifs. Avalokitesvara, the *bodhisattva* of compassion (to the left), has pilgrimage sites, court vignettes, palaces and pre-Muslim-style *stupas* on his robe, while that of Maitreya is decorated with episodes from the life of Gautama Buddha. The robe of Manjushri, destroyer of falsehood, to the right, shows 85 masters of Tantra, the *mahasiddhas*, adopting complex yogic poses in a maze of bold square patterns.

Among the exquisite **murals**, some repaired in the sixteenth century, is the famous six-armed green goddess Prajnaparamita, the "Perfection of Wisdom". Amazingly, when viewed from the centre of the shrine, this – and the multitude of other images that plaster the interior of the Sumtsek – resolves into a harmonious whole.

The Vairocana

An inscription records that Alchi's oldest structure, the **Vairocana**, was erected late in the eleventh century. Its centrepiece is an unlit, hard-to-make-out image of Vairocana, the "Buddha Resplendent", flanked by the four main Buddha manifestations that

introduction to trekking in Ladakh, the perfect acclimatizer if you plan to attempt any longer and more demanding routes. Ponies and guides for the trip may be arranged on spec at either Likkir or Temisgang villages, both of which have small guesthouses and are connected by daily buses to Leh.

THE MARKHA VALLEY

The beautiful **Markha Valley** runs parallel with the Indus on the far southern side of the snowy Stok-Kangri massif, visible from Leh. Passing through cultivated valley floors, undulating high-altitude grassland and snow-prone passes, the winding trail along it enables trekkers to experience life in a roadless region without having to hike for weeks into the wilderness – as a result, it has become the most frequented route in Ladakh. Do not attempt this trek without adequate wet- and cold-weather gear: snow flurries sweep across the higher reaches of the Markha Valley even in August.

The circuit takes six to eight days to complete, and is usually followed anticlockwise, starting from the village of **Spitok** (see page 500), 10km south of Leh. A more dramatic approach via **Stok** (see page 494) affords matchless views over the Indus Valley to the Ladakh and Karakoram ranges, but involves a sharp ascent of **Stok La** (4848m) on only the second day; don't try it unless you are already well acclimatized to the altitude.

PADUM TO LAMAYURU

The trek across the rugged Zanskar Range from **Padum to Lamayuru** usually completed in ten to twelve days, is a hugely popular but very demanding long-distance route, not to be attempted as a first-time trek nor without adequate preparation, ponies and a guide.

LAMAYURU TO ALCHI

The five-day trek from **Lamayuru**, on the Srinagar–Leh highway, to **Alchi** is one of the toughest in the region, winding across high passes and a tangle of isolated valleys past a couple of ancient *gompas*, and offering superb panoramic views of the wilderness south of the Indus Valley. It's very hard to follow in places, so don't attempt it without an experienced guide, ponies and enough provisions to tide you over if you lose your way.

STOK-KANGRI

Visible from most of Leh, **Stok-Kangri** (6120m) is reputed to be the easiest peak above 6000m in the world. Several agents in Leh advertise five-day **climbing expeditions** via the village of Stok with a non-technical final climb for around ₹5000 per head per day for a group of four. It's straightforward to walk up it independently, though you'll need to carry enough food for three or four days.

appear all over Alchi's temple walls, always presented in their associated colours: Akshobya ("Unshakeable"; blue), Ratnasambhava ("Jewel Born"; yellow), Amitabha ("Boundless Radiance"; red) and Amoghasiddhi ("Unfailing Success"; green). The other walls are decorated with six elaborate mandalas, interspersed with intricate friezes.

ACCOMMODATION AND EATING   ALCHI

The number of places to stay has grown as Alchi's fame has spread but prices are generally quite high. Most serve food, so apart from a couple of *dhabas* in the village centre, there is just one independent restaurant.

Heritage Home Right beside Chos-kor entrance ☎01982 227125, ✉heritagehome@rediffmail.com. Pleasantly welcoming mid-range guesthouse with a shady courtyard. The rooms are quite large and decorated in traditional Ladakhi style, and some look straight into the Chos-kor. ₹2350

Lotsava About 50m below the access road ☎01982 227129, ✉stanzindorjey@gmail.com. Very basic guesthouse with good views from the attached and non-

attached rooms, but layers of dust. Meals usually available, no wi-fi. ₹600/₹700

Ule Ethnic Resort Uleytokpo ☎01982 253640, ⊚uleresort.com. Not in Alchi, but a short drive away in Uleytokpo, this resort is made up of sweet little huts and cottages, many of which have wonderful views of the Indus below. Mercifully for a place with little around it, the food here is good. No wi-fi. ₹5700

★ **Zimskhang Holiday Home** On lane to Chos-kor ☎01982 227086, ⊚zimskhang.com. On one side of the lane to Chos-kor is a smart hotel, and on the other a highly recommended garden restaurant, whose mostly veg meals cost ₹150–300. ₹4200

Lamayuru

Daily bus from Leh (3pm, return 2pm next day); also accessible on Leh-Kargil buses • A road now goes right up to the monastery, or take a steep footpath up through the village from the highway • Gompa Daily 8am–1pm & 1.30–6pm • ₹50

If one sight could be said to sum up Ladakh, it would have to be the *gompa* at **LAMAYURU**, 130km west of Leh and 107km east of Kargil. Hemmed in by a moonscape of scree-covered mountains, the whitewashed medieval monastery towers above a scruffy cluster of tumbledown mud-brick houses from the top of a near-vertical, weirdly eroded cliff. A major landmark on the old silk route, the *gompa* numbers among the 108 (a spiritually significant number) founded by the Rinchen Zangpo in the tenth and eleventh centuries. However, its craggy seat, believed to have sheltered Milarepa, a Tibetan Buddhist saint, during his religious odyssey across the Himalayas in the eleventh century, was probably sacred long before the advent of Buddhism, when local people followed the shamanistic Bon cult. Just ten to twenty lamas of the Brigungpa branch of the Kagyu school are now left, as opposed to the four hundred that lived here a century or so ago, though the number increases in summer. Nor does Lamayuru harbour much in the way of art treasures; the main reason visitors make a stop on this section of the Srinagar–Leh road is to photograph the *gompa* from the valley floor (though the line of poplars makes this hard), or to pick up the trail to Zanskar.

ACCOMMODATION AND EATING   LAMAYURU

★ **Dragon** Just off main road at bottom of village ☎01982 224501, ✉dragonskyabu@gmail.com. The old hop-covered block has a range of non-attached rooms, including one covetable glass room, while the newer block contains smarter en suites. The pleasant garden restaurant is makes a good place to eat, and the place is a good

trekking resource too. ₹800/₹2800

Niranjana Near the gompa entrance ☎01982 253355. This imposing four-storey building has carpeted, concrete rooms with good views of the surrounding valleys; the shared bathrooms have hot running water. Its location allows it to be overpriced. ₹1000

Mulbekh

Accessible on Leh-Kargil buses • Gompa Daily 8am–6pm • ₹30

West of Lamayuru, the main road crawls to the top of **Fotu La** (4091m), the highest pass between Leh and Srinagar, drops and then ascends **Namika La** (3760m), so called (it means "Sky-Pillar") because of the jagged pinnacle of rock that looms above it to the south. Once across the windswept ridge, it drops through a dramatic landscape of disintegrating desert cliffs and pebbly ravines to the wayside village of **MULBEKH** – the last sizeable Buddhist settlement along the road before the Muslim Purig settlements around Kargil. The village is scattered around the banks of the River Wakha, lined with poplars and orchards of walnut and apricot trees and would be a sleepy hamlet were it not for the endless convoys of trucks and tourist buses that thunder through while the passes are open. Those visitors who stop at all tend only to stay long enough to grab a chai at a roadside *dhaba* and to have a quick look at the 7m-high **Maitreya** ("Chamba" in Tibetan) **statue** carved from the face of a gigantic boulder nearby. The precise origins of the shapely four-armed Buddha-to-be are not known, but an ancient inscription on its side records that it was carved between the seventh and eighth centuries, well before Buddhism was fully established in Tibet. The single-chambered *gompa* in front of the statue is decorated with particularly beautiful murals, and is dedicated to the thousand-armed Chenrazig (Avalokitesvara).

ACCOMMODATION AND EATING	MULBEKH
Paradise On main road opposite the statue ☎01985 270010. A few shabby non-attached rooms nestle above	a canteen serving *thukpa*, dhal, rice, *momos* and butter tea during the day, and booze by night. ₹500

Kargil

Though it is surrounded by awesome scenery, most travellers don't spend more than a few hours in **KARGIL**, capital of the area dubbed "Little Baltistan", which rises in a clutter of corrugated-iron rooftops from the confluence of the Suru and Drass rivers. As a halfway point between Leh and Srinagar, its mundane hotels once filled up at night with weary bus passengers, who then got up at 4am and careered off under cover of darkness; this has not really been necessary since improvements to the road were made, but some choose to stay on, and many actually end up preferring the place to Leh. Bearded, woolly-hatted old men stroll the streets past wholesalers bearing sacks of grains, spices and tins of ghee, and butchers displaying severed goats' heads on dusty shelves. The town feels more Pakistani than Indian, with the faces and food deriving from Kashmir and Central Asia.

The majority of Kargil's eighty thousand inhabitants, known as **Purig**, are strict Muslims. Unlike their Sunni cousins in Kashmir, however, the locals here are orthodox **Shias**, which not only explains the ubiquitous Ayatollah photographs, but also the conspicuous absence of women from the bazaar; Western women should keep their arms and legs covered and may arouse mild curiosity. You might even spot the odd black turban of an Agha, one of Kargil's spiritual leaders, who still go on pilgrimage to holy sites in Iran and have outlawed male–female social practices such as dancing. Descendants of settlers and Muslim merchants from Kashmir and Yarkand, Purig speak a dialect called **Purgi** – a mixture of Ladakhi and Balti.

Kargil is often used as a jumping-off point for the Suru Valley and the wider Zanskar area; if pressing on further west towards Srinagar, the first place of note you'll come across is Sonamarg (see page 521), now out of Ladakh and inside Kashmir.

Brief history

Had it not been for the daring Indian re-conquest of the region during the 1948 Indo-Pak War, Kargil would today be part of Baltistan, the region across the Line of Control which it closely resembles. Indeed, Kargil is so close to the LoC and Pakistani positions that it served as the logistics centre in the 1999 war (see page 480) and was repeatedly targeted by Pakistani artillery. Aside from the destruction of the odd building, however, much of the town escaped unscathed, as the army bases and airport lie on the outskirts of town. The dust has settled markedly in recent years and, as dialogue continues between India and Pakistan on Kashmir, tourist numbers have been steadily increasing.

7

ARRIVAL AND DEPARTURE

State buses arriving in Kargil from Leh and Srinagar pull in by the river, 150m below the middle of the bazaar, while private buses, minibuses and jeeps share a larger compound further south, just below the bazaar.

By bus Buses to Srinagar (7hr) leave mostly late at night, and to Leh (6hr) early morning. There are also several daily until 2pm to Panikhar (3hr), and afternoon departures to

Mulbekh (1hr 30min). Services to Padum (12–13hr) are confined to a weekly summertime bus from Leh.

By jeep Shared jeeps to Leh (5hr; ₹1000) and Srinagar (6–7hr; ₹900) mostly leave early in the morning. Unfortunately, only whole jeeps can be hired to Padum (9–10hr; at least ₹13,000), but you can try asking around for a shared one.

ACCOMMODATION

Room tariffs soar in July and August when most travellers pass through; rates lower than those given here are usually available at other times.

Baru La On a rise south of the centre ☎94691 90337, ⊕barulahotel.com. The most pleasant place to stay in town by far, with lovely rooms, a garden area (with occasional bonfires), and a viewing terrace. As their website states, "price includes a huge amount of tax, and an excellent breakfast". BB ₹4500

Marjina Down an alley from the main bazaar ☎94191 76212, ⊜saggedmargina@yahoo.com. Reasonably large rooms in a rickety old wooden building – those on the ground floor are cheapest but rather dowdy. No wi-fi. ₹600

Royal Inn South of the centre, by the river ☎01985 232114, ⊕royalinnkargil.com. A fine choice at this price level, and particularly good value given its liability to give discounts at any time. Many of their cosy rooms overlook the river; the deluxe options have particularly fine views. ₹2800

EATING

Eating options are rather limited, but the street food can be delicious – chai, chapattis and omelettes, with hot Kashmiri bread slathered with butter. Spicy shish kebabs are on sale from late in the afternoon.

Las Vegas Middle of the main bazaar ☎94691 93900. One of the more salubrious places (these things are relative), serving mainly non-veg Indian, Kashmiri and Chinese food, such as *rogan josh* and chow mein, for ₹100–200. Daily noon–9pm.

Ruby South end of the main bazaar ☎94197 19903. Popular restaurant serving Kashmiri specialities including *yakhani* (meat boiled in yogurt) and *gustaba* (meat balls), typical of Central Asian cuisine. Most items under ₹150. Daily 10am–8pm.

Tibetan Food Restaurant Middle of the main bazaar ☎94692 21128. All the favourites like *momos* and *thukpa* (₹70–120), dished up in a simple upstairs dining room. Choice can be limited. Daily 10am–9pm.

The Suru Valley

Dividing two of the world's most formidable mountain ranges, the **Suru Valley** winds south from Kargil to the desolate Pensi La, the main entry point for Zanskar. The first leg leads through the broad lower reaches of the Suru Valley, strewn with Muslim villages clustered around metal mosque domes. As you progress southwards, the pristine white icefields and twin pinnacles of **Nun-Kun** (7135m and 7077m, respectively) nose over the horizon. Apart from a brief disappearance behind the steep sides of the valley at **Panikhar**, this awesome massif dominates the landscape all the way to Zanskar.

Panikhar

Sixty-five km south of Kargil, **PANIKHAR** is by no means the largest settlement in the Suru Valley, but is nonetheless a good place to break the long journey to Padum. It's also a minor trekking centre, thanks to its position at the start of the Lonvilad Gali–Pahalgam trail.

The main reason to stop is to hike to nearby **Parkachik La** for panoramic views of the glacier-gouged north face of the mighty **Nun-Kun massif**. The **trail** up to the pass begins on the far side of the Suru River, crossed via a suspension bridge thirty minutes south of the village. It may look straightforward from Panikhar, but the three-hour climb up to the ridge gets very tough indeed towards the top, especially if you're not used to the altitude. However, even seasoned trekkers gasp in awe at the sight that greets them when they finally arrive at the cairns. Capped with a plume of cloud and with snow streaming from its huge pyramidal peak, Nun sails 3500m above the valley floor, draped with heavily crevassed hanging glaciers and flanked by its sisters, multi-pinnacled Kun and saddle-topped Barmal.

ARRIVAL AND DEPARTURE	PANIKHAR

By bus and taxi There are several daily buses from Kargil (2hr 30min), with the last heading back at 5pm, and occasionally shared taxis too, but no services on to Padum bar the weekly (usually) summertime bus from Leh, which is not to be relied upon. **Hitching** If you're looking for a lift to Padum (8–9hr), return to the check post 5km back down on the main road, and try your luck there (the earlier the better).

ACCOMMODATION AND EATING

Apart from the state-run bungalow listed below, your only option here is to homestay, which is incredibly easy to arrange; even if the first person you talk to has no room, they'll probably introduce you to someone who does.

J&K Tourist Bungalow 100m from the bus stand ☎ 01985 259137. Large but rather dowdy attached rooms full of old furniture. The restaurant serves simple veg meals, just about the only food available in the village. ₹500

Rangdum and around

Having wound across a seemingly endless boulder field, closed in on both sides by sheer mountain walls, the road to Zanskar emerges at a marshy open plain surrounded by snow peaks and mountainsides of near-vertical strata. **Juldo**, a tiny settlement whose fodder-stacked rooftops are strung with fluttering prayer flags, marks the beginning of Buddhist **Suru**. The most noteworthy place to break the journey is **RANGDUM**, a village that would be insignificant but for its splendid *gompa*, 5km east.

Continuing south on the main road, one glistening 6000m peak after another appears atop a series of side-valleys, many lined with gigantic folds of rock and ice. The real high point, though, is reserved for the dizzying descent beyond **Pensi La** (4401m), as the road's switchbacks swing over the colossal S-shaped **Darung Drung Glacier**, whose milky-green meltwaters drain southeast into the Stod Valley, visible below.

ACCOMMODATION AND EATING · RANGDUM AND AROUND

J&K Tourist Bungalow Centre of Rangdum. One of the most remote places to stay in India, this government bungalow is predictably basic but provides a roof and very simple food on request. No wi-fi. ₹500

Zanskar

Walled in by the Great Himalayan Divide, **ZANSKAR**, literally "Land of White Copper", has for decades exerted the allure of Shangri-La on visitors to Ladakh. The region's staggering remoteness, extreme climate and distance from the major Himalayan trade routes has meant that the successive winds of change that have blown through the Indus Valley to the north have had little impact here. The annual influx of trekkers and a driveable road have certainly quickened the pace of development, but away from the main settlement of **Padum**, the Zanskaris' way of life has altered little since the sage Padmasambhava passed through in the eighth century.

The nucleus of the region is a Y-shaped glacial valley system drained by three main rivers: the **Stot** (or Doda) and the **Tsarap** (or Lingit) join and flow north as the **Zanskar**. Lying to the leeward side of the Himalayan watershed, the valley sees a lot more snow than central Ladakh: even the lowest passes remain blocked for seven or eight months of the year, while midwinter temperatures can drop to a bone-numbing -40°C. Fifteen thousand or so tenacious souls subsist in this bleak and treeless terrain – among the coldest inhabited places on the planet – muffled up for half the year inside their smoke-filled whitewashed crofts, with a winter's-worth of fodder piled on the roof.

Until the end of the 1970s, anything the resourceful Zanskaris could not produce for themselves (including timber for building) had to be transported into the region over 4000- to 5000-metre passes. In midwinter, they had to be carried along the

---

ORGANIZING TREKS FROM PADUM

Basic **trekking supplies** are sold at the hole-in-the-wall stores along the bazaar. Prices are much higher than elsewhere, so it pays to bring your own provisions with you from Kargil. Most trekkers arrange **ponies** through the tourist office or guesthouse owners, or you could try Zanskar Trek (ⓦzanskartrek.com), who also provide guides (₹600–1000/day). Expect to pay around ₹600 per pony per day, depending on the time of year (ponies transport grain during the harvest, so they're more expensive in early September). If you have trouble finding a horse-wallah in Padum, ask at a neighbouring village, such as Pipiting, a thirty-minute walk north across the fields from Padum, where many of them live.

---

frozen surface of the Zanskar from its confluence with the Indus at Nimmu, and this ten- to twelve-day round trip remains the quickest trekking route from Padum to the Srinagar–Leh road. Finally, in 1980, a driveable dirt track was blasted down the Suru and over Pensi La into the Stot Valley. Landslides and freak blizzards permitting (Pensi La can be snowbound even in August), the bumpy journey from Kargil to Padum can now be completed in as little as ten hours.

Padum

After a memorable trek or bus ride, **PADUM**, 240km to the south of Kargil, comes as a bit of an anticlimax. Instead of the picturesque Zanskari village you might expect, the region's administrative headquarters and principal roadhead turns out to be a desultory collection of typical concrete cubes, oily truck parks and tin-roofed government buildings. The settlement's only real appeal lies in its superb location. Nestled at the southernmost tip of a broad, fertile river basin, Padum presides over a flat patchwork of farmland enclosed on three sides by colossal walls of scree and snow-capped mountains.

Straddling a nexus of several long-distance trails, the town is an important **trekking hub** – during the short summer season, you'll see almost as many weather-beaten Westerners wandering around its sandy lanes as locals – a mixture of indigenous Buddhists and Sunni Muslims. Even so, facilities are still limited to a small (but growing) number of shops, restaurants and guesthouses. Nor is there much to see while you're waiting for your blisters to heal; the only noteworthy sight within easy walking distance is a small **Tagrimo gompa**, fifteen minutes' walk to the west.

ARRIVAL AND GETTING AROUND — PADUM

By bus The private bus from Leh (2 days) via Kargil (12–13hr) is erratic, but usually operates weekly during summer – ask in Leh which day this currently is. The only services within the valley are from Padum to Karsha (1 daily; 1hr), some of which go on to Zangla (2 weekly; 1hr 30min).

By jeep Due to the short season, jeep taxis in Padum (through the Padum Taxi Union office on the main road) are expensive: a trip to Karsha and back will probably cost ₹1500.

INFORMATION

Tourist office The J&K Tourist Office, as you enter the village on the main road (Mon–Sat 10am–4pm; ☎01983 245017), is good for general information and trekking advice.

Services There are no official exchange or ATM facilities in Padum. A few places have wi-fi but connections, but they're still slow.

ACCOMMODATION

★ **Marq** 200m west of the main bazaar ☎01983 245021. The smartest place in town, with bright, spacious rooms, all of which have cable TV and splendid views. Relative luxury with a homely family feel and excellent food. **₹3000**

Mont Blanc South end of the main bazaar ☎01983 245183. Friendly French-run place with simple rooms, all with bathrooms and slight Gallic touches; also ₹150 tent pitches. Good for trekking advice. **₹600**

Rigyal West of the main road ☎94692 24500, ⓦhotelrigyal.com. Relatively new option, with comfortable attached rooms (somewhat amusingly, all ten of them are "standard"), and decent food; they'll also let you camp for ₹200 or so. **₹1800**

EATING AND DRINKING

Food supplies are plentiful in summer, but start to dwindle as autumn approaches. Apart from the guesthouse restaurants, there are some good cheap *dhabas* and the odd noteworthy independent establishment.

Korean Restaurant West end of the main bazaar ☏ 94692 17528. Run by two sisters, this is something out of the ordinary – good Korean staples such as bibimbap for ₹150–250, with degrees of spiciness to suit all palates. Daily 8am–8pm.

Zanskar Restaurant Middle of the main bazaar ☏ 94190 25612. The best of the Zanskari-cum-Tibetan joints, good for egg and local bread brekkies and well-prepared *momos* and *thukpas* later in the day. Most items around ₹100 or under. Daily 7am–9pm.

Karsha

The hike across the fields from Padum to the *gompa* at **KARSHA**, Zanskar's largest Gelug-pa monastery, is the most rewarding and popular side-trip. This cluster of whitewashed mud cubes clinging to the rocky lower slopes of the mountain north of Padum dates from the tenth to the fourteenth century. Of the prayer halls, the recently renovated Du-khang and Gon-khang at the top of the complex are the most impressive, while the small Chukshok-jal, set apart from the *gompa* below a ruined fort on the far side of a gully, contains Karsha's oldest wall paintings, contemporaneous with those at Alchi (see page 501). The tiny village is also a nicer place to stay than Padum.

En route to Karsha, you pass another large *gompa*, **Sani**, lauded as the oldest in Zanskar, and the only one built on the valley floor. Local legend attributes its foundation to the itinerant Padmasambhava (Guru Rinpoche) in the eighth century. Set apart from the temples a little to the north is a 2m-high Maitreya figure, carved out of local stone sometime between the eighth and tenth centuries.

ARRIVAL AND DEPARTURE
KARSHA

On foot The quickest way to get to Karsha on foot (around 2hr–2hr 30min) is to head north from Padum to the cable bridge across the Stot, immediately below the monastery.

By road Karsha can also be reached by road, via the bridge at Tungri, 8km northwest of Padum. There's a daily bus in summer that leaves Padum at 4pm, returning at 7am. Taxis cost around ₹1500 return.

ACCOMMODATION

Some villagers rent rooms to tourists – ask around. It's also possible to nab a room at the monastery itself.

Kashmir

Long before **Kashmir** was immortalized in the eponymous Led Zeppelin song it had already achieved legendary status with Western travellers, from officers of the British Raj to the first hippie overlanders in the 1960s. No stint in the Subcontinent was complete without an idyllic sojourn on the famous houseboats of the capital Srinagar, which sits at the heart of the idyllic **Kashmir Valley**. By the end of the 1980s, the tourist business was booming alongside agriculture, and had in fact overtaken it as the region's main source of income. This all came to an almost overnight halt with the onset of the conflict in 1989 (see page 480). With the situation stabilizing in recent years, visitor numbers have risen again (mostly domestic, thanks to the burgeoning Indian middle class), though they are still well below the 1980s zenith.

There could hardly be a greater contrast than that between the hot and dusty plains around Jammu and the cool green belt of the Kashmir Valley. Apart from the geographical divide, separated as they are by a rise in altitude of more than 1000m, there are huge cultural and religious differences. While the whole area around Jammu is predominantly Hindu, the Kashmir Valley and its capital, Srinagar, are distinctly Muslim, a key factor in the sectarian problems.

Most people content themselves with a visit to **Srinagar**, although the towns of **Gulmarg** and **Pahalgam**, both in prime trekking territory, are regarded as safe these

7

SECURITY CONCERNS IN KASHMIR

Although the situation in Kashmir is calmer than it has been for decades, it is still essential to check the current state of affairs with reputable media sources before travelling (kashmirtimes.com is a good local resource). No tourists have been directly targeted since 1995 (see page 480), but if trouble flares up, as it did in early 2019, you will have to endure a very heavy **military presence** and may even run the risk of getting – quite literally – caught in the crossfire or an act of **terrorism**. You should not necessarily be put off by government advisories, however, as these tend to be extremely cautious, and Kashmir has remained on the list of no-go areas even when at its most peaceful; locals pin the blame for their region's reputation on "the media", and most visits are trouble-free.

Once you are in Jammu and the Kashmir Valley, you will find that **security** is taken very seriously – the vast majority of tourist sites, such as temples, mosques, museums and forts, are heavily guarded. You are usually prohibited from taking bags or electronic items inside; tokens are given when you check them, but if you are not comfortable about leaving cameras or mobile phones in the cloakroom, then lock them in your hotel. Both Jammu and Srinagar **airports** have extra-high security, including at the perimeter fences, and passengers are sometimes not allowed into the terminal until a certain period of time before departure – usually two hours, but occasionally less. At times hand luggage is not permitted on board (and shoes usually have to go in the hold), so it is best to do your research in advance.

days, as is the lovely town of **Sonamarg** on the Kargil road. Nevertheless, before setting off for Kashmir, it is wise to check on the current security situation (see page 510).

The initial impression of the Vale of Kashmir, whether you approach it via the Jawahar Tunnel, which cuts through the mountains from Jammu in the south, or via the Zoji La pass from Kargil to the east, remains one of a lush rural paradise guarded by the grandeur of the surrounding peaks, the mighty **Pir Panjal** range snow-capped except in the very height of summer. Vivid green fields of corn and wheat form a patchwork quilt with fruit orchards and groves of nut trees, principally walnut and almond. These are most often lined with towering poplars and willows, hence the preponderance, on the approach to the capital, of shops selling high-quality cricket bats.

Srinagar

Steeped in tradition, **SRINAGAR** is the summertime administrative capital of J&K, and set in one of the most dramatic locations in India – a mile above sea level, with majestic mountains pressing in on three sides. All too often associated with strife in recent times, this city of almost one million inhabitants is most famous with tourists for the **houseboats** (see page 515) that line the fringes of **Dal and Nageen lakes**, as well as the central section of the **Jhelum River**, a tributary of the Indus. In September 2014, the river flooded vast areas of Srinagar up to first-floor level; the eventual death toll in the valley was nearly two hundred, but mercifully the city is now back on its feet.

Like the rest of Kashmir, Srinagar is predominantly Muslim, even more so since the advent of serious trouble in 1990, when almost all the Hindu Pandits were driven out – though for centuries this region was known for its religious tolerance, where adherents of all the major Eastern faiths lived side by side. As such, away from the lake, most of the sights here are religious in nature, including two venerated mosques – **Jama Masjid**, deep in the heart of the atmospheric **Old City**, and the lakeside **Hazratbal** – and the Sufi shrine of **Makhdoom Sahib**, as well as the **Shankaracharya Mandir**, a Hindu temple atop a hill overlooking Dal Lake.

The bustling centre of Srinagar, which revolves around the two main thoroughfares of Residency Road and Moulana Azad (MA) Road, is not particularly appealing; the bazaar area of **Lal Chowk** at the western end of these streets holds more interest, while the quieter area to the southeast of Dal Gate is even more appealing. Of the city's secular sights, options include the engaging **Sri Pratap Singh Museum** and the Mughal **pleasure gardens** around Dal Lake.

Dal Lake and around

Shikara hire ₹500/hr (₹300 if your bargaining skills are up to it); some houseboats can arrange self-paddle boats for ₹40/hr • Floating market 5.30–7.30am

Srinagar would be a major draw on the strength of its Himalayan scenery alone, but it is the city's serene lakes and grand gardens that make it irresistible. There are actually several large bodies of water dividing the urban sprawl into its constituent neighbourhoods but by far the largest is **Dal Lake**, with a surface area of approximately 21 square kilometres. The lake is usually as flat as a mirror and incredibly photogenic, with the surrounding peaks reflected in its greenish-blue waters, the natural beauty now "enlivened" by cheesy fountains dotted around the fringe. Apart from the

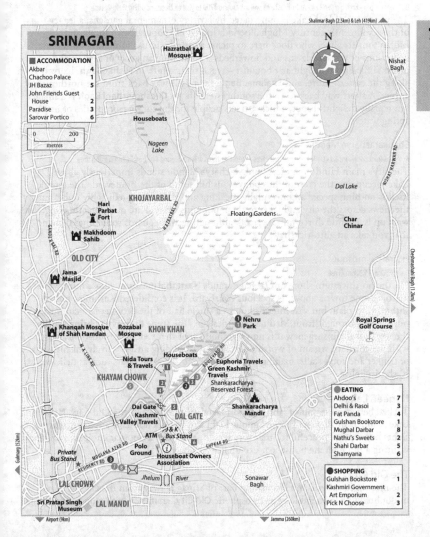

SRINAGAR

Shalimar Bagh (2.5km) & Leh (419km)

7

ACCOMMODATION
Akbar	4
Chachoo Palace	1
JH Bazaz	5
John Friends Guest House	2
Paradise	3
Sarovar Portico	6

0   200   metres

Hazratbal Mosque

Nishat Bagh

Houseboats

Nageen Lake

KHOJAYARBAL

Dal Lake

Hari Parbat Fort

Makhdoom Sahib

Floating Gardens

Char Chinar

OLD CITY

Jama Masjid

Nehru Park

Royal Springs Golf Course

Khanqah Mosque of Shah Hamdan

Rozabal Mosque

KHON KHAN

Nida Tours & Travels

Houseboats

Euphoria Travels
Green Kashmir Travels

KHAYAM CHOWK

Shankaracharya Reserved Forest

Dal Gate

Kashmir Valley Travels

DAL GATE

Shankaracharya Mandir

EATING
Ahdoo's	7
Delhi & Rasoi	3
Fat Panda	4
Gulshan Bookstore	1
Mughal Darbar	8
Nathu's Sweets	2
Shahi Darbar	5
Shamyana	6

ATM
J & K Bus Stand

Polo Ground

Private Bus Stand

MOULANA AZAD RD
RESIDENCY RD

Houseboat Owners Association

GUPKAR RD

Sonawar Bagh

Jhelum River

LAL CHOWK

Sri Pratap Singh Museum

LAL MANDI

SHOPPING
Gulshan Bookstore	1
Kashmiri Government Art Emporium	2
Pick N Choose	3

Gulmarg (52km)

Chesmashahi Bagh (1.2km)

Airport (9km)

Jammu (260km)

houseboats that cover its southern end, nearest the town centre, the lake is famous for its floating gardens, as well as a floating flower and vegetable market – well worth the 4am wake-up you'll need to see it at its best. The best way to tour the lake is on a *shikara*, a colourful flat-bottomed water taxi that is steered with a heart-shaped paddle (see page 515).

Nehru Park

A ₹50 shikara ride from the mainland • Swimming free, water skiing from ₹400 including lesson

Nehru Park is the lake's largest island, but still pretty tiny. Here you'll find pontoons for swimming, and even water skiing facilities, the latter available at rates that must be among the world's lowest. It's also home to the excellent Gulshan Books café (see page 516).

The Mughal gardens

Daily 6am–7pm • Each garden ₹24 • Auto-rickshaws will ask around ₹700 to visit all three, including waiting time

The perimeter of Dal Lake is punctuated by lavishly ornamental gardens, a legacy of the seventeenth-century Mughal period. Incredibly popular with locals and Indian tourists alike, who flock here to picnic and frolic in the fountain pools, these collections of terraced lawns and flowerbeds – containing an array of flowers and plants sufficient to delight any botanist – reach their zenith in **Nishat Bagh**, halfway along the eastern shore, and **Shalimar Bagh**, set a little way back from the northeastern corner. A short way back from the southeastern shore, **Cheshmashahi Bagh** is a smaller but equally delightful spot, which attracts people for the curative properties of its spring waters.

Shankaracharya Mandir

Accessed from Boulevard Rd • Daily 7.30am–5pm • Free • Auto-rickshaws will ask around ₹400, including waiting time

The city's main Hindu temple, **Shankaracharya Mandir** stands imperiously above Dal Lake, occupying the crest of the eponymous hill south of the Boulevard. The temple itself is nothing special architecturally speaking and security is predictably tight, but the views across the city and lakes to the mountains beyond are quite breathtaking. The walk up is a gentle thirty-minute stroll, although security guards sometimes demand that you take an auto-rickshaw.

Hazratbal mosque

Daily 9.30am–5.30pm • Free

On the northwestern shore of Dal Lake stands **Hazratbal mosque**, whose huge white marble dome towers above its spacious courtyard. It is considered Kashmir's holiest shrine, as its plain but vast interior houses a single hair of the prophet Mohammed, purportedly brought from Medina centuries ago. The scene of heavy fighting during the worst of the insurgency, it is now a tranquil spot that welcomes outsiders along with the constant stream of worshippers. The surrounding area is a lively mishmash of trinket and food stalls, making it a good place to snack on treats such as delicious Kashmiri halwa.

Nageen Lake

Tucked between the spit of land behind Hazratbal mosque and the Old City, **Nageen Lake** is much smaller than more famous Dal Lake. It does not have any particular sights but is more peaceful for that very reason, and quite a popular choice for anyone wanting a more serene houseboat experience (see page 513).

The Old City

The most atmospheric and fascinating part of Srinagar away from the lakes is undoubtedly the venerable and atmospheric **Old City**, crammed with wooden buildings displaying the typical Kashmiri architectural style of carved balustrades and ornate frames on windows and doors.

Jama Masjid

Srinagar's largest mosque, **Jama Masjid** stands in the heart of the Old City. Built of sturdy stone and brick with the distinctive pagoda-style wooden minarets unique to Kashmir, it was erected between 1398 and 1402 by Sikander But-Shikoh but has been destroyed by fire and rebuilt several times, most recently in 1961. Look out for the fascinating family tree of the Prophet Mohammed going all the way back to Adam and Eve, which hangs on the wall near the main niche.

Khanqah Mosque of Shah Hamdan

Sitting on the east bank of the River Jhelum, the **Khanqah Mosque of Shah Hamdan** was originally built in 1395 by Shah Sikandar, though the current structure dates from 1732. It is inaccessible to non-Muslims but still worth a visit for the intricate woodcarvings of its exterior. You can also get a glimpse of the equally beautiful interior from the door.

7

Rozabal

A couple of kilometres to the southeast of Jama Masjid, the small square mosque of **Rozabal**, with its simple octagonal dome, is purported to enshrine the tomb of Jesus by those who subscribe to the theory – the subject of Holger Kersten's *Jesus Lived In India* – that Christ actually lived to a ripe old age and died here in Kashmir. The mosque is kept locked but you may be able to peep inside through the gate. Note that this is one place where foreigners sometimes encounter hostility from locals, so it is best to move on if asked.

Makhdoom Sahib

Cable car daily 9am–5pm • ₹50 each way

One of Kashmir's most vibrant places of worship, with frequent live music, the Sufi shrine of **Makhdoom Sahib** is located on the northern edge of the Old City, halfway up towards Hari Parbat Fort on the hill of the same name. The inner shrine housing the tomb of the saint is open to men only. Good views across Nageen Lake and further afield can be enjoyed by all from the nearby steps, though it's now possible to save yourself a gentle walk by taking the cable car.

Hari Parbat Fort

Sat–Thu 10am–3pm • ₹100 (₹50) • Best to arrange a visit through the Tourist Reception Centre (see page 514); bring your passport, or a copy of the visa and picture pages

Atop the eponymous ridge that dominates the Old City, **Hari Parbat Fort** is officially called Durrani Fort, after the emperor who had the current structure built in 1808. It is also known locally as Akbar Fort, however, because the first battlements were constructed here under the reign of Akbar in the late sixteenth century. For many years the fort was completely off limits as a military zone, but it re-opened to the public in 2015, despite an ongoing army presence. Though there are plans for development, there's not much to see inside; the ramparts are the main surviving feature, and you may content yourself to admire them from afar.

Sri Pratap Singh Museum

Tues–Sun 10am–5pm • Free • ☎ 0194 231 2859

The outstanding **Sri Pratap Singh Museum** is in Lal Mandi, south across the Jhelum River from Lal Chowk. The former maharaja's palace (and an adjacent newer wing) house a huge collection that includes archeological findings such as terracotta tiles and Buddhist tablets, decorative arts from enamelware to papier-mâché, textiles, manuscripts and miniature paintings.

WALKING DAL LAKE

On a map, it looks like Dal Lake's perimeter should make ideal **walking** territory – sadly this is not really the case. For most of the stretch, there's a path of sorts running through the greenery separating lake and road, but you'd be forced into the road from time to time by stacked-up piles of weeds pulled from the lake. Far better is what, on maps, looks like a road running clean across the lake; in reality, the eastern segment of this is a dirt track traversed by only the most skilful motorbike drivers, and it's most commonly used as a fishing spot. Brave sorts can start their walk at the **Nishat Bagh** gardens (see page 512); you'll see the "road" branching off to the right after 500m. Padding along the dirt track, and occasionally the wall, you'll have wonderful views of the lake and the mountains. After a few kilometres, you'll see the first of several "floating" villages; accessible by boardwalk, they're usually home to between ten and fifty homes, though most have a mosque, and some have simple shops (and there are even a couple of tailors and salons). When you start to see the first semblances of urbanity, think about hailing an auto-rickshaw; the roads get busier and more confusing, and things get less fun.

Back in town, the **pedestrianized lane** north of Dal Gate also makes for a nice walk, though you'll be offered shikara rides and marijuana every minute or so. Walking the entirety of **Boulevard Rd** is pretty fun; to return to the city centre without meeting any pests whatsoever, return along **Old Gagribal Rd**, sketching a near-parallel to the south; this is, without doubt, the most charming non-lake part of the city, featuring old mansions to the east, then butchers, bakers and (probably) candlestick-makers in a lively area south of Dal Gate.

ARRIVAL AND DEPARTURE

SRINAGAR

By plane Srinagar's airport (📞0194 243 0334) lies 14km south of the city centre. Taxis into town cost ₹700–800; auto-rickshaws around half that.
Destinations Amritsar (1 daily; 1hr 10min); Delhi (1–3 hourly; 1hr 30min); Jammu (1–2 hourly; 40min); Leh (1–2 daily; 55min).

By bus Government buses pull in on Residency Rd, a few minutes' walk south of Dal Gate, while the private bus stand is around 1km further west.
Destinations Delhi (2 daily; 22–24hr); Jammu (10–12 daily; 11–12hr); Kargil (6–8 daily; 10–11hr); Leh (2–4

daily; 16hr, or with overnight stay in Kargil).
By jeep/minibus Jeeps, which also pull in on Residency Rd, run to Jammu (8–9hr; ₹800), Kargil (6–7hr; ₹1000) and Leh (14–15hr; ₹2300) and operate more flexible hours. Shared minibuses are the best way to travel within the Kashmir Valley.
By train Srinagar does have a railway station, but at the time of writing it was only for local services west to Baramulla, and south to Anantnag; by 2020 the stretch to Jammu should have been completed, enabling rail access from the rest of the country.

INFORMATION

Tourist office The surprisingly fancy – though slightly hard to find – Tourist Reception Centre (📞0194 250 2512, ⓦjktourism.org) is beside the government bus stand on Residency Rd, and claims to be open 24hr. Staff are usually helpful, and can assist with bus tickets.

Tours Green Kashmir Travels off Boulevard Rd (📞0194 210 1701, ⓦgreenkashmirtravels.com) can book tickets and arrange treks (see page 517) or give useful advice on them, as can Euphoria Travels on 3rd Cross Rd, just to the south (📞99068 47303, ⓦeuphoriatravels.com).

ACCOMMODATION

Although most foreign tourists stay on houseboats (see box opposite), but there are plenty of conventional hotels and lodges. During the domestic high season (April–June) prices below are likely to double.
Akbar North of Dal Gate (📞0194 250 0507, ⓦhotel akbar.com; map p.511. Quite a grand complex of white, colonial-style buildings set in pleasant, grassy grounds beside Dal Lake. The rooms are spacious and brightly decorated, with quality furniture. ₹4200
Chachoo Palace New Rd, Khon Khan, Dal Lake (📞99068 20423, ⓦhotelchachoopalace.com; map p.511. This quaint hotel – with a wooden balcony, lakeside lawn

and comfortable, attached rooms – has the charm of a houseboat with easier access and cheaper prices. The friendly proprietors can also provide food on request. ₹1000
JH Bazaz Backstreet behind Dal Gate no.2 (📞0194 247 3413, ⓦhotelinsrinagar.co; map p.511. Tucked in the lanes south of the lake, this welcoming and efficient hotel has rooms of different shapes and sizes, a modern annexe and grassy garden. ₹2150
★ **John Friends Guest House** North of Dal Gate (📞99064 75607; map p.511. A real budget winner, located in the lake-lanes north of Dal Gate. As well as a super-quiet atmosphere, it has pretty rooms (some with views) and friendly staff, and they

rent out boats to guests for peanuts. ₹600

Paradise Boulevard Rd, Dal Lake ☎0194 250 0663, ⓦhotelparadisesgr.in; map p.511. Several blocks of rather classy rooms that vary in size. Set just off the

lakefront, and cheaper than its mid-range competitors. Decent restaurant (₹250 extra per meal). ₹2000

★ **Sarovar Portico** Gupkar Rd, behind UN head office ☎0194 250 0314, ⓦsarovarhotels.com; map p.511.

SLEEPING ON A HOUSEBOAT

Few experiences are as romantic as lounging on an exquisitely carved **houseboat**, watching kingfishers diving for their dinner between the floating lilies, or gazing at the moon reflected in the lake's dark waters. These floating hotels of one to four rooms have existed for generations; many originated at the peak of the British Raj, when Victorian families would spend the entire hot season here. They originally chose to stay on boats to get around laws that forbade them from owning land.

CHOOSING A LOCATION

Srinagar has no fewer than 1200 houseboats lining the shores of the two main lakes, Dal and Nageen, and the banks of the Jhelum River – and that's just the official ones. Consequently, it can seem like a bewildering business to know where to start looking.

First, have a think about what you want from your houseboat experience, and where on the two lakes you would like to be based. The default option is staying at one of the many houseboats facing Boulevard Road at the southwestern corner of Dal Lake; the westernmost ones are accessible by footpath, which makes things easier, if a little less romantic, and the rest are a set ₹50 ride by *shikara* from the road. There's another glut of houseboats a little further north; again, some are accessible on foot, and many of these have the benefit of having the city out of eyeshot. Also quiet are the boats on Nageen Lake, which are usually accessible by footpath; there are also some houseboats floating on their lonesome at various points around Dal Lake, though their peace is often interrupted by the lake's perimeter road.

CHOOSING A HOUSEBOAT

Although it's now very easy to book a houseboat stay online, this comes with an element of risk – while the reviews on certain booking engines may be genuine and informative, the boat's purported position on the lake can be way, way off, with obvious implications when trying to actually find it. The best bet remains to hole up in a town hotel for the first night, then either walk or hire a **shikara** to embark on a scouting mission, armed with a few ideas from online research; this way you can compare the prices, amenities and location of a number of boats, though do note that you'll be pestered regularly on the way.

Another approach is to organize your stay through the **Houseboat Owners Association** (daily 8am–6pm; ☎0194 245 0326, ⓦhouseboatowners.org), whose office is opposite the Tourist Reception Centre on Residency Road. They can arrange rooms in different categories of boat from Deluxe Class (₹4000 for a double with full board, though often discounted to ₹2500) down to D Class (₹600 for the same). They do, however, often seem keen to push the boats of their buddies.

HOUSEBOAT TIPS

- The golden rule is to ignore the many **touts** in town who try to get you to commit yourself with all sorts of promises. Never pre-book in Delhi.
- Check with other travellers and on booking websites or forums to see which houseboats have been offering **positive experiences**.
- Always try to **view the houseboat** in person before agreeing to stay there, checking things like bedding, plumbing and security issues.
- Be sure to agree exactly what is included in the **price**, such as the number of meals, drinks or whether a daily *shikara* ride to the shore (if necessary) is part of the deal.
- Make it clear that you do not want to be pestered by **floating salesmen** and that there should be no deterioration in houseboat service if you do turn them away.
- Do not be pressured into accepting **other services** the owner might offer you, such as *shikara* rides round the lake or trekking trips.
- Do not leave **valuables** such as your passport or electronic devices unattended, or even with the houseboat owner for safekeeping.

An excellent choice if you're worried about visiting Srinagar – it's located right behind the UN compound, so security is high. Set across three blocks, the rooms are all plush affairs, while staff are very professional; breakfast-with-a-view is served on the top of the main block. BB ₹5500

EATING

The **local cuisine** of Kashmir is known as *wazwan* and is heavily meat-based, its signature dish being *rogan josh*, richly spiced mutton in a tomato sauce. Dishes often include **saffron**, as the costly spice is grown locally and therefore less expensive than elsewhere. Kashmiris are also famed for their green *kahwa* tea, drunk sweet and often spiced with cardamom or almond. **Alcohol** is still pretty hard to come by, though you may find it in a few flashy hotel bars, and even from some *shikara* salesmen.

RESTAURANTS

★**Ahdoo's** Residency Rd ☎0194 247 1984; map p.511. So smart that you'll forget you're in Srinagar, this first-floor dining room is by far the most appealing place to eat in town. Specializes in Kashmiri wazwan dishes (mostly ₹420), though they offer cheaper Indian mains, and there's a good bakery downstairs too. Daily 10am–10.30pm.

Delhi & Rasoi Boulevard Rd ☎94197 7814; map p.511. Simple pure-veg restaurant with courtyard or interior seating, where you can enjoy south Indian snacks like masala dosa and *uttapam* for around ₹100, or thalis for about double that. Daily 8am–11pm.

Fat Panda Off Boulevard Rd ☎97965 25252; map p.511. For something a little different, hit this pretty place, tucked into the same land as the Paradise. Indian and Thai dishes are woven into a mainly Chinese menu; try filling noodle or rice meals, such as the spicy pad Thai, from ₹230. Daily noon–10pm.

Mughal Darbar Residency Rd ☎0194 248 0007; map p.511. Popular, mildly pretty spot serving a range of tandoori, biryani and traditional *wazwan* dishes, and some fish too. Non-veg items cost ₹200–250. Daily 8am–10.30pm.

Shahi Darbar Khayam Chowk ☎94190 67777; map p.511. The best of a host of small local joints specializing in mutton and chicken kebabs and tikka dishes for ₹160–200. The upstairs room with a delightful carved ceiling is better than the cramped downstairs seating area. Daily 11am–10pm.

Shamyana Boulevard Rd ☎0194 250 1629; map p.511. The best of the Boulevard Rd restaurants, serving a mix of Indian and Kashmiri dishes (try the gushtaba, meatballs in soup, for ₹260), as well as Chinese and even a few Mexican choices (such as chicken enchiladas; ₹410). Local trout also pops up as a special from time to time. Daily 12.30pm–10.30pm.

CAFES AND SWEETSHOPS

★**Gulshan Bookstore** Nehru Park ☎94190 11110; map p.511. You'll have to take a ₹50 shikara ride to this island bookstore, which is more notably also a cafe, with very good coffee (cappuccino ₹100, teas available), and winning views over the lake. Daily 11am–7.30pm.

★**Nathu's Sweets** Boulevard Rd ☎05062 38104; map p.511. Prepare yourself – these are, without doubt, the prettiest Indian sweeties in the state, and you'll want to buy more than you can eat. You can eat them in the outside yard (a restaurant or sorts, but forget about that), or have them packed up into a cute little box; they'll cost ₹25–50 each. Daily 9.30am–9.30pm.

SHOPPING

Kashmir is synonymous with quality carpets, rugs and shawls of various materials, though knowing what is authentic can be a veritable minefield. There are salesmen everywhere, even touting their wares around the lake on *shikaras*. Beware of houseboat owners on commission bringing them to your vessel and be firm that you are not interested if you don't want to buy. Also note that there's a fun floating market on Dal Lake (see page 511).

Gulshan Bookstore Nehru Park ☎94190 11110; map p.511. Although more popular as a café (see page 516), this island bookstore also has plenty of literature pertaining to Kashmir. Daily 11am–7.30pm.

Kashmiri Government Art Emporium Boulevard Rd, Dal Lake ☎0194 250 1266; map p.511. Conveniently-located state-run shop offering a good range of rugs, fabrics, papier-mâché, walnut woodcarvings and bronze sculptures, all at fixed prices. Daily 9am–5pm.

Pick N Choose Residency Rd ☎0194 247 1802; map p.511. Western-style supermarket stocking a host of local goodies, from *kahwa* tea and *halwa* sweets to nuts, dried fruits and pure Kashmiri honey. Daily 8am–11pm.

Gulmarg

Some 56km west of Srinagar and at an elevation of around 2700m, **GULMARG**, whose name means "flower meadow", is a pleasant escape from the city, but can get very crowded with domestic tourists – especially in winter, when it becomes a ski resort

TREKKING IN KASHMIR

Despite being prime trekking territory, the security concerns of recent decades mean that relatively few foreigners take to the hills. The once booming industry is slowly picking up, however, and there have been no unpleasant incidents involving foreign tourists since 1995 (see page 480). Given the tricky terrain and the delicate political situation, however, it is not recommended to set off without at least a **local guide**. Trekking agencies in Srinagar (see page 510) and Aru (see page 520), and some hotels mentioned in the text, can provide fully organized treks with ponies, porters and all the requisite equipment.

Pahalgam and **Aru** are still the main bases for treks, which vary in length and level of difficulty from two-day round trips within the Lidder Valley to the week-long hike to Panikhar in Ladakh's Suru Valley (see page 506). You can also do some good walking from **Sonamarg**, the last main town in Kashmir before the Zoji La pass. Conditions for trekking are pretty hot and uncomfortable in high summer; the shoulder seasons of late spring and early autumn are the optimum time. The best **map** is Sheet 1 in Leomann's *India Himalaya* series. For more general advice about trekking, see Basics (see page 59).

AMARNATH TREK

Kashmir's most trodden route becomes crowded during the July/August full moon with thousands of pilgrims, who flock to see the natural ice lingam in the **Amarnath cave**, at an altitude of 3962m. The trek from Pahalgam usually takes four days and includes overnight stays at Chandanwari (2900m), Sheshnag (3720m) and Panchtarni (3933m). The final stage involves crossing the Mahagunas Pass. After visiting the cave, you can either return the same way or make the more direct descent to Baltal, 8km east of Sonamarg on the Srinagar–Leh road. Naturally, the ascent can also be made from Sonamarg via Baltal.

TULIAN LAKE TREK

For those with limited time, the overnight two-day trek to peaceful **Tulian Lake** (4000m) from Pahalgam is a good way to get a taste of the Kashmiri Mountains. The route winds up through meadows, pine forests and past welcoming gypsy tents, where you may well be offered refreshments. The best place to spend the night is at the Kanimarg base camp.

KOLAHOI GLACIER TREK

The five-day trek from Pahalgam to the impressive but receding **Kolahoi glacier** (3400m) can be shortened by a day if you start in picturesque Aru (2414m; see page 520). The next day's ascent is via alpine meadows and streams to Lidderwat (3049m), before a gentler stage to Satlanjan (3150m), which allows you to conserve energy for the steep climb to the glacier and back to Lidderwat on the following day. You can then walk back down to Aru or Pahalgam itself on the fifth day.

SONAMARG TO WANGAT TREK

This popular route takes you through a beautiful stretch of the mountains via a number of delightful **high altitude lakes**, where fishing is permitted with a permit (available through agents in Srinagar). The first staging post at Nichnai (3620m) affords views of the Thajiwas Glacier (see page 521) before the second day's walking undulates to Kishanar (3819m). On the third day you cross over the 4191m Bazkal Gali pass and descend past Gadsar Lake to overnight at Dubta Pani (3280m). Next day's walking takes in the seven tiered lakes of Satsar en route to the region's largest body of water, Gangabal Lake (3507m), for a final night's camping before the descent to Wangat, where there are buses and jeeps to Srinagar.

of-sorts. The season usually runs from mid-December to mid-March, but in recent years, possibly due to climate change, this has contracted to just over a month, starting in January. Gulmarg is rather spread out, with the taxi rank at the junction its only discernible centre; the meadow itself is 1km wide and more than 3km long, allowing ample room for picnics, pony rides and even one of the world's highest golf courses. The surrounding pine slopes can be ascended for a distant view of **Nanga Parbat** (8126m) to the north, in Pakistan-controlled Baltistan.

Gulmarg Gondola

First phase Daily 9am–5pm in summer, 10am–4pm winter · ₹740 return · Second phase Daily 10am–4pm in summer, 10.30am–3.30pm winter · An extra ₹950 return · ⓦ gulmarggondola.com

Visitors can ascend the slopes on the **Gulmarg Gondola**, the world's second highest cable car at the time of writing. During ski season, the gondola is used to get to the top of Gulmarg's **ski** slopes, which are underused but highly recommended for the quality of powdery snow.

ARRIVAL AND DEPARTURE
GULMARG

By bus Gulmarg is accessible by bus, though you'll have to change in Tangmarg; it'll cost ₹110 in total for the two legs.
By taxi The best way to get to Gulmarg from Srinagar is by shared taxi (₹150), or you can hire a whole vehicle for ₹1850, or more like ₹3000 for a day-trip.

ACTIVITIES

Skiing and trekking Government rates for skiing are displayed on boards around the resort; equipment rental costs ₹1000/day. One private operation that can arrange packages and lessons is Kashmir Alpine (ⓣ 94195 25606, ⓦ kashmiralpine.com), which purports to be the world's smallest ski shop and also runs trekking expeditions during the warmer months.
Other activities Pony riding costs ₹350/hr, and ATVs ₹300 for 15min. In winter, try snow mobiles (₹500 for 15min), or rent ski equipment (₹1000).

ACCOMMODATION

Accommodation is plentiful, but uniformly overpriced; Gulmarg has two high seasons, one between April and June, and another from mid-December to the end of February, and prices outside these times dip accordingly.
Heevan Retreat West of the village ⓣ 01954 254455, ⓦ ahadhotelsandresorts.com. There's a palpable alpine feel at this higher-end option, set back in the woods; there are walnut furnishings and hand-woven curtains in many of its 31 rooms, central heating throughout, and a good restaurant. Due to be rebranded as the Apple Tree by 2020. ₹7,000

★ **The Khyber** South of the gondola ⓣ 01954 254666, ⓦ khyberhotels.com. By far the best hotel this side of Delhi, a large and immaculately designed affair with courteous staff and truly splendid rooms; you should ask for one facing the mountains, which is the same direction that the fitness centre and stunner of a swimming pool are oriented. ₹20,000
New Mount View By the bazaar ⓣ 01954 254622, ⓦ gravityassault.com. Backpacker inn that's just about the cheapest place to stay hereabouts. Rooms are all heated, with attached bathrooms, and rates drop to ₹800 out of season. ₹2200

EATING

Bakshi In the middle of the bazaar ⓣ 01954 254566. Simple and popular canteen-style restaurant specializing in Jain pure-veg dishes, including filling mains for around ₹150; alternatively, try their excellent homemade *kehwa* for ₹50. Daily 8am–9pm.
The Khyber South of the gondola ⓣ 01954 254666, ⓦ khyberhotels.com. Even if you can't afford to stay here, dinner is very affordable, with many of the curries and continental mains going for just ₹750. It's around the same for a hookah in the lounge opposite the restaurant – less than you'll pay at most "standard" places, let alone a five-star hotel. Daily 12.30–3.30pm & 7–11pm.

Pahalgam

Kashmir's number-one trekking base (see page 517), **PAHALGAM** enjoys a stunning location around 100km east of Srinagar, 2139m above sea level in the deep-cut Lidder Valley, whose pine-crested ridges ascend sharply from both banks of the chilly, fast-flowing river. The town mostly occupies the slightly flatter east bank and the lower surrounding slopes. **Main Market**, the central thoroughfare of the modern town, runs parallel to the river and contains most of the facilities, while the **old village** – more pleasant, though with little to do – lies 1.5km north, beyond Pushwan Park with its fancy flowerbeds and topiary. Eager pony-men tout rides at fixed government rates (₹300–350/hr) to various local beauty spots.

Note that Pahalgam becomes extremely busy and security is tightened during the Amarnath pilgrimage (see page 517) in July and August. During that time especially, nearby **Aru** makes a quieter and more relaxing base.

ARRIVAL AND ACTIVITIES
PAHALGAM

By bus/jeep The bus service from Srinagar to Pahalgam is rather unreliable but it is easy to get a bus or shared jeep (2hr; ₹100) to Anantnag (known locally as Islamabad) and another from there to Pahalgam (1hr 30min; ₹80).

Trekking Staff at the *Beach Resort* (see below) can arrange very reliable treks of various lengths.
Pony rides Eager pony-men tout rides at fixed government rates (₹300–350/hr) to various local beauty spots.

ACCOMMODATION

Beach Resort Old village ☎94693 92930. Small guesthouse with newly renovated rooms of varying sizes, the best of which overlook the lush lawn and river. Excellent food is available on request and the welcoming owners also run treks. ₹700
Grand Abdullah Main market ☎97971 26788. A solid mid-range choice, which certainly looks old and alpine from the outside, but has modern rooms with large windows. The owner is a friendly sort who'll be on hand to solve any issues

that you may have regarding treks, pony rides or onward transport. ₹3500
★**Heevan** West of the village ☎0194 250 1323, ⍟ahadhotelsandresorts.com. Located all on its lonesome across the river, this is the most charming place to stay hereabouts, with gorgeous rooms (try to nab one with a river view), filling buffet breakfasts, and staff determined to make their guests' stay enjoyable. ₹9500

EATING

Dana Pani Main Market ☎01936 243234. Clean, modern place, great for filling Punjabi veg meals (₹150–200). Also offers good South Indian cuisine such as dosas. Daily 7.30am–10.30pm.
Paradise Main Market ☎01936 243368, ⍟hotel paradiseandrestaurant.com. Standard but reliable hotel restaurant that does a brisk trade in tasty veg and non-veg Kashmiri staples, such as the signature *rogan josh* (₹360). Daily 7.30am–10pm.

★**The Trout Beat** Pahalgam Hotel, Main Market ☎01936 243252. Trout and chips, masala trout, trout *a l'orange*, tandoori trout – this may sound a bit like Bubba Gump's shrimp, but they're all excellent. The fish are sourced locally, and all dishes cost around ₹650. There's also a good coffee-and-cake wing down the road, but they're often combined into the same space. Daily 8am–10pm.

Aru

Twelve km northwest of Pahalgam, the peaceful village of **ARU** is located in an eponymous valley amid splendidly verdant mountain terrain; hemmed in on all sides by lushly carpeted ridges, it boasts several burbling streams that traverse the grassy meadows.

Aru makes a good base for **local hikes** and longer treks, such as the three-day treks to the Thajiwas Glacier (see page 521) or Amarnath cave (see page 517). The T-shaped village contains half a dozen places to stay, and a few *dhabas* to supplement the guesthouse restaurants. It has a growing reputation as a **relaxed hangout** and is particularly popular with chillum-toting Israelis.

ARRIVAL AND INFORMATION
ARU

By jeep or taxi A seat in a shared jeep should cost around ₹30 from Pahalgam; a whole taxi will cost ₹600 one way.
On foot Traffic from Pahalgam is light, so it's actually quite

easy to walk – it'll take over two hours each way, though.
Trekking The Milky Way guys (see below) are by far your best contact for local trekking.

ACCOMMODATION AND EATING

★**Milky Way** Just off the main bazaar ☎01936 210899, ⍟milkywaykashmir.com. By far the most comfortable place here, with beautifully furnished rooms spread over two buildings beside a lovely lawn. The brothers

who own it serve good food on request, and run reliable treks. ₹2500
Rohella On the road into the village ☎01936 211339, ✉quyoomrohella@gmail.com. Friendly, basic guesthouse

with basic but clean rooms, very popular with Israelis. The pick of the cheapies, it also does decent food. ₹500

Sagar Main bazaar ☎94699 69844. The best of the village *dhabas*, serving up a range of Kashmiri, Indian and Chinese dishes for ₹100–300, as well as simple snacks like pakora. Daily 9am–9pm.

Sonamarg

Located on the Ladakh road, 84km northeast of Srinagar, **SONAMARG** has started to see a return of foreign travellers in recent years. Perched beside the River Sindh and surrounded by forests of pine, fir, beech and sycamore, with towering peaks all around, it is a scenic spot to break the journey to Kargil or Leh (see page 482 for details of the route through Western Ladakh). This is also the place with the best display of spring and early summer flowers. The **Thajiwas Glacier** is just a 4km hike away, and the town is also a good base for the famous Amarnath trek (see page 517).

Sonamarg itself is not particularly attractive, with its main bazaar strung along the vital Srinagar–Leh road, which means there is a constant flow of traffic and a noticeable **military presence**. Most of the more established hotels, restaurants and shops line the north side of the bazaar, with the opposite side given over to government complexes, the bus and taxi stands, plus a couple of the larger new hotels.

7

Thajiwas Glacier

To reach the **Thajiwas Glacier**, take any of the paths on the hillside that run below the treeline from behind the *Glacier Heights* hotel (see below). These unite into a single path as you go on, which skirts the ridge through the woods and emerges after about half an hour above the main car park for vehicles visiting the glacier. It is best to carry on for a while longer before descending to the meadows, which are populated by grazing sheep and picnicking Indian tourists. There is usually a steady stream of people heading along the path into the valley that holds the glacier itself, although climate change means that the ice has rapidly receded in recent years.

ARRIVAL AND INFORMATION — SONAMARG

By bus Frequent buses ply the main route between Srinagar and Ladakh, although those heading east are more liable to be full. Buses take around 3hr to Srinagar, around 5hr to Kargil.

By jeep A seat in a shared jeep to Srinagar should cost around ₹170, while a whole vehicle will cost ₹2400 one way.

ACCOMMODATION AND EATING

Glacier Heights Just above west end of main bazaar ☎0194 241 7215, ⓦhotelglacierheights.in. Attractively designed alpine-style hotel consisting of two blocks. The wood-panelled rooms are large and comfortable, while the bathrooms have unusually powerful showers. ₹3000

Green Town Middle of main bazaar ☎97970 30206. Just about the cheapest place in town, with small but adequate rooms above commercial premises. Rather prone to street noise. ₹500

JKTDC West end of main bazaar ☎98691 37017. Just like its government-run counterpart in Jammu, this is a steady choice for Kashmiri food; a *rogan josh* or kebab will set you back ₹200 or so. Daily noon–3.30pm & 7.30–10.30pm.

Jammu

Despite its location on the easier of the two main overland routes to Kashmir, **Jammu Division** remains somewhat off the tourist radar, and is without doubt the runt of the J&K litter, well behind Ladakh and Kashmir in terms of scenic beauty and cultural interest. Those who pass through are mainly determined overlanders heading to or from Kashmir; **Jammu City** is certainly not without interest, while an hour's ride to its north is the revered shrine of **Vaishno Devi**.

Brief history

Archeological evidence suggests that the area around Jammu, whose name appears in the Mahabharata, was part of the **Harappan** civilization, based in the Indus Valley, one of the oldest in the world. Remains of other powerful kingdoms, such as the **Mauryas** and **Guptas**, have also been found near the city, although the foundation of Jammu itself is credited to the **Raja Jambu Lochan** in the late fourteenth century. It later fell under the control of the **Sikhs** but after their defeat by the British in 1846 became part of the Hindu **Dogra dynasty**. The majority of its people still identify themselves as Dogras, and speak the Dogri dialect.

Jammu City

Known as "the city of temples" because of the many shrines that dot the town, **JAMMU** is an increasingly attractive place, and worthy of at least a full day en route to or from Srinagar. The most revered place of worship in Jammu itself is **Ragunath Temple**, a

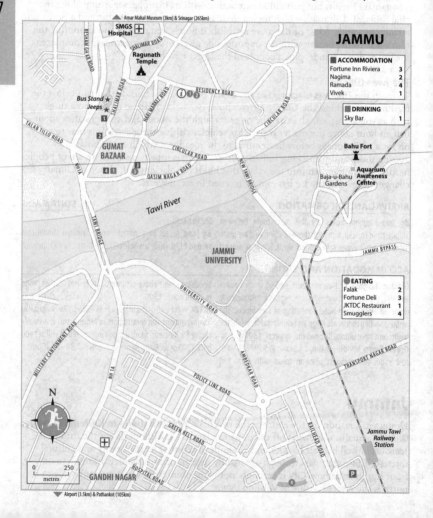

pretty place just north of the Tawi River, which bisects the town. The mildly absorbing
Amar Mahal museum is a little north again, while overlooking the river to its south is
the impressive **Bahu Fort**, from which topple the splendid **Bagh-e-Bahu** gardens.

Ragunath Temple

Daily 6am–10pm • Free • Entrances on south and east sides of complex

If you only have time to visit one of Jammu's many temples, it should be the buzzing
Ragunath, about 10min walk uphill through the commercial lanes east of the
bus stand. Once you've got through the tight security, you enter a large courtyard
surrounded by multiple *shikharas* and two gardens. Within, the inner courtyard houses
the main shrine of Lord Ragunath, an incarnation of Vishnu, and his two consorts,
watched over by an orange-robed statue of Hanuman nearby.

Bahu Fort and around

Fort: daily 9am–1pm & 2–9pm • Free • A ₹150 tuk-tuk ride or half-hour uphill walk from town, and also the terminus of several town bus routes

The town's most imposing attraction is **Bahu Fort**, which stands proudly on a high bluff
above the south bank of the Tawi River. The solid, squat battlements of the fort enclose
some beautifully manicured lawns, although the principal draw for Hindus is the
small **Mata Kali temple** within the complex. Beneath the fort are an **aquarium** and the
lovely **Bagh-e-Bahu Gardens**; on a hot day it makes sense to visit the fort first, then the
aquarium just underneath, then enter the gardens via an adjacent entrance, descending
to the lower exit, and returning to town from there.

Aquarium Awareness Centre

Daily 9am–9pm • ₹30, mobile phone photo permit ₹25

Plonked between the fort and the gardens, the **Aquarium Awareness Centre** contains
a mildly diverting assortment of more than four hundred varieties of fish and other
marine creatures. Hilariously designed with a metallic casing in the shape of a fish, the
museum is entered through its mouth and exited via the tail.

Bagh-e-Bahu Gardens

Daily 9am–9pm • ₹24 • Entrances at top and bottom of gardens

Descending in attractive tiers below the fort, the impressive **Bagh-e-Bahu Gardens**
contain a series of well-tended flowerbeds and decorative pools, which act as swimming
baths for the local monkeys. It's a favourite picnic spot for Indian tourists, as the upper
reaches afford splendid views across the city and river; for refreshments, there's a small
café near the lower entrance.

Amar Mahal Museum

Srinagar Rd, 2km northeast of the bus stand • Tues–Sun 10am–12pm & 3–7pm • ₹50 (₹10)

Housed in a converted palace hanging over the river, and modelled along the lines of
a grand chateau, the **Amar Mahal Museum** is basically an art gallery with some regal
memorabilia. Its most impressive architectural feature is the grandiose Durbar Hall.
Pride of place among the regal artefacts is Maharaja Hari Singh's solid gold throne. The
portraits and miniatures in the gallery date mostly from the early twentieth century
and there is an interesting collection of Nepali *objets d'art* in the Nepal Room.

ARRIVAL AND DEPARTURE   JAMMU CITY

Most travellers use Jammu as a stepping-stone to or from
Srinagar; rides in a jeep (₹800 for a seat, ₹6,000 for the
whole vehicle) usually take an hour or two less than the
buses (from ₹500). Alternatively, you can save most of a day
by flying; ticket prices often dip under ₹2,000.
By plane Jammu's surprisingly busy airport (☏ 0191 243

7843) is 7km southwest of the city; a taxi to the centre or
railway station costs around ₹300. Security is tight, so arrive
with plenty of time in hand.
Destinations Amritsar (1 daily; 1hr); Delhi (1–3 hourly;
1hr 30min); Leh (3 weekly; 55min); Srinagar (1–2 hourly;
40min).

By train Trains from all over India pull into Jammu Tawi station, which sits south of the river. The best night service to Delhi is the *Uttar S Kranti* #12446 (departs 8.43pm; arrives New Delhi 6.45am), while the most convenient daytime service is the *Malwa Express* #12920 (9am; arrives Delhi 6.55pm). Construction of the much-delayed line to Srinagar is set to be completed in 2020.

Destinations Delhi (9–13 daily; 9–14hr); Katra (5–8 daily; 2hr); Pathankot (11–15 daily; 1hr 40min–2hr 35min).

By bus The main bus stand is located north of the river, in the old centre of town. Most buses to Srinagar depart between 5am and 8am, though there are overnight sleeper services too (₹700); state buses often depart from the railway station. City minibuses connect the railway station to the centre of town, via the main bus stand, every few minutes.

Destinations Amritsar (4–5hr); Delhi (9–14hr); Pathankot (2–3hr); Katra (1hr); Srinagar (10–12hr).

By jeep Shared jeep rides to Srinagar (9–10hr) or Katra (1hr) can be organized at one of the numerous travel agencies located where the jeeps gather, just south of the bus stand.

ACCOMMODATION

★ **Fortune Inn Riviera** Gulab Singh Marg ☎ 0191 256 1415, ⌨ fortunehotels.in; map p.522. Excellent mid-range choice with attentive staff, plush rooms, and a decent choice of restaurants and bars. There's a fitness centre on site, and breakfast is included in the rates. ₹5000

Nagima Gumat Bazaar ☎ 0191 256 6008; map p.522. Budget travellers should hunt down this clean and welcoming Sikh-run establishment, containing just ten rooms; the a/c ones cost ₹1000 in theory, but often ₹800 in practice. ₹600

Ramada Gulab Singh Marg ☎ 0191 274 0070, ⌨ ramadajammu.in; map p.522. This is the largest and most luxurious accommodation option in Jammu, with a prime location overlooking the river to the south; it's just about visible from the stylish rooms, most of which face east or west. Breakfast included, and guests usually have other meals (and drinks) within the complex; options include the Sky Bar (see below), sat on the rooftop by the river-facing infinity pool. ₹8450

Vivek Just south of bus stand ☎ 0191 254 7545; map p.522. Simple hotel in a convenient location, with comfortable a/c rooms and a snazzy lobby; the restaurant isn't great, so dine elsewhere, and wi-fi can be scratchy. ₹1800

EATING

Jammu has plenty of cheap snack joints and vegetarian *vaishno dhabas*, especially east of Ragunath Temple. Hotel restaurants remain the best choice if you want meat and more comfortable surroundings; recent years have also witnessed the introduction of Western fast-food outlets, as well as a few independent modern venues catering to local youth.

Falak 7F KC Residency, Residency Rd ☎ 0191 252 0770; map p.522. Set atop a business hotel, this revolving restaurant serves good Indian and international cuisine. Most local mains cost ₹500 for veg and ₹600 for meat; try the *gosht shahi korma*, in a creamy cashew sauce. They also have a decent list of alcoholic drinks. Daily 11.30am–11.30pm.

Fortune Deli Gulab Singh Marg ☎ 0191 256 1415, ⌨ fortunehotels.in; map p.522. The ground-floor café of this hotel (see above) is a good spot for coffee and breakfast; sets cost from ₹220, or try their tasty toasted "eggwiches" (₹150). Daily 7am–11pm.

JKTDC Restaurant Off Residency Rd ☎ 0191 257 9554; map p.522. Tucked into a state hotel, and a little hard to find, this is the best place in town for mutton-centric Kashmiri cuisine; portions of rogan josh or dhaniwal korma go for ₹220, and are best washed down with a cup of kehwa, a yummy tea made with saffron, cardamom and almond. Daily noon–4pm & 7.30–10.30pm.

Smugglers Bahu Plaza Park ☎ 87130 20784; map p.522. One of several modern choices in the double-winged Bahu Plaza complex, this two-level spot claims to serve "illegally healthy" food – an odd way to describe peanut butter pancakes (₹99) or choco-banana smoothies (₹139), although they do have a range of salads too (₹149–319), as well as decent coffee. Daily 10.30am–10.30pm.

DRINKING

Many of Jammu's hotels have bars, and there are some earthier ones south of the bus stand, as well as a fair few liquor stores dotted around town – more in the area east of Ragunath Temple than the relatively Muslim area around the bus stand. The importance of all this may be clear if you've just arrived from alcohol-lite Kashmir; if you're heading that way, you may wish to take the opportunity to cut loose here in Jammu.

Sky Bar 5F Ramada Hotel, Gulab Singh Marg ☎ 0191 274 0070, ⌨ ramadajammu.in; map p.522. Catch the sunset from this lofty bar, sat atop the Ramada (see above). Cocktails go from ₹300, and beers from around half that, or you could indulge in a hookah session (₹800). Daily 7–11pm.

Katra

Around 40km north of Jammu on the way to Srinagar – a route predictably punctuated by army signs spouting militaristic slogans such as "the power behind the punch" – a road branches off to the small, unassuming town of **KATRA**, famed for nearby **Vaishno Devi** temple, the second most visited shrine in India after Tirumala in Andhra Pradesh.

Vaishno Devi temple

13.5km from Katra, a 2hr 30min–3hr 30min walk, ₹700 each way on a pony, or ₹4000 return by palanquin • Free, though donations expected

Lying at a comfortable altitude of 1615m, the revered **Vaishno Devi** temple draws around eight million pilgrims a year. It's a fair hike from Katra, though on a relatively easy and well-trodden path; the cave shrine itself is entered via an ankle-deep stream, whose chilly waters you must brave in order to get *darshan* of the image of the goddess, a triple incarnation of the female Shakti.

ARRIVAL AND DEPARTURE

KATRA

By bus or jeep There are regular buses and jeeps to Katra from Jammu (1hr 20min).

By taxi A taxi from Jammu (1hr) will set you back ₹1450 one way, or ₹2290 return including waiting time.

By train Trains from Jammu take far longer than any other form of transport (5–8 daily; 2hr), but can be of use if you want to get straight here from Delhi (4–7 daily; 12–16hr) or destinations south without stopping in Jammu City itself.

ACCOMMODATION

Saraswati Near Shalimar Park, Katra ☏0191 254 9065, ⓦjktdc.co.in. Nestled below the verdant mountains near the start of the temple hike, this three-storey concrete government block contains a variety of rooms, some of them deluxe with a/c. Standard government restaurant. ₹1000

Patnitop

Regular buses and jeeps from Jammu (2hr 30min) or Srinagar (around 7hr)

Around 110km north of Jammu on the way to Srinagar, just as the pines start to take over from the deciduous forest, the main road passes by **PATNITOP**. This alpine-style resort is popular with lowland Indians for its views and fresh air, as well as its relative accessibility – it's still deemed "safe", even when curfews and rock-hurling see domestic tourism come to a relative standstill in the Srinagar area.

ACCOMMODATION

PATNITOP

Forest View On a hill above the centre of Patnitop ☏94191 60615, ⓦforestviewinn.com. Set amid tall pines around 2km from the highway, this is the nicest place in the area, with 43 rooms across its three floors; all have heating and mod-cons, and many have prime views. Forget the rack rates – you'll probably end up paying half of these. ₹3300

7

Punjab and Haryana

LE CORBUSIER'S BRUTALIST CAPITAL COMPLEX

Punjab and Haryana

Crossed by the five major tributaries of the Indus River, the region of Punjab ("Five Rivers") was split down the middle at Independence, with Indian Muslims fleeing west into Pakistan, and Sikhs and Hindus doing likewise to the east. In 1966, the plains on the Indian side of the border were further divided into the predominantly Sikh Punjab and the 96-percent Hindu Haryana, and both remain governed from the purpose-built capital of Chandigarh. The states of Punjab and Haryana have both prospered on account of their position in the fertile river plain northwest of Delhi, and are often referred to as India's breadbasket. They're somewhat less important to international visitors, though Amritsar's astonishingly beautiful Golden Temple is deservedly one of the country's major draws, and Chandigarh a must-visit for fans – and such people do exist – of brutalist architecture.

The region as a whole is very important to the nation's **economy** – its farmers produce nearly a quarter of India's wheat and one third of its milk and dairy foods, while Ludhiana churns out ninety percent of the country's woollen goods. Helped by remittance cheques from millions of expatriates in the UK, US and Canada, the states' per capita income is almost double the national average.

Punjab contains the vast majority of tourist interest in the two states. Pride of place, of course, goes to the stunning **Golden Temple** in **Amritsar**, a hugely holy city which deserves at least a couple of days of your time – this will also enable a visit to the bizarre border ceremony, which takes place each evening just to the west in **Wagha**. Southeast across the plains, **Patiala** is a far more low-key city, and one which is not yet making the most of its array of sights – unlike Amritsar, you'll see very few tourists knocking about here. There are a few more in nearby **Chandigarh**, the purpose-built state capital; concrete testament to a Corbusier vision, it's also home to the wacky **Rock Garden**.

Chandigarh is also the capital of Haryana state, which has very little to detain the visitor bar the bars and modern high-rise of **Gurgaon**, a city which most, in any case, refer to as part of greater Delhi.

Brief history

Punjab's first urban settlement was the **Harappan** civilization of around 3000 BC, while later on the epic battles in the **Mahabharata** drew on real-life encounters between ancient Punjabi kings at Karnal. Conquered by the Mauryans in the third century BC, the Punjab saw further action as various invaders passed through on their way from the Khyber Pass to Delhi – including the Mughal emperor Babur, who routed Ibrahim Lodi at **Panipat** in 1526.

Sikhism began in the region under the tutelage of Guru Nanak (1469–1539). Based on the notion of a single formless God, the guru's vision of a casteless egalitarian society found favour with both Hindus and Muslims, in spite of Mughal emperor

8

BEST TIME TO VISIT

As ever in northern India, spring (March–April) and autumn (Oct & Nov) are the best times to visit. Winter (Dec & Jan) can be rather nippy, and summer (June–Aug) very hot, although nothing like the south, of course. Summer is also the wettest season, with rainfall peaking in August, but the monsoon is largely spent by the time it gets this far, so it isn't anything like as full-on as it is further south and east.

AMRITSAR'S GOLDEN TEMPLE

Highlights

❶ The Golden Temple, Amritsar One of the great sights, and sounds, of India – *kirtan* (devotional songs) are performed throughout the day and into the night from the breathtaking golden Harmandir. See page 533

❷ Border ceremony, Wagha Shorter and more colourful than a cricket match, the border ceremony is a highly charged event, where thousands of people chant and cheer from the Indian and Pakistani sides. See box, page 539

❸ Brutalist architecture, Chandigarh A whole city designed from blueprints created by Le Corbusier, with the brutalism particularly, well, brutal in the Capital Complex. See page 539

❹ Rock Garden, Chandigarh This bizarre and seemingly haphazard sculpture garden, assembled from rubbish by a local eccentric, offers a curious contrast to the ordered city that surrounds it. See page 541

❺ Patiala A friendly and atmospheric eighteenth-century city, formerly the capital of a princely state, where you can do a heritage tour of the old town and check out one of India's great palatial fortresses. See page 545

❻ Gurgaon Inside Haryana state but essentially a suburb of Delhi, this relatively modern city is where many young folk from the capital come to let their hair down. See page 547

HIGHLIGHTS ARE MARKED ON THE MAP ON PAGE 530

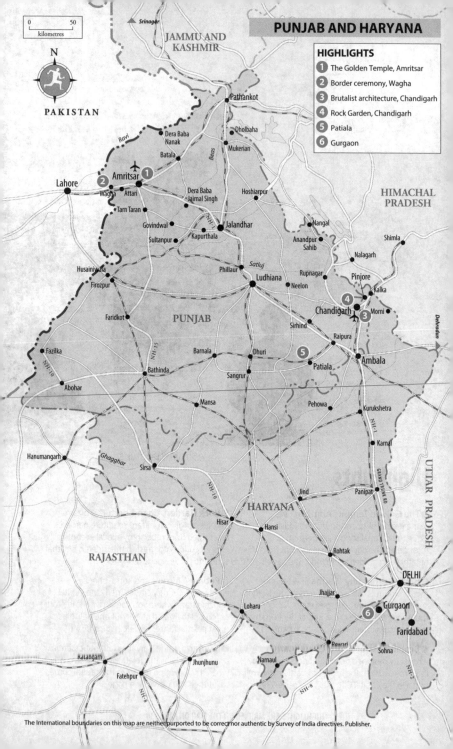

FESTIVALS IN PUNJAB AND HARYANA

Baba Bakala (March). Sikh pilgrimage to Bakala to commemorate the induction of the tenth Sikh guru, Gobind Singh.

Baisakhi (April or early May). Anniversary of the establishment of the Sikh Khalsa by the tenth Sikh guru, Gobind Singh, in 1699, celebrated with a morning of bathing and praying, followed by parades and distribution of sweet *prasad* in the afternoon.

Pinjore Mango Mela (early July). Gorge on mangoes at this annual two-day mango fest held in the Yadavindra Gardens in Pinjore.

Guru Nanak Jayanti (late Oct/early Nov). The birthday of the first Sikh guru is celebrated with a three-day reading of the Granth Sahib (Sikh holy scriptures) and processions in most Punjabi cities.

Harballabh Sangeet Sammelan (last weekend in Dec; ⊕harballabh.org). Held in Jalandhar since 1875, this is the world's oldest festival of Indian classical music, lasting three days, with no admission or accommodation fees.

Aurangzeb's attempts to stamp it out. Indeed, one result of his intolerance was that the Sikhs – eager to avoid a Mughal resurrection – willingly helped the British to quash the great uprising in 1857, though their relationship with the British soured after the **Jallianwalla Bagh massacre** of 1919 (see page 536).

Partition in 1947 brought sectarian hatred to the surface, with an exodus of Muslims from the Indian half of the Punjab, and of Hindus and Sikhs from the Pakistani half, amid great slaughter. After Independence, the Indian part grew wealthy on its agricultural output; militant Sikhs began to press for the creation of an independent state called Khalistan. In 1966, the mainly Hindu area of Haryana was hived off, but that failed to silence the separatists, whose party, the **Akali Dal**, trounced Congress in state elections.

With covert support from the national government (who saw the group as a way to defeat the Akali Dal), a more radical separatist movement led by **Sant Jarnail Singh Bhindranwale** began a campaign of sectarian terror, coming to a head in 1984 with the occupation of Amritsar's Golden Temple. Indira Gandhi's brutal response, **Operation Blue Star** (see page 532), plunged the Punjab into yet another ugly bout of communal violence; four years later, a less threatening occupation of the temple was crushed by **Operation Black Thunder**. Most Akali Dal factions boycotted the 1992 elections, which saw Congress returned on a 22 percent turnout. Chief minister **Beant Singh** was killed by a car bomb in 1995, but that was the militants' last gasp, and subsequent state elections have seen a **return to normality**.

Pathankot

The dusty town of **PATHANKOT**, 270km northwest of Chandigarh and 101km to the northeast of Amritsar, is an important cantonment and railway junction, close to the frontier with Pakistan and near the borders with Himachal Pradesh and Jammu. Pathankot itself is a friendly enough place, but there's nothing special to see here, and most travellers just pass through to pick up bus connections to Dharamsala, Dalhousie, Chamba and Kashmir, or to take the slow train east through the picturesque Kangra Valley.

ARRIVAL AND DEPARTURE   PATHANKOT

By train The slow, narrow-gauge passenger trains to Jogindernagar (daily 2.15am & 10am) wind through the scenic Kangra Valley, and make a pleasant alternative to the busy road to both Dharamsala (change at Kangra) and the Kullu Valley (bus from Joginder Nagar or Baijnath). Destinations Amritsar (11 daily; 2–3hr); Baijnath (2 daily; 8hr); Jogindernagar (2 daily; 9–10hr); Kangra (6 daily; 4–5hr).

By bus Pathankot's bus station is on Railway Rd, 300m west of the railway station.
Destinations Amritsar (every 10min; 3hr); Chandigarh (1–2 hourly; 6hr); Dharamsala (1–2 hourly; 4hr); Jammu (every 10–15min; 3hr); Manali (9 daily; 12hr); Shimla (7 daily; 12 hr).

MICROBREWERIES

If you like a good beer and have had enough of the usual industrial Indian brands, you'll be glad to know that many cities in Punjab and Haryana – including all large cities listed in this chapter – have **microbrewery bars** serving their own beers. Though still generally in the "experimental" phase of ale development, expect quality to increase as time goes by; also note that, like Delhi, the legal drinking age is a ridiculous 25.

ACCOMMODATION

Darshan Guest House Railway Rd (200m east of the railway station) ☎ 94173 17066. The best (and pinkest) of the cheapies along this stretch of Railway Road – like all of them it's rather grimy, but friendly enough, and the rooms are attached, with hot water, although wi-fi reaches up only as far as the first floor. ₹600

Venice 300m east of station, then 400m south of Railway Rd on Dhangu Rd ☎ 0186 222 5061, ⓦ venicehotelindia. com. This is Pathankot's top business hotel, and its most comfortable address, with good rooms ranging from semi-deluxe to super-deluxe (the only real difference being the size), as well as a restaurant and a bar. ₹1500

Amritsar

The Sikhs' holy city of **AMRITSAR** is the largest city in Punjab, and one of the most popular tourist destinations in this whole chunk of India. Sikh pilgrims, domestic tourists and international visitors arrive en masse for one gleaming reason – the fabled **Golden Temple**, whose domes soar above Amritsar's teeming streets, is certainly one of the most captivating sights in the whole country. The temple aside, Amritsar is a little noisy and congested, but its old city in particular is as lively as any in India, and a stretch of it was recently pedestrianized and gentrified, which at least provides temporary escape from the hubbub. Some stay in town for a couple more days than they need – it's the kind of place that grows on you, even if there's not too much else to see other than **Jallianwalla Bagh**, host to the greatest single atrocity of colonial times, and the new **Partition Museum**. Amritsar is also an important staging post for those crossing the Indo-Pakistan frontier at **Wagha**, 29km west – or, much more commonly, for those seeking to witness the astonishing border-closing ceremony, which takes place there each evening (see page 539).

Brief history

Amritsar was founded in 1577 by **Ram Das**, the fourth Sikh guru, beside a bathing pool famed for its healing powers. The land around the tank was granted in perpetuity by the Mughal emperor Akbar to the Sikhs. When merchants moved in to take advantage of the strategic location on the Silk Route, Amritsar expanded rapidly, gaining a grand new temple under Ram Das's son and heir, **Guru Arjan Dev**. Sacked by Afghans in 1761, the shrine was rebuilt by the Sikhs' greatest secular leader, **Maharaja Ranjit Singh**, who also donated the gold used in its construction.

Amritsar's **twentieth-century** history has been blighted by a series of appalling **massacres**. The first occurred in 1919, when thousands of unarmed civilian demonstrators were gunned down without warning by British troops in **Jallianwalla Bagh** (see page 536) – an atrocity that inspired Gandhi's Non-Cooperation Movement. During Partition, Amritsar experienced some of the worst communal blood-letting ever seen on the Subcontinent. In 1983, heavily armed Sikh fundamentalists under the preacher-warrior Sant Jarnail Singh **Bhindranwale** occupied the Golden Temple's Akal Takht, and in early June 1984 Indira Gandhi ordered a paramilitary attack on the temple, code-named **Operation Blue Star**, in which two thousand people were killed, including pilgrims trapped inside.

Indira Gandhi's assassination by her Sikh bodyguards just four months later provoked the worst riots in the city since Partition. But Congress learned little from its mistakes and in 1987, Indira's son Rajiv reneged on an important accord with the main Sikh party, Akali Dal, strengthening the hand of the separatists, who retaliated by occupying the temple again. This time, the army responded with more restraint, leaving **Operation Black Thunder** to the Punjab police. Neither as well provisioned nor as well motivated as Bhindranwale's martyrs, the fundamentalists eventually surrendered.

The Golden Temple

Golden Temple Rd · ⓦ goldentempleamritsar.org · Daily 24hr · Free · Free bus from railway station forecourt (every 30min 4.30am–9pm)

Even visitors without a religious bone in their bodies cannot fail to be moved by Amritsar's resplendent **Golden Temple**, spiritual centre of the Sikh faith and open to all. Built by **Guru Arjan Dev** in the late sixteenth century, the richly gilded **Harmandir** rises from the middle of an artificial rectangular lake, connected to the surrounding white-marble complex by a narrow causeway. Every Sikh tries to make at least one pilgrimage here during their lifetime to listen to the sublime music (*shabad kirtan*), readings from the Adi Granth and also to bathe in the purifying waters of the temple tank – the **Amrit Sarovar** or "Pool of Immortality-Giving Nectar".

The best time to visit is early morning, to catch the first rays of sunlight gleaming on the bulbous golden domes and reflecting in the waters of the Amrit Sarovar. Sunset and evenings are an excellent time to tune in to the beautiful music performed in the Harmandir.

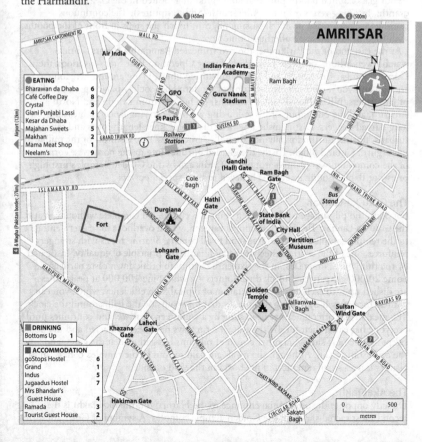

AMRITSAR

8

EATING
Bharawan da Dhaba	6
Café Coffee Day	8
Crystal	3
Giani Punjabi Lassi	4
Kesar da Dhaba	7
Majahan Sweets	5
Makhan	2
Mama Meat Shop	1
Neelam's	9

DRINKING
Bottoms Up	1

ACCOMMODATION
goStops Hostel	6
Grand	1
Indus	5
Jugaadus Hostel	7
Mrs Bhandari's Guest House	4
Ramada	3
Tourist Guest House	2

> **GOLDEN RULES**
>
> Visitors of all nationalities and religions are allowed into the Golden Temple provided they respect a few basic **rules**, enforced by patrolling guards. Firstly, tobacco, alcohol and drugs of any kind are forbidden. Before entering, you should also leave your shoes at the free cloakrooms (you'll receive a numbered metal token, and the process is usually fast), cover your head (cotton scarves are available outside the main entrance, or wear a Kullu hat) and wash your feet in the pool below the steps. **Photography** is permitted around the pool, but not inside any of the shrines.

The Parikrama

The principal north entrance to the temple, the **Darshini Deori**, leads under a Victorian **clock tower** to a flight of steps, from where you catch your first glimpse of the Harmandir, floating serenely above the glassy surface of the Amrit Sarovar. Dropping down as a reminder of the humility necessary to approach God, the steps end at the polished marble **Parikrama** that surrounds the tank, its smooth white stones set with the names of those who contributed to the temple's construction.

The shrines on the north edge of the enclosure are known as the **68 Holy Places**. Arjan Dev, the fifth guru, told his followers that a visit to these was equivalent to a pilgrimage around all 68 of India's most sacred Hindu sites. Several have been converted into a **Gallery of Martyrs**, in which paintings of glorious but gory episodes from Sikh history are displayed.

Four glass-fronted booths punctuate the Parikrama. Seated in each is a priest, or **granthi**, intoning verses from the Adi Granth (Sikh scriptures). The continuous readings are performed in shifts; passing pilgrims touch the steps in front of the booths with their heads and leave offerings of money.

At the east end of the Parikrama, the two truncated **Ramgarhia Minars** – brick watchtowers whose tops were blasted off during Operation Blue Star – overlook the Guru-ka-Langar (see below) and the main bathing **ghats**. Hang around here long enough and you'll see a fair cross-section of modern Sikh society parade past: families of Jat farmers, NRIs (Non-Resident Indians) on holiday from Britain and North America, and the odd group of fierce-looking warriors carrying lances, sabres and long curved daggers. Distinguished by their deep-blue knee-length robes and saffron turbans, the ultra-orthodox **nihangs** (literally "crocodiles") are devotees of the militarist tenth guru, Gobind Singh. Lastly, the gnarled old **Jubi Tree** in the northwest corner of the compound was planted around 450 years ago by the Golden Temple's first high priest, or Babba Buddhaya, and is believed to have special powers.

The Guru-ka-Langar

For Sikhs, no pilgrimage to the Golden Temple is considered complete without a visit to the **Guru-ka-Langar**. The giant communal canteen, which overlooks the eastern entrance to the temple complex, provides **free food** to all comers. Sharing meals with strangers reinforces one of the central tenets of the Sikh faith, the **principle of equality**, instigated by the third guru, **Amar Das**, in the sixteenth century to break down caste barriers. Some 20,000 chapatti and black dhal dinners – a whopping 100,000 at peak times – are dished up here each day in an operation of typical Sikh efficiency, which you can witness for yourself by joining the queues that form outside the hall, around the clock. The meal begins after grace has been sung by a volunteer, or *sevak*, and continues until everyone has eaten their fill. By the time the tin trays have been collected and the floors swept for the next sitting, another crowd of pilgrims has gathered at the gates, and the cycle starts again. Although the meals are paid for out of the temple's coffers, most visitors leave a small donation in the boxes in the yard outside.

The Akal Takht

Directly opposite the ceremonial entrance to the Harmandir, the **Akal Takht** is the second most sacred shrine in the Golden Temple complex. A symbol of God's authority on earth, it was built by Guru Hargobind in the seventeenth century and came to house the Shiromani Gurudwara Parbandhak Committee, the religious and political governing body of the Sikh faith founded in 1925.

During the 1984 siege, **Bhindranwale** and his army used this golden-domed building as their headquarters, fortifying it with sandbags and machine-gun posts. When Indian paratroopers tried to storm the shrine, they were mown down in their hundreds while crossing the courtyard in front of it: the reason why the army ultimately resorted to much heavier-handed tactics to end the siege. Positioned at the opposite end of the Amrit Sarovar, tanks pumped a salvo of high-explosive squash-head shells into the delicate facade, reducing it to rubble within seconds. The destruction of the Akal Takht offended Sikh sensibilities more than any other aspect of the operation. The shrine has been largely rebuilt and now looks almost the same as it did before June 6, 1984. Decorated with elaborate inlay, its ground floor is where the Adi Granth is brought each evening from the Harmandir, borne in a gold-and-silver palanquin.

The Harmandir

Likened by one guru to "a ship crossing the ocean of ignorance", the triple-storey **Harmandir**, or "Golden Temple of God" was built by Arjan Dev to house the Adi Granth, which he compiled from teachings of all the Sikh gurus; it is the focus of the Sikh faith. The temple has four doors indicating it is open to people of all faiths and all four caste divisions of Hindu society. The large dome and roof, covered with 100kg of gold leaf, is shaped like an inverted lotus, symbolizing the Sikhs' concern for temporal as well as spiritual matters.

The long causeway, or **Guru's Bridge**, which joins the Harmandir to the west side of the Amrit Sarovar, is approached via an ornate archway, the **Darshani Deorh**. As you approach the sanctum check out the amazing Mughal-style inlay work and floral gilt above the doors and windows.

The **interior** of the temple – decorated with yet more gold and silver, adorned with ivory mosaics and intricately carved wood panels – is dominated by the enormous **Adi Granth**, which rests on a sumptuous throne beneath a jewel-encrusted silk canopy. Before his death in 1708, Guru Gobind Singh, who revised the Adi Granth, declared that he was to be the last living guru, and that the tome would take over after him – hence its full title, the Guru Granth Sahib. *Granthis* intone continuous readings from the text as the worshippers file past, accompanied by singers and musicians – all relayed by loudspeakers around the complex. Known as Shri Akhand Path, a single continuous reading of the Guru Granth Sahib is carried out in three-hour shifts and takes around 48 hours to complete.

Jallianwalla Bagh

Off Golden Temple Rd • Daily 6.45am–6.30pm • Free

Just 100m northeast of the Golden Temple, a narrow lane leads between two buildings to **Jallianwalla Bagh**, a grassy compound whose prettiness belies a rather gruesome history – this was the site of one of the bloodiest atrocities committed by the British Raj (see page 536), and today the park functions as a memorial to those martyred here. A wall at the southwest corner sports 36 bullet holes created during the massacre; oddly, this has become a popular selfie spot with smiling domestic tourists. Coins are also thrown into Martyrs' Well, housed under a pretty pink structure to the east of the park.

Partition Museum

Town Hall • Tue–Sun 10am–6pm • ₹250 (₹10)

A relatively recent addition to the city is its **Partition Museum**, set in the pretty, red-brick Town Hall buildings; it's the default thing to see in Amritsar when you've seen

THE JALLIANWALLA BAGH MASSACRE

In 1919, a series of one-day strikes, or *hartals*, was staged in Amritsar in protest against the recent **Rowlatt Act**, which enabled the British to imprison without trial any Indian suspected of sedition. When the peaceful demonstrations escalated into sporadic looting, the lieutenant governor of Punjab declared martial law and called for reinforcements from Jalandhar. A platoon of infantry arrived soon after, led by **General R.E.H. Dyer**.

Despite a ban on public meetings, a mass demonstration was called by Mahatma Gandhi for April 13, the Sikh holiday of Baisakhi. The venue was a stretch of waste ground in the heart of the city, hemmed in by high brick walls and with only a couple of alleys for access. An estimated twenty thousand people gathered in Jallianwalla Bagh (see page 535) for the meeting. However, before any speakers could address the crowd, Dyer and his 150 troops, stationed on a patch of high ground in front of the main exit, opened fire without warning. By the time they had finished firing, ten to fifteen minutes later, hundreds of unarmed demonstrators lay dead and dying, many of them shot in the back while clambering over the walls. Others perished after diving for cover into the well that still stands in the middle of the *bagh*.

No one knows exactly how many people were killed. Official estimates put the death toll at 379, with 1200 injured, although the final figure may well have been several times higher; Indian sources quote a figure of two thousand dead. Hushed up for more than six months in Britain, the Jallianwalla Bagh massacre caused an international outcry when the story finally broke. It also proved seminal in the Independence struggle, prompting Gandhi to initiate the widespread civil disobedience campaign that played such a significant part in ridding India of its colonial overlords.

Moving first-hand accounts of the horrific events of April 13, 1919, and contemporary pictures and newspaper reports, are displayed in Jallianwalla Bagh's small **martyrs gallery**. The **well**, complete with chilling bullet holes, has been turned into a memorial to the victims.

8

the Golden Temple and been to the border ceremony, and have run out of things to do. Still, the exhibits are absorbing enough, with a series of artefacts, photos and documents charting the course of the independence movement, the subsequent demands for separation, and finally the partition and its consequences.

ARRIVAL AND DEPARTURE   AMRITSAR

By plane The airport is 12km northwest of town (₹400–500 by taxi, ₹200–300 by auto-rickshaw).
Destinations Delhi (6 daily; 1hr 15min); Mumbai (2 daily; 2hr 40min); Srinagar (1 daily; 1hr).

By train The railway station is centrally located, just north of the old city, though since it faces north you'll have to get across the tracks – time-consuming, even in a vehicle. The fastest trains for Delhi are the daily a/c *Shatabdis* – the #12014 (dep. 5am, arr. 11.15am) and the #12030 (dep. 4.50pm, arr. 11.05pm). If you prefer to travel overnight, there's the #12904 *Golden Temple Mail* (dep. 9.25pm, arr. 7.05am), which continues to Mumbai (arr. 5.20am, two calendar days after

departure). Other trains include the daily #13006 *Amritsar–Howrah Mail* (dep. 6.45pm) via Varanasi (arr. 4.40pm next day) to Kolkata (arr. Howrah 7.20am the day after that).

By bus For Pathankot (every 10min; 3hr) and HP destinations, you are restricted to state transport buses from the large bus stand on Grand Trunk Rd (NH-1), north of the old city, where there are also services to Chandigarh (approximately every 30min; 5–6hr). Most private buses, including a/c services, leave from just north of Gandhi (Hall) Gate. Agencies outside Gandhi (Hall) Gate and on Queens Rd operate deluxe and a/c buses to Chandigarh (5hr) and Delhi (10hr), but Delhi is a long and tiring road journey, and most people prefer to travel by train.

GETTING AROUND

By rickshaw You may find Amritsar too large and labyrinthine to negotiate on foot; if you're crossing town or are in a hurry, flag down an auto-rickshaw. Otherwise, stick to cycle rickshaws, which are the best way to get around the

narrow, packed streets of the old quarter.
By taxi If you've got the app, it's often worth giving Ola taxis a try – they're often the same price as (or even cheaper than) auto-rickshaws, and you won't even need to haggle.

INFORMATION

Tourist information PTDC's tourist office (Tues–Sun 9am–5pm; ☎0183 240 2452, ⓦpunjabtourism.gov.in), at the western exit from the railway station on Queens Rd, is

usually friendly and helpful. They also run a Heritage Walk through the old city (₹75/₹25 per person), starting at the City Hall daily at 8am and finishing at the Golden Temple.

ACCOMMODATION

As well as the places reviewed below, it's also possible to stay at the *niwas* within the Golden Temple complex itself (see page 538)

HOTELS

Grand Queens Rd, opposite railway station ☎0183 256 2424, ⓦhotelgrand.in; map p.533. Kicking around since 1950, this hotel is showing its age a bit, but is generally clean, with attached rooms surrounding a pleasant garden courtyard, though windows all face inward. There's an adjacent bar (see page 538), and they also offer day and night tours, the latter including the Wagha border ceremony. ₹1300

Indus 211/3 Sri Mandir Harmandar Sahib Marg ☎0183 253 5900, ⓦhotelindus.com; map p.533. A decent enough budget hotel, although the "deluxe" (ie, standard) rooms lack windows. The big thing about it is the amazing view over the Golden Temple from the rooftop café-restaurant and the two "luxury" rooms (₹2450). All rooms are in any case pretty cosy, with attached bathrooms, hot water and TV. ₹2000

Mrs Bhandari's Guest House 10 Cantonment ☎0183 222 8509, ⓦbhandari_guesthouse.tripod.com; map p.533. Wonderful old-fashioned rooms with wood fires and bathtubs in a colonial home with lawns, gardens and even a small swimming pool. Three-course meals are available, but pricey. You can camp in the grounds for ₹300/person. Popular with overland package tours, it's become an Amritsar institution. ₹2600

★**Ramada** 117 Hall Bazaar ☎0183 502 5555, ⓦramadaamritsar.com; map p.533. Amritsar has plenty of competition at this price level, but this colonial-yellow wedding-cake of a building is the stand-out for one main reason – it's close, as in very close, to the Golden Temple. Rooms are just as good as you'd expect from the chain, and there's a coffee area by reception, a fitness centre further into the complex, and best of all, a swimming pool on the roof. ₹5500

Tourist Guest House Hide Market, near Bhandari Bridge, Grand Trunk Rd ☎0183 255 3830, ⓦtouristguesthouse.com; map p.533. Popular with budget travellers since hippie trail days and still the city's best-value cheapie, offering a variety of rooms, of which the simplest have shared bathrooms and hot water in buckets; a large attached room with hot water doesn't cost much more. It backs onto the railway line however, so expect trains rattling past at all hours (one of the great sounds of India!). ₹500

HOSTELS

★**goStops Hostel** Tirath Shah Bhatia Rd (inside Sultanwind Gate) ☎74288 82828, ⓦgostops.com; map p.533. Part of a growing chain, this is by far the best hostel in town, with comfy rooms (but "No Gangnam Style" allowed in them, as the signs say), a relaxing common area-cum-kitchen with more power points than you could possibly imagine, and a rooftop with a kick-ass view towards the Golden Temple. Guests find it easy to mingle, and the friendly staff are adept at lassoing together groups for runs to the border ceremony. Breakfast included. Dorm beds ₹300, doubles ₹1200

Jugaadus Hostel Plot no.193, 1st Floor, above Salon 16, Ajit Nagar Main Road (off Sultanwind Rd), Ajit Nagar ☎85688 00020, ⓦjugaadus.com; map p.533. A backpackers' hostel that's hip and laidback in a slightly uptight kind of way – no booze allowed, and wi-fi gets turned off 5–7pm daily to "allow" you to disconnect from the outside world. Still, the atmosphere is great, and furnishings are made from natural or recycled materials. Each dorm has its own bathroom, though not always directly attached (and with no hot water mid-May to mid-Sept), and there's a communal kitchen. Dorm beds ₹400

EATING

For inexpensive food, try the simple vegetarian **dhabas** around the Golden Temple and bus stand, which serve cheap and tasty puris and *chana* dhal. Local specialities include **Amritsari fish** (fillets of river fish fried in a spicy batter – sohal or river sole is the best, but *singara* is cheaper).

RESTAURANTS

★**Bharawan da Dhaba** Near the City Hall ☎0183 253 2575; map p.533. One of the best *dhabas* in Amritsar, founded in 1912 and now a full-sized restaurant, serving simple and inexpensive but good veg curries (₹120–190).

GETTING TO PAKISTAN

For **Pakistan**, take one of the frequent buses to **Attari** (1hr 45min), from where it's just 2km to the border at **Wagha** (home to the famously colourful ceremonies; see page 539), or hire a taxi or auto from Amritsar. Rickshaws are available between Attari and Wagha. You'll have to cross into Pakistan by foot – it can take up to two hours to complete formalities. There is a **cross-border train** – the twice-weekly *Samjhauta Express* to Lahore in the Pakistani part of the Punjab – but whether it runs depends on the political situation, and at present it must be boarded at Delhi or Attari, not in Amritsar.

Their speciality, however, is Amritsari *kulcha* (bread stuffed with potato), which is very buttery and simply wonderful here – it'll cost ₹180 for a set including raita and channa, both pleasingly sweet and creamy. Daily 8am–11pm.

Crystal Crystal Chowk ☎ 0183 222 5555; map p.533. One of the city's most popular restaurants, with Indian, Chinese and Western food served in comfortable surroundings, by waiters in proper uniform. If you've made here, you might as well go for one of the pasta dishes – there are loads of options (mostly ₹480–530), including lasagne and cannelloni, but their chicken dishes are pretty luscious too, and there's cold beer to wash it down. Daily 11am–11.30pm.

Kesar da Dhaba Passian Chowk, between Golden Temple and Durgiana Temple ☎ 0183 255 2103, ⓦ kesardadhaba.com; map p.533. Old-school to the max here, in an establishment that's been going since 1916, and is well hidden away in the back streets (ask around if you get stuck). They have a limited menu of basic veg curries (₹125) and tempting thalis (₹195–295), and the lassis are pretty great too. Daily 11.30am–11pm.

★ **Makhan** Makhan Chowk, 500m north of Mall Rd; map p.533. Everyone in Amritsar seems to recommend this attractive restaurant, which is certainly the best place in town for the city's signature fish – you can have it several ways, including tikka or tandoori-style, but locals prefer it fried (₹360 for sangara, ₹400 for sohal). Served with a mayo-like sauce, it's not unlike a spicy fish and chips, without the chips. Daily 10.30am–11.30pm.

Mama Meat Shop Maqbool Rd, 750m north of Mall Rd; map p.533. One of a clutch of locally renowned *dhabas* that together form an Amritsar institution, frying up

spicy mutton tikka or (for the brave) brain curry, on *tawas* (griddles) out front, at around ₹220 a throw. Wed–Mon noon–9pm.

Neelam's Golden Temple Rd near Jallianwalla Bagh ☎ 0183 253 5727; map p.533. Indian veg dishes, plus some Chinese and Continental, at reasonable prices (mostly under ₹170), including good Punjabi thalis. The main appeal, however, lies in its location on the pedestrianized street – you can walk all the way here from the Golden Temple without fear of getting clonked by a rickshaw. Daily 9am–11pm.

CAFÉS AND SWEET SHOPS

Café Coffee Day East of Golden Temple ☎ 95698 95800; map p.533. Yes, it's a chain café, but there are almost no other decent places to scratch your caffeine cravings in central Amritsar, and this one's smack-bang next to the Golden Temple. Coffees from ₹100. Daily 24hr.

Giani Punjabi Lassi Golden Temple Out Rd, no phone; map p.533. You'll see plenty of lassi spots around the Golden Temple, and most are very good. However, a little further afield, this is even better, one of a trio of super-simple, similarly-named spots with similarly spurious claims to longevity. It's ₹40 for a full cup of the good stuff, ₹25 for a half. Daily 5am–9pm.

Majahan Sweets Chowk Bijli (just off Hall Bazaar) ☎ 0183 254 1078; map p.533. An excellent and long-established sweet shop (since 1947), and a very good place to try local sweet specialities such as lentil-based *badam dal pinni* and savoury *matthi*. Little selection boxes (from ₹130) give you three types of goodies. Daily 8.30am–9.30pm.

DRINKING

There's essentially nowhere to drink within the city gates, though venture outside and it won't be long until you find a liquor store – most of them seem to be called "English Wine & Beer Shop".

Bottoms Up Grand Hotel, Queens Rd ☎ 0183 256 2424,

ⓦ hotelgrand.in; map p.533. This "grand" old dame of a hotel (see page 537) has a decent bar attached to it – nothing special, but the Kingfisher's cold, and it's not too far from the old town.

STAYING AT THE GOLDEN TEMPLE COMPLEX

Undoubtedly the most authentic places to stay in Amritsar are the five **niwas** or pilgrim hostels run by the Golden Temple management committee. Intended for Sikh pilgrims, these charitable institutions also open their doors to foreign tourists. Charges are nominal (by donation, which is at your discretion), but stays are limited to a maximum of three nights.

The first building as you approach on the east side of the temple is the *Guru Arjan Dev Niwas*, which has the check-in counter for Indian citizens. Foreigners have their own dedicated room at the *Sri Guru Ramdas Ji Niwas*, which is the next one along. The *Sri Guru Nanak Niwas* was where Bhindranwale and his men holed up prior to the Golden Temple siege in 1904.

The downside of staying at these *niwas* is that facilities can be basic (*charpoy* beds and communal wash-basins in the central courtyard are the norm) and **security** can be a problem, although lockers are available. Alternatively, private rooms are available by the eastern entrance to the temple itself. It is advisable to book in advance (☎ 0183 255 3957, ⓦ goldentempleamritsar.org) as rooms and beds are almost always at a premium.

BEDLAM AT THE BORDER

Every evening as sunset approaches, the **India–Pakistan border** closes for the night with a spectacular and somewhat Monty Pythonesque show. It takes place at a remote little place 27km west of Amritsar called **Wagha** (the nearest town, 2km away, is Attari), to which hundreds – often thousands – of Indians make their way each evening to watch the popular tourist attraction from what is effectively a small half-stadium. The other (considerably smaller) half is over the border in Pakistan, and it likewise receives crowds each evening – strictly gender-segregated, you'll most likely wonder what they make of the Indian side, at which females are often encouraged to dance like mad to the sound of ear-splitting Indopop.

After the crowd has been built into something of a flag-waving frenzy, guards from both side – all sporting outlandish hats – perform synchronized speed marching along a 100m walkway to the border gate, where they turn and stomp back. Raucous cheering, clapping and much blowing of horns accompanies the spectacle. The guards strut their military catwalk several times and then vanish into the guardhouse. Flags are simultaneously lowered, the gates slammed shut and the crowds on either side rush forward for a massive and congenial photo session. On both sides, more empathy than ever occurs on a cricket pitch permeates the air; photos are taken with the stone-faced guards and then everyone heads home – back to business as usual.

Tourists wishing to watch the bizarre border spectacle can rent taxis for the round trip. You can ask drivers yourself (₹1200–1500 per vehicle), but hotels and hostels – most pertinently goStops (see page 537) – often pool together interested parties. Alternatively, tour-style buses run daily from outside the Town Hall at 2.30pm (₹250 per person), or you can get your butt nice and sore in a cramped auto-rickshaw (₹100 per person).

SHOPPING

Tablas (hand-drums), harmonia and other musical instruments are available at the shops near the Golden Temple. Other possible souvenirs include a pair of traditional *Arabian Nights*-style Punjabi leather slippers (*jootis*), sold at a row of shops opposite the outside of Gandhi (Hall) Gate, and in many places near the Golden Temple.

DIRECTORY

Banks and exchange There are ATMs across town, including several in the railway station forecourt and the bus station, and around Jallianwala Bagh. There's a clutch of forex bureaux opposite the train station on Railway Link Rd, many of which will change Pakistani rupees.
Hospitals The best in the city are Kakkar Hospital, Green Ave (☎0183 250 6015), and Muni Lal Chopra Hospital, 361 Mall Rd (☎0183 222 2072).
Left luggage Baggage can be left for short periods at the Golden Temple's *gurudwaras*, or at the railway station or bus-stand cloakroom.

Chandigarh and around

CHANDIGARH is the state capital of both Punjab and Haryana, but part of neither, being a Union Territory administered by India's federal government. Its history begins in 1947, when Partition placed the Punjab's main city of Lahore in Pakistan, leaving India's state of Punjab without a capital. Nehru saw this as an opportunity to realize his vision of a city "symbolic of the future of India, unfettered by the traditions of the past, (and) an expression of the nation's faith in the future". The job of designing it went to controversial Swiss-French architect Charles-Edouard Jeanneret, alias **Le Corbusier**.

Begun in 1952, Chandigarh was to be a groundbreaking experiment in town planning. Le Corbusier's blueprints were for an orderly grid of sweeping boulevards, divided into 29 neat blocks, or **Sectors**, each measuring 800m by 1200m, and interspersed with extensive stretches of green. Chandigarh's numbered **sectors** are further subdivided into lettered blocks, making route-finding relatively easy. Le Corbusier saw the city plan as a living organism, with the imposing **Capital Complex** to the north as a "head", the shopping precinct (**Sector 17**) a "heart", and the green open spaces as "lungs".

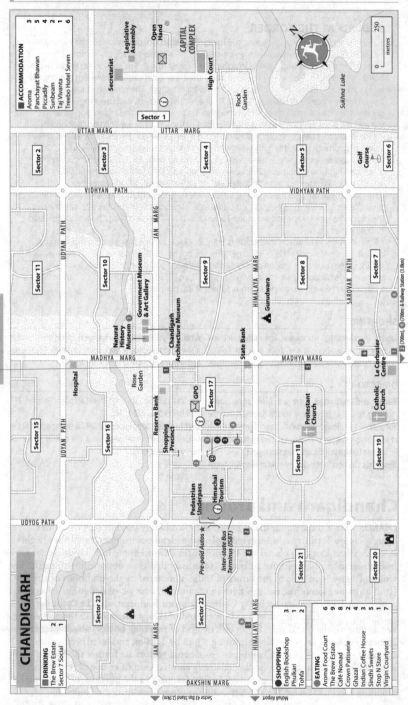

CHANDIGARH

DRINKING
The Brew Estate	2
Sector 7 Social	1

ACCOMMODATION
Aroma	3
Panchayat Bhawan	5
Piccadilly	4
Sunbeam	2
Taj Vivanta	1
Treebo Hotel Seven	6

SHOPPING
English Bookshop	3
Phulkari	1
Tohfa	2

EATING
Aroma Food Court	6
The Brew Estate	9
Café Nomad	8
Crown Patisserie	2
Ghazal	4
Indian Coffee House	3
Sindhi Sweets	5
Stop N Stare	1
Virgin Courtyard	7

CAPITAL COMPLEX

Legislative Assembly
Open Hand
Secretariat
High Court
Rock Garden
Sukhna Lake

Sector 1

UTTAR MARG
UTTAR MARG

Sector 2
Sector 3
Sector 4
Sector 5
Golf Course
Sector 6

VIDHYAN PATH
VIDHYAN PATH

Sector 11
UDYAN PATH
Sector 10
Government Museum & Art Gallery
Chandigarh Architecture Museum
JAN MARG
Sector 9
HIMALAYA MARG
Gurudwara
Sector 8
SAROVAR PATH
Sector 7

Natural History Museum

State Bank

MADHYA MARG
MADHYA MARG
Le Corbusier Centre

Hospital
Rose Garden
Reserve Bank
Shopping Precinct
GPO
Sector 17
Protestant Church
Catholic Church

Sector 15
Sector 16
Sector 18
Sector 19

Pedestrian Underpass
Himachal Tourism
Inter-state Bus Terminus (ISBT)
Pre-paid Autos

UDYOG PATH
UDYAN PATH

Sector 23
Sector 22
Sector 21
Sector 20

JAN MARG
HIMALAYA MARG

DAKSHIN MARG

8

250 metres

Sector 43 Bus Stand (2.9km)
Mohali Airport

(700m) & Railway Station (3.8km)

Some applaud Le Corbusier's brainchild as one of the great architectural achievements of the twentieth century, but detractors complain that the design is self-indulgent and un-Indian. Le Corbusier created a city for fast-flowing traffic at a time when few people owned cars, while his cubic concrete buildings are like ovens during the summer. The city has expanded from the first phase comprising sectors 1 to 30 (there is no Sector 13), through a second phase – sectors 31 to 47 – and is now into the third phase with (half-size) sectors 48 to 61. Satellite towns emulating Chandigarh's grid plan and sterile concrete architecture, such as Panchkula in Haryana and Mohali in Punjab, have sprung up on either side.

Despite Chandigarh's shortcomings, its inhabitants are proud of their capital, which is cleaner, greener and more affluent than other Indian cities of comparable size, and its **rock garden** is Punjab's second-most visited tourist site after the Golden Temple.

The museums

Sector 10 • All Tues–Sun 10am–5pm • ₹10 joint ticket for the Art Gallery and Natural History Museum; ₹10 for the Architecture Museum; ₹5 camera charge for each

Situated in the green belt known as the Leisure Valley, Chandigarh's museums form part of a cultural complex that includes the neighbouring Rose Garden. The **Government Museum & Art Gallery** is best of the lot, housing a sizeable and informatively displayed collection of textiles, Harappan artefacts, miniature paintings and contemporary art, including five original Roerichs and a couple of A.N. Tagore's atmospheric watercolours. The ancient sculptures are the most compelling exhibits, notably the Gandhara Buddhas with their delicately carved "wet-look" *lunghis* and distinctly Hellenic features – a legacy of Alexander the Great's conquests.

A stone's throw to the west, the small but appropriately modernist **Chandigarh Architecture Museum** illustrates the planning and construction of Chandigarh, with models and photographs in a concrete pavilion based on one of Le Corbusier's designs. Beyond that, the **Natural History Museum** has a few stuffed animals, some bits of fossilized mammoths and diorama depictions of early humans, and is thus most popular with school kids.

The Capital Complex

Sector 1 • Guided visits daily at 10am, noon & 3pm • Visitors must obtain permission from office of Chandigarh Tourism at the Complex; arrive half an hour early to allow time for this, or apply in advance online (W chandigarhtourism.gov.in) • Bring passport or other ID

Visits to the **Capital Complex** are by guided tour only – security is tight here, and has been since 1995, when Punjab chief minister Beant Singh was assassinated in front of the Assembly building by Sikh nationalist hardliners. The complex's most imposing edifice is the eleven-storey **Secretariat**, Chandigarh's highest building, which houses ministerial offices for both Haryana and Punjab, and has a roof garden with good views over the city. The resemblance of the adjacent **Legislative Assembly building**, or Vidhan Sabha (home to the legislatures of both states) to a power station is no coincidence: Le Corbusier was allegedly inspired by a stack of cooling towers he saw in Ahmedabad. Opposite the Secretariat is the most colourful building in the complex, the **High Court** (also serving both states), which is said to incorporate elements of the Buland Darwaza in Fatehpur Sikri, and is decorated inside with huge woollen tapestries. North of this is the black, 13m-high **Open Hand monument**, Chandigarh's adopted emblem. Weighing all of 45 tonnes, it revolves on ball bearings like a weather vane and stands for "post-colonial harmony and peace".

The Rock Garden

Uttar Marg, Sector 1 • Daily: April–Sept 9am–7.30pm; Oct–March 9am–6.30pm • ₹20 • W nekchand.com

Close to the Capital Complex, the **Rock Garden** is a surreal fantasyland fashioned from fragments of shattered plates, neon strip-lights, pots, pebbles, broken bangles and assorted urban-industrial junk. The open-air exhibition was a labour of love by

GETTING TO SHIMLA

Chandigarh is an important transport hub for **Shimla**, most swiftly reached by bus from Sector 43 (every 15min; 4hr–4hr 30min). You can also get there on the slower but more congenial Viceroys'"Toy Train"(see page 415) from Kalka, 26km to the northeast and connected to Chandigarh by trains and frequent buses. The scenic 75km journey from Kalka to Shimla takes around 5hr (dep. 4am, 5.10am, 5.30am, 6am & 12.10pm).

retired Public Works Department road inspector **Nek Chand**. Inspired by a recurrent childhood dream, he began construction in 1957. His intention was to create just a small garden, but by the time it was discovered in 1975 – to widespread astonishment – it covered twelve acres. Though it was completely illegal, the city council recognized it as a great artistic endeavour and, in a conspicuously enlightened decision, awarded Chand a salary to continue his work (which he did until his death in 2015), and a workforce of fifty labourers to help. Opened to the public in 1976, the garden now covers 25 acres and contains several thousand sculptures.

The site is a labyrinth of enclosures interconnected by narrow passages, arched walkways, streams, bridges, grottos, waterfalls, battlements and turrets. Stick to the path, or you could end up wandering the maze until the chowkidar finds you at closing time.

Le Corbusier Centre

Sector 19 • Tue–Sun 10am–5pm • Free

Though less interesting (in an architectural sense) than the City Architecture museum, Sector 19's **Le Corbusier Centre** has a more interesting array of exhibits, including a lot of black-and-white photos of the fella himself boating around Sukhna Lake, plans of the envisioned city, and more photos of the buildings during and after creation.

ARRIVAL AND DEPARTURE · CHANDIGARH

Chandigarh is a major regional hub, and also a useful jumping-off point for Shimla, to which there are direct buses, as well as the "Toy Train" from Kalka (see page 415), 26km northeast of Chandigarh and connected to it by trains and frequent buses.

By plane Chandigarh's airport is at Mohali, 8km east of the city. It's ₹500 by auto from the ISBT, ₹1000 by taxi, or ₹20 by local bus #38A from Sector 17 ISBT.

Destinations Delhi (9 daily; 1hr); Mumbai (6 daily; 2hr 35min); Srinagar (2 daily; 1hr).

By train The railway station sits an inconvenient 8km southeast of the centre – it'll cost ₹100 by auto or app taxi, or ₹10 on a local bus. Superfast a/c *Shatabdi* trains run to Delhi (#12046 & #12012 dep. at noon & 6.23pm), and there's a rail reservation centre at the Sector 17 ISBT (Mon–

Sat 8am–8pm, Sun 8am–2pm).

Destinations Amritsar (2 daily; 4hr 20min); Delhi (11 daily; 3hr 30min–5hr); Jodhpur (1 daily; 17hr 45min); Kolkata (1 daily; 30hr 45min); Mumbai (1 daily; 27hr 25min).

By bus The main Inter-state Bus Terminal (ISBT) is on the south edge of the main commercial and shopping district, Sector 17, with regular services to Delhi (via Delhi airport). However, daytime services to Punjab and Himachal Pradesh use the Sector 43 bus stand, connected to the ISBT by frequent local buses (₹10). Tickets can be pre-booked at both terminals, or for less busy services, bought on the bus. There's a prepaid auto-rickshaw counter across the road from the west side of the Sector 17 ISBT (next to the pedestrian underpass exit).

Destinations Delhi (34 daily; 4–5hr); Shimla (every 15min; 4hr–4hr 30min).

GETTING AROUND

On foot Chandigarh is rather spread out, but with actual paths and some quiet inner-sector roads and parks, it can actually be a pleasant place to explore on foot.

By auto-rickshaw Cycle and auto-rickshaws cruise the streets; a prepaid auto from the ISBT to the Rock Garden is ₹56.

By taxi There's a taxi stand (☎ 90410 44555; 24hr) in the northwest corner of Sector 17 ISBT, with others dotted around town. Uber and Ola cabs operate in the city, and are usually about the same price as the auto-rickshaws.

INFORMATION AND TOURS

Tourist information Chandigarh Tourism (⌚ chandigarh tourism.gov.in; ☎ 1800 180 2116) has information booths in Sector 17 (daily 10am–5pm) and at the station (daily 6am–6pm), as well as an office at the Capital Complex (daily 9am–5pm), where they issue visitors' permits for the Complex (see page 533). The Himachal Pradesh tourist office (Mon–Sat 9am–6pm; ☎ 0172 270 7267), at the Sector 17 ISBT, is useful for booking tours and buses to Manali and Shimla.

Tours Chandigarh Tourism run a half-day tour around town in an open-top tourist bus (daily 10am & 2.30pm; ₹50 per person; ☎ 0172 467 2222), departing from the *Shivalik View* hotel in Sector 17 (next to the *Taj Vivanta*).

ACCOMMODATION

Chandigarh's high property prices make **accommodation** here expensive, especially at the bottom end where choice is limited, and places are very often full (so book ahead if possible).

★ **Aroma** Himalaya Marg, Sector 22-C ☎ 0172 401 0000, ⓦ hotelaroma.com; map p.540. A vintage Austin guards the doorway of this attractive-looking hotel, whose rooms are mock-classic, with laminated floors and slightly scuffed walls imitating an old-fashioned feel. They've a good restaurant on site, and more choice in the attached food court (see below). Breakfast included. ₹3300

Panchayat Bhawan Madhya Marg, Sector 18 ☎ 0172 270 0791, ⓔ panchayatbhawan@yahoo.com; map p.540. A hostel, basically, and rather institutional, but well-kept and pretty good value by local standards, with dorms (which are the cheapest accommodation option in town) and large, clean, a/c rooms. Dorms ₹200; doubles ₹1300

Piccadily Himalaya Marg, Sector 22-B ☎ 0172 431 5431, ⓦ thepiccadily.com; map p.540. Despite the missing "L" in the name, this is a rather plush establishment, tastefully refurbished in blue and grey decor, with thickly carpeted corridors and a/c rooms, and an excellent bar (see below) which doubles as a restaurant and coffee shop. Breakfast included. ₹6000

Sunbeam Udyog Path, Sector 22-B ☎ 0172 450 6050, ⓦ hotelsunbeam.com; map p.540. Upmarket hotel opposite the ISBT with swish marble lobby and comfortable rooms, though the decorative brickwork in front of the windows makes them a bit dark. ₹4000

★ **Taj Vivanta** Block 9, Sector 17-A ☎ 0172 661 3000, ⓦ tajhotels.com; map p.540. Chandigarh's poshest option by a long chalk, in a well-designed building whose minimalist modern decor in cool, light colours makes it something like an elegant, beautiful version of one of Le Corbusier's concrete boxes. Ignore the rack rates, which you can usually discount by up to half. ₹14,000

Treebo Hotel Seven 8-A, Sector 7-C ☎ 0172 478 3444, ⓦ hotel7chandigarh.com; map p.540. A good find at this neglected price level, this simple hotel is convenient for Chandigarh's main nightlife area. Staff are well drilled, and rooms clean and pretty comfy, though noise does carry a bit from the reception area. Simple breakfast included, and served in the room. ₹1300

EATING

You'll most likely eat well in Chandigarh, where a number of great international options have popped up in recent years.

RESTAURANTS

Aroma Food Court Himalaya Marg, Sector 22-C ☎ 0172 401 0000, ⓦ hotelaroma.com; map p.540. It may seem a bit dull to eat in a food court, but the one attached to this hotel (see above) is actually pretty good. Ignore the McDonald's and Subway, and try something from the biryani cart, chai (or really tasty samosa chaat) from Chaayos, a milkshake from Keventer's, or coffee from the Café Coffee Day. Daily 7am–midnight.

The Brew Estate 25 Madhya Marg, Sector 26 ☎ 98887 88887; map p.540. Though primarily a bar (see below), this is also a good spot for food, with an extensive menu including great pizzas, burgers and Indian mains (mostly ₹250–425). Daily 11am–midnight.

★ **Café Nomad** 1914 Sarovar Path, Sector 7-C ☎ 0172 654 1569; map p.540. Though little out of the way, this is a real find – not a café at all (though the coffee's okay), but a surprisingly stylish restaurant serving Middle Eastern food. Try something simple like falafel and hummus (₹425), or more adventurous selections like a clay-pot tajine (₹575). Licenced. Daily 11.30am–11.30pm.

Ghazal 189–91 Sector 17-C ☎ 0172 270 4448; map p.540. Refined Punjabi non-veg cuisine, with tasty Punjabi and Mughlai chicken and mutton dishes, as well as freshwater sole fish (sole fish tikka ₹690). The house speciality is a superb creamy, mildly spiced Ghazal special *murg* (a half portion at ₹440 will be more than enough for one), and the place is licenced, with a surprisingly good range of whiskies. Daily 11.30am–4pm & 7.30–11pm.

Indian Coffee House 63–64 Sector 17-E ☎ 0172 270 4504; map p.540. Budget co-op chain with a cheap menu, including masala dosas (₹71), sandwiches and coffee. All dishes are under ₹90. Daily 9am–9pm.

Stop N Stare Sector 10, no phone; map p.540. This snack shack is the only place to eat around the museums, but the food here is super cheap (samosa with channa ₹35, lassis ₹30), and the place is surrounded by greenery. Daily 8am–7pm.

★ **Virgin Courtyard** 1-A Madhya Marg, Sector 7-C ☎ 86990 00999, ⓦ virgincourtyard.com; map p.540. The best choice on this busy side-road, this swanky spot wouldn't

8

look out of place in Delhi, and its candle-lit courtyard is a great evening spot (reservations required). Most of the menu choices are Italian – try something from the bruschetta bar for starters, and a risotto, wood-fired pizza or hand-made ravioli dish for mains (all ₹400–500). They also have an extensive alcohol selection. Daily 11.30am–11.30pm.

CAFÉS AND SWEET SHOPS

Crown Patisserie 14 Sector 17-E, no phone; map p.540. Chandigarh's best coffee spot, a gaily-decorated place tucked up on the first floor, with a small balcony overlooking the pedestrianized shopping area. Coffees from ₹115, and tasty cupcakes on display by the counter. Daily 9.30am–10.30pm.

Sindhi Sweets 110 Sector 17-B ☎0172 507 5222; map p.540. An excellent a/c sweets emporium with several branches around town, all packed to the gunwales with silver-coated confections of all sorts, and translucent *kesar* or *angoora petha* at ₹360/kg. Daily 9am–10.30pm.

DRINKING

Most of the best nightlife action takes place along a strip running down the west flank of Sectors 7 and 26.

★**The Brew Estate** 25 Madhya Marg, Sector 26 ☎98887 88887; map p.540. There are almost too many microbreweries in Chandigarh now, but this attractive venue is just ahead of the rest, with a good selection of craft beer (₹345 for 500ml), of which you'll be given a free sampler set as soon as you've sat down. Awesome cocktails, too, some involving betel leaf, cloves or litchi, and great food available (see above). Daily 11am–midnight.

Sector 7 Social 37 Madhya Marg, Sector 7-C ☎73411 18093, ⊛socialoffline.in; map p.540. The Social team have opened up a branch in Chandigarh, and it replicates the success of their establishments in Delhi. Inventive drinks available (try the banarsi patiala, sugar cane juice and triple-shot of rum; ₹510), and often live music – and, sadly, also often an extortionate "stag entry" fee for unaccompanied males. Daily 9am–1am.

SHOPPING

English Bookshop 30 Sector 17-E ☎0172 270 2542; map p.540. Well-stocked general bookstore with plenty in the way of novels and travel guides, centrally located in the middle of Sector 17's main shopping area. Daily noon–8pm.

Phulkari 27 Sector 17-E ☎0172 270 6246; map p.540. Several states run handicraft emporiums in the Sector 17 shopping complex, among them Punjab, whose Phulkari store stocks a good range of embroidered silk, woodwork and traditional pointed Punjabi shoes. Mon–Sat 10.30am–2pm & 3.30–8pm.

Tohfa 98–100 Sector 17-C ☎0172 402 5152; map p.540. Pile 'em high, flog 'em cheap clothes store full of brightly coloured, jolly Punjabi *phulkaris* and shawls. Mon–Sat 11am–8.30pm, Sun 2–8.30pm.

DIRECTORY

Banks and exchange Several banks around Bank Square in the northeast corner of Sector 17 change money. ATMs are common around town, including at the railway and bus stations.

Hospitals Chandigarh's Government Multi Specialty Hospital is in Sector 16 (☎0172 276 8201), but is not as good as the PGI, Sector 12 (☎0172 275 6565, ⊛pgimer.edu.in).

Left luggage There is a cloakroom in the ISBT (₹10/day; 24hr except 12.30–1pm & 8.30–9pm).

Pharmacies Apollo Pharmacy, 16–17 Sector 34-A ☎0172 258 3578 (24hr).

Pinjore

Buses between Chandigarh and Kalka (every 10min from Chandigarh Sector 43 ISBT, slightly less frequently from Sector 17 ISBT; 1hr) stop right in front of Yadavindra Gardens

PINJORE, 22km north of Chandigarh and 7km south of Kalka on the Shimla road, is one of many sites associated with the exile of the Pandavas as chronicled in the Mahabharata, and is best known for its walled gardens, and it makes a good half-day trip from Chandigarh.

Yadavindra Gardens

Off Kalka-Shimla Rd • Daily 7am–10pm • ₹20 (free)

The **Yadavindra Gardens** originally belonged to the rajas of Sirmaur, but under the Mughals were taken over by Aurangzeb's foster brother, Fidai Khan, who erected three pleasure palaces for his wife amid the cypress trees. Legend tells that the raja reclaimed his summer retreat by sending a female fruit-seller with goitre to the imperial impostors. On being told that the woman's unsightly swelling was caused by the local water, the begum and her entourage fled. The gardens are on seven levels, bisected by waterways with fountains; the best time to visit is in the evening, when it's all aglow with pretty lights. And, as befits former pleasure gardens, there's now an adjacent amusement park, though it's maybe something to avoid.

Bhima Devi Temple

Off Kalka-Shimla Rd • Daily 9am–5pm • Free

Near the gardens, excavated remains of the tenth-century **Bhima Devi Temple** – destroyed during the Muslim conquest of the area – have been assembled in a pleasant park with four exhibition rooms that the caretaker will open for you if he's about. The temple is contemporary with Khajuraho, and one or two of the reliefs are similarly erotic, though well worn.

ACCOMMODATION   **PINJORE**

Tourist Complex Motel Yadavindra Gardens ☎ 01733 231877, ✉ pinjore@hry.nic.in. One of the palaces in the gardens has been converted by Haryana Tourism into a motel, with a range of clean, fresh rooms – nothing fancy, but good value and right next to the site. ₹2000

Patiala

The capital of a princely state under the Raj, and a city with much charm and few visitors, **PATIALA** dates back to the early eighteenth century. It was founded as the capital of a state that featured a unique power-sharing arrangement, in which the maharaja was always a Sikh and the army commander a Muslim. Buffeted by rival powers, be they Hindu, Muslim or Sikh, Patiala's maharajas finally secured their state's survival in 1808 by allying themselves with the British. Like India's other princely states, Patiala was absorbed into the Republic in 1947, but the city remained capital of its own state (the Patiala and East Punjab States Union, aka PEPSU) until 1956. To this day, there's still something special about Patiala, and even the local measure of whisky – the **Patiala peg** – is bigger than a standard peg that you get elsewhere (60ml, versus the normal 30ml). The old city is full of bazaars and temples, and still has its fort and several of its original gates, although the walls are long gone. The tourist board have designated a self-guided "heritage walk" around the city's main sights, with signposts marking out the route, although they're a bit patchy, and a map is more helpful; in addition, most of them those sights been under renovation for quite some time, but hopefully Patiala will soon make some proper use of its past.

Quila Mubarak

Quila Chowk • Tues–Sun 10am–5pm • Durbar Hall ₹10

At the very heart of the old city, the Quila Mubarak was founded in 1763 as a crude mud-walled fortress, but subsequently became the palace of Patiala's maharajas, who embellished and enlarged it. It's certainly impressive, but it has fallen into a terrible state of disrepair and is currently undergoing extensive restoration work. Unfortunately, this includes the **Durbar Hall**, which until recently remained open to the public, and was worth a look on account of its huge mirrors and chandeliers – hopefully it, and the fortress, will open fully in due course.

Shahi Samadhan

Adalat Bazar • Tues–Sun 10am–5pm • Free

Southeast of the Quila Mubarak, at **Shahi Samadhan**, an ornate gateway marks the mausoleum of the founder and first ruler of Patiala, Baba Ala Singh, whose tomb lies inside it. The arch subsequently became a cenotaph for his successors, with memorials inscribed across the top of the gate in Urdu, English and Punjabi.

Kali Devi Temple

Mall Road, 500m southwest of the bus stand • ⓦ maakalidevimandirpatiala.com • Daily 24hr • Free

Being a Sikh didn't stop Maharaja Bhupinder Singh from endowing this Hindu **Kali Devi Temple** in 1936. The six-foot statue of the terrifying Bengali goddess Kali, to whom the temple is dedicated, was brought over from Kolkata and presides over it, tongue out, sword raised, and holding a human head in her hand. During Diwali – which is also Kali Puja – in particular, people come here to make offerings of sweets, coconuts, dhal and even booze to the goddess. The same complex also contains the rather older Raj Rajeshwari temple.

Sheesh Mahal

Old Moti Bagh • Tues–Sun 10am–5pm • Free

To the southwest of the city, the flamboyant **Sheesh Mahal** (Palace of Mirrors) was commissioned in 1847 by Maharaja Narendra Singh, a great patron of the arts, who had it decorated with murals, inlays and the mirrors that give it its name. Since then, alas, it has fallen on hard times and its grandeur has become rather dilapidated; at the time of writing in 2019 it was closed completely, but restoration is promised in the near future.

ARRIVAL AND INFORMATION   PATIALA

By bus The bus stand is at the northern end of the old city. Destinations Ambala (every 10min; 40min); Amritsar (every 30min; 5hr); Chandigarh (every 15min; 1hr 30min).

By train The station, just north of the bus stand, has one daily train to Delhi (dep. 1.53pm, arr. 8.20pm) and one to Amritsar (dep. 10.40am, arr. 4.30pm). The only train to Chandigarh travels inconveniently during the early hours

(dep. 2.30am, arr. 5.10am).

Tourist information The tourist office is at the Punjab State Archive on Mall Road, 300m southwest of the bus stand (Tues–Sun 9am–5pm; ☏ 98727 74777, ⓦ punjabtourism.gov.in). They run guided one-hour heritage walks starting at the Shahi Samadhan (Fri–Sun: March–Nov 8am; Dec–Feb 9am).

ACCOMMODATION

★**Baradari Palace** Baradari Gardens ☏ 0175 230 4433, ⓦ the-baradari-palace.neemranahotels.com. The city's best offering by far: a grand, spacious heritage hotel in a palace built for the maharaja in 1876. Service is excellent – plus points for the free tea and cookies served from 5–6pm – and there's a range of deluxe rooms, each done out in individual style. Discounts usually available off season, and also a good place to eat or drink (see below). ₹6400

Corner Northern end of the bus stand ☏ 0175 654 4054, ⓔ cornerhotel1960@gmail.com. Best of the hotels around the bus station (others are cheaper, but very grubby), and situated on a prominent corner, as its name suggests, this makes for a convenient stay. Some rooms are impressively large, there's hot water, plus a good restaurant in the same building; things can, however, get a little noisy. ₹1400

EATING AND DRINKING

Amritsari Kulcha Anardana Chowk, no phone. There are few notable places to eat in the old town, but this small spot just north of the fortress is great for Amritsar-style kulcha (bread stuffed with stuff, most commonly potato), which goes from a mere ₹60. Daily 9am–3.30pm.

Baradari Palace Baradari Gardens ☏ 0175 230 4433, ⓦ the-baradari-palace.neemranahotels.com. The tile-floored bar of this heritage hotel (see above) is the prime place for a "Patiala peg" – a cheap, large shot of local whisky

will set you back just ₹150. The restaurant is also very fancy, with a good, affordable range of Indian mains. Daily noon–10pm, food noon–3pm & 7–10pm.

The Drew Estate Punjabi Bagh ☏ 78510 00004. Chandigarh's best microbrewery has opened up a branch in little Patiala, and it's actually larger and even more attractive – try some of their tasty beers, or a pizza, burger or curry. Daily 11am–11pm.

Gurgaon

Essentially the only place of note in Haryana state, and now in a slow-motion process of being rechristened "Gurugram", **GURGAON** is effectively a satellite city of Delhi, though it draws young people from the capital in their droves for two big reasons. Firstly, relaxed licencing laws have made for a simply ridiculous number of **brewpubs**, with a full dozen of them staring at each other out in Sector 29. Secondly, and more importantly, a lack of historical and cultural baggage has seen the city become, in parts, more modern than Delhi, especially in the gleaming, high-rise **Cyber City** area – here, in its umpteen bars and eateries, you'll often hear Delhi millennials wondering aloud why their city can't be more like this, and it's not hard to imagine their wishes coming true after the next generational shift.

Kingdom of Dreams

Sector 29 • ⓦ kingdomofdreams.in • Tue–Sun 12.30pm–midnight • ₹600, redeemable against food and drink; show tickets from ₹1200

Gurgaon's only real "sight", the wistfully-named **Kingdom of Dreams** is a sort of Indian Disneyland, arranged like a Bollywood film set. The entry ticket will allow you to roam the family-friendly grounds, which are peppered with places to snack, drink (even booze) or have a full meal; however, for many the highlight is a chance to sample one of the lurid, Bollywood-style shows.

ARRIVAL AND INFORMATION   GURGAON

By metro Delhi's Yellow Line (see page 104) crosses state lines to terminate in Gurgaon's HUDA City Centre station, around 40min from central Delhi; three stations north, at Sikanderpur station, there's an intersection with Gurgaon's own Rapid Metro Line, which provides access to Cyber City.

By train Gurgaon railway station, located over 7km west of the area of interest, is a stop for some trains running between Delhi and Jaipur (4–5hr away).

ACCOMMODATION

Bloom Boutique B1/B near Signature Towers ☏0124 419 7000, ⓦ staybloom.com. A relaxed, attractive option located near the Sector 29 bars (though given the road layout, you'll still need to take a taxi or auto-rickshaw). Rooms are highly comfortable, and there's a decent restaurant by reception, as well as a small fitness centre; the rooftop makes a great place to drink in the evening. ₹5200

EATING

Burma Burma 8/6 Tower C, DLF Cyber City ☏0124 437 2999; Ⓜ Cyber City, ⓦ burmaburma.in. Cyber City's restaurant offerings are essentially a roster of chains that have done well in Delhi. This is one of the best such offerings, with a menu full of Burmese curries, mohinga noodles and the like (all around ₹460); service is slick and the meals very photo-worthy, and there are plenty of teas to try too. Daily noon–3pm & 7–11pm.

Made in Punjab 5–6 Cyberhub, DLF Cyber City ☏81309 11899; Ⓜ Cyber City. Great if you want some Punjabi flair in culinary-cosmopolitan Cyber City. The lamb dishes are highly recommended, with soft meat just falling from the bone; alternatively, go for the chicken tikka, or fill up at the weekday lunch buffet (₹760). Licenced. Daily noon–11.30pm.

DRINKING

Bronx Brewery 38 Sector 29 ☏99711 10974; Ⓜ IFFCO Chowk. The best of the staggering number of brewpubs clustered corral-like in Sector 29. It's a multi-level affair, with each floor having its own ambience; most head straight to the rooftop, to drain one of their slightly oversweet brews. Daily 1pm–1am.

Soi 7 205–208 Cyberhub, DLF Cyber City ☏81302 61166, ⓦ facebook.com/soi7pub; Ⓜ Cyber City. Located in the modern Cyber City mall, this is one of the wider Delhi area's best brew-bars, with their own excellent beers including a lager, a wheat beer and a dark ale (₹325 for 500ml). The cocktails and nibbles are good too. Daily noon–12.30am.

8

Gujarat

MEMBERS OF THE MEGHAWAL TRIBE IN KUTCH

9 Gujarat

Heated in the north by the blistering deserts of Pakistan and Rajasthan, and cooled in the south by the gentle ocean breeze of the Arabian Sea, Gujarat forms India's westernmost bulkhead. The diversity of its topography – forested hilly tracts and fertile plains in the east, vast tidal marshland and desert plains in the Rann of Kutch in the west, with the rocky shoreline jutting into its heartland – can be compared to the multiplicity of its politics and culture. Home to significant populations of Hindus, Jains, Muslims and Christians, as well as tribal and nomadic groups, the state boasts a patchwork of religious shrines and areas steeped in Hindu lore. Gujarat is the homeland of Mahatma Gandhi, born Mohandas Gandhi in Porbandar and a long-time resident of Ahmedabad. In line with his credo of self-dependence, Gujaratis consistently rank at or near the top of the chart in terms of India's economic output, and have fanned around the world to settle abroad.

The region's **prosperity** dates as far back as the third millennium BC, when the Harappans started trading shell jewellery and textiles. The latter, Jain-dominated industry, remains an important source of income to the state. India's most industrialized state, Gujarat also boasts some of the Subcontinent's biggest oil refineries; thriving cement, chemicals and pharmaceutical manufacturing units; and a lucrative yet secretive ship-breaking yard at Alang. Kandla is one of west India's largest ports, while much of the country's diamond cutting and polishing takes place in Ahmedabad and Bhavnagar. Rural poverty remains a serious problem, however, and health and education developments still lag behind economic growth.

Despite Gandhi's push for political change through nonviolent means, his home state has often followed a different course, and Muslim-Hindu tensions have boiled over into violence on a number of occasions. Following the devastating **earthquake** of January 2001, centred in Kutch, Gujarat suffered India's worst **communal rioting** since Partition, with more than a thousand people killed in 2002. Six years later, dozens more died in a string of bomb attacks in Ahmedabad. All these events added to the woes of a state already beleaguered by severe **water shortages** and **drought**. The current scene is less fraught, and Gujarat – and Bhuj in particular – is showing signs of **renewal**; take the splendid new Shree Swaminarayan temple in Bhuj as an example.

Given this, Gujarat has plenty to offer those who take time to detour from its more famous northerly neighbour, Rajasthan. The lure of important **temple cities**, **forts** and **palaces** is balanced by the chance to search out unique **crafts** made in communities whose way of life remains scarcely affected by global trends. Gujarat's **architectural diversity** reflects the influences of its many different rulers – Buddhist Mauryans, Hindu rajas and Muslim emperors.

BEST TIME TO VISIT

The best months to visit Gujarat, climate-wise, are between November and February when the temperature stays a comfortable 17–27°C. Summers (April to May) are dry, sunny and very hot, with temperatures reaching around 41°C in the day and 30°C at night. Monsoon season (July–Sept) keeps temperatures lower, around 30°C, although some areas, like Saurashtra and Kutch, don't actually receive much rain.

AN ASIATIC LIONESS AND HER CUB

Highlights

❶ Ahmedabad Superb Indo-Islamic architecture, bustling bazars and Mahatma Gandhi's Sabarmati Ashram. See page 556

❷ Sun Temple, Modhera This beautiful eleventh-century temple is the finest example of Solanki architecture in the country. See page 566

❸ Kutch Distinct from the rest of Gujarat: traditional embroidery, costume and culture still thrive in this harsh and remote landscape. See page 567

❹ Dwarka Krishna's ancient capital and India's westernmost holy town is always abuzz with pilgrims. See page 581

❺ Gir National Park The last remaining habitat of the rare Asiatic lion and home to a host of other animals. See page 589

❻ Diu West India's most congenial beach venue, this relaxed island has a Portuguese flavour in its colonial architecture. See page 591

❼ Palitana temples Hundreds of sumptuously carved Jain shrines and stunning views from the top of Shatrunjaya Hill. See page 597

❽ Champaner and Pavagadh A Solanki fortress guarding a lost Muslim city and a sacred hill dotted with Hindu and Jain temples. See page 601

HIGHLIGHTS ARE MARKED ON THE MAP ON PAGE 552

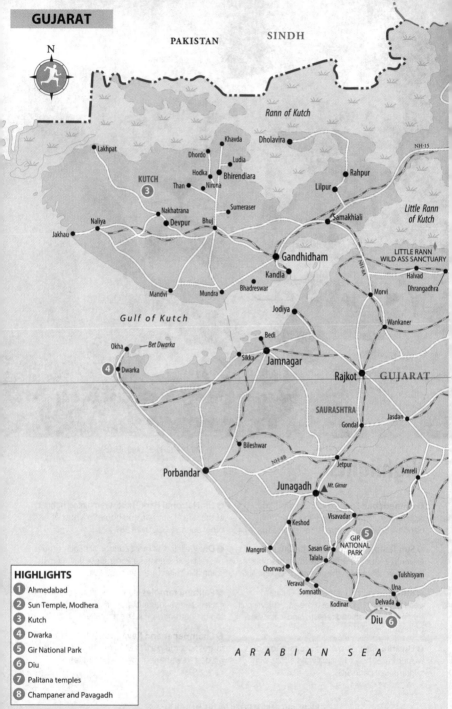

GUJARAT

PAKISTAN   SINDH

N

Rann of Kutch

Lakhpat

Khavda   Dholavira

Dhordo   NH-15

KUTCH   Ludia   Rahpur

Hodka   Bhirendiara

Than   Nirona   Lilpur

Nakhatrana   Sumeraser   Samakhiali

Naliya   Devpur   Bhuj   Little Rann
of Kutch

Jakhau   LITTLE RANN
WILD ASS SANCTUARY

Gandhidham   Halvad

Kandla   Morvi   Dhrangadhra

Mandvi   Mundra   Bhadreswar   Wankaner

Jodiya

Gulf of Kutch   Bedi

Okha   — Bet Dwarka —   Sikka   Jamnagar

Dwarka   Rajkot   GUJARAT

SAURASHTRA

Gondal   Jasdan

Bileshwar

Porbandar   NH-8B   Jetpur   Amreli

Junagadh   Mt. Girnar

Visavadar

Keshod   GIR
NATIONAL
PARK

Mangroi   Sasan Gir   Tulshisyam

Chorwad   Talala   Una

Veraval   Delvada

Somnath   Diu

Kodinar

A R A B I A N   S E A

HIGHLIGHTS

1 Ahmedabad
2 Sun Temple, Modhera
3 Kutch
4 Dwarka
5 Gir National Park
6 Diu
7 Palitana temples
8 Champaner and Pavagadh

The International boundaries on this map are neither purported to be correct nor authentic by Survey of India directives. Publisher.

9

Ahmedabad, state capital until 1970 and the obvious place to begin a tour, harbours the first mosques built in the curious **Indo-Islamic** style, along with richly carved temples and step-wells dating from the eleventh century. Just north is the ancient capital of **Patan** and the Solanki sun temple at **Modhera**, while south is the Harappan site, **Lothal**, home of the world's oldest-known dock. In the northwest, the barren region of **Kutch** was largely bypassed by Gujarat's foreign invaders, and consequently preserves a village culture where crafts long forgotten elsewhere are still practised.

The Kathiawar Peninsula, or **Saurashtra**, is Gujarat's heartland, scattered with temples, mosques and palaces bearing testimony to centuries of rule by Buddhists, Hindus and Muslims. Highlights include the superb Jain temples adorning the hills of **Shatrunjaya**, near Bhavnagar, and **Mount Girnar**, close to Junagadh. The temple at **Somnath** is said to have witnessed the dawn of time, and that at **Dwarka** is built on the site of Krishna's ancient capital. At **Junagadh**, ancient Ashokan inscriptions stand a stone's throw from flamboyant mausoleums and Victorian Gothic-style palaces. There's plenty of scope for spotting **wildlife**, too, including Asia's only lions, found in **Gir National Park**, blackbucks at **Velavadar National Park** and the Indian wild ass in the **Little Rann Sanctuary**. Separated from the south coast by a thin sliver of the Arabian Sea, the island of **Diu**, a Union Territory and not officially part of the state, is fringed with beaches, palm groves, whitewashed Portuguese churches – and, unlike the rest of the region (see box above), bars.

Brief history

The first known settlers in what is now Gujarat were the **Harappans**, who arrived from Sindh and Punjab around 2500 BC. Despite their craftsmanship and trade links with Africans, Arabs, Persians and Europeans, the civilization fell into decline in 1900 BC, largely due to severe flooding. From 1500 to 500 BC, little is known about the history of Gujarat but it is popularly believed the **Yadavas**, Krishna's clan, held sway over much of the state, with their capital at Dwarka. Gujarat's political history begins in earnest with the powerful **Mauryan** empire, established by Chandragupta with its capital at Junagadh and reaching its peak under Ashoka. After his death in 226 BC, Mauryan power dwindled; the last significant ruler was Samprati, Ashoka's grandson, a Jain who built fabulous temples at *tirthas* (pilgrimage sites) such as Girnar and Palitana. Rule then passed among a succession of warring dynasties and nomadic tribes throughout the first millennium AD, among them the native Gurjars (or Gujjar), from whom the modern state would derive its name.

A golden age

In the eleventh and twelfth centuries, Gujarat came under the sway of the **Solanki** (or **Chalukyan**) dynasty, originating from a Gurjar clan, which ushered in a golden era in the state's architectural history. The Solankis built and rebuilt (following the devastating raid of Mahmud of Ghazni in 1027) splendid Hindu and Jain **temples** and **step-wells** throughout the state.

Foreign conquests

Muslim rule in Gujarat was established by the Khalji conquest in 1299. A century later, the **Sultanate of Gujarat** was founded when Muzaffar Shah declared independence from Delhi. Setting up a new capital at Ahmedabad, the Muzaffarid dynasty ruled for two hundred years before the Mughal conquest of Emperor Akbar in the sixteenth century. In the ensuing period, Muslim, Jain and Hindu styles were melded to produce remarkable **Indo-Islamic** mosques and tombs.

In the 1500s, the **Portuguese**, already settled in Goa, turned their attention to Gujarat. Having captured Daman in 1531, they took Diu four years later, building forts and typically European towns. The **British East India Company** set up its headquarters in Surat in 1613, sowing the seeds of a prospering textile industry. British sovereignty over the state was established in 1818 when governors general signed treaties with about two hundred of Saurashtra's princely and petty states. The introduction of machinery upgraded textile manufacture, bringing substantial wealth to the region while putting many manual labourers out of business. Their cause was valiantly fought by Gujarat-born **Mahatma Gandhi** (see page 584), who led the momentous Salt March from Ahmedabad to Dandi. After Partition, Gujarat received an influx of Hindus from Sindh (Pakistan) and witnessed terrible sectarian fighting as Muslims fled to their new homeland.

The birth of modern Gujarat

In 1960, after the Marathi and Gujarati **language riots** (demonstrators sought the redrawing of state boundaries according to language, as had happened in the south), Bombay state was split and Gujarat created. The Portuguese enclaves were forcibly annexed by the Indian government in 1961. After Independence, Gujarat remained a staunch Congress stronghold until the BJP took control in 1991. The communal violence of 2002 pitted Muslim and Hindu neighbours against one another (see box below), but, despite this past infighting, Gujarat remains one of India's most wealthy and prosperous states.

GODHRA AND GUJARAT'S COMMUNAL VIOLENCE

The BJP's landslide victory in the 2002 election was seen by many as a shock, but the events of that year made it much less surprising. After the brutal attack on Hindu pilgrims at **Godhra** on February 27, 2002, when 58 were killed, **riots** rampaged across Gujarat. The death count reached almost one thousand, earning Gujarat's BJP chief minister **Narendra Modi** the moniker "Muslim killer" for standing by as the violence continued. There were even allegations that the officials "were directly involved" and helped to cover up the state's involvement. PM Atal Bihari Vajpayee later apologized and announced a US$31 million rehabilitation package, but a political campaign pledging to prevent another Godhra saw Modi go on to a landslide win.

In 2004, however, following protests against biased state authorities, the Supreme Court ordered further investigation into the riots, calling for a reopening of more than two thousand dismissed cases. In 2007, *Tehelka* magazine published secretly filmed footage of senior Gujarati Hindu politicians, mainly from the BJP, describing their involvement in fanning the riots. The report alleged that Modi ordered the police to side with Hindu rioters and sheltered the perpetrators from justice. Still, he was resoundingly re-elected and his ascension has continued unhindered; on May 26, 2014, he became prime minster, gaining a majority in the Lok Sabha (the lower house of the Indian parliament) – for the first time, for any party, since 1984. The Supreme Court eventually found Modi not guilty, concluding that there was not enough evidence to convict him.

Modi may appear untouchable for now, but others involved in these events have not been as lucky. In 2011, dozens of those guilty of the Godhra fire were convicted and sentenced, and a year later hundreds more of the rioters were convicted, including a former state minister, the first political figure to be officially implicated in the events.

9

FESTIVALS IN GUJARAT

Even the smallest of Gujarat's farming villages explodes into life during their **festivals**, which can celebrate anything from the harvest to various gods or new relationships.

Diu Festival (Dec–Feb; ⓦfestadiu.com). Music, fashion shows and even bungee jumping take place in Diu (see page 591) at Nagoa beach, the fort and an open-air theatre at Sunset Point.

Kite Festival/Uttarayan (14 Jan). The biggest of its kind in the world, this festival marks the beginning of the harvest season (Makar Sankranti) where kite-makers from more than four hundred countries descend on the Sabarmati riverfront in Ahmedabad (see below).

Suth Tera (Feb/March). A one-day event in which fifty thousand pilgrims hike up to the hilltop temple complex of Shatrunjaya (see page 597).

Tarnetar Fair (Aug/Sept). Turbans, embroidered jackets and decorative umbrellas abound at this celebration of youth in Sayla (see page 577), where tribal music and poetry set a backdrop for young men and women to meet their future spouses.

Janmashtami (Aug/Sept). Krishna's birthday is important all over Gujarat, but the "sacred abode" of Dwarka (see page 581) is one of the best places to be to witness the most vibrant celebrations.

Navratri (late Sept/early Oct). In Vadodara (see page 599), thousands of people dance through the night across ten days (*navratri* means "nine nights"), worshipping nine forms of the Hindu goddess Durga.

Ahmedabad

A tangled mass of factories, mosques, temples and skyscrapers, Gujarat's commercial hub, **AHMEDABAD** (pronounced "Amdavad"), sprawls along the banks of the River Sabarmati, about 90km from its mouth in the Bay of Cambay. With an extended population of more than 7.2 million, it is the state's largest city (and was the capital until it was moved to Gandhinagar in 1970) and India's sixth largest – and a metropolis of appalling pollution, dreadful congestion and outbreaks of communal violence.

However, its mix of medieval and modern makes Ahmedabad a compelling place to explore – a wander through the bazars of the **old city** is particularly rewarding. The city is packed with diverse architectural styles throughout, with more than fifty **mosques** and **tombs**, plus Hindu and Jain **temples** and grand **step-wells** (*vavs*). The **Calico Museum of Textiles** is one of the world's finest, while Gandhi's **Sabarmati Ashram** is a must-see for anyone with an interest in the Mahatma.

In 2002, a controversial **canal project** diverted water from the River Narmada into the Sabarmati, which previously had virtually dried up outside the monsoon. This has given the city a cooler feel, but Ahmedabad, which has been plagued by high carbon monoxide levels in the past, has a long way to go before it can breathe easily.

Brief history

When **Ahmed Shah** inherited the Sultanate of Gujarat in 1411, he moved his capital from Patan to Asawal, on the east bank of the Sabarmati, renaming it after himself. It quickly grew as artisans and traders were invited to settle, and its splendid mosques, intended to assert Muslim supremacy, heralded the new **Indo-Islamic** style of architecture. In 1572, Ahmedabad became part of the Mughal Empire and, on the back of a flourishing **textiles trade**, came to be regarded as India's most handsome city. However, two devastating famines, coupled with political instability, led the city into decline. The merchants only returned in 1817, when the newly arrived British lowered taxes. A new wave of prosperity came from the burgeoning opium trade, while the introduction of modern machinery re-established the Ahmedabad as a textile exporter. In the run-up to independence, while **Mahatma Gandhi** was revitalizing small-scale textile production, the "Manchester of the East" became an important seat of political power and a hotbed for religious tension. Nowadays, having largely stepped out of the darkness caused by violent **communal rioting**, Ahmedabad remains a booming economic powerhouse.

The old city

The historic heart of Ahmedabad is the **old city**, an area of about three square kilometres on the east bank of the river, dissected by the main thoroughfares of Relief Road and Mahatma Gandhi (MG) Road, and reaching its northern limits at **Delhi Gate**. It's best to start exploring in the **Lal Darwaja** area, taking in the squat buildings of the original citadel, **Bhadra**, the **mosques** and tombs of Ahmedabad's Muslim rulers, as well as vibrant bazars and pols – labyrinths of high wooden havelis and narrow cul-de-sacs.

Lal Darwaja and around

The solid fortified citadel, **Bhadra Fort**, built of deep red stone in 1411 as Ahmedabad's first Muslim structure, is relatively plain in comparison to the city's later mosques. The palace is now occupied by offices and most of it is off-limits (some of it, at the time of writing in early 2019, due to renovation work), but you can climb to the roof via a winding staircase just inside the main gateway. Across from the fort to the east is **Alif Shah's Mosque**, gaily painted in green and white. Further on, beyond the odoriferous

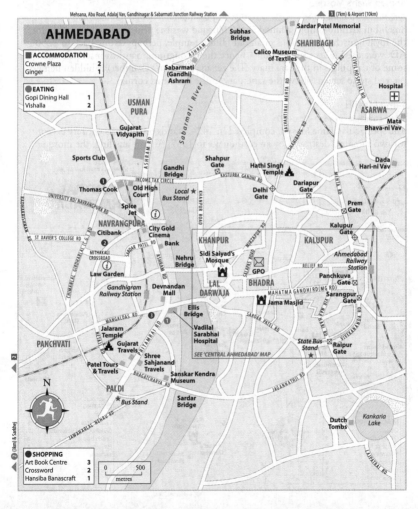

9

meat market in **Khas Bazaar**, is **Teen Darwaja**, a triple gateway built during Ahmed Shah's reign that once led to the outer court of the royal citadel. A trio of pointed arches engraved with Islamic inscriptions and detailed carving spans the busy road below.

Sidi Saiyad's Mosque

Mirzapur Rd, Lal Darwaja • Daily 6am–11pm

Famed for the ten magnificent *jali* (lattice-work) screens lining its upper walls, **Sidi Saiyad's Mosque** sits in the centre of a busy roundabout. Built in 1573, the two semicircular screens on the western wall are its most spectacular, with floral designs exquisitely carved out of the yellow stone. The stonework within depicts heroes and animals from popular Hindu myths – one example of Hindu and Jain craftsmanship influencing an Islamic tradition that rarely allowed the depiction of living beings in its mosques. Women cannot enter this mosque, but the gardens around it afford good views of the screens.

Ahmed Shah's Mosque

Jijabai Marg, west of Bhadra Fort, across from Victoria Gardens • Daily 5am–11pm

Small but artfully simple, **Ahmed Shah's Mosque** was the private place of worship for the royal household. Sections of an old Hindu temple, perhaps dating back to 1250 AD, were used in its construction – hence the incongruous Sanskrit inscriptions on some of the pillars in the sanctuary. The zenana (women's chamber) is hidden behind pierced stone screens above the sanctuary in the northeast corner.

Jama Masjid

Mahatma Gandhi Rd • Daily 6am–10pm • ₹100

The spectacular **Jama Masjid**, completed in 1424, stands today in its entirety except for two minarets destroyed by an earthquake in 1957. Always bustling, the mosque

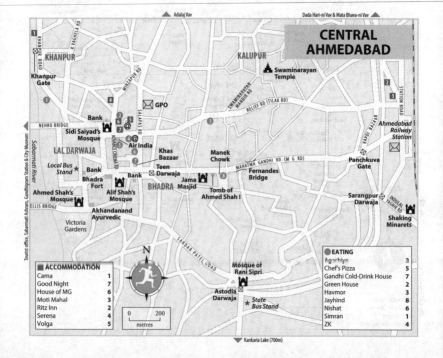

SEWA

Almost ninety percent of women who work in India are self-employed. Outside the protection of labour laws and the minimum wage, they are subject to exploitation, often by unscrupulous banks and lenders. Ahmedabad, however, has maintained a tradition of self-help since the days of Gandhi, achieving global recognition as the base of the ground-breaking **Self-Employed Women's Association**, **SEWA** (☎ 079 2550 6444, ⊚ sewa.org). Founded in the early 1970s, SEWA provides legal advice, training, support and childcare, and runs its own cooperative bank.

Following a major slump in the textile industry in 1984, SEWA set up training centres in weaving, sewing, dyeing and printing, providing efficient machinery. This helped to re-establish many women in the textile labour force, providing an outlet for their products. In 1987, a SEWA protest against *sati* (widow burning) and a campaign to have verbal divorce and polygamy banned in Gujarat resulted in a change in the law. SEWA also strongly opposes female foeticide, which is particularly widespread in Gujarat. With more than a million members nationwide, more than 600,000 of which are in Gujarat, the organization now tackles projects throughout India and overseas.

is busiest on Fridays ("Jama Masjid" literally translates as "Friday Mosque"), when thousands converge to worship. The 260 elegant pillars supporting the roof of the domed prayer hall (*qibla*) are covered with unmistakeably Hindu carvings, while close to the sanctuary's principal arch a large black slab is said to be the base of a Jain idol inverted and buried as a sign of Muslim supremacy.

Immediately outside the east entrance of the mosque, the square **Tomb of Ahmed Shah I**, who died in 1442, stands surrounded by pillared verandas. Women are not permitted to enter the central chamber, the site of his grave, or those of his son and grandson.

Manek Chowk
Manek Chowk Rd, east of Jama Masjid

The jewellery and textile market of **Manek Chowk** is filled with craftsmen working in narrow alleys amid newly dyed and tailored cloth. Further into the market, to the east, and surrounded by the dyers' colourful stalls, is the mausoleum of Ahmed Shah's queen, **Rani-ka-Hazira**. Its plan is identical to Shah's own tomb (see above), with pillared verandas clearly inspired by Hindu architectural tastes.

Mosque of Rani Sipri
Swami Vivekananda Rd, near Astodia Darwaja • Daily 5am–8pm

The small, elegant **mosque of Rani Sipri** was commissioned in 1514 at the queen's orders, when her husband ordered the execution of their son for reasons not fully understood. Her **grave** now also lies in front, sheltered by a pillared mausoleum. The stylish mosque, also known as Masjid-e-Nagira ("Jewel of a Mosque") shows more Hindu influence than any other in Ahmedabad: its pillared sanctuary has an open facade to the east and fine tracery work on the west wall.

Swaminarayan Temple
Swaminarayan Mandir Rd, Kalupur • Daily 6am–7pm • ☎ 079 2213 2170, ⊚ swaminarayan.in

The brightly coloured **Swaminarayan Temple** presents a delicate contrast to the many hard-stone mosques in the city. Both the temple and the houses in the courtyard surrounding it are of finely carved wood, with elaborate and intricate patterns typical of the havelis of north and west Gujarat. The temple's main sanctuary is given over to Vishnu and his consort Lakshmi.

Shaking minarets
Indulal Yagnik Rd, near Sarangpur Darwaja • Daily 8am–6pm

9

The **minarets** are all that remain of the **Sidi Bashir mosque**, built in 1452, which was named after one of Ahmed Shah's favourite slaves. More than 21m high, these are the best existing example of "**shaking minarets**" – built on a foundation of flexible sandstone, probably to protect them from earthquake damage – once a common sight on Ahmedabad's skyline, and now useful protection against the vibration of nearby trains.

Hathi Singh Temple

Shahibaug Rd, north of Delhi Gate • Daily 8am–1pm & 4–8pm

The Jain **Hathi Singh Temple** is easily distinguished by its high, finely carved columns. Built entirely of white marble embossed with smooth carvings of dancers, musicians, animals and flowers, this serene temple is dedicated to Dharamnath, the fifteenth *tirthankara*, or "ford-maker", one of 24 great teachers sanctified by the Jains.

Calico Museum of Textiles

In the Sarabhai Foundation, The Retreat, opposite Shahibagh Underbridge • Compulsory tours (2hr) Thurs–Tues 10.30am & 12.30pm; book in advance as they are each open to twenty people only and fill up quickly • Free • ☎ 079 2286 8172, ⊛ calicomuseum.org • Bus #102 or #105 from Lal Darwaja bus stand; an auto-rickshaw costs ₹100

The **Calico Museum of Textiles** displays India's finest collection of textiles, clothes, furniture and crafts. Highlights of the **morning tour** include exquisite pieces made for the British and Portuguese, an embroidered tent and Shah Jahan's robes from India's royal households. There are *patola* saris from Patan (see page 566) and extravagant *zari* work that gilds saris in heavy gold stitching, bringing their weight to nearly nine kilos. Other galleries are dedicated to embroideries, *bandhani* tie-and-dye, textiles made for overseas trade and woollen shawls from Kashmir and Chamba. The **afternoon tour** includes the galleries of *pichwais* and other temple paintings and decorations, including Jain statues housed in a replica haveli temple and centuries-old manuscripts and mandalas painted on palm leaves.

Dada Hari-ni Vav and around

Haripura, Asarwa, opposite railway yard, northeast Ahmedabad • Daily 8am–6pm • Free • Auto-rickshaw from Lal Darwaja ₹150

Northern Gujarat abounds with remarkable **step-wells** – deep, with elaborately carved walls and broad flights of covered steps leading to a shaft – but **Dada Hari-ni Vav**, just outside the city's old northeast boundaries, is among the finest. While it's a Muslim construction, built in 1500, the craftsmen were Hindu, and their influence is clear in the lavish and sensuous carvings on the walls and pillars. Visit around 11am when the sculpted floral patterns and shapely figurines inside are bathed in sunlight.

Bai Harir's lofty mosque and lattice-walled tomb stand just west of the well, while a couple of hundred metres north of the complex is the neglected **Mata Bhava-ni Vav**, constructed in the eleventh century, before Ahmedabad was founded. It's profoundly Hindu in character, and dedicated to Bhavani, an aspect of Shiva's consort Parvati.

Sanskar Kendra Museum

Bhagatcharya Rd • Tues–Sun 10am–6pm • Free; no photos • ☎ 079 2657 8369 • Bus #33 or #34 from Lal Darwaja bus stand to Sardar Patel Bridge; auto-rickshaw costs ₹120

The **Sanskar Kendra Museum** is worth a visit, covering subjects such as the history of the city, urban growth, sociological development and the activities of Gandhi and the freedom movement. The **Patang Kite Museum** (same hours) in the basement showcases the city's Kite Festival – the world's largest (see page 556).

Sabarmati (Gandhi) Ashram

Ashram Rd • Daily 8.30am–6.30pm • ☎ 079 2755 7277, ⊛ gandhiashramsabarmati.org • Buses #13/1 and #83 connect the ashram to Lal Darwaja

The **Sabarmati (Gandhi) Ashram** is where the Mahatma lived from 1917 until 1930, holding meetings with weavers and Harijans as he helped them find security and

RECOMMENDED TRAINS FROM AHMEDABAD

The services listed below are the most convenient and/or fastest trains from Ahmedabad. All run daily.

Destination	Name	No.	Departs	Arrives
Bhavnagar	*Bhavnagar Express*	12971	5.15am	10.35am
Bhuj	*Sayaji Nagari Express or Dadar Bhuj Express*	19115	11.59pm	7.00+
Delhi	*Swarna J Raj Express*	12957	5.40pm	7.30am+
Dwarka	*Saurashtra Mail*	22945	5.35 am	2.41pm
Jamnagar	*Saurashtra Mail*	22945	5.35am	1138 am
Jodhpur	*Ranakpur Express*	14708	1155 pm	9.45am
Mumbai	*Shatabdi Express*	12010	2.40pm	9.20pm
	Gujarat Mail	12902	10pm	6.25am+
Porbandar	*Saurashtra Express*	19015	7 45 am	5.35am+
Udaipur	*Udaipur City Express*	19944	11.00	9.20am+

+ = next day

re-establish the manual textile industry in Ahmedabad. In keeping with the man's uncluttered lifestyle, the collection of his personal property is modest but poignant – wooden shoes, white seamless clothes and a pair of round spectacles. The ashram itself is no longer operational , but many people come here simply to sit and meditate.

ARRIVAL AND DEPARTURE   AHMEDABAD

BY PLANE
Sardar Vallabhbhai Patel International Airport The airport (☏079 2286 9211),Wahmedabadairport.com 10km north of Ahmedabad, is connected to the centre by prepaid taxis (₹550–700), auto-rickshaws (around ₹200–300) and bus #106 (hourly 7am––10pm; ₹20), which terminates at the local (Lal Darwaja) bus stand in the west of the old city. Free liquor permits can be obtained from the domestic terminal (☏079 2286 0631), from a counter across from the luggage belt (daily 8am–10pm).

Airlines Air India and SpiceJet have offices in the terminal, as well as in town, near Sidi Saiyad's Mosque (☏079 2658 5622) and near Old High Court respectively (☏079 2285 8022). IndiGo also has an office in the airport (☏012 4661 3838).

Destinations Bengaluru (4 daily; 2hr 5min); Delhi (17 daily; 1hr 30min); Jaipur (1 daily; 1hr 5min); Kolkata (3 daily; 2hr 30min); Mumbai (24 daily; 1hr 15min).

BY TRAIN
Ahmedabad is on the Delhi–Mumbai train line, and serves as the jumping-off point for most destinations within Gujarat.

Railway stations The main railway station, Ahmedabad Junction (known locally as Kalupur station), is on Station Rd, a 2km walk (or ₹100 auto-rickshaw ride) from Lal Darwaja; the less-used Gandhigram station, for destinations in Saurashtra, is on the west side of the river, just off Ashram Rd; and a few north- or southbound services also stop at Sabarmati Junction railway station, just northwest of the Sabarmati River. There are reservation centres (Mon–Sat 8am–8pm, Sun 8am–2pm) at all stations.

BY BUS
Bus stands The state bus stand is in the southeast of the old city, on Gita Mandir Rd (☏079 25463409) by Astodia Gate. Reservation centres are located on platforms 1 and 5 (daily 7am–2pm, 2.30–7.30pm & 8–9.45pm). From here, government buses link the entire state and beyond, while a/c "Volvo" buses, operated jointly by the Gujarat State Road Transport Corporation (GSRTC; ☏079 2270 3083, ⓦgsrtc. in) and various private companies, link Rajkot, Vadodara and Bhuj. Numerous private bus agencies near the station and on Paldi Rd, west of Sardar Bridge, offer services throughout the state and into Rajasthan, Maharashtra or Madhya Pradesh.

Agencies Some of the most useful agencies are on Paldi Rd, among them Patel Tours & Travels (☏099 2524 4252, ⓦpateltoursandtravels.com), which has buses to Bhuj (12 daily; 7–8hr), and Gujarat Travels (☏94285 21105, ⓦgujarattravels.co.in) to Mount Abu in Rajasthan (5 daily; 4–6hr). Shree Sahjanand Travels on Satellite Rd (☏079 2657 5988 or T9828 01354, ⓦshreesahjanandtravels.com) serves Diu (1 nightly at 11pm; 9hr) and Mumbai (3 nightly; 10–11hr).

Destinations Bhavnagar (hourly; 4–5hr); Bhuj (20 daily; 7–8hr); Dhrangadhra (every 30min; 3hr); Dwarka (7 daily; 11hr); Gandhinagar (every 45min; 1hr); Jamnagar (12 daily;

9

7hr); Jodhpur (4 daily; 11–13hr); Mehsana (every 30min; 2hr); Mumbai (2 daily; 10hr); Palitana (10 daily; 5–6hr); Rajkot (every 30min; 4hr 30min); Udaipur (12 daily; 10–7hr); Vadodara (every 15min; 2hr).

GETTING AROUND

By bus Ahmedabad AMTS (Ahmedabad Municipal Transport Service; Ⓦamts.co.in) is useful for getting around the city, connecting all parts of town with Lal Darwaja's local bus stand. In addition, Ahmedabad's much-heralded BRTS (Bus Rapid Transit System; Ⓦahmedabadbrts.org), also known as Janmarg, beats the traffic with exclusive lanes and median bus stations.

INFORMATION AND TOURS

Tourist information The helpful tourist office is in HK House, just off Ashram Rd, on the west side of the river (Mon–Sat 10.30am–1.30pm & 2–6pm, closed 2nd & 4th Sat of month; ☎079 2658 9172, or ☎079 2657 8046 Ⓦgujarattourism.com); the attached travel service can book airline tickets and arrange tours.

Tours The Ahmedabad Municipal Corporation (AMC; ☎079 2539 1811, Ⓦahmedabadcity.gov.in) runs non-a/c city bus tours (daily 9am–1pm & 2–5pm; ₹100; ☎079 2550 7739) from platform D of the Lal Darwaja bus stand. Gujarat Tourism, partnered with Pinks Travels, runs a/c city bus tours (daily 12pm–8 pm; ₹430 ☎98250 13563) from the City Civic Centre, opposite the GLS School in the Law Garden, as well as full-day bus tours that take in more than a dozen Hindu and Jain temples (Sun 8am–8pm; ₹300) starting from Jalaram Temple. The *House of MG* hotel (☎079 2550 6946, Ⓦhouseofmg.com) run two heritage walks, one in the morning and one in the evening, both starting at the hotel (daily 7.30–10.30am and 9.30–11pm; call in advance to reserve; rates are ₹413 and ₹295 each respectively). There are other walking tours from Swaminarayan Temple to Jama Masjid as well.

ACCOMMODATION

LAL DARWAJA

Cama Khanpur Rd ☎079 2560 1234, Ⓦcamahotels india.com; map p.558. Large, brightly coloured rooms with baths and carpets, overlooking the Sabarmati. The businessperson clientele is reflected in the 9am checkout time, but the manicured garden, pool, two restaurants, gym, liquor shop (noon–7pm) and 24hr coffee shop make it worthwhile. Breakfast included. **₹4000**

Good Night Opposite Sidi Saiyad's Mosque, Mirzapur Rd ☎079 2550 6997, Ⓦhotelgoodnight.co.in; map p.558. Neat and tidy rooms with private white-tiled bathrooms and TVs; some have a/c. Breakfast included. **₹1800**

★ **House of MG** Opposite Sidi Saiyad's Mosque, Mirzapur Rd ☎079 2550 6946 Ⓦhouseofmg.com; map p.558. This 1920s heritage hotel has spacious, individually decorated rooms fitted with flatscreen TVs, most with four-poster beds. The private courtyards have period furniture and old photos lining the walls, while playful touches like popcorn makers are found in each suite (₹11,000). Two excellent restaurants and an indoor pool complete the package. The hotel also organizes excellent walking tours (see above). **₹8550**

Serena Mirzapur Rd ☎079 2551 0137 or 98250 58906; map p.558. Beyond the unprepossessing exterior are reasonable attached rooms with slightly grubby bathrooms and 24hr checkout; the more expensive have a/c and extra space. A decent budget fall-back option if *Volga* and *Good Night* are full. **₹1350**

Volga Near Ankelsharia Hospital off Relief Rd ☎079 2550 9497, Ⓦhotelvolga.in; map p.558. Friendly service and spotless pastel-shaded attached rooms, each with TV, phone and 24hr checkout; some of the cheaper rooms are a bit stuffy with only internal windows. As quiet as it gets in Lal Darwaja. **₹1400**

AROUND THE RAILWAY STATION

Moti Mahal Kalupur Rd ☎079 2212 1881, Ⓦhotel motimahal.com; map p.558. Very well-kept, clean hotel offering identikit rooms with attached bathrooms and TVs. There's a decent a/c restaurant, too. **₹1350**

Ritz Inn Kalupur Rd ☎079 22123842, Ⓦhotelritzinn. com; map p.558. A three-star establishment with classy Art Deco flourishes and smart service. The charming rooms have black-and-white bathrooms, TVs and writing desks; prices include station transfers. Breakfast included. **₹3500**

OUTSIDE THE CITY CENTRE

Crowne Plaza SG Rd ☎0796 7779000 Ⓦihg.com; map p.557. Service and standards are as high as you'd expect from this international chain, with an excellent restaurant and fantastic breakfast spread included in the rates, outdoor pool, steam room, sauna, Jacuzzi and gym. **₹8400**

Ginger Drive-In Rd, behind Himalaya Mall, 7km north of the centre ☎079 6666 3333, Ⓦgingerhotels.com; map p.557. This slick branch of Tata's chain of stylized hotels is the most useful for the airport, with pared-down a/c attached rooms with coffee makers, fridges and "self check-in". Breakfast included. **₹4300**

EATING

Ahmedabad's most popular **restaurants** are clustered around Relief Rd, Salapose Rd and Badhra; great snack stalls line Khas Bazaar. If you are making only a brief stop in Gujarat, be sure to sample the state's delicious thali.

★ **Agashiye** House of MG, opposite Sidi Saiyad's Mosque, Mirzapur Rd ☎ 079 2550 6946, ⓦ houseofmg. com; map p.558. One of the state's finest restaurants, with a roof terrace, cushions to sit on and an open kitchen: prices are steep (regular thali ₹1200), but the mouth-watering Gujarati thalis are as good as they get. A series of recipe books is on sale, and cookery classes are in the pipeline. Daily noon–3.30pm & 7–10.30pm.

Chef's Pizza Opposite Cadillac hotel, Advance Cinema Rd ☎ 079 7373 9900 or 9173739900 map p.558. The deep-pan pizzas (₹130–300 for a regular) are surprisingly good at this tiny, clean and friendly fast-food joint that's popular among a younger crowd. Also serves burgers, sandwiches and wraps. Daily 11am–11pm.

Gandhi Cold-Drink House Khas Bazaar ☎ 079 2550 7555; map p.558. Friendly, hole-in-the-wall place with plastic chairs out front and a range of refreshing milk and ice cream concoctions (around ₹50), including an Indonesian-style "Royal Faluda",(₹60) unique to Ahmedabad, and a butterscotch lassi (₹40). Daily 10am–11pm.

Gopi Dining Hall Pritamrai Rd, west side of Ellis Bridge ☎ 079 2657 6388 or 9879514277; map p.557. Named by *Newsweek* as one of the 101 Best Places to Eat Around the World in 2012, *Gopi* is a welcoming all-veg place offering generous Gujarati and Kathiawadi thalis with unbeatable prices (₹250–330) and top service. It's very popular, so reserve ahead or be prepared to wait in line. Daily 10.30am–3pm & 6.30–10.00pm.

Green House House of MG, opposite Sidi Saiyad's Mosque, Mirzapur Rd ☎ 079 2550 6946, ⓦ houseofmg. com; map p.558. Cheaper than *Agashiye* (mains from ₹190), and almost as appealing: sit on wooden benches under an ivy-covered pavilion and tuck into snacks, light meals and sorbets, frozen yogurts, ice creams and lassis: try the saffron or rose flavours (₹230). Daily breakfast specials are also fantastic (₹630). Daily 7am–11pm.

Havmor Near Rupam Cinema, Relief Rd ☎ 079 2535 7373, ⓦ havmor.com; map p.558. On one of Ahmedabad's most fume-choked streets, this tidy white-tiled branch of Gujarat's most famous ice-cream company (now one of many in the city) was founded here in 1944 and has spread as far as Punjab and even Pune. It serves South Indian dishes (masala dosa ₹120), fast food (pizza ₹95–180) and lots of ice cream (from ₹70). Daily 11.30am–11pm.

Jayhind Manek Chowk ☎ 079 2214 0714; ⓦ jayhind sweets.com; map p.558. One of the best places to sample Ahmedabad's famous sweets, *Jayhind* has sold wonderful dry-fruit halwa, *ghari* and *mithai* by the kilo, as well as *kaju pista* roll since 1948. See website for sweets and up-to-date rates Daily 8am–8.30pm.

Nishat Khas Bazaar ☎ 079 2550 7335; map p.558. With its huge flashing neon sign, this a/c restaurant is hard to miss. Its mutton *kadai* (₹200) and chicken tikka masala (₹230) are excellent. A cheaper, non-a/c restaurant with the same name is just up the street, serving chicken tikka masala for ₹150, which is just as popular with the locals. Daily 10am–11pm.

Simran FG Tower, Khanpur Rd ☎ 099 2575 8786 or 079255 11002; map p.558. Handy for the big hotels nearby, this a/c restaurant has cosy booths, an old fish tank, and curtains blocking out the bustle of Khanpur Rd; good choices include *tawa jhinga* (prawn curry; ₹190), mutton kebabs (₹280), chicken "lolli-pops" (₹220) and fish curry (₹210). Daily 11.30am–11pm.

★ **Vishalla** Narol Sarkhej Rd, 7km southwest of city centre ☎ 079 2660 2422, ⓦ vishalla.com; map p.557. This fabulous open-air restaurant serves generous portions of pure-veg Gujarati cuisine in a charming village setting, complete with floor seating under thatched-roof huts and a variety of cultural performances. The set lunches (₹560) and dinners (₹690) are served on banana leaves. Don't miss the attached utensil museum (Tues–Sun 3–10pm; ₹100 [₹30]; ⓦ vechaar.com). It's well worth the trip to get here: from Lal Darwaja, take bus #35 or an auto-rickshaw (₹170 return). Tues–Sun 3–10pm.

ZK Relief Rd, opposite Relief Cinema ☎ 079 2550 6121; map p.558. A dimly lit restaurant with a pink-and-maroon colour scheme and an ancient fish tank. Trawling through the exhaustive menu – there's well over two hundred dishes – certainly builds up an appetite: the tandoori items (₹165–290) are particularly good. Daily 11am–11pm.

SHOPPING

You can pick up a selection of clothes and accessories, including saris, shoes and wallets in the lanes of **Lal Darwaja**, while the narrow alleys around **Manek Chowk** are good for fresh vegetables and sweets – and fun to wander around merely to soak up the atmosphere. In the evening, head to the **Law Garden** on the west bank of the river for *cholis* (blouses) and wall hangings.

Art Book Centre Just off Mangaldas Rd, 350m east of Ellis Bridge ☎ 079 2658 2130, ⓦ artbookcenter.net; map p.557. Huge range of books, mainly about arts and architecture of India and beyond, with good prices and friendly staff. Daily 10am–6pm.

Crossword Shri Krishna Complex, near the Mithakali crossroad ☎ 079 2646 8031, ⓦ crossword.in; map p.557. Great selection of books including bestsellers and new titles, plus magazines and DVDs. Daily 10.30am–9pm.

9

Hansiba Banascraft Chandan Complex, CG Rd; T079 2640 5784 map p.557. Official outlet selling handicrafts from the Self-Employed Women's Association (see page 559). Mon–Sat 11am–9pm, Sun 11.30am–7pm.

DIRECTORY

Banks and exchange Foreign exchange is available at, among many other places, the Bank of India on MG Rd, the Central Bank of India opposite Sidi Sayyid's Mosque and the State Bank of India opposite Lal Darwaja bus station (all Mon–Fri 11am–3pm, Sat 11am–1pm); Thomas Cook and CITIBank have branches on Chimanlal Girdharlal Rd.
Cinemas City Gold Cinema (☏ 079 2658 7780 or 079 6605 8392), near the tourist office on Ashram Rd, screens English and Hindi films (tickets ₹250).
Hospitals Vadilal Sarabhai Hospital, Ellis Bridge (☏ 079 2657 7621), is a large government hospital; for traditional treatments, try Akhandanand Ayurvedic, just off Swami Vivekananda Rd (Mon–Sat 8.30am–7.30pm; ☏ 079 2550 7796).
Post office The GPO is on Salapas Rd (Mon–Sat 10am–7.30pm).

Around Ahmedabad

The most obvious day-trips from Ahmedabad are north to **Adalaj**, with its impressive step-well, and beyond to **Gandhinagar**, with its extraordinary Swaminarayan religious complex. South of town, the lake, pavilions and mausoleums of **Sarkhej** make a pleasant break from the crowded city, while further south is the ancient Harappan site at **Lothal**.

Adalaj Vav

19km north of Ahmedabad • Daily 8am–6pm • ₹150 • Connected by frequent buses between Ahmedabad and Gandhinagar; Adalaj village is 1km from the bus stop

One of Gujarat's most spectacular step-wells, **Adalaj Vav** stands in large, well-kept gardens. The monument, built in 1498 and now out of use, is best seen around noon, when sunlight penetrates to the bottom of the five-storey octagonal well-shaft. Steps lead down to the cool depths through a series of platforms raised on pillars. Alive with exquisite sculptures, the walls, pillars, cornices and niches portray erotica, dancing maidens, musicians and animals.

Gandhinagar

The second state capital after Chandigarh to be built from scratch since Independence, uninspiring **GANDHINAGAR** is laid out in thirty residential sectors in an ordered style influenced by the architect **Le Corbusier**. There's little to warrant spending much time here, unless you wish to visit the headquarters of the Swaminarayan sect, **Akshardham**. Just like the version in Delhi, this Hindu revivalist movement promotes Vedic ideals pronounced by Lord Swaminarayan (1781–1830) in what feels rather like a theme park devoted to religion.

Swaminarayan complex

J Rd, Sector 20, west side of Gandhinagar near the Sabarmati • Tues–Sun: park 9.30am–7.30pm; exhibitions 10am–6pm; rides noon–8pm • Free, no cameras or video allowed; audio animatronic shows ₹200 • ☏ 079 2326 0001, ⊕ akshardham.com/gujarat

The Akshardham may advocate simplicity and poverty, but the colossal **Swaminarayan complex** is hugely extravagant. Built of six thousand tonnes of pink sandstone, it houses the gold-leafed statues of Swaminarayan and two other prominent gurus. The rest of the complex is a veritable, if surreal, **theme park**, with a Hall of Holy Relics containing possessions of Swaminarayan and state-of-the-art audio visual shows. On September 24, 2002, 33 people were killed and 72 injured here by Pakistani suicide terrorists. Links were quickly made between the attack and the post-Godhra rioting (see page 555). Today, the only evidence of the **massacre** is the security presence at the entrance.

ARRIVAL AND DEPARTURE

GANDHINAGAR

By bus Buses connect Gandhinagar's ST bus stand (in Sector 11 in the city's centre) with Ahmedabad's ST bus stand (6 daily; 1hr 30min).

By train The station is in Sector 13C /14, about 2km north

of the centre (auto-rickshaw ₹80).
Destinations Ahmedabad (4 daily; 1hr 15min); Gandhinagar Cap (4 daily; 1hr 15min).

ACCOMMODATION AND EATING

Fortune Inn Haveli Plot No 235, Sector 11 ☏ 012 4417 1717, ⓦ fortunehotels.in. Business-oriented, comfortable hotel with modern wood-finished rooms. The hotel's multi-cuisine restaurant, *Orchid*, has a good breakfast buffet, and there is also a gym, wine shop, snooker table, steam room and sauna. Breakfast included. **₹7000**

7WondersHotel Ugati Corporate Park Kudasan ☏ 968 7957 777 ⓦ 7wondershotel.com
A boutique hotel with a restaurant and rooftop bar (not licenced), this three-star property offers deluxe and premium rooms, with breakfast included. **₹4000**

Sarkhej

10km southwest of Ahmedabad • Daily 6am–10pm • Bus #31, #31 Shuttle or #31/3 from Lal Darwaja (45min)

Sarkhej holds a complex of beautiful monuments arranged around an artificial **lake**. On the southwest side of the lake, the square **tomb** of the revered saint Sheikh Ahmed Khattu, the spiritual mentor of Ahmed Shah, who died in 1445, is Gujarat's largest mausoleum. It was constructed by Ahmed Shah's successor, Mohammed Shah, in 1446. The later Sultan Mohammed Beghada (died 1511) added palaces, a harem, a vast lake and, eventually, his own tomb as well. Sarkhej became a retreat of Gujarati sultans and today remains a charming escape from Ahmedabad.

Lothal

80km south of Ahmedabad, near the mouth of the River Sabarmati • **Site** Daily dawn to dusk • Free • **Museum** Daily except Fri 10am–5pm • ₹50 (₹5) • Direct bus from Ahmedabad's ST bus stand (2 daily; 2hr); Ahmedabad's Gandhigram station is connected by a metre-gauge railway to Lothal-Burkhi station (2 daily; 2–3hr), 3km from the site: either walk the rest of the way or take an auto-rickshaw

Near the mouth of the River Sabarmati, by the Gulf of Cambay, is **Lothal**, one of the largest excavated **Harappan** (or Indus Valley) sites (see box below). Foundations, platforms, crumbling walls and paved floors are all that remain of the prosperous sea-trading community that dwelled here between 2400 and 1900 BC, when a flood all but destroyed the settlement. A walk around the **central mound** reveals the old roads that ran past ministers' houses and through the acropolis. The lower town comprised a bazar, workshops and residential quarters. Evidence has been found here of an even older culture, perhaps dating from the fourth millennium BC, known as the **Red Ware**

THE INDUS VALLEY CIVILIZATION

Before the Mauryans took over in the fourth century BC, India's greatest empire was the **Indus Valley Civilization**. Sophisticated settlements dating back to 2500 BC were first discovered in 1924 on the banks of the Indus in present-day Sindh (Pakistan), at **Mohenjo Daro**. Further excavations in 1946 in Punjab revealed the city of **Harappa**, from the same era. In its prime, this great society spread from the present-day borders of Iran and Afghanistan to Kashmir, Delhi and southern Gujarat. It lasted until 1900 BC, when it was destroyed by heavy floods.

A prosperous and literate society, importing raw materials from regions as far west as Egypt and trading ornaments, jewellery and cotton, it also had a remarkable, centrally controlled political system. Each town was almost identical, with complex drainage systems. **Lothal**, close to the Gulf of Cambay in southern Gujarat, was a major port. Although much about this complex society remains unknown, similarities exist between the Indus Valley Civilization and present-day India. For example, like Hindus, the Indus Valley people had a strong custom of worshipping a mother goddess, and there is evidence of phallic worship, still popular among Shaivites.

9

Culture. You can see remains from this period and from the Indus Valley Civilization in the illuminating **museum** adjacent to the site.

Northern Gujarat

North of Gandhinagar, the district of Mehsana was the Solankis' seat of government between the eleventh and thirteenth centuries. Some remains of their old capital, **Anhilawada Patan**, still stand, including the extraordinary **Rani-ki-Vav** step-well, situated just outside the modern city of Patan, home to Gujarat's last remaining *patola* weavers. The big draw here is undoubtedly the ancient Sun Temple at **Modhera**, easily reached from the crowded city of **Mehsana (Mahesana)**; it's also worth visiting the striking shrines at the Jain temple at **Taranga**.

Sun Temple at Modhera

Daily 8am–6pm • ₹200 (₹10) • Modhera is linked by road to Patan (every 30min by bus; 1hr 15min), Zainabad (4 daily; 1hr 30min), Ahmedabad (2 daily; 2–3hr) and Mehsana (every 30min; 45min – or return taxi fare around ₹600)

If you visit just one town in northern Gujarat, make it **MODHERA**, where the eleventh-century **Sun Temple** is the state's best example of Solanki temple architecture. Almost a thousand years old, the temple has survived earthquakes and Muslim iconoclasm; apart from a missing *shikhara* and slightly worn carvings, it remains largely intact. The Solanki kings were probably influenced by Jain traditions; deities and their vehicles, animals, voluptuous maidens and complex friezes adorn the sandy brown walls and pillars. Within the *mandapa*, or pillared entrance hall, twelve *adityas* set into niches in the wall portray the transformations of the sun in each month of the year. Closely associated with the sun, *adityas* are the sons of Aditi, the goddess of infinity and eternity. Modhera's sun temple is positioned so that at the equinoxes the rising sun strikes the images in the sanctuary, which at other times languishes in a dim half-light. In front of the temple, 108 shrines adorn the rim of **Surya Kund**, a 100-square-metre step-well.

Patan and around

The bustling modern town of **PATAN** was built on the ruins of the old city of **Anhilwara**, long-time capital of Gujarat. The old city served several Rajput dynasties between the eighth and the twelfth centuries before being annexed by the Mughals, and fell into decline when Ahmed Shah moved the capital to Ahmedabad in 1411. Little remains now except traces of fortifications scattered in the surrounding fields, as well as the stunning **Rani-ki-Vav**.

While modern Patan has few monuments, in the **Salvivad** area of town you can watch the complex weaving of silk **patola saris**. Once the preferred garment of queens and aristocrats, and an important export of Gujarat, the saris are now made by just one extended family, the Salvis (Salvivado, Patolawala St; ☎098 9877 5748, ⓦpatanpatola.com). They fetch anywhere from one to seven lakhs (₹100,000–700,000) and take around four to six months to produce. For smaller wallets, scarves are also available from ₹6000.

Rani-ki-Vav

2km northwest of Patan • Daily 8am–6pm • ₹200 (₹20)

Gujarat's greatest **step-well**, the **Rani-ki-Vav** (literally "the queen's step-well") was built for the Solanki queen Udaimati in 1050 and extensively restored during the 1980s, re-creating as perfectly as possible the original extravagant carving. Near the well are the remains of the **Sahastralinga Talav**, the "thousand-lingam tank" built at the turn of the twelfth century, but razed during Mughal raids. There's a modest open-air **museum** in the same complex.

ARRIVAL AND DEPARTURE PATAN

Frequent **buses** from the ST bus stand in the centre of Ahmedabad (every 30min; 3hr). Patan connect with Mehsana (every 30min; 1hr 15min) and

ACCOMMODATION AND EATING

Navjivan 46 GIDC, southeast corner of Sidhpur Circle ☎ 027 6623 1035, ⓦ hotelnavjivan.com. A no-frills hotel that has been in business for more than three decades, offering simple and clean rooms (a/c ₹900) with attached bathrooms, and a pure-veg restaurant on site. **₹750**

Tulsi Siddhapur Char Rasta, in the town centre ☎ 027 6622 5440, ⓦ hoteltulsi.in. Bright neon-green lighting makes this place easy to find at night. The decent rooms here have attached bathrooms and TVs; there are both non a/c and a/c options with some suites (₹1700). More impressive are the smart restaurant, serving good Gujarat thalis, and the *paan* parlour at the front of the building. **₹1300**

Ajitanath Temple

Taranga, 56km northeast of Mehsana • Buses from Ahmedabad (3hr 30min) and Mehsana (1hr 30min) drop you off at Timba (near Danta), from where shared jeeps (₹50) ply the remaining 8km to Taranga

Well off the tourist trail, the **hilltop temple complex** at **TARANGA** was built during the Solanki period. Its striking shrines are better preserved than the more famous sites of Mount Abu, Girnar and Shatrunjaya. The **Ajitanath Temple**, built of durable sandstone, is dedicated to the second of 24 *tirthankaras*, whose 5m statue stands just inside, his gaze remarkably calm and unmoving, even for a statue. There is little in the way of tourist facilities here, although you can get an inexpensive lunch (₹150) at one of the *dharamshala* rest houses.

Kutch

Bounded on the north and east by marshy flats and on the south and west by the Gulf of Kutch and the Arabian Sea, the province of **Kutch** (also written Kuchchh or Kachchha) is a place apart. All but isolated from neighbouring Saurashtra and Sindh (Pakistan), the arid landscape is shot through with the colours of the heavily embroidered local dress. Kutchi legends can be traced in sculptural motifs, and its strong folk tradition is still represented in popular craft, clothing and jewellery designs. Few tourists make it here, but those who do are invariably enchanted. Launching from the central city of **Bhuj** – which has now recovered following devastation in the 2001 earthquake – you can explore the region's craft villages, ancient fortresses, medieval ports and isolated monasteries. The treeless salt marshes to the north and east, the Great and Little **Ranns of Kutch**, breathtaking expanses of cracked white earth, can flood completely during a heavy monsoon, effectively turning much of the region into an inland sea from July to September. Home to the rare **wild ass**, the Ranns are also the only region in India where flamingos breed successfully. The southern district of **Aiyar Patti** supports crops of cotton, castor-oil plants, sunflowers, wheat and groundnuts. Northern Kutch, or **Banni**, by contrast, is semidesert with dry shifting sands and arid grasslands.

Brief history

Remains from the third millennium BC in eastern Kutch suggest migrating Indus Valley communities crossed the Ranns from Mohenjo Daro in modern Pakistan to Lothal in eastern Gujarat. Despite being so cut off, Kutch felt the effect of the Buddhist Mauryan Empire, later coming under the control of Greek Bactrians, the

9

KUTCHI PASTORAL GROUPS

Kutch has the most significant population of **pastoral communities** in Gujarat. Each tribe can be identified from its costume, and gains income from farming or crafts such as weaving, painting, woodcarving and dyeing.

The **Rabari**, the largest group, rear cattle, buffalo and camels; sell ghee; weave; and are known for their fine **embroidery**. Most of the men sport a white turban, white cotton trousers tight at the ankle and with baggy pleats above the knee, a white jacket (*khediyun*), and a blanket thrown over one shoulder. Rabari women dress in black pleated jackets or open-backed blouses, full black skirts and tie-dyed head cloths, and always wear heavy silver jewellery and ivory bangles around the upper arms. In **Bhujodi**, near Bhuj, the Rabari weave camel wool into blankets and shawls.

The **Bharvad** tribes infiltrated Gujarat from Vrindavan, close to Mathura in Uttar Pradesh. The men are distinguishable by the peacock, parrot and flower motifs sewn into their *khediyun*, and the women by their bright backless shirts, *kapadun*, rarely covered by veils. Mass marriages take place among the Bharvad every few years.

The wandering **Ahir** cattle-breeders, today prosperous entrepreneurs, came to Gujarat from Sindh, and settled as farmers. The men sport baggy trousers and the *khediyun*, together with a white loosely wound headcloth; the women dress like the Rabaris, with additional heavy silver nose-rings. The children's bright *topis*, or skullcaps, resemble those commonly worn in Pakistan.

The **Charans**, long-established bards of Gujarat, encompass in their clans the Maldharis, who raise prize cattle, and the leather-workers known as Meghwal. They claim descent from a celestial union between Charan and a maiden created by Parvati. The women are often worshipped by other tribes, as their connection with Parvati links them closely to the mother goddess, Ashpura, highly popular in Kutch.

Said to have migrated from Pakistan, the **Jats** are an Islamic pastoral group. The men can be identified by their black clothing, while young Jat girls have dainty plaits curving round the sides of their faces, and wear heavy nose rings.

Western Satraps and the powerful Guptas. The Arab invasion of Sindh in 720 AD pushed refugees into Kutch's western regions, and tribes from Rajputana and Gujarat crossed its eastern borders. Later in the eighth century, the region fell under the sway of the Gujarati capital Anhilawada (now Patan), and by the tenth century the Samma Rajputs, later known as the Jadejas, had infiltrated Kutch from the west and established themselves as rulers, making their capital at **Bhuj**. Jajeda rule was eventually interrupted by a brief period of British domination in the early nineteenth century, and soon afterwards Kutch was absorbed into the Indian Union in 1948. The region has largely retained its customs, laws and a thriving maritime tradition, built originally on trade with Malabar, Mocha, Muscat and the African coast.

Bhuj

In the heart of Kutch, the narrow streets and old bazars of the walled town of **BHUJ** retain a medieval flavour unlike any other Gujarati city. While much of it was reduced to rubble in the **earthquake** of January 2001 (which killed around twenty thousand people, destroyed 1.2 million homes in the region and severely damaged the famed **Aina Mahal**, known as the "Palace of Mirrors"), a US$2 billion reconstruction process resulted in new infrastructure, new businesses and new jobs. And although reconstruction was slow and not always smooth, the city seems to have finally emerged from the tragedy.

Bhuj is overlooked from the east by the old, crumbling fort on Bhujia Hill, while the vast **Hamirsar Tank**, with a small park on an island in its centre, stands on its western edge. The remnants of the **old city** form an intricate maze of streets and alleyways leading to the **palace complex**, guarded by sturdy walls and high heavy gates, enclosing the Aina and Prag mahals.

Aina Mahal

Darbargadh • Daily except Thurs 9am–noon & 3–6pm • ₹100, camera ₹50, video camera ₹100 • ⓦ ainamahalbhuj.com

An eighteenth-century palace built during the reign of Maharao Lakho, and later turned into a museum showcasing the opulence of the royal dynasty, the **Aina Mahal** suffered considerable damage in the 2001 earthquake. Fortunately, despite its roof collapsing, the famed **Hall of Mirrors** remained largely intact; the interior has now been fully restored, but work is ongoing on the exterior. The chief architect of the palace, Ram Singh Malam, was an Indian seafarer who studied in Europe for seventeen years after being rescued from a shipwreck by Dutch sailors off the coast of Africa. His masterpiece was the tiled pleasure chamber at the heart of the palace where the maharaja, soothed by an ingenious system of fountains, would compose poetry and listen to music. Royal heirlooms on display include a couple of original Hogarths; a scroll depicting Nagpanchami Ashwari (an ancient Hindu snake-worshipping festival); and a portrait of Catherine the Great.

Prag Mahal

Darbargadh • Mon–Sat 9am–noon & 3–6pm • ₹50, camera ₹50, video camera ₹100

The once-grand **Prag Mahal**, built in the 1860s and combining Mughal, British, Kutchi and Italian Gothic architectural styles, also suffered damage during the quake. Its main tower appears to be precariously held together by skewed stones. Visitors are currently only allowed inside the cavernous main hall.

Sharad Baug Palace

Sanjog Nagar, west of Hamirsar Tank • Daily 9am–noon & 3–6pm • ₹25, camera ₹25, video camera ₹100

The small but stately **Sharad Baug Palace** was built in 1867 as the retreat of the last maharao of Kutch. Its small porticoed buildings are delicately proportioned and include a plush drawing room, decked with hunting trophies, photographs and old clocks, and a dining room containing Maharao Madansinjhi's coffin. The palace's most appealing feature, however, is its well-tended garden.

Shree Swaminarayan Temple

City Police Station Rd • Mon–Sat 9am–noon & 3–6pm • ☎ 74900 25013 or 028 3225 0231, ⓦ bhujmandir.org

While Bhuj's palaces showcase the grandeur of the old city, the **Shree Swaminarayan Temple** adds an element of modern-day splendour. Only inaugurated in 2010, the temple was built, at a cost of ₹1 billion, to replace the former Shri Swaminarayan Mandir that was all but wiped out by the earthquake. The complex, devoted to the Swaminarayan Sampraday sect of Hinduism, houses beautifully carved marble pillars, golden domes and images of Nar Narayan and Radha Krishna, salvaged from the old temple.

Kutch Museum

Ghanshyam Nagar, southeast of Hamirsar Tank • Daily except Wed 10am–1pm & 2.30–5.30pm • ₹100 (₹20), camera ₹100

The worthwhile **Kutch Museum** is the oldest museum in Gujarat, with two storeys of topographical, historical and cultural exhibits on the region. Kutchi textiles and crafts are showcased, along with life-size mannequins representing major Kutchi communities. There are also some interesting finds from the Indus Valley Civilization at Dholavira, dating back four millennia.

Ram-kund Tank

South of Hamirsar Tank, off Vijayrajji Rd

From the southwest corner of the Hamirsar Tank, a path leads between the Ram Dhun and Satya Narayan temples to the 250-year-old **Ram-kund Tank**. Made of hard grey stone and shaded with trees, it is decorated with skilfully crafted images of Kali, Vishnu, Nag and Ganesh, and bears small niches in the walls where oil lamps once glittered in the dusk as devotees prayed at the evening puja.

9

ARRIVAL AND DEPARTURE

BHUJ

By plane The airport (☎ 028 3224 4147, ⊛ aai.aero) is 4km north of the centre. Daily flights to Mumbai (1hr 30min) and Delhi (4hr) are offered by Air India (☎ 1860 233 1407, ⊛ airindia.in).

By train The railway station is about 1.5km north of Aina Mahal (reservations office Mon–Sat 8am–8pm, Sun 8am–2pm). The best train services to Ahmedabad are the *Sayaji Nagari Express, also called the Bhuj Dadar Express* #19116 (daily; dep. 10.25pm, arr. 5.15am), which continues to Mumbai's Bandra Terminus (arr. 1.45pm), and the *Ala Hazrat Express* #14312 (Tues, Thurs & Sun; dep. 12.45am, arr. 8.35pm), which continues to reach Jaipur and Delhi at 8.35am and 2.35pm respectively, the following day. Several daily trains travel to Gandhidham (1hr), but it's easier to take the bus.

By bus The ST bus stand is on Middle School Rd, about 500m east of Harmirsar Lake. Private operators are strung along Station Rd. Patel Tours and Travels (☎ 099 2524 4252, ⊛ pateltoursandtravels.com), 100m west of the station, has buses to Ahmedabad (9 daily; 8hr), including a nightly a/c sleeper bus (10.45pm). Jay Somnath Travels (☎ 028 3222 1919), opposite *Green Rock*, has buses to Rajkot (6 daily; 7hr).

Destinations Ahmedabad (every 30min; 9hr); Dhordo (2 daily; 2hr 30min); Jamnagar (6 daily; 7hr 15min–8hr 15min); Khavda (4 daily; 2hr); Mandvi (hourly; 1hr 30min).

By shared jeep There's a small shared-jeep stand about 200m east of the bus stand on the opposite side of ST Rd, with regular jeeps departing for Mandvi (45min).

INFORMATION

Tourist information Bhuj's Tourist Information Bureau (☎ 028 3222 4910, ⊛ gujarattourism.com) is on the first floor of the city's Exhibition Hall, opposite Bahumali Bhavan. Also useful is the tourist desk at Aina Mahal (daily except Sat 9am–noon & 3–6pm; ☎ 028 3229 1702 or ☎ 937 423 5379, ⊕ pkumar_94@yahoo.com or ⊕ pramodjethi2013@gmail.com), manned by the friendly

and well-informed Pramod Jethi, who also organizes heritage walks (3hr; ₹700).

Services The State Bank of India on Hospital Rd changes cash, as does ICICI across the street. There are numerous ATMs. Budhbhatti Cycle Stores Centre, near the ST bus stand, rents bicycles (₹70–110/day; ☎ 028 3222 2711).

ACCOMMODATION

The Bhuj House Opposite Camp Police Chowki, Camp Area ☎ 90981 87346, ⊛ thebhujhouse.com. This 150-year-old courtyard home has been immaculately restored into a heritage homestay. The four atmospheric rooms are decked out in Kutchi fabrics, and staff can arrange activities and tours. Rates include breakfast; lunches and dinners also available. **₹1800**

City Guest House Langa St, just off Shroff Bazar ☎ 099 1392 2669, ⊛ cityguesthousebhuj.com. If rupees are tight, head here for no frills but clean rooms – some with attached bathrooms set around a small courtyard. 24hr checkout. **₹550**

★ **Gangaram** Behind Aina Mahal ☎ 02832 222948, ⊛ hotelgangaram.com. Run by the obliging Rajesh Jethi, a mine of information, this travellers' stalwart has clean, attached rooms, some with a/c. There's a roof terrace and a good restaurant (chicken curry ₹150). **₹1100**

Ilark Station Rd ☎ 02832 258999, ⊛ hotelilark.com. A modern red-and-black-glass exterior shields one of the more chic hotels in town: all rooms have laminate floors, large beds and big TVs. There are also two smart restaurants, a bookshop, flower shop and – incongruously – a tree in the lobby. **₹2400**

Kutch Safari Lodge 14km north of Bhuj, overlooking the Gorudra Reservoir ☎ 98250 13392, or ☎ 992 5238 599 ⊛ kutchsafaribhuj.com. This luxurious camp has traditional Kutchi *bhungas* (mud-brick and straw homes) and white concrete huts (₹4200), a pool and a restaurant that often features live music; a good choice if you've got your own vehicle. **₹3900**

Prince Station Rd ☎ 028 3222 0370, ⊛ hotelprince online.com. Long-established mid-range choice with large and spotless attached a/c rooms and suites, a foreign exchange counter, two restaurants and welcoming staff. **₹2850**

Raj Mahel Near ST bus stand, behind Sur Mandir Cinema ☎ 0283 222 3000, ⊛ hotelrajmahalkutch.com. This red-coated hotel in the centre of town gives Bhuj's older hotels a run for their money, with spotless attached rooms, some with a/c and all with 24hr hot water. **₹1200**

Shiv Chhathi Bari, near ST bus stand ☎ 0283 2221 999, ⊛ shivhotel.com. Nicely decorated central lobby area and good modern rooms, all with LCD TV. There's no on-site restaurant but the helpful staff will order a takeaway from a nearby restaurant and bring it to your bedroom. **₹1600**

EATING

Station Rd is the place to pick up the local **snack**, *dhabeli* (spiced lentils and peanuts in a bun). The *Prince* hotel has a

wine shop and can provide **alcohol permits**.

Anando Foods Near the Kutch Museum. ☎ 9825126826

Set under-ground, across from Alfred High School, this hygienic fast food joint serves inexpensive south Indian snacks, Chinese noodles, soups, fried rice, ice cream and pizzas ("Italian" ₹150). Daily 10am–10pm.

Gopi's – The Bite Bazaar ST Rd, 100m west of ST bus stand ☎ 099 7959 5293. With cosy blue booths and plenty of fans, this tiny creamery serves floats, *faloodas*, slushies and genuine thick milkshakes (₹30–₹90). A welcome retreat from the bustle of Bhuj's busy centre. Daily 10am–10.30pm.

Green Rock ST Rd, opposite Gopi's ☎ 028 3225 3644. Smart a/c restaurant with photos of Bollywood and cricket stars on the walls and an all-veg menu of North and South Indian, Chinese and Western dishes. Lunch thalis ₹250. Daily 11am–3pm & 7–10.30pm.

Jesal/Toral Prince hotel, Station Rd. If you're feeling homesick you'll enjoy the fish fingers and beans on toast at *Jesal*. They also serve interesting north Indian fish dishes, plus veg and non-veg Indian and Chinese staples (mains ₹120–350). *Toral*, meanwhile, offers a lavish all-you-can-eat Gujarati thali (₹250). Daily Jesal 7am–3pm & 7–11pm; Toral 11.30am–3pm & 7.30–11.30pm.

Nilam Opposite Prince hotel, Station Rd ☎ 028 3222 4786. Courteous staff serve excellent veg Indian and Chinese food – the sweetcorn and green pepper masala is recommended – plus inexpensive breakfasts and a vegetarian kebab special (₹130) and veg thali (₹250 Daily 11am–10pm.

Park View NK Tower, ST Rd ☎ 028 3222 5655. Overlooking Bhuj's busiest street, this plush and popular a/c restaurant serves Punjabi, South Indian, Chinese and Mexican cuisine, to name just a few. The mouthwatering thalis here may well be the best deal in Bhuj (₹250–₹310), while the Kaju curry (₹150) is also fantastic. Daily 11am–11pm.

Around Bhuj

Bhuj is a useful base for visiting **outlying craft villages**. From Mandvi, Mundra and Kandla on the coast to Hodka, Dhordo and Khavda to the north, Kutch's ethnic diversity, including Rabari, Ahir, Jat, Muthwa, Harijan and Rajput communities, is reflected in its wide-ranging handicrafts. As well as the local villages, sights of interest include the ancient sights of **Dholavira**, the Khanpatha monastery at **Than** and, of course, the vast and desolate **Great Rann of Kutch**.

GETTING AROUND   AROUND BHUJ

By public transport Villages are best reached by private transport; infrequent buses run from Bhuj to Dhordo (2 daily) and Khavda (4 daily).

Taxi and motorbike rental Exploring the area by taxi or motorcycle gives you the most freedom. Most hotels in Bhuj will organize motorbike rental, though many bikes are in a poor state of repair; a better bet is MK Auto (Mon–Sat 10am–8pm; ☎ 098 9898 3999; ₹8000/day with ₹5000 refundable deposit), a motorbike rental place a few metres west of *Green Rock* (see page 571).

Permits Permits are required for many of the outlying villages, and are available for free from the District Superintendent of Police's Office on Ghanshyam Nagar in Bhuj, a 5min walk southeast of the Hamirsar Tank (Mon–Sat 11am–2pm & 3–6pm); the process takes about 15min. Bring photocopies of your passport and visa as well as the originals. In the off-season, you'll need to go to the Bhirandiyara police post (Mon–Sat 9am–6pm) for your permit. It's 50km north of Bhuj, marking the junction where the road turns northwest for Hodka and north for Khavda.

Tours For advice on where to visit, talk to Pramod Jethi (see page 570), who runs tours to the craft villages (₹1400 by car; ₹200 by auto-rickshaw). Ral Laxmi Tours & Travels on Kansara Bazar Rd (Mon–Sat 9am–9pm; ☎ 094 0883 7409) offers a range of regional tours.

Mandvi

The compact town of **MANDVI**, situated on the west bank of a wide tidal estuary, 60km southwest of Bhuj, faces the Arabian Sea to the south and supports a dwindling *dhow*-building industry. Merchants, seamen and later the British settled in this once-flourishing port; though few remained long, they left behind grand European-style mansions. Today, Mandvi has a leisurely feel, its cluttered shops and **markets** stocked with *bandhani* and silver. Shifting sands block the estuary along on its south side, forming a long, uncrowded **beach** that is good for swimming. By the estuary, you can see **dhows** being built by hand: around fifty men spend two years building each ship, the largest of which cost upwards of US$500,000, and are bought by wealthy Gulf Arabs.

9

KUTCHI HANDICRAFTS

Kutch has long been renowned for its distinctive traditional crafts, particularly its **embroidery**, practised by pastoral groups like Hindu Rabaris and Ahirs, and Muslim Jats and Muthwas, as well as migrants from Sindh including the Sodha Rajputs and Meghwal Harijans. Traditionally, each community has its own stitches and patterns, though these distinctions are becoming less apparent with time.

The northern villages of Dhordo, Khavda and Hodko are home to the few remaining communities of **leather embroiderers**, who stitch flower, peacock and fish motifs onto bags, fans, horse belts, wallets, cushion covers and mirror frames. Dhordo is also known for its **woodcarving**, while Khavda is one of the last villages to continue the printing method known as **ajrakh**. Cloth is dyed with natural pigments in a lengthy process similar to batik, but instead of wax, a mixture of lime and gum is used to resist the dye in certain parts of the cloth when new colours are added. Women in Khavda also paint **terracotta pots**.

Rogan painting is practised by only a few artisans at Nirona in northern Kutch. A complex process turns hand-pounded castor oil into coloured dyes that are used to decorate cushion covers, bedspreads and curtains with simple geometric patterns. Craftsmen also make melodic **bells** (once used as a communication system by shepherds) coated in intricate designs of copper and brass. Silver jewellery is common, featuring in most traditional Kutchi costumes, but Kutchi **silver engraving**, traditionally practised in Bhuj, is a dwindling art form. The anklets, earrings, nose rings, bangles and necklaces are similar to those seen in Rajasthan; many are made by the Ahir and Rabari communities living in both areas. The main centres for silver are Anjar, Bhuj, Mandvi and Mundra.

Kutchi clothes are distinctive not only for their fine embroidery and bold designs. The most common form of **cloth** printing is **bandhani** (tie-dye), a practice concentrated in Mandvi and Anjar. Another unique craft is *ilacha* (*mashroo*-weaving), a combination of dyeing and weaving with silk yarn to create designs so detailed and complex as to appear embroidered.

In recent times, the **future** of many local craft centres has become doubtful, especially since the post-earthquake reconstruction of Bhuj and its surrounds. The consequent creation of many largely unskilled labouring jobs, with higher wages, lured many workers away from handicraft making. NGOs like **Kala Raksha** (see page 573) are striving to keep local traditions alive.

Vijay Vilas Palace

8km west of town (turn left after 4km) • Daily 9am–1pm & 3–6pm • ₹100, camera ₹100, video camera ₹250

Mandvi's **Vijay Vilas Palace** is a sandy-coloured domed building bounded by 700 acres of land, built as a summer retreat by Kutch's maharao in the 1940s and now often used as a film set. Behind the decidedly worn facade, European furniture fills the high-ceilinged carpeted rooms, hunting trophies deck the walls and a grand stairway leads to the ladies' quarters on the first floor. The palace estate has a royal pavilion and a long private beach with a hotel (see below).

ARRIVAL AND DEPARTURE   MANDVI

By bus and jeep Regular buses run from Bhuj's ST bus stand to Mandvi's ST bus stand (every 30min; 1hr 30min). Shared jeeps (45min–1hr; ₹100) also link the towns.

ACCOMMODATION AND EATING

HV Beach Hotel Wind Farm Beach ☏ 987 998 444 ⊚ mandvibeachhotel.com. This luxury hotel is right on the beach and has villas with sea views. There are also standard a/c doubles available, together with a multi-cuisine restaurant and free laundry service. **₹16000**

★ **Rukmavati Guest House** On the waterfront near Bridge Gate ☏ 028 3422 3558 or ☏ 942 9040 484 Housed in a former hospital, this is Mandvi's best budget option: all rooms have private bathrooms with solar-heated water while some have a/c (₹1850) and nice balconies. There's a breakfast terrace, small library and friendly manager, Vinod Bhatt, who has loads of local information. **₹900**

Sea View Jain Dharmshala Rd, on the waterfront near ST bus stand ☏ 098 2537 6063, ⊚ hotelseaviewmandvi. com. Although they don't exactly have "sea views", rooms at the front look straight out onto the *dhow* builders. Rooms and suites are decent and brightly lit by large windows; most have a/c. ₹800

Zorba the Buddha First floor of Osho hotel, KT Shah Rd ☏ 098 7919 4555. Set behind the old Bhid Gate downtown, this is the best bet for food other than the *HV Beach Hotel*, offering great service and excellent veg thalis (₹130). Daily 11am–3pm & 7–10pm.

Southeast of Bhuj

The 50km journey **southeast** from Bhuj to **Kandla**, one of the busiest ports on India's west coast, takes you past dry scrubland. In the small village of **BHUJODI**, about 9km out of Bhuj and 1km off the NH-42 eastward, artisans weave thick shawls and blankets on pit looms dug into the floors of squat mud houses. You can buy their products from the small shop run by the Bhujodi Handweaving Co-op Society; then check out the **Kutchi Art Gallery** in town, opposite Ramdevpir Temple (daily 9am–8pm).

Further along on this road are the villages of **PADDHAR**, known for Rabari embroidery, and **DHANETI**, a centre for Ahir embroidery. **Dhamadka** remains a centre for *ajrakh* block-printing, although it has struggled to recover from the 2001 earthquake, after which many of its artisans were moved to the village of **AJRAKHPUR**. Around 10km east of Bhuj, Ajrakhpur is home to the enterprise of UNESCO Award of Excellence-winning Dr Ismail Mohammed Khatri (☏ 028 3229 9786, ✉ dr. ismail2005@gmail.com), who can trace his *ajrakh* block-printing heritage back at least nine generations.

The first main town beyond Bhuj, **ANJAR** was the capital of Kutch until 1548. Badly affected by the earthquake, the town recovered much more slowly than Bhuj, with serious disruption to traditional craftsmaking – Ahir embroidery, *bandhani*, batik and nutcrackers. However, things have improved now, and a **crafts market** is held here every Monday when Rabari people from more than 130 villages set up shop (8.30am–1pm).

North of Bhuj

North of Bhuj are some of the most interesting craft centres in Kutch, their colours accentuated by an increasingly desolate landscape. From the village of **BHIRENDIARA**, 50km north of Bhuj, known for its embroidery and patchwork as well as its beautiful mudwork (*liponkan*) interiors, the road forks. To the northwest is **HODKA**, followed by **DHORDO** at the end of the road, each of which features a cluster of grass-roofed mud huts decorated with traditional clay and whitewash patterns.

Sumeraser Sheikh

South of Bhirendiara and closer to Bhuj is **SUMERASER SHEIKH**, where NGO **Kala Raksha** (☏ 028 0827 7238 or ☏ 942 775 9701 🌐 kala-raksha.org) maintains an archive of antique textiles, a handicraft workshop, a museum and a fixed-price shop. Most of Kala Raksha's participants are women from marginalized communities, and this is a great place to learn about local embroidery, tie-dyeing, patchwork and inlay techniques. Call ahead to arrange a tour.

Kalo Dungar

90km north of Bhuj • Private transport is best; weekend buses depart in the evening from Khavda and return early morning

Kalo Dungar (the Black Hills), Kutch's highest point, rise 462m over the vast salt flats (or inland sea during monsoon season), offering unparalleled views of the Great Rann disappearing into the vast horizon – a truly edge-of-the-world vista. Pleasant pathways and viewing huts have been built along the slopes facing the Rann, and a 400-year-old **temple** nearby marks the spot where Dattreya, the three-headed incarnation of Lords Brahma, Vishnu and Shiva, once offered a band of starving jackals his own body as a meal (it regenerated itself as they ate). The priests here attract today's wild jackals with heaps of boiled rice offered as *prasad*, spilled onto a concrete platform at noon each day while visitors watch from a safe distance. For a donation, the neighbouring *dharamshala* also offers meals and lodgings to Kalo Dungar's trickle of visitors.

9

Banni Grasslands

50km north of Bhuj • Private transport is best; the Centre for Desert and Ocean (see below) offers pick-up from Bhuj

Skirting the southern edge of the Great Rann are the semiarid **Banni Grasslands**, home to a vast array of birds, including flamingos, pelicans, cranes, painted storks and hornbills. Ecologist Jugal Tiwari of the Centre for Desert and Ocean (☎028 3522 1284, or T98252 48135 ⓦcedobirding.com) organizes informative birdwatching trips in the area; the centre also sells local handicrafts.

Than and Dhinodar

60km northwest of Bhuj • Daily bus from Bhuj departs 5pm (2hr); return departs early morning

The Siddha Shree Dhoramnath monastery at **THAN** is home to a Tantric order of Hindu sadhus, known as Kanphata ("split-ear") after the heavy agate rings (*kundals*) they traditionally wear in their ears. This whitewashed complex at the foot of the hill encloses a handful of medieval temples, tombs and domed dwellings. Hardy travellers can spend the night in its *dharamshala* for a small donation. From Than, you can walk up a rocky ravine via an ancient pilgrims' trail to the mountaintop behind (3hr return), where **Dhinodar** is the site of a small painted temple, home to a Kanphata yogi, Hiranath Baba, and his acolytes; take ample water supplies.

ACCOMMODATION AND EATING · NORTH OF BHUJ

Devpur Homestay Darbargadh, Devpur village, 40km northwest of Bhuj ☎028 3528 3065 or 9825711852, ⓦsites.google.com/site/devpurhomestay. A sandstone fort built in 1905 in the Kutchi (or Roha) style and converted into a charming homestay with fancy suites (non-a/c ₹4500, a/c ₹5000) and simple bungalows. Elegant courtyard, a tennis court and a vintage dining room (breakfast included in rates) plus car rental. ₹2800

Shaam-e-Sarhad Village Hodka village, 50km north of Bhuj ☎02832 654124 or 02832 296220, ⓦhodka.in.

This full-board resort is a sustainable tourism project run by the local Halepotra people. "Sunset at the Border", as the name means, offers accommodation in *bhungas* (circular mud huts, ₹5600 for a couple including all meals) or luxury tents, all with attached Western-style toilets and some with a/c. The resort offers craft workshops, birdwatching excursions and trips to local villages. A permit is required to visit, obtainable from Bhuj's District Superintendent of Police's Office. Closed April to mid-Oct. ₹3200

Dholavira

250km northeast of Bhuj • Daily 9am–dusk • No video

In the far north of Kutch, on an island surrounded by snow-white salt flats, the tiny village of **DHOLAVIRA** surrounds the remnants of a Harappan city, perhaps the fifth largest in India, which thrived six thousand or more years ago. Archaeological digs started here in the 1970s after a local farmer ploughed up a small terracotta seal. Soon, the existence of a major planned city with monumental structures, a palace complex and an extraordinary water management system was revealed. Until recently, the archeological remains attracted barely a trickle of visitors, but that changed in 2014 with the creation of an international running event, **Run the Rann** (ⓦruntherann.com), which is bringing in competitors in their hundreds.

ARRIVAL AND DEPARTURE · DHOLAVIRA

By bus There's a daily bus from Bhuj to Dholavira, departing at 2.30pm (7hr 30min) and returning at 5.30am, or there are two daily bus services from Bhuj to Rapar, where you can take a minibus the remaining 90km. Due to the inconvenient schedule, it's best to visit with private transport.

ACCOMMODATION AND EATING

Toran Tourist Complex 1km south of Dholavira site ☎098 2502 6813. The simple *bhunga*-style cottages at the state-run *Toran* hotel are Dholavira's only choice for accommodation, all with attached bathrooms and some with a/c (₹1600). A basic cafeteria offers Gujarati thalis (₹120). ₹600

Little Rann Wild Ass Sanctuary

Entrance to the sanctuary is near Bajana village, a 30min drive from Dasada • Oct–May daily 6am–6pm • ₹1200 (₹350)/vehicle seating up to six, SLR camera ₹600 (₹100)

Spanning 4850 square kilometres, the **Little Rann Wild Ass Sanctuary**, a vast salt-encrusted desert plain that becomes inundated during the rains (July–Sept), is home to an abundance of wildlife, including the endangered Indian **wild ass**. Usually seen in loosely knit herds, this handsome chestnut-brown-and-white member of the horse family is capable of running up to 80 km/h. The sanctuary is also home to wolves, foxes, jackals, jungle and desert cats, blackbuck and nilgai antelopes and the chinkara gazelle. Large flocks of flamingos, pelicans and winter-visiting cranes can be seen at Bajana Lake; October to March is the time to see the migratory birds.

ARRIVAL AND GETTING AROUND   LITTLE RANN WILD ASS SANCTUARY

While the sanctuary headquarters is at **Dhrangadhra** near its southern edge, most tourist facilities are at **Dasada**, 70km to the northeast. Although recommended, hiring a guide is not mandatory.

By train Dhrangadhra is linked by train to Ahmedabad (2 daily; 4hr) and Bhuj (5 daily; 5hr 15min). Dasada is 33km from Viramgam railway station, connected by regular buses and autos/taxis (₹600/₹800); from Viramgam there are frequent trains to Ahmedabad (hourly; 2hr) and Bhuj (4

daily; 6hr).

By bus Dhrangadhra is linked by buses to Ahmedabad (every 30min; 4hr), while buses from Dasada also connect with Ahmedabad (every 30min; 3hr), Patan (2 daily; 3hr) and Bhuj (4 daily; 6hr).

By jeep You can rent a jeep and guide (around ₹4000/day) to take a tour of the sanctuary from Dasada, Dhrangadhra or the resort hotels (see below).

ACCOMMODATION

Desert Coursers Zainabad, 10km west of Dasada ☎099 9830 5501 or 094 2637 2113, ⊚desertcoursers. net. Also known as *Camp Zainabad* after its location, this is a friendly all-in eco-camp offering comfortable thatched-roof *kooba* (traditional hut) accommodation, all meals and one jeep safari. Horse and camel safaris can be arranged (from ₹2000). The camp is also highly involved in numerous laudable social and cultural projects. Free pick-up from Dasada bus station included in rate. **₹6000**

Eco Tour Camp Jogad village, 20km north of Halvad and about 45km northwest of Dhrangadhra ☎027 5428 0560 or 982 554 8090, ⊚littlerann.com. Among the best options for the Little Rann is wildlife photographer

Devjibhai Dhamecha's excellent eco-camp close to Sumera Lake, on the very southern edge of the sanctuary. The camp offers full-board accommodation in their family home in Dhrangadhra, with all meals included. Safaris cost ₹2000/₹3000 for morning and evening respectively. **₹4000**

Rann Riders 2km east of Dasada ☎099 2523 6014, ⊚rannriders.com. This eco-resort has twenty-eight a/c cottages with tiled or living roofs, a restaurant, pool, gardens, several inviting hammocks and a friendly and helpful owner. Accommodation packages include full board and the choice of a jeep, horse or camel safari. Free pick-up from Dasada bus station included in rate. **₹6700**

Saurashtra

SAURASHTRA, or the **Kathiawar Peninsula**, forms the bulk of Gujarat state, a large knob of land spreading south from the hills and marshes of the north out to the Arabian Sea, cut into by the Gulf of Cambay to the east and the Gulf of Kutch to the west. This is Gujarat at its most diverse, populated by cattle-rearing tribes in the countryside and industrialists in urban centres such as **Rajkot**. Fabulous architecture includes the royal palaces at **Wankaner** and **Gondal**, while one of the region's most flamboyant festivals, the **Tarnetar Fair** (see page 556), comes to the town of Sayla in the autumn.

Rajkot

RAJKOT is a typically sprawling, crowded and congested Indian metropolis. Founded in the sixteenth century, Rajkot was ruled by the Jadeja Rajputs until

9

Independence, after which it merged with the Union of Saurashtra, and has since grown into a large industrial centre with a significant middle class. Best known for its association with **Mahatma Gandhi**, Rajkot has few tourist sights other than a **museum** and **Gandhi's family residence** in the **old city**, which is still home to a plenitude of typical Gujarati wooden-fronted houses with intricately carved shutters and stained-glass windows. It also makes a good base for day-trips to nearby palaces.

Kaba Gandhi No Delo

Off Ghikantha Rd, 300m west of Sanganwa Chowk • Mon–Sat 9am–noon & 3–6pm, Sun 10am–noon & 3–6pm • Free • ☎ 028 1222 6544

The Gandhis moved to **Kaba Gandhi No Delo** from Porbandar in 1881 when the Mahatma's father accepted an appointment as the diwan of Rajkot state. Tucked away in the narrow streets off the old city, the house has several rooms lined with artefacts and pictures stringing together the story of Gandhi's life.

Watson Museum

Jubilee Bagh • Mon–Sat 9am–1pm & 3–6pm; closed 2nd & 4th Sat of month • ₹100 (₹10)

Named after Colonel Watson, a British political agent from 1886 to 1893 largely responsible for documenting Saurashtran history, the **Watson Museum** features a somewhat dishevelled collection of artefacts and artworks. Gathered from some of the region's erstwhile royal families, the displays range from Mohenjo Daro relics to medieval statues and manuscripts, nineteenth-century oil paintings and Indus Valley remnants.

Shri Ramakrishna Ashrama

Dr Yagnik Rd • Daily: March–Oct 5am–noon & 4–9pm; Nov–Feb 5am–noon & 3.45–8.45 pm • Free • ☎ 028 1246 5200, ⌨ rkmrajkot.org

An unbelievably peaceful spot in the centre of the chaotic Rajputpara district, **Shri Ramakrishna Ashrama** is dedicated to the man, born to poor Bengali parents, who in the nineteenth century became a religious visionary (*paramahamsa*) and *advaitya* philosopher. The entrance is designed to resemble the Ajanta caves in Maharashtra, with four sculptured columns supporting a keystone denoting a *shivalingam*. Inside are murals showing Ramakrishna's teachings, a *murti* (statue) of the man himself, and steps up to a balcony with great views over the city.

ARRIVAL AND DEPARTURE   RAJKOT

By plane Air India (opposite GEB Office, Dhebar Rd; ☎ 026 5233 0466) have daily flights to Mumbai. The airport is north-west of the centre (₹100 auto-rickshaw ride).

By train Rajkot's railway station is about 2km north of the city centre (₹100 by auto-rickshaw). Plenty of daily trains link Rajkot to Ahmedabad (5hr 30min), including the #19016*Saurashtra Mail* (dep. 1.25am, arr. 06.40am, which continues to Mumbai Central (arr. 07.15pm). Several daily trains also head to Junagadh (2hr 30min) and Veraval (5hr).

By bus From the ST bus stand on Dhebar Rd there are regular state buses to Ahmedabad, Jamnagar and Junagadh. In addition, numerous private bus companies

have offices clustered at Limda Chowk, each operating shuttles to private terminals on the outskirts of town: Eagle Travels (Ring Rd, opposite the Adani Hyper Market; ☎ 079 6155 5555, ⌨ eaglecorporate.com) has comfortable a/c buses to Ahmedabad (hourly; 4hr) and Mumbai (3 daily; 11hr); and Jay Somnath (Gondal Rd, 50m south of the Telegraph Office; ☎ 99798 69669) has buses to Bhuj (daily; 5–6hr).

Destinations (private buses) Ahmedabad (every 30min; 4hr 30min); Jamnagar (every 30min; 2hr 15min); Junagadh (hourly; 2hr 45min).

INFORMATION

Tourist information Rajkot's tourist office (Mon–Sat 10.30am–1.30pm & 2–5.30pm, closed 2nd & 4th Sat of month; ☎ 028122 34507, ⌨ gujarattourism.com) is in Bhavnagar House, off Jawahar Rd north of Sanganwa

Chowk, behind the State Bank of India.
Services. The post office is on Sadar Rd, off Jawahar Rd, opposite Jubilee Gardens.

ACCOMMODATION

Bhabha Kingstone Panchnath Rd, off Jawahar Rd ☎ 760 0071 000, ⓦ hotelbhabhakingstone.com. Stylish property, with exposed brickwork and wood finishes, across from MKG High School. The costlier of the sixteen rooms come with tubs and a/c. ₹1400

Galaxy Jawahar Rd, 100m north of Sanganwa Chowk ☎ 830 679 9999, ⓦ thegalaxyhotelrajkot.com. Sizeable a/c rooms with TVs – but the attached bathrooms could be better. It's on the third floor of a shopping complex. Breakfast included. ₹2250

Imperial Palace Dr Yagnik Rd ☎ 982 506 5544, ⓦ theimperialpalace.biz. Rajkot's classiest hotel attracts cricketers and Bollywood stars with their sophisticated rooms, a pool and fitness suite and an excellent restaurant. Rates include breakfast too. Unusually for Gujarat, it's also wheelchair-accessible. ₹6500

Jyoti Kanak Rd, 200m north of bus stand ☎ 094 2671 9558, ⓦ hoteljyoti.co.in. Smartly decorated business-oriented hotel 500m from Shri Ramakrishna Ashrama. ₹2100

Raviraj Palace Dhebar Rd, opposite Jivan Bank ☎ 090 3334 7840, ⓔ info@hotelravirajpalace.com. Large windows and balconies in fan-cooled and a/c (₹1150) rooms. The four-person a/c rooms (₹1700) are a good deal. ₹900

Regenta RPJ Everest Park, Kalawad Road ☎ 028 1616 7777. Located close to the Sacred Heart Syro Malabar Cathedral, this three-star property offers deluxe rooms of varying standards. As part of the Royal Orchid group, the *Regenta* has a gym, a business centre and a multi-cuisine restaurant. All rooms have mini-bars and coffee-makers. ₹5000

EATING

Look out for the Kathiawadi version of the Gujarati **thali**, spiced with ginger and garlic. Rajkot is also known for **milk sweets** like *thabdi* halwa and the saffron-flavoured *kesar pedas*.

Dhola Maru Grand Regency hotel, Dhebar Rd ☎ 915 2433 497. Elegant hotel restaurant serving Indian, Chinese, Italian and Mexican dishes. The kitchen is an attraction in itself; you can watch cooks prepare your food through its glass walls. Mains are between ₹190–320. Daily 11am–11pm.

Kitchen Stories Regenta, RPJ, Everest Park, Kalawad Road ☎ 028 1616 7777. Besides Italian, cuisines served here include Arabic, Chinese, Mexican and Italian. The breakfast buffet costs ₹450 per head. Dinner is à la carte; mains include falafel sandwich (₹250) and pastas dishes

(₹250–450). A meal for two will cost around ₹800–1000. Daily 7–10.30am & 7–10.30pm.

★ **Lord's Banquet** Kasturba Rd ☎ 940 9484 094. This efficient a/c place, serving superior North Indian food (₹100–190), is where locals go for a treat. You can specify the spiciness of your dish and even the crispiness of your roti. *Paneer* butter masala is ₹150. Daily 12.30–3.30pm & 7.30–11.30pm.

Temptations Kasturba Rd ☎ 0281 247 5010. Next to *Lord's Banquet* and run by the same management, this classy restaurant offers Chinese, Italian, Indian, American and Mexican dishes (*chimichangas* ₹220) as well as snacks and ice cream. Unique renditions of *The Last Supper* adorn the entrance. Dinner or lunch around ₹400 per head. Daily 11am–midnight.

Sayla

In August or September, the quiet pastoral town of **SAYLA** bursts into life with one of Gujarat's most unique and colourful festivals, the **Tarnetar Fair**. To a flurry of Barwhadi tribal songs, dances and battles of poetry in a sport known as *duhas*, the local men strut in colourful turbans and embroidered jackets, and sporting brightly decorated umbrellas. Tarnetar aims to celebrate youth, joy and artistry, and many of the bejewelled young women are there to choose their future husbands. As the tradition goes, women have first choice.

ARRIVAL AND DEPARTURE   SAYLA

By bus Sayla's bus stand lies at the southern entrance to town, 600m north of the busy Rajkot–Ahmedabad highway, 87km from Rajkot (1hr 30min) and 135km from

Ahmedabad (3hr). Several daily buses to both cities depart from here, but more frequent connections are available from the bus stand on the highway itself.

ACCOMMODATION

Bell Guest House Off Sayla Roundabout, NH-8A ☎ 097 2467 8145, ⓦ bellguesthouse.com. Built by Sayla's royal family for British colonial officers, this old bungalow has been

converted into a comfortable homestay offering large a/c, attached rooms and a fine restaurant. The shady grounds are home to a giant chessboard and an aged tennis court. ₹4000

9

Wankaner

The small city of **WANKANER** is named for its setting at the bend of the River Machchhu (*wanka* means "bend" and *ner* means "river"). Overlooking the city from a hill, the flamboyant **Ranjit Vilas Palace** (₹200; call ahead to visit; ☏028 2822 0000) was home to the family that once ruled the state of the same name. Built between 1899 and 1914, it has an arched facade featuring a frenzy of architectural styles, combining Mughal domes with Doric columns, Victorian Gothic arches, stained-glass windows, chandeliers and Franco-Italian window panes that overlook the palace grounds, where stables are stocked with thoroughbred Kathiawadi stallions. The interior is at least as eccentric, with a stuffed animal collection that includes rhinos, Kodiak bears, several now-extinct Indian wildcats, and no less than seventeen tiger heads.

ARRIVAL AND DEPARTURE   WANKANER

By bus Wankaner's bus stand is in the southeast of town; regular buses run to Rajkot (every 30min; 1hr). Be sure to call the palace ahead before visiting and take a taxi there (₹100).

ACCOMMODATION

Royal Oasis 2km from Ranjit Vilas Palace ☏028 2822 000, ⓦwankanerheritagehotels.com. Splurge on the Art Deco splendour of the royal family's summer home, built between 1875 and 1940, offering full board with sumptuous rooms, two fine restaurants and a spacious indoor pool. **₹5500**

Gondal

Once the capital city of a Jadeja Rajput clan, **GONDAL** houses a handful of extravagant royal residences. All contain memorabilia from the life of the widely admired scholar-maharaja Bhagwat Sinhji, responsible for making Gondal one of India's most prosperous states. The city is now a centre for beadwork embroidery, handloom weaving, silverware, brassware and Ayurvedic medicine. Good places for **shopping** include the market on Darbargadh Road and the Udyog Bharati emporium.

Naulakha Museum

Fort Darbargadh • Daily 9am–noon & 3–6pm • ₹230, camera ₹100

Housed in a crumbling riverside palace, the **Naulakha Museum** displays various artefacts from Gondal's glory days, including the royal wardrobe and library and the weighing scale on which Bhagwat Sinhji measured himself against gold to be distributed as charity on his own golden jubilee.

ARRIVAL AND DEPARTURE   GONDAL

By bus The bus stand is near the city centre, about 500m south of *Orchard Palace*; regular buses link Gondal with Rajkot (every 30min; 1hr).

ACCOMMODATION

Orchard Palace Huzoor Palace Complex ☏02825224550 or 079 2630 20191 ⓦheritagepalacesgondal.com. Built as an annexe to the Huzoor Palace, the current royal residence, *Orchard Palace* was the official guesthouse of the maharajas from the late nineteenth century, deriving its name from a neighbouring grove of fruit trees. Although a bit pricey, all rooms have high ceilings, four-posters and period furniture, while the palace itself houses a royal car collection spanning a century. Price includes a guided tour of Gondal's palaces. **₹6100**

Jamnagar

The busy hub of **JAMNAGAR** in northwest Saurashtra, founded in the sixteenth century, was one of the region's most important princely states. **K.S. Ranjitsinhji**, who played cricket for England alongside W.G. Grace, ruled Jamnagar at the start of the twentieth

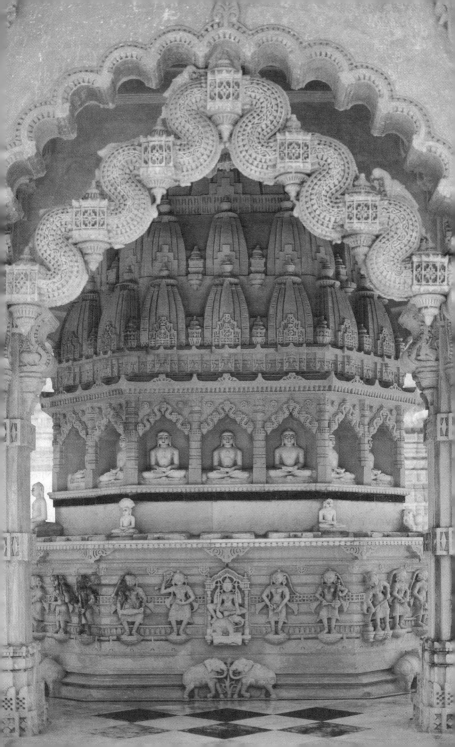

9

century, replacing run-down buildings with attractive constructions that still attest to his prosperous and efficient rule. In recent years, the city has become the world's undisputed refining hub, with the Reliance Industries' refinery just west of town stacking up well over a million barrels of oil each day. Visitors come to Jamnagar for its fabulous mix of architecture and renowned *bandhani* (tie-dye), sold in the markets near the Darbargadh; from October to May, a small number use the city as a base from which to explore the diverse intertidal sea life of the **Marine National Park** (60km west; ☎0288 2679357), India's first national marine park, which encompasses 42 islands strung along 120km of coastline.

The Old City

The most remarkable of Ranjitsinhji's constructions is **Willingdon Crescent**, the swooping arches of its curved facade overlooking the wide streets of Chelmsford Market and the old palace, the **Darbargadh**. In the heart of town, just off Ranjit Road, southwest of Bedi Gate, stands the late nineteenth-century **Ratan Bai Mosque**. This grand, domed prayer-hall, its sandalwood doors inlaid with mother-of-pearl, is the unlikely neighbour to a magnificent pair of **Jain temples**, both decorated with extraordinary **murals**. The more spectacular of the two, **Shantinath Mandir**, is a maze of brightly coloured columns. The outer side of the large dome over **Adinath Mandir** is inlaid with gold and coloured mosaic and both temples have cupolas enriched with a design of mirrors above the entrance porch. The temples form the hub of **Chandni Bazaar**, an almost circular market area enlivened by carved wooden doors, mosaics and balconies.

Ranmal Lake and around

Some of Jamnagar's most interesting sites are set to the east of the man-made **Ranmal Lake**, at the centre of which stands the **Lakhota Palace**, an island fort built in the eighteenth century. It's only accessible from the north side, and upon entering you'll pass a guardroom containing muskets, swords and powder flasks, and the **museum** (daily except Wed and 2nd & 4th Sat of month 10.30am–2pm & 2.30–5.30pm; ₹50 [₹2]) on the upper floor, which holds a mediocre display of paintings, sculpture, folk art and coins.

South of the lake stands the crumbling, circular **Bhujia Fort**, closed since becoming a casualty of the 2001 earthquake. To its northwest, on the edge of the old city, the **Bala Hanuman Temple** has been the scene of round-the-clock nonstop chanting ("Shree Ram, Jai Ram, Jai Jai Ram", a reference to Lord Rama being everywhere) since August 1, 1964, a feat cited in the *Guinness Book of Records*.

ARRIVAL AND DEPARTURE   JAMNAGAR

By plane The airport is 6km west of town – an auto or taxi will cost around ₹100 or ₹200 respectively. Air India (Rathod Nivas Nehru Road ☎ 0288 2550211) operates flights to Mumbai (daily; 1hr).

By train The main railway station is 5km northwest of town. Regular trains connect with Ahmedabad (6–7hr), Rajkot (1hr 30min–2hr) and Dwarka (2–3hr). The # 22946 *Saurashtra Mail* departs at 3.40pm and arrives in Rajkot at 5.45pm, Ahmedabad at 10.40pm, and Mumbai Central at 7.10am. In the other direction, the #22945 *Saurashtra Mail* departs

Jamnagar at 11.40 pmpm and arrives in Dwarka at 2.40pm.

By bus The bus station is 2km west of the town centre; an auto-rickshaw will cost around ₹70. When heading to Rajkot, buses can be hailed from outside the *President* hotel. Private buses leave from Pancheshwar Tower near Teen Batti: Patel Tours & Travels (☎099 2524 4252, ⊚pateltoursandtravels.com) has buses to Ahmedabad (18 daily; 7hr) and Bhuj (5 daily; 6hr).

Destinations (private buses) Ahmedabad (hourly; 7hr); Junagadh (hourly; 4hr 30min); Rajkot (every 30min; 2hr).

INFORMATION

Services Thomas Cook, opposite the town hall, and several banks on Ranjit Rd, change money. Jamnagar's Ayurvedic University (☎028 8255 7324, ⊚ayurveduniversity.com),

1km northwest of Teen Batti, runs a vast array of courses, and offers massage, yoga and mud-therapy treatment sessions.

ACCOMMODATION

Aram Nand Niwas, Pandit Nehru Marg, Bedi Rd ☎ 0288 2551701, ⊕ hotelaram.com. Palatial white building – once the home of a scion of the state's ruling family – whose blue awnings give it something of the feel of a British seaside hotel. Its large a/c rooms and suites (from ₹4200), nostalgic for the days of the Raj and filled with European antiques, have a faded charm. Breakfast included. **₹2000**

Ashiana Third Floor, New Super Market, Bedi Gate Rd ☎ 0288 2559110, ⊕ asashianahotel.com. Jamnagar's best budget option: spacious attached rooms with TV, some with carpets and a/c, set right in the centre of town. The helpful staff can arrange onward bus, train or air tickets. There is a restaurant where you can have some local specialities serving Indian food. **₹650**

President Teen Batti ☎ 028 8255 7491, ⊕ hotel president.in. A well-managed hotel, home to a/c rooms with wood-panelled walls and non-a/c rooms with somewhat grubby bathrooms. All have private balconies and TVs, while there's a currency exchange, a good restaurant and nautically themed decor throughout. Staff can organize birdwatching and sailing trips and visits to the nearby marine park. Free airport transfers. **₹950**

Punit Pandit Nehru Marg, just northwest of Teen Batti ☎ 028 8255 9275, ⊕ hotelpunit.com. A popular place with a small but pleasant roof terrace and airy turquoise rooms, which come with carpets and slightly dated decor. **₹2250**

EATING

★ 7 Seas President hotel, Teen Batti ☎ 028 8255 7491, ⊕ hotelpresident.in. In line with the hotel's maritime theme, with a porthole-like door and paintings of the sea, 7 Seas serves up some of Jamnagar's best non-veg food, with fish curries (₹300) and (mutton) *sheek kebab* curry (₹350), which stands out; the pineapple lassi (₹100) is not to be missed either. Daily 24hr.

Café Paradise Ranjit Rd ☎ 0288 267 0561. Look for the orange sign for this friendly, low-key restaurant, stacked with booths and offering a photo menu of Chinese and Punjabi meals, including chicken biryani (₹170) and chicken

lollipop (₹55/piece). Daily 10am–11pm.

Kalpana Teen Batti ☎ 028 8255 4369. The decor may be ancient, but the tempting veg snacks – burgers, dosas, milkshakes and ice cream (₹60–160) – certainly hit the spot. Daily 9.30am–11pm.

Madras Hotel Old Station Rd, Teen Batti ☎ 02 88254 1057 . A cramped dining room with separate, slightly more spacious a/c area, serving great Punjabi, south Indian (masala dosa ₹80), Jain and Chinese dishes, as well as fresh juices, ice cream and pizzas (₹90–110). Daily 10am–10pm.

Dwarka

Poised at the tip of the peninsula, at India's western edge, **DWARKA** is one of Hinduism's sacred Charm Dham, or "four abodes", thanks to its legendary role as Lord Krishna's capital following his flight from Mathura to the coast. In vivid contrast to the arid expanses further inland, Dwarka is surrounded by fertile wheat, groundnut and cotton fields, while the city itself is a labyrinth of narrow winding streets cluttered with crumbling temples. Today, these still resonate with the bustle of saffron-clad pilgrims and the clatter of celebratory drums. Dwarka really comes to life during the major Hindu **festivals**, especially Janmashtami (Aug/Sept), marking Krishna's birthday.

Dwarkadhish Temple

100m north of Gomti Ghat • Daily 7am–12.30pm & 5–9.30pm • No camera or video camera

Jagat Mandir, the elaborately carved tower of the sixteenth-century **Dwarkadhish Temple**, looms 78m over the town, comprising five storeys and 72 pillars while hoisting a giant flag made from more than 46m of cloth. It is believed that the original structure was built 2500 years ago by Vajranabha, Krishna's grandson, and that it has been destroyed by raging seas and rebuilt no less than six times. Non-Hindus may be required to sign a form declaring respect for the religion before they enter.

ARRIVAL AND DEPARTURE   DWARKA

By train The railway station is 2km northeast of town. Several daily trains connect Jamnagar (16 daily; 2–3hr) and Rajkot (12 daily; 3hr 50min–5hr), while at least one daily train goes to Ahmedabad (9hr). The # 22946*Saurashtra*

Mail departs daily at 1.35pm, travelling to Jamnagar (arr. 3.40pm), Rajkot (arr. 5.45pm), Ahmedabad (arr. 10.40pm) and Mumbai Central (arr. 7.10am).

By bus The bus stand is a 10min walk north of the old

9

city centre on the Okha Rd. More comfortable private bus companies have offices along Bhadrakali Rd, among them Shiv Shakti Travels (opposite *Guruprerna* hotel; ☎02892 234601, ⓦshivshaktibus.com), which has buses to Jamnagar (hourly; 3hr), Rajkot (hourly; 5hr) and Bhuj (7.30pm daily; 11hr).

Destinations (from the main stand) Jamnagar (4 daily; 3hr); Porbandar (3 daily; 3hr); Veraval (daily; 8hr).

INFORMATION AND TOURS

Tours Dwarka Darshan (Vegetable Market; ☎02892 234093) runs tours (8am & 2pm; ₹100) to the underground *jyotirlinga* at the Nageshwar Temple, 16km from Dwarka.

Services There are several banks with ATMs along Bhadrakali Rd.

ACCOMMODATION AND EATING

Guruprerna Opposite Bhadrakali Temple, Bhadrakali Rd ☎089 8072 4314, ⓦhotelsharanam.com. Institutional-style hotel with clean, comfortable rooms, all with attached bathrooms and some with a/c. Its popular a/c restaurant, *Sharanam*, serves generous South Indian thalis (₹200). ₹1300

Purushottam Parotha House Bhadrakali Rd ☎98988 10251. Small but extremely popular diner serving all-veg Punjabi meals, including excellent *paneer* tikka masala

(₹120). Daily noon–10.30pm.

Shri Dwarkesh Bhojnalay Next to HDFC, Bhadrakali Rd. A hole-in-the-wall thali joint offering fantastic Gujarati food for pennies (thali ₹90). Daily 11am–2pm & 6–10pm.

Tulsi Opposite Dr Ambadker Statue, Bhadrakali Rd ☎028 9223 5232. A bland business hotel with mostly clean and modern a/c (₹1450) and fan-cooled rooms with TVs. Hot water 5–10am only. ₹1200

Porbandar

Despite its links to legends of Krishna, **PORBANDAR**, once an international port and princely state capital, owes the bulk of its fame to **Mahatma Gandhi**, born here in 1869. Today, shrouded in a dim haze of excretions from the cement and chemical factories on its outskirts, the town is pretty grimy, despite the flow of remittances from its many emigrants overseas. Still, the Gandhi connection isn't Porbandar's only draw. Several lavish palaces are strung along the coast near the city's Chowpatty Seaface, including **Daria Rajmahal Palace**, now a college, and **Huzoor Palace**, occupied by the descendants of the former maharaja when they visit from London. An impressive old arched pavilion, **Grishmabhawan**, built for eighteenth-century poet Maharaja Sartanji, stands near the bus stand, while Porbandar's lake is a designated bird sanctuary (although you're more likely to spot **flamingos** – along with *dhow*-builders – at the creeks along the coast than here). Meanwhile, more than a thousand **whale sharks** visit the coast each year near Porbandar and Veraval; the Wildlife Trust of India (☎01 2041 43900, ⓦwti.org.in) can help organize dives or trips on research boats.

Gandhi's birthplace

Near Manek Chowk, Kasturba Rd • Daily 10am–noon & 3–6.30pm • Free but guides expect small donation

Porbandar's biggest attraction is **Gandhi's birthplace**, an old three-storey haveli. A floral swastika on the floor marks the exact point where he was born. Faded traces of old paintings adorn some of the walls in the reading and prayer rooms on the upper floors, but little else remains. The neighbouring **Kirti Mandir**, completed in 1950, is a memorial to Gandhi and his wife Kasturba, blending various religious architectural styles and displaying photographs and artefacts from the Mahatma's life.

ARRIVAL AND DEPARTURE

PORBANDAR

By plane Porbandar's airport is 7km east of town (₹90 auto-rickshaw ride). SpiceJet has daily flights to Mumbai (dep. 11.10am; 1hr 20min).

By train The railway station is 1km northeast of the town centre; the daily #19216 *Saurashtra Express* departs at 9.05pm, reaching Ahmedabad at 6.10am and Mumbai at 7.15pm the following day.

By bus The ST bus stand is a short walk south of the town

centre. Private bus offices are strung along MG Rd; Shree Ramkrupa (☎078 7878 0702) and Eagle Travels (☎079 6155 5555, ⓦeaglecorporate.com), both with buses to Rajkot (4hr 30min) and Ahmedabad (10–11hr), are two of the better options.

Destinations Jamnagar (3 daily; 3hr 15min–4hr); Junagadh (3 daily; 4hr).

INFORMATION

Banks The banks along MG Rd change foreign currency, as does JK forex (Mon–Fri 9am–6pm), also on MG Rd, across from Natraj.

Travel agents Thankys Tours & Travel (MG Rd, near Dreamland Cinema; ☎ 028 6224 7153) can book taxis, trains and domestic flights.

ACCOMMODATION

Indraprasth Opposite Swaminarayan Temple, off ST Cross Rd ☎ 028 6224 2681, ⓦ hotelindraprasth.biz. One of the better-value mid-range choices in Porbandar, offering straightforward fan-cooled and a/c attached rooms and suites in warm colours with TVs. ₹1000

Moon Palace MG Rd, 100m east of the main square ☎ 028 6224 1172, ⓦ porbandaronline.com/moonpalace. The rooms here, all attached and with TV, somehow have a European-holiday-home vibe; some have a/c (₹700). Clean, comfortable and good value; suites (₹1900) probably aren't worth the splurge. ₹700

★ **Natraj** MG Rd, close to Moon Palace ☎ 099 2533 3399, ⓦ hotelnatrajp.com. A notch above the competition: surprisingly cool, minimalist, fan-cooled and a/c attached rooms at bargain prices, plus cute suites and a fine restaurant, currency exchange. ₹700

Silver Palace Silver Complex Rani Baug, just off MG Rd ☎ 094 2955 0881. Another good choice despite the somewhat grimy entrance, with spotless fan and a/c (₹1600) rooms with TVs, fridges and various superfluous pieces of furniture, such as padded stools and mini tables. Some have lurid decor, so ask to see a few first. ₹1000

EATING

Moon Palace Moon Palace hotel, MG Rd ☎ 028 6224 1172, ⓦ porbandaronline.com/moonpalace. Popular restaurant serving Gujarati thalis (₹120), Punjabi dishes and Western snacks. It also opens early for breakfast. Daily 7.30am–11pm.

National MG Rd ☎ 098 7942 9988. This unassuming Muslim-run place serves delicious (but small) meat and veg meals (₹50–200) to a steady stream of contented customers. Daily 8am–10.30pm

Natraj Natraj hotel, MG Rd ☎ 099 2533 3399, ⓦ hotelnatrajp.com. Run with the same style and quiet efficiency as the hotel, *Natraj* has an elegant, modern dining room and a varied menu of Indian and Chinese and even decent pizzas (veg ₹115) and pasta dishes – the last a real rarity for Gujarat. Dining is limited to the fast-food menu until dinner begins at 7pm. Daily 11am–1pm.

Swagat MG Rd, 250m east of the main square. A relaxed, softly lit place that offers good-quality, reasonably priced Punjabi and south Indian veg dishes (₹55–100). It can get very busy at weekends. Daily 8.30am–3pm & 5.30–11pm.

Junagadh (Junagarh)

Little-visited **JUNAGADH** (or **Junagarh**) is an intriguing small city with a striking skyline of domes and minarets. Its lively bazars, Buddhist monuments, Hindu temples, mosques, Victorian Gothic-style archways and faded mansions – plus the magnificent Jain temples on **Mount Girnar**, 4km away – make it well worth exploring. Because of the sanctity of Mount Girnar, the **Shivratri Mela** (Feb/March) assumes particular importance here, when thousands of saffron-clad sadhus set up camp in town. Fireworks, processions, chanting, chillum-smoking and demonstrations of body-torturing ascetic practices run for at least five days and nights. In addition, every November, up to a million people take part in the **Parikrama**, a three-day 36km walk around the base of Mount Girnar and the surrounding hills to Bhavnath.

Brief history

From the fourth century BC to the death of Ashoka (c.232 BC), Junagadh was Gujarat's capital under the Buddhist Mauryas. The brief reigns of the Kshatrapas and the Guptas came to an end when the town passed into the hands of the Hindu Chudasanas, who in turn lost out to Muslim invaders. Muslim sovereignty lasted until Independence when, although the nawab of Junagadh planned to unite with Pakistan, local pressure ensured that the city became part of the Indian Union.

Chitta Khana Chowk and around

Junagadh is fairly compact, focused on the busy market area around **Chitta Khana Chowk**. To the north, near the railway station, quiet wide roads lead past the majestic

9

MAHATMA GANDHI – INDIA'S GREAT SOUL

Gujarat's most famous son, **Mohandas Karamchand Gandhi**, was born on October 2, 1869, in Porbandar. Although merchants by caste – Gandhi means grocer – both his grandfather and father rose to positions of political influence. Young Mohandas was shy and sickly, just an average scholar, but from early on he questioned the codes of power around him, even flouting accepted Hindu practice: he once ate meat for a year believing it would give him the physical edge the British appeared to possess. As a teenager, he began to develop an interest in spirituality, particularly the Jain principle of **ahimsa** (nonviolence).

At 19, he moved to London to study law, outwardly adopting the appearance and manners of an Englishman while obeying his mother's wish that he resist meat, alcohol and women. Studying the Bible alongside the Bhagavad Gita, he came to view different religions as a collective source of truth from which all could draw spiritual inheritance.

After a brief spell back in India, Gandhi left again to practise law in South Africa. The plight of his fellow Indians there, coupled with his own indignation at being ejected from a first-class train carriage, fuelled his campaigns for racial equality. Gaining crucial victories for minorities against the usage of indentured labour, his public profile grew. At this time he opted to transcend material possessions, donning the peasant's hand-spun *dhoti* and shawl and taking a vow of celibacy. This turn to ascetic purity he characterized as *satyagraha*, derived from Sanskrit ideas of "truth" and "firmness"; it would become the touchstone of **passive resistance**.

Returning to India with his messianic reputation well established – the poet Tagore named him **"Mahatma"** (Great Soul) – Gandhi travelled the country campaigning for **swaraj** (home rule). He also worked tirelessly for the rights of women and untouchables, whom he called **Harijans** (children of God), and founded an ashram at Sabarmati outside Ahmedabad where these principles were upheld. Gandhi stepped up his activities in the wake of the brutal massacre of protesters at Amritsar, leading a series of self-sufficiency drives during the 1920s, which culminated in the great **salt march** from Ahmedabad to Dandi in 1930. This month-long 386km journey led a swelling band of followers to the coast, where salt was made in defiance of the British monopoly on production. It drew worldwide attention: although Gandhi was promptly imprisoned, British resolve was seen to have weakened. On his release, he was invited to a round-table meeting in London to discuss home rule. The struggle continued for several years and Gandhi served more time in jail, his wife Kasturba dying by his side in 1944.

As the nationalist movement gained strength, Gandhi grew more concerned about the state of Hindu-Muslim relations. He responded to outbreaks of communal violence by subjecting his own body to self-purification and suffering through fasting. After Independence, Partition left him with a deep sense of failure. In a bid to stem the ensuing violence, he again fasted in Calcutta as large numbers of Hindus and Muslims flowed between the new countries. Gandhi's commitment to the fair treatment of Muslim Indians and his intention to visit and endorse Pakistan as a neighbour enraged many Hindu fundamentalists. He survived an attempt on his life on January 20, 1948, only to be shot dead from close range by a lone gunman, nationalist Nathuram Godse, in Delhi ten days later. Prime minister Jawaharlal Nehru announced the loss on national radio: "Friends and comrades, the light has gone out of our lives and there is darkness everywhere."

maqbara monuments, while to the south, congested streets surround Circle Chowk, a fine semicircular terrace between towering Victorian Gothic-style gateways. Nearby is the extravagant **Durbar Hall Museum**, while MG Road continues south to bustling Kalwa Chowk.

Maqbara

MG Rd, opposite the High Courts

Junagadh's chief Muslim monuments, the boldly decorated nineteenth-century **maqbara** (tombs), are unlike any other in Gujarat. These outstanding mausoleums blend European, Indian and Islamic styles, crowned with a multitude of bulbous domes. The most opulent tomb is the 1892 sepulchre of Mahabat Khan II, but more outstanding is that of Vizir Sahib Baka-ud-din Bhar, completed four years later and flanked on each corner by tall minarets hugged by spiral staircases.

Uparkot

Eastern end of Dhal Rd • Daily except 2nd & 4th Sat of month 7am–6pm • ₹100 (₹10)

The imposing fortified citadel of **Uparkot** is perched on a thickly walled mound to the east of the city and colonized by eagles, egrets and squirrels. Legend dates the fort's origins to the time of the Yadavas (Krishna's clan) who fled Mathura to settle in Dwarka, but historians believe it was built by Chandragupta Maurya in 319 BC. Rediscovered and repaired in 976 AD by Muslim conquerors, it regained its defensive importance, withstanding sixteen sieges over the next eight hundred years. A grand sequence of three high gateways cut into solid rock during the Muslim occupation stands at the entrance to the citadel, spanning a cobbled walkway that winds upwards to the summit of the raised fort, where the fort-like **Jama Masjid**, converted from a palace by a conquering Sultan in the fifteenth century, stands abandoned with its unique octagonal courtyard. Climb up to the roof for superb views over the city and Mount Girnar.

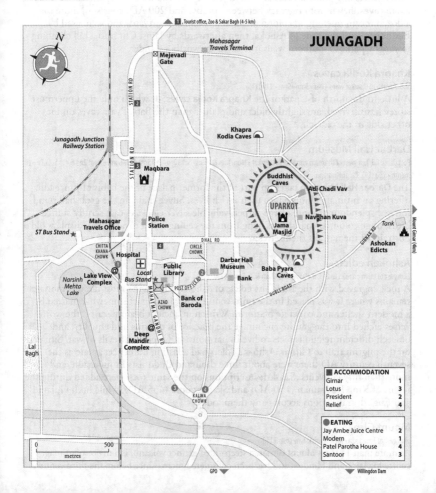

9

The two fierce cannons opposite the mosque were brought here in 1538 after being used in Diu fort against the Portuguese in 1530. About 200m northeast, more than 170 steps descend to the **Adi Chadi Vav** step-well, believed to date from the fifteenth century. As impressive is the eleventh-century **Navghan Kuva** in the southeast of the citadel, consisting of a superb staircase winding around a well shaft to the dimly lit water level more than 52m below.

Buddhist caves
100m north of Jama Masjid • Daily 8am–6pm • ₹100 (₹5)

Near the Jama Masjid is a two-storey complex of monastic cells cut into the rock and arranged around courtyards. These **Buddhist caves** are the most recent of their kind in Junagadh, built in the third or fourth century AD. Worn traces of figurines and foliage can still be made out on the columns in the lower level.

Baba Pyara caves
100m south of Uparkot walls • Daily 9am–5.30pm • ₹100 (₹5)

Two clusters of Buddhist caves are found just beyond the walls of Uparkot. The **Baba Pyara caves**, hewn from the rock between 200 BC and 200 AD, consist of more than a dozen rooms opening to colonnades and a spacious courtyard, and were used by Buddhists until the time of Ashoka, then afterwards by Jains. Cut into a hill climbing towards Uparkot's southern walls, the caves are worth a wander.

Khapra Kodia caves
300m north of Uparkot walls • Daily 9am–5pm • ₹100 (₹5)

A little to the north of Uparkot the **Khapra Kodia caves**, of which only the uppermost storey has survived, are slightly older and plainer than the Baba Pyara caves on the other side of the citadel.

Darbar Hall Museum
Post Office Rd, just west of the main entrance to Uparkot • Mon, Tues & Thurs–Sat 10am–1.15pm & 3–6pm, except 2nd & 4th Sat of each month • ₹50 (₹5), ₹2/photograph

The **Darbar Hall Museum** takes up part of the former palace of the babis of Junagadh, offering an intimate glimpse into their lavish lives. Silver chairs in the great hall stand in regal splendour around a large carpet, valuable silver clocks encase scruffy stuffed birds, huge coloured chandeliers hang from the ceiling and a royal gallery displays old portraits of the nawabs themselves.

Ashokan edicts
2km east of town on road to Girnar • Daily 8am–1pm & 2–6pm • ₹150 (₹10)

A rock engraved with the Buddhist **edicts of Ashoka**, Junagadh's most famous monarch, remains where it was placed in the third century BC, its impact somewhat marred by a modern shelter and concrete platform. Written in ancient brahmi script, the worn verses etched into the granite encourage the practice of dharma and equality, and beseech different religious sects to live in harmony and repent the evils of war. Situated on the pilgrim trail to Girnar, Ashoka's edicts had a lasting influence: as late as the seventh century AD there were about three thousand Buddhists in Junagadh, and more than fifty convents. Sanskrit inscriptions on the same rock were added during the reigns of King Rudraman (150 AD) and Skandagupta (455 AD), while both Gujarati and English translations accompany them today.

Mount Girnar
6km east of Junagadh • An auto-rickshaw costs ₹150

At more than 1116m, **Mount Girnar**, a steep-sided extinct volcano, is a major pilgrimage centre for Jains and Hindus, and has been considered sacred since before the third century

BC. It's best to start the roughly eight-thousand-step ascent around 6am. The trail (6–7hr return), scattered with chai stalls, climbs through eucalyptus forests before zigzagging across the sheer rock face. On a plateau below the summit, the picturesque huddle of Jain temples has been renovated a little since its erection between 1128 and 1500. In the marble **Neminath temple**, the first on the left as you enter the "temple city", Neminath, the 22nd *tirthankara* – said to have died on Mount Girnar after seven hundred years of meditation and asceticism – is depicted as a black figure in the lotus position holding a conch.

The final two thousand steps to the summit of Mount Girnar are worth the effort, offering breathtaking views. At the top, a temple dedicated to the Hindu goddess **Amba Mata** attracts both Hindu and Jain pilgrims. Steps lead down from this temple and then up again along a narrow ridge towards **Gorakhnath Peak**, where a small shrine covers what are supposedly the footprints of the pilgrim Gorakhnath, and further to a third peak where the imprints of Neminath's feet are sheltered by a small canopy. At the most distant point of the ridge, a shrine dedicated to the fierce Hindu goddess **Kalika**, the eternal aspect of Durga, is a haunt for near-naked **Aghora ascetics** who express their absolute renunciation of the world by ritually enacting their own funerals.

ARRIVAL AND DEPARTURE   JUNAGADH (JUNAGARH)

By train Junagadh Junction is just off Station Rd, to the northwest of the town centre. The *Somnath Express* #22958 departs daily at 11.05 pm to Rajkot (arr. 01.10 am) and Ahmedabad (5.25 am).

Destinations Ahmedabad (3–4 daily; 7hr); Delvada for Diu (1 daily at 7.15am; 6hr); Rajkot (11 weekly–7 daily; 2hr 30min); Sasan Gir (1 daily at 7.15am; 2hr 45min); Veraval (9 daily; 1hr 50min).

By bus The long-distance ST bus stand is 300m west of Chitta Khana Chowk. Mahasagar Travels (☎ 028 5262 9340), which has a bus terminal just east of Majevadi Gate, plus offices on Dhal Rd near the railway station and at Kalwa Chowk, operates private buses to Ahmedabad (hourly; 7hr); Rajkot (hourly; 2hr 30min) and Mumbai (1 daily; 17hr); shuttle services are available from city offices to the main terminal. Services to Porbander leave regularly from the local bus stand on Azad Chowk.

Destinations (from ST bus stand) Ahmedabad (hourly; 7hr); Porbandar (hourly; 4hr); Rajkot (hourly; 3hr); Sasan Gir (6 daily; 2hr); Una for Diu (hourly; 4hr 30min); Veraval (hourly; 2hr 30min).

INFORMATION

Tourist information The official tourist office is in the *Girnar* hotel, near the northern Majevadi Gate (☎ 028 5262 1201) but staff at the *Relief* hotel (see below) provide the best information on the town's sites and Gir National Park.

Services The main post office is 2km south of town; there's also a smaller branch on Post Office Rd near Azad Chowk. The State Bank of India opposite the Durbar Hall Museum changes dollars and sterling, and there are several ATMs scattered around town, including the Bank of Baroda near the local bus stand.

ACCOMMODATION

If you're arriving in Junagadh during either **Shivratri Mela** or the **Parikrama** (see page 583), it's advisable to book rooms well in advance.

Girnar 2km north of town, near Majevadi Gate ☎ 028 5262 1201; map p.585. Run (without much enthusiasm) by Gujarat Tourism, the modern *Girnar* has reasonable, attached rooms; some also have balconies and a/c (₹1800–2200) and there's a decent restaurant (thalis ₹120). Autorickshaws from the bus stand cost ₹50–70. ₹1700

Lotus Station Rd ☎ 028 5265 8500, ✆ thelotushotel. com; map p.585. A tranquil contrast to the dust and noise outside, *Lotus* is the town's smartest hotel. The swish rooms have marble floors and beige furniture, along with hot water, TV and refrigerator. Breakfast included. ₹1900

President Station Rd ☎ 028 5262 5661; map p.585. Handy if you have to catch an early train, this place has acceptable attached rooms, some with a/c (₹900). The larger, more expensive rooms face the noisy main road, so opt for one facing the courtyard. ₹800

★ **Relief** Dhal Rd ☎ 028 5262 0280, ✆ reliefhotel.com; map p.585. Welcoming and extremely knowledgeable staff, clean and cheap attached rooms and a superior restaurant (in season) make *Relief* easily the best bet in town for backpackers. ₹850

EATING

Jay Ambe Juice Centre Post Office Rd, 50m south of Circle Chowk, no phone; map p.585. The place to come for fresh fruit juices, milkshakes and ice cream: don't miss the drinks made from Junagadh's famous kesar mangos and

9

the sapodilla shakes (around ₹60). Daily 10am–11pm.
Modern Jayshree Rd opposite the Civil Hospital ☏ 028 5262 0928; map p.585. An a/c dining hall serving bottomless spicy-sweet thalis (₹110). Tourists are unusual here, however, so you may have an audience while you eat. Meal for two will cost around ₹350. Daily 10am–10.30pm.
Patel Parotha House Jawahar Rd, north of Kalwa Chowk ☏ 098 9899 6023; map p.585. A clean and busy

a/c restaurant with big windows overlooking Kalwa Chowk, serving generous Gujarati and Jain thalis (₹120). Daily 9am–11pm.
Santoor MG Rd, northwest of Kalwa Chowk ☏ 028 5262 5090 or 915 266 9368; map p.585. Delicious, reasonably priced Chinese, Punjabi and south Indian dishes (masala dosa ₹70), plus juices from locally grown fruit and milkshakes served in cosy, dimly lit booths. Daily 11am–11pm.

Veraval

Midway between Porbandar and Diu sprawls the chaotic, congested fishing port of **VERAVAL**. While most visitors today use Veraval as a jumping-off point for the area's pilgrimage sites – such as **Somnath**, 6km to the east – it was also once a major port for *hajjis* en route to Mecca. The vicinity's various shrines to Vishnu and connection with Krishna – said to have lived here with the Yadavas – make it equally important for Vaishnavites today.

The city itself has little to hold visitors' interest, although its enormous **fishing harbour**, crammed with a dizzying number of colourful *dhows*, is worth a look. A kilometre along the road to Somnath is **Bhalka Tirtha**, a modest temple marking the spot where Shri Krishna was fatally mistaken for a deer, taking an arrow wound while he slept on a deerskin. Beneath a tree planted in his memory is a marble statue of the reclining deity.

ARRIVAL AND DEPARTURE   VERAVAL

By train Veraval's railway station (☏ 028 7627 1411) is just over 1km north of town. For longer journeys, it's often quicker to change at Rajkot. The *Somnath–Jabalpur Express* #11463 depart at 9.50 am, connecting Junagadh (1hr 30min), Rajkot (4hr) and Ahmedabad (8hr 30min). There are also two daily departures for Sasan Gir (9.45am & 1.55pm; 1hr 30min–2hr) and one for Delvada (4.20pm; 3hr 30min), the nearest station to Diu.

By bus Veraval's bus stand (☏ 028 7622 1666, ⊛ gsrtc.in) is on ST Bus Stand Rd near the centre of town, connecting major cities throughout Gujarat. Several private offices are set nearby, some of which offer overnight bus services.
Destinations Ahmedabad (6 daily; 9hr); Dwarka (4 daily; 6hr); Junagadh (6 daily; 2hr); Porbandar (4 daily; 3hr 30min); Rajkot (6 daily; 4hr); Sasan Gir (every 4hr; 1hr 30min).

ACCOMMODATION AND EATING

Kaveri 2nd Akar Complex, ST Rd ☏ 028 7622 0842, ⊛ hotelkaveri.in. Just to the left when exiting the bus stand, this is the best option in town, with clean, bright and well-appointed a/c (₹1500) and non-a/c attached rooms with TV. ₹700
Sagar Riddhi Siddhi Complex, ST Rd ☏ 028 7622 3939. This smart, a/c vegetarian restaurant near the clock tower offers a varied menu of south Indian, Chinese and Punjabi

dishes (masala dosa ₹8; Punjabi and Gujarati thali ₹120–160). Daily 9am–3.30pm & 5–11pm.
Utsav Opposite the bus stand, ST Rd ☏ 028 7622 2306. Just to the right when exiting the bus stand, this hotel has rooms that are much more habitable than the entrance to the grubby complex would suggest, with views high over the busy road. No a/c, though. ₹750

Somnath

The town of **SOMNATH** consists of little more than a few streets between the bus stand and its giant temple, famed across India as the first of the twelve *jyotirlinga* of Shiva. The temple is visible from all over town, towering over a reclaimed beach, which now has a great market selling nautical trinkets and offering camel rides.

Somnath Temple

Temple Daily 6am–9.30pm • Aarti (prayer) times: 7am, noon & 7pm • Photography prohibited • **Sound-and-light show** 8–9pm • ₹20 • ☏ 028 7665 9093, or 942 821 4914, ⊛ somnath.org

Legend has it that the site of **Somnath Temple**, formerly known as **Prabhas Patan**, was dedicated to Soma, the juice of a plant used in rituals and greatly praised for its enlightening powers (and hallucinogenic effects) in the Rig Veda. The temple itself is believed to have appeared first in gold, at the behest of the sun god; next in silver, created by the moon god; a third time in wood at the command of Krishna; and finally, in stone, built by King Bhimdev, the strongest of the five Pandava brothers from the Mahabharata epic. The earliest definite record, however, dates the temple to the tenth century when it became rich from devotees' donations. Unfortunately, such wealth came to the attention of the brutal iconoclast Mahmud of Ghazni who destroyed the shrine and carried its treasure off to Afghanistan. The next seven centuries saw a cycle of rebuilding and sacking, though the temple lay in ruins for more than two hundred years after a final sacking by Aurangzeb, before the most recent reconstruction began in 1950. Although very little of the original structure remains, the latest reconstruction follows the elegant style of the Solanki period, and merits a visit for its physical and spiritual grandeur.

Prabhas Patan Museum

300m north of Somnath Temple • Daily except Wed and 2nd & 4th Sat of the month 10.30am–5pm • ₹50 (₹5)

The **Prabhas Patan Museum** preserves the scant remains of previous constructions of the Somnath Temple. In addition to the array of carved stone statues lined up in the open courtyard, the museum's collection includes lintels, vials of sacred water, sections of roof pillars, friezes and *toranas* from the tenth to twelfth centuries.

Other temple sites

Tongas and rickshaws gather outside the bus station, ready to take pilgrims to the temple sites east of Somnath. Most important of these is **Triveni Ghat**, mentioned in the epics of the Ramayana and Mahabharata. Also called Triveni Sangam, this newly renovated bathing *ghat* lies at the confluence of the Hiran, Saraswati and Kapil rivers where they meet the Arabian Sea. A dip in the waters here is believed to be highly propitious. Before reaching the confluence, the road passes the ancient **Surya Mandir**, the Sun Temple, probably built during the Solanki period and now cramped by a newer temple and concrete houses built almost against its walls.

ARRIVAL AND DEPARTURE	SOMNATH
By bus and auto-rickshaw Somnath's bus stand is just a few hundred metres east of the temple. Buses run to	Veraval's ST bus stand (every 15–30min; ₹30). Autos will charge around ₹80 for the trip.

ACCOMMODATION AND EATING

Aastha Khodiyar St, behind Central Bank ☎ 094 2818 9792. Just behind Central Bank and very close to the temple, with small but clean, tiled attached rooms, non a/c and all with TVs. ₹600

Bhabha Restaurant Khodiyar St. The original *Bhabha* sits just outside the *Aastha* hotel, while about 200m east is a new restaurant with the same name and owner. Both

are popular, friendly joints offering good breakfasts (₹150). Daily 8.30am–10.30pm.

Mayuram Triveni Rd, southeast of the bus stand ☎ 028 7623 1286. The once-sparkling, tiled rooms here all have attached bathrooms and are among Somnath's best-value options, but be sure to book ahead. ₹800

Gir National Park

Mid-Oct to mid-June daily 6–9am, 9am–noon & 3–5.30pm; late monsoons can delay opening until Nov • Six-person jeep ₹12,000 (₹5300) including permit (from park information centre or buy online), guide, camera and hotel pick-up and drop-off • ☎ 099 7123 1439, ⓦ girnationalpark.in

The **Asiatic lion**, which, on account of hunting, forest-clearance and poaching, has been extinct in the rest of India since the 1880s, survives in the wild in just 1150 square kilometres of the gently undulating Gir Forest. **Gir National Park**, accessed via **Sasan**

9

THE ASIATIC LION

The rare **Asiatic lion** (*Panthera leo persica*) is paler and shaggier than its more common African cousin, with longer tail tassels, more prominent elbow tufts and a larger belly fold. Probably introduced to India from Persia, the lions were widespread in the Indo-Gangetic plains at the time of the Buddha. In 300 BC, Kautilya, the minister of Chandragupta Maurya, offered them protection by declaring certain areas *abharaya aranyas*, "forests free from fear". Later, in his rock-inscribed edicts, **Ashoka** admonished those who hunted the majestic animals.

The lion was favourite game for India's nineteenth-century rulers and by 1913, not long after it had been declared a protected species by the nawab of Junagadh, its population was reduced to twenty. Since then, Gir Forest has been recognized as a sanctuary (1969), and a national park (1975), while the number of lions has swelled to more than five hundred. However, they remain under serious threat from poachers, while illegal timber-felling in the forest is still common. Three major roads and a railway line bisect the park, which also has four temples that attract more than 84,000 pilgrims each year; all this produces noise, pollution and littering. Moreover, when lions stray from the sanctuary – a common occurrence – there have been attacks on humans and livestock. Plans, meanwhile, to create another reserve outside Gujarat, possibly in Madhya Pradesh – to reduce the risk of the cats being wiped out by a particularly contagious disease or infection – continue to be resisted (for political rather than conservation reasons) by the state government. For more information, see ⓦ asiaticlion.org.

Gir, lies 60km southeast of Junagadh and 45km northeast of Veraval, and boasts more than five hundred lions in its 260 square kilometres. The park also shelters around three hundred leopards, as well as sambar (large deer), chousingha (four-horned antelope), chinkara (gazelle), jackal, striped hyena and wild boar. The wildlife shares the land with Maldhari cattle-breeders, many of whom have been relocated outside the sanctuary. Those who remain are paid compensation by the government for the inevitable loss of their livestock to marauding lions. In 2008, it emerged that some tourists had been paying to watch lions devour tethered cattle in cruel – and illegal – "*baitwalla* shows"; if anyone approaches you about one of these shows, inform the park's management team. **Sightings** of the lions aren't guaranteed, although summer is the best time to spot them.

Devalia

Daily except Wed 8–11am & 3–5pm • Mon–Fri ₹2400 (₹150); Sat, Sun & public holidays ₹3000 (₹190) • Jeeps (₹250 return) leave regularly from Sasan Gir

For a guaranteed lion sighting, head for **Devalia**, a partially fenced-off area of the park known as the Gir Interpretation Zone, just 12km from Sasan Gir. You get a surprisingly good impression of the lions "in the wild" here – they still have to hunt for their food, even if the deer have limited space to escape.

ARRIVAL AND INFORMATION   GIR NATIONAL PARK

By public transport Buses and trains connect Sasan Gir to Junagadh (2 daily; 1hr 45min), Rajkot (2 daily; 3hr) and Veraval (2 daily; 1hr). From Diu, head to Una and then catch a bus (2hr 15min).

Park information centre The park's reception centre is in Sasan Gir village, next to *Sinh Sadan Guest House* (daily: mid-Oct to mid-Feb 6.30am–noon & 3–5pm; mid-Feb to mid-June 6.30am–1pm & 4–5.30pm; ☏ 028 7728 5541).

ACCOMMODATION AND EATING

Amidhara Resort Off Railway Station Rd, Sasan Gir ☏ 028 7728 5950 or 704 358 6305, ⓦ amidhararesorts.com. These full-board lodgings are the plushest to be found near Gir, with comfortable attached rooms and private cottages (₹4500–8000). The attractive grounds include a pool, gym, billiards hall, badminton court and restaurant. **₹5000**

Gir Birding Lodge 2km west of Sasan Gir, opposite Bambhafod Naka ☏ 088 8267 7766, ⓦ girnationalpark.com. This full-board option has rooms in the main building and in cottages, complete with wood fittings and four-posters; there's also a fine restaurant. The hotel's friendly naturalist guide takes guests for birdwatching walks, too. **₹5000**

Gir Jungle Resort 3km west of Sasan Gir, 500m east of Bhalchel Village ☏028 7728 5590, ⊕girjungleresort.com. With lovely gardens and pretty rooms that have checked floors and cane furniture, this is among Gir's best options. There's also a pool and an excellent restaurant overlooking the Hiran River. ₹4000

Umang Off Station Rd, Sasan Gir, 100m west of Sinh Sadan ☏028 7728 5728, ⊕sasangirhotels.in. One of the better cheap hotels, in a convenient location, offering twenty bright but spartan attached rooms. ₹1950

Diu

Set off the southern tip of Saurashtra is the tiny island of **Diu**, just 12km long and 3km wide. Under Portuguese control for more than four hundred years, until 1961, it is now governed as a Union Territory from Delhi along with its sister city of Daman (see page 601). The combination of relaxed atmosphere, historic charm, broad beaches and lack of alcohol restrictions makes Diu one of the most popular tourist destinations in the region. While its beaches are admittedly not as idyllic as Goa's, most visitors stay longer than intended.

Diu Town in the east is the island's main focus. A maze of alleys lined with distinctive Portuguese buildings form the hub of the **old town**, while the **fort** stands on the island's easternmost tip, staring defiantly out at the Gulf of Cambay. Along the northern coast, the island's main road runs past salt pans that give way to mudflats sheltering flocks of waterbirds, including flamingos that stop to feed in early spring. The route skirting the south coast passes rocky cliffs and beaches, the most developed of which is **Nagoa Beach**, before reaching the tiny fishing village of **Vankbara** in the very west of the island.

Brief history

The earliest records of Diu date from 1298, when it was controlled by the Chudasana dynasty. Soon after, it fell into the hands of invading Muslims and by 1349 was ruled by Mohammed bin Tughluq who successfully boosted the shipbuilding industry. Diu prospered as a harbour and in 1510 came under the government of the Ottoman Malik Ayaz, who repelled besieging **Portuguese** forces in 1520 and 1521. Aware of Diu's strategic position for trade with Arabia and the Persian Gulf, and having already gained a toehold in Daman, the Portuguese did not relent. Under **Nuno da Cunha**, they once more tried, but failed, to take the island in 1531. However, in 1535, Sultan Bahadur of Gujarat, facing pressure from both the Mughals and Portuguese, allowed Da Cunha to build a fort in Diu. Three years later an Ottoman siege of Diu was repelled, cementing

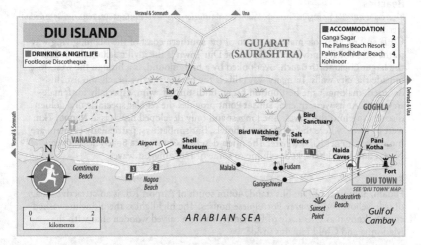

9

Portuguese control of Diu. The Portuguese held sway for more than four centuries, making Diu one of the world's longest-held colonial possessions. They were finally forced out in 1961 by Nehru's government, which, after a swift bombing campaign, declared Diu to be part of India.

Diu Town

Little Diu Town **DIU TOWN** is protected by the fort in the east and a wall in the west. **Nagar Sheth Haveli**, one of the grandest of the town's distinctive Portuguese mansions, is on Makata Road, hidden in the web of narrow streets that wind through the residential **Old Portuguese District**. Fishermen make daily trips from the north coast in wooden boats; their catch is sold in the fish market opposite the bus stand (daily 9am–noon).

Diu's churches

Although the Christian population is dwindling along with the old language, a few old whitewashed **churches** in Diu's Farangiwada (Foreigner's Corner) are still used. Portuguese Mass is celebrated beneath the high ceilings and painted arches of **St Paul's**, widely considered to be India's most elaborate Portuguese church. To the northwest, the church of **St Thomas** now houses a sparsely stocked museum (daily 9am–9pm) and a guesthouse (see page 594), while to the south, the church of **St Francis of Assisi** is partly occupied by the local hospital.

The fort

East end of Fort Rd • Daily 8am–6pm • Free

Diu's serene **fort**, built by Nuno da Cunha in 1535, still stands robust, resisting the battering of the sea on three sides and sheltering birds, jackals and the town jail. Its wide moat and coastal position enabled the fort to withstand attack by land and sea, but there are obvious scars from the Indian government's air strikes in 1961 – notice the hole above the altar of the church in the southwest corner. Now abandoned almost completely to nature, and littered with centuries-old cannonballs, it commands excellent views out to sea and over the island. Just offshore, the curious, ship-shaped old prison known as **Pani Kotha Fort** – connected to the mainland by tunnel, according to lore – is off-limits due to partial collapse, but when the waters are calm, passenger boats (₹50) circle the island from the port for a closer look.

Beaches

Nagoa can be reached by bus from Diu Town – check with the tourist office for up-to-date details; Gomtimata Beach can only be reached by private vehicle

Cliffs and rocky pools make up much of the southern coast of the island, giving way to the occasional sandy stretch. South of Diu Town is the idyllic **Jallandhar Beach**; the larger **Chakratirth Beach**, overlooked by a high mound, is a little to the west, just outside the city walls. In many ways this is the most attractive beach and usually deserted, making it the best option for an undisturbed swim, especially for female travellers. At its western end, **Sunset Point** provides the regular spectacle of a golden disc sinking into the waves. The longest and only developed beach is at **Nagoa**, 7km west of town, where there are several hotels, but sunbathers, particularly women, are more likely to get hassled here. The often deserted **Gomtimata Beach** lies between Nagoa and Vanakbara, and is home to some of Diu's biggest waves.

Fudam

Fudam, 3km west of Diu bus stand, 400m south of Airport Rd, is an attractive village of pale yellow and sky grey Portuguese houses. The highlight is the old whitewashed **church**, known as Our Lady of Remedies, where a carved wooden altar with the Madonna and Child remains inside.

Shell Museum

Just east of the airport on the Airport Rd Nagao Beach Road • Daily 9am–5pm m • ₹30

The **Shell Museum** is the vast personal collection – 42 years in the making – of Captain Devjibhai Vira Fulbaria, who spent a lifetime on the ocean picking up shells wherever he weighed anchor. With 2500 shells and detailed descriptions, this quirky, unexpected exhibit is certainly worth a look.

ARRIVAL AND DEPARTURE — DIU

By plane Diu's airport (ⓘ 028 7525 4743), 6km west of town, has flights to Mumbai with Air India (Mon–Thurs; 2pm; 1hr 5min).

By train The nearest railway station to Diu is at Delvada, 8km up the Diu–Una road. From here, train #52951 Delvada Junagadh Passenger (daily 1110 am) departs for Sasan Gir (arr. 2.54pm) and Junagadh (arr. 5.10pmpm), while the slow #52950 runs to Veraval (daily 8.05am; arr. 11.20am), where there are daily trains for Ahmedabad.

By bus Buses remain the most convenient means of transport, and private buses are most often well worth the slight jump in price. Be warned that some buses may be inundated with drunken passengers on weekend nights,

particularly on Sun. Services arrive and depart from the bus stand by the bridge in Diu Town, just a few minutes' walk to the west of town. State bus services run to Porbandar, Rajkot, Junagadh and Veraval; for Palitana, take a bus to Bhavnagar and change at Talaja. Private tour operators offer more comfortable buses to Ahmedabad and Mumbai. Far better transport connections are found on the mainland, at Una bus stand, connected to Diu by auto-rickshaws and buses (6.30am–8pm; hourly; 40min; ₹30).

Destinations Ahmedabad (daily; 9hr); Bhavnagar (5 daily; 6hr); Junagadh (8 daily; 5hr); Mumbai (6 daily; 19hr); Porbandar (3 daily; 7hr); Rajkot (5 daily; 7hr 30min); Veraval (10 daily; 3hr).

GETTING AROUND

By auto-rickshaw Widely available across the island: ₹50 for trips within town and ₹80 to reach Nagoa Beach.

By bus DMC (Diu Municipal Council) buses depart from the main bus stand to Nagoa Beach at 7am, 11am and 4pm

(returning 30min later), stopping at the airport along the way.

By bike or moped Numerous places near the main square, Bunder Chowk, rent out bikes (₹100/day), as well as mopeds and scooters (₹250–350/day).

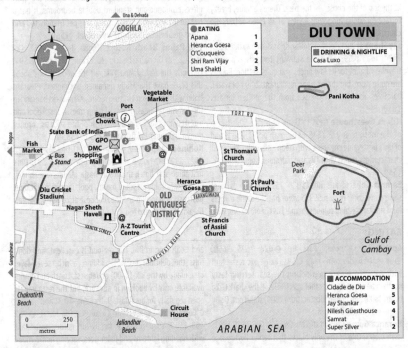

DIU TOWN

● EATING
Apana	1
Heranca Goesa	5
O'Couqueiro	4
Shri Ram Vijay	2
Uma Shakti	3

■ DRINKING & NIGHTLIFE
Casa Luxo	1

■ ACCOMMODATION
Cidade de Diu	3
Heranca Goesa	5
Jay Shankar	6
Nilesh Guesthouse	4
Samrat	1
Super Silver	2

9

INFORMATION

Tourist information The tourist office, next to Bandar Gate at the port (Mon–Sat 10am–1pm & 2–6pm; ☎028 7025 2653, ⓦ diutourism.co.in), offers little beyond maps and brochures. A–Z Tourist Centre (daily 9am–11pm; ☎098 2546 3245, ⓦ atoztraveldiu.com) on Vaniya St near Panchvati Rd in the Old Portuguese District, offers basic information on the island and can arrange car, moped and scooter rental, as well as train, bus and flight tickets.

Services The main post office is on the western side of Bunder Chowk (Mon–Sat 8am–noon & 2–5pm). The State Bank of India nearby exchanges money, while ICICI, Axis and State Bank all have ATMs.

ACCOMMODATION

Prices rise during **festival periods** – particularly Diwali, Holi and New Year's – while in the off-season they come down by as much as seventy percent (some places may even close for the season, so call ahead). Some people, especially women, may be put off at festival times by the rowdy atmosphere.

DIU TOWN

Cidade de Diu Off Collectorate Rd ☎028 7525 4443, ⓦ cidadedediu.in; map p.593. A wedding cake of a building, with clashing paint jobs illuminated by neon lights at night; the rooms are thankfully more tasteful. While the cheaper options are a bit worn, all are brightly painted and clean – the more expensive rooms are much more spacious. ₹1800

Heranca Goesa Behind Diu Museum, Farangiwada ☎028 7525 3851; map p.593. A handful of a/c and non-a/c, attached rooms in the very friendly Goan-style family home of Francisco and Alina: all are immaculate but those at the top of the house are the best. There's a large, breezy terrace for sunbathing with a view of all three of Diu's old churches. ₹800

Jay Shankar Just north of Jallandhar Beach ☎028 7525 2424; map p.593. This old stalwart remains a popular travellers' haunt for its low prices and quiet setting. Rooms are quite worn, but there's a bar, restaurant, 24hr hot water, balconies and views of the sea from the rooftop terrace. ₹850

Nilesh Guesthouse Next to Bank of India, 50m south of the mosque ☎028 7525 2319; map p.593. This is one of Diu's best-value cheapies, with clean although somewhat characterless rooms with TVs and balconies, some with a/c. ₹550

Samrat Collectorate Rd ☎028 7525 2354, ⓦ hotel samratdiu.com; map p.593. *Samrat* has the same owners (and similar clashing colour schemes) as *Cidade de Diu*, with which it shares a pool and bar. The pink and beige rooms here have TV and attached private bathrooms, while some also have a/c (₹2100) and balconies. ₹1500

Super Silver Super Silver Complex ☎028 7525 2020, ⓔ supersilverdiu@yahoo.com; map p.593. A warm welcome and clean, excellent-value attached double occupancy rooms with TVs, some with a/c (₹1500), make *Super Silver* a popular choice with overseas travellers. ₹850

THE REST OF THE ISLAND

Ganga Sagar Nagoa Beach ☎02875 275449; map p.591. While it may be a bit of a dive, *Ganga Sagar* has budget tiled rooms (some a/c), a lively bar (sometimes a tad too lively on weekends), a restaurant, and best of all, a great location right on the beach. ₹1650

Hotel Palms Kodhidhar Beach Nagoa ☎02875 275375 or 082389 63356 ⓦ hotelpalms.co.in; map p.591. Located in the touristy Kodhidhar Beach, the hotel offers economic and standard double bedrooms. It has a restaurant and wheelchair access; it is pet friendly too and offers great views of sunrise and sunset. ₹2550

The Palms Beach Resort Nagoa Beach ☎982 429 4048, ⓦ thepalmsbeachresort.com; map p.591. Formerly the *Hoka Island Villa*, all the good things about this place have thankfully remained unchanged. Pleasant hotel with seventeen enticing rooms, hammocks hanging in the communal areas, groves of palm trees, a small pool and a restaurant offering delicious fish dishes such as coconut prawn and tamarind fish curry (₹350). ₹3550

Kohinoor Airport Rd, 1.5km west of Diu town ☎028 7527 5301, ⓦ hotelkohinoordiu.com; map p.591. Diu's first three-star hotel, this resort has a Mediterranean feel, with comfortable attached rooms, pool, Jacuzzi, restaurant, pastry shop, bar, gym and the *Footloose* disco (see opposite). Breakfast is included too. ₹5000

EATING

Apana Apana hotel, Fort Rd ☎028 7525 3650, ⓦ apanahoteldiu.com; map p.593. Large a/c restaurant with a garden terrace overlooking the sea, serving tasty north Indian cuisine and other specialities – the shark tikka (from ₹300) and grilled lobster (from ₹800) stand out. Daily 7am–4.30pm & 7–11pm.

Heranca Goesa Behind Diu Museum ☎028 7525 3851; map p.593. One of the only places that serves Portuguese and Goan food in Diu. The seafood is excellent, and don't miss the delicious *bebinca* pudding, a rich, seven-layer cake made by the kilo (₹400) on request. Lunch and dinner available only by booking in advance, but the restaurant is open regularly for breakfast. Daily 8am–10.30am.

O'Couqueiro Lane behind Cidade de Diu hotel; ☎982 468 1565; map p.593. A family-run garden restaurant with hanging lanterns and palm trees, serving home-made muesli and yogurt, pasta dishes made with imported Italian olive oil and parmesan, and a handful of Portuguese options (mains ₹395–850). There's a slim selection of books and magazines to read too, and international chill-out music on the sound system. Daily 8am–9pm

★ **Shri Ram Vijay** Just off Bunder Chowk (Main Square), no phone; map p.593. A wonderful slice of small-town Americana transported to Diu Town, this tiny parlour started up in 1933, still serves home-made ice

cream (₹50–60/scoop), sundaes, banana splits, cream sodas and milkshakes. Daily 8.30am–-1.30pm & 3.30–9.30pm.

Uma Shakti Behind vegetable market; map p.593. This hotel restaurant and bar serves good breakfasts of cornflakes, toast or pancakes, as well as more substantial Indian or Chinese meals. The breezy roof terrace, with views over Diu Town, is a great spot for a sundowner. Mains ₹90–210. Daily 9am–10.30pm.

DRINKING AND NIGHTLIFE

The availability of **alcohol** seems to be the greatest Portuguese legacy in Diu. Expect to pay around ₹90 for a Kingfisher.

Casa Luxo Bunder Chowk (Main Square), Diu town; map p.593. Caught in a bit of a 1960s time warp, this is one of Diu's more welcoming bars. Tues–Sat 9am–1pm & 4–9pm.

Footloose Discotheque Kohinoor hotel, Airport Rd, 1.5km west of Diu Town ☎028 7527 5301, ☏hotelkohinoordiu.com; map p.591. In addition to the welcoming, modern *Rio Bar* (daily 11am–3pm & 7–11pm), the *Kohinoor* hotel houses Diu's only nightclub, *Footloose Discotheque*, a/c with a spacious dance floor complete with flashy lighting effects. Sat & Sun 8–11pm.

Bhavnagar

The port of **BHAVNAGAR**, founded in 1723 by the Gohil Rajput Bhavsinghji, whose ancestors came to Gujarat from Marwar (Rajasthan) in the thirteenth century, is an important trading centre whose principal export is cotton. It has also produced a string of artists and writers, notably poet **Jhaverchand Meghani**. For Gujarati industrialists, it serves as the jumping-off point for the massive, controversial and booming ship-breaking yard at **Alang**. The yard, which employs twenty thousand labourers, has been off-limits to foreigners since Greenpeace red-flagged it for environmental damage, toxic spills and hazardous work in the early 2000s.

With few sights of its own, Bhavnagar is nonetheless an obvious place to overnight before heading southwest to the Jain temples of Palitana. The focus of interest is the **old city**, overlooked by delicate wooden balconies and the pillared facades of former merchants' houses, which boasts a fascinating **bazar**, clustered around the Becharaji railway station. The marble temple, **Ganga Devi Mandir**, by the Ganga Jalia Tank in the town centre, has a large dome and intricate latticework on its walls, while the **Takhteshwar Temple**, raised on a hill in the south of town, affords a good view over to the Gulf of Cambay in the east.

Gandhi Smriti and Barton museums

Off Crescent Circle • **Gandhi Smriti Museum** Mon–Sat 9am–1pm & 2–6pm, closed 2nd and 4th Sat of the month • Free • **Barton Museum** Mon–Sat 9am–1pm & 3–6pm, open on Sundays from 9 am-2 pm. closed 2nd and 4th Sat of the month • ₹50 (₹2) • ☎027 8242 4516

In the east of town by the clock tower, the **Gandhi Smriti Museum** exhibits old sepia photos of the Mahatma, who studied here at the Shamaldas Arts College & Sir PP Science Institute. Downstairs, the **Barton Museum** shows off a huge, haphazard collection of Buddhist, Jain and Hindu statues, medieval bronzes, Harappan terracotta and the odd skeleton.

ARRIVAL AND DEPARTURE   BHAVNAGAR

By plane The airport (☏aai.aero) is 5km southeast of town on Airport Rd, a taxi or auto will cost ₹150 or ₹100 respectively.

By train Bhavnagar's railway station is a few hundred metres north of the old city, at the top of Station Rd. The

#19260 *Bhavnagar–Kochuveli Express* train connects to Ahmedabad (5 hr 30 min) on Sun, departing at 7.15am and arriving at 12 50 pm while the daily *Bhavnagar–Bandra Express* #12972 departs at 6.30pm, arriving in Ahmedabad at 11.40pm, Vadodara at 1.47am and Mumbai's Bandra

9

Terminus at 8.35am.

By bus The ST bus stand is on ST Rd, a 10min walk from the centre of Bhavnagar. Private buses are operated by numerous firms along and around Waghawadi Rd, such as Tanna Travels (☎027 8242 5218) at the Aristo Complex, with services to Ahmedabad (almost every hour; 4hr),

Vadodara (7 daily; 4–5hr) and Mumbai (daily at 4pm; 13hr). Destinations Ahmedabad (7 daily; 4hr); Bhuj (6 daily; 11hr); Junagadh (4 daily; 6hr 30min); Palitana (every 30min; 1hr); Rajkot (10 daily; 4hr); Vadodara (8 daily; 6hr); Velavadar National Park (2 daily; 1hr).

ACCOMMODATION

Bluehill Jasunath Chowk, opposite Pil Gardens ☎027 8242 6951, ⊕hotelbluehill.com; map p.596. Spacious, clean rooms with a/c, TVs, desks, fridges and cute separate seating areas. The more expensive ones, including the suites (₹2800–3500) also have views of the stork-filled Pil Gardens. **₹1500**

Nilambagh Palace ST Station Rd ☎027 8242 4241, ⊕heritagehotelsofindia.com; map p.596. Built in 1859 by a German architect for the local crown prince, *Nilambagh Palace* is Bhavnagar's most luxurious hotel, with vast rooms, peaceful gardens, a pool, tennis courts, and remnants of European influence in the chandeliers and period furniture. A separate annexe houses the less atmospheric but still good-value *Narayani Heritage Hotel* (☎027 8251 3535)

₹2000.

★ Sun 'n' Shine ST Station Rd ☎027 8251 6131, 9879535103, ⊕hotelsunshine.com; map p.596. The high expectations generated by the elegant green marble lobby are matched by swish rooms with carpets and bathtubs. Breakfast and airport transfers are included. Choose between deluxe and executive rooms and suites. **₹2000**

Vrundavan Guest House Darbargadh ☎0278 251 9149; map p.596. This rambling and, from the exterior at least, quite dramatic-looking hotel has tired attached rooms with tiny bathrooms and TV, some with a/c. It's not the friendliest place, however. **₹550**

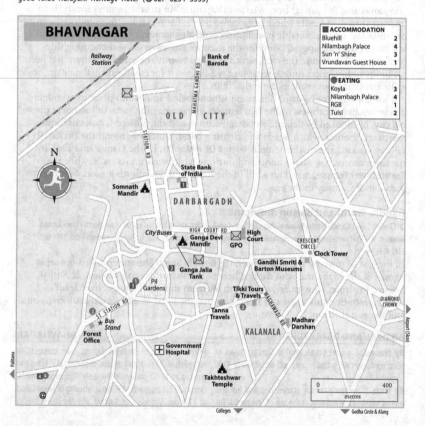

BHAVNAGAR

Railway Station

Bank of Baroda

MAHATMA GANDHI RD

OLD CITY

STATION RD

N

State Bank of India

Somnath Mandir

DARBARGADH

City Buses

HIGH COURT RD

Ganga Devi Mandir

High Court

GPO

CRESCENT CIRCLE

Clock Tower

Gandhi Smriti & Barton Museums

Ganga Jalia Tank

Pil Gardens

Tikki Tours & Travels

WAGHAWADI RD

DIAMOND CHOWK

ST STATION RD

Bus Stand

Tanna Travels

Madhav Darshan

Forest Office

KALANALA

Government Hospital

Palitana

Takhteshwar Temple

0   400
metres

@

Colleges

Godha Circle & Alang

Airport (5km)

EATING

Koyla Apollo hotel, opposite ST bus stand ☎027 8242 5251; map p.596. A shiny orange dining area with glass partitions between the tables and a nice selection of Chinese, North Indian and Punjabi meals, but mainly non vegetarian (butter chicken ₹380). Daily 11am–3pm & 7–10.45pm.

★ **Nilambagh Palace** Nilambagh Palace hotel, ST Station Rd ☎027 8242 4241, ⓦheritagehotelsofindia. com; map p.596. Superb and keenly priced dishes including chicken, mutton, fish and prawn (₹120–400). The real draw, however, is the atmosphere in the stately dining room and on the veranda, where the bustle of the city seems a world away. Daily 7–10am, 1–3pm & 7–10pm.

RGB Sun 'n' Shine hotel, ST Station Rd ☎027 8251 6131, ⓦhotelsunnshine.com; map p.596. Excellent vegetarian Indian Jain and Chinese food – the rich *paneer* dishes are particularly good – as well as ice cream sundaes. Staff are professional and happy to adjust spicing levels to suit personal tastes. Veg *tawa* masala ₹250. Live music Sat and Sun. Daily 7.30–10am & 11.30am–11pm

Tulsi Kalanala Chowk ☎0278 300 4942; map p.596. Appealing veg Chinese and Indian food, including a comforting *chana* masala, and less appealing *muzak* are on offer at the quiet, relaxed *Tulsi*. Steer clear of the handful of Western dishes, however, especially the pineapple and vegetable macaroni. Daily noon–4pm & 7–11pm.

DIRECTORY

Banks and exchange The State Bank of Saurashtra and the Bank of India, both on Amba Chowk, have exchange facilities and ATM.

Hospital The government hospital, Sir T Hospital (ⓦsirthospitalbhavnagar.org) is on Dr Hemantkumar Vaidya Rd.

Post office The GPO is at 336 High Court Rd, with branches just off Station Rd a block south of the railway station, and opposite the southeastern corner of Ganga Jalia Tank.

Blackbuck National Park

Velavadar, 65km north of Bhavnagar • Mid-Oct to mid-June daily 6am–6pm • ₹350 (₹20), plus ₹1500 (₹200)/vehicle, camera ₹250, mandatory guide ₹600 (₹100) • ☎027 8288 0342, ⓦgujarattourism.com • No jeeps available to hire on site; taxis available by Ganga Jalia Tank in Bhavnagar – day-trips ₹2500

Outside the tiny village of **Velavadar**, the 34-square-kilometre **Blackbuck National Park** is Gujarat's own slice of savannah. Bounding through the tall golden grass, however, are not impalas but blackbucks, spiral-horned Indian antelopes of which the park has the country's highest concentration. Prior to Independence their number stood at eight thousand, but habitat loss and hunting cut this figure down to two hundred by 1966. The park's blackbuck now number well over three thousand, making it a laudable success story. It is also home to endangered Indian wolves, striped hyenas, nilgai antelope, jackals, jungle cats and Indian foxes, as well as birds of prey like Stoliczka's bushchat and harrier hawks, at least 1500 of the latter arriving from Siberia each winter.

Palitana

For many visitors, the highlight of a trip to Saurashtra is a climb up the holy hill of **Shatrunjaya**, India's principal Jain pilgrimage site, just outside the dull town of **PALITANA**, 50km southwest of Bhavnagar.

Shatrunjaya

6km south of Palitana • Daily 7am–6pm • Free, camera ₹100 (no photography inside the complex) • Auto-rickshaws (₹80) run from Palitana's bus stand to the foot of Shatrunjaya (10min)

More than nine hundred temples crown **Shatrunjaya**, said to be a chunk of the mighty Himalayas where the Jains' first *tirthankara*, Adinath, and his chief disciple gained enlightenment. While records show that the hill was a *tirtha* as far back as the fifth century, the existing temples date only from the sixteenth century, anything earlier having been lost in the Muslim raids of the 1500s and 1600s.

Climbing the wide steps up Shatrunjaya takes one to two hours, but, as with all hilltop pilgrimage centres, *dholis* (seats on poles held by four bearers; ₹1500–1900

9

return) are available for those who can't make it under their own steam. The views as you ascend are magnificent, and you should allow at least two more hours to see even a fraction of the temples.

The temple complex

The individual **tuks** (temple enclosures) are named after the merchants who funded them. Together they create a formidable city, laid over the two summits and fortified by thick walls. Each *tuk* comprises courtyards chequered in black-and-white marble and several temples whose walls are exquisitely and profusely carved with saints, birds, animals, buxom maidens, musicians and dancers. Many are two or even three storeys high, with balconies crowned by perfectly proportioned pavilions. The largest temple, dedicated to **Adinath**, in the Khartaravasi *tuk* on the northern ridge, is usually full of masked Svetambara nuns and monks, dressed in white and carrying white fly-whisks. The southern ridge and the spectacular **Adishvara** temple in its western corner are reached by taking the right-hand fork at the top of the path. On a clear day the view from the summit takes in the Gulf of Cambay to the south, Bhavnagar to the north and Mount Girnar to the west.

A path leads along the ridge and down into the valley of Adipur, 13km away; it's open for one day only, during the festival of **Suth Tera** (Feb/March), when up to fifty thousand pilgrims come to Shatrunjaya for this unique display of devotion.

Shri Vishal Jain Museum

400m from the start of the steps to Shatrunjaya • Daily 10am–1pm & 3–8.30pm • ₹10, no photos

The **Shri Vishal Jain Museum** displays a haphazard collection of artefacts, including centuries-old Jain idols, artwork and palm-leaf manuscripts, with a small temple set down the stairs towards the back. Despite being labelled only in Gujarati, the exhibits are worth the minuscule entry fee.

ARRIVAL AND INFORMATION   PALITANA

By train Palitana station is 1.5km north of the town centre, with four daily trains to Bhavnagar (1hr 25min).

By bus Regular buses arrive and depart from the bus stand in the north of town, 400m north of the bridge.
Departures Bhavnagar (hourly; 1hr 30min); Junagadh (2 daily; 6hr); Talaja for Diu (hourly in the morning; 1hr); Una for Diu (daily; 4hr 30min).

Tourist information The owner of the *Shravak* hotel, opposite the bus stand, is a good source of regional information.

ACCOMMODATION

Takhatgadh Dharmsala Opposite Shri Vishal Jain Museum ☎ 028 4825 2167. A few hundred metres from the steps to Shatrunjaya, this three-storey *dharamshala* is one of Palitana's best deals, with non-attached a/c (₹650) and fan-cooled rooms, most sleeping three, facing onto a spacious, pink courtyard. ₹400

Vijay Vilas Palace Adpur, 4km from the bus station ☎ 09427182809 , ⊕ heritagehotelsofindia.com. A good option if you have your own vehicle (auto-rickshaw around ₹100), the rooms in this converted 1906 European-style palace guesthouse have four-posters, old dressers and other early twentieth-century paraphernalia, some overlooking the western slopes of Shatrunjaya. There's a great veg restaurant, and an alternate path to the summit starts nearby. No wi-fi. ₹4200

EATING

Bhojan Shala Parshwanath Jain Trust, beside Shri Vishal Jain Museum. This large dining hall on the ground floor of a four-storey yellow block, doubling as a *dharamshala* (₹300 for non a/c and ₹600 for a/c), serves generous and tasty Jain meals (₹60–80). Daily 7.30–9am, 11.30am–1.30pm & 4.30–6pm.

Jagruti Restaurant ☎ 942 6271 900 Opposite the bus stand. The best place to eat other than in Palitana's hotels, this basic but friendly and busy restaurant serves excellent Gujarati meals and snacks for pennies. No thalis but meals with roti and curry or dal *chaval* (rice with a lentil-based curry). Daily 9am–10.30pm.

Southeastern Gujarat

9

Sandwiched between Maharashtra and the Arabian Sea, the seldom-visited
southeastern corner of Gujarat harbours few attractions to entice you off the beaten
path to or from Mumbai. **Vadodara** (Baroda), former capital of the Gaekwad rajas,
is most appealing for its proximity to the old Muslim town of **Champaner** and the
ruined forts and exotic Jain and Hindu temples crowning **Pavagadh Hill**. Further south,
dairy pastures gradually give way to a swampy, malaria-infested coastal strip of banana
plantations and shimmering saltpans cut by silty, sinuous rivers, before reaching the
former Portuguese territory of **Daman**.

Vadodara (Baroda)

VADODARA, also known as **Baroda**, is congested and industrial but with a youthful
vibe owing to the presence of Gujarat's largest university, **Maharaja Sayajirao University**
(MSU). Although its old core retains some interest, with beautiful havelis, palaces and
traditional bazaars, its main draw lies in its being the most convenient base for visiting
the nearby sites of **Champaner** and **Pavagadh**.

Sayaji Bagh
Entrance on Tilak Rd

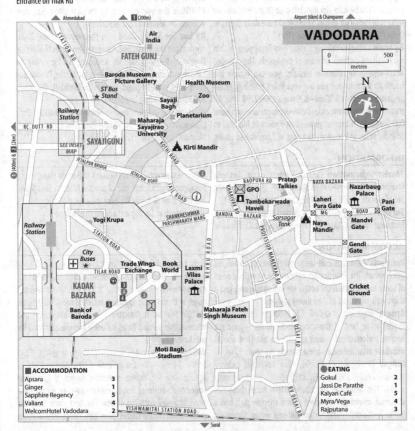

VADODARA

ACCOMMODATION
Apsara	3
Ginger	1
Sapphire Regency	5
Valiant	4
WelcomHotel Vadodara	2

EATING
Gokul	2
Jassi De Parathe	1
Kalyan Café	5
Myra/Vega	4
Rajputana	3

9

Built and dedicated to the people of Vadodara by the beloved reformer Maharaja Sayajirao Gaekwad III, the large green park of **Sayaji Bagh** contains two museums and a planetarium, zoo, a floral clock and vintage toy train. The large Indo-Saracenic **Baroda Museum and Picture Gallery**, reached from University Rd (daily 10.30am–5pm; ₹200 [₹10]; ☎026 5279 3801), originally built to resemble the V&A Museum in London, holds art and textiles from all over the world, plus Gujarati archeological remains and Mughal miniatures.

Laxmi Vilas Palace

Nehru Rd • **Laxmi Vilas Palace** Daily 9.30am–5.30pm; audiotours (1hr) are available • ₹150 (₹25) • **Maharaja Fateh Singh Museum** Tues–Sun 10.30am–4pm • ₹150 (₹30); no photography • ☎026 5242 6372 or 07227 939902

Laxmi Vilas Palace is the most extravagant of Vadodara's palaces, designed by Major Charles "Mad" Mant and commissioned at great expense by Maharaja Sayajirao Gaekwad III in 1890. Audiotours take in its Durbar Hall, armoury and palm-filled mosaic courtyards. The palace grounds are home to the **Maharaja Fateh Singh Museum**, which holds a modest selection of European, Chinese, Japanese and Indian art, including many epic works of Raja Ravi Varma, personally commissioned by the maharaja of Baroda.

ARRIVAL AND DEPARTURE

VADODARA (BARODA)

By plane Civil Airport Harni is 6km northeast of the city (around ₹100 by auto-rickshaw). IndiGo (Harni Rd), and Air India (Old Padra Rd; ☎026 5233 0466) have daily flights to Delhi (1hr 30min) and to Mumbai (1hr).

By train Vadodara railway station is in Sayajigunj, within easy walking distance of most of the hotels. The crowded ticket reservation office is upstairs; you can bypass the hassle for a small fee if you buy your ticket from Yogi Krupa on Station Rd (daily 8.30am–8.30pm; ☎966 2798 198). All trains travelling on the main Delhi–Mumbai line stop here. The Suryanagari Express connecting Bandra at Mumbai to Jodhpur stops at Vadodara and runs to Ahmedabad (daily;

dep. 7.13pm, arr. 9.05 pm), while the *Shatabdi Express* #12010 is the quickest train to Mumbai (Mon–Sat; dep. 4.16pm, arr. Mumbai Central 9.20pm).

By bus The ST bus stand is in the west of town, 300m north of the railway station. However, few buses to Mumbai (frequent; 9–10hr) start at Vadodara, so they may be full when they arrive – the train is far better. Private bus companies with frequent services to Mumbai, Rajasthan and Madhya Pradesh line Station Rd.

Destinations (private buses) Ahmedabad (hourly; 3hr); Champaner (hourly; 1hr 30min–2hr); Diu (3 daily; 9hr); Mumbai (hourly; 8hr); Rajkot (hourly; 6hr).

INFORMATION

Tourist information Gujarat Tourism is on Narmada Bhavan, Jail Rd (Mon–Sat 10.30am–6pm, closed 2nd & 4th Sat of month; ☎026 5242 7489, ⓦgujarattourism.com).

Services Currency exchange is offered at the Trade Wings Exchange Bureau (Alankar Tower, Sayajigunj, opposite

Kalyan restaurant), and at the Bank of Baroda (Suraj Plaza, Sayajigunj), which has one of several ATMs in Sayajigunj. The GPO is on Kharivav Rd, near the centre of town; there's also a branch in Sayajigunj (just south of Kalyan).

ACCOMMODATION

Vadodara's numerous mid-range hotels are often full, so book ahead. The few budget options are in serious need of some loving care. Most hotels are in **Sayajigunj**, just a short walk southeast of the railway station.

Apsara Sayajigunj ☎026 5222 5533; map p.599. Probably the best of the shoestring options – hardly a ringing endorsement – with ramshackle but (just about) habitable attached rooms and a friendly manager. ₹700

Ginger Fatehgunj Camp Rd, 1km north of railway station ☎026 5663 3333, ⓦgingerhotels.com; map p.599. This branch of the über-modern hotel chain has colourful, minimalist, attached rooms, friendly staff and a buffet restaurant. Perks include filtered water dispensers

and a branch of *Café Coffee Day*. ₹2300

Sapphire Regency Sayajigunj ☎026 5236 1130, ⓦsapphireregency.in; map p.599. Business-oriented hotel, with sixty-one sparkling attached rooms and suites (₹4700) that boast flatscreen TVs, stylish bathrooms and white leather seating. Rates include a breakfast buffet. 24hr checkout. ₹1700

Valiant 7th floor, BBC Tower, Sayajigunj ☎026 5236 3480, ⓦhotelvaliant.com; map p.599. Accessed via an aged private lift, *Valiant* is another decent, if somewhat impersonal, business hotel; the twenty-nine rooms have clean attached bath-rooms and TVs, and some have a/c (₹1600).Breakfast included, plus 24hr checkout and room service. ₹1300

WelcomHotel Vadodara RC Dutt (Racecourse) Rd ☎026 5233 0033, ⊛itcwelcomgroup.in; map p.599.

One of Vadodara's few five-stars, with 133 swanky attached rooms, plus an outdoor pool, gym, salon and spa. Rates include a breakfast buffet at its fine restaurant. ₹6700

EATING

Gokul Kothi Rd ☎026 5247 7632; map p.599. Small snack bar serving excellent south Indian dishes, Punjabi and Gujarati thalis (₹130) and ice cream, all at low, low prices (masala dosa ₹65). Daily 11am–3pm & 7–10pm.

Jassi De Parathe Panorama Complex, Alkapuri ☎997 888 1313; map p.599. One of the most sought after and authentic Punjabi eatery. There is a queue here for lunch, especially on weekends. Besides the thalis and the parathas, not to be missed are the *paneer* tikka dry, the dum biriyani and the dal makhani. Wash them down with special Patiala lassi. Daily 10.30am–11pm

Kalyan Café Sayajigunj ☎026 5236 2211 ⊛kalyan hotel.com; map p.599. Lively "veg food mall" with multi-coloured stools and thin, thatched shutters where students come to chat and tuck into anything from chow mein (₹110 to cheeseburgers (₹85), as well as Indian and Chinese

snacks. Daily 7am–11pm.

Myra/Vega Surya hotel, Sayajigunj ☎026 5222 6161, ⊛hotelsurya.com; map p.599. Two superior restaurants under one roof: head to *Myra* for a hearty Gujarati thali (₹240); while *Vega* offers well-prepared curries, Chinese dishes and a good Punjabi lunch buffet (₹300). Vega daily 11.30am–2pm, 3.30–6.30pm & 7.30–11pm; Myra daily 11.30am–2pm & 7.30–11pm.

Rajputana Dhanvantri Complex, Sadar Patel Chowk, Sayajigunj ☎026 5662 2799; map p.599. Tasty north Indian and Chinese dishes (*paneer* butter masala ₹190) served up in eccentric surroundings; the restaurant is kitted out with hanging chains, bells, dolls and fake wood beams. The Royal Lunch (₹240), an all-veg feast, on offer from noon to 3pm. Daily 11am–3pm & 6.30–11pm.

Champaner and around

49km northeast of Vadodara • Daily 8am–6pm • ₹250 (₹20) • Services from Vadodara (every 15min; 1hr 30min) and Ahmedabad (6 daily; 2hr 45min) arrive at Halol, 7km west of Champaner; hourly buses leave Halol for Champaner's bus stand, opposite the south gate

Rising 820m above the plains of Panchmahal, the almost forgotten city – and World Heritage Site – of **CHAMPANER** stands overlooked by the solitary hill of **Pavagadh**. Although the city was fortified centuries earlier, in 1297 the Chauhan rajputs made Champaner their stronghold, fending off three Muslim attacks. It remained Gujarat's capital until 1536, when the courts moved to Ahmedabad, and Champaner fell into decline. When the British arrived in 1803 it was almost completely overrun by the forest.

Some of the massive city walls with inscribed gateways still stand, encompassing several houses, exquisite mosques and Muslim mausoleums, all imbued with a strange, time-warped atmosphere. The largest mosque is the exuberant **Jama Masjid**, east of the walls; two minarets stand either side of the main entrance, and the prayer halls are dissected by almost two hundred pillars supporting a splendid carved roof raised in a series of domes.

Pavagadh

4km south of Champaner • Regular shuttle buses depart from opposite Champaner's southern gate to the end of Pavagadh Hill Rd (halfway up the hill; 15min); otherwise it's a 1hr 30min walk from the trailhead opposite Champaner's southern gate to the halfway point – from here, the trail to the summit is a 2hr walk or quick cable-car ride (7am–11pm; ₹100)

The **patha** (pilgrim's route) ascends 4km from Champaner to **Pavagadh**, passing the old battered gates of the fortress. Roughly midway up, the road ends along with a cluster of snack, souvenir and chai stalls and the cable-car station. Continuing the ascent on foot, pilgrims pass numerous Jain temples and several sacred lakes along the trail to the summit, where the eleventh-century **Kalikamata Temple** stands, along with a shrine to the Muslim saint Sadan Shah on its roof.

Daman

As a Union Territory, independent of the dry state that surrounds it, **DAMAN** is a weekend target for busloads of Gujarati men who come here to drink themselves

9

senseless. The rest of the time it is quiet but generally disappointing, its pair of grubby beaches subject to massive tides. It does, however, offer fantastic **seafood** and some well-preserved **Portuguese churches**, **houses** and **forts**. To the north of the Damanganga River is **Nani** ("Little") **Daman**, home to most of the hotels, restaurants and bars, while on the south side is **Moti** ("Great") **Daman**, the old Portuguese quarter.

Brief history

Straddling the mouth of the **Damanganga River**, Daman made an obvious target for the Portuguese, who took it in 1531 from the Sultanate of Gujarat's Ethiopian governor, Siddu Bapita. The governor of Goa, Dom Constantino de Bragança, cajoled the sultan into ceding the territory 28 years later, after which it became the hub of the Portuguese trans-Arabian Sea trade with East Africa. The British occupation of Sindh in the 1830s strangled the town's opium business and led to decline. Colonial rule, however, survived until 1961 when Nehru lost patience with the Portuguese and sent in the troops.

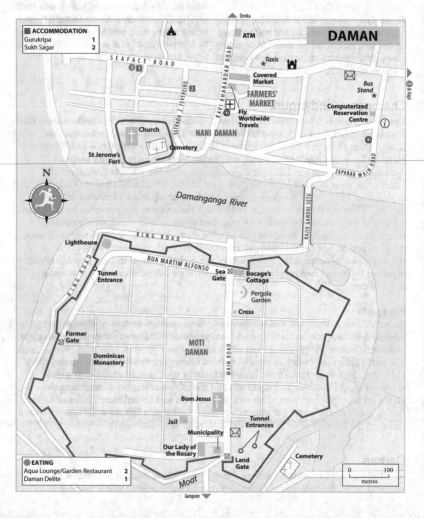

Nani Daman

Most of the action in **Nani Daman** centres on Seaface Road, which runs west from the market past rows of hotels, seedy bars and liquor stores to the **beach**, which is often too polluted for a comfortable swim or sunbathe. To the south and directly behind the quay, the ramparts of **St Jerome's Fort**, erected between 1614 and 1672, offer views of the riverfront, dominated by fishing trawlers. The citadel encircles a Catholic church (now a school) and a walled Portuguese cemetery.

Moti Daman

The town's most impressive monuments lie in the colonial compound of **Moti Daman**. Inside its hefty walls, elegant mansions with verandas and colour-washed facades overlook leafy courtyards. Moti Daman's highlights are its **churches**, among the oldest and best-preserved Christian monuments in Asia. The grandest is the **Church of Bom Jesus** on the main square. Built in 1603, its gigantic gabled Baroque facade opens onto a lofty vaulted hall. Across the square, the **Church of Our Lady of the Rosary** is crammed with ornate woodwork. **Main Road** links Moti Daman's two **gates**, installed in the 1580s following a Mughal invasion. A small cottage next to the northern Sea Gate was once home to the Portuguese poet Bocage, while atop the bastion facing the southern Land Gate is the cell where condemned prisoners spent their final days.

ARRIVAL AND DEPARTURE   DAMAN

By train The nearest station to Daman is at Vapi; train tickets can be reserved at the reservation centre (daily except Wed 9.30am–1.30pm & 4–9pm) opposite Daman's tourist office. The *Shatabdi Express* #12009 north connects Ahmedabad (dep. 8.20am arr. 12.45pm) and the #12010 south serves Mumbai (dep. 6.50pm; arr. 9.20pm).

By bus Daman's main bus stand is east of Seaface Rd in Nani Daman; buses connect to Vapi, 13km east (every 30min; 25min), as do shared taxis (20min; ₹50), private taxis (₹160) and auto-rickshaws (₹120). From Vapi, there are many bus connections, including to Mumbai (12 daily; 3hr 30min–5hr) and Vadodara (14 daily; 4hr 30min–6hr).

INFORMATION

Tourist information The tourist office (Mon–Fri 9.30am–1.30pm & 2–6pm; ☎ 026 0225 0002, ⊚ damandiutourism. com) is on Zapabar Main Rd, just south of the bus stand.
Services There are two post offices: one in Nani Daman 100m west of the bus stand and one in Moti Daman

opposite the Municipal Council Building. Fly Worldwide Travels (daily 10.30am–7.30pm; ☎ 093 2773 2779) in the basement of the *Maharaja* hotel is the best place to change money, and there are several ATMs on Kavi Khabardar Rd.

ACCOMMODATION

Gurukripa Seaface Rd ☎ 026 0225 5046, ⊚ hotel gurukripa.com; map p.602. Though beginning to show its age, *Gurukripa* is well run, boasting large a/c attached rooms, plus a roof garden and the *Daman Delite* (see below) and *Sovereign* restaurants.₹**2000**
Sukh Sagar Estrada 2 Fevereiro ☎ 0260 2255 089

⊚ hotelsukhsagardaman.in; map p.602. This friendly little hotel, tucked away on a quiet street, has no-nonsense, basic but clean, attached, a/c rooms with TV, as well as a multi cuisine budget restaurant and a well-stocked bar.
₹**1300**

EATING

Aqua Lounge/Garden Restaurant Royal Garden hotel ☎ 98240 45633 ⊚ hotelroyalgardendaman.in; map p.602. *Aqua*, Daman's slickest bar lounge, serves beers and cocktails under subtle neon lights with comfy seating. The restaurant, *Garden*, features a high-end terrace space serving tasty – if pricey – tandoori pomfret (₹250) and lobster, as

well as Goan meat and veg specialities. Daily 11am–11pm.
Daman Delite Gurukripa hotel, Seaface Rd ☎ 026 0225 5046, ⊚ hotelgurukripa.com; map p.602. The place to come for a slap-up meal: choose from an extensive seafood menu (prawns ₹250) and finish with a nip of potent Goan *feni* (coconut spirit). Daily 7.30am–11pm.

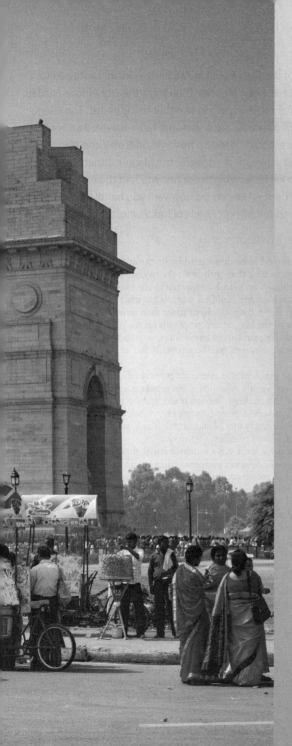

Mumbai

THE GATEWAY TO INDIA

Mumbai

Ever since the opening of the Suez Canal in 1869, the principal gateway to the Indian Subcontinent has been Mumbai (Bombay), the city Aldous Huxley famously described as "the most appalling of either hemisphere". Travellers tend to regard time spent here as a rite of passage to be survived rather than savoured. But as the powerhouse of Indian business, industry and trade, and the source of its most seductive media images, the Maharashtrian capital can be a compelling place to kill time. Whether or not you find the experience enjoyable, however, will depend largely on how well you handle the heat, humidity, traffic fumes and relentless crowds of India's most dynamic, Westernized city.

10

First impressions of Mumbai tend to be dominated by its chronic shortage of space. Crammed onto a narrow spit of land that curls from the swamp-ridden coast into the Arabian Sea, the city is technically an island, connected to the mainland by bridges and narrow causeways. In less than five hundred years, it has metamorphosed from an aboriginal fishing settlement into a megalopolis of more than sixteen million people – India's largest city and one of the biggest urban sprawls on the planet. Being swept along broad boulevards by endless streams of commuters, or jostled by coolies and hand-cart pullers in the teeming bazaars, you'll continually feel as if Mumbai is about to burst at the seams.

The roots of the population problem and attendant poverty lie, paradoxically, in the city's enduring ability to create wealth. Mumbai alone generates one third of India's tax income, its port handles half the country's foreign trade, and its movie industry is the most prolific in the world. Symbols of prosperity are everywhere: from the phalanx of office blocks clustered on Nariman Point, Maharashtra's Manhattan, to the expensively dressed teenagers posing in Colaba's trendiest nightspots.

The flip side to the success story is the city's much-chronicled poverty. Each day, an estimated five hundred economic refugees pour into Mumbai from the Maharashtrian hinterland. Some find jobs and secure accommodation; many more end up living on the already overcrowded streets, or amid the squalor of some of Asia's largest slums, reduced to rag-picking and begging from cars at traffic lights.

However, while it would definitely be misleading to downplay its difficulties, Mumbai is far from the ordeal some travellers make it out to be. Once you've overcome the major hurdle of finding somewhere to stay, you may begin to enjoy its frenzied pace and crowded, cosmopolitan feel.

Nowhere reinforces your sense of having arrived in Mumbai quite as emphatically as the **Gateway of India**, the city's defining landmark. Only a five-minute walk north, the **Prince of Wales Museum** should be next on your list of sightseeing priorities, as much for its flamboyantly eclectic architecture as for the art treasures inside. The

---

BEST TIME TO VISIT

As a coastal city, the temperature in Mumbai hovers around 30ºC for much of the year; the weather is most pleasant from October to March, when it's not too humid. If possible, avoid visiting the city during April and May when it's particularly hot and humid, and during the monsoon (June–Sept), which often causes flooding in the low-lying areas and disruptions to public transport.

HAJI ALI'S TOMB

Highlights

❶ The Gateway of India Mumbai's defining landmark, and a favourite spot for an evening stroll. See page 611

❷ Chhatrapati Shivaji Museum A fine collection of priceless Indian art, from ancient temple sculpture to Mughal armour. See page 614

❸ Maidans (parks) Where Mumbai's citizens escape the hustle and bustle to play cricket, eat lunch and hang out. See page 615

❹ CS (Victoria) Terminus A fantastically eccentric pile, and the greatest railway station ever built by the British. See page 617

❺ Haji Ali's Tomb Mingle with the crowds of Muslim worshippers who flock to the island tomb of Sufi mystic Haji Ali to listen to *qawwali* music on Thursday evenings. See page 623

❻ Elephanta Island Catch a boat across Mumbai harbour to see one of ancient India's most wonderful rock-cut Shiva temples. See page 625

❼ Bollywood blockbusters Check out the latest Hindi mega-movie in one of the city centre's gigantic Art Deco cinemas. See page 641

HIGHLIGHTS ARE MARKED ON THE MAP ON PAGE 610

museum provides a foretaste of what lies in store just up the road, where the cream of Bartle Frere's Bombay – the **University** and **High Court** – line up with the open maidans on one side, and the boulevards of **Fort** on the other. But for the fullest sense of why the city's founding fathers declared it Urbs Prima in Indis, you should press further north still to visit the **Chhatrapati Shivaji Terminus (CST)**, the high-water mark of India's Raj architecture.

Beyond CST lie the crowded bazaars and Muslim neighbourhoods of **central Mumbai**, at their liveliest and most colourful around **Crawford Market** and **Mohammed Ali Road**. Possibilities for an escape from the crowds include an evening stroll along **Marine Drive**, bounding the western edge of downtown, or a boat trip out to **Elephanta**, a rock-cut cave on an island in Mumbai harbour containing a wealth of ancient art.

Brief history

Mumbai originally consisted of seven **islands**, inhabited by small Koli fishing communities. In 1534, Sultan Bahadur of Ahmedabad ceded the land to the **Portuguese**, who subsequently handed it on to the English in 1661 as part of the Portuguese Infanta Catherine of Braganza's dowry during her marriage to Charles II. Bombay's safe harbour and strategic commercial position attracted the interest of the **East India Company**, based at Surat to the north, and in 1668 a deal was struck whereby they leased Bombay from Charles for a pittance.

Life for the English was not easy, however: "fluxes" (dysentery), "Chinese death" (cholera) and other diseases culled many of the first settlers, prompting the colony's chaplain to declare that "two monsoons are the age of a man". Nevertheless, the city established itself as the capital of the flourishing East India Company, attracting a diverse mix of settlers including Goans, Gujarati traders, Muslim weavers and the business-minded Zoroastrian Parsis. The export crisis in America following the Civil War fuelled the great Bombay **cotton boom** and established the city as a major industrial and commercial centre, while the opening of the Suez Canal in 1869 and the construction of enormous docks further improved Bombay's access to European markets, ushering in an age of mercantile self-confidence embodied by the grandiloquent colonial-Gothic buildings constructed during the governorship of **Sir Bartle Frere** (1862–67).

As the most prosperous city in the nation, Bombay was at the forefront of the **Independence** struggle; Mahatma Gandhi used a house here, now a museum, to coordinate the struggle through three decades. Fittingly, the

Goral, Esselworld & Global Vipassana Pagoda

SEE 'THE NORTHERN SUBURBS' MAP

0   2
kilometres

N

ARABIAN
SEA

Basilica of Mt Mary

Rajiv Gandhi Setu
(Bandra Worli
Sea Link)

Juhu
Beach **JUHU**

Santa Cruz

Khar Road

BANDRA

Bandra

Mahim

Matunga Road

Dadar

Parel

Vile Parle

Chhatrapati
Shivaji
Domestic
Airport
(Santa Cruz)

Chhatrapati
Shivaji
International
Airport

Kurla (LTT)

DHARAVI

Chunabhatti

Sion

GTB Nagar

King's Circle

Matunga

Wadala Road

Asiad Bus Stand

■ **DRINKING &
NIGHTLIFE**
AER   5
Café Zoe   3
The Irish House 6
Todi Mill Social 1
Toit Brewery   2
XXO   4

PVR
Phoenix

Elphinstone Road

Currey
Road

Lower Parel

Chinchpokli

Mahalaxmi

Mumbai Central

Grant Road

MALABAR HILL

Charni Road

Marine Lines

Churchgate

Back Bay

Nariman Point **COLABA**

SEE 'MUMBAI' MAP

Byculla

Mumbai
Central
Bus Stand

Sewri

Cotton Green

Reay Road

Dockyard Road

Sandhurst Road

Masjid Bunder

Chhatrapati Shivaji Terminus

Gateway
of India

**GREATER
MUMBAI**

Elephanta Island

Mandwa & Alibag

> **FESTIVALS IN MUMBAI**
>
> **Kala Ghoda Arts Festival** (Feb). The country's largest multicultural festival is held across nine days, with hundreds of events covering literature, performing and visual arts, among many other things.
>
> **Elephanta Festival** (Feb/March). Two- to three-day festival that sees classical Indian dance performed against the backdrop of the eponymous caves.
>
> **Ganesh Chaturthi** (Aug/Sept). Ten days celebrating the beloved elephant-headed god Ganesha: street processions, loud music and lots of dancing culminate in idols of the god being immersed in the sea on the final day.
>
> **Krishna Janmashtami** (Aug). The birthday of Lord Krishna sees mass celebrations in the city, including special decorations and chanting of hymns at temples and homes, and *rangoli* (colourful floor designs).

10

first British colony took pleasure in waving the final goodbye to the Raj, when the last contingent of British troops passed through the Gateway of India in February 1948. Since Independence, Mumbai has prospered as India's commercial capital and the population has grown tenfold, to more than sixteen million, although the modern city has also been plagued by a deadly mixture of **communal infighting** and **terrorist attacks**.

Tensions due to the increasing numbers of immigrants from other parts of the country, and the resultant overcrowding, has fuelled the rise of the extreme right-wing Maharashtrian party, the **Shiv Sena**, founded in 1966 by Bal Thackeray, whose death and cremation in 2012 brought the state to a standstill.

Thousands of Muslim Mumbaikars were murdered by Hindu mobs following the destruction of the Babri Masjid in Ayodhya in 1992–93, while in March 1993, ten massive retaliatory **bomb blasts** killed 260 people. The involvement of Muslim godfather Dawood Ibrahim and the Pakistani secret service was suspected, and both Ibrahim and the Pakistanis have been linked with subsequent atrocities. These include the bomb blasts in August 2003, which killed 107 tourists next to the **Gateway of India**; the subsequent explosions in July 2006, when coordinated bomb blasts simultaneously blew apart seven packed commuter trains across the city; and, most dramatically, the horrific attacks of **November 26, 2008**, when a group of rampaging gunmen ran amok across the city, killing 166 people.

Despite these setbacks, Mumbai has prospered like nowhere else in India as a result of the country's ongoing **economic liberalization**. Following decades of stagnation, the textiles industry has been supplanted by rapidly growing IT, finance, healthcare and back-office support sectors. Whole suburbs have sprung up to accommodate the affluent new middle-class workforce, with shiny shopping malls and car showrooms to relieve them of their income. Even so, corruption in politics and business has drained away investment from socially deprived areas. Luxury apartments in Bandra may change hands for half a million dollars or more, but an estimated seven to eight million people (just under fifty percent of Mumbai's population) live in slums with no toilets, on just six percent of the land.

Colaba

Mumbai's main tourist enclave is the district of **Colaba**, at the far southern end of the peninsula. Even though it's a long, sweaty drive from the airport and far from representative of the city as a whole, most visitors base themselves in the neighbourhood and rarely venture beyond it. As the home of the super-swanky *Taj Mahal Palace* hotel, as well as some of the city's trendiest bars and restaurants, Colaba certainly has its glamorous side. But the dimly lit streets between its dozen or so blocks

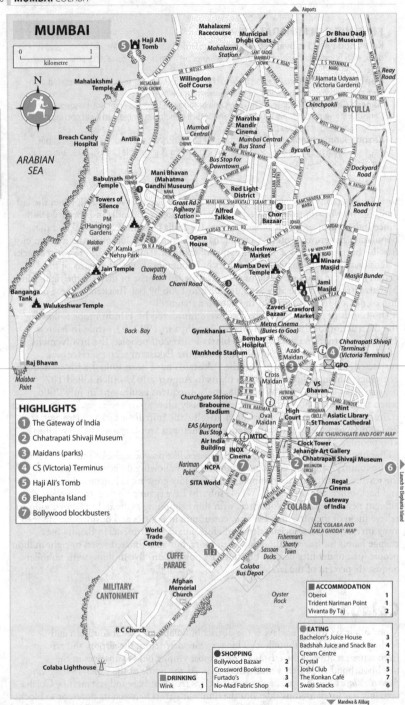

MUMBAI

10

HIGHLIGHTS

1. The Gateway of India
2. Chhatrapati Shivaji Museum
3. Maidans (parks)
4. CS (Victoria) Terminus
5. Haji Ali's Tomb
6. Elephanta Island
7. Bollywood blockbusters

■ **ACCOMMODATION**

Oberoi	1
Trident Nariman Point	1
Vivanta By Taj	2

■ **EATING**

Bachelor's Juice House	3
Badshah Juice and Snack Bar	4
Cream Centre	2
Crystal	1
Joshi Club	5
The Konkan Café	7
Swati Snacks	6

● **SHOPPING**

Bollywood Bazaar	2
Crossword Bookstore	1
Furtado's	3
No-Mad Fabric Shop	4

■ **DRINKING**

Wink	1

MUMBAI OR BOMBAY?

In 1996 Bombay was renamed **Mumbai**, as part of a wider policy instigated by the right-wing Maharashtrian nationalist Shiv Sena Municipality to replace names of any places, roads and features in the city that had connotations of the Raj. The Shiv Sena asserted that the British term "Bombay" derived from the Marathi title of a local deity, Mumba Devi (see page 619). In fact, historians are unanimously agreed that the Portuguese, who dubbed the harbour "Bom Bahia" ("Good Bay") when they first came across it, were responsible for christening the site and that the later British moniker had nothing to do with the aboriginal Hindu earth goddess.

The name change was widely unpopular when it was first imposed, especially among the upper and middle classes, and non-Maharashtrian immigrant communities, who doggedly stuck to Bombay. A couple of decades on, however, "Mumbai" seems to have definitively taken root with the dotcom generation and even outgrown the narrow agenda of its nationalist originators – just as "Bombay" outlived the Raj.

10

of dilapidated colonial tenements are also awash with junkies and touts, and after a day of being hissed at from doorways by sellers of "brown sugar" most people head for the bazaars and brighter lights of uptown.

The Gateway of India

Commemorating the visit of King George V and Queen Mary in 1911, India's own honey-coloured Arc de Triomphe, the **Gateway of India**, is Colaba's principal monument and the landmark most iconic of Mumbai in the Indian imagination. Featured in countless Bollywood movies, it was built in 1924 by George Wittet, whose brief was to combine the grandeur of a Roman triumphal arch with decorative motifs from Hindu and Muslim architecture. The resulting structure, every bit a symbol of "power and majesty", was originally intended to be a ceremonial disembarkation point for passengers alighting from the P&O steamers, but is, ironically, more closely associated with the moment in August 1947 when, amid much pomp and ceremony, the last remaining British soldiers on Indian soil slowly marched to their waiting troop ship as the Union Jack was lowered – to euphoric cheers from a vast crowd. The hour around sunset when thousands of visitors mill about the archway and plaza, munching *bhel puri* and having their photos taken, is the best time to visit.

The Taj Mahal Palace and Tower

Apollo Bunder

Local pride in the face of colonial oppression is the subtext of the **Taj Mahal Palace and Tower** complex, directly behind the Gateway. Its patron, the Parsi industrialist J.N. Tata, is said to have built the old *Taj* as an act of revenge after he was refused entry to what was then the best hotel in town, the "whites only" *Watson's*. The ban proved to be its undoing. *Watson's* disappeared long ago, but the *Taj* still presides imperiously over the seafront, the preserve of Mumbai's air-kissing jet set, visiting cricket teams and heads of state. Lesser mortals are allowed in to experience the tea lounge, shopping arcades and vast air-conditioned lobby (there's also a fabulously luxurious loo off the corridor to the left of the main desk).

Almost as emblematic of Mumbai as the Gateway, the building featured prominently in news coverage of the 2008 terror attacks, in which a team of Islamist jihadis occupied it for three days, killing 31 people. The subsequent refit cost US$40 million and took a year to complete, but has restored the hotel to its glittering former splendour.

COLABA AND KALA GHODA

10

Convocation Hall
HDFC ATM
M G ROAD
B BHARUCHA ROAD
ROPE WALK LN
Knesset Eliyahoo Synagogue
VB GANDHI MARG
SHAHID BHAGAT SINGH MARG
CHAMBER OF COMMERCE LN
A D'MELLO RD
KALA GHODA
SUBHASH CHOWK
VB GANDHI MARG
Chetana Bookstore
HOPE ST
Jehangir Art Gallery
Goethe-Institut
K DUBASH MARG
Chhatrapati Shivaji Maharaj Vastu Sangrahalaya (Prince of Wales Museum)
Secretariat
MAHATMA GANDHI RD
Bombay Natural History Society
S P MUKHERJEE CHOWK (WELLINGTON CIRCLE)
National Gallery of Modern Art (NGMA)
MADAME CAMA RD
NAVAL DOCKYARD
COOPERAGE ROAD
Citibank ATM
Regal Cinema
SHIVAJI MARG
Sahakari Bhandar
BATTERY ST
RAJKAVI BHUSHAN MARG
MTDC Kiosk
Bombay Yacht Club
Boat Ticket Booths
NATHALAL PAREKH MARG
CONVENT ROAD
Bank of Baroda & ATM
Reality Tours
TULLOCH RD
HFDC Bank & ATM
Shivaji Statue
Launch Ticket Booth
NAWROJI F MARG
N PAREKH MARG
BEST MARG
Police Station
MANDLIK ROAD
Gateway of India
BEST MARG
SHAHID BHAGAT SINGH MARG (COLABA CAUSEWAY)
B BEHRAM MARG (MEREWEATHER ROAD)
Taj Mahal Palace & Tower
Bus Depot
J A ALLANA MARG
HENRY RD
P J RAMCHANDANI MARG (APOLLO BUNDER)
CUSROW BAUG
COLABA
WALTON RD
OLIVER STREET
GARDEN RD
ARTHUR BUNDER RD (H N A A MARG)
S B ROAD
Pharmacy
FIRST PASTA ROAD
BHASKARRAO KARGUTKAR ROAD
STRAND ROAD
BRAHMAKUMARIS MARG
V DESAI MARG

Elephanta Island

Manhwa & Alibag

0   100
metres

N

▼ Strand Cinema, Colaba Market & Sassoon Docks   ▼ Colaba Market

SHOPPING
Avante Cottage Crafts	5
Fabindia	2
Good Earth	7
Kitab Khana	1
Nicobar	3
Phillip's Antiques	4
Vaya	6

DRINKING & NIGHTLIFE
Café Marina	4
Café Mondegar	1
Garage Inc	3
Havana	2

EATING
All Stir Fry	7
Bademiya	8
Chetana	5
Churchill	14
Colaba Social	13
Indigo Deli	6
Kailash Parbat	15
Kala Ghoda Café	3
Khyber	4
Leopold's	9
Miss T	11
Olympia Coffee House	10
The Pantry	1
The Sea Lounge	12
Trishna	2

ACCOMMODATION
Abode	4
Aga Bheg's & Hotel Kishan	8
Ascot	12
Backpacker Panda	10
Bentley's	9
Godwin	13
Gordon House	3
Lawrence	1
Moti International	6
Red Shield	7
Sea Palace	11
Sea Shore	14
Taj Mahal Palace and Tower	5
YWCA	2

> ### BOMBAY DUCK
>
> Its name suggests some kind of fowl curry, but **Bombay duck** is actually a fish – to be precise, the marine lizard fish (*Harpalon nehereus*), known in the local dialect of Marathi as *bombil*. How this long, ribbon-like sea creature acquired its English name no one is exactly sure, but the most plausible theory holds that the Raj-era culinary term derives from the Hindustani for mail train, *dak*. The nasty odour of the dried fish is said to have reminded the British of the less salubrious carriages of the Calcutta–Bombay *dak* when it pulled into VT after three days and nights on the rails, its wooden carriages covered in the stinking mould that flourished in the monsoonal humidity.

10

Colaba Causeway

Reclaimed in the late nineteenth century from the sea, Colaba's main thoroughfare, **Shahid Bhagat Singh Marg**, better known as **Colaba Causeway**, leads south from the tourist enclave towards the quieter military cantonment area. Few tourists stray much further down it than the claustrophobic hawker zone at the top of the street, whose shops are fronted by a line of covered incense and knick-knack stalls, but it's well worth doing so, if only to see the neighbourhood's earthy **fresh produce market** a couple of blocks south of the Strand cinema.

Sassoon Docks

Mumbai's wholesale seafood market, **Sassoon Docks**, lies a ten-minute walk beyond the southern end of Colaba Causeway. The greasy quaysides are at their liveliest immediately before and after sunrise, when coolies haul the night's catch in crates of crushed ice over gangplanks, while Koli women cluster around the auctioneers. The stench, as overpowering as the noise, comes mostly from bundles of one of the city's traditional exports, **Bombay duck** (see page 613). Note that **photography** is strictly forbidden as the docks are adjacent to a sensitive naval area.

Afghan Memorial Church of St John the Baptist

Nanabhai Moos Marg • Buses #3, #11, #103, #123 or #125 or #137 from SBS Marg (Colaba) and VT

The **Afghan Memorial Church of St John the Baptist** was built in 1847–54 to commemorate British victims of the ill-fated First Afghan War, in which Elphinstone's expeditionary force was famously wiped out while trying to withdraw from Kabul. Of the 16,500 troops and camp followers who set out on January 1, 1842, only forty survived the massacre, and only one British solider – William Brydon – arrived alive. The battle-scarred colours of the 44th Regiment of Foot are among those displayed inside the church. It's by no means an impressive structure, with plain walls and wooden beams, but there are a few memorial plaques listing officers killed in action during the conflict.

Kala Ghoda and around

Immediately north of Colaba, **Kala Ghoda** ("Black Horse") district is named after the large equestrian statue of King Edward VII that formerly stood on the crescent-shaped intersection of MG Road and Subhash Chowk. Flanked by Mumbai's principal museum and art galleries, the neighbourhood today is something of a "cultural enclave" where small galleries, boutiques and top Indian designers occupy its many historic buildings. Fancy stainless-steel interpretive panels now punctuate the district's walkways, and on Sundays in December and January, the **Kala Ghoda Fair** sees portrait artists, potters and *mehendi* painters plying their trade in the car park fronting the Jehangir Art Gallery.

Chhatrapati Shivaji Museum

MG Rd · Daily 10.15am–6pm · ₹500 (₹85) · ⑩ csmvs.in

The **Prince of Wales Museum of Western India**, or **Chhatrapati Shivaji Maharaj Vastu Sangrahalaya** as it was renamed by the Shiv Sena, ranks among the city's most distinctive Raj-era constructions. It stands rather grandly in its own gardens off MG Road, crowned by a massive white Mughal-style dome, beneath which one of India's finest collections of paintings and sculpture is arrayed on three floors. The building was designed by George Wittet, of Gateway of India fame, and stands as the epitome of the hybrid **Indo-Saracenic** style – regarded in its day as an "educated" interpretation of fifteenth- and sixteenth-century Gujarati architecture, mixing Islamic touches with typically English municipal brickwork.

The foreigners' ticket price includes a good **audio tour**, which you collect at the admissions kiosk inside and takes around one hour to complete. The heat and humidity inside the building can be a trial, but the on-site café serves cold drinks and snacks. To exit the museum and re-enter (which you're entitled to do) you'll have to get your ticket stamped in the admissions lobby first.

Ground floor

The **Key Gallery** in the central hall of the **ground floor** provides a snapshot of the collection's treasures, including the fifth-century-AD stucco Buddhist figures unearthed by archeologist Henry Cousens in 1909. The main **sculpture room** in the east wing displays other fourth- and fifth-century Buddhist artefacts, mostly from the former Greek colony of Gandhara. Important Hindu sculptures include a seventh-century Chalukyan bas-relief depicting Brahma seated on a lotus, and a sensuously carved torso of Mahisasuramardini, the goddess Durga, with tripod raised ready to skewer the demon buffalo.

Upper floors

The main attraction on the **first floor** has to be the museum's famous collection of **Indian painting**, which includes works from the Mughal emperors' private collections. More fine medieval miniatures are housed in the **Karl & Meherbai Khandalavala Gallery**, on the renovated east wing of this floor, along with priceless pieces of Ghandaran sculpture, Chola bronzes and some of the country's finest surviving examples of medieval Gujarati woodcarving. Indian **coins** are the subject of the **House of Laxmi Gallery**, also in the east wing, while the **second floor** showcases a vast array of Oriental ceramics and glassware. Finally, among the grisly **weapons** and pieces of armour stored in a small side gallery at the top of the building, look out for the cuirass, helmet and jade dagger which belonged to the Mughal emperor Akbar.

Jehangir Art Gallery

MG Rd · Daily 11am–7pm · Free

Technically in the same compound as the Prince of Wales Museum, though approached from further up MG Road, the **Jehangir Art Gallery** is Mumbai's longest-established venue for contemporary art, with five small halls specializing in twentieth-century arts and crafts from around the world. You never know what you're going to find – most exhibitions last only a week, exhibits are usually for sale and the artists themselves are often found hanging around their hall.

National Gallery of Modern Art

MG Rd, facing the museum and Mukharji Chowk · Tues–Sun 11am–6pm · ₹500 (₹20) · ⑩ ngmaindia.gov.in

Charting the development of modern Indian art from its beginnings in the 1950s to the present day, the **National Gallery of Modern Art (NGMA)** holds a mix of permanent and temporary exhibitions. The works are arrayed over five wonderfully light, semicircular galleries, interconnected by teak-and-chrome staircases. The installations, in particular, tend to be a lot more adventurous than those you'll find in the Jehangir across the road.

Around Oval Maidan

Northeast of Kala Ghoda stretches the yawning expanse of **Oval Maidan**, where impromptu cricket matches are held almost every day, against a backdrop of giant palms and even taller Raj-era buildings. Green during the monsoons and parched yellow for the rest of year, it is flanked on its eastern side by some of Mumbai's finest Victorian piles, dating from the high point of British power. On its western side is an ensemble of fabulous Art Deco apartment buildings. The entire area was inscribed on the UNESCO World Heritage List in 2018 as a testimony to the various phases of modernization Mumbai has undergone in the last three hundred years.

High Court
Karmaveer Bhaurao Patil Marg

Dominating the east side of Oval Maidan is the **Mumbai High Court**, originally the Old Secretariat, which the Raj historian G.W. Forrest described in 1903 "a massive pile whose main features have been brought from Venice, but all the beauty has vanished in trans-shipment". With its gigantic pitched roofs and balconies shaded by enormous rattan blinds, the building has changed little since. Take a peek inside, where lawyers in black gowns, striped trousers and white tabs bustle up and down the staircases, and office desks are piled high with dusty beribboned bundles of documents – a vision of Indian bureaucracy at its most Dickensian.

Mumbai University
MG Rd

Across AS D'Mello Road from the High Court stand the two major buildings comprising **Mumbai University** (established 1857), which were designed in England by Sir Gilbert Scott, architect of the Gothic extravaganza that is London's St Pancras railway station. Funded by the Parsi philanthropist Cowasjee "Readymoney" Jehangir, whose white marble statue appears in front of it, the **Convocation Hall** greatly resembles a church. Above the entrance, a huge circular stained-glass window features a wheel with spokes of Greek pilasters separating the signs of the zodiac. With all its polished teak and brass, the interior, currently closed to visitors for security reasons, could have been transported from a Victorian public school in the home counties of England. Gilbert Scott's 79.2m-high **Rajabhai Clock Tower** is said to have been modelled on Giotto's campanile in Florence and formerly chimed tunes such as *Rule Britannia* and *Home Sweet Home*.

Fort

East of Oval Maidan stretches the spectacular **Fort** district, site of Mumbai's original British settlement and the first East India Company fort – hence the name. The sloping ramparts, moats and fortified gateways were pulled down in the mid-nineteenth century following the demise of the French threat to British supremacy in India, but this is still the commercial hub of the southern city. It's a great area for aimless wandering, with plenty of old-fashioned cafés, department stores and street stalls crammed in between the imposing Victorian buildings.

Horniman Circle

At the heart of the Fort district lies the spacious **Horniman Circle**, conceived in 1860 as the centrepiece of a newly planned Bombay by the then Municipal Commissioner,

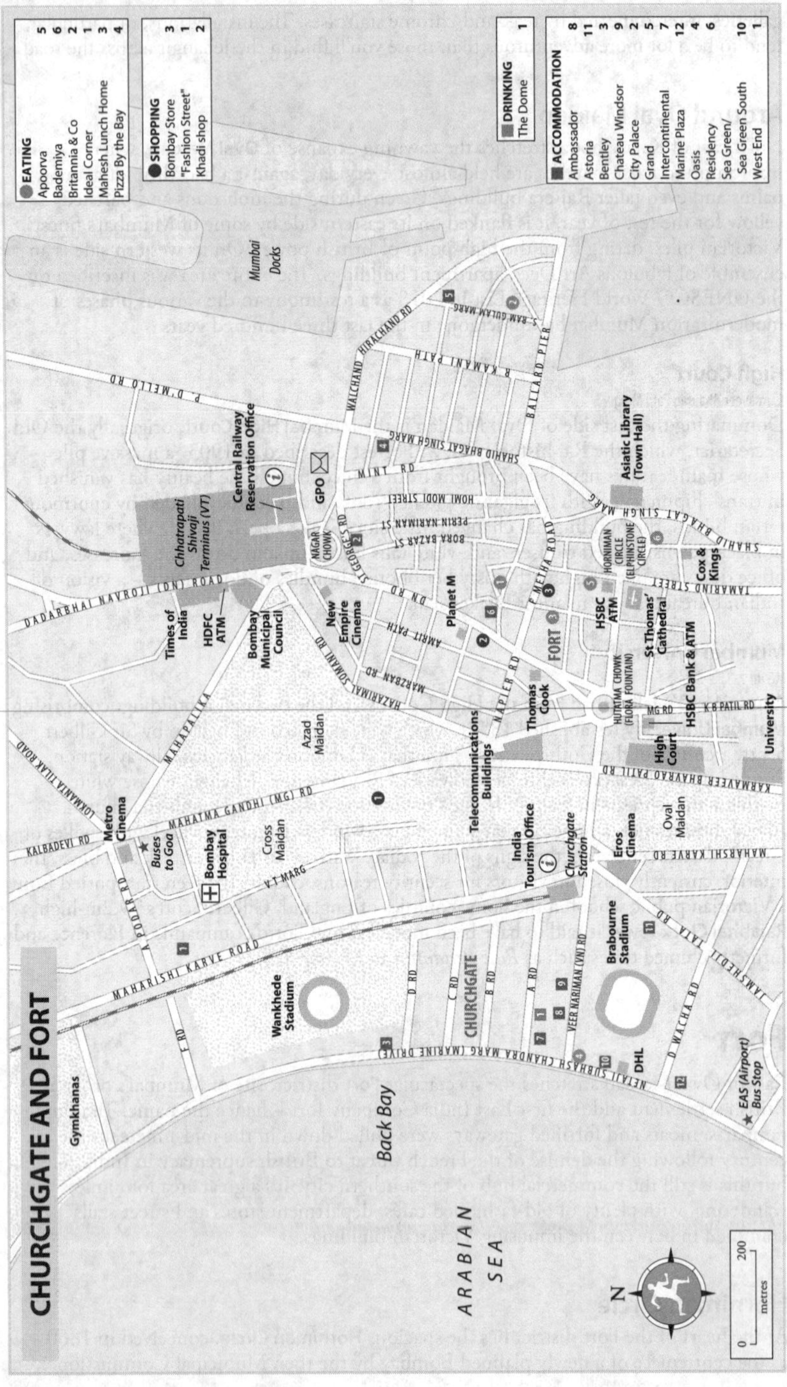

CHURCHGATE AND FORT
EATING
Apoorva 5
Bademiya 6
Britannia & Co 2
Ideal Corner 1
Mahesh Lunch Home 3
Pizza By the Bay 4
SHOPPING
Bombay Store 3
"Fashion Street" 1
Khadi shop 2
DRINKING
The Dome 1
ACCOMMODATION
Ambassador 8
Astoria 11
Bentley 3
Chateau Windsor 9
City Palace 2
Grand 5
Intercontinental 7
Marine Plaza 12
Oasis 4
Residency 6
Sea Green/
Sea Green South 10
West End 1
Mumbai Docks
Chhatrapati Shivaji Terminus (VT)
Central Railway Reservation Office
GPO
Asiatic Library (Town Hall)
Times of India
HDFC ATM
Bombay Municipal Council
New Empire Cinema
Planet M
FORT
HSBC ATM
Horniman Circle (Elphinstone Circle)
Cox & Kings
St Thomas' Cathedral
Hutatma Chowk (Flora Fountain)
HSBC Bank & ATM
Thomas Cook
Telecommunications Buildings
High Court
University
Azad Maidan
Metro Cinema
Buses to Goa
Bombay Hospital
Cross Maidan
India Tourism Office
Churchgate Station
Eros Cinema
Oval Maidan
Brabourne Stadium
Wankhede Stadium
CHURCHGATE
DHL
EAS (Airport) Bus Stop
Gymkhanas
Back Bay
ARABIAN SEA
N
0 200 metres
Dadarbhai Navroji (DN) Road
P. D'Mello Rd
Walchand Hirachand Rd
Shahid Bhagat Singh Marg
R Kamani Path
S Ram Gulam Marg
Ballard Pier
Mint Rd
Homi Modi Street
Perin Nariman St
Bora Bazar St
St George's Rd
Nagar Chowk
DN Rd
Amrit Path
Marzban Rd
Hazarimal Somani Rd
Napier Rd
P Metha Road
Tamarind Street
MG Rd
K B Patil Rd
Karmaveer Bhaurao Patil Rd
Mahapalika
Lokmanya Tilak Road
Kalbadevi Rd
Mahatma Gandhi (MG) Rd
A Podar Rd
V T Marg
Maharshi Karve Road
Maharshi Karve Rd
Jamshedji Tata Rd
D Rd
C Rd
B Rd
A Rd
Veer Nariman (VN) Rd
D Wacha Rd
F Rd
Netaji Subhash Chandra Marg (Marine Drive)

Charles Forjett, on the site of Bombay's "Green". Later, the space served as a cotton market and parade ground. The garden's wrought-iron gates and fences enclose a haven of vegetation where office workers bring their lunches and newspapers. Surrounding it are ranks of grand buildings whose paved arcades, crowned by grim-faced keystone heads, today provide accommodation for families of street sleepers.

The Asiatic Society Library

Shahid Bhagat Singh Marg • Mon–Sat 10am–5pm • ☎ 022 2266 0956, ⊕ asiaticsociety.org.in

The splendid Neoclassical building on the east side of Horniman Circle served as the city's former Town Hall, one of the few buildings in Mumbai that pleased Aldous Huxley: "(Among) so many architectural cads and pretentious bounders," he wrote in 1948, "it is almost the only gentleman." The Doric edifice, dating from 1833, was originally built to house the vast collection of the **Asiatic Society Library**, which is still open to the public. Save for the addition of electricity, little has changed here since the institution was founded. Reading rooms, lined with wrought-iron loggias and teak bookcases, are filled with scholars poring over mouldering tomes dating from the Raj. Among the ten thousand rare and valuable manuscripts stored here is a fourteenth-century first edition of Dante's *Divine Comedy*, said to be worth around US$3 million, which the Society famously refused to sell to Mussolini. Visitors are welcome but should sign in at the Head Librarian's desk on the ground floor.

St Thomas' Cathedral

Veer Nariman Rd • Daily 7am–6pm

Just west off Horniman Circle stands the diminutive **St Thomas' Cathedral**, reckoned to be the oldest British building in Mumbai, blending Classical and Gothic styles. After the death of its founding father, Governor Aungier, the project was abandoned; the walls stood 5m high for forty-odd years until enthusiasm was rekindled in the second decade of the eighteenth century. It was finally opened on Christmas Day, 1718, complete with the essential "cannonball-proof roof". The whitewashed and polished brass-and-wood interior looks much the same at it did in the eighteenth century. Lining the walls are memorial tablets to British parishioners, many of whom died young, either from disease or in battle.

Chhatrapati Shivaji Terminus (Victoria Terminus)

Tours Mon–Fri 3–5pm • ₹200 • Contact Zakir Palekar ☎ 90044 11438

Inspired by St Pancras Station in London, F.W. Stevens designed **Victoria Terminus**, the barmiest of Mumbai's buildings, as a paean to "progress". Built in 1887 as the largest British edifice in India, it's an extraordinary amalgam of domes, spires, Corinthian columns and minarets that was succinctly defined by the journalist James Cameron as "Victorian-Gothic-Saracenic-Italianate-Oriental-St Pancras-Baroque". In keeping with the current re-Indianization of the city's roads and buildings, this icon of British imperial architecture has been renamed **Chhatrapati Shivaji Terminus**, in honour of the famous Maratha warlord. The new name is a bit of a mouthful, however, and locals mostly still refer to it as **VT** (pronounced "vitee").

Few of the three million or so passengers who fill almost a thousand trains every day notice the mass of decorative detail. A "British" lion and Indian tiger stand guard at the entrance, and the exterior is festooned with sculptures executed at the Bombay Art School by the Indian students of John Lockwood Kipling, Rudyard's father. Among them are grotesque mythical beasts, monkeys, plants and medallions of important personages. To minimize the sun's impact, stained glass was employed, decorated with locomotives and elephant images. Above it all, the statue of "Progress" stands atop the massive central dome.

10

DABBAWALAS

Mumbai's size and inconvenient shape create all kind of hassles for its working population. One thing the daily tidal wave of commuters does not have to worry about, however, is where to find an inexpensive and wholesome home-cooked lunch. The members of the **Nutan Mumbai Tiffin Box Suppliers Charity Trust (NMTSCT)**, known colloquially as "**dabbawalas**", see to that. Every day, around 5000 dabbawalas deliver freshly cooked meals from 200,000 suburban kitchens to offices in the downtown area. Each is prepared early in the morning by a wife or mother while her husband or son is enduring the crush on the train. She arranges the rice, dhal, *subzi*, curd and *parathas* into cylindrical aluminium trays, stacks them on top of one another and clips them together with a neat little handle.

This **tiffin box** is the linchpin of the whole operation. When the runner calls to collect it in the morning, he uses a special colour code on the lid to tell him where the lunch has to go. At the end of his round, all the boxes are carried to the nearest railway station and handed over to other dabbawalas for the trip into town. Between leaving the cook and reaching its final destination, the tiffin box will pass through at least half a dozen different pairs of hands, carried on heads, shoulder-poles, bicycle handlebars and in the brightly decorated handcarts that glide with such insouciance through the midday traffic.

WHERE TO FIND THEM

To catch them in action, head for **CST (VT)** or **Churchgate** stations around late morning, when the tiffin boxes arrive in the city centre to a chorus of "*lafka! lafka*" – "hurry! hurry!" – as the dabbawalas rush to make their lunch-hour deadlines. Nearly all come from the same small village near Pune and are related to one another. They collect around ₹2000–4000 per month in total.

One of the reasons the system survives in the face of competition from trendy fast-food outlets is that dabba lunches still work out a good deal cheaper, saving precious rupees for the middle-income workers who use the system. Competition has recently arisen from high-end takeaway joints in Mumbai, some of whom offer freshly prepared gourmet food delivered in tiffin tins. But the dabbawalas are not sitting on their heels in the face of the new competition, with a website (⬥mumbaidabbawala.in) to facilitate booking online and by SMS. An excellent initiative called "Share my Dabba" has also been launched to prevent wastage of uneaten food and distribute it to the needy.

A polished black marble memorial next to the station's main entrance commemorates the 58 passengers and staff gunned down by terrorists during the 26/11 attack (see page 609).

Central Bazaar District

Sir JJ Rd, 1km north of CST (VT) station

Lining the anarchic jumble of streets beyond Lokmanya Tilak Road is Mumbai's bustling **Central Bazaar District** – a fascinating counterpoint to the wide and Westernized streets of downtown. In keeping with traditional divisions of guild, caste and religion, most streets specialize in one or two types of merchandise. If you lose your bearings, the best way out is to ask someone to wave you in the direction of **Mohammed Ali Road**, the busy road through the heart of the district (now surmounted by a gigantic flyover), from where you can hail a cab.

Crawford Market

Crawford (aka Mahatma Phule) **Market**, ten minutes' walk north of CST, is an old British-style covered market dealing in just about every kind of fresh food and domestic animal imaginable. Before venturing inside, stop to admire the **friezes** wrapped around its exterior – a Victorian vision of sturdy-limbed peasants toiling in the fields, as designed by Rudyard Kipling's father, Lockwood, principal of the Bombay School of Art in 1865.

The **main hall** is still divided into different sections: pyramids of polished fruit and vegetables down one aisle, sacks of nuts or oil-tins full of herbs and spices down another. Around the back of the market, in the atmospheric wholesale wing, the pace of life is more hectic. Here, noisy crowds of coolies mill about with large reed-baskets held high in the air (if they are looking for work) or on their heads (if they've found some). Animal lovers should steer well clear of the market's eastern wing, where all kinds of unfortunate creatures are crammed into undersized cages; beyond the pet section, the meat hall is not for the squeamish.

Jama Masjid and Zaveri Bazaar

Sheikh Memon St

The streets immediately **north of Crawford Market** and west of **Mohammed Ali Road** form one vast bazaar area, dominated by the domes and minarets of the chintzy white **Jama Masjid**, or "Friday Mosque" (c.1800). The nucleus of the building is an ancient water tank, which now serves as an ablution pool. Pillars rise directly from the murky green pond to support the main body of the mosque, whose halls are reached by stairways. Cutting north from the Jama Masjid is **Zaveri Bazaar**, the jewellery market where Mumbaikars come to shop for dowries and wedding attire. An estimated 65 percent of all India's gold, silver and precious gems trading is carried out in the brightly lit emporia lining the market's lanes.

Mumba Devi Temple

Sheikh Memon St, Bhuleshwar

An important centre of Devi worship, the **Mumba Devi Temple** rises from one of the most densely populated square miles on the planet – a maze of twisting lanes and alleyways, lined by five- or six-storey wooden-balconied tenement buildings. The present structure, with its tapering polychrome sanctuary tower, dates only from the nineteenth century, but the black-stone deity inside it, patron goddess of the city's Koli fisherfolk, is much older. Originally she occupied a shrine further south, just outside the walls of the East India Company's fort, but that site was commandeered to make way for VT station. Colourful stalls selling floral offerings and other religious paraphernalia line the streets around it, where you'll encounter plenty of saffron-clad sadhus, their foreheads smeared with vibrant red vermilion powder.

Marine Drive

Netaji Subhash Chandra Marg, better known as **Marine Drive**, is Mumbai's seaside prom, an eight-lane highway with a wide pavement built in the 1920s on reclaimed land. The whole 3km stretch – still often referred to by Mumbaikars as the "Queen's Necklace" after the row of lights that illuminates its spectacular curve at night – is a favourite place for a stroll; the promenade next to the sea has uninterrupted views virtually the whole way along, while the peeling, mildewed Art Deco apartment blocks on the land side remain some of the most desirable addresses in the city.

Chowpatty Beach

Situated at the top of Marine Drive, **Chowpatty Beach** is a Mumbai institution. On evenings and weekends, Mumbaikars gather here in large numbers – not to swim (the

10

THE TOWERS OF SILENCE

High on Malabar Hill, screened from prying eyes by a high wall and dense curtain of vegetation (and strictly closed to visitors), stand the seven **Towers of Silence**, where the city's dwindling Zoroastrian community (better known as Parsis) dispose of their dead. Pollution of the four sacred elements (air, water, earth and, holiest of all, fire) contradicts the most fundamental precepts of the 2500-year-old Parsi faith, first imported to India when Zoroastrians fled from Sassanid Persia to escape Arab persecution in the seventh century. So instead of being buried or cremated, the bodies are laid out on top of open-topped, cylindrical towers, called *dokhmas*, for their bones to be cleaned by **vultures** and the weather. The remains are then placed in an ossuary at the centre of the tower.

sea is foul) but to wander, sit on the sand, eat kulfi and *bhel puri*, get their ears cleaned and gaze across the bay while the kids ride a pony or a rusty Ferris wheel.

At the back of the beach, a bronze bust recalls the bravery of Tukaram Omble, the policeman who lost his life capturing terrorist Ajmal Kasab during the 2008 attacks. Omble held on to the gunman's AK47 long enough for his colleagues to overpower the attacker, but was shot several times in the process and later died of his injuries.

Mani Bhavan

19 Laburnum Rd • Daily 10am–5.30pm • Free, with optional donation • ☎ 022 2380 5864, ⓦ gandhi-manibhavan.org • If coming by taxi, ask for the nearby Gamdevi Police Station

A ten-minute walk north from the middle of Chowpatty Beach along Pandita Ramabai Marg, **Mani Bhavan** was Gandhi's Bombay base between 1917 and 1934. Set in a leafy upper-middle-class road, the house has now been converted into a permanent memorial to the Mahatma. The lovingly maintained polished-wood interior is crammed with historic photos and artefacts – the most disarming of which is a friendly letter to Hitler suggesting world peace.

Malabar Hill

Its shirt-tails swathed in greenery and brow bristling with gigantic skyscrapers, **Malabar Hill**, the promontory enfolding Chowpatty Beach at the north end of Back Bay, has been south Mumbai's most desirable neighbourhood almost since the city was founded. The British were quick to see the potential of its salubrious breezes and sweeping sea views, constructing bungalows at the tip of what was then a separate island – the grandest of them the Government House, originally erected in the 1820s and now the seat of the serving governor of Maharashtra, **Raj Bhavan**.

Although none of Malabar's landmarks can be classed as unmissable, its Hindu shrines and surviving colonial-era residences form an interesting counterpoint to the modernity towering on all sides. Bal Gangadhar Kher Marg (formerly Ridge Road) is the district's main artery. You can follow it from Mumbai's principal **Jain Temple** (see map, p.610), with its mirror-encrusted interior dedicated to Adinath, all the way to the tip of the headland, where the famous **Walukeshwar Temple** stands as the city's oldest Hindu shrine surviving *in situ*. According to the Ramayana, Rama fashioned a lingam out of sand to worship Shiva here, which over the centuries became one of the Konkan's most important pilgrimage centres. Today's temple, erected in 1715 after the original was destroyed by the Portuguese, is of less note than the **Banganga Tank** below it – a rectangular lake lined by stone *ghats* and numerous crumbling shrines.

A DHOBI WALA AT WORK

Central Mumbai: Mahalakshmi to Byculla

The centre of Mumbai, beyond Malabar Hill, is mostly made up of working-class neighbourhoods: a huge mosaic of dilapidated tenements, markets and industrial eyesores left over from the Victorian cotton boom. For relief from the urban cauldron, residents travel west to the seashore to worship at the **Mahalakshmi Temple** (if they're Hindus) or the island **tomb of Haji Ali** (if they're Muslims). Both make great excursions from south Mumbai, and can be combined with a foray across town to the recently revamped **Dr Bhau Dadji Lad Museum** in Byculla, calling en route at the **Mahalakshmi dhobi ghats** – one of the city's more offbeat sights.

Mahalakshmi Temple

Just off Bhulabhai Desai Rd • Daily 6am–10pm • Buses #81, #83, #86 or #132 will take you from Colaba to Haji Ali, within a stone's throw of the Mahalakshmi Temple • ☎ 022 2351 4732, ⓦ mahalakshmi-temple.com

Mumbai's busy **Mahalakshmi Temple**, dedicated to the Hindu goddess of wealth and prosperity – the city's most sought-after attributes – stands on the shoreline off the frenetic Bhulabhai Desai intersection. The approach is via an alley lined with stalls selling spectacular floral offerings and devotional pictures. A heavy security cordon has to be crossed before entering the main shrine, where a statue of the *devi* glittering with gold jewellery and bangles, and seated astride a tiger and demon, is propitiated by a constant stream of worshippers. Donations pile so high that the temple pujaris run a

---

DHARAVI: THE £700 MILLION SLUM

Sprawling over 550 acres, **Dharavi**'s maze of dilapidated shacks and narrow, stinking alleyways is home to more than a million people. An average of fifteen thousand of them share a single toilet. Infectious diseases such as dysentery, malaria and hepatitis are rife; and there aren't any hospitals.

Despite the poverty, Dharavi has been described by the UK's *Observer* newspaper as "one of the most inspiring economic models in Asia": hidden amid the warren of ramshackle huts and squalid open sewers are an estimated fifteen thousand single-room factories, employing around a quarter of a million people and turning over a staggering £700 million (US$1 billion) annually. The majority of small businesses in Dharavi are based on **waste recycling** of one kind or another. Slum residents young and old scavenge materials from across the city and haul them back in huge bundles to be reprocessed. Aluminium cans are smelted down, soap scraps salvaged from schools and hotels are reduced in huge vats, leather reworked, disused oil drums restored and discarded plastic reshaped and remoulded. An estimated ten thousand workers are employed in the plastics sector alone. Ranging from ₹3000–15,000 per month, wages are well above the national average, and though Dharavi may not have any health centres, it does hold a couple of banks, and even ATMs.

As India's most iconic slum, Dharavi has also found an unlikely niche in the history of Indian and international **cinema**. The district provided many of the settings for Danny Boyle's multiple-Oscar-winning *Slumdog Millionaire*, as well as several of its leading child actors.

Despite its burgeoning international fame, Dharavi's future remains uncertain. The entire district is living in the shadow of a proposed US$40 billion **redevelopment project** which aims to bulldoze the entire slum. In return for agreeing to eviction, residents will be entitled to apartment space in new multi-storey tower blocks. Schools, roads, hospitals and other amenities have also been promised. Opposition to the scheme among Dharavites has been all but unanimous, however, with slum dwellers insisting any future development should focus not on erecting a swanky new suburb but on improving existing conditions.

You can visit Dharavi yourself by joining one of the "**Slum Tours**" run by Reality Tours and Travels out of Colaba (☎ 9820 822253, ⓦ realitytoursandtravel.com). Tickets for these engaging guided trips start from ₹900 (walking tour), with a longer and more comfortable version with an a/c car for ₹1750.

ANTILIA

If Mumbai is notorious for its poverty, then the city is no less famous for the glittering wealth of its richest inhabitants, and they don't come richer than **Mukesh Ambani**, chairman of the Reliance Industries petrochemical corporation. With a net worth of US$45 billion, Ambani is officially India's richest man, and his towering, futuristic home on Altamount Rd in the Cumballa Hill district of south-central Mumbai is said to be the world's most valuable piece of real estate. The Jenga-like, 27-storey skyscraper – known as **Antilia** – enjoys a majestic view over the Arabian Sea on one side, and Dharavi slum area on the other. Completed in 2010, it cost an estimated US$500–600 million to build, and is valued at somewhere between US$1–2 billion. Six floors are given over to a 168-car parking area. The building boasts nine elevators, three helipads, a glittering ballroom with solid silver balustrades and ceilings festooned with crystal chandeliers, hanging gardens of hydroponic plants and an ice room where the Ambanis can beat the summer heat in flurries of man-made snow.

Reaction to this behemoth on Mumbai's skyline has been mixed, to say the least. While most of the locals and sightseers regard it with wide-eyed wonder, members of India's intelligentsia – from industrialist J.R. Tata to novelist Arundhati Roy – have been less than complimentary, deploring the Ambanis' apparent lack of social conscience.

money-spinning sideline reselling them. While you're here, find out what your future holds by joining the huddle of devotees pressing rupees onto the rear wall of the shrine room. If your coin sticks, you'll be rich.

Haji Ali's Tomb

Just off Lala Lajpatrai Marg • Daily 5am–10pm • Buses #81, #83, #86 or #132 will take you from Colaba to Haji Ali • ☎ 022 2352 9082, 🌐 hajialidargah.in

Occupying a small islet in the bay just north of the Mahalakshmi Temple is the mausoleum of the Muslim saint, Afghan mystic **Haji Ali Bukhari**. The site is a great place to head on Thursday and Friday evenings, when large crowds gather around the promontory to watch the sunset and listen to live qawwali music.

The tomb is connected to the mainland by a narrow concrete **causeway**, only passable at low tide. When not immersed in water, its entire length is lined with beggars supplicating passers-by and chanting verses from the Koran. Non-Muslims are welcome, but all visitors need to keep well covered (a headscarf should be worn by women).

Haji Ali Juice Centre

Daily 5am–2am

The traditional way to round off a trip to the mausoleum is to take a glass or two of fresh fruit juice at the legendary **Haji Ali Juice Centre**, just to the right of the entrance to the causeway. Customers either cram into the tiny dining hall or else order from their cars.

Mahalakshmi dhobi ghats

Bapurao Jagtap Marg • Buses #124 (from Colaba) and #153 (from Haji Ali) go to the dhobi ghats; trains run from Churchgate to Mahalakshmi station. Emerging from the station, turn left and follow the road over the rail tracks – the ghats will be below you on your left (hawkers from the nearby slums will show you the way)

On the face of it, the idea of going out of your way to ogle Mumbai's dirty washing sounds like a very perverse pastime. If you're passing, however, the **Mahalakshmi dhobi ghats**, near Mahalakshmi suburban railway station, are a sufficiently memorable spectacle to break a trip across town to see. Washing from all over the city is brought here each morning to be soaked in concrete vats and thumped by the resident dhobis. A trickle of curious foreign tourists gathers on Mahalakshmi Road bridge for this uniquely Indian photo opportunity.

10

Dr Bhau Dadji Lad Museum

Rani Baug, Dr Ambedkar Rd, Byculla East • Daily except Wed 10am–6pm • ₹100 (₹10) • Free tour 11.30am on weekends • Buses #1, #6 or #7 from Colaba • ☎ 022 2373 1234, ⓦ bdlmuseum.org

Way out in the post-industrial area of Byculla, the **Dr Bhau Dadji Lad Museum** was originally opened in 1872 as the **Victoria and Albert Museum** – "one of the greatest boons the British have conferred on India", according to contemporary reports. The elegant, Palladian-style building, set amid classically planned botanical gardens (now home to a rather depressing zoo) has been restored to its former glory – see the story of the pain-staking process on a video in the café out the back – and houses a collection of fascinating lithographs, prints, documents, uniforms and models relating to the development of Bombay, including a replica of those mysterious Towers of Silence. In the adjacent garden, the carved stone pachyderm after which the Portuguese are said to have named Elephanta Island presides over a collection of forlorn British statues, moved here during Independence beyond the reach of angry mobs.

Gorai

Just beyond the northern limits of Mumbai, **Gorai** is a low-lying, sparsely populated peninsula separated at its tip from the mainland by tidal creek. Among the city's residents, this isolated green belt, settled by Portuguese priests and Catholic converts in the sixteenth century, is famous for two starkly contrasting attractions: if you've a day to kill in Mumbai between flights, and can't face exploring the city, either the **Esselworld** amusement park complex or adjacent **Global Vipassana Pagoda** might be worth considering – though be warned that getting to and from Gorai from downtown can take upwards of two hours at peak times.

Esselworld

Daily 10am–7pm • ₹1050 for adults; ₹750 for children; combined Esselworld & Water Kingdom ₹1390 adult, ₹950 children • ⓦ esselworld.in

Mumbai's answer to Disneyland, **Esselworld** is the first-choice destination for local families who can afford the trip – an island of American-style fun and frolics on the city's green fringe. It consists of two parts: the Esselworld amusement park, with its white-knuckle roller coasters, gentler kiddies' rides, ice rink and bowling alley; and the adjacent Water Kingdom, a vast complex of aqua slides featuring the world's largest wave pool, a huge play lagoon and some brilliant family-friendly rides.

Global Vipassana Pagoda

Daily dawn–dusk • ⓦ globalpagoda.org

Chugging across Gorai Creek on the ferry, you could be forgiven for thinking yourself on a river somewhere in Southeast Asia. From the far bank, the ethereal, gold-painted **Global Vipassana Pagoda** rises like something you'd expect to see shimmering over the waters of Burma's Ayeyarwady Delta. In fact the pagoda was built as a replica of the resplendent Shwedagon Paya in Yangon (Rangoon), Myanmar's most venerated Buddhist monument. Its gleaming golden pinnacle soars 99m – the height of a thirty-storey building – above the shoreline peaks and the adjacent amusement park, making it the world's largest freestanding dome, taller even than Vijayapura's Gol Gumbaz.

An entranceway leads to a cavernous meditation hall measuring 280m in diameter and capable of accommodating eight thousand worshippers. Genuine relics of the Buddha, donated by the government of Sri Lanka and the Mahabodhi Society of Bodh Gaya, are enshrined in the upper dome above the hall. Other structures in the landscaped complex include a 21m-tall seated Buddha carved from a single piece of marble, a massive entrance gateway and towers containing a colossal Burmese-style bell and gong.

ARRIVAL AND DEPARTURE

By train and launch Make for Borivali or Malad station on the suburban train line. You can pick up BEST bus #294 or #247 to Gorai Creek from both stations – or better still, jump in an auto-rickshaw for the 4km trip to the river. Once at the jetty, take the Esselworld launch (₹50), not the cheaper local Gorai ferry, as the latter drops you a long way from the park.

GORAI

By bus Modern Tours and Travels (☎ 022 2353 0888) run a private service (2hr 30min; ₹700 plus ferry) that also runs direct to Esselworld from Colaba each day, departing from outside the Regal Cinema at 8.30am. Book in advance.

By taxi Taxis charge around ₹1000 for the 68km journey from Colaba, and can be in short supply for the return leg.

Elephanta

An hour's ride northeast across Mumbai harbour from Colaba, the island of **Elephanta** offers the best escape from the seething claustrophobia of the city – as long as you time your visit to avoid the weekend deluge of noisy day-trippers. Populated only by a small fishing community, it was originally known as **Gherapura**, the "city of Ghara priests", until the island was renamed in the sixteenth century by the Portuguese in honour of the carved elephant they found at the port – now on display outside the Dr Bhau Dadji Lad Museum in Byculla (see page 624). Its chief attraction is its unique **cave**

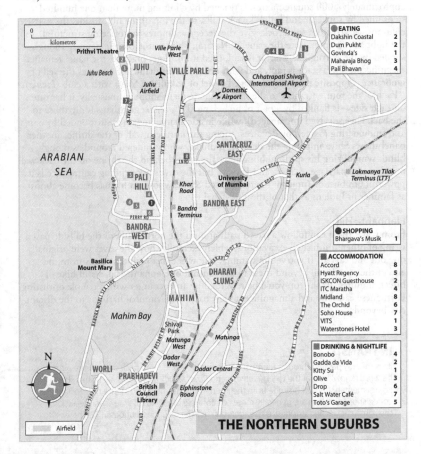

EATING
Dakshin Coastal	2
Dum Pukht	2
Govinda's	1
Maharaja Bhog	3
Pali Bhavan	4

SHOPPING
Bhargava's Musik	1

ACCOMMODATION
Accord	8
Hyatt Regency	5
ISKCON Guesthouse	2
ITC Maratha	4
Midland	8
The Orchid	6
Soho House	7
VITS	1
Waterstones Hotel	3

DRINKING & NIGHTLIFE
Bonobo	4
Gadda da Vida	2
Kitty Su	1
Olive	3
Drop	6
Salt Water Café	7
Toto's Garage	5

THE NORTHERN SUBURBS

10

temple, whose massive **Trimurti** (three-faced) **Shiva sculpture** is as fine an example of Hindu architecture as you'll find anywhere.

ARRIVAL AND INFORMATION

By boat Boats set off every 30min from the Gateway of India (daily 9am–3pm; returning from Elephanta noon–5.30pm; book through the Gateway Plaza kiosks near the Gateway of India); note that boats may be cancelled due to adverse weather conditions during the monsoon. Luxury launches (₹200 return adults; ₹125 children) include a 30min tour with a government guide – ask for your guide at the cave's ticket office on arrival. Ordinary Economy launches (₹125 return adults; ₹95 children) don't include the guided tour and are usually more packed. There's a

ELEPHANTA

tourist tax of ₹5 payable on arrival, and a further admission charge of ₹10.

Information Cool drinks and souvenir stalls line the way up the hill, and, at the top, the MTDC *Chalukya* restaurant offers substandard food and warm beer, served on a terrace with good views out to sea. If you don't want to walk up the 120 steps to the caves there's a miniature train up from the jetty (₹10 return). Note that you cannot stay overnight on the island and that the caves are closed on Mondays.

The cave

Tues–Sun 9.30am–5pm • ₹600 (₹50)

Elephanta's impressive excavated eighth-century **cave**, covering an area of approximately 5000 square metres, is reached by climbing more than one hundred steps lined by souvenir and knick-knack stalls, to the top of the hill. Inside, the massive columns, carved from solid rock, give the deceptive impression of being structural. To the right as you enter, note the panel of **Nataraj**, Shiva as the cosmic dancer. Though spoiled by the Portuguese who, it is said, used it for target practice, the panel remains magnificent: Shiva's face is rapt, and with one of his left hands he removes the veil of ignorance. Opposite is a badly damaged panel of Lakulisha, Shiva with a club (*lakula*).

Each of the four entrances to the simple square main **shrine** – unusually, it has one on each side – is flanked by a pair of huge fanged *dvarapala* guardians (only those to the back have survived undamaged), while inside a large lingam is surrounded by coins and smouldering joss left by devotees. Facing the northern wall of the shrine, another panel shows Shiva impaling the demon Andhaka, who wandered around as though blind, symbolizing his spiritual blindness. The panel behind the shrine on the back wall portrays the marriage of Shiva and Parvati, but the cave's outstanding centrepiece is its powerful 6m bust of **Trimurti**, the three-faced Shiva, whose profile has become almost as familiar to Indians as that of the Taj Mahal.

Elephanta Hill

From Cave 1 you can follow a paved path around the north flank of the hillside past a string of other, unfinished excavations, which exemplify how the caves were originally dug out and carved. If you've the stamina, follow the dirt path that leads from the end of the paved trail beyond these to the summit of **Elephanta Hill**, a stiff hike of fifteen minutes. At the top you'll be rewarded by an encounter with a couple of rusting Portuguese cannons and a magnificent view back over Mumbai harbour to the distant city beyond.

IN TRANSIT

If you're only passing through Mumbai between flights and need to sit out half the night, it's worth knowing that the *Leela Kempinski* and *Royal Meridien* five-stars are both a short, complimentary transfer bus ride from the international terminal at CST. Their a/c restaurants, coffee shops and bars are generally more comfortable places to kill time than the airport, though first-class and business passengers can use the luxurious lounges in T2. There's also a transit hotel on Level 1 of that terminal.

GETTING TO GOA

Easily the best-value way to travel the 500km from Mumbai to Goa is by **plane** – prices often compare favourably with the cost of the same journey on the Konkan Railway, which has two departures daily. If you are on a budget or unable to procure a flight or train ticket, there are several overnight **bus services** with semi-sleeper or sleeper seats.

BY PLANE

Around two dozen flights leave daily from Mumbai's domestic airport for Goa's **Dabolim airport** (code GOI). Flights are currently operated by JetKonnect, IndiGo, SpiceJet, Go Air, and Air India (see page 628). One-way fares start from around ₹2700; check ⓦ expedia.co.in and ⓦ cleartrip.com for the latest deals, or the websites of the airlines themselves for special offers and promotions.

Demand for seats can be fierce around Diwali and Christmas/New Year, when you're unlikely to get a ticket at short notice. At other times, one or other of the carriers should be able to offer a seat on the day you wish to travel – though perhaps not the lowest fares. If you didn't prebook when you purchased your international ticket, check availability as soon as you arrive.

BY TRAIN

The **Konkan Railway** line runs daily express trains from Mumbai to Goa. However, these services are not always available at short notice from the booking halls at CST and Churchgate. Don't, whatever you do, be tempted to travel "unreserved" class on any Konkan service, as the journey as far as Ratnagiri (roughly midway) is overwhelmingly crushed. There are a number of convenient overnight services (see page 628).

Fares range from a bargain-bucket ₹270 for basic second-class seated, to ₹390 for sleeper class, or ₹1530 for two-tier a/c. The priciest first-class tickets cost ₹2795 – roughly what you pay for a low-cost flight off peak.

BY BUS

The Mumbai–Goa bus journey is not as bad as it used to be, thanks to better road conditions, though the journey is still long. Depending on the type of bus you get and the sinuous coastal route, thirteen to fifteen hours is a realistic estimate for the journey time.

Fares start at around ₹840 for a push-back seat on a beaten-up Kadamba (Goan government) and ₹945 on a sleeper. MSRTC a/c coaches cost from ₹540. Tickets for these services are in great demand in season with domestic tourists, so **book in advance** at Mumbai Central. Quite a few **private overnight buses** (around a dozen daily) also run to Goa, costing from around ₹750 for no-frills buses up to ₹1500 for swisher a/c Volvo coaches with berths. Tickets are best booked at least a day in advance through the bus company, or online via ⓦ redbus.in or ⓦ makemytrip.com. Apart from enabling you to compare services, these websites allow you to check departure and pick-up points, which vary between operators. Few leave from south Mumbai. Among those that do is the largest operator for Goa, Paulo Travels (ⓦ paulotravels.com), whose recommended sleeper services from Dhobi Talao Junction on Fashion St at 5.15pm and 7.35pm, are the most comfortable buses to catch, costing ₹900 single and taking 15hr. Alternatively, Neeta Tours & Travels starts from the northern suburbs and has a pick-up point at Kalanagar bus stop in Bandra East near the Western Express highway (ⓦ neetabus.in).

ARRIVAL AND DEPARTURE   MUMBAI

Unless you're travelling by train to or from **Chhatrapati Shivaji Terminus** (formerly Victoria Terminus), be prepared for a long slog to or from the centre. The international and domestic **airports** are way north of the city, and ninety minutes or more by road from the main hotel areas, while from **Mumbai Central** railway or **bus station** you also face a laborious trip across town. At the time of writing in 2019, a brand-new subway was under construction which will connect the northern suburbs of Mumbai to the southern tip of Colaba. It is expected to be completed by 2022, but for now has just cause chaos on Mumbai's already overcrowded roads.

BY PLANE

INTERNATIONAL FLIGHTS

Mumbai's busy international airport, Chhatrapati Shivaji (30km north of downtown; ☎ 022 6685 1010, ⓦ csia.in) was

10

RECOMMENDED TRAINS FROM MUMBAI

All the following trains run daily.

Destination	Name	No.	From	Departs	Arrives
Aurangabad	*Tapovan Express*	#17617	CST	6.15am	1.15pm
Bengaluru (Bangalore)	*Udyan Express*	#11301	CST	8.10am	7.30am*
Bhuj	*Kutch Express*	#22955	Bandra	5.45pm	10am+
Delhi	*Rajdhani Express*	#12951	MC	5pm	8.15am+
Goa (Margao)	*Konkan–Kanya Express*	#10111	CST	11.25pm	9.30am+
	Jan Shatabdi	#12051	Dadar	5.25am	1pm
	Mangalore Express	#12133	CST	10pm	7am+
Kochi (Cochin)	*Netravati Express*	#16345	LTT (Kurla)	11.40am	1pm+
Kolhapur	*Sahyadri Express*	#11023	CST	5.50pm	6am+
Lonavala	*Udyan Express*	#11301	CST	8.05am	10.35am
Nasik	*Pushpak Express*	#12534	CST	8.20pm	11.50pm
Neral (for Matheran)	*Deccan Express*	#11007	CST	7am	8.30am
Pune	*Inrdayani Express*	#22105	CST	5.40am	8.40am

*+ = next day

impressively revamped in 2015, and the iconic T2 (Terminal 2) is (surprisingly) home to India's largest public art programme. Check-in is located in the departure area (Level 4), and all airlines have offices outside the main entrance.

Taxis While many of the more upmarket hotels send out courtesy coaches or chauffeur-driven cars to pick up and drop off their guests, most people arriving in Mumbai use the prepaid taxi desk in the arrivals hall. Choose from no-frills black and yellow cabs or the a/c Cool Cabs (☎76665 54466, ⍶citycoolcab.in). A prepaid taxi will cost ₹600 (or ₹700 a/c), while a Cool Cab is ₹800–1000 to Colaba. Alternatively, there's a choice of fleet taxis like Meru (☎022 4422 4422, ⍶merucabs.com) or Tab Cab (☎022 6363 6363, ⍶tabcab.in) and app-based services such as Ola (⍶olacabs.com) and Uber (⍶uber.com). There's free wi-fi available for booking cabs online, but the latter also has an information desk in the arrivals hall.

DOMESTIC FLIGHTS

confusingly, internal flights also land at both terminals in Mumbai's international airport (26km to the north of downtown; ☎022 6685 1010, ⍶csia.in). Vistara and Air India are the only airlines that use T2 for domestic routes, all others use Terminal 1.

Transfers If you're transferring directly from Terminal 1 to Terminal 2 for an international flight, take the free "fly-bus" that shuttles every 30min between the two terminals; look for the transfer counter in your transit lounge. Note that you may be required to collect and re-check your baggage.

Information and taxis India Tourism and the MTDC both have 24hr information counters in the arrivals hall, and

there's a foreign exchange counter and accommodation desk tucked away near the first-floor exit. The official "prepaid" taxi counter on the arrivals concourse charges around ₹600 to Colaba (₹700 for a/c). Alternatives are Cool Cab (☎76665 54466, ⍶citycoolcab.in) and Meru (☎022 4422 4422, ⍶merucabs.com) or app-based Ola (⍶olacabs. com) and Uber (⍶uber.com). There's free wi-fi available for booking cabs online.

Domestic airlines Air India, Air India Building, Nariman Point (☎1800 180 1407); Air India Express, Air India Building, Nariman Point (☎022 2202 3031); GoAir (☎092232 22111); IndiGo Airlines (☎099103 83838 or ☎1800 180 3838); JetKonnect, Chattrapathi Shivaji International Airport (☎022 6121 1000); SpiceJet (☎096540 03333).

BY TRAIN

Three main rail networks service Mumbai: Western Railways, covering Gujarat, northern Madhya Pradesh and Rajasthan; Central Railways, covering Maharashtra and southern Madhya Pradesh; and the Konkan Railway, running south down the coast to Goa and beyond.

CHHATRAPATI SHIVAJI TERMINUS (CST)

Trains operating between Mumbai and most central, southern and eastern regions work out of Chhatrapati Shivaji Terminus or CST (formerly Victoria Terminus, or VT), the main railway station at the end of the Central Railway line. The station lies a 10- or 15min ride to/from Colaba; taxis wait at the busy rank outside the south exit, opposite the reservation hall.

MUMBAI CENTRAL

The terminus for Western Railway trains from northern India, Mumbai Central, is a 30min ride from Colaba; on arrival, take a taxi from the forecourt, or flag one down on the main road – it should cost around ₹250–300.

OTHER STATIONS

Some trains from south India run out of more obscure stations: Dadar is way up in the industrial suburbs; Kurla, arrival/departure point for a few trains to/from Bengaluru (Bangalore) and Kerala, is even further out, just south of the domestic airport. From either, it's worth asking at the station when you arrive if there is another long-distance train going to Churchgate or CST (Victoria Terminus) shortly after – far better than trying to cram into either a suburban train or bus.

RESERVATIONS

The quickest and most convenient place for foreign nationals to make reservations on any of the networks is the efficient tourist counter (#14) on the first floor of the Western Railway's booking hall, next door to the Government of India tourist office on M Karve Rd, opposite Churchgate station (Mon–Fri 8am–8pm, Sat 8am–2pm; ☎022 2209 7577). Mumbai's other "Tourist Ticketing Facility" is on the ground floor (counter #4) of the a/c Central Railway Reservation Office at CST (VT; Mon–Sat 8am–8pm, Sun 8am–2pm; ☎022 2262 2859). The office is on the right of the main station entrance (as you go in), just off the concourse where taxis pull up. In theory you may be required to produce a foreign currency encashment certificate or ATM slip to buy tickets here, though it's unlikely to be asked for. Tickets for seats on the Konkan Railway can be booked at either Churchgate or CST booking halls.

BY BUS

Although taxis, working from ranks immediately outside both airports and the train stations, are by far the most convenient form of onward transport, there are a number of bus services.

GOVERNMENT SERVICES

Nearly all interstate buses work from Mumbai Central Bus Stand, a stone's throw from the railway station of the same name. Government services use the main Maharashtra State Road Transport Corporation (MSRTC) stand itself.

BOOKING COUNTERS AND RESERVATIONS

States with bus company booking counters (daily 8am–8pm) here include Maharashtra, Karnataka and Goa. Few of their services compare favourably with train travel on the same routes. Reliable timetable information can be difficult to obtain, reservations are not available on standard buses, and most long-haul journeys are gruelling overnighters. Among the exceptions are the deluxe buses run by MSRTC to Pune and Kolhapur; the small extra cost buys you more leg room, fewer stops and the option of advance booking. The only problem is that most leave from the ASIAD bus stand in Dadar, or the MSRTC stand in Thane, 30min and 60min respectively by road or rail north of Mumbai Central.

PRIVATE BUSES

Private services operate from the roadside next to Mumbai Central railway station, a 2min walk west on the opposite side of busy Dr AN Marg (Lamington Rd). They cover most of the same routes as government buses and tend to be faster, more comfortable and easier to book in advance – though again, long-distance services invariably depart at night. Note that fares on services to popular tourist destinations such as Goa and Mahabaleshwar double during peak season.

TIMETABLES

Timetable information is most easily researched online, via websites such as ⓦmakemytrip.com, which compare fares, class of vehicles, journey durations, departure times and – crucially – departure points (services leave from different places and follow different routes out of the city).

Destinations The following refers only to MSRTC (government) services. For timetable information for private buses, check ⓦmakemytrip.com or ⓦredbus.in.

ASIAD Dadar to: Kolhapur (hourly; 10hr); Nasik (hourly; 4–5hr); Pune (every 15min; 4hr).

Mumbai Central to: Aurangabad (3 daily; 10hr); Bengaluru (6 daily; 24hr); Goa (2 daily; 13–16hr); Mahabaleshwar (2 daily; 7hr 30min); Goa (1 daily; 12hr).

BY BOAT

Three companies – PNP, Maldar Catamarans and Ajanta – operate boat services from the Gateway of India to Mandwa jetty, on the far side of Mumbai harbour, from where buses shuttle to nearby Alibag, transport hub for the route southwards down the Konkan coast. Ranging from comfortable a/c catamarans (₹185) to bog-standard launches (₹165 upper deck; ₹135 main deck), the ferries leave roughly every hour; tickets should be purchased in advance from the PNP, Ajanta or Maldar company booths near the Gateway of India, on the north side of Shivaji Marg, next to the MTDC information counter.

GETTING AROUND

During peak hours in Mumbai **gridlock** is the norm, and you should brace yourself for long waits at junctions if you take to the roads by taxi, bus or auto. Local **trains** get there faster, but can be a real endurance test even outside rush hours.

10

A "SUPER-DENSE" CRUSH

The suburban rail network in Mumbai is officially the busiest on the planet. No other line carries as many passengers, nor crams them into such confined spaces. At peak times, as many as 4700 people may be jammed into a nine-carriage train designed to carry 1700, resulting in what the rail company, in typically jaunty Mumbai style, refers to as "**Super-Dense Crush Load**" of fourteen to sixteen standing passengers per square metre. Not all of these actually occupy floor space, of course: ten percent will be dangling precariously out of the doors.

The busiest stretch, a 60km segment between Churchgate terminus and Virar in north Mumbai, transports nearly nine hundred million people each year, the highest of any rail network in the world. **Fatalities** are all too frequent: on average, six hundred die on the rail network annually (that's more than sixteen deaths per day), usually from falling out of the doors, crossing the tracks or because they're hit by overhead cables while riding on the roof.

BY TRAIN

Mumbai's local trains carry an estimated 7.5 million commuters each day between downtown and the sprawling suburbs in the north – half the entire passenger capacity of Indian Railways (see box below). One line begins at CST (VT), running up the east side of the city; the other leaves Churchgate, travelling via Mumbai Central and Dadar to Santa Cruz and beyond. Services depart every few minutes from 5am until midnight, stopping at dozens of small stations. Carriages are packed for most of the day, with passengers dangling precariously out of open doors to escape the crush, so start to make your way to the exit at least three stops before your destination. Peak hours (approximately 8.30–10am & 4–10pm) are the worst of all. Women are marginally better off in the "ladies carriages"; look for the crowd of colourful saris and *salwar kameez* grouped at the end of the platform. Travel during non-peak hours (11am–3.30pm) can be comparatively easier.

METRO

The Mumbai Metro (☎ 022 3031 0900, ⓦ reliancemumbai metro.com) connects Versova in the west to Ghatkopar in the east, a 12km elevated network that stops at twelve stations en route, most importantly Andheri, Western Express Highway and Airport Road, close to the inter-national airport and the clutch of hotels around it. At the time of writing in 2019, a new route stretching to central Mumbai was under construction and is expected to be finished by 2022.

BUSES

BEST (☎ 022 2285 6262, ⓦ bestundertaking.com) operates a bus network of labyrinthine complexity, covering every part of the city. You can check routes and bus numbers on their website; recognizing bus numbers in the street, however, can be more problematic, as numerals are written in Marathi (although in English on the sides). Avoid rush hours at all costs and aim, wherever possible, for the "Limited" ("Ltd") services, which stop less frequently. Buses hardly come to a standstill at stops, so it's not uncommon to run alongside and jump on; tickets are bought from the conductor on the bus.

TAXIS AND CAR RENTAL

With rickshaws banished to the suburbs, Mumbai's ubiquitous black-and-yellow taxis are the quickest and most convenient way to nip around the city centre. In theory, all should have meters; in practice, particularly at night or early in the morning, many drivers refuse to use them. If this happens, either flag down another or haggle out a fare. As a rule of thumb, expect to be charged ₹22 for the first 1.5km and ₹14.84/km thereafter, plus a small sum for heavy luggage (₹10/article). A fifty percent supplement is levied for journeys between midnight and 5am. For more comfort, try a Cool Cab (☎ 022 2216 4466, ⓦ citycoolcab. in), blue taxis with a/c and tinted windows; rates are around forty percent higher than in a normal cab.

CARS WITH DRIVERS

Cars can be rented per 8hr day (₹2000–2500 for non-a/c, or from 3000 for a/c, depending on the car), plus ₹300/day driver allowance if the trip involves an overnight stay (the driver sleeps in the car). A minimum kilometre rate applies (usually 250km), after which there is a charge for every additional kilometre covered. A recommended travel agent who can arrange cars and drivers in Mumbai is Karmic Travels PVT Ltd (☎ 022 2612 4927, ⓦ karmictravels.com). For car hire, try CarJee (☎ 022 2830 1941 or ☎ 96193 78898, ⓦ carjee.com).

INFORMATION

Tourist information The best source of information in Mumbai is the excellent India Tourism (Mon–Fri 8.30am–6pm, Sat 9am–2pm; ☎ 022 2207 4333 or ☎ 022 2207 4334, ⓔ indiatourism-mum@nic.in) on the ground floor of the Air India building on Nariman Point, with exceptionally helpful staff and lots of free maps and brochures. The Maharashtra State Tourism Development Corporation (MTDC) office is in Apeejay House, 4th Floor, 3 Dinshaw Vachha Road (Mon–Fri 10am–5.30pm; ☎ 022 2204 4040, ⓦ maharashtratourism. gov.in).

Listings Check out the "Metro" page in the *Indian Express* or the "Bombay Times" section of the *Times of India*. Both are available from street vendors around Colaba and downtown.

ACCOMMODATION

Finding **accommodation** at the right price when you arrive in Mumbai can be a real problem. Budget travellers, in particular, can expect a hard time finding decent but affordable accommodation. The best low-cost places tend to fill up days or weeks in advance, so you should book well ahead to avoid a stressful, sweaty room hunt. Tariffs in midrange and upmarket places are also especially high for India. State-imposed **luxury tax** (currently ten percent), and **service charges** levied by the hotel itself further bump up bills; both these add-ons are included in the prices quoted in the following reviews. A short ride from the railway stations, **Colaba** makes a handy base and is where the majority of foreign visitors head first. The streets around the Gateway of India are chock-full of accommodation, and the area also offers more in the way of food and entertainment than neighbouring districts. At the western edge of the downtown area, swanky **Marine Drive** (officially Netaji Subhash Chandra Marg) is lined with four- and five-star hotels taking advantage of the panoramic views over Back Bay and the easy access to the city's commercial heart.

COLABA AND KALA GHODA

★ **Abode** First Floor, Lansdowne House, M.B. Marg ⊕ 80 8023 4066 ⓦ abodeboutiquehotels.com; map p.612. A rare find in south Mumbai, this thoughtfully-decorated, exceptional boutique hotel has delightful rooms ranging from basic (en-suite shower, shared toilet) to superior luxury. All are furnished with Indian antiques and receive a turn-down service including a hand-written note. Brilliant breakfast included. ₹5355

Aga Beg's & Hotel Kishan Ground, 2nd & 3rd floor, Shirin Manzil, Walton Rd ⊕ 022 2284 2227; map p.612. Muslim-run pair of budget guesthouses on different floors of the same building. Their differently priced rooms (up to ₹3000) are nice and clean, some jazzily decorated. A/c costs ₹350 extra. ₹1500

Ascot 38 Garden Rd ⊕ 022 6638 5566, ⓦ ascothotel. com; map p.612. One of the oldest and most comfortable small hotels in Mumbai, updated with contemporary glass-and-marble designer interiors and spacious modern rooms. Their Deluxe rooms (₹8151) are twice the size of the Superiors. ₹7434

Backpacker Panda 15, Walton Road ⊕ 917 231 3994, ⓦ backpackerpanda.com; map p.612. India's newest chain of cool backpacker hostels has its flagship in Colaba, with graffiti style art on the walls and a fun, relaxed atmosphere in the communal living space. Dorms ₹950, doubles ₹1800

Bentley's 17 Oliver Rd ⊕ 022 2284 1474, ⓦ bentleys hotel.com; map p.612. Dependable old Parsi-owned

---

TOURS

A number of operators around the Gateway of India offer whistle-stop one-day city "darshan" tours by bus (around ₹175–200 non-a/c, not including admission charges) – an inexpensive but usually very rushed way to cram Mumbai's tourist highlights into a single day. These trips are pitched primarily at Indian visitors, so expect slow drives past the homes of Bollywood stars and the US$200-billion skyscraper of tycoon Mukesh Ambani (see page 623), as well as a crossing of the Worli-Bandra Sea Link bridge. There are, however, some more foreigner-friendly alternatives.

The Bombay Heritage Walks ⊕ 98218 87321, ⓦ bombayheritagewalks.com. Focusing mainly on period buildings and colonial history around Kala Ghoda and Horniman Circle, the excellent guided walks organized by architects Abha Bahl and Brinda Gaitonde last for 2hr and are offered mainly at weekends, though weekday evening outings can sometimes be arranged, depending on availability. Advance bookings essential. ₹3750 minimum for a group of up to five people.

MTDC Maharashtra Tourism's 1hr after-dark tours of downtown Mumbai's illuminated landmarks are on an open-top bus. Tickets bookable at the MTDC kiosk near the Gateway of India, which is also where they leave from. Weekends 7pm & 8.15pm; upper deck ₹180, lower deck ₹60.

Mumbai Magic ⓦ mumbaimagic.com. A range of interesting walking and driving tours delving into various aspects of the city, from colonial architecture to Jewish heritage. Two-hour walking tour ₹3000/person.

Reality Tours and Travels ⓦ realitytoursandtravel. com. Memorable trips out to the huge Dharavi shantytown (see page 622).

World of Bollywood Tours and Travels ⊕ 99305 66780, ⓦ worldofbollywoodtoursandtravels.com. Several excursions and tours in and around Mumbai including a Dharavi Slum Tour (US$70/person), a Bollywood Tour (US$115/150 for half/full day) and City tour.

10

10

favourite in five different colonial tenements, all on leafy backstreets. Rooms are quiet, secure and spacious, if a little worn, though the overall shabbiness isn't compensated for by the rates, which are higher than you'd expect for the level of comfort. Singles ₹2788; doubles ₹3776

Godwin Jasmine Building, 41 Garden Rd ☎022 2287 2050, ⊛hotelgodwin.in; map p.612. Smart three-star with large, international-standard rooms and great views from the rooftop garden restaurant and upper floors (ask for #804, #805 or #806). Not quite in the same league as the nearby (and comparably priced) *Ascot* but a sound choice nonetheless. ₹7552

Gordon House 5 Battery St ☎022 2289 4400, ⊛ghhotel.com; map p.612. Chic designer boutique place behind the Regal cinema. Each floor has a different theme: Scandinavian, Mediterranean and Country, plus there's a Versailles Suite. ₹8850

Lawrence 3rd floor, 33 Sri Sai Baba Marg (Rope Walk Lane), off K Dubash Marg, behind TGI's ☎022 2284 3618 or ☎6633 6107; map p.612. Close to the Jehangir Art Gallery, this is arguably south Mumbai's best rock-bottom choice, with five well-scrubbed doubles (plus two singles and two triples for ₹900 and ₹1800 respectively) with fans, and not-so-clean shared shower-toilets. Be warned though, it's a long slog up three floors of filthy wooden steps if the (decrepit) lift isn't working. No wi-fi. Advance booking essential. ₹3000

Moti International 10 Best Marg ☎022 2202 5714, ✉hotelmotiinternational@yahoo.co.in; map p.612. Quiet and friendly hotel in a characterful old colonial building. Rooms are cosy and clean; most (but not all) have windows. All come with a/c, fridge, TV and complimentary soap and towels. Good value. ₹3500

Red Shield Red Shield House, 30 Boram Behram (Mereweather) Rd, near the Taj hotel ☎022 2284 1824, ✉redshieldhouse_mumbai@iwt.salvationarmy.org; map p.612. Ultrabasic bunk beds in cramped, stuffy dorms (lockers available), or larger doubles. Rates include a basic breakfast, served in a sociable canteen. Maximum one-week stay. Dorms ₹500, doubles ₹1400

Sea Palace Kerawalla Chambers, 26 PJ Ramchandani Marg (Apollo Bunder) ☎022 2284 1828, ⊛seapalacehotel.net; map p.612. Best of the three mid-range hotels at the quiet end of the harbour front, although the rooms come as a bit of a disappointment for the price, with old-fashioned decor and worn furnishings. All are a/c but sea views cost extra. Breakfast and light meals are served in the rooftop café. ₹5400

Sea Shore 4th floor, 1-49 Kamal Mansion, Arthur Bunder Rd ☎022 2287 4238; map p.612. Among the best budget deals in Colaba, with singles for ₹800. The sea-facing rooms with windows are much nicer and cost only ₹100 more than the airless cells on the other side. Friendly management and free, safe baggage store. Non-attached

bath only. *India Guest House* (☎022 2283 3769), one floor below, has very ordinary box rooms with thin partition walls and a hostel-like appeal from ₹500. ₹1200

Taj Mahal Palace and Tower PJ Ramchandani Marg ☎022 6665 3366, ⊛tajhotels.com; map p.612. Perhaps India's most famous hotel and the haunt of Mumbai's *beau monde*, with 560 luxury rooms, shopping arcades, a huge outdoor pool and a good spread of bars and restaurants. The hotel was at the centre of the terrorist attacks of November 2008 (see page 609), but reopened within a month, and has now been restored to its former glory after a US$40-million refit. Prices are considerably more in the *Palace* than the *Tower*. ₹31,500

Vivanta By Taj 90 Cuffe Parade ☎022 6665 0808, ⊛tajhotels.com; map p.610. Modern, business-oriented five-star occupying a seventeen-floor skyscraper just south of Colaba. A much more competitively priced option than its sister concern, the *Taj Mahal Palace and Tower*, though lacking old-world style and atmosphere. There is a large outdoor pool, three restaurants, a spa and gym and steam room. ₹16,000

YWCA 18 Madam Cama Rd ☎022 2202 5053, ⊛ywcaic.info; map p.612. Relaxing, secure and quiet hostel (open to men as well as women) with spotless attached rooms. Singles for ₹2678. Rates include breakfast and a generous buffet dinner – a bargain for south Mumbai. Advance booking online is obligatory with minimum payment of one night's stay. Temporary membership for ₹59. ₹4457

MARINE DRIVE

Ambassador VN Rd ☎022 2204 1131, ⊛ambassadorindia.com; map p.616. Landmark four-star hotel established in 1930 with smart modern rooms and a choice location close to the sea and cafés. The revolving restaurant on the top floor is unfortunately still closed for renovation but there's also a bar, restaurant and bakery on site. ₹12,138

Astoria Jamshedji Tata Rd ☎022 6654 1234, ⊛astoriamumbai.com; map p.616. Smart business hotel in a refurbished 1930s Art Deco building near the Eros cinema. The rooms are nowhere near as ritzy as the lobby but offer good value this close to the centre. ₹7735

Bentley 3rd floor, Krishna Mahal, Marine Drive ☎022 2281 5244, ⊛bentleyhotel.in; map p.616. Not to be confused with *Bentley's* in Colaba (see page 631), this small, friendly guesthouse is near the cricket stadium. The nineteen marble-lined a/c rooms are clean and comfortable, though five share shower-toilets. Rates include Continental breakfast. ₹4046/₹5250

★ **Chateau Windsor** 5th floor, 86 Veer Nariman Rd ☎022 6622 4455, ⊛chateauwindsor.com; map p.616. Impeccably neat and central, with unfailingly polite staff and a selection of attractively renovated rooms – many of them quaintly old-fashioned. Their "penthouse" on the fifth floor is particularly nice, comprising an individual bungalow surrounded by pot plants. Very popular, so reserve well in advance. Singles for ₹5934. **₹7150**

Intercontinental 135 Marine Drive ☎022 3987 9999, ⓦmumbai.intercontinental.com; map p.616. Ultra-chic boutique hotel whose rooms have huge sea-facing windows and state-of-the-art gadgets. There's a rooftop pool, outdoor dining with sheesha, and the *Long & Short* restaurant serves great breakfast buffets (₹750) and brunches, plus the *Dome* (see page 638). **₹25,000**

Marine Plaza 29 Marine Drive ☎022 2285 1212, ⓦhotelmarineplaza.com; map p.616. Ritzy but small luxury hotel on the seafront, with the usual five-star facilities and a (pseudo) Art Deco atrium lobby topped by a glass-bottomed rooftop pool. Sea-view rooms cost ₹2000 extra. **₹17,850**

Oberoi Nariman Point ☎022 6632 5757, ⓦoberoi hotels.com; map p.610. Enjoying a prime spot over-looking Back Bay, this hotel is traditionally the first choice of business travellers to the city – lacking the heritage character of the *Taj Mahal Palace and Tower*, but with fine views from its soaring tower and an atmosphere of glittering opulence throughout. It was severely damaged during the 2008 terror attacks, in which 32 staff and guests lost their lives, but has been fully renovated since. **₹34,000**

Sea Green/Sea Green South 145 Marine Drive ☎022 6633 6525, ⓦseagreenhotel.com & 145-A Marine Drive ☎022 6633 6535, ⓦseagreensouth.com; map p.616. Jointly owned and enduringly popular pair of seafront hotels. Decor is old-fashioned going on shabby, and rates are quite high, although the sweeping bay views from front-facing rooms partly compensate. **₹6070**

Trident Nariman Point Nariman Point ☎022 6632 4343, ⓦtridenthotels.com; map p.610. Sitting next to the *Oberoi* (see opposite) on Nariman Point, the *Trident* has equally spectacular views out to the ocean. One of the city's premier business hotels, with full five-star facilities and trimmings, including sea views from its pool and a dreamy spa. **₹23,800.**

West End 45 New Marine Lines ☎70 6506 7405, ⓦwestendhotelmumbai.com; map p.616. A large economy hotel established in 1948 in the heart of South Mumbai with a/c rooms and suites, great Continental, Tandoori and Mughlai food in the *Gourmet* restaurant, plus a lounge bar. **₹8000**

AROUND CHHATRAPATI SHIVAJI (VICTORIA) TERMINUS

City Palace 121 City Terrace ☎99 3035 9336, ⓦhotel citypalace.net; map p.616. Large and popular hotel bang opposite the station. The twenty economy rooms are tiny and windowless (almost like in a capsule hotel), but have a/c and are perfectly clean. Deluxe rooms higher up

the building are larger and have bird's-eye views. Singles **₹1800**

Grand 17 Shri SR Marg, Ballard Estate ☎022 6658 0500, ⓦgrandhotelbombay.com; map p.616. Characterful British-era three-star near the old docks, almost a century old though nicely refurbished, with well-equipped rooms at competitive rates and a decent restaurant. **₹7000**

Oasis 276 Shahid Bhagat Singh Marg, near the GPO ☎022 3022 7886, ⓦhoteloasisindia.in; map p.616. Very well placed for CST station, and the best-value budget option in this area: rooms have good beds, clean linen and TVs. It's worth splashing out on a top-floor "deluxe" room as they offer better views. Singles from ₹2260, a/c is ₹700 extra. **₹2300**

★ **Residency** 26 Rustom Sidhwa Marg, off DN Rd ☎022 2262 5525, ⓦresidencyhotel.com; map p.616. Great little mid-range hotel, close to the best shopping areas. Its variously priced rooms (all with safe and complimentary breakfast) offer unbeatable value, especially the no-frills "standard" options. Some rooms are cramped and lack external windows, but they're well-furnished and clean, and staff are courteous. Book a fortnight in advance. **₹5581**

JUHU AND AROUND THE AIRPORTS

Accord 32 Jawaharlal Nehru Rd, Near Canara Bank, Santa Cruz (East) ☎022 2611 0560, ⓦhotelaccordindia. com; map p.625. If all you want is a simple, inexpensive, clean, secure, attached room for the night within easy reach of the airport, you won't do better than this place. Don't expect a palace: the decor is faded and the location, amid a tangle of busy roads and overpasses, is dreadful; but they get the basics right. The windows are well sound-proofed; staff are courteous; breakfast is included; and there's a 24hr complimentary transfer car to or from the airport, just 15min away. **₹3500**

Hyatt Regency Airport Rd, Andheri (East) ☎022 6696 1234, ⓦmumbai.regency.hyatt.com; map p.625. Ancient Hindu precepts on architecture and design were incorporated into this ultra-luxurious five-star, right next to the airport. The results are impressive, with floor-to-ceiling windows and rain showers, plus a spa and fitness centre. **₹12,250**

ISKCON Guesthouse Juhu Church Rd, Juhu ☎022 2620 6860, ⓦiskconmumbai.com (follow the "Guest House" link under "Temple" on the drop-down menu); map p.625. Idiosyncratic hotel run by the International Society for Krishna Consciousness. Rooms (some with a/c, ₹500 extra) are very large and impeccably clean and comfortable for the price, though certain restrictions apply (no alcohol, meat or caffeine may be consumed on the premises). Wi-fi costs ₹600/day. Forty days' advance booking is recommended. **₹4820**

ITC Maratha Sahar Rd, Andheri (East) ☎022 2830 3030, ⓦitchotels.in; map p.625. This palatial luxury

10

10

STREET FOOD

Mumbai is renowned for distinctive street foods – especially **bhel puri**, a quintessentially Mumbai masala mixture of puffed rice, deep-fried vermicelli, potato, crunchy puri pieces, chilli paste, tamarind water, chopped onions and coriander. More hygienic, but no less ubiquitous, is **pao bhaji**, a round Portuguese-style bread roll served on a tin plate with griddle-fried, spicy vegetable stew, and **kanji vada**, savoury doughnuts soaked in fermented mustard and chilli sauce. And if all that doesn't appeal, a pit-stop at one of the city's hundreds of **juice bars** probably will. There's no better way to beat the sticky heat than with a glass of cool milk shaken with fresh pineapple, mango, banana, *chikoo* (small brown fruit that tastes like a sweet pear) or custard apple. Just make sure they hold on the ice – which may be made with untreated water.

hotel close to the airport has made an attempt to infuse some Maharashtra character into its decor, and holds a particularly pleasant pool in its central courtyard. Check for early bird offers. ₹23,800

Midland Jawaharlal Nehru Rd, Santa Cruz (East) ☎ 022 2611 0414, ⓦ midland.hotelsofmumbai.com; map p.625. Dependable two-star with well-furnished twin-bedded rooms, just a short ride from the airport. It's right in front of the *Accord* (see above) but not as good value. Breakfast included in the price. ₹6545

The Orchid 70-C Nehru Rd, Vile Parle (East) ☎ 022 2616 4000, ⓦ orchidhotel.com; map p.625. Award-winning "Eco-Five-Star", built with organic and recycled materials and using low-toxin paints. Every effort is made to minimize waste of natural resources, with a water-recycling plant and "zero garbage" policy. Breakfast included. ₹8,330

★ **Soho House** 16, Juhu Tara Rd ☎ 022 6213 3333, ⓦ sohohousemumbai.com; map p.625. The first Asian

outpost of the London-born private members club, *Soho House Mumbai* has a fantastic location right on Juhu Beach. Rooms are beautiful and modern but homely, with antiques and Indian artworks adding a nice touch. Lovely rooftop pool and bar, the latter with glorious ocean views. ₹13,000

VITS Andheri Kurla Rd, International Airport Zone, Andheri (East) ☎ 022 6151 7555, ⓦ vitshotels.com; map p.625. An "Eco-Four-Star at Three-Star prices" is how this environment-friendly hotel describes itself, designed using energy-saving materials and with "green" trimmings such as jute slippers and recycling bins in the rooms. A very comfortable option for the price. ₹6395

Waterstones Hotel Sahar, Andheri (East) ☎ 022 4090 6633, ⓦ waterstoneshotel.com; map p.625. A boutique hotel just five minutes away from the International Airport. Rooms are modern, clean, and there's a terrific bar and grill, a "movie lounge", Olympic-sized pool and a spa. Breakfast and airport transfers included. ₹8000

EATING

Mumbai is crammed with interesting **places to eat**, from glamorous rooftop lounge bars to hole-in-the-wall kebab shops. The cafés, bars and restaurants of **Colaba** encompass just about the full gamut of possibilities, while a short walk or taxi ride north, **Kala Ghoda** and **Fort** are home to some of the best cafés and restaurants in the city, including its last traditional Parsi diners, whose menus (and sometimes decor as well) have changed little in generations. Watch out for the service charges levied on your bill by some of the more expensive places.

COLABA

All Stir Fry Gordon House Hotel; map p.612. Cool modern restaurant specializing in build-your-own meals using a selection of fresh veg, meat, fish, noodles and sauces, flash cooked in a wok in front of you. The wok buffet is ₹1071 for unlimited servings, and there's an extensive *dim sum* menu (₹365–690). Daily 7–10.30am, 12–3.45pm & 7pm–11.30pm.

Bademiya Behind the Taj Mahal Palace & Tower on Tulloch Rd ☎ 022 2284 8038, ⓦ bademiya.com; map

p.612. Legendary Colaba kebab-wala serving delicious flame-grilled chicken, mutton and fish steaks (all at ₹170–250), as well as veg alternatives (₹150), wrapped in paper-thin, piping hot *rotis*, from benches on the sidewalk. Families from uptown drive here on weekends, eating on their car bonnets, but there are also little tables and chairs if you don't fancy a takeaway. For a sit-down meal, try their restaurant on nearby Navroji F Rd (☎ 99 6711 4179) or their fine-dining branch near the State Central Library at Horniman Circle (☎ 022 2265 5657; map p.616). Daily 12pm–late.

Churchill 103 Colaba Causeway; map p.612. Tiny a/c Parsi diner, with a vast choice of filling, Continental comfort food, from pizza to pasta and burgers (₹260–300) – ideal if you've had your fill of spicy food. For dessert or an afternoon treat, check the famous *Churchill* fridge for freshly baked treats such as gooey chocolate cake or blueberry cheesecake (₹105). No alcohol, no washrooms. Most mains ₹390–445. Daily 11am–midnight.

Colaba Social 24, B K Boman Behram Marg ☎ 75 0639 4239 , ⓦ socialoffline.in; map p.612. One of Colaba's

10

coolest hangouts, this place is packed with well-to-do students and young Mumbaikars every night of the week. Great pub-style food in a modern, somewhat hipster warehouse setting. Don't miss the calamari in *cafreal* spices (₹390) and chicken tikka tacos (₹250). Drinks are reasonable too, with Indian wines from ₹300 and beers from ₹170. Daily 9am–1am.

Indigo Deli Ground Floor, Pheroze Building, Chattrapati Shivaji Maharishi Marg ✆022 6655 1010; map p.612. This much-loved gastro café-restaurant is a stalwart of the south Mumbai scene thanks to its menu of Continental comfort foods and NY deli-style staples – from burgers (₹565–725) and hot dogs to thin-crust pizzas and perfect steak frites – served in sleek designer comfort. Pick of the all-day breakfast selection is the chef's special Eggs Benedict (or "Eggs Benny" as it's known here). For dessert, try the organic lime pie (₹395), or croissant bread pudding with brandy sauce. They serve single origin coffees and teas. Most mains ₹565–800. Daily 8.30am–12.30am.

Kailash Parbat 5 First Pasta Rd, just off Colaba Causeway ✆022 2283 1913; map p.612. Popular little chain restaurant (they now even have outposts in Hong Kong) serving build-your-own Punjabi thalis (veg only) from ₹205 and snacks such as *pav bhaji* (₹124) and paneer paratha (₹100). The sweet shop of the same name over the road is the place to go for dessert. Daily 11am–11pm.

The Konkan Café Vivanta By Taj Hotel, Cuffe Parade ✆022 6665 0808; map p.612. Sophisticated five-star hotel restaurant, done up in earthy terracotta red and banana-leaf green hues in homage to a Mangalorean home. They serve fine regional cuisine from coastal Maharashtra, Goa, Karnataka and Kerala. Choose from their thali platters (₹1950) or go à la carte: butter-pepper-garlic crab is to die for. Quite simply some of the most mouth-watering south Indian food you'll ever eat. Daily noon–2.45pm & 7–11.45pm.

Leopold's Colaba Causeway; map p.612. A Mumbai institution that played a starring role in Gregory David Roberts' *Shantaram*, *Leopold's* is the number-one hangout for India-weary Western travellers, who continue to cram onto its small tables for overpriced Indian, Continental and Chinese food. The café was one of the leading targets of the 2008 terror attacks, though its bullet-ridden walls have now been discreetly hidden with pictures. Mains ₹310–570; beer ₹210–510. Daily 7.30am–midnight.

★ **Miss T** 4 Mandlik Rd, Apollo Bandar ✆ ✆022 2280 1144, ⊛miss-t.in; map p.612. Contemporary fine-dining restaurant open for dinner only, serving truly exceptional Southeast Asian food. Soups and salads from ₹450, snacks/starters from ₹550 and sharing plates such as soba noodles and tamarind port from ₹750–2500. Cocktails (₹850) by the head barman are inventive, with flavours such as peanut butter whiskey and caramelised onion cordial. Daily 7pm–1am.

Olympia Coffee House Rahim Mansion, Colaba Causeway ✆022 2202 1043; map p.612. *Fin-de-siècle* Irani café with marble tabletops, wooden wall panels, fancy mirrors and a mezzanine floor for women. Waiters in Peshwari caps and *salwar kameez* serve melt-in-the-mouth kebabs and delicious curd-based dips. It gets crowded at breakfast for cholesterol-packed *masala kheema* (fried mutton mince), which regulars wash down with bright orange chai. A quintessential (and inexpensive) Bombay experience. Mains ₹70–220. Daily 7.30am–midnight.

The Sea Lounge Taj Mahal Palace and Tower; map p.612. Atmospheric 1930s-style lounge café on the first floor of the *Taj*, with fine Gateway and harbour views – good for high tea (from around ₹4500) or a decadent breakfast (₹1160–1225). Daily 7am–midnight.

KALA GHODA

Chetana 34K Dubhash Marg ✆022 2284 4968, ⊛chetana.com; map p.612. Sumptuous pure-veg thalis (Maharashtrian, Rajasthani or Gujarati, with a healthy low-calorie option at lunchtime; ₹499–635) served in a mellow, Indian-style interior (a/c) with booths and traditional art on the walls. You won't find better *desi* cooking at this price anywhere else in south Mumbai. Daily 12.30–3.30pm & 7.30–11.30pm.

Kala Ghoda Café 10 Rope Walk Lane ✆022 2263 3866, ⊛kgcafe.in; map p.612. This café, with a full restaurant at the back, makes a great little pit-stop if you're visiting the nearby museums. High, whitewashed walls, long skylights and wood benches give a feeling of space even though it's pint-sized. The coffee and teas are first rate, and they do freshly baked light bites, sandwiches (₹170–395), salads (₹180–430), soups, waffles and fruit sundaes (₹230–525), as well as more filling main meals like pasta (₹350–575) after 7.30pm. There's a wine bar right at the back too (see below). Free wi-fi. Daily 8am–11.45pm.

★ **Khyber** 145 MG Rd, opposite Jehangir Art Gallery ✆022 4039 6666, ⊛khyberrestaurant.com; map p.612. You enter this romantic Mughlai restaurant through a finely carved, cusp-arched sandstone facade, and the interior is no less enchanting. The cuisine is "Northwest Frontier" style: rich, creamy curries made with sublime blends of spices, and choice cuts of seafood, chicken or mutton kebabs flame-grilled or braised in traditional *tava* pans. Mains ₹495–800. Daily 12.30–4pm & 7.30–11.45pm.

The Pantry Yeshwant Chambers, Ground Floor, Military Square Lane ✆022 2267 8901; map p.612. A great option for a heat-beating light bite or gourmet brunch: with its cement floors, recycled Burmese hardwood table tops, white walls and dabs of pastel colour, the café has a fresh, airy feel and a varied Continental menu (vegan and gluten free options available) including quiche (₹295), vegetable

10

lasagne (₹375) and pizzas (₹450–500), alongside freshly baked pastries. Mains ₹400–600. Daily 8.30am–11.30pm.

Trishna 7 Sai Baba Marg (Ropewalk Lane), Kala Ghoda ☎ 022 2270 3213, ⊛ trishna.co.in; map p.612. Visiting dignitaries and local celebs, from the President of Greece to Bollywood stars, have eaten in this dimly lit Mangalorean restaurant. There are wonderful fish dishes in every sauce going, including the signature butter-pepper-garlic crab (₹1450) and superb pomfret stuffed with green masala (₹1400), plus cheaper north Indian standards. Very small, so book in advance. Mon–Sat noon–3.30pm & 6.30pm–midnight, Sun noon–3.30pm and 7pm–midnight.

CHURCHGATE AND FORT

★ **Apoorva** SA Brelvi Rd ☎ 022 2287 0335; map p.616. Popular Mangalorean restaurant, hidden up a side street off Horniman Circle (look for the tree trunk wrapped with fairy lights). The cooking is authentic and the seafood – simmered in spicy coconut-based gravies – comes fresh off the boat each day. Try their definitive Bombay duck, *surmai* (kingfish) in coconut gravy or delicious prawn *gassi*, served with perfect *sannas* and *appams*. Mains ₹290–1500. Daily noon–4pm & 6.30pm–11.30pm.

★ **Britannia & Co** Shri SR Marg, Ballard Estate ☎ 022 2261 5264; map p.616. Quirky little Parsi restaurant set up in 1923, famous for its quaint period atmosphere and wholesome Irani food, like the mouthwatering berry pulao (chicken, mutton or vegetable), made with deliciously tart dried berries imported from Tehran (₹350/550 veg/non-veg, but portions are gigantic). For afters, there's the house caramel custard (₹170). One of the city's unmissable eating experiences. Mon–Fri noon–4pm & Sat noon–10pm.

Ideal Corner 12 F/G Hornby View, Gunbow St ☎ 022 2262 1930; map p.616. Another Parsi café with a cult following, dishing up delicious home-made specialities like *salli boti* (meat curry with potato stick toppings), *patra ni machi* (fish steamed in banana leaf), lamb or veg dhansak, and exceptional *lagan nu* custard – a Zoroastrian take on the classic British pud, flavoured with rose water and cardamom. Most mains ₹150–200. Daily noon–10pm.

Mahesh Lunch Home 8-B Cawasji Patel St ☎ 022 2287 0938, ⊛ maheshlunchhome.com; map p.616. Much like *Trishna* (see above) only a good bit cheaper and less touristy, this Mangalorean diner in the depths of Fort is famous across the city for its flavoursome seafood specialities, especially the Koliwada prawns (₹520), *pomfret gassi* (₹695) and fish curry (₹455), and the jumbo butter-garlic crab, sold by weight. Reservations recommended on weekends. Mon–Sat 11.30am–4pm & 6.30pm–midnight, Sun 7pm–midnight.

Pizza By the Bay Soona Mahal, 143 Marine Drive ☎ 022 2284 3646, ⊛ pizzabythebay.in; map p.616. This bustling, high-end Italian on the corner of VN Rd and Marine Drive does a brisk trade in authentic pasta (₹870),

pizza (₹720–1050) and freshly baked treats, as well as European-style breakfasts (7–11am). Reserve ahead for a table next to the window for breezy bay views. Long waits on weekends are the norm, even if you book. Count on spending upwards of ₹1500 for three courses. Daily 7am–12.30am.

★ **Swati Snacks** Dalmal Tower, Free Press Journal Marg ☎ 022 6666 6880, ⊛ swatisnacks.com; map p.610. The best place to try Mumbai's favourite street foods in a clean and safe environment, Swati Snacks opened its second restaurant at Nariman Point after 50 years in central Mumbai. Their minimalist canteen lets the food do the talking, with superb snacks like *bhel puri* (₹140) and *panki chatni* (₹190) on the menu. Expect to spend around ₹1000 for two people with drinks. The fresh sugarcane juice (₹170) is addictive. Daily 11.30am–10.45pm.

CHOWPATTY

Bachelorr's Juice House Chowpatty Sea Face, opposite Birla Krida Kendra, near Charni Rd station ☎ 022 2368 8889; map p.610. There's no better antidote to the brouhaha of the nearby beach than a "Strawberry Cream" at *Bachelorr's* – a tall milkshake crammed with whipped cream and pieces of fresh strawberry, which they do in any number of chocolate-based variations. It's hidden under an awning, so look out for the lime piled high on the shelves. Don't miss the green chilli ice cream (₹65). Daily 10.30am–1.30am.

Cream Centre Fulchand Niwas 25/B, Chowpatty Sea Face ☎ 022 2367 9222; map p.610. This immaculately clean, pure-veg fast-food joint facing Chowpatty Beach serves a huge range of Indian snacks, but the best, by far, is their famous *channa batura* (₹560) – a frisbee-sized pillow of deep-fried puri, which you poke with your finger to deflate and use to mop up a bowl of creamy masala chickpeas, diced potatoes and onions. Daily noon–11.30pm.

Crystal 19 Chowpatty Sea Face, near Wilson College ☎ 022 2369 1482; map p.610. Lovers of north Indian home-cooking travel here from across the city to eat *dhaba*-style dhal *makhani*, *alu matar* and other spicy vegetarian dishes, served from a soot-blackened kitchen. For dessert, there's divine *kheer* (cardamom-flavoured rice pudding) and *amras* (mango pulp). A great little budget option if you're not fazed by the grime, with most mains under ₹120. Daily noon–3.30pm & 7–10.30pm.

CRAWFORD MARKET AND THE CENTRAL BAZAARS

Badshah Juice and Snack Bar Opposite Crawford Market, Lokmanya Tilak Rd ☎ 022 2342 1943; map p.610. Delicious kulfi, and dozens of freshly squeezed fruit juices, though most locals come for the *faloodas* (₹85–130) – an incomparable, quintessentially Mumbai mix of vermicelli, basil seeds and tapioca pearls steeped in milk, ice cream and rose syrup. The ideal place to round off a trip to the market. Daily 7am–12.30am.

★**Joshi Club** 381-A Narottamwadi, Kalbadevi Rd ☎022 2205 8089; map p.610. Also known as *The Friends Union Joshi Club*, this eccentric thali canteen serves what many aficionados regard as the most genuine and tasty Gujarati-Marwari meals in the city, on unpromising Formica tables against a backdrop of grubby walls. ₹200 buys you unlimited portions of four vegetable dishes, dhal and up to four different kinds of bread, with all the trimmings (and banana custard). Daily 11am–3pm & 7–10pm.

THE NORTHERN SUBURBS

★**Dakshin Coastal** ITC Maratha, Sahar Rd, near the airport ☎022 2830 3030; map p.625. A far cry from your regular Udupi vegetarian joint, *Dakshin Coastal* showcases the sublime and varied cuisine of the south Indian shoreline. From the sun-dried chillis soaked in buttermilk appetizer to main-course delights such as Keralan-style prawns delicately cooked with raw mango and fresh coconut, everything is packed with intense flavours and exquisitely presented. Count on ₹2000–2500/head for the works. Mon–Sat 7–11.45pm, Sun 12.30–2.45pm.

★**Dum Pukht** ITC Maratha, Sahar Rd, near the airport ITC Maratha, Sahar Rd ☎022 2830 3030; map p.625. One of the few kitchens in India that faithfully re-creates the cuisine of the Muslim nawabs of Hyderabad and Awadh, where chefs developed a technique of slow cooking known as *dum*. If you've a monster appetite, go for the *raan-e-dum*

pukht – a leg of marinated lamb stuffed with spices, baked in dough and finished with a shell of dried fruit, coconut and oven juices. The decor's as regal as the cooking. Count on ₹2000–2500/head for three courses. Daily 7–11.45pm.

Govinda's ISKCON Hare Krishna Mandir, Juhu Tara Rd, Juhu ☎022 2620 0337; map p.625. Sumptuous vegetarian thalis of sattvic cooking (no garlic or onions). Everything's been ritually offered to Krishna before being served, guaranteeing what the management describe as a "transcendental dining experience". At ₹450/head, it's certainly great value for Mumbai and there's often live *bhajan* singing. Daily 7am–3pm & 7.30–10.30pm.

Maharaja Bhog Juhu Tara Road, Opposite Juhu Beach ☎022 2661 7722; map p.625. A superb veg thali restaurant with a menu that changes monthly. You'll be plied with an assortment of twenty different dishes, from breads to veg curries to dessert; don't miss their famous traditional khichdi (rice and lentils cooked in ghee). It's always busy, so get there early to ensure a seat. Thalis ₹600, takeaway available for ₹250. Daily noon– 3.30pm & 7pm–11pm.

Pali Bhavan 10 Adarsh Nagar, Pali Naka, near Costa Coffee, Bandra (West) ☎022 2651 9400; map p.625. An aura of Old India hangs over this quirkily styled restaurant up in Bandra, which delights as much for its decor of sepia photos and antique woodwork as its classy pan-Indian cuisine. The huge menu features dishes from across the country, given classy gourmet twists (₹1500–2000/head). Daily noon– 2.30pm & 6pm–11.30pm.

DRINKING

Mumbaikars have an unusually easy-going attitude to alcohol; popping into a **bar** for a beer is very much accepted, even at lunchtime. **Colaba Causeway** is the focus of the travellers' and local students' social scene but to sample the cutting edge of the city's nightlife, you'll have to venture to the **suburbs**, where the trendiest places have turned the city's draconian licensing laws to their advantage by serving gourmet food to complement the range of beers, wines and cocktails.

★**AER** Four Seasons Hotel, 114 Dr E Moses Rd, Worli ☎022 2481 8000, ⊛fourseasons.com; map p.608. With its all-white, *Miami Vice*-style jigsaw furniture and astounding panoramic views over the city, this alfresco bar on the 34th floor of a luxury skyscraper hotel has become the poster boy of Mumbai's lounge bars, even out-blinging the *Dome* on Marine Drive (see below). Cocktails go from ₹950 and beers from ₹475. A glass of good Indian bubbly costs ₹900. Cover charges after 10pm, ₹2500/head admission on Fri & Sat. Daily 5pm–1.30am.

Bonobo 1 Kennilworth Phase II, 2nd Floor, off Linking Rd, Bandra ☎022 2605 5050; map p.625. *Bonobo* hosts live gigs and DJ sets on Fridays and Saturdays in a (tiny) a/c performance space – from drum 'n' bass to dubstep. A balmy rooftop bar soaks up the overspill, and doubles as a gastro

diner with delicious dishes like picante prawns and calamari (₹354). Drinks ₹250–550. Daily 6pm–1am.

★**Café Marina** Sea Palace Hotel, Kerawalla Chambers, Apollo Bunder, Colaba; map p.612. If lounge-resto isn't your thing, and all you want is a reasonably priced cold beer, and something tasty to munch while savouring an expansive view, this place ticks all the boxes. Overlooking the harbour from a great rooftop vantage point, it offers local and imported bottled beers from ₹475–500. Daily 4pm–midnight.

Café Mondegar Colaba Causeway; map p.612. Draught and bottled beer (₹230–380) and deliciously fruity cocktails are served in this small café-bar. The atmosphere is very relaxed, the music on the famous jukebox tends towards cheesy rock classics and the clientele is a mix of Westerners and local students; murals by famous Goan cartoonist Mario Miranda give the place a cheerful ambience. Breakfast menu till 11.30am. Daily 7.30am–12.30am.

Café Zoe Mathurdas Mills Compound, N.M Joshi Marg, Lower Parel ☎022 2490 2065, ⊛cafezoe.in; map p.608. Set in the compound of an old cotton mill turned creative hub, this light, airy bar has the feel of a European café, probably owing to its Belgian owners. Natural light streams

10

10

through the glass ceiling by day, and at night the place comes alive with well-heeled locals after a quiet drink. Live jazz on Wed, local beers ₹200, Belgian beer from ₹480. Daily happy hour 5–8pm. Daily 7.30am–1.30am.

The Dome Hotel InterContinental, 135 Marine Drive; map p.616. This cool rooftop bar is easily south Mumbai's most alluring spot for a sundowner. Plush white sofas and candlelit tables surround the domed rotunda and a very sexy raised pool, while the views over Back Bay make even the sky-high drink prices (₹1250 plus for a cocktail) feel worth it. ₹2000/head. Daily 5pm–1.30am.

Gadda da Vida Novotel Mumbai, Balraj Sahani Marg, Juhu Beach ☎022 6693 4444, ⓦnovotel.com; map p.625. Beach-front bars are like hens' teeth in Mumbai, but at *Gadda da Vida* (named after a hit from 1970s prog-rock band Iron Butterfly) you can sip your Caipiroska by the poolside as the sun sets over Juhu's churning waves. House DJs spin electro jazz early on, followed by dance anthems as the place fills up. ₹500 for a beer and ₹900 for cocktails. Cover charge ₹1500/per person. Daily 2pm–1.30am.

Garage Inc Apollo Bandar, Colaba ☎022 2283 9393; map p.612. Low vaulted ceilings with renaissance style murals and red-brick pillars make this a cosy bolthole for a drink. Don't come for a romantic date, though; loud pop music blares from speakers while groups of young Mumbaikars drink bottles of beer (from ₹110) or local wines (₹315). Burgers and pizza also served (₹320–580). Daily 9am–1.30am.

Havana Gordon House Hotel, Battery St, Colaba; map p.612. The retro *Polly Esther's* has been revamped into a warm-toned Cuban-style café and bar with wooden railway sleepers and hand-painted signs of Che and Castro, plus a separate cigar room. Beers from ₹199 and cocktails ₹300. Tues–Sun 6pm–1.30am.

The Irish House Phoenix Mills Compound, Senapati Bapat Marg, Lower Parel ☎022 2496 1222, ⓦtheirish house.in; map p.608. Rustic wooden decor and booths create the chatty ambience of a typical Irish pub. Fresh draught beer (₹195) is served out of wooden kegs, and there's an extensive range of bottled beers. Their popular pub grub includes fish 'n' chips (₹495) and BBQ sandwiches (from ₹375). Happy hours 5–8pm. Daily noon–1am.

Olive 4 Union Park Rd, Pali Hill (between Juhu and Bandra) ☎022 4340 8228, ⓦolivebarandkitchen.com; map p.625. If you want to rub shoulders with Mumbai's party crowd, the theme bar night on Thursday evening (aka TGIT or Thank God It's Thursday) is your best bet,

though dress to kill – and come armed with a full wallet. Cocktails are around ₹1000. Mon–Fri 8pm–1am, Sat & Sun 12.30pm–3.30pm & 8pm–1am.

Salt Water Café Rose Minar Annexe, 87 Chapel Rd, next to Mount Carmel Church, Bandra (West) ☎022 2643 4441, ⓦsaltwatercafe.in; map p.625. This smart all-day diner in swanky Bandra is renowned for its relaxed atmosphere, warm-toned designer decor, gastro food and drink-till-you-drop happy hours. From 11am–4pm on weekdays you can down unlimited quantities of sangria for ₹600 and the Sunday brunch is ₹1500/head without alcohol. Daily 9am–1am.

Toit Brewery Zeba Centre, Mathuradas Mill Compound, 242, Lower Parel ☎93 2455 5223, ⓦtoit.in; map p608. The Bangalore-based brewery's Mumbai outlet serves its best beers and ales on draught (₹325 a pint, ₹300 for a sample tray of six) in a large taproom with tables and booths and a convivial atmosphere. Memes and movie posters cover the walls, there's a live band every last Wed of the month and Fri & Sat night sees a DJ play tunes to boozy crowds. The all-you-can-eat-and-drink Sunday brunch (₹2200) is killer. Daily 12pm–1am.

Todi Mill Social Mathuradas Mill Compound, 242, Lower Parel ☎75083 94240 ⓦsocialoffline.in; map p.608. Sister bar to the *Colaba Social* (see page 634), this one sits inside a repurposed 1920s loom mill with all recycled furniture and striking black-painted windows set against exposed red brick. There's an impressive drinks menu including cocktails (₹295), imported bottled beers (₹540) and even mead (₹315). Don't miss the Long Island Iced Tea served in a bong (₹630). Fri & Sat DJs, no cover charge. Daily 9am–1.30am.

Toto's Garage 30 Lourdes Heaven, Pali Junction, Bandra (West) ☎022 2600 5494; map p.625. Neon-lit, garage-themed bar with a VW hanging from its ceiling, belting mostly 80s rock. It's tiny and packed to the gills most of the time with the lads piling in for pitchers of draught beer after work (from ₹200/pint). Daily 6pm–12.30am.

Wink Vivanta by Taj, G.D. Somani Rd, 90 Cuffe Parade ☎022 6665 0808; map p.610. This stylish lounge bar a short hop from Colaba is split into two areas, separated by a Japanese gauze screen: a sleek island bar, famous for its Winktini cocktails (₹895); and a chillout area with brick walls and comfy couches where you can chat and munch on wasabi peas until the DJ cranks up the volume around 11pm. It gets very busy on weekends. Daily 6pm–1am.

NIGHTLIFE

Despite a 1.30am curfew (only clubs within hotels are allowed to carry on later), Mumbai's **clubbing** scene remains the most full-on in India. Dancefloors get as rammed as a suburban commuter train and the cover charges can be astronomical on weekends. Door policies and dress codes tend to be strict ("no ballcaps, no shorts, no sandals"), and, many clubs have a "couples-only" policy. In practice, if you're in a mixed group and don't appear sleazy you shouldn't have any problems.

Drop G1/B, Krystal Building, Waterfield Road, Bandra

PERFORMING ARTS IN MUMBAI

Mumbai is a major centre for traditional **performing arts**, attracting the finest **Indian classical musicians** and **dancers** from all over the country. Frequent concerts and recitals are staged at venues such as Bharatiya Vidya Bhavan, KM Munshi Marg (☎ 022 2363 1261), the headquarters of the international cultural (Hindu) organization, and the National Centre for the Performing Arts, Nariman Point (NCPA; ⓦ ncpamumbai.com). The Royal Opera House (ⓦ royaloperahouse.in), with its fabulous Baroque edifice reopened in 2016 after lying dormant for 25 years and now puts on theatre, concerts and arts festivals throughout the year.

For **drama**, head out to the Prithvi Theatre (☎ 022 2614 9546, ⓦ prithvitheatre.org) on Juhu Church Road, a small but lively venue focusing mainly on Hindi-language theatre, along with some English productions.

10

West ☎ 022 4229 6000 ⓦ facebook.com/DropinMumbai. Brushed concrete floors and walls and bright, contemporary furnishings make this one of Mumbai's coolest clubs. The dancefloor fills up by midnight and the place gets pretty crazy by 1am. Resident DJs play popular techno and hip-hop, and there are frequent gigs by guest artists. Expect to spend around ₹6000 for two people including drinks and entry. Wed–Sun 10pm–1.30am.

★ **Kitty Su** Ground Floor The LaLit Mumbai, Airport Rd, Andheri East ☎ 022 6104 3355, ⓦ kittysu.com; map p.612. Taking shabby chic to a whole new, possibly uncomfortable level, you enter this popular nightclub through a corrugated iron entrance reminiscent of the homes in the nearby Dharavi Slum. Bizarre design choices aside, the club has been a safe space for LGBTQ+ party-goers well before the legalization of gay sex; resident and guest DJs spin techno, dance and pop music for a packed dancefloor throughout the week. Cocktails from ₹1000 and beers ₹600. Cover ₹1000 for women, ₹1500 for men. Daily 10pm–3am.

XXO Level 37, St Regis Hotel, Senapati Bapat Marg, Lower Parel ☎ 022 6162 8422, ⓦ stregismumbai.com. Mumbai's hottest nightclub, spread over two floors (Level 37–38 of the swish *St Regis*, with floor-to-ceiling windows, Osler chandeliers, leather upholstery and foot-tapping house music. Expect to spend ₹6000 for two people including drinks and entry. Wed, Thurs & Sun 7pm–1am, Fri & Sat 7pm–3am.

CINEMA

Not surprisingly for a city obsessed with the movies, Mumbai has hundreds of **cinema houses**, among them a handful of glorious Art Deco halls dating from the twilight of the Raj. However, only a handful regularly screen **English-language** films. The rest feature the latest Bollywood blockbusters, which of course aren't shown with subtitles. For the latest listings go to ⓦ in.bookmyshow.com/mumbai. Alternatively, look for the biggest, brightest hoarding, and join the queue. **Seats** in a comfortable a/c cinema cost ₹150–300, or less if you sit in the stalls.

Eros Cambata Building, 42 M. Karve Rd, opposite Churchgate station ☎ 022 2282 2335, ⓦ erostheatre.com. At the time of writing in 2019, this glorious Art Deco behemoth was closed to the public, with its owners in tentative talks to revive the cinema. The Eros can accommodate over a thousand people and before it closed screened mainly Hindi and Marathi movies, with occasional English-language offerings.

Inox CR2 Mall, 2nd Floor, Barrister Rajni Patel Marg, Nariman Point ☎ 022 6152 2888, ⓦ inoxmovies.com. Another big multiscreen venue, in the retro Mumbai-Art Deco style.

Metro Big MG Rd, Dhobi Talao Junction, Marine Lines ☎ 022 3984 4060 or ☎ 93241 41119, ⓦ inoxmovies.com . Opened by Metro-Goldwyn-Mayer in 1938, this is the granddaddy of the city's movie houses, transformed into a six-screen multiplex in 2006. Facilities are top-notch. Screens mainly Hindi movies, but does show the odd Hollywood hit.

Regal Shahid Bhagat Singh Rd, Colaba ☎ 022 2202 1017. One of Mumbai's oldest and best-loved cinema halls, the Regal showed Laurel and Hardy's *The Devil's Brother* on its opening night in 1933. There's still only one screen, and the auditorium is filled with velvet seats. Shows both Hollywood and Bollywood, mainly to affluent middle-class professionals and students, so the vibe is generally civilized. The handiest cinema if you're based in south Mumbai.

SHOPPING

Mumbai is a great place to shop and prices compare well with other Indian cities. Locally produced **textiles** and export-surplus clothing are among the best buys, as are **handicrafts** from far-flung corners of the country. In the larger shops, rates are fixed and **credit cards** are often accepted; elsewhere, particularly when dealing with street vendors, it pays to haggle. Uptown, the **central bazaars** are better for spectating than serious shopping.

10

ANTIQUES

Bollywood Bazaar Mutton St ☎90 7044 0970; map p.610. The Chor Bazaar area, and Mutton Street in particular, is the centre of Mumbai's antiques trade. And one shop that's worth the trip alone for Indian film fans is the wonderful Bollywood Bazaar, which sells old posters and memorabilia. The priciest pieces are hand-painted specimens dating from the 1950s, but they also stock plenty of repro versions that make great souvenirs. Daily 10am–10pm.

Phillip's Antiques Madame Cama Rd, opposite Regal Cinema ⓦphillipsantiques.com, Colaba; map p.612. Although much more expensive than Chor Bazaar, this famous antique shop is well worth a browse – even if you're not buying. Brass, bronze and wood Hindu sculpture, silver jewellery, old prints and aquatints form the mainstay of its collection. Mon–Sat 11am–7pm.

CLOTHES AND TEXTILES

Mumbai produces the bulk of India's clothes, mostly the lightweight, light-coloured "shirtings and suitings" favoured by droves of uniformly attired office-wallahs. Better-quality cotton clothes (often stylish designer-label rip-offs) are available in shops along Colaba Causeway and Mandlik Marg (behind the *Taj Mahal Palace and Tower*).

Fabindia Jeroo Bldg, 137 MG Road, Kala Ghoda ☎022 2262 6539, ⓦfabindia.com; map p.612. It's worth checking out the local branch of the nationwide Fabindia chain, which has an excellent and very affordable selection of stylish modern Indian-style shirts, *kurtas*, *salwar kameez*, as well as beautifully made items for the home. Daily 10am–8.30pm.

"Fashion Street" MG Rd; map p.616. For cheap Western clothing, you can't beat this long row of stalls strung out along MG Rd between Cross and Azad maidans west of CST, specializing in reject and export-surplus goods ditched by big manufacturers: mainly T-shirts, jeans, summer dresses and sweatshirts. Daily 10am–9pm.

Khadi shop (signed "Mumbai Khadi Gramodyog Sangh") 286 Dr D.N. Marg, near the Thomas Cook office ☎022 2261 7641; map p.616. For traditional Indian clothes, look no further than here. As Whiteaway & Laidlaw, this rambling Victorian department store used to kit out all the newly arrived burrasahibs with pith helmets, khaki shorts and quinine tablets. These days, its old wooden counters and shirt and sock drawers stock dozens of different hand-spun cottons and silks, sold by the metre or made up as vests, *kurtas* or block-printed *salwar kameez*. Mon–Sat 10.30am–6.30pm.

No-Mad Fabric Shop First floor, Mangaldas Market Building, Kitchen Garden Ln ☎22 2209 1787 ⓦno-mad. in; map p610. Once you've navigated the crush of stalls overflowing with fabrics inside Mangaldas market, you'll be relieved to step into this tiny but beautiful air-conditioned store. There isn't a huge range, but this is the place to buy high-end, trendy block-printed fabrics. You'll get the full fabric shop experience: remove your shoes, take a seat on the mattress, order a chai and let the assistants lay out their wares one by one. Daily 11–7pm.

Vaya Tanna House Annexe, Nathalal Parekh Marg ☎022 2202 9115; map p.612. Charming collective of hand-woven and heritage textiles from across India with artisan shawls, saris and fabrics sourced directly from weavers. Mon–Sat 10.30am–7pm.

LIFESTYLE

Bombay Store Western India House, Sir PM Rd, Fort ☎022 2288 5048; map p.616. This department store in the Fort district is a great place to shop for souvenirs, with vibrant displays of traditional handicrafts, textiles, woodwork, silver-ware, repro vintage photos and funky fashion accessories and designer artefacts from the Elephant Company. Mon–Sat 10am–8pm, Sun 11am–6.30pm.

Good Earth 2 Reay House, next to Taj Mahal Palace and Tower Hotel ☎022 2202 1030; map p.612. Fine tableware, luxury bed linen, lanterns and exquisite clothes made from traditional Indian fabrics. Prices reflect its proximity to the *Taj*, but their stock is all original and beautifully displayed. Daily 11am–8pm.

Nicobar Ropewalk Lane, above Kala Ghoda Café, Kala Ghoda ☎84 4809 5484, ⓦnicobar.com; map p.612. Colourful range of contemporary homewares, such as bowls, glasses and plates, designer clothes and accessories from mostly Indian producers. Daily 11am–8pm.

HANDICRAFTS

Regionally produced handicrafts are marketed in assorted state-run emporia at the World Trade Centre, down on Cuffe Parade, and along Sir PM Rd, Fort. The quality is consistently high – as are the prices, if you miss out on the periodic holiday discounts. Mereweather Rd (now officially B Behram Marg), behind the *Taj Mahal Palace and Tower*, is awash with Kashmiri handicraft stores stocking overpriced papier-mâché pots and bowls, silver jewellery, woollen shawls and rugs. Avoid them if you find it hard to shrug off aggressive sales pitches. Down at the south end of Colaba Causeway, around Arthur Bunder Rd, shops with mirrored walls and shelves are stacked with cut-glass carafes full of syrupy, fragrant essential oils. Incense is hawked in sticks, cones and slabs of sticky *dhoop* on the pavement nearby (check that the boxes haven't already been opened and their contents sold off piecemeal).

Avante Cottage Crafts 12 Oriental Mansion, Wodehouse Rd, Colaba ☎022 2202 0873, ⓦavante crafts.com; map p.612. One of the pioneering handicraft retailers in town selling a wide range of metal, wood and stone artefacts, folk paintings and textiles. Daily 10.30am–7.30pm.

BOLLYWOOD REVOLUTION

Film is massive in India. The country produces around 1200 movies annually, half of them in the studios of north Mumbai. Known as **"Bollywood"**, the home of the All-India cinema industry has experienced a sea change over the past decade, as its output has started to reach mass audiences of expat Indians in Europe and North America. The resulting global revenues have financed much higher production standards and a completely new approach to plot, acting styles and scripts – rendering redundant the old cinematic stereotypes of the so-called "masala format", which dominated Indian film for decades.

Big song-and-dance numbers still very much have their place in the modern Bollywood blockbuster, as does melodrama. But the overall tone these days tends to be much more sophisticated, with glamorous foreign locations, more plausible story lines, cutting-edge camera work and even state-of-the-art CGI deployed to wow cinemagoers at home and abroad. Much of it is now developed in-house, helmed by VFX studios like Red Chillies.

Whereas in the past, hit movies tended to incorporate a bit of everything – romance, laughs, fight scenes, chases, lurid baddies, a set of instantly recognizable stock characters and convoluted plots that emphasized traditional values – now the industry is making big bucks from more nuanced genre flicks. The highest grossing movies of the past decade were a cross-border comedy drama (*Bajrangi Bhaijaan*; 2015); a sci-fi comedy satirizing religious dogma (*PK*; 2014); a caper (*Dhoom 3*; 2013); an action flick (*Ek Tha Tiger*; 2012); and a love story (*Bodyguard*; 2011) – radical departures from the Bollywood mainstream. Though "commercial" film-makers like Karan Johar and Rohit Shetty continue to churn out tried-and-tested formulaic films, a crop of directors like Vishal Bhardwaj, Dibakar Banerjee and Anurag Kashyap are unafraid to experiment with themes.

Some elements, however, remain consistent. Not even the most serious Indian movie can do without at least two or three "item numbers" – the set-piece song-and-dance sequences that give all hit films their essential anthems. And the cult of the Bollywood star shows no sign of abating. A-listers in the industry enjoy almost god-like status (only the country's top cricketers come close to matching their exalted mass appeal). Images of the current heartthrobs appear everywhere, from newspapers to cheesy TV ads.

At the top of the heap stands the veteran, white-bearded éminence grise of Bollywood, **Amitabh Bachchan**, whose record-breaking career as a screen hero saw a startling revival in the 2000s after he came out of de facto retirement to host India's version of *Who Wants To Be A Millionaire*, called *KBC* (*Kaun Banega Crorepati*). Only a notch behind him comes **Shah Rukh Khan**, the smouldering lead of countless romantic blockbusters and the man the *Los Angeles Times* dubbed "the world's biggest movie star" in 2011. SRK has great overseas appeal, and the Khan trilogy is completed by Bollywood bad boy **Salman Khan** and **Aamir Khan**, the actor-director-producer behind hits such as *Lagaan*, *Ghajini*, *3 Idiots* and *PK*. Other leading men of the moment include action stars Akshay Kumar and Ajay Devgan, dancing sensation **Hrithik Roshan**, newcomer **Ranveer Singh** and talented **Ranbir Kapoor** who represents the fourth generation of the illustrious Kapoor clan, India's first family of cinema.

Not surprisingly in such an image-obsessed industry, **female leads** tend to have a shorter shelf life than their male counterparts, although contemporary starlets such as **Priyanka Chopra**, **Deepika Padukone**, **Katrina Kaif**, **Anushka Sharma** and **Kangna Ranaut** are tackling increasingly demanding roles in an attempt to prove themselves as serious actresses.

Even so, their off-screen antics and romantic dalliances continue to capture more attention than their acting skills, as do any public appearance of India's biggest celebrity couple, star actor **Abhishek Bachchan** (son of Amitabh) and his wife **Aishwarya Rai**. A former Miss World whose extreme beauty and svelte figure are often credited as spearheading the crossover of Bollywood into Western cinemas, Aishwarya has maintained her great popularity despite having had her first child in 2011. The career trajectory of Bollywood actresses has tended to be downwards after marriage (the assumption being that Indian audiences aren't prepared to accept a married woman, or even worse, a mother, as a romantic heroine). But with several other Bollywood queens – **Madhuri Dixit Nene, Karisma Kapoor, Rani Mukherjee** and **Vidya Balan** – making comebacks after starting a family, the times may well be changing.

10

10

LAUGHTER YOGA

On the principle that laughter is the best medicine, Mumbai doctor Madan Kataria and his wife Madhuri – aka "the Giggling Gurus" – have created a new kind of therapy: *hasya* (laughter) yoga. There are now more than three hundred **Laughter Clubs** in India and many more worldwide; around fifty thousand people join the Laughter Day celebrations in Mumbai on the first Sunday of May each year, with tens of thousands more participating in seventy countries worldwide.

Fifteen-minute sessions start with adherents doing yogic breathing while chanting "Ho ho ha ha", which develops into spontaneous "hearty laughter" (raising both hands in the air with the head tilting backwards), "milkshake laughter" (everyone laughs while making a gesture as if they are drinking milkshake), and "swinging laughter" (standing in a circle saying "aaee-oo-eee-uuu") before the rather fearsome "lion laughter" (extruding the tongue fully with eyes wide open and hands stretched out like claws, and laughing from the tummy). The session then winds up with holding hands and the chanting of slogans ("We are the laughter club member [sic]…Y…E…S!").

Laughter Clubs take place between 6am and 7am at various venues around the city, including Colaba Woods in Cuffe Parade and Juhu Beach. For the full story, go to ⓦ laughteryoga.org.

BOOKSHOPS

Crossword Bookstore Mohammed Bhai Mansion, NS Patkar Marg, Kemp's Corner, a 10min walk north of Chowpatty Beach ☎ 022 6627 2100; map p.610. Mumbai's largest retailer, in a/c premises, complete with its own coffee bar. Daily 11am–8.30pm.

Kitab Khana Somaiya Bhavan, MG Rd ☎ 022 6170 2276; map p.612. Eclectic bookshop in a restored heritage building with high ceilings, polished woodwork and a café. Daily 10.30am–7.30pm.

MUSIC AND MUSICAL INSTRUMENTS

Bhargava's Musik 4/5 Imperial Plaza, 30th Rd, Bandra ☎ 022 2641 1842, ⓦ bhargavasmusik.com; map p.625.

The city's foremost music shop, up in the northern suburb of Bandra, stocks every conceivable kind of Indian instrument, from sitars and sarods to bamboo flutes and *shruti* boxes, as well as Western guitars, strings and drums. Mon–Sat 10.30am–8pm.

Furtado's Jer Mahal, Dhobitalao ☎ 022 6622 5454, ⓦ furtadosonline.com; map p.610. Mostly Western-style woodwind, brass, keyboard and percussion, with a basic stock of Indian instruments. It's more easily accessible than Bhargava's if you're based in south Mumbai. Mon–Sat 10am–8pm.

SPORTS

In common with most Indians, Mumbaikars are crazy about **cricket**. Few other spectator sports get much of a look-in, although the **horseracing** at Mahalakshmi draws large crowds on Derby days. Previews of all forthcoming events are posted on the back pages of the *Times of India*, and in *Time Out Mumbai*.

CRICKET

Cricket provides almost as much of a distraction as movies in the Maharashtrian capital, and you'll see games in progress everywhere, from impromptu sunset knockabouts on Chowpatty Beach to more formal club matches in full whites at the gymkhanas lined up along Marine Drive. The Indian season runs from October through February. Tickets for cup and test matches are almost as hard to come by as seats on commuter trains, but foreign visitors can sometimes gain preferential access to quotas through the Mumbai Cricket Association's offices on the first floor of Wankhede (see below; ☎ 022 2279 5500, ⓦ mumbaicricket.com).

Brabourne Stadium Off Marine Drive. The home of the highly exclusive Indian Cricket Club (membership is by invitation only), history was made in this stadium which has now been side-lined by the newer Wankhede Stadium (see below). Occasional matches are still played here though.

Oval Maidan South Mumbai. This is the place to watch local talent in action, set against a wonderful backdrop of imperial-era buildings. Something of a pecking order applies here: the further from the path cutting across the centre of the park you go, the better the wickets and the classier the games become. Pitches like these are where former India captain Sachin Tendulkar cut his cricketing teeth.

Wankhede Stadium Off Marine Drive. This 45,000-capacity stadium is where major test matches are hosted, amid an atmosphere as intense, raucous and intimidating for visiting teams as any in India.

HORSERACING AND HORSERIDING

Mahalakshmi Racecourse Near the Mahalakshmi Temple, just north of Malabar Hill ⓦarcmumbai.com. This is the home of the Royal Western India Turf Club – a throwback to British times that still serves as a prime stomping ground for the city's upper classes. Race meets are held twice weekly, on Wednesdays and Saturdays between November and March, and big days such as the 2000 Guineas and Derby attract crowds of 25,000. Entrance to the public ground is by ticket on the day. Seats for the colonial-era stand, with its posh lawns and exclusive *Gallops Restaurant* are, alas, allocated to members only. Race cards are posted in the sports section of the *Times of India* and at ⓦrwitclive. com. On non-race days, the Mahalakshmi ground doubles as a riding track. Temporary membership of the Amateur Riding Club of Mumbai, another bastion of elite Mumbai, entitles you to use the club's thoroughbreds for classes. Full details on how to do this, along with previews of forthcoming club polo matches, are posted on the website.

DIRECTORY

Ambulance ⓣ101 for general emergencies; but you're nearly always better off taking a taxi.

Banks and exchange There are dozens of ATMs dotted around the city. All the major state banks downtown change foreign currency (Mon–Fri 10.30am–2.30pm, Sat 10.30am–12.30pm); some (eg the Bank of Baroda) also handle credit cards and cash advances. Thomas Cook's big Dr D.N. Marg branch (Mon–Sat 9.30am–6pm; ⓣ022 4879 5009), between the Khadi shop and Hutatma Chowk, can also arrange money transfers from overseas.

Consulates and high commissions Note that most of India's neighbours, including Bangladesh, Bhutan, Burma, Nepal and Pakistan, only have embassies in New Delhi and/ or Kolkata (Calcutta). All of the following are open Mon– Fri only: Australia, Level 10, A Wing, Crescenzo Building, G Block, Plot C 38-39, Bandra Kurla (ⓣ022 6757 4900, ⓦmumbai.consulate.gov.au); Canada, Indiabulls Finance Centre, 21st Floor, Tower 2, Senapati Bapat Marg, Elphin-stone Rd West (ⓣ022 6749 4444, ⓦcanadainternational. gc.ca); Republic of Ireland, Mafatlal House, 7th Floor, H.T. Parekh Marg, Churchgate (ⓣ022 6635 5635); South Africa, Gandhi Mansion, 20 Altamount Rd (ⓣ022 2351 3725, ⓦdha.gov.za); United Kingdom, Naman Chambers, C/32 G Block, Bandra Kurla Complex, Bandra East (ⓣ022 6650 2222, ⓦgov.uk); US, C-49, G-Block, Bandra Kurla Complex, Bandra East (ⓣ022 2672 4000, ⓦin.usembassy.gov).

Hospitals The best hospital in the centre is the private Bombay Hospital, New Marine Lines (ⓣ022 2206 7676, ⓦbombayhospital.com), just north of the government tourist office on M Karve Rd. Breach Candy Hospital (ⓣ022 2366 7788, ⓦbreachcandyhospital.org) on Bhulabhai Desai Rd, near the swimming pool, is also recommended by foreign embassies.

Internet A couple of cramped 24hr places (₹40/hr) can be found in Colaba on Nawroji F Marg. If you have your own computer, wi-fi access is available at most of the city's mid-and high-end hotels, as well as at local branches of the *Barista* coffee shop chain (there's a branch next to the Regal cinema in Colaba).

Libraries Asiatic Society (see page 617), Shahid Bhagat Singh Marg, Horniman Circle, Ballard Estate (Mon–Sat 10.30am–-7pm); British Council (for British newspapers and magazines), A Wing, 1st floor, Mittal Tower, Nariman Point (Tues–Sat 10am–6pm); Bombay Natural History Society, Hornbill House, next to the Chhatrapati Shivaji Museum (ⓦbnhs.org; Mon–Fri 9.30am–5.30pm), has an international reputation for the study of wildlife in India. Visitors may obtain temporary membership, which allows them access to the library, natural history collection, occasional talks and the opportunity to join organized walks and field trips.

Pharmacies Causeway Chemist on the Colaba Causeway just beyond the corner of Garden Road, is open until 8.30pm.

Police The main police station in Colaba (ⓣ022 2204 3702) is on the west side of Colaba Causeway, near the crossroads with Best Marg.

Postal services The GPO (Mon–Sat 9am–5pm) is around the corner from CST (VT) station, off Nagar Chowk. The parcel office (10am–4.30pm) is behind the main building on the first floor. Packing-wallahs hang around on the pavement outside. DHL (ⓣ1800 111 345) has twenty offices in Mumbai, including a few along Colaba Causeway and one on Marine Drive.

Travel agents The following travel agents are recommended for booking domestic and international flights, and cars with drivers: Cox and Kings India, 16 Bank St, Fort (ⓣ022 2270 9100, ⓦcoxandkings.co.in); Sita World, 11th Floor, Bajaj Bhavan, Nariman Point (ⓦsitatours. com); Thomas Cook, 324 Dr DN Rd, Fort (ⓣ022 6160 3333, ⓦthomascook.in); Karmic Travels, B7 Ground Floor, Shivam Apartments Opp Greater Bank, Sant Janabai Road, Vile Parle East (ⓣ022 2612 4927 or 022 2612 4928).

10

Maharashtra

MINIATURE TRAIN TO MATHERAN

Maharashtra

Vast and rugged, the modern state of Maharashtra is the third largest in India, and one of the most visited by foreign tourists, though most people venture no further than its port capital, Mumbai. As soon as you leave the seemingly endless concrete housing projects, industrial works and swamplands of Mumbai, you enter a different world with a different history. Undoubtedly, Maharashtra's greatest treasures are its extraordinary cave temples and monasteries; the finest of all are found near Aurangabad, renamed after the Mughal emperor Aurangzeb and home to the Bibi-ka-Maqbara, dedicated to his wife. The busy commercial city is the obvious base for visits to the Buddhist caves at Ajanta, with their fabulous and still-vibrant murals, and the monolithic temples of Ellora, where the astonishing Hindu Kailash temple was carved in its entirety from one single rock.

11

Despite Maharashtra's early importance as a centre of Buddhism, Hinduism is very much at the core of the life in the state. Balancing modern industry alongside ancient associations with the Ramayana, the main pilgrimage centre has always been **Nasik**, a handy place to break journeys en route to Aurangabad. One of the four locations of the Kumbh Mela, the city is always a hive of devotional activity, and lies close to one of India's most sacred Shiva shrines, reached from the village of **Trimbak**. In the state's far northeastern corner, the city of **Nagpur** lies close to **Sevagram**, where Mahatma Gandhi set up his headquarters during the struggle for Independence.

Away from the cities, one of the most characteristic features of the landscape is a plenitude of **forts**. Rising abruptly a short distance inland from the sea, the Sahyadri Hills – part of the **Western Ghats** – form a series of huge steps that march up from the narrow coastal strip to the edge of the **Deccan plateau**. These flat-topped hills could easily be converted into forts where small forces could withstand protracted sieges by large armies. Today, visitors can scale such windswept fortified heights at **Pratapgadh** and **Daulatabad**.

During the nineteenth century, the mountains found another use. When the summer proved too much for the British in Bombay, they sought refuge in nearby **hill stations**, the most popular of which, **Mahabaleshwar**, now caters for droves of domestic tourists. **Matheran**, 800m higher, has a special attraction: a rickety miniature train. South of Matheran, a further series of magnificent rock-cut caves clustered around another town, **Lonavala**, provides the main incentive to break the journey to the modern, cosmopolitan city of **Pune**, famous for its **Osho** resort founded by the New Age guru Bhagwan Rajneesh, but most appealing for its atmospheric old town and burgeoning restaurant and bar scene.

BEST TIME TO VISIT

The best time to visit Maharashtra is the October–February period, when it is typically hot and dry (though the eastern side of the state may get a few showers). Temperatures ramp up from March to May, when it can get uncomfortable, and thunderstorms are not uncommon. The monsoon generally hits in June and lasts till September, with July the wettest month; most hotels in the hill station of Matheran (see page 680) close during this period. It is also well worth trying to coincide your visit with one of the state's many festivals (see page 649).

EXPLORING THE AJANTA CAVES

Highlights

❶ Nasik Pilgrimage centre and capital of India's nascent wine industry, this city is a fascinating combination of ancient and modern. See page 650

❷ Ellora caves A World Heritage Site with breathtaking Hindu, Buddhist and Jain caves carved from solid volcanic rock, as well as the stunning Kailash temple. See page 660

❸ Ajanta caves Hidden in a remote horseshoe-shaped ravine, Ajanta's caves contain the finest surviving gallery of art from any of the world's ancient civilizations. See page 668

❹ Gandhi ashram, Sevagram Learn about the great man's life and beliefs at the last ashram he

lived in. See page 675

❺ The Konkan coast This stretch of coastline remains relatively unspoilt with several appealing places to stay, including the small port of Murud-Janjira. See page 678

❻ Miniature train to Matheran Fantastic views across the Western Ghats are revealed during the switchback train journey up to this former British hill station. See page 680

❼ Pune Known as the "Oxford of the East", this sophisticated city is home to an absorbing old town, a riveting museum and some excellent places to eat and drink, plus the Osho ashram. See page 684

HIGHLIGHTS ARE MARKED ON THE MAP ON PAGE 648

To the west, Maharashtra occupies 500km of the **Konkan coast** on the Arabian Sea, from Gujarat to Goa. The little-explored palm-fringed coast winds back and forth with countless inlets, ridges and valleys; highlights include **Murud-Janjira**, whose extraordinary fortress was the only one never conquered by the Mughals, and **Ganpatipule**, the region's chief pilgrimage centre, with kilometres of virtually deserted, palm-fringed beaches. By the time you reach **Kolhapur**, the main town in the far south of the state, famous for its temple and palace, Mumbai feels a world away.

Brief history

Maharashtra enters recorded history in the second century BC, with the construction of its first Buddhist caves. These lay in peaceful places of great natural beauty, and were created with the wealth generated by the nearby caravan trade routes between north and south India.

The region's first Hindu rulers – based in Badami, Karnataka – appeared during the sixth century, and Buddhism was almost entirely supplanted by the twelfth century. Hinduism, in the form of the simple faith of Ramdas, the "Servant of Rama", provided the philosophical underpinning behind the campaigns of the Maharashtra's greatest warrior, **Shivaji** (1627–80), who remains a potent symbol for Maharashtrans. The fiercely independent Maratha chieftain united local forces to place insurmountable obstacles in the way of any prospective invader; so effective were their guerrilla

HIGHLIGHTS

1. Nasik
2. Ellora caves
3. Ajanta caves
4. Gandhi ashram, Sevagram
5. The Konkan coast
6. Miniature train to Matheran
7. Pune

MAHARASHTRA

FESTIVALS IN MAHARASHTRA

Makar Sankranti (Jan). Marks the end of Dakshinayana (the southward movement of the sun) and the start of Uttarayan (the northward movement of the sun; kite-flying, bathing in sacred rivers and/or with sesame oil, lighting oil lamps to honour ancestors, and exchanging sesame sweets all feature in the festivities.

Ratha Saptami (Jan). This festival heralds the start of spring and the harvest, when offerings are made to the sun god, Surya.

Gudhi Padwa (usually March). Hindu celebration marking the start of the new year, the day Brahma created the universe. People raise a bright green or yellow flag outside households and kick off festivities by eating a paste made from neem leaves and jaggery.

Narali Purnima/Raksha Bandhan (Aug). The "coconut festival" marks the end of the monsoon, and heralds the start of the fishing season – it is celebrated enthusiastically by communities on the Konkan coast (see page 678).

Ganesh Chaturthi (Aug/Sept). Dedicated to one of Hinduism's most popular deities, this ten-day festival finishes with a procession and the immersion of large Ganesh effigies into rivers, water tanks or the sea.

Marabats and Badgyas (Aug/Sept). Celebrated with particular fervour in Nagpur (see page 673), where effigies personifying evils such as corruption and bribery are taken on a procession and then burned.

Navarata (Sept/Oct). The "Nine nights" festival dedicated to the worship of Shakti, the mother goddess, and by extension the importance of women generally. A Maharashtran characteristic of the festival is *bondhla*, folk dances performed by girls each evening.

Tripuri Purnima (Nov). The most important Shiva festival after Shivrati, Tripuri Purnima marks the god's victory over the demon Tripurasura. Celebrations include ritual bathing, and in places such as Nasik (see page 650) lit candles are floated on the Godavari River.

11

tactics that he could even take on the mighty Mughals, who by 1633 had got as far as capturing Daulatabad. By the time he died, in 1680, he had managed to unite the Marathas into a stable and secure state, funded by the plunder gleaned through guerrilla raids as far afield as Andhra Pradesh. In response, Mughal Emperor **Aurangzeb** moved his court and capital south to the Deccan, first to Bijapur (now Vijayapura) in 1686 and then Golconda in 1687, but still failed to subdue Shivaji's dynasty. Yet by the end of the eighteenth century the power of both had weakened and the British were able to take full control.

Maharashtra claims a crucial role in the development of a nationalist consciousness. The Indian National Union, originally convened in Pune, held a conference in Bombay in 1885; thereafter it was known as the **Indian National Congress**. This loose congregation of key local figures from around the country changed the face of Indian politics. At first, its aim was limited to establishing a national platform to raise the status of Indians, and it remained loyal to the British. In the long term, of course, it was instrumental in the achievement of Independence 62 years later, with many of the Congress's factional leaders over the years hailing from Maharashtra.

With Independence, the Bombay Presidency, to which most of Maharashtra belonged, became known as Bombay State. Maharashtra as such was created in 1960 from the state's Marathi-speaking regions. Its manufacturing industries, centred on Mumbai and to a lesser extent cities such as Nagpur, Nasik, Aurangabad, Sholapur and Kolhapur, now account for around fifteen percent of the nation's output. Textiles have long been important – the Deccan soils supplied the world with cotton in the nineteenth century after its main source was interrupted by the American Civil War – but this is now also one of the premier high-tech industry regions, especially along the Mumbai–Pune corridor. Still, the majority of Maharashtra's population of around 116 million are still engaged in agricultural pursuits.

Nasik and around

Lying at the head of the main pass through the Western Ghats, the city of **NASIK** (or Nashik) makes an interesting stopover en route to or from Mumbai, 187km southwest. It is one of the four sites of the world's largest religious gathering, the **Kumbh Mela** (see page 269), most recently hosting it in 2015 (it won't return until 2027). Even outside festival times, the *ghat*-lined banks of the **River Godavari** are always animated.

According to the Ramayana, Nasik was where Rama (Vishnu in human form), his brother Lakshmana and wife Sita lived during their exile from Ayodhya, and the arch-demon Ravana carried off Sita from here in an aerial chariot to his kingdom, Lanka, in the far south. The scene of such episodes forms the core of the busy pilgrimage circuit – a lively enclave packed with religious specialists, beggars, sadhus and street vendors touting puja paraphernalia.

However, Nasik has a surprising dearth of historical buildings, and its only real monuments are the rock-cut caves at nearby **Pandav Lena**. Excavated at the peak of Buddhist achievement on the Deccan, these 2000-year-old cells hark back to the days when, as capital of the powerful **Satavahana** dynasty, Nasik dominated the all-important trade routes linking the Ganges plains with the ports to the west.

From Nasik, you can make an interesting day-trip to the highly auspicious village of **Trimbak**, from which a steep climb takes you to **Brahmagiri**, the source of the Godavari. Somewhat in contrast to its religious importance, Nasik is also the centre of Maharashtra's burgeoning **wine region** (see box above).

Ram Kund

Around 1.7km northeast of the Old City Bus Stand

Always buzzing with a carnival atmosphere, the **Ram Kund** is the reason most people come to Nasik, although this sacred bathing tank can look more like an overcrowded municipal swimming pool than one of India's most ancient holy places. Among the Ram Kund's more arcane attributes is its capacity to dissolve bones – whence the epithet of **Astivilaya Tirth** or "Bone Immersion Tank".

Kala Ram Mandir

At the end of the narrow, uphill street opposite the Ram Kund • No fixed opening times • Free

The square around the **Kala Ram Mandir**, or "Black Rama Temple", is the city's second most important sacred area. Among the well-known episodes from the Ramayana to occur here was the event that led to Sita's abduction, when Lakshmana sliced off the nose of Ravana's sister after she had tried to seduce Rama by taking the form of a voluptuous princess. Sita's cave, or **Gumpha**, a tiny grotto known in the Ramayana as Parnakuti ("Smallest Hut"), is just off the square.

The Kala Ram temple itself, at the bottom of the square, houses unusual jet-black deities of Rama, Sita and Lakshmana; these are very popular with visiting pilgrims, as access is free from all caste restrictions. The best time to visit is around sunset, after evening puja, when a crowd, mostly of women, gathers in the courtyard to listen to a traditional storyteller recount tales from the Ramayana and other epics.

Pandav Lena

8km southwest of Nasik • Daily sunrise–sunset • ₹200 (₹10) • An auto-rickshaw costs ₹400-450 return, including waiting time

A steep fifteen-minute climb up one of the precipitous conical hills that overlook the Mumbai–Agra road is **Pandav Lena**, a small group of 24 rock-cut caves famous for their well-preserved Pali inscriptions and fine ancient stone sculpture. Cave 18, the only *chaitya* hall, is one of the earliest, dating from the first century BC, and is

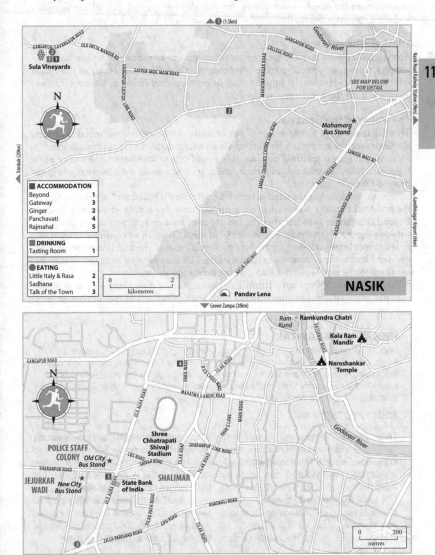

11

■ ACCOMMODATION	
Beyond	1
Gateway	3
Ginger	2
Panchavati	4
Rajmahal	5

■ DRINKING	
Tasting Room	1

● EATING	
Little Italy & Rasa	2
Sadhana	1
Talk of the Town	3

notable for its striking facade, while Cave 3, the largest *vihara*, boasts some superb exterior stonework.

Trimbak

Buses leave regularly from Nasik's Old City Bus Stand (every 30min; 45min). To return, you can catch a bus (which run until around 8pm) or one of the shared taxis that wait outside Trimbak Bus Stand

Crouched in the shadow of the Western Ghats, 28km west of Nasik, the village of **TRIMBAK** – literally "Three-Eyed", another name for Lord Shiva, in Marathi – marks the spot where one of the four infamous drops of immortality-giving *amrita* nectar fell to earth from the *kumbh* vessel during the struggle between Vishnu's vehicle Garuda and the Demons – the mythological origin of the Kumbh Mela (see page 269).

Trimbakeshwar Mandir

Among India's most sacred Shiva centres (it houses one of the twelve holiest Shiva temples, known as *jyotirlingas*), the **Trimbakeshwar Mandir**, in the centre of the village, is closed to non-Hindus. Its impressive eighteenth-century *shikhara*, however, can be glimpsed from the backstreets nearby.

The source of the Godavari

Trimbak is also close to the source of one of India's longest and most venerated rivers, the **Godavari**; the spring can be reached via an ancient trail that cuts through a cleft in an awesome, guano-splashed cliff face. The round trip to **Brahmagiri**, the source of the Godavari, takes between two and three hours. It's a strenuous walk, particularly in the heat, so take enough water.

From the trailhead at the edge of the village, the way is paved and stepped as far as the first level outcrop, where there are some welcome chai stalls and a small hamlet. Beyond that, either turn left after the last group of huts and follow the dirt trail through the woods to the foot of the **rock-cut steps** (20min), or continue straight on to the three **shrines** clinging to the base of the cliff above. The first is dedicated to the goddess Ganga, the second – a cave containing 108 lingams – to Shankar (Shiva), and the third to the sage Gautama Rishi, whose hermitage this once was.

The steps climb 550m above Trimbak to the remains of **Anjeri Fort** – a site that was, over the years, attacked by the armies of both Shah Jahan and Aurangzeb before it fell

---

INDIA'S WINE CAPITAL

With its temperate winters, rich soil and gently undulating landscape, Nasik's arid and dusty hinterland has over the past two decades proved itself to be – incongruously enough – ideal for growing wine grapes, and the city has firmly established itself at the centre of India's fast-expanding wine industry. Note that Maharashtra has eleven "dry days" when it is illegal to sell alcohol; check the Sula website for dates.

TOURS AND TASTINGS

Grover Zampa 32km southwest of Nasik ☎911 220 2586, ⓦgroverzampa.in. Based in the Sanjegaon Valley, Grover Zampa is India's second-biggest wine producer (after Sula), and offers tours and tastings lasting 1hr 30min–2hr (daily 10.30am, 2.30pm & 4pm; ₹400 for the tour, ₹500 for the tour and five tastings, ₹650 for the tour and seven tastings). Book in advance.
Sula Vineyards 14km west of Nasik ☎0253 220 2424, ⓦsulawines.com. The best-established producer,

enthusiastically supported by Mumbai's urban sophisticates, Sula Vineyards is a slick operation that wouldn't feel out of place in the Napa Valley. It runs 30min tours of its winery (hourly daily 11.30am–6.30pm; ₹150 for the tour, ₹400 for the tour and six tastings), concluding with a tasting session. There's also the *Tasting Room* wine bar and the *Soleil* restaurant (see page 654). In February, the vineyard stages a lively festival, SulaFest (ⓦsulafest.com), featuring live bands, DJs, food and, of course, plenty of wine.

into the hands of Shaha-ji Raj, father of the legendary rebel-leader Shivaji. The **source** itself is another twenty minutes further on, across **Brahmagiri Hill**, in the otherwise unremarkable Gaumukh ("Mouth of the Cow") temple. From its rather unimpressive origins, this paltry trickle flows for nearly 1000km east across the entire Deccan to the Bay of Bengal.

ARRIVAL AND DEPARTURE   NASIK AND AROUND

By plane Gandhinagar airport is around 5km southeast of the city and has irregular flights to/from Delhi; a taxi to/ from the city centre costs around ₹350.

By bus Buses from Mumbai pull in at the Mahamarga Bus Stand, 10min by rickshaw from the city centre, while Aurangabad and Pune buses terminate at the central New City Bus Stand. The Old City Bus Stand is around 500m north along the Old Agra Rd (also known as Swami Vivekanand Rd), and is primarily useful for buses to Trimbak; it's an easy walk from either stand to several budget hotels and restaurants.

Destinations Aurangabad (every 1–2hr; 4hr–4hr 30min); Mumbai (roughly hourly; 4hr); Pune (every 30min; 4–5hr); Trimbak (every 30min; 45min).

By train Nasik Road is the nearest railway station, 8km southeast of the centre; local buses regularly ply the route into town, and there is no shortage of shared taxis and auto-rickshaws (₹150–250). There's a ticket booking office (Mon–Sat 8am–8pm, Sun 8am–2pm), near HDFC House, around 1km west of the city bus stands, though it is easier to book online or via a travel agent.

Destinations Agra (3-5 daily; 14hr 25min–20hr 50min); Aurangabad (4–5 daily; 3hr–3hr 40min); Delhi (3–4 daily; 17hr–24hr 30min); Jalgaon (20–23 daily; 2hr 30min–4hr); Mumbai (every 30min–1hr; 2hr 30min–4hr 30min); Nagpur (8–10 daily; 9hr 20min–20hr 15min); Pune (1 daily; 7hr).

INFORMATION

Tourist information The helpful MTDC tourist office (Mon–Sat 10am–5.30pm; ☎0253 257 0059, ⊛maharashtratourism. gov.in) is at T1, Golf Club, Old Agra Rd, most easily reached by cutting across the park opposite the New City Bus Stand.

Banks and exchange The State Bank of India, between the two city bus stands on Old Agra Rd, changes money.

ACCOMMODATION

Most of Nasik's hotels, stretching along the Mumbai–Agra road en route to Pandav Lena, are pitched at business travellers, though there are a few more budget-friendly exceptions around the Old City Bus Stand chowk.

Beyond Sula Vineyards, 14km west of Nasik ☎0253 220 2424, ⊛sulawines.com; map p.651. Each of the super-stylish rooms is named after a grape variety at this tranquil hotel in the grounds of Sula Vineyards. There's also an infinity pool, spa and gym, and you can go hiking or cycling. The rate listed here is for weekends; prices are generally lower during the week. ₹8999

Gateway 7km southwest on the Mumbai–Agra road ☎0253 660 4499, ⊛gateway.tajhotels.com; map p.651. Set amid beautifully landscaped grounds, with a gleaming marble lobby designed in mock-Maratha style, the *Gateway* is one of the most luxurious places to stay in the area, though rooms are somewhat overpriced. Facilities include a pool, gym, restaurant and bar. ₹9600

Ginger Satpur MIDC ☎0253 661 6333, ⊛gingerhotels. com; map p.651. Nasik outpost of this reliable mid-range chain offering efficient service, comfortable if bland rooms, a small gym and a branch of *Café Coffee Day*. The downside is the location, on a busy road 4km northwest of the Mahamarga Bus Stand. It's much cheaper to book online in advance. ₹3100

Panchavati 430 Chandak Vadi ☎0253 257 5771, ⊛panchavatihotels.com; map p.651. Set mercifully off noisy MG Rd a 15min walk from the New City Bus Stand, this complex has rooms to suit most pockets, all of them clean, attached and good value for money, though overall it's a little worn and institutional. At the bottom of the range is the budget *Panchavati Guest House*, followed by the mid-range *Panchavati Yatri*, the slightly smarter *Hotel Panchavati* and, at the top of the range, the *Panchavati Millionaire*. ₹1200

Rajmahal Sharanpur Rd ☎0253 258 0501, ⊛hotel rajmahalnashik.com; map p.651. Solid, centrally located, though not the friendliest hotel, the *Rajmahal* has simple, but clean and fairly modern rooms (ask for one of the quieter ones away from the very noisy main road). Decent value. ₹2400

EATING

Nasik's best-value meals are to be had in its traditional thali restaurants, where for less than the price of a beer you can enjoy carefully prepared and tasty vegetable, pulse and lentil dishes, often including such regional specialities as bajra (wholemeal *rotis*) and bakri (hot oatmeal biscuits).

Little Italy & Rasa Sula Vineyards, 14km west of Nasik ☎0253 223 0575, ⊛sulawines.com; map p.651. Two excellent, if rather pricey, restaurants on

11

> **GOING DOOLALLY**
>
> In the days of the Raj, soldiers who cracked under the stresses and strains of military life in British India were packed off to recuperate at a psychiatric hospital in the small Maharashtran cantonment town of **Deolali**, near Nasik. Its name became synonymous with madness and nervous breakdown; hence the English phrase "to go doolally".

the Sula vineyard. As you'd expect, the former specialises in pasta, risotto and pizza, while the former focuses on contemporary north Indian cuisine. Daily 12.30–3.30pm & 7–10.30pm.

Sadhana Hardev Bagh, Motiwala College Rd ☎ 93739 37310; map p.651. Popular budget joint where misal pav is the order of the day: a reviving mix of lentils, veg and beansprouts in a hearty gravy, topped with puffed rice and served with a soft buttered roll. Mon, Thurs & Sun 8am–

2.30pm, Tues, Wed & Sat 8am-2.30pm & 7-10pm, Fri 8am-2pm & 7-10pm.

Talk of the Town Suyojit Chambers, Trimbak Rd, near the New City Bus Stand ☎ 0253 257 1961; map p.651. One of central Nasik's smarter restaurant-bars with a choice of dining halls, from the family-friendly to the smoky and masculine. The north Indian veg and non-veg dishes (mains ₹200–450) are generally pretty tasty, and there's a long list of alcoholic drinks. Daily 11am–11pm.

DRINKING

Ironically, given that the surrounding region is the country's prime wine region, Nasik's religious associations tend to mean that meat and alcohol are less easily available than elsewhere in Maharashtra, but most of the larger hotels have bars (known as "permit rooms") and several of the more expensive restaurants serve beers and spirits too.

★ **Tasting Room** Sula Vineyards, 14km west of Nasik ☎ 0253 223 0575, ⓦ sulawines.com; map p.651.

This breezy bar looks out over acres of neat rows of vines towards the scenic Gangapur tank. The wine list focuses on Sula's range of whites, reds and rosés (the Merlot-Malbec and the Shiraz are well worth sampling), as well as a small selection from other (mainly New World) producers. A glass of wine costs ₹180–360; there's a ₹100 cover charge. Daily 11am–11pm.

Aurangabad and around

Many travellers regard **AURANGABAD** as little more than a convenient, though largely uninteresting, place in which to kill time on the way to **Ellora** and **Ajanta**, yet given a little effort, this city can compensate for its architectural shortcomings. Scattered around its ragged fringes, the remains of fortifications, gateways, domes and minarets – including those of the most ambitious Mughal tomb garden in western India, the **Bibi-ka-Maqbara** – bear witness to an illustrious imperial past; the small but fascinating crop of **rock-cut Buddhist caves**, huddled along the flanks of the flat-topped, sandy yellow hills to the north, are remnants of even more ancient occupation.

Modern Aurangabad is one of India's fastest growing commercial and industrial centres, specializing in car, soft drink and beer production. It's an upbeat place, boasting plenty of restaurants, bars and interesting shops in the old city. Easy day-trips include the dramatic fort of **Daulatabad**, and, just a little further along the Ellora road, the tomb of Emperor Aurangzeb at the Muslim village of **Khuldabad**.

Brief history

The city was founded in the early seventeenth century by **Malik Ambar**, an ex-Abyssinian slave and prime minister of the independent Muslim kingdom of the Nizam Shahis; many of the **mosques** and palaces he erected still endure, albeit in ruins. Aurangabad really rose to prominence, however, towards the end of the seventeenth century, when **Aurangzeb** decamped here from Delhi. At his behest, the impressive city walls and gates were raised in 1682 to withstand the persistent Maratha attacks that bedevilled his later years. Following his death in 1707, the city was renamed in his honour as it changed hands once again. The new rulers, the **Nizams of Hyderabad**, staved off the Marathas for the greater part of 250 years, until the city finally merged with Maharashtra in 1956.

The old city

The **old city**, laid out on a grid by Malik Amber in the early seventeenth century, still forms the core of Aurangabad's large **bazaar** area. It's best approached via **Gulmandi Square** to the south, along any of several streets lined with colourful shops and stalls. Sections of Aurangzeb's city wall survive, though more impressive is the network of city **gates**, some of which have been restored to something approaching their former glory.

The Panchakki

Panchakki Rd, about 600m northwest of the Central Bus Stand • Daily 6am–9pm • ₹200 (₹10)

On the left bank of the Kham River is an unusual watermill known as the **Panchakki**. Water pumped underground from a reservoir in the hills 6km away drives a small grindstone, once used to mill flour, and collects in an attractive fish-filled tank, shaded by a large banyan tree. The Panchakki forms part of the **Dargah** of Baba Shah Muzaffar, a religious compound built by Aurangzeb as a memorial to his spiritual mentor, a Chishti mystic. The complex makes a lively place to wander around in the early evening with lots of chai shops, *mehendi* (henna hand-painting) artists and souvenir shops.

Bibi-ka-Maqbara

Around 2.5km north of the city centre • Daily 6am-9pm • ₹200 (₹10) • The easiest way to get here is by auto-rickshaw; a round trip encompassing the Bibi-ka-Maqbara and the Aurangabad caves (see page 656) costs ₹350–400

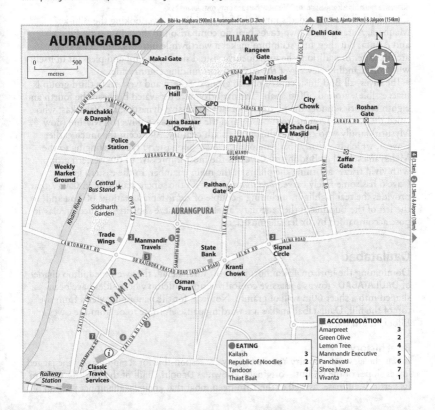

Although it's the most impressive Islamic monument in Maharashtra, Aurangabad's Mughal tomb-garden, the **Bibi-ka-Maqbara**, has always suffered from comparison with the Taj Mahal, built forty years earlier, of which it's an obvious imitation. Completed in 1678, the mausoleum was dedicated by **Prince Azam Shah** to the memory of his mother **Begum Rabi'a Daurani**, Aurangzeb's wife. Lack of resources dogged the 25-year project, and the end result fell far short of expectations. Looking at the mausoleum from beyond the ornamental gardens and redundant fountains in front of it, the truncated minarets and ungainly entrance arch make the Bibi-ka-Maqbara appear ill-proportioned compared with the elegant height and symmetry of the Taj, an impression not enhanced by the abrupt discontinuation of marble after the first 2m – allegedly a cost-saving measure.

An enormous brass-inlaid **door** – decorated with Persian calligraphy naming the maker, the year of its installation and chief architect – gives access to the archetypal *charbagh* garden complex. Of the two entrances to the mausoleum itself, one leads to the inner balcony while the second drops through another beautiful door to the **vault** (visitors may no longer climb the minarets). Inside, an exquisite octagonal **lattice-screen** of white marble surrounds the raised plinth supporting Rabi'a Daurani's grave. Like her husband's in nearby Khuldabad, it is "open" as a sign of humility. The unmarked grave beside it is said to be that of the empress's nurse.

Aurangabad caves

Around 3.5km north of the city centre • Daily sunrise–sunset • ₹200 (₹10) • The most practical way of getting to the caves is by auto-rickshaw; a round trip encompassing the Bibi-ka-Maqbara and caves costs around ₹350

Carved out of a steep-sided spur of the Sahyadri Range overlooking the Bibi-ka-Maqbara, Aurangabad's own **caves** bear no comparison to those in nearby Ellora and Ajanta, but their fine **sculpture** makes a worthwhile introduction to rock-cut architecture. In addition, the infrequently visited site is peaceful and pleasant in itself, with commanding views over the city and surrounding countryside.

The caves, all Buddhist, consist of two groups, eastern and western (a third group is inaccessible), around 500m apart. The majority were excavated between the fourth and eighth centuries, under the patronage of two successive dynasties: the **Vakatkas**, who ruled the western Deccan from Nasik, and the **Chalukyas**, a powerful Mysore (now Mysuru) family who emerged during the sixth century. All except the much earlier Cave 4, which is a *chaitya* hall, are of the *vihara* (monastery) type, belonging to the Mahayana school of Buddhism. **Cave 3** is the most impressive of the western group, with vivid friezes adorning the pillars in the main chamber. In the eastern group, Cave 6 has some finely carved *bodhisattvas*, but it's the superb sculpture in **Cave 7** that provides the real highlight, including a couple of *zaftig* representations of Tara and, to the left of the Buddha in the sanctuary, a celebrated frieze showing a dancer in classic pose accompanied by six female musicians.

Daulatabad

Dominating the horizon 13km northwest of Aurangabad, the awesome hilltop citadel of **DAULATABAD** crowns a massive conical volcanic outcrop whose sides have been shaped into a sheer 60m wall of granite. Not least for the panoramic **views** from the top of the hill, Daulatabad makes a rewarding pause en route to or from the caves at Ellora, 17km northwest.

Brief history

It was the eleventh-century **Yadavas** who were responsible for scraping away the jagged lower slopes of the mount – originally known as **Deogiri**, "Hill of the Gods" – to form its vertical-cliff base, as well as the 15m-deep moat that encircles the upper portion of the citadel. Muslim occupation of Deogiri began in earnest with the arrival in 1327 of Sultan Ghiyas-ud-din **Tughluq**, who decreed that his entire court should decamp here from Delhi, an epic 1100km march that cost thousands of lives, and ultimately proved futile – within seventeen years, drought and famine had forced the beleaguered ruler to return to Delhi. Thereafter, the fortress fell to a succession of different regimes, including Shah Jahan's **Mughals** in 1633, before it was finally taken by the **Marathas** midway through the eighteenth century.

The fortress
Daily 6am–6pm • ₹200 (₹15)

Beyond the formidable sets of outer defences that enclose a series of high-walled courtyards at the foot of the hill, Daulatabad's labyrinthine **fortress** unfolds around the enormous **Chand Minar**, or "Victory Tower", erected in 1435. The Persian blue-and-turquoise tiles that once plastered it in complex geometric patterns have disappeared, but it remains an impressive spectacle, rising from the ruins of the city that once sprawled from its base. The **Jama Masjid**, back along the main path, is Daulatabad's oldest Islamic monument. Built in 1318, the well-preserved mosque comprises 106 pillars plundered from the Hindu and Jain temples that previously stood on the site. It now functions as a Bharatmata temple, much to the chagrin of local Muslims. Adjoining the mosque, the large stone-lined "Elephant" **tank** was once a central component in the fort's extensive water-supply system. Two giant terracotta pipes channelled water from the hills into Deogiri's legendary fruit and vegetable gardens.

From the Chand Minar, the main walkway continues through another set of bastions and fortified walls before emerging close to the **Chini Mahal**, or "Chinese Palace". The impressive **Mendha Tope** ("Ram-headed Cannon"), inscribed in Persian, rests on a squat stone tower just above. From here onwards, a sequence of macabre traps lay in wait for the unwary intruder. First, a moat infested with man-eating crocodiles (now spanned by an iron bridge) had to be crossed to reach the main citadel. Next the attackers would have had to clamber through a maze of claustrophobic, zigzagging passageways, the last of which was closed with an iron cover that could be heated to generate toxic gases.

From the final tunnel, it's a fairly steep ten-minute climb up a broad flight of steps to the **Baradari**, an attractive octagonal pavilion used by Shah Jahan during his visits to Daulatabad. The **views** from the flat roof of the building are superb, but an even more impressive panorama is to be had from the **look-out post** perched on the summit of the hill, marked with another grand cannon.

ARRIVAL AND INFORMATION   **DAULATABAD**

By bus/taxi Although Daulatabad features on the guided tours of Ellora from Aurangabad (see page 658), you'll have more time to enjoy it by travelling here on one of the buses (every 30min; 30min) that shuttle between Aurangabad and the caves. From Daulatabad, it is easy to catch another bus or shared taxi on to Khuldabad and Ellora; the stop is

opposite the main entrance to the fort.

Visiting independently If you're not on a tour, try to arrive early as the place is often overrun, and bring a torch as some of the passages in the fort are pitch-black and hopelessly confusing – one reason why you might also consider hiring a guide (around ₹500).

Khuldabad
22km north of Aurangabad • Tombs sunrise–10pm • Free, but small tips and donations are expected • Buses run every 30min between Aurangabad and Ellora, stopping en route at Khuldabad's small bus stand (30min from Aurangabad, 10min from Ellora), a 10min walk from the tombs

Nestled on a saddle of high ground, **KHULDABAD**, also known as **Rauza**, is an old walled town famous for a wonderful crop of onion-domed **tombs**. Among the Muslim notables deemed worthy of a patch of earth in this most hallowed of burial grounds ("Khuldabad" means "Heavenly Abode") were the Emperor Aurangzeb himself, who raised the town's granite battlements and seven fortified gateways, a couple of nizams, and a fair few of the town's Chishti founding fathers.

Aurangzeb's tomb lies inside a whitewashed **dargah**, midway between the North and South gates. The grave itself is a humble affair decorated only by the fresh flower petals scattered by visitors, open to the elements instead of sealed in stone. The devout emperor insisted that it be paid for not out of the royal coffers, but with the money he raised in the last years of life by selling his own hand-quilted white skullcaps. Aurangzeb chose this as his final resting place primarily because of the presence, next door, of **Sayeed Zain-ud-din**'s tomb, which occupies a quadrangle separating Aurangzeb's grave from those of his wife and second son, Azam Shah. Locked away behind a small door in the mausoleum is Khuldabad's most jealously guarded relic, the **Robe of the Prophet**, revealed to the public once a year on the twelfth day of the Islamic month of Rabi-ul-Awwal, when the tomb attracts worshippers from all over India. Directly opposite Zain-ud-din's tomb is the **Dargah of Sayeed Burhan-ud-din**, a Chishti missionary buried here in 1334. The shrine is said to contain hairs from the Prophet's beard, which magically increase in number when they are counted each year.

ARRIVAL AND DEPARTURE
AURANGABAD AND AROUND

BY PLANE

Chikal Thana airport Aurangabad's airport is 10km east of the city; a taxi to/from the city centre costs around ₹400–450. Most of the smarter hotels offer a pick-up service. Air India run daily flights to Mumbai (1hr) and Delhi (1hr 50min).

BY TRAIN

Aurangabad railway station The railway station is on the southwest edge of the city centre, at the southern end of Station Rd West. As Aurangabad is not on the main line, trains to and from the city are fairly limited (Jalgaon, 166km north, has the nearest mainline station, with services to a far greater range of destinations; see page 673). The quickest train to Mumbai is the #12072 *Jan Shatabdi Express* (daily 6am; 5hr 30min); if you prefer to travel overnight, try the #17058 *Devagiri Express* (daily 11.25pm; 6hr 20min). Destinations Delhi (1 daily; 22hr); Hyderabad/Secunderabad (6–7 daily; 9hr 30min–15hr 30min); Jalgaon (1–3 daily; 4hr 15min–5hr 50min); Mumbai (4–5 daily; 5hr

30min–9hr 30min); Nasik (4–5 daily; 3hr–3hr 40min).

BY BUS

State buses The hectic Central Bus Stand is 2.5km north of the railway station, off Dr Ambedkhar Rd. All the state transport corporation (MSRTC) buses arrive and depart from here.

Destinations Ellora (every 30min; 40min) via Daulatabad and Khuldabad; Jalgaon (every 30min; 3hr 30min–4hr) via Fardapur for Ajanta (2hr 30min–3hr); Mumbai (5–6 daily, including a nightly "luxury" bus; 8–10hr); Nagpur (around 5–6 daily; 12hr); Nasik (every 30min–1hr; 4hr 30min); Pune (every 30min–1hr; 5hr).

Private buses For a little more comfort, numerous private companies run a/c buses to most of the larger destinations; you can save yourself a lot of hassle by heading straight to the calm and efficient Manmandir Travels on Adalat Rd (📞0240 236 5748, 🌐manmandir.co.in), which operates services to a wide range of destinations from its own private terminus – a far cry from the usual bedlam.

GETTING AROUND

By auto-rickshaw Aurangabad's sights lie too far apart to take in on foot. The city is, however, buzzing with auto-rickshaws; longer sightseeing trips work out much cheaper if you settle on a fare in advance (around ₹700/day).

By taxi Taxis can be hailed in the street or found at the

railway station and cars with drivers can be hired through travel agents such as the efficient Classic Travel Services (📞0240 233 7788, 🌐classictravelservicesaurangabad. tripod.com), on the ground floor of the Tourist Reception Centre. Expect to pay around ₹1500/day.

INFORMATION AND TOURS

Tourist Information A booth at the airport (opens to meet incoming flights) provides basic information, while more detailed enquiries are fielded at the Tourist Reception Centre on Station Rd East, where helpful offices of both India Tourism (Mon–Fri 8.30am–6pm, Sat 8.30am–1.30pm; 📞0240 233 1217, 🌐incredibleindia.org) and

MTDC (Mon–Fri plus 1st & 3rd Sat of month 10am–1pm & 1.30–5.45pm; 📞0240 234 3169, 🌐maharashtratourism. gov.in) are on the first floor.

Tour operators Several companies run guided tours of Aurangabad and the surrounding area, all operating similar itineraries and departure times, and all generally rushed. Ellora and City tours usually include the Bibi-ka-Maqbara, Panchakki, Daulatabad Fort, Aurangzeb's tomb at Khuldabad, and the Ellora caves (though not the Aurangabad ones). Ajanta tours go to the caves only, but it's a long round-trip to make in a day – if you want to spend

more time at the site, stay at Fardapur (see page 672) or travel on to Jalgaon (see page 673). Classic Travel Services (see above) runs the best of the tours (₹300–500, excluding entry fees).

ACCOMMODATION

Aurangabad's proximity to some of India's most important monuments, together with its "boom-city" status, ensures a profusion of **hotels**, though standards are variable. For local guesthouses, contact the MTDC.

Amarpreet Jalna Rd ☎0240 233 2521, ⍟amarpreet hotel.com; map p.655. This whitewashed, vaguely Art Deco upper- to mid-range hotel, on a main road just south of the old city, is a reliable choice. Rooms are large and well furnished (if a bit dated), and there's a quality non-veg restaurant and a bar. Good value, especially if you book online. ₹4400

★ **Green Olive** CBS Rd ☎0240 232 9490, ⍟hotel greenolive.com; map p.655. A swish hotel that has set a bench-mark for its competitors: staff are friendly and efficient; the rooms are clean, modern and well equipped (nice toiletries, kettle and so on); there's a great restaurant (try the ₹550 buffet dinner); and rates – particularly if you book online – are very reasonable. ₹4800

Lemon Tree 7/2 Chikalthana ☎0240 660 3030, ⍟lemontreehotels.com; map p.655. Set around a large pool, this is the brightest and cheeriest of the high-end hotels lining the airport road. It has a couple of good restaurants (see below) and the appealing *Slounge* bar. The rate given here is for booking online in advance; rack rates are significantly higher. ₹8600

Manmandir Executive Adalat Rd ☎0240 236 5777, ⍟manmandirmotels.com; map p.655. Well-maintained, low-cost business hotel above a private bus terminus (see above), with a range of sizeable, blandly comfortable rooms (the non-a/c options are particularly good value), plus a reason-able a/c dorm for those on a really tight budget. Dorms ₹300, doubles ₹1500

Panchavati Off Station Rd West ☎0240 232 8755, ⍟hotelpanchavati.com; map p.655. Decent, if unspectacular, hotel on the western edge of the city centre with economical rooms (some with a/c), welcoming staff and a restaurant (whose menu even features a few Korean options). ₹1300

Shree Maya Bharuka Complex, Padampura Rd, off Station Rd West ☎0240 233 3093; map p.655. Friendly and popular place with large, cleanish rooms (some a/c); standards vary, so ask to look at a few. There's also a sociable restaurant with good food. ₹1250

Vivanta Ajanta Rd, 4km north of the centre ☎0240 661 3737, ⍟vivanta.tajhotels.com; map p.655. Part of the Taj group, Aurangabad's most luxurious option is a domed, gleaming-white, wedding-cake confection. Rooms are tastefully finished in dark wood, and all come with bathtubs and a balcony. Facilities include a spa, large pool and croquet on the palm-fringed lawn. ₹8500

EATING

Aurangabad is full of places to eat, with most restaurants serving either strictly vegetarian **Gujarati** food or meat-oriented north Indian dishes. As elsewhere in the state, non-veg places tend to be synonymous with dim lights, drawn curtains and a male clientele – with a few exceptions – while the veg restaurants attract families. **Drinking** is an exclusively male preserve in Aurangabad, usually carried out in the many specially segregated bars (aka "permit rooms"), as well as the larger, more tourist-oriented restaurants and hotels.

Kailash Station Rd East ☎0240 233 8916; map p.655. This pure-veg restaurant serves inexpensive south Indian (including tasty dosas; ₹50–135) and Punjabi food (mains ₹100–150) – plus some so-so Chinese dishes – and is a popular local spot. Daily 9am–11pm.

Republic of Noodles Lemon Tree hotel ☎0240 660 3030; map p.655. If you fancy something a little different, head to this award-winning Southeast Asian restaurant, which has an alfresco dining area by the pool. As well as some classic Thai and Vietnamese dishes, there are a few

more unusual Burmese, Indonesian and Singaporean options. Daily 7am–11pm.

Tandoor Shyam Chambers, Station Rd East ☎0240 232 8481; map p.655. Dominated somewhat surreally by an imposing bust of Egyptian pharaoh Tutankhamun, this travellers' favourite is one of the city's best-established non-veg restaurants. Tandoori chicken and mutton kebabs (₹150-375) are the house specialities, while for monster appetites there's the full-on "sizzling non-veg tandoori platter" (big enough for two; ₹825). Daily 10.30am–4pm & 6.30–11pm.

Thaat Baat Beneath Embassy Hotel, near Vivekanand College, Samarth Nagar Rd ☎0240 233 4666; map p.655. There's a festive air at this fun, family-friendly thali place, where armies of waiters breezily ladle out dollops of tasty pure veg against a backdrop of Rajasthani puppets, paintings and handicrafts. A hearty meal (and soft drink) costs around ₹260. Daily 11am–3.30pm & 7–11pm.

DIRECTORY

Banks and exchange An efficient foreign exchange service is provided at this branch of national chain Trade Wings on CBS Rd (daily 9am–7pm; ☎ 0240 235 7480, ⓦ tradewings.in).

Textiles Aurangabad is famous for its Himroo and Paithani textiles, which are on sale (alongside an array of cheaper imitations) throughout the city; Classic Travel Services runs a tour (see page 658) to the Paithani Weaving Centre.

Ellora

Palaces will decay, bridges will fall, and the noblest structures must give way to the corroding tooth of time; whilst the caverned temples of Ellora shall rear their indestructible and hoary heads in stern loneliness, the glory of past ages, and the admiration of ages yet to come.
Captain Seely, *The Wonders of Ellora*

11

Maharashtra's most visited ancient monument, the **ELLORA** caves, 29km northwest of Aurangabad, may not enjoy as grand a setting as their older cousins at Ajanta, but their amazing wealth of **sculpture** more than compensates – this is an unmissable stop if you're heading to or from Mumbai, 400km southwest. In all, 34 Buddhist, Hindu and Jain caves – some excavated simultaneously, in competition – line the foot of the 2km-long Chamadiri escarpment as it tumbles down to meet the open plains. The site's principal attraction, the colossal **Kailash temple**, rears from a huge, sheer-edged cavity cut from the hillside – a vast lump of solid basalt fashioned into a spectacular complex of colonnaded halls, galleries and shrines.

Brief history

The original reason why this apparently remote spot became the focus of so much religious and artistic activity was the busy **caravan route** that passed through here on its way between the prosperous cities to the north and the ports of the west coast. Profits fuelled a 500-year spate of excavation, beginning midway through the sixth century AD at around the same time that Ajanta, 100km northeast, was abandoned. This was the twilight of the **Buddhist** era in central India; by the end of the seventh century, **Hinduism** had begun to reassert itself. The Brahmanical resurgence gathered momentum over the next three hundred years under the patronage of the Chalukya and Rashtrakuta kings – the two powerful dynasties responsible for the bulk of the work carried out at Ellora, including the eighth-century Kailash temple. A third and final flourish of activity on the site took place towards the end of the first millennium AD, after the local rulers had switched allegiance from Shaivism to the **Jain** faith. A small cluster of more subdued caves to the north of the main group stand as reminders of this age.

Unlike the isolated site of Ajanta, Ellora did not escape the iconoclasm that accompanied the arrival of the **Muslims** in the thirteenth century. The worst excesses were committed during the reign of Aurangzeb who ordered the demolition of the site's "heathen idols". Although Ellora still bears the scars from this time, most of its best pieces of sculpture have remained remarkably well preserved, sheltered from centuries of monsoon downpours by the hard basalt hillside.

The caves

Daily except Tues dawn–dusk • ₹600 (₹40) • If you've come in an auto-rickshaw or a taxi you will also need to buy a ₹15 parking ticket

The **caves** are numbered, following a roughly chronological plan. Numbers 1 to 12, at the southern end of the site, are the oldest, from the Vajrayana Buddhist era (500–750 AD). The Hindu caves, 13 to 29, overlap with the later Buddhist ones and date from between 600 and 870 AD. Further north, the Jain caves – 30 to 34 – were excavated from 800 AD until the late eleventh century. Because of the sloping hillside, most of the cave entrances are set back from the level ground behind open courtyards and large colonnaded verandas or porches.

To see the oldest caves first, turn right opposite Cave 16, the vast Kailash temple, and follow the main pathway down to Cave 1. From here, work your way gradually northwards again, avoiding the temptation to look around Cave 16, which is best saved until late afternoon when the bus parties have all left and the long shadows cast by the setting sun bring its extraordinary stonework to life.

The Buddhist group

The **Buddhist caves** line the sides of a gentle recess in the Chamadiri escarpment. All except Cave 10 are *viharas*, or monastery halls, which the monks would originally have used for study, solitary meditation and communal worship, as well as the mundane business of eating and sleeping. As you progress through them, the chambers grow steadily more impressive in scale and tone. Scholars attribute this to the rise of Hinduism and the need to compete for patronage with the more overtly awe-inspiring Shaivite cave-temples being excavated so close at hand.

Caves 1 to 9

Cave 2 is the first cave of interest, a large central chamber supported by twelve massive, square-based pillars while the aisles are lined with seated Buddhas. The doorway into the shrine room is flanked by two giant, bejewelled *dvarapalas*, or guardian figures: an unusually muscular Padmapani, the *bodhisattva* of compassion, on the left, and an opulent Maitreya, the "Buddha-to-come", on the right. Both are accompanied by their consorts. Inside the sanctum itself, a stately Buddha is seated on a lion throne, looking stronger and more determined than his serene forerunners in Ajanta.

Caves 3 and 4 lack the artifice of Cave 2, though the latter retains some fine capital work. **Cave 5** is the largest single-storey *vihara* in Ellora. Its enormous 36m-long rectangular assembly hall is thought to have been used by the monks as a refectory, and has two rows of benches carved from the stone floor.

Caves 6–9 were excavated at roughly the same time in the seventh century, and are reached via a single door and stairwell cut into the rock. On the walls of the antechamber at the far end of the

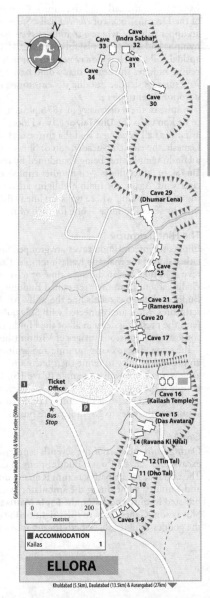

central hall in **Cave 6** are two of Ellora's most famous and finely executed figures: Tara, the buxom female consort of the *bodhisattva* Avalokitesvara, stands to the left; on the opposite side, the Buddhist goddess of learning, Mahamayuri, is depicted with her emblem, the peacock, while a diligent student sets a good example at his desk below. From Cave 6, a short flight of steps leads up to diminutive **Cave 9**, with a fine frieze decorating the facade.

Caves 10, 11 and 12

Excavated in the early eighth century, **Cave 10** is one of the last and most magnificent of the Deccan's rock-cut *chaitya* halls. Steps lead from the left of its large veranda to an upper balcony, where a trefoil doorway flanked by flying threesomes, heavenly nymphs and a frieze of playful dwarfs leads to an interior balcony. Inside the long apsidal hall (which you may need to ask to be unlocked), the rib-vaulting effect on the ceiling imitates the beams that would have appeared in earlier freestanding wooden structures. A slender Buddha sits enthroned in front of a votive *stupa*, the hall's devotional centrepiece.

In spite of the rediscovery in 1876 of its hitherto hidden basement, **Cave 11** continues to be known as the **Dho Tal**, or "Two Floors" cave. Its top storey is a long, columned assembly hall housing a Buddha shrine and, on its rear wall, images of Durga and Ganesh, the elephant-headed son of Shiva – evidence that the cave was converted into a Hindu temple after being abandoned by the Buddhists. **Cave 12** next door – the **Tin Tal**, or "three floors" – is another triple-storey *vihara*, approached via a large open courtyard. Again, the main highlights are on the uppermost level. The shrine room at the end of the hall, whose walls are lined with five large *bodhisattvas*, is flanked on both sides by seven Buddhas – one for each of the Master's previous incarnations.

The Hindu group

Ellora's seventeen **Hindu caves** are grouped around the middle of the escarpment, to either side of the majestic Kailash temple. Excavated at the start of the Brahmanical revival in the Deccan during a time of relative stability, the cave-temples throb with a vitality absent from their restrained Buddhist predecessors. In place of benign-faced Buddhas, huge **bas-reliefs** line the walls, writhing with dynamic scenes from the Hindu scriptures. Most are connected with **Shiva**, the god of destruction and regeneration (and the presiding deity in all of the Hindu caves on the site), although you'll also come across numerous images of Vishnu (the Preserver) and his various incarnations.

The same tableaux crop up time and again, a repetition that gave Ellora's craftsmen ample opportunity to refine their technique over the years leading up to their greatest achievement, the Kailash temple (Cave 16). Covered separately (see page 664), the temple is the highlight of any visit to Ellora, but you'll appreciate its beautiful sculpture all the more if you visit the earlier Hindu caves first. Numbers 14 and 15, immediately south, are the ones to go for if you're pushed for time.

Cave 14

Dating from the start of the seventh century AD, and among the last of the early excavations, **Cave 14** was a Buddhist *vihara* converted into a temple by the Hindus. The entrance to the bare sanctum is guarded by two impressive river goddesses, Ganga and Yamuna, while lining the ambulatory wall behind and to the right, seven heavy-breasted fertility goddesses, the **Sapta Matrikas**, dandle chubby babies on their laps. Shiva's son, Ganesh, sits to their right beside two cadaverous apparitions, Kala and Kali, the goddesses of death. Superb **friezes** adorn the cave's long side walls.

Cave 15

Like its neighbour, the two-storey **Cave 15**, reached via a long flight of steps, began life as a Buddhist *vihara* but was hijacked by the Hindus and became a Shiva shrine. Behind the Natya Mandapa ("Hall of Dance") in the centre of the courtyard, make for the upper level of the main structure to find some of Ellora's most magnificent sculpture. The cave's name, **Das Avatara**, is derived from the sequence of panels along the right wall, which show five of **Vishnu**'s ten incarnations (avatars).

A carved panel in a recess to the right of the antechamber shows Shiva emerging from a lingam. Brahma and Vishnu stand before the apparition in humility and supplication – symbolizing the supremacy of Shaivism in the region at the time the conversion work was carried out. Finally, halfway down the left wall of the chamber as you're facing the shrine, the cave's most elegant piece of sculpture shows Shiva as Nataraja, poised in a classical dance pose.

Caves 17 to 29

Only three of the Hindu caves strung along the hillside north of the Kailash temple are really worth exploring in depth. **Cave 21** – the **Ramesvara** – was excavated late in the sixth century. Thought to be Ellora's oldest Hindu cave, it harbours some well-executed sculpture, including a fine pair of river goddesses on either side of the veranda, two wonderful door guardians and some sensuous loving couples, or *mithunas*, dotted around the walls of the balcony. **Cave 25**, further along, contains a striking image on the exterior ceiling of the main shrine of the sun god **Surya** speeding in his chariot towards the dawn.

From here, the path picks its way past two more excavations, then drops steeply across the face of a sheer cliff to the bottom of a small river gorge. Once under the seasonal **waterfall**, the trail climbs the other side of the gully to emerge beside **Cave 29**, the huge **Dhumar Lena**. Dating from the late sixth century, the cave boasts an unusual cross-shaped floor plan similar to the Elephanta cave in Mumbai harbour. Pairs of rampant lions guard its three staircases while, inside, the walls are covered with huge **friezes**. On the right-hand side of the (southern) entrance, a dice-playing scene shows Shiva teasing Parvati by holding her arm back as she prepares to throw. Left of the exit, Shiva skewers the Andhaka demon, while in the opposite wall panel he foils the many-armed Ravana's attempts to shake him and Parvati off the top of Mount Kailash; look for the cheeky dwarf baring his bum to taunt the evil demon.

The Kailash temple (Cave 16)

Cave 16, the colossal **Kailash temple**, is Ellora's masterpiece. Here, the term "cave" is not only a gross understatement but a complete misnomer. For although the temple was, like the other excavations, hewn from solid rock, it bears a striking resemblance to earlier freestanding structures in south India. The monolith is believed to have been the brainchild of the Rashtrakuta ruler **Krishna I** (756–773). One hundred years and four generations of kings, architects and craftsmen elapsed, however, before the project was completed. Climb up the track leading along the lip of the compound's north-facing cliff to the ledge overlooking the squat main tower, and you'll see why.

The sheer scale is staggering. Work began by digging three deep trenches into the top of the hill using pickaxes and lengths of wood which, soaked with water and stuffed into narrow cracks, expanded to crumble the basalt. Once a huge chunk of raw rock had been exposed in this way, the royal sculptors set to work. In all, around a quarter of a million tonnes of chippings and debris were cut from the hillside, with no room for improvisation or error. The temple was conceived as a giant replica of Shiva and Parvati's Himalayan abode, the pyramidal **Mount Kailash**. Today, all but a few fragments of the thick coat of white-lime plaster that gave the temple the appearance of a snowy mountain have flaked off, to expose elaborately carved surfaces of grey-brown stone beneath. Around the rear of the tower, these have been bleached and blurred by centuries of erosion, as if the giant sculpture is slowly melting in the fierce Deccan heat.

The temple

The main **entrance** to the temple is through a tall stone screen, intended to mark the transition from the profane to the sacred realms. After passing between two guardian river goddesses, Ganga and Yamuna, you enter a narrow passage that opens onto the main forecourt, opposite a panel showing **Lakshmi**, the goddess of wealth, being lustrated by a pair of elephants. Custom requires pilgrims to circumambulate clockwise around Mount Kailash, so descend the steps to your left and head across the front of the courtyard towards the near corner.

From the top of the concrete steps in the corner, all three principal sections of the complex are visible: first, the shrine above the entrance housing Shiva's vehicle, **Nandi**, the bull; next, the intricate recessed walls of the main assembly hall, or **mandapa**, which still bear traces of the coloured plaster that originally coated the whole edifice; and finally, the sanctuary itself, surmounted by the stumpy, 29m pyramidal tower, or **shikhara** (best viewed from above). These three components rest on an appropriately huge raised platform, borne by dozens of lotus-gathering elephants. As well as symbolizing Shiva's sacred mountain, the temple also represented a giant **chariot**. The transepts protruding from the side of the main hall are its wheels, the Nandi shrine its yoke, and the two life-sized, trunkless elephants in the front of the courtyard (disfigured by Muslim raiders) are the beasts of burden.

Most of the main highlights of the temple itself are confined to its side walls, which are plastered with vibrant **sculpture**. Lining the staircase that leads up to the north side of the *mandapa*, a long, lively narrative panel depicts scenes from the Mahabharata, and below this the life of **Krishna**. Continuing clockwise, the majority of the panels around the lower sections around the temple are devoted to **Shiva**. On the south side of the *mandapa*, in an alcove carved out of the most prominent projection, you'll find the finest piece of sculpture in the compound. It shows Shiva and Parvati being disturbed by the multiheaded **Ravana**, who has been incarcerated inside the sacred mountain and is now shaking the walls of his prison with his many arms. Shiva is about to assert his supremacy by calming the earthquake with a prod of his toe. Parvati, meanwhile, nonchalantly reclines on her elbow as one of her handmaidens flees in panic.

From here, head up the steps at the southwest corner of the courtyard to the **Hall of Sacrifices**, with its striking frieze of the seven mother goddesses, the Sapta Matrikas, and their ghoulish companions Kala and Kali (shown astride a heap of corpses). The sixteen-columned assembly hall is shrouded in a gloomy half-light designed to focus worshippers on the presence of the deity within. Using a portable arc light, the chowkidar will illuminate fragments of painting on the ceiling, where Shiva, as **Nataraja**, performs the dance of death.

The Jain group

Ellora's small cluster of four **Jain caves** is north of the main group, just a five-minute walk north along the path from Cave 29 or, alternatively, reachable from the Kailash temple via a curving asphalt road.

Excavated in the late ninth and tenth centuries, after the Hindu phase had petered out, the Jain caves are Ellora's swansong, featuring some fine decorative carving and a few exquisite paintings. Of principal interest is **Cave 32**, the **Indra Sabha** ("Indra's Assembly Hall"), a miniature version of the Kailash temple. The lower of its two levels is plain and incomplete, but the upper storey, guarded by huge *yaksha* and *yakshi* figures facing each other across the veranda, is crammed with elaborate stonework, notably the ornate pillars and the two *tirthankaras* guarding the entrance to the central shrine. The naked figure of Gomatesvara, on the right, is fulfilling a vow of silence in the forest. He is so deeply immersed in meditation that creepers have grown up his legs, and animals, snakes and scorpions crawl around his feet.

The Grishneshwar Mandir

Rising above the small village west of the caves, the cream-coloured *shikhara* of the eighteenth-century **Grishneshwar Mandir** pinpoints the location of one of India's oldest and most sacred deities. The lingam enshrined inside the temple's cavernous inner sanctum is one of the twelve "self-born" **jyotirlingas** ("linga of light"), thought to date back to the second century BC. Non-Hindus are allowed to join the queue for *darshan*, but men have to remove their shirts before entering the shrine itself.

ARRIVAL AND INFORMATION ELLORA

Most visitors use Aurangabad as a base for day-trips to the caves; if you prefer to take in the caves at a more leisurely pace and climb Daulatabad Hill, either spend the night at Ellora or leave Aurangabad early in the morning.

By bus There are regular MSRTC buses (every 30min; 40min) from Aurangabad to Ellora.

By tour Travel agencies in Aurangabad offer tours (see page 658), though these tend to be rather rushed.

By auto-rickshaw/taxi An auto-rickshaw for the round trip from Aurangabad costs about ₹800, including waiting time; a taxi costs around ₹1500.

Guides Official multilingual guides are on hand to take you on a tour of the most interesting caves (groups of up to five people around ₹850).

Tourist information There's a good visitor centre (same opening times as the caves) with displays on the caves, plus temporary exhibitions.

ACCOMMODATION

Apart from the mediocre MTDC canteen inside the complex and the roadside *dhabas* opposite the bus stand, the only place to eat is at the restaurant inside the *Kailas* hotel.

Kailas Opposite the entrance to the caves ☎02437 244543, ⓦhotelkailas.com; map p.661. This small, peaceful hotel has a mix of simple rooms close to the road and smarter cottages (₹4200) facing the caves themselves. There's a decent restaurant, and a range of activities on offer, including trips to local markets, hikes, massages and even paragliding. **₹2750**

Ajanta

Hewn from the near-vertical sides of a horseshoe-shaped ravine, the caves at **AJANTA** occupy a site worthy of the spectacular ancient art they contain. Less than two centuries ago, this remote spot was known only to local tribespeople; the shadowy entrances to its abandoned stone chambers lay buried deep under a thick blanket of creepers and jungle.

The chance arrival in 1819 of a small detachment of East India Company troops, however, brought the caves' obscurity to an abrupt end. Led to the top of the precipitous bluff that overlooks the gorge by a young "half-wild" scout, the tiger-hunters spied what has now been identified as the facade of Cave 10 protruding through the foliage.

The British soldiers had made one of the most sensational archeological finds of all time. Further exploration revealed a total of 28 colonnaded caves chiselled out of the chocolate-brown and grey basalt cliffs lining the River Waghora. More remarkable still were the immaculately preserved **paintings** writhing over their interior surfaces. For, in addition to the rows of stone Buddhas and other **sculpture** enshrined within them, Ajanta's excavations are adorned with a swirling profusion of murals, depicting everything from battlefields to sailing ships, city streets and teeming animal-filled forests to snow-capped mountains. Even if you aren't wholly familiar with the

ROCK-CUT CAVES OF THE NORTHWESTERN DECCAN

The **rock-cut caves** scattered across the volcanic hills of the northwestern Deccan rank among the most extraordinary religious monuments in Asia. Ranging from tiny monastic cells to elaborately carved temples, they are remarkable for having been hewn by hand from solid rock. Their third-century-BC origins seem to have been as temporary shelters for Buddhist monks when heavy monsoon rains brought their travels to a halt. Modelled on earlier wooden structures, most were sponsored by **merchants**, for whom the casteless new faith offered an attractive alternative to the old, discriminatory social order. Gradually, encouraged by the example of the Mauryan emperor Ashoka, the local ruling dynasties also began to embrace Buddhism. Under their patronage, during the second century BC, the first large-scale monastery caves were created at **Karla**, **Bhaja** and **Ajanta**.

THE HINAYANA SCHOOL

Around this time, the austere **Hinayana** ("Lesser Vehicle") school of Buddhism predominated in India. Caves cut in this era were mostly simple worship halls, or **chaityas** – long, rectangular apsed chambers with barrel-vaulted roofs and two narrow colonnaded aisles curving gently around the back of a monolithic **stupa**. Symbols of the Buddha's enlightenment, these hemispherical burial mounds provided the principal focus for worship and meditation, circumambulated by the monks during their communal rituals.

THE MAHAYANA SCHOOL

By the fourth century AD, the Hinayana school was losing ground to the more exuberant **Mahayana** ("Greater Vehicle") school. Its emphasis on an ever-enlarging pantheon of **bodhisattvas** (merciful saints who postponed their accession to nirvana to help mankind towards enlightenment) was accompanied by a transformation in architectural styles. *Chaityas* were superseded by lavish monastery halls, or **viharas**, in which the monks both lived and worshipped, and the once-prohibited image of the Buddha became far more prominent. Occupying the circumambulatory recess at the end of the hall, where the *stupa* formerly stood, the colossal **icon** acquired the 32 characteristics, or **lakshanas** (including long dangling ear-lobes, cranial protuberance, short curls, robe and halo) by which the Buddha was distinguished from lesser divinities. The peak of Mahayana art came towards the end of the Buddhist age. Drawing on the rich catalogue of themes and images contained in ancient scriptures such as the **Jatakas** (legends relating to the Buddha's previous incarnations), Ajanta's exquisite wall **painting** may, in part, have been designed to rekindle enthusiasm for the faith, which was, by this point, already starting to wane in the region.

THE VAJRAYANA SECT

Attempts to compete with the resurgence of **Hinduism**, from the sixth century onwards, eventually led to the evolution of another, more esoteric religious movement. The **Vajrayana**, or "Thunderbolt" sect stressed the female creative principle, **shakti**, with arcane rituals combining spells and magic formulas.

BRAHMANISM

Ultimately, however, such modifications were to prove powerless against the growing allure of Brahmanism. The ensuing shift in royal and popular patronage is best exemplified by **Ellora** where, during the eighth century, many old *viharas* were converted into temples, their shrines housing polished *shivalinga* instead of *stupas* and Buddhas. Hindu cave architecture, with its dramatic mythological **sculpture**, culminated in the tenth century with the magnificent **Kailash temple**, a giant replica of the freestanding structures that had already begun to replace rock-cut caves. It was Hinduism that bore the brunt of the iconoclastic medieval descent of Islam on the Deccan, Buddhism having long since fled to the comparative safety of the Himalayas, where it still flourishes.

narratives they portray, it's easy to see why these paintings are regarded as the finest surviving gallery of art from any of the world's ancient civilizations.

Brief history

Located close enough to the major trans-Deccan trade routes to ensure a steady supply of alms, yet far enough from civilization to preserve the peace and tranquillity necessary for meditation and prayer, Ajanta was an ideal location for the region's itinerant Buddhist monks to found their first permanent monasteries. Donative inscriptions indicate that its earliest cave excavations took place in the second century BC.

In its heyday, Ajanta sheltered more than two hundred monks, as well as a sizeable community of painters, sculptors and labourers employed in excavating and decorating the cells and sanctuaries. Sometime in the seventh century, however, the site was abandoned – whether because of the growing popularity of nearby Ellora, or the threat posed by the resurgence of Hinduism, no one knows. By the eighth century, the complex lay deserted and forgotten, overlooked even by the Muslim iconoclasts who wrought such damage to the area's other sacred sites during the medieval era.

The caves

Tues–Sun 9am–5pm • ₹600 (₹40), "amenities fee" ₹10 • Entry tickets are sold at the booth at the main entrance, a 4km bus ride (a/c bus ₹22, non-a/c bus ₹16 one way) from the Ajanta T-junction

An obvious path leads up from the ticket booth to the grand **Mahayana** *viharas*; if you'd prefer to see the caves in chronological order, however, start with the smaller **Hinayana** group of *chaitya* halls at the bottom of the river bend (caves 12, 10 and 9), then work your way back up, via Cave 17. For help getting up the steps, sedan-chair bearers (around ₹550), or dhooli-wallahs, stand in front of the stalls below, while porters (around ₹200) are on hand to carry bags. Official **guides** make two-hour tours (around ₹1400) which can be arranged through the ticket office; most deliver an interesting spiel but you may well feel like taking in the sights again afterwards at a more leisurely pace.

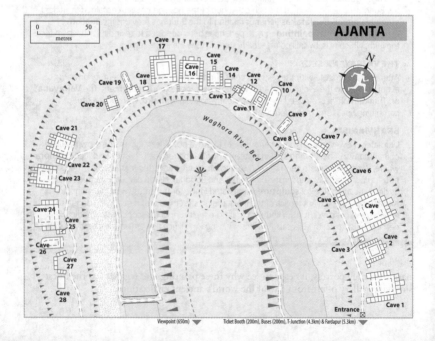

VISITING AJANTA

In spite of its comparative remoteness, **Ajanta** receives an extraordinary number of visitors. If you want to enjoy the site in anything close to its original serenity, avoid coming on a weekend or public holiday – it takes a fertile imagination indeed to picture Buddhist monks filing softly around the rough stone steps when hundreds of riotous schoolchildren and throngs of tourists are clambering over them. Among measures to minimize the impact of the hundreds of visitors who daily trudge through is a ban on flash photography – though the introduction of low-impact lighting has aided close viewing – and strict limits on the numbers allowed into the most interesting caves at any given time. Another significant move to reduce the ecological impact on the area has been the creation of the **Ajanta T-junction** (see page 672).

The best seasons to visit are either during the monsoon, when the river is swollen and the gorge reverberates with the sound of the waterfalls, or during the cooler winter months between October and March. At other times, the relentless Deccan sun beating down on the south-facing rock can make a trip around Ajanta a real endurance test. Whenever you go, take a hat, some sunglasses, a good torch and plenty of drinking water.

11

Cave 1

There's always a queue for **Cave 1**, which contains some of the finest and stylistically most evolved paintings on the site. By the time work on it began, late in the fifth century, *viharas* served not only to shelter and feed the monks, but also as places of worship in their own right. In common with most Mahayana *viharas*, the extraordinary murals lining the walls and ceilings depict episodes from the Jatakas, tales of the birth and former lives of the Buddha.

Left of the doorway into the main shrine stands another masterpiece. **Padmapani**, the lotus-holding form of Avalokitesvara, is surrounded by an entourage of smaller attendants, divine musicians, lovers, monkeys and a peacock. His heavy almond eyes and languid hip-shot *tribhanga* (or "three-bend") pose exudes a distant and sublime calm. Opposite, flanking the right side of the doorway, is his counterpart, **Vajrapani**, the thunderbolt holder. Between them, these two *bodhisattvas* represent the dual aspects of Mahayana Buddhism: compassion and knowledge.

The real focal point of Cave 1, however, is the large sculpted Buddha seated in the shrine room – the finest such figure in Ajanta. Using portable electric spotlights, guides demonstrate how the expression on the Buddha's exquisitely carved face changes according to where the light is held.

On the way out, you should be able to spot this cave's other famous *trompe l'oeil*, crowning one of the pillars (on the fourth pillar on the left as you face the exit): the figures of four apparently separate stags that, on closer inspection, all share the same head.

Cave 2

Cave 2 is another impressive Mahayana *vihara*, dating from the sixth century. Here, the ceiling is decorated with complex floral patterns, including lotus and medallion motifs. Sculpted friezes in the small subsidiary shrine to the right of the main chapel centre on a well-endowed fertility goddess, **Hariti**, the infamous child-eating ogress, and Kubera, the god of wealth. The side walls teem with lively **paintings** of the Jatakas and other mythological episodes. A mural on the left veranda shows the birth of the Buddha, emerging from under his mother's arm, and his conception when a white elephant appeared to her in a dream (bottom left).

Caves 3 to 9

Cave 3 is inaccessible but unfinished **Cave 4**, the largest *vihara* in the complex, is worth a quick look for its 28 pillars and huge Buddha. It's also worth popping into

Cave 6, a two-storey *vihara* with a finely carved doorjamb and lintel around the entrance to its shrine room. Cave 8 is always closed; it contains the generator for the lights.

Cave 9, which dates from the first century BC, is the first *chaitya* you come to along the walkway. Resting in the half-light shed by a characteristic *peepal*-leaf-shaped window in the sculpted facade, the hemispherical **stupa**, with its inverted pyramidal reliquary, forms the devotional centrepiece of the 14m-long hall. The fragments of painting that remain, including the procession scene on the left wall, are mostly superimpositions over the top of earlier snake deities – *nagarajas*.

Cave 10

Although, like Cave 9, marred by the unsightly wire meshing used to keep out bats, the facade of **Cave 10**, a second-century-BC *chaitya* hall – the oldest of its kind in the ravine – is still a grand sight. The cave's main highlights, however, are far smaller and more subdued. Along the left wall, you may be able to pick out the fading traces of painting (now encased in glass) that depict a scene in which a raja and his retinue approach a group of dancers and musicians surrounding a garlanded *bodhi* tree – a symbol of the Buddha (the Hinayanas preferred not to depict him figuratively); it's believed to be the earliest surviving Buddhist mural in India. Elsewhere on the walls is graffiti scrawled by the British soldiers who rediscovered the caves in 1819.

The apsidal-ended hall itself, divided by three rows of painted octagonal pillars, is dominated by a huge monolithic **stupa** at its far end. If there's no one else around, test out the *chaitya*'s amazing acoustics.

Caves 16 and 17

The next cave of interest, **Cave 16**, is another spectacular fifth-century *vihara*, with the famous painting known as the **Dying Princess** near the front of its left wall. The "princess" was actually a queen named **Sundari**, and she isn't dying, but fainting after hearing the news that her husband, King Nanda (Buddha's cousin), is about to renounce his throne to take up monastic orders. The opposite walls show events from Buddha's early life as **Siddhartha**.

Cave 17, dating from between the mid-fifth and early sixth centuries, boasts the best-preserved and most varied paintings in Ajanta. While you wait to enter, have a look at the frescoes on the **veranda**. Above the door, eight seated Buddhas, including Maitreya, the Buddha-to-come, look down. To the left, an amorous princely couple share a last glass of wine before giving their worldly wealth away to the poor. The wall that forms the far left side of the veranda features fragments of an elaborate "Wheel of Life". Inside the cave, the murals are, once more, dominated by the illustrations of the Jatakas, particularly those in which the Buddha takes the form of an animal to illustrate certain virtues. This is also where you'll find the exquisite and much-celebrated portrait of a sultry, dark-skinned princess admiring herself in a mirror while her handmaidens and a female dwarf look on. The chowkidars will demonstrate how, when illuminated from the side, her iridescent eyes and jewellery glow like pearls against the brooding, dark background.

Cave 19

Excavated during the mid-fifth century, when the age of Mahayana Buddhism was in full swing, **Cave 19** is indisputably Ajanta's most magnificent *chaitya* hall, its **facade** teeming with elaborate sculpture. Inside, the faded frescoes are of less note than the sculpture around the tops of the pillars. The standing Buddha at the far end, another Mahayana innovation, is even more remarkable. Notice the development from the stumpier *stupas* enshrined within the early *chaityas* (caves 9 and 10) to this more elongated version. Its umbrellas, supported by angels and a vase of divine nectar, reach right up to the vaulted roof.

CAVE PAINTING TECHNIQUES

The basic **painting techniques** used by the artists of Ajanta to create the caves' lustrous kaleidoscopes of colour changed little over the eight centuries the site was in use, from 200 BC to 650 AD. First, the rough stone surfaces were primed with a thick coating of paste made from clay, cow-dung, animal hair and vegetable fibre. Next, a finer layer of smooth white lime was applied. Before this was dry, the artists quickly sketched the outlines of their pictures using red cinnabar, which they then filled in with an undercoat of *terre-verte*. The **pigments**, all derived from natural water-soluble substances (kaolin chalk for white, lamp soot for black, glauconite for green, ochre for yellow and imported lapis lazuli for blue), were thickened with glue and added only after the undercoat was completely dry. Thus the Ajanta paintings are not, strictly speaking, frescoes (always executed on damp surfaces), but **tempera**. Finally, once dry, the murals were painstakingly polished with a smooth stone to bring out their natural sheen. The artists' only sources of **light** were oil-lamps and sunshine reflected into the caves by metal mirrors and pools of water (the external courtyards were flooded expressly for this purpose), a constraint that makes their extraordinary mastery of line, perspective and shading – which endow Ajanta's paintings with their characteristic otherworldly light – all the more remarkable.

11

Caves 21 to 26

Caves 21 to 26 date from the seventh century, a couple of hundred years after the others, and form a separate group at the far end of the cliff. Apart from the unfinished **Cave 24**, whose roughly hacked trenches and pillars give an idea of how the original excavation was carried out here, the only one worth a close look is **Cave 26**. Envisaged on a similarly grand scale to Cave 19, this impressive **chaitya** hall was never completed. Nevertheless, the sculpture is among the most vivid and sensuous at Ajanta. On the left wall as you enter the cave, the colossal image of **Parinirvarna** (Siddhartha reclining on his deathbed) is the essence of tranquillity. Note the weeping mourners below, and the flying angels and musicians above, preparing to greet the sage as he drifts into nirvana. Two panels down, and in dramatic contrast, the **Temptation of Mara** frieze depicts Buddha ensconced under a *peepal* tree as seven tantalizing sisters try to seduce him. Their father, the satanic Mara, watches from astride an elephant in the top left corner. The ruse to lead the Buddha astray fails, of course, eventually (bottom right) forcing the evil adversary and his daughters to retreat.

The viewpoint

The climb to the **viewpoint** from where the British hunting party first spotted the Ajanta caves is well worth the effort – the panorama over the Waghora gorge and its surrounding walls of bare, flat-topped mountains is spectacular. From the far side of the iron footbridge beneath Cave 8, steps lead up the opposite side of the ravine to a small tin-roofed shelter, where the full majesty of the sheer-sided gorge becomes clear. From here it's a stiff twenty-minute climb straight ahead to the clearly visible viewpoint at the ridge of the hill.

ARRIVAL AND DEPARTURE   **AJANTA**

By bus All MSRTC buses (every 30min; the last one returns around 5pm) between Aurangabad (2hr 30min–3hr), 108km southwest, and the nearest railhead at Jalgaon (1hr), 58km north, stop on request at the Ajanta T-junction, which is 4km from the caves on the main road. Provided that you catch an early enough service up here, it's possible to see the caves, grab a bite to eat, and then head off again in either direction (there are facilities for storing your luggage here).

By taxi A taxi for the round trip from Aurangabad, with waiting time, costs around ₹3000; from Jalgaon you can expect to pay roughly ₹1700.

By tour Travel agencies in Aurangabad offer rather rushed tours (see page 658) of Ajanta.

GETTING AROUND AND INFORMATION

The Ajanta T-junction All vehicles (including taxis and tour buses) must terminate at the Ajanta T-junction, where you'll find a tourist complex with snack joints, toilets and hawker stalls. There is also a very good visitor centre (Tues–Sun 9am–5.30pm) that houses a museum with replicas of four of the caves, plus three restaurants. After paying a ₹10 "amenities fee" to enter the complex, you catch one of the supposedly ecofriendly green buses that regularly ply the route to and from the caves (non-a/c ₹16, a/c ₹22 one way).

ACCOMMODATION

As the first bus from the T-junction to the caves doesn't leave until 9am, there's little advantage in staying locally, though there are some reasonable accommodation options. For food, apart from the uninspiring MTDC dining halls just outside the entrance to the caves and at the *MTDC Ajanta Tourist Resort*, you have a choice of *Padmapani Park*'s pure-veg restaurant and the nearby string of *dhabas* that line the main highway.

MTDC Ajanta Tourist Resort Fardapur ☎02438 244230, ⓦmaharashtratourism.gov.in. Located around 1.5km from the T-junction in the village of Fardapur, this hotel is pretty basic, with spartan rooms with fans or a/c, as well as an unremarkable restaurant. ₹1790

MTDC T-Junction Guest House Close to the tourist complex ☎02438 244230, ⓦmaharashtratourism.gov.in. Set in attractive gardens a short wander from the tourist complex and the bus stop, this faded guesthouse has five spacious, split-level rooms, all a/c, with small verandas. The main drawback is that, apart from the nearby snack stalls, there's nowhere to eat. ₹2016

Padmapani Park Fardapur ☎02438 244280, ⓦhotel padmapaniparkajanta.com. At the edge of Fardapur, a 1km walk from the *MTDC Ajanta Tourist Resort*, is this just-about-adequate, low-cost alternative to the MTDC hotels: rather shabby rooms, but a good restaurant. ₹950

Lonar

Few travellers reach the crater at **LONAR** but those who do find this **meteorite-formed lake** an amazing and tranquil place. Referred to as "Taratirth" in a Hindu legend that correctly claimed it was created by a shooting star, the gigantic hole in the ground was formed about 50,000 years ago when a lump of space rock survived its fiery descent through the atmosphere to bury itself here. As the only such crater formed in basalt rock in the world, the site is not just a geological curiosity but also highly valuable to scientists – NASA has made extensive studies due to its apparent similarity to some lunar and Martian landscapes; though many of the lake's mysteries, such as the extreme alkalinity of its thick, sulphurous water, continue to baffle.

Numerous steep paths lead down to the lake from the rim, the principal one starting around 500m from the *MTDC Holiday Resort* and emerging in the basin near a twelfth-century temple dedicated to Shiva. A complete circuit of the lake, surrounded by forest and home to a rich array of birdlife, takes around three hours. En route you will discover numerous other seemingly lost Shaivite shrines. While huddling along a ravine etched into the crater's northeastern slope – an alternative path back up – is a fascinating cluster of temples, fed by a spring, or *dhar*, supposedly originating from the Ganges. Before leaving, it's well worth searching out the tenth-century Chalukyan **Daitya Sudana** temple in Lonar village, its walls inside and out crawling with a profusion of exquisite carvings of mythological scenes.

ARRIVAL AND INFORMATION

By taxi The easiest way to get to Lonar is by taxi from Aurangabad, which costs around ₹3500 for a day-trip.
By bus There are two morning buses direct from Aurangabad (4hr), with the last bus back around 4pm; services stop in the centre of Lonar village, around 2km from the lake.

Guides For more on the crater, it's worth hiring a local guide; Gajanan Kharat (☎07260 221428) is recommended.

ACCOMMODATION

MTDC Holiday Resort Opposite the crater ☎ 07260 22160, ⓦ maharashtratourism.gov.in. The only accommodation in Lonar is this rather ghostly hotel built for a tourist rush that never came. The attached rooms are comfortable, though uninspiring, but the restaurant has a superbly sited terrace from which to view the lake. ₹2016

Jalgaon

Straddling an important junction on the Central and Western Railway networks, as well as the main trans-Deccan trunk road, NH-6, **JALGAON** is a prosperous market town for the region's cotton and banana growers, and a key jumping-off point for travellers heading to or from the Ajanta caves, 58km south. Even though the town holds nothing of touristic interest, you may find yourself obliged to hole up here to be well placed for a morning departure.

ARRIVAL AND DEPARTURE   JALGAON

By train The railway station, on Station Rd, appropriately enough, is well served by mainline trains between Delhi, Kolkata and Mumbai, and convenient for most cities to the north on the Central Railway. Express services also pass through en route to join the Southeastern Railway.
Destinations Agra (6–7 daily; 14–18hr); Aurangabad (1–3 daily; 4hr 15min–5hr 50min); Bengaluru (1–2 daily; around 24hr); Bhopal (9–10 daily; 7–9hr); Chennai (1-2 daily; 22hr 40min–23hr); Delhi (6 daily; 17hr 15min-21hr 30min); Gwalior (6-7 daily; 12hr 15min–16hr); Mumbai (hourly; 6hr 15min–9hr 20min); Nagpur (11–16 daily; 5hr 10min–8hr 20min); Nasik (20–23 daily; 2hr 30min–4hr); Pune (5–7 daily; 8hr 30min–11hr 10min); Wardha Junction (for Sevagram; 10-16 daily; 5hr 20min–6hr 30min); Varanasi (5–7 daily; 18hr 40min–24hr 40min).
By bus The busy MSRTC Bus Stand is 1.5km across town from the railway station (around ₹40–50 in an auto-rickshaw). There are frequent buses to Aurangabad (every 30min; 3hr 30min–4hr), 160km away, all of which stop at the Ajanta T-junction (1hr). MSRTC also runs buses to Mumbai (1–2 daily; 9–11hr), Nagpur (1–2 daily; 9–10hr) and Pune (4–5 daily; 9–10hr), but preferable are the (generally overnight) buses run by the private companies such as Red Bus (☎ 0257 222 8124, ⓦ redbus.in) and Uncle Travels (☎ 0257 224 1294); tickets can be booked at the travel agents on Station Rd.

ACCOMMODATION AND EATING

★ **Plaza** Station Rd, 2min walk from the railway station ☎ 0257 222 7354, ⓔ hotelplaza_jal@yahoo.com. By far the best place to stay in Jalgaon – in fact one of the best budget hotels in Maharashtra – is this welcoming and very spruce hotel. Immaculately clean rooms feature a cool, white minimalist design; the huge a/c "deluxe" room (₹1200) is particularly good. The owner is very friendly and well informed, and staff will provide tea in your room if you're leaving early in the morning. ₹850

Royal Palace Mahabal Rd, 10–15min auto-rickshaw ride from the railway station ☎ 0257 223 3888, ⓦ hotelroyalpalace.in. The grand marble lobby, decorated with a glitzy chandelier, a reproduction of the *Mona Lisa* and fountain filled with fish, raise expectations that the mid-range rooms fail to match; still, they are comfortable enough, and there's a good restaurant. Book online for a twenty-five percent discount. ₹2950

Nagpur

Capital of the "land of oranges", **NAGPUR** is the focus of government attempts to develop industry in the remote northeastern corner of Maharashtra – most foreign visitors come for business rather than pleasure. In the city itself, the most prominent landmark is the Sitabuldi Fort, standing on a saddle between two low hills above the railway station, though it's closed to the public. North and west of the fort, the pleasantly green Civil Lines district holds some grand Raj-era buildings, dating from the time when this was the capital of the vast Central Provinces region.

ARRIVAL AND DEPARTURE   NAGPUR

Geographically at the virtual centre of India, Nagpur is handily placed for connections all across the country –

though a long way from anywhere.

By plane The airport is around 8km southwest of the centre (around ₹300 by auto-rickshaw, more by taxi).

Destinations Delhi (4 daily; 1hr 30min); Kolkata (3 daily; 1hr 30min); Mumbai (8 daily; 1hr 20min); Pune (3 daily; 1hr 15min).

By train Nagpur's busy central mainline railway station is a short auto-rickshaw (around ₹40–50) ride from the main hotel district along Central Ave. The quickest train to Mumbai is the #12290 *Nagpur CSMT Duronto* (daily 8.40pm; 11hr 25min).

Destinations Bhopal (every 1–2hr; 5hr 15min–8hr 10min); Chennai (9–11 daily; 15hr–19hr 45min); Delhi (every 1–2hr;

13hr 30min–22hr 15min); Hyderabad (6–11 daily; 8hr 25min–11hr 35min); Jabalpur (4–5 daily; 8hr–11hr 10min); Jalgaon (11–16 daily; 5hr 10min–8hr 20min); Kolkata (8-10 daily; 15hr 30min–22hr 15min); Mumbai (every 1-2hr; 11hr-22hr 15min); Nasik (8–10 daily; 9hr 20min–20hr 15min); Pune (3–5 daily; 15hr 10min–27hr 35min); Wardha Junction (for Sevagram; 16–19 daily; around 1hr).

By bus MSRTC buses pull in at the State Bus Stand, 2km southeast of the railway station.

Destinations Aurangabad (6 daily; 12hr); Jabalpur (2–3 daily; 7–8hr); Jalgaon (2–3 daily; 9hr); Pune (4–5 daily; 16hr); Ramtek (every 30min; 1hr 30min); Wardha (every 30min; 2–3hr).

INFORMATION

Tourist information The MTDC tourist office (Mon–Sat 10am–6pm; ☎0712 253 3325, ⓦmaharashtratourism. gov.in) is 2.5km west of the centre on West High Court Rd in Civil Lines, but is only useful for booking accommodation. If you're heading to Madhya Pradesh, you can get information from the helpful MP Tourism office on the fourth floor of the

Lokmat Building, Wardha Rd (Mon–Sat 10am–5pm except 2nd & 3rd Sat of month; ☎0712 244 2378).

Banks and exchange The State Bank of India on Kingsway, near the railway station, changes foreign currency.

ACCOMMODATION AND EATING

Grand Just off Central Ave, around 1km east of the bus stand ☎0712 661 7850. The *Grand* is one of the better budget hotels on Central Ave, though as standards are generally low, this isn't a ringing endorsement. The clean(ish), fan-cooled rooms here are a bit shabby, but OK for a night. ₹800

Naivedhyam 198 Rani Jhansi Chowk, Sitabuldi ☎0712 256 3070. This swish, first-floor restaurant, right in the centre of town, is a Nagpur institution, serving up delicious veg Indian/Chinese food and sizzlers (mains ₹230–350). There are various good-value meal combos, especially at lunchtime (₹240–400). Daily 11am–11pm.

Hotel Peanut Bharti House, 43 Kachipura Garden ☎76209 13141, ⓦpeanuthotel.com. In a relatively peaceful location, the mid-range Peanut offers clean, comfortable, though rather clinical rooms, all with TVs, a/c and private bathrooms. Rates fluctuate, so hunt around

online for the best deal before booking. ₹2200

Pride Wardha Rd, opposite the airport ☎0712 229 1102, ⓦpridehotel.com. One of Nagpur's best top-end hotels, the *Pride* often plays host to visiting cricket teams. The rooms are spacious and well equipped, though some have rather kitsch 1970s-era decor. Facilities include a pool and gym, a clutch of fine cafés/restaurants and an appealing bar. Good online discounts available. ₹5300

Tuli International 1km northwest of the railway station ☎0712 665 3700, ⓦtulihotels.com. Of Nagpur's numerous business-traveller-oriented hotels, this hotel in the quiet Sadar district probably has the most charm; its chandeliered lobby, carpeted corridors and chintzy decor give it an endearingly old-fashioned feel. Rooms are comfort-able and there's a good restaurant, coffee shop and "pub". If you want a bit more luxury, try sister hotel *Tuli Imperial*. ₹4600

Around Nagpur

The trickle of visitors who pass through Nagpur tend to visit en route to Madhya Pradesh, or the Gandhian ashrams at **Sevagram** and **Paunar**, a two-hour journey southwest. The other worthwhile excursion is the ninety-minute bus ride northeast to the hilltop temple complex at **Ramtek**.

Ramtek

The picturesque cluster of whitewashed hilltop temples and shrines at **RAMTEK**, 40km northeast of Nagpur on the main Jabalpur road (NH-7), is one of those alluring apparitions you spy from afar on long journeys through central India. According to the Ramayana, this craggy, scrub-strewn outcrop was the spot where Rama,

Sita and Lakshmana paused on their way back from Lanka. Although few traces of these ancient times have survived, the site's old **paved** pilgrim trails, sacred lake, tumbledown shrines and fine views across the endless plains more than live up to its distant promise.

Ram Mandir and the Kalidas Smarak

Around 4.5km from the bus stand • Kalidas Smarak daily sunrise–sunset • ₹10

On the fringes of the town a flight of stone steps climbs steeply up the side of Ramtek hill to the **Ram Mandir**. Built in 1740, the temple stands on the site of a fifth-century structure, of which only three small sandstone shrines remain. Just beneath the temple complex stands the circular **Kalidas Smarak**, a modern memorial to the great Sanskrit poet, Kalidasa. The pavilion's interior walls are decorated with painted panels depicting scenes from his life and works.

Ambala Lake

Just off the road that runs between the bus stand and the Ram Mandir

Another of Ramtek's sacred sites is Ambala Lake, a holy bathing tank that lies 1.5km along a pilgrims' trail at the bottom of the gully, enfolded by a spur of parched brown hills. Its main attractions are the temples and *ghats* clinging to its muddy banks. More energetic visitors can combine a look with a *parikrama*, or circular tour of the tank, taking in the semi-derelict cenotaphs and weed-choked shrines scattered along the more tranquil north and western shore.

ARRIVAL AND DEPARTURE   RAMTEK

By bus Frequent buses shuttle between Nagpur and Ramtek (every 30min; 1hr 30min). From the bus stand, an auto-rickshaw will take you the 4.5km to the Ram Mandir via Ambala Lake for around ₹200.

Sevagram

9km east of Wardha • **Main ashram compound** Daily 6am–6pm • Free • **Visitors' centre** Daily except Tues 10am–6pm • Free • ☎ 71522 84753, ⓦ gandhiashramsevagram.org

SEVAGRAM, Gandhi's model "Village of Service", is deep in the serene Maharashtran countryside. The Mahatma moved here from his former ashram in Gujarat during the 1936 monsoon, on the invitation of his friend Seth Jamnalal Bajaj. At the centre of the Subcontinent, within easy reach of the Central Railway, it made an ideal headquarters for the national, nonviolent Satyagraha movement, combining seclusion with the easy access to other parts of the country Gandhi needed in order to carry out his political activities.

These days, the small settlement is a cross between a museum and living centre for the promulgation of Gandhian philosophies. Interested visitors are welcome to spend a couple of days here, helping in the fields, attending discussions and prayer meetings, and learning the dying art of hand-spinning. The older ashramites, or *saadhaks*, are veritable founts of wisdom when it comes to the words of their guru, Gandhiji.

Once past the absorbing visitors' centre, which documents Gandhi's life, the real focal point of the ashram is the sublimely peaceful main compound entered a few hundred metres along the road. These modest huts – among them the Mahatma's main residence – have been preserved exactly the way they were when the great man and his disciples lived here in the last years of the Independence struggle. A small shop sells handloomed cloth and other products made on site.

ARRIVAL AND DEPARTURE   SEVAGRAM

By train Wardha Junction railway station, 77km south-west of Nagpur and 9km west of Sevagram, has regular services to/from Nagpur (16-19 daily; around 1hr)and Jalgaon (10-16 daily; 5hr 20min–6hr 30min).

By bus Local buses (every 30min; around 20min) run between Wardha and the crossroads outside the Kasturba Gandhi Hospital, from where it's a 1km walk to the ashram.

Buses also connect Nagpur and Wardha (every 30min; 2–3hr).

By auto-rickshaw An auto-rickshaw from the bus stand to Sevagram and Paunar (see below) costs around ₹350.

ACCOMMODATION

Rustam Bhavan Guest House In the main ashram compound ☏07152 284753, ⊕ghandia shramsevagram.org. If you want to spend some time at the ashram, you can stay in the basic but spotless *Rustam*

Bhavan Guest House, though you will be expected to do a couple of hours' communal work a day. Simple, super-healthy veg meals are on offer. **₹600**

Paunar

Vinoba Bhave's ashram at **PAUNAR**, 3km from Sevagram has a more dynamic feel than its more famous cousin at Sevagram. Bhave (1895–1982), a close friend and disciple of Gandhi, best remembered for his successful Bhoodan, or **land gift**, campaign to persuade wealthy landowners to hand over farmland to the poor, founded the ashram in 1938 to develop the concept of **swarajya**, or "self-sufficiency". Consequently, organic gardening, milk production, spinning and weaving have an even higher profile here than the regular meditation, prayer and yoga sessions. Another difference between this institution and the one up the road is that the *saadhaks* here are almost all female.

In the living quarters, Bhave's old **room** is kept as a shrine. Stone steps lead down from the upper level to a small terrace looking out over the **ghats**, where two small memorials mark the spots where a handful of Gandhi's, and later Bhave's, ashes were scattered onto the river. Every year, on January 30, the *ghats* are inundated with half a million people who come here to mark the anniversary of Gandhi's death.

ARRIVAL AND DEPARTURE
PAUNAR

By bus Paunar can be reached by bus from Wardha (every 30min; 2–3hr); hop off at the old stone bridge, which is close to the ashram.

On foot Alternatively, you can walk the 3km from

Sevagram (see page 675). The path, a cart track that runs over the hill opposite the hospital crossroads, comes out in the roadside village 1km west of the Paunar ashram.

ACCOMMODATION AND EATING

Paunar Ashram 3km from Sevagram ☏07152 288388. As with Sevagram, it is possible to stay in one of the visitors' rooms at the ashram, though you should call in advance

to check there's space. Meals, made from organic, home-grown produce, are available on request. **₹600**

Tadoba Andhari Tiger Reserve

Daily except Tues: March & April 5.30–10am & 3–6.30pm; May & June 5–9.30am & 3.30–7pm; Oct & Nov 6–10am & 2.30–6.30pm; Dec–Feb 6.30–11am & 2–6pm; closed rest of year

Visitor numbers are slowly increasing at the **Tadoba Andhari Tiger Reserve**, 140km south of Nagpur, but it remains a great place to spot a big cat (there are an estimated forty-plus tigers here) without the crowds you get at some of India's other parks. The forests and lakes of the reserve, which spans over 625 square kilometres, are also home to mugger crocodiles, leopards, hyenas, and honey badgers, plus 195 species of bird.

THE AJANTA CAVES

ARRIVAL AND INFORMATION

By car The park is a 2hr drive from Nagpur; a taxi/rental car and driver costs ₹3500–4500.

By bus There are buses (3–4 daily; 3hr 30min–4hr) from Nagpur to the city of Chandrapur, around 5km from the reserve.

Safaris The following prices are all per safari: ₹350 per guide per safari. Vehicle numbers are restricted, so book ahead. Many lodges will do this for you; if not visit ⓦmahaecotourism.gov.in. A range of other activities are available, including hikes in the "buffer zone" around the park, and canoe and boat trips. Book via your lodge.

ACCOMMODATION AND EATING

MTDC Tadoba Moharli gate ☎02168 260318, ⓦmaharashtratourism.gov.in. The best budget option near the park, beside a lake, this lodge has simple, clean but rather austere rooms with either fan or a/c. There's a restaurant and staff can help organize safaris. **₹3500**

Svasara Jungle Kolara gate ☎93700 08008, ⓦsvasararesorts.com. Just 300m from one of the park gates, this top-end resort has twelve luxury suites (each with a private veranda), pool and spa amid expansive grounds. Rates include full board, and the well-informed staff can organize safaris and transfers for you. **₹17,000**

11

The Konkan coast

Despite the gradual appearance of a string of resorts aimed at wealthy urbanites, the coast stretching south from Mumbai, known as the **Konkan**, remains relatively unspoilt. Empty beaches, backed by casuarina and areca trees and coconut plantations, regularly slip in and out of view, framed by the distant Western Ghats, while little fortified towns preserve a distinct coastal culture, with its own dialect of Marathi and fiery cuisine. The number of rivers and estuaries slicing the coast meant that for years this little-explored area was difficult to navigate, but the Konkan railway, which winds inland between Mumbai and Kerala via Goa, now renders it more easily accessible; proposals for a seaplane service from Mumbai have rumbled on for years – check the latest with the MTDC.

Murud-Janjira

The first interesting place to break the journey south is the small port of **MURUD-JANJIRA**, 165km south of Mumbai. A traditional trade centre that once belonged to a dynasty of former Abyssinian slaves known as the Siddis, it still has plenty of attractive wooden houses, some brightly painted and fronted by pillared verandas. The gently shelving beach is wide and generally safe for swimming, though the sea is more inviting further south or north. Currents throughout the region, however, can be strong, and people have drowned here in recent years.

In Murud, the 1661 Kasa Fort sits in the open sea 2km off the beach but cannot be visited, nor can the impressive nineteenth-century palace of the last nawab, which dominates the northern end of the bay. Fine views of the coast and surrounding country-side can be had, however, from the hilltop **Dattatreya Temple**, sporting an Islamic-style tower but dedicated to the triple-headed deity comprising Brahma, Vishnu and Shiva.

Janjira Fort

5km south of Murud · Daily dawn–dusk · Free · Local *hodka* boats (20min) sail to the fort from the Rajpuri jetty, a short auto-rickshaw ride away, though, since they seat twenty and only leave when full, at quiet times you may have to charter the boat yourself (around ₹600)

Just offshore some 5km south of Murud-Janjira stands the imposing sixteenth-century **Janjira Fort**, one of the few the Marathas failed to penetrate, and now a picture of majestic dereliction. The boat trip to the fort is a serene one, and once there you're given an hour so to explore the formidable battlements, though the interior lies mostly in ruins.

ARRIVAL AND INFORMATION

By bus and catamaran or ferry The nearest railhead is Roha, a 2hr bus ride away, which is why most travellers still reach the town via one of the hydrofoil catamarans or regular ferries (roughly hourly; 1hr) from the Gateway of India in Mumbai to Mandawa, on the southern side of Mumbai harbour. Buses meet the boats and shuttle passengers to Alibag (45min), from where you can catch a bus to Murud (every 1–2hr; 2hr). Most direct bus services (every 1–2hr) from Mumbai Central take 6hr; there are also two faster buses (4hr 30min) which must be booked in advance. Buses stop along Murud's main street, Durbar Rd, parallel to the coast.

Banks and exchange Bring enough cash to cover your stay – at the time of writing there was no ATM or currency exchange facilities.

ACCOMMODATION AND EATING

Golden Swan Resort On the edge of town, 1km north of the chowk ☎ 02144 274078, ⟨w⟩ goldenswan.com. This resort is the most comfortable option, with a/c cottages (₹7200) sleeping up to six people and smart a/c rooms (some with views of the sea and the fort); weekend rates (given here) include full board; prices drop by about a third during the week, but only breakfast is included. Bike rental is available. ₹6000

Sea Shell Resort Darbar Rd, next to the police station ☎ 02144 274306, ⟨w⟩ seashellmurud.com. This centrally located, resort-style hotel has decent if rather plain rooms (with fans or a/c) overlooking the sea and a small pool shaded by palm trees, and a restaurant. Staff can arrange dolphin-spotting boat trips. ₹2800

Raigad Fort

100km southeast of Murud-Janjira • Daily 8am-5.30pm • ₹200 (₹15)

Around 100km southeast of Murud-Janjira are the impressive remains of the sixteenth-century **Raigad Fort**. Once the capital of Maratha king Shivaji, the fort was sacked by the British in 1818. Described by some as the "Gibraltar of the East", the fort is perched on top of an 820m rocky hill. It is accessed via some 1450 steps (a 3hr–3hr 30min climb) or a "ropeway" (see below).

ARRIVAL AND DEPARTURE

By taxi Raigad Fort is a challenge to get to without your own wheels; the easiest option is to hire a taxi in Murud-Janjira (around ₹2500–3000 return, with waiting time).

Ropeway If you don't fancy climbing the 1450 odd steps, a ropeway (cable car) runs to the peak (daily 8am--5pm; ₹300 return; ☎ 02145 202122, ⟨w⟩ raigadropeway.com).

Ganpatipule

Some 215km south of Murud-Janjira lies **GANPATIPULE**, a tiny village centred on a modern **Ganapati temple**. Approached via a long covered walkway, the temple is built around a Ganapati *omnar*, a naturally formed – though hardly accurate – image of the elephant god, which attracts thousands of Indian pilgrims each year. Much more impressive is Ganpatipule's spectacular white-sand **beach**, which extends for several kilometres either side of the village. The sea is generally safe for swimming, though you should exercise caution between June and October, when currents can be particularly strong.

ARRIVAL AND DEPARTURE

By train/bus To get to Ganpatipule, either make your way to Ratnagiri (on the Konkan railway and well connected by buses to other cities in the state) and take a local bus (every 30min–1hr; 1hr 30min) the last 32km, or catch one of the direct MSRTC services from Mumbai (1–2 daily; 10hr) or Kolhapur (every 2–3hr; 4hr). Buses usually stop outside the *MTDC Resort*, though at festival times you may be dropped along the main road at the edge of the village, a 1.5km walk or rickshaw ride from the beach.

11

ACCOMMODATION AND EATING

★ **Atithi Parinay** 12km south of Ganpatipule ☎ 90499 81309, ⓦ atithiparinay.com. Owned by an interior designer and her mother, this delightful homestay is a great place to unwind. Choose to stay in a comfortable "Swiss" tent, cottage, bungalow, or very atmospheric treehouse. Home-cooked veg meals are on offer, as are yoga, hiking, beach and river visits, and trips to local palaces, temples and a traditional boat-making centre. ₹5100

MTDC Resort In the centre of Ganpatipule ☎ 02357

235248, ⓦ maharashtratourism.gov.in. Set around neat lawns right at the heart of the village, this state-run resort has reasonable rooms, some with breezy balconies, occupying a row of attractive two-storey villas a stone's throw from the sea; the "Konkani Huts", in a shaded beachside compound a 10min walk north, are poorly maintained and disappointing, however. There's a good restaurant-bar. ₹2750

Malvan, Tarkali Beach and around

In the far south of the Konkan coast, 195km south of Ganpatipule, the scenic town of **MALVAN** is a relaxing place to spend a few days. Just offshore lies the eye-catching Sindhudurg Fort, and 6km to the south is the palm-fringed **Tarkali Beach**, where the Karli River meets the sea. Boat cruises along the river and dive trips to the nearby coral reefs are both popular activities; try the Indian Institute of Scuba Diving and Aquatic Sports (see below); alternatively staff at the *MTDC Tarkali Beach Resort* (see below) can advise on reputable companies (there are several unscrupulous and inexperienced dive shops in and around Malvan).

ARRIVAL AND DEPARTURE

By train/bus The nearest railway station is 40km away in Kudal, from where there are regular buses (every 1–2hr during the day; 1hr). There are also buses to Kolhapur (5–6 daily; 4hr 30min–6hr).
Diving The Indian Institute of Scuba Diving and Aquatic

MALVAN, TARKALI BEACH AND AROUND

Sports has a centre in Tarkali, offering dives (from ₹2500) and a range of PADI courses (from ₹18,000), as well as accommodation: book via Maharashtra Tourism (ⓦ maharashtratourism.gov.in).

ACCOMMODATION AND EATING

★ **Dwarka Homestay** Sawantwadi , 54km southeast of Malvan ☎ 023 6326 6267, ⓦ dwarkahomestay.com. If you want to get away from it all for a few days, head to this charming homestay on a working dairy and fruit farm. Accommodation is simple but comfortable, the food fresh and delicious, and there are plenty of activities on offer, including nature hikes, visits to local potters and bamboo

craftsmen, and fishing trips. ₹2800
MTDC Tarkali Beach Resort Tarkali Beach ☎ 02365 252390, ⓦ maharashtratourism.gov.in. One of the more comfortable options in the area, right on the beach, has attached cabins – large and clean but decorated in the typically unimaginative MTDC style – as well as a decent restaurant serving Indian and Chinese standards. ₹3000

Matheran

The Raj-era hill station of **MATHERAN**, 108km east of Mumbai, is set on a narrow north–south ridge at an altitude of 800m in the Sahyadri Range. From evocatively named viewpoints, at the edge of sheer cliffs that plunge into deep ravines, you can see way across the hazy plains – on a good day, so they say, as far as Mumbai. The town itself, shrouded in thick mist for much of the year, has, for the moment, one unique attribute: cars, buses, motorbikes and auto-rickshaws are banned. That, added to the journey up, on a **miniature train** that chugs its way through spectacular scenery to the crest of the hill, gives the town an agreeably quaint, time-warped feel.

Matheran ("mother forest") has been a popular retreat from the heat of Mumbai since the nineteenth century. These days, few foreign visitors venture up here, and those who do only hang around for a couple of days, to kill time before a flight or to sample the charms of Matheran's colonial-era hotels. The tourist season lasts from mid-September to mid-June (at other times it's raining or misty), and is at its most hectic around Diwali and Christmas, in April and May, and over virtually any weekend. There's really nothing to do but relax, explore the woods on foot or horseback and enjoy the views.

As the crow flies, Matheran is only 6.5km from Neral on the plain below, but the train climbs up on 21km of track with no fewer than 281 curves, said to be among the sharpest on any railway in the world. Sadly, the steam engines that once handled the demanding haul puffed their last in 1980, to be replaced by cast-off diesels from Darjeeling, Shimla and Ooty. The train ride is a treat, especially if you get a window seat, but be prepared for a squash unless you travel first class.

The points and forest walks

Matheran occupies a long, narrow, semicircular plateau, bounded for most of its extent by sheer cliffs. These taper at regular intervals into outcrops, or **points**, revealing through the tree canopy wonderful panoramas of distant hills and plains.

For a quick taster, head south from the main bazaar past *Lords Central* hotel on Matheran's eastern flank to Alexander Point, pressing on beyond it to Chowk Point – the most southerly of the mountain's spurs. This shouldn't take more than a couple of hours return. Another enjoyable route on an old cart track winds around the western rim, past a series of gorgeous British-era bungalows to Louisa, Coronation and Sunset (or Porcupine) points, the last regarded as the choicest place to see the sun go down.

Accurate topographical maps of the mountain and its many paths are all but impossible to come by, although there's a wonderful old British one proudly on display in the dining room of *Lords Central* hotel, which walkers are welcome to consult.

All the viewpoints are walkable, and horses and rickshaws are available (see page 682).

ARRIVAL AND INFORMATION   **MATHERAN**

By train To reach Matheran by rail you must first get to Neral Junction, served by trains from Mumbai (2–3 daily; around 1hr 30min); other trains travel between Mumbai and Karjat, from where you can backtrack to Neral on suburban services. One or two daily fast trains (2hr 40min) travel between Neral and Pune; there are more frequent services between Pune and Karjat. From mid-Oct to mid-June, narrow-gauge trains chug up from Neral to Matheran (2–5 daily; 2hr). During the monsoon services are weather dependent and unreliable. All trains are timed to tie in with incoming mainline expresses, so don't worry about missing a connection if the one you're on is delayed – the toy train should wait. Nevertheless it's worth booking a day in advance at weekends. Matheran railway station is in the town centre on MG Rd, which runs roughly north–south.

By minibus or taxi A taxi from Mumbai (2hr 30min–3hr) to Matheran costs from around ₹2400, one to Pune costs from around ₹2500 (2hr 30min–3hr). Shared taxis and minibuses (both 30min) shuttle regularly between Matheran and Neral. All motorized transport parks at the taxi stand next to the *MTDC Resort* at Dasturi Naka, 2km from central Matheran.

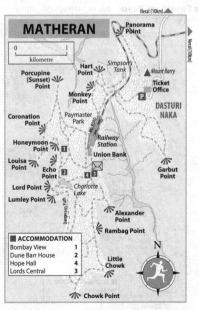

MATHERAN

0 _____ 1
kilometre

Neral (10km)

Panorama Point

Hart Point

Simpson's Tank

Mount Barry

Porcupine (Sunset) Point

Ticket Office

Monkey Point

DASTURI NAKA

Coronation Point

Paymaster Park

Railway Station

Honeymoon Point

Union Bank

Louisa Point

Echo Point

Garbut Point

Lord Point

Charlotte Lake

Lumley Point

Alexander Point

Rambag Point

■ ACCOMMODATION
Bombay View   1
Dune Barr House   2
Hope Hall   4
Lords Central   3

Little Chowk

Chowk Point

Dangerous Path

N

Banks and exchange Neither of Matheran's banks offers foreign exchange, though the ATM at the Union Bank, just south of the station, accepts foreign cards; nevertheless, it is worth bringing some cash with you just in case.

GETTING AROUND

By porter, horse and rickshaw From the taxi stand – after paying the entry toll (₹50 adults, ₹25 children) – you can walk with a porter (around ₹150–300), be led by a rather frail-looking horse (around ₹350) or take a hand-pulled rickshaw (around ₹500) to your hotel; you are expected to haggle. If you're happy to carry your own bags, follow the rail tracks, which cut straight to the middle of Matheran, rather than the more convoluted dirt road. Trips to the town's various viewpoints cost from ₹350 by horse and ₹500 by rickshaw.

ACCOMMODATION

Matheran has plenty of **hotels**, though all are pricey – particularly at weekends, when rates almost double (book ahead), and during peak periods when they become astronomical. Most are near the railway station on MG Rd. Note that 10–11am checkouts are standard, and many places close down during the rainy off-season. The town's hoteliers almost universally refuse beds to "stags" (single male travellers). Most places only have hot water in the morning. Many provide **full** or **half-board** at reasonable rates; there are also numerous thali joints near the station.

Bombay View Southwest of Paymaster Park, 1.5km from the station ☎ 02148 230453, ⊕ bombay viewhotelmatheran.com; map p.681. Housed in a huge converted colonial-era mansion and annexe, this establishment is a notch pricier than the more basic places down by the station, but just about worth the extra. The rooms are dated, but most have plenty of space, as well as forest or garden views. Gujarati and Jain food is on offer. ₹3500

★ **Dune Barr House** 2km southwest of station ☎ 02148 230810, ⊕ dunewellnessgroup.com; map p.681. Hidden away in the woods, just above Charlotte Lake, this sumptuously restored nineteenth-century bungalow is reason enough to visit Matheran. As well as period decor and furnishings, its greatest asset is a huge west-facing veranda smothered in foliage – one of the most perfect spots in India for lunch (₹600) or afternoon tea and biscuits (though beware the pilfering monkeys). ₹7700

Hope Hall MG Rd, opposite Lords Central ☎ 99691 25299, ⊕ hopehallmatheran.com; map p.681. Situated at the quiet end of town and open since 1875, *Hope Hall* has decent-sized, clean, attached "small" and "large" rooms (sleeping up to four and five people respectively; the better ones come with high ceilings and a shared veranda) scattered across a secluded yard. Badminton and table-tennis facilities available. ₹2750

Lords Central MG Rd ☎ 02148 230228, ⊕ matheran hotels.com; map p.681. Though worn at the edges – its wonky verandas, poinsettias, hard beds and tasty (and copious) set meals give it the feel of a 1930s boarding house – eccentric, Raj-era *Lords* is one of Matheran's best-loved institutions, thanks in no small part to its irreverent, anecdote-loving Parsi owners. It also boasts spectacular views from its poolside terrace garden. ₹4750

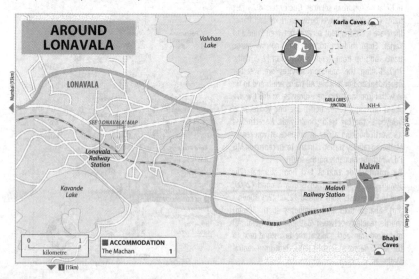

AROUND LONAVALA

N

Karla Caves

Valvhan Lake

Mumbai (93km)

LONAVALA

KARLA CAVES JUNCTION

NH-4

Pune (54km)

SEE LONAVALA MAP

Lonavala Railway Station

Malavli

Kavande Lake

Malavli Railway Station

Pune (54km)

MUMBAI – PUNE EXPRESSWAY

Bhaja Caves

0   1
kilometre

■ ACCOMMODATION
The Machan   1

▼ 1 (15km)

VISITING BHAJA AND KARLA

The two sites lie some 6km apart, to the east of Lonavala, and can be covered by bus and/or train in a day, if you are prepared for a good walk (bring plenty of water), though it is easier to hire an **auto-rickshaw** (around ₹600) or taxi (around ₹1500) for the tour, both of which can usually be found at Lonavala railway station. Avoid weekends if you want to enjoy the caves in peace; Karla, in particular, gets swamped with noisy day-trippers to its Hindu shrine.

Lonavala and around

Forty years ago, **LONAVALA** (also spelt Lonavla), 110km southeast of Mumbai and 62km northwest of Pune, was a quiet town in the Sahyadri Hills. Since then, the place has mushroomed to cope with hordes of weekenders and second-home owners from the state capital, and is now only of interest as a base for the magnificent **Buddhist caves** of **Karla** and **Bhaja**, some of the finest rock-cut architecture in the northwest of the Deccan region. Though not as impressive as Ajanta and Ellora, they have some beautifully preserved ancient sculpture.

11

Bhaja

9km east of Lonavala • Daily 9am-6pmpm • ₹200 (₹15) • Local trains run roughly hourly from Lonavala (20–30min) to Malavli railway station, 2km from the caves; from here follow the road south of the station until it peters out (1.5km), from where it's a steep 10min climb up to the caves

The excavations at **caves** at **BHAJA** are among India's oldest, dating from the late second to early first century BC, during the earliest, Hinayana, phase of Buddhism. You enter the complex opposite Bhaja's apsidal **chaitya** hall, which contains a *stupa* but no figures. Its 27 plain bevelled pillars lean inwards, mimicking the style of wooden buildings, and sockets in the stone of the exterior arch reveal that it once contained a wooden gate or facade. Most of the other caves consist of simple halls – *viharas* – with adjoining cells that contain plain shelf-like beds; many are fronted by rough verandas. Further south, beyond a mysterious dense cluster of fourteen **stupas**, the veranda of the **last cave**, a *vihara*, is decorated with superb carvings, which scholars have identified as the figures of the Hindu gods, Surya and Indra.

Karla

3km north of the Karla Caves junction on the Mumbai–Pune road and 11km from Lonavala • Daily 9am–5.30pm • ₹150 (₹15) • Three morning buses (generally 9am, 10am & 11.30am; 30min) head for the caves directly from Lonavala, with the last bus returning from Karla at 5pm

The rock-cut Buddhist *chaitya* hall at **KARLA** (also Karli), reached by steep steps that climb 110m, is the largest and best preserved in India, dating from the first century AD. Though partially obstructed by a modern Hindu temple housing a shrine to Ekviri, the enormous 14m-high facade of the hall, topped by a horseshoe-shaped window, is still an impressive sight. To the left of the entrance stands a *simhas stambha*, a tall column capped with four lions, while in the porch of the cave, dividing its three doorways, are panels of figures in six couples,

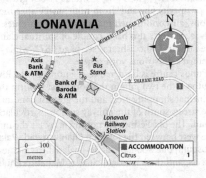

presumed to have been the wealthy patrons of the hall. With their expressive faces and sensuous bodies, it's hard to believe these figures were carved around two thousand years ago.

Two rows of octagonal columns with pot-shaped bases divide the interior into three, forming a wide central aisle and, on the outside, a hall that allowed devotees to circumambulate the monolithic *stupa* at the back. Above each pillar's fluted capital kneel a pair of finely carved elephants, each mounted by two riders, one with arms draped over the other's shoulders. Amazingly, some of the timber rafters supporting the arched roof appear to date from the time when the hall was in use.

ARRIVAL AND DEPARTURE

By bus The Central Bus Stand is just off the old Mumbai–Pune road, but the train is an infinitely preferable way to travel.

By train The railway station is in the south of town, a

10min walk from the bus stand. Lonavala is on the main railway line between Mumbai (every hour or so; 2hr–2hr 30min) and Pune (every hour or so; around 1hr), and most express trains stop here.

ACCOMMODATION

With the odd exception, Lonavala's limited accommodation offers poor value, mainly because demand well outstrips supply for much of the year. **Rates** drop between Oct and March. Numerous shops sell the local sweet speciality, **chikki** – a moreish amalgam of nuts, seeds or coconut set in rock-solid jaggery.

Citrus D Shahani Rd, a 5min auto-rickshaw ride from the bus or railway station ☎02114 279531, ⓦcitrushotels.com; map p.683. Slick, business-traveller-focused hotel, somewhat incongruously tucked into a sleepy backstreet. The minimalist rooms are arranged within lemon-fragranced blocks. There's a

spa, tiny cinema, chic courtyard, and excellent Italian/ Mediterranean restaurant. **₹7000**

The Machan Jambulne, 17km south of Lonavala ☎95940 53113, ⓦthemachan.com; map p.682. Easily the best place to stay in the area (for those with deep pockets), the *Machan* is an "off-grid" (all the electricity is generated by solar and wind power) ecofriendly resort in a rural location surrounding by 25 acres of grounds. Accommodation is provided in luxurious treehouses high above the canopy, making them a haven for birders, as well as in a charming cabin. Massages are available and rates include half-board. **₹14,600**

Pune

At an altitude of 598m, the sophisticated city of **PUNE** (sometimes anglicized as Poona), Maharashtra's second largest, lies close to the Western Ghat mountains (known here as the Sahyadri Hills), on the edge of the Deccan plains as they stretch away to the east. Capital of the Marathas' sovereign state in the sixteenth century, its rulers were deposed by the Brahmin Peshwa family. Pune was – thanks to its cool, dry climate – chosen by the British in 1820 as an alternative headquarters for the Bombay Presidency. Since the colonial days, Pune has continued to develop as a major industrial city and is one of India's fastest growing business and tech centres. Signs of prosperity abound, from multistorey apartment blocks and gated estates, to coffee shops, air-conditioned malls and hip boutiques. Pune, recently voted India's most "liveable city", also has a couple of spiritual claims to fame: Koregaon Park is home to the famous Osho ashram (see page 687), while on the outskirts is *yogarcharya* BKS Iyengar's illustrious yoga centre.

Pune's centre is bordered to the north by the **River Mula** and to the west by the **River Mutha** – the two join in the northwest to form the Mutha-Mula, at Sangam Bridge. The principal shopping area, and the greatest concentration of restaurants and hotels, is in the streets south of the railway station, particularly Connaught and, further south, **MG Road**. The old Peshwa part of town, by far the most interesting to explore, is towards the west between the fortified **Shaniwarwada Palace** and fascinating **Raja Dinkar Kelkar Museum**; old wooden *wadas* – palatial city homes – survive on these narrow, busy streets, and the Victorian, circular **Mahatma Phule Market** is always a hive of activity.

Raja Dinkar Kelkar Museum

1378 Shukrawar Peth • Daily 9.30am–5.30pm • ₹200 (₹50) • ☎ 020 2446 1556

Dinkar Gangadhar Kelkar (1896–1990), aside from being a celebrated Marathi poet published under the name Adnyatwasi, spent much of his life travelling and collecting arts and crafts from all over the country. In 1975, he donated his collection to the Maharashtran government for the creation of a museum dedicated to the memory of his son, Raja, who died at the age of 12. Housed in a huge old-town mansion, the **Raja Dinkar Kelkar Museum** is a wonderful potpourri in which beauty and interest is found in artistic and everyday objects, though the sheer scale of the collection – 21,000 pieces strong – means that only a fraction can be shown at any one time. Paraphernalia associated with *paan*, the Indian passion, includes containers in every conceivable design: some mimic people, animals or fish, others are egg-shaped and in delicate filigree.

Also on show are musical instruments, superb Marathi and Gujarati textiles and costumes, domestic shrines, puppets, ivory games and a model of Shaniwarwada Palace; while curiosities include a suit of fish-scale armour, a collection of intricate noodle-makers and an entire cabinet full of "erotic nut cutters".

11

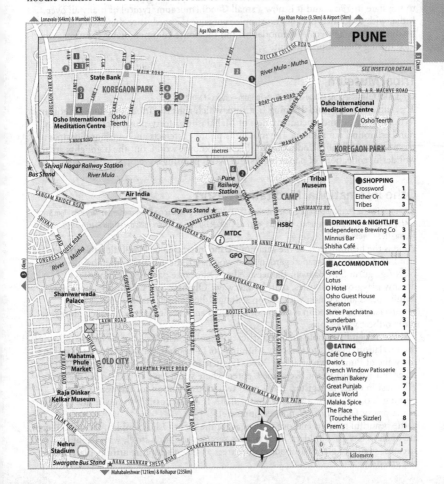

Lonavala (64km) & Mumbai (150km)

Aga Khan Palace (3.5km) & Airport (5km)

Aga Khan Palace

PUNE

DECCAN COLLEGE ROAD

River Mula - Mutha

SEE INSET FOR DETAIL

State Bank

MAIN ROAD

KOREGAON PARK

BOAT CLUB ROAD

DR. A.R. MACHVE ROAD

BUND GARDEN ROAD

Osho International Meditation Centre

Osho International Meditation Centre

Osho Teerth

Osho Teerth

S MAIN ROAD

MANGALDAS ROAD

KOREGAON ROAD

KOREGAON PARK

0   500
metres

Shivaji Nagar Railway Station

Bus Stand

River Mula

Pune Railway Station

SASOON RD

Tribal Museum

●SHOPPING

Crossword	1
Either Or	2
Tribes	3

SANGAM BRIDGE ROAD

Air India

CONNAUGHT ROAD

GARDEN ROAD

CAMP

ABHIMANYU RD.

SHIVAJI ROAD

DR BABASAHEB AMBEDKAR ROAD

City Bus Stand

SANJAY GANDHI RD.

MTDC

DR ANNIE BESANT PATH

HSBC

■DRINKING & NIGHTLIFE

Independence Brewing Co	3
Minnus Bar	1
Shisha Café	2

CONGRESS HOUSE ROAD

River Mutha

MOLEDINA (AMBEDKAR) ROAD

GPO

■ACCOMMODATION

Grand	8
Lotus	5
O Hotel	2
Osho Guest House	4
Sheraton	7
Shree Panchratna	6
Sunderban	3
Surya Villa	1

Shaniwarwada Palace

GURUDWARA ROAD

MAJ J. SHASTRI ROAD

JAWAHARLAL NEHRU PATH

PANDIT RAMABAI ROAD

MAHATMA GANDHI (MG) ROAD

LAXMI ROAD

SHIVAJI ROAD

BOOTEE ROAD

Mahatma Phule Market

OLD CITY

MAHATMA PHULE ROAD

PANDIT NEHRU ROAD

●EATING

Café One O Eight	6
Dario's	3
French Window Patisserie	5
German Bakery	2
Great Punjab	7
Juice World	9
Malaka Spice	4
The Place (Touché the Sizzler)	8
Prem's	1

BAJIRAO ROAD

Raja Dinkar Kelkar Museum

TILAK ROAD

BHAVANI MALA MAN DIR PATH

N

Nehru Stadium

SHANKARSHETH ROAD

0   1
kilometre

Swargate Bus Stand

NANA SHANKAR SHESH ROAD

Mahabaleshwar (121km) & Kolhapur (235km)

Shaniwarwada Palace

1km north of the Kelkar Museum • **Palace** Daily 8am–6pm • ₹200 (₹15) • **Sound-and-light show** Daily except Tues 8pm

In the centre of the oldest part of town only the imposing high walls of the **Shaniwarwada Palace** survived a huge conflagration in 1828. The chief residence of the Peshwas from 1732 until it was captured by the British in 1817, the building has little to excite interest today, though there's a **sound-and-light show** in English. The entrance is through the Delhi gate on the north side, one of five set into the perimeter wall, whose huge teak doors come complete with nasty elephant-proof spikes. The interior of the palace is now grassed over, the seven-storey building entirely absent.

Aga Khan Palace and Gandhi Memorial

5km northeast of the city centre • Daily 9am–5.30pm • ₹300 (₹20) • An auto-rickshaw costs around ₹100–120 from the city centre

In 1942, Mahatma Gandhi, his wife Kasturba and other key figures of the freedom movement were interned at the grand **Aga Khan Palace**, which is set in quiet leafy gardens across the river, 5km northeast of the centre. The Aga Khan donated the palace to the state in 1969, and it is now a small **Gandhi museum**, typical of many all over India, with captioned photos and simple rooms unchanged since they were occupied by the freedom fighters. A **memorial** behind the house commemorates Kasturba, who died during their imprisonment.

Tribal Museum

Koregaon Rd, 1.5km east of the railway station • Daily 10.30am–5.30pm • ₹200 (₹10)

The Tribal Research and Training Institute, which runs the **Tribal Museum**, is dedicated to the protection and documentation of Maharashtra's forty-plus tribal groups, who number around ten million. The museum's photos, artefacts and outdoor dioramas serve as an excellent introduction to this little-known world, but the highlights are the wonderful collections of dance masks and Worli paintings.

Osho International Meditation Resort

17 Koregaon Park Rd, 2km northeast of the railway station • ☎ 020 2401 9999, ⊕ osho.com • **Welcome Center** Daily 9am–1pm & 2–4pm • Registration for first-time visitors ₹1560, one-day pass ₹1890 (₹970), spa/pool entry ₹320/day • **Osho Teerth** Daily 6–9am & 3–6pm • Free with day-pass

Pune is the headquarters of the infamous **Osho International Meditation Resort**. Set amid 28 acres of landscaped gardens and woodland, the ashram of the now-deceased New Age guru, Shri Bagwan Rajneesh, aka "Osho" (see page 687), comprises a dreamy playground of cafés, marble walkways, Olympic-size swimming pool, spas, tennis courts and clinics, with a shop selling Osho paraphernalia. Courses at its multiversity are offered in a variety of therapies and meditation techniques, alongside more offbeat workshops.

This ecofriendly bubble follows a strict door policy, with security beefed up following the revelation of visits to Osho by Mumbai 26/11 conspirator **David Headley**, and in the wake of Pune's own attack in 2010. If you're interested in taking a course, you must take your passport to the Welcome Center, where you'll have to take an on-the-spot HIV test in order to register. You'll need **two robes** (maroon for daywear, white for evenings), on sale at the ashram's "mini-mall". It is also possible to stay inside the resort at the pricey *Osho Guest House* (see opposite).

The beautiful gardens laid out to the east of the main Osho complex, the **Osho Teerth**, are open to day-pass holders. They make a serene place for a stroll, with babbling streams, stands of giant bamboo, mature trees and Zen sculpture artfully placed amid the greenery.

OSHO

It is almost half a century since followers began to congregate around **Bhagwan Rajneesh** (1931–90), the self-proclaimed New Age guru better known to his tens of thousands of acolytes worldwide as **Osho**. Underpinned by a philosophical mishmash of Buddhism, Sufism, sexual liberation, Tantric practices, Zen, yoga, hypnosis, Tibetan pulsing, disco and unabashed materialism, the first Rajneesh ashram was founded in Pune in 1974. It rapidly attracted droves of Westerners, and some Indians, who adopted new Sanskrit names and a uniform of orange or maroon cottons and a bead necklace (*mala*) with an attached photo of the enlightened guru, in classic style, sporting long greying hair and beard.

FULFILMENT, UTOPIANISM AND TAX EVASION

Few early adherents denied that much of the attraction lay in Rajneesh's novel approach to fulfilment. His dismissal of Christianity ("Crosstianity") as a miserably oppressive obsession with guilt struck a chord with many, as did the espousal of liberation through sex. Rajneesh assured his devotees that material comfort was not to be shunned. Within a few years, satellite ashrams were popping up throughout Western Europe, and by 1980 an estimated 200,000 devotees had liberated themselves in 600 meditation centres across 80 countries.

To protect itself from pollution, nuclear war and HIV/AIDS, the organization poured money into a utopian project, **Rajneeshpuram**, on 64,000 acres in Oregon, US. It was at this point that the media really got interested in Rajneesh, now a multimillionaire. Infiltrators leaked stories of strange goings-on at Rajneeshpuram and before long its high-powered female executives became subject to police interest. Charges of tax evasion, drugs, fraud, arson and a conspiracy to poison several people in a neighbouring town to sway a local election vote provoked further sensation. Although he claimed to know nothing of this, Rajneesh pleaded guilty to breaches of US immigration laws and was deported in 1985. Following protracted attempts to resettle in 21 different countries, Rajneesh returned home to Pune, where he died in 1990, aged 59.

POST-RAJNEESH

The ashram went through internal squabbles and financial trouble in the 1990s. At his death, Rajneesh appointed an inner circle to manage the group, though several departed and the Osho "brand" – which sells millions of books each year, supplemented by CDs, DVDs, paintings and photos – is now controlled from Zurich and New York. The Pune ashram wasn't seeing enough of this to meet its costs and consequently has had to relaunch and restyle itself and the pattern of life inside its walls; in its heyday an average stay was three to six months, today people typically stay no more than two weeks.

It was partly due to Osho's enduring popularity with foreigners that the nearby *German Bakery*, Koregaon Park's erstwhile hippie hangout, was targeted for a Mumbai-style terrorist attack in February 2010, which left seventeen dead and around sixty injured – a huge shock for this normally peaceful little enclave. Resolutely, the café itself reopened in 2013 (see page 689).

The 2018 Netflix documentary *Wild Wild Country* provides an illuminating insight into Osho, particularly the controversial Rajneeshpuram years.

ARRIVAL AND DEPARTURE   PUNE

Pune is very well connected, but demand for seats on planes, trains and buses far exceeds supply; book onward transport as soon as you can.

BY PLANE

Lohagaon airport Pune's airport, 10km northeast of the city centre, is a major hub, with regular direct flights to cities throughout India. It's a 15–30min journey to/from the city centre, depending on traffic; a taxi costs ₹300–500. A new international airport is in the pipeline, with work due to begin in 2019.

BY TRAIN

Pune railway station The railway station is in the centre of the city, south of the river; an auto-rickshaw to/from Koregaon Park costs around ₹70–90. It is one of the last stops for numerous long-distance trains to and from Mumbai, so rail services are excellent – despite many of them departing in the early morning; some terminate at Dadar or (worse still) Kurla, so always check first. Some services are much more convenient than others (see box below). Reservations for all trains should be made as far in advance as possible online, via a travel agency or at

TRAINS TO AND FROM PUNE

Of the myriad rail services feeding in and out of Pune, the following are recommended as the fastest and/or most convenient:

Destination	Name	No.	Frequency	Departs	Arrives
Bengaluru	*Vivek Express*	#19568	Fri	10.30pm	4.04pm+
Chennai	*Chennai Express*	#12163	Daily	00.10am	7.45pm
Delhi	*Jhelum Express*	#11077	Daily	5.20pm	8.26pm +
Goa	*Goa Express*	#12780	Daily	4.35pm	5.40am+
Hyderabad/ Secunderabad	*Shatabdi Express*	#12025	Daily except Tues	5.50am	1.39pm
Kolhapur	*Sahyadri Express*	#11023	Daily	10.05pm	6.05am
Mumbai	*Deccan Queen Express*	#12124	Daily	7.15am	10.03am

+ next day

the reservation centre next to the station itself (Mon–Sat 8am–8pm, Sun 8am–2pm).

Destinations Bengaluru (6–8 daily; 17hr 30min–25hr 15min); Chennai (3–4 daily; 19hr 30min–24hr); Delhi (2–4 daily; 19hr 34min–28hr); Ernakulam (for Kochi; 1–2 daily; 27hr 50min–33hr 40min); Hyderabad/Secunderabad (5–9daily; 9hr–13hr 20min); Jalgaon (5–7 daily; 8hr 30min–11hr 10min); Kolhapur (5–6 daily; 6hr 50min–8hr); Lonavala (roughly hourly; 1–2hr); Magdaon (for Goa; 1-2 daily; 12hr 25min-17hr 20min); Mumbai (1–2 hourly; 2hr 30min–5hr); Nagpur (3–5 daily; 15hr 10min–27hr 35min)); Nasik (1 daily; 6hr 20min).

BY SHARED TAXI

For Mumbai, 24hr shared taxis leave from agencies at the taxi stand in front of Pune railway station – they're quicker than the buses, but only take you as far as Dadar.

BY BUS

Pune has three main bus stands. If you're unsure which

station you require for your destination, ask at the enquiries hatch of the City Bus Stand or at the MTDC counter at the railway station. More comfortable private buses depart from offices throughout Pune; tickets can be bought from travel agencies in Koregaon Park.

City Bus Stand Next to the railway station, City Bus Stand is split into two sections, one serving Pune itself (with signs and timetables only in Marathi), the other for destinations south and west. Regular buses to Mumbai (via Lonavala) also leave from here.

Destinations Goa (3–4 daily; 11hr); Kolhapur (hourly; 5–6hr); Mahabaleshwar (hourly; 3hr 30min–4hr); Mumbai (every 15min; 3hr 15min).

Swargate and Shivaji Nagar stands The Swargate Bus Stand, about 5km south, close to Nehru Stadium, services Karnataka and some of the same destinations as City, while the stand next to Shivaji Nagar railway station, 3km west of the centre, runs buses every 30min to points north, such as Aurangabad (5hr) and Nasik (4–5hr).

INFORMATION

Tourist information The MTDC Tourist Office (Mon–Fri plus 1st & 3rd Sat of month 10am–-5.45pm; ☎020 2612 6867, ⍟maharashtratourism.gov.in) is inside "I" block of Central Building (enter between Ambedkar Chowk and Sadhu Vaswani Circle). It also has an information counter (officially the same times) opposite the railway station's first-class booking office and at the airport (opens to meet incoming flights).

ACCOMMODATION

Top-end hotels are springing up all over Pune, but there's a chronic shortage of budget and mid-range places, which explains why prices are high and vacancies like gold dust: book as far in advance as possible.

Grand MG Rd, near the Dr Ambedkar statue ☎020 2636 0728; map p.685. Set behind a dimly lit beer garden, the colonial-era *Grand* doesn't live up to its name, but is an acceptable budget choice: the high-ceilinged doubles in the rear annexe are pretty clean, though scruffy; the bathroomless, wood-partitioned singles, however, are best avoided. ₹1000

Sheraton RBM Rd, just northwest of the railway station ☎020 6641 1111, ⍟marriott.com; map p.685. Previously under the *Le Meridien* banner, this vast cathedral of marble still feels like its most opulent and luxurious. Spacious rooms come with thick honey-coloured carpets and huge beds; the rooftop bar (complete with two-tiered pool) is one of the city centre's most heavenly spaces for an evening drink and is open to non-guests. Rates vary wildly online, and there are often good deals to be had. ₹11,600

Lotus Plot No. 356, Lane No.5, Koregaon Park ☎020 2613 9701; map p.685. In an unassuming salmon-pink block in tranquil, leafy surroundings, this is Koregaon's Park's best-value hideaway. Bright, clean rooms with big windows, comfy beds and balconies. A basic breakfast (included) is served to the rooms, and the location is handy for the city's best restaurants/bars. ₹2700

★ **O Hotel** North Main Rd ☎020 4001 1000, ⓦohotels india.com; map p.685. Goa chic in Pune: outside, a forbidding sandstone-coloured tower block; inside, a designer playground of bold textures, shades and shapes. Rooms are suitably Zen-like, blending simple lines and stylish details with warm, muted tones and natural materials, and facilities include a gorgeous spa and spectacular rooftop infinity pool and bar, plus Indian and Japanese restaurants. ₹7200

Osho Guest House Osho International Meditation Resort, 17 Koregaon Park Rd ☎020 6601 9900, ⓦosho. com; map p.685. Part of the Osho ashram, and open only to attendees, this luxury hotel offers stylish minimalist rooms – though be warned that the hotel is situated above the main auditorium, which, as the ashram likes to put it, can make the 6am meditation session "very hard to resist". Room rates do not include the various registration and pass fees (see page 687). ₹5900

Shree Panchratna 7 Tadiwala Rd ☎020 2605 9999, ⓦhotelshreepanchratna.in; map p.685. Aimed at business travellers and located on a quiet side-street close to the railway station, *Shree Panchratna* is well maintained and efficiently run, if unexciting. The plain rooms all have a/c, kettles, mini-fridges, and a fresh feel; some also have balconies (though no views). There are a couple of onsite restaurants, too. ₹4200

Sunderban 19 Koregaon Park ☎020 2612 4949, ⓦtghotels.com; map p.685. Attractive Art Deco mansion, set behind an immaculate expanse of lawn, and sited beside the Osho ashram. The older rooms in the main house, furnished in swathes of leather and acres of teak and mahogany, are better value than those in the flashier modern garden block; there are often discounts April–Sept. There's a great Italian restaurant (see below) and a spa. ₹4000

Surya Villa 294/1 Koregaon Park ☎020 2612 4501; map p.685. Under the same management as *Lotus* (see above) and slightly cheaper, *Surya Villa* has sizeable if somewhat spartan rooms (with fans or a/c) spread over four floors in a suburban block close to Osho. It's very popular, mainly with long-staying foreign ashramites, and has a good restaurant filled with traveller favourites. ₹2100

EATING

Pune's affluent young things have money to burn these days, and new, innovative places to eat and drink open up every month to relieve them of their tech salaries, the largest concentration of them up at the eastern end of Koregaon Park. Booking is advisable at the smarter places at weekends. In addition to those listed below, several of the hotels have good restaurants, including *Surya Villa* and *O Hotel* (see above); *Shisha Café* (see page 670) also has excellent food.

★ **Café One O Eight** Precious Gem, Lane 6, Koregaon Park ☎90118 04770, ⓦfacebook.com/oneoeightcafe; map p.685. Hip Aussie-style café and yoga studio that's an easy place to while away a few hours. As well as excellent coffee – including a proper flat white – smoothies and fresh juices, there are top-notch all-day-breakfast options, toasted sandwiches (including one with Vegemite), inventive bruschettas and pasta dishes. The food's mostly organic and there are plenty of veggie, vegan and gluten-free options. Daily 7am–10pm.

Dario's Sunderban ☎020 2605 3597, ⓦdarios.in; map p.685. A tranquil, Italian veg restaurant with a lovely patio filled with plants and birdsong. The food – sandwiches, a huge range of salads, risottos, pastas and pizzas, plus crêpes, waffles and pastries for breakfast – is pretty authentic, and it is a great place for a glass of wine or a proper espresso or cappuccino. Mains ₹470–650. Daily 8am–11.30pm.

French Window Patisserie Bungalow 4 Lane 5, Koregaon Park ☎976 6644 202, ⓦfacebook.com/ thefrenchwindowpatisserie; map p.685. This cosy spot is a great choice for a sweet treat at any time of day. In addition to flaky croissants, cream-filled choux buns and decadent cakes, this gem serves savoury snacks and meals (₹125–440), as well as excellent coffee and hot chocolate (₹150–330). Daily 9am–11pm.

German Bakery 291 Koregaon Park ☎020 3939 5552; map p.685. Open again after the 2010 terrorist attack (see page 687), *German Bakery* is a good spot throughout the day with breakfast options, main meals ranging from thin-crust pizzas to bangers and mash, and – of course – plenty of cakes, including *sachertorte* (a rich chocolate cake) and lamingtons. On the downside, it's right on the main road, and the music choices can be questionable. Daily 7.30am–11.45pm.

Great Punjab 5 Jewel Tower, Lane 5, Koregaon Park ☎020 2614 5060; map p.685. One of Koregaon Park's most popular north Indians, offering generous kebabs, grills and tandoori dishes – and a long list of cocktails and spirits – in smart if subdued surroundings. Dedicated carnivores should sample the *karela* kebab, a mountain of succulent tandoori chicken stuffed with a robust mix of minced meat and herbs. Daily 11am–11pm.

Juice World 2436/B East Street Camp ☎ 020 2611 4318; map p.685. Freshly squeezed fruit juices, milkshakes and *faloodas* (₹65–250) are the mainstay of this buzzing haunt just east of the top of MG Rd; lychee, *chikoo* and musk melon are some of the more unusual flavours on offer. It also serves piping-hot snacks and meals such as stuffed *paratha*, tangy Bombay-style *pao bhaji*, and biryani. Daily 11am–11pm.

Malaka Spice Lane 5, Koregaon Park ☎ 07507 486969, ⓦ malakaspice.com; map p.685. This Southeast Asian specialist serves up pretty authentic stir-fries, curries and noodle dishes in arty surroundings. It's relaxed at lunchtime and intimate in the evening when the candlelit covered veranda and garden terrace twinkle with fairy lights. It's also a good spot for a drink. There are a couple of other branches, but this is the most convenient. Daily 11.30am–midnight.

The Place (Touché the Sizzler) 7 Moledina Rd ☎ 020 2613 4632; map p.685. Huge, succulent sizzlers (veg, fish, pork, mutton or beef; ₹350–480), steaks, fish and chips, and veal escalope are among the house specialities of this Parsi-run old-timer in the city centre (somewhat bizarrely, the founder of the restaurant later opened a sizzler restaurant on the Isle of Man). Daily 11.30am–3.30pm & 7–10.45pm.

Prem's Main Rd, Koregaon Park ☎ 020 2615 0081, ⓦ facebook.com/PremsResto.Pune; map p.685. Tucked away from the main road, this cool, modern restaurant-bar is a hit for both its spot-on Indian and Chinese dishes (there are also a few decent Continental options) and its range of beers (including draught Hoegaarden) and spirits – plus "detox" drinks if you've overindulged. Mains ₹325–600. Daily 8am–11pm.

DRINKING AND NIGHTLIFE

Independence Brewing Co 79/1, Zero One Complex, Pingale Vasti, Mundhwa ☎ 020 2688 1500, ⓦ facebook. com/Indebrewco; map p.685. At the forefront of Pune's burgeoning craft beer scene, this swish microbrewery-run bar has an excellent range of bottles and pints, plus good snacks, live sport and a highly convivial atmosphere. Daily 1pm–1.30am.

★ **Minnus Bar** O Hotel ☎ 020 4001 1000, ⓦ ohotels india.com; map p.685. High over the cityscape, the O's lantern-lit rooftop bar is Pune's most elegant spot for a sundowner. Sink into a low-slung white-cushioned sofa, settle onto a beanbag or dip your toes in the infinity pool as you choose from an enterprising list of cocktails (around

₹650–900; beers are cheaper) and soak up the views. Daily noon–11.30pm.

★ **Shisha Café** ABC Farms, Koregaon Park ☎ 020 2688 0050, ⓦ facebook.com/shishajazzcafe; map p.685. One of Pune's most congenial watering holes: a cavernous restaurant-bar filled with plants and capped with a huge thatched roof hung with Persian carpets. Indo-Iranian food, notably kebabs (mains ₹350–650) dominate the menu, and they serve a good range of beers, wines and spirits, plus hookahs and Turkish coffee. The walls are lined with posters of jazz greats, and live jazz and blues bands often play in the evenings. Daily 11am–midnight.

SHOPPING

The Koregaon Park area has several quality – if pricey – clothes and craft shops, especially in the area between Lane 7 and Lane 5. For less expensive options – and a considerably more bustling environment – head to the streets south of the railway station, especially Connaught, which have a wide range of shops and stalls.

Crossword Koregaon Park Plaza mall, Main Rd ☎ 020 6704 0225, ⓦ crossword.in; map p.685. This bookshop chain has numerous stores around town: this one, on the second floor of the mall, is one of the most convenient. It has an extensive range of English-language fiction and non-fiction. Mon–Fri 11am–9pm, Sat–Sun 11am–9.30pm.

Either Or 24 Sohrab Hall, Sassoon Rd ☎ 020 2605 7225, ⓦ facebook.com/eitherorindia; map p.685. This classy shop is an excellent place for souvenir shopping, with an extensive range of textiles, jewellery, household furnishings, crafts and music. Daily 10.30am–8pm.

Tribes Kamdhenu Building, Senepati Bapat Marg ☎ 020 2566 5289, ⓦ tribesindia.com; map p.685. This government-backed shop stocks a wide range of crafts and artworks – including paintings, pottery, textiles, home furnishings and food items – that have been produced by the country's tribal groups. Daily 10am–7pm.

DIRECTORY

Banks and exchange For changing currency, Thomas Cook is at 13 Thacker House, just off General Thimmaya Rd (☎ 020 2634 6171, ⓦ thomascook.in).

Post office The efficient GPO is on Sadhu Vasavani (Connaught) Rd.

Mahabaleshwar and around

The former capital of the Bombay Presidency, the hill station of **MAHABALESHWAR**, 250km southeast of Mumbai, is easily reached from Pune, 120km northeast. The highest point in the Western Ghats (1372m), it is subject to extreme **weather** conditions. Early June brings heavy mists and a dramatic drop in temperature, followed by a deluge of biblical proportions. Tourists tend only to visit between October and early June; during April and May, at the height of summer, the place is packed.

For most foreign visitors, Mahabaleshwar's main appeal is its location midway between Mumbai and Goa, but it has some good **hiking trails**, and a boating lake, and is close to the Pratapgadh fort (see below). Otherwise, the main activity is to amble up and down the pedestrianized **main bazaar** (Dr Sabne Road) and graze on the locally grown **strawberries** for which the town is famous.

Pratapgadh

Around 24km west of Mahabaleshwar • Daily dawn–dusk • Free • Taxis charge around ₹1000 for the return trip to Pratapgadh, with waiting time; state buses (1hr) also do the journey each day, leaving the bus stand around 9.30am and returning around 11am

The seventeenth-century fort of **PRATAPGADH** stretches the full length of a high ridge affording superb views over the surrounding mountains. Reached by a flight of five hundred steps, it is famously associated with the Maratha chieftain, **Shivaji**, who lured the Mughal general Afzal Khan here from Bijapur (now Vijayapura) to discuss a possible truce. Neither, it would seem, intended to keep to the condition that they should come unarmed. Khan attempted to knife Shivaji, who responded by killing him with the gruesome *wagnakh*, a set of metal claws worn on the hand. Today visitors can see Afzal Khan's tomb, a memorial to Shivaji, and views of the surrounding hills.

ARRIVAL AND INFORMATION

MAHABALESHWAR AND AROUND

By bus The State Bus Stand is at the northwest end of the bazaar. There are regular MSRTC buses to/from Mumbai (5–6 daily; around 7hr), Pune (every 30min–1hr; 3hr 30min) and Kolhapur (4–5 daily; 5hr 30min), and one to Panaji in Goa (12hr); for the latter, numerous agents in the bazaar sell tickets for more comfortable private buses.

Entry fees There is a ₹20 entry fee for visitors, collected at toll booths at each end of town.

GETTING AROUND

By taxi Auto-rickshaws are banned in Mahabaleshwar but taxis line up at the west end of the bazaar, charging ₹50–100 for short hops in and around town.

By bike Bikes can be rented from a stall at the *Dreamland* hotel (see below).

ACCOMMODATION

Despite an abundance of hotels, at peak times prices in Mahabaleshwar are well above average. Room rates are a moveable feast, particularly at the lower end of the scale, but fall roughly into three categories: peak months are April and especially May, when as at Diwali, Christmas and New Year, rates at the cheaper places double or even treble and the place is well worth avoiding. Prices quoted are for off-season, which broadly covers most of the rest of the year, bar long weekends ("mid-season"). The cheapest places to stay are on the Main Bazaar and the road parallel to it, Murray Peth. Two points to note: hoteliers in Mahabaleshwar refuse to take in single male travellers ("stags"), and many places close during the monsoon.

Dreamland Below the State Bus Stand ☎02168 260228, ⊛hoteldreamland.com. Large, well-established hotel surrounded by extensive gardens. Rooms range from simple "cottages" to spacious a/c rooms with stupendous views. There's a pool, Jacuzzi and sauna, café and pure-veg restaurant. Prices drop during the week. **₹5000**

MTDC Holiday Resort 2km southwest of the centre ☎02168 260318, ⊛maharashtra.gov.in. A sprawling campus with a wide choice of accommodation, ranging from austere economy rooms through high-ceilinged standard rooms to family-sized suites (₹2600), in a peaceful location; a 10min walk from Mumbai Point. **₹1500**

11

EATING AND DRINKING

Grapevine Western end of Masjid Rd, which is parallel with the main bazaar ☎ 02168 261100. For something a bit different, make for the idiosyncratic *Grapevine*, where a decent list of wines, beers and spirits complements a delightfully eclectic (if expensive) menu ranging from Parsi home-cooking to lamb burgers and fish and chips (mains from ₹180). Daily 9.30am–3pm & 6–10.30pm.

Kolhapur

KOLHAPUR, on the banks of the River Panchaganga 225km south of Pune, is thought to have been an important centre of the Tantric cult associated with Shakti worship since ancient times. The city probably grew around the sacred site of the present-day **Mahalakshmi temple**, still central to the life of the city, although there are said to be up to 250 other shrines in the area. Today it is a major industrial centre, but has retained enough Maharashtran character to make it worthy of a stopover.

Mahalakshmi temple

In the centre of the old town, overlooking the town square • Daily dawn–10.30pm • Free

The **Mahalakshmi temple**, whose cream-painted sanctuary towers embellish the centre of Kolhapur's old town, is thought to have been founded in the seventh century, though what you see today dates from the early eighteenth century. The devout queue around the block from the complex's east gate for *darshan* at the image of the goddess Mahalakshmi, beneath the largest of five domed towers; tourists are welcome to join them.

Rajwada (Old Palace)

Near the Mahalakshmi temple • No fixed opening times • Free

The **Rajwada**, or Old Palace, is still occupied by members of the former ruling Chhatrapati family, though its entrance hall is usually busy with worshippers to its Bhawani temple – you can access it by passing under the pillared porch that extends out into the town square.

Wrestling pit (motibaug)

Close to the Rajwada • **Wrestler training** June–Sept daily except Sat 6–9am & 4–6pm • Free

Kolhapur is famous as a centre for traditional wrestling, or *kushti*. On leaving the Old Palace gates, turn right and head through the low doorway in front of you, from where a path picks its way past a couple of derelict buildings to the *motibaug*, or **wrestling pit**. You can watch wrestlers training; matches take place at the nearby **Khasbag Maidan** stadium.

New Palace

Shahaji Chhatrapati, 2km north of the town centre • Tues–Sun 9.30am–1pm & 2.30–6pm • ₹100 (₹25)

The maharaja's **New Palace** was built in 1884, following a fire at the Rajwada. Designed by Major Mant, founding father of the Indo-Saracenic school of so much British colonial architecture, it fuses Jain and Hindu influences with local touches from the Rajwada while remaining indomitably Victorian, with a prominent clock tower. The present maharaja lives on the first floor, while the ground floor houses the **Shahaji Chhatrapati Museum**, a dozen or so rooms crammed with fascinating memorabilia that demonstrates above all else the Chhatrapati family's extraordinary history of bloodlust: among the maharaja's collection of portraits, costumes, embroidery, riding paraphernalia and old Raj-era photos is an astonishing array of swords (including one that belonged to Mughal emperor Aurangzeb), rifles and torture equipment, a gruesome display cabinet of a huntsman's homeware – fans fashioned from tails, an elephant's-foot table – and, in the final room, a scandalous Who's Who of stuffed endangered species. Rather less macabre is the spectacular church-like Durbar Hall, with its superb carvings and mosaic floor.

ARRIVAL AND INFORMATION   KOLHAPUR

By train The railway station is 400m west from the bus stand on Station Rd, near the centre of town. There are services to Pune (5–6 daily; 6hr 50min–10hr) and Mumbai (3 daily; 9hr 40min–11hr 40min).

Tourist information The MTDC tourist office (Mon–Fri plus 1st & 3rd Sat of month 10am–5pm; ☎0231 269 2935, ⍟maharashtratourism.gov.in) is on Assembly Rd, a 15min walk north of the railway station (ask locally for the Collector's Office).

ACCOMMODATION AND EATING

There's no shortage of decent, good-value **accommodation** in Kolhapur, which is famous for its fiery **cuisine**. In addition to the hotel restaurants – notably *Woodland* and *Padma* – there are good, inexpensive places to eat around Station Square.

Padma Guest House Near Padma Talkies, Laxmipuri ☎0231 264 1387, ⍟padmakolhapur.com. A reliable budget hotel with decent rooms (all with private bathrooms and TVs) and an excellent restaurant specializing in Kolhapuri cuisine – the tongue-tingling mutton curries are not to be missed. ₹600

Tourist Station Rd ☎0231 265 0421, ⍟hoteltourist. co.in. The pick of a row of welcoming mid-range hotels a few minutes' walk east of the bus stand. Rooms (all are attached; a/c costs about ₹650 extra) are unfussy but large and well maintained; ask for one away from the road. It has veg and non-veg restaurants, and a "permit room" (bar). 24hr checkout. ₹1500

★ **Woodland** 204 "E" Ward, Tarabai Park ☎0231 265 0941, ⍟hotelwoodland.net. Decent-value and welcoming mid-range hotel, in a peaceful suburb 2km north of the railway and bus stations. It has spacious and bright a/c rooms, plus a terrific non-veg garden/veranda restaurant, *Sunderban*, and a bar. 24hr checkout. ₹4000

11

Goa

FISHERMEN ON COLVA BEACH

Goa

The former Portuguese enclave of Goa, midway down India's southwest coast, has been a holiday destination since colonial times, when British troops and officials used to travel here from across the country for a spot of "R&R". Back then, the three Bs – bars, brothels and booze – were the big attractions. Now it's the golden, palm-fringed beaches spread along the state's 105km coastline that pull in the tourists – around two million of them each winter. Cheap air travel has made it a major package tour destination for Europeans, and there has been a dramatic rise in the number of newly-affluent domestic visitors in recent years. Luckily, in spite of the increasing chaos of Goa's main resorts, it's still possible to find the odd quiet corner if you're prepared to explore and can avoid the busy Christmas/New Year period. If you know where to go, Goa can still be a wonderful place.

Serving as the linchpin for a vast trade network for more than 450 years, Goa was Portugal's first toehold in Asia. However, when the Portuguese empire began to flounder in the seventeenth century, so too did the fortunes of its capital. Cut off from the rest of India by a wall of mountains and hundreds of kilometres of unnavigable alluvial plain, it remained apart from the wider Subcontinent until 1961, when the exasperated prime minister, Jawaharlal Nehru, finally gave up trying to negotiate with the Portuguese dictator, António de Oliveira Salazar, and sent in the army.

It was shortly after the "Liberation" (or "Occupation" as some Goans still regard it), that the first **hippie travellers** came to the region on the old overland trail. They found a way of life little changed in centuries: back then Portuguese was still very much the lingua franca of the well-educated elite, and the coastal settlements were little more than fishing- and coconut-cultivation villages. Relieved to have found somewhere culturally undemanding to party, the travellers got stoned, watched the mesmeric sunsets over the Arabian Sea and danced like lunatics on full-moon nights. The rave scene reached its peak in the 1990s, with "Goa trance" becoming a fully-fledged musical genre.

Since then, the state has been at pains to shake off its reputation as a druggy drop-out zone, although the dance music scene is still very much in evidence, and its beaches have grown in popularity year on year. Around two dozen stretches of soft white sand indent the region's coast, from spectacular 25km sweeps to secluded palm-backed coves. The level of development behind them varies a great deal; while some are lined by swanky Western-style resorts, the most sophisticated structures on others are palm-leaf shacks.

Which beach you opt for largely depends on what sort of holiday you have in mind. Developed resort towns such as **Calangute** and **Candolim** in the north, and **Colva** and **Benaulim** in the south, offer more accommodation than elsewhere. **Anjuna**, **Vagator** and **Chapora**, where places to stay are generally harder to come by, are the places to aim

---

BEST TIME TO VISIT

The best time to come to Goa is during the dry, relatively cool **winter months** between late November and mid-March. At other times, either the sun is too hot for comfort, or the humidity, clouds and rain make life miserable. During peak season, from mid-December to the end of January, the weather is perfect, with temperatures rarely nudging above 32°C. Finding a room or a house to rent at that time, however – particularly over Christmas and New Year when tariffs double, or triple – can be a real hassle.

PALACIO DO DEÃO, IN SOUTHERN GOA

Highlights

❶ **Old Goa** The belfries and Baroque church facades looming over the trees on the banks of the Mandovi River are all that remain of this once splendid colonial city. See page 707

❷ **Saturday Night Market, Arpora** Cooler and less frenetic than the flea market at Anjuna, with appealing goods for sale and a fun atmosphere. See page 718

❸ **Flea market, Anjuna** Goa's famous tourist bazaar is the place to pick up the latest party gear, shop for souvenirs and watch the crowds go by. See page 719

❹ **Aswem** The hippest spot on the north Goan coast to swim, fine-dine and dance under the stars, with the stars. See page 726

❺ **Palacio do Deão** An extravagant, painstakingly restored colonial-era mansion in south Goa, where you can eat lunch on a leafy garden terrace. See page 734

❻ **Beach shacks** Tuck into a fresh kingfish, lobster or tandoori pomfret, washed down with an ice-cold beer. See page 738

❼ **Sunset stroll, Palolem** Tropical sunsets don't come much more romantic than at this idyllic palm-fringed cove in the hilly deep south. See page 740

HIGHLIGHTS ARE MARKED ON THE MAP ON PAGE 698

for if you've come to Goa to party. However, the bulk of budget travellers taking time out from tours of India end up around **Palolem** in the far south, beyond the reach of the charter transfer buses – though be warned that it too has become a major resort over the past decade, attracting literally thousands of long-stay visitors in peak season. For a quieter scene, you could head for **Patnem**, just over the headland from Palolem, or **Agonda**, further up the coast, where development is limited to a string of more

GOA

MAHARASHTRA

KARNATAKA

ARABIAN SEA

N

HIGHLIGHTS

1. Old Goa
2. Saturday Night Market, Arpora
3. Flea market, Anjuna
4. Aswem
5. Palacio do Deão
6. Beach shacks
7. Sunset stroll, Palolem

0   20
kilometres

KARNATAKA

FESTIVALS IN GOA

With its diverse cultural mix, Goa's festivals range from Christian and Hindu celebrations to hedonistic parties and arty events. The **Christmas and New Year** period attracts many thousands to electronic dance music parties – of which Sunburn is the largest. Outside this period, however, less touristy, more authentic draws – Carnival or Narkasur Parades, for example – go to show that Goa is not all beaches and western dance music.

Goa Carnival (Pre-Lent). Four-day party held throughout the state with parades of colourful floats surrounded by masked revellers (especially in Panjim) as well as live music and street stalls.

Shigmotsav/Gulalotsav (March). Goa's answer to Holi; the state's biggest spring festival. Huge dance troupes perform folk dances in the streets through the night.

Sao Joao (24 June). A Catholic festival celebrated around the world, as a tribute to St John the Baptist. In Goa it occurs during the monsoon season and is marked by colourfully-dressed devotees jumping into drinking wells.

Damodar Saptah (August). More than a hundred years old, this 7-day festival sees thousands of street vendors from across India descend on Vasco de Gama as well as processions, traditional dances and devotional singing.

Narkasur Parades (Oct; eve of Diwali). A festival unique to Goa, when giant demon effigies (*narkasurs*) dance through the streets before being burned to mark the festival of lights. The main parades are in Panjim (see page 702), Margao (see page 732), Mapusa (see page 712), Vasco and Ponda.

International Film Festival of India (IFFI) (Late Nov; ⓦiffi.nic.in). A lively, glittering, contemporary event held in Panjim.

St Francis Xavier's Feast (Dec 3). Ceremonies to commemorate the saint's death attract thousands of pilgrims to Old Goa (see page 707).

Mary Immaculate Conception Church Feast (Early Dec). One of the major festivals in Panjim (see page 702), this three-day event sees street stalls set up around the church, and firework displays.

Christmas/New Year (Dec 25/Jan 1). Celebrated in Goa more than anywhere else in the country. The state heaves with foreign and domestic tourists set to party – and accommodation prices can double or triple.

Sunburn (Dec 27–30; ⓦsunburn.in). The biggest techno/house party of the year in Goa (if not Asia) at five arenas in Vagator. See page 722.

12

upmarket "hut" camps and family guesthouses. The only place where the **hippie scene** endures to any significant extent is **Arambol**, in the far north of the state, where you can dip in to any number of yoga sessions and holistic therapies between spells on the beach.

Some 10km from the state capital, **Panjim**, the ruins of the former Portuguese capital at **Old Goa** are foremost among the attractions away from the coast – a sprawl of Catholic cathedrals, convents and churches that draw crowds of Christian pilgrims from all over India. Another popular day-excursion is to Anjuna's Wednesday **flea market**, a sociable place to shop for souvenirs and dance gear. In the south, the district of Salcete, and its main market town, **Margao**, is also littered with distinctively hybrid buildings in the form of Portuguese-era mansions, churches and seminaries. Finally, wildlife enthusiasts may be tempted into the interior to visit the nature reserves at **Cotigao** and **Netravali** in the far south.

Brief history

Goa's sheer inaccessibility by land has always kept it outside the mainstream of Indian history; on the other hand, its control of the seas and the lucrative spice trade made it a much-coveted prize for rival colonial powers. Until a century before the arrival of the Portuguese, Goa had belonged for more than a thousand years to the kingdom of the **Kadamba** dynasty. They, in turn, were overthrown by the Karnatakan Vijayanagars, the Muslim Bahmanis, and Yusuf Adil Shah of Bijapur, but the capture of the fort at Panjim by **Afonso de Albuquerque** in 1510 signalled the start of a Portuguese occupation that was to last 451 years.

Goa Dourada ("Golden Goa")

As the colony expanded, its splendid capital (dubbed as "Goa Dourada", or "Golden Goa", due to its incredible prosperity) came to hold a larger population than Paris or London. Though the king of Bijapur laid siege for ten months in 1570, and the Marathas came very close to seizing the region, the greatest threat came from other European maritime nations, principally Holland and France. Meanwhile, conversions to **Christianity**, started by the Franciscans, gathered pace when St Francis Xavier founded the **Jesuit** mission in 1542. The Portuguese Inquisition also introduced laws that censored literature and banned any faith other than Catholicism. Hindu temples were destroyed, and converted Hindus adopted Portuguese names, such as Da Silva, Correa and De Sousa, which remain common in the region. Thereafter the Portuguese colony, whose trade monopoly had been broken by its European rivals, fell into a gradual decline which was hastened by the unhealthy, disease-ridden environment of its capital.

"Liberation"

Despite certain moves towards independence, such as the restoration of Hindus' right to worship and the final abolition of the dreaded Inquisition in 1820, the nineteenth century saw widespread civil unrest. During the British Raj many Goans moved to Bombay, and elsewhere in British India, to find work.

The success of the post-Indian Independence Goan struggle for freedom owed as much to the efforts of the Indian government, which cut off diplomatic ties with Portugal, as to the work of freedom fighters such as **Menezes Braganza** and **Dr Cunha**. After a "liberation march" in 1955 resulted in a number of deaths, the state was blockaded. Trade with Bombay ceased, and the railway was cut off, so Goa set out to forge international links, particularly with Pakistan and Sri Lanka: that led to the building of Dabolim Airport, and a determination to improve local agricultural output. In 1961, Prime Minister Jawaharlal Nehru finally sent in the armed forces. Mounted in defiance of a United Nations resolution, "**Operation Vijay**" met only token resistance, and the Indian army overran Goa in two days. Thereafter, Goa (along with Portugal's other two Indian enclaves, Daman and Diu) became part of India as a self-governing **Union Territory**, with minimum interference from Delhi. In 1987 Goa eventually became an official Indian state while Diu and Daman functioned as independent Union Territories.

Goa today

After Independence Goa continued to prosper, bolstered by iron-ore exports and a booming tourist industry. However, dominated by issues of statehood, the status of Konkani (Goa's official language) and the ever-rising levels of immigration, its political life has been dogged for decades by chronic **instability**, with frequent changes of government and chief ministers, interrupted by occasional periods of "**President's Rule**" when the state had to be governed directly from New Delhi.

At the start of the 21st century, renewed fears over the pace of change on the coastal strip started to dominate the news. A sudden influx and just as sudden disappearance of **Russian charter tourists** has now been replaced by high-rolling **property developers** from Delhi and Mumbai who have provoked a backlash from successive ruling coalitions, with a state-sponsored land grab of expatriate property. Hundreds of resident Europeans had their assets confiscated, and fled. A series of high-profile attacks on, and unexplained deaths of foreigners has done little to improve the state's image abroad. Meanwhile, as ever-improving infrastructural links with the rest of India render Goa's borders more porous, the survival of the region as a culturally distinct entity continues to hang in the balance.

ARRIVAL AND DEPARTURE   GOA

TO AND FROM MUMBAI
By plane A couple of dozen flights shuttle between

Mumbai and Goa's Dabolim Airport daily, with fares from as low as ₹3000 if you book well in advance with one of the no-

EASY RIDING

Zipping round Goa on a **rented motorbike** is very much part of the Goa experience for most people, but before you take to the road there are a few things to consider. Officially, you need an international **driver's licence** to rent and ride anything, but in practice a standard licence will probably suffice if you're stopped and asked to produce your papers by the local police. All rented motorcycles should carry special yellow-and-black **licence plates**; make sure yours does, to avoid harassment by Goa's notoriously corrupt traffic cops. Although recent changes mean that police checks on foreigners have reduced considerably, if you are caught without a licence the bike owner will be fined ₹10,000 so they are very unlikely to rent to you without seeing one. Make sure the lights and brakes are in good shape, wear a helmet, and be especially vigilant at night. Rates for motorbikes vary according to season, duration of rental and vehicle; most owners also insist on a **deposit** and/or passport as security. The cheapest bike, a scooter-style **Honda Activa** 100cc which has automatic gears, costs ₹250–350 per day. Other options include the perennially stylish **Enfield Bullet** 350cc, although these are heavy and – at upwards of ₹700-1000 per day – the most expensive bike to rent. It's worth bearing in mind that road traffic accidents are the biggest cause of death of foreigners in India, so if you're not an experienced motorcyclist they are best avoided. **Fuel** is sold at service stations around the state (known locally as "petrol pumps"). In smaller settlements, including the resorts, it's sold in mineral-water bottles at general stores or through backstreet suppliers – but you should avoid these as some bulk out their petrol with low-grade kerosene or industrial solvent, which makes engines misfire and smoke badly.

frills airlines – or as much as ₹40,000 on New Year's Eve. Try SpiceJet, IndiGo, Go Air or JetKonnect (see page 37). Flying with Air India will set you back around ₹4000–8000 each way. The cheaper flights are usually at inconvenient times.

By train Seven or so more trains run daily on the Konkan Railway from Mumbai, the most convenient being the overnight *Mangalore Junction Express* (#12133), which departs from CST at 10pm and arrives in Goa at 7.05am the following morning. Travelling to Mumbai, the service to go for is the overnight *Konkan Kanya Express* (#10112), which departs from Margao/Madgaon (see page 732) at 6pm (or Karmali, near Old Goa, 11km west of Panjim, at 6.32pm), arriving at Mumbai CST at 5.50am the following day. The other fast train from Goa to CST, the *Mandovi Express* (#10104), departs Margao/Madgaon at 9.15am (or Karmali at 9.50am) and arrives at 9.40pm the same evening. Note that all Konkan trains book up within days of the seats being released.

By bus A fleet of night buses covers the 500km between Goa and Mumbai – a terrible 16hr journey, best avoided. If you have to go this way, choose Paulo Travels, which offers a range of services from no-frills buses for ₹600 to swisher a/c Volvo coaches with berths (₹1425). For tickets, contact their office just north outside the Kadamba bus stand, Panjim (☎0832 2277036, ⊕paulobus.com). In south Goa, the firm's main outlet is just north of the bus station in Margao (☎0832 273 3355). Information on all departures and fares is available online.

TO AND FROM HAMPI

By train The most stress-free and economical way to travel between Goa and Hosapete, the jumping-off place

for Hampi, is the *Vasco–Howrah Express* (#18048), which departs Vasco da Gama every Tues, Thurs, Fri and Sun at 7.10am (Margao/Madgaon 7.50am), arriving 7hr 38min later. Fares range from ₹235 for a seat in a second-class sleeper compartment to ₹890 for second-class a/c – the comfiest option. Tickets can be bought on the day, but arrive at Margao/Madgaon by at least 6.30am, as the "queues" are invariably more like rugby scrums. There are also trains from Hosapete to Goa via Hubballi (see page 1163).

By bus The bus journey covering the same route is no cheaper than the train (sleeper class) and is far more gruelling. Two or three clapped-out government services leave Panjim's Kadamba stand (platform #9) each morning for Hosapete, the last one at 10.30am. Brace yourself for a long, hard slog; all being well, it should take 9 or 10hr, but delays and breakdowns are frustratingly frequent.

TO AND FROM GOKARNA

By train The fastest and most convenient way to travel along the coast between Goa and Gokarna is on the Konkan Railway. The *Madgaon–Mangaluru Passenger* (#56641) leaves Margao/Madgaon at 1pm, passing through the market town of Canacona/Chaudi at 1.52pm en route to Gokarna Rd, the town's railhead, where it arrives at 3.35pm. The return train (#56640) leaves Gokarna Rd at 10.11am, stopping at Canacona/Chaudi at 11.38pm, and arriving at Margao/Madgaon at 12.40pm. As this is classed as a passenger service, you don't have to buy tickets in advance; just turn up at the station 30min before departure and pay at the regular ticket counter.

GETTING AROUND

By local bus Although often crowded, local buses can get you most places in Goa, and for shorter journeys cost only

12

₹10–15. Most services run from around 6am until around 7pm, though often later for inter-urban routes.

By taxi Most foreign visitors travel around Goa in white or yellow-and-black Maruti van taxis or the slightly cheaper auto-rickshaw. Fares are often posted at ranks and the official per-kilometre rates for all taxis and rickshaws can be found at ⊕ goatourism.gov.in/inside-goa – you should always clearly settle the fare before you start your journey.

By motorcycle taxi If you're not weighed down with luggage, motorcycle taxis – known throughout Goa as "pilots" – offer a faster alternative and generally cost less than half the taxi rate. Just remember that with motorcycle taxis there are old pilots and there are bold pilots, but no old, bold pilots – it's always best to choose a more mature driver (as well as haggle hard on the rate).

By bike A cheaper alternative is to rent a bicycle (gearless, Indian-made cycles) which are on offer in all the resorts for around ₹150–200/day.

By motorbike Many people travel around Goa by motor-bike, but there are some things to note (see box, page 701).

Central Goa

Known as the *Velhas Conquistas* ("Old Conquests"), the land wedged between the Mandovi and Zuari rivers in Central Goa was the first territory to be colonized by the Portuguese in the early sixteenth century, and still retains a more Christian feel than outlying districts. Gabled, whitewashed churches dominate most village squares, and you'll see plenty of old-style Portuguese dresses worn by Catholic women.

The Lusitanian atmosphere is most discernible of all in the older districts of the state capital, **Panjim**, and although the town attracts far fewer visitors than the coastal resorts, it certainly deserves a day or two's break from the beach, if only to visit the remains of **Old Goa**, a short bus ride away upriver. Further inland, the forested lower slopes of the Western Ghats, cut through by the main Panjim–Bengaluru (Bangalore) highway, shelter the impressive **Dudhsagar falls**, reachable only by 4WD jeep, and a small, but beautifully situated, medieval Hindu temple at **Tambdi Surla**.

Panjim

Stacked around the sides of a lush terraced hillside at the mouth of the River Mandovi, **PANJIM** (also known by its Marathi name, **Panaji** – "land that does not flood") was for centuries little more than a minor landing stage and customs house, protected by a hilltop fort and surrounded by stagnant swampland. It only became state capital in 1843, after the port at Old Goa had silted up, and its rulers and impoverished inhabitants had fled the plague.

Today, the town ranks among the least congested and hectic of any Indian capital. Conventional sights are thin on the ground, but the backstreets of the old quarter, **Fontainhas**, have retained a faded Portuguese atmosphere, with their colour-washed houses, *azulejo*-tiled street names and Catholic churches.

Panjim's annual hour in the spotlight comes at the end of November each year when it hosts the **International Film Festival of India**, or **IFFI** (⊕ iffi.nic.in), during which a galaxy of Bollywood glitterati, and the odd foreign director, turn up to strut their stuff.

Fontainhas

The town's oldest and most interesting district, **Fontainhas**, comprises a dozen or so blocks of Neoclassical houses nestled at the foot of leafy Altinho Hill on the eastern edge of Panjim, across the creek from the bus stand. Many have retained their traditional coat of ochre, pale yellow, green or blue – a legacy of the Portuguese insistence that every Goan building (except churches, which had to be white) should be colour-washed after the monsoons. While some have been restored, the majority remain in a state of charismatic decay.

One of the district's oldest structures is the **Chapel of St Sebastian**, which stands at the centre of Fontainhas, at the head of a small square. The eerie crucifix inside, brought here

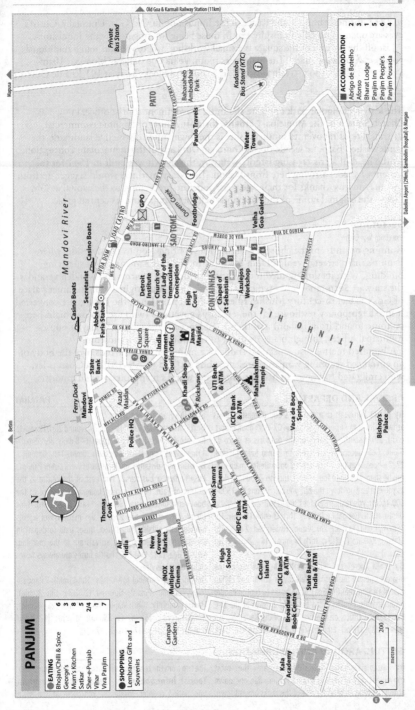

PANJIM

● EATING
Bhojan/Chilli & Spice	6
George's	3
Mum's Kitchen	8
Satkar	5
Shere-Punjab	2/4
Vihar	1
Viva Panjim	7

■ SHOPPING
Lembranca Gifts and Souvenirs	1

■ ACCOMMODATION
Abrigo de Botelho	2
Afonso	3
Bharat Lodge	1
Panjim Inn	5
Panjim People's	6
Panjim Pousada	4

Old Goa & Karmali Railway Station (11km)

Mapusa

Betim

Dabolim Airport (29km), Bambolim (hospital) & Margao

12

Map labels:

Private Bus Stand
Babasaheb Ambedkhar Park
Kadamba Bus Stand (KTC)
PATO
Paulo Travels
Water Tower
Mandovi River
Casino Boats
Secretariat
Casino Boats
GPO
Ouem Creek
SÃO TOMÉ
Footbridge
Velha Goa Galeria
Abbé de Faria Statue
Detroit Institute
Church of our Lady of the Immaculate Conception
High Court
FONTAINHAS
Chapel of St Sebastian
Azulejos Workshop
State Bank
Church Square
India Government Tourist Office
Jama Masjid
ALTINHO HILL
Ferry Dock
Mandovi Hotel
Azad Maidan
Khadi Shop
Rickshaws
UTI Bank & ATM
Mahalakshmi Temple
ICICI Bank & ATM
Vaca de Boca Spring
Bishop's Palace
Police HQ
Thomas Cook
Ashok Samrat Cinema
HDFC Bank & ATM
Air India
Market
New Covered Market
High School
Caculo Island
ICICI Bank & ATM
State Bank of India & ATM
INOX Multiplex Cinema
Campal Gardens
Broadway Book Centre
Kala Academy

PATTO BRIDGE
BHARAT CAUSEWAY
RUA DE OUREM
RUA 31 DE JANEIRO
ARMADA PORTUGUESA
RUA DE OUREM
31 JANEIRO ROAD
MG RD
AVDA DOM JOÃO CASTRO
MG RD
RUA JOSÉ FALCÃO
DR RS RD
CUNHA RIVARA ROAD
CUNHA RIVARA ROAD
OHMUZ RD
OHMUZ ROAD
MALACCARD
DR P PISURLEKAR RD
MAHATMA GANDHI ROAD
AVNDA DE ANGLO
DR DADA VAIDYA ROAD
SWAMI VIVEKANANDA ROAD
DR ATMARAM BORKAR ROAD
DR P SHIRGAONKAR RD
KHANDVE KELESKAR RD
GANA PINTO ROAD
GEN COSTA ALVARES ROAD
HELIODORO SALGADO ROAD
GEN BERNARDO GUEDES ROAD
DR BANDODKAR MARG
DR BRAGANZA PEREIRA ROAD

N

200 metres
0

CENTRAL GOA

in 1812, formerly hung in the Palace of the Inquisition in Old Goa. Unusually, Christ's eyes are open – allegedly to inspire fear in those being interrogated by the Inquisitors.

Just off the bottom of the square is a small workshop where you can watch traditional Goan *azulejos* being made. The main sales room, **Velha Goa Galeria** (Mon–Sat 10am–9pm; ☎0832 2711468, ⊛velhagoa.net), is a couple of blocks away at 191 Rua de Ourem.

Church Square

The leafy rectangular park opposite the India Government tourist office, known as **Church Square** or the **Municipal Gardens**, forms the heart of Panjim's commercial district. Presiding over its southeast side is the town's most distinctive landmark, the whitewashed Baroque facade of the **Church of Our Lady of the Immaculate Conception**. At the head of a crisscrossing laterite walkway, the church was built in 1541 for the benefit of sailors arriving here from Lisbon. The weary mariners would stagger up from the quay to give thanks for their safe passage before proceeding to the capital at Old Goa – the original home of the enormous bell that hangs from its central gable.

Secretariat

Avda Dom João Castro

Running north from the church, Rua José Falcão brings you to the riverside, where Panjim's main street, Avenida Dom João Castro, holds the town's oldest surviving building. With its sloping tiled roofs, carved-stone coats of arms and wooden verandas, the stalwart **Secretariat** looks typically colonial. Yet it was originally the summer palace of Goa's sixteenth-century Muslim ruler, the Adil Shah. Later, the Portuguese converted it into a temporary resthouse for the territory's governors (who used to overnight here en route to and from Lisbon) and then a residence for the viceroy. Today, it houses municipal offices, though plans are afoot to transform it into a museum.

A hundred metres east, a peculiar statue of a man holding his hands over the body of an entranced reclining woman represents **Abbé de Faria** (1755–1819), a Goan priest who emigrated to France to become one of the world's first professional hypnotists.

ARRIVAL AND DEPARTURE
PANJIM

By plane European charter planes and domestic flights arrive at Dabolim Airport (☎0832 254 0796, ⊛goanairport.com), 29km south of Panjim on the outskirts of Vasco da Gama, Goa's second city. Prepaid taxis into town (45min; ₹790), booked at the office directly opposite the main exit, can be shared by up to four people, though if you turn right as you exit and go down the hill, you can get one for ₹500–600. Motorcycle taxis are about ₹300–350.
Destinations Bengaluru (8 daily; 1hr); Chennai (1 daily; 1hr 35min); Delhi (13 daily; 2hr 30min); Hyderabad (2 daily; 1hr 30min); Kolkata (1 daily; 3hr); Mumbai (16–18 daily; 1hr 15min).

By train There's no railway station in town itself; the nearest one, on the Konkan Railway, is at Karmali (11km east of Panjim near Old Goa). State buses to central Panjim await arrivals. Bookings can be made in town at the KRC Reservations Office, on the first floor of the Kadamba bus stand, Panjim (Mon–Fri 8am–6pm; ₹10 booking fee). Book

as far in advance as possible.
Destinations Gokarna Rd (3–4 daily; around 2hr); Hosapete for Hampi (4 weekly; 7hr); Mumbai (6–8 daily; 8hr 35min–11hr 40min); Pune (1–3 daily; 12hr 30min–14hr 40min).

By bus Long-distance and local buses work out of Panjim's busy Kadamba bus stand, 1km east of the centre in the district of Pato. Tickets can be bought in advance at the booking counters here (daily 9–11am & 2–5pm). Trips for private services are sold by the many travel agents immediately outside the station. Buses tend to depart in the afternoon/evening, and arrivals are in the morning. Within Goa, note that KTC shuttle buses are always faster than normal services.
Destinations Arambol (3–4 daily; 1hr 45min); Calangute (every 30min; 45min); Gokarna (2 daily; 5hr 30min); Hampi (1 nightly; 10hr); Mapusa (every 15min; 25–40min); Margao (every 15min; 45–55min); Mumbai (12 daily/nightly; 16hr); Pune (7–8 daily; 12hr).

GETTING AROUND AND INFORMATION

By auto-rickshaw Auto-rickshaws are the most convenient way of getting around Panjim; flag one down at the roadside or head for one of the ranks around town.

The trip from the bus stand to Fontainhas costs around ₹50.
Tourist information The Government of Goa tourist information counter, inside the concourse at the main

GOAN FOOD AND DRINK

Not unnaturally, after 451 years of colonization, Goan **cooking** absorbed a strong Portuguese influence – palm vinegar (unknown elsewhere in India), copious amounts of coconut, tangy *kokum* and fierce local chillies also play their part. Goa is the home of the famous **vindaloo** (from the Portuguese *vinho d'alho*, literally "garlic wine"), originally an extra-hot and sour pork curry, but now made with a variety of meat and fish. Other **pork** specialities include spicy *chouriço* sausages; *sorpotel*, a hot curry made from pickled pig's liver and heart; *leitão*, suckling pig; and *balchao*, pork in a rich brown sauce. Another traditional Goan Catholic dish is mutton *xacuti*, made with a sauce of lemon juice, peanuts, coconut, chillies and spices. The choice of **seafood**, often cooked in fragrant masalas (such as the sour and spicy *ambotik*), is excellent – clams, mussels, crab, lobster, giant prawns – while **fish**, depending on the type, is either cooked in wet curries, grilled, or baked in a *tandoor*. Chicken dishes include *cafrea*, a spicy stew with origins in Africa. *Sanna*, like the south Indian *idli*, is a steamed cake of fermented rice flour, but here sweetened with palm toddy. Sugar fiends will adore *bebinca*, a rich, delicious, solid egg custard with coconut, and the toffee-like *dodol*.

As for **drinks**, locally produced wine, spirits and beer are cheaper than anywhere in the country, thanks to lower rates of tax. The most famous and widespread **beer** is Kingfisher, which tastes less of glycerine preservative than it does elsewhere in India, but you'll also come across pricier Fosters, brewed in Mumbai and nothing like the original. Goan **port**, a sweeter, inferior version of its Portuguese namesake, is ubiquitous, served chilled in large wine glasses with a slice of lemon. Local **spirits** – whiskies, brandies, rums, gins and vodkas – come in a variety of brand names for less than ₹50–150 a shot, but, at half the price, local speciality **feni**, made from distilled cashew or from the sap of coconut palms, offers strong competition. Cashew *feni* is usually drunk after the first distillation, but you can also find it double-distilled and flavoured with ginger or cumin, producing a smooth liqueur.

12

Kadamba bus stand (daily 9am–5pm; ☎0832 2437430 ⊚ goatourism.gov.in) is useful for checking train and bus timings, but little else. The more reliable India Government tourist office is across town on Church Square (Mon–Fri 9.30am–6pm, Sat 9.30am–1pm; ☎0832 222 3412, ⊚ incredibleindia.org).

ACCOMMODATION

The heritage properties in the atmospheric and peaceful Fontainhas are the best places to stay, while more modern and expensive hotels cluster in the area around 18th of June Rd. Finding a room can be a problem during Dussehra (Sept & Oct), Diwali (mid-Nov), the IFFI film festival in late Nov, and over Christmas and New Year. Note that checkout times vary.
Abrigo de Botelho Rua de Natal, Fontainhas ☎98221 00867, ⊚hadbgoa.com; map p.703. The newest of the district's heritage boutique hotels, set on a quiet corner in one of the prettiest backstreets. Its rooms, which come in three categories (₹3000–5000), are all a/c, large and tastefully decorated, with beautiful wood and tiled floors. Complimentary breakfast is served in a secluded rear garden. ₹3000
★**Afonso** St Sebastian Chapel Square, Fontainhas ☎0832 222 2359 or ☎97643 00165, ⊚afonsoguest house.com; map p.703. This refurbished colonial-era house in a picturesque square is a safe bet if you can't quite afford the *Panjim Inn* down the road. Spotless attached rooms, (₹3000) friendly owners and leafy rooftop terrace with views and cool ceramic mosaic floors – though someone's gone overboard with the textured wall paint. There is no breakfast but there are popular restaurants close by. ₹2500
Bharat Lodge Sao Tome Rd, near the GPO ☎0832 222 4862, ✉thebharatlodge@gmail.com; map p.703. Good-value budget guesthouse, located at the heart of the old quarter in a terracotta-washed, 150-year-old building that has retained many of its original features despite extensive modernization. The ten rooms are large for the price, have quiet fans and good-sized bathrooms: ask for no. 106 or 102 if they're vacant. A/c ₹2000. No breakfast. ₹1500
★**Panjim Inn/Panjim Pousada** E–212, Rua 31 de Janeiro, Fontainhas ☎0832 222 6523, ⊚panjiminn.com; map p.703. Grand three-hundred-year-old townhouse, managed as a homely heritage hotel, with period furniture, antique photos, balconies and a veranda where meals and drinks are served. Their adjacent three-storey wing over-looking the river is in the same style, but with better views, while the *Pousada* annexe over the road has two lovely rear side rooms sharing a wooden balcony that overlooks a secret courtyard. Buffet breakfast available. ₹6500
Panjim People's Rua 31 de Janeiro, Fontainhas ☎0832 222 6523, ⊚panjiminn.com; map p.703. Sister to the *Panjim Inn*, in a former high school opposite the original house. It's more upmarket than their other two buildings, with rooms fitted with antique rosewood furniture, gilded pelmets, lace curtains and bathtubs. Rates include buffet breakfast. ₹6500

EATING

Catering for the droves of tourists who come here from other Indian states, as well as fussy, more price-conscious locals, Panjim is packed with good **places to eat**. Most are connected to a hotel, but there are also plenty of other independently-run establishments offering quality food for far less than you pay in the coastal resorts. If you're unsure about which regional cooking style to go for, head for The Fidalgo Food Enclave, in the *Hotel Fidalgo* on 18th June Rd, which hosts six different outlets, from Goan to Gujarati.

Bhojan/Chilli & Spice Hotel Fidalgo, 18th June Rd ☎ 0832 222 6291; map p.703. Authentic, pure-veg Gujarati thali joint, in the a/c restaurant complex of a popular upscale hotel. You won't eat finer Indian vegetarian cuisine anywhere in Goa. ₹350 for the works. For equally superb non-veg, north Indian food (kebabs, curries, tandoori and the like), head next door to *Chilli & Spice* (around ₹800 for mains). Daily noon–3pm & 7.30–11pm.

George's Emilio Gracia Rd ☎ 0832 242 6820; map p.703. This great little Goan-Catholic café serves proper local food (though at slightly more than local prices, thanks to the guidebooks), on cramped tables near the Immaculate Conception church. Grab a seat under a fan and tuck into calamari chilli fry, prawn-curry-rice, or the superb and spicy beef tongue roast (mains ₹200–350). They also do good-value fish curry rice meals (₹200). Mon–Sat 11am–3.30pm & 6.30–10.30pm

★ **Mum's Kitchen** Dr D Bandodkar (DB) Marg (Panjim–Miramar Rd) ☎ 9822175559, ⌨ mumskitchengoa.com; map p.703. The owners of this great Goan restaurant in the suburb of Miramar, 10min by auto from the centre of Panjim, collected old family recipes from mothers, grandmas and aunties across the state in an attempt to revive disappearing culinary traditions. The results, such as *kombdechem sukhem* (spicy boneless chicken) are as authentic and flavour-packed as any you'll encounter in Goa. Around ₹500–600/person. Daily 11am–11pm.

Satkar 18th June Rd ☎ 0832 222 1922; map p.703. Popular vegetarian, south Indian snack and juice joint. There's a huge range of dishes, including Chinese and north Indian, but most people go for their fantastic masala dosas (₹50) and piping hot, crunchy Goan samosas (₹50) – the best in town. Daily 7am–10.30pm.

Sher-e-Punjab Above Hindu Pharmacy, Cunha Rivara Rd, Church Square ☎ 0832 2227204 or ☎ 0832 242 5657; map p.703. This north Indian restaurant, an old Panjim favourite, occupies a funky, glass-sided dining hall overlooking the square. Steer clear of the Goan and Chinese menu – Mughlai is the thing here: chicken, mutton and *paneer* (₹275–450) prepared in the *tandoor* or steeped in rich, spicy and creamy sauces, which you scoop up with flaky naan breads. There's another branch near *Satkar*. Daily noon–3.30pm & 7–11pm.

Vihar Near the petrol station on MG Rd ☎ 0832 2225744; map p.703. Very clean, and one of the best places in town for south Indian snacks (₹25–1000); they serve hearty thalis (₹120–160) and good north Indian food, too. It's more conveniently situated than its competitors if you're staying in Fontainhas, though it does suffer from traffic noise; best avoided during rush hours. Daily 7am–10pm.

★ **Viva Panjim** 178 Rua 31 de Janeiro, behind Mary Immaculate High School, Fontainhas ☎ 0832 2422405; map p.703. Award-winning traditional Goan home-cooking – *xacutis*, vindaloo, prawn *balchao*, *cafrea*, *ambotik* and delicious freshly grilled fish – served by a charming local woman, Linda de Souza, in a pretty colonial-era backstreet. This place should be your first choice for dinner if you're staying in Fontainhas. Most mains ₹250-300. Mon–Sat 11.30am–3pm & 7–10.30pm, Sun 7–10.30pm.

SHOPPING

The main shopping area in the city is on and around 18th June Rd, though there are a few more interesting shops in Fontainhas.

Lembranca Gift and Souvenirs 7 Durga Chambers, 18th June Road ☎ 0832 2421779; map p.703. Souvenirs, gifts, knick-knacks and a variety of crafts including ceramics and tiles are available here. Daily 9.30am–8pm

DIRECTORY

Banks and exchange Nearly all the banks in town have ATMs, where you can make withdrawals using Visa or MasterCard. The most efficient place to change currency is Thomas Cook, near the Air India/Indian Airlines office at 8 Alcon Chambers, Dr D Bandodkar (DB) Marg (April–Sept Mon–Sat 9am–6pm; Oct–March also Sun 10am–5pm; ☎ 832 663 9257).

British Consular Assistant The British High Commission of Mumbai has a one-woman Consular Section in Panjim – a useful contact for British nationals who've lost passports, got into trouble with the law or need help dealing with a death. It's on the far western end of town, opposite the five-star *Marriott Hotel* at 303–304 Casa del Sol, Miramar (Mon–Thurs 9.30am–3pm, Fri 9.30am–12.30pm; ☎ 832 6636777).

Cinema Panjim's swanky multiplex, the 1272-seater INOX, is in the northwest of town on DB Marg (☎ 80802 11111 ⌨ inoxmovies.com). It screens all the latest Hindi blockbusters and some Hollywood movies.

Hospital The state's main medical facility is the new Goa Medical College, aka GMC (☎ 0832 245 8700, ⌨ gmc.goa. gov.in), 7km south on NH-17 at Bambolim, where there's also a 24hr pharmacy. Ambulances (☎ 102) are likely to get you there a lot less quickly than a standard taxi. Conditions are grim by Western standards. Less serious cases can receive attention at the Vintage Hospital, next to the fire brigade headquarters in Panjim's St Inez district (☎ 0832

564 4401 to 4405). Better medical facilities are available in Margao, less than an hour away by road (see page 732).

Pharmacies Hindu Pharma, near the tourist office on Church Square (Mon–Sat 9am–8pm; ☎0832 222 3176), stocks a phenomenal range of Ayurvedic, homeopathic and allopathic medicines.

Old Goa

Just 10km from Panjim, and at one time a byword for oriental splendour, Portugal's former capital in India, **OLD GOA**, was virtually abandoned following malaria and cholera epidemics from the seventeenth century onwards. Today, despite its UNESCO World Heritage Site status, you need considerable imagination to picture the once-great city at its zenith, when it boasted a population of several hundred thousand. The maze of twisting streets, piazzas and ochre-washed villas has vanished, and all that remains is a score of cream-painted churches and convents. Foremost among the surviving monuments is the tomb of **St Francis Xavier**, the legendary sixteenth-century missionary, whose desiccated remains are enshrined in the **Basilica of Bom Jesus** – the object of veneration for Catholics from across Asia and beyond.

Viceroy's Archway

Old Goa's grandest mansions formerly lined the riverfront, and the best direction from which to approach the site is still from the north. Begin your tour at the **Viceroy's Archway** (1597), which would have been the first structure to greet new arrivals in the seventeenth century. Constructed to commemorate Vasco da Gama's first landfall in India, it features a Bible-toting figure resting his foot on the cringing figure of a "native" on one side, and a statue of Da Gama himself on the other.

12

Church of St Cajetan

A short way up the lane from the Archway, the spectacular domed **Church of St Cajetan** (1651) was modelled on St Peter's in Rome by monks from the Theatine Order. While it boasts a Corinthian exterior, non-European elements are also evident in the decoration, such as the cashew-nut designs in the carving of the pulpit.

The Sé (St Catherine's Cathedral)

The Portuguese viceroy Redondo (1561–64) commissioned the **Sé**, or **St Catherine's Cathedral**, southwest of St Cajetan's, to be "a grandiose church worthy of the wealth,

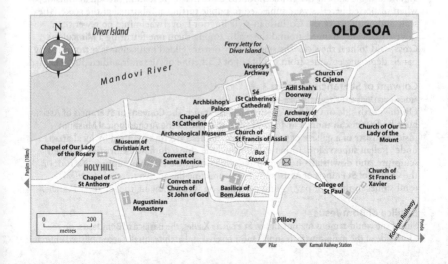

ST FRANCIS XAVIER

Francis Xavier, the "Apostle of the Indies", was born in 1506 in the old kingdom of Navarre, now part of Spain. When the Portuguese king, Dom Joao III (1521–57), received reports of corruption and dissolute behaviour among the Portuguese in Goa, it was Xavier whom the Jesuit Order selected to restore the moral climate of the colony.

Arriving after a year-long journey, the young priest embarked on a programme of missionary work throughout southern India, converting an estimated thirty thousand people – primarily by performing such miracles as raising the dead and curing the sick with a touch of his beads. Subsequent missions took him further afield to Sri Lanka, Malacca (Malaysia) and Japan, before his death from dysentery on the island of San Chuan (Sancian), off the Chinese coast in 1552.

Although credited with converting more people to Christianity than anyone other than St Paul, Francis Xavier owes his subsequent canonization principally to the legend surrounding the fate of his mortal remains, which, when exhumed in China a year after burial, were found to be in a perfect state of preservation. His body was later removed and taken to Old Goa, where it has remained ever since, enshrined in the **Basilica of Bom Jesus**.

PLUNDERED RELICS

St Francis's incorruptible corpse, however, has never rested entirely in peace. Chunks of it have been removed over the years by **relic hunters** and curious clerics: in 1614, the right arm was dispatched to the pope in Rome (where it allegedly wrote its name on paper); a hand was sent to Japan, and parts of the intestines to Southeast Asia. One Portuguese woman, Dona Isabel de Caron, even bit off the little toe of the cadaver; apparently, so much blood spurted into her mouth, it left a trail to her house and she was discovered.

Every ten years (the next is due in 2024), the saint's body is carried in a three-hour ceremony from the Basilica of Bom Jesus to the Sé cathedral, where visitors file past, touch and photograph it. Around a quarter of a million pilgrims flock to view the corpse, these days a shrivelled and somewhat unsavoury spectacle.

power and fame of the Portuguese who dominated the seas from the Atlantic to the Pacific". Today it stands larger than any church in Portugal, although it was beset by problems, not least a lack of funds and the motherland's temporary loss of independence to Spain. It took eighty years to build and was not consecrated until 1640.

On the Tuscan-style exterior, the one surviving tower houses the **Golden Bell**, cast in Cuncolim (south Goa) in the seventeenth century. During the Inquisition its tolling announced the start of the gruesome autos-da-fé that were held in the square outside, when suspected heretics were subjected to public torture and burned at the stake. The scale and opulence of the Corinthian-style interior is overwhelming; no fewer than fifteen altars are arranged around the walls, among them one featuring a **Miraculous Cross**, said to heal the sick. The staggeringly ornate, gilded main **altar** is surrounded by panels depicting episodes from the life of St Catherine of Alexandria (died 307 AD).

Convent of St Francis of Assisi

Archeological Museum Daily except Fri 10am–6pm • ₹10

On the north side of Old Goa's central square stands the **Convent of St Francis of Assisi**, built by Franciscan monks in 1517. Today, the core of the **Archeological Museum** inside consists of a gallery of **portraits** of Portuguese viceroys, painted by local artists under Italian supervision. Other exhibits include coins, domestic Christian wooden sculpture, and downstairs in the cloister, pre-Portuguese Hindu sculpture. Next door, the **Church of St Francis of Assisi** (1521) features fine decorative frescoes, *hidalgos'* tombstones in the floor paving and paintings on wood showing the life of St Francis.

Basilica of Bom Jesus

Site of the world-famous mausoleum of St Francis Xavier, the **Basilica of Bom Jesus**, on the south side of the main square, is India's most revered and architecturally accomplished church.

Work on the building was started in 1589 and took sixteen years to complete. In 1964, it became the first church in South Asia to be promoted to a Minor Basilica, by order of Pope Pius XII, and today forms the main focus for Christian worship in the old colonial capital.

Is it believed that the design of the basilica is derived from the Gesù, the Jesuits' headquarters in Rome, and, with its idiosyncratic blend of Neoclassical restraint and Baroque extravagance, is typical of the late Renaissance. The sumptuous **facade**, the most ornate in Goa, is dominated by the IHS motif, standing for Iesus Hominum Salvator ("Jesus Saviour of Men") – a feature of all Jesuit churches.

The interior

The **interior** is positively plain by comparison to the exterior, but no less impressive, dominated by a massive gilt altarpiece and a huge central statue of St Ignatius Loyola, founder of the Jesuit Order, accompanied by the Infant Jesus. Swathed in lush gold leaf, the gigantic **reredos** filling the far end of the nave remains the basilica's most arresting feature. Its undisputed treasure, however, is to be found in the south transept: the **mausoleum of St Francis** was installed in 1698, a century and a half after his death, gifted to the Jesuits by the last of the Medicis, Cosimo III (1670–1723), Grand Duke of Tuscany, in exchange for the pillow on which the saint's head was laid to rest. It took Florentine sculptor Giovanni Batista Saggini a decade to design and was made from precious marble and coloured jaspers shipped from Italy.

Holy Hill

If the heat hasn't got the better of you, head west up the lane leading from the bus stand to take in the cluster of monuments on **Holy Hill**, some of which date from the earliest phase of Christian building in Goa.

12

Convent of Santa Monica

The lane winds uphill, passing the weed-choked **Convent of Santa Monica** on the right. This was the only Goan convent at the time of its construction in 1627, and the largest one in Asia in its era. It housed around a hundred nuns and offered accommodation to women whose husbands were called away to other parts of the empire. As they had to remain away from the public gaze, the nuns attended Mass in the choir loft of the adjacent **chapel**, where a Miraculous Cross rises above the figure of St Monica at the altar.

Museum of Christian Art

Daily 9.30am–5pm • ☎ 0832 228 5299 • ₹20

Next door to the Convent of Santa Monica stands Goa's foremost **Museum of Christian Art**. Exhibits include processional crosses, ivory ornaments, damask silk clerical robes and some finely sculpted wooden icons dating from the sixteenth and seventeenth centuries, among them an unusual statue of John the Baptist wearing a tiger-skin wrap (in the style of the Hindu god Shiva).

Chapel of Our Lady of the Rosary

Crowning the very top of the Holy Hill, the **Chapel of Our Lady of the Rosary**, constructed in 1526 in the Manueline style (after the Portuguese king Manuel I, 1495–1521), features Ionic plasterwork with a double-storey portico, cylindrical turrets and a tower that commands fine views across the river from the terrace where Albuquerque surveyed the decisive battle of 1510. Its cruciform interior is unremarkable, except for the marble tomb of **Catarina a Piró**, believed to have been the first European woman to set foot in the colony. A commoner, she eloped here to escape the scandal surrounding her romance with Portuguese nobleman Garcia de Sá, who later rose to be governor of Goa. Under pressure from no less than Francis Xavier, Garcia eventually married her, but only in *articulo mortis* as she lay on her deathbed. Her finely carved tomb, set in the wall beside the high altar, incorporates a band of intricate Gujarati-style ornamentation, probably imported from the Portuguese trading post of Diu.

ARRIVAL AND DEPARTURE

Given how short the trip is, and the high each-way charges levied by local **taxis** (₹400) and **auto-rickshaws** (₹250), this is one excursion that's eminently doable by public transport. Just 15–20min by road from the state capital, Old Goa is served by **buses** every 10min from Panjim's Kadamba bus stand (₹10).

Tambdi Surla

Six or seven hundred years ago, the Goan coast and its hinterland were littered with scores of richly carved stone temples. Only one, though, made it unscathed through the Muslim onslaught and the religious bigotry of the Portuguese era. Erected in the twelfth or thirteenth century, the tiny **Mahadeva temple** at **TAMBDI SURLA**, 65km from Panjim and deep in the interior of Goa, owes its survival to its remote location in a tranquil clearing deep in the forest at the foot of the Western Ghats, which enfold the site in a wall of impenetrable vegetation.

The temple, dedicated to Shiva, was built from the finest weather-resistant grey-black basalt, carried across the mountains from the Deccan Plateau and richly carved in situ by the region's most accomplished craftsmen.

Despite its remoteness, Tambdi Surla sees large numbers of visitors, especially on weekends, when it becomes the target for numerous school trips – so if you want to enjoy the site's essential tranquillity come during the week.

ARRIVAL AND DEPARTURE

By bus A single daily bus leaves Panjim's Kadamba bus stand at 10.50am and arrives at the temple at 1.10pm. The return bus leaves late afternoon.

By taxi To get to Tambdi Surla you have to follow the course of NH-4 east from the central Goan town of Ponda, which, used by streams of iron-ore trucks, is a nightmare on a scooter or motorbike. Go by taxi if you can afford it: drivers charge around ₹3000 for a return trip from the coast.

Dudhsagar waterfalls

Measuring a mighty 600m from head to foot, the famous **Dudhsagar waterfalls**, on the Goa–Karnataka border, are some of the highest in India, and a spectacular enough sight to entice a steady stream of visitors from the coast into the rugged Western Ghats. The Konkani name for the falls, which literally translated means "sea of milk", derives from clouds of foam kicked up at the bottom when the water levels are at their highest. Overlooking a steep, crescent-shaped head of a valley carpeted with pristine tropical forest, Dudhsagar is set amid impressive **scenery** that is only accessible on foot or by jeep.

The **best time to visit** is immediately after the monsoons, from October until mid-December, when water levels are highest, although the falls flow well into April.

ARRIVAL AND INFORMATION

By jeep The only practical way to get to Dudhsagar and back is by 4WD jeep from Colem/Kulem (get to Colem by train from Vasco, Margao and Chandor, or by taxi from the north coast resorts for around ₹3000). Look for the "Controller of Jeeps" in Colem, near the station. The cost of the onward 30–40min trip from Colem to the falls, across rough forest tracks and three river fords, is ₹2100/six-person jeep (you may have to wait for the vehicle to fill up); the drive ends with an enjoyable 10min hike.

Entrance fee The park entrance fee is ₹20, with an extra ₹300 for a camera.

North Goa

Development in North Goa is concentrated mainly behind the 7km strip of white sand that stretches from the foot of **Fort Aguada**, crowning the peninsula east of Panjim, to

SWIMMING IN GOA: A WARNING

Be very careful where you swim in Goa. Many places are subject to vicious **currents** (even in relatively shallow water) and during the season at least one tourist a week drowns here – often after they have consumed drugs or alcohol. It's safest to stick to the beaches with lifeguards and flags indicating the safe areas to swim. Swimming anywhere during the **monsoon** would be suicidal.

Baga creek in the north. Encompassing the resorts of **Candolim**, **Calangute** and **Baga**, this is Goa's prime charter belt and an area that most independent travellers steer well clear of.

Since the advent of mass tourism in the 1980s, the alternative "scene" has drifted progressively north away from the sunbed strip to **Anjuna** and **Vagator** – site of some of the region's loveliest beaches – and scruffier **Chapora**, which still has the feel of a fishing village (although overfishing means few boats actually go out these days). Further north still, **Arambol** has thus far escaped any large-scale development, despite the completion of the new road bridge across the Chapora River. **Aswem** and **Mandrem**, just south of Arambol, are this stretch of coast's hot tips: still reasonably off-track, though rapidly filling up.

ARRIVAL AND DEPARTURE   NORTH GOA

North Goa's market town, Mapusa, is the area's main jumping-off place if you're arriving overland from out of state. Travelling here by train via the **Konkan Railway**, get off at Tivim (Thivim), 12km east of Mapusa, from where you'll have to jump in a bus or taxi for the remaining leg.

12 Mapusa

MAPUSA (pronounced "Mapsa") is the district headquarters of Bardez *taluka*. A dusty collection of dilapidated, mostly modern buildings ranged around a busy central square, the town is of little more than passing interest, although it does host a lively daily fresh produce **market**. Anjuna's market may be a better place to shop for souvenirs, but Mapusa's is much more authentic. Local specialities include strings of spicy Goan sausages (*chouriço*), bottles of toddy (fermented palm sap) and large green plantains from nearby Moira.

Whatever you're looking for in the Mapusa market, it's a good idea to arrive as early in the morning as possible to beat the heat. After 11am temperatures can be stifling.

ARRIVAL AND DEPARTURE   MAPUSA

By train Tivim (Thivim), the nearest railway station to Mapusa, is 12km east in the neighbouring Bicholim district. Buses should be on hand to transport passengers into town. The Konkan Railway's *Konkan Kanya Express* #10111 arrives in Tivim from Mumbai's CST at around 9am, leaving plenty of time to find accommodation in the coastal resorts west of Mapusa.
Destinations Cancona (for Palolem; 3 daily; 1hr 30min–2hr); Gokarna Rd (Fri; 2hr 30min); Mumbai (5–7 daily; 8hr 20min–11hr 30min).

By bus You can pick up local services to Calangute, Baga, Anjuna, Vagator, Chapora and Arambol. These leave from

the Kadamba bus stand, a 5min walk west of the main square, where all state-run services from Panjim also pull in. Destinations Anjuna (hourly; 30min); Arambol (every 30min; 1hr); Calangute (every 30min; 30min); Chapora (every 30min; 30–40min); Mumbai (24 daily; 16hr); Panjim (every 10–15min; 25min); Pernem (6 daily; 1hr 45min); Vagator (every 30min; 25–35min).

By taxi Motorcycle taxis hang around the square to whisk lightly laden shoppers and travellers to the coast for around ₹150. Taxis charge considerably more (around ₹300), but you can split the fare with up to five people.

EATING

Café SF Xavier Municipal Market ☎ 98221 01475. For quick, authentic Goan food, you won't do better than *Café SF Xavier*, which has been here since the Portuguese era. It serves scrumptious veg patties and beef "chops" (rissoles), as well as spicy meals of fish, prawn and chicken curry, and other local standards such as *cafrea* and *xacuti*. Most mains cost less than ₹350. Vegetarians can try the local pav (bread)

with bhajji, a spicy and tangy curry. Mon–Sat 9am–9pm.
Ruchira Fifth floor, Hotel Satyaheera, by the roundabout, past the taxi stand ☎ 832 226 3869. The best and most comfortable of the eating options around the main intersection, serving decent but expensive local and Indian dishes such as Goan chicken chilli fry and prawn biryani (₹250–450). Daily 11am–11pm.

SHOPPING

Other India Bookstore Above the Mapusa Clinic
☎ 0832 226 3305, ⓦ otherindiabookstore.com. Hidden
away above the Mapusa Clinic, this bookstore is a treasure
trove with a vast range of titles relating to ecology, the
environment and Goa in general; a full stock list is available
online. Mon–Fri 9am–5pm, Sat 9am–1pm.

Candolim and around

CANDOLIM is prime package-tourist country, and not a resort that sees many backpackers,
but, with a few pleasant places to stay in the village by the fort, it can make a good first
stop if you've just arrived in Goa – and its predominantly more mature clientele make
it much less rowdy than Calangute/Baga. The busy strip running through the middle
of town holds a string of banks and handy shops where you can stock up with essentials
before moving further afield, and there are some great places to eat and drink, frequented
mostly by boozy, middle-aged Brits and, increasingly, domestic tourists.

Fort Aguada

The one sight worth seeking out in the area is **Fort Aguada**, crowning the rocky
flattened headland to the south, at the end of the beach. Built in 1612 to protect the
northern shores of the Mandovi estuary from Dutch and Maratha raiders, the bastion
encloses several natural springs, the first source of drinking water available to ships
arriving in Goa after the long sea voyage from Lisbon. The ruins of the fort can be
reached by following the main drag south from Candolim as it bears left, past the
turning for the *Vivanta Resort*; keep going for 1km until you see a right turn, which
runs uphill to a small car park. Panoramic views extend from the top of the hill where
a four-storey Portuguese **lighthouse**, erected in 1864 and the oldest of its kind in Asia,
looks down over the vast expanse of sea, sand and palm trees.

12

Sinquerim Beach

From the base of the walled *Vivanta Resort* on the northern flank of the headland, a
rampart of red-brown laterite juts into the bay at the bottom of what's left of **Sinquerim
Beach**, which was virtually wiped out by a series of particularly heavy monsoon
storms in 2009. This was among the first places in Goa to be singled out for upmarket
tourism. The Taj group's *Vivanta* resort, among the most expensive hotels in India,
lords it over the sands from the slopes below the battlements.

ARRIVAL AND GETTING AROUND   CANDOLIM AND AROUND

By bus Buses from and to Panjim and Calangute stop every
10–15min or so at the stand by the crossroads in the middle
of Candolim and a few head south here to the Sinquerim
terminus by the fort; you can also flag them down from
anywhere along the main road to Calangute.
Destinations Calangute (every 15min; 15min); Panjim

(every 15min; 25min).
By motorbike During the season there is often a dearth
of motorcycles for rent, in which case search for one in
Calangute. The nearest petrol pump lies 5km east on the
main Panjim road, just beyond Nerul.

INFORMATION AND ACTIVITIES

Banks and exchange There are lots of ATMs dotted along
the main drag and you can change money at any number of
private exchange places in Candolim, although their rates
are unlikely to be as competitive as those in Calangute.

Scuba diving Dive Goa, at the SinQ Beach Club, offers
diving trips (☎ 93250 30110, ⓦ divegoa.com). One
introductory dive along with training session in the pool
costs ₹5500. They also conduct diving certification courses.

ACCOMMODATION

Candolim is charter-holiday land, so **accommodation**
tends to be expensive for most of the season. That said, if
bookings are down you can find some great bargains here, and
Sinquerim, east of the fort, is a genuinely nice place to stay.

★ **Dona Florina** Monteiro's Rd, Escrivao Waddo
☎ 99230 49076, ⓦ donaflorina.co.in; map p.714. Large
guesthouse in a superb location, overlooking the beach in a
secluded corner of the village. Its friendly owner has added

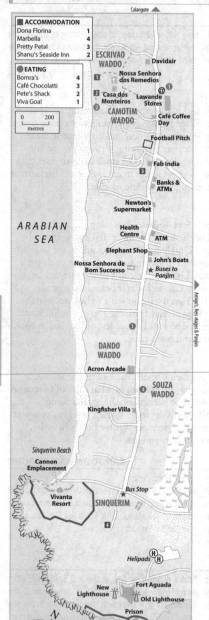

ACCOMMODATION

Dona Florina	1
Marbella	4
Pretty Petal	3
Shanu's Seaside Inn	2

EATING

Bomra's	4
Café Chocolatti	3
Pete's Shack	2
Viva Goa!	1

0   200
metres

Calangute

ESCRIVAO WADDO

Davidair

Nossa Senhora dos Remedios

Casa dos Monteiros

Lawande Stores

CAMOTIM WADDO

Café Coffee Day

Football Pitch

Fab India

Banks & ATMs

Newton's Supermarket

Health Centre

ATM

Elephant Shop

Nossa Senhora de Bom Successo

John's Boats

Buses to Panjim

ARABIAN SEA

Amigo's, Reis Magos & Panjim

DANDO WADDO

Acron Arcade

SOUZA WADDO

Kingfisher Villa

Sinquerim Beach

Cannon Emplacement

Vivanta Resort

SINQUERIM

Bus Stop

Helipads

New Lighthouse

Fort Aguada

Old Lighthouse

Prison

N

CANDOLIM & FORT AGUADA

a breezy rooftop terrace with ceramic mosaic floors where guests can practise yoga. Non a/c single rooms are ₹1200 but it's well worth paying the extra for an a/c double with idyllic sea views. No car access but parking is 500 metres away. **₹2000**

Marbella Sinquerim ☎ 98221 00811, ⓦ marbellagoa. com; map p.714. Individually-styled suites and spacious rooms in a beautiful house built to resemble a traditional Goan mansion. There are six rooms, starting with rates of ₹4500. Everything is gorgeous, especially in the top-floor "Penthouse" (₹7800), and the whole place is screened by a giant mango tree. Unashamedly romantic. **₹4500**

Pretty Petal Camotim Waddo ☎ 96375 56149, ⓦ prettypetalsgoa.com; map p.714. Thirteen very large modern rooms, all with fridges, good mattresses, balconies and relaxed communal areas overlooking lawns. Their top-floor apartment, with windows on four sides and a huge balcony, is the best choice, though more expensive at ₹2200. Use of swimming pool included which is about half a km away on foot. Rates are ₹1800 for non a/c and ₹2000 for a/c. **₹1800**

Shanu's Seaside Inn Escrivao Waddo ☎ 98230 25281, ⓦ shanu.in; map p.714. Eighteen good-sized, well-furnished rooms with narrow balconies right overlooking the dunes, some of them with uninterrupted views of the sea. The a/c rooms cost double. Ask the hospitable owners for no. 120 or 110 (or failing that 111, 107). Breakfast (₹150–350) is served in your room. **₹990**

EATING

Candolim's numerous beach **cafés** are a cut above your average seafood shacks, with pot plants, high-tech sound systems and prices to match. The further from the *Vivanta* complex you venture, the lower the prices become. Fancier places serving more ambitious cuisine line busy Fort Aguada Rd, alongside a string of enduringly popular local joints.

★ **Bomra's** 247 Fort Aguada Rd, Souza ☎ 97675 91056; map p.714. Understated, relaxed place, on a dimly-lit gravel terrace by the roadside. From the outside you'd never know this was one of Goa's gastronomic highlights, but the food – contemporary Burmese and Kachin cuisine with fusion food– is superb. The menu is reassuringly short; try their aromatic-flavoured pickle tea-leaf salad for a starter, and tamarind pork curry or chicken curry or snapper with lemongrass and galangal for a main. They also do fantastic cocktails and, for dessert, delicious ginger crème brûlée. Count on ₹1200–1400 for three courses. Daily noon–2.30pm & 7–11pm.

Café Chocolatti 409 Fort Aguada Rd, Dando Waddo ☎ 93261 12006; map p.714. Nazneen, the British-raised owner of this delightful café in south Candolim, has conjured up a chocoholic heaven. Order a perfect cup of freshly ground coffee or a milkshake to drink in the garden,

12

and indulge in gourmet Belgian-style truffles, tinged with chilli, mocha and orange, a succulent marmalade brownie, or crunchy almond-flavoured Italian biscuits, all priced between ₹95–180. ₹350 for coffee and a treat. Their decent full English breakfast is ₹490. Daily 10am–9pm.

Pete's Shack Sequeira Beach ⊙98230 25281; map p.714. One beach shack that deserves singling out, because it's always professional and serves great healthy salads with real olive oil, mozzarella and balsamic vinegar (₹280–430). All the veg is carefully washed in chlorinated water first, so the food is safe and fresh. The same applies to their seafood sizzler and barbecue grilled dishes all in

the range of ₹300–500. For dessert, try the wonderful home-made *matka kulfi* (served in an earthenware pot) or a cooling mint lassi. Daily 8am–10pm.

Viva Goa! Fort Aguada Rd, Ana Waddo ⊙0832 248 9677; map p.714. Tasty, no-nonsense Goan food fresh from the market – mussel-fry, barramundi (*chonok*), lemonfish (*modso*) and sharkfish steaks fried *rechado* style in chilli paste or in millet (*rawa*) – served on a roadside terrace. It used to be a locals' place, but the customers are mostly tourists these days, and although not as authentic as it used to be, it's good value with most seafood mains around ₹200–500. Daily 11am–3.30pm & 6.30–11.30pm.

Calangute and Baga

A 45-minute bus ride up the coast from Panjim, **CALANGUTE** was, in Portuguese times, where well-to-do Goans would come for their annual *mudança*, or change of air, in May and June, when the pre-monsoon heat made life in the towns insufferable. It remains the state's busiest resort, but has changed beyond recognition since the days when straw-hatted musicians in the beachfront bandstand would regale smartly dressed strollers with Lisbon *fados* and Konkani *dulpods*. Mass package tourism, combined with a huge increase in the number of Indian visitors (for whom this is Goa's number-one beach resort), has placed an impossible burden on the town's rudimentary infrastructure. Hemmed in by four-storey buildings and swarming with traffic, the market area, in particular, has taken on the aspect of a typical makeshift Indian town of precisely the kind that most travellers used to come to Goa to get away from. That said, the south end of the beach around **Maddo Waddo** is quite mellow and there are marginally fewer domestic lager louts than in Baga to the north.

Baga

BAGA is pretty much an extension of Calangute, though the scenery in the far north is somewhat more varied and picturesque. Overlooked by a rocky headland draped in vegetation, a small tidal **river** flows into the sea at the top of the village, past a spur of soft white sand where ranks of brightly coloured fishing boats are moored.

Since the package boom, Baga has developed more rapidly than anywhere else in the state and today looks less like the Goan fishing village it was in the early 1990s and more like a small-scale resort on the Spanish *costas*, with a predominantly young, male, Indian clientele. These "stags", lured to Goa by advertising hinting at cheap booze, hard partying and erotic encounters with exotic foreign women, can be annoying. Beyond the rowdy bars where they hang out, however, you'll find a crop of excellent **restaurants** and some lively **nightlife**.

ARRIVAL AND INFORMATION

CALANGUTE AND BAGA

By bus Buses from Mapusa (every 30min; 30min) and Panjim (every 15min; 45min) pull in at the small bus-stand-cum-market-square in the centre of Calangute. Some continue to Baga, stopping at the crossroads behind the beach en route.

By taxi From Mapusa a taxi should cost around ₹400 and from Panjim around ₹500, with motorcycle taxis costing around half that and rickshaws somewhere in between.

Banks and exchange There are more than 27 ATMs along the main streets, all of which will give cash with Visa or MasterCard. Private currency changers on the same street (many of which also do money wiring) include Wall Street Finances (Mon–Sat 9.30am–6pm), opposite the *Plantain Leaf* and in the shopping complex on the beachfront, who exchange cash at bank rates.

ACCOMMODATION

In spite of the encroaching mayhem, plenty of travellers get hooked on Calangute's mix of market town and beach

resort, returning year after year to stay in little family guesthouses in the fishing waddo. Nowhere is far from the

12

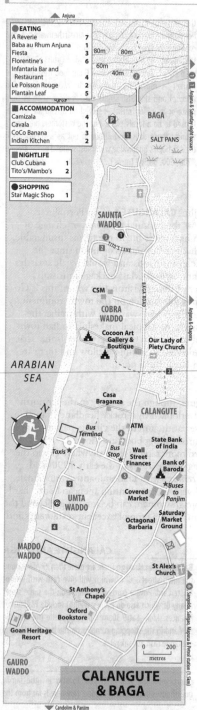

EATING

A Reverie	7
Baba au Rhum Anjuna	1
Fiesta	3
Florentine's	6
Infantaria Bar and Restaurant	4
Le Poisson Rouge	2
Plantain Leaf	5

ACCOMMODATION

Camizala	4
Cavala	1
CoCo Banana	3
Indian Kitchen	2

NIGHTLIFE

Club Cubana	1
Tito's/Mambo's	2

SHOPPING

Star Magic Shop	1

CALANGUTE & BAGA

---

shore, but sea views are a rarity. Accommodation is harder to find in Baga, as even rooms in smaller guesthouses tend to be booked up well before the season gets under way. The majority of family-run places lie around the north end of the beach, where nights have been a lot more peaceful since Goa's premier club, *Tito's*, acquired soundproofing.

Camizala 5–33B Maddo Waddo ☎96891 56449; map p.716. A lovely, breezy haven amid the brouhaha of Calangute, with four non a/c rooms, common verandas and sea views. About as close to the beach as you can get, and the waddo is quiet. Cheap, considering the location, and a popular long-stay option. They own another two-star hotel by the sea called *Delta House Horizon View* with six a/c rooms priced at ₹2500. **₹800**

Cavala Baga Rd ☎83900 55518, ⓦcavala.com; map p.716. Modern hotel in tastefully traditional laterite, with a pool in a plot across the road, surrounded by banana groves. Some rooms have separate balconies front and back; and most of the views look across open fields. Rooms range from simple non a/c doubles to luxurious suites (₹7250). **₹3800**

★**CoCo Banana** 1195 Umta Waddo ☎99608 03790, ⓦcocobananagoa.com; map p.716. Very comfortable, spacious chalets, all with bathrooms, fridges, fans, mosquito nets, kettles and *extra-long mat*tresses. It is run by a welcoming Goan-Swiss couple, Walter and Marina Lobo, who have been here for more than 35 years – a chat with the former about the cultural history of Goa is reason enough to stay here. They also have a few quieter rooms closer to the beach. The a/c rooms cost ₹1500 and the non a/c rooms are **₹1400**

Indian Kitchen Behind Our Lady of Piety Church ☎98221 49615, ⓦindian-kitchen-goa.com; map p.716. Highly decorated guest-house with crazy mosaic tiling, brightly patterned walls and lanterns. The rooms, all attached, have fridges and TV – and, amazingly for a budget hotel, there's a little pool to the rear. They also have more expensive a/c rooms (₹3500) and quieter chalets round the back (₹2100). **₹880**

EATING

This has long been a destination where people come to eat as much as to stroll on the beach, and even if you stay in resorts elsewhere you'll probably be tempted down here for a meal.

A Reverie Near Goan Heritage Resort, Gauro Waddo ☎98231 74927 or 98235 05550; map p.716. Over-the-top gourmet place on the south side of Calangute, centred on a grand, multilevel, terracotta-tiled canopy. Both the gastronomic menu and ambience are about as extravagant as Goa gets, but the prices aren't top whack (around ₹2000/head, plus drinks). Signature dishes include the little BBQ (beef or lamb steak cooked at the table), and lobster cooked in a risotto, poached or with spices. Reservations recommended. Daily 7–11.30pm.

Baba au Rhum Anjuna Calangute–Anjuna Road ☎98228 66366; map p.716. This cool French patisserie-cum-pizzeria hidden deep in the expat enclave of Arpora is a bit off the beaten track, but worth hunting out for its crumbly croissants, baguettes, pain au raisin, fruit salads, juices and perfect café au lait, served on heavy wood tables, with infectious World grooves playing in the background. To find it, turn left off the main Calangute–Anjuna road when you see their signboard. Around ₹500 for pizzas with desserts and pastries at around ₹250. Wed–Mon 9am–11pm

Fiesta Tito's Lane ☎0832 227 9894, ⓦ fiestagoa. com; map p.716. Baga's most sumptuously decorated restaurant is nestled inside an old 1930s mansion by the sea – but you only get views of a lush garden. The contemporary Italian and Mediterranean food is as delectable as the decor. Try their carpaccio of beef for starters, followed by the succulent wood-fired pizzas (₹400–750). Most starters and mains ₹350–1100. Reservations recommended. Daily 7pm–midnight.

Florentine's 4km east of St Alex's Church at Saligao, next door to the Ayurvedic Natural Health Centre ☎0832 227 8122; map p.716. It's well worth venturing inland to taste Florence D'Costa's legendary chicken *cafreal* (₹380; half portion available) made to a jealously guarded family recipe that pulls in crowds of locals and tourists from across north Goa. The restaurant is a down-to-earth place, with prices to match, serving only chicken, some seafood and only a couple of vegetarian snacks, including mushroom and *gobi* (cauliflower) *manchurian*. Daily 11.30am–3pm & 6.30–10.30pm.

Infantaria Bar and Restaurant Next to St John's Chapel, Baga Rd ☎9222 02526; map p.716. A bakery that also morphs into a popular bar and restaurant with live music every evening. It gets packed out for its stodgy croissants, freshly baked apple pie and traditional Goan sweets (such as *dodol* and home-made *bebinca*). Top of the savouries are the prawn, chicken and veg patties (₹120), which locals buy by the box-load. Dinner for two with drinks is in the range of ₹800. Daily 7.30am–midnight.

★**Le Poisson Rouge** Baga Creek ☎98238 50276, ⓦ gregorybazire.com; map p.716. An established fixture on north Goa's gastronomic map, this Gallic-run restaurant is situated in an elegantly styled palm garden lit by pretty tea lights. An ever-changing menu mixes classic French technique with local flavour – check the website for the latest offerings. Around ₹1500/head for three courses, plus extra for wine. Reservations recommended. Daily 7–10.30pm.

Plantain Leaf Market area ☎72649 20949; map p.716. The best Udupi-style restaurant outside Panjim, if not all Goa, where waiters in matching shirts serve the usual range of delicious dosas and other spicy snacks in a clean, cool marble-lined canteen. Try their definitive idli and *vada* breakfasts, delicious masala dosas (₹80), or the cheap and filling set thalis (₹150; deluxe version ₹200). Daily 8am–midnight.

12

NIGHTLIFE

Nightlife is centred around Baga and the various bars and clubs along Tito's Lane, named after *Tito's* club, the most famous club in Goa, if not India. This is where the Indian "stags" come to fulfil their Goa fantasies, so single women may feel uncomfortable with the level of attention –the flipside is that single women will rarely have to pay for entry or drinks. Otherwise, take your pick from the string of shacks lined up along the beach or bars on Baga Road, which stay open until the last punter staggers home.

Club Cubana Arpora ☎91582 57000, ⓦ clubcubana goacom; map p.716. *Cubana*, which occupies a hilltop just inland from the strip, is the most civilized nightspot in the area, especially for women. Only couples are admitted (₹2000 for two, includes drink); and there's even a ladies-only dance floor. The music's so-so, but the vibe is much more chilled than male-dominated *Tito's*. Jeeps shuttle punters up the hill, and you can wallow in a swimming pool. On Wed women get in for free (₹800 admission for guys). Daily 9.30pm–late

Tito's/Mambo's Tito's Lane, Saunta Waddo ⓦtitos. in; map p.716. Baga's legendary nightlife is largely attributable to *Tito's* and its various offspring, including the latest, more techno-orientated, *Mambo's*. Every night hundreds of revellers, many of them single men from other states, are lured in by TV images of women in skimpy dancewear and a thumping sound-and-light system. This can make for an uncomfortably loaded atmosphere for women. Biggest nights are Fri and Sat; music genre is lounge till

---

SEXUAL HARASSMENT IN GOA

While the vast majority of harassment of female tourists in Goa is relatively harmless (though unacceptable) – the surreptitious use of cell phones to take photos of scantily clad women on beaches, for example (report them to the beach police and they'll be forced to delete the pictures), or unwanted attempts at conversation by large groups of men – there have been more serious cases of sexual crimes. Women should avoid walking alone in remote places (or on the beach), especially after dark, and never accept drinks from strangers.

SATURDAY NIGHT BAZAARS

One of the few genuinely positive improvements to the north Goa resort strip over the last fifteen years has been the Saturday Night Market (⊚snmgoa.com), held on a plot inland at Arpora, midway between Baga and Anjuna. Originally the brainchild of an expat German called Ingo, it's run with great efficiency and a sense of fun that's palpably lacking these days from the Anjuna flea market (see opposite). The balmy evening temperatures and pretty lights are also a lot more conducive to relaxed browsing than the broiling heat of mid-afternoon on Anjuna beach. Although far more commercial than its predecessor in Anjuna, many old Goa hands regard this as far truer to the original spirit of the flea market. A significant proportion of the stalls are taken up by foreigners selling their own stuff, from reproduction of Indian pop art to antique photos, the latest trance party gear, stunning antique and coconut-shell jewellery and techno DJ demos. There's also a mouth-watering array of ethnic food and a stage featuring live music from around 7pm until 3am, when the market winds up, as well as a couple of trendy bars with live music or DJs. Admission is free.

The night market from which Ingo's splintered – Mackie's (⊚mackiesnitebazaar.com) – lies nearby, close to the riverside in Baga. Spurned by the expatriate designers and stallholders, it is not quite as lively as its rival, though in recent years has made an effort to close the gap, with better live acts and more foreign stallholders.

11pm, then hip-hop, house, techno and, at *Tito's*, Bollywood hits. At both, entry and drinks are usually free for women. Otherwise you might pay anything from ₹1000 to ₹3000 including drinks (₹1500 for couples), depending on how busy they are. At Christmas, prices can soar above ₹3500. Nov & Dec daily 10pm–3am; off-season closes earlier.

12

SHOPPING

Star Magic Shop Tito's Ln, opp. Kamaki Restaurant ☎91581 83113; map p.716. It rains magic in this colourful shop, which is filled with tricks and treats. Plenty of quirky gifts like "magic" cards, lights, notebooks and other souvenirs. Daily 9am–midnight.

Anjuna

ANJUNA, the next sizeable village up the coast from Baga, was, until a few years back, the last bastion of alternative chic in Goa – where the state's legendary full-moon parties were staged each season, and where the Beautiful Set would rent pretty red-tiled houses for six months at a time, make trance mixes and groovy dance clothes, paint the palm trees fluoro colours and spend months lazing on the beach. A small contingent of fashionably attired, middle-aged hippies still turn up, but thanks to a combination of the Y2K music curfew (see page 721) and overwhelming growth in popularity of the flea market, Anjuna has seriously fallen out of fashion with the party crowd.

As a consequence, the scattered settlement of old Portuguese houses and whitewashed churches, nestled behind a long golden sandy beach, nowadays more closely resembles the place it was before the party scene snowballed than it has for a decade or more. There is, however, a downside to staying here: levels of substance abuse, both among visitors and locals, remain exceptionally high, and the village suffers more than its fair share of dodgy characters.

The beach

The north end of Anjuna beach, just below where the buses pull in, is no great shakes by Goan standards, with a dodgy undertow and lots of even dodgier people selling hash, as well as parties of whisky-filled day-trippers in constant attendance. The vibe is much nicer at the far, southern end, where a pretty and more sheltered cove accommodates a mostly twenty-something tourist crowd. A trance soundtrack thumps from the shacks behind it, cranking up to become proper parties after dark, when Curlie's and neighbouring Shiva Valley take turns to max their sound systems, hosting international DJs through the season. Chai ladies and food stallholders sit in wait on the sands, just like in the raves of old, and on Thursdays, when they seem to have come to an arrangement with authorities, the party continues till daylight. Every other night things grind to a halt at 10pm sharp.

Flea market

The biggest crowds gather on Wednesdays after Anjuna's flea market, held in the coconut plantation behind the southern end of the beach, just north of Curlie's. Along with the Saturday Night Market at Arpora (see page 718), this is the place to indulge in a spot of souvenir shopping. Two decades or so ago the weekly event was the exclusive preserve of backpackers and the area's seasonal residents, who gathered here to smoke chillums and to buy and sell party clothes and jewellery. These days, however, it's more mainstream. Pitches are rented out by the metre, drugs are banned and the approach roads to the village are choked all day with air-conditioned buses and Maruti taxis ferrying in tourists from resorts further down the coast. Even the beggars have to pay baksheesh to be here. The mayhem is, however, fun to experience at least once.

What you end up paying for the exotic merchandise on offer – from Rajasthani handicrafts to south Indian stone carving and everything in between – largely depends on your ability to haggle. Prices are sky-high by Indian standards. Be persistent, though, and cautious, and you can usually pick things up for a reasonable rate (except from the Western designers, who are not so fond of haggling).

Even if you're not spending, the flea market is a good place just to sit and watch the world go by. Mingling with the suntanned masses are bands of strolling musicians, mendicant sadhus and fortune-telling bulls. And if you happen to miss the show, rest assured that the whole cast reassembles every Saturday at Baga/Arpora's night markets.

12

ARRIVAL AND DEPARTURE   ANJUNA

By bus Buses from Mapusa (hourly; 30–40min) drop passengers at various points along the tarmac road across the top of the village, which turns north towards Chapora at the main Starco's crossroads. If you're looking for a room on spec, get off here as it's close to many of the guesthouses.

ACCOMMODATION

Anjuna Beach Resort De Mello Waddo ☎0832 227 4499 or ☎98221 76753 (Joseph), ⌨anjunabeachresort.com; map p.719. This place offers 23 spacious, comfortable rooms with balconies, fridges, attached bathrooms and solar-heated water in two concrete blocks ranged around a pool. Those on the upper floors are best. There's also a block of apartments for long-stayers; both are very good value, though the complex is showing signs of age. There is a restaurant as well. Room rates rise to around ₹3200 for deluxe categories. **₹2500**

Anjuna Palms De Mello Waddo ☎98226 86817 (Felix), ⌨anjunapalms.com; map p.719. Cosy budget guesthouse just a 10min walk from the beach, tucked away behind an old Portuguese-era house next door to the Oxford Arcade, with more character than most. It offers family rooms with three and four beds in the range of ₹1000–1250. All rooms open into a garden courtyard. **₹900**

Banyan Soul Peqqem Peddem, off Flea Market Rd ☎98207 07283, ⌨thebanyansoul.com; map p.719. Leafy, chic hotel on the quiet, southeastern fringes of the

ANJUNA

SHOPPING
Artjuna House ... 1

ACCOMMODATION

Anjuna Beach Resort	1	Manali	4
Anjuna Palms	2	Pebbles Guest House	8
Banyan Soul	9	Renées	7
Blue Nest	3	Yoga Magic	6
Granpa's Inn	5		

EATING

Artjuna	4
Café Eva	3
German Bakery	5
Laguna Anjuna	1
Villa Blanche	2
Xavier's	6

NIGHTLIFE
Curlie's/Shiva Valley ... 1

YOGA IN ANJUNA

Thanks to the presence on its fringes of two world-class centres, Anjuna is a great place to develop your **yoga** skills.

Lou Ferguson Yoga Jungle Shala Tito's White house, Anjuna ☎ 7262 076805, ⊛ loufergusonyoga.com. Brahmani or Vinyasa yoga is taught here, as well as private sessions in Restorative Yoga and meditation. Classes are held three days a week from Tuesday to Thursday and classes for beginners are held on Tuesday. There are several retreats and teacher training courses as well. See website for details.

Purple Valley 142 Bairo Alto Assagoa ⊛ yogagoa. com. If you're looking for a fully-fledged retreat or course, you won't do better than *Purple Valley*, which has accommodation for up to forty guests and what must be one of the loveliest yoga *shalas* (practice areas)

in India. Their teachers were all students of the late Ashtanga guru, Shri K. Pattabhi Jois. Just 15 minutes by car from Anjuna.

Satsanga Retreat Verla Canca, 4km inland from Anjuna ☎ 0832 247 2823, ⊛ satsangaretreat.com. Offering retreats, yoga holidays and teacher training, *Satsanga* describes itself as a "home away from home" – but with palm trees, tropical gardens and a swimming pool, located in a small village between Anjuna and Mapusa. The yoga space is beautiful and there are plenty of chill-out areas and hammock spots. Ayurvedic food and massage are on offer too.

village, near the German Bakery. Shaded by an old banyan tree, the twelve rooms are attractively decorated – though small for the price – and each has a private outdoor sitout that's well screened from the neighbours. Some travellers find this place a bit overpriced and boxed-in, others love its tucked-away feel. Breakfast is extra and is around ₹200–300 per head. **₹3000**

Blue Nest Soronto Waddo ☎ 97630 63379; map p.719. Joseph and Cecilia's little row of four old-fashioned rooms, with pitched-tiled roofs and wood rafters, is close to the main road through the village, but you wouldn't know it. Neatly painted, they're large for the price and have good thick mattresses, as well as nice little tiled verandas looking out into woodland. No wi-fi. **₹500**

Granpa's Inn Gaun Waddo ☎ 0832 227 3270, ⊛ granpasinn.com; map p.719. *Granpa's* occupies a lovely 200-year-old house set in half an acre of lush gardens, with a kidney-shaped pool and shady breakfast terrace. They offer three categories of rooms: standard rooms and suites in the main house and pool side routes. Very popular despite the high tariffs, so book well ahead. **₹4500**

Manali South of Starco's crossroads ☎ 0832 227 4421; map p.719. Anjuna's most popular all-round budget guesthouse offers recently renovated, simple, clean attached rooms with fans, Services include a money exchange, book shop and wi-fi. Booking recommended. Rates for a/c rooms are in the region of ₹900. **₹500**

Pebbles Guest House Anjuna Flea Market Rd, Monterro

Waddo ☎ 099236 49993, ⊛ anjunapebblesgoa.com; map p.719. Barely 700 metres from the beach, this simple no frills guest house has ten large and spacious a/c rooms with attached bathrooms. There is also a slightly bigger room that they call a penthouse which has a kitchenette and attached bathroom and can house a family or a group of three (₹2700). **₹1800**

Renées Monteiro Waddo ☎ 0832 227 3405 or 98504 62217; map p.719. This is a little gem of a guesthouse. Swathed in greenery, welcoming and family run, it holds just eight rooms, most of them surprisingly spacious, with garden-facing balconies. A few have simple kitchenettes and fridges. It's a tad pricier than the competition but worth it. Different categories of rooms with a/c up to ₹1500. Medical services provided on request. **₹700**

★ **Yoga Magic** ☎ 0832 652 3796 or 8806111252, ⊛ yogamagic.net; map p.719. Innovative "Canvas Ecotel", offering low-impact luxury on the edge of Anjuna in Rajasthani hunting tents. They have standard lodges to swankier suites (₹7700–14400) and they are all decorated with block-printed cotton and furnished with cushions, silk drapes and solar halogen lights. Loos are of the biodegradable, non-smelly compost kind. Rates vary according to season (low, high and peak) and there are separate rates for sharing and single occupancies. They also have a separate yoga package. All prices include breakfast, and there's a pool. **₹5,500**

EATING

Responding to the tastes of its visitors, Anjuna boasts a good crop of quality cafés and restaurants, many of which serve healthy vegetarian dishes and juices. If you're hankering for a taste of home, call in at Orchard Stores on the southeastern side of the village, or the rival Oxford Arcade, on the opposite, north side, which both serve the expatriate

and tourist community with a vast range of pricey imported delights and organic produce from around India.

Artjuna 972 Monteiro Waddo, on the flea market road ☎ 0832 227 4794, ⊛ artjuna.com; map p.719. Pretty little garden café serving delicious salads, pesto omelettes, sandwiches of all varieties, a few sweet treats (₹130–420) and great coffee. There's a play area for kids, yoga, and a beautiful shop. Mon–Sun 7am–10.30pm.

Café Eva Anthony St, De Mello Waddo ☎ 073500 56717; map p.719. Cosy and comfortable beach café serving breakfast dishes throughout the day besides sea food. Their homemade desserts are excellent. A meal for two is around ₹500–700. Daily 9am–8pm.

★ **German Bakery** South Anjuna, on the road to Nirvana Hermitage ☎ 70579 01002, ⓦ german-bakery. in; map p.719. The original and inimitable outlet of this much-copied wholefood café-restaurant, hidden away in a tree-shaded garden on the south side of the village, is Goa's ultimate travellers' hangout. Sitting beneath old trees strung with Tibetan prayer flags and Pipli lanterns, you can eat lovely crunchy salads (₹200–300). There is a full menu of Italian, Indian and Asian dishes and seafood, and, of course, the bakery's famous cakes and coffee. There is accommodation available as well. Daily 8am–11pm.

Laguna Anjuna De Mello Waddo, close to the flea market ☎ 0832 227 4131, ⓦ lagunaanjuna.com; map p.719. Pretty poolside restaurant in a chic little boutique hotel, offering large Goan fish thalis (₹400), and a full range Indian delights such as chicken *dhansak* (₹450), with other mains at ₹250–600. Daily 8am–11pm.

Villa Blanche Assagao ☎ 98221 55099, ⓦ villablanche-goa.com; map p.719. A short drive from Anjuna on the road to Mapusa, this great bistro-cum-bakery serves terrific light bites, including smoked salmon bagels with capers (₹450), heavier mains such as German-style beef meatballs (₹440), and everything from healthy sprout salads to home-made ice cream. On Sunday it hosts a popular brunch (10am–4pm) which just keeps on giving for ₹800; booking is essential. Mon–Sat 9am–11pm, Sun 10am–4pm.

Xavier's South Anjuna ☎ 99231 33200; map p.719. Nestled in the palm forest just inland from the flea market, Xavier's has formed the hub of the south Anjuna alternative scene for decades, and is still going strong. Most people come for the seafood, kebabs, tikkas and tandoori dishes (₹350–450), but they also serve tasty Chinese grub. Look for the sign on the left off the market lane. Daily 11am–3pm & 6.30–11pm.

NIGHTLIFE

Anjuna is far from being the rave spot it once was, but at least one big party is still held in the area around the Christmas/New Year full-moon period. The rest of the time, serious tranceheads make the trek up to Vagator (see page 722) or Aswem (see page 726).

Curlie's/Shiva Valley South beach, Anjuna ⓦ curlies goa.com; map p.719. A pair of adjacent shacks that together form the focus of a rather heavy, druggy scene,

12

THE DARK SIDE OF THE MOON

Lots of visitors come to Goa expecting to be able to party on the beach every night, and are dismayed when most places to dance turn out to be mainstream clubs they probably wouldn't look twice at back home. The truth is that the full-on, elbows-in-the-air beach party of old, when tens of thousands of people would space out to huge techno sound systems under neon-painted palm trees, is – for now – pretty much a thing of the past in Goa.

Goa's coastal villages saw their first big parties back in the 1960s with the influx of hippies to Calangute and Baga. Much to the amazement of the locals, the preferred pastime of these wannabe sadhus was to cavort naked on the sands together on full-moon nights, amid a haze of chillum smoke and loud rock music. At first the villagers took little notice of these bizarre gatherings, but with each season the scene became better established, and by the late 1970s the Christmas and New Year parties, in particular, had become huge events, attracting travellers from all over the country.

In the late 1980s, the local party scene received a dramatic shot in the arm with the coming of Acid House and techno. LSD and ecstasy became the preferred dance drugs as the rock and dub scene gave way to rave culture, with ever-greater numbers of young clubbers pouring in for the season on charter flights. Goa soon spawned its own distinctive brand of psychedelic music, known as Goa Trance, cultivated by artists such as Goa Gill, Juno Reactor and Hallucinogen.

The golden era for Goa's party scene, and Goa Trance, was in the early 1990s, when big raves were held two or three times a week in beautiful locations around Anjuna and Vagator. For a few years the authorities turned a blind eye. Then, quite suddenly, the plug was pulled: during the run-up to the Y2K celebrations a ban on amplified music was imposed between 10pm and 7am. Nearly twenty years later, the curfew is still officially in place but routinely flaunted: some places pay backhanders to stay open until the early hours, while during an election year it's early to bed for everyone again. Today's rave scene is limited to a few es*tablished*, ab*ove-boa*rd clubs – notably the *Nine Bar* and *Hilltop* in Vagator (see page 724), and *Marbela Beach* at Aswem (see page 727). The recent drop in foreign tourist numbers, however, has led to talk of the legislation being changed.

with large, mixed crowds of both Indian and Western tourists gathering from sunset until 10pm. A small dance area between the two hosts trance parties every Thurs from sunset till very late. Drinks at regular shack prices; admission free. Daily sunset–10pm.

SHOPPING

Artjuna House 972 Monteiro Vaddo ✆0832 227 4794, ⓦartjuna.com; map p.719. Chock full of everything from cute kids' clothes to antique furniture, Artjuna's delightful boutique offers an eclectic mix of jewellery by expat designers, as well as tribal adornments. They also do a fantastic collection of women's clothes and create unique leatherwork – all displayed in a lovely Portuguese villa. There's a nice little café too. Daily 8am–10.30pm.

DIRECTORY

Banks and exchange ATMs are clustered along the Mapusa Rd near the Bank of Baroda, which itself will make encashment against Visa cards, but doesn't offer foreign exchange.

Post office The village post office is on the Mapusa Rd near the bank.

Vagator

Barely a couple of kilometres of clifftops and parched grassland separate Anjuna from the southern fringes of **VAGATOR**. Spread around a tangle of winding back lanes, this is a more chilled, undeveloped resort that appeals, in the main, to southern European beach bums who come back year after year.

With the red ramparts of **Chapora fort** looming above it, Vagator's broad sandy beach – known as "**Big Vagator**" – is undeniably beautiful. However, a peaceful swim or lie on the sand is out of the question here as it's a prime stop for bus parties of domestic tourists. A much better option, though one that still sees more than its fair share of day-trippers, is the next beach south. Backed by a steep wall of crumbling **palm-fringed** laterite, **Little** (or "Ozran") **Vagator** beach is actually a string of three contiguous coves. To reach them you have to walk from where the buses park above Big Vagator, or drive to the end of the lane running off *the mai*n Chapora–Anjuna road (towards the *Nine Bar*), from where footpaths drop sharply down to a wide stretch of level white sand (look for the mopeds and bikes parked at the top of the cliff). Long dominated by Italian tourists, the southernmost – dubbed "**Spaghetti Beach**" – is the prettiest, with a string of well-established shacks, at the end of which a face carved out of the rocks, staring serenely skywards, is the most prominent landmark. Relentless racquetball, trance sound systems and a particularly sizeable herd of stray cows are the other defining features.

ARRIVAL AND INFORMATION

VAGATOR

By bus Buses from Panjim and Mapusa, 9km east, pull in every 15min or so at the crossroads on the far northeastern edge of Vagator, near where the main road peels away towards Chapora. From here, it's a 1km walk over the hill and down the other side to the beach.

ACCOMMODATION

Bethany Inn Just south of the main road ✆98223 85154; map p.723. Ten immaculate, self-contained rooms with minibar fridges, balconies and attached bathrooms; plus four additional a/c options in a new block, with big TVs, larger balconies and more spacious tiled bathrooms (up to ₹2500). ₹1600

★ **Boon's Ark** Near Bethany Inn ✆0832 2274045 or ✆98221 75620, ⓦboonsark.com; map p.723. Honest, clean, family-run place offering modern rooms with excellent beds, stone shelves, fridges and pleasant little verandas opening on a well-tended courtyard garden. Owners Peter and Jessie Hungu also offer room service, money exchange and bikes to rent. A/c ₹500 extra. ₹1800

Dolrina Vagator Beach Rd ✆7774075583; map p.723. Nestled under a lush canopy of trees near the beach, Vagator's largest budget guesthouse has 12 rooms and two dorms set amidst the greenery. There are three categories of non a/c rooms, including a couple of larger family options and dorms for up to six people (can be as much as ₹3000 in high season). Long term stays can be negotiated at discounted prices. Breakfast can be served in your room. ₹700

★ **Jackie's Daynite** Beach Rd ✆0832 227 4320 or 98221 33789; map p.723. The best all-round budget place in the village, perfectly placed within easy reach of both the *Nine Bar* and *Hilltop*. Jackie De Souza has been running a shop here for almost forty years, and added rooms behind. Room rates depend on the season and there are four categories, with a/c more expensive. They're clean and great value, though often booked, so reserve in advance. **₹900**

Vista Mare Little Vagator clifftop ☏ 97670 64192, ⊚ vistamarevagator.com; map p.723. Lovely big rooms

behind a (quiet-ish) restaurant on the cliff top, boasting a/c, king-size beds, spacious attached bathrooms, marble-topped tables and huge verandas. A top location and they also have a six person room for ₹7000. **₹4000**

Yellow House Big Vagator ☏ 98221 25869; map p.723. Henriquita Moniz and son Jubert renovated this guesthouse behind Big Vagator beach, which now looks better than ever after more than twenty years in business.

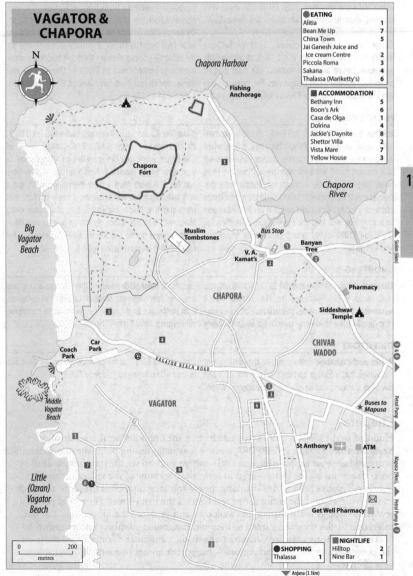

VAGATOR & CHAPORA

N

Chapora Harbour

Fishing Anchorage

Chapora Fort

Chapora River

Big Vagator Beach

Muslim Tombstones

Bus Stop

Banyan Tree

V. A. Kamat's

CHAPORA

Pharmacy

Siddeshwar Temple

Coach Park

Car Park

@ VAGATOR BEACH ROAD

CHIVAR WADDO

Middle Vagator Beach

VAGATOR

Buses to Mapusa

St Anthony's

ATM

Little (Ozran) Vagator Beach

Get Well Pharmacy

0 — 200 metres

● EATING

Alitia	1
Bean Me Up	7
China Town	5
Jai Ganesh Juice and Ice cream Centre	2
Piccola Roma	3
Sakana	4
Thalassa (Mariketty's)	6

■ ACCOMMODATION

Bethany Inn	5
Boon's Ark	6
Casa de Olga	1
Dolrina	4
Jackie's Daynite	8
Shettor Villa	2
Vista Mare	7
Yellow House	3

● SHOPPING

Thalassa	1

■ NIGHTLIFE

Hilltop	2
Nine Bar	1

Siolim (6km)

Petrol Pump

3 & 4

Mapusa (9km)

Petrol Pump & 7

12

Anjuna (3.1km)

It's peaceful and secluded, despite the proximity of the surf, and the 13 rooms are neat and pleasantly furnished (a/c room ₹1800). There is a restaurant that serves breakfast but it isn't complimentary. ₹1000

EATING

Bean Me Up Near the petrol pump ☎ 0832 227 3479, ⓦ beanmeup.in; map p.723. North Goa's only raw and vegan joint – the last word in Goan gourmet healthy eating. Design-your-own salads and fresh juices, various tofu, tempeh and combos steeped in creamy sauces, and pizzas from a real wood-fired oven. Mains (₹180–350) come with steamed spinach, fresh brown bread and hygienically-washed greens. Daily 8am–11pm.

China Town Chapora crossroads, next to Bethany Inn ☎ 98221 42230; map p.723. This small roadside restaurant, tucked away just south of the main drag, is perennially popular for its budget eats. The menu includes tasty in addition to a large Chinese selection and all the usual Goa-style travellers' grub. A meal for two is about ₹400. Daily 9am–11pm.

★ **Thalassa (Mariketty's)** Ozran clifftop ☎ 98500 33537, ⓦ thalassagoa.com; map p.723. Stylish and hospitable, Thalassa serves high-end, flavoursome and scrupulously-authentic Greek food, with excellent service, against a backdrop of swaying palms and rippling ocean. Try to get there in time for the stunning sunset from the large (and popular) terrace. Especially recommended are the kebabs – you can often see them spit-roasting a whole lamb as you enter. Count on ₹1200 for three courses plus drinks; double that if you have seafood. Booking essential. Daily 9am–11.30pm.

NIGHTLIFE

Hilltop Vagator ☎ 0832 2273665, ⓦ facebook.com/hilltopgoa; map p.723. *Hilltop's* big night is Sun, when bumper crowds take to its pretty, circular dancefloor, set in a coconut grove just back from the clifftop. The PA is heavy duty, the palm trunks painted regulation neon, chai mamas ring the arena with their flickering kerosene lamps and freshly baked nibbles, and overseas DJs do the honours on stage. They also host their own night market on Fri. Admission ₹1000–1500, though occasionally free. Fri & Sun 4–10pm.

Nine Bar Above Small Vagator beach ☎ 96231 02102, ⓦ club9bar.com; map p.723. The spiritual home of Goa trance, where you can space out on a large open-air dancefloor as the sun sets behind a curtain of palm trees and DJs spin beats from a chest-thumping rig. It's got a very welcoming vibe and admission is free – but note that photography is strictly prohibited. They play trance every Mon, with different dance genres on one or two other nights a week during the season. Daily 9am–sunset for food; 5pm–sunrise on party nights.

SHOPPING

Thalassa Ozran clifftop ☎ 98500 33537, ⓦ thalassago.com; map p.723. Attached to the popular Greek restaurant of the same name, this boutique offers a range of stylish beach and evening wear, from beautiful floaty dresses to hand-made textiles. There is also a selection from resident designer Martino Caramia, who favours light cotton and bright colours – perfect attire for sipping sundowners. Daily 11am–11pm.

DIRECTORY

Banks and exchange *Bethany Inn*, on the north side of the village, has a foreign exchange licence (for cash and travellers' cheques), and an efficient travel agency (Vikings Trail; ☎ 3222 73731) in the office on the ground floor. The nearest ATM is in Anjuna (see page 722).

Chapora

Huddled in the shadow of a Portuguese fort on the opposite, northern side of the headland from Vagator is **CHAPORA**, north Goa's main fishing port. The anchorage and boatyard below its brown-walled citadel – where you can see the mostly now disused boats drawn up on the shore – used to form the backbone of the village's economy, but there's always been a hard-drinking, heavy-smoking hippie tourist scene alongside it, revolving around the coffee shops and bars on the main street. For a brief period a few years back, Russian mafia types took over and squeezed the hippies out, but like migrating turtles they've returned to their old hangout in numbers undiminished by Goa's recent changes. Today Chapora remains the commuter dormitory for those on the party scene in Vagator and Anjuna – many rent houses or rooms long-term here, year after year.

Chapora fort

Chapora's chief landmark is its venerable old **fort**, most easily reached from the Vagator side of the hill. At low tide, you can also walk around the bottom of the headland, via the anchorage and the secluded coves beyond it to Big Vagator, then head up the hill from there. The red-laterite bastion, crowning the rocky bluff, was built by the Portuguese in 1617 on the site of an earlier Muslim structure (thus the village's name – from Shahpura, "town of the Shah"). Deserted in the nineteenth century, it lies in ruins today, although the views up and down the coast from the weed-infested ramparts are still superb.

ARRIVAL AND DEPARTURE
CHAPORA

By bus Buses run between Chapora and Panjim (3 daily), and from Mapusa (every 15min), with departures until 7.30pm. Most drop passengers at the old banyan tree at the far end of the main street, where the motorcycle pilots all hang out.

ACCOMMODATION

Chapora specializes in long-term rentals of rooms and houses (by the week or month) to repeat visitors; these economical options can be found by asking around the village.

Casa de Olga ☎0832 227 4355, ✉eadsouza@yahoo.co.in; map p.723. By far the most comfortable guesthouse in Chapora, this immaculate, red-and-white-painted little place, near the fishing anchorage, is run with great efficiency and enthusiasm by hosts Edmund and Elisa. Their nicest rooms are in a new block to the rear, which are all attached and have good-sized balconies; Rates can go up to ₹1500 for rooms with attached bathrooms, hot showers and a quiet spot around the back. **₹600**

Shettor Villa Off the west side of the main street ☎0832 227 3766 or ☎98221 58154, ✉brianlive@hotmail.com; map p.723. More basic than Casa de Olga, with five attached rooms with fans, ranged around a sheltered backyard; there's also a (sometimes noisy) rooftop restaurant where you can use the wi-fi. **₹500**

EATING

Alitia On the main street ☎7262 076857; map p.723. Chapora's main street is a bit of a low-key bar-hopping zone most nights for locals and foreign residents; this tiny shack is a good place to refuel on tasty crêpes, waffles and toasties (₹150–350), made with fresh or imported ingredients like mozzarella, chorizo and smoked ham. Outstanding coffee, too. Daily dusk–dawn.

Jai Ganesh Juice and Ice cream Centre Just up from the banyan tree ☎9823686262; map p.723. The focal point of the tourist scene, where Chapora's resident Westerners watch the world go by over fresh fruit juices and milkshakes (₹50–90) and perhaps a cheese or chocolate croissant (₹90). Daily 8am–sunset.

Piccola Roma 1km southwest of Chapora on the Mapusa Rd ☎5078 06821; map p.723. One of the few restaurants in the area that stays open year-round, this Indian-run joint serves very good Italian food with particularly good wood-oven pizza (₹210–550). They also deliver within 5km. Daily noon–11pm.

Sakana 1km southwest of Chapora on the Mapusa Rd, opposite Piccola Roma ☎98901 35502; map p.723. Generally considered one of the best Japanese places in Goa, this smart and stylish joint decorated with paper lanterns and red tablecloths serves fresh sashimi (from ₹450), veg and non-veg sushi (₹200–370) and a set menu of king fish or tuna teriyaki (₹600–650). Daily noon–midnight.

12

Morjim

Relatively isolated, the village of **MORJIM** was where Goa's first Russian tourists headed in the early noughties. Once dubbed "Morjimograd" by other foreign visitors, it has now reverted to a mixed resort, attracting more middle-aged Brits and Indians than Russians. That said, the atmosphere in the guesthouses and restaurants along and behind the beach can feel less than friendly (probably as few Russians speak any English), and most Western travellers find the experience of staying here disconcerting – not to mention eye-wateringly expensive. Many prefer to continue north to the more culturally-mixed resorts of Aswem and Mandrem.

Morjim beach itself is dramatic and well worth at least a walk, especially in the early morning, when you may see teams of fishermen hauling giant handnets from the surf. The spit at its southern end, opposite Chapora fort, is also a great birding hot spot.

ARRIVAL AND DEPARTURE

By bus Half a dozen buses a day skirt Morjim en route to Panjim, the first at 7am; heading the other way, you can pick up a direct bus from Panjim at 5pm, and there are hourly services from Mapusa via Siolim after 11am. They'll drop you on the main road, a 5min walk from the beachfront area at Vithaldas Waddo.

ACCOMMODATION

Because of the unwelcoming vibe, the hotels and guesthouses immediately behind the beach, in the dunes and along the beachfront road, are best avoided. One really nice option, however, stands on the riverfront south of the village.

★ **Jardin d'Ulysse** Facing the riverbank on the village's south side ☎ 98225 81928, ✉ ulyssemorjim@gmail.com. Delightful Goan/French-run place comprising five a/c "cottages" with tiled roofs, ochre-washed floors and kitchenettes. Down in the front garden, a small restaurant whips up an eclectic menu of steaks, scrumptious lasagne, Tibetan *momos* and salads for mostly French and British travellers – at least ₹500/head for a meal without drinks. Owners Fleur and Gilbert are charming, always on hand to help arrange excursions, boat trips and scooters. **₹4700**

EATING

★ **Sublime** Morjim beach ☎ 98224 84051, ⊕ facebook.com/SublimeMorjim. Run by celebrity chef, Chris Saleem Agha Bee, this funky little gastro beach shack in the heart of Morjim rustles up stylish, innovative cuisine deploying novel combos of fresh local ingredients: try the fish carpaccio (₹310) or ginger batter calamari (₹290) for starters, and Asiatic beef with wasabi mashed potatoes (₹60) for mains. Ample veggie options include the popular mega organic salad (₹350). Booking essential. Daily noon–3pm & 6–11pm.

Aswem

Pretty **ASWEM**, the next settlement north of Morjim, could hardly be described as a proper resort. Officially inside the Coastal Protection Zone, its beachfront holds few permanent buildings and most of the accommodation is in temporary structures. And yet, over the past few seasons, the s*trip* of soft white sand nestled beneath its *mand* of slender palms has become the place to see and be seen by India's hip set – Mumbai millionaires, Bollywood A-listers and international celebs are regularly spotted in the swanky resorts and clubs in the dunes. A more down-to-earth scene holds sway around the headland to the south, which is family friendly, with lots of children playing on the beach. How long this stretch can hold out against the rising tide of bling, however, is anyone's guess.

ARRIVAL AND DEPARTURE

By bus Buses from Panjim (3 daily; 1hr 30min) cover the quiet stretch of road running parallel to the beach inland, from where a 5min walk across paddy fields brings you to the shacks and hut camps attached to them. More frequent buses can be caught from the stop 2km away in Morjim.

ACCOMMODATION

With accommodation either ultrabasic or staggeringly expensive, most visitors ride up to Aswem for the day on scooters and decamp after sunset. A handful of places, however, offer reasonable value.

Anahata ☎ 98225 90123, ⊕ anahataretreat.com. This spot, in the coconut plantation under the Ajoba temple just north of *La Plage* restaurant, is arguably the finest place on the coast here. The place holds sixteen octagonal huts made from dark mango wood and five rooms described as "Anahata Villas", costing around ₹18,000. The cheapest are in the garden, with some on the beach (₹11000) and others with sea views (₹13500). They're large, well-spaced, have wraparound verandas, and are naturally cross-ventilated, with quality beds and simple, relaxing decor. There is also a yoga space and a great restaurant and lounge area on the beach. **₹9500**

Leela Cottages Near La Plage ☎ 0840 792 4040, ⊕ leelacottage.com. Beautiful designer huts, cottages, suites and beach houses of various sizes and prices, grouped in a gated property under the palms. The interiors are furnished with antiques collected from all over India. It's just a stone's throw from the beach, but far enough away from the restaurants to remain quiet (and free from cooking smells). There is a yogashala, a spa and a couple of restaurants serving both Indian and Continental cuisine. **₹7000**

Nifa Aswem Morjim Rd, opposite the Madji Organic Café ☎ 0832 224 4400 or ☎ 98221 33370, ⊕ hotelnifa.com. A cheaper alternative set back on the roadside inland, *Nifa* has clean, comfortable, fan and a/c (₹2500) rooms as well as sea-facing options (₹3500) a short walk from the beach. There is a small pool on site. ₹1200

Otter Creek ☎ 98700 11500, ⊕ aseascape.com. You have to cross a rickety footbridge to reach these three luxury tents, nestled on the riverbank just behind the dunes, in the thick of a coconut plantation. Each is fitted with a bamboo four-poster, with a fridge and mini bar, attached bathroom, verandah and a jetty facing the creek. The rates vary according to low and high seasons. They are also closed during the monsoons in the months of May to October. The magic of this is place is that you are right near the sea

shore and there are five beach houses as well. All details on website. ₹2500

★ **Yab Yum** ☎ 0832 651 0392, ⊕ yabyumresorts.com. A campus of beautiful domed structures made from palm thatch, mango wood and laterite, with curvy moulded concrete floors and purple walls. Large and attractively furnished inside, the rooms have beds on platforms and comfy mattresses, glitter balls, paper lanterns and muslin drapes. Accommodation varies from non a/c tents to standard a/c cottages (₹11,500) to a super-chic suite on the beach housing four people (₹25,600). ₹10,700

EATING

Agni Café Leela Cottages, near La Plage ☎ 0840 792 4040, ⊕ leelacottage.com. This restaurant specialises in Mughalai and tandoori cuisine with an occasional Mexican or Continental dish. There are vegetarian and non-vegetarian combo meals (₹450-550) and ala carte dishes as well. Vegan food and organic dishes are available on request. Daily 8.30am–10.30pm.

Gopal Just south of La Plage ☎ 98221 47416. Once the only shack on Aswem beach, now almost hidden by its more famous neighbour *La Plage*, Gopal still commands a loyal following of customers who want simple Indian food. It offers a typical Goan menu, focussing on sea food – fish/prawn curry rice and a bit of everything from all over the world, be it Indian Chinese or tandoori. Mains cost ₹350-500. Daily 8am–10pm.

Elevar Leela Cottages ☎ 91303 52188. Nestled inside *Leela Cottages*, this chic restaurant serves European and Italian cuisine with a dash of Indian flavour and a focus on seafood. Try their mustard marinated fish or their mezze platter. A meal for two with drinks costs in the region of

₹1500–1700. While the liquid centred chocolate cake is highly recommended, you can also opt for the chef's special, which is a personalised dessert served at your table after a consultation with the chef. Daily 11.30am–10.30pm.

★ **La Plage** Aswem beach ☎ 98221 21712. Nestled in a shady coconut grove, *La Plage* does a brisk trade in Gallic-Mediterranean snacks and drinks, served up by Nepali waiters in black lunghis. The menu changes a little each season and the restaurant is reworking its entire menu for the next festive season along with the rates. However mains would be around ₹600. Their chocolate thali with five choco-rich desserts at ₹700 is not to be missed. Booking essential for dinner and Sun lunch. Daily 8.30am–11pm.

Roma Aswem beach road, before Anahata ☎ 92268 93536. Pretty, Italian-run garden restaurant with delicious wood-fired pizzas (₹260–450), and an interesting (and similarly priced) selection of home-made pasta, including very good ravioli with mushroom sauce. A cut above the usual Italian dishes, and they have a children's play area too. Daily 11am–midnight.

NIGHTLIFE

Aswem has emerged as a new face of Goan nightlife, with a few chic beachfront clubs where you can jump off the dancefloor straight on to the sand. In addition to *Marbela Beach* there are a couple of other choices – such as *Club Fresh* – but whether they are good or not depends very much on which crew are on the decks in any one year.

Marbela Beach Aswem ⊕ marbelabeach.com. Probably

the chicest club in Goa, this white-themed resort on the beachfront features a lounge bar, champagne bar and three open-air dancefloors blasting dance mixes into the night air from outsized PAs. At the time of writing, only the accommodation, with the bar and night club under renovation. Check the website for more details.

SHOPPING

Jade Jagger Aswem beach, south of La Plage. Aswem is renowned for its designer boutiques. This place features beautifully chic and eye-wateringly expensive beach

creations from the renowned designer, with floaty dresses and jewellery set with precious stones. Thurs–Tues noon–6.30pm.

Mandrem

From the far side of the creek bounding the edge of Aswem, a magnificent and largely empty beach stretches north towards Arambol – the last unspoiled stretch of the north Goan coast. Whether or not **MANDREM** can continue to hold out against the developers remains to be seen, but for the time being, nature still has the upper hand here. Olive ridley marine turtles nest on the quietest patches, and you're more than likely to catch a glimpse of one of the white-bellied fish eagles that live in the casuarina trees – their last stronghold in the north of Goa.

ARRIVAL AND INFORMATION   MANDREM

By bus Connected by regular buses from Mapsua (9 daily; 1hr 30min), the market area at Madlamaz is easy to reach by public transport, but getting to the beach area is trickier as auto-rickshaws are few and far between. Ask your guesthouse or hut camp for help.

Services A couple of small grocery stores, internet cafés, ATMs and travel agents are on hand.

ACCOMMODATION

Most of the village's accommodation is tucked away inland at Junasa Waddo, where a growing number of small guesthouses, hotels and yoga retreats cater to a mixed, peace-and-quiet-loving crowd – costs are generally higher than at Arambol, however.

Ashiyana Junasa Waddo ⊚ashiyana-yoga-goa.com. If you like your yoga retreats to be drop-dead gorgeous, look no further than here. Perched on the banks of the Mandrem River facing the sea from the middle of an old coconut *mand*, the centre offers world-class yoga, massage, meditation and *satsang* tuition with accommodation in Indonesian-style boutique treehouses and ecolodges. Some of them boast glorious sea views, and there's a wholefood-Ayurvedic-veg restaurant on site (guests only). Rates vary depending on accommodation and they include workshop sessions and meals. There is also a per person rate of ₹650 for just a yoga session or a meal. ₹8000

The Mandala Just upriver from Ashiyana ☎98115

00069, ⊛themandalagoa.com. Beautifully-painted murals adorn the buildings at *Mandala*, a "back-to-nature boutique resort". There are four categories of rooms, starting with the large and spacious Panomandala suite with a private terrace overlooking the lagoon, There are also villas, eco beach huts and you can stay in the main house at the Art House double a/c bedrooms. The villas are like two tiered bamboo chalets based on the design of Kerala houseboats. Yoga classes and workshops are conducted as well. Email for rates, which change seasonally.

Villa River Cat ☎0822 224 7928 or 98236 10001, ⊛villarivercat.com. Quirky riverside hotel, screened from the beach by the dunes, with distinctive hippie-influenced décor and furniture. The fifteen rooms including wooden cottages are all individually designed: mosaics, shells, devotional sculpture and hammocks set the tone. Host Rinoo Seghal is an animal-lover, so brace yourself for the menagerie of cats and dogs. ₹3015

EATING

★ **Café Nu** Junnaswada, small track before D'Souzas Residency ☎98506 58568. Lovely open-sided restaurant in a pretty garden, serving sublime, light gourmet bites. There are plenty of fish dishes (₹400–600), a popular steak (₹600) and for the health-conscious, a copious variety of salads (₹200-400). The Bonbon dessert (₹290) is legendary. Booking essential for dinner. Daily 11.30–2.30pm & 6–10.30pm.

O'Saiba Mandrem beach. Great views from this beach shack, which serves up high-quality versions of the usual Indian and tandoori food. Expect delicious seafood including *hariyali* king prawn and fish curry, fish tikka with fresh mint sauce and a flavoursome palak paneer (₹250) and a fair number of Western favourites (prices ₹500–800). Daily 7am–11pm.

Arambol

ARAMBOL, 32km northwest of Mapusa, is easily the most populous village in the far north, and the area's main tourist hub. Traditionally a refuge for a hard-core hippie fringe, it nowadays attracts a lively and eclectic mix of travellers, the majority of whom stick around for the season, living in rented rooms, hut camps and small houses scattered behind the magnificent white sand beach. As in most of north Goa, there's also a showing of young, often quite alternative, Russians here, joining the spiritually inclined types from northern Europe who have long formed Arambol's mainstay. The overall vibe is inclusive and positive, with plenty of live music, lots of relaxed places to eat and drink, and more opportunities to learn new yoga poses and reshuffle your chakras than you could get through in several lifetimes. Beach life is generally laidback too – except on weekends, when day-tripping drinkers descend en masse in SUVs from nearby Maharashtra.

The village and beaches

Arambol's main drag is a winding road lined cheek-by-jowl with clothes and bedspread stalls, travel agents, internet cafés and souvenir shops. The lane bends downhill to the main beach – one of the most picturesque in south India, dotted with wooden outriggers. The best view of it is from the crucifix and small **Parasurama shrine** on the hilltop to the north, which is an especially serene spot at sunset. **After dark**, when the Hula-Hoopers, fire jugglers and *bhajan* singers have turned homewards, the candles and fairy lights of the shacks illuminate the beachfront to magical effect.

Swimming is possible here during the daytime, but less inspiring than around the headland at Paliem or "Lakeside" beach, reached by following the track through a series of rocky-bottomed coves. The path emerges at a broad strip of soft white sand hemmed in by cliffs. Behind here a small freshwater lake extends along the bottom of the valley into the jungle, lined with sulphurous mud, which, when smeared over the body, dries to form a surreal, butter-coloured shell.

Keep following the path around the back of the lake and you'll soon come to Paliem's famous **banyan tree**, a monster specimen with giant runners extending more than 60m – a popular chillum-smoking spot. Keen walkers can continue over the cliffs immediately north – Arambol's prime parascending venue – to reach the generally quiet **Kerim beach**.

ARRIVAL AND DEPARTURE
ARAMBOL

By bus Buses run between Panjim and Arambol, via Mapusa's main town stand, every 30min until noon, and every 90min till 8pm, terminating at the small bus stop on the main road in Arambol. A faster private minibus service from Panjim bus stand arrives daily opposite the chai stalls at the beach end of the village. If you're heading for the Chapora/Vagator/Anjuna area, taking the same bus to Siolim and a taxi (₹300) or rickshaw (₹200) from there will save you changing at Mapusa.

By taxi Taxis charge ₹1500–1650 for the run from Dabolim airport to Arambol, and ₹700–800 for the 30min trip from the nearest railhead at Tivim (Thivim).

ACTIVITIES

Posters pinned to palm trees and café noticeboards around Arambol advertise an amazing array of activities, from **kitesurfing** to **reiki**. Good places to get a fix on what's happening are the noticeboard at Lamuella (see page 731) and *Double Dutch's* "Bullshit Info" corner (see page 731), which displays details for just about everyone who *does* anything – including their own popular *dokra* bronze-casting workshops, held annually each January.

Dance Temple of Dance Girkar Waddo, signposted off the road close to the Kundalini Rooftop Garden, offers tribal fusion to contemporary, salsa, Bollywood and belly dance styles, and hosts a festival (Feb 9–11) with workshops and performances.

Paragliding Tandem rides from the clifftops above Lakeside beach, run by an ever-changing

12

● SHOPPING	
Lamuella	1

■ NIGHTLIFE	
Ash	1
Surf Club	2

■ ACCOMMODATION		● EATING	
Arun Huts	4	Cheeky Monkey	6
Famafa	3	Double Dutch	7
Go-Ym	6	Dylan's (Toasted and Roasted)	9
Ivon's	5	Fellini's	4
The No Name		Lamuella	5
Guest House	2	The No Name Guest House	2
Om Ganesh		Relax Inn	3
Naik Guest House	1	Rice Bowl	1
Surf Club	7	Sai Deep	8

YOGA IN ARAMBOL

Yogis and yoga classes are ubiquitous in Arambol, and of varying quality. Here are two of our favourites.

Sharat Yoga Modlo Waddo ☎98166 11075, ⓦhiyogacentre.com; map p.729. Iyengar yoga teacher Sharat holds five-day sessions (Nov–March, courses start on Wed; ₹5500) in his studio. To find it, head for the *Priya Guest House* and follow the "HIYC" signs from there. Accommodation, in a comfortable tent with attached bathroom, is ₹750 a night for single occupancy and ₹900 for double. There are also luxurious rooms available and prices range from ₹750-1200 for single occupancy and ₹1500-1800 for double occupancy.

Viriam Kaur's Kundalini Yoga Kundalini Rooftop Garden, Girkar Waddo ☎96375 55880, ⓦorganickarma.co.uk; map p.729. These classes, held in the leafy rooftop garden, have a strong following – not least because it's among the few places in India where you can learn Kundalini yoga. Also trained in Western and Ayurvedic massage, Viriam and her partner Adam Divine offer individual sessions and training, plus workshops and courses on chakra healing and other therapeutic techniques.

combination of Indian and international fliers. Costs include all equipment and full instruction. For more information, go to the Western India Paragliding Association shack, just in front of the lake.

ACCOMMODATION

The cost of accommodation in Arambol has risen sharply over the past few seasons, reflecting the village's popularity with more affluent hippies, but it's still nearly all pitched at budget travellers: no-frills, Goan-run guesthouses and expat-inspired hippie-chic predominate here.

Arun Huts Near Narayan Temple ☎81919 00095; map p.729. Quirky little hut camp, run by local beautician, Mrs Mala Singh, in the thick of Arambol village. Just 60m from the sea, it comprises two rows of neatly painted wood huts, fitted with decent mattresses, attached shower toilets and fans. The whole earth-floored compound is smothered in banana trees, palms and flowers, and very atmospheric, especially in the evening. ₹1000

Famafa Khalcha Waddo ☎96049 21200, ⓦfamafa rambolgoa.com; map p.729. Large, anodyne concrete place just off the main drag; very close to the beach and great value. One of the few places with hot showers. They don't take bookings and operate a 10am checkout, so get here early for a room. Double a/c rooms are ₹500 extra. ₹500

Go-Ym Bag Waddo, close to Atman ☎95031 12167, ⓦgo-ym.com; map p.729. Large mid-range resort with fifteen tiled, vibrantly-coloured cottages close to the beach. The tastefully decorated rooms have comfortable beds. ₹2550

Ivon's Girkar Waddo ☎0832 224 2672 or ☎98221 27398; map p.729. The pick of the budget bunch: immaculately clean, tiled 25 rooms, all with attached bathroom (with hot water) some fronted by good-sized tiled balconies opening onto the dunes or a well-groomed family compound. Wi-fi in their restaurant next door. Rates increase during peak season. ₹900

The No Name Guest House Main Street Kalcha Waddo ☎70308 38396, ⓦthenonamebrand.com; map p.729. Open since 1989, this cheerful guest house has 12 large clean non a/c rooms in different categories which cost the same for both single and double occupancies. Breakfast included. There is an open kitchen and you can even watch your dishes being prepared. Grab a coffee and a sandwich and you can even have a co working space here with thatched roof and comfortable tables and stools. ₹2500

Om Ganesh Naik Guest House Rooms and cottages in the cove between the village and Lakeside beach ☎94212 57688, or book at the Om Ganesh stores on the main drag ☎0832 229 7614; map p.729. There are 25 rooms in the main guest house and the cottages, located just south of Lakeside beach have superb sea views from the verandas. Rates vary wildly according to demand, and advance booking with a deposit is all but essential by mid-season. Rates double during peak season. ₹1000

The Surf Club Kepker Vado Dando South end of the beach ☎9975054051, ⓦthesurfclubgoa.com; map p.729. Simple, clean, very good eight rooms at the quietest end of the beach, located both on the ground and first floor. The rooms upstairs are much larger and lighter than those downstairs and one of them offers a great view of sunset. Email the club for rates. There is also a restaurant and bar with live music. Email for rates.

EATING

Thanks to its annually replenished pool of expat gastronomic talent, Arambol harbours a handful of unexpectedly good restaurants – not that you'd guess from their generally lacklustre exteriors. The village's alternative, Western European contingent cares more about flavours than fancy decor, and prices in the village reflect this. The more affluent short-term visitors, meanwhile, tend to gravitate towards the fancier seafood joints along the beachfront, where the day's catch is displayed on cold trays for selection, then grilled alfresco in front of you. Prices can be eye-popping, so get a quote before you order.

Cheeky Monkey Arambol beach ☎98508 23926; map p.729. A cut above your average beach shack, offering a great variety of salads, home-made pastas and stir-fried noodle dishes. Try the beetroot salad (₹270), mushroom ravioli (₹230) and the only dessert on the menu, a knockout chocolate pudding with cinnamon ice cream (₹250). Daily 9am–11pm.

★ **Double Dutch** Main St, halfway down on the right (look for the yellow signboard) ☎70838 89420; map p.729. Spread under a palm canopy in the heart of the village, this laidback café is the hub of alternative Arambol. Renowned for its melt-in-the-mouth apple pie (₹210), it also offers a tempting range of home-bake buttery biscuits, cakes, healthy salads (₹110–230) and sumptuous main meals (from ₹200–400), including popular dishes like Indonesian noodles (₹250) and perennially popular "mixed stuff" (stuffed mushrooms and capsicums with sesame pesto; ₹320). Daily 7am–11pm.

Dylan's (Toasted and Roasted) Behind Kinara restaurant and Golden Hands jewellers ☎96047 80316; map p.729. Owner Raj insists that it's not just about the coffee and the cookies, but both are exceptional – he also sells ground coffee and beans. In the evening, as well as serving a decent veg thali (₹150), he hosts regular concerts and art shows. Mon–Sat 9am–11pm.

Fellini's Main St ☎98814 61224; map p.729. Italian-run place serving delicious wood-fired pizzas (₹230–450), and authentic pasta or gnocchi with a choice of more than twenty sauces. It gets horrendously busy in season, so get here early if you want snappy service. Daily 11am–11pm.

★ **Lamuella** Main St ☎98224 86314; map p.729. Hiding behind the boutique of the same name, *Lamuella* serves healthy breakfasts, toasties, hummus plates and filling salads during the day, as well as energizing juice combos and herb teas. After sunset you can order from an eclectic menu with amazing home-made mushroom ravioli and fish and cheese (₹370-420), with chocolate fondant ice cream for dessert (₹180). Daily 8.30am–11pm.

The No Name Guesthouse Main Street Kalcha Waddo ☎70308 38396, ⊛thenonamebrand.com; map p.729. This guest house has a lovely open kitchen that serves European and Mediterranean cuisine that is vegetarian and vegan. Try their salads, homemade pasta, hummus and paella. They have a set menu every day and breakfast is served from 9am till 1pm (₹450). Set meals from ₹650. Daily 9am-9pm

Relax Inn North end of beach; map p.729. Top-quality seafood straight off the boats, and authentic pasta (you get even more expat Italians in here than at Fellini's) – try the vongole (clam) sauce. Inexpensive (most mains around ₹200–300), but expect a wait as they cook to order. Daily 8–10.30pm.

Rice Bowl North end of beach ☎70306 07427; map p.729. This cliffside place serves the best Chinese food in Arambol, with a perfect view of the beach to match, and a pool table (₹120/hr). Any of their tasty noodle dishes are safe bets, as are the Japanese and Tibetan specialities (₹190–350). Daily 8am–11pm.

Sai Deep At the bottom end of the village ☎90490 51266; map p.729. This little *dhaba* has a devoted following. They serve copious fruit salads as well as a good travellers' breakfast menu of pancakes, eggs and curd all at rock bottom prices – the veg thali is a mere ₹70. Daily 8.30am–8.30pm.

NIGHTLIFE

Many of the shacks on the beach have occasional live music, though *Dylan's* has the most going on, with some kind of (usually) low-key performance most nights.

Ash Girkar Waddo ☎885509 60772; map p.729. With amazing art work, this Russian-run open-air venue hosts two or three events a week during the season, with everything from Russian shamanic singers to gypsy folk musicians and Sufi bands – the musicianship is of a

consistently high standard. Event nights only 6.30–11pm.

Surf Club South end of the beach ☎99750 54051, ⊛thesurfclubgoa.com; map p.729. Secret little hippie drinking establishment decorated with some trippy tiles, this place has a great vibe and hosts some very good psychedelic rock acts every week or so on its small stage. Daily 8am–10pm.

SHOPPING

Lamuella Opposite Shiv Krupa Store, Main St; map p.729. In the heart of Arambol, *Lamuella* holds a great collection of clothes for women and children – with a few options for men – mostly from expat local designers.

They also stock beautiful jewellery for every budget and homeware from fair-trade collectives in India. There's a café in the back garden. Daily 10am–10pm.

DIRECTORY

Banks and exchange There is an ATM close to the bus stand, and several places along the main village lane change money and do cash advances on debit and credit cards: try SS Travels, opposite Om Ganesh General Store.

Post office On the east side of the village, 1km out on the Querim–Arambol–Agarwada Rd, just before the petrol pump.

12

South Goa

Backed by a lush band of coconut plantations and green hills, Goa's south coast is fringed by some of the region's finest **beaches**. An ideal first base if you've just arrived in the region is **Benaulim**, 6km west of the state's second city, **Margao**. The most traveller-friendly resort in the area, Benaulim stands slap in the middle of a spectacular 25km stretch of pure white sand. Although increasingly carved up by Mumbai time-share companies, low-cost accommodation here remains plentiful and of a consistently high standard. Nearby **Colva**, by contrast, has degenerated over the past decade into an insalubrious sink resort. Frequented by huge numbers of day-trippers, and boasting few discernible charms, it is best avoided.

With the gradual spread of package tourism down the coast, **Palolem**, a ninety-minute drive south of Margao along the main highway, is Goa's most happening beach, attracting droves of sun seekers from November through March. Set against a backdrop of forest-cloaked hills, its bay is spectacular, though the crowds can feel overwhelming in high season. For a quieter scene, try **Agonda**, just up the coast, or **Patnem**, immediately south of Palolem. Among the possible day-trips inland, a crop of Portuguese-era mansions at **Chandor** and **Quepem** are your best options; and in the far south, the **Cotigao Wildlife Sanctuary** affords a rare glimpse of unspoiled forest and its fauna.

Margao

The capital of prosperous Salcete *taluka*, **MARGAO** – referred to in railway timetables and on some maps by its official government title, **Madgaon** – is Goa's second city, and if you're arriving in the state on the Konkan Railway, you'll almost certainly have to pause here to pick up onward transport by road. Surrounded by fertile rice paddy and plantain groves, the town has always been an important agricultural market, and was once a major religious centre, with dozens of wealthy temples and *dharamshalas* – however, most of these were destroyed when the Portuguese absorbed the area into their **Novas Conquistas** ("New Conquests") during the seventeenth century. Today, Catholic churches still outnumber Hindu shrines, but Margao has retained a cosmopolitan feel due to a huge influx of migrant labour from neighbouring Karnataka and Maharashtra.

12

Largo de Igreja and around
It's a short auto-rickshaw ride from the centre to **Largo de Igreja** (Church Square), at the north end of town, where **Church of the Holy Spirit** is the main landmark of Margao's dishevelled colonial enclave. Built by the Portuguese in 1675, the church ranks among the finest examples of late Baroque architecture in Asia, with an interior dominated by a huge gilt reredos dedicated to the Virgin.

Just northeast, overlooking the main Ponda road, stands one of the state's grandest eighteenth-century *palacios*, **Sat Burzam Ghor** ("Seven Gables house"). Just three of its original seven high-pitched roof gables remain, but the mansion is still an impressive sight, its facade decorated with fancy scrollwork and huge oyster-shell windows.

Market area
Colonial-era vestiges aside, the main reason to come to Margao is to shop at the town's **market**, the hub of which is a labyrinthine covered area and shopping centre, and the open-air **Gandhi Market** just south. Just up the road, on the southeast side of the town's hectic main square, **Praça Jorge Barreto**, stands the little government-run **Khadi Gramodyog** shop, which sells the usual range of hand-spun cottons and raw silk by the metre, as well as ready-made traditional Indian garments.

ARRIVAL AND DEPARTURE   **MARGAO**

By train Margao's huge railway station, Madgaon Junction, lies 3km south of the centre, its reservation office (Mon–Sat

8am–4.30pm, Sun 8am–2pm; ☎0832 271 2940) divided between the ground and first floors. Tickets for trains to

Mumbai are in short supply, so make your reservation as far in advance as possible. If you're catching the train to Hosapete (for Hampi) get here early to avoid long queues. Several principal trains stop in Margao at unsociable times of night, but there's a 24hour information office and a round-the-clock prepaid auto-rickshaw and taxi stand outside the exit.

Destinations Canacona/Chaudi (6–7 daily; 30–45min); Gokarna (2 daily; 1hr 30min–2hr 30min); Hosapete (4 weekly; 7hr); Mangaluru (4–5 daily; 5–6hr); Mumbai (3 daily; 9hr 30min–11hr 50min).

By bus All interstate and state buses arrive at and depart from the Kadamba bus stand, 3km north of the centre, with auto-rickshaws charging around ₹100 to get into town. Buses to destinations on the south coast also stop in front of the *Kamat Hotel*, on the east side of Praça Jorge Barreto. Paulo Travel's deluxe coach to and from Hampi works from a lot 300m or so north of the Kadamba bus stand, on the left just before the large yellow government building.

Destinations Agonda (4 daily; 2hr); Benaulim (every 30min; 15min); Chandor (hourly; 45min); Canacona/Chaudi (every 30min; 1hr 40min); Gokarna (2 daily; 4hr 30min); Hampi (1 nightly; 10hr); Mangaluru (5 daily; 7hr); Mapusa (10 daily; 2hr 30min); Mumbai (2 daily; 16–18hr); Panjim (every 30min; 50min); Panolem (every 30min; 2hr); Pune (1 daily; 12hr).

ACCOMMODATION

Nanutel Rua Padre Miranda ☎0832 272 9999, ⊛nanuhotels.in; map p.733. With Colva and Benaulim so close, it's hard to think of a reason why you'd want to stay in Margao, but if you're stuck then this three-star multi-storey block, north of Praça Jorge Barreto, is a possibility. Pitched at visiting businesspeople, it has 55 comfortable central a/c rooms and a small pool with friendly staff. Breakfast included. **₹6500**

EATING

After a browse around the market, most visitors make a beeline for Longuinho's, once the hangout of Margao's English-speaking middle classes (now it's mostly tourists), before heading home. If you are on a tight budget, try one of the south Indian-style pure-veg cafés along Station Road.

Café Coffee Day Shop 18/19 Vasanth Arcade, Da Costa Rd near Popular High School ☎078880 23611; map p.733. India's answer to *Starbucks* has a super-cool a/c branch tucked away off Praça Jorge Barreto, popular with college kids. Aside from a good latte (₹116), it serves spicy savouries and sandwiches; ₹210) and a sinful brownie (₹105 185). Daily 9.30am–10.30pm.

Longuinho's Luis Miranda Rd ☎0832 2739908; map p.733. Old-fashioned café serving meat, fish and veg mains (₹140–200), with cheaper freshly baked savoury snacks, cakes and drinks. The food isn't up to much these days – though they do a decent Bombay duck (₹140–120) – and the 1950s Goan atmosphere has dwindled with the tourist trade, but it's a pleasant enough place to catch your breath over a beer. Daily 8.30am–10.30pm.

Tato Tucked up an alley off the east side of Praça Jorge Barreto, and opposite the yellow government building north of the Kadamba bus stand ☎97654 98690; map p.733. The town's brightest and best south Indian café chain serves the usual range of hot snacks (including especially good samosas at breakfast, and masala dosas from noon. For a proper meal, climb the stairs to their cool a/c floors, where you can order wonderful thalis veg (₹150), (fish ₹180) and north Indian dishes, as well Udupi nibbles (₹20–170). Tues–Sun 11am–3.30pm & 6.30–10.30pm.

12

DIRECTORY

Cinema Margao boasts south Goa's principal cinema, the INOX Osia Multiplex (☎080802 111116), out in the north of town in the Osia Commercial Arcade. It screens Hollywood as well as Bollywood releases; tickets cost ₹120–300.

Hospitals Hospicio (☎0832 270 5664 or ☎0832 270 5754), Rua Do Miranda, and the Apollo Victor Hospital, in the suburb of Malbhat (☎0832 272 8888, ⊛apollovictorhospital.com).

Post office The GPO is at the top of Praça Jorge Barreto.

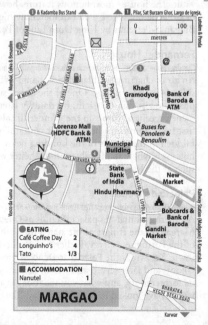

MARGAO

Around Margao

For a good dose of quirky colonial architecture, head **inland from Margao**, where villages such as **Loutolim** and **Chandor** are littered with decaying old Portuguese houses, most of them empty – the region's traditional inheritance laws ensure that old family homes tend to be owned by literally dozens of descendants, few of whom are willing or can afford to maintain them.

Braganza-Perreira/Menezes-Braganza house

Chandor • Daily except holidays, no set hours – just turn up 10am–noon or 3–6pm, go through the main entrance, up the stairs and knock at either of the doors • Recommended donation ₹200/person • ☏ 0832 278 4201 or ☏ 98221 60009

Thirteen kilometres east of Margao across Salcete district's fertile rice fields lies sleepy **Chandor** village, a scattering of tumbledown villas and farmhouses ranged along shady tree-lined lanes. The main reason to venture out here is to see the splendid **Braganza-Perreira/Menezes-Braganza house**, regarded as the grandest of Goa's colonial mansions. Dominating the dusty village square, the house, built in the 1500s by the wealthy Braganza family for their two sons, has a huge double-storey facade, with 28 windows flanking its entrance. Braganza de Perreira, the great-grandfather of the present owner, was the last knight of the king of Portugal; more recently, Menezes Braganza (1879–1938), a journalist and freedom fighter, was one of the few Goan aristocrats actively to oppose Portuguese rule. Forced to flee Chandor in 1950, the family returned in 1962 to find their house, amazingly, untouched. The airy tiled interiors of both wings contain a veritable feast of **antiques**.

Exploring the house

The house is divided into two separate wings, owned by different (and contrasting) branches of the old family. Furniture enthusiasts and lovers of rare Chinese porcelain, in particular, will find plenty to drool over in the **Menezes-Braganza wing** (to the right as you face the building). Next door, in the Braganza-Perreira wing, an ornate oratory enshrines St Francis Xavier's diamond-encrusted toenail, retrieved from a local bank vault. The house's most famous feature, however, is its ostentatiously grand ballroom, or **Great Salon**, where a pair of matching high-backed chairs, presented to the Braganza-Perreiras by King Dom Luís of Portugal, occupy pride of place.

Fernandes House

Chandor • Mon–Sat 10am–5pm; phone in advance • A donation of around ₹200/person is expected • ☏ 0832 278 4245

An air of charismatic dilapidation hangs over the **Fernandes House**, on the south side of Chandor village. One of the oldest surviving palacios in Goa, its core is of pre-conquest Hindu origin, overlaid by later accretions. Sara Fernandes, the present owner, receives visitors in the wonderful **salon** that extends the length of the building's first floor, abutting a bedchamber containing its original, ornately carved four-poster. Hidden in the bowels of the building below, a narrow passage fitted with disguised gun holes was where the family used to shelter when attacked by Hindu rebels and bandits such as the Ranes.

Palacio do Deão

Quepem • Guided tours daily except Wed 10am–5pm • Free • ☏ 98231 75639, ⟨w⟩ palaciododeao.com

A superb colonial-era palacio stands at **Quepem**, a thirty-minute drive southeast of Margao on the fringes of the state's iron-ore belt. In 1787, a high-ranking member of the Portuguese clergy, Father José Paulo de Almeida, built a country house in the town. Known as the **Palacio do Deão**, it grew to become one of the grandest in the colony, and later served as a retreat for its viceroys. The palacio was recently restored to its former glory, and what you see today is a faithful approximation of how the house would have looked in José Paulo's day. The engaging guided tour lasts around half an

12

hour, winding up on the lovely rear terrace overlooking the river where you can enjoy a delicious Goan lunch, dinner or afternoon tea (by prior arrangement, at least a day in advance; around ₹500).

Colva

A hot-season retreat for Margao's moneyed middle classes since long before Independence, **COLVA** is the oldest and largest – and least appealing – of south Goa's resorts. Its outlying waddos are pleasant enough, dotted with colonial-style villas and ramshackle fishing huts, but the beachfront is dismal: a lacklustre collection of concrete hotels, souvenir stalls and flyblown snack bars strewn around a bleak central roundabout. The atmosphere is not improved by the heaps of rubbish dumped in a rank-smelling ditch that runs behind the beach, nor by the stench of drying fish wafting from the nearby village. Benaulim, just a five-minute drive further south, has a far better choice of accommodation and range of facilities, and is altogether more salubrious.

Benaulim

The predominantly Catholic fishing village of **BENAULIM** lies in the dead centre of Colva beach, scattered around coconut groves and paddy fields 7km west of Margao. Two decades ago, the settlement had barely made it onto the backpackers' map. Nowadays, though, affluent holiday-makers from metropolitan India come here in droves, staying in the huge resort and time-share complexes mushrooming on the outskirts, while long-staying, heavy-drinking Brit pensioners and thirty-something European couples taking time out of trips around the Subcontinent make up the bulk of the foreign contingent.

Benaulim's rising popularity has certainly dented the village's old-world charm, but time your visit well (avoiding Diwali and the Christmas peak season), and it is still hard to beat as a place to unwind. The seafood is superb, accommodation and motorbikes cheaper than anywhere else in the state, and the **beach** is breathtaking, particularly around sunset, when the brilliant white sand and churning surf reflect the changing colours to magical effect. Shelving away almost to Cabo da Rama on the horizon, it is also lined with Goa's largest, and most colourfully decorated, fleet of **wooden outriggers**, which provide welcome shade during the heat of the day.

Goa Chitra

Tues–Sun 9.15am–6pm, last tour 5.15pm • ₹300 • ☎ 0832 2772910 , ⓦ goachitra.com • To get to Goa Chitra by bike or motorcycle, head east from Maria Hall crossroads towards Margao, and take the first turning on your left at a fork after 1.5km; when you reach the T-junction ahead, turn sharply right – the museum lies another 500m on your right

Conventional sights are thin on the ground along this stretch of coast, though one exception stands out on the eastern fringes of Benaulim: a splendid new ethnographic museum, **Goa Chitra**. Set against a backdrop of a working organic farm, the exhibition comprises a vast array of antique agricultural tools and artefacts, ranging from giant cooking pots and ecclesiastical robes to tubas and sugar-cane presses. The idea is to promote appreciation of the region's traditional agrarian lifestyle – a world of knowledge and skills fast disappearing.

ARRIVAL AND DEPARTURE   BENAULIM

By bus Buses from Margao run every 20min or so from the Kadamba bus stand to the Maria Hall crossroads in Benaulim. There is a taxi and auto-rickshaw rank at the crossroads, from where you can pick up transport to the beach, 1.5km west.

By motorbike or bicycle Signs offering motorbikes for rent are dotted along the lanes off Maria Hall crossroads:

rates are standard, descending in proportion to the length of time you keep the vehicle (₹250–350/day is about average for a Honda Activa). Worth bearing in mind if you're planning to continue further south is that motor-bikes are much cheaper to rent (and generally in better condition) here than in Palolem. Bicycle rental costs around ₹100/day.

ACCOMMODATION

Aside from the unsightly time-share complexes and five-stars that loom in the fields around the village, most of Benaulim's accommodation consists of small budget guesthouses, scattered around the lanes 1km or so back from the beach.

Anthy's Sernabatim ☏ 0832 277 1680 or ☏ 99228 54566, ✉ anthysguesthouse@rediffmail.com; map p.737. Nicely furnished rooms right on the sea, with high ceilings, tiny bathrooms and breezy verandas. It also boasts a restaurant and bar. A/c ₹400 extra. ₹1600

Blue Corner Sernabatim ☏ 98504 55770, ⓦ blue-corner-goa.com; map p.737. Popular hut camp on the beach, run by an enthusiastic young crew. Large palm-leaf structures with fans, mosquito nets, attached shower-toilets and plywood sitouts. Rates are ₹1350 for non a/c

coco huts. Quiet and secure, and the bar-restaurant is one of the most lively places on the beach in the evenings. ₹1350

★**Heaven Goa** 1 Ambeaxir, Sernabatim ☏ 98906 96202, ⓦ heavengoa.in; map p.737. Welcoming Swiss-run guesthouse in a block of a dozen or so rooms occupying a plum spot, 10min back from the sea beside a lily pond alive with frogs, egrets and water buffalo. The rooms are spacious and well set up (with wooden shelves, mosquito nets, shiny tiled floors and balconies over-looking the water). Eight rooms offer a/c for ₹400 more. Unbelievable value in this bracket. ₹1250

L'Amour Beach Rd ☏ 0832 277 0404, ⓦ lamour beachresortgoa.com; map p.737. Benaulim's oldest hotel comprises a comfortable 21-room complex; the rooms are fan-only but chalets (₹3000) are spacious, a/c and cool,

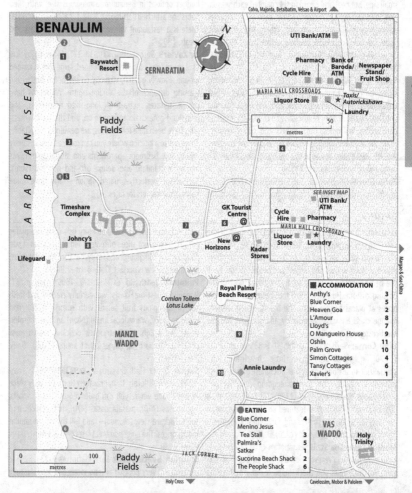

Colva, Majorda, Betalbatim, Velsao & Airport

BENAULIM

Baywatch Resort

SERNABATIM

ARABIAN SEA

Paddy Fields

Timeshare Complex

Johncy's

Lifeguard

Comlan Tollem Lotus Lake

MANZIL WADDO

Royal Palms Beach Resort

Annie Laundry

Paddy Fields

JACK CORNER

VAS WADDO

Holy Trinity

UTI Bank/ATM

Pharmacy   Bank of Baroda/ATM
Cycle Hire   Newspaper Stand/Fruit Shop

MARIA HALL CROSSROADS   Taxis/Autorickshaws
Liquor Store
                              Laundry

0   50
metres

SEE INSET MAP
UTI Bank/ATM
Cycle Hire   Pharmacy
MARIA HALL CROSSROADS
Liquor Store   Laundry

GK Tourist Centre

New Horizons

Kadar Stores

ACCOMMODATION	
Anthy's	3
Blue Corner	5
Heaven Goa	2
L'Amour	8
Lloyd's	7
O Mangueiro House	9
Oshin	11
Palm Grove	10
Simon Cottages	4
Tansy Cottages	6
Xavier's	1

● EATING	
Blue Corner	4
Menino Jesus Tea Stall	3
Palmira's	5
Satkar	1
Sucorina Beach Shack	2
The People Shack	6

0   100
metres

Holy Cross

Cavelossim, Mobor & Palolem

Mangao & Goa Chitra

12

with ceramic tiled floors and little verandas opening onto a central garden. Reasonable rates (a/c rooms cost ₹500 extra). ₹1500

Lloyd's 1554/A Vas Waddo ☎0832 277 1492, ✉lloydtouristrooms@gmail.com; map p.737. With its garish yellow exterior, this place on the beach side of the village stands out in more ways than one. The rooms are really big for the price, with high ceilings, quality beds and fans, plus neat mozzie screens over the windows. Also various-sized a/c apartments (from ₹2500) upstairs for longer stays. Non a/c rooms for long stays ₹800

O Mangueiro House 1685/A, Vas Waddo (next to Carina Beach Resort) ☎0832 277 0408 or ☎99225 42217, ✉mangogrovegoa.com; map p.737. One of the oldest budget guesthouses in Benaulim, run by the affable Mr Caetano. Just 400m from the beach, the rooms are on the small side, but neat and clean, freshly painted each season, and with quality mattresses. Some have tiny balconies opening onto a sandy courtyard; others face the road. Standard rooms ₹650, studio apartments are ₹900 and large self-contained apartments for four cost ₹1600. No wi-fi or breakfast. ₹650

Oshin Mazil Waddo ☎98223 82819, ✉oshinsholiday care@rediffmail.com; map p.737. Large complex of old-style budget rooms set well back from the road. Opening onto leafy terraces, they're spacious and clean with attached bath-rooms, balconies, fresh towels and complimentary soap; those on the top floor afford views over the treetops. A notch above most places in this area, and good value, but quite a walk from the beach. ₹1500

Palm Grove Tamdi-Mati, 149 Vas Waddo ☎0832 277 0059, ✉palmgrovegoa.com; map p.737. Secluded

hotel surrounded by beautiful gardens, offering three classes of a/c rooms, ranging from ropy to luxurious. A 10- to 15min walk (or bike ride) back from the beachfront, but very pleasant and the management is welcoming. Rates vary based on categories. ₹3800

Simon Cottages Ambeaxir, Sernabatim ☎0832 277 0581, ✉simoncottages@yahoo.com; map p.737. Perennially among the best budget deals in Benaulim, in a quiet spot 1km from the beach at the unspoiled north side of the village. Twelve huge rooms on three storeys with shower-toilets and verandas, opening onto a sandy courtyard. ₹500

Tansy Cottages Beach Rd ☎0832 277 0574, ✉tansycottages@yahoo.in; map p.737. Not the best of locations, and the shocking green-and-purple paintwork is hard to live with, but the rooms are some of the nicest budget options in Benaulim: a generous size, with tiled floors and attached bathrooms. Rates for a/c are ₹400 extra. There is a restaurant where you can have breakfast and meals. ₹800

★**Xavier's** Sernabatim ☎0832 277 1489, ✉jovek@ vsnl.in; map p.737. Well-maintained, large rooms ranged around a lovely garden, virtually on the beach but within walking distance of the village centre. All rooms have private terraces, extra-thick king-sized mattresses, and low-slung cane chairs to lounge on, and the local owners, who have been here for decades, are genuinely hospitable. There is also a kitchen where you can cook, as well as family rooms, two bedroom apartments and studio apartments alongside standard and deluxe a/c and non a/c rooms. A peaceful, perfectly-situated option – and great value Contact the owners for rates.

EATING

Benaulim's proximity to Margao market, along with the presence of a large Christian fishing community, means its restaurants serve some of the tastiest, most competitively priced seafood in Goa. The largest and busiest shacks flank the beachfront area, where *Johncy's* catches most of the passing custom. However, you'll find better food at lower prices at places further along the beach, which seem to change chefs annually; wander by and see who has the most customers.

Blue Corner Sernabatim ☎73500 14885 or ☎98504 55770; map p.737. Great little beachside joint specializing in seafood and authentic Chinese dishes. House favourites include "fish tomato eggdrop soup" (₹160), scrumptious "dragon potatoes" (₹180) and, best of all, their "Dave's steak" (₹450). Also featured on the eclectic menu are tasty Italian dishes, sizzlers and, for homesick veggies, a pretty good cauliflower cheese (₹220). Daily 7.30am–late.

Menino Jesus Tea Stall Sernabatim ☎0832 2789697; map p.737. If you've ever wondered what beach shacks were like thirty years ago, check this place out. It's where the

local rickshaw drivers refuel on spicy fish-curry-rice plates (₹180), piping-hot slices of millet-fried mackerel and *pao bhaji* for just ₹50. Rough and ready, but the food's delicious, and the sea view is perfect. Daily 6am–7.30pm.

Palmira's Beach Rd ☎0832 277 1309; map p.737. Benaulim's best breakfasts: wonderfully creamy and fresh set curd, copious fruit salads with coconut (₹80), real espresso (₹50), warm local bread (*bagri*) and the morning paper. For a light lunch, try their delicious prawn toast (₹120) or tomato or ginger-carrot soups (₹100). Daily 7am–10pm.

Satkar Maria Hall Crossroads ☎93261 29443; map p.737. No-frills locals' Udupi canteen that's the only place in the village where you can order regular Indian snacks – samosas (₹10), masala dosas (₹70), hot pakoras and spicy chickpea stew (*channa*) – and full thalis – at regular Indian prices. The *bhaji pau* breakfast (₹70) is a must. Daily 8am–9.30pm.

Sucorina Beach Shack Sernabatim ☎98224 82456; map p.737. Very popular among locals and tourists, they

12

are virtually round the clock serving full English breakfast with toast, omelette and bacon. They specialise in Goan curries and cuisine and seafood. Try their shredded beef and their king fish and prawn curries (mains around ₹250–350). Daily 8am–11pm.

The People Shack South end of beach ☏ 98221 84936; map p.737. Nadia and Vinod from Himachal Pradesh have run this welcoming little shack for more than a decade, and

can claim one of the most loyal clienteles in the village, most of whom come for the Italian dishes, prepared with home-made pasta, fresh herbs, olive oil and proper cheese. The prawn lasagne (₹450) and moussaka (₹350) also get the thumbs up and they do a zingy, fresh-mint mojito (₹150). During the day, a kids' play area is an additional attraction. They also run a restaurant called *Garden Retreat*. Daily 8am–late.

DIRECTORY

Banks and exchange The Bank of Baroda (Mon–Fri 9am–2pm, Sat 9–11.30am) on Maria Hall crossroads has an ATM, as does the UTI Bank. Currency may be changed at the two travel agents GK Tourist Centre, at the crossroads in the village centre, and New Horizons, diagonally opposite. It's worth comparing rates at the two.

General stores You'll find a couple of well-stocked general stores near the Maria Hall crossroads.

Internet GK Tourist Centre and New Horizons each have broadband connections (₹50/hr).

Laundry Annie's, opposite Palm Grove hotel, offers an inexpensive same-day laundry service. The Frank Bela laundry on the Maria Hall crossroads charges slightly more.

Pharmacy There is a pharmacy at the Maria Hall crossroads.

Agonda

AGONDA, 10km northwest of the market town of **Chaudi** (known to outsiders as **Canacona**), comes as a pleasant surprise after the chaos elsewhere in Goa. Accommodation in this predominantly Catholic fishing village is in small-scale, family-run guesthouses and upper-end hut camps, the restaurant scene is relatively unsophisticated, and the clientele easy-going and health-conscious. Granted, you don't get a dreamy brake of palm trees as a backdrop, but the surrounding hills and forest are exquisite, and the sand is as clean as any in the state.

The smart money says Agonda could all too soon go the way of Palolem, but for the time being the village deserves to be high on the list for anyone seeking somewhere quiet and wholesome, with enough amenities for a relaxing holiday and plenty of local atmosphere.

12

ARRIVAL AND DEPARTURE   AGONDA

By bus Agonda is served by four daily buses from the nearest market town, Canacona/Chaudi (20–30min); two run to Margao (2hr). Most services stop at the junction on

the main Palolem road, 1km east (you can usually find a rickshaw for the trip into the village), but a couple go as far as the church in the centre of Agonda.

ACCOMMODATION

Agonda gets packed in peak season, and over Christmas and New Year you'll be lucky to find a bed anywhere on spec. Tariffs rocket after fifty percent or more at this time, but after Jan 15 settle back down again and remain on a par with those in Patnem and Palolem. Except for the upscale camps (which require payment in advance online) few places accept advance bookings so you'll probably have to plod around to find somewhere that suits, or else phone ahead from the comfort of a café table (though note that mobile coverage tends to be patchy hereabouts).

★ **Agonda White Sand Beach Huts** 90m north of St Anne's Church ☏ 0832 2647049 ⊛ agondavillas.com. This campus of stylish huts has raised the bar in Agonda. Made of local wood, thatch and bamboo, with stone-tiled floors, the cottages are furnished like chic hotel rooms – though ranged around a busy bar-restaurant – and there's

a minimum stay of three nights. For greater seclusion, and unparalleled luxury on the beach, treat yourself to a stay in one of their gorgeous villas (three nights ₹9000) – huge, five-star boutique chalets in Balinese and Keralan styles, with decadent open-to-sky bathrooms and uninterrupted sea views from private terraces. Standard a/c doubles ₹4500

Chris-Joana Just south of St Anne's Church ☏ 0832 264 7306 or 94211 55814, ✉ chrisjoana92@yahoo.com. Smart modern house on the roadside. Its bargain rooms are clean, light and airy, with decent beds – two have a/c for ₹2500. Go for one on the rear side, overlooking the rooftops and creek toward coconut plantations; the front ones get warm in the afternoons. ₹1000

Jardim A Mar Doval Kazan ☏ 94208 20470, ✉ info@jardim-a-mar.com, ⊛ jardim-a-mar.com. Professionally run "palm-tree-garden resort", offering both rustic and seaside rooms and cosy beachside huts including those that can accommodate a family of four. They are nicely decorated with Rajasthani quilts and block print throws. Partly German-owned, it has a slicker feel than most of the competition. You can email them for the rates.

★ **Kaama Kethna Gurawal** 2km southeast of Agonda, off the Palolem road ☎0832 22647958, ⓦkaamakethna.com. This German-run ecotourism and permaculture project just outside the village – a 15min cycle from the beach – offers simply furnished treehouses (₹1500–2500), built high in the cashew canopy from palm leaf panels and wood, plus a few bamboo huts with spacious terraces at ground level. The site is wonderfully quiet, with colourful birds and monkeys flitting through the branches. Food grown on the farm is served in their little restaurant; they also offer yoga and meditation courses and natural therapies. ₹1000

Monsoon Guesthouse 1km north of St Anne's Church ☎96733 63235. Low-slung thatched huts (prices vary depending on size and season) and rooms in a secluded, peaceful setting behind the north end of the beach. Efficiently run by the resident German owner, it offers a pleasant parachute-shaded chill out terrace and dining area with a tiled roof. Family-friendly (no bar). Prices are especially high over Christmas. ₹1500

EATING

Agonda's restaurants are as much hangouts as places to eat. Most are furnished with relaxing cane chairs, pretty Himalayan lanterns and lounge areas with bolsters, and are on or near the beach.

Agonda White Sand 900m north of St Anne's church. ☎0832 2647049 ⓦagondawhitesand.com One of the more sophisticated menus including eggs rösti for breakfast (₹300) steaks with peppercorn or blue cheese sauce (₹550), seafood, tandoori chicken and cashew brown rice with beetroot raita (₹200) for lunch and dinner , as well as a good range of cocktails (₹300–400). Daily 8am–late.

Fatima Corner and Thali Opposite the bank at the main junction. The place for tourists to get a local-food fix, this shady little restaurant has a pleasant vibe and serves the usual mix of Indian and Continental dishes as well as excellent thalis (₹120/₹50). Also popular for its set breakfasts (₹150–200). Daily 8am–9pm.

Jardim A Mar Doval Kazan ☎94208 20470, ⓦjardim-a-mar.com. A café-restaurant that ticks all the boxes: it's right on the sand, well shaded (under palms and a Ladakhi parachute), with comfy cane chairs and silk cushions scattered on lounge mats. And it's a great breakfast spot, churning out fresh fruit juices, proper coffee, grilled baguettes and, the house speciality, rice pudding, as well as a popular all-day menu. Around ₹200–500 for a main meal. Daily 7am–11pm.

Madhu's North side of beach. ☎94238 13442. For years the best tandoori outfit on the beach: great for fresh local fish and Indian dishes alike (₹140–300). It's inexpensive and always *busy*, so get here early. The chicken tikka *malai* kebab (₹250) is especially good. Daily 8am–11pm.

Monsoon Guesthouse 1km north of St Anne's Church ☎96733 63235. One for the healthy eaters: great houses and copious fresh salads for break*fast* (₹150–280); pasta (₹150–350), Tibetan *momos* (₹220), seared fish steaks (₹400–600) and a focused selection of curries the rest of the day. Served on a small sandy terrace on the beach. Daily 8am–10.30pm.

DIRECTORY

Banks and exchange There are ATMs at the junction opposite St Anne's church.

Internet A string of places along the tarmac lane leading north of the church offer internet access.

Palolem

Nowhere else in peninsular India conforms so obediently to the archetypal image of a paradise beach as **PALOLEM**, 35km south of Margao. Lined with a swaying curtain of coconut palms, the bay forms a perfect curve of golden sand, arcing north from a giant pile of boulders to a spur of the Sahyadri Hills, which tapers into the sea draped in thick forest. Palolem, however, has become something of a paradise lost over the past decade. It's now the most popular resort in Goa among independent foreign travellers, and is deluged from late November. Visitor numbers become positively overwhelming in peak season, when thousands of people spill across a beach backed by an unbroken line of shacks and Thai-style hut camps.

Basically, Palolem in full swing is the kind of place you'll either love at first sight or want to flee from as quickly as possible. If you're in the latter category, try smaller, less frequented **Patnem** beach, a short walk south around the headland, where the shack scene is more subdued and the sands marginally emptier.

ARRIVAL AND DEPARTURE

PALOLEM

By bus Regular buses run between Margao and Palolem, stopping at the end of the lane leading from the main street to the beachfront. Frequent services also run between Margao and Karwar (in Karnataka) via the nearby market town of Canacona/Chaudi (every 30min; 2hr), 2km southeast across the rice fields.

By train Canacona/Chaudi is also the nearest railhead to Palolem; the station lies a short way north of the main bazaar. Rickshaws charge ₹80–100, taxis ₹200–250, for the ride to the beach.

GETTING AROUND AND ACTIVITIES

Bike rental A stall halfway along the main street charges around ₹50–100/day.

Surf canoes Available for rent at various places along the beach for ₹200/hr – great for paddles to Monkey Island at the top of the bay, or, weather permitting, around the headland to "Butterfly Beach".

Trekking Goa Jungle Adventure (☎98504 85641, ⓦ goajungle.com or ⓦ facebook.com/goajungleadventure) runs guided treks to natural swimming sites and features a mix of trekking, canyoning, swimming and abseiling in the mountain area inland from Palolem. You will need to be reasonably fit. Full-day trips ₹1990–3690, including transport and equipment.

ACCOMMODATION

The local municipality's strict enforcement of a rule banning new concrete construction in Palolem (it went so far as to bulldoze without warning the entire resort a few years back) has ensured that most of the village's accommodation consists of simple palm-leaf huts.

Ciaran's Camp Centre of Palolem beach ☎0832 264 3477, ⓦ ciarans.com; map p.741. "Camp" understates the sophistication of this compact resort whose coir, coconut wood and terracotta-tiled chalets are ranged around a neatly manicured central lawn. You've a choice of sea-facing or super-plush a/c rooms (₹5500). Also available are jungle huts with sea view starting at ₹3500. The whole place is exceptionally well run, with a popular double-decker bar-restaurant on site, safe lockers and a pair of friendly large hounds. **₹3500**

Cozy Nook North end of the beach, near the island ☎98223 82799, ⓦ cozynookgoa.com; map p.741. One of the most attractive set-ups in Goa, comprising bamboo huts in three styles. The nicest are the Robinson Crusoe-esque deluxe options, which have balconies. The sea-facing ones (₹4500) are ramshackle and jazzy, decked out in Rajasthani furniture; the semi-deluxe only have upper-floor rooms. Opening onto the lagoon on one side and the beach on the other, the site occupies a prime spot at the scenic north end of the bay. Email the hosts for current rates, which change on a regular basis. **₹3500**

Dream Catcher North end of the beach behind Cozy Nook ☎0832 264 4873 or 77700 89572, ⓦ dreamcatcher.in; map p.741. Individually styled, very glam Keralan-style huts in a neatly swept, sandy compound, with more space, better mattresses, nicer textiles, bigger windows and sturdier foundations than most, in a plum position by the riverside. There's also a shaded yoga shala for classes (₹500), and a "chillout-ambient bar". Prices are on the high side, to say the least (starting from ₹3250 for a standard hut and rising to ₹9900 for a luxury hut. **₹3250**

12

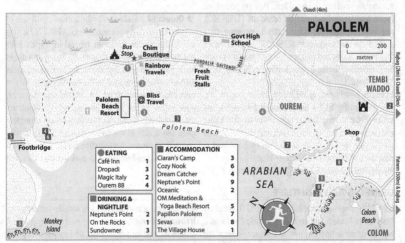

PALOLEM

● EATING	
Café Inn	1
Dropadi	3
Magic Italy	2
Ourem 88	4

■ DRINKING & NIGHTLIFE	
Neptune's Point	2
On the Rocks	1
Sundowner	3

■ ACCOMMODATION	
Ciaran's Camp	3
Cozy Nook	6
Dream Catcher	4
Neptune's Point	9
Oceanic	2
OM Meditation & Yoga Beach Resort	5
Papillon Palolem	7
Sevas	8
The Village House	1

Map labels: Chaudi (4km), Bus Stop, Chim Boutique, Govt High School, PUNDALIK GAITONDI ROAD, Rainbow Travels, Fresh Fruit Stalls, Palolem Beach Resort, Bliss Travel, Ourem, TEMBI WADDO, Palolem Beach, Shop, Footbridge, ARABIAN SEA, Monkey Island, Colom Beach, COLOM, Rajbag (2km) & Chaudi (5km), Patnem (500m) & Rajbag

12

Neptune's Point South Palolem ☎91584 32629, ⓦ neptunepoint.com; map p.741. *Neptune's* occupies the sweet spot atop the boulder headland dividing Palolem and Patnem, and its huts, stacked up on the hillside under giant coconut palms, make the most of the stupendous views. They're basic by today's standards, but comfortable enough, and having the sea on three sides is a unique selling point. The only downside is the Saturday night party, held on the premises, which brings in big crowds. Seaview cottages range between ₹3250-9500.

Oceanic Tembi Waddo ☎0832 264 3059, ⓦ hotel-oceanic.com; map p.741. A 10min walk inland from the beach (and also reachable via the backroad to Canacona/Chaudi), *Oceanic* is a popular hotel. Its marble-floored rooms are stylishly designed, fresh, cool and relaxing, with large mosquito nets, block-printed bedspreads and bedside lamps. The best rooms go for up to ₹4000. There's also a pool and a good restaurant. ₹1500

★ **OM Meditation & Yoga Beach Resort** Far northern end of Palolem beach, on the far side of the creek (look for the rickety footbridge to the right as you head for the island) ☎0832 264 3550 or 9822 382799, ⓔcozynook. goa@gmail.com; map p.741. Run by the guys at *Cozy Nook* (where you can access wi-fi), this isolated tent camp is a silent space with music and noise prohibited – there's also a small yoga area. The tents are quite well equipped, with comfortable beds, and the attached bathrooms are open to the sky. Email the hosts at *Cozy Nook* for room rates.

Papillon Palolem Qurem Rd ☎98904 95470, ⓦpapillonpalolem.com; map p.741. Run by *Heaven*, this beach bar and restaurant on the beach offers accommodation as well. Cosy and quiet, there are 20 comfortable wooden huts, of which four of them are deluxe beach front huts. Hot showers, mosquito nets, ceiling fans are provided in all the huts. Rates vary according to seasons and can start from ₹1200-4500 for the standard huts to ₹2000-9500 for the deluxe categories. ₹1200

Sevas Far southern end of the beach, on the hill dividing Palolem from Colom ☎0832 264 3977 or 94220 65437, ⓦsevaspalolemgoa.com; map p.741. Beautiful "ethnic" huts with Mangalorean tiled roofs and tiled flooring with hygienic squat-style loos and bucket baths. There are bamboo huts and wooden huts. They also offer massages and yoga classes, and there's a pleasant restaurant. Breakfast costs ₹150–200. ₹800

The Village Resort #196, near Government High School ☎0832 2645767, ⓦthevillageresortpalolem. com; map p.741. This boutique guesthouse, on the fringes of Palolem and 10mins from the beach, is the most comfortable and stylish place to stay in the area. Furnished with four-posters and vibrant silk bed covers, the a/c rooms are either "cosy" or large (costing up to ₹4500 during peak season) and the designer bathrooms palatial. A shady rear garden serves as a common breakfast area, and you can enjoy your tea on the verandah. ₹2500

EATING

Palolem's restaurants reflect the cosmopolitan make-up of its visitors. Each year, a fresh batch of innovative, ever more stylish places opens, many of them managed by expats.

Café Inn Pundalik Gaitondi Rd ☎0750 732 2799; map p.741. The best coffee in Palolem, made with a proper Italian coffee machine, is served here. They get packed out for an international range of set breakfasts (₹250–500), and have a small but eclectic menu, including tasty smoked chicken sandwiches (₹250–300), tortilla wraps (₹280–350), cakes and pastries. The best reason to come here, though, is for the Belgian waffles (₹220-280). Daily 8am–11pm.

Dropadi Beachfront ☎0832 264 4555; map p.741. This place enjoys both a top location and Palolem's best Indian chef, who specializes in rich, creamy Mughlai dishes and tandoori. Go for the superb *murg makhini* (₹350), crab masala with spinach (₹700) or tandoori jumbo prawns in basil sauce (₹500 each). Daily noon–11pm.

Magic Italy Beach Rd ☎88057 67705; map p.741.

Italian-run and on the busy approach to the seafront, this is in the running to be south Goa's number-one Italian restaurant, serving authentic home-made ravioli and tagliatelle (₹380–450) and scrumptious, large wood-fired pizzas (from ₹200-600). Reservation recommended. Daily 5–11pm.

★ **Ourem 88** On a lane running behind south side of beach (behind Rococo Pelton Bar) ☎86988 27679; map p.741. Tiny garden restaurant run by Brit expats Jodie and Brett, serving cleverly-thought-out Euro gastro dishes made from fresh local ingredients. Try their superb steak with béarnaise sauce, melt-in-the-mouth chicken Kiev or oven-baked barramundi filet in a herb and parmesan crust, leaving room for the divine chocolate *fondata*. Absolutely the finest dining in Palolem, though prices are reasonable given the quality of the cuisine (around ₹2000 for two people three courses, not including drinks). By reservation only (several days beforehand in peak season). Tues–Sun 6.30–11pm.

DRINKING AND NIGHTLIFE

Goa's 10pm amplified music ban (see page 721) is officially observed in Palolem, although *On the Rocks* has found a way of circumventing the rule and Neptune's Point has

seemingly come to an arrangement with the authorities.

Neptune's Point South side of beach; map p.741. A dreamy location for a sundowner. On Saturdays, they host techno dance parties (9pm–4am; ₹800). Drinks won't break the bank either. Daily 11am–late.

On the Rocks Southern end of the beach ☎77986 80842, ⓦsilentnoise.in; map p.741. On the rocky promontory at the far south end of the bay, the *Silent Noise* collective stages weekly headphone parties here on Sat nights (₹600), where the music is broadcast digitally to individual headsets instead of through PAs. You've a choice of house, electro and big beats on three separate channels, synced with live AV screens, lights and lasers. Can be a bit weird when you don't have headphones on, but many people seem to enjoy it. They also run a Wed afternoon market and other events. Sat 9pm–4am.

Sundowner Opposite Monkey Island, across the estuary at the north of the beach ☎78875 67384; map p.741. As indicated by the name, this eco-friendly open-air bar is the top spot for a sunset tipple with its sweeping view across the bay, although you may have to wade across the estuary to get there – there is a rickety bridge slightly inland and you can clamber around the rocks if you can't find the crossing point. They have a new restaurant specialising in Western food such as stone-baked pizzas. Yoga and massages available as well as four accommodation huts. Daily 10am–midnight.

DIRECTORY

Banks and exchange Several agents in Palolem are licensed to change money; LKP forex in the Palolem Beach Resort offers competitive rates. Sai Baba, Sun Moon Travel and Rainbow Travels on the main street all do cash advances against Visa and MasterCard. The nearest ATMs are 2km away towards the market town of Canacona/Chaudi on the main road.

Doctor Dr Sandheep, at the private Dhavalikar Hospital (☎88888 88888 or 0832 2643910), 2km out of Palolem at Devabag on the road to Agonda.

Internet Among a few cybercafés along the main road, Bliss Travel, on the left near the main entrance to the beach, charges ₹50/hr for the village's fastest broadband.

Pharmacy Palolem's main pharmacy is 1km out of the village on the Chaudi Rd, to your right just after the Agonda turning. It's closed on Sun, but out of hours you can call at the pharmacist's house immediately behind the shop.

12

South of Palolem

If the bright lights of Palolem start to lose their allure, wander around the headland to the south, where the Hindu fishing hamlet of **Colom** offers a more sedate scene. The shacks and bar strip resurfaces in earnest once around the next promontory at **Patnem**, but even in peak season the beach here rarely gets packed. Finally, to the south of Patnem, **Rajbag** is a worthwhile destination for a hike, but little more, thanks to the massive luxury resort behind it.

Colom

Once across the creek and boulder-covered spur bounding the south end of Palolem beach, you arrive at **COLOM**, a largely Hindu fishing village scattered around a series of rocky coves. Dozens of long-stay rooms, leaf huts and houses are tucked away under the palm groves and on the picturesque headland running seawards. This is the best place in the village to start an accommodation hunt – the lads at the *Boom Shankar* bar (see page 744) will know of any vacant places – but be warned that most of the rooms here can be basic.

Patnem

A string of hut camps and shacks lining the beach south of Colom, **PATNEM** is one of the mellower spots in these parts. The beach, curving for roughly 1km to a steep bluff, is broad, with little shade, and shelves quite steeply at certain phases of the tide, though the undertow rarely gets dangerously strong. On the headland dividing Patnem from Colom, the **Harmonic Healing & Eco Retreat Centre** (☎98225 12814, ⓦharmonicingoa.com) hosts daily yoga, reiki, pilates and Thai massage classes, as well as lessons in Bollywood dance and classical Indian singing, in a greenery-swathed site with panoramic views of the beach.

Rajbag and beyond

At low tide, you can walk around the bottom of the steep-sided headland dividing Patnem from neighbouring **RAJBAG**, another kilometre-long sweep of white sand.

Sadly, its remote feel has been entirely overwhelmed by the massive five-star hotel recently erected on the land behind it – much to the annoyance of the locals, who campaigned for four years to stop the project.

It's possible to press on even further **south from Rajbag** by crossing the Talpona River via a hand-paddled ferry, which usually has to be summoned from the far bank (fix a return price in advance). Once across, a short walk brings you to **Talpona beach**, backed by low dunes and a line of straggly palms. From here, you can cross the headland at the end of the beach to reach **Galjibag**, a remote white-sand bay that's a protected nesting site for olive ridley marine **turtles**. A strong undertow means swimming isn't safe here.

ARRIVAL AND DEPARTURE
SOUTH OF PALOLEM

By train The nearest railway station is Canacona/Chaudi.

By auto-rickshaw or taxi Most beaches can be reached by auto-rickshaw from Canacona/Chaudi for around ₹75. Auto-rickshaws and taxis for the return trip hang around along the beachfront lane.

By bus Patnem's bus stop is 1km or so closer to Canacona/Chaudi than Palolem's, with buses starting at the Kadamba bus stand at the north end of Chaudi's bazaar and dropping passengers at the end of the short lane leading to Patnem beach.

ACCOMMODATION

April 20 North end of Patnem beach ☎ 99609 16989, ⓦ goyam.net. Luxury, two-storey wooden bungalows painted pretty pastel colours, with tariffs ranging up to ₹5000, depending on size and time of year. Partly screened by casuarina trees, each is smartly furnished and fitted with bathrooms, mosquito nets and swings on sea-facing balconies; those at the front are the village's number-one des reses. ₹2500

Boom Shankar Colomb ☎ 97651 87294 or ☎ 9986773345. Simply furnished, clean, attached rooms on the southern edge of the village, with lots of lounging space and fine views across the cove. They can also help you root out longer-term rentals in houses nearby. The restaurant is right on the beach. ₹1500

Home Middle of Patnem beach ☎ 0832 264 3916, ⓦ homebeachresort.com. A chic little local-run guesthouse within sight of the beach, comprising an annexe of attached rooms under Mangalorean tiles, pleasantly decked out with textiles, coconut mats, lampshades and other touches to justify their tariffs. There are four category rooms starting with family garden view rooms to partial sea view rooms. No wi-fi. ₹2500

★ **Laguna Vista** Just east of Colomb beach ☎ 85549 498110, ⓔ agunavistapatnem@gmail.com. Basic but beautifully-located thatched huts on their own quiet cove, with fans, loos, comfy mattresses, mozzie nets, fresh towels, safe lockers and perfect sunset views. There's a lovely yoga shala on site and a relaxing lounge-resto. ₹4000

Namaste Patnem ☎ 97642 43700. A standout choice among the string of budget traveller camps in Patnem, this dependable, lively budget option is run by the amiable Satay. Fan rooms cost up to ₹3000 depending on size and comfort of the hut, time of year and how far back you are from the sand, and there are also a/c options (₹3500 all have individual shower-toilets) and service apartments close by (₹2000–3000). ₹3000

Papaya's Patnem ☎ 99230 79447, ⓦ papayasgoa.com. A delightfully green oasis, where water is recycled to keep the plants in their prime and power comes from solar panels. The eco-huts have four-posters, thick mattresses, breezy little sitouts and shaggy palm-frond fringes made from locally-sourced materials. ₹4000

EATING AND DRINKING

It's a safe bet you'll spend a few hours each day in one or other of the cafés in Colom or behind Patnem beach, and a couple of commendable places are tucked away just inland.

April 20 North end of Patnem beach ☎ 99609 16989. This swanky beachside restaurant, an offshoot of the popular *Dropadi* in Palolem (see page 742), does superb seafood prepared in rich north Indian tandoori style: crab makhini, avocado prawns and tandoori sea bass (₹500–600) are their signature dishes. Daily 8am–11pm.

Boom Shankar Colom. *Boom Shankar* does a great range of food – including its perennially-popular fresh mozzarella and tomato salads (₹210) and inexpensive seafood dishes (₹190–380) – and, with a terrace overlooking the bay and gorgeous views, is the perfect place for a sundowner. They are located right on the beach. Daily 11am–late.

Capital Patnem beach, opposite Patnem Chai Shop ☎ 99235 33015. It's worth ambling up the lane from the beach for a meal at Capital. The roadside location isn't up to much, but they do fantastic salads (₹250–350) and a knockout spinach-mushroom cheeseburger (₹300), to name but two of the healthy, freshly prepared dishes on an extensive multicuisine menu. Daily 8.30am–11pm.

Casa Fiesta Patnem beach ☎ 98239 28548. Popular place near the centre of the beach, offering an appetizing menu of world cuisine: hummus, Greek salad, Mexican specialities and fish *pollichathu*. Mains (mostly under ₹400) come with delicious roast potatoes. They also have one of the most impressive selections of fresh fish on the beach, though for considerably more. Daily 8am–11pm.

★ **Home** Middle of Patnem beach. Patnem's nicest beach café, serving meze, freshly baked bread, Swiss röstis (₹210), fresh salads (₹190–290), proper Italian espresso and wonderful desserts (banoffee pie, warm apple tart with cream and legendary brownies are all ₹150). It's a particularly pleasant option for breakfast, with Chopin on the sound system and sparrows chirping in the palms. Daily 8.30am–9.30pm.

Laguna Vista Colom ⓣ 99230 94676. Full-flavoured, healthy, organic meals made from local ingredients and served on a dreamy, wave-lapped terrace by a young crew. The menu is eclectic and international – bruschetta, crunchy salads, chapatti wraps, falafels and Indian dishes – and prices restrained (count on ₹550 for two courses). Daily 7.30am–11pm.

Papaya Middle of Patnem beach. Italian, Indian and Asian cuisine with a speciality in seafood. Succulent grilled seafood steaks and potato wedges (₹250) are the big hit at Papaya, but they also do a roaring trade in zingy Thai curries (₹300) and prawns with more- roasted potatoes and mushrooms (₹350). There is a bar as well which serves beers, cocktails and wines. Daily 8am–11pm.

Patnem Chai Shop At the end of the lane leading from Patnem beach, on the corner. ⓣ 99234 90794. The village chai shop is famous hereabout for its crunchy samosas (₹10), *bhaji pao* (₹15), banana bread (₹8) and delicious tea, attracting as many discerning expats as locals to its tiny interior. Daily 6.30am–6.30pm.

Cotigao Wildlife Sanctuary

The **Cotigao Wildlife Sanctuary**, 10km southeast of Canacona/Chaudi, was established in 1969 to protect a remote and vulnerable area of forest lining the Goa–Karnataka border. Best visited between October and March, Cotigao is a peaceful and scenic park that makes a pleasant day-trip from Palolem, 12km northwest. Encompassing 86 square kilometres of mixed deciduous woodland, the reserve is certain to inspire tree lovers, but less likely to yield many wildlife sightings: its tigers and leopards were hunted out long ago, while the gazelles, sloth bears, porcupines and hyenas that allegedly lurk in the woods rarely appear. You do, however, stand a good chance of spotting at least two species of monkey, a couple of wild boar and the odd gaur (the primeval-looking Indian bison), as well as plenty of birdlife.

A network of trails winds from the trailhead 3km beyond the centre to various named sites in the forest, but aren't waymarked and are very hard to follow. It is worth noting that some visitors complain about walking for hours without seeing anything of interest.

ARRIVAL AND INFORMATION — COTIGAO WILDLIFE SANCTUARY

By bus Any of the buses running south on the NH-17 to Karwar via Canacona/Chaudi will drop you within 2km of the gates. However, to explore the inner reaches of the sanctuary, you really need your own transport.

Interpretative Centre You have to pay entry fees (₹20, plus ₹100 for a car, ₹30 for a motorbike; ₹30 for a camera permit) at the reserve's small interpretative centre. The wardens here will show you how to get to a 25m-high treetop watchtower, overlooking a waterhole that attracts a handful of animals around dawn and dusk.

ACCOMMODATION AND EATING

Cottages ⓦ goatourism.gov.in. Book through the Deputy Conservator of Forests in Margao. You can stay in the sanctuary at one of four cottages, in the compound behind the main reserve gates. ₹800

Eating Food and drink may be available by prior arrangement (at least 4hr), and there's a shop at the nearest village, 2km inside the park.

Kolkata and West Bengal

VICTORIA MEMORIAL, KOLKATA

13 Kolkata and West Bengal

Unique among Indian states in stretching all the way from the Himalayas to the sea, West Bengal is nonetheless explored in depth by few foreign travellers. That may have something to do with the exaggerated reputation of its capital, Kolkata (Calcutta), an enthralling, sophisticated and friendly city that belies its popular image as poverty-stricken and chaotic. The rest of Bengal holds an extraordinary assortment of landscapes and cultures, ranging from the dramatic hill station of Darjeeling, within sight of the highest mountains in the world, to the vast mangrove swamps of the Sundarbans, prowled by elusive Royal Bengal tigers. The narrow central band of the state is cut across by the huge River Ganges as it pours from Bihar into Bangladesh and here the Farakka Barrage controls the movement of south-flowing channels such as the River Hooghly, the lifeline of Kolkata.

At the height of British rule, in the nineteenth and early twentieth centuries, Bengal flourished both culturally and materially, nurturing a uniquely creative blend of West and East. The **Bengali Renaissance** produced thinkers, writers and artists such as Bankim Chandra Chatterjee and **Rabindranath Tagore**, whose collective influence still permeates Bengali society more than a century later.

Not all of Bengal is Bengali, though; the Nepalese-led separatist movement for the creation of an autonomous "Gurkhaland" in the Darjeeling area has focused on sharp differences in culture. Here, the Hindu Nepalese migration eastward from the nineteenth century onwards has largely displaced the indigenous tribal groups of the north, though Lamaist Tibetan Buddhism continues to flourish. In the southwest, on the other hand, tribal groups such as the Santhals and the Mundas still maintain a presence, and itinerant Baul **musicians** continue the region's traditions of song and dance, most often heard around Tagore's university at **Shantiniketan**; Tagore's own musical form, Rabindra Sangeet, is a popular amalgam of influences including folk and classical. Other historical specialities of Bengal include its ornate **terracotta temples**, as seen at Bishnupur, and its **silk** production, concentrated around **Murshidabad**, the state's last independent capital.

Bengal's own brand of Hinduism emphasizes the **mother goddess**, who appears in such guises as the fearsome Kali and Durga, the benign Saraswati, goddess of learning, and Lakshmi, the goddess of wealth. The most mysterious of all is Tara, an echo of medieval links with Buddhism; her temple at **Tarapith** is perhaps the greatest centre of Tantrism in the entire country.

BEST TIME TO VISIT

The climate of **Kolkata** – and much of west and lowland north Bengal – is at its best during the short winter (Nov–Feb), when the daily maximum temperature hovers around 27°C, and the markets are filled with fresh vegetables and flowers. Before the monsoons, however, the heat hangs unbearably heavily; the arrival of the rains in late June brings relief, but usually also floods that turn the streets into a quagmire. After a brief period of post-monsoon high temperatures, October and November are quite pleasant; this is the time of the city's biggest festival, Durga Puja (see page 753).

The best seasons to visit **Darjeeling** and the mountainous areas of **north Bengal** are after the monsoons and before winter (late Sept to late Nov), and spring (mid-Feb to May).

Highlights

❶ Victoria Memorial This monument to the British Empire in Kolkata is a dizzying blend of Mughal and Italian architecture and one of the most striking buildings in India. See page 758

❷ Eden Gardens Enjoy the chaos and spectacle of a match at Kolkata's legendary cricket ground. See page 760

❸ Kumartuli A fascinating warren of lanes in Kolkata where artisans model lavish images of goddesses and demons out of straw, clay and *pith*. See page 763

❹ Sundarbans Float through the endless mangrove forests, home to a profusion of wildlife, including the majestic Bengal tiger. See page 778

❺ Shantiniketan This tranquil university town exudes the spirit of its founder, the poet and philosopher Rabindranath Tagore. See page 781

❻ Darjeeling A charming hill station with Raj-era relics, spectacular views and – of course – famously fine tea. See page 790

❼ Toy Train Take a leisurely journey on this Victorian railway, partly steam-driven, past the tea gardens that carpet the steep hillsides around Darjeeling. See page 795

❽ Singalila trek This trek, close to Darjeeling, features unforgettable mountain vistas, especially beautiful in April and May, when the rhododendrons are in bloom. See page 800

HIGHLIGHTS ARE MARKED ON THE MAP ON PAGE 750

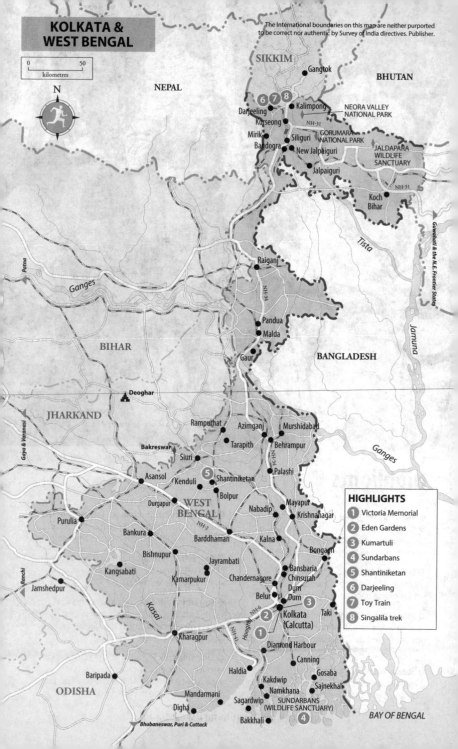

Brief history

Although Bengal was part of the Mauryan Empire during the third century BC, it first came to prominence in its own right under the Guptas in the fourth century AD. So dependent was it on trade with the Mediterranean that the fall of Rome caused a sharp decline, only reversed with the rise of the Pala dynasty in the eighth century.

After a short-lived period of rule by the highly cultured Senas, based at **Gaur**, Bengal was brought under Muslim rule at the end of the twelfth century by the first Sultan of Delhi, Qutb-ud-din-Aibak. Sher Shah Suri, who briefly usurped power from the Mughals in the mid-sixteenth century, developed the infrastructure and built the Grand Trunk Road, running all the way to the Northwest Province on the borders of his native Afghanistan. Akbar reconquered the territory in 1574, before the advent of the Europeans in the eighteenth century.

The arrival of the Europeans

The Portuguese, who were the first to set up a trading community beside the Hooghly, were soon joined by the British, Dutch, French and many others. Rivalry between them eventually resulted in the ascendancy of the **British**, with the only serious indigenous resistance coming from the tutelary kingdom of **Murshidabad**, led by the young Siraj-ud-Daula. His attack on the fledgling British community of Calcutta in 1756 culminated in the infamous **Black Hole** incident (see page 760), when British prisoners suffocated to death. Vengeance, in the form of a British army from Madras under **Robert Clive**, arrived a year later. The defeat of Siraj-ud-Daula at the **Battle of Plassey** paved the way for British domination of the entire Subcontinent. Bengal became the linchpin of the British East India Company and its lucrative trading empire, until the company handed over control to the Crown in 1858.

Twentieth-century Bengal

Up to 1905, Bengal encompassed Orissa (now Odisha) and Bihar; it was then split down the middle by Lord Curzon, leaving East Bengal and Assam on one side and Orissa, Bihar and West Bengal on the other. The move aroused bitter resentment, and the rift it created between Hindus and Muslims was a direct cause of the second Partition, in 1947, when East Bengal became East Pakistan. During the war with Pakistan in the early 1970s that resulted in the creation of an independent **Bangladesh**, up to ten million refugees fled into West Bengal. Shorn of its provinces, and with the capital moved from Calcutta to Delhi in 1911, the story of West Bengal in the twentieth century was largely a chronicle of decline.

The state's political life has been dominated by a protracted – and sometimes violent – struggle between the **Congress** and, more recently, the breakaway **Trinamool Congress**, against the major left-wing parties: the Marxist Communist Party of India, or **CPI(M)**, and the Marxist-Leninist **Naxalites** (Communist Party of India [ML]). In the 1960s and 1970s, the latter launched an abortive but bloody attempt at revolution. Bolstered by a strong rural base, the CPI(M) and allies emerged victorious in 1977 under the enigmatic Jyoti Basu, weathering the collapse of world communism, and heralding the decades-long dominance by the **Left Front**.

Bengal today

This long dominance by the CPI(M) came to a dramatic end in 2011, when the firebrand politician, **Mamata Banerjee**, who had honed her political skills supporting the oppressed poor in two notorious campaigns against industrialization, swept to power. While she inherited a state of political and industrial turmoil, **Didi**, or "Sister" as she is commonly known, has yet to redress the imbalance in the infrastructure and there are many who feel that she has been neither able to transcend the grassroots struggle that brought her to prominence, nor to comprehend the complexities of what was once, and still is, a dynamic industrial powerhouse.

13

FESTIVALS IN KOLKATA AND WEST BENGAL

Most of Bengal's Hindu festivals are devoted to forms of the mother goddess, **Shakti**.

Jaidev Mela (early Jan). Baul minstrels gather to commemorate Joydeb, the revered author of the *Gita Govinda*, held in the village of Kendubilwa (Kenduli), near Shantiniketan. See page 781.

Ganga Sagar Mela (mid-Jan). During the winter solstice of Makar Sankranti, thousands of Hindu pilgrims and sadhus gather for a three-day festival at Sagardwip, 150km south where the Ganges meets the sea. See page 780.

Dover Lane Music Festival (Jan/Feb). A week-long festival in south Kolkata, attracting many of the country's best musicians.

Saraswati Puja (Jan/Feb). Popular and important festival, dedicated to the goddess of learning and staged throughout Bengal.

Chinese New Year (Jan/Feb). Celebrated with a week-long festival of dragon dances, firecrackers and fine food, concentrated around Chinatown and the suburb of Tangra.

Muharram (dates determined by the lunar calendar; see ⓦ when-is.com). Shi'ite Muslims mark the anniversary of the martyrdom of Hussein by severe penance.

Durga Puja (Sept/Oct). At the onset of winter, Durga Puja (known elsewhere as Dasara or Dussehra) is the Bengali equivalent of Christmas. It climaxes on Mahadashami, the tenth day, when the images of goddess Durga are immersed in the river. See page 753.

Lakshmi Puja (Oct/Nov). Held five days after Mahadashami on the full moon, to honour the goddess of wealth.

Christmas (Dec 25). Park Street and New Market are adorned with fairy lights and the odd Christmas tree.

Poush Mela (late Dec). Held in Shantiniketan (see page 781), the *mela* brings in Bauls, the wandering minstrels who attract large audiences.

In Kolkata – booming with expatriate wealth and a surge in business confidence, though nothing like in Delhi or Mumbai – political turmoil can seem a world away. Meanwhile in the north of the state, ethnic political groups are calling for autonomy from Bengal. The fabric and future shape of the current state is by no means certain.

Kolkata

One of the four great urban centres of India, **KOLKATA** is, to its proud citizens, the equal of any city in the country in charm, variety and interest. As the showpiece capital of the British Raj, it was the greatest colonial city of the Orient, and descendants of the fortune-seekers who flocked from across the globe to participate in its eighteenth- and nineteenth-century trading boom remain conspicuous in its cosmopolitan blend of communities. Despite this, there has been a rise in Bengali nationalism over the last twenty years, and in 2001 the city was officially renamed as Kolkata (its precolonial Bengali name).

Since Indian Independence, mass migrations of dispossessed refugees caused by twentieth-century upheavals within the Subcontinent have tested the city's infrastructure to the limit. The resultant suffering – and the work of Mother Teresa in drawing attention to its most helpless victims – has given Kolkata a reputation for poverty that sells the city short. Although it undoubtedly faces huge challenges, they are no greater than in other cities of comparable size in India and around the world. In fact, though Kolkata's mighty Victorian buildings stand peeling and decaying, and its central avenues are choked by traffic, the city exudes a warmth and buoyancy that leaves few visitors unmoved. Kolkata is expanding rapidly, with shopping malls, hip cafés and restaurants, and satellite towns springing up all around the city. The downside of all this development, however, partly resulting from the huge increase in traffic, is some of the worst air pollution in the world, with one of the most chaotic road systems in the country.

13

In terms of the city's cultural life, Kolkata's Bengalis exude a pride in their artistic heritage and like to see themselves as the **intelligentsia** of India. The city is home to a multitude of **galleries** and huge Indian classical music festivals, with a thriving Bengali-language **theatre** scene and a cinematic tradition brought world renown by director Satyajit Ray. It also has an enviable literary tradition, hosting a world-famous book fair (see page 775) and producing a string of award-winning authors.

Visitors still experience Kolkata first and foremost as a colonial city with the chief bastion of imperialism at its heart – the **Writers' Building**, the seat of state government – little changed over the decades. Grand edifices in a profusion of styles litter the old city and several venerable Raj-era institutions continue to survive, such as the racecourse, the reverence for cricket and several exclusive gentlemen's clubs. Kolkata's crumbling, weather-beaten buildings and slightly anarchic streets can create an intimidating first impression. With time and patience, though, this huge metropolis unravels its secrets, providing a fascinating conglomerate of styles and influences.

The **River Hooghly**, spanned by the remarkable cantilever Howrah Bridge, is not all that prominent in the life of the city. Instead its heart is the green expanse of the **Maidan**, which attracts locals from all walks of life for recreation, sports, exhibitions and political rallies. At its southern end stands the white marble **Victoria Memorial**, and close by rise the tall Gothic spires of **St Paul's Cathedral**. Next to the busy **New Market** area looms the eclectic **Indian Museum** housing one of the largest collections in Asia, ranging from natural history to art and archeology. Further north, the district centred on BBD Bagh is filled with reminders of the heyday of the East India Company, dominated by the bulk of the **Writers' Building**, built in 1780 to replace the original structure that housed the clerks or "writers" of the East India Company; nearby stand **St Andrew's Kirk** and the pillared immensity of the **GPO**.

The city's old **Chinatown**, a short walk north of BBD Bagh, is a sad reminder of a once flourishing community, while on the edge of the frenetic, labyrinthine markets of **Barabazaar**, **synagogues** and the **Armenian church** are remnants of a once thriving cosmopolitan trade. The renowned temple of **Kalighat** is away to the south. Across the river, south of the marvellous **Howrah railway station**, lies the tranquillity of the **Botanical Gardens**.

Brief history

By the time the remarkable **Job Charnock** established the headquarters of the **East India Company** at **Sutanuti** on the east bank of the Hooghly in 1690, the riverside was already dotted with trading communities from European countries. A few years later, Sutanuti was amalgamated with two other villages to form the town of **Calcutta**, whose name probably originated from *kalikutir*, the house or temple of Kali (a reference to the **Kalighat** shrine). With trading success came ambitious plans for development; in 1715 a delegation to the Mughal court in Delhi negotiated trading rights, creating a territory on both banks of the Hooghly of around 15km. Later, it became entangled

---

DURGA PUJA

She has no temple but the two-week **Durga Puja** is Kolkata's most lavish festival (Sept/Oct). A symbol of victory over evil, the ten-armed **Durga** is commonly depicted sitting on a lion slaying the demon Mahisasura who assumed the shape of a buffalo. During the celebrations images of the goddess are placed in elaborate marquees called *pandals*, supported by large donations and the local communities, which block off small streets for days. After the puja, the images are taken to the river for immersion, before being quickly fished out again with cranes to avoid pollution caused by the materials and paints used in the statuary. *Pandals* worth visiting during Durga Puja, beside the popular one at Kumartuli, include those at Mohammed Ali Park near Chittaranjan Avenue, MG Marg crossing and the nearby College Square. Baghbazaar's *pandal* is the oldest, and renowned for its simple elegance.

13

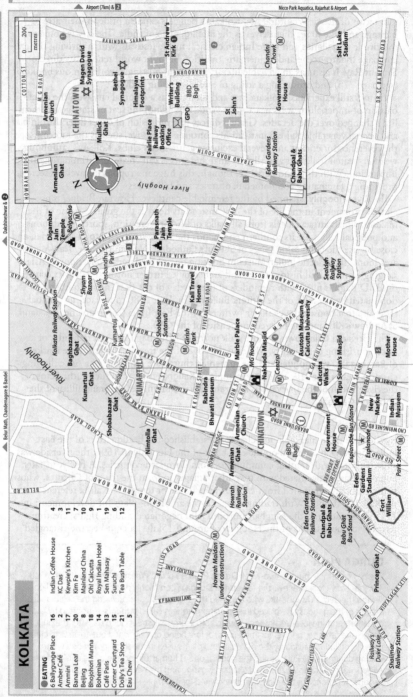

KOLKATA

● EATING

6 Ballygunge Place	16	Indian Coffee House	4
Amber Café	2	KC Das	3
Ammini	17	Kewpie's Kitchen	11
Banana Leaf	20	Kim Fa	7
Beijing	8	Mainland China	10
Bhojohori Manna	18	Oh! Calcutta	9
Bohemian	14	Royal Indian Hotel	1
Café Paris	13	Sen Mahasay	19
Corner Courtyard	15	Suruchi	6
Dolly's Tea Shop	21	Tea Bush Table	12
Eau Chew	5		

Botanical Gardens

Dakshineshwar & 2

Belur Math, Chandernagore & Bandel

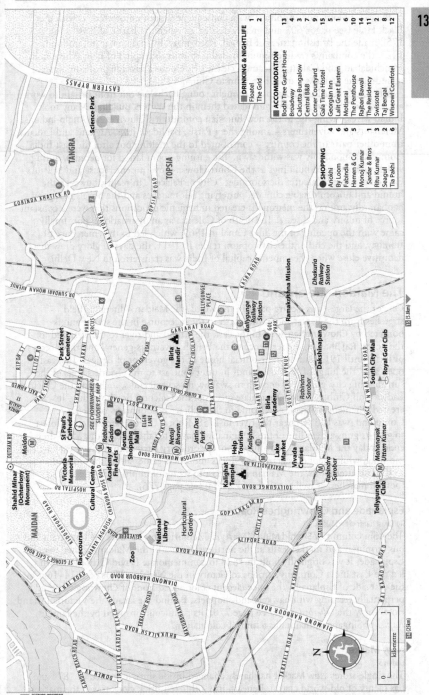

EASTERN BYPASS

Science Park

TANGRA

GOBINDA KHATICK RD

TOPSIA

TOPSIA ROAD

MAA FLYOVER

DR SUNDARI MOHAN AVENUE

KASBA ROAD

BALLYGUNGE PLACE

Dhakuria Railway Station

Ballygunge Railway Station

GARIAHAT ROAD

Ramakrishna Mission

GOL PARK

PARK CIRCUS

SHAKESPEARE SARANI

Park Street Cemetery

Birla Mandir

SYED AMIR ALI AVENUE

B. GUNGE CIRCULAR RD

Dakshinapan

RIPON ST
ELLIOT RD

PARK STREET

MIRZA GHALIB ST
PARK ST

RAFI AHMED

SEE CHOWRINGHEE & SUDDER ST. MAP

SARAT BOSE ROAD

B. GUNGE CIRCUL AR RD

HAZRA ROAD

RASHBEHARI AVENUE

SOUTHERN AVENUE

Birla Academy

Rabindra Sarobar

Royal Golf Club

South City Mall

PRINCE ANWAR SHAH ROAD

OUTRAM RD

St Paul's Cathedral

Maidan

Shahid Minar (Ochterlony Monument)

MAIDAN

HOSPITAL RD

Victoria Memorial

Academy of Fine Arts

Cultural Centre

Rabindra Sadan

Forum Shopping Mall

ELGIN LANE

Netaji Bhavan

PADDA PUKUR RD

Jatin Das Park

ASHUTOSH MUKHERJEE ROAD

Kalighat

Help Tourism

Lake Market

Vivada Cruises

Rabindra Sarobar

PRATAPADITYA RD

Kalighat Temple

TOLLYGUNGE ROAD

Mahanayak Uttam Kumar

Tollygunge Club

ACHARYA JAGDISH CHANDRA BOSE ROAD

KIDDERPORE ROAD

Racecourse

Zoo

National Library

Horticultural Gardens

BELVEDERE ROAD

ALIPORE ROAD

GOPALNAGAR RD

CHETLA CRD

STATION ROAD

ST GEORGE'S GATE ROAD

CANAL ROAD

DIAMOND HARBOUR ROAD

EKBALPUR ROAD

BHUKAILASH ROAD

MAYURBHANJ ROAD

DIAMOND HARBOUR ROAD

N SARKAR AVENUE

RAI BAHADUR ROAD

GARDEN REACH ROAD

CIRCULAR GARDEN REACH ROAD

DOMEN AV

TARATALA ROAD

Botanical Gardens

15 (5.8km)

14 (25km)

N

0   kilometre   1

13

in the web of local power politics, with consequences both unforeseen, as with the Black Hole (see page 760), and greatly desired, as when the Battle of Plassey in 1758 made the British masters of Bengal. Recognized by Parliament in London in 1773, the company's trading monopoly led it to shift the capital of Bengal here from Murshidabad, and Calcutta became a clearing house for a vast range of commerce, including the lucrative export of opium to China.

At first, the East India Company brought young bachelors out from Britain to work as clerks or "writers" and accommodated them in the **Writers' Building**. Many took Indian wives, giving rise to the new Eurasian community known as the **Anglo-Indians**. Merchants and adventurers – among them Parsis, Baghdadi Jews, Afghans and Indians from other parts of the country – contributed to the melting pot after the East India Company's monopoly was withdrawn. The ensuing boom lasted for decades, during which such splendid buildings as the Court House, Government House and St Paul's Cathedral earned Calcutta the sobriquet "City of Palaces". In reality, however, the humid and uncomfortable climate, putrefying salt marshes and the hovels that grew haphazardly around the metropolis created unhygienic conditions that were a constant source of misery and disease. The death of Calcutta as an international port finally came with the opening of the Suez Canal in 1869, which led to the emergence of Bombay, and the end of the city's opium trade. In 1911, the days of glory drew to a definitive close when the imperial capital of India was transferred to New Delhi.

The Maidan and around

One of the largest city-centre parks in the world, the **Maidan** – literally "field" – stretches from the Esplanade in the north to the racecourse in the south, and is bordered by **Chowringhee Road** to the east, the Strand and river to the west and to the north, **Raj Bhavan**, the residence of the British governors-general and the viceroys of India until 1911 and now the official home of the governor of Bengal. This vast open area, the lungs of Kolkata, stands in utter contrast to the chaotic streets of the surrounding city, and is big enough to swallow up several clubs, including the Calcutta Ladies Golf Club and the immaculate greens of the Calcutta Bowling Club. It was created when **Fort William**, now home to the military headquarters of the Eastern Command, was laid out near the river in 1758; Robert Clive cleared tracts of forest to give its guns a clear line of fire. Originally a haven for the elite, with a strict dress code, today the Maidan is a favourite spot for ordinary citizens to come to exercise each morning, while shepherds graze their flocks and riders canter along the old bridleways. In the late afternoons, the Maidan plays host to scores of impromptu cricket and football matches, as well as games of kabaddi (see page 776).

Esplanade and Chowringhee Road
Northeast corner of the Maidan

The 46m column of **Shahid Minar** (Martyrs' Memorial) towers over the busy tram and bus terminals and market stalls at the northeast corner of the Maidan, known here as Esplanade. It was originally built in 1828 to commemorate David Ochterlony, who led the East India Company's troops to victory in the Nepalese Wars of 1814–16. On the east side of Esplanade, the once-elegant colonnaded front of **Chowringhee Road** is perpetually teeming with hawkers and shoppers. Behind the facade the Victorian **Grand Hotel** (now the *Oberoi Grand*; see page 770), its palm court inspired by the famous *Raffles* of Singapore, maintains a hint of colonialism.

New Market
Lindsay St

The single-storey **New Market** has barely changed inside since it opened in 1874 and has plenty of old-world charm. Beneath its Gothic red-brick clock tower, the market

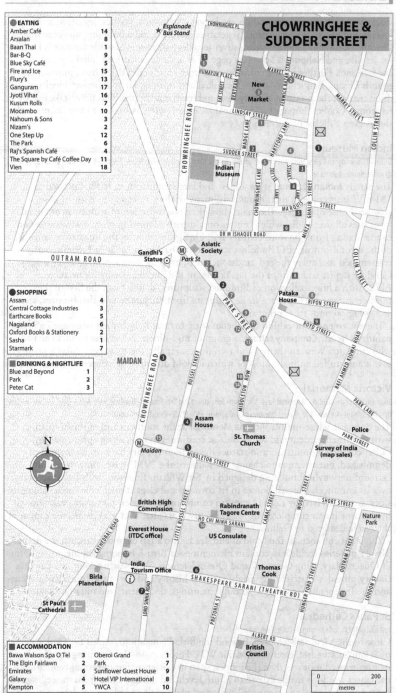

CHOWRINGHEE & SUDDER STREET

13

EATING

Amber Café	14
Arsalan	8
Baan Thai	1
Bar-B-Q	9
Blue Sky Café	5
Fire and Ice	15
Flury's	13
Ganguram	17
Jyoti Vihar	16
Kusum Rolls	7
Mocambo	10
Nahoum & Sons	3
Nizam's	2
One Step Up	12
The Park	6
Raj's Spanish Café	4
The Square by Café Coffee Day	11
Vien	18

SHOPPING

Assam	4
Central Cottage Industries	3
Earthcare Books	5
Nagaland	6
Oxford Books & Stationery	2
Sasha	1
Starmark	7

DRINKING & NIGHTLIFE

Blue and Beyond	1
Park	2
Peter Cat	3

ACCOMMODATION

Bawa Walson Spa O Tel	3	Oberoi Grand	1
The Elgin Fairlawn	2	Park	7
Emirates	6	Sunflower Guest House	9
Galaxy	4	Hotel VIP International	8
Kempton	5	YWCA	10

Esplanade Bus Stand

New Market

Indian Museum

Asiatic Society

Gandhi's Statue

Pataka House

Assam House

St. Thomas Church

Police

Survey of India (map sales)

Maidan

Nature Park

British High Commission

Rabindranath Tagore Centre

Everest House (ITDC office)

US Consulate

India Tourism Office

Birla Planetarium

Thomas Cook

St Paul's Cathedral

British Council

0   200
metres

13

stocks a vast array of household goods, luggage, garments, textiles, jewellery, knick-knacks and books as well as meat, vegetables and fruit and a booming flower market. **Chamba Lama** sells Tibetan curios, silver jewellery and bronzes while **Sujata's** is known for its silk, and **Nahoum & Sons** (see page 772) is a renowned Jewish bakery and confectioner. Further up the corridor, condiment stalls offer dried fruit, miniature rounds of salty Bandel cheese (both smoked and unsmoked) and *amshat*, blocks of dried mango; the produce, poultry, fish and meat market nearby is unmistakeable by its aroma. Coolies, hoping for commission, eagerly offer assistance to any shopper who shows even a flicker of uncertainty.

Indian Museum

Corner of Chowringhee Rd and Sudder St • Tues–Sun: March–Nov 10am–5pm; Dec–Feb 10am–4.30pm • ₹500 (₹20) • ☏ 033 2286 1699, ⓦ indianmuseumkolkata.org

The stately **Indian Museum** is the oldest and largest museum in India, founded in 1814. Visitors come in their thousands, many of them referring to it as the *jadu ghar* or "house of magic". The main showpiece is a collection of **sculptures** obtained from sites all over India, which centres on a superb Mauryan polished-sandstone **lion capital** dating from the third century BC. One gallery houses the impressive remains of the second-century BC Buddhist **stupa from Bharhut** in Madhya Pradesh, partly reassembled to display the red-sandstone posts, capping stones, railings and gateways. Carvings depict scenes from the Jataka tales of the Buddha's many incarnations. Along with a huge collection of Buddhist sculptures, dating from the first to the third centuries, you'll also see stone sculpture from **Khajuraho** and Pala bronzes, and archeological finds from other sites.

There is an excellent exhibit of Tibetan *thangkas* and Kalighat *pat* (see page 765) and paintings by the **Company school**, a group of mid-nineteenth-century Indian artists who emulated Western themes and techniques. Finally, there's a spectacular array of fossils and stuffed animals, most of which look in dire need of a decent burial.

Victoria Memorial

Southern end of the Maidan • **Memorial** Tues–Sun 10am–5pm, closed 2nd Sat of month • **Gardens** Daily: March–Sept 5.30am–6.15pm; Oct–Feb 5.45am–5.45pm • ₹10 • Tickets to memorial and gardens ₹500 (₹30) • ⓦ victoriamemorial-cal.org

The dramatic white-marble **Victoria Memorial** at the southern end of the Maidan, with its formal gardens and watercourses, continues to be Kolkata's pride and joy. Other colonial monuments and statues throughout the city have been renamed or demolished, but attempts to change the name of the "VM" have come to nothing. This extraordinary hybrid building designed by Sir William Emerson, with Italianate statues over its entrances, Mughal domes in its corners, and elegant open colonnades along its sides, was conceived by Lord Curzon to commemorate the empire at its peak, though by the time it was completed in 1921, twenty years after Victoria's death, the capital of the Raj had shifted to Delhi.

The main entrance, at the Maidan end, leads into a tall chamber beneath the dome. The 25 **galleries** inside still contain mementoes of British imperialism including statues of Queen Mary, King George V and Queen Victoria. Well worth seeing, the **Calcutta Gallery** provides a fascinating insight into the history and life of the Indians of the city and the Independence struggle through paintings, documents and old photographs.

St Paul's Cathedral

Just east of the Victoria Memorial • Daily 10am–6pm

Close to the Victoria Memorial, beyond the Birla Planetarium, stands the Gothic edifice of **St Paul's Cathedral**, erected by Major W.N. Forbes in 1847. Measuring 75m by 24m, its iron-trussed roof was then the longest span in existence. For improved ventilation, the lancet windows inside extend to plinth level, and tall fans hang from the ceiling. The most outstanding of the many well-preserved memorials and plaques to long-perished

KOLKATA'S ART GALLERIES   13

Bengal has a lively tradition of contemporary art, and with increased prosperity and speculation in fine art, galleries showing a high standard of work are burgeoning throughout the city. Exhibitions are listed in *The Telegraph*'s Sunday supplement, *Graphiti*, and *Explocity*, a free listings magazine available at the tourist office, some hotels and online (ⓦexplocity. com). Besides the Academy of Fine Arts and the Ashutosh Museum, the following are worth checking out.

Aakriti Art Gallery 1st floor, Orbit Enclave, 12/3A Hungerford St ☏ 033 2289 3027, ⓦaakritiartgallery. com. A well-designed modern Indian art gallery with big-name exhibitions and a shop. Mon–Sat noon–7pm.

Birla Academy of Art and Culture 108 Southern Ave ☏ 033 2466 2843, ⓦbirlaart.com. Ancient and modern art with regular exhibitions of contemporary Indian artists. Tues–Sun 4–7pm.

Galerie 88 28B Shakespeare Sarani ☏ 033 2290 2274, ⓦgalerie88.in. Private gallery specializing in contemporary Indian paintings plus specialist exhibitions and some big names. Also stocks art supplies. Mon–Sat 10am–7pm.

Rabindranath Tagore Centre ICCR, 9A Ho Chi Minh Sarani ☏ 033 2287 2680, ⓦtagorecentreiccr.org. Art and craft exhibitions in this government-run, cultural establishment with a number of galleries and auditoria. Mon–Sat 10am–7pm.

imperialists is the stained glass of the west window, designed by Sir Edward Burne-Jones in 1880 to honour Lord Mayo, assassinated in the Andaman Islands. The original steeple was destroyed in the 1897 earthquake; after a second earthquake in 1934 it was remodelled on the Bell Harry Tower at Canterbury Cathedral.

The Academy of Fine Arts

Cathedral Rd • Daily 3–8pm • Free

South of the cathedral, the **Academy of Fine Arts** is a showcase for Bengali contemporary arts. As well as temporary exhibitions, it holds permanent displays of the work of artists such as Jamini Roy and Rabindranath Tagore (see page 782). A café and pleasant grounds enhance the ambience.

The Cultural Centre: Rabindra Sadan, Nandan and Sisir Mancha

1 AJC Rd • Daily 9am–8pm

Immediately south of the Academy of Fine Arts, the **Cultural Centre** features the large auditorium of **Rabindra Sadan** which, occasionally and especially in winter, features programmes of Indian classical music. Next door, **Nandan**, designed by Satyajit Ray, is a lively film centre and pays homage to the rich tradition of Bengal's film-making. Also within the complex, Bengali theatre is celebrated with its own auditorium, **Sisir Mancha**.

Park Street

Renamed by the CPI(M) as Mother Teresa Sarani – though few locals use this name – **Park Street** is packed with restaurants, cafés and bars, and has long been the hub of cosmopolitan and even hedonistic Calcutta. Once famous for its live music, including a renowned jazz club now sadly gone, the western or Maidan end of the strip continues to support some of the liveliest nightlife in the city. The street also has been important in the history of the city, housing the Asiatic Society, the Survey of India and the iconic Raj-era monoliths of the Park Street Cemetery.

Asiatic Society

1 Park St • **Reading Room** Mon–Fri 10am–8pm, Sat 10am–5pm • Free • ☏ 033 2229 0779, ⓦasiaticsocietykolkata.org

Close to Chowringhee Road, the **Asiatic Society**, established in 1784 by Orientalists including Sir William Jones, houses a huge collection of around 150,000 books and

13

THE BLACK HOLE OF CALCUTTA

Built in 1868 on the site of the original Fort William – destroyed by Siraj-ud-Daula in 1756 – the **GPO** on the west side of the square hides the supposed site of the **Black Hole of Calcutta**. On a hot June night in 1756, 146 British prisoners were forced by Siraj-ud-Daula's guards into a tiny chamber with only the smallest of windows for ventilation; most had suffocated to death by the next morning. By all accounts, the guards were unaware of the tragedy unfolding and, on hearing the news, Siraj-ud-Daula was deeply repentant. A **memorial** to the victims that formerly stood in front of the Writers' Building was moved in 1940 to the grounds of St John's Church, south of the GPO.

60,000 manuscripts, some dating back to the seventh century. The society has a **reading room** open to the public as well as a **gallery** of art and antiquities that holds paintings by Rubens and Reynolds, a large coin collection and one of Ashoka's stone edicts.

Park Street Cemetery

Around 2km east of the Maidan • Mon–Fri 8am–4.30pm, Sat 8–11am • Donation or buy guide pamphlet ₹100

The disused **Park Street Cemetery** is one of the city's most haunting memorials to its imperial past. Inaugurated in 1767, it is the oldest in Kolkata, holding a wonderful concentration of pyramids, obelisks, pavilions, urns and headstones, beneath which many well-known figures from the Raj lie buried including Sir William Jones of the Asiatic Society. The epitaphs make poignant reading.

Central Kolkata

The commercial and administrative hub of both Kolkata and West Bengal is **BBD Bagh**, which die-hard Kolkatans still refer to as **Dalhousie Square**. The new official name, in a fine piece of irony, commemorates three revolutionaries hanged for trying to kill Lieutenant-Governor General Lord Dalhousie.

Beyond the headquarters of Eastern Railways on Netaji Subhash Road, you come to the heart of Kolkata's **commercial district**, clustered around the Calcutta Stock Exchange at the corner of Lyon's Range, which started out as a gathering of traders under a *neem* tree in the 1830s. The warren of buildings houses all sorts of old colonial trading companies, including some still bearing Scottish names.

St John's Church

Just south of the GPO • Daily 8am–5pm • ₹10 • ☏ 033 2243 6098

Of the eighteenth- and nineteenth-century British **churches** dotted around central Kolkata, the most interesting is **St John's**, just south of the GPO. Erected in 1787, it houses memorials to British residents, along with an impressive painting of *The Last Supper* by Johann Zoffany, in which prominent Calcuttans are depicted as apostles. In the grounds, Kolkata's oldest graveyard holds the tomb of **Job Charnock**, the city's founding father, who earned eternal notoriety for marrying a Hindu girl he saved from the funeral pyre of her first husband; he is one of the few colonialists still cherished among Bengalis.

Eden Gardens

West of Esplanade Bus Stand • Daily dawn–dusk • Free

Eden Gardens, the imposing site of the world-famous **cricket** ground (officially known as the **Ranji Stadium**), lies near the river close to Chandpal Ghat and has been described as the "Coliseum of Cricket". Watching a test match here is an unforgettable experience as the 66,000-seat stadium resounds to the roar of the crowd. Next to the stadium, towards the river, the pleasant palm-fringed **gardens** are a picture of tranquillity with a **Burmese pagoda** set against a little lake.

The synagogues of BethEl and Magen David

Pollock St and Synagogue St (both off Brabourne Rd) • Mon–Thurs & Sun 10am–5pm • Gain permission from *Nahoum & Sons* (see page 772) in New Market; staff can arrange a guide to visit either of the synagogues

Now protected monuments, a short distance north of BBD Bagh and on the edge of Barabazaar, the **synagogues** of **BethEl** and **Magen David** are reminders of the once flourishing community that played such an important role in the commercial life of the city. While the Jewish community has all but disappeared from Kolkata, the two synagogues remain lovingly preserved. Buried in the heart of a busy electrical goods market, BethEl's exterior, emblazoned with the Star of David, hides an immaculate, lofty hall with aisles awaiting a lost congregation. A short distance away, Magen David's church-like appearance is similar. Both feature striking stained glass, common throughout the synagogues of India.

13

North Kolkata

The amorphous area of **north Kolkata**, long part of the "native" town rather than the European sectors of the "white town", was where the city's prosperous nineteenth-century Bengali families created their little palaces, or *raj baris*, many of which are now in advanced and fascinating states of decay.

Barabazaar

North of BBD Bagh

The area known as **Barabazaar** has hosted a succession of trading communities; the Portuguese were here before Job Charnock landed at the fishing village that stood close by, and it later became home to Marwari and Gujarati merchants. The small, hectic lanes south of MG Road are lined with shops and stalls selling everything from glass bangles to textiles.

At the northwest corner of Barabazaar, near Howrah Bridge, is Kolkata's oldest church, the **Armenian Church of Our Lady of Nazareth** (Sun 9am–11pm). Founded in 1724 by Cavond, an Armenian from Persia, it was built on the site of an Armenian cemetery in which the oldest tombstone dates to 1630. The Armenian community was already highly influential at the courts of Bengal by the time the British arrived, and played an important role in the early history of the East India Company. Later they helped start the lucrative jute industry and still have a small community in the city.

Nakhoda Masjid

East of Barabazaar on Rabindra Sarani (formerly Chitpore Rd)

The huge red **Nakhoda Masjid**, whose two lofty minarets rise to 46m, is the great Jama Masjid (Friday mosque) of the city. Completed in 1942, it was modelled on Akbar's Tomb at Sikandra near Agra; its four floors can hold ten thousand worshippers. The traditional Muslim market sells religious items along with clothes, dried fruit and sweets such as *firni*, which is made of rice.

Chinatown

Rabindra Sarani

Until relatively recently, the chaotic jumble of streets to the south along Rabindra Sarani housed a thriving **Chinatown**, restaurants, temples, markets, opium dens and all. A handful of Chinese families continue to live around the decaying environs of Chhatawala Gully, where a small early-morning **street market** (daily 6–7am) offers home-made pork sausages, noodles and jasmine tea. Today, the main focus of the city's Chinese community is at Tangra on the eastern edge of the city, where dwindling numbers continue to nurture some of its customs and industries.

Marble Palace

North of MG Rd, on tiny Muktaram Babu St off Chittaranjan Ave • Tues, Wed & Fri–Sun 10am–3pm • Free; no photography

13

The ornate **Marble Palace** holds a lavish collection of statues, European antiques, Ming vases, and paintings by Rubens and Gainsborough. To join one of the free guided tours of this extraordinary pile, get a pass from the tourist offices at BBD Bagh or Shakespeare Sarani (see page 768). To the north of Marble Palace, **Sonagachi**'s warren of lanes is one of Kolkata's red-light districts.

Rabindra Bharati Museum (Tagore's House)

Dwarkanath Tagore Lane • Tues–Sun 10.30am–5.00pm • ₹150 (₹10) • ☎ 033 2269 5242, ⊛ rbu.ac.in

A short walk northeast of the Marble Palace, the small campus of Rabindranath Tagore's liberal arts university, **Rabindra Bharati**, preserves the house where he was born and died as the **Rabindra Bharati Museum**, or Tagore's House. A fine example of a nineteenth-century *raj bari*, the museum holds a large collection of Tagore's paintings.

College Street

The heart of Calcutta University and surrounded by its hallowed institutions, **College Street** is famed for its book vendors – forming one of the largest second hand book markets in the world. While the emphasis is primarily on textbooks, browsing unearths far more. No trip is complete without a visit to the frenetic **Indian Coffee House** (see page 772), which maintains its reputation as a meeting place for the intelligentsia.

Asutosh Museum of Indian Art

Centenary Building • Mon–Fri 11am–4pm • ₹10

In the Centenary Building just inside Calcutta University's College Street gateway, the **Asutosh Museum of Indian Art** is dedicated to the arts of Bengal, with a superb collection from eighth-century Pala-dynasty sculpture to nineteenth-century painted scrolls and contemporary art. Few people come this way; you are more than likely to have the museum to yourself and a few officious staff.

River Hooghly

Until silting rendered it impractical for large ships, the **River Hooghly**, a distributary of the Ganges, was responsible for making Calcutta a bustling port. The *ghats* that line the river's east bank serve as landings and places for ritual ablutions but, unlike in Varanasi, hold no mythological significance. Around 2km north of Howrah Bridge, beyond the cremation grounds of **Nimtolla Ghat**, lies **Kumartuli Ghat** and its community of artisans and sculptors. A short distance further north lies **Baghbazaar Ghat** where overladen barges of straw arrive for the artisans of Kumartuli. Baghbazaar, the Garden Market, stands on the original site of **Sutanuti**, its grand but decaying mansions epitomizing the long-vanished lifestyle of the Bengali gentry, the *bhadra log* (lampooned by Rudyard Kipling in *The Jungle Book*, whose monkey troupe he called the "bandar log").

The ghats

South of Howrah Bridge • Boat trips from Princep Ghat around ₹300/hr

South of Howrah Bridge, in its shadow, set behind the busy flower market of **Mullick Ghat**, the **Armenian Ghat** is most animated at the first light of dawn, when traditional gymnasts and wrestlers, devotees of Hanuman the monkey god, come to practise. As the Strand – separated from the river by the Circular Railway line – heads south, it passes several warehouses, **Millennium Park** and Fairlie Place and comes to another cluster of *ghats*. Frequent ferries (7.30am–8pm) from **Chandpal Ghat** provide an easy alternative to Howrah Bridge and connect with several other useful *ghats* such as **Shibpur** (for the Botanical Gardens) and **Shobabazaar** (for Kumartuli). **Babu Ghat**, near a messy bus terminus and identified by its crumbling colonnade, is used for early morning bathing, attended by pujaris (priests) and heavy-handed masseurs. Further

---

HOWRAH BRIDGE

13

One of Kolkata's most famous landmarks (officially called Rabindra Setu, though few people use this new name), **Howrah Bridge** is 97m high and 705m long, spanning the river in a single leap to make it the world's third longest cantilever bridge. Erected with a maze of girders during World War II in 1943 to give Allied troops access to the Burmese front, it was the first bridge to be built using rivets. Joining the streams of pedestrians who walk across it each day is a memorable experience. **Vidyasagar Setu**, the second Hooghly bridge, built 3km south to relieve the strain, was 22 years in the making. It's a vast toll bridge with Spaghetti Junction-style approaches high enough to let ships pass below.

---

south towards **Princep Ghat**, between Fort William and the river, the Strand comes into its own as a leafy promenade, pleasant during the early evenings with cafés, food stalls and boat rides from the small jetty near *Scoops* café.

Kumartuli

Just north of Shobabazaar

A short walk north of Shobabazaar Ghat, lies the warren of **Kumartuli**, where a community of *kumars* or "potters" hand-craft lavish statues of voluptuous goddesses used for the city's religious festivals. In the days leading up to the great pujas, especially that of Durga Puja (see page 753), Kumartuli is a fascinating hive of activity. Statues take form from straw and river clay before being spray-painted and then clothed in all their finery. Although *pith* (banana tree marrow) is still used to decorate the statues, modern materials have made an impact. The community is also accessible from Shobabazaar Metro Station – emerge from the west exit and walk west along a lane to Rabindra Sarani and an entrance to Kumartuli.

Botanical Gardens

Shibpur, 10km south of Howrah station • Tues–Sun 5.30am–5pm • ₹50 (₹10) • ☎ 033 6732 3135, ⓦ bgci.org • Buses #C6 (from Esplanade), #T9 (from Park St), #6 minibus (from Dharamtala via Howrah); taxis from the central Sudder St area cost ₹300–350 one way

The **Botanical Gardens** at Shibpur, on the west bank of the Hooghly, are populated by countless bird species. These huge gardens are best seen in the winter and spring, and early in the morning, before the heat of the day sets in. Their most famous feature is the world's largest **banyan tree**, 24.5m high and an astonishing 420m in circumference. The Orchid House, the Herbarium and the Fern Houses are also worth seeing, and there's an attractive riverside promenade.

South Kolkata

South of the Maidan and Park Street, Kolkata spreads towards posh and rapidly expanding **suburbs** such as **Alipore** and **Ballygunge**, which are both within easy distance of the centre. The thoroughfare that starts life as Chowringhee at Esplanade proceeds past **Kalighat** to **Tollygunge**, following the Metro line that terminates near the luxurious *Tollygunge Club*, the mansion of an indigo merchant now surrounded by immaculate golfing fairways and bridle-paths; note that only members or their guests are allowed to stay at the club. Northeast of Tollygunge, beyond a white-tiled mosque built in 1835 by descendants of Tipu Sultan, lies the parkland of Rabindra Sarobar, known locally as "the Lakes", a popular spot for early evening walks.

Alipore

Around 3km southwest of Park St • **Zoo** Daily except Thurs 9am–5pm • ₹20 (plus ₹5 for the aquarium) • ☎ 033 2479 1150, ⓦ kolkatazoo. in • **National Library** Mon–Fri 9am–8pm, Sat & Sun 9.30am–6pm • Free

In the suburb of Alipore, which starts around 3km southwest of Park Street, elegant triple-arched gates just south of the popular **zoo** and **aquarium** lead to Belvedere, the

13

MOTHER TERESA

Canonized by Pope Francis in September 2016, **Mother Teresa** (1910–97) is undoubtedly Kolkata's most famous citizen. Born Agnes Gonxha Bojaxhiu to Albanian parents, she grew up in Skopje in the former Yugoslavia. Joining the Sisters of Loreto, an Irish order, she was sent as a teacher to Darjeeling, where she took her vows in May 1931 and became Teresa. While working in Kolkata, she was moved by the terrible poverty around her; in 1948 she changed her nun's habit for the simple blue-bordered white sari that became the uniform of the **Missionaries of Charity**.

The best known of their many homes and clinics is **Nirmal Hriday** at 251 Kalighat Rd, a hospice for the destitute. Despite local resistance, Mother Teresa chose its site by Kalighat temple in the knowledge that many poor people come here to die next to a holy *tirtha* or crossing-place. Her piety and single-minded devotion to the poor won her international acclaim, and she was awarded the Nobel Peace Prize in 1979. However, she also attracted significant controversy thanks to her fierce anti-abortion stance and was accused of disregarding advances in medicine in favour of saving souls. The late journalist and author Christopher Hitchens wrote a searing polemic, *The Missionary Position*, describing her as "a fanatic, a fundamentalist, and a fraud", alleging misappropriation of donations, questioning her choice of friends (including the likes of brutal Haitian dictator Papa Doc), and challenging her regressive attitudes to contraception and reproductive rights.

If you're interested in the work of the Missionaries of Charity, they can be contacted at **Mother House**, near Sealdah Station at 54A AJC Bose Rd (📞033 2249 7115; closed Thurs; 🌐 motherteresa.org). Mother Teresa is buried here, and along with her tomb there is a small museum dedicated to her life. They run orientation workshops (a brief introduction to their work) on Mondays, Wednesdays and Fridays from 3pm to 5pm at nearby Shishu Bhavan, 78 AJC Bose Rd, which is an orphanage and a dispensary for children.

The appalling poverty highlighted by Mother Teresa has led to a number of NGO charities developing in the city. Established in 1979, **Calcutta Rescue** is a nonreligious organization that runs clinics, schools and a creche in Kolkata, as well as an outreach programme to help people in need further afield in West Bengal. For more information visit them online at 🌐 calcuttarescue.org or call 📞033 2217 5675.

An organization dedicated to the welfare and rehabilitation of street and slum children, **Hope** relies on volunteers and donors for its many projects throughout the city and further afield. For more information call 📞033 2472 2904 or visit 🌐 hopefoundation.ie.

former residence of the lieutenant-governor of Bengal, presented to Warren Hastings by Mir Jafar, and now serving as the **National Library**. When the capital shifted to Delhi, this library was left behind; today it houses a huge collection of books, periodicals and reference material, as well as rare documents in an air-conditioned chamber. Day-membership to the reading room is available with ID and two photographs.

Kalighat
5km south of Park St off Ashutosh Mukherjee Rd (an extension of Chowringhee Rd)

Kolkata's most important temple, **Kalighat**, stands at the heart of a diverse and animated area, part residential, part bazaar. The destitute, hoping for charity from pilgrims, line the temple approaches and prostitutes linger on the thoroughfares and bridges, offering their services in tragic, grimy circumstances. The typically Bengali temple itself, built in 1809 of brick and mortar but capturing the sweeping curves of a thatched roof, is dedicated to Kali, the Divine Mother, a form of Shakti. According to legend, Shiva went into a frenzy after the death of his wife Sati, dancing with her dead body and making the whole world tremble. In an attempt to stop him, Vishnu took his solar discus and chopped the disintegrating corpse into 51 bits. The spot where each piece fell became a *pitha*, a sacred site for the female principal of divinity – Shakti. The shrine here marks the place where her little toe fell.

Open all hours, the temple is tended by avaricious priests who will try to whisk you downstairs to confront the dramatic monolithic image of the terrible goddess with her

13

huge eyes and bloody tongue. The courtyard beyond the main congregational hall is used for sacrificing goats on special occasions. **Nirmal Hriday**, Mother Teresa's home for the destitute and dying, is on the northwest corner of the complex.

Ballygunge

East of Kalighat is **Ballygunge**, one of the most sought-after neighbourhoods in Kolkata for the city's wealthier residents. Alongside scores of expensive houses are a series of shopping malls, an increasing number of art galleries (including the Birla Academy of Art and Culture), and an array of fancy restaurants and Western-style coffee shops. Head here if you want a break from the chaos of the city centre, or a glimpse into the lives of wealthy Kolkatans.

ARRIVAL AND DEPARTURE

KOLKATA

BY PLANE

Netaji Subhash Bose International Airport Kolkata's airport (☎ 033 2511 8787), 20km north of the city centre, is officially called Netaji Subhash Bose International Airport, but is still universally known by its old name of Dum Dum. Its key amenities include money-exchange and a prepaid taxi booth, an accommodation booking counter, a railway reservation desk, useful taxi counters and a city coach counter.

Flights Kolkata has excellent domestic services to cities across the country on AirAsia, IndiGo, SpiceJet and other companies. Check *Graphiti, The Telegraph's* Sunday supplement, for current flight (and train) information.

GETTING INTO TOWN

By taxi A prepaid taxi from the airport to the central Sudder St area costs around ₹400 (expect to pay more if you're travelling in the opposite direction); several other operators offer smarter (and more expensive) a/c cars into town. The transport counters at the domestic terminal are clustered together near the exit in the arrivals lounge.

By bus Express Volvo a/c coach services connect the airport with various points in the city, the most useful being the V1, which travels to Esplanade, handy for accessing the metro and the Sudder St area. Luggage allowance is one bag plus hand luggage per person, as these are essentially commuter coaches.

By Metro and Circular Railway An alternative is to take a taxi (around ₹300) or shuttle bus to the Dum Dum

Metro station (5km), and then the Metro (see page 767) into town; Sudder St is a short walk from Park Street station. Bear in mind that you can't take large items (bikes, sports equipment etc) onto the Metro system. Dum Dum is also a terminus for the Circular Railway to Eden Gardens (Chandpal Ghat) (daily 7.50am–6.45pm) from where Sudder St is a short taxi ride away.

BY TRAIN

Kolkata has three main railway stations: Howrah, Kolkata and Sealdah, with two others, Santragachi and Shalimar, as subsidiary hubs. Unfortunately, none of the stations is currently linked to the Metro system, though the east–west line, under construction at the time of writing, will have stations at Howrah and Sealdah.

Howrah Howrah – the point of arrival for most major trains from the south and west – stands on the far bank of the Hooghly, 2km west of the centre. To reach the central downtown area, traffic has to negotiate Howrah Bridge – the definitive introduction to the chaos of the city. Avoid the touts and taxis outside the station building, and head straight for the prepaid taxi booth, from where the fare to the central Sudder St and Park St areas is ₹150–200. Minibuses and buses also operate from Howrah to destinations all over the city, but tend to be very crowded. A good alternative is to follow the signs from the station gate and take a ferry across the Hooghly to Babu Ghat or the adjacent Chandpal Ghat, close to BBD Bagh, and pick up a metered taxi or bus from there.

KALIGHAT PAINTINGS

Early in the nineteenth century, Kalighat was in its heyday, drawing pilgrims, merchants and artisans from all over the country. Among them were **scroll painters** from elsewhere in Bengal, who developed the distinctive style now known as **Kalighat pat**. Adapting Western techniques, using paper and water-based paints instead of tempera, they moved away from religious themes to depict contemporary subjects. By 1850, Kalighat **pat** had taken a dynamic new direction, satirizing the middle classes in much the same way as today's political cartoons. They serve as a witty record of the period, filled with images of everyday life, and can be found in galleries and museums around the world, and in the Indian Museum (see page 758) as well as the Birla Academy and Ashutosh Museum in Kolkata.

13

RECOMMENDED TRAINS FROM KOLKATA

Destination	Name	No.	From	Departs	Arrives
Bhubaneswar	*Falaknuma Express*	#12703	Howrah	7.25am	1.50pm
Bolpur	*Kanchenjunga Express*	#15657	Sealdah	6.35am	9.14am
Chennai	*Coromandel Express*	#12841	Howrah	2.50pm	5.20pm+
Delhi	*Rajdhani Express**	#12301	Howrah	4.55pm	10am+
Gaya	*Mumbai Mail*	#12321	Howrah	10pm	5.22am+
Guwahati	*Saraighat Express*	#12345	Howrah	3.50pm	9.35am+
Mumbai	*Howrah Mumbai Duronto Express**	#12262	Howrah	8.20pm	10.30am+
New Jalpaiguri**	*Darjeeling Mail*	#12343	Sealdah	10.05pm	3.24pm+
Prayagraj	*Kalka Mail*	#12311	Howrah	7.40pm	9.25am+
Puri	*Puri Express*	#12837	Howrah	10.35pm	7.10am
Raxaul	*Mithila Express*	#13021	Howrah	3.45pm	8.30am+ (for Birganj in Nepal)
Varanasi	*Amritsar Mail*	#13005	Howrah	7.10pm	9.12am+

*A/c only
**Connect here for transport to Siliguri, Darjeeling, Kalimpong, Sikkim and Gangtok.
+ next day

Kolkata Kolkata station (or Terminus, also known as Chitpur station) lies 1km from Shyambaazaar Metro station, from where it is a convenient seven stops south to Park St (for Sudder St hotels). There isn't a prepaid booth but auto-rickshaws to Shyambaazaar are available and there is a taxi rank. The Circular Railway connects the station with Eden Gardens (handy for the Sudder St area).

Santragachi Several major trains stop here in transit but the station, 7km to the west of Howrah, is also the terminus for a few long-distance trains on the Southeastern Railways network. Taxis and buses are available and there is an a/c Volvo bus (V2) all the way to the airport via Park Circus.

Shalimar Shalimar, the city's newest station, lies 5km to the south of Howrah and across Vidyasagar Setu Bridge from central Kolkata, with a handful of trains along the Southern Railways network. There is an occasional and irregular ferry service to Garden Reach and Babu Ghat, plus plenty of taxis.

Sealdah Sealdah station, with its own prepaid taxi booth in the car park, is on the eastern edge of the centre close to the Sudder St area. Once the main terminus for trains from the north, Sealdah now shares this role with Kolkata station.

BOOKING TICKETS

Centralized information on train connections is available on ☎ 033 2230 3545 or 033 2230 3535. For general reservation enquiries, call ☎ 033 2230 3496. You can also book online or through agents around Sudder St – the latter is by far the easiest and quickest option.

Railway Reservation Offices Of the numerous computerized booking offices throughout the city the convenient ones are: Fairlie Place (BBD Bagh), Howrah and Sealdah stations, Bentinck St (Esplanade) and Alexandra Court, 61 Chowringhee Rd, Rabindra Sadan (Mon–Sat 8am–8pm, Sun & hols 9am–2pm).

Foreign Tourist Office The tourist office on the first floor of the Eastern Railways office, in the northwest corner of BBD Bagh at 6 Fairlie Place, books tourist quota train tickets (Mon–Sat 10am–5pm, Sun & hols 10am–2pm; ☎ 033 2222 4206). You'll need to bring proof of encashment (an exchange or ATM receipt) to reserve a berth if paying in rupees.

BY BUS

While the main highways and expressways to the west and northwest of the city are relatively quick, having undergone modernization in recent years, much of the state's roads are in appalling condition. Buses are generally cheaper but can be a painful experience, especially on the northern route to Siliguri (for Darjeeling).

Esplanade bus stand The largest, the most chaotic but also most convenient of Kolkata's bus terminals less than 500m north of the tourist hub of Sudder St, Esplanade is not a single terminal but rather a collection of bus services to numerous points throughout the state. These include the Rocket Bus travelling the 560km route to Siliguri (7pm; 13hr; Santanu Booking Counter ☎ 9331062749), which offers reclining seats as well as a sleeper section (single travellers will be required to share). Among the most efficient and luxurious services from the terminus is Royal Cruiser (☎ 033 2252 1415, ⓦ royalcruiser.com), which has its office within the Esplanade Metro station (entrance opposite *Grand Hotel*), with a/c Volvo buses to Siliguri (7pm) and Puri (9pm) among other key destinations. Several buses from here head to Basanti and the Sundarbans (especially early morning) and for points south to Diamond Harbour and beyond.

Babu Ghat bus stand Some long-distance buses from the south, including Puri and Ranchi, terminate at Babu Ghat bus stand, not far from Fort William on the east bank. State transport companies (Odisha Roadways ☏ 943 314 34280;

West Bengal State Transport ☏ 033 241 6388) have their booths here. Among the private companies, the Dolphin (☏ 94332 36077, ⊛ dolphinbusservice.com) service to Puri departs at 9pm and arrives in Puri at 7am; the bus is a basic "sleeper" but some sleeper coaches offer separate bunk sections – do check first; others have reclining seats.

GETTING AROUND

The **Metro**, India's first and Kolkata's pride and joy, provides a fast, clean and efficient way to get around. The river is also used for transport, with the *ghats* near Eden Gardens at the hub of a **ferry** system. You can beat the traffic by jumping on one of the frequent ferries from Chandpal Ghat to Howrah station, though they're crowded at rush hour. Metered **taxis** remain the most convenient mode of transport and radio cabs (private taxis) provide more comfort at a price. There is a bewildering plethora of **buses** plying the city and the few trams left are a reminder of bygone days. While using public transport, be wary of **pickpockets**, especially on crowded buses.

By Metro The Russian-designed Metro (⊛ kmrc.in), inaugurated in 1984, is still every bit as good as its inhabitants proudly claim, with trains operating punctually every few minutes. Services run 7am–9.45pm Mon–Sat and 3–9.45pm on Sun. Tickets are inexpensive, starting at ₹5. Single tickets work on a token system and are valid for 90min from purchase – touch the token on the turnstile to enter and drop into the slot to exit. Smart Cards allow multiday travel and cost ₹100 (refundable) plus charges from ₹100. Recharge machines are available at certain stations including Park Street.

By bus Kolkata supports a vast and complicated bus network

ONWARD TRAVEL: TO BANGLADESH AND THE ANDAMAN ISLANDS

TO BANGLADESH

Kolkata is the main gateway to Bangladesh from India. The Bangladesh Consulate is at 9 Circus Ave (Mon–Fri 9am–5pm; ☏ 033 2247 5208, ext 207 for visa section, ⊛ bdhc-kolkata.org). **Visas** on arrival can now be obtained at the Petrapole-Benapole border for USD50, but you may experience delays. You can always obtain a visa in advance, which will generally be issued on the same day if you submit your passport before 10am. You can reach Bangladesh by train or road or a combination of the two, and there are several daily **flights** from Kolkata to Dhaka.

Departing Kolkata station, the *Maitree Express* (#13108/9; departs Tues, Sat & Sun 7.10am, arrives 6pm) – buy tickets from the Foreign Tourist Bureau, Fairlie Place (see page 766) – is the only direct **train** to Dhaka and you need a visa to book. An alternative is to take an early train from Sealdah to Bangaon (₹20) and cross the border to take another train from Benapole. Numerous travel agents around Sudder and Marquis streets sell tickets for private buses to Dhaka, which depart from the Esplanade stand, but some involve a change at the border.

Private **buses** such as Shyamoli Paribahan, 10 Marquis St (☏ 033 2252 0693, ⊛ shyamolibusservice.com), to Dhaka depart from Esplanade while government-run WBSTC and BRTC buses operate from Esplanade and Salt Lake International Karunamoyee terminal (☏ 033 2359 8448), a roughly ₹200 taxi ride from the centre, to Dhaka (Tues, Thurs & Sat from 5.30am; 12hr); you will need to show your visa to book, or you can use these services to reach the border (₹300) and catch an onward bus to Dhaka in Benapole.

TO THE ANDAMAN ISLANDS

Flights with Air India, Go Air and Spicejet serve Port Blair. To go by **ship** (there are three to four sailings a month), you'll need to book through the Shipping Corporation of India, 13 Strand Rd (☏ 033 2248 2354, ⊛ shipindia.com); the journey takes three to five days, so bring plenty to read and food to supplement the dull meals. Free thirty-day permits are granted on arrival.

TO ARUNACHAL PRADESH

Kolkata is a good place to apply for a Restricted Area Permit. The Deputy Resident Commissioner, Govt. of Arunachal Pradesh is at CE-109, Sector-1, Salt Lake City, Kolkata. (Mon–Fri 9am–5pm, ☏ 033 2334 1243 and 2358 9865). Permits take up to five working days to be issued, but can generally be sent to your email as you travel. Bring two photographs and ₹3500 in cash.

13

(for route information, check ⊚ calcuttayellowpages.com/busroute.html), in operation each day roughly between 5am and 11pm, and subject to overcrowding and the occasional pickpocket. Most buses stop far from the kerb, making getting on and off a hazard. Useful routes include: #S8 from Howrah via Esplanade to Gariahat; #S17 from Chetla near Kalighat via Esplanade to Dakshineshwar; and #5 and #6, which both travel via Howrah and the Esplanade–Chowringhee area, and stop at the Indian Museum at the head of Sudder St. Buses with an "S" prefix denote special express buses, which charge marginally more. The a/c Volvo buses run on several useful routes including the #VS1 from Esplanade to the airport and the #V1 between Tollygunge (via Gariahat) and the airport. These are commuter buses, so getting on with luggage mid-route can be a problem when the buses are full. In addition, there are private brown-and-yellow minibuses which travel at inordinate speeds. Their destinations are painted boldly in Bengali and English on their sides and route numbers are occasionally visible; #128 connects Howrah with Esplanade.

By tram Kolkata's cumbersome trams, barely changed save for a lick of paint since they started operating in 1873, have been largely phased out, but certain routes linger on and a "new" model has been introduced with high glass windows. Female travellers can take advantage of the rush-hour women-only coaches. Routes include, among many others, #1, Esplanade to College St.

By taxi Painted either yellow or black and yellow, taxis in Kolkata are extremely good value, especially on long journeys (around ₹400 from the airport to Sudder St), but a few drivers can be unwilling to take you on short journeys or to areas they don't like the sound of. There's a 25 percent night-time surcharge (10pm–6am). Up to two pieces of luggage are free, but there's an additional charge for further pieces and for placing bags in the boot. Most cabs have working meters and tend to use them in conjunction with the conversion charts they are obliged to carry. Prepaid taxis are available at some railway stations and the airport.

Private taxis Several private taxi companies, also referred to as radio cabs, with vehicles at the airport and railway stations as well as the major hotels, provide more safety and luxury with a/c and printed receipts. Firms include Bengal Cabs (☎ 99035 95337, ⊚ bengalcabs.com) and Mega Cabs (☎ 90909 09090, ⊚ megacabs.com).

By rickshaw Despite efforts to ban them, Kolkata still has human-drawn rickshaws, though they're only available in the central areas of the city, especially around New Market where some pullers supplement their meagre income by acting as touts and pimps. Most of the rickshaw-pullers are Bihari pavement-dwellers, who live short and very hard lives. Haggle for a realistic price but feel free to give a handful of baksheesh too.

By ferry The ferry system provides a pleasant alternative to the city's manic roads. The most useful ferry terminal is Chandpal Ghat near Eden Gardens and a short taxi ride from Sudder St, from where, along with Howrah station, you can get ferries downriver to Shibpur for the Botanical Gardens and upriver to Shobabazaar, useful for visiting Kumartuli.

INFORMATION

India Tourism office 4 Shakespeare Sarani, off Chowringhee Rd (Mon–Fri 9am–6pm, Sat 9am–1pm; ☎ 033 2282 5813, ⊚ incredibleindia.org). Provides general information on Kolkata, West Bengal and destinations further afield, and can assist with itineraries. Get your Marble Palace (see page 761) pass here.

West Bengal Tourist Bureau (WBTDC) 3/2 BBD Bagh East (Mon–Sat 10.30am–4.30pm; ☎ 033 2248 5168). Arranges tours of Kolkata and package trips throughout West Bengal; also issues permits and books tours and accommodation in WBTDC lodges across the state.

State tourist offices The most useful of the many offices representing other states in Kolkata are those that cover the northeastern states and assist in securing permits for these areas (see page 862) and the Andaman and Nicobar islands. Andaman and Nicobar, 2nd Floor, DP-7, Sector 5 (☎ 033 2357 4897); Arunachal Pradesh, Block CE, 109 Sector 1, Salt Lake (☎ 033 2321 3627); Assam, 8 Russel St (☎ 033 2229 5094); Manipur, 26 Rowland Rd (☎ 033 2475 8075); Meghalaya, 120 Shantipally, EM Bypass (☎ 033 2441 2159); Mizoram, 24 Old Ballygunge Rd (☎ 033 2461 5887); Nagaland, 11 Shakespeare Sarani (☎ 033 2282 5247);

WHAT'S IN A NAME?

Though most of the old British **street names** in Kolkata were officially changed years ago, habits die hard and some of the original names continue to be widely used in tandem with the new. The most important of these is Chowringhee or Jawaharlal Nehru Road (still called Chowringhee). Other name changes to note are BBD Bagh (still often referred to by its old name of Dalhousie Square or simply "Dalhousie"), Mirza Ghalib Street (Free School St), Dr Mohammed Ishaque Road (Kyd St), Muzaffar Ahmed Street (Ripon St), Ho Chi Minh Sarani (Harrington St), AJC Bose Road (Lower Circular Rd), Shakespeare Sarani (Theatre Rd), Rabindranath Tagore Street (Camac St), Lenin Sarani (Dharamtala) and Rabindra Sarani (Chitpore Rd).

Odisha, 41 & 55 Lenin Sarani (☎ 033 2249 3653); Sikkim, 41 Middleton St (☎ 033 2281 5328); Tripura, 1 Pretoria St (☎ 033 2282 5703).
Listings Newspapers such as *The Telegraph* and *The* *Statesman* remain the primary source of information on what's on. *Explocity Kolkata* (ⓦ explocity.com) is a free listings magazine available at the tourist office and some hotels (and online).

TOURS

WALKING TOURS
If you want to devise your own walking itineraries, the *A–Z* of the city, *Eicher Kolkata City Map*, makes an excellent companion.
Calcutta Walks 9A Khairu Place, Chandni Chowk ☎ 98301 84030, ⓦ calcuttawalks.com. Very well organized and well-informed high-end agency that concentrates on walks and tours of the city (including one on the back of a Royal Enfield motorbike; from ₹2000).
Help Tourism 67A Kali Temple Rd, Kalighat ☎ 033 2455 0917, ⓦ helptourism.com. Help's walking tours provide a great insight into the historic heart of the city. They are 4–5hr long and prices start at ₹1500.
Kali Travel Home 5A Ishwar Chakraborty Lane, Burtola ☎ 94321 45532, ⓦ traveleastindia.com. A welcoming agency, run by two Australian aficionados of the old city. Tours (from ₹700) give you an in-depth view of Kolkata, warts and all.
Walks of Kolkata F25, 1st floor Kamalalaya Centre, 156A Lenin Sarani ☎ 98317 61003, ⓦ walksofkolkata. com. Themed walks and tailor-made itineraries with lots of flexibility, including tours for individuals, from ₹3000.

RIVER CRUISES
Assam Bengal Navigation Company 3B Dirang Arcade, GNB Rd, Guwahati ☎ 0361 266 7871, ⓦ assam bengalnavigation.com. Luxurious operators with an international network providing multiday cruises along the Hooghly as well as in Assam and elsewhere on converted river steamers.
Vivada Cruises 14 Southern Ave ☎ 033 2463 1990 or ☎ 98839 33033, ⓦ vivadacruises.com. Along with cruises along the Hooghly, Vivada also provides a multiday cruise to Varanasi and wildlife cruises on the Sundarbans; it also charters boats.

TOUR OPERATORS
Help Tourism. Ethically minded, this pioneering agency has helped establish several wildlife projects and offers a wide range of tours, including to the Sundarbans and wildlife-viewing in north Bengal.
Himalayan Footprints 77 Netaji Subhas Rd ☎ 98300 33896, ⓦ abouthimalayas.com. Informative and flexible wildlife tours, nature treks and trips to the Sundarbans, Sikkim and Darjeeling.
Kali Travel Home. This knowledgeable Australian agency is keen to share its enthusiasm for the city and for Bengal with tailor-made guided tours, cooking classes and farm stays.

TRAVEL AGENT
Thomas Cook 1st Floor, 19B Shakespeare Sarani ☎ 033 6652 6241, ⓦ thomascook.in. Deals with domestic tours and international flights and foreign exchange.

ACCOMMODATION

As soon as you arrive in Kolkata, taxi drivers are likely to assume that you'll be heading for Sudder St, near New Market, where you'll find a heady mix of travellers, businessmen and Bangladeshis in transit. As the main travellers' hub in Kolkata and close to all amenities, the area is a sociable place to stay, with numerous hotels, though if you're after more luxury, you may have to look further afield. Note that budget hotels in Kolkata are generally pretty poor quality: it is well worth spending a bit more here to avoid the grottiest rooms.

SUDDER STREET, NEW MARKET, ESPLANADE AND AROUND
Bawa Walson Spa O Tel 5A Sudder St ☎ 033 2252 1512; map p.757. A relatively new addition to the strip, this chain hotel offers smart, modern and tastefully decorated rooms, though they are overpriced unless you manage to score one of the regular online offers. *The Courtyard* restaurant serves platter meals including tandoori. **₹3500**
Broadway 27A Ganesh Chandra Ave ☎ 033 2236 3930, ⓦ broadwayhotel.in; map p.754. Established in 1937, this old hotel, near Chandni Chowk Metro station, offers basic non-a/c rooms on the edge of the commercial district; cheaper rooms come with shared baths. The Art Deco restaurant and bar downstairs exudes a faded atmosphere. 24hr checkout. **₹1100**
★**The Elgin Fairlawn** 13A Sudder St ☎ 033 2252 1510, ⓦ elginhotels.com/fairlawn.php; map p.757. Chock-full of memorabilia, this famous and old-fashioned family-run hotel exudes a charmingly faded and eccentric Raj atmos-phere. The rooms are large and clean, though a little bare. Non-residents can drink in the lush garden bar, which is a very popular spot for a sundowner. Breakfast is included. **₹4700**
Emirates 11/1 Kyd St ☎ 033 2217 8487; map p.757. New budget boutique hotel boasting a series of clean,

13

large and luminous rooms with all the bells and whistles the category commends. There's a rooftop, a restaurant, and a new wing was being built when we visited. Breakfast included. ₹2500

Galaxy 3 Stuart Lane ☎033 2252 4565; map p.757. This small, economical hotel, with a handful of rooms of varying degrees of modernity, is clean and good value despite the lack of light and position, with hot water and an a/c option too. ₹980

Georgian Inn 1 Doctor Lane ☎98300 68355; map p.754. Although brightly coloured, clean, and featuring fans or a/c, the rooms at this low-cost guesthouse are cramped and cell-like. But, at this price point, there are few better options around. ₹1000

Kempton 3 Marquis St ☎033 4017 7888, ⚲hotel kempton.in; map p.757. Just around the corner from Sudder St, this business-traveller-oriented hotel, with its smart modern design and decor, is very good value, given the quality on offer. Facilities include a 24hr coffee shop and a multicuisine restaurant. ₹4200

★ **Lalit Great Eastern** 123 Old Court House St ☎033 4444 7777, ⚲thelalit.com; map p.754. In a historic building, which first opened in the 1840s and subsequently became known as "The *Savoy* of the East" the *Lalit Great Eastern* has been restored to its former glory, with Victorian, Edwardian and "contemporary" wings. A lovely pool and spa, an array of eating and drinking options, and smart service make it an excellent choice. ₹7100

Oberoi Grand 15 Chowringhee Rd ☎033 2249 2323, ⚲oberoihotels.com; map p.757. If money is no object, this is the place to stay. The white Victorian facade of this luxurious hotel, established in 1938, is very much part of the fabric of the city. Service is attentive, and the interior has an elegant modern-meets-traditional style; facilities include a swimming pool, spa, and excellent Thai and Indian restaurants; security is very tight. ₹15,680

Hotel VIP International 51 Mirza Ghalib St ☎033 2217 6495, ⚲vip-international.hotels-kolkata.com; map p.757. Ideally situated in walking distance to both the New Market and Park Street, this mid-range hotel has large rooms with comfortable beds and was being upholstered at time of research. There's a restaurant downstairs, whose Lucknowi-style kebabs and biriyanis are excellent, yet a bit overpriced. Breakfast included. ₹4200

PARK STREET, CHOWRINGHEE AND AROUND

Park 17 Park St ☎033 2249 9000, ⚲theparkhotels. com; map p.757. Modern five-star hotel, recently renovated, in a good location on cosmopolitan Park St; as well as comfortable, stylish rooms, there is a pool, gym, spa, and good food at the three restaurants, plus a popular nightclub and a bar with live music. ₹8000

Sunflower Guest House 7 Royd St ☎033 2229 9401, ⚲sunflowerguesthouse.com; map p.757. A large, well-

maintained old building managed by one of the city's *rajbari* families; most of its spotless rooms – all with attached bathrooms – are on the top four floors, with the penthouse rooms providing good views; there's a small roof garden. ₹800

YWCA 1 Middleton Row ☎033 2222 9703, ⚲ywca calcutta.org; map p.757. Open to both female and male travellers, and especially good for longer stays, this clean, central hostel with plain but adequate rooms, some a/c, off Park St, is built around a pleasant courtyard with a tennis court. Book well in advance. Breakfast included. ₹1250

SOUTH KOLKATA

★ **Bodhi Tree Guest House** 48/44 Swiss Park ☎033 2424 3871, ⚲bodhitreekolkata.com; map p.754. A stunning little boutique guesthouse, with just six impeccably designed rooms, across the tracks from the lakes and close to the Rabindra Saravar Metro station; there's a tranquil garden courtyard, and plenty of contem-porary art on display. ₹2500

Central B&B Flat 28, 7th floor, Lansdowne Court, 5B Sarat Bose Rd ☎98364 65400, ⚲centralbnb.com; map p.754. The rooms and apartment here are as functional as the name: clean, spacious, well-equipped (TVs, kettles, a/c and so on; the apartment has a kitchenette), and good views from the seventh floor. Good location too, a short walk from Park St and Ballygunge. Rooms ₹3400, apartment ₹4700

Corner Courtyard 92 Sarat Bose Rd ☎99039 99567, ⚲thecornercourtyard.com; map p.754. An immaculately-decorated boutique hotel, situated in a colonial-era house close to Kalighat, with seven charming rooms – each has a different colour scheme, but all have four-poster beds and period furnishings. There's a lush roof terrace and a fine restaurant (see below). ₹4000

Motisarai 259 Darga Rd, Park Circus ☎98364 10333, ⚲motisarai.com; map p.754. Small and homely boutique hotel set half an hour walk south of the New Market. Rooms are luminous and squeaky-clean, with a/c, coffemakers and LED TVs, and surround an intimate common room where meals are served. Breakfast is included, and guests can also use the kitchen for self-catering. ₹2400

★ **The Penthouse** 52d Hindustan Park Rd ☎98301 35801; map p.754. This homestay exceeds all expectations with its homely, well-furnished and large ensuite rooms. There is a pretty rooftop strewn with sofas, chairs, and dim lights that's perfect to rest after a day trawling the city. Breakfast included. ₹2950

The Residency 50/1C Purna Das Rd ☎98300 94188 map p.754. This welcoming place is located in a residential area just off Gol Park and within walking distance of the lakes and Gariahat. Rooms are spotless and come with a/c, TV and all mod cons. ₹3000

Wiseowl Comfotel 66/2B Purna Das Rd ☎033 2464 6422, ⚲wiseowlcomfotel.com; map p.754. Situated in a pleasant part of town, handy for Kalighat, the lakes and Gariahat, and increasingly lively with good restaurants and trendy shops, this guesthouse has spacious rooms in classic Kolkata style; there is a popular coffee shop down-stairs and the top floor hosts an American-style steak house. Breakfast is included and served in the room. ₹2600

ELSEWHERE IN AND AROUND THE CITY

★**Calcutta Bungalow** 5 Radha Kanta Jew St, Fariapukur, Shyam Bazar ☎98301 84030, ⓦcalcutta bungalow.com; map p.754. Carefully renovated by the people behind Calcutta Walks, this heritage boutique hotel offers beautifully furnished rooms, some with exposed bricks and terraces, housed into a historical home on the edge of a park. Bicycle rental is available and continental breakfast is included. ₹6900

Gala Time Hostel Patuli Township J-11 ☎9830113370, ⓦgalatimehostel.com; map p.754. Kolkata's first self-proclaimed backpacker hostel is far from the centre and yet well-located close to a metro station. The mixed dorms are clean and functional, there's a common kitchen and guests love the good vibes. You may reconsider booking in the hot season though, because the dorms are fan only. Breakfast included. ₹380

★**Rajbari Bawali** Hasnecha, Bawali ☎98303 83008, ⓦtherajbari.com; map p.754. After 9 years of dedicated renovation work, this collapsing Zamindar residence got a new lease of life as one of Kolkata's most luxurious heritage properties. The large, high-ceilinged rooms, all fitted with four poster beds and antiques, dot the perimeter of the residence, overlooking a beautiful garden cum water pond. The restaurant, an open-air verandah, is surrounded by trees and set next to a charming swimming pool. It's the perfect getaway from Kolkata's hustle, and yet only about an hour drive from the city centre. Full board included. ₹7000

Swissotel City Centre, New Town ☎033 6626 6666, ⓦswissotel.com/kolkata; map p.754. Modern luxury hotel with all the usual amenities and very well placed for the airport. There are a number of good restaurants, cafés and bars, a health centre and a rooftop swimming pool from where you can watch the planes fly by. The shopping mall next door offers alternative dining and designer brands. ₹8075

Taj Bengal 24B Belvedere Rd, Alipore ☎033 2223 3939, ⓦtaj.tajhotels.com; map p.754. Opulent show-piece hotel and still one of the prime addresses in the city, attempting to amalgamate Bengali features with the usual *Taj* grandeur. Excellent range of restaurants, including Chinese and Indian, and a pool and nightclub. Peak season rates can be astronomical but at other times there are good deals to be had online. Breakfast included. ₹16,030

EATING

Although locals love to **dine out**, traditional Bengali cooking was, until relatively recently, restricted to the home; however, some excellent restaurants now offer the chance to taste this wonderful fish- and seafood-based cuisine; *Kewpie's* (see page 773) is a great place to get an overview. Chinese, spiced and cooked to local tastes, is also popular: the city has a rich tradition including its own Chinatown at **Tangra** on the road to the airport. You'll also find several good south Indian restaurants, numerous joints offering varying standards of Western cuisine, as well as rich Mughal cooking and the not-to-be-missed *kati* roll (sometimes referred to as "kathi roll" or just "roll"; they are *parathas* stuffed with chicken, mutton, *paneer*, egg or spiced potato, spiked with chilli and lime, and rolled in a sheaf of paper), which is an integral part of Kolkata's cuisine; *Kusum* (see page 772) and *Nizam's* (see page 772) are classic places to sample them. Coffee culture is growing with the usual chain cafés throughout the city and there is a handful of purveyors of fine tea. Numerous patisseries and confectioneries work hard to keep up with demand. Restaurants and cafés around **Sudder St** cater for Western travellers while roadside chai shops and street food stalls around BBD Bagh are extremely popular for lunch.

SUDDER STREET, NEW MARKET, ESPLANADE AND AROUND

Amber 11 Waterloo St ☎033 2248 6746; map p.754. A Kolkata landmark that refuses to fade away, the dimly lit *Amber* spreads out across three floors, with a bar downstairs. The menu focuses on Mughal and tandoori cuisine (mains ₹300–450): try the mutton *reshmi* kebab or the barbecued prawns. If you're feeling more adventurous, go for the brain curry. *Amber* has a sister café in south Kolkata (see page 772). Daily noon–11pm.

Arsalan 119A Ripon St ☎033 2227 7493, ⓦarsalan restaurants.com; map p.757. Large restaurant that serves a selection of Chinese and other food; you're best off sticking to its Mughal cuisine (mains ₹140–265) – such as the kebabs and excellent biryanis (try the rich mutton Lucknow biryani) – for which it is famous. There are several other branches dotted around the city. Daily 10am–10pm.

Baan Thai Oberoi Grand hotel, 15 Chowringhee Rd ☎033 2249 2323, ⓦoberoihotels.com; map p.757. Although expensive – expect to pay upwards of ₹2600 per person – this restaurant offers by far the best Thai cooking in town, with dishes such as *Kai yang* (barbecued chicken with lemongrass) and *yam phet yang* (roast duck salad with rambutan and water chestnuts), as well as standards such as red, green and penang curries, satay and *tom yum* soup. Mon–Fri 7–11.30pm, Sat & Sun 12.30–3pm & 7–11.30pm.

Blue Sky Café Sudder St ☎033 2252 2958; map p.757. Budget travellers' haunt halfway down the strip on a corner, providing all the old favourites, including good breakfasts (₹35–190). Clean and well run, with a/c, it's a popular meeting place. Daily 6.30am–11pm.

13

Eau Chew P32 Mission Row Extension, Ganesh Chandra Ave ☎033 2237 8260; map p.754. A legendary family-run restaurant and a remnant from the heyday of Chinatown: ignore the unprepossessing location – above a petrol station – and gloomy interior, and focus on the authentic, reasonably priced food (mains ₹150–230). The "chimney soup", cooked slowly around a metal coal-burning container, is especially good; alternatives include roast duck or pork. Daily 11.30am–2.30pm & 6–10pm.

Indian Coffee House 15 Bankim Chatterjee St, just off College St ☎09007 798519; map p.754. Atmospheric, historic café in the heart of the university area where students and intellectuals continue to meet. It's good for a snack or light meal (₹25–70) and a break from trawling the bookshops of College St, though the coffee itself isn't great. Daily 8am–8pm.

★ **Nahoum & Sons** F-20, New Market ☎033 6526 9936; map p.757. Hidden away in the New Market, surrounded by sari and pashmina stores, this legendary Jewish bakery and confectioner sells delicious fruitcakes and buns, cashew macaroons, lemon tarts, cheese straws and chicken puffs (from ₹25). Mon–Sat 8am–8pm.

Nizam's 22–23 Hogg St ☎98361 94669; map p.757. The owners of *Nizam's* invented the legendary *kati* roll. They moved to the current location in the 1930s, and while the current surroundings are grotty, to say the least, the signature dishes (₹25–70) are seriously good. If you want something a bit more substantial – or in addition to your *kati* roll – go for the other house speciality, biryani (₹140–200). Daily 10am–11pm.

★ **Raj's Spanish Café** 7 Sudder St ☎033 2252 3456, ⓦfacebook.com/rajspanishcafe; map p.757. Tucked away in the far right corner of the courtyard, this is the most traveller-friendly place on the strip, with the usual breakfast menu and great coffee; there is a good selection of Spanish, Mexican and Italian dishes including burritos, veg lasagne, and gazpacho (mains ₹100–175). Daily 7.30am–10pm.

PARK STREET, CHOWRINGHEE AND AROUND

Amber Café 2A Middleton Row ☎033 4000 7490; map p.757. Bright and popular family restaurant run by the owners of celebrated *Amber*; no alcohol and disappointing coffee, but the food is good, with sandwiches, platter meals (from ₹265) and specialities such as chicken tikka masala wrap. Daily noon–11pm.

Bar-B-Q 43 Park St ☎033 2229 9345; map p.757. A long-standing favourite, offering competent Chinese and much-lauded tandoori cuisine (mains ₹140–390) in pleasant a/c surroundings with a bar downstairs (Kingfisher from ₹160); the special lunch menu includes Persian delicacies such as *chelo* kebabs on rice. Daily noon–11pm.

Bistro by the Park 2A Middleton Row ☎033 2229 6494. Tasteful and fresh decor in this popular modern bistro with a varied menu including chicken satay, Caesar salad, and *bhetki* fish in a yogurt, lime, ginger and chilli marinade (₹285–495); a great lunch spot. Daily noon–11pm.

Fire and Ice Kanak Building, 41 Chowringhee Rd ☎033 2288 4073, ⓦfireandicepizzeria.com; map p.757. A trendy bistro and bar – the offshoot of a famous Kathmandu restaurant – serving some of the best Italian cuisine in Kolkata, including authentic thin-crust pizzas (₹495–695), pasta, risottos, and – for dessert – tiramisu and gelato. There's a good range of cocktails too (₹400–650). Daily noon–11pm.

Flury's 18 Park St, on the corner of Middleton Row ☎033 4064 6053, ⓦflurys.com; map p.757. A Kolkata landmark, this once-legendary Swiss teashop and patisserie, founded in 1927, has been completely revamped. Little of the old atmosphere remains, but it's still a popular place and worth visiting for all-day English breakfasts (₹418) or cakes, patties, home-made chocolates and pastries – try the rum balls. Other branches at Alipur, South City Mall and Salt Lake, Sector 3. Daily 8am–9pm.

Jyoti Vihar 3A/1 Ho Chi Minh Sarani ☎033 2282 9791; map p.757. One of the most popular south Indian joints in town can get packed, especially at lunchtime. It is an eat-and-run place, split between two cramped floors, but its reputation is justified with excellent dosas (₹55–95). Daily noon–8pm.

★ **Kusum Rolls** Just off Park St ☎98310 66077; map p.757. Since 1971 this street-side stall serves some of the best *kati* rolls (₹30–160) in Kolkata, and has a loyal following of lunching office workers and students. It's a three-man operation: the first one cooks the *parathas*, another adds the filling – chicken, mutton, *paneer*, omelettes or liver, or a combination thereof – while a third takes the money and hands out napkins. Mon–Sat noon–7/8pm.

Mocambo 25B Park St, entrance around the corner on Mirza Ghalib St ☎033 2265 4300; map p.757. A Kolkata institution, dating back to the 1950s, with a hugely varied menu featuring everything from steak in mushroom sauce to chicken Kiev, lobster Thermidor to fish Florentine. Smart, yet relaxed. Expect to pay from ₹700. Daily noon–11pm.

One Step Up 18A Park St ☎033 2229 5339; map p.757. Modern, conveniently located restaurant whose menu jumps from Italy to Burma, Thailand to Morocco; all are well prepared, though inevitably the Indian food stands out (mains ₹215–350). Good for an early evening drink too. Daily noon–11pm.

The Park 17 Park St ☎033 2249 3121, ⓦtheparkhotels.com; map p.757. This top-end hotel has a well-deserved reputation for some of the finest dining in town. *Zen*, a Terence Conran restaurant, serves dishes from Thailand, China, Japan and Indonesia, while *Saffron* specializes in contemporary Indian cuisine; *Someplace Else*, meanwhile, has a fun pub atmosphere. Expect to pay from ₹900 for a night out. Daily noon–11pm.

13

SWEETSHOPS

Bengalis have a notoriously sweet tooth, and milk-based treats such as the small and dry *sandesh* are a regional speciality. Though the white *rosogulla*, the brown (deep-fried) *pantua* and the distinctive black *kalojam*, all in syrup, are found elsewhere in north India, the best examples are made in Kolkata. Others worth trying are *lal doi* – a delicious red steamed yogurt made with jaggery – or white *mishti doi*, yogurt made with sugar. Sweetshops serve savoury snacks in the afternoons such as deep-fried pastry strips called *nimki* (literally "salty"); *shingara*, a delicate Bengali samosa; and *dalpuri*, *paratha*-like bread made with lentils.

Ganguram 46C Chowringhee Rd ☎80134 10402, ⓦganguram.com; map p.757. Perhaps the most famous sweets company in town, with this branch close to the Victoria Memorial and several others scattered around the city; try *mishti doi* and *sandesh*. Daily 8am–9pm.

KC Das 11 Esplanade East and 57A Ripon St ☎033 2554 4007, ⓦkcdas.co.in; map p.754. Another famous sweetshop with a takeout counter, café and a/c mezzanine; try the *rosogulla*. Other branches include Block B, Laketown. Daily 7.30am–7.30pm.

Sen Mahasay 171H Rashbehari Ave ☎033 2334 8271; map p.754. Next to Gariahat Market, renowned for its *sandesh*; there are several other branches throughout the city including Shyambazaar. Daily 11am–11pm.

Vien 34B Shakespeare Sarani ☎033 2297 4810; map p.757. Small, popular sweetshop, with excellent *sandesh* among other offerings. Daily 7am–10pm.

The Square by Café Coffee Day Chowringhee Mansion, Park St ☎1800 102 5093, ⓦcafecoffeeday. com; map p.757. Conveniently-located branch of the nationwide chain, with a spacious modern-chic lounge, a/c seating area, reasonably quick wi-fi, tasty snacks, and reliably good coffee (from ₹100). Very popular with young Kolkatans and couples. Daily 9am–12am.

SOUTH KOLKATA

6 Ballygunge Place 6 Ballygunge Place ☎033 2460 3922, ⓦsavourites.in; map p.754. Located in an atmospheric old townhouse, *6 Ballygunge Place* specializes in quality Bengali cuisine (mains ₹250–500). Dishes include *posto narkel bora* (coconut and poppy seed dumplings) and *kankrar jhal* (spicy crab curry). Daily 12.30–3.30pm & 7–10.30pm

★ **Ammini** 21C Monohar Pukur Rd ☎033 3221 6769, ⓦfacebook.com/Amminikolkata; map p.754. Smart, modern bistro in a residential part of town, serving excellent and great-value south Indian cooking (mains ₹90–200). Try the Keralan chicken curry. Tues–Sun 11.30am–10.30pm.

Banana Leaf 73 Rashbehari Ave, Lake Market ☎033 2464 1960, ⓦbananaleaf.in; map p.754. Plain decor and a fast turnaround for this extremely popular restaurant that cooks up some of the best south Indian food in town. The dosas, *uttapams*, *idlis* and *vadas* (₹52–140) are all good. Mon–Fri 8am–10pm, Sat & Sun 7am–10pm.

Bhojohori Manna 18/1A Hindustan Rd ☎033 2466 3941, ⓦbhojohorimanna.com; map p.754. A popular local chain serving Bengali food, with a huge menu – highlights include the fish, crab and *chingri* (prawn) curries, the *kosha mangsho* (mutton curry), and the *thalas* (thalis; from ₹160). Expect to queue. There's a small branch on

nearby Ekdalia Rd and another at 11A Esplanade next to *KC Das*. Daily noon–9pm.

Bohemian 32/4 Old Ballygunge First Lane, Bondel Rd ☎033 6460 1001; map p.754. Hip restaurant with a modern take on Bengali cuisine in a simple but chic environment. The extensive menu features creative dishes such as Sundarbans-style barbecued pomfret with onion chutney, braised pork with smoked pineapple and cumin, and Darjeeling tea *panna cotta*. Mains ₹400–700. Daily noon–3pm & 7–11pm.

Café Paris 1/1 Ashutosh Chowdhury Ave ☎99039 20380, ⓦfacebook.com/pariscafekolkata; map p.754. A favourite of Ballygunge's wealthy residents, *Café Paris* is a good spot throughout the day for its superior coffee and hot chocolate, Western-style cakes (from red velvet to macarons), crêpes, paninis, salads and pasta dishes (mains ₹250–300). Mon–Sat 7am–11pm.

Corner Courtyard 92 Sarat Bose Rd ☎99039 99567, ⓦthecornercourtyard.com map p.754. Inside the hotel of the same name (see above), the sunny, stylishly decorated *Corner Courtyard* is an elegant place for a lunch or dinner. The creative menu (₹400–650) features dishes such as quinoa, bean and coriander croquettes, Jamaican jerk chicken, and spicy lamb sliders; good pizzas and desserts too. Daily noon–11pm.

Dolly's Tea Shop Dakshinapan Shopping Centre, Dhakuria; map p.754. Run by the eponymous Dolly, India's former "tea ambassador", this small but iconic tea shop lights up this cheerless mall, with rattan furniture, a peaceful ambience and a great selection of teas (from ₹60) and snacks including sandwiches and cakes. Mon–Sat 10am–6pm.

★ **Kewpie's Kitchen** 2 Elgin Lane ☎033 2486 1600, ⓦfacebook.com/kewpies.kitchen; map p.754. Private

13

home with a restaurant annexe, offering traditional Bengali food fit for a *jamai babu* (son-in-law) first entering his wife's home – try the *lucci* (puris) and the fish and prawn preparations including *malai chingri* (prawns in cream) and *dab-er-chingri* (prawns in green coconut). Prices are relatively high – the set *thalas* (thalis) cost ₹400–900 – but it's worth every rupee. If you fancy trying some of the dishes at home, pick up a copy of Kewpie's English-language cookbook, *Bangla Ranna*. Tues–Sun 12.30–3pm & 7–11pm.

Oh! Calcutta Forum Mall, Elgin Rd ☎033 3099 0301, ⊕facebook.com/ohcalcuttakol; map p.754. Considerably less raunchy than the play of the same name, this Kolkata institution, on the fourth floor of a shopping centre, serves top-notch Bengali cuisine (mains ₹240–650) – the *chingri* dishes are particular highlights – in sophisticated surroundings. Daily 12.30–3pm & 7.30–11pm.

Suruchi 89 Elliot Rd ☎033 3085 9068; map p.754. Run by the All Bengal Women's Union, a charity that provides support for sex workers and their families, *Suruchi* is a good place to taste Bengali home-cooking – try the *mocha chingri* (prawns with banana flower). There's an unpretentious atmosphere, and reasonable prices (from ₹100); recommended for lunch despite its poor location. Mon–Fri 10.30am–5.45pm.

Tea Bush Table 5B Ashton Rd, near the Samilton hotel, off Sarat Bose Rd ☎033 4001 3937; map p.754. A trendy café with chic design and an inventive menu including an extensive list of teas from the traditional to Oriental exotic varieties, such as Pu-erh from China. They serve all-day breakfasts as well as sandwiches, salads and pasta. Expect to pay from ₹100 for tea and around ₹500 for a meal. Mon–Fri 11am–11pm, Sat & Sun 9am–11pm.

ELSEWHERE IN THE CITY

Beijing 77/1 Christopher Rd, Tangra ☎033 3099 0161; map p.754. Owned by a celebrated restaurateur, this place has an extensive menu featuring favourites such as Peking chicken and steamed fish and Meifoon noodles. The bar is well stocked. Expect to pay around ₹800 for a hearty meal and drinks (more if you go for the seafood). Daily noon–11.00pm.

Kim Fa 47 South Tangra Rd ☎033 2325 2895; map p.754. This small Chinese restaurant is still one of Tangra's best, serving excellent Hakka cuisine and popular with the local community. Try the Thai soup, *kung pao* chicken or the chilli king prawns, which can be quite potent (mains ₹130–900). Daily 6–11pm.

Mainland China 3A Gurusaday Rd ☎033 2287 2206; map p.754. Chic Chinese restaurant with elegant service and excellent seafood; widely considered the city's finest, though it can be a little inconsistent. Expect to pay around ₹1200 for a night out. Daily noon–3pm & 7–11pm.

Royal Indian Hotel Near Nakhoda Masjid, Rabindra Sarani ☎033 3099 0251; map p.754. No trip to this area is complete without a visit to this legendary Muslim restaurant for a biryani (from ₹180) or a chicken or mutton *champ* (chop) cooked in aromatic spices and accompanied by *rumali* roti (thin "handkerchief" bread). It's basic, but there is an a/c room which charges more. Daily 11am–11pm.

DRINKING AND NIGHTLIFE

The formerly tense, all-male atmosphere of Kolkata's bars is becoming a thing of the past, with designer-style places attracting a young, professional clientele. As well as the places listed below, several restaurants – notably *Bar-B-Q* (see page 772) – and many of the big hotels are a good option for a quiet drink; some of the hotels also have nightclubs. Most clubs do not allow single males and charge entry fees (from around ₹500).

Blue and Beyond 9th floor, Lindsay hotel, 8A Lindsay St ☎033 7199 8727; map p.757. The terrace up here is probably the best spot for a relaxing drink (beer from ₹155, glass of wine ₹390) and a nibble at dusk, with the bustle of New Market below yet out of earshot. Daily noon–11pm.

Floatel 9/10 Kolkata Jetty, Strand Rd ☎033 2213 7777, ⊕floatelindia.com; map p.754. The *Anchor Bar* at water level is a fine place to languish in a/c-cooled splendour and watch crowded ferries passing by. The bar-restaurant upstairs with its expansive deck catches the refreshing river breeze, but is sometimes booked for events. Daily noon–11pm.

The Grid Ground Haute Street Corporate Park, 86A Topsia Rd ☎84440 00888, ⊕ jointhegrid.in; map p.754. Kolkata's first microbrewery is the perfect place to relax with a beer, enjoy the cosy industrial-chic environment, and sample a concoction of local and international titbits. Daily noon–midnight.

Park 17 Park St ☎1800 102 7275, ⊕theparkhotels. com; map p.757. This hotel is brimming with bars and discos. *Tantra* remains one of the liveliest nightclubs in town, starting at 7pm most days and 4pm on weekends, and attracting a well-heeled crowd with celebrities and fashion shows and live music on Sundays (cocktails from ₹500). Other options include Trincas, with food and live music, and the poolside *Aqua*, which serves food while DJs pump out lounge music in the evenings. Daily noon–11pm.

Peter Cat 18A Park St ☎033 2229 8841; map p.757. This long-term favourite with diners and drinkers alike maintains a good reputation as a bar, offering drinks from cocktails to beer, as well as for its food (mains ₹160–400) including the much-lauded *chelo* kebab (an Indian-Iranian chicken kebab served on buttered rice). Daily noon–11pm.

ENTERTAINMENT

CINEMA

Cinemas showing English-language films several times each day can be found along Chowringhee near Esplanade and New Market. All are a/c, and many are fine examples of Art Deco. The Kolkata Film Festival (wkff.in) takes place in mid-Nov with films shown at venues throughout the city.

CLASSICAL MUSIC

Kolkata has an unassailable reputation as the most discerning centre of classical Indian music in the country. The main concert season runs from winter to spring, with the huge week-long Dover Lane Music Conference (wdoverlanemusicconference.org), held in south Kolkata around the end of Jan and early Feb, attracting many of India's best musicians. Other popular venues for single- and multiday festivals include Rabindra Sadan. Of the many nonreligious festivals each year, the Ganga Utsav, held over a few weeks around the end of Jan at Diamond Harbour, involves music, dance and theatrical events.

Music classes One of the country's leading north-Indian classical music research institutes, Sangeet Research Academy in Tollygunge (☎033 2377 3395, witcsra.org) offers long-term courses in various music forms and a three-month short-term residential course. It also hosts free Wednesday-evening concerts as well as occasional concerts on Saturdays.

SHOPPING

Compared to Delhi and Mumbai, Kolkata has a fairly limited tourist shopping scene. However, there are many lively **markets**, including the wide-ranging **New Market**, as well as local institutions such as **Barabazaar** to the north and **Gariahat Market**, with its produce market best in the early mornings, in south Kolkata. Modern **shopping malls** – good for books, clothes, designer labels, leather, jewellery and restaurants – include Forum, 10/3 Elgin Rd (wforumcourtyard.com); Emami Shoppers City at Lord Sinha Rd; South City Mall on Prince Anwar Shah Rd, south Kolkata; City Centre II at Rajarhat near the airport. Typical **Bengali handicrafts** to look out for include **metal** *dokra* items from the Shantiniketan region northwest of the city: animal and bird objects are roughly cast by a lost-wax process to give them a wiry look. Long-necked, pointy-eared terracotta horses from Bankura, in all sizes, have become something of a cliché. *Kantha* **fabrics** display delicate line stitching in decorative patterns. Bengal boasts several good centres of cotton and **silk** weaving, producing legendary **saris** such as the Baluchari style from Murshidabad.

BOOKS

The month-long Kolkata Book Fair (wkolkatabookfair.net), held at the Milan Mela ground off the EM Bypass in Jan and Feb, is one of the biggest of its kind in the world and is an excellent opportunity to pick up books at a discount. The shops and the roadside stalls of College St are well worth a browse, with an occasional rare gem turning up amid stacks of science and computer studies books.

Earthcare Books 10 Middleton St ☎033 2229 6551, wearthcarebooks.com; map p.757. Tucked away at the back of a yard, this small and modest but focused bookshop specializes in books on green issues, and publishes several titles itself too. Mon–Sat 10am–7pm.

Oxford Books & Stationery 17 Park St ☎033 2229 7662, woxfordbookstore.com; map p.757. A smart a/c bookshop with a small music section and the *Cha Bar* café upstairs. Nice atmosphere, but the collection is relatively limited. Mon–Sat 10am–8pm.

Seagull 31A SP Mukherjee Rd ☎033 2476 5869, wseagullindia.com; map p.754. Small bookshop owned by interesting and creative publishers; its resource centre, a block away, has a library and holds special exhibi-tions and events. Mon–Sat 10am–6pm.

Starmark Emami Shoppers City, 3 Lord Sinha Rd ☎81001 20120, wstarmark.in; map p.757. Extensive bookshop with an adequate range from fiction and travel to magazines as well as music and DVDs in a popular shopping complex. Other branches include South City Mall and City Centre, Salt Lake. Mon noon–8.30pm, Tues–Fri 10am–8.30pm, Sat 10am–9pm, Sun 10.30am–9pm.

TEXTILES AND HANDICRAFTS

Good selections of most handicrafts, including textiles and saris, can be found in various state emporia, many of which, such as Gujari (Gujarat), are located in the large Dakhsinapan shopping complex south of Dhakuria Bridge near Gol Park and the lakes. Offering fixed (if slightly high) prices, these are the simplest places to start shopping.

Assam 8 Russel St ☎033 2229 5094; map p.757. Part of Assam House, selling handicrafts and textiles from Assam including fabrics in *pat* and *moga*, two techniques of silk manufacturing. Mon–Sat 10am–5pm.

Central Cottage Industries 7 Jawaharlal Nehru Rd, Chowringhee ☎033 2228 3205, wcottageemporium. in; map p.757. Part of the national chain, with handicrafts, jewellery, silver, and fabrics from all over India, though service is apathetic and the stock is a bit faded. Mon–Sat 9.30am–6pm.

Nagaland 13 Shakespeare Sarani ☎033 2282 1967; map p.757. A fine assortment of Naga shawls, with red bands and white and blue stripes on black backgrounds. As with Scottish tartan, certain patterns denote particular tribes. Mon–Sat 10am–5pm.

13

Sasha 27 Mirza Ghalib St ☎ 033 6458 9421, �ⓦ sasha world.com; map p.757. This women's self-help group has a good collection of handicrafts and textiles including *kantha*. Mon–Sat 10am–7pm.

FABRICS AND CLOTHES

Along with several designer boutiques, a wide range of fabric is available to buy and outlets can direct you toward good (and very cheap) tailors; there are several around Mirza Ghalib St and New Market. You can still get shoes made to order at one of the few remaining Chinese shoe shops around Bentinck St.

Anokhi 2nd Floor, Forum Mall, 10/3 Elgin Rd ☎ 033 2283 7251, ⓦ anokhi.com; map p.754. This branch of the national chain is renowned for its chic Rajasthani hand-printed cottons with a wide range from clothing to furnishing, though it's not cheap. Daily 10am–8pm.

By Loom 58B Hindusthan Park ☎ 033 2419 8727, ⓦ byloom.co.in; map p.754. A small but stunning selection of handicrafts, textiles and saris fusing traditional handlooms and contemporary design to great effect. Mon–Sat 10am–7pm.

Fabindia 16 Hindusthan Park near Gariahat ☎ 033 2465 6954, ⓦ fabindia.com; map p.754. Good selection of hand-printed *kurtas* and *salwar kameez* as well as shirts, fabrics and furnishings from this trendy chain boutique; they use natural dyes which run, so use a cool wash and separate colours. There are various other branches around town – check the website for details. Mon–Sat 11am–8.30pm.

Ritu Kumar 4 Woodburn Court Rd ☎ 033 2283 7310, ⓦ ritukumar.com; map p.754. Chic boutique for *salwar kameez* from a designer who started out here in Kolkata before rising to international fame dressing the likes of Princess Diana and Jemima Khan. Mon–Sat 10am–7pm.

Tia Pakhi 49/13 Hindustan Park ☎ 033 4000 1783, ⓦ tiapakhi.com; map p.754. Small but delightful selection of gifts and home furnishings featuring traditional craft with contemporary design, in this increasingly chic part of town. Mon–Sat 10am–7pm.

MUSICAL INSTRUMENTS

Kolkata is renowned for its sitar and sarod makers – expect to pay upwards of ₹12500 for a decent instrument, much more for a premium one. Shops around Sudder St are strongest on Western instruments, but their traditional instruments are invariably of inferior quality and may be beyond tuning; Rabindra Sarani (Chitpore Rd) has a concentration of shops of varying quality, many catering to the wedding-band trade. Kolkata must produce more tabla players than any other city; tabla makers can be found next to Kalighat Bridge and at Keshab Sen St off College St.

Hemen & Co Triangular Park, Rashbehari Ave ☎ 033 2466 2607; map p.754. The legendary Hemen & Co has made sarods for some famous musicians and makes pricey instruments to order; it's now run by the son of the original owner. Mon–Sat 10am–8pm.

Monoj Kumar Sardar & Bros 8A Lalbazaar St, opposite the police station ☎ 033 2237 5835, ⓦ monojkrsardar. com; map p.754. Monoj Kumar Sardar & Bros makes good sitars and sarods to order; it also has a small selection of off-the-shelf instruments. Mon–Sat 10am–8pm.

SPORTS

Sport is enthusiastically followed in Kolkata, with **football** matches (Atlético de Kolkata are the local Indian Super League team; they won the first competition in 2014) and **cricket** matches both drawing huge crowds (the Kolkata Knight Riders are the local IPL team). There are two major stadium complexes, **Ranji** at Eden Gardens (see page 760) and **Salt Lake** on the eastern edge of the city.

Hindusthan International Hotel 235-1 AJC Bose Rd ☎ 033 2247 2394, ⓦ hhihotels.com. This hotel allows non-residents to use its **swimming pool** on a daily basis (₹500).

The Maidan Home to the Calcutta Bowling Club and the Ladies Golf Club, is a favourite venue for impromptu cricket

and football matches, and the scene of regular race meets in winter and spring run by the Calcutta Turf Club, which also has *polo* on the grounds at the centre of the racecourse. The curious sport of *kabaddi*, a fierce form of tag played by two teams on a pitch the size of a badminton court, can also be seen around here.

Royal Calcutta Golf Club 18, Golf Club Road, Tollygunge ☎ 033 2473 1352, ⓦ rcgc.in. Across the road from the superbly equipped Tollygunge Club — where (with the right connections) you might get to use the pool and tennis courts — this elite golf club is the world's second oldest after St Andrews in Scotland, dating back to 1829. Daily 6am–11pm.

DIRECTORY

Ambulance Call ☎ 102, or the Red Cross ☎ 033 2248 3636; St John's Ambulance Brigade ☎ 033 2476 1935; or Belle Vue clinic.

Banks and currency exchange Kolkata airport has a 24hr branch of the State Bank of India (SBI), as well as Thomas Cook at the international terminal. There are numerous private foreign-exchange bureaux around Sudder

St, New Market and in the vicinity of Park St, some offering very competitive rates. Banks that offer foreign exchange around the centre include SBI, 38B Chowringhee Rd and 1 Strand Rd; Standard Chartered Bank, 41 Chowringhee Rd, and Citibank, 43 Chowringhee Rd. Other currency exchange bureaux include Thomas Cook, 19B Shakespeare Sarani

13

(☏ 033 6652 6625, ⓦ thomascook.in; other offices at Salt Lake and Lake Gardens), and American Express, 21 Old Court House St, near the West Bengal Tourist Office (☏ 033 2248 9491, ⓦ americanexpress.com).

Consulates Bangladesh, 9 Circus Ave (Sheikh Mujib Sarani) (☏ 033 4012 7500); Bhutan, 48 Tivoli Court, 1A Ballygunge Circular Rd (☏ 033 4012 3999); Canada, Duncan House, 31 Netaji Subhash Rd (☏ 033 2242 6820); China, EC-72 Sector 1, Salt Lake (☏ 033 4004 8169); Germany, 1 Hastings Park Rd, Alipur (☏ 033 2479 1141); Myanmar (Burma), 57K Ballygunge Circular Rd (☏ 033 2485 1658); Nepal, 1 National Library Ave, Alipore (☏ 033 2456 1224); Singapore, 8 AJC Bose Rd (☏ 033 2247 4990); South Africa, 225D AJC Bose Rd (☏ 033 2247 4107); Sri Lanka, Nicco House, 2 Hare St (☏ 033 2248 5102); Thailand, 18B Mandeville Gardens (☏ 033 2440 7836); UK, 1A Ho Chi Minh Sarani (☏ 033 2288 5172); US, 5/1 Ho Chi Minh Sarani (☏ 033 3984 2400).

Hospitals Cheap, government-run hospitals are notoriously mismanaged, and private medical care, if expensive by comparison, is infinitely superior. In case of serious illness, you are best advised to contact your consulate. Good private clinics/hospitals include Belle Vue, 9 Loudon St (☏ 91630 58000, ⓦ bellevueclinic.com), Ruby Hospital, EM Bypass, Kasba (☏ 033 3987 1800, ⓦ rubyhospital.com); and Woodlands Multispecialty Hospital, 8/5 Alipore Rd (☏ 033 4033 7000, ⓦ woodlandshospital.in).

Permits and visas The Foreigners' Registration Office is at 237A AJC Bose Rd (☏ 033 2247 0549).

Pharmacies Deys Medical Stores, 6 Lindsay St and 20A Nelly Sengupta Sarani (☏ 033 2249 9810, ⓦ deysmedical.com); Dhanwantary Clinic, 65 Diamond Harbour Rd (☏ 033 2449 1756, ⓦ dhanwantary.com).

Police ☏ 100. The central police station is on Lal Bazaar St, BBD Bagh (☏ 033 2241 3230). Others include Park St (☏ 033 2226 8321).

Postal services The GPO, on the west side of BBD Bagh, houses the poste restante and a philatelic department. If you're staying in the Sudder St area, the New Market Post Office, Mirza Ghalib St, is much more convenient. Sending parcels is easiest from the large and friendly post office on Park St, where enterprising individuals will handle the entire process for you for a negotiable fee.

Around Kolkata

There are several worthwhile attractions around Kolkata. The Hindu temples of **Dakshineshwar** and **Belur Math**, and even the great Vaishnavite centres of **Nabadip** and **Mayapur** further north, can be taken in as day-trips on local trains from Kolkata's Sealdah and Howrah railway stations.

Dakshineshwar

20km north of central Kolkata • Daily: Oct–March 6am–12.30pm & 3–8.30pm; April–Sept 6am–12.30pm & 3.30–9pm • Free • Local trains run from Sealdah to Dakshineshwar

At the edge of Kolkata, 20km north of Esplanade on the east bank of the river, the popular temple of **Dakshineshwar** stands in the shadow of Bally Bridge. Built in 1855, it was a product of the Bengali Renaissance, consecrated at a time when growing numbers of middle-class Hindus were questioning their faith. Typical Bengali motifs – a curved roof reminiscent of local village huts, nine chhatris and beehive cupolas – dominate the design. The mystic and influential religious philosopher **Ramakrishna** once officiated here, and his room, beside the main gate, now houses a collection of his personal effects. His life is beautifully portrayed in Romain Rolland's biography, *The Life of Ramakrishna*. Not far from the main temple, **Yogoday Satsanga Math** is the headquarters of the Self-Realization Fellowship, founded in California in 1925 by the author of *Autobiography of a Yogi*, **Paramahansa Yogananda**.

Belur Math

Across the bridge from Dakshineshwar, 3km south along the west bank of the Hooghly • Daily: April–Sept 6–11.30am & 4–7pm; Oct–March 6.30am–noon & 3.30–6pm • Free • ☏ 033 2654 1144, ⓦ belurmath.org • Belur Math is best visited along with a trip to Dakshineshwar; local trains run from Howrah (5 daily; 25min)

The serene forty-acre riverfront campus of **Belur Math** was founded by a disciple of Ramakrishna, **Swami Vivekananda**, and completed (after his death) in 1938. The monastery houses temples and museums dedicated to the Mission. It incorporates elements from several world religions; the gate is inspired by early Buddhist sculpture, the windows by Islamic architecture, and the ground plan is based on the Christian cross. After the *math* closes in the evenings, you may stay for **aarti** (evening worship), held at the Sri Ramakrishna Temple, followed by meditation till around 8pm.

Nabadip and Mayapur

An important centre for Vaishnava pilgrimage, the little town of **NABADIP** (or Nawadip) lies on the west bank of the Hooghly, around 100km north of Kolkata. Once the eleventh-century capital of Bengal under the Sen dynasty, Nabadip was also the home of Hindu sage **Sri Chaitanya** (1486–1533) and its temples are alive with his devotees singing *kirtan* (devotional song). A 50km *padakrama*, or foot pilgrimage, links the various Vaishnava sites spread across nine islands. Nabadip may be a Vaishnava town, but its most atmospheric temple is the **Kali Bari** at Poramatolla, tucked into the folds of one of the most impressive banyan trees you are ever likely to see.

Across the river from Boral Ghat, the jetty at Nabadip, the Vaishnava centre of **Mayapur**, run by the Hare Krishna sect of ISKCON, draws huge crowds at weekends, visitors thronging to the labyrinthine temple complex where a gigantic basilica is under construction. One way of exploring the area is on the afternoon boat ride that takes in some of the holy islands, but this is part pilgrimage and is accompanied with lectures.

ARRIVAL AND INFORMATION
NABADIP AND MAYAPUR

By train Several trains from Howrah run to Nabadip, 2.5km from the main Boral Ghat (around ₹50 by cycle rickshaw). An alternative is to take a train from Sealdah to Krishnagar, then a bus or auto-rickshaw to Mayapur Ghat and then a ferry.

Tourist information ISKCON's Mayapur Tourism Centre, opposite Gada Bhavan (⊕03472 245219, ⓦvisitmayapur. com), also organizes transport from Kolkata and you can book online.

ACCOMMODATION

ISKCON's Shri Mayapur Dham ⊕03472 245219, ⓦvisitmayapur.com. The well-run Mayapur complex has a huge variety of accommodation from simple pilgrim rooms to a/c splendour in one of several guesthouses. You can book online. Besides the two dining halls with set meal times, there is a restaurant open till 9pm; the entire site is vegetarian and alcohol is forbidden. **₹900**

The Sundarbans and the Gangetic Delta

South of Kolkata down to the coast, the Hooghly fringes one of the world's largest estuarine deltas, the **Sundarbans**, a 10,000-square-kilometre expanse of mangrove swamp and forested islets formed by silt swept down from the Himalayas and home to the world's largest population of **tigers**. Closer to the city, the former colonial port of **Diamond Harbour** is a popular weekend break and lies en route to **Sagardwip**, a sacred island where the Ganges reaches the sea. The expansive **beaches** of the delta provide quiet respite and are within easy reach of Kolkata.

Sundarbans Tiger Reserve

Daily Sept–March dawn–dusk • All visitors need to pay an entry fee (₹50) to the national park at Sajnekhali

The cluster of mangrove-covered islands known as the **Sundarbans** or "beautiful forest", lie in the Ganges Delta, stretching east from the mouth of the Hooghly to Bangladesh. They are home to the legendary **Royal Bengal tiger**, which has adapted remarkably well to this watery environment, swimming from island to island and covering distances of as much as 40km in one day. The region has been designated a UNESCO World Heritage Site and its abundant wildlife also includes saltwater crocodiles, Gangetic dolphins, otters and monitor lizards. All the half-million or so people sharing this delicate ecosystem, regardless of religion, worship Bonbibi, the goddess of the forest, and her Muslim consort, Dakshin Rai, supreme ruler of the Sundarbans. (Amitav Ghosh's excellent novel *The Hungry Tide* brings this world vividly to life.)

Along with a crocodile and turtle hatchery, the Project Tiger compound at **Sajnekhali** also houses a shrine to Bonbibi. There is a **watchtower** here, but others like Dobanki, where an aerial walkway skirts the top of the mangroves, and Netidhopani, which sits near the ruins of a 400-year-old temple, are far more attractive. As getting to the Sundarbans on your own is a laborious process, you might want to opt for an all-inclusive package tour. Be aware, though, that tiger sightings are rare.

ARRIVAL AND DEPARTURE

By organized tour WBTDC organize two- and three-day packages with the option of staying either on the boat, at the *Sunderban Tiger Camp* or at the *Sajnekhali Tourist Lodge* (from ₹3000). However, the cruises can get crowded and noisy. A better option, in season, Vivada Cruises (☎033 2463 1990, ⊛vivadacruises.com) offers luxury cruises to the Sundarbans. Alternatively you can arrange your own boat at Gosaba Ghat in Godhkali (see below). Tailor-made tours by private operators (from around ₹20,000 for a three-day itinerary) are more peaceful and leisurely: try Kali Travel Home (see page 769), or Himalayan Footprints (see page 769), which runs its own camp and boats. Help Tourism (see page 769) also has a deservedly good reputation.

SUNDARBANS TIGER RESERVE

By public transport Travelling independently, and not through a pre-arranged tour package, is an adventure in itself – take a train to Canning from Sealdah, a shared taxi from Canning to Godhkali, a ferry to Gosaba Bazaar, a rickshaw or cycle van to Pakhirala Tigar Mor (6km), and finally a ferry to Sajnekhali. Alternatively, take an early bus from Kolkata's Babu Ghat to Basanti (around 6 daily; 3hr; from 6.45am), an auto to Godhkali (Gosaba Ghat), a ferry to Gosaba Bazaar, and then as above. Scheduled ferries cross the estuarine channel from Pakhirala to Sajnekhali (generally 7am & 6pm) or you could negotiate a country boat; boats are also available at Godhkali or Dayapur near Gosaba.

GETTING AROUND

By boat All transport within the reserve is by boat, which can be rented from the Boatman Association with the help of the lodge staff (from ₹1000 depending on your itinerary).

You have to take along a Project Tiger guide (₹800 [₹500]) and pay an entry fee of ₹340. The loud diesel motors scare wildlife away, but when they cut their engines the silence is awesome.

ACCOMMODATION

The only accommodation within the reserve is at the *Tourist Lodge* at Sajnekhali. All other accommodation is on the fringes but some of these are well managed with attractive tours (see page 769) arranged from Kolkata.

Sajnekhali Tourist Lodge Sajnekhali; reservations: WBTDC, 3/2 BBD Bagh, Kolkata ☎97325 09925, ⊛wbtdcl.com. This ramshackle lodge, raised on stilts, is devoid of all charm except for its unique access to the core forest; rooms are basic, over-priced and only the most expensive have a/c; rates include basic thali meals. The institutional atmosphere adds to a certain feeling of incarceration and you are best advised to remain upstairs after dark to avoid wild animal encounters. The boat ride option is thoroughly recommended. The compound also houses the Project Tiger office as well as a shrine to Bonbibi, and monitor lizards roam freely. No wi-fi. ₹2500

Sunderbans Jungle Camp & Sundergaon Earth Villa

Bali Island ☎033 2455 0917, ⊛helptourism.com. Run by Help Tourism (see page 769) partly in conjunction with conservationist Belinda Wright, the camp on the edge of the reserve is a tasteful mix of rustic tradition and contemporary comfort. It has its own boat and employs local villagers. The all-inclusive package includes engagement with the community along with wildlife tours, and pick-up from Kolkata. ₹32,000

Sunderban Tiger Camp Opposite Sajnekhali, near Gosaba ☎87777 21013, ⊛sunderbantigercamp.com. Well-organized and popular place offering packages that include pick-up from south Kolkata and boat excursions. There are also daily cultural dances, movie screenings and village walks. Accommodation is in tented rooms, modern a/c rooms with verandahs, and more comfortable cottages. All have a/c and hot water, and all meals are included. Tented room ₹5000, huts ₹800, cottages ₹15,000

Along the Hooghly to the sea

South of Kolkata the Hooghly merges with the delta, gaining girth rapidly as it approaches Sagardwip and the islands at the river's mouth. The river scenery is particularly popular with city folk at the weekends, who come to enjoy the breeze of

13

Diamond Harbour, 50km south of Kolkata. At the far southern end of the delta, the casuarina-lined beaches provide a welcome retreat from the grime of Kolkata.

Hindus revere **Sagardwip**, also known as Sagar Island, as the point where the Ganges meets the sea. At the mouth of the Hooghly, it is accessible by ferry from Harwood Point near Diamond Harbour and from Namkhana further south. The confluence is venerated at the **Kapil Muni Temple**, on an island that bears the brunt of the savage Bay of Bengal cyclones and is gradually being submerged. On Makar Sankranti (mid-Jan), during the **Sagar Mela**, hundreds of thousands of pilgrims from all over India descend on the island, cramming into the water to bathe. Facilities are limited at the best of times, but alternatives include Diamond Harbour and the island beaches such as **Bakkhali** at the western reaches of the Sundarbans.

ARRIVAL AND DEPARTURE

To Diamond Harbour The trip down to Diamond Harbour from the city, by bus or train from Sealdah station, is a popular day's excursion for Kolkatans who come to enjoy the river cruises.

To Sagardwip Direct buses from Esplanade travel to Harwood Point during the *mela*; the island can also be reached from Namkhana (3hr) on the suburban railway network from Kolkata's Sealdah station, from where the quiet casuarina-lined beach at Bakkhali is easily accessible.

ALONG THE HOOGHLY TO THE SEA

Once on Sagardwip, the temple is a further 32km from the ferry, and can be accessed by bus or taxi.

For Sagar Mela WBTDC (see page 768) organize a coach trip as well as a cruise (from ₹5000/person) to visit the *mela*. The advantage of the cruise is that you can stay on the boat and avoid the crush.

To Bakkhali Trains from Sealdah travel to Namkhana where a rickshaw takes you to a ferry and a bus to Bakkhali.

ACCOMMODATION

DIAMOND HARBOUR

Ganga Kutir Resort & Spa Raichak ☎ 85840 40624, ⓦ raichakonganges.com. Luxurious resort from one of Bengal's leading Marwari developers, *Ganga Kutir* has classy rooms, a spa and gourmet restaurant, and a swimming pool that blends into the river scenery. The sister concern, *Ffort*, is older, with a more traditional ambience. **₹7500**

SAGARDWIP AND AROUND

Sagardwip has limited accommodation, especially during the *mela*, with only a handful of lodges, ashrams and *dharamshalas* offering basic accommodation; you'll find much greater choice at Bakkhali. Bring mosquito repellent, and if staying at Sagardwip, bring your own sleeping bag.

Bakkhali Tourist Lodge Bakkhali ☎ 97325 10150, ⓦ wbtdcl.com. Extensive government-run lodge, with elaborate garden and kitsch sculptures of a flock of flamingos. The a/c rooms and cottages are generously sized, and the lodge is the only accommodation here with direct access to the expansive beach beyond the casuarina trees. It has its own restaurant, and there are other places to eat in the vicinity. No wi-fi. Doubles **₹1900**, cottages **₹2500**

Bharat Seva Ashram Near Kapil Muni Temple, Sagardwip. Basic *dharamshala* near the temple, geared towards pilgrims and almost impossible to book during the *mela*; there are simple rice restaurants nearby for food. You are expected to give a donation, as suggested here, to the caretaker. No wi-fi. **₹300**

Mandarmani Beach

Some 180km southwest of Kolkata, not far from the Odishan border, is the village of **Mandarmani**, home to one of the most beautiful beaches in the region. The 13km-long stretch of sand is populated by red crabs and local fishermen but relatively few tourists, though there are several resort-style hotels, restaurants and souvenir stalls.

ARRIVAL AND DEPARTURE

By train The nearest railhead is Digha, linked to Howrah by daily trains (2–3 daily; 2hr 30min–3hr); the 30km journey

MANDARMANI BEACH

from Digha to Mandarmani costs around ₹600 in a taxi.

ACCOMMODATION

Anutri Beach Resort 30km east of Digha ☎ 93314 28678, ⓦ anutribeach.com. Smart resort, right on the

sand, ideal for days of relaxation on the beach. The rooms are comfortable, if rather bland (the more expensive ones have sea views), and there's a swimming pool (complete with bar), restaurant and children's playground; at the time of research there were also plans for a spa and another bar. **₹3200**

13

Central Bengal

A low-lying rural region where the pace of life is in stark contrast to that of Kolkata, **central Bengal** has a few sights to tempt tourists off the Kolkata–Darjeeling route. **Shantiniketan**, built on the site of Rabindranath Tagore's father's ashram, is a haven of peace, and a must for anyone interested in Bengali music, art and culture. The other highlights of the region include a cluster of exquisite terracotta temples in **Bishnupur**, the ruins of **Gaur**, the region's seventh-century capital, and the palaces of **Murshidabad**, capital of Bengal's last independent dynasty. With the Maoist insurgency affecting the borders of Jharkhand and Odisha, the southwestern districts of Bengal have become too dangerous to visit.

Bishnupur

A sleepy backwater town 150km northwest of Kolkata, **BISHNUPUR** is a famous centre of Bengali learning, renowned above all for its exquisite **terracotta temples**. It was the capital of the Malla rajas, under whose patronage one of India's greatest schools of **music** developed. The roots of Bishnupur's long tradition of temple building are in the basic form of the domestic hut translated into temple architecture. Built of brick and faced with finely carved terracotta decoration, the temples combine striking simplicity of form with vibrant texture.

The temples

All daily dawn–dusk • ₹250 (₹10) pass for all sites

Several temples lie scattered in a wide area around Bishnupur. **Raas Mancha**, built in 1587 by Bir Hambir in a unique pyramidal style, is used to display the images of Krishna and Radha during the annual Raas festival. Nearby, the well-preserved **Shyamarai**, built in 1643, is a particularly fine example of terracotta art, while the smaller **Jorbangla** has fine detail. The unassuming tenth-century **Mrinmoyee temple** encloses the auspicious *nababriksha*, nine trees growing as one. To the north of town and dating from 1694, the **Madan Mohan**, with its domed central tower and scenes from the life of Krishna, is one of the largest.

ARRIVAL AND DEPARTURE   BISHNUPUR

By train Of the express trains that connect Kolkata to Bishnupur, the *Rupashi Bangla Express* (#12883, returning #12884) is the most convenient for a day-trip, departing Santragachi at 6.25am, arriving at 9.37am.

ACCOMMODATION

Basudah 16km outside Bishnupur ☎97321 00950, ⓦtraveleastindia.com. A rural idyll in an adobe farmhouse, devoted to organic farming, conservation and research. This is the best way to see Bengali village life in all its simplicity. Kali Travel Home (see page 769) arranges the recommended three-day package from Kolkata, which includes transport. **₹18,500**

Bishnupur Tourist Lodge Near Raas Mancha ☎033 2210 3199, ⓦwbtdcl.com, reserve via the WBTDC (see page 768). Sprawling, state-run complex, with a range of fair-sized plain rooms from basic doubles to larger a/c options, is the most convenient for visiting the sites. The restaurant serves standard Bengali meals. Book well ahead during the festival season. **₹750**

Shantiniketan

Despite rapid growth and encroachment into the tribal Santhal habitat, the peaceful haven of **SHANTINIKETAN**, 136km northwest of Kolkata, remains a world away from the clamour and grime of the city. Founded by Nobel Laureate **Rabindranath Tagore** (see box below) in 1921 on the site of his father's ashram, both the settlement and its liberal arts university **Visva-Bharati** were designed to promote the best of Bengali culture. Towards the end of the Bengali Renaissance, Tagore's vision and immense talent inspired a whole way of life and art; the university and school still operate under this momentum.

Centred around the **Uttarayan** complex of buildings, designed by Tagore, the university is very much in harmony with its surroundings, despite its recent growth as Kolkatans have settled or built holiday homes nearby. Well-known graduates include Indira Gandhi and Satyajit Ray, and departments such as **Kala Bhavan** (art) and **Sangeet Bhavan** (music) still attract students from all over the world.

The renowned **Bauls**, Bengal's wandering minstrels, who play a unique style of folk music, gather during the afternoon at the informal **shanibarer haat** (Saturday market) held under the trees by Shantiniketan's canal, where Shantal tribals also gather to sell their crafts. The large fair of **Poush Mela**, between December 22 and 25, attracts numerous Bauls each year.

Kala Bhavan Archive

Daily except Tues 10am–5pm • Free, with special permission from the head of department

The **Kala Bhavan Archive** houses twentieth-century Bengali sculpture and painting, including works by eminent artists such as Abanendranath and Gaganendranath Tagore, Nandalal Bose and Rabindranath Tagore himself, as well as a collection of Chinese and Japanese art.

Vichitra Museum

Uttarayan • Mon & Thurs–Sun 10.30am–1pm & 2–4.30pm, Tues 10.30am–1pm • ₹10

Also known as the Rabindra Bhavan Museum, the **Vichitra Museum** captures the spirit of Rabindranath Tagore's life and work with a collection of his paintings, manuscripts and personal effects, though it's probably only really of interest to aficionados.

ARRIVAL AND DEPARTURE   SHANTINIKETAN

By train Bolpur, 3km south of Shantiniketan, is the nearest railway station, on the main line between Kolkata and Darjeeling, served by several trains via Burddhaman (or Burdwan). The best train for Bolpur from Kolkata is the *Shantiniketan Express* #12337, which leaves Howrah at 10.10am and terminates at Bolpur at 12.25pm, returning to Howrah again some 30min later. Baul singers occasionally busk in second-class carriages. If you're heading on from Shantiniketan to Darjeeling, the best of the daily express trains is the *Darjeeling Mail* #12343, which stops late at night (12.28am) in Bolpur but arrives in New Jalpaiguri (NJP) at 8am the next morning. The best daytime train is the *Kanchenjunga Express* #15657, which departs at 9.14am and arrives at NJP at 6.15pm. Reservations are available from the Shantiniketan reservations counter (Mon–Sat 10am–3pm) near the post office, though this has limited

RABINDRANATH TAGORE

The Bengali poet and literary giant **Rabindranath Tagore** (1861–1941) has inspired generations of artists, poets and musicians. He developed an early interest in theatre, and set his poems to music – this was to become, as Rabindra Sangeet, one of the most popular musical traditions in Bengal. Introduced to England and the West by the painter William Rothenstein and the poet W.B. Yeats, Tagore had his collection of poems, *Gitanjali*, first published in translation in 1912, and the following year was awarded the Nobel Prize for Literature. Though he preferred to write in Bengali, and encouraged authors in other Indian languages, he was also a master of English prose. Not until he was in his 70s did his talent as an artist and painter emerge, developed from scribblings on the borders of his manuscripts. Tagore was an enormous inspiration to many, including his students, the illustrious painter Nandalal Bose, and later the film-maker Satyajit Ray, who based several of his films on the works of the master.

quotas; the computerized reservations counter at Bolpur station offers more choice.

By bus The main bus stand is at Jamboni, 2km west towards Surul with connections to Kendubilwa (Kenduli) and Rampurhat (Tarapith) among other destinations.

By cycle rickshaws or bike Cycle rickshaws are the chief means of transport in the area and generally very reliable, but the best way to experience Shantiniketan is to cycle – ask at your hotel or at one of the bicycle shops along the main road.

ACCOMMODATION

The Shantiniketan area holds a reasonable amount of accommodation, with several options along the noisy main Shantiniketan–Bolpur Rd, and more appealing places around the fringes of the campus and especially Shyambati where there is a small choice. Expect to pay a lot more during Poush Mela, when you are advised to book well ahead.

Babli Farm Illambazaar Rd ☎03463 271285, ⓦbablifarm.wordpress.com. An agricultural and forestry project that works with the local community to develop a balanced ecosystem. The farm features beautiful, traditional cottages, and a dorm, as well as a healthy menu in its restaurant – this is open to non-residents but it's advisable to book ahead. No wi-fi. Dorms ₹250, cottages ₹1800

★ **Rare Earth Farms & Homestay** Bautijole, Bolpur ☎80173 20752 and 98301 19546, ⓦfacebook.com/

rareearthfarmsandhomestay. Set amid peaceful countryside, this rustic yet modern farmhouse offers impeccable and charming rooms paired with very attentive service. Meals (₹400) are prepared in a firewood oven, using their own organically grown vegetables, and it's a delight to kick back at night, enjoying nature and the sound of crickets. They organise pickups at Bolpur railway station. Breakfast included. ₹3500

Shantiniketan Tourist Lodge Bolpur Tourist Lodge Rd ☎97321 00920, reservations ☎033 2334 4062, ⓦwbtdcl.com. Large state-run place midway between Bolpur and Shantiniketan, with some a/c rooms, good-value cottages, a pleasant garden and a restaurant. The a/c rooms, however, are a bit overpriced. Cottages ₹2000, rooms ₹900

EATING

Alcha Ratan Palli ☎83730 60755, ⓦalchashop.com. A delightful little garden café that combines a bookshop, a library (refundable deposit), a gallery and a small but excellent boutique selling clothes and furnishings; it's also good for breakfasts, grilled sandwiches, snacks and cakes (₹50–200). Daily 8–10.30am & 4–8pm.

Ghare Baire Gitanjali Complex, Siuri Rd ☎99325

88220. This is as smart as it gets in Shantiniketan, with a pleasant ambience and an eclectic menu including mocktails, Chinese dishes for when you need to get away from *dhal bhaat*, and south Indian food. But the Bengali cuisine (mains ₹200–3000) is best – try the special thali with fish or mutton or the more economical vegetarian version. Daily noon–8pm.

Tarapith

One of the most important centres of Tantric Hinduism, **TARAPITH** is easily visited on a day-trip and features in William Dalrymple's book *Nine Lives*. The temple and the cremation ground, in a grove beside the river littered with shrines 50km north of Shantiniketan, are popular with Tantric sadhus, and it's not uncommon to witness rituals involving skulls and cremation ashes. The temple, in a perpetually busy courtyard, is dedicated to the mysterious and feared goddess Tara, who appears here with a silver face and large eyes. The lanes leading to the temple are a hive of activity where pilgrims procure offerings and liaise with temple priests (*panda*) to officiate in deeply personal ceremonies.

ARRIVAL AND DEPARTURE
TARAPITH

By train The *Ganadevta Express* #13017 departs Howrah at 6.05am, passing through Bolpur near Shantiniketan (8.44am) and arriving at Rampurhat railway station, 8km north of Tarapith, at 10.12am; the 4.35pm *Rampurhat Express* #12348 returns via Shantiniketan. Buy tickets in

advance – as the time of departure approaches, the station and the footbridges become uncomfortably chaotic.

By auto-rickshaw Shared *tempos* (auto-rickshaws), the main mode of public transport, regularly ply the path between Tarapith and Rampurhat station (around ₹50).

ACCOMMODATION AND EATING

Amantran Rampurhat Rd, 3km from the temple ☎03461 253133, ⓦamantrangrouptarapith.com. This

welcoming place offers a wide selection of sleeping options including economical, small non-a/c cottages. There's a

13

good restaurant and bar, pleasant garden with a small lake and a non-chlorinated swimming pool. ₹900
Sonar Bangla Rampurhat Rd ☎97321 27224, ⓦhotelsonarbangla.com/tarapith. This is the most luxurious hotel in the town centre with an incongruous resort-like atmosphere, with a large landscaped garden and pool. The non-a/c rooms are overpriced; the best, and most expensive, rooms are those clustered around the pool; all are rather garish. The restaurant has an extensive menu but service is slow. ₹2240

Kendubilwa

The town of **KENDUBILWA**, also known as **Kenduli**, 42km west of Shantiniketan on the bank of a wide shallow river, is the birthplace of **Jaidev**, the author of *Gita Govinda*, and the spiritual home of the Bauls. Its small terracotta temple is engulfed each year in mid-January when the **Jaidev Mela** attracts streams of pilgrims, as well as a collection of yogis and sadhus who gather among the banyan trees to hear the **Bauls** perform through the night. Over the years the *mela* has grown to include a wide range of stalls and a funfair. During the *mela*, special buses leave regularly from Bolpur (2hr).

Murshidabad

Set in the brilliant green landscape of rural Bengal and close to the commercial town of **Behrampur**, **MURSHIDABAD**, 219km north of Kolkata, represents the grand and final expression of independent Bengal before the arrival of the British. Several eighteenth-century monuments along the banks of the Hooghly stand as melancholic reminders of its days as the last independent capital of Bengal.

Established early in the eighteenth century by the **Nawab Murshid Quli Khan**, Murshidabad was soon eclipsed when the forces of Siraj-ud-Daula were defeated by Robert Clive at the Battle of Plassey in 1757, as a result of which the British came to dominate Bengal from the new city of Calcutta. Clive described Murshidabad as equal to London, with several palaces and seven hundred mosques; today most of its past glory lies in ruins, though it is still renowned for cottage industries, especially silk weaving.

Murshidabad's intriguing mixture of cultures is reflected in its architectural styles, which range from the columned **Hazarduari** to the **Katra Mosque**, built by Murshid Quli Khan in the style of the mosque at Mecca. A large oxbow lake, the **Moti Jheel** or **Pearl Lake**, guards the desolate ruins of Begum Ghaseti's palace, where Siraj-ud-Daula reigned before his defeat, and which was subsequently occupied for a while by Clive. To the south and across the river, **Khushbagh**, the **Garden of Delight**, holds the tombs of many of the nawabs, including Alivardi Khan and Siraj-ud-Daula.

Hazarduari

Lalbagh • Mon–Thurs & Sat 10am–4.30pm • ₹250 (₹10) • ⓦ murshidabad.net

Hazarduari, the nawab's Italianate palace, designed by General Duncan Macleod of the Bengal Engineers, with its mirrored banqueting hall, circular durbar room, armoury and library of fine manuscripts, is now a museum; some of the paintings are in dire need of restoration, but the portrait collection is excellent.

ARRIVAL AND DEPARTURE
MURSHIDABAD

The main transport hub for Murshidabad is Behrampur, 11km to the south. Auto-rickshaws (around ₹50), cycle rickshaws and ferries provide access to the sites of Murshidabad.

By train Trains run to Behrampur from stations in Kolkata (up to 11 daily; 4–6hr), including the *Hazarduari Express* #13113 (6.50am from Kolkata station) which also stops at Murshidabad (10.42am); there is more choice from Azimganj, 20km and around ₹800–1000 taxi-ride away.

By bus Most long-distance buses arrive and depart from Behrampur station with connections to Kolkata's Esplanade (every 1–2hr; 5–6hr), as well as Malda (every 1–2hr; 3hr 30min).

By ferry A regular short ferry service (daily 1–2 hourly 8am–5pm; around 20min) from near Hazarduari in Lalbagh is the only direct means of access to places across the river, including Khushbagh.

A COLONIAL GOVERNMENTAL BUILDING IN KOLKATA

13

ACCOMMODATION

Manjusha Near Hazarduari ☎03482 70321, ⊚hotel manjusha.com. This is a welcoming place, beautifully situated, overlooking the timeless river. However, the rooms are disappointingly dingy. The catering is poor but a short walk along the river leads to restaurants. However, the early morning boat ride, which can be arranged here, to Khushbagh is thoroughly recommended. ₹700

Sunshine Panchanantala, Behrampur ☎94752 27453, ⊚hotelsunshine3star.com. With a handy location close to the main highway and away from the chaos of central Behrampur, yet not far from Murshidabad if you have transport. It's been recently renovated, and now boasts comfortable, large rooms, and there's a good restaurant too. ₹2200

Malda and around

Famous for its delicious mangoes, the large, rather unattractive commercial town of **MALDA**, located some 340km north of Kolkata, makes a good base to explore the historic sites of **Gaur** and **Pandua**, both of which were once capitals of Bengal.

Gaur

Spread across a landscape of lush paddy fields, **Gaur**, 16km south of Malda, was the seventh-century capital of King Sasanka, and then successively belonged to the Buddhist Palas and the Senas. The latter, the last Hindu kings of Bengal, were violently displaced by the Muslims at the start of the thirteenth century. Gaur was sacked in 1537 by Sher Shah Suri, and its remaining inhabitants wiped out by plague in 1575.

The city lay buried in silt for centuries, but excavations have revealed the extensive remains of a city that once boasted more than a million inhabitants. Recent finds include a vast brick **palace** complete with waterways and a mint. A *ghat* with chains for anchoring barges suggests that the River Ganges may have once flowed past the palace. Elsewhere, Gaur's sites include various large tanks, such as the 1.5km long **Sagar Dighi** from 1126, and the extensive embankments. **Dakhil Darwaza**, an impressive red-brick gateway built in 1425 during the Muslim period, leads into the **Fort**, in the southeast corner of which a colossal wall encloses the ruins of the old palace. The **Qadam Rasul Mosque** nearby was built in 1531 to contain the Prophet's footprint in stone.

Pandua

The splendid **Adina Masjid** at **PANDUA**, 18km north of Malda, was built around 1370 and was the largest mosque in the Subcontinent in its day. It now lies in ruins, but these still betray the origin of much of the building materials – carved basalt masonry from earlier Hindu temples was used to support 88 brick-built arches and 378 identical small domes, the design following that of the eighth-century mosque of Damascus. Other monuments include the **Eklakhi mausoleum** – one of the first square brick tombs in Bengal, with a carved Ganesh on the doorway, and **Qutb Shahi Masjid**, or the Golden Mosque.

ARRIVAL AND GETTING AROUND   MALDA AND AROUND

By train Malda Town railway station, near the centre, is on the main line between Kolkata and north Bengal, served by several good trains such as the *Kanchenjunga Express* #15657/15658 (from Sealdah; daily 6.35am, arrives 1.35pm, and then continues on to New Jalpaiguri at 6.15pm).

By taxi Taxis to both Gaur and Pandua charge around ₹3000 for the day.

ACCOMMODATION AND EATING

Golden Park NH-34, 8km north of town ☎03512 262251, ⊚hotelgoldenpark.com. Malda's smartest hotel, outside town but convenient for a visit to Pandua, offers clean, comfortable rooms, a/c and a decent restaurant; coffee shop and bar; facilities include a travel desk. The hotel is popular for events including weddings, but at other times can feel soulless. ₹2000

Purbanchal NH-34 ☎03512 266183. One of a clutch of budget business hotels dotted around the town centre, with a range of rooms including some a/c; choose one away from the highway to avoid noise. The hotel has one of the better restaurants in town and a dimly lit bar. ₹900

Darjeeling and North Bengal

13

North Bengal, where the Himalayas soar from the flat alluvial plains towards Nepal, Sikkim and Bhutan, holds some magnificent mountain panoramas, as well as a number of India's most attractive **hill stations**. Most visitors pass as quickly as possible through **Siliguri** en route to **Darjeeling**, **Kalimpong** and the small, mountainous state of Sikkim. If you've time on your hands, it's worth making a detour east of Siliguri to explore the sub-Himalayan **Dooars**, with its patchwork of tea gardens and forests that encompasses the **Jaldapara Wildlife Sanctuary**, home to the one-horned rhino, bison and wild boar.

The region has its fair share of political turmoil. The Gurkhaland movement, centred around Darjeeling, and the Kamtapuri Liberation Front, which purports to represent most of north Bengal south to Malda, has called for a complete break from the state of West Bengal. Occasional strikes can paralyse the Darjeeling hills and affect traffic. Tourist traffic is usually allowed to exit the district, but you may have to pay an exorbitant fee to the taxi driver. You should check the press and with your hotel before travelling to the region.

Siliguri and New Jalpaiguri

A major commercial hub and Bengal's second city, ever-expanding **SILIGURI** has a thriving tea-auction centre and serves as the gateway to Darjeeling, Kalimpong, Sikkim and Bhutan. Together with its main railway station, **New Jalpaiguri** – commonly referred to as NJP – and the airport at **Bagdogra**, it forms an unavoidable link between the rail and air connections to Kolkata and Delhi, and the roads up into the mountains. The border with Nepal at **Kakarbitta** nearby is open to tourists, though the bus journey from here to Kathmandu is an arduous one.

Most tourists pass straight through Siliguri, but travel connections may mean that you have to stop overnight. Besides teeming bazaars such as Bidhan Market, there's little of interest to see save the impressive **Tashi Gomang Stupa** (daily 5am–noon & 1–5pm) inside the **Salugara Monstery** in the small Tibetan enclave 2km or so from the centre on Sevoke Road. The **Darjeeling Himalayan Railway**'s (see page 795) route to Darjeeling leaves at 8.30am daily, climbing up the Himalayan foothills all the way to **Ghoom**.

ARRIVAL AND DEPARTURE   **SILIGURI AND NEW JALPAIGURI**

BY PLANE OR HELICOPTER
Bagdogra airport, 12km west of Siliguri, is served by flights from Delhi, Kolkata, Guwahati, Bhutan and Bangkok. Helicopters to Gangtok (daily 11am & 2.30pm; ₹3500) leave from Bagdogra, weather permitting, only with a full load of five passengers and with a maximum baggage allowance of 10kg; reserve in advance via the Sikkim Tourism Development Corporation, which has a counter at the airport (☎03592 201372, ⊛sikkimstdc.com), or at the Tourist Service Agency (TSA) in Pradhan Nagar, the lane opposite Siliguri bus terminal (☎0353 251 0872 or 09434 467236).

BY TRAIN
New Jalpaiguri (NJP) station Siliguri has its own railway station, but the New Jalpaiguri (NJP) station, 4km east, is the main rail junction in the region, with trains to and from Kolkata, Delhi and Assam. Reservations can be made online, at the station itself, or at the Central Railway Booking Office

(daily 8am–4pm), Bidhan Rd, near Kanchenjunga Stadium in Siliguri. The best train to Kolkata is the *Darjeeling Mail* #12344 (departs 5.35pm; 10hr 36min), which terminates at Sealdah. The most convenient train for Delhi is the efficient *Rajdhani Express* #12423 (departs 1.15pm; 21hr); it also passes through Patna (8hr 35min), which has connections for Gaya/Bodhgaya. The *Rajdhani* #12435 (Mon & Fri; departs 12.15pm; 13hr 25min) stops at Varanasi; on other days take the *Rajdhani* #12423 (departs 1.15pm) and change at Mughal Sarai (11hr 52min). For Guwahati, take the *Saraighat Express* #12345 (departs 2.00am; 7hr 55min).
Auto-rickshaws and taxis Cycle and auto-rickshaws (around ₹60 and ₹150) ply the route between NJP and Siliguri, battling through the often-gridlocked market, while shared Vikrams (auto-taxis) are an even cheaper alternative; totos (e-rickshaws) will charge ₹100-150, and taxis charge around ₹500. Use the prepaid booth outside the main station for local and long-distance journeys in auto-rickshaws as well as taxis.

13

BY TAXI

Taxis booked through the prepaid counter at Bagdogra airport run directly to Siliguri (from ₹500), Darjeeling (from ₹2000), Kalimpong (from ₹2000) and Gangtok (from ₹2400), though you can often negotiate cheaper fares from the stand outside the gates with returning taxis.

BY BUS OR SHARED JEEP

Tenzing Norgay Bus Terminal Most buses arriving at Siliguri terminate at the Tenzing Norgay Bus Terminal on Hill Cart Rd at Pradhan Nagar, close to most hotels and taxis to Darjeeling. Overnight Volvo "luxury" buses to Kolkata (12hr) are an alternative to the train and have the advantage of depositing you in Esplanade, near the central Sudder St area. However, the roads are dire, so be prepared for a severe rattling. Gupta Tour & Travels (☏ 97331 08246, ⊕ guptatravelsagency.co.in), opposite the *Heritage* hotel, Pradhan Nagar, are more comfortable but usually need prior booking; cheaper alternatives include the Rocket Bus, booked at TNBT (☏ 0353 251 8879). Standard buses run from Siliguri to Kolkata, Patna and Guwahati, although the train is far more comfortable. Frequent buses also travel to Chalsa and Madarihat, convenient for the wildlife sanctuaries.

To Darjeeling and Kalimpong The easiest way to get to Darjeeling is by shared jeep. These depart from in front of NJP station, and Sevoke More and Tenzing Norgay Bus Terminal in Siliguri, where jeep transport syndicates have their own ticket booths and the prices are fixed. Shared taxis to Darjeeling depart when full (3–5hr; ₹200-250). For a bit more comfort, take two seats up in front or a whole taxi (negotiate with returning taxis for reduced rates). Shared taxis to Kalimpong (3–5hr) depart from Panitanki More across the bridge while buses to Kalimpong depart from around the bus terminal.

To Sikkim Regular buses and shared jeeps run to Gangtok from around the bus terminus in Pradhan Nagar. Sikkim Nationalized Transport, opposite the bus terminus (daily 6am–4pm; ☏ 0353 251 1496, ⊕ sntd.in), runs bus services to Gangtok (several departures between 8.30am–3.00pm), and other points in Sikkim. Get a Sikkim permit (see page 832) from Sikkim Tourism next door or get one at the border (carry two photographs and photocopies of your passport and Indian visa); shared jeeps are also obtainable here and on the main road outside the gates. There are also helicopter flights from Bagdogra (see page 834).

To Kathmandu To reach Kathmandu in Nepal, travel to Panitanki, the crossing (24hr) on the Indian side of the border, and use a cycle rickshaw (around ₹50) to get to the Nepalese side at Kakarbitta (daily 7am–7pm), where there is a decent choice of accommodation if you arrive late. Shared taxis, regular buses from the terminal or outside it and taxis (around ₹1000) travel to Panitanki, where you can pick up a Nepalese visa for US$25/40/100 in cash for 15, 30 or 90 days. Kakarbitta offers a greater choice of onward buses to Kathmandu (17hr), or you could make a stop at the tea estates of Ilam and Dhankuta nearby. For a lot more luxury, take a Buddha Air (about US$140; book online; ⊕ buddhaair.com) flight from Bhadrapur (25km and a 45min taxi ride from Kakarbitta) to Kathmandu.

INFORMATION AND TOURS

Tourist information West Bengal's Tourist Office (WBTDC; Mon–Fri 10.30am–4pm; ☏ 0353 251 7561), opposite the Tenzin Norgay bus station, books rooms in tourist lodges in places such as Jaldapara Wildlife Sanctuary and offers wildlife package tours; at the next desk, the Forest Department officer books forest lodges such as at Lava near Neora Valley. There are information-only tourist counters at NJP station and Bagdogra airport.

Sikkim Tourism Opposite the bus stand in the same compound as Sikkim Nationalized Transport, the Sikkim Tourist Office (SNT Colony, Hill Cart Rd; Mon–Sat 10am–4pm; ☏ 0353 251 2646, ⊕ sikkimtourism.gov.in), provides information and Sikkim permits (see page 832).

Tour operators Siliguri's best private tour operator, Help Tourism, 1st Floor, Malati Bhavan, 143 Hill Cart Rd (☏ 0353 253 5896, ⊕ helptourism.com), organizes wildlife tours, village homestays, and treks and tours off the beaten track.

ACCOMMODATION

It is worth noting that some of the cheap hotels around the bus terminal – the *Delhi* and the *Shere-e-Punjab* in particular – have dubious reputations, especially in their treatment of female guests.

Marina's Motel Naxalbari Rd, Bagdogra ☏ 0353 211 0726, ⊕ marinasmotel.com. A pleasant mid-range option, handy both for the airport (free transfers are provided) and the Nepal border at Kakarbitta. It offers comfy rooms, a peaceful garden, and several places to eat and drink. ₹3300

Nirvana 18 Patel Rd, Pradhan Nagar ☏ 9832 014001.

Right behind *Khana Khazana* restaurant, this conveniently located multistorey block offers a bit more comfort than the similar *Apsara* next door. The small, carpeted rooms come with private bathrooms. ₹900

Sinclairs Pradhan Nagar ☏ 0353 251 7674, ⊕ sinclairs hotels.com/siliguri. Smart old hotel that remains popular for its convenient location near the cross-roads to Darjeeling and for all points including the airport. Comfortable, if a bit overpriced, with large refurbished rooms, a good restaurant, a garden and a (summer only) swimming pool. ₹4700

13

Vinayak Hill Cart Rd ☎0353 243 3131, ⓦvinayakonline. com. A reliable low-cost hotel conveniently located in the centre of town yet close to the taxi stands, with a choice of small but adequate rooms; the cheapest options only have fans. The restaurant downstairs serves good Bengali food. ₹999

EATING

City Centre Uttorayan Complex, NH-31 ⓦsiliguri. citycentremalls.in. This shopping mall, handy for the airport, has a food court, a branch of *Café Coffee Day* and several other decent restaurants, along with the usual mix of shops including a Crossword bookshop, and a cinema. Daily noon–9pm.

Khana Khazana Pradhan Nagar, opposite the bus terminal ☎0353 251 7516, ⓦfacebook.com/Khana Khazanasiliguri. A very pleasant restaurant and a good stop for travellers as it is handy for bus and taxi connections.

Serving everything from dosas to pizzas (mains ₹70–180), this is still one of the best options in town. Daily 9am–10pm.

★ **Punjabi Kadhai** Siddhi Arcade, Sevoke Rd ☎0353 254 5678, ⓦpunjabikadhai.in. Perhaps the best place to eat in Siliguri, situated around 1km from the centre, this restaurant serves top-notch Punjabi cuisine (as well as less-good Chinese and "fusion" food): the award-winning kebabs – marinated overnight and then fired in the *tandoor* – are not to be missed. Expect to pay ₹400–500/person for dinner. Daily noon–10pm.

DIRECTORY

Banks and exchange State Bank of India, Mangaldeep Building, Hill Cart Rd, or Cox & Kings, Ganeshayan Building, Sevoke Rd (☎98510 00802, ⓦcoxandkings.com)

Hospitals Neotia Getwel, Uttorayon (☎0353 305 3030, ⓦneotiagetwelsiliguri.com). With state-of-the-

art facilities, this is by far the best hospital in the region, servicing the hills and Sikkim as well.

Post office The main post office is on Kacheri Rd, with branches near the Central Railway Booking Office and the bus terminal.

Jaldapara Wildlife Sanctuary

Daily mid-Sept to mid-June dawn–dusk • A ₹200 (₹50) fee is payable at the entrance to the park (camera ₹50) • Jeep safaris are also available from ₹2200/jeep maximum 6 people • Access to Gorumara is via Lataguri (₹200 [₹80]) by jeep

Apart from the Darjeeling hills, most of North Bengal is well off the beaten track, and few travellers make detours from the Darjeeling–Sikkim–Nepal route. Probably the best reason to do so is to visit one of a string of **wildlife sanctuaries** that, along with tea gardens, carpet the **Dooars** along the southern approaches to the Himalayas.

The largest of these, **Jaldapara Wildlife Sanctuary**, 124km from Siliguri, was established in 1943 to protect wildlife from the encroachment of tea cultivation. Set against a backdrop of forested foothills on the banks of the River Torsa, Jaldapara's 216 square kilometres hold large tracts of tall elephant grass, are best explored at dawn, but we do not recommend taking an elephant ride. Around fifty highly endangered one-horned rhinoceros, as well as wild elephants, sambar and hog deer reside in the sanctuary.

ARRIVAL AND INFORMATION

JALDAPARA WILDLIFE SANCTUARY

By train The closest railway station is at Madarihat, 7km from the reserve and 1km from the sanctuary gates, with a limited service from both Siliguri and NJP. From here taxis run to *Hollong* in the heart of the forest for around ₹200. Alternatively, more trains travel via New Mal Junction to Hasimara 18km from the reserve including *Kanchan Kanya* (#13149; departs Siliguri Junction 8am, arrives 10.23am). The nearest station to Lataguri, the entry point to Gorumara

is New Mal Junction (30km), with a choice of transport including buses and taxis.

By bus A handful of buses and trains run from Siliguri and NJP to Madarihat and in season there is a handy tourist bus departing NJP around 8.30am via Siliguri, Gorumara and Lataguri to arrive around 2.20pm at *Jaldapara Tourist Lodge*. Enquire at the tourist office at Siliguri.

ACCOMMODATION AND EATING

You can book the *Hollong Forest Lodge* and the *Jaldapara Tourist Lodge* through the WBTDC tourist offices in Kolkata (see page 768) or Siliguri (see page 788 or directly online at ⓦwbtdcl.com). The WBTDC also offers all-inclusive packages from Siliguri (from around ₹9000), including

transport, accommodation, meals (and elephant rides – which we don't recommend).

Gach Bari Resort Dhupjhora Elephant Camp ☎90076 66411, ⓦjaldapara.org/gachbari-resort.html. While it is far from luxurious, this most atmospheric of the forest

13

lodges, in the form of a basic treehouse, provides a good chance of seeing wildlife from the veranda. Don't expect room service or hot water, and book well in advance – the phone number given is for the Forest Officer, who manages reservations. There are also some spartan cottages and a restaurant in the garden. No wi-fi. ₹1800

Hollong Forest Lodge ☎ 03563 262228, ⓦ north bengaltourism.com. Extremely popular due to its location – it's the only lodge within the sanctuary itself – the state-run *Hollong Forest Lodge* has a handful of simple, fan-cooled rooms and a communal veranda that's great for wildlife spotting. Book well in advance. No wi-fi. ₹2500

Jaldapara Jungle Camp Birpara, Madarihat ☎ 09733 267517, ⓦ jaldaparacamp.com. A welcoming place around 3km from the sanctuary, with comfortable wood-built jungle cabins, a well-ordered campus and the *Aranya Restaurant* serving good Bengali cooking. Staff will arrange safaris and transport. No wi-fi. ₹1300

Jaldapara Tourist Lodge ☎ 03563 262230, ⓦ wbtdcl. com. An extensive state-run complex. Rooms (with either fan or a/c) in the newer block are more comfort-able than those in the more atmospheric old wing. There are also some cottages. Book well in advance. Doubles ₹1600, cottages ₹2600

Kurseong

Around 30km southeast of Darjeeling and about 37km north of Siliguri, connected by both road and rail, is bustling **KURSEONG**. Less touristy and with a slightly warmer climate than its more famous neighbour – though, admittedly, less picturesque – the town is a pleasant place to break your journey. Surrounded by tea estates, the hill station still has a sprinkling of Raj-era buildings, most notably a clutch of English-style boarding schools, as well as several Buddhist monasteries.

ARRIVAL AND DEPARTURE   KURSEONG

By train/taxi Kurseong is linked to Darjeeling and to Siliguri by the Toy Train (see page 795). A taxi from Siliguri costs in the region of ₹2000.

By jeep There are two daily direct *sumos* to Gangtok (7.30am and 1pm; ₹300) and several to Siliguri and Darjeeling.

ACCOMMODATION AND EATING

In addition to the option listed below, you can also stay at the Makaibari Tea Estate (see page 799), located around 3km below the bazaar.

Cochrane Place 1 km below the bazaar ☎ 099320 35660, ⓦ cochraneplacehotel.com. If you want to stay

the night in Kurseong, try *Cochrane Place*, a rambling old villa with grand views, plenty of railway and Raj memorabilia, atmospheric if creaky rooms, and good Anglo-Indian food. Good tours of local villages and tea estates are on offer. ₹4000

Darjeeling

Part Victorian holiday resort, part major tea-growing centre, **DARJEELING** (from *Dorje Ling*, "the place of the thunderbolt") straddles a ridge 2200m up in the Himalayas, almost 600km north of Kolkata. Over seventy years since the British departed, the town remains as popular as ever with holiday-makers from the plains, and promenades such as the Mall and the Chowrasta still burst with life. The greatest appeal for visitors has to be its stupendous mountain vistas – with Kanchenjunga (the third highest mountain in the world) and a vast cohort of ice-capped peaks dominating the northern horizon. However, the infrastructure created under the Raj has been unable to cope with the ever-expanding population, leading to acute shortages of water and electricity, and chaos on the hopelessly inadequate roads. Still, Darjeeling remains a colourful and lively, cosmopolitan place, with good shopping and dining, plenty of walks in the surrounding hills, and attractions such as the **Toy Train** and colourful Buddhist monasteries. The best seasons to visit – and to attempt the magnificent trek to Sandakphu to see Everest – are after the monsoons and before winter (late Sept to late Nov), and spring (mid-Feb to May).

Brief history

Until the nineteenth century, Darjeeling belonged to **Sikkim**. However in 1817, after a disastrous war with Nepal, Sikkim was forced to concede the right to use the site as a health sanatorium to the **British**, who had helped to broker a peace settlement. Darjeeling soon became the most popular of all hill resorts, especially after the Hill Cart Road was built in 1839 to link it with Siliguri. **Tea** arrived a few years later, and with it an influx of Nepalese labourers and the disappearance of the forests that previously carpeted the hillsides. The town's growing economic significance led Britain to force a treaty on the Sikkimese in 1861, thereby annexing Darjeeling

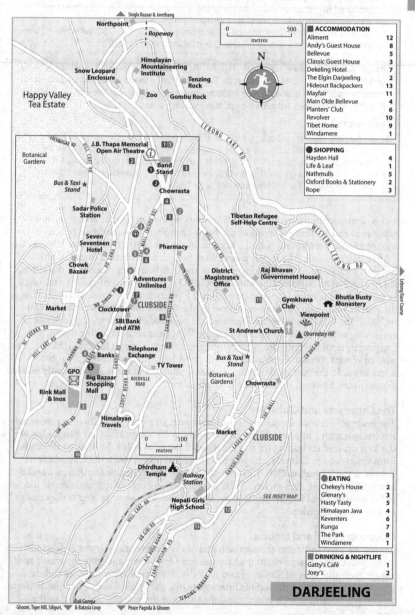

ACCOMMODATION

Aliment	12
Andy's Guest House	8
Bellevue	5
Classic Guest House	3
Dekeling Hotel	7
The Elgin Darjeeling	2
Hideout Backpackers	13
Mayfair	11
Main Olde Bellevue	4
Planters' Club	6
Revolver	10
Tibet Home	9
Windamere	1

SHOPPING

Hayden Hall	4
Life & Leaf	1
Nathmulls	5
Oxford Books & Stationery	2
Rope	3

EATING

Chekey's House	2
Glenary's	3
Hasty Tasty	5
Himalayan Java	4
Keventers	6
Kunga	7
The Park	8
Windamere	1

DRINKING & NIGHTLIFE

Gatty's Café	1
Joey's	2

DARJEELING

13

DARJEELING TEA

Although the original appeal of Darjeeling for the British was as a hill resort with easy access from the plains, inspired by their success in Assam they soon realized its potential for growing **tea**. Today, the Darjeeling tea industry continues to flourish, producing China Jat, China Hybrid and Hybrid Assam. A combination of factors, including altitude and sporadic rainfall, have resulted in a relatively small yield – only three percent of India's total – but the delicate black tea produced here is considered to be one of the finest in the world. It is also some of the most expensive with varieties fetching more than ₹18,000 a kilo at auction.

Grades such as Flowery Orange Pekoe (FOP) or Broken Orange Pekoe (BOP) are determined by quality and length of leaf as it is withered, crushed, fermented and dried.

Happy Valley Tea Estate off Lebong Cart Rd ☎ 80177 00700, ⊛ ambootia.com. To watch the process for yourself, call in at the *Happy Valley Tea Estate*; it's a 30min walk from town. Just follow the signs from the Hill Cart Rd near the District Magistrate's office; it's worth phoning ahead to make sure there is someone to show you round. Tues–Sat 8am–noon & 1–4.30pm, Sun 8am–noon.

BUYING TEA

As for **buying**, numerous shops on the Mall, at Chowrasta and the Rink Mall offer try-before-you-buy, with the menu set clearly by the seasons (otherwise known as "flushes"). See the "Shopping" section (see page 797) for where to make your purchase; expect to pay ₹300–600 for 100g of a good-quality tea. You can taste life on a tea plantation either through the luxurious *Glenburn TE* or at *Makaibari* (see page 799).

and Kalimpong. In the early 1900s, Darjeeling's reputation grew as one of the most glamorous and far-flung outposts of the British Empire. Subsequently it became a mountaineering centre and played a key role in the conquest of the greater Himalayas.

After Independence, the region joined West Bengal, administered from Calcutta, but calls for autonomy grew, taking shape in the **Gurkhaland** movement of the 1980s, led by the **Gurkha National Liberation Front (GNLF)**. The subsequent violent campaign ended a decade later and, once in power, GNLF politicians grew complacent, fuelling discontent and leading to their overthrow by the **Gorkha Jana Mukti Morcha (GJMM)** in 2007. The GJMM victory reinvigorated the push for an autonomous Gurkhaland, employing wildcat strikes designed to cripple West Bengal's hold on the region. Despite unhappiness with the West Bengal government, support for the GJMM, who adminster through Gurkhaland Territorial Administration (GTA), is far from unanimous. In the past local opposition was vigorously and sometimes violently put down. Today, however, the situation is much calmer.

The Chowrasta and Clubside

The heart of Victorian Darjeeling is the **Chowrasta**, an expansive traffic-free promenade resplendent with a bandstand, high above the busy bazaar on Hill Cart Road. One of the four main roads leading off it is the **Nehru Road** (also called the **Mall**), it descends from Chowrasta to **Clubside**, the area below the prestigious **Planters' Club**, otherwise known as the **Darjeeling Club**. Established in 1868, this venerable institution was the centre of Darjeeling high society. Today, visitors are welcome to stay and sample the faded ambience and facilities such as the bar and snooker room, as long as they buy temporary membership.

Observatory Hill and around

Taking the right fork from the northern end of the Chowrasta, near the bandstand, brings you to the **viewpoint** from where you can survey the Kanchenjunga massif and almost the entire state of Sikkim. From near the *Windamere Hotel* steps, ascend the pine-covered hillside to the top of **Observatory Hill**, the original site of the Bhutia Busti monastery. Streaming with prayer flags, the shrine at the summit, dedicated to the wrathful Buddhist deity Mahakala, whom Hindus worship as Shiva, reflects a garish hybrid of styles. Another faded Raj-era -institution, the **Gymkhana Club**, stands near Observatory Hill; temporary memberships are available (see page 797).

A steep but pleasant walk down from near Government House, or a circuitous taxi ride, leads to the **Tibetan Refugee Self-Help Centre** (Mon–Sat 9am–4.30pm). Founded in 1959 after the Chinese invasion of Tibet, it houses around seven hundred refugees, most of whom make carpets or Tibetan handicrafts. The community also has a hospital and a school. Tourists are welcome to watch the activities; the shop sells handicrafts and carpets, which they will ship for you. Around the same altitude, and a short distance away, is the small, picture-postcard **Bhutia Busti Monastery** (daily 8am–6pm) re-established here from its original site on Observatory Hill. An alternative approach is the pleasant 1km walk downhill along the steep CR Das Road from the Chowrasta. Linked to Phodong in Sikkim, the *dukhang* (prayer hall) houses a venerated copy of the **Tibetan Book of the Dead** – the *Bardo Thodol*.

Darjeeling Zoo (Padmaja Naidu Zoological Park)

Birch Hill • Daily except Thurs 8.30am–4pm • ₹100 (₹30), including HMI ticket, camera ₹10

The promenade north from the Chowrasta leads to Darjeeling's well-maintained **zoo**. Its snow leopard breeding centre (closed to the public), established in 1986, is the only place in the world to have successfully bred this endangered species, while Project Panda has produced a number of red pandas.

Himalayan Mountaineering Institute

Birch Hill • **Museum** Daily except Thurs 8.30am–4.30pm • Included in zoo ticket price

The **Himalayan Mountaineering Institute** (HMI) (see page 794), reached via the zoo and covered by the same ticket, is one of India's most important training centres for mountaineers. Its first director was **Sherpa Tenzing Norgay**, Sir Edmund Hillary's climbing partner on the first successful ascent of Everest, who lived and died in Darjeeling, and is buried in the Institute's grounds. In the heart of the leafy complex, the **HMI Museum** is dedicated to the history of mountaineering, with equipment old and new, a relief map of the Himalayas, and a collection of costumes of hill people.

The **Everest Museum** in the annexe recounts the history of ascents on the world's highest peak, from Mallory and Irvine's ill-fated 1924 expedition to Tenzing and Hillary's triumph in 1953 and the record-breaking 20hr 24min climb by Kaji Sherpa in 1998.

Northpoint and the Ropeway

Northpoint, a 10–15min walk beyond the zoo • Daily in season 10am–2pm • ₹150 return

Below the HMI at Northpoint, where the views of Sikkim open out, and near the Gothic ramparts of **St Joseph's College**, the cable car or **Ropeway** has restarted its operation after a terrible accident in 2003. A popular day-trip destination, the cable car (20min one way) travels down past tea gardens to Tukvar Tea Estate towards Singla and the Sikkim border.

Lloyd Botanical Gardens

Chowk Bazaar • Mon–Sat 8am–5pm • Free

Lochnagar Road winds down from the bus stand in the bazaar to enter the **Lloyd Botanical Gardens**, resplendent with pines, willows and maples that cover the hillside. A quiet spot with tended flowerbeds and meandering walkways, the gardens were established in 1878 and feature a central glasshouse filled with ferns and orchids and other flowers.

Nipponjan Myohoji Buddhist Temple (Peace Pagoda)

AJC Bose Rd • Daily 4.30am–7pm • Prayers 4.30–6am & 4.30–6pm

13

Heading out of town on AJC Bose Road, just past Lal Kothi, you come to the discreetly hidden **Nipponjan Myohoji Buddhist Temple**, usually referred to as the Peace Pagoda, a peaceful spot for meditation, yoga or tai chi, with great views over the valley to Kanchenjunga. The temple itself has a small museum upstairs.

ARRIVAL AND DEPARTURE
DARJEELING

Virtually all travellers arriving in Darjeeling from the plains come via Siliguri, whether by the Toy Train (see box opposite) or by road. Jeeps and buses stop at the **bus stand** in the lower half of the town, from where it's a bit of an uphill trek to the main hotel area. Most taxis and some jeeps drop you off at **Clubside** near the **Mall** (officially Nehru Rd), at the upper end of town. Porters are available (from ₹100) at the bus stand and bazaar, but be aware that some act as touts. Darjeeling is best explored on foot – in fact, much of it is closed to all vehicles.

By plane The nearest airports to Darjeeling are Bagdogra, 100km to the south (see page 787) — allow at least 3hr to get there by taxi – and Pakyong, 79km away, in Sikkim.

By train Darjeeling is famous for its spectacular Toy Train (see box). Railway reservations (daily 8am–2pm) for selected main-line trains out of NJP can be made at Darjeeling's station a couple of days before departure,

though booking online or via one of the town's travel agencies is easier.

By bus Due to poor road conditions, it is best to avoid the handful of buses and minibuses that run to Siliguri from the bus stand near Chowk Bazaar. For overland bus travel to Kathmandu, head to the border town of Kakarbitta in Nepal to get a choice of coaches (see page 788).

By taxi/jeep In the mornings, jeeps run regularly to Gangtok (for Sikkim; foreigners need two photographs and photocopies of their passport information page and Indian visa to get permits at the border), Siliguri, Mirik, and Kalimpong, and are by far the most efficient way to travel, especially if you pay for two front seats for yourself. Book in advance if you can at the jeep stand (next to the bus stand); each route has its own syndicate, and some have two or three. A private taxi to either Bagdogra and Pakyong airports, or Kalimpong, costs around ₹2000/2500.

INFORMATION

Permits Foreigners planning to head on to Sikkim need a permit. You can apply online (W sikkimpts.azurewebsites. net) or through a painless formality at the Rangpo border checkpoint, where all Gangtok-bound jeeps stop. You will need to bring a photocopy of your passport and visa plus two passport photos. Initial thirty-day permits are extendable to a maximum of three months once you're in

Gangtok (see page 830). Permits are free and single-entry only; you cannot re-enter within three months.

GTA Tourism 4 Silver Fir, Bhanu Sarani, 100m north of Chowrasta (daily: March–May, Oct & Nov 9am–1pm & 2–5pm; rest of year 10am–4.30pm; ☏ 0354 225 4879, W gtatourism.com), provides information on treks and tours, transport and whitewater rafting on the Teesta River.

ACCOMMODATION

Darjeeling has hundreds of hotels, which places a considerable strain upon the infrastructure, particularly

the water supply. Some budget places only provide water in buckets, sometimes charging extra if you want it hot. If

---

DARJEELING TOUR AND ADVENTURE OPERATORS

Darjeeling is brimming with tour and trek operators, and some of the budget hotels provide cost-effective trekking services for the Singalila Ridge.

Adventures Unlimited 142 Dr Zakir Hussein Rd ☏ 99330 70013, W adventuresunlimited.in. This excellent agency offers both motorbike and mountain-bike tours, as well as motorbike and mountain-bike rental; it also organizes rafting and kayaking on the Teesta River, rock climbing and trekking, plus homestays.

Himalayan Mountaineering Institute ☏ 0354 225 4087, W hmidarjeeling.com. Basic and advanced mountaineering courses, including a women-only expedition. Basic trips, centred around the Institute's Chaurikhang Base Camp at the foot of Rathong Glacier in Sikkim, are run with military precision and last 28

days ($650 [₹4000]). However, this is an economical and unique introduction to Himalayan mountaineering. The more rewarding advanced course requires previous mountaineering experience; to join either course, you must be aged between 17 and 40 and should be fit. Apply at least three months in advance.

Himalayan Travels 18 Gandhi Rd ☏ 0354 225 6956 or 94342 09847, W facebook.com/Himalayan TravelsDarjeeling. An efficient organization run by the affable K.K. Gurung, one of the first and most experienced operators in town, offering tours and treks throughout Darjeeling, Sikkim and Bhutan.

THE DARJEELING HIMALAYAN RAILWAY: THE TOY TRAIN

Completed in 1881, the small-gauge (610mm) **Darjeeling Himalayan Railway** (commonly known as the **Toy Train**) was designed as an extension of the North Bengal State Railway, climbing from **New Jalpaiguri**, via **Siliguri**, for a tortuous 88km up to **Darjeeling**. Given UNESCO World Heritage status in 1999, the Toy Train follows the Hill Cart Road, crossing it at regular intervals and even sharing it with traffic. Although no longer an essential mode of transport, the train is certainly a tourist attraction, and currently runs daily from New Jalpaiguri at 8.30am, reaching Darjeeling at 3.35pm. Diesel engines are now de rigueur on the long route.

Weather permitting, coaches with large viewing windows provide magnificent vistas as the journey progresses and the scenery gradually unfolds; second class can be fun but crowded.

Some travellers may find the entire route from Siliguri painfully slow. The section from Kurseong is well worth the time, however; alternatively you could take the short ("Joy") ride from Darjeeling to Ghoom.

"JOY RIDES" TO GHOOM

In season (March–May, Oct & Nov), six steam-driven **"Joy Ride"** tourist trains leave Darjeeling at 9.40am, 10am, 12.10pm, 12.20pm, 4.05pm and 4.10pm; they then travel up to Ghoom, where they stop for just 15min (not enough time to view the monasteries). At its highest point at Jorebungalow near Ghoom (2438m), 7km short of Darjeeling, the dramatic panorama of the Kanchenjunga Range is suddenly revealed. Just beyond Ghoom, the train does a complete circle at the Batasia Loop (another method used to gain rapid height is the **reversing stations** where the track follows a "Z" shape) with another brief stop for views of the Himalayas. Although sold as a package, you could return on the regular diesel service. Alternative transport back to Darjeeling includes buses or shared jeeps, or you can take the top road for a quiet walk back, enjoying stupendous views along the way and a visit to the **Peace Pagoda** in the woods above the Dali Gompa.

JUNGLE SAFARI FROM SILIGURI TO TINDHARIA

An on-demand, diesel-hauled **Jungle Safari Special** train departs Siliguri Junction at 10.30am, traveling to Tindharia via Rongtong and back to Siliguri Junction (arrival at 3.20pm). It passes through magnificent Mahananda Wildlife Sanctuary, rolling over the Chunbhatti Loop, and three Z-reverses. For more information and bookings, contact Darjeeling Himalayan Railway (☎ 90020 41955, ⓦ dhr.in.net).

INFORMATION

Train times At the time of research, passenger train #52541 left New Jalpaiguri daily at 8.30am, stopping at Kurseong at 12.46pm, Ghoom at 2.51pm, and then arriving at Darjeeling at 3.35pm. From Darjeeling, train #52540 left daily at 8am, reaching New Jalpaiguri at 3.10pm. The regular Toy Train (#52587) departed Kurseong daily at 6.30am, stopping at Ghoom at 8.30am and then arriving in Darjeeling at 9.05am. For the return journey, services left Darjeeling at 10.15am (#52544) and 3.35pm (#52588). Check the latest schedules at ⓦ dhr.in.net/train-schedule.php.

Booking tickets For more information on the Toy Train, contact the Darjeeling Himalayan Railway Society (ⓦ dhr.in.net) or, in India, the Director at Elysia Building, near Himali School, Kurseong 734203 (☎ 0354 200 5734, ⓦ dhr.in.net). Book ahead as there are rarely more than three coaches on a train.

you visit during the winter months, make sure your room is adequately heated. Off-season (late June to Sept & late Nov to Feb) **discounts** can be up to fifty percent.

Aliment 40 Dr Zakir Hussein Rd ☎ 81163 47274; map p.791. Popular, low-cost hotel with decent though rather gaudy rooms, all with private bath-rooms and hot water, spread across five floors. The in-house restaurant is one of the best in this part of town with an eclectic menu. ₹3500

Andy's Guest House 102 Dr Zakir Hussein Rd ☎ 0354 225 3125; map p.791. Run by a retired couple, and essentially a comfortable family home, this is the best of the budget guesthouses: safe, with large, immaculate rooms and great views towards Kalimpong and Bhutan, but no restaurant. Hot water is time-managed and doors close early. It was under renovation at the time of writing, so the price stated here may increase a little. ₹1000

Bellevue Chowrasta ☎ 0354 225 4075, ⓦ bellevue hotel-darjeeling.com; map p.791. Dominating the Chowrasta, this once-grand hotel, linked to Tibetan nobility, is now rather musty and faded. Still the large, wood-panelled rooms with fireplaces have a certain charm, and its location couldn't be more central. ₹2200

13

Classic Guest House CR Das Rd ☏0354 225 7025, ⓦclassicguesthouse.in; map p.791. This excellent spot, just a couple of minutes below Chowrasta, offers five clean, large and comfortable wood-lined rooms with verandas and dramatic views. Despite its proximity to the centre and good restaurants, it is peaceful and quiet. ₹3000

★ **Dekeling Hotel** 51 Gandhi Rd ☏0354 225 4159, ⓦdekeling.com; map p.791. In a central location, approached up steep steps, with running hot water, heaters and a range of rooms – some have great views and the timbered ones upstairs are charming (though low-ceilinged). The new wing at the back is the most comfortable and a bit quieter in the early mornings. The Tibetan owners are especially helpful and there is a welcoming log fire in winter; it sits above a fine restaurant, *Dekevas*, too. Smarter sister property *Dekenling Resort*, a 10min walk away, has comfortable suites (from ₹3640) with fireplaces, good home-cooking and a garden. ₹1610

★ **The Elgin Darjeeling** 32 HD Lama Rd ☏0354 225 7226, ⓦelginhotels.com/darjeeling.php; map p.791. Dating back some 125 years, this premier heritage hotel has a rather formal atmosphere that captures the old-fashioned spirit of Darjeeling. There are elegant rooms, a well-equipped spa, and good restaurant and bar. Rates include full board. ₹12,200

Hideout Backpackers 10 A Rock Ville, Near Water Tank ☏97331 18521, ⓦhideoutdarjeeling.business. site; map p.791. Finally Darjeeling has a budget hostel offering clean mixed-dorms with shared bathrooms and water heaters. There's a social atmosphere, friendly owners, and a nice rooftop with superb views of the mountains. A continental breakfast is included, and they offer cycling and walking tours. ₹600

Mayfair Below Government House, The Mall ☏0354 225 6376, ⓦmayfairhotels.com; map p.791. Once a maharaja's summer retreat, now a luxury hotel, whose wood-panelled rooms and suites ooze class. Facilities include restaurants, a bar and health spa; the gardens are immaculate, and the garden restaurant offers great views. Rates include board. ₹11,000

Main Olde Bellevue Above Bellevue, 1 Nehru Rd, Chowrasta ☏0354 225 4178, ⓦbellevueheritagehotel. com; map p.791. A large property with rooms overlooking Nehru Rd in two new blocks and an old rambling chalet with plenty of atmosphere, wooden rooms and creaky floors. It's on the top of the hill, with great views, and close to all amenities. ₹2500

Planters' Club The Mall ☏0354 225 4349 or ☏94340 48572, ✉thedarjeelingplantersclub@rediffmail. com; map p.791. A local landmark (also known as the *Darjeeling Club*) with old-fashioned rooms, coal fires, a billiard room, bar, restaurant and library. Residential guests must take temporary membership (₹50); non-guests can use the facilities for ₹225. ₹1800

Revolver 110 Gandhi Rd ☏98000 05455, ⓦrevolver. in; map p.791. A delightful oddity, this Beatles-themed hotel has five rooms, four named after the bandmates and one after manager Brian Epstein; rooms are simple and comfortable, and the owners have avoided being kitsch. The restaurant, mean-while, specializes in the food of Nagaland (and Lavazza coffee) and there's a library of books, music and films (many devoted to the Fab Four) to delve into. There is a sister café in Gangtok. ₹1400

Tibet Home Manjushree Centre, 12 Gandhi Rd ☏0354 225 2977, ✉slg_mctc1988@sancharnet.in; map p.791. This non-profit Tibetan cultural centre and museum offers eight large, comfortable and well-appointed rooms with attached bathrooms and hot water. Students of the centre get discounts. Book well in advance of your visit. ₹2500

Windamere Observatory Hill ☏0354 225 4041, ⓦwindamerehotel.com; map p.791. The most iconic and celebrated of Darjeeling's hotels has accommodated a pantheon of rich and famous guests in its old-world cottages decked out with Raj memorabilia; it also has a modern wing with comfortable suites but less character. Rates include full board. Even if you're not staying here, it's worth visiting for high tea (see opposite). Doubles ₹13,500, cottages ₹16,500

EATING

Chekey's House Dr Zakir Hussain Rd, blue door opposite Kalden Café; map p.791. This hole in the wall local eatery, catered to locals, has been serving delicious Tibetan food for years. Chekey and her family cook fresh momos, thukpas, thentuk and juicy meat-filled sha phaley, served with a fiery-hot, homemade chutney, that are cheap and authentic. A meal will set you back a mere ₹100. Daily 8am–9.30pm.

Glenary's The Mall ☏0354 225 4122, ⓦfacebook.com/ glenarysdarjeeling; map p.791. One of Darjeeling's most reputable eating places, with a patisserie and tearoom on the ground floor, a restaurant upstairs serving tasty sizzlers,

great tandoori and Raj-era dishes such as shepherd's pie (mains ₹150–350), and a pub-bar-coffee shop downstairs. Look out for the red British telephone box near the entrance. Daily 8am–9pm.

Hasty Tasty The Mall; map p.791. Tasty? Yes. Hasty? Not so much. Regardless, this veg Indian joint is rightly popular, often packed with Indian holiday-makers. You can get a good meal for less than ₹150, with economical thalis and dosas among the highlights. Daily 11am–8pm.

★ **Himalayan Java** The Mall ☏0354 225 4731, ⓦhimalayanjava.com; map p.791. A long-standing Kathmandu favourite, now expanding overseas, *Himalayan*

Java serves the best coffee in town – from ristrettos to iced caramel macchiatos (₹90–160), all produced from organic Nepalese beans. There's also a tasty array of cakes, pastries and snacks. A fine spot to spend an afternoon. Daily 8am–8pm.

Keventers Clubside ☎98320 41448; map p.791. A landmark café serving fried, British-style breakfasts that include sausages and bacon, as well as toasted sandwiches, plus milk-shakes, hot chocolate and coffee (drinks ₹80–140). The terrace above the crossroads is excellent for people-watching (if the weather is amenable), though service is notoriously poor. A delicatessen downstairs sells cheese, ham and sausages. Daily 8am–8pm.

Kunga Gandhi Rd ☎96798 89365; map p.791. Minute Tibetan restaurant, popular with locals and tourists, and serving excellent *momos* (dumplings filled with chicken, pork, beef or veg, steamed or fried, and served with a fiery chilli sauce; ₹125–150) and thick *thukpa* soups. The salted butter tea, however, is very much an acquired taste. Daily 8am–9pm.

The Park 41 Laden La Rd ☎0354 225 4989; map p.791. *The Park* offers some of the finest north Indian and tandoori dishes in Darjeeling, as well as decent Thai food, and tasty chicken *momos*. Prices are reasonable (mains ₹120–380). Daily noon–3pm & 6–11pm.

Windamere Observatory Hill ☎0354 225 4041, ⓦwindamerehotel.com; map p.791. The classic place to sample a British-style high tea (₹900), which is taken on the lawn or in one of the stately sitting rooms in front of the fire and surrounded by photos of Darjeeling in its colonial heyday. As well as a pot of tea, you'll get a platter along the lines of the following: two types of sandwiches, a scone with cream and jam, a slice of sponge cake, a couple of coconut macaroons, and some biscuits. Daily 4–6pm.

DRINKING AND NIGHTLIFE

In addition to the options here, the *Windamere* and *Planters' Club* are both atmospheric places for a drink, especially the veranda at the latter.

Gatty's Café Dr Zakir Hussain Rd ☎99330 70013, ⓦfacebook.com/gattyscafe; map p.791. The closest one gets to a nightclub in Darjeeling with a lively motorbike theme (the owner Gautam also runs motorbike tours), this café-bar is a great place for a beer in the evening, and the tempo picks up after 9pm, when there's often live music (cover charges of ₹150 sometimes apply). There's also a large screen to watch the football. Daily 6–11.30pm.

Joey's Opposite Rink Plaza, ☎92326 92573, ⓦfacebook.com/joeyspubdarjeeling; map p.791. Run by musician Puran Gongba – a mean guitarist and something of a local celebrity – this small and intimate pub is a popular rendezvous for visitors, expats and locals alike. Not renowned for its food but rather its beer (₹200–300), ambience and chat. Daily noon–10pm (though sometimes stays open an hour or so later).

ENTERTAINMENT

Cinema Inox Rink Mall ☎0354 225 7183. A modern multiplex with three auditoria and the latest from Bollywood and Hollywood; it can be loud so, depending on the film, you might want to take earplugs.

Gymkhana Club Just north of Observatory Hill, near St Andrew's Church ☎0354 225 4342, ⓦdarjeeling gymkhanaclub.com. Visitors can buy temporary memberships (day ₹100, week ₹600) at this Raj-era club, dating back over 100 years, and take advantage of an array of facilities, including a gym, tennis, badminton and squash courts, table tennis, billiards and – bizarrely – roller skating, plus a library and bar. Daily 7am–9.30pm.

SHOPPING

Hayden Hall 42 Laden La Rd ☎0354 225 3228, ⓦhaydenhall.org; map p.791. Run by an NGO that supports women who have fled abusive relationships, this shop sells a range of hand-made carpets, jumpers, bags and other items. A colourful statue of the Virgin Mary stands by the entrance. Mon–Sat 10am–6pm.

Life & Leaf Chowrasta; map p.791. An excellent place to pick up quality souvenirs, this fair-trade shop sells a strong selection of handicrafts and produce from the local area, including organic tea and honey. Mon–Sat 10am–7pm.

Nathmulls Suite 21, Chachan Mansions, Laden La Rd Chowrasta ☎0354 225 6437, ⓦnathmulltea.com; map p.791. This family-run tea business was founded in 1931, so they know their stuff: there are scores of varieties on offer here (if you can't decide ask for a tasting) as well as an array of tea paraphernalia (pots, cups and so on). Mon–Sat 10am–8pm.

Oxford Books & Stationery Chowrasta ☎0354 225 4325, ✉mayaprimlani@gmail.com; map p.791. Easily the best-stocked bookshop in town, with a strong selection of novels, maps, non-fiction and coffee-table books, with northeast India titles particularly well represented. If you buy more than you intended, they will even ship books home for you. Daily 10am–7pm.

Rope NB Singh Rd (below Clubside); map p.791. A good selection of trekking gear (much of it genuine), including jackets and sleeping bags, but it's on the expensive side. Inexpensive knock-offs, mainly made in Nepal and varying in quality, are available from stores across town. Daily 9am–5pm.

13

DIRECTORY

Banks and exchange The State Bank of India on Laden La Rd and HDFC at Rink Mall offer foreign exchange. Licensed private foreign-exchange vendors offer an alter-native but charge a bit more than the bank rate. Among these, the *Mohit* and *Seven Seventeen* hotels are both on HD Lama Rd. Poddar's, 8 Laden La Rd near the GPO, is also good for cash advances on credit/debit cards.

Hospital Planters' Hospital, *Planter's Club*, The Mall (☎ 0354 225 4327) is the best bet in an emergency.

Post office The main post office (Mon–Fri 9am–5pm, Sat 9am–noon) is on Laden La Rd.

Tibetan studies The Manjushree Centre of Tibetan Culture, 12 Gandhi Rd (☎ 0354 225 2977, ⌨ manjushree-culture.org), founded in 1988 to preserve and promote Tibetan culture, offers part-time Tibetan language classes (Mon–Sat 4–6pm) and more intensive three-, six- and nine-month courses and holds seminars, talks, video shows and exhibitions. The Chagpori Medical Institute at Takdah (en route to Teesta) runs excellent long courses in Tibetan medicine; ask at the Manjushree Centre.

Around Darjeeling

An unmissable part of the Darjeeling experience is the early-morning mass exodus to **Tiger Hill** to watch the sunrise. This can easily be combined with a visit to the old monastery of **Ghoom**, and the huge monastery at **Sonada** on Hill Cart Road towards Siliguri.

Tiger Hill

7.5km southeast of Ghoom, 9.5km southeast of Darjeeling • Viewing tower ₹20–40 • Jeeps from ₹100/seat or around ₹1200 for the whole vehicle, reserved from *Clubside* (see page 794)

In good weather and in the high season a couple of hundred jeeps and taxis packed with tourists leave from *Clubside* in Darjeeling around 4am each morning, careering 12km through Ghoom to catch the dramatic sunrise at **Tiger Hill**. This incredible viewpoint (2585m) on the eastern extremity of the Singalila Range provides a 360-degree Himalayan panorama, with the steamy plains bordering Bangladesh to the south, the Singalila ridge with Everest beyond to the west, Kanchenjunga and Sikkim to the north, and the Bhutan and Assam Himalayas trailing into the distance to the northeast. From left to right, the **peaks** include: Lhotse (which actually looks higher than Everest); Everest itself; Makalu; then, after a long gap, the rocky summit of Kang on the Sikkim–Nepal divide; the prow of Jannu in Nepal; Rathong; tent-like Kabru south and north; Talung; Kanchenjunga main, central and south; Pandim; Simvo; horned Narsing; and the fluted pyramid of Siniolchu. If you're feeling energetic you could opt to walk back from Tiger Hill visiting the *gompas* of Ghoom on the way.

Senchal Wildlife Sanctuary

Senchal, 8.5km southeast of Darjeeling • Daily dawn–dusk • ₹100 • ☎ 0354 54308

Tiger Hill also gives access to the small **Senchal Wildlife Sanctuary**, which, at just 38 square kilometres is home to a variety of fauna including barking deer, jackals, wild boar, the occasional black bear and a leopard. It is best to explore on foot or by mountain bike – Adventures Unlimited (see page 794) rents out bikes and can give advice or arrange a trip to the sanctuary.

Ghoom and other monasteries

Often obscured in cloud, **Ghoom** (or Ghum; 2438m), 8km south of Darjeeling, with its charming little railway station and tiny bazaar on the edge of Jorebangla, holds several interesting monasteries. The most venerated of these is **Yiga Choling**, or the Old Ghoom Monastery (signposted from the bazaar), tucked off the main thoroughfare above a brash resort. Built in 1850 by Sharap Gyatso, a renowned astrologer, the monastery consists of a single chambered temple and a few residential buildings. Inside the prayer hall is a huge figure of Maitreya, the Buddha of the future – a statue of an exceptionally high standard of workmanship, with fine detail above and around the bronze face.

Back on the main road, the **Shakya Choling** *gompa* has expanded in recent years; while **Samten Choling**, a small but colourful *gompa* on a bend in the main road to Darjeeling, is sometimes included on the jeep tours to Tiger Hill.

Thupten Sanga Choling
Midway between Ghoom and Darjeeling • No fixed opening times • Free

Halfway between Ghoom and Darjeeling on the main road stands the imposing **Thupten Sanga Choling**, otherwise known as the **Dali Gompa**, inaugurated by the Dalai Lama in 1993. This is a very active **Drukpa Kagyu** *gompa* with two hundred monks. The huge meditation hall is richly decorated with exquisite murals and ceiling mandalas.

Sonada Monastery
2km south of Ghoom • No fixed opening times • Free • ☎ 0354 246 6716, ⓦ paldenshangpa.org

Down the Hill Cart Road towards Kurseong, the influential **Sonada Monastery** or **Samdrub Darjay Choling**, founded in the 1960s, was the seat of **Kabje Kalu Rinpoche**, who developed a large American and French following. Today the monastery continues under the tutelage of his incarnate Yangsi Kalu Rinpoche. Rooms are occasionally available for those looking for a retreat.

ACCOMMODATION	**AROUND DARJEELING**

Glenburn Tea Estate Off the road to Kalimpong, 35km northeast of Darjeeling ☎ 033 2288 5630, ⓦ glenburn teaestate.com. You can get a taste of the opulence of a tea-manager's lifestyle – at a price – with a stay at this estate, which offers all-inclusive packages including airport transfers, tours, tastings and all meals. The extensive estate, en route to Kalimpong, stretches down the hillside to the Rangeet River, and offers riverside camping and fishing. ₹43,710

Makaibari Tea Estate Pankhabari Rd, Kurseong ☎ 033 2248 6017, ⓦ makaibari.com. The pioneering owner of this organic tea estate offers homestays around the plantation in the workers' houses. Expect rustic but comfortable rooms and meals, and a family atmosphere; rates go directly to the host family and the community. Plenty of activities, including trekking, tea picking (and tasting) and birdwatching, and there are also opportunities to volunteer. No wi-fi. ₹2000

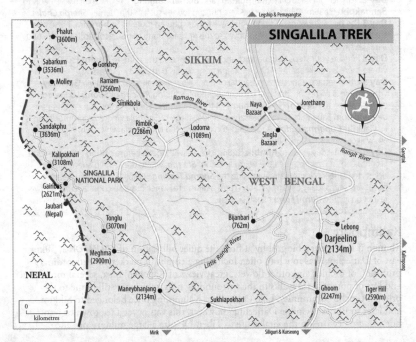

SINGALILA TREK: THE MANEYBHANJANG–PHALUT TRAIL

The single ridge of the **Singalila Range** rises near Darjeeling and extends all the way to the summit of Kanchenjunga. Unfortunately, although some longer trails have been opened in Sikkim (see page 832), there is currently no provision to link them to the initial lower sections of the ridge to **Sandakphu** (3636m) and **Phalut** (3600m) in Darjeeling District.

Easily accessible from Darjeeling, the later stages of the Maneybhanjang–Phalut trail provide magnificent views of the higher ranges; lightweight expeditions are possible as there are trekking huts and lodges (₹150–1000) and simple food stalls along the way. The walking is demanding and you should bring your own sleeping bag and warm clothes as the weather can be unpredictable.

Maneybhanjang, a small town and roadhead 27km from Darjeeling, is the usual starting point for the route, with the finest views found along the **Sandakphu–Phalut** section of the trail while trekking north. You will need to get an **entry fee** from the Forestry Department (₹300 [₹100]) to enter the **Singalila National Park**, and regulation states that you have to take a **guide** (around ₹1200/day) – available through the Highlander Guides and Porters Welfare Association (☎97340 56944, ⦿highlanderguidesandporters.com). Take an early shared jeep to Maneybhangjang from Chowk Bazaar in Darjeeling to start the trek the same day.

Several organizations arrange porters, from ₹900/day as well as **guides**, from ₹1200 (more for an English-speaking guide), as part of all-inclusive packages (from ₹2000/day); most will also **rent out equipment**. The **best time** to trek is after the monsoon (Oct & Nov), and during spring (Feb–May). It gets hot at the end of April and into May, but this is an especially beautiful season, with the rhododendrons in bloom. Several permutations are possible, including a trek to the Sikkim border at Jorethang.

THE CLASSIC ROUTE

Day 1 Start from Maneybhanjang with a sharp climb to **Meghma**; the trail eases to the hut at **Tonglu** (3070m). One variation bypasses Tonglu to Tumling where there are lodges, including the *Shikar Lodge*, but most strong walkers should be able to press on to Gairibas, or to Kalipokhari where there are a couple of lodges including *Sherpa*.

Day 2 From Tonglu head on to **Kalipokhari** and **Bikhebhanjang**. The trail then rises steeply to **Sandakphu** (3636m), which has a trekkers' hut and lodges such as the friendly *Sherpa Chalet*.

Day 3 The panorama opens out as you leave Sandakphu en route to **Sabarkum**. There's no shelter or food here, but if you drop down to the right for thirty minutes to **Molley**, you'll find a trekkers' hut.

Day 4 Retrace your steps to Sabarkum and continue along the ridge to **Phalut** (3600m), where there is a trekkers' hut. The panorama from here is particularly impressive.

Day 5 Either retrace your steps to Sandakphu or follow the trail from Phalut via **Gorkhey**, where there is plenty of choice of accommodation including *Pasang* or *Shanti Lodge*. You could walk on to **Ramam** (2560m), home of the welcoming *Sherpa* hotel, among others, or descend from Sabarkum to the pleasant riverside village of Sirikhola where accommodation is available at *Goparma Lodge*. A road is being constructed to Sirikhola which when open will allow access back to Darjeeling.

Day 6 The final day leads to **Rimbik** (2286m); check with locals before setting off as the route is confusing. In Rimbik there's the warm and cosy *Sherpa*, where they'll help arrange bus tickets to Darjeeling; alternatives include the *Sherpa Tenzing*. Rimbik is a roadhead served by buses and jeeps (daily 6–7am & noon–1pm) heading to Darjeeling; you could also set off by taxi or on foot to *Karmi Farm* near Bijanbari.

Kalimpong

Though it may seem a bit grubby at first, the quiet hill station of **KALIMPONG**, 50km east of Darjeeling, has much to offer, including a colourful market, an extraordinary profusion of orchids and other flowers, great views of Kanchenjunga, several monasteries and lots of potential for walks in the surrounding hills, which are still home to the original **Lepcha** community. Like Darjeeling, Kalimpong once belonged to Sikkim, and later to Bhutan. Unlike Darjeeling, however, this was never a tea town or resort but a trading centre on the vital route to Tibet. Despite a large military presence,

Kalimpong's recent history has been one of neglect, decaying infrastructure and water shortage. A deep-rooted dissatisfaction has simmered for several years, spearheaded by the Gurkhaland movement (something documented in Kiran Desai's excellent Booker Prize-nominated novel *The Inheritance of Loss*; see page 1222), but political uncertainties and wildcat strikes have not detracted from Kalimpong's charm. The 2011 **earthquake** (see page 830) devastated parts of the town, but today its quiet leafy avenues offer a breath of fresh air after the razzmatazz of Darjeeling.

Tenth Mile

Market area

Kalimpong spreads along a curving ridge to either side of its main market area, known as **Tenth Mile**. Though there are few of the curio and tourist emporia so abundant in Darjeeling, there are plenty of places selling Buddhist handicrafts and religious paraphernalia, which attract wholesale buyers from all over India. Silk brocade, Tibetan incense, made-to-order monks' attire and silver bowls predominate.

Rinkingpong Hill

4km southwest of town

Rinkingpong Hill, also known as **Durpin Dara**, looms above Kalimpong and is best visited at dawn. At its highest point, **Zong Dog Palri Phodrang Gompa**, also known as Durpin ("telescope") Monastery, built in 1957 to house three copper statues brought from Tibet in the 1940s, was modelled on Guru Rinpoche's mythical "pure realm" palace and consecrated by the Dalai Lama. Despite the communication masts and the army campus next door, the *gompa*'s roof is a great place to take in the sunrise accompanied by the chanting of the monks below; you are welcome to sit in for the prayers.

The wooded roads leading up Rinkingpong Hill hide several interesting old manor houses. **Morgan House** was built for a British jute merchant but now serves as a tourist lodge, where tea on the lawn captures the atmosphere of the period; the views are stunning.

St Teresa's Church

2km above town

St Teresa's Church was built in 1929 by a Swiss missionary and borrows heavily from vernacular Buddhist monastic

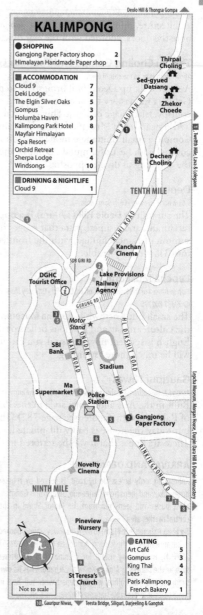

KALIMPONG

Deolo Hill & Thongsa Gompa

● SHOPPING
Gangjong Paper Factory shop — 2
Himalayan Handmade Paper shop — 1

■ ACCOMMODATION
Cloud 9 — 7
Deki Lodge — 2
The Elgin Silver Oaks — 5
Gompus — 3
Holumba Haven — 9
Kalimpong Park Hotel — 8
Mayfair Himalayan
 Spa Resort — 6
Orchid Retreat — 1
Sherpa Lodge — 4
Windsongs — 10

■ DRINKING & NIGHTLIFE
Cloud 9 — 1

Thirpai Choling
Sed-gyued Datsang
Zhekor Choede
Dechen Choling

TENTH MILE

Twelfth Mile, Lava & Lolegaon

RISHI ROAD
K D PRADHAN RD
Kanchan Cinema
SDB GIRI RD
Lake Provisions
DGHC Tourist Office
Railway Agency
GURUNG RD
Motor Stand
SBI Bank
OGDEN RD
MAIN ROAD
H L DIKSHIT ROAD
PRINTAN RD
Stadium
Ma Supermarket
Police Station
Gangjong Paper Factory
RINKINGPONG RD
Novelty Cinema
NINTH MILE
Lepcha Museum, Morgan House, Durpin Dara Hill & Durpin Monastery
Pineview Nursery
N
St Teresa's Church
Not to scale

● EATING
Art Café — 5
Gompus — 3
King Thai — 4
Lees — 2
Paris Kalimpong
French Bakery — 1

Gauripur Niwas, Teesta Bridge, Siliguri, Darjeeling & Gangtok

13

> ### HORTICULTURE
>
> Kalimpong is renowned for its **horticulture**, especially its orchids, cacti, amaryllis, palms and ferns. There are around fifty nurseries, such as **Pineview** on Atisha Road (Mon–Sat 9am–5pm; ₹10), which specializes in exotic cacti. Although Kalimpong blossoms all year long, the **best time** to see orchids in bloom is between mid-April and mid-May, when a **flower festival** is usually held.

architecture, mimicking a Bhutanese *gompa*. There's beautiful carving inside and out: note the doors, adorned with the eight sacred Buddhist symbols.

Thirpai Choling Gompa and Thongsa Gompa
Above Tenth Mile, to the east of town

A short walk up Deolo Hill brings you to the **Thirpai Choling Gompa**, a breakaway Gelugpa monastery founded in 1892 and recently renovated, which once venerated the controversial image of Dorje Shugden, a deity proscribed by the Dalai Lama.

Also near Tenth Mile and below the main road, the meditation halls of **Thongsa Gompa**, a small Bhutanese monastery founded in 1692, completely renovated, are covered with beautiful murals. Some of these are sexually explicit, depicting *yabyum*, the coupling of divine opposites.

Deolo Hill
9.5km north of town • Daily 9am–6pm

The summit of **Deolo Hill** (1704m) is a popular picnic spot, with a lodge and restaurant, and a superb vista that ranges from the steamy Teesta Valley far below to the summit of Kanchenjunga, with the frontier ridge and the passes of Nathula and Jelepla into Tibet clearly visible.

Lepcha Museum
1km southeast of the town centre, off HC Dixit Rd • Officially Mon–Fri 10.30am–4.30pm, though opening hours are a little erratic • Free • ☎ 99337 802295

The small but worthwhile **Lepcha Museum** has a collection of exhibits that illuminate the culture, music and religious beliefs of the Lepcha indigenous community. Little English is spoken, however, so if you can find someone to interpret for you, the visit will be much more rewarding.

Gauripur Niwas
Around 2km southwest of the town centre, en route to the army golf course

Built in the Arts and Crafts style in the 1930s, **Gauripur Niwas** was a summer residence of Rabindranath Tagore (see page 782). The Nobel Laureate wrote several poems here, but today the house is badly dilapidated, partly as a result of the 2011 earthquake. There are hopes that it will be restored in the not too distant future.

ARRIVAL AND DEPARTURE   KALIMPONG

Kalimpong, only accessible by road, is served by regular buses, taxis and jeeps from Darjeeling, Siliguri and Gangtok. Most buses and jeeps run from the Motor Stand in the central market area.

By jeep A shared jeep (1pm) to the NJP railway station, booked in advance through the Railway Agency on Rishi Rd (☎ 03552 259954), is especially useful for evening train departures such as the *Darjeeling Mail* to Kolkata. Each route has its own syndicate and ticket office; vehicles depart when full. Bear in mind that the last reliable transport links are mid-afternoon.

Destinations Darjeeling (2hr 30min–4hr); Gangtok (3hr); Siliguri (2hr 30min). Other destinations include NJP, Lava, Kakarbitta (Nepal border), Pelling and Ghezing.

By taxi Himalayan Travellers (☎ 94341 66498) is good for reserved taxis and the Motor Transport Syndicate (☎ 99327 66064) runs services to Darjeeling (7am–3pm).

By bus Although slower than jeeps, buses to Siliguri are generally more comfortable; similarly, the bus to Gangtok is worth considering, rather than a shared jeep (around 7am; 3–4hr).

INFORMATION AND TOURS

Tourist information The erratically staffed GTA tourist office, just off Damber Chowkh (daily 9.30am–5pm; ☎ 03552 257992), provides general information. A better bet is the helpful Travel Help Desk at *Sherpa Lodge* (see page 804; ☎ 89720 29913).

Tour operators Gurudongma Tours and Treks (☎ 03552 255204, ⊛ astonishingindiatours.com) specializes in ornithological, culinary, birdwatching, rafting and trekking trips and has its own farmhouse (see box). Travel Help Desk organizes village tours, local walks, trips to the Neora Valley and mountain-bike tours.

Mondo Challenge, an educational charity that welcomes volunteers, also runs one-, two- and three-day village treks (☎ 03552 255423, ⊛ mondochallenge.wix.com/kalimpong). Not for the faint-hearted, the Swedish-run Himalayan Eagle (*Himalayan Eagle Resort*, Lower Chibbo village, 3km outside Kalimpong; ☎ 9635 156911, ⊛ himalayaneagle.in) offers tandem paragliding flights from near Deolo. Its sister agency, Himalayan Bike Tours (⊛ himalayanbiketours.se), organizes motorbike tours of the region.

ACCOMMODATION

Cloud 9 Ringkingpong Rd ☎ 98320 39634, ⊛ cloudnine kalimpong.weebly.com; map p.801. This guesthouse, above the lively bar-restaurant of the same name, has five simple but well-kept rooms with grand views across the distant town. The real draw, however, is the welcoming owner Binodh, a great source of local knowledge. ₹1500

Deki Lodge Tirpai Rd ☎ 03552 255095, ⊛ dekilodge. yolasite.com; map p.801. A 10min walk from the Motor Stand, this clean and very friendly Tibetan-run hotel offers a wide choice of rooms, all of which have attached hot-water bathrooms. There's a small book exchange and laundry facilities. ₹1250

The Elgin Silver Oaks Ringkingpong Rd ☎ 03552 255296, ⊛ elginhotels.com; map p.801. One of the grandest addresses in Kalimpong, with a central location, spacious, classically decorated rooms, and a good restaurant. The garden is a pleasant setting for tea in the afternoon or something a little stronger in the evenings. Rates include full board. ₹10,400

Gompus Damber Chowk ☎ 72101 01502, ⊖ gompuskpg@gmail.com; map p.801. This popular place bang in the centre of town has been completely revamped into a smart, mid-range business hotel with large rooms all with TV and modern plumbing. It's spread across three floors above a popular restaurant-bar. ₹1800

★ **Holumba Haven** 8.5 Mile, near the Fire Station ☎ 03552 256936, ⊛ holumba.com; map p.801. Beautifully presented cottages set in a plant nursery resplendent with tree ferns and complete with a menagerie of birds. Some cottages come with their own kitchens, or you can have home-cooked meals (₹200–350) with the informative and extremely welcoming owners. This is essentially a homestay and so doesn't provide all the amenities of a hotel. ₹1000

Kalimpong Park Hotel Ringkingpong Rd ☎ 80164 80665, ⊛ kalimpongparkhotel.com; map p.801. This charming mid-range option, surrounded by gardens and located 1km uphill from the town centre, is based in a former maharaja's summer palace and retains many period

---

VILLAGE TOURISM AND HOMESTAYS

Offering the chance to explore the rural landscape and experience local culture, organized **village tourism** is becoming increasingly popular. The main operators include Gurudongma and Holumba in Kalimpong, Help Tourism (see page 769) in Siliguri, and Himalayan Footprints in Gangtok (see page 769).

Farm House and Wise Elephant Samthar Plateau, 80km from Kalimpong ☎ 94340 47372, ⊛ awake andshine.org. These homestays, run by Gurudongma, are in tranquil and rustic yet luxurious developments on the beautiful Samthar Plateau, an 80km drive from Kalimpong. The rate shown here is for full board. There are also a number of less expensive and luxurious homestays available in the region; visit the website for more details. ₹2500

Gurung Guest House Tinchuley Village, near Takdah ☎ 9733 326309, ⊛ tinchuley.com. Situated 28km from Kalimpong near Takdah, this well-run

guesthouse, with some delightful wood-lined rooms plus a modern block and a cottage, provides a comfortable retreat with a small tea and cardamom plantation and nature trails nearby. Full meal plan is ₹650/day. Doubles ₹2016, cottage ₹3540

Turuk Kothi Sikkim, 35km from Kalimpong ☎ 89673 89545, ⊛ turukkothiheritage.com. Across the border into Sikkim, 35km from Kalimpong, this grand manor house has six attractive cottages set in an idyllic plantation that dates back to the late nineteenth century. Rates are for full board. ₹6000

13

features. Rooms are comfortable and good value, and the lovely bar is an atmospheric spot for an evening drink. ₹3300

Mayfair Himalayan Spa Resort Upper Cart Rd ☏03552 255248, ⓦmayfairhotels.com/mayfair-kalimpong; map p.801. In a house once owned by explorer and author David Macdonald – who served on Sir Francis Younghusband's mission to Lhasa and helped the thirteenth Dalai Lama to escape from Tibet in 1910 – this historic hotel is full of Tibetan memorabilia and set amid exquisite, leafy gardens in an unspoilt spot above town. The modern cottages are luxurious but lack the ambience of the old house with its large wood-panelled rooms. ₹7500

Orchid Retreat 12 Mile ☏03552 274517, ⓦtheorchid retreat.com; map p.801. A family-run plant nursery that has been partly converted into a comfortable homestay; beyond the initial modern buildings the grounds drop steeply away into a lush garden decorated with tree ferns

and exotic flora, where a handful of wooden chalets built in vernacular style provide a quiet haven. Some 65 species of bird have been spotted here. ₹3000

Sherpa Lodge Ongden Rd ☏89720 29913; map p.801. In a convenient – if noisy and fume-filled – central location, this cheapie has reasonable budget rooms, though hot water is only provided via a bucket. The owner runs an information and travel desk on the ground floor. ₹80

★ **Windsongs** 8 Mile ☏03552 255387, ⓦwindsongs kalimpong.com; map p.801. A palm nursery and family home with a handful of comfortable attached rooms. However, the cottage (₹5500) in the manicured garden is the best spot here (and in town): from the bathtub you can gaze through the window at the most impressive view in the hills – from the Teesta to the top of Kanchenjunga (a distance of around 8000m). Doubles ₹4500, cottage ₹4500

EATING

Art Café Just off the main road ☏97495 48034, ⓦfacebook.com/artcafekalimpong; map p.801. Run by a fashion designer and florist, this hip café-boutique-plant-shop is a peaceful spot for a coffee (₹40–100), snack or light meal. It is located on the first floor of a shopping complex, surrounded by banks. Mon–Sat 10am–6pm.

Gompus Damber Chowk; map p.801. A popular restaurant and bar right in the centre of town, with a wide-ranging menu but best known for its Tibetan *momos* and *thukpa*; mains will set you back ₹110–220. Daily 8am–9pm.

King Thai Ma Supermarket, near the police station ☏87592 65948; map p.801. Despite the name, this restaurant-bar serves up reasonable Chinese and Indian food (mains ₹110–320), rather than Thai cuisine. In the evenings it doubles up as a bar; local bands occasionally

play, though it can get rowdy, and fights sometimes break out. The decor consists of an Americana mural, Beatles photos and classic film posters. Daily noon–9/10pm.

Lees Above Maya Liang, SBG Rd; map p.801. Authentic Chinese restaurant owned by and named after the chef. Try the steamed golden chicken or spare ribs; it's best to come for lunch as he closes early in the evenings. Expect to pay around ₹300. Daily noon–6pm.

★ **Paris Kalimpong French Bakery** SDB Giri Rd ☏80167 51311; map p.801. This French-run bakery and coffee shop is a very welcome surprise: delicious, authentic baguettes, croissants, pains au chocolat and quiches, as well as proper Lavazza coffee (₹40–100). It also provides work – as waiters – for local hearing-impaired youths. Daily 8am–6.30pm.

DRINKING AND NIGHTLIFE

In addition to *Cloud 9*, several of the restaurants and hotels have good bars, notably *Gompus* and the *Kalimpong Park Hotel* (see above). *King Thai* also doubles up as a bar.

Cloud 9 Ringkingpong Rd ☏98320 39634; map p.801. Below the guesthouse of the same name, this welcoming

bar-restaurant has occasional live music (the Beatles feature heavily) and a charming owner, Binodh. The food's good too: beyond the standard menu, the chef can – with notice – produce a special Bhutanese feast. Daily noon–10pm.

SHOPPING

Markets On Wednesdays and Saturdays, Tenth Mile gets very lively as villagers flock in from the surrounding areas for the principal weekly markets.

Traditional paper workshops The Gangjong Paper Factory (Mon–Sat 9am–4.30pm) welcomes visitors to its

handmade paper workshop down steps off Printam Rd; access to Himalayan Handmade Paper, on KD Pradhan Rd near Thirpai, is easier and it also has a shop. Mon–Sat 9am–5pm.

DIRECTORY

Hospital Adarsha Nursing Home, SD Giri Rd (☏89679 68474), is one of the best medical centres for emergencies.

Post office The main post office is near the town centre, above the bazaar area just behind the police station.

Around Kalimpong

Although the **Lepchas**, the original inhabitants of the area, have lost their traditional way of life in most parts of Darjeeling and Sikkim, their lifestyle has remained relatively untouched in the unspoilt forest-covered hills and deep river valleys to the south of Kalimpong.

Lava and Neora Valley National Park

35km east of Kalimpong • Daily Oct–May dawn–dusk • Travel agencies in Kalimpong can arrange guides and permits (₹200 [30]) as well as transport for a multiday trek through the sanctuary staying at remote forest resthouses; they can also advise on treks around Lava • The Forest Department (☎ 03561 24907), 1km above Lava on the Kalimpong road also manages permits

Lying on an old trade route to Bhutan, the small town of **Lava** (2184m) with a colourful Tuesday market, 35km from Kalimpong and accessible by shared jeep, makes an ideal base for exploring the nature trails of **Neora Valley National Park**. An 88-square-kilometre reserve stretching along a narrow river valley, with a huge variation in wildlife and abundant orchids and birds, the park has been designated a tiger reserve but sightings are extremely rare. As well as black bear and red panda Neora Valley is home to packs of wild dogs.

Lava is also convenient for approaching the **Rachela Pass** (3152m) on the Sikkim–Bhutan border, which provides excellent views of the Chola Range including Chomalhari (7314m), the sacred mountain of Bhutan.

Walking around Lava

Pleasant **trails** lead west from Lava towards **Budhabare**, a market town in the Git River Valley, which has a sprinkling of Lepcha, Gurkha and Bhutia villages. The track continues through forest to **Kafer Lolegaon** where the sunrise is legendary and there is a Heritage Forest walk along a canopy trail. You can get here via a rough road from Kalimpong, but if you're fit, you could walk the trail that crosses the Relli River near the village of the same name and climbs directly to Kalimpong. Alternatively, you could **cycle** through the area – ask at the Travel Help Desk in Kalimpong (see page 803) for routes.

ARRIVAL AND DEPARTURE

LAVA AND NEORA VALLEY NATIONAL PARK

By jeep or bus The crossroads at the centre of Lava serves as a shared taxi stand with regular connections to Kalimpong and also to Siliguri; buses make the same journey. The turn-off to Kafer Lolegaon is 5km away on the Kalimpong road. There is less transport on this route and so

it is best to travel early. Jeeps from Lava to the gate of Neora Valley NP (15km) charge the earth (around ₹3000–3500). **Into the park** The road into the park is too rutted to take ordinary vehicles. If you're driving, leave the vehicle by the park gates where there is a café and the checkpost to register your permit. Access into the park is on foot.

ACCOMMODATION AND EATING

Lava has limited **accommodation** within the town but the surrounding area offers a choice from forest bungalows to places with a bit more luxury. Further afield, Lolegaon has a handful of hotels to choose from. There are a few basic **restaurants** around the taxi stand in the centre.
Forest Rest House Lava ☎ 03552 255780, ⑩ wbfdc. com. On the edge of town and a short drive off the main Kalimpong road, this state-run lodge is a pleasant and quiet place to stay. Booking can be a pain: it is theoretically possible online, though often easier if you book in at the tourist office in Siliguri (see page 788), the WBFDC office in Kalimpong (off Rinkingpong Rd) or the West Bengal tourist office in Kolkata (see page 768). No wi-fi. ₹1100

Neora Valley Jungle Camp Kolakham, Lava ☎ 0353 253 5896, ⑩ helptourism.net. The most luxurious accommodation in the vicinity of the park, and run by experienced wildlife experts, this is hardly a camp but rather a collection of tasteful stone and wood cottages with expansive views of Sikkim. Transport there from Lava is extra. ₹5500
Paradise Lava Bazaar, Lava ☎ 9932 889565, ⑩ paradise groupofhotels.net/lava/. One of Lava's better hotels, with partially wood-panelled rooms with TV and attached bathrooms (and hot water when electricity allows); there is also a decent restaurant. The owners also have a similarly priced branch at Rishyap, a pleasant 4km walk away through the woods. ₹1100

Bihar and Jharkhand

BUDDHIST MONKS VISIT THE MAHABODHI TEMPLE

Bihar and Jharkhand

Bihar occupies the flat eastern Ganges basin, south of Nepal, between
Uttar Pradesh and West Bengal. To its south, Jharkhand, occupying the
hilly Chotanagpur plateau north of Odisha, was hewn out of Bihar in 2000,
following agitation by its tribal majority. Both states are beset by poverty, lack
of infrastructure, inter-caste violence, corruption and general lawlessness.

14

Although visitors are usually unaffected by the banditry and guerrilla war, tourists and
Buddhist pilgrims have on occasion been robbed and few travellers spend much time
here, which is a shame, because the region offers a fascinating mix of **religious history**.
The **safety situation** has improved significantly, but check with your government's
foreign ministry and the local press (⊕patnadaily.com and ⊕bihartimes.in are good
sources of information) before travel; local state and tourist authorities tend to
downplay safety concerns.

Patna

PATNA, Bihar's capital, dates back to the sixth century BC, but shows few signs today
of its former glory as the centre of the Magadhan and Mauryan empires. A sprawling
metropolis hugging the south bank of the Ganges, Patna stretches for around 15km in
a shape that has changed little since Ajatasatru (491–459 BC) shifted the Magadhan
capital here from Rajgir. The first Mauryan emperor, **Chandragupta**, established himself
in what was then **Pataliputra** in 321 BC, and pushed the limits of his empire as far
as the Indus; his grandson **Ashoka** (274–237 BC), one of India's greatest rulers, held
sway over even greater domains. To facilitate Indo-Hellenic trade, the Mauryans built
a Royal Highway from Pataliputra to Taxila, Pakistan, which later became the Grand
Trunk Road. The city experienced two revivals, first when the first Gupta emperor,
Chandra Gupta, made it his capital early in the fourth century AD, and then again
when it was rebuilt in the sixteenth century by Afghan ruler Sher Shah Suri.

Buddha Smirti Park

Fraser Rd • Tues–Sun 9am–7pm • Park ₹10; Pat Kaman Stupa ₹50; museum ₹40; meditation centre free

Slap-bang in the middle of town, the 22-acre **Buddha Smirti Park** stands on the site
once occupied by Bankipur Central Jail. The park was inaugurated by the Dalai Lama
in 2010, and its trees include saplings taken from the Bodhi tree in Bodhgaya. The
big **stupa** in the middle houses an urn supposedly containing ashes from the body of
Buddha himself, which were unearthed at Vasihali. This being a Buddhist site, there's
also a **meditation centre**, and a **museum** illustrating the life of Buddha and the history
of Buddhism.

BEST TIME TO VISIT

The monsoon hits Bihar and Jharkhand in early June, lasting until September, and the very
best time to visit is immediately after that, in October and November. November is also the
time of the Sonepur Mela (see page 815). Bihar and Jharkhand can get quite chilly from
December through February, especially at night, although daytime temperatures remain
comfortable. From March, temperatures start to rise and the heat then gets progressively
stickier and more debilitating until the monsoon breaks it.

A MAHOUT WASHES AN ELEPHANT DURING SONEPUR MELA

Highlights

❶ Sonepur Mela This month-long festival and cattle fair is a spectacular gathering of pilgrims, sadhus and animals. See page 815

❷ The Mahabodhi Temple A cutting from the tree under which the Buddha attained enlightenment is the focal point of Bodhgaya's renowned temple, which really does have an air of calm, meditative holiness about it. See page 817

❸ Mahakala Caves Climb a path to see the caves where Buddha underwent years of bodily mortification before realizing that this was not the true path to enlightenment. See page 819

❹ Rajgir A dusty Buddhist pilgrimage town filled with shrines, as well as therapeutic hot springs, and a chairlift to take you up to the Peace Pagoda on a hill. See page 821

❺ Nalanda The site of a fifteen-hundred-year-old university, from the days when Buddhism dominated India, strewn with the remains of ancient *stupas* and monasteries. See page 821

HIGHLIGHTS ARE MARKED ON THE MAP ON PAGE 810

Golghar

Danapur–Banikpur Rd • Tues–Sun 10am–5.30pm • Laser show: Fri, Sat & Sun 7.15pm; ₹30

Patna's most notable monument is the **Golghar**, also called "the round house", a huge colonial-era grain store built in 1786 to avoid a repetition of 1770's terrible famine; thankfully, it never needed to be used. Overlooking the river and Gandhi Maidan, its two sets of stairs spiralling up to the summit were designed so indentured workers could carry grain up one side, deliver their load through a hole at the top, and descend down the other. Sightseers now clamber up for mighty views of the river and the city. On Friday, Saturday and Sunday nights, there's a sound-and-light laser show illustrating the history of Bihar and the Golghar.

BIHAR & JHARKHAND

HIGHLIGHTS

1. Sonepur Mela
2. The Mahabodhi Temple
3. Mahakala Caves
4. Rajgir
5. Nalanda

The International boundaries on this map are neither purported to be correct nor authentic by Survey of India directives. Publisher.

FESTIVALS IN BIHAR AND JHARKHAND

Makar Sankranti Mela (mid-Jan). Pilgrims from across India gather in Rajgir to bathe in the hot springs and herald the coming of spring.

Sarhul (March). Popular village celebration among the *Adivasi* peoples of Jharkhand, welcoming the new blossom on the sal trees with music and dancing.

Pataliputra Mahotsava (March). Patna celebrates its illustrious history with music, dancing and public events.

Chatth Puja (March/April and Oct/Nov). An ancient festival dedicated to the Vedic sun god Surya, celebrated twice a year.

Patna Sahib Mahotsav (May). Annual cultural festival put on by Bihar Tourism around Patna's Harimandir Sahib.

Rajgir Mahotsav (Nov). Three-day festival of dance and music in Rajgir.

Sonepur Mela (Nov/Dec). Huge annual sadhu gathering at the confluence of the Gandak and the Ganges at Sonepur.

Gandhi Museum

Ashok Rajpath, just northwest of Gandhi Maidan • Daily except Sat 10am–6pm • Free • ⟨w⟩ gandhisangrahalaypatna.org

Patna's **Gandhi Museum** is really more like a book in museum format, consisting largely of text and photos illustrating, in one room, the Mahatma's life, and in another, the history of the Independence movement in Bihar. One or two of Gandhi's personal effects are also on display, but are labelled in Hindi only.

Patna Museum

Buddha Marg • Tues–Sun 10.30am–4.30pm • ₹250 (₹50), phone ₹20, camera ₹100, video camera ₹500

The **Patna Museum** (Jadu Ghar), although faded and run down, has an excellent collection of sculptures. Among its most famous exhibits is a polished sandstone female attendant, or *yakshi*, holding a fly-whisk, dating back to the third century BC. There are also Jain images from the Kushana period, a group of Buddhist *bodhisattvas* from Gandhara (in northwest Pakistan), some freakishly deformed stuffed animals and a gigantic fossilized tree thought to be two hundred million years old.

Harimandir Sahib

Harimandir Gali (off Ashok Rajpath), Haji Ganj

In Haji Ganj, an old part of town 10km east of Gandhi Maidan, congested lanes lead to **Harimandir Sahib**, the second holiest of the four great Sikh shrines known as *takhts* (thrones). Set in an expansive courtyard off the main road, the dazzling white onion-domed marble temple is dedicated to Guru Gobind Singh, born in Patna in 1660. Visitors can explore the courtyard and even venture inside where devotional music is often playing. Remove your shoes and cover your head before entering. Shared auto-rickshaws cost ₹15 from Gandhi Maidan Bus Stand.

Qila House

Jalan Ave • Visits by appointment only (visiting times Mon–Sat 9–11am, Sun 10am–4pm; call or email 48hr ahead on ☎ 0612 222 5070 or ✉ visit@jalanmuseum.com) • ⟨w⟩ quilahouse.com

A short way northeast of Harimandir Sahib, the private **Qila House** (or Jalan Museum) holds a fine collection of art, including Chinese paintings and Mughal filigree work in jade and silver. Among the antiques are porcelain items that once belonged to Marie Antoinette, and Napoleon's four-poster bed.

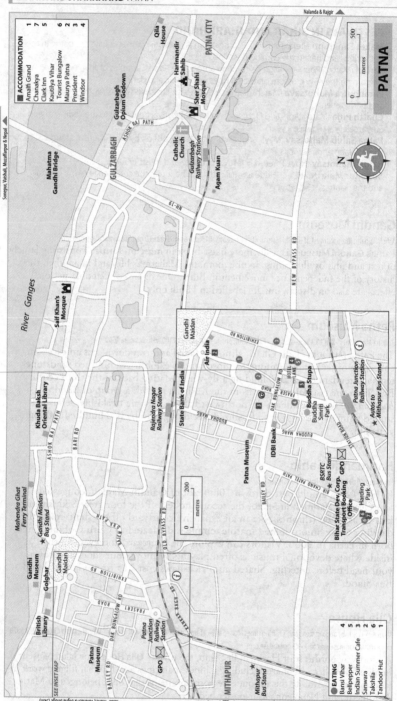

PATNA

ACCOMMODATION
Amalfi Grand 1
Chanakya 7
Clark Inn 5
Kautilya Vihar 6
Tourist Bungalow 2
Maurya Patna 3
President
Windsor 4

EATING
Bansi Vihar 4
Bellpepper 5
Indian Summer Cafe 3
Sanwara 2
Takshila 6
Tandoor Hut 1

Saif Khan's Mosque

Midway between Harimandir Sahib and Gandhi Maidan stands **Saif Khan's Mosque**, also called "the mosque of stone". That is indeed what it is made from, but the stone is hidden behind layers of whitewash, with pretty green highlights. The mosque was commissioned in 1621 by the son of the Mughal emperor Jahangir, Parwez Shah, who was governor of Bihar at the time (although it doesn't actually look very Mughal).

ARRIVAL AND DEPARTURE

By plane Patna's airport is 5km west of town (around ₹275 by taxi, ₹100 by auto). Flights serve Delhi (10 daily with Air India, IndiGo and Go Air), Kolkata (5 daily with Go Air and IndiGo), Ranchi (3 daily with Go Air and IndiGo) and Lucknow (2 daily with IndiGo).

By train All mainline train services arrive either at Patliputra or at Patna Junction station, 10km apart, both set in the west of the city. Patna Junction is the most important railway station in the region, and has a foreigners' reservation window (No. 7) on the upper floor of the booking office. The best train to Kolkata (Howrah) is the a/c *Janshatabdi Express* #12024 (Mon–Sat; dep. 5.45am, arr. 1.25pm); overnight services include the *Vibhuti Express* #12334 (daily; dep. 10.35pm, arr. 7.30am). For destinations beyond Kolkata, the *Northeast Express* #12506 leaves Patna at 10.20pm daily, reaching New Jalpaiguri (for Darjeeling) at 8.20am and Guwahati at 4.50pm. In the other direction, to Varanasi, the *Shramjeevi Express* #12391 (daily; dep. 10.50am, arr. just after 3pm) is a good option. The *Rajdhani Express* #12309 at 7.25pm (arr. 7.40am next day) and the *Sampark Kranti Express* #12393 at 6pm (arr. 8.35am next day) are the pick of several daily trains to New Delhi.

LALU AND THE CASTE WARS: POLITICS IN BIHAR

For years, Bihar languished at the bottom of almost every measure of development, from literacy rates to GDP. Author William Dalrymple described it as, "the most ungovernable and anarchic state in India", even though it is blessed with ample coal and iron deposits and large tracts of arable land. The problem was caused by a disastrous combination of virulent inter-caste conflict and criminal misgovernance.

After Indian Independence, Bihar was ruled by a mafia of high-caste landowners, with the lower castes – who together with the *dalits* and tribal people make up more than seventy percent of the state's population – marginalized to the point of persecution. All that seemed set to change in 1991 when a rabble-rouser from a lowly caste of buffalo milkers, **Lalu Prasad Yadav**, united the "backward castes", the Muslims and the *dalits* under a banner of social justice, winning that year's state election by a landslide. In power, Lalu delighted with his common touch; he spontaneously unclogged traffic congestion in Patna by walking the streets with a megaphone and filled the grounds of his official residence with buffalo.

Unfortunately Lalu proved little better than his predecessors. His cabinet of caste brethren included men wanted for murder and kidnapping, and violence remained the main tool of political persuasion – as one election candidate said: "Without one hundred men with guns you cannot contest an election in Bihar." Much of the state degenerated into virtual civil war as the upper castes, lower castes, Maoist (Naxalite) guerrillas, police and private armies clashed violently.

Lalu's career appeared to be over in 1997, when he was imprisoned for a short spell for embezzling billions of rupees. He responded by getting his illiterate wife **Rabri Devi** proclaimed chief minister. Even though his RJD party was toppled in the 2005 state elections, Lalu went on to serve as minister for railways from 2004 to 2009.

At state level, however, things changed. In 2005 a Janata Dal (U)–BJP coalition under Lalu's chief opponent Nitish Kumar took power, and the situation began to improve, with less obvious domination by organized crime.

Nitish held power for ten years, during which things did improve in the state (literacy went up and unemployment down, for example), with Lalu his main opponent. But in the 2014 Lok Sabha election the BJP swept the board and it looked like the 2015 state elections would herald the end of Nitish's rule. He subsequently joined together with Lalu and the local Congress Party, and divvied up the state assembly seats in an anti-BJP block, so that each candidate had a straight run against the BJP. Thus united, Nitish and Lalu swept jointly into power, giving the BJP its first major electoral setback since the 2014 general election, and beginning a new chapter in Bihar's chequered political history.

14

For Mumbai, the *Rajendra Nagar* #12142 leaves daily at 11.10am, arriving at 3.30pm the next day. Seven daily trains cover the 2–3hr journey to Gaya, of which the fastest is the 6am *Janshatabdi* #12365 (arr. 7.55am), which continues on to Ranchi (arr. 1.55pm). Only one inconvenient weekly train links Patna directly with Puri, and no trains arrive in Gaya at a convenient time for the daily *Purshottam Express* #12802 (which leaves Gaya at 1.30pm, arriving in Puri at 5.25am), so take a bus to Gaya for that, or change at Howrah instead.

By bus For all destinations it's wise to stick to daytime services. State-run buses to Sonepur, Muner and Hajipur (for Vaishali) use the Gandhi Maidan Bus Stand. Private buses leave from the chaotic Mithapur Bus Stand, 2km south of the railway station (shared autos connect the two), where there is no enquiry office or departure board, and you'll have to depend on touts to guide you to a bus. For Nalanda and Rajgir, you usually have to change at Bihar Sharif. Private companies offer bus tickets to Kathmandu with a voucher for the bus across the border, but it's better to make your own way to Raxaul (see page 816), cross the border, and find a bus on the Nepali side. The best services to Raxaul and Ranchi are the twice daily a/c buses run by Bihar State Roadways (BSRTC) from their stand in Bir Chand Patel Path (📞0612 250 6099, 🌐gauravluxury.com). They also offer handy tours to Nalanda and Rajgir leaving at 7am and returning at 8pm (₹750).

INFORMATION

Tourist information The Bihar State Tourism Development Corporation is at *Kautilya Vihar Tourist Bungalow* (Mon–Sat 10am–5pm; 📞0612 222 5411, 🌐bstdc.bih.nic.in), with a booth at Patna Junction (supposedly daily 8am–8pm, but often closed; 📞0612 222 2622). Bihar Tourism can arrange tours and car rental. India Tourism are in the Institution of Engineers Building, near R-Block roundabout, Hardinge Rd (📞0612 657 0640, ✉itopat@gmail.com).

Internet Internet Point, G-6, ground floor, Hem Plaza, Fraser Rd (Mon–Sat 10am–10.30pm, Sun noon–6pm; ₹20/hr); Windsornet at the *Windsor* hotel (daily 7am–9.30pm; ₹50/hr).

ACCOMMODATION

Amalfi Grand Opp Pillar No. 4, Bailey Road Behind SBI 📞612 259 1001, 🌐amalfigrand.com; map p.812. One of Patna's newest 4-star hotels has well-appointed rooms clad in wood, with facilities including a meeting room and a restaurant. It's not far from the airport and Patliputra Junction. Breakfast included. ₹2200

Chanakya Bir Chand Patel Path 📞0612 222 0590, 🌐hotelchanakyapatna.com; map p.812. This looming hotel has tastefully furnished beige- and apricot-coloured attached rooms. There's also a currency exchange and two good restaurants, one serving Indian and Chinese, and *Takshila*, serving Mughal and Afghan dishes. Breakfast included. ₹7000

Clark Inn Jamal Rd 📞0612 309 2107, ✉clarkinn@gmail.com; map p.812. Best of the cheapies near the station; looks quite grand from the outside and the rooms are quite a reasonable size, with attached bathrooms and hot water. ₹800

Kautilya Vihar Tourist Bungalow Bir Chand Patel Path 📞0612 222 5411, 🌐bstdc.bih.nic.in; map p.812. The Bihar State Tourism Development Corporation's rambling hotel has grimy corridors but large double rooms, if rather bare, and a relaxed rooftop restaurant. Avoid the grotty dorms (₹200) unless you are really broke. ₹1600

Maurya Patna Fraser Rd, South Gandhi Maidan 📞0612 220 3040, 🌐maurya.com; map p.812. Service can be impersonal at this five-star, but the luxurious rooms – decorated in a range of styles, from colonial to oriental – swimming pool and fine restaurants tend to make up for it. ₹16,000

President Off Fraser Rd 📞0612 220 9203, 🌐hotelpresidentpatna.com; map p.812. Its decor may not have been updated since the 1970s, but *President* remains a good option. Although the rooms are a little stuffy, they're clean and quite a decent size, and the management is also a good source of transport information. ₹1700

Windsor Exhibition Rd 📞0612 220 3250, 🌐hotelwindsorpatna.com; map p.812. A reassuringly well-run mid-range hotel, good value, with nicely furnished, modern attached rooms, an internet café and the excellent *Bellpepper* restaurant (see below). ₹3200

EATING

There are several decent **restaurants** strung along Fraser Rd. Keep an eye out for *littis* – baked balls of spiced chickpea dough – a Bihari speciality sold by street vendors. Alcohol was banned in Bihar in April 2016.

Bansi Vihar Fraser Rd 📞0612 222 4804; map p.812. A low-ceilinged, dimly lit dining hall packed with locals, who come to sample tasty south Indian snacks, primarily dosas, of which there are 23 varieties (₹80–165), as well as *uttapams* and the odd Chinese dish. Daily 8am–10.30pm.

★ **Bellpepper** Hotel Windsor, Exhibition Rd 📞0612 220 3250; map p.812. A cosy and intimate little place serving excellent tandoori dishes such as chicken *malai tikka* (₹285) and kebabs such as chicken *seekh* kebab (₹290). Daily 7.30–10am, 12.30–3.30pm & 7.30–10.30pm.

Indian Summer Café Satya Narain Building, Exhibition Rd 📞74886 02318, 🌐indiansummercafe.com; map p.812. A modern diner, with its own bakery, serving Western, Chinese and Indian dishes — with yummy fusions like *butter chicken phulka tacos* (₹295) — trendily-decorated with exposed brick walls and naked bulbs. Their locally-produced lychee honey makes for a great souvenir. Daily 11am–11pm.

Sanwara Om Complex, S.P. Verma Rd ☎ 93041 16049; map p.812. Vegetarian Indian plus the obligatory Chinese dishes in a modern, clean restaurant with cloths on the tables. Tasty offerings include *malai kofta* for ₹185 or *paneer pasanda* for ₹230. Daily 11am–10.30pm.

Takshila Hotel Chanakya, Bir Chand Patel Path ☎ 0612 222 0590; map p.812. A top-notch restaurant specializing in Mughlai and Afghan meat dishes, with kebabs, Peshwari-style tandoori chicken (₹535 for half a bird), and in the evenings, set menus at ₹725 veg, or ₹825 non-veg. Daily 12.30–3.30pm & 7.30–11pm.

Tandoor Hut BSFC Building, Fraser Rd ☎ 93868 51333; map p.812. Popular takeaway restaurant with a full range of veg and non-veg curries and Chinese dishes. They do meal boxes (effectively, thalis in a box) at ₹170 veg ₹190 non-veg, or ₹150/₹170 for Chinese, and they deliver orders over ₹300. Daily 11am–11pm.

Around Patna

Patna is a good base for exploring Nalanda, Rajgir and **Vaishali**, and **Sonepur**, north of Patna, is worth visiting for its *mela*, usually held in November.

Vaishali

Set amid paddy fields 55km north of Patna, the quiet village of **VAISHALI** was the site of the Buddha's last sermon. Named after King Visala, who is mentioned in the Ramayana, Vaishali is also believed by some historians to have been the first city-state in the world to practise a democratic, republican form of government. After leaving his family and renouncing the world, Prince Gautama (Buddha) studied here, but eventually rejected his master's teachings and found his own path to enlightenment. He returned to Vaishali three times and on his last visit announced his final liberation – *Mahaparinirvana* – and departure from the world, in around 483 BC. A hundred years later, the second Buddhist Council was held in Vaishali and two *stupas* erected.

A small but well-presented **archeological museum** (daily except Fri 9am–5pm; ₹10; ⓦ vaishalimuseum.org) provides a glimpse into the ancient Buddhist world. A short path next to the Coronation Tank (Abhishekh Pushkarni) leads off to the remains of the **stupa** where the ashes of the Buddha were reputedly found in a silver urn.

Two kilometres north among the ruins of **Kolhua** (daily sunrise–sunset; ₹100 [₹5]), the remarkably well-preserved **Ashokan Pillar** was erected by the Mauryan emperor (273–232 BC) to commemorate the site of Buddha's last sermon. Known locally as *Bhimsen-ki-lathi* (Bhimsen's Staff), the 18.3m-high pillar, made of polished red sandstone, is crowned by a lion sitting on an inverted lotus, which faces north towards Kushinagar, where Buddha died.

ARRIVAL AND DEPARTURE   **VAISHALI**

Most people take in Vaishali as a **day-trip** from Patna, and the best way to do that is to hire a taxi (Bihar Tourism can sort you one for around ₹2500). You could take a bus from Gandhi Maidan Bus Stand to Hajipur, then one to Lalganj

---

SONEPUR MELA

If you're in Bihar between early November and early December, don't miss the **Sonepur Mela**, staged 25km north of Patna, across the Gandhi Bridge, at the confluence of the Gandak and the Ganges. Cattle, elephants, camels, parakeets and other animals are brought for sale, pilgrims combine business with a dip in the Ganges, sadhus congregate, and festivities abound. The event is memorably described by Mark Shand in his quixotic *Travels on My Elephant* (see page 1221). The Bihar State Tourism Development Corporation in Patna (see page 814) organizes tours and maintains a tourist village at Sonepur during the *mela*.

14

and one from there to Vaishali, but that would take too long to do the round trip in one day, and buses back to Patna dry up early. There is no accommodation in Vaishali as such, but Hajipur has a handful of very simple hotels.

The road to Nepal

Some 55km north of Vaishali, **KESARIYA** (Kessaputta) has an impressive five-terraced eighth-century *stupa* said to have been built on top of another erected by the Buddha's Licchavi disciples after he announced he was to attain nirvana and gave them his begging bowl as a souvenir. To get to Kesariya, take a bus (3hr) from Vaishali to **Chakia**, 20km away, then a taxi or rickshaw to the site.

In 1917, **MOTIHARI**, a poor and lawless town 298km north of Patna, was the site of one of Gandhi's first acts of civil disobedience – he refused bail after being arrested for protesting the plight of local farmers, who were being forced to grow indigo for the British textile industry. There's a small **museum** with photos and items such as Gandhi's walking stick and slippers. Motihari was also the birthplace of **George Orwell**, whose father worked here as a government opium agent; the house where he was born is now a museum. For those wanting to stay, Motihari has *dharamshalas*.

Raxaul

The border crossing for **Nepal** is at **RAXAUL**, a grubby, mosquito-infested town with limited amenities. There's a mosque and a couple of temples and cinemas here, but you're much better off staying over the border in Birganj.

ARRIVAL AND ACCOMMODATION   RAXAUL

By train On Thursdays and Saturdays there's an over-night service, the *Raxaul–Howrah Express* (dep. 8.15pm, arr. 12.15pm). Otherwise, the *Mithila Express* #13022 leaves Raxaul for Howrah (Kolkata) at 10am daily, arriving at 4am. Coming the other way, it's more conveniently timed, leaving Howrah at 3.45pm to reach Raxaul at 8.30am. For Delhi, the *Satyagrah Express* #15273 leaves Raxaul daily at 9.05am, pulling into Old Delhi at 9.20am the next day.

By bus Gaurav (ⓦ gauravluxury.com) run an a/c bus from Ranchi via Gaya and Patna, where it can be picked up at the BSRTC bus stand (see page 814) at 6.05am, arriving at 12.20pm.

Crossing the border The border between Raxaul and the Nepalese town of Birganj, 5km away (₹50 by auto-

rickshaw), is open 6am to 10pm, but if you need to buy a Nepalese visa (US$25 for 15 days, US$40 for 30 days, US$100 for 90 days, payable in US dollars, plus two passport photos), you must arrive by 6pm. From Birganj bus park (1km east of town) there are frequent buses to Kathmandu (9hr), and less frequently to Pokhara (11hr), and jeeps to Kathmandu (6hr). Simara airport, north of Birganj, has flights to Kathmandu. The foreign exchange bureaux in Birganj will change Indian to Nepalese rupees or vice versa, and most will change US dollars to local currency.

Kaveri Main Rd ⓣ 06255 221148. If you do have to spend the night, this functional hotel is about the best Raxaul has to offer. ₹500

Gaya

GAYA, 100km south of Patna, is a transit point for visitors to **Bodhgaya**, 13km away. Gaya has no real tourist attractions but many Hindus come here to honour their parents a year after death by offering *pinda* – funeral cakes – at the massive **Vishnupad temple** (no entry to non-Hindus). Pilgrims also bathe at the riverside *ghats*. **Brahmajuni Hill**, 1km southeast of the Vishnupad temple, is said to be where Buddha preached his fire sermon.

ARRIVAL AND ACCOMMODATION   GAYA

By train Most people arrive by train. Auto-rickshaws will take you to Bodhgaya from the station (₹200, though you may find a shared one), or you can take a cycle rickshaw to Kacheri Bus Stand and continue to Bodhgaya by shared auto

14

MADHUBANI PAINTINGS

Jitwarpur, a village on the outskirts of the small town of **Madhubani**, in northern Bihar, is home to a vibrant tradition of folk art. Madhubani **paintings** by local women were originally decorations for the outside of village huts. Illustrating mythological themes – including images of local deities as well as Hindu gods and goddesses – the paintings were eventually transferred onto handmade paper, often using bright primary colours to fill the strong black line drawings. **Fabrics** printed with Madhubani designs have become very chic; these days they tend to be professionally made elsewhere, and are sold in the expensive boutiques of India's major cities, although you can still pick them up cheaply in Madhubani itself.

Buses connect Patna to Madhubani (5hr 30min), where there are some basic hotels; rickshaws can take you on to Jitwarpur.

(₹30). If you arrive after dark, stay overnight in Gaya as the route between the two can be unsafe.

Ajatsatru Station Rd (opposite the station) ⊙ 0631 222 2961, ⊚ ajatsatruhotel.com. The standard rooms are quite basic, although they have attached bathrooms with water heaters, and there are cleaner and more cheerful (but still overpriced) a/c rooms (₹1360). The downstairs restaurant has decent Indian and Chinese food (daily 7am–midnight;

veg biryani ₹90, chicken biryani ₹140). **₹700**

Akash Close by on Laxman Sahay Rd ⊙ 0631 222 2205. Simple rooms with attached bathrooms, but hot water comes in a bucket (free on request). The place looks like it's half-built, but it's been like that for some years. They have their own generator, so there's electricity even during Gaya's frequent power cuts, but no wi-fi. **₹600**

Bodhgaya and around

The world's most important Buddhist pilgrimage site, **BODHGAYA**, 13km south of Gaya, is wonderfully relaxed, with an array of monasteries, temples and retreats. Its focal point is the **Mahabodhi Temple**, where Buddha attained enlightenment.

The temple dates from the seventh century AD and flourished up to the sixteenth century, when it fell into the hands of Hindu priests, who professed to be baffled by its origins. In the early nineteenth century, British archeologists rediscovered its significance, and Bodhgaya has since been rejuvenated by overseas Buddhists, who have built monasteries, temples and shrines on the site. From November to February, Bodhgaya is home to an animated community of exiled **Tibetans**, often including the Dalai Lama, as well as a stream of international Tibetophiles. Meditation courses (see page 819) attract others, while large monasteries from places like Darjeeling bring their followers to attend ceremonies and lectures. From mid-March to mid-October, the region becomes oppressively hot and Bodhgaya returns to its quiet ways.

The Mahabodhi Temple is also sacred to Hindus, who regard Buddha as an incarnation of Vishnu, and dominate the management, despite protests from the Buddhist world. The dispute is exacerbated by the contrasting forms of worship: Buddhists have a solitary inward approach; Hindus prefer spectacle and noisy ceremony.

Mahabodhi Temple

Daily 5am–9pm • Camera ₹100, video camera ₹300–500 • Shoes, bags and phones must deposited at a cloakroom near the entrance

The elegant single spire of the **Mahabodhi Temple** rises to a lofty height of 55m, and is visible throughout the surrounding countryside. Within the temple complex, which is liberally sprinkled with small *stupas* and shrines, the main brick temple stands in a hollow encircled by a stone railing dating from the second century BC. Shoes are tolerated within the grounds but not inside the temple (so best leave them at the cloakroom before entering the site). Unlike most popular temples in India, this UNESCO World Heritage Site exudes an atmosphere of peace and tranquillity. Extensively renovated during the nineteenth century, it is supposed to be a replica of a seventh-century structure that in turn stood on the site of Ashoka's original third-century-BC shrine. Inside the temple, a single chamber holds a large gilded image of the Buddha, while upstairs is a balcony and a small, plain meditation chamber.

The Bodhi Tree

At the rear of the temple to the west, the large **Bodhi Tree** grows out of an expansive base, attracting scholars and meditators, but it's only an off-shoot of the one under which the Buddha attained enlightenment. Many legends surround the destruction of the original, but it is generally thought that Ashoka, when he sent his daughter Sangamitra to Sri Lanka as an emissary of Buddhism, had sent a cutting with her. This was planted at Anuradhapuram, and a cutting from that was later brought back to Bodhgaya and replanted. Pilgrims tie coloured thread to its branches and Tibetans accompany their rituals with long lines of butter lamps. A sandstone slab with carved sides next to the tree is believed to be the **Vajrasana**, or "thunder-seat", upon which Buddha sat facing east.

Animesh Lochana Temple

The small white **Animesh Lochana Temple** to the right of the compound entrance marks the spot where Buddha stood and gazed upon the Bodhi Tree in gratitude. Numerous ornate *stupas* from the Pala period (seventh to twelfth centuries) are littered around the grounds and next to the temple compound to the south is a rectangular lotus pool where Buddha is believed to have bathed.

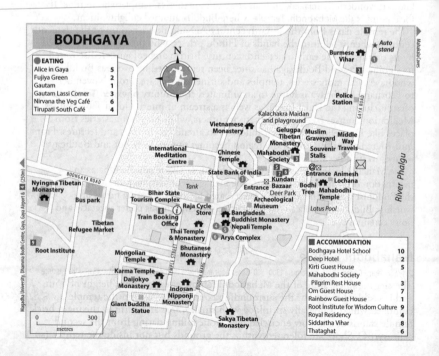

BODHGAYA

EATING

Alice in Gaya	5
Fujiya Green	2
Gautam	1
Gautam Lassi Corner	3
Nirvana the Veg Café	6
Tirupati South Café	4

ACCOMMODATION

Bodhgaya Hotel School	10
Deep Hotel	2
Kirti Guest House	5
Mahabodhi Society Pilgrim Rest House	3
Om Guest House	7
Rainbow Guest House	1
Root Institute for Wisdom Culture	9
Royal Residency	4
Siddartha Vihar	8
Thataghat	6

14

MEDITATION COURSES IN BODHGAYA

Dhamma Bodhi International Meditation Centre ☎0631 220 0437, ⍵bodhi.dhamma.org. A Vipassana centre with regular courses throughout the year, run on a donation basis.

International Meditation Centre ☎0631 220 0707, ✉bsatypla@gmail.com. Vipassana courses for beginners and advanced students; the courses are free,

but you pay for food and lodging (₹500/day).

Root Institute for Wisdom Culture ☎0631 220 0714, ⍵rootinstitute.com. A real haven, offering residential courses, drop-in meditation classes, one-day workshops, and longer courses on Buddhism, yoga and meditation between October and March; book well in advance.

Archaeological Museum

Daily except Fri 9am–5pm • ₹10

Bodhgaya's **Archaeological Museum**, west of the Mahabodhi Temple complex, has a collection of locally discovered sculptures. Its prize exhibit is the stone balustrade that once surrounded the Bodhi Tree in the Mahabodhi Temple. The pink-sandstone parts date from the first or second century BC, but the granite ones are newer, dating from the sixth or seventh century AD.

Mahakala Caves

12km northeast of Bodhgaya • No buses: access by auto-rickshaw from Bodhgaya

In remote, almost desert-like surroundings on the far side of the Falgu River, sit the **Mahakala** (or Dungeshwari) **Caves**, where Buddha did the severe penance that led him to see the futility of extreme asceticism. Realizing that the key to enlightenment was a "middle path" between self-denial and self-indulgence, he walked down to Bodhgaya, where he achieved nirvana. A short climb from the base of the impressive cliff leads to a Tibetan monastery and the three caves.

ARRIVAL AND INFORMATION · BODHGAYA AND AROUND

By plane Gaya's international airport (☎0631 221 0129) is around 12km west of Bodhgaya, and is connected by Air India to Varanasi (daily; 35min), Kolkata (2 weekly; 1hr 5min) and Delhi (weekly; 1hr 40min).

By auto There are auto-rickshaws to Bodhgaya from outside Gaya railway station (₹200; less if you can find a shared one), and shared autos from Kacheri Bus Stand, a couple of kilometres south (₹40). An auto from the airport is around ₹400.

By bus From Bodhgaya, you'll need to travel back to Gaya for most onward services, although, especially in

season, there are private buses from Kalchakra Maidan to destinations such as Ranchi, Raxaul, Varanasi, Siliguri and even Thimpu.

Tourist information The main tourist office in the Bihar State Tourism Corporation complex (daily 10am–5pm; ☎0631 220 0672) is distinctly unenlightening but has a computerized train reservation booth next door (Mon–Sat 8am–noon & 12.30–2pm). Middle Way Travels (☎99736 52641, ⍵facebook.com/middleway.travels), near the entrance to the temple, can arrange local tours and car rental, and book train, bus and flight tickets.

ACCOMMODATION

Outside the pilgrimage season (Nov–Feb) discounts of up to fifty percent are available in most hotels. Many **monastery guesthouses** welcome tourists, subject to the same rules as the pilgrims – in particular no smoking, alcohol or sex.

MONASTERIES

Mahabodhi Society Pilgrim Rest House Bodhgaya Rd ☎9163 1220 0742, ✉mbsibuddhagaya@gmail. com; map p.818. Very popular with pilgrims and often full. Rooms take three or six people and have attached

bathrooms and hot water. In high season (Dec–Jan) prices can go up to ₹2500. Wi-fi only available on the ground floor. Three-person ₹1000, six-person ₹1200

Root Institute for Wisdom Culture ☎0631 220 0714, ⍵rootinstitute.com; map p.818. The simple but charming little double rooms are normally booked up from Dec–Feb, but there's usually dorm space, although people doing courses at the institute take priority. Note that members of opposite sexes may not share rooms even if married, and there is no wi-fi access. Dorms ₹250; doubles ₹900/₹1500

14

HOTELS

★ **Bodghaya Hotel School** Katorva Road, behind the Great Buddha statue ☎ 631 220 0044, ⊕ thebodhgaya hotelschool.com; map p.818. Excellent value at this charming minimal-chic guesthouse on the edge of town – part of the Agragami India Project to train unemployed locals in hospitality. Rooms are large, squeaky-clean and light, there's a restaurant serving Indian and continental food, and a nice rooftop with good views over the surrounding countryside. Breakfast is included. ₹2700

Deep Hotel Gaya Rd, near the Burmese Vihar ☎ 0631 220 0463, ⊕ deephotel.in; map p.818. One of Bodhgaya's best budget lodges, offering a warm welcome and sociable atmosphere. Rooms are reasonably spacious and clean, with attached bathrooms and 24hr hot water. ₹750/850

Kirti Guest House Close to Kalchakra Maidan ☎ 0631 220 0744, ⊕ kirtihouse744@yahoo.com; map p.818. The Dalai Lama beams benevolently over the reception at this serene guest-house run by the Tibetan Monastery and accessed over a short bridge. The rooms are fresh and bright, with discounts off season. ₹2250

Om Guest House Bodhgaya Rd ☎ 99340 57498; map p.818. A long-standing travellers' hotel, *Om* delivers spick-and-span, if rather small, rooms with attached bathrooms

and salmon pink walls in a central location, but no wi-fi. ₹500

Rainbow Guest House Gaya Rd, near the Burmese Vihar ☎ 0631 220 0308, ⊕ rainbowbodhgaya@hotmail. com; map p.818. Not very central, with attached but otherwise spartan rooms, (reasonably) hot water and friendly staff, at monastery guesthouse prices but without the religious strictures. ₹600

★ **Royal Residency** Domuhan Rd (Bodhgaya Rd) ☎ 0631 220 1156, ⊕ theroyalresidency.co; map p.818. An immaculate but pricey option favoured by well-heeled Japanese visitors. The rooms boast sleek wooden floors and fittings, cream-coloured walls and minimalist decor. There's also excellent dining and, for a minimum of thirty takers, they'll heat up a Japanese-style communal bath. ₹600

Siddartha Vihar Bihar State Tourism Corporation complex ☎ 0631 220 0445, ⊕ bodhgaya.bstdc@gmail. com; map p.818. The state-run hotel is pretty decent value, with spacious if rather plain, attached doubles, all with a/c. ₹1500

Thataghat off a side road near the Mahabodi Society ☎ 92644 27601, ⊕ hoteltathagatbodhgaya.com; map p.818. Good mid-range choice in the midst of town, with classy rooms and a dimly lit, bamboo-furnished boutique ambience. Breakfast included. ₹3500

EATING

During November and February, **Tibetan tent restaurants** spring up throughout town – follow the crowds to find the best ones.

Alice in Gaya Arya Complex (south side, downstairs) ☎ 72960 28888, ⊕ facebook.com/aliceingaya; map p.818. Hip cafe serving an interesting, if slightly overpriced, mix of Thai (*pad thai* ₹240) and Western food (fish & chips ₹450), strong coffees (from ₹100), cakes and pastries. Daily 9am–10pm.

Fujiya Green Kalchakra Maidan ☎ 99340 58923; map p.818. An ever-popular Tibetan restaurant housed in a cross between a hut and a tent, with a vast array of *momos* (stuffed dumplings; ₹50–100) and hearty *thukpa* (noodle soup; ₹40–90). Daily 7am–9.30pm.

Gautam Gaya Rd, opposite the Burmese Vihar; map p.818. Hole-in-the-wall restaurant serving traveller-oriented food, with big breakfasts, banana pancakes (₹50) and cinnamon rolls (₹25) as well as real oat porridge, Indian veg curries and thalis. Daily 7am–8pm.

Gautam Lassi Corner Happy Place, Kundan Bazar

☎ 99342 90977; map p.818. A bustling, low-key refreshment kiosk, relocated after the 2013 bomb destroyed its original premises, which does a brisk trade in refreshing lassis (flavoured with syrups such as rose and pineapple; ₹50), coffee, and freshly squeezed juices (₹40). Daily 7am–9pm.

Nirvana the Veg Café Opposite the Thai temple, ground floor of Maya Heritage Hotel ☎ 0631 220 0071; map p.818. Mid-range restaurant serving an eclectic menu of North and South Indian, Chinese, sandwiches (from ₹105) and decent pizzas (₹295) in a sleek, high-ceilinged sala. A meal will set you back around ₹500. Daily 9am–10.30pm.

Tirupati South Café Arya Compex, ☎ 0631 220 0530, ⊕ facebook.com/tirupatisouthcafe; map p.818. The place to go for a healthy dose of simple, tasty South Indian veg delicacies, including big dosas, thalis, plus a selection of Chinese and North Indian favourites. A meal will set you back about ₹200. Daily 8am–10pm.

DIRECTORY

Banks and books Middle Way Travels (see page 819) is among travel agents who'll change cash; it also sells new and used books in English.

Bicycle rental The Raja Cycle Store, next door to the *Embassy* hotel (☎ 99317 11505).

Internet Computer World, Arya Complex (daily 9am–9pm; ₹40/hr); Shivam Internet Cafè, Bodhgaya Rd (daily 9am–9pm; ₹40/hr).

Rajgir

Eighty kilometres northeast of Bodhgaya, the small market town of **RAJGIR** nestles in rocky hills that witnessed the meditations and teachings of both the Buddha and Mahavira, the founder of Jainism. The capital of the Magadha kingdom before Pataliputra (Patna), Rajgir was also where King Bimbisara converted to Buddhism. Rajgir is also regarded as a health resort because of its **hot springs**, 1km south of town, which can get unpleasantly crowded, especially as the neighbouring **Laxmi Narayan Temple** has become a popular destination for Hindus not wishing to miss out on Rajgir's Buddhist and Jain pilgrimage fest.

At **Venuvana Vihara**, a Japanese shrine marks the spot where a monastery was built for Buddha to live in, while at **Griddhakuta** (Vulture's Peak), on Ratnagiri Hill, 4km south of the town centre (buses can drop you at the turn-off), Buddha set in motion his second "Wheel of Law". The massive modern **Vishwashanti Stupa** (Peace Pagoda), built by the Japanese, dominates Ratnagiri Hill and can be reached by a rickety chairlift (daily 8.15am–1pm & 2–5pm, last ticket 4.30pm; ₹60). Griddhakuta is actually halfway down the hill, so you may prefer to wander down from here rather than climb back up to take the chairlift. Look out for the 26 Jain shrines on top of these hills, reached by a challenging trek attempted almost solely by Jain devotees. On an adjacent hill, in the **Saptaparni cave**, the first Buddhist council met to record the teachings of the Buddha after his death.

The Jains also have a shrine at **Virayatan**, 1km east of Venuvana Vihara, beyond Griddhakuta, which was established in 1973 to commemorate the 2500th anniversary of the birth of Mahavira. They run courses here but the main attraction for casual visitors is the gallery of diorama tableaux (daily 8am–6.30pm) illustrating the lives of the 24 *tirthankaras*.

ARRIVAL AND GETTING AROUND   RAJGIR

Consider visiting on weekdays, when the site is less crowded.
By train There are three daily trains from Patna, one of which starts in Delhi.
By bus Rajgir is connected by bus to Gaya (2hr), Nalanda (15min) and sometimes Patna (2hr 30min direct, although you usually have to change at Bihar Sharif, 25km away).

By tonga A popular way to visit the sights in Rajgir is to take a tonga (horse-drawn carriage) for up to six people (eight at a pinch). Costs are typically around ₹600–800 for a half-day tour, but you'll have to haggle, and make it clear to the driver exactly which sights you want to visit and how long you'll want to spend at each.

ACCOMMODATION AND EATING

Green Hotel Opposite the Japanese temple complex, 1.5km south of the bus stand ☏ 98358 58246. A small restaurant ("hotel" does not imply accommodation) with a relaxed atmosphere, serving reasonably-priced food including a choice of thalis (₹100–300 veg, ₹210–400 non-veg). Daily 8am–10pm.

★ **Indo Hokke** 4km west of the bus stand ☏ 06112 255245, ✉ indohokkehotel@gmail.com. A unique hotel fusing Japanese and Indian architectural influences. It has Japanese- and Western-style rooms, a communal Japanese bath (if there's sufficient demand), and the outstanding *Lotus* restaurant, which serves Indian, Chinese and Japanese

dishes. Breakfast included. **₹6500**
Raj By the bus stand ☏ 93043 76445. Cheapest of the hotels by the bus stand, with a choice of rooms at the front (brighter but noisier) or back (quieter but darker), small and simple but attached, with hot water in a bucket on request. Non a/c **₹700**, a/c **₹1500**
Nalanda Regency 200m east of the bus stand ☏ 70700 94800, ⊕ hotelnalandaregency.com. Well-maintained mid-range hotel with neat, decent sized a/c and non-a/c rooms, and large bathrooms. There's a restaurant and a relaxing garden whose selling point is the Olympic-sized swimming pool. Breakfast included. **₹4500**

Nalanda and around

Daily: March–Sept 9am–5.30pm; Oct–Feb 9am–4.40pm • ₹600 (₹40) • video camera ₹25

Founded in the fifth century AD by the Guptas, the great monastic **Buddhist university** of **NALANDA** attracted thousands of international students and teachers until it was

14

sacked by the Afghan invader Bhaktiar Khilji in the twelfth century. Courses included philosophy, logic, theology, grammar, astronomy, mathematics and medicine.

Excavations have revealed nine levels of occupation on the site, dating back to the time of the Buddha and Mahavira in the sixth century BC. The **site** is strewn with the remains of *stupas*, temples and eleven monasteries, their thick walls impressively intact. Nalanda is now part of the modern Buddhist pilgrimage circuit, but even casual tourists will appreciate taking the time to walk through the extensive site, or climb its massive 31m **stupa** for commanding views. Informative booklets available at the ticket booth render the numerous guides unnecessary.

Nalanda Museum (daily except Fri 9am–5pm; ₹5) houses antiquities found here and at Rajgir, including Buddhist and Hindu bronzes and a number of undamaged statues of the Buddha. **Nava Nalanda Mahavihara**, the Pali postgraduate research institute, houses many rare Buddhist manuscripts, and is devoted to study and research in Pali literature and Buddhism.

ARRIVAL AND GETTING AROUND · NALANDA AND AROUND

By train The railway station, 2km east of the bus stop, is served by three daily trains each way between Rajgir and Patna.

By bus Buses every 30min or so between Rajgir and Bihar Sharif (25km northeast, change here for Patna) stop at the turning to Nalanda, from where rickshaws are available for the remaining 2km to the gates of the site. From Patna, Bihar State Roadways (BSRTC) runs tours to Nalanda and Rajgir (₹750) leaving at 7am and returning at 8pm from their stand in Bir Chand Patel Path (☎0612 250 6099, ⊛gauravluxury.com).

ACCOMMODATION AND EATING

Hotel Shubam International 700m west of Nalanda road's junction ☎99736 19507 or 99733 65709. In the middle of peaceful countryside, away from Nalanda's traffic-clogged main road, this new hotel has large and airy rooms that are very good value for the area. There's a restaurant serving veg and non-veg Indian mains (from ₹100), and nice views of Nalanda and the surrounding paddy fields from the rooftop. Non a/c ₹900, a/c ₹1800

Tourist Cafeteria By the site entrance ☎99736 19507. This canteen run by the Bihar State Tourism Development Corporation serves veg and non-veg food, both Indian and Western, including chicken biryani (₹150), or American chop suey (₹160). Nothing special, but good enough. Daily 7am–10pm.

Jharkhand

Carved out of Bihar in 2000, after years of agitation by its largely *Adivasi* population, **JHARKHAND** yields almost forty percent of India's minerals, but suffers from extreme poverty, lawlessness and Naxalite (Maoist guerrilla) activity, and is rarely visited by tourists. Although the area around the capital, Ranchi, and the main tourist attraction, Palamau (Betla) National Park, are now safe to visit, it's vital to check the **security situation** before venturing out of those areas, and you should avoid travelling at night by road anywhere in the state.

Ranchi

Jharkhand's capital, **RANCHI** was Bihar's summer capital under the colonial regime, and must be the most laidback state capital in the country. Its main hub is **Firayalal Chowk**, two kilometres north of the train station, a busy road junction now renamed **Albert Ekka Chowk** after a hero of the 1971 Indo-Pakistani War whose statue now stands in the middle of it. Ranchi's top shopping and commercial thoroughfare, **Main Road** (officially Mahatma Gandhi Marg), runs north and south from here, crossing the rail line some 500m west of the station. Ranchi itself isn't exactly thick with sights, but there are a couple of places worth seeing within easy striking distance.

Jagganathpur Temple

11km southwest of town (around ₹400 by auto for the round trip) • Daily 5am–9pm

Like its more famous counterpart in Puri, the **Jagganathpur Temple** is dedicated to the triad of Jagganath, Balabhadra and Subhadra, and like the one in Puri, it has a **Rath Yatra** festival in June or July in which their images are hauled out on chariots, attracting thousands of devotees. Built on a hilltop and originally dating from 1691, the temple even looks like a smaller version of the one in Puri, with a 30-metre-high *daul* (main tower). Unlike the one in Puri, however, non-Hindus are allowed to go inside.

14

ARRIVAL AND INFORMATION
RANCHI

By train The railway station, 2km south of the city centre, has three daily trains to Gaya, four to Patna, and two to Kolkata. The #18109 *Rourkela–Jammu Tawi Express* trundles up to Old Delhi daily, but some days of the week have faster trains to Delhi.

By air Birsa Munda Airport, 7km southeast of town, has flights to Patna (with IndiGo), Kolkata (IndiGo), Delhi (Air India, IndiGo and Go Air) and Mumbai (IndiGo and Go Air).

Tours The tourist office is at 5 Main Road (☎ 0651 645 2307; Mon–Fri 8am–5pm), but you're better off going to Suhana Travels on Station Rd (☎ 0651 329 3808, ✉ suhana_jharkhandtour@yahoo.co.in), a travel agent whose proprietor is happy to dish out information and offers overnight trips to Palamau (Betla) National Park or the Jain temples at Parasnath.

ACCOMMODATION AND EATING

★ **Chanakya BNR Hotel** ☎ 0651 246 1241, ⊚ chanakya bnrranchi.com. The best accommodation in Ranchi is at this beautiful old low-rise railway hotel set around lawns, built at the beginning of the twentieth century and now completely refurbished and super-elegant. Breakfast included. ₹13,300

Eat Hotel Beena Inn, Station Rd ☎ 95344 11111. Bright, modern café where you can get espresso-based coffees (cappuccino ₹75), teas, shakes, smoothies, and also snacks and good food (veg or chicken noodles ₹75–125). Daily 8am–11pm.

Sunny Station Rd ☎ 0651 246 1359. Reliable diner

offering a range of veg curries, south Indian veg snacks (masala dosa; ₹50) and thalis (₹120–170), with ice cream for afters. Daily 7am–10pm.

Yatri Niwas At the railway station (up the stairs to the left of the main entrance) ☎ 0651 246 2925, ✉ yatriniwasranchi@gmail.com. The best-value cheapie near the station – and it's very near indeed – offering clean and bright attached and non-attached rooms as well as dorm beds, but hot water comes by the bucket and there's no wi-fi. 24hr checkout. Dorm ₹300; double ₹700/₹900

Palamau (Betla) National Park

170km west of Ranchi • ₹300 per vehicle, compulsory guide ₹100/hr per vehicle, camera permit ₹150, video camera permit ₹250, jeep rental ₹800/hr (up to 8 people), elephant safari ₹400 per elephant (up to 4 people) • ⊚ palamu.nic.in

In a remote corner of Jharkhand, the beautiful *sal* forests of the **PALAMAU NATIONAL PARK** cover around eight hundred square kilometres of hilly terrain. Although part of **Project Tiger** (see page 1215), Palamau has been hard hit by drought, and at the time of writing, there were no tigers or leopards. If lucky, you may still see elephants, *nilgai* (antelope), *gaur* (bison) and wild boar. The park is open all year, but October to April is the best time to visit, although it can be rather chilly then, especially in the morning. Most visitors take a **jeep safari to explore the park**. However, make sure you check the situation before you visit — in recent years, Palamau has seen movements of local guerrillas who spill in from the troubled north-eastern forests of bordering Chhattisgarh, and the park can sometimes be closed to tourists.

ARRIVAL AND ACCOMMODATION
PALAMAU NATIONAL PARK

By train and bus The nearest railway station is at Daltonganj, but train timings are not tremendously convenient and it's better to get there from Ranchi by bus (every 30min; 5hr). From Daltonganj you need to take a shared jeep, a bus or an auto for the 25km journey to the park's entry point at Betla.

★ **Tree House** inside the park entrance ☎ 06562 222

650. Can be booked up months ahead so reserve well in advance. This wonderful two-room lodge is, as stated, in a tree house. No wi-fi. ₹1000

Van Vihar outside the park entrance ☎ 06562 226 513. State-run lodge offering a choice of rooms. It's recently been given a facelift, but is still a bit rustic, although the staff are very helpful. No wi-fi. ₹900

Sikkim

RUMTEK MONASTERY, SIKKIM

Sikkim

The tiny and beautiful state of Sikkim lies to the south of Tibet, sandwiched between Nepal to the west and Bhutan to the east. Measuring just 65km by 115km, Sikkim's landscape ranges from swelteringly hot valleys just 300m above sea level, to lofty snow-capped peaks such as Kanchenjunga (Kanchendzonga to the locals) which, at 8586m, is the third-highest mountain in the world. A small but growing network of tortuous roads penetrates this rugged and beautiful Himalayan wilderness. In 2018, Sikkim became a role-model for India, and the world, by becoming the first-ever organic state, and earning a Future Policy Gold Award from the United Nations Food and Agriculture Organisation.

15

For centuries, Sikkim was an isolated, independent Buddhist kingdom, until war with China in the early 1960s led the Indian government to realize the area's strategic importance as a crucial corridor between Tibet and Bangladesh. As a result of its annexation by India in 1975, Sikkim has experienced dramatic changes. Now a fully-fledged Indian state, it is predominantly Hindu, with a population made up of 75 percent **Nepalese Gurungs**, and less than twenty percent **Lepchas**, its former rulers. Smaller proportions survive of **Bhutias**, of Tibetan origin, and **Limbus**, also possibly of Tibetan origin, who gave the state its name – *sukh-im*, "happy homeland". Nepali is now the lingua franca, and the Nepalese are socially and politically the most dominant people in the state. However, the people of Sikkim continue to jealously guard their freedom and affluence and remain untouched by the Nepalese Gurkhas' autonomy movement in neighbouring Darjeeling. Although only Sikkimese can hold major shares in property and businesses, partnerships with Indian (non-Sikkimese) entrepreneurs and subsidies to indigenous Sikkimese industry have led to prosperity – fuelled by its special status within the union.

   Historically, culturally and spiritually, Sikkim's strongest links are with Tibet. The main draws for visitors are the state's off-the-beaten-track **trekking** and its many **monasteries**, more than two hundred in all, mostly belonging to the ancient **Nyingmapa** sect. **Pemayangtse** in West Sikkim is the most historically significant, and houses an extraordinary wooden mandala depicting Guru Rinpoche's Heavenly Palace. **Tashiding**, a Nyingmapa monastery built in 1717, surrounded by prayer flags and *chortens* and looking across to snow-capped peaks, is considered Sikkim's holiest. **Rumtek** is the seat of the **Gyalwa Karmapa** – head of the **Karma Kagyu** lineage – and probably the wealthiest monastery in Sikkim. The capital, **Gangtok**, a colourful, bustling cosmopolitan town, is home to a bewildering array of trekking agents only too happy to take payment (in dollars) and arrange the necessary permits.

BEST TIME TO VISIT

Summer, from April to mid-June, is characterized by warm weather and clear skies, but no mountain views. From late September to November, temperatures are moderate, cherry blossoms are in bloom and the skies intermittently clear for views of Kanchenjunga — which can be seen up to mid-January, despite fog from mid-December. An influx of tourists during these two high spells means higher hotel rates, especially in Gangtok and Pelling. Discounts are possible during low season, from December to March, when it's freezing and the fog plays spoilsport. The monsoon lasts from June to September, when road conditions deteriorate and landslides are common. Winter can be bitterly cold in the northern reaches, but still a good time to travel. Check for road closures when it snows.

RED PANDA IN SIKKIM

Highlights

❶ Chaam Experience this mysterious and colourful lama dance, held in most monasteries around the harvest festival of Losung (early Dec). See page 829

❷ Rumtek One of Sikkim's most venerated monasteries, Rumtek is home to the Black Hat sect and hosts a spectacular festival in February. See page 838

❸ Pemayangtse A wonderful, highly venerated seventeenth-century monastery perched on a commanding ridge with glorious views. See page 846

❹ Varshey Rhododendron Sanctuary Magnificent views and gentle trails through a botanical paradise. See box, page 847

❺ Dzongri and Singalila trails High-altitude treks through rhododendron forests, across meadows and past remote lakes with breathtaking views of mighty Kanchenjunga. See page 847

❻ Monastery Trail: West Sikkim You won't need porters or special permits to walk this rewarding circuit from Pelling to Khecheopalri, Yuksom and Tashiding, staying at village homestays en route. See page 849

❼ Tashiding An especially sacred monastic complex on a conical hill with marvellous views. See page 850

❽ Yumthang Walk through this spectacular rhododendron-filled valley with icy pinnacles towering overhead. See page 854

HIGHLIGHTS ARE MARKED ON THE MAP ON PAGE 828

Sikkim's soaring mountain walls and steep wooded hillsides, carved by torrential rivers such as the **Teesta** and the **Rangit**, are a botanist's dream. The lower slopes abound in **orchids**, sprays of cardamom carpet the forest floor, and the land is rich with apple orchards, orange groves and terraced paddy fields (to the Tibetans, this was Denzong, "the land of rice"). At higher altitudes, monsoon mists cling to huge tracts of lichen-covered forests, where countless varieties of rhododendron carpet the hillsides and giant magnolia

SIKKIM

HIGHLIGHTS

1. Chaam
2. Rumtek
3. Pemayangtse
4. Varshey Rhododendron Sanctuary
5. Dzongri and Singalila trails
6. Monastery Trail: West Sikkim
7. Tashiding
8. Yumthang

0 — 20 kilometres

CHINA

Kangchengyao (6889m)

Pauhunri (7125m)

Gurudogmar

Chopta Valley

Thangu

Chombu (6362m)

Yume Samdong (Zero Point)

Fluted Peak (6084m)

Nepal Peak (6910m)

G R E A T H I M A L A Y A

8 Yumthang (3645m)

Green Lake (4850m)

Tangchung Khang (6010m)

Lama Wangden (5868m)

Kanchenjunga (8586m)

Zemu Glacier

Lachen (2977m)

Lachung (2734m) Lachung

NEPAL

Siniolchu (6887m)

Simvo (6812m)

Kyeshong La (3790m)

DZONGU

Teesta

CHINA

Talung Glacier

KANCHENDZONGA NATIONAL PARK

Chungthang (1579m)

TIBET AUTONOMOUS REGION

Rathong (6678m)

Kabru (7338m)

Pandim (6691m)

Goecha La (4940m)

Japuno (5935m)

Narsing (5825m)

Tolung

Kokthang (6147m)

Zemanthang (4453m)

Samiti Lake

Singhik

Tosar Lake

Kangla (5200m)

Chaurikhang

Dzongri La (4400m)

Thansing (3930m)

Mangan

SIKKIM

Lampokhari Lake

5 Dzongri (4030m)

Tsokha

Labrang

Danfeybhir Tar (4400m)

Khecheopalri Lake

Bakhim

6 Yoksum (1780m)

Rangit Trail

Phodong

Phensang

Nathu La (4328m)

Chewabhanjang (3170m)

3 7 Tashiding

Ralang

Lingdum

Tsomgo Lake (3767m)

Serathang

Pelling

Pemayangtse

Maenam (3235m)

Rumtek 2

Gangtok

4 Uttarey (1695m)

Gyalshing

Legship

Kewzing

1

Ravangla

Temi Tea Garden

Ranipool

Assam Lingzey

Varshey (3030m)

Hee

Rinchenpong

Damthang

Tendong (2757m)

NH-31A

Singtam

Pakyong Airport

Aritar

Dentam

Hilley

Samdruptse

Rangpo

Phalut

Soreng

Naya Bazaar

Namchi

BHUTAN

Sombare

Daramdin

Jorethang

Melli

WEST BENGAL

Teesta

Kalimpong

WEST BENGAL

Darjeeling

Teesta Bazaar

The international boundaries on this map are neither purported to be correct nor authentic by Survey of India directives. Publisher.

FESTIVALS IN SIKKIM

Maghey Mela (14 Jan). One of Sikkim's most famous festivals, celebrated in Jorethang with grand shows of archery, paragliding, hot air ballooning and river rafting.

Losar (in/around Feb). The Tibetan New Year, celebrated with grand monastic dances.

Bumchu Festival (Feb/March). Lamas gather at Tashiding, where a vessel containing holy water is opened and examined – the water level indicates the future of the state.

Pang Lhabsol (Aug/Sep–15th day of 7th Tibetan month). Commemoration of the consecration of Mount Kanchenjunga as the guardian deity of Sikkim, celebrated with colourful Tibetan masked dances (*chaams*) and Sikkimese *pangtoed* (warrior dance).

Dasain (Dussehra; Sept–Oct). The Nepali community celebrates this ten-day Hindu festival marking the victory of good over evil; the goddess Durga is worshipped and her idol immersed in a river.

Namchi Mahotsav (Oct). Three-day South Sikkim festival with folk dances, flower exhibitions, handicraft markets and food stalls.

Tihar (Diwali; Oct–Nov). The Nepali version of Diwali, this is an elaborate five-day affair, when houses are cleaned, adorned with marigolds and lit up.

Temi Autumn Carnival (Nov). Three days of traditional dances, music and adventure sports in Sikkim's only historical tea garden.

Losung (Dec). Marks the end of the harvest season. Spectacular *chaam* take place at various monasteries (see pages 832, 839 and 842).

Red Panda Winter Festival (Dec/Jan). A nine-day food and culture fiesta set in Gangtok's Titanic Park, MG Marg.

15

trees punctuate the deep verdant cover. Higher still, approaching the Tibetan plateau, larch and dwarf rhododendron give way to meadows abundant with gentians and potentilla. Sikkim's forests and wilderness areas are inhabited by a wealth of fauna, including extremely elusive snow leopards, *tahr* (wild goat on the Tibet plateau), *bharal* (blue sheep), black bear, flying squirrels and the symbol of Sikkim – the endangered **red panda**.

Brief history

No one knows quite when or how the **Lepchas** – or the Rong, as they call themselves – came to Sikkim, but their roots can be traced back to the animist Nagas of the Indo-Burmese border. **Buddhism**, which arrived from Tibet in the thirteenth century, took its distinctive Sikkimese form four centuries later, when three Tibetan monks of the old Nyingmapa order, disenchanted with the rise of the reformist Gelugpas, migrated south and gathered at Yoksum in western Sikkim. Having consulted the oracle, they sent to Gangtok for a certain Phuntsog Namgyal, whom they crowned as the first **chogyal** or "righteous king" of Denzong in 1642. Both the secular and religious head of Sikkim, he was soon recognized by Tibet, and set about sweeping reforms. His domain was far larger than today's Sikkim, taking in Kalimpong and parts of western Bhutan.

Over the centuries, territory was lost to the Bhutanese, the Nepalese and the **British**. Sikkim originally ceded Darjeeling to the East India Company as a spa in 1817, but was forced to give up all claim to it in 1861 when the kingdom was declared a protectorate of the British. **Tibet**, which perceived Sikkim as a vassal state, objected and invaded in 1886, but a small British force sent in 1888 to Lhasa helped the British consolidate their hold. By importing a Nepalese labour force to work the tea plantations of Sikkim, Darjeeling and Kalimpong, the British sought to diminish the strong Tibetan influence and helped alter the ethnic make-up of the region, with the new migrants soon outnumbering the indigenous population.

After Indian Independence, the reforming and intensely spiritual eleventh chogyal, **Tashi Namgyal**, strove hard until his death in 1962 to prevent the dissolution of his kingdom. Officially Sikkim was a protectorate of India, and the role of India became increasingly crucial, with the Chinese military build-up along the northern borders that culminated in an actual invasion early in the 1960s. His son **Palden Thondup**, the last

EARTHQUAKES, LANDSLIDES AND DAMS

Although **earthquakes** are a common occurrence throughout the Himalayas, the one that struck in September 2011 – with its epicentre at Mangan, 42km northwest of Gangtok – was particularly destructive, leaving around sixty people dead and a trail of devastation as far away as Gangtok. The effects of the magnitude 6.9 quake were felt throughout the region, in Nepal and as far away as Kolkata. Much of the destruction took place around **hydroelectric** projects and led to disrupted roads and infrastructure. To compound the state's communication nightmare, unseasonal rains in 2012 resulted in deadly **landslides** and loss of life, and North Sikkim was virtually cut off from the rest of the state for several weeks.

Industrialization and the construction of dams and numerous hydroelectric projects on Sikkim's rivers, such as the **Teesta**, have brought pressure on the state's diminishing indigenous population, threatening their lifestyle and heritage, particularly in Dzongu, the heartland of Lepchas. Although the voice of their **protest** is now all but lost, the destruction of habitat and the extraordinary strain on the state's fragile road system is self-evident. For more information, visit ⓦ weepingsikkim.blogspot.com.

15

chogyal, married twice; his second wife was an American, Hope Cook, whose reforms as *gyalmo* (queen) did not prove popular at home and irritated the Indian government. The embattled *chogyal* eventually succumbed to the demands of the Nepalese majority, and Sikkim was **annexed** by India in 1975 after a referendum with an overwhelming 97 percent majority. The *chogyal* remained as a figurehead until his death in 1981.

The state continues to be treated with care by the Indian government, partly through a lingering sense of unease among the disaffected Sikkimese minority and an increasingly complex ethnic patchwork but, more importantly, because Sikkim remains a bone of contention between India and China. Today, the **Sikkim Democratic Front** forms the government of Sikkim; generous government subsidies and loans have helped to ensure that people remain generally contented, while extensive road-building is bringing benefits to remote communities despite the many landslides in recent years.

Gangtok

Capital of Sikkim, the overgrown and colourful hill-town of **GANGTOK** (1870m) occupies a rising ridge in the southeast of the state, on what used to be a busy trade route into Tibet. Today, rapid development means an ugly assortment of concrete multi-storey buildings is growing virtually unchecked, and the urban sprawl retains only a few traditional Sikkimese architectural elements. However, a short amble soon leads you away from the congested centre to bring you occasional glimpses of the snow-capped Himalayas, and on a good day you can see Kanchenjunga, the horned peak of Narsing (5825m) and the fluted pyramid of Siniolchu (6887m) poking above the surrounding hills.

While modern Gangtok epitomizes the recent changes in Sikkimese culture, politics and society, its Buddhist past is the root of its appeal for visitors, evident in the collection at the **Institute of Tibetology** and the charming **Enchey Monastery**, as well as the impressive **Rumtek Monastery** (see page 838), 24km west of town. However, the **palace** on the tree-lined promenade, the **Ridge** above town, used by the chogyals between 1894 and 1975, is now out of bounds, part-occupied by the government and a closed chapter in Sikkim's heritage. Sikkim's pride and joy, **orchids**, are nurtured at several sites in and around Gangtok, and celebrated at the Flower Show Complex, also on the Ridge.

Most of the town itself looks west; one explanation for the lack of development east of the ridge is that tradition dictates that houses face northwest, towards Kanchenjunga, Sikkim's guardian.

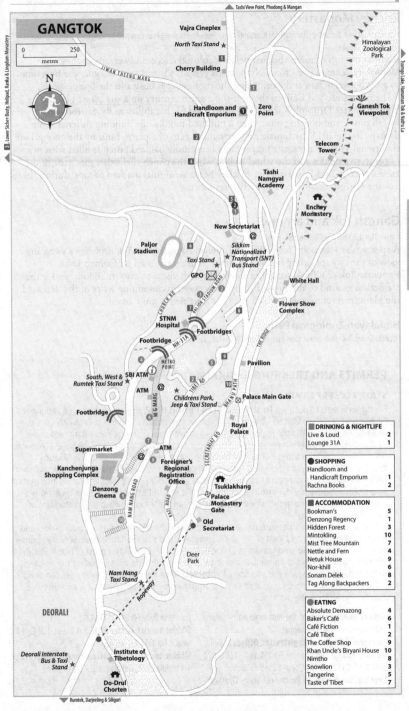

GANGTOK

Tashi View Point, Phodong & Mangan

Vajra Cineplex

North Taxi Stand ★

Cherry Building

JIWAN THEENG MARG

0   250
metres

N

Lower Sichey Busty, Helipad, Ranka & Lingdum Monastery

Handloom and
Handicraft Emporium

Zero
Point

Himalayan
Zoological
Park

Tsomgo Lake, Hanuman Tok & Nathu La

Ganesh Tok
Viewpoint

Telecom
Tower

Tashi
Namgyal
Academy

Enchey
Monastery

New Secretariat

Paljor
Stadium

Taxi Stand

GPO

Sikkim
Nationalized
Transport (SNT)
Bus Stand

White Hall

CHURCH RD

PALJOR STADIUM ROAD

Flower Show
Complex

THE RIDGE

STNM
Hospital

Footbridges

Footbridge

NH-31A

Pavilion

METRO
POINT

SBI ATM

South, West &
Rumtek Taxi Stand

ATM

TIBET RD

BHANU PATH

Palace Main Gate

M G MARG

Childrens Park,
Jeep & Taxi Stand

Footbridge

SECRETARIAT RD

Royal
Palace

Supermarket

ATM

Kanchenjunga
Shopping Complex

NAM NANG ROAD

TIBET ROAD

Foreigner's
Regional
Registration
Office

Tsuklakhang

Denzong
Cinema

Palace
Monastery
Gate

Old
Secretariat

Deer
Park

Nam Nang
Taxi Stand

Ropeway

DEORALI

Deorali Interstate
Bus & Taxi
Stand

Institute of
Tibetology

Do-Drul
Chorten

Rumtek, Darjeeling & Siliguri

15

■ DRINKING & NIGHTLIFE	2
Live & Loud	
Lounge 31A	1

● SHOPPING	
Handloom and	
Handicraft Emporium	1
Rachna Books	2

■ ACCOMMODATION	
Bookman's	5
Denzong Regency	1
Hidden Forest	3
Mintokling	10
Mist Tree Mountain	7
Nettle and Fern	4
Netuk House	9
Nor-khill	6
Sonam Delek	8
Tag Along Backpackers	2

● EATING	
Absolute Demazong	4
Baker's Café	6
Café Fiction	1
Café Tibet	2
The Coffee Shop	9
Khan Uncle's Biryani House	10
Nimtho	8
Snowlion	3
Tangerine	5
Taste of Tibet	7

Enchey Monastery

3km northeast from the centre • Daily daylight hours until 5pm • Free • A picturesque hour-long walk heading north from the Ridge and Flower Show Complex

Right at the top of town and just below a colossal telecom tower, sits **Enchey Monastery**, a small two-storey Nyingmapa *gompa*. Visitors are welcome; the **best time** to go is between 7am and 8am, when the monastery is busy and the light is good.

The monastery was built in the mid-nineteenth century on a site blessed by the Tantric master Druptob Karpo, who was fabled for his ability to fly. Surrounded by tall pines, and housing more than a hundred monks, the building suffered some damage in the 2011 earthquake, but remains a gem of a place. Built by the chogyal on traditional Tibetan lines, the prayer hall's beautifully painted porch is filled with murals of protective deities and the wheel of law, while the conch shells that grace the doors are auspicious Buddhist symbols. Enchey holds an annual **masked *chaam***, during the Losung festival, usually held in early December.

Ganesh Tok and around

A steep 1km climb past the TV tower from Enchey

A spectacular **viewpoint** festooned with prayer flags, **Ganesh Tok** provides a sweeping view of the city sprawling below. A further 5km up the road to Tsomgo Lake, **Hanuman Tok** (2300m) is another viewpoint with vistas of eastern Sikkim, and is the cremation ground of the Royal Family, with *chortens* containing relics of the deceased; the Hanuman temple after which the spot is named is more recent.

Himalayan Zoological Park

Opposite Ganesh Tok • Daily except Thurs 9am–3.30pm • ₹100 (₹20), car ₹50

PERMITS AND TREKKING IN SIKKIM

STATE ACCESS PERMIT

Foreigners need to obtain a **Restricted Area Permit** (**RAP**; previously known as an Inner Line Permit or ILP) to visit Sikkim. Permits can now be obtained online at Ⓦ sikkimilp.in, or in advance along with your Indian visa, but agencies abroad charge exorbitant fees so are best avoided. If obtained within India, Sikkim permits are **free** and can be arranged through the tourism agencies listed below, trekking operators (see page 835) or at the **Sikkim border** at Melli and Rangpo in a dedicated office. In order to apply, you'll need two passport photographs, and photocopies of your passport and Indian visa. Check the latest information at Ⓦ sikkimtourism.gov.in. Permits are date-specific and initially valid for thirty days from entry (no return within three months); **extensions** are normally available up to a maximum of sixty days.

As well as Gangtok and its surroundings in East Sikkim, the RAP covers all of South Sikkim and most areas in the east and west of the state, apart from most high-altitude treks. Sensitive border areas, like Tsomgo Lake (also known as Changu or Tsangu) in East Sikkim, most of North Sikkim except for Mangan and its immediate vicinity, and all high-altitude treks including the Singalila Ridge and Dzongri, require the additional **Protected Area Permit** (**PAP**); foreigners can only enter these areas in groups of at least two accompanied by representatives of approved travel agents who arrange the permits.

Airport immigration At the four main entry points: Delhi, Mumbai, Kolkata, Chennai.

Foreigners' Regional Registration Offices In Delhi, Mumbai, Kolkata and Chennai (Ⓣ 011 2671 1384, 022 2262 1169, 033 2290 0549, or 044 2345 4970).

New Sikkim House 14 Panchsheel Marg, Chanakya-puri, New Delhi (Ⓣ 011 2611 5171).

Sikkim tourist centre SNTC Bus Stand, Hill Cart Rd, Siliguri (Ⓣ 0354 251 2646).

Sikkim tourist information centre Sikkim House, 4/1 Middleton St, Kolkata (Ⓣ 033 2281 7905).

Visitors come to the 506-acre **Himalayan Zoological Park** in the hope of catching a glimpse of the red pandas (which are especially easy to spot), snow leopards, bears and Tibetan wolves that roam the extensive open-air enclosures.

The Ridge

Midway between MG Marg and Enchey

The quiet leafy promenade of the **Ridge** is a popular spot, with the Flower Show Complex and a small park at the northern end, and at the southern end, the **Royal Palace**. The Secretariat, south of the compound, was devastated by the 2011 earthquake and, at the time of writing, was still being rebuilt.

Tsuklakhang

At the far end of the Royal Palace compound, best accessed through the rear gates of the compound

Tsuklakhang, the chapel in the Royal Palace, is currently out of bounds. A **lama dance**, known as *kagyat*, usually takes place here at the end of December, during which the main gates are open to the public (though some years it's in Pemayangtse; see page 846). Across the lawns lies the **Royal Palace**, used by the chogyals (Sikkim's former rulers) until 1975. Following the state's annexation by India, the palace lies mostly abandoned, a prisoner of circumstance.

Institute of Tibetology

2km south of the centre of Gangtok, in Deorali • Mon–Sat 9am–4pm • ₹10 • ⊕ tibetology.net

South of Gangtok at Deorali, the lower part of town, set in wooded grounds, is the museum-cum-library of the **Institute of Tibetology** with an impressive and invaluable

15

TREKKING AND MOUNTAINEERING PERMITS

High-altitude trekking in Sikkim remains a restricted and expensive business. Firstly, foreigners have to acquire **trekking permits** (aka **Protected Area Permits** or **PAP**), which also act as entry permits for these areas. These are only available from the Sikkim Tourism offices in Gangtok, but can be arranged through trek operators (see page 835).

Carefully check documents and itineraries – you don't want to be rushed, especially at altitude – before you set off. Trekking parties consist of a minimum of two people; tour operators charge an official daily rate of US$60 to US$150 per head per day, depending on group size and route.

While most major peaks require permission from the Indian Mountaineering Foundation (**IMF**) in Delhi (see page 121) with at least three months' notice, as well as **mountaineering** permits, the Sikkim government, through the appropriate **Gangtok trekking operator**, hands out permits for the following treks: Frey's Peak (5830m) near Chaurikhang on the Singalila Ridge; Thingchenkang (6010m) near Dzongri and Jopuno (5935m) in West Sikkim; and Lama Wangden (5868m) and Brumkhangse (5635m) in North Sikkim. Recommended Gangtok agents include Namgyal Treks and Tours (see page 835).

The high-altitude treks most commonly offered by the operators are the Dzongri–Goecha La route, plus its variation starting from Uttarey (see page 847) and the Singalila Ridge (see page 851). The exhilarating trek from Lachen to Green Lake is possible, but permission must be obtained from Delhi (most easily arranged through a Gangtok agent) at least two months in advance. At the moment, Dzongri still bears the brunt of the trekking industry in the state, and the pressure is beginning to tell severely on the environment.

Low-altitude hikes often come without the restriction of permits, and makes Sikkim an alluring destination for quiet walks off the beaten track. The **rhododendron trails** around Varshey, West Sikkim, for example, are particularly pleasant. A word of warning: avoid trekking unaccompanied in forest areas due to the risk of **black bears**.

Some areas, such as Nathu La on the border with Tibet in East Sikkim, and Gurudongma Lake in North Sikkim remain completely off-limits to foreigners.

collection of books and rare manuscripts, as well as religious artefacts such as exquisite *thangkas* (scrolls) and a photography archive. You can also get here from the upper town via the ropeway cable car.

Do-Drul Chorten

About 50m east of the Institute of Tibetology

Within the same complex as the Institute of Tibetology, an imposing whitewashed *chorten*, known as the **Do-Drul Chorten** – one of the most important in Sikkim – dominates a large, lively monastic seminary on the brow of a hill. The *chorten* is capped by a gilded tower, whose rising steps signify the thirteen steps to nirvana; the sun and moon symbol at the top stands for the union of opposites and the elements of ether and air, surrounded by 108 prayer wheels. Behind the monastic complex, a prayer hall houses a large image of **Guru Rinpoche** (Padmasambhava) who brought Buddhism to Tibet at the request of King Trisong Detsen in the eighth century AD. He later travelled through Sikkim hiding precious manuscripts (*termas*) in caves, for discovery at a future date by *tertons*. Curiously, part of the head of the image projects into the ceiling; belief has it that the image is slowly growing.

15

ARRIVAL AND DEPARTURE   GANGTOK

BY ROAD

Shared jeeps and taxis are far more popular and efficient than buses for accessing Gangtok. Due to occasional agitation in neighbouring Darjeeling, the busy route to and from Siliguri in West Bengal sometimes sees closures, though the authorities endeavour to keep it open.

By jeep Most travellers arrive by jeep from Siliguri (4hr 30min), the current transport centre for the railhead at New Jalpaiguri (NJP; 117km). Jeeps to North Sikkim depart from the Vajra stand until 1pm.

Destinations from Mainline taxi stand: Darjeeling (5hr; ₹250); Kalimpong (3–4hr; ₹150), New Jalpaiguri (NJP; ₹250); Siliguri (5–6hr; ₹200).

Destinations from taxi stand near MG Marg: Gyalshing (4–5hr; ₹200); Jorethang (3–4hr; ₹150); Pelling (5–6hr; ₹300); Rumtek (1hr; ₹50).

Destination from Vajra taxi stand: Mangan (3hr; ₹130).

BY BUS

If you're determined to suffer the buses, you can choose between the state carrier, SNT (Sikkim Nationalized Transport), or a number of private operators. All buses run by SNT use the SNT Bus Stand on Paljor Stadium Rd, but passengers may prefer to be dropped off earlier at Metro Point, MG Marg, which is more convenient for the tourist office and most hotels. Non-SNT buses stop at the Mainline

Stand, Deorali, 2km south of the centre.

Destinations Bagdogra airport, via Siliguri (daily 5.30am; 5–6hr); Kalimpong (daily at 7.30am; 4hr); Namchi (twice daily at 7.30am and 2pm; 3hr); Pakyong (daily at 3.30pm; 1hr); Siliguri (hourly 7.30am to 9.30pm, 1pm and 2pm; 5–6hr); New Jalpaiguri (daily at 7.15am; 5hr).

BY TRAIN

The nearest railway station, New Jalpaiguri (NJP), is 117km away. SNT has a train reservations counter (Mon–Sat 8am–2pm), but the reservations quota for Gangtok is highly inadequate so you are advised to book in Siliguri or online.

BY AIR

By plane SpiceJet (Ⓦ spicejet.com) flies to Pakyong airport, 32km southeast of Gangtok, from Guwahati (1h5min) and Kolkata (1h25min). Coming from elsewhere you must fly to Bagdogra (124km) in West Bengal and reach Sikkim by shared taxi.

By helicopter Sikkim Tourism Development Corporation (STDC; see below) sells tickets for the helicopter flight (subject to weather conditions; daily 10am and 11am; ₹3500; 35min; ☎03592 203960) to Bagdogra. Note that the flights only operate with a full load of five passengers and baggage allowance is a mere 10kg.

GETTING AROUND

By taxi Shared local taxis are the most common way of travelling the main highway (Gangtok to Deorali around ₹20). After 8pm, taxis become scarce but reserved taxis are available from stands near the SNT Bus Stand; the Private Bus Stand at Deorali; the Lal Bazar supermarket; Children's Park between MG Marg and Tibet Rd; and the Main Line jeep stand. All taxis carry a rate chart, and drivers are generally honest.

By the ropeway With terminals at the old Secretariat, Nam Nang and Deorali, the ropeway (daily 8am–4.30pm) provides a spectacular view of the southern city, though it's an expensive way to get around by local standards (₹170 return, no one-way fare) and is not particularly useful for most accommodation. While it's scheduled to run every 12min, in practice it waits to fill up before moving on.

TREKKING, TOUR AND ADVENTURE OPERATORS

All high-altitude treks in Sikkim (see page 851) have to be conducted in groups and be arranged through the following **travel agents** or **tour operators**, all based in Gangtok, who will also secure the necessary permits. Note that payment for treks is in US dollars.

Blue Sky Tours & Travels Tourism Building, MG Marg ☏ 87983 04933, ⊛ blueskysikkim.com. Helpful agency specializing in West Sikkim; also operates tours to North Sikkim and the Green Lake trek.

Hub Outdoor Bojoghari, Near Tashi Viewpoint ☏ 94342 03848, ⊛ huboutdoor.in. Great adventure operator with an outdoor gear outlet that specializes in trekking and mountain-biking adventures. They also rent mountain bikes for ₹800/day.

Khangri Tours & Treks Tibet Rd ☏ 98320 46820, ⊛ khangrii.com. Owner Tsering Dorjee is an experienced trekking guide who can arrange cultural and monastic tours and treks throughout Sikkim – he pioneered some of the routes himself.

Namgyal Treks & Tours Tibet Rd ☏ 03592 203701 or 94340 33122, ⊛ namgyaltreks.com. Namgyal Sherpa is an exceedingly capable and experienced high-altitude trek and expedition operator, recognized by both the Sikkim and Central Government tourist offices.

Sikkim Adventure 6th Mile, Tadong ☏ 03592 251250, ⊛ sikkim-adventure.com. Sailesh Pradhan runs a plant nursery and is an extremely knowledgeable botanist and a specialist guide for trips focused around Sikkim's rich flora, including rhododendron and orchid trails.

Sikkim Tours & Travels Church Rd ☏ 03592 202188, ⊛ sikkimtours.com. Owner Lukendra is tremendously helpful and experienced, and specializes in nature tours, birdwatching, homestays and treks; he also offers trips off the beaten path and mountain-bike tours.

Tag Along Journeys Abhilasha, next to Nepali Sahitya Parishad, Development Area ☏ 75509 25535, ⊛ tagalong.asia. Tour operator catering to young, adventurous backpackers, offering trekking, mountain biking and road trips with knowledgeable local guides.

Tashila Tours and Travels Below TNSS School Hall ☏ 03592 202978, ⊛ tashila.com. Experienced operator offering trekking, kayaking and river-rafting expeditions, plus cultural and monastery tours.

15

INFORMATION AND TOURS

Tourist office STDC (Mon–Fri 10am–5pm; ☏ 03592 209090) is next to the tourist office on MG Marg.
Helicopter flights STDC sell tickets for their spectacular helicopter flights that operate on demand (from ₹9500/15min flight; entire aircraft charter ₹1200/min) over Gangtok and to West Sikkim, Yumthang, Gangtok and, the most breathtaking of them all, a 90min Kanchenjunga trip up the Zemu Glacier. Cameras aren't allowed on some routes.

ACCOMMODATION

Gangtok's **hotels** are expensive in high season (broadly speaking April–June and Sept–Nov), but offer discounted rates at other times. As the town has spread, so has the choice of accommodation, with some excellent hotels and guesthouses springing up along the highway at Deorali, and a growing number of alternatives within striking distance of town.

CENTRAL GANGTOK

Denzong Regency Cherry Banks ☏ 03592 201566, ⊛ denzongregency.com; map p.831. In a very pleasant location with quiet grounds; away from the bustle of the bazaar but yet within easy walking distance, this luxurious hotel exudes a sense of Sikkimese history and offers large suite-like rooms with balconies. High level of service. ₹8,500

Mintokling Bhanu Path (Tashiling Rd) ☏ 03592 208553, ⊛ mintoklingsikkim.com; map p.831. Run by an old Sikkimese family, in a quiet location near the palace, high above the market yet within pleasant walking distance. Its airy garden rooms have good views over the valley to the mountains. ₹3000

Mist Tree Mountain Tibet Rd ☏ 03592 205489, ⊛ hotel misttreemountain.com; map p.831. Smack in the centre of town, this mid-range hotel clings on the hillside and has large, well-appointed rooms with wooden floor panels, Buthanese rugs, and breathtaking views of Gangtok and the valley. The attached *Zaiqa Restaurant* is perfect for a romantic meal with 180 degrees views of Kanchenjunga. Breakfast included, and walk-ins get up to a 30 percent discount. ₹4300

★ **Netuk House** Tibet Rd ☏ 03592 206778, ⊛ netuk house.com; map p.831. A family home near the centre, which has been extended into a boutique hotel offering an authentic Sikkimese experience. The traditional rooms are warm, atmospheric and beautifully-presented, plus there's a pleasant roof terrace and decent restaurant with home-cooked local meals. ₹2665

15

Nor-khill Paljor Stadium Rd ☎03592 205637, ⓦelginhotels.com; map p.831. Luxurious former royal guesthouse of the chogyal, this landmark hotel is one of the finest addresses in town. Plush rooms in grand Sikkimese style and there's a good restaurant and cosy bar, but the location – overlooking the sports stadium – is poor, and you will need transport. Price includes one meal (lunch or dinner). ₹12,000

AROUND GANGTOK

Bookman's 1km north of Metro Point, Development Area ☎03592 204336, ⓦbookmans.in; map p.831. In a peaceful location above the iconic Rachna Books (see page 837) and opposite the new Secretariat, this trendy little B&B has just three rooms, all with attached baths and cosy interiors. Downstairs, *Café Fiction* (see below) does a great Western breakfast for ₹200. ₹1600

★ **Hidden Forest** Middle Sichey Busty ☎03592 205197, ⓦhiddenforestretreat.org; map p.831. A 2km taxi ride from the SNT bus terminus and Paljor Stadium brings you to this peaceful idyll, with organic food, a pleasant terrace garden and sublimely comfortable cottages in a family-run nursery that specializes in orchids and azaleas. ₹3000

Nettle and Fern Jiwan Theeng Marg, Development Area ☎03592 204355, ⓦnettleandfernhotel.com; map p.831. A smart little hotel with friendly staff and cosy wood-panelled rooms, all with heating, plush interiors, and tea and coffee facilities. The American-style restaurant and bar is a lively spot, with good desserts and a range of international cuisines. Discounts of up to 30 percent are possible off-season. It's close to the taxi stand and a ₹20 taxi ride or 20min walk to MG Marg. Rates include breakfast. ₹3500

★ **Tag Along Backpackers** Abhilasha, Next to Nepali Sahitya Parishad, Development Area ☎75509 25535, ⓦtagalong.asia; map p.831. Finally Gangtok has a sparkling clean hostel catering to backpackers, run by two energetic, friendly sisters. The colourful dorms are all en suite, bright, with plugs, reading lights, and luggage storage under the bunks. On the ground floor, the eco-friendly *Travel Café* has a bakery and is a good place to meet like-minded travellers and locals. Breakfast is included. Dorms ₹800

EATING

Though Gangtok has mushroomed into a modern town with hip eateries and bars, most places still wrap up by 9pm.

Absolute Demazong NH-31A, Hungry Jack Complex ☎83487 61655, ⓦfacebook.com/hungryjackplaza; map p.831. On the upper floors of a nondescript building, this large restaurant is a good bet for local food and drink. Cane furniture lends a rustic vibe, and traditional set meals include rice, vegetables, a meat curry and local drinks such as *so-chang* (millet beer) or the Nepali liquor *raksi*. There's a selection of Bhutanese dishes along with the usual Indian and Chinese; expect to pay ₹900 for two. Live music on some evenings. Daily 11am–9.30pm.

Baker's Café MG Marg ☎03592 220195, ⓦfacebook. com/bakerscafeindia; map p.831. Modern patisserie a short walk from the tourist office, with a tempting selection of cakes, croissants and pizzas, as well as good coffee (₹80) and fruit drinks. Daily 9am–8pm.

Café Fiction Rachna Books, Development Area ☎03592 204336, ⓦfacebook.com/cafefiction; map p.831. Below the celebrated bookshop and *Bookman's* B&B, the bright and airy café is a gathering point for travellers and creative types, with frequent live music and poetry readings. The menu is small but eclectic, with a great French Press coffee (₹80), Vietnamese and Nepalese dishes and good breakfast choices. Mon–Sat 10am–7pm.

Café Tibet NH-31A, past the hospital; map p.831. This lively café, serving pizzas and burgers, croissants, cakes and ice cream, is popular with students. *Momos*, noodles and other Tibetan items are also on the menu; expect to pay around ₹150 for a meal. Daily 10am–8pm.

The Coffee Shop New Market, MG Marg ☎03592 201300; map p.831. Bright and cosy first-floor restaurant with a pleasant balcony overlooking the busy market street. The menu features Italian dishes, burgers, coffee, baked treats and a selection of wines and beers. Meals ₹400. Daily 10am–8.30pm.

Khan Uncle's Biryani House MG Marg ☎99324 80018, ⓦfacebook.com/KhanUncleGtk; map p.831. Popular takeaway restaurant dishing up good, inexpensive Kolkata and Hyderabadi-style chicken biryanis, saucy *momos*, and Chinese food. There's cheap coffee (₹30), too. Daily 11am–9pm.

Nimtho New Market, MG Marg ☎03592 205324, ⓦfacebook.com/nimthosikkim; map p.831. This mid-range restaurant, attractively decked out to resemble the kitchen of a rural Nepali mud home, serves good traditional Sikkimese, Nepali and Tibetan cuisine. Try the delicious *churpi ko jhol*, a Sikkimese special cheese soup (₹110). There is also a good selection of beers and spirits. A meal will set you back ₹500. Daily 10am–10pm.

Snowlion Hotel Tibet, Paljor Stadium Rd ☎03592 203468; map p.831. Superb Tibetan and Indian food, with a selection of Sikkimese and Japanese dishes. Expensive by local standards, at around ₹800 a meal or more, but highly recommended. Interesting choices include the Tibetan sweet *momo* and Japanese *suriyaki*. Daily noon–9pm.

Tangerine Chumbi Residency hotel, Tibet Rd ☎03592 206618; map p.831. Plush, elegant yet affordable restaurant serving Indian, Chinese and Sikkimese specialities, including the intriguing *churpi ningro* (cheese

FOOD AND DRINK

Sikkimese food is a melange of Nepalese, Tibetan and Indian influences; rice is a staple, eaten with dhal, forest vegetables and pickles, including the supremely hot, fire-engine-red **dalley** chilli pickle. **Churpi**, a fresh cow-milk cheese, is generally made with a fern called **ningro**. **Gyakho** is a traditional chimney stew served on special occasions. **Phing** (glass noodles), **shisnu** (nettle soup), **gundruk** (fermented spinach), **gyathuk** (soup with handmade macaroni and local herbs; usually with beef) are other typical specialities, along with chicken, pork and beef dishes. **Khodo** (millet pancake) and **fafar roti** (buckwheat pancake) are generally eaten for breakfast. Tibetan dishes including *momos* and *thukpa* are found easily.

Restaurants in Gangtok serve alcohol; Hit and Dansberg are the local Sikkimese **beer** brands. Look out for **tomba**, a traditional drink usually served in winter, consisting of fermented millet served in a wooden or bamboo mug and sipped through a bamboo straw. The mug is periodically topped up with hot water; once it's been allowed to sit for a few minutes, you're left with a pleasant warm, watery drink that's best on a cold evening. **Chaang** is a local millet beer, milky and fermented, found more commonly in homestays.

15

and fern; ₹100) and *phing shymo* (rice noodles with oyster mushroom). The adjacent lounge bar is good for a relaxing drink. Expect to pay ₹600 for a meal for two. Daily 11am–9pm.

Taste of Tibet MG Marg; map p.831. At the corner of MG Marg, this upstairs restaurant is very popular with travellers and locals for its reasonable, wholesome local cuisine. There's the ubiquitous *momos*, *thukpa* and chow mein, while more uncommon options include the Tibetan *shyaphale* (meat pie; ₹190) and beef chilli. Daily 11am–9pm.

DRINKING AND NIGHTLIFE

Live & Loud Tibet Rd ☎03592 205024; map p.831. A hip bar/restaurant with large sofas and live music, busy on weekends when it gets packed-out for bands from around the region. There's both indoor and balcony seating, and the menu features the usual Chinese and Indian fare. Entry fee on gig nights ₹300. Daily noon–11pm.

Lounge31A Zero Point, NH31A ☎83718 71883; map p.831. Long-standing Gangtok American-style bar perched on Zero Point's hilltop, with amazing sunset views over the city. Expect beers on tap, finger food, a few Indian and continental mains, and the odd karaoke night. Daily noon–11pm.

SHOPPING

The town's best shopping areas are the **Main Market**, stretching for 1km along the pedestrianized MG Marg, and the local produce bazaar in the concrete **Kanchenjunga Shopping Complex (Lal Bazar)**. Here, stalls sell dried fish, *dri* (female yak) cheese (*churpi*), and yeast for making the local beer, *tomba*; on Sundays, there's a *haat* (bazaar) when people from surrounding areas sell traditional wares from the villages. Curio shops on **MG Marg** and on **Paljor Stadium Rd** sell turquoise and coral jewellery, plus religious objects such as silver ritual bowls and beads.

Handloom and Handicraft Emporium NH-31A, north of the centre ☎03592 203126; map p.831. Workshops and a retail outlet for traditional Sikkimese handicraft including carpets, hand-loomed fabrics, *thangka* paintings and wooden objects; prices are fixed and you can visit the workshops. Mon–Sat 10am–4pm.

Rachna Books Development Area, 1km north of Metro Point ☎03592 204336, ⓦfacebook.com/rachnabooks; map p.831. This cosy wooden-floored bookshop with couches and large windows invites you to linger over its varied collection of books. The shop hosts poetry and other readings, seminars, art exhibitions and even concerts. The owner, Raman, is a keen jazz aficionado and music is central to the theme, with the great *Café Fiction* downstairs. Mon–Sat 10am–7pm.

DIRECTORY

Banks and exchange If you're travelling into the interior, note exchange facilities are few and far between beyond Gangtok.

Hospital The STN Memorial Hospital, on the junction of NH-31A and Paljor Stadium Rd, has a 24hr emergency wing and an ambulance service (☎03592 2222994); Central Referral Hospital, 5th Mile, Tadong (☎03592 231137), has more facilities. Find pharmacies along MG Marg.

Internet Gangtok has several internet cafés (around ₹40/hr) clustered around Tibet Rd.

Police ☎ 100.

Post office The main branch is on Paljor Stadium Rd.

Around Gangtok

The most obvious destinations for day-trips from Gangtok are the great Buddhist monasteries of **Rumtek** to the southwest, and **Phodong** to the north. Indian tourists flock to **Tsomgo Lake** and beyond, to the Tibetan border at **Nathu La**.

Tsomgo Lake and around

Tsomgo Lake (pronounced "Changu"), 35km northeast of Gangtok and just 20km from the Tibetan border at **Nathu La**, is a scenic spot at an altitude of 3750m. It is popular with Indian and foreign visitors alike, all of whom need permits arranged through travel agents (see box, page 832). Indian visitors flock here to sample the high-mountain environment and, hopefully, experience the thrill of snow in the colder months. It's possible to visit the **Kyongnosla Alpine Sanctuary** (3350m) en route, where a profusion of wild flowers bloom between May and August and migratory birds stop over in winter on their annual migration from Siberia to India. Only Indian nationals are allowed up to the trade post at **Serathang** and **Nathu La** (4130m), where, at a motley collection of border buildings, they try to catch a glimpse of Chinese soldiers.

Lingdum (Ranka)

14km west of Gangtok, on the road to Rumtek • Free • Shared taxi ₹50; taxis only run till mid-afternoon

The most rewarding route to Rumtek from Gangtok is via the impressive **Zum Gharwang** *gompa* of **Lingdum** (also called **Ranka**), completed in 1998. A haven of peace surrounded by deep woodland, Lingdum is a grand example of modern monastic architecture, with an expansive terrace and courtyard. Inside, delicate and detailed murals, with a predominance of pastel colours, depict the life of the Buddha. Adrenaline junkies will find several paragliding outfits here.

Rumtek

Visible from Gangtok, and a popular 24km day-trip southwest of the capital, **RUMTEK** is one of Sikkim's largest and most impressive *gompas* and the main seat of the **Karma Kagyu** lineage – also known as the **Black Hat** sect – founded during the twelfth century by the first Gyalwa Karmapa, Dusun Khyenpa (1110–93).

Foreigners need to register passport details at the **checkpoint** off the village bazaar; even Indians and locals are sometimes asked for ID.

The main temple

Daily 6am–5pm • ₹10 • ☎ 03592 252329 • No photography allowed

The **main temple**, with its ornate facade covered in intricate, brightly painted wooden latticework, overlooks the expansive **courtyard**. Large red columns support the high roof of the **prayer hall**, where the walls are decorated with murals and *thangkas*. Visitors may attend daily rituals here, when lines of monks sit chanting.

Karma Shri Nalanda Institute of Buddhist Studies and Golden Stupa

The **Karma Shri Nalanda Institute of Buddhist Studies**, behind the main temple, built in 1984 in traditional Tibetan style, is the most ornate of all the buildings of Rumtek. Monks spend a minimum of nine years studying here, followed by an optional three-year period of isolated meditation. The ashes of the sixteenth Karmapa are contained in a gilded 4m-high *chorten* or *stupa*, studded with turquoise and coral, which sits in the **Golden Stupa** hall opposite the Institute.

THE KARMA KAGYU AND RUMTEK

Dusun Khyenpa established the Tsurphu monastery in central Tibet near Lhasa, which became the headquarters of the **Karma Kagyu** for eight centuries until the Chinese invasion of Tibet in 1959. The sixteenth **Karmapa**, Rangjung Rigpe Dorje, fled Tibet for Sikkim, where he was invited to stay at the old Rumtek *gompa*. Within a couple of years, the Karmapa had begun building a monastery at **Rumtek**, which was to become his new seat, on land donated by the Sikkimese King Chogyal Tashi Namgyal. One of the great Tibetan figures of the twentieth century, the sixteenth Karmapa was very influential in the spread of Tibetan Buddhism to the West, setting up over two hundred Karma Kagyu centres and raising funds for the rebuilding of Tsurphu. When he died in 1981, he left behind a wealthy monastery and a huge and lucrative international network, but one bitterly divided by an ugly squabble over his rightful successor. Two reincarnate Karmapas have now emerged as the main contenders to the throne – one blessed by the Dalai Lama and ensconced in Dharamsala, the other in nearby Kalimpong. A heavily armed security presence at Rumtek keeps the peace, but is a sad intrusion into the otherwise impressive monastery.

15

Old Rumtek gompa

From the entry gate to Rumtek, take the path going downhill to the left (15min walk)

A flower-and prayer-flag-lined path leads to the simple **Old Rumtek gompa**, the original monastery, founded in 1740 and recently renovated. The quiet setting, surrounded by empty outbuildings in traditional Sikkimese alpine style, with latticed wooden windows, is a world away from the charged atmosphere of the main complex.

ARRIVAL AND DEPARTURE   RUMTEK

By jeep If you don't arrange your own transport (₹1200 for a private car), the best way to get to Rumtek is in one of the shared jeeps that leave Gangtok, when full, from the private taxi stand near Metro Point. Few shared taxis travel after 2pm, and those that do will charge a lot more after dark. Destination Gangtok (1hr; ₹50).

ACCOMMODATION AND EATING

Rumtek has a limited choice of budget **accommodation**, but an increasing number of more upscale resorts offering a quiet alternative to crowded Gangtok. In Rumtek itself, noodles and chai are available at the **teashops** clustered near the monastery gate and at the **bazaar**.

The Bamboo Retreat Sajong, 1km before the monastery gates ☎03592 252516, ⊛ bambooretreat. in. A boutique hotel where Swiss chic meets formal Sikkimese style, set against a backdrop of forest with views towards Gangtok and Nathu La in the far distance. Each bedroom has a unique colour scheme according to feng shui elements. There's an organic vegetable and herb garden, a library and traditional meditation hall, plus mountain bikes available for hire. Rates include breakfast and taxes. ₹4700

Sungay Between the checkpoint and monastery gates ☎98006 03242 or 86095 76992. A welcoming guest-house, not to be confused with the far more basic *Sangay*, which is closer to the monastery. This is by far the best of the budget options, boasting large, clean rooms, good home-cooking, an expansive terrace and a garden. All rooms have attached baths with hot water; the more expensive (₹800) have balconies with views. ₹500

Teen Taley Eco Garden Resort Lower Sajong ☎03592 252256, ⊛ sikkimresort.com. Around 2km from Rumtek and spread over six acres, this place is geared towards families, with a small farm and guided walks, mountain bikes for hire, pony riding and a pick-your-own vegetable garden. The wood-lined cottages and suites use a blend of vernacular and modern architecture. ₹4100

Phodong and Labrang

38km north of Gangtok on the Mangan road • Free • Shared taxi ₹150 from Gangtok's Vajra taxi stand

The road to **Phodong**, another living but far less ostentatious monastery, passes Kabi Lunchok, a pleasant wooded spot marking a historic treaty between the Lepchas and the Bhutias, and some spectacular waterfalls.

On a high spur of 3km above the small Phodong Bazar, Phodong commands superb views, with a simple, square main temple and several outhouses. Built in the early eighteenth century, this was Sikkim's pre-eminent Kagyu monastery until the growth of Rumtek in the 1960s. It too hosts colourful lama dances, similar to the *chaam* of Rumtek, each December.

A rough road leads a further 4km up from Phodong to another renovated old monastery – the unusual octagonal **Labrang**. A cluster of *chortens* between these two monasteries marks the ruins of **Tumlong**, Sikkim's capital city for most of the nineteenth century.

South Sikkim

Ignored by most travellers en route to higher trekking trails and the great *gompas* of West Sikkim, **southern Sikkim** nevertheless offers quiet charm, its lichen-covered forests draped with a stunning array of orchids and inhabited by rare and endangered animals. The region is dominated by the great, forested peak of **Maenam** – towering high above the town of **Ravangla** – a challenging day-trek and famous for its plants and flowers and for the tremendous view from its summit. Easier options such as the delightful jungle walk to the lesser heights of **Tendong** are just as rewarding, while high above the district capital **Namchi**, the gigantic statuary of **Samdruptse** and **Solophok** are clearly visible from as far away as Darjeeling. Sikkim's sole tea garden, the organic **Temi Tea Estate**, welcomes visitors and provides a good base from which to explore the area and its villages, among which **Chalamthang** is rising as an interesting eco-tourism destination.

Namchi and around

Some 79km southwest of Gangtok and pleasantly situated on a saddle at 1676m above sea level, busy **NAMCHI** is the administrative centre for South Sikkim. The area around town is a magnet for domestic tourists, but Namchi itself has little to offer save a handful of monasteries, including the Nyingmapa **Doling Gompa**, **Shirdi Sai Baba Mandir**, and the impressive statues of **Samdruptse** and **Siddhesvara Dham** on nearby Solophuk Hill.

Chalamthang

42km southeast of Gangtok • Private taxis charge ₹3500 from Bagdogra airport or New Jalpaiguri, or ₹250 for a shared jeep. From Singtam, a shared jeep costs ₹50.

Perched high above Singtam, **Chalamthang** village put itself firmly on South Sikkim's tourist map by striving to become the state's cleanest village, and promoting community-based homestay tourism with a 100 percent organic, vegetarian lifestyle, where all food is grown in the garden (entry ₹30), manned by an 88-year old warden. You can hike to **Devi Mandir**, a Shiva temple sheltered under a 200-year-old tree, the **Ban Jakhri Cave**, or the **Deorali Dara** viewpoint, with breathtaking views of the Teesta River as it snakes into the surrounding valleys and mountain ranges. A 160-year-old traditional Nepali house stands as a memorial to Sikkim's architectural heritage.

Samdruptse

8km north of Namchi • Daily 8am–5pm • ₹30 • Accessed via a steep, gruelling climb past Ngadak Monastery, or an easier jeep ride (₹250) to the ornamental Rock Garden, from where a scenic ropeway (₹150 return) climbs to the statue. By 2020, the ropeway will be connected all the way to Namchi's District Hospital • Taxis from Namchi's Central Park to the car park near the statue cost ₹500.

High above town, the gigantic 41m statue of Guru Rinpoche (Padma Sambhava) known as **Samdruptse** sits on a ridge, gazing south towards Darjeeling. Inaugurated by the Dalai Lama in 2004, the statue cost ₹67,600,000 (around US$16 million) to build, and is large enough to contain a meeting hall.

Siddhesvara Dham

5km southwest of Namchi • Daily 8am–7pm • ₹50 • taxis from Namchi's Central Park to the entrance cost ₹500

Also known as **Char Dham** ("four abodes"), this hilltop temple complex features a towering 33m-high statue of Lord Shiva surrounded by life-size models of the four sacred Vaishnavite Hindu Temples found at Badrinath, Dwaraka, Puri and Rameswaram.

Temi Tea Garden

18km north of Namchi • Daily 8am–5pm • All SNT buses from Siliguri or Gangtok to Namchi stop at Temi Tea Estate en route. Shared jeeps leave from Siliguri SNT bus stand (₹250), Singtam (₹100), or Namchi Car Parking Plaza (₹100).

Sikkim's only organic tea estate opened in 1969 under direct supervision of the Chogyal of Sikkim, and has delivered top-quality tea worldwide ever since. **Temi Tea Garden** is sprawled over 177 hectares in a gradient slope between 1450m and 1920m of height, graced by breathtaking views of Kanchenjunga. Visitors can take a tea-making and tasting tour in the factory (₹500), soar above the tea gardens on a zipline (₹300), paraglide (₹3500), bike around the estate (₹400/hr including mountain bike), and enjoy cultural nights with masked dances and bonfires (₹3600/4 persons).

Tendong Hill

15km north of Namchi

Faint forest trails lead north from Samdruptse through the forest to **Tendong Hill** (2623m) where a small monastery sanctifies the sacred spot revered by the Lepchas, who believe that the hill saved them from the great flood that once submerged the Earth. An easier and more direct route to Tendong than from Namchi starts from the hamlet of **Damthang**, 14km north of Namchi on the Ravangla road and accessible by shared taxi, from where it's a 6km trek along a pleasant brick-paved trail through dense, protected forest. On a clear day, the views from the Tendong summit stretch from the plains of Bengal to the high Himalayas, and in good weather it's worth camping at the top to catch the sunrise. Beware of **black bears** — don't go alone.

ARRIVAL AND DEPARTURE

NAMCHI AND AROUND

By jeep Namchi is well connected to all points in Sikkim as well as Siliguri, Kalimpong and Darjeeling, and jeeps are frequent between 6am and 5pm. The main transport hub is the multi-storey Car Parking Plaza below Central Square where all jeeps, taxis and buses converge; use the prepaid booths.

Destinations Darjeeling (2hr30min; ₹220); Gangtok (2hr; ₹190); Kalimpong (3hr; ₹150); Pakyong (3hr; ₹200) Ravangla (40min; ₹80); Singtam (45min; ₹130); Siliguri (3hr; ₹200).

By train The Car Parking Plaza has an advanced railway reservation office, useful for Tatkal tickets from New Jalpaiguri station.

INFORMATION AND TOURS

Information The Sikkim Tourism office is on Alley Rd, below Dak Bungalow (Mon–Fri 9am–5pm), ☏ 953595 264557.

Services There are several internet cafés in the bazaar (₹30/hr).

Tours For tailor-made journeys in South Sikkim, such as food tours covering tea-harvesting and learning how to make traditional meals, or for arts and crafts tours, contact Kamalan (☏ 97110 08524, ⊛ kamalan.travel).

ACCOMMODATION AND EATING

Namchi and its surroundings offer an increasing choice of accommodation. Most places are clustered around the pedestrianized main square, Central Park, resplendent with two magnificent trees including a pipal (sacred fig, also called the *bodhi* tree) with an aquarium built around it. For more atmospheric stays, however, it's best to leave the town behind.

Aansham Kutir Homestay Below Temi Bazaar, Temi, ☏ 74782 37552, ⊛ aanshamkutir.com. The seven well-appointed rooms — four en suite (₹1500) and three with immaculate shared bathrooms — surround the garden of this lovely Nepali family home. It's an ideal place to relax, hike, and learn about local life. Meals are excluded — breakfast is ₹120, veg thali ₹200, and non-veg meal ₹250. **₹800**

15

Chalamthang Homestay Chalamthang village ☏ 8902232559, ⌨ chalamthanghomestay.com. This beautiful homestay sits high on a ridge with fantastic views of the Singtam valley, and fully embodies Chalamthang's village green lifestyle. Rooms are large and comfortable and include two simpler budget options (₹700); meals are deliciously home-cooked, and guests are treated as part of the family. Price includes full board. **₹2500**

Crumbs n Whips 100m from main square on Jorethang Rd, above Sikkim Bank, Namchi ☏ 89274 11039, ⌨ facebook.com/CrumbsNWhips. Hip and central bakery with a good selection of pizzas (₹200), sandwiches, good veggie burgers, and other Western comfort foods — wash it all down with good barista coffee (₹70. A meal will set you back ₹500. Daily 9am–9pm.

Dungmali Solophok Rd, 3.5km from Namchi Bazaar ☏ 86702 44061. To reach this welcoming family-run guesthouse with organic kitchen garden and adjacent woodland, take a taxi from the stand in town (₹120). Most rooms benefit from the great views, and the home-cooking is wholesome. It's within walking distance of Siddhesvara Dham, and staff can arrange tours of the region. **₹2500**

Orchid Villa Gangchung Temi, ☏ 97331 54928, ⌨ orchidvillasikkim.com. The comfortable and clean wood-floored rooms at this homely resort, overlooking two orchid greenhouses, are very good value. The family's home-cooked food is delicious, and the rooftop is a great spot for uncluttered Kanchenjunga views. Breakfast is included, and ₹500 extra covers all meals. **₹1500**

15

Ravangla and around

Spread across a high saddle, 65km west of Gangtok and 52km east of Pelling, the sleepy market town of **RAVANGLA** (also known as Ravang and Rabang) makes for a convenient stopover, especially for anyone interested in trekking through one of the last remaining **rhododendron forests** in south-central Sikkim. The fabulous **Maenam Sanctuary** remains a botanist's dream, covering the flanks of the gigantic forested peak which looms over the town.

Ravangla itself has a sizeable Tibetan settlement, with a handicrafts centre and shop at the **Kheunpheling Carpet Centre** in the refugee camp to the south. Steps north of the bazaar lead to a completely renovated **Nyingmapa monastery** and behind it, the lavish Buddha Park. Down the road is Chodzo Lake, a green, manmade pond surrounded by cartoonish statues of Himalayan animals. It hosts a yearly festival, and otherwise sees a number of locals who come to enjoy the paddle boat joyrides and simple restaurants.

Buddha Park (Tathaghata Tsal)

1km north of Ravangla on the way to Ralang • Daily 9am–5pm • Entry ₹200 (₹50).

Dominated by a grandiose 40m-high seated statue of Sakyamuni Buddha, this well-manicured park was built between 2006 and 2013 to celebrate the 2550th birthday of Lord Gautama Buddha. A temple under the main statue houses a glass-covered golden Buddha and murals depicting his life.

Mane Chorkeling Monastery

A short, steep walk from the north end of Ravangla Bazaar leads to the lavishly renovated Nyingmapa **Mane Chorkeling Monastery** with a landscaped garden, which, along with the old chapel within the grounds, is dedicated to Shakyamuni and Guru Rimpoche, accompanied by a host of stucco images of the wrathful protectors.

This is the site of the annual three-day **Pang Lhabsol festival** in late August, which celebrates the worship of Kanchenjunga and draws thousands of Sikkimese to enjoy the traditional sports and **Pangtoed Chaam**, masked dances that are unique in that they are performed by lay people, not by monks.

Maenem

Summit is 10km from Ravangla bazaar • Guide ₹1000 for a day's trek, arranged through hotels in town or at the forest gate 1km above town where you pay an entry fee to the sanctuary (₹50)

The summit of **Maenam** (3235m) is home to a small chapel to Guru Rinpoche (Padma Sambhava) and boasts superlative views, especially of the horned summit of Narsing (5825m). Feasible as a day-trek, the stiff 1000m **ascent** of Maenam (2hr 30min–4hr)

NARSING AND RANGIT TRAILS

Numerous trails and permutations cover this corner of Sikkim, forming the watershed dominated by the elegant peak of Narsing (5825m; climbing not permitted) and offering the promise of a **high-altitude trek** without the restriction of a special permit. The region abounds with high mountain **lakes** as well as **hot springs** along the Rangit River, best accessed via Ralang and the village of Borong or from Tashiding (see page 850). However, the area is most famous for its **holy caves** including **Lhar Rinchen Nying Phug** (3785m), one of the four in Sikkim associated with Guru Rinpoche, which lies en-route to the mountain lakes of Panchpokhari (3–4 days). The little-visited trek starts at **Labdang**, connected to **Tashiding** (13km) by jeep. Local **guides** are available at Labdang (from ₹500/day) and through *Sanu* homestay in Tashiding (see page 852), while complete itineraries are available through hotel *Zumthang* in Ravangla (see below).

starts with steps rising from the bazaar up to the *gompa* before trailing off through the sanctuary where you may even be lucky enough to glimpse wildlife, including the elusive red panda, black bear and a variety of birds. The route through the forest is confusing, so you may want to take a local guide. To catch the sunrise from the dilapidated shelter, bring a good sleeping bag, food and water.

15

Ralang

13km north of Ravangla • Shared jeeps travel here from Ravangla on demand (₹50), though not usually after dark, which can be as early as 4pm

Monasteries in the vicinity of Ravangla include the old and the new *gompas* at **Ralang**. The old *gompa*, **Karma Rabtenling**, is linked to the ninth Karmapa and was founded in 1730. The new Ralang monastery, **Palchen Choeling**, built in 1995 in much the same style as Rumtek, is one of the largest temple buildings in Sikkim with numerous resident monks.

ARRIVAL AND DEPARTURE   RAVANGLA AND AROUND

Note that you can't be assured of regular transport much after noon.

By bus The shortest route to Darjeeling is via Namchi, where you may have to change for a jeep or bus.

Destinations Namchi (9am; 1hr); Siliguri (6.30am; 4hr).

By jeep Jeeps leave from the stand at the crossroads towards the southern end of the market. Gangtok jeeps leave at 7am, 8am, 11am, noon; jeeps to other destinations leave intermittently from around 7am till 2pm.

Destinations Gangtok (4hr; ₹200); Namchi (via Legship and Gyalshing; 3hr; ₹70); Pelling (1hr 30min; ₹180).

ACCOMMODATION

Annexe at Mount Narsing Village Resort 3km west of Ravangla, off Kewzing Rd ☎ 81452 94900, ⓦ mtnarsingresorts.com. A quiet idyll in a stunning location, a steep 20min walk (or precarious jeep drive) up from the main resort, on the dirt track veering left off the road leading to Kewzing. Comfortable chalets, built partly of local materials, are ringed around the main lodge, with a restaurant boasting an open fire. Their tour operation Yuksom Tours & Travels specializes in this region. Full board available. ₹2750

Bon Farmhouse Kewzing Busti, 8km west of Ravangla ☎ 97359 00165, ⓦ sikkimbonfarmhouse.com. In an idyllic spot surrounded by terraced fields, Chewang Rinchen Bonpo's family farmhouse has well-furnished wood-lined rooms, marrying rustic vernacular style with modern amenities. The Bonpos also offer birding walks and monastic tours. Breakfast included and dinner is ₹300 extra. ₹4000

Buddha Retreat 500m down the road from Buddha Park ☎ 03592 20258, ⓦ yangthangheritage.com. Luxe boutique hotel in walking distance to the Sakyamuni Buddha, with 18 large and luminous wooden-floored rooms named after Himalayan peaks, and traditional-chic decorations. The large hall leads to a restaurant and a spa, and breakfast is included. ₹4499

Zumthang Kewzing Rd ☎ 97330 61311, ⓦ hotel zumthang.webs.com. On the outskirts of Ravangla, this delightful family-run homestay offers warm, clean rooms, some with balconies, and good home-cooked meals. Pema is very informative about the area and can organize Buddhist retreats, day-treks and tours of the region. ₹1500

15

SIKKIM HOMESTAY TRAIL

Homestays in rural Sikkim offer unique insights into various ethnic customs, cuisines and lifestyles, such as those of the Chhetris, Gurungs and Bhutias communities. Set within forested hillsides, there's ample opportunity for treks, village walks and birdwatching, and you'll eat home-cooked meals, interact with locals and observe customs. A convenient homestay trail is from **Hee Bermiok** in West Sikkim to Darap, 8km from Pelling, on to **Kewzing** in South Sikkim, covering forest treks via Kecheopalri, Pemayangtse and Tashiding. Eco-travel agent **Kipepeo** (📞 99300 02412, 🌐 kipepeo.in) works with local communities and can organize tours and homestay accommodation across rural Sikkim.

ACCOMMODATION

Daragaon Village Retreat Darap, 8km from Pelling 📞 95939 76152. Away from Pelling yet easily accessible by a 10min drive, Darap village is home to Gurung, Rai, Limboo and Bhutia communities. Shiva Gurung's hilltop homestay offers warm, bamboo-lined rooms with attached baths and hot water, two friendly dogs, evening bonfires accompanied by *tomba*, and insights into the Buddhist family's way of life. A good base for the low-altitude Rani Dunga trek and the challenging Goechala trek. ₹2800

Dhungay Homestay Hee Bermiok 📞 97332 69413, 🌐 dhungayhomestay.com. A traditional Chhetri household in a Sherpa-dominated village, high on the mountain-side with an organic garden. Wooded rooms have attached baths, and local cuisine is eaten in a common dining space. Ganesh arranges day-treks and village walks; handy for the Singalila rhododendron forests. ₹2800

Kewzing Homestays Kewzing village 📞 97493 24860. The homestays here, in a lush Bhutia village on the fringes of Ravangla in South Sikkim, operate on a community-based model under the Kewzing Tourism Development Committee (KTDC). Traditional homes set within bamboo forests near the Kewzing monastery have been developed into homestays and accommodate guests on a rotational basis. Rooms range from basic doubles with common baths to more luxurious wood-panelled styles; price includes full board. There are great mountain views, birdwatching opportunities and hikes to Maenam and Tendong, among others. ₹3600

West Sikkim

The beautiful land of **West Sikkim**, characterized by great tracts of virgin forest and deep river valleys, is home to ancient monasteries such as **Pemayangtse** and **Tashiding** and the rapidly developing tourist hub and hill station of **Pelling**. The old capital, **Yoksum**, lies at the start of the trail towards Dzongri and Kanchenjunga. In the far west, along the border with Nepal, the Singalila Range rises along a single ridge, with giants such as Rathong and Kabru culminating in Kanchenjunga itself. Only two **high-altitude trails** are currently easily accessible but require permits (see page 832), and are expensive; however, several **low-altitude treks** with numerous variations provide appealing alternatives.

Gyalshing and Legship

The bustling market town of **GYALSHING** (pronounced and also known as **Geyzing**), 110km west of Gangtok, is the administrative centre and transport hub of western Sikkim, and a good place to stock up on provisions and extend **permits**, which you can do through the Superintendent of Police (Mon–Sat 10am–4pm) at **Tikjuk**, midway between Gyalshing and Pelling. There are a handful of **hotels** around the main square in the centre of Gyalshing should you miss connections. At the bottom of the climb up to Gyalshing, **LEGSHIP** (14km) is an important regional road junction and the gateway to western Sikkim. Nestling deep in the shadows of the Rangit Valley, Legship is dull with little to see save a temple across the river and grubby hot springs down the road, but you may find yourself here waiting for onward transport.

Pemayangtse

2km east of Pelling • Daily 7am–5pm • ₹50 (₹20) • No photography • Shared jeeps from Gyalshing ply regularly until mid-afternoon (₹30; 10min); from Pelling, book a reserved taxi (around ₹100) or walk for around 30min

The hallowed monastery of **Pemayangtse**, perched at the end of a ridge, with a grand panorama of the entire Prek River watershed including the Kanchenjunga massif, is poised high above the Rangit River. It's a 9km journey along the main road from Gyalshing; or you can take a steep, 4km short cut, walking through the woods past a line of *chortens* and the otherwise uninteresting remains of Sikkim's second capital, **Rabdantse** (daily 7am–5pm; ₹50/₹20), now made into a pleasant park.

Pemayangtse, the "Perfect Sublime Lotus", was founded in the seventeenth century by Lhatsun Chempo and is one of the three lamas of Yoksum. Extended in 1705 by his reincarnation, it's one of the most important *gompas* in Sikkim and belongs to the Nyingmapa sect. The views and the surrounding woods create an atmosphere of meditative solitude.

The main gompa

Surrounded by outhouses featuring intricate woodwork on the beams, lattice windows and doors, the **main gompa** itself is plain in comparison. Built on three floors, it centres around a large hall which contains images of Guru Rinpoche and **Lhatsun Chenpo** (the latter was an enigmatic Tibetan lama who is the patron saint of Sikkim), and an exquisite display of *thangkas* and murals. On the top floor, a magnificent wooden sculpture carved and painted by Dungzin Rinpoche, a former abbot of Pemayangtse, depicts Sang Thok Palri, the celestial abode of Guru Rinpoche, rising above the realms of hell. The extraordinary detail includes demons, animals, birds, Buddhas and *bodhisattvas*, *chortens* and flying dragons, and took him just five years to complete.

Pelling and around

The rapidly swelling town of **PELLING**, situated 2085m above sea level, is most notable for its expansive views north towards the glaciers and peaks of Kanchenjunga. High above forest-covered hills, in an amphitheatre of cloud, snow and rock, the entire route from Yoksum over Dzongri La to the Rathong Glacier can be seen. Frenetic building activity has somewhat detracted from Pelling's quiet charm, and the area is a magnet for Bengali travellers; the main drag from the crossroads to Lower Pelling is chock-full of hotels and not much else. However, on a clear day, you can gaze in awe at the world's third-highest peak from any of the numerous hotel terraces in Upper Pelling, and there's easy access to attractive walks in the hinterland. One noticeable element missing is a bazaar, although a few shops are now beginning to appear.

Sanga Choling

4km north from Upper Pelling • Daily 7am–5pm • Taxis from Pelling charge ₹200

A new road blasted up the steep ridge from near the helipad just above Pelling makes a good 4km walk to reach the small but highly venerated Nyingmapa monastery of **Sanga Choling**, one of the oldest *gompas* in Sikkim and another of Lhatsun Chenpo's creations. Gutted by fire, it was rebuilt in 1948 and houses some of the original clay statues including a stunning Samantha Bhadra. Next to the monastery is the world's tallest statue of Chenrezing — a 42m-high rendition of Amitabha, the earthly manifestation of the eternal Buddha — opened on 1 November 2018. At the bottom of its grand staircase, a skywalk and a café cater to tourists.

ARRIVAL AND DEPARTURE   **PELLING**

By jeep Shared jeeps depart from the crossroads of Upper Pelling, also called Zero Point; shared jeeps from here to Gangtok only run in season, and it's advisable to book beforehand through your hotel or an agent. Father Travels (see below) runs a direct jeep service to Gangtok and Siliguri (both daily 7am; ₹350). You can also wait for 2/3 daily

WEST SIKKIM HIKES

The numerous **trails** crisscrossing through West Sikkim's wonderful profusion of orchid and rhododendron forests, waterfalls, terraced hillsides and river valleys, give independent walkers the opportunity to explore the region without the headache of red tape (permits) and the expense of tour operators and expedition costs. Apart from the occasional forest lodge or guesthouse, a growing network of **homestays** allows intrepid trekkers to wander off the beaten track, especially along the **Monastery Trail** (see page 849) from Pelling. On the western boundaries of the state, the rhododendron forests are best seen around Varshey.

RHODODENDRON WALKS

The Singalila Range's rhododendron forests, lauded by the famous botanist Sir J.D. Hooker, who travelled here in 1848, are best visited between mid-April and mid-May when the flowers are in full bloom. Of these forests, the **Varshey Rhododendron Sanctuary** (aka Barsey or Varsey) covers 104 square kilometres, ranges in altitude from 2840m to 4250m and is home to black bear, red panda and pheasant. Entry to the forest is via **Hilley**, **Soreng** or **Dentam** and entry permits (₹100 (₹50), tents and camera extra) for the sanctuary are available from forestry departments at **Hilley**, **Soreng**, **Uttarey** and **Gangtok**. The most popular route is the 8km round trip from Hilley to **Varshey** (3030m), which offers majestic views. You can extend the walk to Uttarey (3–4 days with tented accommodation), from where you can either take transport out or continue on foot to the small town of Dentam. From Dentam, a river-valley trail leads to the quiet village of **Rinchenpong** (4–5hr), a good base for West Sikkim village walks; another trail from Dentam leads east up the ridge to **Pelling** (4–5hr).

There are numerous permutations and possibilities for trekking around Varshey including an extension (with prior arrangement with tour operators and the appropriate permits) into the long high-altitude **Singalila Ridge trek** to **Dzongri** and beyond (see page 851).

15

ACCOMMODATION

Choice of accommodation by the sanctuary itself is limited; it's best to look a bit further afield such as at Soreng, Rinchenpong bazaar and Kaluk, where there is increasing choice.

Guras Kunj Lodge Varshey ☏ 95938 82002, ✉ info. guraskunj@gmail.com. Very handy for the sanctuary, this well-situated but absolutely basic trekker's hut offers just one en suite triple-bed room and a dorm. Full board. Dorms ₹900; triples ₹1200

Nagbeli Uttarey ☏ 97332 10853, ⊕ nagbeliresort. com. Above the small Uttarey Bazaar and handy for the rhododendron treks, the hotel, popular with Bengali travellers, has small, comfortable rooms some in a concrete block and others in a wooden chalet set in a colourful garden. Trekking guides and permits can be arranged. ₹1500

★ **Yangsum Farm** Rinchenpong ☏ 94341 79029, ⊕ yangsumheritagefarm.com. The sylvan environs of this working hill-farm, 3km below the bazaar, provide a quiet retreat with large, comfortable rooms furnished in local Tibetan style with modern amenities and good home-cooking. Thendup can arrange decent village and forest walks and all-inclusive treks including guides for the Singalila trails. Rates include taxes. Full board. ₹6500

Yuksom-bound jeeps that stop in Pelling between 12 and 2pm. Shared taxis to Kecheopalri (₹100) and Yuksom (₹100) can be arranged through tour operators, who will pick up guests from their hotels; the regular route to Yuksom via Tashiding entails a change at Gyalshing – leave as early as possible to make the connections.

Destinations Gangtok (7am; 4hr; ₹350); Gyalshing (regularly 7am–5pm; 20min; ₹50); Ravangla (7am; 2hr; ₹250); Siliguri (7am; 6hr; ₹350).

By bus A single bus leaves for Siliguri via Gyalshing from Lower Pelling. Book in advance between 6 and 7pm at SNT, *Hotel Saredena*, Upper Pelling (☏ 97332 12625).

Destination Siliguri (7am; 6hr; ₹300).

INFORMATION AND TOURS

Information The tourist information centre near the helipad (daily 10am–4pm) is good for general and travel information, as is the excellent local website, ⊕ gopelling. in. Avoid the pretend tourist information centre above the crossroads. For the best in local trekking and transport

information, consult *Hotel Garuda* (see page 848).

Tours Tour operators such as Destination Treks & Tours (☏ 96097 76494) at the crossroads and Father Travels in Lower Pelling (☏ 77972 83512) can arrange day-trips by jeep (from ₹1500 for half-day and around ₹2000 for a

15

full day). *Hotel Garuda* provides reliable travel services (₹2500 car rental for a full day, maximum 10 people) and

can arrange local treks, village tours and logistics for the Monastery Trail (see page 849).

ACCOMMODATION

Most of Pelling's **hotels**, whose rates rise steeply in the high seasons (March–May & Sept–Nov) are spread along a 2km stretch of road between Upper, Middle and Lower Pelling. Lower Pelling gears itself more towards the domestic market, while Upper Pelling offers the finest views and has several attractive options and new luxury developments away from the concrete jungle.

The Elgin Mount Pandim Just below Pemayangtse Monastery ☎ 03595 250756, ⓦ elginhotels.com. Darjeeling-style elegance has turned this old government hotel into the most luxurious address in western Sikkim. Every room has a view of the snowy peaks, there's a good multicuisine restaurant, and the unspoilt location makes this the ideal base from which to explore the area. ₹8950

★ **Garuda** The crossroads, Upper Pelling ☎ 03595 258319 & 97330 76484, ⓔ hotelgaruda.pelling@ gmail.com. A long-popular travellers' haunt with a decent restaurant, great travel desk and wi-fi (lobby only), this charming family-run hotel offers a wide range of rooms, from dorms to deluxe balconied suites. The hotel's comments books contain useful trekking information and travellers' tips, and Tshering is full of stories of Pelling in the old days. Thirty percent discount available off-season. Dorms ₹250; doubles ₹600

Hotel Kabur On the edge of town towards Pemayangtse, Upper Pelling ☎ 097759 72112, ⓦ hotel kabur.com. This charming hotel has a good restaurant that spills onto a sociable terrace with great mountain views. Few storeys of clean, large wood-panelled rooms cling to the slope beneath. Those with a view (₹800) are perfect for early morning views of Kanchenjunga. ₹600

Norbhu Ghang Upper Pelling ☎ 03595 258272, ⓔ norbughang.com. Traditional Sikkimese-style cottages, with Buddhist decor and set in pretty gardens, are spread across this expansive hotel, one of Pelling's plushest resorts. The location high above town promises good views from most of the wood-lined rooms, which are heated and have modern amenities. The new *Retreat & Spa* is an extension of the original property, with more luxurious offerings. Rates include breakfast. ₹6500

Phamrong Upper Pelling ☎ 94323 24780, ⓦ retreat hotels.in/hotel-phamrong-retreat-pelling/. Conveniently located at the crossroads, this old favourite has a wide range of comfortable wood-panelled rooms with running hot water. The suites on the fourth floor are charming and have good views, but involve quite a schlep, as there's no lift. The restaurant serves Sikkimese, Indian and Chinese food. Breakfast is included, and good-value deals are available in low season. ₹2850

EATING

Many of Pelling's best **restaurants** are in hotels, but traditional Sikkimese food is rather rarer than *dhal bhat* due to the strong Bengali presence. Upper Pelling has several cafés, and for fine dining try the conservative menu at *The Elgin Mount Pandim*.

Big Bowl Zero Point ☎ 96478 76717. A multicuisine restaurant attached to Destination Treks & Tours, where there's comfortable seating and an extensive menu featuring the standard Indian and Chinese fare. Breakfast offerings are varied, including porridge and pancakes. Around ₹250 a head for lunch or dinner. Daily 8am–9pm.

Garuda The crossroads, Upper Pelling ☎ 03595 258319. A popular restaurant and bar on the ground floor of the *Garuda* hotel, with a cosy fireplace and a view of the street. There's a mix of Indian, Tibetan and Chinese dishes, as well as traditional Sikkimese meals which include cheese soup and meat curries; try the spinach *momos*. There's beer, too. Expect to pay around ₹500 for a meal. Daily 7am–9.30pm.

Havmor Upper Pelling ☎ 97342 30378. Good south Indian dhaba dishing up a range of dosas (from ₹90), sandwiches (₹100), a few North Indian paratas and rice pulaus (from ₹100). Daily 9am–9pm.

Lotus Bakery 500mt out of town on the road to Pemayangtse ☎ 94745 32034. Run by the Denjong Pema Choeling Academy, this grassroots bakery has good chai (₹20), apple rolls (₹40), cookies (₹10) and other baked treats that are great for breakfast or tea time. Daily 7am–5pm.

Melting Point Middle Pelling ☎ 97333 07934. One of the few good restaurants not part of a hotel, this bright and cheerful place has comfortable couches indoors and a pleasant veranda with mountain views, though its popularity means you may not get a seat outside. There's a bar with ample choice, including some Tibetan specialities (₹150) such as *gyathuk* (noodle soup), *falay* (stuffed patty) and *thenthuk* (soup with noodles, meat and veggies). Daily 11.30am–8pm.

DIRECTORY

Internet There's an internet café at the post office during office hours (₹40/hr).

Post office The post office is in Upper Pelling just above the crossroads.

THE MONASTERY TRAIL

You won't need a guide for this rewarding circuit which has come to be known as the **Monastery Trail**, taking in the highlights of western Sikkim including several holy places and monasteries. Don't expect a totally wild experience, as parts of the trail nowadays are along paved roads. Do ask advice from hotel *Garuda* in **Pelling** (see page 848) on the most scenic route, and pick up a rough map of the trail. Each section takes between four and seven hours, and the growing network of **homestays** allows trekkers to find comfortable accommodation. Most walkers start the popular three-to-four-day trail from Pelling via **Darap** to **Khecheopalri** (see page 849), then continue to **Yuksom** (with a steep descent and a knee-grinding ascent to the small town) where there are some decent hotels and homestays. Continuing from Yuksom takes in monasteries such as Dubdi (above Yuksom), Hongri and Sinon before descending to **Tashiding** (see page 850). To return to Pelling, walk down to Sakyung from where there is an unrelenting ascent to Pelling. Along with several extensions, alternative routes from Tashiding include walking to Borong, Ralang and **Ravangla** (see page 842) with a dip in a hot spring along the Rangit River; the advantage of this variation is that it would help you get on to the road for Gangtok. For trail information in Tashiding, ask at *Sanu's* homestay (see page 852), or go through Red Panda in Yoksum.

15

Khecheopalri Lake

32km from Pelling • 6am–6pm • ₹10 • Regular jeep services from Gyalshing (90min; ₹100) via Pelling (1hr; ₹100) drop passengers off at the stand at the bazaar (around 15min walk to the lake) – Deepen Pradhan of *Lake View Nest* can organize transport to Khecheopalri; guides are available for exploring the area for around ₹500/day

Surrounded by forests and hidden in a mountain bowl (2000m) 33km northwest of Pelling, **Khecheopalri Lake**, known as the "Wishing Lake", is sacred to the Lepchas. A footpath leading to the right from the police booth at the tiny bazaar and road-head, past the picturesque *anni gompa* (nunnery), leads to the lake, which attracts pilgrims of all faiths. Legend has it that if a leaf drops onto the lake's surface, a guardian bird swoops down and picks it up, thereby maintaining the purity of the water. The path going left from the police booth in the bazaar leads to the small **Khecheopalri Gompa** (1km) that serves a scattered farming community occupying the plateau above the lake, with great views of Mount Pandim (6691m).

The village homestays and natural serenity make Khecheopalri a place to linger for a day or more, and walks include those to sacred caves such as **Dufuk**.

ACCOMMODATION AND EATING

★ **Lake View Nest Homestay** Kecheopalri Gompa ☎ 97359 45598, ✉ lakeviewnest@gmail.com. Welcoming homestay on the plateau near the *gompa*, with comfortable rooms and a modern shared bathroom downstairs. Wholesome home-cooked food, great views and a glimpse of pastoral life abound. Chumden, the owner, will organize guides, birdwatching tours, and give advice on walks in the region. It's a 20min uphill walk from the jeep stand; turn left

from the police booth and walk a slightly descending trail for 200m. Price includes three meals. ₹1500
Pala Homestay Kecheopalri Gompa (contact through Lake View Nest Homestay). Near the *gompa*, the owner – a local lama and father of *Lake View Nest*'s Chumden – offers very basic traditional wooden rooms and shared bathrooms; he also organizes meditation courses. Price includes two meals. ₹800

Yoksum

The sleepy, spread-out hamlet of **YOKSUM** at the end of the road which runs north of Pelling and at the entrance to the Rathong Chu gorge, 40km north of Pemayangtse, holds a special place in Sikkimese history. This was the spot where three lamas converged from different directions across the Himalayas to enthrone the first religious king of Sikkim, Chogyal Phuntsog Namgyal, in 1642. Named the "Great Religious King", he established Tibetan Buddhism in Sikkim. Lhatsun Chenpo (see page 846) is supposed to have buried offerings in Yoksum's **Norbugang Chorten**, a vast white stupa built with stones and earth from different parts of Sikkim, to be found in **Norbugang Park** a kilometre north of Yoksum, which also houses the **Coronation Throne**, a simple stone throne of the first chogyal. In front of the throne, a large footprint embedded in a rock belongs to one of the lamas. **Kathok Lake**, a small pond nearby at the top end of town, was also part of the original ceremony, but it's disappointing and pretty scummy these days.

The village's main role these days is as the start of the high-altitude **Dzongri Trail** (see page 851), but unless you have a trekking permit, you're not supposed to venture any further and the authorities are quite vigilant. So long as you're not carrying a backpack, they may allow a day-trip along the main trail to the Prek River and its convergence with the Rathong – a 28km round trip.

Dubdi Monastery

It's best to enquire in the bazaar or the KCC office (see box page 852) before you set out, as it's often closed

High above Yoksum, prayer flags announce the site of the **Dubdi Monastery**, built in 1701 and one of the oldest of its kind in Sikkim. To get here, walk past the bazaar to the hospital at the top of the village, where the road ends. A path from here threads past waterwheels and a small river, and rises through the forest to arrive at the *gompa* on an expansive shelf.

15

ARRIVAL AND INFORMATION
YOKSUM

By jeep There are no buses to or from Yoksum itself, but the regular jeep services (book the night before at the bazaar) start early (6.30–7.30am); you're unlikely to get any shared transport after 1pm.
Destinations Gangtok (4–5hr; ₹350); Gyalshing (1hr; ₹150); Pelling (1hr; ₹150); Ravangla (2.5hr; ₹250).
Information Kangchendzonga Conservation Committee (KCC), Gompa Rd (daily 10am–4pm; ☎9832 452527), provide information and will assist with homestays and

other travel-related enquiries.
Trekking Of the few operators, Dhan Raj Gurung of Red Panda in the bazaar (☎97331 96470, ✉sikkimtraveler@gmail.com) is a knowledgeable, enthusiastic and experienced operator who rose through the ranks and knows the area well. He can arrange Dzongri Trail permits with two days' notice and is reasonably priced at US$60/head for two. He can also arrange local guides (₹700 per day) and offers internet use. KCC can also help arrange guides.

ACCOMMODATION AND EATING

Most options are around the small market area. The KCC at the Visitors Information Centre, at the head of town, organizes several **homestays** (from ₹600 full board) around the village. Besides hotel restaurants, the only other **places to eat** are cafés along the main drag, which serve snacks and basic meals.
Dragon 100m south of the bazaar (☎97359 34578, ✉yukland@ymail.com. On the main drag leading to Yoksum's tiny market, this cosy family-run establishment has a little lawn space and a sunny terrace. Accommodation is simple, but clean and comfortable, with attached rooms upstairs and a shared bathroom for the rooms downstairs. The restaurant offers traditional food and a bar. ₹800/₹600
Dzongri Bazaar (☎97331 58258. A centrally located, rustic wood building with a handful of rooms (shared baths) and hot water. Facilities are basic, but there's a restaurant

that offers all meals, and staff can arrange guides for trails. Accommodation options include a dorm and single, double and triple rooms. Dorms ₹250; doubles ₹600
Tashi Gang Just above the bazaar (☎99330 07720, ✉hoteltashigang@gmail.com. The oldest and the best of Yoksum's mid-range hotels tastefully amalgamates traditional Sikkimese style with modern amenities. Rooms are comfortable, with wooden floors and Buddhist art; some have balconies. There's also a decent restaurant and a large lawn with good views. ₹2500
Yuksum Residency Bazaar (☎99331 33330, ✉yuksumresidency@gmail.com. This central and plush hotel, with a strong Buddhist theme, has a little too much marble for a mountain village and can get rather chilly. It offers a high level of comfort, and the more expensive rooms are wood-lined and thus warmer. ₹3200

Tashiding

Considered the holiest in Sikkim, the beautiful *gompa* of **Tashiding** occupies the point of a conical hill 19km southeast of Yoksum, high above the union of the Rangit and the Rathong rivers. "The Devoted Central Glory" was built in 1717, after a rainbow

WEST SIKKIM HIGH-ALTITUDE TREKS

Two **high-altitude treks** are currently allowed in Sikkim. The first, from **Yoksum** to **Dzongri**, in the shadow of Kanchenjunga, passes through huge tracts of forest and provides incredible mountain vistas; all-inclusive rates from a decent agency are from around US$50 per head per day including **permits**. The second, the **Singalila Ridge**, explores the remote high pastures of the Singalila frontier range with breathtaking views of the massif. Trekkers for either route must have special permits, travel in groups of at least two and organize the trip with an authorized agency (see page 832). General advice on trekking equipment and health issues is given in Basics (see page 59).

THE DZONGRI TRAIL

Although Dzongri is the junction of several trails, the prescribed route onwards leads to **Goecha La** via Zemanthang and Samiti Lake. Well-marked and dotted with basic accommodation, the trail, also used by yak herders, is at its best in May when the rhododendrons bloom.

DAY 1 It takes approximately six hours to climb the 16km from **Yoksum** (1780m) to **Tsokha** (3048m). The forested trail begins gently before arriving at the Prek River above its confluence with the Rathong. The next 4.5km involve a knee-grinding ascent, entering the lichen zone and cloud forests, past the *Forest Rest House* at **Bakhim** (2684m) to the Tibetan yak herders' settlement of Tsokha where there are a couple of trekkers huts.

DAY 2 This day can be spent acclimatizing to the altitude at Tsokha, perhaps with a 5km trek towards Dzongri, to a watchtower with superb views of Kanchenjunga and Pandim.

DAY 3 The 11km section from **Tsokha** to **Dzongri** (4030m) takes at least five hours, rising through beautiful pine and rhododendron forests to **Phedang Meadows** (3450m), before continuing to the hut at Dzongri.

DAY 4 Once again, it's worth staying around Dzongri for further acclimatization. This gives you the opportunity to climb Dzongri Hill above the hut for views of Kanchenjunga's craggy south summit and the black rocky tooth of Kabur, a holy mountain towering above Dzongri La (4400m), a pass that leads to the HMI base camp, 12km away at Chaurikhang, and the Rathong Glacier (a recommended variation).

DAY 5 The 8km trek from **Dzongri** to **Thangsing** (3841m) takes around four hours, descending against an incredible backdrop of peaks to a rhododendron forest, crossing a bridge and continuing through woods to *Trekkers Hut* at **Thangsing** at the end of a glacial valley.

DAY 6 The 10km short, sharp shock up to **Samiti Lake** (4303m) takes around three hours, through alpine meadows traversing glacial moraine before arriving at the emerald-green **Samiti Lake** (local name Sungmoteng Tso). If you are still going strong, you could continue to **Zemanthang** (4453m), where there's a trekkers hut.

DAY 7 This is the climax of the trek and its most difficult section by far, due to the high altitude. From **Samiti Lake**, the 14km round-trip climb takes around four hours up to **Goecha La** and two to three hours back down again. The trail follows glacial moraine to Zemanthang, before a final grinding rise following cairns and the occasional prayer flag to the narrow defile at Goeche La (5000m), where Kanchenjunga South is visible on a clear day.

DAY 8 Most of the long 24km hike from **Samiti Lake** back to **Tsokha** is downhill and takes around eight hours, involving a short-cut after the bridge to avoid Dzongri. There are several variations to this finish.

THE SINGALILA RIDGE

Itineraries for **Singalila Ridge** treks range between ten and nineteen days, and though more expensive due to the area's remoteness, they prove exceptionally rewarding, with views from Everest to the huge Kanchenjunga massif ahead. It's best done from south to north, facing the views as the trail rises towards the snows through remote alpine pastures and past hidden lakes. The most common variation starts from the road-head at **Uttarey** (1965m), 28km to the west of Pelling, and ascends to **Chewabhanjang** (3170m) on the Sikkim–Nepal frontier. Thereafter, the trail rarely descends below 3500m, high above the tree line; the highest point of the trail is the **Danfeybhir Tar**, a pass at 4400m. The route descends to **Gomathang** (3725m), a yak-herders' shelter on the banks of the Boktochu, then passes through delightful forests of silver fir and rhododendron before arriving at the welcome sight of the bungalow at **Dzongri** which connects with the main trekking trails.

15

15

CONSERVATION AND THE KANCHENJUNGA NATIONAL PARK

Established in 1996 with the help of the Sikkim Biodiversity and Ecotourism Project, the **Khangchendzonga Conservation Committee (KCC)** aims to promote ecological awareness to locals and visitors alike. The KCC's main concern is the impact of tourism on the fabric of the **Kanchenjunga National Park**, and their initiatives include keeping trails clean, planting trees, promoting eco-awareness, training local workers as porters and guides and organizing self-help initiatives. Conservation has also been embraced by the Sikkim government, which has put in place a code of conduct, banning the use of wood for fuel in preference to kerosene; however, wood fires continue to be part and parcel of the Sikkim landscape. For more information on the KCC, contact their coordinator Pema Chewang Bhutia at Visitors Information & Biodiversity Centre, Gompa Road, Yoksum (☎97331 49975, 98324 52527 or 9733 158268, ✉ kcc_sikkim@hotmail.com). They also arrange low-altitude trail **guides** for ₹1000 a day.

was seen to connect the site to Kanchenjunga. While a paved road has eaten its way through the forest to the monastery, the climb is still recommended – the well-marked path leaves the main road near an impressive *mani* wall (inscribed with the Buddhist mantra *Om mani padme hum*: "Hail the jewel in the lotus" in silver paint) and leads steeply past rustic houses and fields, and along a final flag-lined approach.

On the fifteenth day of the first month of the Tibetan New Year, devotees from all over Sikkim gather in Tashiding for the **Nyingmapa Bhumchu festival**, when they are blessed with the holy water from an ancient bowl, which – legend has it – never dries up. Oracles consult the water's level to determine the future.

On the popular **Monastery Trail** (see page 849), Tashiding provides a good base from which to explore the **treks** along the watershed of Mount Narsing and the Rangit River, with several holy lakes and caves a few days' walk away.

ARRIVAL AND DEPARTURE
TASHIDING

By jeep Leaving from the bottom of the main street of Tashiding's tiny Sinek Bazaar, 3km below the monastery, one or two timetabled jeeps (7–9am) and a handful of unscheduled jeeps run to the destinations below. The last regular shared jeeps depart at 8am.
Destinations Gangtok (7.30am & noon; 4–5hr; ₹350); Gyalshing (1hr; ₹200); Legship (40min; ₹100); Siliguri (5–6hr; ₹350); Yoksum (1hr; ₹100).

On foot Several trails through the forests and along stretches of roads make trekking an alternative option to public transport; the route to Yuksom climbs up to Sinon Gompa before traversing high ground, while the route to Pelling descends to Sakyung before a final relentless climb. You can also walk to Ravangla via Borong and Ralang. For more details and numerous other trekking possibilities including guides, consult Sanu at her homestay.

ACCOMMODATION AND EATING

Accommodation around Tashiding's Sinek Bazaar is generally disappointing, though there are some good homestays on the footpath up to the monastery and a few in the compound itself. Additionally, at the time of writing, a clutch of new homestays were due to open.
Mount Siniolchu Guesthouse At the top end of the bazaar ☎97333 42511. This simple guesthouse has just three wooden rooms, with plain beds and shared baths downstairs. It's a welcoming place, close to the bazaar cafés and a short walk from the taxi stand at the crossroads. ₹500
★**Sanu Homestay** 300m uphill through the monastery entrance gates ☎96350 60062, ✉ sanu bhutia79@gmail.com. This excellent village homestay in the monastery complex offers a warm welcome and good home-cooking from an organic garden. The shared

bathroom outside features hot showers but squat toilets. Sanu is a font of knowledge for the area and can help arrange treks, guides or just directions for those wanting to go it alone. Sanu can also arrange for shared taxis to pick up guests from the doorstep. Her sister next door runs the *Sonam* homestay, where Sanu accommodates guests if hers is full. Rate includes dinner, breakfast and snacks for two. ₹1500
Yatri Niwas Tourist Lodge 10min winding walk above the bazaar ☎98326 23654. In a good location, 2.5km from the monastery, this government lodge offers a decent degree of comfort. The large rooms all have attached baths and hot water, and there's food to order and a pleasant garden. ₹2000

North Sikkim

A fragile road etches its way up the Teesta Valley and splits at Chungthang with one branch bearing northwest to Lachen and beyond, the other due north to Lachung, to the beautiful valley of Yumthang and eventually Zero Point on the high plateau.

The huge **earthquake** of 2011, with its epicentre near the capital Mangan, severed the roads to North Sikkim and left over sixty people dead. Then, a year later, unexpected late-season rains caused deadly **landslides** that once again isolated the region for several weeks Travellers to North Sikkim need to show their permits at Tong, from where the stretch of road to Chungthang has greatly improved in recent times.

ESSENTIALS   NORTH SIKKIM

Monsoons Every year throughout the monsoon, landslides take out stretches of road – at the height of the tourist season around five hundred jeeps battle their way up and down the tortuous and inadequate roads to and from Gangtok.

Permits Access to much of North Sikkim is restricted: visitors are only allowed in with the necessary permits, and some areas along the borders remain completely out of bounds. Groups armed with Protected Area Permits can go as far north as Thangu, past Lachen, at the edge of the plateau. Only Indians – similarly armed – can travel further on to the spectacular lake of Gurudongma, on the Tibetan plateau. North of Mangan, foreigners are only allowed up in groups of two or more, and need to book travel through a registered operator. Jeep tours include transport and homestay accommodation. North Sikkim permits (extendable through the Superintendent of Police in Mangan) are only valid for five days and a further seven for trekking.

15

Mangan

Travelling north past Phodong, the highway reaches the town of **MANGAN**, 67km north of Gangtok, the district capital of North Sikkim and perched high above the Teesta Valley. Recovering after the devastating earthquake of 2011 which all but demolished the bazaar and destroyed **Rinzing Gompa**, Mangan is nevertheless a convenient stop on an arduous route to the north (note that it's the furthest you can go without a Protected Area Permit. The town itself has little interest other than its busy bazaar, a handful of hotels and the District Collector's office, which is a relatively easy place to get a **permit** if you haven't already picked one up in Gangtok.

ARRIVAL AND INFORMATION   MANGAN

By jeep Share taxis from Gangtok's Vajra stand depart for Mangan 8am to 1pm. From Mangan to Dzongu and beyond, share taxis ply irregularly – it's best to reserve ahead. Destinations Dzongu (1hr; ₹500); Gangtok (2hr 30min; ₹250).

Tours and permits You can get PAPs from the District Collector's office, 2km above town (Mon–Sat 10am–4pm; ☎03592 234856; ₹20 share taxi from bazaar). Khangri Treks & Tours of Gangtok (☎98320 46820) arrange treks, permits and tours of the area.

ACCOMMODATION

The Planter's Home Pentok, 15min walk above town ☎03592 234286, ⬤theplantershome.com. Sister to the *Sonam Delek* in Gangtok, this hotel features very comfortable cottages with large wood-panelled rooms all with attached baths and tea- and coffee-makers. There's a restaurant, bar and fireplace in the main cottage, offering the usual fare along with some local specialities. ₹3000
Tamarind Bazaar ☎03592 234297. Mid-market splendour bang in the centre of town, with marble lobbies, a vegetarian restaurant, and large, clean rooms. Rates include breakfast and taxes. ₹3500
Tshana Residency NH-31A, 300m south of the bazaar ☎94344 45079. On the highway, this welcoming family home offers traditional wood-lined rooms with attached baths, hot water and TVs. The more expensive rooms are large and comfortable (₹2000); meals available. ₹800

Dzongu

Few visit the magnificent, untouched valley and pristine heart of Sikkim – the Lepcha homeland of **Dzongu**, which branches northwest from Mangan towards Kanchenjunga. At the heart of the valley, the ancient *gompa* of **Tholung**, devastated by the 2011 earthquake, has been rehoused in a new *gompa* and is home to ancient treasures of the chogyals; these are displayed every three years to the public with the next exhibition, known as Kamsel, due in April/May 2020. Few roads penetrate Dzongu, and the only way to get to Tholung is on foot from the road-head (20km; 5hr). A few good **homestays** allow visitors to explore the pastoral life of the region, which is abundant with forest walks, challenging **treks** and **mountain-bike** trails.

ACCOMMODATION   DZONGU

Homestays are able to arrange necessary permits and provide all logistics from Mangan including transport.

Dzongu Lee Lingdong ☎96098 64255 ☜dzongulee homestay.yolasite.com. A comfortable Lepcha family home in traditional style but with modern amenities in the non-attached rooms. Wholesome food is on offer, as is a variety of walks and activities. Hot springs nearby are another plus. Rates include three meals, tea and snacks. ₹3000

Mayal Lyang Passingdan ☎94344 46088, ☜maya llyang.com. A traditional mountain home with simple colourful rooms, shared bathroom and a lush garden. Good home-cooked meals are served with fresh vegetables from the family's fields. Camping, treks and walks can be arranged. Rates are all-inclusive. ₹4000

Sohar Dho Tingvong ☎95937 83043, ☻tingvong homestay@gmail.com. Nestled among the terraced fields, with a backdrop of forests and mountain views, Dupden Lepcha's welcoming home offers warm, comfortable rooms with shared baths and trekking services. Full board, with free drinks and snacks. ₹2400

Lachung and around

The road forks at the grubby town of **CHUNGTHANG**, 40km north of Mangan – the road to the right climbs rapidly to the group of small settlements of **LACHUNG**, the "big pass", a mere fifteen kilometres west of Tibet. Across the river from the main cluster of settlement, **Lachung Monastery** is a two-storey Tibetan-style *gompa* belonging to the Nyingmapa sect, and worth visiting especially for its wonderful murals.

As the road north ascends past yak pastures, it enters the **Shingba Rhododendron Sanctuary**, announcing the start of **Yumthang** (3645m), 25km north of Lachung, with spectacular rock and ice pinnacles towering to 6000m on either side. This beautiful tree-lined valley does not have accommodation but boasts somewhat neglected hot **sulphur springs**. A pleasant purpose-made **walking trail** leads 10km along the valley floor, back to the sanctuary gates – due to the high altitude and problems with acclimatization, descent rather than ascent is recommended. Past Yumthang, the road continues up the valley and emerges on the high plateau land at **Yumesamdong** or **Zero Point** (the end of the road), at an altitude of 4770m with a backdrop, weather permitting, of the snowy sentinels along the Tibet border.

Lachen and around

The road which forks left from Chungthang leads 26km to **LACHEN** and a further 36km to **THANGU**, tantalizingly close to the Tibetan plateau and as far as foreign tourists are allowed to go. This is the route to the sacred **Gurudongma Lake**, considered blessed by Guru Rinpoche and the source of the River Teesta, set against a spectacular backdrop of icy peaks. A short day-hike (5km each way) from Thangu (no special trekking permit needed) leads to the picturesque **Chopta Valley** (4400m). There are a couple of homestays in Lachen (contact Rinzing on ☎94745 28499), but note that foreign tourists must be travelling through a registered tour operator and with a guide.

Several interesting **high-altitude treks** are now open to group tours in this isolated region, including the challenging **Lachen to Green Lake** trek (4850m; 9 days), which offers great views of Mount Siniolchu (6887m) across the Zemu glacier and the gigantic east face of Kanchenjunga. Permits take anywhere from a month or even two to be issued.

15

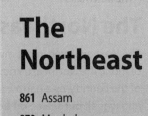

The Northeast

KAZIRANGA NATIONAL PARK, ASSAM

The Northeast

The least explored, most mysterious and arguably the most beautiful region of India, the Northeast, known as the "Seven Sisters", is connected to the rest of the country by a narrow stretch of land between Bhutan and Bangladesh, and was all but sealed off from the outside world until relatively recently. Arunachal Pradesh shares an extremely sensitive frontier with Chinese-occupied Tibet and, together with Nagaland, Manipur and Mizoram, a 1600km-long border with Myanmar.

Many insurgencies, caused by a vast ethnic diversity, have fractured the region since Independence, with tribal groups pushing for autonomy as well as fighting each other. A huge influx of Bangladeshis in the last decade and the displacement of many indigenous people has created further tension. Though there has been improvement in security in some areas, others remain disturbed with occasional clashes and armed conflict on the fringes. **Permits** (see page 862) are required for travel in Arunachal Pradesh, while some other areas, such as the Manipur Hills and Nagaland's eastern fringes, may still experience the occasional unrest. However, tourists are not a target of violence, and the extraordinary diversity of peoples and spectacular landscapes make a visit to the region well worth the effort. One of the world's wettest monsoon belts, the area also boasts an astounding array of flora and fauna, estimated to represent fifty percent of India's entire biodiversity.

Until the 1960s, the region comprised just two states, the North East Frontier Agency – now Arunachal Pradesh – and Assam, but separatist pressures further divided it into the seven states, now officially joined by an eighth: Sikkim. **Assam** consists of the flat Brahmaputra valley. Its capital, **Guwahati**, has two of India's most important ancient temples and is the gateway to the region, while an encounter with a one-horned rhino in the magnificent **Kaziranga National Park** is a highlight of any trip to the Northeast.

The other six states occupy the surrounding hills, and are quite distinct from the rest of India in landscape, climate and peoples. **Meghalaya** has beautiful lakes and includes the wettest places on earth, Cherrapunjee and Mawsynram. Its capital, **Shillong**, retains some of the colonial atmosphere from its days as east India's summer capital. Majestic **Arunachal Pradesh**, one of India's most remote states, is inhabited by a fascinating range of peoples, many of Tibetan origin. In the state's northwestern corner, close to Bhutan, lies the Buddhist monastery of **Tawang**, in sight of the mountainous border with Tibet, while in the far northeast is the remote wilderness of **Namdapha National Park**. To the south, the lush mountains of **Nagaland** are home to fourteen distinctive tribal groups. **Mizoram**, in the Lushai Hills, is predominantly Christian and has one of the highest literacy rates in India.

After years of insurgency and factionalism, **Manipur** – perhaps the most fractured of all the Northeast states and unsafe for travel off the beaten track (see page 891) –

BEST TIME TO VISIT

Weather conditions are best from November to April, although the high-altitude areas of Arunachal, Meghalaya and Nagaland are extremely cold by December, and winter fog can disrupt road journeys. It rains heavily from May to the end of September, particularly in Meghalaya, but travel during this period has its own charm. In major cities such as Guwahati, Tezpur and Shillong, accommodation rates are not affected by the low season, but Kaziranga, Manas and the remote parts of Arunachal, Nagaland and Assam do offer off-season discounts.

Highlights

① Kaziranga National Park, Assam Spot the rare one-horned rhino on a dawn jeep safari deep into the jungle where, with luck, you can see wild elephant or even tigers. See page 868

② Living root bridges, Meghalaya In India's wettest state, entwined roots of the rubber tree form magnificent natural bridges, some centuries old, across waterways. See page 875

③ Tawang Monastery, Arunachal Pradesh In a remote corner that was once Tibet, the largest Buddhist monastery in India maintains an ancient, unbroken tradition. The quiet chapel commemorating the sixth Dalai Lama lies close by. See page 880

④ Namdapha National Park, Arunachal Pradesh A beautiful, remote wildlife park, bordering Burma, with habitat from steamy foothills up to the snow line, and home to a huge variety of wildlife including the Hoolock gibbon and elusive big cats. See page 883

⑤ Hornbill Festival, Nagaland An unmissable occasion and the highlight of the Northeast calendar, bringing together all the Naga tribes in their finery with music, dance and martial art displays. See page 884

⑥ Dzükou Valley, Nagaland Trek to a remote plateau of rolling green hills that is carpeted with flowers in the wet season. See page 886

HIGHLIGHTS ARE MARKED ON THE MAP ON PAGE 860

THE NORTHEAST

HIGHLIGHTS

1. Kaziranga National Park, Assam
2. Living root bridges, Meghalaya
3. Tawang Monastery, Arunachal Pradesh
4. Namdapha National Park, Arunachal Pradesh
5. Hornbill Festival, Nagaland
6. Dzükou Valley, Nagaland

CHINA

TIBET
AUTONOMOUS
REGION

West Siang River

DANAROSHA

Tuting

Roing
Bhismaknagar

Parasuram-
kund

Siang (Dihong) River

Dibong

Lohit River

NAMDAPHA
NATIONAL
PARK

Pasighat

Tezu

Namsai

Miao

Mechuka

Along

Pasighat

Oiramghat

Murkong Selek

DIBRU-SAIKHOWA
NATIONAL PARK

Digboi

NH-37

Ledo

Margherita

ARUNACHAL
PRADESH

Daporijo

Tinsukia

**Bogibeel
Bridge**

Dibrugarh

*Nyegi
Kangsang*

Hapoli
(Ziro)

Sibsagar

Shangnyu

Gori Chen

Harmuti

North
Lakhimpur

Jorhat

Mariani

Mon

MYANMAR
(BURMA)

Itanagar

Nimatighat

Majuli

NAGALAND

Dirang
Munna
Bomdila

Seppa

Naharlagun

Sangrua

Longkhum

Mokokchung

Sela Pass

Bangachangsa

Tawang

Rupa

Tipi

Bokakhat

Tuensang

Wokha

Kiphire

Tuophena

Kalaktang

Bhalukpong

Tezpur

**KAZIRANGA
NATIONAL PARK**

Dimapur

Kohima

Kisama

Mt Saramati

NAMERI
NATIONAL PARK

Nagaon

Khonoma

Kigwema

Ukhrul

BHUTAN

Lumding

Zhakama

Viswema

POBITORA WILDLIFE SANCTUARY

NH-39

MANAS
NATIONAL
PARK

Nalbari

Madan
Kamdev

Maibong

*Cachar
Hills*

MANIPUR

Imphal

NH-31

Hajo

Guwahati

Nartiang

Haflong

*Loktak
Lake*

Barpeta

Sualkuchi

*Lake
Barapani*

NH-44

Moirang

Moreh

ASSAM

Shillong

Jowai

Mawlynnong

Silchar

KEIBUL LAMJAO
NATIONAL PARK

Brahmputra

Mawphlang

*Khasi
Hills*

Dawki

*Jaintia
Hills*

NH-31

Mawsynram

Cherrapunjee

Tamabil

Lalaghat

MEGHALAYA

Sylhet

Dharmanagar

Kolasib

Champhai

*GARO
HILLS*

Williamnagar

Kailashahar

Aizawl

Siju

Kumarghat

Zokhawthar

Tura

Baghmara

Unakoti

MIZORAM

TRIPURA

NB-54

BANGLADESH

Akhaura

Agartala

SEPAHIJALA
NATURE RESERVE

Kamala Sagar

Udaipur

Gumti

Comilla

Neermahal

Dhaka

Trishna

*CHITTAGONG
HILL TRACTS*

Noakhali

Chittagong

N

0   100
kilometres

The International boundaries on this map are neither purported to
be correct nor authentic by Survey of India. Publisher.

FESTIVALS IN THE NORTHEAST

RELIGIOUS FESTIVALS

Yaoshang (March). Manipur's version of Holi is celebrated with the *thabal chongba* folk dance.
Aoling Monyu (April). Konyak festival in the Mon region of Nagaland marking the arrival of spring.
Bihu (mid-April). The major festival of Assam, celebrated with singing, dancing and feasts in the villages, to mark the New Year and the onset of spring.
Chapchar Kut (March). In spring before the new sowing season begins, this is the biggest harvest festival in Mizoram.
Moatsu (May). Celebrated by the Ao tribe in Nagaland after the sowing season.
Dree (July). The Apatanis of Ziro in Arunachal observe this agrarian festival in which animal sacrifices are common.
Nongkrem (first week Nov). In Meghalaya, the Khasi tribe give thanks for the harvest over five days. Young men and women in traditional attire and heavy ornaments perform songs and dances at Smit, near Shillong.
Raas Leela (Nov). For three days, Majuli Island comes alive with masked performances to celebrate the life of Lord Krishna.
Torgya (Nov/Dec/Jan) and **Losar** (Tibetan New Year; Feb). Arunachal Pradesh festival of the Monpa people in Bomdila and Tawang, with colourful *chaam* (masked dances) and religious ceremonies.

MUSIC AND CULTURAL FESTIVALS

Ziro Festival of Music (Sept). Four-day Central Arunachal outdoor music festival with *apong* (rice beer) and indie music, camping under the stars in the Ziro Valley (wzirofestival.com).
Tawang Festival (end of Oct). Three days of tribal performances, masked dances and Buddhist rituals to promote Arunachal's prominent hill station.
NH7 Weekender (Oct/Nov). This popular multiday urban music festival held its first Shillong edition in 2015 and is now slated to be an annual feature. Indian global artists spanning rock, funk, electro and more perform on various stages (wnh7.in/weekender).
Sangai Festival (21-30 November). Held annually in several locations in Imphal and Moirang (see page 892), this festival celebrates the rebirth of Manipur with a smorgasbord of dance, sport, polo and an international expo (wsangaifestival.gov.in).
Hornbill Festival (first week Dec). Held annually in Nagaland at the Naga Heritage Village in Kisama (see page 885), this is among the Northeast's largest occasion, showcasing the dance, music, food, games and intriguing culture of different local tribes (whornbillfestival.com).

16

resurfaced as a rewarding destination and a gateway to Southeast Asia. Even **Tripura**, with its long history of insurgency, is far more settled today, with rail links and a good road system; that said, you are still advised to exercise caution if travelling in the eastern hills. The people of Manipur are closely related to the neighbouring Burmese population. Tripura, bordered by Bangladesh on three sides (having been cut off from the Bangladeshi plains during the 1947 Partition) is distinctly Bengali to the west, while hill tribes make up the majority in the east.

Assam

Assam is dominated by the mighty **River Brahmaputra**, and its vast, lush valley sandwiched between the Himalayan foothills to the north and the Meghalayan hills and plateau to the south. An attractive state carpeted by plantations, forests and paddy fields, Assam is one of India's few **oil** regions, and produces around sixty percent of the nation's **tea**. However, the industry is not as profitable as it once was, and for the marginalized *baganiyas* (tea workers), mainly *adivasis* – tribal people brought in from central India by the British to work as indentured labourers on the plantations – depressingly little has changed since colonial times.

ACCESS, PERMITS AND TOUR OPERATORS

The Indian Government is currently investing to boost both local and international tourism to the region, and **regulations** have become quite relaxed. However, check the latest information with the Indian Embassy, Consulate, tourist office or visa agency before travelling. It is best to get **permits** while in India through a tour operator (see below) or by yourself in Guwahati (see page 865).

PERMITS

Currently **Arunachal Pradesh** is the only one of the seven states that requires foreign visitors to obtain **Restricted** or **Protected Area Permits** (US$50 for a maximum of thirty days) prior to entry. Parties should theoretically consist of a minimum of two, accompanied by a travel agent, though in practice you can get away with saying the second person was "delayed". Allow up to five working days to obtain the permit. **Mizoram** and **Manipur** currently only require registration on arrival at the entry point at the border. Indian nationals do require Inner Line Permits for Nagaland if travelling beyond Dimapur (₹100; ☻home.nagaland.gov.in/inner-line-permit-ilp), Mizoram (₹120; ☻mizoram.nic.in/more/ilp.htm) and Arunachal Pradesh (₹100) prior to entry. Those Indians travelling to Mizoram by road will also need an ILP, but for those arriving by air, permits are issued on arrival. ILPs for Arunachal can be obtained online at ☻arunachalilp.com.

Make several **photocopies** of your passport and permits while travelling through the region. To obtain **Inner Line Permits**, Indian citizens should apply with two passport photographs to representatives of the state governments concerned. Applications should only take a day to process, and can be extended for up to six months in the relevant state capital. Passes are valid for the full period they are allocated for, no matter how many times you enter and exit a state.

RECOMMENDED TOUR OPERATORS

Explore Nagaland Main Rd, Midland, Kohima, Nagaland ☎98563 43037, ☻explorenagaland.com. Well-organized tour operator whose services range from arranging local guides to entire itineraries.

Greener Pastures First Choice, H. S Road, Dibrugarh ☎94767 27547, 84040 02125, ☻thegreenerpastures.com. Experienced tour operator with fixed and tailor-made eco-friendly tours that focus on wildlife, tribes, Buddhism and trekking.

The Holiday Scout Syndicate Press Building, Kakaling Road, Bomdila ☎95406 98458, ☻theholidayscout.com. Arunachal-based tour operator organising a range of excellent customised tours, from rural homestays to photography tours and women-only adventures.

Himalayan Holidays Bomdila ☎03782 222017 or ☎94360 45063, ☻himalayan-holidays.net. They focus on western Arunachal and Tawang but have a good network throughout the Northeast and offer a number of treks.

Jungle Travels India GNB Rd, Silpukhuri, Guwahati, Assam ☎0361 266 7871, ☻jungletravelsindia.com. Offering wildlife and tailor-made tours, including luxury river cruises through its sister outfit, Assam Bengal Navigation.

Purvi Discovery Jalannagar, Dibrugarh, Assam ☎0373 230 1120, ☻purvidiscovery.com. Upmarket operator that specializes in tea tours as well as wildlife, birding, golf, riding and tribal culture.

Social divisions and ethnic strife have lead to long-term **instability** in the state. The separatist group United Liberation Front of Asom (**ULFA**) began an armed struggle for independence in 1985, and in the early 1990s Assamese nationalism sparked opposition from Bodos, Cachars and other ethnic minorities. Bangladeshi migration into Assam has been a bone of contention for indigenous Assamese, resulting in the deadly clashes of 2012 between migrant Bangladeshis and Bodos that left several dead in the western districts of the state. Despite the seemingly insurmountable ethnic tensions, occasional violence reported in the press, *bandhs* and political in-fighting, the situation has vastly improved, as has the infrastructure. More and more visitors are enjoying the delights of the local **wildlife** and **tea plantations**, as tourists are rarely embroiled in the strife that underlies the social fabric of Assam.

Guwahati

The state capital, **GUWAHATI** (or Gauhati), lies on the banks of the mighty **Brahmaputra**. Although some of the old town still retains its character, Guwahati is a sprawling city of shopping malls and bazaars. As the main gateway to the region, you may well need to stay here briefly. Guwahati's main attractions are the **Kamakhya**, **Navagraha** and **Umananda** temples, while northwest of the city are the silk village of **Sualkuchi**, the pilgrimage site of **Hajo** and **Manas National Park**.

As the primary hub for the region's lucrative tea industry, Guwahati's **Assam Tea Auction Centre** at Dispur is the largest trade centre in the world for the CTC (crush, tear and curl) tea so characteristic of Assam. Elsewhere, the bustling markets of **Paltan Bazaar**, **Pan Bazaar** and **Fancy Bazaar**, Guwahati's main shopping areas, are bunched in the centre on either side of the railway, with the older residential areas north of the tracks spread along the riverside. Assamese **silk**, wooden rhinos and other crafts are sold at several shops on GNB Road.

Kamakhya temple

Kamakhya, 8km west of the centre / Paltan Bazaar • Daily 8am–1pm & 3–8pm • Shared taxi or bus to temple gate (₹10) from foothill

On the commanding Nilachal Hill, overlooking the river, the important Kali temple of **Kamakhya**, with its beehive-shaped *shikhara*, is a good example of the distinctive Assamese style of architecture. As one of the *shakti pithas*, it marks the place where

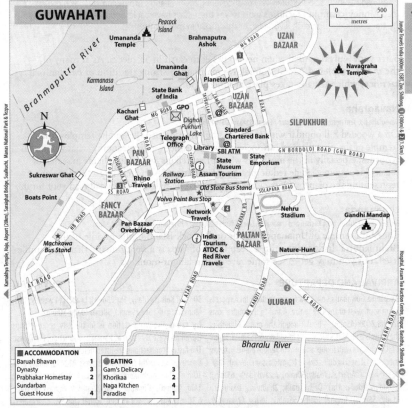

WARNINGS AND TRAVEL ADVICE

WARNINGS

Sporadic violence does plague **Assam**. In 2014, a **curfew** was imposed after violent clashes between a Bodo faction and *adivasi* tribes around the Kokrajar, Sontipur and Chirang districts. The region is prone to **strikes** known as *bandhs* (lockouts) when shops, restaurants and public transport shut down – check the news and ask travel agencies in the Northeast for advice before and while travelling. Avoid **driving** any distance at night, even through Assam, due to the threat of banditry often in the guise of insurgency.

TRAVEL ADVICE

Although **roads** in the Assam valley are well-maintained along the Brahmaputra up to Pasighat and Roing, and there is a good stretch from Tezpur to Tawang, elsewhere – especially in the hills of Nagaland and the interior of Arunachal Pradesh – roads are generally in a terrible state and journeys can prove tedious and painfully slow. If arranging **car** rental, ensure you rent a large vehicle such as a Sumo or Bolero for the mountains of Arunachal Pradesh.

Trains along the valley from Guwahati to Upper Assam and Dimapur are reasonable, and there is a rail-link to Naharlagun in central Arunachal (see page 876). At the time of research, the railway was being extended from Dibrugarh to Pasighat, and should be operational by the time you read this.

Flights are the most convenient mode of travel, with major airports at Guwahati, Agartala (Tripura), Aizawl (Mizoram), Dibrugarh, Silchar, Dimapur and Imphal.

Some of the **ferries** along the Brahmaputra are useful, especially those connecting Majuli Island with the north and south shores of the Brahmaputra (see page 869), while upmarket cruises provide a languid and leisurely way of discovering the river and surrounding areas (see page 865).

Money-changing facilities most towns these days have banks and **ATM**s, but you should travel with enough cash if you plan of striking off in the countryside.

Sati's yoni (vulva) landed when her body fell to earth in 51 pieces. As at many of the *shakti* temples of Assam, Kamakhya maintains a strong tradition of *bali* (animal sacrifice) which usually takes place around noon.

Navagraha

Navagraha Rd, 3km northeast of the centre / Paltan Bazaar • Daily 8am–6pm

On a wooded hill popular with monkeys, the single-domed **Navagraha** temple – the "temple of the nine planets", an ancient seat of astrology and astronomy – has wonderful acoustics, especially in the mornings when priests chant prayers for clients in search of solace. Housed in a single red dome, the central lingam is encircled by a further eight representing the planets. Outside the temple, fortune-tellers (*jyotish*) will read your future.

Umananda

Ferries leave regularly from Kachari and Umananda Ghat (10min each way; ₹30 return) • Daily 10am–4.30pm

The Shiva temple of **Umananda** stands on Peacock Island in the middle of the Brahmaputra. Its location atop a steep flight of steps is more dramatic than the temple itself, but you may get to see some rare golden langur monkeys.

ARRIVAL AND DEPARTURE

GUWAHATI

By plane Guwahati's Lok-Priya Gopinath Bordoloi Airport is 20km southwest of the city centre. A taxi to the centre costs around ₹600 (45min) – book through the prepaid booth in the arrivals hall. ASTC's a/c airport bus (daily 6.15am–3.30pm; ₹130) connects with flights and runs to various points in town; check the latest schedules online (@ astc.assam.gov.in).
Destinations Agartala (daily; 50min); Aizawl (daily; 65min); Bagdogra (daily; 1hr); Delhi (daily; 2h50min); Dibrugarh (daily; 55min); Imphal (daily; 55min); Jorhat (2 weekly; 50min); Kolkata (daily; 1hr 25min); Lilabari (4 weekly; 1hr); Mumbai (daily; 3hr 25min;); Silchar (daily; 50min).

By train The main station is in the city centre; trains travelling west also stop at Kamakhya Junction, 8km west. The fastest connections are listed below.
Destinations Delhi (*Rajdhani Express* #12423; daily; 27hr 10min); Dibrugarh (*Kamrup Express* #15959; daily 3.50pm; 14hr 10min); Dimapur (*Jan Shatabdi Express* #12067; 6.30am Mon–Sat; 4hr 10min); Jorhat (*Jan Shatabdi Express*

#12067; 6.30am Mon–Sat; 6hr 50min); Kolkata (Howrah; *Kamrup Express* #15960; daily 7.45am; 22hr); Lumding (*Jan Shatabdi Express* #12067; 6.30am Mon–Sat; 3hr).

By bus The Interstate Bus Terminus (ISBT) is inconveniently located on NH-37, 9km east of town. Private and public buses leave from here to destinations throughout the Northeast. You can book tickets and check schedules online (w astcbus. in). A handful of private bus companies are based in hectic

and chaotic Paltan Bazaar to the south of the station.

Destinations Bomdila (daily 6am; 9hr); Dimapur (daily; 11hr); Imphal (daily; 12–15hr); Itanagar (daily; 10–11hr); Kaziranga (hourly; 5hr); Siliguri (5–7 daily; 12hr); Tezpur (1–2 hourly; 4–5hr).

By taxi Shared taxis and Sumos to Shillong (3hr 30min) and other destinations depart when full from the old bus stand, opposite *Hotel Tibet* in Paltan Bazaar.

INFORMATION AND TOURS

Tourist office Assam Tourism is on Station Rd next to the *Tourist Lodge* (Mon–Sat, closed 2nd & 4th Sat of the month: March–Oct 10am–5pm; t 0361 254 7102, w assamtourism. gov.in). The state's commercial wing, ATDC (4th floor, Asom Paryatan Bhavan, AK Azad Rd, Paltan Bazaar; t 0361 263 3654), along with their Red River travel services downstairs, offers a range of practical services. Next door, the India Tourism office (Mon–Fri 9.30am–5pm; t 0361 273 7554) provides information on the Northeast and general tourism. **Tours and travel** Nature-Hunt, first floor, 96 Barthakur Mill Rd, Ulubari (t 0361 245 0330 or 99575 77417, w naturehunttours.

com), arranges wildlife and adventure tours as well as luxury tented accommodation in Kaziranga. Greener Pastures (t 94357 47471, w thegreenerpastures.com) offers a range of tours off the beaten track, including food tours in Guwahati and wildlife tours at Manas and Kaziranga. Network Travels, Paltan Bazaar (t 0361 260 5335, w networktravelindia.com), arranges tours, permits and bus and plane tickets.

Cruises For those with time (and money), the Assam Bengal Navigation Company runs cruises on the Brahmaputra; book direct (t 0361 266 7871, w assambengalnavigation.com), or through Jungle Travels India (see page 862).

ACCOMMODATION

Baruah Bhavan 40 MC Rd, Uzan Bazaar t 0361 254 1182, w baruahbhavan.com; map p.863. A comfortable family home close to the river, converted into a luxurious guesthouse with five twin rooms and one double; each room has its own theme. They serve good home-cooked food, and there's a garden and roof terrace, the latter very

pleasant in the evenings. ₹2500

Dynasty SS Rd, Fancy Bazaar, Lakhtokia t 0361 251 6021, w dynastyhotel.in; map p.863. Expectations are raised by the imposing palm-shaded entrance, water feature and opulent lobby, though not quite met by the smart but overpriced rooms. Of the hotel's four restaurants

16

FOOD AND DRINK

Meat-based dishes, smoked, dried and pungent flavours, a liberal use of chilli and the distinct lack of typical Indian masala defines cuisine in the Northeast. The food is mostly **mild**, owing to the lack of spices that grow in the region, aside from some local herbs. **Rice** is a staple and the Tibetan **momos** and **thukpa** are ubiquitous. For **drinks**, salty yak-butter tea and local brews (known by various names including *raksi*, *chang* and *apong*) made of millet, maize or rice are recommended to keep off the chill.

In **Assam**, try the *xaag* (leaf vegetables), fish *tenga* (a souring agent), *pitika* (a pungent vegetable mash) and *khorika* (meat on a skewer).

Meghalaya tends to go heavy on the pork, with dishes such as *doh neiiong* (pork with black sesame seeds) and the staple *jadoh* (rice cooked in meat stock with pork). Meghalayan cooking also features liberal use of seasonal mustard leaves and mushrooms.

At local markets in **Arunachal** you'll find strings of *churpi* (fermented rock-hard yak's cheese), *lai patta* (mustard spinach) and dried river fish. *Churpa*, popular in Arunachal kitchens, is a pungent cheese stew with meat and vegetables.

Naga cuisine consists of smoked, dried meats, bamboo shoot, *anishi* (dry yam leaves) and *akhuni* (fermented soy bean); wild herbs are used as flavouring agents. The star, of course, is the *bhut jolokia* or the king chilli, among the hottest in the world.

Thalis are common in **Manipur**, with side dishes such as *singju* (raw papaya and chickpea salad) and *iromba* (fish and veg chutney) accompanying rice and fish or meat curries.

Mizo cuisine is fairly bland, consisting of forest vegetables and smoked meats; *bai* (vegetable stew with dry soy bean) is a staple.

Fish is abundant in **Tripura**, and *berma*, a pungent fermented fish paste, is used as flavouring.

and bars, *Tandoor* is the best and the *Roof Top* barbecue is a good spot to hang out in the evenings. There's a gym and spa. It's bang in the middle of the bazaar, so be prepared for some noise. ₹3800

★**Prabhakar Homestay** House 2, Bylane 2, K. P. Barua Road, Chandmari ☎0361 2650053, ⚲prabhakar homestay.com; map p.863. A luxurious homestay with five immaculate rooms in the charming villa of Shiela and Mahesh Bora. She's a scholar and daughter of Assam's former Chief Conservator of Forests, while he, a mining engineer, now makes paper from rhino and elephant dung.

Clever conversations make guests feel at home, helped by delicious home-made dinners (₹700). Breakfast included. ₹4800

Sundarban Guest House Just off Buddha Hall, ME Rd, Paltan Bazaar ☎0361 273 0722, ⚲sundarbanguest house.com; map p.863. At the end of a lane off a strip full of small hotels, this popular and friendly place, by a canal, is the pick of the budget lodges with character-less but good-value basic rooms with TVs. The corridors are brightened up with houseplants, framed photos and religious posters. ₹850

EATING

Gam's Delicacy GS Rd, 2km south of the centre ☎82560 20001; map p.863. Ignore the unprepossessing location beneath an overpass – *Gam's Delicacy* is the place to come for authentic regional cuisine. Huge portions of duck, pigeon, pork, chicken and freshwater fish are served with banana flowers, sesame seeds and bamboo shoots (mains from ₹110). Daily noon–3.30pm & 6.30–10pm.

Khorikaa GS Rd, opposite Bora Service Petrol Pump ☎98649 82948; map p.863. Legendary Assamese thali restaurant run by celebrated chef Atul Lahkar. Located upstairs, with a canteen-like atmosphere, it gets packed at lunch and is a must for anyone keen to sample authentic local cuisine. Try the duck with bamboo shoots (₹180). Daily 10.30am–4pm & 7–10.30pm.

Naga Kitchen GS Rd, opposite Pantaloons (7km southeast of the centre) and RG Baruah Rd, opposite Doordarshan (4km east of the centre) ☎98642 68266; map p.863. Pleasant, relaxed and trendy restaurant with two branches in the city, serving Chinese, seafood and, of course, Naga cuisine. Try their Naga speciality of smoked pork with bamboo shoots and *akhuni* (₹210). Daily 10am–10pm.

★**Paradise** Maniram Dewan Rd, Krishna Nagar, Silphukuri ☎94355 48812, ⚲facebook.com/paradise guwahati; map p.863. Consistently dishing up hearty thalis and Assamese specialties, this simple joint is a popular choice to taste some authentic, less spicy, local food. Punjabi and other North Indian dishes are also available. A meal will set you back around ₹300. Daily 11am–11pm.

Hajo and Sualkuchi

HAJO, 38km northeast of Guwahati, is a pilgrimage site for Hindus, Buddhists and Muslims, with a mix of religious temples, including the Hindu **Hayagriba-Madhava Mandir**. Muslims believe visiting the **Poa Mecca Mosque** here four times is equivalent to a pilgrimage to Mecca. Nearby, the town of **SUALKUCHI** is renowned for its golden *muga* **silk**, named after the rich amber colour of the *muga* cocoon, exclusive to Assam.

Manas National Park

Oct–March 9am–5pm • ₹650 (₹100); vehicle ₹300, camera ₹200 (₹100), video camera ₹1000 • Contact tourist office at Guwahati for info (see page 865); 2hr jeep safaris (₹2500 for 6 people) can be arranged at the park's headquarters

Manas National Park, 80km west of Guwahati on the border with Bhutan, has been on UNESCO's list of endangered World Heritage Sites since 1992. Troubled by insurgency and poachers and plagued by development, the park's population of large mammals had sadly declined – sightings of tigers and elephants are now relatively rare. However, several rhinos have been relocated successfully from Kaziranga and a recent photographic audit between India and Bhutan counted fourteen tigers. Consisting of two ranges, Bansbari and Koklabari, Manas is well worth visiting for its varied natural beauty, with buffalo and rhino grazing on expansive stretches of sand and grass, and *sal* forests flanking the Manas River.

ARRIVAL AND DEPARTURE   MANAS NATIONAL PARK

By train and bus The main town, somewhat confusingly called Barpeta Road, is 40km from the park and has good train (daily; 3–4hr) and road (multiple daily; 4–5hr) links

to Guwahati.
By taxi Taxis are available at the station in Barpeta Road to take you up to the park.

GETTING AN ARUNACHAL PRADESH PERMIT IN GUWAHATI

Regardless of what most tour operators will tell you, often inflating the price, Guwahati is a very easy place to get an Arunachal Pradesh Restricted Area Permit by yourself. The Deputy Resident Commissioner office (☏ 361 222 9506) is located on a side street of G.S. Road, about 30 minutes by bus (₹10) south of the train station and Paltan Bazaar, and not far from *Naga Kitchen*. Get off at the Manasha Mandir stop and proceed down a turnoff to the right, across from the HDFC Bank. The office is open Mon to Fri 10am–5pm but you can apply for a permit up to 2pm. You will need a copy of your passport, Indian visa and entry stamp, one filled-in application form (available at the office) and ₹3,450 in cash. Permits are usually prepared within three working days – and often delivered to your accommodation by the overzealous and courteous commissioner – but they can also be sent to your e-mail as you travel. Print and make several photocopies for the entry checkpoints and the few hotels which sometimes require them for registration.

ACCOMMODATION

Manas has a handful of **lodges** including at Mathanguri – the area of the park on the banks of the Manas River and the last point up to which you can take personal vehicles – and some in Barpeta Road.

Bansbari Lodge ☏0361 266 7872, ⊛assambenga lnavigation.com/bansbari-lodge. The most comfortable of Manas's places to stay and conveniently close to the park gates, *Bansbari Lodge* offers an all-inclusive package covering meals, two daily jeep safaris, full board, a guide and park entry fees (₹9500). They can arrange transport to Guwahati airport or train station. Foreign visitors pay a premium; Indians pay around a third. **₹4,500**

Tezpur   16

TEZPUR, 174km northeast of Guwahati, is a busy administrative and commercial hub on the north bank of the Brahmaputra. It is a convenient and sometimes essential stop en route to Arunachal Pradesh and provides good road links to Kaziranga National Park (83km) on the south bank across the 3km long Kolia Bhomora Bridge. Eco-camp **Ugroshore**, set on an empty river island facing Ganesh Ghat, is a new reason to linger longer.

ARRIVAL AND INFORMATION   TEZPUR

By bus State buses go from Tezpur's ASTC bus stand is on Jenkins Rd. An alternative transport hub for those passing through is Mission Charali 4km to the north. Most transport to Guwahati and Bhalukpong in West Arunachal stops here. Destinations Guwahati (1–2 hourly; 4–5hr); Jorhat (hourly; 4hr); Itanagar (1–2 daily; 5hr); Kaziranga (hourly; 2hr).

By Sumo/shared taxi Jenkins Rd is lined with Sumo stands, with daily services to the destinations below. If heading to Tawang in West Arunachal, a break at Bomdila or Dirang is recommended; shared taxis also travel to Itanagar (8–10hr; ₹800). Travel early in the day.

Destinations Bomdila (6am; 5hr; ₹500); Dirang (6.30am; 6hr; ₹500); Tawang (10hr; ₹1200).

Tourist information The tourist office (daily except Sun and 2nd & 4th Sat of month 10am–5pm; ☏03712 221 016) is in the *Prashanti Tourist Lodge* on Jenkins Rd.

ACCOMMODATION

KF Mission Charali, 4km north of the bus station ☏03712 255203, ⊛kfhotels.com. Next to the busy and convenient crossroads, *KF* is a welcome surprise. Immaculate, contemporary rooms with slick bathrooms, modern art, flats creen TVs and tea/coffee-making facilities make this "boutique" hotel one of Assam's most stylish. There is a bright patisserie, department store and an ice-cream parlour on the ground floor, an a/c multicuisine restaurant upstairs (meals ₹450) and a dimly lit, smart bar. **₹2700**

★**Ugroshore** 500m south from the ASTC bus stand ☏88768 09850, ⊛facebook.com/ugro.shore. Experience life on a blissful, inhabited riverine island facing Tezpur's main ghat at this eclectic eco-campsite featuring wooden chalets (₹3500) and tents (₹500 if bringing your own). Prices include boat transfers and activities like morning trekking, water sports, evening river dolphin spotting, yoga classes, and a bonfire. Meals are about ₹500 for two. They also offer boat transfers to Kaziranga National Park (₹1500 per person). **₹1500**

★**Wild Mahseer** Sonitpur, 30km north of Tezpur ☏022 67060861 or ☏98336 31377, ⊛wildmahseer.com. These five luxurious colonial-era bungalows based in the peace and quiet of the Addabari Tea Estate are handy for the journey to Tawang (see page 880) and provide an unparalleled homestay experience. Prices include full board and activities including walks through the tea gardens or cycling and hiking in the area. Good discounts available off-season (May–Oct). Cash only. **₹11,900**

Kaziranga National Park

A World Heritage Site covering 430 square kilometres on the southern bank of the Brahmaputra, **Kaziranga National Park**, 217km northeast of Guwahati, occupies a vast valley floor against a backdrop of the Karbi Anglong Hills. Its rivulets, shallow lakes and semi-evergreen forested highlands blend into marshes and flood plains covered with tall elephant grass teeming with deer and wild buffalo. However, the big draw is the park's famous yet highly endangered one-horned **rhinos**, best observed early on a winter's morning. **Tiger** sightings are relatively rare, despite the park's official claim to have the highest density of tigers of any park in the world.

We recommend you only stick to jeeps, which take you deeper into the forest than elephants, but are far more humane to ride. The abundant **birdlife** includes egrets, herons, storks, fish eagles, kingfishers and a grey pelican colony.

During the monsoons (June–Sept), the Brahmaputra bursts its banks, **flooding** the low-lying grasslands and causing animals to move to higher ground within the park. In 2012, monsoon floods ravaged Kaziranga, leading to a huge death toll among the animals, including several rhinos. Traditional animal migration routes have also been choked by overdevelopment around Kaziranga. To compound the extreme pressures on the park, population growth in the region has led to **land encroachment** and **poaching**, the latter of which is now endemic. In 2018 poachers killed six rhinos for their horns, in spite of the park's deployment of surveillance drones. So far, the authorities have proved incapable of protecting the park's wild inhabitants.

ARRIVAL AND DEPARTURE   KAZIRANGA NATIONAL PARK

Kaziranga consists of five directional ranges, with the administrative centre at **Kohora**. Major towns nearby include Jorhat (100km), which has access to the railway network, and Majuli and Tezpur (54km) – useful if you're travelling to West Arunachal.

By plane Jorhat is the nearest airport (90km; 1hr 30min). Taxis charge around ₹3000 to the park.

Destinations Guwahati (2 weekly; 55m); Kolkata (5 weekly; 2hr 30min).

By bus State and private buses all stop at Kohora, the main gate, on the NH-37 (AT Rd), while Network Travels serves as the pick-up and drop-off point.

Destinations Dibrugarh (5–7 daily; 6hr); Guwahati (hourly; 5hr); Jorhat (hourly; 1hr 30min); Tezpur (hourly; 2hr).

INFORMATION

Tourist information For park information, visit the tourist office (daily 10am–5pm; ☏ 03776 262423) in *Bonani* lodge, in the *Tourist Complex*, Kohora. This is where you book park entry and rides; they can also book transport to and from the park. The current tourist officer has been very proactive in developing trekking and ecotourism in the nearby Karbi hills. Check ⊕ kaziranga.assam.gov.in for more information.

Opening hours Kaziranga is open from Nov to early April (daylight hours). Avoid visiting on Sundays, when it gets busy with noisy groups.

Park entry and safaris Entrance fee ₹500 (₹100), vehicle ₹300, camera ₹200 (₹100), video camera ₹1000. The park offers jeep safaris (7.30–10am & 1.30–3pm; ₹1750–2750

per jeep/6 persons, depending on which of the four park ranges you visit) and although they can be a bit cramped, they allow you to travel deeper into the park. Book safaris at least the day before at the *Tourist Complex* at Kohora or ask your hotel to arrange. For the latest rates, visit ⊕ kaziranga. assam.gov.in.

Travel and tours Himalayan Footprints (see page 862) arranges full packages in Kaziranga and also tours and transport throughout the Northeast. Jungle Travels India (see box, page 862) provides exclusive, upmarket holidays in and around Kaziranga with multiday cruises on the Brahmaputra. Ugroshore organises boat transfers on the Brahmaputra from Tezpur to the park.

ACCOMMODATION AND EATING

Kaziranga has a large selection of places to stay with numerous "resorts" cropping up south of the main highway. Accommodation is now reaching saturation point; an alternative is to seek out one of several **homestays** around Bogorijuri. There is a selection of **restaurants** along the highway but most of the lodges and resorts have their own catering. If you get a chance, try local **Karbi cuisine** which

consists of simple, oil-free meals cooked in bamboo containers. **Diplu River Lodge** Kuthuri ☏ 0361 266 7871, ⊕ dipluriverlodge.com. Slightly difficult to locate but beautifully designed, this place has a rustic look and luxurious feel, with cottages raised up on stilts. There's a high level of service and they offer well-organized tours, safaris and boat rides (booked through the luxury brand of Assam Bengal

16

Navigation). Rates halve for Indians, and are a fraction of the price during the monsoon (May–Oct; ₹9975/person). The peak-time price includes safaris, park entry and camera fees, transfers, all meals and cultural activities. **₹36,000**

Nature-Hunt Eco Camp Kohora ☏ 94355 15011, ⓦ naturehunttours.com. A young and enthusiastic team run this small resort tucked into a corner of a tea-garden nursery, where accommodation is in the form of rustic cottages and luxury tents with adjacent bathrooms. There are bonfires in the evenings, a restaurant serving local cuisine and a range of tours and safaris on offer. **₹2800**

Tourist Complex Kohora ☏ 03776 262429. There are four state-run lodges in this complex. *Aranya* (₹1600) is the most comfortable, offering a range of cottages with clean rooms, some with balconies, plus they have a decent restaurant and bar. *Bonani* (₹1200) has a vaguely colonial feel, with large, worn rooms (some with a/c) and – unsettlingly – several animal skulls dotted around. *Bonoshree* (₹800) has tatty but acceptable doubles, and *Jonaki Kareng* (☏ 70867 32356; ₹2400), in the same complex but not government run, has large pleasant doubles, good service and is well located near the main entrance gate. **₹800**

Pobitora Wildlife Sanctuary

40km east of Guwahati • Daily 7am–4pm • ₹500 (₹100), jeep ₹300, camera ₹500 (₹50) • Hire a private vehicle from Guwahati for around ₹3000/day; local buses from Jagiroad, the nearest railhead, stop nearby

The **Pobitora Wildlife Sanctuary** is located in the flood plains of the Brahmaputra. Though much smaller than Kaziranga, at just 39 square kilometres, the park has a high density of rhinos and possibilities of multiple sightings. The best time to visit is between November to February, and a visit can be done as a day-trip from Guwahati.

Upper Assam

Around 310km northeast upriver from Guwahati, **Jorhat** has an airport and road connections to Kaziranga, Nagaland, Guwahati, Kolkata and northern Arunachal Pradesh. The city is noteworthy as a transport hub alone – you will almost certainly have to wade through Jorhat at some point on a trip to the Northeast.

The unique Vaishnavite culture of **Majuli**, reputedly the world's largest river island, and **Sibsagar**, former capital of the Ahoms, are also close by. Further north, **Dibrugarh** is full of **tea plantations** to explore and is the gateway to northern Nagaland and eastern Arunachal Pradesh. There is good birdwatching at **Dibru-Saikhowa National Park**, while **Digboi** has an interesting oil museum and war memorial.

Majuli

Within striking distance of Jorhat, **MAJULI** is often described as one of the largest inhabited river islands in the world, but **erosion** in recent years is threatening its claim and, indeed in the long run, its future. Regardless of its precise status, Majuli is a fascinating place and a true gem of the Northeast, largely because of its unique Vaishnavite **satras** (Hindu monasteries), though it is also a haven for birdwatchers.

There are 22 *satras* – institutions that contain elements of a temple, monastery, school and centre for the arts – on Majuli: each consists of a prayer hall (*namghar*), surrounded by living quarters for devotees, and *ghats* for bathing. Music, song and dance are essential elements of the devotional life of the *satras*, and you may be lucky enough to catch one of the performances which are sometimes arranged for large parties of visitors. The **Natun Samaguri Satra** is particularly famous for its long tradition of Assamese mask-making. Since the mid-17th century, this satra produced the headgear used in the colourful *Raas Leela* festival (held for three days in mid-November) and for *Bhaona*, a style of Assamese street theatre.

Majuli is also home to the Mising, Assam's only riverine tribal community, who still live in traditional bamboo stilt houses.

ARRIVAL AND INFORMATION   **MAJULI**

By ferry Ferries for Majuli's Kamalabari Ghat leave from Nimatighat (8.30am, 9.30am, 10.30am, 1pm, 2pm, 3pm; 2hr

30min; ₹20, vehicle ₹700), accessible by bus or taxi (₹500–800; 40min) and shared taxi (₹30; 1hr) from Jorhat. As the ferry timings only give you a few hours on the island, it is inadvisable to visit on a day-trip. You'll get more out of the experience if you stay overnight, with return ferries to Nimatighat running at 7am, 7.30am, 8.30am, 10.30am, 12.30pm, 1.30pm, 3pm. A word of warning: the ferries can get uncomfortably crowded, with people sitting on the corrugated roof and vehicles loaded on the back, and the single cabin can feel low in the water. It is also possible to travel north from Majuli, with two morning ferries from Luhitghat, 3km north of Garamur; they arrive at Khabalughat on the north bank, from where there are buses to north Lakhimpur, and from there, buses on to Itanagar or Tezpur, Sumos to Ziro, and a train to Guwahati.

By train The closest railhead to Jorhat is Mariani junction, from where buses, taxis and shared taxi ply the 30min route to Jorhat.

Guides Parag Saikia (☎95775 01010) is a reliable tour guide for the area. Jyoti Narayan Sarma of Majuli Tourism, NLK Rd, Garamur (☎94356 57282, ⓦmajulitourism.com), is the most organized and commercial of Majuli's tour operators and can coordinate tours beyond the island.

ACCOMMODATION

La Maison de Ananda Goromur, behind the post office ☎99571 86356, ⓦfacebook.com/lamaisondeananda. One of Majuli's oldest traveller haunts offers relaxed and homely bamboo cottages, with tastefully decorated verandahs filled with Assamese terracottas and cushions, and luxury concrete en suite rooms with a boutique feel. Breakfast is ₹150 extra. ₹900

Ygradasill Bamboo Cottage Bamungaon ☎88767 07326, ⓦfacebook.com/Bedamajuli. This series of bamboo cottages on stilts, built around a pond and surrounded by Majuli's countryside, are the loving work of Beda, an amiable local who helps the community find work placements through his NGO Amar Majuli. The cottages, albeit rustic, are charming and have en suite bathrooms with hot showers. There's a restaurant and breakfast is included. ₹1500

16 Meghalaya

Meghalaya, one of India's smallest states, occupies the plateau and rolling hills between Assam and Bangladesh. Its people are predominantly Christian, belonging to three main ethnic groups, the Garos, Jaintias and the matriarchal Khasis – throughout these hills, women do most of the work and the household management. The state has a high literacy rate, and children are taught in English. Much of Meghalaya ("the land of the rainclouds") is covered with lush forests, rich in orchids; these "blue hills" bear the brunt of the Bay of Bengal's monsoon-laden winds and are among the wettest places on earth. Stupendous waterfalls are a standard feature of the state, many of them on the outskirts of the capital, **Shillong**; however, the most dramatic falls plummet from the plateau to the south, around **Cherrapunjee**.

Meghalaya's hills rise to almost 2000m, making for a pleasantly cool year-round climate. The **Jaintia Hills** offer good walking and caving, and the state is laced with historical sites such as **Nartiang** near **Jowai**, which has an impressive collection of monoliths. Elsewhere, the **sacred forests**, crucibles of biodiversity to be found throughout the Khasi Hills, remain jealously protected. To the south of Shillong, walks through pristine forests and across some of the most intriguing features of the region, the **living root bridges** around the village of **Mawlynnong** and **Nongriat**, make the **East Khasi Hills** one of the highlights of the Northeast. Although the state has seen its share of political turmoil since its inception in 1972, all in all Meghalaya remains a charming land of misty forests and hospitable people, and has become a hit with Indian tourists.

Shillong and around

SHILLONG was known to the British as "the Scotland of the East", an impression first brought to mind by **Barapani** (or **Umiam**), the picturesque loch-like reservoir 23km from town on the Guwahati highway, and the sight of the local Khasi women wearing gingham and tartan shawls. At an altitude of around 1500m and with its rolling hills of conifers and pineapple shrubs, Shillong became a popular hill station for the British, who built it on the site of a thousand-year-old Khasi settlement and made it Assam's capital in 1874.

Sadly, with uncontrolled growth, choking traffic jams and water shortages – despite the rain – the city today has lost much of its charm. Some of the original Victorian town around the centre, known as the European Ward, however, is still preserved, with garden villas and the sylvan environs of **Ward Lake**. North of the polo ground is one of Asia's oldest golf courses, founded in 1898 by a group of British civil servants.

Siat khnam, a local sport and popular gambling tradition, involves teams of Khasi men firing arrows at a target while punters throughout the city bet on the final two digits of the total. Daily (except Sun) games start around 3.30pm opposite Nehru Stadium. Of the town's markets, including the busy **Police Bazaar** in the centre, the **Iewduh** (Mon–Sat) or Bara Bazaar, is Meghalaya's oldest and most traditional market, run mainly by women. For some respite from the city, head to **Tripura Castle**, from where a short uphill walk takes you into pine-forested hills.

Shillong Peak

10km southwest of the centre • Share taxi ₹50 from the centre

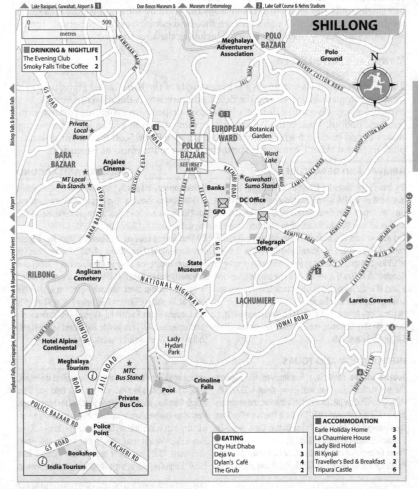

SHILLONG

DRINKING & NIGHTLIFE
The Evening Club	1
Smoky Falls Tribe Coffee	2

EATING
City Hut Dhaba	1
Deja Vu	3
Dylan's Café	4
The Grub	2

ACCOMMODATION
Earle Holiday Home	3
La Chaumiere House	5
Lady Bird Hotel	4
Ri Kynjai	1
Traveller's Bed & Breakfast	2
Tripura Castle	6

Shillong Peak (1965m), the highest point in Meghalaya, offers panoramic views of the city below from its popular promenade, as well as being home to the last four *ilex khasiana*, a high-altitude tree on the verge of extinction. At the base, among a handful of teashops and souvenir stalls, throngs of domestic tourists pose for pictures in rented traditional Khasi costumes. It's a short uphill walk to the viewpoint on the peak.

Don Bosco Museum

Mawlai, 3km northwest of Police Bazaar • Mon–Sat 9am–5.30pm (Dec & Jan till 4.30pm) • ₹200 (₹100) • ☎ 03642 550260, ⊛ dbcic.org

Despite the overtly Christian message, the sparkling **Don Bosco Museum** offers a fascinating insight into the region's tribal groups. Well-organized galleries each have dedicated themes ranging from prehistory, costumes and musical instruments to modern art. The contemporary seven-storey building features an extraordinary, caged Sky Walk on the curving roof, with grand views of the city.

Wankhar Entomology Museum

2km west of Police Bazaar • Mon–Sat 11am–4pm • ₹150 (₹50) • ☎ 36425 44473

The small family-run **Museum of Entomology** (or Butterfly Museum) is dedicated to moths and butterflies, with more than ten thousand exhibits lovingly preserved. There's also a sizeable display of endemic insects, including the large rhinoceros beetle.

Mawphlang Sacred Forest

25km southwest of Shillong

The **sacred forest** at **Mawphlang** is a prime example of the Khasi sacred grove, preserved from time immemorial to protect the delicate biodiversity. A thick layer of humus harbours a huge diversity of flora, while the trees, draped with lichen, are covered with ferns and orchids. Visitors should not pick anything, not even a fallen leaf. Mawphlang makes a good base from which to trek the picturesque **David Scott Trail**, a British-built pony track that skirts Cherrapunjee before dropping to the plains of Bangladesh.

ARRIVAL AND DEPARTURE

SHILLONG AND AROUND

By bus Public buses for Guwahati depart from the MTC bus stand on Jail Rd, which also has a railway reservation counter. Private bus firms have offices nearby and run services all over the Northeast, often departing from the bus park in front of Shillong's Jawaharlal Nehru Stadium, north of Police Bazar. For Aizawl, you may prefer to travel to Silchar and then continue by jeep. The border crossing to Bangladesh at Dawki is served by a few private buses and a fleet of taxis/Sumos, which also run to Cherrapunjee and Mawsynram, from Bara Bazaar.

Destinations Aizawl (1–2 daily; 18hr); Cherrapunjee (2hr); Dawki (4–5hr); Guwahati (hourly; 4hr); Mawsynram (3hr); Silchar (2–3 daily; 10hr);

By helicopter Choppers fly from Shillong to Guwahati airport (₹1500; 30min). There's a 10kg luggage allowance, and you pay ₹300 for each extra kg. Book at the counter inside the MTC Bus station (Mon–Sat 8am–5pm; ☎ 87949 44764).

By taxi Shared taxis run to Guwahati from Police Bazar and Kacheri Rd (3hr 30min; ₹200). Private taxis to Guwahati airport run early in the mornings (₹2000) and Guwahati's Paltan Bazaar (₹1500); rates are much higher in the afternoons. Book through agents around Police Point, at Meghalaya Tourism (see below) or at Khasi Hills Taxi Cooperative on Kacheri Rd. Happy Fleet (⊛ facebook.com/happyfleet6427) run private and shared cars between Shillong, Dimapur and Kohima in Nagaland.

INFORMATION AND TOURS

Tourist offices Meghalaya Tourism, Jail Rd, opposite the bus station (Mon–Sat 9am–5pm; ☎ 0364 222 6220, ⊛ megtourism.gov.in), provides information and organizes tours; they also arrange taxis. The India Tourism office is on the corner of GS Rd at the Police Bazaar Circle (Mon–Fri 9.30am–5.30pm; ☎ 0364 222 5632).

Tours Cultural Pursuits at *Hotel Alpine Continental* on Thana Rd, Police Bazaar (☎ 98560 41205, ⊛ culturalpursuits.com),

arrange good-value tailor-made tours throughout the region, including homestays in Khasi villages. Their treks and tours include Garo Wangala and the David Scott Trail to Cherrapunjee. Meghalaya Tourism also run good-value yet occasionally hit-or-miss day-trips in tourist buses to Cherrapunjee (8am–4.30pm; from ₹350); Mawlynnong, Riwai's root bridge and Dawki (8am–8pm; ₹500); and a city tour (8.30am–2.30pm; from ₹300). Meghalaya Adventurers' Association, at the Mission

SARI-CLAD WOMEN HEAD TO THE MONASTERY ON MAJULI ISLAND

Compound near the Synod Complex (☎ 0364 254 5621, ⊛ bit.ly/2LzhEbp), offers trips to explore the spectacular caves of the region. Pathfinders Adventures (☎ 84149 21822 or 70052 84852, ⊛ facebook.com/pathfinderadventuresindia) organise guided, fully customisable tours in private SUVs, highlighting lesser-known attractions and hiking.

Internet Internet cafés are thin on the ground (from ₹30/hr) – try the xerox shops along Jail Road and Police Bazaar.

Car and Motorbike rental Visiting Meghalaya by car, scooter or Enfield is an increasingly popular option. Pathfinders Adventures rents well-maintained scooters for ₹700/day. You can also book cars, Royal Enfields, scooters or chauffeur cabs online through Shillong-based operator Autorides (☎ 872 994 9548, ⊛ autorides.in).

ACCOMMODATION

Shillong has a wide range of **accommodation**. Note that staying on GS Rd can be noisy; for a quiet and central location, look around the European Ward area. Further afield, Umiam Lake offers scenic tranquillity, while in the village of Mawphlang you can gain an insight into Khasi life by staying in a homestay.

Earle Holiday Home Oakland Rd ☎ 98633 02149; map p.871. Central and popular, with a range of clean but twee rooms (think lino floors and garish bed covers) in a traditional Meghalayan house or a more modern annexe. There's a good restaurant too. ₹800

La Chaumiere House Upper Lachaumiere ☎ 0364 250 1239, ⊛ facebook.com/LachaumiereHouseShillong; map p.871. A family run, grand manor house with pleasant lawns and home comforts, and an adjacent cottage in the grounds; set in a residential area yet close to all amenities. ₹4000

Lady Bird Hotel Police Bazar, Umsohsun Rd ☎ 70850 61137, ⊛ ladybirdhotel.com; map p.871. Very central and modern hotel, with minimal-chic rooms equipped with warm wood flooring, plush beds, LED TVs, and all the amenities flashpackers expect. It's quiet in spite of being just a 3min walk from Police Bazar. Staff are very friendly, and a continental buffet breakfast is included. ₹2500

★ **Ri Kynjai** 20km north of Shillong ☎ 98624 20300, ⊛ rikynjai.com; map p.871. Set in 45 acres of forest in a spectacular location beside Umiam Lake, the region's best hotel has luxury rooms and stunning cottages. The latter are raised on stilts, have traditional "upturned boat" roofs, fire-places and Jacuzzis. The restaurant specializes in northeastern cuisine and there's a spa. ₹9500

★ **Travellers Bed & Breakfast** Buddhist Temple Rd, 100mt beyond Buddha Vihar Polo ☎ 98621 58574; map p.871. Set in a residential area not far from the Polo Ground, this homely guesthouse has large, neat rooms with hot water, a/c, electric kettles, desks and chairs, and immaculately clean en suite bathrooms. Shoestringers can use the functional 8-bed dorm with shared toilets, one of the best value budget accommodations in town. Breakfast is only included with the doubles. Doubles ₹2016, Dorms ₹ ₹350

Tripura Castle Tripura Castle Rd, 3km south of town ☎ 03642 501111, ⊛ tripuracastle.com; map p.871. Also known as *Royal Heritage*, this beautiful hotel is set in an inspiring hilltop location, next to the maharaja of Tripura's former summer home. The charming rooms have wooden floors and brass fireplaces, while the Maharaja Suite has a mahogany bed once slept in by Tagore, an iconic Bengali poet and composer. There's a decent restaurant and bar. The recently developed annexe next door is equally comfortable. ₹5500

EATING

City Hut Dhaba Earle Holiday Home ☎ 03642 220386; map p.871. A cabin-like dining room with an extravagant water feature, City Hut Dhaba has a menu of more than three hundred items, including interesting dishes like duck cubes in tawa masala. Expect to pay around ₹700 for a meal. Daily 11am–9.30pm.

Deja Vu Nongkynrih, Laitumkhrah ☎ 03642 502777; map p.871. A bit out of the way, this Cantonese-style restaurant serves a concoction of Chinese, Thai curries, and Western bar food. At ₹280, the combo meals with drinks (think veg fried rice or noodles, pork ribs, French fries and a virgin mojito) are great value. Daily noon–10.30pm.

★ **Dylan's Café** Tripura Castle Rd, Dhankheti ☎ 03642 500 116, ⊛ dylanscafeshillong.com; map p.871. The Northeast's first tribute café is dedicated to Bob Dylan, who had a huge impact on Shillong's music scene – believe it or not, since 1972 local musicians celebrate the birthday of the American songwriter with a tribute gig. A menu of hearty burgers, all day breakfast platters, pancakes and desserts – together with walls tiled with vintage vinyl records – make it a unique local favourite. A meal will set you back ₹500. Daily 11.30am–10pm.

The Grub Laitumkhrah, Main Road ☎ 70850 69008, ⊛ facebook.com/thegrubcafebakery; map p.871. Among the most popular in Shillong's new wave of Western-style cafés, it's a cosy place to get your cuppas, pastries, burgers and some Italian pastas. Expect to pay around ₹600 for a meal. Daily 1pm–9pm.

DRINKING AND ENTERTAINMENT

The flourishing local **music scene** has earned Shillong the nickname "rock city". For performances, look out for posters.

MEGHALAYA'S LIVING ROOT BRIDGES

Deep within the wet tropical forests of Meghalaya's Khasi Hills, gnarled, moss-covered roots of the Indian rubber tree (*Ficus elastica*) stretch across waterways, forming unique **"living" bridges**. The consistently high rainfall swells rivers and streams, which leads to the decay of wooden bridges, stranding locals. Over generations, the indigenous Khasi people have created alternatives by directing entwined **rubber-tree roots** such that they grow into sturdy bridges. Some of these tangled webs are nearly 200 years old and up to 30m long.

The Evening Club The Eee Cee Hotel, Police Bazar ☎ 08837 271206, ⓦ facebook.com/eveningclubshillong; map p.871. More of a mid-range bistro than a real live music club, this welcoming bar hosts rock, jazz and acoustic bands (₹250 cover charge) and has a good selection of beers and spirits. Daily 11am–11pm.

Smoky Falls Tribe Coffee Police Bazar ☎ 84160 69751, ⓦ facebook.com/NaLaBri; map p.871. This central hole in the wall coffee shop uses strong local brews (from ₹60), all grown by Meghalaya's indigenous tribes, pastries (₹100), and is popular with the young Shillong crowd. Daily 11am–11pm.

Cherrapunjee and around

CHERRAPUNJEE, 56km south of Shillong in the Khasi Hills, is a spread-out settlement with the town of **Sohra** at its centre. It has achieved fame as the wettest place on earth: the highest daily rainfall ever recorded fell here in 1876 – 104cm in 24 hours. The area's numerous waterfalls are most impressive during the steamy monsoon season when awesome torrents plunge down to the Bangladeshi plains, often obscured by rain clouds.

Every eight days a **market** is held here, with tribal jewellery, honey and local produce on offer. Of the various points of interest, the **Noh Kalikai** and **Weisawdong waterfalls**, **Bangladesh viewpoint**, **Mawsmai village and cave** and **Mawjinbuin cave** near Mawsynram, which is even wetter than Cherra itself, are all within a few kilometres.

16

Nongriat

65km southwest of Shillong • entry fee ₹20 • camera ₹20 • Motorbike parking ₹50 per night

The most spectacular living root bridge is the **Umshiang Double Decker Bridge** at the **NONGRIAT** village, where two bridges run one above the other across the Umshiang River. To get to the double-decker bridge it's a knee-grinding trek from the **Tyrna** village, set at the top of more than 3000 steps. It's not for the faint-hearted: the dizzying staircase tumbles down through the forest, past natural swimming holes, and across two suspended metallic bridges. Roughly halfway down, a 3min side path leads to the **long bridge** (entry ₹10, camera ₹20), a single decker root bridge strewn across the river. Because this trek is usually crowded with Indian tourists who visit as a gruelling day-trip, staying overnight in Nongriat to rest your legs and enjoy the village's eerie remoteness is recommended. Cherrapunjee Holiday Resort (see below) can arrange guides.

ARRIVAL AND DEPARTURE   CHERRAPUNJEE AND AROUND

On a tour An easy way of seeing all the sights around Cherrapunjee, albeit in a rush, is to join Meghalaya Tourism's day-trip (see page 872) from Shillong.
By taxi A taxi for the day from Shillong costs ₹3000.

By Sumo Shared Sumos to Cherrapunjee market ply regularly from Shillong's Bara Bazaar (2hr; ₹70), where you change to a shared jeep to Tyrna (1hr; ₹40) and start hiking down to Nongriat

ACCOMMODATION

★ **Cherrapunjee Holiday Resort** Laitkynsew Village ☎ 94361 15925, ⓦ cherrapunjee.com. Around 12km from Sohra, this friendly and welcoming place makes an ideal base for exploring the area. Sitting on a ledge looking down to villages, hills and the Bangladesh plains in the distance, the main building has six large, comfortable rooms set around a central hall and restaurant. There's also a new annexe with higher-end rooms. The restaurant offers a range of dishes, from local cuisine to *dhal bhaat* and a lot more. They have useful information on hikes and treks.

Rates include breakfast. ₹4650

Serene Homestay Nongriat ☏ 94778 70423. Thanks to backpacker hype, this homestay has become a proper guesthouse, losing its family vibe in pursuit of tourist dollars. Regardless of the cold atmosphere and occasional rudeness, their 6-dorm beds with decent shared toilets (₹300) are basic, but still the best option in Nongriat. There are double rooms, and a veg rice and *dhaal* dinner costs ₹130 extra. No wi-fi. ₹800

Mawlynnong

86km southeast of Shillong • ₹10 entry fee • Meghalaya Tourism (see page 872) runs a day-trip from Shillong (8am–8pm; ₹500 by bus, ₹3000 by car)

Reputedly the cleanest village (in Asia), **MAWLYNNONG**, in the East Khasi Hills, is a victim of its own hype. Once a marvel of community ecological awareness where all rubbish is carefully recycled and processed, the village has turned into an overpriced tourist trap, and is best enjoyed in the evenings, after the tourist hordes have left. A bamboo walkway, the Sky View, climbs to the forest canopy providing views of treetops and the distant plains of Bangladesh. Nearby Riwai village is also a good place to see a 100-year-old living root bridge (₹20 entry fee) if you don't mind fending off selfie-sticks.

Mawryngkhang Bamboo Trek

56km southeast of Shillong in Wahkhen village • ₹500/group for a guided tour • Buses and shared jeeps depart from Bara Bazaar in Shillong to Pomlum village (1hr 30min; ₹90), 15km away from Wahkhen; Pathfinders Adventures (see page 872) organise direct trips from Shillong.

This two to three-hour circuit to a sacred boulder called **U Mawryngkhang**, the legendary "King of Rocks", was completely hand-made by Wahkhen village's engineers to promote tourism to their remote home. You'll walk over rickety bamboo-and-cane bridges, soaring above patches of forest, a river, and deep gorges. If you suffer vertigo, avoid climbing the last 100mt-high bamboo ladder to the rock's top.

Dawki

96km southeast of Shillong • Buses and irregular shared jeeps depart from Bara Bazaar in Shillong before 11am (2hr 30min), likewise departing from Dawki to Shillong before 11am; Meghalaya Tourism runs a day-trip from Shillong (8am–8pm; ₹500 by bus); a private taxi to and from Shillong costs ₹3000

DAWKI, 35km from Mawlynnong, is the most important of the Meghalaya–Bangladesh **border crossings to Tamabil**, two and a half hours from Sylhet. The town holds nothing of interest, but you can take a boat (₹700 for 3 people) on a scenic part of the Umngot river separating India from Bangladesh. The real attraction is the crystal-clear water and suspended bridge at nearby **Shnongpdeng**, the source of the river, seven kilometers away. Shillong-based Pioneer Adventure Tours (☏ 98560 06437, ✆ pioneeradventuretour.com) organise river camping (₹3000 inclusive of four meals, barbecue, bonfire and boat transfers), scuba diving, river rafting, caving, zip lining, rock climbing and rappelling (from ₹300). If you are going to cross the border, note that there's no Bangladesh visa office in Meghalaya, so you will need to acquire a visa beforehand; Kolkata has a consulate. Note that there are no official currency exchange facilities at the crossing.

Arunachal Pradesh

Arunachal Pradesh, "the land of the dawn-lit mountains", is one of India's last unspoilt wildernesses. A wealth of fascinating cultures, peoples and **tribes** – plus a staggering five hundred species of orchid – are found in its glacial terrain, alpine meadows and subtropical rainforests.

The capital, **Itanagar**, is north of the Brahmaputra across from Jorhat. In the far west of the state, the road from **Bhalukpong** on the Assamese border to the monastery of **Tawang** climbs steadily through rugged hills, streams and primeval forests, crossing the dramatic **Sela Pass** (4300m) midway. Along the route lie the Buddhist towns of **Bomdila** and **Dirang**. In the far northeast, both cloud and snow leopards reside in **Namdapha National Park**. Arunachal's remote and unspoilt central highlands, home to myriad tribes, hides some of the best the Himalayas have to offer, including the mysterious Buddhist land of **Pemako**.

Despite the region's beauty, tourism has been discouraged here because of the extremely sensitive borders with Chinese-occupied Tibet in the north and Myanmar in the east. In 1962, the Chinese invaded Arunachal Pradesh, reaching the outskirts of Tezpur in Assam, a 300km incursion that India has never forgotten. Since then, a strong military stance has been adopted in the area with China laying claim to much of the state. All visitors require a **permit** (see page 862) to enter the state.

Itanagar

Just under 400km northeast of Guwahati, **ITANAGAR**, the state's quiet capital, is of little interest but an important transport hub for anyone heading to the central plateau. You may find you need to spend a night or two here organizing permits and logistics. Surrounded by low, wooded hills, the town spreads along a 4km stretch of road running between Zero Point, where the better hotels are located, and Ganga Market, the animated main bazaar, which has cheaper accommodation and the bus station. Six kilometres west of town, **Gyakar Sinyi** (Ganga Lake), cupped in a jungle hollow, is a popular picnic spot.

16

ARRIVAL AND DEPARTURE
ITANAGAR

By train A rail link to Naharlagun (15km from Itanagar) connects central Arunachal to Delhi by the *Naharlagun–New Delhi AC SF Express* #22411; and Guwahati by the *Naharlagun–Guwahati Intercity Express* #15618.
Destinations Delhi (Tues 9.10pm; 38hr 30min); Guwahati (daily 9.30pm; 9hr 20min).

By bus State and private buses connect Itanagar with Guwahati and destinations throughout the state, but be aware that most roads are in terrible condition.

Destinations Bomdila (30m daily; 12–14hr; ₹600); Guwahati (daily; 10–11hr); Pasighat (6.15am and 2pm; 5hr; ₹380); Ziro (daily; 6hr; ₹200).

By Sumo/jeep Sumos and shared jeeps are quicker than buses, and their hub is in nearby Naharlagun.
Destinations from Naharlagun Aloo (6am and 5pm; 8hr; ₹1000); Daporijo (6am; 8hr; ₹1000); Guwahati airport (3am; 8hr; ₹1500); Pasighat (5hr; ₹450); Ziro (5.30am and 10.30am; 4hr; ₹350).

INFORMATION AND TOURS

Tourist office There's an intermittently open tourist office (ⓦ arunachaltourism.com) behind the Akash Deep complex in Ganga Market.

Tour operators Abor Country Travels & Expeditions, B Sector, below Raj Bhavan (ⓣ 94360 53870, ⓦ aborcountry travels.com), organizes treks, white-water rafting expeditions

and tours. Highly recommended, The Holiday Scout (see page 862) conducts offbeat and customised cultural, photographic, and women-focused tours.

Websites ⓦ arunachaltourism.com is a good introduction to what to see and do in the state. ⓦ chaloarunachal.com offers plenty of local insider knowledge

---

ARUNACHAL PRADESH'S TRIBAL GROUPS

Arunachal Pradesh is stunningly diverse, with 26 major **tribal groups**, each with its own culture, dialect, dress, social structure and traditions. Polygamy remains common among many of them, as does the religious blend of Hindu, Buddhist and animist beliefs. The main ethnic groups include Monpas, Sherdukpens, Apatani, Wanchos, Noctes, Tangsas, Singphos, Khamptis, Mishmis, Mijis, Galos, Padams, Miwongs, Tagins and Puroiks. However, within all the groups, tradition is slowly giving way to modern influences, particularly among the younger generation, who increasingly wear Western clothes, watch Bollywood flicks and eat Chinese food.

ACCOMMODATION

Pybss Hotel D-Sector, Near Civil Secretariat ☏ 03602 292178, ⓦ pybsshotel.com. Modern 3-star hotel with a range of good-value rooms and suites with plush beds, TVs, and in walking distance to BB Plaza Shopping Mall. There's a gym for guests and breakfast is included. ₹2950

Waii International Near State Museum, Gompa Rd ☏ 03602 291471, ⓦ waiiinternational.com. Itanagar's best hotel has large, elegant rooms with marble tiles, wooden furnishings and plush king size beds. The Olympic size swimming pool is a nice place to cool off. Breakfast is included. ₹5500

West Arunachal

Bordered by Bhutan and Tibet, the isolated hills and valleys of **West Arunachal** climb to some of the remotest glaciers and peaks in the Himalayas. Most of the 6000m-plus mountains – except **Gori Chen** (6488m) and **Nyegi Kangsang** (7047m) – remain completely unknown. The main road, the best in the state, runs from **Bhalukpong** on the Assamese border to near the Tibet frontier at **Tawang**, ending high in the mountains at one of Asia's largest monasteries. On this spectacular journey you rise from the steamy foothills to the high market town of **Bomdila** with its Buddhist monasteries and occasional yak; further on lies **Dirang**, an ancient fortress town, before the climb up through the **Sela Pass** to Tawang.

Bomdila

Set on a spur of the Thagla Ridge at 2530m, the dividing line between rainforests to the south and subalpine valleys to the north, freezing **BOMDILA** is a quiet, pleasant, spread-out settlement with a handy bazaar in the lower town and quiet walks above. A few kilometres beyond Bomdila, the snow-covered peaks of Gori Chen (6488m) and Kangto (7042m) come into view, weather permitting. There are a handful of **Tibetan Buddhist monasteries** in town – the oldest of which is at the end of the bazaar in the lower town, and houses a large blue Medicine Buddha statue. You can take a walk on the hill beyond the town to Shiva's **Nag Mandir**, and then proceed to Nyingmapa **Rizing Woselling Monastery**, crowned by a giant statue of the Second Buddha Padmasambhava. In the afternoons, you may see Sange Lama and his young novice monks use human bones for their entrancing *pujas*.

Bomdila Monastery

No fixed hours; roughly daylight hours • Free • A round trip from and to the Sumo stand costs around ₹150–200

The largest *gompa*, known as the **Bomdila Monastery** (Gentse Gaden Rabhyel Ling), high above town, was inaugurated by the Dalai Lama in 1997. The *gompa* holds a spectacular *chaam* (festival of lama masked dance) around mid-November which attracts plenty of local people including **Monpa** women in distinctive pink knitted gowns and yak-hair hats.

ARRIVAL AND INFORMATION   BOMDILA

There are just two routes out of Bomdila: onward and upward towards Tawang, and back down to Bhalukpong. All transport arrives at the **Sumo stand** in the middle of town, where there are some convenient hotels. There are travel offices in the Sumo stand, one SBI ATM, and an internet café, though electricity and bandwidth is a problem.

By bus State buses, for those who are willing to take a severe rattling, run from the bus station in the lower part of town, but get cancelled frequently. It's better to use Network Travels' (☏ 84030 77666, ⓦ networktravels.com) a/c night service to Guwahati.

Destinations Guwahati (daily 3.30pm; 10hr).

By shared taxi/jeep These are the most common forms

of transport to and from Bomdila; you should pre-book at the Sumo offices on the ground floor of the Urban Shopping Complex, and be prepared for early departures. For Itanagar, catch the night service leaving at 3.30pm.

Destinations Dirang (11am; 1hr 30min; ₹150); Itanagar (6am; 10hr; ₹700); Tawang (6am; 6hr; ₹500); Tezpur (5.30am; 5hr; ₹400).

Tourist office Tourist information (☏ 03782 222049 or 94366 71949) is at the *Tourist Lodge*, but the desk is not always manned.

Tours The Holiday Scout (see page 862), Syndicate Press Building, Kakaling Road, arranges customised sightseeing, photography trips and treks.

ACCOMMODATION

★ **Doe-Gu-Khil** Bomdila Monastery ☎ 81190 26374. A wonderful, quiet spot within the monastery compound and just below the main complex, with spotless and well-presented rooms set around a courtyard. The food is vegetarian, since it's in the monastery complex. You will need to book early for the *chaam*. ₹900

Lungta Residency Next to Urban Shopping Complex ☎ 03780 222555. Central hotel, perfectly located for early

morning departures, rooms are clean and well-appointed and there is a popular restaurant. Breakfast included. ₹1420

Tsepal Yangjom Main Bazaar ☎ 03782 223473. In the lower market, this established hotel has comfortable wood-panelled rooms and the best restaurant in town (daily 9am–8pm) serving local, Chinese and Indian cuisine – try the boiled chicken with bamboo shoots and *lai patta* (mains around ₹150). ₹1800

Dirang

Ninety minutes beyond Bomdila, the predominantly Monpa township of **Dirang** sits at a much lower altitude of 1497m, thus enjoying a more equitable climate. The settlement lies along the highway to Tawang, separated into Old and New Dirang and punctuated with kiwi orchards and a handful of ancient *gompas*. The Dirang River, flanked by terraced fields, flows parallel to the highway in the valley below.

Old Dirang

The ancient fortress town of **OLD DIRANG** (1690m), also known as **Dirang Dzong**, or "**fort**", commands the lower river valley. Take the steps up just before the bridge to the walled medieval settlement where within the warren of stone houses and lanes shared by human and livestock alike, and besides the odd TV dish, time seems to have stood still. The *dzong* stands more or less abandoned in the centre of the settlement and is often locked. The rest of Old Dirang, with several medieval buildings and a 500-year-old Khastong *gompa* above town, is worth a wander, past the odd tethered yak and with the strong aroma of local brew wafting through the alleyways.

New Dirang

NEW DIRANG, 5km further up the valley from Old Dirang, is the uninspiring main market and transport hub, with fruit orchards on the outskirts and a yak-breeding farm. There are several **monasteries** in the area, including the **Kalachakra** *gompa*, dedicated to the Wheel of Life, and the old **Thupsung Dhargye Liung** *gompa*, belonging to one of the oldest Tibetan Buddhism sects. Further up the road towards Tawang, a footpath leads down to **hot springs**, a popular bathing spot for local villagers, but in pretty dire condition when we visited. About 8km away, the **Sangti Valley** is the winter home of the black-necked crane and a popular place for birdwatching. There are several homestays, a sheep farm, and a new *gompa* that should be completed by the time you read this.

ACCOMMODATION   DIRANG

Old Dirang is the best place to stay, unless you need to catch an early-morning Sumo from the market. *Sangyela* and *Snow Lion Hotel*, both along the main bazaar, don't look like much from the outside but have serviceable, clean rooms that can accommodate up to 3 guests for ₹1000.

★ **Dirang Boutique Cottages** Near Old Dirang's Power House ☎ 76409 67387, ⓦ facebook.com/dirang boutiquecottages. These eight charming rooms, housed in rustic stone cottages, set on a bend of the Siang River, have plenty of local charm. Outside, a stone pathway connects

the cottages to an exquisite open-air area for bonfires and basking in the high-altitude sun. Breakfast is included. ₹2500

Sang Nima Tsering Homestay On the main road, Old Dirang ☎ 70853 18416. The large, clean rooms here face a spacious courtyard shared with a local Monpa family. Breakfast (included) and dinner (₹300 veg/₹350 non veg), lovingly prepared by owner Sang Nima, are consumed around a traditional stove inside the home's common kitchen. The momo-making classes (₹500) are fun. No wi-fi. ₹2000

The Sela Pass and around

4hr drive from Dirang

The spectacular road from Dirang to **Tawang** rises steadily from the river valley through alpine scenery past waterfalls and grazing yaks. The endless switchbacks climb up to the dramatic 4300m **Sela Pass**, where you can have tea and samosas in front of a *bukhari* (wood-fired oven) at the *Prahri Café* by the gate. The pass is snowed in for around six months a year, though ill-equipped jeeps still brave the journey. Of the many memorials to those who lost their lives during the 1962 Chinese invasion, the most impressive is the **Jaswant Singh Memorial**, 13km beyond the pass that commemorates a battle when a tiny Indian contingent held off the Chinese army for several days before finally being overrun.

Tawang

180km northwest of Bomdila

The great Buddhist monastery of **TAWANG**, the largest in India, dominates the land of the Monpas. Perched at around 3500m and looking out onto a semicircle of peaks that are snow-capped for much of the year, the monastery teeters on the edge of Tibet and peers down to Bhutan. This feels like the end of the road, with long cold nights and plenty of snow in winter. A bone of contention between India and China, Tawang has always been of special significance to Tibetans and the Dalai Lama who fled Tibet in 1959 and travelled surreptitiously through here on his way into exile. His pre-incarnation, the **Sixth Dalai Lama**, was born on the outskirts of the town.

The three-day **Torgya festival** in January, shortly before Losar (Tibetan New Year), celebrates the life of the first king of Mon; a *chaam* dance wards off evil spirits. The **Tawang Festival**, in late Oct, showcases cultural performances.

Tawang Monastery

A few kilometres beyond town • Roughly daylight hours

Established by Merak Lama Lodre Gyatso in 1680 under the auspices of the Fifth Dalai Lama, when this area was part of Greater Tibet, the highly influential **Tawang Monastery** is a huge fortress-like complex with a warren of buildings. It houses around five hundred monks and is renowned for its collection of priceless manuscripts and *thangkas*. There is a small **museum** (entry fee ₹20) filled with Buddhist ornaments and relics, and a vast library. Rebuilt in the 1990s, the main *dukhang* (temple hall), dominated by an 8m-high statue of Shakyamuni along with spectacular murals, was consecrated by the present **Dalai Lama** whose 2009 visit brought much displeasure to the Chinese government. The abbot, Gyalshey Rimpoche, has declared the entire region free from the slaughter of animals – one reason why so many yaks wander freely in these parts.

Urgyelling

5km south of town

As you descend south from Tawang a fork in the road, adorned by ceremonial gates, leads to the small monastery of **Urgyelling**. Turn left and down the hill behind the car repair shop, and then keep to the left looking for the gate, as it's not well sign-posted. Set in peaceful grounds, the chapel commemorates the birth here of the **Sixth Dalai Lama**, Tsanyang Gyatso, in 1683. The monastery was sacked when Tsanyang was deposed, but he prophesied he would return and that when one of the three grand trees he planted died, catastrophe would befall Tibet. In 1959, one of the trees died in a storm; that very year, the fourteenth (and present) Dalai Lama, fleeing Tibet, sought refuge at this very spot.

ARRIVAL AND INFORMATION   TAWANG

By bus At the time of research, Tawang only had one daily bus to Tezpur (11.30am; 10hr; ₹650)

By helicopter On Mon and Fri, Pawan Hans (⚙ booking. pawanhans.co.in) run scenic chopper flight connecting Guwahati to Tawang (10.10am; 1hr 10min; ₹3500)

By jeep Daily jeeps run from Tawang to Bomdila, Dirang,

Guwahati and Tezpur – book in advance from ticket agents near the bus stand; transport leaves early from the Old Market. Destinations Bomdila (6am; 4/5hr; ₹500); Dirang (6am; 4hr; ₹500); Guwahati (6am; 14hr; ₹1400); Tezpur (10hr; ₹850).

By taxi A one-way taxi trip to the monastery from town costs around ₹250, but it's worth asking the driver to wait as it can be difficult to find one for the return leg; it is also a pleasant, but long, walk. A taxi to Bomdila costs ₹5000.

Tourist office The *Tourist Lodge* (Mon–Sat 9am–4pm; ☎03794 222359) has a small tourist office, but Himalayan Holidays (Mon–Sat 5am–7pm; ☎03794 223151), opposite *Hotel Gorichen*, Old Market, is a better source of information.

ACCOMMODATION AND EATING

Dolma Khangsar Near monastery gates ☎03794 223271 or 94360 51011, ⍟dolmahotels.com. Excellent wood-panelled, suite-like rooms with hot-water bathrooms, in a welcoming family home with good vegetarian cooking and in a great location next to the monastery. Double-roomed cottages by the vegetable garden (₹3300/room) are good for larger groups. A brisk 3km walk up from the bazaar (or a taxi ride). ₹1750

Hotel Mon Paradise Nehru Market ☎03794 222443, ⍟hotelmonparadise.com. The closest Tawang comes to a boutique hotel offers 19 large rooms with wooden floor tiles, flat TVs, and attached bathrooms. Breakfast is not included. ₹2500

Mon Valley Restaurant Old Market ☎84158 15411. With deep red and black walls, and large windows overlooking the valley, this busy restaurant is a popular favourite. Tibetan, North Indian and Chinese dishes are cooked fresh on order, so the service can be slow, but the local specialities like beef thentuck and thukpa (₹80) are well worth the wait. They also have milkshakes (₹70) and coffee. Around ₹150 a head. Daily 8am–8pm

★ **Tenzin Paying Guest House** 5km from the bazar, on the main road ☎03794 222893. This quiet family-run hotel has four storeys of warm wood-panelled rooms, hot-water bathrooms and a serene garden. It's run by a former lama (now a teacher at Tawang Monastery), his wife, and three energetic daughters, who keep everything squeaky clean and run an excellent, inexpensive kitchen. A meal will set you back ₹200, and breakfast costs an additional ₹150. ₹1500

Central and East Arunachal

16

Pristine forests mark the watersheds of the Siang, Dibang and Lohit rivers – an unspoilt wilderness gradually opening up to visitors in search of exploration and adventure. The town of **Ziro** (**Hapoli**) makes a good base for exploring this land of rainclouds, forests, swirling paddy terraces and the fascinating **Apatani villages** where animist beliefs and the worship of **Donyi-Polo** (sun and moon) are still very much alive. The Apatanis are just one of the many **tribes** inhabiting these remote forests and hills of Central Arunachal. Beyond Ziro, the fragile highway etches through forested hills to the settlement of **Along**. Further south, the River Siang, battling through the jungles, merges into the mighty Brahmaputra at **Pasighat**, close to the urban centres of Upper Assam. Further east, the remote valleys of the **Dibang** and **Lohit** rivers, inhabited by the Mishmi, Singpho and Khampti tribes, descend from snow-covered passes through subtropical forests where, in the far east corner of the state, the pristine **Namdapha National Park** harbours a huge variety of fauna and flora.

Ziro (Hapoli)

The quiet, yet slowly expanding town of **HAPOLI** – still known widely by its former name **ZIRO** – 150km north of Itanagar, is surrounded by the terraced fields and rolling pine-clad hills of the Apatani plateau, 1780m above sea level. Besides the colourful market, where you will come across local delicacies such as dried rat and other unusual meat, Ziro provides a base for exploring the surrounding hills and village communities. It's best to base yourself in **Old Ziro** (a scenic 7km walk or a ₹250 taxi ride from Hapoli's sumo stand), which is made up by the interconnected Apatani villages of Hari, Biirii, Mudang Tage, Bulla, Hija, Ditta, Bamin Michi and Hong. Here you can still see Apatani women with bamboo nose-plugs and five lines tattooed across their faces and chins — a tradition banned in the 1980s. It will completely disappear in the next 20 years, with the last of these 200-odd remaining elders. The **Talley Valley Wildlife Sanctuary**, renowned for its clouded leopards, makes a good two-day trek.

ARRIVAL AND INFORMATION   ZIRO (HAPOLI)

The **road** from Naharlagun to Ziro is paved and in good condition, but proceeding onwards in any direction may be a challenge. During the monsoons the roads become almost impassable.

By bus Irregular state buses depart from the bazaar.
Destinations Daporijo (3 weekly; 8hr); Guwahati (2 weekly;
15hr); Itanagar (3 weekly; 4hr).
By Sumo Shared Sumos depart from the bazaar in the
mornings to Daporijo, Naharlagun/Itanagar, and North
Lakhimpur in Assam. For Guwahati, change in Itanagar.
Royal Tours & Travels (☏ 0378 822 5577) run direct jeeps to
Naharlagun's railway station.
Destinations Daporijo (10.30am; 8–10hr; ₹600); Itanagar
(5 daily until 11.30am; 10hr; ₹350); New Lakhimpur
(5.30am, 9am, 10am, 11am; 5hr; ₹330).

Tours and information Most hotels offer guide services,
necessary to make sense of the local traditions, for ₹1500
per day. A car with driver costs ₹2500 per day. NGOs such
as NgunuZiro (☏ 94362 24834, ✉ NgunuZirohomestay2@
gmail.com, ⌨ facebook.com/NgunuZiro) provide vital
information and assistance for exploring the area and local
tours. Other established tour operators in the region include
The Holiday Scout (☏ 95406 98458; ⌨ theholidayscout.
com), based in Bomdila, and Greener Pastures (☏ 94767
27547, ⌨ thegreenerpastures.com).

ACCOMMODATION

Dogingdo Homestay Hari village, 4km from the centre
☏ 87299 02206. Welcoming homestay with large, clean
en suite rooms equipped with TVs, tables and chairs, and
mosquito nets, set below the family's loft-like wooden
traditional kitchen. It's in walking distance to the other
four Old Ziro Apatani villages. Hearty breakfasts and home-
cooked dinners are included. No wi-fi. ₹1200

Ziro Palace Inn Biirii, midway between the old and
new towns ☏ 99493 44788, ⌨ ziropalaceinn.com. The
most luxurious hotel in Ziro has very large, bright rooms
with plush beds, balconies, and living room areas furnished
with LED TVs, tables and leather couches. It's close to the
Ziro Festival's grounds and fills up fast, so book ahead.
Breakfast included. ₹2950

Along and Pasighat

East of Ziro, the River Siang, having started life as the Tsangpo on the Tibet plateau,
tumbles through the lush rainforests around the small towns of **ALONG** and **PASIGHAT**,
to eventually form the Brahmaputra. Few visitors travel this tortuous road through the
land of the Adis and the Mishmis, but there are numerous opportunities for **trekking**
and river adventures, especially in **MECHUKA**, including some of the most challenging
white-water in the Himalayas.

ARRIVAL AND DEPARTURE ALONG AND PASIGHAT

By car The towns can be reached from Itanagar (7hr to
Along; 5hr to Pasighat); the easiest routes are via North
Lakhimpur along the Brahmaputra valley on the NH-52
rather than the hill roads through Ziro. From Pasighat, you
can reach Dibrugarh via the 5km-long Bogibeel Bridge,
India's longest road and railway bridge.
By bus Buses ply from the Pasighat bus stand, around
1km from the centre. Network Travels (☏ 0361 260
5335, ⌨ networktravelindia.com) and Shapna Tours
(☏ 8257073011) run bus services to Siliguri, Guwahati,
Itanagar and Dimapur in Nagaland.
Destinations from Pasighat Dimapur (11.30am; 15hr;
₹950); Guwahati (1pm and 1.30pm; 9hr; ₹660); Itanagar

(6.15am and 2pm; 5hr; ₹380); Siliguri (6.30am; 15hr; seat
₹900, sleeper ₹2000).
Destinations from Along Daporijo (10hr; daily; ₹500);
Itanagar (11hr; daily; ₹800).
By jeep Shared jeeps run to and from Pasighat Sumo
counters situated along the main road, and about 200mt
from the bust station.
Destinations from Pasighat Along (5.30am; 5hr; ₹400);
Dibrugarh (5am; 5hr; ₹400); Guwahati (1pm; 8hr; ₹650).
By train At the time of research, the new rail link between
Dibrugarh in Assam and Pasighat via the Bogibeel Bridge
was about to start operations.

ACCOMMODATION AND EATING

★ **The Lhoba** 5km north of the Main Bazaar, Pasighat
☏ 124580558 76298 41592, ⌨ facebook.com/
thelhobha. Experience authentic Mising hospitality in an
orange farm set on a secluded bend of the Siang river, where
four charming thatch-and-bamboo cottages sit before an
ocean of pink elephant grass. A Mising longhouse caters to
large groups (₹600/person), and there's a campsite (₹1000
per tent, ₹500 if you bring your own). Breakfast is included,
and dinner costs around ₹500. They will pick up guests from

the sumo stand. No wi-fi. ₹3000
The Bean LIC Building, next to bus station, Pasighat
☏ 93663 88097, ⌨ facebook.com/CafeAtBean. Hip
café serving good brews, teas, milkshakes (₹100) and
Western-styled finger food (from ₹80). A cosy place to meet
Pasighat's young and sophisticated, and use some decent
free wi-fi. Daily 9am–7pm.

16

Namdapha National Park

Oct–April daylight hours • ₹350 (₹50), ordinary camera ₹100, camera with a zoom lens ₹500, video camera ₹1000

The beautifully remote **NAMDAPHA NATIONAL PARK**, covering an area of 1985 square kilometres, is unique for its massive range of altitudes (200–4500m) and its huge biodiversity. Close to the Burmese border, Namdapha is home to tigers, leopards (clouded and snow), elephants, red pandas, deer and the endangered Hoolock gibbon, although you are unlikely to spot any big wildlife on a short visit.

ARRIVAL AND INFORMATION

NAMDAPHA NATIONAL PARK

16

By bus Buses to and from Miao, 25km from the park entrance, pass through Margherita, 64km southwest, and the convenient Tinsukia, 40km further southwest in Assam, where rail services run to Guwahati. Dibrugarh is a further 47km beyond Tinsukia, with connections to central and east Arunachal.

Destinations from Miao Dibrugarh (daily; 6hr); Margherita (daily; 3hr); Tinsukia (daily; 4hr).

By car and taxi Taxis from Miao to the entry gates at Deban charge ₹2000, and vehicles are charged a ₹500 parking fee.
By jeep Jeeps are not allowed in the National Park.
Information The park headquarters are at Miao (ask for the Field Director's office; ☎94366 32806), where you can book forest rest-houses. The best source of information is ⓦnamdaphanationalpark.in, run by the Nature Conservation Foundation.

ACCOMMODATION

Namdapha Jungle Camp Miao, Upper Colony ☎94362 28763. Run by a local NGO involved in conservation, this guesthouse has just four comfortable rooms and a caretaker who will provide simple meals. All rooms have hot water in the attached bathrooms. Book in advance and they will look after your entire itinerary. No wi-fi. ₹800

Nagaland

On the Myanmar border, south of Arunachal Pradesh and east of Assam, **Nagaland** is physically and conceptually at the very edge of the Subcontinent. Home to the fiercely independent Nagas, its hills and valleys only opened up to tourism in 2000. One of India's most beautiful states, it was once renowned for its head-hunters but is now ninety percent Christian.

A visit to a Naga village provides a fascinating insight into a rapidly disappearing way of life. Most tour operators arrange guided trips; it is a good idea and far more informative to use a guide than going solo as some Nagas are tired of having their homes on show. If you do visit, bring a gift and offer money for the village to the chief (or *angh*).

Traditional Angami villages surround the capital of **Kohima**, including **Khonoma**. From **Mon** you can see various Konyak villages such as Shangnyu and Longwa, which straddles the India-Myanmar border. The Ao tribe inhabits **Mokokchung**, while **Tuensang** is home to six different tribes. The state's terrain is also ideal for trekking and mountain biking.

THE NAGAS

Naga warriors have long been feared and respected, and have practised **head-hunting** within living memory. They are also skilful farmers, growing twenty different species of rice. They differentiate between the soul and the spirit, believing the soul resides in the nape of the neck, while the spirit, in the head, holds great power and brings good fortune. Heads of enemies and fallen comrades were once collected to add to those of the community's own ancestors. The heads were kept in the men's meeting house (*morung*) in each village, which was decorated with fantastic carvings of animals, elephant heads and tusks – you can still see examples in many villages. After decades of Christianity, dominated by the Baptists, age-old traditions were fading away and festivals such as the Hornbill (see page 861) have recently been introduced in an attempt to reinstate traditional Naga culture. Today, music is an important feature of modern Naga youth culture.

Politically, Nagaland has seen a series of violent insurgencies and a powerful **independence movement**. The Naga were brought within the Indian union when, following a series of Naga raids on Assamese villages, the British sought to push them back into the hills. Despite two victories over the British, the **Angami Naga** were made to sign a truce in 1879 and went on to be loyal to the British; during World War II the Nagas fought valiantly against the Japanese. At the time of Independence, the Nagas found their land divided, with the larger area falling to Burma; India's promise of self-determination never materialized, and today sections of Naga society still yearn for autonomy while politicians wrangle. Though a ceasefire is officially in place, violence occasionally flares up and the politics of independence have disintegrated into a quagmire of inter-political rivalries that pays little heed to the wellbeing of the Naga people.

16

Naga festivals are tribe-specific, characterized by ritualistic dances and songs in traditional attire. A good time to visit is during the **Hornbill Festival** (ⓦhornbillfestival.com), held in the first ten days of December, which showcases Naga art, dance, music and sport (see page 861). Indians need a **permit** to visit Nagaland beyond Dimapur (see page 862).

Dimapur

For most, bustling **DIMAPUR**, 74km northwest of Kohima, the main gateway to the state, comes as a disappointing introduction, feeling much like a typically busy Indian town. Don't let this put you off though, as Nagaland has a lot more to offer than Dimapur would lead you to believe. Almost unavoidable, the town provides all the vital air, road and train connections linking Nagaland to the other states of the Northeast, especially Assam and Manipur. On the riverside edge of town are the **Kachari ruins**, fertility symbols dating back to the thirteenth-century Kachari kingdom.

ARRIVAL AND DEPARTURE   DIMAPUR

By plane Dimapur's airport is 4km northeast of town, off the Kohima road, currently serviced by Air India and Indigo. There are direct connections only to Dibrugarh and Kolkata. Destination Dibrugarh (2 weekly; 45min); Kolkata (daily; 1hr 30min).

By train Dimapur is Nagaland's sole railhead. Destinations Delhi (*Brahmaputra Express* #14056; daily; 40hr); Dibrugarh (*Kamakhya-Dibrugarh Intercity Express* #15605; daily; 10hr); Guwahati (*Jan Shatabdi Express* #12068; Mon–Sat 4.55pm; 4hr 30min); Jorhat (*Jan Shatabdi Express* #12067; Mon–Sat 10.45am; 2hr 35min); Simaluguri, for Sibsagar (*Kamakhya-Ledo Intercity Express* #15603; daily; 4hr 10min); Tinsukia (*Kamakhya-Ledo*

Intercity Express #15603; daily; 7hr 15min).

By bus State and private buses run to Kohima, Imphal and Mon from the Nagaland State Transport stand adjacent to the station. Private buses to other destinations leave from Blue Hill, opposite the railway station. Destinations Guwahati (daily; 11hr); Imphal (daily; 9hr); Itanagar (daily; 13hr); Jorhat (daily; 5hr); Kohima (several daily; 4hr).

By shared taxi The main transport hub is the railway station, from where shared taxis, marked yellow, regularly wait; services slow down after mid-afternoon. Destinations Kohima (3hr; ₹250); Mon (10–12hr; ₹700).

ACCOMMODATION AND EATING

★ **Jumping Bean** 1st Floor, Ana-Ki, near Tata Parking,   Circular Rd. With a refreshingly varied menu, from oriental and Korean through to great sandwiches, pasta and coffee, this popular bistro is a hub for the town's lively contemporary music scene. Gigs happen frequently, especially around the Hornbill Festival. Daily 10am–6pm.

Niathu Resort 7th Mile, Chumukedima ☏84159 21118, ⌨niathu.niathugroup.com. The most luxurious of Dimapur's hotels, the resort consists of cottages with an oblique reference to Naga traditional style coupled with large areas of marble flooring, modern amenities, a bar and a multicuisine restaurant. There's a swimming pool (₹500), a gym and pleasant gardens. It's also handy for the airport. **₹3700**

Tragopan Circular Rd ☏03862 230291, ⌨hotel tragopan.in. A popular business hotel across the tracks, with comfortable rooms and a decent restaurant. **₹1500**

Kohima and around

KOHIMA, Nagaland's capital, was established below the large Angami **Kohima Village** by the British in the nineteenth century and has been developing and spreading rapidly over the last few years. Traditional Naga villages – including **Khonoma**, 20km beyond Kohima, **Jakhema** and **Kigwema** – are just a short drive away, though Kohima itself is an increasingly cosmopolitan place, with traditional markets being replaced by modern shopping centres. Elsewhere the strength of Christianity is nowhere better epitomized than in the soaring gabled rooflines, inspired by the *morung* of the new Catholic cathedral to the south of the city.

Kohima Village

The large Angami settlement of **Kohima Village** is set on a high hill overlooking modern Kohima. A few of the buildings still sport the traditional pitched roofs and crossed "house-horns" on the gables – a mark of seniority – and its tightly knit labyrinth of lanes maintains a strong Naga feel.

World War II Cemetery

Spread over two large hills, Kohima forms a pass that played a strategic role during World War II. The Imphal–Dimapur highway – the route along which the Japanese hoped to reach the plains of India – crosses the saddle at the foot of the **World War II Cemetery** at the heart of Kohima. Located on the site of the battle that climaxed over the District Commissioner's tennis court, the cemetery stands as a tribute to the Allies who died during the three-month Battle of Kohima, which ended in June 1944 with a death toll of more than ten thousand soldiers. A plaque towards the bottom of the cemetery bears the poignant message "When you go home, tell them of us and say, for your tomorrow, we gave our today".

Kisama and around

10km south of Kohima

The **Naga Heritage Village** at **Kisama**, a showcase of Naga arts and crafts, is well worth the visit to see the collection of *morung* from most of the tribes of Nagaland. It is a beautiful spot, right under the wooded **Japfu Peak** (3048m), which makes a rewarding day-**trek** (Oct–May) from near Kisama and provides grand views of Kohima and beyond, especially at sunset or sunrise. The nearby Angami village of **Kigwema**, 3km further on, feels untouched and is well worth a walk through, with a guide.

Khonoma

20km northwest of Kohima

Khonoma and a rewarding day out, is where the Angami warriors made their final stand against the British in 1879. It's a rare animist village that celebrates the festival of Sekrenyi (Purification of the Soul) in late February. Renowned as a "green village" where tradition is carefully preserved, Khonoma is surrounded by magnificent swirls of rice terraces irrigated by a complex system of bamboo water pipes. Several houses around Khonoma offer homestay facilities (see page 886).

16

Dzükou Valley

25km south of Kohima • Entry ₹100 • Camera ₹200 • Shared Sumos leave Kohima's BOC Market to Viswema (₹50). From here, taxis to cover the 8km distance to the trek's starting point cost about ₹1000, or you can walk. It's another 3hr to the valley proper • A second, more demanding 5hr-long trek over steep rock-hewn steps starts 3km outside Jakhama village, but it's best to use this route to descend.

The scenic **Dzükou Valley**, part of the Khonoma Nature Conservation and Tragopan Sanctuary, straddles the Nagaland and Manipur border, and is graced with rolling green hills that blanket with thousands of colourful flowers in the wet season. Temperatures drop in the winter but the weather is clear and the valley remains green. There's only one extremely basic government-run guesthouse (₹50 for pitching your tent or floor space in one of two dormitory halls; ₹300 for a private room) which rent out sleeping pads, blankets, pots and cooking gear (₹50 per piece) and sell simple *thalis* for ₹200. Bring your own sleeping bag and some provisions from Kohima.

ARRIVAL AND DEPARTURE

By bus Buses drop you at the stand in the town centre. From the Nagaland State Transport (NST) stand, there are state buses to Dimapur, Mokokchung and Imphal. Show up at least an hour before your departure time, as tickets cannot be reserved and sell out very quickly. Tickets for private buses can be bought from agents in the centre.
Destinations Dimapur (hourly; 4hr); Imphal (7.30am; Mon–Sat; 6hr); Mokokchung (daily; 7hr);

KOHIMA AND AROUND

By Sumo Frequent Sumos to Dimapur and twice-daily Sumos to Mokokchung (6am & 10am) depart from the taxi stand 200m up from the bus station.
Destinations Dimapur (3hr; ₹250); Mokokchung (5hr; ₹300).
By car From Kohima, roads lead west to the railhead and airport at Dimapur (see page 884), north to Mokokchung and south to Imphal. From Mokokchung, the road continues to Jorhat in Assam.

INFORMATION AND TOURS

Tourist office The tourist office (Mon–Fri 10am–4pm; ⓦ tourismnagaland.com) is on Officer's Hill.
Guides and tours Explore Nagaland's Nino Zhasa (ⓣ 98563 43037) arranges tours of Kigwema and guides for trekking to Japfu. For wildlife tours, contact Gurudongma Tours & Treks (see page 862); for adventure treks contact Abor Country (see page 877); and for homestays and customised private tours by car, contact Happy Fleet (ⓣ 70050 73676, ⓦ facebook.com/happyfleet6427).

ACCOMMODATION

To stay here during the Hornbill Festival in the first week of December, you should book well in advance. There are several homestays around the city, and during Hornbill several families welcome guests into their homes.
Central Guesthouse Kohima 200m from the NST stand ⓣ 094028 00057 or 76288 42222, ⓦ facebook. com/ebguesthousekohima. Finally Kohima has a budget backpacker haunt, perfectly located in the centre of town. A sociable common room with great views of the city leads to simple, yet clean, dorms and three private rooms with shared bathrooms. Breakfast IS included and their café has decent meals for ₹200. Dorms ₹300, Doubles ₹700
★ **Green Wood Villa** Kipfüzha Sector, Kigwema ⓣ 98563 43037. A contemporary house close to the Heritage Village at Kisama, with all the comforts of home and great views from the roof garden; Nino organizes tours across Nagaland as well as treks up to Japfu peak (see page 885). She can also arrange homestays in Kohima. This is the best place to stay for the Hornbill Festival, but do book well in advance. There's a dorm and annexe too, and good off-season discounts. Dorms ₹1500, doubles ₹3500
The Heritage Officers Hill, near DC Bungalow ⓣ 94360 00044, ⓔ theheritagekohima@gmail.com. Once the District Commissioner's bungalow, this grand manor is set within extensive grounds south of the cemetery. Inside is a handful of beautiful wood rooms with large bathrooms, fireplaces, high ceilings and plenty of colonial charm. Meals are available to order. Run by the affable Thejal, who also runs the *Dream Café* in town. ₹2800
★ **Razhü Pru** Mission Compound ⓣ 03702 290291, ⓦ razhupru.com. A lovely old British-era manor-house, conveniently located 200m uphill past the Kohima Village gates. Large rambling rooms are well decorated throughout with Naga art, and the place has a great atmosphere and a fireplace. The restaurant serves good multicuisine meals including Naga dishes (₹500 per head). ₹2500

EATING

Traditional **Naga cooking** is based around rice with boiled vegetables, bamboo shoots and meat, and the infamous Naga chilli. Everything, besides hotels, shuts down by 7pm and there is a state-wide ban on alcohol. Most places are closed Sundays.
Aradura Spur Café Aradura Inn ⓣ 03702 241079. A relaxed

and elegant restaurant and café with soft sofas, dining areas and an open kitchen, serving a multicuisine menu alongside Naga dishes. It's a popular hangout for young people, and the hilltop location affords great views. Daily 10am–6pm.

★ **Chingtsüong** Razhü Point, Main Town ☎ 94360 01855. *Chingtsüong* ("come and eat"), with its bamboo-and-cane interiors and weapons on the wall, has plenty of atmosphere, and is the place to come if you're looking for an authentic Naga meal. Try the smoked pork with *anishi* (dried yam leaves; ₹100). The owner will keep the restaurant open in the evenings, with prior booking, for larger groups. Mon–Sat 9am–5pm.

The Continent Razhü Point, Main Town ☎ 90772 38022. Elegant and hip Western-style bistro cum café with wood-panelled walls, large sofas, wall windows and padded chairs. They serve cakes and a variety of cuisines, from Tibetan to Chinese, plus a small selection of beef steaks. A meal will set you back around ₹500. Daily 10am–6pm.

Dream Café Jasokie Place, Main Town. At the back of the UCO building, off the crossroads near the bottom of the cemetery, this small café and patisserie, owned by a renowned local musician (also owner of *The Heritage*), is a great meeting place, with pizzas, cakes and coffee. It's popular, and sometimes you will need to wait for a space. Around ₹200 a head. Mon–Sat 10am–6pm.

Mon and around

In the far northeast of Nagaland, 70km southeast of Sibsagar in Assam, **MON** is the regional capital of the **Konyak** tribe, mainly attractive as a base for visits to the surrounding villages. Look out for older Konyaks with elaborate and iconic facial tattoos and goat-horn earrings.

In April, the Konyaks celebrate the six-day spring **Aoling festival**, turning out in all their finery to mark the new year. A bumpy 23km drive northeast from Mon, **Shangnyu** is a typical Naga village where the welcoming *angh's* (chief's) home is packed with horns and animal skulls; the village also has a small but interesting museum. Another gruelling 42km drive east from Mon is **Longwa**, an interesting Konyak Naga village whose chief, *angh Nowano IV's*, home lies right across the India-Myanmar border. As locals say, their chief "rules from Myanmar, and sleeps in India", where his bedroom is located. From Longwa, you can trek to the nearby villages of Phuka, Weting and Nyanyu.

ARRIVAL AND DEPARTURE

MON AND AROUND

By bus and jeep Buses and jeeps to Mon run from Dibrugarh via Sonari in Assam (ask at your hotel for schedules; at least 7hr), bypassing the need to go through Dimapur and Kohima – but be prepared for dreadful roads after the border at Tizit, and check current permit regulations before you set off.

ACCOMMODATION

Helsa Cottage 15min walk from Mon taxi stand/market ☎ 98623 45965. A welcoming place run by a Konyak family, with large rooms and hot water provided in buckets, which you can take into the attached bathrooms. The food is reasonable and they can arrange guides. You must reserve in advance in April as it's a busy period of local festivals. No wi-fi. ₹1500

Mokokchung and around

160km north of Kohima (5hr by jeep)

A vibrant hill-town southwest of Mon, **Mokokchung** is Nagaland's third-largest urban centre, yet remains a quiet backwater in terms of tourism. Just 104km from Jorhat and more easily accessible from Assam than Kohima or Dimapur, Mokokchung makes a good base for exploring the surrounding Ao villages, including **Longkhum**, 17km away, which has a small museum and a guesthouse.

Tuensang

Tuensang, 115km east of Mokokchung, lies at the centre of a region inhabited by six different tribes – the Phom, Khiamniungan, Chang, Yimchunger and Sangtam. From here it's a two-day drive to **Thanamir**, and the start of a stunning two-day trek between tribal villages to **Mount Saramati**, Nagaland's highest peak (3826m), near the Burmese border. En route, there are basic places to stay at **Kiphire**. Check the security situation with your tour operator before setting off.

Mizoram

Heading south from Assam into **Mizoram**, "land of the highlanders", a winding mountain road takes you into forests and bamboo-covered hills. Mizoram is a gentle pastoral land, and the **Mizos** are a welcoming people who see very little tourism. Whitewashed churches dot the landscape, giving it more of the feel of a Central American country than a state squashed between Burma and Bangladesh.

The Mizos, who migrated from the Chin Hills of Burma, regularly raided tea plantations in the Assam Valley right into the late nineteenth century; only in 1924 did the British finally manage to bring about some semblance of control. They opened up what were then the **Lushai Hills** to missionaries who converted much of the state to Christianity. **Aizawl**, the capital, is a large sprawling city built on impossibly steep slopes. In the heart of the state, traditional Mizo communities occupy the crests of a series of ridges, each village dominated by its chief's house and *zawlbuk*, or bachelors' dormitory. An egalitarian people, without gender or class distinctions, the Mizos remain proud of their age-old custom of *Tlawmgaihna*, a code of ethics that governs hospitality. They enjoy a 95 percent literacy rate and are culturally more influenced by the Christian West than by mainstream India; music is an important part of Mizo life and an integral part of the Mizo Christian service. Indians need a **permit** to enter (see page 862).

Aizawl

One of India's remotest state capitals, **AIZAWL** (1250m), with the Tropic of Cancer passing straight through it, perches precariously on the steep slopes of a sharp ridge. Although the views are of hills rather than snowy mountains, it has something of the feel of a Himalayan hill station. There are few monuments or temples, but the markets are interesting and there are some extraordinary churches, including the imposing **Solomon's Temple**, which looks a bit like a cardboard cut-out, at Chawlhhmun. Everything closes on Sunday, when many people go to church dressed in their best. **Zarkawt** is the downtown area, where **Bara Bazaar** (Mon–Sat 6am–3pm) is the city's main attraction: everything from Mizo music to bespoke shoes can be bought here.

The **Durtlang Hills** immediately north of Aizawl, and **Luangmual**, 7km west of the centre, provide pleasant **walking** country – both are easy day-trips.

ARRIVAL AND DEPARTURE   **AIZAWL**

The easiest way of travelling to Mizoram is by air, as the overland routes are long and tedious. To the north, the busy commercial hub of **Silchar**, 180km away in Assam, provides the most convenient transport hub.

By plane Aizawl's Lengpui airport is 35km west of the city. A taxi to the airport costs around ₹1500. Prepaid tickets for shared taxis (₹300) are sold at the arrivals hall; taxis leave for town when full, so you may have to wait for an hour or so.

Destinations Guwahati (daily; 1hr 15min); Imphal (3 weekly; 50min); Kolkata (daily; 1hr 30min).

By Sumo The only recommended road out of Mizoram

BAMBOO, RATS AND REVOLUTION

Mizoram's two main species of bamboo flower every 48–50 years, attracting hordes of rats that devour crops, leading to famine. The first time this happened, in 1959, the government was seriously unprepared, which led **Laldenga** to found the **Mizo Famine Front** (MFF) to combat famine. It transformed into the **Mizo National Front** (MNF), a guerrilla group fighting for secession. The government's heavy-handed response in 1967 boosted support for the MNF who relied on essential Pakistani assistance, which came to an end with Bangladeshi independence. The MNF eventually came to the negotiating table and statehood was granted in 1986 in return for an end to the insurgency. Mizoram is now the most peaceful of the "seven sisters". However, in 2007 the bamboo began to flower again, the rat population grew and crops were destroyed; thankfully, this time the famine was not as devastating.

from Aizawl leads to Silchar, with Sumos the best way to travel; there are several ticket agents in Zarkawt. Buy tickets from the counters at Zarkawt.

Destinations Guwahati via Silchar (14–18hr; ₹1500); Shillong (14–18hr; ₹1200); Silchar (4–6hr; ₹500).

By bus Private bus companies in Zarkawt run services to Silchar and beyond. Buses leave for Luangmual from outside the Salvation Army Temple.

Destinations Guwahati (daily; 14–18hr); Shillong (daily; 14–18hr); Silchar (multiple daily; 7hr).

INFORMATION AND TOURS

Tourist office There's a tourist office at the New Secretariat Complex in Khatla (Mon–Fri 9am–5pm).

Tours and transport Staff at *David's Clover* hotel are extremely good at arranging transport around Mizoram for guests. Maliana of Evergreen Tours & Travels, Chanmari Chaltland Rd (☎96120 80159, ⓦevergreenmz.com), provides guides, organizes treks and adventure tour packages, including overland tours to Myanmar.

ACCOMMODATION

★ **David's Clover** 300m north of Hrangbana College, Chanmari ☎03892 305736, ⓦdavidscloverhotel.com. This recently renovated, central, family-run, mid-range hotel is run on a B&B basis. It offers comfortable rooms and a gym; each room has a TV and fridge. The owners, and especially Dolly, are extremely helpful and will arrange transport and suggest itineraries; the *David's Kitchen* restaurant is good for local Mizo cuisine. **₹2750**

Regency B49 Zarkawt Main St ☎03892 349334, ⓦregencyaizawl.com. The fanciest address in town, with lavish marble interiors, provides a promising introduction, but the rooms themselves are uninspiring. There is wi-fi, a good travel service and the restaurant is trendy and bright. **₹2806**

Ritz Near Machhunga Point, Bara Bazaar ☎03892 310409. A good option, popular with business travellers. Staff are friendly, and there's a range of rooms, all with wi-fi, as well as the excellent *Blue Berry* multicuisine restaurant. **₹1200**

EATING

The best restaurants are in hotels, and there are a couple of good cafés around. For local cuisine, mild by Indian standards, try the modest restaurants around Bara Bazaar. The state is dry and most eateries not attached to hotels close by around 7pm.

Magnolia 1st floor, Regency Hotel, Zarkawt ☎03892 349334. This is the smartest restaurant in town, with bright-yellow walls featuring Mizo decor and white-leather chic. The menu offers a variety of dishes, from pasta to tandoori. Try the sesame oven-roasted fish or the seafood bisque. Around ₹800 a head. Daily noon–9pm.

Zo Foods Near Vanapa Hall ☎03892 328726, ⓦfacebook.com/zofood. Popular restaurant with ethnic décor and specialised in authentic Mizo food. Try the pork stew and pork bamboo shoot rice, two excellent choices. A meal will set you back around ₹350. Daily 7am–9pm.

16

Manipur

Manipur, stretching along the border with Burma, centres on a vast lowland area watered by the lake system south of its capital **Imphal**. This far corner is home to the **Meithei**, who despite their own fascinating version of Vaishnava Hinduism, remain resolutely independent in their thinking. With its myriad **tribes**, including Naga, Manipur feels closer to Southeast Asia – and you can indeed cross into Myanmar from here – than mainstream India and many locals speak neither English nor Hindi. Manipur's **matriarchal society** means that women do most of the work and also champion political causes, with well-publicized protests against the violation of women and the people of Manipur by paramilitary groups stationed in the state. The strength of Manipuri women is no better exemplified than by the universal popularity and success of the inspiring boxer and five-times World Champion and Olympic medallist, Mary Kom.

Although the vale of Imphal is now all but devoid of trees, the outlying hills are still forested and shelter exotic birds and animals like the spotted linshang, Blyth's tragopan and even the clouded leopard, as well as numerous varieties of orchid. The unique natural habitat of **Loktak Lake** is home to the sangai deer – a symbol of Manipur.

Manipur's **history** can be traced back to the founding of Imphal in the first century AD. After long periods of independent and stable government, the state was incorporated into India at the end of the Indo-Burmese war in 1826, before coming under British rule in 1891. During **World War II**, much of Manipur was occupied by the Japanese, with 250,000 British and Indian troops trapped under siege in Imphal for three months. Thanks to a massive RAF airlift, the Allies held out, and when Japanese troops received the order to end the Imphal campaign, it was in effect the end of the campaign to conquer India. Manipur became a fully-fledged Indian state in 1972.

Imphal and around

Encircled by distant hills, Manipur's capital, **IMPHAL** (785m), lies at the northern end of the lake district and sprawls around the extensive grounds of what was once the medieval fortress of **Kangla**. Closed to the public for years due to it being a paramilitary camp, the large park behind the boulevard of Kanglawat holds some remains of the old fort, taken by the British following the war of 1891. The **Polo Ground** adjacent to Kangla plays an important role in Manipuri tradition; according to popular legend, the Manipuri game of Sagol Kangjei is the inspiration for modern polo, and every November the **Sangai Festival** features an international polo tournament.

Close to the main gates of Kangla, the **Shaheed Minar** memorial commemorates the failed Meithei revolt against British occupation in 1891, while a short distance south is the **State Museum** (Tues–Sun 10am–4pm; ₹20), a showcase for Manipuri culture with tribal art and costumes and a historical collection, along with stuffed animals.

Khwairamband bazaar

Kangchup Rd • Daily around 9am to late afternoon

At the heart of Imphal, the fascinating **Khwairamband bazaar**, also known as *ima keithel* (mother's market), now rehoused in four buildings and spilling on the kerb outside, is run by more than three thousand Meithei women, making it the largest female-run market in Asia.

Shri Shri Govindjee

Southeast of Kangla, the Vaishnavite temple of **Shri Shri Govindjee**, where priests perform rituals addressing the deities according to the times of day, is well worth a visit, especially in the afternoon when you may be lucky to catch a glimpse of a **Manipuri dance** rehearsal in the hall opposite. Nearby lies the old **Royal Palace**, closed to the public.

War cemetery and memorial

The Commonwealth War Graves Commission immaculately maintains the **Imphal War Cemetery** (daily: March–Sept 9am–4.30pm; Oct–Feb 9am–4pm), 500m north of the *Tourist Lodge* on Imphal Road, while south of the city near Bishnupur, a **Japanese memorial** stands as a poignant reminder of the war.

Andro Heritage Village

25km from east of Imphal • Buses (₹30)leave from Andro Parking in Imphal's Wangkhai area

Nestled in the verdant foothills of the Nongmaiching Hills, the ancient village of ANDRO has transformed into an interesting heritage village. The Meitei-styled temple to **Panam Ningthou**, the village's governing deity, is 1.5km from Andro Bazaar. It houses the "sacred fire of Andro", one of the Meitei's holiest sites, which has been kept burning since the 1st century AD. The **Mutua Bahadur Museum**, (Mon–Fri 10am–5pm; ₹20) a cultural complex established in 1993, has model houses of Manipur's various ethnic groups — including the Meitei, Kuki, Tangkhul, Kabui and Mao.

ARRIVAL AND DEPARTURE	IMPHAL

By plane Imphal airport, 6km to the south, is well connected to Guwahati and Kolkata and sees a handful of flights to Aizawl. There are no airport bus connections to the city centre; reserved taxis charge around ₹500, shared autos

SAFETY IN MANIPUR

Manipur has been racked by waves of **violence** through insurgency, drug- and arms-trafficking across the Burmese border, and brutal factional **conflict**. Some governments, including that of the UK, still advise against all but essential travel to the state (see ⦿gov.uk/foreign-travel-advice); but at the time of writing, the situation has greatly improved and travel to the vale of Imphal is generally safe. You can arrive **by air** or **by road** from Kohima and Dimapur without a permit, but your passport will be registered and stamped upon arrival at the airport or at road checkpoints. It is recommended you seek the advice of a local tour operator, and a local guide, if heading into the hills and border regions.

₹10. Foreigners currently do not need permits but must enter passport details at the desk just inside the arrivals hall.

Destinations Agartala (4 weekly; 50min); Aizawl (4 weekly; 50min); Guwahati (4 daily; 50min); Kolkata (4 daily; 1hr 30min); Silchar (3 weekly; 35min).

By bus and Sumo The AOC (Assam Oil Corporation) corner on Dimapur Rd is the main hub, with buses and unscheduled Sumos to Dimapur (215km), the closest railhead (via Kohima), and Guwahati. The roundabout across the bridge opposite Khwairamband bazaar has buses to Moirang.

Bus destinations Dimapur via Kohima (7hr; ₹600); Guwahati (12–15hr; ₹800); Kohima (5hr; ₹600); Moirang (1hr; ₹100).

By shared taxi Winger shared taxis (large vans) are a bit faster than buses and Sumos, and ply round the clock to Dimapur and Moirang. Share taxis to Silchar leave from Wahengbam Leikai Jiri parking.

Destinations Dimapur (6hr; ₹800); Silchar (9–11hr; ₹600).

By taxi A reserved taxi to Dimapur costs ₹7000.

INFORMATION

Tourist office The state tourist office (Mon–Sat 9.30am–4.30pm; ⦿manipurtourism.gov.in) is at the Directorate of Tourism building, off the main Dimapur Rd. The India Tourism office is on Jail Rd (Mon–Fri 9.30am–5pm).

Banks & ATMs The State Bank of India on MG Ave has a foreign exchange service.

Tours Seven Sisters (MG Ave; ☎97061 23401, ⦿sevensistersholidays.com) offers tours and books road and air transport. Khuibo Tours & Travel, Yaiskul Chingakham Leirak (☎94368 91270, ⦿khuibotours.com), offers itineraries and guides around Manipur, including Loktak Lake.

ACCOMMODATION

Imphal has a few decent hotels, where you will find the best restaurants, but there are no bars – Manipur is another of the Northeast's dry states and everything, outside of hotels, shuts down around 7pm.

Aheibam Homestay Iroishemba Forest Gate, 5km west of the Khwairamband bazaar ☎0873 187 1324, ⦿facebook.com/ImphalHomestay. Charming homestay set under Imphal's only hill, and run by Milan, an experienced local guide and eco-farmer. The two rooms are non-attached, set around a sunny courtyard, and a perfect spot to experience simple Manipuri family life. Breakfast is included, and meals are available on request (₹400). Shared autos from the town centre only cost ₹10. **₹1000**

★ **The Classic** North AOC, Dimapur Rd ☎0385 244 3967, ⦿theclassichotel.in. Opposite the Kangla grounds, this is the most opulent of Imphal's hotels, with a swish lobby, two good restaurants and great breakfasts. Both a/c and non-a/c rooms are comfortable and have modern amenities; service is friendly and they also have a useful travel desk. **₹1740**

Loktak Lake and around

60km south of Imphal • Keibul Lamjao National Park daily 9am–5pm • ₹20

South of Imphal, Lotak Lake is home to a unique community of fishermen who live on circular floating atolls of matted vegetation, called *phumdis*. Much of the lake is taken up by the **Keibul Lamjao National Park**, a floating park located on the largest *phumdis*, home to the endemic and endangered sangai deer that live on the reed beds. Avoid the hill at **Sendra**, which is now a paramilitary camp surrounded by litter. You can drive up to **Sendra Island** and get a boat to the national park and the *phumdis*. The park has a viewing tower on a hill with views down to the reed beds; it is a good 1.5km past the gate. You will need binoculars and lots of patience to catch sight of any wildlife.

16

CROSSING OVER INTO MYANMAR

Since May 2018, the once off-limits **border** between Manipur and Myanmar has opened to independent travelers. If you are travelling on foot or by bicycle, all you need is a Myanmar Evisa (Ⓦevisa.moip.gov.mm) which costs 50USD, is valid for 28 days, and takes up to 3 days. **Shared jeeps** to the border town of Moreh (several daily between 7am and 11am; 3hr; ₹300) start from Imphal's Sumo stand at Moirang Khom. Burmese taxis continue from the Myanmar entry checkpoint to Tamu. From here, buses proceed to Mandalay. If you are overlanding with your own car or motorbike, however, you will still need a special permit on top of a Myanmar Evisa, and you will need to cross in a convoy of vehicles. Milan Sanji of Aheibam Homestay (☎87318 871324, Ⓦtourmanipur.com) can organise all the necessary documents. You can also consult Horizons Unlimited (Ⓦhorizonsunlimited.com) or Overland to Asia Facebook Group (Ⓦbit.ly/2s0nRE3) to organise a convoy. Finally, check the news for the current **security situation** before you set off.

Moirang

3km from the lake and 45km south of Imphal

On the way to Loktak, the small town of **MOIRANG** is the traditional centre of Meithei culture, with a temple devoted to the pre-Hindu deity **Thangjing**. In April 1944, the Indian National Army planted its flag at Moirang, having fought alongside the Japanese against the British Indian Army for the cause of Independence. The **INA Memorial Complex** (Tues–Sun 10am–4pm) commemorates the event.

16

Tripura

Surrounded by Bangladesh on three sides, the lush mountains, hills and valleys of **TRIPURA** became part of India in 1949. Its fate and culture has been closely entwined with Bengal, while indigenous ethnic groups form around thirty percent of the population, mostly around the northern and eastern districts. Partition and the subsequent creation of East Pakistan (now Bangladesh) in 1948, followed by war, famine and military regimes, forced millions of Bangladeshis to flee into Tripura. Indigenous people, such as the Tripuri (a Tibeto-Burman ethnic group), became outnumbered, causing resentment and **conflict** over the decades. In 2013, elections returned the CPI(M) government, making Tripura one of the last Communist-run states in India. Today, **Agartala**, the capital, is a relaxed city with a palace and a few temples. A handful of wildlife sanctuaries, such as **Gumti**, **Rowa**, **Trishna** and **Sepahijala**, protect the state's few remaining forests, while to the northeast the medieval Shaivite rock carvings of **Unakoti** are now accessible after years of strife.

Agartala and around

Agartala, Tripura's capital, is a laidback administrative centre. Its main attraction is the gleaming white **Ujjayanta Palace**, completed in 1901. Set amid formal gardens and artificial lakes, this huge building, now home to the State Legislative Assembly, covers around eight hundred acres. Across the road, one of many temples nearby and open to the public, the **Jagannath Temple**'s orange tower rises from an octagonal plinth.

Kamala Sagar lake, 27km south of Agartala, is overlooked by a small Kali temple. Twenty-eight kilometres along the road south to Udaipur, the **Sepahijala** nature reserve and botanical gardens (9am–5pm closed Fri; ₹20, camera ₹10) is actually a vast **zoo** dedicated to the preservation of animals such as the Hoolock gibbon, capped langur and slow loris. With a bit of luck, you may spot clouded leopard.

Boxanagar

43km southeast of Agartala • Direct buses to Boxanagar leave from Agartala's Nagerjala Bus Stand. In Boxanagar, catch an auto or walk 10min to reach the site.

The red brick stupas of **Boxanagar** date back to the 6th century and are a well-preserved, albeit remote, sign of early Buddhist influence over the region. You can visit and climb the base structure of two stupas, and peek across the nearby border into Bangladesh.

Tripura Sundari
55km southeast of Agartala

Of particular note in **Udaipur**, a town of lakes and temples, is **Tripura Sundari**, a sixteenth-century temple dedicated to Kali. It is also one of the *shakti pithas*, marking where Sati's right foot landed when her body fell to earth in 51 pieces. Animal sacrifices are common.

Neermahal
55km south of Agartala • Take a boat from the Rudrasagar lakeshore (10min; ₹25)

The red-and-white fairy-tale water palace at **Neermahal** stands in the waters of Lake Rudrasagar in Melaghar. The former royal palace, accessible by boat, was built in 1930 as a summer home for Maharaja Bir Bikram Kishore, blending Hindu and Islamic styles. Today, the ravages of time are apparent on its frontage.

ARRIVAL AND INFORMATION | AGARTALA

By plane Agartala airport, 12km north of the centre, has direct flights to Guwahati, Kolkata, Imphal and Silchar serviced by Air India, Spice Jet and Indigo. Plans to upgrade the airport and link it to Bangladesh are currently underway. Autos (₹150) and taxis (₹400) run from the airport to the centre of Agartala.

Destinations Guwahati (daily; 50min); Imphal (Mon, Thurs & Sat; 45min); Kolkata (daily; 1hr).

By train Agartala has limited connections to Lumding and Silchar in Assam. However, at the time of writing, all rail services were suspended.

By bus and Sumo Buses drop off at the Chandrapur bus stand (also known as ISBT) or one of the private company offices on LN Bari Rd. Buses leave from ISBT for the gruelling journey to Silchar, Shillong and Guwahati; book tickets in advance to avoid frequent stoppages and changes. Buses and Sumos to Udaipur leave from Nagarjala.

Bus destinations Guwahati (daily; 20hr); Shillong (daily; 17hr); Silchar (daily; 12hr); Udaipur (every 20min; 2hr).

Information and tours The tourist office (TTDC), at the Palace Compound (Mon–Fri 10am–5pm; ☎0381 232 5930, ⓦ tripuratourism.nic.in), organize good-value multi-day tours and day car rental (₹9/km).

ACCOMMODATION

Executive Inn 9 Mantri Bari, Chowmuhani ☎72101 01502, @hotelexecutiveinn@yahoo.com. Set in the market, this little hotel is in need of a makeover, but provides good-value, comfortable accommodation. Rooms are a bit dingy downstairs, but lighter on the top floor. Staff offer helpful travel advice and there's a good restaurant too – *Blossom* – with Indian food. ₹1500

Ginger Khejurbagan, Airport Rd ☎0381 241 1333, ⓦ gingerhotels.com. Efficient chain-hotel 15min from the airport, with clean rooms, modern amenities (including a gym), welcoming staff and attractive full-board packages for multi-night stays. There is a decent restaurant and a *Coffee Café Day* downstairs. Staff at the travel desk can organize tours. Rates include taxes. ₹4205

CROSSING OVER INTO BANGLADESH

Agartala is 2km from the **border** with Bangladesh. There is no official currency exchange at the border so it's advisable to change your rupees in town. Rickshaws on the Bangladeshi side can take you to Akhaura Junction, 4km away, from where there are **trains** to Comilla, Sylhet and Dhaka. **Buses** to Dhaka (1 daily Mon–Sat; 4hr; from ₹350) start from the Tripura Road Transport Corporation (TRTC) stand in Krishnanagar (Agartala) and further continue to Kolkata (10hr; ₹1800–2000). **Visas** for Bangladesh (required) are checked at the border crossing; entry formalities are carried out again on the Bangladeshi side border. The Bangladeshi Embassy, Kunjaban, near Circuit House in Agartala (Mon–Thurs 8.30am–1pm & 2–4.30pm, Fri 8.30am–noon & 2–4.30pm; ☎0381 232 4807), issues visas. Check the news for the current **security situation** before booking.

16

Odisha

TRADITIONAL BOATS ON CHILIKA LAKE, ODISHA

17 Odisha

Despite being one of India's poorest states, Odisha – formerly known as Orissa – boasts a rich and distinctive cultural heritage. Its coastal plains have the highest concentration of historical and religious monuments – Odisha's principal tourist attractions. Puri, site of the famous Jagannath temple and one of the world's most spectacular devotional processions, the Rath Yatra, combines the heady intensity of a Hindu pilgrimage centre with the more hedonistic pleasures of the beach. Konark, just up the coast, has the ruins of Odisha's most ambitious medieval temple, whose surfaces writhe with exquisitely preserved sculpture, including some eyebrow-raising erotica. The ancient rock-cut caves and ornate temples of Bhubaneswar, the state capital, hark back to an era when it ruled a kingdom stretching from the Ganges delta to the mouth of the River Godavari.

Away from the central "Golden Triangle" of sights, foreign travellers are few and far between, though you'll see plenty of Bengali tourists travelling throughout coastal Odisha. In the winter, the small islands dotted around **Chilika Lake**, a huge saltwater lagoon south of Bhubaneswar, is good for birdwatchers. Further north, in the **Bhitarkanika Sanctuary**, a remote stretch of beach is the nesting site for rare olive ridley **turtles**.

From the number of temples in Odisha, you'd be forgiven for thinking Brahmanical Hinduism was its sole religion. In fact, almost a quarter of the population are **adivasi** (literally "first"), or "tribal" people, thought to have descended from the area's pre-Aryan aboriginal inhabitants. In the more inaccessible corners of the state many of these groups have retained unique cultural traditions and languages, though dam builders, missionaries, "advancement programmes" initiated by the state government, and the activities of Maoist rebels continue to threaten their way of life. Tourism poses another danger (see page 924).

Brief history

Other than scattered fragmentary remains of prehistoric settlement, Odisha's earliest archeological find dates from the fourth century BC. The fortified city of **Sisupalgarh**, near modern Bhubaneswar, was the capital of the **Kalinga** dynasty, about which little is known. In the third century BC, the ambitious Mauryan emperor **Ashoka** routed the Kalingan kingdom in a battle so bloody that the carnage was supposed to have inspired his legendary conversion to **Buddhism**. Rock edicts erected around the empire extol the virtues of the new faith, **dharma**, as well as the principles that Ashoka hoped to instil in his vanquished subjects. With the demise of the Mauryans, Kalinga enjoyed something of a resurgence. Under the imperialistic **Chedi** Jain dynasty, vast sums were spent expanding the capital and on carving elaborate monastery caves into the nearby

---

BEST TIME TO VISIT

The best time to visit Odisha is the October–March period – especially November, December and January – when the weather is warm and dry. It gets uncomfortably hot in April–May, and the monsoon generally hits in June and lasts until the end of September. The first couple of months of the rainy season are also sweltering, but this is when Odisha's most famous festival, the **Rath Yatra** (see page 915), takes place.

SUN TEMPLE AT KONARK

Highlights

❶ Bhubaneswar Hidden in the suburbs of the state capital are around five hundred temples with unique architecture and elaborate sculptures, including the majestic Lingaraj Mandir. See page 899

❷ Udaigiri and Khandagiri Among Odisha's premier historical sites, these 2000-year-old sandstone caves, once occupied by Jain monks, feature fascinating carvings and friezes. See page 907

❸ Satkosia Tiger Reserve Located in central Odisha, this little-visited, very scenic reserve is set around the beautiful Mahanadi River and the eponymous gorge. See page 907

❹ Olive ridley turtles Endangered olive ridley turtles journey to Gahirmatha beach for one night in February or March to lay their eggs – an unforgettable scene. See page 912

❺ Puri With one of India's holiest temples and a small, laidback traveller scene, Puri is an essential stop-off for pilgrims and backpackers alike. See page 913

❻ Rath Yatra Pilgrims flock to Puri to celebrate Lord Jagannath during the frenetic midsummer "Car Festival". See page 915

❼ Konark Dating back to the thirteenth century, this elegant Hindu temple sits astride a huge stone chariot and is decorated by some extraordinary erotic carvings. See page 919

HIGHLIGHTS ARE MARKED ON THE MAP ON PAGE 898

17

hills of **Khandagiri** and **Udaigiri**. During the second century BC, however, the kingdom gradually splintered into warring factions and entered a kind of dark age. The influence of Buddhism waned, Jainism all but vanished, and **Brahmanism**, disseminated by the teachings of the Shaivite zealot Lakulisha, started to resurface as the dominant religion.

A golden age

Odisha's golden age, during which the region's prosperous Hindu rulers created some of South Asia's most sophisticated art and architecture, peaked in the twelfth century under the **Eastern Gangas**. Fuelled by the gains from a thriving trade network (which extended as far east as Indonesia), the Ganga kings erected magnificent **temples** where Shiva worship and arcane tantric practices adopted by earlier Odishan rulers were replaced by new forms of devotion to Vishnu. The shrine of the most popular royal deity of all, Lord Jagannath, at Puri, was by now one of the four most hallowed religious centres in India.

In the fifteenth century, the **Afghans of Bengal** swept south to annexe the region, with Man Singh's **Mughal** army hot on their heels in 1592. That even a few medieval Hindu monuments escaped the excesses of the ensuing iconoclasm is miraculous, and **non-Hindus** have never since been allowed to enter the most holy temples in Puri and Bhubaneswar. In 1751 the **Marathas** from western India ousted the Mughals as the dominant regional power. The East India Company, meanwhile, was also making inroads along the coast, and 28 years after Clive's victory at Plassey in 1765, Odisha finally came under **British rule**.

Post-Independence

Following **Independence**, the state saw rapid **development**. Discoveries of coal, bauxite, iron ore and other minerals stimulated considerable industrial growth and

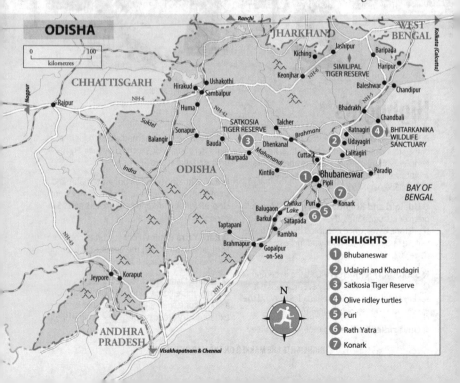

ODISHA

0 ——— 100
kilometres

HIGHLIGHTS

1. Bhubaneswar
2. Udaigiri and Khandagiri
3. Satkosia Tiger Reserve
4. Olive ridley turtles
5. Puri
6. Rath Yatra
7. Konark

FESTIVALS IN ODISHA

Makar Mela (mid-Jan). Pilgrims descend on a tiny island in Chilika Lake to leave votive offerings in a cave for the goddess Kali.

Adivasis Mela (Jan 26–Feb 1). Bhubaneswar's "tribal" fair is a disappointing cross between New York's Coney Island and an agricultural show, though it does feature good live music and dance.

Magha Saptami (Jan/Feb). During the full-moon phase of Magha, a small pool at Chandrabhaga beach, near Konark, is swamped by thousands of worshippers in honour of Surya, the sun god and curer of skin ailments.

Panashankranti (early April). In various regions, on the first day of Vaisakha, saffron-clad penitents carrying peacock feathers enter trances and walk on hot coals.

Chaitra Parba (mid-April). Santals (the largest of Odisha's many *adivasi* groups) perform *Chhou* dances at Baripada in Mayurbhunj district, northern Odisha.

Ashokastami (April/May). Bhubaneswar's Car Festival (a procession of temple chariots), when the Lingaraj deity takes a dip in the Bindu Sagar tank.

Sitalasasthi (May/June). Commemorating the marriage of Shiva and Parvati, celebrated in Sambalpur and Bhubaneswar.

Rath Yatra (June/July). The biggest and grandest of Odisha's festivals. Giant images of Lord Jagannath, his brother Balabhadra and his sister Subhadra make the sacred journey from the Jagannath temple to Gundicha Mandir in Puri. See box, p.901.

Bali Yatra (Nov/Dec). Commemorates the voyages made by Odishan traders to Indonesia. Held at full moon on the banks of the River Mahanadi in Cuttack.

Konark Festival (early Dec). A festival of classical dance featuring Odishan and other regional dance forms in the Sun Temple at Konark.

improvements to infrastructure. Despite such urban progress, however, Odisha remains a poor rural state, heavily dependent on agriculture to provide for the basic needs of its inhabitants.

Events of recent years have damaged the state's reputation. Violent **Maoist** (Naxalite) activity in rural areas has increased, drawing an often equally violent response from government forces. In March 2012, two Italian travellers visiting tribal areas in the Kandhamal area were kidnapped by Naxalites and held for almost a month, before being released unharmed. There have also been regular attacks on the state's **Christian minority** by Hindu fundamentalists, who, in 2008, killed at least seventy people and forced tens of thousands from their homes.

An ongoing campaign by environmental and human rights groups, meanwhile, has been vociferous in its opposition to the multinational corporation **Vedanta**, which wants to develop a bauxite mine on Niyamgiri mountain in eastern Odisha, considered sacred by the local *adivasi* community.

GETTING AROUND
ODISHA

Travelling around Odisha presents few practical problems if you stick to the more populated coastal areas. **NH-5** and the **Southeast Railway**, which cut in tandem down the coastal plain via Bhubaneswar, are the main arteries of the region. A branch line also runs as far as Puri, connecting it by frequent, direct express **trains** to Delhi, Kolkata and Chennai. **Buses** are often the only way to reach some of the more remote inland areas.

Bhubaneswar

With its featureless 1950s architecture, **BHUBANESWAR** may initially strike you as surprisingly dull for a city with a population of around a million and a history of settlement stretching back more than two thousand years. However, the southern suburbs harbour the remnants of some of India's finest medieval **temples**, which are made all the more atmospheric by the animated religious life that continues to revolve around them, particularly at festival times.

17

Brief history

Bhubaneswar first appears in history during the fourth century BC, as the capital of ancient **Kalinga**. It was here that Ashoka erected one of the Subcontinent's best-preserved rock edicts – still in place 5km south of **Dhauli**. Under the **Chedis**, ancient Kalinga gained control over the thriving mercantile trade in the region and became the northeast seaboard's most formidable power.

Bhubaneswar then declined, re-emerging as a regional force only in the fifth century AD, when it became an important Shaivite centre. Coupled with the formidable wealth of the **Sailodbhavas** two centuries later, the growing religious fervour fuelled an extraordinary spate of temple construction. Between the seventh and twelfth centuries some seven thousand shrines are believed to have been erected around the **Bindu Sagar** tank. Most were razed in the Muslim incursions of the medieval era, but

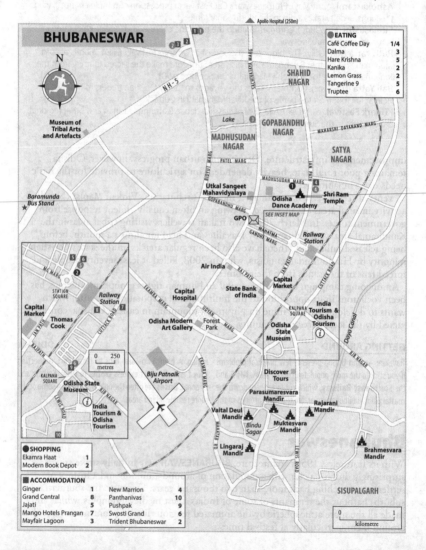

ODISHAN TEMPLES

Odishan temples constitute one of the most distinctive regional styles of religious architecture in south Asia. They were built according to strict templates set down one thousand years or more ago in a body of canonical texts called the *Shilpa Shastras*. These specify not only every aspect of temple design, but also the overall symbolic significance of the building. Unlike Christian churches or Islamic mosques, Hindu shrines are not simply places of worship or objects of worship in themselves – re-creations of the "Divine Cosmic Creator-Being" or the particular deity enshrined within them. For a Hindu, to move through a temple is akin to entering the very body of the god glimpsed at the moment of *darshan*, or ritual viewing, in the shrine room. In Odisha, this concept also finds expression in the technical terms used in the *Shastras* to designate the different parts of the structure: the foot (*pabhaga*), shin (*jangha*), torso (*gandi*), neck (*kantha*), head (*mastaka*) and so forth.

THE DEUL

Most temples are made up of two main sections. The first and most impressive of these is the **deul**, or sanctuary tower. A soaring, curvilinear spire with a square base and rounded top, the *deul* symbolizes Meru, the sacred mountain at the centre of the universe. Its intricately ribbed sides, which in later buildings were divided into rectangular projections known as *raths*, usually house images of the accessory deities, while its top supports a lotus-shaped, spherical *amla* (a motif derived from an auspicious fruit used in Ayurvedic medicine as a purifying agent). Above that, the vessel of immortality, the *kalasha*, is crowned by the presiding deity's sacred weapon, a wheel (Vishnu's *chakra*) or trident (Shiva's *trishul*). The actual deity occupies a chamber inside the *deul*. Known in Oriya as the **garbha griha**, or inner sanctum, the shrine is shrouded in womb-like darkness, intended to focus the mind of the worshipper on the image of God.

THE JAGAMOHANA

The **jagamohana** ("world delighter"), which adjoins the sanctuary tower, is a porch with a pyramidal roof where the congregation gathers for readings of religious texts and other important ceremonies. Larger temples, such as the Lingaraj in Bhubaneswar and the Jagannath in Puri, also have structures that were tacked on to the main porch when music and dance were more commonly performed as part of temple rituals. Like the *jagamohana*, the roofs of the **nata mandir** (the dancing hall) and **bhogamandapa** (the hall of offerings) are pyramidal. The whole structure, along with any smaller subsidiary shrines (often earlier temples erected on the same site), is usually enclosed within a walled courtyard.

AN EVOLVING STYLE

Over the centuries, Odishan temples became progressively grander and more elaborate. It's fascinating to chart this transformation as you move from the earlier buildings in Bhubaneswar to the acme of the region's architectural achievement, the stunning Sun Temple at **Konark** (see page 919). Towers grow taller, roofs gain extra layers, and the **sculpture**, for which the temples are famous all over the world, attains a level of complexity and refinement unrivalled before or since.

enough survived for it to be possible in even a short visit to trace the evolution of Odishan architecture from its small, modest beginnings to the gigantic, self-confident proportions of the **Lingaraj** – the seat of Trimbhubaneshwara, or "Lord of Three Worlds", from which the modern city takes its name. A relative backwater until after Independence, Bhubaneswar was only declared the new state capital after nearby Cuttack reached bursting point in the 1950s.

The temples

Of the five hundred or so **temples** that remain in Bhubaneswar only a handful are of interest to anyone but the most ardent temple-phile. They are quite spread out in the south of the city, but it's possible to see the highlights in a day by auto-rickshaw

17

(see page 905). The majority are active places of worship, so dress appropriately, remove your shoes (and any leather items) at the entrance and seek permission before taking photographs, particularly inside the buildings. The resident priest will expect a donation if he's shown you around, but don't believe the astronomical amounts recorded in the ledgers you'll be shown. Entry is free to all temples except the Rajarani.

The central group
Just west of Lewis Rd, around 2.5km south of the railway station

The compact **central group** includes some of Bhubaneswar's most celebrated temples, most notably the eye-catching **Parasuramesvara Mandir** and the exquisite, tenth-century **Muktesvara Mandir**.

Parasuramesvara Mandir

The best-preserved and most beautiful early example in the central group, the lavishly decorated **Parasuramesvara Mandir** stands in the shade of a large banyan tree. Dating from around 650 AD, the shrine's plain, rectangular assembly hall (*jagamohana*), simple stepped roof and squat beehive-shaped tower (*deul*) typify the style of the late seventh century. Besides the sheer quality of the building's exterior sculpture, Parasuramesvara is significant in marking the then-recent transition from Buddhism to Hinduism. Look out for panels depicting Lakulisha, the proselytizing Shaivite saint whose sect was largely responsible for the conversion of Odisha to Hinduism in the fifth century. More graphic assertions of Hindu supremacy mark corners of the *deul*, where rampant lions crouch or stand above elephants, symbols of the beleaguered Buddhist faith.

Muktesvara Mandir

Erected in the mid-tenth century, the **Muktesvara Mandir** is often described as the gem of Odishan architecture for its compact size and exquisite sculptural detail. It stands in a separate walled courtyard, beside the small **Marichi Kund** tank (whose waters are believed to cure infertility). The temple was constructed two hundred years after the Parasuramesvara, and represents the new, more elaborate style that had evolved in Bhubaneswar. Its *jagamohana* sports the more distinctively Odishan pyramidal roof, while the *deul*, though similar in shape to earlier sanctuary towers, places more emphasis on vertical rather than horizontal lines. Directly facing the main entrance, the ornamental **torana** (gateway), topped by two reclining female figures, is Muktesvara's masterpiece.

On the edge of Muktesvara's terrace, the unfinished **Siddhesvara** was erected at around the same time as the Lingaraj, but is far less imposing.

The eastern group
Just east of Lewis Rd, around 2.5km south of the railway station

The two key temples in the **eastern group** are the **Rajarani Mandir**, widely considered to be one of the most beautiful temples in Bhubaneswar, and the **Brahmesvara Mandir**, which continues to host a living deity in its eleventh-century shrine.

Rajarani Mandir
Daily sunrise–sunset • ₹200 (₹100)

Although it was never completed, the twelfth-century **Rajarani Mandir** ranks among the very finest of Bhubaneswar's later temples. From the far end of the well-watered gardens in which it stands, the profile of the *deul* dominates first impressions. The best of the sculpted figures for which Rajarani is famous surround the sides of the tower, roughly 3m above the ground, where the **dikpalas** ("guardians of the eight directions"), separated from one another by exquisite female *nayikas*, protect the main shrine.

17

Brahmesvara Mandir

Unlike most of its neighbours, the eleventh-century shrine within **Brahmesvara Mandir** still houses a living deity, as indicated by the saffron pennant flying from the top of the sanctuary. Here, as at Rajarani, *dikpalas* preside over the corners, with a fierce Chamunda on the western facade (shown astride a corpse and holding a trident and severed head), while curvaceous maidens admire themselves in mirrors or dally with their male consorts. An inscription, now lost, records that one Queen Kovalavati once made a donation of "many beautiful women" to this temple, recalling that **devadasis**, the dancers-cum-courtesans who were to become a prominent feature of Odishan temple life in later years (see page 922), made an early appearance here. Non-Hindus are barred from the central shrine, whose majestic Nandi bull has testicles well-polished by years of propitious rubbing from worshippers.

The Bindu Sagar group

West of the central group around the Bindu Sagar

The largest group of temples is clustered around the **Bindu Sagar** ("ocean drop tank"). This small artificial lake, mentioned in the Puranas, is said to contain nectar, wine and water drawn from the world's most sacred rivers. It's main bathing place both for pilgrims visiting the city and for the Lingaraj deity, who is taken to the pavilion in the middle once every year during Bhubaneswar's annual **Car Festival** (Ashokastami) for his ritual purificatory dip. The hours around sunrise and sunset are the most evocative time for a stroll here, when the residents of the nearby *dharamshalas* file through the smoky lanes to pray at the *ghats*.

Lingaraj Mandir

Immediately south of the Bindu Sagar stands Odisha's most stylistically evolved temple. Built early in the eleventh century by the Ganga kings, one hundred years before the Jagannath temple at Puri, the mighty **Lingaraj Mandir** has remained a living shrine. For this reason, foreign visitors are not permitted inside, but there is a **viewing platform** overlooking the north wall of the complex, from where all four of the principal sections of the building are visible. The two nearest the entrance, the *bhogamandapa* (hall of offering) and the *nata mandir* (hall of dances), associated with the rise of the *devadasi* system (see page 922), are both later additions. Beautiful **sculpture** depicting the music and dance rituals that would once have taken place inside the temple adorns its walls.

The immense 45m *deul* is the literal and aesthetic high point of the Lingaraj. The rampant lion projecting from the curved sides of the tower, and the downtrodden elephant beneath him, once more symbolize the triumph of Hinduism over Buddhism. On the top, the typical Odishan motif of the flattened, ribbed sphere (*amla*) supported by gryphons, is crowned with Shiva's trident. As in the Brahmesvara temple, the long saffron pennant announces the living presence of the deity below.

The **shrine** inside is unusual. The powerful 2.5m-thick Svayambhu ("self-born") lingam that it contains, one of the twelve *jyotirlingas* in India, is known as "Hari-Hara" because it is considered half Shiva, half Vishnu – an extraordinary amalgam thought to have resulted from the ascendancy of Vaishnavism over Shaivism in the twelfth and thirteenth centuries. Unlike other lingams, which are bathed every day in a concoction prepared from hemlock, Svayambhu is offered a libation of rice, milk and bhang by the brahmins.

Vaital Deul Mandir

The **Vaital Deul** temple, one of the group's oldest buildings, is a real feast of Tantric art. The building was erected around 800 AD in a markedly different style from most of its contemporaries in Bhubaneswar, drawing heavily on earlier Buddhist influences. Among the panels of Hindu deities encrusting its outer walls, you can make out examples of some of India's earliest erotic sculpture.

17

Once you have proceeded past the four-faced lingam post at the main entrance (used for tethering sacrificial offerings), your eyes soon adjust to the darkness of the **interior**, whose grotesque images convey the macabre nature of the esoteric rites once performed here. Durga, in her most terrifying aspect as **Chamunda**, peers out of the half-light from behind the grille at the far end of the hall – her withered body, garlanded with skulls and flanked by an owl and a jackal, stands upon a rotting corpse. In front of her a man picks himself up from the floor, having filled his skull-cup with blood from the decapitated body nearby.

Odisha State Museum

Lewis Rd • Tues–Sat 10am–5pm • ₹100 (₹10) • ☎ 0674 243 1597, ⊛ odishamuseum.nic.in

The **Odisha State Museum** has a collection of "tribal" artefacts, manuscripts and archeological finds, including pre-twelfth-century Buddhist statues and reproductions of **chitra muriya**, the folk murals seen in village houses around Puri. The museum's real highlight, however, is its collection of antique **painting** and illuminated **palm-leaf manuscripts** (see page 920). Only New Delhi's National Museum holds finer examples of this traditional Odishan art form.

Museum of Tribal Arts and Artefacts

NH-5, close to the Baramunda bus stand • Tues–Sat 10am–5pm • Free • ☎ 0674 256 3649

The anthropological **Museum of Tribal Arts and Artefacts** exhibits the distinctive cultures and art of the 62 different tribal groups spread throughout Odisha. Filling the gardens outside are somewhat idealized replicas of *adivasi* dwellings, decorated with more authentic-looking murals. The **library** reputedly holds copies of all the books and journals ever compiled on the *adivasi* groups of Odisha. Opposite the museum is Asia's largest **cactus collection**, home to more than one thousand species.

Odisha Modern Art Gallery

132 Forest Park, Surya Nagar • Mon–Sat 11am–1.30pm & 4–8pm, Sun 4–8pm • Free • ☎ 98610 93875, ⊛ odishaartgallery.org

The **Odisha Modern Art Gallery** showcases the work of the state's best contemporary and most underprivileged artists. Original works are available to buy from around ₹500 to well over ₹15,000 – alternatively you can settle for a less expensive print.

ARRIVAL AND DEPARTURE
BHUBANESWAR

By plane Biju Patnaik airport is 2–3km southwest of the city centre; there's a prepaid taxi counter (around ₹250 to the city centre) in the arrivals lounge; auto-rickshaws are cheaper – there are normally a few in the far reaches of the airport car park. Air India (Raj Path, near New Market; ☎ 0674 253 0380), IndiGo (at the airport; ☎ 0124 661 3838) and Air Asia (at the airport; ☎ 01860 500 8000) have direct daily flights to Bengaluru (7–8 daily; 2hr 5min), Delhi (12 daily; around 2hr 30min), Hyderabad (5 daily; 1hr 30min), Kolkata (9 daily; 1hr 10min) and Mumbai (4 daily; 2hr 35min).

By train Bhubaneswar railway station, in the centre of the city, is on the main Howrah–Chennai train line.

Destinations Brahmapur (Berhampur; 11–17 daily; 2hr 20min–2hr 50min);
Chennai (3–7 daily; 20hr 30min–21hr 15min); Cuttack (every 30min–1hr; 30–45min); Gaya (for Bodhgaya; 3–4 daily; 11hr 30min–17hr); Kolkata (16–20 daily; 6–8hr); Puri

(around 20 daily; 1hr 15min–2hr 15min); Visakhapatnam (16–19 daily; 6hr 30min–7hr 30min).

By bus Long-distance state buses terminate at the inconveniently situated Baramunda Bus Stand, 5km from the centre on the western edge of the city, though not before making a whistle-stop tour of the centre. Ask to be dropped at Station Square (look for a statue of a horse in the middle of a large roundabout), close to most of the budget hotels. If you are heading to Puri or Pipli, you can shave up to an hour off your journey by flagging down a bus from outside the State Museum, rather than getting on at the bus stand, though they are invariably jam-packed at this stage. (Minibuses also run to Puri/Pipli, but tend to travel dangerously fast.)

Destinations Baleshwar (Balasore; 7–8 daily; 3hr 30min–4hr 30min); Brahampur (Berhampur; 7–8 daily; 4–5hr); Cuttack (every 30min–1hr; 30min); Konark (hourly; 1hr 30min–2hr); Puri (every 30min–1hr; 1hr 15min–2hr), via Pipli (45min–1hr 15min).

GETTING AROUND AND INFORMATION

By auto-rickshaw/car Bhubaneswar is too spread out to explore on foot and is best seen by auto-rickshaw; a day's temple-viewing, with waiting time, costs ₹500–900. The OTDC (see below) can organize car (and driver) hire; rates start at around ₹150/hr.

Tourist information The Odisha Tourism office (daily except Sun & 2nd Sat of month 10am–5pm; ☏0674 243 1299, ⚇odishatourism.gov.in) is on the second floor of the Paryatan Bhavan building, just off Lewis Rd. India Tourism has an office (daily except Sun & 2nd Sat of month 9am–6pm; ☏0674 243 2203, ⚇incredibleindia.org) on

the same floor. Odisha Tourism also has an office at the train station (officially daily 24hr, though this is more of a vague aspiration than a reality) and at the airport (opens to meet incoming flights).

Tours The Odisha Tourism Development Corporation (OTDC), which handles state-run tours and accommodation, has an office at the *Panthanivas* hotel (☏0674 243 0764, ⚇panthanivas.com). It offers city tours and guided half- and full-day trips (from ₹355, excluding entry fees) to various destinations throughout the state, including one that takes in Pipli, Puri and Konark (₹440).

ACCOMMODATION

While the better-class hotels are spread out all over the city, the budget places – which are generally fairly poor – are mainly grouped around the **railway station** or near the busy **Kalpana Square** junction at the bottom of Cuttack Rd, a 5min auto-rickshaw ride away.

Ginger Joydev Vihar, Nayapalli, 8km from the railway station ☏1860 266 3333, ⚇gingerhotels.com; map p.900. The city's best mid-range hotel offers unfussy service and modern if characterless a/c rooms with flat-screen TVs. There's an on-site restaurant, a branch of *Café Coffee Day*, a small gym and an ATM. Book online for the best rates. **₹4,900**

Grand Central Old Station Rd ☏9437 001152, ⚇hotel grandcentral.com; map p.900. In a convenient if unprepossessing location, *Grand Central* is a solid choice, with comfortable a/c rooms with TVs; the more expensive ones come with tubs and minibars. The superb restaurant serves fine dosas. **₹3600**

Jajati MG Marg, top end of Station Square ☏0674 250 0352, ✉sahuramesh2003@hotmail.com; map p.900. A popular hotel with a lime-green exterior located within striking distance of the railway station. Although frayed around the edges, the rooms (which come with either a/c or fans) are acceptable for a night if rupees are tight.**₹850**

Mango Hotels Prangan 692 Cuttack Rd ☏0674 711 9000, ⚇staymango.com; map p.900. Aimed primarily at business travellers, and somewhat bland as a result, *Mango Hotels Prangan* is nevertheless a good choice thanks to its clean, functional rooms, efficient staff and central location. **₹4700**

Mayfair Lagoon 8-B Jaydev Vihar, 4km from the railway station ☏0674 236 0101, ⚇mayfairhotels.com; map p.900. This luxury hotel (the better of the two *Mayfair* hotels in the city) is something of an oddity: sumptuous cottages and super-expensive villas with four-poster beds and Jacuzzis surround an ornamental lake; the

attractive grounds, meanwhile, are filled with kitsch life-sized models of wild animals. Four excellent restaurants and a fine bar are added perks. Cottages **₹9500**, villas **₹64,000**

New Marrion 6 Jan Path ☏0674 238 0850, ⚇hotel newmarrion.com; map p.900. Smart, upper-mid-range hotel with good-value rooms, a curvy pool, Thai-style spa, money-changing facilities and a travel agency, as well as several good restaurants and a Scottish-themed bar. Online prices can be up to fifty percent lower than the rack rates. **₹5310**

Panthanivas Lewis Rd ☏0674 243 2314, ⚇panthanivas. com; map p.900. An institutional OTDC-run hotel close to the museum and temples with dated but large and comfortable a/c rooms. There are a couple of good restaurants, and the 8am checkout is negotiable when they're not too busy. **₹1600**

Pushpak 68 Buddha Nagar ☏0674 231 0185; map p.900. Despite the rather dusty exterior, the friendly *Pushpak* is the pick of the Kalpana Square hotels. The rooms are large and clean, and have either fans or a/c; those at the front suffer from road noise. There are three restaurants, a bar, an ice-cream parlour out front, and an ATM on site. 24hr checkout. **₹2300**

Swosti Grand 103 Jan Path ☏0674 301 9000, ⚇swosti. com; map p.900. The older and cheaper of the city's two *Swosti*s shows its age, but remains a reliable option. The slightly over-priced a/c rooms have tubs, minibars and thoughtful touches such as hairdryers and kettles. There's also a good travel agency, a couple of restaurants and a bar. **₹3300**

Trident Bhubaneswar CB-1 Nayapalli, 4km from the railway station ☏0674 230 1010, ⚇tridenthotels.com; map p.900. The city's top hotel is exquisitely furnished with antique textiles, stone and metalwork. Facilities include fourteen acres of gardens dotted with mango and cashew trees, an excellent restaurant, an efficient travel centre, exchange facilities, a pool and even a running track. **₹13,500**

EATING

The few restaurants that specialize in traditional **Odishan cuisine**, or include some Odishan dishes on their menus,

are well worth seeking out. Look out for *chenna poda* (cheesecake stuffed with almonds), *raswadi* (thickened milk

17

with balls of curd) and *gajar ka halwa* (a rich sweet made from grated carrots).

Café Coffee Day New Marrion hotel ☎98802 63333, ⓦcafecoffeeday.com; map p.900. This Indian chain serves the best coffee (from around ₹100) in Bhubaneswar, as well as teas, smoothies and milkshakes, plus a selection of (pricey) sandwiches, pastries, snacks, cakes and cookies. There are several other branches, including at *Ginger* hotel (see above). Daily 8am–11pm.

Dalma 157 Madhusudan Nagar ☎92384 459237; map p.900. Named after the state's signature dish (potato, *brinjal* and other vegetables cooked in dhal; they also offer a deluxe version with added shrimps), this modest restaurant is the place to go for traditional regional cuisine. The fish curry is excellent, and there are some fine crab and prawn dishes. There are a couple of other branches away from the centre. Daily 11.30am–3.30pm & 7–10.30pm.

Hare Krishna Jan Path, just north of the junction with MG Marg ☎0674 253 4188; map p.900. Waiters in dinner jackets rather than *dhotis* serve ISKCON food (the Hare Krishna movement's cuisine, without garlic or onions): vegetarian and delicious. Most mains ₹140–300. The restaurant can be a little hard to find – it's located inside the Lal Chand jewellery store. Daily 10am–3pm & 7–10pm.

Kanika Mayfair Lagoon ☎0674 666 0101, ⓦmayfair hotels.com; map p.900. Specializing in traditional Odishan food, this is one of the city's best restaurants and one of two in the *Mayfair Lagoon* worth visiting. If you fancy a post-dinner drink and dance, head to the *Mayfair's* British-style pub and club. Mains ₹250–600. Daily noon–3pm & 7.30–11pm.

Lemon Grass Mayfair Lagoon ☎0674 666 0101, ⓦmayfairhotels.com; map p.900. The second of two excellent restaurants in this hotel. This one serves top-quality Thai, Chinese, Japanese and Indonesian cuisine amid decor that steers just the right side of Far Eastern pastiche. Mains ₹200–575. Daily 11.30am–3pm & 7–11pm.

Tangerine 9 Jan Path, just north of the junction with MG Marg ☎0674 253 3009; map p.900. Modern restaurant with well over 250 Indian and Chinese dishes (₹100–410) on offer: if you're having trouble deciding, opt for one of the tasty kebabs or the tandoori pomfret. Daily noon–3.30pm & 7–10.30pm.

Truptee 67 Buddha Nagar, Kalpana Square ☎0674 231 4565; map p.900. Subterranean veg restaurant, with a gloomy aspect and rather murky fish tank: the inexpensive food, however, is much brighter, ranging from south Indian idly, vada and dosas to north Indian veg classics (mains ₹100–160). Daily 7am–10.30pm.

SHOPPING

Ekamra Haat Madhusan Marg, northwest of the railway station; map p.900. A permanent craft market with more than fifty stalls selling goods from across the state and beyond. Daily 9am–9pm.

Modern Book Depot At the top of Station Square; map p.900. A modest little bookshop, just up from the railway station, with a small collection of English-language fiction. Opening times are erratic. Mon–Sat 10am–6pm.

DIRECTORY

Banks and exchange The State Bank of India (Mon–Fri 10am–4pm, Sat 10am–2pm, closed 2nd Sat of month) on Raj Path changes foreign currencies, as does Thomas Cook (Mon–Fri 9am–5pm, Sat 10am–2pm, closed 2nd Sat of month; ☎0674 253 9893, ⓦthomascook.in), at 57 Ashok Nagar, Jan Path.

Dance Dance lessons can be arranged through the Odisha Dance Academy, Quarter 4R-8, Unit 8 (☎0674 256 0458, ⓦorissadanceacademy.org), while the Utkal Sangeet Mahavidyalaya, Odisha's premier college of performing arts, on Sachivalaya Marg (☎0674 250 3956, ⓦusmodisha. com), hosts regular music, dance and drama events.

Hospitals and pharmacies Capital Hospital (☎0674 239 1983, ⓦcapitalhospital.nic.in) is at Udyan Marg, Unit 6, Ganga Nagar, near the airport, while the more modern Apollo Hospital (☎0674 715 0382, ⓦapollohospitals.com) is at Plot 251, Old Sainik School Rd. The former has a well-stocked pharmacy. The Red Cross (☎0674 240 2005 or 0674 239 2005) provides a 24hr ambulance service.

Police station Raj Path, near the State Bank of India (☎0674 253 3732).

Post office On the corner of MG Marg and Sachivalaya Marg (Mon–Sat 9am–7pm).

Travel agents Discover Tours (463 Lewis Rd; ☎91241 101770, ⓦorissadiscover.in), is a reliable operator for cultural and wildlife tours. The *New Marrion*, *Swosti* and *Trident* hotels all have good in-house agencies.

Around Bhubaneswar

Several places around Bhubaneswar can be easily visited as a day-trip. Fifteen minutes by auto-rickshaw out of the centre, the second-century BC caves at **Khandagiri** and **Udaigiri** offer a glimpse of the region's history prior to the rise of Hinduism. **Dhauli,** just off the main road to Puri, boasts an even older monument: a rock edict dating from the Mauryan era, commemorating the battle of c.260 BC that gave emperor Ashoka control of the eastern seaports, and thus enabled his missionaries to export the state religion across Asia. **Pipli**, 20km south, is famous for its appliqué work and colourful lampshades.

Nandankanan Zoological Park

20km north of Bhubaneswar • Tues–Sun: April–Sept 7.30am–5.30pm; Oct–March 8am–5pm • ₹100 (₹50) • ☎ 0674 246 6077, ⓦ nandankanan.org • Buses run from Kalpana Square in Bhubaneswar (every 30min–1hr; 1hr)

The **Nandankanan Zoological Park**, one of India's better zoos, is a good place for families to spend a few hours. Its animal collection includes rhinos, giraffes, Asiatic lions and some white tigers, there's a botanical garden and you can rent paddle boats. The toy train and cable car are being modernized and are scheduled to reopen in 2019-20.

Udaigiri and Khandagiri caves

6km west of Bhubaneswar • Daily sunrise–sunset • ₹200 (₹15) • The OTDC in Bhubaneswar (see page 905) runs day-trips to the caves that also take in Dhauli or you can take a bus (every 30min–1hr; 30–45min) from Bhubaneswar's Old City Bus Stand near Capital Market

More than two thousand years ago, caves chiselled out of the malleable yellow sandstone of a pair of low hills 6km west of Bhubaneswar were home to a community of **Jain monks**. Nowadays, they're clambered over by langur monkeys and occasional parties of tourists. Though by no means in the same league as the caves of the Deccan, **Udaigiri** and **Khandagiri** rank among Odisha's foremost historical monuments.

Inscriptions show that the **Chedi** dynasty, which ruled ancient Kalinga from the first century BC, was responsible for the bulk of the work. There are simple monk's cells, as well as royal chambers where the hallways, verandas and facades are encrusted with **sculpture** depicting court scenes, lavish processions, hunting expeditions, battles and dances. The later additions (from medieval times, when Jainism no longer enjoyed royal patronage in the region) are more austere, showing the 24 heroic Jain prophet-teachers, or *tirthankaras*.

From Bhubaneswar, the caves are approached via a road that follows the route of an ancient **pilgrimage path**. As you face the hills with the highway behind you, Khandagiri ("Broken Hill") is on your left and Udaigiri ("Sunrise Hill") is on your right.

SATKOSIA TIGER RESERVE

Spanning almost a thousand square kilometres in central Odisha, some 125km northwest of Bhubaneswar, the **Satkosia Tiger Reserve** (Oct–May daily dawn–dusk; ₹1000 (₹20), camera ₹100 (₹20), access to nature trails ₹100 (₹20); ☎ 06764 236218, ⓦ satkosia.org) is a beautiful, forested riverine landscape, with the Mahanadi River and the stunning Satkosia gorge at its heart.

Few foreign travellers make it out to the reserve, which encompasses the Satkosia Gorge Wildlife Sanctuary and the Baisipalli Wildlife Sanctuary, and tourism is in its infancy. However, if you make it here you'll be amply rewarded: the reserve has large communities of gharial and mugger crocodiles, and 164 species of bird, as well as a handful of elusive tigers. Boat trips, hikes and jeep safaris are all on offer.

Getting to the reserve independently is a bit of a drag and most people visit on an organized tour. Trains (5–6 daily; 2hr 5min–3hr 50min) run from Bhubaneswar to the town of Angul, from where buses (3–4 daily; 2hr 30min–3hr) head to Tikarpada via the main park gate at Pampasar (where you pay the entry fees). At Tikarpada, looking over the Mahanadi River, you will find the *Tikarpada Nature Camp* (₹1700 per person full board in tents; book via the park authorities), one of several camps run in partnership with local communities (more details are available at ⓦ satkosia.org).

17

Udaigiri

The **Udaigiri** caves occupy a fairly compact area around the south slope of the hill. **Cave 1** (Rani Gumpha or "Queen's Cave"), off the main pathway to the right, is the largest and most impressive of the group. A long frieze across the back wall shows rampaging elephants, panicking monkeys, sword fights and the abduction of a woman, perhaps illustrating episodes from the life of Kalinga's King Kharavela. **Caves 3 and 4** contain sculptures of a lion holding its prey and elephants with snakes wrapped around them, and pillars topped by pairs of peculiar winged animals. **Cave 9**, up the hill and around to the right, houses a damaged relief of figures worshipping a long-vanished Jain symbol. The crowned figure is thought to be the Chedi king, Vakradeva, whose donative inscription can still be made out near the roof. Inside the sleeping cells of all the caves, deep grooves in the stone wall at the back and in the floor were designed to carry rainwater down from the roof as an early air-conditioning system.

To reach **Cave 10**, return to the main steps and climb towards the top of the hill. Its popular name, "Ganesh Gumpha", is derived from the elephant-headed Ganesh carved on the rear wall of the cell on the right. From here, follow the path up to the ledge at the very top of Udaigiri hill for good views and the ruins of an old **chaitya hall**, probably the main place of worship for the Jain monks who lived below.

Below the ruins are **Cave 12**, shaped like the head of a tiger, and **Cave 14**, the Hathi Gumpha, known for the long **inscription** in ancient Magadhi carved onto its overhang. This relates in glowing terms the life history of King Kharavela, whose exploits brought in the fortune needed to finance the cave excavation.

Khandagiri

The caves on the hill opposite Udaigiri, **Khandagiri** can be reached either by the long flight of steps leading from the road, or by cutting directly across from Hathi Gumpha via the steps that drop down from Cave 17. The latter route brings you out at **Caves 1 and 2**, known as Tatowa Gumpha ("Parrot Caves") for the carvings of birds on their doorway-arches. Cave 2, excavated in the first century BC, is the larger and more interesting. On the back wall of one of its cells, a few faint lines in red Brahmi script are thought to have been scrawled two thousand years ago by a monk practising his handwriting. The reliefs in **Cave 3**, the Ananta Gumpha ("Snake Cave"), contain the best of the sculpture on Khandagiri hill, albeit badly vandalized in places. **Caves 7 and 8**, left of the main steps, were former sleeping quarters, remodelled in the eleventh century as sanctuaries. Both house reliefs of *tirthankaras* on their walls as well as Hindu deities which had become part of the Jain pantheon by the time conversion work was done. From the nineteenth-century **Jain temple** at the top of the hill there are clear views across the sprawl of Bhubaneswar to the white dome of Dhauli.

Dhauli

8km south of Bhubaneswar • No fixed opening times • Free • Unless you're on a tour, getting to Dhauli involves a 2km walk – get off the bus from Bhubaneswar's Baramunda Bus Stand (every 30min–1hr; 30–45min) at Dhauli Chowk, and make your way along the avenue of trees to the rock edict, from where the road begins its short climb up the hill

The gleaming white **Vishwa Shanti Stupa** on **Dhauli Hill**, 8km south of Bhubaneswar on the Pipli road, overlooks the spot where the Mauryan emperor **Ashoka** defeated the Kalingas in the decisive battle of 260 BC. Apart from bringing the prosperous Odishan kingdom to its knees, the victory also led the emperor, allegedly overcome by remorse at having slain 150,000 people, to renounce the path of violent conquest in favour of the spiritual path preached by Gautama Buddha. Built in 1972, the modern *stupa*, which eclipses its older predecessor nearby, is a memorial to this legendary change of heart, and the massive religious sea-change it precipitated.

After his conversion, Ashoka set about promulgating the maxims of his newly found faith in **rock edicts** installed at key sites around the empire. One such inscription, in ancient **Brahmi**, the ancestor of all non-Islamic Indian scripts, still stands on the roadside at the foot of Dhauli hill, etched in a rock featuring a beautifully carved figure of an elephant (symbolizing Buddhism). The Dhauli edict includes a mixture of rambling philosophical asides, discourses on animal rights and tips on how to treat your slaves. Particularly of note are the lines claiming the Buddhist doctrine of nonviolence was being recognized by "the kings of Egypt, Ptolemy and Antigonus and Magas", which proved for the first time the existence of a connection between the ancient civilizations of India and the West. The inscription diplomatically omits the account that crops up elsewhere describing how many Kalingas Ashoka put to the sword before he finally "saw the light".

Pipli

A 15min drive beyond Dhauli on the road to Puri • Buses between Bhubaneswar and Puri pass through Pipli (every 30min–1hr; 1hr–1hr 30min to/from Bhubaneswar, 30min–1hr to/from Puri)

Splashes of bright colour in the shopfronts along the main street announce your arrival in **PIPLI**, Odisha's **appliqué** capital (see page 920). Much of what the artisans now produce is shoddy kitsch compared with the painstaking work traditionally undertaken for the Jagannath temple. Express enough interest and you'll be shown some of the better-quality pieces for which Pipli is justly famed. Bedspreads, wall hangings and small chhatris (awnings normally hung above household and temple shrines) are the most authentic goods on offer. The shops do not open early; the best time to wander around is in the evening, when gas lamps and devotional music make the experience much more atmospheric.

ACCOMMODATION AROUND BHUBANESWAR

Gajlaxmi Palace Borapada, Dhenkanal, a 2hr drive northwest of Bhubaneswar ☏09861 011221, ⓦgajlaxmipalace.com. If you want to get away from it all, head to this royal palace in the little-visited, densely forested area of Dhenkanal. Accommodation is simple, but very comfortable (there are just two rooms) and delicious food is available. Among the activities on offer are birdwatching, fishing, hiking and visits to tribal villages. Pick-ups available from Bhubaneswar. Rates include full board. ₹6500

Kila Dalijoda Mangarajpur, 1hr drive north of Bhubaneswar ☏09438 667086, ⓦkiladalijoda.com. A fine alternative to the Gajlaxmi Palace, located in a pretty village, Kila Dalijoda is a charming 1930s mansion that once functioned as a royal hunting lodge. The interior features atmospheric rooms (simpler cottages are available too) with vintage furnishings, and everything from cycle rides to nature walks are on offer. Pick-ups available from Bhubaneswar. Meals available. Doubles. ₹5500, cottages ₹4500

Northeastern Odisha

Cuttack, Odisha's second city in the north of the state, straddles the Mahanadi River. Devoid of attractions, it detains few travellers on the long journey to or from Kolkata. Once clear of Cuttack's polluted outskirts, however, you soon find yourself amid the flat paddy fields, palm groves and mud-walled villages of the **Mahanadi Delta**. Twisting through it is one of India's busiest transport arteries; the main railway line and NH-5 follow the path of the famous pilgrim trail, the **Jagannath Sadak**, which once led from Kolkata to Puri.

The area's biggest attraction is **Bhitarkanika Wildlife Sanctuary**, 130km northeast of Bhubaneswar, which has outstanding natural scenery, an abundance of fauna and flora and is visited by the endangered olive ridley turtles. **Similipal Tiger Reserve**, close to the state border with West Bengal, is also impressive.

17 Ratnagiri, Udayagiri and Lalitgiri

95km northeast of Bhubaneswar • Daily sunrise–sunset • ₹300 (₹25) • The three sites are relatively inaccessible by public transport, so it is better to hire a car and driver for a day (around ₹1500) or take an organized tour (the OTDC office in Bhubaneswar offers one for ₹820)

Nestled among picturesque verdant hills 95km northeast of Bhubaneswar are the remains of three Buddhist universities, **Ratnagiri**, **Udayagiri** and **Lalitgiri**. The sites lie around 10km apart and are best reached in a day-trip or by hiring a car and driver.

Ratnagiri

Museum daily except Fri 10am–5pm • ₹5

RATNAGIRI, the most impressive of the sites, lies 20km from the main road on top of a hill overlooking the River Keluo. When Chinese chronicler Hiuen T'sang visited the university in 639 AD, it had already been a major Buddhist centre for at least two hundred years. In those days the sea reached much further inland, and would have been visible from this point – which may in part account for the choice of location. **Missionaries** were trained in such places before being sent away to China and Southeast Asia.

Two **monasteries** lie below the enormous *stupa* at the top of the hill. The larger and better-preserved one, dating from the seventh century, has a paved courtyard surrounded by cells and a beautifully carved doorway made from local blue-green chlorite stone. The shrine inside houses a majestic Buddha. A **museum** contains the antiquities and architectural remains collected from the excavations at all three sites.

Udayagiri

Ten kilometres back towards the main road from Ratangiri, **UDAYAGIRI** is the largest Buddhist complex in Odisha. Its main structure is a large *stupa*, better preserved than its counterpart at Ratnagiri. Of the two monasteries here, which flourished between the seventh and twelfth centuries, only one has been excavated. It features a large seated Buddha in its central shrine and an intricately carved entrance, along with an inscribed step-well. More rock-cut sculptures adorn the crest of the hill behind the monastery.

Lalitgiri

The turning for **LALITGIRI** is about 10km further along the main road towards Paradip. Most of the ruins of the four monasteries here are thought to date from around the ninth century, although inscriptions on an apsidal temple suggest that the site may have been occupied as early as the first century AD. Excavations in 1982 of the large *stupa* at the top of the hill revealed a gold casket containing a fragment of bone, believed to be a relic of the Buddha. The hilltop also provides grand panoramic views.

Bhitarkanika Wildlife Sanctuary

Aug to mid-May daily dawn–dusk • Entry permits ₹1000 (₹20)

Covering 672 square kilometres overlying the Brahmani–Baitarani delta, the mangrove forests and wetlands of the **Bhitarkanika Wildlife Sanctuary** constitute one of the richest ecosystems of its type in India. As well as more than two hundred species of bird, it's a refuge for saltwater crocodiles, monitor lizards, rhesus monkeys and a host of other reptiles and mammals, and incorporates the olive ridley turtle nesting beaches at Gahirmatha, Rushikulya and Devi. The best time to visit is between November and March, when most of the migratory birds that flock to the sanctuary are in situ, although the nesting season for the herons usually ends around the middle of November. If you're hoping to witness the arrival of olive ridley turtles, check first at the tourist office in Bhubaneswar (see page 905) to find out exactly when they are expected. Other highlights include the crocodile conservation programme at Dangmar Island and the heronry at Bagagahana.

SORTING FRESH FISH ON THE BEACH IN PURI

17

OLIVE RIDLEY TURTLES

Every year around February or March, a strip of beach at the end of Odisha's central river delta witnesses one of the world's most extraordinary natural spectacles. Having swum right across the Pacific and Indian oceans, hundreds of thousands of female **olive ridley marine turtles** crawl onto the sand to nest. Almost as soon as the egg laying is complete, they're off again into the surf to begin the journey back to their mating grounds on the other side of the world.

No one knows quite why they travel such distances, but for local villagers the arrival of the giant turtles was traditionally something of a boon: turtle soup for breakfast, lunch and dinner, and extra cash from market sales. Over the years the annual slaughter began to turn into a green gold rush, and turtle numbers plummeted drastically until the Bhitarkanika Wildlife Sanctuary on **Gahirmatha beach**, 130km northeast of Bhubaneswar, was set up in 1975 at the personal behest of Indira Gandhi. Weeks before the big three- or four-day invasion, coastguards monitor the shoreline and armed rangers aim to keep poachers at bay. For wildlife enthusiasts it's a field day.

Over the last twenty years, however, **environmental threats** have impacted on the turtles' habitat. Local families cultivate land within the sanctuary, while illegal prawn farms, fishing trawlers, industrial pollution, and distracting night-time light from nearby settlements are additional hazards.

However, there are some positive signs. Further fishing restrictions have been put in place, conservation organizations, including Greenpeace and the WWF, are monitoring the area, and the number of turtles nesting along the Odishan coast has generally risen over the last few years – more than 700,000 nested here in 2017.

ARRIVAL AND INFORMATION

To minimize costs if you're visiting the sanctuary independently, it is possible to use the small port of Chandbali as a base for day-trips. The hassle of reaching one of Bhitarkanika's entry points and obtaining permits, boat transportation and accommodation, means it's much easier to take an organized trip.

By bus or train Chandbali is linked by bus to Bhubaneswar, 130km away (6–8 daily; 4–5hr). Alternatively, head to Bhadrak, the nearest railhead, 60km away (around 24 trains daily between Bhadrak and Bhubaneswar; 1hr 10min–5hr); regular buses (around 5–6 daily; 1hr 30min–

BHITARKANIKA WILDLIFE SANCTUARY

2hr) connect Bhadrak and Chandbali.

By boat There are several agents based around the jetty in Chandbali who can arrange park entry permits and boats (₹3000–4000/day; be prepared to haggle). If you want to obtain the permit yourself you'll need to contact the elusive Assistant Conservator of Forests, also based at the jetty (☎06786 220372).

Tours Discover Tours in Bhubaneswar (see page 906), Heritage Tours in Puri (see page 917) and Nature Camp (see below) all arrange tours to the sanctuary.

ACCOMMODATION

You can stay at one of the inexpensive forest lodges at Dangmal, Ekakula, Gupti or Habalikathi, though these are very basic options suitable only for very hardy travellers. You have to bring your own food and water, which the chowkidar will cook for you, and unless you use an agent, the only way to book this accommodation is in advance through the Divisional Forest Officer in the less-than-accessible outpost of Rajnagar (☎06729 272460).

Ayanyanivas Chandbali ☎06786 220397, ⊕panthanivas. com. Located near the jetty in Chandbali, the OTDC-run *Ayanyanivas* is fine for a night or two, despite an institutional

air. It has scruffy but acceptable rooms (with either fans or a/c), as well as a low-cost eight-bed dorm and a so-so restaurant. Dorms ₹330, doubles ₹800

Nature Camp Bankuala Village ☎0674 653 3812, ⊕bhitarkanikatour.com. Also known as *Bhitarkanika Village Retreat*, *Nature Camp* is the best place to stay in the area: accommodation is provided in comfortable "Swiss" tents with attached bathrooms, and there is a good restaurant. Rates include meals, transfers to/from Bhubaneswar, and trips to the sanctuary; various other packages are also available. ₹8344 per person

Similipal Tiger Reserve

Mid-Nov to mid-June daily dawn–dusk • Entry fee ₹100 (₹100), camera ₹200 (₹50), payable at the Pithabata entrance • ⊕ similipal.org

Once a royal hunting ground, **Similipal Tiger Reserve** remains – despite suffering serious problems – one of the last wildernesses left in eastern India, home to tigers, leopards, wild elephants and 231 species of bird. In 2009, Maoist rebels launched an attack in the park: several buildings were blown up, vehicles were set on fire and tourists were robbed. The park was subsequently closed, most of the forestry department officials fled their posts, and illegal logging, hunting and poaching increased. The reserve is open again now, but despite a crackdown, rebel groups remain active and the security situation is prone to change: check with Odisha Tourism in Bhubaneswar for the latest before setting off.

ARRIVAL AND INFORMATION | SIMILIPAL TIGER RESERVE

By train Independent travellers should head to the town of Baripada, around 25km east of the park's Pithabata entrance; there are some basic lodges, and you can organize onward transport to the park. The *BBS BPO Express* #12892 (daily; departs 5.10pm; 4hr 45min) runs from Bhubaneswar to Baripada; the *BGY BBS Express* #12891 (daily; departs 5.10am; 4hr 50min) does the return journey.

Tours The easiest way to visit the park is on an organized tour – try Discover Tours in Bhubaneswar (see page 906) or Heritage Tours in Puri (see page 917).

Puri

As the home of Lord Jagannath and his siblings, **PURI** ranks among Hindu India's most important sacred sites, visited by a vast number of pilgrims each year. The crowds peak during the monsoons for **Rath Yatra**, the famous "Car Festival", when millions pour in to watch three giant, multicoloured chariots being drawn up the main thoroughfare. At the centre of the maelstrom, the **Jagannath temple** soars above the town's medieval heart and colonial suburbs like some kind of misplaced space rocket. Non-Hindus aren't allowed inside its bustling precincts, but don't let this deter you; Puri's streets and beach remain the focus of intense devotional activity year-round, while its bazaars are crammed with collectable religious souvenirs associated with Lord Jagannath.

Three distinct types of visitor come to Puri: middle-class Bengalis lured by the combined pleasures of puja and promenade; a few young Western and Japanese backpackers enjoying the low-key traveller scene at this former hippie trail favourite; and thousands of pilgrims, mainly from rural eastern India, who flock in to pay their respects to Lord Jagannath. Over the years the three have staked out their respective

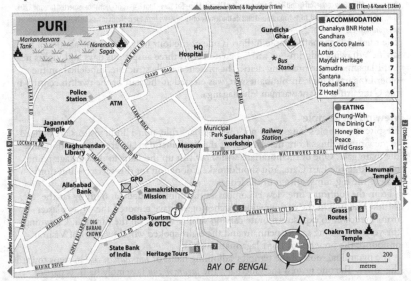

PURI

Bhubaneswar (60km) & Raghuratpur (11km)

(11km) & Konark (33km)

■ ACCOMMODATION	
Chanakya BNR Hotel	5
Gandhara	4
Hans Coco Palms	9
Lotus	3
Mayfair Heritage	8
Samudra	7
Santana	2
Toshali Sands	1
Z Hotel	6

● EATING	
Chung-Wah	3
The Dining Car	4
Honey Bee	2
Peace	5
Wild Grass	1

MITHAM ROAD

Markandesvara Tank

Narendra Sagar

ATHAR WALA RD

HQ Hospital

Gundicha Ghar

Bus Stand

GRAND ROAD

HOSPITAL ROAD

Police Station

ATM

CLARKE ROAD

GARANTI RD

Jagannath Temple

COLLEGE ROAD

Raghunandan Library

TEMPLE RD

Municipal Park

Sudarshan workshop

Railway Station

Museum

STATION RD

WATERWORKS ROAD

LOCKNATH RD

GPO

Allahabad Bank

Ramakrishna Mission

K.P. RD

Hanuman Temple

Odisha Tourism & ODTC

SWARGADWAR RD

HADISAHI RD

GOPAL BALLABH RD

KACHHERI ROAD

DIG BARANI CHOWK

V.I.P. RD

State Bank of India

Heritage Tours

MARINE DRIVE

CHAKRA TIRTHA ICTI RD

Grass Routes

Chakra Tirtha Temple

N

BAY OF BENGAL

Swargadwar Cremation Ground (350m), Night Market (400m) & 9 (1km)

150m) & Sanskrit University (1.7km)

0   200
metres

17

ends of town and stuck to them. It all makes for a rather bizarre and intoxicating atmosphere, where you can be transported from the intensity of Hindu India to the sea and back to the relative calm of your hotel veranda at the turn of a bicycle wheel.

Brief history

Until the seventh and eighth centuries, Puri was little more than a provincial outpost along the coastal trade route linking eastern India with the south. Then, thanks to its association with the Hindu reformer **Shankaracharya** (Shankara), the town began to feature on the religious map. Shankara made Puri one of his four *mathas*, or centres for the practice of a radically new, and more ascetic form of Hinduism. Holy men from across the Subcontinent came to debate the new philosophies – a tradition carried on in the city's temple courtyards to this day. With the arrival of the **Gangas** at the beginning of the twelfth century, this religious and political importance was further consolidated. In 1135, Anantavarman Chodaganga founded the great temple in Puri, and dedicated it to **Purushottama**, one of the thousand names of Vishnu – an ambitious attempt to integrate the many feudal kingdoms recently conquered by the Gangas. Under the Gajapati dynasty in the fifteenth century Purushottama's name changed to **Jagannath** ("Lord of the Universe"). Henceforth **Vaishnavism** and the devotional worship of Krishna, an incarnation of Vishnu, was to hold sway as the predominant religious influence in the temple. Puri is now one of the four most auspicious pilgrimage centres, or *dhams*, in India.

Western-style leisure **tourism**, centred on the town's long sandy beach, is a comparatively new phenomenon. The British were the first to spot Puri's potential as a resort. When they left, the Bengalis took over their bungalows, only to find themselves sharing the beach with an annual migration of young, chillum-smoking Westerners attracted to the town by its abundant hashish. Today, few vestiges of this era remain. Thanks to a concerted campaign by the municipality to clean up Puri's image, the "scene" has dwindled to little more than a handful of cafés, and is a far cry from the swinging hippie paradise some still arrive here hoping to find.

The Jagannath temple

Northwest of the town centre, off Grand Rd · **Raghunandan Library** Mon–Sat 9am–1pm & 4–6pm · Donation expected (around ₹20 is fine); when the library is closed, touts hang around outside the temple offering views from the rooftops of nearby buildings – try not to pay more than ₹50

The mighty **Jagannath temple** in Puri is one of the four holy *dhams*, or "abodes of the divine", drawing pilgrims, or *yatris*, here to spend three auspicious days and nights near Lord Jagannath, the presiding deity. The present temple structure, modelled on the older Lingaraj temple in Bhubaneswar, was erected at the start of the twelfth century by the Ganga ruler Anantavarman Chodaganga.

Viewing the temple

Despite the temple's long-standing "caste no bar" rule, non-Hindu visitors are obliged to view proceedings from the flat roof of the **Raghunandan Library**, directly opposite the main gate. One of the librarians will show you up the stairs to the vantage point overlooking the East Gate. You should make a donation for this service – but don't believe the big sums written in the ledger.

From the rooftop a fine view encompasses the immense **deul**, at 65m by far the loftiest building in the entire region. Archeologists have removed the white plaster from the tower to expose elaborate **carving** similar to that on the Lingaraj. Crowning the very top, a long scarlet pennant and the eight-spoked wheel (*chakra*) of Vishnu announce the presence of Lord Jagannath within.

The pyramidal roofs of the temples' adjoining halls, or *mandapas*, rise in steps towards the tower. The one nearest the sanctuary, the *jagamohana* (assembly hall), is part of

THE JAGANNATH DEITIES AND RATH YATRA

Stand on any street corner in Odisha and you'll probably be able to spot at least one image of the black-faced **Jagannath deity**, with his brother **Balabhadra** and sister **Subhadra**; each figure is legless, with undersized arms and prominent eyes. The origins of this peculiar symbol are shrouded in **legend**. One version relates that the image of Lord Jagannath looks the way it does because it was never actually finished. King Indramena, a ruler of ancient Odisha, once found the god Vishnu in the form of a tree stump washed up on Puri beach. He carried the lump of wood to the temple and, following instructions from Brahma, called the court carpenter Visvakarma to carve out the image. Visvakarma agreed – on condition that no one set eyes on the deity until it was completed. The king, however, unable to contain his excitement, peeped into the workshop; Visvakarma, spotting him, downed tools and cast a spell on the deity so that no one else could finish it.

RATH YATRA

The Jagannath deities are also the chief focus of Puri's annual Car Festival, the **Rath Yatra** – just one episode in a long cycle of rituals that begins in the full moon phase of the Oriya month of Djesto (June/July). In the first of these, the **Chandan Yatra**, special replicas of the three temple deities, are taken to the **Narendra Sagar** where for 21 consecutive days they are smeared with *chandan* (sandalwood paste) and rowed around in a ceremonial, swan-shaped boat. At the end of this period, in a ceremony known as **Snana Yatra**, the three go for a dip in the tank, after which they head off for fifteen days of secluded preparation for Rath Yatra.

The Car Festival proper takes place during the full moon of the following month, Asadho (July/Aug). Lord Jagannath and his brother and sister are placed in their chariots and dragged by 4200 honoured devotees through the assembled multitudes to their summer home, the **Gundicha Ghar** (Garden House), 1.5km away. If you can find a secure vantage point and escape the crush, it's an amazing sight. The immense chariots are draped with brightly coloured cloth and accompanied down Grand Road by elephants, the local raja (who sweeps the chariots as a gesture of humility and equality with all castes) and a cacophony of music and percussion. Each chariot has a different name and a different-coloured cover, and is built anew every year to rigid specifications laid down in the temple's ancient manuals. Balabhadra's *rath*, the green one, leads; Subhadra is next, in black; and lastly, in the 13m-tall chariot with eighteen wheels and a vivid red and yellow drape, sits Lord Jagannath himself. It takes eight hours or more to haul the *raths* to their resting place. After a nine-day holiday, the sequence is performed in reverse, and the three deities return to the temple to resume their normal lives.

Conventional wisdom has it that the procession commemorates Krishna's journey from Gokhul to Mathura; historians cite the similarity between the *raths* and temple towers to claim it's a hangover from the time when temples were made of wood. Whatever the reason for the Car Festival, its devotees take it very seriously indeed. Early travellers spoke of fanatics throwing themselves under the gigantic wheels as a short cut to eternal bliss (whence the English word "**juggernaut**", meaning an "irresistible, destructive force"). Contemporary enthusiasts are marginally more restrained, but like most mass gatherings in India, the whole event teeters at times on the brink of complete mayhem.

the original building, but the other two, the smaller *nata mandir* (dance hall) and the *bhogamandapa* (hall of offerings) nearest the entrance, were added in the fifteenth and sixteenth centuries. These halls still see a lot of action during the day as worshippers file through for *darshan*, while late every night they become the venue for devotional music. Female and transvestite dancers (*maharis* and *gotipuas*) once performed episodes from Jayadev's Gita Govinda, the much-loved story of the life of Krishna, for the amusement of Lord Jagannath and his siblings. Nowadays, piped songs have replaced the traditional theatre.

The kitchens

Outside the main building, at the left end of the walled compound surrounding the temple, are the **kitchens**. The food prepared here, known as *mahaprasad*, and blessed by Lord Jagannath, is said to be so pure that even a morsel taken from the mouth of a

17

dog and fed to a brahmin by a Harijan (a lower-caste *dalit*) will cleanse the body of sin. Devotees mill around carrying pieces of broken pots full of dhal and rice; they can only offer food to the deity from an imperfect pot as Lord Jagannath is the only perfection in this world.

The temple employees

Among the ten thousand or so daily recipients of the *mahaprasad* are the six thousand employees of the temple itself. These **servants** are divided into 96 hereditary and hierarchical orders known as *chhatisha niyoga*, and include the priests who minister to the needs of the deities (teeth cleaning, dressing, feeding, getting them ready for afternoon siesta, and so forth), as well as the teams of craftspeople who produce all the materials required for the daily round of rituals.

The bazaar

Grand Rd, near the Jagannath temple

The crowded streets around the Jagannath temple buzz with activity – commercial as much as religious. **Grand Road**, Puri's broad main thoroughfare, is lined with a lively **bazaar**, many of its stalls specializing in *rudraksha malas* (Shaivite "rosaries" made of 108 beads), Ayurvedic cures and the ubiquitous images of Lord Jagannath. Look out too for the wonderful "religious maps" of Puri.

Swargadwar

Around 2.5km west of the town centre

The **Swargadwar** cremation ground, one of India's most auspicious mortuary sites, is situated well beyond the south corner of the beach. Although anyone can watch the ceremonies from a respectful distance, over-inquisitive tourists are definitely not welcome.

The Markandesvara tank

North of the Jagannath temple • To get here, follow the temple's north wall up to a little road junction in the far corner, then turn right and stick to the same narrow twisting backstreet for about 1km; the journey is best attempted by bike

The **Markandesvara tank**, a large, steep-sided bathing place, is said to have been the spot where Vishnu once resided in the form of a *neem* tree while his temple was buried deep under a sand dune. There's no sign of the tree, but the temples on the south side are worth a look, particularly the smaller of the group, which contains images of the Jagannath trio.

Narendra Sagar

East of the Markandesvara tank • To get here, retrace your route from Markandesvara tank down the lane as far as the first road junction, then bear left and continue for another 1km or so

The **Narendra Sagar** is Puri's most holy tank. A small temple stands in the middle, joined to the *ghats* by a narrow footbridge. During the annual **Chandan Yatra**, a replica deity of Lord Jagannath, Madan Mohan, is brought here every day for his dip. The temple itself is plastered with vivid **murals** that you can photograph on payment of the set fee listed nearby. The list also advertises the range of services offered by the temple pujaris, including the unlikely sounding "throw of bone" and "throw of hair" – references to the tank's role as another of Puri's famous mortuary ritual sites.

Sudarshan workshop

Station Rd • No fixed opening hours

The **Sudarshan workshop** is one of the few traditional stone-carvers' yards left in Puri. The sculptors and their apprentices are more interested in pursuing their art than selling it to tourists, but gladly direct potential customers to the factory **shop** next door. Most of the pieces here are large religious icons carved out of khondalite – the multi-coloured stone used in the Sun Temple at Konark.

The beach
South of the town centre

If a peaceful swim and a spot of sunbathing are your top priorities, you're likely to be disappointed with **Puri beach**; the stretch in front of the fishing village is a 3km-long open-air toilet and rubbish dump, though the "Model Beach" project, a cleaned-up stretch of sand near the *Mayfair Heritage* hotel (see page 918), is attempting to change this. The beach beyond the Sanskrit University, 3km further east, is generally a better bet.

In the west end of town, along **Marine Parade**, the atmosphere is more akin to a British Victorian holiday resort. This stretch is very much the domain of the domestic tourist industry and the beach is cleaner here. It's a pleasant place to stroll and becomes highly animated after sunset when the nightly souvenir market gets going.

Local fishermen sometimes patrol the beach as **lifeguards**; recognizable by their triangular straw hats and *dhotis*. However, the **undertow** claims victims every year, so weak swimmers should be careful. When not saving lives, the fishermen are busy at the CT Road end of the beach, engaged in the more traditional industries of mending nets and boats.

Note that there have been reports of attacks and **muggings** on quieter stretches of the beach, so take care and avoid entirely after dark.

ARRIVAL AND DEPARTURE   PURI

By train Trains arriving at Puri's end-of-line station, in the north of town, are often greeted by fired-up rickshaw-wallahs sprinting alongside in the race to catch a foreigner. (You'll encounter a similar frenzy at the bus stand and the Jagannath temple, caused by competition for the commission offered by the hotels.) Puri is joined to the main Kolkata–Chennai routes by a branch line of the busy Southeastern rail network, but there is a far greater range of services from Bhubaneswar and Khurda Rd, 44km away. An auto-rickshaw into the centre costs around ₹50.
Destinations Bhubaneswar (around 20 daily; 1hr 15min–2hr 15min); Gaya (for Bodhgaya; 2 daily; 15hr 10min–16hr 15min); Kolkata (around 12 daily; 8hr 15min–16hr);

Varanasi (3 weekly; 20hr 30min).
By bus The bus stand is in the north of the city, a 10min rickshaw ride from the centre through the bumpy back streets. Minibuses and jeeps also run to Bhubaneswar and Konark, though often travel dangerously fast. An auto-rickshaw into the centre costs around ₹80.
Destinations Bhubaneswar (roughly hourly; 1hr 30min–2hr 30min); Konark (roughly hourly; around 1hr); Satapada on Chilika Lake (every 30min–1hr; 1hr 30min–2hr).
By car The tourist office and the town's travel agencies (see below) can organize cars and drivers; expect to pay around ₹1700 for a round trip to Konark and ₹2000 to Satapada.

GETTING AROUND

By bike Puri is fairly spread out but flat, so bicycles (around ₹50–60/day) are ideal for getting around and exploring the maze of streets around the Jagannath temple. There are several places to rent them on Chakra Tirtha (CT) Rd between the *Gandhara* and *Z*.
By moped/motorbike Mopeds and motorbikes (around

₹400/day) are rented out by a couple of travel agents and shops along CT Rd for full or half-days and are useful for trips up the coast to Konark; standards vary, however.
By rickshaw and auto-rickshaw Auto-rickshaws and cycle rickshaws are both common in Puri.

INFORMATION AND TOURS

Tourist information The main Odisha Tourism office is on the corner of VIP and CT roads (daily except Sun & 2nd Sat of month 10am–5pm; ☏ 06752 222664); there's also a (fairly unhelpful) counter at the railway station (officially

daily 24hr).
Tours The OTDC, which has a booking counter close to the main Odisha Tourism office, offers a range of tours, including one taking in the main sights of Konark (₹300)

17

and another that visits Chilika Lake (₹355). Gandhara Travel at the *Gandhara* hotel (see below) also offers tours, including to Konark during the dance festival, as well as flight and train bookings. Heritage Tours (📞 06752 223656, 🌐 heritagetoursorissa.com), based at the *Mayfair Beach Resort*, is well established and reliable, offering a wide range of tours throughout the state and beyond. Grass Routes on CT Rd (📞 06752 220560, 🌐 grassroutesjourneys. com) arranges excellent themed-tours of Puri and the surrounding area, including bike tours, paddleboard trips to Konark, and Chilika Lake birdwatching trips, plus cookery classes.

ACCOMMODATION

Virtually all of Puri's **hotels** are on or near the beach, where a strict distinction is observed: those aimed at domestic tourists are lined up behind Marine Drive, the promenade on the west end of the beach, while budget-conscious Westerners are sandwiched further east around CT Rd between the high-rise resort hotels and the fishing village, an area sometimes referred to as **Pentakunta**. The less expensive hotels are quiet during the summer months, but the pricier accommodation tends to be booked solid well in advance of Rath Yatra. Checkout is 8am for most hotels, although off-season this rule is less rigidly enforced.

Chanakya BNR Hotel CT Rd 📞 06752 223006, 🌐 chanakyabnrpuri.com; map p.913. A must for Rajophiles, this renovated hotel – formerly the *South Eastern Railway Hotel* – retains much of the old-world charm that once made it the premier bolthole for Calcutta's burra- and memsahibs. The rooms are comfortable, and there's an atmospheric restaurant (see opposite). Check out the old train engine in the neatly manicured gardens out front. **₹4500**

★**Gandhara** CT Rd 📞 06752 224117, 🌐 hotel gandhara.com; map p.913. The best mid-range hotel in town and consequently very popular, so advance bookings are a must year-round. All the spick-and-span rooms are attached, some have a/c and a few have sea views. There's a swimming pool, restaurant, honesty bar, internet café, money exchange, efficient travel agency, and – bizarrely – a tank of piranhas. **₹1200**

Hans Coco Palms Marine Drive, 2km west of the town centre 📞 06752 230038, 🌐 hanshotels.com/cocopalms-puri; map p.913. A modern complex in a superb setting outside town; all the rooms are a/c and overlook the sea. There's a pool, bar and restaurant, and the beach here is pleasant. Book online for the best deals. **₹7100**

Lotus CT Rd 📞 06752 224433, 🌐 hotellotuspuri.com; map p.913. One of the better budget joints, *Lotus* has sparsely furnished, but clean rooms, all attached – the quads (₹1200) are good value if you're in a group. A/c rooms are twice the price of fan-cooled ones. There's also a good pure-veg restaurant, *Harry's*, on the premises. **₹875**

Mayfair Heritage Off CT Rd 📞 06752 227800, 🌐 mayfairhotels.com/mayfair-puri; map p.913. The best-value top-end hotel in Puri has elegant, classically designed rooms and cottages surrounded by palm trees, a pool and an appealing stretch of beach to the front. Facilities include a gym, spa, bar and a fine restaurant. If you want even more luxury, head to neighbouring sister hotel Mayfair *Waves* (rooms from ₹13,500). Doubles **₹11,000**, cottages **₹12,000**

Samudra Off CT Rd 📞 06752 222705, 🌐 samudrapuri. com; map p.913. This well-run, whitewashed hotel is one of the better lower- to mid-range options in Puri with a bewildering range of rooms, the better and more expensive of which are on the second floor and have sea-facing balconies. The cheapest rates exclude breakfast. **₹900**

Santana At the end of CT Rd 📞 06752 251491, 🌐 india santana.com; map p.913. A small, pleasant hotel with a good set-up for travellers (it's particularly popular with Japanese visitors). The economy rooms are narrow and cell-like, but the more expensive ones (from ₹1500) are larger and have a/c. All have bright mauve, green or purple walls and wonderfully clashing orange curtains. **₹900**

Toshali Sands Konark Rd, 9km north of town 📞 06752 250571, 🌐 toshalisands.com; map p.913. Spread across 25 acres, this self-styled "ethnic village" resort has attractive a/c rooms and cottages (from ₹8000) grouped around a garden and a pool. Popular with tour groups, it also has a good restaurant, gym, sauna, hot tub and Ayurvedic spa. Rates include free pick-up from Puri railway station. **₹5250**

Z Hotel CT Rd 📞 06752 222554, 🌐 zhotelindia.com; map p.913. A Puri institution, the *Z* (pronounced "jed") is based in a mansion once owned by the raja of Serampore. Once a popular backpacker haunt, a revamp has pushed it into the mid-range category. The best rooms have partial sea views, and there's a pleasant garden area perfect for a sundowner. **₹2200**

EATING

Most of the **restaurants** along CT Rd offer inexpensive thalis, and there's good **fresh fish** to be had, though better food can be found at the smarter hotels. An interesting alternative is the sacred food, or *mahaprasad*, the creation of four hundred cooks in the Jagannath temple kitchens and available from stalls in the nearby Anand Bazaar.

Chung-Wah Lee Garden Hotel, VIP Rd 📞 06752 229986; map p.913. Run by a Chinese-Indian family originally from Kolkata, *Chung-Wah* offers suitably authentic food (including a range of tempting fish and prawn dishes), big portions and a quick turnover. Mains ₹100-300. Daily noon–3pm & 6.30–10.30pm.

The Dining Car Chanakya BNR hotel ☎ 06752 223006, Ⓦchanakyabnrpuri.com; map p.913. A stately, a/c restaurant with high ceilings and evocative black-and-white photos of the Southeastern Railway in years gone by. The menu features the usual Indian and Chinese staples, as well as a few attempts at Western dishes, such as fish and chips (mains ₹140–300). Daily 1–3pm & 8–11pm.

★**Honey Bee** CT Rd; map p.913. This peaceful, a/c bakery-pizzeria is ideal for homesick travellers. The thin-crust pizzas (₹200–550) are surprisingly authentic, there's an inventive range of sandwiches, salads and soups (including gazpacho), and even bacon is on offer. In addition, there's a proper coffee machine (coffee ₹65–90) and tempting home-made cakes, pastries and breads. Daily 8.30am–2pm & 6–10pm.

Peace Just off CT Rd; map p.913. "Famous in Puri – unheard of anywhere else" is the self-deprecating slogan of this friendly traveller stalwart, with tables in a shady garden. The menu has good breakfast options, juices, tasty Indian and Chinese food, fresh fish and seafood, and variable attempts at Western dishes, plus backpacker classics such as banana pancakes. Previously located on CT Rd, the restaurant has recently moved to a side street, near the Pink House hotel. Daily 8am–10.30pm.

★**Wild Grass** Corner of VIP Rd and College Rd, 2km from CT Rd ☎ 09437 023656; map p.913. Set in a garden that appears to be growing into a jungle (though there is also an a/c dining room), *Wild Grass* has an excellent selection of dishes from Odisha, Puri and the Chilika region – try the crab masala, deep-fried pumpkin flowers, or fish cooked in a mustard sauce (₹50–280). Cookery classes, which include a trip to the market, cost around ₹1200. Daily noon–3pm & 7–10pm.

SHOPPING

Crafts and markets Several shops on Temple Rd stock a good range of local crafts at fixed prices, and there's a lively evening market on the beach off Marine Drive, south of *Puri* hotel. Some 11.5km outside Puri, off the road to Bhubaneswar, is Raghurajpur, a village where artisans specialize in traditional Odishan arts and crafts: it's a good place to pick up paintings, carvings, wooden toys and papier-mâché masks.

DIRECTORY

Banks and exchange The State Bank of India on VIP Rd, changes dollars, sterling and euros. You can also change money at Allahabad Bank on Temple Rd, 200m up from the GPO towards the temple, and at the *Gandhara* hotel.

Hospitals Puri's main "HQ" hospital (☎ 06752 223742) is outside the town centre on Grand Rd. Hotels such as the *Mayfair* can help find doctors in an emergency.

Police The main police station is on Grand Rd, near the Jagannath temple. There is another branch at the Kacheri–VIP road junction (☎ 06752 222025).

Post office The GPO, which has poste restante, is on Kacheri Rd.

Konark

Time runs like a horse with seven reins,
Thousand-eyed, unageing, possessing much seed. Him the poets mount; His wheels are all beings.
The Artharva Veda

If you see only one temple in Odisha, it should be **KONARK**, 35km north of Puri and one of India's most visited ancient monuments. Standing imperiously in its compound of lawns and casuarina trees, this majestic pile of oxidizing sandstone is considered to be the apogee of Odishan architecture and one of the finest religious buildings anywhere in the world.

The temple is all the more remarkable for having languished under a huge mound of sand since it fell into neglect around three hundred years ago. Not until the dune and heaps of collapsed masonry were cleared away from the sides, early in the twentieth century, did the full extent of its ambitious design become apparent. In 1924, the Earl of Ronaldshay described the newly revealed temple as "one of the most stupendous buildings in India which rears itself aloft, a pile of overwhelming grandeur even in its decay". A team of seven galloping horses and 24 exquisitely carved wheels found lining the flanks of a raised platform showed that the temple had been conceived in the form of a colossal chariot for the sun god **Surya**, its presiding deity.

Equally sensational was the rediscovery among the ruins of some extraordinary **erotic sculpture**. Konark, like Khajuraho, is plastered with loving couples locked in

17

ingenious amatory postures drawn from the *Kama Sutra* – a feature that may well explain the comment made by one of Akbar's emissaries, Abul Fazl, in the sixteenth century: "Even those who are difficult to please," he enthused, "stand astonished at its sight."

Apart from the temple, a small **museum** and a fishing **beach**, Konark **village** has little going for it. Sundays and public holidays are particularly busy here: aim to stay until sunset after most of the tour groups have left, when the rich evening light works wonders on the natural colours in the khondalite sandstone.

Brief history

Inscription plates attribute the founding of the temple to the thirteenth-century Ganga monarch **Narasimhadeva**, who may have built it to commemorate his military successes against the Muslim invaders. Local legend attributes its aura of power to the two very powerful magnets said to have been built into the tower, with the poles placed in such a way that the idol was suspended in midair.

The temple's 70m tower became a landmark for European mariners sailing off the shallow Odishan coast, who knew it as the "**Black Pagoda**", and the frequent incidence of shipping disasters along the coast was blamed on the effect of the aforesaid magnets on the tidal pattern. The tower also proved to be an obvious target for raids on the region. In the fifteenth century, Konark was sacked by the Yavana army, causing sufficient damage to allow the elements to get a foothold. As the sea receded, sand slowly engulfed the building and salty breezes set to work on the spongy khondalite, eroding the exposed surfaces and weakening the superstructure. By the end of the nineteenth century, the tower had disintegrated completely, and the porch lay buried

ODISHAN ART AND ARTISTS

Few regions of India retain as rich a diversity of **traditional art forms** as Odisha. While a browse through the bazaars and emporia in Puri and Bhubaneswar provides a good idea of local styles and techniques, a trip out to the **villages** where the work is actually produced is a much more memorable way to see it. Different villages specialize in different crafts – a division that harks back to the origins of the caste system in Odisha. Patronage from the nobility and wealthy temples during medieval times allowed local artisans, or *shilpins*, to refine their skills over generations. As the market for arts and crafts expanded, notably with the rise of **Puri** as a pilgrimage centre, **guilds** were formed to control the handing down of specialist knowledge and separate communities established to carry out the work. Today, the demand for **souvenirs** has given many old art forms a new lease of life.

STONE SCULPTURE

With modern temples increasingly being built out of reinforced concrete, life for Odisha's stone sculptors is getting tougher. To see them at work, head for Pathuria Sahi ("Stonecarvers' Lane") and the famous Sudarshan workshop on Station Road in **Puri** (see page 913), where master craftsmen and apprentices still fashion Hindu deities and other votive objects according to specifications laid down in ancient manuals.

PAINTING

Patta chitra, classical Odishan painting, is closely connected with the Jagannath cult. Traditionally, artists were employed to decorate the inside of the temples in Puri and to paint the deities and chariots used in the Rath Yatra. Later, the same vibrant colour schemes and motifs were transferred to lacquered cloth or palm leaves and sold as sacred souvenirs to visiting pilgrims. In the village of **Raghurajpur** near Puri, where the majority of the remaining artists, or *chitrakaras*, now live, men use paint made from the local mineral stones. Specialities include sets of *ganjiffa* – small round cards used to play a trick-taking game based on the struggle between Rama and the demon Ravana, as told in the Ramayana.

PALM-LEAF MANUSCRIPTS

Palm leaves, or *chitra pothi*, have been used as writing materials in Odisha for centuries. Using a up to its waist, prompting one art historian of the day to describe it as "an enormous mass of stones studded with a few *peepal* trees here and there".

Restoration only really began in earnest in 1901, when British archeologists set about unearthing the immaculately preserved hidden sections of the building and salvaging what they could from the rest of the rubble. Finally, trees were planted to shelter the compound from the corrosive winds, and a museum opened to house what sculpture was not shipped off to Delhi, Kolkata and London.

The temple

Daily dawn–dusk • ₹500 (₹30)

The main entrance to the **temple** complex on its eastern, sea-facing side brings you out directly in front of the **bhogamandapa**, or "hall of offerings". Ornate carvings of amorous couples, musicians and dancers decorating the sides of its platform and stocky pillars suggest that the now roofless pavilion, a later addition to the temple, must originally have been used for ritual dance performances.

To get a sense of the overall scale and design, stroll along the low wall that bounds the south side of the enclosure before you tackle the ruins proper. As a giant model of Surya's war chariot, the temple was intended both as an offering to the Vedic sun god and as a symbol for the passage of time itself – believed to lie in his control. The seven **horses** straining to haul the sun eastwards in the direction of the dawn (only one is still intact) represent the days of the week. The **wheels** ranged along the base stand for the twelve months, each with eight spokes detailed with pictures of the eight ideal stages of a woman's day.

sharp stylus called a *lohankantaka*, the artist first scratches the text or design onto the surface of palm leaves, then applies a paste of turmeric, dried leaves, oil and charcoal that, when rubbed off, emphasizes the etching. Palm-leaf flaps are often tied onto the structure so an innocent etching of an animal or deity can be lifted to reveal *Kama Sutra* action. The best places to see genuine antique palm-leaf books are the National Museum in **New Delhi** or the State Museum in Bhubaneswar.

TEXTILES

Distinctive textiles woven on handlooms are produced throughout Odisha. Silk saris from **Brahmapur** and **Sambalpur** are the most famous, though **ikat**, which originally came to Odisha via the ancient trade links with Southeast Asia, is also typical. It is created using a tie-dye-like technique known as *bandha*, also employed by weavers from the village of **Nuapatna**, 70km from Bhubaneswar, who produce silk *ikats* covered in verses from the scriptures for use in the Jagannath temple.

APPLIQUÉ

The village of **Pipli** (see page 909) has the monopoly on appliqué, another craft rooted in the Jagannath cult. Geometric motifs and stylized birds, animals and flowers are cut from brightly coloured cloth and sewn onto black backgrounds. Pipli artists are responsible for the chariot covers used in the Rath Yatra as well as for the small canopies, or chhatris, suspended above the presiding deity in Odishan temples.

METALWORK

Tarakashi (literally "woven wire"), or silver filigree, is Odisha's best-known metalwork technique. Using lengths of wire made by drawing strips of silver alloy through small holes, the smiths create distinctive ornaments, jewellery and utensils for use in rituals and celebrations. The designs are thought to have come to India from Persia with the Mughals, though the existence of an identical art form in Indonesia, with whom the ancient Odishan kingdoms used to trade, suggests that the technique itself may be even older. *Tarakashi* is now only produced in any quantity in **Cuttack** and is dying as an art form.

ODISSI DANCE

Even visitors who don't normally enjoy classical dance cannot fail to be seduced by the elegance and poise of Odisha's own regional style, **Odissi**. Friezes in the Rani Gumpha at Udaigiri (see page 908) attest to the popularity of dance in the Odishan courts as far back as the second century BC. By the time the region's Hindu "golden age" was in full swing, it had become an integral part of religious ritual, with purpose-built dance halls, or *nata mandapas*, being added to existing temples and corps of dancing girls employed to perform in them.

DEVADASIS

Devadasis, literally "wives of the god", were handed over by their parents at an early age and symbolically "married" to the deity. They were trained to read, sing and dance and, as one disapproving early nineteenth-century chronicler put it, to "make public traffic of their charms" with male visitors to the temple. Gradually, ritual intercourse (a legacy of the Tantric influence on medieval Hinduism) degenerated into pure prostitution, and dance, formerly an act of worship, grew to become little more than a form of commercial entertainment. By the colonial era, Odissi was all but lost.

RESURGENCE

Its resurgence followed the rediscovery in the 1950s of the **Abhinaya Chandrika**, a fifteenth-century manual on classical Odishan dance. Like Bharatanatyam, India's most popular dance style, Odissi has its own highly complex language of poses and steps. Based on the *tribhanga* "hip-shot" stance, movements of the body, hands and eyes convey specific emotions and enact episodes from well-known religious texts – most commonly the **Gita Govinda** (the Krishna story). Using the *Abhinaya* and temple sculpture, dancers and choreographers were able to reconstruct this grammar into a coherent form and within a decade Odissi was a thriving performance art once again. Today, ironically, dance lessons with a reputed guru have become *de rigueur* for the young daughters of Odisha's middle classes.

LIVE PERFORMANCES

Unfortunately, catching a **live performance** is a matter of being in the right place at the right time. The only regular recitals take place in the Jagannath temple. If, however, you're not a Hindu, the annual **festival of dance** at Konark, in the first week of December, is your best chance of seeing Odisha's top performers. If you're keen to learn, check out the several dance academies in Bhubaneswar that run **courses** for beginners (see page 906).

The sanctuary tower

With the once-lofty **sanctuary tower** now reduced to little more than a clutter of sandstone slabs tumbling from the western wing, the **porch**, or *jagamohana*, has become Konark's real centrepiece. Its impressive pyramidal roof, rising to a height of 38m, is divided into three tiers by rows of lifelike statues – mostly musicians and dancers serenading the sun god on his passage through the heavens. Though now blocked up, the huge cubic **interior** of the porch was a marvel of medieval architecture. The original builders ran into problems installing its heavy ornamental ceiling, and had to forge 10m iron beams as support – a considerable engineering feat for the time.

Sculpture and erotica

Marvellously elaborate **sculpture** embellishes the temple's exterior with a profusion of deities, animals, floral patterns, bejewelled couples, voluptuous maidens, mythical beasts and aquatic monsters. Some of Konark's most beautiful **erotica** is to be found in the niches halfway up the walls of the porch; look for the telltale pointed beards of sadhus, clearly making the most of a lapse in their vows of chastity. Many theories have been advanced over the years to explain the lascivious scenes here and elsewhere on the temple. The most convincing explanation is that the erotic art was meant as a kind of metaphor for the ecstatic bliss experienced by the soul when it fuses with the divine cosmos – a notion central to **Tantra** and the related worship of the female principle, **shakti**, which were prevalent throughout medieval Odisha.

Carved wheels and friezes
Moving clockwise around the temple from the south side of the main staircase, you pass the intricately carved **wheels** and extraordinary **friezes** that run in narrow bands above and below them. These depict military processions (inspired by King Narasimhadeva's tussles with the Muslims) and hunting scenes, featuring literally thousands of rampaging elephants. In the top frieze along the south side of the platform, the appearance of a giraffe proves that trade with Africa took place during the thirteenth century.

The Surya statue
Beyond the porch, a double staircase leads to a shrine containing a **statue of Surya**. Carved out of green chlorite stone, this serene image – one of three around the base of the ruined sanctuary tower – is considered to be one of Konark's masterpieces. The other two statues in the series are also worth a look, if only to compare their facial expressions which, following the progress of the sun around the temple, change from wakefulness in the morning (south) to heavy-eyed weariness at the end of the day (north). At the foot of the western wall there's an altar-like platform covered with carvings: the kneeling figure in its central panel is thought to be King Narasimhadeva.

Konark dance festival
In early December, the temple hosts one of India's premier **dance festivals**, drawing an impressive cast of both classical and folk dance groups from all over the country. For the exact dates and advance bookings, contact the Odisha Tourism offices in Bhubaneswar or Puri.

The archeological museum
Near the *Yatrinivas* hotel, a 10min walk from the temple compound • Daily except Fri 10am–5pm • ₹10

The **archeological museum** has lost most of its best pieces to Delhi, but still has fragments of sculpture, much of it erotic. Outside, a small shed in the northeast corner of the enclosure houses a stone architrave bearing images of **nine planet deities**, the Navagrahas. This originally sat above one of the temple's ornamental doorways and is now kept as a living shrine.

Chandrabhaga beach
3km south of the temple compound

Chandrabhaga beach is a quiet and clean alternative to Puri's dirty sands. Although it is far from ideal for swimming or sunbathing, the beach is nonetheless a pleasant place to wander in the late afternoon and watch the fishermen and their catch.

ARRIVAL AND INFORMATION KONARK

By bus, jeep and minibus Regular buses (roughly hourly; around 1hr) travel the 33km between Puri and Konark; the last one back to Puri leaves around 6.30pm. Jeeps and minibuses also shuttle along this route, though they are often driven recklessly. From Bhubaneswar, there are hourly buses (2–3hr) to Konark; some involve a change at Pipli.
By auto-rickshaw From Puri, an auto-rickshaw will do the return journey to Konark, with waiting time, for about ₹800–900.

By car A car (and driver) for the Puri–Konark round trip, including waiting time, costs from ₹1700.
On a tour The OTDC offices in Puri and Bhubaneswar offer several tours that visit Konark; prices start at ₹300.
Tourist information The Odisha Tourism office is in the *Yatrinivas* hotel (daily except Sun & 2nd Sat of month 10am–5pm; ☏ 06758 236821, ⓦ odishatourism.gov.in).

17

THE ADIVASI OF SOUTHWESTERN ODISHA

Most of Odisha's **adivasi** groups live in the remote southwest of the state. Once you have ventured over the pass above the hot springs of Taptapani (see page 926), the appearance of pots attached to sago palms and windowless mud huts with low thatched roofs indicates that you have arrived in the traditional land of the **Saoras**. Further west around the Koraput and Jeypore area live the **Dongria Kondh**, the **Koya** and the **Bondas**.

So-called "tribal tourism" was very popular in this region, but it has been heavily restricted since 2012 after a series of reports highlighting exploitative, unethical and degrading "human safaris" in Odisha (particularly involving the Bondas) and the Andaman Islands. The situation was exacerbated by the kidnapping of two Italian travellers (see page 899). *Adivasi* villages saw little or no share of the spoils of the tours, a situation they were – and continue to be – justifiably angry about. Whichever way you look at it, turning up in an isolated and **culturally sensitive** place with a camera is a pretty unsound way of "meeting" the locals, and a glance from a car is hardly likely to enlighten you on traditions that have existed for centuries.

That said, and although many areas remain off-limit to tourists, it is possible to visit with a responsible operator.

INFORMATION AND TOURS

Odisha Tourism offices in Bhubaneswar (see page 905) and Puri (see page 917) can advise on responsible travel agencies and guides working in this region, and provide up-to-date information on what areas it is possible to visit.

Several operators run sensitive tours that benefit – or, at least, don't actively harm – local communities in southwestern Odisha. They include Desia Koraput (☎94370 23656, ⓦdesiakoraput.com), which runs four- to seven-day tours (from ₹12,000 per person) in the Koraput Valley; activities include cookery classes, hiking, craft classes, and visits to markets and farms. Volunteering placements can also be organized. Accommodation is clean and simple. Another option is Chandoori Sai (☎94395 28602, ⓦchandoorisai.com), an Australian-run operator with a guesthouse in Goudaguda, a village 40km from Koraput known for its handicrafts. Transfers can be organized or you can travel by public transport – contact for details.

ACCOMMODATION AND EATING

Few people stay in Konark, but the **accommodation** here is convenient if you want to enjoy the temple in peace after the day-trippers have left. For **food** you have a choice between the row of thali and tea stalls opposite the temple or a more substantial meal in one of the hotel restaurants.

Labanya Lodge Just outside the village on the beach road ☎06758 236824, ⓦlabanya.eodisha.com. The *Labanya Lodge* is the most backpacker-friendly place in Konark, with a small garden, internet access and bikes for rent. The spartan rooms vary though, so make sure you look at a few. ₹1000

Lotus Eco Village Ramchandi beach, 7km southwest of Konark ☎06758 236161, ⓦlotusresorthotels.com.

The most stylish place to stay in the area, this peaceful complex is designed to look like a traditional village and sits right on the beach. Accommodation is in snug wood-panelled cottages and more spacious villas, and there's a restaurant and small spa. Deer can sometimes be spotted in the adjoining woodland. Cottages ₹5310, villas ₹6550

Yatrinivas A 10min walk from the temple compound ☎06758 236820, ⓦpanthanivas.com. A conveniently located OTDC-run hotel, *Yatrinivas* has pleasant gardens and a decent restaurant that is often packed out with tour parties at lunchtime. The a/c rooms are plain and rather dated but fine for a night. ₹1200

Southeastern Odisha

Along the stretch of coast between Puri and Andhra Pradesh/Telangana there are a couple of scenic detours that may tempt you to break the long journey south. Three hours south of the capital, at the foot of a barren, sea-facing spur of the Eastern Ghats, is India's largest saltwater lake. **Chilika**'s main attractions are the one million or so migratory birds that nest here in winter. Seventy kilometres further on, **Gopalpur-on-Sea** is a low-key beach town. **Brahmapur** (formerly Berhampur), 16km inland, is southeastern Odisha's biggest market town, and the main transport hub for the sinuous route west through the hills to the spa station of **Taptapani** and "tribal districts" beyond.

Chilika Lake

Were it not for its glass-like surface, **Chilika Lake**, Asia's largest lagoon, could easily be mistaken for the sea; from its mud-fringed foreshore you can barely make out the narrow strip of marshy islands and sand-flats that separate the 1100-square-kilometre expanse of brackish water from the Bay of Bengal. Come here between December and February, and you'll see a variety of **birds**, including flamingos, pelicans, painted storks, fish eagles, ospreys and kites, many of them migrants from Siberia, Iran and the Himalayas. Chilika is also one of the few places in India where the **Irrawaddy dolphin** can be spotted.

The best way to see the lake and the birdlife is on a boat trip. Unfortunately, tourists are currently banned from visiting Nalabana Island, a bird sanctuary, which has dramatically reduced the chances of seeing the migratory species close up. It's still possible to see them from further away, however, on a boat cruise or by visiting some of Chilika's other islands.

The fishing villages and fabled island "kingdom" of **Parikud** on the eastern side of the lake are generally passed up in favour of the boat ride to the *devi* shrine on **Kalijai** island. Legend has it that a local girl once drowned here on the way to her wedding across the lake, and that her voice was subsequently heard calling from under the water. Believing the bride-to-be had become a goddess, local villagers inaugurated a shrine to her that over the years became associated with **Kali**. Each year at Makar Sankranti, after the harvest, pilgrims flock to the tiny island from all over Odisha and West Bengal to leave votive offerings in the sacred cave where the deity was enshrined.

Satapada, on the coastal side 45km from Puri, is the best place to stay on the lake; the surrounding waters offer the best chance of seeing dolphins. The scenery around **Barkul** is less impressive than at Satapada, and you're further from most of the islands, but it does have the lake's best accommodation. **Rambha**, 135km from Bhubaneswar, is well placed for walks around the more scenic southern corner of the lake and for boat rides to Parikud.

ARRIVAL AND DEPARTURE
CHILIKA LAKE

By bus Satapada is linked to Puri by daily buses (every 30min–1hr; 1hr 30min–2hr). To get to Barkul, take a bus from Puri or Bhubaneswar towards Brahmapur (6–7 daily; 3hr 30min–4hr) and get off at Balugaon, where you can get an auto-rickshaw for the remaining 7km to Barkul.

INFORMATION AND TOURS

Tourist information Satapada is home to an informative visitor centre (daily 10am–5pm; ₹10), while the *Yatrinivas* hotel (see below) houses the tourist office (daily except Sun & 2nd Sat of month 10am–5pm; ☏ 0675 262077).

Tours Travellers can take trips on OTDC motor launches (from ₹180) or cheaper rowing boats from Barkul and Satapada; it costs around ₹800–2500/hr to rent a motorboat for yourself. The manager at the Barkul *Panthanivas* can help with arrangements. Alternatively, numerous travel agencies, including the *Gandhara's* in-house travel agency (see page 918) in Puri and the OTDC offices in Bhubaneswar and Puri run day-trips to Chilika.

ACCOMMODATION AND EATING

Panthanivas Barkul ☏ 06756 222488, ⓦ panthanivas. com. The OTDC-run *Panthanivas* offers spacious, though dated and rather unkempt, rooms and a good restaurant; especially recommended is the *chinguri charchari* (shrimp with fried vegetables). If you plan to visit between Sept and March, book ahead at the Bhubaneswar or Puri OTDC offices, or online. **₹1000**

Swosti Chilika Resort 10km south of Barkul ☏ 93374 76478, ⓦ swostihotels.com. Easily the most luxurious place to stay around Chilika Lake, with sister hotels in Bhubaneswar (see page 905) and Gopalpur-on-Sea (see page 926), Swosti offers swish en suites overlooking the manicured gardens or the lake, plus an excellent restaurant, spa, games room and swimming pool. **₹6000**

Yatrinivas Satapada ☏ 06752 262077, ⓦ panthanivas. com. Run by the OTDC, *Yatrinivas* provides the best accommodation in Satapada, though this is far from a ringing endorsement; some rooms have a/c private balconies overlooking the well-tended gardens that run down to the lake, and the restaurant serves thalis and fresh fish. **₹650**

17

Gopalpur-on-Sea

More than two thousand years ago, when the Kalingas were accruing wealth from the pearl and silk trade with Southeast Asia, **GOPALPUR-ON-SEA**, formerly the ancient port of Paloura, must have been a swinging place. Today, the only time you're likely to encounter much action is during festivals and holidays. For the rest of the year, its desultory collection of seafront hotels stands idle, left to the odd backpacker and some industrious fishermen (*katias*). Paradise it certainly isn't, but if you're looking for a spot to unwind and enjoy the warm sea breezes, this is as appealing a place as any. **Sunbathing** on the beach will quickly make you the centre of attention, but the uncrowded sands, punctuated by coconut groves, sleepy lagoons and tiny creeks, are good for a rejuvenating walk.

ARRIVAL AND DEPARTURE   GOPALPUR-ON-SEA

By train or bus Getting to Gopalpur-on-Sea is easiest via the town of Brahmapur (Berhampur), which is connected to Bhubaneswar by numerous trains (11–17 daily; 2hr 20min–2hr 50min) and buses (7–8 daily; 4–5hr).
By auto-rickshaw, jeep and minibus Minibuses and jeeps depart when full from Brahmapur's centrally located

bus stand for the 16km trip (around 30min) to Gopalpur. You'll be dumped at the top of the main street, a 10min walk from the seafront and most of the hotels. Alternatively an auto-rickshaw straight to your hotel from Brahmapur costs around ₹350–400.

ACCOMMODATION AND EATING

Standards are fairly low at Gopalpur's **hotels**: it's worth haggling – only during holiday and festival times are they likely to be full. As for **eating**, there's a surprising dearth of seafood, though some restaurateurs can be cajoled into cooking the odd pomfret or prawn curry, given sufficient warning.
Mayfair Palm Beach Resort Overlooking the beach ☎0680 666 0101, ⍟mayfairhotels.com. Easily the smartest hotel in town, the *Mayfair* is housed in a building that dates back to 1914. The rooms, however, are decidedly modern, and many boast sea views. There's also a pool, spa, gym, games room, and an excellent restaurant and bar. ₹11,000
Motel Mermaid On the north side of the beach ☎0680

224 2050 or 99381 05760. A friendly, family-run place, popular with holidaying Kolkatans, with plain, somewhat scruffy rooms and private sea-facing balconies. With advance notice, non-residents can enjoy delicious Bengali thalis. ₹750
Swosti Gopalpur Palm Resort Near the lighthouse ☎0680 224 2453, ⍟swostihotels.com/gopalpur-palm-resort. One of Gopalpur's more comfortable hotels, if slightly overpriced. Its a/c rooms are pleasant, but nothing special, and most lack a view of the sea. The restaurant, however, is strong on seafood: the *chengudi malai* (prawns in coconut cream) and *macha tarkari* (fish curry) are both worth a try. Good discounts available online. ₹3600

Taptapani

The spa village of **TAPTAPANI**, nestled in the Ghats 51km west of Brahmapur, is little more than a line of dingy snack stalls and mildewed bungalows deep in the forest. Pilgrims, however, come here in large numbers for the legendary **hot springs**, which are believed to cure infertility. The boiling sulphurous water bubbles out of a cleft in the mountainside and is piped into a small pool, where little rocks smeared with vermilion and hibiscus petals mark the presence of the living deities believed to reside in the water (it is prohibited to dip any part of the body into the pool).

ARRIVAL AND DEPARTURE   TAPTAPANI

By bus Regular buses (roughly hourly; 1hr 15min–2hr)   travel between Brahmapur and Taptapani.

ACCOMMODATION AND EATING

Panthanivas Just down the hill from the springs ☎06816 255031, ⍟panthanivas.com. You can enjoy the hot springs in privacy at the atmospheric OTDC-run

Panthanivas as the water is pumped straight into capacious sunken bathtubs in some of the more expensive rooms (all of which are a little drab). Despite the fine views, the place is rarely full, which is just as well, as there's nowhere else to stay in the vicinity (book in advance just to be on the safe side). There's also a decent restaurant. ₹1100

Andhra Pradesh and Telangana

GIANT STATUE OF BUDDHA ON LAKE HUSSAIN SAGA

Andhra Pradesh and Telangana

Although Andhra Pradesh and the recently created state of Telangana
together occupy a great swathe of eastern India, stretching more than
1200km along the coast from Odisha to Tamil Nadu and reaching far inland
from the fertile deltas of the Godavari and Krishna rivers to the semi-arid
Deccan Plateau, most foreign travellers simply pass through en route to
their better-known neighbours. This is understandable, as places of interest
are few and far between, but the sights that the two states do offer are
absorbing enough to warrant at least a brief stop-off.

18

A major high-tech hub and, for the time being, the joint capital of both states, **Hyderabad**
is an atmospheric, predominantly Muslim city with lively bazaars, the eclectic Salar Jung
Museum, impressive Chowmahalla Palace and the mighty **Golconda Fort. Warangal**, 150km
northeast, has Muslim and Hindu remains from the twelfth and thirteenth centuries, while
the region's Buddhist legacy is preserved in museums at sites such as **Nagarjunakonda** and
Amaravati. In the east, the city of **Vijayawada** has little to recommend it, though it is a
convenient access point for Amaravati. Similarly, in the northeast, the fast-growing city of
Visakhapatnam is little more than a handy place to break up a long trip, but between the
two the delightful region around the **Godavari Delta** is well worth a detour. By contrast, the
temple town of **Tirupati** in the far southeast is a fascinating, impossibly crowded pilgrimage
site. In the southwest, **Puttaparthy** attracts a more international pilgrim crowd, who still
flock to the ashram of the late spiritual leader Sai Baba.

Although modern industries have grown up around the capital, and shipbuilding,
iron and steel are important on the coast, most people in Andhra Pradesh and
Telangana remain poor. Away from the Godavari and Krishna deltas, where the soil is
rich enough to grow rice and sugar cane, the land is in places impossible to cultivate,
which has contributed to the desperate plight of many farmers (see page 932).

Brief history

The earliest accounts of the region, from the third century BC, refer to a people known
as the Andhras. The **Satavahana dynasty** (second century BC to second century AD),
also known as the Andhras, came to control much of central and southern India from
their second capital at Amaravati on the Krishna. They enjoyed extensive international
trade and were great patrons of Buddhism. Subsequently, the Pallavas, the Chalukyas
and the Cholas all held sway. By the thirteenth century, the Kakatiyas of Warangal were
under constant threat from Muslim incursions; while later on, after the fall of their city
at Hampi, the Hindu Vijayanagars transferred operations to Chandragiri near Tirupati.

The next significant development was in the mid-sixteenth century, with the rise of
the Muslim **Qutb Shahi dynasty**. In 1687, the son of the Mughal emperor Aurangzeb
seized Golconda. Five years after Aurangzeb died in 1707, Hyderabad's viceroy declared
independence and established the Asaf Jahi dynasty of **nizams**. In return for allying

---

BEST TIME TO VISIT

As with the rest of the south, the ideal time to come to Andhra Pradesh and Telangana
is during the winter months from December to mid-March. April to June is blazing hot,
particularly inland towards the Deccan Plateau. The southern part of Andhra Pradesh misses
most of the main summer monsoon but is hit by the northeast monsoon between September
and November, when cyclones can create havoc, especially in the coast areas.

CHARMINAR, HYDERABAD

Highlights

❶ Hyderabad A predominantly Islamic city, as well as a focal point of twenty-first-century high-tech India, with a compelling combination of monuments, museums and bazaars. See page 933

❷ Golconda Fort Set in a lush landscape just west of Hyderabad, the Qutb Shahi dynasty's capital boasts a dramatic and well-preserved fort with amazing acoustics. See page 937

❸ Warangal This sleepy town features two important Hindu monuments: a rambling medieval fort and an exquisitely carved thousand-pillared Shiva temple. See page 942

❹ Nagarjunakonda Now surrounded by a vast artificial lake, this peaceful place boasts various Buddhist monuments, including a huge statue, and a fine museum. See page 943

❺ The Godavari Delta With a mixture of verdant hills, mangrove swamps and the lush Konaseema area, this is a fine region to explore. See page 946

❻ Tirumala Hill The world's most visited pilgrimage centre, crowned by the crowded, vibrant and colourful Venkateshvara Vishnu temple. See page 948

HIGHLIGHTS ARE MARKED ON THE MAP ON PAGE 932

with the British against Tipu Sultan of Mysore, the nizam dynasty was allowed to retain a certain degree of autonomy even after the British had come to dominate India.

During the Independence struggle, harmony between Hindus and Muslims in Andhra Pradesh disintegrated. **Partition** brought matters to a climax, as the nizam wanted to join other Muslims in the soon-to-be-created state of **Pakistan**. In 1949 the capital erupted in riots, the army was brought in and Hyderabad state was admitted to the Indian Union. Andhra Pradesh state was created in 1956 from Telugu-speaking regions (although Urdu is widely spoken in Hyderabad) that had previously formed part of the Madras Presidency on the east coast and the princely state of Hyderabad to the west. Today almost ninety percent of the population is Hindu, with Muslims largely concentrated in the capital.

In 1999, the pro-business Telugu Desam party eventually wrested the power long held by Congress, and over the following five years there was huge development around Hyderabad, most famously, **HITEC City**. However, rural areas – where drought and economic crisis led to thousands of farmer suicides – were neglected. In 2004 Congress regained control of the state government, although they were also criticized for not doing enough to help farmers, and suicides have continued with alarming frequency, though numbers have fallen in recent years.

In December 2009, following a high-profile hunger strike, the Indian government surprisingly bowed to pressure from the Telangana Rashtra Samithi (TRS) party

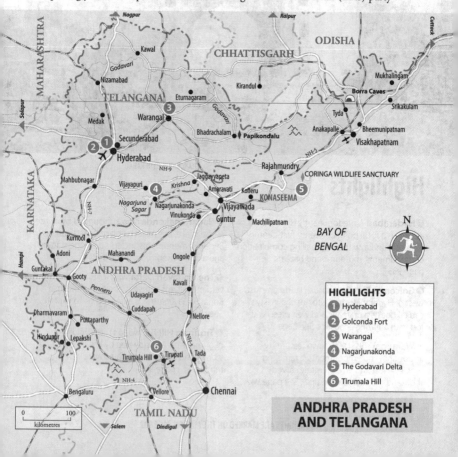

HIGHLIGHTS
1. Hyderabad
2. Golconda Fort
3. Warangal
4. Nagarjunakonda
5. The Godavari Delta
6. Tirumala Hill

ANDHRA PRADESH AND TELANGANA

FESTIVALS IN ANDHRA PRADESH AND TELANGANA

Sankranti (Jan). Celebrated all over both states with lively music and dance, especially in the Konaseema region (see page 946).

Antarvedi Chariot Festival (Jan/Feb). Impressive temple chariot festival celebrating the marriage of Lord Narasimha and the goddess Lakshmi in the East Godavari district (see page 946).

Muharram (Oct/Nov). The sacred month of the Muslim New Year is celebrated with verve by the large Shia population in Hyderabad.

Vaikunta Ekadashi (Dec/Jan). One of the most important festivals at Tirumala (see page 948), when Vishnu's victory over the demon Muran is commemorated.

18

and announced plans to carve a new state, **Telangana**, out of northwestern Andhra Pradesh. Despite widespread protests, strikes and political resignations a commission was set up to examine the practicalities of the issue, and in July 2013 a resolution was unanimously passed in Congress agreeing to the bifurcation. Almost a year later, on June 2, 2014, Telangana officially ceded from Andhra Pradesh to become India's twenty-ninth state, with Hyderabad serving – in a rather complicated arrangement – as capital of both states until the new Andhran capital at Amaravati is complete.

Hyderabad/Secunderabad

A melting pot of Muslim and Hindu cultures, the joint capital of Andhra Pradesh and Telangana comprises the twin cities of **HYDERABAD** and **SECUNDERABAD**, with a combined population of around eight million. Secunderabad, of little interest, is the modern administrative city founded by the British, whereas Hyderabad, the old city, has teeming **bazaars**, **Muslim monuments**, the absorbing **Salar Jung Museum** and magnificent **Chowmahalla Palace**. Hyderabad declined after Independence, with tensions often close to the surface due to lack of funding. Nowadays, although the overcrowded old city still suffers from substandard amenities, the conurbation as a whole is booming. In recent years Hyderabad has overtaken Bengaluru to become India's foremost computer and **IT centre**.

The Hyderabad metropolitan area has three distinct sectors: **Hyderabad**, divided between the old city and newer areas towards HITEC City; **Secunderabad**, the modern city; and **Golconda**, the old fort. The two cities are basically one big sprawl, separated by an artificial lake, **Hussain Sagar**. The most interesting area, the **old city** south of the River Musi, holds the bazaars and **Charminar**, the city's principal landmark, as well as the Salar Jung Museum and Chowmahalla Palace. North of the river, the traditional shopping areas are found around **Abids Circle** and **Sultan Bazaar**. Four kilometres west of Hyderabad railway station lies the posh **Banjara Hills** district, full of gleaming malls and fancy restaurants. Beyond here is the exclusive residential area of **Jubilee Hills**, while a further 4km brings you to **HITEC City**.

Brief history

Hyderabad was founded in 1591 by **Mohammed Quli Shah** (1562–1612), 8km east of Golconda, the fortress capital of the Golconda empire. Unusually, the new city was laid out on a grid system, with huge arches and stone buildings that included Hyderabad's most famous monument, **Charminar**. At first it was a city without walls; these were only added in 1740 as defence against the Marathas. Legend has it that a secret tunnel linked the city with the spectacular **Golconda Fort**, 11km away.

For the three hundred years of Muslim reign, there was harmony between the predominantly Hindu population and the minority Muslims. Hyderabad was the most important focus of Muslim power in south India at this time; the princes' fabulous wealth derived primarily from the fine gems, particularly diamonds, mined in the

▲ Secunderabad (6km), 🚇 (6km), 🚇 (6km) & 🚇 (5km)

HYDERABAD

0	500
metres	

N

Hussain Sagar

Buddha Statue

Lumbini Park

Indira Park

Thomas Cook

SECRETARIAT ROAD

AP Tourism & APTDC

British Library

Birla Mandir
BM Birla Science Centre

Air India

Stadium

OLD MLA QUARTERS ROAD

India Tourism

HIMAYATNAGAR ROAD

UNIVERSITY ROAD

NEHRU NAGAR

INDIRA PARK ROAD

A.P. State Museum

Public Gardens

NAMPALLY

Nampally Railway Station

Bank

ABIDS ROAD

RAJA REDDY ROAD

KING KOTHI ROAD

Bank

Ek Minar

Yusufian Dargah

STATION ROAD

ABIDS CIRCLE

TILAK ROAD

SULTAN BAZAAR

VIR SAVARKAR ROAD

Kacheguda Railway Station

MAHIPATRAM ROAD

MUKARRAMJAHI ROAD

GOSHAMAHAL ROAD

JAMBAGH ROAD

STREET NO.5

PUTLIBOWLI RD

MAMARANI JHANSI ROAD

BHAGYA REDDY ROAD

TURREBAZAAR ROAD

KACHEGUDA STATION ROAD

GOSHAMAHAL

JAWAHARLAL NEHRU ROAD

MAULVI ALAUDDIN ROAD

Mahatma Gandhi Bus Stand

River Musi

OLD MALAKPET

VIJAYAWADA ROAD

State Library

Hospital

CITY COLLEGE ROAD

SARDAR PATEL ROAD

Salar Jung Museum

High Court

CHATTA BAZAR RD

RAJENDRA NAGAR ROAD

Nizam's Museum

DABEERPURA ROAD

Charkaman (Four Arches)

Charminar

Mecca Masjid

PATTHARGATTI

KALI KAMAN ROAD

LAD BAZAAR ROAD

RATHKHANA STREET

▼ 🚇 (3km), Airport (17km) & Chowmahalla Palace (300m)

● SHOPPING	
Ankur	2
Chenetha Bhavan	6
Higginbothams	4
Lepakshi	5
Sheela's	4
Sri Mahalaxmi	1
Utkalika	3

● EATING	
Bikanerwala	3
Chef Inam's Steak House	4
Fusion 9	2
Kamat Hotel	8
Paradise Food Court	1
Salzburg Street	6
Shadab	10
Sher-e-Punjab	7
Shezan	9
Via Milano	5

■ DRINKING & NIGHTLIFE	
10 Downing Street	1
Coco's Bar & Grill	5
Liquids et Cetera	3
Spoil Pub	4
Syn	2

■ ACCOMMODATION	
Amrutha Castle	5
Baseraa	1
DM Residency	10
Golden Glory Guest House	4
Quality Inn Residency	6
Rajmata	7
Sai Prakash	11
Sri Laxmi Lodge	8
Sri Sai Ganesh Lodge	2
Taj Banjara	3
Taj Falaknuma Palace	12
Taj Mahal	9

18

Kistna Valley at Golconda. The famous **Koh-i-Noor** diamond was found here – the only time it was ever captured was by Mughal emperor Aurangzeb, when his son seized the Golconda Fort in 1687. It ended up, cut, in the British royal crown.

Since the creation of **Telangana** in 2014, Hyderabad has been leading a double life as joint capital of the new state as well as Andhra Pradesh. Officially it belongs to Telangana, as evidenced by the fact that government offices bear the new state's name, but it will continue to act as the administrative centre of Andhra Pradesh until the latter's new capital is created at Amaravati (see page 945). This transition is supposed to be complete by the mid-2020s but that seems overly optimistic.

18

The old city

By far the most atmospheric part of Hyderabad is the **old city**, immediately south of the River Musi. This is easily the most Islamic enclave in south India, where the majority of women wear full black burqa and many men sport fine beards. This is where you will find the city's liveliest and most interesting bazaars, as well as many of its most important sights, from the eclectic **Salar Jung Museum**, through the majestic minarets of **Charminar** to the extensive complex of **Chowmahalla Palace**.

Salar Jung Museum

Daily except Fri 10am–5pm • ₹500 (₹20), camera ₹50 • ⊛ salarjungmuseum.in

The unmissable **Salar Jung Museum**, on the south bank of the River Musi opposite the ornate bulbous domes of the Osmania General Hospital, houses part of the huge collection of Salar Jung, one of the nizam's prime ministers, and his ancestors. A well-travelled man of wealth, he bought whatever took his fancy from both East and West, from the sublime to, in some cases, the ridiculous. His extraordinary hoard includes Indian jade, miniatures, furniture, lacquerwork, Mughal opaque glassware, fabrics, bronzes, Buddhist and Hindu sculpture, manuscripts and weapons. At the time of writing, it was planned to reorganize the somewhat haphazard collection into geographical themes with the use of two new buildings that have been constructed either side of the old one. The museum gets very crowded at weekends, especially on Sunday.

Charminar

Daily 9am–5.30pm • ₹100 (₹10)

A maze of bazaars teeming with people, the old city has at its heart **Charminar** or Four Towers, a triumphal arch built at the centre of Mohammed Quli Shah's city in 1591 to commemorate an epidemic of the plague. It features four graceful 56m-high minarets, housing spiral staircases to the upper storeys. The (now defunct) mosque on the roof is the oldest in Hyderabad. The yellowish colour of the building is due to a special stucco made of marble powder, gram and egg yolk. In the evening (7–9pm), the edifice is attractively lit up. The **Charkaman**, or Four Arches, north of Charminar, were built in 1594; the western arch, **Daulat-Khan-e-Ali**, was at one time adorned with rich gold tapestries.

Lad Bazaar

Charminar marks the beginning of the fascinating **Lad Bazaar**, which leads to Mahboob Chowk, a market square featuring a mosque and Victorian clock tower. Lad Bazaar specializes in everything you could possibly need for a Hyderabadi marriage, including bangles, rosewater, herbs, spices and cloth. You'll also find silver filigree jewellery, antiques, *bidri*-ware, hookah paraphernalia and, in the markets near Charminar, **pearls** – so beloved of the nizams that they ground them into powder to eat. Hyderabad is still the centre of India's pearl trade.

Nizam's Museum

Daily except Fri 10am–5pm • ₹80 (₹10)

18

Just over 1km northeast of Charminar, the faded and peeling white-painted facade of the **Nizam's Museum** does not hold much promise but behind its solid wooden doors there is quite a treasure-trove of royal family memorabilia. The first two of the four rooms display a motley collection of silver boxes, model planes and boats, Koranic inscriptions, cylindrical caskets, china and glass objects, photos and paintings, plus larger pieces such as thrones. The third room proclaims itself to be the **City Museum** and showcases some quite detailed and very informative historical displays from the Megalithic era to the present day, while the last room has numerous costumes in long dark-wood cabinets.

Mecca Masjid

Daily 8am–noon & 3–8pm

Southwest, behind Charminar, the **Mecca Masjid** was constructed in 1598 and can hold three thousand devotees, with room for up to ten thousand more in the courtyard. On the left of the courtyard are the tombs of the nizams, while the ornamental walls and lattice archways delight throughout the building. In May 2007, the mosque was rocked by a powerful bomb; the incident killed fourteen people. The perpetrators were never caught and since this and subsequent bombings, security has been very tight throughout the city.

Chowmahalla Palace

Khilwat 20-4-236, Motigalli • Daily except Fri 10am–5pm • ₹200 (₹50), camera ₹50 • ⓦ chowmahalla.co.in

The 150-year-old **Chowmahalla Palace**, southwest of the Mecca Masjid, was built between 1857 and 1869 by the nizams to entertain royal visitors and official guests. Inspired by the Shah's palace in Tehran, it is actually a complex of four palaces, other imposing edifices, elegant courtyards and fountain-filled gardens.

The grand **Kilwat Mubarak** (Durbar Hall) is the most impressive building, containing a hall dominated by opulent chandeliers and other rooms full of furniture, ornaments, costumes, china crockery and displays on the history of the nizams. The oldest part is the southern courtyard, where you can visit the two-storeyed **Aftab Mahal**, which houses more costumes and some intricate wall hangings, as well as the smaller Afzal Mahal, Mahtab Mahal and Tahniyat Mahal. At the rear of the complex there is a collection of carriages and vintage motorcars.

North of the river

The area around Hyderabad Deccan railway station, known locally as Nampally, and north towards Hussain Sagar contains some interesting nooks and crannies. Just south of the station itself, tucked in the lanes behind the striking bulbous yellow dome of the **Ek Minar mosque**, the atmospheric **Yusufian Dargah** is the shrine of a seventeenth-century Sufi saint of the venerable Chishti order. About 1km north of the station, set in tranquil public gardens, the **Telangana State Museum** (daily except Fri & 2nd Sat of month 10.30am–5pm; ₹10, camera ₹20, video ₹100) displays a modest collection of bronzes, prehistoric tools and weapons.

Kala Pahad Hill

The **Birla Venkateshvara Mandir** (daily 7am–noon & 3–9pm; no photography) on **Kala Pahad ("black mountain") Hill**, north of the public gardens, is open to all. Constructed in 1976, the temple itself is not of great interest, but affords fine views and is a notable landmark, tapering towards the sky in elegant fashion. Nearby is the mildly diverting **BM Birla Science Centre** (daily 10.30am–8pm, closes 3pm on Fri; ₹50; ⓦbirlasciencecentre.org), which has a lot of satellite hardware and photos, sensory perception machines and a small dinosaur display, plus a **planetarium** (English shows at 11.30am, 4pm & 6pm; ₹50). In a very unscientific manner, the centre also incorporates the **Nirmala Birla Gallery of Modern Art**, featuring the works of Indian painters such as Krishnan Kanna and Amitava Dhar.

Hussain Sagar

Hussain Sagar, the large expanse of water separating Hyderabad from Secunderabad, lends a welcome air of tranquillity to the busy conurbation, and the pedestrianized sections of its banks are popular areas for a stroll, especially at sunset. In the centre of the artificial lake stands a large stone statue of the **Buddha Purnima** ("Full Moon Buddha"), erected in 1992. Regular **boats** (₹60 return) chug out to the statue from Lumbini Park (daily 9am–9pm; ₹10), just off Secretariat Road, which offers some shady spots and also has a toy railway. The park was the site of one of two bombs that exploded in August 2007, claiming 44 lives, so security is predictably tight.

Golconda Fort

Daily 9am–5.30pm • ₹200 (₹15), video ₹25 • Sound-and-light show: English: March–Oct 7pm, Nov–Feb 6.30pm; 1hr; ₹130 • Bus #66G from Charminar via Nampally

Golconda, 122m above the plain and 8km west of old Hyderabad, was the capital of the seven Qutb Shahi kings from 1518 until the end of the sixteenth century, when the court moved to Hyderabad itself. Well preserved and set in thick green scrubland, it is one of India's most impressive forts, boasting 87 semi-circular bastions and eight mighty gates, complete with gruesome elephant-proof spikes. Set aside a day to explore the fort, which covers an area of around four square kilometres.

Entering the **fort** by the Balahisar Gate, you come into the Grand Portico, where guards clap their hands to show off the fort's acoustics. To the right is the **mortuary bath**, where the bodies of deceased nobles were ritually bathed prior to burial. If you follow the arrowed anticlockwise route, you pass the two-storey residence of ministers Akkana and Madanna before starting the stairway ascent to the Durbar Hall. Halfway along the

steps, you arrive at a small, dark cell named after the court cashier **Ramdas**, who while incarcerated here produced the clumsy carvings and paintings that litter the gloomy room.

Nearing the top, you come across the small, pretty mosque of Ibrahim Qutb Shah; beyond here is an even tinier temple to Durga. The steps are crowned by the three-storey **Durbar Hall** of the Qutb Shahis, on platforms outside which the monarchs would sit and survey their domains.

The ruins of the **queen's palace**, once elaborately decorated with multiple domes, stand in a courtyard centred on an original copper fountain that used to be filled with rosewater. You can still see traces of a "necklace" design on one of the arches, at the top of which a lotus bud sits below an opening flower with a cavity at its centre that once contained a diamond. At the entrance to the **palace** itself, four chambers provided protection from intruders. Passing through two rooms, the second of which is overgrown, you come to the **Shahi Mahal**, the royal bedroom. Originally it had a domed roof and niches on the walls that once sheltered candles or oil lamps. Golconda has a nightly **sound-and-light show**.

Tombs of the Qutb Shahi kings

Daily except Fri 9.30am–4.30pm • ₹20 • Bus #123 or #142S from Charminar

There are no less than seventy monuments, including the famous **tombs of the Qutb Shahi kings** about 1km north of Golconda Fort's outer wall. Set in peaceful and beautifully landscaped gardens, the forty mausoleums commemorate commanders, relatives of the kings, dancers, singers and royal doctors, as well as all but two of the Qutb Shahi kings. Now whitewashed, they were once brightly coloured in turquoise and green. Other buildings include more than twenty mosques, five step-wells, some pavilions and a hammam. The whole complex is in the process of undergoing a ten-year conservation programme at the expense of the Aga Khan Foundation.

The western suburbs

Most of Hyderabad's newfound wealth is concentrated in the city's western suburbs. The nearest of these is **Banjara Hills**, around 4km from Nampally, which comprises spacious residences in quiet streets surrounding Road No.1, a glitzy strip of trendy shops, restaurants and bars. The Western appearance and dress, particularly of the young women here, is a sharp contrast to the niqabs and saris ubiquitous in the old city. Several kilometres further west, you enter the even leafier and more upmarket district of **Jubilee Hills**, which is largely residential.

The upturn in Hyderabad's fortunes was driven by its becoming a high-tech hub in the late 1990s, earning it the nickname "Cyberabad", although it is also home to other industries including car manufacture. **HITEC City** itself is several square kilometres of modern blocks and complexes about 10km from the city centre. Although strict security prevents casual visits by those with no business within the complexes, you can get a flavour by touring the area, which is bordered on the south and west by a large lake and beautiful rock formations, reminiscent of Hampi.

Nehru Centenary Tribal Museum

Mon–Sat 10.30am–5pm • ₹120 (₹20) • ☏ 040 2339 1270

Around half a kilometre west of Banjara Hills Road No.1, the **Nehru Centenary Tribal Museum** offers an interesting glimpse into tribal culture and customs. Displays include musical instruments, costumes, agricultural equipment, a bullock cart and a depiction of a traditional dance by the Khond and Bagata peoples. Live performances occasionally take place – call for details.

Ramoji Film City

Daily 9am–5.30pm • Tours from ₹1150 • **Sahas Adventure Park** Daily 9am–5.30pm • ₹1000 • Combined ticket ₹1600 • ⓦ ramojifilmcity.com

Ramoji Film City (RFC), 25km east of central Hyderabad, is the world's largest film studio complex. Covering nearly two thousand acres, with around five hundred set locations, it can produce up to sixty movies simultaneously. Although you cannot see films actually being made, you can tour the facades, enjoy rides such as the Ramoji Tower simulated earthquake and watch a dance and stunt show. The adjacent **Sahas Adventure Park** is packed with activities such as zip-lining, zorbing, quad biking and other adrenaline-filled fun. The easiest way to get here is on a tour from Hyderabad.

ARRIVAL AND DEPARTURE

By plane Modern and efficient Rajiv Gandhi International Airport (⊛hyderabad.aero) is around 20km south of central Hyderabad. Until the metro connection is complete, the airport is only linked to the city by taxis (about ₹1000) and Pushpak Airport Liner buses (every 10–15min; ₹106–265); heading to the airport, you can catch these from the Secretariat.

Destinations There are frequent international flights and excellent domestic connections to Bengaluru (17–21 daily; 1hr 5min–1hr 15min); Chennai (13–16 daily; 1hr 5min–1hr 40min); Delhi (23–25 daily; 2hr 5min–2hr 45); Goa (8–10 daily; 1hr 15min–1hr 45min); Kochi (5–7 daily; 1hr 25min–1hr 45min); Kolkata (10–11 daily; 2hr–2hr 35min); Mumbai (19–21 daily; 1hr 25min–1hr 35min) and many other cities.

By train Many long-distance trains terminate at Secunderabad; your ticket is valid for any connecting train to Hyderabad (Nampally) railway station. The two stations are also linked to each other – and other points in the city, such as Banjara Hills and HITEC City – by the overground Hyderabad Metro (or MMTS). The railways reservations office at Hyderabad (daily 8am–8pm) is to the left as you enter the station: counter 211 is for tourists. The Secunderabad reservation complex is more than 400m to the right as you exit the station: counter 34 is for foreigners. Most northeast-bound services call at Warangal, Vijayawada and Visakhapatnam. A few services depart from Kacheguda station, around 3km east of Nampally.

By bus The long-distance Mahatma Gandhi Bus Stand occupies an island in the River Musi, 3km southeast of Nampally railway station.

Destinations From the long-distance bus stand, regular bus services run to destinations throughout the state and beyond, including Bidar (hourly; 4hr), Tirupati (12 daily; 12hr), Vijayapuri for Nagarjunakonda (6 daily; 4hr), Vijayawada (every 15min; 6hr) and Warangal (every 15min; 3hr). Various "deluxe" private buses depart for Bengaluru, Chennai, Mumbai and other major cities from outside Hyderabad (Nampally) railway station.

INFORMATION AND TOURS

Tourist information The AP Tourism (daily 9am–6pm; ☎040 2340 5656, ⊛aptourism.gov.in) and Telangana Tourism (daily 7am–9pm; ☎1800 4254 6464, ⊛telanganatourism.gov.in) offices are next to each other on Secretariat Rd, near the huge flyover. The APTDC office also in the same complex (daily 7am–8pm; ☎040 2345 3036, ⊛aptdc.gov.in) and the other APTDC office, on Sardar Patel Rd, Secunderabad (☎040 2789 3100), exist principally to book their tours. The Incredible India office is in the new tourist plaza at Begumpet (Mon–Fri 9am–5pm; ☎040 2326 1360), along with the offices of many other states.

Guided tours Telangana Tourism operates a number of good-value guided tours. The times quoted below are when tours set off from the Secunderabad office; the pick-up time in Hyderabad is 15–20min later. There's a Heritage-

RECOMMENDED TRAINS FROM HYDERABAD

Destination	Name	No.	From	Departs	Arrives
Bengaluru	*Bangalore Express*	12785	Kacheguda	7.05pm	6.25am*
Chennai	*Charminar Express*	12760	Hyderabad	6.30pm	8.15am*
Ernakulam	*Sabari Express*	17230	Hyderabad	11.15am	1.15pm*
Kolkata	*East Coast Express*	18646	Hyderabad	9.50am	4.10pm*
Mumbai	*VSKP LTT Express*	11020	Secunderabad	1.05pm	4.40am*
	Mumbai Express	17032	Hyderabad	8.40pm	1.05pm*
Tirupati	*Rayasaleema Express*	17429	Hyderabad	5.25pm	6.15am*
Trivandrum	*Sabari Express*	17230	Hyderabad	11.15am	6.50pm*
Vijayawada	*East Coast Express*	18646	Hyderabad	9.50am	4.30pm
Visakhapatnam	*Janmabhoomi Express*	12806	Secunderabad	7.10am	7.40pm

*Denotes next day arrival

18

cum-Museum city tour (daily 7.30am–7.30pm; non-a/c ₹300, a/c ₹400); a Ramoji Film City tour (daily 7.30am–6.30pm; non-a/c ₹1500, a/c ₹1800 including entry); and several fascinating heritage walks, mostly departing from Charminar (on demand 7.30–9am; ₹50, including breakfast; ☎ 040 2345 0444). The Nagarjuna Sagar tour (Sat & Sun 7.30am–10pm; ₹650 excluding entry) is a rushed but convenient way to reach this fascinating area.

ACCOMMODATION

The area to the east of **Hyderabad (Nampally) railway station** has the cheapest accommodation, but you're unlikely to find anything acceptable for less than ₹500: avoid the grim little collection of five lodges with "Royal" in their name. A little over 1km north of Secunderabad railway station, several decent places can be found on **Sarojini Devi Rd**.

HYDERABAD

Amrutha Castle 5-9-16 Saifabad, opposite the Secretariat ☎ 040 4443 3888, ⊛ amruthacastle.com; map p.934. This extraordinarily kitsch hotel, which looks like a fairy castle, is undoubtedly a fun place to stay. The turreted attached rooms have faux wooden beams, fortified doors and paintings of famous royals. Although there's no moat, you can take a dip in the rooftop pool. Cheaper rates online. ₹4800

★ **DM Residency** 5-8-196/B Nampally ☎ 040 6644 7734, ⊛ dmresidency.com; map p.934. Set back from the Nampally hubbub, this new hotel is kept scrupulously clean by the overtly helpful staff. The rooms are comfortable, with flat-screen TVs. Good single and a/c rates. ₹1500

Golden Glory Guest House Road No.3, Banjara Hills ☎ 040 2355 4765, ⊛ goldengloryguesthouse.com; map p.934. Billing itself as a business and family guesthouse, this modest place with neat modern rooms, some with balconies, is one of the more affordable places in the area. A/c rooms are not much more than non-a/c. Complimentary breakfast. ₹1300

Quality Inn Residency Public Garden Rd, Nampally ☎ 040 4006 8050, ⊛ qualityinn.chobs.in; map p.934. A business traveller-oriented chain hotel with central a/c and comfortably furnished attached rooms. Convenient for the station and the veg restaurant is very good. ₹3300

Rajmata Nampally High Rd, opposite railway station ☎ 040 6666 5555, ✉ royalrajmata@gmail.com; map p.934. Set back from the road, the popular *Rajmata* has a slightly over-priced collection of relatively clean, attached rooms: all have TVs and some also boast a/c. ₹1000

Sai Prakash Station Rd ☎ 040 2461 1726, ⊛ hotelsai prakash.in; map p.934. The vast marble lobby gives way to keenly-priced a/c rooms with flat-screen TVs and contemporary floral motifs on the walls: the bathrooms are decidedly cramped, but it has two decent restaurants. ₹1450

Sri Laxmi Lodge Gadwal Compound, Station Rd ☎ 040 6663 4200; map p.934. Down a small lane opposite the *Sai Prakash*, *Sri Laxmi* is one of the city's better shoestring options. The rooms – if not always the sheets – are clean and have attached showers and squat toilets. A TV costs ₹50 extra. No wi-fi. ₹500

Taj Banjara Road No.1, Banjara Hills ☎ 040 6666 9999, ⊛ tajhotels.com; map p.934. In a pleasant lakeside location, with all the usual top-notch facilities including a pool, three classy restaurants and a 24hr coffee shop. Online specials with particularly good weekend rates. ₹6400

★ **Taj Falaknuma Palace** Road Fatima Nagar, Falaknuma ☎ 040 6666 9999, ⊛ tajhotels.com; map p.934. The opulent and beautiful former residence of the nizams is now a top-notch Taj Hotel, with superb grounds, rooms, restaurants, and exceptional service. A real treat if you can afford it. ₹38,400

Taj Mahal 4-1-999 Abids Rd ☎ 040 6651 1122, ⊛ tmh group.in/abids; map p.934. This classy white-and-pale-green 1920s heritage building has a patio garden, spiral staircase and plenty of character. The rooms themselves are plainer, but feature high ceilings, a/c, flat-screen TVs and fridges; the pricier upper-storey rooms are better. ₹3500

SECUNDERABAD

Baseraa Sarojini Devi Rd ☎ 040 2770 3200, ⊛ baseraa. com; map p.934. The smartest hotel within walking distance (around 15min) of the station, *Baseraa* boasts modern attached rooms with a/c, cable TV and minibars. ₹2900

Sri Sai Ganesh Lodge St John's Rd ☎ 040 2780 6633; map p.934. With some a/c rooms, this modern concrete-and-glass hotel with largish attached rooms is one of the best options in the immediate station area. No wi-fi. ₹1300

EATING

HYDERABAD

Bikanerwala 6-3-190/Z Road No.1, Banjara Hills ☎ 040 6666 1111; map p.934. At this bustling fast-food joint the focus is firmly on north Indian cuisine, with authentic *bhel puri*, *chana bhatura* and *aloo tikki* (₹60–180) on offer, as well as sweets. Daily 8.30am–11.30pm.

Chef Inam's Steak House Road No.12, Banjara Hills ☎ 040 6999 4858; map p.934. American-roadhouse-style joint serving a dozen different chargrilled steaks for ₹600–1000, plus a variety of burgers, kebabs, chicken and seafood dishes, as well as Boston Creameries ice cream. Daily 11am–midnight.

★ **Fusion 9** 6-3-249/A Road No.1, Banjara Hills ☎ 040 6557 7722, ⊛ fusion9.in; map p.934. Expensive (mains

HYDERABADI AND ANDHRA CUISINE

Hyderabadi cooking is derived from Mughlai court cuisine, featuring sumptuous meat dishes with northern ingredients such as cinnamon, cardamom, cloves and garlic. The city is also the home of the world-famous biryani, where mutton, chicken or veg is mixed with rice and spices including nutmeg and cloves. **Andhra cuisine** encompasses traditional southern vegetarian dishes with an array of flavourings such as cassia buds, peanuts, coconut, tamarind leaves, mustard seeds and red chillies. Fish and prawns are commonly eaten in coastal areas.

₹450–750) but quality cuisine from regions as diverse as Mexico, Europe, the Middle East and Southeast Asia, served in a smart modern lounge. There's a smart deli below and the same owners have several other outlets – check the website. Mon–Sat 12.30–3.30pm & 7–11.30pm, Sun 1–4pm & 7–11.30pm.

Kamat Hotel Station Rd, opposite Sai Prakash hotel ☎ 040 2320 3351; map p.934. At this conveniently located branch of the hygienic veggie chain, waiters in white shirts with red lapels serve up inexpensive veg dosas, *idlis*, *vadas*, thalis and mains (₹50–190). Daily 7am–10pm.

Salzburg Street Amrutha Castle hotel, 5-9-16 Saifabad ☎ 040 4443 3880; map p.934. Overlooking the lobby's water feature, this restaurant has unusual, but well-executed, options such as wok-tossed garlic prawns for ₹500 and the Korean-Indian fusion *kimchi paneer* as well as some more traditional Indian and Chinese dishes. Most mains ₹250–400. Daily 7.30–10.30am, 12.30–3pm & 7.30–11pm.

Shadab High Court Rd, Old City ☎ 040 2456 1648; map p.934. While there are some fine meat and fish tandoori items on the menu, the main reason to visit the *Shadab* hotel is for its excellent mutton and chicken biryanis (₹150–200), some of the best in the city. You may have to queue for a table, but it's worth the wait. Daily 5am–11pm.

Sher-e-Punjab Corner of Nampally High Rd and station slip road ☎ 040 2320 4448; map p.934. In a convenient, if not particularly appealing location, this popular basement restaurant offers tasty north Indian veg and non-veg food from ₹150, while a full tandoori chicken goes for ₹350. Daily 10am–10.30pm.

Shezan MJ Rd, Nampally ☎ 040 2461 7867; map p.934. People flock to this hotel restaurant for the excellent and gut-busting biryanis, a snip at ₹190. Some Western and Chinese dishes are also served in the tiered open-air dining hall. Daily noon–11pm.

Via Milano 1259 Road No.36, Jubilee Hills ☎ 040 6455 5544; map p.934. Swish Italian bar-restaurant that does a range of pasta, risotto, pizza and main courses for ₹400–500. On the third floor above equally trendy *Eat India* and *Urban Asia*. Daily noon–11pm.

SECUNDERABAD

★ **Paradise Food Court** Sarojini Devi Rd ☎ 040 6631 3721, ⌖ paradisefoodcourt.in. This very popular modern multi-restaurant complex, with several other branches all over the city, bashes out fine Hyderabadi cuisine, as well as Chinese. The biryanis are recommended, but don't miss out on the succulent mutton kebabs. Mains ₹240–430. Daily 8am–11pm.

DRINKING AND NIGHTLIFE

There are plenty of **bars**, particularly along Road No.1 in Banjara Hills and the burgeoning Jubilee Hills area further west, although a lot of young professionals in Hyderabad prefer to party in each other's homes in comparison with Bengaluru.

10 Downing Street 10–12 Kundanbagh, Begumpet ☎ 040 6455 6010, ⌖ 10ds.in; map p.934. This popular chain bar north of Hussain Sagar manages to look as English as the name suggests, with wood panels and comfy booths. Different theme every night. Daily 11am–11pm.

★ **Coco's Bar & Grill** 217 Road No.2, Banjara Hills ☎ 040 2354 0600; map p.934. Airy rooftop terrace with comfortable, cushioned bamboo armchairs, where you can enjoy a beer or cocktail while listening to the nightly live music. Daily noon–midnight.

Liquids et Cetera Road No.1, Banjara Hills ☎ 040 6625 9907, ⌖ facebook.com/liquidsclubetc; map p.934. Trendy nightclub that hosts theme nights such as "Bollywood Bling" on Sundays. Attracts celebrities from the Mumbai entertainment scene. Daily 8pm–2am.

Spoil Pub Road No.1, Jubilee Hills ☎ 040 3316 5657; map p.934. Popular pub that offers a range of entertainment from "Ladies Nite" to "House of Noise". Cheap snacks and happy hour drinks until 8.30pm. Daily 2–11pm.

Syn Taj Deccan hotel, Road No.1, Banjara Hills ☎ 040 6666 3939; map p.934. Although some of the food is overpriced for the quality, futuristic *Syn* features a *teppanyaki* counter and a slick bar that, alongside the usual range of alcoholic drinks, also serves "detox cocktails". Daily noon–11pm.

SHOPPING

All the shops listed below operate core hours of Mon–Sat 10am–8pm, sometimes later. Lad Bazaar (see page 935) in the old city remains the most absorbing place to browse

for anything from saris to spices.

Ankur 6-1-84 Secretariat Rd ☎ 040 2323 4901; map p.934. A huge range of beautiful silks and saris of varying

18

18

quality and extent can be found at this well-stocked shop.

Chenetha Bhavan A little south of the railway station, Nampally ☎040 2460 2845; map p.934. This modern shopping complex is stuffed with handloom shops, specializing in both clothes and carpets.

Higginbothams 9 Lal Bahadur Stadium ☎040 2323 7918; map p.934. The main Hyderabad branch of the venerable national chain has a diverse collection of novels, reference and academic books.

Lepakshi Gunfoundry, MG Rd ☎040 2323 5028; map p.934. The flagship branch of the AP government emporium stocks a wide range of handicrafts from all over

the state.

Sheela's 17 Lal Bahadur Stadium Complex ☎040 2323 6944; map p.934. Keenly priced souvenir shop selling lots of jewellery, leather bags and various handicrafts.

Sri Mahalaxmi 1264 Road No.36, Jubilee Hills ☎96768 04991; map p.934. Upmarket jewellers displaying a dazzling range of pearls and large pieces in brightly lit cases.

Utkalika Opposite DGP Office, Saifabad ☎040 2324 0510; map p.934. This government of Odisha handicrafts emporium has a modest selection of silver filigree jewellery, handloom cloth, ikat tie-dye, Jagannath papier-mâché figures and buffalo bone carvings.

DIRECTORY

Banks and exchange State Bank of Hyderabad, MG Rd, and Federal Bank, first floor, Orient Estate, MG Rd, exchange foreign currency; both open Mon–Fri 10.30am–2.30pm, the latter also Sat 10.30am–12.30pm. Alternatively try Thomas Cook (☎040 2329 6521) at Nasir Arcade, Secretariat Rd, or LKP forex (☎040 2321 0094) on Public Gardens Rd, a 10min walk north of Nampally station; both open Mon–Sat 9.30am–6pm. ATMs are ubiquitous.

Hospitals The government-run Gandhi Hospital is in Secunderabad (☎040 2770 2222); the private CDR Hospital is in Himayatnagar (☎040 2322 1221); and there's a Tropical Diseases Hospital in Nallakunta (☎040 2766 7843).

Library You must be a member or a British citizen to use the British Library, Secretariat Rd (Tues–Sat 11am–7pm; ☎040 2323 0774).

Pharmacies Apollo Pharmacy (☎040 6060 2424) has branches throughout the city, some open 24hr.

Police ☎040 2323 0191. In an emergency call ☎100.

Travel agents Sagar Tours & Travels, with branches in Afzal Gunj and Lakdi-Ka-Pul (☎98480 82716, ⊛sagartravels hyderabad.com); Sri Sai International Travels in Ameerpet (☎040 2374 2604, ⊛srisaitravels.com); Travel World in Secunderabad (☎040 2781 6018, ⊛travelworld-india. com).

Telangana

The principal places of interest in the rest of Telangana lie about the same distance in opposite directions from the capital. As you head north from Hyderabad, the landscape becomes greener and hillier, sporadically punctuated by photogenic black-granite rock formations. There is little to detain visitors here except **Warangal**, which has a medieval fort and a Shiva temple, and nearby **Palampet**, with its Kakatiya temple. South of the capital, swathes of flat farmland stretch into the centre of the state, where the **Nagarjuna Sagar** dam has created a major lake with the important Buddhist site of **Nagarjunakonda**, now an island, in its waters.

Warangal and around

WARANGAL – "one stone" – 150km northeast of Hyderabad and just about possible to visit as a day-trip, was the Hindu capital of the Kakatiyan empire in the twelfth and thirteenth centuries. Like other Deccan cities, it changed hands many times between the Hindus and the Muslims – something reflected in the remains you see today.

Warangal's **fort** (daily 9am–5pm; ₹100 [₹5]), 4km south of the city, is famous for its two circles of fortifications: the outer made of earth with a moat, and the inner of stone. Four roads into the centre meet at the ruined Shiva temple of **Swayambhu** (1162). At its southern gateway, another Shiva temple, from the fourteenth century, is in much better shape; inside, the remains of an enormous lingam came originally from the Swayambhu shrine. Also inside the citadel is the **Shirab Khan**, or **Audience Hall**, an early eleventh-century building very similar to Mandu's Hindola Mahal.

Some 6km north of town just off the main road beside the slopes of Hanamkonda Hill, the largely basalt Chalukyan-style "**thousand-pillared**" **Shiva temple** (daily 6am–6pm) was constructed in 1163. A low-roofed building on several stepped stages, it features superb carvings and shrines to Vishnu, Shiva and Surya, the sun god. They lead off the *mandapa*, whose numerous finely carved columns give the temple its name. In front, a polished Nandi bull was carved out of a single stone. A Bhadrakali temple stands at the top of the hill.

Palampet

PALAMPET, around 70km northeast of Warangal, is a remote village that is worth the effort to get to for its splendid thirteenth-century **Ramappa temple**. Created by the same Kakatiyan artisans who built the Hanamkonda temple near Warangal, the temple is built on a 1.8m-high cruciform plinth and crowned by a central *shikhara*, delicately carved with scenes from the Puranas, while the inner sanctum boasts a 2.7m-tall lingam. There is also an impressive Nandi statue and bathing tank.

18

ARRIVAL AND INFORMATION

WARANGAL AND AROUND

By train There are at least twenty services daily between Hyderabad and Warangal, taking 2–3hr.

By bus There are buses every 15–30min between Warangal and Hyderabad, taking around 3hr. There is no direct bus from Warangal to Palampet, so change in Mulugu.

Getting around The easiest way to cover the sites near Hanamkonda.

Warangal is to rent a bike from one of the stalls on Station Rd (₹50/day). An auto-rickshaw to either the fort or the temple costs around ₹130, if you negotiate hard.

Tourist information There's a Telangana Tourism office (☏0870 257 1339; Mon–Sat 10am–5pm) at Nakalgutta in Hanamkonda.

ACCOMMODATION AND EATING

Ashoka Main Rd, Hanamkonda ☏0870 257 8491, ⓦhotelashoka.in. Near the thousand-pillared temple, this place has carpeted a/c rooms with TV and fridge but dodgy service. The restaurant provides Indian and Chinese standards; there's also an attached bar. **₹3000**

Bharati Mess Station Rd, Warangal. The best of the simple vegetarian restaurants in the station area, offering huge and wholesome unlimited refill meals for around ₹80, all made with fresh ingredients. Daily 7am–10pm.

Grand Gayatri Station Rd, Warangal ☏70950 19949, ⓦhotelgrandgayatri.com. Best hotel in the station area,

offering warmly furnished rooms of various sizes and prices. Decent north India restaurant too. **₹1999**

Harita Kakatiya Main Rd, Hanamkonda ☏0870 256 2236, ⓦtelanganatourism.gov.in. Not far from the thousand-pillared temple, this government hotel is the best in the area, with large spacious a/c rooms and a good restaurant. **₹1850**

Vijaya Lodge Station Rd, Warangal ☏0870 225 1222. The pick of the basic lodges near the station, quite large and modern with fairly hygienic rooms, many of them with shared bathrooms. Simple but decent restaurant. **₹350/₹600**

Nagarjunakonda

NAGARJUNAKONDA, or "Nagarjuna's Hill", 166km south of Hyderabad and 175km west of Vijayawada, is all that remains of the vast area, rich in archeological sites, that was submerged when the huge Nagarjuna Sagar dam was built across the River Krishna in 1960. Ancient settlements in the valley had first been discovered in 1926, and extensive excavations carried out between 1954 and 1960 uncovered more than one hundred sites dating from the early Stone Age to late medieval times. Nagarjunakonda was once the summit of a hill, where a fort towered 200m above the valley floor; now it is just a small oblong island near the middle of Nagarjuna Sagar Lake. The new border between Telangana and Andhra Pradesh runs right through the lake and both states claim it as their own in tourist literature. It certainly falls more within the compass of Hyderabad, eventually to be solely the capital of Telangana, which manages the local resort (see page 944).

Several Buddhist monuments have been reconstructed, in an operation reminiscent of that at Abu Simbel in Egypt, and a **museum** exhibits the more remarkable ruins of the valley. **VIJAYAPURI**, the village on the shore of the lake, overlooks the colossal dam itself, which produces electricity for the whole region, and is the jumping-off point for visiting **Nagarjunakonda island** (daily 9am–5pm). Boats arrive on the northeastern edge of the island, at what remains of one of the gates of the fort, built in the fourteenth century and renovated by the Vijayanagar kings in the mid-sixteenth century. Low, damaged, stone walls skirting the island mark the fort's edge, and you can see ground-level remains of the

Hindu temples that served its inhabitants. Well-kept gardens lie between the jetty and the museum, beyond which nine Buddhist monuments from various sites in the valley have been rebuilt. West of the jetty, there's a reconstructed third-century-AD bathing *ghat*.

The stupas

The **maha-chaitya**, or *stupa*, constructed at the command of King Chamtula's sister in the third century AD, is the area's earliest Buddhist structure. It was raised over relics of the Buddha – said to include a tooth – and has been reassembled in the southwest of the island. Nearby, a towering **Buddha statue** stands beside a ground plan of a monastery that enshrines a smaller *stupa*. Close by are other **stupas**; the brick walls of the *svastika chaitya* have been arranged in the shape of swastikas, common emblems in early Buddhist iconography.

The museum

Daily except Fri 10.30am–5pm • ₹100 (₹5)

The **museum** houses stone friezes decorated with scenes from the Buddha's life, and statues of the Buddha in various postures. Earlier artefacts include metal axe-heads and knives (dating from the first millennium BC). Later exhibits include inscribed pillars from Ikshvaku times. Medieval sculptures include a thirteenth-century *tirthankara* (Jain saint) and a seventeenth-century Ganesh.

ARRIVAL AND INFORMATION   NAGARJUNAKONDA

By bus Nagarjunakonda can easily be reached from Hyderabad (4hr; all the regular Macherla services stop at Vijayapuri) or Vijayawada (6hr; a direct service runs daily at 11am and frequent services leave from Guntur).

By boat Tickets for boats to the island (daily 9.30am, 11.30am & 1.30pm; 45min; ₹100) go on sale 25min before

departure. Each boat leaves the island 90min after it arrives, so if you want to see the ruins and museum in detail, take a morning boat and return in the afternoon.

Tourist information The AP Tourism office (Mon–Sat 10am–5pm; ☏ 08680 277364) is near the bus stand.

ACCOMMODATION

Accommodation at Vijayapuri is limited and there are two distinct settlements 6km apart on either side of the dam. For easy access to the sites it's better to stay near the jetty on the right bank of the dam; ask the bus driver to leave you at the launch station.

Haritha Vijay Vihar Resort On the near side of the dam as you approach the lake from Hyderabad ☏ 08680

277362, ⊛ harithahotel.com. APTDC runs the comfortable all-a/c *Vijay Vihar*, complete with swimming pool. Rooms are over 50 percent more expensive at weekends. ₹1600

Nagarjuna Motel Complex 500m beyond the boat jetty ☏ 08642 278188. This functional but drab-looking concrete complex has minimally adequate rooms, some with a/c, and a basic restaurant. ₹700

Eastern and northern Andhra Pradesh

One of India's least visited areas, **eastern Andhra Pradesh** is sandwiched between the Bay of Bengal in the east and the red soil and high peaks of the Eastern Ghats in the north. Its sole architectural attraction is the ancient Buddhist site of **Amaravati**, gradually being transformed as the new capital of Andhra Pradesh (see page 945), near the business hub of **Vijayawada**, whose sprinkling of historic temples is far overshadowed by impersonal, modern buildings. For anyone with a strong desire to explore, however, pockets of natural beauty along the coast and in the hills of eastern Andhra Pradesh can offer rich rewards, especially the **Godavari Delta** around Rajahmundry. At the northern tip of the state, the nondescript industrial port city of **Visakhapatnam** is a useful place to break up a journey to northern India.

Vijayawada

Almost 450km north of Chennai, a third of the way to Kolkata, **VIJAYAWADA** is a bustling commercial centre on the banks of the Krishna Delta, 90km from the coast.

This mundane city, alleviated by a mountain backdrop of bare granite outcrops and some urban greenery, is seldom visited by tourists, but is an obvious stop-off point for a visit to nearby **Amaravati**. The **Kanaka Durga** (also known as Vijaya) **temple** on Indrakila Hill in the east, dedicated to the city's patron goddess of riches, power and benevolence, is the most interesting of Vijayawada's handful of temples. Across the river, roughly 6km southwest of town, is an ancient, unmodified cave temple complex at **Undavalli** (daily 9am–5pm; ₹100 [₹5]) a tiny rural village on the local #301 bus service to Amaravati. There are shrines to all three of the *trimurti*, with the reclining Vishnu statue on the upper level being the most impressive feature.

18

ARRIVAL AND INFORMATION VIJAYWADA

By train Vijayawada's railway station, on the main Chennai–Kolkata line, is in the centre of town: the daily *East Coast Express* #18645 (11.15am; 5hr 55min) is a convenient service to Hyderabad (Secunderabad).

By bus The Pandit Nehru bus stand is 1.5km west of the station, on the other side of the Ryes Canal. The efficient #301 bus to Amaravati via Undavalli (every 20–30min;

1hr 30min) leaves from platform 47. There are also regular services to Hyderabad (every 15min; 6hr) and Visakhapatnam (hourly; 6–9hr).

Tourist information There's a tourist office (Mon–Sat 10am–5pm; ☏ 0866 252 3966) at the railway station, and APTDC has an office in the town centre at the *Hotel Ilapuram* complex, Gandhi Nagar (same times; ☏ 0866 257 0255).

ACCOMMODATION AND EATING

Monika Lodge Just off Elluru Rd about 300m northeast of the bus stand ☏ 0866 257 1334. Cheap, no-frills lodge, with small attached rooms, some a/c, perfectly salubrious enough for a night. No wi-fi. ₹600

Narayana Swamy Atchutaramaiah St ☏ 0866 257 1221. Good-value lodge, with spotless rooms, some with a/c and TV. If full, try the similar *Sitara* nearby on the other side of the road. ₹975

Raj Towers Elluru Rd ☏ 0866 257 1311. Mid-range hotel

in a tall modern block, which offers pleasantly furnished a/c rooms with cable TV and has a decent restaurant. The owner also has the budget *Hotel Comforts* opposite. ₹2200

Swarna Palace Corner of Atchutaramaiah St and Elluru Rd ☏ 0866 257 7222, ✉ swarnapalace@rediffmail.com. Reliable place, with spacious and comfortable singles that can sleep two, though the a/c rooms cost over twice as much. Its fourth-floor *Palace Heights* restaurant serves hearty portions of Indian, Chinese and Continental food, and there's a bar. ₹950

Amaravati

Daily except Fri 10am–5pm • ₹100 (₹5); museum ₹2

For centuries **AMARAVATI**, 33km from Vijayawada, has been little more than a village on the banks of the Krishna. All that is rapidly changing, however, as this is the location that has been chosen to be the brand-new **capital** of Andhra Pradesh, following the secession of Telangana (see page 942). Eventually, an ultramodern city of gleaming skyscrapers will emerge from the quiet fields, although at the time of writing there were a lot more foundations than floors above ground level.

Amidst this building frenzy, Amaravati remains famous as the site of a Buddhist settlement formerly known as Chintapalli, where a *stupa* larger than those at Sanchi was erected over relics of the Buddha in the third century BC, during the reign of Ashoka. The *stupa* no longer stands, but its size is evident from the mound that formed its base. There was a gateway at each of the cardinal points, one of which has been reconstructed, and the meticulously carved details show themes from the Buddha's life. A Kalachakra initiation programme was conducted by the Dalai Lama here in January 2006 to commemorate 2550 years since the Buddha's birth.

Exhibits at the small but fascinating **museum** date from the third century BC to the twelfth century AD and include Buddha statues with lotus symbols on the feet, tightly curled hair and long ear lobes – all traditional indications of an enlightened teacher.

ARRIVAL AND DEPARTURE AMARAVATI

By bus Bus #301 runs every 20–30min from Vijayawada to Amaravati (1hr 30min). The excavated site and museum are

less than 1km from the bus stand but it's better to jump off when the bus turns onto the main street.

ACCOMMODATION AND EATING

RKS Rest House Temple St ☎08645 255516. Typical of the handful of basic lodges dotted around the temple, this place offers no creature comforts but is OK for a night. ₹450

The Godavari Delta

A previously uncharted region that is just beginning to open up to tourism, though still mostly aimed at domestic visitors, is the enchanting **Godavari Delta**, where the mighty river ends its journey of almost 1500 miles across India from its source in the Western Ghats. The best base for exploration of the area is **Rajahmundry**, roughly halfway between Vijayawada and Visakhapatnam. From there, you can take a trip upriver to the verdant **Papikondalu Hills**, delve into the lush **Konaseema** region to the south or visit the **Coringa Wildlife Sanctuary** to the southeast.

Rajahmundry

Busy but not unpleasant **RAJAHMUNDRY** sprawls along the east bank of the Godavari, still 80km from the sea, yet the river is so wide at this point that it takes over five minutes to cross it by rail or road. Although the main reason to come here is to explore the rural areas that surround it, the lively riverfront merits a stroll. Being the last major town on India's second holiest river, the banks are a riot of temples, shrines and bathing *ghats*, always bustling with pilgrims and locals alike.

Papikondalu Hills

As the best spots in the green riverside **Papikondalu Hills** to the north of Rajahmundry are only accessible by boat, it is best to take a tour (see opposite) to reach them. You are first taken 35km by road to the muddy jetty at **Polavaram** and then transferred onto a double-decker boat that sedately cruises upstream to **Bhadrachalam**, visiting some temples en route and giving you the option to stay overnight in rustic bamboo huts at **Kolluru**, beside a tributary where you can bathe in the clear rushing waters.

Konaseema

Billing itself as Andhra's answer to the renowned Keralan backwaters (see page 1080), **Konaseema** is a palm-rich region of fertile islands and grassy marshes created by the seven mouths of the Godavari. This sleepy area, home to water buffalo, farmers and fishermen, is just waking up to tourism, especially around the nearby villages of **Razole** and **Dindi**, around 50km south of Rajahmundry, which offer waterfront resorts and houseboats for groups.

Coringa Wildlife Sanctuary

Daily 7am–6pm • ₹200 (₹10)

Roughly 45km southeast of Rajahmundry, the **Coringa Wildlife Sanctuary** contains the largest area of **mangrove swamps** in India apart from the Sundarbans (see page 778). There's a boardwalk through the muddy groves and a small jetty for boat trips when the tide is high enough, plus an ugly concrete viewing platform that does allow great views all around. Among the birdlife to be spotted here is the ubiquitous egret, the open-billed stork, kingfishers and even the Brahminy kite, while the elusive otter is the most notable resident mammal. The surrounding bay is also a major breeding ground for the olive ridley turtle.

ARRIVAL AND INFORMATION   THE GODAVARI DELTA

By train Rajahmundry's railway station, on the main east-coast line, is on the south side of the city centre: all of the 15–20 daily trains between Vijayawada (2hr 30min–3hr) and Visakhapatnam (3hr–3hr 30min) stop here.

By bus The bus stand is 3km northeast of the station. There are regular services to Dindi (hourly; 2hr), Hyderabad (every 30min–1hr; 9–10hr), Razole (hourly; 2hr), Vijayawada (every 15–30min; 3–4hr) and Visakhapatnam (every 30min–1hr; 3hr 30min–4hr 30min). For Coringa Wildlife Sanctuary, you can take a bus to Kakinada (every 15–30min; 1hr 30min and get an auto-rickshaw or Yanam-bound bus from there.

Tourist information and tours The best source of information and place to book tours of the region is the efficient Konaseema Tourism office (daily 8am–8pm; ☎80087 57111, ⊛konaseematourism.com), 200m north of Rajahmundry railway station.

ACCOMMODATION AND EATING

Foodway 200m north of Rajahmundry railway station ☎99599 84550. Better than the fast-food-joint appearance suggests, this modern place serves a range of special thalis and biryanis plus other Indian and Chinese dishes, all under ₹200. Daily 11am–10pm.

Haritha Coconut Country Resort Dindi ☎98487 80524, ⊛aptdc.gov.in. Unusually attractive government resort with large rustic rooms, a multicuisine restaurant, swimming pool, and a couple of luxury two-room house-boats for rent. ₹2400

★**Podarillu Resort** Razole ☎80087 27333, ⊛konaseema

tourism.com. Spacious a/c rooms with uninterrupted views across the tranquil waters. The huge ground-floor bathrooms have shrubs growing in the sandy soil. Food by arrangement. ₹3200

Sri Ishwarya Residency Opposite Rajahmundry railway station ☎0883 243 7315. Standard station-area lodge with decent-sized rooms that are clean enough. Rather haphazard service. No wi-fi. ₹750

Transit Bay 200m north of Rajahmundry railway station ☎0883 244 1000. Modern hotel with central a/c and smart business-oriented rooms painted in bright colours. Overlooks the tracks, so suffers from train noise. ₹1400

Visakhapatnam and around

Andhra Pradesh's second largest city, 650km east of Hyderabad and 350km north of Vijayawada, **VISAKHAPATNAM** (commonly known as Vizag) is a busy port and home to major shipbuilding, oil refining and steel industries. Apart from having a decent beach, some interesting temples and a couple of museums, for most travellers it only serves to break up a long journey along the east coast. Those who do linger in the area, however, can enjoy the seaside area of **Waltair** and will be rewarded by visiting outlying places such as **Bheemunipatnam**, **Mukhalingam** and the **Borra caves**.

Kursura Submarine Museum

Beach Rd • Tues–Sat 2–8.30pm, Sun 10am–12.30pm & 2–8.30pm • ₹40, camera ₹50, video ₹200 • ☎0891 256 3429

Housed in a decommissioned submarine named INS *Kursura*, which is now landed like a beached whale in a dry dock on the seafront, the **Kursura Submarine Museum** is mainly of interest to nautical fanatics. It gives you the chance to see the inner workings of the vessel and get an idea of what life must have been like on board.

Vishaka Museum

Beach Rd • Mon–Thurs 11am–7pm, Sat & Sun noon–8pm • ₹10 • ☎0891 255 0316

The surprisingly well-laid-out and well-labelled **Vishaka Museum** covers seafaring from ancient times to post-Independence, with plenty of paintings and naval equipment, though with perhaps a little too much emphasis on and glorification of military prowess.

Kailashagiri Hill and beach

The best beach for swimming is below **Kailashagiri Hill**, several kilometres north of the port. The popular hilltop park boasts fantastic coastal and city vistas, and a hilarious viewing deck in the shape of the *Titanic*'s bow, as well as the usual modest funfair paraphernalia and stalls. The park is also linked to the coast road and fine sandy beach by a **cable car** (₹30 one way).

Around Visakhapatnam

Various traces of older civilizations lie within a day's journey of the city. At **Bheemunipatnam**, 30km north, you can see the remains of a Dutch fort and a peculiar cemetery with slate-grey pyramidal tombs. You'll need a car to get to **Mukhalingam**, 100km north of Bheemunipatnam, where three Shaivite temples, built between the sixth and twelfth centuries, rest in low hills. Their elaborate carvings and well-preserved towering *shikharas* display slight local variations from the otherwise standard Odishan style.

18

Ninety kilometres inland on a minor road that winds through the Eastern Ghats and the Araku forest, **Borra** boasts a set of dark and eerie limestone **caves**, pierced with age-old stalactites and stalagmites (daily 10am–1pm & 2–5pm; ₹40).

ARRIVAL AND INFORMATION

VISAKHAPATNAM AND AROUND

By train Visakhapatnam's railway station, on the main Chennai–Kolkata line, is close to the port. The best service in both directions is the superfast *Coromandel Express* #12842 (10.10pm) to Bhubaneswar (6hr 30min) and Kolkata (13hr 45min); #12841 (4.20am) to Chennai (12hr 40min) and Vijayawada (5hr 35min).

By bus Regular buses for Vijayawada (every 30min; 6–8hr), Rajahmundry (every 30min–1hr; 3hr 30min–4hr 30min) and Hyderabad (hourly; 11–13hr) leave from the bus stand, south of the city centre.

Tourist information The APTDC office is in the RTC Complex in the city centre (Mon–Sat 9am–5pm; ☎0891 278 8820).

ACCOMMODATION

VISAKHAPATNAM

Gateway Beach Rd ☎0891 662 3670, ⓦthegateway hotels.com. The top-end Taj Hotels-run *Gateway* has recently renovated sea-facing attached rooms and an excellent Chinese restaurant. Good online deals. ₹7000

Haritha Hotel Beach Rd ☎0891 256 2333, ⓦaptdc. gov.in. This mid-range APTDC hotel offers comfortable, if slightly institutional, standard and a/c rooms. Breakfast included. ₹1600

★ **Karanths Hotel** 33-1-55 Patel Marg, Visakha patnam ☎0891 256 0347. By far the best place if you're just overnighting between trains and want to stay by the station. Very clean attached rooms with cable TV and polite service. No wi-fi. ₹600

The Park Beach Rd, Visakhapatnam ☎0891 304 5678,

ⓦ theparkhotels.com. This branch of the nationwide chain is Visakh's classiest hotel, with elegantly furnished rooms and all mod cons, including fine dining, lush gardens and a pool. Breakfast included. ₹11,000

YMCA Beach Rd, Visakhapatnam ☎0891 275 5826, ⓦymcavizag.org. The reliable and predictably popular *YMCA*, which boasts a splendid seaside location, has a few economical attached rooms and a dorm. No wi-fi. Dorms ₹150, doubles ₹800

AROUND VISAKHAPATNAM

Jungle Bells Tyda ⓦaptdc.gov.in. This mid-range APTDC hotel has fair-sized rustic rooms and is the nearest place to Borra caves. Buffet breakfast included. ₹1200

EATING

Flying Spaghetti Monster Waltair Rd, Visakhapatnam ☎0891 276 6652, ⓦfsm.in. An unexpected find for such a city, serving pizzas, pasta, and some Mexican dishes for ₹350–600. Daily noon–10.30pm.

Sandy Lane Beach Rd, Visakhapatnam ☎0891 273 6997. Housed in an attractive Raj-era mansion and with seating at the back of the beach, this bar-restaurant offers chilled beer and fresh seafood for ₹150–300. Daily 11am–11pm.

Southern Andhra Pradesh

The further south you travel from the fertile lands watered by the great Krishna and Godavari rivers, the less hospitable the terrain becomes, especially in the rocky southwest of the state. For Hindus, the main attraction in southern Andhra Pradesh is the **Venkateshvara temple**, outside **Tirupati**, India's most popular Vishnu shrine, where several thousand pilgrims come each day to receive *darshan*. **Puttaparthy**, the community founded by the deceased spiritual leader **Sai Baba**, and the **Oneness University** (see page 949) are the only other places in the region to attract significant numbers of visitors. All three places are closer to Chennai in Tamil Nadu and Bengaluru in Karnataka than to other points in Andhra Pradesh.

Tirumala Hill and Tirupati

Set in a stunning position, surrounded by wooded hills capped by a ring of vertical red rocks, the **Sri Venkateshvara temple** at **Tirumala**, 170km northwest of Chennai, is said to be one of the richest places of pilgrimage in the world, and is certainly the most popular, drawing more devotees than Rome or Mecca. With its many shrines and *dharamsalas*, the whole area around Tirumala Hill, an enervating drive 700m up in the Venkata Hills, provides a fascinating insight into contemporary Hinduism practised on a large scale.

The road trip up Tirumala Hill is a lot less terrifying now that there's a separate route down; the most devout, of course, climb the hill by foot. The steep **trail** starts at Alipuri, 4km from the centre of Tirupati; all the pilgrim buses pass through – look out for a large Garuda statue and the soaring *gopura* of the first temple. There are drinks stalls all along the route, which is covered for most of the way. The walk takes at least four hours, and an early start is recommended. When you get to the top, you will see barbers giving pilgrims tonsures as part of their devotions.

At the bottom of the hill, the **Sri Kapileswaraswami** temple at Kapilateertham is the only Tirumala temple devoted to Shiva.

The Venkateshwara temple

General entry free; *sarvadarshanan* ₹50; special entry and *e-darshan* ₹300 • ⑩ tirumala.org

The **Venkateshwara temple** (aka Sri Vari) dedicated to **Vishnu** and started in the tenth century, has been renovated to provide facilities for the thousands of pilgrims who visit daily; weekends, public holidays and festivals are even busier. Unless your visit is intended to be particularly rigorous, you should buy one of the **special darshan** tickets, as this can reduce the time it takes to get inside by quite a few hours, perhaps even more than a day. All types of tickets can be purchased from booths near the temple entrance and even in advance online. Before entering the temple non-Hindus have to sign a declaration of faith in Lord Venkateshwara and provide photocopies of the picture and visa pages from their passports, along with the originals. Note that **no electronic devices** are allowed inside the temple.

At the entrance is a colonnade, lined with life-sized copper or stone statues of royal patrons. The *gopura* gateway leading to the inner courtyard is decorated with sheets of embossed silver; a gold *stambha* (flagstaff) stands outside the inner shrine next to a gold upturned lotus on a plinth. Outside, opposite the temple, is a small museum, the **Hall of Antiquities** (daily 8am–8pm). Your *darshan* tickets entitle you to enter the museum via shorter queues opposite the exit.

THE ONENESS UNIVERSITY AND TEMPLE

A few kilometres from the small town of Tada, around 70km east of Tirupati, lies the startling complex of the **Golden City**, home to the **Oneness University**. The focal point of this community is the stunning and gigantic three-storey **Oneness Temple**, built in brilliant white marble and visible for miles around. The largest pillarless hall in Asia, it is capable of housing up to five thousand people. The huge edifice has an impressive meditation hall on the upper storey and beneath it areas for communal worship and events, most notably *darshan* with the founders of the Oneness Movement, **Sri Bhagavan** (born March 15, 1949 in Natham, Tamil Nadu) and his partner **Amma** (born August 15, 1954 in Sangam, Andhra Pradesh). Often referred to as Kalki Bhagavan, as many followers have declared him to be the tenth incarnation of Vishnu, the guru has always disavowed this title, concentrating instead on promoting his core message of seeking union with the divine.

After the couple married in 1976, they founded the Jeevashram school in 1984, originally located at Satyaloka, a remote location in the Eastern Ghats near the Andhra and Karnataka borders. Here they developed the philosophy of Oneness, wherein every individual feels connected to all that is and gradually awakens to a state of higher consciousness. This is achieved by the process of **deeksha blessing**, whereby divine energy is transferred directly to the recipient by a gentle touching of the head around the crown chakra. In the early 1990s, the school relocated to **Nemam**, in Tamil Nadu north of Chennai, before finding its new home at the Golden City at the turn of the millennium.

The temple is not open to casual visitors but those genuinely interested can arrange a visit in advance and be given a tour. You can find out more about the movement and get details on the four-week-long **deepening process** at the university by logging onto ⑩omoneness. com. If you do arrange to go independently, it is better to hire a taxi from Tirupati or Chennai as the complex is very difficult to reach by public transport.

18

Tirupati

The hill is 11km as the crow flies from its service town of **TIRUPATI**, but double that by road. The town is almost entirely modern and pretty unappealing, as well as being predictably crowded with the constant flow of pilgrims. A five-minute walk from the railway station, the one temple in Tirupati itself that's definitely worth a look is **Govindarajaswamy**, whose modern grey *gopura* is clearly visible from many points in town. The inner sanctum is open to non-Hindus and contains a splendid, large, black reclining Vishnu. In its own compound by the side entrance stands the fine little Venkateshvara Museum of Temple Arts (daily 8am–8pm; ₹5). The temple's impressive bathing tank lies 200m to the east.

Tiruchanur Padmavati temple

Between Tirupati and Tirumala Hill, the **Tiruchanur Padmavati temple** is another popular pilgrimage halt. A gold *vimana* tower with lions at each corner surmounts the sanctuary, which contains a black stone image of goddess Lakshmi with one silver eye. A ₹50 ticket allows you to jump the queue to enter the sanctuary.

Chandragiri Fort

Daily except Fri 10am–5pm • ₹100 (₹5) • **Sound-and-light show (in English)** Nov–Feb 7.30pm, March–Oct 8pm; 45min; ₹40

In the sixteenth century, **Chandragiri**, 11km southwest of Tirupati, became the third capital of the Vijayanagars. It was here that the British negotiated the acquisition of the land to establish Fort St George, the earliest settlement at what is now Chennai. The original fort, thought to date from around 1000 AD, was taken over by Haider Ali in 1782, followed by the British in 1792. A small **museum** is housed in the main building, the Indo-Saracenic Raja Mahal. Another building, the **Rani Mahal**, stands close by, while behind that is a hill with two freestanding boulders that was used as a place of public execution during Vijayanagar times. There's a nightly **sound-and-light show**.

ARRIVAL AND DEPARTURE

By plane There are flights to Bengaluru (2 daily; 1hr) and Hyderabad (12–14 daily; 1hr–1hr 15min) from the airport, 14km outside Tirupati.

By train Trains from Chennai (7–11 daily; 2hr 35min–4hr) pull in at Tirupati's central railway station. There are several connections to Hyderabad (6–10 daily; 11hr 15min–15hr 15min).

TIRUMALA HILL AND TIRUPATI

By bus The bus stand is 500m east of the train station. From Hyderabad it's a long haul (8–10 daily; 12–15hr). Frequent express bus services run to Chennai (every 15–30min; 3hr 30min–4hr). There are hourly buses to both Kanchipuram (5hr), two of which continue to Mamallapuram (7hr), and Bengaluru (7hr).

GETTING AROUND AND INFORMATION

By bus A special section at the back of Tirupati bus stand has services every few minutes to Tirumala Hill; you can also access the hill via a local bus stop outside the railway station.

Tourist information The AP Tourism office (daily 7am–9pm; ☏ 0877 225 5385) is on the second floor of the Sri Devi Complex, Tilak Rd.

ACCOMMODATION AND EATING

Unless you're a pilgrim seeking accommodation in the *dharamshalas* near the temple, all the decent places to stay are in Tirupati. Eating is almost exclusively vegetarian, and there are many cheap "meals" places in town and on Tirumala Hill.

Annapurna 349 G Car St, opposite the railway station ☏ 0877 225 0666. On a busy corner, this modern hotel has spacious, sparsely furnished attached rooms with tiled floors, TVs and either fans or a/c. The a/c restaurant serves south Indian snacks, thalis, Chinese and north Indian dishes. ₹1200

Bhimas Deluxe 34–38 G Car St, near the railway station ☏ 0877 222 5521, ⊕ bhimasdeluxehotels.com. Despite an unappealing grey colour scheme, the attached a/c rooms

with TV here are a decent choice; 12hr "transit rooms" are available for two thirds of the regular rate. ₹1900

Mayura 209 TP Area ☏ 0877 222 5925, ⊕ mayura hotels@yahoo.co.in. The best of the mid-range hotels opposite the bus station, offering average rooms with clean bathrooms and TV. No wi-fi. ₹1800

★**The Orchid** Fortune Kences hotel, opposite the bus stand ☏ 0877 225 5855. The excellent ₹799 evening buffet is one of the few places to enjoy non-veg food, with superb chicken and lamb dishes, followed by a great range of desserts. À la carte available too. Daily 7–11pm.

Sindhuri Park Opposite the bathing tank ☏ 0877 225 6430, ⊕ hotelsindhuri.com. One of the smartest places

SHRI SATYA SAI BABA

Born on November 23, 1926, in Puttaparthy, **Satyanarayana Raju** allegedly displayed prodigious talents from an early age. His apparently supernatural abilities initially caused some concern to his family, who took him to Vedic doctors and eventually to be exorcised. Having been declared possessed by the divine rather than the diabolical, at the age of 14 he calmly announced he was the new incarnation of **Sai Baba**, a saint from Shirdi in Maharashtra who died eight years before Satya was born.

Gradually his fame spread and a large following developed. In 1950 the **ashram** was inaugurated and a decade later Sai Baba was attracting international attention; he still has millions of devotees worldwide, more than five years after his death on April 27, 2011. Just 5ft tall, with a startling Hendrix-style Afro, his smiling, saffron-clad figure can be seen on posters, photos and murals all over south India. Though his **miraculous powers** reportedly included the ability to materialize *vibhuti*, sacred ash, with curative properties, Sai Baba always claimed this to be unimportant, emphasizing instead his message of **universal love**. During his last years a number of ex-followers made serious accusations about coercion and even sexual abuse on the part of the guru himself, which have been vehemently denied.

Predictably, following the passing of the guru, there have been further rumours of corruption by the trustees of his organization, casting its future into some doubt. Whatever your feelings about the divinity of Sai Baba, the atmosphere around the ashram remains undeniably peaceful. You can find out more about the Satya Sai Organisation at ⊛saibaba.ws.

18

in the town centre, this all-a/c hotel has comfortable – if unremarkable – attached rooms with good views of the tank and temple. The restaurant offers a good range of Indian *paneer* and veg dishes, as well as banana splits for dessert. ₹2499

Sri Vignesh Residency 191 Railway Station Rd ☎0877 645 2547. The bright yellow exterior rather masks the dingy interior. Still, the cell-like rooms are among the best budget deals in town. No wi-fi. ₹500

Puttaparthy

Deep in the southwest of the state, amid the arid rocky hills bordering Karnataka, a thriving community has grown up around the once insignificant village of **PUTTAPARTHY**, birthplace of spiritual leader **Sai Baba**. Centring on **Prasanthi Nilayam** (Abode of Peace), the ashram where Sai Baba used to reside most of the year, the town has schools, a university, hospital and sports centre that offer up-to-date and free services to all. The ashram itself is a huge complex, with canteens, shops, a museum and library, and a vast assembly hall. The museum (daily 10am–noon) contains detailed displays on the world's major faiths and presents a positive Unitarian message.

ARRIVAL AND DEPARTURE   PUTTAPARTHY

By train The railway station, named Sri Satya Sai Prasanti Nilayam, is 8km from town on the main north–south route but it is only served by infrequent passenger trains. For express services go to Dharmavaram, 42km away, connected to Puttaparthy by regular buses.

By bus Buses from Bengaluru (every 30min–1hr; 4hr), Hyderabad (5–8 daily; 12–13hr), Tirupati (hourly; 6–7hr) and Chennai (8–12 daily; 8–9hr) stop at the stand outside the ashram entrance.

ACCOMMODATION AND EATING

Many visitors stay in the ashram accommodation, which is strictly segregated by sex, except for families. Costs are minimal, and although you can't book in advance, you can enquire about availability at the secretary's office (☎08555 287583). Outside the ashram, many of the hotels are overpriced. The ashram also has a canteen open to non-residents.

Bamboo Nest Chitravathi Rd ☎99064 34576. Delicious Tibetan *momos* (dumplings) and *thukpas* (thick noodle soups) are available at this popular and sociable haunt.

Most items under ₹150. Daily 9.30am–2pm & 4.30–9pm.
Chaitanya International Main Rd ☎08555 287265. Gaily painted an ochre-yellow, this functional concrete building has comfortable and good-value rooms and is close to all the action. ₹1000
Sai Towers Near the ashram entrance ☎0855 287270, ⊛saitowers.com/hotel. Charges a lot for its smallish fan and a/c rooms, except for some much cheaper singles, but has a good veg restaurant downstairs. ₹2500

The Andaman Islands

THE IDYLLIC HAVELOCK ISLAND

The Andaman Islands

India's most remote state, the Andaman Islands are situated more than 1000km off the east coast in the middle of the Bay of Bengal, connected to the mainland by flights and ferries from Kolkata, Chennai and Visakhapatnam. Thickly covered by deep green tropical forest, the archipelago supports a profusion of wildlife, including some extremely rare species of bird, but the principal attraction for tourists lies in the beaches and the pristine reefs that ring most of the islands. Filled with colourful fish and kaleidoscopic corals, the crystal-clear waters of the Andaman Sea feature some of the world's richest and least spoilt marine reserves – perfect for snorkelling and scuba diving. Although parts of the archipelago still see few visitors, the Andamans are now firmly on the tourist circuit.

19

For administrative purposes, the Andamans are grouped with the **Nicobar Islands**, 200km further south, which until 2018 were strictly off limits to all foreigners and most Indians. At the time of writing some were opening up but it was unclear if any paperwork was still required and there is precious little tourist infrastructure on any of them, so they are not covered here. Approximately two hundred islands make up the Andaman group and nineteen the Nicobar. They are of varying size, the summits of a submarine mountain range stretching 755km from the Arakan Yoma chain in Burma to the fringes of Sumatra in the south. All but the most remote are populated in parts by **indigenous tribes** whose numbers have been slashed dramatically as a result of nineteenth-century European settlement and, more recently, rampant **deforestation**, now banned – at least in theory.

With the timber-extraction cash cow now largely tethered, **tourism** has gradually been replacing tree-felling as the main source of revenue on the Andamans. However, the extra visitor numbers are already beginning to overtax an already inadequate infrastructure, aggravating seasonal water shortages and sewage disposal problems. Given India's track record with tourism development, it's hard to be optimistic about how these issues will be managed. Consequently, it's no small mercy that plans to allow flights from Southeast Asia and even further afield to enter India at Port Blair seem to be on permanent hold, as the impact on this culturally and ecologically fragile region could be catastrophic.

The point of arrival for boats and planes is the small but busy capital, **Port Blair** in **South Andaman**, which holds almost half the total population. The only island to have fully developed a tourist infrastructure is **Havelock**, although its smaller neighbour **Neil** is heading in the same direction; these two are the only inhabited islands of **Ritchie's Archipelago**. The other places where foreigners can spend the night are on the large islands of **Middle** and **North Andaman**, connected to South Andaman by the Andaman Trunk Road (ATR), diminutive **Long Island** and remote **Little Andaman**, a long voyage to the south.

BEST TIME TO VISIT

The Andaman Islands enjoy a consistently warm climate, rarely departing from the parameters of 22–32°C all year round, even at night, while humidity never drops below seventy percent. There is a lot of rain from May to September and they also catch the northeast monsoon in the autumn, with occasionally violent cyclones prone to hit during either period, so the ideal months to visit from a climatic perspective are December to April. Increased tourism, however, means that Diwali and the Christmas/New Year periods are busy, with prices at their peak. Not all accommodation in the more remote parts such as Little Andaman opens outside peak season.

Highlights

❶ **Wandoor** The white sandy beach and islets of the Mahatma Gandhi National Marine Park are the most popular day-trip destination from capital Port Blair, and a good appetizer for more remote parts. See page 964

❷ **Havelock** For the best diving and partying, head for Havelock, still relaxed and convivial despite being the most developed of the Andamans. See page 966

❸ **Scuba diving** The Andamans' beautiful coral reefs teem with vivid underwater life. See page 969

❹ **Long Island** This is the place to head to get an idea of what Havelock was like two decades ago and a chance to unwind in a friendly, laidback village. See page 970

❺ **North Andaman** The long haul by bus or boat from Port Blair is worthwhile for the backdrop of thick rainforest and the dazzling tropical beaches when you arrive. See page 972

❻ **Little Andaman** As very few travellers make it to the archipelago's southernmost island, you may well have the stunning forest-fringed beaches to yourself. See page 973

HIGHLIGHTS ARE MARKED ON THE MAP ON PAGE 956

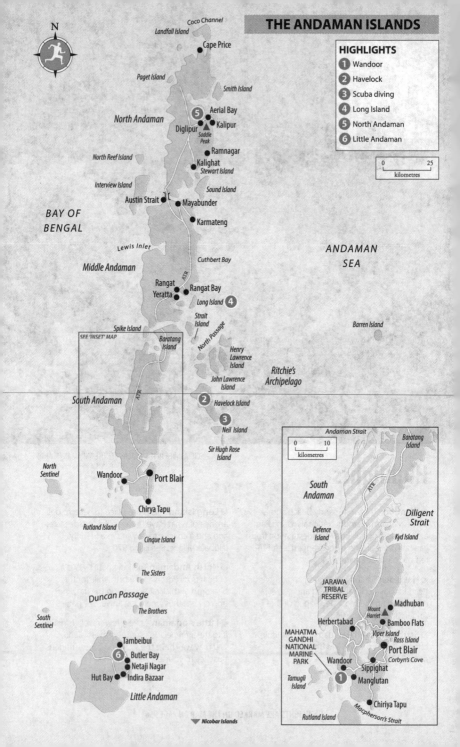

The outlying islands are richest in natural beauty, with the beaches of **Smith** and the coral around **Cinque** of particular note. Such spots are not always easy to reach, as connections and transport can be erratic, frequently uncomfortable and severely limited.

Brief history

The earliest mention of the Andaman and Nicobar islands is found in **Ptolemy's** geographical treatises of the second century AD. Other records from the Chinese Buddhist monk I'Tsing some five hundred years later and Arabian travellers who passed by in the ninth century depict the inhabitants as fierce and cannibalistic. It is unlikely, however, that the Andamanese were cannibals, as the most vivid reports of their ferocity were propagated by Malay pirates who held sway over the surrounding seas, and needed to keep looters well away from trade ships that passed between India, China and the Far East.

During the eighteenth and nineteenth centuries, **European missionaries** and trading companies turned their attention to the islands with a view to colonization. A string of unsuccessful attempts to convert the Nicobaris to Christianity was made by the French, Dutch and Danish, all of whom were forced to abandon their plans in the face of hideous diseases and a severe lack of food and water. Though the missionaries themselves seldom met with any hostility, several fleets of trading ships that tried to dock on the islands were captured and their crews murdered by Nicobari people.

In 1777, the British Lieutenant Archibald Blair chose the South Andaman harbour now known as **Port Blair** as the site for a **penal colony**, although it was not successfully established until 1858, when political activists who had fuelled the Mutiny in 1857 were made to clear land and build their own prison. Out of 773 prisoners, 292 died, escaped or were hanged in the first two months. Many also lost their lives in attacks by Andamanese tribes who objected to forest clearance, but by 1864 the number of convicts had grown to three thousand. The prison continued to confine political prisoners until 1945 and still stands as Port Blair's prime "tourist attraction" (see page 958).

During World War II the islands were occupied by the **Japanese**, who tortured and murdered hundreds of indigenous islanders suspected of collaborating with the British, and bombed the homes of the Jarawa tribe. British forces moved back in 1945, and at last abolished the penal settlement. After **Partition**, refugees – mostly low-caste Hindus from Bengal – were given land in Port Blair and North Andaman, where the forest was clear-felled to make room for rice paddy, cocoa plantations and new industries. Since 1951, the population has increased more than tenfold, further swollen by repatriated Tamils from Sri Lanka, ex-servicemen given land grants, economic migrants from poorer Indian states including thousands of Bihari labourers, and the legions of government employees packed off here on two-year "punishment postings". This replanted population greatly outnumbers the Andamans' indigenous people (see page 960), who currently comprise around 0.5 percent of the total.

INFORMATION

THE ANDAMAN ISLANDS

Health It's worth pointing out that a minority of travellers fall sick in the Andamans. The dense tree cover, marshy swamps and high rainfall combine to provide the perfect breeding ground for mosquitoes, and malaria is endemic in even the most remote settlements. Sand flies are also ferocious in certain places and tropical ulcer infections from scratching the bites are a frequent hazard.

Restricted areas In 2018 the need to obtain a 30-day restricted area permit for the Andamans was scrapped and travellers can now stay for as long as their Indian visa is valid. Tribal areas are still off limits, although some of the Nicobar Islands can now be visited.

Time Despite being so far east, the islands run on Indian time, so the sun rises as early as 4.30am in summer and darkness falls soon after 5pm.

South Andaman

South Andaman is the most heavily populated of the Andaman Islands – particularly around the capital, **Port Blair** – thanks in part to the drastic thinning of tree cover to make way for settlement. Foreign tourists can only visit its southern and east-central reaches – including the beaches at **Corbyn's Cove** and **Chiriya Tapu**, the fine reefs on the western shores at **Wandoor**, 35km southwest of Port Blair, and the environs of **Madhuban** and **Mount Harriet**, on the east coast across the bay from the capital. With your own transport it's easy to find your way along the narrow bumpy roads that connect small villages, weaving through forests and coconut fields, and skirting the swamps and rocky outcrops that form the coastline.

Port Blair

An odd combination of refreshingly scenic hills and characterless tin-roofed buildings tumbling towards the sea in the north, east and west, and petering out into fields and forests in the south, **PORT BLAIR** merits only a short stay. There's little to see here – just the **Cellular Jail** and a few small **museums** – but as it's the point of arrival for the islands and the place with the most facilities, you may well find yourself staying longer than you'd ideally want to. The hub of the town's activities and facilities is the cluster of streets known as Aberdeen Bazaar. Generally, street names are in short supply all over town, and are rarely used.

Cellular Jail

GB Pant Rd • **Jail and museum** Tues–Sun 9am–noon & 2–5pm • ₹30, camera ₹200, video ₹1000 • **Sound-and-light show** Mon, Wed & Fri 6.45pm • ₹50

Port Blair's only firm reminder of its gloomy past, the sturdy brick **Cellular Jail**, overlooks the sea from a small rise in the northeast of town. Built between 1896 and

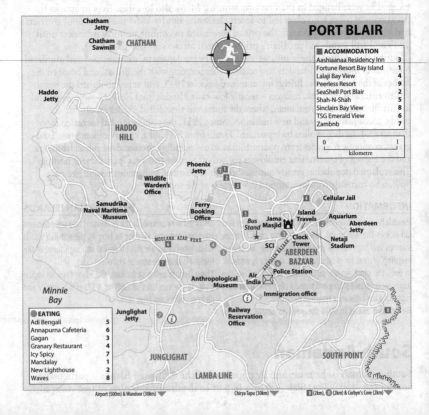

1905, its tiny solitary cells were quite different and far worse than the dormitories in other prison blocks erected earlier. Only three of the seven wings that originally radiated from the central tower now remain. Visitors can peer into the 3m by 3.5m cells and imagine the grim conditions in which the prisoners lived. Cells were dirty and poorly ventilated, drinking water was limited to two glasses per day, and the convicts were expected to wash in the rain as they worked clearing forests and building prison quarters. Food, brought from the mainland, was stored in vats where the rice and pulses became infested with worms; more than half the prison population died long before their twenty years' detention was up. Protests against conditions led to several hunger strikes, and frequent executions took place at the gallows that still stand in squat wooden shelters in the courtyards, in full view of the cells. The **sound-and-light show** outlines the history of the prison, and a small **museum** by the entrance gate exhibits lists of convicts, photographs and grim torture devices.

Anthropological Museum

MG Rd • Tues–Sun 9am–1pm & 1.30–4.30pm • ₹20, camera ₹20

On the south side of the centre, close to the Directorate of Tourism, the **Anthropological Museum** has exhibits on the Andaman and Nicobar tribes, including weapons, tools and rare photographs of the region's indigenous people taken in the 1960s. Among the most striking of these is a sequence featuring the Sentinelese, taken on April 26, 1967, when a party of Indian officials made the first contact with the tribe. After scaring the aborigines, the visitors marched into one of their hunting camps and made off with the bows, arrows and other artefacts now displayed in the museum.

19

Samudrika Naval Maritime Museum

Haddo Rd, Delanipur • Tues–Sun 9am–noon & 2–5pm • ₹50

To the northwest of town in the area known as Delanipur, the **Samudrika Naval Maritime Museum** is an excellent primer if you're heading off to more remote islands, with a superlative shell collection and informative displays on various aspects of local marine biology. One of the exhibits features a cross-section of the different corals you can expect to see on the Andamans' reefs, followed by a rundown of the various threats these fragile organisms face, from mangrove depletion and parasitic starfish to clumsy snorkellers.

ARRIVAL AND DEPARTURE   PORT BLAIR

Port Blair is the departure point for all flights and ferry crossings to the **Indian mainland**; it is also the hub of the Andamans' inter-island bus and ferry network. **Booking tickets** for boats (especially back to Chennai, Kolkata or Visakhapatnam) can be time-consuming, and many travellers are obliged to come back here well before their permit expires to make reservations before heading off to more pleasant parts of the islands again. Port Blair has an efficient computerized Southern Railways reservation office near the Secretariat (Mon–Sat 8.30am–1pm & 2–4pm) – useful for travellers intending to catch onward **trains** from their port of arrival on the mainland.

BY PLANE

Veer Savarkar airport The smart airport terminal is less than 4km south of town at Lamba Line. Taxis and auto-rickshaws are on hand for short trips into town (₹70–100), while mid- or upper-range hotels usually have shuttle buses to collect guests. Local buses also frequently ply the route to town from outside the shop on the far side of the main road, barely 100m from the terminal building.

To and from the mainland Port Blair is currently served by flights from Chennai (5–6 daily; 2hr 10min–2hr 20min), Delhi (4 weekly; 3hr 45min), Kolkata (6 daily; 2hr 15min), Mumbai (1 daily; 3hr 25min) and Visakhapatnam (5 weekly; 2hr). Flights at peak times like Diwali, Christmas and New Year through to February can be heavily subscribed, so book early. These periods also see prices soar as high as ₹20,000 one way; at other times they can be as low as ₹5000. The Air India office (☎03192 233108) is diagonally opposite the tourist office. SpiceJet and Go Air can only be booked online or through travel agents such as the efficient Island Travels (Mon–Sat 9am–6pm; ☎03192 233034, ⊛islandtravelsandaman. com), between the clock tower and marina.

Inter-island services There is an inexpensive (₹2500–4000) helicopter service connecting Port Blair with Havelock, Diglipur and Little Andaman but tourists can only book tickets one day in advance and seats are often taken up by officials. Flights are also prone to cancellation due to bad weather and there is a 6kg baggage limit. Contact the Secretariat in Port Blair to check (☎03192 230093).

19

BY BOAT

Jetties Port Blair has two main jetties: boats from the mainland moor at Haddo Jetty, nearly 2km northwest of Phoenix Jetty, arrival point for inter-island ferries. The Director of Shipping Services (DSS; ☎03192 245555) at Phoenix Jetty has the latest information on boats and ferries, but you can also check details of forthcoming departures in the shipping news column of the local newspaper, the *Daily Telegrams*. Boats can get cramped and uncomfortable, sometimes lacking shade outside and space inside; take adequate supplies of food and water, as minimal sustenance is sold on board.

To and from the mainland Services to and from Chennai (see page 980) can be relied upon to leave in each direction once every week to ten days, while those to and from Kolkata (see page 767) sail roughly every two weeks; boats to and from Visakhapatnam are altogether more erratic, averaging once a month in each direction – call the Shipping Office there on ☎0891 256 5597 for more information. Although much cheaper than flying (from ₹2500), sea crossings are long (3–5 days), uncomfortable and often delayed by bad conditions. Tickets for all three mainland ports (Chennai, Kolkata and Visakhapatnam) are handled by the DSS and go on sale a week in advance of departure at the allotted booths within the Computerized Reservation Centre (Mon–Fri 9am–1pm & 2–4pm, Sat 9am–noon) at Phoenix Jetty. When they do go on sale, it's wise to be there to join the fray ahead of time. Make sure you get a ticket before your permit expires, as you will need to show it to get the fifteen-day extension (see page 957).

Inter-island services Most of the islands open to foreign tourists are accessible by government-run boats from Phoenix Jetty. Details of sailings to and from Port Blair for the following two to five days are posted in the

---

NATIVE PEOPLE OF THE ANDAMAN AND NICOBAR ISLANDS

Quite where the **indigenous population** of the Andaman and Nicobar islands originally came from is a puzzle that has preoccupied anthropologists since Alfred Radcliffe-Brown conducted his famous fieldwork among the Andamanese at the beginning of the twentieth century. Asian-looking groups such as the Shompen may have migrated here from the east and north when the islands were connected to Burma, or the sea was sufficiently shallow to allow transport by canoe, but this doesn't explain the origins of the black populations, whose appearance suggests African roots.

The survival of the islands' first inhabitants has long been threatened by traders and colonizers, who introduced disease and destroyed their territories through widespread tree-felling. Thousands also died from addiction to the alcohol and opium that the Chinese, Japanese and British exchanged for valuable shells. Many have had their populations decimated, while others like the Nicobarese have assimilated to modern culture, often adopting Christianity. The indigenous inhabitants of the Andamans, divided into *eramtaga* (those living in the jungle) and *ar-yuato* (those living on the coast), traditionally subsisted as hunter-gatherers, living on fish, turtles, turtle eggs, pigs, fruit, honey and roots. For more information on the islands' original inhabitants, visit Survival International's website, ⓦ survival-international.org.

THE GREAT ANDAMANESE

Although they comprised the largest group when the islands were first colonized, only around fifty **Great Andamanese** now survive. In the 1860s, the Rev Henry Corbyn set up a "home" for the tribe to learn English on Ross Island, insisting that they wear clothes and attend reading and writing classes. Five children and three adults from Corbyn's school were taken to Calcutta in 1864, where they were shown around the sights but treated more as curiosities themselves. Within three years, almost the entire population had died, victims of either introduced diseases or addiction. In recent years the surviving Great Andamanese were forcibly settled on Strait Island, north of South Andaman, as a "breeding centre", where they were forced to rely on the Indian authorities for food and shelter. Sadly, the last speaker of Bo, one of the oldest Andamanese languages, died in 2010.

THE JARAWAS

The **Jarawas**, who were shifted from their original homes when land was cleared to build Port Blair, currently number around three hundred and live on the remote western coasts of Middle and South Andaman. They are hemmed in by the Andaman Trunk Road (ATR), which since the 1970s has cut them off from hunting grounds and freshwater supplies. During the 1980s and 1990s, encroachments on their land by loggers, road builders and settlers met with fierce

Daily Telegrams newspaper. More details of boat services between destinations outside the capital appear in the relevant accounts of this guide. The only way to guarantee a passage is to book tickets in advance at the Inter-Island booths in the Computerized Reservation Centre at Phoenix Jetty, though any unsold tickets are issued prior to departure on the quay. You can avoid these scrums by paying an agent such as Island Travels to get a ticket for you. Fares are still reasonable, even allowing for the two-tier pricing system for islanders and non-islanders: Havelock, for example, costs ₹850, Little Andaman just ₹500. Havelock and Neil also have a smart private catamaran service, the *Makruzz* (1–2 daily; 2hr; from ₹1400; ⊛makruzz.com), as well as two upmarket private *Green Ocean* ferries (1 daily; 2hr 30min; from ₹1050; ⊛greenoceancruise.com).

Destinations Aerial Bay on North Andaman (3 weekly; 8–9hr); Havelock (3–4 daily; 2hr–3hr 30min); Hut Bay on Little Andaman (5–6 weekly; 6–9hr); Long Island (4 weekly; 5–6hr); Neil (2–3 daily; 2hr); Rangat on Middle Andaman (4 weekly; 6–7hr).

BY BUS
Buses connect Port Blair with most of the major settlements on Middle and North Andaman via the Andaman Trunk Road. From the bus stand in the centre of town, there are government services to Rangat (3 daily; 6hr), Mayabunder (2 daily; 9hr) and Diglipur (2 daily; 11hr). Several private companies, including Ananda (☎03192 233252), who have an office near the bus stand, run deluxe or video coach services to the same destinations; these leave from outside the bus stand between 5am and 10am. Tickets for both categories of service are cheap at ₹200–400.

19

resistance, and dozens, possibly hundreds, of people died in **skirmishes**, mostly on or near the ATR. Some more amicable **contact** between settlers and tribals was subsequently made through gift exchanges at each full moon, although the initiative was later cancelled. These meetings nevertheless led to some Jarawas becoming curious about what "civilization" had to offer, and they started to hold their hands out to passing vehicles and even visiting Indian settlements near their territory. Despite the authorities trying to minimize contact, it is still common for Jarawas to approach buses, and some private vehicles ignore the rules and stop for photo shoots. The government has increased Jarawa land by 180 square kilometres, but lodged an ongoing appeal over a 2002 Indian Supreme Court order to close the ATR – a ruling made following protests by international pressure groups such as Survival International. A disturbing legal reversal made early in 2013 has also once again allowed "human safaris" to take place.

THE ONGE

Relations with the **Onge**, who call themselves the **Gaubolambe**, have been relatively peaceful. Distinguished by their white-clay and ochre body paint, they continue to live in communal shelters and construct temporary thatched huts on Little Andaman. The remaining population of just under one hundred retain their traditional way of life on two small reserves. Contact with outsiders is limited to an occasional trip into town to purchase liquor, and visits from rare parties of anthropologists. The reserves are strictly off-limits to foreigners, but you can learn about the Onge's traditional hunting practices, beliefs and rituals in Vishvajit Pandya's wonderful ethnographic study, *Above the Forest*.

THE NICOBARESE AND OTHER TRIBES

On the Nicobars, the most assimilated and numerous tribe, the **Nicobarese**, are of Mongoloid descent and number well over twenty thousand. They live in villages, ruled by a headman, and have largely cordial relations with the Indian settlers. By contrast, only very limited contact is ever had with the isolated **Shompen** tribe of Great Nicobar, whose population of around four hundred manage to lead a traditional hunting-and-gathering existence. The most elusive tribe of all, the **Sentinelese**, live on North Sentinel Island west of South Andaman. Following the first encounter with Indian settlers in 1967, some contact was made with them in 1990, after a team put together by the local administration left gifts on the beaches every month for two years, but subsequent visits have invariably ended in a hail of arrows and a self-appointed American missionary made the news by getting killed after landing there in late 2018. Since the early 1990s, the authorities have effectively given up trying to contact the Sentinelese, who are estimated to number around one hundred. Flying in or out of Port Blair, you pass above their island, ringed by a spectacular coral reef. It's reassuring to think that the people sitting at the bottom of the plumes of smoke drifting up from the forest canopy still manage to resist contact with the outside world.

19

GETTING AROUND

By taxi and auto-rickshaw Taxis gather opposite the bus stand in central Port Blair. They all have meters and there's a prepaid booth, but negotiating the price before leaving is the usual practice. Expect to pay at least ₹140 for a trip from the centre of town to Corbyn's Cove; auto-rickshaws try to charge just as much as taxis but a ride within town shouldn't cost more than ₹60.

By bus Local buses run from the bus stand frequently to Wandoor (hourly) and less so to Chiriya Tapu (every 2hr), so they can be used for day-trips.

By motorbike It's pleasant to rent a motorbike or scooter but there are few outlets – try Green Island Tours & Travels (☎03192 230226), near the clock tower in Aberdeen Bazaar. The only petrol pumps are on the crossroads west of the bus stand and on the airport road.

INFORMATION AND TOURS

Tourist information The counter at the airport (☎03192 232414) hands out a useful general brochure, but trying to get more than basic tour and hotel information from the main A&N Directorate of Tourism office (Mon–Sat 8am–8pm; ☎03192 232747, ⚑andamantourism.gov. in), situated on a hill south of Aberdeen Bazaar, can be frustrating. Further southwest on Junglighat Main Rd, the Incredible India office (Mon–Fri 8.30am–5pm; ☎03192 233006, ⚑incredibleindia.org) is not much better.

Permits If you intend to visit Interview Island (see page 971), you must first obtain a free permit from the Chief Wildlife Warden, whose office (☎03192 233270) is next to the zoo in Haddo.

Hospital The main hospital for the whole archipelago is GB Pant Hospital on GB Pant Rd (☎03192 232102).

Services It's wise to stock up on rupees in Port Blair as the banks and agencies here are the only places on the islands officially allowed to exchange cash. There are several ATMs dotted around the town (and now a couple on Havelock too).

Tours A couple of smart private tourist boats such as the MV *Mark Marina* (☎96795 38188) conduct various harbour cruises (2–7hr; ₹300–1200) from Phoenix Jetty around the harbour, taking in North Bay, Viper and Ross islands (see opposite).

ACCOMMODATION

Port Blair boasts numerous places to stay in most budget ranges. The abundance of options means availability is only an issue around Christmas and New Year, when prices are also hiked; they drop during the monsoon season.

Aashiaanaa Residency Inn Marine Hill ☎94742 17008, ✉shads_maria@hotmail.com; map p.958. An attractive ochre-coloured building, very conveniently located for Phoenix Jetty. There is a selection of decent-sized, mostly attached rooms, some with balconies. ₹50/hr. **₹600/₹750**

Fortune Resort Bay Island Marine Hill ☎03192 234101, ⚑fortunehotels.in; map p.958. Port Blair's swishest hotel is elegant and airy with polished dark wood. All rooms have carpets and balconies overlooking Phoenix Jetty. There's a good restaurant, gardens and an open-air seawater swimming pool. Check for online deals. **₹12,500**

★ **Lalaji Bay View** RP Rd ☎03192 230551, ⚑lalaji bayview.com; map p.958. Popular budget guesthouse on a bayside hill above Aberdeen Bazaar, which offers good-value attached rooms, the cheapest ones windowless. It also has a good sociable rooftop restaurant that serves beer, but service is slow. ₹50/hr. **₹900**

Peerless Resort Corbyn's Cove ☎03192 229263, ⚑peerless hotels.co.in; map p.958. The setting is lovely, with a white-sand beach opposite, and gardens of palms, jasmine and bougainvillea, but the balconied a/c rooms and cottages are a bit tatty for the prices they charge. There's a bar and mid-priced restaurant with an average evening buffet. **₹5750**

★ **SeaShell Port Blair** Marine Hill ☎03192 242773, ⚑seashellhotels.net; map p.958. Excellent modern hotel, suitable for business travellers and tourists alike. Spacious, beautifully furnished and decorated rooms with great showers and flat-screen TVs. The more expensive rooms have balconies overlooking the sea. **₹9000**

Shah-N-Shah Mohanpura ☎03192 233696, ✉apsara tours786@yahoo.com; map p.958. Conveniently located between the bus stand and Phoenix Jetty, this is very basic but friendly, with mostly attached rooms and a travel agent. Cheap single occupancy. No wi-fi. **₹500/₹700**

Sinclairs Bay View On the coast road to Corbyn's Cove ☎03192 227824, ⚑sinclairshotels.com; map p.958. Clifftop hotel offering spotless carpeted rooms with balconies, large bathrooms and dramatic views, as well as a much-improved restaurant. **₹8500**

TSG Emerald View 25 Moulana Azad Rd ☎03192 246488, ⚑tsghotelsandresorts.com; map p.958. Smart mid-range place with a sparkling new lobby and spacious, colourfully furnished a/c rooms, boasting all mod cons. Also has a decent restaurant. **₹5700**

Zambnb Prem Nagar ☎99320 89772, ⚑zambnb.com; map p.958. Handy for the airport or Phoenix Jetty, this smart modern place has spacious and colourfully-decorated rooms. Breakfast included. **₹2499**

EATING

★ **Adi Bengali** Moulana Azad Rd ☎99332 50583; map p.958. Simple but sparkling clean place serving tasty

Bengali dishes such as fish masala, a snip at ₹100. Also offers chicken and a range of veg dishes. Daily 7am–10pm.

Annapurna Cafeteria Aberdeen Bazaar, towards the post office ☎03192 234199; map p.958. Port Blair's best south-Indian joint, serving a range of huge crispy dosas, plus north Indian and Chinese meals, delicious coffee and wonderful *pongal* at breakfast. The lunchtime thalis are also good. Mains ₹80–175. Mon–Sat 6.30–10.30am & 3.30–10.30pm.

Gagan Aberdeen Bazaar, opposite the clock tower ☎03192 212140; map p.958. Simple canteen with a decent range of north and south Indian veg and non-veg dishes for around ₹80–200, including tasty fried fish. Daily 7am–10pm.

Granary Restaurant Islanderr Inn, Moulana Azad Rd ☎03192 234234; map p.958. Colourful ground-floor restaurant in a modern hotel, serving a standard range of Indian and Chinese food for ₹120–240 and a ₹450 evening buffet. Daily 8am–3pm & 6–10pm.

Icy Spicy Island Arcade, Junglighat ☎03192 232704, ⓦicyspicy.in; map p.958. Gleaming modern basement dining hall, which serves a range of tasty fast food (mostly ₹100–250), such as *chaat*, as well as South Indian favourites and pizza. Daily 11am–10pm.

Mandalay Fortune Resort, Marine Hill ☎03192 234101; map p.958. À la carte main courses (₹300–500) or, when demand allows, a reasonable dinner buffet for around ₹750, can be enjoyed in the airy open restaurant with great bay views. Service can be a bit lax for its class. The adjacent *Nico Bar* is a decent bet for a drink. Daily noon–10.30pm.

★ **New Lighthouse** Near Aberdeen Jetty ☎03192 237356; map p.958. Popular place with outdoor seating and an airy rooftop, where you can catch the sea breeze while feasting on some of the cheapest lobster and other seafood (₹180–400) in the Andamans. Daily 11am–10.30pm.

Waves Peerless Resort, Corbyn's Cove ☎03192 229263; map p.958. Rather pricey but very congenial alfresco hotel restaurant under a shady palm grove, and one of the few places in town you can order a beer with your meal. Most dishes ₹300–600. Daily 11am–11pm.

19

Around Port Blair

At some point, you're almost certain to find yourself killing time in Port Blair, waiting for boats to show up or tickets to go on sale. Rather than wasting days in town, it's worth exploring the **coast** of South Andaman which, although far more densely populated than other islands in the archipelago, holds a handful of easily accessible beauty spots and historic sites. Among the latter, the ruined colonial monuments on **Viper** and **Ross islands** can be reached on daily harbour cruises or regular ferries from the capital (see opposite). For **beaches**, head to nearby **Corbyn's Cove**, or cross South Andaman to reach the more pleasingly secluded **Chiriya Tapu**, which is easily accessible on a day-trip if you rent a motorbike or scooter, and is the jumping-off point for Cinque. By far the most rewarding way to spend a day out of town, however, is to catch the tourist boat from **Wandoor** to **Jolly Buoy** or **Red Skin islands** in the **Mahatma Gandhi National Marine Park** opposite, which boasts some of the Andamans' best snorkelling. The other area worth visiting is **Mount Harriet** and **Madhuban** on the central part of South Andaman, north across the bay from Port Blair.

Viper Island

First stop on the harbour cruises from Port Blair is generally **Viper Island**, named not after the many snakes that doubtless inhabit its tangled tropical undergrowth, but a nineteenth-century merchant vessel that ran aground on it during the early years of the colony. Lying a short way off Haddo Jetty, it served as an isolation zone for the main prison, where escapees and other convicts were sent to be punished. Whipping posts and crumbling walls, reached from the jetty via a winding brick path, remain as relics of a torture area, while occupying the site's most prominent position are the original gallows.

Ross Island

₹20 • Several daily boats from Phoenix Jetty (see page 960) • **Sound-and-light show**, including government boat 4.15pm, returns 7.15pm; ₹250

Eerie decaying colonial remains are to be found on **Ross Island**, at the entrance to Port Blair harbour, where the British sited their first penal settlement in the Andamans. Originally cleared by convicts wearing iron fetters, Ross witnessed some of the most brutal excesses of British colonial history, and was the source of the prison's infamy as **Kalapani**, or Black

> ### A WALK ON THE WET SIDE
>
> One new activity that has started up in recent years is **sea walking** at North Bay. In this rather peculiar piece of fun, people are fitted into a large and rather unwieldy space-type helmet, which is connected to a non-pressurized oxygen source on the surface, and lowered down for a stroll around the seabed at a depth of five to eight metres. A sea walk of up to twenty minutes costs from ₹3500 and can be organized through Sea Link Adventures at 43 MA Rd, Phoenix Bay (☎96795 78661, ⓦsealinkadventures.com).

Water. Of the many convicts transported here, distinguished by their branded foreheads, the majority perished from disease or torture before the clearance of the island was completed in 1860. Thereafter, it served briefly as the site of Rev Henry Corbyn's **Andaman Home** – a prison camp created with the intention of "civilizing" the local tribespeople – and then the headquarters of the revamped penal colony before the British were forced to evacuate by the Japanese entry into World War II. Little more than the hilltop **Anglican church**, with its weed-infested graveyard, has survived the onslaught of tropical creepers and vines. There is a sound-and-light show every evening, but only in Hindi.

Corbyn's Cove

The best beach within easy reach of the capital lies 6km southeast, at **Corbyn's Cove**, a small arc of smooth white sand backed by a swaying curtain of palms. There's a large hotel here, *Peerless Resort* (see page 962), but the water isn't particularly clear, and bear in mind that lying around scantily-clothed may bring you considerable attention from crowds of local workers.

Chiriya Tapu

For a little isolation, take a bus 30km south of Port Blair to **Chiriya Tapu** ("Bird Island"), at the tip of South Andaman. The walkable track running beyond this small fishing village leads through thick jungle overhung with twisting creepers to a large bay, where swamps give way to shell-strewn beaches. Other than at lunchtime, when it often receives a deluge of bus parties, the beach offers plenty of peace and quiet, forest walks on the woodcutters' trails winding inland and easy access to an inshore reef. However, the water here is nowhere near as clear as at outlying spots in the archipelago.

Cinque Island

Cinque, two hours south of Chiriya Tapu, actually comprises two islets, joined by a spectacular sand isthmus with shallow water either side that covers it completely at high tide. The main incentive to come here is the superb diving and snorkelling around the reefs. However, heaps of dead coral on the beach attest to damage wreaked by the Indian navy during the construction of the swish "cottages" overlooking the beach. Rumour has it that these were built for the visit of a Thai VIP in 1996, but local government officials now use them as bolt holes from Port Blair.

Although there are no **ferries** to Cinque, it is possible to charter a dinghy and boatman for around ₹3000 per day from Chiriya Tapu. Foreigners are not allowed to stay the night.

Wandoor

Much the most popular excursion from Port Blair is to **WANDOOR**, 30km southwest. The long white **beach** here is littered with the dry, twisted trunks of trees torn up and flung down by annual cyclones. It's fringed not with palms but with dense forest teeming with birdlife. You should only snorkel here at high tide, as the coral is easily damaged when the waters are shallow.

ACCOMMODATION   **WANDOOR**

Sea Princess Beach Resort 500m back from the car park ☎03192 280002, ⓦseaprincessandaman.com. This smart resort, set in nicely landscaped grounds, offers luxury cottages, rooms and suites. The restaurant is also very pleasant. ₹7499 **Wandoor Paradise Resort** On the beach ☎ 94342 72135.

The only budget option in Wandoor are the two ramshackle huts here, though the seaside location is made less idyllic because the restaurant is mainly a drinking den. No wi-fi. ₹600

The Mahatma Gandhi National Marine Park

Park entry ₹500 (₹50), camera ₹25 • Boats from Wandoor Tues–Sun 10am; ₹500

Most people take a cruise around the fifteen islets comprising the **Mahatma Gandhi National Marine Park**, which boasts one of the richest coral reefs in the region. From the jetty at Wandoor, the boats chug through broad creeks lined with dense mangrove swamps and pristine forest to either **Red Skin Island** or, more commonly, **Jolly Buoy**. The latter, an idyllic deserted island, boasts an immaculate shell-sand beach ringed by a bank of superb coral. The catch is that the boat only stops for around an hour, which isn't nearly enough time to explore the shore and reef. While snorkelling off the edges of the reef, beware of **strong currents**.

Mount Harriet and Madhuban

Park entry ₹250 (₹25) • Passenger ferries from Chatham Jetty every 30min, vehicle ferries from Phoenix Jetty 8 daily

The richly forested slopes of **Mount Harriet** make for some decent exercise and can easily be visited on a day-trip from Port Blair. From the ferry landing at **Bamboo Flats**, it's a pleasant 7km stroll east along the coast and north up a path through trees hung with thick vines and creepers to the 365m summit, which affords fine views back across the bay. An intermittent bus service runs between Bamboo Flats and Hope Town, where the uphill path starts, and saves you the 3km coastal stretch. Alternatively, jeeps and taxis are available to take you all the way to the top, but they charge at least ₹500. The Mount Harriet National Park checkpoint is on the road so you probably won't be asked if you take the path. It's 2.5km from the checkpoint up to the resthouse and viewing tower at the summit. If you have strong legs, you can reach the small settlement of **Madhuban** on the coast northeast of the mountain by the 16km round route via Kala Patthar (Black Rock) and back via the coast. There is a decent beach at Madhuban but not much else.

Neil

Tiny, triangular-shaped **Neil** is the most southerly inhabited island of **Ritchie's Archipelago**, barely two hours northeast of Port Blair on a fast ferry. The source of much of the capital's fresh fruit and vegetables, its fertile centre, ringed by a curtain of stately tropical trees, comprises vivid patches of green paddy dotted with small farmsteads and banana plantations. The beaches are mediocre by the Andamans' standards but worth a day or two en route to or from Havelock and, as it is far less developed with little more than ten accommodation options, some visitors prefer it to its busier neighbour for more extended stays.

Neil boasts five **beaches**, all of them within easy cycling distance of the small bazaar just up the lane from the jetty. The best place to swim is **Neil Kendra**, a gently curving bay of white sand on the north coast which straddles the jetty and is scattered with picturesque wooden fishing boats. This blends into **Bharatpur** to the east and **Lakshmanpur**, which continues for nearly 3km west: to get to Lakshmanpur by road, head right when the road from the jetty meets the bazaar and follow it for around twenty minutes until it dwindles into a surfaced track, then take a right. Wrapped around the headland, the beach is a broad spur of white-shell sand, with shallow water offering good snorkelling, although footing is difficult when entering the water at any time other than high tide.

Exposed to the open sea and thus prone to higher tides, **Sitapur** beach, 6km southeast of Neil Kendra, is also appealing and has the advantage of a sandy bottom extending into the sea. The ride there across Neil's central paddy land is pleasant, but there are no facilities beyond the two new guesthouses on intermediate **Ram Nagar** beach.

19

ARRIVAL AND DEPARTURE

By boat Neil is well connected with Havelock (2–4 daily; 1hr 30min) and Port Blair (2–4 daily; 2hr), plus there are

NEIL

four weekly ferries to Long Island (4hr 30min) and Rangat (5hr 30min–6hr).

GETTING AROUND

By bus An hourly bus runs between the bazaar and Sitapur. You can also rent bicycles (₹60/day) or mopeds (₹300/day)

at guesthouses or stalls in the market.

ACCOMMODATION

A-N-D Beach Resort 250m east of the jetty, Neil Kendra ☎ 96795 25789. Tucked along the path behind the beach, this welcoming place has some very cheap huts with common bathrooms and a few attached ones, as well as a decent restaurant. No wi-fi. **₹400/₹600**

Breakwater Ram Nagar ☎ 95318 52332. Ever-expanding group of mostly attached bamboo huts, plus some larger concrete rooms, arranged around a patch of open land behind the beach. The restaurant does good food and is a sociable gathering place. No wi-fi. **₹400/₹700**

★ **Emerald Gecko** Sitapur ☎ 95318 61054, ⊛ emerald-gecko.com. Great newish offshoot of the Havelock favourite, with large and sturdy bungalow-style and two-storey bamboo huts, plus a sociable and fine-quality restaurant. No wi-fi. **₹2650**

Kalapani Ram Nagar ☎ 94742 74991. Though not quite as appealing as those at nearby *Breakwater*, the huts here are perfectly habitable and some of them have shared facilities. Free cooking lessons. No wi-fi. **₹300/₹600**

SeaShell Lakshmanpur ☎ 03192 242773, ⊛ seashell hotels.net. The latest venture from the *SeaShell* group is by far Neil's most upmarket resort, with superbly furnished thatched cottages set in lush landscaped gardens. Look for online deals in advance. Breakfast included. **₹10,500**

★ **Tango Beach Resort** Lakshmanpur ☎ 03192 282634, ⊛ tangobeachandaman.com. This friendly place right on the beach offers a range of accommodation from small non-attached bamboo huts to larger ones with verandas and the pricey Lagoon suites. It also has a new rooftop restaurant. No wi-fi. **₹600/₹1000**

EATING

Blue Sea Ram Nagar beach ☎ 94760 13330. This joint just back from the beach offers keenly priced seafood, plus pasta, Indian dishes and filling sizzlers for around ₹100–300. Daily 8.30am–11pm.

Chand Restaurant In the bazaar ☎ 94742 22395. Small *dhaba*-style establishment, which serves up tasty, albeit somewhat oily, food. It's mostly Indian, with a range of thalis, including fish, for under ₹200, plus some Western dishes. Daily 6am–10.30pm.

Garden View Near Sitapur ☎ 99332 21552. Friendly family restaurant in a field just beside the main road, which does fresh fish curry for ₹175, as well as a lot of veggie and some chicken dishes. Daily 7am–10pm.

★ **Gyan Garden** 400m west of the bazaar ☎ 99332 93078. Far and away the best place to eat, this delightful and welcoming garden restaurant cooks fresh fish (₹160–250) and home-grown veg dishes are also a speciality. Daily 8am–10pm.

Havelock

Havelock is the largest island in Ritchie's Archipelago, and the most intensively cultivated, settled – like many in the region – by Bengali refugees after Partition. Thanks to its regular ferry connections with the capital, it is also visited in far greater numbers than anywhere else in the Andamans. In peak season, several thousand tourists can be holed up here at one time, with hordes of well-heeled Indians now greatly outnumbering the traditional foreign backpacker crowd. This has led to an explosion in upmarket accommodation and mostly Kashmiri-owned tourist shops.

The east coast

Havelock's hub of activity is not **Jetty village**, which just has a few stalls, a couple of dowdy lodges, the odd restaurant and the police station, but the **Main Bazaar**, which you come to if you follow the road straight ahead from the jetty for 2km, passing Beach #2 on the way. Here you'll find a greater variety of shops and places to eat, the only bank and the island's main junction.

If you take the left turn through the busier strip of Main Bazaar, the road leads on past **beaches #3 and #5**, where most of the beach huts and resorts are located. As on Neil's north coast, these east-facing beaches, though exquisitely scenic, have fairly thin strips of golden-white sand, and when the sea recedes across the lumps of broken coral and rock lying offshore, swimming becomes all but impossible. After Beach #5 the road continues south for several kilometres before turning slightly inland and eventually petering out at **Kalapathar** beach. The entire southern half of Havelock consists of impenetrable forest.

The west coast

The right turn from the island's main junction leads 9km through paddy fields and other crops before dropping through some spectacular woodland to **Radhnagar** (Beach #7), a 2km arc of perfect white sand, backed by stands of giant *mowhar* trees and often touted as the most beautiful in India. The water is a sublime turquoise colour and, although the coral is sparse, marine life here is diverse and plentiful, especially among the rocks around the corner from the main beach (accessible at low tide). The main drawback, which can make sunbathing uncomfortable, is a preponderance of pesky sand flies. Another hazard, around the lagoon at the far northern end, is saltwater **crocodiles**.

As the nesting site for a colony of olive ridley **turtles** (see page 912), Radhnagar is strictly protected by the Forest Department, whose wardens ensure tourists don't light fires or sleep on the beach. There's not much accommodation here, but a clutch of *dhabas* provides ample sustenance for day-trippers.

A couple of kilometres before the road descends to Radhnagar, a path on the right leads over a hill and down through some scattered settlements to far wilder **Elephant Beach**, although the only trunks you are likely to spot are those of huge fallen trees. Snorkelling here is good, and coral reefs are accessible from the shore, but it can be tough to find the way; look out for the start of the path at a sharp bend in the road with a Forest Department noticeboard and then keep asking the way whenever you see a local.

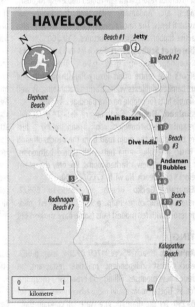

ARRIVAL AND INFORMATION
HAVELOCK

By boat Havelock's main jetty is on the north side of the island, at the village known as Beach #1. If you've booked accommodation in advance, most places arrange a pick-up.

Destinations Ferries: Long Island (4 weekly; 4hr–4hr 30min); Neil (2–4 daily; 1hr 30min); Port Blair (3–5 daily; 2hr–3hr 30min); Rangat (4 weekly; 5hr–5hr 30min). There are also one or two daily *Makruzz* catamaran sailings for Port Blair.

■ ACCOMMODATION		● EATING	
Barefoot at Havelock	5	Anju-coco	4
Barefoot Scuba Resort	3	Barefoot Bayside Brasserie	1
Dreamland Resort	7	Blackbeard's Bistro	7
Emerald Gecko	8	Café del Mar	2
The Flying Elephant	9	Fat Martin	5
Green Valley	4	Full Moon Café	3
SeaShell Havelock	1	Nala's Kingdom	1/8
Sea View	2	Red Snapper	6
Wild Orchid	6		
		■ DRINKING & NIGHTLIFE	
		Cicada	1

19

19

Tourist information When staffed, the small tourist office just outside the jetty gates is moderately helpful (daily 8am–5pm; ☎ 94742 22245).

Services The only place to change money is the State Co-operative Bank (Mon–Fri 9am–1pm, Sat 9–11am), at the Main Bazaar, 2km inland of the main jetty, although there are now two ATMs en route. Numerous places now offer satellite internet connections, but charge as much as ₹300/hr.

GETTING AROUND

By bus From the jetty buses run hourly from 6.30am to Radhnagar (aka Beach #7), the last returning at 6pm. Another service runs several times daily to Kalapathar, passing down the east coast, where the bulk of the accommodation is located.

By bike You can rent a scooter, motorbike (around ₹400/day) or cycle (₹60/day) at the guesthouses.

ACCOMMODATION

With the only fully developed tourist scene in the Andamans, Havelock now has over a hundred accommodation establishments to choose from, although the number of basic beach huts has dwindled in favour of luxuriously-furnished cottages to satisfy the domestic tourists. Prices can rise by 50 percent from mid-December to mid-January, and drop considerably between May and October.

Barefoot at Havelock Radhnagar ☎ 03192 220191, ⊛ barefoot-andaman.com; map p.967. Havelock's most luxurious resort, with fan-cooled duplexes, "Nicobari" cottages, a/c "Andaman" villas and top-quality a/c Rajasthani tents. The fine restaurant and bar area are also attractive timber-and-thatch structures. ₹10,500

★ **Barefoot Scuba Resort** Beach #3 ☎ 03192 282343, ⊛ diveandamans.com; map p.967. The home of Barefoot's dive centre offers luxury Rajasthani tents and smart bamboo duplexes with attached bathrooms, as well as humble huts for people on dive packages. ₹4500

Dreamland Resort Radhnagar ☎ 94742 24164, ⊛ dreamlandresorthavelock.com; map p.967. Just 200m back along the main road from the beach, offering ten basic, pale blue raffia huts with shared bathrooms, plus some smart new attached rooms. The only cheapie at Havelock's best beach. No wi-fi. ₹700/₹1500

★ **Emerald Gecko** Beach #5 ☎ 95318 60527, ⊛ emerald-gecko.com; map p.967. The nicest mid-range resort, with ten modest huts (some have showers but share toilets) and half a dozen superbly designed two-tier cottages. Breakfast included. No wi-fi. ₹1650/₹2650

The Flying Elephant Kalapathar ☎ 95318 61903, ⊛ flying-elephant.in; map p.967. The most remote place to stay on the island, with five spacious duplexes and four huge bungalows, connected by an elevated boardwalk, plus a yoga room. There's a restaurant on the opposite side of the road. No wi-fi. ₹3300

Green Valley Beach #5 ☎ 94760 02984, ⊛ greenvalleyhavelock.in; map p.967. Now only consisting of sturdy plywood huts with comfy furnishings. All are rather overpriced, especially the non a/c ones. ₹2950

SeaShell Havelock Beach #2 ☎ 03192 211830, ⊛ seashellhotels.net; map p.967. Arranged around a manicured lawn barely 1km from the jetty, there are five types of a/c lodgings from traditional villas to chalets, which offer all mod cons including flat screen TVs. ₹9500

Sea View Beach #3 ☎ 94342 98979; map p.967. Very simple but spacious eco-friendly bamboo huts, all with attached bathrooms and mosquito nets. The restaurant does decent, mostly Indian food. No wi-fi. ₹600

★ **Wild Orchid** Beach #5 ☎ 95318 35655, ⊛ wildorchidandaman.com; map p.967. Easily the best value higher-end resort, for its classy cottages (some with a/c), splendidly constructed timber restaurant and lounge, and all-round laidback atmosphere. Breakfast included. No wi-fi. ₹7499

EATING

★ **Anju-coco** Beach #5 ☎ 94760 07284; map p.967. Havelock's best independent roadside restaurant, in expanded new premises. Filling ₹50 breakfasts, cheap fish and chips, Tibetan momos and more adventurous dishes for ₹200–250. Try the dramatic Fire Waterfall cocktail. Daily 8am–10.30pm.

Barefoot Bayside Brasserie Main jetty ☎ 94742 24212; map p.967. Smart upper-storey wooden deck with film posters and expensive food. Most mains around ₹300 and seafood sizzlers up to ₹800. Inexpensive lunchtime thalis served downstairs. Daily 11am–4.30pm & 6–10pm.

Blackbeard's Bistro Emerald Gecko, Beach #5 ☎ 03192 206084; map p.967. The lovely open dining area has a bar and furniture created from recycled timber, and often offers rare dishes such as ceviche as well as fresh fish cooked in delicious and imaginative sauces for ₹350–400. Daily 7–10.30am, noon–2pm & 6–9.30pm.

Café del Mar Barefoot Scuba Resort, Beach #3 ☎ 03192 282343; map p.967. Convivial joint serving Indian, Chinese and Western dishes. Excellent meat and seafood specials for ₹200–300. Daily 6.30am–9pm.

Fat Martin At Andaman Bubbles Beach #5 ☎ 94760 71965; map p.967. Gradually expanding around the dive shop, this place rustles up superb masala dosas for ₹90, as well as main courses ranging from ₹150–400. Daily 7am–8pm.

SCUBA DIVING IN THE ANDAMAN ISLANDS

The seas around the Andaman Islands are some of the world's most unspoiled. Marine life is abundant, with an estimated 750 species of fish existing on one reef alone, and parrot, trigger and angel fish living alongside manta rays, reef sharks and loggerhead turtles. Many species of fish and coral are unique to the area, and fascinating ecosystems exist in ash beds and cooled lava based around the volcanic Barren Island. For a quick taste of marine life, you could start by **snorkelling**; most hotels can supply masks and snorkels, though some equipment is in dire need of replacement. The only way to get really close, and venture out into deeper waters, is to **scuba dive**. The main centre for **diving** has always been Havelock, although the number of accessible sites has been severely reduced. There are also operators on Neil, Long and South Andaman. Since 2013 the **decompression chamber** at the naval base in Port Blair has been open to any divers with suspected bends, boosting safety.

PRICES AND COURSES

Prices are very similar at all the centres, with certified divers paying around ₹5500–7000 for two tanks; more economical packages, often including accommodation and food, are available for multiple dives, while Discover Scuba introductory dives start at ₹3500. **Courses** cost from ₹20,000 for a basic four-day PADI open-water qualification, ₹21,000 for advanced or ₹56,000 to go all the way up to Divemaster, including all the tanks.

DIVING ADVICE

Underwater, it's not uncommon to come across schools of reef shark, which rarely turn hostile, but one thing to watch out for and avoid is the **black-and-white sea snake**. Though these seldom attack – and, since their fangs are at the back of their mouths, would find it difficult to get a grip on any human – their bite is twenty times deadlier than that of the cobra.

Increased tourism inevitably puts pressure on the delicate marine ecosystem, and poorly funded wildlife organizations can do little to prevent damage from insensitive visitors. Ensure your presence in the sea around the reefs does not harm the coral by observing the following **Green Coral Code** while diving or snorkelling:

- Never touch or walk on living coral, or it will die.
- Try to keep your feet away from reefs while wearing fins; the sudden sweep of water caused by a flipper kick can be enough to destroy coral.
- Always control the speed of your descent while diving; enormous damage can be caused by divers landing hard on a coral bed.
- Never break off pieces of coral from a reef, and remember that it is illegal to export dead coral from the islands, even fragments you may have found on a beach.

DIVE CENTRES

Andaman Bubbles Beach #5, Havelock ☎ 03192 282140, ⊛ andamanbubbles.com. Top-quality centre with excellent equipment and nitrox diving.

Barefoot Scuba Beach #3, Havelock ☎ 94742 63120, ⊛ barefootscuba.in. A PADI 5-star-rated operator with expert divemasters. Offers cheap accommodation with multiple dive packages. Another branch in Diglipur.

Dive India Beach #5, Havelock ☎ 03192 214247, ⊛ diveindia.com. One of the more established operations on Havelock. It has another branch on Neil, too.

India Scuba Explorers Neil Kendra, Neil ☎ 99332 71450, ⊛ indiascubaexplorers.com. Small but professional German-run dive centre.

Infiniti Live-Aboard Chiriya Tapu, South Andaman ☎ 65315 90988, ⊛ infinitiliveaboard.com. Reliable company run by a team of enthusiastic mainlanders with a smart boat with sleeping facilities, good for getting to Cinque and other more distant sites.

Lacadives Chiriya Tapu, South Andaman ☎ 96196 90898, ⊛ lacadives.com. After nearly twenty years of experience in the Lakshadweeps, Lacadives now explore the reefs around South Andaman.

19

★ **Full Moon Café** Island Vinnie's, Beach #3 ☎ 01392 282222.; map p.967. Wide menu, including some genuinely spicy Indian cuisine, plus many Western favourites and fresh seafood, mostly ₹180–450. Try the succulent fish tikka. Daily 7am–11pm.

Nala's Kingdom Main jetty ☎ 01392 282233; map p.967. The most salubrious place in the jetty area, serving Bengali, south Indian, Chinese and various fish dishes for under ₹200. Great thalis too. New branch at Beach #5. Daily 7am–4pm & 7–9.30pm.

★ **Red Snapper** Wild Orchid, Beach #5 ☎03192 282472; map p.967. Excellent upmarket seafood, meat and veg menu, served in classy surroundings. Most dinners are in the ₹400–600 range. Occasional recitals of traditional Bengali music. Daily 7–10.30am, noon–2.30pm & 6.30–9pm.

DRINKING AND NIGHTLIFE

Cicada Beach #5 ☎94742 67689; map p.967. The island's only dedicated nightspot, set amid the palm groves inland from the road, has recorded and occasional live music, as well as great cocktails. Only operates in the dry months. Daily 9pm–midnight.

Long Island

Just off the southeast coast of Middle Andaman, **Long Island** is attracting a growing number of travellers, with a couple of excellent beaches in **Marg Bay** and **Lalaji Bay**. Both of these are most easily approached by chartering a fisherman's dinghy from the jetty (around ₹500 each way), if you can find one, although Lalaji can be reached on foot by following the red arrows across the island and then turning left along the coast. You should not attempt this at high tide, and even when the sea is out it's quite an obstacle course of rocks and fallen trees.

The main settlement by the jetty has the island's only facilities, which amount to a handful of shops, a couple of basic *dhabas*, and the only two places to stay.

ARRIVAL AND DEPARTURE   LONG ISLAND

By boat Long Island has four weekly ferries to and from Havelock (4hr–4hr 30 min), Neil (5hr–5hr 30min), Port Blair (6–7hr) and Rangat (1hr), as well as a small local ferry connection with Yeratta (2 daily; 1hr 15min), 9km from Rangat.

ACCOMMODATION AND EATING

Blue Planet Signposted with blue arrows from the jetty ☎03192 215923, ⊛blueplanetandamans.com. Around a dozen adjoining rooms of varying sizes, some attached, arranged compactly around the courtyard restaurant whose centrepiece is a giant *padauk* tree. Also a couple of larger cottages and campsite nearby, with tents for rent from ₹200. ₹350/₹900

Forest Office Guesthouse Near the jetty ☎03192 278532. Some people see if there is any availability at the Forest Office's guesthouse, which has a couple of spartan rooms, usually occupied by officials. ₹500

Hotel GKR Opposite the village football pitch ☎94742 08368. A very basic restaurant that serves south Indian snacks, fish fry and fairly skimpy thalis for ₹120. Daily 6am–9pm.

Middle Andaman

For most travellers, **Middle Andaman** is a gruelling rite of passage to be endured en route to or from the north. The sinuous Andaman Trunk Road, hemmed in by walls of towering forest, winds through kilometres of jungle, and crosses the strait that separates the island from its neighbour, **Baratang**, by means of a rusting flat-bottomed ferry. The island's frontier feeling is heightened by the knowledge that the impenetrable forests west of the ATR comprise the **Jarawa Tribal Reserve** (see page 960). Of its two main settlements, the more northerly **Mayabunder**, the port for alluring **Interview Island** (see page 971), is slightly more appealing than characterless inland **Rangat** because of its pleasant setting by the sea, but neither town gives any reason to dally. Baratang, meanwhile, has some interesting mud volcanoes and limestone caves, which can be accessed on the boat trips that run daily except Sunday according to demand (₹350).

Rangat

At the southeast corner of Middle Andaman, **RANGAT** consists of a ramshackle sprawl around two rows of chai shops and general stores divided by the ATR, which is now at least paved. However, as a major staging post on the journey north, it's impossible to avoid – just don't get stranded here if you can help it.

ARRIVAL AND DEPARTURE   RANGAT

By boat The four weekly ferries from Port Blair via Havelock, Long Island and Neil dock at Rangat Bay, 8km east, from where you can take a bus or auto-rickshaw into town; there are also small daily ferries to Long Island from nearby Yeratta.

By bus Rangat is served by two daily government buses to Port Blair (6–7hr) as well as some private services, which pass through in the morning from further north. There are several daily buses to Mayabunder (2hr 30min–3hr) and Diglipur (4hr 30min–5hr).

ACCOMMODATION AND EATING

APWD Rest House ☎03192 274237. The Andaman Public Works Department (APWD)'s *Rest House*, pleasantly situated up a winding hill from the bazaar with views across the valley, is the best place to stay and eat, providing good, filling fish thalis (₹100). No wi-fi. **₹650**

Aroma Restaurant Main Rd ☎9474273527. Other than a couple of *dhabas*, this first-floor place, offering north and south Indian and Chinese staples for under ₹150, is the only place to eat in town. Daily 11am–10pm.

Hawksbill Nest 15km north at Cuthbert Bay (aka RRO)

☎03192 279159. The rooms (some a/c) are characterless but comfortable at this A&N Tourism hotel, which is invariably empty. Buses between Rangat and Mayabunder stop here on request and there is a fine beach nearby. No wi-fi. Dorms **₹150**, doubles **₹600**

Sea Shore Lodge ☎03192 274464. If you have an early ferry out of Rangat Bay, it's better to stay down near the jetty at the friendly *Sea Shore Lodge*. Basic meals can be had from the motley conglomeration of stalls between the lodge and the jetty. No wi-fi. **₹700**

19

Mayabunder

Only 70km north of Rangat by road, **MAYABUNDER** is perched on a long promontory right at the top of the island and surrounded by mangrove swamps. Unfortunately, the bus journey from Rangat can exceed three hours due to continual stops on the surprisingly populated route. Home to a large minority of former Burmese **Karen** tribal people who were originally brought here as cheap logging labour by the British, the village is more spread out and more appealing than Rangat. At the brow of the hill, before it descends to the jetty, a small hexagonal wooden structure houses the **Forest Museum** (Mon–Sat 8am–noon & 1–4pm; free), which holds a motley collection of turtle shells, snakes in formaldehyde, dead coral and a crocodile skull.

ARRIVAL AND DEPARTURE   MAYABUNDER

By bus Some of the buses from Port Blair (9–10hr) and Rangat (2hr 30min–3hr) now continue over the bridge to Diglipur on North Andaman (2hr from Mayabunder).

ACCOMMODATION AND EATING

Anmol Lodge Middle of the bazaar in the village centre ☎03192 262695. This once humble lodge has been fully renovated so all rooms are now attached, with cable TV and some a/c. Food must be pre-ordered. No wi-fi. **₹750**

APWD Rest House Next door to the Forest Museum ☎03192 273211. The rooms (some a/c) are large and very comfortable, plus there's a pleasant garden and gazebo

overlooking the sea, and a dining room serving good set meals (around ₹100). Often booked up by officials. No wi-fi. **₹600**

Sea'N'Sand 1km south of the centre ☎03192 273454, ✉thanzin_the_great@yahoo.co.in. Nicely located by the sea, this very welcoming Karen-run lodge has a range of simple rooms, mostly attached and some with a/c, as well as a reasonable restaurant. **₹400/₹800**

Interview Island

Mayabunder is the jumping-off place for **Interview Island**, a windswept nature sanctuary off the remote northwest coast of Middle Andaman – if you've come to the Andamans to watch

wildlife, it should be top of your list. Large and mainly flat, it is completely uninhabited save for a handful of unfortunate forest wardens, coastguards and policemen, posted here to ward off poachers. Foreigners aren't permitted to spend the night on the island, and to do a day-trip you must first obtain a ₹500 **permit** from the Forest Museum in Mayabunder. The only way to reach Interview is to charter a private fishing dinghy from Mayabunder jetty for around ₹5000. Arrange one the day before and leave at first light. Ask your boatman to moor by the **beach** at the southern tip of the island, which has a perennial freshwater pool inside a low cave; legend has it that the well, a nesting site for white-bellied **swifts**, has no bottom. At the forest post, where you have to sign an entry ledger, ask the wardens about the movements of Interview's feral **elephants**, descendants of trained elephants deserted here by a Kolkata-based logging company after its timber operation failed in the 1950s. **Saltwater crocodiles** are found on the island's eastern coastline.

North Andaman

19

Shrouded in dense jungle, **North Andaman** is the least populated of the region's large islands, crossed by a single road linking its scattered Bengali settlements. Although parts have been seriously logged, the total absence of driveable roads into northern and western areas has ensured blanket protection for a vast stretch of convoluted coastline, running from Austin Strait in the southwest to the northern tip, Cape Price; it's reassuring to know at least one extensive wilderness survives in the Andamans.

Despite the completion of the ATR's final section and the bridge from Middle Andaman, the main settlement of **DIGLIPUR** continues to exist in relative seclusion, though this may well change if the projected airport out towards Kalipur ever opens. Known in the British era as Port Cornwallis, North Andaman's largest settlement is another disappointing market town where you're only likely to pause long enough to pick up a local bus further north to the coast. Unless you are catching a boat (to Smith or Ross islands or back to Port Blair) straightaway from the port of **Aerial Bay**, 9km northeast, it's better to continue another 9km to **Kalipur**, where there's an excellent deserted beach, backed by lush forest and covered in photogenic driftwood. Swimming is best at high tide because the water recedes across rocky mud pools. Offshore snorkelling is also excellent, especially along the reef that runs towards the islet barely 500m away.

It's possible to walk from Kalipur to **Saddle Peak**, the highest mountain in the Andamans at 737m, which rises dramatically to the south, swathed in lush jungle. A permit (₹250/25) to make the three- to four-hour climb must be obtained from the Range Officer at the forest checkpost near the start of the ascent, but don't attempt it without a guide and plenty of drinking water. Another enjoyable day-trip is to the **limestone caverns**, 12km south near Ramnagar beach, best accessed by dinghy from Kalipur. You can arrange a dinghy, or guide for the Saddle Peak climb, at *Pristine Beach Resort* (see opposite).

Smith and Ross islands

Many tourists find their way up here in order to explore the various **islands** dotted around the gulf north of Aerial Bay, particularly **Smith** and **Ross** (not to be confused with its namesake near Port Blair), whose white sandbars, coral reefs and flora are splendid. At low tide it is possible to walk between the two islands. You can organize the requisite ₹500 permit from the Wildlife Information booth at Aerial Bay and rent a boat (₹2500) for the return trip yourself, or through one of the area guesthouses – try *Pristine Beach Resort*.

ARRIVAL AND DEPARTURE	**NORTH ANDAMAN**
By boat There are three boats a week in each direction from Aerial Bay to Port Blair (7–9hr). **By bus** Several buses a day leave in the early morning for	Port Blair (11–12hr) via Mayabunder (2hr) and Rangat (4hr 30min–5hr). There are 10–12 daily buses from Diglipur to Aerial Bay (20min) and Kalipur (45min).

ACCOMMODATION AND EATING

DIGLIPUR

APWD Rest House ☎ 03192 272203. On the hill above the main road, the *APWD Rest House* offers the village's nicest accommodation. ₹600

Maa Yashoda On the main road ☎ 99332 55086. This selection of ultra-basic rooms above a shop have bathrooms but not a lot else. ₹400

KALIPUR

★ **Pristine Beach Resort** ☎ 03192 271793, ⓦ andamanpristineresorts.com. Easily the most congenial place to stay on North Andaman, with a huge range of options from small but tidy huts through sturdy duplexes to luxury cottages, all set in lovely grounds near the beach. Very good restaurant too (most dishes ₹150–300). ₹1000

Turtle Resort ☎ 03192 272553. Typically institutional A&N Tourism hotel, which enjoys a prime location on a hilltop above the bay. The rooms are plain but large. Dorms ₹150, doubles ₹600

Little Andaman

Little Andaman is the furthest point south in the archipelago that foreigners can travel to on their tourist permit. Most of the island has been set aside as a tribal reserve for the **Onge** and is thus off-limits. It was also the only island open to foreigners to sustain extensive damage in the 2004 **tsunami**, but although a number of buildings were destroyed, and 64 people died, Little Andaman has recovered well. Relatively few visitors make it down here, although a slight improvement in tourist infrastructure renders it increasingly worthwhile for those who do. Still, it is worth noting that boats can be infrequent outside peak months and not all accommodations operate outside high season.

The main settlement, **INDIRA BAZAAR**, is 2km north of the jetty at **Hut Bay**, which curves gradually round in a majestic 8km sweep, the quality of the sand and beauty of the adjacent jungle increasing the further north you go. The top stretch is named **Netaji Nagar** after the village on the island's only road, which runs behind it. En route, you can detour 1km inland at the huge signpost about 2.5km north of Indira Bazaar to see the **White Surf Waterfalls** (daily dawn–dusk; ₹20). Made up of three 10- to 15m-high cascades, it's a relaxing spot; you can clamber into the right-hand fall for a soothing shower – yet crocodiles are said to inhabit the surrounding streams. Over the headland at the top of Hut Bay, 12km or so from the jetty, lies the smaller but equally picturesque crescent of **Butler Bay**. There's not much to do here but swim, sunbathe or look around the slightly eerie remains of the government beach resort, which was swept away by the tsunami – that is unless you've brought your surfboard with you: Little Andaman has a cult reputation among surfers for having some of the best conditions anywhere in South Asia.

ARRIVAL AND DEPARTURE   LITTLE ANDAMAN

By boat Daily ferries from Port Blair arrive at Hut Bay, the faster ones making the voyage in less than 6hr.

GETTING AROUND

Bicycles (₹50/day) and **mopeds** (₹300/day) can be rented through the guesthouses, but are in very short supply.

ACCOMMODATION AND EATING

Blue View Netaji Nagar ☎ 97344 80842. A motley mixture of huts and rooms, all with shared facilities, spaced around open ground, plus a good seafood restaurant (dishes ₹150–250). Only opens from late Nov to May. No wi-fi. ₹500

Greenwood Island Resort Hut Bay ☎ 94342 72338, ⓦ greenwoodandaman.in. The most comfortable resort on the island, with sturdy but attractive and comfortably furnished rooms, wood panelled on the outside. Decent restaurant too. No wi-fi. ₹800

★ **Jina Resort** Netaji Nagar ☎ 94760 38057. Pleasant and welcoming place with a sociable eating area and great banana leaf fish (₹200) on the menu. There are huts and rooms of varying sizes but all are non-attached. Only opens from late Nov to May. No wi-fi. ₹300

Palm Grove Indira Bazaar ☎ 94342 99212. Decent government-run restaurant which offers a limited menu of fish, chicken and veg dishes, mostly Indian. Filling thalis go for ₹130. Daily 7am–9pm.

Tamil Nadu

TWO HINDU PILGRIMS AT CAPE COMORIN

Tamil Nadu

When Indians refer to "the South", it's usually Tamil Nadu they're talking about. While Karnataka and Andhra Pradesh are essentially cultural transition zones buffering the Hindi-speaking north, and Kerala and Goa maintain their own distinctively idiosyncratic identities, the peninsula's massive Tamil-speaking state is India's Dravidian Hindu heartland. Traditionally protected by distance and the military might of the southern Deccan kingdoms, the region has, over the centuries, been less exposed to northern influences than its neighbours. As a result, the three powerful dynasties dominating the south – the Cholas, the Pallavas and the Pandyans – were able, over a period of more than a thousand years, to develop their own unique religious and political institutions, largely unmolested by marauding Muslims.

The most visible legacy of this protracted cultural flowering is a crop of astounding **temples**, whose gigantic gateway towers, or *gopuras*, still soar above just about every town. It is the image of these colossal wedge-shaped pyramids, high above the canopy of dense palm forests, or against patchworks of vibrant green paddy fields, which Edward Lear described as "stupendous and beyond belief". Indeed, the garishly painted deities and mythological creatures sculpted onto the towers linger long in the memory of most travellers.

The great Tamil temples, however, are merely the largest landmarks in a vast network of **sacred sites** – shrines, bathing places, holy trees, rocks and rivers – interconnected by a web of ancient pilgrims' routes. Tamil Nadu harbours 274 of India's holiest Shiva temples, and 108 are dedicated to Vishnu. In addition, five shrines devoted to the five Vedic elements (Earth, Wind, Fire, Water and Ether) are to be found here, along with eight to the planets, as well as other places revered by Christians and Muslims. Scattered from the pale orange crags and forests of the Western Ghats, across the fertile deltas of the **Vaigai** and **Kaveri** rivers to the Coromandel coast on the Bay of Bengal, these sites were celebrated in the hymns of the Tamil saints, composed between one and two thousand years ago. Today, so little has changed that the same devotional songs are still widely sung and understood in the region and it remains one of the last places in the world where a classical culture has survived well into the present.

> ## BEST TIME TO VISIT
>
> Tamil Nadu can be visited year-round, although by far the most popular time is between December and March, when the skies are mostly blue and the weather not as hot as it becomes from April to June, especially on the inland plains. Coastal areas, however, only ever vary a few degrees either side of 30°C but humidity levels are consistently high from April through September.
>
> The main summer monsoon largely misses Tamil Nadu but the state does receive plenty of precipitation during the northeast monsoon season from October to early December, when violent cyclones can be a threat, sometimes causing floods and wreaking havoc with transport links.
>
> During the hotter months, the hill stations of the Western Ghats provide welcome respite from the heat but they can be pretty chilly, at least at night, in the winter. The Christmas and New Year period gets busy and prices are higher then and for local festivals, of which the state has many.

FRENCH COLONIAL ARCHITECTURE

Highlights

❶ Mamallapuram Stone-carvers' workshops, a long sandy beach and wonderful Pallava monuments have made this a top tourist attraction. See page 993

❷ Puducherry Former French colony that has retained the ambience of a Gallic seaside town: croissants, a promenade and gendarmes wearing *képis*. See page 1007

❸ Thanjavur Home to some of the world's finest Chola bronzes, this town is dominated by the colossal tower of the Brihadishwara Temple. See page 1020

❹ Madurai The love nest of Shiva and his consort Meenakshi, this busy city's major

temple hosts a constant round of festivals. See page 1029

❺ Kanyakumari At the southern tip of the Subcontinent, Kanyakumari marks the sacred meeting point of the Bay of Bengal, Indian Ocean and Arabian Sea. See page 1039

❻ The Ghats The spine of southern India, excellent for trekking through lush mountains and tea plantations from its refreshingly cool hill stations. See page 1041

❼ Mudumalai Wildlife Sanctuary This densely forested park is becoming increasingly popular for its wild elephants and excellent accommodation. See page 1052

HIGHLIGHTS ARE MARKED ON THE MAP ON PAGE 978

The Tamils' living connection with their ancient Dravidian past has given rise to a strong **movement**. With a few fleeting lapses, one or other of the pro-Dravidian parties has been in power here since the 1950s, spreading their anti-brahmin, anti-Hindi proletarian message to the masses, principally through the medium of movies. Indeed, since Independence, the majority of Tamil Nadu's political leaders have been drawn from the state's prolific **cinema** industry.

TAMIL NADU

HIGHLIGHTS

1. Mamallapuram
2. Puducherry
3. Thanjavur
4. Madurai
5. Kanyakumari
6. The Ghats
7. Mudumalai Wildlife Sanctuary

FESTIVALS IN TAMIL NADU

Pongal (mid-Jan). One of the most colourful and important Tamil festivals, celebrating the harvest, when thresholds are decorated with beautiful designs.

Thiruvaiyaru Thyagaraja Aradhana (Jan). A five-day celebration of Carnatic classical music at Thiruvaiyaru, near Thanjavur, in honour of the great Carnatic composer-saint. See page 1020.

Teppam Floating Festival (Jan/Feb). Worshippers take boats to the shrine in the middle of the great bathing tank in Madurai. See page 1029.

Mamallapuram Dance Festival (Jan–Feb). Month-long classical dance performances against the wonderful backdrop of Arjuna's Penance.

Natyanjali Dance Festival (Feb/March). Five-day dance festival at the great temple in Chidambaram, with occasional offshoots in Kumbakonam and Thanjavur.

Chithirai (April/May). Maybe the most important Madurai festival, celebrating the marriage of the principal deities of the great Meenakshi-Sundareshwar Temple. See page 1031.

King Rajaraja's birthday (Oct). Vibrant ten-day affair when Thanjavur's magnificent Brihadishwarar temple is decked out fully to celebrate its creator's birthday. See page 1020.

Kartigai Deepam (Nov/Dec). Especially lively in Tiruvannamalai, where pilgrims circumambulate Arunachala.

Chennai festival season (Dec–Feb). A series of Indian classical concerts and dance performances takes place at various venues throughout the city.

With its seafront fort, grand mansions and excellence as a centre for the performing arts, the state capital **Chennai** is nonetheless a hot, chaotic, noisy Indian metropolis that still carries faint echoes of the Raj. However, it can be used as a base for visiting **Kanchipuram**, a major pilgrimage and sari-weaving centre, filled with reminders of an illustrious past.

Much the best place to start a temple tour is in nearby **Mamallapuram**, a seaside village that – quite apart from some exquisite Pallava rock-cut architecture – boasts a long and lovely beach. Further down the coast lies the one-time French colony of **Puducherry**, which is a Union Territory and not part of Tamil Nadu administratively, and is now home to the famous Sri Aurobindo ashram; nearby, **Auroville** has carved out a role for itself as a popular New Age centre. The road south from Puducherry puts you back on the temple trail, leading to the tenth-century Chola kingdom and the extraordinary architecture of **Chidambaram, Gangaikondacholapuram, Kumbakonam** and **Darasuram**. For the best Chola bronzes, however, and a glimpse of the magnificent paintings that flourished under Maratha rajas in the eighteenth century, travellers should head for **Thanjavur**. Chola capital for four centuries, the city boasts almost a hundred temples and was the birthplace of Bharatanatyam dance, famous throughout Tamil Nadu.

In the very centre of Tamil Nadu, **Tiruchirapalli**, a commercial town just northwest of Thanjavur, held some interest for the Cholas, but reached its heyday under later dynasties, when the temple complex in neighbouring **Srirangam** became one of south India's largest. Among its patrons were the Nayaks of **Madurai**, whose erstwhile capital further south, bustling with pilgrims, priests, peddlers, tailors and tourists, is an unforgettable destination. The deeply rural area of **Chettinadu** to the northwest hides many delightful villages with splendid mansions, a fine break from the temple trail. **Rameshwaram**, on the long spit of land reaching towards Sri Lanka, and **Kanyakumari** at India's southern tip are both important pilgrimage centres, and have the added attraction of welcome cool breezes and vistas over the sea.

While Tamil Nadu's temples are undeniably its major attraction, the hill stations of **Kodaikanal** and **Udhagamandalam** (**Ooty**) in the west of the state are popular destinations on the well-beaten tourist trail between Kerala and Tamil Nadu. The verdant, cool hills offer mountain views and gentle trails through the forests and tea and coffee plantations. You can also spot wildlife in the teak forests of **Mudumalai Wildlife Sanctuary** and bamboo groves of **Indira Gandhi Wildlife Sanctuary**, situated in the Palani Hills.

20

Brief history

Since the fourth century BC, Tamil Nadu has been shaped by its majority **Dravidian** population, a people of uncertain origins and physically quite different from north Indians. The influence of the powerful *janapadas*, established in the north by the fourth and third centuries BC, extended as far south as the Deccan, but they made few incursions into **Dravidadesa** (Tamil country). Incorporating what is now Kerala and Tamil Nadu, Dravidadesa was ruled by three dynasties: the **Cheras**, who held sway over much of the Malabar Coast (Kerala), the **Pandyas** in the far south and the **Cholas**, whose realm stretched along the eastern Coromandel Coast.

In the fourth century, the **Pallava** dynasty established a powerful kingdom centred in **Kanchipuram**. By the seventh century, the successors of the first Pallava king, Simhavishnu, were engaged in battles with the southern Pandyas and the forces of the Chalukyas, based further west in Karnataka. This was also an era of social development. **Brahmins** became the dominant community. The emergence of *bhakti*, devotional worship, placed temples firmly at the centre of religious life, and the inspirational *sangam* literature of saint-poets fostered a tradition of dance and music that has become Tamil Nadu's cultural hallmark.

In the tenth and eleventh centuries, the Cholas experienced a profound revival, ploughing their new wealth into the construction of splendid and imposing temples. Subsequently, the **Vijayanagar Dynasty**, based in Hampi (Karnataka), resisted Muslim incursions from the north and spread to cover most of south India by the sixteenth century. This prompted a new phase of architectural development, including the introduction of colossal *gopuras*. In Madurai, the Vijayanagar governors, **Nayaks**, set up an independent kingdom whose impact spread as far as Tiruchirapalli.

Simultaneously, the south experienced its first significant wave of **European settlement**. First came the Portuguese, followed by the British, Dutch and French. The Western powers soon found themselves engaged in territorial disputes, most markedly between the French, based in **Pondicherry**, and the British, whose stronghold since 1640 had been Fort St George in **Madras**. It was the British who prevailed, confining the French to Pondicherry.

As well as occasional rebellions against colonial rule, Tamil Nadu also saw anti-brahmin protests, in particular in the 1920s and 1930s. **Independence** in 1947 signalled the need for state boundaries, and by 1956 the borders had been demarcated on a linguistic basis. Thus in 1965 Madras Presidency became **Tamil Nadu**.

Since Independence, Tamil Nadu's industrial sector has mushroomed. The state was a Congress stronghold until 1967, when the **DMK** (Dravida Munnetra Kazhagam), championing the lower castes and reasserting Tamil identity, won a landslide victory on a wave of anti-Hindi and anti-central government sentiment. Power has ping-ponged back and forth between the DMK and the breakaway party AIADMK ever since (see page 982).

Chennai

In the northeastern corner of Tamil Nadu on the Bay of Bengal, **CHENNAI** (still commonly referred to by its former British name, **Madras**) is India's fourth largest city, with a population nudging ten million. Hot, congested and noisy, it's the major transport hub of the south and a tourist destination in its own right. The attractions of the city are diverse; it boasts fine specimens of **Raj architecture**, pilgrimage sites connected with the apostle, **Doubting Thomas**, superb **Chola bronzes** at its state museum, and plenty of classical music and dance performances.

Geographically, Chennai divides into three main sectors. North of the River Cooum stands **Fort St George**, site of the first British outpost in India, and **George Town**, the commercial centre, which developed during British occupation. George Town's principal landmark is **Parry's Corner**, located at the southern end of Rajaji Salai. Sandwiched between the Cooum and Adyar rivers is **central Chennai**, the modern, commercial heart of the metropolis, crossed and served by the city's main thoroughfare, **Anna Salai**. East of Anna Salai is the atmospheric old Muslim quarter of **Triplicane** and beyond is the long straight **Marina** with its massive beach, fishing boats and hordes of domestic tourists, saris and trousers hitched up, enjoying a paddle. Further south along

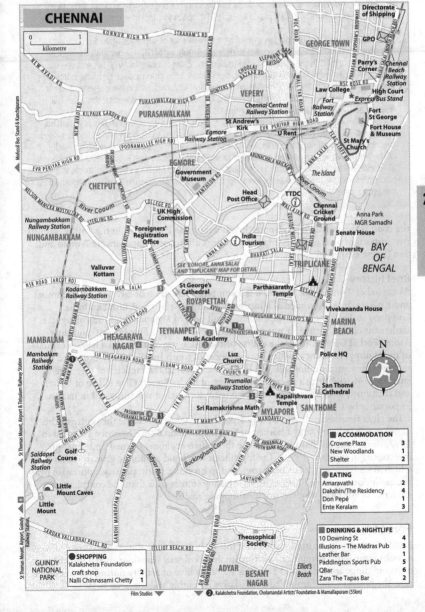

ACCOMMODATION
Crowne Plaza	3
New Woodlands	1
Shelter	2

EATING
Amaravathi	2
Dakshin/The Residency	4
Don Pepé	1
Ente Keralam	3

DRINKING & NIGHTLIFE
10 Downing St	4
Illusions – The Madras Pub	3
Leather Bar	1
Paddington Sports Pub	5
QBar	6
Zara The Tapas Bar	2

SHOPPING
Kalakshetra Foundation craft shop	2
Nalli Chinnasami Chetty	1

OF MOVIE STARS AND MINISTERS

One notable difference between the Chennai-based Tamil movie industry and the mainstream Bollywood movies from Mumbai is the influence of **politics** on Tamil films. Traditional folk ballads about low-caste heroes vanquishing high-caste villains were perfect propaganda vehicles for the nascent Tamil nationalist movement, the Dravida Munnetra Kazhagam (**DMK**). It is no coincidence that the party's founding father, **C.N. Annadurai**, was a top script- and screenplay-writer. He and his colleagues used the popular film genres of the time to convey their political ideas to the masses and this politicization of the big screen created the **fan clubs**, or *rasigar manrams*, that play a key role in mobilizing support for the nationalist parties in elections.

Perhaps the most influential fan club of all time was that of superstar Marudur Gopalamenon Ramachandran, known to millions simply as "**MGR**". He generated fanatical grass-roots support in the state and rose to become chief minister in 1977. His eleven-year rule is still regarded by liberals as a dark age of chronic corruption, police brutality, political purges and rising organized crime. When he died in 1987, two million people attended his funeral and even today, MGR's statue, sporting trademark sunglasses and lamb's-wool hat, is revered across Tamil Nadu at roadside shrines.

MGR's political protégée, and eventual successor, was teenage screen starlet **Jayalalitha**, a convent-educated brahmin's daughter whom he recruited to be both his leading lady and mistress. After 25 hit films together, Jayalalitha followed him into politics, becoming leader of the AIADMK, the party MGR set up after being expelled from the DMK in 1972. Despite allegations of fraud and corruption Jayalalitha enjoyed two spells as chief minister in the early noughties and assumed power for her third stint in 2011. Her death in 2016 was mourned by the entire state.

20

the coast is the district of **Mylapore**, inhabited by the Portuguese in the 1500s, with its two important places of pilgrimage and tourist attractions, **Kapalishvara Temple** and **San Thomé Cathedral**.

Brief history

As capital of Tamil Nadu, Chennai is a comparatively modern creation, like Mumbai and Kolkata. It was founded as a fortified trading post by the **British East India Company** in 1639, north of the ancient Tamil port of **Mylapore** and the Portuguese settlement of San Thomé. It was completed on St George's Day in 1640 and thus named **Fort St George**. Over the course of the following century and a half, as capital of the **Madras Presidency**, which covered most of south India, the city expanded to include many surrounding villages. It was briefly lost to the French but three years later, in 1746, the British re-established control under **Robert Clive** (Clive of India) and continued to use it as their southern base, although it was surpassed in national importance by Calcutta.

The city's renaissance began after Independence, when it became the centre of the Tamil **movie industry**, and a hotbed of **Dravidian nationalism**. Renamed Chennai in 1997, the metropolis has boomed since the Indian economy opened up to foreign investment in the early 1990s. The flip side of this rapid economic growth is that Chennai's infrastructure has been stretched to breaking point: poverty, oppressive heat and pollution are more likely to be your lasting impressions than the conspicuous affluence of the city's modern marble shopping malls.

Fort St George

Fort St George is quite unlike any other fort in India. Facing the sea amid state offices, it looks more like a complex of well-maintained colonial mansions than a fort. Many of its buildings are today used as offices and are a hive of activity during the week. It is now the house of the Tamil Nadu Legislative Assembly and the Secretariat.

The fort was the first structure of Madras town and the first territorial possession of the British in India. Construction began in 1640 but most of the original buildings were damaged during French sieges and replaced later that century. The most imposing structure is the slate-grey-and-white eighteenth-century colonnaded **Fort House**.

Fort Museum

York St • Daily except Fri 9am–5pm • ₹100 (₹5), no photography

The modestly proportioned **Exchange Building** houses the excellent **Fort Museum**. The collection within faithfully records the central events of the British occupation of Madras with portraits, regimental flags, weapons, East India Company coins, medals, stamps and thick woollen uniforms that make you wonder how the Raj survived as long as it did. The first floor is now an **art gallery**, where portraits of prim officials and their wives sit side by side with fine sketches of the British embarking at Chennai in

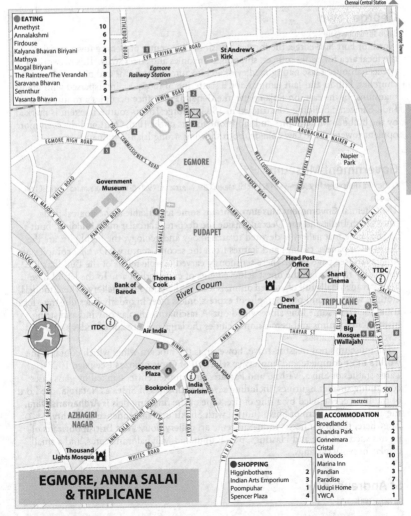

EATING

Amethyst	10
Annalakshmi	6
Firdouse	7
Kalyana Bhavan Biriyani	4
Mathsya	3
Mogal Biriyani	5
The Raintree/The Verandah	8
Saravana Bhavan	2
Sennthur	9
Vasanta Bhavan	1

SHOPPING

Higginbothams	2
Indian Arts Emporium	3
Poompuhar	1
Spencer Plaza	4

ACCOMMODATION

Broadlands	6
Chandra Park	2
Connemara	9
Cristal	8
La Woods	10
Marina Inn	4
Pandian	3
Paradise	7
Udupi Home	5
YWCA	1

EGMORE, ANNA SALAI & TRIPLICANE

0 — 500 metres

20

aristocratic finery, attended by Indians in loincloths. Also on display are etchings by the famous artist **Thomas Daniell**, whose work largely defined British perceptions of India at the end of the eighteenth century.

St Mary's Church

St Thomas St • Daily 9am–5pm

South of the Fort Museum, past the State Legislature, stands the oldest surviving Anglican Church in Asia, **St Mary's**, built in 1678 and partly renovated after the battle of 1759. It's distinctly English in style, crammed with plaques and statues in memory of British soldiers, politicians and their wives. The grandest plaque, made of pure silver, was presented by Elihu Yale, former governor of Fort St George (1687–96) and founder of Yale University. A collection of photographs of visiting dignitaries, including Queen Elizabeth II, is on display in the entrance porch.

George Town

Bus no 18 from Anna Salai

North of Fort St George, the former British trading centre of **George Town** remains the focal area for banks, offices, shipping companies and street stalls. This network of streets harbours a fascinating medley of architecture: eighteenth- and nineteenth-century churches, Hindu and Jain temples and a scattering of mosques, interspersed with grand mansions. In the east, on Rajaji Salai, the **General Post Office** occupies a robust earth-red Indo-Saracenic building constructed in 1884. George Town's southern extent is marked by the bulbous white domes and sandstone towers of the **High Court** and the even more opulent towers of the **Law College**, both showing strong Islamic influence.

Government Museum

Pantheon Rd • Daily except Fri 9.30am–5pm • ₹250 (₹15), camera ₹200, video camera ₹500 • ⊕ chennaimuseum.org • Bus #23C from Anna Salai

The Chennai **Government Museum** contains some remarkable archeological finds from south India and the Deccan. Inside the deep-red, circular **main building**, built in 1851, the first gallery is devoted to archeology and geology; the highlights are the dismantled panels, railings and statues from the second-century AD *stupa* complex at **Amaravati** (see page 945). These sensuously carved marble reliefs of the Buddha's life are widely regarded as the finest achievements of early Indian art. To the left of here high, arcaded halls full of stuffed animals lead to the **ethnology gallery**, where models, clothes, weapons and photographs of expressionless faces in orderly lines illustrate local tribal societies, some long since wiped out. A fascinating display of wind and string **instruments**, drums and percussion includes the large predecessor of today's sitar and several very old tablas.

The museum's real treasure-trove, however, is the modern wing, which contains the world's most complete and impressive selection of **Chola bronzes** (see page 1023). Large statues of Shiva, Vishnu and Parvati stand in the centre, flanked by glass cases containing smaller figurines, including several sculptures of Shiva as **Nataraja**, the Lord of the Dance, encircled by a ring of fire. One of the finest models is **Ardhanarishvara**, the androgynous form of Shiva (united with Shakti in transcendence of duality). Elsewhere, the magnificent Indo-Saracenic **art gallery** houses old British portraits of figures such as Clive and Hastings, plus Rajput and Mughal miniatures, and a small display of ivory carvings.

St Andrew's Kirk

Off Periyar EVR High Rd

Just northeast of Egmore Station, **St Andrew's Kirk**, consecrated in 1821, is a fine example of Georgian architecture. Modelled on London's St Martin-in-the-Fields, it's one of just three churches in India with a circular seating plan, laid out beneath a huge dome painted blue with gold stars and supported by a sweep of Corinthian columns. Marble plaques around the church give a fascinating insight into the kind of people who left Britain to work for the imperial and Christian cause. A staircase leads onto the flat roof, surrounding the dome, from where you can climb further up into the steeple past the massive bell to a tiny balcony affording excellent views of the city.

The Marina

One of the longest city beaches in the world, the **Marina** (Kamaraj Salai) stretches 5km from the harbour at the southeastern corner of George Town to near San Thomé Cathedral. Going south, you'll pass the Indo-Saracenic **Presidency College** (1865–71), one of a number of stolid Victorian buildings that make up the **University**, as well as adjacent **Vivekananda House** (see below).

Today the **beach** itself is a sociable stretch, peopled by idle paddlers, picnickers and pony-riders; every afternoon crowds gather around the beach market. However, its location, just a little downstream from the port, which belches out waste and smelly fumes, combined with its function as the toilet for the fishing community, detract from its natural beauty.

Vivekananda House
Tues–Sun 10am–12.15pm & 3–7.15pm • ₹10 • ⓦ vivekanandahouse.org

Housed in a splendidly rotund and ornate stone building, the nineteenth-century Madras depot of the Tudor Ice Company has been converted into the interesting **Vivekananda House** museum, which gives an excellent account of the life of the nineteenth-century saint, Swami Vivekananda, who stayed here for some time in 1897. Now a branch of the Sri Ramakrishna Math organization (see page 986), the museum contains attractive visual displays of Hindu beliefs, as well as photographic and detailed textual material on Vivekananda's life.

Mylapore
Buses #4, #5 or #21 from the LIC building on Anna Salai

Long before Madras came into existence, **Mylapore**, south of the Marina, was a major settlement; the Greek geographer Ptolemy mentioned it in the second century AD as a thriving port. During the Pallava period (fifth to ninth centuries) it was second only to Mamallapuram. Its two outstanding sights are venerable **San Thomé Cathedral** and the mighty **Kapalishvara Temple**, while the **Sri Ramakrishna Math** also warrants a visit.

San Thomé Cathedral
San Thomé High Rd • Daily 6am–8pm • ⓦ santhomechurch.com

An important stop on the St Thomas pilgrimage trail, **San Thomé Cathedral** marks the eastern boundary of Mylapore, lying close to the sea at the southern end of the Marina on San Thomé High Road. Although the present neo-Gothic structure dates from 1896, it stands on the site of two earlier churches built over the tomb of St Thomas. The saint's **relics** are kept inside the nave, accessed by an underground passage from the small **museum** at the rear of the courtyard, and are the object of great reverence. The museum itself houses stones inscribed in Tamil, Sanskrit (twelfth-century Chola) and early Portuguese, and a map of India, dated 1519.

Kapalishvara Temple
N Mada St • Daily 6am–noon & 4–9.30pm

The huge **Kapalishvara Temple** sits just under 1km west of the San Thomé Cathedral, off RK Mutt Road. Seventh-century Tamil poet-saints sang its praises, but the present structure, dedicated to Shiva, probably dates from the sixteenth century. The huge (40m) *gopura* towering above the main east entrance, plastered in stucco figures, was added in 1906. Surrounding an assortment of busy shrines, where priests offer blessings for devotees and non-Hindus alike, the courtyard features an old tree where a small shrine to Shiva's consort, Parvati, shows her in the form of a peahen (*mayil*) worshipping a lingam.

Sri Ramakrishna Math

31 Ramakrishna Math Rd · Temple daily 5–11.45am & 3–9pm · W chennaimath.org

A short walk south of the Kapalishvara Temple, lie the peaceful and extensive grounds of the **Sri Ramakrishna Math**, an active place of study for devotees wishing to follow the teachings of the famous nineteenth-century master. The focus of interest for the casual visitor is the **Universal Temple of Sri Ramakrishna**, an elegant construction combining architectural motifs from Hindu, Buddhist and Jain temples, as well as European churches, while the manicured forecourt echoes the Islamic themes of the Mughals. Within the temple itself are a series of prayer halls, approached by steps, and the inner sanctum contains a solid marble statue of Ramakrishna seated on a lotus.

Little Mount Caves

Little Mount, off Mount Rd. Bus #18A, #18B, or #52C from Anna Salai

St Thomas is said to have sought refuge from persecution in the **Little Mount Caves**, 8km south of the city centre. Entrance to the caves is beside steps leading to a statue of Our Lady of Good Health. Inside, next to a small natural window in the rock, are impressions of what are believed to be St Thomas' handprints, created when he made his escape through this tiny opening. Behind the new circular church of Our Lady of Good Health is a natural **spring**. Tradition has it that this was created when Thomas struck the rock, so the crowds that came to hear him preach could quench their thirst; samples of its holy water are on sale.

St Thomas Mount

Mount Rd · Take a suburban train to Guindy railway station and walk from there

It's said that St Thomas was speared to death while praying before a stone cross on **St Thomas Mount**, 11km south of the city centre. **Our Lady of Expectation Church** (1523), at the summit of the Mount, can be reached by 134 granite steps marked with the fourteen Stations of the Cross, or by a road which curls its way to the top, where a huge old banyan tree provides shade for devotees who come to fast, pray and sing. Inside the church, St Thomas' cross is rumoured to have bled in 1558, while the altar is said to mark the exact spot of the apostle's death; the painting of the Madonna and Child above the altar is attributed to St Luke.

Theosophical Society headquarters

Adyar Bridge Rd, Besant Nagar (south of Mylapore) · **Grounds** Mon–Sat 8.30–10am & 2–4pm **Bookshop** Mon–Sat 9.30am–12.30pm & 2.30–5.30pm **Library** Tues–Sun 9am–5pm · Free · W ts-adyar.org · Buses #5, #5C or #23C from George Town/Anna Salai

The **Theosophical Society** was established in New York in 1875 by American Civil War veteran Colonel Henry S. Olcott and the eccentric Russian aristocrat Madame Helena Petrovna Blavatsky, who claimed to have occult powers. Based on a fundamental belief in the equality and truth of all religions, the society in fact propagated a modern form of Hinduism, praising all things Indian and shunning Christian missionaries. Needless to say, its two founders were greeted enthusiastically when they transferred their operations to Madras in 1882, establishing their headquarters near Elliot's Beach in Adyar.

The society's buildings still stand today, sheltering several shrines and an excellent **library** of books on religion and philosophy. The collection includes 800-year-old scroll pictures of the Buddha; rare Tibetan xylographs; exquisitely illuminated Korans; a giant copy of Martin Luther's *Biblia* printed in Nuremberg three hundred years ago; and a thumbnail-sized Bible in seven languages. Anybody is welcome to look around, but to gain full use of the library you have to register as a member.

The 270 acres of woodland and gardens surrounding the society's headquarters make a serene place to sit and restore the spirits. In the middle, a vast 400-year-old **banyan tree**, said to be the second largest in the world, can provide shade for up to three thousand people at a time.

Kalakshetra Foundation

Kalakshetra Rd, Thiruvanmiyur, 15km south of the centre • Daily 8.30–11.30am, except 2nd & 4th Sat of month • ₹500 (₹100) • Ⓦ kalakshetra.in • Take one of the many city bus routes to Thiruvanmiyur bus stand, 500m away

Set in delightfully landscaped and shady grounds, the **Kalakshetra Foundation** was created in 1936 and has since established itself as the prime cultural organization for the study and performance of traditional Tamil song and dance. Visitors are welcome to quietly witness the morning classes and, of course, are encouraged to attend an evening performance whenever they are scheduled. The small **Rukmini Devi Museum**, named after the dancer whose success inspired the foundation, contains her personal collection of artistic objects, from stone and brass sculptures to delicate fabrics and fine paintings; unfortunately, at the time of writing it was closed for major refurbishment. There is also a great craft centre, complete with shop (see page 992).

Cholamandal Artists' Village

Injambakkam, 24km south of the centre • Daily 9am–6.30pm • Grounds free; museum ₹20 • Ⓦ cholamandalartistvillage.com • Any ECR bus destined for Mamallapuram and Puducherry passes close to the entrance

Tucked beside the beach in the sprawling southern suburbs of Chennai, the **Cholamandal Artists' Village** was established in the mid-1960s to encourage contemporary Indian art. In a country where visual culture is so comprehensively dominated by convention, fostering innovation and artistic experimentation proved no easy feat. Despite an initially hostile response from the Madrasi establishment (who allegedly regarded the tropical storm that destroyed the artists' first settlement as an act of nemesis), the village has prospered. Today, Cholamandal's thirty-strong community has several studios and a large **museum** filled with paintings, sketches, sculpture and metalwork, as well as a shop selling work produced here.

ARRIVAL AND DEPARTURE   CHENNAI

BY PLANE

Chennai airport The airport, in Tirisulam, 16km south-west of the city centre on NH-45, is comprehensively served by international and domestic flights. The new international and domestic terminals are a short walk from each other, on opposite sides of the old terminal. Facilities at both are much better on the air side than the land side. The Tamil Nadu Tourist Information Centre at the arrivals exit can book accommodation.

Getting into town The quickest and cheapest way to get into town is by suburban train (see below) from Tirisulam station, 400m from the airport on the far side of the road, to Park, Egmore and North Beach stations (30–40min). There are prepaid taxi counters at both terminals for the ever-congested ride to the main hotels or railway stations; from the main road, rickshaws charge ₹400, not much less than taxis. Taxis straight down the coast to Mamallapuram cost around ₹1300. Buses #70 and #70A go to Mofussil Bus Stand (see below) in Koyambedu suburb, from where you can connect to other destinations.

Airlines, international Air India ☎044 2345 3303, airport ☎044 2256 6002; American Airlines ☎91-124-

20

2567222; British Airways ☎ 1860 180 3592; Emirates ☎ 044 6683 4400; Gulf Air ☎ 044 22566446; Lufthansa ☎ 044 22569393; Qatar Airways ☎ 91-79-3061-6000; Singapore Airlines ☎ 044 45921921; Sri Lankan Airlines ☎ 044 4392 1100; Thai Airways ☎ 044 4206 3311. Most offices are open Mon–Fri 10am–5pm, Sat 10am–1pm.

BY TRAIN

Chennai has two main long-distance railway stations – Egmore and Central, both on the north side of the city centre and just 1.5km apart. Egmore station is the arrival point for most trains from Tamil Nadu and Kerala; its booking office, up the stairs left of the main entrance, handles bookings for both stations. There is also an efficient tourist reservation counter (Mon–Sat 8am–8pm, Sun 8am–2pm) on the first floor of the Moore Market Complex (next to the main Central station building), which sells tickets for trains from both stations. Both stations have left-luggage offices. The occasional service for southern Tamil Nadu leaves from the suburban Tambaram station.

BY BUS

Mofussil Bus Stand Buses from all long-distance destinations use the huge Mofussil Bus Stand, inconveniently situated in the suburb of Koyambedu, more than 10km west of the centre. Mofussil is linked to other parts of Chennai by a host of city buses, which depart from the well-organized platforms outside the main terminal: buses #27, #15B, #15F and #17E go to the Egmore/Central area and Parry's Corner; bus #27B also goes on to Triplicane; while buses #70 and #70A link the bus stand with the airport. Note that all express ECR buses from Mamallapuram, Puducherry and other coastal towns to the south of Chennai stop at Guindy suburban railway station; taking a train in from there saves time.

Destinations The six platforms at Mofussil are each divided into thirty-odd bays, with frequent services to destinations throughout Tamil Nadu and neighbouring states, including Bengaluru (every 15–30min; 8–10hr); Chengalpattu (every 5–10min; 1hr 30min–2hr); Chidambaram (20 daily; 6–7hr); Coimbatore (every 30min; 11–12hr); Kanchipuram (every 20min; 1hr 30min–2hr); Kanyakumari (10 daily; 15–17hr); Kodaikanal (1 daily; 14–15hr); Kumbakonam (every 30min; 7–8hr); Madurai (every 20–30min; 10hr); Mamallapuram (every 15–30min; 2hr); Puducherry (every 15–30min; 4–5hr); Rameshwaram (3 daily; 13–14hr); Thanjavur (20 daily; 8–9hr); Thiruvananthapuram (6 daily; 18–20hr); Tiruchirapalli (every 15–30min; 8–10hr); Tirupati (every 30min–1hr; 4–5hr); Tiruvannamalai (every 20–30min; 4–5hr); Udhagamandalam (Ooty) (2 daily; 14–15hr).

BY BOAT

Boats leave Chennai every week/ten days for Port Blair, capital of the Andaman Islands. The first thing you'll need to do is contact the Shipping Corporation of India at 17 Rajaji Salai, Jawahar Building, George Town (☎ 044 2523 1401, ⊛ shipindia.com) to find out when the next sailing is and when tickets go on sale, usually up to a month prior to departure. There are no ticket sales on the day of sailing. Permits for up to thirty days are given on arrival in Port Blair. The Andaman Information Centre (Mon–Fri 10am–5.30pm, Sat 10am–1pm; ☎ 044 2533 3952) is in the Tamil Nadu Tourism Complex, 2 Wallajah Rd, Triplicane. For more details, see the Andaman Islands chapter (see page 954).

GETTING AROUND

Chennai's sights and facilities are spread over such a wide area that it's impossible to get around without using some form of **public transport**. Most visitors jump in auto-rickshaws, but outside rush hours you can travel around comfortably by **bus** or on the suburban **train** (Mass Rapid Transit System; see below). At the time of writing, the section of the new Chennai metro (⊛ chennaimetrorail.gov. in) between Koyambedu and Alandur was up and running, as was the line from Little Mount to the airport.

By train If you want to travel south from central Chennai to Guindy (Deer Park) or the airport, the easiest way to go is by suburban train (aka the MRST). Services run every 15min (on average) between 4.30am and 11pm, prices are minimal, and they only get overcrowded during rush hours (around 7–9am & 4–6pm). Buy a ticket before boarding. City trains travel between Beach (opposite the GPO), Fort, Park (for Central), Egmore, Nungambakkam, Kodambakkam, Mambalam (for T Nagar and silk shops), Saidapet (for Little Mount Church), Guindy, St Thomas Mount and Tirisulam (for the airport).

By bus Local bus routes radiate out from the amalgamated Express and Broadway bus stands, between Central train station and George Town. On Anna Salai and other major thoroughfares buses have dedicated stops, but on smaller streets you have to flag them down, or wait with the obvious crowd. Numbers of services to specific places of interest in the city are listed in the relevant accounts, while those to and from the Mofussil Bus Stand are listed in "Arrival and departure".

By rickshaw Auto-rickshaw drivers in Chennai are notorious for demanding high fares from locals and tourists alike. The diversions and one-way systems in place due to the construction of the metro are having a considerable effect on journey times and hence rickshaw prices. It's worth asking two or three drivers to compare prices and then haggle. If you need to get to the airport or station early in the morning, expect to pay up to ₹500. Arrange in advance.

By taxi Chennai's yellow-top Ambassador taxis have meters but drivers often refuse to use them, so prepare yourself for some hard bargaining. At around ₹200 from

RECOMMENDED TRAINS FROM CHENNAI

Destination	Name	No.	From	Departs	Arrives
Bengaluru	*Shatabdi Express*	#12007	Central	6am*	10.50am
	Double Decker	#22625	Central	7.25 am	5pm
Coimbatore	*Kovai Express*	#12675	Central	6.15am	1.45pm
	Cheran Express	#12673	Central	10.10pm	6.15am+
Hyderabad	*Charminar Express*	#12759	Central	6.10pm	8am+
Kanyakumari	*Kanyakumari Express*	#12633	Egmore	5.15pm	6.20am+
Kochi/Ernakulam	*Alleppey Express*	#22639	Central	09.05pm	8.40am+
	Trivandrum Mail	#12623	Central	7.45pm	7.08am+
Kodaikanal Road	*Pandian Express*	#12637	Egmore	9.40pm	4.40am+
Madurai	*Vaigai Express*	#12635	Egmore	1.40pm	9.25pm
	Pandian Express	#12637	Egmore	9.40pm	5.45am+
Mettupalayam (for Ooty)	*Nilagiri Express*	#12671	Central	08.55 pm	6.15am+
Mumbai	*Mumbai Express*	#11042	Central	12.20am	1.35pm+
	Chennai Express	#12164	Egmore	6.45 am	6am+
Mysuru	*Shatabdi Express*	#12007	Central	6am*	1pm
	Mysore Express	#22682	Central	11.30pm	8.20am+
Rameshwaram	*R'waram Express*	#22661	Egmore	5.50pm	4.35am+
Thanjavur	*Trichy Express*	#16795	Egmore	8.00am	2.15pm
Tiruchirapalli	*Guruvayur Express*	#16127	Egmore	08.15am	1.30pm
	Vaigai Express	#12635	Egmore	1.40pm	6.30pm
Thiruvananthapuram	*Trivandrum Mail*	#12623	Central	7.45pm	12.15pm +
Tirupati	*Sapthagiri Express*	#16057	Central	6.25am	9.40am

*Except Wed; a/c only, + next day

Central station to Triplicane, they're practically pricing themselves out of business. For this reason, more reliable and economical radio taxis such as Bharati Call Taxi (☎044 2814 2233) are popular.

By car Private cars (with driver) can be booked at any of the city's upmarket hotels, through TTDC or with one of the numerous private tour agents (see below).

INFORMATION

Tourist information The Tamil Nadu Tourism Development Office, 2 Wallajah Rd, Triplicane (theoretically open 24hr; ☎044 2533 3333, ⊛tamilnadutourism.org), houses several other state tourist offices including the office of the Andamans. You can pick up Chennai and Tamil Nadu maps here. The India Tourism Office, 154 Anna Salai (Mon–Fri 9.15am–5.45pm; ☎044 2846 1459, ⊛incredibleindia. org), is far more helpful and provides information, maps and brochures for the whole of India.

Services A useful and centrally located travel agent and exchange facility is Thomas Cook, 112 Nungambakkam High Road, Eldorado (Mon–Sat 9.30am–6pm; ☎044 2825 5909).

ACCOMMODATION

Finding an inexpensive **place to stay** in Chennai can sometimes be a problem. With the 24hr checkout system it's difficult to predict availability and some of the cheaper places don't take advance bookings. The good news is that standards in the cheapies are better than in other cities. Most of the mid-range and inexpensive hotels are around the railway station in **Egmore** and further east in **Triplicane**. The bulk of the top hotels are in the south of the city and several offer courtesy buses to and from the airport.

EGMORE

Chandra Park 9 Gandhi Irwin Rd, opposite the station ☎044 2819 1177, ⊛hotelchandrapark.com; map p.983. Clean-cut business hotel with central a/c, foreign exchange, 24hr coffee shop, bar, and a rather disappointing restaurant. The spacious, light and well-furnished standard rooms are a very good deal and single standard rooms cost ₹1500. Taxes included. Double ₹1650.

Marina Inn 55/31 Gandhi Irwin Rd ☎044 2819 2919, ⊛marinainn.in; map p.983. Very smart business-style hotel with central a/c, which is around 200m on the right as you exit Egmore station. The double rooms, though not big, are all tastefully decorated and very clean and all have LCD TVs; there is also a pretty decent multicuisine restaurant and bar. Single rooms cost in the range of ₹1700–₹1900 for non a/c. A/c and all include taxes. A/c doubles ₹2000

20

20

CHENNAI TOURS

One good way to get around the sights of Chennai is on a TTDC **bus tour**; bookings are taken at its office. They're good value, albeit rushed, and the guides can be very helpful. The TTDC **half-day tour** (daily 8am–1pm or 1.30–6.30pm; ₹300 non-a/c, ₹375 a/c) takes in Fort St George, the Government Museum (Birla Planetarium on Fri), the Snake Park, Kapalishvara Temple, and Marina Beach. TTDC also offers good-value **day-trips**, including visits to Mamallapuram, Kanchipuram (daily 6.30am–7pm; ₹825 non-a/c, ₹1025 a/c), and Puducherry (Sat & Sun 6.30am–7pm; ₹750 non-a/c, ₹925 a/c), with meals included in the tariff; check at the office for other itineraries and further details.

Storytrails (☎ 044 4501 0202, ⓦ storytrails.in) conducts a number of fascinating and expertly led, themed **walking tours**, with enticing titles such as Bazaar Trail, Spice Trail, British Blueprints and Steeple Chase. Prices vary according to the number of people but reckon on around ₹1000 per person for a small group. A perennially popular tour among bikers is the one offered by the **Royal Enfield motorcycle factory** around 18km north of the centre in Tiruvottiyur (every 2nd & 4th Sat of month 10am; ₹600 per person; ☎ 1800 210 0007, ⓦ royalenfield.com).

★ **Pandian** 15 Kennet Lane ☎ 04428191010, ⓦ hotel pandian.com; map p.983. Very smart two-star hotel with spotless, brightly coloured rooms, breakfast included and free wi-fi. There are some singles (from ₹1400 for non a/c and ₹2200 for a/c). Double **₹2600**

Udupi Home 1 Halls Road ☎ 044 28192030 ⓦ udupi home.com; map p.983. One of the old and traditional three star hotels with comfortable rooms, clean and spacious with a very good vegetarian restaurant. Highly recommended and very close to the railway station. Free Wi-fi. Rates start with **₹2300** per night for an a/c double room.

★ **YWCA** 1086 Periyar EVR High Rd ☎ 044 2532 4234, ⓦ ywcamadras.org; map p.983. Attractive hotel in quiet gardens, behind Egmore station, with spotless, spacious rooms, safe-deposit, and a good restaurant. A highly-recommended, safe and friendly place; book in advance. Rates include a buffet breakfast. Singles vary from ₹1500–₹2100 for a/c and non a/c. Double **₹1900**

ANNA SALAI AND TRIPLICANE

Broadlands 18 Vallaba Agraharam St, Triplicane ☎ 044 2854 5573, ✉ broadlandshotel@yahoo.com; map p.983. Reception is in an old whitewashed house, from which stretches a maze of corridors, outbuildings and courtyards. This is a budget travellers' enclave with character. There's a wide range of rooms, some with private balconies, with singles from ₹550. Double **₹1000**

Connemara Binny Rd ☎ 0446 600 0000, ⓦ tajhotels. com; map p.983. Dating from the Raj era, this whitewashed Art Deco five-star near Anna Salai, owned by Taj Hotels, is a Chennai institution and has just reopened after a two year renovation. The large heritage rooms feature Victorian decor, dressing rooms and verandas overlooking the pool; suites go up to ₹100,000. There's also a health club, 24hr coffee shop, two excellent restaurants

(see opposite) and a bar. A heritage category room is in the range of ₹16,000. Double **₹11,000**

Cristal 34 CNK Rd, Triplicane ☎ 044 2851 3011; map p.983. Down a lane off Quaide Milleth Salai (opposite the *Firdouse* hotel) and thus a little quieter, this is as cheap as it gets in Chennai. Rooms are tiled and all have attached showers. The a/c rooms start at ₹800, depending on size and facilities. Ideal for backpackers but not recommended for families. No wi-fi. **₹400**

La Woods 1 Woods Rd ☎ 04428460677, ⓦ lawoods hotel.com; map p.983. Good-value, mid-range hotel with central a/c. The comfortable and nicely decorated rooms have modern plumbing, lighting and media hub, while Italian marble flooring throughout gives a bright and airy feel. Breakfast included. Rates from ₹3000 for single occupancy. Double **₹5500**

★ **Paradise** 17/1 Vallaba Agraharam St, Triplicane ☎ 044 2859 4252, ⓦ paradiseguesthouse.co.in; map p.983. A friendly and dependable hotel, offering inexpensive rooms with attached bathrooms, TVs, and a choice of Western or Indian loos. There are two blocks, old and new, right next to each other; rooms in the new block are slightly bigger and cleaner. There's also a large roof terrace, travel facilities and exchange. Good value. Ideal for backpackers, but not recommended for families. **₹1200**

OUTSIDE THE CENTRE

Crowne Plaza 132TTK Rd ☎ 0442 4994101, ⓦ crowneplaza.com; map p.981. The last word in American-style executive luxury, with great online deals. There are several excellent restaurants (see below), a 24hr coffee shop, gym and spa. The spacious rooms with plush furnishings make it a first-rate choice. Standard room rates begin at ₹8000 for single occupancy including breakfast. Double **₹9000**

New Woodlands 72–75 Dr Radhakrishnan Salai ⊕ 044 2811 3111, ⊛ newwoodlands.com; map p.981. Sprawling complex of spacious, self-contained apartments called cottages (a/c ₹4000–₹7500) and clean, reasonably sized rooms in the main block. There are also two good restaurants and a swimming pool. ₹2500

Shelter 19–21 Venkatesa Agraharam St, Mylapore ⊕ 044 4924 1919, ⊛ hotelshelter.com; map p.981. A stone's throw from the Kapalishvara Temple, this sparklingly clean luxury three-star hotel with good restaurants and a bar is better value than most upmarket places. All rooms are a/c. ₹4500

EATING

Chennai offers the complete range of dining options you would expect from a major city, ranging from dirt-cheap vegetarian "meals" joints to high-class Westernized hotel restaurants, with some unique independent venues in between.

EGMORE

Kalyana Bhavan Biriyani 139/140 Marshalls Rd ⊕ 044 2819 3111; map p.983. As the name suggests, this is a specialist biryani place, serving tasty plain, chicken and mutton versions (₹180–200) on banana leaves, accompanied by aubergine sauce and a semolina sweet. Daily 11am–4pm & 6–9pm.

Mathsya 1 Halls Road ⊕ 044 28192030 Casa Major Road; map p.983. This famous vegetarian restaurant serving both south and north Indian cuisine is always crowded and is open for breakfast, lunch and dinner. Try their popular dosais and the thalis or meals, especially the traditional Udupi thali. Daily 6am–12am.

Saravana Bhavan 21 Kennet Lane ⊕ 044 2819 2055, ⊛ saravanabhavan.com; map p.983. This famous south Indian fast-food chain is an institution in Chennai, with more than twenty branches dotted around the city, plus more state wide and international locations. Try one of the many set meals (around ₹150) and finish with freshly made *ladoo* or *barfi* from the sweets counter. Daily 6am–10pm.

★ **Vasanta Bhavan** 20 Gandhi Irwin Rd ⊕ 044 2819 2354; map p.983. One of the best-value joints around the station, with ranks of attentive waiters and delicious pure-veg food – ₹100 for a generous thali, plus great dosas and so on. It's busy, spotlessly clean, and its coffee and sweets are delicious too. Daily 6am–10.30pm.

ANNA SALAI AND TRIPLICANE

Amethyst Next to Corporation Bank, White's Rd ⊕ 044 4599 1633, ⊛ amethystchennai.com; map p.983. Delightfully lush garden café with tables set among ferns and palms along a veranda and in an a/c hall. There are toasted sandwiches (from ₹225), a range of coffees, fresh veg and fruit juices (from ₹120) and filling main courses such as bangers and mash for around ₹400. Daily 10am–10pm.

★ **Annalakshmi** 1st floor, Sigapi Achi Building (behind Air India office), 18/3 Rukmani Lakshmipathy Rd ⊕ 044 2852 5109; map p.983. This beautifully decorated restaurant is a charitable venture run voluntarily by Sivananda devotees, whose profits go to the community. You can choose between pricey set menus with different Ayurvedic properties or order à la carte dishes for around ₹250–400. Tues–Sun noon–2pm & 7–8.45pm.

Firdouse 307 Triplicane High Road ⊕ 044 4215 7174; map p.983. One of Triplicane's best, with an extensive menu of north and south Indian food: *aloo parathas*, a range of chicken dishes, vegetarian options and biryanis, all in the ₹100–200 range; also caramel custard. Clean, with a separate a/c dining area. Daily 11am–midnight.

Mogal Biriyani Triplicane High Rd, near the junction with Wallajah Rd; map p.983. A tiny *dhaba*, the best of many such places on this road, with few tables but serving up tasty chicken in tandoori, kebab and biryani for under ₹100. Daily 11am–11pm.

The Raintree/The Verandah Connemara hotel, Binny Rd ⊕ 044 6600 0000; map p.983. Occupying a classy wooden building at the rear of the compund, *The Raintree* specializes in set Chettinad meals from ₹1450, while *The Verandah* is a high-quality multicuisine restaurant, with meals for around ₹1000. Both daily: The Raintree 12.30–3pm & 7.30pm–midnight; The Verandah 24hr.

Sennthur 154 Anna Salai, opposite Spencer Plaza ⊕ 91766 23490; map p.983. Large, centrally-located "banana-leaf" restaurant very popular with locals. There are two main eating areas, non-a/c at the front and a slightly more expensive a/c hall at the back. "Meals" are served from 11.30am–3.30pm (standard meals ₹70; specials with extra dishes and dessert ₹100); also north Indian dishes. Daily 7am–11pm.

OUTSIDE THE CENTRE

Amaravathi Corner of Cathedral and TTK roads ⊕ 044 2811 7000; map p.981. One of four dependable options in this complex of regional speciality restaurants, south of the downtown area. This one does excellent Andhra food, including particularly tasty biryanis (from ₹300). Daily noon–4pm & 7–11pm.

★ **Dakshin/The Residency** Crowne Plaza hotel, 132 TTK Rd ⊕ 044 2499 4101; map p.981. The *Dakshin* is one of the country's top south Indian restaurants, serving a range of unusual dishes, including seafood in marinated spices, Karnataka mutton biryani and *appam*. Live Carnatic music in the evenings. Book in advance and expect to pay at least ₹1000 for a meal with starter and drink. *The Residency*

20

serves multicuisine, including Southeast Asian, Chinese and European dishes. Daily 12.15–3pm & 7.15–11pm.

Don Pepé 1st floor, above Hot Breads, 73 Cathedral Rd ☎044 2811 0343; map p.981. Swish a/c Tex-Mex joint, serving a predictable menu of fajitas, enchiladas, tortillas and burritos, plus a selection of average pasta dishes (dubbed "Euro-Mex"). Meat dishes cost in the region of ₹300–400. Daily 11am–10pm.

Ente Keralam 1 Kasturi Estate, First St, Poes Garden ☎044 42328585, ⍟entekeralam.in; map p.981. Food is served in seven separate rooms at this top-notch Kerala restaurant, giving it a homely feel. Try a backwater speciality, Karimeen fish (₹400–600 depending on size), one of the veggie coconut curries (₹200) or the meat dishes (around ₹350). The lunchtime menu offers sixteen dishes for ₹250. Daily noon–3pm & 7–11pm.

DRINKING AND NIGHTLIFE

Chennai's bar and club scene has been growing along with the disposable income of the local middle class. Triplicane, however, is almost dry and Egmore doesn't offer much, so most of the major nightspots are located in the top-end hotels dotted around the south side of the city. Expect cover charges including a drink of up to ₹1000 per person. Check out ⍟whatshot.in/chennai for the latest trends.

10 Downing St Kences Inn, 50 North Boag Rd, T Nagar ☎044 28152152, ⍟10ds.in/chennai; map p.981. As you might guess from the name, there's an austere English feel to the decor at this chain pub but there's no holds barred on the fun front, with ladies' nights on Wednesdays and karaoke Thursdays. Daily 11am–11pm.

Illusions – The Madras Pub 105 Dr Radhakrishnan Salai, Mylapore ☎044 4214 4449; map p.981. First-floor bar with snazzy modern design in its artwork and furniture. Popular with clubbers and celebrities for its mix of rock, hip-hop and Bollywood nights. Daily 12.30–3pm & 6.30pm–midnight.

Leather Bar Park hotel Plot 601, Anna Salai ☎044 42676000, ⍟theparkhotels.com; map p.981. A

favourite of Chennai's young, moneyed crowd – especially at weekends – this smart hotel bar gains its name from the black leather furniture throughout. The wide range of drinks includes plenty of cocktails, which you can sip alfresco on the spill-out terrace area. Daily 11am–midnight.

Paddington Sports Pub 132 Chamiers Rd, Nandanam ☎044 24348440, ⍟gotopaddington.co.in; map p.981. Large sports bar complete with billiards room, smart restaurant area and a goalpost-shaped bar. They also serve Indian and Chinese food. Daily 11am–11pm.

QBar Hilton Chennai, 10th Floor, 124/1 Jawaharlal Nehru Salai, Guindy ☎044 22255555; map p.981. Poolside rooftop club with an ambient soundtrack provided by the resident DJ. They serve a good selection of beers and wines, cocktails and mocktails. Daily noon–11pm.

Zara The Tapas Bar 71 Cathedral Rd, Gopalapuram ☎044 2811 1462; map p.981. A dizzying mishmash of neon lighting, TV screens flashing images and trendy decor, where you can sample good cocktails and snack on the idiosyncratic take on tapas. Themed club nights, such as Retro Thursdays. Daily 11am–11pm.

ENTERTAINMENT

Cinema There is plenty of entertainment on offer in Chennai, including a number of high-quality cinemas showing English, Hindi and, of course, Tamil films, such as the swish Sathyam chain (⍟spicinemas.in).

Music The annual Carnatic music festival runs from

mid-December to mid-February, with the main concerts taking place at the music academy on TTK Rd. You can find details of other classical music and dance performances at ⍟kutcheribuzz.com.

SHOPPING

Higginbothams 116 Anna Salai ☎044 2852 0640; map p.983. One of the largest stores of the nationwide bookseller, packed with hardbacks and paperbacks on every subject imaginable. Very strong history, philosophy and religion sections. Mon–Sat 9am–8pm, Sun 10.30am–7.30pm.

Indian Arts Emporium 152 Anna Salai ☎044 2846 0560; map p.983. This jointly-managed row of several crafts shops has a wide range of bronzes, ornaments, silks and carpets. Mon–Sat 10.30am–7.30pm, Sun 10.30am–4pm.

Kalakshetra Foundation craft shop Kalakshetra Rd, Thiruvanmiyur ☎044 2452 5423, ⍟kalakshetra.in; map

p.981. The shop here sells a huge array of quality handmade crafts, from silk and silk/cotton saris to larger woven items and accessories such as bags. Mon–Sat 9am–5pm.

Nalli Chinnasami Chetty 9 Nageswaran Rd, T Nagar ☎044 2434 4115, ⍟nallisilks.com; map p.981. Huge branch of this famous silk shop, selling an array of saris and other items, including some of Kanchipuram's best products. Daily 9am–9pm.

Poompuhar 108 Anna Salai ☎044 2852 0624, ⍟tnpoompuhar.org; map p.983. Tamil Nadu's official state handicrafts showroom stocks all sorts of souvenirs, from small trinkets to huge bronze Nataraj replicas. Mon–Sat 10am–8pm.

Spencer Plaza Anna Salai ☎044 2849 1001; map p.983. Chennai's original mall with its glass-roofed atrium is packed with hundreds of shops, from chains such as Bata to small independent clothes outlets. Also boasts forex agents and fast food aplenty. Daily 9.30am–9.30pm.

DIRECTORY

Banks and currency exchange Chennai has plenty of banks, though the major hotels offer exchange facilities to residents only. Thomas Cook (Mon–Sat 9am–6pm) has offices at the G-4 Eldorado Building, 112 Uttar Gandhi Salai. There are forex agents at the airport and in Spencer Plaza (see above).

Consulates Australia, 9th Floor, Express Chambers, 49–50 Whites Rd, Royapettah ☎044 4592 1300; Canada, Suite No 205, Hotel Park Hyatt, 39 Velachery Road, Little Mount, Guindy, ☎044 71000201; New Zealand, 132 Cathedral Rd ☎044 2811 2472; South Africa, 234 NSC Bose Rd ☎044 2530 6789; Sri Lanka, 56 Sterling Rd, Nungambakkam ☎044 2824 1896; UK, 20 Anderson Rd, Nungambakkam ☎044 4219 2151; US, Gemini Circle, Anna Salai ☎044 28112000.

Hospitals Chennai's best-equipped private hospital is the Apollo, 21 Greams Lane (☎044 2829 3333, ⓦchennai. apollohospitals.com). For an ambulance, try ☎102, but it's usually quicker to jump in a taxi.

Post office Chennai's main post office is opposite Shanti theatre on Anna Salai (Mon–Sat 8am–8pm, Sun 10am–5pm). There are smaller branches in both Egmore and Triplicane.

Travel agents Reliable agents include Macro Hawk Flight Travels, Munoth Centre, 343 Triplicane High Rd ☎044 2852 8585, ⓔmacrohawk05@yahoo.com; Thomas Cook, Eldorado Building, 112 Nungambakkam High Rd ☎044 2827 5052, ⓦthomascook.in; Trade-wings, 713 Anna Salai ☎044 4203 7101, ⓦtradewingstravels.in; and Welcome Tours & Travels, 150 Anna Salai ☎044 2846 0677, ⓦallindiatours.com.

The northeast

20

Fazed by the heat and air pollution of Chennai, most visitors head down the Coromandel coast to India's stone-carving capital, **Mamallapuram**. En route, it's worth stopping at **Dakshina Chitra**, a folk museum around 30km south of Chennai, where traditional buildings from across south India have been beautifully reconstructed. Further inland, **Kanchipuram** is an important pilgrimage and silk-sari-weaving town from where you can loop southwest to the atmospheric temple town of **Tiruvannamalai**, situated at the base of the sacred mountain, Arunachala. Along the coast, you can breakfast on croissants and espresso coffee in the former French colony of **Puducherry**, which is a Union Territory and not administratively a part of Tamil Nadu. A short way north, **Auroville**, the Utopian settlement founded by followers of the Sri Aurobindo Ghose's spiritual successor, The Mother, provides a New Age haven for soul-searching Westerners and an economy for the local population.

Mamallapuram and around

Scattered around the base of a colossal mound of boulders 58km south of Chennai is the small seaside town and UNESCO World Heritage Site of **MAMALLAPURAM** (formerly Mahabalipuram). From dawn till dusk, the rhythms of chisels chipping granite resound down its sandy lanes – evidence of a stone-carving tradition that has endured since this was a major port of the Pallava dynasty, between the fifth and ninth centuries. It is only possible to speculate about the purpose of much of the boulder sculpture, but it appears that the friezes and shrines were not made for worship at all, but rather as showcases for the talents of local artists. Due in no small part to the maritime activities of the Pallavas, their style of art and architecture had wide-ranging influence, spreading from south India as far north as Ellora, as well as to Southeast Asia.

Mamallapuram's monuments divide into four categories: open-air **bas-reliefs**, structured **temples**, man-made **caves** and **rathas** ("chariots" carved in situ from single boulders to resemble temples or the chariots used in temple processions). The famous bas-reliefs, **Arjuna's Penance** and the **Krishna Mandapa**, adorn massive rocks near the centre of the village, while the beautiful **Shore Temple**, one of India's most photographed monuments, presides over the beach. Sixteen man-made caves and monolithic structures, in different stages of completion, are scattered through the area, but the most complete of the nine *rathas* are in a group, named after the five Pandava brothers of the Mahabharata.

Given the coexistence of so many stunning archaeological remains with a long sandy **beach**, it was inevitable this would become a major destination for Western travellers, with the inevitable presence of Kashmiri emporia, beach hawkers, budget hotels and fish restaurants – and more recently hordes of Chennai-escapees descending at the weekends as well. The sandy hinterland and flat estuarine paddy fields around Mamallapuram also harbour a handful of sights well worth making forays from the coast to see. You can take any coastal bus between Mamallapuram and Chennai, or rent a moped for the day.

The Shore Temple

Daily 6am–6pm (ticket office closes 5.30pm) • ₹600 (₹40), includes Pancha Pandava *rathas* if visited on the same day

With its unforgettable silhouette, visible for kilometres along the beach, Mamallapuram's **Shore Temple** dates from the early eighth century and is considered to be the earliest stone-built temple in south India. Today, due to the combined forces of wind, salt and sand, much of the detailed carving has eroded, giving the whole temple a soft, rounded appearance.

The taller of the towers is raised above a cell that faces out to sea – don't be surprised to see mischievous monkeys crouching inside. Approached from the west through two low-walled enclosures lined with small Nandi (bull) figures, the temple comprises two lingam shrines (one facing east, the other west), and a third shrine between them housing an image of the reclining Vishnu. Recent excavations, revealing a tank containing a structured stone column thought to have been a lantern, and a large Varaha (boar incarnation of Vishnu) aligned with the Vishnu shrine, suggest that the area was sacred long before the Pallavas chose it as a temple site.

Arjuna's Penance

Mamallapuram's most celebrated bas-relief, **Arjuna's Penance** (also referred to as the "Descent of the Ganges"), lies directly west of the bus stand behind the modern Talasayana Perumal Temple. The surface of this rock erupts with detailed carving, most notably endearing and naturalistic renditions of animals. On the left-hand side, Arjuna, one of the Pandava brothers and a consummate archer, is shown standing on one leg. He is looking at the midday sun through a prism formed by his hands, meditating on Shiva, who is represented by a nearby statue fashioned by Arjuna himself. The Shiva Purana tells that Arjuna made the journey to a forest on the banks of the Ganges to do penance, in the hope that Shiva would part with his favourite weapon, the *pashupatashastra*, a magic staff or arrow. Shiva eventually materialized in the guise of Kirata, a wild forest-dweller, and picked a fight with Arjuna over a boar they both claimed to have shot. Arjuna only realized he was dealing with the deity after his attempts to drub the wild man proved futile; narrowly escaping death at the playful hand of Shiva, he was finally rewarded with the weapon. To the right of Arjuna, a natural cleft represents the **Ganges**, complete with *nagas* – water spirits in the form of cobras. You may well see sudden movements among the carved animals: lazing goats often join the permanent features.

Ganesha Ratha and Krishna's Butter Ball

Just north of Arjuna's Penance a path leads west and uphill to a single monolith, the **Ganesha Ratha**. Its image of Ganesh dates from this century; some say it was installed at the instigation of England's King George V. The sculpture at one end, of a protecting demon with a tricorn headdress, is reminiscent of the Indus Valley Civilization's

4000-year-old horned figure known as the "proto-Shiva". Further north up the hill, precipitously balanced on the top of a ridge, is a massive, natural, almost spherical boulder called **Krishna's Butter Ball**. Picnickers and goats often rest in its perilous-looking shade.

Varaha Mandapa II Cave

On the hill behind Arjuna's Penance, southwest of the Ganesha Ratha, is the **Varaha Mandapa II Cave**, whose entrance hall has two pillars with horned lion-bases and a cell flanked by two *dvarapalas*, or guardians. One of four **panels** shows the boar-incarnation of Vishnu, who stands with one foot resting on the *naga* snake-king as he lifts a diminutive Prithvi – the Earth – from the primordial ocean. Another is of Gajalakshmi, the goddess Lakshmi seated on a lotus being bathed by a pair of elephants. Trivikrama, the dwarf brahmin who becomes huge and bestrides the world

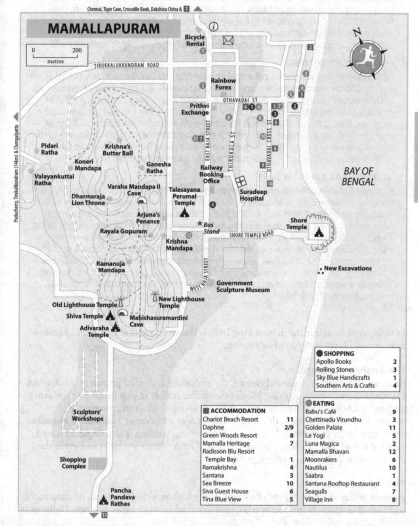

MAMALLAPURAM

Chennai, Tiger Cave, Crocodile Bank, Dakshina Chitra &

0   200 metres

TIRUKKALUKKUNDRAM ROAD

Bicycle Rental

Rainbow Forex

Prithvi Exchange

OTHAVADAI ST

Pidari Ratha

Krishna's Butter Ball

Koneri Mandapa

Ganesha Ratha

Valayankuttai Ratha

Varaha Mandapa II Cave

Dharmaraja Lion Throne

Arjuna's Penance

Rayala Gopuram

Krishna Mandapa

Ramanuja Mandapa

Railway Booking Office

Talasayana Perumal Temple

Bus Stand

Suradeep Hospital

SHORE TEMPLE ROAD

Shore Temple

BAY OF BENGAL

New Excavations

Government Sculpture Museum

Old Lighthouse Temple

New Lighthouse Temple

Shiva Temple

Mahishasuramardini Cave

Adivaraha Temple

Puducherry, Tirukkalikundram (14km) & Chengalpattu

EAST RAJA STREET

TIRUKULA ST

OTHAVADAI CROSS ST

WEST RAJA STREET

Sculptors' Workshops

Shopping Complex

Pancha Pandava Rathas

20

● SHOPPING

Apollo Books	2
Rolling Stones	3
Sky Blue Handicrafts	1
Southern Arts & Crafts	4

■ ACCOMMODATION

Chariot Beach Resort	11
Daphne	2/9
Green Woods Resort	8
Mamalla Heritage	7
Radisson Blu Resort Temple Bay	1
Ramakrishna	4
Santana	3
Sea Breeze	10
Siva Guest House	6
Tina Blue View	5

● EATING

Babu's Café	9
Chettinadu Virundhu	3
Golden Palate	11
Le Yogi	5
Luna Magica	2
Mamalla Bhavan	12
Moonrakers	6
Nautilus	10
Saabra	1
Santana Rooftop Restaurant	4
Seagulls	7
Village Inn	8

THE TEMPLES OF TAMIL NADU

No Indian state is more dominated by its **temples** than Tamil Nadu, where temple architecture catalogues the tastes of successive dynasties and testifies to the centrality of religion in everyday life. Most temples are built in honour of Shiva, Vishnu and their consorts; all are characterized not only by their design and sculptures, but also by constant activity: devotion, dancing, singing, pujas, festivals and feasts. Each is tended by Brahmin priests, recognizable by their *dhotis* (a garment tied around waist that covers the lower body until the legs), a sacred thread draped over the right shoulder, and marks on the forehead. One to three horizontal (usually white) lines distinguish Shaivites; vertical lines (yellow or red), often converging into a near-V shape, are common among Vaishnavites.

DRAVIDA ARCHITECTURE

Dravida, the temple architecture of Tamil Nadu, first took form in the Pallava port of **Mamallapuram**. A step-up from the cave retreats of Hindu and Jain ascetics, the earliest Pallava monuments were **mandapas**, shrines cut into rock faces and fronted by columns. This sculptural skill was transferred to freestanding temples, **rathas**, carved out of single rocks and incorporating the essential elements of Hindu temples: the dim inner sanctuary, the *garbhagriha*, capped with a modest tapering spire featuring repetitive architectural motifs.

CHOLA ARCHITECTURE

Pallava themes were developed in Karnataka by the Chalukyas and Rashtrakutas, but it was the Shaivite **Cholas** who spearheaded Tamil Nadu's next architectural phase, in the tenth century. In **Thanjavur**, Rajaraja I created the Brihadishvara Temple principally as a status symbol; its proportions far exceed any attempted by the Pallavas. Set within a vast walled courtyard, the sanctuary, fronted by a small *mandapa*, stands beneath a sculpted *vimana* that soars more than 60m high. Most sculptures once again feature Shiva, but the *gopuras* on each side of the eastern gateway to the courtyard were an innovation, as were the lions carved into the base of the sanctuary walls, and the pavilion erected over Nandi in front of the sanctuary.

VIJAYANAGAR ARCHITECTURE

By the time of the thirteenth-century **Vijayanagar** kings, the temple was central to city life, the focus for civic meetings, education, dance and theatre. The Vijayanagars extended earlier structures, adding enclosing walls around a series of **prakaras**, or courtyards, and erecting freestanding *mandapas* for use as meeting halls, elephant stables, stages for music and dance, and ceremonial marriage halls (*kalyan mandapas*). Raised on superbly decorated columns, these *mandapas* became known as **thousand-pillared halls**. **Tanks** were added, doubling as water stores and washing areas, and used for festivals when deities were set afloat in boats.

Under the Vijayanagars, the *gopuras* were enlarged and set at the cardinal points over the high gateways to each *prakara*, to become the dominant feature. **Madurai** is the place to check out Vijayanagar architecture.

in three steps to defeat the demon king Bali, is shown in another panel, and finally a four-armed Durga is depicted in another.

The Krishna Mandapa

Immediately south of Arjuna's Penance, the enormous bas-relief known as the **Krishna Mandapa** shows Krishna raising Mount Govardhana aloft in one hand. The sculptor's original intention must have been for the rock above Krishna to represent the mountain, but the seventeenth-century Vijayanagar addition of a columned *mandapa*, or entrance hall, prevents a clear view of the carving. Krishna is also depicted seated milking a cow, and standing playing the flute. Other figures are *gopas* and *gopis*, the cowboys and -girls of his pastoral youth.

The lighthouses

Around 300m south of Arjuna's Penance, at the highest point in an area of steep paths, unfinished temples, ruins, scampering monkeys and massive rocks, the **New Lighthouse** affords fine views east to the Shore Temple, and west across paddy fields and flat lands littered with rocks. Next to it, the **Olakanesvara** ("flame-eyed" Shiva), or **Old Lighthouse Temple**, used as a lighthouse until the early twentieth century, dates from the Rajasimha period (674–800 AD).

Mahishasuramardini Cave

Nestling between the two lighthouses is the **Mahishasuramardini Cave**, whose central image portrays Shiva and Parvati with the child Murugan seated on Parvati's lap. Shiva's right foot rests on the back of the bull Nandi, and Parvati sits casually, leaning on her left hand. On the left wall, beyond an empty cell, a panel depicts Vishnu reclining on the serpent, his attitude of repose contrasted with the weapon-brandishing demons, Madhu and Kaithaba. Other figures seek Vishnu's permission to chase them. Opposite, an intricately carved panel shows the eight-armed goddess Durga as Mahishasuramardini, the "crusher" of the buffalo demon Mahishasura. The panel shows Durga riding a lion, in the midst of the struggle. Accompanied by dwarf *ganas*, she wields a bow and other weapons; Mahishasura, equipped with a club, can be seen to the right, in flight with fellow demons.

Government Sculpture Museum

West Raja St • Daily 9.30am–5pm • ₹10

The small **Government Sculpture Museum**, located on the main road south of the bus stand, has a rather motley collection of unlabelled Pallava sculpture found in and around Mamallapuram, some of it quite colourful and attractive. Many of the best pieces stand on the front lawn, perfectly visible from the road. The building itself, though modern, is also appealing and resembles a temple more than a museum.

Pancha Pandava Rathas (Five Rathas)

Daily 6am–6pm (ticket office closes 5.30pm) • ₹250 (₹10) including the Shore Temple on the same day

In a sandy compound 1.5km south of the village centre stands the stunning group of monoliths known as the **Pancha Pandava Rathas**, the five chariots of the Pandavas. Dating from the period of Narasimhavarman I (c.630–670 AD), they consist of five separate freestanding sculptures that imitate structured temples, plus some beautifully carved life-sized animals.

The "architecture" of the *rathas* reflects a variety of styles and stands almost as a model for much subsequent development in the southern style. Carving was always executed from top to bottom, enabling the artists to work on the upper parts with no fear of damaging anything below. Intriguingly, it's thought that the *rathas* were never used for worship.

The southernmost and tallest of the *rathas*, named after the eldest of the Pandavas, is the pyramidal **Dharmaraja**. Set on a square base, the upper part comprises a series of diminishing storeys, each with a row of pavilions. Four corner blocks, each with two panels and standing figures, are broken up by two pillars and pilasters supported by squatting lions. Figures on the panels include Ardhanarishvara (Shiva and female consort in one figure), Brahma, the king Narasimhavarman I and Harihara (Shiva and Vishnu combined). The central tier includes sculptures of Shiva Gangadhara and one of the earliest representations in Tamil Nadu of the dancing Shiva, Nataraja, who became all-important in the region. Alongside, the **Bhima** *ratha*, the largest of the group, is the least complete. Devoid of carved figures, the upper storeys, as in the Dharmaraja, feature false windows and repeated pavilion-shaped ornamentation.

The Arjuna and Draupadi *rathas* share a base. Behind the **Arjuna**, the most complete of the entire group and very similar to the Dharmaraja, stands a superb unfinished sculpture of Shiva's bull Nandi. **Draupadi** is unique in terms of rock-cut architecture, with a roof that appears to be based on a straw-thatched hut. There's an image of Durga inside, but the figure of her lion vehicle outside is aligned side-on and not facing the

20

image, suggesting this was not a real temple. To the west, close to a life-sized carving of an elephant, stands the *ratha* named after the twin brothers **Nakula and Sahadeva**.

Tiger Cave

Main highway, 4km north of Mamallapuram • Daily sunrise–sunset • Free

Set amid trees close to the sea, the extraordinary **Tiger Cave** contains a shrine to Durga, approached by a flight of steps that passes two subsidiary cells. Following the line of an irregularly shaped rock, the cave is remarkable for its elaborate exterior, which features multiple tiger or lion-heads surrounding the entrance to the main cell. If you sit for long enough, the section on the left with seated figures in niches above two elephants begins to resemble an enormous owl. These animals which resembled a tiger or lion were mythical yalis and it is often referred to as Yali Mandapa.

Crocodile Bank

14km north of town on the road to Chennai • Tues–Sun 8.30am–5.30pm • ₹60, camera ₹20, video camera ₹100 • **Night Safari** Sat & Sun 7–8.30pm • ₹200 • ⓦ madrascrocodilebank.org ⓔ info@madrascrocodilebank.org

The **Crocodile Bank** at Vadanemmeli was set up in 1976 by the American zoologist Romulus Whittaker to protect and breed indigenous crocodiles. The Bank has been so successful (from fifteen crocs to five thousand in the first fifteen years) that its remit now extends to saving endangered species, such as turtles and lizards, from around the world.

Low-walled enclosures in its garden compound house hundreds of inscrutable crocodiles, soaking in ponds or sunning themselves on the banks. Breeds include the fish-eating, knobbly-nosed gharial, and the world's largest species, the saltwater *Crocodylus porosus*, which can grow to 8m in length.

There are **feeding demonstrations** at 11.30am, 12.30pm, 4.30pm and 5.30pm on Sundays. The temptation to take photos is tempered by the sight of those hungry saurians clambering over each other to snap up the chopped flesh, within centimetres of the top of the wall. Another attraction is the weekend **Night Safari**, when the crocodiles are far more active, which has to be booked at least 48 hours in advance.

Another important field of work is conducted with the collaboration of local Irula people, whose traditional expertise is with snakes. Cobras are brought to the bank for **venom collection**, to be used in the treatment of snakebites. Elsewhere, snakes are repeatedly "milked" until they die, but here only a limited amount is taken from each snake, enabling them to return to the wild. To visit this section costs an extra ₹5.

Dakshina Chitra

Main Coast Rd • Daily except Tues 10am–6pm • ₹200 (₹100), camera ₹20, video camera ₹75 • ⓣ 044 2747 2603, ⓦ dakshinachitra.net

Occupying a patch of sand dunes midway between Chennai and Mamallapuram, **Dakshina Chitra**, literally "Vision of the South", is one of India's best-conceived folk museums, devoted to the rich architectural and artistic heritage of Kerala, Karnataka, Andhra Pradesh and Tamil Nadu. Set up by the Chennai Craft Foundation, the museum exposes visitors to many disappearing traditions of the region, which you might otherwise not be aware of, from tribal fertility cults and Ayyannar field deities to pottery and leather shadow-puppets.

A selection of traditional buildings from across peninsular India has been painstakingly reconstructed using original materials. Exhibitions attached to them convey the environmental and cultural diversity of the south, most graphically expressed in a wonderful textile collection featuring antique silk and cotton saris from various castes and regions. Snacks are available on site.

ARRIVAL AND DEPARTURE	MAMALLAPURAM AND AROUND

By train The nearest railway station is in Chengalpattu, 29km to the northeast for mainline trains to Chennai, Tiruchirapalli and beyond. There are frequent bus connections from Chengalpattu to Mamallapuram (see opposite).

By bus The bus stand is in the centre of the village in front of the Talasayana Perumal Temple. There are services roughly every 30min to Chennai (4.15am–10pm; 2hr), six daily to Kanchipuram (2hr) and regular services to Chengalpattu (for Tiruvannamalai and better connections to Kanchipuram). Mamallapuram lies just off the East Coast Rd between Chennai and Puducherry; buses between the two run every 15–20min but don't come in to Mamallapuram – you need to either walk or take an auto-rickshaw (₹50) the 1.5km northwest to the bus stop on the East Coast Rd.
By taxi Taxis to and from the centre of Chennai cost around ₹1600 or ₹1300 to and from the airport. Puducherry is a ₹2000 ride.

GETTING AROUND AND INFORMATION

By bike and motorbike By far the best way to get to the important sites is by bicycle. You can rent bikes from shops on East Raja St for ₹20/hr or ₹75/day. Scooters and Enfield motorcycles can also be rented for around ₹400/day – check at your guesthouse.

Tourist information The Government of Tamil Nadu Tourist Office (Mon–Fri 10am–5.45pm; ☎ 044 2744 2232) is one of the first buildings you see in the village, on your left as you arrive from Chennai, but is not much use. A better resource is ⊚ mahabalipuram.co.in.

ACCOMMODATION

Mamallapuram village has dozens of guesthouses and small hotels in the budget and mid-range categories but it suffers badly from aggressive touting by a small number of places; ignore the touts and walk to your chosen destination – it's a small place. The more luxurious resorts are dotted along the coast, mostly to the north.
Chariot Beach Resort 69 Five Rathas Rd ☎ 86680 95606, ⊚ chariotbeachresorts.com; map p.995. A luxurious resort at the southern end of town with massive garden area, unobstructed sea views and a 57m swimming pool. All rooms are spacious and beautifully furnished, and there's also the option of luxurious cottages (₹12,000) and sea-view suites (₹21,200). Doubles from ₹**7500**
Daphne Fishermans Colony (reception at Daphne's Hotel Othavadai, Cross St) ☎ 98942 82876, ⊚ hotel daphne1@yahoo.com; map p.995. The very last guesthouse on the beach strip with just nine rooms on three floors, a roof terrace and sea views. The place in the village is fine too. There is a small café where you can buy toast and pancakes and there are restaurants in the village. ₹**900**
★ **Green Woods Resort** 12 Othavadai Cross St ☎ 044 2744 2212, ⊚ greenwoods_resort@yahoo.com; map p.995. Very friendly and extremely good value family-run place, set round a leafy courtyard garden, which does attract mosquitoes. There's a wide range of very clean rooms (the best a/c rooms cost just ₹1400), some with swing chairs, private balconies, terraces and TVs, plus excellent Ayurvedic massage on site. No restaurant or café here so you have to venture out for breakfast. ₹**700**
Mamalla Heritage 104 East Raja St ☎ 044 2744 2060, ⊚ hotelmamallaheritage.com; map p.995. Efficient, modern hotel on the main road through the village with comfortable and spotless a/c rooms overlooking a courtyard. There's a choice of standard and slightly bigger deluxe (₹3300) rooms, for double occupancy with breakfast and all with fridge and TV, and there are two very good restaurants on site. ₹**2400**
Radisson Blu Resort Temple Bay 57 Kovalam Rd, 1km north of the village ☎ 044 2744 3636, ⊚ radissonb.

com; map p.995. A luxurious resort with a swimming pool and excellent restaurant, which backs right onto the beach. There are eight different categories of room, from standard doubles to sea-view villas with Jacuzzi and sit-out areas (₹26,000). An ultra luxury experience would be a three bed bungalow with private pool and jacuzzi at ₹125,000. ₹**5600**
Ramakrishna 8 Othavadai St ☎ 04427 442331, ⊚ hotel ramakrishna.com; map p.995. Bigger than many of the surrounding hotels, its rooms have been completely refurbished with hardwood floors, new bathrooms, a/c and flat screen TVs. There's also a breezy rooftop restaurant. ₹**200**
Santana 178 Othavadai St ☎ 97910 77352, ⊚ babus antana@rediffmail.com; map p.995. Six sizeable and spotless first-floor rooms; the seafront one is a gem, sandwiched in between its popular ground-floor beachside restaurant and roof terrace. It also offers a travel service. ₹**1000**
★ **Sea Breeze** Othavadai Cross St ☎ 044 2744 3035, ⊚ hotelseabreeze.net; map p.995. The only bona fide beach resort within the village, featuring a range of a/c rooms whose prices vary according to size and view – the large sea-view rooms with private balcony and king-size beds are the best. The swimming pool is open to non-residents (₹400/day) and there's an Ayurveda centre. Breakfast included. ₹**3000**
Siva Guest House 2 Othavadai Cross St ☎ 044 2744 3534, ⊚ sivaguesthouse.com; map p.995. A small but clean and tidy lodge with just fifteen rooms, which are spread over three floors. Mandala-patterned bedsheets add colour and there is a choice of non-a/c and a/c rooms. Good value. ₹**750**
Tina Blue View 48 Othavadai St ☎ 044 2744 2319; map p.995. Established family guesthouse with simple turquoise and whitewashed rooms, some in the main block and others in an annexe in the pleasant garden. All rooms have attached bathrooms and mosquito nets. There are also some single rooms. ₹**700**

20

20

EATING

Mamallapuram is crammed with small restaurants specializing in **seafood** – tiger prawns, pomfret, tuna, shark and lobster – usually served marinated and grilled with chips and salad; always establish in advance exactly how much it will cost. As this is a travellers' hangout, there are also numerous places offering the usual array of pasta, pancakes and bland Indian dishes. **Beer** is widely available, but it's pricey (₹180–200) and there are no dedicated bars. If you want to enjoy real Indian food, head to the *dhabas* by the bus stand and the banana-leaf places on East Raja St.

Babu's Café 7, Othavadai Cross St ☏ 99449 60639; map p.995. A seafood café and restaurant, it has a great atmosphere, a lively host and a great cook in Babu. One of the most crowded eateries in Mamallapuram, don't miss the calamari here. They also serve vegetarian food and gluten free meals. A meal for two costs in the range of ₹300. Daily 9am–10.30pm.

Chettinadu Virundhu 10 East Raja St ☏ 73584 45177; map p.995. Smart new canteen-style place with an a/c area, serving a range of tasty recipes from the Chettinad region for ₹150–300, plus other Indian and Chinese standards. Dosas with chicken, mutton and meat are the specialities here. Daily 11.30am–4pm & 6.30–10.30pm.

★ **Golden Palate** Mamalla Heritage hotel, 104 East Raja St ☏ 044 2744 2060; map p.995. Blissfully-cool café with a/c and tinted windows, serving the best veg food in the village: ₹210 "meals" at lunchtime (noon–3pm), north Indian tandoori in the courtyard in the evenings and wonderful ice-cream sundaes. *Wok To Dhaba*, a nearby restaurant, serves mainly meat and chicken dishes and Indian Chinese and costs ₹800 for two people. Golden Palate daily 7am–10.30pm; Wok To Dhaba daily noon–4pm & 7–10.30pm.

★ **Le Yogi** 19 Othavadai St ☏ 98405 75571; map p.995. Run by a French/Indian couple, this relaxed place is a good spot to chill, serving French crêpes (around ₹170), a range of salads with brown sesame bread, pasta dishes for up to ₹300, plus good coffee and lassis. Daily 8am–11pm.

Luna Magica Bajanai Kovil St, Fisherman Colony ☏ 98401 00519; map p.995. Beach restaurant serving top-notch seafood, kept alive in a tank and sold by weight. They specialize in tiger prawns and lobster in a choice of tasty sauces such as tomato or garlic butter and also offer fish curry, plus grilled fish, shark and tuna steaks for ₹200–350. Red wine and cold beer are available, but expensive. Daily 7.30am–10pm.

Mamalla Bhavan Shore Temple Rd, opposite the bus stand. ☏ 044 27442250; map p.995. A very popular pure-veg and "meals" joint that's invariably packed. At ₹105, the unlimited lunchtime "meals" (11.30am–3.30pm) are a bargain, and they also serve good south Indian breakfasts including *pongal*, masala dosas and coffee. Daily 6.30am–9.30pm.

Moonrakers 34 Othavadai St ☏ 044 2744 2115; map p.995. Cool jazz and blues sounds, great fresh seafood and slick service ensure this place, with its three floors, is often packed with travellers. The owners are constantly touting passers-by for custom. Good seafood platter (fish, prawns, calamari) for ₹700. Daily 11.30am–11.30pm.

Nautilus Othavadai Cross St; map p.995. Popular café/restaurant run by a French chef. The menu features soups, a wide range of French salads (₹180), ratatouille and non-veg mains such as seafood, beef and the usual travellers' favourites for ₹300–500. Daily 9am–11pm.

Saabra 5/4 Kovalam Rd ☏ 97911 78900; map p.995. First-floor joint that does great veg, egg and chicken *kaati* rolls for ₹60, as well as Indian and Chinese dishes such as tandoori and biryanis for ₹100–200. Daily 11am–10pm.

Santana Rooftop Restaurant Santana hotel, 178 Othavadai St ☏ 94442 90832; map p.995. The breezy rooftop is much nicer than the ground-floor dining area, especially if you can get a front seat. Lobster per kilo, fish dishes, calamari and seafood platters with rice and salad go for ₹300–600. Daily 7am–11pm.

Seagulls Tina Blue View, 48 Othavadai St ☏ 044 2744 2319; map p.995. A large and pleasant rooftop restaurant serving a decent, extensive seafood menu including tuna steak with chips and salad, seafood platters, fish and prawn curries, veggie dishes and chicken, all in the ₹250–400 range. Daily 7am–11pm.

Village Inn Thirukulam St, off Othavadai St ☏ 94441 16406; map p.995. A small, pleasant restaurant with cane furniture and classical Indian music, dishing up grilled seafood for around ₹500 upwards plus cheaper fish curry, biryanis and veggie dishes. One of the cheaper places for beer. Daily 9am–10.30pm.

SHOPPING

Apollo Books 150/1 Fisherman Colony ☏ 044 2744 2992; map p.995. Excellent and friendly bookshop, owned by knowledgeable Apollo himself, who stocks a fine range of literature and titles on art, history, culture and religion. Daily 10am–8pm.

Rolling Stones 4 Othavadai Cross St ☏ 80561 13998; map p.995. Tiny stone-carving shop, whose charming owner not only sells his work at fair prices but offers carving lessons so you can make your own piece. Daily 9am–9pm.

Sky Blue Handicrafts 8 Othavadai St ☏ 044 2744 3729; map p.995. Easily the friendliest and most reputable Kashmiri shop in the village, where you can find lots of authentic fabrics, dresses, bags and silver jewellery. Daily 8am–10pm.

VEDANTHANGAL BIRD SANCTUARY

One of India's most spectacular bird sanctuaries lies roughly 1km east of the village of **Vedanthangal**, 30km from the east coast and 86km southwest of Chennai. The **sanctuary** is busiest with birdlife between December and February, when it's totally flooded. The rains of the northeast monsoon, sweeping through in October or November, bring local and migratory waterbirds, including some that nest and settle here until the dry season (usually April), when they leave for wetter areas. Abundant trees on mounds above water level provide perfect nesting spots, alive by January with fledglings. Visitors can watch the avian action from a path at the water's edge, or from a watchtower (fitted out with strong binoculars). Try to come at sunset, when the birds return from feeding. Common Indian **species** to look out for are openbill storks, spoonbills, pelicans, black cormorants, and herons of several types. You may also see ibises, grey pelicans, migrant cuckoos, sandpipers, egrets (which paddle in the rice fields), and darting bee-eaters.

ARRIVAL AND DEPARTURE

By bus Getting to Vedanthangal can present a few problems. The nearest town is Maduranthakam, 8km east, on NH-45 between Chengalpattu and Tindivanam, from where there are hourly buses to the sanctuary. Alternatively, direct services run every hour or two from Chengalpattu.

By taxi Taxis make the journey from Maduranthakam for ₹500 but cannot be booked from Vedanthangal.

INFORMATION

Opening hours Daily 6am–6pm. The best months to visit are Nov–Feb, although weekends and holidays can be crowded and noisy.

Entry fees Entry to the sanctuary is ₹100 (camera ₹500, video camera ₹1000).

Accommodation To arrange accommodation in the *Forest Department Guest house*, call the Wildlife Warden in Chennai (☎044 2235 1471 or ☎044 2220 0335 or call the Forest Ranger (☎98404 84529).

Southern Arts & Crafts 72 East Raja St ☎044 2744 3675, ⓦsouthernarts.in; map p.995. Smart showroom for stone carving, bronzes, paintings and other local artefacts. Daily 9am–8pm.

DIRECTORY

Banks and exchange Two of the best places to change money are Prithvi Exchange, 23/12 East Raja St (daily 9.30am–7pm; ☎044 2744 3265), and The Rainbow Forex, 14 Othavadai St (daily 9.30am–9pm; ☎91767 04374).

Hospital If you need medical treatment, Suradeep Hospital 15, Thirukulam St (☎044 2744 2448), is highly recommended.

Surfing A relatively new activity in Mamallapuram, available through Mumu Surf School (☎97898 44191, ⓦmumusurfer.wix.com/indiasurfing), where you can take lessons from ₹750 per person, depending on group size. If you know what you're doing, board rental goes from ₹250/hr.

Travel agents Delhi-based Hi! Tours at 125 East Raja St (☎044 2744 3260, ⓦhi-tours.com) offer car rental, ticketing and other services. Travels Partners (☎98403 77033, ✉travelspartners@gmail.com) on Othavadai St provide friendly service.

Kanchipuram

KANCHIPURAM is situated on the Vegavathi River 70km southwest of Chennai. Ask any Tamil what Kanchipuram (aka "Kanchi") is famous for, and they'll probably say silk saris, shrines and saints – in that order. A dynastic capital throughout the medieval era, it remains one of the country's seven holiest cities, sacred to both Shaivites and Vaishnavites, and among the few surviving centres of goddess worship in the south. Year round, pilgrims pour through for a quick puja stop on the Tirupati tour circuit and, if they can afford it, a spot of shopping in the sari emporia. For non-Hindu visitors, however, Kanchipuram holds less appeal. Although the temples are undeniably impressive, the town itself is unremittingly hot, with only basic accommodation and amenities. Some people prefer to visit Kanchipuram as a **day-trip** from Chennai or Mamallapuram, both of which are a two-hour bus ride away.

Established by the **Pallava** kings in the fourth century AD, Kanchipuram served as their **capital** for five hundred years, and continued to flourish throughout the Chola,

Pandya and Vijayanagar eras. Under the Pallavas, it was an important scholastic forum, and a meeting point for Jain, Buddhist and Hindu cultures. Its **temples** dramatically reflect this enduring political prominence, spanning the years from the peak of Pallava construction to the seventeenth century, when the ornamentation of the *gopuras* and pillared halls was at its most elaborate. You might need to be a little firm to resist the attentions of pushy puja-wallahs, who try to con foreigners into overpriced ceremonies. If you've come for silk, head for the shops that line Gandhi and Thirukatchininambi roads.

Ekambareshvara Temple
North Mada St • Daily; closed noon–4pm • Camera ₹20, video camera ₹100

On the north side of town, Kanchipuram's largest temple and most important Shiva shrine, the **Ekambareshvara Temple** – also known as Ekambaranatha – is easily identified by its colossal whitewashed *gopuras*, which rise to almost 60m. The main temple contains some Pallava work, but was mostly constructed in the sixteenth and seventeenth centuries, and stands within a vast walled enclosure beside some smaller shrines and a large fish-filled water tank.

The entrance is through a high-arched passageway beneath an elaborate *gopura* in the south wall which leads to an open courtyard and a majestic "thousand-pillared hall", or *kalyan mandapa*. This faces the tank in the north and the sanctuary in the west that protects the emblem of Shiva (here in his form as **Kameshvara**, Lord of Desire), Prithvi lingam (one of five lingams in Tamil Nadu that represent the elements, in this case *Prithvi*, the Earth). Behind the sanctum, accessible from the covered hallway around it, an eerie, bare hall lies beneath a profusely carved *gopura*, and in the courtyard a venerable **mango tree** represents the tree under which Shiva and Kamakshi were married. This union is celebrated during a festival each April, when many couples are married in the *kalyan mandapa*.

Sankaramadam
Raja St • Daily; closed noon–4pm

Kanchipuram is the seat of a line of holy men bearing the title **acharya**, whose line dates back perhaps as far as 1300 BC to the saint Adi Sankaracharya. The 68th acharya, the highly revered Sri Chandrasekharendra Sarasvati Swami, died in January 1994 at the age of 101. Buried in the sitting position, as is the custom for great Hindu sages, his mortal remains are enshrined in a *samadhi* at the **Sankaramadam**, a *math* (monastery for Hindu renouncers) down the road from the Ekambareshvara Temple. Lined with old photographs from the life of the former swami, with young Brahmin students chanting Sanskrit verses in the background, it's a typically Tamil blend of simple sanctity and garish modern glitz. The *math*'s two huge elephants are available to bestow blessings upon visiting pilgrims for a small fee.

Kailasanatha Temple
Western outskirts • Daily; closed noon–4pm

The **Kailasanatha Temple**, the oldest structure in Kanchipuram and the finest example of Pallava architecture in south India, is situated among several low-roofed houses just over 1km west of the town centre. Built by the Pallava king Rajasimha early in the eighth century, its intimate size and simple carving distinguish it from the town's later temples. Usually quieter than its neighbours, the shrine becomes the focus of vigorous celebrations during the **Mahashivratri festival** each March. Like its contemporary, the Shore Temple at Mamallapuram, it is built of soft sandstone, but its sheltered position has spared it from wind and sand erosion, and it remains remarkably intact, despite some rather clumsy renovation work.

ELEPHANT AT THE MUDUMALAI WILDLIFE SANCTUARY

Kamakshi Amman Temple

Raja St • Daily; closed noon–4pm • ⓦ kanchikamakshi.com

Built during Pallava supremacy and modified in the fourteenth and seventeenth centuries, the **Kamakshi Amman Temple**, north of the bus stand, combines several styles, with an ancient central shrine, gates from the Vijayanagar period, and high, heavily sculpted, creamy *gopuras* set above the gateways.

This is one of India's three holiest shrines to Shakti, Shiva's cosmic energy depicted in female form, usually as his consort. The goddess Kamakshi, a local form of Parvati, shown with a sugar-cane bow and arrows of flowers, is honoured for having lured Shiva to Kanchipuram, where they were married, and thus having forged the connection between the local community and the god. In February or March, deities are wheeled to the temple in huge wooden "cars", decked with robed statues and swaying plantain leaves.

ARRIVAL AND DEPARTURE   KANCHIPURAM

By train The railway station in the northeast of town sees twelve daily passenger services from Chengalpattu (originating in Chennai, Arakkonam, Tirupati and Puducherry) and two express trains (the weekly *Mumbai–Madurai Express* and biweekly *Mumbai–Nagercoil Express*).

By bus Buses from Chennai, Mamallapuram and

Chengalpattu stop at the stand in the town centre just off Kosa St.

Destinations Chennai (every 10–15min; 1hr 30min–2hr); Madurai (4 daily; 8–9hr); Puducherry (hourly; 3–4hr); Tiruchirapalli (12 daily; 7–8hr); Tiruvannamalai (10 daily; 3–4hr).

GETTING AROUND

By bike The best way to get around Kanchi is by bicycle. Most of the main roads are fairly wide and traffic just about

manageable. Bikes are available (₹10/hr) from stalls at both the west and northeast entrances to the bus stand.

20

ACCOMMODATION

Aruna Residency 15 Ulakalanthar Maada St, tucked away 50m down from the main junction ☏ 044 2722 4274, ✉ arunamahal@gmail.com; map p.1004. A large, quiet mid-range place that offers very good deals on single occupancy rooms. The double rooms, complete with TV, are a good size, light and airy. ₹2000

Jothis Residency 53 & 56 KS Murugesa Mudalyar Nagar, Tollgate ☏ 86810 08899, ⓦ jothiresidency. com; map p.1004. Located behind one of the most famous temples, the shrine of Varadaraja Perumal, *Jothis* has 18 clean and comfortable double-occupancy a/c rooms. There are two separate restaurants, offering both vegetarian and non vegetarian cuisine. ₹2350

MM 65/66 Nellukkara St ☏ 044 2722 7250, ⓦ mmhotels.com; map p.1004. Large, clean, medium-priced hotel, situated right in the heart of the town. The wood-panelled a/c rooms for double occupancy (₹2350) have armchairs but are a little on the small side; the non-a/c rooms are plainer but slightly bigger. ₹1560

Raja's Lodge 20-B Nellukkara St ☏ 044 2722 2603; map p.1004. One of the best budget options in town, although little English is spoken. The rooms are on the small side and somewhat dingy. Double rooms with a/c are ₹1500. Restaurant downstairs. ₹850

Map legend:

KANCHIPURAM

■ ACCOMMODATION

Aruna Residency	2
Jothis Residency	5
MM	1
Raja's Lodge	4
Silk City	3

● EATING

| Neo Sri Rama Café | 1 |
| Saravana Bhavan | 2 |

Silk City 1st Floor, 77 Nellukara St ☎ 044 2722 7573, ✉ hotelsilkcity@gmail.com; map p.1004. Brand-new hotel in a central location with immaculate, spacious a/c rooms. A kettle, TV and towels are provided in all rooms, and the large attached bathrooms are spotless. Excellent value. No alcohol or wi-fi. **₹1500**

EATING

Neo Sri Rama Café 20 Nellukkara St ☎ 044 2722 2435; map p.1004. Great value, if slightly dingy, restaurant, churning out filling unlimited "meals" for only ₹55. Tiffins or snacks only in the evenings. The sort of place where you are likely to attract the interest of locals. Daily 7am–10.30pm.
Saravana Bhavan 504, Gandhi Road ☎ 044 2722 2506; map p.1004. Located near the bus stand, this popular chain of eateries offer your standard vegetarian fare of both south and north Indian cuisine and the speciality is the variety of dosas and meals during lunch (₹100–300). Daily 7am–10pm.

Tiruvannamalai

Synonymous with the fifth Hindu element of Fire, **TIRUVANNAMALAI**, 100km southwest of Kanchipuram, ranks, along with Madurai, Kanchipuram, Chidambaram and Trichy, as one of the five holiest towns in Tamil Nadu. Its name, meaning "Red Mountain", derives from the spectacular extinct volcano, **Arunachala**, which rises behind it, and which glows an unearthly crimson in the dawn light. This awesome natural backdrop, combined with the colossal **Arunachaleshvara Temple** in the centre of town, make Tiruvannamalai one of the region's most memorable destinations. Well off the tourist trail, it's a perfect place to get to grips with life in small-town Tamil Nadu, especially for anyone with an interest in Hinduism.

Mythology identifies Arunachala as the place where Shiva asserted his power over Brahma and Vishnu by manifesting himself as a lingam of fire, or **agni-lingam**. The event is commemorated each year at the rising of the full moon in November/ December, when a vast vat of two thousand litres of ghee and a 30m-wide wick is lit by priests on the summit of Arunachala. This symbolizes the fulfilment of Shiva's promise to reappear each year to vanquish the forces of darkness and ignorance with firelight.

The sacred Red Mountain is also associated with the famous twentieth-century saint, **Sri Ramana Maharishi**, who chose it as the site for his 23-year meditation retreat. A crop of small ashrams have sprung up on the edge of town below Sri Ramana's Cave, some of them more authentic than others, and the ranks of white-cotton-clad foreigners floating between them have become a defining feature of Tiruvannamalai.

Arunachaleshvara Temple

Daily; closed noon–4pm

Known to Hindus as the "Temple of the Eternal Sunrise", the enormous **Arunachaleshvara Temple**, built over a period of almost a thousand years, consists of three concentric courtyards whose gateways are topped by tapering *gopuras*, the largest of which cover the east and north gates. The best spot from which to view the precinct, a breathtaking scene, set against the sprawling plains and lumpy, granite Shevaroy Hills, is the path up to Sri Ramana Maharishi's meditation cave, Virupaksha (see below), on the lower slopes of Arunachala. To enter the temple, however, head for the huge eastern gateway, which leads through the thick outer wall carved with images of deities, local saints and teachers. In the basement of a raised hall to the right before entering the next courtyard is the Parthala lingam, where Sri Ramana Maharishi is said to have sat in a state of Supreme Awareness while ants feasted on his flesh.

The caves

Opposite the western entrance of the temple complex, a path leads up a holy hill (15min) to the **Virupaksha Cave**, where the Maharishi stayed between 1899 and 1916. He personally built the bench outside and the hill-shaped lingam and platform inside, where all are welcome to meditate in peace. When this cave became too crowded,

20

THE PRADAKSHINA

During the annual Kartigai festival, Hindu pilgrims are supposed to perform an auspicious circumambulation of Arunachala, known as the **pradakshina** (*pra* signifies the removal of all sins, *da* the fulfilment of desires, *kshi* freedom from the cycle of rebirth, and *na* spiritual liberation). Along the way, offerings are made at a string of shrines, tanks, temples, lingams, pillared meditation halls, sacred rocks, springs, trees and caves related to the Tiruvannamalai legends. Although hectic during the festival, the paved path linking them all together is quiet for most of the year, and makes a wonderful day-hike, affording fine views of the town and its environs.

Ramana shifted to another, hidden away a few minutes further up the hill. He named this one, and the small house built onto it, **Skandasramam**, and lived there between 1916 and 1922. The inner cave here is also set aside for meditation, and the front patio affords splendid views across the temple, town and surrounding plains.

Sri Ramana ashram

Main Rd • ⓦ sriramanamaharshi.org

The caves can also be reached via the pilgrims' path winding uphill from the **Sri Ramana ashram**, 2km south of the temple along the main road. This simple complex is where the sage lived after returning from his retreat on Arunachala, and where his body is today enshrined. The *samadhi* has become a popular place for Sri Ramana's devotees on pilgrimage, but interested visitors are welcome to stay in the dorms here. There's also an excellent bookshop (daily 8–11am & 2–6pm) stocking a huge range of titles on the life and teachings of the guru, as well as quality postcards, calendars, devotional music and DVDs.

ARRIVAL AND INFORMATION   TIRUVANNAMALAI

By train The railway station, 500m east of the temple, is on the main Tirupati–Madurai line, with a daily service in each direction.

By bus Buses arrive at the town bus stand on Chinnakadai St, 1km north of the temple. Coming from the coast, it's easiest to make your way on one of the numerous buses from Tindivanam, which pass through Gingee. There are excellent bus connections to Chennai (every 10min; 4hr), Chengalpattu (every 10min; 2hr 30min; change for Mamallapuram), Puducherry (every 30min; 3hr), Trichy (hourly; 4–5hr) and Kanchipuram (every 2hr; 2hr 30min).

Services There is intermittent internet access at the Image Computer Centre, 52 Car St, and Sri Sai, 14-A Kadambarayam St. There are a few ATMs and a couple of Western Union offices but the best place to change money is the India Boutique/Forex, 138 Raj Chettiyar Complex on Chengam Rd, near the ashram (ⓣ 04175 238248).

ACCOMMODATION

Arunachala 5 Vada Sannathi St ⓣ 04175 228300, ⓦ hotelarunachala.in. Large, clean and comfortable hotel situated right outside the main temple entrance. There is a choice of non-a/c and a/c rooms, all of which are a good size and have TVs. Not the quietest place to stay, but certainly atmospheric. ₹1000

Park 26 Kosmadam St ⓣ 04175 222471. Reliable budget option a 5min walk from the junction of North and East Car streets. The rooms are fairly basic but clean, with TVs and buckets but no showers. You have a/c and non-a/c rooms with varying rates. There's a vegetarian canteen on the ground floor. No wi-fi. ₹500

Ramakrishna 34-F Polur Rd, 5min from the bus station on the main Gingee road (turn right out of the bus station and veer left at the fork) ⓣ 04175 250003, ⓦ hotelramakrishnatiruvannamalai.com. One of the best places in town, with sizeable, clean rooms with TV, en suite bathrooms, and a choice of Indian or Western loos. There are also larger deluxe rooms and a/c rooms from ₹1500–₹2200. Excellent a/c restaurant next door to the reception (see opposite). ₹950

SASA Lodge Chinnakadai St, almost opposite the bus stand ⓣ 04175 252293. One of the cheapest lodges in town, painted a bright blue and white. Rooms (some with a/c; ₹1300) are basic and clean enough, but most of them are windowless. They have attached toilets as well. There is no restaurant but there is service available where they will buy breakfast from other eateries close by and deliver to your room. The front-facing rooms have light but are rather noisy. No wi-fi. ₹450

Trishul 6 Kanagarayar St ☎04175 222219, ⓦhotel trishul.com. Tucked away down a lane off Kosmadam St near the *Park* in a quiet location away from the hustle, this hotel has a rooftop terrace with views of the temple, a good restaurant and a bafflingly dark a/c bar. Choice of decent-sized non-a/c and a/c rooms. ₹1500

EATING

Nala Residency 21 Anna Salai ☎04175 222322. A couple of hundred metres beyond the *Park*, this hotel restaurant has an extensive menu (veg and non-veg) and serves quality food. Veggie dishes cost under ₹185 and chicken dishes around ₹250. Try the delicious paneer or cottage cheese butter masala. Daily 7.30am–midnight.

★**Ramakrishna** 34-F Polur Rd ☎04175 250005. Excellent food served quickly and efficiently in a/c comfort. Good breakfasts, excellent eleven-dish "meals" (11am–3pm; ₹120) and a range of north and south Indian food available in the evenings. Daily 6.30am–10.30pm

Udipi Brindhavan Car St ☎04175 222693. Located down a small lane opposite the temple's east entrance, this long and narrow *eatery* is a typical Udupi restaurant, serving very cheap lunchtime "meals" (11am–4pm; ₹100) and excellent *parathas*. Daily 6am–11pm.

Vickys Trishul hotel 6 Kanagarayar St ☎04175 222219. Posh a/c ground-floor restaurant with a vaguely oriental vibe and decor, and a wall-length aquarium. Prices range between ₹150 and ₹250 for veg, chicken, the usual lunchtime "meals" option, and tandoori in the evenings. Daily 7.30am–10.30pm.

Gingee Fort

Daily 9am–5pm · ₹100 (₹5) · ⓦ gingeefort.com · The half-hourly buses between Tiruvannamalai (1hr) and Puducherry (2hr) all stop on demand right by the gate of the fort

An epic landscape of huge boulder hills, interspersed by lush splashes of rice paddy≈and banana plantations, stretches east of Tiruvannamalai towards the coast. The scenery peaks at **GINGEE** (pronounced "*Shinjee*" and also spelt Senji), 37km east of the Red Mountain, where the ruins of Tamil Nadu's most spectacular **fort** sprawl over a vast swathe of sun-scorched granite, left to the mercy of the weeds and tropical weather. Only on weekends, when bus parties pour around the most accessible monuments, does the site receive more than a trickle of visitors.

Bisected by the main Tiruvannamalai–Puducherry road, Gingee Fort comprises three separate citadels, crowning the summits of three dramatic hills: **Krishnagiri** to the north, **Rajagiri** to the west and **Chandrayandurg** to the southeast. Connecting them to form an enormous triangle, 1.5km from north to south, are 20m-thick walls, punctuated by bastions and gateways giving access to the protected zones at the heart of the complex. A network of raised, paved paths links the site's principal landmarks. From the road, head south to the main east gate, where a snaking passage emerges, after no fewer than four changes of direction, inside the **palace** enclave. Of the many structures that were unearthed by archeologists here, the most distinctive is the square seven-storey **Kalyana Mahal tower**, focal point of the former governor's residence; featuring an ingenious hydraulic system that carried water to the uppermost levels, it is crowned by a tapering pyramidal tower.

It's hard to imagine such defences ever being overrun, but they were on numerous occasions following the fort's foundation by the Vijayanagars in the fifteenth century. The Muslim Adil Shahis from Bijapur (now Vijayapura), Shivaji's Maharatas and the Mughals all conquered Gingee, using it to consolidate the vulnerable southern reaches of their respective empires. The French also took it in 1750, but were ousted by the British after a bloody five-week siege eleven years later.

Puducherry

First impressions of **PUDUCHERRY** (**Pondicherry**, also often referred to simply as Pondy), the former capital of French India, can be unpromising. Instead of the leafy boulevards and *pétanque* pitches you might expect, its messy outer suburbs and bus stand are as cluttered and chaotic as any typical Tamil town. Closer to the seafront, however, the atmosphere grows tangibly more Gallic, as the bazaars give way to rows of

20

houses whose shuttered windows and colour washed facades wouldn't look out of place in Montpellier. For anyone familiar with the British colonial imprint, the town can induce culture shock with its richly ornamented Catholic churches, French road names and policemen in De Gaulle-style *képis*, and *boules* played in the dusty squares. Many of the seafront buildings were damaged by the 2004 tsunami, but Puducherry's tourist infrastructure remained intact.

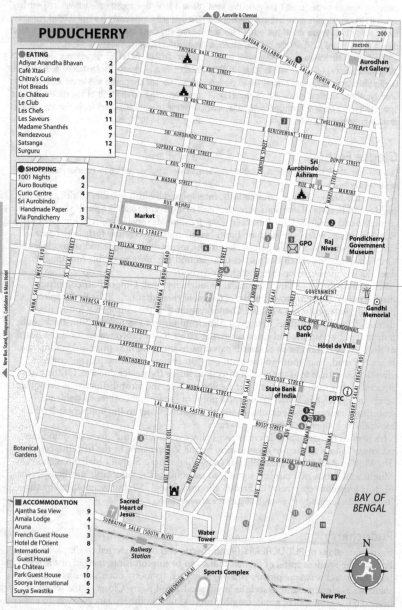

PUDUCHERRY

EATING

Adiyar Anandha Bhavan	2
Café Xtasi	4
Chitra's Cuisine	9
Hot Breads	3
Le Château	5
Le Club	10
Les Chefs	8
Les Saveurs	11
Madame Shanthés	6
Rendezvous	7
Satsanga	12
Surguru	1

SHOPPING

1001 Nights	4
Auro Boutique	2
Curio Centre	4
Sri Aurobindo Handmade Paper	1
Via Pondicherry	3

ACCOMMODATION

Ajantha Sea View	9
Amala Lodge	4
Aruna	1
French Guest House	3
Hotel de l'Orient	8
International Guest House	5
Le Château	7
Park Guest House	10
Soorya International	6
Surya Swastika	2

Map labels: Auroville & Chennai; SARDAR VALLABHAI PATEL SALAI (NORTH BLVD); THIYAGA RAJA STREET; P KOIL STREET; MA KOIL STREET; ID KOIL STREET; KA COVIL STREET; SRI AUROBINDO STREET; SUPRAYA CHETTIAR STREET; C KOIL STREET; A MADAM STREET; RUE NEHRU; Market; RANGA PILLAI STREET; VELLAJA STREET; NIDARAJAPAYER ST; SS PILLAI STREET; BHARATI STREET; ANNA SALAI WEST BLVD; SAINT THERESA STREET; MAHATMA GANDHI ROAD; SINNA PAPPARA STREET; LAPPORTH STREET; MONTHORSIER STREET; C MUDHALIAR STREET; LAL BAHADUR SASTRI STREET; Botanical Gardens; RUE ELLAMMAN KOIL; RUE MOULLAI; Sacred Heart of Jesus; SUBBAIAH SALAI (SOUTH BLVD); Water Tower; Railway Station; DR AMBEDKAR SALAI; Sports Complex; MISSION STREET; CANTEEN STREET; R OERICHEMONT STREET; L THOLLANDAL STREET; RUE DE LA MARINE; L MARTIN STREET; DUPUY STREET; Sri Aurobindo Ashram; GPO; Raj Nivas; Pondicherry Government Museum; COTCLAVER STREET; GINGEE SALAI; Y SIMONEL STREET; GOVERNMENT PLACE; Gandhi Memorial; RUE MAHE DE LABOURDONNAIS; UCO Bank; Hôtel de Ville; SURCOUF STREET; State Bank of India; PDTC; AMBOUR SALAI; BUSSY STREET; RUE SUFFREN; RUE ROMAIN ROLAND; RUE DUMAS; RUE DE BAZAR SAINT LAURENT; RUE DE LA BOURDONNAIS; GOUBERT SALAI (BEACH RD); New Pier; BAY OF BENGAL; New Bus Stand, Villupuram, Cuddalore & Mas Hotel; New Bus Stand, Villupuram, Cuddalore & Mass Hotel; Aurodhan Art Gallery

20

Brief history

Known to Greek and Roman geographers as "Poduke", Puducherry was an important staging post on the second-century maritime trade route between Rome and the Far East. When the Roman Empire declined, the Pallavas and Cholas took control and were followed by a succession of colonial powers, from the Portuguese in the sixteenth century to the French, Danes and British, who exchanged the enclave several times after the various battles and treaties of the Carnatic Wars in the early eighteenth century. Puducherry's heyday, however, dates from the arrival of the French governor Joseph **Dupleix**, who accepted the governorship in 1742 and immediately set about rebuilding a town decimated by its former British occupants. It was Dupleix who instituted the street plan of a central grid encircled by a broad oblong boulevard, bisected north to south by a canal dividing the "Ville Blanche", to the east, from the "Ville Noire", to the west.

Although relinquished by the French in 1954 – when the town became the headquarters of the **Union Territory of Pondicherry**, administering the three other former colonial enclaves scattered across south India – Puducherry's split personality still prevails. The seaside promenade, **Goubert Salai** (formerly Beach Road), has the forlorn look of an out-of-season French resort, complete with its own white Hôtel de Ville. Many visitors are grave Europeans in white Indian costume, busy about their spiritual quest. It was here that **Sri Aurobindo Ghose** (1872–1950), a leading figure in the freedom struggle in Bengal, was given shelter after it became unwise for him to live close to the British in Calcutta. His ashram attracts thousands of devotees from all around the world, most particularly from Bengal.

20

Goubert Salai

Puducherry's beachside promenade, **Goubert Salai**, is a favourite place for a stroll, though there's little to do other than watch the world go by. The Hôtel de Ville, today housing the Municipal Offices building, is still an impressive spectacle, and a 4m-tall Gandhi memorial, surrounded by ancient columns, dominates the northern end. Nearby, a French memorial commemorates French Indians who lost their lives in World War I.

Just north of the Hôtel de Ville, a couple of streets back from the promenade, is the leafy old French-provincial-style square now named **Government Place**. On the north side, the impressive, gleaming white **Raj Nivas**, official home to the present lieutenant-governor of Puducherry Territory, was built late in the eighteenth century for Joseph Francis Dupleix.

Pondicherry Government Museum

Ranga Pillai St • Tues–Sun 10am–1pm & 2–5pm • ₹50 (₹2) • 🌐 art.puducherry.gov.in/museum.html

The **Pondicherry Government Museum** is opposite Government Place. The archaeological collection includes Neolithic 2000-year-old remains from Arikamedu, a few Pallava (sixth- to eighth-century) and Buddhist (tenth-century) stone sculptures, bronzes, weapons and paintings. Alongside are a bizarre assembly of French salon furniture and bric-à-brac from local houses, including a velvet S-shaped "conversation seat".

Sri Aurobindo Ashram

Rue de la Marine • Daily 8am–noon & 2–6pm • Free, no children under 3, no photography • 🌐 sriaurobindoashram.org

The **Sri Aurobindo Ashram** is one of the best-known and wealthiest ashrams in India. Founded in 1926 by the Bengali philosopher-guru, Aurobindo Ghosh, and his chief disciple, personal manager and mouthpiece "The Mother", it serves as the headquarters of the Sri Aurobindo Society, or SAS. Today the SAS owns most of the valuable property and real estate in Puducherry, and wields what many consider to be a disproportionate influence over the town. The **samadhi**, or mausoleum, of Sri

Aurobindo and "The Mother" is covered daily with flowers and usually surrounded by supplicating devotees with their hands and heads placed on the tomb. Inside the main building, an incongruous and slightly bourgeois-looking Western-style room, complete with three-piece suite and Persian carpet, is where "The Mother" and Sri Aurobindo chilled out. The adjacent bookshop sells a range of literature and tracts, while the building opposite hosts frequent cultural programmes.

Botanical Gardens

Subbaiyah Salai • Daily 10am–6pm • Free; aquarium ₹10

Established in 1826, the **Botanical Gardens** offer many quiet paths to wander. The French planted nine hundred species here, experimenting to see how they would do in Indian conditions; one mahogany tree, the *Khaya senegalensis*, has grown to a height of 25m. You can also see an extraordinary fossilized tree, found about 25km away in Tiravakarai. The aquarium inside the gardens is uninspiring.

ARRIVAL AND DEPARTURE — PUDUCHERRY

By air Puducherry has recently opened its airport to public with just two daily flights to and from Hyderabad and Bengaluru, both operated by Spice Jet.

By train Puducherry's railway station is in the south, a 5min walk from the sea off Subbaiyah Salai. There are daily express and passenger trains to Chennai and Tirupati and weekly fast express trains to Bhubaneswar (Wed), Mangaluru (Tues), New Delhi (Wed) and Howrah, Kolkata (Wed).

By bus All buses pull into New Bus Stand, which lies on the western edge of town. From here, auto-rickshaws charge at least ₹50 into the old town, taxis double that; but you can jump in a *tempo* to central Ambour Salai for ₹10.

Destinations Bengaluru (4 daily; 10–11hr); Chennai (every 15–20min; 2hr 30min–3hr); Chidambaram (every 20min; 2hr); Coimbatore (10 daily; 9hr); Kanchipuram (10 daily; 3–4hr); Kanyakumari (hourly; 12–13hr); Madurai (hourly; 9–10hr); Mamallapuram (every 15–20min; 1hr 30min–2hr); Thanjavur (hourly; 5hr); Tiruchirapalli (every 30min; 5hr 30min–6hr); Tiruvannamalai (every 30min; 3hr).

20

GETTING AROUND

By auto-rickshaw Puducherry is well served by auto-rickshaws, which can negotiate the narrow and chaotic streets efficiently.

By bicycle/scooter You can rent a bicycle for ₹75/24hr from one of the many stalls dotted about town, such as Sri Durga Pharameshwari Cycle Stores, 106-B Mission St (T 98941 21133), and JDR, 47 Mission St (T 0413 319 4888), which also rents scooters (₹400/24hr), useful for trips further afield such as Auroville.

INFORMATION AND TOURS

Tourist information The Puducherry Tourism Development Corporation (PTDC) office is at 40 Goubert Salai (daily 8.30am–7.30pm; T 0413 233 9497, W pondytourism.in).

The staff are extremely helpful, providing leaflets and a city map, and information about Auroville.

Tours PTDC run city tours to all the main attractions (half-day 1.30–5.30pm, non-a/c ₹150, a/c ₹200; full-day 9.30am–5.30pm, non-a/c ₹250, a/c ₹300), a fine Heritage Walking Tour (daily 8am–12.30pm; free) and can help arrange car rental.

Services Muthu Forex, 161 Mission St (T 0413 222 4239), has a Western Union transfer facility. Thomas Cook is at 2A Rue Labourdonnais (T 0413 222 4008). Other places to change money include the State Bank of India, 15 Suffren St, and UCO Bank on Rue Mahe de Labourdonnais.

ACCOMMODATION

Puducherry's **basic lodges** are concentrated around the main market area, Ranga Pillai St and Rue Nehru, while trendy boutique hotels now punctuate the French quarter. Guesthouses belonging to the Sri Aurobindo Ashram offer good value for money but are not overly welcoming, with a lot of regulations, curfews and overpowering "philosophy of life" notices.

Ajantha Sea View 50 Goubert Salai T 0413 234 9032, W ajanthaseaviewhotel.com; map p.1008. Just about the only hotel on the seafront, whose large and comfortable, if slightly faded, rooms all have balconies with direct or partial sea views. ₹3700

Amala Lodge 92 Ranga Pillai St T 0413 233 8910; map p.1008. This centrally-located hotel is one of the best of the budget options. The rooms, some with shared bathrooms, are clean enough but a little bit on the small side. There is also a three-bed room available with a/c for ₹800. No wi-fi. ₹500

Aruna 3 Zamindar Garden, SV Patel Rd ☎0413 233 7756, ✉hotelarunapondy@gmail.com; map p.1008. Located on a quiet side street, in the northern part of town. It has pleasant double rooms (some a/c; ₹1350) with TV and balcony, some of which catch the morning sun. **₹850**

French Guest House 38 Ambour Salai ☎0413 222 7770; map p.1008. Clean, reasonably-sized rooms, including some family suites, in a welcoming centrally located hotel with a comical Eiffel Tower mural. The a/c rooms are slightly cleaner and brighter and cost ₹900, just ₹200 more than non a/c rooms. No wi-fi. **₹700**

★ **Hotel de l'Orient** 17 Rue Romain Rolland ☎0413 234 3067, ⊛neemranahotels.com; map p.1008. A beautiful, UNESCO heritage-accorded French house, boasting sixteen individually decorated rooms with French antiques, tiled balconies and long shuttered windows overlooking the leafy courtyard restaurant. Four categories of room with the most expensive, featuring an anteroom and four-poster bed, costing ₹8500. **₹3500**

International Guest House 47 NSC Bose Salai ☎0413 233 6699, ✉ingh@aurosociety.org; map p.1008. The largest Aurobindo establishment in town, with dozens of very large, clean rooms. No TV, no a/c, no wi-fi. It's a good budget option but typically institutional, with a 10.30pm curfew. Often full, so best book in advance. Rooms in the new wing are slightly more expensive with a/c at ₹1680. **₹700**

★ **Le Château** 11A Rue Romain Rolland ☎0413 222 9500, ⊛lechateau.co.in; map p.1008. No detail has been overlooked in the conversion of this colonial house into a very smart but reasonably priced boutique hotel. The balconied, all a/c rooms are well-appointed and there's a fine ground-floor restaurant. Two categories of rooms – classic and superior. **₹4500**

Park Guest House Goubert Salai ☎0413 223 3644, ✉parkgh@sriaurobindoashram.org.in; map p.1008. Another Sri Aurobindo Society place with the same strict rules (no alcohol and a 10.30pm curfew), for ashram visitors only. Spotless and very comfortable rooms (a/c only ₹1500) with mosquito nets and sitouts, overlooking garden and sea. Bike rental and restaurant but no TV or wi-fi. **₹800**

Soorya International 55 Ranga Pillai St ☎0413 222 7485, ⊛hotelsooryainternational.com; map p.1008. Decent, all a/c hotel, located in the centre of town. Good-sized, comfortable standard rooms and bigger deluxe rooms complete with sofa and balcony costing around ₹1500. It also has a multi cuisine restaurant. No wi-fi. **₹1000**

Surya Swastika 11 Eswaran Koil St ☎0413 234 3092, ✉suryaswastika@gmail.com; map p.1008. A traditional Tamil guest-house in a quiet corner of town, with nine basic rooms dotted around a covered central courtyard. A/c rooms ₹800. Quintessential budget travellers' place – incredibly cheap, friendly and clean enough. **₹450**

EATING

If you've been on the road for a while and are hankering for healthy salads, fresh coffee, crusty bread, cakes and real pastry, you'll be spoilt for choice in Puducherry. **Beer** is available just about everywhere (except the SAS-owned establishments) and is much lower than the regular Tamil Nadu price, starting at around ₹80 a bottle.

Adyar Anandha Bhavan Rue Nehru ☎0413 222 3333; map p.1008. Very popular pure-veg restaurant with three counters under one brightly lit roof. Samosas, chaat and snacks on the left, a sweet counter in the centre and veggie dishes to the right, all under ₹100. Pay first and show receipt. Daily 7am–11pm.

Café Xtasi 245 R D Mission Street ☎99947 00098; map p.1008. Cosy and comfortable, this popular café is known for its authentic thin crust wood fired pizza. Burgers and chicken nuggets also available. ₹900 for two. Daily 11am -11pm.

Chitra's Cuisine 31 Suffren Street ☎95977 12635; map p.1008. One of the only purely Indian restaurants in this part of town, this place serves Chinese besides north Indian. You can also get seafood dishes here that are very popular. Usually crowded during lunch. A meal for two is around ₹500. Daily noon–11.30 pm

Hot Breads 42 Ambour Salai ☎0413 222 786, ⊛hotbreads.in; map p.1008. Squeaky-clean *boulangerie-café* popular with French expats. Classic fresh croissants, crusty baguettes and delicious savoury pastry snacks are available; their aromas waft temptingly out onto the street. Great breakfast combos for ₹70–120, plus pizza, burgers and hot dogs later on. Daily 7.30am–9.30pm.

La Chateau 11A Rue Romain Rolland ☎0413 222 9500; map p.1008. A stylish and cosy restaurant serving French, Italian and Indian cuisine on the rooftop of this hotel. A meal for two costs ₹1200. Daily noon–11pm.

★ **Le Club** 38 Rue Dumas ☎0413 233 9745, ⊛leclubraj. com; map p.1008.One of the best-known restaurants in town. The menu is predominantly French and features their famous *coq au vin*, *steak au poivre* and seafood dishes (all around ₹500-600). No alcohol. Daily noon–3.30pm and 6.45–10.45pm.

Les Chefs 27 Yanam Vengadachalam Ranga Pillai Road ☎73387 75757, ⊛leschefsrestaurant.com; map p.1008. A very eclectic set of dishe, from fish biriyani to bamboo beef biriyani, *Les Chefs* offers north and south Indian, Mexican, French and Italian cuisine. Mains from ₹500–600. Daily noon–3pm and 6.30–11pm.

Les Saveurs 36 Dumas St ☎0413 2339100; map p.1008. French and Italian cuisine with an emphasis on seafood. Their speciality is the marinated baby octopus (₹350). Don't miss the delicious crepes as well. Breakfast deals cost ₹250-400. Daily 8am–10pm.

20

★**Madame Shanthés** 40A Rue Romain Rolland ☎0413 222 2022; map p. 1008. Very friendly rooftop restaurant, with lovely ambience and evening illuminations, that serves tasty French, Indian and Chinese dishes. The speciality is seafood: pasta *marinara* (₹380) and a superb, excellent-value seafood platter. meat dishes, such as chicken stroganoff for ₹450. Daily noon–11pm.

★**Rendezvous** 30 Rue Suffren ☎0413 222 7677, ⓦrendezvouscafe.co.in; map p.1008. This delightful restaurant has been completely revamped with white leather seating and sleek decor. The quality of the Indo-Gallic cuisine is superb, with seafood costing around ₹650–2000. The fine cocktails are two for one from 6pm. Mon–Thurs dinner only, from 6.30–10.30pm. Fri–Sun 12.30–3.30pm and 6.30–10.30pm.

Satsanga 54 Rue Labourdonnais ☎0413 222 5867; map p.1008. The food here is prepared by the French *patron*: organic salads, tzatziki, garlic bread, sauté potatoes and *tagliatelle alla carbonara* complement the fresh fish and French beef dishes, mostly under ₹500. Also a wide Indian menu. Two dining areas – courtyard or rooftop. Tues–Sun noon–3pm & 6–11pm.

Surguru 104 SV Patel Salai ☎0413 222 9022; map p.1008. Located in the popular *Surguru Hotel*, this is one of the most popular pure-veg restaurants, serving both south and north Indian cuisine. "Meals" at lunch vary from ₹140-200.A la carte dishes with biriyani, rotis and curries are served at dinner and cost around ₹500 for two. Daily 7am–10.30pm

SHOPPING

1001 Nights 40A Rue Romain Rolland ☎98400 90073; map p.1008. A jewellery store with other accessories like acarpets, rugs, gifts and souvenirs, this Kashmiri shop is fairly busy as both tourists and locals throng here. Daily 9am–9pm.

Auro Boutique 12A JN Street ☎88708 31840; map p.1008. A beautiful and unique collection of artifacts, candles, home décor products, pottery, gifts and other hand-made items from Auroville. Daily 9.30am –7.30pm

Curio Centre 40 Rue Romain Rolland ☎0413 222 5676; map p.1008. Classy, if slightly ramshackle, old place with high ceilings. In between the larger items of furniture, you can discover some unusual ornaments. Daily 9.30am–8pm.

Sri Aurobindo Handmade Paper 50 Sardar Vallabhai Patel Salai ☎0413 233 4763, ⓦsriaurobindopaper.com; map p.1008. Something of an institution, this place sells colourful paper gifts and all sorts of stationery from within a leafy compound where you can also witness the traditional manufacturing process. Mon–Sat 9am–5.30pm, Sun 10am–1pm.

Via Pondicherry 38 Rue Romain Rolland ☎0413 222 3319, ⓦviapondicherry.com; map p.1008. Created and run by a vivacious classical dancer and designer, this little shop is a veritable swirl of colour, with all sorts from bags to shawls and bright decorations. Daily 9am–1pm & 3–8pm.

Auroville

The most New Age place anywhere in India must surely be **AUROVILLE**, the planned "City of Dawn", 10km north of Pudicherry, straddling the border of the Union Territory and Tamil Nadu. Founded in 1968, Auroville was inspired by "The Mother", the spiritual successor of Sri Aurobindo. Around 1700 people live in communes (two thirds of them non-Indians), with such names as Fertile, Certitude, Sincerity, Revelation and Transformation, in what it is hoped will eventually be an ideal city for a population of fifty thousand. Architecturally experimental buildings, combining modern Western and traditional Indian elements, are set in a rural landscape of narrow lanes, deep red earth and lush greenery. Income is derived from agriculture, handicrafts, alternative technology, educational and development projects and Aurolec, a computer software company.

Considering how little there is to see here, Auroville attracts a disproportionately large number of day-trippers – much to the chagrin of its inhabitants, who rightly point out that you can only get a sense of what the settlement is all about if you stay a while. Interested visitors are welcomed as paying guests in most of the communes (see below), where you can work alongside permanent residents.

The Visitor Centre

Daily 9am–5.30pm • ☎0413 262 2239, ⓦauroville.org

The **Visitor Centre** is the focal point of any tourist visit to Auroville. You need to get tickets here for an exterior viewing of Matri Mandir (see below), but before they are issued, you're shown a short video presentation about the village. The adjacent bookshop has plenty of literature on Auroville and it's worth checking the notice board, which has details of **activities** in which visitors may participate (including yoga, reiki and Vipassana meditation, costing around ₹200/session). The nearby **Bharat Niwas** houses a permanent exhibition on the history and philosophy of the settlement. There are also three quality handicraft outlets and several pleasant vegetarian cafés serving snacks, meals and cold drinks.

Matri Mandir

Mon–Sat 10am–noon & 2–4pm, Sun 10am–noon • Free • Tickets available from the Visitor Centre • To obtain "concentration entry" for the Matri Mandir to meditate on the crystal, you must book two days ahead

Begun in 1970, the space-age **Matri Mandir** – a gigantic, almost spherical high-tech meditation centre at the heart of the site – was conceived as "a symbol of the Divine's answer to man's inspiration for perfection". Earth from 124 countries was symbolically placed in an urn, and is kept in a concrete cone in the amphitheatre adjacent to Matri Mandir, from where a speaker can address an audience of three thousand without amplification. The focal point of the interior of the Matri Mandir is a 70cm crystal ball symbolizing the neutral but divine qualities of light and space.

ARRIVAL AND INFORMATION   AUROVILLE

Auroville lies 15km north of Puducherry, off the main Chennai road; you can also get here via the coastal highway, turning off at the village of Chinna Mudaliarchavadi.

By bus Buses from Puducherry run every 20–30min but as Auroville is spread over some fifty square kilometres it's best to come with your own transport.

By auto-rickshaw or taxi From Puducherry to Auroville costs around ₹300 for the 30min journey in an auto-rickshaw or around ₹400 in a taxi.

Tours Alternatively, there's the PTDC half-day tour from Puducherry (see page 1007).

ACCOMMODATION AND EATING

The information desk at the Visitor Centre is a good place to enquire about accommodation or you can contact the Auroville guest accommodation service (☏0413 262 2704, ⦿guesthouses.auroville.org). This should be done months ahead for the peak winter months. Officially there's no lower limit on the time you have to stay, but visitors are encouraged to stick around for at least a week and to help out on communal projects. There are many excellent privately-run restaurants dotted around the ashram and a café at the Visitor Centre.

Central Tamil Nadu: the Chola heartland

To be on the banks of the Cauvery listening to the strains of Carnatic music is to have a taste of eternal bliss. Tamil proverb

Continuing south of Puducherry along the Coromandel coast, you enter the flat landscape of the **Kaveri** (aka Cauvery) **Delta**, a watery world of canals, dams, dykes and rivulets that has been intensively farmed since ancient times. Just 160km in diameter, it forms the verdant rice-bowl core of Tamil Nadu, crossed by more than thirty major rivers and countless streams. The largest of them, the River Kaveri, known in Tamil as Ponni, "The Lady of Gold" (a form of the Mother Goddess), is revered as a conduit of liquid *shakti*, the primordial female energy that nurtures the millions of farmers who live on her banks and tributaries. The landscape here is one endless swathe of green paddy fields, dotted with palm trees and little villages of thatched roofs and market stalls; it comes as a rude shock to land up in the hot and chaotic towns.

This mighty delta formed the very heartland of the **Chola** empire, which reached its apogee between the ninth and thirteenth centuries, an era often compared to classical Greece and Renaissance Italy both for its cultural richness and the sheer scale and profusion of its architectural creations. Much as the Cholas originally intended, every visitor is immediately in awe of their huge temples, not only at cities such as **Chidambaram**, **Kumbakonam** and **Thanjavur**, but also out in the countryside at places like **Gangaikondacholapuram**, where the magnificent temple is all that remains of a once-great city. Exploring the area for a few days will bring you into contact with the more delicate side of Chola artistic expression, such as the magnificent **bronzes** of Thanjavur.

Chidambaram

CHIDAMBARAM, 58km south of Puducherry, is so steeped in myth that its history is hard to unravel. As the site of the *tandav*, the cosmic dance of Shiva as **Nataraja**, King of the Dance, it's one of the holiest sites in south India, and a visit to its **Sabhanayaka Nataraja Temple** affords a fascinating glimpse into ancient Tamil religious practice and belief. The legendary king **Hiranyavarman** is said to have made a pilgrimage here from Kashmir, seeking to rid himself of leprosy by bathing in the temple's Shivaganga tank. In thanks for a successful cure, he enlarged the temple. He also brought three thousand brahmins, of the Dikshitar caste, whose descendants, distinguishable by top-knots of hair at the front of their heads, are the ritual specialists of the temple to this day.

Few of the fifty *mathas* (monasteries) that once stood here remain, but the temple itself is still a hive of activity and hosts numerous **festivals**. The two most important are ten-day affairs, building up to spectacular finales: on the ninth day of each, temple chariots process through the four Car streets in a **car festival**, while on the tenth there is an **abhishekham**, when the principal deities in the Raja Sabha (thousand-pillared hall) are anointed. For exact dates (one is in May/June, the other in Dec/Jan), contact any TTDC tourist office and plan well ahead, as they are very popular. Other local festivals include fire-walking and *kavadi* folk dance (dancing with decorated wooden frames on the head) at the Thillaiamman Kali (April/May) and Keelatheru Mariamman (July/Aug) temples respectively.

Chidambaram revolves around the Sabhanayaka Nataraja Temple and the busy market area that surrounds it, along North, East, South and West Car streets. The town also has a large student population, based at Annamalai University to the east, a centre of Tamil studies.

Sabhanayaka Nataraja Temple

Daily 4am–noon & 4–10pm

For south India's Shaivites, the **Sabhanayaka Nataraja Temple**, where Shiva is enthroned as Lord of the Cosmic Dance (Nataraja), is the holiest of holies. Its huge *gopuras*, whose lights are used as landmarks by sailors far out to sea in the Bay of Bengal, soar above a 55-acre complex, divided by four concentric walls. The oldest parts now standing were built under the Cholas, who adopted Nataraja as their chosen deity and crowned several kings here. If you have the time the best way to tackle the complex is to work slowly inwards from the third enclosure in clockwise circles.

Frequent **ceremonies** take place at the innermost sanctum, the most popular being at noon and 6pm, when a fire is lit, great gongs are struck and devotees rush forward to catch a last glimpse of the lingam before the doors are shut. On Friday nights before the temple closes, during a particularly elaborate puja, Nataraja is carried on a palanquin accompanied by music and attendants carrying flaming torches and tridents. At other times, you'll hear ancient devotional hymns from the Tevaram.

The gopuras

The west *gopura* is the most popular entrance, as well as being the most elaborately carved and probably the earliest (c.1150 AD). Turning north (left) from here, you come to the colonnaded **Shivaganga tank**, the site of seven natural springs. From the broken pillar at the tank's edge, all four *gopuras* are visible. In the northeast corner, the largest building in the complex, the **Raja Sabha** (fourteenth- to fifteenth-century) is also known as "the thousand-pillared hall"; tradition holds that there are only 999 actual pillars, the thousandth being Shiva's leg. During festivals the deities Nataraja and Shivakamasundari are brought here and mounted on a dais for the anointing ceremony, *abhishekha*.

The importance of **dance** at Chidambaram is underlined by the reliefs of dancing figures inside the east *gopura*, demonstrating 108 *karanas* (a similar set is to be found in the west *gopura*). A *karana* is a specific point in a phase of movement prescribed by the extraordinarily comprehensive Sanskrit treatise on the performing arts, the *Natya Shastra* (c.200 BC–200 AD) – the basis of all classical dance, music and theatre in India.

The second enclosure

To get into the square **second enclosure** head for its western entrance (just north of the west *gopura* in the third wall), which leads into a circumambulatory passageway. Once beyond this second wall you may become disorientated as the roofed inner enclosure sees little light and is supported by a maze of colonnades.

Govindaraja shrine

The innermost **Govindaraja shrine** is dedicated to Vishnu – no surprise, as most Shiva temples have a Vishnu shrine inside them, though no Vaishnavite temple has a shrine for Shiva. The deity is attended by non-Dikshitar brahmins who, it is said, don't always get along with the Dikshitars. From outside the shrine, non-Hindus can see through to the most sacred part of the temple, the **Kanaka Sabha** and the **Chit Sabha**, adjoining raised structures, roofed with copper and gold plate and linked by a hallway. The latter houses bronze images of Nataraja and his consort Shivakamasundari; behind and to the left of Nataraja, a curtain, sacred to Shiva and strung with rows of leaves from the *bilva* tree, demarcates the most potent area of all. Within it lies the **Akashalingam**, known as the *rahasya*, or "secret", of Chidambaram: made of the most subtle of the elements, Ether (*akasha*) – from which Air, Fire, Water and Earth are born – the lingam is invisible, signifying the invisible presence of God in the human heart.

A crystal lingam, said to have emanated from the light of the crescent moon on Shiva's brow, and a small ruby Nataraja are worshipped in the Kanaka Sabha. They are ritually bathed in the flames of the priests' camphor fire or oil lamps six times a day. This inner area is where you're most likely to hear **oduvars**, hereditary singers from the middle, non-brahmin castes, intoning verses of ancient Tamil poetry. The songs with which they regale the deities at puja time, drawn from compilations such as the Tevaram or earlier Sangam, are believed to be more than a thousand years old.

20

ARRIVAL AND INFORMATION   CHIDAMBARAM

By train The railway station is just over 1km southeast of the centre. There are daily trains to Chennai Egmore (5hr 30min–6hr) and Tiruchirapalli (3hr 30min) via Thanjavur (2hr 30min).

By bus Buses from Chennai, Thanjavur, Mamallapuram and Madurai pull in at the bus stand, about 500m from the temple.

Destinations Chengalpattu (every 20–30min; 4hr 30min–5hr); Chennai (every 20–30min; 5–6hr); Coimbatore (8 daily; 7hr); Kanchipuram (hourly; 7–8hr); Kanyakumari (4 daily; 9–10hr); Kumbakonam (every 10min; 2hr 30min); Madurai (6 daily; 7hr 30min–8hr); Puducherry (every 15–20min; 2hr); Thanjavur (every 15–20min; 3hr); Tiruchirapalli (every 30min; 4hr 30min); Tiruvannamalai (hourly; 3hr 30min).

Tourist information The TTDC tourist office (Mon–Fri 9.45am–5.45pm; ☏04144 238739) is next to *Vandayar Gateway Inn* hotel on Railway Feeder Rd. Friendly, helpful staff but not a lot of printed info.

Services None of the banks in Chidambaram change money, although the *Saradharam* hotel, near the bus stand, will.

ACCOMMODATION

Akshaya 17/18 East Car St ☏04144 220192, ⓦhotel-akshaya.com. Pleasant, clean, mid-range hotel, with a garden backing right onto the temple wall. There's a choice of non a/c and a/c rooms, both standard and deluxe categories (₹2600), though the non a/c are much better value, and there are a couple of restaurants. **₹1300**

Arudhra Residency 20/9 East Sannidhi Street ☏ 93446 46902. Located close to the temple, this 2-star hotel has good sized clean rooms and is extremely convenient for a temple visit. There is no restaurant, but the closest eatery is a 5min walk away. **₹1200**

Mansoor Lodge 91 East Car St ☏ 94433 39446, ✉ mansoorlodge@rediffmail.com. A cheap, friendly and good-value hotel, right opposite the temple. Rooms with a/c are ₹1200. They have tiled floors, clean bathrooms and a TV. No wi-fi. **₹750**

Raja Rajan 162 West Car St ☏ 97905 16358. Close to the west gate of the temple, this tall skinny building is another budget option with clean rooms and tiled bathrooms. There

are some cheap singles (₹300) and good-value a/c rooms (₹900). No wi-fi. **₹400**

Sabanayagam 7 East Sannathi St, off East Car St ☏ 04144 220896. Despite its flashy exterior, this is a run-of-the-mill budget place located 10m down the main temple entrance lane. Rooms (some windowless; a/c ₹1600) are clean, with a choice of Western or Indian toilets, but off dim corridors. No wi-fi. **₹600**

Saradharam 19 Venugopal Pillai St, opposite the bus stand ☏ 04144 221336, ⊛ hotelsaradharam.co.in. Large, clean, well-kept rooms, some with balconies, in a modern building; a/c rooms (₹2250) include breakfast. The hotel also has three decent restaurants (including the multicuisine *Anupallavi*), a garden, cocktail lounge, laundry service and foreign exchange. **₹990**

EATING

Palagaram.com West Car St (just north of west gate) ☏ 04144 224228. Oddly-named but smart, new a/c vegetarian restaurant, where you can enjoy a variety of filling set meals for ₹100–₹200. Daily 7.30am–10.30pm.

Pallavi 19 Venugopal Pillai St, opposite the bus stand ☏ 04144 221336. Located inside the *Hotel Saradharam*, this vegetarian restaurant serves traditional south Indian tiffins and meals, which are all within ₹100. The hotel also has a separate kitchen and restaurant serving meat and other non-veg dishes at the multicuisine restaurant, Anu Pallavi. Daily 7.30am–10pm

Southern Spice Vandayar hotel, 12 VGP St ☏ 04144 225374. This comfortable a/c dining hall offers a range of Indian and Chinese food in the ₹150–300 bracket. Daily 7am–10pm.

Sri Krishna Vilas 93 East Car St ☏ 94432 12328. Simple but very good, south Indian food served in a clean environment with deities adorning the walls and early morning pujas. Small range of breakfast dishes including tasty *pongal*. No menu as such – just ask for what you want – but all items ₹50 or less. Daily 7.15am–2pm & 4–10pm.

Gangaikondacholapuram

Devised as the centrepiece of a city built by the Chola king Rajendra I (1014–42) to celebrate his conquests, the magnificent **Brihadishwara Temple** (a replica of the Tanjore temple) stands in the tiny village of **GANGAIKONDACHOLAPURAM** in Ariyalur District, 35km north of Kumbakonam. The tongue-twisting name means "the town of the Chola who took the Ganges". Under Rajendra I, the Chola Empire did indeed stretch as far as the great river of the north, an unprecedented achievement for a southern dynasty. Apart from the temple and the rubble of Rajendra's palace, 2km east at Tamalikaimedu, nothing of the city remains. Nonetheless, this is among the most extraordinary archeological sites in south India, outshone only by Thanjavur, and the fact that it's devoid of visitors most of the time gives it a memorably forlorn feel. Note there are scarcely any facilities beyond a couple of stalls, so avoid getting stuck here when the temple is closed.

Brihadishwara Temple

Daily 6am–noon & 4–8pm

Dominating the village landscape, the **Brihadishwara Temple** sits in a well-maintained grassy courtyard, flanked by a closed *mandapa* hallway. Over the sanctuary, to the right, a massive pyramidal tower (*vimana*) rises 55m in nine diminishing storeys.

Turning right (north) inside the courtyard, before you reach a small shrine to the goddess **Durga**, containing an image of Mahishasuramardini (the slaying of the buffalo demon), you come across a small well, guarded by a lion statue, known as Simha-kinaru and made from plastered brickwork. King Rajendra is said to have had Ganges water placed in the well to be used for the ritual anointing of the lingam in the main temple. The lion, representing Chola kingly power, bows to the huge Nandi respectfully seated before the eastern entrance of the temple, in line with the *shivalingam* contained within.

Directly in front of the eastern entrance to the temple stands a small altar for offerings. Two parallel flights of stairs ascend to the *mukhamandapa* or porch, which leads to the long pillared *mahamandapa* hallway, the entrance of which is flanked by a pair of large guardian deities. Immediately inside the temple a guide can show you the way to the tower, up steep steps. If you enter alone, a torch is useful because parts of the interior are extremely dark. On either side of the temple doorway, sculptures of Shiva in his various benevolent (*anugraha*) manifestations include him blessing Vishnu, Devi, Ravana and the saint Chandesha. In the northeast corner, an unusual square stone block features carvings of the nine planets (*navagraha*). A number of **Chola bronzes** (see page 1023) stand on the platform; the figure of Karthikeya, the war god, carrying a club and a shield, is thought to have had particular significance

The base of the main temple sanctuary is decorated with lions and scrollwork. Above this decoration, running from the southern to the northern entrance of the *ardhamandapa*, a series of sculpted figures in plastered niches portray different images of Shiva. The most famous is at the northern entrance, showing Shiva and Parvati garlanding the saint Chandesha, who here is sometimes identified as Rajendra I.

Archeological Museum
Daily except Fri 10am–1pm & 2–5.45pm • Free

Two minutes' walk northeast along the main road (turn right from the car park), the tiny **Archeological Museum** contains Chola odds and ends discovered locally. The finds include terracotta lamps, coins, weapons, tiles, bronze, bangle pieces, palm-leaf manuscripts and an old Chinese pot.

20

ARRIVAL AND DEPARTURE	**GANGAIKONDACHOLAPURAM**

By bus Although it is marginally closer to Chidambaram, bus connections are better to and from Kumbakonam (every 15–30min; 1hr 30min). Some Trichy-to-Chidambaram services also stop here.

Kumbakonam and around

Sandwiched between the Kaveri (Cauvery) and Arasalar rivers, 74km southwest of Chidambaram and 38km northeast of Thanjavur, is **KUMBAKONAM**. Hindus believe this to be the place where a water pot (*kumba*) of *amrita* – the ambrosial beverage of immortality – was washed up by a great deluge from atop sacred Mount Meru in the Himalayas. Shiva, who just happened to be passing through in the guise of a wild forest-dwelling hunter, for some reason fired an arrow at the pot, causing it to break. From the shards, he made the lingam that is now enshrined in **Kumbeswara Temple**, whose *gopuras* today tower over the town, along with those of some seventeen other major shrines. A former capital of the Cholas, who are said to have kept a high-security treasury here, Kumbakonam is the chief commercial centre for the Thanjavur region. The main bazaar, **TSR Big Street**, is especially renowned for its quality costume jewellery.

The main reason to stop in Kumbakonam is to admire the exquisite sculpture of the **Nageshwara Swami Shiva Temple**, which contains the most refined Chola stone carving still in situ. The town also lies within easy reach of the magnificent Darasuram and Gangaikondacholapuram temples, both spectacular ancient monuments that see very few visitors. The village of Swamimalai, just a bike ride away, is the state's principal centre for traditional **bronze casting**.

Kumbeswara Temple
Nageshwaram Rd • Daily 6am–noon & 4–8pm

Surmounted by a multicoloured *gopura*, the east entrance of Kumbakonam's seventeenth-century **Kumbeswara Temple**, home of the famous lingam from which the town derived its name, is approached via a covered market selling a huge assortment of cooking pots, a local speciality, as well as the usual glass bangles and trinkets. At the gateway, you may meet the temple elephant, with a painted forehead and necklace of bells. Beyond the flagstaff, a *mandapa* houses a fine collection of silver *vahanas*, vehicles of the deities, used in festivals, and *pancha loham* (compound of five metals) figures of the 63 Nayanmar poet-saints.

Sarangapani Temple

Off ISR Big St • Daily 6am–noon & 4–8pm • ⊛ srirangapanitemple.org

The principal and largest of the Vishnu temples in Kumbakonam is the thirteenth-century **Sarangapani Temple**, entered through a ten-storey pyramidal *gopura* gate, more than 45m high. The **central shrine** dates from the late Chola period, with many later accretions. Its entrance, within the innermost court, is guarded by huge *dvarapalas*, identical to Vishnu whom they protect. Between them are carved stone *jali* screens, each different, and in front of them stands the sacred, square *homam* fireplace. During the day, rays of light from tiny ceiling windows penetrate the darkness around the sanctum, designed to resemble a chariot with reliefs of horses, elephants and wheels. A painted cupboard contains a mirror for Vishnu to see himself when he leaves the sanctum sanctorum.

Nageshwara Swami Shiva Temple

Daily 6am–noon & 4–8pm

The small **Nageshwara Swami Shiva Temple**, in the centre of town, is Kumbakonam's oldest, founded in 886 and completed a few years into the reign of Parantaka I (c.907–940). First impressions are unpromising, as much of the original building has been hemmed in by later Disney-coloured additions, but beyond the main courtyard, occupied by a large columned *mandapa*, a small *gopura*-topped gateway leads to an inner enclosure where the earliest Chola shrine stands. Framed in the main niches around its sanctum wall are a series of exquisite stone figures, regarded as the finest

20

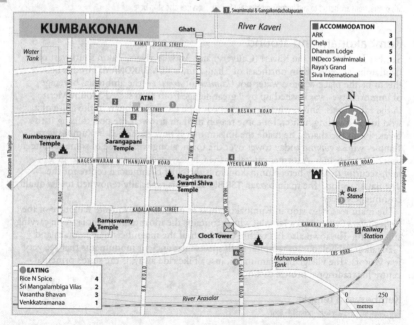

KUMBAKONAM

surviving pieces of **ancient sculpture** in south India. With their languid stance and mesmeric, half-smiling facial expressions, these modest-sized masterpieces far outshine the more monumental art of Thanjavur and Gangaikondacholapuram.

Mahamakham
Indira Gandhi Rd • Daily 6am–noon & 4–8pm

The most famous and revered of many sacred **water tanks** in Kumbakonam, the **Mahamakham** in the southeast of town is said to have filled with ambrosia (*amrit*) collected from the pot broken by Shiva. Every twelve years, when Jupiter passes the constellation of Leo, it is believed that water from the Ganges and eight other holy rivers flows into the tank, thus according it the status of *tirtha*, or sacred river crossing. At this auspicious time, as many as four million pilgrims come here for an absolving bath; the last occasion was in early 2016.

Airavateshwara Temple
Temple daily 5am–7pm • From central Kumbakonam it is a short bus, auto-rickshaw or an easy 4km bike ride (on the Thanjavur route) southwest; the route is flat enough, but keep your wits about you on the Thanjavur Main Rd

The **Airavateshwara Temple**, built by King Rajaraja II (c.1146–73), stands in the village of **Darasuram**, now more of a suburb of Kumbakonam. This superb, if little-visited, Chola monument ranks alongside those at Thanjavur and Gangaikondacholapuram as UNESCO World Heritage Sites; but while the others are grandiose, emphasizing heroism and conquest, this is far smaller, exquisite in proportion and detail, and said to have been decorated with *nitya-vinoda*, "perpetual entertainment", in mind. At this temple, Shiva is called Airavateshwara because he was worshipped here by Airavata, the white elephant belonging to Indra, king of the gods.

Darasuram's finest pieces of sculpture are the Chola black-basalt images adorning wall niches in the *mandapa* and inner shrine. These include images of Nagaraja, the snake-king, with a hood of cobras, and Dakshinamurti, the "south-facing" Shiva as teacher, expounding under a banyan tree.

20

Swamimalai
8km west of Kumbakonam on the NH-22 route to Trichy • Temple daily 5am–noon & 4–10pm • ⦿ swamynathaswamytemple.tnhrce.in • To reach Swamimalai by bicycle from Darasuram, head northwest and ask frequently for directions through the convoluted country lanes

SWAMIMALAI, 8km west of Kumbakonam, is revered as one of the six sacred abodes of Lord Murugan, Shiva's son, whom Hindu mythology records became his father's religious teacher (*swami*) on a hill (*malai*) here. The site of this epic role-reversal now hosts one of the Tamils' holiest shrines, the **Arulmigu Swaminatha Swamy Temple**, crowning the hilltop of the centre of the village, but of more interest to non-Hindus are the **bronze-casters'** workshops dotted around the bazaar and the outlying hamlets.

Known as **sthapathis**, Swamimalai's casters still employ the "lost wax" process perfected by the Cholas to make the most sought-after temple idols in south India. Their finished products are displayed in numerous showrooms along the main street, from where they are exported worldwide, but it is more memorable to watch the *sthapathis* in action, fashioning the original figures from beeswax and breaking open the moulds to expose the mystical finished metalwork inside.

ARRIVAL AND DEPARTURE KUMBAKONAM AND AROUND

By train Kumbakonam's small railway station, in the southeast of town 2km from the main bazaar, is well served by trains in both directions, and has a 24hr left-luggage office and decent (non-a/c and a/c) retiring rooms.

By bus The hectic bus stand is in the southeast of town, just northwest of the railway station. All the timetables are in Tamil, but there's an enquiry office with English-speaking staff. Buses leave for Gangaikondacholapuram (every 15-–30min; 1hr 30min), Puducherry (hourly; 4hr) and Thanjavur (every 5–10min; 1hr 30min), many going via Darasuram. Frequent services run to Chennai (every 30min; 7–8hr), Trichy (every 5–10min; 2hr 30min), and there's a daily service to Bengaluru at 6pm (11hr).

ACCOMMODATION

ARK 21 TSR Big St ☎ 0435 242 1942, ✉ info@hotelark. com; map p.1018. Centrally located hotel with five floors and fifty spacious and very clean rooms (a/c from ₹1400) and suites, all with TV and decent-sized bathrooms. There's also an a/c bar serving overpriced beer. ₹1000

Chela 9 Ayekulam Rd ☎ 0435 243 0336, ⊚ hotelchela. com; map p.1018. Large mid-range place located between the bus stand and the centre, with a pale green mock-classical front. The good-sized clean rooms (a/c ₹1400) have pleasant bathrooms and TVs, plus there's a multicuisine restaurant and bar. ₹900

Dhanam Lodge 188 Kamaraj Rd ☎ 0435 242 3864; map p.1018. Good, basic but perfectly clean budget lodge, with compact rooms. The rooms have a/c and those with four beds are priced at ₹1600. Equally convenient for the bus stand and train station. No wi-fi. ₹1300

INDeco Swamimalai In the hamlet of Thimmakkudy, 6km west of Kumbakonam ☎ 0435 248 0044, ⊚ indecohotels.com; map p.1018. Set in its own grounds, this heritage resort is in a beautifully restored nineteenth-century Brahmin's mansion, modern facilities in teak and rosewood-furnished rooms. Suites cost ₹6500. One restaurant, a small swimming pool and massage. Good online deals. ₹3500

Raya's Grand 23/25 Mahamaham Tank West ☎ 0435 242 6611, ⊚ hotelrayas.com; map p.1018. Brand-new business-oriented hotel with large, lavishly furnished a/c rooms , all with mini-fridges and large flat-screen TVs. Great views of the tank from the 'suite' rooms at the front, which are priced at ₹4150. ₹2520

Siva International 104/5 TSR Big St ☎ 0435 242 4014; map p.1018. This huge hotel complex is one of the tallest buildings in town. The rooms (a/c ₹1100) are a good size and it's clean enough, but there are some grungy corridors. Great views from the rooftop. No wi-fi. ₹800

EATING

Rice N Spice 23/25 Mahamaham Tank West ☎ 0435 242 6611; map p.1018. A very traditional restaurant housed in *Raya's Grand* hotel which serves Indian vegetarian and Chinese dishes. Try the *pulav* dishes here, made with rice and vegetables, as well as the curries with chapathis and phulkas. A meal for two is ₹300. Daily 6am–10.30pm

Sri Mangalambiga Vilas Adi Kumbeshwara Temple Complex ☎ 93443 01418; map p.1018. A small eatery infused with over 100 years of history, serving traditional, authentic south Indian vegetarian tiffins or snacks and meals for less than ₹80. Don't miss their rava dosas and fluffy idlis (₹10) and good filter coffee. Daily 6am–10pm

Vasantha Bhavan Bus stand ☎ 0435 6533996; map p.1018. Good veg restaurant serving a full range of south Indian breakfasts to fuel any onward journey. "Meals" are served from 11am (₹80) and there's plenty of chai and coffee. Daily 6am–midnight.

Venkkatramanaa 40 Gandhi Park North ☎ 0435 2400736; map p.1018. Huge and very popular restaurant, adorned with pictures of Sri Ramana. There's no English menu, but the staff are friendly and helpful. A small range of dishes including "meals" and south Indian specials, all ₹100 or less. Daily 5am–9.45pm.

Thanjavur

One of the busiest commercial towns of the Kaveri Delta, **THANJAVUR** (aka Tanjore), 55km east of Tiruchirapalli and 35km southwest of Kumbakonam, is nevertheless well worth a visit. Its history and treasures – among them the breathtaking **Brihadishwara Temple**, Tamil Nadu's most awesome Chola monument and a UNESCO World Heritage Site – give it a crucial significance to south Indian culture. The home of the world's finest Chola bronze collection, it holds enough of interest to keep you enthralled for at least a couple of days plus it's a good base for short trips to nearby Gangaikondacholapuram, Darasuram and Swamimalai.

Thanjavur divides into two sections, separated by the east–west **Grand Anicut Canal**. The **old town**, north of the canal and once entirely enclosed by a fortified wall, was chosen, between the ninth and the end of the thirteenth century, as the capital of their extensive empire by all the Chola kings save one. None of their secular buildings survive, but you can still see as many as ninety temples, of which the Brihadishwara most eloquently epitomizes the power and patronage of Rajaraja I (985–1014), whose military campaigns spread Hinduism to the Maldives, Sri Lanka and Java. Under the Cholas, as well as the later Nayaks and Marathas, literature, painting, sculpture, Carnatic classical music and Bharatanatyam dance all thrived here. Quite apart from its own intrinsic interest, the Nayak **royal palace compound** houses an important library and museums including a famous collection of bronzes.

Of major local **festivals**, the most lavish celebrations at the Brihadishwara Temple are associated with the birthday of King Rajaraja, in late October. A five-day celebration of **Carnatic classical music** is held each January at the Panchanateshwara Temple at **Thiruvaiyaru**, 13km away, to honour the great Carnatic composer-saint, Thyagaraja.

Brihadishwara Temple

Temple Daily 6am–8pm • **Museum** Daily 9am–6pm • Free • ☎ 04362 274476, ⓦ brihadeeshwarartemple.com

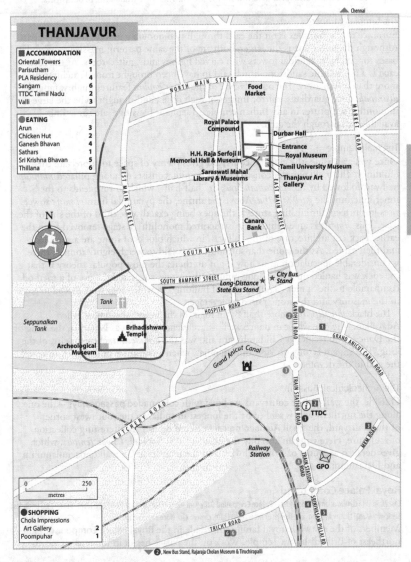

THANJAVUR

ACCOMMODATION
Oriental Towers	5
Parisutham	1
PLA Residency	4
Sangam	6
TTDC Tamil Nadu	2
Valli	3

EATING
Arun	3
Chicken Hut	2
Ganesh Bhavan	4
Sathars	1
Sri Krishna Bhavan	5
Thillana	6

SHOPPING
Chola Impressions	
Art Gallery	2
Poompuhar	1

20

Chennai

NORTH MAIN STREET · Food Market · MARKET ROAD · Royal Palace Compound · Durbar Hall · Entrance · H.H. Raja Serfoji II Memorial Hall & Museum · Royal Museum · Tamil University Museum · Saraswati Mahal Library & Museums · Thanjavur Art Gallery · WEST MAIN STREET · EAST MAIN STREET · Canara Bank · SOUTH MAIN STREET · SOUTH RAMPART STREET · Long-Distance State Bus Stand · City Bus Stand · Tank · HOSPITAL ROAD · GANDHIJI ROAD · GRAND ANICUT CANAL ROAD · Seppunalkan Tank · Brihadishwara Temple · Archeological Museum · Grand Anicut Canal · TRAIN STATION ROAD · TTDC · KUTCHERY ROAD · MICA ROAD · Railway Station · GPO · TRAIN STATION ROAD · SRINIVASAM PILLAI RD · TRICHY ROAD

N

0   250
metres

▼ New Bus Stand, Rajaraja Cholan Museum & Tiruchirapalli

Thanjavur's skyline is dominated by the huge tower of the **Brihadishwara Temple**, nicknamed the Big Temple, which for all its size and UNESCO World Heritage status lacks the grandiose excesses of later periods. The temple was constructed as much to reflect the power of its patron, King Rajaraja I, as to facilitate the worship of Shiva. Profuse **inscriptions** on the base of the main shrine provide incredibly detailed information about the organization of the temple, showing it to have been rich, both in financial terms and in ritual activity. No fewer than four hundred female dancers, **devadasis** (literally "slaves to the gods", married off to the deity), were employed, and each provided with a house. Other staff – another two hundred people – included dance teachers, musicians, tailors, potters, laundrymen, goldsmiths, carpenters, astrologers, accountants and attendants for all manner of rituals and processions.

The temple entrance

Entrance to the complex is on the east, through two **gopura** gateways some way apart. Although the outer one is the larger, both are of the same pattern: massive rectangular bases topped by pyramidal towers with carved figures and vaulted roofs. At the core of each is a monolithic sandstone lintel, said to have been brought from Tiruchirapalli, more than 50km away. The outer facade of the inner *gopura* features mighty, fanged *dvarapala* door guardians, mirror images of each other, and thought to be the largest monolithic sculptures in any Indian temple. "Elephant blessings" are sometimes available just through the arch.

The main temple

Once you are inside, the gigantic **courtyard** gives plenty of space to appreciate the buildings. The **main temple**, constructed of granite, consists of a long pillared *mandapa* hallway, followed by the *ardhamandapa*, or "half-hall", which in turn leads to the inner sanctum, the *garbha griha*. Above the shrine, the pyramidal 61m *vimana* tower rises in thirteen diminishing storeys, the apex being exactly one third of the size of the base. This *vimana* is an example of a "structured monolith", a stage removed from the earlier rock-cut architecture of the Pallavas, in which blocks of stone are assembled and then carved. As the stone that surmounts it is said to weigh eighty tonnes, there is considerable speculation as to how it got up there; the most popular theory is that the rock was hauled up a 6km-long ramp. Others have suggested the use of a method comparable to the Sumer Ziggurat style of building, in which logs were placed in gaps in the masonry and the stone raised by leverage.

The black *shivalingam*, more than 3.5m high, in the **inner sanctum**, is called Adavallan, "the one who can dance well" – a reference to Shiva as Nataraja, the King of the Dance, who resides at Chidambaram and was the *ishtadevata*, chosen deity, of the king. The lingam is only on view during pujas, when a curtain is pulled back to reveal the god to the devotees.

The Archeological Museum

Outside, the walls of the courtyard are lined with **colonnaded passageways** – the one along the northern wall is said to be the longest in India. In the southwest corner of the courtyard, the small **Archaeological Museum** houses an interesting collection of sculpture. Here you can also buy the excellent ASI booklet, *Chola Temples*, which gives detailed accounts of Brihadishwara and the temples at Gangaikondacholapuram and Darasuram.

Royal Palace Compound

East Main St (a continuation of Gandhiji Rd) • **Palace Compound** Daily 9am–6pm • Free • **Durbar Hall** Daily 10am–5pm • ₹200 (includes Saraswati Mahal Library Museum and Thanjavur Art Gallery) (₹10), camera ₹30, video camera ₹100

Members of the erstwhile royal family still reside in the **Royal Palace Compound**, 2km northeast of Brihadishwara Temple. Work on the palace began in the mid-sixteenth

CHOLA BRONZES

Originally sacred temple objects, **Chola bronzes** are the only art form from Tamil Nadu to have penetrated the world art market. The most memorable bronze icons are the **Natarajas**, or dancing Shivas, performing the cosmic dance. The image of Shiva, standing on one leg, encircled by flames, with wild locks caught in mid-motion, has become almost recognizably Indian.

The principal icons of a temple are usually stationary and made of stone. Frequently, however, ceremonies require an image of the god to be led in procession outside the inner sanctum, and even through the streets. According to the canonical texts known as *Agamas*, these moving images should be made of metal. Indian bronzes are made by the **cire-perdue ("lost wax")** process, known as *madhuchchishtavidhana* in Sanskrit. Three layers of clay mixed with burned grain husks, salt and ground cotton are applied to a figure crafted in beeswax, with a stem left protruding at each end. When that is heated, the wax melts and flows out, creating a hollow mould into which molten metal – a rich five-metal alloy (*panchaloha*) of copper, silver, gold, brass and lead – can be poured through the stems. After the metal has cooled, the clay shell is destroyed, and the stems filed off, leaving a unique completed figure, which the caster-artist, or *sthapathi*, remodels to remove blemishes and add delicate detail.

Those bronzes produced by the few artists practising today invariably follow the Chola model; the chief centre is now **Swamimalai** (see page 1019). Original Chola bronzes are kept in many Tamil temples, but as the interiors are often dark it's not always possible to see them properly. Important **public collections** include the Royal Palace Compound at Thanjavur (see below), the Government Museum at Chennai (see page 984) and the National Museum, New Delhi (see page 95).

20

century under Sevappa Nayak, the founder of the Nayak kingdom of Thanjavur; additions were made by the Marathas from the end of the seventeenth century onwards. Dotted around the compound are several reminders of Thanjavur's past under these two dynasties, including an exhibition of oriental manuscripts and a superlative museum of **Chola bronzes**. Unfortunately, many of the palace buildings remain in a sorry state, despite various promises of funds for renovation.

Remodelled by Shaji II in 1684, the **Durbar Hall**, or hall of audience, houses a throne canopy decorated with the mirrored glass distinctive of Thanjavur. Although damaged, the ceiling and walls are elaborately painted. Five domes are striped red, green and yellow, and on the walls, friezes of leaf and pineapple designs and trumpeting angels in a night sky show European influence. The **courtyard** outside the Durbar Hall was the setting for one of the more poignant moments in Thanjavur's turbulent history when, in 1683, the last of the Nayak kings gave himself up to the king of Madurai. Its most imposing structure, the Sarja Madi or "seven-storey" bell tower, built by Serfoji II in 1800, is closed to the public due to its unsafe condition.

Saraswati Mahal Library Museum

Daily 10am–1pm & 1.30–5pm • Free

The **Saraswati Mahal Library** holds one of the most important oriental manuscript collections in India, used by scholars from all over the world. The library is closed to the general public, but a small **museum** displays a bizarre array of books and pictures from the collection. Among the palm-leaf manuscripts is a calligrapher's *tour de force* in the form of a visual mantra, where each letter in the inscription "Shiva" comprises the god's name repeated in microscopically small handwriting. Most of the Maratha manuscripts, produced from the end of the seventeenth century, are on paper; they include a superbly illustrated edition of the Mahabharata. Sadists will be delighted to see the library managed to hang on to its copy of the explicitly illustrated **Punishments in China**, published in 1804. Next to it, full rein is given to the imagination of French artist **Charles Le Brun** (1619–90), in a series of pictures on the subject of physiognomy.

Animals such as the horse, bullock, wolf, bear, rabbit and camel are drawn in painstaking care above a series of human faces which bear an uncanny, if unlikely, resemblance to them. You can buy postcards of this scientific study and exhibits from the other palace museums in the **shop** next door.

Thanjavur Art Gallery

East Main St • Daily 9am–1 & 3pm–6pm • ₹60 (₹7), camera or video camera ₹100 (₹30)

A magnificent collection of **Chola bronzes** – the finest of them from the Tiruvengadu hoard, unearthed in the 1950s – fills the **Thanjavur Art Gallery**, a high-ceilinged audience hall with massive pillars, dating from 1600. The elegance of the figures and delicacy of detail are unsurpassed. A tenth-century statue of Kannappa Nayannar (#174), a hunter-devotee, shows minutiae right down to his embroidered clothing, fingernails and the fine lines on his fingers. The oldest bronze, four cases left of the main doorway (#58), shows Vinadhra Dakshinamurti ("south-facing Shiva") who, with a deer on one left hand, would have originally been playing the *vina* – the musical instrument has long since gone. However, the undisputed masterpiece of the collection shows Shiva as Pasupathinath, Lord of the Animals (#86), sensuously depicted in a skimpy loincloth, with a turban made of snakes. Next to him stands an equally stunning Parvati, his consort (#87), but the cream of the female figures, a seated, half-reclining Parvati (#97), is displayed on the opposite side of the hall.

ARRIVAL AND INFORMATION

THANJAVUR

By train Thanjavur's railway station is located south of the old town, canal and Brihadishwara temple complex.
Destinations Chennai Egmore (5 daily; 7–8hr); Kumbakonam (10 daily; 45min–1hr 15min); Madurai (2 daily; 3hr 55min–4hr 40min); Rameshwaram (1 daily; 8hr 5min); Trichy (10 daily; 1hr–1hr 50min).
By bus Most buses, including those from Madurai, Tiruchirapalli and Kumbakonam, terminate at the New Bus Stand, 6km southwest of the centre. Rickshaws into town from here cost ₹150, or you can jump on one of the #57, #74 or #75 buses that shuttle to and from the centre every few

minutes. Buses from northern destinations such as Chennai, Puducherry and Kumbakonam pass through town, so you can get off near the temple.
Destinations Kumbakonam (every 5min; 1hr 30min); Madurai (every 15min; 6hr); Trichy (every 5min; 1hr 30min).
Tourist information The TTDC tourist office (Mon–Fri 10am–5.45pm; ☎04362 230984) is located in the compound of *TTDC Tamil Nadu* hotel on Gandhiji Rd.
Services You can change money at Canara Bank on South Main St.

ACCOMMODATION

Oriental Towers 2889 Srinivasam Pillai Rd ☎04362 230450, ⓦhotelorientaltowers.com; map p.1021. Huge hotel-cum-shopping complex, with small swimming pool, a multicuisine restaurant and luxurious a/c rooms. Four rooms on each floor have good temple views, while deluxe rooms are larger. Good value. ₹2600
Parisutham 55 Grand Anicut Canal Rd ☎04362 231801, ⓦhotelparisutham.com; map p.1021. Luxurious hotel with spacious, a/c rooms, a large palm-fringed pool, Ayurvedic treatments, multicuisine restaurant, craft shop, foreign exchange and travel agent. It's popular with tour groups, so book ahead. ₹3600
PLA Residency 2886 Srinivasam Pillai Rd ☎04362 278391, ⓦplaresidency.com; map p.1021. Small but immaculate rooms with large flat-screen TVs and lovely attached bathrooms with modern plumbing and serious shower heads. It's worth paying an extra ₹200 for the bigger exec double that costs ₹2200. Good rooftop restaurant, and

a new annexe two doors along. ₹2000
Sangam Trichy Rd ☎04362 239451, ⓦsangamhotels. com; map p.1021. Luxury four-star hotel on the road in from the bus stand, with comfortable a/c rooms, an excellent restaurant, pool (₹250 for non-residents), and beautiful Tanjore paintings – the one in the lobby is worth a trip here in itself. Deluxe rooms cost ₹8100 and suites are priced at ₹10,000. ₹5300
TTDC Tamil Nadu Gandhiji Rd ☎04362 231325, ⓦttdconline.com; map p.1021. A 10min walk from the railway station, this state-run hotel, once the raja's guesthouse, manages to maintain lots of character. Large, comfortable and very clean a/c rooms with a sofa and armchairs, all of them set around a pleasant enclosed garden. A/c rooms are ₹1600. Includes complimentary breakfast. ₹1300
★ **Valli** 2948 MKM Rd ☎04362 231580, ⓔarasu_tnj@ rediffmail.com; map p.1021. At the end of an industrial

lane, this friendly hotel has clean rooms, some with a/c, with a choice of Indian or Western loos, a rooftop terrace and convenient but rather average restaurant. The best budget option in town. Deluxe rooms ₹1600. **₹750**

EATING

Arun Court Rd ☏ 04362 277310; map p.1021. Conveniently located on the corner of Gandhiji and Court roads, this small pure-veg south Indian restaurant has an extensive menu featuring nearly 100 dishes, most of which cost around ₹60–70. Fine masala dosas too. Daily 6.30am–10pm.

Chicken Hut 82 Gandhiji Rd ☏ 04362 231133; map p.1021. Far superior to the average fast-food joint, serving Indian Chinese, pizza and burgers as well as, of course, tasty fried chicken – four-piece meal only ₹330. Burgers and pizzas ₹100–₹300. Daily 11.30am–3pm & 6.30–10.30pm.

Ganesh Bhavan 2905 Srinivasam Pillai Rd ☏ 98426 59222; map p.1021. Large, clean, south Indian *dhaba* situated on the first floor. Serves a wide range of vegetarian dishes, a selection of noodle dishes (around ₹100), masala dosas (₹60), and tandoori food after 4pm. Daily 7am–10.30pm.

Sathars 167 Gandhiji Rd ☏ 04362 231041; map p.1021. The most popular non-veg restaurant in town, serving a variety of chicken and prawn dishes for ₹150–230, and a few cheaper veggie favourites. There are three separate sections, including an a/c hall upstairs. Daily 12.30–4.30pm & 6.30–11.30pm.

★**Sri Krishna Bhavan** 68A VAC Nagar Trichy Rd ☏ 04362 233344; map p.1021. Clean and popular pure-veg restaurant, which serves delicious, unlimited thalis for just ₹85 and a good range of curries and breads. Its a/c hall is open from 10am. Daily 7am–10pm.

★**Thillana** Sangam hotel, Trichy Rd ☏ 04362 239451; map p.1021. Swish multicuisine restaurant known for its superb lunchtime south-Indian thalis (₹350). In the evening, the extensive à la carte menu, featuring superb *chettinad* specialities (₹300–₹500), is served up with live Carnatic music. Daily noon–3pm & 7–11pm.

SHOPPING

Chola Impressions Art Gallery 26 Chelliah Nagar Tamil University ☏ 78750 54510; map p.1021. A private art gallery and emporium, where you can buy Thanjavur dolls and paintings. They also have classes for those who are interested. Open 24 hours.

Poompuhar Gandhiji Rd ☏ 04362 230060, ⊛ tnpoompuhar.org; map p.1021. This state government shop near the TTDC hotel is a safe bet for reasonable prices on replica bronzes and an array of other handicrafts and souvenirs. Daily 10am–8pm. Closed Sun.

20

Tiruchirapalli (Trichy) and around

TIRUCHIRAPALLI – more commonly referred to as Trichy – stands in the plains between the Shevaroy and Palani hills, just under 100km north of Madurai. Dominated by the dramatic Rock Fort, it's a sprawling commercial centre with a modern feel. Most of its business is in the southern **Trichy Junction** district, where the **bazaars**, immediately north of the Junction, heave with locally made cigars, textiles and fake diamonds, made into inexpensive jewellery and sewn into dance costumes. Head north along Big Bazaar Road and you're confronted by the dramatic profile of the **Rock Fort**, topped by the seventeenth-century Vinayaka (Ganesh) Temple. There are several British churches dotted around the town, the most notable of which is **Our Lady of Lourdes**, west of the Rock Fort, which is modelled on the basilica of Lourdes.

North of the fort, the River Kaveri marks a wide boundary between the crowded business districts and the somewhat more serene temples beyond the river. The spectacular **Ranganathaswamy Temple** in **Srirangam**, 6km north of central Trichy, is so large it holds much of the village within its courtyards. Also north of the Kaveri is the elaborate **Sri Jambukeshwara Temple**.

Brief history

The precise date of Trichy's foundation is uncertain, but though little early architecture remains, it is clear that between 200 and 1000 AD control of the city passed between the Pallavas and Pandyas. The Chola kings who gained supremacy in the eleventh century embarked upon ambitious building projects, reaching a zenith with the Ranganathaswamy Temple. In the twelfth century, the Cholas were ousted by the

Vijayanagar kings of Hampi, who then stood up against Muslim invasions until 1565, when they succumbed to the might of the sultans of the Deccan. Less than fifty years later the Nayaks of Madurai came to power, constructing the fort and firmly establishing Trichy as a trading city. After almost a century of struggle against the French and British, who both sought lands in southeast Tamil Nadu, the town came under British control until it was declared part of Tamil Nadu State in 1947.

The Rock Fort

Daily 6am–8pm • ₹20 video camera • ☎ 0431 270 4621, ⓦ trichyrockfort.tnhrce.in • Bus #1 from outside the railway station or Dindigul Rd

The massive sand-coloured rock on which Trichy's **Rock Fort** rests towers to a height of more than 80m, its irregular sides smoothed by wind and rain. The Pallavas were the first to cut into it, but it was the Nayaks who grasped the site's potential as a fort, adding only a few walls and bastions as fortifications. From the entrance, off China Bazaar, a long flight of red-and-white-painted steps cuts steeply uphill, past a series of Pallava and Pandya rock-cut temples (closed to non-Hindus), to the **Ganesh**

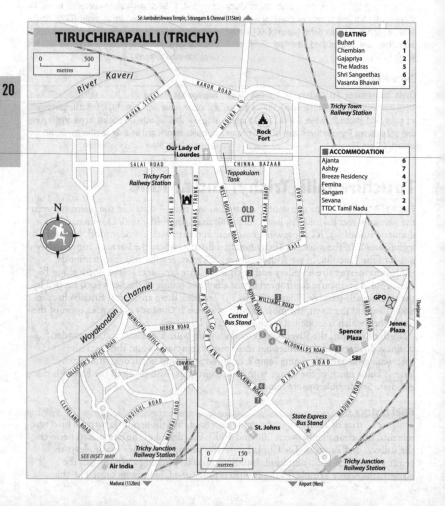

Temple crowning the hilltop. The views from its terrace are spectacular, taking in the Ranganathaswamy and Jambukeshwara temples to the north, their gopuras rising from a sea of palm trees, and the cubic concrete sprawl of central Trichy to the south.

Sri Ranganathaswamy Temple

Srirangam • Daily 5.30am–9pm • Free, camera ₹50, video camera ₹100; official guides ₹300/2hr • ⓦ srirangam.org • Frequent buses from Trichy pull in and leave from the southern gate

The **Sri Ranganathaswamy Temple** at **Srirangam**, 8km north of Trichy Junction, is among the most revered shrines to Vishnu in south India, and also one of the largest and liveliest. Enclosed by seven rectangular walled courtyards and covering more than sixty hectares, it stands on an island defined by a tributary of the River Kaveri. This location symbolizes the transcendence of Vishnu, housed in the sanctuary reclining on the coils of the snake Adisesha, who in legend formed an island for the god, resting on the primordial Ocean of Chaos.

The temple complex

A gateway topped with an immense and heavily carved gopura, completed in the late 1980s, leads to the outermost courtyard, the latest of seven built between the fifth and seventeenth centuries. Most of the present structure dates from the late fourteenth century, when the temple was renovated and enlarged after a disastrous sacking in 1313.

The first **three courtyards** form the hub of the temple community, housing ascetics, priests, musicians and souvenir shops. On reaching the fourth wall, the entrance to the temple proper, visitors remove footwear and can purchase camera and video camera tickets before passing through a high gateway, topped by a magnificent gopura and lined with small shrines to teachers, hymn-singers and sages. In earlier days, this **fourth** *prakara* would have formed the outermost limit of the temple, and was the closest members of the lowest castes could get to the sanctuary. It contains some of the finest and oldest buildings of the complex, including a temple to the goddess **Ranganayaki** in the northwest corner where devotees worship before approaching Vishnu's shrine. On the eastern side of the prakara, the heavily carved "thousand pillared" kalyan mandapa, or hall, was constructed in the late Chola period. The pillars of the outstanding **Sheshagiriraya Mandapa**, south of the kalyan mandapa, are decorated with rearing steeds and hunters, representing the triumph of good over evil.

To the right of the gateway into the fourth courtyard, a small **museum** houses a modest collection of stone and bronze sculptures and some delicate ivory plaques. For ₹10, you can climb to the roof of the fourth wall from beside the museum and take in the view over the temple rooftops and gopuras, which increase in size from the centre outwards.

Inside the gate to the fifth courtyard – the final section of the temple open to non-Hindus – is a pillared hall, the **Garuda Mandapa**, carved throughout in typical Nayak style. Maidens, courtly donors and Nayak rulers feature on the pillars that surround the central shrine to Garuda, the man-eagle vehicle of Vishnu.

20

ARRIVAL AND DEPARTURE	TIRUCHIRAPALLI (TRICHY) AND AROUND
By plane Trichy's airport is 8km south of the centre and has daily flights to and from Chennai, Bangalore, Kochi and frequent services to Sri Lanka, Singapore, Malaysia and the Gulf states. The journey into town, by taxi (around ₹350) or bus (#7, #28, #59, #63 or #K1) takes less than 30min.	Destinations Bengaluru (1 daily; 9hr 15min); Chengalpattu (6–7 daily; 4hr–5hr 30min); Chennai (16–17 daily; 5hr 40min–7hr 55min); Coimbatore (4 daily; 4hr 50min–5hr 20min); Ernakulam for Kochi (2 daily; 10hr 30min–14hr); Kanyakumari (3 daily; 7hr 30min–9hr); Kodaikanal Rd (3–4 daily; 1hr 50min–2hr 15min); Madurai (11–14 daily;
By train The main railway station, Trichy Junction, which has given its name to the southern district of town, is within easy reach of most hotels and restaurants.	2hr 20min–3hr 15min); Thanjavur (10 daily; 38min–1hr 40min).

By bus There are two main bus stands in Trichy, State Express and Central, both served by a mixture of state and private buses. The efficient local city service (#1) that leaves from the platform on Rockins Rd, opposite the Shree Krishna restaurant, is the most convenient way of getting to the Rock Fort, the temples and Srirangam. Auto-rickshaws are also widely available.

Destinations Chengalpattu (every 15–30min; 7–8hr); Chennai (every 15–30min; 8hr 30min–9hr 30min); Coimbatore (every 30min; 5hr); Kanchipuram (3 daily; 7hr); Kanyakumari (every 30min; 10–11hr); Kodaikanal (8–10 daily; 5–6hr); Madurai (every 20–30min; 4–5hr); Puducherry (every 30min; 5–6hr); Thanjavur (every 10min; 1hr–1hr 30min); Tiruvannamalai (5 daily; 6hr).

INFORMATION

Tourist information The tourist office (Mon–Fri 10am–5.30pm; ☎ 0431 246 0136), which offers travel information but no maps, is just outside the Tamil Nadu hotel, opposite the Central Bus Stand.

Services There are many places to change money, such as the Highway forex office (Mon–Sat 10am–6pm) in the Plaza and the State Bank of India on Dindigul Rd.

ACCOMMODATION

Ajanta 6A Rockins Rd ☎ 0431 241 5501; map p.1026. A huge, 85-room complex centred on its own Vijayanagar shrine, and with an opulent Tirupati deity in reception, which is popular with pilgrims. The rooms (deluxe a/c ₹2200; good-value singles ₹540) are fairly spartan but clean. No wi-fi. ₹ **₹900**

Ashby 17A Rockins Rd ☎ 0431 246 0652, ⊛ ashbyhotel. com; map p.1026. This atmospheric Raj-era place is first choice for most foreign tourists, though it's seen better days. The rooms (a/c ₹1700) are large and cleanish, with cable TV and mosquito coils, and there's a decent little restaurant and bar. Free wi-fi only in ground floor rooms, otherwise it's not available. **₹950**

Breeze Residency 3/14 McDonald's Rd ☎ 0431 404 5333, ⊛ breezeresidency.com; map p.1026. This large, centrally located a/c hotel boasts good-sized, comfortably furnished rooms, a nicely decorated foyer, swimming pool and a very good restaurant, *The Madras*, and 24 hour coffee shop called *The Clock*. **₹3000**

★ **Femina** 109 Williams Rd, near Central Bus Stand ☎ 0431 241 4501, ⊛ feminahotel.net; map p.1026. Well-maintained, sprawling block of double a/c rooms some with balconies offering views of the Rock Fort. The

hotel has a flashy marble lobby and houses two plush restaurants, travel services, shops, a pool, fitness centre and 24hr coffee bar. **₹2700**

Sangam Collector's Office Rd ☎ 0431 241 4700, ⊛ sangamhotels.com; map p.1026. Trichy's top hotel, with all the facilities expected of a four-star: a very nice swimming pool and an excellent restaurant, *Chembian* (see below), with live music at weekends. Suites ₹11000–₹15000. **₹4275**

Sevana 5 Royal Rd ☎ 0431 241 5201, ⊖ hotelsevana @ gmail.com; map p.1026. Set in its own grounds 100m back from the main road, this hotel lacks character but offers clean, spacious doubles with king-size beds and towels provided. There's a good-value discount for non a/c single-occupancy rooms. No wi-fi. **₹750**

TTDC Tamil Nadu McDonald's Rd ☎ 0431 241 4346, ⊛ ttdconline.com; map p.1026. One of TTDC's better hotels, and just far enough from the bus stand to escape the din. There are two categories of a/c room (standard and larger deluxe), all with cable TV, but the non-a/c rooms are better value. Suites and family rooms are available at ₹2775–₹3350. Complimentary breakfast. **₹1050**

EATING

Buhari Annamalai Complex, McDonald's Rd ☎ 98424 66221; map p.1026. Refreshingly cool, a/c, north Indian restaurant with yellow walls, serving chicken, mutton, fish and veg dishes, with or without gravy, plus some Chinese. Daily 11.30am–11pm.

Chembian Sangam hotel, Collector's Office Rd ☎ 0431 424 4555; map p.1026. This excellent restaurant offers a range of delicious Indian dishes as well as unusually good Western and Chinese cuisine, in an atmospheric, beautifully decorated dining hall. Non-veg mains around ₹500–₹650. Live Carnatic music at weekends. Daily 11.30am–3.30pm & 7–11pm.

Gajapriya Royal Rd, ground floor of the Gajapriya hotel; map p.1026. Non-veg north Indian and noodle

dishes are specialities of this small but blissfully cool and clean a/c restaurant, where meat dishes cost ₹100–150. Dingy bar next door. Daily 6.30–11pm.

The Madras Breeze Residency, 3/14 McDonald's Rd ☎ 0431 404 5333; map p.1026. Worth a visit for its excellent-value weekday lunchtime (₹350) and dinner buffets (₹450), which feature a wide range of Indian and Chinese dishes and a few random Mexican treats thrown into the mix. Prices higher at weekends. Daily 12.30–3.30pm & 7–11pm.

Shri Sangeethas 2 VOC Road, near Central Bus Stand ☎ 0431 420 0405; map p.1026. Casual, simple vegetarian restaurant which is part of a chain that you will see across the city. Meals during lunch are very filling at (₹95) but if you fancy a special meal, with few sweets and desserts, it is about ₹50 more. Daily 6.30am–11.30pm

Vasanta Bhavan Abhirami hotel complex, 10 Rockins Rd, opposite Central Bus Stand ☏ 0431 241 5001; map p.1026. Trichy's best-known south Indian restaurant,

serving up unbeatable-value lunchtime "meals" (₹90) and the standard range of snacks the rest of the day. The fast-food counter serves fine dosas and uttapams all day. Daily 6am–11pm.

Madurai

One of the oldest cities in South Asia, **MADURAI**, on the banks of the River Vaigai, has been an important centre of worship and commerce for as long as there has been civilization in south India. It was often described as "the Athens of the East" and indeed, when the Greek ambassador Megasthenes visited in 302 BC, he wrote of its splendour and described its queen, Pandai, as "a daughter of Herakles". The Roman geographer Strabo also wrote of Madurai, complaining that the city's silk, pearls and spices were draining the imperial coffers of Rome. It was this lucrative trade that enabled the **Pandyan** dynasty to erect the mighty **Meenakshi-Sundareshwarar temple**. Although now surrounded by a sea of modern concrete cubes, the massive gopuras of this vast complex, writhing with multicoloured mythological figures and crowned by golden finials, remain the greatest man-made spectacle of the south. No fewer than 15,000 people pass through its gates every day and on Fridays (sacred to the goddess Meenakshi) numbers swell to more than 25,000, while the temple's ritual life spills out into the streets in an almost ceaseless round of festivals and processions.

Although considerably enlarged and extended through the ages, the overall layout of Madurai's **old city**, south of the River Vaigai, has remained largely unchanged since the first centuries AD, comprising a series of concentric squares centred on the

20

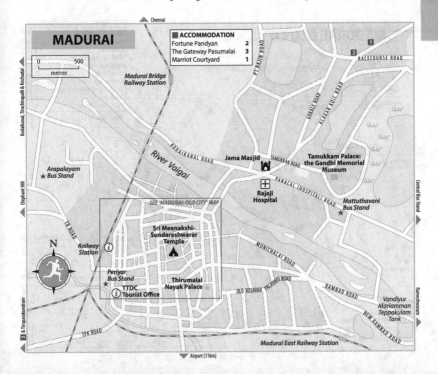

massive **Meenakshi Temple**. Aligned with the cardinal points, the street plan forms a giant mandala, whose sacred properties are activated during the regular mass clockwise circumambulations of the central temple. **North of the river**, Madurai becomes markedly more mundane and irregular. You're only likely to cross the Vaigai to reach the city's more expensive hotels or the Gandhi Museum.

Brief history

Although invariably interwoven with myth, the traceable history and fame of Madurai stretches back well over two thousand years. Numerous natural **caves** in local hills, and boulders often modified by the addition of simple rock-cut beds, were used both in prehistoric times and by ascetics such as the Ajivikas and Jains, who practised withdrawal and penance.

Madurai appears to have been capital of the Pandyan Empire without interruption for at least a thousand years. It became a major commercial city, trading with Greece, Rome and China, and yavanas (a generic term for foreigners) were frequent visitors to Pandyan seaports. The Tamil epics describe them walking around town with their eyes and mouths wide open with amazement. Under the Pandya dynasty, Madurai also became an established seat of Tamil culture, credited with being the site of three **sangams**, "literary academies", said to date back ten thousand years and which supported some eight thousand poets.

The Pandyas' capital fell in the tenth century, when the **Chola** king Parantaka took the city. In the thirteenth century, the Pandyas briefly regained power until the early 1300s, when the notorious **Malik Kafur**, the Delhi Sultanate's "favourite slave", made an unprovoked attack during a plunder-and-desecration tour of the south, and destroyed much of the city. Forewarned of the raid, the Pandya king, Sundara, fled with his immediate family and treasure, leaving his uncle and rival, Vikrama Pandya,

20

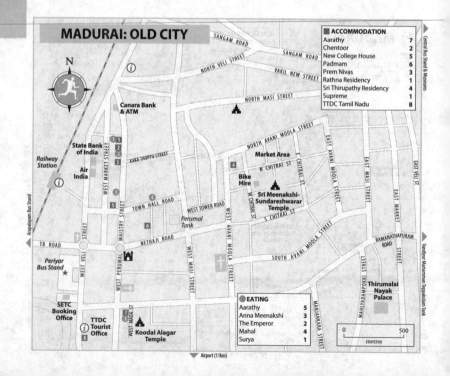

MADURAI: OLD CITY

N

Central Bus Stand & Museums

SANGAM ROAD
SANGAM ROAD
NORTH VELI STREET
VAKIL NEW STREET
NORTH MASI STREET

Canara Bank & ATM

Railway Station

Arapalayam Bus Stand

State Bank of India
KAKA THOPPU STREET
Air India
WEST MARKET STREET
TOWN HALL ROAD
WEST TOWER ROAD
Perumal Tank
MAISTRY STREET
NETHAJI ROAD
TB ROAD
Periyar Bus Stand
WEST VELI STREET
WEST PERUMAL STREET
WEST MASI STREET
WEST AVANI MOOLA STREET

NORTH AVANI MOOLA STREET
Market Area
N CHITRAT ST
CHITRAT ST
Bike Hire
W CHITRAT ST
Sri Meenakshi-Sundareshwarar Temple
S CHITRAT ST
EAST AVANI MOOLA STREET
EAST MASI STREET
EAST VELI STREET
EAST MARKET

SOUTH AVANI MOOLA STREET
RAMANATHAPURAM ROAD
Thirumalai Nayak Palace
MAHAVADAPOKKI STREET
MANJANAKARA STREET
STREET

SETC Booking Office
TTDC Tourist Office
WEST MADA ST
Koodal Alagar Temple

Vandiyur Mariamman Teppakulam Tank

0 — 500 metres

Airport (11km)

to repel Kafur. Nevertheless, the latter returned to Delhi with booty said to consist of "six hundred and twelve elephants, ninety-six thousand mans of gold, several boxes of jewels and pearls and twenty thousand horses".

Shortly after this raid Madurai became an independent Sultanate. In 1364, it joined the Hindu **Vijayanagar** Empire, ruled from Hampi and administered by governors, the **Nayaks**. In 1565, the Nayaks asserted their own independence. Under their supervision and patronage, Madurai enjoyed a renaissance, being rebuilt on the pattern of a lotus centring on the Meenakshi Temple. Part of the palace of the most illustrious of the Nayaks, **Thirumalai** (1623–55), survives today. The city remained under Nayak control until the mid-eighteenth century when it was gradually taken over by the British. A hundred years later the British de-fortified Madurai, filling its moat to create the four Veli streets that today mark the boundary of the old city.

Sri Meenakshi-Sundareshwarar Temple

Daily 4am–12.30pm & 4–10pm • No shorts or cameras or mobiles.

Enclosed by a roughly rectangular 6m-high wall, in the manner of a fortified palace, and with modern security measures to match, the **Sri Meenakshi-Sundareshwarar Temple** is one of the largest temple complexes in India. Much of it was constructed during the Nayak period between the sixteenth and eighteenth centuries, but certain parts are very much older.

For the first-time visitor, confronted with a confusing maze of shrines, sculptures and colonnades, and unaware of the logic employed in their arrangement, it's very easy to get disorientated. Quite apart from the estimated 33,000 sculptures to arrest your attention, the life of the temple is absolutely absorbing, with the endless round of puja ceremonies, loud nagaswaram and tavil music, weddings, brahmin boys under religious instruction in the Vedas, the prostrations of countless devotees and the glittering market stalls inside the east entrance. If you're braving the heat of late spring, check when the stunning **Chithirai festival** is taking place to celebrate the marriage of Meenakshi and Sundareshwarar (Shiva), marked by vivid chariot processions. Even if you're not lucky enough to see a festival procession, something is always going on to make this one of the most compelling places in Tamil Nadu. Approximately fifty priests live and work here, recognizable by the white dhotis tied between their legs and silk cloth worn around their waists. You can roam freely within the complex but the main shrines can only be entered by Hindus.

20

The entrance

Madurai takes the **gopura**, prominent in all southern temples, to its ultimate extreme. The entire complex has no fewer than twelve such towers. Built into the outer walls, the four largest reach a height of around 46m and are covered with a profusion of gaily painted stucco gods and demons.

The most popular entrance, on the east side, leads directly to the Shiva shrine. Another entrance nearby, through a towerless gate, leads to the adjacent Meenakshi shrine deep inside. In the **Ashta Shakti Mandapa** ("Eight Goddesses Hallway"), a market sells puja offerings and souvenirs. Sculpted pillars illustrate different aspects of the goddess Shakti, and Shiva's 64 miracles at Madurai.

Golden Lotus Tank

Continuing straight on from the Ashta Shakti Mandapa, you cross East Ati Street and having passed through the seven-storey **Chitrai gopura** you then enter a passageway which leads to the eastern end of the **Pottamarai Kulam** ("Golden Lotus Tank"), where Indra bathed before worshipping the shivalingam. From the east side of the tank you can see the glistening gold of the Meenakshi and Sundareshwarar vimana towers. Facing Meenakshi, just beyond the first entrance and in front of the sanctum

MEENAKSHI: THE GODDESS WITH FISH-SHAPED EYES

The goddess Meenakshi of Madurai emerged from the flames of a sacrificial fire as a 3-year-old child, in answer to the Pandyan king Malayadvaja's prayer for a son. The king, not only surprised to see a female, was also horrified that she had three breasts. In every other respect, she was beautiful, as her name, Meenakshi ("fish-eyed"), suggests; fish-shaped eyes are classic images of desirability in Indian love poetry. Dispelling his concern, a mysterious voice told the king that Meenakshi would lose the third breast on meeting her future husband.

In the absence of a male heir, the adult Meenakshi succeeded her father as Pandyan monarch. With the aim of world domination, she embarked on a series of successful battles, culminating in the defeat of Shiva's armies in his Himalayan abode, Mount Kailash. Shiva then appeared on the battlefield and upon seeing him, Meenakshi immediately lost her third breast thus fulfilling the prophecy. They then travelled to Madurai, where they were duly married. They assumed a dual role – firstly as king and queen of the Pandya kingdom, with Shiva assuming the title Sundara Pandya, and secondly as the presiding deities of the Madurai temple, into which they subsequently disappeared.

Today, their shrines in Madurai are the focal point of a hugely popular fertility cult centred on their "coupling". The temple priests maintain that this ensures the preservation and regeneration of the universe, so every night the pair are placed in Sundareshwar's bedchamber – but not before Meenakshi's nose ring is carefully removed so that in the heat of passion it won't cut her husband. However, fidelity is never taken for granted, and has to be ritually tested each year when the beautiful goddess Cellattamman is brought to Sundareshwar "to have her powers renewed". After she is spurned, she flies into a fury that can only be placated with the sacrifice of a buffalo.

sanctorum, stands Shiva's bull-vehicle, Nandi. At around 9pm, the moveable images of the god and goddess are carried to the **bed chamber**. Here the final puja ceremony of the day, the **lalipuja**, is performed, when for thirty minutes or so the priests sing lullabies (lali), before closing the temple for the night.

Every Friday (6–7pm) Sundareshwar and Meenakshi are brought to the sixteenth-century **Oonjal Mandapa**, where they are placed on a swing (oonjal) and serenaded by members of a special caste, the Oduvars.

Sundareshwarar shrine

Walking back north, past the Meenakshi shrine and through a towered entrance, you arrive at the Sundareshwarar shrine. Inside is the huge monolithic Ganesh, **Mukkuruni Vinayaka**, thought to have been unearthed during excavation of the Mariamman Teppakulam tank. Chubby Ganesh is well known for his love of sweets and during the annual **Vinayaka Chaturthi festival** (Sept), a special prasad (food offering) is concocted using 300 kilos of rice, ten kilos of sugar and 110 coconuts.

North of the flagstaffs are statues of Shiva and Kali in the throes of a dance competition; a nearby stall sells tiny **butter balls** for visitors to throw at the deities "to cool them down".

The Thousand Pillar Hall

Art Museum Daily 6.30am–12.30pm & 4–9pm • ₹5

Leaving through the east gateway of the Sundareshwarar shrine you come to the fifteenth-century **Ayirakkal Mandapa** (thousand-pillared hall) in the northeast corner, which now houses the temple **Art Museum**. Throughout the hall, large sculptures of strange mythical creatures and cosmic deities rear out at you from the broad stone pillars, some of which have startlingly metallic-like musical tones when tapped.

Vandiyur Mariamman Teppakulam

Ramnad Rd • Bus #4 or #4A

At one time, the huge **Vandiyur Mariamman Teppakulam** tank in the southeast of town, with its constant supply of water, flowing via underground channels from the Vaigai, was always full. Nowadays it is only filled during the spectacular Teppam **floating festival** (Jan/Feb), when pilgrims take boats out to the goddess shrine in the centre. Before their marriage ceremony, Shiva and Meenakshi are brought in procession to the tank, where they float on a beautifully illuminated raft pulled by devotees, which encircles the shrine. The boat trip is the overture to a seduction that reaches its passionate conclusion later that night in the temple. This traditionally makes the Teppam the most auspicious time of year for young couples to get married.

Thirumalai Nayak Palace

Mahlyadampokki St • **Palace** Daily 9am–5pm • ₹50 , camera ₹30, video camera ₹100, includes Palace Museum • **Sound-and-light show** English 6.45–7.35pm, ₹50; Tamil 8–8.50pm, ₹25; tickets issued 15min before the show • T0452 233 2945 • Bus #4, #14 or #47

Today only a quarter of the seventeenth-century **Thirumalai Nayak Palace**, located 1.5km southeast of the Meenakshi Temple, survives. Much of it was dismantled by Thirumalai's grandson, Chockkanatha Nayak, and used to build a new palace at Tiruchirapalli. The remains were renovated in 1858 by Lord Napier, then governor of Madras, and once again in 1971 for the Tamil World Conference. The palace originally consisted of two residential sections, a theatre, private temple, harem, royal bandstand, armoury and gardens. The **Palace Museum** in an adjacent hall includes unlabelled Pandyan, Jain and Buddhist sculptures, terracottas and an eighteenth-century print of the palace in a dilapidated state. A nightly **sound-and-light show** (in both English and Tamil) recalls the story of the Tamil epic, Shilipaddikaram, and the history of the Nayaks.

Tamukkam Palace: the Gandhi Memorial Museum

Tamukkan Rd • Daily except Fri 10am–1pm & 2–5.45pm • Free • Bus #1, #2A, #22, #24, #44 & #77 (from Periyar bus stand 20min)

Across the Vaigai, 5km northeast of the centre near the Central Telegraph Office, stands **Tamukkam**, the seventeenth-century multipillared and arched palace of Queen Rani Mangammal. Built to accommodate such regal entertainment as elephant fights, Tamukkam was taken over by the British, used as a courthouse and collector's office, and in 1955 became home to the Gandhi and Government museums. The **Gandhi Memorial Museum** charts the history of India since the landing of the first Europeans, viewed in terms of the freedom struggle. The perspective is national, but where appropriate, reference is made to the role played by Tamils. Wholeheartedly critical of the British, it states its case clearly and simply, quoting the condemnation by Englishman John Sullivan of his fellow countrymen's insulting treatment of Indians. One chilling artefact, kept in a room painted black, is the bloodstained dhoti the Mahatma was wearing when he was assassinated. Next door to the museum, the **Gandhi Memorial Museum Library** houses a reference collection, open to all, of fifteen thousand books, periodicals, letters and microfilms.

20

ARRIVAL AND DEPARTURE   **MADURAI**

By plane Madurai's small domestic airport (☏0452 269 0433), 12km south of the centre, is served by direct domestic flights to and from Chennai (10 daily; 1hr 5min–1hr 20min), Bengaluru (1 daily; 1hr 20min), Hyderabad (1 daily; 1hr 50min), Mumbai (1 daily; 2 hours 30 min) and Delhi (1 daily; 3 hours) as well as international connections to Colombo (1–2 daily; 1hr) , Singapore (1 daily; 4 hours) and Dubai (3hr 5min). To get to the airport, catch a taxi (around ₹400) or take city bus #10A from the Periyar Bus Stand.

By train The reservations office is to the left of the main hall. There's a prepaid auto-rickshaw and taxi booth outside the main entrance. Madurai is well connected with most major towns and cities in south India and some beyond. It's possible to reach the railhead for Kodaikanal by train, but the journey is much faster by express bus.

Destinations Bengaluru (2–3 daily; 9hr 15min–10hr 50min); Chennai (10–13 daily; 7hr 40min–11hr 40min); Delhi (2 weekly; 41hr 45min); Ernakulam for Kochi (1 daily; 11hr); Kanyakumari/Nagercoil (6–8 daily; 4hr 25min–6hr

20

RECOMMENDED TRAINS FROM MADURAI

Destination	Name	No.	Departs	Arrives
Bengaluru	*Bangalore Express*	#17236	11.55pm	9.30am+
Chennai	*Vaigai Express*	#12636	7am	2.35pm
	Pandian Express	#12638	8.40pm	4.55am+
Nagercoil	*Guruvayur Express*	#16127	4.15pm	9.25pm
Rameshwaram	*Rameshwaram Express*	#16734	4.00pm	9.30pm (only on Thursdays)
Trichy	*Vaigai Express*	#12636	7am	8.55am
				+ Next day

20min); Mumbai (5 weekly; 34hr 55min–36hr 15min); Rameshwaram (3–4 daily; 3hr 40min–4hr 30min); Trichy (11–15 daily; 1hr 55min–3hr 40min); Trivandrum (3 daily; 6hr 50min–7hr 40min).

By bus The Central Bus Stand is the arrival point for all services except those from Kerala and west Tamil Nadu, which arrive at Arapalayam Bus Stand. The Central Bus Stand is 7km from the centre, east of the river, and is connected to the centre by city buses #700 and #75, while Arapalayam Bus Stand is in the northwest, about 2km from the railway station. Periyar Bus Stand, on West Veli St, is for local city buses. Next to Periyar is the Tamil Nadu State Express reservation office (8am–2pm & 4–8pm) for a/c buses to Chennai and other destinations including several Keralan towns and Bengaluru.

Destinations (from the Central Bus Stand unless otherwise stated): Chengalpattu (every 20–30min; 8–9hr); Chennai (every 20–30min; 10–11hr); Chidambaram (6 daily; 7hr 30min–8hr); Coimbatore (Arapalayam stand, every 30min; 5–6hr); Kanchipuram (4 daily; 9–10hr); Kanyakumari (every 30min; 5hr 30min–6hr); Kochi/Ernakulam via Kottayam (Arapalayam stand, 9 daily; 9hr 30min–10hr); Kodaikanal (Arapalayam stand, hourly; 4hr–4hr 30min); Kumbakonam (8 daily; 6hr–6hr 30min); Kumily, for Periyar Wildlife Sanctuary (Arapalayam stand, hourly; 5hr); Mysuru (5 daily; 10–11hr); Puducherry (hourly; 9–10hr); Rameshwaram (every 30min–1hr; 4hr); Thanjavur (every 30min; 4–5hr); Thiruvananthapuram, Kerala (hourly; 7–8hr); Tiruchirapalli (every 30min; 4–5hr); Tirupati (4 daily; 15hr). There are no direct services from Madurai to Ooty – you need to change in Coimbatore.

GETTING AROUND

By bike Cheap bike rental is available at SV, West Tower St, near the west entrance to the temple, or the stall on West Veli St, opposite the *Tamil Nadu* hotel.

By taxi If you want a taxi to see the outlying sights, head to the rank outside the main railway station, which abides by government set rates; a 5hr city tour will cost around ₹1500.

INFORMATION

Tourist information The TTDC tourist office, on West Veli St (Mon–Fri 10am–5.45pm, plus Sat 10am–1pm during festivals; ☎0452 233 4757), is useful for general information and maps, and can provide information on car rental and approved guides. In the main hall of the railway station itself you'll find a very helpful branch of the Tourism Department information centre (daily 6.30am–8.30pm).

Services The State Bank of India at 6 West Veli St can change cash.

ACCOMMODATION

Aarathy 9 Perumal Koil, West Mada St ☎0452 233 1571 ⓦhotelaarathy.com; map p.1030. Popular hotel in a great location over-looking the Koodal Alagar Temple; it's often booked up. All rooms (a/c from ₹1350) have TV. Good a/c restaurant which serves pure vegetarian. ₹750

Chentoor 106 West Perumal Maistry St ☎0452 307 7777 ⓦhotelchentoor.in; map p.1030. Good-value tower-block hotel with very nice, clean all-a/c rooms with TV and king-size beds. The Star Suite goes for ₹4150. Also has a good rooftop restaurant called *Emperor*. ₹2350

Fortune Pandyan Racecourse Rd, north of the river ☎0452 4356789, ⓦfortunehotels.in; map p.1029. Smart, a/c hotel with a range of large, comfortable rooms

all with TV and lavishly decorated with period-style furnishings. Quiet and relaxed, but some way from the centre. Good restaurant, a bar, exchange facilities and travel agency. Suites are ₹10,000–₹15,000. ₹5000

★ The Gateway Pasumalai 40 TPK Rd, Pasumalai Hills ☎0452 663 3000, ⓦthegatewayhotels.com; map p.1029. Madurai's most exclusive hotel, a beautifully refurbished colonial house in 25 acres of manicured gardens in the hills, overlooking the city from 6km away. Superior rooms in the old building are the most atmospheric, but the executive rooms have the best views. There is a gourmet restaurant, swimming pool, tennis court and bar. Good early-bird online specials. ₹5525

Marriott Courtyard Alagar Koil Rd ☎ 0452 5244555, ⓦ marriott.com map p.1029. Situated in its own grounds, this plush, centrally a/c hotel which was earlier called Sangam is now rebranded as a Marriott property. It has very comfortable rooms (deluxe ₹7000 with bath and sofa), a bar and currency exchange. There is a decent swimming pool, nice gardens and an excellent restaurant. ₹3750

New College House 2 Town Hall Rd ☎ 0452 234 2971, ⓔ collegehouse_mdu@yahoo.co.in; map p.1030. This huge, maze-like place which is over a century old, has more than 140 rooms, and one of the town's best "meals" restaurant, called *Anna Meenakshi*. A/c rooms are at ₹1500. No wi-fi but a browsing centre on the ground floor. ₹800

Padmam 1 Perumal Tank West St ☎ 0452 234 0702, ⓔ hotel_padmam@hotmail.com; map p.1030. Clean, comfortable, modern hotel in a central location with a rooftop restaurant. All rooms have TV, some have small balconies and a few are a/c (₹1800). The front rooms, which overlook the ruined Perumal tank and have views of the temple *gopuras*, are more expensive. Luxury suites are ₹2350. Breakfast is extra, at ₹150 per head. ₹1330

Prem Nivas 102 West Perumal Maistry St ☎ 0452 234 2532; map p.1030. The swanky exterior belies a slightly grubby interior, although bed linen is clean and the rooms (a/c ₹2020) are a reasonable size, with flatscreen TVs. ₹990

Rathna Residency 109 West Perumal Maistry St ☎ 0452 437 4444, ⓦ hotelrathnaresidency.com; map p.1030. This is a standard mid-range hotel with central a/c and clean, decent-sized rooms. There's also a money exchange facility and a good restaurant, *The Sangam*. Breakfast included. ₹2220

★ **Sri Thirupathy Residency** 20 West Avani Moola St ☎ 0452 234 7431; map p.1030. This small hotel, right next to the temple, has spotless non-a/c doubles and is a popular choice with travellers. The "deluxe" a/c rooftop room (₹2000) has a great view of the western *gopura*. Book in advance. Wi-fi only in reception. ₹660

Supreme 110 West Perumal Maistry St ☎ 0452 234 3151, ⓦ hotelsupreme.in; map p.1030. A large, central hotel in a seven-storey block with comfortable a/c rooms (₹3300) some of which have temple views. There are good facilities, including foreign exchange, a travel counter, and two restaurants (see below). Lukewarm reception. ₹2500

TTDC Tamil Nadu Unit I West Veli St ☎ 0452 233 7471, ⓦ ttdconline.com; map p.1030. Situated a little out of the way from the atmosphere of the temples and the bazaar, this hotel offers spacious rooms overlooking a leafy courtyard. The non-a/c rooms are very good value; the a/c rooms (from ₹1400) are larger and very comfortable. No wi-fi. ₹900

EATING

When the afternoon heat gets too much, head for one of the juice bars dotted around the centre, where you can order freshly squeezed pomegranate, pineapple, carrot or orange juice for around ₹30 a glass. And the drink that Madurai is famous for is a cold beverage which is milk based and topped with dry fruits called *jigarthanda* at around ₹50 a glass. Madurai is hardly a drinking town, but most of the pricier hotels have a bar, perhaps the most eccentric being the *Apollo 96*, a sci-fi-themed extravaganza at the *Supreme* hotel (see above).

Aarathy Aarathy hotel, 9 Perumal Koil, West Mada St ☎ 0452 233 1571; map p.1030. This place serves south Indian breakfasts (7–10.30am), very good lunchtime "meals" (11.30am–3.30pm; ₹110) and a good range of vegetarian dishes (4.30–10.30pm). There's an a/c dining room and tables in a courtyard. Daily 6am–10.30pm.

★ **Anna Meenakshi** West Perumal Maistry St; map p.1030. One of the best-value places to eat in the centre, this upmarket branch of *New College House*'s more traditional canteen serves good pure-veg food. Delicious coconut and lemon rice "meals" (₹85), banana-leaf "meals"

(₹120), plus north Indian meals for just ₹5 more. Daily 6am–11pm.

★ **Hotel Chentoor**, 106 West Perumal Maistry St ☎ 0452 307 7777; map p.1030. With a lovely breeze and great city and temple views, this multicuisine rooftop restaurant is a great place to eat. They serve good Indian food, including biryanis, chicken dishes (₹150–250) and Chinese cuisine. Daily 6am–11pm.

Mahal 21 Town Hall Rd ☎ 0452 234 2700; map p.1030. Well-established and nicely decorated street-level restaurant serving small but tasty portions of fish and chips, plus half tandoori chicken for ₹225 and cheap south Indian veg snacks. Daily noon–10.30pm.

Hotel Supreme, 110 West Perumal Maistry St ☎ 0452 234 3151; map p.1030. This is one of Madurai's most popular rooftop restaurants, with great views of the city and temple. The pure-veg food is average and the service a little lax, but it's still worth checking out. A/c hall on ground floor. Main courses ₹150–280. Daily 4pm–midnight.

SHOPPING

Old Madurai is crowded with textile and tailors' shops, particularly in West Veli, Avani Moola and Chitrai streets, and Town Hall Rd. At the tailors' shops near the temple, locally produced textiles are generally good value, and tailors pride themselves on turning out faithful copies of

favourite clothes in a matter of hours. South Avani Moola Street is packed with jewellery, particularly gold shops, while stores on West Veli Street sell crafts, oil lamps, Meenakshi sculptures and *khadi* cloth and shirts.

20

Chettinadu

The tranquil rural area known as **Chettinadu** occupies a swathe of land about equidistant from Madurai to the southwest and Trichy and Thanjavur to the north. It is the traditional home of the **Chettiars**, also known as the Nagarathas, a merchant community who date back to the Chola empire and came to prominence in the nineteenth century, when they played an important role in the British trade routes to countries on the Subcontinent and Southeast Asia. The great wealth accumulated during this period allowed them to build lavish **mansions** and notable temples in their 96 villages, of which 72 remain, plus the larger towns of **Karaikudi** and **Pudukottai**. These urban areas grew from villages and provide the gateway to the area, especially the former.

It would take days if not weeks to explore the area thoroughly, so it is best to base yourself at one of the most picturesque villages, such as **Kanadukathan**, 15km north of Karaikudi, en route to Pudukottai. Many of the mansions here and in other villages fell into disrepair when their owners emigrated but have recently been beautifully refurbished as heritage hotels, often by returning Chettiars themselves. Chettinadu is also renowned for its **cuisine** (see box), with examples of it often to be found on Indian menus worldwide.

Kanadukathan

Set amid vivid rice paddies and sugar cane fields, just a couple of kilometres off the main highway, **KANADUKATHAN** epitomizes the effortless class that is exuded by most Chettinad villages. It takes barely ten minutes to walk from one side of it to the other, during which time your eye will marvel at the ornate architecture of the houses and mansions on display. Some heritage houses, usually bearing the owner's initials, such as CVRM and VVR, can be entered by paying a small fee to the janitor. The main attraction, just a block the other side of the large temple bathing tank from the central crossroads, is the Maharaja Palace. This large two-storey edifice is not open to the public but you can admire the startling white walls and arches, counterpointed by vivid flashes of reds and blues from outside.

ARRIVAL AND DEPARTURE   **KANADUKATHAN**

By bus Kanadukathan is most easily accessed from Karaikudi (every 15–30min; 30min).

FOOD IN TAMIL NADU

As befits the heartland of the south, Tamil Nadu's **cuisine** is typical of south India's finest, especially the rice-based thali, known throughout the state simply as **"meals"**. This inexpensive lunchtime feast comprises a pile of rice, often served on a section of **banana leaf**, accompanied by a papad and a selection of dishes in tiny metal pots. These can vary but usually include the likes of sambhar (a spicy lentil soup) or rasam (a peppery tamarind juice soup), kootu (vegetable curried with more lentils), spicy potato fry, kosumari salad (grated carrot and coconut in lime juice), medu vadai (lentil dumpling), mango or lime pickle, and curd. Often there is a pot of a sweet concoction such as akkaravadisal (made with rice and lentils) thrown in for good measure. These meals are sometimes "limited"(i.e. a fixed amount) but more often "unlimited", which means they keep coming round dolloping more on your plate (or leaf) until you beg them to stop.

One of the most celebrated types of Tamil cooking is **Chettinad** cuisine, renowned for its skilful use of aromatic spices such as tamarind, star aniseed, a lichen called *kalpasi*, fennel seeds, fenugreek and whole red chillies. Chettinad chicken and Chettinad fish are the dishes most commonly found on menus outside India. Another item seen throughout India that originated here is Chicken 65, so called because the combination of spices was said to preserve the meat for 65 days on long commercial sea voyages.

By taxi As the Chettinadu villages are spread over a wide area, many people choose to hire a vehicle and driver for their visit from Madurai, Trichy or Thanjavur – reckon on around ₹2500/day.

ACCOMMODATION AND EATING

★ **Chettinadu Mansion** Three blocks behind the palace ☎ 04565 273080, ⓦ chettinadmansion.com. This splendid 1902 mansion has been converted into a luxury hotel while preserving many of its original features, such as the classy halls, period furniture and family photos. Quality food is available to guests. The gentlemanly owner lives on the premises and his less expensive *Chettinad Court* is nearby. Breakfast included. ₹6650

Chettinadu Narayana Vilas 2 blocks behind the palace ☎ 04565 283199, ⓦ chettinadunarayanavilas.

com. Attractive, characterful mansion decorated in warm, vibrant colours. The smart bedrooms have a modern feel and the Chettinad cooking is excellent. Breakfast included. ₹5000

Visalam On the main village street ☎ 04565 273301, ⓦ cghearth.com. The largest local mansion has been taken over by this eco-conscious luxury chain, which has created top-notch rooms, quality dining and drinking areas in the lush grounds, plus a sizeable pool. Breakfast included. ₹16,300

Rameshwaram

The sacred island of **RAMESHWARAM**, 163km southeast of Madurai and less than 20km from Sri Lanka across the Gulf of Mannar, is, along with Madurai, south India's most important pilgrimage site. Rameshwaram is mentioned in the Ramayana as the place where the god Rama, as an incarnation of Vishnu, worshipped Shiva, and consequently attracts followers of both Vishnu and Shiva. The **Ramalingeshwara Temple** complex, with its magnificent pillared walkways, is the most famous on the island, but there are several other small temples of interest, such as the **Gandhamadana Parvatam**, sheltering Rama's footprints, and the **Nambunayagi Amman Kali Temple**, frequented for its curative properties. **Danushkodi** (Rama's Bow) at the eastern end is where Rama is said to have bathed. The boulders peppering the sea between here and Sri Lanka, making "Rama's bridge" (Rama Sethu), were strategically placed by Hanuman's monkey army so they could cross to Lanka in their search for Rama's wife Sita, after her abduction by the demon king Ravana. The town offers uncommercialized **beaches** (not India's most stunning) where you can unwind, bathe and do ablutions.

Rameshwaram, whose streets radiate out from the vast block enclosing the Ramalingeshwara Temple, is always crowded with day-trippers and ragged mendicants who camp outside the Ramalingeshwara and the **Ujainimahamariamman**, the small goddess shore temple. An important part of their pilgrimage is to bathe in the main temple's sacred tanks and in the sea; the narrow strip of beach is shared by groups of bathers, relaxing cows and mantra-reciting swamis sitting next to sand lingams. As well as fishing – prawns and lobsters for packaging and export to Japan – shells are a big source of income in the coastal villages.

20

Ramalingeshwara Temple

The core of the **Ramalingeshwara** (or Ramanathaswamy) **Temple** was built by the Cholas in the twelfth century to house two much-venerated **shivalingams** associated with the Ramayana. After rescuing his wife Sita from the clutches of Ravana, Rama was advised to atone for the killing of the demon king – a Brahmin – by worshipping Shiva. Rama's monkey lieutenant, Hanuman, was despatched to the Himalayas to fetch a Shivalingam, but when he failed to return by the appointed day, Sita fashioned a lingam from sand (the Ramanathalingam) so the ceremony could proceed. Hanuman eventually made it back bearing a lingam and in order to assuage the monkey's guilt Rama decreed that in future, of the two, Hanuman's should be worshipped first. The lingams are now housed in the inner section of the Ramalingeshwara, but can only by viewed by Hindus. Much of what can be visited dates from the 1600s, when the temple received generous endowments from the Sethupathi rajas of Ramanathapuram.

The temple is enclosed by high walls, which form a rectangle with huge pyramidal gopura entrances on each side. Each gateway leads to a spacious closed ambulatory, flanked on either side by continuous platforms with massive pillars set on their edges. These corridors are the most famous attribute of the temple, their extreme length – 205m, with 1212 pillars on the north and south sides – giving a remarkable impression of receding perspective. Before entering the inner sections of the temple, pilgrims are expected to bathe at each of the 22 temple **tirthas** (tanks) in the temple – hence the groups of dripping-wet pilgrims, most of them fully clothed, making their way from tank to tank, to be soaked by bucket-wielding temple attendants. Monday is Rama's auspicious day, when the Padilingam puja takes place. Festivals of particular importance at the temple include **Mahashivaratri** (ten days during Feb/March), **Brahmotsavam** (ten days during March/April) and **Thirukalyanam** (July/Aug), celebrating the marriage of Shiva to Parvati.

ARRIVAL AND INFORMATION

By train The railway station is 1km southwest of the centre; trains from Chennai and further afield all terminate here. There are daily services to Chennai Egmore (13hr 30min) via Trichy (5hr 30min) and Thanjavur (6hr 25min).

By bus The NH-49 links Madurai to Mandapam on the coast and the impressive 2km-long Indira Gandhi Bridge links the mainland to the island of Rameshwaram. Frequent services from Madurai (every 30min–1hr; 4hr), Trichy (hourly;

7–8hr) and beyond arrive at the bus stand 2km west of the centre. Local bus #1 (every 10min) connects the bus stand, temple and railway station.

Tourist information The main TTDC tourist office, a dilapidated two-storey peach-coloured building next to the bus stand (daily 10am–5.45pm; ☎04573 221371) gives out information about guides, accommodation and boat trips, but opens rather erratically.

ACTIVITIES

Kitesurfing This thrilling watersports activity can be enjoyed at several locations around the island, between Rameshwaram and Danushkodi, from around ₹2500/hr

with Quest Asia (☎98203 67412, ⌨Quest-Asia.com), who can also provide accommodation with full board.

ACCOMMODATION

Accommodation in Rameshwaram comprises a mixture of basic old lodges in the streets round the temple and newer hotels, mostly in the direction of the transit points. The temple authorities also provide pilgrim rooms; ask at the Devasthanam Office, East Car St (☎04573 221223). During holidays and festivals, rooms are like gold dust and just as pricey.

Daiwik NH-49 near the bus stand ☎04573 223222, ⌨daiwikhotels.com. This is one of several new hotels on the main highway into town. Immaculate, spacious and comfortable a/c rooms with king-size beds and flatscreen TVs. On-site massage and restaurant. They can also arrange sightseeing on request. **₹4000**

Island Star 41A South Car St ☎95859 92772 This is a fair-sized hotel with clean and pleasantly appointed rooms, most of which have sea views. The non-a/c rooms are quite good value and four-bed rooms are ₹700. There is a new lodge close by which offers a/c rooms for ₹1200 and non a/c for ₹700. Car parking also available. No wi-fi. **₹500**

Hotel Sethu Maharaja 7 Middle St ☎98946 21271, ✉hotelmaharajas@gmail.com. Located near the west gate of the temple, this hotel has clean and comfortable

rooms with attached bathrooms and TV. Some rooms have temple views from the balcony. Only non a/c rooms are available for now. No wi-fi ₹605

Sri Kumaran Delux 1/54 West Car St ☎90800 50040. Smart modern lodge that backs right onto the temple near the west *gopura*. The rooms are compact but neat and a/c rates are ₹1300 while non a/c is ₹900. Just a few minutes away is another lodge owned by the same group, called *Sri Kumaran Residency* which offers a/c rooms with sea view at ₹1500. No breakfast. **₹1300**

★**TTDC Tamil Nadu** Near the beach, 500m from the corner of North Car and East Car streets ☎04573 221277, ⌨ttdconline.com. The best option in the temple area of Rameshwaram, situated in its own grounds, with restaurant and bar. There are some sea-facing rooms as well for ₹3500. Most rooms have two to four bedrooms and both a/c and non a/c are available. Rates vary from ₹1000 for non a/c double occupancy to ₹2700–₹3300 for a/c depending on categories. Taxes are extra and breakfast is included. **₹1000**

Vinayaga 5 Railway Feeder Rd ☎96298 66611, ⌨vinayagahotel.com. A pleasant hotel in a three-storey block just 100m from the railway station precinct. Clean and well kept, with 45 light, spacious and airy a/c rooms in the

price range of ₹2500 for single occupancy. Breakfast included. Away from the temple area but quieter for it. **₹3500**

EATING

Ahaan Restaurant, Daivik Hotel NH-49 near the bus stand ☎04573 223222, ☮daiwikhotels.com Upscale, traditional and pure vegetarian with vegan and gluten free options. It includes traditional north and south Indian cuisine besides Indian Chinese.Try the buffet here for lunch or dinner at ₹300–₹400. Daily 7am–10.30pm

Abhirami Shore Rd, near the east entrance to the main temple ☎04573 221178 Reasonably clean south-Indian veg joint on the way to the seashore, with street views from the tables. Lunchtime "meals" are served from 11.30am–3pm at the pilgrim price of ₹50. Daily 6.30am–11.30pm.

Aryaas Residency 43 C West St ☎94432 21441. Clean and traditional south-Indian-style restaurant serving good south Indian breakfasts. "Meals" available from 11.30am–3.30pm (₹80) plus pure-veg dishes costing under ₹100. Daily 6.30am–11pm.

Ganesh Mess Middle St, off Car St West ☎99940 63984. A small restaurant with just a few tables and pleasant and friendly service. The lunchtime "meals" cost ₹70 and they also serve masala dosas (₹55) and other south Indian snacks throughout the day. Daily 7.15am–10.30pm.

Saravana Bhavan 6 Middle St, off Car St West ☎04573 222733. Spotless franchise of the ever-popular and reliable chain, churning out copious quantities of snacks and meals, all under ₹100. This one also has a good bakery. Daily 7am–10.30pm.

TTDC Tamil Nadu Near the beach. Gigantic, noisy, high-ceilinged glass building serving all-you-can-eat pure veg breakfast, lunch and dinner buffets (from ₹100–150). There is also an a/c bar in the grounds opposite reception. Daily 7.30–10am, 12.30pm–2.30pm & 7.30–9.30pm.

Kanyakumari

At the southernmost extremity of India, **KANYAKUMARI** is almost as compelling for Hindus as Rameshwaram. It's significant not only for its association with a virgin goddess, Devi Kanyakumari, but also as the meeting point of the Bay of Bengal, Indian Ocean and Arabian Sea, thus regarded as a holy *sangam*. Watching the sun rise and set from here is the big attraction, especially on full-moon day in April, when it's possible to see both the setting sun and rising moon on the same horizon. Although Kanyakumari is in the state of Tamil Nadu, most foreign visitors arrive on day-trips from Kerala. While the place is of enduring appeal to pilgrims and those who just want to see India's tip, some may find it bereft of atmosphere, its magic obliterated by ugly concrete buildings and hawkers. Kanyakumari was devastated by the 2004 tsunami, although the seafront and jetty have since been rebuilt.

Kumari Amman Temple

Sannathi St • Daily 4.30am–12.15pm & 4–8.15pm

The shoreline **Kumari Amman Temple** is dedicated to the virgin goddess **Devi Kanyakumari**, who may have originally been the local guardian deity of the shoreline but was later absorbed into the figure of Devi, or Parvati, consort of Shiva. The image of Devi Kanyakumari inside the temple wears a diamond nose stud of such brilliance that it's said to be visible from the sea. Male visitors must be shirtless and wear a dhoti before entering the temple; non-Hindus are not allowed in the inner sanctum. It is especially auspicious for pilgrims to wash at the bathing *ghat* here.

Gandhi Mandapam

Daily 7am–7pm

Resembling a prewar British cinema, the **Gandhi Mandapam**, 300m northwest of the Kumari Amman Temple, was actually conceived as a modern imitation of an Odishan temple. It was so designed that at noon on October 2, Mahatma Gandhi's birthday, the sun strikes the auspicious spot where his ashes were laid prior to immersion in the sea.

The rocks

Ferry every 20min; daily 7.45am–4pm • ₹34, 150 people/boat

Possibly the original sacred focus of Kanyakumari were the two **rocks**, about 60m apart, jutting out of the sea 500m off the coast. They can be reached by the Poompuhar ferry service leaving from the jetty on the east side of town. Known as the Pitru and Matru tirthas, they attracted the attention of the Hindu reformer Vivekananda (1862–1902), who swam out to the rocks in 1892 to meditate on the syncretistic teachings of his recently dead guru, Ramakrishna Paramahamsa. Incorporating elements of architecture from around the country, the 1970 **Vivekananda Memorial** (daily 8am–4pm; ₹20; ⊕vivekanandakendra.org) houses a statue of the saint. The footprints of Devi Kanyakumari can also be seen here, at the spot where she performed her penance. The other rock features an imposing 40m-high statue of the ancient Tamil saint and poet **Thiruvalluvar**, who is revered throughout the state.

Wandering Monk Museum (Vivekananda Puram)

Beach Rd, just round the corner from Rock St • Daily 8am–noon & 4–8pm • ₹10

The small **Wandering Monk Museum** is dedicated to the life and teachings of Vivekananda, one of the first Hindu masters to take the teachings of *advaita* non-dualism to the West. The recently modernized exhibition in English, Tamil and Hindi concentrates on providing a meticulously detailed account of the *swami's* odyssey around the Subcontinent at the end of the nineteenth century, using a series of attractively illustrated panels.

ARRIVAL AND INFORMATION

KANYAKUMARI

By train Trains from all over the Subcontinent (even once a week from Jammu – at 70hr the longest rail journey in India) stop at the railway station in the north of town, 2km from the seafront, although even more services terminate at Nagercoil, only 10km away and connected by frequent buses.

Destinations from Kanyakumari or Nagercoil: Bengaluru (2–3 daily; 14hr–20hr 50min); Chennai (3 daily; 13hr 30min–15hr 50min); Coimbatore (3 daily; 11hr 5min–12hr 20min); Ernakulam for Kochi (5–7 daily; 5hr 10min–7hr 30min); Madurai (6–8 daily; 4hr 10min–7hr 40min); Mumbai (1–4 daily; 29hr 50min–45hr 45min); Thiruvananthapuram (7–9 daily; 1hr 30min–2hr 10min); Tiruchirapalli (3–4 daily; 7hr 10min–8hr 40min).

By bus The Express Bus Stand, near the lighthouse on the west side of town, has frequent services to Thiruvanantha-puram and Madurai, plus regular buses to more distant destinations. Changing in Nagercoil sometimes gives you more options too.

Destinations Chennai (8 daily; 15–17hr); Kovalam (10–12 daily; 2hr); Madurai (every 30min; 5hr 30min–6hr); Puducherry (1 daily; 11–12hr); Rameshwaram (3 daily; 10hr); Thiruvananthapuram (every 30min–1hr; 2hr 30min–3hr); Tiruchirapalli (every 30min; 10–11hr).

Tourist information The main Tamil Nadu tourist office on Beach Rd (Mon–Fri 10am–1pm & 2–5.45pm; ☏ 04652 246276) has maps and brochures.

ACCOMMODATION

Maadhini East Car St ☏ 04652 246787, ⊕ hotel maadhini.com. Large hotel right on the seafront above the fishing village. Comfortably-furnished rooms (a/c ones at ₹2950), some with fine sea views. It has one of the best restaurants in town (see opposite), an a/c bar and a rooftop terrace. Wi-fi in lobby only. ₹950

Manickam Tourist Home North Car St ☏ 04652 246387, ⊕ hotelmanickam.com. Large hotel block and sister hotel to the *Maadhini* (same owners). It has spacious, clean rooms (a/c ₹1800) some with balconies and sea views. Non a/c rooms are almost half the price. Avoid the basement rooms. Also has a rooftop terrace. Wi-fi in lobby. ₹800

Samudra Sannathi St ☏ 04652 246162, ✉ hotel samudra@yahoo.com. Smart hotel towards the bottom of Sannathi St, near the temple entrance. It has forty well-furnished deluxe rooms (a/c ₹2020), all facing the sea. All rooms have cable TV and the hotel also has its own generator. ₹800

Hotel Seaview 2/17 East Car St ☏ 04652 247841. ⊕ hotelseaview.in. This 3 star hotel is a popular choice, with spacious rooms, most of which are sea-facing, except the standard rooms. Rates vary depending on the categories. There are also family rooms with four beds which can be booked. Try online deals for better rates. There's also a multicuisine veg and non veg restaurant. ₹3000

TTDC Tamil Nadu Near the lighthouse on Seafront ☏ 04652 246257, ⊕ ttdconline.com. Up the hill and a little further from the temple and main drag. Choice of rooms (a/c ₹3200) in the main block or separate family cottages (₹2580). The on-site restaurant (7.30–10pm) serves veg and non-veg. No wi-fi. **₹1500**

EATING

Archana Maadhini East Car St ☎04652 246787. A comfortable a/c basement dining-hall option that has an extensive veg and non-veg multicuisine menu for ₹100–300. In the evening you can also eat in the alfresco courtyard and they boast the town's widest selection of ice creams. Daily 7am–10.30pm.

The Curry Hotel Gopinivas, Grand East Car St, near the seashore ☎04652 246262. One of the most popular multicuisine restaurants at the rooftop of this hotel by the seashore. Serves both vegetarian and non vegetarian Indian food and Indian Chinese. Chicken and sea food dishes cost around ₹150-₹250, while vegetarian dishes are around ₹100-₹150. Daily 7am–11 pm.

The Ocean, Hotel Seashore 2/12 East Car St ☎04652 246704. Located in the 7th floor of this hotel, *The Ocean* gives you great views while treating you to some delicious seafood all in the price of ₹300-₹500. The multicuisine restaurant also serves vegetarian dishes. No meals and buffet only for breakfast. Daily 7am–11pm

Saravana Bhavan Sannathi St ☎04652 246357. Opposite the Samudra, to which it belongs, this very large dining hall is arguably the best of Kanyakumari's many "meals" restaurants, although service can be slow. Serves the usual snacks in the morning and evening and ₹160 "meals" at lunchtime. Daily 6.30am–10pm.

Sebaa 2/19 South Car St ☎04652 246396. On the corner with East Car St, this pleasant restaurant serves up pure vegetarian but only north Indian cuisine, with chapathis (₹10 each) and puris served in the morning and thali (₹100) for lunch and dinner, besides curry and other dishes. If you like prawn and fish curries, they have a tie up with a neighbouring restaurant called *Jam Jam* and it can be served on your table. Prices in the range of ₹150–200. Daily 8am–10.30pm.

The Ghats

20

Around sixty million years ago, what is today called peninsular India was a separate land mass drifting northwest across the ocean towards Central Asia. Geologists believe this mass originally broke off from the African continent along a fault line. This line is still discernible today as the north–south ridge of volcanic mountains, known as the **Western Ghats**, which stretch 1400km down the west coast of India. Rising to a height of around 2500m, it is India's second highest mountain chain after the Himalayas.

Forming a natural barrier between the Tamil plains and coastal Kerala and Karnataka, the Ghats (literally meaning "steps", but also refers to mountain ranges) soak up the bulk of the southwest monsoon, which drains east to the Bay of Bengal via the mighty Kaveri and Krishna river systems. The massive amount of rain that falls here between June and October (around 2.5m) allows for an incredible **biodiversity**. Nearly one third of all India's flowering plants can be found in the dense evergreen and mixed deciduous forests cloaking the Ghats, while the woodland undergrowth supports the Subcontinent's richest array of wildlife.

It was this abundance of game, and the cooler temperatures of the range's high valleys and grasslands, that attracted the British away from the withering summer heat on the southern plains. They also realized the economic potential of the local climate, fertile soil and plentiful rainfall. As the forests were felled to make way for tea plantations, and the region's many tribal groups – among them the Todas – were forced deeper into the mountains, permanent **hill stations** were established. Today, as in the days of the Raj, these continue to provide welcome escapes from the incessant heat, as well as romantic getaways for the emergent Indian middle classes and nostalgia for foreign tourists.

The best known of the hill resorts is **Udhagamandalam** (formerly Ootacamund, and known just as "**Ooty**") nestling in the **Nilgiris** (from *nila-giri*, "blue mountains"). The ride up to Ooty on the **miniature railway** via Coonoor is fun, and the views are breath taking, but the town centre suffers from heavy traffic pollution and actually has little to offer. Further south and reached by a scenic switchback road, the other main hill station is **Kodaikanal**. The lovely walks around town provide views and fresh air in abundance, while the bustle of Indian tourists around the lake makes a pleasant change from life in the city.

The forest areas lining the state border harbour Tamil Nadu's principal **wildlife sanctuaries**, **Indira Gandhi** and **Mudumalai**, which comprise part of the vast **Nilgiri Biosphere Reserve**, the country's most extensive tract of protected forest. Road building, illegal felling, hydroelectric projects and overgrazing have whittled away large parts of this huge wilderness area over the past two decades, but what's left is still home to an array of wildlife. The main route between Mysuru and the cities of the Tamil plains wriggles through the Nilgiris, and you may well find yourself pausing for a night or two along the way. Whichever direction you're travelling in, a stopover in the dull textile city of **Coimbatore** is hard to avoid.

Kodaikanal

Perched on top of the Palani range, around 120km northwest of Madurai, **KODAIKANAL**, also known as **Kodai**, owes its perennial popularity to its hilltop position which, at an altitude of 2133m, affords breath taking views over the blue-green reaches of the Vaigai plain. Raj-era bungalows and flower-filled gardens add atmosphere, while short walks out of the centre lead to rocky outcrops, waterfalls and dense *shola* forest. With the more northerly wildlife sanctuaries and forest areas of the Ghats closed to visitors, Kodai's outstandingly scenic hinterland also offers south India's best **trekking** terrain.

After a while in the south Indian plains, a retreat to Kodai's cool heights is more than welcome. However, in the height of summer (April–July) when

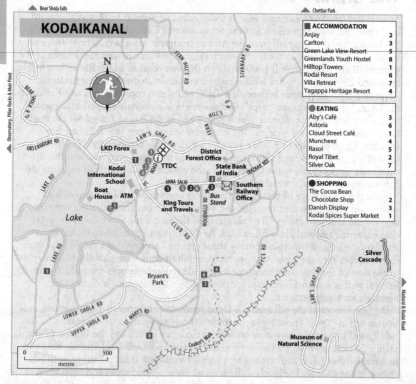

temperatures compete with those in the lowlands, it's not worth the trip – nor is it a good idea to come during the monsoon (Oct–Dec), when the town is shrouded in mist and prone to heavy downpours. From January to early March the nights are chilly so the **peak tourist season** runs from April to June, when prices soar.

The lake

Kodai's focal point is its **lake**, sprawling like a giant amoeba over sixty acres just west of the town centre. This is a popular place for strolls or bike rides along the 5km path that fringes the water's edge; a leisurely circumambulation is a very pleasant way to while away an hour or two and also makes a good excuse for an evening indulging in Kodai's locally made chocolate. Pedal boats (₹70–140) and rowing boats (₹245 for a 4 seater for 30 mins) and Shikara boat (₹415 for 30 mins) can be rented on the eastern shore. Horse riding is also an option here – ₹100 to be led along the lakeside for 1km and ₹500 for an hour's ride. Shops, restaurants and hotels are concentrated in a rather congested area east of and downhill from the lake. The only monuments to Kodai's colonial past are the neat **British bungalows** that overlook the lake, and Law's Ghat Road on the eastern edge of town. The British first moved here in 1845, to be joined later by members of the American Mission, who set up schools for European children.

Bryant's Park

Park Daily 9am–6.30pm, last entry 6pm • ₹30, camera ₹50, video camera ₹100 • **Coaker's Walk** Daily 7am–7pm • ₹10 ₹ 20 to visit telescope house

Southeast of the lake is **Bryant's Park**, with tiered flowerbeds, rhododendrons, pine, eucalyptus and wattle. A flower show is held here in May. On the opposite side of the road a path, known as **Coaker's Walk**, skirts the precipitous hillside, winding from the *Villa Retreat* to *Greenlands Youth Hostel* (10min), offering remarkable views that stretch as far as Madurai on a clear day.

Pillar Rocks and Bear Shola Falls

One of Kodai's most popular natural attractions is the **Pillar Rocks**, 7km south of town, where a series of granite cliffs rise more than 100m above the hillside. To get here, follow the westbound Observatory Road from the northernmost point of the lake (a steep climb) until you come to a crossroads; the southbound road passes the gentle **Fairy Falls** on the way to Pillar Rocks. Some 2km west of the lake, the signposted **Bear Shola Falls** is now barely a trickle of water but remains a popular picnic and photo-stop for local tourists.

Museum of Natural Science

3km down Law's Ghat Rd • Daily except Tues 10am–5pm • ₹10, camera ₹10

Downhill and southeast of the town centre, within the premises of Sacred Heart College, the **Museum of Natural Science** has a very uninviting array of stuffed animals. However, the spectacular orchid house contains one of India's best collections, which can be viewed by appointment only; ask at the tourist office (see page 1044).

Chettiar Park

On the very northeast edge of town, around 3km from the lake at the end of a winding uphill road, **Chettiar Park** has an abundance of trees and flowers all year round. Every twelve years it is also flushed with a haze of pale-blue **Kurinji blossoms** (the next flowering is due in 2030). These unusual flowers are associated with the god Murugan, the Tamil form of Karttikeya (Shiva's second son), and god of Kurinji, one of five ancient divisions of the Tamil country. A temple in his honour stands just outside the park.

20

ARRIVAL AND DEPARTURE

By train Tickets for onward rail journeys from Kodai Rd can be booked at the Southern Railway office, at the GPO – follow signs for the Philatelic Counter (Mon–Fri 9.30am–1.30pm & 2.30–3.30pm, Sat 9.30am–noon). Several travel agents in town, such as King Tours and Travels on Woodville Rd (☎04542 243357, ⊕kodaikingtravels.com), can reserve trains, buses and planes within south India.

By bus The buses from Madurai and Dindigul that climb the steep road up to Kodai pull in at the stand in the centre of town. There are two roads to Kodaikanal: the less-used

route from Palani is by far the more spectacular approach, and during the monsoon may be the only one open. Unless you're travelling long distances the bus is more convenient than the train, as the nearest railhead, Kodai Rd, is 3hr away by bus. The TNSTC reservation counter (daily 10am–1pm & 2–4pm) is at the bus station.

Destinations Coimbatore (2 daily; 6hr); Madurai (15 daily; 4hr); Palani (10 daily; 3hr). There are also daily ultra-deluxe SETC departures to Bengaluru (5.30pm; 12hr), Chennai (6.30pm; 12hr) and Kanyakumari (9am; 10hr).

GETTING AROUND

By taxi Taxis line Anna Salai in the centre of town, offering sightseeing at high fixed rates (₹900/half-day).

By bike Bicycles are a popular and convenient way to travel both in and around Kodaikanal. They can be rented from

the bike stall on Anna Salai or from numerous stalls around the lake (₹20/hr or around ₹100/day). While freewheeling downhill is fun, what goes down must come up, so walking is usually the best bet.

INFORMATION

Tourist information The tourist office (Mon–Fri 10am–5.45pm; ☎04542 241675) on PT Rd is minimally helpful. *Greenlands Youth Hostel* (see below) can arrange treks of varying lengths, such as the 5hr trek in the hills around Kodaikanal itself or the three-day trek of moderate

difficulty across the mountains to Munnar in Kerala. Rates depend on group numbers.

Services There are several foreign exchange places; the State Bank of India and Canara Bank are both on Anna Salai.

ACCOMMODATION

Kodaikanal's inexpensive **lodges** are grouped at the lower end of Anna Salai. It is worth asking whether blankets and hot water are provided (the latter should be free, but you may be charged in budget places).

Anjay Anna Salai ☎04542 241089, ⊕hotelanjay.com; map p.1042. Simple, clean and pleasant hotel centrally located near the bus stand. Rooms are smarter than you'd expect from the outside, all with balconies and TV; the deluxe rooms (₹1445–₹1785) have the best views. **₹700**

Carlton Off Lake Rd ☎04542 240056, ⊕kraheja hospitality.com; map p.1042. The most luxurious hotel in Kodaikanal – a spacious, tastefully-renovated and well-maintained colonial house overlooking the lake. All rooms have a lake view and exude Raj-era charm. There are also cottages within the grounds, a restaurant, bar and comfortable lounge. **₹11,250**

Green Lake View Resort 11/213 Lake Rd ☎04542 242384, ⊕greenlakeviewresort.com; map p.1042. Pleasant resort set in its own extensive grounds on a quiet corner of the lake with lovely gardens and swings. There is a wide range of different rooms priced according to size and hot water availability. Breakfast not included. You can pay ₹600 more for a deluxe room with breakfast. No wi-fi. **₹2360**

★ **Greenlands Youth Hostel** Coaker's Walk, off St Mary's Rd ☎04542 241099, ⊕greenlandskodaikanal. com; map p.1042. An attractive old stone house with unrivalled views and sunsets from its deep verandas.

There's a variety of decent-sized rooms with wooden beds, colourful linens and attached bathrooms, plus also a dorm. Very popular with groups, so book ahead. Dorms are ₹600 per head and a double standard room is about ₹1900. Breakfast not included, no wi-fi. **₹1900**

Hilltop Towers Club Rd ☎04542 240413, ⊕hilltopgroup. in; map p.1042. Decent hotel, 5min from the lake, with modern, comfortable rooms featuring arched doors, large beds and TV. There's also a cosy and romantic honeymoon suite with a circular bed, plus three good restaurants and a bakery. **₹2100**

Kodai Resort Noyce Rd, near Coaker's Walk ☎04542 241301, ⊕kodairesorthotel.com; map p.1042. Large complex of fifty incongruous-looking but pleasant cottages housing comfortable bedrooms with king-sized beds, TVs and huge individual roof terraces with good views. Also a health club, restaurant and resident emu. **₹7000**

Villa Retreat Coaker's Walk, off Club Rd ☎04542 240940, ⊕villaretreat.com; map p.1042. Comfortable old stone house, with more character than most, situated in lovely gardens that afford superb views. Though a touch over-priced, rooms (priced according to views, up to ₹7600) have 24hr hot water; some also have real fires. Wi-fi in lobby. **₹4150**

Yagappa Heritage Resort Noyce Rd ☎04542 241235 ⊕yagappaheritageresort.com; map p.1042. Good mid-range budget option with very clean rooms in three buildings, set around a lawn-cum-courtyard with views to the rear. There's a choice of standard and deluxe rooms (with balcony) and a small dining area for guests only. **₹2250**

EATING

Aby's Café PT Rd ☎98429 12398; map p.1042. This started as popular eatery for students and backpackers, serving cheap homemade sandwiches and pizzas. Now you can get anything from *dal chawal* (rice with lentils) to pastas and parathas. All in the price range of ₹55–₹200. Fri–Wed 11am–7.45pm.

Astoria Anna Salai ☎04542 240524; map p.1042. Large clean dining area that dishes up ample servings of south Indian "meals" (₹120–160) and all the usual snacks and standard menu items. Daily 7am–10pm.

Cloud Street Café PT Rd ☎04542 246425; map p.1042. Large, pleasant, upstairs café with travellers' vibe and second-hand book swap. Veggie breakfasts with mushrooms, tomatoes and beans are served until 11.30am, after which there are wood-fired pizzas (from ₹480), pasta, cakes and chocolate brownies. Daily 9am–9pm.

★**Muncheez** PT Rd ☎04542 240046; map p.1042. A café and restaurant serving wraps, pizzas, pastas and some delicious desserts (no longer a take-away joint). All prices in the range of ₹100–₹250. Daily 11am–9.30pm.

Rasoi Anna Salai, above the Cocoa Bean ☎98651 04664; map p.1042. Tiny first-floor *dhaba* with just eight tables, serving delicious Punjabi and Gujarati food for ₹150–200: excellent *aloo parathas*, a range of north Indian vegetarian dishes, limited Punjabi thalis and unlimited Gujarati thalis. Daily 10am–10pm.

★**Royal Tibet** J's Heritage Complex, PT Rd ☎04542 2241586; map p.1042. Small, friendly Tibetan joint, serving thick homemade bread and particularly tasty *momos*, soups and noodles. There's a range of chicken, mutton, beef and vegetarian dishes, including some Indian and Chinese, all for under ₹180. Daily noon–4pm & 5.30–9pm.

Silver Oak Carlton hotel, off Lake Rd ☎04542 240056; map p.1042. Splash out at Kodai's top hotel on its evening buffet spread (veg and non-veg; ₹1060), rounded off with a *chhota* peg of Scotch in the bar. Lunchtime buffet also available, as are à la carte items. Daily 7.30–10am, 12.30–3pm & 7.30–10.30pm.

SHOPPING

The Cocoa Bean Chocolate Shop No 6, Maratha Complex ☎075982 40414; map p.1042. Kodai's speciality with a variety of handmade chocolates besides several spices, tea and coffee powders and gourmet foods are sold here. Prices start at ₹400 for chocolates. Must try the fruit and nut varieties. Open from 9am–9pm.

Danish Display Anna Salai ☎04542 242455; map p.1042. Lots of handicrafts and trinkets to be found here, from religious items to wood and bronze ornaments, plus colourful clothes and scarves. Mon–Sat 9.30am–9pm, Sun 11.30am–9pm.

Kodai Spices Super Market Anna Salai ☎98653 88756; map p.1042. All sorts of spices, herbs, honey and nuts can be found here, good for travels or the cupboard at home. Daily 9am–9pm.

Indira Gandhi (Anamalai) Wildlife Sanctuary

Indira Gandhi (Anamalai) Wildlife Sanctuary is a 958-square-kilometre tract of forest on the southern reaches of the Cardamom Hills, 37km southwest of the busy junction town of **Pollachi**. Vegetation ranges from *shola*-grassland to dry deciduous to tropical evergreen, and the sanctuary is home to lion-tailed macaques (black-maned monkeys), gaur, sambar, spotted and barking deer, sloth bear, as well as leopards and tigers. Birds such as hornbills and frogmouths are also seen here. It's possible to **trek** through the giant creaking stands of bamboo with a guide and the Forestry Department also runs **safari tours** by minibus and **elephant safaris**. For reservations, contact the park reception office.

ARRIVAL AND DEPARTURE   INDIRA GANDHI (ANAMALAI) WILDLIFE SANCTUARY

By bus There are good bus connections between Pollachi and both Coimbatore and Palani. From Pollachi there are three buses a day (6.15am, 11.15am & 3.15pm) up to the park's reception centre (☎04259 238360) at Top Slip.

By car/taxi Rented cars/taxis, available at Pollachi, run to the official entrance at the Sethumadai checkpost from 6.30am–6pm daily. Private vehicles can drive into the park with prior permission from the Field Director, Wildlife Warden Office, 178 Meenkarai Rd, Pollachi (☎04259 225356).

ACCOMMODATION AND EATING

The Forestry Department runs six **resthouses**, ranging from the basic *Hornbill* to the luxurious *Pillar Top*. Most are within easy walking distance of the reception centre and should be booked in advance through the Field Director in Pollachi. The canteen next to the reception centre serves basic **meals** and drinks and the local shop has equally basic provisions.

20

Coimbatore

Visitors tend only to use the busy industrial city of **COIMBATORE** as a stopover on the way to Ooty, 90km northwest. Once you've climbed up to your hotel rooftop to admire the blue, cloud-capped haze of the Nilgiris in the west, there's little to do here other than kill time wandering through the nuts-and-bolts bazaars, lined with lookalike textile showrooms, "General Traders" and shops selling motor parts.

ARRIVAL AND DEPARTURE
COIMBATORE

By train For Ooty, catch the daily #12671 *Nilagiri Express* at 5.15am, which gets into Mettupalayam at 6.15am, in time to connect with the Toy Train (see page 1050) for Ooty.

By bus Coimbatore has half a dozen bus stands, linked to each other and the railway station by local buses from the busy Central Bus Stand, 2km north of the railway station. The Thiruvalluvar Bus Stand is the main state and interstate station, while most buses to and from Ooty, Coonoor and Mettupalayam use the Mettupalayam New Bus Stand 4km

north of town. The south of town holds a fourth bus stand, Ukkadam, which serves Palani, Pollachi, Madurai, Trichy and towns in northern Kerala.

Destinations Chennai (every 30min–1hr; 7–8hr); Kodaikanal (4 daily; 6hr); Madurai (every 30min; 5–6hr); Udhagamandalam (Ooty) (every 30min; 3hr 30min–4hr); Palani (hourly; 2hr 30min–3hr); Pollachi (every 30min; 1hr); Tiruchirapalli (every 30min; 5hr).

ACCOMMODATION AND EATING

Annapoorna Gowrishankar 2, Government Arts College Road, ☎0422 4392116 ⊛ sreeannapoorna.com. A legendary family-run hotel with restaurants and sweet shops scattered around the city. They have over 15 branches. Known for its traditional south Indian vegetarian fare, they are extremely popular for their dosas. Try the Paper Roast dosa which can cover about two tables and can feed over five people and costs ₹185.

City Tower 56 Sivasamy Rd ☎0422 423 6999, ⊛ hotelcitytower.com. A smart high-rise hotel, 5min walk south of the Central Bus Stand, with decent rooms featuring leatherette and vinyl. The "executive" rooms are more spacious and have a minibar and balcony Rates vary for double occupancy across different categories. Quality multicuisine restaurant. <u>₹2100</u>

KK Residency 7 Shastri Rd ☎0422 430 0222, ⊛ hotelkkresidency.com. Large, business-style hotel in a tower block behind the Central Bus Stand, with very clean a/c rooms, good deals for single occupancy (₹1400) and two good restaurants. <u>₹1600</u>

New Vijaya Lodge 8/81 Geetha Hall Rd ☎0422 230 1570, ⊜ newvijayalodgemka@yahoo.com. Close to the railway station and one of the best (of many) budget options on this street. Rooms (₹900 for single) are clean, simple and compact, with TV, a/c, hot water in the mornings and towels provided. <u>₹1300</u>

TTDC Tamil Nadu 2 Dr Nanjappa Rd ☎0422 230 2177, ⊛ ttdconline.com. Conveniently located opposite the Central Bus Stand, with clean, pleasant rooms (a/c ₹1800). There's a tourist information service and its own very good restaurant next door. Often fully booked, so phone ahead.

Coonoor

At an altitude of 1858m, **COONOOR**, a scruffy bazaar and tea-planters' town on the Nilgiri Blue Mountain Railway (see page 1050) lies at the head of the Hulikal ravine, on the southeastern side of the Dodabetta mountains, 27km north of Mettupalayam and 19km south of Ooty. Thanks to its proximity to its more famous neighbour, Coonoor has avoided Ooty's over commercialization, and can make a pleasant place for a short stop.

Coonoor consists of two "levels", **Lower Coonoor**, with its small but atmospheric hill market, which specializes in leaf tea and fragrant essential oils and **Upper Coonoor**, with its old Raj-era bungalows and narrow lanes with flower-filled hedgerows. At the top lies **Sim's Park**, a lush botanical garden on the slopes of a ravine with hundreds of rose varieties (daily 7am–6.30pm; ₹30, camera ₹50, video camera ₹100).

Around the town, rolling hills and valleys carpeted with spongy green tea bushes and stands of eucalyptus and silver oak offer some of the most beautiful scenery in the Nilgiris, immortalized in many a Hindi-movie dance sequence. Cinema fans from across the south flock here to visit key locations from their favourite blockbusters, among them **Lamb's Nose** (5km) and **Dolphin's Nose** (9km), former British picnicking spots with

COONOOR'S TEA ESTATES

Visible from far away as tiny orange or red dots amid the green vegetation, **tea-pickers** work the slopes around Coonoor, carrying wicker baskets of fresh leaves and bamboo rods that they use like rulers to ensure that each plant is evenly plucked. Once the leaves reach the factory, they're processed within a day, producing seven grades of tea. **Orange pekoe** is the best and most expensive; the seventh lowest grade, a dry dust of stalks and leaf swept up at the end of the process, will be sold on to make instant tea. To visit a tea or coffee plantation, contact **UPASI** (United Planters' Association of Southern India) at Glenview House, Coonoor (☎0423 223 0270, ⊛upasi.org), just along from *Vivek Tourist Home*. Or you can go directly to one such as **High Field Estate** (Mon–Sat 9am–5pm; free; ☎0423 223 0023), less than 2km past Sim's Park; it also has a fine shop.

paved pathways and dramatic views of the Mettupalayam plains. If you take an early morning bus to Dolphin's Nose, it's possible to walk the 9km back into town via Lamb's Nose – a very pleasant scenic amble that takes you through tea estates and dense forest.

ARRIVAL AND DEPARTURE

COONOOR

By train The railway station is in Lower Coonoor across the bazaar from the bus station. There are four trains daily to Ooty (7.45am, 10.40am, 12.35pm & 4.30pm) and one daily service to Mettupalayam at 3.15pm, which arrives at 5.30pm. The ticket office is open daily 7.30am–5.30pm.

By bus Buses to and from Mettupalayam, Coimbatore, Kotagiri and Ooty all use the bus stand, a large blue building at the entrance to Lower Coonoor. Local buses run to Dolphin's Nose every 2hr, starting at 7am.

ACCOMMODATION

There are a few decent places to stay in Coonoor but it's spread over a wide area, so it's best to arrive early to look for a room; you'll need an auto-rickshaw to find most of the hotels. Those around the bus stand are either not worth staying in or won't accept foreigners. Expect to pay around ₹60 from the bus stand to Bedford Circle or jump on a bus bound for Kotagiri.

Gateway (By Taj Group) Church Rd, Upper Coonoor ☎0423 222 5400, ⊛tajhotels.com. Luxurious colonial-era hotel with spectacular views from the gardens. Ayurvedic treatments, excellent lunchtime buffets and a range of sports and activities. A suite room costs around ₹14,000 and includes breakfast. **₹8000**

SunValley Homestay Stanley Park, Ottupattarai, Coonoo ☎0423 2206029 ⊛sunvalleyhomestay.com. Over 20 spacious, comfortable rooms are available in this charming homestay which offers views of the blue mountains and the tea plantations. A multicuisine restaurant, gym, indoor and outdoor games and activities. Rates include breakfast. **₹3800**

Velan (aka Ritz) Ritz Rd, Bedford Circle ☎0423 223 0784, ⊛velanhotels.com. Characterful mid-range hotel, set in a great location on the outskirts of town. It has deep balconies, fine views and spacious rooms – the standard rooms have tiled floors, while the deluxe suites (₹3000) have wooden floors. Good restaurant. **₹2000**

Vivek Tourist Home 42 Figure of Eight Rd, near Bedford Circle ☎0423 223 0658, ⊛hotelvivek.com. Clean rooms in a slightly institutional atmosphere; some have tiny balconies overlooking the lawn and tea terraces. Standard rooms have hot water by bucket only in the morning; deluxe rooms with a view (₹2200) have 24hr hot showers. **₹1100**

★**YWCA Guest House** Wyoming, near Nankem hospital, 500m down from Bedford Circle ☎0423 223 4426, ⊛ywcaagooty.com. There are only eleven rooms – six doubles, five singles (₹700– ₹1200) – in this Victorian-era house, full of character on a bluff overlooking town. Superb home-cooked meals are available at very reasonable rates, and there's a flower garden with fine views of the tea terraces. No alcohol. **₹1900**

EATING

Dragon Bedford Circle ☎0423 223 2158. Chinese restaurant serving up authentic Chinese dishes including spring rolls, a range of chop suey, chow mein and a few Indian dishes, all in the ₹100–200 range. Daily 10am–4pm & 6.30–10pm.

★**Hyderabad Biriyani House** Cash Bazaar, Lower Coonoor ☎0423 223 2223. Brand new first-floor

restaurant and a splendid selection of filling biryanis for around ₹300 as well as other veg, chicken, mutton, fish and prawn dishes. Large and jumbo biriyanis that serve over five people are in the range of ₹700–1000. Daily 11am–11pm.

Khana Khazana Bedford Circle ☎90035 57477. Clean restaurant with pleasant decor serving a range of exclusive vegetarian, specialising in North Indian cuisine. There

20

are also south Indian dishes including a selection of spicy Chettinad dishes. Mini meals (₹180–₹220) are a favourite here. Daily 7.30am–9.30pm

Sri Ramachendra Lunch Home Cash Bazaar, Lower

Coonoor ☎ 0423 220 6740. Simple pure-veg place serving traditional south Indian breakfasts and great lunchtime "meals" for only ₹90. Could do with a lick of paint but clean enough. Daily 6.30am–9.30pm.

Kotagiri

Forming the third point of an almost equilateral triangle with Coonoor and Ooty, **KOTAGIRI** is another tea town, which sees far fewer visitors than its more famous neighbours. It is for that very reason that it is worth making the detour here, in order to stroll along the ridges draped with vivid green tea plantations or among the locals busying themselves in the lively little bazaar on the hill above the bus stand. Further downhill to the south, the town's most notable building is the huge yellow 1867 **St Mary's Church**, built by an order of Franciscan nuns.

ARRIVAL AND DEPARTURE KOTAGIRI

By bus Kotagiri is served by buses from Coonoor (every 20–30min; 1hr) and Ooty (every 30min–1hr; 1hr 15min).

ACCOMMODATION AND EATING

Suthy's Resort On the main road into town ☎ 04266 272444, ⓦ suthysresorts.com. Surprisingly palatial two-storey building with unique floral designs in the guest rooms and elsewhere. Smart multicuisine restaurant and superb views across the valley. **₹2000**

Top Hill Lodge Uphill from the bazaar ☎ 04266 271473. Large block perched on a hill, which offers average-sized, cleanish rooms at good value, though service is a little lackadaisical. No restaurant or wi-fi. **₹600**

Udhagamandalam (Ooty)

In the early nineteenth century, when the British burra sahib John Sullivan first ventured into this region of the Nilgiris through the Hulikal ravine and "discovered" **UDHAGAMANDALAM** (anglicized to **Ootacamund**, abbreviated to Ooty), the territory was the traditional homeland of the pastoralist **Toda** hill tribe. Until this moment, the Todas had lived in almost total isolation from the cities of the surrounding plains and Deccan plateau lands. Sullivan quickly realized the agricultural potential of the area, acquired tracts of land for ₹1 per acre from the Todas, and set about planting flax, barley and hemp, as well as potatoes, soft fruit and, most significantly, **tea**, all of which flourished in the mild climate. Within twenty years, the former East India Company clerk had made a fortune. Needless to say, he was soon joined by other fortune-seekers, and a town was built, complete with artificial lake, churches and stone houses that wouldn't have looked out of place in Surrey or the Scottish Highlands. **Ooty** was the "Queen of Hill Stations" and the most popular hill retreat in India outside the Himalayas.

By a stroke of delicious irony, the Todas outlived the colonists whose cash crops originally displaced them – but only just. Having retreated with their buffalo into the surrounding hills and wooded valleys, they continue to preserve a more-or-less traditional way of life, albeit in greatly diminished numbers. Until the mid-1970s "Snooty Ooty" continued to be "home" to the notoriously snobbish British inhabitants who chose to "stay on" after Independence. Since then, visitors have continued to be attracted by Ooty's cool climate and peaceful green hills, forest and grassland. However, indiscriminate **development** and a deluge of domestic holiday-makers mean that the quaint vestiges of the Raj have been somewhat diluted and are now few and far between.

Situated 2286m above sea level, the town sprawls over a large area with plenty of winding roads and steep climbs. The focal point is **Charing Cross**, a busy junction at the end of **Commercial Road**, the main shopping street running south to the Big Bazaar and municipal vegetable market.

Botanical Gardens

Woodhouse Rd • Daily 7am–6.30pm • ₹30, camera ₹50, video camera ₹100 • ☎ 0423 244 2545

A little way north of Charing Cross, the **Botanical Gardens**, laid out in 1847 by gardeners from London's Kew Gardens, consist of fifty acres of immaculate lawns, lily ponds and beds, with more than a thousand varieties of shrubs, flowers and trees. There's a refreshment stand in the park, and shops in the small Tibetan market sell ice creams and snacks. The **Rose Garden** (same hours and fees), south of Charing Cross along a lane off Etienne's Road, has 2800 varieties of rose and is the largest collection in the whole of India. It's worth a visit for any budding botanists

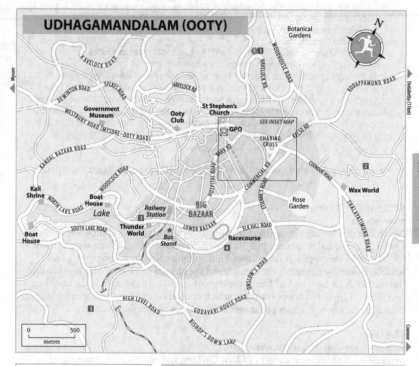

UDHAGAMANDALAM (OOTY)

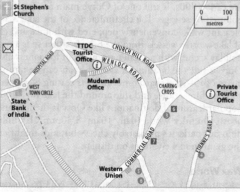

ACCOMMODATION	
Co-operators Guest House	6
Hills Palace	7
King's Cliff	1
Reflections Guest House	3
Sherlock	2
WH Ferrnhills Royale Palace	5
YWCA Anandagiri	4

EATING	
Chandan	3
Hyderabad Biriyani House	5
Preethi Palace	4
Secret	1
Shinkows	2
Willy's	6

THE NILGIRI BLUE MOUNTAIN RAILWAY

The famous narrow-gauge **Nilgiri Blue Mountain Railway** climbs up from Mettupalayam (departs 7.10am) on the plains, via Hillgrove (17km) and Coonoor (27km) to Udhagamandalam, a journey of 46km that passes through sixteen tunnels, eleven stations and nineteen bridges. It's a slow haul of four and a half hours or more – sometimes the train moves little faster than walking pace, and always takes at least twice as long as the bus – but the **views** are absolutely magnificent, especially along the steepest sections in the Hulikal ravine.

The line was built between 1890 and 1908, paid for by the tea-planters and other British inhabitants of the Nilgiris. It differs from India's two comparable narrow-gauge lines, to Darjeeling and Shimla, for its use of the so-called **Swiss rack system**, by means of which the tiny locomotives are able to climb gradients of up to 1 in 12.5. Special bars were set between the track rails to form a ladder, which cogs of teeth, connected to the train's driving wheels, engage like a zip mechanism. Because of this novel design, only the original locomotives can still run the steepest stretches of line, which is why the section between Mettupalayam and Coonoor has remained one of South Asia's last functioning **steam routes**. The chuffing and whistle screeches of the tiny train, echoing across the valleys as it pushes its blue-and-cream carriages up to Coonoor (where a diesel locomotive takes over) rank among the most romantic sounds of south India, conjuring up the determined gentility of the Raj era. Even if you don't count yourself as a trainspotter, a boneshaking ride on the Blue Mountain Railway should be a priority. Note that the two reserved carriages get booked months in advance but there are 80 seats in two unreserved carriages that are sold on the morning of the journey (be in the queue from 5.30am).

20

and gardeners, particularly in season, when the flowers proudly flaunt their petals and perfumes.

St Stephen's Church
Mysore–Ooty road

Northwest of Charing Cross, the small Gothic-style **St Stephen's Church** was one of Ooty's first colonial structures, built in the 1820s on the site of a Toda temple; timber for its bowed teak roof was taken from Tipu Sultan's palace at Srirangapatna and hauled up here by elephant. The area around the church gives some idea of what the hill station must have looked like in the days of the Raj. To the right is the rambling and rather dilapidated **Spencer's store**, which opened in 1909 and sold everything a British home in the colonies could ever need; it's now a computer college.

The lake
Boathouse daily 9am–6pm • ₹10, camera ₹20, video camera ₹125

Situated in the southwest corner of Ooty, the long and narrow **lake**, constructed in the early 1800s, is still one of Ooty's main tourist attractions, despite being somewhat polluted by sewage. The circumference of the lake is about 4.5km and makes for a very pleasant walk, conveniently peppered with juice and chai stalls. Renting one of a range of lake-worthy vessels from the busy **boathouse** is a quintessential part of the domestic holiday scene, with a small percentage of foreigners also choosing to brave the waters. Once inside the boathouse, various boats can be rented (pedal boats ₹120–200, rowing boats ₹145–185, charter motor boats seating 8–15 people ₹420–1800). Back outside, you can hire a horse and ride around the lake for ₹400 per hour. Another increasingly popular feature of destinations like Ooty is theme parks and North Lake Road now boasts Thunder World (daily 10am–8.30pm; ₹10, unlimited rides ₹300), India's largest dinosaur park. It's predictably cheesy but kids might enjoy the various rides and seeing the giant model creatures on display.

Wax World
Dodabetta Rd • Daily 9.30am–6.30pm • ₹50, camera ₹10 • ☎ 97903 43296, ⓦ waxworld.in

A kilometre from Charing Cross, **Wax World** is a rather lifeless exhibition of twenty famous and infamous social and political figures, mostly from the twentieth century. Interesting in its own way, and with helpful guides to commentate, you may pick up the odd historical nugget. Watch out for the "disturbing scene". There are no Bollywood divas or sports heroes as yet but freedom fighters find themselves immortalised.

ARRIVAL AND DEPARTURE UDHAGAMANDALAM (OOTY)

By train Ooty's station for the miniature Nilgiri Blue Mountain Railway (see box opposite) from Coonoor and Mettupalayam is near Big Bazaar and close to the bus station. The station has a booking office (6.30am–7pm), where you can buy tickets for the little train, and a reservation counter (daily 8am–12.30pm & 2.30–4.30pm) for booking onward services to most other destinations in the south. Four trains daily (9.15am, 12.15pm, 2pm & 6pm) pootle down the narrow-gauge track to Coonoor but only the 2pm train continues down to Mettupalayam, on the main broad-gauge network, arriving at 6.30pm. If you are Chennai-bound you can connect with the daily #12672 *Nilagiri Express*, which departs at 7.45pm.

By bus Buses from all destinations arrive at the bus stand, in the southwest of Ooty, near the racecourse and Big Bazaar. Auto-rickshaws and taxis are available just outside the bus stand. There is an enquiry office (daily 7am–8pm) on the left side of the station (as you enter) on the first floor. Both Tamil Nadu and Karnataka State Transport run regular and super-deluxe state buses out of Ooty.
Destinations Bengaluru (9 daily; 7–8hr), Masingudi (4 daily; 2hr–2hr 30min), Mettupalayam (every 10 min; 2hr), Mysuru (every 30min; 4hr 30min–5hr) and other destinations in Tamil Nadu and Kerala. Private buses to Mysuru, Bengaluru and Kodaikanal can be booked at the bigger hotels and agents dotted around the town.

INFORMATION

Tourist information The TTDC tourist office (Mon–Fri 10am–5.45pm; ☏0423 244 3977) is next door to the TTDC *Hotel Tamil Nadu* just above Wenlock Rd. You can book tours here, including a mammoth day-trip (daily 9am–8pm; (₹2500/car) that includes Kamarajasagar Dam, Mudumalai and a jungle ride. There's also a day-trip around Ooty and Coonoor (daily 9am–6pm; ₹1800/car), which goes to Ooty Lake, Doddabetta Peak, the Botanical Gardens, Sim's Park, Lamb's Nose, Dolphin's Nose and a tea garden. There's an erratically opening private tourist information

centre (Mon–Fri 10am–1pm & 2–6pm) in the clock tower building at Charing Cross that gives out leaflets and hotel information. The Mudumalai Forest Ranger Officer's office (Mon–Fri 10am–1pm & 2–5.45pm; ☏0423 244 4098, ⓦmudumalaitigerfoundation.in) is just up behind the TTDC office.

Services The State Bank of India on West Town Circle changes currency, as does the Western Union Office on Commercial Rd.

ACCOMMODATION

Ooty's **accommodation** is a lot more expensive than in many places in India and during the peak season (April and May) prices can rise by thirty to a hundred percent. It also gets very crowded, so you may have to hunt around.
Co-operators Guest House Commercial Rd, just along from Charing Cross ☏0423 244 4046; map p.1049. This centrally-located hotel is a good budget option. Set slightly back from the main road, the Raj-era building has clean rooms and yellow-and-turquoise balconies overlooking a courtyard. No wi-fi. ₹800
Hills Palace Commercial Rd ☏0423 244 6483, ⓦeghplanet.com; map p.1049. Centrally-located place set back from the main road and insulated from the traffic noise. Friendly, with spotlessly clean rooms, with 24hr hot water and TV. Cheaper rates during weekdays. ₹1500.
King's Cliff Havelock Rd ☏0423 245 2888, ⓦlittlearth. in; map p.1049. Imposing ancestral mansion with nine lavishly furnished rooms, executive, standard and deluxe, each with a Shakespearean theme. The place is full of

character and has a stylish lounge and dining room. ₹4000
Reflections Guest House North Lake Rd ☏0423 244 3834, ⓔreflectionsin@yahoo.co.in; map p.1049. Homely, relaxing guesthouse by the lake, just 5min walk from the railway station. Rooms open onto a small terrace and most have lake views. Limited food menu. Easily the best budget option in Ooty, but it's small and fills up quickly, so book in advance. ₹1000
★**Sherlock** Tiger Hill Rd, 3km east of Charing Cross ☏0423 224 4000, ⓦlittlearth.in; map p.1049. Beautifully landscaped Victorian mansion with stunning views from the grassy terrace. All thirteen rooms, standard or deluxe, are tastefully furnished and have sit outs. Friendly service and good food, too. ₹3500
WH Ferrnhills Royale Palace Fernhills Post Nilgiris ☏0423 244 3910 ⓦwelcomheritagehotels.in; map p.1049. This 19th-century summer palace of the Mysore Maharajas, set amidst 50 acres of lush greenery with dense forests and beautiful gardens, is perfect for a luxury stay.

20

Rates include breakfast and one choice of meal. If you fancy sleeping like a Maharaja for the night, the suite costs ₹35,200. **₹11,900**

YWCA Anandagiri Etienne's Rd ☎0423 244 4262, ⊕ywcaagooty.com; map p.1049. Charming 1920s building set in spacious grounds near the racecourse. There are seven different types of room (tariffs vary according to size and hot water availability), bungalows and four dorms. Excellent value and popular, so book ahead. No wi-fi. Dorms **₹200**, doubles **₹800**

EATING

Chandan Nahar hotel, Commercial Rd, near Charing Cross. ☎0423 244 2173; map p.1049. A south Indian garden restaurant and a café serve traditional meals and tiffins. Main courses ₹250–350. Daily 12.30–3.30pm & 7.30–10.30pm.

Hyderabad Biriyani House Walsham Rd ☎0423 244 5080; map p.1049. Small, brightly lit, modern restaurant in the thick of the market which dishes up excellent filling biryanis and a range of other dishes for around ₹180–300. Daily noon–10.30pm.

★ **Preethi Palace** Etienne's Rd near Charing Cross ☎0423 244 2789; map p.1049. Excellent and very popular restaurant serving great lunchtime "meals" (Bengali ₹140, north Indian and Gujarati ₹200) and a range of delicious pure-veg Jain food throughout the day. Daily 7am–10pm.

Secret King's Cliff hotel, Havelock Rd ☎0423 245 2888; map p.1049. Extensive menu of more than two hundred quality dishes, including quail, chicken, seafood and veggie as well as delicious home-baked desserts, served in atmospheric surroundings. Expect to pay ₹350–500 for a main course. Daily noon–3pm & 7–10pm

Shinkows 42 Commissioners Rd ☎0423 244 2811; map p.1049. Good-value, authentic Chinese restaurant serving decent-sized portions on the spicy (and pricey) side – main meat and fish courses are around ₹400, veggie dishes ₹200–300. Daily noon–4pm & 6.30–10pm.

Willy's KRC Arcade, Walsham Rd ☎0423 244 8646; map p.1049. Second-floor café with a laidback ambience and 70s-style dolphin mural, where you can chill out over a coffee, cake, toasted sandwich or Indian snack (all under ₹120) and browse the impressive lending library. No Wi-fi. Daily 10am–10pm.

Mudumalai Tiger Reserve

Elephant Camp Daily 8.30–9am & 4.30–6pm • ₹2400 • **Vehicle safari tour** Daily 7–10am & 3–5.30pm; 45min ₹300/person, 2hr30min jeep safari ₹5000, camera ₹50 video camera ₹150 • ☎0423 244 4098, ⊕mudumalaitigerfoundation.in.

Set 1140m up in the Nilgiri Hills, the **Mudumalai Tiger Reserve** covers 322 square kilometres of deciduous forest, split by the main road from Ooty (64km to the southeast) to Mysore (97km to the northwest). Occupying the thickly wooded, lower northern reaches of the hills, it boasts one of the largest populations of elephants in India, along with wild dogs, gaur (Indian bison), common and Nilgiri langurs and bonnet macaques (monkeys), jackals, hyenas, sloth bears and even a few tigers and leopards. The abundant local flora includes the dazzling red flowers of the Flame of the Forest.

The main focus of interest by the park entrance at **Theppakkadu** is the **Elephant Camp** show, where you can watch the sanctuary's elephants being fed and bathed. This is also the starting point for the government **safari tour**, either on elephant back (which we do not recommend, due to the negative impact this has on the animals) or by vehicle, which is the only way of accessing the official park limits. It is worth noting that the nearby Nagarhole and Bandipur parks are much cheaper, with the same price for both Indians and tourists.

ARRIVAL AND DEPARTURE   MUDUMALAI WILDLIFE SANCTUARY

By bus The main route to Mudumalai from Ooty plied by buses to Mysore and Bengaluru takes 2hr 30min to reach Theppakkadu. The alternative route, a tortuous journey of very steep gradients and hairpin bends, shoiuld only be attempted by taxis, 4WD and minibuses.

ACCOMMODATION

Forest Resthouses Theppakkadu & Masinagudi ☎0423 244 4098, ⊕mudumalaitigerfoundation.in. The Forest Department has a selection of rustic resthouses in or just outside the park, including some basic but nonetheless pleasant wood houses. Best budget option. There are also very expensive suites for ₹24,000. Restaurants and canteens are available. No wi-fi. Dorms **₹350** doubles **₹1750**

★ **Jungle Hut** Bokkapuram, 6km southwest of

Masinagudi ☎ 0423 252 6463, ⓦ junglehut.in. A combination of eco friendly huts, cottages and luxury tents which includes three sumptuous buffet meals and unlimited tea and coffee. They can also arrange treks and plantation visits at extra cost. Wi-fi only in lobby. ₹8500

Misty Grove Resort Calicut, Mysore–Ooty Road, Nadugani, 20 kms from Mudhumalai ☎ 097512 60516, ⓦ mistygroveresort.com. Nestled in lush greenery and surrounded by forests, there are 20 rooms of different categories, as well as cottages, including breakfast. The resort also arranges activities such as treks. ₹4000

Secret Ivory Masinagudi ☎ 94432 04102, ⓦ secret ivory.com. Luxury guesthouse with just eight rooms and a treehouse (₹4800). They serve delicious farm-fresh veg, grown on their own land and also organize treks. Meals are priced between ₹250–400 per person. Wi-fi in lobby. ₹3200

Wild Haven Chadapatti, 6km south of Masinagudi ☎ 0423 252 6490, ⓦ wildhaven.in. This lodge is in open land with great mountain views. There is a choice of simple, spacious double rooms in a stone block or in cottages. Breakfast included but other meals only available for large groups. ₹3645

20

Kerala

VARKALA BEACH

21 | Kerala

The state of Kerala stretches for 550km along India's southwest coast, divided between the densely forested mountains of the Western Ghats inland and a lush, humid coastal plain of rice paddy, lagoons, rivers and canals. Its intensely tropical landscape, fed by the highest rainfall in peninsular India, has intoxicated visitors since the ancient Sumerians and Greeks sailed in search of spices to the shore known as the Malabar Coast. Equally, Kerala's arcane rituals and spectacular festivals – many of them little-changed since the earliest era of Brahmanical Hinduism – have dazzled outsiders for thousands of years.

Travellers weary of India's daunting metropolises will find Kerala's cities smaller and more relaxed. The most popular is undoubtedly the great port of **Kochi** (Cochin), where the state's long history of peaceful foreign contact is evocatively evident in the atmospheric old quarters of Mattancherry and Fort Cochin. In Kerala's far south, the capital, **Thiruvananthapuram** (Trivandrum), is gateway to the nearby palm-fringed beaches of **Kovalam** and **Varkala**, and provides visitors with varied opportunities to sample Kerala's rich cultural and artistic life.

One of the best aspects of exploring Kerala, though, is the actual travelling – especially by **boat**, in the spellbinding Kuttanad region, around historic **Kollam** (Quilon) and **Alappuzha** (Alleppey); travellers are increasingly setting out from **Kumarakom** too. Cruisers and beautiful wooden barges known as *kettu vallam* ("tied boats") ply the **backwaters**, offering tourists a window on village life in India's most densely populated state. Furthermore, it's easy to escape the heat of the lowlands by heading for the **hills**, which rise to 2695m. Roads pass through landscapes dotted with churches and temples, tea, coffee, spice and rubber plantations, and natural forests, en route to wildlife reserves such as **Periyar**, where herds of mud-caked elephants roam freely in vast tracts of jungle.

Kerala is short on the historic monuments prevalent elsewhere in India, and most of its ancient **temples** are closed to non-Hindus. Following an unwritten law, few buildings in the region, whether houses or temples, are higher than the surrounding trees, which in urban areas often creates the illusion that you're surrounded by forest. Typical features of both domestic and temple architecture include long, sloping tiled and gabled roofs that minimize the excesses of rain and sunshine, and pillared verandas; the definitive examples are Thiruvananthapuram's **Puttan Malika Palace**,

BEST TIME TO VISIT

The period from **December to February** is generally considered to be the best time to visit Kerala, especially if you're planning some beach time – the skies are blue and the humidity isn't too fierce. From March the heat builds up until the skies open in June for the state's first **monsoon**, which lasts until August and is more intense than October's "retreating" monsoon. A word of warning, however, for budget travellers. Kerala's **accommodation** is pricey (though it tends to be of a high standard) and in high season cheap places to stay are thin on the ground everywhere, but especially in the hill stations and backwater areas, where it's not uncommon to pay upwards of ₹2000 for a room in a modest guesthouse. March, April and May are good months to negotiate discounts and the best time to hike in the cooler climes of the Western Ghats.

Summer is noted for its festivals (see page 1059), including the traditional snake boat races held during monsoon.

A RICE BARGE CRUISING ON THE BACKWATERS

Highlights

❶ Varkala Chill out in a clifftop café, sunbathe on the beach or soak up the atmosphere around the town's busy temple tank. See page 1071

❷ The backwaters Explore the beautiful waterways of Kerala's densely populated coastal strip on a rice barge or punted canoe, following the narrow, overgrown canals right into the heart of the villages. See page 1080

❸ Hiking around Munnar The tea plantations, grassy mountains and dazzling viewpoints around Munnar are the perfect antidote to the heat and humidity of the coast. See page 1091

❹ Fort Cochin Dutch, Portuguese, British and traditional Keralan townhouses line the backstreets of Malabar's old peninsular port.

Stay in a heritage hotel, see the fisherman hauling their catch at sunrise and take in a performance of *kathakali* – elaborately costumed ritual theatre. See page 1094

❺ Temple festivals Parades of extravagantly decorated elephants, backed by drummers and firework displays, form the focal point of Kerala's Hindu festivals, among them Thrissur's famed Puram; you can also see intimate *theyyem* spirit-possession rituals in the north of the state. See pages 1107 and 1115

❻ Wayanad Engage a local guide to take you on foot to explore the dense forests and grasslands that cover this isolated mountain region. See page 1112

HIGHLIGHTS ARE MARKED ON THE MAP ON PAGE 1058

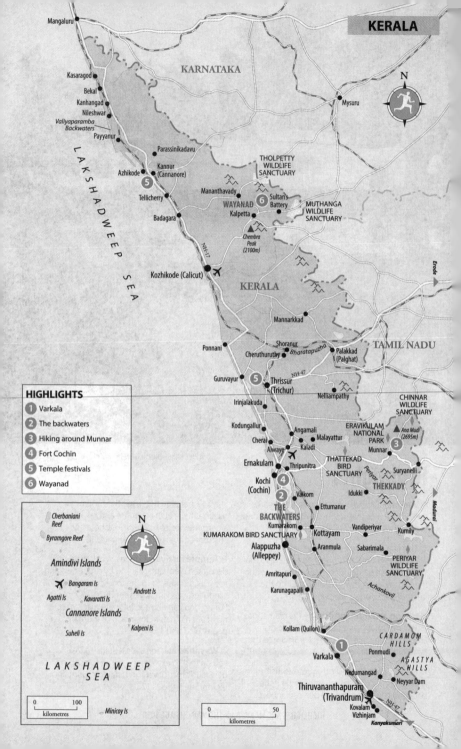

and **Padmanabhapuram Palace**, in neighbouring Tamil Nadu but easily reached from the capital.

As well as **festivals**, **theatre** and **dance** also abound; not only the region's own female classical dance form, **mohiniyattam** ("dance of the enchantress"), but also the martial-art-influenced **kathakali** dance drama, which has for four centuries brought gods and demons from the Mahabharata and Ramayana to Keralan villages. Its two-thousand-year-old predecessor, the Sanskrit drama **kudiyattam**, is still performed by a handful of artists, while localized rituals known as **theyyem** (see page 1115), where dancers wearing decorative masks and hats become "possessed" by temple deities, remain a potent ingredient of village life in the north of the state.

Brief history

Ancient Kerala is mentioned as the land of the **Cheras** in a third-century-BC Ashokan edict, and in several even older Sanskrit texts, including the Mahabharata. Pliny and Ptolemy also testify to thriving trade between the ancient port of Muziris (now known as Kodungallur) and the Roman Empire. Kodungallur is also tipped to be where one of the twelve disciples, St Thomas, first set foot in 52 AD; today Christians account for some 21 percent of Kerala's population. Little is known about the region's early rulers, whose dominion covered a large area, but whose capital, Vanji, has not so far been identified. At the start of the ninth century, King Kulashekhara Alvar – a poet-saint of the Vaishnavite *bhakti* movement known as the *alvars* – established his own dynasty. His son and successor, Rajashekharavarman, is thought to have been a

---

FESTIVALS IN KERALA

Huge amounts of money are lavished upon many, varied, and often all-night **festivals** associated with Kerala's temples. Fireworks rend the air, while processions of caparisoned elephants are accompanied by some of the loudest (and deftest) drum orchestras in the world. Thrissur's famous **Puram** festival (see page 1107) is the most astonishing, but smaller events take place throughout the state, with everyone welcome to attend. Between December and March it's possible to spend weeks hopping between village **theyyems** in northern Kerala, experiencing rituals little altered in centuries (see page 1115). The **snake boat races** in June, August and September are an incredible sight, while **Christmas** sees paper lanterns and fairy lights decorating homes and churches. Kerala's Hindu festivals are fixed according to the Malayalam Calendar, so dates change from year to year – see ⓦ keralatourism.org.

Swathi Sangeetotsavam (Jan). Held in honour of composer Sri Swathi Thirunal (maharaja of Travancore 1813–46), free evening performances of Karnatic and Hindustani music take place on the raised porch of Thiruvananthapuram's Puttan Malika Palace (see page 1063), with spectators seated on the lawn.

Maha Shivrati (Usually early March; the moonless night). The night of the worship of Shiva is an all-night vigil at temples across the state. A *shivalingam* rises out of the banks of the River Periyar near Kochi, attracting thousands of devotees.

Vishu (Mid-April). A festival of lights and fireworks on Hindu New Year's Day. On this day it's believed that the first object seen is auspicious, so items including rice, fruit, flowers and gold are set out in homes.

Nehru Trophy Snake Boat Race (Second Sat in Aug). The most spectacular of the boat races attracts huge crowds to Punnamda Lake near Alappuzha (see page 1077). Following a grand procession, the magnificently decorated longboats – each carrying more than one hundred oarsmen rowing to the rhythmic *vanchipattu* ("song of the boatman") – compete in knockout rounds. Similar races can be seen at Aranmula (Aug–Sept) and Champakulam (June–July).

Onam (Ten days in Aug or Sept). Kerala's harvest festival is marked by singing, *kathakali*, *pookalam* (floral "carpets"), traditional food and in Thrissur, *pulikali* (the dance of the tigers). Four of the days are state holidays.

21

saint of the parallel Shaivite movement, the *nayannars*. The great Keralan philosopher **Shankaracharya**, whose *advaitya* ("non-dualist") philosophy influenced the whole of Hindu India, was alive at this time.

Eventually, the prosperity acquired by the Cheras through trade with China and the Arab world proved too much of an attraction for the neighbouring **Chola** empire, which embarked upon a hundred years of sporadic warfare with the Cheras at the end of the tenth century. Around 1100, the Cheras lost their capital at Mahodayapuram in the north, and shifted south to establish a new capital at Kollam (Quilon).

Direct trade with Europe commenced in 1498 with the arrival in the capital, Calicut, of a small Portuguese fleet under **Vasco da Gama** – the first expedition to reach the coast of India via the Cape of Good Hope and Arabian Sea. After an initial show of cordiality, relations between him and the local ruler, or Zamorin, quickly degenerated, and da Gama's second voyage four years later was characterized by appalling massacres, kidnapping, mutilation and barefaced piracy. Nevertheless, a fortified trading post was soon established at Cochin from which the Portuguese, exploiting old enmities between the region's rulers, were able to dominate trade with the Middle East. This was gradually eroded away over the ensuing century by rival powers France and Holland. An independent territory was subsequently carved out of the Malabar Coast by Tipu Sultan of Mysore, but his defeat in 1792 left the British in control right up until Independence.

Kerala can claim some of the most startling **radical** credentials in India. In 1957 it was the first state in the world to democratically elect a communist government, and still regularly returns communist parties in elections. Due to reforms made during the 1960s and 1970s, Kerala currently has the most equitable land distribution of any Indian state. Poverty appears far less acute than in other parts of the country, with life expectancy and per capita income well above the national averages. Kerala is also justly proud of its reputation for healthcare and education, with **literacy** rates that stand, officially at least, at 96 percent for men and 92 percent for women. Industrial development is negligible, however: potential investors from outside tend to fight shy of dealing with such a politicized workforce.

Thiruvananthapuram

Kerala's capital, **THIRUVANANTHAPURAM** (still widely known as **Trivandrum**), is set on seven low hills just a couple of kilometres inland from the Arabian Sea. Despite its administrative importance – demonstrated by wide roads, multistorey office blocks and gleaming white colonial buildings – it's an easy-going state capital by Indian standards, with enclaves of traditional red-tiled gabled houses breaking up the bustle of its modern concrete core, and a swathe of parkland spreading north of the centre. Although its principal sight, the **Sri Padmanabhaswamy temple**, is closed to non-Hindus, the city holds enough of interest to fill a day. Foremost among its attractions is the splendid **Puttan Malika Palace**, one of the state's best museums, and a typically Keralan market, **Chalai Bazaar**.

Both the palace and bazaar are in the oldest and most interesting part of the city, the **Fort** area in the south. At the opposite, northern side of the centre, the **Sri Chitra Art Gallery** and **Napier Museum** showcase painting, crafts and sculpture in a leafy park. In addition, schools specializing in the martial art *kalarippayat* and the dance/theatre forms of **kathakali** and **kudiyattam** offer an insight into the Keralan obsession with physical training and skill.

Sri Padmanabhaswamy temple

Padmanabha, the god Vishnu reclined on a coiled serpent with a lotus flower sprouting from his belly button, is the presiding deity of the **Sri Padmanabhaswamy**

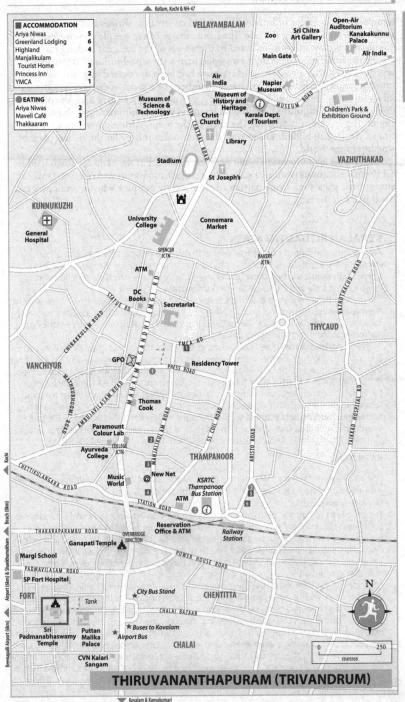

THIRUVANANTHAPURAM (TRIVANDRUM)

21

temple, a vast complex of interlocking walled courtyards, shrines and ceremonial walkways in the south of the city. The iconic image of the temple's seven-tiered, Tamil-style *gopura* gateway, reflected in the waters of the adjacent bathing tank, graced the front pages of many newspapers across the world in June 2011 when it was discovered that a vast horde of **treasure** had been discovered in vaults below its inner sanctum. Sealed inside the secret chambers were sacks of diamonds, a thousand kilograms of gold, thousands of pieces of gem-encrusted jewellery and, the pièce de résistance, an exquisite 1m-tall gold **image of Vishnu** shimmering with precious stones. Experts are still debating the value of the items, with estimates ranging from US$40–200 billion. Either way, the find makes this by far the richest place of worship in the world.

Non-Hindus are unfortunately not permitted inside, but the main approach road to Sri Padmanabhaswamy, with its stalls full of religious souvenirs and offerings, makes an atmospheric place for a stroll, particularly in the early morning when worshippers take ritual baths in the tank.

KERALAN RITUAL THEATRE

Among the most magical experiences a visitor to Kerala can have is to witness one of the innumerable ancient drama rituals that play such an important role in the cultural life of the region. **Kathakali** is the best known; other less publicized forms, which clearly influenced its development, include the classical Sanskrit **kudiyattam**.

Many Keralan forms share broad characteristics. A prime aim of each performer is to transform the mundane into the world of gods and demons; his preparation is highly ritualized, involving otherworldly costume and mask-like make-up. In *kathakali* and *kudiyattam*, this preparation is a rigorously codified part of the classical tradition.

One-off **performances** of various ritual types take place throughout the state, building up to fever pitch during April and May before pausing for the monsoon (June–Aug). Finding out about such events requires a little perseverance, but it's well worth the effort; enquire at tourist offices, or buy a Malayalam daily paper such as the *Malayalam Manorama* and ask someone to check the listings for temple festivals – most of the action invariably takes place within the temples. Tourist *kathakali* is staged daily in **Kochi** (see page 1093) but to find authentic performances, contact **performing arts schools** such as Thiruvananthapuram's Margi (see page 1064) and Cheruthuruthy's Kerala Kalamandalam (see page 1108); *kudiyattam* artists work at both, as well as at Natana Kairali at Irinjalakuda, which is accessible from Thrissur (see page 1106).

KATHAKALI

Here is the tradition of the trance dancers, here is the absolute demand of the subjugation of body to spirit, here is the realization of the cosmic transformation of human into divine.
Mrinalini Sarabhai, classical dancer

The image of a *kathakali* actor in a magnificent costume with extraordinary make-up and a huge gold crown has become Kerala's trademark. Traditional performances, of which there are still many, usually take place on open ground outside a temple, beginning at 10pm and lasting until dawn, illuminated by the flickers of a large brass oil lamp centre-stage. Virtually nothing about *kathakali* is naturalistic, because it depicts the world of gods and demons; men play both the male and female roles.

Standing at the back of the stage, two musicians play driving rhythms, one on a bronze gong, the other on heavy bell-metal cymbals; they also sing the dialogue. Actors appear and disappear from behind a hand-held curtain and never utter a sound, save the odd strange cry. Learning the elaborate hand gestures, facial expressions and choreographed movements, as articulate and precise as any sign language, requires rigorous training which can begin at the age of 8 and last ten years. At least two more **drummers** stand left of the stage; one plays the upright *chenda* with slender curved sticks, the other plays the *maddalam*, a horizontal barrel-shaped hand drum. When a female character is "speaking", the *chenda* is replaced by the hourglass-shaped *ettaka*, a "talking drum" on which melodies can be played. The drummers keep their eyes on the actors, whose

Puttan Malika Palace

Tues–Sun 8.30am–1pm & 3–5.30pm • ₹30; guided tour only

The **Puttan Malika Palace**, immediately southeast of the Sri Padmanabhaswamy temple, became the seat of the Travancore rajas after they left Padmanabhapuram at the end of the nineteenth century. The cool chambers, with highly polished plaster floors and delicately carved wooden screens, house a crop of dusty royal heirlooms, including a solid crystal throne gifted by the Dutch. The real highlight, however, is the elegant Keralan architecture itself. Beneath sloping red-tiled roofs, hundreds of wooden pillars, carved into the forms of rampant horses (*puttan malika* translates as "horse palace"), prop up the eaves, and airy verandas project onto the surrounding lawns.

The royal family have always been keen patrons of the arts, and the **Swathi Sangeetotsavam festival**, held in the grounds in January, continues this tradition (see page 1059).

every gesture is reinforced by their sound, from the gentlest embrace to the gory disembowelling of an enemy.

Although it bears the unmistakeable influences of *kudiyattam* and indigenous folk rituals, *kathakali*, literally "story-play", is thought to have crystallized into a distinct theatre form during the seventeenth century. The plays are based on three major sources: the **Hindu epics** the Mahabharata, Ramayana and the Bhagavata Purana. While the stories are ostensibly about god-heroes such as Rama and Krishna, the most popular characters are those that give the most scope to the actors – the villainous, fanged, red-and-black-faced *katti* ("knife") antiheroes; these types, such as the kings Ravana and Duryodhana, are dominated by lust, greed, envy and violence. David Bolland's *Guide to Kathakali*, widely available in Kerala, gives invaluable scene-by-scene summaries of the most popular plays and explains in simple language a lot more besides.

When **attending a performance**, arrive early to get your bearings before it gets dark, even though the first play will not begin much before 10pm. (Quiet) members of the audience are welcome to visit the dressing room before and during the performance. The colour and design of the mask-like make-up, which specialist artists take several hours to apply, reveal the character's personality. The word *pacha* means both "green" and "pure"; a green-faced *pacha* character is thus a noble human or god. Red signifies *rajas*, passion and aggression; black denotes *tamas*, darkness and negativity; and white is *sattvik*, light and intellect. Once the make-up is completed, elaborate wide skirts are tied to the waist, and ornaments of silver and gold are added. Silver talons are fitted to the left hand. The transformation is complete with a final prayer and the donning of waist-length wig and crown. Visitors new to *kathakali* will almost undoubtedly get bored during such long programmes, parts of which are very slow indeed. If you're at a village performance, you may not always find accommodation, so you can't leave during the night. Be prepared to sit on the ground for hours, and bring some warm clothes. Half the fun is staying up all night to witness, just as the dawn light appears, the gruesome disembowelling of a villain or a demon *asura*.

KUDIYATTAM

Three families of the Chakyar caste and a few outsiders perform the Sanskrit drama **kudiyattam**, the oldest continually performed theatre form in the world. Until recently it was only performed inside temples and then only in front of the uppermost castes. Visually it is very similar to its offspring, *kathakali*, but its atmosphere is infinitely more archaic. The actors, eloquent in sign language and symbolic movement, speak in the compelling intonation of the local Brahmins' Vedic chant, unchanged since 1500 BC.

A single act of a *kudiyattam* play can require ten full nights; the entire play takes forty. A great actor, in full command of the subtleties of gestural expression, can take half an hour to do such a simple thing as murder a demon, berate the audience or simply describe a leaf fall to the ground. Unlike *kathakali*, *kudiyattam* includes comic characters and plays. The ubiquitous Vidushaka, narrator and clown, is something of a court jester, and traditionally has held the right to criticize openly the highest in the land without fear of retribution.

21

CVN Kalari Sangam

S St, East Fort • Mon–Sat 9.30–12.30pm, 4.30pm–6.30pm • ☎ 0471 247 4182, ⊚ cvnkalari.in

Around 500m southeast of the temple in East Fort, the redbrick **CVN Kalari Sangam** ranks among Kerala's top **kalarippayat** gymnasiums. It was founded in 1956 by C.V. Narayanan Nair, one of the legendary figures credited for the martial art's revival, and attracts students from across the world. Every morning except Sunday you can watch fighting exercises in the sunken *kalari* pit that forms the heart of the complex. Foreigners may join courses, arranged through the head teacher, or *gurukkal*, although prior experience of martial arts and/or dance is a prerequisite.

Chalai Bazaar

Thiruvananthapuram's main source of fresh produce and everyday items is the kilometre-long **Chalai Bazaar**, which runs east from MG Road in East Fort, from opposite the main approach to the temple. Lined with little shops selling flowers, incense, spices, bell-metal lamps and fireworks, it's a great area for aimless browsing (most shops open daily 10am–8pm). On your left (north side) as you enter the street, look out for **United Umbrella Mart**, which sells brightly coloured temple parasols used in elephant processions. Further down on the opposite side of the road, the delightfully old-fashioned **Ambal Coffee Works** is another source of authentic Keralan souvenirs.

Margi School

West Fort • ☎ 0471 247 8806, ⊚ margitheatre.org

Thiruvananthapuram has for centuries been a crucible for Keralan classical arts, and the **Margi School**, at the western corner of the Fort area, is one of the foremost colleges for **kathakali** dance drama and the more rarely performed **kudiyattam** theatre form (see page 1062). Most visitors venture out here to watch one of the authentic *kathakali* or *kudiyattam* performances staged once each month in its small **theatre**, details of which are posted on the school's website.

To reach Margi, head to the SP Fort Hospital on the western edge of Fort and then continue 200m north; the school is set back from the west side of the main road in a large red-tiled and tin-roofed building, behind the High School (the sign is in Malayalam).

Napier Museum

LMS Vallayambalam Rd • Tues–Sun 9am–5pm • ₹200

A minute's walk east from the north end of MG Road, opposite Kerala Tourism's information office, brings you to the entrance to Thiruvananthapuram's **public gardens**. As well as serving as a welcome refuge from the noise of the city, the park holds the city's best museums. Give the dusty and uninformative Natural History Museum a miss and head instead for the more engaging **Napier Museum**. Built at the end of the nineteenth century, it was an early experiment in what became known as the "Indo-Saracenic" style, with tiled, gabled roofs, garish red-, black- and salmon-patterned brickwork, and a spectacular interior of stained-glass windows and loud turquoise, pink, red and yellow stripes. Highlights of the collection include fifteenth-century Keralan woodcarvings, terrifying Ceylonese (Sri Lankan) masks, a carved temple chariot (*rath*) and Chola and Vijayanagar bronzes.

Sri Chitra Art Gallery

Next to Zoological Gardens • Tues–Sun 9am–5pm • ₹200

You pass through the main ticket booth for the city's depressing, faded zoo to reach the **Sri Chitra Art Gallery**, which shows paintings from the Rajput, Mughal and Tanjore schools, along with pieces from China, Tibet and Japan. The meat of the collection, though, is made up of works by the celebrated artist **Raja Ravi Varma** (1848–1906), a local aristocrat who achieved fame and fortune as a producer of Hindu mythological prints – forerunners of India's quirky calendar art. Varma's style was much criticized by later generations for its sentimentality and strong Western influence, but in his time he was regarded as the nation's greatest living artist.

Also on view at the Sri Chitra, in rooms to the rear of the main building, are a couple of minor **Tagores**, and some striking, strongly coloured Himalayan landscapes by the Russian artist-philosopher and mystic, **Nicholas Roerich**, who resided in the Kullu Valley for two decades until his death in 1947.

ARRIVAL AND DEPARTURE   THIRUVANANTHAPURAM

BY PLANE
Beemapalli airport Connected to most major Indian cities, as well as Sri Lanka, the Maldives and the Middle East, Beemapalli airport lies 6km southwest of town. You'll find a Kerala Tourism information booth (in theory 24hr), ATM, Vodafone stand (where you can buy an Indian SIM) and a Thomas Cook foreign exchange facility just before the exit of the arrivals concourse.

GETTING INTO TOWN
By shuttle The best way to get to and from the airport is on the a/c airport bus (₹30), which runs between the arrivals concourse and the City bus stand in East Fort. See ⓦ aanavandi.com for the schedule.

By auto-rickshaw and taxi Auto-rickshaws can get you into the centre for around ₹150 and there's also a handy prepaid taxi service (pay before departure; ₹350 for Thiruvananthapuram railway station, ₹500 for Kovalam's Lighthouse Beach).

BY BUS
Interstate buses The long-distance KSRTC Thampanoor bus station is opposite the railway station in the south-east of the city, within walking distance of most of the city's budget accommodation. This is the place to catch services to Varkala as well as long-distance buses heading north up the coast (to Kollam, Alappuzha, Ernakulam or Thrissur).

For the latter aim for the 6am or 5.30pm "super-deluxe a/c" specials – you can buy tickets for all long-distance routes at the reservations hatch, main bus stand concourse (daily 6am–10pm). The Tamil Nadu bus company, TNSRTC, has its own counter on the same concourse. Numerous private bus companies also run interstate services; many of the agents are on Aristo Rd near the *Greenland Lodging*.

Local services Local buses (including those for Kovalam) depart from City bus stand, in East Fort, a 10min walk south from the KSRTC Thampanoor and railway stations. Services to Kovalam leave from the stand on the roadside – be prepared for a crush if you attempt this journey in the late-afternoon rush hour.

Destinations Alappuzha/Alleppey (every 15–20min; 3hr 30min); Ernakulam/Kochi (every 30min; 5hr); Kanyakumari (5 daily; 2hr 15min); Kollam/Quilon (every 15–20min; 1hr 40min); Kovalam (from East Fort; every 20–30min); Kumily/Periyar (3 daily; 7hr 45min); Madurai (8 daily; 7hr); Neyyar Dam (hourly; 1hr 30min); Varkala (8 daily; 90min).

BY TRAIN
Kerala's capital is well connected by train with other towns and cities. Although you can buy a ticket just before departure, getting seats at short notice on long-haul journeys can be a problem, so make reservations as far in advance as possible from the efficient computerized

RECOMMENDED TRAINS FROM THIRUVANANTHAPURAM

The following trains are recommended as the fastest and/or most convenient from Thiruvananthapuram.

Destination	Name	No.	Departs	Arrives
Alappuzha	*Netravati Express**	#16346	daily 9.30am	12.12pm
Chennai	*Chennai Mail**	#12624	daily 2.55pm	7.40am+
Ernakulam/Kochi	*Jan Shatabdi*	#12076	daily 6am	9.25am
Kanyakumari	*Kanyakumari Express*	#16381	daily 10.10am	12.50pm
Kollam	*Kerala Express*	#12625	daily 11.15am	12.20pm
Madurai	*Anantapuri Express*	#16724	daily 4.10pm	11pm

*via Kollam, Varkala, Kottayam and Ernakulam, + = next day

21

booking office at the station (24hr). There's a handy prepaid auto-rickshaw counter on the arrivals concourse. Destinations Alappuzha/Alleppey (7 daily; 2hr 15min–3hr); Chennai/Madras (4 daily; 16hr–17hr 30min); Ernakulam/Kochi (20 daily; 3hr 25min–5hr 15min); Kanyakumari (3 daily; 2hr 40min–3hr); Kollam/Quilon (24 daily; 55min–1hr 20min); Madurai (5 daily; 6hr 50min–10hr 50min); Varkala (24 daily; 35min).

INFORMATION AND TOURS

Tourist information In addition to at the airport, Kerala Tourism has an information counter at the KSRTC Thampanoor bus station (Mon–Sat 10am–5pm; ☎0471 232 7224), while in Vellayambalam on Museum Rd, next to the unremarkable Museum of History and Heritage, KTDC hosts a visitor reception centre where you can book accommodation in their hotel chain and tickets for various guided tours (daily 7am–9pm; ☎0471 232 1132).

Tours Most of the KTDC tours, including the city tours (daily 1.30–6.45pm; ₹400), are too rushed, but if you're really pushed for time and want to reach the tip of India, try the Kanyakumari tour (daily 7.30am–9pm; ₹700), which takes in Padmanabhapuram Palace (except Mon), Suchindram Temple and Kanyakumari in Tamil Nadu.

ACCOMMODATION

Accommodation is a lot cheaper in Thiruvananthapuram than at nearby Kovalam Beach. That said, this is one city where budget travellers should consider spending a bit more than they might usually.

Ariya Niwas Manorama Rd, Thampanoor ☎0471 233 0789, ✉ariyanivas.tvm@gmail.com; map p.1061. Large, spotless and airy rooms with comfy beds and great views from its upper floors. Good value, 24hr checkout, 2min walk from the railway station, with an excellent restaurant on the ground floor (see below). A/c ₹1100 extra. ₹1070

Greenland Lodging Aristo Rd, Thampanoor ☎0471 232 3196; map p.1061. An efficient lodge with immaculate rooms (some a/c). The best low-cost option near the bus stand and railway station – book ahead. ₹800

Highland Manjalikulam Rd, Thampanoor ☎0471 233 3200, ⊚highland-hotels.com; map p.1061. The rooms in this lower- to mid-range option fail to live up to the promise of the six-storey concrete-and-tinted-glass facade, but it's well managed, a short walk from the stations, and easy to find. A/c ₹700 extra. ₹1700

Manjalikulam Tourist Home Manjalikulam Rd, Thampanoor ☎0471 233 0776, ⊚manjalikulam.com; map p.1061. Don't be fooled by the shining glass-and-marble ground floor – above lurks a basic budget place offering variously priced rooms, all of them clean and with good, comfy mattresses. No single occupancy. A/c ₹500 extra. ₹700

Princess Inn Manjalikulam Rd, Thampanoor ☎0471 233 9150, ✉princess_inn@yahoo.com; map p.1061. Well-scrubbed, respectable cheapie close to the stations. One of the more welcoming and better-value small hotels in this busy enclave, though it's a bit more of a plod up the lane from Station Rd than some. A/c ₹400 extra. ₹1500

★ **YMCA** YMCA Rd, near the Secretariat ☎0471 233 0059, ⊚ymcatvm.org; map p.1061. Neat, smartly-furnished rooms at good rates. The "deluxe" options (₹1600) are enormous and have high ceilings, quiet fans (some with a/c), TVs and spacious bathrooms. Not the bargain it once was, but you'll still need to book at least two weeks in advance. No wi-fi. ₹800

EATING

Freshly cooked dosas, *idli-vada-sambhar*, biryanis and other traditional snacks are available at street-side cafés across town, including the perennially popular **Indian Coffee House** chain, which runs several branches in the city centre – most famously the circular *Maveli Café* next to the KSRTC bus stand in Thampanoor.

★ **Ariya Niwas** Ariya Niwas hotel, Manorama Rd, Thampanoor; map p.1061. Top-class south Indian vegetarian thalis (₹100) dished up on banana leaves in a scrupulously clean non-a/c dining room on the hotel's ground floor, or in the pricier a/c dining hall on the first storey. Hugely popular with everyone, and deservedly so: there's nowhere better to eat in the city. Daily 10am–10.30pm.

Maveli Café Next to the bus station on Station Rd, Thampanoor ☎0471 233 3517; map p.1061. Part of the *Indian Coffee House* chain, this bizarre redbrick, spiral-shaped café (designed by the renowned expatriate British architect, Laurie Baker) is a Thiruvananthapuram institution. Inside, waiters in the trademark *ICH pugris* serve dosas (₹40), *vadas*, greasy omelettes, mountainous biryanis (meat ₹105, ₹veg 55) and china cups of the usual (weak and sugary) filter coffee. An obligatory pit stop, though a grubby one. Daily 7am–10pm.

Thakkaaram Pulimood Junction, Press Rd ☎86 0631 4422; map p.1061. On the ground floor of Naaz Tower, this cool and clean non-veg a/c restaurant serves mouth-watering Malabari food in booths that look like train carriages. The menu is tricky to navigate, but you can't go wrong with the *kozhi chuttathu* (chargrilled chicken; ₹400 for half) and roti fresh from the *tandoor* (₹30). Great lunchtime biryani specials too (₹229 with tea and dessert). Daily noon–11pm.

DIRECTORY

Banks and exchange A string of big banks along MG Rd have ATMs and change currency; there are additional ATMs next to the information counter across the road from the railway station, and immediately outside the station exit, next to the reservations hall. Thomas Cook has a foreign exchange counter at the airport and at its travel agency on the ground floor of the Soundarya Building (near the big

Raymond's tailoring store), MG Rd (Mon–Sat 9.30am–6pm).

Hospitals SP Fort Hospital (☎ 0471 245 0540), just down the road from the Margi School in West Fort, has a 24hr casualty and specialist orthopaedic unit; the private Cosmopolitan Hospital in Pattom (☎ 0471 252 1252) is also recommended.

Internet New Net on Manjalikulam Rd charges ₹30/hr and is convenient if you're staying in Thampanoor.

Kovalam

You have to envy the travellers who discovered **KOVALAM** back in the 1970s. Before the appearance of the crowds and sunbeds that nowadays spill over the resort's quartet of beaches, not to mention the warren of hotels, shops and restaurants crammed into the palm groves behind them, this must have been a heavenly location. Four decades of unplanned development, however, have wrought havoc on the famous headland and its golden sand bays. Virtually every conceivable patch of dry ground behind the most spectacular of them, **Lighthouse Beach**, has been buried under concrete, but it's still a popular base for Ayurveda and yoga. The proximity of Kovalam to the city means domestic tourism is booming; closest to the bus and taxi stand, **Howah Beach** in particular attracts a lot of day-trippers, who leave behind a trail of rubbish.

Kovalam beaches

Kovalam consists of **four coves**, each with markedly different characters. It takes around 45 minutes to an hour to walk from one end of them to the other, but there's no shortage of potential pit stops along the way to restore your energies.

Lighthouse Beach

The largest and most developed cove at Kovalam, known for obvious reasons as **Lighthouse Beach**, is where most foreign tourists congregate. Lined by a paved esplanade, its seafront of shops and hotels extends along the full length of the bay, overlooked by the eponymous **lighthouse** at the southern end (daily 3–5pm; ₹25 [₹10], camera ₹20). You can scale the 142 spiral steps and twelve ladder rungs to the observation platform for a fine view.

Hawah Beach

A small rocky headland divides Lighthouse Beach from **Hawah Beach** (or **Eve's Beach**) – almost a mirror image of its busier neighbour, although backed for most of its length by empty palm groves. In the morning, before the sun-worshippers arrive, it functions as a base for local fishermen, who hand-haul their massive nets through the shallows, singing and chanting as they coil the endless piles of rope.

Kovalam Beach

Kovalam Beach, the third of the coves, is dominated from on high by the angular chalets of the five-star *Leela* resort. Coachloads of excited Keralan day-trippers descend here on weekends, but at other times it offers a peaceful alternative to the beaches further south. To get there, follow the road downhill past the bus terminus.

Samudra Beach

The most northerly of Kovalam's quartet, **Samudra Beach** was until recently a European package-tourist stronghold. Nowadays the large hotels clustered just beyond it, on the far side of a low, rocky headland, host mainly metropolitan Indian and Russian holiday-makers.

WARNING: SWIMMING SAFETY IN KOVALAM

Due to unpredictable rip currents and a strong undertow, especially during the monsoons, **swimming** from Kovalam's beaches is not always safe. The introduction of blue-shirted lifeguards has reduced the annual death toll, but at least a couple of tourists still drown here each year, and many more get into difficulties. Follow the warnings of the safety flags at all times and keep a close eye on children. There's a first-aid post midway along Lighthouse Beach.

ARRIVAL AND INFORMATION   KOVALAM

By bus Buses from Thiruvananthapuram loop through the top of the village before coming to a halt outside the gates of the *Leela* resort, on the promontory dividing Hawah and Kovalam beaches. If you don't intend to stay at this northern end of the resort, get down just after *Hotel Blue Sea* where the road bends – a lane branching to the left drops steeply downhill towards the top of Hawah Beach. The bus journey generally takes 30 to 45 minutes. Heading in the other direction (into the city) pick up the bus from outside the gates of the *Leela*. Long-distance services heading down the coast towards Kanyakumari stop at Kovalam Junction on the main highway.

By auto-rickshaw or taxi You can cover the 14km from Thiruvananthapuram more quickly by auto-rickshaw (₹250) or taxi (₹650).

Tourist information The friendly tourist office (daily 10am–5pm, closed Sun in low season; ☏ 0471 248 0085, ⊚ keralatourism.org), just inside the *Leela* resort gates, close to where the buses pull in, stocks the usual range of glossy leaflets and can offer up-to-date advice about cultural events in the area.

ACCOMMODATION

Kovalam is chock-full of **accommodation** in all categories. Little of it could be considered great value by Keralan standards, but you may be able to pick up last-minute discounts outside the Dec/Jan high season. Expect to be plagued by commission touts as you arrive; to avoid them, approach via the back paths.

★ **Amruthamgamaya (Amrutham)** Panagodu, near Venganoor, 6km northeast ☏ 0880 6020629 or 09967 222152, ⊚ amruthamgamaya.com; map p.1068. A great option if you want to base yourself away from the busy coastal strip, but within striking distance of the beaches.

It's essentially an Ayurveda centre, but with comfortable accommodation in beautiful, large rooms overlooking a terraced garden. Veg meals are served on a high rooftop overlooking a sea of palm trees, and there's a gorgeous pool. Great value, but tricky to find: phone ahead for directions. Rates are for double occupancy and include superb Keralan food. Half board ₹8000, full board ₹8500

Beach Hotel II Above Fusion restaurant, Lighthouse Beach ☏ 0471 248 6575, ⊚ thebeachhotel-kovalam. com; map p.1068. Stylish, German-run hotel at the quiet end of Lighthouse Beach with an outdoor pool. Its twelve

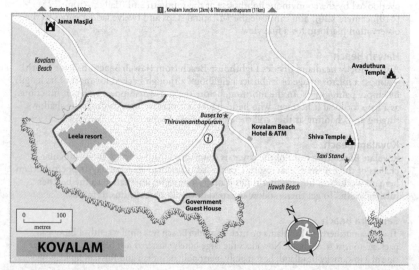

Samudra Beach (400m)   ⊞ , Kovalam Junction (2km) & Thiruvananthapuram (11km)

Jama Masjid

Kovalam Beach

Avaduthura Temple

Buses to ★ Thiruvananthapuram
ℹ️

Leela resort

Kovalam Beach Hotel & ATM

Shiva Temple

Taxi Stand ★

Hawah Beach

Government Guest House

0   100
metres

N

KOVALAM

rooms (some a/c) all have big, sea-facing balconies, and are light, spacious and airy, with terracotta-tiled floors and block-printed cotton bedspreads. Not to be confused with its sister concern, *Beach Hotel I*, below *Waves* restaurant, which isn't nearly as nice. A/c ₹1000 extra. **₹5000**

Beach House Resort Lighthouse Beach ☎ 81292 27212 (Naza); map p.1068. Tiny, garish yellow place on the seafront offering large rooms with kitchenettes that have a fridge. The two rooms below the penthouse each have a breezy balcony and sea view. A/c 800 extra. **₹2000**

Dream Palace Homestay Lighthouse Beach ☎ 0471 248 4774, ⓦ dreampalacekovalam.com ⓔ info@dream palacekovalam.com; map p.1068. Half a dozen pleasant rooms in a modern block set a 3min walk back from the beachfront, with marble floors, dark varnished furniture, sprung mattresses, kitchenettes, fancy headboards and tiny balconies. Excellent value. **₹1000**

Maharaju Palace 30m behind Lighthouse Beach ☎ 99468 54270, ⓦ maharajupalace.com; map p.1068. This Dutch-owned guesthouse, a block in from the beach, offers boutique style at affordable rates. Occupying a modern house in a well-kept tropical garden, its rooms are clean and decorated with Indian handicrafts and comfy cane chairs on the verandas. Breakfast included. **₹3000**

Sky Palace Lighthouse Beach ☎ 75598 34334; map p.1068. Basic but comfortable option two blocks back from the waterfront, just a thirty-second walk from the beach. The very clean rooms, opening onto a sociable common veranda, are a good size, with gleaming floors and crisp white sheets. **₹2500**

Surya Lighthouse Beach ☎ 94953 06932, ⓦ surya kovalam.com; map p.1068. Professionally run, budget travellers' guest-house down a narrow lane from the seafront. It's secure and quiet, with pleasant rooms for the price. If it's full, try the *White House* next door (see below). **₹5000**

Swapnatheeram (formerly Sri Krishna Palace) Lighthouse Beach ☎ 98466 99991, ⓦ swapnatheeram. com; map p.1068. Great-value mid-range place run by an friendly local family, a 1min walk from the beach. Their thirteen rooms are spacious and clean, with complimentary towels and soap – some, which cost a little more, have sea views. Breakfast included. **₹2200**

White House Lighthouse Beach ☎ 80897 91293, ⓔ whitehousekovalamag@gmail.com; map p.1068. Basic guesthouse fronting a leafy plot. Quiet, clean and set back from the beach. Rooms 203 and 204 are the pick of the crop. A/c ₹600 extra. **₹1600**

EATING

Lighthouse Beach is lined with identikit cafés and restaurants specializing in **seafood**: pick from displays of fresh fish, lobster, tiger prawns, crab and mussels that are then weighed, grilled over a charcoal fire or cooked in a *tandoor* (traditional clay oven), and served with rice, salad or chips. Meals are **pricey** by Indian standards and service is often painfully slow, but the food is generally very good and

the ambience convivial. **Nightlife** in Kovalam is sedate, revolving around the beachfront cafés. Beer and spirits are served in most places, albeit in discreet china teapots from under the table due to tight liquor restrictions.

★ **Fusion** Lighthouse Beach; map p.1068. Along with *Waves* further along the main beach, this is the liveliest place in Kovalam, with three innovative menus (Eastern,

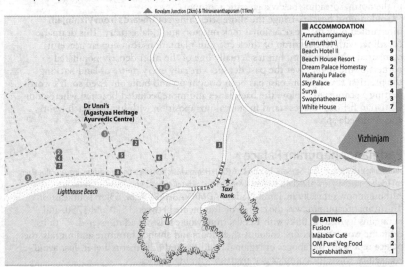

▲ Kovalam Junction (2km) & Thiruvananthapuram (11km)

Dr Unni's
(Agastyaa Heritage
Ayurvedic Centre)

Lighthouse Beach

LIGHTHOUSE ROAD

★ Taxi
Rank

Vizhinjam

■ **ACCOMMODATION**
Amruthamgamaya (Amrutham)	1
Beach Hotel II	9
Beach House Resort	8
Dream Palace Homestay	2
Maharaju Palace	6
Sky Palace	5
Surya	4
Swapnatheeram	3
White House	7

● **EATING**
Fusion	4
Malabar Café	3
OM Pure Veg Food	2
Suprabhatham	1

21

Western and fusion), served on a first-floor terrace overlooking the bay. Try the fish fillet sautéed in coconut jus, one of the Keralan seafood specialities, or home-made tagliatelle and chilli pesto. Most mains ₹200–550. Daily 8am–10pm.

Malabar Café Lighthouse Beach; map p.1068. Deservedly one of the most popular spots on the beachfront, serving a jack-of-all-trades menu of pizzas, burgers, superb tandoori seafood and choose-your-own lobsters, as well as Keralan staples such as fish *pollichathu* (₹350) and fish curry with tapioca (₹350). Most other mains ₹120–350. Daily 7.30am–10.30pm.

OM Pure Vegetarian Food Behind Lighthouse Beach and Surya resort; map p.1068. The place to go for excellent veg thalis (₹200) on an outdoor covered terrace. Delightful service from the lovely owner. Try the dal makhani (₹180) and good-value snacks like pakora (₹70–100). Daily 7am–11pm.

Suprabhatham Behind Lighthouse beach, next to a small Shiva temple; map p.1068. Simple, popular vegetarian café-restaurant in a shaded courtyard, where you can order Indian breakfasts (*idli* ₹80), as well as an extensive multicuisine menu. Daily 8am–11pm.

DIRECTORY

Banks and exchange There's an ATM in the *Kovalam Beach Hotel*, on the road leading up from the southern end of Hawah Beach; otherwise, the nearest are up at Kovalam Junction, 2km inland on the national highway (roughly ₹100 return in an auto-rickshaw), where both ICICI and Canara Bank have sub-branches. Pheroze Framroze, near the entrance to the *Leela* resort and bus stand, offers competitive rates for currency and travellers' cheques.

Tailors Dozens of little tailor shops are crammed in to the alleyways behind Lighthouse Beach; Suku's (near *Keerthi* restaurant) is recommended. You can have light cotton clothes made to measure, or ask them to copy your favourite garment from home, using a wide choice of coloured calico.

South of Kovalam

A tightly packed cluster of tiled fishermen's huts, **VIZHINJAM** (pronounced "Virinyam"), on the opposite (south) side of the headland from Lighthouse Beach, was once the capital of the Ay kings, the earliest dynasty in south Kerala. A number of simple small shrines survive from those times, and can be made the focus of a pleasant afternoon's stroll through coconut groves, best approached from the centre of the village rather than the coast road – brace yourself for the sharp contrast between hedonistic tourist resort and workaday fishing village. Note, too, another stark divide: between the Christian quarter to the south, with its towering Catholic church, and Muslim quarter to the north, spreading below a gigantic mosque.

Golden-sand beaches fringe the shore stretching **southwards from Vizhinjam**, interrupted only by the occasional rock outcrop and tidal estuary. This dramatic coastline, with its backdrop of thick coconut plantations, can appear peaceful compared with Kovalam, but it's actually one of the most densely populated corners of the state. Over the past decade, virtually every metre of land backing the prettiest stretches of coast has been bought up and built on. Even so, it's worth renting a scooter to explore the back lanes and more secluded beaches, where poor Christian fishing villages stand in surreal juxtaposition with luxury beach resorts and Ayurveda spas.

Padmanabhapuram Palace

50km southeast of Kovalam • Tues–Sun 9am–4.30pm • ₹300 (₹35) • Frequent buses along the main highway from Thiruvananthapuram and Kovalam; hop on any service heading to Nagercoil or Kanyakumari and get off at Thakkaly (sometimes written Thuckalai)

Although now officially in Tamil Nadu, **PADMANABHAPURAM**, 63km southeast of Thiruvananthapuram, was the capital of Travancore between 1550 and 1750, and maintains its historic links with Kerala, from where it is still administered. With its exquisite wooden interiors, coconut-shell floors and antique furniture and murals, the **palace** represents the apogee of regional building, and fully merits a visit. Just **avoid weekends**, when the complex gets overrun with bus parties.

21

AYURVEDA IN KERALA

"Health tourism" is very much a buzz phrase in Kerala, and resorts such as Kovalam and Varkala are packed with places to de-stress and detox – the majority of them based on principles of **Ayurveda medicine**. The Keralan approach to India's ancient holistic system of medicine has two distinct elements: first, the body is cleansed of toxins generated by imbalances in lifestyle and diet; secondly, its equilibrium is restored using herbal medicines, mainly in the form of plant oils applied using a range of different **massage** techniques. A practitioner's first prescription will often be a course of **panchakarma** treatment – a five-phase therapy during which harmful impurities are purged through induced vomiting, enemas and the application of medicinal oils poured through the nasal cavity. Other less onerous components, tailored for the individual patient, may include: *dhara*, where the oils are blended with ghee or milk and poured on to the forehead; *pizhichi*, in which four masseurs apply different oils simultaneously; and, the weirdest looking of all, *sirovashti*, where the oils are poured into a tall, topless leather cap placed on the head. Alongside these, patients are prescribed special balancing foods, and given vigorous full-body massages each day.

Standards of both treatment and hygiene vary greatly between establishments, as do the prices. Female travellers also sometimes complain of sexual harassment at the hands of opportunistic male masseurs; cross-gender massage is forbidden in Ayurveda. The application of dodgy oils that can cause skin problems is another risk you might be exposed to at a backstreet clinic. Your best bet is to follow tips from fellow travellers and, if you're unsure, check the state of any treatment rooms in advance.

ACCOMMODATION   **SOUTH OF KOVALAM**

Should you decide to prolong exploring the Vizhinjam coastline and its surrounds, you can choose from a few lovely resorts and **heritage properties**.

Bethsaida Hermitage Pulinkudi ☎0471 226 7554, ⓦbethsaidahermitage.com. An "ecofriendly Ayurveda beach resort" with a difference. The huge, well-furnished rooms in brick cottages or imposing modern blocks, two large pools, à la carte restaurant and prime location next to a beautiful cove are standard for the area – here, however, the profits support a church-run orphanage, a great initiative that's been doing a fine job for more than two decades. A/c ₹2500 extra. **₹8000**

Thapovan Nellikunnu ☎0471 248 0453, ⓦthapovan. com. This German-run heritage resort comprises two parts: one in a grove by the seashore, and another higher up the cliffside. The latter's elevated position and views across the palm canopy to Vizhinjam give it the edge. The traditional teak chalets and gardens are lovely. A/c ₹2000 extra. **₹7500**

Travancore Heritage Chowara ☎0471 226 7828, ⓦthe travancoreheritage.com. The centrepiece of this extravagant complex is a splendid 150-year-old mansion, fronted by a kidney-shaped pool and sun terrace. Below it are sixty relocated antique bungalows (₹15,000–25,000), some boasting alfresco garden bathrooms and their own plunge pools. **₹12,000**

Varkala and around

Devout Hindus have for hundreds, and possibly thousands, of years travelled to **VARKALA**, 54km north up the coast from Thiruvananthapuram, to scatter ashes of recently-deceased relatives on **Papanasam beach**. The beach, 4km from Varkala town itself, is dramatically set against a backdrop of superb, burnt-clay-coloured cliffs, which, coupled with comparatively low-key development, makes this a more appealing place to spend a beach holiday than Kovalam. Tightly crammed along the rim of crumbling North Cliff, its row of restaurants and small hotels stare out across a vast sweep of ocean – a view that can seem almost transcendental after sunset, when a myriad tiny fishing boats light up their lanterns.

Papanasam beach

Known in Malayalam as Papa Nashini ("sin destroyer"), Varkala's beautiful white-sand **Papanasam beach** (also known just as **Varkala beach**) has long been associated with ancestor worship. Devotees come here after praying at the ancient Janardhana Swamy

21

Temple on the hill to the south, then perform mortuary rituals on the beach, directed by specialist pujaris (priests). The best time to watch the rites is in the **early morning**, just after sunrise – though out of respect, it's best to keep your camera in your bag.

Western sun-worshippers keep to the northern end of the bay, where whistle-happy lifeguards ensure the safety of **swimmers** by enforcing the no-swim zones beyond the flags: the undercurrent is often strong, claiming lives every year. **Dolphins** are often seen swimming quite close to the coast, and, if you're lucky, you may be able to swim with them by arranging a ride with a fishing boat. Sea otters can also occasionally be spotted playing on the cliffs by the sea.

North Cliff

Few of Varkala's Hindu pilgrims make it as far as the **North Cliff** area, the focus of a well-established tourist scene where bamboo and palm-thatch cafés, restaurants and souvenir shops jostle for space close to the edge of the mighty escarpment that plunges vertically to the beach below. Several steep flights of steps cut into the rock provide shortcuts from the sand, or you can also get here via the gentler path that starts from the beachfront.

1, 2, 3, 4, 5 & Odayam (1km)

0 100 metres

ACCOMMODATION

Blue Water	1
Cliff Lounge	9
Deshadan	8
The First Place	2
Keratheeram Beach Resort	7
KR House	12
Maadathil Cottages	3
Mektoub	4
Oceanic	6
Oceano	11
Palm Tree Heritage	5
Villa Jacaranda	10

Sharanagati Yoga

NORTH CLIFF

Tibetan Market

Khan's Cookery

Durga Temple

KURAKANNI JUNCTION

Varkala Cultural Centre

Edava (6km) & Kappil Beach (7km)

ARABIAN SEA

Papanasam Beach

EATING

Café del Mar	1
Coffee Temple	4
Juice Shack	2
Little Tibet	3
Sri Padmam	5
Suprabhatam	6

BEACH ROAD

Temple Tank

TEMPLE JUNCTION

Mahindra 2-Wheelers

Soul and Surf

Janardhana Swamy Temple

Perumkulam Pond

SOUTH CLIFF

Varkala Town, Station, Shivgiri Mutt &

VARKALA BEACH

Anchengo

South Cliff

Dotted with mid-range hotels and guesthouses, the clifftop area running south of the main beachfront – known locally as **South Cliff** – is a much quieter neighbourhood of leafy lanes and large residential houses – a legacy of the lingering presence of numerous clean-living Brahmin families. The beach below the cliff, reached via rock-cut steps from several of the hotels, largely disappears at low tide, but offers a blissfully secluded spot to swim when the water recedes, though you should watch out for the sharp laterite boulders lurking in the surf.

Janardhana Swamy Temple

Varkala's ancient **Janardhana Swamy Temple** is reached by heading up the lane that climbs steeply south from the beachfront area. **Non-Hindus** are not permitted to enter the inner sanctum of the shrine, but you can peep over the perimeter walls from the encircling path – a pleasant stroll in the morning, when the temple elephant is led around the lanes on her exercise walk.

Enshrining a form of Vishnu, the temple is adorned with brightly painted images of Hanuman, Rama's monkey general. Among its treasures is a bell salvaged from a Dutch ship that was wrecked on the beach in the eighteenth century – the ship's captain donated it in a gesture of thanksgiving after his entire crew escaped with their lives.

North of Varkala

Just **north of Varkala** the shoreline grows a lot less densely populated, though the large, gaudily painted houses dotted around its hinterland of leafy lanes bear witness to the considerable affluence flooding in with remittance cheques from the Gulf States. You can comfortably walk the kilometre or so from the north end of Varkala cliff as it descends to **ODAYAM**, a mixed Hindu and Muslim village where a cluster of resorts and modest guesthouses has sprung up around the small black-sand beach. Room rates are on the high side, but it can be well worth paying for the extra seclusion when Varaka's clifftop area is firing on all cylinders.

Around 7km north is **Kappil Beach**, a scenic spot where the sea meets the backwaters. A narrow road separates the pretty stretch of sand from Edava-Nadayara Lake, where **Priyadarshini Boat Club** has rowing boats and pedalos to rent (☎0470 266 2323).

ARRIVAL AND DEPARTURE — VARKALA

By train The town's railway station – Varkala-Sivagiri – is 500m north of the central junction, served by express and passenger trains from Thiruvananthapuram, Kollam and most other Keralan towns on the mainline.

Destinations Alappuzha/Alleppey (3 daily; 2hr); Ernakulam/Kochi (hourly; 3hr 30min–4hr 30min); Kollam/Quilon (every 30min; 25min); Thiruvananthapuram (every 30min; 1hr).

By bus While some buses from Thiruvananthapuram's Thampanoor stand, and from Kollam to the north, continue on to within walking distance of the beach and clifftop area, most terminate in Varkala town.

Destinations from Varkala Junction Alappuzha/Alleppey (daily; 3hr 30min); Kollam/Quilon (3 daily; 1hr); Thiruvananthapuram (every 30min; 1hr 30min–2hr).

GETTING AROUND

By bus and auto-rickshaw Auto-rickshaws between the town and beach shouldn't cost more than ₹100, and frequent local buses also cover the route (₹5).

By motorcycle Scooters may be rented from Mahindra 2-Wheelers (Mon–Sat 9.30am–5pm; ☎98467 01975), near Temple Junction, and Wheels of South India, a business of no fixed abode that works up in North Cliff (☎98470 80412 or 93879 74698). The nearest petrol pump is in Varkala town – 300m north of the main circle, on the left side of Station Rd as you head towards the railway station.

By taxi Unni (☎98466 90300) is recommended for airport drops and local sightseeing day-trips.

ACTIVITIES

Yoga and meditation Many guesthouses offer morning yoga for around ₹300–400; just ask around to find a good class. For a real retreat, Sharanagati Yoga (☎90486 94762, ⓦsharanagati-yogahaus.com), on the Thiruvambadi road behind North Cliff, offers expert tuition in both yoga and meditation. Most students sign up for an all-inclusive package (₹4800/day, plus ₹1200 for anyone sharing the same room), covering two daily yoga and two daily meditation sessions, all (vegetarian) meals and comfortable accommodation.

Surfing Although Varkala has a reputation for surf that dumps you right on the sand, it's an undeveloped scene and you won't be fighting to get on a wave. Husband-and-wife team Ed and Sofie set up Soul and Surf (☎99617 11099, ⓦsoulandsurf.com) in 2010 and offer lessons (₹2500/1hr 30min), board rental (₹1500/day) and surf packages with accommodation on South Cliff (from ₹4850/day).

ACCOMMODATION

Varkala offers a wide choice of **accommodation**. The hotels up on **North Cliff** are most people's first choice, with more inspiring views than those lining the road to the beach, but there are some even better options on quieter **South Cliff** if you don't mind being away from the thick of things. For greater seclusion and a vivid taste of the area's lush palm forest and paddy fields, try **Odayam**, 1km north along the coastal path. All areas are accessible by road. You're likely to be able to negotiate a discount if you contact the hotel direct – and don't forget that rates plummet outside high season.

NORTH CLIFF

Cliff Lounge ☎90202 01785, ⓦclifflounge.com; map p.1072. This mid-range place is set back behind the strip but with uninterrupted sea views from its spacious double rooms, which are clean and simple, and with balconies. It has a focus on Ayurvedic medicine, with a clinic on site

21

(w motherayurvedics.com). ₹1000 extra for a/c. **₹2000**

Deshadan ☎ 47032 04242, w deshadan.com; map p.1072. The smartest of Varkala's small resorts, a 10min walk from the clifftop. Centred on a great little swimming pool, its fourteen rooms are tastefully styled. A pair of two-bedroomed cottages (₹8000) in the garden suit families well. Quality Ayurveda centre on site. Dorms ₹1500, doubles **₹4500**

Keratheeram Beach Resort ☎ 73566 53034, w facebook.com/ keratheeram; map p.1072. Set back a bit from the clifftop strip, this nice budget hotel feels secure and private. The downstairs rooms have their own hammocks and the whole place has a chilled-out vibe, particularly on the covered rooftop area where you can do yoga in the morning (donation requested). **₹2500**

Oceanic ☎ 0470 260 1413 or ☎ 98460 96912, w oceanic varkala.com; map p.1072. Pleasant rooms, with flowering climbers trailing from its balconies, close to the clifftop. Among the better-run, better-value budget options close to the strip. ₹500 extra for a/c. **₹1500**

SOUTH CLIFF

KR House ☎ 0470 260 6400 or ☎ 93497 41998, e ramachandran.krhouse@yahoo.co.in; map p.1072. A gem of a budget place, in a plum spot, with comfy mattresses, spotless bathrooms and balconies overlooking a narrow garden running to the cliff edge, from where a flight of steps drops steeply down to the beach. It's quiet, and run with great efficiency. **₹1000**

★ **Oceano** ☎ 93493 92022 or ☎ 4703 251546, w the oceanoresort.com; map p.1072. Set on the highest stretch of secluded South Cliff, rooms in this Ayurveda resort are light, cool, stylish and good value, with spectacular views from the pricier sea-facing suites (₹10,800). You eat meals (including a complimentary breakfast) in thatched gazebos on the cliff edge, from where steps lead to the beach. Ayurveda packages from ₹10,000/day, extra night **₹2700**

Villa Jacaranda Temple Rd West ☎ 0470 261 0296, w villa-jacaranda.biz; map p.1072. Bijou boutique guesthouse nestled amid the leafy lanes near the temple. It's small (just four rooms), with cool wooden furniture, crisp white sheets, fresh jasmine flowers in your room and a fragrant garden. Room 4 – which costs a little extra – has expansive sea views from its private terrace. **₹3550**

ODAYAM

Blue Water ☎ 94468 48534, w bluewaterstay.com; map p.1072. A nicely set up, welcoming option, comprising fourteen varnished palm-wood chalets with tiled roofs – not all that spacious, but comfortably furnished, with floating flowers in terracotta pots, cane blinds and silk throws on the beds. All have sea views. The open-sided restaurant, overlooking the waves at the bottom of a terraced plot, is also the best place to eat and drink hereabouts. **₹6500**

The First Place ☎ 0470 299 2090 or ☎ 97469 83783, w thefirstplace.dinstudio.se; map p.1072. Eco-friendly Swedish-run guest-house on the bluff overlooking the beach, with its own shady garden. The rooms aren't large, but they're nicely done – freshly painted with little wooden shelves, glossy red-oxide floors and mozzie nets – with Scandinavian touches that give them a boutique feel. Home-cooked Indian food and an outdoor space for yoga. High season only. **₹3000**

Maadathil Cottages Manthara Temple Rd ☎ 97461 13495 (Muhajir), w maadathilcottages.com; map p.1072. Row of locally owned and run holiday cottages in traditional Keralan style (gabled, red-tiled roofs, wood railings and split-cane blinds) in a sweet spot under the coconut trees behind Odayam beach. There's a pricier, larger cottage with a lovely rear veranda looking on to a lotus pond filled with egrets and butterflies. **₹6500**

Mektoub ☎ 94479 71239, e mektoubexperience@gmail. com; map p.1072. A perfect place to soak up the unspoiled vibe that still holds sway in Odayam. In an idyllic setting between coconut groves and paddy fields, it comprises a campus of red-laterite buildings with spacious rooms and sea-facing verandas. Bargain rates considering the level of comfort, and owner Rafik is a great cook. It's hard to find; call ahead to be met. **₹4000**

★ **Palm Tree Heritage** ☎ 99460 55036, w palmtree heritage.com; map p.1072. Stylish, part-Swedish-owned boutique place right behind the beach, set in well-watered gardens. The architecture is delightful and the interiors cool and comfortable, blending traditional, handmade Keralan woodwork and modern comforts, including luxurious bathrooms. The food's terrific, and Babu and his staff are unfailingly courteous. Simple non-a/c bamboo huts ₹7000, doubles **₹4500**

EATING

Varkala's clifftop **café-restaurants** specialize in locally caught seafood (you'll also find plenty of Italian, Thai and Mexican dishes on offer – but they won't taste much like the real thing). Prices are high, even by Keralan standards, and service painfully slow, but the superb location more than compensates. Although alcohol is available in just about all the clifftop places, due to Varkala's religious importance **beer** tends to be served in discreet teapots. Once the restaurants finish serving, **nightlife** is generally low-key.

★ **Café del Mar** North Cliff; map p.1072. The most professionally run place to eat on North Cliff, with an Italian coffee machine and polite, uniformed service. It offers the usual mixed menu, but they can actually cook everything on it. Made with imported cheeses, the Italian dishes are especially good) and there are plenty of light bites and healthy salads. Most mains ₹250–400. Daily 7.30am–late.

Coffee Temple North Cliff ⓦ coffeetemple.in; map p.1072. Hot contender (along with *Café del Mar*) for the crown of "Best Coffee in Varkala" and with a loyal following. The cakes are uninspiring *German Bakery* fare, but the Western menu is a hit. Espresso from ₹100. Free filter water. Daily 6am–10pm.

Juice Shack North Cliff ⓣ 99952 14515; map p.1072. Fresh juices churned out by the larger-than-life, resplendently-bearded Umesh and his team. They also do a range of healthy snacks (wraps and crunchy salads; ₹200) and host popular buffets (non-veg ₹500) on Wed and Sat (buy your ticket in advance). Daily 7am–11.30pm.

Little Tibet North Cliff; map p.1072. Decorated with cheerful prayer flags and Buddhist *thangkas*, this large bamboo and palm-thatch place catches the breezes at a prime cliff-edge location. Mexican and Italian specialities are offered, but most people come for the tasty Tibetan

momo dumplings (₹150–230) and *thukpa* soup (₹150). Very friendly, professional service. Daily 9am–10pm.

Sri Padmam Temple Junction; map p.1072. This dingy-looking café on the temple crossroads serves freshly made, cheap and tasty south Indian veg food (including ₹90 "meals" at lunchtime). You can walk through the front dining room to a large rear terrace affording prime views of the tank – particularly atmospheric at breakfast time. Daily 6am–9pm.

Suprabhatam Varkala town; map p.1072. The cheapest and best pure veg joint in Varkala, just off the main roundabout in a dining hall lined with coir mats. Their dosas and other fried snacks aren't great, but the lunchtime "unlimited" rice-plate "meals" (noon–3pm; ₹45), featuring the usual *thoran*, *avial*, dhal, *rasam*, buttermilk, curd, *papad* and red or white rice, pull in streams of locals and foreigners alike. Daily 8am–9pm.

DIRECTORY

Banks There's an ATM on Temple Junction, and several banks up in Varkala town, just off the main roundabout.

Cookery classes Khan's Cookery offers daily classes in a spruce little kitchen behind *Little Tibet* on North Cliff (₹600/₹800 for veg/non-veg; book on ⓣ 98956 33896).

Internet There's free wi-fi with a good connection at *Coffee Temple* (see above).

Post office Just north of Temple Junction (Mon–Sat 10am–5pm), near the *Sri Padmam* restaurant.

Kollam (Quilon)

Sandwiched between the sea and Ashtamudi ("eight inlets") Lake, **KOLLAM** (pronounced "Koillam", and previously known as **Quilon**), was for centuries the focal point of the Malabar's spice trade. Phoenicians, Arabs, Greeks, Romans and Chinese all dispatched ships to the city, before the rise of Calicut and Cochin eclipsed the port. These days, it's a workaday market town and busy transport hub for the southern backwater region, with surprisingly few vestiges of its former prominence. Many travellers stay overnight here, however, en route to or from Alappuzha on the excursion boats that leave each morning from its lakeside ferry jetty. If the traffic in the centre gets too much, take a short auto-rickshaw ride south to the main **beach**, or a couple of kilometres west along the coastal road to the **Thangassery Lighthouse** (daily 10am–5pm; ₹25), which is well worth the climb to the top for views of the fishing harbour.

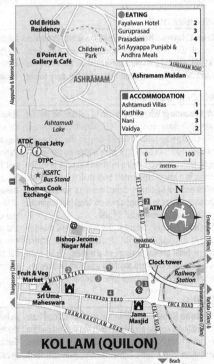

KOLLAM (QUILON)

● **EATING**
Fayalwan Hotel	2
Guruprasad	3
Prasadam	4
Sri Ayyappa Punjabi & Andhra Meals	1

■ **ACCOMMODATION**
Ashtamudi Villas	1
Karthika	4
Nani	3
Vaidya	2

21

In the evening, a stroll through the town's traditional **bazaar**, with its old wooden houses and narrow backstreets lined by coir warehouses, rice stores and cashew traders, is a pleasant diversion.

Old British Residency and around

Residency Rd, Ashtamudi Lake

Of the few surviving colonial vestiges, the only one worth a detour is the former **British Residency**, a magnificent 250-year-old mansion on the shores of the lake, now only open for official events. Among the last monuments surviving in India from the earliest days of the Raj, it perfectly epitomizes the openness to indigenous influences that characterized the era, with typically Keralan gable roofs surmounting British pillared verandas. There are no set visiting hours – just turn up and ask the manager if you can have a look around.

Just nearby, another colonial-era building has been transformed into the **8 Point Art Gallery & Café**, which is a great place for a break.

ARRIVAL AND DEPARTURE   KOLLAM (QUILON)

By train Kollam's busy mainline railway station lies east of the clock tower that marks the centre of town, and is easily reached by auto-rickshaw. Note that most Thiruvananthapuram-bound trains do not stop in Varkala. Destinations Alappuzha/Alleppey (8 daily; 1hr 15min–2hr); Ernakulam/Kochi (every 30min; 3–4hr); Thiruvananthapuram (hourly; 1hr 30min–2hr); Varkala (hourly; 20–30min).

By bus The KSRTC bus stand is on the west side of town, near the boat jetty on Ashtamudi Lake. You can book express buses in advance but not local or "limited stop" services. Destinations Alappuzha/Alleppey (hourly; 2hr); Ernakulam/Kochi (hourly; 3hr–3hr 20min); Thiruvananthapuram (hourly; 1hr 45min).

By boat There are some backwater ferry services from Kollam (see page 1080).

INFORMATION

Tourist information The District Tourism Promotion Council (DTPC) has a tourist office (daily 8am–7pm; ☎ 0474 274 5625, ⊚ dtpckollam.com) at the KSRTC bus stand, where you can book tickets for the daily tourist backwater cruises (see page 1080) and other tours. The local Alappuzha Tourism Development Council office (ATDC; daily 8am–8pm; ☎ 47722 64462, ⊚ atdcalleppey.com), across the road, offers comparable services.

ACCOMMODATION

★ **Ashtamudi Villas** 2km north of Kollam, on the far side of Thevally Bridge ☎ 98471 32449, ⊚ ashtamudi villas.com; map p.1075. Buried deep in the backwaters on the outskirts of town, this place is right on the water's edge, with hammocks strung between the palm trees. The rooms, in a row of eco-friendly brick chalets, are spacious, bright and cool (get the detached one if it's available). You can phone ahead to arrange a pick-up. Local tours arranged from here are recommended. ₹1500

Karthika Paikkada Rd, near the Jama Masjid mosque ☎ 0474 275 1821; map p.1075. Large, popular, central budget hotel offering a range of acceptably clean, plain rooms (some a/c) ranged around a courtyard that centres, rather unexpectedly, on three huge nude figures. ₹600

Nani Opposite the clock tower ☎ 0474 275 1141, ⊚ hotelnani.com; map p.1075. A decent hotel, in a quirky, Keralan-gabled redbrick tower block near the railway station. The comfortably furnished, standard rooms are the real bargain, though couples might appreciate the extra space of the "executive" deluxe options (₹4000). ₹2500

Vaidya Residency Rd, Chinnakkada ☎ 0474 274 8432, ⊚ thehotelvaidya.com; map p.1075. This place is fine if you just want somewhere comfortable to crash for a night and aren't fussy about the view. The business-orientated, characterless rooms have no balconies and zero outlook, but are clean, and huge for the price. The standard ones (referred to as "deluxe") are the best value. ₹1950

EATING

Fayalwan Hotel Main bazaar; map p.1075. Come here for traditional Keralan breakfasts (₹60) and the best mutton biryani in town (lunchtime only; ₹140). It's run by the third generation of the same family and the walls still sport pictures of traditional wrestlers – the *fayalwans* after which the restaurant is named. Daily 8am–9pm.

Guruprasad Main bazaar; map p.1075. Cramped and sweaty, but offering wonderfully old-school "meals" (₹50):

21

BACKWATER CRUISES FROM KOLLAM

DTPC run popular **cruises from Kollam to Alappuzha** (10.30am; 8hr; ₹400) on alternate days, with stops for lunch and tea. Tickets can be bought on the day from their tourist office at the boat jetty on Ashtamudi Lake, and at some of the hotels. They also offer exclusive overnight *kettu vallam* cruises, and half-day canal trips to nearby **Monroe Island** (daily 9am–1pm & 2–6.30pm; ₹600), as well as guided village tours taking in Ayurveda factories, coir-makers, boat-builders and bird-nesting sites.

You may find that you get a far better impression of backwater life by hopping between villages on the very cheap **local ferries**. DTPC have timetables and route information; tickets are sold on the boats themselves.

blue-and-cream walls, framed ancestral photos and Hindu devotional art provide the typical backdrop for great pure-veg rice plates and Udupi-style snacks (₹18–35). Daily 7am–9pm.

★ **Prasadam** Nani hotel, opposite the clock tower. ☎0474 275 1141, ⊚hotelnani.com; map p.1075. Kollam's best food, served in plush a/c comfort. Traditional south Indian thalis are the most popular lunchtime options from an exhaustive menu, but this is also great for fresh local seafood and backwater cuisine, like the *karimeen pollichathu* (white fish steamed in banana leaf; ₹225) and

a blow-out seafood platter. Daily 7.30–10am, noon–3pm & 7–10.30pm.

Sri Ayyappa Punjabi & Andhra Meals Main bazaar, near Dhanya Super Market; map p.1075. Situated down a tiny alleyway off Kollam's main bazaar, this place is a real hidden gem. Look for the sign just east of the Indian Bank, on the north side of the road. Superb Punjabi cuisine (a rarity in these parts) includes a delicious *paneer* butter masala (₹100) and dhal fry (₹60), hot naan breads and heavenly lassis. Mon–Sat 8.30am–3.30pm, 6.30pm–10.30pm, Sundays 6.30pm–10.30pm.

DIRECTORY

ATM ATMs can be found in the smart Bishop Jerome Nagar shopping mall just south of the main road between the jetty and the clock tower. The efficient Axis bank also has a dependable ATM next to the *Vaidya* hotel, and there's a

Thomas Cook Exchange on the crossroads not far from the boat jetty.

Internet Cyber.com, just south of the clock tower on the first floor of Yeskay Towers, charges just ₹35/hr.

Alappuzha (Alleppey)

From the mid-nineteenth century, **ALAPPUZHA** (or "**Alleppey**") served as the main port for the backwater region. Spices, coffee, tea, cashews, coir and other produce were shipped out from the inland waterways to the sea via its grid of canals and rail lines. Tourist literature loves to dub the town as "the Venice of the East", but in truth the comparison does few favours to Venice. Apart from a handful of colonial-era warehouses and mansions, and a derelict pier jutting into the sea from a sun-blasted and dirty **beach**, few monuments survive, while the old canals enclose a typically ramshackle Keralan market of bazaars and noisy traffic.

That said, Alappuzha makes a congenial place to while away an evening en route to or from the **backwaters**. Streams of visitors do just that during the winter season, for the town has become Kerala's pre-eminent **rice boat cruising** hub, with an estimated four hundred *kettu vallam* moored on the fringes of nearby Vembanad and Punnamada lakes. To cash in on the seasonal influx, the local tourist offices lay on excursion boats for day-trips, while in mid-December the sands lining the west end of town host a popular **beach festival**, during which cultural events and a procession of fifty caparisoned elephants are staged with the dilapidated British-built pier as a backdrop. Alappuzha's really big day, however, is the second Saturday of August, in the middle of the monsoon, when it serves as the venue for one of Kerala's major spectacles – the **Nehru Trophy snake boat race** (see page 1059).

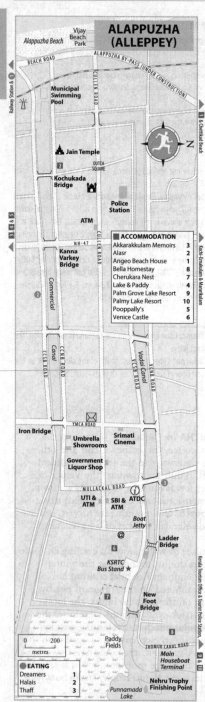

ALAPPUZHA (ALLEPPEY)

Alappuzha Beach · Vijay Beach Park

BEACH ROAD · ALAPPUZHA BY-PASS (UNDER CONSTRUCTION)

CULLEN ROAD

Railway Station &

Municipal Swimming Pool

Jain Temple

DUTCH SQUARE

Kochukada Bridge

Police Station

ATM

NH-47

Kanna Varkey Bridge

CULLEN ROAD

Commercial Canal

CCNB ROAD

CCSB ROAD

Vadai Canal

VCNB ROAD

VCSB ROAD

YMCA ROAD

Iron Bridge

Umbrella Showrooms

Srimati Cinema

Government Liquor Shop

MULLACKAL ROAD

UTI & ATM

SBI & ATM · ATDC

Boat Jetty

@

Ladder Bridge

KSRTC Bus Stand ★

New Foot Bridge

SHOMUR CANAL ROAD

Paddy Fields

Main Houseboat Terminal

Nehru Trophy Finishing Point

Punnamada Lake

Kochi-Ernakulam & Maraikulam

Kerala Tourism Office & Tourist Police Station

0 — 200 metres

■ ACCOMMODATION

Akkarakkulam Memoirs	3
Alasr	2
Angeo Beach House	1
Bella Homestay	8
Cherukara Nest	7
Lake & Paddy	4
Palm Grove Lake Resort	9
Palmy Lake Resort	10
Pooppally's	5
Venice Castle	6

● EATING

Dreamers	1
Halais	2
Thaff	3

ARRIVAL AND DEPARTURE   ALAPPUZHA (ALLEPPEY)

By bus The KSRTC bus stand is at the northeast edge of town, 1min from the boat jetty. For Fort Cochin, catch any of the fast Ernakulam services along the main highway and get down at Thoppumpady (7km south), from where local buses run the rest of the way.

Destinations Ernakulam/Kochi (hourly; 1hr 30min); Kollam/Quilon (hourly; 2hr 30min); Thiruvananthapuram (hourly; 4hr 15min).

By boat The main boat jetty is on Vadai Canal, close to the KSRTC bus stand, from where the daily tourist ferries to and from Kollam run, as well as cheaper local (and less direct) ferries to and from Kottayam (dep. 7.30am, 9.35am, 11.30am, 2.30pm & 5.15pm). Regular services also connect Alappuzha with Champakulam, where you pick up less frequent boats to Neerettupuram and Kidangara, and back to Alappuzha. This round route ranks among Kuttanad's classic trips; the tourist offices can help you make sense of the timetables (also found at ⊕ swtd.gov.in).

By train The station, on the main Thiruvananthapuram–Ernakulam line, lies 3km southwest across town, on the far side of Alappuzha's main waterway, Commercial Canal. As the backwaters prevent trains from continuing directly south beyond Alappuzha, only a few major daily services and a handful of passenger trains depart from here. For points further north along the coast, take the *Jan Shatabdi Express* (#12076) and change at Ernakulam, as the after-noon *Alleppey–Cannanore Express* (#16307), which runs as far as Kozhikode and Kannur, arrives at those destinations rather late at night. It is, however, a good bet if you want to get to Thrissur.

Destinations Ernakulam/Kochi (15 daily; 1hr–1hr 30min); Thiruvananthapuram (4 daily; 3hr–4hr 30min); Varkala (6 daily; 2hr–3hr).

INFORMATION

Tourist information The town has several rival tourist departments, all of them eager to offer advice and book you onto their houseboat tours. The most conveniently situated – at the jetty itself on Boat Jetty Rd – are the DTPC tourist reception centre (daily 9am–5pm; ☎ 0477 225 1796) and ATDC office (☎ 0477 226 4462, ⊕ atdcalleppey.com). Both ATDC and DTPC sell tickets for their ferries, backwater cruises and charter boats, and can help you fathom the intricacies of local ferry timetables. Though many of the houseboat booking agencies dotted around town call themselves "tourist information offices" they're nothing of the kind; their sole purpose is to sell their cruises. The Kerala Tourism Office is further east on the water's edge next to the police station (☎ 0477 226 0722, ⊕ keralatourism.org)

Services You can change money at the Ahalia Money Exchange (daily 9.30am–6pm, ☎ 0477 223 9911) office on Church Rd. Both Axis bank and the State Bank of India on Cullen Rd have reliable ATMs.

21

DAY-CRUISES AND CANOE TRIPS AROUND ALAPPUZHA

The obvious destination for a day-trip from Alappuzha is **Vembanad Lake** on the town's north and eastern fringes: **Punnamada Lake** (also called Punnamada Kayal) is the local section of this vast waterway. Reaching either from town is most straightforward by water. For short cruises, it's possible to charter diesel-powered motorboats (₹400/hr), but a better option would be to dispense with engines altogether and opt for a guided village tour in a hand-paddled canoe. Aside from being more "green", these allow you to penetrate narrow waterways beyond the range of the other tourist boats. DTPC offers its own punted tours, carrying two people for ₹250/hr.

A recommended private operator who's been ferrying tourists around Alappuzha's off-track backwaters for years is **Mr K.D. Prasenan** (☎93888 44712), based at the *Palm Grove Lake Resort* on the Punnamada Kayal, 3.5km north of the boat jetty (see below). He offers tours in a slender 10m boat (₹500/hr for two people).

Alternatively, **Paddyland** tours charges ₹1000 per person for an 8hr trip, which includes a transfer to and from town on the ferry, and breakfast and lunch in the boatman's home. Contact Mr Joseph on ☎94465 84905, ⊛paddylandtours.com.

ACCOMMODATION

There are some great **homestay** possibilities if you're willing to travel to the outskirts and pay a little more, along with some good options a taxi ride away in the surrounding **backwaters** and further up the coast. Nearly everywhere, whatever its price bracket, has some kind of tie-in with a houseboat operator: good-natured encouragement tends to be the order of the day rather than hard-sell tactics, but you may be able to negotiate a reduction on your hotel tariff if you do end up booking a backwater trip. Whenever you come, and wherever you choose to stay, brace yourself for clouds of **mosquitoes**.

ALAPPUZHA TOWN

Alasr Commercial Canal, North Bank Rd, west of Kochukada Bridge ☎99470 66699; map p.1078. Bona fide heritage hotels offering rooms for less than ₹1500 are as rare as hen's teeth in Kerala, but *Alasr* is just that – a splendid two-hundred-year-old merchant's mansion overlooking one of Alappuzha's main canals, offering a range of huge, affordable room. They can be tricky to get hold of: use ⊛booking.com to book. **₹1300**

★ **Bella Homestay** Near Nehru Trophy Finishing Point ☎90617 93196 or 0477 223 0201, ⊛bellakerala.com; map p.1078. Tucked away in a leafy, quiet backstreet, this homestay in a modern house within walking distance of the main houseboat terminal is a great mid-range option. The impeccably clean rooms are spacious and individually furnished with splashes of colour, the welcome from Keralan-Polish hosts Biju and Natasha is warm, and the breakfasts are great. **₹2500**

Cherukara Nest 9 774 Cherukara Building ☎0477 225 1509 or ☎99470 59628, ⊛cherukaranest.com; map p.1078. 1940s "heritage" home, on a quiet canal road just a short walk around the corner from the KSRTC bus stand. Breakfast is served in a courtyard under a huge mango tree.

Eco-friendly houseboat cruises are a sideline. A/c ₹600 extra. **₹1000**

Palm Grove Lake Resort Punnamada Kayal, 3.5km north of boat jetty ☎09526 940 909, ⊛palmgrove lakeresort.com; map p.1078. Near where the canal meets Punnamada Lake, this relaxed resort overlooks the water – a perfect, tranquil spot from which to watch the snake boat races. Shaded by areca and coconut palms, its pretty cottages have gabled tile roofs, private outdoor showers and sitouts opening onto the garden. **₹3500**

Palmy Lake Resort Thathampally, 2km north of boat jetty ☎0477 223 5938, ⊛palmyresort.com; map p.1078. Spacious, neatly painted red-tiled "cottages" (a/c and non-a/c), grouped behind a modern family home on the northeastern limits of town. It isn't actually on the lake, but offers exceptional value; all rooms have private pillared verandas opening onto a restful garden. **₹1000**

Venice Castle Behind Canara Bank, close to KSRTC bus stand ☎0477 223 7779 or 99470 84414, ⊛venicecastle. com; map p.1078. Substantial, modern Keralan home a stone's throw from the bus stand and town centre, but sheltered behind a screen of lush greenery. Huge rooms for the price, and well aired, with comfy beds, decent bathrooms and views over mango and palm trees. A/c ₹300 extra. **₹1700**

CHETTIKAD

Angeo Beach House Chettikad Beach, Priyadarsini Rd, Thumpoly ☎80867 52586; map p.1078. A simple and secluded homestay right on the beach. The charming hosts cook great Keralan food – though only their son Martin, who runs *Dreamers* in Alappuzha (see page 1081), speaks English. Each of the three rooms has a veranda and there's a hammock and a little sitout in the shaded garden. They plan to add a couple of bamboo huts, too. **₹3800**

21

ALAPPUZHA BACKWATERS

Akkarakkulam Memoirs Chennamkary ☏ 0484 600 3300; map p.1078. One of the few proper heritage hotels in the backwaters (as opposed to homestays), in a recently converted Syrian-Christian mansion overlooking the Pamba River. Great value, and the rates include a sunset cruise, use of a rowing boat, bicycles, night fishing tours and guided walks around the area. ₹5500

Lake & Paddy Pamba riverside, 2.5km east of town centre at Chungam; map p.1078. Tiny and colourful budget guest-house, run by hospitable brothers, situated right on the Pamba River with rice fields to the rear. Two lovely tile-floored cottages make the most of the green views (₹1000); two other cheapie rooms in the main house are bamboo lined and share a bathroom. A fantastic location for watching village and river life roll by, and easily reached by auto-rickshaw or government ferry from Alappuzha. ₹650

Pooppally's Ponga, Pooppally, on the Pamba River ☏ 0477 276 2034 or 0477 329 0800, ⊚ pooppallys. com; map p.1078. This old ancestral mansion is a typically Syrian-Christian home with double-gabled roof and guest rooms in twin wings opening on to a central courtyard garden next to the river. They're not overly large, but have delightful wood-pillared verandas. If it's free, splash out on the romantic, 200-year-old *nalukettu* (₹5000), which sits on stilts above a pond in the back garden. *Pooppally's* is accessible by ferry or road. ₹4000

KUTTANAD: THE BACKWATERS OF KERALA

One of the most memorable experiences for travellers in India is the opportunity to take a boat journey on the **backwaters of Kerala**. The area known as **Kuttanad** stretches for 75km from Kollam in the south to Kochi in the north, sandwiched between the sea and the hills. This bewildering labyrinth of shimmering waterways, composed of lakes, canals, rivers and rivulets, is lined with dense tropical greenery and preserves rural Keralan lifestyles that are completely hidden from the road.

The region's bucolic way of life has long fascinated visitors. And the ever entrepreneurial Keralans were quick to spot its potential as a visitor destination – particularly after it was discovered that foreigners and wealthy tourists from India's cities were prepared to pay vast sums in local terms to explore the area aboard converted **rice barges**, or *kettu vallam*. Since its inception in the early 1990s, the houseboat tour industry has grown exponentially in both size and sophistication, and has brought with it major environmental drawbacks as well as increased prosperity. You can, however, explore this extraordinary region in lower-impact ways, too.

TOURIST CRUISES

The most popular excursion in the Kuttanad region is the full-day journey between **Kollam** and **Alappuzha**. All sorts of private hustlers offer their services, but the principal boats are run on alternate days by the ATDC and the DTPC. The double-decker boats leave from both Kollam and Alappuzha daily, departing at 10.30am (10am check-in); tickets (₹400) can be bought in advance or on the day at the ATDC/DTPC counters, other agents and some hotels. Both companies make three stops during the 8hr journey, including one for lunch, and another 3hr north of Kollam at the **Mata Amritanandamayi Math** at Amritapuri (where "Amma" offers devotees her trademark hugs). Although this is by far the main backwater route, many tourists find it too long, with crowded decks and intense sun. There's also something faintly embarrassing about being cooped up with a crowd of fellow tourists, madly photographing any signs of life on the water or canal banks, while gangs of kids scamper alongside the boat screaming "one pen, one pen".

VILLAGE TOURS AND CANOES

Quite apart from their significant environmental impact, most boats are too wide to squeeze into the narrower inlets connecting small villages. To reach these more idyllic, remote areas, therefore, you'll need to charter a punted **canoe**. The slower pace means you cover less distance in an hour, but the experience of being so close to the water, and those who live on it, tends to be correspondingly more rewarding. You'll also find more formal "**village tours**" advertised across the Kuttanad area, tying together trips to watch coir-makers, rice farmers and boat-builders in action, with the opportunity to dine in a traditional Keralan village setting.

EATING

In addition to the **restaurants** listed here, most of Alappuzha's homestays and guesthouses provide meals for guests, usually delicious, home-cooked Keralan cooking that's tailored towards sensitive Western palates.

★ **Dreamers** Alappuzha beach ☎ 80867 52586, ⓦ dreamersrestaurant.com; map p.1078. With its sea view and rustic decor, this place is a cross between a treehouse and dune shack. The menu includes fresh pasta and pizza (₹250–300) – *Dreamers* is part-owned by an Italian – plus fresh salads and local seafood (the roast crab is a winner). Springsteen, Clapton and Rihanna dominate a rather random soundtrack. Daily noon–11pm.

Halais CCSB Rd; map p.1078. Proper Keralan-Muslim restaurant that's been an Alappuzha institution for generations. Much of its old-world character disappeared in a recent face-lift, but the food's as delicious as ever. Nearly everyone comes for their chicken biryanis (₹180) or their blow-out "meals" (₹380), to be enjoyed with the legendary house date pickle. Daily 9am–10.30pm.

Thaff YMCA Junction; map p.1078. It looks a bit down on its luck from the outside, but this is the best place in town for inexpensive non-veg Indian food, from local fish to chicken and mutton specialities, and all the standard veggie dishes. Intense Keralan flavours and rock-bottom prices are guaranteed, with chicken biryanis for ₹120 and pomfret from ₹180. Daily 7.30am–10pm.

KETTU VALLAM (HOUSEBOATS)

Whoever dreamed up the idea of showing tourists around the backwaters in old rice barges, or **kettu vallam**, could never have imagined that, more than three decades on, nine hundred or more of them would be chugging around Kuttanad waterways. These **houseboats**, made of dark, oiled jackwood with canopies of plaited palm thatch and coir, are big business, and almost every accommodation seems to have one. The flashiest are fitted with a/c rooms, Jacuzzis and widescreen plasma TVs on their teak sun decks and have bottles of imported wine in their fridges. At the opposite end of the scale are rough-and-ready transport barges with gut-thumping diesel engines, cramped bedrooms and minimal washing facilities.

Rates vary hugely depending on the quality, more than double over Christmas and New Year, and halve off-season during the monsoons. In practice, ₹7500–18,000 is the usual bracket for a trip on a two-bedroom, a/c boat with a proper bathroom, including three meals, in early December or mid-January. The cruise should last a minimum of 22 hours, though don't expect to spend all of that on the move: running times are carefully calculated to spare gas. From sunset onwards you'll be moored at a riverbank.

You'll save quite a lot of cash, and be doing the fragile ecosystem a big favour, by opting for a more environmentally friendly **punted** *kettu vallam*. Rice barges were traditionally propelled by punt, and though it means you travel at a more leisurely pace, the experience is silent (great for wildlife-spotting) and altogether more relaxing.

Houseboat operators work out of **Kollam** and **Kumarakom**, but most are in **Alappuzha**, where you'll find the lowest prices – but also the worst congestion on more scenic routes. Spend a day shopping around for a deal (your guesthouse or hotel-owner will be a good first port of call), or if you're in Alappuzha, head to the main houseboat terminal at 9am to meet returning *kettu vallam* and question travellers as they disembark. Always check the boat over beforehand. It's also a good idea to get the deal fixed on paper before setting off, and to withhold a final payment until the end of the cruise in case you're not satisfied.

Dependable operators include: **Lakes and Lagoons** (☎ 0477 226 6842, ⓦ lakeslagoons.com); **Angel Queen** (☎ 98951 89095, ⓦ angelqueencruise.in); Xandari Riverscapes (☎ 0484 6503 044 or 0484 311 5036, ⓦ xandari.com); and the upmarket **Spice Routes Luxury Cruises** (☎ 0484 266 5314 or 86060 00430, ⓦ spiceroutes.in).

LOCAL FERRIES

Kettu vallam may offer the most comfortable way of cruising the backwaters, but you'll get a much more vivid experience of what life is actually like in the region by jumping on one of the local ferries that serve its towns and villages. Particularly recommended is the trip from **Alappuzha to Kottayam** (dep. 7.30am, 9.30am, 11.30am, 2.30 & 5.15pm; 2hr 30min; ₹20), which winds across open lagoons and narrow canals, through coconut groves and islands. Arrive early to get a good place with uninterrupted views.

Good places to aim for from Alappuzha include Neerettupuram, Kidangara and Chambakulam; all are served by regular daily ferries, but you may have to change boats once or twice along the way, killing time in local cafés and toddy shops (all of which adds to the fun, of course).

21

THREATS TO THE BACKWATER ECOSYSTEM

The **African moss** that often carpets the surface of the narrower waterways may look attractive, but it is a symptom of the many serious **ecological problems** currently affecting the region, whose population density ranges from between two and four times that of other coastal areas in southwest India. This has put growing pressure on land, and consequently a greater reliance on fertilizers that eventually work their way into the water and cause the build-up of moss.

Illegal land reclamation poses the single greatest threat to this fragile ecosystem. In little more than a century, the total area of water in Kuttanad has been reduced by two-thirds, while mangrove swamps and fish stocks have been decimated by pollution and the spread of towns and villages around the edges of the backwater region. Tourism adds to the problem, as the film of oil from motorized ferries and houseboats spreads through the waters, killing yet more fish, which has in turn led to a reduction of more than fifty percent in the number of bird species found in the region.

Mararikulam

Fourteen kilometres north of Alappuzha a number of high-end eco-resorts have sprung up in the fishing village of **MARARIKULAM**; the attraction here is that there's little to do except lounge on the uninterrupted stretch of white-sand **beach**. One nearby place of interest is sixteenth-century **St Andrew's Basilica** (ⓦarthunkalchurch.org; ₹50 donation requested) 6km north in **Arthungal** – not to be missed in January when Christian pilgrims flock here for the Feast of San Sebastian.

ARRIVAL AND DEPARTURE   MARARIKULAM

By bus Buses from Alappuzha drop passengers at St Augustine's church, a short walk from the beach (frequent; 40min). For services further afield, you'll need to get an auto-rickshaw up to the main highway, NH-47.
By taxi Cars line up outside *Marari Beach Resort*. Laiju is a recommended local driver (ⓣ 99463 83081).

ACCOMMODATION

Most visitors will have booked into one of the expensive resorts in advance; those listed below are independent, local options. Note that the lane from St Augustine's church (on Beach Rd) towards the beach is lined with budget **homestays** that usually have space.
Arakal Heritage Chethy, 3km north of Marari Beach ⓣ0478 286 5545, ⓦarakal.com. Three-hundred-year-old heritage home tucked away in a shady spot at the far end of Marari Beach. Individual cottages have bags of Keralan character, with traditional gabled roofs and dark-wood antique furniture – one even has a mango tree growing through it. Mini and Abi are wonderful hosts who will arrange cookery classes and lend you a canoe to paddle in the backwaters. Full board. ₹8300
Marari Austin Beach Villa Marari Beach ⓣ94475 04293, ⓦmarariaustinbeachvilla.com. Right on the beachfront, this solid option has four rooms, the slightly pricier two on the first floor with a terrace and a/c (₹3000 extra). Rooms and bathrooms are spotless and there's solar hot water. Breakfast included. ₹6820
Marari Arapakal Beach Villa Marari Beach ⓣ99474 40334, ⓦmararirapakalbeach.com. These two newish buildings in the grounds of a family home might not have much character, but they're clean and secure and just a few minutes' walk from the beach. Dominic also owns a more basic shack right on the beach with two rooms for the same price. Breakfast included. ₹2500
★ **Marari Dreamz** Mararikulam ⓣ87144 14309, ⓦmararidreamz.com. Somehow the location on the wrong side of Beach Rd doesn't seem to matter. Behind a standard suburban facade this lovely hideaway has large and very private rooms; each comfort-ably sleeps three and has its own shady veranda in the garden. There are bicycles and motorbikes to rent and young hosts Allwyn and Jency go out of their way to look after guests. ₹3000

Kottayam and around

Some 76km southeast of Kochi and 37km northeast of Alappuzha, **KOTTAYAM** is a compact, busy Keralan town strategically located between the backwaters and the mountains of the Periyar Wildlife Sanctuary. The many **rubber plantations** around town, introduced by British missionaries in the 1820s, have for more than a century formed the bedrock of a booming local economy, most of it controlled by landed **Syrian Christians**. Author Arundhati Roy grew up in nearby **Ayemenem**, the magical setting for her acclaimed novel *The God of Small Things* and partway towards vast **Vembanad Lake**, where the **Kumarakom Bird Sanctuary** spreads across a cluster of islands.

Kottayam's churches

The presence of two thirteenth-century **churches** on a hill 5km northwest of the centre (accessible by auto-rickshaw) attests to the area's deeply rooted Christian heritage. Two eighth-century Nestorian stone crosses with Palavi and Syriac inscriptions, on either side of the elaborately decorated altar of the **Valliapalli** ("big") church, are among the earliest solid traces of Christianity in India. The visitors' book contains entries from as far back as the 1890s, including one each from the Ethiopian king, Haile Selassie, and a British viceroy. The apse of the nearby **Cheriapalli** ("small") church is covered with lively paintings, thought to have been executed by a Portuguese artist in the sixteenth century. If the doors are locked, ask for the key at the church office (9am–1pm & 2–5pm).

Kumarakom

A twenty-minute bus ride west of Kottayam brings you to the shores of **Vembanad Lake**, where the **Kumarakom Bird Sanctuary** forms the focus of a line of ultra-luxurious resorts on the water's edge. A **backwaters cruise** hereabouts is a much better bet for peace and quiet than in Alappuzha or Kollam, although you will have to pay a little more if you want to arrange things from here: your hotel or homestay will be able to help.

Kumarakom Bird Sanctuary

Daily dawn–dusk · ₹150 (₹50); guide ₹300

The small **Kumarakom Bird Sanctuary** in the wetlands is a good place to spot domestic and migratory birds such as egrets, osprey, flycatchers and racket-tail drongos, as well as glimpses of otters and turtles in the water. There's a paved walkway for a lot of the route, but it does get tricky in parts. The best time to visit is between November and May before the sun rises; the one and only official guide can't be booked in advance and is snapped up by 6.30am.

Bay Island Driftwood Museum

Outskirts of Kumarakom village · Tues–Sat 10am–5pm, Sun 11.30am–5pm · ₹50 · ⓦ bayislandmuseum.com

Birds, or representations of them, feature prominently in the area's most bizarre visitor attraction, the **Bay Island Driftwood Museum**, just off the main road, in which lumps of driftwood sculpted by the sea are displayed in an idiosyncratic gallery.

Ettumanur

12km north of Kottayam · Admission is free for foreigners, but you'll need to buy a camera ticket (₹20, video ₹50) from the counter on the left of the main gateway

Another possible day-trip from Kottayam is the magnificent Mahadeva (Shiva) temple at **ETTUMANUR**, on the road to Ernakulam, whose entrance porch holds some of Kerala's most celebrated medieval **wall paintings**. The most spectacular depicts Nataraja (Shiva) executing a cosmic *tandava* dance, trampling evil in the form of a demon underfoot.

ARRIVAL AND INFORMATION

By train Kottayam railway station, 2km north of the centre, sees a constant flow of traffic between Thiruvananthapuram (3hr 30min) and points north, including Ernakulam/Kochi (1hr 30min). There's a prepaid auto-rickshaw stand outside the main entrance.

By bus Kottayam's KSRTC bus stand, 500m south of the centre on TB Rd (not to be confused with the private stand for local buses on MC Rd), is an important stop on routes to and from major towns in south India.

Destinations Ernakulam/Kochi (hourly; 1hr 45min); Kollam/Quilon (daily; 2hr 45min); Kumily/Periyar (daily;

KOTTAYAM AND AROUND

3hr); Madurai (2 daily; 7hr); Thiruvananthapuram (hourly; 4hr).

By ferry The public ferry leaves for Alappuzha (2hr 30min) at 7am, 9am, 11am, 1.30pm and 3.30pm.

Tourist information DTPC maintains a tiny tourist office at the jetty (daily 10am–6pm; ☎ 0481 256 0479).

Services The best place to change money is the Canara Bank on KK Rd, which also has one of several ATMs around the main square. Internet facilities are available at Intimacy (₹30/hr), also on KK Rd, just north of the KSRTC bus stand.

ACCOMMODATION

Akkara Mariathuruthu ☎ 0481 251 6951, ⓦ akkara.in. Just a 15min drive out of town, this welcoming homestay occupies an ancestral Syrian-Christian homestead sitting proudly on the riverbank – an idyllic, typically Keralan building, with traditional gabled architecture and interiors. In 2016 they opened an Ayurvedic centre on site and packages are available. Access is by road or dugout canoe. A/c ₹500 extra. **₹2800**

Arcadia TB Rd ☎ 0481 256 9999, ⓦ arcadiahotels.net. The town's top hotel, occupying its tallest building – a towering, white, angular monster block just south of the centre. Its rooms look much nicer from the inside, however, and are very good value (especially the "standard doubles"); there's also a fantastic rooftop pool on the fourteenth floor, as well as a restaurant (*Déja Vu*) and bar (*Ice Lounge*). **₹2500**

Backwater Breeze Cheepumkal, 5km north of Kumarakom, near the bird sanctuary ☎ 99954 99320, ⓦ backwaterbreeze.com. Ajish and his family live

downstairs, with the four large guest rooms upstairs sharing a veranda overlooking the canal towards Vembanad Lake. Breakfast is included and there's a restaurant next door where you can order dinner. A/c ₹500 extra. **₹2500**

★ **GK's Riverview** Thekkakarayil, Kottaparambil, near Pulikkuttssery, 4km by water from Kumarakom ☎ 94471 97527. Award-winning rustic homestay, buried deep in the watery wilds between Kottayam and Kumarakom. The accommodation comprises four comfortable a/c guest rooms in a separate block behind a family home, overlooking paddy fields. Charming hosts George and Dai are mines of information about the area; they'll pick you up from Kottayam if you phone ahead. Half board **₹3000**

Homestead KK Rd ☎ 0481 256 0467. This long-standing hotel is the best mid-priced option, though the beds in the economy rooms are rock hard and it's well worth shelling out an additional ₹200 for a "deluxe" with more space, better furniture and thicker mattresses. **₹1250**

EATING

Anand KK Rd. For a delicious, pure-veg thali or Udupi snack, you won't do better than this place on the ground floor of the *New Anand Lodge*, just off the northeast side of the main square. Of the two rooms the a/c family hall is more relaxing (though both are a little rough around the edges) and meals only cost ₹10 more. A range of rice meals for under ₹100, and scrumptious masala dosas for ₹45.

Daily 6.30am–9pm.

Meenachil Homestead Hotel KK Rd. Quality non-veg Keralan food such as *kozhi* (chicken) *varutha* curry (₹140) and Chinese duck (₹120) is served on the a/c floor; the cheaper "Thali" section downstairs opens earlier for breakfast, as well as serving set Keralan "meals" for ₹105 (veg) and ₹140 (fish) at lunchtime. Daily 8am–9.30pm.

Periyar and around

One of the largest national parks in India, the **Periyar Wildlife Sanctuary** (also known as the Periyar Tiger Reserve) occupies 925 square kilometres of the Cardamom Hills region of the Western Ghats. The majority of its visitors come in the hope of seeing **wild elephants** – or even a rare glimpse of a **tiger** – grazing the shores of the reservoir at the heart of the reserve. Daily safari boats ferry day-trippers around this sprawling, labyrinthine lake, where sightings are most likely at the height of the dry season in April. However, for the rest of the year, wildlife is less abundant than you might expect given Periyar's overwhelming popularity.

21

Just a few hours by road from the Keralan coastal cities and Madurai in Tamil Nadu, Periyar ranks among India's busiest reserves, attracting thousands of visitors over holiday periods. The park's ageing infrastructure, however, has struggled to cope with the recent upsurge in numbers. Just how overburdened facilities had become was horribly revealed in September 2009 when an excursion boat capsized on the lake, killing 45 tourists. Since that **Thekkady disaster**, strict restrictions have been imposed, but the lake safari experience hasn't improved; most foreign visitors leave disappointed, not merely with the park, but also its heavily commercialized surroundings and apparent paucity of wildlife.

That said, if you're prepared to **trek** into the forest, Periyar can still be worth a stay. Elephant, sambar, Malabar giant squirrel, gaur, stripe-necked mongoose and wild boar are still commonly spotted in areas deeper into the park, where birdlife is also prolific. Another selling point is Periyar's much vaunted **ecotourism** initiative. Instead of earning their livelihoods through poaching and illegal sandalwood extraction, local Manna people are these days employed by the Forest Department to protect vulnerable parts of the sanctuary. Schemes such as "Border Hiking", "Tiger Trail" and "Jungle Scout" tours, in which visitors accompany tribal wardens on their duties, serve to promote community welfare and generate income for conservation work.

In addition, the area **around Periyar** holds plenty of engaging day-trip destinations, such as **spice plantations**, as well as lots of scope for **trekking** in the surrounding hills and forest. It's also a lot cooler up here than down on the more humid coast, and many foreign visitors are glad of the break from the heat.

Kumily

As beds inside the wildlife sanctuary are in short supply, most visitors to Periyar stay in nearby **KUMILY**, a typical High Range town, centred on a hectic roadside market, 1km or so north of the main park entrance (known as **Thekkady**). Hotels and Kashmiri handicrafts emporia have spread south from the bazaar to within a stone's throw of the park, and tourism now rivals the spice trade as the area's main source of income. That said, you'll still see plenty of little shops selling local herbs, essential oils and cooking spices, while in the busy **cardamom sorting yard** behind the *Spice Village* resort, rows of Manna women sift through heaps of fragrant green pods using heart-shaped baskets.

Periyar Wildlife Sanctuary

Daily 6am–6pm • ₹450 (₹33) • ⓦ periyartigerreserve.org

Centred on a vast artificial **lake** created by the British in 1895 to supply water to the drier parts of neighbouring Tamil Nadu, the **Periyar Wildlife Sanctuary** lies at altitudes of between 900m and 1800m, and is correspondingly cool: temperatures range from 15°C to 30°C. The royal family of Travancore, anxious to preserve favourite hunting grounds from the encroachment of tea plantations, declared it a forest reserve, and built the Edapalayam Lake Palace to accommodate their guests in 1899.

Seventy percent of the protected area, which is divided into core, buffer and tourist zones, is covered with evergreen and semi-evergreen forest. The **tourist zone** – logically enough, the part accessible to casual visitors – surrounds the lake, and consists mostly of semi-evergreen and deciduous woodland interspersed with grassland, both on hilltops and in the valleys. Although excursions on the lake (either by diesel-powered launch or paddle-powered bamboo raft) are the standard ways to experience the park, you can get much more out of a visit by **walking** with a local guide in a small group away from the crowd. However, avoid the period immediately after the monsoons, when **leeches** make hiking virtually impossible. The **best time to visit** is between December and April, when the dry weather draws animals from the forest to drink at the lakeside.

Bamboo rafting trips

By far the best option for wildlife viewing from the lake is to sign up for one of the
Forest Department's excellent **bamboo rafting trips**, which start with a short hike from
the boat jetty at 8am, with the half-day trip returning at 2pm and the full-day option
at 5pm. The rafts carry four or five people and, because they're paddled rather than
motor-driven, can approach the lakeshore in silence, allowing you to get closer to the
grazing animals and birds. Tickets cost ₹2000 per person for a full day and may be
booked in advance from the ecotourism centre on Ambadi Junction (see below). Note
that during busy periods places sell out quickly, so reserve as far ahead as possible.

Boat tours

Although **boat tours** are considerably less expensive than the bamboo rafting trips, they
can come as a disappointment. It's unusual to see many animals – engine noise and
the presence of dozens of other people make sure of that. To maximize your chances of
sighting elephants, wild boar or sambar grazing by the water's edge, take the 7.30am
service (for which you'll need to wear warm clothing in winter).

Trips are run by the **Forest Department** and **KTDC** and depart at the same times
(7.30am, 9.30am, 11.15am, 1.45pm & 3.30pm; ₹250). Since the 2009 Thekkady
disaster, however (see page 1086), only twenty people are permitted to travel on the
upper decks and tickets sell out very fast; you'll need to be at the lakeside at least two
hours before the scheduled departure time (or 1hr 30min for the 7.30am boat) or book

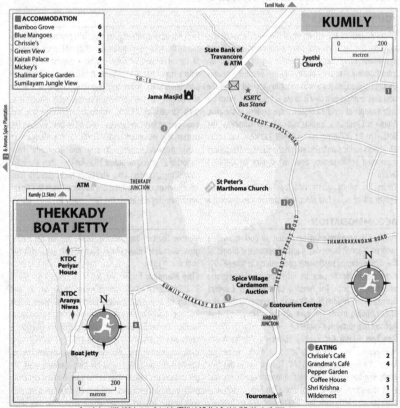

ACCOMMODATION	
Bamboo Grove	6
Blue Mangoes	4
Chrissie's	3
Green View	5
Kairali Palace	4
Mickey's	4
Shalimar Spice Garden	2
Sumilayam Jungle View	1

KUMILY

Tamil Nadu

State Bank of
Travancore
& ATM

Jyothi
Church

SH-19

Jama Masjid

KSRTC
Bus Stand

THEKKADY BYPASS ROAD

& Aroma Spice Plantation

ATM

THEKKADY
JUNCTION

Kumily (2.5km)

**THEKKADY
BOAT JETTY**

St Peter's
Marthoma Church

THAMARAKANDAM ROAD

KTDC
Periyar
House

KTDC
Aranya
Niwas

KUMILY THEKKADY ROAD

Spice Village
Cardamom
Auction

Ecotourism Centre

AMBADI
JUNCTION

Boat jetty

Touromark

● EATING	
Chrissie's Café	2
Grandma's Café	4
Pepper Garden Coffee House	3
Shri Krishna	1
Wildernest	5

Forest check post (400m) & Park entrance, Periyar Lake, KTDC Hotels & Thekkady Boat Jetty (2.5km) (see inset)

21

online in advance (⊚periyarfoundation.online). Sales counters are just above the main **visitor centre** (daily 6am–6pm; ☎04869 224571), next to the boat jetty; the Forest Department will issue two seats per person. You'll need to fill in an indemnity form, and wear a life-jacket at all times.

Walks and treks

Although you can – leeches permitting – trek freely around the fringes of Periyar, access to the sanctuary itself on foot is strictly controlled by the Forest Department. Their community-based ecotourism programme offers a variety of structured **walking tours**, ranging from short rambles to three-day expeditions, all guided by local Manna tribal wardens. Tickets should be booked in advance from the ecotourism centre on Ambadi Junction (see below), where you can also pick up information on the trips.

ARRIVAL AND INFORMATION   PERIYAR AND AROUND

By bus Buses from Kottayam (daily; 3hr). Auto-rickshaws will run you from here to the visitor centre inside the park for around ₹60–70, stopping at the park entrance at Thekkady where you can pay the reserve fee.

Tourist information To book any of Periyar's popular eco tours (see below), you'll have to walk down the Thekkady Rd to the ecotourism centre on Ambadi Junction (daily 6.30am–9pm, last tickets sold at 7.30pm; ☎85476 03066)

– or better still, book in advance on ⊚periyarfoundation. online.

Services Both the State Bank of Travancore (which has an ATM), near the bus stand, and the Thekkady Bankers in the main bazaar can change currency and travellers' cheques. Internet facilities are available around Thekkady Junction for about ₹40/hr.

TOURS AND TREKS

Tours As well as the attraction of the wildlife sanctuary, tours to tea factories and spice plantations are offered by almost every hotel and tourist agency in Kumily. Unfortunately, many places have become heavily commercialized, so it's worth shopping around; often the best way to organize a tour is to ask at your hotel. There are only a couple of certified organic spice gardens in the area, Aroma at Chelimada, a short walk west of Kumily on the Kottayam Rd (₹250/person; ☎04869 222805), and Manu Abraham's idyllic plantation out on the Kumily–Attapallum main road (₹300/person; book in advance on ☎94464 02276).

Treks The windy, grassy ridgetops and forests around Periyar afford many fine treks, with superb views over the

High Range guaranteed. One especially rewarding half-day trip is the hike up Kurusamalai (3hr), the peak towering to the northwest of Kumily, whose summit is crowned with a Holy Cross. As the summit falls within the national park boundaries, you're only permitted to hike to it under the auspices of the ecotourism centre, who market it as their "Cloud Walk" (₹300). Although hilly, this area is also good cycling territory; you can rent bikes from stalls in the market, and Touromark (☎99477 66076, ⊚exploreperiyar. com), midway between Kumily and Thekkady, have imported 21-speed mountain bikes for rent. They also offer guided trips, ranging from 4hr/15km hacks through local spice gardens, coffee plantations and woodlands to a three-night/four-day ride across the Cardamom Hills to Munnar.

ACCOMMODATION

Kumily has **accommodation** to suit all pockets, with a number of small homestay guesthouses on the fringes of the village offering particularly good value; the three KTDC-run hotels inside the park are either ludicrously expensive or shabby, or both. The forest department has a decent campsite, just beyond Vallakkadavu checkpoint; they also offer camping inside the park on their "Tiger Trail" trek (contact the ecotourism centre).

Bamboo Grove Off Kumily Thekkady Rd; book via the ecotourism centre ☎04869 224571, ⊚periyar foundation.online; map p.1087. Though not in the park itself, *Bamboo Grove* is run by the forest department and aims to support local communities. The fifteen individual cottages are a little dark, but they're clean and set in lovely

gardens. The two-day package (₹4000 per day per hut) is great value as it includes food, a jungle trek, tribal visit and boat tour. **₹1500**

Blue Mangoes Bypass Rd ☎04869 224603 or 97449 95253; map p.1087. Simple rooms (with sitouts and balconies) in a clean modern block, plus a larger family "cottage". Rock-bottom rates, but good bedding and a quiet location. Owner Bobby speaks excellent English. **₹1500**

Chrissie's Bypass Rd ☎0486 922 4155 or 94476 01304, ⊚chrissies.in; map p.1087. Smart four-storey hotel below the bazaar, run by Adel and his long-standing staff. It's pricier than most homestays in the area, but you get more privacy and better views, and homely interiors decorated with unique artwork. There's also a yoga *shala* and small

THE AYAPPA CULT

Throughout December and January, Kerala is packed with huge crowds of men wearing black *dhotis*; you'll see them milling about railway stations, driving in overcrowded and gaily decorated jeeps and cooking a quick meal on the roadside by their tour bus. They are pilgrims on their way to the Sri Ayappa forest temple (also known as Hariharaputra or Shasta) at **Sabarimala**, in the western section of Periyar, around 200km from both Thiruvananthapuram and Kochi. The **Ayappa devotees** can seem disconcertingly ebullient, chanting "*Swamiyee Sharanam Ayappan*" ("Give us protection, god Ayappa") in a lusty call-and-response style reminiscent of English football fans.

Ayappa – the offspring of a union between Shiva and Mohini, Vishnu's beautiful female form – is primarily a Keralan deity, but his appeal has spread phenomenally in the last thirty years across south India, to the extent that this is said to be **the largest pilgrimage in the world**, with as many as 40 to 50 million devotees each year. Pilgrims are required to remain celibate, abstain from intoxicants, and keep to a strict vegetarian diet for 41 days before setting out on the four-day walk through the forest from the village of **Erumeli** (61km, as the crow flies, northwest) to the shrine at Sabarimala. Less-keen devotees take the bus to the village of Pampa, and join the 5km queue. When they arrive at the modern temple complex, pilgrims who have performed the necessary penances may ascend the famous eighteen **gold steps** to the inner shrine. There they worship the deity, throwing donations down a chute that opens onto a subterranean conveyor belt, where the money is counted and bagged.

The pilgrimage reaches a climax during the festival of Makaravilakku or **Makar Sankranti**, when massive crowds congregate at Sabarimala. On January 14, 1999, 51 devotees were buried alive when part of a hill crumbled under the crush of a stampede. The pilgrims had gathered at dusk to catch a glimpse of the final sunset of **makara jyoti** ("celestial light") on the distant hill of Ponnambalamedu.

Although males of any age and even of any religion can take part in the pilgrimage, **females** between the ages of 9 and 50 are barred.

pool on the rooftop, and a popular little café-restaurant on the ground floor (see below). **₹3100**

Green View Bypass Rd 📞 0486 922 4617 or 94474 32008, 🌐 sureshgreenview.com; map p.1087. One of Kumily's most popular homestays, just off the Thekkady Rd. The seventeen rooms range from basic with bucket hot water to large with solar-heated showers and balconies looking across the valley to Kurusamalai Mountain (₹2000); the rooftop where you can do yoga shares the same view. A lovely rear garden attracts lots of wild birds. **₹1500**

Kairali Palace Bypass Rd 📞 98951 87789, 📧 nithee shmeera@gmail.com; map p.1087. Extremely attractive homestay in a fusion building that blends traditional and modern styles, with gabled roofs and wooden railings wrapped around the airy first-floor terrace. It has just two rooms, both well-furnished for the price. **₹1000**

Mickey's Bypass Rd 📞 04869 223196 or 94472 84160; map p.1087. One of the oldest guesthouses in Kumily, whose smiling owner, Sujata, offers a range of rooms and cottages, all with balconies or sitouts. **₹950**

Shalimar Spice Garden Murikaddy, 6km from Kumily 📞 04869 222132, 🌐 shalimarkerala.net; map p.1087. Teak huts in traditional Keralan style with elephant-grass roofs, whitewashed walls, chic interiors and verandas looking straight onto forest, on the edge of an old cardamom and pepper estate. Facilities include a beautiful Ayurveda centre, an outdoor pool set amid the trees and an open-sided restaurant where you can fine dine at rough-hewn granite tables. **₹17,300**

★ **Sumilayam Jungle View** On the eastern edge of town 📞 04869 223582 or 94461 36407, 🌐 jungleview. webs.com; map p.1087. The best-value budget homestay in Kumily, a 10min plod (or short auto-rickshaw ride) from the bus stand – literally on the Tamil Nadu–Kerala border. The clean, bright guestrooms are comfort-ably furnished; those on the upper storey open onto a marble-floored veranda just metres from jungle. Free nocturnal wildlife-spotting walks in the gardens are offered by your welcoming host, Mr Ramachandran. **₹1000**

EATING

You're more likely to take **meals** at your guesthouse or hotel than eat out in Kumily, but for a change of scene the following places are the best options within walking distance of the bazaar.

Chrissie's Café Bypass Rd 📞 0486 922 4155, 🌐 chrissies. in. This relaxing expat-run café, on the ground floor of *Chrissie's* hotel, pulls in a steady stream of foreigners through-out the day and evening for its delicious pizzas

21

(₹175–250), made with Kodai mozzarella, and Middle Eastern options; check out the specials board. They also do healthy breakfasts with unlimited drinks (₹200), home-made cakes and proper coffee. Count on ₹400–500/head. Daily 8am–9pm.

Grandma's Café Bypass Rd ☎ 99953 17261; map p.1087. This arty café is adored by backpackers for its laidback vibe and tasty grub; try the *ularthiyathu* with mushrooms (₹160) or prawns (₹330). Service can be a little slow, but for distraction there's a projector for films and most nights a campfire is lit. Daily 7.30am–10.30pm.

Pepper Garden Coffee House Thamarkandam Rd ☎ 99614 39789; map p.1087. In a garden filled with cardamom bushes behind a prettily painted blue-and-green house, a former park guide and his wife whip up tempting travellers' breakfasts (date and raisin pancakes, porridge with jungle honey, fresh coffee and Nilgiri tea), in addition to home-cooked lunches of veg fried rice, curry and dhal, using mostly local organic produce. Mains ₹65–150. Daily 8.30am–9.30pm.

Shri Krishna Bypass Rd; map p.1087. Run by a Bihari family, this pure-veg restaurant serves authentic north Indian dishes, including cheap and filling Gujarati and Marwari thalis (₹70–110), served on the usual tin trays or leaves. Daily 8am–9pm.

Wildernest Thekkady Rd ☎ 0486 922 4030, ⓦ wildernest-kerala.com; map p.1087. Filling Continental buffet breakfasts (fruit, juices, cereals, eggs, toast, peanut butter, home-made jams and freshly ground coffee; ₹250) served in the ground-floor café of a stylish small hotel (rooms ₹4500; those on the first floor with terraces are best). They also serve afternoon tea and cakes (including a delicious, very British, warm plum cake). Daily 8am–7pm.

Munnar and around

MUNNAR, 130km east of Kochi and 110km north (4hr 30min by bus) of the Periyar Wildlife Sanctuary, is the centre of Kerala's principal tea-growing region. A scruffy agglomeration of corrugated-iron-roofed cottages and tea factories, its centre on the valley floor fails to live up to its tourist-office billing as "hill station", but there's plenty to enthuse about in the surrounding mountains, whose lower slopes are carpeted with lush tea gardens and dotted with quaint old colonial bungalows. Above them, the grassy ridges and crags of the High Range offer superlative **trekking** routes, many of which can be tackled in day-trips from the town – though note that peninsular India's highest peak, **Ana Mudi** (2695m), is closed to visitors for the time being.

It's easy to see why the pioneering Scottish planters who developed this hidden valley in the 1870s and 1880s felt so at home here. At an altitude of around 1600m, Munnar enjoys a refreshing **climate**, with crisp mornings and sunny blue skies in the winter – though as with all of Kerala, torrential rains descend during the monsoons. Munnar's greenery and cool air draw streams of well-heeled honeymooners and weekenders from south India's cities. However, increasing numbers of foreign visitors are stopping for a few days too, enticed by the superbly scenic bus ride from Periyar, which takes you across the high ridges and lush tropical forests of the Cardamom Hills, or for the equally spectacular climb across the Ghats from Madurai.

Clustered around the confluence of three mountain streams, Munnar town is a typical hill bazaar of haphazard buildings and congested market streets; the daily vegetable **market** in the main bazaar is a good place for a wander (closed Wed).

Kanan Devan Hills Tea Museum

Nallathany Rd • Tues–Sun 10am–4pm • ₹95, camera ₹25 • ⓦ kdhptea.com/TeaMuseum.html

Although it doesn't physically demonstrate how tea is made, the **Kanan Devan Hills Tea Museum**, 2km northwest of the centre, is worth a visit for its collection of antique machinery and exhibition of photos of the area's tea industry, ranging from 1880s pioneers to the modern Tata tea conglomerate. The highlight of the visit is a short audio-visual presentation outlining how tea was introduced to the region and how it is processed today, rounded off with a tasting session; and there's a shop selling various KDH products.

HIKING AROUND MUNNAR

Although south India's highest peak, Ana Mudi, is off-limits due to the Nilgiri tahr conservation programme (see page 1092), several of the other summits towering above Munnar can be reached on day-treks. The hiking scene is surprisingly undeveloped and it makes sense to use the services of a guide, particularly for **Meesapulimalai Peak** (2640m), which can be accessed from Silent Valley or Kolukkumalai estates and could easily be incorporated into a multiday excursion. Always check whether transport to and from the trailhead is included.

OPERATORS

Greenview Pleasure Holidays ⓦ munnartrekking. com. The owner of the *Green View* guesthouse (see page 1092) and his enthusiastic young team lead groups of two or more on nearby routes; rates range from ₹650/ person for soft treks up to ₹1250 for longer, more challenging outings.

Kestrel Adventures ⓣ 94470 31040, ⓦ kestrel adventures.com. This professionally run local adventure company arranges treks (₹4200 for 2–3hr for two people at Chinnar, including transport), sightseeing by jeep (₹2000 for a full day) and mountain biking (₹6100 for two people for a full day off-road – plus tax and jeep rental).

KFDC The Kerala Forest Development Corporation (see page 1092) arranges 24hr treks (₹9000), including basic overnight accommodation in Silent Valley and transfers in packed jeeps.

Kolukkumalai ⓦ kolukkumalai.in. Your best bet for multiday bespoke trips on Meeshapulimalai and the surrounding grasslands. English-speaking guides and delicious food – plus you can opt to stay in a mountain hut nestled in the highest tea estate in the world. Prices start at ₹3000 for a day-trek (plus transport and accommodation).

Around Munnar

Buses wind their way up to the aptly named **Top Station**, a hamlet famed for its views and meadows of **Neelakurunji plants**, and to the more distant nature sanctuaries of Eravikulam and Chinnar, where you can spot Nilgiri tahr, elephants and many other wild animals. To reach the most remote attractions, however, you might want to hire a taxi for the day.

Top Station

34km northeast of Munnar • 10 daily buses (from 5.30am; 1hr 30min); jeep taxis do the return trip for ₹1200

One of the most popular **excursions** from Munnar is the long climb through some of the Subcontinent's highest tea estates to **TOP STATION**, a tiny hamlet on the Kerala–Tamil Nadu border which, at 1600m, is the highest point on the interstate road. The settlement takes its name from the old aerial **ropeway** that used to connect it with the valley floor, the ruins of which can still be seen in places.

Eravikulam National Park

13km northeast of Munnar • Daily 8am–4.30pm; closed for calving season Feb through March, check ahead • ₹400 (₹120), tickets can be purchased in advance (additional ₹50) online to avoid the queues • ⓦ eravikulam.org

Encompassing 100 square kilometres of moist evergreen forest and grassy hilltops in the Western Ghats, **Eravikulam National Park** is the last stronghold of one of the world's rarest mountain goats, the **Nilgiri tahr**. Its innate friendliness made the tahr pathetically easy prey during the hunting frenzy of the colonial era. Today, however, numbers are healthy, and the animals have regained their tameness, largely thanks to the efforts of the American biologist Clifford Rice, who studied them here in the early 1980s. Unable to get close enough to observe the creatures properly, Rice followed the advice of locals and attracted them using salt, and soon entire herds were congregating around his camp. The tahrs' salt addiction also explains why so many hang around the park gates at **Vaguvarai**, where visitors – despite advice from rangers – slip them salty snacks.

You're almost guaranteed sightings of tahr from the minute you enter the park gates, reached by shuttle bus (₹20). From there, you can walk a further 1500m up a winding single-track road before the rangers turn you around, but expect to do so in the company of hundreds of other tourists on weekends – a rather hollow experience.

21

THE NEELAKURUNJI PLANT

Apart from the marvellous views over the Tamil plains, the hills around Munnar are renowned for the very rare **Neelakurunji plant** (*Strobilanthes*), which flowers only once every twelve years. Huge crowds climb up to Top Station and other viewpoints to admire the cascades of violet blossom spilling down the slopes (the next flowering is due in Sept/Oct 2030). Views are best before the mist builds at 9am.

Chinnar Wildlife Sanctuary

58km north of Munnar • Daily 6am–7pm • ₹100 (₹10) • ⓦ chinnar.org • Any bus running between Munnar and Udumalpet will stop at the sanctuary

Although it borders Eravikulam, the **Chinnar Wildlife Sanctuary** is far less visited, not least because its entrance lies a two-hour drive from Munnar along winding mountain roads. The reserve, in the rain shadow of the High Range and thus much drier than its neighbour, is one of the best spots in the state for birdwatching, with 225 species recorded to date. But the real star attractions are the resident **grizzled giant squirrels**, who scamper in healthy numbers around the thorny scrub here, and the near-mythical "**white bison of Manjampatti**", thought to be an albino Indian gaur.

Members of local tribal communities (who won't be fluent in English) act as guides for popular day-treks that might take in prehistoric rock art, dolmen sites or a waterfall – all of which can be arranged on spec at a counter next to the Chinnar Forest Check Post. For multiday treks you can camp or book a bed in the thirty-bed dormitory, but this needs to be arranged in advance at the Forest Information Centre in Munnar or with Kestrel Adventures (see page 1091).

ARRIVAL AND INFORMATION
MUNNAR

By bus State-run and private buses pull into the town bus stand in the modern main bazaar, near the river confluence and Tata headquarters; state buses continue through town, terminating nearly 3km south. For most hotels you should ask to be dropped off at Old Munnar, 2km south of the centre, near the ineffectual DTPC tourist office (daily 8.30am–7pm; ⓣ 04865 231516).
Destinations Ernakulam/Kochi (daily; 3hr); Kottayam (3 daily; 5hr).

KFDC office Based in the Rose Gardens, 2km east on Mattupetty Rd (ⓣ 0486 523 0332, ⓦ munnar. kfdcecotourism.com), KFDC can arrange a whistlestop day-tour around Munnar (₹1000/person) as well as multiday treks (see page 1091).
Forest Information Centre Near Mount Carmel Church in the centre of Munnar town (ⓣ 0486 523 1587). Drop in to organize trips to Chinnar Wildlife Sanctuary.

ACCOMMODATION

Munnar's **accommodation** costs significantly more than elsewhere in the High Range region, reflecting the high demand for beds from middle-class tourists from the big cities. Rooms at the low end of the scale are in particularly short supply; the few that exist are blighted by racket from the bus stand and bazaar. There are some options outside town that would suit travellers with their own transport.
Anaerangal Camp at Suryanelli 25km east of Munnar on the Periyar road ⓣ 8086 694 102, ⓦ campanaerangal. com. Half a dozen spacious fixed tents, fitted with beds and bathrooms, facing a magnificent panorama of mountain peaks, lake and forest. Keralan food, prepared at kitchens on site, is included in the rate, along with trekking to the lake and nearby peak, plantation visits and an evening camp fire. An inspiring location, but not the quality outfit it once was. ₹4000
Green Valley Vista Chekuthan Mukku, Chithirapuram, 8km south of Munnar ⓣ 0486 5263 261 or 94474 32008,

ⓦ greenvalleyvista.com. On the main road (ask the bus to drop you at the stop 20m away), so it's worth paying a bit extra for the larger quieter rooms at the back, which have the added advantage of gorgeous valley views. Sister to the *Green View* in Kumily, it offers the same good-value, clean rooms but with a bit less character. ₹2750
Green View Sri Parvati Amman Kovil St, near the KSRTC bus stand ⓣ 0486 523 0189 or 94478 25447 (Deepak), ⓦ greenviewmunnar.com. Clean and friendly budget guesthouse on the valley floor, down a side road just off the main drag, with rooms of various sizes – the best of them, no. 402, is a tiny double with big windows and hill views. Pitched squarely at foreign backpackers, it's run by an enthusiastic, competent young crew who do a sideline in guided day-treks (see page 1091). They have some quieter properties outside town; enquire about *River Green Villa* and *Greenwoods Cottage*. ₹1600

★ **High Range Club** Kanan Devan Hills Rd ☎ 0486 523 0253, ⓦ highrangeclubmunnar.com. This old Raj-era club, founded by British planters in 1909, must have been a nightmare of suffocating imperialism in its heyday. Now the faded colonial ambience, with lounges filled with 1940s furniture and moth-eaten hunting trophies, feels undeniably quaint (though there *is* still a dress code on Sat evenings). The club's guest wing holds three kinds of rooms and cottages (₹3500–4500), varying in size and comfort. Breakfast, lunch and dinner available for an extra ₹745. ₹4000

JJ Cottage Sri Parvati Amman Kovil St, near the KSRTC bus stand ☎ 94968 22163. Next door to *Green View*, and very much in the same mould, though it's been open longer, charges more and tends to get booked up earlier. Like its neighbour, the nicest of its clean, variously sized rooms is the one at the top (front side), which has wood-panelled walls and fine views. A warm family welcome is guaranteed. ₹800

★ **Rosegardens** Karadipara, near the viewpoint on NH-49, 10km southwest of Munnar ☎ 0486 4278 243 or 94473 78524, ⓦ rosegardensmunnar.com. This gem of a homestay has five rooms, all with terraces. It's the two-acre setting that steals the show and hosts Tomy and Rajee are justly proud of their beautiful gardens. There's no TV here – instead you have meals with the family and plenty of peace and quiet. Trekking and cookery courses can be arranged, and there's decent driver accommodation. ₹5600

Zina Cottages Kad ☎ 0486 523 0349 or 94471 90954, ⓦ zina-cottage.business.site. British-era stone bungalow, nestled amid tea gardens high on the hillside above Munnar. The basic rooms can be chilly, but the flower-filled front terrace has magnificent views across the town to Ana Mudi, and the young host will fill you in on local walks over flasks of hot tea in his sitting room. Come here less for creature comforts than for atmosphere, of which it has plenty. ₹900

EATING

The **thattukada** (hot food stall market) just south of the main bazaar, opposite the taxi stand, gets into its stride around 7.30pm and runs through the night, serving delicious, piping-hot Keralan food – dosas, *parathas*, *iddiappam*, green-bean curry, egg masala – ladled onto tin plates and eaten on rough wood tables in the street.

Guru Bhavan Mattupetty Rd ☎ 94972 31184. This place, a 10min uphill walk from the bazaar, is packed out with locals enjoying veg and non-veg (mostly) south Indian dishes; veg "meals" are stupendous value at ₹60. Drop by in the morning for cheap and delicious breakfast staples like *idli* and dosas. Daily 7am–10pm.

Saravana Bhavan Munnar Market. The best pure-veg south Indian restaurant in town, serving the standard range of tasty Udupi dosas (₹30–50) and thali meals (₹70) – in addition to popular mini-*idli* plates and delicious buttermilk. Tucked away down a narrow side street, but there's a large sign on the roadside in the main bazaar, directly behind the Gandhi statue. Daily 8am–9pm.

Kochi (Cochin)

Spreading across islands and promontories between the Arabian Sea and the backwaters, **KOCHI** (long known as **Cochin**) is Kerala's prime tourist destination. Its main sections – modern **Ernakulam** and the old peninsular districts of **Mattancherry** and **Fort Cochin** to the west – are linked by bridges and a complex system of ferries. Although some visitors opt to stay in the more convenient Ernakulam, the overwhelming majority base themselves in Fort Cochin, where the city's complex history is reflected in an assortment of architectural styles. Spice markets, Chinese fishing nets, a synagogue, a Portuguese palace, India's first European church and seventeenth-century Dutch homes can all be found within an easy walk.

Brief history

Kochi sprang into being in 1341, when a flood created a safe natural port that swiftly replaced Muziris (now Kodungallur, 50km north) as the chief harbour on the Malabar Coast. The royal family moved here in 1405, after which the city grew rapidly, attracting Christian, Arab and Jewish settlers from the Middle East. The history of **European** involvement from the early 1500s onwards is dominated by the aggression of the Portuguese, Dutch and British, who successively competed to control the port and its lucrative spice trade. From 1812 until Independence in 1947 it was administered by a succession of *diwans*, or finance ministers. In the 1920s, the British expanded the port to accommodate modern ocean-going ships, and Willingdon Island, between Ernakulam and Fort Cochin, was created by extensive dredging.

21

Old Kochi: Fort Cochin and Mattancherry

Old Kochi, the thumb-shaped peninsula whose northern tip presides over the entrance to the city's harbour, formed the focus of European trading activities from the sixteenth century onwards. With high-rise development restricted to Ernakulam across the water, its twin districts of **Fort Cochin**, in the west, and **Mattancherry**, on the headland's eastern side, have preserved an extraordinary wealth of early colonial architecture, spanning the Portuguese, Dutch and British eras – a crop unparalleled in India. As you approach by ferry, the waterfront, with its sloping red-tiled roofs and ranks of peeling, pastel-coloured *godowns* (warehouses), offers a view that can have changed little in centuries.

Closer up, however, Old Kochi's historic patina has started to show some ugly cracks. The spice trade that fuelled the town's original rise is still very much in evidence. But over the past twenty years an extraordinary rise in visitor numbers has had a major impact. Thousands of tourists pour through daily in winter, and with no planning or preservation authority to take control, the resulting rash of new building threatens to destroy the very atmosphere people come here to experience. That said, tourism has also brought some benefits, inspiring renovation work to buildings that would otherwise have been left to rot.

Fort Cochin

Fort Cochin, the grid of old streets at the northwest tip of the peninsula, is where the Portuguese erected their first walled citadel, Fort Immanuel, which the Dutch East India Company later consolidated with a circle of well-fortified ramparts. Only a few fragments of the former battlements remain (the outline of the old walls is traced by the district's giant rain trees, some of which are more than two centuries old), but dozens of other evocative European-era monuments survive.

A good way to get to grips with Fort Cochin's many-layered history is to pick up the free **walking-tour maps** produced by Kerala Tourism. They lead you around some of the district's more significant landmarks, including the early eighteenth-century Dutch Cemetery, Vasco da Gama's supposed house and several traders' residences.

Walking around the old quarter you'll come across several small exhibition spaces and **galleries** – evidence of Fort Cochin's newfound status as one of India's contemporary art hubs. The scene takes centre stage between mid-December and March when the **Kochi-Muziris Biennale** (⊕kochimuzirisbiennale.org) draws artists and collectors from across the country with its mix of film, art, performance art and new media hosted by half a dozen different venues.

Chinese fishing nets

Daily 6.30–11am & 5–7pm

Probably the single most familiar photographic image of Kerala, the huge, elegant **Chinese fishing nets** lining the northern shore of Fort Cochin add grace to the waterfront view. Traders from the court of Kublai Khan are said to have introduced them to the Malabar region. Known in Malayalam as *cheena vala*, they can also be seen throughout the backwaters further south. The nets, which are suspended from poles and operated by levers and weights, require at least four men to control them. If you linger, the fishermen will beckon you over to help (for a small tip).

Church of St Francis and around

Parade Ground · Daily 8.30am–6.30pm · Free

South of the Chinese fishing nets on Church Road (the continuation of River Road) is the large, typically English **Parade Ground**. Overlooking it, the **Church of St Francis** was the first built by Europeans in India. Its exact age is not known, though the stone structure is thought to date back to the early sixteenth century. The facade, meanwhile, became the model for most Christian churches in India. Vasco da Gama was buried here in 1524, but his body was later removed to Portugal. Under the Dutch, the church was renovated and became Protestant in 1663, then Anglican with the advent of the British in 1795. Inside, the earliest of various tombstone inscriptions placed in the walls dates from 1562.

Mattancherry

Mattancherry, the old district of red-tiled riverfront wharves and houses occupying the northeastern tip of the headland, was once the colonial capital's main market area – the epicentre of the Malabar's spice trade, and home to its wealthiest Jewish and Jain merchants. Like Fort Cochin, its once grand buildings have lapsed into advanced states of disrepair, with most of their original owners working overseas. When Mattancherry's Jews emigrated en masse to Israel in the 1940s, their furniture and other un-portable heirlooms ended up in the **antique shops** for which the area is now renowned – though these days genuine pieces are few and far between.

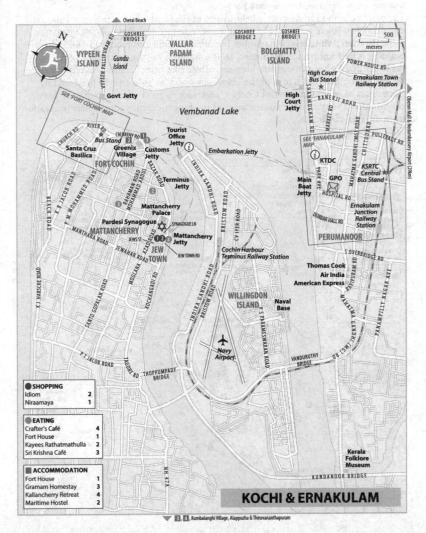

KOCHI & ERNAKULAM

● **SHOPPING**
Idiom	2
Niraamaya	1

● **EATING**
Crafter's Café	4
Fort House	1
Kayees Rathatmathulla	2
Sri Krishna Café	3

■ **ACCOMMODATION**
Fort House	1
Gramam Homestay	3
Kallancherry Retreat	4
Maritime Hostel	2

3, **4**, Kumbalanghi Village, Alappuzha & Thiruvananthapuram

21

Mattancherry Palace

Jew Town Rd • Daily except Fri 10–5pm • ₹5

The sight at the top of most itineraries is **Mattancherry Palace**, on the roadside a short walk from the Mattancherry Jetty, 1km or so southeast of Fort Cochin. Known locally as the Dutch Palace, the two-storey building was actually erected by the Portuguese, as a gift to the raja of Cochin, Vira Keralavarma (1537–61) – though the Dutch did add to the complex. While its squat exterior is not particularly striking, the interior is captivating, with some of the finest examples of Kerala's underrated school of **mural** painting, along with Dutch maps of old Cochin, coronation robes belonging to past maharajas, royal palanquins, weapons and furniture.

Paradesi Synagogue

Synagogue Lane, Jew Town • Sun–Thurs 10am–noon & 3–5pm • ₹5

The neighbourhood immediately behind and to the south of Mattancherry Palace is known as **Jew Town**, home of a vestigial Jewish community whose place of worship is the **Paradesi (White Jew) Synagogue**. Founded in 1568 and rebuilt in 1664, the building is best known for its interior, an incongruous hotchpotch paved with hand-painted eighteenth-century blue-and-white tiles from Canton. An elaborately carved Ark houses four scrolls of the Torah, on which sit gold crowns presented by the maharajas of Travancore and Cochin, testifying to good relations with the Jewish community. The synagogue's oldest artefact is a fourth-century copperplate inscription from the raja of Cochin.

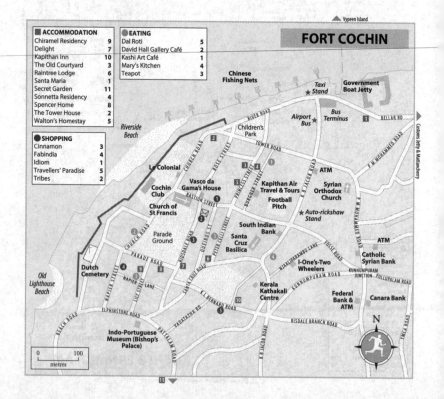

ACCOMMODATION		EATING	
Chiramel Residency	9	Dal Roti	5
Delight	7	David Hall Gallery Café	2
Kapithan Inn	10	Kashi Art Café	1
The Old Courtyard	3	Mary's Kitchen	4
Raintree Lodge	6	Teapot	3
Santa Maria	1		
Secret Garden	11		
Sonnetta Residency	4		
Spencer Home	8		
The Tower House	2		
Walton's Homestay	5		

SHOPPING	
Cinnamon	3
Fabindia	4
Idiom	1
Travellers' Paradise	5
Tribes	2

FORT COCHIN

21

KATHAKALI IN KOCHI

Kochi is the only city in Kerala where you are guaranteed the chance to see live **kathakali**, the state's unique form of ritualized theatre (see page 1062). Whether in its authentic setting, in temple festivals held in winter, or at the shorter tourist-oriented shows that take place year-round, these mesmerizing dance dramas – depicting the struggles of gods and demons – are an unmissable feature of Kochi's cultural life.

Four venues in the city currently hold daily shows, each preceded by an **introductory talk** at around 6.30pm. You can watch the dancers being made up if you arrive an hour or so beforehand; keen photographers should turn up well before the start to ensure a front-row seat. **Tickets** (usually around ₹250) can be bought at the door. Most visitors only attend one performance, but you'll gain a much better sense of what *kathakali* is all about if you take in at least a couple. The next step is an **all-night recital** at a temple festival.

Greenix Village Opposite Fort House, Fort Cochin ☎0484 221 7000, ⓦgreenix.in. You've a choice between a short *kathakali* recital (₹350) or longer "kaleidoscope" culture show (₹650) combining excerpts from *kathakali* plays with displays of *mohiniyattam* dance, *kalarippayat* martial art and, on Sun, *theyyem*, set against a combination of live and pre-recorded music. Performances aren't of the highest standard, but costumes and acts change in quick succession and the make-up is particularly stunning. Note that it costs ₹50 extra to take photos.

Kerala Folklore Museum Theyvara, near Kundanur Bridge, southeastern edge of Ernakulam ☎70347 77499, ⓦkeralafolkloremuseum.org. The most atmospheric venue – an a/c theatre decorated with wonderful Keralan murals and traditional wooden architecture – though it's a long trek across town if you're staying in Fort Cochin and sadly you have to book the entire theatre for an exclusive (and eye-wateringly expensive) show. Most visitors tour the museum downstairs and just take a peek at the theatre.

Kerala Kathakali Centre Bernard Master Lane, near Santa Cruz Basilica, just off KB Jacob Rd, Fort Cochin ☎0484 221 5827, ⓦkathakalicentre.com. Popular performances in a dedicated a/c theatre from a company of graduates from the renowned Kerala Kalamandalam academy. You usually get to see three characters, and the music is live. Shows (₹350) 6–7.30pm (make-up 5pm), plus classical music recitals at 8pm every night except Sat (₹300) and *kalarippayat* martial art daily at 4pm (₹300).

Ernakulam

With its fast-paced traffic, broad streets and glittering gold emporia, **ERNAKULAM** has more of a big-city feel than Thiruvananthapuram – despite the fact it's marginally smaller. Other than the contemporary art on display at the small **Durbar Hall Art Gallery** on Durbar Hall Road (daily 11am–7pm; free), and the remarkable **folklore museum** on the southern outskirts, there's little in the way of sights – if you spend any time here, it'll probably be to eat at one of the area's famous Keralan **restaurants**.

Running parallel to the seafront, roughly 500m inland, **Mahatma Gandhi (MG) Road** is its main thoroughfare, where you'll find some of the largest textile stores, jewellery shops and hotels.

Kerala Folklore Museum

Theyvara, near Kundanur Bridge • Daily 9.30am–6pm • ₹200 • ☎70347 77499, ⓦ keralafolkloremuseum.org • Auto-rickshaws charge around ₹200 for the trip out to the museum from the Main Boat Jetty in Ernakulam – ask for Riviera Junction, or Kundanur Bridge

Ernakulam's one outstanding visitor attraction is the **Kerala Folklore Museum**, on the distant southeast fringes of the city. Housed in a multi-storey laterite building encrusted with traditional wood- and tile-work, the collection of antiques includes dance-drama masks and costumes, ritual paraphernalia, musical instruments, pieces of temple architecture, 3000-year-old burial urns, cooking utensils, portraits and ancestral photographs – to name but a few of the categories amassed by founder and avid antiques collector, George Thaliyath.

Its crowning glory is an exquisitely decorated **theatre** on the top floor, decorated with swirling Keralan temple murals and dark wooden pillars. It's only open for exclusive, prearranged *kathakali* performances.

21

RECOMMENDED TRAINS FROM KOCHI/ERNAKULAM

The trains listed below are recommended as the fastest and/or most convenient services from Ernakulam. If you're heading to **Alappuzha** for the backwater trip to Kollam, take the bus, as the only trains that can get you there in time invariably arrive late.

Destination	Name	No.	Station	Departs	Arrives
Bengaluru (Bangalore)	*Kanyakumari–Bangalore Express*	#16525	ET	daily 6.05pm	7.25am+
Kozhikode (Calicut)	*Netravathi Express*	#16346	EJ	daily 2.05pm	6.40pm
Madgaon (Margao)	*Netravathi Express*	#16346	EJ	daily 2.05pm	4.35am+
Mumbai	*Mangala Ldweep*	#12617	EJ	daily 1.15pm	12.50pm+
Thiruvananthapuram	*Jan Shatabdi*	#12081	EJ	daily 5.25pm	9.35pm
Varkala	*Sabari Express*	#17230	ET	daily 1.20pm	5.13pm

EJ = Ernakulam Junction
ET = Ernakulam Town
+ = next day

ARRIVAL AND DEPARTURE

By plane Kochi's international airport (W cial.aero) – one of India's most modern and efficient – is at Nedumbassery, near Alwaye (aka Alua), 29km north of Ernakulam. A prepaid taxi into town costs around ₹800 and takes 45min or so, traffic permitting. Modern, comfortable a/c airbuses also cover the route more or less hourly, running to Fort Cochin (9 daily; 45min–1hr 30min; ₹100).

By train There are two main railway stations, Ernakulam Junction, near the centre, and Ernakulam Town, 2km further north. The Cochin Harbour Terminus, on Willingdon Island, serves the island's luxury hotels. Ernakulam Town lies on Kerala's main broad-gauge line and sees frequent services to and from Thiruvananthapuram via Kottayam, Kollam and Varkala. In the opposite direction, trains connect Ernakulam and Thrissur, and Chennai across the Ghats in Tamil Nadu. Since the opening of the Konkan Railway, a few express trains travel along the coast all the way to Goa and Mumbai. Although most long-distance express and mail trains depart from Ernakulam Junction, a couple of key services leave from Ernakulam Town. To confuse matters further, a few also start at Cochin Harbour station, so be sure to check the departure point when you book your ticket. The main reservation office, good for trains leaving all the stations, is at Ernakulam Junction.

GETTING AROUND

By ferry Kochi's dilapidated ferries provide a cheap and relaxing way to reach the various parts of the city. The most popular route for visitors is the one connecting Ernakulam's Main Boat Jetty and Fort Cochin/Mattancherry's Customs Jetty (5.50am–9.30pm; every 20–30min). Also leaving from Ernakulam are ferries to Bolghatty Island (6.30am–9pm; every 30min) and Vypeen Island (7am–9.30pm; every 30min). The latter has two routes – one direct, and another slower service via Willingdon Island. From Fort Cochin's Government Jetty (10min walk west of Customs Jetty),

KOCHI (COCHIN)

Destinations Alappuzha/Alleppey (15 daily; 1hr–1hr 30min); Bengaluru (3 daily; 11hr 20min–13hr 30min); Chennai (6 daily; 12–15hr); Goa (2 daily; 12hr 25min–15hr); Kozhikode/Calicut (9 daily; 3hr 20min–4hr 40min); Mumbai (3 daily; 20hr 45min–27hr); Varkala (hourly; 3–4hr).

By bus The KSRTC Central bus stand (☎0484 236 0531), beside the railway line east of MG Rd and north of Ernakulam Junction, is for state-run long-distance services. Reservations for services originating here can be made up to twenty days in advance. There are also two stands for pricier private services: the Kaloor Stand (rural destinations to the south and east) is across the bridge from Ernakulam Town railway station on the Alwaye Rd, while the High Court Stand (buses to Kumily, for Periyar Wildlife Reserve, and north to Thrissur, Guruvayur and Kodungallur) is opposite the High Court ferry jetty. The Fort Cochin bus terminus serves tourist buses, local services to Ernakulam and the airport bus.

Destinations Alappuzha/Alleppey (hourly; 1hr 50min); Coimbatore (10 daily; 4–5hr 20min); Kottayam (hourly; 2hr); Kozhikode/Calicut (hourly; 5hr 30min); Munnar (daily; 2hr 15min); Thiruvananthapuram (every 30min; 6hr); Thrissur (every 15min; 2hr 20min).

you can also hop on a flat-bottomed vehicle ferry across the harbour mouth to Vypeen Island (6.30am–9pm; every 10min). Tickets should be purchased prior to embarkation from the hatch (separate queues for ladies and gents).

By bus KSRTC is in the process of upgrading its ageing fleet with new, state-of-the-art, low-floored Volvo buses, coloured bright green or orange. The new vehicles – used on prime routes such as the run between Fort Cochin and the airport – are cleaner and more comfortable, but there remain plenty of the old rust buckets in circulation and they're invariably crammed to bursting point. Frequent services run throughout the day between Ernakulam and Fort Cochin, though the ferry is a lot more enjoyable. If you miss the last boat back at 9.30pm, don't wait around for a bus (departures are sporadic and horrendously packed at that time of night); jump in an auto-rickshaw instead (₹350).

By bike Bicycles can be rented from many hotels and guesthouses in Fort Cochin.

By motorbike I-One's-Two Wheelers, at 1/946-A Njaliparambu (the lane opposite the entrance to the Kerala Kathakali Centre, near the Basilica in Fort Cochin) has Enfields for rent, as well as a few automatic Honda Activas. You'll need to leave your passport as security. Contact Ivan Joseph (☎ 98471 55306, ⓦ rentabikecochin.com).

INFORMATION

Tourist information India Tourism's main office (Mon–Fri 9am–5.30pm, Sat 9am–noon; ☎ 0484 266 9125, ⓦ incredibleindia.org), providing reliable information and qualified guides for visitors, is inconveniently situated on Willingdon Island, between the *Vivanta by Taj Malabar Hotel* and Tourist Office Jetty; they also have a desk at the airport. KTDC's reception centre, on Shanmugham Rd, Ernakulam (daily 8am–6.30pm; ☎ 0484 235 3234, ⓦ ktdc.com), books rooms in their hotel chain and organizes sightseeing and backwater tours.

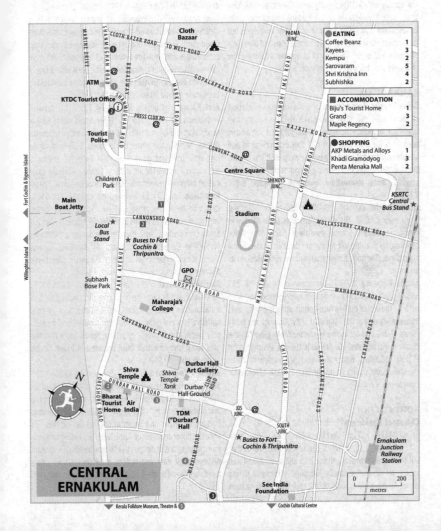

EATING

Coffee Beanz	1
Kayees	3
Kempu	2
Sarovaram	5
Shri Krishna Inn	4
Subhishka	2

ACCOMMODATION

Biju's Tourist Home	1
Grand	3
Maple Regency	2

SHOPPING

AKP Metals and Alloys	1
Khadi Gramodyog	3
Penta Menaka Mall	2

CENTRAL ERNAKULAM

0   200
metres

21

TOURS AND BACKWATER TRIPS

Backwater trips KTDC offers day-trips into the backwaters south of Kochi (daily 8.15am–5.30pm; ₹1250). The cost includes hotel pick-up, transfer to the departure point 5km north of Alappuzha, a morning cruise (in a motorized boat) on the open backwaters, a village tour, a Keralan lunch buffet and an afternoon trip through narrow waterways in a much smaller punted canoe. In a similar vein are the community-based tours run by the villagers of Kumbalanghi

on Kallancherry Island, 14km south of Fort Cochin (☎ 93884 84424), profits from which go to the farmers, coir producers and fishermen who show you around (see page 1104).

Cruises If you are pushed for time, KTDC's half-day Kochi boat cruise (daily 9.30am–1pm & 2.30–6pm; ₹300) is a good way to orient yourself, but it doesn't stop long in either Mattancherry or Fort Cochin. Book at the reception centre on Shanmugham Rd.

ACCOMMODATION

Most foreign visitors opt to stay in **Fort Cochin**, with its uncongested backstreets and charming colonial-era architecture. There are, however, drawbacks: room rates are grossly inflated (especially over Christmas and New Year), with few options at the budget end of the scale. **Ernakulam** may suffer a dearth of historic ambience, but it's far more convenient for travel connections and offers lots of choice and better value in all categories. Wherever you choose to stay, book well in advance.

ERNAKULAM

Biju's Tourist Home Corner of Cannonshed and Market roads ☎ 0484 236 1661, ⊚ bijustouristhome.com; map p.1099. A friendly, efficiently run budget hotel just a 5min walk from the boat jetty, with 27 spotless, well-aired and sizeable rooms that cater to a business crowd. It has its own clean water supply and offers a cheap same-day laundry service. Phone reservations accepted. A/c ₹500 extra. ₹1390

Grand MG Rd ☎ 0484 238 2061, ⊚ grandhotelkerala. com; map p.1099. The most glamorous place to stay in central Ernakulam. Spread over three floors of a 1960s building, its relaxing a/c rooms are done in retro-colonial style blinds. The good hotel restaurant warrants a visit in its own right. ₹3500

Maple Regency XL/1511 Cannonshed Rd ☎ 0484 235 5156 or 0484 237 1711, ⊚ hotelmapleregency.com; map p.1099. The best of the few rock-bottom options in the streets immediately east of the Main Boat Jetty. Although the thirty cheap, clean, non-a/c rooms in the main block are OK, the couple of old ancestral bungalows in the rear are much nicer (₹1050, ₹1820 a/c). *Boat Jetty Bungalow* next door is run by the same outfit and it's worth checking a couple of rooms for comparison. ₹780

FORT COCHIN

Chiramel Residency 1 296 Lilly St ☎ 0484 221 7310 or ☎ 94478 18930, ⊚ chiramelhomestay.com; map p.1096. A great seventeenth-century heritage homestay, with welcoming owners and five lofty and carefully restored rooms set around a fancily furnished communal sitting room. All have big wooden beds, teak floors and modern

bathrooms. There's a cheaper, newer block too, with a similarly nice communal feel. Breakfast included. ₹4180

Delight Ridsdale Rd, opposite the parade ground ☎ 0484 221 7658 or 98461 21421, ⊚ delighthomestay. com; map p.1096. Occupying an annexe tacked onto a gleaming three-hundred-year-old Portuguese mansion, David and Flowery's homestay holds seven spacious, comfortable and well-aired rooms, all equipped with new bathrooms and quiet ceiling fans. Some open onto a lovely courtyard garden; another has a long veranda overlooking the parade ground. Breakfast included. ₹3000

Fort House 6A Calvathy Rd ☎ 0484 221 7103, ⊚ hotel forthouse.com; map p.1095. Stylishly simple rooms flank a sandy courtyard littered with pot plants and votive terracotta statues. Those in the better block (rooms 1–6) have comfy king-sized beds and good showers in their chic wet-room bathrooms – though the a/c units can be noisy. Avoid the older budget block on the west side. Rates include breakfast. ₹8260

Kapithan Inn 931 KL Bernard Rd ☎ 0484 221 6560, ⊚ kapithaninn.com; map p.1096. Scrupulously clean, very nicely furnished rooms in a friendly homestay behind Santa Cruz Basilica, with four smarter, larger a/c cottages (₹2500) to the rear (large enough for families). Various rooms at varying rates, but all are a real bargain, plus there's a lovely rooftop space. A/c ₹500 extra. ₹1100

Maritime Hostel 2/227 Calvathy St ☎ 0484 656 7875, ⊚ thelosthostels.com; map p.1095. It's unusual to find a backpacker hostel in Kerala and this one, in a colonial building, is a real gem. There's both a mixed and female-only dorm, plus a couple of private rooms (note that the girls' room isn't en suite). Dosa breakfast included. Dorms ₹400, doubles ₹1500

The Old Courtyard 1/371–2 Princess St ☎ 0484 221 5035, ⊚ oldcourtyard.com; map p.1096. Another delightful heritage hotel, with eight rooms around a seventeenth-century courtyard, framed by elegant Portuguese arches and bands of original *azulejo* tiles. For once the decor and antique furnishings (including romantic four-posters) are in keeping with the building – though perhaps a bit dark and lacking mod cons. Upper-storey rooms are less disturbed by noise from the courtyard café. ₹5700

Raintree Lodge Peter Celli St ☎97477 21091, ⓦfortcochin.com; map p.1096. Five outstandingly smart rooms furnished in modern style (three of them with tiny balconies) in a cosy guesthouse that's within easy walking distance of the sights, but still tucked away. The really nice thing about this place is its plant-filled roof terrace, which has panoramic views. No breakfast, however. ₹3800

Santa Maria 1/306 opposite Brunton Boatyard, Bellard Rd ☎0844 844 4604, ⓦbackpackerpanda.com; map p.1096. Part of the excellent Backpacker Panda hostel chain, a clean, friendly place to stay with both dorms and private rooms, just a few minutes' walk from the fishing nets. Exceptional value. A/c 100 extra. Dorms ₹390, doubles ₹650

★ **Secret Garden** 745 Bishop Garden Lane, near Pattalam Market ☎0484 221 6658 or 98955 81489, ⓦsecretgarden.in; map p.1096. This unique place is run by Icelandic architect, Thóra Guðmundsdóttir. Huge rooms with high wooden ceilings, hand-carved beds and brightly painted traditional Indian murals open onto balconies fronting a garden with sizeable pool. Morning yoga the can be arranged, and there are books and bicycles to borrow. Family rooms are particularly good value. ₹9500

Sonnetta Residency 387 Princess St ☎0484 221 5744 or ☎98955 43555, ⓦsonnettaresidency.com; map p.1096. This small, old-fashioned guesthouse has to be one of the cleanest places to stay in Kerala. It lacks character, and has no outside sitting space, but is efficiently run and provides a secure, convenient base, with some of the cheapest a/c rooms (₹500 extra) in the district. ₹1120

Spencer Home 298 Parade Rd ☎0484 221 5049, ⓦhotelspencerhomes.com; map p.1096. Warm-toned wood pillars and gleaming ceramic tiled floors line the verandas fronting this Portuguese-era house's eleven immaculate rooms, which open onto a painstakingly kept garden. Peaceful and good value for the area. A/c ₹1000 extra. ₹2500

The Tower House 320–321 Tower St ☎0484 221 6960, ⓦneemranahotels.com; map p.1096. Graceful period house perfectly situated opposite the Chinese fishing nets. The airy interiors are scrupulously of-the-era, and there's a secluded pool. Don't expect the slick service of other places in this bracket, but note that rates plummet in the off season. ₹10,500

★ **Walton's Homestay** 39 Princess St ☎0484 221 5309 or 99959 55915, ⓦwaltonshomestay.com; map p.1096. Among Cochin's most characterful home-stays, run by philosopher and local historian, Christopher Edward Walton, in a centuries-old Dutch house. The rooms, many of which open onto a delightful rear garden, have been beautifully renovated, with modern bathrooms, ceiling fans, solar-powered hot water and comfy beds (a/c ₹400 extra). Book-swap library available; breakfast on the terrace is included. ₹1900

KUMBALANGHI VILLAGE

Gramam Homestay Neduveli House, North Kumbalanghi ☎0484 224 0278 or 94471 77312, ⓦgramamhomestay.com; map p.1095. Welcoming homestay offering accommodation in a beautifully-converted coconut warehouse, slap on the banks of a lagoon. Chill in a hammock under the palms, go for cycle and canoe rides around the village, watch local fishermen and toddy tappers at work and generally soak up the peaceful rural atmosphere. Hosts Jos and Lyma provide breakfast (and dinner on request) and there's a self-catering cottage too. Double ₹3500, cottage ₹6500

★ **Kallancherry Retreat** Kumbalanghi village ☎0484 224 0564, ⓦkallancherryretreat.com; map p.1095. Charming little family homestay, a world away from the crowded streets of Fort Cochin, set under palm trees on the banks of a huge lagoon just a 30min ride out of town. The rooms are squeaky clean and have balconies. ₹2500

EATING

Foreign tourists tend to congregate at the pavement joints along **Tower Rd** near the Chinese fishing nets, drinking warm beer disguised in teapots. Your rupees will stretch further in **Ernakulam**, where you'll find some of the best traditional food in all south India.

ERNAKULAM

Coffee Beanz Shanmugham Rd ☎0484 485 6757; map p.1099. Trendy a/c cappuccino bar, patronized in the main by well-heeled students from the local management college shrieking into their mobiles over a full-on MTV soundtrack. The din notwithstanding, it's a good spot to beat the heat and grab a good coffee or quick meal (burgers, grilled sandwiches, dosas and fish curries, mostly under ₹200). Daily 12pm–10.30pm.

Kayees Durbar Hall Rd ☎0484 235 4321; map p.1099. This salubrious branch of the city's most famous Muslim restaurant is a modern dining hall in the heart of the downtown area, with an a/c section on the first floor. Everyone comes for the Malabari biryanis (veg, chicken or mutton; ₹150–190), served with mellow palm-date pickle and Arabian tea. Pay for your meal token in advance. Daily 11am–10pm.

Kempu Ground floor, Bharat Tourist Home, Durbar Hall Rd ☎0484 329 5090, ⓦbharathotel.com; map p.1099. The decor is soothing, and the south Indian bites dependably good. Try their *bonda* – spicy vegetable and peanut balls (₹35), served with coconut-chilli *chatni*. A good place for a coffee break after a shopping trip on nearby MG Rd. Mon–Sat 3pm–2am, Sun 3pm–12am.

21

★**Sarovaram** Bypass Rd, Kudunnur ☎0484 230 5519; map p.1099. People travel from across the city for *Sarovaram*'s famous lunchtime *sadyas* (noon–2.30pm; ₹170), served on banana leaves. The pure veg food is unrivalled in the city and the atmosphere is much more Keralan, though it's a long trek across town – you might want to combine it with a trip to the Folklore Museum (see page 1097), about 15min away in a rickshaw. Daily 7am–10.30pm.

Shri Krishna Inn Warriam Rd ☎99613 61999; map p.1099. The sumptuous south Indian thalis served in this smart, dimly lit a/c vegetarian restaurant are on a par with nearby *Subhiksha*'s, but the decor is more appealingly traditional, with lathe-turned wooden pillars and earthy-toned Keralan murals setting the tone. As well as unlimited thalis (₹140–180), they do a huge range of ice creams. Daily 7.30am–11pm.

Subhiksha Bharat Tourist Home, Durbar Hall Rd ☎0484 230 5519, ⓦbharathotel.com; map p.1099. The same banana leaf *sadyas* as at *Sarovaram* (₹180 unlimited), served in more contemporary surroundings, with incongruous music and a/c. It's a great place for crowd-watching, especially on Sun when everyone appears in their best saris and shirts for the big family meal. Daily 7am–3.30pm & 7–11pm.

FORT COCHIN

★**Dal Roti** 1 293 Lilly St; map p.1096. The first choice among Fort Cochin's hungry travellers. You'll know why as soon as you taste their signature *kati* rolls – deliciously flaky wraps filled with egg, chicken or vegetables – or good-value thalis (₹170 for the delicious veg option). The food is authentic north Indian and full of smoky, spicy flavours you don't get to enjoy that often in Kerala. Wed–Mon noon–3.30pm & 6.30–10pm.

David Hall Gallery Café Parade Ground ⓦdavidhall.in; map p.1096. Delicious pizzas (₹300–400; noon–3pm & 6–9pm only), made in a proper pizza oven and served alfresco in a lovely green oasis behind the David Hall art space. They also serve freshly ground coffee, quality teas and juices. Daily 12pm–9pm.

Fort House 6A Calvathy Rd ☎0484 330 6337, ⓦhotel forthouse.com; map p.1096. Carefully prepared Keralan specialities – including delicious seafood options and not-so-traditional roast chicken – served on a romantic, candlelit jetty. The food is consistently good, and not too pricey (most mains ₹350–450), and the location's perfect for watching the ships chugging in and out of the docks. Daily 7.30am–7.30pm.

Kashi Art Café Burgher St ⓦkashiartgallery.com; map p.1096. Cool, open-air gallery café, with floors made from pebbles and railway sleepers, patronized mainly by well-heeled metropolitan Indian tourists. Freshly ground espresso (₹80) is the big draw, along with their famous house cakes (the old-fashioned chocolate gateau is legendary; ₹130), but they also do light meals and savoury snacks – expect perfunctory service. Daily 8.30am–7.30pm.

Mary's Kitchen 1/957 KB Jacob Rd ☎94460 14385; map p.1096. This small rooftop restaurant across from Santa Cruz Basilica is lovingly run by husband-and-wife team Mary and Martin. Everything is home-cooked from scratch and it's the place to come for true Keralan specialities, particularly at breakfast. *Kozhukkotta* (coconut dumplings) and banana *ada* (steamed rice-flour parcels made with coconut and jaggery) are fresh and filling – and remarkably cheap (₹75). Ask about cookery classes. Daily 8am–10pm.

Teapot Peter Celli St ☎0484 221 8035; map p.1096. With its massive collection of teapots from around the world and funky little mezzanine floor, this backstreet tearoom gives *Kashi* some much-needed competition. Quality teas (₹80) and coffees (₹60) are the mainstay, but they also do light meals (₹200–300) and delicious home-made cakes. A generous breakfast with tea or coffee for ₹240. Daily 8.30am–9.30pm.

MATTANCHERRY

Crafters Café Next to Heritage Arts shop, Jew Town Rd ☎0484 222 3346, ⓦcrafters.in; map p.1095. Handy pit stop if you're visiting the nearby synagogue. Tables on their wonderful little blue-pillared balcony are great for people-watching as you enjoy a plate of delicious butterfly prawns (₹280), *appam* with coconut-veg stew (₹150) or a freshly cut sandwich (₹100–160). They also do proper espresso and cakes. Daily 9.30am–6.30pm.

★**Kayees Rhatmathulla** Rahtmathulla Hotel, New Rd; map p.1095. This Muslim joint in the backstreets of Mattancherry is legendary across the state for its fragrant biryanis, prepared fresh each morning according to a traditional, closely guarded Malabari recipe. Get there before 1pm to avoid disappointment. You've a choice of chicken, prawn, fish, veg or mutton (₹100–195) biryanis, accompanied by the wonderful house date pickle. Daily 8am–9pm.

★**Sri Krishna Café** Mattancherry Palace/Cheralai Rd; map p.1095. Typical south Indian, pure-veg restaurants are thin on the ground on this side of the water, so it's worth jumping in a rickshaw from Fort Cochin to eat at this famous old Udupi café in the temple district of Mattancherry, where traditional Keralan "meals" cost ₹80. Daily 8am–9.30pm.

SHOPPING

While serious shopping in **Ernakulam** tends to be focused on MG Rd and the **mega malls** to the north of the city (see box below), over in the tourist enclave of Fort Cochin, a combination of lookalike Kashmiri emporia (best avoided)

KOCHI'S SHOPPING MALLS

Kochi's massive **shopping malls** are prime leisure destinations for the city's well-heeled middle classes (daily 10am–10pm). On Ernakulam's MG Road, **Centre Square** (ⓦcentresquarekochi.com) has a food court and the eleven-screen Cinépolis, plus the usual international, air-conditioned stores. Some 7km north of the centre, around Edapally Junction and spread over six storeys, the **Oberon** (ⓦoberonmall.com) used to be the high temple of modern Keralan consumerism until it was usurped by the colossal **LuLu Mall** (ⓦlulumall.in), a sixteen-acre complex 2km further north, with a seven-screen multiplex, eighteen food outlets and parking for three thousand cars.

and more individual boutiques, handicraft and curio shops cater for the passing foreign trade; the **Ethnic Passage** next to the synagogue in Jew Town has a number of these under one renovated two-thousand-year-old roof. **Jew Town** is also the hub of an established **antiques** scene, with some of the largest and most spectacular showrooms in India – a legacy of the post-1960s exodus of the district's Jewish population to Israel. Some approach the scale of small museums, with chunks of temple masonry, carved wood pillars, religious sculpture, doors and windows. **Original art** by local painters also features prominently in the galleries of Jew Town.

AKP Metals and Alloys Broadway, Ernakulam ⓦakp metallodrome.com; map p.1099. The city's largest metal-ware emporium, showcasing a vast selection of traditional Keralan items in brass, copper, silver and bell metal. Mon–Sat 9.30am–8pm.

Cinnamon Trinity Hotel, 658 Ridsdale Rd, Parade Ground, Fort Cochin ☎0484 221 7124; map p.1096. The Fort Cochin branch of the hip Bengaluru lifestyle chain sells clothes, shoes and items for the home from a range of top Indian designers in a light and airy boutique. Women's garments are particularly striking: unusual pieces in gorgeous natural colours. Mon–Sat 10am–7pm.

Fabindia 279(I), Napier St, near Parade Ground, Fort Cochin ☎0484 221 7077, ⓦfabindia.com; map p.1096. Specializing in garments made from traditional Indian textiles, the nationwide chain boasts five branches in the city, the most convenient of them in Fort Cochin. Browse a huge range of vibrant *kurtas*, tops, skirts, bedspreads and cushion covers – all at reasonable (fixed) rates. Mon–Sat 10.30am–9.30pm.

Idiom Bastion St near Princess St, Fort Cochin; map p.1096. The best place to browse for books on travel, Indian and Keralan culture, flora and fauna, religion and art; they also have an excellent range of fiction. There's a second branch in Mattancherry (map p.1095). Mon–Sat 10am–9pm.

Khadi Gramodyog Bhavan Pallimuku, MG Rd, Ernakulam; map p.1099. The usual assortment of climate-friendly, hand-spun cotton and silk, sold by length or as ready-made garments, as well as items for the home, incense, honey, sandalwood and other village handicrafts at fixed prices. Mon–Sat 10.30am–6.30pm.

Niraamaya Behind the Pardesi Synagogue, Mattan-cherry ⓦayurvastraonline.com; map p.1095. This innovative little boutique in Jew Town sells clothes made from organic cotton infused with healing Ayurvedic herbs. Dyed in subtle colours, they're perfect for the sticky Keralan heat. Also bed linen and yoga mats from natural materials. Another branch on Quiros St in Fort Cochin. Mon–Sat 9am–5pm.

Penta Menaka Mall Marine Drive, Ernakulam; map p.1099. The best place in the city for electronic goods, computer/video games and movies – at a fraction of the price you'd pay back home (they're mostly pirated). Daily 10.30am–9.30pm.

Travellers' Paradise KL Bernard Master Rd, Fort Cochin ⓦbloominthenaturalway.com; map p.1096. French designer Sophie Debiève set up this collective to market original pieces made by local Keralan women The range includes original household linen, bags and cards. The adjoining *Masters Art Café* is a nice place to have a breather. Mon–Sat 10am–6pm.

Tribes Next to Head Post Office, Fort Cochin ⓦtribes india.com; map p.1096. Jewellery, textiles, paintings, terracotta and stone work, metal crafts and organic food products produced by tribal communities across the country. Profits go towards development projects in the artists' communities. Mon–Sat 9am–5pm.

DIRECTORY

Banks All the major south Indian banks have branches on MG Rd in Ernakulam. In Kochi, head to Kunnumpuram Junction for banks; ATMs are dotted everywhere around town.

Cinemas The largest multiplex in Kochi is Cinépolis, on the sixth floor of Centre Square Mall. It has eleven screens, swanky VIP sofas, a "7D screen" and shows all the latest Hollywood and Bollywood offerings.

Hospitals The six-hundred-bed Medical Trust Hospital on MG Rd (☎0484 235 8001, ⓦmedicaltrusthospital.com) is one of the state's most advanced private hospitals and has a 24hr casualty unit and ambulance service.

21

Laundry The municipal laundry in Fort Cochin is the Dhobi Khanna, on the south side of the district, a 3km/₹40 rickshaw ride from the tourist enclave. ₹10–15 for shirts; ₹25 for trousers. Allow 24hr.

Taxis Ashik Taxis (☏ 92881 57145 or 96567 98481) cover the entire state, and offer day-trips at fair prices. If you'd like to hire a car and driver for a few days or more, get in touch with Baiju (☏ 94468 27117), who is reliable and friendly and speaks great English.

Around Kochi

While the majority of visitors use the city as a base for day-trips into the surrounding backwaters and satellite villages, there's nothing to stop you doing the opposite, basing yourself in quiet backwater locations out of town – such as **Vypeen Island** to the north, or **Kumbalanghi** to the south – and travelling in to see the sights by bus, taxi or auto-rickshaw. There is some outstanding homestay accommodation in Kumbalanghi village (see page 1101).

Backwater trips

Coir-production, rope-making, toddy-tapping, fishing and crab-farming are the main sources of income in the **backwater villages** south of Kochi. Easily reachable via the national highway, they're scattered over an expanse of huge lagoons and canals, flowing west behind a near continuous beach.

You can dip into the region for a day on one of the popular trips run out of Fort Cochin by KTDC, or with a community-based tourism initiative based at Kumbalanghi village – an award-winning project where proceeds are shared among the locals. The cost of the latter tour is ₹1400 (or ₹800 without lunch). You also have to budget for transport to and from the village. The trip is most easily done by auto-rickshaw (₹350–400 each way); if travelling by bus, head for Perumamapadappu, aka "Perumbadapu" on Google maps, and catch an auto from there for the remaining couple of kilometres.

Thripunitra

Some 12km southeast of Ernakulam and a short bus or auto-rickshaw ride from the bus stand just south of Jos Junction on MG Road, the small suburban town of **THRIPUNITRA** is worth a visit for its dilapidated colonial-style **Hill Palace**, now an eclectic museum, as well as its fabulous **temple festival**, held in October or November.

Hill Palace
Tues–Sun 9.30am–12.30pm, 2pm–4.30pm • ₹30

The royal family of Cochin at one time had around forty palaces – the **Hill Palace** was confiscated by the state government after Independence, and has slipped into dusty decline over the past decades. One of the museum's finest exhibits is an early seventeenth-century wooden *mandapa* (hall) featuring carvings of episodes from the Ramayana. Of interest too are the silver filigree jewel boxes, gold and silver ornaments, and ritual objects associated with grand ceremonies. Artefacts in the **bronze gallery** include a *kingini katti* knife, whose decorative bells belie the fact that it was used for beheading, and a body-shaped cage in which condemned prisoners would be hung while birds pecked them to death.

Sri Purnathrayisa Temple
Performances of theatre, classical music and dance, including all-night **kathakali**, are held over a period of eight days during the annual **Vrishikolsavam** festival (Oct/Nov) at the **Sri Purnathrayisa Temple** on the way to the palace. Inside the temple compound, both in the morning and at night, massed drum orchestras perform *chenda melam* in procession with fifteen caparisoned elephants.

LAKSHADWEEP

Visitors to Kerala in search of an exclusive tropical paradise may well find it in **Lakshadweep** (ⓦlakshadweep.nic.in), the islands that lie between 200km and 400km offshore in the deep blue of the Arabian Sea. The smallest Union Territory in India, Lakshadweep's 27 tiny, coconut-palm-covered coral islands are the archetypal tropical hideaway, edged with pristine white sands and surrounded by calm lagoons where average water temperature stays around 26°C all year. Beyond the lagoons lie the **coral reefs**, home to sea turtles, dolphins, eagle rays, lionfish, parrotfish, octopus, barracudas and sharks. Only ten of the islands are inhabited, with a total **population** of just over 65,000, the majority of whom are Malayalam-speaking Sunni Muslims said to be descended from seventh-century Keralan Hindus who converted to Islam.

Theoretically, it's possible to **visit** Lakshadweep year round; the hottest time is April and May, when temperatures can reach 33°C; the monsoon (May–Sept) attracts approximately half the rainfall seen in Kerala, in the form of passing showers rather than deluges, although the seas are rough. Concerted attempts are being made to minimize the ecological impact of tourism in the islands; all visits must be arranged in Kochi through the **Society for Promotion of Recreational Tourism and Sports (SPORTS)** on IG Rd, Willingdon Island (☎0484 235 5387, ⓦlakshadweeptourism.com). At the time of writing, basic but pricey **accommodation** – run by the Lakshadweep department of tourism – was available on Kadmat, Kavaratti, Bangaram, Thinnakara and Minicoy. Access by plane is to the gateway island of **Agatti** (Mon–Sat; daily 1hr 30min), from where you'll be transferred by speedboat; or you can travel by sea from Kochi (14–18hr). SPORTS also offers a five-day **cruise** package taking in Kavaratti, Kalpeni and Minicoy (₹30,500/person). Meals are included, and permits taken care of, but diving costs extra. Week-long **diving** courses are available in Kadmat, Kavaratti and Minicoy from ₹20,000/person.

Cherai Beach

The closest beach to Kochi worth the effort of getting to is **Cherai**, 25km north on **Vypeen Island**. A 3km strip of golden sand and thumping surf, it's sandwiched on a narrow strip of land between the sea and a very pretty backwater area of glassy lagoons. Chunky granite sea defences prevent the waves from engulfing the ribbon of fishing villages that subsist along this strip. Nowhere, however, is the sand more than a few metres wide at high tide, and the undertow can get quite strong. Even so, Cherai is gaining in popularity each year, and a row of small resorts and guesthouses has sprung up to accommodate the trickle of mainly foreign travellers who find their way up here from Fort Cochin.

ARRIVAL AND DEPARTURE

CHERAI BEACH

By ferry and bus To get to Cherai, you can jump on the car ferry (*jangar*) across to Vypeen Island from the jetty next to Brunton Boatyard in Fort Cochin, then transfer onto the hourly bus waiting on the other side, or catch one of the more frequent buses from opposite the High Court Jetty in Ernakulam.

By scooter Alternatively, you can hire a scooter and ride up – in which case, a preferable route to the main road is the more picturesque coastal lane hugging the sea wall; you can pick this up by turning west (left) down a bumpy backroad at Nayarambalam, 1km north of Narakkal, or via any of the lanes peeling left further on.

ACCOMMODATION

Brighton Beach House 3/783 Palli Fort, Convent Beach Rd, 2.5km north of Cherai ☎99474 40449, ⓦbrightonbeachhouse.org. Fairly basic rooms (some a/c) opening on to a yard right next to the sea wall, a 5min drive north of the main beachfront. Meals and sundowners are served in a small gazebo-cum-sun-terrace overlooking the sand, which is particularly narrow here. A/c ₹800 extra. **₹2300**
La Dame Rouge Kizhakke Veedu, Manapilly ☎0484 2481 062 or 92494 10523, ⓦladamerouge.com. This small, French-owned boutique guesthouse is a true labour of love – beautifully designed and run by host Marco, a

former consular official who's been here for decades. The rooms and duplex suites are exquisitely decorated, with colour-washed walls, four-posters and Indian antiques – and the location, near a huge backwater, is superb. Canoe trips to the local market, Ayurvedic massages and fragrant Indo-Gallic fusion cooking are all on offer. Half board **₹8000**
Kuzhupilly Beach House Kuzhupilly, 4.5km south of Cherai ☎0484 2531456 or 94471 07028, ⓦkuzhupilly-beach-house.business.site. Little budget guesthouse just 30min by taxi from the Vypeen–Fort Cochin ferry dock, but over-looking a deserted stretch of beach and back-waters. The best rooms

(₹2500) are on the upper floor and have fine sea views. Delicious, authentic Keralan home-cooking is on offer, along with bicycles and canoe tours. You can get most of the way there by bus (much cheaper); phone ahead for instructions. ₹2000

Ocean Breath Cherai ☎ 93492 88868, ⊛ cheraihotels.

com. The best-value budget option in Cherai, and the one with most Keralan atmosphere. No sea views (it's set back across the road from the sea wall) but the rooms are pleasant, with high, traditional Keralan ceilings and carved gables, shiny ceramic floors and small sitouts. ₹1350

Thrissur (Trichur)

THRISSUR (Trichur), a busy market hub and temple town roughly midway between Kochi (74km south) and Palakkad (79km northeast) on the NH-47, is a convenient, albeit traffic-clogged, base for central Kerala. Close to the Palghat (Palakkad) Gap – an opening in the natural border made by the Western Ghats – Thrissur presided over the main trade route into the region from Tamil Nadu and Karnataka and for years was the capital of Cochin state.

Today, Thrissur is home to several influential art institutions and prides itself on being the cultural capital of Kerala. One of the state's principal Hindu temples, **Vadukkunnathan**, is here too, at the centre of a huge circular *maidan* that hosts all kinds of public gatherings, not least Kerala's most extravagant, noisy and sumptuous festival, **Puram**. The town derives most of its income from remittance cheques sent by expatriates in the Gulf – hence the predominance of ostentatious modern houses in the surrounding villages. The hinterland also serves as a storehouse, dotted with communities and pilgrimage sites where both contemporary party politics and ancient art traditions are pursued with great enthusiasm, despite the disruptive impact on local life of mass out-migration.

Vadakke Madham Brahmaswam

Thakkemadham Rd • Daily 10am–5pm • Donation requested • ☎ 0487 244 0877

The mighty Vadukkunnathan Temple, in the centre of the Round, may be closed to non-Hindus, but you can gain a sense of how ancient its roots are at the nearby **Vadakka Madham Brahmaswam**, five minutes' walk west of the temple, where young Namboodiri Brahmin boys attend **chanting** classes at a traditional *madham*, or college. Wearing traditional white *mundu*, sacred threads and ash marks on their skin, the students sit cross-legged in traditional Keralan halls while they repeat verses from three-thousand-year-old texts modelled for them by their gurus. If you'd like to visit, telephone ahead to ensure classes will be in progress.

Basilica of Our Lady of Dolours

Church Rd • **Tower** Tues–Fri 9am–1pm & 2–6pm, Sat & Sun 10am–1pm & 2–7.30pm • ₹20 • ⊛ doloursbasilicathrissur.com

Not to be outdone by the scale of the Hindu temple across town, the vast Indo-Gothic **Basilica of Our Lady of Dolours** (**Puthan Pally** in Malayalam) dominates the skyline southeast of the Round, thanks to its gigantic 79m-high belfry – the tallest in India. Take the lift to the top, where superb views extend across the palm forest surrounding Thrissur, but coming down choose the stairs so you can view the artwork adorning the walls; an eclectic mix of wood, stained glass and brass depict stories from the Bible.

Archeological Museum

Karunkaram Nambiar Rd • Tues–Sun 10am–5pm • ₹20

Of the town's **museums**, grouped to the north of the Round, the only one worth visiting – not least for the splendid Keralan architecture of the former palace it's housed in – is the **Archeological Museum**, opposite the Priya Darshini bus stand, a five-minute walk north of the Round on Karunkaram Nambiar Road. Former residence of the Cochin royal family, the two-hundred-year-old **Shaktan Thampuran Palace** is beautifully decorated with

THRISSUR PURAM

Thrissur is best known to outsiders as the venue for Kerala's biggest annual festival, **Puram**, which takes place on one day in the Hindu month of Medam (April–May; ask at a tourist office or check online for the exact date). Inaugurated by Shaktan Tampuran, the raja of Cochin, between 1789 and 1803, the event is the culmination of eight days of festivities spread over nine different temples to mark obeisance to Lord Shiva, at the peak of the summer's heat. Like temple festivals across Kerala, it involves the stock ingredients of caparisoned elephants, massed drum orchestras and firework displays, but on a scale and performed with an intensity unmatched by any other.

Puram's grand stage is the long, wide path leading to the southern entrance of **Vadukkunnathan Temple** on the Round. Shortly after dawn, a sea of onlookers gathers here to watch the first phase of the 36-hour marathon – the **kudammattom**, or "Divine Durbar" – in which two majestic **elephant processions**, representing Thrissur's Tiruvambadi and Paramekkavu temples, advance towards each other down the walkway, like armies on a medieval battlefield, preceded by ranks of drummers and musicians. Both sides present thirteen tuskers sumptuously decorated with gold caparisons (*nettipattom*), each ridden by three young Brahmins clutching objects symbolizing royalty: silver-handled whisks of yak hair, circular peacock-feather fans and colourful silk umbrellas fringed with silver pendants. At the centre of the opposing lines, the principal elephant carries an image of the temple's presiding deity. Swaying gently, the elephants stand still much of the time, ears flapping, seemingly oblivious to the crowds and huge orchestra that plays in front of them, competing to create the most noise and greatest spectacle. When the music reaches its peak around sunset, the two groups set off towards different districts of town. This signals the start of a spectacular **firework display** that begins with a series of deafening explosions and lasts through the night, with the teams once again trying to outdo each other to put on the most impressive show.

If you venture to Thrissur for Puram, be prepared for packed buses and trains, and book **accommodation** well in advance. As is usual for temple festivals, many men use the event as an excuse to get hopelessly drunk. Women are thus advised to dress conservatively and only to go to the morning session, or to watch with a group of Indian women – and at all times avoid the area immediately in front of the drummers, where the "rhythm madmen" congregate.

intricate wood- and tile-work. Exhibits include fifteenth- and eighteenth-century hero stones, a fearsome selection of beheading axes and a massive iron-studded treasury box.

ARRIVAL AND INFORMATION

THRISSUR (TRICHUR)

The principal point of orientation in Thrissur is the **Round**, a road (subdivided into North, South, East and West) which circles the Vadukkunnathan Temple complex and maidan in the town centre.

By train On the main line to Chennai and other points in neighbouring Tamil Nadu, and with good connections to Ernakulam/Kochi and Thiruvananthapuram, the railway station is 1km southwest.

Destinations Ernakulam/Kochi (every 30min; 1hr 20min); Kozhikode/Calicut (12 daily; 2hr 15min–3hr 40min); Thiruvanantha-puram (hourly; 6hr–8hr).

By bus The KSRTC long-distance bus stand is opposite the station. The Shakthan Thampuran bus stand, on TB Rd, around 1km from Round South, serves local destinations south such as Irinjalakuda, Kodungallur and Guruvayur.

Tourist information The primary purpose of the volunteer-run DTPC tourist office (Mon–Sat 10am–5pm; ☏0487 232 0800), on Palace Rd opposite the Town Hall (5min walk off Round East), is to promote the Puram festival, but they also hand out maps of Thrissur.

ACCOMMODATION

Thrissur has plenty of competitively priced mid-range hotels but only a couple of decent budget ones. If you're planning to be here during **Puram**, book well in advance and bear in mind that room rates soar – some of the more upmarket hotels, and those overlooking the Round, charge up to ten times their usual prices.

Ashoka Inn TB Rd ☏0487 244 4333, ⓦashokainn.co.in. Best value among the business-oriented three-stars in the Shakthan Thampuran bus stand district, in a gleaming, glass-sided tower block with spacious, impeccably clean rooms. Breakfast included. ₹4100

Gurukripa Heritage Chembottil Lane ☏89215 48909, ⓦgurukripaheritage.in. Run with great efficiency by the venerable Mr Venugopal, the *Gurukripa*, just off Round South, offers a variety of simple rooms, (including several great-value singles) ranged around a long inner courtyard. ₹2500

★ **Kuruppath** Mannadiara Lane, off Kuruppam

Rd ☎94952 60000 or 0487 242 4696, ⊛kuruppath heritage.com. An impeccably restored heritage bungalow, cowering amid the high-rise tower blocks in the heart of town, just a stone's throw from Round South. Filled with dark wood and antique tiles, the interiors are light, cool and astonishingly peaceful, considering the location. ₹2200

EATING AND DRINKING

There are plenty of dependable places to eat in Thrissur, with many hotels and busy "meals" joints lining the Round. In the evening, from 8.30pm, you can also join the auto-rickshaw-walas, hospital visitors, itinerant mendicants, Ayappa devotees and students who congregate at the popular *thattukada* **hot food market** on the corner of Round South and Round East, opposite the Medical College Hospital. The rustic Keralan cooking – omelettes, dosas, *parathas*, *iddiappam*, bean curries and egg masala – is freshly prepared, delicious and unbelievably cheap.

Akshaya Luciya Palace, Marar Rd, just off the southwest corner of the Round ⊛hotelluciyapalace.com. Fairly bland hotel restaurant where waiters in bow ties serve quality Keralan meals at lunchtime (₹195) in a blissfully cold a/c dining hall. From 7.30pm you can order from an exhaustive multicuisine menu, sitting outside in a pleasant garden illuminated by fairy lights. Beer is permitted with meals. Daily 7am–1am.

★ **Bharath Hotel** Chembottil Lane, 50m down the road from the Elite Hotel ☎0487 242 1720. Thrissur's top pure-veg place, packed from 7.30am onwards. The food is unfailingly fresh and delicious, and the queues stretch out the door on weekends. Be sure to leave room for the *ada*, a mix of sugar cane, coconut and rice steamed in a banana leaf (which tastes disconcertingly like old-fashioned British treacle pudding and costs just ₹38). Daily 6.30am–10.30pm.

DIRECTORY

Banks There are ATMs all over the centre of town. The best place to change money and travellers' cheques is the UTI Bank in the City Centre Shopping building (Mon–Fri 9.30am–3.30pm, Sat 9.30am–1.30pm) on Round West. The UAE Exchange & Financial Services (Mon–Fri 9.30am–6pm, Sat 9.30am–2pm) in the basement of the *Casino Hotel* building also changes currency and travellers' cheques.

Internet Available for ₹30/hr at Hugues Net on the top floor of the City Centre Shopping building and at SS Consultants next to the *Luciya Palace* hotel.

Post office The main post office is on the southern edge of town, just off Round South.

Around Thrissur

Guruvayur, 19km west of Thrissur, is the site of south India's most revered Krishna temple, with hundreds of thousands of Hindu pilgrims pouring in all year to worship at the shrine. As usual, non-Hindus are barred from entering, but there is a cultural institution that has opened its doors to visitors; learn all about *kathakali* in **Cheruthuruthy**'s Kerala Kalamandalam.

Cheruthuruthy

CHERUTHURUTHY, on the banks of the Bharatpuzha (aka "Nila") River 32km north of Thrissur, is internationally famous as the home of **Kerala Kalamandalam** (☎0488 4 26 2418, ⊛kalamandalam.org), the state's flagship training school for *kathakali* and other indigenous Keralan performing arts. The academy was founded in 1927 by the revered Keralan poet Vallathol (1878–1957), and has since been instrumental in the large-scale revival of interest in unique Keralan art forms. Non-Hindus are welcome to attend *kathakali*, *kudiyattam* and *mohiniyattam* performed in the school's wonderful **theatre**, which replicates the style of the wooden, sloping-roofed traditional *kuttambalam* auditoria found in Keralan temples. You can also sit in on classes, watch demonstrations of mural painting, and visit exhibitions of costumes by signing up for the fascinating "**a day with the masters**" cultural programme (Mon–Sat 9.30am–1pm; ₹1400, including lunch).

ARRIVAL AND DEPARTURE   CHERUTHURUTHY

By train Served by express trains to and from Mangalaru, Chennai and Kochi, the nearest mainline railway station is Shoranur Junction, 3km south.

By bus Buses heading to Shoranur from Thrissur's Priya Darshini (aka "Wadakkancheri") stand pass through Cheruthuruthy.

21

River Retreat Heritage Ayurvedic Resort 2km from Kalamandalam ☏04884 264444, ⊛riverretreat.in. Accommodation in Cheruthuruthy is limited to the luxurious *River Retreat Heritage Ayurvedic Resort*, former palace of the raja of Cochin. The three-star hotel and Ayurveda spa occupies an idyllic position on the banks of the Nila, where you can swim in a crystalline pool, partly shaded by coconut palms. ₹5800

Kozhikode (Calicut)

Formerly one of Asia's most prosperous trading capitals, the busy coastal city of **KOZHIKODE** (Calicut), 225km north of Kochi, occupies an extremely important place in Keralan legend and history. It's also significant in the chronicles of European involvement on the Subcontinent, as Vasco da Gama landed at nearby Kappad beach in 1498. After centuries of decline following the Portuguese destruction of the city, Kozhikode is once again prospering thanks to the flow of remittance cheques from the Gulf – a legacy of its powerful, Moppila-Muslim merchant community, who ran the local ruler's (Zamorin's) navy and trade. The recent building boom has swept aside most monuments dating from the golden age, but a few survive, notably a handful of splendid Moppila **mosques**, distinguished by their typically Keralan, multi-tiered roofs.

The Moppila mosques

The three most impressive mosques lie off a backroad running through the **Muslim** quarter of **Thekkepuram**, 2km southwest of the maidan (the auto-rickshaw-walas will know how to find them). Start at the 1100-year-old **Macchandipalli Masjid**, between Francis Road and the Kuttichira Tank, whose ceilings are covered in beautiful polychrome stucco and intricate Koranic script. A couple of hundred metres further north, the eleventh-century **Jama Masjid**'s main prayer hall, large enough for a congregation of 1200 worshippers, holds another elaborately carved ceiling. The most magnificent of the trio of mosques, however, is the **Mithqalpalli** (aka **Jama'atpalli**) **Masjid**, hidden down a lane behind Kuttichira tank. Resting on 24 wooden pillars, its four-tier roof and turquoise walls were built more than seven hundred years ago.

By plane Kozhikode's international airport (⊛aai.aero), at Karippur, 23km south of the city, is primarily a gateway for emigrant workers flying to and from the Gulf, but also has direct flights to many other Indian cities, including Mumbai, Delhi, Kochi, Chennai and Hyderabad. A taxi from the airport into town costs around ₹550.
Destinations Chennai (1–2 daily; 1hr 30min); Cochin (daily; 45min); Mumbai (3 daily; 1hr 40min–2hr).
By train The railway station, near the centre of town, is served by coastal expresses, slower passenger trains and superfast express trains to and from Goa, Mumbai, Kochi and Thiruvananthapuram.
Destinations Bengaluru (daily; 12hr 30min); Chennai (4 daily; 12–18hr); Goa (2 daily; 8–11hr 30min); Kannur (every

30min–1hr; 1hr 20min–1hr 45min); Ernakulam/Kochi (10 daily; 4–5hr); Mumbai (2 daily; 22hr); Thiruvananthapuram (7 daily; 7hr 50min–11hr).
By bus There are three bus stands. Government-run services pull in at the KSRTC bus stand, on Mavoor Rd (aka Indira Gandhi Rd). Private long-distance – mainly overnight – buses stop at the New Moffussil private stand, 500m away on the other side of Mavoor Rd. The Palayam bus stand, off MM Ali Rd, just serves the city.
Destinations Bengaluru (19 daily; 7–10hr); Kannur (hourly; 1hr 30min–3hr); Kalpetta/Wayanad (every 30min; 2hr); Kottayam (12 daily; 4–7hr); Ooty (3–4 daily; 5hr 30min–6hr); Thrissur (every 30min; 3hr 30min).

Tourist information KTDC's tourist information booth (officially daily 9am–7.30pm; ☏0495 270 0097), at the railway station, has information on travel connections and sights, but opening hours are erratic.

ACCOMMODATION

Hotels in Kozhikode are plentiful, except at the bottom end of the range, where decent places are few and far between. This is one city where travellers on tighter budgets might be tempted to **upgrade**. The beach is a great place to stay, though you'll need to head into town for the best places to eat.

Alakapuri Guest House Chinthavalappu Junction, MM Ali Rd, near the Palayam bus stand ☏ 0495 272 0219, ⊛ hotelalakapuri.com. Opening on to a large central garden, the rooms in this popular place range from old-fashioned, spartan, a/c doubles to more spacious "cottages" with polished wood chairs, pillared sitouts and sofas (₹3700). All are neatly painted and clean. In the evening, you can eat on the lawn or in their cavernous dining hall under the watchful gaze of a giant plaster elephant. ₹1960

Beach Hotel Beach Rd, 2km west of the centre ☏ 0495 276 2056, ⊛ beachheritage.com. Dating from 1890, the premises of the colonial-era Malabar English Club, with its closely cropped lawns and high-pitched tiled roofs, now house a heritage hotel with loads of lovely character. The six rooms come with balconies or private patios, split-cane blinds, paddle fans and a/c. Those on the upper floor are larger and have the best sea views. Good value. ₹4200

Calicut Tower Markaz Complex, off IG Rd ☏ 86069 49132, ⊛ alhindcalicuttower.com. This ninety-room tower block, tucked away down a quiet side street close to the KSRTC bus station and popular mainly with visiting Gulf Arab medical tourists, offers by far the best value in Kozhikode's lower-mid-range bracket. Impeccably clean, with shiny tiled floors and well-scrubbed bathrooms, its "standard a/c" rooms (just ₹300 pricier than the stuffier non-a/c options) are huge for the price. Strictly no alcohol. ₹2700

★ **Harivihar** 4km north of the centre in the residential suburb of Bilathikulam ☏ 96562 02250, ⊛ harivihar.com. Ancestral home of the Kadathanadu royal family, converted into a particularly desirable heritage homestay. Set among lawns, herb beds, lotus ponds and an original laterite-lined bathing tank (which guests are welcome to use), the mansion is a model of traditional Keralan refinement. Distractions include short courses in yoga, astrology, cookery and Indian mythology, but the focus is the top-grade Ayurvedic centre. Generously sized rooms make the Ayurveda yoga 21-day retreats an even nicer prospect. ₹8300

Sea Queen Beach Rd ☏ 0495 236 6604, ⊛ seaqueen hotel.com. This modern four-storey building is a good option if your budget can stretch to one of the pleasant, spacious a/c rooms, the best of which is the sea-facing "a/c-deluxe" (no. 213; ₹3300). The non-a/c rooms are fusty and not nearly as nice. Breakfast, served alfresco on the rooftop, is included in the price (there's an a/c restaurant up there too). ₹2700

EATING

Kozhikode is famous for its **Moppila cuisine**, which has its roots in the culinary traditions of the city's former Arab traders. Fragrant chicken biryanis and seafood curries with distinctive Malabari blends of spices crop up on most non-veg restaurant menus. **Mussels** are also big news here; deep-fried in their shells in crunchy, spicy millet coatings, they're served everywhere during the season (Oct–Dec; at any other time, they'll have been imported and won't be as fresh). Finally, no Kozhikode feast is complete without a serving of the city's legendary **halwa**: a sticky Malabari sweet made from rice flour, coconut, jaggery (unrefined sugar) and ghee, it comes in a dazzling variety of colours and flavours.

★ **Paragon** Off the Kannur Rd ☏ 0495 276 7020, ⊛ paragonrestaurant.net. Paragon has been a city institution since it opened in 1939. Don't be put off by the gloomy setting beneath a flyover: the Malabari cooking here is as good as you'll find anywhere. Seafood dishes are the speciality – especially fish tamarind, fish-mango curry, pollichathu and mollee – but there are dozens of alter-natives. Whatever you order, make sure it's accompanied by their famously light appam and paratha combo. Most mains ₹150–225. Daily 6am–11.45pm.

Sagar Mavoor/IG Rd ⊛ facebook.com/calicutsagar. Another old favourite of Calicut's middle classes, now with two branches. Both are housed in distinctive laterite buildings, with non-a/c on the ground floor, and brighter a/c "family" dining halls on the floors above. Ignore the generic north Indian/Chinese/multicuisine menu. Everyone comes for the Malabari dishes such as egg curry, fish korma and, best of all, the flavour-packed chicken pollichathu. Most mains under ₹200. Daily 7am–midnight.

Zain's Hotel Convent Cross Rd ☏ 0495 236 6311. An unassuming, red-painted family house down a dingy lane in the west end of town is hardly what you'd expect the Holy Grail of Moppila cuisine to look like, but people travel from across the city to eat here. You'll find a choice of biryanis (fish, chicken or mutton; ₹150–250), various fiery seafood curries and a range of different pathiris – the definitive Malabari rice-flour bread. Most mains ₹150–200. Daily 12.30pm–11.30pm.

DIRECTORY

Banks and exchange The UAE Exchange on Bank Rd, next to Hyson Heritage (Mon–Sat 9.30am–1.30pm & 2–6pm, Sun 9.30am–1.30pm), changes cash and travellers' cheques, while the Union Bank of India and the State Bank of India, opposite each other on MM Ali Rd, are two of many large branches with ATMs.

Internet Available at the Hub, on the first floor of the block to the right of Nandhinee Sweets, MM Ali Rd, and at Internet Zone, near KTDC Malabar Mansion (both ₹40/hr).

21

Wayanad

The seven mountains encircling the hill district of **Wayanad**, 70km inland from Kozhikode, enfold some of the most dramatic scenery in all of south India. With landscapes varying from semitropical savanna to misty tea and coffee plantations, and steep slopes that rise through dense forest to distinctive, angular summits of exposed grassland, the region ranges over altitudes of between 750m and 2100m. Even at the base of the plateau, scattered with typically ramshackle Indian hill bazaars, it's cooler than down on the plains.

The main Mysuru–Kozhikode highway, NH-17, slices through Wayanad. Since the late 1990s, it has been the source of new income in the form of overstressed dot-com executives and their families from Bengaluru and Delhi, with numerous high-end resorts, eco-hideaways and plantation stays springing up to service the screen-weary. Even if you can't afford to stay in one of these bijou retreats, however, there are plenty of reasons to venture up here. Abutting the Tamil Nadu and Karnatakan borders, the twin reserves of **Muthanga** in the southeast and **Tholpetty** in the north collectively comprise the **Wayanad Wildlife Sanctuary** – part of the world-famous Nilgiri Biosphere and one of the best places in India to spot wild **elephant**.

Southern Wayanad

If you're travelling on all but the most flexible of budgets, you'll probably have to stay in the district's capital, **Kalpetta**. A hectic market hub straddling the main road, the town has little to commend it as a place to hang out, but does have budget accommodation, as well as good transport connections to points east. The other centres are **Mananthavady** and **Sulthan Bathery**, which is closest to **Muthanga Wildlife Sanctuary**.

Muthanga Wildlife Sanctuary
40km east of Kalpetta • Daily 7–10am & 3–5pm • ₹450, plus jeep entry ₹80 and hire ₹600

Part of a network of protected reserves with neighbouring states, **Muthanga Wildlife Sanctuary** is noted primarily for its elephants, but also shelters Indian bison (gaur), deer, wild boar, bear and a handful of tigers. There is currently no trekking allowed inside the sanctuary.

Edakkal Caves
28km east of Kalpetta, near Adikavala • Tues–Sun 8am–4pm • ₹40

The prehistoric rock art site of **Edakkal**, which means "stone in between", was rediscovered in 1894 and is now overrun most days. It's a 1km hike up to the entry gate, after which there are a *lot* of stairs to navigate, but it's worth it to see where people etched human figures and animals – and geometric symbols of the sun – more than six thousand years ago. In nearby Adikavala, the **Wayanad Heritage Museum** (daily 9am–5.30pm; ₹20) gives a bit of background.

ARRIVAL AND DEPARTURE   **SOUTHERN WAYANAD**

By bus Some buses will terminate at either Kalpetta or Sulthan Bathery, but it's easy to hop on a local bus between the two (30min). Most services for Kannur depart from Mananthavady, 30km north of Kalpetta.

Destinations Kozhikode/Calicut (every 30min; 2hr); Mysuru (Karnataka; hourly; 2hr 15–5hr); Ooty/Udhagamandalam (Tamil Nadu; 3–4 daily; 4hr; daylight hours only).

INFORMATION AND TOURS

DTPC office Close to *Green Gates* hotel in North Kalpetta (Mon–Sat 10am–5pm; ☎0493 620 2134, ⊛wayanad tourism.org). Staff will help with permits, tours and trekking.

Wayanad Nature Tours By far the best guide is Sabu (☎99612 84874, ⊛wayanad-naturetours.com) who can

take you to tea estates and tribal villages, into forests to spot wildlife or on a challenging trek into the mountains (though you could only ascend halfway up Chembra Peak at the time of writing). His website is a useful resource, updated daily with the latest from Wayanad.

ACCOMMODATION

★ **Aranyakam** Valathur–Rippon, Meppadi ☎ 04936 280261 or 94477 81203, ⓦ aranyakam.com. Rooms and suites in a handsome Keralan-style bungalow, with wood floors and verandas on both sides, the rear ones just a few metres from the coffee bushes. Best options, if you can stretch to them, are their two huts (₹6500/₹8000), which look across a spectacular wilderness of pristine forest and mountain. **₹5300**

Chandragiri Inn Main Rd, Kalpetta ☎ 98478 02000, ⓦ chandragiriinn.com. The best cheapie in Kalpetta, in a modern block at the north end of town, and the only place with beds under ₹750 that you'd want to sleep in. It has three kinds of room, varying in size from tiny to small, but they're well-scrubbed and aired. **₹600**

Green Gates TB Rd, North Kalpetta ☎ 04936 202001, ⓦ greengateshotel.com. Tucked away in its own lush grounds 300m north of the DTPC office, with rooms in the main multi-storey block (ask for a balcony; ₹5000), or more private cottages to its rear (₹6800). There's a pool (the only area with wi-fi), plenty of chillout space in the gardens and an Ayurveda centre. The most comfortable option in Kalpetta, but not a great location. Half board option for ₹800 extra. **₹3800**

Mint Flower Chungam Sulthan's Battery ☎ 0494 6222 206 or 97452 22206, ⓦ hotelmintflower.com. This modern mid-range hotel on the main road through town has 36 spotless rooms; the more expensive ones have huge bath-rooms. South Indian breakfast included, but the food highlight is the cheap snacks – samosas are ₹38 – at the bakery out front. Wi-fi in reception only, a/c ₹300 extra. **₹1450**

Tranquil Kappamudi Estate, Kolaggappara ☎ 99475 88507, ⓦ tranquilresort.com. The crème de la crème of Wayanad's homestays, set amid 400 acres of rambling coffee, cardamom and vanilla plantations. The planter's bungalow itself holds eight comfy rooms (from ₹13,275), all opening on to a glorious veranda wrapped in manicured gardens, and there are two palatial treehouses (from ₹20,300) as well as a large pool. The cooking's terrific, and the Dey family are perfect hosts. **₹13,275**

North Wayanad

The teak forest takes over completely as you climb towards the northern limits of Wayanad, tracked by the savanna-grass summits of the Brahmagiri massif. Some travellers use the pot-holed trunk road cutting north towards Mysuru to reach the Nagarahole National Park or the Kodagu (Coorg) district in neighbouring Karnataka. But the majority of people who venture up here do so for a glimpse of wild elephants at the **Tholpetty Wildlife Sanctuary**, on the state border.

Tholpetty Wildlife Sanctuary

25km northeast of Mananthavady • Daily 7–10am & 3–5pm • ₹300, plus jeep entry ₹75 and hire ₹600 • Taxis charge ₹850 for the trip (with waiting time) from Mananthavady and the frequent KSRTC buses to Kutta will drop you off at the sanctuary entrance

Forming the northern sector of the Wayanad reserve, **Tholpetty Wildlife Sanctuary** is one of the best parks in south India for sighting elephant, as well as bison, boar, sambar, spotted deer, macaques and Nilgiri langurs. Tigers also inhabit the reserve and their pug marks are commonly encountered along the muddy margins of forest trails; numbers are steadily increasing, although you'd be lucky to see one in the flesh.

The Forest Department runs 24km **jeep safaris** from the park's main gates along a network of rutted tracks, passing through stands of old teak and bamboo groves. There is currently no trekking allowed inside the sanctuary.

Sree Thirunelli

30km northwest of Mananthavady • A dozen buses daily connect Mananthavady to Thirunelli; jeeps will run you out there for around ₹550

One of Wayanad's most celebrated temples, **Sree Thirunelli**, lies in a remote part of the district, reached via a bumpy backroad winding west off the Kogadu road. Set amid an awesome amphitheatre of mountains draped in vegetation, the temple is an unusual mix of Keralan tiled roofs and north Indian-style pillared halls. The forest road is a good one to drive at dusk to spot elephants.

ACCOMMODATION

NORTH WAYANAD

Enteveedu Kayakkunnu, Pananaram ☎ 0493 522 0008, ⓦ enteveedu.co.in. Meaning "my own home", this wonderful out-of-the-way place halfway between Kalpetta and Mananthavady has large comfortable rooms; one has three double beds, others interconnect so you can book as a family or group. Shared sitout areas look over the

21

surrounding paddy fields and coffee plantations. Breakfast included, veg meals ₹250. A/c ₹500 extra. ₹3920 **Wildlife Resort** 500m from the Tholpetty Forest Check Post ☎ 97447 70500 or 9 846 603 147, ⓦ wildlife resorts.in. The most comfortable option within easy walking distance of the Tholpetty National Park gate. Its recently built laterite, red-tiled "cottages", set in steeply sloping gardens just off the main road, are bland, and a tad overpriced, but well furnished with good mattresses and private sitouts. ₹3500

The far north

The beautiful coast **north of Kozhikode** is a seemingly endless stretch of coconut palms, wooded hills and virtually deserted beaches. The small fishing towns ranged along it hold little of interest for visitors, most of whom bypass the area completely – missing out on some exquisite, quiet coves, and the chance to see **theyyem**, the extraordinary masked trance dances that take place in villages throughout the region between November and May (see page 1115).

The only village in Kannur district where you can be guaranteed a glimpse of *theyyem* is **Parassinikadavu**, a thirty-minute drive north of Kannur, where temple priests don elaborate costumes, dance and make offerings to the god Muthappan each morning and evening. With an early enough start, it's possible to catch the morning session and still have time to continue north to explore the little-visited **Valiyaparamba backwater** region.

Pressing on further north into Kasaragod district, it's worth splashing out on a night in one of the boutique retreats that have sprung up recently – the loveliest of them near the roadside town of **Nileshwar**, at the head of the Valiyaparamba backwaters. Larger hotel complexes, pitched at wealthy holiday-makers from Bengaluru, are beginning to appear further north still around **Bekal Fort**, where you can walk along impressive ramparts overlooking kilometres of empty coast.

Kannur (Cannanore)

KANNUR (Cannanore), a large, predominantly Moppila Muslim fishing and market town 92km north of Kozhikode, was for many centuries the capital of the Kolathiri rajas, who prospered from the maritime spice trade through its port. India's first Portuguese Viceroy, Francisco de Almeida, took the stronghold in 1505, leaving in his wake an imposing triangular bastion, **St Angelo's Fort**. This was taken in the seventeenth century by the Dutch, who sold it a hundred or so years later to the Arakkal rajas, Kerala's only ruling Muslim dynasty.

These days, the town is the largest in the northern Malabar region – a typically Keralan market and transport hub jammed with giant gold emporia and silk shops, and seething with traffic. Land prices are booming ahead of the opening of an international airport, which will doubtless see more skyscrapers rise on the outskirts. Kannur's few sights can be slotted into a morning, but increasing numbers of travellers are using the beaches to the south as bases from which to venture into the hinterland in search of **theyyem** rituals.

St Angelo's Fort
Daily 8am–6pm • Free, car park ₹10

Accessed through a gateway on its northern side, **St Angelo's Fort** remains in good condition and is worth visiting to wander the gardens and scale the massive laterite ramparts, littered with British cannons, for views over the town's massive Norwegian-funded fishing anchorage.

Arakkal Heritage Museum
Tues–Sun 10am–5.00pm • ₹50

The somewhat dilapidated whitewashed building facing the beachfront below the fort – once the raja and bibi of Arrakal's palace – now houses the government-run **Arakkal**

THEYYEM

Theyyem (or *theyyam*) – the dramatic spirit-possession ceremonies held at village shrines throughout the northern Malabar region in the winter – rank among Kerala's most extraordinary spectacles. More than four hundred different manifestations of this arcane ritual exist in the area around Kannur alone, each with its own distinctive costumes, elaborate jewellery, body paints, face make-up and, above all, gigantic headdresses (*mudi*).

Unlike in *kathakali* and *kudiyattam*, where actors impersonate goddesses or gods, here the performers actually become the deity being invoked, acquiring their magical powers. These allow them to perform superhuman feats, such as rolling in hot ashes or dancing with a crown that rises to the height of a coconut tree. By watching the *theyyem*, members of the audience believe they can partake of the deity's powers – to cure illness, conceive a child or get lucky in a business venture.

Traditionally staged in small clearings (*kaavus*) attached to village shrines, *theyyem* rituals are always performed by members of the lowest castes; Namboodiri and other high-caste people may attend, but they do so to venerate the deity – a unique inversion of the normal social hierarchy. Performances generally have three distinct phases: the *thottam*, where the dancer, wearing a small red headdress, recites a simple devotional song accompanied by the temple musicians; the *vellattam*, in which he runs through a series of more complicated rituals and slower, elegant poses; and the *mukhathezhuttu*, the main event, when he appears in full costume in front of the shrine. From this point on until the end of the performance, which may last all night, the *theyyem* is manifest and empowered, dancing around the arena in graceful, rhythmic steps that grow quicker and more energetic as the night progresses, culminating in a frenzied outburst just before dawn, when it isn't uncommon for the dancer to be struck by a kind of spasm.

Increasing numbers of visitors are making the journey up to Kannur to experience *theyyem*, but **finding rituals** requires time, patience and stamina. The best sources of advice are local guesthouse owners, who can check the Malayalai newspapers for notices; ⓦ keralatourism. org/theyyamcalendar is also useful. Anyone pushed for time might consider a trip out to **Parassinikadavu** (see page 1117), where a form of *theyyem* is staged daily.

Heritage Museum. Here documents, weapons, various pieces of four-hundred-year-old rosewood furniture and other heirlooms relating to the family's history are displayed – though they're somewhat upstaged by the old building itself, with its high-beamed ceilings and original floorboards.

Folklore Museum

Chirakkal, 5km north of Kannur town • Mon–Fri 10am–4.30pm • ₹10 • ☏ 0497 277 8090 • Rickshaws charge ₹200–300 for the trip, and buses run every 30min from the Padanna Paalam bus stand on the north edge of Kannur town

Extravagant costumes worn in *theyyem* and other less-known local art and ritual forms, including the Muslim dance style *oppana*, dominate the collection of the **Folklore Museum**, in the village of **Chirakkal** just off NH-17. Housed in the 130-year-old palace, the engaging collection also features masks and weapons used in *patayani* rituals performed in local Bhadrakali temples, and displays of *todikkalam* murals.

ARRIVAL AND DEPARTURE   KANNUR (CANNANORE)

Straddling the main coastal transport artery between Mangalaru in Karnataka and Kochi/Thiruvananthapuram, Kannur is well connected by bus and train to most major towns and cities in Kerala.

By train The busy railway station, right in the centre of town, is Kannur's principal landmark, and the best place to pick up auto-rickshaws and taxis for trips further afield. Kerala Tourism has an info counter on the main concourse (Mon–Sat 9am–4pm; ☏ 0497 270 3121) where you can

find out about homestays and *theyyem* rituals.

Destinations Goa (2 daily; 7hr–9hr); Ernakulam/Kochi (9 daily; 5hr 30min–6hr 30min); Kozhikode/Calicut (every 30min–1hr; 1hr 20min–1hr 45min); Mangalaru (hourly; 2–3hr); Mumbai (2 daily; 18–21hr).

By bus Most local services, including those from other towns in Malabar, work out of the New Bus Stand, a 5min walk southeast of the railway station; the hub for long-distance Kerala state services is the KSRTC stand, a short

21

KANNUR COOPERATIVES

Local guesthouse owners can point you towards **handloom weaving workshops** dotted around nearby villages – a legacy of the old calico cotton trade. A couple that are used to receiving visitors (Mon–Sat) are the **Kanhirode Co-operative**, 13km northeast of Kannur on the main road to Mattanur (☎ 0497 285 7865, ⓦ weaveco.com), which employs around four hundred workers to make upholstery and curtain fabrics, plus material for luxury shirts and saris, and **Lokanath Weavers Co-operative**, 3km east of Kannur on the Edapally–Panvell Hwy (☎ 0497 272 6330, ⓦ lokfab.com). The **Kerala Dinesh Beedi Co-operative** in Thottada 7km south of Kannur (☎ 0497 270 1699, ⓦ keraladinesh.com) makes an interesting visit to see workers deftly rolling thousands of skinny Indian cigarettes – though you can't actually buy them here.

hop by auto-rickshaw north. Fleets of private buses – the most garishly painted coaches in India – also cover the same routes.

Destinations The following refers only to Kerala and Karnataka State Transport Corporation services: Ernakulam/Kochi (4–6 daily; 8hr); Kozhikode/Calicut (hourly; 1hr 30min–3hr); Madurai (1 nightly; 12hr); Mangalaru (8 daily; 3–5hr); Mysuru (6 daily; 5–6hr).

ACCOMMODATION

Kannur's noisy and congested centre is jammed with **hotels**, but you'll find better options further east in the cantonment district behind **Baby Beach**, and further north at **Palliyamoola Beach** (a ₹75 ride away), where a number of small resorts and homestays stand close to the sea. Southeast of town down the coast, a string of four spectacular beaches hold even more desirable places to stay.

Blue Mermaid Thottada Beach ☎ 94973 00234, ⓦ bluemermaid.in. Gorgeous homestay resort comprising a modern block of spacious, well-furnished a/c rooms, a detached cottage on the headland (₹3800) and a romantic bamboo honeymoon lodge (₹4000) – all in a heavenly setting overlooking one of the area's loveliest beaches. Keralan meals and yoga lessons on site. Half board **₹4000**

Chera Rocks 14km south at Chera Kalle, Tayeechery ☎ 94476 43211 or 0490 234 3211, ⓦ cherarocks.com. If you're dreaming of a room where you can watch the moonlight on the waves and fall asleep to the sound of surf crashing through the coconut trees, look no further. Here is a pretty three-bedroom cottage huddled in a palm grove behind an idyllic beach, and less pricey "deluxe" rooms occupying a white house set back just behind it. Rates include full board and station pick-up. **₹4500**

★ **Costa Malabari** 10km south near Thottada village ☎ 94477 75691. Three traditional Keralan bungalows, surrounded by cashew and coconut groves on the bluff above pretty Thottada Beach. *Costa Malabari II* is the pick of the crop (and costs ₹1500 more than *I* & *III*), perched on a clifftop where a flight of rickety wooden steps descends to a golden-sand cove. The food, which is included and served on a picturesque veranda, gets rave reviews. Pick-up from Kannur by arrangement. **₹4200**

Ezhara Beach House Near Ezhara Moppila School, Ezhara Kadappuram, Kuttikkagam ☎ 0497 283 5022 or 98468 19941, ⓦ ezharabeachhouse.com. Tucked under the palms, this slightly shabby, blue-painted bungalow is incredibly private and the sort of place travellers pitch up and stay for weeks. It's a stone's throw from an empty beach, but visitors are asked to respect the fact it's in a Muslim village and cover up. Hyacinth is a great host; you get a whole floor to yourself. Half board **₹3500**

★ **Kannur Beach House** Thottada ☎ 98471 86330 or 98471 84535, ⓦ kannurbeachhouse.com. Sandwiched on a sliver of land between a river and the beach, this friendly little guesthouse has a sublime location and the rooms, with their antique wooden doors and windows, luminous interiors and lovely verandas, are perfect havens. Half board **₹4000**

Palm Grove Heritage Mill Rd, near Government Guesthouse, Kannur town ☎ 0497 270 3182, ⓦ palmgroveheritageretreat.com. Dating from the 1930s, this former palace once belonged to the last raja of Arikkal but now accommodates an offbeat hotel, with a choice of bargain rooms or threadbare suites in the old portion, and large, modern, good-value doubles in the two adjacent, multi-storey blocks that sometimes host conferences. Breakfast not included. A/c ₹500 extra. Doubles **₹900**, suites **₹1120**

EATING

Geetha Station Rd. For a real Keralan experience stop at this diminutive, slightly grubby four-table "bakery" opposite the railway station exit. The menu isn't in English so you'll have to point at what you want from the glass case (samosa, buttery *paratha*, *ela ada*...). The masala curry is spicy, the chai sweet and strong, and you'll have lunch for two for under ₹100. Daily 7am–9pm.

Parassinikadavu

The **Parassini Madammpura** temple in the village of **PARASSINIKADAVU**, 20km north of Kannur beside the River Valapatanam, is visited in large numbers by Hindu pilgrims for its **theyyem** rituals (daily 6.30–8.30am & 5.45–8.30pm). Elaborately dressed and accompanied by a traditional drum group, the resident priest, or *madayan*, becomes possessed by the temple's presiding deity – Lord Muthappan, Shiva, in the form of a *kiratha*, or hunter – and performs a series of complex offerings. The two-hour ceremony culminates when the priest/deity dances forward to bless individual members of the congregation – an extraordinary spectacle, even by Keralan standards.

ARRIVAL AND DEPARTURE   PARASSINIKADAVU

By bus and taxi Regular local buses leave Kannur for Parassinikadavu from around 7am, dropping passengers at the top of the village. If you want to get here in time for the earliest *theyyem*, however, you'll have to fork out for one of the Ambassador taxis that line up outside Kannur bus stand (around ₹500 return). Cabbies sleep in their cars, so you can arrange the trip on the spot by waking one up; taxis may also be arranged through most hotels. Either way, you'll have to leave around 4.30am – or else spend the night nearer the temple.

ACCOMMODATION

Thai Resort 80m from the temple ☎0497 278 4242, ⓦthairesort.in. Shaded by coconut trees, seven circular stone cottages are dotted around a well-kept garden with cool, comfortable rooms. They're a bit gloomy, but well aired, and the location's perfect. **₹2200**

Thapasya Heritage Temple Rd ☎0497 278 2944 or 94470 65108, ⓦthapasyaheritage.com. Situated on the hillside just south of the village, this is by far the best-value budget option within walking distance of the temple, and is very popular because of it. The building's modern, the beds have crisp linen and comfy mattresses, and the bathrooms are clean. A/c ₹1500. **₹800**

Valiyaparamba

If you were overwhelmed by the crowded backwaters in the south and are yearning for quiet white-sand beaches and coconut trees, push on 50km north of Kannur to one of the quietest stretches of coast in the state. The **Valiyaparamba backwaters** centre on a small, 30km delta fed by four rivers and their various bands and tributaries. Though local ferries crisscross this fascinating necklace of lagoons and islets, and a few companies organize houseboat trips from Ayitti Jetty, Valiyaparamba holds comparatively few permanent dwellings and traffic on its waterways largely consists of country fishing boats. It makes a wonderful region for off-track explorations; foreign tourists are few and far between.

ACCOMMMODATION

★**Kanan Beach Resort** Nileswar ☎0467 228 8880 or 86062 08880, ⓦkananbeachresort.com. Of all the swanky resorts in the area, this has the most Keralan character. The self-contained, gable-roofed cottages – the size of small villas – come with a kitchen and sea- and sunset-facing verandas. There's a quiet pool and the location in a coconut grove alongside the beach is unbeatable. **₹16,550**

Valiyaparamba Retreat Oriyara village, 15km north of Payyanur, ☎98450 22056, ⓦvretreat.in. This three-bedroom house facing the backwater on the northern side of Valiyaparamba has a welcoming host, tasty food and all the basics for a comfy stay. Regular buses run to Oriyara (30min) from the nearest railway station at Payyanur. Full board **₹4200**

Bekal

BEKAL, 24km north of Nileshwar and the Valiyaparamba backwaters, is popular among Keralans as a weekend day-trip destination, with huge **Bekal Fort** (daily 8am–5.30pm; ₹100) standing on a hot and dusty promontory north of palm-fringed **Bekal Beach**. Both spots are great for people-watching in the late afternoon as families in their Sunday best stroll and paddle in the sea.

Karnataka

VERDANT FOREST IN THE COORG DISTRICT OF KARNATAKA

Karnataka

Created in 1956 from the princely state of Mysore, Karnataka – a derivation of the word *karu nadu* meaning "black soil" in the local language, Kannada – marks a transition zone between central India and the Dravidian deep south. Along its borders with Maharashtra, Andhra Pradesh and Telangana, a string of medieval walled towns studded with domed mausoleums and minarets recall the era when this part of the Deccan was a Muslim stronghold. The coastal and hill districts that dovetail with Kerala are, in contrast, quintessential Hindu south India, lush with tropical vegetation and soaring temple *gopuram*. In between are scattered several extraordinary sites, notably the ruined Vijayanagar city at Hampi, whose lost temples and derelict palaces stand amid an arid, rocky landscape of surreal beauty.

Fed by the southwest monsoon (see box below) and draped in dense deciduous forests, the **Western Ghats**, recognized among the world's top eight biodiversity hotspots (see page 1151), run in an unbroken line along the state's palm-fringed coast, impeding the path of the rain clouds east. As a result, the landscape of the interior – comprising the southern apex of the triangular Deccan trap, known as the **Mysore Plateau**, is considerably drier. Three of south India's most sacred rivers, the Kaveri (also spelt Cauvery), Tungabhadra and Krishna, flow across this sun-baked terrain, draining east to the Bay of Bengal.

Karnataka's principal attractions are concentrated at opposite ends of the state, with a handful of less-visited places dotted along the coast between Goa and Kerala. Road and rail routes dictate that most itineraries take in the brash state capital, **Bengaluru (Bangalore)**, a go-ahead, modern city that epitomizes the aspirations of the country's new middle class, with glittering malls, fast-food outlets and nightlife unrivalled outside Mumbai. The state's second city, **Mysuru (Mysore)**, appeals more for its Raj-era ambience, nineteenth-century palaces and vibrant produce and incense markets. It also lies within easy reach of several important historical monuments.

A clutch of unmissable sights lie further northwest, dotted around the dull railway town of **Hassan**. Around nine centuries ago, the Hoysala kings sited their grand dynastic capitals here, at the now middle-of-nowhere villages of **Belur** and **Halebidu (Halebid)**, where several superbly crafted temples survive intact. More impressive still, and one of India's most extraordinary sacred sites, is Gomateshwara, the 18m Jain colossus at **Sravanabelagola**, which stares serenely over idyllic Deccan countryside.

West of Mysuru, the Ghats rise in a wall of thick jungle cut by deep ravines and isolated valleys. Within, the coffee-growing district of **Kodagu (Coorg)** offers an entrancing, unique culture and lush, misty vistas. Most Coorg agricultural produce

---

BEST TIME TO VISIT

Coastal Karnataka is one of the wettest regions in India, its climate dominated by the seasonal monsoon, which sweeps in from the southwest in June, dumping an average of 4m of rain on the coast before it peters out in late September. October to April is therefore the best time to visit. **Bengaluru and Mysuru**, to the south of the Deccan Plateau, have a temperate climate with mild weather most of the year. The **northern tracts** and the coast get really hot in summer (April–June), with monsoon bringing some respite between July and October.

Highlights

❶ Bengaluru (Bangalore) Booming silicon city offers the best shopping, nightlife and dining this side of Mumbai, not to mention a few great parks, plus the odd palace and temple. See page 1124

❷ Mysuru (Mysore) The sandalwood city oozes relaxed, old-world charm and has lots to see, including the opulent palace and a photogenic market. See page 1134

❸ Halebidu and Belur Two wonderfully ornate and architecturally unique Hoysala temples set deep in the slow-paced Karnataka countryside. See pages 1144 and 1146

❹ Gokarna This vibrant Hindu holy town is blessed with atmospheric temples and exquisite crescent beaches and is ideal for serious unwinding. See page 1159

❺ Hampi The crumbling remains of the Vijayanagar kingdom, scattered among a stunning boulder-strewn landscape bisected by the Tungabhadra River. See page 1165

❻ Vijayapura (Bijapur) Known as the "Agra of the South" for its splendid Islamic architecture, most famously the vast dome of the Gol Gumbaz. See page 1176

❼ Bidar Rarely visited Muslim outpost in the remote northeast of the state, famed for *bidri* metalwork and magnificent medieval monuments. See page 1181

HIGHLIGHTS ARE MARKED ON THE MAP ON PAGE 1122

FESTIVALS IN KARNATAKA

Hampi Utsav (early Nov). Celebrated since Vijayanagar times and revived by the Government of Karnataka, this three-day festival is a cultural showcase of music, dance, costume dramas, puppet shows, fireworks, processions and *kushti* (wrestling) that once received royal patronage.

Makar Sankranti (mid-Jan). The transition of the sun into the zodiacal sign of Makara (Capricorn) is when the harvest festival (*suggi habba*) is celebrated. Temple festivities, cultural programmes and kite-flying, especially in northern Karnataka, mark the occasion.

Bangalore Karaga (April). Bengaluru's oldest festival is celebrated over eleven days around the Dharmaraya Swamy Temple in the old city. The festival honours Draupadi, considered a form of Shakti, and is named after the *karaga* or large floral pyramid borne by the appointed carrier during a night-time procession to the accompaniment of music and acrobatics.

Mysore Dasara (Sept/Oct). The biggest of them all, Karnataka's *naada habba* (state festival) culminates in a grand procession on its tenth and final day (see page 1138).

Kadalekai Parishe (Dec/Jan). Bengaluru's unique groundnut fair, held near the Bull Temple in Basavanagudi (see page 1127) with rural produce on sale.

22

is shipped out of **Mangaluru (Mangalore)**, a useful stopover on the journey along Karnataka's beautiful **Karavali coast**. Interrupted by countless mangrove-lined estuaries, the state's 320km-long coastline contains plenty of fine beaches. Attractions of the coastal belt include the famous Krishna temple at **Udupi**, an important Vaishnavite centre, **Jog Falls** – India's second highest cataract – set amid some of the region's most spectacular scenery, though for many the region's biggest draw is the atmospheric Hindu pilgrimage town of **Gokarna**, further north up the coast, a well-established hideaway for Western budget travellers owing to its string of exquisite beaches.

However, the state's undisputed highlight lies in the hinterland of **northern Karnataka**: the UNESCO-listed ghost city of Vijayanagar, better known as **Hampi**. Scattered around boulder hills on the south banks of the Tungabhadra River, the ruins of this once splendid capital provide a magical setting, often prompting travellers to overstay. The main access point to Hampi is **Hosapete (Hospet)**, from where buses leave for the journey north across the rolling Deccan plains to **Badami**, **Aihole** and **Pattadakal**, the last another UNESCO World Heritage Site. Now lost in countryside, these tiny villages – once capitals of the **Chalukya** dynasty – are still littered with ancient rock-cut caves and finely carved stone temples.

Further north, in one of Karnataka's most remote and poorest districts, craggy hilltop citadels and crumbling wayside tombs herald the formerly troubled buffer zone between the Muslim-dominated northern Deccan and the Dravidian-Hindu south. **Bijapur**, capital of the Bahmanis – now formally **Vijayapura** – harbours south India's finest collection of Islamic architecture, including the world's second largest freestanding dome, the Gol Gumbaz. The first Bahmani capital, **Gulbarga** (now **Kalaburagi**) site of a famous Muslim shrine and theological college, has retained little of its former splendour but the more isolated **Bidar**, where the Bahmanis moved in the sixteenth century, deserves a detour en route to or from Hyderabad. Perched on a rocky escarpment, its crumbling red ramparts include Persian-style mosaic-fronted mosques, mausoleums and a sprawling fort complex evocative of Samarkand on the Silk Route.

Brief history

Like much of southern India, Karnataka has been ruled by successive Buddhist, Hindu and Muslim dynasties. The influence of Jainism has also been marked; India's very first emperor, **Chandragupta Maurya**, is believed to have converted to Jainism in the fourth century BC, renounced his throne and fasted to death at Sravanabelagola, now one of the most visited Jain pilgrimage centres in the country.

During the first millennium AD, this whole region was dominated by power struggles between the various kingdoms controlling the western Deccan. The period between the third and fifth centuries saw the rise of dynasties like the **Satavahanas**, the **Kadambas** and the **Gangas** of Talakad. From the sixth to the eighth centuries, the **Chalukya** kingdom of Vatapi (Badami) included Maharashtra, the Konkan coast on the west and the whole of Karnataka. The **Rashtrakutas** and the **Hoysalas** dominated until the thirteenth century, when the Deccan kingdoms were overwhelmed by General Malik Kafur, a convert to Islam.

By the medieval era Muslim incursions from the north laid the foundation of the **Bahmani** Sultanate and forced the hitherto warring and fractured Hindu states of the south into close alliance, with the mighty **Vijayanagar** kings emerging as overlords. Their lavish capital, Vijayanagar, ruled an empire stretching from the Bay of Bengal to the Arabian Sea and south to Cape Comorin. The Bahmani Sultanate split into five independent kingdoms in 1490 but joined forces as a confederacy, the Deccan Sultanate, in 1565 at the Battle of Talikota, and laid siege to Vijayanagar, plundering its opulent palaces and temples.

Thereafter, a succession of Muslim sultans held sway over the north, while in the south of the state, the independent **Wadiyar rajas** of Mysore, whose territory was comparatively small, successfully fought off the Marathas. In 1761, the brilliant Muslim campaigner Haider Ali, with French support, seized the throne. His son, Tipu Sultan, turned Mysore into a major force in the south before he was killed by the British at the **battle of Srirangapatnam** in 1799. After Tipu's defeat, the British restored the Wadiyar family to the throne. Apart from a further half-century of colonial rule in the mid-nineteenth century, they kept it until Karnataka was created by the merging of the states of Mysore and the Madras Presidencies in 1956.

Bengaluru (Bangalore) and around

The political hub of the region, **BENGALURU** is a world apart from the rest of the state and in many ways India's most Westernized urban centre. Once a sleepy cantonment, the charming, verdant "Garden City" of just over 600,0000 people at Independence has been completely transformed by the technology boom into both a trendy, racy business hub and a bustling, smog-choked megalopolis of nearly twelve million, perhaps the fastest growing city in India. These days, signs of the West are thick on the ground: big-brand fashion stores and branches of *CCD* or *Barista* on nearly every corner; a swanky international airport and ultramodern metro (still far from completion); and legions of hard-working, free-spending twenty- and thirty-somethings in designer T-shirts and miniskirts.

Despite its lush environs and cosmopolitan air, Bengaluru's few attractions are no match for those elsewhere in the state. That said, it's an efficient transport hub, well served by plane and bus, and paired with first-rate shopping, dining and nightlife, and a calendar packed with big-ticket events in music, dance, art, literature, theatre or folk arts, this vibrant city can still deliver a few days' respite from south India's more taxing inconveniences.

The centre of modern Bengaluru lies about 4km east of Kempe Gowda Circle (and the bus and railway stations), near **MG Road**, where you'll find most of the mid-range accommodation, restaurants, shops, tourist information and banks, although **Indiranagar** further east is the up and coming area for leisure. Leafy **Cubbon Park**, and its less than exciting museums, lie on its eastern edge, while the oldest, most "Indian" part of the city extends south from the railway station, a warren of winding streets at their most dynamic in the hubbub of the **City** and **Gandhi markets**. Bengaluru's tourist attractions are spread out: monuments such as **Tipu's Summer Palace** and the **Bull Temple** are some way south of the centre. Most, if not all, can be seen on a half-day tour, but if you explore on foot, be warned that Bengaluru has some of the worst pavements in India.

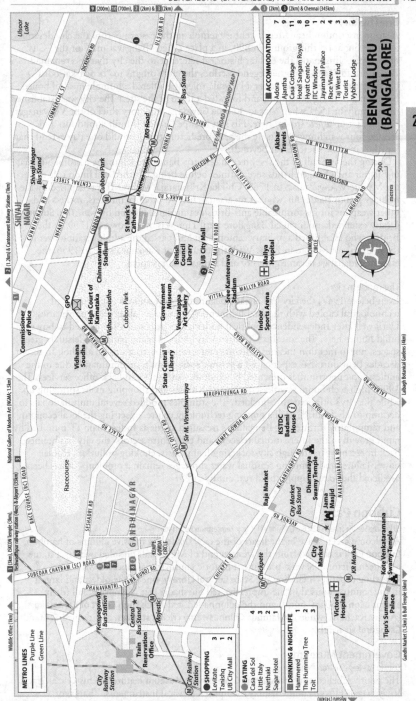

BENGALURU (BANGALORE)

22

Ulsoor Lake

★ Bus Stand

SHIVAJI NAGAR

Shivaji Nagar Bus Stand ★

Commissioner of Police

Cubbon Park

St Mark's Cathedral

Chinnaswamy Stadium

High Court of Karnataka

GPO ⊠

Vidhana Soudha

Vidhana Soudha

Cubbon Park

State Central Library

Government Museum

Venkatappa Art Gallery

British Council Library

UB City Mall ⓘ

Sree Kanteerava Stadium

Mallya Hospital ✚

Indoor Sports Arena

Akbar Travels

Racecourse

GANDHINAGAR

KEMPE GOWDA CIRCLE

KSTDC Badami House ⓘ

Raja Market

City Market Bus Stand

Dharmaraya Swamy Temple

Jama Masjid

Chickpete Ⓜ

City Market

KR Market Ⓜ

Victoria Hospital ✚

Kote Venkataramana Swamy Temple

Tipu's Summer Palace

Kempegowda Bus Station

Central ★ Bus Stand

Train Reservation Office

City Railway Station

Majestic Ⓜ

City Railway Station Ⓜ

Sir M. Visvesvaraya Ⓜ

METRO LINES
— Purple Line
— Green Line

0   500   metres

N

◄ Wildlife Office (11km)

◄ 1 (3km), ISKCON Temple (3km), Yeshwantpur railway station (4km) & Airport (35km)

◄ National Gallery of Modern Art (NGMA; 1.5km)

◄ 2 (1.2km) & Cantonment Railway Station (1km)

Lalbagh Botanical Gardens (4km) ►

Gandhi Market (1.5km) & Bull Temple (6km) ►

▼ Mysun (145km)

■ ACCOMMODATION
Adora	7
Ajantha	9
Casa Cottage	11
Hotel Sangam Royal	8
Hyatt Centric	10
ITC Windsor	1
Jayamahal Palace	2
Race View	4
Taj West End	3
Tourist	5
Vybhav Lodge	6

● SHOPPING
Levitate	3
Tanishq	1
UB City Mall	2

◆ EATING
Casa del Sol	4
Little Italy	3
Narthaki	1
Sagar Hotel	2

■ DRINKING & NIGHTLIFE
Hammered	1
The Humming Tree	2
Toit	3

22

Brief history

A stone inscription near a tenth-century temple in the eastern part of the city describes a battle fought on this ground in 890, in a place called "Bengaval-uru," or the "City of Guards". This marks the earliest historical reference to the city that was **renamed** Bengaluru in 2006. (Another legend ascribes the city's origins to "benda-kal-ooru", or "village of boiled beans", after a Hoysala ruler was offered a humble meal of boiled beans on a hunting expedition and founded a town at the site.) The city was established more firmly in 1537 when Magadi **Kempe Gowda**, a feudatory chief of the Vijayanagar Empire, set up a *pete* (town) here. His son Kempe Gowda II built a mud fort and erected four watchtowers outside the *pete*, predicting that it would one day extend that far (the city now stretches far beyond).

During the first half of the seventeenth century, Bangalore fell to the Muslim Sultanate of Bijapur and changed hands several times before being returned to Hindu rule under the Mysore Wadiyar rajas. In 1758, Chikka Krishnaraja Wadiyar II was deposed by the military genius **Haider Ali**, who set up arsenals here to produce muskets, rockets and other weapons for his formidable anti-British campaigns. He and his son, **Tipu Sultan**, greatly extended and fortified Bangalore until Tipu was overthrown in 1799 by the British, who established a military cantonment and passed the administration over to the maharaja of Mysore in 1881. With the creation of Karnataka state in 1956, the erstwhile maharaja became governor and Bangalore the capital.

The modern city

Even before 1947, the city had already begun to transform into a scientific and technological capital with the establishment of numerous colleges and universities. Until well after Independence, political leaders, film stars and VIPs flocked to buy or build homes here. The so-called "Garden City" offered many parks and leisurely green spaces, not to mention theatres, cinemas and a lack of restrictions on alcohol. In recent decades Bengaluru has experienced a **seismic societal shift**, predominantly due to the endless job opportunities presented by computer software and back-office services. The 1990s high-tech boom saw skyscrapers, swish stores and shopping malls springing up, while the city's infrastructure buckled. The stumbles prodded several multinationals to decamp to Hyderabad, itself a growing technology centre, upsetting the local economy and temporarily threatening Bengaluru's treasured status as India's main IT hub. Led by rapid growth in the international telecom and call-centre sectors, the city has bounced back in recent years, though sky-rocketing living costs, choking pollution, regular power failures and crippling seasonal water shortages remain a problem – it has been predicted the water supply could run out by 2025.

Cubbon Park

Ⓜ Vidhana Soudha or buses #296B, #114B and #114C from Kempegowda Bus Station

A welcome green space in the heart of the city, shaded by massive clumps of bamboo, **Cubbon Park** is entered from the western end of MG Road, presided over by a statue of Queen Victoria. Several prominent historic landmarks are located within its sprawling expanse, including the **State Central Library**, one of the oldest and largest in the country, housed in the impressive red Sheshadri Iyer Memorial Hall (daily except Mon 8.30am–6pm), and the colonnaded, red-brick **High Court of Karnataka** (Attara Kacheri), while the famous **Chinnaswamy cricket stadium** and domed **St Mark's Cathedral** sit nearby.

Government Museum

Kasturba Rd • Tues–Sun 10am–5pm • ₹10

The poorly labelled and maintained **Government Museum** features prehistoric artefacts, Vijayanagar, Hoysala and Chalukya sculpture, musical instruments, Thanjavur paintings and Deccani and Rajasthani miniatures. It includes the adjacent **Venkatappa Art Gallery**, which exhibits twentieth-century landscapes, portraits, abstract art, wood sculpture and occasional temporary art shows.

Vidhana Soudha

On the northwest edge of Cubbon Park • No public entry

Built in 1956, Bengaluru's vast State Secretariat, **Vidhana Soudha**, is the largest civic structure of its kind in the country. Kengal Hanumanthaiah, chief minister at the time, wanted a "people's palace" that, following the transfer of power from the royal Wadiyar dynasty to a legislature, would "reflect the power and dignity of the people". In theory its design is entirely Indian, but its overall effect is not unlike the bombastic colonial architecture built in the so-called Indo-Saracenic style.

22

Lalbagh Botanical Gardens

Daily 6am–7pm • ₹20 • Ⓜ Lalbagh or buses #25, #25A & #25B and #25E from Kempegowda Bus Station • ☎ 080 2657 1925

Inspired by the splendid gardens of the Mughals and the French botanical gardens at Puducherry in Tamil Nadu, Sultan Haider Ali set to work in 1760 laying out the **Lalbagh Botanical Gardens**, 4km south of the centre. Originally covering forty acres, just beyond his fort – where one of Kempe Gowda's original watchtowers can still be seen – the gardens were expanded under Ali's son Tipu, who introduced numerous exotic species of plants, and today they house an extensive horticultural seedling centre. The British brought in gardeners from Kew in 1856 and built a military bandstand and a glasshouse, based on London's Crystal Palace, which hosts wonderful flower shows. Now spreading over 240 acres, the gardens are pleasant to visit during the day, but tend to attract unsavoury characters after around 6pm. Great sunsets and city views can be had from the central hill, which is topped by a small shrine.

Tipu's Summer Palace and around

KR Market • Daily 10am–6pm • ₹100 (₹5) • Buses #15E, #31 & #31E and #210A from Kempegowda Bus Station

Just southwest of the crowded City Market (aka KR Market), near the fairytale-like **Jama Masjid** – whitewashed and rambling and still in regular use – lies **Tipu's Summer Palace**, a two-storey, mostly wooden structure built in 1791. Similar in style to the Daria Daulat Bagh at Srirangapatna (see page 1142), the palace is in a far worse state, with most of its painted decoration destroyed. Next door, the **Kote Venkataramana Swamy Temple**, dating from the early eighteenth century, was built by the Wadiyar rajas.

Bull Temple

Basavanagudi • Daily 7.30am–1.30pm & 2.30–8.30pm • Buses #15E, #31, #210A and #210E from Kempegowda Bus Station

Lying 6km south of the Kempegowda Bus Station, in the Basavanagudi area, Kempe Gowda's sixteenth-century **Bull Temple** houses a massive monolithic Nandi bull, its grey granite made black by the application of charcoal and oil. The temple is approached along a path lined with mendicants and snake charmers; inside, for a small donation, the priest will offer you a string of fragrant jasmine flowers.

Don't miss the **Dodda Ganesha Temple** (daily 6.30am–12.30pm & 5.30–8.30pm), featuring a mammoth monolith of Ganesha, 5.5m tall and 5m wide, below the Bull Temple.

Sri Radha Krishna Mandir (ISKCON temple)

Hare Krishna Hill, Chord Rd • Daily 7.15am–1pm & 4.15–8.30pm • Buses #78A, #78E, #19E, 258CC from Kempegowda Bus Station

22

Some 8km north of the centre lies ISKCON's (International Society of Krishna Consciousness) gleaming temple, a hybrid of ultramodern glass and vernacular south Indian architecture. Also known as **Sri Radha Krishna Mandir**, it's a huge, lavish showpiece crowned by a gold-plated dome. Barriers guide visitors on a one-way journey through the well-organized complex to the inner sanctum, an octagonal hall resplendent with colourfully painted ceilings and golden images of the god Krishna and his consort Radha. Collection points throughout and inescapable merchandizing on the way out are evidence of the organization's highly successful commercialization.

National Gallery of Modern Art (NGMA)

Manikyavelu Mansion, 49 Palace Rd • Daily 11am–6.30pm; 1hr guided tours Wed 11am & Sat 3pm • ₹500 (₹20) • ☎ 080 2234 2338, ⓦ ngmaindia.gov.in

Set in a former Wadiyar mansion, the beautifully designed and laid out **National Gallery of Modern Art** (one of three in India – the others are in Delhi and Mumbai) is a fabulous repository of 17,000 paintings, sculptures and graphic prints capturing Indian art from the early eighteenth century to present times.

Around Bengaluru

While most visitors push straight on to Mysuru, there are several places of interest within easy reach of Bengaluru, especially for those with interest in folk culture, wildlife or spiritual renewal.

Nrityagram Dance Village

Hesaraghatta • Tues–Sun 10am–2pm • Village entrance fee ₹100; guided tours with lunch and performance (book in advance) ₹1500/person (minimum ten) • ☎ 080 2846 6313, ⓦ nrityagram.org

Anyone wishing to see or study classical dance in a rural environment should check out **Nrityagram Dance Village**, a delightful, purpose-built model village 30km northwest of Bengaluru, designed by the award-winning architect Gerard de Cunha and founded by the late Protima Gauri. Gauri had a colourful career in media and film, and eventually came to be renowned as an exponent of Odissi dance (see page 922). Attracting pupils from all over the world, the school hosts regular performances and lectures on Indian mythology and art, and also offers courses in different forms of Indian dance.

Nandi Hills

Daily 6am–10pm • ₹10 • ☎ 080 2659 9231 • You can stay at Nehru Nilaya (bookings via ⓦ nandihillsreservations.in) or KSTDC's Mayura Pine Top (☎ 0815 6250906, ⓦ karnatakaholidays.net) • Regular government buses from Kempegowda Bus Station (2hr)

Some 60km north of Bengaluru in Chikkaballapur district, **Nandi Hills** is named after the hilltop shrine of Yoga Nandishwara, dedicated to Shiva. The erstwhile summer retreat of Tipu Sultan and the British, the hills rise to almost 1500m and offer panoramic views and invariably pleasant weather. You can hike to **Tipu's Drop**, a dreaded 600m clifftop from which convicts were hurled to their death by Tipu Sultan, while other draws include the spring-fed Amrita Sarovar tank and *Nehru Nilaya*, the guesthouse where ex-PM Jawaharlal Nehru stayed.

Bannerghatta National Park

Daily 9.30am–5pm • Zoo ₹80; Butterfly Park ₹30; bus safari adults₹400 (₹260), children ₹300 (₹130); boating ₹60; camera ₹20, video camera ₹200 • ⓦ bannerghattabiologicalpark.org • Bus BIG-10 AC4 from MG Rd, #365/#V365 from Kempegowda Bus Station or #366 from City Market; buses stop at Nagamanna Doddi, 400m from the park

The key attraction of the 104-square-kilometre **Bannerghatta National Park**, 22km south of Bengaluru, is a compact "biological park", which houses a zoo, butterfly enclosure, crocodile farm, reptile park and aviary. Safaris are organized to see lions, tigers, herbivores and sloth bear in a wilderness habitat.

ART OF LIVING INTERNATIONAL CENTRE

Ved Vignam Maha Vidya Peeth (daily 9am-6.30pm; ☎ 080 6726 2626, ⓦ artofliving.org), the main centre of the **Art of Living** organization founded in 1982 by **Sri Sri Ravi Shankar** (not to be confused with the great sitar maestro), occupies 24 acres of lush, green, hilly land 21km south of Bengaluru on Kanakapura Road in Udayapura. Its centrepiece is the splendid, lotus-like **Vishalakshmi Mantap temple**, which is surrounded by more shrines, an amphitheatre and an ashram boasting lodgings, restaurants and a host of other facilities including a wellness centre, bookshop, Ayurvedic spa and even a wedding hall. The organization – now with centres worldwide and NGO status – was founded by the guru after he discovered **Sudarshan Kriya**, a powerful stress-reducing breathing technique that is the focal point of his teachings. Those interested in courses or volunteering can register through the website, or simply drop in to attend regular events like music, meditation and *darshan* led by the guru (most Wed & Sat 4.30pm). Get here by taking bus #211A, #211B, #211C or #211F from Kempegowda Bus Station or #213 or #214D from City Market.

22

Janapada Loka Folk Arts Museum

On the Mysuru road · Daily except Tues 9am–5.30pm · Museum ₹100 (₹20); video show ₹5; boating ₹10 · ☎ 96866 01166 · Any Bengaluru–Mysuru bus, except nonstop express services, can drop you here

The **Janapada Loka Folk Arts Museum**, 53km southwest of Bengaluru, gives a fascinating insight into the region's culture. The collection is impressive: there's an amazing array of hunting implements, weapons, ingenious household gadgets, masks, dolls and shadow puppets, plus carved wooden *bhuta* (spirit) sculptures and larger-than-life temple procession figures, manuscripts, musical instruments and *yakshagana* theatre costumes. A small **restaurant** serves simple food, and the adjacent *Kamat Lokaruchi* restaurant is a popular stopover for Bengaluru–Mysuru travellers.

ARRIVAL AND DEPARTURE	BENGALURU (BANGALORE) AND AROUND

BY PLANE

Airport Bengaluru International Airport (ⓦ bengaluru airport.com) is 35km northeast of the city in Devanahalli. It's the busiest in south India and the most spacious in the country, with top-notch facilities. Until the much-discussed high-speed rail link is up and running, you can get into the city by Meru Airport Taxi (₹900–1000; ☎ 080 4422 4422, ⓦ merucabs.com) or efficient a/c Vayu Vajra bus; the most useful routes to visitors are the round-the-clock #9 to/from Central Bus Stand (every 20–50min; 45min–1hr 15min; ₹250) and #7A to/from MG Rd (11 daily; 50min–1hr 20min; ₹250). KSRTC (see page 1130) also runs direct FlyBus services from the airport to Mysuru (20 daily; 4hr), Madikeri (2 daily; 6hr 45min) and Tirupati (2 daily; 6hr 30min), plus an overnight service (departing 9pm) to Kundapur on the coast (10hr), via Mangaluru and Udupi.

Airlines Air India (☎ 080 6678 5161); Go Air (☎ 080 4740 6091); Indigo (☎ 080 6678 5450); SpiceJet (☎ 1 800 180 3333).

Destinations Chennai (17–22 daily; 50min–1hr); Delhi (38–42 daily; 2hr 30min–3hr 30min); Goa (9–11 daily; 1hr–1hr 20min); Hyderabad (24–27 daily; 1hr–1hr 25min); Kochi (12–14 daily; 1hr–1hr 20min); Mumbai (32–34 daily; 1hr 35min–2hr); Trivandrum (4–5 daily; 1hr 10min–1hr 20min).

BY TRAIN

Stations Bengaluru is well connected by train to all parts of India. Bangalore City railway station is west of the centre, near Kempe Gowda Circle, opposite the main bus stands; for the north of the city, it's better to board or disembark at Bangalore Cantonment station north of the centre. Bangalore City has prepaid auto-rickshaw and taxi booths in the forecourt, and is connected (via Majestic station) to MG Road and points east in the city by Namma Metro's Purple Line. Trains to Goa and a handful of trains to other destinations leave from Yeshwanthpur railway station (☎ 080 2337 7161) in the north of the city, on the Namma Metro's Green Line.

Bookings The computerized reservation office at Bangalore City (Mon–Sat 8am–2pm & 2.15–8pm, Sun 8am–2pm; ☎ 132) is in a separate building, to the left as you approach the station; counter 14 is for foreigners.

BY BUS

Government buses Long-distance government buses, including those from other states like Goa and Maharashtra, arrive at the busy Central Bus Stand, opposite the railway station (☎ 77609 90562, ⓦ ksrtc.in). There is a comprehensive timetable in English in the centre of the Central Bus Stand concourse. Most services can be booked

22

RECOMMENDED TRAINS FROM KSR BENGALURU

Destination	Name	No.	Departs	Arrives
Chennai	Shatabdi Express	12008	4.25pm	9.40pm°
	Sanghamitra Express	12295	9am	3.15pm
Delhi	Karnataka Express	12627	7.20pm	10.30am**
Ernakulam	Ernakulam Express	12677	6.15am	4.55pm
Hosapete	Hampi Express	16592	10.05pm	7.10am*
Hyderabad	Kacheguda Express	12786	6.20pm	5.40am*
Mumbai	Udyan Express	11302	8.45pm	8.15pm*
Mysuru	Shatabdi Express	12007	11am	1pm°
	Tippu Express	12614	3.15pm	5.45pm
Trivandrum	Kanyakumari Express	16526	8pm	1.25pm*

* Next day arrival; **arrival two days later; ° except Wed

in advance at the computerized counters near Bay 13 (daily 7.30am–7.30pm).

Private buses Tickets for the numerous private bus companies can be bought from the agencies on Tank Bund Rd, on the opposite side of the bus stand from the train station; operators include Sharma (☎080 2670 2447, ⊛sharmatransports.com), Vijayanand Travels or VRL (☎080 2297 1245, ⊛vrlbus.in), Paulo (☎080 2238 4040, ⊛paulotravels.com), SRS (☎080 2680 1616, ⊛srsbooking.

com) and National (☎080 2660 3112, ⊛nationaltravels. in), which all advertise a multitude of destinations, including sleeper coaches to Goa and Mumbai.

Destinations Chennai (hourly; 6–7hr); Hassan (every 15–30min; 4hr); Hosapete (3 daily; 10hr); Hyderabad (8 daily; 15–16hr); Madikeri (hourly; 6hr); Mangaluru (every 30min–1hr; 9–10hr); Mumbai (2–4 daily; 23–24hr); Mysuru (every 10–15min; 3hr); Ootacamund (6 daily; 7hr 30min–8hr); Puttaparthy (every 30min–1hr; 4hr); Tirupati (hourly; 7hr).

GETTING AROUND

By bus Bengaluru's extensive bus system radiates from the Kempegowda Bus Station (☎080 222 2542), near City railway station. Most buses from platform 17 travel past MG Rd. Along with regular buses, BMTC (☎1800 425 1663, ⊛mybmtc.com) also operates a deluxe express service, Pushpak, on a number of set routes (#P109 terminates at Whitefield, by the famous Sai Baba ashram) as well as a handful of night buses. Other important city bus stands include the City Market Bus Stand at Kalasipalayam (☎080 2295 2333), near the railway station, and Shivaji Nagar (☎080 2295 2324) to the northeast of Cubbon Park.

By metro In June 2017, the first phase of Bengaluru's Namma Metro (⊛bmrc.co.in) was completed. The east–west Purple Line links the main train and bus stations (via City Railway and Majestic stations) with points east including Cubbon Park, MG Road and Indiranagar. The north–south Green Line travels south via Yeshwantpur before intersecting with the Purple Line at Majestic and continuing south via Chikpete, KR Market and Lalbagh. Trains run every 10–15min from 6am to 10pm, and tickets cost ₹10–60. Payment is by single-use tokens or Varshik smart cards, which give a slight discount.

By auto-rickshaw The easiest way of getting around is by metered auto-rickshaw, which can now even be summoned by app (⊛mgaadi.com). Fares start at ₹25 for the first kilometre and ₹13/km thereafter; one-and-a-half or double-meter rates usually apply 10pm–5am, and there's an extra surcharge of ₹20 to suburban areas. Most meters do work and drivers are usually willing to use them, although you will occasionally be asked for a flat fare, especially during rush hour. Expect to pay ₹120–150 from the Kempegowda Bus Station to MG Rd.

By taxi You can book chauffeur-driven cars and taxis through several agencies including EZI Drive (☎080 4240 0000, ⊛ezidrive.in) or Carzonrent (☎88822 22222, ⊛carzonrent.com), or use Ola or Uber.

Car rental Avis has outlets at the airport and the Oberoi hotel, 37–39 MG Rd (☎080 2558 5858, ⊛avis.com). Hertz (☎080 4330 2201, ⊛hertz.com) has counters at the airport and on Swami Vivekananda Rd, east of MG Rd. Zoom (⊛zoomcar.com) is a decent Indian self-drive option. For long-distance car rental and tailor-made itineraries, try one of the travel agents listed in the Basics chapter or any KSTDC office.

INFORMATION AND TOURS

India Tourism For information on Bengaluru, Karnataka and neighbouring states, go to the excellent India Tourism Office (Mon–Fri 9.30am–6pm, Sat 9am–1pm; ☎080 2558 5417), in Triumph Tower, 48 Church St, where you can pick

up free maps for both city and state.

KSTDC Apart from booths at the City railway station (daily 7am–8pm; ☎080 2287 0068) and at the airport, Karnataka State Tourist Development Corporation

(⑩karnatakatourism.org) also has an office at Badami House, NR Square (daily 6am–10pm; ☎080 4334 4334), where you can book tours (⑩kstdc.co).

Listings For information about what's on, pick up the twice-monthly listings magazine *Travel & Shop* (⑩travelandshop. in), available at most hotels and tourist offices, or the online guide *Time Out Bangalore* (⑩timeout.com/bangalore).

National parks information For information on any of Karnataka's national parks, call at the Wildlife Office, Forest Department, Aranya Bhavan, Malleswaram (☎080 2334 1993), or try Jungle Lodges & Resorts, Floor 2,

Shrungar Shopping Centre, off MG Rd (☎080 2559 7021, ⑩junglelodges.com). The latter, a quasi-government body, promotes ecotourism through a number of upmarket forest lodges.

Walking tours Bangalore Walks (⑩bangalorewalks. com) organizes engaging theme-based walks (₹500, plus optional breakfast ₹200) regularly around the city. Bengaluru by Foot (☎080 4120 3095, ⑩bengalurubyfoot. com) lead a range of fascinating cultural and food tours in and around Bengaluru (from ₹600), as well as in Mysuru.

22

ACCOMMODATION

Due to the great number of business visitors it receives, Bengaluru offers a wealth of upmarket lodgings, as well as serviced apartments. Decent **budget accommodation** is also available, mostly concentrated around the Central Bus Stand and railway station.

MG ROAD AND AROUND

Ajantha 22-A MG Rd ☎080 2558 4321, ⑩hotelajantha. in; map p.1125 Decent option, with 61 basic yet large rooms and four spacious cottages (₹2800), located at the end of a quiet lane but close to all the action. Complimentary breakfast at the veg restaurant. ₹1750

★**Casa Cottage** 2 Clapham St ☎080 2227 0754, ⑩casacottage.com; map p.1125. Tranquillity awaits at these cottages, set in well-maintained grounds just over 1km south of MG Rd. The cottages and apartments are enormous, comfort-able and well appointed, and the free breakfasts are excellent. Great online deals. ₹2700

Hyatt Centric 1/1 Swami Vivekananda Rd ☎080 2555 8888, ⑩bangalore.hyatthotels.hyatt.com; map p.1125. This ultra-luxurious hotel is a secluded sanctuary, with an

infinity pool, Jacuzzi and gym, plus breezy, safari-themed *Liquid Lounge* bar. Some of the spacious rooms have marble baths and views of Ulsoor Lake; suites have large garden balconies. Online deals available. ₹13,750

★**Octave Suites** Toucan Plaza, 65 Residency Rd ☎080 4174 5599, ⑩octavehotels.com; map p.1131. Excellent boutique hotel with spacious suites, all boasting modern furniture and design in vivid colours. Good restaurant and pub on the premises too. ₹2400

The Park Residency Pinto Towers, 36 Residency Rd ☎080 2558 2151, ⑩parkresidency.net; map p.1131. This concrete behemoth offers good value, considering the central location, with clean, sizeable rooms, all with fridge, TV and some a/c. Hearty Indian or Continental breakfast included. ₹2200

Shangrila 182 Brigade Rd ☎080 4112 1622, ✉shangrila_htl@yahoo.co.in; map p.1131. A welcoming Tibetan-run lodge that's right in the thick of things; the comfy standard rooms are decent value and the a/c ones are a great deal. Good Tibetan/Chinese restaurant, too. No wi-fi. ₹1100

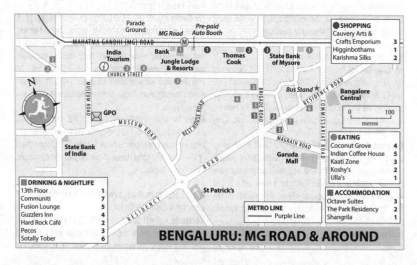

BENGALURU: MG ROAD & AROUND

22

AROUND THE RAILWAY STATION AND CENTRAL BUS STAND

Adora 47 SC Rd ☏ 080 2220 0024, ⓦ facebook.com/hoteladora; map p.1125. Above a quality south Indian veg restaurant, this large hotel is a top budget place and popular backpacker choice. Though bland, the rooms are clean and sizeable, and some have a/c. Wi-fi only in lobby. ₹950

Hotel Sangam Royal 5 1st Cross, Annamma Temple Extension ☏ 080 4171 3999, ⓔ hotelsangamroyal; map p.1125. Good value budget hotel on a quiet sidestreet near the pedestrian underpass from the station, with simple but adequate rooms. All rooms are attached, with TV. Wi-fi only in lobby. ₹800

Tourist Ananda Rao Circle, Race Course Rd ☏ 080 2226 2381; map p.1125. One of Bengaluru's best all-round budget lodges, with four floors wrapped round a courtyard and a veg restaurant. Small rooms, long verandas, friendly family management and no reservations, so it fills up fast. No wi-fi. ₹450

Vybhav Lodge 42 SC Rd ☏ 080 2287 3997; map p.1125. A tad grubby and frayed at the edges but not a bad fall-back. All the rooms are extremely compact and the cell-like attached singles with TV are very inexpensive. No wi-fi. ₹750

NORTH OF THE CENTRE

ITC Windsor 25 Golf Course Rd ☏ 080 2226 9898, ⓦ itchotels.in/hotels/itcwindsor.aspx; map p.1125. Ersatz palace, now a luxurious five-star, mainly for overseas businesspeople with rates to match. Facilities include a gym, pool, Jacuzzi, fine restaurant and popular Irish pub, *Dublin*. ₹7500

Jayamahal Palace 1 Jayamahal Rd ☏ 080 4058 0444, ⓦ jayamahalpalace.com; map p.1125. A charming heritage hotel tucked in a leafy precinct near Cantonment railway station. The large rooms have parquet flooring and balconies overlooking lawns. ₹2500

Race View 25 Race Course Rd ☏ 080 4069 6111; map p.1125. Large business hotel with sizeable wood-panelled rooms. Those at the front do overlook the racecourse but also the busy road. The a/c rooms cost just a little more. No wi-fi. ₹1250

Taj West End Race Course Rd ☏ 080 6660 5660, ⓦ tajhotels.com; map p.1125. Begun as a British-run boarding house in 1887, these lodgings were later upgraded with fabulous gardens and long colonnaded walkways. The old wing is bursting with character, with broad verandas over-looking acres of grounds. Good online deals. ₹10,900

EATING

Bengaluru's profusion of cafés and restaurants makes up for its deficit of tourist sights with a gastronomic variety unparalleled in south India. Around **MG Rd**, and in **Indiranagar** (east of the centre) and the southeastern suburb of Koramangala, pizzerias, burger chains, ritzy ice-cream parlours and gourmet restaurants stand cheek by jowl with regional cuisine from Andhra Pradesh, Tamil Nadu, Kerala, Bengal and Punjab, besides Mumbai *chaat* cafés and snack bars. Stand-up local eateries called **darshinis** are popular for a quick bite. In addition to the places below, many of the establishments listed under "Drinking and nightlife" also serve good food.

MG ROAD AND AROUND

★ **Casa del Sol** 3rd floor, Devatha Plaza, 131 Residency Rd, 3km south of MG Rd ☏ 080 4151 0101; map p.1125. The ₹275 lunch buffet is worth every paise and the Sunday brunches are festive, all-you-can-drink affairs. An evening cocktail on the cool, comfortable terrace is a real treat. Daily 11am–11pm.

Coconut Grove 86 Church St ☏ 080 2559 6262; map p.1131. Mouthwatering gourmet cuisine from Kerala, Chettinad and Coorg. Veg, fish and meat preparations are served in traditional copper thalis on a leafy terrace, and there's a wide range of seafood dishes. Main dishes ₹500–700. Its *Coco Grove* cocktail bar is a good spot for a drink. Daily 12.30–3.30pm & 7–11.30pm.

Indian Coffee House Church St ☏ 080 2558 7088, ⓦ indiancoffeehouse.com; map p.1131. Now occupying incongruous modern premises but still old-fashioned at heart, with turbaned waiters serving tasty finger foods (₹35–70) and fine filter coffee. The perfectly fluffy scrambled eggs are superb. Daily 8am–8.30pm.

Kaati Zone Church St ☏ 080 6566 0000, ⓦ kaatizone.com; map p.1131. Fast, clean and wallet-friendly, the popular chain serves delicious *kaati* rolls (from ₹120), biryani, curry meals and "Rolls-Rice". It has a busy outlet at the airport with dine-in and delivery stores across town. Daily 11am–11pm.

★ **Koshy's** St Mark's Rd ☏ 080 2221 3793; map p.1131. A popular hangout for theatre folk, artists and old-timers, this atmospheric colonial-style café with pewter teapots and cotton-clad waiters serves tasty Indian specialities and international favourites. The fish biryani, beef fry and chilli pork are legendary, all under ₹400. Its adjacent sister concern, *Jewel Box*, is more upmarket with a/c. Daily 9am–11pm.

Ulla's 1st floor, Public Utility Building, MG Rd ☏ 080 2558 7486; map p.1131. Superb pure-veg restaurant, with a terrace and indoor section. Excellent lunchtime thalis (₹50–120) and a good choice of curries, plus Bombay *chaat*. Daily 9am–10pm.

AROUND THE RAILWAY STATION AND CENTRAL BUS STAND

Narthaki Just off SC Rd ☏ 94485 53274; map p.1125. The best restaurant in the railway station and bus stand area. Veg meals are served on the first floor, while the restaurant-cum-bar on the second offers a full range of Indian and Chinese dishes. The chicken chilli is a belter. Mains ₹200–280. Daily 11.30am–11.30pm.

Sagar Hotel 48 SC Rd ☎ 080 2291 4197; map p.1125. First-floor Andhra-style family restaurant serving filling biryanis for little more than ₹100, as well as dishes from other parts of India. There's an a/c bar upstairs. Daily 11.30am–4pm & 6.30–11pm.

DRINKING AND NIGHTLIFE

Bengaluru's progressive outlook has fostered a thriving nightlife for urban youth and tourists alike. A night on the town generally kicks off with a bar crawl along the old colonial quarter of **Brigade Rd**, **Residency Rd** and **Church St**, which are lined with scores of swish **pubs**. Drinking alcohol does not have the seedy connotations it does elsewhere in India; you'll even see young Indian women enjoying a beer with their mates. While some prefer an elegant tipple in five-star hotels, it's the latest crop of microbreweries serving craft beer that are now all the rage. Most **clubs** operate a couples-only policy.

★ **13th Floor** 13th Floor, Ivory Tower, 84 MG Rd ☎ 080 4178 3355; map p.1131. Sip your poison and take in the sunset view (or glittering city lights) from a fine vantage point: classy and cosmopolitan, with cool postmodern decor, *13th Floor* is an absolute must. Come early because it fills up fast (happy hour till 7pm). Daily 5–11pm.

★ **Communiti** 67–68 Brigade Solitaire, Residency Rd ☎ 080 4099 9755, ⊛ communiti-pub.business.site; map p.1131. The best central microbrewery by far, which serves a wicked IPA and other fine beers in its cool spacious interior or airy wooden deck. Pizza, burgers and filling sandwiches go for ₹300–400. Daily 11.30am–1am.

Fusion Lounge 185 Deena Complex, Brigade Rd ☎ 080 4114 2912; map p.1131. Dazzling high-tech lounge-cum-nightclub with different spaces for pricey but excellent food, DJ nights, karaoke and live performances. Daily 11.30am–11.30pm (till 1am Fri & Sat).

Guzzlers Inn 48 Rest House Rd, off Brigade Rd ☎ 080 4112 2513; map p.1131. Long-established watering hole serving up classic rock, live sports, draught beer and good affordable Indian food. Half-price afternoon happy hour extends till 8pm on weekdays. Daily 11am–11.30pm.

Hammered 18 Ali Askar Rd, off Cunningham Rd ☎ 95902 10210, ⊛ hammeredpub.in; map p.1125. Massive modern pub spread over two floors and presided

INDIRANAGAR

★ **Little Italy** 1135 100 Ft Rd, Indiranagar, 2km east of MG Rd ☎ 080 2520 7171, ⊛ littleitaly.in; map p.1125. Fantastic vegetarian Italian food – try the risottos or tomato-based pasta dishes (₹400–500) – served on the bamboo-bordered terrace or in the elegant dining room. There's also an extensive wine list. Daily noon–3.30pm & 6.30–11pm.

over by an equally huge tree. Everything from ethnic food, via fine ales and cocktails to a variety of hookah flavours. Daily 11am–1am.

★ **Hard Rock Café** 40 St Mark's Rd, at Church ☎ 080 4124 2222, ⊛ hardrock.com/cafes/bengaluru; map p.1131. This gorgeous, multi-room space inside an old stone library is well established as the buzzing nexus of Bengaluru nightlife, not to mention the finest bar and grill in town. With high vaulted ceilings, grey stone walls and subtle accents, it feels both lived in and new. Daily noon–11pm.

★ **The Humming Tree** 12th Main Rd, Indiranagar ☎ 98866 18386, ⊛ bit.ly/HummingTreeBangalore; map p.1125. A popular venue for music gigs with a lounge bar serving drinks and good food in a friendly atmosphere. Daily noon–11.30pm (till 1am Fri & Sat).

Pecos 34 Rest House Rd, off Brigade Rd ☎ 080 2558 6047, ⊛ pecospub.com; map p.1131. Three dank levels of rock posters and ageing wood make up the definitive Bengaluru dive. The tunes are hard-driving, the beer's cheap and the Indian grub ain't half bad. Daily 10.30am–11pm.

Sotally Tober 65 Residency Rd ☎ 080 4374 1160, ⊛ sotallytober.com; map p.1131. Trendy new gastropub whose irreverent atmosphere is reflected in the jokey name. Board games available to play while you sup a vast range of mostly imported beers – over 300 from Canada alone. Daily noon–midnight (till 1am Thurs–Sat).

★ **Toit** 100 Ft Rd, Indiranagar II Stage ☎ 90197 13388, ⊛ toit.in; map p.1125. A lively, loud brewpub across multiple levels with warm brick and wood interiors and eclectic decor. Terrific finger food is on offer and a drinks menu encompassing branded Belgian and German beer to cocktail pitchers. It's always crowded, so reserve a table or grab a stool near the bar. ₹750 entry on Wed, Fri & Sat. Daily noon–11pm.

SHOPPING

The bustling area around **MG Rd** is the hub of Bengaluru shopping, with lots of stores along its main section selling designer goods a little cheaper than in the West, as well as quality Indian clothing and accessories, and handy including UB City (see page 1134), Bangalore Central and Garuda Mall. **Dickenson Rd** and **Commercial St** nearby

are particularly strong on good jewellery and clothing. The free *Travel & Shop* magazine carries a huge list of establishments. At occasional **flea markets** like Kitsch Mandi (⊛ facebook.com/Kitsch.Mandi/) and Soul Santhe (⊛ sundaysoulsante.com) you can find the traveller's garb and trinkets so evident in places like Hampi or Gokarna,

22

and Raja Market and the crowded lanes of **Chickpet** are atmospheric for shopping for ethnic items.

Cauvery Arts & Crafts Emporium 49 MG Rd ☎080 2558 1118, ⓦcauveryhandicrafts.net; map p.1131. This state government-run outlet sells all manner of wooden toys and gadgets, sandalwood sculptures, inlaid rosewood coffee tables, metalwork, carpets, rugs and hundreds of other gift items. Daily 10am–9pm.

Higginbothams 74 MG Rd ☎080 2558 6574; map p.1131. The main Bengaluru branch of the venerable national chain has a diverse collection of fiction, plus academic and reference books. Daily 9.30am–8.30pm.

Karishma Silks 45 MG Rd ☎080 2558 1606; map p.1131. Vast, colourful range of pure silks, embroidered saris, cottons and *salwar kameez*, to suit most budgets. Daily 10.15am–8.45pm.

Levitate India 777i 100 Ft Rd, Indiranagar ☎080 6452 8190, ⓦlevitateindia.com; map p.1125. A quirky lifestyle boutique selling handwoven cotton scarves, handcrafted leather footwear, funky bags and trinkets, besides kitsch and retro Bollywood posters. Lots of stuff under ₹500. Daily 11am–10pm.

Tanishq 121 Dickenson Rd ☎080 2555 0907, ⓦtanishq. co.in; map p.1125. If you have money to splash out on some really special jewellery, head for this treasure-trove of diamonds, gold and silver. Daily 10am–8pm.

UB City Mall Vittal Mallya Rd ⓦubcitybangalore.in; map p.1125. Upmarket global luxury brands from Louis Vuitton to Jimmy Choo, fancy pubs, fine dining, an art gallery and Angsana spa announce where and how the rich come to roost and splurge.

DIRECTORY

Banks and exchange Thomas Cook, 70 MG Rd (☎1800 209 9100); TT Forex, 180 Cunningham Rd (☎080 2225 1201); Weizmann Forex Ltd, 56 Residency Rd (☎080 6628 4463) are all open Mon–Sat 10am–6.30pm. Banks have better rates; the State Bank of Mysore on MG Rd is the most convenient. There are ATMs all over, especially in the MG Rd area.

Hospitals Victoria Hospital, near City Market (☎080 2670 1150); Mallya (☎080 2227 7979), close to MG Rd.

Internet Internet cafés are widely available across the city, and generally charge ₹20–30/hr. They're usually open until 9pm or later.

Libraries The British Council (English-language) library, 23 Kasturba Rd Cross (Mon–Sat 10.30am–6.30pm; ☎080 2248 9220), has newspapers and magazines that visitors

are welcome to peruse in a/c comfort.

Pharmacies Most pharmacies attached to hospitals are open 24/7; try Al-Siddique Pharma Centre, opposite Jama Masjid near City Market, and Janata Bazaar, in the Victoria Hospital.

Police ☎100.

Post office On the corner of Raj Bhavan Rd and Cubbon Rd, at the northern tip of Cubbon Park (Mon–Sat 10am–7pm, Sun 10.30am–1.30pm).

Travel agents For flight bookings and train, bus or hotel reservations, try Akbar Travels at 131 Brigade Rd, Shoolay Circle (☎080 2222 7645, ⓦakbartravels.com). For customised tours and adventure trails contact Nirmala Travels at Netkallappa Circle, SC Rd (☎080 2662 1007, ⓦnirmalatravels.com).

Mysuru (Mysore)

A centre of sandalwood-carving, silk and incense production, and dotted with palaces and gardens, **Mysore**, officially renamed **MYSURU** in 2014, is one of south India's more appealing cities and its cultural capital, attracting about 2.5 million visitors each year. Nevertheless, it remains a charming, old-fashioned place, changed by neither an IT boom nor its now well-established status as a top international yoga destination. That said, the erstwhile capital of the Wadiyar rajas can be underwhelming at first blush: upon stumbling off a bus or train you're not so much embraced by the scent of jasmine blossoms or gentle wafts of sandalwood as smacked by a cacophony of tooting, careening buses, bullock carts, bikes and tongas. Still, give it a few days and Mysuru will cast a spell on you.

In addition to its established tourist attractions, chief among them the **Mysore Palace**, Mysuru is a great city simply to stroll around. The evocative, if dilapidated, pre-Independence buildings lining market areas such as **Ashoka Road** and **Sayaji Rao Road** lend an air of faded grandeur to a busy centre that teems with vibrant street life.

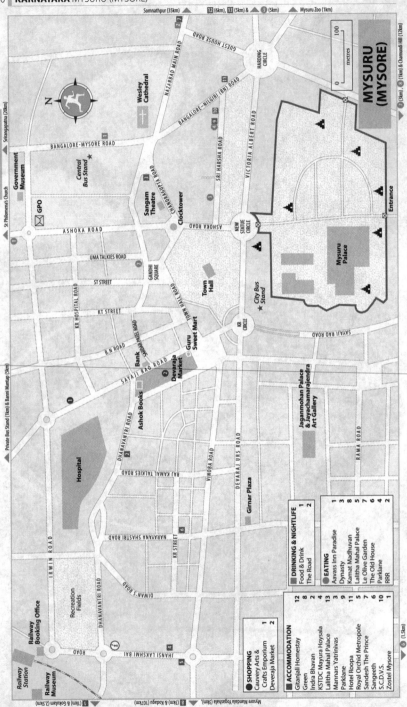

MYSURU (MYSORE)

Somnathpur (35km) · 12 (6km), 13 (5km) & 9 (5km) · Mysuru Zoo (1km)

7 (3km), 8 (1km) & Chamundi Hill (12km)

SHOPPING
Cauvery Arts & Crafts Emporium ... 1
Deveraja Market ... 2

ACCOMMODATION
Gitanjali Homestay ... 12
Green ... 8
Indra Bhavan ... 2
KSTDC Mayura Hoysala ... 13
Lalitha Mahal Palace ... 3
Mannars Yatrinivas ... 9
Parklane ... 11
Hotel Roopa ... 5
Royal Orchid Metropole ... 7
Sandesh The Prince ... 6
Sangeeth ... 10
S.C.D.V.S. ... 1
Zostel Mysore ... 4

DRINKING & NIGHTLIFE
Food & Drink ... 1
The Road ... 2

EATING
Aavass Inn Paradise ... 1
Dynasty ... 3
Kamat Madhuvan ... 8
Lalitha Mahal Palace ... 5
Le Olive Garden ... 7
The Old House ... 4
Parklane ... 2
RRR ... 10

Brief history

In the tenth century Mysuru was known as Mahishur – "the town where Mahishasura, the demon buffalo was slain" (by the goddess Durga; see page 1138). Presiding over a district of many villages, the city was ruled from about 1400 until Independence by the Hindu **Wadiyars**. Their rule was only broken from 1761, when the Muslim Haider Ali and his son Tipu Sultan took over. Two years later, the new rulers demolished the labyrinthine old city to replace it with the elegant grid of sweeping, leafy streets and public gardens that survive today. However, following Tipu Sultan's defeat in 1799 by the British colonel Arthur Wellesley (later the Duke of Wellington), Wadiyar power was restored. As the capital of Mysore state, the city thereafter dominated a major part of southern India. In 1956, when Bangalore became capital of newly formed Karnataka, its maharaja was appointed governor. Following the demise in 2013 of Srikantadatta Narasimharaja Wadiyar, who had held the now titular role since 1974, his 23-year-old nephew Yaduveer Krishnadatta Chamaraja Wadiyar was ceremonially crowned as Mysuru's new king on May 28, 2015.

22

Mysuru Palace

There are four gates in the perimeter wall with public entrances via the northern and southern gates • Daily 10am–5.30pm • ₹70; shoes must be left at the stall • **Sound & Light** show Mon–Sat 7pm; ₹70 • ☎ 0821 2421051, Ⓦ mysorepalace.gov.in

Mysuru's centre is dominated by the walled maharaja's palace, popularly known as **Mysuru Palace**, a fairytale spectacle topped with a shining brass-plated dome. It's especially magnificent on Sunday nights and during festivals, when it is illuminated by nearly 100,000 lightbulbs. The palace was completed in 1912 for the 24th Wadiyar raja, on the site of the old wooden palace that had been destroyed by fire in 1897. In 1998, after a lengthy judicial tussle, the courts decided in favour of formally placing the main palace in the hands of the Karnataka state government but the royal family, who still hold a claim, have lodged an appeal, which is ongoing. Twelve temples surround the palace, some of them of much earlier origin.

Entrance area and outer buildings

An extraordinary amalgam of styles from India and around the world crowds the lavish interior. Entry is through the Gombe Thotti or **Dolls' Pavilion**, once a showcase for the figures featured in the city's lively Dasara celebrations and now a gallery of European and Indian sculpture and ceremonial objects. Halfway along, the brass **Elephant Gate** forms the main entrance to the centre of the palace, through which the maharaja would drive to his car park. Decorated with floriated designs, it bears the Mysore royal symbol of Ganda-Berunda, a mythical double-headed eagle, now the state emblem. To the north, past the gate, stands a ceremonial elephant *howdah*. Elaborately decorated with 84kg of 24-carat gold, it appears to be inlaid with red and green gems – in fact the twinkling lights are battery-powered signals that would have let the *mahout* know when the maharaja wished to stop or go.

The main halls

Walls leading into the octagonal **Kalyana Mandapa**, the royal wedding hall, are lined with a meticulously detailed frieze of oil paintings, executed over a period of fifteen years by four Indian artists, illustrating the great Mysore Dasara festival (see page 1138) of 1930. The hall itself is magnificent, a cavernous space featuring cast-iron pillars from Glasgow, Bohemian chandeliers and a domed ceiling featuring multi-coloured Belgian stained glass arranged in peacock designs.

Climbing a staircase with Italian marble balustrades, past an unnervingly realistic figure of Krishnaraja Wadiyar IV, lounging comfortably with his bejewelled feet on a stool, you come into the **Public Durbar Hall**, an orientalist fantasy like something from *One Thousand and One Nights*. A vision of brightly painted and gilded colonnades,

22

> ## MYSURU DASARA FESTIVAL
>
> Following the tradition set by the Vijayanagar kings, the ten-day festival of **Dasara** (Sept/Oct), to commemorate the goddess Durga's slaying of the demon buffalo, Mahishasura, is celebrated in grand style at Mysuru. Scores of cultural events include concerts of south Indian classical (Carnatic) music and dance performances in the great Durbar Hall of the **Mysore Palace**. On Vijayadashami, the tenth and last day of the festival, a magnificent procession of mounted guardsmen on horseback and caparisoned elephants – one, carrying the palace deity, Chamundeshwari, on a gold *howdah* – marches 5km from the palace to Banni Mantap, site of a sacred banyan tree. There's also a floating festival in the temple tank at the foot of **Chamundi Hill**, and a procession of chariots around the temple at the top. A torchlit parade (Jamboo Savari) takes place in the evening, followed by a massive firework display and much jubilation on the streets.

open on one side, the massive hall affords views out across the parade ground and gardens to Chamundi Hill. The maharaja gave audience from here, seated on a throne made from 280kg of solid gold, though these days the hall is only used during the Dasara festival, when it hosts classical concerts. The smaller Ambavilas, or **Private Durbar Hall**, features especially beautiful stained glass and gold-leaf painting. Before leaving you pass two embossed silver doors – all that remains of the old palace.

Residential Museum

Behind the Private Durbar Hall • Daily 10am–5.30pm • ₹60

Privately owned by the present scion of the royal family, and housed within the residential part of the palace, the **Residential Museum** displays royal treasures, paintings, musical instruments, children's toys, furniture, trousseaux and armoury.

Jayachamarajendra Art Gallery

300m west of Mysore Palace • ☎ 0821 2423693

Built in 1861, the three-storey **Jaganmohan Palace** was used as a royal residence until 1915, when it was turned into a picture gallery and museum, the **Jayachamarajendra Art Gallery**, by Maharaja Krishnaraja Wadiyar IV. Most of the "contemporary" art in the collection dates from the 1930s, when a revival of Indian painting was spearheaded by E.B. Havell and the Tagore brothers, Rabindranath and Gaganendranath, in Bengal. At the time of writing the gallery was closed long-term for a complete renovation.

Government Museum

Irwin Rd • Tues–Sun 10am–5.30pm • Free • ☎ 0821 242 4673

Occupying a two-storey building that was once home to the Duke of Wellington, the **Government Museum** is devoted to anthropology on the ground floor, with photos, artifacts and jewellery of various tribal groups, mainly from the Himalaya and northeastern India. Upstairs there is a collection of statues and a modest selection of modern art. The grounds are strewn with large terracotta sculptures.

Mysuru Zoo

Zoo Main Rd, 1km east of Mysore Palace • Daily except Tues 8.30am–5.30pm • ₹60 (₹80 Sat, Sun & hols), camera ₹20, video camera ₹150 • ☎ 0821 2520302, ⊛ mysorezoo.info

Officially named Sri Chamarajendra Zoological Gardens, **Mysuru Zoo** is one of the oldest and best in India. Established as far back as 1882, it was opened to the public in 1902 and has grown to encompass 245 beautifully landscaped acres, with spacious compounds for most of the animals that live here. The zoo boasts all the usual big mammals, including leopards and tigers, and there are also many species of bird and reptile to be admired, though some of their cages do not make viewing the animals easy. The zoo even has a very cheap canteen and an admirable policy of charging a deposit on water bottles, which can be claimed back at the exit. As always, it pays to visit early morning or late afternoon when the animals are most active.

Chamundi Hill

Temple Daily 7am–2pm, 3.30–6pm & 7–9pm • Free but special entrance ₹10 • Bus #201 from the City stand

22

Chamundi Hill, 12km southeast of the city, is topped with a temple to the chosen deity of the Mysore rajas – the goddess Chamundi, or Durga, who slew the demon buffalo Mahishasura. It's a pleasant, easy bus trip to the top; the walk down takes about thirty minutes. Take drinking water, especially in the middle of the day – the walk isn't very demanding, but by the end of it, after more than a thousand steps, your legs are likely to be a bit wobbly.

Inside the twelfth-century **temple**, which is open to non-Hindus, is a solid gold Chamundi figure. Outside, in the courtyard, stands a fearsome, if gaily coloured, statue of Mahishasura. Overlooking the path down the hill, the magnificent 5m **Nandi**, carved from a single piece of black granite in 1659, is an object of worship himself, adorned with bells and garlands. Minor shrines, dedicated to Chamundi and the monkey god Hanuman, among others, line the side of the path; at the bottom, a little shrine to Ganesh lies near a chai shop. From here you can pick up an auto-rickshaw or bus back into the city, but at weekends the latter are often full. If you walk on towards the city, passing a temple on the left with a big water tank (the site of the floating festival during Dasara), you'll reach the main road between the *Lalitha Mahal Palace* (see page 1140) and the centre; there's a bus stop, and often auto-rickshaws, at the junction.

ARRIVAL AND DEPARTURE
MYSURU (MYSORE)

By train The railway station is 1.5km northwest of the centre. For long hauls, the best way to travel is by train, usually with a change at Bengaluru (14–16 daily; 2–3hr); the fastest service is the a/c *Shatabdi Express* #2008 (daily except Wed 2.15pm; 2hr), which continues to Chennai (7hr 10min). The Hampi Express #16592 goes daily via Bengaluru to Hosapete (7pm; 12hr 10min). There are 2–5 daily express

services to Hassan, of which the *Talguppa Intercity Express* #16206 (6am; 1hr 50min) is the fastest.

By bus Mysuru has three bus stands: major long-distance KSRTC and other state services pull in to Central, near the heart of the city, where there are advance booking counters. The Private stand is about 1km northwest of here and a host of agents there can make bookings for private buses

YOGA IN MYSURU

Despite the passing in 2009 of its founder, Sri Pattabhi Jois, the world-renowned **Ashtanga Yoga Institute** (☎98801 85500, ⓦ kpjayi.org), 3.5km northwest of town in Gokulam, is still a revered pilgrimage destination for devotees. The surrounding neighbourhood has in recent years turned into a bustling expat haven, filled with cafés, guesthouses, restaurants and internet cafés. The institute doesn't offer drop-in classes; students must register for a minimum of one month (around ₹30,000), and book at least two months in advance.

There are several other centres clustered around Gokulam, including Bharath Shetty's popular **IndeaYoga** (☎0821 241 6779, ⓦ yoga-india.net) at 144E 7th Main Rd, which offers early morning courses of between two and eight weeks' duration, and **Yoga Bharata**, 810 Contour Rd (☎0821 424 2342, ⓦ yogabharata.com), who welcome drop-ins (₹300 per class) and offer courses of one to four weeks (from ₹2000).

Some 3km south of town, **Mysore Mandala Yogashala**, at 897/1 Narayan Sastry Rd, Lakshmipuram (☎0821 425 6277, ⓦ mandala.ashtanga.org; closed Mon & Sat), is a self-contained retreat, offering excellent instruction, an organic café, well-tended garden, cultural events and drop-in classes. Two-hour Ashtanga classes (₹500) run at 6am, 8.30am and 4.30pm, with the slightly less strenuous ninety-minute Hatha classes (₹400) at 7am and 4.30pm.

22

to many destinations. Local buses, including services for Chamundi Hill and Srirangapatna, stop at the City stand, next to the northwestern corner of Mysore Palace.

Destinations from Central Bus Stand Channarayapatna (for Sravanabelagola; hourly; 2hr 30min); Hassan (every 15–30min; 3hr); Hubballi (4–6 daily; 9hr); Kochi (7 daily;

11–12hr); Madikeri (every 30min–1hr; 3hr); Mangaluru (every 30min–1hr; 7hr); Ootacamund (via Bandipur National Park; 8 daily; 5hr).

Destinations from Private Bus Stand Overnight services to Goa leave at 4pm and 5pm, getting to Panjim at 9am and 10am respectively.

INFORMATION AND TOURS

Karnataka Tourism The helpful Karnataka Tourism office (Mon–Sat 9.30am–5.30pm; ☎ 0821 242 2096) is located at the Department of Tourism, *Hotel Mayura Hoysala*, 2 Jhansi Lakshmi Bai Rd, Metropole Circle. They run marathon city bus tours (8.30am–8.30pm; ₹230) for a minimum of twelve passengers, and rushed tours of Belur, Halebidu and Sravanabelagola.

Bike tours MYcycle Tours (☎ 98867 05179, ⦿ bit.ly/ MYcycle) organizes rickshaw rides and cycling trips covering Mysuru and Srirangapatna (3hr; ₹1500).

ACCOMMODATION

Finding a room is only a problem during Dasara (see page 1138) and the Christmas/New Year period, when the popular places are booked up weeks in advance and prices predictably soar. Checkout is generally noon.

★ **Gitanjali Homestay** Siddharthanagar, 6km east of the centre ☎ 0821 247 4646, ⦿ gitanjalihomestay.com; map p.1136. Run by a Coorg family, this peaceful homestay located at the base of the Chamundi Hills has four rooms in a cottage-style unit with a large common veranda opening out to a garden. Excellent home-cooked Kodava cuisine. **₹4500**

★ **Green** Chittaranjan Palace, 2270 Vinoba Rd, Jayalakshmipuram ☎ 0821 251 2536, ⦿ green hotelindia.com; map p.1136. This former royal palace among landscaped gardens on the western outskirts has been refurbished as an elegant, eco-conscious two-star hotel. The 31 rooms are a decent size, and facilities include lounges, verandas, a croquet lawn and well-stocked library. All profits go to charities and environmental projects. Book in advance to arrange a pickup. **₹4125**

Indra Bhavan Dhanavantri Rd ☎ 0821 242 3933, ✉ hotelindrabhavan@gmail.com; map p.1136. A dilapidated old lodge full of character, with attached singles (₹350) and doubles. The "ordinary" rooms are a little grubby, but the good-value "deluxe" ones have clean tiled floors, TVs and open onto a wide common veranda. Two good veg restaurants. No wi-fi. **₹500**

KSTDC Mayura Hoysala 2 Jhansi Lakshmi Bai Rd ☎ 0821 242 6160, ⦿ karnatakaholidays.net; map p.1136. Reasonably priced rooms and suites in a colonial-era mansion (a/c rooms ₹2750). There's a terrace restaurant and beer garden, which is good value, but the food is uninspiring. The budget *Yatri Niwas* (☎ 0821 2423492) in the same compound offers rooms for ₹900. Rate includes tax. No wi-fi. **₹1120**

Lalitha Mahal Palace T. Narasipur Rd, 5km east of the city ☎ 0821 252 6100, ⦿ lalithamahalpalace.co.in; map p.1136. On a slope overlooking the city in the distance, this white Neoclassical palace was built in 1931 to accommodate the maharaja's foreign guests. Now it's a Raj-style fantasy, decked with stunning period furniture and popular with tour groups. Rooms range from the cute turret rooms to the "Viceroy Suite" (₹25,000). The tea lounge, restaurant and pool are open to non-residents (₹400). **₹3500**

Mannars Yatrinivas Chandragupta Rd ☎ 0821 2521148, ⦿ mannarsyatrinivas.com; map p.1136. Budget hotel near the Central Bus Stand and Gandhi Square. Spruced up of late but overall still very plain; of its 24 rooms only the "deluxe" have TV (₹1400). Deservedly popular with back-packers but no advance booking. **₹850**

★ **Parklane** 2720 Sri Harsha Rd ☎ 0821 243 0400, ⦿ parklanemysore.com; map p.1136. A complete overhaul has trans-formed the *Parklane* into a swish yet affordable boutique hotel. Appealingly misshapen rooms, all with a/c, contemporary furnishings and most with balconies, encircle a sky-lit atrium. **₹1680**

Hotel Roopa 2724-C Bangalore–Nilgiri Rd ☎ 0821 244 0044, ⦿ hotelroopa.com; map p.1136. Bright modern hotel block with compact but comfy rooms at surprisingly reasonable prices and a good complimentary buffet breakfast. Centrally located near the station, and ideal for the palace. **₹845**

Royal Orchid Metropole 5 Jhansi Lakshmi Bai Rd ☎ 0821 425 5566, ⦿ royalorchidhotels.com; map p.1136. Luxurious heritage hotel set in pleasant gardens built in 1920 by the maharaja of Mysore. Its thirty rooms have high ceilings and a sense of grandeur. There's also a small outdoor pool and gym. The fine *Tiger Trail* multicuisine restaurant serves buffet breakfast (included) and lunch in the central courtyard; the *Shikari* restaurant hosts barbecue dinners. **₹4250**

Sandesh The Prince 3 Nazarbad Main Rd ☎ 0821 243 6777, ⦿ sandeshtheprince.com; map p.1136. Smart, stylish four-star with comfortable, well-furnished rooms and an impressive, sky-lit foyer. Facilities include travel desk, foreign exchange, outdoor pool (₹300/day to non-residents) with barbecue, and an excellent Ayurvedic centre and beauty parlour. **₹4700**

Sangeeth 1966 Narayana Shastri Rd, near the Udipi Krishna temple ☎0821 242 4693; map p.1136. One of Mysuru's best all-round budget deals: bland and a bit boxed in, but friendly and very good value, with a rooftop restaurant. ₹500

S.C.D.V.S. Sri Harsha Rd ☎0821 242 1379, ⓦhotelscvds. com; map p.1136. Friendly modern lodge with some a/c rooms and cable TV in most. Some of the upper-storey rooms have balconies overlooking the palace. ₹1050

Zostel Mysore 2639/1 Valmiki Rd ☎022 4896 2269, ⓦzostel.com; map p.1136. West of the railway station, this bright modern branch of the growing hostel chain has ultra clean 4-, 6- and 8-bedded dorms, plus some private rooms. Dorm from ₹449, double ₹1450

22

EATING

Mysuru has scores of **places to eat**, from numerous south Indian "meals" joints dotted around the market to the opulent Lalitha Mahal Palace. To sample the renowned **Mysore pak**, a sweet, rich crumbly mixture made of ghee and maize flour, queue at Guru Sweet Mart, a small stall at KR Circle that's considered to be the best sweetshop in town. Another speciality is the soft, fragrant mallige idli, named after the delicate jasmine flower for which the city is known.

Aavass Inn Paradise Ashoka Rd ☎0821 252 5443; map p.1136. Small sparse canteen at the back of a hotel, serving South Indian breakfasts and meals for under ₹100. Stand-up snack bar out front. Daily 7am–10.30pm.

Dynasty Palace Plaza hotel, Sri Harsha Rd ☎0821 241 7592; map p.1136. Dynasty offers a wide range of Indian, Chinese and Continental fare (mains ₹180–300), served either in the ground-floor dining hall or breezy covered rooftop terrace, great in the evening. Full bar. Daily 7.30am–11pm.

Kamat Madhuvan Near Gun House, Nanjangud Rd ☎99800 04507; map p.1136. A traditional veg place 1km south of the palace, serving and north Karnataka cuisine such as jolada roti (flatbread), plus thalis (veg ₹150, special ₹215), to a sound-track of light classical music in the evening. Daily 7am–10.30pm.

Lalitha Mahal Palace T. Narasipur Rd ☎0821 252 6100, ⓦlalithamahalpalace.in; map p.1136. Sample the charms of this palatial five-star hotel with a hot drink in the atmospheric tea lounge, or an à la carte lunch in the grand dining hall, accompanied by live sitar music. Buffet dinners for around ₹1000 on special occasions. The old-style bar also boasts a full-size billiards table. Daily 12.30–3pm & 8–11pm.

★ **Le Olive Garden** The Windflower Spa, Maharana-pratap Rd, 3km southeast of town ☎0821 252 2500; map p.1136. Excellent, reasonably priced Indian, Chinese and Western dishes served to the sound of falling water and croaking frogs at this quasi-jungle hideaway. Daily noon–11pm.

The Old House Jhansi Lakshmi Bai Rd, RTO Circle, 2km west of the palace ☎0821 233 3255; map p.1136. Overlooking a leafy garden, this lovely café and patisserie serves wood-fired pizzas, pastas, salads and juices, besides a variety of fresh breads from the in-house bakery. Drop by at the adjoining Maya boutique, housed in a charming colonial building, for knick-knacks. Daily 7.30am–10pm.

★ **Parklane** Sri Harsha Rd ☎0821 243 0400, ⓦparklanemysore.com; map p.1136. Congenial courtyard restaurant-cum-beer balcony, with reasonably priced veg and non-veg (meat sizzlers are a speciality for around ₹400), fake trees and live Indian classical music every evening. The hotel rooftop space is a real stunner, with full bar, pool and fantastic views. Daily 8am–11pm.

★ **RRR** Gandhi Square ☎0821 244 1979; map p.1136. Superb Andhra canteen with a small but plush a/c room at the back. Gets packed at lunchtimes and at weekends, but it's well worth the wait for its excellent chicken biryani, fried fish and set menus served on banana leaf. Daily 11.30am–4.30pm & 7–11pm.

DRINKING AND NIGHTLIFE

Food & Drink Maharaja Shopping Complex, Bangalore–Mysore Rd ☎92415 57015; map p.1136. Advertising itself as a music bar, this joint is still more of a drinking den, with a wide selection of drinks and a jarring mixture of Western and Indian sounds. Daily noon–11pm.

The Road Sandesh The Prince, 3 Nazarbad Main Rd ☎0821 243 6777; map p.1136. Lined with plush booths – several of which are inside faux classic cars – this upmarket, American road trip-themed restaurant/club serves a good lunch menu before the tables are cleared at 7pm and patrons take to the circular wooden dancefloor, usually to guest DJs (₹300–400 cover at weekends). Daily noon–11.30pm.

SHOPPING

Cauvery Arts and Crafts Emporium Sayaji Rao Rd ☎0821 252 1258, ⓦcauverycrafts.com; map p.1136. Souvenir stores spill over with the famous sandalwood in Mysuru but the best place to get a sense of what's on offer is this government-run store, which stocks a wide range of local crafts that can be shipped overseas. Daily 10.30am–8pm.

Devaraja Market Sayaji Rao Rd; map p.1136. One of

south India's most atmospheric produce markets: a giant complex of covered stalls groaning with bananas (the delicious Nanjangud variety), luscious mangoes, blocks of sticky jaggery and conical heaps of lurid *kumkum* powder. Daily 5.30am–8.30pm.

Around Mysuru

Mysuru is a jumping-off point for some of Karnataka's most popular destinations. At **Srirangapatna**, the fort, palace and mausoleum date from the era of Tipu Sultan, the "Tiger of Mysore", while the superb Hoysala temple of **Somnathpur** is an architectural masterpiece. Nagarahole National Park (see page 1151) is also accessible within three hours of the city.

Srirangapatna

The island of **Srirangapatna**, in the River Kaveri, 20km northeast of Mysuru, measures 5km by 1km. Long a site of Hindu pilgrimage, it is named after its tenth-century Sriranganathaswamy Vishnu temple. The Vijayanagar kings built a fort here in 1454, and in 1616 it became the capital of the Mysore Wadiyar rajas. However, Srirangapatna is more famously associated with **Haider Ali**, who deposed the Wadiyars in 1761, and his son **Tipu Sultan**. During his seventeen-year reign – which ended with his death in 1799, when the future Duke of Wellington took the fort at the bloody battle of "Seringapatnam" – Tipu posed a greater threat than any other Indian ruler to British plans to dominate India. Born in 1750, of a Hindu mother, he inherited his father Haider Ali's considerable military skills, but was also an educated, cultured man, whose lifelong desire to rid India of the hated British invaders naturally brought him an ally in the French. He obsessively embraced his popular name of the **Tiger of Mysore**, surrounding himself with symbols and images of tigers; much of his memorabilia is decorated with the animal or its stripes, and, like the Romans, he is said to have kept tigers for the punishment of criminals.

Sri Ranganathaswamy temple

300m east of station • Daily 7.30am–1pm & 4–8pm

At the heart of the fortress, the great temple of **Sri Ranganathaswamy** still stands proud and virtually untouched by the turbulent history that has flowed around it, and remains, for many devotees, the island's prime draw. Developed by succeeding dynasties, it consists of three distinct sanctuaries and is entered via an impressive five-storeyed gateway and a hall built by Haider Ali. The innermost sanctum, the oldest part of the temple, contains an image of a reclining Vishnu.

Daria Daulat Bagh

2km east of the station • Daily 9am–5pm Fri • ₹100 (₹5)

The former summer palace, the **Daria Daulat Bagh**, literally "wealth of the sea", was built in 1784 to entertain Tipu's guests. At first sight, this low, wooden colonnaded building set in an attractive formal garden fails to impress. But the superbly preserved interior is remarkable, with its ornamental arches, tiger-striped columns and floral decoration on every centimetre of the teak walls and ceiling. A much-repainted mural on the west wall relishes every detail of Haider Ali's victory over the British at Pollilore in 1780.

Gumbaz mausoleum

3km east of Daria Daulat Bagh • Daily except Fri 9am–5pm • Free

An avenue of cypresses leads from an intricately carved gateway to the **Gumbaz mausoleum**. Built by Tipu Sultan in 1784 to commemorate Haider Ali, and later also to serve as his own resting place, the lower half of the grey-granite edifice is crowned by a dome of whitewashed brick and plaster, spectacular against the blue sky. Ivory-inlaid rosewood doors lead to the tombs of Haider Ali and Tipu, each covered by a pall (tiger stripes for Tipu), and an Urdu tablet records Tipu's martyrdom.

ARRIVAL AND GETTING AROUND SRIRANGAPATNA

Srirangapatna is a small island, but places of interest are quite spread out; tongas, auto-rickshaws (around ₹300 for a 2hr tour) and bicycles are available on the main road near the bus stand.

By train All the Mysuru–Bengaluru trains pull in to the station near the temple and fort, taking only 15min from Mysuru.

By bus Frequent buses (including #307, #313 and #316) leave from Mysore City Bus Stand (30min); #316 drops you near the Gumbaz.

ACCOMMODATION AND EATING

Mayura River View 3km south of the railway station ☎ 08236 252114, ⊛ karnatakaholidays.net. The KSTDC hotel-cum-restaurant occupies a pleasant spot beside the River Kaveri. Its rooms and cottages (all a/c) are overpriced, however. ₹1680

New Amblee Holiday Resort 2km east of the railway station ☎ 08236 252357, ⊛ ambleeresort.in. Located along the banks of the picturesque Kaveri River, this hotel offers luxury and deluxe rooms with or without a/c. ₹1600

Somnathpur: Keshava Vishnu temple

Daily 9am–5.30pm • ₹100 (₹5)

Built in 1268, the exquisite **Keshava Vishnu temple**, in the sleepy hamlet of **SOMNATHPUR**, was the last important temple to be constructed by the Hoysalas; it is also the most complete and the finest example of this singular style (see page 1145). Somnathpur itself, just ninety minutes from Mysuru by road, is little more than a few neat tracks and some attractive simple houses with pillared verandas.

Built on a star-shaped plan, like other Hoysala shrines, the Keshava temple is a *trikutachala*, "three-peaked hills" type, with a tower on each shrine. Its high plinth (*jagati*) provides an upper ambulatory, which allows visitors to marvel at the profusely decorated walls. Among the many superb images here is a life-size statue of Krishna playing the flute, and as at Halebidu, a lively frieze details countless episodes from the Ramayana, Bhagavata Purana and Mahabharata. Unusually, the temple is autographed, bearing the signatures of its sculptors. Outside the temple stands a flagstaff (*dhvajastambha*), which may originally have been surmounted by a figure of Vishnu's bird vehicle Garuda.

It's best to visit as early as possible, as the black stone gets hot in the day, making it tough to walk barefoot.

ARRIVAL AND DEPARTURE SOMNATHPUR

By bus There are no direct buses from Mysuru to Somnathpur. Private buses run from Mysuru to Tirumakudal Narasipur (1hr), from where there are regular buses to Somnathpur (20min).

ACCOMMODATION AND EATING

There is nowhere to stay near the temple and the only food available is biscuits or maybe a samosa or fruit from a street-seller.

Hassan and around

The nondescript town of **HASSAN**, 118km northwest of Mysuru, is visited in large numbers because of its proximity to the Hoysala temples at **Belur** and **Halebidu**, both northwest of the town, and the Jain pilgrimage site of **Sravanabelagola** to the southeast. Some travellers end up staying a couple of nights but with a little forward

22

planning you shouldn't have to linger for long, as Belur, Halebidu and Sravanabelagola, deep in the serene Karnataka countryside, offer more appealing surroundings.

ARRIVAL AND INFORMATION HASSAN

By train The railway station, served by regular trains from Mysuru (10 daily; 2–3hr), is 2km east of the town centre on BM Rd. There are also several daily trains to Mangaluru (5–6hr), one of them overnight.

By bus Hassan's KSRTC Bus Stand is in the centre of town, at the northern end of Bus Stand Rd, and served by frequent buses from Mysuru (every 15–30min; 3hr). In order to see the surrounding sights by bus, you'll need at least two days. Belur and Halebidu can be comfortably covered in one day; it's best to take one of the earliest hourly buses to Halebidu (1hr) and move on to Belur (30min), from where services back to Hassan are more frequent (6.30am–6.15pm; 1hr

10min). Sravanabelagola, however, is in the opposite direction, and not served by direct buses; you have to head to Channarayapatna (every 30min from 6.30am; 1hr), aka "CR Patna", on the main Bengaluru highway and pick up one of the regular buses (30min) or any number of minibuses from there.

By car Apart from taking a tour, the only way to see Sravanabelagola, Belur and Halebidu in one day is by car, which some visitors share; most of the hotels can fix this up for around ₹2500/day.

Tourist information AVK College Rd (Mon–Sat 10am–5.30pm; ☏ 08172 268862).

ACCOMMODATION AND EATING

DR Karigowda Residency BM Rd, under 1km west from railway station ☏ 96868 41686. Immaculate budget hotel: friendly, comfortable and amazing value. Single occupancy possible; a/c ₹200 extra. No wi-fi. ₹750

Harsha Mahal Below Harsha Mahal Lodge, Harsha Mahal Rd ☏ 08172 268533. Excellent veg canteen that serves freshly cooked *idli*, dosas and other south Indian fare. Meals ₹50. Daily 6.30am–9.30pm.

Hoysala Village Belur Rd, 6km northwest of the centre ☏ 95910 77400, ⊛ hoysalavillageresorts.com. Ethnically designed and decorated luxury cottages and suites in a quiet rural setting, with a multicuisine restaurant and a

pool. ₹9000

Southern Star BM Rd, 500m from the train station ☏ 08172 251817, ⊛ hotelsouthernstar.com. Newish hotel with a variety of rooms and all mod cons. It's better value than most and the *Hoysala* multicuisine restaurant is excellent. ₹2970

Suvarna Gate Suvarna Regency, PB 97, BM Rd ☏ 08172 264006. This plush non-veg restaurant and bar with a few tables overlooking the garden is one of Hassan's finest. The varied menu is not cheap, with most curries going for at least ₹200. Daily 7am–11pm.

Halebidu (Halebid)

Now little more than a scruffy village of brick houses and chai stalls, **HALEBIDU** (formerly **Halebid**), 32km northwest of Hassan, was the second capital of the powerful Hoysala dynasty, which held sway over south Karnataka from the eleventh until the early fourteenth centuries and its peak stretched from coast to coast. Once known as **Dora Samudra** (Gateway to the Sea), the capital city became *Hale-bidu*, or "Old City", after successive raids by the Delhi sultanate between 1311 and 1326 reduced it to rubble. Despite the sacking, several large Hoysala temples (see page 1145) survive, two of which, the **Hoysaleshvara** and **Kedareshvara**, are superb, covered in exquisite carvings. Note that Belur has superior facilities to those found in Halebidu, making it a far better base for exploration of the Hoysala region.

Hoysaleshvara temple

Temple Daily 6am–6pm • Free **Archeological museum** Daily except Fri 10am–5pm • ₹5

The **Hoysaleshvara** temple, in the centre of the village, was started in 1121 and still unfinished even after a century of work; this possibly accounts for the absence here of the type of towers that feature at Somnathpur. Two large, ornately carved idols of Nandi, the bull, face its double shrine, with a Ganesha figure to the south. Each shrine contains a lingam.

Hoysaleshvara also features many Vaishnavite images. The **sculptures**, which have a fluid quality lacking in the earlier work at Belur, include Brahma aboard his swan, Krishna holding up Mount Govardhana and Vishnu (Trivikrama) spanning the world

---

HOYSALA TEMPLES

The **Hoysala** dynasty, who ruled southwestern Karnataka between the eleventh and thirteenth centuries, built a series of distinctive temples centred primarily at three sites: **Belur** and **Halebidu**, close to modern Hassan, and **Somnathpur**, near Mysuru. At first sight, and from a distance, the buildings, all based on a star-shaped plan, appear to be modest structures, compact and even squat. Yet on closer inspection, their profusion of fabulously detailed and sensuous sculpture, covering every centimetre of the exterior, is astonishing. Detractors often class Hoysala art as decadent and overly fussy, but anyone with an eye for craftsmanship will be sure to marvel.

The intricacy of the carvings was made possible by the material used in construction: a soft **soapstone** that on oxidization hardens to a glassy, highly polished surface. The level of detail, similar to that seen in sandalwood and ivory-work, became increasingly free and more fluid as the style developed, and reached its highest point at Somnathpur. Beautiful bracket figures, often delicate portrayals of voluptuous female subjects, were placed under the eaves, fixed by pegs top and bottom. A later addition (except possibly in the Somnathpur temple), these serve no structural function.

Another technique more usually associated with wood is the unusual treatment of the massive stone **pillars**: lathe-turned, they resemble those of the wooden temples of Kerala. They were probably turned on a horizontal plane, pinned at each end, and rotated with the use of a rope. It may be no coincidence that, to this day, wood-turning is still a local speciality.

---

in three steps. One of the most remarkable images is of the demon king **Ravana** shaking Shiva's mountain abode, Mount Kailash, populated by numerous animals and figures with Shiva and Parvati seated atop. You'll also come across the odd erotic tableau featuring voluptuous, heavily bejewelled maidens. A narrative frieze, on the sixth register from the bottom, follows the length of the Nandi *mandapas* and illustrates scenes from the Hindu epics.

A small **archeological museum** next to the temple houses a collection of Hoysala art and other finds from the area.

The Jain basadis
600m south of the Hoysaleshvara temple

Halebidu's Jain *basadis* (temples) stand virtually unadorned; their only sculptural decoration consists of ceiling friezes inside the *mandapas* and elephants at the entrance steps, where there's an impressive donation plaque. The thirteenth-century temple of **Adi Parshwanatha** is dedicated to the 23rd *tirthankara*, Parshvanath, while the sixteenth-century **Vijayanatha** is dedicated to the sixteenth *tirthankara*, Shantinath. The chowkidar will demonstrate various tricks made possible by the carved pillars' highly polished surfaces; some are so finely turned they sound metallic when struck.

Kedareshvara temple
400m east of the *basadis* • Daily 6.30am–6pm • Free

With its magnificently carved outer walls, tower, doorway and ceiling, the Shaivite **Kedareshvara temple**, built in 1219, has been described by architectural historian James Fergusson as "a gem of Indian architecture". The multitude of sculpted friezes at the base of the exterior depict elephants, horses, lions, mythical animals, swans and scrolls illustrating stories from Hindu epics, while the upper sections bear 180 finely carved images of gods and goddesses standing under elegantly designed floral arches. Inside, the ceilings are of most interest, replete with dancing images and other carvings.

ARRIVAL AND DEPARTURE   **HALEBIDU (HALEBID)**

Buses run until 7pm to Hassan (every 30min–1hr; 1hr) and   to Belur (hourly; 30min).

22

ACCOMMODATION

Mayura Shantala Halebeedu Opposite Hoysaleshvara temple ☎08177 273224, ⓦkarnatakaholidays. net. KSTDC hotel set in a small garden offering three comfortable, if overpriced, doubles with verandas, plus a four-bed room – all should be booked in advance. This is also the only place to eat, apart from a handful of daytime chai stalls. No wi-fi. ₹1000

Belur

BELUR, 37km northwest of Hassan, on the banks of the Yagachi River, was the Hoysala capital prior to Halebidu, during the eleventh and twelfth centuries. Still in active worship, the **Chennakeshava temple** is a fine and early example of the singular Hoysala style, built by King Vishnuvardhana in 1117 to celebrate his conversion from Jainism, victory over Chola forces at Talakad and his independence from the Chalukyas. Today, its grey-stone *gopura*, or gateway tower, soars above a small, bustling market town – a popular pilgrimage site from October to December, when busloads of Ayappan devotees stream through en route to Sabarimala. The **car festival** held around March or April takes place over twelve days and has a pastoral feel, attracting farmers from the surrounding countryside who conduct a bullock cart procession through the streets to the temple.

Chennakeshava temple

West of the bus stand • Daily 7.30am–7.30pm; main shrine opens for worship 8–10am, 11am–1pm, 2.30–5pm & 6.30–7.30pm

Chennakeshava temple stands in a huge walled courtyard, surrounded by smaller shrines and columned *mandapa* hallways. Both the sanctuary and *mandapa* are raised on the usual plinth (*jagati*), creating the jagged star shape. The quantity of **sculptural decoration**, if less mature than in later Hoysala temples, is staggering. The bracket figures depict celestial nymphs with intricately carved make-up, ornaments and hair, such detail being exclusive to Belur. Notable are the stunning sculpture of Darpanasundari ("lady with a mirror"), the pillars in the Navaranga hall and the 2m-high statue of Sri Keshava depicted with four hands.

Within the same enclosure, the **Kappe Channigaraya temple** has some finely carved niche images and a depiction of Narasimha (Vishnu as man-lion) killing the demon Hiranyakashipu. A few metres west, fine sculptures in the smaller **Viranarayana** shrine include a scene from the Mahabharata of Bhima killing the demon Bhaga.

ARRIVAL AND INFORMATION   BELUR

By bus Buses from Hassan and Halebidu arrive at the small bus stand in the middle of town, a 10min walk west along the main street from the temple.

Bike rental There are auto-rickshaws available, but a good way to explore the area, including Halebidu, is to rent a bicycle (₹5/hr) from one of the stalls around the bus stand.

Tourist information The tourist office (Mon–Sat 10am–5pm) is located within the KSTDC *Mayuri Velapuri* compound on Temple Rd.

ACCOMMODATION AND EATING

Kalpavriksha Just off Temple Rd ☎98276 30455. Just about the only place to eat meat in Belur, this small bar and restaurant offers a standard range of Indian and Chinese main courses for around ₹100–180, as well as south Indian snacks. Daily 7am–10pm.

Mayura Velapuri Temple Rd ☎08177 222209, ⓦkarnatakaholidays.net. This KSTDC hotel is a clean and comfortable place to stay, with five non-a/c and eight a/c rooms. The two dorms are rarely occupied, except in the March–May pilgrim season. Dorms ₹150, doubles ₹1000

Sumukha Residency Temple Rd ☎08177 222181. Close to the temple and bus stand, this fairly modern and comfortable place has singles for ₹350 and a/c rooms for ₹850. No wi-fi. ₹500

Vishnu Lodge Main Rd, near the bus stand ☎08177 222263. Above a great veg restaurant and sweet shop, this is the best-value place, with sizeable rooms (some with TV) but tiny attached bathrooms where hot water is only available in the mornings. No wi-fi. ₹500

Sravanabelagola

The sacred Jain site of **SRAVANABELAGOLA**, 49km southeast of Hassan and 93km north of Mysuru, consists of two hills and a large tank. On one of the hills, Indragiri (also known as Vindhyagiri), stands an extraordinary 18m-high monolithic statue of a naked male figure, **Gomateshvara**. Said to be the largest freestanding sculpture in India, this tenth-century colossus, visible from kilometres away, makes Sravanabelagola a key pilgrimage centre. At the **Mahamastakabhisheka** or "great head anointing ceremony", held every twelve years, devotees congregate to pour libations over the statue. The next will be held in February 2018. Spend a night or two in the village, and you can climb Indragiri Hill before dawn to enjoy the serene spectacle of the sun rising over the sugar cane fields and outcrops of lumpy granite that litter the surrounding plains – an unforgettable sight.

Sravanabelagola is linked in tradition with the Mauryan emperor Chandragupta, who starved himself to death on the second hill around 300 BC, in accordance with a Jain practice. The hill was renamed Chandragiri, marking the arrival of Jainism in southern India. At the same time, a controversy regarding the doctrines of Mahavira, the last of the 24 Jain **tirthankaras** (literally "ford-makers", who assist the aspirant to cross the "ocean of rebirth"), split Jainism into two separate branches – *svetambara*, "white-clad" Jains, more common in north India, and *digambara*, "sky-clad", who usually go naked and are associated with the south.

The monuments at Sravanabelagola probably date from no earlier than the tenth century, when a General Chavundaraya is said to have visited Chandragiri in search of a Mauryan statue of Gomateshvara. As a result of a vision in the rock face, having failed to find it, he decided to have one made. From the top of Chandragiri he fired an arrow across to Indragiri Hill; where the arrow landed, he had a new Gomateshvara sculpted from a single rock.

Indragiri Hill

Gomateshvara is approached from the tank between the two hills south of the main road by 612 steps, cut into the granite of **Indragiri Hill**, which pass numerous rock inscriptions on the way up to a walled enclosure. Shoes must be deposited at the stall to the left of the steps, and you can leave bags at the site office nearby. Take plenty of water if it's hot, as there is none available on the hill. Entered through a small wagon-vaulted *gopura*, the **temple** is entirely dominated by the towering figure of Gomateshvara. With elongated arms and exaggeratedly wide shoulders, his proportions may seem unnatural but depict the idealized physical features possessed by great thinkers and sages. The sensuously smooth surface of the white granite is finely carved: particularly the hands, hair and serene face. As in legend, ant hills and snakes sit at his feet and creepers appear to grow on his limbs.

Chandragiri Hill

Leaving your shoes with the keeper at the bottom, take the rock-cut steps to the top of the smaller **Chandragiri Hill**, north of the main road. Fine views stretch south to Indragiri and, from the north on the far side, across to a river, paddy and sugar cane fields, palms and the village of Jinanathapura, where there's another ornate Hoysala temple, the Shantishvara *basadi*.

Rather than a single large shrine, as at Indragiri, Chandragiri holds a group of *basadis* in late Chalukya Dravida style, within a walled enclosure. Caretakers will take you around and open up the closed shrines. Save for pilasters and elaborate parapets, all the temples have plain exteriors. Named after its patron, the tenth-century **Chavundaraya** temple is the largest of the group, dedicated to Parshvanath. Inside the twelfth-century **Chandragupta**, superb carved panels in a small shrine tell the story of Chandragupta and his teacher Bhadrabahu. Traces of painted geometric designs survive and the pillars feature detailed carving. Elsewhere in the enclosure stands a 24m-high *manastambha*,

22

22

"pillar of fame", decorated with images of spirits, *yakshis* and a *yaksha*. No fewer than 576 inscriptions dating from the sixth to the nineteenth centuries are dotted around the site, on pillars and on the rock itself.

Bhandari Basadi and monastery (math)

The road east from the foot of the steps at Chandragiri leads to two interesting Jain buildings in town. To the right as you face the hill, the **Bhandari Basadi** (1159), housing a shrine with images of the 24 *tirthankaras*, was built by Hullamaya, treasurer of the Hoysala raja Narasimha. Two *mandapa* hallways, where naked *digambara* Jains may sometimes be seen discoursing with devotees clad in white, lead to the shrine at the back.

At the end of the street, the *math* (monastery) was the residence of Sravanabelagola's senior *acharya*, or guru. Thirty male and female monks are attached to the *math*; normally a member of staff will be happy to show visitors around. Among the rare palm-leaf manuscripts in the library, some more than a millennium old, are works on mathematics and geography, and the Mahapurana, hagiographies of the *tirthankaras*. Next door, a covered walled courtyard edged by a high platform on three sides has a chair placed for the *acharya*. A collection of tenth-century bronze *tirthankara* images is housed here, and vibrant murals detail the various lives of Parshvanath. The hills where the *tirthankaras* stood to gain *moksha* are represented in a model, somewhat resembling a jelly mould, with tacked-on footprints.

ARRIVAL AND INFORMATION   **SRAVANABELAGOLA**

By bus You can reach Sravanabelagola from Hassan with one change of bus, although many people choose the easier option of a tour from Mysuru or Bengaluru.

Bike rental Crisscrossed by winding back roads, the idyllic countryside around Sravanabelagola is mostly flat and thus perfect cycling terrain. Bicycles are available for rent at Saleem Cycle Mart, on Masjid Rd, opposite the northeast corner of the tank.

ACCOMMODATION AND EATING

There are plenty of *dharamshalas* to choose from if you want to stay. Managed by the temple authorities, they offer simple, scrupulously clean rooms, many with their own bathrooms and sitouts, set around gardens and courtyards, and costing under ₹300 per night. The 24hr office of the Shravanabelagola Digambara Jain Managing Committee (☏ 08176 257258), located inside the *SP Guest House*, next to the bus stand clock tower, allocates rooms.

Hotel Raghu Opposite the main tank ☏ 08176 257238. Very simple attached rooms but clean enough and the only private option around, with some a/c rooms. It also has the best of the many small local restaurants – try the excellent thali. **₹650**

Kodagu (Coorg)

The hill region of **Kodagu**, formerly known as **Coorg**, lies 100km west of Mysuru in the Western Ghats, its eastern fringes merging with the Mysore plateau. India's leading coffee-producing region, Kodagu is also the birthplace of the River Kaveri and home to the martial Kodavas, whose customs, language and appearance set them apart from their neighbours. Its rugged mountain terrain is interspersed with cardamom valleys and fields of lush paddy, as well as coffee plantations, making it one of south India's most beautiful areas. Yet much has changed since Dervla Murphy spent a few months here with her daughter in the 1970s (the subject of her classic travelogue, *On a Shoestring to Coorg*) and was entranced by the landscape. **Homestays** have given tourism in Kodagu a big boost, and larger hotel chains and resorts have moved in to cater to weekend visitors, making the main towns feel much more crowded.

Nonetheless, the countryside is still idyllic and the climate refreshingly cool, even in summer. Many visitors **trek** through the unspoilt forest tracts and ridges that fringe the district. On the eastern borders of Kodagu around Kushalnagar, large **Tibetan settlements** have transformed the once barren countryside of Bylakuppe into fertile farmland dotted with monasteries, some of which house thousands of monks. To its south, and three hours southwest of Mysuru, **Nagarahole National Park** can be rewarding if visited at the right time of year.

If you plan to cross the Ghats between Mysuru and the coast, the route through Kodagu is definitely worth considering. A good time to visit is during the festival season in early December, or during the **Blossom Showers** around March and April when the coffee plants bloom with white flowers that scent the air.

22

Brief history

The first records of a kingdom here date from the eighth century, when it prospered from the salt trade passing between the coast and the cities on the Deccan. Under the Hindu **Haleri rajas**, the state repulsed invasions by its more powerful neighbours, including Haider Ali and his son Tipu Sultan. A combination of hilly terrain, absence of roads (a deliberate policy on the part of defence-conscious Kodagu kings) and the tenacity of its highly trained warriors ensured Kodagu was never conquered.

In 1834, after ministers appealed to the British to help depose their despotic king, Chikkaviraraja, Kodagu became a princely state with nominal independence, which it retained until the creation of Karnataka in 1956. **Coffee** was introduced during the Raj and, despite plummeting prices on the international market, this continues to be the linchpin of the local economy, along with pepper and cardamom. Although Kodagu is Karnataka's wealthiest region, despite being its smallest, and provides the highest tax revenue, it does not reap the rewards – some villages are still without electricity – and this, coupled with the distinct identity and fiercely independent nature of the Kodavas, has given rise to movements for autonomy, such as the **Codava National Council**.

Madikeri (Mercara) and around

Nestling beside a curved stretch of craggy hills, **MADIKERI**, capital of Kodagu, undulates around 1300m up in the Western Ghats, roughly midway between Mysuru and the coastal city of Mangaluru. The gradually increasing number of foreigners who travel up here find it a pleasant enough town, with red-tiled buildings and undulating roads that converge on a bustling bazaar, but most move on to home and plantation stays in the verdant Coorg countryside within a couple of days.

Omkareshwara temple

1km northwest of bus stand

The red-roofed **Omkareshwara temple**, built in 1820 and dedicated to Shiva, features an unusual combination of Hindu features, Islamic-influenced domes and even Gothic elements. The annual Teppothsava or boat festival takes place in November or December.

Madikeri Fort

1km northwest of bus stand • Tues–Sun 10am–5.30pm • **Museum** Tues–Sun 9am–5pm, except 2nd Sat • Free

Housed within the old **Madikeri Fort**, the original mud **palace** of Haleri king Muddu Raja was rebuilt in stone by Tipu Sultan in 1781 and further modified by the British in the nineteenth century; it now serves as government offices. The fort also houses the old prison and an ancient Kote Ganapati temple, as well as St Mark's Chapel, which has been converted into a small **museum** containing British memorabilia, Jain and Hindu deity figures and weapons.

Around 2km north of the fort and temple, at Gaddige, the huge square **tombs of the rajas**, with Islamic-style gilded domes and minarets, are also worth a look.

22

THE KODAVAS

Theories abound as to the origins of the **Kodavas**, or **Coorgs**, who today comprise less than one sixth of the hill region's population. Fair-skinned and with their own language and customs, they are thought to have migrated to southern India from Kurdistan, Kashmir or even Greece, though no one knows exactly why or when. One popular belief holds that this staunchly martial people, who since Independence have produced some of India's leading military brains, are a branch of Indo-Scythians; some even claim connections with Alexander the Great's invading army. Whatever their origins, the Kodavas have managed to retain a distinct identity distinct from the freed plantation slaves, Moplah Muslim traders and other immigrants who have settled here. Their language is Dravidian, yet their religious practices, based on ancestor veneration and worship of nature spirits, sacred groves (*devarakadu*) and the river, differ markedly from those of mainstream Hinduism. Land tenure in Kodagu is also quite distinctive: women have a right to inheritance and ownership, and, are also allowed to remarry.

Spiritual and social life for traditional Kodavas revolves around the **ain mane**, or ancestral homestead. Built on raised platforms to overlook the family land, these large, detached houses, with their beautiful carved wood doors and beaten-earth floors, generally have four wings and courtyards to accommodate various branches of the extended family, as well as shrine rooms, or **Karona Kalas**, dedicated to the clan's most important forebears. Key religious rituals and rites of passage are always conducted in the *ain mane*, rather than the local temple. However, you could easily travel through Kodagu without ever seeing one, as they are invariably away from roads, deep in the plantations.

Raja's Seat and around

The Kodagu kings chose an ideal vantage point from which to watch the sunset: **Raja's Seat** (daily 6am–8pm; ₹5), a grassy park and garden on the western edge of town, fills up just before dusk for a water-and-light show at 7pm. Nearby, **Gandhi Mantap** marks the site where Mahatma Gandhi addressed the townsfolk in 1934.

Abbi Falls

8km southeast of the town • Auto-rickshaws charge around ₹400 for the return journey including waiting time

The pleasant road to **Abbi Falls**, Madikeri's famous 21m cascade, winds through the hill country and makes for a good day's outing. A gate near the car park leads through a private coffee and cardamom plantation to the base of the cascade (fenced off to dissuade swimming). Viewed from a hanging bridge, the falls are at their best during and after the monsoons.

ARRIVAL AND INFORMATION

MADIKERI AND AROUND

By bus Madikeri has regular bus connections with Bengaluru (hourly; 6hr), Hassan (6–8 daily; 4hr), Mangaluru (every 30min–1hr; 4hr) and Mysuru (every 30min–1hr; 3hr). The KSTRC state bus stand is at the lowest part of town, towards its eastern side, below the main bazaar; private buses from villages around the region pull into a car park 100m west.

Tourist information Coorg Travel World (☏ 08272 224394, ⊛ coorgtravelworld.com), on Main Rd, and Coorg SR Tours & Travels (☏ 08272 222717, ⊛ coorgsrtravels.com), near the bus stand, both arrange treks, tours and homestays. For information on Kodagu's forests and booking forest bungalows contact the Deputy Conservator of Forests (☏ 08272 228305) at the fort. To arrange coffee plantation visits, contact the Codagu Planters Association on Mysore Rd (☏ 08272 226273, ⊛ cpa.org.in).

ACCOMMODATION

Kodagu has a huge range of stay options from rustic cottages to ritzy resorts, though its charm lies in the profusion of traditional homestays, many in plantation bungalows, which offer the legendary hospitality of the Kodavas. For more see ⊛ coorghomestays.com.

IN AND AROUND TOWN

★ **Caveri** School Rd ☏ 08272 225492. Below the private bus stand, this large hotel has been upgraded but remains good value, with spacious and nicely furnished double rooms. There's a ground-floor restaurant, serving the spicy

local delicacy *pandi* (pork) curry, and adjacent bar. ₹1000
Chitra School Rd ⊕ 08272 225372, ⊚ hotelchitra.co.in.
Good-value hotel near the private bus station. Neat, well-kept rooms have cable TV, and there's also an excellent veg restaurant-cum-bar downstairs. No wi-fi. ₹950
Coorg International Convent Rd ⊕ 08272 228071,
⊚ coorginternational.com. A 10min rickshaw ride west of the centre, this large hotel has comfortable Western-style rooms, a multicuisine restaurant, exchange facilities, and shops. Wi-fi only in the lobby. Breakfast included. ₹4500
Daisy Bank Heritage Inn General Thimaya Rd (aka Mysore Rd) ⊕ 08272 321172. Housed in a converted mansion, the original *East End Hotel* has nine double rooms with high ceilings and subtle decor. All rooms, named after flowers, have spotless bathrooms and flat-screen TVs; prices vary according to size. No wi-fi. ₹1300
★ **Gowri Nivas** New Extension ⊕ 94481 93822,
⊚ gowrinivas.com. Bops and Muthu's charming homestay in the heart of town has two rooms in a separate cottage and one in the main house, decorated with lovely artefacts. Delicious Kodava cuisine is on offer. ₹4000
Mayura Valley View Raja Rd ⊕ 08272 228387,
⊚ karnatakaholidays.net. A stiff walk up past Raja's Seat,

this KSTDC hotel offers large old-fashioned rooms, many with excellent views. The restaurant serves booze and has an open terrace with epic views. ₹2250

OUTSIDE TOWN

★ **Palace Estate** Near Nalaknad Palace, Kakkabe, 35km southwest of Madikeri ⊕ 98804 47702, ⊚ palaceestate.co.in. Set at the base of Thadiyendamol, Coorg's loftiest mountain, this pioneering homestay is a 1hr 15min drive from Madikeri. A backpacker favourite, it has panoramic views, home-style food, warm hosts and a private waterfall, making it the perfect spot to linger. There's even a single room for ₹1400. ₹3600
★ **Rainforest Retreat** 13km north of Madikeri, near Galibeedu village ⊕ 08272 265636, ⊚ rainforestours. com. Informed hosts and botanists Sujata and Anurag Goel run a 20-acre organic farm, with warmly furnished eco cottages and two tents (₹2000) set amid lush rainforest. Produce such as pepper, cardamom and coffee are sold under their "Don't Panic, It's Organic" brand, with profits going to their NGO, WAPRED, which fosters environmental awareness and sustainable agriculture in the region. Tariff includes breakfast and a plantation walk. ₹3000

22

EATING

Athithi Opposite the Town Hall ⊕ 99010 40200. Tucked just off the main road, this place has an outdoor terrace, as well as indoor seating, where you can enjoy south Indian and tandoori pure-veg cuisine for ₹70–180. Daily 7am–10pm.
★ **Choice** Junior College Rd ⊕ 08272 225585. This popular three-storey restaurant has had a facelift, with the addition of a spacious roof "garden" upstairs. Tuck into huge portions of Indian and Chinese food; the American chop suey is a winner at ₹190. Daily 8am–10pm.
★ **East End** General Thimaya Rd ⊕ 08272 229996. Though the landmark hotel has shifted to a new building behind East End petrol pump, the restaurant has retained

the same flavours and menu as before. Try the *keema* ball curry or biryanis for lunch (around ₹200), or snacks like *keema dosa* and mutton cutlet. Daily 8am–10pm.
Karavali Fish Land Down the lane opposite the Fort ⊕ 98457 89989. Sparkling-clean family restaurant that specializes in fish, including a great-value ₹70 thali, although there are plenty of a la carte veg and meat options too. Daily 8am–10.30pm.
West End Near KSRTC bus stand, Kohinoor Rd. A grubby hole-in-the-wall bar and restaurant popular among locals for spicy *pandi* curry, served with *akki otti* (rice rotis) roasted on a wood fire. Daily 9.30am–10.30pm.

Nagarahole National Park

90km south from Madikeri • ₹1000 (₹200), video camera ₹1000 payable at check post

Nagarahole ("Snake River") **National Park,** together with Bandipur and Tamil Nadu's Mudumalai national parks, forms the **Nilgiri Biosphere Reserve,** one of India's most extensive tracts of protected forest. Straddling Kodagu and Mysore districts, the park extends 640 square kilometres north from the River Kabini, which has been dammed to form a picturesque artificial lake. During the dry season (Feb–June), this perennial water source attracts large numbers of animals to its muddy riverbanks and grassy swamps, or *hadlus*, making it a potentially prime spot for sighting gaur (Indian bison), elephant, *dhole* (wild dog), deer, boar, and even the odd tiger or leopard. The forest here is of the moist deciduous type – thick jungle with a 30m-high canopy – and more impressive than Bandipur's drier scrub. The park is best avoided altogether during the monsoon season.

ARRIVAL AND INFORMATION

By bus Buses from Mysuru's Central stand go to Hunsur (2 daily; 3hr), 10km from the park's north gate, where you can find transport, mostly in the form of jeeps, to the Forest Department's two guesthouses. From Madikeri, there are regular buses to the southern entrance at Kutta (hourly; 2hr); buses headed for Kozhikode stop there too. Auto-

NAGARAHOLE NATIONAL PARK

rickshaws and jeeps from the Kutta stand drop you at the park entrance and reservation office.

Tours Jeep safaris cost ₹3000–5000 depending on group size. Bus tours (6–9am & 4–6.30pm; ₹100) can be arranged at the visitor centre.

ACCOMMODATION

Forest Department guesthouses Inside the park; bookings through the Project Tiger office in Mysuru ☎0821 248 0901 or Forest Department in Hunsur ☎0822 252 041. These simple rustic cabins are scantily furnished and you must arrive (either by jeep or rented vehicle) at the park gates well before dusk – the road through the reserve to the lodges closes at 6pm, and is prone to "elephant blocks". ₹500

The Jade Manchalli, Kutta ☎08228 244396, ⓦthejade coorg.com. Kabir and Megha's heritage homestay is just 10km from the park's southern entrance and a great base for trekking in the Brahmagiri range to Irpu Falls. The classy rooms overlook the garden and hills. Excellent Kodava cuisine; breakfast and dinner included. ₹3700

Jungle Inn Veerana Hosahalli, Hunsur ☎08222 246022, ⓦjungleinn.in. Close to the park's northern entrance, this highway lodge has a mix of rooms of different sizes plus huge Swiss tented cottages. Staff can arrange pick-up from Hunsur. ₹3500

Kabini River Lodge Approached via the village of Karapura, east of the park ☎08228 264403, ⓦjunglelodges.com. Set in its own leafy compound overlooking the Kabini reservoir, this former maharaja's hunting lodge offers all-in deals that include meals, forest entry charges and safaris around the park with expert guides. It's impossible to reach by public transport, so you'll need to rent a car to get here. Choose from cottages, rooms and tented cottages. All-inclusive from ₹22,420

Mangaluru (Mangalore)

Most visitors dismiss **Mangalore**, now officially renamed **MANGALURU**, as a stopover between Goa and Kerala, or as a strategic hub from which to access Coorg and Hassan. However, this bustling multicultural town is packed with history and some visit just to relish its famed coastal cuisine.

Named after the ancient temple of Mangaladevi at Bolar, 3km from the city centre, Mangalore was one of the most famous ports of south India and frequented by Arab traders. It was already well known overseas in the sixth century as a major source of pepper; the fourteenth-century Muslim writer Ibn Battuta noted its trade in pepper and ginger and the presence of merchants from Persia and Yemen. In the mid-1400s, the Persian ambassador Abdu'r-Razzaq saw Mangalore as a lucrative "frontier town" of the Vijayanagar Empire, which was why it was captured by the Portuguese in 1529, and later Tipu Sultan and the British. Nowadays, the modern port, 10km north of the city proper, is principally known for the processing and export of coffee and cocoa (mostly from Kodagu), and cashew nuts (from Kerala). It is also a centre for the production of *beedis* (local cigarettes).

Mangaluru's strong Christian influence can be traced back to the arrival of St Thomas further south. Some 1400 years later, in 1526, the Portuguese founded one of the earliest churches on the coast, although today's **Rosario Cathedral**, with a dome based on St Peter's in Rome, dates only from 1910. Closer to the centre, on Lighthouse Hill Road, fine restored fresco, tempera and oil murals by the Italian Antonio Moscheni adorn the Romanesque-style **St Aloysius College Chapel**, built in 1882.

Manjunatha temple

Atop the Kadri Hill, 3km north of the centre

Mangaluru's tenth-century **Manjunatha temple** is believed to be the oldest Shiva temple in the city and an important centre of the tantric **Nathapanthi cult**, a divergent form of Hinduism and similar to cults in Nepal. Enshrined in the sanctuary are a number of superb **bronzes**, including a 1.5m-high seated Matsyendranatha, made in 958 AD. To see it up close, visit at *darshan* times (6am–1pm & 4–8pm), although the bronzes can be glimpsed through the wooden slats on the side of the sanctuary. If possible, time your visit to coincide with *mahapuja* (8am, noon & 8pm) when the priests give a fire blessing to the accompaniment of raucous music. Opposite the east entrance, steps lead via a reddish-coloured path to a curious group of minor shrines. Beyond this complex stands the **Shri Yogishwar Math**, a hermitage set round two courtyards.

Ullal

10km south of Mangaluru • Local bus #44A runs to Ullal from the junction at the south end of KS Rao Rd (centre of town)

To escape the city for a few hours, head to the suburb of **ULLAL**, where a long sandy **beach** stretches for kilometres, backed by wispy casuarina trees. It's a popular place for a stroll,

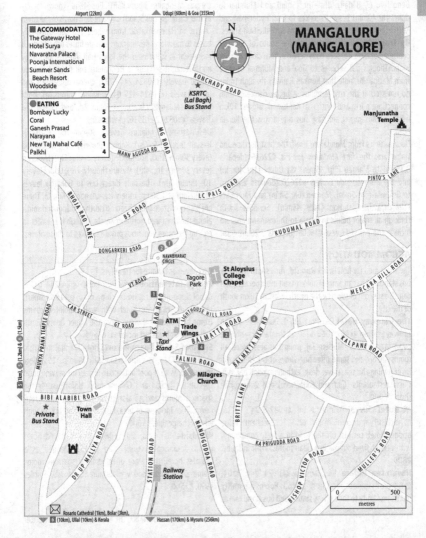

particularly in the evening when Mangaloreans come out to watch the sunset, but a strong undertow makes swimming difficult, and at times unsafe. You might be better off using the pool at the *Summer Sands Beach Resort* (see below), immediately behind the beach. Towards the centre of Ullal, and around 700m from the main bus stand, is the *dargah* of **Seyyid Mohammad Shareeful Madani**, a sixteenth-century saint who is said to have come from Medina in Arabia, floating across the sea on a handkerchief. The extraordinary nineteenth-century building with garish onion domes houses the saint's tomb, which is one of the most important Sufi shrines in southern India. Visitors are advised to follow custom and cover their heads and limbs and wash their feet before entering.

ARRIVAL AND DEPARTURE
MANGALURU (MANGALORE)

By plane Bajpe airport, 22km north of the city (bus #22 or #47A or taxis for ₹450–500), has regular flights to Bengaluru (7–8 daily; 1hr–1hr 15min) and Mumbai (6 daily; 1hr 40min) besides services to Goa, Hyderabad and Kochi. There are also daily connections with the Gulf States.

By train The railway station, to the south of the city centre on Station Rd, sees daily services from cities all over India. Though rail services to Goa and Mumbai operate from Mangaluru, note that Konkan Railway through trains do not stop at the city terminus. A better choice of train connections north and south is at Kankanadi, around 10km north, or Kasaragod, an easy bus ride across the Kerala border.

Destinations From Mangaluru itself, the best northbound trains are: the fast *Madgaon Express* #22636 (departs 8.15am) to Margao (5hr 45min) via Udupi (1hr 40min) and the *Matsyaganda Express* #12620 (departs 2.25pm) to Gokarna (4hr 5min), Margao (6hr 5min) and Mumbai's Lokmanya Tilak station (14hr 45min). Services south through all major points in Kerala to Thiruvananthapuram include the *Ernad Express* #16605 (departs 7.20am; 13hr 40min) and the *Malabar Express* #16630 (departs 6.15pm; 15hr 15min).

By bus Mangaluru's busy KSRTC Bus Stand (known locally as the "Lal Bagh" Bus Stand) is nearly 3km north of the town centre, in Hampankatta, from where you can catch city buses to most local destinations. Private buses use the much more central stand near the Town Hall. Agents for luxury and overnight services to Bengaluru and beyond include Anand Travels (☎0824 244 6737, ⊛anandbus.com) and Ideal Travels (☎0824 425 0499, ⊛idealtravels.co), both opposite Milagres Church on Falnir Rd, and Vijayanand Travels (☎0824 249 3536, ⊛vrlbus.in).

Destinations Bengaluru (every 30min–1hr; 9–10hr); Hassan (hourly; 5–6hr); Kannur (hourly; 3hr); Kasaragod (every 30min; 1hr); Kozhikode (every 1–2hr; 5hr); Madikeri (every 30min–1hr; 4hr); Mysuru (hourly; 7hr); Udupi (every 10–15min; 1hr). The only direct bus to Gokarna leaves Mangaluru at 1.30pm; otherwise, change at Kumta. There are plenty of state buses heading north to Udupi and south along the coast into northern Kerala, though it is easier to pick up the more numerous private services to those places.

ACCOMMODATION

The main area for hotels, **KS Rao Rd**, runs south from the bus stand and has an ample choice to suit most pockets. You can also stay out of town by the beach in **Ullal**, 10km south of the city.

The Gateway Hotel Old Port Rd, 1.5km west of the railway station ☎0824 666 0420, ⊛thegatewayhotels. com; map p.1153. Modern Taj group business hotel; all rooms are a/c and some offer fine views of the Netravathi River joining the sea. Travel desk, exchange, pool, bar, two classy restaurants (*Gad* and *Cardamom*) and 24hr coffee shop. ₹6000

★**Hotel Surya** Balmatta Rd ☎0824 242 5736, ⊛hotelsuryamlr.com; map p.1153. Excellent value budget hotel, set just off the road in a leafy compound, with decent sized simple but clean rooms. Wi-fi in lobby. ₹800

Navaratna Palace KS Rao Rd ☎0824 244 1104, ⊛navaratnapalace.com; map p.1153. Rooms are musty but its proximity to the railway station and bus stand makes it a convenient choice for travellers. ₹1499

Poonja International KS Rao Rd ☎0824 244 0171, ⊛hotelpoonjainternational.com; map p.1153. Smart, mostly a/c, high-rise hotel with well-appointed rooms (some a/c) and good views from the upper floors. South Indian buffet breakfast included. ₹1699

Summer Sands Beach Resort Chota Mangalore, Ullal ☎88613 73737, ⊛summersands.in; map p.1153. Near the beach, with a pool and a bar-restaurant serving local specialities, Indian and Chinese food. Unfortunately the spacious rooms and villa-style cottages are rather run-down. Price inclusive of breakfast, dinner and tax, though wi-fi is chargeable. ₹5600

Woodside Balmatta Rd ☎0824 244 0296, ⊛hotel woodsidemangalore.com; map p.1153. Pegged as a business hotel, this place offers unfussy spacious rooms (some a/c) and a good veg restaurant, *Xanadu*. Singles ₹990. ₹1500

STATUE OF NANDI, THE ABODE OF SHIVA, AT HALEBIDU

EATING

Bombay Lucky Near North Police Station, Mohammed Ali Rd, Bunder, under 2km west of the railway station ☎0824 242 3710; map p.1153. Dating back to 1917, this late-opening restaurant, legendary for its Muslim cuisine, has been renovated but the quality remains high. Try the ghee rice, chicken korma, chicken or mutton biryani (₹150) or *bheja* (brain-fry) chicken or mutton fry, washed down with Suleimani (lemon) tea. Reasonably-priced and lightning-quick service. Daily 9.30am–midnight.

Coral Ocean Pearl hotel, Navabharat Circle ☎0824 241 3800, ⓦtheoceanpearl.in; map p.1153. As the name suggests, there's an excellent seafood selection here and at reasonable prices despite the luxury hotel setting, including delicious fish thalis (lunchtime only; ₹350) and *koliwada* (crunchy, fried) prawns (₹650). Daily noon–3pm & 7–11pm.

Ganesh Prasad Down a lane running off KS Rao Rd ☎0824 425 5932; map p.1153. Classic pure-veg canteen, churning out all the south Indian favourites, from crispy dosas to gut-busting lunchtime "meals" (₹70). Daily 7am–9.30pm.

Narayana Near Indian Overseas Bank, Azizuddin Rd, Bunder ☎0824 244 0891; map p.1153. A humble yet popular place near the harbour dishing out the best fish curry in town, served with boiled rice, and a choice of fried fish, all under ₹150. Always packed like a tin of sardines. Daily 12.30–3.30pm & 7–9.30pm.

New Taj Mahal Café Kodialbail, KS Rao Rd ☎0824 426 9335; map p.1153. This Mangalore institution (since the 1920s) is a great choice for and early breakfast. Try local savouries like *ambade* (lentil fritters), *kadle upkari* (spiced chickpeas), *thuppa* dosa (slathered with clarified butter), *godi* (wheat) halwa and banana halwa, all under ₹100. Daily 6am–9.30pm.

Palkhi Balmatta Rd ☎0824 244 4929; map p.1153. This airy family rooftop restaurant offers a wide menu of north Indian, Chinese and Continental cuisine, with main courses around ₹250. Daily noon–3.15pm & 7–11.15pm.

North of Mangaluru: coastal Karnataka

Whether you travel the **Karnataka (Karavali) coast** on the Konkan Railway or along the busy NH-17, southern India's smoothest highway, the route between Goa and Mangaluru ranks among the most scenic anywhere in the country. Crossing countless palm- and mangrove-fringed estuaries, the railway line stays fairly flat, while the recently upgraded road, dubbed by the local tourist board as "The Sapphire Route", scales several spurs of the Western Ghats, which here creep to within a stone's throw of the sea, with spellbinding views over long, empty beaches and deep blue bays. Highlights are the pilgrim town of **Udupi**, site of a famous Krishna temple, and **Gokarna**, another important Hindu centre that provides access to exquisite unexploited beaches. A decent inland road winds through the mountains to **Jog Falls**, India's biggest waterfall, which can also be approached from the east.

Udupi

UDUPI (also spelt Udipi), on the west coast, 60km north of Mangaluru, is one of south India's holiest Vaishnavite centres. The Hindu saint **Madhva** (1238–1317) was born here, and the **Krishna temple** and *mathas* (monasteries) he founded are visited by hundreds of thousands of pilgrims each year. The largest numbers congregate during the late winter, when the town hosts a series of spectacular **car festivals** and gigantic, bulbous-domed chariots are hauled through the streets around the temple. Even if your visit doesn't coincide with a festival, Udupi is a good place to break the journey along the Karavali coast. Thronging with pujaris and pilgrims, its small sacred enclave is wonderfully atmospheric.

The Krishna temple and mathas

Udupi's **Krishna temple** lies five minutes' walk east of the main street, surrounded by the eight **mathas** founded by Madhva in the thirteenth century. Legend has it that the idol enshrined within was discovered by the saint himself after he prevented a shipwreck. The grateful captain of the vessel offered Madhva his precious cargo as a reward, but the holy man asked instead for a block of mud, which he broke open to

---

KAMBLA

If you're anywhere between Mangaluru and Bhatkal from October to April and come across a crowd gathering around a waterlogged paddy field, chances are they're there to watch the spectacular rural sport of **Kambla**, or **buffalo racing**. It's a centuries old tradition unique to Dakshina Kannada, the southernmost district of coastal Karnataka.

Two contestants, usually local rice farmers, take part in the race, riding on a wooden plough-board tethered to a pair of buffaloes. The object is to reach the opposite end of the field first, but points are also awarded for style, and riders gain extra marks – and roars of approval from the crowd – if the muddy spray kicked up from the plough-board splashes the special white banners, or *thorana*, strung across the course at a height of 6–8m. In simpler formats of the competition contestants may be tugged by a single buffalo, connected by a rope or even hold the animal's tail.

Generally, race days are organized by wealthy landowners on fields specially set aside for the purpose. Villagers flock in from all over the region, as much for the fair (*shendi*), as the races themselves: men huddle in groups to watch cockfights (*korikatta*), women haggle with bangle sellers and kids roam around sucking sticky *kathambdi goolay*, the local bonbons. It is considered highly prestigious to be able to throw such a party, especially if your buffaloes win any events or, better still, come away as champions. Pampered by their doting owners, racing buffaloes are massaged, oiled and blessed by priests before big events, during which large sums of money are often won and lost. In recent years, however, the sport has come under the scanner of animal activists leading to a request for a ban on the practice by the Animal Welfare Board of India, though time will tell whether a law will be enforced.

22

expose a perfectly formed image of Krishna. Believed to contain the essence (*sannidhya*) of the god, this deity draws a steady stream of pilgrims, and is the focus of almost constant ritual activity. It is looked after by *acharyas*, or pontiffs, from one of the *mathas* on a two-year rotation system. They perform pujas (5.30am–8.45pm) that are open to non-Hindus; men are only allowed into the main shrine bare-chested.

ARRIVAL AND INFORMATION
UDUPI

By train Udupi's railway station is at Indrali on Manipal Rd, 3km west from the centre, and there are at least five trains in each direction daily.

By bus Udupi's three bus stands are dotted around the amorphous square in the centre of town: the KSRTC and private stands form a practically indistinguishable gathering spot for the numerous services to Mangaluru and more long-distance buses to Mysuru and Bengaluru and between northern Kerala and Goa. There are hardly

any direct buses to Gokarna or Jog Falls, so you usually have to change at Kumta or Honnavar for both. The City stand is down some steps to the north and handles private services to local villages.

Tourist information There's a tourist information centre near the temple in the Krishna Building, on Car St (☎ 0820 429 3222), and a tourist office at Rajasadri, Manipal End Point (Mon–Sat 10am–5.30pm; ☎ 0820 257 4868).

ACCOMMODATION

As a busy pilgrimage town, Udupi offers ample inexpensive **accommodation**, which is only likely to approach capacity during a major festival.

Durga International Just west of City Bus Stand ☎ 94484 26665. Airy and efficient lodge with a variety of attached rooms, all with TV and some with a/c, on the upper storeys of a modern block. Also has a good multicuisine restaurant. Wi-fi in lobby. ₹1000

★ **OYO Janardana** Next to KSRTC Bus Stand ☎ 0820 252 3880, ⊛ janardanahotel.in. Recently spruced up, with nicely furnished attached rooms of different sizes, all with cable TV and some a/c. ₹1000

Sriram Residency Opposite the GPO ☎ 0820 253 0761, ⊛ hotelsriramresidency.in. Plushest place in the centre, though costing no more than most, with a smart lobby and comfortable a/c rooms. One of the two restaurants serves fine non-veg, and there's a bar too. ₹1400

Sri Vidyasamudra Choultry Opposite Krishna temple ☎ 0820 252 0820. Foreigners are welcome in this ultra-basic lodge for pilgrims. The front rooms overlooking the temple are incredibly atmospheric. No wi-fi. ₹200

Vyavahar Lodge Kankads Rd ☎ 0820 252 2568. Basic but friendly and clean lodge between the bus stands and temple. Singles are just ₹300. No wi-fi. ₹500

EATING

As you might expect of the **masala dosa**'s birthplace, there are many fine, simple south Indian restaurants in Udupi, where you can sample these and other veg favourites. The vast majority of places are pure veg: for non-veg food or alcohol, you'll have to try a posh hotel restaurant such as the *Sriram Residency*.

Diana Jodukatte, Ajjarkad, 1.5km southwest of the Krishna temple ☎0820 252 0505. This long-established restaurant on the first floor of the *Diana* hotel is the birthplace of the *gadbad* ice cream (₹90), a famous dish invented hurriedly (*gadibidi* is Kannada for confusion) when several layers of different ice creams were mixed with chopped nuts and chewy dried fruit. Local snacks like dosas, *poori kurma* (veg curry with fried bread) and veg cutlets

are also available, besides tandoori and Chinese. Daily 8am–9pm.

Mitra Samaj Car St ☎98801 99678. Established in 1949, this cramped place shares wall space with the Chandra-mouleshwara shrine close to the Krishna temple. Try the bullet *idlis* (available only after 2pm), *goli bajji* (a spongy, fried snack, after 4pm) or dosa served with typical Udupi *sambhar* (₹60). Daily 5.30am–9pm.

Pooja Below Janardana hotel ☎7204 022221. Formerly called *Adarsha*, this pure-veg eatery rustles up tasty south Indian tiffin, filling masala dosa, *upma* (thick semolina or rice-flour porridge) and wholesome thalis (₹80). Daily 6am–9pm (Sun till 4pm).

Jog Falls

Vehicle entry fee ₹10 per person • Musical fountain and laser show Mon–Sat 7.15–8.15pm, Sun 7.15–9.15pm

Hidden in a remote, thickly forested corner of the Western Ghats 240km northeast of Mangaluru, **Jog Falls** are the highest waterfalls in India. Today, however, they are rarely as spectacular as they were before the construction of a large dam upriver, which impedes the flow of the River Sharavati over the sheer red-brown sandstone cliffs. Still, the surrounding scenery is gorgeous, with dense scrub and jungle carpeting sparsely populated, mountainous terrain. The views of the falls from the opposite side of the gorge are also impressive, though during the monsoons mist and rain clouds tend to envelop the cascades. Another reason not to come during the wet season is that the extra water, and abundance of leeches at this time, make the excellent hike to the floor valley a trial; if you can, head up here between October and January. The trail starts just below the bus park and winds steeply down to the water, where you can enjoy a refreshing dip. The whole patch opposite the falls has been landscaped for appealing viewing, with its own entrance gate and reception centre.

ARRIVAL AND INFORMATION

By bus Jog Falls is connected by the well-paved NH-206 that crosses the Ghats from the coast south of Kumta (6 buses daily to the falls from Kumta; 3hr), which is connected by frequent buses to Gokarna. Coming from the south, it is slightly quicker to connect at Honnavar (4–6 daily; 2hr 30min). On the inland side, there are hourly services to Shivamogga (Shimoga), from where you can change onto

buses for Hosapete and Hampi. Change at Sagar (40km) instead for buses to Udupi, Mysuru, Hassan and Bengaluru.

Tourist information The tourist office (Mon–Sat 10am–1.30pm & 2.30–5.30pm), upstairs at the new reception centre, opens rather erratically but can supply information on transport and vehicle rental.

ACCOMMODATION AND EATING

Apart from the standard government canteen at the *Mayura Gerusoppa Jogfalls* hotel, the only other food options are at the enclave of small chai stalls and shops that cluster around the reception centre.

JMJ Homestay More than 1km southeast of the reception centre, beyond the canal ☎94822 08755. Friendly homestay with four comfortable, rustic rooms. Food served on request. No wi-fi. ₹550

Matthuga Homestay Talavata, BH Rd, 8km from Jog Falls ☎98807 99975, ⓦmatthuga.in. Popular homestay,

close to nature, set in a plantation bungalow with lovely attached rooms and cottages (₹2900). Fixed pure-veg menu (breakfast ₹80; lunch/dinner ₹130). No TV, no wi-fi. ₹1800

Mayura Gerusoppa Jogfalls 200m west of reception centre ☎08186 244732, ⓦkarnatakaholidays.net. Predictable concrete KSTDC hotel whose vast, old-fashioned a/c and non-a/c rooms are comfortable enough but grossly overpriced, especially at weekends. It has two blocks: the more basic *Tunga*; and *Sharavati*, with better views of the falls. No wi-fi. Tunga ₹1000, Sharavati ₹2520

PWD Inspection Bungalow 400m west of the reception centre ☎08186 244333. Nicely situated on a hillock above the main road, with four spacious a/c attached rooms and five decent non-a/c rooms. No wi-fi but food is made on request (veg ₹75, non-veg ₹400). **₹500**

Gokarna

Among India's most scenically situated sacred sites, **GOKARNA** lies between a broad white-sand beach and the verdant foothills of the Western Ghats, 230km north of Mangaluru. Yet this compact little coastal town – a Shaivite centre for more than two millennia – remained largely "undiscovered" by Western tourists until the early 1990s, when it began to attract dreadlocked and didgeridoo-toting neo-hippies fleeing the commercialization of Goa, just over 60km north. Now it's firmly on the tourist map, although the town retains a charming local character, as the Hindu pilgrims pouring through still far outnumber the foreigners who flock here in winter.

A hotchpotch of wood-fronted houses and red terracotta roofs, Gokarna is clustered around a long L-shaped bazaar. Its broad main road – known as **Car Street** – runs west to the town beach, which is a sacred site in its own right. Hindu mythology identifies it as the place where Shiva was reborn from the underworld after a period of penance through the ear of a cow, or *go-karna*, thus giving the town its name.

Gokarna is also the home of one of India's most powerful *shivalingas* – the **atmalinga**, which took root here having being carried off by Ravana, the evil king of Lanka, from Shiva's home on Mount Kailash. It is said Ravana's brute force distorted the *shivalingam* to resemble the shape of a cow's ear – another theory behind the town's name.

The temples

The *atmalinga* (or *pranalinga*) is enshrined in the medieval **Shri Mahabaleshwar temple**, at the far west end of the bazaar. It is regarded as so auspicious that a mere glimpse of it will absolve a hundred sins, even the murder of a brahmin. Pilgrims shave their heads, fast and take a ritual dip in the sea before *darshan*. For this reason, the tour of Gokarna

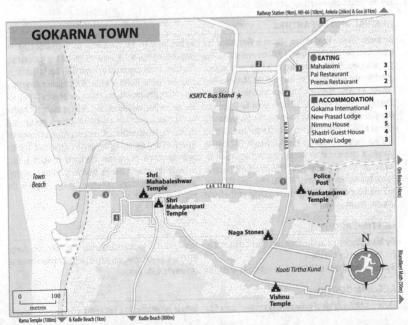

GOKARNA TOWN

Railway Station (9km), NH-66 (10km), Ankola (26km) & Goa (61km)

KSRTC Bus Stand ★

EATING	
Mahalaxmi	3
Pai Restaurant	1
Prema Restaurant	2

ACCOMMODATION	
Gokarna International	1
New Prasad Lodge	2
Nimmu House	5
Shastri Guest House	4
Vaibhav Lodge	3

MAIN ROAD

Town Beach

Shri Mahabaleshwar Temple

CAR STREET

Shri Mahaganpati Temple

Police Post

Venkatarama Temple

Naga Stones

Kooti Tirtha Kund

Vishnu Temple

Om Beach (4km)

Bhandikeri Math (50m)

N

0   100
metres

Rama Temple (100m) & Kudle Beach (1km)   Kudle Beach (800m)

22

traditionally begins at the beach, followed by a puja at the **Shri Mahaganpati temple**, a stone's throw east of the Mahabaleshwar shrine, to propitiate the elephant-headed god Ganesh. Foreign tourists are not allowed into the inner sancta of the main two temples but the parts you can visit are still extremely atmospheric. One interesting holy place you can get right into is **Bhandikeri Math**, a short way east of the bathing tank. This three-hundred-year-old temple and learning centre has shrines to the deities Bhavani Shankar, Uma Maheshwari and Maruthi.

The beaches

While Gokarna's numerous temples, shrines and tanks are the big draw for Indian pilgrims, most Western tourists head for the beautiful **beaches** to the south of the more crowded town beach. Beyond the lumpy, reddish black-coloured headland that overlooks the town, lie a series of sandy strips connected by short seaside walks and motley shacks offering varied cuisine.

To pick up the trail, take a left off Car Street beside the Shri Mahaganpati temple and follow the narrow cemented road for twenty minutes uphill and across a rocky plateau to **Kudle Beach**. This wonderful 1km-long sweep of golden-white sand sheltered by a pair of steep-sided promontories is now punctuated by dozens of restaurant-cum-accommodation ventures. This is the longest and broadest of Gokarna's beaches, with decent surf too, though the water can be dangerous.

It takes around twenty minutes more to hike over the headland from Kudle to exquisite **Om Beach**, so named because its distinctive twin crescent-shaped bays resemble the auspicious Om symbol. Apart from the luxury resort set well back from the beach, a mixture of modest concrete rooms and flimsy huts populate the palm groves, usually belonging to restaurants. Large groups of male travellers tend to descend on the beach at weekends – female sunbathers may prefer to press on further south.

Gokarna's two most remote beaches lie another thirty-minute walk over the rocky hills. **Half Moon** and **Paradise** beaches are mainly for intrepid sun-lovers happy to pack in their own supplies. If you're looking for near-total isolation – a sense of Goa perhaps thirty years ago – these are your best bet.

ARRIVAL AND DEPARTURE

GOKARNA

By train Gokarna Road railway station is 9km inland but buses, taxis and auto-rickshaws (₹300) are available to take you into town. Gokarna Road has two daily trains in each direction: the southbound services are the *Matsyagandha Express* #12619 (departs 3.08am) and the *Madgaon Passenger* #56641 (departs 3.37pm), both to Udupi and Mangaluru; the same trains north are the *Matsyagandha Express* #12620 (departs 6.40pm) to Margao and Mumbai and the *Madgaan Passenger* #56640 (departs 10.11am) to Margao. A couple of other weekly expresses also call here, such as the *Maru Sagar Express* #12978 (dep. Sat 7.15pm) to Ernakulam and *Poorna Express* #11098 (dep. Tues 11.24am) to Pune, but more regular express connections can be found in either Kumta or Ankola.

By bus The KSRTC Bus Stand, 300m north of Car St, is within easy walking distance of Gokarna's limited accommodation. The town is well connected by direct daily bus to Goa (from 3hr) and several towns in Karnataka, including Bengaluru (13–14hr), Hosapete/Hampi (10hr) and Mysuru (13hr), via Mangaluru (6hr) and Udupi (5hr). You can change at Ankola on the main highway for more services north into Goa and Hubbali for Hosapete/Hampi. For more buses to Hosapete/Hampi, all destinations further south on the coast and the best connections to Jog Falls, change at Kumta. It is best to avoid the private sleeper services to Hampi, as they are cramped and invariably involve a change of bus in the middle of the night.

GETTING AROUND

By bike Bicycles are available for rent from a stall next to *Pai Restaurant* for ₹50/day.
By auto-rickshaw and taxi Auto-rickshaws and taxis

cost ₹200–250 to Om Beach, while auto-rickshaws charge ₹100 to take you along the paved path that goes almost all the way to Kudle Beach.

ACCOMMODATION

There is a better range of **guesthouses** than of bona fide **hotels** in Gokarna. As a last resort, you can nearly always find a bed in one of the spartan **dharamshalas** dotted around town. There's an increasing number of options at the **beaches**, from basic huts to swanky resorts. Prices can double over the Christmas/New Year period.

GOKARNA TOWN

Gokarna International On the main road into town ☎08386 256622, ✉hotelgokarn@yahoo.com; map p.1159. Popular mid-scale place in a four-storey block on the edge of town, offering good value, from no-frills singles to deluxe, carpeted a/c doubles. The better ones (₹1400) have balconies overlooking the palm tops. Restaurant and bar on the premises. **₹866**

New Prasad Lodge On the lane near the bus stand ☎08386 257135; map p.1159. Very clean budget place with no frills but a convenient location. The pricier rooms have cable TV and balconies. **₹1000**

★**Nimmu House** Southwest of Car St, towards Kudle Beach ☎08386 256730, ⊛nimmuhouse.in;

map p.1159. This foreigners' favourite is in a great leafy location but prices spike in peak season. Double rooms in the attractive modern block are spacious, attractive and many have balconies with beach views, while those in the old wing are much plainer. New restaurant and segregated dorms on upper floor. Dorm **₹400**, doubles **₹800**

Shastri Guest House 100m east of the bus stand ☎08386 256220, ✉narasimha.shastri@gmail.com; map p.1159. Tucked behind the Shastri Clinic on the main road, this quiet but rather shabby place offers attached plus a handful of non-attached rooms with rock-bottom single rates (₹200), as well as four roomier cottages (₹800) up the hill. Only slightly more in high season. No phone or online bookings. **₹400**

Vaibhav Lodge Off the main road, a few minutes from the bus stand ☎08386 256714, ✉vaibhavnivas97@ gmail.com; map p.1159. Friendly, cheap and justifiably popular guesthouse pitched at foreigners, with a rooftop café-restaurant; rock-bottom rooms with shared facilities and some attached with TV. **₹500**

▲ NH-66 (10km), Railway Station (9km), Ankola (26km) & Goa (61km)

GOKARNA: BEACHES

SEE 'GOKARNA TOWN' MAP

Shri Mahabaleshwar

Town Beach

Gokarna Town

Kooti Tirtha Kund

Shri Mahaganpati

Vishnu Temple

Bhandikeri Math

Rama Temple & Spring

Kudle Beach

Om Beach

Half Moon Beach

Paradise Beach

N

■ ACCOMMODATION	
Gokarna International Beach Resort	5
Hostelavie	1
Namaste Café	7
Namaste Yoga Farm	2
Nirvana Café	8
Sea Rock Café	4
Strawberry Farm House	3
SwaSwara	6

● EATING	
Dolphin Bay	5
Little Paradise Inn	1
Munchies	2
Oasis Café	4
Sunset Café	3

0   500
metres

22

22

GOKARNA BEACHES

★ Gokarna International Beach Resort Kudle Beach ☏ 08386 257843, ⊛ gokarnabeachresort.com; map p.1161. Set back from the beach in a small garden dotted with coconut trees, this compact hotel offers simple comforts in neat laterite cottages and rooms fitted with small kitchenettes and verandas, some of them sea-facing. Rates drop as low as ₹800 off season. **₹2400**

Hostelavie Kudle Beach Rd ☏ 90082 42838, ⊛ hostelavie.com; map p.1161. One of the dozen or so places that have sprouted up on the road to Kudle Beach, with both segregated and mixed dorms and a self-service laundry. Dorm **₹550**

Namaste Café Northwest end of Om Beach ☏ 08386 257141, ⊛ namastegokarna.com; map p.1161. One of the more popular beach options. Each room has a different theme: in one, everything is round (including the bed); another resembles a rustic log cabin. There's also a pleasant, shaded restaurant. The same folk also run *Namaste Sanjeevini*, a pricier option on Kudle Beach with a/c and non-a/c (₹4000) and more budget-conscious *Namaste Samudra*. **₹1200**

Namaste Yoga Farm Above Kudle Beach ☏ 08386 257454, ⊛ spiritualland.com; map p.1161. Sea-view cottages, rooms and tree houses amid lush greenery, with an organic vegetable patch. Dressed with good linen, rugs and cheery curtains, plus well-equipped bathrooms, the clean, airy spaces guarantee secluded relaxation. Besides complimentary yoga and chi qong, Thai massages are available. **₹3000**

Nirvana Café Southeast end of Om Beach ☏ 08386 257401, ⊜ suresh.nirvana@gmail.com; map p.1161. A dozen bamboo huts with solid attached brick bathrooms (not all attached), neatly arranged behind a congenial restaurant with raised concrete loungers. **₹500/₹1000**

★ Sea Rock Café Central Kudle Beach ☏ 99167 29466; map p.1161. Very simple but good value concrete bungalows and rooms in a more modern block, all attached. The restaurant does fine special lassis. **₹500**

Strawberry Farm House North end of Kudle Beach ☏ 97423 73105; map p.1161. Ten sturdy concrete rooms painted a cheery yellow, all very clean but sparse inside. Handily placed for town but rather overpriced. **₹1500**

SwaSwara Above Om Beach ☏ 08386 257133, ⊛ swaswara.com; map p.1161. The first luxury resort in Gokarna, this CGH Earth property offers beautifully designed wood villas spread over terraces on a hillside overlooking the bay. There's a pool, yoga dome and an Ayurvedic treatment centre, all set in extensive gardens. Minimum five-night stay; all-inclusive packages per villa **₹€2400**

EATING

Gokarna town offers a good choice of **places to eat**, with a string of busy "meals" joints along Car St and the main road. The beaches now have a plethora of places offering travellers' favourites. Look out for the local sweet speciality *gadbad*.

GOKARNA TOWN

Mahalaxmi At the beach end of Car St ☏ 99450 59215; map p.1159. Service can be rather slow, but you won't feel much need to hurry, waiting on this sea-view rooftop perch. The menu includes tasty veg curries or veg with a creamy cheese sauce (all under ₹100). Daily 8am–10pm.

Pai Restaurant Main Rd ☏ 08386 256755; map p.1159. An excellent spot for fresh and tasty veg thalis (₹70), masala dosas and crisp *vada*s, plus teas and coffees any time of day. Daily 7am–9.30pm.

★ Prema Restaurant Car St, 150m west of the Mahabaleshwar temple ☏ 94810 52117; map p.1159. Welcoming and hugely popular veg canteen with a varied menu encompassing delicious dosas, superb toasted English muffin sandwiches, lots of other veg dishes and the best *gadbad* in town. Daily 8am–9pm.

GOKARNA BEACHES

Dolphin Bay Southeastern Om Beach ☏ 98452 65608; map p.1161. Typically laidback place at the back of the beach, offering Western and Indian food, plus a fine range of lassis. Fish costs ₹250–400. Daily 8am–10pm.

★ Little Paradise Inn Central Kudle Beach ☏ 95351 94383; map p.1161. Welcoming and highly relaxing hangout, with seating on the sand and an upstairs wooden chill-out deck. Huge menu of India, Chinese and Continental cuisine, mostly in the ₹200–400 range. Daily 8am–11pm.

Munchies South-central Kudle Beach ☏ 96482 37456; map p.1161. One of the newer and most relaxing spots on Kudle, with pleasant shady seating and known for its pancakes, banoffee pie and garlic cheese naan. Also offers tasty grilled seafood and curries in the ₹180–300 range. Daily 8am–11pm.

Oasis Café South-central Kudle Beach; map p.1161. You can dig your feet in the soft sand at this friendly hangout, nicely decorated with colourful lanterns and wall hangings. A range of offerings from lamb to *momos*, plus Thai dishes at only around ₹200–250. Daily 8am–11pm.

Sunset Café Southern Kudle Beach ☏ 98868 97597; map p.1161. This very popular restaurant offers a range of veg, chicken and seafood dishes such as calamari sizzler for ₹350, and guarantees prime sunset views accompanied by Arabian Sea breezes. Daily 8am–10.30pm.

Hubballi (Hubli)-Dharwad

Karnataka's second most industrialized city, **Hubli**, now officially known as **HUBBALLI**, just east of the Ghats and 418km northwest of Bengaluru, has little of interest except for its transport connections to Mumbai, Goa, the coast of Uttar Kannada (North Canara), Hampi and other points in the interior. Its twin city, the cultural hub of **DHARWAD**, 20km northwest, has a little more to offer fans of Indian classical music.

22

Gangothri

Dharwad Yellapur Rd, Shukravarpet • Regular KSRTC buses and taxis ply between Hubballi and Dharwad

The birthplace of several renowned Indian classical singers, Dharwad's biggest attraction is **Gangothri**, the childhood home of Dr Gangubai Hangal (1913–2009), a doyenne of Hindustani classical music who broke boundaries of tradition, gender and stereotype with her deep powerful voice. Her greatness lay in her simplicity, and her humble home has been converted into a museum showcasing her life, musical achievements and memorabilia.

ARRIVAL AND DEPARTURE · HUBBALLI (HUBLI)-DHARWAD

By train Hubballi's railway station is right in the town centre and is well connected.

Destinations Bengaluru (8–12 daily; 8hr 5min–11hr 45min); Hassan (*Dharwar Mysore Express* #17302 dep. 9.40pm; 6hr 20min); Hosapete (6–9 daily; 2hr 20min–3hr 5min); Mumbai (2–5 daily; 14hr 30min–18hr); Pune (3–5 daily; 10hr 55min–14hr).

By bus Hubballi's efficient KSRTC Bus Stand is 2km south of the centre, and can be reached by bus from the railway station or the chaotic City Bus Stand, about 1km west of the station. There are connections to most towns in Karnataka, most usefully to Ankola (every 30min–1hr; 3hr 30min–4hr) for Gokarna; handy if you do not happen to coincide with one of the four daily direct buses.

ACCOMMODATION

Ajanta JC Nagar Rd ☎ 0836 236 2216. This no-frills lodge near the station has a range of rooms, including very cheap singles with shared bathroom, and various doubles. ₹450
Shri Renuka Lodge Opposite the City Bus Stand ☎ 0836 225 3615. This large and well-organized lodge offers a range of reasonable rooms, some with a/c, and has

its own veg restaurant. ₹500
Swarnaa Paradise Station Rd ☎ 80712 65999, ⓦ swarnaaparadise.com. Conveniently located right outside the railway station, this smart business hotels has nicely designed all a/c rooms of varying sizes. ₹1800

EATING

Don't leave Dharwad without picking up a box of Dharwad *pedha*, a caramel-brown, milk-based sweet dusted with caster sugar, which can be bought at Babusingh's Thakur Pedha in Line Bazar or numerous outlets of Mishra Pedha.
Basappa Khanavali Opposite Civil Court, PB Rd ☎ 93426 79111. This 1930 pure-veg eatery serves excellent North Karnataka thalis for ₹80, served with *bhakri* (*jowar roti*). Gets rather busy at lunchtime. 10.30am–3.30pm & 7.30–10.30pm.

Kamat Hotel ☎ 0836 236 2845, ⓦ kamatyatri.in. The two branches of the famous south Indian food chain dish out excellent vegetarian meals and snacks. One is by the traffic island at the bus stand end of Lamington Rd, the other opposite the railway station. Both daily 7am–10pm.
Megh Darshini Subhash Rd ☎ 0836 243 5147. A popular restaurant serving excellent south Indian fare, with budget meals and generously large puris. Daily 7am–10pm.

Hosapete (Hospet)

Charmless **Hospet**, now reverted to its traditional name of **HOSAPETE** ("New City"), about ten hours from both Bengaluru and Goa, is of little interest except as the jumping-off place for the extraordinary ruined city of **Hampi** (Vijayanagar), 13km northeast. If you arrive really late, or want a more upmarket hotel, it makes sense to stay here and catch a bus or auto-rickshaw out to the ruins the following morning.

22

ARRIVAL AND DEPARTURE

By train Hosapete's railway station is 1.5km north of the centre. Note that the Hosapete-based auto-rickshaws that gather on the forecourt charge at least ₹250 to Hampi but if you walk a short way along the road, you can usually bargain a returning Hampi auto down to around ₹100. Hosapete has one direct train daily to Bengaluru, the overnight *Hampi Express* #16591 (dep. 9.15pm; 8hr 55min); change at Guntakal Junction (3hr) for numerous south-bound and northbound expresses. For connections to the coast and Goa, take the *Amaravathi Express* #18047 (dep. Mon, Wed, Thurs & Sat 6.20am; 7hr 35min) or head west to Hubballi (4 daily; 3–4hr). For connections to Badami and Vijayapura, change at Gadag (4 daily; 1hr 20min–2hr).

By bus The bus stand is in the centre, just off MG (Station) Rd, which runs south from the railway station. Bookings for long-distance routes can be made at the ticket office on the

bus stand concourse (daily 8am–noon & 3–6pm), where there's also a left-luggage facility. Regular buses run the 30min route to Hampi, some via Kamalapura, until around 7.30pm. There are KSRTC buses to destinations throughout the state, but journeys are slow so the only ones worth taking are to Gadag (every 30min; 2hr), Hubballi (every 30min; 3hr) or Guntakal (hourly; 2hr 30min–3hr), for the better rail and road connections in those towns. Many tourists opt for the apparently easy option of a private sleeper coach to Goa or Gokarna which depart between 7 and 8pm (9–10hr; around ₹1000), operated by Paulo Travels (☎ 08394 225867, ☞ paulotravels.com) from beside the hotel *Priyadarshini*. Unfortunately, these are usually overbooked, overcrowded and, if you are travelling to Gokarna, you will be offloaded for a transfer at Ankola in the wee hours.

INFORMATION

Tourist information The tourist office at the Rotary Circle (Mon–Sat: April & May 8am–1.30pm; June–March 10am–5.30pm; ☎ 08394 228537) offers limited information and sells tickets for KSTDC tours of Hampi.

Services Full exchange facilities are available at the *Malligi* hotel. Enfield motorbikes are available for rent (or sale) from Bharat Motors (☎ 08394 224704) near Vijaya Talkies cinema.

ACCOMMODATION

Hampi International Station Rd ☎ 08394 222067, ☞ hotelhampiinternational.com; map p.1164. Snazzy modern business hotel right by the station with central a/c and stylish rooms, a plush restaurant and a pleasant bar. ₹2500

Krishna Palace MG Rd ☎ 08394 294300, ☞ krishna palacehotel.com; map p.1164. Offering a bit of luxury surprising for Hosapete, this central and snazzy a/c hotel has

smartly furnished rooms and an ostentatious lobby, plus spa massages. Sadly, the restaurant food disappoints. ₹5000

Malligi 10/90 JN Rd, a 2min walk southeast of the bus stand ☎ 08394 228101, ☞ malligihotels.com; map p.1164. A 40-year-old institution that's been renovated from a tourist home to swanky hotel with several blocks of luxurious a/c rooms and suites separated by manicured lawns. There is also a large outdoor swimming pool (₹100/hr for non-residents), two smart restaurants, a gym and spa, in addition to a small bookshop and an efficient travel service. ₹1400

Priyadarshini MG Rd ☎ 08394 228838, ☞ priyadarshinihotels.com; map p.1164. Large and bland, but spotless and decent value, especially the a/c rooms (some with balconies). Two good restaurants: the veg *naivedyam* and, in the garden, the excellent non-veg *manasa*, which has a bar. ₹1200

Pushpak Lodge MG Rd ☎ 08394 421380; map p.1164. With basic but clean attached rooms, this is the best low-priced lodge in town and is conveniently, if noisily, located right by the bus stand. ₹500

EATING

Shanbhag Next to the bus station; map p.1164. The excellent Udupi restaurant at this old hotel is a perfect pit stop before heading to Hampi, particularly since it opens early for breakfast. Daily 6.30am–9.30pm.

HOSAPETE (HOSPET)

■ ACCOMMODATION	
Hampi International	1
Krishna Palace	3
Malligi	5
Priyadarshini	2
Pushpak Lodge	4

● EATING	
Shanbhag	1

Tungabhadra Dam (15km)

Hampi (Vijayanagar)

Among a surreal landscape of golden-brown boulders and leafy banana fields, the ruined "City of Victory," **Vijayanagar**, better known as **HAMPI** (the name of the main local village), spills from the south bank of the River Tungabhadra. This once dazzling Hindu capital was devastated by a six-month Muslim siege in the second half of the sixteenth century. Only stone, brick and stucco structures survived the ensuing sack – monolithic deities, crumbling houses and abandoned temples dominated by towering *gopuras* – as well as the irrigation system that channelled water to huge tanks and temples, some of which are still in use today.

22

Thus, Hampi's monuments appear a lot older than their four or five hundred years. With its wooden superstructure burnt and past buried in ruins, excavations by the Archaeological Survey of India (ASI) can only piece together the fragmented history of this sophisticated city. Grappling with years of encroachment and the constant tussle between preservation and modernization, the Hampi World Heritage Area Management Authority (HWHAMA) has controversially pressed ahead with plans to revamp **Hampi Bazaar** and the adjoining "heritage zone" (see page 1169). Yet, at least for the time being, the serene riverside setting and air of magic that still lingers over the site, sacred for centuries before a city was founded here, make it one of India's most extraordinary locations. Many find it difficult to leave and spend weeks chilling out in cafés, wandering to whitewashed hilltop temples and gazing at the spectacular sunsets.

Although spread over 26 square kilometres, the **ruins** of Vijayanagar are mostly concentrated in two distinct groups: the designated **Sacred Centre** around Hampi Bazaar and the nearby riverside area, encompassing an enclave of temples and *ghats*; and the **Royal Enclosure** – 3km south of the river, just northwest of **Kamalapura** village – which holds the remains of palaces, pavilions, elephant stables, guardhouses and temples. Between the two stretches is a long boulder-choked hill and scores of banana plantations, fed by ancient irrigation canals.

Brief history

According to the Ramayana, the region was once the mythical Kishkinda, ruled by the monkey king Bali, with his brother Sugriva and their ambassador, Hanuman. The unpredictably placed rocks – some balanced in perilous arches, others heaped in colossal, hill-sized piles – are said to have been flung down by their armies in a show of strength. It was here that Lord Rama raised his monkey army to rescue Sita from demon king Ravana's clutches.

While Hampi's mythic status was grand, its chronological evolution into the capital of a vast empire was no less extraordinary. The rise of the **Vijayanagar Empire** seems to have been a direct response, in the first half of the fourteenth century, to the expansionist aims of Muslims from the north, most notably Malik Kafur and Mohammed-bin-Tughluq. Two Hindu brothers from Andhra Pradesh, Harihara and Bukka, who had been employed as treasury officers in Kampili, 19km east of Hampi, were captured by the Tughluqs and taken to Delhi, where they supposedly converted to Islam. Assuming them to be suitably tamed, the Delhi sultan despatched them to quell civil disorder in Kampili, which they duly did, only to abandon both Islam and allegiance to Delhi shortly afterwards, preferring to establish their own independent Hindu kingdom. Within a few years they controlled vast tracts of land from coast to coast. In 1343, guided by their spiritual guru Vidyaranya Swami, they founded their new capital, Vijayanagar, on the southern banks of the River Tungabhadra, a location long considered to be sacred by Hindus.

The city's most glorious period was under the reign of **Krishna Deva Raya** (1509–29), when it enjoyed a near monopoly of the lucrative trade in Arabian horses and Indian spices passing through the coastal ports and was the most powerful Hindu capital in the Deccan. Travellers such as the Portuguese chronicler Domingo Paez, who stayed for

22

two years after 1520, were astonished by its size and wealth, telling tales of markets full of silk and precious gems, bejewelled courtesans, ornate palaces and fantastic festivities. Records reveal how it was once larger than Rome, with palaces grander than those of Lisbon.

Thanks to its natural features and massive fortifications, Vijayanagar was virtually impregnable. Yet in 1565, following his interference in the affairs of local Muslim sultanates, the regent Rama Raya was drawn into a battle with a confederacy of Muslim forces to the north and ultimately defeated. Rama Raya was captured and suffered a grisly death at the hands of the **sultan of Ahmadnagar**. Vijayanagar then fell victim to a series of destructive raids, and its days of splendour were brought to an abrupt end.

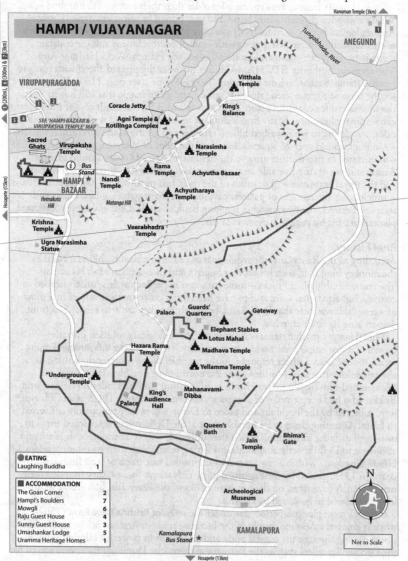

HAMPI / VIJAYANAGAR

ANEGUNDI

Hanuman Temple (3km)

Tungabhadra River

VIRUPAPURAGADDA

Vitthala Temple

King's Balance

Coracle Jetty

Agni Temple & Kotilinga Complex

SEE 'HAMPI BAZAAR & VIRUPAKSHA TEMPLE' MAP

Sacred Ghats

Virupaksha Temple

Narasimha Temple

Bus Stand

Rama Temple

Achyutha Bazaar

HAMPI BAZAAR

Nandi Temple

Achyutharaya Temple

Hemakuta Hill

Matanga Hill

Krishna Temple

Veerabhadra Temple

Ugra Narasimha Statue

Palace

Guards' Quarters

Gateway

Elephant Stables

Lotus Mahal

Hazara Rama Temple

Madhava Temple

Yellamma Temple

"Underground" Temple

Palace

King's Audience Hall

Mahanavami-Dibba

Queen's Bath

Jain Temple

Bhima's Gate

EATING

Laughing Buddha	1

ACCOMMODATION

The Goan Corner	2
Hampi's Boulders	7
Mowgli	6
Raju Guest House	4
Sunny Guest House	3
Umashankar Lodge	5
Uramma Heritage Homes	1

Archeological Museum

KAMALAPURA

Kamalapura Bus Stand

N

Not to Scale

Hosapete (13km)

Hampi Bazaar and around

Hampi's long, straight main street, **Hampi Bazaar**, runs east from the entrance to the Virupaksha temple, and is lined by the remains of Vijayanagar's ruined, columned bazaar. While the Bazaar has been cleared of all shops under a restoration initiative (see page 1169), the area north of the temple towards the river still houses a maze of restaurants, hotels and other businesses.

The Virupaksha temple

Daily 6.30am–12.30pm & 2–8.30pm • ₹2 but free during *aarti* (daily 6.30–8am & 6.30–8.30pm)

Dedicated to a form of Shiva known as Virupaksha ("the terrible-eyed one"), the **Virupaksha temple** dominates the village, drawing a steady flow of pilgrims, with its 50m-high nine-storey tower, the tallest *gopura* in Karnataka, acting like a beacon. The temple is at its liveliest during *aarti* (worship). The small three-headed Nandi outside the main entrance supposedly represents the past, present and future of Hampi. In the 1565 siege, Nandi's third head, representing the future, was defaced; Hampi never regained its glory.

The complex consists of two courts, each entered through a towered *gopura*. From the smaller *gopura* near the ticket counter you enter the inner court, surrounded by a colonnade which is usually filled with pilgrims dozing, singing religious songs or receiving blessings from the temple elephant, Lakshmi. In the middle, the principal temple is approached through a *mandapa* hallway whose carved columns feature rearing animals. Rare Vijayanagar-era paintings on the *mandapa* ceiling include aspects of Shiva, a procession with the sage Vidyaranya, the ten incarnations of Vishnu and scenes from the Mahabharata. In a side passage of the main shrine, guides show the inverted image of the *gopura*, illustrating an early example of a pin-hole camera.

The riverside

The sacred **ford** in the river is reached from the Virupaksha's north *gopura*; you can also get there by following the lane around the impressive temple **tank**. A *mandapa* overlooks the steps that originally led to the river, now some distance away. A small **motorboat** (₹50 [₹10]) runs from this part of the bank, ferrying villagers to the fields and tourists to the increasingly popular enclave of **Virupapuragadda**. The road left from the sacred ford through the village eventually loops back towards the hilltop Hanuman temple, about 5km east, and on to Anegundi – a recommended circular walk.

Matanga Hill

The place to head for sunrise is the boulder hill immediately east of Hampi Bazaar. From the end of the main street, an ancient paved pathway winds up a rise, topped by the magnificent Achyutharaya temple (see below) on the eastern ridge of **Matanga Hill**. The views improve as you progress up towards the small Veerabhadra temple at its summit, which provides an extraordinary vantage point. Muggings have been reported along this path early in the morning, so be vigilant if there are only one or two of you.

The riverside path

Walking east from the Virupaksha temple along the length of Hampi Bazaar, turn left before the huge monolithic **Nandi** statue to get to Vitthala temple. This riverside path, peppered by conch-blowing sadhus and ragged mendicants, winds past cafés and numerous shrines, including a Rama temple – home to hordes of fearless monkeys. Beyond at least four Vishnu shrines, a paved and colonnaded **bazaar** leads due south to the **Achyutharaya temple** (aka Tiruvengalanatha), whose beautiful stone carvings – among them some of Hampi's famed erotica – are being restored by the ASI. Back on the main path again, make a short detour across the rocks leading

22

to the river to see the little-visited waterside **Agni temple**; next to it, the Kotilinga complex consists of 1008 tiny lingas, carved on a flat rock. As you approach the Vitthala temple, to the south is an archway known as the **King's Balance**, where the rajas were weighed against gold, silver and jewels to be distributed to Brahmins and the needy on festive occasions.

Vitthala temple

22

Daily 6am–6pm • ₹600 (₹40); ticket also valid for the Lotus Mahal (see page 1171) on the same day

Although the area of the **Vitthala temple** does not show the same evidence of early cult worship as Virupaksha, the ruined bridge to the west probably dates from before Vijayanagar times. The bathing *ghat* may be from the Chalukya or Ganga period, but as the temple has fallen into disuse it seems that the river crossing (*tirtha*) here lacks the sacred significance of the Virupaksha site. Now part of the UNESCO World Heritage Site, the Vitthala temple was built for Vishnu, who according to legend was too embarrassed by its ostentation to live here.

The **Saptasvara Mandapa** (Open Dancing Hall) features slender monolithic granite musical **pillars** which were constructed so as to sound the notes of the scale when struck. Today, due to vandalism and erosion from being repeatedly beaten, heavy security makes sure that no one is allowed to touch them. Guides, however, will happily demonstrate the musical resonance of other pillars on an adjacent structure. Outer columns sport characteristic Vijayanagar rearing horses, while friezes of lions, elephants and horses on the moulded basement display sculptural trickery – you can transform one beast into another simply by masking one portion of the image.

In front of the temple, to the east, a stone representation of a wooden processional **rath**, or chariot, houses an image of Garuda, Vishnu's bird vehicle. Now cemented, at one time the chariot's wheels revolved.

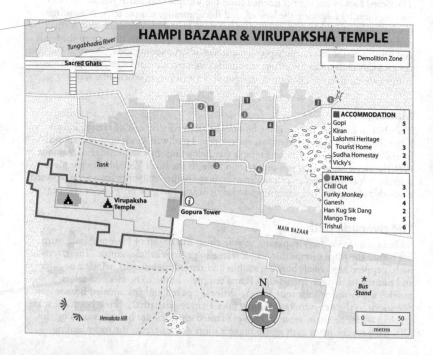

HAMPI BAZAAR & VIRUPAKSHA TEMPLE

Tungabhadra River

Sacred Ghats

Demolition Zone

Tank

Virupaksha Temple

Gopura Tower

MAIN BAZAAR

■ ACCOMMODATION
Gopi	5
Kiran	1
Lakshmi Heritage Tourist Home	3
Sudha Homestay	2
Vicky's	4

● EATING
Chill Out	3
Funky Monkey	1
Ganesh	4
Han Kug Sik Dang	2
Mango Tree	5
Trishul	6

N

Bus Stand

Hemakuta Hill

0   50
metres

SACRILEGE IN A SACRED SETTING?

Until 2011, the local people of Hampi Bazaar had lived a peaceful and largely idyllic existence amid the Vijayanagar ruins. Indeed, in recent decades many had been making a decent living from tourists who came to hang out in the cafés and guesthouses while marvelling at the sights. All that changed abruptly when a long-pending **government scheme** to fence off the whole 26-square-kilometre area in order to protect its UNESCO World Heritage status finally got out of legal gridlock and began to be implemented, and residents were forced to move out of the bazaar to a rehabilitation area 4km away. Amid protests, the **bulldozers** cleared a 30–40m swathe of modern buildings flanking the bazaar and the main lane from the temple to the river. Ironically, even the tourist office was flattened.

While the heritage conservation project may take years to complete, locals who run guesthouses near the river and on the opposite bank feel they are living on borrowed time, fearing the next round of demolition. With authorities having to comply to strict conservation norms and locals facing displacement with paltry **compensation packages**, Hampi is in a Catch-22 situation. For travellers who have been enchanted by Hampi over the years it is heartbreaking that the magic of staying amid the ruins seems certain to disappear.

Anegundi and beyond

With more time, and a sense of adventure, you can head across the River Tungabhadra to **ANEGUNDI** (also spelt **Anegondi**), a fortress town predating Vijayanagar, and its fourteenth-century headquarters. The most pleasant way to get here is to take a coracle from the ford 1.5km east of the Vitthala temple; these circular baskets, which are today reinforced with plastic sheets, also carry bicycles, which are a good way to visit Hampi's many monuments. A contentious bridge was constructed at this point but collapsed some years ago. A new one is being built outside the core heritage zone, at Bukkasagar, further downstream.

Forgotten temples and fortifications litter Anegundi village and its quiet surroundings. The ruined **Huchchappa-matha** temple, near the river gateway, is worth a look for its lathe-turned black stone pillars and fine panels of dancers. **Aramane**, a ruined palace in the centre, stands opposite the home of the descendants of the royal family; also in the centre, the **Ranganatha temple** is still active. A huge wooden temple chariot stands in the village square. Limited **accommodation** is available here in village houses and you can get basic snacks at the local stalls.

Pampa Sarovar

To complete a five-kilometre loop back to Hampi from Anegundi (the simplest route if you have wheels), head left (west) through the old gateway just north of the village, which winds through sugar cane fields and eventually comes out near Virupapuragadda. En route you can visit the Vali Kila fort, a Durga temple and the sacred **Pampa Sarovar**, signposted down a dirt lane to the left. The small temple above this square bathing tank is dedicated to the goddess Lakshmi and holds a cave containing a footprint of Vishnu. If you're staying around Anegundi, this quiet spot is best visited early in the evening during *aarti*.

Hanuman temple

A worthwhile detour off the road north of the river leading west from Anegundi is the hike up to the tiny whitewashed **Hanuman temple**, perched on the rocky hilltop of Anjanadri. Believed to be the birthplace of Hanuman (also called Anjaneya, the son of Anjana), the spot holds a strange attraction for monkeys. The steep climb takes around thirty minutes and affords superb views over Hampi, especially at sunrise and sunset. Further west of Anjanadri, you reach an impressive old **stone bridge** dating from Vijayanagar times. The bridge no longer spans the river but just beyond it to the west, back at Virupapuragadda, the motorboat (₹50 [₹10]) returns you to the Virupaksha temple.

Hemakuta Hill and around

Directly above Hampi Bazaar, **Hemakuta Hill** is dotted with pre-Vijayanagar temples that date from the ninth to eleventh centuries. Aside from the architecture, the main reason to clamber up is to admire the **views** of the ruins and surrounding countryside. With views across the boulder-covered terrain and banana plantations, the sheer western edge of the hill is Hampi's top sunset spot, attracting crowds of tourists most evenings, along with entrepreneurial chaiwalas and little boys posing for photos in Hanuman costumes.

A couple of interesting monuments lie on the road leading south towards the southern group of ruins. The first of these, a walled **Krishna temple complex** to the west of the road, dates from 1513. Although dilapidated in parts, it features some fine carving and shrines.

Hampi's most-photographed monument stands just south of the Krishna temple in its own enclosure. Depicting Vishnu in his incarnation as the Man-Lion, the monolithic **Ugra Narasimha** statue, with its bulging eyes and crossed legs strapped into yogic pose, is one of Vijayanagar's greatest treasures.

The southern and royal monuments

The most impressive remains of Vijayanagar, the city's **royal monuments**, lie some 3km south of Hampi Bazaar, spread over a large expanse of open ground. Before tackling the ruins proper, it's a good idea to get your bearings with a visit to the small **Archeological Museum** (daily except Fri 10am–5pm; free) at Kamalapura, which can be reached by bus from Hosapete or Hampi. Among the sculptures, weapons, palm-leaf manuscripts and paintings from Vijayanagar and Anegundi, the highlight is a superb scale model of the city, giving an excellent bird's-eye view of the entire site.

Bhima's Gate

The route to the monuments is well signposted. After 200m or so you reach the partly ruined massive **inner city wall**, made from granite slabs, which runs 32km around the city, in places as high as 10m. Just beyond the wall, the **citadel area** was once enclosed by another wall and gates, of which only traces remain. To the east, the small *ganigitti* ("oil-woman's") fourteenth-century **Jain temple** features a simple stepped pyramidal tower of undecorated horizontal slabs. Beyond it is **Bhima's Gate**, once one of the principal entrances to the city, named after the Titan-like Pandava prince and hero of the Mahabharata. Like many of the gates, it is "bent" with two 90° turns, a form of defence against any frontal assault. Bas-reliefs depict such episodes as Bhima avenging the honour of his wife, Draupadi, by killing the general Dushasana. Draupadi vowed she would not dress her hair until Dushasana was dead; one panel shows her tying up her locks, the vow fulfilled.

Queen's Bath

To the west of the Jain temple, the plain facade of the 15m-square **Queen's Bath** belies its glorious interior, open to the sky and surrounded by corridors with 24 different domes. Eight projecting balconies overlook the now dry tank; traces of Islamic-influenced stucco decoration survive. Women from the royal household would bathe here and umbrellas were placed in shafts in the tank floor to protect them from the sun. The water supply channel can be seen outside.

Mahanavami-Dibba

Northwest of the Queen's Bath is **Mahanavami-Dibba** or "House of Victory", built to commemorate a successful campaign in what is now Odisha. A 12m pyramidal structure with a square base, it is said to have been where the king gave and received honours and gifts. From here he watched the magnificent parades, music and dance performances, martial arts displays, elephant fights and animal sacrifices that made celebration of the ten-day Dasara festival famed throughout the land. Carved reliefs decorate the sides of the platform.

King's Audience Hall
To the west of the Mahanavami-Dibba, another platform – the largest at Vijayanagar – is thought to be the basement of the **King's Audience Hall**. Stone bases of a hundred pillars remain, in an arrangement that has caused speculation as to how the building could have been used; there are no passageways or open areas.

Lotus Mahal
Daily 6am–6pm • ₹600 (₹40); ticket also valid for the Vitthala temple on the same day

The two-storey **Lotus Mahal**, in the north of the compound and part of the **zenana enclosure**, or women's quarters, was designed for the pleasure of Krishna Deva Raya's queen: a place where she could relax, particularly in summer. Displaying a strong Indo-Islamic influence, the pavilion is open on the ground floor, whereas the inaccessible upper level contains windows and balcony seats. A moat surrounding the building is thought to have provided water-cooled air via tubes.

Elephant Stables
Just northeast of the Lotus Mahal, the **Elephant Stables**, a series of high-ceilinged, domed chambers entered through arches, are the most substantial surviving secular buildings at Vijayanagar – a reflection of the high status accorded to elephants, both ceremonial and in battle.

Hazara Rama temple
To the west of the compound, on Hemakuta Hill, is the small **Hazara Rama** ("One thousand Ramas") temple. Thought to have been a private palace shrine, the rectangular enclosure features a series of medallion figures and bands of detailed friezes showing scenes from the Ramayana.

ARRIVAL AND INFORMATION   HAMPI (VIJAYNAGAR)

By bus Buses from Hosapete terminate close to where the road joins the main street in Hampi Bazaar, halfway along its dusty length.

Tourist information Numerous private agencies can also help with most travel-related enquiries and bookings.

Services Stalls such as Pampa (☏94805 10464), diagonally opposite *Vicky's* guesthouse, has motorbikes and scooters for rent (around ₹400/day). Most guesthouses rent bicycles (₹150/day) but the bumpy terrain does make cycling hard work. There are no ATMs or banks but agents can offer exchange; rates are rather poor, so it's better to stock up on cash in Hosapete.

ACCOMMODATION

Hampi Bazaar remains the best place to stay for access to the sites, choice of restaurants and other facilities. There are no fancy hotels but a number of guesthouses of varying size and calibre. Some travellers, especially Israelis, prefer to stay across the river in **Virupapuragadda**, which is now well developed and has caught up in price. Still, prices are pretty low most of the year apart from the Christmas to mid-January peak, when they at least double.

HAMPI BAZAAR

Gopi Centre of the village ☏08394 241695, ⊛gopi-guesthouse.com; map p.1168. One of the more established places with small, simple rooms in the old building and smart but more expensive a/c options (₹1500) in another block round the corner. ₹800

Kiran Beside the river ☏94481 43906, ⊜gowdakiran96@yahoo.co.in; map p.1168. The basic rooms here are compact but clean enough and among the cheapest left in the area. The rooftop restaurant has fine views of the river and the temple. ₹600

★**Lakshmi Heritage Tourist Home** Down the lane towards the river ☏08394 241456; map p.1168. There's nothing heritage about this modern guesthouse, whose smart a/c rooms have big mirrors around the headboards.

22

Those downstairs are better. A tad noisy, but has hot running water all the time. Good discounts at slack times. ₹800

★ **Sudha Homestay** Northeast end of the village ☎94499 81492, ✉hampiabdul@gmail.com; map p.1168. One of the nicest, friendliest places to stay. The rooms vary in size but are generally larger and decorated more nicely on the slightly pricier upper storey. ₹600

Vicky's Just east of the village centre ☎94802 43226, ✉vikkyhampi@yahoo.co.in; map p.1168. Small, clean attached rooms in one of the village's oldest lodges. The lodge's *Top Secret* restaurant has relocated to diagonally opposite. ₹800

ACROSS THE RIVER

The Goan Corner 500m inland and east of boat crossing, Virupapuragadda ☎08762 626999, ⊛thegoancorner. wordpress.com; map p.1166. Large complex between lush paddy fields and attractive boulders with 36 rooms in thatched huts plus a 24-bed "million star" rooftop dorm. The lively restaurant has a good view of the boulders. Dorm ₹300; ₹600/₹800

Hampi's Boulders Narayanpet, Bandi Harlapur ☎94480 34202, ⊛hampisboulders.com; map p.1166. Overlooking a bend in the River Tungabhadra, this small, quirky resort hotel is the best upscale option, a 30min drive from Hampi Bazaar. There are four grades of cottages, from non-a/c to executive suites (₹15,000), moulded around giant boulder outcrops, with palms and mango trees for shade. Meals are so-so south Indian buffets but they have a natural rock-cut swimming pool. ₹9500

★ **Mowgli** Far west end of main road, Virupapuragadda ☎08533 287033, ⊛mowglihampi.com; map p.1166.

The smartest option right across the river, offering thirty rooms and cottages, including two with a/c, with comfy sitouts and private balconies, some with garden and river views, as well as a welcoming restaurant, set against a gorgeous paddy and river backdrop. ₹1200

Raju Guest House Main road, Virupapuragadda ☎94802 93002, ✉mailvenkatasim@gmail.com; map p.1166. Attached rooms on two storeys ranged around a small courtyard, with the *Evergreen* roof restaurant above it. ₹700

★ **Sunny Guest House** Near the village crossroads, Virupapuragadda ☎94485 66368, ⊛sunnyguesthouse. com; map p.1166. Nicely landscaped gardens with brightly painted bungalows and two sets of compact rooms, some with piped hot water. Their *Sheesh Besh* restaurant is a popular hangout. ₹800

Umashankar Lodge Main road, Virupapuragadda ☎94495 32394, ✉rameshhampi@gmail.com; map p.1166. Cosy, popular spot with small but clean attached rooms (the upstairs ones rather overpriced) set round a leafy courtyard. Has a shaded garden restaurant. ₹800

Uramma Heritage Homes Anegundi ☎08533 267792, ⊛urammaheritagehomes.com; map p.1166. Quaint rustic homestays in renovated heritage homes. Choose from the seven *Uramma Cottages*, set within a farm, each with thatched roof and traditional food on offer, or individual rural villas such as beautiful two-room *Uramma House*. Nearby *Peshegar House* has five doubles with shared baths and common dining in the garden courtyard. *Peshegar House* ₹1200, *Uramma Cottage* ₹4500

EATING

Hampi has a plethora of traveller-oriented **restaurants**, either in the bazaar, although guesthouse rooftop restaurants above the first floor have been banned, or among the growing row of joints in Virupapuragadda. As a holy site, the main village is strictly alcohol-free and almost entirely vegetarian. There are no such restrictions on the other side of the river.

Chill Out Centre of Hampi Bazaar ☎94820 48655; map p.1168. One of the cooler hangouts, with cushioned seating and bright decoration. Veg sizzlers go for ₹180. Daily 8am–10.30pm.

Funky Monkey Pushpa Homestay, Hampi Bazaar ☎08394 241775; map p.1168. First floor restaurant with a relaxed vibe, great river views, decent Continental food (₹200–300) and beverages like herbal teas and passion fruit lemonade. Daily 8am–10.30pm.

Ganesh East West end of Hampi Bazaar; map p.1168. This upstairs family restaurant is one of the best places for authentic Indian food (₹120–200); there are even some genuinely spicy dishes on request. Daily 7am–10pm.

★ **Han Kug Sik Dang** Towards the river, Hampi Bazaar ☎94487 95096; map p.1168. Courtyard restaurant specialising in Korean dishes such as tasty kimchi. Try the excellent Korean thali, a snip at ₹200. Daily 8am–10.30pm.

Laughing Buddha Main road, Virupapuragadda ☎94827 67374; map p.1166. Good for set breakfasts, pizza, pasta and Tibetan dishes for ₹180–300, with a relaxed atmosphere and film screenings every evening. Daily 8am–10pm.

★ **Mango Tree** Centre of Hampi Bazaar ☎94487 65213; map p.1168. Relocated from its riverside spot, this famous place is renowned for its veg food, especially banana pancakes and pasta dishes (around ₹100). Daily 7.30am–9.30pm.

Trishul Southeast side of Hampi Bazaar ☎94484 81332; map p.1168. Featuring chicken, tuna, lasagne, pizza and apple crumble, plus Mexican and Israeli cuisine, this is one of Hampi's widest menus, promising the rare treat of non-veg dishes. Daily 7am–11pm.

Badami, Aihole and Pattadakal: Monuments of the Chalukyas

Now quiet villages, **Badami**, **Aihole** and **Pattadakal**, the last a UNESCO World Heritage Site, were once the capital cities of the **Chalukyas**, who ruled much of the Deccan between the fourth and eighth centuries. The astonishing profusion of **temples** in the area beggars belief. Badami's and Aihole's cave temples, stylistically related to those at Ellora, are some of the most important of their type. Among the many freestanding temples are some of the earliest in India, and at Pattadakal, uniquely, it is possible to see both northern (*nagara*) and southern (Dravida) architectural styles side by side, besides the *vesara*, a fusion of the two.

Badami

Surrounded by a yawning expanse of flat farmland, **BADAMI**, capital of the Chalukyas from 543 to 757 AD, extends east into a gorge between two red sandstone hills, topped by an ancient fortified complex. The southern hill is riddled with cave temples, while the northern one is studded with early structural temples and fort remains. Beyond the village, to the east, is an artificial lake, **Agastya Teertha**, said to date from the fifth century. Badami's selection of hotels and restaurants makes it an ideal base from which to explore the Chalukyan remains at Aihole and Pattadakal, as they do not possess such facilities. Be aware that the whole Badami area is home to numerous troupes of monkeys, especially around the monuments, and they will crawl all over you if you carry food.

Southern Fort cave temples

Daily sunrise–sunset • ₹100 (₹5)

Badami's earliest monuments are a group of sixth-century **caves** cut into the hill's red sandstone, each connected by steep steps leading up the hillside.

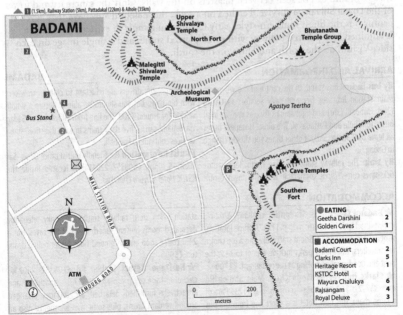

BADAMI

1 (1.5km), Railway Station (5km), Pattadakal (22km) & Aihole (35km)

Upper Shivalaya Temple

North Fort

Bhutanatha Temple Group

Malegitti Shivalaya Temple

Archeological Museum

Agastya Teertha

Bus Stand

N

Cave Temples

Southern Fort

ATM

RAMBURG ROAD

MAIN STATION ROAD

0   200
metres

● EATING	
Geetha Darshini	2
Golden Caves	1

■ ACCOMMODATION	
Badami Court	2
Clarks Inn	5
Heritage Resort	1
KSTDC Hotel Mayura Chalukya	6
Rajsangam	4
Royal Deluxe	3

22

About 15m up the rock face and reachable after forty steps is **Cave 1**, dedicated to Shiva. The entrance is through a triple opening into a long porch raised on a plinth guarded by images of Shiva's dwarf attendants, the *ganas*. On the right is a striking 1.5m-high image of an eighteen-armed Nataraja illustrating 81 dance postures. Guides dramatically point out certain arm positions to highlight various *mudras*.

A little higher, **Cave 2** is a Vishnu shrine that holds some impressive sculpture and painting. Climbing again, steps and slopes lead upwards past a natural cave containing a smashed image of the Buddhist *bodhisattva*, Padmapani (he who holds the lotus), before steps on the right lead up to the fort.

Cave 3 (578 AD), another Vishnu shrine, stands beneath a 30m-high perpendicular bluff, and holds an image of Vishnu seated on a coiled snake. The oldest and largest of the group, with a facade measuring 21m from north to south, it is also considered to be the finest for the quality of its sculptural decoration. Treatment of the pillars is extremely elaborate, featuring male and female bracket figures, lotus motifs and medallions portraying amorous couples.

To the east of the others, **Cave 4** is a Jain temple that overlooks Agastya Teertha and the town. It's a simpler shrine, dating from the sixth century. Lining the walls are figures of the 24 *tirthankaras*, both seated and standing and mostly without their identifying emblems. Here, the rock is striped.

After seeing the caves it is possible to climb up to the fort and walk east where, hidden in the rocks, a carved panel shows Vishnu reclining on the serpent Adisesha, attended by a profusion of gods and sages. Continuing, you can skirt the gorge and descend on the east to the Bhutanatha temples at the lakeside.

North Fort

North of Agastya Teertha, a number of structural temples can be reached by steps. The small **Archeological Museum** (daily except Fri 10am–5pm; ₹2) contains sculpture from the region. Although now dilapidated, the **Upper Shivalaya temple** is one of the earliest Chalukyan buildings. Scenes from the life of Krishna decorate the base and various images of him can be seen between pilasters on the walls. Only the sanctuary and tower of the **Lower Shivalaya** survive. Perched on a rock, the **Malegitti Shivalaya** (late seventh century) is the finest southern-style, early Chalukyan temple in existence. Its shrine is adjoined by a pillared hallway with small pierced stones and a single image on each side: Vishnu on the north and Shiva on the south.

ARRIVAL AND INFORMATION

By bus Badami bus stand, in the centre of the village on Main Station Rd, sees frequent daily services to Gadag (2hr), Hubballi (3hr) and Vijayapura (4hr), as well as local buses to Aihole and Pattadakal. The direct Hosapete buses all leave by 8.30am (5hr); at other times you should change in Gadag.

By train The railway station is 5km north; large auto-rickshaws-cum-*tempos* connect it with the town centre for ₹10/person; drivers are reluctant to cram in travellers with big bags, but you should be able to secure a whole vehicle for around ₹100. The line from Vijayapura to Gadag via Badami carries five daily trains in each direction; some services continue to Hubballi.

Tourist information The friendly tourist office (Mon–Sat 10am–5.30pm; ☎08357 220414) is located inside the KSTDC Hotel Mayura Chalukya.

ACCOMMODATION

★ **Badami Court** Main Station Rd ☎08357 220207, ⓦhotelbadamicourt.com; map p.1173. A prime location, superior a/c rooms and efficient staff make this a top choice for travellers. Additional perks include a pool to beat the heat and good-quality cooking at the restaurant. ₹2700

★ **Clarks Inn** Veerpulakeshi Circle, Main Station Rd ☎08357 220150, ⓦclarksinn.in; map p.1173. Part of a large chain, this new hotel is a short hop from the bus station (2km from railway station). Swanky, elegantly decorated rooms present superb views of the caves. Has a 24hr coffee shop on the ground floor. Super online deals, too. ₹5000

★ **Heritage Resort** Station Rd ☎08357 220250, ⓦtheheritage.co.in; map p.1173. Spacious and attractively furnished detached a/c cottages arranged around verdant lawns, plus some non-a/c rooms. Also an excellent multicuisine restaurant. ₹2400

KSTDC Hotel Mayura Chalukya Ramdurg Rd ☎ 08357 220046, ⓦ karnatakaholidays.net; map p.1173. This renovated government hotel has 26 sizeable rooms, the majority of which are a/c, plus pleasant gardens and a bar-restaurant. ₹1000

Rajsangam Opposite the bus stand ☎ 08357 221991, ⓦ hotelrajsangam.in; map p.1173. Spacious singles,

deluxe doubles, suites with balconies and two good restaurants: the *Banashree* serves pure-veg food and the *Shubashree* is non-veg and has a bar. ₹1500

Royal Deluxe 50m north of the bus stand ☎ 08357 220114; map p.1173. Good-value newish lodge, built of brightly painted concrete and marble, with simply furnished but clean attached rooms, all with flat-screen TVs, and a veg restaurant. ₹1000

EATING

Geetha Darshini 100m south of the bus stand ☎ 90363 56378; map p.1173. This is a small but top-notch south Indian joint whose *idlis*, *vadas* and dosas are out of this world and all under ₹100. Daily 6am–9pm.

Golden Caves Just opposite the bus stand ☎ 94487

29812; map p.1173. Good, inexpensive non-veg Indian and Chinese food, served indoors or in the airy courtyard, though service is slow. Try the tandoori chicken (full: ₹500), thali (₹90) or good-value fish. Daily 8am–11.30pm.

Aihole

No fewer than 125 temples, dating from the Chalukyan and the later Rashtrakuta periods (sixth to twelfth centuries), are found in the tiny village of **AIHOLE** (Aivalli), near the banks of the River Malaprabha. Lying in clusters within the village, in surrounding fields and on rocky outcrops, many of the temples are remarkably well preserved. Reflecting both its geographical position and spirit of architectural experimentation, Aihole boasts northern (*nagara*) and southern (Dravida) temples, as well as variants that failed to survive subsequent stylistic developments.

Two of the temples are **rock-cut caves** dating from the sixth century. The Hindu **Ravalaphadi cave**, northeast of the centre, a Shiva shrine with a triple entrance, contains fine sculptures of Mahishasuramardini, a ten-armed Nateshan (the precursor of Nataraja) dancing with Parvati, Ganesh and the Sapta Matrikas ("seven mothers"). A two-storey cave, plain save for decoration at the entrances and a panel image of Buddha in its upper veranda, can be found partway up the hill to the southeast, overlooking the village. At the top of that hill, the Jain **Meguti** temple, which may never have been completed, bears an inscription on an outer wall dating it to 634 AD. You can climb up to the first floor for fine views of Aihole and the surrounding country.

Durga temple

In the Archaeological Survey compound near the centre of the village • Daily 6am–6pm • ₹100 (₹5)

The late seventh- to early eighth-century **Durga temple**, one of the most unusual, elaborate and large in Aihole, stands close to others on open ground. The horseshoe-shaped shrine derives its name not from the goddess Durga but from the Kannada *durgadagudi*, meaning "temple near the fort". A series of pillars – many featuring amorous couples – form an open ambulatory path around the whole building. Other sculptural highlights include the decoration on the entrance to the *mandapa* hallway and niche images on the outer walls.

Archeological Museum

Just outside the entrance to the Durga temple • Daily except Fri 10am–5pm • Free

The small **Archeological Museum** displays a modest collection of early Chalukyan sculpture and sells the booklet *Glorious Aihole*, which includes a site map and accounts of the monuments.

Ladh Khan temple

A short way south of the Durga temple, beyond several other shrines

The **Ladh Khan** temple, perhaps the best known of all at Aihole, was one of the early temple prototypes. Originally a royal assembly and marriage hall dating back to the fifth century, it was named after the Muslim soldier who later made it his home. Inside are a Nandi bull and a small sanctuary containing a *shivalingam* next to the back wall. Both may have been later additions, with the original inner sanctum located at the centre.

ARRIVAL AND DEPARTURE	AIHOLE

Six daily **buses** run to Aihole from Badami (1hr 30min) via Pattadakal (45min) from 5.30am to 9pm; the last bus returns around 6pm.

22

Pattadakal

On a bend in the River Malaprabha 22km northeast of Badami, the village of **PATTADAKAL** served as the ceremonial site of Chalukyan coronations between the seventh and eighth centuries; in fact, it may have been used solely for such ceremonies (*pattada kallu* means "coronation stone" in Kannada). Like Badami and Aihole, the area boasts fine Chalukyan architecture, with particularly large mature examples; as at Aihole, both northern and southern styles can be seen. Pattadakal is connected by regular state buses and hourly private buses to Badami (45min) and Aihole (45min).

Temple compound

Daily 6am–6pm • ₹250 (₹10)

Pattadakal's main group of monuments stand together in a well-maintained **temple compound**, next to the village, and have been designated a UNESCO World Heritage Site. The site is used for a major annual **dance festival** at the end of January or early February.

Earliest among the temples, the **Sangameshwara**, also known as **Shri Vijayeshwara** (a reference to its builder, Vijayaditya Satyashraya; 696–733), shows typical southern features. To the south, both the **Mallikarjuna** and the enormous **Virupaksha**, side by side, are in the southern style, built by two sisters who were successively the queens of Vikramaditya II (733–46). Along with the Kanchipuram temple in Tamil Nadu, the Virupaksha was probably one of the largest and most elaborate in India at the time. Interior pillars are carved with scenes from the Ramayana and Mahabharata, while in the Mallikarjuna the stories are from the life of Krishna.

The largest northern-style temple, the **Papanatha**, further south, was probably built after the Virupaksha in the eighth century. Outside walls feature reliefs from the Ramayana (some of which bear the sculptors' autographs), including Hanuman's monkey army on the south wall.

Vijayapura (Bijapur) and the north

The dry and dusty far northern region of Karnataka is as distinct culturally as it is in landscape. Predominantly Muslim, at least in the larger settlements, it boasts some wonderful Islamic architecture and shrines in the venerable city of Vijayapura (Bijapur), bustling **Kalaburagi (Gulbarga)** and rather forlorn **Bidar**.

Vijayapura (Bijapur)

Boasting some of the Deccan's finest Muslim monuments, **Bijapur** – now officially **VIJAYAPURA** – is often billed as "the Agra of the South". The comparison is partly justified: for more than three hundred years, this was the capital of a succession of powerful rulers, whose domed mausoleums, mosques, colossal civic buildings and fortifications recall a lost golden age of unrivalled prosperity and artistic refinement. Yet there the similarities between the two cities end. A provincial market town of around 300,000 inhabitants, modern Vijayapura is a world away from the urban frenzy of Agra. With the exception of the mighty **Gol Gumbaz**, which attracts busloads of day-trippers, its historic sites see only a slow trickle of tourists, while the ramshackle town centre is surprisingly laidback, dotted with peaceful green spaces and colonnaded mosque courtyards. In the first week of February the town hosts an annual **music festival**, which attracts several renowned musicians from both the Carnatic (south Indian) and the Hindustani (north Indian) classical music traditions.

Unlike most medieval Muslim strongholds, Bijapur lacked natural rock defences and had to be strengthened by the Adil Shahis with huge **fortified walls**. Extending some 10km around the town, these ramparts, studded with cannon emplacements (*burjs*) and watchtowers, are breached in five points by *darwazas*, or strong gateways, and several smaller postern gates (*didis*). In the middle of the town, a further hoop of crenellated battlements encircled Bijapur's **citadel**, site of the sultans' apartments and durbar hall, of which only fragments remain. The Adil Shahis' **tombs** are scattered around the outskirts, while most of the important **mosques** lie southeast of the citadel.

Brief history

Still generally known as Bijapur, a name that stuck until the city's rechristening in 2014, Vijayapura (the Chalukyas' "City of Victory") was established around the tenth century. Taken by the Vijayanagar Empire, it passed into Muslim hands for the first time in the thirteenth century with the arrival of the sultans of Delhi. The Bahmanis administered the area for a time, but it was only after the local rulers, the **Adil Shahis**, won independence from Bidar by expelling the Bahmani garrison and declaring this their capital that Bijapur's rise to prominence began.

Burying their differences for a brief period in the late sixteenth century, the five Muslim dynasties that issued from the breakdown of Bahmani rule – based at Golconda, Ahmadnagar, Bidar and Gulbarga – formed a military alliance to defeat Vijayanagar. The spoils of this campaign, which saw the total destruction of Vijayanagar (Hampi), funded a two-hundred-year building boom in Bijapur during which the city's most impressive monuments were built. However, old enmities between rival Muslim sultanates on the Deccan soon resurfaced, and the Adil Shahis' royal coffers were gradually squandered on fruitless and protracted wars. By the time the British arrived on the scene in the eighteenth century, the Adil Shahis were a spent force, locked into a decline from which they and their capital never recovered.

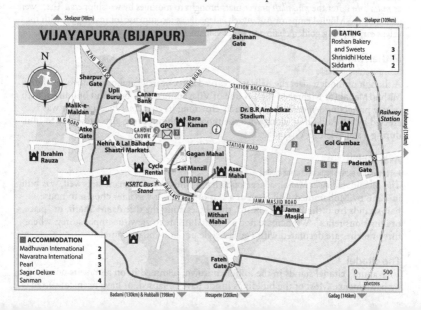

Gol Gumbaz

Daily 6am–6pm • ₹200 (₹15)

The vast **Gol Gumbaz** mausoleum, Vijayapura's most famous building, soars above the town's east walls, visible for kilometres in every direction. Inspired by a seven-storey structure in Arabia and built for muezzins to offer *azaan* (call to prayer) from its summit, the original name Bol Gumbaz was corrupted over the years to Gol Gumbaz.

The cubic tomb, enclosing a 170-square-metre hall, is crowned with a single hemispherical **dome**, only 5m smaller than St Peter's in Rome, once the largest in the world. Spiral staircases wind up the four seven-storey octagonal towers that buttress the building to the famous **Whispering Gallery**, a 3m wide passage encircling the interior base of the dome from where, looking carefully down, you can get a real feel of the sheer size of the building. Arrive here just after opening time to avoid the bus tours and to experience the extraordinary acoustics. The **view** from the mausoleum's ramparts, which overlook the town and its monuments to the dark-soiled Deccan countryside beyond, is superb.

Set on a plinth in the centre of the hall below are the gravestones of the ruler who built the Gol Gumbaz, **Mohammed Adil Shah**, along with those of his wife, daughter, grandson and favourite courtesan, Rambha. At one corner of the grounds stands the simple gleaming white shrine to a Sufi saint of the Adil Shahi period, **Hashim Pir**, which attracts *qawwals* (singers of devotional *qawwali* music) each February to the annual three-day *urs*.

Jama Masjid

A little under 1km southwest of the Gol Gumbaz • Modest clothing is advised – no shorts or skirts

The **Jama Masjid** was commissioned by Ali Adil Shah, the ruler credited with constructing the city walls and complex water supply system, as a monument to his victory over the Vijayanagar Empire at the battle of Talikota in 1565. Still an active place of worship, it is widely regarded as one of the finest mosques in India.

Simplicity and restraint are the essence of the colonnaded prayer hall below, divided by gently curving arches and rows of thick plaster-covered pillars. Aside from the odd geometric design and trace of yellow, blue and green tile-work, the only ornamentation is found in the mihrab, or west- (Mecca-) facing prayer niche, which is smothered in gold leaf and elaborate calligraphy. The marble floor of the hall features a grid of 2500 rectangles, known as *musallahs* (after the *musallah* prayer mats brought to mosques by worshippers). These were added by the Mughal emperor Aurangzeb, allegedly as recompense for making off with the velvet carpets, long golden chain and other valuables that originally filled the prayer hall.

Mithari Mahal

800m west of the Jama Masjid

Although of modest size, the delicately carved three-storey gatehouse known as the **Mithari Mahal** (or Mehtar Mahal) is one of Vijayapura's most beautiful buildings, with ornate projecting windows and minarets crowning its corners. Once again, it was erected by Ali Adil Shah, along with the mosque behind, using gifts presented to him during a state visit to Vijayanagar.

Asar Mahal

Just beyond the eastern battlement of the citadel

The dilapidated **Asar Mahal**, a large open hall fronted by a stagnant step-well, was built in 1646 by Mohammed Adil Shah as a seat of justice. It was later chosen to house hair strands from the Prophet's beard, thereby earning the title **Asar-i-Sharif**, or "place of illustrious relics". Women are not permitted inside to view the upper storey, where fifteen niches are decorated with Persian-style pot-and-foliage murals.

The citadel

Vijayapura's **citadel** stands in the middle of town, hemmed in on all but its north side by battlements. Most of the buildings inside have collapsed, or have been converted into government offices, but enough remain to give a sense of how imposing this royal enclave must once have been.

The best-preserved monuments lie along, or near, the citadel's main north–south artery, Anand Mahal Road, reached by skirting the southeast wall from the Asar Mahal. The latter route brings you first to the **Gagan Mahal**. Originally Ali Adil Shah's "Heavenly Palace", this now-ruined hulk later served as a durbar hall for the sultans, who would sit in state on the platform at the open-fronted north side, watched by crowds gathered in the grounds opposite. West off Anand Mahal Road, the five-storey **Sat Manzil** was the pleasure palace of the courtesan Rambha. In front stands an ornately carved water pavilion, the **Jal Mandir**, now left high and dry in an empty tank.

Malik-e-Maidan and Upli Buruj

Guarding the principal western entrance to the city is the Burj-i-Sherza ("Lion Gate"), one of several bastions that punctuate Vijayapura's battlements. This one sports a colossal cannon, known as the **Malik-e-Maidan**, literally "Lord of the Plains". It was brought here as war booty in the sixteenth century, and needed four hundred bullocks, ten elephants and an entire battalion to haul it up the steps to the emplacement. Inscriptions record that the cannon, whose muzzle features a relief of a monster swallowing an elephant, was cast in Ahmadnagar in 1551.

A few more discarded cannons lie atop the watchtower, a short walk northeast of the Malik-e-Maidan. Steps wind around the outside of the oval-shaped **Upli Buruj**, or "Upper Bastion", to a gun emplacement that affords unimpeded views over the city and plains.

Ibrahim Rauza

Under 1km west of the ramparts • Daily 6am–6pm • ₹100 (₹5)

Set in its own walled compound, the **Ibrahim Rauza** represents the apogee of Bijapuri architecture. Whereas the Gol Gumbaz impresses primarily by its scale, the appeal of this tomb complex lies in its grace and simplicity. It's also a haven of peace, with cool, colonnaded verandas and flocks of iridescent parakeets careening between the mildewed domes, minarets and gleaming golden finials.

Opinions differ over whether the tomb was commissioned by Ibrahim Adil Shah (1580–1626), or his favourite wife, Taj Sultana, but the former was the first to be interred here, in a gloomy chamber whose only light enters via a series of exquisite pierced-stone windows. Made up of elaborate Koranic inscriptions, these are the finest examples of their kind in India. More amazing stonework decorates the exterior of the mausoleum, and the equally beautiful **mosque** opposite, the cornice of whose facade features a stone chain carved from a single block. The two buildings, bristling with minarets and cupolas, face each other from opposite sides of a rectangular raised plinth, divided by a small reservoir and fountains. Viewed from on top of the walls that enclose the complex, you can see why its architect, Malik Sandal, added a self-congratulatory inscription in his native Persian over the tomb's south doorway, describing his masterpiece as "A beauty of which Paradise stood amazed".

ARRIVAL AND INFORMATION

By train The railway station is just east of the Gol Gumbaz, outside the old city walls, and 3km northeast of the bus stand. Departing at 4.55pm, the daily *Golgumbaz Express* #16536 links Vijayapura with Badami, Gadag, Hubballi and Bengaluru (15hr 5min), while the *Basava Express* #17308 (dep. 4.35pm) runs daily via Kalaburagi (5hr 20min) to Bengaluru (18hr 10min). Destinations Badami (3–4 daily; 2hr 20min–2hr 55min); Bengaluru (2–3 daily; 15hr 5min–18hr 10min); Gadag (3–6 daily; 4hr 10min–4hr 40min); Hubballi (3–5 daily, 5hr 55min–7hr).

By bus State and interstate buses from as far afield as

Mumbai and Aurangabad pull into the KSRTC Bus Stand on the southwest edge of the town centre. KSRTC run deluxe buses to Bengaluru, Hubballi, Mumbai and Hyderabad. Heading to Badami, it is often quicker to take the first bus to Bagalkot and change there. VRL runs private services to Bengaluru (3 buses from 7pm) and operates other overnight buses to Mangaluru (via Udupi) and Mumbai. These can be booked through Vijayanand Travels, terrace floor, Shastri Market, Gandhi Chowk (☎08352 251000, ⬥vrlbus.in) or its other branch just south of the bus stand.

Destinations Aurangabad (12hr); Badami (4hr); Bagalkot

(2hr); Bengaluru (13hr); Hubballi (6hr); Hyderabad (10hr); Kalaburagi (4hr); Mangaluru (15hr); Mumbai (12hr).

Tourist information The tourist office (Mon–Sat 10am– 5.30pm; ☎08352 250359) behind the *Hotel Adil Shahi* annexe on Station Rd, can help with arranging itineraries and guides.

GETTING AROUND

By bus Frequent local buses, largely uncrowded, connect the bus stand with the Gol Gumbaz and the train station.

By auto-rickshaw Auto-rickshaws don't have meters and charge a minimum of ₹30; although most of Vijayapura is covered by a fare of ₹80, they are a much more expensive way of getting around the monuments, when they charge at least ₹400 for a 4hr tour.

By tonga or tempo Tongas are available from near the bus stand, while *tempos* ply the main road between the bus stand, the Gol Gumbaz and the train station.

By bike Vijayapura is flat, relatively uncongested, and generally easy to negotiate by bicycle; rickety Heros are available for rent from stalls outside the bus stand for ₹15/hr.

ACCOMMODATION

Madhuvan International Station Rd ☎08352 255571; map p.1177. With a bright yellow exterior and a variety of rooms, from overpriced ordinary doubles to more comfortable a/c options, this is a safe bet. The veg restaurant serves good-value thalis at lunchtime. Currency exchange available for guests. **₹1500**

Navaratna International Just off Station Rd ☎08352 222771; map p.1177. The huge, shiny-tiled rooms at this quiet hotel are great value for this price. Good service, veg and non-veg restaurants and a popular palm-shaded dining (and drinking) area. **₹850**

★**Pearl** Station Rd ☎08352 256002, ⍟hotel pearlbijapur.com; map p.1177. Bright, modern hotel with

clean, sizeable rooms. The front ones have balconies and those at the top afford views of the Gol Gumbaz. The smart attached annexe at the back has quality a/c rooms. **₹1200**

Sagar Deluxe Near Bara Kaman ☎08352 259236, ⍟hotelsagardeluxebijapur.com; map p.1177. A budget option close to the action yet tucked away on a quiet side street. Simple but adequate rooms, including cheap singles and great-value a/c. **₹800**

Sanman Station Rd ☎08352 251866; map p.1177. Best value among the real budget places, if a tad grubby, and right opposite the Gol Gumbaz. The more expensive rooms have TV and the rooftop restaurant/bar offers excellent evening views of the mausoleum. **₹550**

EATING

Roshan Bakery and Sweets MG Rd; map p.1177. Among other goodies, this popular place whips up the perfect budget takeaway brunch: flaky croissants filled with boiled egg or veg. Most items cost ₹25 or less. Daily 7am–9pm.

Shrinidhi Hotel Ashram Rd ☎98441 45240; map p.1177. Probably the best choice for good south Indian veg

food, from *vada*, dosa and snacks to full-on thalis for just ₹100. Daily 7am–8pm.

★**Siddarth** Gandhi Chowk ☎93416 11635; map p.1177. Above the main market, this sprawling rooftop bar-restaurant offers tasty non-veg Indian cuisine such as tandoori chicken for around ₹300, plus a good selection of booze. Daily 10am–10pm.

Kalaburagi (Gulbarga)

Gulbarga, officially renamed **KALABURAGI**, around 150km northeast of Vijayapura, was the founding capital of the Bahmani Sultanate and the region's principal city before the court moved to Bidar in 1424. Later captured by the Adil Shahis and Mughals, it has remained a staunchly Muslim town, and bulbous onion domes and mosque minarets still soar prominently above its ramshackle concrete-box skyline. The town is also famous as the birthplace of the Sufi saint, Hazrat Gesu Daraz (1320–1422), whose tomb, situated next to one of India's foremost Islamic theological colleges, is a major shrine.

In spite of Kalaburagi's religious and historical significance, its **monuments** pale in comparison with those at Vijayapura, or even Bidar. Unless you're particularly interested in medieval Muslim architecture, few are worth breaking a journey to see.

The Dargah

The one monument that warrants a look is the **Dargah**, a tomb complex on the edge of town around 2km northeast of the train station. Approached via a broad bazaar, this marble-lined enclosure centres on the tomb of **Hazrat Gesu Daraz Banda Nawaz**, or "the long-haired one who brings comfort to others". The saint was spiritual mentor to the Bahmani rulers, and it was they who erected his beautiful double-storeyed mausoleum, now visited by thousands of Muslim pilgrims each year. Women are not allowed inside, and men must wear long trousers. The same applies to the neighbouring tomb, whose interior has retained its exquisite Persian paintings. The Dargah's other important building, open to both sexes, is the **madrasa**, founded by Banda Nawaz and enlarged during the two centuries after his death.

ARRIVAL AND DEPARTURE   KALABURAGI (GULBARGA)

22

By train Kalaburagi's mainline railway station lies 1.5km east of the bus stand, along Mill Rd. Station Rd, the town's other main artery, runs due north of here past the lake to the busy Chowk crossroads, at the heart of the bazaar.
Destinations Bengaluru (5–9 daily; 10hr 35min–16hr 40min); Chennai (3–4 daily, 13hr 35min–16hr 50min); Hyderabad/Secunderabad (7–11 daily; 3hr 40min–8hr 5min); Mumbai (10–12 daily; 9hr 55min–12hr); Pune

(12–16 daily; 5hr 15min–7hr 40min).
By bus Daily KSRTC buses from Vijayapura, Bidar and beyond pull in to the State Bus Stand on the southwest edge of town. Frequent local buses such as #206 run from the bus stand via the crossroads near the station to the Dargah.
Destinations Hourly to Vijayapura (4hr) and Bidar (3hr); less frequently further afield.

ACCOMMODATION

Central Park Station Rd, 1km north of the railway station ☎08472 273231. Clean, modern business hotel whose simple but smart rooms have TV; some have a/c. Good veg restaurant. ₹900
Golden Regency Opposite GESCOM, Station Rd, 1km north of the railway station ☎08472 266688, ⓦ goldenregency.in. Centrally located modern hotel with

large, neat rooms and complimentary breakfast. Singles for ₹940. ₹1350
Heritage Inn SB Temple Rd ☎08472 224093. Modern hotel next to Gulbarga's deserted fort with deluxe rooms and suites, separate veg and non-veg restaurants, a bar and complimentary breakfast and pick-up/drop. ₹1500

EATING

Kamat The venerable chain restaurant has several branches in Kalaburagi including a pleasant one at Station Chowk, specializing in veg "meals"; try *jolada roti*, an unleavened local bread made from sorghum cooked either hard and crisp or soft like a chapatti. Daily 7am–10pm.

Rajdhani Mill Rd ☎97417 37143. Most of the mains such as chicken and mutton cost under ₹200 at this simple basement restaurant on the way towards the station from the bus stand. Daily 11am–11pm.

Bidar

Lost in the far northeast of Karnataka, **BIDAR**, 284km northeast of Vijayapura, is a provincial backwater, known for its fighter-pilot training base, gently decaying monuments and the most important Sikh shrine in Karnataka. The town, half of whose 210,000-strong population is Muslim, has a gritty charm, with narrow red-dirt streets ending at arched gates and open vistas across the plains. Littered with tile-fronted tombs, rambling fortifications and old mosques, it merits a visit if you're travelling between Hyderabad (150km east) and Vijayapura, although you should expect little in the way of Western comforts, and lots of curious approaches from locals.

In 1424, following the break-up of the Bahmani Sultanate into five rival factions, **Ahmad Shah I** shifted his court from Gulbarga to a less constricted site at Bidar. Revamping the town with a new fort, splendid palaces, mosques and ornamental gardens, the Bahmanis ruled from here until 1487, when the Barid Shahis took control. They were succeeded by the Adil Shahis from Vijayapura, and later the Mughals under Aurangzeb, who annexed the region in 1656, before the nizam of Hyderabad acquired the territory in the early eighteenth century.

The heart of Bidar is its medieval **old town**, encircled by crenellated ramparts and eight imposing gateways (*darwazas*). This predominantly Muslim quarter holds many Bahmani-era mosques, havelis and *khanqahs* – "monasteries" set up by the local rulers for Muslim cleric-mystics and their disciples.

22

Mahmud Gawan's madrasa

The highlight of the old town is the impressive ruins of **Mahmud Gawan's madrasa**, whose single minaret soars high above the city centre. The distinctively Persian-style building, originally surmounted by large bulbous domes, once housed a world-famous library. However, this burnt down after being struck by lightning in 1696, and several of the walls and domes were blown away when gunpowder stored here by Aurangzeb's occupying army caught fire and exploded. Today, the madrasa is little more than a shell, although its elegant arched facade has retained large patches of the vibrant Persian glazed tile-work that once covered most of the exterior surfaces.

The Fort

At the far north end of the street running past the madrasa

A rambling, crumbling Monument Valley to the fifteenth-century Bahmani Sultanate, the Bidar **Fort** retains a serene, austere beauty. Though locals have incorporated the vast rolling spaces into their lives – young boys play cricket in the grassy turf, terraces are planted with rice, and scooters and small trucks ply its roads – its appeal remains undiminished.

The fort was founded by the Hindu Chalukyas and strengthened by the Bahmanis in the early fifteenth century. Despite repeated sieges, it remains largely intact, encircled by 10km of ramparts that drop away in the north and west to 300m cliffs. The main southern entrance is protected by equally imposing man-made defences: gigantic fortified gates and a triple moat formerly crossed by a series of drawbridges. You can complete the round of **the ramparts** in ninety minutes, taking time out to enjoy the views over the red cliffs and across the plains.

Rangeen Mahal

The first building of note inside the fort is the exquisite **Rangeen Mahal**, on the left after the third and final entrance gateway. Mahmud Shah built this "Coloured Palace" after an unsuccessful uprising of Abyssinian slaves in 1487 forced him to relocate to a safer site inside the citadel. The palace's relatively modest proportions reflect the Bahmanis' declining fortunes, but its interior comprises some of the finest surviving Islamic art in the Deccan, with superb woodcarving above the door arches and Persian-style mother-of-pearl inlay on polished black granite surfaces. If the doors to the palace are locked, ask for the keys at the nearby **ASI Museum** (daily 8am–1pm & 2–5pm; free).

Solah Khamb Masjid

Opposite the ASI Museum

An expanse of gravel is all that remains of the royal gardens, overlooked by the austere **Solah Khamb** mosque (1327), Bidar's oldest Muslim monument, whose most outstanding feature is the intricate pierced-stone calligraphy around its central dome. From here, continue west through the ruins of the former royal enclosure – a rambling complex of half-collapsed palaces, baths, zenanas and assembly halls – to the fort's west walls.

Ashtur: the Bahmani tombs

As you look from the fort's east walls, a cluster of eight bulbous white domes floats alluringly above the trees in the distance. Nearly 5km east of Bidar (leave the old town via Dulhan Darwaza gate) and dating from the fifteenth century, the mausoleums at **Ashtur** are the final resting-places of the Bahmani sultans and their families, including the son of the ruler who first decamped from Gulbarga, Ala-ud-din Shah I. His tomb is by far the most impressive, with patches of coloured glazed tiles on its arched facade, and a large dome whose interior surfaces bear sumptuous Persian paintings. Reflecting sunlight onto the ceiling with a small pocket mirror, the chowkidar picks out the highlights, among them a diamond, barely visible among the bat droppings.

The tomb of Ala-ud-din's father, the ninth and most illustrious Bahmani sultan, Ahmad Shah I, stands beside that of his son, decorated with Persian inscriptions.

22

BIDRI

Bidar is renowned as the home of a unique damascene metalwork technique known as **bidri**, developed by the Persian silversmiths who came to the area with the Bahmani court in the fifteenth century. These highly skilled artisans engraved and inlaid their traditional Iranian designs onto a metal alloy composed of lead, copper, zinc and tin, which they blackened and polished. The resulting effect – swirling silver floral motifs framed by geometric patterns and set against black backgrounds – has since become the hallmark of Muslim metalwork in India.

Bidri objets d'art are displayed in museums and galleries all over the country. But if you want to see pukka *bidri*-walas at work, take a walk down Bidar's **Siddiq Talim Road** (or Chaubara Road), which cuts across the south side of the old town, where skull-capped artisans tap and burnish vases, goblets, plates, spice boxes, betel-nut tins and ornamental hookah pipes, as well as less traditional objects – coasters, ashtrays and bangles – that crop up (at vastly inflated prices) in silver emporiums as far away as Delhi and Kolkata.

Beyond this are two more minor mausoleums, followed by the partially collapsed tomb of Humayun the Cruel (ruled 1458–61), cracked open by a bolt of lightning. Continuing along the line, you can chart the gradual decline of the Bahmanis as the mausoleums diminish in size, ending with a sad handful erected in the early sixteenth century, when the sultans were no more than puppet rulers of the Barid Shahis.

Gurudwara Nanak Jhira Sahib

1km north of bus stand • Headscarves are mandatory, and provided just outside the shrine

Guru Nanak, the founder of Sikhism, came to Bidar during his second Udasi (sacred journey) in 1512, when the region was in the grips of a famine. Since Bidar had brackish water, forcing its denizens to travel far away for potable water, the Guru uttered a mantra ("Sat kartar"), shifted a stone with his wooden sandal, and a spring (*jhira*) miraculously emerged from a laterite trap in the hill, which now fills the water tank known as **Amrit Kund** (Pool of Nectar). Built in 1948 beside the spring and recently expanded, the **Gurudwara Nanak Jhira Sahib** is the largest in Karnataka and open to people of all faiths. Drop by at the **Sikh Museum**, to the left of the *gurudwara* entrance, where pictures and paintings depict key events in Sikh history, and don't leave without having a meal at the *langar* (free community kitchen), run by volunteers for pilgrims round the clock.

ARRIVAL AND DEPARTURE   BIDAR

By train Bidar lies on a branch line of the main Mumbai–Secunderabad–Chennai rail route and can only be reached by slow passenger train.

By bus Most visitors arrive by bus at the KSRTC Bus Stand on the far northwestern edge of town, around 2km from the centre. The best connections are with Kalaburagi (every 15min; 3hr) and Hyderabad (every 30min; 4hr).

ACCOMMODATION AND EATING

Extremely grubby lodges predominate in Bidar but the good news is that none of the handful of better **hotels** listed below cost very much. These are generally the best **places to eat** too, along with the odd basic veg restaurant.

Ashoka Near Deepak Theatre, Basaveshwara Circle, 2km southeast of bus stand ☎ 08482 227621. Standard business hotel with reasonably comfortable, good-value deluxe rooms, some of them a/c. The restaurant serves both veg and non-veg. No wi-fi. ₹700

Mayura Opposite the bus stand ☎ 08482 228142. Ugly concrete block but with large rooms; deluxe a/c rooms are ₹1000. The restaurant food is tasty but it doubles as a slightly unsavoury bar. No wi-fi. ₹650

Rohit Inside gurudwara arch, near town police station ☎ 08482 223425. Great Punjabi cuisine close to Gurudwara Nanak Jhira Sahib, including excellent *dal makhani* (₹100) and *paneer* dishes. Daily 12.30–10pm.

Sapna International Udgir Rd, 300m north of the bus stand ☎ 94802 39377, ⓦ hotelsapnacontinental.com. Bidar's nicest lodgings, with big, clean rooms and a good non-veg restaurant. ₹1400

Udupi Krishna On Dr Ambedkar Circle ☎ 92065 77811. A very humble place but undoubtedly one of the best independent restaurants in town, serving up unlimited pure-veg thalis for lunch and south Indian breakfasts, all under ₹100. Daily 6.30am–9.30pm.

MURAL IN KERALA

Contexts

History

India's history is as complex and as multifaceted as you would expect from such a huge, populous and culturally varied country – a place that was home to one of the world's earliest civilizations and the birthplace of four major global religions, as well as having spawned more dynasties, monarchs and kingdoms than even the most determined historian can keep track of. Broadly speaking, the history of India divides into two parts: the history of the Aryan north, heavily influenced by successive waves of invaders from the uplands of Central Asia, and the much more self-contained history of the Dravidian south.

The Indus Valley Civilization

The earliest human presence in the Indian Subcontinent can be traced back to the Early, Middle and Late **Stone Ages** (400,000–200,000 BC), when the country was first settled by seminomadic hunters and gatherers. Village settlements gradually developed over the next four thousand years across the Indus Valley as their inhabitants began to use copper and bronze, domesticate animals, make pottery and trade with their neighbours.

By around 2500 BC, the village settlements of the Indus Valley had begun to develop into one of the world's earliest civilizations – roughly contemporaneous with those of Sumer and ancient Egypt. Known variously as the **Indus Valley Civilization** or the **Harappan Civilization**, this first great Subcontinental culture spread across a sizeable proportion of what is now southern Pakistan and the periphery of western India. Much of what is known about it comes from the remains of two great cities on the Indus, **Harappa** in the north and **Mohenjo Daro** in the south (both in present-day Pakistan). Laid out on a grid, both cities boasted large houses made from uniformly sized baked bricks, an elaborate system of covered drains (the world's first urban sanitation system) and large granaries. The absence of royal palaces and the large numbers of religious figurines found at both sites suggest that the Indus Valley Civilization was a theocratic state of priests, merchants and farmers.

The Indus Valley Civilization displayed remarkable longevity, surviving for a thousand years until its sudden demise around 1700 BC, probably caused by a catastrophic series of floods.

The Vedic Age (1500–600 BC)

The written history of India begins with the invasions of the charioteering **Indo-European** or **Aryan** tribes, which dealt the final death blow to the enfeebled Indus Civilization. The arrival of the Aryans marks the beginning of the so-called **Vedic Age**, named after the earliest Indian literature, the Vedas (see page 1205). The Aryans

10,000–3000 BC	2400 BC	1700 BC	1500–1000 BC
Spectacular Mesolithic rock art is created in Bhimbetka, central India.	Harappan people construct India's oldest known port city, at Lothal in Gujarat.	Natural disasters and climate change precipitate the demise of the Harappan civilization.	The world's oldest surviving sacred texts, the Vedas, are composed in northern India.

were one of the various nomadic tribes who emerged out of the vast steppes of Central Asia, marauding and eventually colonizing Europe, the Middle East and the Indian Subcontinent.

Aryan culture was diametrically opposed to that of the Indus Civilization. Seminomadic hunters and pastoralists when they first reached the Subcontinent, the Aryans gradually adopted the farming techniques learned from the peoples they conquered as they spread eastwards into India.

The Aryans' hymns, written down in the Vedas, describe the intertribal conflicts characteristic of the period, but also express an underlying sense of solidarity against the indigenous peoples, whom the Aryans referred to as **Dasas**. Originally a general term for "enemies", it came to denote "subjects" as they were colonized within the expanding land of the Aryans. The Aryans began to emphasize purity of blood as they settled among the darker aboriginals, and their original class divisions of nobility and ordinary tribesmen were hardened to exclude the Dasas. At the same time, the priests, the sole custodians of the increasingly complex religion and sacrificial rituals, began to claim high privileges for their skill and training. By 1000 BC, Aryan society had become divided into four classes, or **varnas** (literally "colour"): priests (Brahmins), warriors (kshatriya), peasants (*vaishya*) and serfs (*shudra*), a division that still survives today. The first three classes covered the main divisions within the Aryan tribes; the Dasas and other non-Aryan subjects became the *shudras*, who served the three higher classes. Many of India's most important religious texts and epics also date from this period, including the Sama, Yajur and Atharva Vedas, Brahmanas and the Upanishads (see page 1205), while the **Mahabharata** and the **Ramayana** (see page 1206) also claim to relate to this era.

By the fifth century BC the scattered states of north India had been consolidated into five great kingdoms: Magadha, Kashi, Koshala, Vatsa and the republic of the Vrijjis. Eventually, **Magadha** emerged supreme, under Bimbisara (543–491 BC), who was also, according to legend, a personal friend and great patron of the **Buddha**, his almost exact contemporary. Bimbisara's son and successor Ajatashatru (491–461 BC) moved the capital of Magadha to **Pataliputra** (the forerunner of modern Patna) and either annihilated the other kingdoms in the Ganges valley or reduced them to the status of vassals. In the middle of the fourth century BC, the **Nanda** dynasty usurped the Magadhan throne; Mahapadma Nanda conquered Kalinga (Odisha and the northern coastal strip of Andhra Pradesh) and gained control of parts of the Deccan. The disputed succession after his death coincided with significant events in the northwest; out of this confusion the first of India's empires was born.

The Mauryan Empire (320–184 BC)

North India's burgeoning prosperity was by now beginning to attract the attention of ambitious rulers in Central Asia – something that was to become a recurrent theme in Indian history over the next thousand years. **Darius I**, the third Achaemenid emperor of Persia, had already conquered the kingdom of Gandhara (in what is now northern Pakistan and eastern Afghanistan) around 520 BC. Far more significant, however, was the later invasion by **Alexander the Great**, who defeated Darius III, the last Achaemenid, crossed the Indus in 326 BC, and then overran the Punjab. Alexander

C. 1000 BC	C. 563–483 BC	326 BC	265–232 BC
Rise of the caste system.	Lifetime of Gautama Buddha, founder of the Buddhist faith.	Alexander the Great crosses the Indus and stays in India with his Macedonian army for two years.	Reign of the Mauryan emperor Ashoka.

was in India for just two years, and although he left garrisons and appointed satraps to govern the conquered territories, their position following his death in 323 BC became increasingly untenable.

The disruption caused by Alexander's brief incursion was seized upon by **Chandragupta Maurya**, the ruler of Magadha, who had overthrown the last of the Nanda dynasty in around 320 BC. Chandragupta is said to have met Alexander the Great and was probably inspired by his exploits; his 500,000-strong army drove out the Greek garrisons in the northwest and annexed all the lands east of the Indus.

From about 297 BC onwards, Chandragupta's son Bindusara extended the empire as far south as Mysore, before being succeeded in around 269 BC by his son, **Ashoka**, the most famous of India's early rulers. Ashoka ruthlessly consolidated his power for the first eight years of his reign, but then – allegedly sickened by the terrible carnage caused by his conquests – abruptly converted to Buddhism and renounced the use of violence in favour of the law of moral righteousness, or dharma. His adoption of Buddhism, however, did not interfere with his imperial pragmatism, and he continued to govern the newly acquired territory with a firm military hand. By the end of his reign, Ashoka's empire stretched from Assam to Afghanistan and from Kashmir to Mysore; only the three Dravidian kingdoms of the Cholas, Cheras and Pandyas in the southernmost tip of the Subcontinent remained independent. After Ashoka's death in 232 BC, the empire began to fall apart, and in 184 BC the last of the Mauryans, Brihadratha, was assassinated by one of his generals, bringing to an end nearly 140 years of Mauryan rule.

The age of invasions (184 BC–320 AD)

The five hundred years following the collapse of the Mauryan Empire are the most complex and confusing in Subcontinental history, marked by political fragmentation and a new and seemingly endless series of **invasions** from the northwest. The period is sometimes referred to as India's "Dark Age", although despite the lack of any unified central power it was also one of economic dynamism and considerable cultural achievement.

The first invaders were the **Bactrian Greeks** of Gandhara, who occupied the Punjab and extended their power as far as Mathura in Uttar Pradesh.

Yet the arrival of newcomers from Central Asia soon threatened the Greek position in Bactria. Large-scale movements of central Asian Yueh-Chi nomads had precipitated the migration of the **Shakas** (Scythians), from the Aral Sea area, who displaced the **Parthians** (Pahlavas) from Iran, who in turn wrested control of Bactria from the Greeks (who henceforth administered their Indian territories from a new capital in Kabul). The finer details of these various population movements remain unclear, and they were probably more in the nature of migrations than invasions. Whatever the details, both the Yueh-Chi and Shakas continued to drift slowly in the direction of India, finally arriving during the first century AD. The Shakas were the first to arrive, establishing themselves in northwestern India until the coming of the **Kushan** branch of the Yueh-Chi, who drove the Shakas off into Gujarat and Malwa (the area around Ujjain).

Despite the disintegration of the Mauryan Empire and the proliferation of rival kingdoms, the period from 200 BC to 300 AD was also one of unprecedented

261 BC	Mid-2nd century BC	1st and 2nd century AD
Terrible loss of life at the Battle of Kalinga (in modern-day Odisha) prompts Ashoka's conversion to Buddhism.	First rock-cut cave monasteries excavated in the Deccan region.	Andhra Dynasty erects magnificent *stupas* around India, the greatest at Sanchi.

economic wealth and cultural development. Urban centres began to develop all over India, while external trade, both overland and maritime, opened up lines of communication with the outside world stretching as far as Arabia and Southeast Asia by sea, and China and the Mediterranean by land via the **Silk Route**.

The rise of the south

Meanwhile, the first great kingdom of southern India was flexing its muscles. Between the second century BC and the second century AD the **Andhra** or **Satavahana** dynasty, which originated in the region between the Godavari and Krishna rivers (modern-day Andhra Pradesh and Maharashtra), began to make inroads into much of south and central India. The dynasty survived until the middle of the third century, when its territories were carved up by rival dynasties including the Pallavas, who took control of their territories in Andhra Pradesh.

Further south, the three kingdoms of the **Cheras** on the Malabar Coast in the west, the **Pandyas** in the central southern tip of the peninsula, and the **Cholas** on the east coast of Coromandel – together comprising much of present-day Tamil Nadu and Kerala – had been developing almost completely independently of north India. Society was divided into groups based on the geographical domains of hills, plains, forest, coast and desert rather than class or *varna*, though brahmins did command high status. Although agriculture, pastoralism and fishing were the main occupations, trade in spices, gold and jewels with Rome and southeast Asia underpinned the region's prosperity.

From the middle of the first century BC, however, conflicts between the three states intensified. This enervating warfare rendered them vulnerable; early in the fourth century AD, the **Pallavas** overran the Chola capital of Kanchipuram, and by 325 AD had taken control of Tamil Nadu. The Pallavas remained a dominant power in the south until the ninth century AD, and thus became one of the longest ruling dynasties in Indian history.

The Guptas (320–650)

During the fourth century AD, a second great Indian empire began to emerge in the north: the **Guptas**. The parallels with the earlier Mauryan Empire are striking. Both were founded in the year 320 (BC and AD respectively) by a king named Chandragupta (though the later king is usually written as two words, Chandra Gupta), and both emerged from within the famous old kingdom of Magadha. **Chandra Gupta** (reigned c.320–335) appears to have been the ruler of a minor statelet within the old Magadhan kingdom, acquiring considerable new territory through intermarriage with the famous Licchavi clan, one of the Mauryas' principal enemies six hundred years previously. Chandra Gupta thus found himself master of a powerful kingdom in the Gangetic plain, which controlled the vital east–west trade route. His son and heir, **Samudra Gupta** (c.335–376 AD), expanded the frontiers of his realm from Punjab to Assam, while the empire reached its apogee under his successor, **Chandra Gupta II** (376–415 AD), who subjugated the Shakas in Gujarat and reunified the whole of northern India, with the exception of the northwest.

375–415 AD	460–477 AD	543 AD	700–728 AD
The Golden Age of Classical India during the reign of Chandra Gupta II.	Ajanta's finest cave paintings are commissioned by Emperor Harishena.	Chalukya Dynasty found their capital at Badami, erecting India's first freestanding stone temples.	Pallava Dynasty builds the famous Shore Temple at Mamallapuram.

The era of these three imperial Guptas, along with the subsequent reign of Harsha Vardhana (606–647 AD) of Kanauj, is generally seen as the **Classical Age** of Indian history, one of cultural and artistic brilliance, religious ferment and political stability. Secular **Sanskrit literature** reached its perfection in the works of Kalidasa, the greatest Indian poet and dramatist, who was a member of Chandra Gupta II's court. The cave paintings of **Ajanta** and **Ellora** inspired Buddhist artists throughout Asia, and Yashodhara's detailed analysis of painting in the fifth century prescribed the classical conventions for the new art form. In **sculpture**, the images of the Buddha produced in Sarnath and Mathura embodied the simple and serene quality of classicism. In **architecture**, the Gupta era saw the birth of a new style of **Hindu temple** which would become India's classic architectural form. The era of the Guptas produced great thinkers as well: six systems of **philosophy** evolved, which refuted Buddhism and Jainism. One of them, **Vedanta**, has continued as the basis of all philosophical studies in India to this day.

The Guptas performed Vedic sacrifices to legitimize their rule, and patronized popular forms of Hinduism, such as devotional religion (*bhakti*) and the worship in temples of images of Vishnu, Shiva and the goddess Shakti, deities who were attracting increasing numbers of devotees during this era. Buddhism continued to thrive, however, with thousands of monks dwelling at Mathura as well as hundreds in Pataliputra itself.

The Gupta Empire remained relatively peaceful during the long reign of Kumara Gupta (c.415–455), who succeeded Chandra Gupta II, but by the time Skanda Gupta (c.455–467) came to the throne, western India was again threatened by invasions from Central Asia, this time by the **White Huns**, nomads from Central Asia who had already established themselves in Bactria. Skanda managed to repel White Hun raids, but after his death their disruption of central Asian trade seriously destabilized the empire. By the end of the fifth century, the Huns had wrested the Punjab from Gupta control, and further incursions early in the sixth century dealt a death blow to the Gupta Empire, which had completely disintegrated by 550 AD.

Kingdoms of central and south India (500–1250)

Meanwhile, significant events were taking place in central and south India. The history of the period was dominated by three major kingdoms: the **Pallavas**, who had supplanted the Satavahanas in the Andhra region and made Kanchipuram their capital back in the fourth century; the **Pandyas** of Madurai, who had -established their own regional kingdom by the sixth century; and the **Chalukyas** of Vatapi (Badami in Karnataka), who had expanded into the Deccan in the middle of the sixth century. All three kingdoms intermittently fought one another, but their military strength was so evenly matched that none was able to gain ascendancy.

The Chalukyas were eventually overthrown in 753 by Dantidurga, the founder of the **Rashtrakuta** kingdom (whose rulers also tried their luck in the north, briefly gaining possession of Kanauj). The Pallavas survived their arch-enemies by about a hundred years, then succumbed to a combined attack of the Pandyas and the **Cholas**. The Cholas were a major new force in Tamil Nadu, conquering the Thanjavur region in the ninth century and taking Madurai from the Pandyas in 907, before being defeated by the Rashtrakutas in the middle of the tenth century, who were themselves replaced by the revived Chalukyas in 973 AD.

757–790 AD	788–820 AD	**Early 11th century**
Excavation of Kailash temple at Ellora in Maharashtra.	The philosopher Adi Shankara spreads the doctrine of Vedanta, the most widely followed tradition in Hinduism today.	The Cholas establish an empire stretching from the far south of India to Sumatra.

Ultimately, the chief beneficiaries of this dynastic back-and-forth were the Cholas, who were able to regain lost territories and expand further during the eleventh and twelfth centuries. The great Chola kings **Rajaraja I** (985–1014) and **Rajendra I** (1014–1044) launched a series of campaigns against the Cheras, Pandyas and Chalukyas, and by the end of the eleventh century the Cholas were supreme in the south, although incessant campaigning had exhausted their resources. Ironically, their destruction of the Chalukyas sowed the seeds of their own downfall. Former Chalukya feudatories, such as the **Yadavas** of Devagiri in the northern Deccan and the **Hoysalas**, around modern Mysuru, set up their own kingdoms; the latter attacked the Cholas from the west while the Pandyas directed a new offensive from the south. By the thirteenth century, the **Pandyas** had superseded the Cholas as south India's major power, while the Yadavas and Hoysalas controlled the Deccan until the advent of the Delhi sultans in the fourteenth century.

Despite constant political and military conflicts, this period was very much the classical age of the south. The ascendancy of the Cholas was complemented by the crystallization of Tamil culture; the religious, artistic, and institutional patterns of this period dominated the culture of the south and influenced developments elsewhere in the Subcontinent. In the sphere of religion, for instance, the great philosophers Shankara and Ramanuja, as well as the Tamil and Maharashtrian saints, had a significant impact on Hinduism in north India.

Kingdoms in north India (650–1250)

In north India, Harsha Vardhana's death was followed by a century of confusion, with assorted kingdoms competing to control the Gangetic valley. In time, the **Pratihara-Gurjaras**, from western India, and the **Palas**, of Bihar and Bengal, emerged as the main rivals, although both were weakened by repeated incursions from the Deccan by the **Rashtrakutas**, who briefly occupied Kanauj in 916. The Pratiharas regained their capital, but the tripartite struggle sapped their strength and they were unable to repel the invasion of Kanauj by Mahmud of Ghazni in 1018. The struggle for possession of Kanauj depleted the resources of all three competing powers and resulted in their almost simultaneous decline, while various smaller feudatory kingdoms began to assert their independence. Kingdoms emerged in Nepal, Kamarupa (Assam), Kashmir and Odisha, all with their own cultural identities, customs, literatures and histories. The Eastern Gangas of **Kalinga** (roughly equivalent to modern Odisha) also achieved political independence and unity in the twelfth century.

Meanwhile, in the west, the celebrated **Rajputs** began to emerge as a new element within Indian society. Their origins remain the subject of considerable speculation, although they probably descended from the various invaders who arrived in India between the third and sixth centuries, including the Pratihara-Gurjaras, Huns and Shakas and perhaps others. Whatever their origins, they acquired respectable Hindu genealogies and were given kshatriya status. By the tenth century, the most important Rajput clans, like the Chauhans of Ajmer, the Guhilas of Chittaurgarh, the Chandellas of Bundelkhand, and the Tomaras of Haryana (who founded modern Delhi in 1060), had all established small regional kingdoms spread across modern-day Rajasthan, Gujarat, Madhya Pradesh and other parts of the north.

1000–27	1192	1198
The Muslim warlord Mahmud of Ghazni mounts seventeen bloody incursions into Hindu India from Afghanistan.	Muhammad of Ghor defeats Prithviraj III at the Battle of Tarain, laying the foundations of the Delhi Sultanate.	Qutbu'd-din Aibak erects the Qutub Minar victory tower in Delhi, marking the start of Muslim rule in India.

The Rajputs fought among each other incessantly, however, and failed to grasp the significance of a new factor, which entered the politics of north India at the start of the eleventh century. **Mahmud of Ghazni** (971–1030), a Turkish chieftain who had established the powerful Ghaznavid kingdom at Ghazni in Afghanistan, made seventeen plundering raids into India between 1000 and 1027, looting Mathura, Kanauj and Somnath, among other places. The powerful Rajput clans of northern India were still busy fighting one another almost two centuries later when **Muhammad of Ghor** (1162–1206) seized Ghaznavid possessions in the Punjab at the end of the twelfth century, and then turned his attention towards the wealthy lands further east. **Prithviraj III**, the legendary hero of the Chauhans of Ajmer, patched together an alliance to defeat the Turkish warlord at Tarain (north of Delhi) in 1191; but Muhammad returned the next year with a superior force and defeated the Rajputs. He had Prithviraj executed before returning home, leaving his generals to complete his conquest.

The Delhi Sultanate (1206–1526)

Muhammad of Ghor was assassinated in 1206 and his empire immediately disintegrated, leaving his Turkish general **Qutbu'd Aiback**, a former slave, as the autonomous ruler of Muhammad's former Indian territories. Aiback thus became the founder of the so-called "Slave Dynasty", the first part of which would eventually come to be known as the **Delhi Sultanate**, which would remain the major political force in the north until the early sixteenth century. The sultanate marked an important turning-point in Indian history. Islam rather than Hinduism suddenly became the religion of the country's rulers, while Delhi, rather than Kanauj or Pataliputra, became the most important city in the north.

Aiback's son-in-law **Iltutmish** (1211–36) extended the sultanate's territories from the Sind to Bengal by the time he died, but a period of confusion followed, with five different rulers in just six years. Not until **Ghiyas-ud-din Balban** took effective control in 1246 did the sultanate attain any degree of stability, despite repeated threats from yet another set of foreign interlopers, the **Mongols**, who had been launching raids into western India from around 1220 and continued to attack the edges of the sultanate.

Ghiyas-ud-din's death in 1287 was followed by the inevitable period of dynastic mayhem that only ended in 1290, when Aiback's Slave Dynasty came to an end, replaced by the **Khalji** dynasty. The Khalji family had entered India with Muhammad of Ghor, and subsequently carved out their own Muslim fiefdom in Bengal and Bihar. The first Khalji sultan, the elderly Feroz Shah I, was soon done away with by the implacable **Ala-ud-din Khalji** (1296–1315), one of the most fearsome of all Indian rulers. A hard man for hard times, Ala-ud-din was faced immediately by a series of further Mongol attacks. Delhi was besieged twice and its hinterlands plundered before the invaders suffered a resounding defeat at the hands of the new sultan in 1300, after which they left him alone. Having seen off the Mongols, Ala-ud-din set out to conquer Gujarat and Rajasthan in a series of expeditions between 1299 and 1311, before turning his attention to the Deccan and the south. Even so, his military campaigns were more a question of exacting tribute and raising funds than of building a stable empire.

A fresh imperial impetus came from the **Tughluq** dynasty, which succeeded the Khaljis in 1320. Under **Mohammed bin Tughluq** (1325–51), the sultanate reached

1325–51	1498	1510
Mohammed bin Tughluq forces the entire population of Delhi to march 1200km south to a new capital at Daulatabad.	Vasco da Gama completes the sea route across the Arabian Sea to land in Calicut on the Malabar Coast (Kerala).	Portuguese admiral Alfonso Albuquerque takes the strategically vital port of Goa.

its largest extent, comparable in size to Ashoka's empire, although the onerous taxes required to finance Mohammed's military campaigns provoked a series of revolts, while the new Hindu kingdom of **Vijayanagar** took advantage of the decline of the sultanate's authority to extend its influence from its capital near **Hampi**. **Firoz Shah Tughluq** (1351–88) reversed the fortunes of the sultanate to some extent, thanks to the comparative mildness of his rule, but arguments over the succession after his death in 1388 further weakened the sultanate, as did an attack by the ruthless **Timur**, the Central Asian despot known to the West as Tamerlane, who sacked Delhi in 1398. By the end of the fourteenth century, the Delhi Sultanate had been reduced to just one of several competing Muslim states in northern India.

The greatly weakened sultanate was next taken over by the Afghan-descended Khizr Khan (1414–21), whose **Sayyid** dynasty ruled until 1444, to be succeeded by the **Lodis**, under whom the sultanate experienced a modest revival. **Sikander Lodi** (1489–1517) was particularly energetic and successful, annexing Jaunpur and Bihar, but his successor, Ibrahim, was unable to quell dissension among his Afghan feudatories, one of whom enlisted the support of Babur, the ruler of Kabul, who defeated Ibrahim at Panipat in 1526.

The early Mughal Empire (1526–1605)

For Babur – the founder of India's most famous dynasty, the **Mughals** – India appears to have been something of an afterthought. A direct descendant of Timur (and also distantly related to Genghis Khan), Babur was born in Uzbekistan and spent most of his life in Afghanistan, where he seized control of Kabul. It was only relatively late in life, hearing of the military weakness of the Lodis, that he decided to attack India.

His battle-hardened forces easily routed the very last Delhi sultan, Ibrahim Lodi, at the Battle of Panipat in 1526, which gave him tenuous control of Delhi and Agra, although his position remained unsafe until his troops had first defeated a far stronger Rajput force led by Rana Sanga of Mewar, at the Battle of Kanwaha in 1527, and then the allied forces of assorted Afghan chiefs. Shortly afterwards, his failing health forced him to retire to Agra, where he died in 1530.

Humayun, his son and successor, was a volatile character, alternating between bursts of energetic activity and indolence. He subdued Malwa and Gujarat, only to lose both while he indulged himself in the harem in Agra. The Afghan-descended **Sher Shah Suri** (also known as Sher Khan or Sher Khan Sur) of south Bihar soon assumed the leadership of the Afghan opposition and, after two resounding defeats, Humayun was forced to seek refuge in Persia in 1539. He returned fifteen years later, however, to annihilate the forces of Sher Shah Suri's successor, Sikander Sur. Humayun died the following year after a fall in the Purana Qila in Delhi, leaving his 13-year-old son **Akbar** to succeed to the throne.

Fortunately for the young emperor, Humayun's experienced general **Bairam Khan** was on hand to serve as guardian and regent to help him through the difficult early years of his reign. Bairam first overcame the challenge of the Hindu general Hemu at the second Battle of Panipat in 1556, recovered Gwalior and Jaunpur, and handed over a consolidated kingdom of north India to Akbar in 1560. Akbar's own first military campaigns were against the **Rajputs**; and within a decade he had subdued all the Rajput

1526	1569	1600	1615
Babur defeats Ibrahim Lodi's forces at the Battle of Panipat to found the Mughal dynasty.	Humayun's successor, Akbar, builds Fatehpur Sikri.	The British East India Company is formed.	Sir Thomas Roe, British ambassador to the Mughal court, negotiates trade rights with Jahangir.

domains except Mewar (Udaipur) by a clever combination of diplomacy and force. By the end of his reign in 1605 he controlled a broad sweep of territory stretching from the Bay of Bengal to Kandahar in Afghanistan.

In 1565, Akbar had the small fort built by Sikander Lodi in **Agra** demolished and replaced by the magnificent new Agra Fort, the centrepiece of a newly revitalized city that would henceforth rival Delhi as the major centre of Mughal power. Not content with this, in the late 1560s, he embarked on the creation of an entire new city, the remarkable but short-lived **Fatehpur Sikri**, which served for a brief period as the capital of the empire.

Akbar was as clever a politician and administrator as he was a successful general. In addition to involving Hindu landowners and nobles in political life, Akbar adopted a conscious policy of religious toleration aimed at widening his power base, abolishing the despised poll tax on non-Muslims (*jizya*) and tolls on Hindu pilgrimages.

The later Mughals (1605–1761)

The reign of **Jahangir** (1605–27) was a time of brisk economic and expansionist activity conjoined with artistic and architectural brilliance. Jahangir himself was a contradictory character: an alcoholic and a sadist, but also a notable connoisseur of art as well as an able and determined military commander who succeeded in extending the bounds of the already very considerable domains bequeathed to him by Akbar.

Jahangir's son **Shah Jahan** came to power in 1628, having already proved himself an outstanding commander during his father's reign. Despite his considerable military abilities, however, it is as perhaps the greatest patron of architecture the world has ever known that Shah Jahan is best remembered. In 1648 he officially moved the Mughal capital from Agra back to Delhi, celebrating the translocation with the construction of the new city of **Shahjahanabad** (now better known as Old Delhi), though it was in Agra that he left his greatest mark, with his myriad embellishments to the city's fort and, pre-eminently, in the creation of the **Taj Mahal**.

Shah Jahan's reign witnessed the entry of a new force into Indian history: the **Marathas**, a potent military power in central India. A group of militant Hindus from Maharashtra in central India, the Marathas had carved out a kingdom of their own under their inspirational chief, **Shivaji**, and soon began to turn their attentions northwards. Shah Jahan had responded to the Maratha threat by sending his third son, the ambitious young **Aurangzeb**, to the Deccan to take charge of Mughal interests in the region, although his military successes were repeatedly undermined by Shah Jahan's oldest son and preferred heir **Dara Shikoh**, who was anxious to destabilize Aurangzeb's military exploits lest they create a threat to his own prestige. The anticipated struggle between the two brothers erupted in 1658 when Shah Jahan fell suddenly and seriously ill. Shah Jahan recovered, but not before Aurangzeb had seen off Dara Shikoh, wiping out his army in a series of encounters that culminated in a rout at Ajmer. The thirty-year reign of the ailing emperor ended ignominiously. Aurangzeb had him incarcerated in Agra Fort, where he remained until his death in 1666.

Though lacking the charisma of Akbar or Babur, Aurangzeb evoked an awe of his own and proved to be a firm and capable administrator, who retained his grip on the increasingly unsettled empire until his death at the age of 88. In contrast to the

1658	1659	1666
Aurangzeb, last, most devout and austere of the great Mughal emperors, ascends to the throne after murdering his brothers.	The Maratha warlord, Shivaji, defeats the sultan of Bijapur to become the most powerful chief in peninsular India.	Shivaji and his son, Sambhaji, escape from Aurangzeb's court by hiding in a box of sweets.

extravagance of the other Mughals, Aurangzeb's lifestyle was pious and disciplined. However, his religious dogmatism ultimately alienated the Hindu community whose leaders had been so carefully cultivated by Akbar. Hindu places of worship were again the object of iconoclasm and the *jizya* tax on non-Muslims was reintroduced.

The chief threat to Mughal rule in this period came from the Maratha chief, Shivaji, who established a compact and well-organized kingdom in western India, while the nearby Muslim kingdoms of Bijapur and Golconda allied themselves with him. Meanwhile, Guru Tegh Bahadur, the leader of the important new **Sikh** religion, was executed in 1675 for refusing to embrace Islam; his son, Guru Gobind, transformed the religious community into a military sect that became increasingly powerful in Punjab. Aurangzeb's confrontation with the Rajputs over the Jodhpur succession in 1678 resulted in another war, and the alienation of most of his Rajput partners in the empire.

Aurangzeb's attention, however, was turning steadily south. In 1681 he transferred his base to the Deccan, where he spent the rest of his extremely long life overseeing the subjugation of the Bijapur and Golconda kingdoms and trying to contain the increasingly belligerent Marathas. In 1689, he succeeded in capturing and executing Shivaji's son, and by 1698 the Mughals had overrun almost the whole of the peninsula.

Aurangzeb's son, Bahadur Shah, succeeded in 1707 but reigned for just five years. His death in 1712 marked the beginning of the end for the Mughals, as their empire disintegrated. By the 1720s the rulers of Hyderabad, Avadh (Lucknow) and Bengal were effectively independent; the Marathas overwhelmed the rich province of Malwa in 1738; Hindu landholders everywhere were in revolt; and **Nadir Shah** of Persia dealt a serious blow to the empire's prestige when he invaded India, defeated the Mughal army and sacked Delhi in 1739.

The East India Company (1600–1857)

India's trading potential had attracted European interest ever since 1498, when Vasco da Gama landed on the Malabar (Keralan) Coast. During the ensuing century Portuguese, Dutch, English, French and Danish companies had all set up coastal trading centres, exporting textiles, sugar and indigo. British interests in India were formalized by the creation of the **East India Company**, granted a royal charter by Elizabeth I in 1600, whose representatives arrived at Surat in Gujarat in 1608, quickly establishing 27 trading posts around the country, including Fort George and Fort William (out of which the cities of Madras and Calcutta would subsequently develop), as well as at the fledgling settlement of Bombay.

It was in the south that European trading initiatives first took on a political significance, after the onset of the War of the Austrian Succession in 1740. Armed conflict between French and English trading companies along the south Indian coast soon developed into a minor war over the succession of the nizam of Hyderabad. Sporadic fighting continued until the end of the Seven Years' War in Europe and the Treaty of Paris in 1763 put an effective end to French ambitions in India. Meanwhile, **Robert Clive**'s defeat of the rebellious young nawab of Bengal at Plassey in 1757 had decisively augmented British power; by 1765 the enervated Mughal emperor legally recognized the Company by granting it the revenue management of Bengal, Bihar and Orissa (now Odisha).

1739	1757	1799
With the Mughal dynasty in decline, the Persian king Nadir Shah sacks Delhi, slaughtering tens of thousands.	Robert Clive's victory over the nawab of Bengal at Plassey lays the foundation for two centuries of British rule in India.	Tipu Sultan is killed at the Battle of Srirangapatna, securing British control of the far south.

For the next thirty years, the British in India contented themselves with developing trade and repulsing Indian offensives against their three major settlements in Calcutta, Bombay and Madras, though by the end of the century the defeat of **Tipu Sultan** of Mysore, the Company's best-organized and most resolute enemy, and the subjugation of the nizam of Hyderabad, resulted in the annexation of considerable territories, and by 1805 nearly all the other rulers in India recognized British suzerainty. A long-drawn-out series of conflicts between the British and Marathas (the so-called three "Maratha Wars" of 1774–1818) finally extinguished the Marathas as an effective military threat.

Following the subjugation of the Marathas, the British established a series of treaties with the rulers of Rajasthan and with most of India's other surviving independent kingdoms, collectively known as the so-called **princely states**, stretching from Hyderabad in the south to Kashmir in the north. Under these treaties, the various kingdoms retained their autonomy more or less intact and received a guarantee of military protection in exchange for pledging their loyalty to the British Crown and agreeing to certain political, mercantile and financial concessions. The much-abused city of Delhi, the traditional capital of north India, fared less well, as the British established their capital at the burgeoning new city of **Calcutta**. Not until 1911 would Delhi recapture its mantle as the north's imperial city.

The 1857 uprising

The new British **colony**, however, was in a state of social and economic collapse as a result of the almost incessant conflicts of the previous hundred years. The controversial "Doctrine of Lapse", whereby autonomous states were gradually annexed, was widely resented. In addition, the Company's policy, after 1835, of promoting European literature and science (with English replacing Persian as the official state language), the suppression of local customs such as *sati* and child marriage, and the deployment of Indian troops overseas (resulting in loss of caste) were increasingly perceived as part of a covert British attack on traditional Hindu and Muslim religious and cultural practices.

The final spark which ignited a full-blown uprising by the Indian army was supplied when troops were issued with cartridges for a new Enfield rifle rumoured to have been smeared in cows' and pigs' grease (polluting to both Hindus and Muslims). The resultant **1857 uprising** (traditionally referred to by the British as the "Indian Mutiny" or "Sepoy Rebellion", and, in India, as the "First War of Independence") began with a rebellion of Indian troops (sepoys) at Meerut on May 10, 1857, and Delhi was seized the next day. The rebellion quickly spread across most of central northern India, where mutineers seized Lucknow and Kanpur. The British authorities were caught by surprise, though control was gradually reasserted. Delhi and Kanpur were both retaken in September, and the final recapture of Lucknow in March 1858 effectively signalled the end of the uprising. Bloody reprisals ensued.

The Raj and Indian nationalism (1857–1947)

The uprising had important consequences for subsequent British rule in the Subcontinent. The governing powers of the East India Company were abolished

1857	1911	1915	1919
A rebellion by sepoy troops triggers a full-scale uprising against British rule in northern India, suppressed with much brutality.	Delhi succeeds Calcutta as the British capital.	Gandhi returns to India from South Africa.	British troops open fire on unarmed civilians during a demonstration in Amritsar, killing 379 people.

and the British Crown assumed the direct administration of India in the same year. Henceforth, British India was no longer merely a massive trade operation, but a fully-fledged independent kingdom, or **Raj**, as the period of British rule in the Subcontinent subsequently became known.

As a British colony, India assumed a new position in the world economy. Its trade (though not the population as a whole) benefited from the railways developed by the British, and Indian businessmen began to invest in a range of manufacturing industries. However, India subsidized the British economy as a source of cheap raw materials and as a market for manufactured goods, and its own economy and agriculture remained chronically underdeveloped. British civil servants dominated the higher echelons of the administration, often introducing policies contrary to Indian interests and cultural traditions. Public demonstrations eventually forced the British to sanction the creation of the **Indian National Congress** party (usually known simply as "Congress") in 1885, and by 1905 Congress had adopted self-government as a political aim. In 1906, concerns about the predominantly Hindu Congress led to the foundation of the **All-India Muslim League** to represent the country's Muslims.

The Morley-Minto Reforms of 1909 paved the way for Indian participation in provincial executive councils and made allowance for separate Muslim representation. At the **Great Durbar** of 1911, held in honour of the new king, George V, the capital was moved back to **Delhi**, with the construction of yet another imperial city, so-called "New" Delhi, to celebrate the relocation (though it wasn't finished until 1931). A few years later, the Royal Proclamation of 1917 promised a gradual development of dominion-style self-government; and two years later the Montagu-Chelmsford Reforms attempted to implement the declaration.

At this point an British-educated lawyer, **Mohandas Karamchand Gandhi** (see page 1198) – better known as the Mahatma, or "Great Soul" – took up the -initiative, espousing a political philosophy based on non-violence and the championing of the so-called "untouchables", whom he renamed the Children of God (Harijan). Gandhi began by organizing India-wide one-day strikes and protests, though these were mercilessly crushed by the government – as in the infamous incident (see page 536) in 1919 when troops under General Dyer dispersed a meeting at Jallianwalla Bagh in Amritsar by firing on the unarmed crowd, killing 379 and wounding 1200.

By 1928 Congress was demanding complete independence. The government offered talks, but the more radical elements in Congress, now led by the young **Jawaharlal Nehru**, were in a confrontational mood. Gandhi, in turn, led a well-publicized 386km "salt march" from his ashram in Sabarmati to make salt illegally at Dandi in Gujarat in defiance of a particularly unpopular British tax. This demonstration of nonviolent civil disobedience (*satyagraha*) fired the popular imagination, leading to more processions, strikes, and mass imprisonments over the next few years, which in turn led to the formulation of the new **Government of India Act** in 1935, although this still fell short of offering the country complete independence. Congress remained suspicious of British intentions, and despite Gandhi's overtures refused to accommodate Muslim demands for representation. **Mohammed Ali Jinnah**, who assumed the leadership of the Muslim League in 1935, initially promoted Muslim–Hindu cooperation, but he soon despaired of influencing Congress and by 1940 the League passed a resolution demanding an independent Pakistan.

1930	1931	Aug 15, 1947
Gandhi leads "Salt Satyagraha" to protest against British rule. Sixty thousand are imprisoned in its wake.	The Gandhi–Irwin Pact secures the release of all political prisoners.	India is partitioned as Nehru is sworn in as the country's first prime minister – more than a million people are killed and many millions more are displaced.

Confrontations between the government, Congress and the Muslim League continued throughout World War II, despite the promise, in 1942, by a Britain increasingly reliant on Indian troops, of post-war independence. Gandhi introduced the **Quit India** slogan and proposed another campaign of civil disobedience; Jinnah, meanwhile, preached his "two nations" theory and inspired mass Muslim support with his rhetoric against "Hinduization". A spate of terrorist activities across the country left a thousand dead and sixty thousand imprisoned. By the end of the war, the British government accepted that complete independence for India could no longer be postponed.

Unfortunately, British attempts to find a solution that would preserve a united India while allaying Muslim fears disintegrated in the face of continued intransigence from both sides, and they gradually realized that the division – or so-called **Partition** – of the existing country of India into separate Muslim and Hindu states was inevitable. **Lord Mountbatten** was appointed viceroy to hastily supervise the handover of power, yet few preparations were made for what would be one of the biggest mass migrations in history. The Subcontinent was **partitioned** on August 15, 1947, and Pakistan came into existence. The new boundaries cut through both Bengal and the Punjab; Sikhs, Muslims and Hindus who had been neighbours became enemies overnight. More than five million Hindus and Sikhs from Pakistan, and a similar number of Muslims from India, were involved in the ensuing two-way exodus, and the atrocities cost more than a million lives. Mahatma Gandhi, who had devoted himself to ending the communal violence after Partition, was **assassinated** in January 1948 by a Hindu extremist antagonized by his defence of Muslims.

India under Nehru (1947–64)

Jawaharlal Nehru, India's first and longest-serving prime minister, proved to be a dynamic and extremely popular leader during his seventeen years in office, building the foundations of a democratic secular nation, and guiding the first stages of its agricultural and industrial development. The franchise was made universal for all adults and, with 173 million eligible to vote, in 1951 India became the **world's largest democracy**.

Despite Independence, there was still the problem of the 562 **princely states** within India, covering no less than forty percent of the country's total area, and which remained technically autonomous under the terms of ongoing British treaties. At Independence rulers of several of these states had yet to decide whether they were going to join India or Pakistan. Nehru's able deputy prime minister, Sardar Vallabhai Patel, was made responsible for encouraging the rulers of the recalcitrant statelets to join the new India, including sending a detachment of Indian troops into the territory of the Muslim nizam of **Hyderabad**, who had resisted joining the union even though the majority of his state's population was Hindu. Some parts of the Subcontinent retained their independence for even longer. The **French** enclaves at Pondicherry and Chandernagar were not incorporated until the 1950s, while the Portuguese refused to accept the new situation, until in 1961 Nehru finally sent in the army to annex **Goa**.

The most serious legacy of Partition concerned the Himalayan state of **Kashmir**. At Independence, Kashmir's Hindu Maharaja Hari Singh remained undecided as to

Jan 30, 1948	**1948**	**1961**
Gandhi is shot at point-blank range by a Hindu fanatic while attending a prayer meeting in Delhi.	Indian troops and Pakistani insurgents clash for the first time in Kashmir, leading to the fateful partition of the region.	451 years of Portuguese rule in Goa come to an end as Nehru orders in the Indian army.

which of the two new countries he wished to join. Jinnah naturally assumed Kashmir would join Pakistan, given that three-quarters of its inhabitants were Muslim; Nehru was equally determined to keep it for India. Meanwhile, the maharaja continued to prevaricate. Events reached a head in October 1947, when Islamic partisans from Pakistan's tribal areas suddenly arrived in the Kashmir valley to encourage the maharaja to join with Pakistan. Hari Singh, fearing he was about to be overthrown, immediately determined to join India instead. Shortly afterwards Indian troops were airlifted into the valley, and began to battle with the Islamic insurgents. Although war was never officially declared, and no regular Pakistani military units were involved, the fighting is usually described as the **First Indo-Pakistan War**. By the time the UN brokered a ceasefire in 1948, Pakistani insurgents had secured a sizeable slice of Kashmiri territory, which Pakistan retains to this day.

Elsewhere in the region, Nehru attempted to promote Asian unity by following a policy of peaceful **nonalignment**, although this was repeatedly threatened by **Chinese aggression**. The Chinese invasion of Tibet in 1950 brought the Chinese right up to India's border (and a flood of refugees into India itself, including the Dalai Lama, who arrived in 1959), while in 1962 Chinese troops brushed aside Indian border patrols and began to move down into Assam. This "invasion" (although it was really more a show of force) ended soon afterwards, and while the humiliating inability of the Indian army to repel the interlopers did not officially spell the end of India's policy of nonalignment, Nehru immediately signed a defence treaty with the US, and the Chinese retained small areas of Indian territory in Kashmir and Assam which they still hold.

Indira Gandhi (1966–84)

In 1946, the whole nation mourned Nehru's death which prevented him from witnessing the restoration of India's military prestige in the **Second Indo-Pakistan War** of 1965. Pakistani leader General Ayub Khan, perhaps wishing to test the resolve of new Indian premier **Lal Bahadur Shastri**, launched a series of skirmishes into disputed areas of Gujarat, and followed this up with attempts to infiltrate Kashmir and provoke a pro-Pakistani uprising. Full-scale fighting broke out in Kashmir and to the south, and the Indian army responded by driving Pakistani forces back to within 5km of a virtually defenceless Lahore before a ceasefire was agreed, with both sides returning to their previous borders. Despite this triumph, Lal Bahadur Shastri died shortly afterwards, in January 1966, leaving Nehru's daughter **Indira Gandhi** to establish herself as the new leader of Congress.

The 49-year-old Indira – or "Mrs Gandhi", as she is often called (though no relation to the Mahatma; she acquired her surname through marriage to a Parsi named Feroze Gandhi, who had died in 1960) – was initially chosen as a popular but easily manipulated figurehead by Congress chiefs. Gandhi herself had different plans. She moved rapidly to shore up her own power, and then – after consolidating her mandate in fresh elections in 1971 – launched Congress along a populist socialist path, nationalizing the banks, abolishing the former maharajas' privy purses, and introducing new legislation on corporate profits and land holdings. By this time, India was experiencing massive industrial growth and had also made a spectacular agricultural

1966	June 26, 1975–March 21, 1977	1984
Nehru's niece, Indira Gandhi, becomes leader of the Congress Party and India's third prime minister.	In response to widespread civil unrest, Indira Gandhi declares a "State of Emergency", suspending elections and civil liberties.	Militant Sikhs occupy the Golden Temple in Amritsar. Indira Gandhi orders in the troops. A massacre ensues.

breakthrough with its **Green Revolution**, becoming self-sufficient in food by the early 1970s thanks to the introduction of high-yield grains.

Gandhi also had to deal with the increasingly chaotic situation in **East Pakistan** (present-day Bangladesh), which had declared independence from (West) Pakistan in 1971. Pakistani troops had been sent in to bring the East Pakistanis back into line, causing a mass exodus of refugees into India. Gandhi astutely waited until she had the moral support of the international community before launching -simultaneous attacks in West and East Pakistan on December 4. By December 15, Pakistani forces in Bangladesh had capitulated.

Back at home, Gandhi was proving less successful. After widespread agrarian and industrial unrest against the rate of inflation and corruption within the Congress Party, she declared a **State of Emergency** on June 26, 1975, suspending all civil rights, censoring the press and imprisoning some twenty thousand of her opponents, real or imagined. The "Emergency" lasted eighteen months, characterized by the enforced sterilization of millions of men from deprived communities and brutal slum-clearances in Delhi and elsewhere. When she finally released her opponents and called off the Emergency in January 1977, the bitterness she had engendered resulted in her ignominious defeat in the March elections. The ensuing **Janata** coalition under Morarji Desai fell apart within two years, and his premiership was terminated by a vote of no confidence in 1979. Gandhi, now apparently forgiven, swept back into office in January 1980.

Four years afterwards, Gandhi made the second, fatal, mistake of her career. A group of rebels demanding a separate Sikh nation – Khalistan – took control of the **Golden Temple** in Amritsar early in 1984, from where they organized a campaign of violence, killing hundreds of Hindus and moderate Sikhs. Gandhi sent in the tanks in June 1984, but two days of raging combat desecrated the Sikhs' holiest shrine as well as giving Khalistan its first martyrs. In October that year, Gandhi's Sikh bodyguards took revenge by assassinating her at her house in Delhi. The city was then engulfed in massive communal **rioting**, during which Hindu mobs went about Delhi systematically murdering Sikhs – according to some reports locating their victims with the help of electoral rolls supplied by Congress politicians.

Communal conflict (1984–95)

Following Gandhi's death, it was left to her sole surviving son, **Rajiv Gandhi** (a former pilot), to take up leadership of Congress. He came to power in December 1984 on a wave of sympathy boosted by his reputation as "Mr Clean", an image given added meaning by the **Bhopal** gas tragedy (see page 349) just two weeks before the elections. The opposition subsequently rallied under the leadership of **V.P. Singh**. Elections in 1989 did not give Singh's Janata Party a majority, but he managed to form a coalition government with the support of the "Hindu first" Bharatiya Janata Party, or **BJP**, led by **L.K. Advani**.

Singh was immediately confronted by problems in the Punjab and Kashmir, but it was an even more emotive issue that brought down his government in less than a year. Advani's populist BJP were demanding that the Babri Masjid mosque in **Ayodhya**, built by Babur on the supposed site of the birthplace of Rama, god-hero of the

Oct 31, 1984	1984	Dec 3, 1984
Indira Gandhi's Sikh bodyguards take revenge by shooting dead the prime minister, unleashing a communal bloodbath.	Rajiv Gandhi, Indira's eldest son, succeeds his mother and initiates a period of sweeping economic reforms.	2200 die after toxic gas escapes from an American-owned fertilizer plant in Bhopal, Madhya Pradesh.

Ramayana, should be replaced by a Hindu temple. Advani set off towards Ayodhya in October 1990, accompanied by thousands of supporters, with the avowed intention of destroying the mosque. Singh ordered Advani's arrest, and the inevitable withdrawal of the BJP from his coalition government resulted in a vote of no confidence.

New elections were called. Shortly afterwards, while campaigning in Tamil Nadu in May 1991, Rajiv Gandhi was assassinated by Tamil Tigers seeking revenge for India's military opposition to their "freedom fight" in Sri Lanka. It was left to **P.V. Narasimha Rao** to steer Congress through the elections and form a new coalition government, which immediately embarked on a far-reaching programme of **economic liberalization**, dismantling trade barriers and allowing Western multinationals to enter the Indian market for the first time.

At the same time, the BJP increased its seats in the Lok Sabha (the Lower House of Parliament) from eighty to 120 and Advani became leader of the opposition, amid growing popular support for the rebuilding of Rama's temple in Ayodhya. The situation finally came to a head in December 1992, as Hindu extremists incited crowds of fanatical devotees to tear down the Babri Masjid at Ayodhya in a blaze of publicity. The demolition was followed by terrible **riots** in many parts of the country, especially Bombay and Gujarat, where Muslim families and businesses were targeted. A few months later, a massive series of bomb blasts ripped through **Bombay**, killing 260 people and destroying some of the city's most important commercial buildings. No one claimed responsibility, though the attacks were thought to have been orchestrated by Islamic groups in retaliation for Hindu violence against their fellow Muslims.

Against this backdrop of uncertainty, the rise of right-wing Hindu-fundamentalist parties gathered pace. The BJP took advantage of the power struggle in the Congress Party to rekindle regional support. Their new rallying cry was **Swadeshi** – a campaign against the Congress-led programme of economic liberalization and, in particular, the activities of newly arrived companies such as Coca-Cola, Pepsi and KFC.

The rise of the BJP (1996–2004)

The BJP emerged from the **general election** of May 1996 as the single largest party but were unable to muster a majority and were ousted a couple of weeks later by the hastily formed **Unified Front (UF)** coalition. The UF soldiered on until March 1998, after which the **BJP** finally struggled to power as the head of a new conservative coalition government under **Atal Bihari Vajpayee**.

This time, the party managed to stay in office for thirteen months, as opposed to the thirteen days of its previous spell in government. The BJP had promised change and the restoration of national pride, and one of its early acts in government was to conduct five underground **nuclear tests** in May 1998, provoking Pakistan to respond in kind. There was a chorus of world criticism, and US-led financial **sanctions** were imposed on both nations.

Ongoing tensions in **Kashmir** did little to calm local and international fears. In May 1999, at least eight hundred Pakistani-backed mujahedeen crept across the so-called Line of Control (the de facto border) overlooking the Srinagar–Leh road near **Kargil** and began to occupy Indian territory. India moved thousands of troops into the area,

May 21, 1991	1992	Dec 1992–Jan 1993
Rajiv Gandhi assassinated by Tamil Tiger suicide bomber while campaigning near Chennai.	A mob of Hindu extremists destroy the Babri Masjid mosque in Ayodhya, sparking riots and killings across India.	Scores die in a spate of communal disturbances in Bombay. Terrible reprisal bombings take place two months later.

and within days the two countries were poised on the brink of all-out war. In the event the conflict was contained, and by July 1999 the Indian army had retaken all the ground previously lost to the militants.

Shortly afterwards, the Congress Party, reinvigorated under the leadership of **Sonia Gandhi**, the Italian-born widow of the former prime minister Rajiv, collaborated with the Jayalalitha's AIADMK to bring about the downfall of the BJP government. At the start of the campaign, Congress hopes were high that, with a Gandhi once again as party leader, it could revive the popular support lost after years of infighting and corruption scandals. Unfortunately for them, the wave of **patriotism** that swept India after the Kargil victory in Kashmir was a godsend for Vajpayee (cynics argued it may well have been the hidden policy behind the army's uncompromising response to the crisis). Riding high on the feel-good factor, his party inflicted the biggest defeat Congress had sustained since 1947.

At the end of 2000, Vajpayee announced the **creation of three new states:** Jharkhand, Chhattisgarh and Uttaranchal (later changing its name to Uttarakhand), carved out of Bihar, Madhya Pradesh and Uttar Pradesh respectively.

Meanwhile, the wider world started to become aware of India's burgeoning **high-tech revolution**, centred at first on **Bangalore** which, by the mid-1990s had become a major player in the international software market. Its pre-eminence was challenged at the turn of the millennium by the even more spectacular emergence of **Hyderabad** (nicknamed "Cyberabad"), and more recently by Delhi's satellite cities of Gurgaon and Noida. Unfortunately, the rural poor see little of this newly generated wealth, exacerbating the wealth gap, which commentators quickly christened the "digital divide".

To the brink of war

During late 2001, **Indo-Pak relations** and the Kashmiri question returned to the fore as India entered one of the most volatile periods in its history. In October, the **State Assembly building in Srinagar** was destroyed by Islamist suicide car-bombers, and then in December, three Muslim gunmen stormed the **Parliament Building** in New Delhi, killing several police guards before they were picked off by army marksmen. Pakistani involvement was inevitably suspected. Then, in early 2002, a Muslim mob in **Godhra**, Gujarat, attacked a trainload of Hindu activists returning from Ayodhya: 38 died and 74 were injured. In the reprisal killings that followed, around two thousand people (mostly Muslims) were slaughtered.

Anti-Muslim sentiment was further fuelled only a month later when an Islamist suicide squad commandeered a tourist bus and used it to attack the **Kaluchak** army cantonment near Jammu. Coming hot on the heels of yet another promise by Pakistan to clamp down on cross-border militancy, the atrocity provoked outrage in Delhi. Vajpayee, bowing to the hawks on the right of his party, called for a "decisive battle", initiating a massive build-up of troops on the border. An estimated million men at arms were involved in the ensuing standoff as India and Pakistan edged to the brink of war, until US diplomacy diffused the crisis.

In 2003, the Archaeological Survey of India released its long-awaited **report on Ayodhya**. To no one's surprise, the ASI panel of "experts", appointed by the BJP government, declared they'd found evidence to show there had been a temple, in effect condoning the tearing down of the mosque.

May 1996	**May 11, 1998**	**1999**	**Jan 26, 2001**
A far-right Hindu nationalist party, the BJP, wins the general election.	India detonates its first atomic bomb. Pakistan follows suit soon after.	India and Pakistan on the brink of war after insurgents occupy Kargil, in Ladakh.	20,000 die and 167,000 are injured after a massive earthquake devastates northwest Gujarat on India's Independence Day.

The return of Congress (2004–2014)

Despite continuing sectarian troubles, with India booming as never before, Vajpayee and his BJP-led coalition decided to cash in on the perceived feel-good factor and call a snap **election** in **May 2004**. Congress gained the largest share of the vote and **Sonia Gandhi** was duly invited to form a government, but stunned supporters by "humbly declining" the invitation and stepping down. Former finance minister, 71-year-old **Manmohan Singh**, stepped into the breach and was named as prime minister, the first Sikh to lead the country. As the architect of the important liberalizing economic reforms enacted during the early 1990s, Singh seemed like the perfect candidate to oversee India's continuing economic and technological growth. In April 2007 the country launched its first commercial space rocket, and the following month saw the government announce the strongest economic growth figures (an impressive 9.4 percent) for twenty years.

Terrorist violence continued to plague the country, however. A series of bomb attacks in 2005–2007 culminated in November 2008 with the "26/11" coordinated assaults by Pakistani gunmen in Mumbai, who murdered 164 people. Images of the burning *Taj Palace* hotel and the blood-spattered concourse of CST station were beamed live around the world, producing global outrage, and raising questions about India's security.

Elections in 2009 were won by a Congress-led coalition, with Manmohan Singh becoming the first Indian leader since Nehru in 1952 to be returned directly to power after a five-year term. At the end of the year, the government announced that it would agree to the secession of a new state, **Telangana**, from Andhra Pradesh. Strong opposition delayed the move, but in 2014 Andhra Pradesh was formally split and Telangana became India's 29th state.

Meanwhile, a series of **corruption scandals** emerged in 2010–11 (notably around India's hosting of the Commonwealth Games), and undermined confidence in the administration. Protests at the abysmal standards in public life and regular misappropriation of government funds coalesced around a social activist from Maharashtra, **Anna Hazare**, who staged a series of high-profile, Gandhian-style hunger strikes to lobby for a strengthening of anti-corruption legislation. A watered-down anti-corruption law in 2011 took the sting out of the movement but the plight of India's poor, the big losers in every government corruption case, remained centre-stage in 2012, as more than a hundred thousand peasant farmers marched to Delhi from all over the country to lobby for greater land rights.

Fears over India's **faltering economy** dominated the news in late 2012, as growth rates remained stubbornly sluggish at just over 6 percent. Those who identified corruption and government inefficiency as the culprits felt vindicated after a massive electricity blackout in July paralyzed the country, leaving 700 million people without power.

The yawning gulf between middle-class-urban and rural-peasant India was underlined by the **Delhi rape case** in 2012, when a young student died after being brutally gang raped on a bus (see page 74). Galvanized by the atrocity, people poured on to the streets protesting at police indifference to sexual violence and poor treatment generally of women in India. Demonstrations across the country garnered worldwide media attention. Yet when, just weeks later, the bodies of three young girls were discovered in a Maharashtran village well, a veil of silence seemed to fall over the

Dec 2001	2008	Nov 2008	2010
Islamist gunmen attack the Indian parliament building in protest at the government's Kashmir policy.	Tata launch the US$2500 "Nano", the world's cheapest car.	Terrorists launch a bloody attack on Mumbai; 164 die.	Growth rates exceed ten percent as the Indian economy goes into overdrive despite recession elsewhere in the world.

Indian media. Only after local mothers blocked the national highway did the police mount an investigation, in the course of which tests proved the girls had been raped before being murdered.

Return of the BJP (2014–)

The **general election** of 2014 resulted in a landslide victory for the BJP, led by former – and controversial – Gujarat chief minister **Narendra Modi**, who now became prime minister. The anti-corruption movement had largely fizzled out, although the Aam Aadmi Party that arose out of it did well in Delhi and the Punjab. Seen as more business-friendly than Congress, the BJP launched initiatives such as the Digital India programme, designed to roll out internet access and increase the number of IT industry jobs. Falling oil prices helped the Indian economy, and a slowdown in China from the end of 2015 allowed India to outstrip its neighbour in economic growth, keeping it on course to become the world's third largest economy (after the US and China) by around 2035. The fall in inflation enabled the national government to cut subsidies on energy and agriculture, but for the poor, life remains hard. A hike in the price of lentils, for example – a basic staple food for the majority – forced several state governments in 2015 to import and sell lentils from abroad at subsidized prices. The following year, in a surprise move, the government controversially withdrew ₹500 and ₹1000 notes from circulation. Ministers claimed this would help to tackle corruption, yet all it seemed to do was spark chaos. In 2017, the government quietly admitted that economic growth had slowed as a result (though it remained at a healthy 7.5 percent in 2018).

Despite the strength of the economy and a burgeoning middle-class, grinding **poverty** continues to blight the lives of millions in rural and urban India. As of 2018, around 71 million Indians lived in absolute poverty, though rates are declining. This is far from the only challenge the country faces. The rise of the BJP has been accompanied by increasing **sectarian sentiment** – and sometimes violence – directed largely against Muslims, but also against other religious minorities, most notably Christians, as well as secular voices, human rights activists and journalists. And while the Telangana question may have been settled, **agitation for statehood and secession** continues in several areas, including Kashmir, North Bengal and the Northeast, while the Naxalite (Maoist guerrilla) insurgency across central India, though reduced to some extent, has not gone away. **Gender inequality** is also a huge problem, and sex-selective abortions are actually most prevalent in affluent states such as Haryana. Among the country's urban middle classes, the status of women, both at home and in the workplace has improved greatly since Independence, but in rural areas the lot of women has improved little, with domestic violence and rape still horrifyingly commonplace and rarely punished. One positive piece of news, however, has been in the realm of LGBTQ rights, with a landmark Supreme Court ruling in September 2018 overturning a colonial-era ban on homosexuality.

Meanwhile, the always volatile relationship with **Pakistan** is a source of uncertainty, and the threat from Islamic militants remains alive and well. Tensions between the two countries threaten to boil over into all-out war during a tense stand-off in early 2019, but the situation was eventually diffused. Relations with another neighbour,

Dec 2012–Feb 2013	May 2014	November 2016
Crowds take to the streets across the country to express outrage at the rape and murder of a young student on a moving bus in Delhi.	BJP wins overall Lok Sabha majority in the general election.	The Modi government withdraws ₹500 and ₹1000 notes from circulation, sparking chaos across India.

Nepal, were blighted by what the Nepalis saw as an economic blockade of the country by Modi's administration. Increasingly, Nepal is turning to China for help.

India's economic boom, far from alleviating the plight of the poorest, seems only to have increased **disparities in wealth.** Whether the country can continue to evolve at its present pace and achieve its longed-for position on the global stage will be determined not merely by the power of its economy, but also by the extent to which it is able to balance the needs of rich and poor, and curb the corruption endemic in public life. Whether the state can meet these challenges, along with those of sectarian strife, secessionism and gender inequality remains to be seen, but it is nonetheless apparent that, in the long term, and despite the serious challenges it faces, India is still on the up.

In May 2019, the BJP won a landslide victory at the **general election,** increasing their majority in the Lok Sabha (parliament's lower house), from 282 to 303. In doing so, Narendra Modi became the first Indian prime minister since 1971 to win a single-party majority at two consecutive elections. The failure of the Indian National Congress to secure a minimum ten percent of the seats in the Lok Sahba means that India is without an official opposition party. The turnout was over 67 percent, the highest in the country's history; a record number of women participated in the elections too. With over 900 million people eligible to vote, the 2019 Indian general elections were – in theory – the largest democratic exercise in history.

September 2018	February 2019	May 2019
In a groundbreaking ruling, the Supreme Court decriminalises homosexuality.	India and Pakistan engage in a tense stand-off, following a suicide attack that killed over forty Indian security personnel.	Narendra Modi's BJP win a landslide victory in the general election.

Religion

Four out of five Indians are Hindus, and Hinduism permeates every aspect of life in the country, from the commonplace details of daily life up to national politics. After Hindus, Muslims are the largest religious group, and have been an integral part of Indian society since the twelfth century. The more recently established Sikh faith was founded in reaction to the caste laws and ritual observances of Hinduism and now boasts millions of adherents. The far older Jain religion also still commands a sizeable following, and there are also small communities of Buddhists, Christians, Iranian-descended Zoroastrians, or Parsis, together with more than two million members of the Baha'í Faith.

Hinduism

Hinduism is the product of several thousand years of evolution and assimilation. It has no founder or prophet, no single creed, and no single prescribed practice or doctrine; it takes in hundreds of gods, goddesses, beliefs and practices, and widely variant cults and philosophies. Some are recognized by only two or three villages, others are popular right across the Subcontinent. Hindus call their beliefs and practices **dharma**, which defines a way of living in harmony with natural and moral law while fulfilling personal goals and meeting the requirements of society.

The Vedic age

The origins of Hinduism date back to the arrival of the **Aryans** (see page 1185). The Aryans believed in a number of gods associated with the elements, including **Agni**, the god of fire, **Surya**, the sun god, and **Indra**, the chief god. Most of these deities faded in importance in later times, but Indra is still regarded as the father of the gods, and Surya was widely worshipped until the medieval period.

Aryan religious beliefs were first set down in a series of four books, the **Vedas** (from the Sanskrit word *veda*, meaning "knowledge"). Transmitted orally for centuries, the Vedas were finally written down, in Sanskrit, between 1000 BC and 500 AD. The earliest and most important of the four Vedas, the **Rig Veda**, contains more than a thousand hymns to various deities, while the other three (the Yajur Veda, Sama Veda and Atharva Veda) contain further prayers, chants and instructions for performing the complex sacrificial rituals associated with this early Vedic religion.

The Vedas were followed by further religious texts, including the **Brahmanas**, a series of commentaries on the Vedas for the use of priests (brahmins) and, more importantly, the **Upanishads**, which describe in beautiful and emotive verse the mystic experience of unity of the soul (*atman*) with Brahma, the absolute creator of the universe, ideally attained through asceticism, renunciation of worldly values and meditation. In the Upanishads the concepts of **samsara**, a cyclic round of death and rebirth characterized by suffering and perpetuated by desire, and **moksha**, liberation from *samsara*, became firmly rooted. As fundamental aspects of the Hindu world view, both are accepted by all but a handful of Hindus today, along with the belief in **karma**, the certainty that one's present position in society is determined by the effect of one's previous actions in this and past lives.

Hindu society

The stratification of Hindu society is rooted in the **Dharma Sutras**, a further collection of scriptures written at roughly the same time as the later Vedas. These defined four

THE MAHABHARATA AND THE RAMAYANA

Eight times as long as the *Iliad* and *Odyssey* combined, the **Mahabharata** was written around 400 AD and tells of a feuding kshatriya family in northern India during the fourth millennium BC. The chief character is **Arjuna**, who, with his four brothers, represents the **Pandava** clan, supreme fighters and upholders of righteousness. The Pandava clan are resented by their cousins, the evil **Kauravas**, led by Duryodhana, the eldest son of Dhrtarashtra, ruler of the Kuru kingdom.

When Dhrtarashtra hands his kingdom over to the Pandavas, the Kauravas are understandably less than overjoyed. The subsequent battle between the Pandavas and Kauravas is described in the sixth book, the famous **Bhagavad Gita**. Krishna steps into battle as Arjuna's charioteer. Arjuna is in a dilemma, unable to justify the killing of his own kin in pursuit of a rightful kingdom. Krishna consoles him, reminding him that his principal duty is as a warrior, and convincing him that by fulfilling his dharma he not only upholds law and order by saving the kingdom from the grasp of unrighteous rulers, he also serves the gods in the spirit of devotion and thus guarantees himself eternal union with the divine in the blissful state of *moksha*.

The Pandavas finally win the battle and Yudhishtra, one of the five Pandava brothers, is crowned king. Eventually Arjuna's grandson, Pariksit, inherits the throne, and the Pandavas trek to Mount Meru, the mythical centre of the universe and the abode of the gods, where Arjuna finds Krishna's promised *moksha*.

THE RAMAYANA

The Ramayana tells the story of **Rama**, the seventh of Vishnu's eight incarnations. Rama is the oldest of four sons born to Dasaratha, the king of Ayodhya, and heir to the throne. When the time comes for Rama's coronation, Dasaratha's scheming third wife Kaikeyi has her own son Bharata crowned instead, and has Rama banished to the forest for fourteen years. In an exemplary show of filial piety, Rama accepts the loss of his throne and leaves the city with his wife Sita and brother Laksmana.

One day, Suparnakhi, the sister of the demon **Ravana**, spots Rama in the woods and instantly falls in love with him. Being a virtuous husband, Rama rebuffs her advances, while Laksmana cuts off her nose and ears in retaliation. In revenge, Ravana kidnaps Sita, who is borne away to one of Ravana's palaces on the island of **Lanka**.

Determined to find Sita, Rama enlists the help of the monkey god **Hanuman**, and the two of them gather an army and prepare to attack. After much fighting, Sita is rescued and reunited with her husband. On the long journey back to Ayodhya, Sita's honour is brought into question. To prove her innocence, she asks Laksmana to build a funeral pyre and steps into the flames, praying to Agni, the fire god. Agni walks her through the fire into the arms of a delighted Rama. They march into Ayodhya guided by a trail of lights laid out by the local people. Today, this illuminated homecoming is commemorated by Hindus all over the world during **Diwali**, the festival of lights. At the end of the epic, Rama's younger brother gladly steps down, allowing Rama to be crowned as the rightful king.

hierarchical classes, or **varnas** (from *varna*, meaning "colour", perhaps a reference to difference in appearance between the lighter-skinned Aryans and the darker indigenous Dravidian population). Each *varna* was assigned specific religious and social duties, with Aryans established as the highest social class. In descending order the *varnas* are: **brahmins** (priests and teachers), **kshatriyas** (rulers and warriors), **vaishyas** (merchants and cultivators) and **shudras** (menials). The first three classes, known as "twice-born", are distinguished by a sacred thread worn from the time of initiation, and are granted full access to religious texts and rituals. Below all four categories, groups whose jobs involve contact with dirt or death (such as undertakers, leather-workers and cleaners) were classified as **untouchables** or **dalits** (*dalit* meaning oppressed). Though discrimination against *dalits* is now a criminal offence, in part thanks to the campaigns of Mahatma Gandhi, they continue to face extreme prejudice.

Within the four *varnas*, social status is further defined by **jati**, classifying each individual in terms of their family and job (for example, a *vaishya* may be a jewellery seller, cloth merchant, cowherd or farmer). A person's *jati* determines his **caste**, and lays restrictions on all aspects of life from what sort of food he can eat, religious obligations and contact with other castes, to the choice of marriage partners. There are almost three thousand *jatis*; the divisions and restrictions they have enforced have repeatedly been the target of reform movements and critics.

A Hindu has three **aims in life**: to fulfil his social and religious duties (dharma); to follow the correct path in his work and actions (*karma*); and to gain material wealth (*artha*). These goals are linked with the four traditional stages in life. The first is as a child and student, devoted to learning from parents and guru. Next comes the stage of householder, expected to provide for a family and raise children. That accomplished, he may then take up a life of celibacy and retreat into the forest to meditate alone, and finally renounce all possessions to become a homeless ascetic, hoping to achieve the ultimate goal of *moksha*. The small number of Hindus who follow this ideal life assume the final stage as saffron-clad **sadhus** who wander throughout India, begging for food and retreating to isolated caves, forests and hills to meditate. They're a common feature in most Indian towns and many stay for long periods in particular temples. Not all have raised families: some assume the life of a sadhu at an early age as *chellas*, pupils of an older sadhu.

The main deities

Alongside the Vedas and Upanishads, the most important Hindu religious texts are the **Puranas** – long mythological stories about the Vedic gods – and the two great epics, the **Mahabharata** and **Ramayana** (see page 1206), thought to have been completed by the first century AD, though subsequently retold, modified and embellished on numerous occasions and in various different regional languages. The Puranas and the two great epics helped crystallize the basic framework of Hindu religious belief, which survives to this day, based on a supreme triumvirate of deities. **Brahma**, the original Aryan godhead, or "creator", was joined by two gods who had begun to achieve increasing significance in the evolving Hindu world-view. The first, **Vishnu**, "the preserver", was seen as the force responsible for maintaining the balance of the cosmos whenever it was threatened by disruptive forces, incarnating himself on earth nine times in various animal and human forms, or avatars, to fight the forces of evil and chaos, most famously as Rama (the god-hero whose exploits are described in the Ramayana) and as Krishna (who appears at the most significant juncture of the Mahabharata). The second, **Shiva**, "the destroyer" (a development of the Aryan god Rudra, who had played a minor role in the Vedas), was charged with destroying and renewing the universe at periodic intervals, though his powers are not merely destructive, and he is worshipped in myriad forms with various attributes. The three supreme gods are often depicted in a trinity, or *trimurti*, though in time Brahma's importance declined, and Shiva and Vishnu became the most popular deities – the famous Brahma temple at Pushkar is now one of the few in India dedicated to this venerable but rather esoteric god.

Depicted in human or semi-human form and accompanied by an animal "vehicle", other gods and goddesses who came alive in the mythology of the Puranas are still venerated across India. River goddesses, ancestors, guardians of particular places and protectors against disease and natural disaster are as central to village life as the major deities.

Practice and pilgrimage

In most Hindu homes, a chosen deity is worshipped daily in a shrine room. Outside the home, worship takes place in temples and consists of **puja** – sometimes a simple act of prayer, but more commonly a complex process when the god's image is circumambulated, offered flowers, rice, sugar and incense, and anointed with water, milk or sandalwood paste (which is usually done on behalf of the devotee by the temple priest). The aim in puja is to take **darshan** – glimpse the god – and thus receive his or

HINDU GODS AND GODDESSES

VISHNU

With four arms holding a conch, discus, lotus and mace, **Vishnu** is blue-skinned, and often shaded by a serpent, or resting on its coils, afloat on an ocean. He is usually seen alongside his half-man-half-eagle vehicle, Garuda. **Vaishnavites**, often distinguishable by two vertical lines of paste on their foreheads, recognize Vishnu as supreme lord, and hold that he has manifested himself on earth nine times. The most important avatars are **Rama** and **Krishna**, the hero of the Bhagavad Gita. The cult of Krishna evolved into the popular *bhakti* movement – the attempt to achieve *moksha* through devotion to god, and without the intercession of officiating brahmin priests, finding expression in emotional songs concerning the quest for union with the divine. Krishna is represented in various ways: most popularly he is shown as the playful cowherd who seduces and dances with cowgirls (*gopis*), giving each the illusion that she is his only lover. He is also pictured as a small, chubby, mischievous baby, known for his butter-stealing exploits. Like Vishnu, Krishna is blue, and often shown dancing and playing the flute.

SHIVA

Shaivism, the cult of **Shiva**, was also inspired by *bhakti*, requiring selfless love from devotees in a quest for divine communion, but Shiva has never been incarnate on earth. He is presented in many different aspects, such as **Nataraja**, Lord of the Dance, **Mahadev**, Great God, and **Maheshvar**, Divine Lord, source of all knowledge. Though he does have several terrible forms, his role extends beyond that of destroyer, and he is revered as the source of the whole universe.

Shiva is often depicted with four or more faces, holding a trident, draped with serpents, and bearing a third eye in his forehead. In temples, he is identified with the lingam, or phallic symbol, resting in the yoni, a representation of female sexuality. Whether as statue or lingam, Shiva is accompanied by his bull-mount, Nandi, and often by a consort, who also assumes various forms, and is looked upon as the vital energy, **shakti**, that empowers him.

While Shiva is the object of popular devotion all over India, as the terrible **Bhairav** he is also the god of the Shaivite **ascetics**, who renounce family and caste ties and perform extreme meditative and yogic practices.

OTHER GODS AND GODDESSES

Chubby and smiling, elephant-headed **Ganesh**, the first son of Shiva and Parvati, is invoked before every undertaking (except funerals). Seated on a throne or lotus, his image is often placed above temple gateways, in shops and houses; in his four arms he holds a conch, discus, bowl of sweets (or club) and a water lily, and he's always attended by his vehicle, a rat. Ganesh is regarded by many as the god of learning, the lord of success, prosperity and peace.

Durga, the fiercest of the female deities, is an aspect of Shiva's more conservative consort, Parvati (also known as Uma), who is remarkable only for her beauty and fidelity. Among Durga's many aspects, each a terrifying goddess eager to slay demons, are Chamunda, Kali and Muktakeshi, but in all her forms she is Mahadevi (Great Goddess). Statues show her with ten arms, holding the head of a demon, a spear and other weapons; she tramples demons underfoot, or dances upon Shiva's body.

The comely goddess **Lakshmi**, Vishnu's consort, is usually shown sitting or standing on a lotus flower, and sometimes called Padma (lotus). Lakshmi is the embodiment of loveliness and grace, and the goddess of prosperity and wealth. She appears in different aspects alongside each of Vishnu's avatars, including Sita, wife of Rama, and Radha, Krishna's favourite *gopi*. In many temples she is shown as one with Vishnu, in the form of Lakshmi Narayan.

India's great monkey god, **Hanuman**, features in the Ramayana as Rama's chief aide in the fight against the demon-king of Lanka. Depicted as a giant monkey clasping a mace, Hanuman is seen as Rama and Sita's greatest devotee – as his representatives, monkeys find sanctuary in temples all over India.

The most beautiful Hindu goddess, **Saraswati**, the wife of Brahma, sits or stands on a water lily or peacock, playing a lute, sitar or *vina*. She is revered as the goddess of music, creativity and learning.

Closely linked with the planet Saturn, **Shani** is feared for his destructive powers. His image, a black statue with protruding blood-red tongue, is often found on street corners; strings of green chillies and lemon are hung in shops and houses each Saturday (*Saniwar*) to ward off his evil influences.

her blessing. Worshippers leave the temple with *prasad*, an offering of food or flowers taken from the holy sanctuary. **Temple ceremonies** are conducted by priests who tend the image in daily rituals in which the god is symbolically woken, bathed, fed, dressed and, at the end of each day, put back to bed. In many villages, shrines to *devatas*, village deities who function as protectors, are more important than temples.

Strict rules address **purity and pollution**, the most obvious of them requiring high-caste Hindus to limit their contact with potentially polluting lower castes. Above all else, **water** is the agent of purification, used in ablutions before prayer and revered in all rivers, especially Ganga (the Ganges). *Ghat*s, steps leading to the water's edge, are common in all river- or lakeside towns, used for bathing, washing clothes and performing religious rituals.

India also has a wealth of **pilgrimage** sites visited by devotees eager to receive *darshan* and attain merit.

Islam

Muslims – some fourteen percent of the population – form a significant presence in almost every town, city and village. The belief in only one god, Allah, the condemnation of idol worship and the observance of their own strict dietary laws and specific festivals all set Muslims apart from their Hindu neighbours, with whom they have coexisted, not always peacefully, for centuries.

The first Muslims to settle in India were traders who arrived on the southwest coast in the seventh century. Much more significant was the invasion of north India under **Mahmud of Ghazni** (see page 1191), while more raids from Central Asia followed in the twelfth century, resulting in the partial colonization of India, while the invading Muslims set themselves up in Delhi as sultans.

Many Muslims who settled in India intermarried with Hindus, Buddhists and Jains, and the community spread. A further factor in its growth was missionary activity by **Sufis**, who stressed the attainment of inner knowledge of God through meditation and mystical experience. Their use of music, particularly *qawwali* singing, and dance, shunned by orthodox Muslims, appealed to Hindus, for whom singing played an important role in religious practice. Muslims are enjoined to pray five times daily. They may do this at home or in a **mosque** – always full at noon on Friday, for communal prayer (the only exception being the Druze of Mumbai, who hold communal prayers on Thursday).

The position of **women** in Islam is a subject of great debate. It's customary for women to be veiled – though in larger cities many women don't cover their heads – and in strictly orthodox communities most wear a *burqa*, usually black, that covers them from head to toe. Like other Indian women, Muslim women take second place to men in public, but in the home they wield great influence. Contrary to popular belief, polygamy is not widespread and, while it does occur, several sects actually stress monogamy as a duty. In marriage, women receive a dowry as financial security.

Buddhism

Buddhism was born on the Indian Subcontinent, developing as an offshoot of – and a reaction to – Hinduism, with which it shares many assumptions about the nature of existence. For a time it became the dominant religion in the country, though from around the fourth century AD onwards it was gradually eclipsed by a resurgent Hinduism (which cleverly re-appropriated the Buddha, claiming him to be an incarnation of Vishnu), and the subsequent arrival of Islam more or less finished it off. Today Buddhists make up only a tiny fraction of the population – outside north India's numerous Tibetan refugee camps, only Ladakh and Sikkim now preserve a significant Buddhist presence.

The founder of Buddhism, **Siddhartha Gautama**, known as the **Buddha** ("awakened one"), was born into a wealthy kshatriya family in Lumbini, north of the Gangetic plain in present-day Nepal, around 566 BC. Brought up in luxury as a prince, he married at an early age, but renounced family life when he was 30. Unsatisfied with the explanations of worldly suffering proposed by religious gurus, and convinced that asceticism did not lead to spiritual realization, Siddhartha spent years wandering the countryside and meditating. His enlightenment is said to have taken place under a *bodhi* tree in **Bodhgaya** (Bihar). Soon afterwards he gave his first sermon in **Sarnath**, near Varanasi. For the rest of his life he taught, expounding **dharma**, the true nature of the world, human life and spiritual attainment. Before his death (c.486 BC) in Kushinagara (UP), he had established the **Sangha**, a community of monks and nuns who continued his teachings.

The Buddha's world-view incorporated the Hindu concept of *samsara*, and *karma* and *moksha*, which Buddhists call **nirvana** (literally "no wind"). The most important concept outlined by the Buddha was that all things are subject to the inevitability of **impermanence**. There is no independent inherent self, due to the interconnectedness of all things, and our egos are the biggest obstacles on the road to enlightenment.

Tibetan Buddhism

Buddhism was introduced to **Tibet** in the seventh century AD, and integrated to a certain extent with the indigenous **Bon** cult. Practised largely in Ladakh, along with parts of Himachal Pradesh and Sikkim, Tibetan Buddhism recognizes the historical Buddha alongside a host of other Buddhas past and to come, and incorporates elaborate rituals into its worship. There is also a heavy emphasis on teachers, known as lamas, and reincarnated teachers, known as *tulkus*. The **Dalai Lama**, the head of Tibetan Buddhism, is the fourteenth in a succession of incarnate *bodhisattvas*, the representative of Avalokitesvara (the *bodhisattva* of compassion), and the leader of the exiled Tibetan community based in Dharamsala. With as many as 150,000 Tibetan **refugees** now living in India, including the Dalai Lama and the Tibetan government in exile, Tibetan Buddhism is probably the most accessible and flourishing form of Buddhism in India, and there are numerous opportunities for study. Tibetan Buddhist devotees hang prayer flags, turn prayer wheels, and set stones carved with mantras (religious verses) in rivers, thus sending the word of the Buddha with wind and water to all corners of the earth.

Jainism

The number of **Jains** in India is small – accounting for less than one percent of the population – but has been tremendously influential for at least 2500 years. A large proportion of Jains live in Gujarat, and all over India they are commonly found working as merchants and traders. Similarities to Hinduism, and a shared respect for nature and nonviolence, have contributed to the decline of the Jain community through conversion to Hinduism, but there is no antagonism between the two religions.

Focused on the practice of **ahimsa** (non-violence), Jains follow a rigorous discipline to avoid harm to all **jivas**, or "souls", which exist in humans, animals, plants, water, fire, earth and air. They assert that every *jiva* is pure and capable of achieving liberation from existence in this universe. However, *jivas* are obscured by **karma**, a form of subtle matter that clings to the soul, which is born of action and binds the *jiva* to physical existence. For the most orthodox Jain, the only way to dissociate *karma* from the *jiva* is to follow the path of asceticism and meditation, rejecting passion, attachment and impure action.

The Jain doctrine is based upon the teachings of **Mahavira**, or "Great Hero", the last in a succession of 24 **tirthankaras** ("crossing-makers") said to appear on earth every 300 million years. Mahavira (c.599–527 BC) was born as Vardhamana Jnatrputra into a kshatriya family near modern Patna. Like his near-contemporary the Buddha,

Mahavira rejected family life at the age of 30 and spent years wandering as an ascetic in an attempt to conquer attachment to worldly values.

His teachings were written down in the first millennium BC and Jainism prospered throughout India. Not long after, there was a schism. On the one hand the **Digambaras** ("sky-clad") believed that nudity was an essential part of world renunciation, and that women are incapable of achieving liberation from worldly existence. The **Svetambaras** ("white-clad"), however, disregarded the extremes of nudity, incorporated nuns into monastic communities and even acknowledged a female *tirthankara*. Today the two sects worship at different temples, but the number of naked Digambaras is minimal. Many Svetambara monks and nuns wear white masks to avoid breathing in insects, and carry a "fly-whisk", sometimes used to brush their path; none will use public transport and they often spend days or weeks walking barefoot to a pilgrimage site.

Sikhism

Sikhism, India's youngest religion, remains dominant in the Punjab, while its adherents have spread throughout northern India. The movement was founded by **Guru Nanak** (1469–1539), who was born into an orthodox Hindu kshatriya family near Lahore. Nanak was among many sixteenth-century poet-philosophers, sometimes referred to as *sants*, who formed emotional cults, drawing elements from both Hinduism and Islam. Nanak declared that "God is neither Hindu nor Muslim and the path which I follow is God's"; he regarded God as **Sat**, or truth, who makes himself known through gurus. Though he condemned the rituals of brahmins, Nanak did not attack Islam or Hinduism – he simply regarded the many deities as names for one supreme God, and encouraged his followers to shift religious emphasis from ritual to meditation. In common with Hindus, Nanak believed in a cyclic process of death and rebirth (*samsara*), but asserted that liberation (*moksha*) was attainable in this life by all women and men regardless of caste, and that religious practice could and should be integrated into everyday practical living.

Guru Nanak was succeeded by **Guru Angad**, who continued to lead the community of Sikhs (literally, "disciples"), the so-called **Sikh Panth**, and wrote his own and Nanak's hymns in a new script, **Gurumukhi**, which is today used as the script of written Punjabi. Eight further gurus successively led the Sikh Panth after Guru Angad's death in 1552, gradually developing Sikhism into a powerful independent religious movement. **Guru Ram Das** (1552–74) founded the sacred city of **Amritsar**; his successor, **Guru Arjan Dev**, compiled the gurus' hymns in a book called the **Adi Granth**, built the Golden Temple to house it and also became Sikhism's first martyr when Jahangir executed him. Throughout their history, the Sikhs have had to battle to protect their faith and their people, especially against the Mughals; Aurangzeb had **Guru Teg Bahadur** beheaded in 1675, an event that heralded the era of his son and successor, **Guru Gobind Singh**, who was to revolutionize the entire movement.

Gobind Singh, the last leader, was largely responsible for moulding the community as it exists today. In 1699, he founded the brotherhood of the **Khalsa**. The aims of the Khalsa are to assist the poor and fight oppression; to have faith in one god and to abandon superstition and dogma; to worship god; and to protect the faith with steel. The Khalsa requires members to renounce tobacco, halal meat and sexual relations with Muslims, and to adopt the **five Ks**: *kangha* (comb), *kirpan* (sword), *kara* (steel bracelet), *kachcha* (short trousers) and *kesh* (unshorn hair) – the last requirement means that Sikh men are usually instantly recognizable thanks to their luxuriant beards and distinctive turbans. Less visibly, Guru Gobind Singh replaced traditional caste names with Singh for men (meaning "lion" – although this name is not unique to Sikhs, being a common Hindu surname as well) and Kaur ("princess") for women. Finally, Guru Gobind Singh also compiled a standardized version of the Adi Granth, which contains the hymns of the first nine gurus as well as poems written by Hindus and Muslims, and installed it as his successor, naming it **Guru Granth Sahib**. This became the Sikh's spiritual guide, while political authority rested with the Khalsa.

Demands for a separate Sikh state – **Khalistan** – and fighting in the eighteenth century, and later after Independence, have burdened Sikhs with a reputation as military activists, and their bravery and martial traditions mean that they continue to make up an important part of the Indian army. Despite this, Sikhs regard their religion as one devoted to egalitarianism, democracy and social awareness. Though to die fighting for the cause of religious freedom is considered to lead to liberation, the use of force is officially sanctioned only when other methods have failed.

Christianity

The **Apostle Thomas** is said to have arrived in Kerala in 54 AD, and according to popular tradition the Church of San Thome is the oldest Christian denomination in the world, with many tales of miracles by "Mar Thoma", as Thomas is known in Malayalam. According to tradition, Thomas was martyred in 72 AD at Mylapore in **Madras**. The tomb has since become a major place of pilgrimage, while the Portuguese added the Gothic **San Thome Cathedral** to the site in the late nineteenth century.

From the sixteenth century onwards, the history of the Church in India is linked to the spread of foreign Christians across the Subcontinent. In 1552, St Francis Xavier arrived in the Portuguese trading colony of **Goa** to establish missions to reach out to the Hindu "untouchables". In 1559, at the behest of the Portuguese king, the Inquisition arrived in Goa. Jesuit missionaries carried out a bloody and brutal campaign to "cleanse" the small colony of Hindu and Muslim religious practice. Early British incomers took the attitude that the Subcontinent was a heathen and polytheistic civilization waiting to be proselytized and made significant numbers of converts – as Christianity is intended to be free of caste stigmas, it can be attractive to those seeking social advancement, and of the two million Christians in present-day India, most are *adivasi* (tribal) and *dalit* (untouchable) people.

The position of Christians in Indian society remains uncertain. In early 1999, Christian communities in some areas, notably in Gujarat and Orissa, were subject to forced "reconversions" and attacks. These were allegedly carried out by Hindu extremists incensed by proselytizing evangelists targeting low-caste Hindus. Following an international outcry, some states passed laws banning "forced conversions", but in December 2002, a riot was only narrowly averted after police acted to prevent 1500 *dalit* people from attending a mass-conversion in Chennai.

The **Hindu influence** on Christianity remains marked, in any case, and in many churches you can see devotees offering the Hindu *aarti* (a plate of coconut, sweets and rice), and women wearing *tilak* dots on their foreheads. In the same way that Hindus and Muslims consider pilgrimage to be an integral part of life's journey, Indian Christians have numerous devotional sites, including St Jude's Shrine in **Jhansi** and the Temple of Mother Mary in **Mathura**. This sharing of traditions works both ways. At Christmas, for instance, you can't fail to notice the brightly coloured paper stars and small Nativity scenes glowing and flashing outside schools, houses, shops and churches throughout India.

Zoroastrianism

Of all India's religious communities, Western visitors are least likely to come across – or recognize – **Zoroastrians**, who have no distinctive dress and few houses of worship. Most live in Mumbai, where they are known as **Parsis** (Persians) and are active in business, education and politics. Zoroastrian numbers – roughly ninety thousand – are rapidly dwindling due to a falling birth rate and absorption into wider communities.

The religion's founder, **Zarathustra** (Zoroaster), lived in Iran around the sixth or seventh century BC, and was the first religious prophet to expound a dualistic philosophy, based on the opposing powers of good and evil. For him, the absolute, wholly good and wise God, **Ahura Mazda**, together with his holy spirit and six emanations present in earth, water, the sky, animals, plants and fire, is constantly at odds with an evil power, **Angra Mainyu**, who is aided by **daevas**, or evil spirits. Five daily prayers, usually hymns, uttered by Zarathustra and standardized in the **Avesta**, the main Zoroastrian text, are said in the home or in a temple, before a fire, which symbolizes truth, righteousness and order. For this reason, Zoroastrians are often, incorrectly, called "fire-worshippers".

Wildlife

India's vast range of habitats support a staggering range of wildlife, with around 65,000 species of fauna including 1200 birds and 340 mammals (India is the only country in the world where you can see both wild lions and tigers) plus a staggering 13,000 varieties of flowering plant. The lush deodar and rhododendron forests of the lower Himalayas are home to bears and blackbucks, while the fabled snow leopard and yak inhabit the higher mountains. Down on the Gangetic plain, the warm climate, forests and numerous lakes and rivers support a rich array of birdlife, while the Sundarbans mangrove swamps in the east are famous for their population of unusual swimming tigers. Camels, both wild and domesticated, can be found in the deserts of Rajasthan, while elsewhere in the west the dry climate supports spotted deer, leopards and the famous Asiatic lion. Further south, the dry Deccan plateau is thick with sandalwood forests, the home of wild elephants, while at the very southern tip of India you'll find elephants, butterflies and jewel-like birds under the canopy of the teak and rosewood rainforest.

Mammals

The Indian **elephant**, distinguished from its African cousin by its long front legs and smaller ears and body, is still widely used as a beast of burden in many parts of the country. Elephants have worked and been tamed in India for three thousand years, and there is still a sizeable population of wild elephants across the country. Another pachyderm, the lumbering **one-horned rhinoceros**, retains a tenuous foothold in the northeast of the country, with around eleven hundred living in the protected Manas and Kaziranga wildlife sanctuaries in Assam.

Indian **tigers** are fast becoming extinct in the wild (see page 1215), but you still stand a reasonable chance of coming across one in a national park – for the next few years at least. The other **big cats** have fared even worse than the tiger. The **Asiatic lion** now clings on in just one tiny patch of Gujarat, while the ghostly grey- and black-spotted **snow leopard** of the Himalayas is so rare as to be almost legendary. Only the plains-dwelling **leopard** (also known as the panther) can still be commonly found, especially in forested places near human settlement where domestic animals make easy prey. Other indigenous felines include the rare multi-coloured marbled cat, the miniature leopard cat, the jungle cat, the fishing cat, and a kind of lynx called the caracal.

Deer and antelope, the larger cats' prey, are much more abundant. The often solitary sambar is the largest of the **deer**. Smaller and more gregarious are *chital* (spotted deer), while other deer include the elusive mountain-loving muntjac (barking deer) and the *para* (hog deer). The smallest deer in India is the nocturnal chevrotain, known because of its size (just 30cm high), as the mouse deer. **Antelopes** include the nilgai ("blue cow"), the endangered blackbuck and the unique forest-dwelling four-horned chowsingha (swamp deer). The desert-loving gazelle is known as the *chinkara* ("the one who sneezes") due to the sneeze-like alarm call it makes.

The most common **monkeys** are the feisty red-bottomed rhesus macaque and the black-faced "Hanuman" langurs, often found around temples. Wild monkeys include the Assamese macaque and pig-tailed macaque in the northern hills, and the bonnet macaque in the steamy tropical jungles of the south.

THE INDIAN TIGER: SURVIVAL OR EXTINCTION?

Few animals command such universal fascination as the **tiger**, and India is one of the very few places where this rare and enigmatic big cat can still be glimpsed in the wild, stalking through the teak forests and terai grass – a solitary predator, with no natural enemies save one.

As recently as the beginning of the twentieth century, up to 100,000 tigers still roamed the Subcontinent, even though tiger hunting had long been the "sport of kings". It was the trigger-happy British who brought tiger hunting to its most -gratuitous excesses, however. Photographs of pith-helmeted, bare-kneed burra sahibs posing behind mountains of striped carcasses became a hackneyed image of the Raj.

In the years following Independence, **demographic pressures** nudged the Indian tiger perilously close to extinction. As the human population increased in rural districts, more and more forest was cleared for farming, depriving large carnivores of their main source of game and of the cover they needed to hunt. Forced to turn on farm cattle as an alternative, tigers were drawn into direct conflict with humans; some animals, out of sheer desperation, even turned man-eater and attacked human settlements. **Poaching** has taken an even greater toll. The black market has always paid high prices for dead animals – a tiger pelt alone can fetch US$125,000 in China – and for the various body parts believed to hold magical or medicinal properties.

Numbers had plummeted to below two thousand by 1973, the year in which India's ambitious **Project Tiger** (Ⓦ projecttiger.nic.in) was inaugurated. Nine areas of pristine forest were set aside for the remaining tigers. Demand for tiger parts did not end with Project Tiger, however, and the poachers remained in business, aided by organized smuggling rings. India's worst-case conservation scenario was finally played out in 2005, when it was discovered that the entire population of big cats at Sariska Tiger Reserve had mysteriously vanished at the hands of poachers.

Well-organized guerrilla groups operate in some remote national parks, where inadequate numbers of poorly armed and poorly paid wardens offer little more than token resistance. Project Tiger officials are understandably reluctant to jeopardize lucrative tourist traffic by admitting that sightings are nowadays quite rare, but the superstitious demand for supposedly medicinal tiger products continues to make poaching highly lucrative.

Today there are 48 Project Tiger sites and a 2014 survey estimated there were 2226 tigers in India, an apparent **rise of 30 percent** in four years. The increase was hailed by politicians as a huge success, but taken with a pinch of salt by scientists, who suggest that it may at least partly be explained by improved survey methods. They further point out that the number of tigers killed by poachers also went up in that time. The upshot is that, while conservation efforts do appear to be bearing some fruit, the tiger is still endangered as a species, both in India and worldwide.

The shaggy **sloth bear** is hard to spot in the wild, although you may see captive bears being forced to dance near tourist sites; other bears include the black and brown varieties. Of the **canines**, the scavenging striped hyena and the small pest-eating Indian fox are fairly common, though the desert-dwelling Indian wolf is under threat of extinction.

The wild **buffalo** has a close genetic relationship with the domesticated water buffalo. More exotic members of the cow family are the hill-loving **gaur**, an Indian bison which stands 2m across at the shoulders, and the nimble, mountain-dwelling **yak**.

Reptiles

The 238 species of **snake** in India (of which fifty are poisonous) extend from the 10cm-long worm snake to nest-building king cobras and massive pythons. Poisonous snakes include the majestically hooded cobra, the yellow-brown Russell's viper, the small krait and the saw-scaled viper. **Lizards** are also common, with every hotel room seeming to have a resident gecko to keep the place free of insects. The colourful garden lizard and Sita's lizard are both found throughout India. Olive ridley marine turtles nest at remote beaches along the east and southwest coasts. **Crocodiles** are common throughout the Subcontinent.

Birds

You don't have to be an aficionado to enjoy India's abundant **birdlife**. The country has a spectacular array of resident avifauna, while its geographical location also attracts many migratory species from colder countries to the north during the winter months.

Three common species of **kingfisher** frequently crop up amid the paddy fields and wetlands of the coastal plains. Other common and brightly coloured species include the grass-green, blue and yellow **bee-eaters**, the stunning **golden oriole** and the brilliant-blue **Indian roller**. **Hoopoes**, recognizable by their elegant black-and-white tipped crests, also flit around fields and villages, as do several kinds of **bulbuls, babblers** and **drongos**. Paddy fields and ponds often teem with water birds. The most ubiquitous of these is the snowy-white **cattle egret**, which can often be seen riding on the backs of cows and buffalo. Look out, too, for the mud-brown **paddy bird**, India's most common heron, distinguished by its pale green legs, speckled breast and hunched posture.

Common birds of prey such as the **brahminy kite** and the **pariah kite** are widespread around towns and fishing villages, where they vie with raucous gangs of house **crows** and **white-eyed jackdaws** for scraps. Pink-headed **king vultures** and the **white-backed vulture**, which has a white ruff around its bare neck and head, also show up whenever there are carcasses to pick clean. A bird whose call is a regular feature of the Western Ghat forests is the wild ancestor of the domestic chicken – the **jungle fowl**. Finally, among India's abundant **forest birds**, one species every enthusiast hopes to glimpse is the magnificent **hornbill**, with its huge yellow beak sporting a long curved casque on top.

Music

India is home to a staggering variety of different musical traditions, both ancient and modern, ranging from archaic styles of Hindu devotional chanting to the eclectic sounds of contemporary film scores. For many outsiders, the country's aural signature is provided by north Indian classical music, one of the world's most instantly recognizable sounds, with its twanging tanpuras and complex tabla beats. There's also Bollywood's huge treasury of film songs, or *filmi*, to explore, as well as a rich folk music tradition.

Indian classical music: ragas and talas

Underlying all Indian classical music is the concept of the **raga** (or *raag*, from the Sanskrit word meaning "colour"). Put simplistically, a raga is simply a musical scale or mode (loosely equivalent to the "key" of a piece of Western music), -determining which notes can and can't be played during a particular piece. The raga defines the basic musical material and expressive content of each particular piece, meaning that while Indian classical musicians are renowned for their **improvisation**, this only takes place within strictly defined limits – the mark of a good performer is his or her ability to improvise extensively without stepping outside the boundaries of the chosen raga.

Just as the raga organizes melody, so the rhythm of a piece is organized using metric cycles known as **talas**. A *tala* is made up of a number of beats, with each beat being defined by a combination of rhythm pattern and timbre. There are literally hundreds of *talas*, the most common being the sixteen-beat *teen tala* (four times four beats).

The performance of a raga follows a set pattern. First comes the **alap**, a slow, meditative introduction in free rhythm which explores the chosen raga, carefully introducing its constituent notes one by one. In the next two sections, the **jor** and the **jhala**, the instrumentalist introduces a rhythmic element, developing the raga through a series of increasingly complex variations. Only in these and the final section, the **gat**, does the percussion instrument – usually the tabla or (in south India) the *mridangam* – enter. The soloist introduces a short, fixed phrase (known as "the composition") to which he returns between flights of improvisation. The *gat* itself is subdivided into three sections: a slow tempo passage known as *vilambit*, increasing to a medium tempo section called *madhya*, and leading finally to the fast, concluding *drut*.

Musical instruments

The best-known Indian instrument is the **sitar**. This has six or seven main strings, plucked with a plectrum, along with between eleven and nineteen sympathetic strings. The curved neck allows the player to alter the pitch by pulling strings sideways across the fret to provide the pitch-bends so characteristic of Indian music. The **surbahar**, effectively a bass sitar, is played in the same way. Smaller than a sitar, the **sarod** has two resonating chambers connected by a metal fingerboard, and ten metal strings, plucked with a fragment of coconut shell (plus a further fifteen sympathetic strings underneath).

The **sarangi** is a fretless bowed instrument with a very broad fingerboard and three or four main strings of gut, plus anything up to forty sympathetic metal strings. Some claim it is the most difficult musical instrument to play in the world. The *sarangi* is capable of a wide range of timbres and its sound is likened to that of the human voice, meaning that it is often used to accompany vocal recitals. The word **bansuri** refers to a wide variety of bamboo (*banse*) flutes, either end-blown or side-blown. The **shehnai**,

INDIAN CLASSICAL MASTERS

There's a huge variety of Indian – especially north Indian – classical music available, including recordings by many of the country's leading virtuosos of the past fifty years. Perhaps the best-known and most recorded Indian classical artist is sitar player **Ravi Shankar** (1920–2012), who made numerous solo recordings, as well as duetting with artists ranging from Ali Akbar Khan (see below) to Yehudi Menuhin. Other legendary sitar players include **Nikhil Banerjee** (1931–86) and **Vilayat Khan** (1928–2004), while it's also worth searching out recordings by **Imrat Khan** (b.1935, and younger brother of Vilayat), the acknowledged master of the soulful *surbahar* (bass sitar).

Rivalling Ravi Shankar for recorded legacy is the internationally revered *sarod* virtuoso **Ali Akbar Khan** (1922–2009), while the hauntingly atmospheric music of **Hariprasad Chaurasia** (b.1938), India's leading master of the *bansuri* (bamboo flute), is also essential listening for anyone with even a passing interest in Subcontinental music. Less well known, but equally rewarding, are the recorded performances of **Sultan Khan** (1940–2011) and **Ram Narayan** (b.1927), two of modern India's greatest masters of the *sarangi*, while recordings by leading *shehnai* virtuoso **Bismillah Khan** (1916–2006) are also worth looking out for – albeit the instrument is something of an acquired taste. Many notable recordings also feature **Alla Rakha** (1919–2000), perhaps the finest tabla virtuoso of recent years. For **Carnatic** music, try some of the many recordings by violin wizard L. Subramanian, saxophone supremo Kadri Gopalnath, or the much rarer recordings by **Sundaram Balachander** (1927–90), one of the twentieth century's leading exponents of the soulful *veena*.

traditionally used for wedding music, is a double-reed, oboe-type instrument with up to nine finger holes.

The **tabla** is a set of two small drums, tuned to the tonic, dominant or -subdominant notes of the raga and played with the palms and fingertips to produce an incredible variety of sounds and timbres. Predating the tabla, the **pakhavaj** is nearly 1m long and was traditionally made of clay, although wood is now more popular. It has two parchment heads, each tuned to a different pitch.

The instruments of **Carnatic music** include the **vina**, which resembles the sitar but has no sympathetic strings; the **mridangam** double-headed drum; and the enormous **nadaswaram** (or *nagaswaram*), a kind of metre-long oboe, commonly used during temple ceremonies. The **violin** (slightly modified to suit Indian musical requirements) is also widely used.

Finally, perhaps the most ubiquitous but self-effacing of all Indian musical instruments is the **tanpura** (or *tambura*), a type of fretless lute with (usually) four or five wire strings. It's the tanpura that supplies the instantly recognizable, buzzing drone that underpins all Indian classical music. The tanpura is traditionally played by an advanced student of the lead performer – considered a rare and special honour for the pupil concerned.

Classical vocal music

Dhrupad is the oldest and most austere form of north Indian classical music. *Dhrupads* typically consist of two sections: a long and entirely wordless introductory *alap* during which the singer(s) vocalize a sequence of syllables deriving from the mantra "Hari Om Narayana Taan Tarana Tum", followed by a much shorter and faster section sung to the accompaniment of a *pakhavaj* drum. During the eighteenth century the rather severe *dhrupad* was largely displaced by the much more flamboyant **khayal** – described as the "bel canto of Indian music" – a form that allows for far greater displays of virtuosity. *Khayal* is typically accompanied by tabla and harmonium, along with a bowed instrument such as a *sarangi* or violin, which mirrors the vocal line.

Thumri are essentially love songs, written from a female perspective and sung in a language known as Braj Bhasha, a literary dialect of Hindi particularly associated with

Lucknow. The singer is always accompanied by the tabla, as well perhaps as the tanpura, the *sarangi* or the *surmandal*, and sometimes the violin or harmonium. Still more song-like than the *thumri* is the **ghazal**. In some ways the Urdu counterpart of *thumri*, the *ghazal* was introduced to India by Persian Muslims and is a poetic rather than a musical form – many favourite *ghazals* are drawn from the works of great Urdu poets.

Carnatic music

Southern India's classical music – known as **Carnatic** (or "Karnatak") music – is essentially similar to Hindustani classical music in its overall concept but differs in many details, usually ascribed to the far greater Islamic influence in the north. To the Western ear, Carnatic music is emotionally direct and impassioned, without the restraint that characterizes much of the north's music.

Song is at the root of south Indian music, and forms based on song are paramount, even when the performance is purely instrumental. The vast majority of the texts are religious, and the temple is frequently the venue for performance. The most important form is the *kriti*, a devotional song, hundreds of which were written by the most influential figure in the development of Carnatic music, the singer **Thyagaraja** (1767–1847).

Folk music

There are many kinds of **Indian folk music** (*Lok Sangeet*), but the main regional strands are those of Rajasthan, the Punjab (spread across both India and Pakistan), and Bengal. In **Rajasthan**, music is always played for weddings and theatre -performances, and often at local markets or gatherings. There is a whole cast of professional musicians who perform this function, and a wonderful assortment of earthy-sounding stringed instruments like the *kamayacha* and *ravanhata* that accompany their songs.

Bengal is best known for the music of the **Bauls**, an order of wandering mystics and musicians who subscribe to a syncretic mix of Sufi and *bhakti* Hindu mystical beliefs expressed primarily through song, typically accompanied by the *ektara*, a one-stringed drone instrument.

The **Punjab** is most closely associated with **bhangra**. This was originally a kind of folk dance, performed as part of harvest festival celebrations and accompanied by music on the *dhol* and *dholki* drums, *ektara* and *tumbi* (a kind of single-string guitar); but since the 1980s has become a global pop phenomenon both in its traditional form and in contemporary dance, house and hip-hop fusions, created mainly by Asian musicians in the UK.

Filmi

Indian **popular music** is intimately bound up with the country's massive film industry. Music plays a crucial role in Bollywood movies and up until the 1990s virtually all Indian popular music consisted of songs, known as **filmi**, taken from the soundtracks to these movies. The most striking feature of these Bollywood filmi is their incredibly eclectic style, offering a fascinating snapshot of changing musical fashions over the past five decades, all seen from a uniquely Indian point of view.

Early film scores tended to be rooted in Indian folk and classical music, but from the 1960s onwards Bollywood film composers such as the famous **R.D. Burman** began to soak up an incredible range of musical influences in their work, from big band rock'n'roll to the techno and electronic creations of the innovative **A.R. Rahman**. Bollywood filmi are performed by so-called **playback singers**, the invisible artists who record the songs that the film's actors and actresses then mime along to. Many of these singers have achieved massive fame in their own right, including the legendary Asha Bhosle and her sister Lata Mangeshkar, along with male singers such as Kishore Kumar and Mohammed Rafi.

Books

India is one of the most written-about places on earth, and there are a bewildering number of titles available covering virtually every aspect of the country, ranging from scholarly historical dissertations to racy travelogues. Books marked ★ are particularly recommended.

HISTORY, SOCIETY AND REPORTAGE

Charles Allen *Plain Tales from the Raj*. First-hand accounts from erstwhile sahibs and memsahibs of everyday British India, organized thematically.

A.L. Basham *The Wonder That Was India*. This veritable encyclopedia by one of India's foremost historical authorities positively bristles with erudition.

Oliver Blach *India Rising: Tales from a Changing Nation*. Part reportage, part travel writing, *India Rising* is a personalized account of the modern nation state drawn from a broad cast of everyday lives, ranging from millionaire entrepreneurs to slum dwellers. A vivid account of the contradictions and challenges at the heart of India's rise, and its extraordinary potential.

Katherine Boo *Behind the Beautiful Forevers*. Award-winning investigative journalist Boo spent three years exploring the Annawadi slum near Mumbai airport, and her account, tracing the impact of a violent crime on the community, races along with an almost cinematic intensity.

Elizabeth Bumiller *May You Be the Mother of a Hundred Sons*. Lucid exploration of the Indian woman's lot, drawn from dozens of first-hand encounters in the 1990s – since when surprisingly little has changed.

David Burton *The Raj at Table*. Vividly evokes the quirky world of British India – commendable both for its extra-ordinary recipes and as a marvellous piece of social history.

Liz Collingham *Curry*. Original and entertaining account of Indian history seen through its food, from Mughlai biryanis to Mulligatawny soup.

Larry Collins and Dominique Lapierre *Freedom at Midnight*. Readable, if shallow, account of Independence, highly sympathetic to the British and, particularly, to Mountbatten, who was the authors' main source of information.

Anne de Courcy *The Fishing Fleet*. The hitherto untold story of the many British women who, in response to a dearth of eligible bachelors at home, travelled to India in the late nineteenth century in search of husbands. Drawing on mainly unpublished memoirs, diaries and letters, the narrative yields a vivid picture of the Raj at its height from the female perspective.

★ **William Dalrymple** *The Last Mughal*. Masterful account of Delhi's part in the 1857 uprising. Using Urdu as well as English sources, Dalrymple tells us what it was like for the insurgents, the British, the Mughal court and – most importantly – the ordinary people of Delhi.

★ **William Dalrymple** *Nine Lives: In Search of the Sacred in Modern India*. The stories of nine different people who follow contrasting religious paths through the vortex of rapid social and cultural change. Each of Dalrymple's subjects is beautifully defined, revealing a wealth of insight into both India's past and present.

★ **William Dalrymple** *White Mughals*. Compelling account of the previously forgotten story of British political officer James Achilles Kirkpatrick's marriage to the great-niece of the nizam of Hyderabad's prime minister.

Siddartha Deb *The Beautiful and the Damned: Life in the New India*. Another brilliant portrait of the country, this time focusing on a handful of individuals whose tragicomic lives epitomize some of the tensions underlying India's modern metamorphosis.

Louis Fischer *The Life of Mahatma Gandhi*. Veteran American journalist Louis Fischer knew his subject personally, and his book provides an engaging account of Gandhi as a man, politician and propagandist.

Patrick French *India*. A snapshot of the modern nation divided into themes (politics, economy and religion). Drawing on encounters with Indians from contrasting backgrounds, it manages to be scholarly yet wide-ranging at the same time – and a highly enjoyable read.

Patrick French *Liberty or Death*. The definitive account (and a damning indictment) of the last years of the British Raj.

M.K. Gandhi *The Story of My Experiments with Truth*. Gandhi's fascinating record of his life, including his spiritual and moral quests and gradual emergence to the fore of national politics.

Bamber Gascoigne *The Great Mughals*. Concise, entertaining and eminently readable account of the lives of the first six great Mughals.

★ **Sujatha Gidla** *Ants Among Elephants*. A searing account of what it is like to be a so-called "untouchable" in India, Gidla uses her own family's story to eviscerate the brutalities of the caste system. The result is a remarkable, unsentimental, knockout punch of a book.

Anand Giridharadas *India Calling*. An intimate portrait of the country written from the perspective of a young American born of Indian parents who emigrated to the US in the 1970s. It's particularly revealing of the impact of new technology and economic change on families.

Christopher Hibbert *The Great Mutiny*. Account of the 1857 uprising, told entirely from the British point of view, in easy prose and with some compelling first-hand material from the British side.

John Keay *The Honourable Company: A History of the English East India Company*. Readable and balanced account of the East India Company and its strange role in Subcontinental history.

★ **John Keay** *India: A History*. One of the best single-volume histories currently in print. Keay manages to coax clear, impartial and highly readable narrative from five thousand years of fragmented events, enlivened with plenty of quirky asides.

John Keay *Into India*. As an all-round introduction to India, this book – originally written in 1973 but reissued in 1999 – is the one most often recommended by old hands, presenting a wide spread of history and cultural background, interspersed with lucid personal observations.

Edward Luce *In Spite of the Gods*. The most authoritative account of the state of the nation currently in print, packed full of sobering statistics and myth-busting facts that challenge common misconceptions about the country.

★ **Suketu Mehta** *Maximum City: Bombay Lost and Found*. Acclaimed portrait of India's largest city, mixing memoir and travelogue, along with penetrating insights into the history, society and people of Mumbai.

Geoffrey Moorhouse *India Britannica*. A balanced, lively survey of the rise and fall of the British Raj.

Palagummi Sainath *Everybody Loves a Good Drought*. A classic report on India's poorest districts, telling the stories of individual villages that are usually lost in a maze of development statistics.

Amartya Sen *The Argumentative Indian*. A provocative and sharply written collection of essays on identity, religion, history, philosophy and – above all – what it means to be Indian.

Mala Sen *Death By Fire*. Later made into a controversial film, this book uses the infamous Roop Kanwar *sati* case as a springboard to explore some of the wider issues affecting women in contemporary Indian society.

Shashi Tharoor *Inglorious Empire*. A fiercely-argued polemic from politician, diplomat and author Tharoor, sharply rebutting the notion that British colonialism in the sub-continent was a force for good.

Mark Tully *India: the Road Ahead*. Few commentators understand India as well as Mark Tully, the veteran BBC correspondent, who has written a string of books cataloguing the country's rapid change. This is his most recent, but they're all worth hunting out, from *No Full Stops* (1992) to *India In Slow Motion* (2003) and *India's Unending Journey* (2008).

TRAVEL

James Cameron *An Indian Summer*. Affectionate and humorous description of the veteran British journalist's visit to India in 1972, and his marriage to an Indian woman.

★ **William Dalrymple** *City of Djinns*. Dalrymple's account of a year in Delhi sifts through successive layers of the city's past using a blend of inspired historical sleuth-work and interviews with a cast of characters ranging from Urdu calligraphers to local pigeon fanciers. *The Age of Kali* (published in India as *In the Court of the Fish-Eyed Goddess*) is a collection of essays drawn from ten years' travel in India.

Alexander Frater *Chasing the Monsoon*. Frater's wet-season jaunt up the west coast and across to Shillong took him through an India of muddy puddles and grey skies: an evocative account of the country as few visitors see it, now something of a classic.

Tim Mackintosh-Smith *The Hall of a Thousand Columns*. Quirky, learned and entertaining travelogue following the footsteps of Ibn Battuta through the Delhi of the Tughluq sultan Muhammad Shah and thence south to Kerala, with lashings of offbeat Subcontinental Islamic history en route.

V.S. Naipaul *An Area of Darkness*. One of the finest (and bleakest) books ever written about India: a darkly comic portrait based on a year of travel around the Subcontinent in the early 1960s – dated, but still essential reading. Naipaul followed this up with *India: A Wounded Civilisation*, a damning analysis of Indian society written during the Emergency of 1975–77, and the slightly sunnier *India: A Million Mutinies Now*, published in 1990.

Monisha Rajesh *Around India in 80 Trains*. Echoing Jules Verne's classic story, British-Indian travel writer Rajesh covers 40,000km – the circumference of the earth – in her railway journey across India, riding on everything from toy trains to hospitals on wheels.

Tahir Shah *Sorcerer's Apprentice*. A journey through the weird underworld of occult India. Travelling as an apprentice to a master conjurer and illusionist, Shah encounters hangmen, baby renters, skeleton dealers, sadhus and charlatans.

Mark Shand *Travels on My Elephant*. Award-winning account of a 965km ride on an elephant from Konark in Odisha to Bihar, and full of incident, humour and pathos. For the sequel, *Queen of the Elephants*, Shand teamed up with an Assamese princess who's the country's leading elephant-handler.

Eric Shipton and H.W. Tilman *Nanda Devi: Exploration and Ascent*. Two classics of Himalayan mountaineering literature published in a single volume, recounting the famous expeditions of 1934 and 1936. Shipton's, in particular, is a masterpiece: beautifully written and enthralling from start to finish.

FICTION

Aravind Adiga *The White Tiger*. Brilliantly dark satire on the "New" India, set largely in Delhi and featuring the relationship between a wealthy employer and his impecunious but murderously ambitious servant.

Mulk Raj Anand *Untouchable* and *Coolie*. First published in 1935, *Untouchable* gives a memorable worm's-eye view of the brutal life of an untouchable sweeper, while the subsequent *Coolie* (1936) describes the death of a 15-year-old child labourer.

Chetan Bhagat *One Night at the Call Centre*. A heart-warming tale by India's most popular novelist about six employees in a Gurgaon call centre. Like most of Bhagat's novels – including *2 States*, about a Punjabi man who wants to marry a Tamil woman, and *Revolution 2020*, about private tuition colleges and corruption – it's never too heavy, but makes some serious points about the problems faced by young, urban Indians.

★ **Vikram Chandra** *Sacred Games*. More than a decade elapsed between the publication of Chandra's award-winning debut novel, *Red Earth and Pouring Rain*, inspired by the life of Anglo-Indian soldier James Skinner, and this, his second offering – an epic, page-turning tale of friendship and betrayals, love and violence set in modern Mumbai.

Anita Desai *Fasting, Feasting*. One of India's leading female authors' eloquent portrayal of the frustration of a sensitive young woman stuck in the stifling atmosphere of home while her spoilt brother is packed off to study in America.

Kiran Desai *The Inheritance of Loss*. This Booker Prize-winning novel, partly set in the Himalayan town of Kalimpong, with the Gorkhaland movement as a backdrop, tells the haunting stories of a judge, an orphaned girl and a cook, each one trapped by their dreams.

E.M. Forster *A Passage to India*. Set in the 1920s, this withering critique of colonialism is memorable as much for its sympathetic portrayal of middle-class Indian life as for its insights into cultural misunderstandings.

Amitav Ghosh *The Hungry Tide*. The history and myths of the Sundarbans are brought dramatically to life in this beautifully written novel, which centres on the relationship between a marine biologist – an American of Indian descent – and a Bengali businessman.

Amitav Ghosh *Sea of Poppies*. This first instalment in Ghosh's *Ibis* trilogy centres around the opium trade in the early nineteenth century. Full of fascinating historical detail, with engaging characters who speak an array of local English vernaculars, it's an excellent depiction of Bengal under Company rule.

Rudyard Kipling *Kim*. Cringingly colonialist at times, of course, but the atmosphere of India and Kipling's love of it shine through in this story of an orphaned white boy. Kipling's other key works on India are two books of short stories: *Soldiers Three* and *In Black and White*.

★ **Rohinton Mistry** *A Fine Balance*. Magnificent, gut-wrenching novel focusing on two friends who leave their lower-caste rural lives for the urban opportunities of the big smoke. Mistry's *Such a Long Journey* is an acclaimed account of a Mumbai Parsi's struggle to maintain personal integrity in the face of betrayals and disappointment.

R.K. Narayan *Gods, Demons and Others*. Classic Indian folk tales and popular myths told through the voice of a village storyteller. Many of Narayan's beautifully crafted books, full of touching characters and subtle humour, are set in the fictional south Indian territory of Malgudi.

Gregory David Roberts *Shantaram*. Entertaining, albeit rather overlong, semi-autobiographical account of an escaped Australian convict taking refuge in India (mainly Mumbai), with memorable, if occasionally clichéd, depictions of the country and its people.

★ **Arundhati Roy** *The God of Small Things*. Haunting Booker Prize-winner about a well-to-do south Indian family caught between the snobberies of high-caste tradition, a colonial past and the diverse personal histories of its members. Her follow-up novel, *The Ministry of Utmost Happiness*, was published in 2017, 20 years later. Although it doesn't quite hit the heights of her debut, it's still well worth a read, interweaving the stories of a diverse cast of characters to illuminate the dark side of modern India.

★ **Salman Rushdie** *Midnight's Children*. This story of a man born at the very moment of Independence, whose life mirrors that of modern India itself, won Rushdie the Booker Prize and the enmity of Indira Gandhi, who had it banned in India. Set in Kerala and Mumbai, *The Moor's Last Sigh* was the subject of a defamation case brought by Shiv Sena leader, Bal Thackeray.

★ **Vikram Seth** *A Suitable Boy*. Vast, all-embracing tome set in UP shortly after Independence; wonderful characterization and an impeccable sense of place and time make this an essential read for long train journeys.

William Sutcliffe *Are You Experienced?* Hilarious novel sending up the backpacker scene in India. Wickedly perceptive and very readable.

Vikas Swarup *Q&A*. Filmed by Danny Boyle as *Slumdog Millionaire*, this is the story – in turn funny, shocking and heart-warming – of how an illiterate slum dweller's life experiences enable him to answer a series of difficult questions on a high-prize TV quiz show.

Tarun J. Tejpal *The Alchemy of Desire*. Set mainly in the Himalayas, this sensuous tale focuses on two lovers, mixing its exploration of human relationships with wider reflections on India in the twentieth century.

ART, ARCHITECTURE AND RELIGION

Roy Craven *Indian Art*. Concise general introduction to Indian art, from Harappan seals to Mughal miniatures.

★ **Diana L. Eck** *Banaras – City of Light*. Thorough disquisition on the religious significance of Varanasi, and a

good introduction to the practice of Hindu cosmology.

Dorf Hartsuiker *Sadhus: Holy Men of India*. The weird world of India's itinerant ascetics exposed in glossy colour photographs and erudite but accessible text.

Stephen P. Huyler *Meeting God*. Unrivalled overview of the beliefs and practices of contemporary Hinduism, accompanied by fine photographs.

George Michell *The Hindu Temple*. A reasonable primer, introducing Hindu temples, their significance and architectural development.

Wendy O'Flaherty (translator) *Hindu Myths*. Translations of key myths from the original Sanskrit texts, providing an insight into the foundations of Hinduism.

Paramahansa Yogananda *Autobiography of a Yogi*. Uplifting account of religious awakening and spiritual development by one of the most internationally influential Hindu masters.

Language

No fewer than 22 major languages are officially recognized by the Indian constitution, while numerous minor ones and more than a thousand dialects are also spoken across the country. When independent India was organized, the present-day states were largely created along linguistic lines, which help the traveller make some sense of the complex situation. Considering the continuing prevalence of English, there is rarely any necessity to speak a local language, but some theoretical knowledge of the background and learning at least a few words of one or two can only enhance your visit.

The main languages of northern India, including the country's eastern and western extremities, are all **Indo-Aryan**, the easternmost subgroup of the Indo-European family that is thought to have originated somewhere between Europe and Central Asia several millennia BC, before tribal movements spread its progeny in all directions. The oldest extant Subcontinental language is Sanskrit, one of the three "big sisters" (along with Latin and Greek) upon which philologists have created the model of proto-Indo-European language. It's known to have been spoken early in the second millennium BC, although it was not written down until much later, and is the vehicle for all the sacred texts of Hinduism. Sanskrit remained the language of the educated until around 1000 AD and gradually developed into the modern tongues of northern India: Hindi, Urdu, Bengali, Gujarati, Marathi, Kashmiri, Punjabi and Oriya.

North India

Hindi is the pre-eminent language in the north, and the main language in the states of Uttar Pradesh, Madhya Pradesh, Rajasthan, Haryana, Bihar and Himachal Pradesh, as well as being widely used as a second language in other states. Hindi is very closely related to **Urdu**, the main language of Pakistan. Both Hindi and Urdu developed in tandem around the markets and army camps of Delhi (the term Urdu derives from the Turkish word for "camp") during the establishment of Muslim rule around the start of the second millennium AD. Whereas Hindi later returned to the Sanskrit roots of its Hindu speakers, however, and adopted the classical **Devanagari** script, Urdu became culturally more closely linked with Islam and is written in **Perso-Arabic** script. The vocabulary of each also reflects these cultural and religious ties. The scripts of Punjabi, Bengali and Gujarati are among those that have developed out of Devanagari and still bear some resemblance to it.

Other important languages spoken in north India include **Bengali** (West Bengal and Tripura), **Nepali** (West Bengal and Sikkim), **Gujarati** (Gujarat), **Punjabi** (Punjab, Delhi), **Kashmiri** and **Dogri** (Kashmir), **Assamese** and **Bodo** (Assam), **Oriya** (Odisha) and **Maithili** (Bihar).

South India

The four most widely spoken south Indian languages, **Tamil** (Tamil Nadu), **Telugu** (Andhra Pradesh), **Kannada** (Karnataka) and **Malayalam** (Kerala) all belong to the Dravidian family, the world's fourth largest group of languages. These and related minor languages grew up quite separately among the non-Aryan peoples of southern India over thousands of years, and the earliest written records of Tamil date back to the third century AD. The exact origins of the Dravidian group have not been established, but it is likely that Dravidian languages were spoken further north in prehistoric times before being driven south by the Aryan invaders.

INDIAN ENGLISH

During the British Raj, **Indian English** developed its own characteristics, many of which have survived to the present day. It was during this period that Indian words also entered the vocabulary of everyday English, among them veranda, bungalow, sandal, pyjamas, shampoo, jungle, turban, caste, chariot, chilli, cardamom, pundit and yoga. The traveller to India soon becomes familiar with other terms in common usage that have not spread so widely outside the Subcontinent: *dacoit, dhoti, panchayat, lakh* and *crore* are but a few. A full list of Anglo-Indianisms can be found in the famous Hobson-Jobson Anglo-Indian dictionary.

Perhaps the most endearing aspect of Indian English is the way it has preserved forms now regarded as highly old-fashioned in Britain. Addresses such as "Good sir" and questions like "May I know your good name?" are commonplace, as are terms like "tiffin" and "cantonment". This type of usage reaches its apogee in the more flowery expressions of the media, which regularly feature in the vast array of daily newspapers published in English. Thus headlines often appear such as "37 perish in mishap", referring to a train crash, or passages like this splendid report of a bank robbery: "The miscreants absconded with the loot in great haste. They repaired immediately to their hideaway, whereupon they divided the iniquitous spoils before vanishing into thin air."

Language in India since Independence

With **Independence** it was decided by the government in Delhi that Hindi should become the **official language** of the newly created country. A drive to teach Hindi in all schools followed and more than half the country's population are now reckoned to have a decent working knowledge of the language. However, there has always been strong **resistance** to the imposition of Hindi in certain areas, especially the **Tamil-led** Dravidian south, and the vast majority of people living below the Deccan plateau have little or no knowledge of it.

This is where **English**, the language of the ex-colonists, becomes an important means of communication. Not surprisingly, given India's rich linguistic diversity, **English** remains a **lingua franca** for many people. It is still the preferred language of law, higher education, much of commerce and the media, and to some degree political dialogue; and for many educated Indians, not just those living abroad, it is actually their first language. All this explains why Anglophone visitors can often soon feel surprisingly at home despite the huge cultural differences. It is not unusual to overhear everyday contact between Indians from different parts of the country being conducted in English, and stimulating conversations can often be had, not only with students or businesspeople, but also with chai walas and shoeshine boys.

USEFUL HINDI WORDS AND PHRASES

GREETINGS

Hello (slightly formal; not used for Muslims) Namaste/Namaskar

Hello (formal; to a Muslim) As salaam alaykum (in reply) Alaykum as salaam

Goodbye Namaste

Goodbye (to a Muslim) Khudaa haafiz

See you later Phir mileynge

How are you? (formal) Aap kaise hai?

How are you? (familiar) Kya hal hai?

brother (informal; not to be used to older men) bhaaii

sister (informal; not to be used to older women) diidi

sir sahib

sir (Muslims only) hazur

BASIC WORDS

yes (informal/more formal) haa/ji haa

no (informal/more formal) nahi/ji nahi

OK acha/tiik hai

I/me mai

you (formal) aap

you (familiar; and to children) tum

and/more aur

how? kaise?

how much? kitna?

thank you dhanyavad/shukriya

(formal; Indians don't usually say thank you during everyday transactions. There's no direct Hindi equivalent to the English word "please")

good acha
very good bahut acha
bad buraa
big barra
small chhota
hot garam
hot (spicy) mirchi
cold thanda
clean saaf
dirty gandaa
open khulaa
expensive mehngaa
please come aiiye
go jao
run (also "take a run" or "scram") bhaago
enough bas

BASIC PHRASES

My name is... Mera naam...hai
What is your name? (formal) Aapka naam kya hai?
What is your name? (familiar, and to children)
    Tumhara naam kya hai?
I'm from... Mai...se hu
We're from... Hum...se hal
Where do you come from? Aap kaha se aate hai?
I understand Samaj gayaa
I don't understand Samaj nahin aayaa
I don't know Maluum nahi
I don't speak Hindi Mai Hindi nahi bol sakta hu
Please speak slowly Dhiire boliye
Sorry Ma'af kiijiye
It is OK? Tiik hai?
How much is this? Yeh kitne ka hai?
**I don't need it (literally "not needed"); useful
    response to persistent touts** Nahi chai'iya
Do you have...? ...hai?
I/we like it Acha lugta hai
I'm fine Tiik hai
What work do you do? Kya kam karte hai?
Do you have any brothers or sisters? Bhaai behan hai?
Oh dear! Arey!

GETTING AROUND

Where is the...? ...kaha hai?
I want to go to... Mai...jaana chaata hu
Where is it? Kaha hai?
How far? Kitna duur?
Which is the bus for Agra? Agra ki bas kaha hai?
What time does the train leave? Gaarii kab jayegi?
Stop! Ruko!
Wait! Thehero!

ACCOMMODATION

I need a room Mujhe kamra chai'eeye

How much is the room? Kamra kitne ka hai?
I am staying for one night Mai ek raat ke liiye
    theheroonga

HEALTH

I have a headache Sir me dard hai
I have a pain in my stomach Mere pate me dard hai
The pain is here Dard yaha hai
Where is the doctor's clinic? Daktar ka clinic kaha hai
Where is the hospital? Haspital kaha hai?
Where is the pharmacy? Dawaaii khana kaha hai?
medicine dawaaii
ill bimar
pain dard
stomach pate
eye aankh
nose naak
ear kaan
back piith
foot paao

NUMBERS AND TIME

zero shunya
one ek
two do
three tiin
four char
five paanch
six che
seven saat
eight aath
nine nau
ten das
eleven gyaarah
twelve baarah
thirteen terah
fourteen chaudah
fifteen pandrah
sixteen solah
seventeen satrah
eighteen ataarah
nineteen unniis
twenty biis
thirty tiis
forty chaaliis
fifty pachaas
sixty saath
seventy sattar
eighty assii
ninety nabbe
one hundred ek sau
one thousand ek hazaar
one hundred thousand ek lakh
ten million ek crore

today aaj
tomorrow/yesterday kal
day din
afternoon dopahar
evening shaam
night raat
week haftaah
month mahiinaa

year saal
Monday somvaar
Tuesday mangalvaar
Wednesday budhvaar
Thursday viirvaar
Friday shukravaar
Saturday shanivaar
Sunday ravivaar

FOOD AND DRINK GLOSSARY

BASICS

khaana food
chawaal rice
chamach spoon
chhoori knife
kanta fork
plate plate
chini sugar
chini nahi no sugar (e.g. in tea)
kali mirch black pepper
gur jaggery (unrefined sugar)
namak salt
mirch pepper
mirchi chilli hot
mirchi kam less hot
garam hot
thanda cold
dahi yogurt
dhal curried lentils, sometimes reduced to a kind of
broth; traditionally served as an accompaniment to
all Indian meals
garam masala spice mix (literally "hot spices") added to
dishes as hot seasoning
ghee clarified butter; often used instead of cooking oil,
or to flavour food
gravy any kind of curry sauce; nothing to do with
British gravy
jeera cumin
lal mirch red pepper
masala generic term indicating either a spice mixture
or something spicy
methi fenugreek
paan betel nut
paneer unfermented cheese
sabji any vegetable

DRINKS

bhang lassi lassi with pounded cannabis leaf
botal vaala paani mineral water
chai tea
doodh milk
falooda traditional Mughlai dessert, usually made with
milk, ice cream, nuts and sweets

kaapi or **kaafi** coffee
lassi yogurt drink, served either plain or flavoured with
salt or fruit
pani water
peenay ka pani drinking water (not mineral water)

MEAT AND FISH

chingri prawns
gosht meat, usually mutton
keema minced meat
macchi fish
murg chicken

VEGETABLES AND FRUIT

aam mango
alu potatoes
baingan or **brinjal** eggplant (aubergine)
bhindi okra (ladies' fingers)
chana chickpeas
gaajar carrot
gobi cauliflower
kaddoo pumpkin
kela banana
mooli large radish (daikon)
mutter peas
palak spinach
piaz onions
sabji vegetables (literally, "greens")
santaraa orange
seb apple
sag spinach
tamatar tomato

DISHES AND COOKING TERMS

alu baingan potato and aubergine; usually mild to
medium
alu gobi potato and cauliflower; usually mild
alu methi potato with fenugreek leaves, usually
medium-hot
alu mutter potato and pea curry; usually mild
baingan bharta baked and mashed aubergine mixed
with onion
bhindi bhaji gently spiced, fried okra

bhuna roasted and then thickened-down medium-hot curry sauce

biryani rice baked with saffron or turmeric, whole spices and meat (sometimes vegetables), and often hard-boiled egg; rich

chana masala spicy chickpeas; usually medium-hot

cutlet fried cutlet of minced meat or chopped vegetables

dhal gosht meat cooked in lentils; usually hot

dhal makhani lentils cooked with cream

dhansak curry sauce made from reduced lentils; usually medium-hot

dopiaza onion-based sauce; medium-mild

dum steamed in a casserole; the most common dish is *dum aloo*, with potatoes

jalfrezi dish cooked with tomatoes and green chilli; medium-hot to hot

karahi cast-iron wok that has given its name to a method of cooking with dry spices to create dishes of medium strength

karhi dhal-like dish made from dahi and gram flour

kofta balls of minced vegetables or meat in a curried sauce

korma mild sauce made with curd (and perhaps cream)

malai kofta vegetable balls in a rich cream sauce; usually medium-mild

momo Tibetan dumplings

mooli Keralan fish curry

mughlai masala Mughal-style mild, creamy sauce

mulligatawny classic Anglo-Indian-style vegetable soup; moderately spicy

murg makhani butter chicken

mutter paneer paneer and peas curry

palak paneer paneer and spinach

pathia thickened curry with lemon juice; hot

pomfret a flatfish popular in Mumbai and Kolkata

pongal spicy rice and dhal

pulau rice, gently spiced and pre-fried

raita chilled yogurt flavoured with mild spices, sometimes with the addition of small pieces of cucumber and tomato; usually eaten as an accompaniment to a main course

rasam south Indian-style spicy soup

rogan josh deep-red lamb curry, a classic Mughlai dish; medium-hot

sambhar soupy lentil and vegetable curry with asafoetida and tamarind

shahi paneer "royal" paneer; slightly more elaborate version of standard paneer curry, sometimes including fruit and nuts

seekh kebab minced lamb grilled on a skewer

shami kebab small minced lamb cutlets

tarka dhal lentils with a masala of fried garlic, onions and spices

thali combination of vegetarian dishes, chutneys, pickles, rice and bread served as an all-in-one meal

vindaloo Goan vinegared meat (sometimes fish) curry, originally pork; very hot

BREADS AND PANCAKES

appam* south Indian-style rice pancake speckled with holes, soft in the middle

bhatura soft bread made of white flour and traditionally accompanying *chana*; common in Delhi

chapatti unleavened bread made of whole wheat flour

dosa* crispy south Indian rice pancake; can be served in various forms, the best known of which is the masala dosa, when the dosa is wrapped around a filling of spicy potato curry

idli south Indian steamed rice cake, usually served with *sambhar*

kaathi filled wraps

kachori small thick cakes of salty deep-fried bread

loochi delicate puri often mixed with white flour; cooked in Bengal

Mughlai paratha *paratha* with egg

naan white leavened bread kneaded with yogurt and baked in a *tandoor*

papad or **poppadum*** crisp, thin, chickpea-flour cracker

paratha or **parantha** whole wheat bread made with butter, rolled thin and griddle-fried; a little bit like a chewy pancake, sometimes stuffed with meat or vegetables

puri crispy, puffed-up, deep-fried whole wheat bread

rava a type of spiced dosa with cumin

roti loosely used term; often just another name for chapatti, though it should be thicker, chewier, and baked in a *tandoor*

uttapam* thick, south Indian-style rice pancake often cooked with onions

*south Indian terminology; all other terms are either in Hindi or refer to north Indian cuisine.

SNACKS (CHAAT), SWEETS AND DESSERTS

barfi or **burfi** traditional sweet made with milk; a bit like fudge

bhaji or **bhajia** pieces of vegetable deep-fried in chickpea batter, served as a main course or a street snack

bhel puri mix of puffed rice, potato and crunchy puri with tamarind sauce; a Mumbai speciality, though now popular nationwide

gulab jamun classic Indian sweet made from deep-fried dough balls served in syrup

halwa traditional sweet made from lentils, nuts and fruit, baked in a large tray and cut into small squares

jalebi flour batter, deep-fried and soaked in sugar syrup

kheer delicate, Mughal-style rice pudding

kulfi Indian-style ice cream, often flavoured with pistachio

ladoo or **ladu** sweets made from small balls of gram flour and semolina

namkeens savoury snacks of the Bombay mix variety

pakora pieces of vegetable deep-fried in chickpea batter; a popular street snack

raj kachori a crisp puri usually filled with chickpeas and doused in curd and sauce

rasgulla curd cheese balls flavoured with rosewater; a popular dessert

samosa parcels of vegetable and potato (and sometimes meat) wrapped up in triangles of pastry and deep-fried

vada* doughnut-shaped, deep-fried lentil cake (also spelt *vadai, vade, wadi*, etc)

vada pao* a *vada* served in a bun with chutney

Glossary

aarti evening temple puja of lights

adivasi official term for tribal person

ahimsa non-violence

amrita nectar of immortality

anda literally "egg": the spherical part of a *stupa*

angrez general term for Westerners

apsara heavenly nymph

arak or **araq** liquor distilled from rice or coconut

asana yogic seating posture; small mat used in prayer and meditation

ashram centre for spiritual learning and religious practice

asura demon

atman soul

avatar reincarnation of Vishnu on Earth, in human or animal form

ayah nursemaid

Ayurveda ancient system of medicine employing herbs, minerals and massage

baba respectful term for a sadhu or an old man

bagh garden, park

baithak reception area in private house

baksheesh tip, donation or alms

bandh general strike

bandhani tie-dye

baniya another word for shopkeeper/trader/merchant

baniyan a cotton vest

banyan vast fig tree, used traditionally as a meeting place, or shade for teaching and meditating

baoli or **baori** step-well

bastee or **bustee** slum area

beedi Indian-style cigarette, with tobacco rolled in a leaf

begum a Muslim woman of high status

betel leaf chewed in paan, with the nut of the areca tree; also loosely applies to the nut

bhajan song in praise of god

bhakti religious devotion expressed in a personalized or emotional relationship with the deity

bhang pounded marijuana leaf, often mixed in lassi

Bharat Hindi name for India

Bharat Mata literally "Mother India"; a representation of India personified as a maternal goddess

bhawan or **bhavan** building, house, palace or residence

Bhotia Himalayan people of Tibetan origin

bhumi earth

bindu seed, or the red dot (also bindi) worn by women on their foreheads as decoration

BJP Bharatiya Janata Party ("Indian People's Party"): right-wing Hindu political party

bodhi enlightenment

bodhi tree or **bo tree** *peepal* tree (*Ficus religiosa*), associated with the Buddha's enlightenment

bodhisattva in Buddhism an enlightened being

brahmin priest; a member of the highest caste group

burj tower or bastion

burqa a loose robe worn by orthodox Muslim women that covers the entire body

burra sahib colonial official, boss, or a man of great importance

cantonment area of town occupied by military quarters

caste social status acquired at birth

cella chamber, often housing the image of a deity

cenotaph ornate tomb

chaat snack

chaddar literally a sheet, can also mean a shawl

chaitya Buddhist temple or *stupa*

chajja sloping dripstone eave

chakra discus; focus of power; energy point in the body; wheel, often representing the cycle of death and rebirth

chandan sandalwood paste

chandra moon

chang Ladakhi beer made from fermented millet, wheat or rice

chappal sandals or flip-flops (thongs)

charas hashish

charbagh Persian-style garden divided into quadrants

charpoy traditional Indian bed; wooden-framed, with rope stretched across it

chhatri domed stone pavilion, often erected over a tomb

chillum cylindrical pipe for smoking *charas* or ganja

Chishti a follower of the Sufi saint Khwaja Muin-ud-din Chishti of Ajmer

choli short, tight-fitting blouse worn with a sari

chor robber

chorten monument, often containing prayers, texts or relics, erected as a sign of faith by Tibetan Buddhists

choultry quarters for pilgrims adjoined to south Indian temples

chowk crossroads or courtyard

chowki police post

chowkidar watchman/caretaker

coolie porter/labourer

crore ten million

CPI Communist Party of India

CPI(M) Communist Party of India (Marxist)

dabba box; lunch box

dacoit bandit

dalit "oppressed", "out-caste"; the self-chosen name for those considered to be from the lowest strata of society

dargah tomb of a Muslim saint

darshan vision of a deity or saint; receiving religious teachings

darwaza gateway; door

dawan servant

deg cauldron for food offerings, often found in *dargahs*

deul Odishan temple or sanctuary

deva god

devadasi temple dancer

devi goddess

devta deity

dhaba food hall selling local dishes

dham important religious site, or a theological college

dharamshala rest house for pilgrims

dharma sense of religious and social duty (Hindu); the law of nature, teachings, truth (Buddhist)

dhobi laundryman

dholak double-ended drum

dhoop thick pliable block of strong incense

dhoti white ankle-length cloth worn by males, tied around the waist, and hitched up through the legs

dhurrie woollen rug

digambara literally "sky-clad": a Jain sect, known for the habit of nudity among monks, though this is no longer commonplace

diwan or dewan chief minister

diwan-i-am public audience hall

diwan-i-khas hall of private audience

Dravidian family of south Indian languages (including Tamil, Kanada and Malayalam) probably also spoken in the north in ancient times

du-khang main temple in a *gompa*

dukka tank and fountain in courtyard of mosque

dupatta scarf worn (sometimes as a veil) with *salwar kameez*

durbar royal audience or council of state

dvarapala guardian image placed at sanctuary door

dzo domesticated half-cow half-yak

Eve-teasing sexual harassment of women, either physical or verbal

fakir ascetic Muslim mendicant

feni Goan spirit, distilled from coconut or cashew fruits

finial capping motif on temple pinnacle

gandharvas Indra's heavenly musicians

ganj area or neigbourhood

ganja marijuana bud

garbhagriha temple sanctuary, literally "womb-chamber"

garh fort

gari vehicle or car

ghat mountain, landing platform, or steps leading to water

ghazal verse form common in Urdu poems and songs

godown warehouse

go-khang temple in a *gompa* devoted to protector (gon) deities

gompa Tibetan, or Ladakhi, Buddhist monastery

goonda ruffian

gopi young cattle-tending maidens who feature as Krishna's playmates and lovers in popular mythology

gopura towered temple gateway, common in south India

guru teacher of religion, music, dance, astrology etc

gurudwara Sikh place of worship

haj Muslim pilgrimage to Mecca

hajji Muslim engaged upon, or who has performed, the haj

hammam sunken Persian-style bath

Harijan title – "Children of God" – given to "untouchables" by Gandhi

hartal strike

haveli elaborately decorated mansion

hijra eunuch or transvestite

Hinayana literally "lesser vehicle": the name given to the original school of Buddhism by later sects

howdah bulky elephant-saddle, sometimes made of pure silver, and often shaded by a canopy

hypostyle a building or room in which the roof is -supported by columns (usually numerous) rather than walls, arches or vaulting

idgah area laid aside in the west of town for prayers during the Muslim festival Id-ul-Zuha

Imam Muslim leader or teacher

imambara tomb of a Shi'ite saint or congregational hall for Shi'ite religious commemorations

Indo-Saracenic overblown Raj-era architecture that combines Muslim, Hindu, Jain and Western elements

ishwara god

iwan the main (often central) arch in a mosque

jagirdar landowner

jali latticework in stone, or a pierced screen

Jama Masjid Friday (congregational) mosque

janapadas small republics and monarchies; literally "territory of the clan"

jangha the body of a temple

jarokha small canopied balcony, often containing a window seat

Jat major north Indian ethnic group; particularly numerous in eastern Rajasthan around Bharatpur

Jataka popular tales about the Buddha's life and teachings

jati caste, determined by family and occupation

jawab a building constructed to mirror another building opposite it, thus creating symmetry

jawan soldier

jhuta soiled by lips: food or drink polluted by touch

-ji suffix added to names as a term of respect

johar old practice of self-immolation by women in times of war

jyotirlinga twelve sacred sites associated with Shiva's unbounded lingam of light

Kailasa or **Kailash** mountain in western Tibet: Shiva's abode and the traditional source of the Ganges and Brahmaputra; the earthly manifestation of the "world pillar", Mount Meru

kalasha pot-like capping stone characteristic of south Indian temples

kama satisfaction

karma weight of good and bad actions that determine status of rebirth

katcha crude, weak, not pukka

kavad small decorated box that unfolds to serve as a travelling temple

khadi home-spun cotton; Gandhi's symbol of Indian self-sufficiency

khan honorific Muslim title

khana dwelling or house

khejri small tree found throughout the desert regions of Rajasthan

kirtan hymn-singing

kot fort

kothi residence

kotla citadel

kotwali police station

kovil term for a Tamil Nadu temple

kshatriya the warrior and ruling caste

kumkum red mark on a Hindu woman's forehead (widows are not supposed to wear it)

kund tank, lake, reservoir

kurta long men's shirt worn over baggy pyjamas

lakh one hundred thousand

lama Tibetan Buddhist monk and teacher

lathi heavy stick that can be used for support or as a weapon

lingam phallic symbol in places of worship, representing the god Shiva

liwan prayer hall or covered area of a mosque

loka realm or world, e.g. *devaloka*, world of the gods

lunghi male garment; long wraparound cloth worn tucked in around the waist flowing down to the ankles

madrasa Islamic school

maha great or large

mahadeva literally "great god", and a common epithet for Shiva

mahal palace; mansion

mahant in Hinduism, a high-ranking pandit; in Sikhism, the manager of a *gurudwara*

maharaja (maharana, maharawal) prince, especially one who rules

maharani the wife of a maharaja, or the woman holding the rank of maharaja

Mahatma great soul

Mahayana "Great Vehicle": a Buddhist school that has spread throughout Southeast Asia

mahout elephant driver or keeper

maidan large open space or field

makara crocodile-like animal featuring on temple doorways and symbolizing the River Ganges. Also the vehicle of Varuna, the Vedic god of the sea

mala necklace, garland or rosary

mandala religious diagram

mandapa hall, often with many pillars, used for various purposes such as weddings or dances

mandi market

mandir temple

mantra sacred verse, often repeated as an aid to meditation

mardana area for use of men in a haveli or palace

marg road

masjid mosque

mataji "mother"; it is also used as a polite form of address to an older woman or a female sadhu

math or **mutt** Hindu or Jain monastery

mayur peacock

medhi terrace

mehendi henna

mela festival

memsahib respectful address to European women

mihrab niche in the wall of a mosque indicating the direction of Mecca

minaret tower of a mosque, from which the call to prayer is issued

minbar pulpit in a mosque from which the Friday sermon is read

mithuna amorous couples in Hindu and Buddhist figurative art

mohalla neighbourhood

moksha blissful state of freedom from rebirth aspired to by Hindus, Sikhs and Jains

mudra symbolic hand gestures used in meditation and dance that also feature in Hindu, Buddhist and Jain art

muezzin man behind the voice calling Muslims to prayer from a mosque

mullah Muslim teacher and scholar

muqarna a style of Islamic moulded vaulting

nadi river

naga mythical serpent; alternatively, a person from Nagaland

nala gorge cut by a seasonal stream

natak drama

natya dance

nautch dance

nawab Muslim landowner or prince

Naxalites Maoist insurgents

nilgai blue bull

nirvana (or, in Pali, *nibbana*) Buddhist equivalent of *moksha*

nizam title of Hyderabad rulers

NRI non-resident Indian: someone entitled to Indian nationality but resident abroad

nullah stream gorge in the mountains

om or **aum** symbol denoting the origin of all things, and ultimate divine essence, used in meditation by Hindus and Buddhists

paan betel nut

pada foot, or base; also a poetic meter

padma lotus; another name for the goddess Lakshmi

pagoda multi-storeyed Buddhist monument

paisa There are a hundred paise in a rupee

pali original language of early Buddhist texts

panchayat village council

parikrama ritual circumambulation around a temple, shrine or mountain

Parsi Zoroastrian

phulkari flowery Punjabi embroidered fabric used for shawls, head scarfs and dupattas

pietra dura inlay work, traditionally consisting of semiprecious stones set in marble; particularly associated with Agra

pir Muslim holy man

pol fortified gate

pradakshina patha processional path circling a monument or sanctuary

prakara enclosure or courtyard in a south Indian temple

pranayama breath control, used in meditation

prasad food blessed in temple sanctuaries and shared among devotees

prayag auspicious confluence of two or more rivers

puja worship

pujari priest

pukka (literally "ripe" or "mature") proper; done right; correctly so-called

punkah type of manually operated ceiling fan, widely used during the Raj era, hand-pulled by a punkah-wala

punya religious merit

purdah (literally "curtain") hiding of women from men, including wearing a veil

purnima full moon

pyjama men's baggy trousers

qawwal hypnotic Sufi chant

qibla the Mecca-facing wall of a mosque

qila fort

raag or **raga** series of notes forming the basis of a melody

Raj rule; monarchy; in particular the period of British imperial rule 1857–1947

raja a ruler or landlord

Rajput princely rulers who once dominated much of north and west India

rakshasa demon

rangoli geometrical pattern of rice powder laid before houses and temples

rani a queen or princess of a raja

rath chariot

rawal chieftain or ruler of a minor principality

rinpoche literally "precious one", a highly revered Tibetan Buddhist lama, considered to be a reincarnation of a previous teacher

rishi "seer"; philosophical sage or poet

rudraksha beads used to make Shiva rosaries

rumal handkerchief, particularly finely embroidered in Chamba state (HP)

saadhak a person who is engaged in an all-encompassing course in spirituality to achieve realization of the self and God

sadar "main"; e.g. Sadar Bazaar

sadhu Hindu mendicant holy man

sagar lake

sahib respectful title for gentlemen

salwar kameez long shirt and baggy ankle-hugging trousers worn by Indian women

samadhi final enlightenment; a site of death or burial of a saint

sambar species of Asian deer

samsara cyclic process of death and rebirth

sangam sacred confluence of two or more rivers, or an academy

sangeet music

sannyasi homeless, possessionless ascetic (Hindu)

sarai resting place for caravans and travellers who once followed the trade routes through Asia

sari dress for Indian women: a length of cloth wound around the waist and draped over one shoulder

sati immolation of a widow on her husband's funeral pyre in emulation of Shiva's wife (now banned)

satyagraha Gandhi's campaign of nonviolent protest, literally "grasping truth"

scheduled castes official name for "untouchables"

sepoy infantry private, an Indian soldier in the British army during the colonial period

seva voluntary service in a temple or community

shaikh Muslim holy man or saint

Shaivite Hindu recognizing Shiva as the supreme god

shankha conch, symbol of Vishnu

shastra treatise

sheesh mahal "glass palace"; usually a room or apartment decorated with mirrors

shikar hunting

shikhara temple tower or spire common in north Indian architecture

shloka verse from a Sanskrit text

shri or **sri** respectful prefix; another name for Lakshmi

shudra the lowest of the four *varnas*; servant

singh or **singha** lion

sitout veranda

soma unidentified drug used in early Vedic and Zoroastrian rituals

stambha pillar, or flagstaff

sthala site sacred for its association with legendary events

stupa large hemispherical mound, representing the Buddha's presence, and often protecting relics of the Buddha or a Buddhist saint

suchalaya toilet

sulabh convenient toilet

surma black eyeliner, also known as kohl

sutra or **sutta** verse in Sanskrit and Pali texts (literally "thread")

svetambara "white-clad" sect of Jainism that accepts nuns and shuns nudity

swami master; title for a holy man

swaraj "self-rule"; synonym for independence, coined by Gandhi

tala rhythmic cycle in classical music; in sculpture a *tala* signifies one face-length

tandoor clay oven

tank square or rectangular water pool in a temple complex, for ritual bathing

tanpura the instrument producing the drone that accompanies all Indian classical music

tempo three-wheeled taxi

terma precious manuscript (Tibetan Buddhist term)

thakur usually Rajput landowner

thangka Tibetan religious scroll painting

Theravada "Doctrine of the Elders": the original name for early Buddhism, which persists today in Sri Lanka and Thailand

thug member of a north Indian cult of professional robbers and murderers

tiffin light meal

tiffin carrier stainless-steel set of tins used for carrying meals

tilak red dot smeared on the forehead during worship, and often used cosmetically

tirtha river crossing considered sacred by Hindus, or the transition from the mundane world to heaven; a place of pilgrimage for Jains

tirthankara "ford-maker" or "crossing-maker": an enlightened Jain teacher who is deified – 24 appear every 300 million years

tola the weight of a silver rupee: 180 grains, or approximately 11.6g

tonga two-wheeled horse-drawn cart

topi cap

torana arch, or freestanding gateway of two pillars linked by an elaborate arch

trimurti the Hindu trinity

trishula Shiva's trident

tuk fortified enclosure of Jain shrines or temples

tulku reincarnated teacher of Tibetan Buddhism

untouchables former term for *dalit*, now considered pejorative

urs Muslim saint's-day festival

vahana the "vehicle" of a deity: the bull Nandi is Shiva's *vahana*

vaishya member of the merchant and trading caste group

varna literally "colour"; one of the four caste groupings: brahmins, kshatriyas, *vaishyas* and *shudras*

vav step-well, common in Gujarat

Vedas sacred texts of early Hinduism

vedika railing around a *stupa*

vihara Jain or Buddhist monastery

vimana tower over temple sanctuary

waddo south Indian term meaning ward or subdivision of a district

wala suffix implying occupation, e.g. rickshaw-wala

wazir chief minister to the king

yagna Vedic sacrificial ritual

yaksha pre-Vedic folklore figure connected with fertility and incorporated into later Hindu iconography

yakshi female *yaksha*

yali mythical lion

yantra cosmological pictogram, or instrument used in an observatory

yatra pilgrimage

yatri pilgrim

yogi (female: yogini) practitioner of yoga

yoni symbol of the female sexual organ, set around the base of the lingam in temple shrines

yuga aeon: the present age is the last in a cycle of four *yugas*, *kali-yuga*, a "black age" of degeneration and spiritual decline

zamindar landowner

zenana women's quarters; segregated area for women in a mosque, haveli or palace

Small print and index

A ROUGH GUIDE TO ROUGH GUIDES

Published in 1982, the first Rough Guide – to Greece – was a student scheme that became a publishing phenomenon. Mark Ellingham, a recent graduate in English from Bristol University, had been travelling in Greece the previous summer and couldn't find the right guidebook. With a small group of friends he wrote his own guide, combining a contemporary, journalistic style with a thoroughly practical approach to travellers' needs.

The immediate success of the book spawned a series that rapidly covered dozens of destinations. And, in addition to impecunious backpackers, Rough Guides soon acquired a much broader readership that relished the guides' wit and inquisitiveness as much as their enthusiastic, critical approach and value-for-money ethos. These days, Rough Guides include recommendations from budget to luxury and cover more than 120 destinations around the globe, from Amsterdam to Zanzibar, all regularly updated by our team of roaming writers.

Browse all our latest guides, read inspirational features and book your trip at **roughguides.com**.

Rough Guide credits

Editors: Tom Fleming and Tatiana Wilde
Commissioning editor: Rebecca Hallett
Cartography: Carte and Katie Bennett
Managing editor: Rachel Lawrence

Picture editors: Aude Vauconsant
Cover photo research: Aude Vauconsant
Senior DTP coordinator: Dan May
Head of DTP and Pre-Press: Rebeka Davies

Publishing information

Eleventh edition 2019

Distribution

UK, Ireland and Europe
Apa Publications (UK) Ltd; sales@roughguides.com
United States and Canada
Ingram Publisher Services; ips@ingramcontent.com
Australia and New Zealand
Woodslane; info@woodslane.com.au
Southeast Asia
Apa Publications (SN) Pte; sales@roughguides.com
Worldwide
Apa Publications (UK) Ltd; sales@roughguides.com
Special Sales, Content Licensing and CoPublishing
Rough Guides can be purchased in bulk quantities
at discounted prices. We can create special editions,
personalised jackets and corporate imprints tailored to
your needs. sales@roughguides.com.

roughguides.com
Printed in Poland by Pozkal
All rights reserved
© 2019 Apa Digital (CH) AG
License edition © Apa Publications Ltd UK
A catalogue record for this book is available from the
British Library
The publishers and authors have done their best to
ensure the accuracy and currency of all the information
in **The Rough Guide to India**, however, they can accept
no responsibility for any loss, injury, or inconvenience
sustained by any traveller as a result of information or
advice contained in the guide.

Help us update

We've gone to a lot of effort to ensure that this edition of
The Rough Guide to India is accurate and up-to-date.
However, things change – places get "discovered", opening
hours are notoriously fickle, restaurants and rooms raise
prices or lower standards. If you feel we've got it wrong
or left something out, we'd like to know, and if you can
remember the address, the price, the hours, the phone
number, so much the better.

Please send your comments with the subject line
"Rough Guide India Update" to mail@uk.roughguides.
com. We'll credit all contributions and send a copy of the
next edition (or any other Rough Guide if you prefer) for
the very best emails.

Acknowledgements

Nick Edwards: Nick would like to thank all at Greenwoods Resort, Mani at Secret Ivory and Nasi at Vicky's for hospitality
and helpful info. Heartfelt thanks to Manzoor for over 25 years of friendship. Cheers to fellow intrepid travellers Gina,
Annette, Maureen, Janet, Jackie and Ian for excellent company through TN and parts of Karnataka. Love as always to Maria
for braving the UK winter back home, with just Gandalf for company.
Marco Ferrarese: First of all, thanks to my wife Kit Yeng Chan for the good company on another crazy trip through our
beloved Northeast India. My gratitude also goes to: Vaivhav Todi and Greener Pastures for their support with permits
and arrangements. Sange Tsering and the Holiday Scout family for the swell times in Arunachal. Bro George Nathaniel,
SH Rahman and Shamim for treating us like family in Kolkata and the Sundarbans (plus all the great hotel connections).
Government of West Bengal Tourism Department. Elizabeth Clarke and Shubhana Rai at Windamere Hotel in Darjeeling.
Madam Mrinalini Shrivastava and her amazing driver Ugen Buthia for helping out beyond belief and gratitude with
research in Sikkim and North Bengal. Anjan Khanal, Jeet, their friends and the kettle moonlight dance in Gangtok and
Lingmoo. Pallab Kakoty and the Ugroshore team. Jason and Professor Breejesh in Shillong. Brother in arms Ryan Davies,
King of Lucknow. Rahul Kumar in Patna (thanks for taking me all over Bihar!). Kamen, Ajoy, Okit and Are the pig in Loba
Pasighat. Milan Sanji in Imphal. Vedant Chawla in Agra. And Mario Cicotto for the good company and sweet lassis in
Varanasi. At last, cheers to the hundred chai, paratha and lassi wallas who made my life much richer. This was a dream
research trip, and I can't wait to come back to you, my friends. But no thanks to the sleeper class ladyboys and their evil eye.
Shafik Meghji: A huge thanks to: my fellow authors; Tom Fleming at Rough Guides; Nina Meghji for all her help with the
research; Rebecca Hallett; Katie and Jehan Bhujwala at Shergarh; and Jennifer Jones at GEC PR.
Rachel Mills: Thank you to the editorial team at RG HQ for a wonderful commission to the Himalayas and Robin Temple
for braving the mountain roads with me.
Martin Zatko: Martin would like to thank Anil K Prajapati for his extremely kind assistance with accommodation and
transport through Rajasthan and beyond, Meenakshi Sachdev Varma for organising tons of stuff in Kashmir and Ladakh,
and Sania Siddiqui for her stellar company in and around Delhi.

Photo credits
(Key: T-top; C-centre; B-bottom; L-left; R-right)

ABOUT THE AUTHORS

Nick Edwards After years studying Classics and Modern Greek at Oxford, Nick spent many years living in Athens and Pittsburgh and has clocked up a total of well over four years in India. Now living back in his native southeast London with spouse Maria, he is able to devote more time to his beloved Spurs, obscure psychedelic sounds, discovering pastures new and promoting Oneness.

Marco Ferrarese lives in Penang, Malaysia since 2009, from where he covers Malaysia, India and the larger Southeast Asian region for a number of international publications that include Rough Guides, Travel + Leisure Southeast Asia, BBC Travel, *South China Morning Post* and *Nikkei Asian Review*. He first came to India in 2010, and since then has seen more India than most Indians do in a lifetime. He and his Malaysian wife Kit Yeng still call Penang home, even though they are on the road in India, Nepal and Pakistan for most of their time. Know more about Marco and his books at ⓦmarcoferrarese.com and ⓦmonkeyrockworld.com

Lottie Gross is a travel writer and editor who has travelled to countless places in India in search of the best masala chai (the train walas can't be beat). She also writes about the Europe, Africa and North America but has a soft spot for her home in the UK, where she travels mostly with her dog. She has been published in *The Telegraph, National Geographic Traveller*, Mashable, *AFAR* and many more.

Shafik Meghji An award-winning travel writer, journalist and author based in south London, Shafik Meghji has been exploring India since 2003. He has co-authored more than 35 Rough Guides, and writes regularly for publications around the world, including BBC Travel, Adventure.com and *The Guardian*. Shafik is a member of the British Guild of Travel Writers and a fellow of the Royal Geographical Society. ⓦshafikmeghji.com. Twitter: @ShafikMeghji.

Rachel Mills is a freelance writer and editor based by the sea in Kent. She is a co-author for Rough Guides to New Zealand, Canada, Vietnam, Ireland and England, as well as India, and regularly writes for *The Telegraph*, DK Travel, *AFAR* and ⓦloveEXPLORING.com. You can follow her travels on Instagram and Twitter @rachmillstravel.

Lakshmi Sharath is a traveller, travel writer and blogger from Bangalore India. Her forte lies in storytelling and she has written for several publications in India on travel. She also blogs at ⓦlakshmisharath.com

Martin Zatko has been in a near-constant state of motion since 2002. During some of his more productive moments, he has written or contributed to the Rough Guides to Korea, China, Japan, Taiwan, Vietnam, Myanmar, India, Fiji, Australia, Turkey, Morocco, Greece and Europe.

Index

Map symbols

The symbols below are used on maps throughout the book

International boundary	Fuel station	Escarpment
State/union territory boundary	Hospital	Cliff
Major road	Golf course	Waterfall
Minor road	Statue	Hot spring
Unpaved road	Viewpoint	Swimming pool
4WD-only road	Lighthouse	Swamp/paddy field
Pedestrian road	National park/wildlife sanctuary	Palm tree
Steps	Country park	Winery
Footpath	Trekking hut	Synagogue
Railway	Museum	Hindu/Jain temple
Ferry route	Monument	Mosque/Muslim monument
River/coastline	Fortress	Buddhist temple/monastery
Wall	Palace	Stupa
Cable car/ropeway	Haveli	Shrine
Airport	Bridge	Church (regional)
Domestic airport	Ghat	Church (town)
Helipad	Entrance gate	Building
Metro station	Boat	Market
Bus/taxi stand	Mountain range	Stadium
Parking	Mountain peak	Christian cemetery
Point of interest	Cave	Muslim cemetery
Post office	Rocks	Park
Tourist office	Pass	Beach
Internet access	Excavations	Glacier

Listings key

Accommodation	Eating
Drinking/nightlife	Shopping

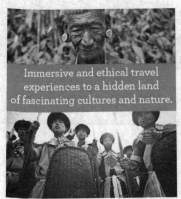
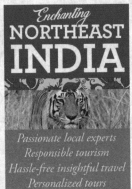

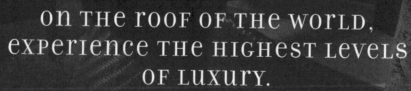